WISDEN

CRICKETERS' ALMANACK

2013

EDITED BY LAWRENCE BOOTH

WISDEN

CRICKETERS' ALMANACK

2013

150th EDITION

John Wisden & Co

An imprint of Bloomsbury Publishing Plc

JOHN WISDEN & CO
An imprint of Bloomsbury Publishing Plc
50 Bedford Square, London WC1B 3DP

WISDEN CRICKETERS' ALMANACK
Editor **Lawrence Booth**
Co-editor **Hugh Chevallier**
Deputy editors **Steven Lynch** and **Harriet Monkhouse**
Assistant editor **James Coyne**
Contributing editor **Richard Whitehead**
Production co-ordinator **Peter Bather**
Chief statistician **Philip Bailey**
Proofreader **Charles Barr**
Database and typesetting **Stephen Cubitt**
Publisher **Charlotte Atyeo**
Consultant publisher **Christopher Lane**

Reader feedback: almanack@wisden.com

www.wisden.com

www.wisdenrecords.com

Follow Wisden on Twitter @WisdenAlmanack
and on Facebook at Wisden Sports

Typeset in Times New Roman and Univers by David Lewis XML Associates, Bungay NR35 1JB
Printed by CPI Group (UK) Ltd, Croydon CR0 4YY

A CIP catalogue record for this book is available from the British Library

Published by John Wisden & Co, an imprint of Bloomsbury Publishing Plc, 2013

EDITIONS

Cased ISBN 978-1-408175-65-1 £50
Soft cover ISBN 978-1-408175-63-7 £50
Large format ISBN 978-1-408175-64-4 £60
Leatherbound ISBN 978-1-408192-29-0 £270

A Taste of Wisden 2013

"No one was sure when England had been so utterly outflanked, though Hastings 1066 was a possibility."
England v South Africa 2012, First Test, page 355

* * *

"In late March, the ECB sent schools advice on how to cope with drought conditions. On April 6, the day after widespread hosepipe bans were announced, the rain started."
Schools Cricket, 2012, page 769

* * *

"The familiar yellow and brown dust jackets, whose colouring always makes me think of streaks of yeast extract over the lid of a Marmite jar…"
Volume control, page 49

* * *

"It meant receiving an email from a contributor saying, 'Hope you've enjoyed your year of being George Lazenby.'"
What editing Wisden meant to me, page 32

* * *

"They hold so many wooden spoons – a record 15 – that a kitchen drawer has often seemed more useful than a trophy cabinet."
Derbyshire in 2012, page 441

* * *

"Ramps and Test cricket: it was never really going to work out. Wrong genius, wrong time."
Retirements, page 191

* * *

"He was once in charge of transport on an army exercise in which he started with 400 vehicles, and returned with 401."
Obituaries, page 241

* * *

"I heard an elderly member assert that Pietersen was 'the closest thing to Jessop I've ever seen'. Since the Croucher played his last Test in 1912, the claim seemed a touch implausible, yet heads nodded approvingly."
It's tough being Kevin, page 67

LIST OF CONTRIBUTORS

Timothy Abraham
Andrew Alderson
Tanya Aldred
David Rayvern Allen
Chris Aspin
Mike Atherton
Philip August
Simon Barnes
Rupert Bates
Greg Baum
Benedict Bermange
Scyld Berry
Edward Bevan
Rahul Bhattacharya
George Binoy
Paul Bolton
Stephen Brenkley
Daniel Brettig
Gideon Brooks
Tim Brooks
Colin Bryden
Ian Callender
Don Cameron
Brian Carpenter
Simon Cleaves
Rex Clementine
Patrick Collins
Mike Coward
Tony Cozier
John Crace
Jon Culley
John Curtis
Steve Davies
Geoffrey Dean
Tim de Lisle
Ralph Dellor
Norman de Mesquita
William Dick
George Dobell
Anjali Doshi
Barney Douglas
Philip Eden
Paul Edwards
Mark Eklid
Matthew Engel
Peter English
John Etheridge
Warwick Franks
Alan Gardner
Mark Geenty
Haydn Gill
Nagraj Gollapudi
Julian Guyer
Gideon Haigh
Duncan Hamilton
Graham Hardcastle
David Hardy
Ed Hawkins
Murray Hedgcock
Douglas Henderson
Paul Hiscock
Richard Hobson
Myles Hodgson
Jesse Hogan
David Hopps
Steve James
Paul Jones
Abid Ali Kazi
Patrick Kidd
Jarrod Kimber
Stephen Lamb
Richard Latham
Jonathan Liew
Simon Lister
Neil Manthorp
Vic Marks
Ali Martin
Christopher Martin-Jenkins
James Martin-Jenkins
Suresh Menon
Andrew Miller
Alison Mitchell
Mohammad Isam
R. Mohan
Benj Moorehead
Paul Newman
Peter Oborne
Michael Peel
Mark Pennell
Sam Peters
Dileep Premachandran
Derek Pringle
Andrew Radd
Paul Radley
Kaushik Ramakrishnan
S. A. Rennie
Barney Ronay
Christian Ryan
Chloe Saltau
Osman Samiuddin
Faraz Sarwat
Neville Scott
Mike Selvey
Shahid Hashmi
Utpal Shuvro
Mehluli Sibanda
Ant Sims
Richard Spiller
Fraser Stewart
Andy Stockhausen
Chris Stocks
Pat Symes
Bruce Talbot
Sa'adi Thawfeeq
Alan Tyers
Sharda Ugra
Anand Vasu
Telford Vice
John Ward
David Warner
Chris Waters
Tim Wellock
Richard Whitehead
Tim Wigmore
Simon Wilde
Martin Williamson
Andy Wilson
Dean Wilson
Robert Winder
John Woodcock
Graeme Wright

Photographers are credited as appropriate. Special thanks to Patrick Eagar, Graham Morris and Philip Brown. **Cartoons** by Nick Newman. **Cricket Round the World** contributors are listed after their articles.

The editor also acknowledges with gratitude assistance from the following: Robin Abrahams, Julie Bacon, Derek Barnard, Julien Bergeaud, Andrew Bunbury, Abi Carter, Adam Cassidy, Stephen Chalke, Marion Collin, Clare Connor, Terry Cooper, Brian Croudy, Nigel Davies, Ted Dexter, Frank Duckworth, M. L. Fernando, Ric Finlay, Alan Fordham, David Frith, Ghulam Mustafa Khan, Norman Gifford, Richard Gray, Sojida Gulomnabieva, Andrew Hignell, David Hughes, Nick Humphrey, Julia and John Hunt, David Kendix, Rajesh Kumar, Eileen Langley, Tony Lewis, Grahame Lloyd, John McKenzie, Roger Mann, Mahendra Mapagunaratne, Ian Marshall, Robin Martin-Jenkins, Ken Medlock, Rangam Mitra, Roy Morgan, Adam Mountford, Graham Napier, Vladimir Ninkovic, Francis Payne, Neil Priscott, Qamar Ahmed, Clive Radley, Neil Robinson, Andrew Samson, Christopher Saunders, Shahriar Khan, Clare Skinner, Chris Smith, Paul Smith, Jeremy Snape, Micky Stewart, Maggie van Reenen, Predrag Vukanovic, Charlie Wat, Beth Wild and Alan Williams.

The production of *Wisden* would not be possible without the support and co-operation of many other cricket officials, county scorers, writers and lovers of the game. To them all, many thanks.

PREFACE

The American satirist Ambrose Bierce once wrote a review consisting of a single line: "The covers of this book are too far apart." As far as we know, *Wisden* escaped his censure, although it may have helped that he appears to have vanished on Boxing Day 1913 in Chihuahua, Mexico – where sales of the Almanack have always been disappointing. I trust Ambrose would have appreciated that the 150th edition was never going to be one of the slimmer volumes. A special Part One marks the milestone, and the Comment section – including Notes by the Editor – now makes up Part Two.

For the sake of simplicity after a year in which England played bilateral series against five different opponents, we have included all their matches in one section, so there is no longer any need to jump around to piece together the chronology; since recent editions have included special Ashes sections, this seemed like the logical next step. An extended Part Eight now includes the section formerly known as "Law and Administration".

The cover has been tweaked too, with pride of place given to the Eric Ravilious wood engraving that first appeared on *Wisden* 75 years ago. The familiar photo jacket will return next year.

Wisden has adapted in other ways. The first *Wisden India Almanack*, edited by Suresh Menon, was published in December, and this year has already included the launch of *The Nightwatchman*, a new quarterly magazine. Along with our regular online publication, *Wisden EXTRA*, it means the long-form writing that is central to *Wisden* is now more available, all year round, than ever.

The compilation of *Wisden 2013* required another frighteningly dedicated team effort. Hugh Chevallier, our co-editor, was a beacon of strength and sagacity; deputy editors Harriet Monkhouse and Steven Lynch were their tireless, eagle-eyed selves; assistant editor James Coyne was indispensable. Christopher Lane deserves special mention for his contributions to the 150th section.

At Bloomsbury, my thanks go to Charlotte Atyeo and Richard Charkin for trusting us to get on with the job. Peter Bather processed proofs with his customary good humour, and Stephen Cubitt and Mike Hatt typeset as diligently as ever. Thanks, too, to Philip Bailey for his painstaking statistical work, and to Lee Clayton and Les Snowdon on the *Daily Mail* sports desk for allowing me once more to sink so many hours into *Wisden*. Natasha Fletcher was a constant source of support.

Among this year's pages are reflections of the future and the past. For the first time, *Wisden* is publishing the best article received from a reader – a competition we hope will become a tradition. We are confident the much-missed Christopher Martin-Jenkins would have approved, and are honoured to be able to run one of CMJ's final pieces, his appreciation of Jacques Kallis, at last a Cricketer of the Year. One institution on another: it felt about right for the 150th.

LAWRENCE BOOTH
Earlsfield, March 2013

CONTENTS

Part One – Wisden's 150th

Part Two – Comment

Part Three – The Wisden Review

Part Four – England International Cricket

Part Five – England Domestic Cricket

Statistics

LV= County Championship

One-day County Competitions

OTHER ENGLISH CRICKET

EUROPEAN CRICKET

Part Six – Overseas Cricket

MAJOR ICC TOURNAMENTS

CRICKET IN AUSTRALIA

CRICKET IN BANGLADESH

CRICKET IN INDIA

CRICKET IN NEW ZEALAND

CRICKET IN PAKISTAN

CRICKET IN SOUTH AFRICA

CRICKET IN SRI LANKA

CRICKET IN THE WEST INDIES

CRICKET IN ZIMBABWE

OTHER OVERSEAS INTERNATIONAL CRICKET

Part Seven – Records and Registers

RECORDS

BIRTHS AND DEATHS

REGISTERS

Part Eight – Administration and the Almanack

SYMBOLS AND ABBREVIATIONS

*	In full scorecards and lists of tour parties signifies the captain. In short scorecards, averages and records signifies not out.
†	In full scorecards signifies the designated wicketkeeper. In averages signifies a left-handed batsman.
‡	In short scorecards signifies the team who won the toss.
MoM/PoM	In short scorecards signifies the Man/Player of the Match.
MoS/PoS	In short scorecards signifies the Man/Player of the Series.
D/L	Signifies where a result has been decided under the Duckworth/Lewis method for curtailed matches.

Other uses of symbols are explained in notes where they appear.

FIRST-CLASS MATCHES

Men's matches of three or more days' duration are first-class unless otherwise stated. All other matches are not first-class, including one-day and Twenty20 internationals.

SCORECARDS

Where full scorecards are not provided in this book, they can be found at Cricket Archive (www.cricketarchive.co.uk) or ESPNcricinfo (www.cricinfo.com). Full scorecards from matches played overseas can also be found in the relevant *ACS Overseas First-Class Annual*.

RECORDS

The entire Records section (pages 1247–1396) can now be found at www.wisdenrecords.com. The online Records database is regularly updated and, in many instances, more detailed than in *Wisden 2013*. Further information on past winners of tournaments covered in this book can be found at www.wisden.com/almanacklinks

Wisden's 150th

WISDEN'S TEN MOMENTS IN TIME

And the game changed for ever

Which of W. G. Grace's feats was the most resounding? And which aspect of Twenty20's gold rush best captured its impact on the modern game? These were the kinds of questions to which *Wisden* hoped to find a convincing answer when it chose the ten most seminal moments in the years spanning the Almanack's 150 editions. The list that emerged contains some that will come as a surprise: among readers who entered our competition to guess the ten, no one managed more than six. But then consensus would have spoiled the fun.

We stipulated that a moment could not be an era – though an era could be sparked by a moment, which we interpreted loosely, to avoid the reduction of everything *ad absurdum* and so awarding pride of place to the Big Bang. So West Indies' 15-year reign didn't count, but the series which triggered it – their thrashing by Australia in 1975-76 – did. And we made a plea for "lasting resonance". Don Bradman's duck in his final Test innings in 1948 felt like a one-off shock; Bodyline, a tactic designed to tame him, reached beyond the skeleton of statistics and deep into cricket's bone marrow. Few entrants were brave enough to omit it.

Otherwise, the *Wisden* team were guided by judgment and a little gut instinct. Who changed batting for ever: Grace in 1871 or Bradman in 1930? We went for Grace, who – as Ranjitsinhji explained – invented an entire methodology, of which Bradman would become the most ruthless exemplar. Was the first Gillette Cup in 1963 more significant for one-day cricket than India's 1983 World Cup win? We thought so, but only just.

Or did this clash with the choice of the Indian Premier League's first auction, in 2008, ahead of Twenty20's appearance on the county scene in 2003? We deferred to impact: in 1963, part of an otherwise forgettable decade for cricket, the Gillette Cup stood out; but the gates to Twenty20 mega-wealth opened widest at the IPL auctions, rather than five years earlier around the shires.

After Bodyline, readers' most common picks were Kerry Packer's World Series Cricket, the Oval Test of 1882 that spawned the sport's greatest and oldest rivalry (though it seems *Wisden* did not refer to the "Ashes" until the late 1920s), the Basil D'Oliveira affair, and the exposure as a cheat of Hansie Cronje. Many others failed to make the cut, though no individual wore more hats than Sachin Tendulkar (Old Trafford 1990, the first double-century in one-day internationals, 100 hundreds, and so on). In fact, Tendulkar does feature – as the victim of the first TV run-out – but, for our purposes, individuals were secondary to moments, not vice versa.

The three readers who came closest to matching our choice in the competition trailed on page 25 of *Wisden 2012* were Annette Rabaiotti from London, Richard Kemp from Leeds, and Peter Handford from Western Australia. They each win a £100 voucher to spend on sports books published by Bloomsbury. Twenty-five runners-up each receive a copy of the *Fire in Babylon* DVD.

THE TEN MOMENTS

W. G. Grace (1871)
The Oval (1882)
Bodyline (1932-33)
The Gillette Cup (1963)
Basil D'Oliveira (1968)
Australia 5 West Indies 1 (1975-76)
World Series Cricket (1977-78)
Technology's entrance (1992-93)
Hansie Cronje (2000)
The IPL auction (2008)

1871: W. G. Grace rewrites the record books

At first, bowlers held the upper hand in first-class cricket, helped by rough, almost unprepared pitches. Then came WG. He had hinted at exceptional talent, but in 1871, the year he turned 23, Grace reshaped the game. No one had previously made 2,000 runs in a season. Now he made 2,739, a record that stood for 25 years. The next-best was Harry Jupp's 1,068, and of the 17 first-class centuries that year, WG made ten. Batting was never quite the same again.

Grace buried the quaint notion that scoring on the leg side was ungentlemanly. He batted in a way we would recognise today: usually a decisive movement forward or back, bat close to pad, although he was also a master of what Ranjitsinhji called a "half-cock stroke", which we would probably term playing from the crease. In his *Jubilee Book of Cricket*, Ranji wrote: "He revolutionised cricket, turning it from an accomplishment into a science… He turned the old one-stringed instrument into a many-chorded lyre, a wand… Until his time, a man was either a back player like Carpenter or a forward player like Pilch, a hitter like E. H. Budd or a sticker like Harry Jupp. But W. G. Grace was each and all at once." STEVEN LYNCH

From Wisden 1872: *MCC and Ground v Surrey at Lord's*

In cold dry weather this match was played out in two days, MCC and G the winners by an innings and 23 runs. There was some superb batting by both Mr W. Grace and Jupp; in fact, it is the opinion of many that the 181 by Mr Grace and the 85 by Jupp in this match are their most skilful and perfect displays of batting on London grounds in 1871. Mr Grace was first man in at 12.10; when the score was 164 for four wickets Mr Grace had made exactly 100 runs; when he had made 123 he gave a hot – a very hot – chance to short square leg, but he gave no other chance; he was much hurt by a ball bowled by Skinner when he had made 180, and at 181 Southerton bowled him, he being fifth man out with the score at 280. Mr Grace's "timing" and "placing" the ball in this innings was truly wonderful cricket; he appeared to hit "all round" just where he chose to, and placing a field for his hit was as useless as were the bowler's efforts to bowl to him. Mr Grace's hits included a great on-drive past the pavilion for six, four fives (all big drives), and 11 fours.

The 1882 Australians, whose victory at The Oval sparked cricket's most famous death notice. *Back row:* Joey Palmer, Harry Boyle, Billy Murdoch (*captain, seated*), Percy McDonnell, Fred Spofforth, Tom Horan, Sammy Jones. *Front row:* Charles Beal (*manager*), George Giffen, Alick Bannerman, Tom Garrett, Hugh Massie, George Bonnor. Palmer and McDonnell did not play at The Oval, where Jack Blackham (absent) kept wicket.

1882: The Ashes are born

The history of England v Australia, the mother of all Test series, was first distilled into a minuscule urn-shaped vessel, then pressure-cooked to create a hyper-contest for the 21st century. But time and distance cannot diminish the role played in the creation myth by a single game. The Oval 1882 was a microcosm of the tension that has never left the Ashes.

Australia's indomitability was summed up by their first-day recovery from 30 for six and Fred Spofforth's demonic bowling – inspired, legend has it, by W. G. Grace's caddish run-out of Sammy Jones. More than 2,000 Tests have taken place since, but Australia's seven-run victory remains in the top ten tightest wins.

The paroxysms of the umbrella-gnawing spectator resonate with fans on all sides of all sporting divides, as does the *Sporting Times's* mock obituary shortly afterwards, the first truly memorable example of English cricket's gallows humour. England had lost to Australia before, but only ever while out of sight, out of mind, on the other side of the globe. This was an awakening in every sense. A rivalry that, according to the newspaper, was dead as soon as it began would attain a life of its own. ANDREW MILLER

From Wisden 1883: *the run-out of Jones in Australia's second innings, leaving them 114 for seven and with their overall lead 76…*

> Jones was run out in a way which gave great dissatisfaction to Murdoch and other Australians. Murdoch played a ball to leg, for which Lyttelton ran. The ball was returned, and Jones having completed the first run, and thinking wrongly, but very naturally, that the ball was dead, went out of his ground. Grace put his wicket down, and the umpire gave him out. Several of the team spoke angrily of Grace's action, but the compiler was informed that, after the excitement had cooled down, a prominent member of the Australian eleven admitted that he should have done the same thing had he been in Grace's place. There was a good deal of truth in what a gentleman in the pavilion remarked, amidst some laughter, that "Jones ought to thank the champion for teaching him something".

… and England's run-chase

> England, wanting 85 runs to win, commenced their second innings at 3.45 with Grace and Hornby. Spofforth bowled Hornby's off stump at 15, made in about as many minutes. Barlow joined Grace, but was bowled first ball at the same total. Ulyett came in, and some brilliant hitting by both batsmen brought the score to 51, when a very fine catch at the wicket dismissed Ulyett. Thirty-four runs were then wanted, with seven wickets to fall. Lucas joined Grace, but when the latter had scored a two he was easily taken at mid-off. Lyttelton became Lucas' partner, and did all the hitting. Then the game was slow for a time, and 12 successive maiden overs were bowled, both batsmen playing carefully and coolly. Lyttelton scored a single, and then four maiden overs were followed by the dismissal of that batsman – bowled, the score being 66. Only 19 runs were then wanted to win, and there were five wickets to fall. Steel came in, and when Lucas had scored a four, Steel was easily caught and bowled. Read joined Lucas, but amid intense excitement he was clean bowled without a run being added. Barnes took Read's place and scored a two, and three byes made the total 75, or ten to win. After being in a long time for five Lucas played the next ball into his wicket, and directly Studd joined Barnes the latter was easily caught off his glove without the total being altered. Peate, the last man, came in, but after hitting Boyle to square leg for two he was bowled, and Australia had defeated England by seven runs.

1932-33: Bodyline divides two nations

Lucky was the young sheep-station owner, Ian McLachlan senior, who spent the Sunday after Bodyline's fever-pitch Adelaide Saturday in the company of Douglas Jardine and others. A beach excursion to Victor Harbour; that night, McLachlan and Jardine roomed together.

"It's going to muck up cricket," said McLachlan, as lights went out, "because you're going to have cricketers playing in things like baseball masks."

"Oh, don't be silly, laddie."

Bumper bombardments and throat-side field settings did not become the new normal, nor did baseball masks (nor, yet, helmets). Spin bowling survived as cricket's guileful art. Even Don Bradman – as exotic as a nine-legged octopus, his fast yet failsafe 1930 mega-scoring having triggered Bodyline's genesis – half-faltered only briefly. He put ointment on his bruises and for the rest of his days averaged 100.12.

What lingered was psychological, a suspicion of the English gentleman, a sense that, while Australians wish to win, the English will break bones/rules/morality to win, a slow-blooming independence. Australia's ride through our current decade's economic travails is something Treasurer Wayne Swan attributes partly to "an enduring determination for our country never again to be at the whim of anyone". That determination's cause, Mr Treasurer? "I believe, Bodyline." CHRISTIAN RYAN

From Wisden 1933*: Notes by the Editor (Stewart Caine)*

The ball to which such strong exception is being taken in Australia is not slow or slow-medium but fast. It is dropped short and is alleged in certain quarters to be aimed at the batsman rather than at the wicket. It may at once be said that, if the intention is to hit the batsman and so demoralise him, the practice is altogether wrong – calculated, as it must be, to introduce an element of pronounced danger and altogether against the spirit of the game of cricket. Upon this point practically everybody will agree. No one wants such an element introduced. That English bowlers, to dispose of their opponents, would of themselves pursue such methods, or that Jardine would acquiesce in such a course, is inconceivable.

To the abuse of this Law may fairly be traced the trouble which has arisen in Australia during the tour now in progress. In suggesting, as has the Australian Board of Control, that bowling such as that of the Englishmen has become a menace to the best interests of the game, is causing intensely bitter feelings between players and, unless stopped at once, is likely to upset the friendly relations between England and Australia, the Commonwealth cricket authorities seem to have lost their sense of proportion. The idea that a method of play to which, while often practised in the past by Australian as well as English bowlers, no exception had been taken in public could jeopardise the relations of the two countries, appears really too absurd.

From Wisden 1934*: The MCC team in Australasia*

Suffice it to say here that a method of bowling was evolved – mainly with the idea of curbing the scoring propensities of Bradman – which met with almost general condemnation among Australian cricketers and spectators and which, when something of the real truth was ultimately known in this country, caused people at home – many of them famous in the game – to wonder if the winning of the rubber was, after all, worth this strife.

1963: The Gillette Cup is launched

Like sex (according to Philip Larkin, at least) one-day cricket, in the manner in which we now know it, began in 1963. The year before, a pilot competition – the four-team Midlands Knock-Out Cup – had attracted some attention, but now all the counties were involved. In a 65-over-a-side knockout format (just imagine: 130 overs a day) was born the great-great-grandfather of all the World Cups, Premier Leagues and Big Bashes we see today.

So too, simultaneously, came the notion that county cricket could attract sponsorship. The story has it that those from Gillette charged with negotiating a deal arrived at their meeting at Lord's with a substantial figure in mind, and departed having apparently financed the competition from the petty-cash box.

But it was a beginning. Crowds flocked to the matches, ponderous though the first format was, and the Lord's final was established as the county game's day out. Such success spawned new competitions: the Gillette (still the name many think of when speaking of county one-day cricket) was reduced to 60 overs a side; then came the 40-over John Player League, the 55-over Benson and Hedges Cup, and finally Twenty20. The genie was out of the bottle. MIKE SELVEY

From Wisden 1964: The Knock-Out Cup

> The new Knock-Out competition aroused enormous interest. Very large crowds, especially in the later rounds, flocked to the matches and 25,000 spectators watched the final at Lord's, where Sussex narrowly defeated Worcestershire by 14 runs in a thoroughly exciting match. It says much for the type of cricket that tremendous feeling was stirred up among the spectators as well as the cricketers, with numerous ties being decided in the closest fashion. At Lord's, supporters wore favours, and banners were also in evidence, the whole scene resembling an Association Football Cup Final more than the game of cricket, and many thousands invaded the pitch at the finish to cheer Dexter, the Sussex captain, as he received the Gillette Trophy from the MCC President, Lord Nugent.
>
> There were two points which invite criticism. Firstly, the majority of counties were loath to include even one slow bowler in their sides and relied mainly on pace; and secondly the placing of the entire field around the boundary to prevent rapid scoring – Dexter used this tactic in the final – became fairly common. The success of the spinners at Lord's may have exploded the first theory.
>
> There is no doubt that, provided the competition is conducted wisely, it will attract great support in the future and benefit the game accordingly.

1968: The D'Oliveira Affair exposes apartheid

The story of Basil D'Oliveira is one of the most romantic in the history of sport. A non-white man is prevented by apartheid from displaying his exceptional cricketing talents in his native South Africa. So he travels to Britain, where he endures a period of misery and loneliness before his genius is fully recognised and he is selected to play for England.

This part of the story is a fairytale come true. But D'Oliveira's selection for England was more than a dream: it was also a political statement, because it smashed the apartheid myth about the superiority of the white race. Elements of the British cricketing establishment were sympathetic to the apartheid regime, and he was initially omitted by MCC's selectors from the tour party for South Africa in 1968-69, despite having made 158 against Australia in the final Test of the summer. But when seamer Tom Cartwright pulled out of the trip, D'Oliveira was chosen to replace him. South Africa cancelled the tour.

The consequences of the international row that followed were enormous. Large sections of the British public were educated about the brutality and ugliness of racism. South African sporting links with England were broken off. The isolation of the apartheid regime deepened. Through it all, D'Oliveira maintained his integrity, and displayed a palpable decency in a crisis that transcended sport and helped bring an unspeakably evil social system to an end. PETER OBORNE

From Wisden 1969*: The D'Oliveira Case, by Michael Melford*

To the non-cricketing public, D'Oliveira's omission immediately after his innings at The Oval was largely incomprehensible. It was easy for many to assume political motives behind it and a bowing to South Africa's racial policies.

More knowledgeable cricketers were split between those who agreed that on technical grounds D'Oliveira was far from an automatic choice and who were doubtful if he would be any more effective in South Africa than he had been in the West Indies, and those who thought that after his successful comeback to Test cricket, it was "inhuman" not to pick him.

Some holding the latter opinion were also ready to see non-cricketing reasons for the omission… Much was said which was regretted later – four out of 19 members of MCC who resigned in protest applied for reinstatement within a few days – and Lord Fisher of Lambeth, the former Archbishop of Canterbury, was prompted to write to the *Daily Telegraph* condemning a leader "which appeared to cast doubt on the word of the selectors".

A group of 20 MCC members, the number required to call a special meeting of the club, asserted this right, co-opting the Rev. D. S. Sheppard as their main spokesman. For three weeks the affair simmered like an angry volcano.

1975-76: Defeat in Australia sparks West Indies' pace revolution

Their heaviest and most humiliating defeat created the philosophy that led to West Indies' domination through the 1980s and beyond. The 5–1 thrashing in Australia, inflicted mainly by the menacing pace of Dennis Lillee and Jeff Thomson, supported by Gary Gilmour and Max Walker, convinced captain Clive Lloyd of the effectiveness of "three or four quick bowlers on your side". He noted that every West Indian had "at some time or other felt the pain of a cricket ball, sent down at great speed, thudding into their bodies"; his players were "determined never to let it happen again".

India's record 406 for four to win the Port-of-Spain Test two months later, against a team containing only one genuine fast bowler, reinforced Lloyd's opinion. From George Francis, Learie Constantine, Herman Griffith and Manny Martindale before the war, to Wes Hall, Roy Gilchrist and Charlie Griffith two generations later, the resources had always been available. Now, through the vagaries of nature, and fired by competition, they exploded in profusion, mostly imposing giants who worked in tandem. In their 82 Tests in the 1980s – West Indies won 43 and lost eight – 16 fast bowlers gathered 1,257 wickets. Between June 1980 and February 1995, they went unbeaten in Test series. It was the greatest dynasty in the history of the game. TONY COZIER

From Wisden 1977*: West Indies in Australia, by Henry Blofeld*

Australia was the first time [Clive Lloyd] had found himself under real pressure as a captain and he did not find the going easy. When the strain was greatest he did not seem able to control his own nerves as he would have liked when batting and as captain he was never prepared to speak firmly to his batsmen and to tell them how he expected them to try to play the fast bowling on the steep bouncing pitches.

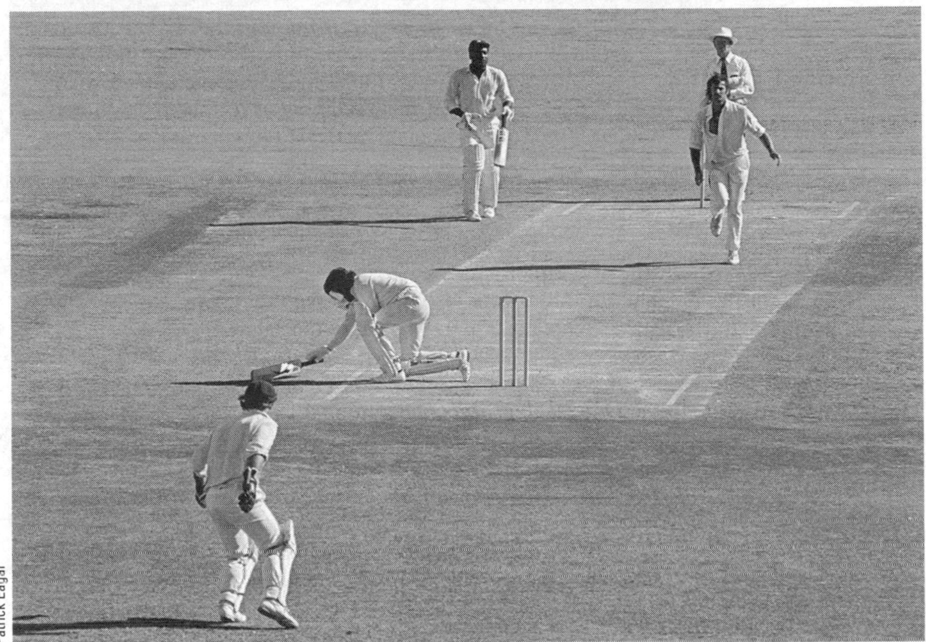
Patrick Eagar

The school of hard knocks: Alvin Kallicharran is hit by Dennis Lillee, December 1975. Viv Richards is the non-striker, Rod Marsh the keeper.

1977-78: World Series Cricket shakes the foundations

When media mogul Kerry Packer approached the Australian Cricket Board in June 1976 with a handsome offer to televise Australian cricket, the administrators dismissed him without misgivings, content with their existing relationship with the national broadcaster. They underestimated Packer's determination. Taking advantage of growing disgruntlement about pay and conditions, he secretly recruited dozens of players from Australia, West Indies, South Africa, England and Pakistan to participate in a punishing schedule of made-for-TV matches in Australia, including the first played at night under lights and in coloured clothing with white balls.

Administrators were immediately hostile, their rhetoric turning into bans and court actions, and World Series Cricket was slow to take off in the 1977-78 season, despite boasting the cream of the world's players. But in 1978-79 it became a success, as the official Australian team, denuded of talent, were badly beaten in the Ashes. Forced to sue for peace, the ACB agreed to welcome back their prodigal sons and award broadcast rights to Packer's Nine Network – rights they have retained to this day. The legacy of the enterprise was growingly acute understanding of the value of the sport as a television property, which others might exploit if cricket failed to do so, and better pay for elite cricketers. GIDEON HAIGH

From Wisden 1978*: Notes by the Editor (Norman Preston)…*

As things stand at the time of writing at the New Year no solution would appear to be in sight and the cricket authorities, particularly those in England, who spend thousands of pounds raising young talent to the top level, run the risk of losing players to any rich entrepreneur, for Packer could be only the first in the line. I feel that those who signed for Packer were placed in a dilemma – loyalty to those who nurtured them or the attraction of financial reward for playing another kind of cricket that excludes them from first-class recognition because it is outside the bounds of the International Cricket Conference.

... and The Packer Case, by Gordon Ross

At this point the only cricketing subject being discussed from the highest committee room in the land to the saloon bar of the tiniest inn, was "Packer", and from all the multifarious points raised, one was likely to be proved the dominant factor in the end. In this age of extreme partisanship, had non-partisanship cricket any future? Does the world not want to see England beat Australia, or Arsenal beat Tottenham, or England beat Wales at Twickenham – or vice versa, according to particular loyalties? Could a collection of players, however great, stimulate public interest, when there was nothing on the end of it, except a considerable amount of money for the participants? The fact that tennis players and golfers are a constant attraction was irrelevant; they are individuals playing for no one but themselves. And moreover, the whole crux of this matter was linked to big business – the business of television, and not so much to the furtherance of cricket or cricketers.

1992-93: Technology takes its bow

Some events develop significance later, others are recognised immediately. This belonged in the second category. There was surprisingly little resistance to the use of television replays for line decisions on India's trip to South Africa late in 1992. But it still felt bizarre to have finally reached this point after the embarrassment TV had been causing umpires for decades.

On the second day of the First Test at Durban, Jonty Rhodes swooped at backward point and flicked an airborne throw to Andrew Hudson at short leg. Umpire Cyril Mitchley was "almost certain" Sachin Tendulkar had been run out but, having been a consultant during the system's trials, had no hesitation in referring it. Third umpire Karl Liebenberg held his breath: there were no fixed cameras at square leg, and everything depended on the midwicket cameraman. But the shot was there. Liebenberg pressed the green light (for "go", which in those days meant "out"), and Tendulkar's dismissal had taken just 34 seconds longer than normal. "I felt instantly the game had changed for ever – and for the better," said South African captain Kepler Wessels.

After domestic use of the referral system revealed its imperfections, fixed cameras – known as the Pana-eye – were implemented in South Africa two years later. They became standard after that. Today, we have the Decision Review System, when money and politics allow. Even the umpires have accepted that their word is no longer necessarily final – a profound shift in the game's psyche. NEIL MANTHORP

From Wisden 1994*: The Indians in South Africa, by Richard Streeton*

The tour will be remembered for the introduction of ICC's scheme for independent umpires and even more for the South African board's experiment using television replays to settle difficult line decisions. It was a successful innovation, welcomed by most players and officials after some initial reservations. Hitherto, for as long as the game has been played, batsmen have received the benefit of an umpire's doubt. When officials on the field felt unable to decide, a third umpire in the pavilion watched video replays to rule on run-outs and stumpings (and hit-wicket decisions, though none arose). A green light signalled that the batsman must go, and red that he was not out. Invariably the crowd buzzed with excitement as they waited and at some grounds they were able to watch the big-screen replays at the same time.

2000: Hansie Cronje admits to match-fixing

The unmasking of Hansie Cronje marked the end of cricket's jolly, even deluded, innocence – both because of the nature of the offence and the identity of the offender. Cronje was a national captain of enviable standing, the prototypical hard-but-fair, principled, devout all-round competitor. He was exposed as the ultimate con artist, the betting mafia's perfect partner, ready to manipulate the scripts behind scorecards. These extremes of his persona contained the game's essential truths, its well-disguised lies and the distance it had travelled in the last few decades of the 20th century.

With Cronje came the deadening awareness that cricket's ethos could be easily corrupted by its best practitioners; that players from all over the world, not merely from the shadowy Orient, could be primed to participate in a world of faux cricket; that the simplest of temptations – starting with friendly free dinners, a wad of cash and, ridiculously, tragically, a leather jacket – could lure respected pros into a dragnet of organised crime. Through his acts and, as importantly, his confession, Cronje became living proof that an old, much-loved game had been poisoned at its very roots. Cricket remains sullied by the cynicism. SHARDA UGRA

From Wisden 2001*: Notes by the Editor (Graeme Wright)…*

> Cronje's worst crime was not against cricket – accepting the bookies' bribes or trying to fix matches – but against morality and decency. It was in the way he ensnared the two most vulnerable members of his team, Herschelle Gibbs and Henry Williams. Cronje's white team-mates could afford to send him on his joking way with a rejection; he was just the captain, one of the boys. For Gibbs and Williams, however, even in the rarefied atmosphere of the new South Africa, Cronje was the white man in charge. It takes more than a rainbow for generations of social conditioning and economic deprivation to be washed away.

… and A Game in Shame, by Mihir Bose

> Cricket corruption, like taxes and poverty, may always be with us. But after cricket's *annus horribilis* of 2000 we can, for the first time, understand how a combination of players' greed, dreadful impotence and infighting by cricket administrators, and a radical shift in cricketing power from England to the Indian subcontinent helped create cricket's darkest chapter.

2008: The first IPL auction puts a price on everything

The Australian seamer Nathan Bracken put it best: "You want to know what you're worth – and you don't want to know what you're worth." In no dressing-room did the tussle for players' services cause as many ructions as it did in Australia's. At a glittering auction in Mumbai on February 20, 2008, Cameron White got more money than the recently retired Shane Warne and Glenn McGrath, while David Hussey was considered a more valuable prospect than Ricky Ponting or Matthew Hayden. "It's probably only me and Matty that will have any reason to be jealous of anybody else," wrote Ponting in a newspaper column after Andrew Symonds went for $1.35m.

There were raised eyebrows in India as well, with Sreesanth and Ishant Sharma getting far more lucrative contracts than Anil Kumble, who had carried the country's bowling for more than a decade. The traditional yardsticks of a player's worth were disregarded, as the franchises' bean-counters spoke of "marketability" and other imponderables. Lalit Modi and his cohorts constantly emphasised "bigger, better, faster, more". It seemed futile to deny this was more seductive than "smaller, worse, slower, less". DILEEP PREMACHANDRAN

From Wisden 2009*: Notes by the Editor (Scyld Berry)*

> The IPL is a clever mixture of ingredients because its administrators have understood their market – their mass market. Although it is impossible to be sure from such a recent perspective, it looks as though the supranational IPL is the single biggest change in cricket not merely since the advent of the limited-overs game in the 1960s but of fixtures between countries in the 19th century: that is, since the invention of international or Test cricket.
>
> Above all, until the time of writing, the IPL has had luck on its side. As the world went into economic crisis, the IPL gave every appearance of bucking the trend. The two auctions of players which it staged, the second on February 6 this year, must have appealed to anyone who has played Monopoly: they gave the franchise-owners the feeling they had power over the world's finest cricketers, and everyone else the illusion. At a time of the most serious recession since the 1930s, Andrew Flintoff and Kevin Pietersen were signed for two years at $1.55m per six-week tournament (or pro rata for the number of games they played). The IPL radiated wealth, well-being, exuberance, and prospects for future growth: in a word, hope.

FIVE CRICKETERS OF 1864–88

Too good, too soon

SIMON WILDE

With the exception of eight wartime years, Wisden *has been choosing its Cricketers of the Year ever since editor Charles Pardon introduced the award in 1889. That means the Almanack went through 25 editions – exactly one-sixth of its life – before the honour was first bestowed (to* six *Great Bowlers of the Year). Who, then, might rank as the most deserving cases for the quarter-century between* Wisden's *first edition in 1864 and Pardon's brainwave?*

It was a time of great change for cricket. Overarm bowling was legalised. County clubs replaced travelling teams as the game's power bases, and competed on an annual, if ad hoc, basis to identify champions. And international matches took off. The first Tests were played in Melbourne in 1876-77, triggering a regular exchange of tours between England and Australia. These contests became the ultimate gauge of ability, although the annual meetings between the Gentlemen and the Players at Lord's were almost as significant.

Unless W. G. Grace was batting, bowlers were largely dominant. Pitches and outfields were often rough, and individual centuries rare for everyone except Grace: Richard Daft, an expert player of fast bowling, managed just seven hundreds in a career spanning more than 30 years.

Grace was still good enough to be named a Cricketer of the Year in 1896 at the age of 47. Other leading players from 1864 to 1888 who were later recognised by *Wisden* included Johnny Briggs, George Lohmann and Bobby Peel (all among the first picks in 1889); Billy Barnes, William Gunn and Arthur Shrewsbury (all 1890); and Walter Read (1893). Among Australians honoured were the great bowling partnership of J. J. Ferris and Charles "The Terror" Turner, both selected in 1889; Jack Blackham, recognised as the first great wicketkeeper, in 1891; and all-rounder George Giffen, in 1894.

If Grace was the batsman by which every bowler was measured, then ALFRED SHAW (1842–1907) is a must-pick. There was no shortage of bowlers capable of operating for hours on end and cutting swathes through batting line-ups, but none was as consistently accurate as Shaw, who took more than 2,000 first-class wickets at 12 apiece in a career almost exactly spanning this period (he started in 1864 and stopped playing regularly after 1886). "He was a remarkably good 'head' bowler," said the Lancashire and England batsman Dick Barlow, "with a wonderful capacity for finding out a batsman's weak points; and could vary his bowling according to the state of the wicket as could no other bowler I ever saw." No one has taken 2,000 so cheaply, and the cost of his 186 wickets in 1880 – 8.54 each – is the lowest for any bowler claiming 100 in a season.

A short-built purveyor of medium-pace who spun the ball or made it break off the pitch, Shaw was accepted as the best bowler in England between 1870 and 1880. Grace said he did not find it difficult to keep him out on a good wicket, but had to be patient to score off him. Yet this was to damn with faint praise: Shaw took Grace's wicket 49 times, more than any bowler. Perhaps more pertinently, relations were not cordial after Shaw turned down Grace's terms for a tour of Australia in 1873-74, objecting to the second-class facilities on offer for the pros. Three years later, in Melbourne, he bowled Test cricket's first ball.

Shaw was as much entrepreneur as player, and acted as joint-promoter of four tours of Australia between 1881-82 and 1887-88, on the first of which he was captain. He also arranged the first British Lions rugby trip, to Australasia in 1888. Perhaps galvanised by the riches the supposedly amateur Grace had accrued, Shaw championed the professionals' cause, and led a strike at Nottinghamshire in 1881, demanding contracts that would guarantee a benefit season, which for many was an essential means of survival. The dispute did not stop him later captaining Nottinghamshire – in an era when amateur leadership was the norm – and taking them to four straight titles.

The fragmented organisation of early Tests meant few players commanded regular places in national sides, but one who did was GEORGE ULYETT (1851–98) of Yorkshire. He toured Australia five times, played in 25 of England's first 33 matches, and was good enough to be selected for either his aggressive batting or round-arm fast bowling; he was also a fine fielder. He once hit a ball over the roof of the old pavilion at Lord's, and split Charles Bannerman's finger during his 165 in the first-ever Test, forcing him to retire hurt. In that game, the Melbourne *Argus* said Ulyett was "pitching his cannon shots… not more than halfway down". One of the few Tests he missed was Australia's first in England, in 1880, when he and others refused to play in protest at a recent riot during a match in Sydney – an unexpected stand for a fun-loving man nicknamed "Happy Jack".

He once hit a ball over the roof of the old pavilion at Lord's

In the period up to mid-1888, only three men scored more Test runs and only three took more wickets than Ulyett; overall, he gave 949 runs and 50 wickets to England's cause. Their first Test victory was aided by a pair of Ulyett fifties, and he bowled with genuine speed to rout Australia at Lord's in 1884, claiming seven for 36.

Billy Bates, a fellow Yorkshire professional, made 656 runs and took 50 wickets in 15 Tests between 1881 and 1887, but all those games took place in Australia. Bates lost out on selection at home to amateurs who were rarely free to tour. One such was ALLAN GIBSON STEEL (1858–1914), known by his initials because he had six brothers, three of whom played, like he did, for Lancashire. He was restricted by his work as a barrister to one tour of Australia, in 1882-83 (averaging, in the Tests, 45 with bat and 17 with ball), but played in England's first nine home Tests, contributing strongly in Ulyett's absence to a win in 1880, and leading them to a 3–0 trouncing of Australia in 1886. Like Ulyett, Steel was a genuine all-rounder – an attacking middle-order batsman

"FIVE CRICKETERS, 1864-88"

A. Shaw

G. Ulyett

A. G. Steel

W. L. Murdoch

F. R. Spofforth

Images: www.therogermanncollection.co.uk Design: Nigel Davies

and a leg-spinner who could turn it both ways; unlike Shaw, he was more interested in wickets than maidens.

Steel was educated at Marlborough and Cambridge, and in his first full season of first-class cricket, in 1878, claimed 164 wickets at 9.43 apiece. For eight years, he rivalled Grace as the most glamorous cricketer in England. As the journalist and broadcaster Alan Gibson – who always included Steel in his all-time XIs on account of his Christian names – later wrote: "He used to wear a pill-box cap, a lavish moustache, a shirt buttoned to the neck, and a swaggering sash – at least that was how he liked to be photographed, the pattern of a Victorian gentleman/cricketer."

In 1884, Steel became the first to score Test centuries in both England and Australia, as well as the first to score a Test century at Lord's, where he has pride of place at the top of the honours board. His record with the ball was less remarkable in Tests (29 wickets at 20) than in first-class cricket (789 at under 15). But as late as 1926, the historian H. S. Altham stated: "Even today he must be written down as the best leg-break bowler in history."

After the last of Steel's 13 England appearances, in 1888, only one batsman had scored more Test runs at a better average – WILLIAM LLOYD MURDOCH (1854–1911). Armed with a small physique, quick footwork and stylish off-side strokes, Billy Murdoch was the outstanding Australian batsman of his era, a prolific accumulator on good pitches – his 211 on a flat'un at The Oval in 1884 was Test cricket's first double-century, and its highest score until 1903 – but technically good enough to cope in all conditions. He was the nation's champion, and it was his run-out that triggered that riot in Sydney. "He always thought he was going to make a century," said C. B. Fry. "At least he did not think he was *not* going to, no matter whether he had a month of minute scores behind him."

He fell out with the authorities over gate receipts

Murdoch made 153 in the first Test ever played in England, in 1880, and scored more than 1,300 first-class runs on each of three subsequent visits. He led Australia on all of them, and was the first successfully to combine captaincy with consistent personal performances. A qualified solicitor, he gave up serious cricket after marrying into a mining family in the mid-1880s, having fallen out with the Australian authorities over the share of gate receipts awarded to players. But he was lured back to lead the 1890 Ashes trip. He became a close friend of Grace, and joined an English tour of South Africa in 1891-92, appearing in one match now deemed of Test status.

Murdoch played in 16 of Australia's first 17 Tests. The only one he missed was the very first, when his omission – as possible wicketkeeper – prompted Australia's best bowler to withdraw his services. FREDERICK ROBERT SPOFFORTH (1853–1926) was without question the greatest Test bowler of this period, and a key figure as Australia challenged England's notion of supremacy.

Fred Spofforth began as an underarm bowler, but changed after watching the English cricketers on their 1863-64 tour. After his boycott of the inaugural

Test, he took four wickets in the Second. In 1878, he caused a sensation by claiming ten as the Australians dismissed MCC twice in a day at Lord's, for 33 and 19. He would henceforth be known as The Demon. Injury prevented him from playing in the 1880 Test, but in 1882 he bowled Australia to their famous win at The Oval after England – including Grace, Ulyett and Steel – had been left 85 to win. Incensed by Grace's devious run-out of Sammy Jones, who had left his crease to repair a divot, Spofforth urged his team on with the words: "Boys, this thing can be done." And he saw that it was, taking seven for 44 to clinch victory by seven runs.

A bank clerk who later became a tea merchant, Spofforth was essentially a medium-pacer from 1878, but he was a lean 6ft 3in and bowled with such skilful intensity that he struck dread into many batsmen. About two-thirds of his 853 first-class wickets were taken on five tours of England. He dismissed Grace 20 times, took the first Test hat-trick and, at the end of his last Test in January 1887, had picked up more wickets (94 at 18 each) than anyone.

Spofforth and Murdoch both eventually settled in England and, like the three Englishmen, played beyond the advent of the Cricketers of the Year. Ulyett and Steel appeared in their final county games in 1893. Spofforth, who turned out occasionally for Derbyshire and in festival matches, played his last first-class match in 1897, as did Shaw. Murdoch, who qualified for and captained Sussex, enjoyed a fine season in that year, when he scored 1,283 runs and led the county to sixth in what was now a properly constituted Championship of 14 teams. He might have been an imaginative inclusion among a Five, but *Wisden* – which had yet to pick an overseas county player – ignored his claims. No longer.

Simon Wilde is cricket correspondent of The Sunday Times *and editor of* Wisden Cricketers of the Year 1889–2013, *to be published in October 2013.*

WHAT EDITING WISDEN MEANT TO ME

A cottage industry

John Woodcock (1981–86)

Almost from the first moment I could read, I seem to have had a copy of *Wisden* at my bedside, and could never be separated from it as a cricket writer. But the thought of editing it had never occurred to me – until the seed was planted in the Long Room at Lord's at the wedding reception of Brian Johnston's daughter, nine days after Norman Preston, the Almanack's tenth editor, had died. Also at the reception was the managing editor of the then publishers, Queen Anne Press; the idea was floated, and things moved on from there.

That I managed to do the job at the same time as being the cricket correspondent of *The Times* was due to two people – Graeme Wright, who was to become my successor, and Christine Forrest, a neighbour of his and as dependable as she was receptive. Technically and administratively they were indispensable. For the first time in its history, *Wisden* was a cottage industry, operating from under my thatched roof in the Hampshire village of Longparish.

As the voice of cricket, it imposes on the editor a singular responsibility. If that sounds self-important, nothing that Sir Donald Bradman said in his letter to me on my appointment made me think otherwise: there was no doubting his affection and respect for the great work, nor the delight he took from his own collection.

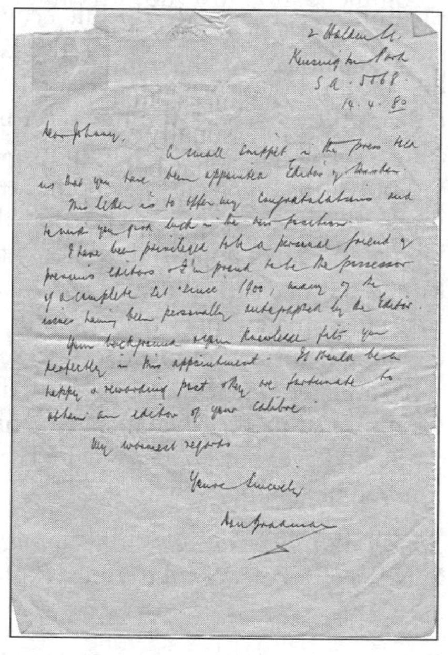

Dear Johnny,

A small snippet in the press told us that you have been appointed Editor of Wisden.

This letter is to offer my congratulations and to wish you good luck in the new position.

I have been privileged to be a personal friend of previous editors & I'm proud to be the possessor of a complete set since 1900, many of the issues having been personally autographed by the Editor.

Your background & your knowledge fits you perfectly in this appointment. It should be a happy & rewarding post & they are fortunate to obtain an editor of your calibre.

My warmest regards

Yours Sincerely

Don Bradman

It must still be fun choosing the Five Cricketers of the Year and keeping the cognoscenti guessing while about it, and the annual encyclical (dubbed Notes by the Editor) remains the one universally quoted cricket article of the year. But if offered the job again today, I'd know I would not be up to it. For one thing, like old John Wisden, I don't have an email; for another, I might submit to the need to put Twenty20 cricket in its place, and that would never do.

Graeme Wright (1987–92, 2001–02)

Being editor of *Wisden* was never my ambition, however much I was enjoying my involvement in the Almanack as assistant editor, first to Norman Preston, then to John Woodcock, and as the director of John Wisden & Co responsible for publishing it. However, the editorship, coming on John Woodcock's recommendation in 1986, was an honour not easily declined.

From a practical viewpoint, it enabled me to continue streamlining the day-to-day systems of the Almanack and, while meeting demands to build the value of the business, maintain a sensible cover price. What I might have wanted to do personally was very much secondary to what was best for the book. It was not what being editor meant to *me*, therefore, but what *Wisden* meant to others – not only current readers but readers in the future.

It seemed to me that the Almanack served manifold purposes. It was a book of record as well as records, it was literary and, most importantly, it had become an institution. Within the game, and indeed beyond the world of cricket, *Wisden* was trusted. Its continuity, its independence and the balance of its writing had won it the rare cachet of integrity. Posited between cricket's political and economic byplay and its passionate grassroots support, *Wisden Cricketers' Almanack* had established itself in the public consciousness as a voice of reason and the champion of everything, real and mythical, that cricket is meant to represent.

Maintaining this integrity and promoting the Almanack were what being editor of *Wisden* meant to me. There was nothing egotistical about it, that's for sure. But it was an immensely enjoyable time, thanks to the support, company and friendship of everyone involved in cricket, particularly the writers worldwide, but no less the administrators who, I see looking back, all too often bore the brunt of my Notes.

Matthew Engel (1993–2000, 2004–07)

Fallible memory suggests I took the call on the Bakelite phone we had received as a retro wedding present. It always crackled. But I was convinced I heard Graeme Wright ask if I wanted to be editor of *Wisden*, an idea that had never previously crossed my mind. I said yes instantly. Well, you would, wouldn't you? I never regretted it, even when wrestling with the Minor Counties before an icy December dawn, or enduring a particularly ghastly board meeting.

The book was on the up: John Woodcock had beefed up its cricketing and literary heft; Graeme had transformed its internal systems. But I sensed there was a fascinating challenge: making sure the book kept pace with the changing game, while remaining true to itself.

That much I hope we achieved in my first term. I made a comeback because I perceived a second challenge: adjusting to the fact that, in my three-year

Patrick Eagar

Matthew Engel, John Woodcock and Graeme Wright.

absence, the internet had gone from novelty to necessity. This task was thwarted by decisions taken well over my head, and remains ongoing.

The title "editor of *Wisden*" opened doors far beyond cricket. Within the game, the job ensured my opinions were always heard and sometimes listened to; now and again they even made a difference. It gave me a seat in the Test match press box, but the freedom to slope off. More than anything, I loved wandering round the county grounds, watching, enjoying the crack, and scrawling the odd note, that just might – the next April – blossom into a Note.

Mostly, the task was internal, but I loved that too: good writers wanted to be in *Wisden*, and it was a joy reeling them in. There was pleasure to be had even on a micro-level. I have spent years being absurdly proud that I changed *Wisden* house style for numbers so that, more elegantly, we used "ten" in text instead of "10". I have just been told by *Wisden's* deputy editor, Harriet Monkhouse, that I didn't actually do that. Having Harriet to correct my false memories was a special delight. I had a terrific team, and we laughed a lot.

Tim de Lisle (2003)

Editing *Wisden* meant a lot, despite, or because of, doing it only once. It meant driving a classic car, and feeling even greater respect for the engineers. (To the long-suffering permanent staff, it was probably more like an episode of *Yes, Minister*.) It meant receiving an email from a contributor saying, "Hope you've enjoyed your year of being George Lazenby." It meant being infamous for 15 minutes, when we announced that *Wisden* would have its first cover photograph. To Ian Wooldridge of the *Daily Mail*, this was "scarcely less heretical than slapping a picture of Judas Iscariot on future editions of the Holy Bible".

It meant standing on the shoulders of giants. John Woodcock had brought wisdom to the Almanack, Graeme Wright had widened its horizons, and Matthew Engel had added wit and waspishness. But there was still something missing. Ever since the social revolution of the 1960s, *Wisden* had been out of tune with the times, a curious fate for a yearbook.

We tried to make it brighter, livelier and more penetrable. We took the best section of the book, the front, and doubled it. We encouraged subscribers to order another copy for a tenner, for their son or nephew – or daughter or niece. And we made sure the cover reflected the previous year in cricket rather than just the ways of previous *Wisdens*.

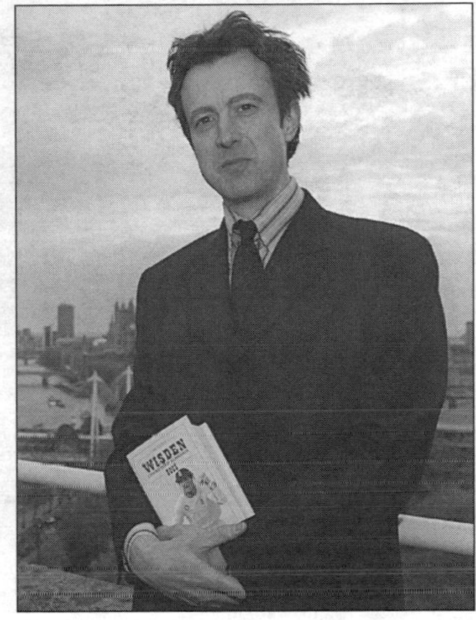

Paul Gilham, Getty Images

Tim de Lisle.

The designer was Nigel Davies, who has done more than anyone to make cricket publishing visually literate. He left most of the furniture in place, from the stumpy stature to the funny old font. The cover star was Michael Vaughan, in a shot chosen for its joy. It was black and white, to avoid clashing with the perennial primrose. Giles Smith in the *Daily Telegraph* said I had tried "to bring the Almanack kicking and screaming into the 1920s".

Scyld Berry (2008–2011)

In my four years, I tried to give cricketers more of a voice. I brought in the records of every Test player, so those of the past could be heard; and asked former players to write, when it was not the time for reporters to report; and had county players interviewed to follow them through their season. *Wisden* had always been strong on the what, where and when; less so on the how and why, perhaps because most editors had not played the game themselves. And I tried to do what it said on the tin, to make it a *cricketers'* almanack, as well as a cricket followers'. That is how it started when John Wisden, the former Sussex professional bowler, provided a player's view.

I also tried to make it the home of creative cricket writing by introducing longer feature articles than had been known before, insofar as the budget allowed. The revisionist assessment of Sir Donald Bradman on the centenary of his birth was the first; another the article on the 1911 All-India tour of England, the most extraordinary of all cricket tours, which took three years to come to print. And I tried to give Test cricket the primacy it deserves by commissioning eminent former players from various countries to act as selectors and pick their World XI for each year.

Lawrence Booth and Scyld Berry.

Many of the most interesting aspects of cricket have yet to be scientifically explained. As the batsman hits a cover-drive off a fast bowler, what goes on in his brain, because it is a physical impossibility for the untrained brain to react in time? Why do bowlers, often left-arm spinners, get the yips? So much remains to be unearthed. The Test-match game is the thing, and what the ball does is its essence.

Lawrence Booth (2012–)

I picked up my first *Wisden* in 1990, having just turned 15, from Blackwell's, Broad Street, Oxford. It cost £15.50 (you've got to love the 50p), which probably made it the most expensive book I had ever bought. But until I'd stumbled across old copies of the Almanack in my school library a couple of years earlier – Mr Noll, the head of history who doubled up as librarian, was a cricket nut – I hadn't even known it existed. Now I was hooked. And if anyone had told me I'd be editing the thing a couple of decades later, I'd have questioned their sanity.

The job was just too implausible to have counted as an adolescent dream and, when the possibility cropped up out of the blue, I may have kept my composure. Matthew Engel, whose editorship I had been lucky enough to work under, once compared editing *Wisden* to a tropical garden – so much pruning and chopping. Wonder of wonders, I'd been allowed in to smell the orchids. Thanks to Scyld Berry, the place was pristine.

What have I had to do in the first two years? Maintain the book's exacting standards, of course, which – it turns out – does not happen overnight. But also extend its relevance beyond its pages. Our website now bears some of the strain. Facebook and Twitter play their part too; Sydney Pardon would have been a formidable tweeter.

Above all, the internet means we have to fine-tune the relationship in *Wisden* between words and numbers. It's always struck me how many people think of it as a book of stats, when it contains so many interesting stories too. Changing perceptions is one task. Another is to remind myself that the age of instant comment still has room for the more considered perspective – perhaps more than ever before.

THE CRICKET REPORTING AGENCY

Boy! Copy! Telegram!

MURRAY HEDGCOCK

No celebration of 150 editions of *Wisden* would be complete without acknowledging the major role played in its life by the Cricket Reporting Agency. The agency were equally at home in the scullery and at high table, overseeing the Almanack's editorial production from 1887 until 1965, and providing seven editors until 1980. They are *Wisden*'s unsung heroes.

Charles Pardon founded the CRA on April 17, 1880, taking with him staff from the Sporting Press Agency, which had employed him as a reporter but folded following the death a year earlier of the owner, George Kelly King. There were various homes for the new agency. The first reference in *Wisden* came at the end of the 1891 preface, which placed them at 112 Fleet Street. Later, they moved down the road to No. 85, where they were a tenant of the Press Association at Byron House, until it was demolished in 1935. The new building would be occupied by Reuters, though the CRA (and PA) – after a temporary spell round the corner at 23 St Bride Street – returned to the new premises to rent office space.

Agency reporting is traditionally factual, straightforward and reliable, qualities which were to characterise the early style of *Wisden* itself. But there was also a financial imperative not to waste words: the length of agency reports determined their cost, and press telegrams were not cheap. The charge was one shilling for every 75 words transmitted between 9am and 6pm, and for every 100 words between 6pm and 9am.

Press reports were originally sent from the local post office or, increasingly, from a dedicated telegraph office at the ground itself. A row of small uniformed messenger boys sat at the back of the press box, chattering animatedly as they waited to be despatched with newspaper copy on a stentorian shout of "Boy!", "Copy!" or "Telegram!" But this was no simple task either. *Wisden 1893* carried a study of facilities for journalists, written by a future editor, Stewart Caine, who described the shortcomings of some counties: "When telegraph wires were extended to the ground, no effort was made to place the press box and the telegraph office in proximity."

Overseas scores for early *Wisdens* were taken initially from Australian and other newspapers, arriving in the UK many weeks or months after the games had finished. It was not until 1928-29 that a CRA staff man was sent to cover an MCC tour. The reports by Sydney Southerton, another editor-to-be, on the 4–1 defeat of Australia were well received, lively and forthright, and in 1932-33 Southerton was meant to go again. But after some debate with PA, Reuters insisted on sending their own man: Gilbert Mant, a hard-working 30-year-old Australian on the London staff, who had reported little cricket, and now kept strictly to his brief to refrain from comment.

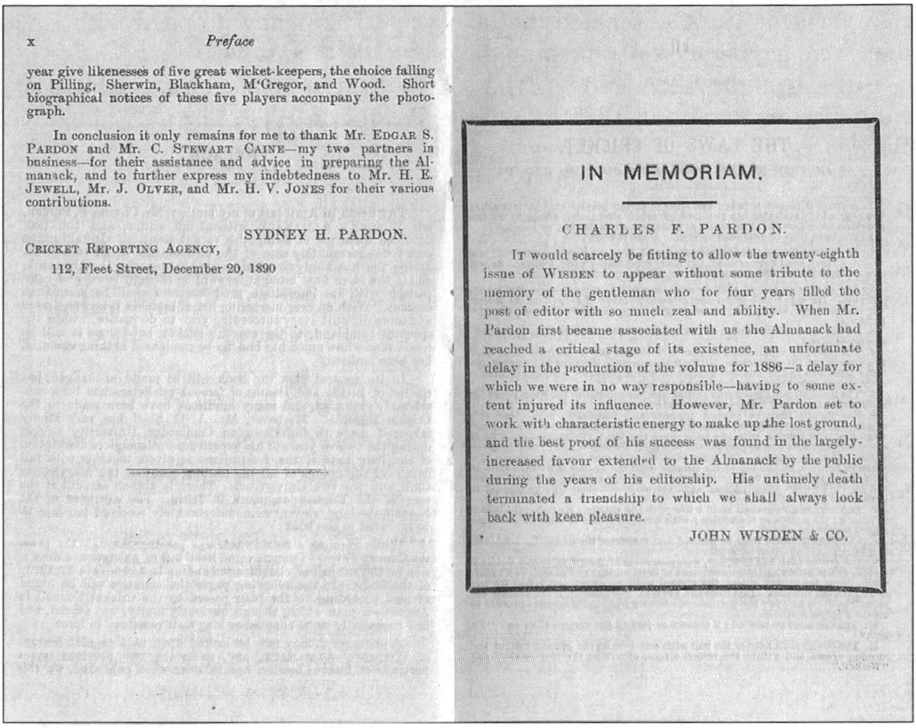

x *Preface*

year give likenesses of five great wicket-keepers, the choice falling on Pilling, Sherwin, Blackham, M'Gregor, and Wood. Short biographical notices of these five players accompany the photograph.

In conclusion it only remains for me to thank Mr. Edgar S. Pardon and Mr. C. Stewart Caine—my two partners in business—for their assistance and advice in preparing the Almanack, and to further express my indebtedness to Mr. H. E. Jewell, Mr. J. Olver, and Mr. H. V. Jones for their various contributions.

SYDNEY H. PARDON.

Cricket Reporting Agency,
112, Fleet Street, December 20, 1890

IN MEMORIAM.

CHARLES F. PARDON.

It would scarcely be fitting to allow the twenty-eighth issue of Wisden to appear without some tribute to the memory of the gentleman who for four years filled the post of editor with so much zeal and ability. When Mr. Pardon first became associated with us the Almanack had reached a critical stage of its existence, an unfortunate delay in the production of the volume for 1886—a delay for which we were in no way responsible—having to some extent injured its influence. However, Mr. Pardon set to work with characteristic energy to make up the lost ground, and the best proof of his success was found in the largely-increased favour extended to the Almanack by the public during the years of his editorship. His untimely death terminated a friendship to which we shall always look back with keen pleasure.

JOHN WISDEN & CO.

First and last: the spread of the 1891 *Wisden* that acknowledges the role of the CRA, and announces the death of Charles Pardon.

Sixty years later, Mant wrote of his dilemma over England's tactics. Saying he was "sickened" by Bill Woodfull's injury in the Adelaide Test, he added: "I was in a hopeless catch-22 situation… If I showed the slightest sign of taking sides about Bodyline, or suggesting it was a threat to cricket, my reports would be censored, and I would probably be replaced. That was when I felt that Sydney Southerton should have been there instead of me. Southerton, writing under a byline, would probably have been able to speak his mind about the general atmosphere… So, reluctantly, I joined Jack Hobbs [reporting via a ghostwriter for the *News Chronicle* and *Star*] in not rocking the boat… I was to some extent leading the British public astray. It has been on my conscience ever since." Southerton was to make a scathing attack on Bodyline, sight unseen, in his editor's Notes in 1934, which leaves one to wonder how differently the series might have been presented to England had he, not Mant, reported from Australia.

The CRA sent journalists on tour more regularly after the war. In 1955, one of them, Reg Hayter – the agency's chief cricket reporter – went on to launch his own agency, a high-pressure training school for many sportswriters who graduated to Fleet Street. But the CRA sent no one to South Africa in 1964-65 and – with their future in some doubt – they were taken over by PA in 1965. Terry Cooper, who was signed by the CRA in 1962, married one of the agency's secretaries, and later reported on cricket and rugby for PA until his retirement in 1999, explained the takeover: "The penny dropped with PA – they were paying us for something they could do themselves."

But it was the CRA editors who set the firmest stamp on the Almanack, from Charles Pardon in 1887 to Norman Preston in 1980. The only non-CRA *Wisden* editor in that time was Haddon Whitaker, who presided over four Almanacks during the Second World War. Pardon himself worked on only four editions, but longevity was generally a hallmark: his brother Sydney worked on 39, Caine 47, Southerton at least 32, Wilfrid Brookes 15, Hubert Preston 51 (he missed the 1916–1920 editions while on military service), and his son Norman 47. Between them, the seven CRA men edited 90 *Wisdens*.

Because of the influence exerted on the agency from their foundation by Charles and his two brothers, the CRA were often known simply as Pardon's. The trio had tackled their new roles with youthful enthusiasm (Charles was 30, Sydney 25, Edgar 20), and were rewarded in 1886 when Wisden's owner, Henry Luff, invited the CRA to compile the following year's Almanack, with Charles as editor. So began the association that would sustain Wisden for nine decades. When Charles died, aged 40 – Edgar would die eight years later – Sydney stepped in and, over the next 35 editions, forged the Almanack's reputation as cricket's most authoritative voice. On his death in 1925, *Wisden* described him as "the man who shaped the Almanack into the publication it is today".

He collapsed after proposing the toast at the Ferrets Club dinner

The CRA also campaigned for a more satisfactory method of deciding the County Championship than simply awarding it to the team suffering fewest defeats – the method used from 1865 to 1886. The agency proposed one point for a win, and half a point for a draw. But this produced its own problems, notably in 1889, when Surrey, Lancashire and Nottinghamshire all finished on $10^1/_2$. Reacting promptly, the counties and MCC devised a new system which, with adjustments, still applies today.

After the Pardons came Caine. He had been at the CRA from the word go, was close to the Pardons, and edited Wisden's *Rugby Football Almanack* for the three years that it ran from 1924 to 1926. Sydney Southerton was the son of the round-arm slow bowler James Southerton, who was the oldest player to make a Test debut – at 49 years 119 days at Melbourne in 1876-77, in Test cricket's inaugural match – and the first Test cricketer to die, a little over three years later. Sydney was working as a ship's steward when he met Jack Blackham's 1893 Australians aboard the *Liguria* en route to England. He was engaged as scorer for the tour, and Sydney Pardon, impressed by his work, employed him at the end of the season as the CRA's statistician. Widely known as "Figure Fiend", Southerton later became a partner, editing *Wisden* in 1934 and 1935. His end was sudden: at the age of 60, he collapsed and died after proposing the toast to "Cricket" at the Ferrets Club dinner at The Oval in 1935.

In fact, five of the seven CRA men to edit *Wisden* died while still in the job. The exceptions were Wilfrid Brookes, who resigned abruptly after the last of his four Almanacks in 1939, having overseen the major revamp of the 75th edition, and was hardly heard of again until his obituary was published in

Wisden 1956; and Hubert Preston, who did not edit the first of his eight *Wisdens* until he was 74 – comfortably the oldest starting age for any of its editors.

The Preston dynasty had begun in 1944, when Hubert was appointed editor. He learned his trade at the *Manchester Guardian's* London office and had a brief spell farming in Canada. He joined the CRA in 1895, became a partner in 1920, and did not retire until 1951. By then, the CRA had four partners: the two Prestons, plus Ebenezer Eden, who was credited in 50 Almanacks up to 1975, and Harry Gee, who worked on the 1934–1971 editions. Leslie Smith, who first contributed to *Wisden* in 1935, was never a partner, but played a central role. He died in 2011, aged 97.

CRA stalwart and editor of *Wisden:* Sydney Pardon.

Norman Preston, who joined the agency in 1933, succeeded his father in 1952, and would guide *Wisden* through 29 editions. Following Hubert's death in 1960, Neville Cardus wrote in *Wisden* that he was "with [Sydney] Pardon and Stewart Caine, the most courteous and best-mannered man ever to be seen in a press box on a cricket ground". Preston, Eden and Gee all accepted positions at PA after the merger in 1965, but when Preston retired in 1968, *Wisden's* association with PA came to an end, though he continued to edit the Almanack as a freelance until his death in 1980.

Today, the contribution of the agency to cricket reporting is commemorated by the Sydney Pardon press box at The Oval. On the first floor of the new OCS Stand, opened in 2005, it houses up to 70 journalists – all heirs of the pioneers of the Cricket Reporting Agency.

Murray Hedgcock is a London-based Australian journalist who came to England in 1953, hoping to see Australia retain the Ashes. They did not – but he has remained loyal and optimistic at every succeeding series.

Additional research: Christopher Lane

BEHIND THE SCENES AT WISDEN

A production in five acts

ROBERT WINDER

Wisden has endured bombing and bankruptcy – but the Almanack never missed a year. Not all its heroes have been cricketers, however, and not all have been honoured or thanked. Here are five men who, inadvertently or otherwise, helped shape Wisden.

When John Wisden died in 1884, single and childless, **Henry Luff** acquired his company. As well as publishing the Almanack, John Wisden & Co were primarily a sports-equipment retailer, with a shop near Leicester Square: its spirit lives on in the red tiling above a fast-food joint in Cranbourn Street. But without Luff, the book might have folded. There was keen competition (from, among others, James Lillywhite), and the 1886 edition nearly failed to come out altogether, eventually emerging in December with a sheepish apology: "Messrs John Wisden & Co desire to express their regret at the delay which has occurred in its publication – a circumstance due to the long-continued indisposition of the Compiler [the editor, George West]." Only decades later, when *Wisden* had grown into a collector's item, would the importance of not skipping an edition become clear: Luff's determination had helped preserve the continuity on which the value of the whole set depended.

Luff strengthened the sports company by making it a manufacturer, and rejuvenated the book by handing it to a new generation. The Pardon brothers ran the Cricket Reporting Agency, which placed journalists at matches to submit copy to newspapers. They were responding to the same technical advances that had played midwife to *Wisden* itself: wireless telegraphy and industrial-age printing. In 1887, Charles Pardon became editor; his brother Sydney, younger by five and a half years, took over in 1891, and remained until 1925. In availing himself of this fresh blood, Luff – who died in 1910 – placed the Almanack in the hands of a dynasty that turned it into an institution.

Charles Pardon edited only four editions, but his third – in 1889 – launched a feature that would become an essential part of the Almanack's appeal. The Cricketers of the Year was inspired by another new technology (photography), and Pardon included medallion portraits of "Six Great Bowlers", provided by prominent photographers E. Hawkins & Company of Brighton. *Wisden* went on to make an annual award to the season's leading players, later prompting Sydney Pardon to declare that this was "proving so acceptable… there is no likelihood of the Almanack ever again being published without one".

This showed that *Wisden* was not only a careful keeper of scores and records, and a stern Victorian preacher when it came to Laws and etiquette, but a wholehearted celebrant of individual feats. This may have cut across the classic ideology of team spirit, but in reality it was a central part of cricket's

Sport & General, PA Photos

A new chapter: Ken Medlock (*fourth right*) hands the gleaming Wisden Trophy to MCC president Lord Nugent at Lord's in 1963. At the presentation are MCC's curator Diana Rait Kerr, assistant secretary (cricket) Donald Carr, Nugent, assistant secretary (administration) Jim Dunbar, club superintendent Dick Gaby, secretary Billy Griffith, Medlock, former *Wisden* editor Haddon Whitaker, *Wisden* editor Norman Preston and Co-operative Wholesale Society secretary Jack Taylor.

fabric. The quality of the images meant that "the faces will be easily recognised" – no small matter at a time when cricket followers only rarely glimpsed their heroes. Sydney Pardon would go on to be the grandest editor of them all (for 35 years), but Charles's innovation has been a *Wisden* hallmark ever since – a little touch of Oscar in the spring.

When in 1938 John Wisden & Co appointed Whitaker's – owners of another famous almanack – as publishers of *Wisden*, **Haddon Whitaker** took charge. Along with *Wisden's* own editor, Wilfrid Brookes, he instigated a thorough overhaul, introducing many elements – such as the yellow cover and the wood engraving by Eric Ravilious – that would become permanent. At the outbreak of the Second World War, Brookes resigned, and Whitaker became editor. As during the previous war, there was little cricket to describe; inevitably, the main event was an expanded Obituary. And against a background of strict paper rationing, wartime sales shrank to barely 4,000 a year.

On December 30, 1940, the Whitaker's office near St Paul's was destroyed in the worst night of the Blitz. Yet somehow *Wisden*, as per the motto of the time, kept calm and carried on. In 1943, Whitaker appointed Hubert Preston, a long-time *Wisden* aide, as editor for the 1944 edition, and thus the Almanack

WISDEN – A TIMELINE

1826 John Wisden (JW) is born in Brighton.

1850 JW takes ten wickets in an innings for North v South at Lord's. All are bowled – still a unique feat in first-class cricket. He also sets up in business, selling cricket gear in Leamington.

1852 JW and Jemmy Dean form the United All-England Eleven.

1855 JW opens his "cricket and cigar" shop at 2 New Coventry Street, London.

1859 JW plays in the USA and Canada on the first overseas tour by an English team.

1863 JW retires from the game.

1864 JW publishes his first *Cricketer's Almanack*. The editor for the first 16 editions is W. H. Knight.

1870 The title is changed to *John Wisden's Cricketers' Almanack* (the second apostrophe moved in 1869).

1872 Wisden's shop moves to 21 Cranbourn Street, London; it remains open until 1928.

1880 The first of seven editions edited by George West.

1884 JW dies in his flat above the Cranbourn Street shop. The business is bought from his estate by Henry Luff.

1887 The first of four editions edited by Charles Pardon, and the first to have its content compiled by the Cricket Reporting Agency.

1889 *Wisden* selects its first Cricketers of the Year ("Six Great Bowlers").

1891 The first of 35 editions edited by Sydney Pardon.

1896 The first hardback edition. JW & Co open their second London shop – in Great Newport Street.

1901 Sydney Pardon starts "Notes by the Editor".

1910 Henry Luff dies. His son, Ernest, takes over the business.

1911 JW & Co receive a royal warrant to certify their "appointment as Athletic Outfitters to the King" (George V).

1914 JW & Co are incorporated as a limited company with their shares divided among several investors.

1920 JW & Co merge with Duke & Son, a sports manufacturer specialising in cricket balls.

1923 JW & Co publish their first *Rugby Football Almanack*. It lasts three editions.

1924 The Almanack exceeds 1,000 pages for first time.

1926 The first of eight editions edited by Stewart Caine.

1934 The first of two edited by Sydney Southerton.

1936 The first of four edited by Wilfrid Brookes.

1938 J. Whitaker & Sons Ltd ("Whitaker's") become *Wisden's* publisher and immediately conduct a thorough overhaul. Changes include dropping "John" from the title, the introduction of yellow linen covers for the limp version (technically, it was not a paperback), and adding Eric Ravilious's wood engraving of top-hatted cricketers to the front cover.

1939 Because of failings in the equipment business, JW & Co go into receivership.

1940 The first of four editions edited by Haddon Whitaker. The Notes in all four are written by Raymond Robertson-Glasgow. Whitaker's offices are destroyed in the Blitz.

1943 JW & Co are bought out of receivership by the Co-operative Wholesale Society.

1944 Wisden's factory in Mortlake is destroyed by a bomb. Although still published by Whitaker's, *Wisden* is moved to the Sporting Handbooks imprint, in which JW & Co have a half share. The first of eight editions edited by Hubert Preston.

1952 The first of 29 edited by Hubert Preston's son, Norman.

1957 Whitaker's buy JW & Co's half share in Sporting Handbooks, who continue to publish *Wisden* under licence.

1960 Facsimiles of early editions are produced for the first time.
1961 JW & Co amalgamate their Duke and Wisden cricket-ball manufacturing business with those of Gray-Nicolls, Surridge and Ives in a joint venture company, Tonbridge Sports Industries. The Great Newport Street shop is closed.
1963 The 100th edition is marked by the introduction of the Wisden Trophy, to be contested in all future Test series between England and West Indies.
1965 The CRA merge with the Press Association. The hardback version has a dust jacket for the first time.
1968 Norman Preston retires from PA, thus ending the PA/CRA editorial arrangement with the Almanack, which had been responsible for 82 editions. Preston continues to edit *Wisden* on a freelance contract.
1970 Grays of Cambridge Ltd purchase JW & Co (including their stake in Tonbridge Sports Industries) from the Co-operative Wholesale Society.
1979 Queen Anne Press (a division of Macdonald and Jane's Publishers which, in 1982, came under Robert Maxwell's control) succeed Sporting Handbooks as *Wisden*'s licensed publishers. The magazine *Wisden Cricket Monthly* is launched, published under licence from JW & Co.
1981 The first of six editions edited by John Woodcock.
1984 The centenary of John Wisden's death is commemorated with the unveiling of a new headstone for his grave in London's Brompton Cemetery.
1985 McCorquodale plc purchase JW & Co from Grays and re establish JW & Co as *Wisden*'s own publisher.
1986 Grays of Cambridge buy back 50% of JW & Co to become joint owners with McCorquodale (who are later acquired by Bowater plc).
1987 The first of eight editions edited by Graeme Wright.
1988 Colour photographs are included for the first time.
1993 The first of 12 editions edited by Matthew Engel. Paul Getty purchases JW & Co from Grays and Bowater. The combined total of pages in all editions exceeds 100,000.
1995 A limited-edition leatherbound version is introduced.
1998 An Australian *Wisden Almanack* is launched, lasting eight editions.
1999 The (British) Almanack exceeds 1,500 pages for first time.
2000 *Wisden* names Five Cricketers of the Century: Don Bradman, Garry Sobers, Jack Hobbs, Shane Warne and Viv Richards.
2001 Wright returns as editor, while Engel takes a sabbatical. Wisden Online is launched.
2003 The only edition edited by Tim de Lisle features *Wisden's* first cover photograph and names its first Book of the Year. JW & Co buy *The Cricketer* magazine (which is merged with *Wisden Cricket Monthly* to form *The Wisden Cricketer*) and the website Cricinfo (into which Wisden Online is integrated). Paul Getty dies. His son, Mark, takes control of JW & Co.
2004 Engel returns as editor. *Wisden* introduces a new annual accolade: the Leading Cricketer in the World.
2006 A large-format version is introduced. Across all formats, *Wisden* sells over 50,000 copies.
2007 Cricinfo is sold to ESPN; *The Wisden Cricketer* to BSkyB.
2008 The first of four editions edited by Scyld Berry. The Wisden Schools Cricketer of the Year award is introduced. Bloomsbury Publishing plc purchase JW & Co from Mark Getty.
2009 Claire Taylor is the first woman to be named a Cricketer of the Year.
2011 *The Shorter Wisden* ebook is introduced.
2012 The first edition edited by Lawrence Booth. The 2013 – and first – edition of *Wisden India Almanack* is launched in late December.
2013 The 150th edition is published.

Compiled by Christopher Lane

entered a new era. It was the start, too, of a second *Wisden* dynasty: his son Norman took over in 1952 and edited the book until his death in 1980. But if it hadn't been for Haddon Whitaker, they might never have got the chance. With pleasing modesty, Whitaker later referred to himself as an "interloper" among the distinguished line of cricket reporters who came before and after.

As the chief engineer of the Co-operative Wholesale Society's retail empire, **Ken Medlock** was cut from a different cloth. In 1960, he was elected to the main board. A keen club cricketer for Birch Vale in the Peak District, he was surprised to see on the agenda of his debut board meeting in Manchester a proposal to dissolve John Wisden & Co, which the Co-op had bought out of receivership in 1943. Even though he was the new boy on the team, Medlock took a deep breath. "We must be out of our minds," he said. "Don't you realise we are talking about liquidating the most famous name in cricket?"

After a flutter of consternation, Medlock arrived at the John Wisden & Co works in Penshurst, Kent, where he found elderly craftsmen and a dispirited management. He moved fast, replacing staff and streamlining product lines until, a decade later, it could be sold to Grays of Cambridge. None of this concerned the Almanack directly, whose contract with Whitaker's assured its immediate future. But Medlock's influence was profound. In 1963, the Almanack's centenary year, he and his friend Sir Learie Constantine gained permission from MCC to award the Wisden Trophy to the winners of England–West Indies series. As Medlock's trophy celebrated its 50th birthday, the man himself (born in 1914) was not far off his 100th.

At the height of his bad-boy fame, Mick Jagger did not always boast of his fondness for cricket, but he spent hours following it on television at home in Chelsea. Even when he visited his reclusive American neighbour, **Paul Getty**, he would – as Getty later put it – insist on watching "this ridiculous game".

Getty's own life had been stalked by tragedy. In 1971, his second wife, Talitha Pol, died from an overdose, and two years later the older of two sons from his first marriage, John Paul Getty III, was kidnapped in Italy. When the initial ransom demand was refused, the boy's right ear was hacked off and sent to a newspaper in Rome. But the "ridiculous game" to which Jagger had introduced the older Getty would at least, in time, play a consoling part in his life.

Armed with a colossal inheritance from his family's oil interests, Getty went on to befriend cricket's leading personalities, finance new architecture at Lord's, and build his own, Gatsbyish, ground at his Wormsley home in the Chilterns. In 1993, when *Wisden* was seeking a new owner, he stepped in. It did not need saving, as such: it was a profitable enterprise in its own right. But it did need a devoted and steady proprietor – and it found one. Under Getty's wing (and the editorship of Matthew Engel) the Almanack grew in prestige as the game entered the electronic age. Jagger's oblique place in the story reminds us that cricket's relationship with rock music long predates the snatches of "Another one bites the dust" that blast across today's Twenty20 grounds.

Robert Winder is author of The Little Wonder: A History of Wisden.

WISDEN'S TOP-HATTED GENTS

Engraved in the memory

RUPERT BATES

They were never honoured as Cricketers of the Year. But a batsman and a wicketkeeper – both nameless, both virtually faceless – have adorned *Wisden* now for 76 springs. The wood engraving of the Victorian duo in top hats is one of the sport's most charming and recognisable images. And yet cricket knows little of its creator.

Also celebrated for his watercolours, book illustrations, ceramics and lithography, Eric Ravilious was commissioned to produce the engraving by Robert Harling, the typographer asked to redesign the 1938 *Wisden*. Harling knew Ravilious had a "special enthusiasm for the game" – though no doubt his deep Wealdean Englishness and sense of tradition helped too – and wrote: "His engraving of mid-19th century batsman and wicketkeeper remains an ideal graphic introduction to one of England's most durable publications."

The engraving briefly lost its cover-star status in 2003, when a photograph of Michael Vaughan relegated it to the spine of the book's jacket, incurring the displeasure of some traditionalists. It was immediately restored to the cover in 2004, while staying on the spine as well. And so, for ten editions now, including this one, Ravilious's creation has been more visible than ever.

Educated at Eastbourne School of Art, he won a scholarship to the Royal College of Art. But Ravilious died in 1942 aged 39 when, as an official war artist and honorary captain in the Royal Marines, his plane was lost on a search-and-rescue mission off Iceland. And while it was clear he was never going to decorate *Wisden* through his on-field achievements, he did leave his indelible mark. In the words of cricket bookseller John McKenzie, the engraving "remains the face of *Wisden*".

> "The engraving remains the face of *Wisden*"

A preparatory sketch from a Ravilious scrapbook has another cricketer in the frame, dressed in top hat, waistcoat and bow tie, with a marquee in the background. Although he wrote many letters to family and friends, he appears never to have explained the inspiration behind the engraving. One theory is that he gained it from a pub sign in Sussex, the county in which he spent most of his life and which provided the backdrop to some of his greatest work, including watercolour landscapes of his beloved South Downs. The Cricketers Arms in Berwick, near Firle – a village where he spent much time – has a top-hatted Victorian batsman on its sign. And the one at the Bat and Ball Inn in Hambledon, admittedly some 60 miles away in Hampshire, also depicts a batsman and wicketkeeper.

But Anne Ullmann, Ravilious's daughter (he also had two sons), insists: "My father soaked up ideas for work wherever he went, but *never* copied –

Courtesy of the Fleece Press

Portrait of the young artist: Eric Ravilious.

and I don't believe for one minute that the design was a copy. He may have seen an inn sign with cricketers or, as the sketch suggests, he may have watched a match played in mid-19th century costume. Or he may just have been playing around with ideas for the engraving. But what remains is one hell of a cracking design, and I pray it may represent *Wisden* for many years to come."

Whatever the origin, we do know for certain that Ravilious played cricket, if at a lowly level. In 1935, he wrote of turning out for the Double Crown Club, a dining club for printers and book designers, against the village team at Castle Hedingham in Essex, where he lived for a while. He said the game went on "a bit too long for my liking and I began to get a little absent-minded in the deep field after tea". He made one not out in defeat, and bowled a few overs. "It all felt like being back at school, especially the trestle tea with slabs of bread and butter, and that wicked-looking cheap cake." He went on to record the comment of the Double Crown captain Francis Meynell that his bowling was "of erratic length, but promising, and that I should have been put on before. Think of the honour and glory there."

"It is, you might say, one of the pleasures of life, hitting a six"

In another game at Castle Hedingham, with his wife Tirzah (a talented artist herself) "in charge of the strawberries and cream", Ravilious talked of hitting three sixes. "It is, you might say, one of the pleasures of life, hitting a six."

Courtesy of the Ravilious family

Before they were famous: Ravilious's sketch suggests he considered including a third figure – and that the top hats, at least for the players, may have been an afterthought.

A shy man, but amusing and invariably cheerful, Ravilious enjoyed the Bohemian company of his artistic friends, who talked of his "Pan-like charm" and the sense that he was always "slightly somewhere else" – no doubt sketching in his head at fine leg, whistling "Better than a Nightingale" below his boater, oblivious to the ball heading his way. Yet it seems no other cricket theme danced on his easel or wood block. Instead, there is a rich and varied output of beautifully observed landscapes, street scenes, ceramic designs for Wedgwood – including a mug to commemorate the coronation of King George VI – and, in his last years, images of war. The *Daily Telegraph* called his death "the greatest artistic loss Britain suffered in the Second World War". And in 2011, the art critic of *The Observer*, Laura Cumming, called him "the lost genius of British art".

Ravilious saw only five of the Almanacks to carry his engraving. Yet his work – in many ways a distillation of Englishness – lives on.

Rupert Bates, a sports and property writer, is Eric Ravilious's great-nephew.

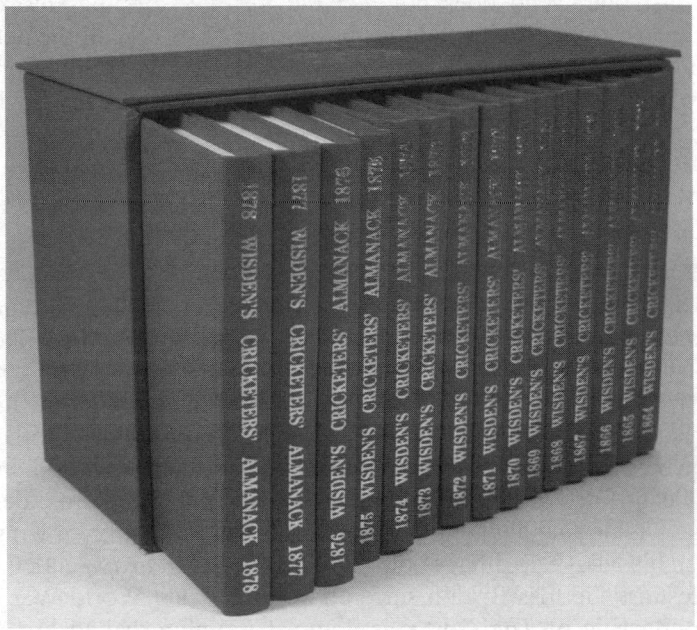

COLLECTING WISDEN

Volume control

PATRICK KIDD

Like kisses and cars, everyone remembers their first *Wisden* – and few people stick at just one. Who does not feel the thrill of dipping into an ancient volume and reading of tales, famous or obscure? I still recall the delight when I bought the 1977 Almanack, looked up what Essex were doing on the day I was born, and saw that, not only did a young G. A. Gooch, my boyhood hero, make a century, but their opener, who made 40, was my future form tutor, M. S. A. McEvoy.

As a *Wisden* collector, though, I am a rank amateur, with a set going back no further than 1950. I look with envy at those who own eight yards' worth of Almanacks, from the fragile early softbacks, through the chocolate hardbacks, the salmon-pink cloth covers and, since 1965, the familiar yellow and brown dust jackets, whose colouring always makes me think of streaks of yeast extract over the lid of a Marmite jar.

To build a full collection now, especially in good condition, is costly. Tim Knight, of Knight's Sporting Auctions in Norwich, estimates a complete set would cost £300,000, but could fluctuate wildly, depending on quality. "Condition is everything," he says. "I've seen 1900 hardbacks differ by a couple of thousand pounds." Knight says the type of book also matters: "In 2008 we sold an 1896, the first year *Wisden* was in hardback, for £22,000. Exactly the same book with soft covers can be bought for a few hundred."

Sir Tim Rice, the lyricist, bought a complete set from Surrey cricket bookseller John McKenzie in the early 1970s for £750, using what he calls "my ill-gotten gains" from the musical *Jesus Christ Superstar*. "I was fairly relaxed about such a serious investment," he says now; the *Sunday Times* described the purchase as "little short of insanity".

Few in those days cared about collecting a shelf-load of reference books. McKenzie had bought his own full set at Sotheby's a year or two earlier for £420. "I keep them out of sentimentality," he says. "They're the only ones I won't sell." He was aware of one set around that time, not complete but with every *Wisden* from 1879, going for just £66.

"People just didn't want to know about cricket," McKenzie says. "Booksellers would store them in warehouses." In 1981, after the *Wisden* market started to boom, he optimistically tried to sell an entire set for £10,000. "I couldn't get a bid. Now you can get that for one edition." His 2012 catalogue featured a rebacked 1869 for £18,000, an 1866 with original soiled wrapper for £12,000, and a 1916, which contains the obituaries of W. G. Grace, Victor Trumper and the poet Rupert Brooke, for £8,000.

The first *Wisden* cost one shilling. The same book would now set you back at least £20,000 – or almost £180 a page. The 1875, which had a shorter print run than previous years, is also highly cherished. Wartime Almanacks are at a premium, especially 1941, when only 800 hardback copies were printed. Of the post-war years, 1971 can sell for up to £100 because fewer copies were printed: a paper shortage didn't help, but it was also thought England's series the previous summer against a Rest of the World XI, who stepped in for the ostracised South Africans, would entice fewer readers.

The *Wisden* market peaked from 2004 to 2009. "That was very buoyant," Knight says. "It has maybe dropped a little, but the market is holding up well. If anything is recession-proof, it may be *Wisdens*."

The collectors are a curious fraternity: obsessive, pernickety and knowledgable but also, in the main, supportive of each other. Many seasoned collectors mentor newer members of the tribe, helping them to understand what to pay and where to find rare editions.

Chris Ridler started collecting in earnest in 2005, when a family member gave him a 1950 hardback to supplement a collection he had built back to 1976. Early on, he sold some shares and went to an auction with £60,000 to spend. "I was outbid on everything but an 1891," he recalls. After that, he made it his business to study the market properly. "The most important part about collecting is knowing which books are rare," he says. He also advises never to buy a hardback after 1965 without a dust jacket: "You'll only end up buying the original one day, and then have a spare that no one wants."

Ridler completed his full set in September 2010 with the purchase of his second 1875 copy. He had sold the first, when there were still a few gaps in his collection, for a record eBay price of £15,000 to fund a website, www.wisdenauction.com, where collectors can seek and trade copies. He upgrades his copies when he finds better-quality ones. "I went from paperbacks

to hardbacks, then to those in top-notch condition," he says. A lot of the early ones were rebound, and Ridler is ten original covers short. "They were really fragile," he says. "The books were only 1cm wide and they fell apart."

He envies those who started earlier and could get bargains. Ridler, who has studied dealers' catalogues going back 35 years, says that in the early 1980s one dealer sold a softback 1896 for £65 and a hardback of the same year for £90. "Today a paperback would be worth £400 and the hardback £25,000," he says. "You wouldn't want to be the person who chose to save £25."

One of his favourite copies is from 1941. He had been bidding on this rarity on eBay but, as the auction neared its end, he had to attend an antenatal class. Asking his mentor to help out, Ridler instructed him to go up to £650 and was delighted to win the auction for £620. The book was then lost in the post.

Devastated, Ridler did at least get his money back, but for his next birthday his wife, Catherine, found another copy as a surprise present. The record fetched at auction for a 1941 was £2,300 in 2007, but Ridler will not sell the copy his wife bought, even though he has since acquired a better-condition one for £1,200. Ridler needed a friend again to complete his set: he was umpiring in a club match as the 1875 edition was auctioned. At tea, he switched on his phone to discover he had paid £12,000. An 1875, rebound without covers, sold in December 2012 for £22,500.

One day I flicked through a *Wisden* at a book sale. I was hooked

Sometimes people pay a premium for sets with special provenance. Sir Pelham Warner's bound set, given to him by Wisden – the company – as a wedding present, sold for £7,800 at auction in 1980, while W. G. Grace's set of the first 38 *Wisdens* fetched £94,000 in 1996. The set in the MCC library was acquired in 1944 from the estate of Sir Julien Cahn, the eccentric philanthropist, who had been given the books up to 1931 by cricket historian F. S. Ashley-Cooper.

Occasionally you come across individual Almanacks that once had an important owner. The most famous is E. W. Swanton's 1939 edition, stamped "not subversive", that sustained him for three and a half years in a Japanese prisoner-of-war camp, and is now in the Lord's museum.

Ridler's collection includes editions owned by John Arlott (1864) and George Duckworth (1933), a 1936 signed from Wilfrid Brookes to Norman Preston (the seventh and tenth editors), and a 1941 signed from Hubert Preston (the ninth) to a young Reg Hayter, the cricket journalist.

There are *Wisden* collectors all around the world. Darren Harold from New Zealand says the internet has made it possible for him to build a collection, although the postal costs are immense. "Being overseas, I can't just pop into a second-hand bookshop to browse, and there are very few *Wisden* collectors in New Zealand, so most of my buying is from the UK," he says. Like Ridler, he uses a mentor.

Harold admits that, when he was young and devouring biographies of his favourite cricketers, he had no interest in the Almanacks: "I figured *Wisdens* were bed-time reading for British anoraks. But one day I flicked through a copy at a book sale. I was hooked – the words brought contests to life."

Hugh Chevallier

A small part of the bigger picture: 21 well-thumbed editions from the Wisden office.

He began his collection with a boxful bought off an elderly man who was going into a rest home, and he now has a complete set back to 1921. He is less worried about quality, though. "It's about the cricket for me, not the cover," he says. The oddest volume he owns is a 1963 centenary edition bound in psychedelic pink.

Everyone has their own motivations for building a collection, but perhaps the most important advice Ridler can give a collector is to actually read the books, which he does regularly, even taking them on flights. "After completing my set, I picked up my 1864 and started to read it," he says. "It was quite nerve-racking to open a book that cost £11,000, but it seems a waste just to keep them on the shelves."

Patrick Kidd writes for The Times. *He bought his first* Wisden *in 1995.*

1864 AND ALL THAT

A foreign country

HUGH CHEVALLIER

The original *Wisden* was an eccentric little volume. Only 85 or so of the book's 116 pages were devoted solely to cricket. In the main, these contained scorecards from remarkable matches played over the previous 50 or 60 years. The first card that readers encountered, on page 27, was of a match from 1855 – nine years earlier – in which the Earl of Winterton's Shillinglee side dismissed the 2nd Royal Surrey Militia for nought. Also in *Wisden's* first offering were the Laws of Cricket, dates of various players' first games at Lord's, and "long scores" (centuries) hit in "great matches" since 1850.

But the volume's principal eccentricity lay either side of that crickety core. The first 12 pages were taken up by a calendar of notable dates and phases of the moon, so justifying the term almanack (in which such information was traditionally found). Some of these calendar entries had a cricketing bent: February 15 recalled a match on ice in 1838, while modesty did not prevent July 15 celebrating the day "John Wisden bowled all the wickets in the 2d in. of the South, in the match at Lord's, North v South" – though there was not enough room to mention it had happened in 1850. Some had little sporting connection: "Papal supremacy destroyed by Act of Parliament, 1559" declared April 8. Sometimes it was hard to tell: "Israel Haggis, of Cambridge, b. 1811", read January 23.

Meanwhile, several of the last 15 pages – despite a notice "to the Reader" that complained of "the confined nature of an Almanack" – were given over to wide-ranging trivia. These ran an unlikely course, from notable dates in the history of China ("the opium dispute commenced, 1834") to the "brass bell weighing 17cwt… cleft by the hammer while ringing, from the effect of the severe frost on January 4, 1861". And in the spirit of those trivia, *Wisden 2013* here presents its own eclectic collection of abstruse facts, illustrating how the world has changed since the first editions were offered for sale.

JANUARY, 1864.

Moon's Changes.

Last Quarter, 2nd, 7h. 39m. morn.
New Moon, 9th, 7h. 16m. morn.
First Quarter, 15th, 11h. 6m. even.
Full Moon, 23rd, 10h. 3m. even.

1	Fri.	British Museum closes. S. Baldwinson b. 1823.
2	Sat.	Fred. Bell, of Cambridge, b. 1830.
3	**Sun.**	*2nd Sunday after Christmas.* [ætat 30.
4	Mon.	James Dean b. 1816. E. Macniven, Esq., d. 1830,
5	Tues.	Dividends due at Bank.
6	Wed.	Epiphany. Twelfth Day.
7	Thurs.	H. Beagley b. 1805. [ætat 47.
8	Fri.	British Museum re-opens. W. Hillyer d. 1861,
9	Sat.	Fire insurance expires.
10	**Sun.**	*1st Sunday after Epiphany.* John Berry b. 1824.
11	Mon.	Plough Monday. Hilary Law Term begins.
12	Tues.	James Cobbett b. 1804. Edmund Hinkly b. 1819.
13	Wed.	Cambridge Lent Term begins. Thomas Lord d. 1832, ætat 74. W. Denison b. 1801.
14	Thurs.	Oxford Lent Term begins.
15	Fri.	James Adams, of Essex, b. 1811.
16	Sat.	John Bickley, of Notts, b. 1819.
17	**Sun.**	*2nd Sunday after Epiphany.*
18	Mon.	Old Twelfth Day.
19	Tues.	Alfred Mynn, Esq., b. 1807. [1826.
20	Wed.	Bartholomew Good b. 1812. George Anderson b.
21	Thurs.	John Small d. 1836, ætat 70. Louis XVI. guillotined, 1793.
22	Fri.	Charles Brown, of Notts, b. 1815.
23	Sat.	Israel Haggis, of Cambridge, b. 1811.
24	**Sun.**	*Septuagesima Sunday.*
25	Mon.	Conversion of St. Paul. Princess Royal m. 1858.
26	Tues.	Dr. Edward Jenner, who introduced vaccination, d. 1823.
27	Wed.	Frederick Wells d. 1849, ætat 53.
28	Thurs.	The Sikhs defeated at Aliwal by Sir Harry Smith,
29	Fri.	George III. d. 1820. [1846.
30	Sat.	Martyrdom of King Charles I.
31	**Sun.**	*Sexagesima Sunday.*

The first Arabian Horse introduced into Britain, 1121.

B

The way we were: among other things, page 1 of *Wisden 1864* warned of the expiry of fire insurance on January 9.

	Then (1860s unless stated)	*Now*
Price of (first-class) stamp	1d (less than ½p)	60p
Price of *The Times*	3d (1¼p)	£1
Price of *Wisden*	One shilling (5p)	£50
Pages of *Wisden*	116 (1864)	1,584
Roast dinner, Simpson's-in-the-Strand	Two shillings (10p, 1850)	£25.75
Cab fare, Charing Cross to Lord's	Two shillings (10p, 1879)	*c.* £15
B&B in a City of London boarding house/ hotel	Three shillings (15p)	£80–£150
Top-of-the-range Jaques croquet set	5 guineas (£5.25)	£5,000
Top-of-the-range bat	21 shillings (John Wisden & Co)	£375 (Chase Cricket)
Membership of MCC	£3	£452
Housemaid's salary	£10–£25 (1879)	£10,400 (35 hours at adult minimum wage for 48 weeks)
Teacher's salary	£75 (female)	£21,588–£36,387
London to Sydney	*c.* 60 days (on *SS Rangitoto*)	*c.* 23 hours by air
London to Madras (Chennai) by ship	65 days (via Cape of Good Hope)	21 days (via Suez Canal, opened 1869)
London to Paris by rail	10 hours 30 minutes (rail–ferry–rail)	2 hours 15 minutes (Eurostar)
Cost per mile of underground rail projects	£347,000 (London underground, opened 1863)	£200m (for Crossrail)
Standard single cash fare, London underground	3d (1¼p)	£4.50
Annual journeys, London underground	12m	>1bn
Toll roads in London	178 (tolls 2d–6d, 1–2½p)	1 (Dulwich College Rd, £1)
Universities in UK	11	134
Population of London	2,803,921	8,173,194
Population of England and Wales	20,281,587	56,100,000
Mortality (deaths per 1,000 per year)	23 (London, 1879)	6.55 (men), 4.67 (women) (UK)
Prison population	18,000	86,000
Cost per prisoner per year	£26 13 shillings (£26.65)	£36,173
Ticket price, dress circle, Haymarket Theatre	5 shillings (25p)	£25–£57.50

Also in 1864...

Five pirates were publicly hanged at Newgate prison... an explosion at a gunpowder depot at Erith on the south bank of the Thames killed at least eight and was felt as far away as Cambridge and Guildford... and war finally resolved the Schleswig–Holstein question (that had famously perplexed so many).

PART TWO

Comment

Wisden Honours

THE LEADING CRICKETER IN THE WORLD

Michael Clarke (pages 97–99)

The Leading Cricketer in the World is chosen by the editor of *Wisden* in consultation with some of the world's most experienced cricket writers and commentators. The selection is based on a player's class and form shown in all cricket during the calendar year, and is merely guided by statistics rather than governed by them. There is no limit to how many times a player may be chosen. A list of past winners can be found on page 99; a notional list, backdated to 1900, appeared on page 35 of *Wisden 2007*.

FIVE CRICKETERS OF THE YEAR

Hashim Amla (page 118)
Nick Compton (page 120)
Jacques Kallis (page 122)
Marlon Samuels (page 124)
Dale Steyn (page 126)

The Five Cricketers of the Year are chosen by the editor of *Wisden*, and represent a tradition that dates back to 1889, making this the oldest individual award in cricket. Excellence in and/or influence on the previous English summer are the major criteria for inclusion as a Cricketer of the Year. No one can be chosen more than once. A list of past winners can be found on page 1508.

WISDEN SCHOOLS CRICKETER OF THE YEAR

Thomas Abell (page 769)

The Schools Cricketer of the Year, based on first-team performances during the previous English summer, is chosen by *Wisden's* schools correspondent in consultation with the editor of *Wisden* and other experienced observers of schools cricket. The winner's school must be in the UK, play cricket to a standard approved by *Wisden's* schools correspondent and provide reports to this Almanack. A list of past winners can be found on page 771.

WISDEN BOOK OF THE YEAR

Bookie Gambler Fixer Spy by Ed Hawkins (page 155)

The Book of the Year is selected by *Wisden's* guest reviewer; all cricket books published in the previous calendar year and submitted to *Wisden* for possible review are eligible. A list of past winners can be found on page 169.

WISDEN–MCC CRICKET PHOTOGRAPH OF THE YEAR

was won by Anthony Au-Yeung (opposite page 96)

The Wisden–MCC Cricket Photograph of the Year is chosen by a panel of independent experts; all images on a cricket theme photographed in the previous calendar year are eligible.

Full details of past winners of all these honours can be found at www.wisden.com

NOTES BY THE EDITOR

On an overcast, late August afternoon in the ECB's clean-cut offices at Lord's, English cricket tried to put a brave face on a miserable month. Andrew Strauss looked wistful but resolute as he resigned the captaincy following the loss of a Test series and the No. 1 ranking, both to South Africa. Beside him sat Alastair Cook, in the same sensible grey suit that spoke of a very British response to a crisis, of keeping calm and carrying on. Kevin Pietersen hovered in spirit, if not in person. And next up for the Test team was a tour of India, perhaps the last place to sort out a domestic. As the room filled with uncharitable thoughts of a hospital pass from a man who played fly-half at university, Cook did well not to drop the ball.

Things were about to get worse. After flunking their World Twenty20 defence in Sri Lanka (though without Cook), England were thrashed in the First Test at Ahmedabad, leaving them one defeat away from matching the record eight they had suffered in 1984, 1986 and 1993, an era when English summers were nothing without a fiasco or three. Exasperatingly, they were being made to look fools by Asia's spinners yet again. Would someone please change the record? Did anyone even know how?

Even now, the answers seem implausible. In a heady fortnight, England won at Mumbai, then Kolkata. Soon, Christmas was coming early: on December 17, in a wood-panelled conference room at the Vidarbha Cricket Association Stadium in Nagpur, Cook could finally relax. A turgid draw had secured a 2–1 win, instantly established his authority and drawn some sort of line under the year's traumas. Crisis management wasn't supposed to be this straightforward.

England have won Test series from unpromising positions before: the Ashes of 1954-55, 1981 and 2005; India in 1984-85 and Sri Lanka in 2000-01. But there may never have been a set of circumstances so loaded in the opposition's favour. Others would have battened down the hatches and waited for spring. Cook came out fighting, bloody-minded but with a clarity of thought, taking on India's slow bowlers with a more open stance, lighter footwork and straighter hitting. Only freak occurrences could stop him: a first-over stumping, a first-ever run-out, a pair of umpiring gaffes.

In the course of three hundreds, a trio to rank with any by an England cricketer, he grew into a leader of men – first equalling, then breaking, the national record of 22 centuries in Tests, which seemed to have stood since biblical times. Throw in the 2010-11 Ashes, and he had now scored 1,328 runs at an average of 102, with six hundreds, in England's two most significant away wins of the modern era. For once, Bradmanesque felt not like a cliché, but the only adjective up to the job.

As with all good captains, Cook coaxed and cajoled. Matt Prior fed off his defiance during the follow-on at Ahmedabad. At Mumbai, Pietersen – now cock of the walk, not elephant in the room – compiled his own third hall-of-fame innings of the year, after Colombo and Headingley. Monty Panesar, mistakenly omitted at first, settled into a mesmeric groove. James Anderson and Steven Finn found reverse swing in Kolkata. Graeme Swann chipped away, troubling not merely left-handers. By the time Jonathan Trott and Ian Bell were grinding out hundreds at Nagpur, England had rediscovered the joys of team spirit.

Victory in India was as stirring as it was unexpected, for earlier in the year there had been a damning hint of the malaise that struck after 2005. By their own admission, England were complacent at the start of 2012 in the UAE against Pakistan. And in the First Test against Sri Lanka at Galle in March, they tested out Einstein's definition of insanity, sweeping straight balls again and again while appearing to expect a different result. After brushing aside West Indies in the first part of the summer, they were then outclassed by South Africa, who spent the year establishing themselves as the world's best Test team, and the start of 2013 confirming it.

The defeat at Lord's prompted Strauss to suggest that England preferred being "hunter" rather than "hunted", which said a lot about the national sporting psyche. But they had been seduced by talk of a legacy: committing the oldest crime in cricket's book, they took their eye off the ball. Cook demanded his players refocus, and so joined Douglas Jardine, Tony Greig and David Gower as the only England captains to win a Test series in India. The London Olympics didn't hand out gold medals for pleasant surprises but, in the most memorable year for British sport, the cricketers had finally chipped in.

We *really* need to talk about Kevin

Tea was approaching on the second day at Nagpur when Anderson bowled Virender Sehwag for a duck and ran straight into the arms of Pietersen at backward point. The explanation was disappointingly simple, a case of falling headlong into the nearest embrace. But the symbolism! After a year in which Pietersen bestrode social media like a virtual colossus, here was the strangest thing: a real-life exchange with a previously hostile team-mate, and not a BlackBerry or an "LOL" in sight. It felt like a modern morality tale.

There were moments in 2012 when Pietersen's behaviour appeared to recall the Italian footballer Giorgio Chinaglia, who was once asked if it was true he had played with Pelé. "No," he said. "Pelé played with me." Cricket, some suspected, existed only as an extension of Pietersen's whims (and unlike team, cricket definitely had an "i" in it). Emboldened by a lucrative new Indian Premier League deal, he was arrogant, attempting to bulldoze over the terms of his central contract. He was self-pitying, claiming he had never been looked after. And he was a man apart, sending silly texts to the South Africans.

What happened next was a mishmash in many genres. A soap opera became a panto when Pietersen was booed at a county match in Southampton. His team-mates cast themselves in a Whitehall farce, giggling in the wardrobe as Pietersen was mocked on a fake Twitter account. Other nations enjoyed a comedy in several acts, not least when his role at the World Twenty20 was confined to a TV studio. And over in the Theatre of the Absurd, ECB chairman Giles Clarke spoke of reintegration – cricket's noun of the year. Then there was Nagpur's Bollywood hug. We await the musical.

The inner workings of the English game were thrust into the spotlight. Despite armchair diagnoses, only the dressing-room knew just how troublesome Pietersen had become; for outsiders to lecture Andy Flower on man-management was plain ludicrous. But as his exile dragged on, the ECB began to look petty, if they showed their faces at all. Pietersen's pursuit of Twenty20's riches at the expense of the Test side – the format which had made his name – was unattractive, although these attitudes can filter down from the top. And if there was a have-cake-and-eat-it feel to his simultaneous grouse about excessive cricket and his yearning for the IPL, it was hard to ignore a wider truth: a bloated schedule has asked the players to make unfair choices. The dilemma is not going away, however much English cricket wishes it would.

Earlier in the year, there had been a hint of double standards, too. When Stuart Broad branded county newspaper reporters "liars", "muppets" and "jobsworths" – on Twitter, naturally – the slurs evaporated into cyberspace. Yet when Pietersen questioned the commentary credentials of Nick Knight, who works for Sky Sports, bankrollers of the English game, he was fined. Insults were being graded by the supposed importance of their victims.

But all was not lost. In India, England were a better, more watchable, team for the inclusion of a fully engaged Pietersen. And, painful though the process was, the ECB had waylaid his international retirement. More than that, they may have saved a man from himself. Pietersen, it turned out, needed England more than he realised, just as England were acknowledging they would prefer not to live without Pietersen; no one said marriages of convenience were easy. Yet amid it all were perhaps the stirrings of a realisation – that while hero-worship at the IPL may feed the ego, a long Test career is more likely to nourish the soul.

Tired but not emotional

Strauss deserved better than the finale he got, but his response to the turmoil that dominated the run-up to the Lord's Test against South Africa showed why he had been one of England's most respected captains. Diplomatic and authoritative, he emitted just the right sort of anger – steam, not lava. And when he told team-mates of his retirement, he did so by letter. He treated others with respect as a matter of course; usually, they returned the favour.

Like Cook, Strauss had inherited a mess involving Pietersen, and set about the repair work with diligence and honesty. Between England's defeat on his first trip in charge, in the West Indies in early 2009, and the loss to Pakistan nearly three years later, Strauss led them to seven Test series wins and a draw. He won the Ashes home and away, becoming only the second Englishman – after Len Hutton – to achieve the feat in two full series against a full-strength Australia. All that had been missing was victory in Asia and against South Africa, though even the 1–1 draw there in 2009-10 was cast in his own unflappable image.

It was odd to think that, less than a month before everything unravelled, England might have topped the world rankings in all three formats had it not rained in Birmingham during the one-day thrashing of Australia. While it's true that Strauss quit Twenty20s in 2009 and 50-over internationals in 2011, he could claim some credit for creating a dressing-room which had grown to expect success. That – and not the confusion at Lord's – was his true gift to the English game.

Yet there was a regret that went beyond the events of the summer. Strauss had been full-time captain for only three and a half years. Graeme Smith, his resilient South African counterpart, took charge in April 2003. Smith did assume the job as a far younger man, but there was a more significant discrepancy: in the period in which Strauss captained in 45 Tests, Smith did so in 27. Neither figure was ideal. South Africa don't play enough series of four games or more; England play too much full stop. Even without the burdens of the limited-overs roles, Strauss had every right to be worn out. Here's wishing Cook a prosperous reign. It may be too much to hope for a long one.

The roaring forties

It is often said, usually by bowlers, that cricket is a batsman's game. But South Africa's pace attack have blithely ignored the maxim. Not long before they dismantled England, Dale Steyn, Vernon Philander and Morne Morkel had blown Australia away for 47 at Cape Town. Then, at the start of 2013, they humiliated New Zealand (45 at Cape Town) and, with the help of Jacques Kallis, Pakistan (49 at Johannesburg). There had been only 17 totals of under 50 in Tests before this trail of destruction, and 11 of those came before the Second World War. England's nadir against the South Africans last summer was a positively zenith-like 240, which history may yet record as some kind of triumph.

The power of three

Perhaps we should have been surprised they were playing South Africa at all. In between their 2012 meeting and the next, in 2015-16, England will have played 24 Tests against either Australia or India. By the end of the 2015 Ashes, the Australians will have visited this country for bilateral series five summers out of seven. And when Australia arrived in India in February 2013, it was for the fifth Border–Gavaskar Trophy series in six years. The main reason given for England's hosting of Australia for five one-day internationals last season was mutual back-scratching: Australia are hosting England in a pre-World Cup triangular tournament in 2014-15. The third nation? That will be India.

The players from these three teams may grow sick of the sight of each other, but the accountants will probably not. Last summer's downgrade of South Africa's visit to a three-Test series for the first time in 18 years was a woeful piece of planning that could not be explained away entirely by the Olympics.

Part of the charm of the big series resides in its sense of occasion. But ten straight Ashes Tests from July to January will be less of an occasion, more of a routine. And if the cycle of two series against Australia every four years was disturbed to spare England winters containing both an Ashes and a World Cup, then no such excuse can be made for Australia's swift return here in 2015. Not since the start of the 20th century, when only three sides played Test cricket, have 15 Ashes matches been crammed into so short a span.

Last year, we fretted about Twenty20 overkill. That process continued when Sri Lanka cancelled Test series against West Indies and South Africa in 2013 because of the IPL and their own 20-over league, while South Africa themselves replaced the Boxing Day Test with a game of Twenty20 against New Zealand. Now we face another extreme: over the next three years, one of the most durable encounters in all sport will be stretched to its limit. Administrators will point to full houses as proof that all is well. But a little of the magic will be lost.

Ever increasing circles

It remains to be seen how Australia's talented but injury-prone seamers cope with ten successive Ashes Tests, although Michael Clarke has done his best to portray rotation as a necessary evil. The Australian hierarchy have even come up with a condescending piece of jargon for their policy. All hail "informed player management". England, who are resigned to it as well, prefer the less slippery "rotation". You get the gist.

Yet you wonder about the point of it all if, fitness permitting, teams are disinclined to field their strongest side – a basic principle of international sport which, thanks to the schedule, has been made to look like a hopeless ideal. England's one-day defeat in India in January 2013 rang hollow without Trott, Anderson, Broad and Swann. Spectators wondering which star players they *won't* be seeing any time soon may sympathise with the French existentialist philosopher who once asked for a coffee without cream. "We're out of cream," said the waitress. "Would you like it without milk instead?"

Even Andy Flower admitted defeat in November, agreeing to hand England's limited-overs coaching duties to Ashley Giles. This was presented as a piece of forward thinking by the ECB. And in the circumstances it probably was: if an HGV needed to get from Portsmouth to Aberdeen and back in 24 hours, you'd hope for two drivers. But when cricket's talent has to job-share to stay awake at the wheel, you know something is wrong.

A turn for the worse?

Comparisons flowed with Jim Laker and Tony Lock while Swann and Panesar were harvesting their 19 wickets at Mumbai in November. Swann is now at Nottinghamshire and Panesar at Sussex but, like Surrey's Laker and Lock, they were once team-mates, at lowly Northamptonshire. This is relevant, for what happened at the Wankhede came with a health warning – and not just for India's batsmen.

The county circuit has not traditionally offered spinners much solace. Swansea used to do a bit, as did the Essex outgrounds and Old Trafford. But Wantage Road would rag square – excessively so in the end, and Swann and Panesar had to learn about bowling on less helpful pitches too. But show them a turner, especially one with the pace that was on offer in Mumbai, and they will show you how to exploit it.

The spinner's paradise has now vanished from county cricket altogether. Last season, the weather didn't help. Neither did a fixture list in which half the Championship matches were over by June 9, when slow bowlers in England are still coming out of hibernation. But it is also a question of attitude. Points penalties just aren't worth the risk, and since Northamptonshire were caught out in 1998 even their pitches have retreated into the Stepford Wives blandness of the domestic game. Just as endemic is a culture in which captains prefer the safety-first of medium-pace: among English-qualified spinners who will still be playing in 2013, only Chris Nash of Sussex and Steven Croft of Lancashire finished in the top 30 of last summer's national averages. And even Nash and Croft would not describe themselves as frontline spinners.

Slow bowlers on the up, such as David Wainwright, Danny Briggs and Simon Kerrigan, are battling a system in which not one of the 18 first-class headquarters in England can be regarded as spin-friendly; the gradual disappearance of outgrounds further precludes variety. If England are to keep winning Tests in India, this has to change – with pitch liaison officers instructed to show more leniency to turners than seamers. Peter Such, appointed last summer as the ECB's spin guru, is aware of the conundrum, and will need to bring to his job all the resolve he once showed while making a 72-minute duck for England.

Cricket's crown princes

Of course, you have to be careful what you wish for. In India, it turns out, they have a different problem: the wrong *kind* of spin. Throughout the Test series against England, their captain M. S. Dhoni pleaded for the magic formula that would help his side exact revenge for the 2011 whitewash. But no groundsman could play the sorcerer's apprentice. After India had taken the lead at somnolent Ahmedabad, Mumbai was too quick, Kolkata ended up helping England's seamers, and Nagpur died a slow death.

Dhoni claimed that India's defeat, only their fourth in a home Test series in a quarter of a century, was nothing compared with the pain of the first-stage exit at the 2007 World Cup, which was either disingenuous or deeply worrying. But the result was the lesson the cricketing world wanted India to learn: power has its uses – and its limits. When Prabir Mukherjee, Eden Gardens' 83-year-old curator, refused to do the BCCI's bidding, he also set an example to the non-Indian members of the ICC.

We may, though, have to defer our hope that power will spawn responsibility. Interviewed by ESPNcricinfo shortly before the Mumbai Test, BCCI president N. Srinivasan was asked about the IPL's global impact, and whether his board should be "thinking about world cricket". He got full marks for brutal honesty: "There's a lot that the BCCI is doing for Indian cricket." Srinivasan was also asked about the possibility of an IPL window, which would restore at least some order to the Future Tours Programme. He replied: "You must understand that it is not ICC who can offer a window. The FTP is among ten members, so ten members decide." Srinivasan knows very well how votes tend to be cast at the ICC – and why.

Last summer, the people of Liechtenstein went to the polls to vote on the right of Crown Prince Alois to veto the results of referendums: three-quarters wanted the veto to remain. The ICC's Full Members had already undergone their Liechtenstein moment when no one properly challenged the BCCI's instant rejection of the Woolf Review, which had called for the game's governing body (the ICC, that is, not the BCCI) to adopt greater transparency and an independent executive board, among other doomed proposals. As long as a majority of Full Member nations remain in India's pocket, administrators can peddle the illusion that cricket's politics operate in a free world.

And then there were not very many

It seems inadequate to talk about Sachin Tendulkar in terms of an era: in cricket's geology he's a one-man eon. But his struggles against England came after the Test retirements of Rahul Dravid, V. V. S. Laxman and Andrew Strauss. Ricky Ponting and Mike Hussey quickly followed. One day soon, we will be without Jacques Kallis and Mahela Jayawardene. An age of distinguished batsmen, brought up before Twenty20 asked a generation to recalibrate their loyalties, will soon die out.

But these names go beyond nostalgia. They are or were not just prolific run-getters, but ambassadors; and if Ponting occasionally belonged to the plainer-speaking school of diplomacy, his concern for cricket's well-being was in his genes. When these men speak, others listen; they are not rent-a-quotes. Dravid was already a member of MCC's world cricket committee before he retired, and Strauss has an executive role written all over him. The appointment of Anil Kumble as chairman of the ICC's cricket committee was a good move. But too many slip through the net. It would be a shame if they are allowed to drift away from the running of the game, which needs more globally respected former players to reassert cricket's integrity.

This is not mere window-dressing. Cricket's fight against corruption continues to strike an underwhelming note. Once more, the most revealing work into the subcontinent's betting markets came from a journalist: Ed Hawkins's *Bookie Gambler Fixer Spy* is *Wisden's* Book of the Year. But its suggestion of foul play at the 2011 World Cup semi-final between India and Pakistan met a predictable fate: the ICC rejected the claim, the BCCI expressed outrage. The suggestion may be wrong, but we are yet to hear how the tweet sent to Hawkins by an Indian bookmaker could so accurately map out the course of the Pakistan innings that day in Mohali.

To dismiss him as a publicity-seeker, as some did, was facile: the book has yet to be written whose author hopes for poor sales. And the moral high horse is no place to keep in touch with events on the ground – recently retired players are closer to reality than any ex-businessman, lawyer or even policeman. Cricket owes it to itself to listen. Yet the perception is that our sport is concerned primarily with safeguarding its reputation – and all too willing to turn a blind eye.

Still hazy after all these years

In August, the Surrey spinner Murali Kartik was jeered at Taunton after he Mankaded Somerset's Alex Barrow. Kartik had already warned Barrow about backing up too far, and was not breaking any law. Still, Surrey later said sorry, compelled by some nebulous nod to the spirit of cricket. It was the wrong way round, like the English habit of apologising after someone has stepped on your foot. The contrition should have been Barrow's, for trying to pinch a few yards that weren't his to pinch.

It is unclear whether this topsy-turviness has its roots in the historical subservience of prole bowlers to bourgeois batsmen; or in the fact that the man who gave his name to the deed in the late 1940s, India's Vinoo Mankad, was cheeky enough to enact it at Sydney, a bastion of cricket's white ruling classes. Either way, it's time to move on – and for the batsmen to stop acting hard done by.

Players applaud the spirit of cricket in theory, but struggle with it in practice. Occasionally the notion can act as a corrective; mainly it is too vague, which may be why MCC's Spirit of Cricket Cowdrey Lecture usually addresses its theme only in the loosest sense. After delivering last year's speech, Tony Greig chatted on stage with Mark Nicholas, Derek Underwood and Stuart Broad. Up cropped the subject of walking – a spirit of cricket favourite. The four pros were unanimous: walking was a waste of time. Not for them the conceit that cricket should have to elevate itself above the standards of everyday life.

Greig's death in late December inadvertently reawakened the debate. His alliance with Kerry Packer to set up World Series Cricket was regarded as the ultimate betrayal of the game's spirit. Yet by forcing the national boards to accept they had been paying their best players less than was fair, Greig did a favour to every cricketer who succeeded him. The jeers at Taunton suggest the spirit of cricket remains an elusive notion.

Growing pains

Jim Troughton definitely smelled of champagne as he emerged from a raucous dressing-room on a sunny September afternoon in Worcester. Fair enough, too, for his Warwickshire side had just secured the Championship with a round of matches to spare, and the players were drinking not just to celebrate, but to forget the pain of 2011, when Lancashire pipped them to the title on the final afternoon. But this whiff of glory was more noticeable for being slightly incongruous: county cricket and glamour rarely rub shoulders, and they will do so even less from 2014, when the Twenty20 Cup is due to take place throughout the summer, not in a block in June and July, as previously.

In fact, there is something to be said for this. With most games scheduled for Friday evenings, spectators may finally be able to get to grips with the calendar. The threat of the jet stream again heading south and staying put will be less serious for a competition not played in one go. And counties may be obliged to employ fewer overseas players, since Twenty20 specialists are less likely to pop in and out – a trend that has damaged the rapport between them and their clubs and fans.

But this is an issue that has been fought over by 18 counties, all with their own priorities. And so there is a flip side. Twenty20 without glamour is like Test cricket without the forward defensive, or one-day internationals without another paranoid tweak of the playing regulations. Other countries stage their Twenty20 domestic tournaments in a block, which – like it or not – suits the format's biggest stars, their suitcases never quite unpacked. The Morgan Review proposed the change from 2014; it did so with the best of intentions, and the counties are acutely conscious of the need for stardust. But the tournament risks evoking a nice cuppa rather than a glass of bubbly. Ten years after it first hit the county scene, our Twenty20 cricket could be heading for middle age before it has reached its teens.

Are you sitting comfortably?

The tiff between *Test Match Special* and *Test Match Sofa*, a group of friends who began providing ball-by-ball commentary on the web in 2009, might normally have been dismissed as a piece of media self-importance. But it was more than that. For while *TMS* were far from flattered by what they regarded as *Sofa's* imitation, they knew there was no law to stop them. At first, the ECB were annoyed too, fearing a dilution of the radio rights, for which the BBC had paid – but at the start of 2012 the deal was renewed, for six years.

Naturally, the friction has suited the underdog. But were *Sofa* really treading on *TMS's* toes – or even endangering the ECB's earnings? And why has no one followed *Sofa's* lead, as some have feared? (Answer: because live commentary takes time, effort and money.) Besides, the two have different audiences; it's hard to imagine that all the 20,000 or so who tuned in on a daily basis to *Sofa* during the India–England Tests had come from *TMS's* large and loyal listenership.

TMS retains four major advantages: its history, its stars, its professionalism, and its status as a rights-holder, which allows access to venues, players and the big-match buzz. To fret over *Sofa* is like Barbra Streisand falling out with the manager of the local karaoke bar. *Sofa* needn't be seen as a menace, either to a radio institution whose longevity is part of its appeal, or to the ECB's bottom line. Cricket needs all the friends it can get. It ought to be the richer for two disparate voices, united by one passion.

What's come to perfection perishes

You may have noticed that *Wisden* is celebrating its 150th edition – in plain English, its sesquicentennial. A certain amount of self-regard is inevitable, but not, we trust, too much. Anyway, you never know what is lurking among the family silver.

The Almanack has always striven for accuracy, while being forlornly aware that this is far from the same thing as perfection. In 1950, the report of Cambridge University's match against Yorkshire recorded three debutants for the county: the third of them was Fred Trueman, "a spin bowler". In 1976, praise was lavished on "the amazing Kallicharran", after Viv Richards ran out three Australians in the World Cup final. And in 2009, the name of the Haileybury bowler was given as J. W. D. Hughes-D'Aeth, when it should have been W. J. D. Hughes-D'Aeth, as any fule kno.

But these things happen in a publication that has been weighing in at 1,000 pages for 90 years, and at 1,500 since 1999; this year's edition takes the total number in the Almanack since 1864 to 133,491. The miracle is that these things don't happen more often. If you find an error in the 150th, please be gentle.

THE KP SUMMER

It's tough being Kevin

PATRICK COLLINS

A few weeks after the close of the 2012 season, Geoffrey Boycott used his pulpit in the *Daily Telegraph* to tell Kevin Pietersen some home truths. Cricket, he said, was a unique sport in the way it accommodated individuals within a team framework. He explained: "There is room for talented people because nobody wants to watch 11 robots. There is even room for awkward so-and-sos, as long as everyone is clear about the team objective and the individual doesn't put 'I' before 'team'." And he concluded: "When Alexandre Dumas wrote *The Three Musketeers*, their motto was exactly what it should be in cricket: 'All for one and one for all.' I think Kevin has forgotten that."

It was easy to imagine the derision in the Pietersen camp. Here was Boycott, the ultimate awkward so-and-so, championing the cause of the collective. Why, it was practically a definition of hypocrisy. Who could take him seriously? The answer, I suspect, is a substantial majority of the cricket-following public.

The English game has always revered its gifted nonconformists. From the likes of Compton and Trueman, through to Botham and Flintoff, special indulgence has been granted to those who ruffle the feathers and raise the spirits. Some may have feet of clay, others may be characters verging on caricatures, yet affectionate memory cherishes the purple passage, the golden hour. Pietersen has given us many such moments, yet affection continues to elude him. There are reasons for this, and most of them involve self-absorption, self-promotion and a distressing absence of self-awareness. Boycott's analysis feels uncomfortably accurate.

Clearly, things would have been far easier had the player not possessed so much talent. A mundane Test cricketer would have been cast aside with sympathetic platitudes and sighs of relief. Terms such as "difficult" and "disruptive" would have been murmured at unattributable briefings, and the phrase "not a team player" would have carried the force of a professional obituary.

But Pietersen is different, his ability unquestioned and his Test record formidable. He has achieved the kind of eminence which enables him to be known by his finest innings. There was the 158 to secure the 2005 Ashes at The Oval, and the nerveless 227 at Adelaide in 2010-11. Then, in 2012, came three of the finest innings the modern game has known: in Colombo, at Headingley, and most dramatically, most violently, at Mumbai.

His batting has also evoked comparisons with some of the great ones, most frequently Hammond and Dexter. Once, as I passed a bibulous lunch in the Harris Garden at Lord's, I heard an elderly member assert that Pietersen was

Andres Leighton, AP/PA

Flying the flag: Man of the Tournament Kevin Pietersen after England win the 2010 World Twenty20.

"the closest thing to Jessop I've ever seen". Since the Croucher played his last Test in 1912, the claim seemed a touch implausible, yet heads nodded approvingly.

In fairness, the richness of Pietersen's talent can unhinge even the most sober of judges. When the mood is upon him, he bats like a demented philanthropist. His improvisations are stunning, his imagination is beguiling. He invents strokes, seemingly on a whim, and he has the eye, the timing and the grizzly strength to bring them off with a flourish. On such days, he reduces the science of field placing to a quivering lottery.

Similarly the bowling. One recalls the bellowing bewilderment of Dale Steyn as Pietersen flipped him through midwicket en route to his 149 at Headingley. Allan Donald, South Africa's bowling coach, described the performance as "the innings of a bit of a genius". No, reservations about Pietersen do not concern his skills.

Yet reservations exist, and they are both real and relevant. Indeed, they may be traced back to when he left his native land. He departed with a flounce, citing an unconvincing quarrel with the quota system. Certainly the move to England opened up the kind of commercial opportunities which were less easily available at home, yet his instincts and his attitudes remained essentially South African. As one of his former colleagues put it: "He even retained that famous South African sense of humour."

So his course was set. Aware that an English mother and four years' residence would enable him to play Test cricket for his adopted country, he worked unsparingly on his game. Just as nobody ever questioned Pietersen's ability, they never doubted his diligence. He had a proper respect for his own burgeoning talent, and he refined it over hour upon arduous hour in the county nets at Nottingham.

But still popularity evaded him. Some tell us he has always wanted to be loved. Others, more perceptively, observe he has a strange way of showing it. In the course of a distinguished career, Jason Gallian played three Tests for England and scored more than 15,000 first-class runs, yet he is destined to be chiefly remembered as the Nottinghamshire captain who hurled Pietersen's kit from the dressing-room balcony at Trent Bridge.

Earlier in the match, Pietersen had told his skipper he wasn't happy, that the pitch wasn't up to his standards, and that he wanted to leave. He said he was surprised and disappointed at Gallian's reaction. He joined his chum Shane Warne at Hampshire in the winter of 2004, won his first Test cap the following season, and made just one Championship appearance for the county in the next five years. "Geographically, it just doesn't work," explained Pietersen, helpfully. "I live in Chelsea." Before joining Surrey, he thanked all and sundry "for the support I have had during my time at the Rose Bowl". Once again, he seemed surprised when his departure was not widely mourned.

In this respect, as in many others, his reactions resemble those of the professional footballer. Loyalty to club or country is often lightly bestowed. When Pietersen first started playing for England, he said: "You are brought up to be loyal to the country you are in, but I have never been totally patriotic to South Africa." Upon touring that country, he announced: "I just sat back and laughed at the opposition, with their swearing and 'traitor' remarks… Some of them can hardly speak English. My affiliation is with England. In fact, I'm going to get a tattoo, with three lions and my number underneath… No one can say I'm not English."

The power of the trite gesture: kiss a badge, choose a tattoo, assert your allegiance with a needle. As football long since discovered, it is a crashingly simple and curiously effective ploy

England were swift to embrace this stunning talent. He announced himself during that tumultuous Ashes series of 2005, and set a pace which rarely faltered. Occasionally, there would be criticism of a reckless dismissal, but his sheer weight of runs provided an eloquent response. They gave him celebrity status, and he greeted it like an old mate. No longer Kevin Pietersen, he became "KP", maker of headlines and friend of the famous. The brighter the spotlight, the more he appeared to relish it. As England captain, Michael Vaughan handled him astutely. "You can see how he winds people up, but he just needs managing," Vaughan would say.

Philip Brown

Off-message? Pietersen and his smartphone.

Managing him was one thing, but giving him the keys to the train set was quite another. The captaincy of England demands all manner of qualities which

Pietersen quite clearly has never possessed. And yet, in the face of all the evidence, he was chosen to succeed Vaughan. He lasted for three Tests and five months before the ECB sacked him, a removal they presented as a resignation. The details of his ham-fisted attempt to depose coach Peter Moores are now the stuff of history, although when they come to write the textbook of witlessly incompetent coups, they may well find space for the Pietersen Manoeuvre, which involves issuing a "back me or sack me" ultimatum before disappearing on a winter-sun holiday in South Africa.

As ever, the small incidents stuck in the mind. There was his eager espousal of the terminally naff. He once asked for a meeting with Simon Cowell, and emerged, star-struck, to declare: "That guy's a legend!" Then, shortly before the infamous Stanford tournament in Antigua, he fatuously insisted he would be as keyed up as on the first morning of an Ashes series. Little things, yet they illustrated an attitude which was hopelessly ill-suited to the task of leading the national team.

> "I never said this before, but I got rid of the captaincy for the good of English cricket"

England were fortunate in that the entire, turbulent affair enabled them to give the job to the man who ought to have had it in the first place, and Andrew Strauss became one of the finest Test captains of the modern era. Yet they were also fortunate in Pietersen's response to his reduction to the ranks. Piqued, he simply toiled at his technique. His consolation came in his enormously lucrative association with the Indian Premier League, a competition which helped lift him from mere affluence to genuine wealth.

And Strauss appreciated the efforts his predecessor was making. "Nine-tenths of my time as England captain, I found him a good guy to have in my team," he would say. "He set the right example in practice, and I felt he could have been far more resentful of me in the sense that he had been removed as captain before I took over." From time to time, Pietersen's real feelings would emerge, as in the aftermath of the successful Ashes defence in 2010-11: "You know what, I have never said this before, but I got rid of the captaincy for the good of English cricket, and we would not be here today if I had not done what I did then." Thus was history bizarrely rewritten.

By now, there were rumours that Pietersen was not getting on with colleagues. This was not a complete surprise. Graeme Swann's clunking conviction that he has a talent to amuse is not to every taste while, on his day, Stuart Broad appears capable of out-preening Pietersen. But nothing prepared us for the sky falling in during the second half of 2012.

Again, the bare bones are familiar. Pietersen announced his retirement from one-day internationals, which instantly invoked a clause in his central contract preventing him from playing Twenty20 cricket for England too. The storm broke at the close of the Headingley Test, as Pietersen threw a titanic strop at the press conference. It was part-truculent: "I've gotta go home. I'm not waiting for Strauss." It was part-paranoid: "You're gonna make me out to be the bad guy." But it was mostly bathetic, gloriously so: "It's tough being me." He suggested that the next Test, at Lord's, might be his last. It was evidently

THE PIETERSEN SAGA

Excommunication and reintegration

May 31 Pietersen announces his retirement from all limited-overs international cricket with immediate effect, because of "the intensity of the international schedule".

Jun 10 Pietersen suggests the ECB alter their central contracts to allow him to play Twenty20 while skipping one-day internationals.

Jul 13 After hitting 234* for Surrey at Guildford, Pietersen confirms negotiations are in progress for a possible return in all formats. But he adds: "I cannot keep playing every single day's cricket. I've never been looked after."

Jul 18 England omit Pietersen from their provisional squad of 30 for the World Twenty20.

Aug 4 Pietersen makes 149* on the third day of the Second Test at Headingley, pointedly raising his bat in the direction of his wife, Jessica, rather than his team-mates.

Aug 6 Appearing alone in the post-match press conference, Pietersen launches an extraordinary outburst. "I can't give any assurances that the next Test won't be my last," he says. "I'd like to carry on, but there are obstacles. It's tough being me playing for England."

Aug 9 A parody Twitter account – @KevPietersen24 – which lampoons Pietersen's personality, is closed down by its owner Richard Bailey, a club cricketer from Melton Mowbray and a friend of Stuart Broad and Alex Hales.

Aug 10 Pietersen is reported to have sent derogatory text messages about Andrew Strauss to South African players during the Headingley Test. South Africa's tour manager Mohammad Moosajee insists the texts contained "friendly banter". Matt Prior phones Pietersen to try to break the impasse.

Aug 11 Pietersen posts a video on YouTube unconditionally pledging himself to England in all forms of cricket, and retracting his demand to play a full season in the next IPL.

Aug 12 England delay their squad announcement for the Lord's Test for five hours, then leave Pietersen out after he fails to deny the texts story.

Aug 14 Pietersen apologises to the ECB by email for what he terms "provocative texts". Broad denies he is behind the parody Twitter account.

Aug 19 Pietersen plays his first match since Headingley, for Surrey against his former county Hampshire in the CB40 at Southampton. He is booed by sections of the crowd.

Aug 24 ESPN STAR Sports confirm they have signed Pietersen for a studio analysis role during the World Twenty20.

Aug 29 Strauss retires, maintaining the Pietersen saga has nothing to do with his decision.

Sep 7 The ECB award a new round of central contracts; Pietersen's name is missing.

Sep 18 Pietersen is left out of England's Test squad to tour India in November.

Oct 3 Pietersen appears alongside ECB chairman Giles Clarke at a press conference in Colombo, pledging himself to England, and signs a four-month central contract. Clarke says: "In our society we believe that, when an individual transgresses and then apologises, it is important that they should be given a real opportunity to be reintegrated into our society."

Oct 7 In a radio interview, ECB chief executive David Collier says members of the South Africa team "provoked" Pietersen into sending the texts, prompting an angry response from Cricket South Africa. Eight days later, Collier apologises.

Oct 18 Pietersen, after meeting Andy Flower, Alastair Cook and other senior players in Oxford, is added to the Test squad for India.

Nov 19 England lose heavily in Ahmedabad – Pietersen makes 17 and 2 – but go on to win the series 2–1 after a swashbuckling 186 from Pietersen in the Second Test at Mumbai.

Jan 9 ECB announce Pietersen has signed a full central contract.

Research by James Coyne

designed to threaten, but came out in the manner of Miss Violet Elizabeth Bott: "I'll scream and scream until I'm sick!"

Then the claim that he had insulted his own captain in text messages to the South Africans tossed a gallon of petrol on to the flames. Strauss was widely acknowledged as a figure of dignity and gravitas, the kind of individual rarely found in public life, far less in international sport. Unconvincingly, Pietersen insisted the texts were "provocative" without being derogatory, but the uncomfortable reality had already dawned. Hence his celebrated YouTube clip, in which a disembodied voice, apparently his agent's, fed him some gentle full tosses masquerading as questions, and he answered with a series of wooden clichés.

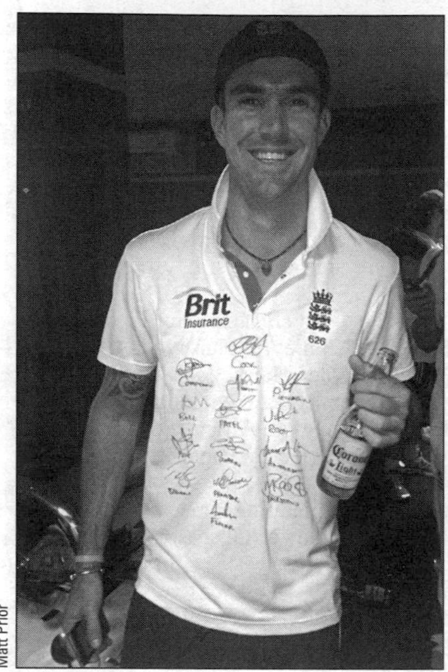

Matt Prior

All smiles: the very model of a team man, after England won the Test series in India, December 2012.

He renounced his decisions. He would play whenever, and in whatever form, England requested: "I can't wait to play in Straussy's 100th Test match next week. These things make me happy." Headingley had been a mistake: "I am who I am in terms of shooting from the hip occasionally. I bat like that [self-conscious smile, reeking of rehearsal]." It was sensationally awful.

Pietersen was dropped for Straussy's 100th Test, with the skipper remarking that his place was "untenable". Warne, sounding not at all like a crass Australian stereotype, suggested the two men could have "gone down the pub and had a beer. And if they'd punched the absolute whatever out of each other to sort it out, so be it". Strauss announced his retirement, insisting it had absolutely nothing to do with the Pietersen affair. Before making his retirement public, he spent half a day composing personal, handwritten letters to every player. He didn't write to Pietersen; instead, he made do with a text message.

Pietersen was left out of the squad for the one-day matches with South Africa, as well as the World Twenty20 but, after some faintly demeaning negotiations, he was brought back for England's tour of India. The new captain, Alastair Cook, gritted his teeth and said: "Time hopefully will be a healer, and we will be able to move on."

Much was made of Pietersen's "reintegration", and the extraordinary innings at Mumbai represented stunning evidence of how much he had to offer the England cause. An abiding image of the celebrations which followed their series victory is of Pietersen grinning at the camera, the autographs of his team-mates scrawled across his shirtfront. The picture positively screamed "reintegration", and the message was convincingly conveyed.

Yet, awkwardly, some recalled his character traits, his unfortunate habit of listening only to bad advice, of taking unsound decisions, of allowing ego to overrule judgment. And they recalled the assessment of a wise old pro. During the summer, Derek Pringle had cast a cold eye over the central character in this dubious drama and delivered a sombre verdict. "Like Shakespeare's seven ages of man, cricketers have three phases of their playing life," he wrote. "At first, they play for love and experience, then, as they begin to improve, they play for glory, before they spend their dotage chasing the money. Pietersen is a brilliant batsman, but he has entered that last phase."

Of course, the man who became KP will dismiss such caution. He plays on because it makes him happy, because it's important to him, because he really, truly believes he is English. The old pros and the awkward so-and-sos, they'll never understand. It's tough being Kevin.

Patrick Collins, five times winner of the Sports Writer of the Year award, is chief sports writer for the Mail on Sunday.

TENDULKAR'S 100 HUNDREDS

The glory was in the number

SIMON BARNES

I would have preferred 99. I thought that was enough. But on March 16, 2012, Sachin Tendulkar reached his 100th international hundred, a century of centuries. And I think there would have been more elegance – perhaps, paradoxically, more sense of completion – if he had stopped before he got there.

He had collected 51 centuries in Test cricket and another 49 in one-dayers, each an unprecedented figure on its own. When combined, they ask for a redefinition of such inadequate concepts as excellence. If you look long enough at a fine Islamic rug, you will eventually find the purposed error: the deliberate imperfection which shows that the humble artist had no thoughts of beating God at his own game; a humility concealing the arrogant thought that, without such a flaw, people might genuinely have mistaken the artist's work for God's.

A flaw humanises and, by doing so, reminds us that something great has been performed by someone just like us: a person who bleeds when pricked, sleeps in a bed at night, eats, digests and defecates. "Cricket is my religion, and Sachin is its God," as the Indian cliché goes. The fact is that Tendulkar was born as we were and will die as we will ourselves. It's harder for humans to do things in real life than it is for a god in a story. Shouldn't we celebrate Tendulkar for his humanity, for what he achieved, despite the inevitable fallibility of humankind?

After all, Sir Donald Bradman left cricket on 99, not a hundred. Tendulkar and Bradman have long been twinned in one of sport's impossible comparisons. Would Bradman have worn a helmet and played the Dilscoop had he been a 21st-century cricketer? Would Tendulkar have gourmandised in the manner of the Don? In a game obsessed with statistics like almost no other, Bradman has a Test average with a number that sings out to cricket followers like a line of poetry: 99.94. The poetry is all in the missing 0.06 – the six lost hundredths.

For a long while, it seemed as if Tendulkar's ultimate stat would have the same sort of humanising fallibility, the not-quite-purposed flaw. For unending months, the figure of 99 overshadowed everything he did. He claimed he wasn't thinking about it; certainly, he did all he could not to. But everyone else in India was mad on the subject. He couldn't order a paratha on room service without the floor-boy asking when the 100th hundred was going to come.

India's tour of England in 2011 was memorable for the hundred that never was. I could feel in my bones during that series – and I don't think I was alone – that the 100th hundred would eventually come as a moment of supreme bathos. The situation demanded it. I even predicted it would be against Bangladesh or Zimbabwe. I didn't, though I should have done, suggest it

Laurence Griffiths, Getty Images

Man of the century: this hundred, Tendulkar's 58th, came in the Second Test against England at Ahmedabad in December 2001.

would come in a losing cause, as Bangladesh beat India by five wickets at Mirpur in the Asia Cup. The only glory of that day was in the number itself.

Which is not to say that numbers lack glory. Sport's all-time great numbers include ten, for Pele. The figure 147 haunts snooker, to the extent that players will chase the maximum break at the expense of mere victory. Four, as in minutes and a mile, was a compelling number in athletics; similarly another type of ten, as in seconds and 100 metres. One is a magic number in golf, just as 100 is in cricket. Baseball has .400, for the batting average that has become extinct. These days, even the finest hitters average in the .300s (you get a baseball average by adding up the number of times the player hits the ball and safely reaches first base, then dividing by the number of at-bats).

The lost .400 average demonstrates one of sport's eternal truths: that while the great players are always great, overall standards tend to rise. Dare we suggest that duffers were more common when Bradman batted? After all, of his 6,996 Test runs, 1,968 came at home against modest attacks from India, South Africa and West Indies, and at an average of 140. And though it's true Tendulkar has made five hundreds in nine Test innings against Bangladesh, he has faced a wider variety of attacks and conditions. It may be no surprise that his average is *merely* in the mid-50s. Bradman got more bad balls to hit, just as the batters from baseball's golden age got more sluggable pitches. The same principle holds true in English football: in 1927-28, Dixie Dean scored 60 league goals; in the Premier League season of 2011-12, the top scorer was Robin van Persie, with 30.

Perhaps Tendulkar's century of centuries will become another of those lost standards: something that says important things not just about the person who achieved them, but about the times in which the record was achieved. It's not precisely that no one could ever be as good as Bradman – just that no one will

Nick Wilson, Getty Images

Fizzing and burning: Steve Redgrave (*third from left*) wins Olympic gold No. 5, at Sydney 2000.

have the same opportunity to collect such an average. And perhaps that will be the same with Tendulkar's century. For what international career in this intense age will ever last as long as his?

Other sports throw up records that seem unbeatable. When Mark Spitz won seven swimming gold medals at the Munich Olympic Games of 1972, it seemed like a record for all time. But Michael Phelps managed eight at Beijing in 2008. He now has 18 golds over three Games, and 22 medals all told. Multiple medal-winning is more possible in swimming than in any other Olympic sport, but those figures – 18 and 22 – will take a great deal of beating. Phelps and Spitz stand out over the narrative of swimming like Tendulkar and Bradman in cricket. The numbers tell the story.

There are those who believe Sir Steve Redgrave's five golds in five successive Olympics is an even finer achievement. Rowing is an endurance event and it is hugely demanding: doubling up – and Redgrave tried that in 1988, when he won gold and a much-forgotten bronze – is considered next to impossible. Five is a number that fizzes and burns across Olympic history.

Oddly, cricket's big numbers are more readily compared with the numbers amassed by athletes in individual sports. That's because cricket, not quite uniquely, is a team game based on individual duels. It has always tended to celebrate the individual above the team. Every cricket follower knows that the highest individual Test innings is Brian Lara's 400 not out against England in 2003-04 (a few can tell you, without pausing for breath, that the highest team score is 952 for six declared, by Sri Lanka against India in 1997-98).

There are two categories of statistical measures in sport: the first for one-off, or season-long, performances; the other for career-long achievements. We are obsessed by the notion of greatness in sport, and we traditionally measure this in terms of career. Tendulkar and Bradman stand out by whatever stats you care to call up, but it is their career-defining figures, the 99.94 and the 100, that really count.

I once conducted an argument in the pages of *The Times* with the cricket correspondent, Mike Atherton. I suggested Andrew Flintoff was a great cricketer, because he was great for a single summer that changed English cricket. Atherton said that wasn't good enough for greatness. I'm prepared to argue my point to this day, but I have to concede that the popular measure of sporting greatness must span an entire career. (What about Bob Beamon, then?)

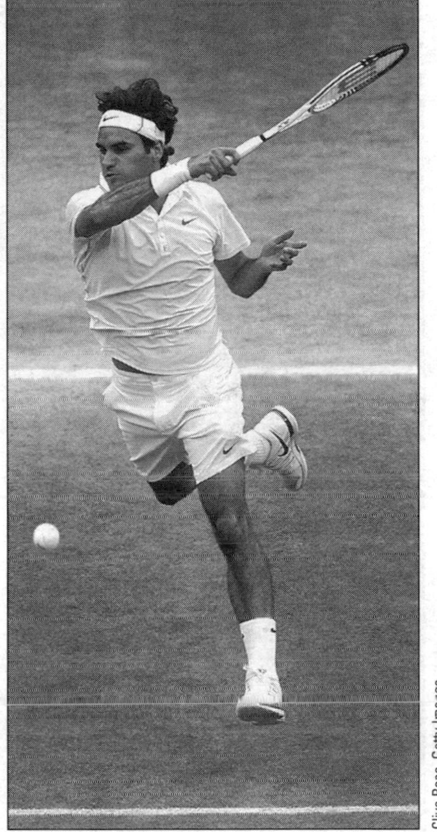
Clive Rose, Getty Images

Sweet seventeen: Roger Federer leads the way in tennis Grand Slam titles.

So, as we look for career-long stats relating to individuals, we must look first to golf. Golf is not a sport in the manner of cricket, since it requires no running about and no physical risk. Still, it is a pleasant pastime for people who are too old for sport or who lack the taste for it. The number we use to measure a golfer is 18: the major tournaments won by Jack Nicklaus.

Everyone in golf expected that number to be overhauled with insolent ease by Tiger Woods, who collected 14 while dominating that sport as no individual had ever done (as Bradman had dominated cricket, in fact). But then came the incident in November 2009 – unforgettably summed up in the headline "crouching tiger, hidden hydrant" – that precipitated Woods's personal crisis. At the end of 2012, he remained stuck on 14. His lifetime achievement will be measured by how close he gets to, or by how far he surpasses, the figure of 18.

In tennis, the measure of greatness is the number of singles victories in the grand slam tournaments. The open-era champion here is Steffi Graf on 22, with Martina Navratilova and Chris Evert on 18 each. In the men's game, Roger Federer is the leading all-time player with 17. Of the top four currently playing, Rafael Nadal has 11 and Novak Djokovic six. Andy Murray has one: in another era, one less stuffed like a Strasbourg goose with talent, he would surely have collected more. Yet we measure him not by his ability, but by his number.

When Federer was at the top, he was considered to be the finest player to have lifted a racket – tennis's Bradman, nothing less. Before him came Pete Sampras. Sampras was no artist, like Federer. He had a game of brutal, pared-down simplicity: the last great serve-and-volleyer. People said that he was boring. I used to reply: well, if you find excellence boring, find something more your size. I believe wrestling is rather amusing.

I loved watching Sampras, especially at Wimbledon, as he made his inevitable march on the previous highest total of slams. He eventually passed Roy Emerson's 12, winning 14 before he retired. Perhaps the finest tennis match I have seen was the Wimbledon final of 1999, when Andre Agassi, at the very peak of his game, played a perfect match against Sampras. But Sampras simply moved beyond perfection and beat him – impossibly, unforgettably – in straight sets.

He won the match on a second-serve ace. Afterwards, an American journo asked: "What was going through your mind at the time, Pete?" There was a baffled pause, before Sampras said: "There was absolutely nothing going through my mind at the time."

David Munden, Popperfoto/Getty Images

No-mindedness: Sachin Tendulkar in 2002.

And I was enlightened. I was enlightened in the sudden manner of a Zen follower. It was in that Zen doctrine of no-mind – the notion that too much thought gets in the way of truth – that Sampras had his being. He is, or was, the Zen master of sport. I wrote this, and later received a letter of agreement: "And I am a Zen master myself…"

There is something of the same quality in Tendulkar's batting. It is by no means complete, and against England before Christmas every run was a struggle. But Tendulkar at his peak had, more than any other batsman I have watched, the ability to play the ball rather than the situation, to immerse himself in the moment rather than the myriad distractions. There was always that touch of serenity about him: each shot not forced, but the inevitable consequence of the question set by the bowler.

Which is why the final, slightly sordid, journey to the 100th hundred was so painful to watch. It was as if Tendulkar had set aside his strongest asset – his indifference, his serenity, his no-mindedness – and was, at the end of it all, hamstrung by numbers. Tendulkar and Bradman have each left a single unforgettable, and perhaps unbeatable, magic number. I'd still have preferred it had they both been 99.

Simon Barnes is chief sports writer of The Times.

THE FASTEST SPELL OF ALL?

Jeff Thomson is annoyed

CHRISTIAN RYAN

Jeff Thomson, running late, rolls over, sits upright, thinks of the many annoyances and injustices in his life, remembers how he hates liars and cheats, gets out of bed. He often drinks Scotch instead of beer because beer hangovers wake him up feeling bloated and lethargic. This morning he is in a lousy mood, cranky, but loose, which for Thomson is the optimum state of being for a day's fast bowling. Without a glance in a mirror, he stuffs his white clothes under an arm and leaves the house on the last day of 1973.

The first inkling that this day's cricket may not be like other days comes when opening batsman Rob Jeffery shapes to play a hook shot. Jeffery is young, 20, and in the space where his two front teeth should be are two false teeth, the real ones having been knocked clean out when, aged 16, he hooked and top-edged fast bowler Dave Gibson of the Waverley club. "Please pick up my teeth," said Jeffery, seeing the teeth sitting pitchside, as he was helped off. Today he has a mouthguard on, no helmet; the cricket helmet's invention is four years away. He, a left-hander, notices that when Thomson bowls, the ball gives the impression it is following him. Jeffery's plan, same as Jeffery's plan always is, is to step back in his crease and hook behind square. He goes to do exactly this, thinking "I'm in position but this ball's on to me quicker than what a ball's ever been" – except the thought is barely half hatched, some kind of skating premonition, because this ball actually is on him, on his right shoulder, bulleting into it, a blast of agony, then Jeffery feels his legs crumpling from beneath and his body toppling backwards on to the stumps.

Until this instant, the nine batsmen yet to bat have sat at ease, on the grass, sort of watching, sort of not bothering. Now, heads lift. Some players hop to their feet. The captain Barry Knight, who played 29 times for England, feels his mind coil back to a day it hasn't alighted on in years – Ilford, 1957, Essex against West Indies, quiet morning, the kid Roy Gilchrist bowling. Next ball whipped clear of batsman, stumps, wicketkeeper and rebounded, with an echoey pock, off the sightscreen.

Jeffery, safely on the sidelines, does not take his pads off, just sits, pads on; minutes later he sees, with a surprise, he's shaking.

John Pym got the best view – 22 yards away, non-striker's end – of the Jeffery ball. Pym, unlike Jeffery, is no step-back-and-attacker. If an hour and a half's batting is up and the ball a bit bruised, Pym's job is done. He has faced Thomson many times. Since the last time, he has read something batsman-turned-classy-journo John Benaud wrote: something about 23-year-old Jeff Thomson having turned himself into the world's fastest bowler. So that week Pym asked Barry Knight to lug the bowling machine into the practice nets and switch the setting to a click under 100 miles an hour. *One–oh–oh.*

Straight away, even before Jeffery's been hit and gone, Pym realises, "Unbelievable. This ball's coming down at least ten per cent faster than the machine." Pym concocts a strategy: he'll hover on tiptoes, weightless, poised to duck or weave or block, and he will not swing his bat back at all because there is simply no time. Then the Jeffery ball explodes before his eyes. Pym's thinking now, "I've got to do something, otherwise I'm gunna be target practice here." He re-schemes things: he'll afford himself a wafer backswing, six inches, enough to deflect the screaming ball behind square leg or through the slip cordon and no glorious-uncertainty-of-cricket way known will a fielder risk laying a hand on it. The first time he tries this the bat jabs back five of the preconceived six inches when – how is this happening? – the ball's too fast for his swing, it has clipped the bat's inside edge, leg stump's cartwheeling. Pym is walking off, disbelieving. "Not fair" – the feeling punches him in the guts, then, "Oh well, at least I'm alive."

Thomson has been annoyed all season. This is round ten, at Bankstown Oval, of the Sydney first-grade competition of 1973-74. It is Mosman against Bankstown, two suburbs separated by Sydney Harbour Bridge and 20-odd miles of motorway. Every cricketer in this city hears it said that the state selectors won't cross the bridge to see Bankstown's players. Thomson, the fourth of Don and Doreen Thomson's five sons, grew up on Market Street, Bankstown. Two-thirds of Bankstown houses are fibro-cement constructions. In Mosman, the verandah posts are sculpted timber, and the roofs terracotta-tiled, "red-tiled roofs of comfort" the poet Henry Lawson called them, and jacaranda-lined avenues wind up hills and in semi-circles.

Bankstown bat first, scoring 186. Sometime before play the pitch, uncovered, was gently rained on. When the ball bounces, it puts a dent in the mud-like surface, and as the mud slowly dries these dents are effectively cemented in, which is the recipe for a pitch that's pockmarked and lumpy, but later on in the afternoon, not yet. Thomson, the No. 8, crouches bent-kneed and fidgety, hacking his bat up and down in readiness like a weed-cutter's rusty shears. Yet his 29 out of 186 is Bankstown's second-top score. One swing of Thomson's sends the ball orbiting high above the fieldsmen, 20 metres beyond the fence and into the nearby high school, a furious swipe.

Reasons for annoyance centre on an October evening when the New South Wales XI for the season's opening interstate match was about to be announced. Leg-spinner Kerry O'Keeffe told Thomson you're not in it, "oh, that'd be bullshit," Thomson replied, but then the selectors confirmed it. Thomson's previous first-class game had been for his country against Pakistan. None for 100, he'd taken; with a broken left foot, he'd bowled. Now he was considered not good enough for the state. Thomson carries inside him an urgent sense of right and wrong. Sometimes he leaps wrongly to the conclusion he's been wronged; this time, no doubt, he'd been wronged, right? He rang his Bankstown captain Dion Bourne to say meet me down at Bankstown Sports Club.

"The pricks," said Thomson. He talked about how upset he felt, about knocking people's arms, legs, heads flying. He said it again. "Pricks."

When Thomson bowls, the climax of a weird shuffling trot that verges on pony-like, his feet perform a last-second cross-shoe slide, then his right leg tilts

Patrick Eagar

Jeff Thomson: the human slingshot.

and braces, his elongated left leg kicks out horizontally at the batsman, and his left arm points skywards, fingers and thumb at full stretch – so completing his temporary self-transformation into a human slingshot – and by this stage his long hair is standing up on end, his white flannels tend to be flapping out around his backside, and his eyes fix so insistently on their target that the muscular torsion this involves is visible when freeze-framed, hollowing out his cheeks and sending a crooked leer ripping across his face. It is – no other word works – beautiful. Here is one subsidiary word – eerie: the ball, dangling low, behind his back, is almost but never quite within the batsman's sight line.

A cricket player's physicality expresses itself mysteriously.

Behind every cricketer is another cricketer.

Thomson's dad, Don, bowled with the same action. Years away Thomson's own boy, Matt, will have the same action. Two other sons do not bowl often but when they do it is with the same action.

Imagine adding annoyance and a miscarriage of justice and a simmering two-month thirst for vengeance to that action. At Coogee, Drummoyne and Marrickville ovals, the wickets and casualties mounted. Against Balmain, he clipped a chunk of Balmain wicketkeeper Kerry Thompson's ear off and the ball kept going. "A little piece of your ear's missing," Dion Bourne offered helpfully, "down near the fence with the ball."

The Pym ball was an inswinging yorker. Next in is Billy King. "Same ball to Kingy," silly mid-off Barry Thebridge wanders over to tell Thomson. "He won't get behind 'em." Thomson does not really need to be told. People have been underestimating Thomson's IQ for years. They still underestimate it. But he ranked in the top five students at Condell Park Primary and had his pick of high schools – and one day in the future, in Perth, he will win not only the Fastest Bowler in the World competition but the $A1,000 bonus prize for *most accurate*.

Thomson bowls the same ball again. This time it is off stump that's cartwheeling.

Greg Bush, the non-striker, who overheard the Thebridge–Thomson conversation, smiles at Thomson: "Pretty impressive."

The hat-trick ball climbs off one of the dents in the pitch and misses Barry Hyland's shoulder. Hyland is batting at five instead of his regular three because he is wearing new glasses. When Thomson's next over begins it is Bush on strike. Bush turns and peers round. Something he has never seen: the slips and wicketkeeper are stationed nearer to the sightscreen than the pitch. This is Bush's sixth first-grade match. At 18 he balances studying law with playing cricket, the thing that he loves, and 14 years from this day he will encounter the massive Barbadian Wayne Daniel on a wet Manly Oval wicket. Daniel will rifle a ball up his armpit, and he will hear Daniel's mouth in his ear, "Hey, man, what you get behind the ball for, man, you're mad?" That will seem like nothing next to facing Thomson today. No chance of a backswing: time only for a short-armed bunt. Even so Bush, a left-hander, is managing to discern the blur coming at him, and because Thomson is angling the ball across and away from him he feels comfortable. He gets away two scoring shots: a forward punch off a full toss, when Thomson slips a little in his run-up, and a backward jab off a short one.

The Mosman line-up, four years on. *Standing:* J. M. A. Tait (*honorary secretary*), R. F. Jeffery, R. J. Ewing, A. J. Skilbeck, J. D. Love, B. C. Hyland, J. E. Pym, I. Crawford, W. P. Corbett (*scorer*). *Seated:* R. G. Saywell, G. M. Bush, B. R. Knight, N. W. L. Bergin (*president*), D. J. Colley (*captain*), A. R. Border, D. M. Felton.

Hyland's new glasses are worrying him. Bush pokes towards gully, tries for a single, Hyland shouts no. It is overcast but not cold. The honking traffic is loud and the atmosphere dead. A hundred people, rough count, are present. The sightscreens are too low to cover the bowlers' arms. Bush has a reputation for not scaring. Next ball, the ball after Hyland's "no", is the first ball on the line of Bush's body. It pitches on leg stump, neither full nor short. One small step lands Bush squarely behind it. This ball leaps. It has its own mind. Bush thrusts his gloves and bat handle up, up to about nose level. But the ball is like a wave breaking, over the top it crashes. Bush staggers and falls. He puts a hand to his right eye. "Have a look," he hears. He looks: blood on the glove. Thomson walks back to his bowling mark, and stands. Bush's eye, people notice, looks to be sort of hanging, not sitting correctly in its socket, the most shocking and grotesque cricketing injury, everybody knows, that they ever have seen or will see.

Bush's team-mates, on the boundary, heard the thud, then a crack.

Garie Beach, Norah Head, Maroubra, The Entrance: at a string of far-from-stress escape hatches along the coast of New South Wales, Thomson and his friend Lenny Durtanovich, later Pascoe, would surf and talk to girls. Thomson cannot remember a time in his life when he did not want a boat. As a kid he asked for toy boats, while dreaming of the real thing. Later, older, still not a boat owner, he and Greg, the third brother, would select some ocean rocks to stand on, and fish off them, sometimes through the night, a metal spike to cling to when the surf turned treacherous on top of them. Thomson played many sports, not just the working-class ones. In his Bankstown backyard flattened by five boys' footfall he gouged holes in the grass, and put soup cans in the holes, to create a golf course. Beach excursions with Lenny happened Saturdays – days of no school, or work, days of invariably turning up late for cricket.

Durtanovich and Thomson were Punchbowl High partners in shooting pigs, catching fish, pulling birds, taking wickets. Durtanovich shook out eight for 21, Punchbowl v Birrong. Thomson smashed that with nine for three, Punchbowl v Belmore. Occasionally Thomson would catch sight of Alan Davidson or Graham McKenzie bowling on TV – "like watching fuckin' paint dry". Davidson's inswinger dipped devastatingly late. McKenzie had a Mona Lisa of an outswinger. Not impressed, was Thomson: "pace and more pace" was more fun and also bothered batsmen. He was six when he bowled his first bumper. At 12 he'd get through 50 eight-ball overs on a Saturday, spread across Under-14s, 16s and C-grade, jogging from venue to venue on days Dad didn't drive him. At 14 he bowled a ball that sent a wicketkeeper flying. Once, when Wes Hall ventured to the far-out western Sydney sticks to teach Australian children how to throw, Thomson threw further than Wes.

Twenty was a complicated age. Those fond of Thomson – and not many who glimpsed a layer beneath the bloodthirsty persona were not – believed that if not for the Bankstown postcode he'd have been opening the nation's struggling Test attack with young Dennis Lillee of Western Australia. Instead that summer, 1970-71, Thomson was dropped from Bankstown first grade to third grade for an afternoon (he took ten for 31) when club officials tired of the surf/girls preoccupation and the lateness.

Thomson's attitude to cricket was: "I mean, you have to play all afternoon, so what's the hurry to get there?"

In the middle of Bankstown Oval lies a red pool. David Colley, the incoming batsman, sees it on his slow walk out. Greg Bush's blood. Sort of "squeezey" looking, like squirted sauce. Sick feeling in the stomach. Red blood on white creaseline. Try not to step in it. Colley gave Bush a lift to the ground that morning. Try not to get your friend's blood on you. Blood on the creaseline, behind it, in front of it. Red splash in the line of all three stumps. Got to know where middle stump is. Colley asks the umpire for middle and marks the spot with his boot. Red on white boot.

Colley's presence today has been playing on every player's mind. Colley is one of three fast bowlers – Steve Bernard and Gary Gilmour are the others – in the New South Wales team. Tapping his bat in blood he hears voices from behind. "This is the one we want, Thommo, this one's yours." They think Thommo should be picked for New South Wales before Colley. Thomson thinks Thommo should be picked. What else is Thomson thinking? – the usual stuff against Mosman – "pack of jerks"; "fancy bats"; "elegant and clever". Colley himself got thinking, before heading out to bat, "I'll try to stir Thommo up. Make him bowl short and go crazy and try to kill me. Might be my best chance." So he put his New South Wales sweater on. Thomson sees the sweater. The day is, still, not cold. The fieldsmen standing closest think they see white in Colley's face. Colley, inside – "I'm not going to dog it" – is fixed tight on a plan, to go back, and across, get yourself behind the ball when it comes…

The ball is fairly full and swinging in. Colley is a long way away, maybe a metre away, the place where he's backed away. Leg and middle stumps are out of the ground. Colley sees nothing – too quick – hears nothing, and seconds later will remember nothing of this. Still, now, he cannot find the memory, and nearly 40 years have gone.

Lying on a stretcher in the corridor between the teams' change-rooms, Bush hears a roar, and knows: Colley out, first ball.

Colley returns, looks around, thinks that's strange – three batsmen, all of them out, have not unbuckled their pads. The three sit still, smiling, but not happy smiles, or normal.

One, Pym, is having hazily philosophical thoughts, like what are we doing here, this is supposed to be a game, and another, Jeffery, is thinking he does not want to bat again today, over and over he thinks this, aware that the thought is surely futile, such is the speed of batsmen's comings and goings.

Sandy Morgan, at No. 7, once a Queensland all-rounder, is next in. He feels no nerves. He has clarity. Thomson shuffles up to bowl and Morgan steps away two paces to leg. Morgan is like a flashing neon white flag. But he does not get paid for cricket, he is fresh-embarked on a stockbroking career that is shaping up promising, and the Test aspirations he had he has left behind. So he steps away two paces, bat waving, "There are the stumps, Jeff, knock 'em over, don't hit me." Morgan survives a ball but not many.

Bush, still on the corridor floor, hears the excited shouts.

Once, on a terrace outside Roselands Shopping Centre, schoolboys Thomson and Durtanovich had a disagreement about who had broken more batsmen's fingers lately.

All day a complicating fear has dangled over proceedings. A year ago at this ground Barry Knight bowled a beamer at Thomson's head from 16 yards and everyone's been wondering if Thomson is plotting retaliation. Knight had his reasons: Thomson had earlier flung at the head of Mosman's last man Bill Carracher two that bounced plus another that didn't. Also, Knight did not (the long version goes) mean it – simply tore in off the long run thinking bumper, until the realisation hit him that an ageing Englishman's attempted bumper might provoke mere laughs, which was when drifting into his subconscious came a seething Trevor Bailey, his idol, beaming a New Zealander from the front creaseline, and Knight decided good idea, front creaseline, still thinking bumper, but then five or six strides from delivery his thinking got scrambled, *bumper* turning to *beamer*, and in his distraction he skipped past the umpire, past the front creaseline, and staggered several yards on accidentally. Anyhow, Thomson ducked.

Knight is the new batsman. Thomson does not retaliate. Knight gets behind the ball, protecting his stumps. The fieldsmen, noticing this, are impressed. But before Knight can think of a run he pops up a catch.

Since first learning cricket, aged eight, on London's Wanstead Flats with some older boys, and in the street against a lamp-post, and with his friend George Catchpole on a wooden pitch his dad built from disused doors, Knight has either practised his batting or batted in actual matches, be it at street, net, club, county, Test or grade level, virtually every dry day. Conservative estimate

(Barry's): 200 balls a day, 73,000 balls a year, which makes, pushing 36 years of age, 2.04 million balls faced in a cricket-devotional lifetime so far. Not one of the two million-plus compared with facing Thomson, that creeping-hysteria sensation of having no reaction time, of hoping and trying to bob on the back foot and somehow pick the ball out of your swimming line of vision – actually, thinks Knight, as he slopes off Bankstown Oval, a tremor of recognition, "I've had this feeling before." On a drab day in Peterborough, 1956, a teenaged Knight passed Essex team-mate Geoff Smith on his way to the wicket. Smith was whimpering, on a stretcher. The ball had struck him under his pad's knee-roll, the jolt shifting the knee out of alignment: Smith lbw b Tyson 0. Knight faced five Tyson balls, none straight. Two bumpers, a beamer, one pitched up outside off, another pitched up and scudding leg side – Knight knows this because he turned and looked, *afterwards*. When the five balls were flying at him he could make out only the faintest shadow, or no shadow. Exact same thing facing Thomson.

Frank Tyson managed five or six overs at that top velocity. Thomson, word on the circuit has it, is good for a dozen or 20.

The ambulance driver, trying to reach Bush in the corridor, cannot get through the gates. It is New Year's Eve and Bush has a date with the girl who

---

MOSMAN v BANKSTOWN 1973

At Bankstown, December 31, 1973. Bankstown won on first innings. Toss: unknown.

Bankstown

*D. Bourne c Morgan b Racklyeft	9
C. Jones run out	16
R. Lamaro c Bush b Colley	1
J. Dunn c King b Colley	0
T. McDonald lbw b Morgan	13
M. Fisher c Cornforth b Colley	61
S. M. Small c Carracher b Morgan	27
J. R. Thomson c Knight b Carracher	29
B. J. Thebridge c Jeffery b Morgan	4
T. T. Radanovic c Pym b Racklyeft	14
†I. Gorman not out	3
Extras	9
(44.7 overs)	186

Colley 3-35; Racklyeft 2-65; Morgan 3-41; Knight 0-34; Carracher 1-2.

Mosman

Batsman	First innings	Second innings	
J. E. Pym b Thomson	3	– not out	50
R. F. Jeffery hit wkt b Thomson	1	– c Gorman b Lamaro	7
G. M. Bush retired hurt	4		
W. King b Thomson	0	– (3) c and b Radanovic	46
B. C. Hyland b Lamaro	1	– (4) not out	2
D. J. Colley b Thomson	0		
O. J. Morgan b Thomson	0		
*B. R. Knight c McDonald b Thomson	0		
†R. Cornforth b Thebridge	60		
A. Racklyeft st Gorman b Radanovic	21		
W. Carracher not out	0		
Extras	4	Extras	5
(26.3 overs)	94	(2 wkts, 18 overs)	110

Thomson 6-31; Lamaro 1-23; Thebridge 1-31; Radanovic 1-5. *Second Innings*—Lamaro 1-22; Small 0-19; Thebridge 0-25; Radanovic 1-8; McDonald 0-1; Fisher 0-5. *Second innings bowling is 25 runs short.*

lives next door. He wonders about stitches; if they are needed, what might his face look like? The ambulance driver gives up. Bush is carried out to the street. At Bankstown Hospital he is X-rayed and let go. The date is off, Bush and the girl next door stay in, but there is more cricket to look forward to, a one-dayer, and he'll play if he gets the all-clear in the morning from his nearest hospital. There, an eye specialist interrupts his holidays to say: "Look up. Look right. Look left." Bush obeys, or thinks he does. The eye does not budge. The bone beneath it, the orbit bone, is smashed – that was the crack team-mates heard – and also sunken, rendering his two eyes crooked. Trapped and tangled in broken bone are the surrounding muscles. The eyeball's a blood clot. Bush will recover and play on, for decades. But first, a delicate operation, then a month in a bed in an old people's annexe of Royal North Shore Hospital, lying perfectly still, lest the eye bleed and he blind himself, listening to every ball of Australia and New Zealand on radio.

Pym is laying bets with team-mates on whether Thomson can bowl six byes – can actually bowl a cricket ball out of the ground.

Thomson has a strained calf, or groin, maybe slipped in his run-up again. Might have figures of six for four. No full scorecard is available. Four men bowled, one caught, one hit on the shoulder and out hit wicket; one more hit in the eye and hospitalised. But, now, Thomson must stop.

He will bowl many more fast spells. But on December 13, 1975, something – something inside, and barely traceable – changes. A flatmate of Thomson's, 22-year-old wicketkeeper Martin Bedkober, is batting in a Brisbane grade match. He lets a short ball hit his chest. The bowler is a medium-pacer. Bedkober waves help away, then falls. Not long after, he is dead: a blood clot, in the spot where the ball struck, the hospital doctor cannot push oxygen through. Thomson will think, after this, "There's no point trying to knock a bloke out."

On the afternoon before Christmas, 1976, Pakistan's Zaheer Abbas spoons up an attempted pull shot in Adelaide. The bowler Thomson dives for the catch, midwicket Alan Turner dives simultaneously, and they crash. Neither man gets up for a while – and Thomson's right shoulder bone is wrenched five centimetres away from the joint. He will bowl again in his life, many times, but with a longer run-up, and without the same serene elasticity in the moment before delivery. Seldom will a ball, neither full nor short, leap with the steep menace of old.

First, his psyche; a year after, his shoulder. He is reduced, cut down – this man who on the last day of 1973 bowled faster probably than anyone in the universe ever has, and faster, perhaps, than the universe wanted him to bowl.

Christian Ryan lives in Melbourne, writes and edits, and is the author of Golden Boy. *His latest book is a pictorial collection of essays,* Australia: Story of a Cricket Country.

CRICKET AND SEXUALITY

The hardest decision of my life

STEVE DAVIES

I'd always known I was gay, but for a long time it wasn't an issue. It helped that I was good at sport, because at school that was a route to popularity. But when I started touring with England, the dynamic changed. I couldn't face long trips away from home trying to hide my sexuality the whole time. So before the last Ashes series, I made sure my team-mates knew. That was two and a half years ago. And it was the best decision I've ever made – even if it was the hardest thing I've ever done.

But I knew I had to: it was eating me up inside. When I was at home I felt all right, because I was with my family, and I'd told them when I was 19. I hated being on tour, though. The actual cricket was fine, but the social situations were not. If you go out in the evenings as a sports team, you sometimes attract interest from girls, and I found that uncomfortable. A two-week trip would feel like two years. And the Ashes tour was going to last three and a half months. I'd had a couple of instances where I'd been out in gay clubs and been recognised, and I knew I couldn't go on like that. Keeping it quiet all that time would have been horrific.

The players' response was amazing, and Australia turned out to be a very special trip. My life has changed since I came out. I feel so much more confident and happy. And I can now count Elton John among my friends, which is something not many cricketers can say…

Your sexuality is no one's business but your own: whether you choose to come out or not is an incredibly personal matter. No one should be made to do it, and you've got to choose a moment you feel completely comfortable with. But hopefully I've proved that, since the announcement was made publicly in February 2011, being a gay cricketer is not an issue – that it can be done.

I think it's difficult telling people you're gay in the sporting world. But it's getting a lot easier, to the point where I honestly don't think people care. Being a cricketer helps, because it's a decent world, and I haven't had a single jibe. In fact, the banter has been good, in both the England and Surrey dressing-rooms, and I occasionally like to get a reaction out of team-mates by pretending to take offence on behalf of the gay brethren. One county colleague – I won't name and embarrass him – has even learned a thing or two: he thought all gay guys were as camp as Christmas. I hope I've opened one or two eyes.

I've been asked why, if coming out as a cricketer isn't an issue, other professionals haven't followed suit. I can see it's a bit of a contradiction: if something really isn't taboo, why the silence? I think it goes beyond cricket, both because sexuality is still an issue in some parts of society, and because of the personal nature of the decision.

Everyone has a different set of circumstances. Being gay and not being able to tell anyone can be a lonely place. I know a few people who have told their

Nigel French, PA Photos

"Being a gay cricketer is not an issue" – Steve Davies on coming out.

parents and then been kicked out of their own homes. But the ingredients were there for me to tell people. I'm lucky to have a supportive and loving family, and the way Andy Flower and Andrew Strauss handled breaking the news to my England team-mates was brilliant. But I can't pretend I didn't have sleepless nights worrying about their reaction.

What has been encouraging, apart from the indifference in the cricket world, is the response from elsewhere. I was hoping my story would help others, and I got plenty of support on Facebook, Twitter and in letters. One guy aged 21 and really into his sport wrote to me saying he was gay and that no one knew about it. He said he felt fake socialising with his friends, and that my story helped a lot. Plenty have said that. It makes me feel like I can do some good.

The one thing that does annoy me at times is when people say: "You must know whether so-and-so is gay." I don't – and I don't think I have what some people call a "gaydar". I also find the idea that I might be attracted to my team-mates in the shower a ridiculous one. They're more like family to me.

The truth is, I don't know if there are other gay county cricketers out there. If there are, I do hope they will look at my experience and realise that coming out is not necessarily an ordeal. But I would stress again that the decision has to feel right. And I'm certainly not here to lecture them.

The process has been surreal at times. When the story broke, I went to buy the papers at my local garage, and could see my face on the front pages from 30 yards away. That was an uncomfortable time. But it turned out to be the right thing to do. Now, I just want to be recognised as a good cricketer. If people aren't mentioning my sexuality by the time I retire, I'll be happy with that.

Steve Davies has kept wicket for England in eight one-day internationals. He was talking to Lawrence Booth.

150 YEARS OF YORKSHIRE COUNTY CRICKET CLUB

No laughing matter

DUNCAN HAMILTON

At the rump end of 1933, an impish, greying and bandy-legged middle-aged man travelled by bus and on foot across the high-ridged toe of the Yorkshire Dales to make an unannounced house call. Under his arm he carried a brown paper parcel, which contained a belated wedding gift. He'd bought it especially for the groom; whether the bride liked it, wanted it or would find any practical use for it was immaterial.

The recipient was Bill Bowes, and the generous giver Emmott Robinson, who told Bowes on the doorstep what the thick wrapping concealed, so ruining the element of surprise. "I've brought you a weather glass, Bill," he said. "It's same make as mine, an' tha wants to look at it night and morning. It's seldom that I've been let down, an' it's nice to know when there's a sticky wicket in t'offing." Robinson wasn't being flippant: he spoke solemnly. As though regarding the barometer as the bowler's equivalent of the philosopher's stone, he began an elaborate description of its benefits. "He instanced matches when Yorkshire had sent the other side in to bat," remembered Bowes. "Occasions when a little more confidence in the barometer would have helped, and left the house with a parting injunction, *'Be sure that tha makes good use of it.'*"

From a first-floor window in my home I can follow the curve of the rutted lane along which Robinson went, clutching that parcel. Poking between the trees I can see the Indian-red tiles of the roof of Bowes's old semi-detached, which overlooks the Wharfe valley. And, passing the front door, I imagine the two of them standing beneath the lintel. In my mind's eye, Bowes nods his surprised thanks and the garrulous Robinson gossips away in front of him.

It's an ostensibly minor moment; an obscure exchange that, I suppose, seems insignificant amid the brass-band-and-bunting celebrations arranged for Yorkshire's sesquicentennial summer of 2013. Landmark anniversaries are essentially about the remembrance of things past and, since history is made up of the biography of Great Men, Yorkshire have a lot to draw on. Old ghosts will be summoned: Lord Hawke and Wilfred Rhodes, F. S. Jackson and J. T. Brown, Schofield Haigh and Alonzo Drake. But I think the vignette about Robinson and the barometer contains something subliminally telling, and is useful in understanding three fundamental aspects about Yorkshire: how seriously they take their cricket; what it required to achieve the unmatched glory of 30 official Championships won outright, and another that was shared, grudgingly, during those 150 crowded years; and, improbable as this seems, why the county's long period of trophy-austerity turned so poisonous and militantly rebellious.

No one was more authoritative about Yorkshire than J. M. Kilburn, who as correspondent of the *Yorkshire Post* counts as the Herodotus of Tyke territory.

Impish and greying: Emmott Robinson.

He either saw or knew, with a casual familiarity, almost everyone now honoured in Headingley's impressive museum. George Hirst coached him, speaking in a voice so hoarse that any instruction must have sounded like gravel pouring down a chute. He observed a padded-up Herbert Sutcliffe writing his correspondence in immaculate copperplate, stopping unperturbedly in mid-sentence when the pavilion bell obliged him to go out and bat. He counted Len Hutton as a friend; and Hutton reciprocated, also counting him as an educational tutor. He wrote about Brian Close as a callow teen, saw almost all Geoffrey Boycott's formative innings, and Ray Illingworth's first, tweaked delivery. He said some of his grandest days were spent admiring "the rampant" Fred Trueman flattening the stumps.

Kilburn always maintained that Yorkshire's success was based on what he called "the many strivers, the bread and butter cricketers". Robinson belongs in that category. Statistically he doesn't rank among the greatest of the club's great. He didn't make his debut until 1919, aged 35, when he was called up to fill one of those tragic gaps created by the First World War. He retired, aged 47, in 1931 after taking 100 wickets in only one season and scoring 1,000 runs just twice. He was one of those figures whom P. G. Wodehouse – fond of the cricketing idiosyncratic – could have invented if God had not got there first. His cap was askew. He wore loose, wrinkled whites, each creased trouser leg rolled up as though, like a Scarborough holiday-maker, he was about to paddle into the North Sea. But, as the ultra-professional, Robinson had a scrupulous devotion to his business. Every evening he wrote his observations into cheap notebooks, compulsively accumulating intelligence which, he said, comprised: "Wheer t'batsmen got t'runs, how they got out, their best shots, state o' t'wicket an' stuff like that." He lived Yorkshire cricket 24 hours a day during the summer and thought about it all winter.

Robinson strikes me as the personification of Yorkshire cricket's character. In approach, opinion and belief he also represents the way in which Yorkshire are seen by outsiders – and how they relish seeing themselves: earnest, thrifty, ruthlessly efficient and hard-bitten, intolerant of failure and possessing a never-give-summat-away-for-nowt attitude that no dictionary definition of competitiveness has ever adequately captured. Those attributes are not, and never were, exclusive to Yorkshire; but Yorkshire – through Robinson and his ilk, before and afterwards – embodied them more than the other counties, and treated the game with the greatest profundity.

The barometer is proof. Robinson thought minutiae mattered. He'd been schooled to explore and exploit *any* advantage, however minuscule. He was

STRONG YORKSHIRE, STRONG ENGLAND?

An old saw cuts no ice

CHRIS WATERS

When eyebrows were raised over the make-up of the England squad for his first Test as chairman of selectors, Raymond Illingworth of Pudsey was unequivocal: "Just tell them that a strong Yorkshire is a strong England." Among his choices were the Yorkshire pair of Craig White and Richard Stemp, along with Worcestershire's Bradford-born wicketkeeper Steve Rhodes.

It was hard to be entirely sure whether Illingworth's remark was tongue-in-cheek, but it served to cement a cliché. For the idea that a strong Yorkshire does indeed mean a strong England is so deeply embedded in the game's culture that, in some parts of the country – especially north of Derbyshire and south of Durham – it practically passes as established fact.

Perhaps it would have been churlish to point out that, by the time Illingworth trotted out the mantra ahead of the Trent Bridge Test against New Zealand in 1994, Yorkshire and England had provided a grim twist. Yorkshire finished 13th that summer, and no higher than eighth between 1981 and 1995 – a period when first West Indies, then Australia, were the strapping Blutos of international competition and England more like Popeye shorn of his spinach. But has the national side really done better in those eras when Yorkshire have prospered, and vice versa? Or is it a myth to rival the Cottingley Fairies?

As with many a cliché, no one seems to know where it actually comes from. Enquiries to eminent cricket historians elicit blank responses and tentative replies. "Didn't someone like Lord Hawke say it?" Possibly. But if Ashes supremacy is the yardstick of English strength, the cliché is manifestly more fiction than fact, even dating back to Hawke's day. When Yorkshire achieved their best run under his captaincy, with four titles in five years around the turn of the century, England lost four successive Ashes series, despite fielding Yorkshire's George Hirst, Wilfred Rhodes, Jack Brown, Stanley Jackson and Ted Wainwright.

And when Yorkshire won four consecutive titles in the roaring '20s, England began the decade with three botched Ashes campaigns, even though their side included Yorkshiremen Herbert Sutcliffe, Percy Holmes, Abe Waddington and Arthur Dolphin. In the not-so-roaring '30s, when the county secured seven Championships, Australia relinquished the Ashes only once, during Bodyline. In those years, Yorkshire supplied Len Hutton, Maurice Leyland, Bill Bowes, Hedley Verity and Arthur Wood, all of whom played when Hutton made 364 at The Oval in 1938.

A more apposite theme continues to emerge: "When one team is strong, the other is not." When England regained the Ashes in 1953 after a 20-year gap, it was the first of three successive wins against Australia, which along the way featured Hutton, Willie Watson, Bob Appleyard, Johnny Wardle and – when he was not in the disciplinary doghouse – Fred Trueman. Yet the Championship decade was dominated by Surrey, who claimed seven straight titles.

Australia regained the urn in 1958-59, before grimly holding on to it for another five series, yet in 1959 Yorkshire chose the moment to embark on a run

Strength in numbers? The England team who demolished Australia by an innings and 579 runs at The Oval in 1938 contained five Yorkshire faces... *Standing:* Bill Edrich, Arthur Fagg (*twelfth man*), **Bill Bowes, Len Hutton,** Joe Hardstaff, Denis Compton, **Arthur Wood.** *Seated:* **Hedley Verity,** Ken Farnes, Wally Hammond (*captain*), **Maurice Leyland,** Eddie Paynter.

of seven titles in ten seasons, a period in which Trueman, Illingworth, Brian Close and Geoffrey Boycott all represented their country. That sequence ended in 1968, when Australia kept the urn with a 1–1 draw in England. Sure enough, by the time England next seized the Ashes, under Illingworth in 1970-71 – they went on to relinquish them only three times until 1989 – Yorkshire's fortunes were already on the wane.

Even as England achieved the most celebrated Ashes series victory of all, in 2005, Yorkshire were competing in the Championship's lower flight. Four years earlier, the club had won their only title since 1968 at a time when – guess what? – England had not long fallen to the foot of the unofficial world rankings. And when England climbed to No. 1 in 2011, Yorkshire were relegated. The Test side two summers ago contained only one Yorkie – Tim Bresnan, the personification of a strong Yorkshireman, if not a strong Yorkshire.

Debatable at best, delusional at worst, the famous old saying grows increasingly inapt. Nowadays, how can any county – not just Yorkshire – be strong if England spirit away their best players and systematically erode the significance of the Championship? To judge by the composition of contemporary England teams, perhaps it is time to modernise the maxim. How about: "A strong South Africa is a strong England"?

Chris Waters is cricket correspondent of the Yorkshire Post. *His book,* Fred Trueman: The Authorised Biography, *was* Wisden's *Book of the Year in 2012.*

reminding Bowes of his duty to do the same, thus perpetuating the Yorkshire credo forged when Victoria was Queen, and "Spy" decorated *Vanity Fair* with caricatures of Grace and Spofforth. It hinged on two connecting philosophies: the impossibility of being *too* eager to win, and the indisputable fact that nothing else bloody mattered. However hoary and tattered by overuse, it is obligatory to quote that sentence synonymous with Yorkshire – "we don't play for fun" – simply because the stony phrase is convenient shorthand to explain their approach without the need for much elaboration. The more interesting aspect is how it became the first tenet of their faith.

The judgment of posterity constantly shifts. But Yorkshire are what they are because of Lord Hawke. When he became captain in 1883 every one of the regular XI counted as an alcoholic except Louis Hall, who was a teetotaller. Sir Home Gordon, Hawke's bosom buddy, described Yorkshire as "easy-going, self-indulgent", and "far too polite to run a man out". Hawke turned them into the Championship's first superpower through the imposition of his will and personality, which was benevolently patriarchal on the surface and harder than metamorphic rock beneath. Gordon insisted he once heard a Yorkshireman triumph in a cricketing debate over a Lancastrian with the finality of this declaration: "I know more than you anyhow, for I've shook 'ands with Lord 'Awke and that's more than you ever did."

The keystone of Hawke's success was a move so obviously sensible that you can only suppose his predecessors must have considered it as well, but were too timid or bone idle to implement the thought. Hawke decided to treat a pro like a pro, as opposed to some inferior subspecies. He secured winter payments for them and awarded "mark money" (dependent on his own scoring system of achievement) and decent bonuses to those he called "my dear boys". Just as a gentleman ought to do, he spoke about the morality of playing "in the proper spirit" and the need for "sportsmanlike unselfishness". But Hawke made Yorkshire slickly businesslike and gave them a corporate-style uniformity of purpose. When circumstances demanded, he also knew how to handle the axe: the boozers and the backsliders were got rid of – Hawke just cut them down. He sacked Joe Preston, so fond of his ale that he died at 26; Hawke's diagnosis of the cause was the coldly euphemistic "he had too many friends". Ted Peate went too, after gluttonous overindulgence caused him to swell to 16 stone. Also booted out was the perpetually inebriated Bobby Peel, who – it was claimed – tried to bowl from stump to sightscreen in a beery fug after assuring Hawke: "I'm in fine fettle this morning, m'lud." Peel is said – surely apocryphally – to have then urinated against the same sightscreen on his slow, zigzagged slump back to whence he had drunkenly come.

The inking of the plates to produce John Wisden's first Almanack and the official formation of Yorkshire were as near as dammit simultaneous and nicely serendipitous. *Wisden* has always been there to record that life at Yorkshire is seldom in equilibrium, and that their politics are complicated and often acrimoniously personal. In a game of word association the instant response to the utterance of "Yorkshire cricket" is likely to include the following: rows, rifts, rivalries, recriminations, upheavals, crises, civil wars. Even Hawke experienced these in the arm-wrestle between Leeds and Sheffield

Benevolently patriarchal – but harder than metamorphic rock: Lord Hawke (*centre*) makes a surprising appearance at Bethnal Green in 1910.

to determine which represented the beating heart in the Yorkshire body. This wasn't a polite kerfuffle of Victorian manners. In the 1890s, there were calls to sack a committee that reformers condemned as "effete" and "out of touch", which is archaeological proof – were any still needed – that trouble at t'mill brewed well before the more recent winters of discontent.

Everyone is entitled to be stupid on occasions; but Yorkshire, it must be said, have been guilty of abusing the privilege because of their tendency to always have breath to spare for a good argument. Think of the early to mid-1950s, when dressing-room disharmony – as much as the Surrey of Lock and Laker – left the county barren of titles. Think of the end of that decade, when Johnny Wardle dabbled with high explosives by disputing the decisions of his captain, Ronnie Burnet, and inevitably blew himself up. "Doesta think tha's been a fool, Johnny?" asked a pitman bluntly when Wardle spoke at a South Yorkshire Miners Institute in the aftermath of his sacking. "Aye, I have," he confessed. And think of some of the unedifying spectacles of the late 1960s, the 1970s and the early to mid-1980s, which led to the club looking like a ramshackle vehicle bearing an illustrious name. A lot of grown men, who ought to have known better, behaved like the stereotypical I've-had-it-tougher-than-thee Yorkshireman satirised by *Monty Python*.

Headingley became the cricketing equivalent of the House of Medici. Divisive scheming obstructed the business of winning the Championship. The web of macho, ideological power struggles and score-settling became so convoluted that the club strangled themselves with it. The bickering sounded puerile and self-serving then, and most of the decisions taken seem to defy every principle of common sense when analysed now.

Close was abruptly given the option of resignation or the sack after leading them to four Championships and two Gillette Cups. "How long have I got to decide?" he asked. "Ten minutes," came the reply. The committee had already prepared different statements to accommodate whichever answer he gave. In shock, Close later vomited. Illingworth was regarded as a rebel for wanting the security of a contract, and despatched with the curt, cruel instruction that he could "take any other bugger" with him when he left. John Hampshire found the sour atmosphere intolerable, and announced he was off to discover "if it was possible once more to find joy… in cricket". Trueman felt so isolated from Yorkshire – a jobsworth attendant even denied him access to the car park – that he wouldn't walk through the gate on principle.

In the matter of Boycott, the county seemed never to tire of hearing their own voice; nor did Boycott himself. His admirers worshipped him from the prayer mat. His detractors regarded him as the Tudors regarded Richard III. This provided splendid entertainment for the sort of voyeur who instinctively rubbernecks at a motorway pile-up. My favourite quote from the interminable period when the pro- and anti-Boycott factions were trying to reduce one another to pulp didn't come from a player or an official. Illingworth, back at Headingley as team manager, was told by Mrs Illingworth, sick of the strife and animosity her husband had to endure: "The day you come home from Yorkshire and tell me you're finished will be the happiest of my life."

Yorkshire struggled to cope with their loss of supremacy and had what was tantamount to a full breakdown. If there's a plea of mitigation to be made for those torturous seasons, it is this. No county feel the weight of their past as Yorkshire do, or the obligation to maintain their reputation. No county have such a regal sense of entitlement. And no county so strongly believe that identity, ego, independence and self-worth are at stake in their cricket. As a polymath, John Arlott could express this sentiment and mean it: "I've enjoyed cricket more and served it better for realising it was never the be-all and end-all of everything." No one ever said that in Pudsey.

The fact that Yorkshire have won only one Championship in 44 years makes winning another urgent. The current president, Mr G. Boycott of Fitzwilliam, is adamant about that. On assuming office he declared: "I know what the members value and that is Championship cricket." He was repeating only what Hutton and Sutcliffe and Rhodes had said before him; and what Hawke said before any of them. But I can hear someone – who long ago toted a barometer across God's Own Country purely for the sake of his beloved club – saying a loud "Amen" in agreement.

Duncan Hamilton is the award-winning author of Harold Larwood: The Authorized Biography of the World's Fastest Bowler.

Anthony Au-Yeung, photosport.co.nz

THE WISDEN–MCC CRICKET PHOTOGRAPH OF 2012 Anthony Au-Yeung won the award for his image of Zimbabwe's Tatenda Taibu aiming for a run-out in a Twenty20 international against New Zealand at Auckland, February 11.

The third Wisden–MCC Cricket Photograph of the Year, in association with Park Cameras, the leading Canon professional dealer, attracted more than 350 entries. Any image with a cricket theme taken during 2012 was eligible. The independent judging panel, chaired by former *Sunday Times* chief photographer Chris Smith, comprised award-winning photographers Patrick Eagar and Eileen Langley, the Essex all-rounder Graham Napier, and art director of *The Cricketer* Nigel Davies. For more details, go to www.lords.org/photooftheyear

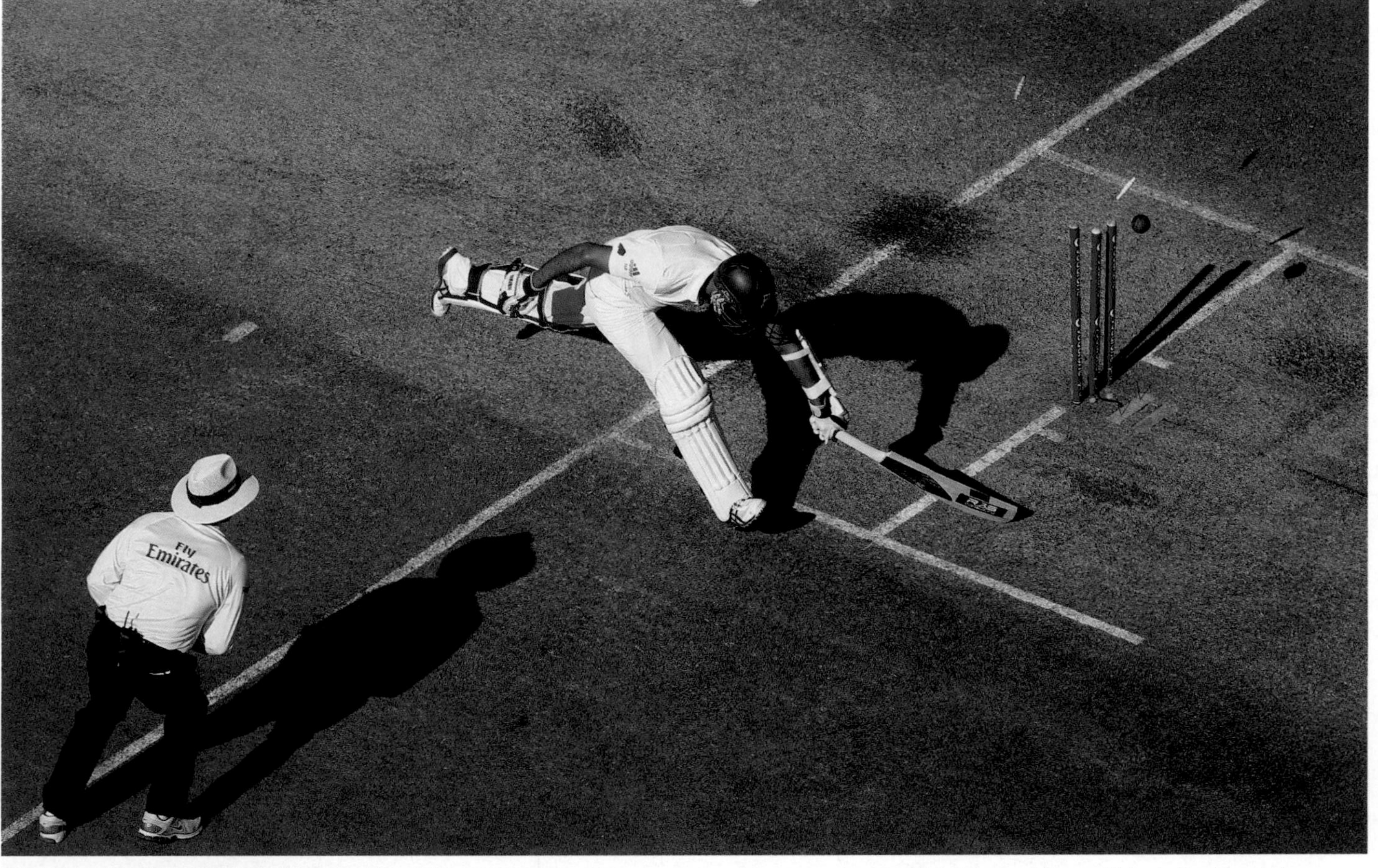

Robert Cianflone, Getty Images

THE WISDEN–MCC CRICKET PHOTOGRAPH OF 2012 Robert Cianflone was one of two runners-up for his image of South Africa's Hashim Amla surviving an attempted run-out, in the Third Test against Australia at Perth, December 1.

Somenath Mukhopadhyay

THE WISDEN–MCC CRICKET PHOTOGRAPH OF 2012 Somenath Mukhopadhyay was the other runner-up for his image of boys playing cricket in West Bengal, India, December 8.

Mark Ralston, AFP/Getty Images

LET THE GAMES BEGIN In July, cricket was part of the London Olympics' opening ceremony; in the days ahead, Lord's became the home of archery.

PA Photos

Adnan Abidi, Reuters

CRICKET, CRICKET EVERYWHERE In India, impromptu games take place on the dried-up riverbed of the Ganges at Patna, and in the campus of the Lady Wellington College in Chennai after the sport was banned from the city's Marina Beach.

C. Suresh Kumar

Cameron Spencer, Getty Images

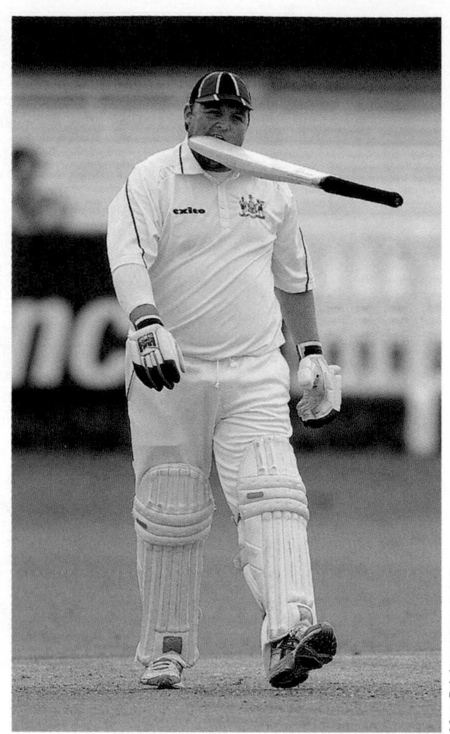

Matt Bright

BEST-LAID PLANS Sri Lanka's Farveez Maharoof loses a chunk of bat at Adelaide (though the string that kept it together clings on); Ashley Leat of Incogniti CC seems to sink his teeth into willow after being dismissed at Lord's; while Matt Prior and Rob Quiney are startled to see where the ball has ended up, in a Big Bash League game. (The image of Leat, taken by Matt Bright, was shortlisted for the Wisden–MCC Cricket Photograph of the Year 2012.)

Michael Dodge, Getty Images

Carl de Souza, AFP/Getty Images

NEW CONVERTS In Mombasa, Kenya, a Maasai tribesman bowls in a practice session in March (see Cricket Round the World, page 1227), while girls at a school in Brunei Darussalam watch their instructor attentively (this image was the ICC Photo of the Year for 2012).

Hj Rusdi Hj Abdul Latif

Hamish Blair, Getty Images

THE LEADING CRICKETER IN THE WORLD Michael Clarke.

THE LEADING CRICKETER IN THE WORLD, 2012

Michael Clarke

GREG BAUM

At Bangalore in 2004, after the 23-year-old Michael Clarke had made a fizzing century on debut for Australia, team-mate Darren Lehmann declared he should play every Test for the next ten years, even if it meant forfeiting his own place. At Brisbane six years later, when Clarke stood in as one-day skipper against England, he became the first Australian captain in living memory to be booed by a home crowd. In 2012, he passed 200 four times in Tests, a feat not achieved even by Don Bradman – and the hallelujahs rang out.

Excitement, disappointment, re-endearment, respect: this is the not uncommon J-curve for a major cricketer. In Clarke, the plotted points read something like this: infatuation, disillusionment, rehabilitation and, last year, awe. It is a capital J-curve, exaggerated in proportion to his talent.

Clarke arrived with a gift, but in public estimation then acquired baggage, and has taken until recently to shed it. Like Steve Waugh, he is from Sydney's unpretentious western suburbs. Unlike Waugh, he was seen to develop pretensions – glamour girlfriend, fast car, endorsements portfolio – until it seemed Australia saw more of him straddling the centrefold crease than the batting crease. In a country in which the buzzword for two decades or more has been aspiration, this would not have mattered, except it led to a presumption that he was neglecting his cricket and squandering his privilege.

Clarke's rise coincided with Australia's decline. This made him an easy scapegoat, most acutely at the end of the 2010-11 Ashes fiasco. When a dressing-room altercation two years earlier with the flinty Simon Katich finally became known, the public sided with Katich, believing the scrapper had taken the pretty boy down a notch. And when Clarke decamped briefly from a tour of New Zealand to deal with the break-up of his relationship, the late Peter Roebuck tore strips off him for dereliction of duty.

In Cricket Australia's high office, Clarke was thought to lack the necessary gravitas. To this day, it is hard to imagine him delivering a Bradman-style dissertation, or even a Mark Taylor-style reflection. He speaks plentifully, but with a side-of-the-mouth tic, and an almost perverse resolve to stick to the team-first dictum, even when a little personal elaboration would cause no offence. He is no one's idea of a statesman.

But nor is he the shallow and indolent playboy of popular imagination. He works hard at his game; the legacy is a chronically sore back. He spurned the modern cynosure of the Indian Premier League at its formation to stay home with his ill father. When he suspected Twenty20 was retarding his development, he gave it away at international level altogether. Fortified, Clarke began to answer critics and doubters in the only idiom he knew: runs, runs, and more runs.

In Clarke's batting maturity, five precepts are evident. The first is range. With an unerring eye, he affronts the ball on the rise as assuredly as anyone can ever have done. Yet he also plays so late that bowlers and slips throw up their hands in anticipation of the lbw that rarely comes. For bowlers, there is almost no margin for error; for Clarke, a repertoire lacking only the hook shot.

The second is the natural's gift of timing. Late in 2012 against Sri Lanka, while hampered by injury at Hobart and Melbourne, he would stab down on yorkers with no thought other than of survival, yet still the ball would squirt from his bat like a pip from an orange.

The third is a delightfully twinkle-toed approach to spin bowling, so at odds with the modern modus of swatting from the crease.

The fourth is temperament. He is capable of batting for hours and days at a consistent tempo, through lulls, beyond spurts and notwithstanding scares. Sometimes, even when compiling an enormous score, he looks oddly vulnerable, almost inept, particularly to bowling aimed at his head. But he shrugs off these moments as he might flies, regards a gram of luck as the reasonable corollary of kilograms of estimable batting, and his innings rolls on.

The fifth, encompassing all four, is strength of character, irreconcilable with his erstwhile image, but now undeniable. Immediately on returning to New Zealand after sorting out his domestic crisis, he answered the howling reproof with a century.

In the wake of the Ashes, Clarke replaced Ricky Ponting as Test captain and, as Australian cricket modernised, he was made a selector too. This imposed on him a heft of responsibility few previous captains have had to bear, liable to crush a faint mind. His stream of runs increased to an outpouring. In his first 21 matches in charge, he averaged 69, with eight hundreds.

Moreover, he quickly revealed himself as an intuitive and adventurous leader in the Taylor mould. Never, if he can help it, does he let a match stand still, or simply run its course. He makes judicious declarations, sets designer fields, rotates bowlers often, and is unafraid to tear up the rulebook, trusting instead in his instinct. When trying to bowl out stubborn Sri Lanka at Hobart, he gave an over to wicketkeeper Matthew Wade. In the bald context of this essay, perhaps that sounds gimmicky. In the match, it altered the rhythms. Australia won.

In 2012, we witnessed a full flowering of the lavish batting talent announced so spectacularly all those years ago in Bangalore. The year began with 329 not out against India, the biggest Test innings ever played at the SCG, curtailed only by his own declaration, with Bradman's (and Taylor's) 334 one hit away. Even then, some suspected he was playing for public favour. A double-century followed at Adelaide before, at the start of the 2012-13 season, free-hitting back-to-back doubles against South Africa. He rounded off the year with his first century in a Boxing Day Test, against Sri Lanka, compiled while nursing a pinched hamstring that reduced him to walking between the wickets, but made no appreciable difference to the sweetness of his strokeplay. His score, 106, was also his calendar-year average; only Bradman, Sobers and Ponting before him had reached New Year's Eve on such a plane. And his 2012 Test aggregate of 1,595 placed him nearly 350 runs clear of his nearest rival, Alastair Cook.

As 2013 began, Clarke deserved to feel content: all the caps fitted. He was 31 – prime batting age – rich in form and circumstance, with a low-profile wife and few of his old affectations. He had earned rave reviews as a batsman and captain; under him, an experimental Australian team had lost only one of seven series, to top-ranked South Africa. The ambivalence of public and critics was forgotten, except in one detail: a perception that he should bat higher than No. 5. While an in-form Ponting was ahead of him, it didn't matter, but a succession of greenhorns had since been exposed. Clarke could reasonably answer that it had been decades since the best batsman axiomatically arrived at No. 3. But No. 4 seemed sensible.

Still, mountains loomed. The retirements of Ponting and Mike Hussey a month apart left Clarke as the only fixture in Australia's batting order, isolating him as no one had been since Allan Border, and imposing on him an Atlas-size burden, as a still-insubstantial team contemplated two Ashes series. Though his own man as captain, he depended on Ponting for almost grandfatherly support; that is gone. More even than Ponting ever was, Clarke is both captain and batting fulcrum. And it looks like being the making of him.

THE LEADING CRICKETER IN THE WORLD

2003	Ricky Ponting (A)	2008	Virender Sehwag (I)
2004	Shane Warne (A)	2009	Virender Sehwag (I)
2005	Andrew Flintoff (E)	2010	Sachin Tendulkar (I)
2006	Muttiah Muralitharan (SL)	2011	Kumar Sangakkara (SL)
2007	Jacques Kallis (SA)	**2012**	**Michael Clarke (A)**

Players can be chosen more than once for this award.

50 YEARS OF TOURING ENGLAND

The ride of a lifetime

TONY COZIER

Nepotism has got itself a bad name, so I'll plump for "fatherly favouritism" as the catalyst for my career, which has tracked cricket's most exciting, erratic and exasperating team for more than half a century. This year, sober to relate, marks 50 since I first covered a West Indies tour of England.

Jimmy Cozier was, at various times, editor of three West Indian papers, before setting up his own, the Barbados *Daily News*, in 1960. In England in 1950, he had been the lone Caribbean chronicler of a series that first established West Indies as a genuine force. Presumably he considered his only son his logical successor. His present on my eighth birthday was the 1948 *Wisden*; seven years later, he got permission for me to be excused from school in Barbados so I could file for St Lucia's *The Voice* (circulation 2,500) during the Kensington Oval Test against Australia. He sent me off to university in Ottawa to study for a journalism degree, but the arctic winters and lack of cricket on the curriculum prematurely ended that venture.

So I recognised he was a soft touch when I put it to him that I should cover West Indies in England in 1963 for the *Daily News*. The deal was that the paper would look after the flight and provide a modest stipend, beyond which I would fend for myself. It meant staying in YMCAs and B&Bs unless I could bunk up with school friends who had gone on to further studies in the UK; at 23, it was hardly an imposition.

I spent the summer criss-crossing the counties, hitching a ride in the team's baggage van or the Ford Zephyr of Roy Lawrence, the melodious Jamaican who was the West Indian voice on *Test Match Special*. My daily reports were tapped out by typewriter on to special mustard-coloured cable forms (specimens still available at any reputable museum), and filed at the nearest post office – in London I tended to use the Embankment – for transmission to Barbados. It was a tiresome business.

On the back of the 1960-61 tour of Australia, that 1963 trip proved another triumph. Frank Worrell, in his final series, was again the revered, level-headed leader of the brilliant young brigade he had nurtured: Garry Sobers, Rohan Kanhai, Wes Hall, Lance Gibbs, now joined by Charlie Griffith. Denis Compton rated it "undoubtedly the best cricketing side in the world". As soon as Basil Butcher stroked the winning runs in the final Test to secure the inaugural Wisden Trophy, created to mark the 100th edition of the Almanack, the Oval outfield was engulfed in a joyous tsunami, it seemed, of every one of the thousands of West Indians who had made their homes in south London a decade earlier. By the end of the summer, MCC had altered West Indies' tour cycle to England from six or seven years to three or four. Worrell's knighthood in the New Year's honours was the perfect way to top things off. It all made for good copy. Circulation at the *Daily News* took an upturn. Cozier senior was delighted. My future was set.

Through the bad times that have overtaken West Indies cricket, and even through the good, when they twice stood unquestionably at the pinnacle of the world game (first in the mid-1960s, then for 15 years until the mid-1990s), there have been confusion and controversy. This was inevitable, perhaps, given the existence of a dozen nations, all with their own governments, anthems and flags, and united only by a game bequeathed to them by British colonialism.

So there has never been a dull moment. And without the initial paternal push, I might otherwise have been confined to some humdrum occupation. The alternative has taken me to vastly different locations: they don't get more disparate than Peshawar and Dunedin, or Chittagong and Canberra. I've delighted in the constantly passing parade of great players and great matches. As a television commentator, I've been first-hand witness to the revolutionary changes instituted by Kerry Packer's World Series Cricket, as well as the Twenty20 tournaments that have transformed cricket's character. And, before the elimination of Test-match rest days, there was always the fun of Sunday games on English village greens with press teams or Brian Scovell's intrepid Woodpeckers.

By the time I returned to England in 1966, radio commentary had been added to my roster. When Roy Lawrence, by now head of Radio Jamaica's sports coverage, was summoned back for the Commonwealth Games in Kingston in August, *TMS* agreed to his recommendation that I should fill in for the Headingley Test. The prospect of joining famous men whose voices we had listened to since schooldays was intimidating; a combination of the presence of an even younger first-timer by the name of Christopher Martin-Jenkins, the relaxed ambience, and a West Indies innings victory proved an ideal introduction. Like the entire summer, the match was dominated by the incomparable Sobers (174 runs, eight for 80). He was later eulogised in a calypso by the Mighty Sparrow as "the greatest cricketer on earth or Mars". I certainly have seen none better.

I've been on *TMS* for every West Indian tour of England since, and it has led to many similar assignments elsewhere. There have been the predictable clashes with passionate fans back home, but only once has the *TMS* connection caused any strife. BBC Radio Four used to insist on having a commentator at the ground from 8am to set the scene for the day's play. I had drawn the short straw for the final day

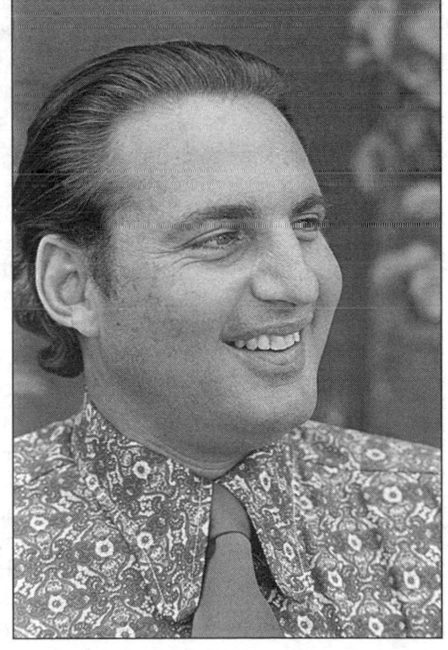

Patrick Eagar

Tony Cozier, 1973.

FIVE WISDEN TROPHY MOMENTS

TONY COZIER

Wes Hall – Lord's, 1963

On a dank June morning, Wes Hall had slept in and missed breakfast, so his captain Frank Worrell gave him two hard-boiled eggs and a packet of salt on the bus ride to Lord's for the last day of the Second Test. Somehow, this helped sustain him through a 24-over spell from the Pavilion End, lasting from the delayed start at 2.20 to the dramatic final over: Colin Cowdrey, arm in plaster from a break inflicted by a Hall thunderbolt the previous day, came in at No. 11, before David Allen kept out Hall's last two deliveries.

Garry Sobers – Lord's, 1966

It was Sobers's summer – batting, bowling, catching, captaining. He would rate the unbeaten 163 in the second innings at Lord's as his best, above even his 254 for the World XI at Melbourne five years later. When he was joined at 95 for five midway through the fourth day by his cousin David Holford, West Indies were just nine ahead. "The only way you were going to get out of this was to play shots," he reasoned, typically. "You couldn't defend for a day and a half." He told Holford the pitch was like Kensington Oval back home, and there should be nothing to worry him. Nothing did. When Sobers declared next day, Holford was 105, their stand a record 274, and the match safe.

Michael Holding – The Oval, 1976

It was a parched summer – with the Oval outfield as barren as the Sahara, and the pitch as flat as a runway. There were double-hundreds for Viv Richards and Dennis Amiss, and 1,507 runs at nearly 54 a wicket. Yet Michael Holding, driven by flawless rhythm and Tony Greig's pre-series promise to make West Indies "grovel", glided in from the Nursery End to destroy England twice with pace and pinpoint accuracy. Of his 14 wickets, 12 were either bowled (Greig twice) or lbw. Awesome.

Gordon Greenidge – Lord's, 1984

At lunch on the final day, MCC president Alex Dibbs hosted West Indian High Commissioners and journalists at lunch. By then, West Indies – needing 344 after David Gower's declaration – were 82 for the run-out of Desmond Haynes. The consensus was a draw, but sheer bluster prompted me to counter with: "We'll piss it" – or words to that effect. And, incredibly, West Indies did, with 11 overs and nine wickets to spare, as Gordon Greenidge pummelled a commanding 214 alongside the unflappable Larry Gomes.

Malcolm Marshall – Headingley, 1984

Within an hour of the start, Malcolm Marshall had copped a double fracture of his left wrist fielding at gully; the team doctor advised he would be out for ten days. But an unexpected twist changed the plan. Gomes was on 94 when Joel Garner was ninth out. Assuming the innings was over, the players headed for the pavilion – only to find Marshall coming the other way. Left arm in plaster, his box forgotten in the rush, and batting exclusively with his right hand, he saw Gomes to his landmark. Ten minutes later, Marshall was back, fracture still strapped, to embark on figures of seven for 53. It was daring typical of a team that took the series 5–0.

of the 1984 Lord's Test, but I'd forgotten my special MCC pass, and the ageing steward – protecting the North Gate as if with his life – refused me entrance. Panicking that I'd miss my slot, I pressed the accelerator and moved slowly forward, only for the steward, by now red-faced with indignation, to throw himself across the bonnet. The intervention of his West Indian colleague, whom I'd known from Barbados, saved the day. "Just pay the £10 parking fee, Tony," was his common-sense solution. The report lasted 90 seconds.

Such was West Indies' command in Wisden Trophy contests in those days that you turned up wondering not if they would win, but by how much. The transformation has been abrupt and complete. From 1973 to 1989-90, they won 25 Tests to England's two, among them a pair of 5–0 blackwashes. Since 2000, the count favours England 17–2, including a 4–0 whitewash. This is one reason – along with health and safety – why West Indians no longer swarm across the outfields at The Oval and Lord's. It is no longer *their* team, as it was their grandparents'. While the current generation have gravitated to football and athletics, the disenchantment is left to their relations back home. And for all the happiness over last year's victory at the World Twenty20 in Sri Lanka, an overall revival is likely to be a long time coming.

It was the most miserable tour I have been on

Even with the debilitating combination at domestic level of a weak board, a militant players' union, poor pitches, erratic umpiring and constant changes of captain (nine since 2000) and coach (six in the same span), it is difficult to comprehend the speed at which West Indies have plunged from a position of pride to virtual irrelevance.

The 2000 series in England typified another factor: attitude. It was, without doubt, the most miserable tour I have been on. West Indies' innings victory in the First Test at Edgbaston prompted such complacency that it was followed by three defeats – and this was a team including Brian Lara, Curtly Ambrose and Courtney Walsh. The indignity of 54 all out at Lord's, 50 years after their historic maiden victory in England at the same ground, followed by defeat in two days at Leeds, left Lester Armoogam – an elderly Trinidadian who followed them round the world – in tears. The response of some players after the Headingley humiliation was to head off to Manchester on the scheduled fourth day to watch Trinidad's Dwight Yorke in action for United.

The debate had once been simply over which team were stronger: those of the 1960s, fashioned by Worrell, the father figure venerated by his players, or those moulded by Clive Lloyd, his 1980s equivalent. Now we wonder whether they will ever pull themselves out of their slump. Between 1976 and 1988, West Indies did not lose a Test in the Wisden Trophy, home or away. The origins of this period of dominance were in the 5–1 drubbing in Australia in 1975-76, inflicted by a fast-bowling quartet spearheaded by Dennis Lillee and Jeff Thomson. From there on, Lloyd packed his teams with West Indian Lillees and Thomsons. A host of worthy contenders couldn't get a game, except with English counties – or on two rebel tours of South Africa.

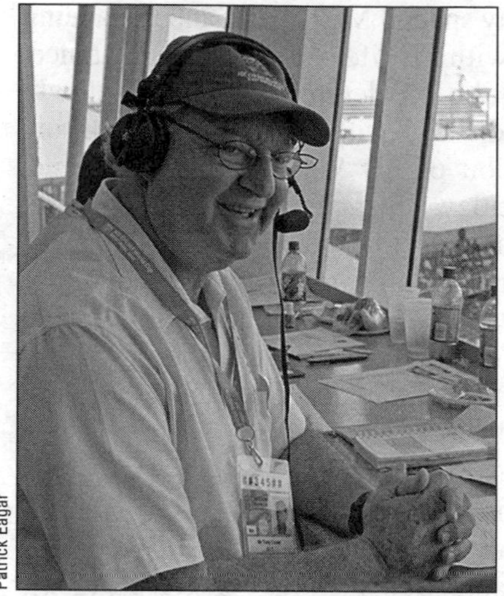
Patrick Eagar

Home service: Tony Cozier at Kensington Oval, in the press box named after him.

There was always one straightforward motivation for those playing under Worrell and Lloyd – winning. There was another significant element when the opponents were England, especially in front of their newly domiciled kith and kin from the 1950s. There had long been images of joyous, guitar-strumming calypsonians parading across Lord's following the historic 1950 victory; now, boisterous cavorting West Indians rejoicing at yet another victory became a regular feature on English grounds. "History does come into play," said Viv Richards, who wore his heart on his sleeve and the Rastafarian colours on his wristband. "These were the colonial masters who had passed the game on to us. There was obviously a lot of passion whenever we played." That passion was further fired by the boast of England captain Tony Greig prior to the 1976 series that he would make them "grovel". It was an ill-chosen word from a white South African at the height of the global resistance to apartheid. As a consequence, Greig's stumps were regularly rearranged by Michael Holding, Andy Roberts and Wayne Daniel, and West Indies won 3–0.

Along the way, I've found myself having to clarify my racial background, confusing to those unaware of the Caribbean's cosmopolitan mix. A dumbfounded waitress once put it: "Hey, youse is a black voice coming from a white mouth!" I am white, born and bred in Barbados, and my accent is the same as those she would have heard from West Indian settlers on any British street. Of course, I couldn't be seen on radio, prompting one racist letter-writer, enraged by a ferocious spell of West Indian pace, to address me as "you black bastard". He insisted: "You should go back to where you came from." It particularly amused Henry Blofeld.

Even London bobbies were fooled. The Saturday of the 1976 Lord's Test was the only day washed out during that drought summer. It gave me the chance to catch up in the bar under the grandstand with expat friends from home. Soon I was surrounded by West Indians stridently arguing about the game, as they tend to. Spotting me in the corner as the only white face in a sea of black, two policemen broke through: "You all right, sir?" They were smartly sent on their way by the Caribbean congregation.

Certainly, I have never found my colour an issue among the players. Reds Perreira, who worked on radio for several tours, and I were often the only West Indians relaying the news back home. The days of Holding, Ian Bishop, Jeffrey Dujon and other former Test players doing commentary were still some way off. So too was the distrust of the media by those who interpret any description of a reckless stroke or a wayward spell as a threat to their now lucrative livelihoods.

It was clearly an advantage to have been roughly the same vintage as the modest stars of the 1960s, played club cricket against some, and known most as friends. And for three decades they were winning – it didn't matter what was said about them. Indeed, Reds and I often found ourselves treated virtually as members of the support staff, invited to their Christmas celebrations in Australia and India, and included in a separate team photo for our albums. As the generation gap widened, such camaraderie has understandably turned to respect for age and longevity. At least, I hope that's what it is.

Tony Cozier has covered the West Indian team in all the major cricket countries (and some minor ones) since 1962, including every Wisden Trophy series bar one.

CHRISTOPHER MARTIN-JENKINS, 1945–2013

Flowing conversation

MIKE SELVEY

We called him The Major. There was nothing secret to it, nothing to do with a military bearing, or clipped diction and moustache to match. One day he blustered his way into the press box. "Hampshire won," he announced to nobody in particular. "Did it, Major?" we chorused, echoing Basil Fawlty. And so The Major he became – or sometimes, to a very select few, Stork, which is considerably more obscure and will remain so.

The Major became a legend, the stories told and retold, embellished, enhanced, and even invented. He could be calamitous. Things happened to him that simply did not to other people. Pick someone to play him in a biopic and it would have to be Rowan Atkinson. It was a trait I first encountered on the 1976-77 tour of India, when he was a young BBC correspondent. Seeking to travel by cab to the local studio of All India Radio, he found himself sitting an hour later outside a remote refinery belonging to Oil India.

This sort of thing continued right through our acquaintance, whether he was inadvertently shedding golf clubs like confetti through the centre of Bridgetown as we raced madcap for a tee-time in our mini-moke, late as ever; or snipping through the wire of his Walkman headphones while attending to his newspaper cuttings and wondering why the music had stopped; or going to the wrong hotel – or, on one occasion, the wrong international ground in London for a match he was late for in any case.

He was notoriously (and often infuriatingly) tardy, to the extent that his memorial service at St Paul's should have been scheduled as "11.15am for 11" as a mark of respect – with directions to the wrong church. The famous incident in which he mistook a TV remote control for his mobile phone and actually tried to dial on it really did happen, although as the sole witness I can say it was rarely in the manner or location in which the story is often told. His capacity to render laptops unusable – merely by looking at them, it seemed – was uncanny, as if he had mystic powers, the sort of thing that should have been harnessed by the secret service. He would laugh at all this, of course, rather revelling in his reputation, not least because he understood the affection behind the ribbing. He even played up to it.

And then comes the other side of him. In an appreciation elsewhere, I suggested cricket had lost perhaps the best friend it has ever had, a thought I stand by. He was a prolific writer on the game, not just as a most respected and authoritative correspondent for the *Daily Telegraph* and then *The Times*, but in his numerous books and as editor of *The Cricketer*. He championed the sport, and all who played it, with remarkable zeal.

Surely, though, it is as a supreme broadcaster that he will be best remembered. Once he had stumbled, tripped and fumbled his way into his

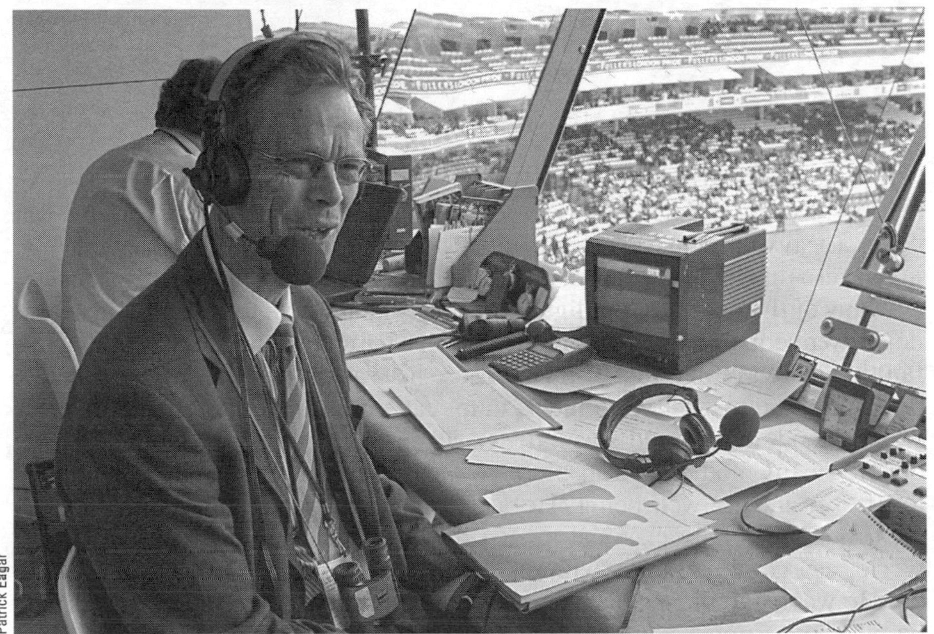

Patrick Eagar

Lucid and knowledgable: Christopher Martin-Jenkins in the *TMS* box at Lord's, 2003.

commentary position, and dumped down the big A4 leatherbound desk diary in which he scrawled his notes, his cricket commentaries were a benchmark for lucidity, knowledge, observation and humour.

Working with him as a summariser, which I was fortunate enough to do for the best part of a quarter of a century, was a joy. There are commentators who insist on taking each over uninterrupted, then hand over for a breather. Some dip into the summariser's time as well. But with The Major it became a conversation, rather than a series of disjointed interjections. Very quickly I got to understand how he worked, when it was appropriate to speak, and when to let him go so that it flowed seamlessly. That was his skill, not mine, for he controlled it all, using his deep knowledge of cricket and cricketers not to pontificate, but to draw things from me, in the way an advocate might a witness.

Only once did I see him flummoxed. Like many cricketers, I used rhyming slang by habit, so if I were to say that someone was having treatment on their Vanburn, you might surmise Holder, or shoulder. During one commentary stint, he thought he would have a stab. "I've been having some trouble with the old Conrad," he said. At first it stunned me, and then I corpsed – so badly I had to leave the commentary box. He meant Conrad Black. I am sorry to say my only thought was of a former West Indies opener by a different surname.

Mike Selvey is the cricket correspondent of The Guardian.

A bank of happy memories

JAMES MARTIN-JENKINS

"Any relation?" It's a question I've been asked almost daily, it seems, for nearly 40 years. "Yes," I reply; and gladly, too. For being the "son of" was never a heavy burden. Rather, life with CMJ was invariably fun and interesting; it was also unusual, privileged, and – needless to say – dominated by cricket.

Many of the qualities highlighted by his colleagues in tributes following his death were equally evident at home. He was hard-working, conscientious to a fault, and always in a rush – less because he was disorganised, more because he took on too many commitments in his eagerness not to let people down. He was a good mimic and even better joke-teller; competitive; enthusiastic; devoted to my mother; and absolutely – though never unthinkingly – committed to cricket and its well-being. He also enjoyed many of life's other refined pleasures, especially classical music, decent wine (less so food), the natural world, and good literature, without ever becoming an expert, or pretending to be. He was punctilious about grammar and properly pronounced vowels. But he was not a snob – anything but. He was liberal, fair and decent, plus God-fearing (increasingly so), thoughtful and kind.

For so accomplished a public performer, he was rather shy in social situations, and far from garrulous. Perhaps that's not unusual. But his job – and therefore my childhood – certainly was. Most of my friends had a dad who worked in an office and came home every evening, or at least at the weekend, and certainly at Christmas. I didn't. Most families went on summer holidays, too. Save for a few days in Devon snatched between Tests, we didn't.

Then again, most children didn't hear or see their dad on radio or TV on a regular basis, as my siblings and I did. And my access to a game I was born to love was a rare treat indeed. What fun it was to accompany dad to a match – to Chelmsford, say, or Southampton or Hove – standing as still as a statue in the back of the commentary box, or playing cricket on the outfield in the tea break, or being introduced to and getting autographs from my playing heroes, then watching and waiting (there was always a lot of waiting), while he recorded or wrote his report of the day's play. We were normally the last to leave the ground, often well after dusk.

Then there was touring with the England team as a child, sometimes for several weeks. Who else can boast of learning to walk in Australia and to swim in India, of being thrown into a pool by Ian Botham, of standing in the commentary box as England won the Ashes at the MCG in 1986-87 and the one-day series at the WACA that followed, then returning to Melbourne in 1992 to witness Wasim Akram blow away England and win Pakistan a World Cup final? I can, and more. I batted against Trevor Bailey on the beach in Barbados, then met two of the Three Ws at a cocktail party the next evening. And I bowled to Sir Len Hutton in his garden.

So I have a lot to thank him for. And a bank of happy memories – shared, I hope, by my children, who are old enough, just, to remember him as the

Not a rabbit in sight: Robin, Judy, Lucy, CMJ, James and Sandy the dog, Naldrett House, 1984.

concerned and caring grandfather he was. (The modern world's ready supply of video and other archives, plus my father's excellent autobiography, will help them fill in the gaps.) They may recall his near obsession with golf, which he took up too late in life to have been as good as he would have liked, and the practice putting green he installed at home in an attempt – vain, it transpired – to improve his short game. They may also recall his ongoing battle – equally in vain – with the many rabbits that used to attack his beloved lawn.

What's likely to be my enduring feeling? Pride – when he wrote well or spoke eloquently, when he stuck to his guns on an unfashionable point, when people laughed, nodded vigorously in agreement, or exclaimed to me, as so many have: "Don't you look and sound exactly like him!"

I didn't always agree with everything he said, and rarely sought his advice on matters outside sport, but how fortunate to be able to wake every day and read or listen to what the old man had to say. It saved on phone bills, anyway. And yes, he may have had a wonderful collection of faux swear words, but he did occasionally swear in private, and with the proper words too – mostly at the rabbits…

James Martin-Jenkins is a partner in a business-intelligence firm, and a keen sportsman. He lives in London with his wife, Nicola, and their three young children.

A full obituary of Christopher Martin-Jenkins will appear in Wisden 2014.

CRICKET AND CORRUPTION

For the better – or worse?

ED HAWKINS

Never meet a hero, they reckon. But what of a villain? Say hello to Vinay, from Bhopal, capital of the central Indian state of Madhya Pradesh. He is an illegal bookmaker, which also makes him a scourge of the game, and a malevolent, match-fixing mobster. Right?

When I met Vinay in a hotel lobby, the reputation of his brethren – there are estimated to be more than 70,000 bookies in India – preceded him. All, bar those who work at racecourses (where gambling, so the argument goes, is based on skill rather than luck, and therefore socially acceptable) are illegal. It is said – by the ICC, corruption officers, national boards and player bodies – that the illegal bookies are dangerous men from the underworld. People fear them. And so, in truth, did I, as I waited for Vinay, nervously tapping my feet to inane pan-pipe music.

Yet when he arrived, I immediately felt at ease. There was no cloak, no dagger. His smile was brilliant, his handshake warm, his enquiry after my health genuine. We had already exchanged emails, Twitter messages and phone calls. What followed was a crash course in India's vast gambling industry. Over several weeks as part of my research for a book on corruption in cricket, I would spend time living with him and his family, and watch him run his business (he also owned a construction firm); I would hide from the police, learn how bookies control betting markets, and hear of fixes before they happened. When we parted, I told Vinay of my initial apprehension. "Me?" he guffawed. "This is too much amusement for me. I hope you know me now, ya? But perhaps I understand why you were like this. Bookmakers in India are supposed to be all bad. No. We are trying to make our living in a corrupt country, and we do this by taking any opportunity we can."

The backdrop to my visit was the sound of exploding myths. Chief among them was the notion that it is possible to place a bet on a no-ball, a misconception that called into question the precise nature of the conviction of Salman Butt, Mohammad Asif and Mohammad Aamer in the spot-fixing trial of November 2011 – though there is no doubt that the *News of the World* sting showed them to be corruptible. But preconceived notions about corruption in cricket simply collapsed, for it is just not possible to bet on the minutiae of a match: a batsman scoring a certain amount of runs, a fielder being placed in a particular position, a bowler operating from a specific end – or even sending down a pre-designated no-ball. Why? Because just as Indian bookies are not the threatening hoodlums of popular depiction, neither are they knuckle-dragging imbeciles. "Do you think we're fools?" asked Vinay. "If someone says they want this no-ball bet for big monies, and I'm Ladbrokes in London, I tell them to go away. No bookmaker in the world takes this bet."

Betfair: the scene of millions of gambling exchanges every day.

One does not need to be invited into Vinay's home to understand that any bookie worth his salt would suspect that this customer had inside information. Yet throughout the Southwark trial of the three Pakistanis and their agent, there was a wilful acceptance that the *News of the World* would have been able to place a bet on the timing of a no-ball, had they so wished. This was clear from the sentencing remarks by Mr Justice Cooke: "Bets could be placed on these no-balls in unlawful markets, mostly abroad, based on inside advance knowledge of what was going to happen… Individuals in India were making £40,000–£50,000 on each identified no-ball. On three no-balls, therefore, the bookmakers stood to lose £150,000 on each bet by a cheating punter."

In fact, this is impossible. The illegal Indian market is highly organised and, crucially, uniform. It offers only four markets for its gamblers: match odds, innings runs (known as *lambi*), brackets (the number of runs scored in a certain amount of overs), and lunch favourite (essentially, betting that the team who are favourites at lunch in a Test, or at the innings break in a limited-overs match, will go on and win the game). In the case of the *lambi* and brackets, a spread is set for the number of runs to be scored, and gamblers bet over or under.

The odds for these markets are provided by four syndicates, who have reached the top of the food chain through their expertise in the field. They charge a fee to bookmakers to use those odds, then take a cut of the profits from all over the country. Think of the syndicates as wholesalers, and the bookies as convenience-store owners, who buy the goods, then sell them on. Vinay is what is known as a first-tier bookmaker. Occasionally, because he is highly regarded, he acts as one of the syndicate heads, who are often based in Mumbai or Dubai, sending out odds to bookies lower down the chain; bookmakers from the second, third or fourth tiers have fewer customers, and receive the odds via SMS, with the syndicate able to reach hundreds of them at once using bulk messaging software. "All bookies in India are connected," said Vinay. "They will send on the prices to even more."

Because the syndicates are so dominant, the potential for the manipulation of markets is obvious. And it is certainly more profitable than paying a bowler to overstep. "The Indian market is very big and powerful," Vinay told me just before England's one-day international against India at Hyderabad in October 2011. "There are much smarter ways to manipulate betting. Look, I'll show you."

"You see: India 1.85 now on Betfair – we have moved the market"

On his laptop he logged on to Betfair, the person-to-person betting exchange with more than 4m customers around the globe. After it was announced India had won the toss, he sent updated odds to 200 bookmakers across the country. On the match-odds market, India were favourites at 1.95 (even money would be 2.00). These decimal odds translate into the traditional fractional odds used in the UK as 20-21: in other words, if you bet £21 you can win £20.

"Now watch how I move the Betfair market," said Vinay. When he sends the SMS to his cohorts instructing them to lower the odds, they flood Betfair with money – or, to be precise, with people prepared to place bets at these odds. He explained: "It is currently India 1.95. Watch how they become 1.85 in line with our odds… wait, you'll see here how it works… we want to get India short." Vinay was keen to price India as short as possible because he knew most of his punters would back the home team. Since an Indian victory would have been certain to cost him money, he wanted to discourage punters from backing them. Seconds later, he chirped: "There, you see: India 1.85 now on Betfair. We have moved the market." And all this from a text message which simply read: "India 85".

This, of course, is not corruption – just the sheer weight of (illegal) Indian money. Yet no matter what wagers are struck, the bookmaker and the syndicates are able to avoid losses by using betting exchanges to hedge their bets. For example, a bookie may have accepted a wager from any Tom, Dick or Hari of £10 on England to win at even money. This has the potential to cost the bookie £10. However, when England's odds during the game drift to 6-4 (greater than even money) – either because momentum has shifted towards India, or because Vinay has manipulated the market from a hotel room in Bhopal – the bookie can lay off, or hedge, his bets. The original bet risks him £10. But by placing a wager himself on England at odds of 6-4 for £10, he stands to win £15 if he's successful: £15 minus £10 is a guaranteed profit of £5. (In the case of an Indian win, Vinay would have hedged his position too, although – because of the amount of money wagered on India – he would be merely seeking to reduce his losses to a manageable level.) Now consider the potential when four or five figures are involved.

Hedging is not illegal, but it shows that corruption is not an exact science: there is more than one method and more than one protagonist. The assumption that it is largely bookmakers who fix matches would appear to be wrong. Vinay worries that punters close to players or officials do the fixing, costing *him* money. Yet there seems little doubt that the all-powerful syndicates have massive influence, as well as the funds and organisational ability, to fix elements of matches – or even the results themselves.

The bookies and the professional punter can be considered enemies, in the mould of the old-fashioned pork-pie-hat-wearing odds-maker and his traditional chancer customer. It is a war for inside information: who knows more? The only consistent loser is the less clued-up customer, who is in effect betting blind. The syndicate operates a subtle fix. By sending out false odds via their bookies, they tempt customers into taking them. Vinay gave the example of how, armed with prior knowledge that a well-known Test match in 2011 would *not* end in a draw – when a draw looked at one stage the only possible result – the odds were set so that more people would bet on the stalemate. This is a ruse that hundreds of thousands fall prey to, and the money tots up.

The professional punter can do likewise, but he is a simpler operator. His original way of making money from fixes, which would have been used in the days of Hansie Cronje – and before the betting exchanges were commonplace – is less sophisticated. It requires much poking and prodding of contacts up and down the country, hoping minions will then place the bets correctly. It is a system that primarily takes advantage of the sheer size of the industry: a few lakh in Mumbai (one lakh equals 100,000), a few more in Delhi, a few more somewhere else. Next week, mix it all up again in an attempt not to draw attention to the scale of the enterprise – and hope you don't get found out.

> If it sounds like insider trading, that's what it amounts to

"The punter will have his friends placing the bets all over," said Vinay. "There is a big connection. Some punters are connected like the bookmakers are connected. If a punter has 50 friends, he can get 50 bets." The aim of fragmenting his bets by placing many smaller ones instead of a couple of large ones is to prevent the bookmaker from suspecting inside knowledge.

The subtle nature of the sting fuels the belief that a wide array of markets are available to bet on in India. But it is not because there is a betting market for fielding positions that a syndicate or punter has cajoled a captain into moving a fielder from third man (there is no such market). It is because, without a third man in the first ten overs of a one-day international, more runs are likely to be scored. This allows the syndicate to set false odds on a bracket, knowing that, if they offer runs in the first ten overs at, say, 70–75, most gamblers will bet under. Similarly, a punter who has a close friendship with a batsman might have arranged for him to score fewer than 25. This will give him an edge when it comes to the *lambi*, bracket and match odds. If it sounds like insider trading on the stock market, that is precisely what it amounts to.

Unfortunately for cricket and the ICC's Anti-Corruption and Security Unit, it is almost impossible to prove. The fixes are so minute – at least in terms of the impact on the match result – as to be virtually undetectable. How, for example, could the ACSU prove in court that a batsman has scored deliberately slowly for just one over in a Twenty20 match to sate a syndicate or a punter playing the brackets?

But the ACSU do not help themselves by failing to grasp how the illegal market in India works. They were embarrassed when Ravi Sawani, their former boss, admitted in the Southwark trial he had not heard of the term "bracket". They should also be pilloried for failing to grasp the nuances of spot-fixing, wrongly believing there are manifold markets for bookmakers or gamblers to exploit. Yet we should not simply criticise the governing body. Rarely are players, the collective, admonished. "It's down to them to take ownership," said an ACSU source. "A few players have said: 'There should be more ACSU people.' No, we should have 20 guys on the field naming the two who are at it."

There is hope – but only a little. If India's bookmakers were legalised, they would have to operate exactly like Ladbrokes or William Hill. That would mean an end to the credit system, where bookies accept customers on trust. Instead, they would need money in their account to wager. And to have an account, they would have to hand over their personal details. When accounts are kept and verified, you have a paper trail. If you have a paper trail, you have no rogue punters setting up fixes with their friends in cricket teams. At a stroke, the potential for corruption would be reduced by half.

Vinay is not convinced: "People say: 'Legalise betting in India and fixing will stop.' Yes. We are ready to pay tax. I'm tired of paying off the police. But it will not stop fixing. Never."

Ed Hawkins is the author of Bookie Gambler Fixer Spy: a journey to the corrupt heart of cricket's underworld. *It is* Wisden's *Book of the Year for 2013 (see Cricket Books, page 155).*

WISDEN WRITING COMPETITION WINNER, 2012

South African Time

BRIAN CARPENTER

It is a warm evening in south London, with just a hint of the hazy stickiness that infuses the capital's air when the temperature and humidity climb. It is July 2012 and the sunshine comes as welcome relief after weeks of sullen skies and intense rain.

The Oval is tense as Kevin Pietersen searches for the fluency and restless innovation which are the leitmotifs of his best batting. The South African attack is fast, skilful and persistently accurate. On 14, Pietersen is dropped at second slip by Jacques Kallis. It is an illusory release of pressure.

He has added only two runs before his stumps are shattered by Morne Morkel, a gangling young Afrikaner with gentle features which contrast sharply with the coltish aggression of his bowling, where pace and bounce are all. Pietersen, with his proud, upright bearing and composed demeanour, leaves the field. The mood is heavy with the scent of unburdened emotion and thwarted ambition.

One of the South African team is Hashim Mahomed Amla, a 29-year-old from Durban who is now among the world's greatest batsmen. He has met Pietersen before. In 1999, Amla and Pietersen played for KwaZulu-Natal against England. Pietersen saw himself as a shackled, repressed talent, forced to bowl off-spin while dreaming of a better life abroad; Amla was 16, saturnine and clean-shaven, yet to become the wearer of the second-most-celebrated beard in cricket history.

A few months later, Pietersen left South Africa. Amla stayed, endured dark times and eventually flourished. His batting is a potent amalgam of technical precision, fluid timing and understated power. In 2012, in England, this is as good as the batsman's art can get.

The history of South African Test cricket is weighed down by unfulfilled expectations and denied promise. Great, great players – Pollock, Procter, Richards, van der Bijl – went to their cricketing graves without an extended opportunity to display their talents on the widest stage. But this is to say nothing of the legions of cricketers who, because of their race, were denied the chance to stand even on the rung below.

Once upon a time, Amla would have been the player required to leave his homeland to realise his potential and live out his dreams. It would have been the destiny of Pietersen, with his expensive Pietermaritzburg education and his apparently inviolable sense of self-certainty, to wear the national cap.

Amla is a modest, reserved, devout man. He wastes little emotion but, as he leaves the field at the close of a day on which he has completed the highest individual score by a South African Test batsman, he exudes calm satisfaction. His place in history is secure.

Cricket is a game of conjunctions, of ironies, of veiled resonances. When Hashim Amla was a boy, his country didn't have an international team. Now, for him and his nation, the feeling of belonging is sweet.

This is their time.

Brian Carpenter grew up watching Middlesex and England in the 1970s and 1980s. He is now often to be found on Gimblett's Hill at Taunton or in the Warner Stand at Lord's. He blogs at differentshadesofgreen.blogspot.com

THE COMPETITION – THIS YEAR AND NEXT

Wisden received more than 100 entries for its first writing competition. They arrived from all corners of the globe, all ages, and both genders. The standard was almost invariably high, and the business of judging tricky. In the end, though, the editorial team were at one in selecting Brian Carpenter as the first winner of what is intended to become **an annual award**. The prize is publication, adulation, and an invitation to the launch dinner.

There are one or two minor changes of housekeeping for the **2013 competition**, and the basic rules are given below. Anyone who has not been commissioned for *Wisden* before can take part. Entries, which should not have been submitted before and are restricted to a maximum of two per person, must be:

1. the entrant's own work;
2. unpublished in any medium;
3. received by November 30, 2013;
4. between 480 and 520 words (excluding the title);
5. neither libellous nor offensive;
6. related to cricket, but not a match report.

Articles should be emailed to almanack@wisden.com, with "Writing Competition" as the subject line. Alternatively, they can be posted to: Writing Competition, John Wisden & Co, 13 Old Aylesfield, Golden Pot, Alton, Hampshire GU34 4BY. Please provide your name, address and telephone number. Bloomsbury staff and those who, in the editor's opinion, have a working relationship with *Wisden* are ineligible. The editor's decision is final. Once again, we look forward to reading your contributions.

THE 2012 ENTRANTS

Brian Baker; Andrew Bloxham; Keith Booth; Geoffrey Brooks; Michael Burnett; Malcolm Burr; Gordon Campbell; Jonathan Campion; Brian Carpenter; Paul Caswell; Jeff Chandler; Matthew Cheadle; Simon Cleverley; Terry Coffey; David Cohen; Angus Cooper; Gerry Cotter; Terry D'Arcy; Martin Davies; Tim Day; Ewan Day-Collins; Viraj R. Deshpande; Aditya Deuskar; Ethan Dwinger; Phillip Edwards; Simeon Edwards; Giles Falconer; Keith Feaver; Alex Fein; Stewart Francis; David Fraser; Allan Garley; Stephen Gibbs; Tony Giles; Yaron Gottlieb; Ian Gray; James Greenbury; Rory Gribbell; Jon Guard; P. J. Hadcock; Mike Harfield; Brian Harwood; Mike Hill; M. J. Holmes; Irfan Nazir; Georgia Isaac; Nilesh Jain; Steve Jennings; Philip Jones; Shyam Krishnan; James Lawrence; Roger Lewis; Amy Lofthouse; Howell Lovell; Michael Mackenzie; Edmund Martin; David Matthews; Neil Matthews; Paul Mercer; Keith Miller; Peter Miller; Greg Morrissey; David Moyes; Nayeem Islam; John Newth; Murrell Osborne; Ken Payne; David Pennington; Lionel Pike; David Potter; Samanta Priyanka; Ravi Kumar Putcha; Satish Kumar Putcha; Partab Ramchand; Keith Riches; Chris Rigby; Martin Roe; Mark Sanderson; Apurv Sardeshmukh; Christopher Sharp; C. J. A. Slater; Alan Smith; Chris Smith; Stuart Smith; Joshua Spink; Michael Strong; Tom Stuttard; S. B. Tang; James Thomson; Fergal Tobin; Denis Vaz; Malcolm Watson; John West; Robert West; Alan White; Reg White; Simon White; Trevor Woolley; Peter Yarlett; Zeeshan Mahmud.

FIVE CRICKETERS OF THE YEAR

The Five Cricketers of the Year represent a tradition that dates back in Wisden *to 1889, making this the oldest individual award in cricket. The Five are picked by the editor, and the selection is based, primarily but not exclusively, on the players' influence on the previous English season. No one can be chosen more than once. A list of past Cricketers of the Year appears on page 1508.*

Hashim Amla

NEIL MANTHORP

Hashim Amla enjoyed one of the most productive tours of England ever seen. In all three formats he was prolific, top-scoring in eight of his 11 international innings. His triple-century in the First Test at The Oval was as career-defining as it was nation-defining: he was the first South African to reach the landmark. It was an epic, and the fact that it laid the platform for a famous series win marked it out for eternal fame. By the time he added another century, in the Third Test at Lord's, he had edged past even Jacques Kallis as the wicket England craved most.

Amla produced yet another hundred in the one-day series, at Southampton, prompting coach Gary Kirsten to purr: "The pitch was extremely awkward, the bowling very good. To make 150 out of 287 rates it very highly, probably in the top three one-day innings for South Africa." Accolades kept coming his way as the year progressed; by the end, he had scored 1,950 runs in all internationals, at an average of nearly 63.

Inevitably, there was much talk of his heritage and its historical significance. But Amla, a 30-year-old, third-generation South African, downplays the situation without demeaning it. "The post-apartheid era has been around for a long time, so we are accustomed to seeing people of all races representing South Africa," he says. "I understand that older generations may find some satisfaction in my achievements, but it is not a factor for me or the team. We were just little boys when Nelson Mandela was released from prison."

A simple question reveals his essence: does he see himself as a role model? "You *are* a role model as an international sportsman. The only choice is whether you are a good or a bad one. I would like to be a good one." And Amla means to be a role model to everyone, irrespective of colour, creed or religion.

On the subject of natural talent, a condition he is accused of possessing with every new example of genius, he smiles knowingly: "There's no substitute for hard work. Even those players who make it look easy, they all train hard. There's such a thing as natural talent, and no such thing as natural success."

Minor frailties in his technique were exposed when he made a false start to his international career back in 2004-05. He played round his front pad, and was dropped after two Tests at home to England amid whispers of tokenism.

He also struggled against the short ball, and spent close to 100 hours in Kingsmead's indoor school facing thousands of bouncers from a bowling machine at full pace. After 15 Tests, he averaged 25 – a figure he has since doubled. That was not, as Amla says, a result of natural talent.

And yet he clearly has something. Whereas others see fielders, Amla sees gaps. It accounts for his occasionally extraordinary shot selection, such as leaping towards cover and flicking decent deliveries through the leg side from outside off stump. "Sometimes you need to hit the ball where the bowler doesn't want you to," he says, trying hard not to sound confrontational. "I'm sure it does upset bowlers, but that's not my aim. I just want to score runs."

The wrist skills which characterise his run-making are not, in fact, a legacy of his Indian heritage. His grandparents emigrated from Gujarat 60 years ago, but his blood is "South African green", and his subcontinental batting skills are all self-taught. It is Amla's ability to manoeuvre himself, at times unobtrusively, into unorthodox positions that makes his batsmanship appear less outrageous than it really is. Only the most discerning observe his ability to toy with the bowler and create scoring opportunities. The off-stump guard he took to Graeme Swann during the Oval Test was a classic of the genre; by the end of the series, Swann was bowling without a slip.

Nothing to them, earthquake to social historian

HASHIM MAHOMED AMLA, born in Durban on March 31, 1983, encounters awe on a regular basis, but he does not encourage it. Awe, he feels, should be reserved for those with a special dispensation in life, not for a cricketer who – like him – happens to lead a simple existence according to the principles of his religion. He does not enjoy the spotlight, nor when his cricket is linked to his Muslim faith. He sees his religion, personality and cricket as existing concurrently, but separately, and finds it peculiar that people should seek a special explanation for his ability to cope with, say, the tension of a Lord's century or a steepling catch in the deep with a series at stake. Amla's Twitter lexicon is more Durban hipster than cricketer: were he not a batsman, he'd be a surfer.

His aura and influence within the team are as profound as they are unintended. The way he goes about his daily life has changed the perspective of team-mates. On tour, Morne Morkel has been known to appease his own stresses and strains just by spending time in Amla's hotel room. An Afrikaner in the room of a Muslim: nothing to them, earthquake to social historians. Even the traditional drinkers in the squad adore Amla for his non-judgmental approach. Despite refusing to wear the logo of the national sponsor – Castle Lager – he thoroughly endorses personal choice. He has gone out of his way to make team-mates aware he is neither disapproving nor uncomfortable when they celebrate victories in the traditional way.

Captaincy is a tricky subject. He's very good at it, and everyone wants him to do it, but he's only reluctantly willing, not keen. Amla understands the political expediency and other benefits of occupying a position of national leadership. But he also understands his game well enough to know that the most likely result is fewer runs. He was Under-19 captain when South Africa were beaten by Australia in 2002, and had the captaincy of KwaZulu-Natal thrust upon him at the age of 21. The first worked, the second didn't.

A glorious 2012 has left him thinking of nothing but the next innings. "Things have a way of sorting themselves out. For now I am simply loving the game. This *Wisden* honour is very, very special. I do not regard myself in the same company as many previous winners." The modesty would have England's bowlers ruefully shaking their heads.

Nick Compton

RICHARD LATHAM

When Somerset declared on 512 for nine against Worcestershire on the penultimate day of the County Championship, Nick Compton was on 155 and six runs adrift of a first-class average of 100. This was a feat only four men had achieved in an English summer since the war (five, if you include Australian tailender Bill Johnston, who was dismissed once in 17 innings in 1953). In the event, he ended up settling for a first-class average of 99.60 and – in case sceptics wondered whether his stats had been misleadingly massaged by a huge 236 against Cardiff MCCU at the start of April – a Championship figure of 99.25. Among batsmen who had played at least ten innings, that average placed him 26 runs ahead of the next best. His first-class tally of 1,494 runs was 280 more than second-placed James Hildreth, a Somerset team-mate – despite Compton missing three matches with a back injury.

It was a gargantuan effort in a summer which, certainly in the matches played before the break for Twenty20 cricket in mid-June, was tailor-made for seam bowling. The fact that he had missed out on another statistical landmark earlier in the season barely seemed to matter. Compton had been robbed by rain of the chance to become the first player since Graeme Hick in 1988 to score 1,000 runs before the end of May, having chalked off nine of the 59 needed against Worcestershire at New Road when the heavens opened on May 31. On June 1, he was finally out for 108.

His early-season performances, which included 99 against Middlesex, 133 against Worcestershire and an unbeaten 204 against Nottinghamshire, had made their impression. In September, Compton's immense powers of concentration and exemplary technique won him the reward he most coveted: a place in England's Test squad for the tour to India, where he was an able lieutenant as Alastair Cook's opening partner, even if the big score he craved eluded him.

NICHOLAS RICHARD DENIS COMPTON was born in Durban, South Africa, on June 26, 1983. His parents Richard – who played first-class cricket for Natal and was the son of England's Denis – and Zimbabwean mother Glynis had backgrounds in public relations and journalism. Early education was at Clifton Preparatory School, Durban, and Compton made his first cricketing trip to England on a school tour aged 12. After periods at Hilton College and Durban High School, where he played under Hashim Amla, the opportunity arose to study at Harrow on a sports scholarship. He immediately helped secure a first victory in 25 years over Eton at Lord's – "a magical day" – and by his third year he was captain, while also securing a contract with Middlesex. He began a social science degree at Durham University, but a persistent groin problem, which eventually led to surgery, curtailed his cricket; he never completed the course.

Once fully fit, Compton took well to county cricket, and was a three-times winner of Middlesex's Young Player of the Year award – named after his grandfather. In 2006, he scored 1,313 first-class runs and was selected for the England A tour to India and Bangladesh, working under Andy Flower – then a batting coach – at Loughborough. In Bangladesh, he topped the averages, and his career appeared to be blossoming. But a shock was around the corner. The following season he managed only 385 Championship runs, and was dropped by Middlesex.

"It was a shattering experience," he says. "I felt I was close to playing for England at the start of the summer, and being left out by Middlesex – unjustly, in my opinion – hit me hard. The next 14 months were really tough." After only three Championship appearances in 2008, Compton decided to head to Australia during the winter to try to regain his confidence.

In the summer of 2009 Compton regained a regular first-team place. It was then that Somerset stepped in. "Even though I had enjoyed a better season with Middlesex, I felt the time was right to cut my ties," he says. "I wanted to push myself and play in the first division of the Championship."

Leaving London for the quiet of the West Country proved more taxing than Compton had expected. He struggled to fit into an established batting line-up, and found socialising difficult, admitting to feeling "pretty lonely at times". Asked to be the rock which would allow more free-scoring players like Marcus Trescothick, Hildreth, Craig Kieswetter and Peter Trego to play their shots, he lost sight of natural strengths.

"I found I was trying to impress the other batsmen, which made me feel pressurised," he says. "After three months, I changed my whole mindset, concentrating more on occupying the crease, and my form improved." In the winter, he played first-class and Twenty20 cricket in Zimbabwe, enjoying success in both formats before returning to Taunton intent on forging a regular first-team place. A solid summer brought 1,010 Championship runs – only Trescothick made more for Somerset – including a top score of 254 not out against Durham at Chester-le-Street. "I was proud of that season. I felt I had put down a marker, and that only fine-tuning was necessary to bring further improvement."

That fine-tuning involved hours of the most arduous practice, both at Taunton and with his batting coach Neil Burns, the former wicketkeeper. Compton makes a habit of facing bowling machines set at 99mph for two- or three-hour sessions, having dimmed the lights in the indoor nets. "The aim is to make conditions as uncomfortable as possible and see how long I can maintain concentration. There is a fear factor, and it's often very cold too. You get hit and there are times when you just want to walk away, but I figure if I can handle that, nothing in games is going to intimidate me."

While Compton is immensely proud of his grandfather's achievements, he is very much his own man. Coming from a cricketing family, he had a bat in his hand from as early as he can remember, but he never received coaching from Denis. "He did offer me one piece of advice when I was playing in his back garden one day. My dad was giving me some underarm throwdowns, and my grandfather was sitting on his porch, probably sipping a port or brandy. I was tapping the ball back with a high elbow and he yelled out: 'For God's sake, hit the bloody thing!'"

Jacques Kallis

CHRISTOPHER MARTIN-JENKINS

The best, most classical and most durable all-rounder of his generation, and arguably of all time, was the mighty difference between South Africa and England in the summer of 2012. His presence gave the tourists an enviable balance, leaving England – who dared not bat their wicketkeeper Matt Prior at No. 6 to accommodate an extra bowler – outgunned.

Kallis's implacable alliance with Hashim Amla made possible England's humiliation at The Oval, where his unbeaten 182 was as easy to miss as any such score could be. He also bowled with shrewdness and calculated venom, undermining England's first innings with the vital wickets of Kevin Pietersen and Ian Bell, and swallowed fast, flying catches at second slip.

Only a Lord's century remained out of reach, though last summer he was not helped by two contentious decisions. Overall, he was for South Africa what he had been for at least 15 years: a pillar and a rock. At last, the claim in 2012 that he had never quite received the credit he deserved felt wrong; but the comparisons with Garfield Sobers did not.

Born in Cape Town on October 16, 1975, JACQUES HENRY KALLIS was quickly recognised as a special talent at his school, Wynberg Boys' High, a couple of miles from Newlands, his spiritual home. Indeed, the school's cricket field was renamed "The Jacques Kallis Oval" in 2009. He first played for his country, against England in the Durban Test of 1995-96, at the age of 20. Batting at No. 6, he made a single in a rain-ruined draw, and did not get a bowl, but his bit part proved misleading: other than a spell out of the Twenty20 side, he has been an essential selection ever since. That Oval hundred was the 43rd of his Test career (only Sachin Tendulkar has more), to go with 17 in one-day internationals. Injuries have been rare, perhaps because of a bowling action reminiscent of Alec Bedser: sideways on, with the left arm leading, a full turn of a strong frame, and a surging follow-through.

Like Jack Nicklaus, the greatest of golfers, he has kept extraordinary command of his emotions, his expression inscrutable until he takes another wicket or reaches another century. Then a wide smile lights his even wider face. He has been a model not just of batting and bowling technique, but of the game's chivalrous spirit: England recall Kallis walking at a crucial moment in a World Cup game at Chennai in 2011, having accepted the fielder's word that a potentially contentious slip catch had carried. Yet he is as intensively competitive as anyone. He is, in fact, driven by his will to succeed.

Massive strength and a temperament as cool as an igloo have made him the most consistently formidable all-round cricketer since the era of Botham, Imran, Hadlee and Kapil – and, like them, Kallis has done things his own way. He ascribes his longevity to managing his fitness: "I've always tried to listen to my body and pick up early warning signs. In the early days I trained all day and bowled in the nets. I was in my mid-twenties when I realised I had to change."

As a batsman he quickly learned to switch off between deliveries; a monumental calm has always pervaded his cricket. Once set, often from the first ball, he looks unmovable, as he confirmed during his unbroken stand of 377 with Amla. Impressive rather than exciting, and utterly orthodox, he rarely looks hurried; his bat appears broader than the Laws allow. Only his strike-rate has drawn criticism: just occasionally, he has seemed wrapped up in personal battles, and once or twice in mid-career he failed to produce the gear-change his team needed.

His omission from the 2007 World Twenty20 may have focused the mind, for barely a week after the tournament he dominated Pakistan's Test bowlers on their notoriously slow pitches, scoring 155 and 100 not out at Karachi, then 59 and 107 not out at Lahore. Soon after, at home to New Zealand, he scored 186 and 131 in successive innings.

To select from his achievements feels invidious, but a few feats capture him best. In 2001-02, he went 1,241 minutes – nearly 21 hours – between Test dismissals. Two years later, he made centuries in five successive Tests, one short of Don Bradman's record. Depicted by some, at times fairly, as a reluctant bowler, he finished the England tour with 555 international wickets, to say nothing of 319 catches.

Short but intensive preparation has been vital to these insatiable performances. "The key," he explains, "is to treat every ball you bowl or face as if it's the real thing. With that intensity you can do your preparation in 20 balls rather than an hour or two. I learned a long time ago that physical preparation for international cricket takes place a long time before the match. It's mental preparation that counts on the eve of the match.

"I've never had to question my motivation, never questioned the reason I go to work every day. I stay fresh by getting as far away from cricket as possible between tours and games. I don't watch any cricket and I certainly don't talk about it."

His escape to private life is easier in Cape Town than it would be if home were Kolkata or Mumbai. "I prefer to play golf than watch cricket," he admits. "I do whatever I can to make the game feel fresh again the next time I play." And his willingness to muck in was exemplified when, as part of a team-bonding exercise before the England tour, Kallis – who loathes heights – jumped ten feet into an Alpine lake.

How much longer Kallis will devote to the game is, inevitably, uncertain. The calamitous ending to the career of Mark Boucher, his close friend, gave him reason to consider his future early in the England tour. But Gary Kirsten, long a team-mate and now the national coach, has a plan. After managing Sachin Tendulkar's cricketing autumn while coaching India, Kirsten hoped he could persuade Kallis to play at the 2015 World Cup. It would be a record-equalling sixth, and he would be 39. Whenever he does decide to call it a day, cricket will have lost a true phenomenon.

Marlon Samuels

TONY COZIER

The transformation of Marlon Samuels from troubled underachiever to elite performer read like a Hollywood script. The steady improvement of West Indies after years of similar frustration was no coincidence. Together they served as a reminder that, for all the headlines gathered by Samuels's fellow Jamaican Usain Bolt and the other Caribbean medallists at the London Olympics, it was cricket that first established the region's reputation for sporting excellence.

The performances of Samuels in England surprised many, if not the man himself. In three Tests, he failed to pass 50 only once in five innings, averaged more than 96, and made the stump mike essential listening with his ice-cool rejoinders to the sledging. More runs at home to New Zealand soon after confirmed this was no fluke and, by the time he was winning the World Twenty20 final almost on his own, he had established himself in the upper echelons of global batsmanship. A maiden Test double-hundred followed in Bangladesh. It was some turnaround – and only a little of the sheen was removed when he became involved in a petty altercation with Shane Warne in Australia's Big Bash League early in 2013.

Fast-tracked into the Test team at the age of 19 after only seven first-class matches, Samuels was restricted to 29 caps and an average of 29 over the next eight years because of his cavalier approach. He was also forced to remedy his flawed off-spinner's action. When he was found guilty of links with a Dubai-based bookmaker ahead of a one-day international at Nagpur in January 2007, and banned for two years, even from club cricket, the feeling was that Samuels – who protested his innocence – might have been swayed towards another profession. His good looks and lithe physique had already earned him work as a male model. Instead, the affair stiffened his resolve.

"All I ever wanted to do was play international cricket and make a name for myself," he says. "The two years that were taken away enabled me to look at myself. I never thought of quitting. I made up my mind that I was going to come back and show them that nothing could break me that easily."

He adopted a rigorous routine. Morning work in the gym from eight to 11 was followed by afternoon sessions in the nets against the bowling machine or willing friends, then yoga in the evening. Though never a heavy drinker, he gave up alcohol altogether. His suspension ended in May 2010, and his form in the Caribbean's regional four-day competition the following year (853 runs at 65) guaranteed a swift recall to international cricket. He inevitably took time to readapt, and even turned down the chance to play at the 2011 World Cup, telling the selectors he was "not 100% ready". And there were further problems when he signed belatedly for Pune Warriors ahead of the 2012 Indian Premier League, knowing the tournament clashed with a home Test series against Australia.

But the West Indies Cricket Board agreed to his suggested compromise – skip Australia, play the first half of the IPL, then rejoin his international team-mates in England. His reason for preferring the chill of a northern spring to the challenge of facing Australia on home territory revealed an ambition not previously obvious: "England, not Australia, were the No. 1 team at the time, and I felt that, if I could dominate against them, it would push me closer to being No. 1 in the world."

Immediately, it became clear this was no braggadocio. Scores of 31 and 86 at Lord's, 117 and 76 not out at Trent Bridge, and 76 at Edgbaston were compiled with the effortless elegance that had always typified his batting; now he came with diligence too. Two months later in the Caribbean, on the 50th anniversary of Jamaica's independence he made 123 in a first-innings total of 209 against New Zealand in his native Kingston, then carried West Indies to a 2–0 triumph with a second-innings 52. In October in Colombo, his breathtaking 78 off 56 balls paved the way for victory over Sri Lanka in the final of the World Twenty20. No one – not even Chris Gayle and his Gangnam Style dancing – embodied their renaissance better than Samuels.

Those who remembered him as a boy prodigy were surprised only that his talents had taken so long to bear fruit. MARLON NATHANIEL SAMUELS, born in Kingston to Philip and Daphne on January 5, 1981, was nurtured at Melbourne, one of Jamaica's most renowned clubs, and Kingston College – a school with a rich sporting tradition and a cricket coach, Roy McLean, whom Samuels credits with first recognising, then shaping, his rare ability. He hoped one of the first initiatives of his new Marlon Samuels Foundation would be to renovate Kingston College's facilities.

His parents had no special love for cricket, but he and his four brothers (plus three sisters) enjoyed the advantage of living within walking distance of Melbourne, where they could rub shoulders with Michael Holding and Courtney Walsh. Robert, the eldest, and ten years Marlon's senior, was a solid left-handed opener who went on to captain Jamaica and play six Tests, against New Zealand and Australia in the late 1990s. Twins David and Daniel were useful club players. But Marlon was the special one.

By the age of 15, he had reeled off 16 hundreds for college and club, and Jamaica included him in their Red Stripe Cup side a year later, with Walsh captain and Robert an opener. But dismissed for two and one on debut, Marlon was immediately consigned to the youth team. The West Indies selectors were more convinced, though, picking him for two successive Under-19 World Cups, and two matches against the touring Pakistanis in 1999-2000. When Shivnarine Chanderpaul succumbed to injury on the tour of Australia later that year, Samuels was summoned. They might as well have tossed him to the saltwater crocs.

But their hunch was justified: in his second Test, at the MCG, he made an unbeaten 60 out of 165, then 46 out of 109. He would beat even Brian Lara to the top of West Indies' series averages. *Wisden* remarked on his "impressive cool". But in the years ahead there was too much cool and not enough substance. Viv Richards, then the travelling chief selector, wanted to send him home from a tour of India in 2002-03 for breaking the team curfew. The board disagreed, and at Eden Gardens he scored his maiden Test hundred in his only innings of the series. His first one-day international century quickly followed, at Vijayawada. Yet Samuels soon dissolved into irritating inconsistency. And he was perplexed and unsettled by it all.

"I never knew when I'd be playing from one match to the next, so I couldn't plan my game as I wanted," he says. "I kept hearing I was left out for some attitude problem, but they never explained to me what it supposedly was. I just kept on hearing that I was too cool, too laid back."

It was no coincidence that he approached his best in South Africa, in 2007-08, almost as soon as Gayle, a compatriot and trusted friend, took over the captaincy. Samuels compiled his second Test hundred, at Durban, and averaged 52. Then in quick succession came the problem with his action and the ICC ban. His future was in obvious doubt. Yet his spirited resurrection ensures it no longer is.

Dale Steyn

TELFORD VICE

It took a girl of no more than ten years old to cut to the chase of what it means to be Dale Steyn. "How do you manage to have fun and look so angry at the same time?" she asked him earnestly at a sponsor's farewell before South Africa flew to Australia late in 2012 to defend the No. 1 ranking earned so emphatically in England a couple of months previously.

How indeed? Not for Steyn the despising sneer of Allan Donald, Makhaya Ntini's brooding brow or Shaun Pollock's cool detachment from the blood-in-the-boots business of fast bowling. Instead, like some demented cartoon elf, Steyn's eyes flash frequently with dark wonder at the fact that he is armed with a skill that could kill.

Everyone who faced him in South Africa's Test series in England survived to tell the tale, but only in a manner of speaking. Fifteen times he dismissed his quarry. And he did so as he always has, with deliveries that seemed almost unfair. How could they swing so sharply at such extreme pace? Their violence was clinical, just like his career strike-rate of 41 balls per wicket – bettered only by four men, including team-mate Vernon Philander, in Test history.

Two other factors played a part as well. One was the almost other-worldly experience undergone by Steyn and the rest of the squad before the tour, with South African explorer Mike Horn in the Swiss Alps. Clambering over mountains and glaciers, they appeared to stumble across aspects of their characters they never knew existed. The other was the cruel fate of Mark

Boucher, whose career was ended when a bail hit him in the eye on the first day of the trip, at Taunton.

"Going to Switzerland was a revelation for us, and the Mark Boucher incident left a deep impression," says Steyn. "I probably realised things aren't as bad on the cricket field as I sometimes make them out to be."

In short, reality bit like it had rarely bitten before. They stopped being a mere team, becoming instead a band of men united in a cause. "Something changed," he says. "I definitely saw that. There's great bonding and camaraderie between the guys, and it showed in England. We can handle those tough times because we can overcome them."

Quite simply, he looked the world's best fast bowler

It was earlier on that fateful day at Taunton that Steyn laid down his marker for the bigger battle to come. He took the new ball, and his first delivery hooked away wickedly from Arul Suppiah's bat. Steyn completed his follow-through with a forlorn raise of the hand, as if to say: "If only he was good enough to get an edge."

Several of those who tangled with Steyn in the summer were indeed good enough – and they paid the price. After crucially halting England's serene progress on the second morning of the series, at The Oval, he took five wickets in the second innings on a pitch still lacking demons, as South Africa dispelled bumptious English doubts about whether they belonged on the same field. Another four crashed in the first innings at Lord's, among them the linchpin wickets of Alastair Cook and Jonathan Trott; between them, the pair fell seven times to Steyn in the series.

To see him slay another victim with what seemed an utter lack of effort was to see a man live up to his billing. Quite simply, he looked like the world's best fast bowler, and performed accordingly. More than that, he looked as if he had been doing so for most of his life. He is, it has been said before and will be said again, a natural – a bundle of fast-twitch fibres and aggressive intent lurking in a body perfect for its role.

It's hard to imagine that DALE WILLEM STEYN was not already a fast-bowler-in-waiting when he was born on June 27, 1983, in Phalaborwa, a town of fewer than 13,000 souls, in the rural north-east of South Africa. But much needed to be done if he was to fulfil that destiny as spectacularly as he has. Throughout his career, he has been among the best conditioned of South Africa's players; happily, serious injury has left him alone. But the confident, wisecracking athlete he would become is a far cry from the unsure young bowler he once was.

Initially, Steyn seemed spooked by his own powers, hesitant to let fly with all the velocity he had at his disposal. This was most apparent in his first three Tests, against England at home in 2004-05. He bowled tentatively, taking eight wickets at 52. The eight no-balls he sent down in nine overs in England's second innings at the Wanderers sealed his fate: he was dropped.

Perhaps it was not the done thing for country kids to hold the spotlight on the world stage. It was certainly not the done thing for them to play cricket at a high level. But Phalaborwa is also a place of extremes: its open-cast copper mine is, at almost 2km across, Africa's widest man-made hole, and summer temperatures reach 47˚C. Steyn's confidence duly caught up with the rest of him. Soon, the man emerged in full.

An important moment arrived shortly after lunch on the first day at Centurion against New Zealand in November 2007, when he put opening batsman Craig Cumming in intensive care with a delivery that hit him in the face and caused 23 fractures. Steyn made a cursory check on his prone opponent, turned on his heel, and went back to his mark to await his next target.

In March 2008, in his 20th Test, Steyn reached 100 wickets more quickly than any South African. A month later, the ICC put him on top of their bowling rankings, where he has remained. He was also the ICC's Test Player of the Year in 2008. Those are the prizes of his carefully aimed anger. Off the field, he has a penchant for retro trainers, fishing, and midnight dashes for ice-cream. That's where the fun comes in. But don't be fooled.

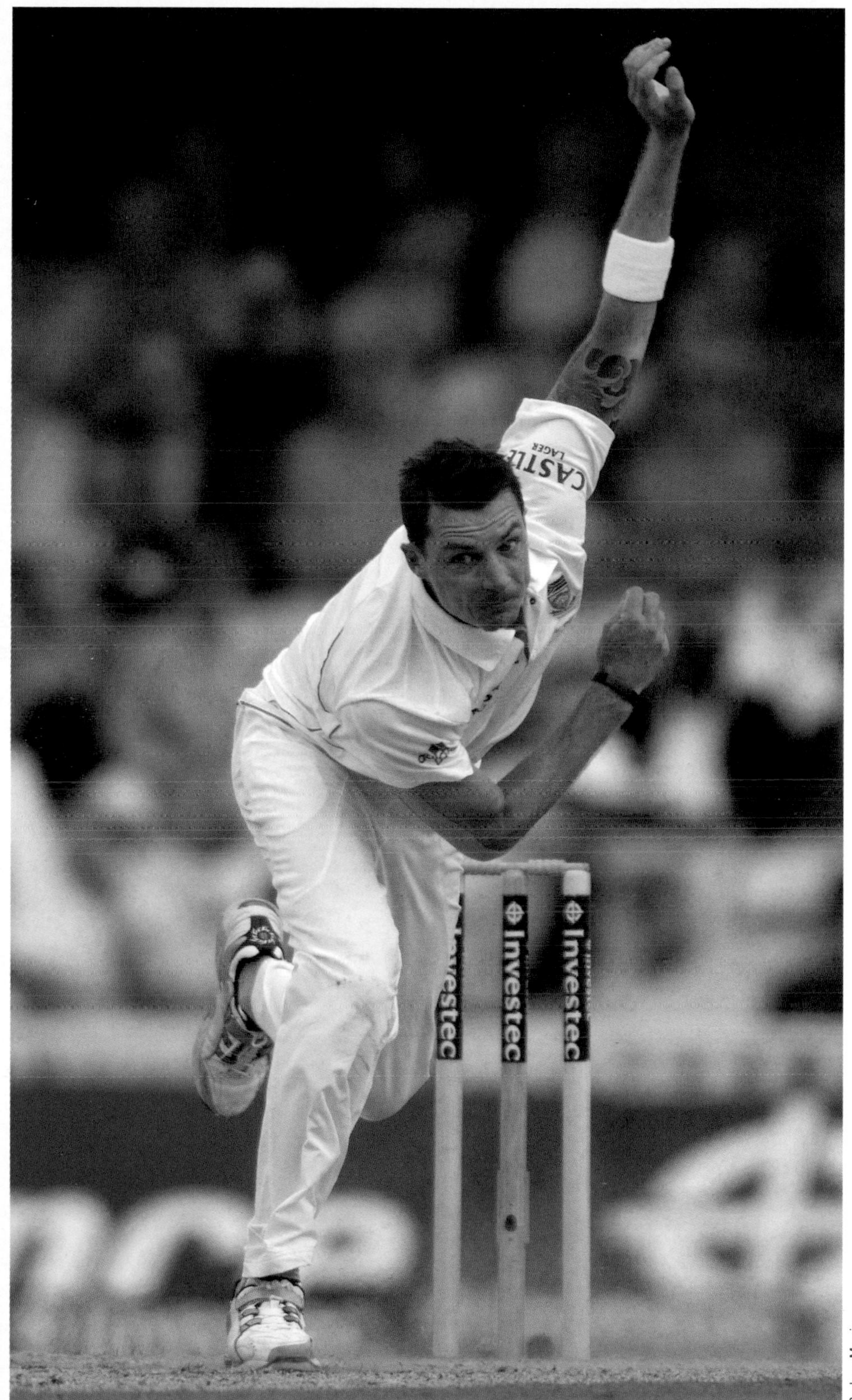

Graham Morris

FIVE CRICKETERS OF THE YEAR Dale Steyn.

FIVE CRICKETERS OF THE YEAR Hashim Amla.

Michael Steele, Getty Images

FIVE CRICKETERS OF THE YEAR Nick Compton.

FIVE CRICKETERS OF THE YEAR Jacques Kallis.

Graham Morris

FIVE CRICKETERS OF THE YEAR Marlon Samuels.

ANOTHER DAY AT THE OFFICE Mike Atherton broadcasts from the Nagpur stadium motorcycle park after a dispute with the BCCI left Sky Sports without a studio. Inside the ground, Virender Sehwag attracts rather more attention as he goes about his business.

David Rogers, Getty Images

WHERE'S THE CRICKET? The wettest summer in 100 years stole countless days from the fixture list: Leicester's Grace Road resembled a lake during an Under-19 international. On a fine evening at The Oval in November, the Royal Engineers and the Wanderers re-enact the first FA Cup final, held at the ground 140 years earlier.

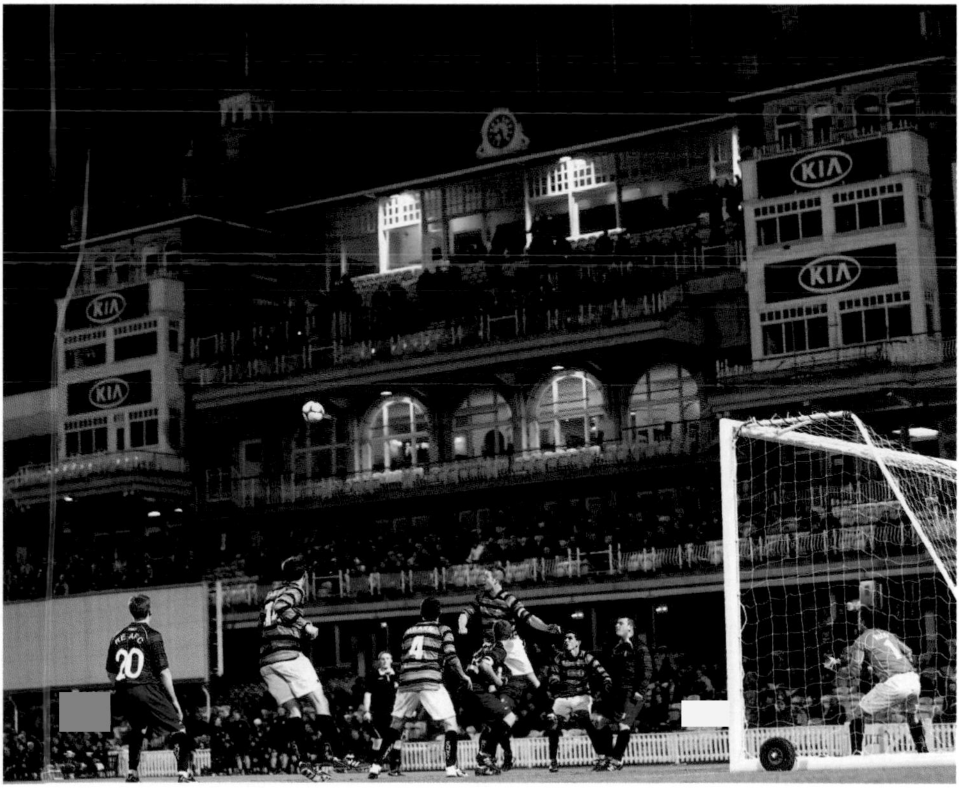

Luke MacGregor, Reuters

Sang Tan, AP/PA Photos

R & R – THAT'S RETIREMENT AND REINTEGRATION Andrew Strauss, after quitting all cricket in late August, watches Alastair Cook, his successor as England captain, field questions. Five weeks later, ECB chairman Giles Clarke and Kevin Pietersen announce peace has broken out.

Gareth Copley, Getty Images

FAREWELL (1): DRAVID AND LAXMAN

Two southern gentlemen

RAHUL BHATTACHARYA

"Nusrat singing, Laxman and Dravid batting – TV on mute, and yoga." A note from an acquaintance in Mumbai had this description of his perfect day. Rahul Dravid and V. V. S. Laxman marked their Test debuts within six months of one another in 1996 with accomplished half-centuries. Sixteen years later, they announced their retirements in accomplished press conferences, also within six months of each other. But this note came not on the occasion of a batting feat or a retirement. It was, in Indian shorthand, an ode to long-form cricket – and the pair that most profoundly summoned its sensation.

Consider the correspondent's other passions. A partnership of Laxman and Dravid could contain both the incantatory rapture of Nusrat Fateh Ali Khan and the meditative discipline of yoga. One might say Laxman was the rapture and Dravid the discipline, but that would not only be partially false, it would be to miss the point. The beauty of a *jugalbandi*, a duet between classical soloists, is in the interplay. A *jugalbandi* is a duet in the same way as a batting partnership: not simultaneous, but one performer at a time, in improvisatory rotation. The great sitar player Ustad Vilayat Khan said the idea was to both showcase and subdue oneself. As he hands over to his partner, the artist must judge how much to dissolve the tune. Dravid and Laxman dissolved into one another more harmoniously, more significantly, than any other Indian duo.

Separately, theirs were brilliant careers. Dravid's was colossal. He played 164 Tests, faced more deliveries than anyone in history (31,260), and made more runs (13,288) than all but two. He became the first man to 200 catches, most of them snaffled at first slip. For a supposed misfit in one-day internationals, he still racked up over 10,000 runs at nearly 40. Though he enjoyed neither, he kept wicket or opened the innings with courage and competence, whenever needed. In a tumultuous stint as captain, he oversaw a first-round World Cup exit and Test series victories in the West Indies and England.

Laxman, who when picked for India still hadn't ruled out returning to medical studies to become a doctor like his parents, scored close to 9,000 runs in 134 Tests. Against Australia, the premier team of the era, he struck ten sublime international centuries, including one that may just be the greatest innings in all cricket. Like Dravid, he caught well at bat–pad, then in the slips. Sometimes vice-captain, he was seen by younger team-mates as the avuncular bridge between generations. They called him *mama*, or uncle. These are the bare facts.

Part of their harmony was that Laxman and Dravid were similar and dissimilar in equal measure. They were both from southern India – Laxman from Hyderabad, Dravid from Bangalore – and were both gentlemen (south

Indians will think this a tautology). Raised on matting wickets, they enjoyed bounce and back-foot play. They were tall, wristy, hit the ball along the ground, and possessed what cricket watchers refer to as "temperament".

For all that, they could give off very different impressions: Dravid seemed to care a little too much, Laxman not enough. This may be because Dravid perspired heavily and tended to grimace, whereas Laxman looked always a serene stroller in pleasant climes. It may be because Dravid committed himself to sincere footwork, whereas Laxman (against pace) trusted his hands and the curvy abstractions of what he once told me was his "bat flow".

Sporting impressions are rarely false. It's just that sportswriters, like cartoonists, exaggerate the features. As with David Gower, the game looked easy in Laxman's lovely hands. He was Goweresque in only that respect. He was not to be spotted swooping in a biplane over his team-mates, or sozzled at an official reception. He was a diligent man, who worked all career at ironing out any incriminating casualness from his strokes; a religious man, who can quote verses from the *Bhagavad Gita*, and in the early years could be seen muttering a prayer (to the saint Sai Baba) as he faced up.

Meanwhile Dravid, given to over-intensity, honed relaxation into a fine art. Before matches, he willed himself away from self-torture through video analysis and training sessions, to long lunches, long sleep, and slow living. Waiting to bat, he watched the game only briefly. He was no contest, it is true, for Laxman, who was fond of showering when the man before him went in, and thereafter might be found lying under a table listening to music on headphones.

Hamish Blair, Allsport/Getty Images

How about that, friend? Laxman and Dravid batted through the fourth day against Australia at Kolkata, March 14, 2001. They would add 376 in all.

When his turn arrived, Dravid strode out briskly to the centre. On certain days, with chest and arm guards in place, his back erect and knees high for a man with pads, it could be said he marched out. Laxman appeared sometimes belatedly, somewhat gingerly (bad knees), with a pacific, Mona Lisa quasi-smile, and collar turned up in the Hyderabadi way. At the crease they were calm, immersed in their work like artistes. They were happy to bat for hours, days. Occasionally Dravid responded to sledging, though in an upstanding kind of manner. Laxman seemed not to notice at all. While fielding in the slips they talked to each other, Dravid told journalist Nagraj Gollapudi, "about kids, house construction, plumbers, electricians, running errands".

The mammoth partnership has usually been the preserve of those in successive batting positions. Only seven pairs in Test history have put together two or more triple-century stands, as Dravid and Laxman did. These have been either openers – Herschelle Gibbs and Graeme Smith – or batted close together: Bill Ponsford and Don Bradman, Kumar Sangakkara and Mahela Jayawardene, Younis Khan and Mohammad Yousuf, Hashim Amla and Jacques Kallis, Ricky Ponting and Michael Clarke. But Dravid and Laxman batted at opposite poles of the middle order, at first drop and fourth. Three-hundred-and-something runs for the *fifth* wicket suggests more than appetite: it suggests valour.

Valour was scarce in the times we refer to. To understand Indian cricket at the turn of the century, consider the sequence: clean-swept in Australia, clean-swept at home by South Africa, the resignation of a deflated captain (Sachin Tendulkar), the naming of the previous captain (Mohammad Azharuddin) and several players in a match-fixing scandal. To passionate fans, cricket felt desperate; to others, it felt wholly discredited.

Kolkata, 2001: it was a day short of the Ides of March. But the 14th was no less portentous for Australia's Caesar, Steve Waugh. On that day two years previously, a beleaguered West Indies side had risen again in Kingston: from 37 for four overnight, Brian Lara and Jimmy Adams batted almost all day and overturned a series. Australia had advanced since, revivified by the phenomenon of Adam Gilchrist, the tank–sniper combination of Matthew Hayden and Justin Langer, and Waugh's own ruthless ambition. Forget losses: they barely did draws. Going into Kolkata they had racked up a world record 16 straight Test wins. The latest of those was a three-day demolition of India in Mumbai. And in Kolkata, a quartet of Glenn McGrath, Jason Gillespie, Michael Kasprowicz and Shane Warne had bowled Australia to a 274-run lead.

The rest is an Indian fairytale: Laxman the last man out in the first innings for a dashing 59, asked to keep his pads on by his captain and the coach, swapping positions with a struggling Dravid in the follow-on, the two coming together in the second innings with Laxman almost upon his century but India still behind Australia's first-innings total.

And then the batting, and batting, and more beautiful batting, over a short evening, the whole of March 14, and then some more. Laxman curling the ball through imperceptible gaps, Dravid regaining lost form through pure unblinking will, Laxman now flick-pulling the fast bowlers as if tossing frisbees, now driving them on the rise, sinuous jabs that raced improbably across the big green outfield, Dravid now blocking, now shouldering arms, now leaning back to cut, the old

DRAVID IN TESTS

	T	R	HS	100	Avge	Ct
v Australia†	33	2,166	233	2	38.67	47
v Bangladesh	7	560	160	3	70.00	13
v England	21	1,950	217	7	60.93	30
v New Zealand	15	1,659	222	6	63.80	17
v Pakistan	15	1,236	270	5	53.73	19
v South Africa	21	1,252	148	2	33.83	21
v Sri Lanka	20	1,508	177	3	48.64	16
v West Indies	23	1,978	146	5	63.80	26
v Zimbabwe	9	979	200*	3	97.90	21
Total	**164**	**13,288**	**270**	**36**	**52.31**	**210**

† *Includes one Test for the ICC World XI in 2005-06; Dravid scored 0 and 23.*

Home record: 70 Tests, 5,598 runs at 51.35; 15 hundreds
Away record: 94 Tests, 7,690 at 53.03; 21 hundreds

One-day internationals: 344 matches, 10,889 runs at 39.16; 12 hundreds
Twenty20 internationals: 1 match, 31 runs at 31.00

LAXMAN IN TESTS

	T	R	HS	100	Avge	Ct
v Australia	29	2,434	281	6	49.67	36
v Bangladesh	3	117	69*	0	39.00	1
v England	17	766	75	0	30.64	19
v New Zealand	10	818	124*	2	58.42	10
v Pakistan	15	775	112*	1	43.05	15
v South Africa	19	976	143*	1	37.53	18
v Sri Lanka	13	900	104	2	47.36	11
v West Indies	22	1,715	176*	4	57.16	13
v Zimbabwe	6	280	140	1	40.00	12
Total	**134**	**8,781**	**281**	**17**	**45.97**	**135**

Home record: 57 Tests, 3,767 runs at 51.60; 8 hundreds
Away record: 77 Tests, 5,014 runs at 42.49; 9 hundreds

One-day internationals: 86 matches, 2,338 runs at 30.76; 6 hundreds

sureness slowly redeveloping, Laxman inside-outing Warne miraculously from far outside leg stump, now whipping him against the turn, Dravid, fully restored, emboldened to come down the track himself and wrist Warne across his break, all of this in the huge sound and growing belief of a hundred thousand in Eden Gardens, an energy that must be experienced to be understood.

Laxman batted ten and a half hours for 281. Dravid was run out for 180 after nearly seven and a half. Together they put on 376. These were runs made in some discomfort: Laxman had been listing, much like a ship, and his back had to be realigned by the physio during the intervals; Dravid, battling the high humidity of Kolkata and his own rate of perspiration, cramped with dehydration. Around their necks both wore strips of towel drenched in ice-water, and they returned to a dressing-room installed with drips. India won the Test, magically, then the series. If a virtue of sport is to make a people cast aside their troubles, not by fantasy but aspiration, here it was.

Hamish Blair, Getty Images

Shot for the ages: Rahul Dravid cuts the winning four at Adelaide in 2003-04, a breakthrough Indian victory forged by his own hand.

Three seasons on, the Indian team were finding their way in the world – but not yet in Australia. At Adelaide, they were 85 for four, trailing by 471, doomed to a ritual humiliation. Despite the absence of Warne and McGrath, the task didn't look hard: it looked hopeless. India hadn't won a Test in Australia for 23 years. Of the 26 Tests that Steve Waugh had captained at home, Australia had won 21 and lost one (a dead rubber in the 2002-03 Ashes). Soon the familiar chemistry between our like-and-unlike couple began to galvanise into something close to inevitability.

Here, Dravid played the lead. He was back at No. 3, and in the form of his life. The previous year he had hit Test centuries in four successive innings, three of them in England, including a defensive tour de force at Headingley. Sunny Adelaide allowed him to be more expansive. His handsomest stroke, the front-foot drive through cover, he repeatedly demonstrated, bending low on his left knee like a skater and letting his arms arc out. Astonishingly, he brought up his century with a miscued pull – for six. He even surprised himself when, late in the collaboration, he looked at the scoreboard to find he had outscored his partner. "Yeah, jeez, not bad for a blocker, huh?" he told the sportswriter Rohit Brijnath.

This time they put on 303: Laxman 148, Dravid 233. In a neat inversion, as Laxman had set up Kolkata with a first-innings fifty, here Dravid anchored a hard fourth-innings chase with 72 not out. When he cut the winning runs to the boundary, Waugh made a point of retrieving the ball from the gutter and handing it over. Waugh retired after the series, and to write a foreword to his autobiography he invited Dravid, a much younger man who had once sought him out to ask how to take his game to a higher plane.

There was much more to Dravid and Laxman than these two partnerships – and also, of course, often much less. Laxmanophiles were bewildered that a batsman of his calibre should average so far below 50, appalled (and secretly charmed) by his running between the wickets, and plain frustrated when the ball seamed about and he poked to slip; against England he averaged 30. Likewise, Dravid partisans could try to construct defences for his unflattering averages against Australia and South Africa, the best bowling attacks of the time – but how to enjoy his most tuneless offerings, the 16-off-114-balls variety, except by wilful perversity? (Dravid, who had not just the cussedness but also the humour to perpetrate these innings, once raised his bat to applause from an Australian crowd after a single.)

Indians place on a pedestal the twin epics because of what they were, and also because of their associations. To think of Dravid's 233 at Adelaide is also to think of his monumental 270 in Rawalpindi, 148 at Headingley, or 93 at Perth – all setting up ground-breaking overseas victories. To think of Laxman's Kolkata masterpiece is also an oblique tribute to its younger brothers: from late 2010 alone, extraordinary fourth-innings chases against Australia and Sri Lanka, and a third-innings 96 in Durban when nobody else in the match touched 40.

Team success cannot and should never be a necessary or a sufficient condition for a cricketer's accomplishments, but in the Indian instance it felt urgent. The Indian side of the 2000s was up against a history of flickering achievement amid lethargic underperformance. Of the batting line-up instrumental in overturning that history, Dravid was the spine and Laxman the nerve. Their runs were tough, elegant and vital. Their manner was classic. The echoes of Kolkata and Adelaide rang down the decade, in far-flung venues and memories, and in notes from cricket watchers to one another.

Rahul Bhattacharya is the author of Pundits from Pakistan *and* The Sly Company of People Who Care, *winner of the 2012 Ondaatje Prize.*

FAREWELL (2): ANDREW STRAUSS

Skilful juggler, born leader

SCYLD BERRY

No modern captain has had such a beneficial effect on the England team as Andrew Strauss. Nasser Hussain changed losers into draw-ers, then Michael Vaughan changed draw-ers into winners. But when Strauss took over as the official captain in January 2009, he not only turned losers into winners in a few short months, but changed the collective culture, for good – in both senses of the word. A group of individuals who had often put self-interest first were transformed by his vision into a team dedicated to England and excellence.

Retaining the Ashes in 2010-11 by winning 3–1 (all three by an innings) was Strauss's proudest achievement. Regaining them in 2009, after inheriting a crisis, was his cleverest. By then, the legacies of Vaughan and his coach Duncan Fletcher had evaporated. He had a resentful predecessor in Kevin Pietersen, no permanent coach, and the uncomfortable knowledge that he had been chosen as a last resort, in the absence of any succession planning. Why Strauss should have been regarded as a last resort is puzzling, given how well he had led the side when filling in for Vaughan in 2006. Perhaps it was a result of his self-effacement, his refusal to blow his own trumpet, and of modern society's inability to recognise true worth.

In any event, when Strauss's team left for the West Indies for his first series as full-time leader, it was the only case in modern times of a captain – not a manager or coach – being in overall charge of an England tour. In an emergency, Strauss was to decide. This was a measure of the chaos in English cricket after the sudden and simultaneous departures of Pietersen and the coach Peter Moores.

Strauss, however, is a skilful juggler: he can keep three cricket balls on the go. He was lucky, too, in having Andy Flower, of like mind, elevated from batting coach to team director after a caretaker role in the Caribbean. Even so, it was a magnificent achievement to regain the Ashes in 2009. Australia scored eight centuries to England's two; Australia had three bowlers who took 20 wickets or more, England none; Australia averaged 40 runs per wicket, England 34. These stats add up to the biggest steal in Ashes history. And by The Oval, it was a patchwork that Strauss led into the field: Andrew Flintoff was on his last legs, Alastair Cook and Paul Collingwood had played only one innings of note apiece, and Pietersen was not even there, absent injured since the Second Test at Lord's.

Yet Strauss took England over the line, leading from the front, changing the culture. For example, he instituted the practice after a day's play of toasting a team-mate who had scored a hundred or taken five wickets, following a brief speech by someone who volunteered. He understood the importance of celebrating as a side.

The man manager: Andrew Strauss with Monty Panesar.

He had read up on Churchill before taking over, and learned from Vaughan how to put his players at ease so they performed their best. Still, Strauss was a born leader. He did not have to raise his voice: everyone listened because he was so clear in thought and word. Graeme Swann, who stood at second slip alongside him, said: "It was a calming, almost fatherly feeling to know that, in the middle of a maelstrom, he would make the right decision."

Strauss was manifestly not in it for his own glory: it was typical that the England record he set was for the most catches (121) by a non-wicketkeeper, which benefited the team far more than his reputation. He was in it to instil his values and beliefs about what was best for England – but only after listening, not dictating. He had a sense of humour, at least until the job weighed him down in 2012, and therefore of perspective. He never forgot what a privilege it was to represent what became his country from the age of six, or the sacrifices his family made. His manners were always exemplary: he was never confrontational, never thought himself above the law, never looked down on anyone. He would talk with, and ask a polite question of, even the most anorakish England fan. And he became statesmanlike in his pronouncements about wider issues, such as match-fixing, or those beyond sport.

Cricket was not an end in itself. He did not love batting like, say, his former partner Marcus Trescothick, which is why he retired from all cricket as soon as he had finished with England. For him, cricket was the means for undertaking challenges and stretching himself. It could have been another sport. When his prep-school headmaster sent a letter to the warden of Radley College, Dennis Silk, about the 11-year-old preparing to enrol there, he wrote four pages on the promising rugby of this young fly-half. Only as a postscript did he add: "He also has the makings of a useful cricketer."

It was this love of a challenge which enabled Strauss to compose two or three of the most valuable innings ever played for England. His 129 in the deciding Oval Test of 2005 kept them in the game, when no other specialist batsman made 50 in their first innings: typical, again, that everyone forgets Strauss and recalls Pietersen's 158 in their second. His 161 at Lord's in 2009 gave England the psychological lead; and they were soothed by his brace of 55 and 75 at The Oval in the last Test. So long as Strauss was in, England were winning on all these momentous occasions. One false move and they would assuredly have lost the match and series; yet Strauss walked the tightrope while millions watched, without looking down.

MOST SUCCESSFUL ENGLAND CAPTAINS

	T	*W*	*L*	*D*	*W%*
J. M. Brearley	31	18	4	9	58.06
M. P. Vaughan	51	26	11	14	50.98
P. B. H. May	41	20	10	11	48.78
A. J. Strauss	**50**	**24**	**11**	**15**	**48.00**
L. Hutton	23	11	4	8	47.82
R. Illingworth	31	12	5	14	38.70
N. Hussain	45	17	15	13	37.77
E. R. Dexter	30	9	7	14	30.00
M. C. Cowdrey	27	8	4	15	29.62
G. A. Gooch	34	10	12	12	29.41
M. A. Atherton	54	13	21	20	24.07
M. J. K. Smith	25	5	3	17	20.00
W. R. Hammond	20	4	3	13	20.00
A. C. MacLaren	22	4	11	7	18.18
D. I. Gower	32	5	18	9	15.62
M. W. Gatting	23	2	5	16	8.69

Qualification = 20 Tests.

In 100 Tests, Strauss scored 7,037 runs at 40.91, with 21 hundreds. In 127 one-day internationals, he scored 4,205 runs at 35.63, with a strike-rate of 80.98, and six hundreds. In four Twenty20 internationals, he scored 73 runs at 18.25, with a strike-rate of 114.06. He held 121 catches in Tests, 57 in one-day internationals, and one in Twenty20 internationals.

Once Strauss got the team culture right, everything flowed from there – like hanging wallpaper properly from the picture rail. His record as England's Test captain by the start of 2012 was 21–5. He had led England to No. 1 in the rankings by supplanting India 4–0. Sir Leonard Hutton and Michael Brearley, if you count the 1978-79 tour of Australia during World Series Cricket, had been the only other England captains to win Ashes series home and away (Percy Chapman won the Oval Test of 1926 after Arthur Carr had drawn the first four, then won again in Australia). But they played when England were the only country with a professional domestic circuit. Strauss made them No. 1 on a level playing field.

The invisible centurion: Andrew Strauss at The Oval, September 2005.

Clive Rose, Getty Images

Self-doubt set in last year. Trying to retain their status – an arithmetical calculation – may have distracted England from winning the next Test. His playing of spin improved after the 3–0 defeat by Pakistan in the UAE – and he was already the only England batsman to score two centuries in a Test in Asia – but the mental side was more important to him than technical competence. He felt he was past his prime; and he had shown by resigning the one-day captaincy after the 2011 World Cup that he would never linger once he had concluded he had given his best.

He was still enthused by the problem-solving side of captaincy, at which he was masterful. But he felt worn down by attending not only to every player, but to all the members of the management team, and had too little energy left for his own game. And that was before Pietersen rocked the boat with his "provocative" texts to the South African tourists, so that instead of concentrating on squaring the series at Lord's and celebrating his 100th Test, it was back to fire-fighting. Of all England captains, Strauss did not deserve his end to be like his beginning.

Only Hutton, from my reading of England's history, has had such a beneficial effect. He took over in a similar state of chaos in 1952, as both the last resort and the first professional captain since the 19th century. England had been thumped by Australia since the Second World War, and had thumped no one in return, yet he transformed them into the team of the 1950s. Both Hutton and Strauss conserved runs in the field, identified players of inner strength, and built a team in their own image.

Both were criticised for being too cautious. Let Strauss speak for both in response: "Based on my own experience, if you starve batsmen of runs they will get edgy, and are likely to get themselves out. That was my philosophy, but if a bowler came up and said, 'I want an extra catcher,' I would say, 'Perfect, let's go along with it.' Normally, though, the bowler hated going for runs. Jimmy Anderson, for example, felt his best way was to starve batsmen, and the way to get the best out of a player is to let him do what he wants. You don't tell Jonathan Trott to score more quickly, because he averages 50 and knows what he's doing.

"It's very easy for commentators and the public to say, when the ball flies through fifth slip: 'You should have had a fielder there.' But that is a bit facile. It is your strategy that wins you games and series, and the most important part of captaincy is to create an environment in which you make best use of the players you have."

Hutton and Strauss: archetypal northern pro and southern amateur type. Poles apart on the surface but, from what I saw when ghosting them, very similar: both outwardly calm, quiet and shrewd problem-solvers who knew their own mind and the direction in which England's cricket should head. I like to think of it as an endorsement, or seal of approval, that Hutton's grandson Ben was Strauss's best man.

When Hutton looked back on his captaincy, after half the Establishment had hoped he would fail so that an amateur could be reinstated, he used to say, with the pauses that were characteristic of his speech: "I never… I never wanted… I never wanted to make… a smell." And, miraculously in this age of intense media scrutiny, Strauss did not do so either: there was no howler, no on-field incident that went undefused, no gesture to any umpire or opponent, not a single word out of place in a press conference or captured on a stump mike. He was dutiful, and selfless in his service to his players and country, until the last.

Scyld Berry, editor of Wisden 2008–11, *is the cricket correspondent of the* Sunday Telegraph, *where he ghosted Andrew Strauss's column.*

FAREWELL (3): RICKY PONTING

The very essence of desire

GIDEON HAIGH

"Catch, Ted," said Ricky Ponting. "Catch, Ted."

It was late in Australia's morning training session ahead of next day's Perth Test against South Africa. The small knots of onlookers had moved on; only a handful of players remained. Still in his pads, Ponting was sitting on a bench after a long stint facing net bowlers and throwdowns, and watching a helmeted Ed Cowan practise his short-leg catching with coach Mickey Arthur. "Catch, Ted," he would repeat as each hit went in. "Catch, Ted."

Nothing so unusual about that. In his long career, Ponting had made a habit of being among the last to leave training. Except that, unbeknown to those beyond the team and their immediate circle, he had just a couple of hours earlier confided that this, his 168th appearance – equalling Steve Waugh's national record – would be his farewell Test. It remained at that stage Australian cricket's best-kept secret. "Catch, Ted," he repeated. "Catch, Ted."

After one last surveillance of the practice area, Ponting shouldered his backpack, tucked two bats under his arm, and began wending his way to the dressing-room – the same one from which he had emerged 17 years earlier, a fresh-faced youngster of 20, to make his Test debut against Sri Lanka. Twenty minutes later, it was official. Amid a gathering sense of anticipation and occasion, Ponting walked into a room in the bowels of the WACA, accompanied by his wife, his daughters and finally his team-mates, who ringed the back wall. There had been tears earlier, Ponting admitted: "I tried to tell them a lot, but I didn't get much out. As I said to the boys this morning, they've never seen me emotional, but I was this morning." Now he was more composed, and there was relatively little theatre, certainly when compared to the lusty salaams that accompanied the departures of his eminent contemporaries Steve Waugh and Shane Warne. Fifteen minutes later, the journalists were composing their obsequies. It had all been disarmingly matter-of-fact – very much the Ponting vein.

And thus did an era pass that had been a long time in the fading: the era of Australian dominance, of which Ponting, and not merely his bustling, bristling batting, but his hairy-armed, spitting-in-his-hands presence, had been a personification. Australia had ceded their No. 1 Test ranking in August 2009, and their No. 1 one-day ranking three years later. Since then, all that had remained had been Ponting – and now he, too, was to go.

He had opened up in that time a sizeable gap between him and the next-highest Australian Test run-scorer, Allan Border. And even if his form had been more variable than of yore, an Australian order with his name in it could not help bear a strong look; he drew, of course, on a massive estate of international runs in all conditions and all climes. But the clock had been running down. He had passed the captaincy on to his dauphin, Michael Clarke, with promising results. Yet the wins were coming harder, and wins were what mattered to Ponting above all else.

"Seriously," he had said to Cowan just before the Sheffield Shield final earlier in the year, "you don't really think I give a toss about hundreds, do you?" Cowan had joked to Ponting about the possibility he might emulate Sachin Tendulkar and score a hundred international hundreds. In reply, Ponting had enumerated all the trophies and garlands Australia had won in his career – a lengthy list. Winning: it wasn't everything, but to Ponting it had always been the main thing.

Shaun Botterill, Getty Images

Young thruster: Ricky Ponting scores 96 on Test debut, against Sri Lanka at Perth, December 1995.

The Test would not be kind to Ponting in either individual or collective terms. He was pushing string uphill with his batting, and made only four and eight. He looked on in the field as Australia gave up 569 in South Africa's second innings. The tributes flowed almost for the game's duration. An especially moving one came on the final day, when South Africa's captain Graeme Smith formed his fielders into two lines so as to applaud him to the wicket, partner Cowan joining in; when he was out, every member of the visiting team went to him individually to shake his hand; there were further impressive displays of cricketing confraternity as the game ended. But you got the feeling Ponting would have swapped them all for a win, even just for a few extra runs.

If desire could be bottled, it would be distilled from essence of Ponting. Sometimes in his career, more of that had seeped out than even he could handle. He had a way of remonstrating with umpires that recalled the Mike Gatting school of diplomacy, although it often looked worse than it was: Ponting tended to be a barrack-room lawyer rather than a potty-mouthed pouter. The first thing he expressed when he sat down at the end of the match, in the same room in which he had started it, was his disappointment at the result and regret that he had not made a few more: "It has been a hard week, and we haven't got the result we were after and I haven't got the result I was after." The desire was still there; it's just that the capabilities could no longer stretch to the same height.

Now he was prepared to take questions about his career, about which he had earlier been reticent. His daughter Emmy was sitting on his knee and, in the way little children have of objecting passively to their parents doing something when they should be available for play, stuck her fingers in her ears. Everyone

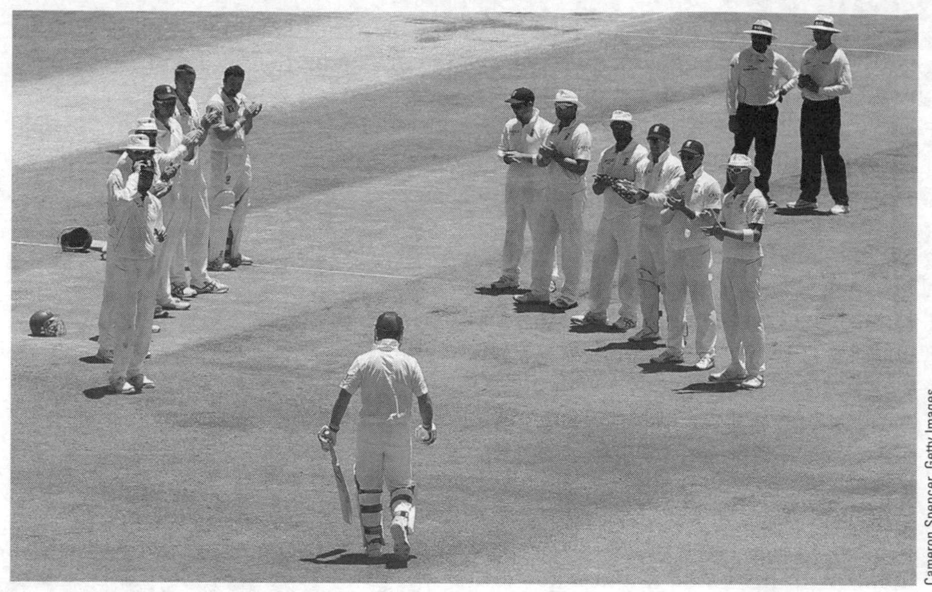
Cameron Spencer, Getty Images

In the V: Ponting walks to the middle for Australia one last time, as the South Africans (and Ed Cowan) show their respect.

else in the room, though, was spellbound. Normally, press conferences take place in a fairly formulaic fashion: they pretend to answer; we pretend to listen. Ponting's press conferences, though, were not like this. He was one cricketer who always gave straight answers to straight questions, and the impression of having thought about them. This was no exception. And as he spoke, there was otherwise complete silence. You could almost hear the tape recorders rolling.

In due course, he began to recite some thanks. Family. Friends. Management. Sponsors, some of whom had been with him from the very beginning, when a local bakery had sponsored his performances at Mowbray Cricket Club in Tasmania. He thanked that club too, with a cough and a sniff. "It's getting a bit harder." No – there would be no tears. "The Mowbray Cricket Club, if they see me up here like this at the moment, they'll be all over me. That's the place I learned the game, and the person I am was moulded from my background and my upbringing. What you've seen over 17 years is a result of my early days at the Mowbray Cricket Club. Thanks to the boys back there."

Cricket Australia. Cricket Tasmania. The pragmatist and the fantasist in Ponting showed through when he revealed that he knew when his next training was, for the Hobart Hurricanes in the Big Bash League, and that as a result he would be in the vicinity of Bellerive Oval for the next Test. "Who knows, I might even be around for the first day of the game," he joked. "If I am, I might even join in the warm-up with the boys and see if there's just one more chance!"

"The boys": they came up a lot. It is funny how athletes always use the words when they are talking about team-mates. Once in a while, it's "the guys", but usually discussion circles back to "the boys". I dare say a detractor of sport would decide this is because sport keeps athletes in a state of arrested development, of perpetual childhood; maybe there's some truth in that. But it is perhaps also this that allows them to express themselves: when adult doubt and cynicism set in, it is time to go.

RICKY PONTING'S INTERNATIONAL RECORD

As a player	*M*	*I*	*NO*	*R*	*HS*	*100*	*50*	*Avge*	*SR*	*Ct*
Tests	168	287	29	13,378	257	41	62	51.85	58.72	196
ODIs*	375	365	39	13,704	164	30	82	42.03	80.39	160
T20Is	17	16	2	401	98*	0	2	28.64	132.78	8

* Includes one match for the ICC World XI in which Ponting hit 115 and held one catch.

As captain	*P*	*W*	*L*	*D*	*NR*
Tests	77	48	16	13	–
ODIs†	229	164	51	2‡	12
T20Is	17	7	10	–	–

† Ponting also led the ICC World XI to victory over the Asian Cricket Council XI in 2004-05.
‡ Two ties in ODIs.

Not that Ponting finished his career as anything other than an adult. His wiry frame and sun-burnished face were those of a man who had seen the world; there was knowhow and wisdom on the game he loved in his every utterance. But to see him to the very end throwing himself around at training, standing in the huddle, singing the team song, enjoying the banter, was to be reminded how sport preserves in us the happiest parts of ourselves.

The boys: how he would miss them. And how they would miss him: not just his run-getting, but his body-and soul commitment to the commonweal, audible in his voice as he watched Cowan taking his catches, always upbeat, always encouraging, always urging them on. Now he was off to see them one last time as a player, with a final: "Thanks, everyone." It was we, of course, who should have been doing the thanking.

Gideon Haigh is a journalist. His latest book is On Warne.

THE EVOLUTION OF THE ONE-DAY GAME

Five decades of hits and giggles

TANYA ALDRED

The cricketer of 1963 wore a woolly jumper, collected his wages in old money, and tidied his short hair to the side with a neat parting. But he was also a revolutionary. On May 1 – a year after the experimental four-county Midlands Knock-Out Cup – Lancashire and Leicestershire stepped out for the first match of the Gillette Cup at Old Trafford. It rained, and the one-day game had to be finished on day two, with Lancashire winning by 101 runs and Brian Statham taking five for 28. But something had changed for ever: that September, 23,000 attended the first Lord's final, where Sussex squeezed out Worcestershire.

Fifty years later, domestic one-day cricket has pulled on a bewildering number of costumes: 65 overs, 60, 55, 50, 45, 40 and 20. There have been coloured clothes, floodlights, pinch-hitters, Jacuzzis and miked-up fielders. Revitalised, endangered, usually a muddle, it has given immense pleasure.

Five men who loved playing it share their memories here, one from each decade. Norman Gifford, now back as Worcestershire's spin-bowling coach, is lyrical about the 1960s; David Hughes clever on Lancashire's golden 1970s; Clive Radley modest about Middlesex in the 1980s; and Paul Smith idiosyncratic on Warwickshire's dominance of the 1990s. Jeremy Snape completes the story as he recalls his time at Gloucestershire and Leicestershire.

Ken Saunders, Sport & General/PA Photos

Half a smile: Norman Gifford holds the match award after Worcestershire lost the first Gillette Cup final to Sussex, in 1963.

The 1960s – Norman Gifford

When the Gillette Cup started, we just played it like a normal three-day game, with three slips and a gully. Worcester had a strong side, and it wasn't until we reached the final that we came up against a team doing anything different. The Sussex captain Ted Dexter would put some thought into who he wanted to bowl, and what field he was after. It was a bit of a shock: for someone of his stature to do that was significant.

Being at Lord's for that first final was a tremendous experience. For those of us who hadn't played Test cricket, it was a completely new experience: there weren't many watching the Championship in the 1960s. I was Man of the Match, even though we lost, and picked up a gold medallion.

During the decade, totals got bigger, and the game evolved. Batsmen became more inventive. When it started, they valued their wickets above all. The need to get runs on the board was foreign to them – they had demons to overcome. Similarly, line-and-length bowlers found it difficult. People assumed medium-pacers and fast bowlers would be the most effective, but it soon became clear we spinners were important too.

People remember the '60s as a dull time for Championship cricket, although for us – winners in 1964 and '65 – it was exciting. But for sides at the bottom it could be run-of-the-mill. The one-day stuff suddenly gave them an opportunity to win something.

Standards of fitness are far greater now, but the equipment is better too. The boots for the quick bowlers used to be heavy and awkward, and the bats smaller. We certainly weren't acrobats. When the 40-overs John Player League was introduced in 1969, it was viewed by players as Twenty20 was in 2003.

But I loved all the one-day competitions, and wouldn't have played as long as I did without them. I went to five finals – but lost all bloody five!

Gifford played for Worcestershire and Warwickshire between 1960 and 1988. He took four for 33 against Sussex in the first Gillette Cup final.

The 1970s – David Hughes

A lot of our guys had come out of the Lancashire and Yorkshire leagues, which were real cut-throat jobs, so we were steeled in one-day cricket. Most of our pre-season training involved visits to RAF Sealand in north Wales, and the instructors used to put us through it.

We had lots of all-rounders, whereas many counties were picking the teams they had done in the 1960s, full of specialists. The quality of our fielding kept us apart: we didn't carry anyone, we all had strong arms, and we were quick. We won a lot of games by saving runs. And in Farokh Engineer and Clive Lloyd we had two of the best overseas players in the business.

Under Jack Bond's captaincy we won five one-day trophies, including a hat-trick of Gillette Cups from 1970. We had huge crowds – maybe 25,000 – for most of our games. Other teams were getting 5,000, and some were intimidated by the Old Trafford atmosphere. Lancastrians can be a noisy bunch.

We were one of the few sides that looked in depth at who we were up against, where they scored their runs, what sort of bowling they had. We didn't have the technology, but we did have a great camaraderie with the umpires, and we used them to find out what other pitches were like, who didn't fancy the short ball, and so on. One of the first things Jack introduced was a lengthy team sit-down to discuss the opposition.

Jack retired in 1972, and David Lloyd took us to three successive finals in 1974–76. Half of that great team then retired, and we never really recovered. But we were there at the beginning of tactics in one-day cricket. Mind you, we didn't have all the background staff they have now. We always had trainers, a doctor and a physio, but no one for the mind. We didn't need people telling us what great players we were.

The 1971 semi-final against Gloucestershire is one of my most precious memories. The nine o'clock news was postponed, and it was really dark. In fact, the more I talk about it, the darker it gets! There were 25,000 people there: our late chairman Cedric Rhoades took the sightscreens out to fit in more spectators, and the kids on the grass pushed the rope in. It was such a dramatic climax.

Hughes played for Lancashire between 1967 and 1991. He hit 24 in an over from off-spinner John Mortimore to win that 1971 Gillette Cup semi-final.

The 1980s – Clive Radley

We were a little bit ahead of our time in one-day cricket, without really knowing it. But it certainly wasn't through any deep thinking about the game. Mike Brearley preferred to cajole – or possibly bollock – players on an individual basis. He was less formulaic than those who had gone before. Don't give him too much credit, though: we had a great side.

Our bowling was capable of both getting wickets and keeping batsmen quiet: Philippe Edmonds, John Emburey, Wayne Daniel, Mike Selvey and Vintcent van der Bijl. The seamers were very good at the death, too.

Things got more athletic as the decade went on, and we started doing a bit more in the gym in pre-season. Fielding circles arrived in 1981. Before that, we could put everyone back on the boundary in the last ten overs and close the game down. Seam bowlers used to be hidden in the field: they'd stick out a size 11, or let someone else chase. Now, they had to start putting in a dive.

I was fairly fit even in my forties, and the slide I used in order to ground my bat between runs just developed naturally as it seemed the quickest way to get back down the other end; it didn't damage the old knees because I didn't bat in studs. My forte was nicking and nudging. Mike Gatting and Roland Butcher were good at smacking the ball, so if they were going at five an over and I was going at three, we were doing well.

The first person to play the reverse sweep in county cricket must have been Mushtaq Mohammad, against Fred Titmus. He told me he'd got fed up with six–three leg-side fields. It was a great stroke, and I must have batted with Gatt while he got 300 runs with it. But after he got out in the 1987 World Cup final, he didn't play it for another two years. I wish I'd played it myself, but I had my method, and there wasn't much time to practise.

I never took part in any game that matched our Benson and Hedges Cup final against Essex in 1983. They were 127 for one chasing 197, and the Middlesex supporters had left the ground. We had given the game up, and everyone was round the bat. I caught Keith Fletcher at silly point off Edmonds, and the rest collapsed. It was just one of those days.

Radley played for Middlesex between 1964 and 1987. He won the match awards in the 1983 Benson and Hedges Cup and 1984 NatWest Trophy finals.

The 1990s – Paul Smith

Warwickshire's one-day success wasn't a fluke. We had every character and skill imaginable, and then this bloke came along with a massive passion for what he did: Bob Woolmer. Chalk and cheese were Woolmer and Dermot Reeve, our captain. Woolly would say: "Why don't you go to bed at ten o'clock, like I do?" Reeve wanted to go out and enjoy himself. But it worked.

Tactically, we were miles ahead of the rest. We had the balls to do what they could have done but didn't want to. In the 1990s in general, you had to be in people's faces, and we played a different type of cricket, with lots of reverse sweeps and tip-and-run. And we had big strikers of the ball. It wasn't popular. I remember our batsmen reverse-sweeping, and the commentators saying it wasn't in the spirit of the game. Brian Lara said we should look at where the gaps were, not the fielders. It made you think very differently.

Woolmer provided a sprinkling of gold dust. People think of his computers, but they forget about the hours he spent in the nets, in the middle, in restaurants – all that time with the guys, talking to them, thinking about them.

We turned up at Old Trafford once, and Woolly took out a tennis racket and hit catches to us. The crowd were shouting: "Aww, don't you want to hurt your hands?" But they didn't realise that, from 50 feet up, a tennis ball will bounce out, so it was teaching us about soft hands. He also introduced warm-downs, even though they were the last thing we wanted to do.

Graham Morris

Band on the run: Paul Smith claims a couple of stumps (and the Gold Award) at the end of the 1994 Benson and Hedges Cup final.

Woolly said to us at the start of the 1994 season that we could win all four competitions. I thought he was barking mad. But we nearly did. Shortly after, Jason Ratcliffe moved from Warwickshire to Surrey, and he reckons it took other counties five years to catch up with us.

Smith played for Warwickshire between 1982 and 1996. He was part of the winning team in four Lord's finals and won the Gold Award in the 1994 Benson and Hedges Cup final.

The 2000s – Jeremy Snape

During my time at Northamptonshire, the focus was on talent. But at Gloucester we trained as a team – and to a different intensity. The fielder went from being someone who defends the ball to someone who attacks the batsman. We would stand in a ring, like fishermen tightening the net. The batsman would hit it hard to point, and the fielder would return the ball just as hard to Jack Russell, who would take it in front of the batsman's face. It was oppressive and claustrophobic. Our coach John Bracewell shifted our mindset, from cricketers to athletes who play cricket.

We saw ourselves as underdogs. We worked exceptionally hard, and there was me, Martyn Ball and Kim Barnett trying to take pace off the ball, on slow, knee-high wickets, with big outfields, and batsmen caught in the deep. We played ugly cricket – but we won.

When I moved to Leicestershire before the 2003 season, we weren't challenging in the Championship, so we focused on Twenty20. We worked out how to pace the initial impetus phase of an innings, the building phase, and the crescendo. We caught other sides out. Everyone was thinking fast bowlers should bowl as fast as they can, but that creates pace and angles. And batsmen thought they had to be ultra-aggressive, whereas we'd worked out the value of players like Darren Maddy and Brad Hodge – one a hitter, the other a rotator.

It was a time of innovation, too. I was in the nets with H. D. Ackerman when he asked me to help him practise his six hitting. So I pulled out the pin and bowled a looping hand grenade. He said: "Don't be stupid, I can't hit that!" A light bulb went on, and the moon-ball was born. Batsmen would think: "I can't get out to that, it's only 40mph…"

Twenty20 has definitely benefited the wider game. In my early career, a yorker could land anywhere under a batsman's feet. Now, it has to be on the white line of the batting crease to compensate for batsmen's power and scoop shots. And people are much more comfortable in high-pressure run-chases: they get 250 in 50 overs easily. In the 1990s and early 2000s, it was all about protein shakes and bleep tests; in the last six to eight years, it's been more pitch-maps and Hawk-Eye. There are no secrets now. The only competitive advantage is what goes on inside players' heads.

Snape played for Northamptonshire, Gloucestershire and Leicestershire between 1992 and 2008. He won four Lord's finals with Gloucestershire, and the Twenty20 Cup twice with Leicestershire.

Tanya Aldred writes about sport for the Daily Telegraph.

A QUESTION OF TALENT

Art and graft

MIKE ATHERTON

Boy, he looked good. Sitting there in his crisp, grey suit, hair slicked back, tanned, square of jaw, he looked as if he could have played for another decade. But Mark Ramprakash had decided enough was enough. The runs had not flowed with their customary ease and, midway through his 26th summer in the first-class game, it was time to reflect on what had gone, rather than speculate about what was to come.

Rightly, the valedictories were gushing. This was a batsman, after all, who had scored over 35,000 first-class runs at an average of 53, and joined the elite group of those who have made more than 100 first-class hundreds. Because of the impact an expanded international game has had on appearances in domestic cricket, he could well be the last member of the club. At every level except the very top, he made batting look easy. He was a fine player.

Many pieces were written about Ramprakash in the days after his retirement, and many included the phrase "the most talented player of his generation". A few suggested his talent was unfulfilled, which seemed a little harsh, even if it reflected his travails in over a decade of Test cricket. The implication was that he had underperformed, a view based on a perception of the ability he was blessed with.

Talent. We have a curious relationship with it in English cricket. If it is generally defined as possessing either a natural gift, or a capacity for success, then our game invariably tags as talented those who enjoy the gift, but not necessarily the success. Many England cricketers who have struggled to establish themselves in the international game – Chris Lewis, Mark Lathwell, Owais Shah and Ravi Bopara, to name four recent examples – are routinely described as being among the most talented players of their time.

The notion of a natural gift has taken a battering in recent years, thanks in particular to the work of one scientist. The Swedish psychologist K. Anders Ericsson has gone a long way towards deconstructing the myths of talent by showing that elite performance is almost always the result of ferocious hard work, relentless self-improvement and specific, rigorous practice – all within a cultural context in which the appetite for self-improvement can flourish. In other words, few have reached the top without putting in the hours.

Ericsson's work is now widely accepted, but there are still some who believe in inherent or inheritable gifts. For sports such as basketball, which require genetically linked physical advantages, it is hard not to sympathise with this view. But whichever side of the divide you tread, it should be obvious that the term tends to be applied retrospectively. In describing someone as talented, we do not really mean they have some innate predisposition to perform; rather, it is a convenient way of explaining their achievements (or even, in English cricket, their shortcomings).

Bob Thomas, Getty Images

A natural: two days before his 19th birthday, Mark Ramprakash strokes Middlesex to victory in the 1988 NatWest Trophy final.

In looking for examples of talent, we nearly always exaggerate the importance of an eye-catching moment, or a graceful style. Aesthetics outweigh almost everything else. Ramprakash's feats were far from modest, but it was his elegance – the ease with which he appeared to play, the extra time he appeared to enjoy – that encouraged the notion he was unusually talented.

Very few observers, by contrast, would describe South Africa's Graeme Smith as naturally gifted. With his wide, ungainly stance, strangling grip, and closed-face back-lift, he makes batting look hard work. And yet his method makes perfect sense. In an era where bowling at fourth stump is accepted practice, and when fielders in the arc between wicketkeeper and point often outnumber the rest, Smith's refusal to hit in areas traditionally regarded as left-handers' strengths gives him an advantage. More than 8,500 Test runs at nearly 50 as an opening batsman suggest he possesses talents that transcend mere aesthetics (or their absence).

Most of us are prone to this weakness of falling for the kind of talent that a moment of brilliance implies: a breathtaking stroke, a scintillating piece of fielding. As a result, we underestimate the gifts given to those who achieve consistently, if not spectacularly. After watching a young Dwayne Smith, the West Indian all-rounder who had made a rapid century on Test debut, smash a length ball from Steve Harmison over midwicket and out of the ground in Trinidad some years ago, I turned to my companion and said: "I've just seen the next great West Indian batsman." One shot was enough to fool me. All through the disappointing years that followed, I kept expecting what I thought was exceptional talent to blossom. It never did.

We are apt to hold too narrow a definition of what constitutes talent. One of Ramprakash's contemporaries was Graham Thorpe. More than a decade ago in Colombo, I watched him score a hundred against Sri Lanka's spinners in conditions that could not have been more testing, with the sun beating down and the pitch disintegrating into dust. His strokeplay was not eye-catching; in fact, the innings was devoid of any flowing shots at all. But what an innings it was – one of the finest I ever saw from an England player.

That day, Thorpe revealed so many different aspects of *his* talent. He played the ball off the pitch later than any of his team-mates. It takes a particular gift to let the ball keep coming and coming until the bowler is almost yelping with success, but he adopted a kind of French-cricket technique, keeping his back-lift low, and turning the blade with his wrists at the last moment to pierce gaps that most others would have needed satellite navigation to find. His talent was to adapt to his surroundings.

As for my own career, I take an innings of 99 at Headingley against South Africa in 1994 as one that revealed my own special – for want of another word – talent. It was after the dirt-in-the-pocket match at Lord's and, in the intervening week, I had to cope with an unusual degree of public interest, with a tabloid tracking my every movement. Between Tests, I had not been able to practise, and there had been no county match for Lancashire.

The attention was not on my batting, but on my captaincy and character. I had been forced to sit through two torturous televised press conferences, and to listen to a range of critics, from the comedian Jimmy Tarbuck to the chairman of the Headmasters' Conference, who sought my resignation. It was an uncomfortable time, and before I walked out to bat, I had not given a moment's thought to the innings. I scratched around for a couple of hours before lunch, and forced myself into some kind of rhythm by dint of nothing more than pure bloody-mindedness. But what I had managed to do, between walking to the middle and facing the first ball, was to put the events of the previous fortnight to the back of my mind. I am certain that, in the same circumstances, not many of my contemporaries could have played that innings, that day.

The ability to shut out the noise and the clamour is something I see now – to a far greater degree – in Alastair Cook. It is not an aptitude that stands out, is easily recognised, or regarded as exceptional. Hidden from view it may be but, set against the requirements for success at international level, with all its pressures, it is a talent as important as the ability to play a good-looking cover-drive. It is only now, after over 7,000 Test runs and more hundreds than any other England player, that observers (I have been more guilty than most) are starting to think of him as gifted.

Barring injury, illness or misfortune, Cook – who is only just entering his prime – will probably become the greatest batsman England have ever produced; greatest, that is, in terms of run-scoring, record-breaking and hundred-making. The adjectives that accompany most of his innings are hard-working, focused, driven, effective, pragmatic – as if these attributes, and Cook's supreme thirst for self-improvement, are not identifiable talents in themselves.

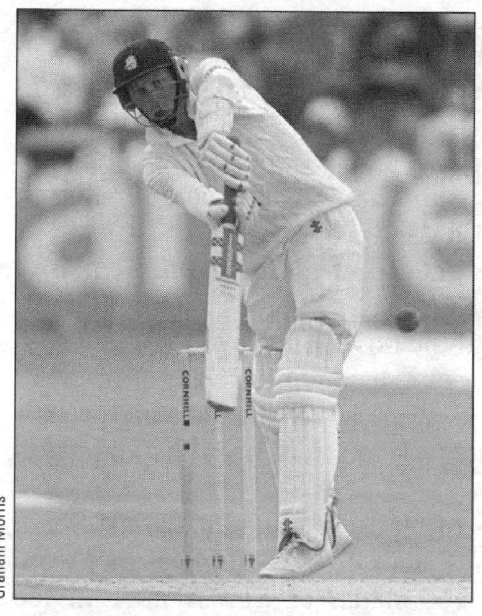

Graham Morris

The end of pure bloody-mindedness: Mike Atherton falls for 99, against South Africa.

They are submerged beneath a game that sometimes stands out only for its ordinariness. Yet Andy Flower has commented upon his world-class facility to score through the leg side and off his hip, a gift those at Essex quickly recognised; his ability to shut out extraneous detail, and his concentration levels, speak of a particular talent too. The way he out-thought and outmanoeuvred India's spinners during consecutive hundreds in Ahmedabad, Mumbai and Kolkata over the winter revealed a cricketing intelligence not shared by many of his team-mates. His hundred in Mumbai was certainly less spectacular than Kevin Pietersen's, but can we really say Cook is less talented? He simply possesses different strengths.

Talent may or may not be innate but, in all its facets, it certainly exists to be developed, honed and crafted. The more humdrum aspects of the game – the ability to work hard, stay focused, adapt to circumstance, bring your best game to the crease time and again, despite all the distractions – are all gifts, just as much as sweet ball-striking.

One of the sweetest strikers in the English game right now is Bopara. The consensus is that he is more naturally gifted than Cook but, as he sat at home over the winter, watching him compile hundred after hundred, how Bopara must have wished for some of his talents – the ability, for example, to put a run of bad scores behind him, or to compile the kind of ugly runs that would keep him in the team from one game to the next until form returns, as Cook did memorably against Pakistan at The Oval in 2010.

In one of his more poetic moments, Friedrich Nietzsche said: "All great artists and thinkers are great workers, indefatigable not only in inventing but also in rejecting, sifting, transforming and ordering." Cook is indefatigable in ordering his gifts, but no doubt it will be his Essex team-mates, Shah and Bopara, who are remembered as the more talented.

Being tagged as supremely talented also diminishes Ramprakash's achievements, because the implication is that the game came easily to him. If it looked that way, it was on the back of unstinting hard work. Having played with him for over a decade, I would not disagree with anybody who called Ramprakash the most dedicated batsman of his generation. As for the most talented? Well, that depends on your definition.

Mike Atherton is cricket correspondent of The Times. *He played 115 Tests for England, and captained them in 54.*

PART THREE

The Wisden Review

CRICKET BOOKS, 2012

Stealing Christmas

JOHN CRACE

Cricket may be some way off the dodgy expenses claims and cosy kitchen suppers with powerful members of the media that have been enjoyed by politicians in recent years, but it can hardly lay claim to utter transparency in all its affairs. To many outsiders, the sport's governing bodies still look suspiciously like old boys' clubs, and their decision-making processes often have all the openness of a group of cardinals at a papal conclave. So, as a gesture of candour, I propose to break with tradition, name my cricket book of the year up front, and declare an interest, for my choice is published by Bloomsbury, the owners of *Wisden*. You will have to take my word for it that no money has changed hands; but then any of you who have had business dealings with Bloomsbury shouldn't find that too hard to believe.

Hundreds of millions of pounds were definitely changing hands in other areas of the game, and this was the subject of **Bookie Gambler Fixer Spy** by Ed Hawkins. This wasn't the best-written book of the year – after a while, the breathless present tense becomes rather too, well, breathless – but it was far and away the most important, because it tried to get to the heart of the betting scandals that continue to dog the game.

Listen to the ICC and cricket's anti-corruption units, and you might imagine skulduggery was largely a thing of the past. Journalist and betting expert Ed Hawkins thought so too, until he started hearing rumours from Indian bookmakers that it was alive and kicking. One game in particular was brought to his attention: the 2011 World Cup semi-final between India and Pakistan at Mohali. According to his sources, "India would score more than 260… then pak will cruise to 100, then lose 2 quick wickets, at 150 they will be 5 down and crumble and lose by a margin of over 20 runs." As Hawkins and an old friend, Cherenne, sat down to watch the match on television, they grew progressively quieter. It's true that India made exactly 260 rather than more, but Pakistan reached 100 for two, slipped to 106 for four, lost their fifth wicket at 142, and were all out one ball before the end of the final over for 231. "You've stolen Christmas from me," Cherenne said as she left. "I'm never watching a game with you again."

Hawkins was halfway through a one-man, heart-of-darkness voyage in investigative gonzo journalism to see what else he could uncover. And it hadn't taken him long to make considerable progress after heading to India and meeting a host of spivs, runners, fixers and Mr Bigs, whose real names remain unclear. The evidence he discovered was damning on a circumstantial level, if not conclusive proof. But that was neither here nor there, for the advantage Hawkins has over other writers who have tried to get to the bottom of match-fixing is that he understands the mathematical nuances of betting.

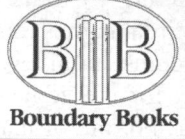

The big scams, such as the Cronje affair and, allegedly, the 2011 World Cup semi-final, may be the easiest for the lay person to grasp. But what Hawkins shows is that, because of the phenomenal amount of money wagered at any one time on even the most insignificant televised match, a very small amount of information can nudge the odds firmly in the bookmakers' favour. It's all about probability. A bookie with the right algorithms can make a fortune in marginal, high-volume bets from knowing something as simple as who will bat first. Throw in the knowledge of a bent, bought player, and it's a licence to print money.

In the process, Hawkins also exposes the 2010 Pakistan spot-fixing scandal – for which the cricket authorities were quick to claim the moral high ground – as something of a show trial. The whole purpose of the no-ball scam was not to influence the betting, but merely to prove that Salman Butt, Mohammad Aamer and Mohammad Asif could be got at. Bookmakers follow betting patterns on a second-by-second basis: if anyone tried to place a bet on something as specific as a no-ball, it would be rejected as abnormal. Whatever else bookies may be, as Hawkins points out, they are not stupid. But others appear to be. The real importance of this book lies in its existence. Over the past 15 years, the cricket authorities have spent millions of pounds on various match-fixing investigations and have uncovered very little. Armed with what was almost certainly an extremely modest advance, Hawkins on his own has uncovered substantially more, in less time.

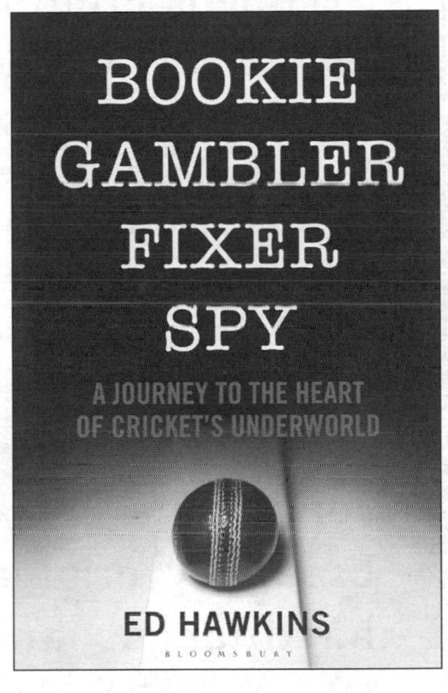

I can't remember Gideon Haigh ever constructing a duff sentence, and **On Warne** more than maintains his reputation as the most literary of the current breed of Australian cricket writers. There have been countless biographies – not to mention autobiographies – of "the greatest spin bowler who ever lived"™, and Haigh sensibly eschews this route, despite having spent more time with Warne over the years than many of his predecessors. Instead, as the title suggests, he has opted for something rather bolder: a philosophical treatise on the meaning of being Shane Warne; a deconstruction of genius.

If some of the material feels relatively familiar – the betting scandals, the weight-loss drugs, the infighting in the Australian dressing-room – Haigh's approach casts them in a new light. While never less than forensic in his analysis, he makes us reconsider the sheer physical exertion and contortion in imparting so many revolutions on a ball, hour after hour, year after year; the burden of being every captain's go-to bowler; the expectation of being asked

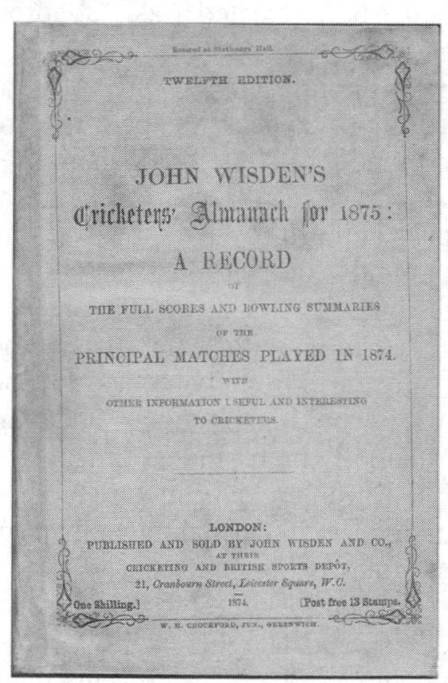

TWELFTH EDITION.

JOHN WISDEN'S
Cricketers' Almanack for 1875:
A RECORD
OF
THE FULL SCORES AND BOWLING SUMMARIES
OF THE
PRINCIPAL MATCHES PLAYED IN 1874.
WITH
OTHER INFORMATION USEFUL AND INTERESTING
TO CRICKETERS.

LONDON:
PUBLISHED AND SOLD BY JOHN WISDEN AND CO.,
AT THEIR
CRICKETING AND BRITISH SPORTS DEPÔT,
21, *Cranbourn Street, Leicester Square, W.C.*

One Shilling.] 1874. [Post free 13 Stamps.

W. H. CROCKFORD, JUN., GREENWICH.

consistently to win the unwinnable; and the sheer absurdity of finding a unique talent in someone who would be just as happy sitting on a beach, drinking beer with his mates.

My only small reservation is that Haigh perhaps loves his subject just a bit too much. Plenty have queued up to knock Warne for his off-field behaviour and, as an author, Haigh is within his rights not to join in. But, while never avoiding the difficult issues, he does tend to give Warne the benefit of the doubt. Take the incident in which Warne and Mark Waugh were found to have accepted money from an Indian bookmaker on the 1994-95 tour of Sri Lanka in exchange for information about pitch conditions and team selection. Haigh's view is that it was an act of naivety on a very demanding tour, no real harm was intended or done and, however badly Warne and Waugh might have acted, they looked like saints in comparison with the Australian board's handling of the situation.

All of which may, or may not, be true, but it rather misses the central point that Warne and Waugh *did* take the money on offer, and should have known better; deep down, they probably did. But why did no one else in the Australian team do the same? Why did they not even think to ask their team-mates whether they thought it was a good idea? Haigh is equally lenient in regard to Warne's diet, drinking, gambling and womanising, his attitude being that countless other cricketers have done the same or worse; that Warne's behaviour away from cricket is a personal matter; and that he gets more flak simply because of his celebrity. These are valid points, but they close down the argument rather than open it up. The aim is not to pass moral judgment on Warne – as far as I'm concerned, he can do pretty much what he likes – but to understand him. Why is he so self-destructive? Is there a relationship between his personality flaws and his bowling genius? I'm fairly sure there might be, if you looked carefully enough.

The link between Yorkshire cricket and manliness had just been smashed

With its subtitle of "Manliness, Yorkshire Cricket and the Century that Changed Everything", Max Davidson's wonderfully entertaining **We'll Get 'Em In Sequins** nails its quirkiness to the mast from the off. Which immediately requires a second disclaimer for mentioning another Bloomsbury title so soon. I haven't been got at. Honest. Nor is it a coincidence. Rather it's a matter of common sense. Cricket has become far more of a niche market in recent years, as book sales have declined substantially and mainstream publishers have become cautious about commissioning anything at all. So when a publisher does commission a talented writer with a proven backlist, it shouldn't come as a total surprise if the book turns out to be a good one.

When Davidson saw Darren Gough competing in tight-fitting spandex and sequins under strobe lighting on BBC TV's *Strictly Come Dancing*, he realised that the long-established link between Yorkshire cricket and testosterone-heavy displays of manliness had just been smashed in front of his eyes. "Was that thunder in the distance?" he writes. "No, it was generations of Yorkshire fast bowlers turning in their graves. What had gone wrong? Or – depending whether you were Old Yorkshire or New Yorkshire – what had gone right? Wasn't there something rather exhilarating in a 90mph fast bowler and lusty tail-end batsman who could also do a nifty foxtrot in an outfit that glittered like a Christmas tree?"

We'll Get 'Em in Sequins is divided into chapters on seven of the greatest cricketers to play for Yorkshire – George Hirst, Herbert Sutcliffe, Hedley Verity, Fred Trueman, Geoffrey Boycott, Gough and Michael Vaughan – and can be read pleasurably in that way. Cumulatively though, the book amounts to rather more, as what emerges is an intelligent and touching social history of a sport and a county that were dragged, at times kicking and screaming, from the repression of the Edwardian era, via the Angry Young Men of the post-war period and the reluctance to engage with women's rights and social diversity, through to the all-singing, all-dancing man hugs of the early 21st century.

Davidson's approach does have its minor drawbacks. I'm all for seeing cricketers as rooted within the social mores of their time – not enough writers have done this – but they are also individuals responsible for their own actions. Even by the standards of their day, Trueman and Boycott took boorishness and self-centredness to new levels. My favourite chapter by far, though, is the one on Verity, in which Davidson perfectly captures his reserve, dignity and self-sacrifice. The description of Verity's war service is almost unbearably moving, and it remains a goal of mine to visit his grave in Sicily.

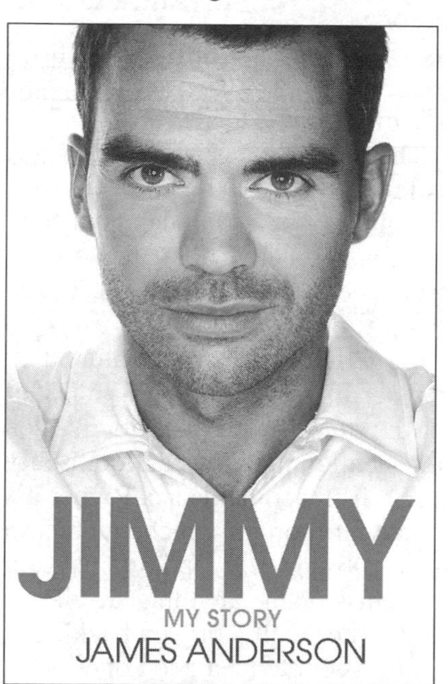

One of the perennial genres of cricket writing is the ghosted autobiography of the senior, well-established international, and this year's pick of the bunch is James Anderson's **Jimmy: My Story**. I don't know Anderson at all, but he has always come across as a nice bloke, even when he was larging it up as the tyro with the red streak in his hair. And his book, the story of his rise, fall and rise again as an England player, does nothing to disprove the notion. Here is a thoughtful, determined and quite gentle man working hard to develop his skills and maximise his success as a bowler.

The inevitable downside of this sort of book is that it feels as if it has been written by committee, with his agent checking every chapter to make sure Anderson has been outspoken enough to secure a newspaper serialisation deal, but not so much that he will risk offending the ECB or any of his current team-mates. As a result, we get a lot of cod psychology about how a man called James – a laid-back guy who wouldn't say boo to a goose – has to turn himself into fearsome Jimmy, the lairy geezer who is never short of a few insults for opposition batsmen. The first time he describes the process, it's quite interesting. By the fourth or fifth, I'm ready to skip a few pages.

More troublesome are the diplomatic omissions. By far the biggest story in the England camp over the past 12 months has been Kevin Pietersen's falling out, and subsequent rehabilitation, with the squad. And as a long-term member of the England team, Anderson is ideally placed to offer an insider's-eye view. We get nothing. Nada. I appreciate that the book's deadline may have predated the denouement of the Pietersen affair, but KP had long been an accident waiting to happen, and Anderson's unwillingness to offer anything but total admiration for him leaves the reader in an unconvincing no-man's-land. Describing his match-winning 151 in Colombo early in 2012, Anderson writes: "At that point things could have gone either way, but he well and truly took the game out of the Sri Lankans' reach by playing one of the innings that has made him as popular as he is with England fans." But what about Pietersen's popularity within the team? Surely relations must have been fairly toxic by then.

> "I never felt comfortable playing under Vaughan"

The other fascination with this genre is the way in which history gets rewritten. When England beat Australia in 2005 for the first time in 18 years, the consensus was that the success was partly down to Michael Vaughan's captaincy. Seven years later, Anderson has become the first player to offer an alternative view, claiming Vaughan never made him feel relaxed. "I actually felt alone and isolated when I most needed support," he writes. "Good captains get players to perform above themselves at times by putting their players at ease, and although a lot has been made of Vaughan's laconic style, I never felt comfortable playing under him. I never felt like he rated me: the language that he used with me was seldom positive and I didn't like that." I can't help feeling that, in seven years' time, Anderson will have something more insightful to say about Pietersen when he writes his inevitable second autobiography. If you can wait that long, that should be the one to buy.

Which brings us to that other long-time cricket favourite, the post-retirement, second-career-as-a-commentator, doyen-of-the-game's memoir, complete with a foreword by Sir Ian Botham – though why so many continue to ask him for his endorsement is never entirely clear. Botham is so competitive – or possibly insecure – that he can't resist putting his subject down, even when he's trying to be nice. His contribution to **Jackers, A Life in Cricket** by Robin Jackman (with Colin Bryden) is a case in point. "I am always happy when we are in the same town for a few days as there aren't many people who are easier to take money off on a golf course," writes Botham. "If he drills a good drive, it goes about the distance of my wedge!" With friends like these…

There again, it has to be said that, though Jackman might have a good story to tell, he doesn't seem to be in any hurry to do so, preferring to act as the after-dinner raconteur with tales, not always entertaining, of beer- and gin-soaked evenings with other players. Each to his own, however, and I dare say there are some who will find this an entertaining and quick read. Personally, I could have done with a great deal more self-analysis. It may not be easy for

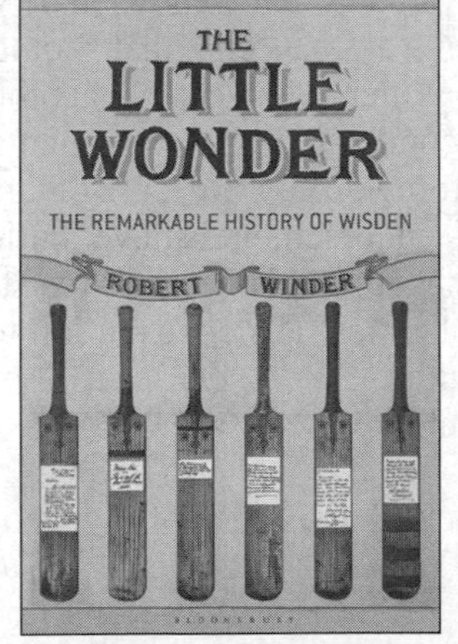
THE
LITTLE
WONDER
THE REMARKABLE HISTORY OF WISDEN
ROBERT WINDER

Jackman to accept that his career was defined as much by what happened off the pitch during the 1980-81 England tour to the West Indies as it was by his performances on it. But that is the way it is: more people will remember Jackman for being the man whose decision to play club cricket in South Africa in the 1970s eventually led to the cancellation of the Georgetown Test.

Jackman is quite eloquent on the manoeuvrings that surrounded that tour and eventually kept it on track. But on his choice to play in South Africa, he is almost entirely silent. The country were banned from Test cricket in 1970, after the ICC recognised what most other countries and sports had grasped many years before: that the apartheid regime was morally and politically repugnant. Jackman must have been aware of this, so why did he choose to spend his winters away from Surrey playing cricket there? Was he not that bothered that the black population was being brutally repressed, kept out of key jobs (cricket included), and forced to live in segregated squalor? Or did he just think it was nothing to do with him, and everything would be OK so long as he kept the money – and his eyes shut? He never says.

The flawed man whose father was an alcoholic

He's also silent on his decision to settle in South Africa after giving up cricket in England, other than to say he had met a lovely South African woman, Vonnie, whom he married. It wasn't as if he was returning to the country of his birth. He had been brought up in the Home Counties and, given the fallout from that 1980-81 West Indies tour, I would have expected Jackman to harbour at least some reservations about emigrating to an apartheid state once he had become aware of other people's strength of feeling. But no. Instead, he writes about the black resistance groups in Zimbabwe as terrorists, with seemingly no understanding of the decades of white colonialism that had sparked the guerilla wars. I don't expect politics to be every cricketer's strong suit, but this is ridiculous, and Jackman leaves me with the feeling – rightly or wrongly – that, however much progress South Africa has made since readmission, it is still dominated by a white cabal.

A rather more revealing and intimate portrait of a South African cricketer from roughly the same era comes in the shape of David Tossell's **Tony Greig**. For the last 30 years or so, the former England captain and all-rounder had, as Gideon Haigh pointed out, "been barely remembered as a cricketer", while Mike Atherton contended: "Greig remains one of the most underrated England cricketers of the post-war period."

Three things defined Greig in the public memory: his ill-advised declaration that he was going to make the 1976 West Indians "grovel"; his leading role in Kerry Packer's World Series Cricket revolution; and his nationality. All three rightly take centre stage in Tossell's book, but so too does Greig himself, the flawed man whose father was an alcoholic, who suffered from epilepsy since he was 11, who took all criticism – fair or unfair – head on, without ever asking anyone to make excuses for him. And, along the way, we learn that Greig was a better cricketer than he was given credit for. His Test batting average of 40 was higher than both Botham's and Andrew Flintoff's; his bowling average was poorer than Botham's, but on a par with Flintoff's. Furthermore, Greig achieved six five-wicket hauls, to Flintoff's three – and in fewer Tests. All of which suggests he ought to be remembered as being among the three best English all-rounders of the post-war era.

The real pleasure of this book, though, is that Greig's story has been told by a first-rate sportswriter. This is no ghosted part-work, overfilled with self-justification and interminable anecdotes of parties and tour drinking bouts which so often are passed off as intimacy and self-revelation. Greig appears to have given Tossell carte blanche to write what he wanted, and encouraged his family to have their say – not all of it flattering. The book unwittingly became a fitting tribute to a man who died at the end of 2012, and was unusual in putting his integrity before legacy. Above all, it comes with the ring of truth. Yes, Greig never denied that qualifying for England was an act of career pragmatism, but never once was he an apologist for apartheid. Nor did he downplay, or have any regrets about, his mercenary role in the professionalisation of cricket. All that's missing is any sense of gratitude from many of the players whose financial futures he was instrumental in securing.

By the end of the book, Greig is still not an easy man to like, but it's impossible not to feel the ice round him melt a little. He was so gloriously difficult. We tend these days to want to package our sports stars into easy, media-friendly compartments. Even in his late sixties, Greig refused to be pigeon-holed. South African, Australian or English? His idiosyncratic TV commentary consistently failed the Tebbit Test everywhere he went.

There again, Icki Iqbal's utterly charming **The Tebbit Test: The Memoirs of a Cricketing Fanatic** exposes the jingoism at the heart of this infamous proposition. In 1990, Norman Tebbit – a former Tory cabinet minister – argued that ethnic minorities in Britain revealed their true nationality by the cricket team they supported. It's unlikely you will have heard of Icki Iqbal, so let me fill you in. He was born in 1945 in Pakistan to a well-off, middle-class family, and has been obsessed with cricket ever since 1954, when the Pakistanis began to make their presence felt in international cricket. He moved to England in the mid-1960s, worked hard as an actuary, and is now as British as anyone. He even supports England.

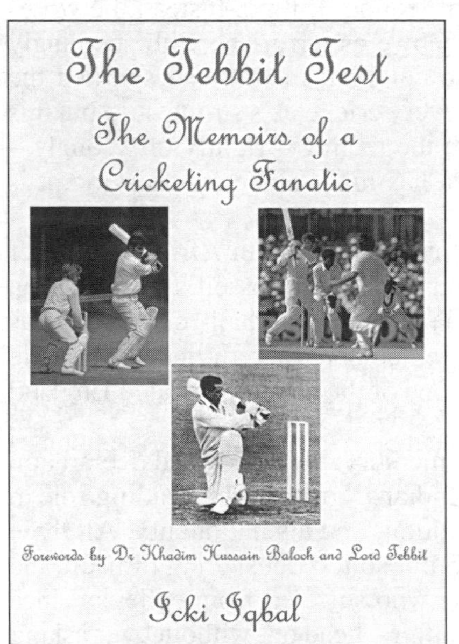

But his journey hasn't been quite as straightforward as Tebbit might have liked. Almost every sentence of this book speaks of a man with a Pakistani soul. His enthusiasm for English cricket is based partly on familiarity, but largely on disillusionment caused by corruption in the subcontinental game. Iqbal has become fed up with defending the indefensible. Had he not lost his faith in Pakistani cricket, there's little reason to believe he would have transferred allegiance.

And why should he? Multiculturalism is one of Britain's great success stories. Partisanship is hot-wired into every true cricket fan, and shouldn't be readily transferable. I have my own sliding scale of prejudice in international cricket. When England are playing, I always support them. If not, my pecking order runs Pakistan, West Indies, India, Sri Lanka, New Zealand, Australia and South Africa. I've no idea how many Tebbit Tests I fail along the way, but I'm really not bothered. In my world, the main test is just being passionate about cricket. If you are, then you're welcome.

Social history is also central to **Gentlemen & Players: The Death of Amateurism in Cricket** by Charles Williams. Few sports have reflected the English class structure quite so rigidly, and Williams offers a faithful account of the development of the modern game through the social make-up of county cricket. What's most astonishing about the Gentlemen–Players divide is not that it ever disappeared, but that it took so long to do so. The idea of a posh amateur being able to tell a county which dates he fancied playing on during his summer holidays is beyond parody. Class barriers were coming down throughout Britain after the Second World War, but cricket managed to maintain them until 1962. Then again, MCC were in charge…

For Williams, the inevitable and necessary end of cricket's class divide is not without its losses, for he believes something of the game's spirit went with it. I'm not so sure. If the only way a sport can retain its ethos is by hanging on to inequality, then it was probably not as pure as it was cracked up to be. Moreover, as Williams's book makes clear, it was more often than not the Gentlemen who were the most ruthlessly professional.

Phil Tufnell never got close to the genius of Shane Warne on the field, but he is more than his equal along the dodgy road of post-cricket celebrity, where the boundaries between being laughed with and laughed at become increasingly blurred. Warne should take **Tuffers' Cricket Tales** away with him on a Trappist retreat for a week before it is too late and, on his re-emergence, vow never again to take fashion advice from Liz Hurley or adopt a haircut that looks 20 years younger than his body.

I realise I'm stepping even closer to grumpiness than usual here, and I concede there is something to be said for live and let live. Tuffers is clearly having a good time in his new life, and a lot of people seem to get pleasure out of it, so what's the harm? Well… it just all seems so trivial. I want to remember Tufnell as the man who spun out West Indies at The Oval, not as some half-wit on reality TV. And this book of recycled anecdotes, packaged in a series of bite-sized paragraphs under subheadings such as "Puking in Ealing" and "The Crepe Suzette Pan of Uncertainty", has clearly been published with his new fan base in mind.

The thing is, I don't believe a word of it. This new cor-blimey geezer feels like a total reinvention. He was born Philip Clive Roderick Tufnell, and went to an independent school. Was his laddish persona a self-cultivation? If so, his performances as a pundit on *Test Match Special* take on a darker meaning. Tuffers's role on *TMS* is to be the informed bloke calling out from a sea of

posh establishment voices, the man of the people who may frequently get his words and thoughts confused, but has a heart of gold and speaks the truth to Joe Public. If Tuffers isn't really like that at all, then his shtick is insincere and patronising. I know I'm being harsh, but I feel disappointed. I loved watching Tufnell bowl, and I can't bear the fact that, if he carries on putting his name to books like this, he'll principally be remembered as having sold out.

Not that there's anything wrong with wanting to make cricket funny. It's the trying too hard that's the problem. The game itself is so shot through with hubris that only those running it seem not to notice. Left to its own devices, humour will almost always find a way to land a laugh.

A few years ago, the actor and stand-up comic Miles Jupp performed a one-man show about his efforts to become a cricket journalist covering an England Test tour; he has now extended that riff into **Fibber in the Heat**, a gentle – and genteel – unrequited love affair.

> Jupp's words resonate with eternal truths, failure and laughter

Like many of us who are blessed with next to no natural ability for cricket, but have a borderline-obsessive desire to follow it, Jupp wondered – during a career break from playing Archie the Inventor in the touring production of the children's show *Balamory: Live!* – whether he might be able to combine his passion for cricket with something that could loosely be called a job. And so, having maxed out his almost non-existent contacts book, he eventually found himself with two letters inviting him to contribute the occasional freelance report for the *Western Mail* and BBC Radio Scotland during England's 2005-06 trip to India.

As it happens, I found myself doing something rather similar in 1992, when I managed to persuade the Pakistan cricket team to let me hang around with them during the 1992 World Cup in Australia and New Zealand so I could write a book about Wasim Akram and Waqar Younis. I can therefore testify that every word Jupp writes resonates with eternal truth, failure and laughter – though in my case it took several years to appreciate just how much funnier everyone else found the experience than I did.

Jupp lives constantly on the verge of being found out. He'd like to write several probing features for the Cardiff-based *Western Mail* about how Welsh-born Simon Jones's injury has unbalanced the squad, but his day-to-day preoccupations are far more mundane: worrying if he has the right accreditation, worrying that the other hacks have made separate travel arrangements, worrying whether he's going to get into the press box and find there's nowhere for him to sit, worrying that no one is going to invite him out in the evenings and that he will be spending night after night feeling homesick in the not-very-nice hotel he can barely afford. Worrying, always worrying.

It has to be said that Jupp came rather closer to making it as a proper member of the British cricket media corps than I ever did, but he fails for much the same reason. At heart, he is just too much of a fan to be a reporter. I never could get used to the po-faced silence of the press box, where cheering a century was the last word in poor form. I knew the game was up when I found myself celebrating with Wasim inside the Pakistan dressing-room at the MCG after he had just bowled his country to victory in the final, rather than trying to get a few quotes I could sell. I just couldn't imagine ever wanting to go back into the press box. And yes, that night I too failed the Tebbit Test.

Marcus Berkmann set the benchmark for heroic tales of failure in amateur cricket with his 1995 book *Rain Men*. It chronicled the weekly incompetence and petty rivalries of his nomadic team, the Captain Scott XI, and established a new – and welcome – sub-genre of cricket writing in which the terminally useless and unfit, who make up 90% of the world's players, get their day in print. Sustaining interest and comedy in people known to nobody but the author and a few close friends is a hard act to pull off. Since Berkmann, many writers have met with varying levels of success.

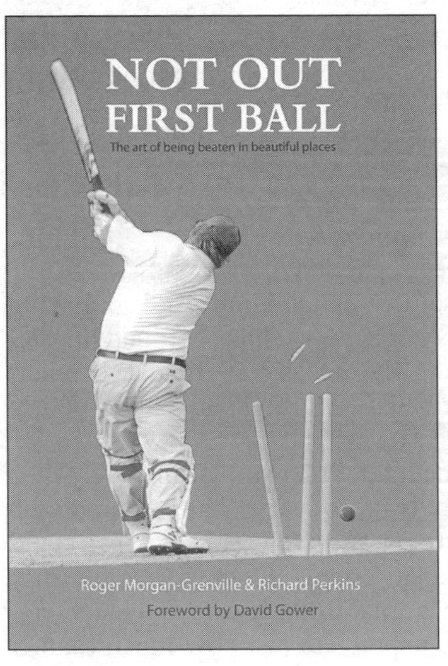

One of the typical problems with this sort of book is being able to believe that the team are quite as bad as portrayed. Amateur cricketers are prone to self-deprecation, and I've lost count of the number of times over the 30 years I've been playing for the particularly useless Hemingford Hermits that opposing captains have said before the start, "Oh we're really not very good at all – seven of our best players are on holiday," only to find we are 13 for five after six overs. So I've become deeply suspicious of cricket writers bearing gifts of false modesty. I will, though, make an exception for **Not Out First Ball**, by Roger Morgan-Grenville and Richard Perkins, a book that oozes charm and humour from the very first page and, most importantly, describes failures of the terminally delusional so accurately that I could almost believe one of the more disloyal members of the Hermits – and disloyalty is written into the team's DNA – had written a *roman à clef*.

Every familiar character is writ large. The captain who has never quite been able to come to terms with the fact he is no longer head boy of his minor public school; the fast bowler whose shoulders went 20 years ago, and can now only pitch one ball in six; the opening batsman who can't get the ball off the square, and is invariably one not out after ten overs; the wicketkeeper who can no longer bend his knees. Then there's the sledging. Why would anyone want to undermine the opposition when there's so much more fun to be had from rubbishing your own mates? If the White Hunter Cricket Club doesn't exist, it ought to. And if it does, the Hemingford Hermits will give you a game.

I shouldn't end, though, without a brief salute to the pamphlets that cricket enthusiasts continue to self-publish. A special mention should be made of

Triumph at Wattle Flat: When Castlemaine Beat the Poms, by Richard Mack. I've no idea what spurs a man on to research a minor game between the first English side to tour Australia in 1861 and a Castlemaine XXII, and then write it up in such depth. But I'm glad that men like Richard Mack exist. Cricket – and cricket writing – wouldn't be the same without them.

John Crace is the author of ten books on subjects from cricket and football to fatherhood and literature. He is also a TV reviewer and columnist for The Guardian.

WISDEN BOOK OF THE YEAR

Since 2003, *Wisden's* reviewer has selected a Book of the Year. The winners have been:

2003 *Bodyline Autopsy* by David Frith
2004 *No Coward Soul* by Stephen Chalke and Derek Hodgson
2005 *On and Off the Field* by Ed Smith
2006 *Ashes 2005* by Gideon Haigh
2007 *Brim Full of Passion* by Wasim Khan
2008 *Tom Cartwright: The Flame Still Burns* by Stephen Chalke
2009 *Sweet Summers: The Classic Cricket Writing of JM Kilburn* edited by Duncan Hamilton
2010 *Harold Larwood: The Authorized Biography* by Duncan Hamilton
2011 *The Cricketer's Progress: Meadowland to Mumbai* by Eric Midwinter
2012 *Fred Trueman: The Authorised Biography* by Chris Waters
2013 ***Bookie Gambler Fixer Spy*** **by Ed Hawkins**

WISDEN SPORTS WRITING

This high-quality series brings the excellence of *Wisden* into areas the Almanack has never reached. Combining the best name in sport with the finest sports writing, there are now six titles available.

Sit Down and Cheer

"A book to relish for all those addicted to TV sport"

Jon Champion, ESPN

Martin Kelner puts down the remote control and tells the story of how sport on TV developed from its adventurous, accident-prone, early days, as well as talking to those who made it happen.

Among the Fans

"A masterful piece of writing"

Daily Telegraph

Patrick Collins joins fans at a variety of sports such as snooker, speedway and darts – and at venues including Twickenham, Wimbledon and Cheltenham.

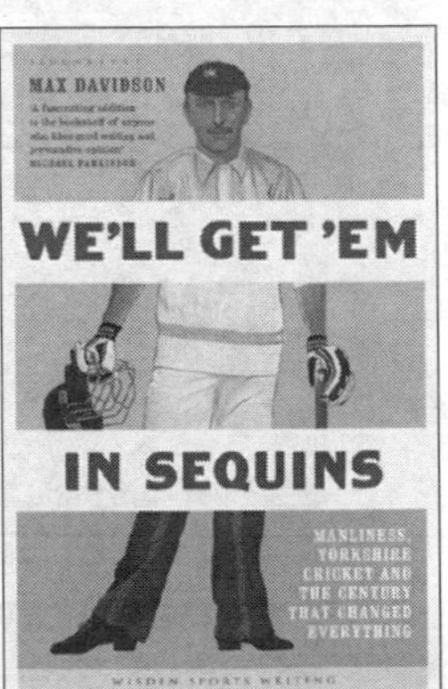

We'll Get 'Em in Sequins

Max Davidson studies seven of Yorkshire's greatest cricketers. He explains how they epitomise their era and traces the changing idea of masculinity the embody.

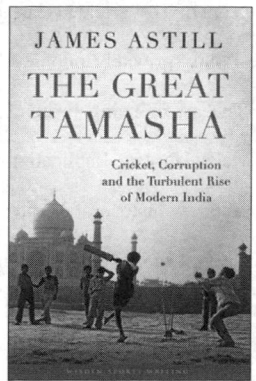

BOOKS RECEIVED IN 2012

GENERAL

Babb, Colin **They Gave Crowd Plenty Fun** West Indian Cricket and its Relationship with the British-Resident Caribbean Diaspora Foreword by Lord Bill Morris of Handsworth (Hansib, paperback, £8.99)

Baxter, Peter **Can Anyone Hear Me?** Testing times with Test Match Special on Tour (Corinthian Books, £16.99)

Benson, Richard **Leather on Willow** The Pocket Book of Cricket (Summersdale, £4.99)

Brookes, Ian **Essex CCC On This Day** History, Facts & Figures from Every Day of the Year (Pitch Publishing, £9.99)

Carroll-Smith, Adam **Chasing Sachin** (Pitch Publishing, paperback, £9.99)

Curr, Alan **Cricket on Everest** The world record attempt for the highest-altitude game of cricket (Matador, paperback, £9.99)

Davidson, Max **We'll Get 'Em In Sequins** Manliness, Yorkshire Cricket and the Century That Changed Everything (Wisden Sports Writing, £18.99)

Davies, Peter **Bats, Balls and Bedrooms** 36 of the Best at the Headingley Lodge Hotel (Cricket Heritage Publications, paperback, more details from peterdavies80@hotmail.co.uk)

Davies, Peter **Dances, Dinners and Ducks** Cricket in Huddersfield, Dewsbury and Batley in the 1950s (Cricket Heritage Publications, paperback, more details from peterdavies80@hotmail.co.uk)

Davies, Peter **From Adwalton and Ajmal to YEB and Young Star** The Centenary History of the Dewsbury & District Cricket League 1912–2012 Foreword by Stan Gostellow (available through the author, peterdavies80@hotmail.co.uk, or 01924 500135, paperback, £5)

Davies, Peter **George Herbert Hirst** Mirfield Cricket Club 1891 (Cricket Heritage Publications, paperback, more details from peterdavies80@hotmail.co.uk)

Davies, Peter **Ramsdens and Clarksons** The History of King Cross Cricket Club 1878–2011 (Cricket Heritage Publications, paperback, more details from peterdavies80@hotmail.co.uk)

Edwards, Alan **Hampshire CCC On This Day** History, Facts & Figures from Every Day of the Year (Pitch Publishing, £9.99)

Frith, David **Cricket's Collectors** A survey of past and present collections of cricket books and memorabilia (The Cricket Memorabilia Society, limited edition of 150, £58)

Halford, Brian **Warwickshire CCC On This Day** History, Facts & Figures from Every Day of the Year (Pitch Publishing, £9.99)

Hawkins, Ed **Bookie Gambler Fixer Spy** A Journey to the Heart of Cricket's Underworld (Bloomsbury, £16.99)

Hawkins, John **Trumper's Team in Queensland 1906** (Christopher Saunders, paperback, limited edition of 150, £20)

Iqbal, Icki **The Tebbit Test** The Memoirs of a Cricketing Fanatic Forewords by Dr Khadim Hussain Baloch and Lord Tebbit (DDKM Publishing, £15)

James, Steve **The Plan** How Fletcher and Flower transformed English Cricket (Bantam, £20)

Jupp, Miles **Fibber in the Heat** Following England in India – A Blagger's Tale (Ebury Press, paperback, £11.99)

Knox, Malcolm **Never A Gentleman's Game** The scandal-filled early years of Test cricket (Hardie Grant, £20)

Mack, Richard **Triumph at Wattle Flat** When Castlemaine Beat the Poms (privately published, paperback, more information from skills@impulse.net.au)

Morgan-Grenville, Roger and Perkins, Richard **Not Out First Ball** The art of being beaten in beautiful places (Bene Factum Publishing, £9.99)

Neal, Patrick J. A. **George Herbert Hirst** Mirfield Cricket Club 1891 (Cricket Heritage Publications, paperback, more details from peterdavies80@hotmail.co.uk)

Odendaal, André, and Reddy, Krish and Samson, Andrew **The Blue Book** A history of Western Province Cricket (Fanele, £27.95)

Quelch, Tim **Bent Arms & Dodgy Wickets** England's Troubled Reign as Test Match Kings during the Fifties (Pitch Publishing, £16.99)

Rodwell, Tom **Third Man in Havana** Finding the Heart of Cricket in the World's Most Unlikely Places Foreword by Courtney Walsh (Corinthian, £14.99)

Tufnell, Phil **Tuffers' Cricket Tales** (Headline, £16.99)

Warner, David **The Sweetest Rose** 150 years of Yorkshire County Cricket Club 1863–2013 (Great Northern Books, £17.99)

White, Simon **The effing c-word** Cricket: a user's guide (The White Words, paperback, £7.99)
Williams, Charles **Gentlemen & Players** The Death of Amateurism in Cricket (Weidenfeld & Nicolson, £25)
Wood, Charles **Bats, Pads & Gladiators** A Miscellany of Gloucestershire Cricket (Halsgrove, £12.99)

BIOGRAPHY

Barker, Tony **Keith Carmody** Keith Miller's Favourite Captain (ACS, paperback, £12)
Bonnell, Max and Sproul, Andrew **Tibby Cotter** Fast Bowler, Larrikin, Anzac (Walla Walla Press, $A34.95)
Booth, Keith **Tom Richardson** A Bowler Pure and Simple (ACS, paperback, £12)
Brodkin, Stuart **A. N. Hornby** The Boss (ACS, paperback, £11)
Chalke, Stephen **Micky Stewart and the changing face of cricket** (Fairfield Books, £18)
Haigh, Gideon **On Warne** (Simon & Schuster, £16.99)
Hill, Alan **The Valiant Cricketer** The Biography of Trevor Bailey Foreword by Doug Insole (Pitch Publishing, £16.99)
Jenkinson, Neil **C. B. Llewellyn** A Study in Equivocation (ACS, paperback, £12)
Murtagh, Andrew **A Remarkable Man** The Story of George Chesterton Forewords by Tom Graveney and Lord MacLaurin (Shire Publications, £25)
Tossell, David **Tony Greig** A reappraisal of English cricket's most controversial captain (Pitch Publishing, £14.99)

AUTOBIOGRAPHY

Anderson, James, with Gibson, Richard **Jimmy** My Story (Simon & Schuster, £19.99)
DeFreitas, Phil, with Clements, Derek **Daffy** The Autobiography of Phil DeFreitas Foreword by Sir Trevor McDonald (Apex Publishing, £15.99)
Jackman, Robin, with Bryden, Colin **Jackers** A Life in Cricket Foreword by Sir Ian Botham (Pitch Publishing, paperback, £12.99)
Martin-Jenkins, Christopher **CMJ** A Cricketing Life (Simon & Schuster, £25)
Nixon, Paul, and Colman, Jon **Keeping Quiet** Paul Nixon The Autobiography Forewords by Steve Waugh and Sir Viv Richards (The History Press, £17.99)

ANTHOLOGY

Levison, Brian, comp. **All In A Day's Cricket** An anthology of outstanding cricket writing Foreword by Christopher Martin-Jenkins (Constable, £20)

ILLUSTRATED

Broad, Stuart **My World in Cricket** (Simon & Schuster, £20)
Meredith, Anthony **Lord's Through Time** (Amberley, paperback, £14.99)

FICTION

Gibbs, Peter **Settling the Score** (Methuen, paperback, £7.99)
Lawrenson, Andy **Tales From Cow-Shot Corner** (Green Chain Publishing, paperback, £7.99)
Murari, Timeri N., **The Taliban Cricket Club** (Allen & Unwin, paperback, £9.99)
Quinn, Anthony **Half of the Human Race** (Vintage, paperback, £7.99)

TECHNICAL

Davis, Mark and Collins, Sam **Batting** How to Play, Coach and Win (John Wisden & Co, paperback, £14.99)
Davis, Mark and Collins, Sam **Bowling** How to Play, Coach and Win (John Wisden & Co, paperback, £14.99)

STATISTICAL

Bailey, Philip **First-Class Cricket Matches 1939/40–1945** (ACS Sales, Blue Bell House, 2–4 Main Street, Scredington, Sleaford, Lincolnshire NG34 0AE, email: sales@acscricket.com, £23)
Bailey, Philip and Bryant, John **Bangladesh First-Class Matches 2006/07 and 2007** (ACS, £9)
Bailey, Philip and Bryant, John **Sri Lanka First-Class Matches 2006/07 and 2007** (ACS, £10)
Bailey, Philip and Bryant, John **Zimbabwe First-Class Matches 2006 and 2006/07** (ACS, £8)
Webb, Tony ed. **The Minor Counties Championship 1906** (ACS, £14)

HANDBOOKS AND ANNUALS

Bailey, Philip ed. **ACS International Cricket Year Book 2012** (ACS, paperback, £26)
Bryant, John ed. **ACS Overseas First-Class Annual 2012** (ACS, paperback, £60)
Full scorecards for first-class matches outside England in 2011-12.
Bryden, Colin ed. **SA Cricket Annual 2012** (CSA, www.sacricketshop.co.za, R199 plus p&p)
Clayton, Howard ed. **First-Class Counties Second Eleven Annual 2012** (ACS, £10)
Colliver, Lawrie ed. **Australian Cricket Digest** Statistics by Ric Finlay (paperback, $A25 + p&p; more information from lawrie.colliver@gmail.com)
Harman, Jo ed. **The Cricketers' Who's Who** Foreword by Andrew Strauss (Pitch Publishing, paperback, £19.99)
Lynch, Steven ed. **The Wisden Guide to International Cricket 2013** (John Wisden & Co, paperback, £9.99)
Marshall, Ian ed. **Playfair Cricket Annual 2012** (Headline, paperback, £7.99)
Payne, Francis and Smith, Ian ed. **2012 New Zealand Cricket Almanack** (Hodder Moa, $NZ55)

REPRINTS AND UPDATES

Cardus, Neville **A Fourth Innings with Cardus** (Souvenir Press, paperback, £18.99)
Cardus, Neville **Cardus on Cricket** Introduction by Rupert Hart-Davis (Souvenir Press, paperback, £14.99)
John Wisden's Cricketers' Almanack for 1864 to 1878 (box set) (facsimile editions, Willows Publishing, 17 The Willows, Stone, Staffordshire ST15 0DE, tel: 01785 814700, email: jenkins.willows@ntlworld.com, £750 + £25 p&p, or £50 p&p overseas)
McKinstry, Leo **Jack Hobbs** England's Greatest Cricketer (Yellow Jersey Press, paperback, £9.99)
Tossell, David **Grovel!** The Story & Legacy of the Summer of 1976 Foreword by Tony Greig (Pitch Publishing, paperback, £12.99)
Waters, Chris **Fred Trueman** The Authorised Biography (Aurum, paperback, £8.99)
Wisden Cricketers' Almanack for 1939 and **1946** (facsimile editions, Willows Publishing, address as above. £60 each (original linen cover), £65 (original hardcloth cover); all editions + £4 p&p, or £12 p&p overseas)

PERIODICALS

All Out Cricket ed. Phil Walker (PCA Management/TriNorth, £4.25; £34.15 for 12 issues. Subscriptions: www.alloutcricket.com/subscribe)
SPIN ed. Matthew Pryor (The Cricket Publications Company, £3.95. Subscriptions: www.spincricket.com)
The Cricketer (monthly) ed. Andrew Miller (The Cricketer Publishing, £3.95. Subscriptions: www.thecricketer.com or ring 0844 815 0864)
The Cricket Paper (weekly) ed. David Emery (Greenways Publishing, £1.50; £20 for ten issues. From www.thecricketpaper.com)
The Cricket Statistician (quarterly) ed. Simon Sweetman (ACS, £3 to non-members)
The Journal of the Cricket Society (twice yearly) ed. Andrew Hignell (from D. Seymour, 13 Ewhurst Road, Crofton Park, London, SE4 1AG, £5 to non-members)

THE CRICKET SOCIETY AND MCC BOOK OF THE YEAR AWARD

The Cricket Society Literary Award has been presented since 1970 to the author of the cricket book judged best of the year. The 2012 award, made by the Cricket Society in association with MCC, was won by Chris Waters for **Fred Trueman The Authorised Biography** (Aurum); he received £3,000.

CRICKET IN THE MEDIA

The goldfish bowl

JONATHAN LIEW

The world of cricket media is a smaller one than many of the men and women who inhabit it – men, mostly – would like to admit. Peer inside the press box at a Test match, and you will find friends and enemies sitting side by side, former team-mates and foes brushing against one another as they queue for the sweet trolley. The analogy of the goldfish bowl is apposite – not least because cricket journalists continue to eat for as long as you keep feeding them.

In such an environment, where information and disinformation spread like contagion, where a rumour can be halfway across the ground before the truth has got its pads on, it is unsurprising that beefs develop. In that respect, 2012 was a more rancorous year than most. Nourished by the onrush of social networks, the cyclic plod of quotes-driven journalism, and the unshakeable fondness of the press for writing about themselves – guilty as charged, by the way – the media, more often than is customary, became the story.

In April, as Andrew Strauss struggled for form in Sri Lanka, Graeme Swann turned his irritation on the assembled press corps. "It's obvious there's been a little bit of a witch-hunt towards him that I think is unjustified," he said. "He hasn't shown any signs of being under any pressure. We only realised he was under scrutiny because some of us can read."

For while the world of cricket media remains small, its reach and penetration are now unprecedented. Online newspaper articles can be shared over oceans and across national borders. Tweets and television broadcasts ping across the globe at all hours of day and night. Throw enough opinions at the dressing-room and, eventually, some will slip under the door.

Ex-players, especially recent ex-players, can sometimes provide the most injurious criticism, and perhaps Michael Vaughan's verdict on Strauss's captaincy struck a nerve in the England camp. "If he clings on to the job and doesn't score runs, then he runs the risk of it turning nasty," he wrote in the *Daily Telegraph*. "My fear is that if he carries on and has a poor start against West Indies, then the selectors might have to remove him from the team."

In truth, the tone of Strauss's inquisitors was never quite as shrill as his supporters claimed. "There is nothing fundamentally so wrong with Strauss's technique that a little serious time and reflection in the nets is not likely to solve," wrote James Lawton in *The Independent*. "Removing him from the captaincy, or pushing him towards resignation, would surely stand out as remarkable folly even by the old standards of English cricket."

Of course, we all know how Strauss's story ended. Indeed, at his final press conference he revealed he had been considering retirement for six to 12 months. Perhaps, in hindsight, there were cracks beginning to appear in his immaculate edifice. Back in Sri Lanka, he responded with uncharacteristic

exasperation to the assertion by Bob Willis on Sky Sports that he had given up the England one-day captaincy at the behest of his wife. A surer-footed Strauss would have thrown Willis's comments out with the rubbish. Instead, he bit. "That was pretty disappointing," he said, "considering the person in question knows neither me nor my other half." Whether he was referring to his wife or Andy Flower, of course, is a matter of tangential discussion.

May brought more shenanigans, as Kevin Pietersen was censured for tweeting criticism of Sky's Nick Knight. It was a classic non-story, utterly extraneous to the game itself. But with Fleet Street struggling to drum up much interest in a one-sided series against West Indies, it could scarcely have been more perfectly timed. A delighted *Daily Mail* emblazoned "SKYGATE" on its back page, following up the next day with a "SKYGATE EXCLUSIVE", in which Paul Newman revealed Pietersen had "held clear-the-air talks with Nick Knight to thrash out their differences" and "explained his feelings face-to-face".

Cricket maintained a dignified detachment from the orgy of precious metal

Surprisingly, given all the air-clearing, difference-thrashing and feeling-explaining, this particular storm blew over quickly enough. More of Pietersen later – you can be assured of that – but the Knight rumpus turned out to be a neat portent of the summer to follow, when cricket had to shout like never before in order to be heard.

In the larger sporting patchwork of 2012, after all, cricket was the merest stitch, the Basil D'Oliveira Trophy proving no match for Team GB's deluge of gold, silver and bronze. While Britain held the biggest sporting party in its history, cricket bumbled along at the peripheries, maintaining a dignified detachment from London's orgy of precious metal. In truth, it was not until England's win in India at the fag end of the year that cricket enjoyed anything like a firm grip on the nation's consciousness.

To every action there is an equal and opposite reaction, and there was a snide subtext to the giddy euphoria that greeted the Olympics. Football suffered most harshly, but cricket received its sideways glances too. "Cricket and rugby, with their positive celebration of alcoholic excess, should be taking a hard look at how they regard their paying customers," wrote Richard Whitehead in *The Times*. "London 2012 has reminded us of one long-forgotten thing: that watching sport can be, above all, about pure, innocent fun."

Beyond the soul-searching, our national summer sport was faced with the dilemma of whether to ingratiate itself with the ecstatic throngs, or tough it out until the Olympic tsunami subsided. Some cross-breeding did occur: Jonathan Agnew chuckled his way through the archery at Lord's, while Mike Atherton, cricket correspondent of *The Times*, wrote a number of fine Olympic-themed essays.

Given London 2012's immense drain on resources and space, most of the dailies deserve praise for operating a near full-strength cricket service. Coverage of the county game was generally threadbare, though there was nothing exceptional in that. But when the national press gathered at Headingley

for the Second Test against South Africa, they were rewarded for their fidelity with the story of the year.

On August 6, Usain Bolt destroyed the field in the 100 metres, Jason Kenny triumphed in the men's sprint cycling, and Britain's showjumpers won their first Olympic gold for 60 years. But it was a measure of the gravity of the Pietersen saga that, the following morning, *The Sun*, *Daily Mirror* and *Daily Star* all found space for it on their back pages.

Pietersen's collision with the media had been brewing all summer. It began in July with an interview in the *Daily Mail*, when he spoke for the first time about his retirement from one-day internationals. "I've read and seen that we had heated discussions," he said. "Well, that's a lie. Whoever told the media that is a liar."

The suggestion that Pietersen had demanded to be excused from Test duty to play in the Indian Premier League had generated a tranche of negative comment. "It takes a vaulting arrogance to believe you can return to a forum that has made its negotiating position extremely clear with a new set of conditions," a seething Derek Pringle wrote in the *Daily Telegraph*. "By doing that, he brings his mercenary instincts, which many feel were his prime motivation when first qualifying for England, to the fore."

Daily Mirror

Despite other events in the sporting universe, the *Daily Mirror* finds room for Kevin Pietersen on its back page.

Now, after it emerged he had sent questionable texts to the opposition, it was open season. Suddenly, all the old preconceptions began to resurface. "Suggestions that Pietersen is not the only one seriously at fault are far from convincing enough to enlist sympathy for the transplanted South African," wrote Hugh McIlvanney in *The Sunday Times*. And in the *Daily Telegraph* there was this from Peter Oborne: "Pietersen is the latest white South African to use his selection for the England cricket team to promote his personal ambitions. Ultimately, Pietersen has not much idea of what it means to be British."

Perhaps the most astonishing philippic came from Michael Henderson, a long-standing and now gleeful detractor. "Those of us who have never accepted

the CRICKET paper

Issue 1: Wednesday, May 16, 2012

ISSN 2049-5749

COLIN CROFT EXCLUSIVE: Time for West Indies batsmen to deliver pages 6-7

8-page club section

Adams: Fluke phone call took me to Notts page 3

Stewart: England bowlers are best ever page 8

Nixon: We need own English Prem League page 17

Strauss: I'm not in a bad place the way Vaughan was

West Indies politics had Sarwan set to retire

By Daniel Schofield

RAMNARESH Sarwan was so disillusioned with the politics of West Indies cricket that only his father's intervention prevented him retiring from the game earlier this year.

It is not without irony that in the same week the West Indies were being beaten by ten wickets by England Lions that Sarwan was

Fighting back in cricket's foothills: the first edition of *The Cricket Paper* was published in May.

him as a bona fide Englishman," he trilled in the *Daily Mail*, "have been expecting this balloon to go up since the moment he made his Test debut against Australia in 2005."

But the best was yet to come. On a late-night discussion show on BBC Radio 5 Live the following week, Henderson embarked on a deeply addled, barely comprehensible, hugely entertaining ten-minute tirade that began as a broadside against Pietersen and ended up insulting virtually the entire cricket-loving public. "Everybody loathes Pietersen," he asserted confidently, before turning on Pietersen's defenders, who included fellow guest Paul Burnham of the Barmy Army. "I think people know who I am in this game," he continued. "I know seven ex-England captains. I spent three days in the MCC president's box – no riff-raff there." It was a bizarre outburst, characterised by frequent interruptions and curt answers, and it ultimately told us a good deal more about Henderson than Pietersen.

There were rare voices of calm amid the collective lunacy. Vic Marks wrote a considered defence of Pietersen in *The Guardian*: "There has been a whiff of witch-hunt about his omission, as a cricketing establishment closes ranks on an outsider. Some seem to be relishing his comeuppance." But it was a measure of Pietersen's estrangement from the media that, when he chose to break his silence, it was via his personal YouTube channel. In September, omitted from England's World Twenty20 squad, he flew out to Sri Lanka to work as a pundit for ESPN STAR Sports. It felt like a divorce, and in more ways than one.

Of course, we know how Pietersen's story ended too. His match-winning century at Mumbai completed a bizarre cycle of disintegration and reintegration, with his celebrity friend Piers Morgan among the first to exult. "He's a consummate professional," he wrote in his *Mail on Sunday* column. "He's also a great, loyal friend, someone who'll go the extra mile to help you if he can. We had breakfast together in Chelsea a few weeks ago…"

As the year ended, the media were forced to contemplate their own relationship with Pietersen. His talent had never been in doubt; nor had his flaws. But which outweighed the other? The answer, it seemed, was almost entirely determined by events. Even as the praise flowed like wine – a *Guardian* leader marvelled at the "concentrated focus that produced a dazzling, inventive, brilliant series of strokes" – there remained a suspicion that Pietersen's next peccadillo would see the tide turn against him yet again. One fancies it will ever be thus.

The fixation with Pietersen may also be seen as a symptom of the increasingly narrow purview of newspaper sport desks. England or nothing; KP or nothing. It is certainly true that the wailing over Pietersen drowned out a number of worthwhile stories. The climax of the County Championship was one notable example.

But in cricket's foothills, the shires were fighting back. The *Daily Mirror* website and ESPNcricinfo launched county blogs for the first time, their coverage augmenting existing online offerings from *The Times*, *The Guardian* and the *Daily Telegraph*. In May came the launch of *The Cricket Paper*, a new weekly offering from Greenways Publishing priced at £1.50. Its tone was refreshingly sober, its scope – "from Test match to village green" – satisfyingly broad.

Even in the traditional outlets, there were frequent affirmations that cricket journalism need not be hewn from the same changeless rockface. Peter Hayter's moving interview with James Taylor in the *Mail on Sunday*, in which the young England batsman shared his memories of his friend Alex Wilson, who died in a tragic accident in late 2009, was touching and brilliant. Scyld Berry's lament on the decline of state school cricket in the *Sunday Telegraph*, meanwhile, was superbly researched and powerfully argued.

On such fare does the goldfish bowl roll on: dwindling but defiant, frequently vilified but unstintingly vital. One fancies that this, too, will ever be thus.

Jonathan Liew writes for the Daily Telegraph.

CRICKET AND BLOGS, 2012

On the outside looking in

S. A. Rennie

In 1956, Len Hutton – newly retired and hired by the London *Evening News* to give his thoughts on the Ashes – was barred from the Lord's press box because he wasn't deemed a proper sportswriter. E. M. Wellings, the paper's cantankerous cricket correspondent, objected to Sir Len's use of a ghostwriter, forcing one of England's greatest captains to go and do his work outside, like a naughty schoolboy. The landscape has changed considerably: nowadays, bloggers get press passes, while ghosted columns and autobiographies are old hat. But the debate over what constitutes cricket journalism continues.

Some regard today's bloggers with the same disdain. Last year, evidence came in a tirade from an employee of the United States of America Cricket Association against ESPNcricinfo writer Peter Della Penna for his criticisms of the administration – or, as USACA's unofficial Facebook page put it, his "unethical, journalistic bias". Ending up with a verbal pitchmap that resembled Mitchell Johnson's bowling on a bad day, the page administrator – USACA executive secretary Kenwyn Williams – sprayed his invective in the direction of anyone who dared register disagreement (and, in many cases, their disbelief). This broadside was also directed at Cricinfo's executive editor Martin Williamson: "In the USA, journalists need to be QUALIFIED and belong to an organisation that endorses their profession… I beg Peter and Martin to prove to me they are qualified as journalists. They are internet bloggers and have NO journalistic privilege. NONE!!!"

Williams was dismissed for his role in this social-media meltdown, and the Facebook page deleted. But when the worst insult that can be aimed at a journalist is to call him a blogger "using the internet to spew venom", it reflects the common view that a blogger is a mere hobbyist, undeserving of consideration or courtesy.

Even if you *are* a blogger whose work is deemed worthy of inclusion on, say, the website of a national newspaper, there is no guarantee you'll be paid. With the print media scrabbling around for a viable business model, newspapers are now "partnering" with bloggers. In the case of *The Guardian*, this means reproducing articles from blogs on a section of their website called the Guardian Sport Network. Cricket blogs include "99.94" at **nestaquin.wordpress.com**, and **theoldbatsman.blogspot.co.uk**. This has ruffled a few feathers in the blogging community. One of the writers of "99.94" was forced to defend himself against the accusation he was taking jobs away from professional journalists, and admitted he felt uneasy. Others wondered if the failure to pay people for their work was rather un-*Guardian*.

And yet one man's "open journalism" is another's free content. Exposure and increased site traffic are the carrots dangled in front of aspiring journalists,

even if exposure won't pay the bills. As Ant Sims pointed out at **wicketmaiden.com/cricket-bloggers-write-free-profit**: "Next time you're at the shop, rattle off all the sites you are writing for for free, tell them about the exposure it's getting you and try using it as currency."

If remuneration is seen as one validation of a blogger's worth, recognition by the sport's great and good is another sign that the genre is being taken more seriously. In March, Sky's Mike Atherton interviewed Mohammad Aamer on his release from prison after the Lord's no-ball saga. I wasn't entirely satisfied by some of Aamer's responses, and wrote an article about it at **www.legsidefilth.com/?p=634**. I was pleasantly surprised when Atherton not only responded in the comments section, but was happy to answer questions raised by others.

Bloggers may often feel as if they are writing in a vacuum, even if they begin only with the objective of writing for themselves, or believe there is something that needs to be said that no one else has. But Atherton's comment that "some of the best cricket writing at the moment is on blogs" received plenty of attention. Jarrod Kimber, at **blogs.espncricinfo.com/sadisthour** wrote: "Atherton's comments don't legitimatise cricket blogging. But I think, to bloggers, tweeters and all those who chat about cricket for no money, they know that, if they produce quality and act like normal human beings, people like Atherton will feel comfortable enough to interact with them."

One recent trend has been the rise of collectives, communities of cricket bloggers run either by fans or, on a more commercial basis, by professional media organisations. **thesightscreen.com** features a variety of writers, including Kimber, Jon Hotten and Masuud Qazi, whose article comparing the Pakistan–England series to chaos theory was inspired off-the-wall analysis.

But as bloggers become assimilated into collectives, commercial endeavours and the mainstream media, they risk diluting the independence of unaffiliated observers who are on the outside, looking in. The lone blogger may be an endangered species, but notables include Freddie Wilde, whose blog at **fwildecricket.blogspot.co.uk** features his entertaining "Twitter at the Tests". Scott Oliver at **reversesweeper.blogspot.co.uk** takes a more academic and philosophical approach, combining tales of league cricket with and against Imran Tahir, Tino Best and Rangana Herath, with references to David Hume and non-linear thermodynamics. As you do.

By far the best newcomer this year, though, has been Darren Harold, who writes as "A Cricketing Buddha" at **donningthewhites.blogspot.com**. His five-part series on New Zealand's *Wisden* Cricketers of the Year is full of scholarly enthusiasm for his country's cricketing history, and is a must-read. In his essay "Why blog? Why not?" he says: "I try to write a number of pieces that give me a reason to go back in time, often inside my own memory banks, and read about the deeds of some of my heroes, and their heroes." With his passion for the game's past, and an understanding of its ties to the present, Harold's blog encapsulates everything that is best about amateur cricket writing.

S. A. Rennie blogs at legsidefilth.com.

KEVIN PIETERSEN AND TWITTER

A beer with Barack

JARROD KIMBER

Whether Kevin Pietersen was texting in Afrikaans, saying sorry or having his genius mocked, it all seemed to end up on Twitter. This was strange, because his own tweets were not that exciting.

He warned Roman Abramovich, Chelsea FC's oligarch owner, not to sell Frank Lampard: "Lamps shows who the boss is today. YOU DARE, Roman!" He congratulated his old mate Yuvraj Singh on his comeback after cancer: "@yuvsingh09 great stuff pie chucker… Be strong champ!!!! #yuvstrong". And when Sachin Tendulkar retired from one-day cricket, he ventured the view that Tendulkar had been a pretty good player: "Statistics NEVER lie! They tell a very true story. Well done Sachin! What an incredible ODI career #thebest".

But give Pietersen a smartphone and a way of conversing with the world, and you could hardly expect him to stay out of trouble all the time. "Can somebody please tell me how Nick Knight has worked his way into the commentary box for the Tests??" he fumed in May. "Ridiculous." It felt odd for anyone to worry about Knight, who is more likely *not* to pass judgment on anything, and take his time doing it. But then Pietersen did not always appear to have thought things through: during the Indian Premier League, he would chat on Twitter to the league's former commissioner Lalit Modi, who just happened to be mid-lawsuit with ECB chairman Giles Clarke – Pietersen's boss.

Somehow it seemed appropriate that, even when he wasn't on Twitter, he was – in a manner of speaking. The fake account @KevPietersen24 became a social-media sensation, claiming to speak directly from his ego. Many seemed happy to suspend disbelief, and the account was followed – and commented on – by England players. At one point Pietersen himself got involved in the fun, retweeting a doctored tweet which purported to show the US president Barack Obama suggesting a beer with the fake KP. In a strange summer no one dared rule out the possibility.

But the account began to annoy him, not least because he suspected team-mates had set it up. In fact, it had been started by a friend of Stuart Broad – and, to complicate matters, on an evening when Broad was with his friend, Richard Bailey, aka @Bailsthebadger. Broad was tweeting pictures of Bailey too. Bailey admitted: "Yes the parody was me. It was for humour purposes only and as soon as I realised it was upsetting people I took it down."

Alas for Bailey – and the England dressing-room – Piers Morgan, the former editor of the *Daily Mirror* and a friend of Pietersen, would not let the matter lie. Having outed Bailey in the first place, Morgan tweeted: "Broad can collude with parody KP account, Swann can slag KP off in a book – no action taken. Total, shameful hypocrisy."

It was one of many tweets from Morgan defending Pietersen that must have confused his followers in America, where he hosted a chat show on CNN. Thanks to Morgan – in his own mind, at least, which was all that mattered – and England's desire to win in India, Pietersen returned to the fold. After the series was sealed at Nagpur, Matt Prior tweeted: "Love this! @kevinpp24 is so reintegrated he's walking around with all our names on his shirt!" And if it was on Twitter, who could doubt it?

RETIREMENTS

Guts among the glitter

STEVE JAMES

We should have known that **Andrew Strauss** would call it a day at the end of the 2012 season. The signs had been there: the gradual decline in form that had not quite been arrested by two centuries against West Indies in May; and the various pieces of symbolism that attached themselves to the final Test of the summer, at Lord's – his 100th as a player, 50th as captain, and at his home ground, where his Test career had begun eight years earlier. Even so, like all the best-timed retirements, it still felt like a bit of a surprise.

It was presumed that Strauss would oversee Ashes series in 2013 and 2013-14 – if not by the man himself. As he put it: "I'd run my race." In truth, the race had been run in his own mind long before he misjudged a straight one in his final innings. But, in a move as classy and understated as the letters he handwrote to all but one of his team-mates to tell them of his decision, he offered his intentions only to his closest confidants. There was never going to be the circus of a farewell series that might have shifted focus away from the team.

Strauss achieved nearly all an England Test captain could hope for, principally Ashes victories home and away, and the No. 1 ranking. He also made 21 Test centuries, leaving only Wally Hammond, Colin Cowdrey and Geoffrey Boycott ahead of him at the time. The Kevin Pietersen saga alone threatened to spoil the dignified manner of his departure.

By contrast, another Middlesex product, **Mark Ramprakash**, made only two Test hundreds. But he scored 68 more first-class centuries than Strauss (114 to 46), though he did play in 461 matches to Strauss's 241 in a 26-year career culminating in 11 seasons at Surrey after he left Middlesex in 2001. Ramprakash should be remembered as a great of the county game, and I have seen no better technician. But at international level, he was granted 52 Test caps, and must be considered a failure. One is left to wonder what might have been had he played under a central contract, or been made England captain when he was interviewed for the job along with Nasser Hussain in 1999.

Another cricketer of passion and longevity, **Robert Croft**, felt he had more to give. But eventually, at 42, he called time, having taken over 1,000 first-class wickets and scored more than 10,000 runs – a unique achievement among Glamorgan cricketers. I played alongside him in 1989, when he made his debut against Surrey at The Oval, and also five years later at the same ground, when we played in a Second XI match, after being dropped by captain Hugh Morris. For us both it was a significant and timely jolt from our reveries. Two years later, Croft made his Test debut, again at The Oval.

To use his favourite rugby analogy, he always said playing for Glamorgan was like representing Wales, with England akin to the British Lions. He won

21 Test caps, and was never less than passionate, as witnessed by his battling batting to save the Old Trafford Test against South Africa in 1998.

Jonathan Batty spent most of his career at The Oval, but never did receive England's call. I played against him there in 1999, when his cheekbone was broken by a vicious delivery from Simon Jones, bowling at a ferocious pace in tandem with the equally hostile Jacques Kallis. Batty, a dependable wicketkeeper and useful batsman, played in Surrey's next Championship match – the guts among their glitter. At one stage, he accepted the tricky task of captaining the glamour boys, which said much for his character. He finished his playing days a popular figure at Gloucestershire.

Will Jefferson wound up at Leicestershire, but it was at Essex that his huge promise as an opener emerged (and at 6ft 10½in, he was the tallest-ever specialist first-class batsman). In their two-day match against the touring Australians in 2005 – when Alastair Cook (214) and Ravi Bopara (135) made names for themselves – it is easily forgotten that Jefferson hit a quick 64. He played superbly in Leicestershire's 2011 Twenty20 triumph, success which he ascribed to the soothing powers of Bikram yoga, but a rare hip condition ended his career at the age of 32.

Charl Willoughby played at Leicestershire and Somerset (as well as gaining two Test caps for South Africa), before finishing his career at Essex. A left-armer, he was not quick. But he possessed the rare skill of late swing, to the extent that, in six seasons for Somerset, he claimed 347 wickets, often when Taunton was at its flattest.

Michael Di Venuto won two Championships, in 2008 and 2009, with Durham. He had retired from Australian state cricket in 2008, but continued in the county game, spending six years in the North-East after spells with Derbyshire and Sussex. He was a top-notch left-hander, and was unfortunate to have been limited to nine one-day internationals by Australia's batting riches. Di Venuto took advantage of his heritage to play for Italy in the 2012 World Twenty20 qualifying tournament, but with modest returns.

Ben Scott, a wicketkeeper with Surrey, Middlesex and Worcestershire, was as silky as any gloveman of his generation – including James Foster – but was often discarded in favour of better batsmen. Another keeper, the South African-born **Gerard Brophy**, could certainly bat, and in four years at Northamptonshire and seven at Yorkshire (where, remarkably, he received a benefit season) he scored over 5,000 first-class runs.

Yet another wicketkeeper, **Paul Dixey**, left the game aged only 24, having played just 22 first-class matches for Kent and Leicestershire. And **James Cameron**, a useful Zimbabwean-born all-rounder, was 26 when he informed Worcestershire he wanted to pursue a career in finance. Derbyshire's off-spinner **Jake Needham**, just 25 and surprisingly deprived of opportunities given his natural ability to spin the ball, had already announced he would do the same.

MARK RAMPRAKASH

Farewell, then, the 1990s

BARNEY RONAY

Last summer, with his retirement still reassuringly distant, Mark Ramprakash gave a speech at Lord's in which he confided that, if he could go back and change any aspect of a magisterial, furiously intense, operatically unyielding 26-season career, he would perhaps like to have "taken things a little less seriously".

For the confirmed Rampraphile it was hard to know how to respond. Certainly, as career retrospectives go, it's up there with Eric Cantona announcing that perhaps he shouldn't have bothered being quite so enigmatic; Jean-Paul Sartre coming out in his dotage against berets and casual sex; or The Clash wishing they'd just been a little less cross about everything and spent more time on *The Kenny Everett Show*.

A Ramprakash who takes things a little less seriously. This is, of course, not just alarming and undesirable. It is also pretty much unimaginable. Across all disciplines there is a certain kind of sportsman who becomes, inexorably, public property – just as Ramprakash has long been cherished as an object of private fascination for a generation of diffuse, faithful, still painfully expectant career Rampraphiles.

Even now it seems inconceivable that an English summer will be allowed to take place unaccompanied, for the first time in a quarter of a century, by the quiet certainty that at any given moment on some distant patch of green ringed by sparsely peopled plastic seats, Ramprakash will be taking guard, dipping his knees, rehearsing with machine-gun ferocity that crisply laundered off-drive, entirely gripped by the prospect of another six-month odyssey of largely overlooked first-class run-harvesting.

Naturally, Ramprakash will be defined to a degree by the greatness-shaped hole at the centre of his career, as a talent that remained forever sputtering and smoking on the launch pad of what should have been a brilliant Test-match span. This is the ex-pro's line, the baffled captain's verdict: if only Ramps could have relaxed a little, laughed it up, taken a chill pill.

This is also to misunderstand completely his broader appeal. If Ramprakash had a cricketing superpower, it was the ability to dust everything he touched – every cobwebbed outground, every deathly four-day draw – with that distinct and indissoluble sense of gravity: he took guard 1,221 times with the same glowering, insatiable intent, and remained almost to the very end the most vibrantly promising 41-year-old batsman in England.

It was all terribly serious. I can remember watching, gripped, as Ramprakash played out three consecutive maiden overs of lard-arsed roundarm all-sorts on some dying September afternoon at a deserted Oval, bat raised like a lance, front knee flexed, off stump painstakingly aligned, a cricketing Don Quixote still toting about the imprint of his own vanishing greatness. Oh aye. It were proper champion.

You see, though. This is what watching Ramprakash could do to you. Or at least, it could if you'd been there – and at an appropriately impressionable age – right from the start. Because with Ramprakash's passing something else has disappeared from view. Farewell, then, the 1990s. For English cricket you were the worst of times – and also the worst of times. The most obviously talented batsman of England's shredded generation, Ramprakash was also the last man standing, the last reminder of that peculiar drowned world, and nobody speaks to the ruined grandeur of a lost decade quite like Ramps.

For the adolescent spectator it was a genuinely compelling era to follow cricket in earnest. Presided over by mute, baffled men, with a Test team of tubby indispensables leavened by the usual sweating, ruined debutants, each on-field humiliation seemed to peel away a fresh layer of frowsty pre-Victorian infrastructure, the whole sorry edifice crumbling away before our eyes like a lath and plaster wall in the process of being cheerfully torn down by an Australian with a jackhammer.

Emerging into this, the young Ramprakash seemed an almost shockingly hopeful figure. Making his Test debut at 21 he looked, even then, curiously complete, rock-star handsome, the only modern person in English cricket, coming out to bat already goggle-eyed with epic-scale obsession. At which point everything started to go wrong. Ramps and Test cricket: it was never really going to work out. Wrong genius, wrong time.

Those who carry the scars of the 1990s can fantasise about the productivity of a young Ramprakash nestled within the velvet embrace of the current England regime (a two-year bedding-in period, then 23 Test hundreds, 40 hundreds, 80 hundreds). Instead Ramprakash's career was a masterpiece of departures. First dropped in August 1991, he was dropped in total 12 times, remaining on the verge of being recalled by the England team – broken only by those tortured interludes when he was actually *in* the England team – for 18 years, or the entire adult life, to that point, of this writer.

In between there were the horribly involving failures: a series against Pakistan where he seemed to have become, at last, entirely immobile at the crease, unable even to twitch or flinch or blink as the ball thudded into the pads; followed by the driven-to-distraction dismissals of an extended mid-career congealment (I managed to crash my first car while listening in dismay to the *Test Match Special* description of one particularly rank caught behind off Nathan Astle's slow-medium slingers).

There were two high-class Test hundreds, the second a brilliant 133 against Australia's greatest Test attack, before that extended backwoods flowering at Surrey. The TV highlights reel that accompanied news of Ramprakash's retirement paid due respect here, the Test-match footage rapidly dwindling into a succession of wobbly county-ground shots: unworthy bowlers thrashed through the pigeons at extra cover, half-track pies despatched with snake-hipped fury into semi-deserted stands, and finally that 100th hundred, celebrated by holding up a disappointingly small bottle of champagne in front of not very many people at all.

And yet he embraced the smaller stage with inspirational zeal. What Stakhanovite commitment! What reproachful tenacity! In scoring 50,651 career runs Ramprakash ran at least 380 miles, or the entire length of England, with a bat in his hand. To the last there remained a purity to his cricket, and in his departure an accompanying sense of wider ending.

Let's face it: no one is going to do this again in a hurry. The list of those who have scored 100 first-class hundreds runs from W. G. Grace (1895) to M. R. Ramprakash (2008). Currently, domestic cricket looks so fractured and frayed, so distracted by the promiscuous global whirligig of format-shift and calendar-overload that it seems possible the list may in fact now be closed for ever.

With Ramprakash's departure, the 1990s may have finally receded, but he remains a perhaps unexpectedly ennobling presence: cuffs buttoned, defensive bat gymnastically thrust, unslakable in his absolute conviction that this – all of this – really, really matters.

Barney Ronay is a sportswriter and columnist for The Guardian.

CAREER FIGURES

Players not expected to appear in county cricket in 2013

(minimum 40 first-class appearances)

BATTING

	M	*I*	*NO*	*R*	*HS*	*100*	*Avge*	*1,000r/ season*
J. N. Batty	220	345	38	9,673	168*	20	31.50	1
I. D. Blackwell	210	319	26	11,595	247*	27	39.57	4
G. L. Brophy	126	198	26	5,520	185	8	32.09	–
S. J. Cook	141	186	31	2,577	92*	0	16.62	–
R. D. B. Croft	407	599	107	12,880	143	8	26.17	–
M. J. Di Venuto	336	591	42	25,200	254*	60	45.90	10
J. du Toit	41	65	3	1,944	154	4	31.35	–
N. J. Edwards	73	125	4	3,849	212	4	31.80	1
A. J. Ireland	41	61	17	257	29	0	5.84	–
W. I. Jefferson	119	212	14	7,096	222	17	35.83	2
R. H. Joseph	62	84	32	535	36*	0	10.28	–
A. McGrath	257	429	30	14,698	211	35	36.83	3
M. N. Malik	90	120	42	768	41	0	9.84	–
Naved Arif	43	56	14	759	100*	1	18.07	–
S. A. Newman	135	230	4	8,630	219	16	38.18	4
G. T. Park	47	79	10	2,354	178*	4	34.11	1
M. R. Ramprakash	461	764	93	35,659	301*	114	53.14	20
B. J. M. Scott	103	160	28	3,474	164*	4	26.31	–
B. M. Shafayat	142	236	9	6,868	161	11	30.25	1
S. D. Snell	44	72	7	1,701	127	1	26.16	–
A. J. Strauss	241	424	25	17,046	241*	46	42.72	5
N. S. Tahir	56	65	16	751	53	0	15.32	–
W. P. U. J. C. Vaas	227	300	59	6,223	134	4	25.82	–
R. A. White	112	190	17	5,706	277	8	32.98	1

BOWLING

	R	*W*	*BB*	*Avge*	*5I*	*10M*	*Ct/St*
J. N. Batty	61	1	1-21	61.00	–	–	605/68
I. D. Blackwell	14,295	398	7-52	35.91	14	–	66
G. L. Brophy	7	0	–	–	–	–	301/22
S. J. Cook	10,993	342	8-63	32.14	12	–	34
R. D. B. Croft	41,229	1,175	8-66	35.08	51	9	177
M. J. Di Venuto	484	5	1-0	96.80	–	–	417
J. du Toit	436	6	3-31	72.66	–	–	32
N. J. Edwards	194	2	1-16	97.00	–	–	67
A. J. Ireland	3,715	122	7-36	30.45	4	1	9
W. I. Jefferson	60	1	1-16	60.00	–	–	127
R. H. Joseph	5,572	174	6-32	32.02	7	1	12
A. McGrath	4,779	134	5-39	35.40	1	–	181
M. N. Malik	8,381	235	6-46	35.66	7	–	11
Naved Arif	4,413	181	7-66	24.38	10	1	13
S. A. Newman	90	0	–	–	–	–	99
G. T. Park	974	18	3-25	54.11	–	–	43
M. R. Ramprakash	2,202	34	3-32	64.76	–	–	261
B. J. M. Scott	1	0	–	–	–	–	271/31
B. M. Shafayat	663	8	2-25	82.87	–	–	128/10
S. D. Snell	15	0	–	–	–	–	104/3
A. J. Strauss	142	3	1-16	47.33	–	–	228
N. S. Tahir	4,163	139	7-107	29.94	2	–	7
W. P. U. J. C. Vaas	19,027	772	7-28	24.64	34	4	57
R. A. White	1,071	18	2-30	59.50	–	–	67

CRICKETANA

What am I bid?

DAVID RAYVERN ALLEN

As the auction merry-go-round continues to spin, it becomes increasingly difficult to discern who is actually doing the bidding. The internet – even the humble telephone – offers anonymity, and not just for the big spenders. At all the major cricket auctions, from London to Cardiff via Nottingham, Leicester, Chester or Ludlow, sales rarely have as many as 30 people in the room. And even when bids are seemingly placed in person, the *real* purchaser may often be hiding behind a frontman, occasionally two. A decoy can be useful when highly desirable items are on offer – and when serious money and the thrill of the chase allow an auction house to assume an air of machismo and flirt with the world of espionage…

Not that everyone warms to the drama of the saleroom. The book dealer Christopher Saunders claims there are too many cricket auctions: "They tend to devalue the product, particularly when eBay is a continuous auction." There is a counter-argument: since cricket booksellers issue an average of two or three catalogues a year, why shouldn't there be as many sales? Saunders also bemoans the damage caused by VAT at 20% and high postage charges: "It costs £5.40 to send a catalogue to Australia or New Zealand. It becomes prohibitive." One man's misfortune, of course, is another's opportunity, and there are bargains available. "With the market for run-of-the-mill items in the doldrums, there has been no alternative but to reduce prices." Yet the illustrated catalogues produced by Saunders, Surrey dealer John McKenzie and others are inviting, and there are plenty of high-end items to pore over: Saunders was offering juvenilia, runs of Almanacks and much offbeat material in between.

McKenzie, meanwhile, was celebrating 40 years in business with his 174th cricket catalogue. Some of the 918 entries were exceptionally scarce: early F. S. Ashley-Cooper booklets; a first edition of James Dance's *Cricket: An Heroic Poem* (from 1744); the Rev. John Duncombe's parody *Surry Triumphant* (1773); and a second edition of Thomas Boxall's *Rules and Instructions for playing at the Game of Cricket* (*c.*1801–02). None was especially cheap, but many items found buyers.

The chances are high that those buyers will be men: Saunders counts only ten women among his thousand or so active clients. But they seem unperturbed at entering what is widely seen as a male preserve, and collecting for themselves. However, McKenzie thinks there may be vicarious purchasing at work: "It's difficult to quantify. They could be buying for their husbands."

Whoever is doing the purchasing, there are traps, especially online, for the unwary. The old adage – if something looks too good to be true then it probably is – still applies. "Customers ring me," says McKenzie, "and declare they've purchased an original autograph of, say, Victor Trumper or Joe Darling for

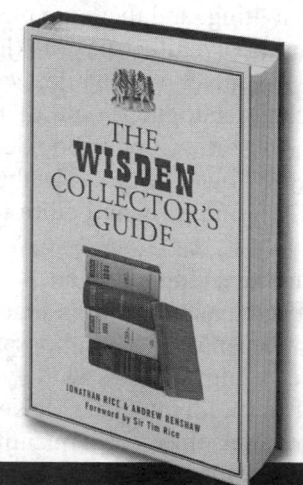

less than £50 – and they don't realise they are almost certain to be fakes." These deceptions can emanate from almost anywhere in the world. It remains a case of *caveat emptor*, wherever the sale takes place.

In his March auction, Trevor Vennett-Smith sold a striking oil painting, thought to be by A. L. "Toby" Grace, of a boy doing homework and looking longingly out of a window at a game of cricket. The painting was probably commissioned by bat-makers Gunn and Moore for their showroom, before being passed to Nottinghamshire and England star Reg Simpson, a director of the firm. It raised over £7,000 after premium and VAT had been added.

Vennett-Smith also sold the extensive personal paper-based archive of former England captain Freddie Brown. There had been doubt about ownership but, once this was resolved, the two albums – containing telegrams, dinner menus, letters, snapshots, scorecards and the like from his playing career – fetched around £18,000. In November, the first half of Denijs Morkel's archive came up for sale. He played 16 Tests for South Africa between 1927-28 and 1931-32, before moving to Nottingham, where he captained Sir Julien Cahn's XI, made guest appearances for MCC and played a few wartime (non-first-class) games at Trent Bridge. The scrapbook, containing unusual ephemera, went for £2,700 on the hammer.

The focal point of Tim Knight's March sale was two exceptional watercolour portraits of W. G. Grace by Louisa Townsend, an inaugural member of the Royal Society of Miniature Painters. She had painted Grace in 1915, the year of his death, and this appeared as a frontispiece in his Memorial Biography, edited by Lords Hawke and Harris, together with Sir Home Gordon. The larger of the two watercolours on sale at Knight's was a very similar portrait, showing Grace in a striped dark suit. This fetched £20,000 on the hammer, while the exquisite miniature in a cameo oval mount and ornate gilt frame realised £15,000.

Another outstanding feature of the auction was a fine collection of nine early 19th-century English School studies of young cricketers. These ranged from a somewhat naive oil of a youngster with dog and bat, to a watercolour-and-pencil painting from the circle of Henry Edridge that showed a youth nonchalantly leaning on his bat. The prices also ranged widely, from a few hundred pounds to nearly £5,000. Some were acquired by MCC. In Knight's summer sale, *The Log of a Trip in the Earl of Sheffield's Yacht, the Heloise, to Boulogne and back by "One of the Team", July 1890* had an estimate of £1,000–£1,500. When the gavel fell, bidding had reached an extraordinary £14,000. Also sold during the year were a couple of important sets of photographs: nine sepia action prints of WG by the pioneer of sports photography in Britain, George Beldam; and an album belonging to Frank Gilligan. Each made £4,000.

The highlight of Christie's cricket year was the sale of Victor Trumper's collection of photos from the 1909 Australian "confines of lunacy" tour of England (Trumper's last), plus a few images from 1902. The album was a gift from the tour manager, Frank Laver. The winning bid was £13,000.

In an Olympics-crazy year, any mention of a gold medal guaranteed attention. Graham Budd Auctions (in association with Sotheby's) sold "a rare and historic gold medal presented by the Melbourne Cricket Club" to the English cricketer E. F. S. Tylecote to commemorate the first Ashes series in 1882-83. It fetched £3,000 in May.

As 2012 drew to a close, Mullock's three-day, 2,560-lot sale at Ludlow found a lone bidder competing against an absent opponent to secure one of the scarcest of all *Wisdens*. The 1875 edition carried an estimate of £2,000–£3,000. From the podium, John Mullock nursed the bidding carefully, increasing the total by small amounts. Gradually the would-be purchasers dropped out, leaving the auction-room warrior – watched closely by his anxious partner beside him – together with his unknown online adversary.

The hush was tangible, the tension crackling. Nearly ten minutes had passed since bidding began: "£12,000… 12,200… 400… 600… 800… £13,000…" And still it went on… The pause before the next figure was offered grew longer from both sides. Mullock's gavel was about to descend. The online bidder had waited too long. Everybody in the room was about to cheer, when – in the nick of time – another bid came over the ether. "£18,800… £18,800… for the third time, £18,800. Going once, going twice…" Crash! The room bidder's arm had dropped. The price had gone too far, and a murmur of sympathy went round. But who *was* the winner? It turned out to be a private collector in Australia, so there was a degree of satisfaction for some that the contest had been between two individuals and did not involve a corporate body. For lovers of cricketana – and spectacle – such a titanic struggle is what auctioneering is all about.

CRICKET AND THE WEATHER, 2012

Thank heavens for small mercies?

PHILIP EDEN

When I remarked in these pages last year that "sooner or later… a very wet April and May is bound to come along", I little realised it was round the corner. May's rainfall was actually close to the average, but April, June and July were all exceptionally wet. Indeed, both April and June set records, and in rainfall statistics for England and Wales that date back to 1766 there is no other instance of two record months occurring in the same year.

According to the Wisden Summer Index (see page 1597 of *Wisden 2004* for the exact formula), this was the worst summer since 1987 and the ninth-worst since 1900. The total rainfall for May to August, averaged over England and Wales, was the third-highest recorded and the highest since 1917. The number of dry days, meanwhile, was the fourth-lowest, and the lowest since 1924. Flooding, however, was less widespread than in 2007, because the rain in 2012 tended to be spread out over longer periods, whereas five years before it was concentrated into single days. Temperatures, although subdued, were not especially low; similarly, the number of sunshine hours was consistently poor – though again nowhere near a record. We should, perhaps, be thankful for small mercies.

The English season began earlier than ever, with the first university matches being played on March 31, but ended early too: the previous ten had all extended beyond September 16. Frustratingly, March had been a dry month with an unequalled spell of warmth and sunshine towards its end. The rains, though, had already set in by the time the Championship started on April 5, and practically every match scheduled during April was seriously interrupted. In two instances, at The Oval and at Bristol, four-day games were wholly washed out.

May 17 marked the beginning of a dry fortnight – and the start of the Test series against West Indies. The First Test was played under cloudy skies with a cold wind, but the Second, which finished a day early on May 28, was warm and sunny throughout. The Third, in mid-June, was strafed by frequent rain.

There were further dry interludes in late-July, coinciding with the First Test against South Africa, while August was largely dry and rather warm in East Anglia and South-East England; other parts of the country were much less fortunate. The first ten days of September were also dry and warm, before the weather tailed off.

> "New Zealand descended towards defeat with the certainty of a sunset – all that changed was the position from which it was viewed."
> South Africa v New Zealand, 2012-13, Second Test, page 1082.

The meteorological statistics, averaged over England and Wales, for the 2012 season, were:

	Average max temperature (°C)	*Difference from normal (1981–2010) (°C)*	*Total rainfall (mm)*	*% of normal*	*Total sunshine (hours)*	*% of normal*
April	10.7	–1.7	143	230	137	88
May	16.5	+0.1	59	96	209	103
June	17.1	–2.2	160	235	126	66
July	18.8	–2.3	117	204	166	83
August	20.7	–0.6	94	130	169	86
September	17.0	–1.3	90	109	171	118
2012 season	**16.8**	**–1.3**	**663**	**167**	**978**	**90**

Each summer has slightly different regional variations, though in most years northern and western counties are cooler, cloudier and damper than those in the east and south. The Wisden Summer Index compares the summer county by county. In essence, an index over 650 indicates a good summer; one below 500 a poor one. Values for the summer of 2012 against the average for the standard reference period of 1981–2010 were:

	2012	*Normal*	*Difference*
Derbyshire	417	578	–161
Durham	342	523	–181
Essex	515	638	–123
Glamorgan	388	553	–165
Gloucestershire	432	593	–161
Hampshire	522	643	–121
Kent	500	653	–153
Lancashire	395	528	–133
Leicestershire	439	583	–144
Middlesex	540	668	–128
Northamptonshire	454	613	–159
Nottinghamshire	427	588	–161
Somerset	443	618	–175
Surrey	545	673	–128
Sussex	497	663	–166
Warwickshire	429	553	–124
Worcestershire	463	613	–150
Yorkshire	442	558	–116

The bad weather during 2012 was spread fairly evenly across the country, with every county recording a deficit of 116 or more. Yorkshire, Hampshire, Essex, Middlesex and Surrey had the lowest deficits, while Durham and Somerset had the largest. Only four counties scored above 500, while three scored below 400, with Durham's 342 comfortably the lowest.

Taking a national view, 2012's index of 455 was 127 points below the year before, and 48 lower than 2007 – the previous worst of the 2000s. The last six summers, 2007–2012, represent the poorest run since 1977–82.

2001	632	2004	541	2007	503	2010	610
2002	506	2005	623	2008	525	2011	582
2003	647	2006	633	2009	568	2012	455

Highest: 812 in 1976
Lowest: 309 in 1879

CRICKET PEOPLE

Dealing in millimetres

ALI MARTIN

Simon Taufel does not like the word "retirement". He insisted upon its removal from the media release announcing his decision to step down from the ICC Elite Panel of Umpires. The 41-year-old Taufel instead "moved on" to become ICC Umpire Performance and Training Manager after 13 years, 74 Test matches, 174 one-day internationals and 34 Twenty20s. For much of that time, he was widely regarded as the best umpire in the world.

A reputation for accuracy, and an ability – according to his friend and fellow Australian umpire Daryl Harper – to turn the panel's workshops into "Simonars", make his next step a logical one. "I have a passion for development and helping others achieve their goals," says Taufel, who intends to spend more time with his wife and their three children. The Lahore terrorist attack on March 3, 2009, in which six policemen and two civilians were killed midway through a Test between Pakistan and Sri Lanka, changed his outlook. Part of the convoy of players and officials ambushed by gunmen near the Gaddafi Stadium, Taufel witnessed the death of his driver, Zafar Khan.

"He was simply taking some people to a Test match, and then his wife and children lose him for ever," he reflects. "That is just not fair. There were lessons for cricket to learn that day, sure, but for me it was about more than that. Life and families are precious."

Five Umpire of the Year awards from 2004 to 2008 demonstrate the respect commanded by Taufel, who made his international debut at Sydney in January 1999 and stood down after October's World Twenty20 final in Colombo. Alastair Cook even apologised to him once after a day's play for referring one of his decisions, despite Cook being proved correct. Taufel recognises that the Decision Review System helps the dialogue between players and officials, as well as the chance to improve the accuracy of umpires: "We used to deal in centimetres, now it's millimetres."

And his favourite decisions? Taufel is especially proud to have had the "courage and knowledge of Law" to give Inzamam-ul-Haq out obstructing the field in a one-day international between Pakistan and India at Peshawar in February 2006. He also mentions working with Billy Bowden and TV official Ian Gould to rule that Sri Lanka's Angelo Mathews had turned a potential six into a three with an astonishing piece of fielding on the boundary during a 2009 World Twenty20 match at Trent Bridge. A former seamer in Sydney's Northern Suburbs, Taufel hopes others are encouraged to take up what is now a full-time profession; his 13 years as an umpire were juggled with a job in the printing industry. He says: "When it came to finishing, I always aimed to have people ask 'why did you?' rather than 'why don't you?' If people talk about my time and the subject of umpiring positively, then I'm satisfied."

"A labour of hate" is how **Jim Cumbes** jokingly describes the legally fraught redevelopment of Old Trafford, from a rundown but historic ground to a striking modern venue that hosts an Ashes Test in 2013. Having retired in December after 25 years at Lancashire – as commercial manager, then chief executive – Cumbes is proud of his legacy, and the battle won to get there.

A dual sportsman from 1965 to 1982, he bowled seam for four first-class counties, and was a top-flight goalkeeper in England and North America. Reflecting on his most illustrious opponents, he verges on blasphemy: "Pelé was just a magically dynamic attacking player, but I think George Best edged him. He was good enough to star anywhere on the pitch."

Cumbes was approached by Tranmere Rovers, West Bromwich Albion and Worcestershire for commercial-manager roles as his playing career drew to a close. New Road appealed most, only for Worcestershire chairman Ralph Matkin to pass away on the morning they were due to discuss the matter. But the offers he was receiving meant Cumbes felt "someone was trying to tell me something", and he played on for a season as Warwickshire's Second XI captain in 1982 in tandem with commercial duties, before going full-time during five years of off-field success that prompted Lancashire's interest.

"I was the only county commercial manager, and my approach was simple: try new things and repeat those that worked," he says. He became chief executive in 1998, and would test out his level-headed outlook during an arduous legal battle in 2011, in which the owners of the nearby White City retail park called for a judicial review into the £70m redevelopment of Old Trafford and the surrounding area. Cumbes and Lancashire, who had pressed on with the building work while the lawyers fought it out, emerged victorious that July.

By the end of the season, captain Glen Chapple, coach Peter Moores and director of cricket Mike Watkinson had taken a team tipped for the drop, and playing home fixtures on outgrounds, to the Championship. But the relegation that followed in 2012 has done little to dampen Cumbes's optimistic spirit: "The talent's there to bounce back, and our ground's now a world-class arena."

Towering over all England's international venues is **Mike Hutton**, a man whose indifference to heights and Arctic conditions ensures television audiences are treated to stunning aerial views from the camera known as a cherry picker, 55 metres above the ground. A professional cameraman since 1977, Hutton's first taste of cricket came on West Indies' tour of India in 1994-95. And he volunteered for the loftiest job in the sport ten years ago, after a colleague's heart condition prevented him from continuing. "It is an absolute privilege: the game, the views, the teamwork," says Hutton, who has not looked back, and is not especially fussed about looking down either.

The rolling Hampshire countryside and the Isle of Wight in the distance are what make the Ageas Bowl his favourite location to shoot from the platform on top of the crane, manned at ground level by colleague Steve Allan.

Asked, as he often is, about the danger of becoming a human lightning rod, the 62-year-old Hutton employs North Yorkshire phlegm: "I have picked up a good knowledge of clouds and can see storms developing from a fair distance. Sometimes you get a twinge of vertigo, but on the whole I'm fine with it."

CRICKET IN THE COURTS

Carpeted in Kidderminster

STANFORD JAILED FOR 110 YEARS

Allen Stanford, 62, the corrupt financier once hailed as the saviour of cricket, was sentenced to 110 years in jail by a court in Houston, Texas. Judge David Hittner described Stanford's corrupt $7bn Ponzi scheme as "one of the most egregious frauds ever presented to a trial jury in federal court".

The judge ordered Stanford to forfeit $5.9bn in assets, though investigators found very little of his fortune. At least 30,000 people were said to have lost money as a result of bogus investments by the Stanford International Bank. Many of his victims – including one woman whose family lost $4m – were in court to hear Assistant US Attorney William Stellmach tell the judge: "From beginning to end, he's treated his victims like roadkill. Allen Stanford doesn't deserve anyone's sympathy and he doesn't deserve your honour's mercy."

In 2006 Stanford was knighted by the Antigua government. In 2008 he flew into Lord's by helicopter where a Perspex case ostensibly containing $20m in cash was waiting – the purse for a Twenty20 match between a team of West Indians and an England XI. He was fawned on by the game's leading officials. Within a year US investigators had gone public with their allegations, and Stanford was in jail.

Stanford blamed his downfall on "Gestapo tactics" by prosecutors which provoked a run on his banks. He said: "I am and will always be at peace with the way I conducted myself." Sentencing him on March 6, Hittner made most of the 13 separate sentences consecutive rather than concurrent, which means Stanford will die in jail unless the conviction is overturned or he is pardoned.

SWANN FINED

England off-spinner Graeme Swann was fined £1,383 by Kidderminster magistrates on June 1 for speeding and failing to respond after his Jaguar was caught doing 74mph on a 50mph stretch of road in Herefordshire. Swann was said to have sent no reply to five letters requesting the name of the driver.

He told the court he had written to West Mercia Police after the first letter, saying his agent was driving, but had not received the other four. Philip Worrall, defending, said they were probably not delivered because they were addressed to West Bridgend, Nottingham, not West Bridgford. "We find the prosecution more credible," said magistrate Tim Morris.

CAIRNS WINS TWITTER LIBEL TRIAL

The former New Zealand all-rounder Chris Cairns won £90,000 damages at the High Court in London on March 26 after suing the former Indian Premier League commissioner Lalit Modi for accusing him of match-fixing. This was said to be the first libel case involving a Twitter message.

Modi was estimated to be facing a bill of £1.4m, including legal costs, after a 24-word tweet sent in 2010 claimed Cairns had a record of fixing. Mr Justice Bean said Modi had "singularly failed" to provide evidence to back up his claim, or even to show there were reasonable grounds for suspicion. He also criticised the aggressive nature of the defence, which included Modi's counsel calling Cairns a liar 24 times; the judge said this had led him to increase the damages by £15,000. An appeal was thrown out in October.

The allegation stemmed from Cairns's time captaining Chandigarh Lions in the Indian Cricket League, the failed rival to the IPL. Cairns faced criticism for bringing the case in the UK, where there were estimated to be between 35 and 100 people who read the tweet. Padraig Reidy of the pressure group Index on Censorship called his decision "one of the most clear-cut cases of libel tourism we have seen"; libel lawyer Mark Stephens called the case "ridiculous" and said it should have been struck out.

JOSHI JAILED FOR SEX OFFENCES

The Indian off-spinner Uday Joshi, who made his name playing for Sussex in the 1970s, was jailed for six years on March 9 for sexually abusing a boy while playing and coaching in Northern Ireland in 1979.

A 45-year-old man gave evidence at Belfast Crown Court about three incidents that took place when, as a 13-year-old, he and Joshi stayed in the same house. Joshi denied all the allegations and said nothing untoward had happened, but he was convicted unanimously after a five-day trial.

Judge Gemma Loughran said she accepted that the offences had been wholly out of character for Joshi, a 67-year-old married father of two, but said they had left the victim with a chronic adjustment disorder and anxiety. Joshi was barred for life from working with children. On December 19, an appeal was dismissed. He took 557 first-class wickets in a 17-year career, mainly for Sussex and Gujarat.

AZHARUDDIN'S LIFE BAN OVERTURNED

Twelve years after being banned for life for match-fixing by the Indian cricket authorities, the former national captain Mohammad Azharuddin had the ban set aside by the Andhra Pradesh High Court on November 9. The court said he had not been given the chance to state his case, and that the claims were unsubstantiated. Asked whether he regretted playing 99 Tests and not 100, Azharuddin said, "Maybe I was destined to play 99 Test matches and that's what the Almighty wanted. I would not like to dwell on the past. I am an MP and would like to focus on the development of my constituency, Moradabad."

SACKED EXECUTIVE AWARDED EIGHT-FIGURE SUM

Tim Wright, the British former chief executive of IPL franchise Deccan Chargers, was awarded £10.5m on July 16 by the High Court in London for breach of contract when he was dismissed in 2009. The Chargers' owners, the

Deccan Chronicle, did not attend the trial because they disputed the court's jurisdiction, and were subsequently reported to be in financial difficulties. Wright insisted the contract was subject to UK law.

LIFE SENTENCE FOR NZ CRICKET BAT KILLER

A New Zealander admitted bashing his de facto stepfather to death with a bat, before going on to play cricket the next day. Christopher Glenn Gleeson, 25, was jailed for life, with a minimum of 11 years four months, in the High Court at Christchurch on April 17. Gleeson pleaded guilty, but offered no explanation.

CRICKET AND THE LAWS IN 2012

Fatal distraction

FRASER STEWART

Steven Finn has demolished many stumps during his career, but it was his disruption of the wrong set that caused a stir in 2012. While Finn had occasionally broken the non-striker's wicket with his knee throughout his career, the quirk came to a head during the Second Test against South Africa at Headingley. On the first morning, he knocked into the wicket during his delivery stride at least twice before umpire Steve Davis signalled dead ball when it happened again. It was from this delivery that Graeme Smith edged to Andrew Strauss at slip – but the dismissal didn't count.

At the time, no specific Law dictated that a bowler should be penalised for accidentally disturbing the non-striker's stumps, and rarely was dead ball called on such occasions. However, Davis chose to apply Law 23.4(b)(vi), which states that either umpire should signal dead ball when "the striker is distracted by any noise or movement, or in any other way, while he is preparing to receive, or receiving a delivery. This shall apply whether the source of the distraction is within the game or outside it. The ball shall not count as one of the over."

Jeff Crowe, ICC's match referee at Headingley, confirmed to MCC that Finn had broken the wicket at least twice prior to the Smith incident. Both batsmen complained it was a distraction, and Finn was told to move over. Davis himself was also said to have found it distracting. Law 23.4(b)(iv) states that the umpire should call dead ball if "one or both bails fall from the striker's wicket before the striker has had the opportunity of playing the ball". The reference to the *striker's* wicket indicates dead ball should not automatically be called if the wicket at the bowler's end is disturbed.

Whether the striker is distracted is a moot point. Smith hit two subsequent balls for four when Finn had broken the wicket, only for a call of dead ball to cancel out the runs. If the striker really feels he is distracted, he can pull away, though this may not always be possible with a bowler as fast as Finn.

The ICC introduced a directive to their umpires that such incidents should result in a warning at the first occasion, followed by the call of dead ball on subsequent occasions (although Finn, deemed a repeat offender, was told during the one-day series in India in January 2013 that he would get no warning, and was subsequently denied the wicket of Suresh Raina at Mohali, with Davis again the umpire). But MCC felt this directive was unfair to batsmen, who could be denied runs. And there is no reason why the second breaking of the wicket should be more distracting than the first.

After discussing the matter at length, MCC decided in February 2013 to change the Law so that, from October, a no-ball will automatically be called should the bowler break the stumps during the act of delivery. This removes the burden from the umpire to rule whether the batsman really has been distracted.

The players' knowledge of the Laws is sometimes questionable – and ignorance can definitely be costly. When Jonny Bairstow was caught by Gautam Gambhir at silly point on the stroke of lunch on the third day of the Second Test against India at Mumbai in November, it was via Gambhir's chest and the grille of his helmet. Law 32.3 states "it is not a fair catch if the ball has previously touched a protective helmet worn by a fielder". But by the time TV replays showed what had happened, Bairstow had left the field and lunch was almost over.

In scenes reminiscent of those described here last year, when Ian Bell was reprieved after being initially given run out during the Trent Bridge Test against India in 2011, the England management attempted to have the decision overturned during the interval. India chose not to withdraw the appeal, as was their prerogative: unlike the more complicated circumstances of the Bell run-out, this was nothing more than an umpiring error. However, had Bairstow known the Law – he admitted he didn't – he could at least have mentioned to the umpire that he felt the ball had struck the helmet (Gambhir said he was unaware of the Law too). He would then have been reprieved by the third umpire.

Cook later confirmed it was a "brain fade"

Then, in Kolkata, Alastair Cook was run out in bizarre circumstances, taking evasive action at the non-striker's end as Virat Kohli threw the ball from midwicket. Cook had backed up a couple of metres down the pitch, but turned to regain his ground after seeing no run was possible. He was leaning towards his crease in order to tap his bat down but, just inches before doing so, took evasive action as the ball passed him. It hit the stumps – and Cook was out for 190.

The Laws do contain a section designed to protect a batsman from being out if he is attempting to avoid injury. The relevant part of Law 38.2 says a batsman is not run out if "he has been within his ground and has subsequently left it to avoid injury, when the wicket is put down". The key is the first six words: Cook had not returned to his crease before taking evasive action, and the umpires could not therefore enact Law 38.2(a). Had he tapped his bat down, *then* taken evasive action, he would have been protected. His reaction suggested he was aware of his blunder, and he later confirmed it was a "brain fade".

The running out of the non-striker by the bowler remains one of the most emotive dismissals, and tempers frayed when Surrey's Murali Kartik removed Somerset's Alex Barrow that way in a Championship match. The Laws allow the bowler to run out the non-striker before he enters his delivery stride, which starts when the back foot is planted. The ICC and the ECB have altered this for their regulations, with the aim of keeping the non-striker in his ground for longer. The ECB's wording is: "The bowler is permitted, before releasing the ball and provided he has not completed his usual delivery swing, to attempt to run out the non-striker."

Neither the Laws nor the regulations state that a warning should be given, although convention suggests it is preferable. But Kartik had already warned

Barrow: while the affair was unsavoury to many, Kartik had done nothing wrong. The bowler is normally painted as the villain in such a scenario, but it is the batsman who is gaining an unfair advantage, whether wilfully or inadvertently.

With TV umpires often scrutinising no-balls at the fall of a wicket, many have questioned whether the no-ball Law is too strict, and the bowler should get the benefit of the doubt on in marginal cases. Law 24.5 explains that the bowler's front foot must land with some part of the foot, whether grounded or raised, behind the popping crease. Law 9.3 additionally defines the popping crease as the back edge of the crease marking. If the bowler's heel is on the line, and nothing behind it, then the delivery is a no-ball. It also makes no difference how thick the markings are: it is the back edge of the line that matters.

There has to be a precise point at which the delivery goes from being fair to unfair. You could redefine the Law, but you would only be shifting the problem, not solving it: the umpire would have to check whether the line was touched, or completely overstepped. It would be the same problem, but moved to a different area. The problem here is not with the Law, but with bowlers overstepping. MCC accept that a centimetre here or there won't necessarily give the bowler an unfair advantage. But unless there is a clear point at which fair becomes unfair, the confusion will only increase. Shades of grey may have been all the rage in 2012 but, in the case of the no-ball, black and white is essential.

Fraser Stewart is Laws manager at MCC.

The current code of the Laws appears in Wisden 2011, *page 1200, and on the MCC website (www.lords.org).*

OBITUARIES

The obituaries section includes those who died, or whose deaths were notified, in 2012, unless otherwise stated. Deaths in 2013 – including Christopher Martin-Jenkins, who died on January 1 – will feature in next year's Almanack.

ABEYNAIKE, RANIL GEMUNU, who died on February 21, aged 57, was a true all-rounder – player, coach, groundsman and commentator. A handy batsman and a slow left-armer with a rather jerky action, he took six wickets for the Sri Lanka Board President's XI against a strong Pakistan touring team in January 1976, and played against Tony Greig's 1976-77 MCC side, before several seasons with Bedfordshire. In 1982-83 – the year after Sri Lanka's inaugural Tests – he scored 171 for the Sinhalese Sports Club against the Police, sharing a big opening stand with Arjuna Ranatunga. Abeynaike made another hundred a fortnight later, but never cracked the Test side. He later became groundsman and general manager at Colombo's SSC, although he was better known as a TV commentator. "He talked a lot of common sense about the game," said Ian Chappell. "And he did the best pitch reports I've heard."

AKBAR, SAEED SHAHID, died on November 28, aged 54. Shahid Akbar was a youthful prodigy who never fulfilled the promise which prompted 1970s contemporaries to imagine him opening India's batting with Sunil Gavaskar. A wristy left-hander and superb fielder, he played 31 first-class matches, mostly for Hyderabad, with a best of 97 (run out) against Tamil Nadu at Madras in 1977-78.

ALAGANAN, R. BALU, who died on October 11, aged 87, captained Madras (now Tamil Nadu) to their inaugural Ranji Trophy title in 1954-55. In the final, against Holkar at Indore, Alaganan made 56 not out from No. 9 in the second innings, adding 77 for the last wicket with M. K. Murugesh; Madras won by 46 runs. Alaganan surprised some by retiring after that triumph, which came in only his sixth first-class match and at the age of 30. He turned instead to administration – he was the state association's vice-president for 25 years from 1961, and assistant manager on some Indian tours – and commentary, becoming a popular voice on All India Radio.

ALEXANDER, LEONARD JAMES, who died on July 22, aged 90, kept wicket for Tasmania in nine matches between 1946-47 and 1951-52. In the last of them, at the MCG, he allowed no byes in Victoria's innings of 647.

ALI, ASHRAF RAJA, died of a suspected heart attack on October 21, aged 36. Raja Ali was a member of the Railways team who won two Ranji Trophies. A big-hitting left-hander who started his career with Madhya Pradesh, Ali averaged almost 40 in first-class cricket, with nine centuries, three of them (including his highest, 148 against his former MP team-mates) during Railways' first title season in 2001-02. He also made 80 in the successful 2004-05 final against Punjab. "I used to call him *Sankat Mochan* [crisis man]," said the former Indian leg-spinner Narendra Hirwani. "I still wonder how he kept his cool under pressure." Ali played some one-day games for Central Zone, whose players wore black armbands during the Duleep Trophy final in Chennai which coincided with news of his death.

ALIMUDDIN, who died on July 12, was an early star of Pakistan cricket, winning 25 Test caps between 1954 and 1962. Well-built and attacking by nature, he scored an unbeaten 103 against India at Karachi in 1954-55, when his partnership of 155 with his captain Abdul Hafeez Kardar came at almost a run a minute – an unheard-of rate in the usually sepulchral matches between the two countries at that time. He made 109 against England in 1961-62, also at Karachi, after a period out of favour, and scored 12 other centuries in a long career that stretched to 1967-68, after which he had a brief spell as national coach. "He was not just a stylish player but a very decent human being," said Hanif Mohammad, a frequent opening partner. "He was very good company, and

Getty Images

First steps: Alimuddin (*left*) and Hanif Mohammad walk out to bat against Indian Gymkhana at Osterley on the first day of Pakistan's maiden tour of England, in 1954.

entertained us through his songs." If Alimuddin's published date of birth (December 15, 1930) is correct, he was 81 when he died – but that would mean he made his first-class debut in a Ranji Trophy semi-final in India in February 1943 at the age of 12, which players from the time discount. It seems likely he was five or six years older: Nasim-ul-Ghani, a Test team-mate, suggested he was nearer 90. Alim eventually settled in London, where he worked for Pakistan International Airlines – the uncertainty about his age caused problems with his pension; it was restored after Pakistan's president intervened.

ANANDAPPA, IGNATIUS, who died on July 4, aged 73, was a club off-spinner who later turned to umpiring. He stood in three Tests – the first, against Australia in Colombo in August 1992, was also Muttiah Muralitharan's debut – and seven one-day internationals in Sri Lanka in the 1990s.

ATHAR ZAIDI, SYED HUSSAIN, who died on November 30, aged 66, was a stocky umpire from Lahore who stood in eight Tests and ten one-day internationals between 1984 and 2002. Aleem Dar, now on the ICC's elite panel, credited Athar with persuading him to take on the job: "He taught me all the basic principles needed to become a good professional umpire."

BEAUMONT, RICHARD, collapsed on the field on August 4, shortly after taking five wickets for Pedmore against Astwood Bank in the Worcestershire County League. He was airlifted to hospital, but pronounced dead shortly after arrival. He was 33. "There was no sign of what was to happen," said Astwood Bank's captain Steve Adshead, the former Gloucestershire wicketkeeper. "He had been bowling really well."

BHAGALIA, SALIM, who died in November, aged 90, was one of the best fast bowlers to emerge from South Africa's Indian community in the 1940s, although he was denied the chance of first-class cricket by his government's policies. A left-armer with a fiery temper, Bhagalia spearheaded Transvaal's successful bid for the national non-white competition in 1951. A knee injury finally forced him to retire at 59.

BHIKANE, KISHOR PRAKASH, was killed while returning from a club game on March 4, when his motorcycle – which he had been awarded as the best bowler of the Maharashtra Premier League Twenty20 tournament in 2011 – collided with a truck near Latur, on the road between Pune and Mumbai. Bhikane, 24, was a medium-pacer who had played three first-class and several limited-overs matches for Maharashtra.

BLAKE, Rev. Canon PETER DOUGLAS STUART, who died on December 11, 2011, aged 84, showed enormous promise as a stylish batsman and an imaginative, enthusiastic captain at Eton in 1945. Three years later, he became the first post-war player to be capped by Sussex. "I think they saw him as future captaincy material," said Hubert Doggart, a contemporary at Hove. But Blake's priorities were to change: he served in the army in Germany immediately after the war, and listened to evidence in the trials of Nazi war criminals from the Ravensbruck concentration camp. He decided his future lay in the church and, after reading theology at Oxford, was ordained in 1955, later becoming rector of Mufulira in Northern Rhodesia (now Zambia). He had a notable career in Africa, working with young people and supervising the building of two churches. At Eton, where he was also a successful boxer, Blake had carried the batting in his final year, scoring nearly 800 runs, including five centuries, although *Wisden* noted that the club sides among the opposition were not as strong as usual. He played for Sussex between 1946 and 1951, and Oxford University from 1950 to 1952 (captaining them in his final year), scoring 2,067 runs at 22 in 58 matches, including three hundreds and a career-best 130 against Worcestershire in the Parks in 1952.

BRIDGE, DEREK JAMES WILSON, who died on March 13, was a pillar of Dorset cricket, playing for the county for 20 years from 1949, as captain from 1954 to 1966. He later served as their secretary and president, and was also president of the Minor Counties Cricket Association from 1997 to 2002. An off-spinner, Bridge dismissed Cyril Washbrook with the first ball he bowled for Dorset, and in all took 429 wickets for them, in addition to scoring 3,705 runs: he took eight for 35 against Oxfordshire in 1962. Bridge was an Oxford Blue – but for rugby, rather than cricket: he was an England triallist and represented the Barbarians. He did play one first-class match for Oxford University, and three for Northamptonshire, in 1947. He later became a schoolmaster, and ran the cricket at Sherborne for 21 years.

BURGIN, ERIC, who died on November 16, aged 88, was a medium-pacer from Sheffield who played a dozen matches for Yorkshire, nine of them in 1952, when they finished second in the Championship to Surrey – despite Burgin's six for 43 in a nine-wicket victory over the eventual champions at Headingley. Shortly before that, in the Roses match at Old Trafford, Burgin had opened the bowling with Fred Trueman – whom he had coached at Sheffield United CC – and took five for 20 with what *Wisden* called "accurate inswingers", as Lancashire were skittled for 65. Trueman, who cut down his pace when he saw how his partner was bowling, ended up with five for 26. But Burgin was already 28, and other, faster, bowlers moved ahead of him the following season, when he made only one Championship appearance – although he did have the satisfaction of dismissing Australia's openers, Arthur Morris and Graeme Hole, at Bradford. Burgin was also a useful footballer, a centre-half, who captained York City. He later served on Yorkshire's general committee.

BYRNE, PETER EDWARD, who died on December 9, aged 70, was a familiar face in the media centre at Lord's, as a scorer and knowledgeable statistician, and for some years provided the facts and figures for Middlesex's match programmes. He was married to Lilian, MCC's famously volatile receptionist, until her death in December 2006. A vice-president of The Cricket Society since 2009, he was also passionate about football – unusually following both Spurs and Arsenal – and an authority on ice hockey.

CARR OF HADLEY, LORD (Leonard Robert), PC, who died on February 17, aged 95, was Secretary of State for Employment, and then Home Secretary, in Edward Heath's Conservative government (1970–74). In 1976, after 26 years as an MP, Robert Carr became a life peer, and was soon appointed chairman of Prudential Assurance; he was a familiar figure at cricket presentations for the tournaments sponsored by the company, which included the World Cups of 1979 and 1983. He was also president of Surrey in 1985-86.

CARRIGAN, AUBREY HERBERT, died on May 23, aged 94. Aub Carrigan was a key member of the Queensland side for seven seasons after serving as a gunner in the Second World War. His team-mate Ken Archer remembered him as "no stylist, but with a powerful bottom hand, particularly when he was cutting, a good competitor and a good athlete". He made a habit of scoring runs against touring teams, hitting a neat 100 in quick time against Freddie Brown's 1950-51 England side, followed next season by 169 out of 253 while he was at the crease against the West Indians, when he hammered the point boundary every time leg-spinner Wilf Ferguson dropped short. Carrigan's medium-paced bowling was useful enough to be given the new ball occasionally: he took four for 95 against South Australia in 1948-49. In addition, he was a versatile and gifted fieldsman. Made captain for his final season in 1951-52, he led Queensland out of the cellar to joint-second in the Sheffield Shield, before spending a successful summer as professional with Church in the Lancashire League. Talented in a number of sports, Carrigan played on the wing in Australian Rules football, appearing in five national carnivals; he also won a state table tennis championship after entering on the day of the tournament following a casual suggestion from a friend. In later life, he represented Queensland at lawn bowls.

PA Photos

"More than a handful": Ray Carter.

CARTER, RAYMOND GEORGE, died on November 13, aged 79. Ray Carter was a versatile bowler who could switch from pace to off-spin, a development initially forced on him when he returned to Warwickshire in 1955 after National Service to find competition for fast-bowling spots. "He was tall and slender, with long arms and legs," remembered his former team-mate Billy Ibadulla. "Depending on conditions, he could change to brisk off-break bowling – and on helpful pitches he could be more than a handful." In 1957, Carter took five for 56 against Nottinghamshire with his quicker stuff, then seven for 57 with off-cutters a fortnight later to set up victory over Gloucestershire at Bristol. He took 70 wickets that year, and 81 in 1958, with a career-best seven for 39 against Worcestershire at Edgbaston – a "devastating" piece of fast-medium bowling, according to *Wisden*, which included a spell of 8.4–6–7–5. Thereafter, he was increasingly troubled by a back injury, which forced his retirement in 1961.

CHERRY, HUGH, who died on October 14, aged 81, devoted much of his life to Warwickshire, as a committee member and manager of the Under-19 side for more than 40 years. Jim Troughton, who captained the county to the 2012 Championship, was one of many to emerge from the youth system set up largely by Cherry. "He played an integral part in the development of lots of young cricketers," said Troughton. "They owe Hugh a debt of gratitude. He was loved by all the guys, and he didn't mind having the mickey taken out of his distinctive Yorkshire accent."

CHESTERTON, GEORGE HERBERT, MBE, who died on November 3, aged 90, was one of a vanished breed of amateurs whose season did not begin until his teaching duties were over for another year. Yet Chesterton was unlike many of his kind in two crucial respects: first, his talent was such that no professional resented his late-summer arrival; second, he put in long days of toil as a bowler, rather than lording it as a batsman. His first-class career stretched from 1948 (when he represented Free Foresters) until 1966 (MCC), but his reputation rests chiefly on his seven seasons with Worcestershire in the 1950s. Contemporaries compared his bowling to Derek Shackleton or, later, Tom Cartwright: naggingly accurate medium, sometimes quicker, off 12 paces. Mainly, he swung the ball away, but the odd one came in. "God knows how," he confided to his biographer, the former Hampshire cricketer Andy Murtagh.

Chesterton began a 76-year association with Malvern College as a pupil in 1936, but the school moved to Blenheim Palace three years later when their buildings were requisitioned by the War Office. At Blenheim, he was hauled before the Duke of Marlborough after breaking a window in the long library while practising his catching. He joined the RAF after school, trained as a pilot in Canada, and danced with Katharine Hepburn and Gypsy Rose Lee on an R & R visit to New York. He flew Sterling bombers, dropping SOE agents into the occupied countries, and towing gliders on D-Day, and into the "cauldron of horror" at Arnhem. Chesterton took up a deferred place at Brasenose College and made his Oxford debut in 1949, playing in a celebrated win over the New Zealanders. One of his earliest victims had been the young Tom Graveney: "He was deceptive, bowling inswingers and little cutters, slightly quicker than he looked."

Lewis Whyld, PA Photos

A Malvern institution: George Chesterton receives his MBE.

Chesterton took five for 22 in the victory over Yorkshire, and afterwards was approached by a reporter who, appraising his features, called to his colleague: "Don't bother with the camera, Charley – he's 27, not 17."

He returned to Malvern in 1950 to teach geography and coach cricket, and his first appearance for Worcestershire came that August. Thirty wickets in six games – including six for 61 against Lancashire at Old Trafford and six for 59 against Somerset at New Road – confirmed he was no makeweight. "He was amazing," said Peter Richardson, his captain in 1956 and '57. "You could use him as an opening bowler, but also as a stock bowler: he had enormous energy. He bowled beautifully – and he did it all with a smile on his face." Chesterton had been offered the chance to succeed Ronnie Bird as Worcestershire captain in 1955 but, although he was keen and the school were willing to grant him time off, it would have hampered his ambitions to become a housemaster: teaching always came first. He played his final game for the county in 1957, having taken 168 wickets at under 20 in 47 matches, but continued to represent MCC on tours of Ireland until 1966. His best figures – seven for 14 – had come at Dublin's College Park in 1956. His overall record was 263 wickets at 22.78 in 72 matches.

Chesterton was an institution at Malvern: housemaster, deputy head, then acting-headmaster in his final year, 1982. He also wrote a history of the school, and lived in a house behind the tennis courts until his death. He founded the Chesterton Cup for Midlands schools, was schools sport correspondent of *The Times*, president of the Cricketer Cup, and club president of Worcestershire between 1990 and 1993. He was also the co-author, with Hubert Doggart, of *Oxford and Cambridge Cricket* (1989), wrote a wartime memoir, and was the subject of Murtagh's 2012 biography, *A Remarkable Man*. He received his MBE from the Queen two weeks before he died.

CLARK, GEORGE, who died on September 2, aged 85, served Essex for 29 years, principally as a dressing-room attendant at Chelmsford. He was a man who believed there was no crisis that could not be eased by a cup of tea. Ronnie Irani remembered: "When I arrived for my first day at Essex and walked through the gates, he said, 'I can't believe Lancashire have let you go, and I am so happy you've joined Essex.' As a young man who had just left home for the first time and travelled over six hours on the train, his words always stayed with me." Irani was even prepared to tolerate Clark sitting next to him to smoke his roll-up cigarettes. He was, said Nasser Hussain, "Essex through and through".

COLEMAN, ROBERT GORDON, who died on August 21, aged 90, was a journalist who worked mainly for the Melbourne *Herald*. He wrote several books, including one that threw fresh light on the Pyjama Girl Murder (a notorious crime in 1930s Australia), and *Seasons in the Sun*, a huge history of the Victorian Cricket Association.

COOPER, GRAHAM CHARLES, who died on April 18, aged 75, played more than 250 matches for Sussex over 15 years from 1955. "Coop had a talent with both bat and ball, with a certain cocky bravado," remembered Ted Dexter, his captain for many years. "But I always thought he was a little short of confidence. Nevertheless, he was a survivor, and clung on to a place in a decent side for quite a few seasons." Capped in 1961, Cooper usually went in after Sussex's strokemakers, and often shored up the innings from No. 7, where he scored both his first-class hundreds: 141 against Warwickshire in 1960, and 142 against Essex at Hove in 1963 after entering at 55 for five. He was able to use the long handle if required: in the second year of the Gillette Cup, in 1964, he and Jim Parks rescued Sussex, the holders, against Durham (then a Minor County) by piling on 134 in an hour. Cooper was also a handy off-spinner: he finished with exactly 100 wickets, including five for 16 against Warwickshire at Edgbaston in 1961, and five for 13 against Oxford University in 1963. Among the victims was the Nawab of Pataudi, soon to be Cooper's county captain.

Bob Thomas, Getty Images

Sussex, 1969: Graham Cooper is second from the right in the back row; Tony Greig, who also died in 2012, towers over his team-mates.

COURY, LEROY ARTHUR, died on October 22, aged 76. Coury's leg-breaks and googlies, allied to Edgar Gilbert's left-arm spin, played an important part as St Kitts dominated the annual Leewards Islands tournament, which predated the smaller territories' introduction into the Caribbean's domestic first-class competition (as Combined Islands) in 1966. Coury played seven first-class matches for the Leewards, the last against the touring Australians in 1965. A businessman of Lebanese descent, he was a benefactor to several young cricketers, and a long-standing member of the St Kitts Cricket Association.

COWLEY, TERENCE JOHN, died on January 30, aged 83. In another time and another place, Terry Cowley would surely have worn the Baggy Green – but he played for Tasmania when their cricket was largely ignored by the mainland. Local cricket historian Rick Smith is unequivocal in nominating him among the best bowlers ever to represent them. Cowley – who started in 1948-49, and was captain for his last five seasons, from 1956-57 – moved the ball both ways in the air and off the pitch at a pace which was as deceptively sharp as it was chokingly accurate. Australia's wicketkeeper Don Tallon, on his way to England in 1953, grumbled after facing him: "Bloody hell, you spend all your time playing against Alec Bedser, and you come down here for a couple of social games and have to face him all over again." He took five for 92 against the 1958-59 MCC tourists, and two seasons later castled Garry Sobers in successive matches. In Launceston grade cricket, where his geniality and wisdom made him a revered figure, Cowley took 908 wickets at just over ten apiece. His younger brother, Ian, played four games for Tasmania in the early 1960s.

COX, CLIFFORD, died on February 4, aged 79. Lancashire-born Cliff Cox became a pillar of cricket in Canada, opening the batting for the national team and captaining them in the annual match against the United States in 1969 and 1970. He later served on the Canadian cricket board, and was a strong advocate of the women's game. An MCC touring team played a match in his memory at the picturesque Brockton Point ground in Vancouver in July 2012.

COXON, ALAN JOHN, who died on November 7, aged 82, was a left-arm medium-pacer who played 17 times for Oxford University between 1951 and 1954. His only Blue came in his second year, when he entered at 127 for seven in the follow-on and made 43 not out – the next-highest score of his career was 16 – as Oxford salvaged an unlikely draw against an attack led by Cuan McCarthy and John Warr, two Test fast bowlers. Hubert Doggart, in the Varsity Match history he co-wrote with George Chesterton, recalled "Coxon, Oxford's No. 9, heading a short-pitched ball from McCarthy with remarkable insouciance to cover point". Coxon played only one further first-class match, for MCC against his former university at Lord's in 1958. He was employed by the brewers Guinness for many years, supervising their operations in Nigeria and, later, working in the Far East and South America.

CRAWFORD, MICHAEL GROVE, who died on December 2, aged 92, was Yorkshire's treasurer for 30 years, and the club's chairman at the time of Geoff Boycott's sacking in 1983. This was overturned by the membership, and the committee resigned; Boycott played on for three more years. "He was a real gentleman," said Robin Smith, a recent Yorkshire president, "an urbane and friendly person of unquestioned integrity." The softly spoken Crawford had been a proficient all-round sportsman, a football Blue at Cambridge and a batsman good enough to score several half-centuries for Yorkshire's Second Eleven, which he captained in 1951. He also played one Championship match in August that year, skippering against Worcestershire at Scarborough in the absence of Norman Yardley: Yorkshire went down to an eight-run defeat which harmed their title chances (they eventually finished second, behind Warwickshire). In 1952 he shared leadership duties in the Second Eleven with Ronnie Burnet, and their paths would cross again six years later when Crawford – who captained Leeds CC throughout the 1950s – was asked to take charge of the first team as Yorkshire doggedly searched for a suitable amateur captain. He declined because of the demands of his accountancy business: 39-year-old Burnet got the job instead, and led Yorkshire to the Championship in 1959.

CURRAN, KEVIN MALCOLM, died after collapsing while jogging in Harare on October 10, aged 53. Kevin Curran's performance in Zimbabwe's sensational victory over Australia in their first match in senior international competition, at the 1983 World Cup, established a template for his career. On that seismic day at Trent Bridge, he made vital runs, took a key wicket and contributed to a fine fielding performance; Curran was not a player to be kept out of the action for long. Duncan Fletcher rightly gained the plaudits for his 69 and four wickets in that game, but Curran made 27 in a sixth-wicket partnership of 70 with his captain to rescue Zimbabwe from early calamity, then removed Allan Border. Later in the tournament, he made 62 against West Indies at Edgbaston, then hit 73 and claimed three for 65 – both one-day international career-bests – against India at Tunbridge Wells. Fletcher recalled: "Kevin always genuinely believed that any difficult situation was a challenge to be overcome." Curran also played in the 1987 World Cup in India and Pakistan, but made little impact: his international career ended after 11 matches, with 287 runs at 26, and nine wickets at 44.

Instantly recognisable by his surfer-style blond hair, Curran was a hard-hitting presence in the middle order, bowled fast-medium (and occasionally quicker), and was an electrifying presence in the field. "As a youngster, his returns to the keeper would be scrappy – until it was run-out time," said Fletcher. "Then the ball would be right above the stumps from the outfield, or a direct hit when closer in." In England, Curran was best known for the 15 seasons he spent with Gloucestershire and Northamptonshire, when he was one of the best all-rounders in the domestic game. An Irish passport – his paternal grandfather had emigrated to Southern Rhodesia in 1902 – meant he did not count as an overseas player, and he joined Gloucestershire in 1985, when his 52 wickets helped their rise from last in the Championship to third. *Wisden* felt a pace attack of Courtney Walsh, David Lawrence and Curran might be the most formidable the county had ever deployed. He was admirably consistent, passing 1,000 runs in four successive seasons, and adding

Patrick Eagar

Give me the ball: Kevin Curran on his way to three for 41 in the 1992 NatWest Trophy final. Leicestershire's James Whitaker and umpire David Constant look on.

65 wickets in 1988, and 60 in 1990, after which Gloucestershire released him amid stories of dressing-room disharmony. Senior coach Eddie Barlow insisted Curran's departure was "in the best interests of the club".

He decamped to Northamptonshire, where his friend Allan Lamb was captain: "He was an abrasive sort of player, but an excellent team man. He got up people's noses a bit, and you definitely wanted him on your side." Curran contributed fully to four successive top-five Championship finishes, and took three for 41 in the NatWest Trophy final victory over Leicestershire in 1992. "He always felt he was better than anybody else, and I liked that," said Lamb. "He would always say 'give me the ball' if we needed a wicket, or 'I'll bat at three'." Lamb also remembered a subtle motivator: "He got on really well with Curtly Ambrose, and he was good for him. Sometimes he'd say: 'I think I'm bowling faster than you this morning, Curtly.'"

In 1993, Curran finished second in the first-class bowling averages, with 67 wickets at 19, including a career-best seven for 47 against Yorkshire at Harrogate. He succeeded Rob Bailey as Northamptonshire captain at the end of the 1997 season after topping 1,000 runs that summer – including a career-best 159 against Glamorgan at Abergavenny – but the club endured a poor time under his leadership, and he was relieved of the post a year later. He returned for just one more season. He played for Natal in 1988-89, and Boland in 1994-95 and 1997-98, and finished his career in 1999 with 15,740 runs in 324 games at nearly 37, including 25 centuries, and 605 wickets at 27. When Zimbabwe achieved Test status in 1992, Curran was completing a ten-year residency qualification in the UK, and decided not to return. He did, however, fill a number of key roles in Zimbabwe cricket, initially as assistant coach of the national team, then as Phil Simmons's successor as head coach, between 2005 and 2007. He had also coached Namibia and been head of the Zimbabwe Cricket Academy. He went on to become a national selector, and at the time of his death was coach of Mashonaland Eagles.

He leaves three sons, who all inherited their father's talent. Tom played for Surrey Second Eleven in 2012, Sam was Zimbabwe's junior cricketer of the year in 2011, and Ben has also displayed great potential. Mashonaland chief executive Vimbai Mapukute said of Curran: "I have yet to meet a man more passionate about cricket in this country."

CURRIE, MARGARET JOYCE, died on October 5, aged 80. Joyce Currie (later Inness) was a bowler from Christchurch, quite speedy for women's cricket in the 1950s, who played three Tests for New Zealand. She opened the bowling in a soggy draw at The Oval in 1954, and won two further caps when England toured in 1957-58, taking three for 36 in the First Test at Christchurch. During her England tour Currie claimed six for 22 – from 20 overs – against the West at Torquay.

DALVI, MADHAV MANGESH, who died on October 1, aged 87, made a remarkable start to his first-class career late in 1947, following innings of 81, 63 not out and 67 in a Bombay festival tournament with 150 not out on his Ranji Trophy debut, for Bombay against Sind, then hitting 143 against Maharashtra. Thus after four matches he averaged 168. He couldn't keep that up, although he did score 110 in the 1948-49 Ranji Trophy final victory over Baroda. He lost his place in a strong side in the late 1950s, but reappeared as Vidarbha's captain in 1961-62, making centuries in what turned out to be his last two first-class games before a car accident ended his playing career.

DHARMA, PANDIAN KUMAR, was found dead at his home in Chennai on June 20. He was 20, and had seemingly committed suicide. Dharma made two one-day appearances for Tamil Nadu, and the day before his death had been playing a club final at the Chidambaram Stadium, in which he was apparently disappointed to take only one wicket. "He was a promising youngster who turned into a fine all-rounder," said Sridharan Sriram, the former Indian one-day player who was Dharma's club captain.

DICK, IAN ROBINSON, died on September 5, aged 86. He captained the Western Australian Colts against the 1950-51 MCC tourists, and later that season played as a batsman against Queensland in what was to be his only state match, despite scoring nearly 9,000 runs for his club, South Perth. A gifted hockey player, Dick played for WA from 1946 to 1959, and represented Australia in all their internationals for a decade from 1948, captaining them in the 1956 Melbourne Olympics, when he scored the first goal of the tournament. His brother, Alec, played once for WA in 1948-49, and he was a cousin of Alex Robinson, who also died in 2012.

FORMSTONE, GEORGE HAYNES, died on December 30, aged 81. Haynes Formstone, from Wrexham, devoted his life to cricket in Denbighshire, where he was honorary secretary for more than 50 years and rarely missed a game. A special match to celebrate his half-century was staged at Brymbo in July 2006.

FORTE, Major JOHN KNOX, MBE, who died on August 9, aged 96, kept cricket alive in Corfu, where he was the British vice-consul from 1958 to 1971. His initiatives included an appeal to readers of the *Daily Telegraph*, which produced 50 bats and 350 balls, and a pleasant history of cricket on the island, *Play's the Thing*, in 1988. This included tales of a batsman who was a heavy scorer, even though his ample stomach forced him to bat one-handed, and an unsuccessful attempt to introduce women's cricket, which was soon banned by the military governor after a lady batsman was smacked on the nose by a bouncer. By 2012 there were 14 cricket clubs in Greece, 11 of them on Corfu. Forte (pronounced "Fort") also produced several travel books and guides, which helped popularise the island as a holiday destination. As a 15-year-old Bradfield schoolboy, he had taken two for four at Lord's.

FUARD, MOHAMED ABDAL HASSAIN, died on July 28, aged 75. Abu Fuard was a prime mover behind Sri Lanka's push for Test status: he enlisted the help of prominent politicians, including the cabinet minister Gamini Dissanayake, who joined the national cricket board and added gravitas to the Sri Lankan delegation at the ICC. Sri Lanka finally became a Test-playing country in 1981-82 – "the greatest day in the life of Abu Fuard", according to his friend, the journalist Elmo Rodrigopulle. As a player, Fuard had been a tall, canny off-spinner, armed with what would probably now be called a doosra. In April 1961 he impressed the Australian team en route for England, dismissing Bill Lawry and Bob Simpson; their captain, Richie Benaud, said he wished he could take Fuard with him for the Ashes. In all, he represented Sri Lanka (then Ceylon) for 15 years, taking six for 31 for the Board President's XI against an International XI, composed mainly of English county players, in March 1968. He was Sri Lanka's manager/coach at the inaugural World Cup in 1975, and assistant manager for the next one, in 1979, when they beat India; he was also in charge when Sri Lanka won their first Test, against India in Colombo in September 1985. Fuard had a ten-year spell as a national selector, for a while chairing the panel, and was also instrumental in redeveloping grounds – particularly the Asgiriya Stadium in Kandy – to make them suitable for international cricket.

GAUNT, RONALD ARTHUR, died on March 30, aged 78. Red-haired and robust, Ron "Pappy" Gaunt – whose nickname came from the American bantamweight boxer "Pappy" Gault – was arguably the cream of the crop of fast bowlers who made life miserable for visiting batsmen on the peppery Perth pitch in the second half of the 1950s. Broad-shouldered and unrelenting, he had a smooth action which hid a wicked bumper among his customary outswingers. John Rutherford, Western Australia's first home-grown Test cricketer, remembered him as "fit as a bull and the quickest bowler in the state team of his time". He recalled the 20-year-old Gaunt's first match, against Queensland in 1955-56, when he bowled Neil Harvey's older brother, Mick, with a lightning full toss which sent stumps and bails hurtling towards the keeper. The following season he cut a swathe through New South Wales at Sydney: a career-best seven for 104 was made up exclusively of Test players. As a left-handed batsman, he generally aimed to hit the ball as hard as he could in the arc between long-on and midwicket; occasionally it worked, and he took 20 off an over of Ian Crowden's off-breaks at Hobart in 1961-62.

But it was Gaunt's misfortune to be competing for a Test spot with Alan Davidson, Ray Lindwall, Ian Meckiff and Graham McKenzie: his three caps were spread over six years. Called to South Africa as an injury replacement in 1957-58, he bowled Dick Westcott in his first over at Durban, but had to wait nine hours for his next success, eventually removing the somnolent Jackie McGlew. A side strain robbed him of a month's cricket early in the 1961 tour of England, but good form later on, including six for 50 against Somerset, earned him a chance in the final Test at The Oval, where he removed Raman Subba Row, Ted Dexter and Ken Barrington. John Arlott enthused that Gaunt "made the ball dart and dive about like a swallow chasing flies". And finally, at Adelaide in 1963-64, after being flayed by Eddie Barlow and Graeme Pollock, Gaunt rebounded by dismissing Colin Bland and Peter Carlstein in successive overs. These three appearances, plus two second-string tours of New Zealand were scant reward for his talents.

In 1960 Gaunt, who worked as a sales representative for Walpamur Paints, took his colour cards across the Nullarbor Plain to Melbourne, in search of further employment and cricket opportunities. There he cut his run-up significantly – and his pace slightly – without reducing his effectiveness, and became an important element of the Victorian attack for four seasons. He remained a significant influence at the Footscray club, where his wise advice helped shape four future Australian bowlers in Alan Hurst, Merv Hughes, Colin Miller and Tony Dodemaide, who praised Gaunt's "patient and knowledgeable" skills as a coach.

GHOSH, HAROLD, who died on January 17, aged 75, had a long career in Indian domestic cricket, which stretched from December 1951, when he was 15, until 1974-75. Initially a left-arm spinner, Ghosh became a solid left-hand batsman who made four Ranji Trophy centuries, the highest an undefeated 166 for Railways against a Delhi side including the young Bishan Bedi, on Christmas Day 1965. The nearest he came to representative honours were two matches for North Zone against touring teams in the 1960s.

GIBSON, DAVID, died on June 7, aged 76. Tall, well-built and able to generate pace and bounce from a rhythmic run-up and a side-on action that made the purists purr, David Gibson had what it took to become a fast bowler at the highest level. He was useful with the bat, too, and his athletic movement around the field hinted at a man who had represented England schools' rugby XVs at full-back. But Gibson's career was stalled at a key moment by a knee injury, and he was never quite the same bowler. Instead, he became a respected coach, all the while leaving former Surrey team-mates to wonder what might have been. The full promise of Gibson, who hailed from Mitcham, was underlined on his Championship debut, at the age of 21, against Gloucestershire at Bristol in July 1957. He took ten for 132 but, such was Surrey's strength in the year of a sixth successive title, that he played just once more that summer; they were match figures he would never better.

He made a more substantial contribution in 1958, deputising when illness sidelined Alec Bedser. He claimed 37 wickets, and came to the fore as Surrey began to rebuild when their years of domination ended. In 1960, Gibson took 90 wickets at 17, including seven for 26 against Derbyshire at The Oval. It remained his career-best, and earned him his county cap. There were 95 wickets in 1961, when he was in with a chance of international recognition. "The selectors were certainly looking closely at him after those two outstanding seasons," said Micky Stewart. But he suffered his first serious knee injury in 1962, and attention switched elsewhere. He recovered sufficiently to have another magnificent season in 1965, taking 86 wickets at 20 and scoring 996 runs at 34. Against Leicestershire at The Oval he was bowled by Peter Marner two short of what would have been his only first-class century. "He had the ability to bat at six or seven if he had really wanted to," said Stewart. Further knee trouble in 1966, however, more or less put paid to his career. There were just a handful of appearances thereafter, including a remarkable performance for the Second Eleven at Guildford in 1969, when he finished with figures of 16.4–10–13–10 as Sussex were skittled for 35. Bob Willis and Robin Jackman remained wicketless.

PA Photos

What might have been: David Gibson, 1963.

Gibson, nicknamed "Hoot" in tribute to an American cowboy actor called Hoot Gibson, retired at the end of that summer, after taking 552 wickets at 22 in 185 matches, and scoring 3,143 runs at almost 19. He had already taken MCC coaching qualifications and, at the behest of Stewart, the county's new cricket manager, he returned to The Oval in 1979 as county coach. Stewart said: "He was very good technically with bowlers – excellent at getting the information across in a way that could be understood." Later, Gibson emigrated to Australia and moved to Bowral. One day in 2007, he arrived at the Bradman Museum and offered his services, mentioning that he "knew a bit about the game". He became a popular guide, and a kindly coach to children visiting the nets. "We were honoured to have such a distinguished Pommy in our midst," said the curator David Wells. "Ill health forced his withdrawal from volunteering, but he did manage to attend the opening of the International Cricket Hall of Fame in November 2010, and I vividly remember him proudly wearing his Surrey blazer."

GIFFORD, JOSHUA THOMAS, MBE, who died on February 9, aged 70, was a giant in British horse racing. In the first half of his career, Josh Gifford was champion National Hunt jockey on four occasions; in the second, he became one of racing's most successful trainers, for ever associated with the storybook triumph of Aldaniti in the 1981 Grand

National. Yet visitors to Gifford's yard in Findon, on the Sussex Downs, were often left wondering if he hadn't chosen the wrong sport. There were cricket pictures on the walls of his home, cricket books on the shelves, and a faithful dog called Sobers. He regretted, he said, not making more of the talent he showed as a boy and, although a batsman, remained proud of dismissing Brian Lara in a charity match. He had his own wandering XI and, every September, Alan Lee – the former cricket correspondent of *The Times* who now covers racing – took a team to the lovely sloping ground at Findon, where Gifford was by turns cussed opening batsman and generous host. "Despite being so late in the season," said Lee, "the sun shone every time for 21 years."

GLASGOW, CARL VIDAL, who died on March 23, aged 69, was secretary and legal adviser to the Windward Islands Cricket Board for many years, and managed the Windward Islands team. Julian Hunte, the West Indies board president, called him "one of the stalwarts of cricket development in these islands".

GODSON, ALFRED THOMAS, died on May 4, aged 94. Fred Godson umpired 29 first-class matches, all at the Adelaide Oval, between 1961-62 and 1973-74. In November 1969, it was the genial Godson and his fellow umpire Col Egar who recalled John Inverarity (now Australia's chief selector) after he was bowled by an abruptly deviating ball from Greg Chappell in a Sheffield Shield match between South Australia and Western Australia. A swallow was found near the pitch; the umpires called dead ball for the dead bird; Inverarity resumed his innings, and took his score from nought to 89.

GOURLEY, IAN, who died on December 7, 2012, aged 70, was a stalwart of the Woodvale club in Belfast. For some years he was treasurer of the Irish cricket board, and also served as chairman and president of the Northern Cricket Union in Ulster.

GOVENDER, JUGOO, who died on September 6, aged 74, was an off-spinning all-rounder and fine slip fielder who played 42 matches now considered first-class, mainly for Natal's non-white side in the 1970s. He scored 74 against Eastern Province in February 1978, after taking five for 27 against Transvaal in the previous match. Govender, who became a headmaster, was also a talented footballer.

GREGG, DONALD MALCOLM, died on September 26, nine days after his 88th birthday. He made his debut for South Australia, aged 30, on Christmas Day 1954, having lost his youth to war: he was 25 before he played top-grade club cricket in Adelaide. Although he lacked real speed, he was accurate, and his ability to swing the ball late both ways helped him to three five-fors, the best of them five for nine in South Australia's inaugural match against Tasmania, in 1956-57. He had an admirer in Bill O'Reilly, who praised him for bowling "tenaciously" and "carrying the fight right up to the batsman". He was a member of the South Australian Metropolitan Fire Service for nearly 50 years.

GREIG, ANTHONY WILLIAM, died on December 29, aged 66. For a brief few years in the mid-1970s, Tony Greig was arguably the leading all-rounder in Test cricket – a belligerent middle-order batsman capable of match-turning hundreds, a wicket-taking bowler (in two styles) who bristled with attacking intent, and a magnificent fielder in any position. By 1975, he was pouring those attributes into gung-ho leadership of England. Throw in his iridescent stage-presence, and it is easy to see why he was talked of as cricket's first superstar.

Greig's on-field credentials are worth re-establishing, for in the decades that followed his sensational defection to Kerry Packer's World Series Cricket in 1977, they were easily overlooked. Instead he was recast as the man who preferred the Australian dollar to the England captaincy, the rebel who led a sport towards enslavement by television, and the broadcaster who coarsened the art of commentary. Typical was *Daily Mail* columnist Quentin Letts's scabrous piece on him in his 2009 book *50 People Who Buggered Up Britain*. Perhaps he was resented the more for being the harder to pin down: he was raised

Patrick Eagar

Exuding charisma: Tony Greig celebrates Ian Davis's wicket in the 1977 Centenary Test at Melbourne.

in South Africa, but played for England; embraced as a commentator in Australia, having been lionised as a player in India; and loved in Sri Lanka for his unfailing endorsement of the island and their cricketers.

Greig was born in Queenstown in the Eastern Cape to a Scottish father and South African mother. His was an archetypal white middle-class South African upbringing (although his parents were liberal in matters of race), and a young Greig barely paused for breath between games of cricket, tennis and rugby. At home he played cricket for hours with "Tackies", the family gardener, who had an inexhaustible appetite for bowling. The only blot on a sunny landscape was epilepsy, first revealed when he collapsed playing tennis aged 14. In the main, Greig managed to control the illness for the rest of his life.

He attended the local Queen's College, a favourite winter destination for Sussex cricketers, who returned to Hove with glowing reports. It was the influence of Mike Buss that secured a trial, and Greig set off for the south coast soon after his first-class debut for Border in February 1966, aged 19. Opportunities were rationed, but he made a century in each innings for Colonel L. C. Stevens' XI against Cambridge University at Eastbourne, and took three West Indian wickets for A. E. R. Gilligan's XI at Hastings. Sussex offered him a contract and, with some reluctance, his father heeded Greig's pleas to put cricket before a place at a South African university. Permission came with a proviso: he had four years to reach the top. It was a mission that began spectacularly on his Championship debut, against Lancashire at Hove in May 1967. Coming to the wicket with Sussex 34 for three against an attack led by Brian Statham and Ken Higgs, he made 156, showing scant regard for the principles of early-season batting in England. Two months later, he took eight for 25 against Gloucestershire.

He passed 1,000 runs and 50 wickets in each of his first three seasons with Sussex and, if centuries and five-fors proved elusive, his true qualities transcended statistics – an unshakable confidence, a desire to attack in any situation, and a talent for inspiring those around him. At 6ft 7½in, and strikingly blond, he also exuded charisma. "He was just so different," said team-mate Peter Graves. "He had that boyish exuberance. And he was noisy."

By 1970, Greig had completed his residency and – while his former countrymen embarked on their 22-year exile – was selected for England against the Rest of the World at Trent Bridge. Characteristically undaunted, he took four for 59 on his first day in international cricket, then hit two of his first three balls for four. But he was less successful at Edgbaston and Headingley, and was dropped for the final match. His next career boost came from an unlikely source. Garry Sobers was leading a Rest of the World squad to Australia in 1971-72 and, when Mike Procter withdrew, he suggested to Don Bradman, overseeing the tour, that Greig should take his place. Arriving in Adelaide, Greig survived a mortifying moment when he palmed off his luggage on the bespectacled, cardigan-wearing figure who greeted him. Only later did he twig: the bagman was Bradman. But it was a successful trip. Greig played in all five of the unofficial Tests and, by the time the Australians arrived in England in 1972, the selectors gave him another chance.

Greig was a ray of light in the First Test at a gloomy Old Trafford, top-scoring twice, with 57 and 62, taking four wickets, and exciting Jack Fingleton: "Greig was an outstanding success, proving himself England's best all-round gain in years." Thereafter, his performances were less eye-catching, but further mature displays came that winter in India. At Delhi, he shared a Christmas Day stand of 101 with his captain Tony Lewis, helping England to victory; at Calcutta, he took his first Test five-wicket haul; at Bombay, he made his first century. "We sat down for a long chat over a glass of wine at the end of the tour," Lewis said. "One thing we had in common was that we were both always looking ahead of the game, not back on it. We both believed in trusting your luck and obeying your gut instinct."

So began the years of Greig's pomp. From the trademark upturned collar, everything about him seemed designed to attract attention: at the crease, he held his bat high in defiance of the textbook (Bradman tut-tutted), and used his tremendous reach to get on the front foot as often as possible. His cover-driving of fast bowlers was a display of power and elegance. When bowling, his hectic approach was a mass of pumping legs and jutting elbows. In the field, he was seldom far from the action, staring batsmen down from close in, or grasping edges in the slips.

He was appointed vice-captain to Mike Denness for the tour of the West Indies in 1973-74, but in the First Test in Trinidad, his combativeness backfired. Fielding the final ball of the second day at silly point, Greig spotted that Alvin Kallicharran, unbeaten on 142, had begun to walk off, and threw down the non-striker's stumps. Having not yet called time, umpire Douglas Sang Hue had no option but to uphold the appeal. The England team left the field to a fusillade of boos, and things might have turned nasty had the scoreboard operators altered the number of wickets. Even so, the presence of angry supporters outside the ground persuaded Sobers to drive Greig back to the hotel. An evening of intense diplomatic activity ensued, ending with Kallicharran's reinstatement. England issued a statement apologising for Greig's "instinctive action", and next morning he reluctantly agreed to shake Kallicharran's hand.

When England returned to the Queen's Park Oval for the final Test, still trailing 1–0, Greig produced perhaps his most unlikely match-winning performance, taking eight for 86 in West Indies' first innings with brisk off-breaks. He had experimented with them in the Second Test in Jamaica, but purely as a defensive measure. Now, the extra bounce at Port-of-Spain made them a viable attacking weapon, and he added five for 70 in the second innings as England squared the series. Alan Knott called it the finest off-spin bowling he had kept to, but for Derek Underwood it paradoxically marked the end for Greig as an effective Test bowler: "At Trinidad he just hit the right rhythm and pace, but after that he never knew what to do, or what to bowl, on any particular day or wicket."

Another thrilling performance followed later that year, this time with the bat, at Brisbane. Arriving at 57 for four, with Jeff Thomson and Dennis Lillee in full cry, Greig launched an extraordinary counter-attack, driving with savage intent and cutting anything short over the heads of an astonished slip cordon. He scored 110. "It was one of the best half-dozen innings I ever saw," said John Woodcock. Greig's relish for a battle was never more obvious than when he infuriated Lillee by treating bouncers with an exaggerated trembling of the knees, and signalling his own boundaries. His colleagues were impressed by his impudence but appalled by the likely consequences: "Think of the poor bastard at the other end," Underwood told him. It is easy to imagine the television mogul Kerry Packer noting this bravura performance and luminous screen presence.

When England's shell-shocked team quickly embarked on a home series with Ian Chappell's bruisers, Denness was on borrowed time, and resigned halfway through the First Test. Greig's captaincy credentials had been buffed by, among others, E. W. Swanton (an improbable, but staunch, supporter), Ian Wooldridge and *Wisden*, although Greig himself felt he had been offered the role only because there were no alternatives. Keen to add backbone to England's fragile batting, he sought the opinion of umpires, who told him Northamptonshire's No. 3, David Steele, was the man to stand up to Lillee and Thomson. It proved a shrewd move: in contrasting styles, Greig and Steele restored national pride on a sunlit first day at Lord's. Greig made 96, Steele 50 and, though the match was drawn and Australia protected their 1–0 lead for the rest of the summer, there was a seismic shift in atmosphere. "He was such a great competitor," said Steele.

With no England tour that winter, Greig accepted an offer to play grade cricket for Waverley in Sydney, where his on-field success became almost incidental to business contacts and promotional deals. Back in England, he gave an interview to the BBC's *Sportsnight* programme ahead of the 1976 West Indies series. Irked by what he saw as the journalist's emphasis on the qualities of the opposition, he retorted: "I'm not really sure they're as good as everyone thinks they are." Next came a comment destined for folklore: "If they get on top, they are magnificent cricketers. But if they are down, they grovel, and I intend – with the help of Closey and a few others – to make them grovel." From any previous England captain, the remark might have been dismissed as crass psychology; from a white South African, it was just crass. The West Indians were furious. During a long, hot summer, England's optimism of 1975 drained away in a 3–0 defeat, although Greig responded with a typically feisty century in the Fourth Test at Headingley, before finally grovelling himself, on hands and knees, in front of jubilant West Indian supporters at The Oval.

If Greig had learned something about public relations, he soon put it to good use in India. His charm offensive began before a ball was bowled, when he ostentatiously praised the local umpires. Ahead of one game, he made his men don blazers and jog around the outfield, waving to the crowd. If Greig was in the middle when a firecracker went off, he would fall to the ground as if he had been shot, and he encouraged Derek Randall to play to the gallery too. Thought was also given to the serious business of winning matches. Underwood recalled: "Before we left for India he said to me, 'You are going to win us the series. If you don't want to play in any of the games outside the Tests, just let me know and I'll make sure you don't have to.' Nobody had spoken to me like that before."

Greig's leadership was inspirational, never more so than in the Second Test at Calcutta, where he batted for more than seven hours with a fever and in a state of near-exhaustion to score 103. It was his second truly great Test innings – and this time in a winning cause. The series was secured when England went 3–0 up at Madras, to complete Greig's finest hour as captain. Before the party left India, Gubby Allen wondered aloud to friends: "Is he really too good to be true?"

An answer of sorts was around the corner. At the Centenary Test in Melbourne, Greig again showed slick PR skills with a letter to the *Age* newspaper, thanking the city for its hospitality. But he immediately boarded a flight to Sydney: Packer, owner of Channel Nine, wanted to see him. Infuriated with the Australian Cricket Board's refusal to sell him the TV rights to Test cricket, Packer was plotting to set up his own breakaway series – and the telegenic Greig was vital to the plan.

Greig was offered $A90,000 for three years, with the guarantee of a job for life at the Packer organisation. He wanted time to think it over, but did not need long. Returning to London, he was ambushed by Eamonn Andrews for *This is Your Life*, but found time to make contact with Packer's other English targets. Two days later, he flew to Trinidad to help recruit West Indians and Pakistanis playing a Test there. Packer's heist remained secret for a few more weeks, long enough for the Australian touring party to arrive in England to defend the Ashes in 1977. Sussex players noted that the dressing-room attendant was suddenly taking a lot more calls for "Mr Greig". Eventually, as the news leaked in Australia, Greig issued a statement on May 8, announcing a "massive cricket project" for the next Australian summer. He then headed for Hove, hit 50 from 36 balls against Yorkshire, and told Geoff Boycott in the car park to keep an eye on the morning papers.

Retribution was swift. By the end of the week he had been stripped of the England captaincy while, curiously perhaps, retaining his place in the team, now led by Mike Brearley. It was an odd summer. Against a distracted, divided Australian side, England won easily, with Greig making 91 at Lord's and 76 at Old Trafford. Brearley was appreciative. "When he was dismissed as captain, he might have shown more resentment, or have been only moderately co-operative," he wrote. "In fact, he could not have been more helpful." Elsewhere, there were less kind words: he was, wrote Woodcock, not English "through and through", and his cloak-and-dagger defection severed many alliances; Greig always regretted not being able to forewarn Alec Bedser, Ken Barrington and Swanton. County dressing-rooms containing Packer players could be chilly places, but Graves insisted there was no problem at Hove: "We wished him well because it was obviously his future." Tony Lewis saw it differently, calling his behaviour a "betrayal".

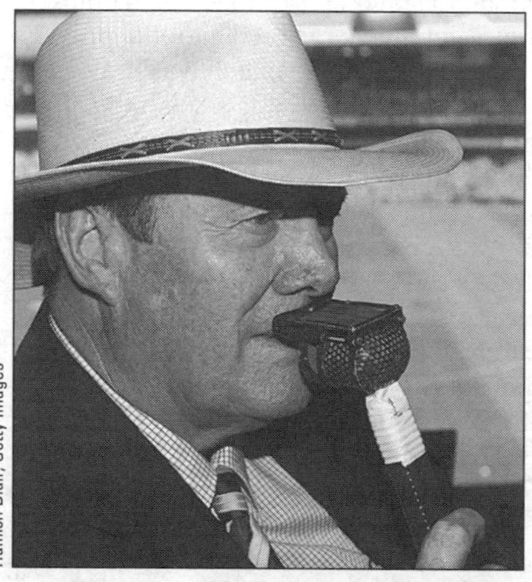

Hamish Blair, Getty Images

International success: Tony Greig – born in South Africa, captain of England, hero in Sri Lanka, commentator in Australia.

As far as his Test career was concerned, though, that was that. In 58 matches, he made 3,599 runs at 40, with eight hundreds, and took 141 wickets at 32, with six five-fors. Among men to have played at least 25 Tests, only Greig, Aubrey Faulkner and Jacques Kallis have averaged 40 or more with the bat and 33 or fewer with the ball. Overall, in 350 first-class matches, Greig scored 16,660 runs at 31, and took 856 wickets at under 29.

He had never disguised his intention to become "the first millionaire cricketer". Catching the militant mood of the 1970s, he once stood up at a Professional Cricketers' Association meeting and suggested a work-to-rule on Sundays. But it was Packer who provided his route to those riches, and the pair strode down the Strand shoulder to shoulder when the WSC players took the authorities to the High Court after they had been banned from the first-class game; the players won. Greig was also at the forefront of promoting WSC in Australia, to the extent that his role as World XI captain became almost secondary. His form was wretched, leading to Ian Chappell's barb that the World XI was "the best bunch of cricketers I've seen – with one exception". Underwood said: "Out there he was an administrator as well as a cricketer. If there was a problem, he had the job of sorting it out."

When a peace deal was brokered after two disrupted Australian summers, Packer's offer of a job for life came good. For the next three decades, Greig was integral to Channel Nine's coverage. His excitable style – "He's gone, goodnight Charlie!" – did not please everyone, but his voice became almost as familiar as Richie Benaud's, and his sparring with Bill Lawry was central to Australian humorist Billy Birmingham's *Twelfth Man* parodies.

In the summer of 2012, Greig was invited by MCC president Phillip Hodson, his brother-in-law, to give the Spirit of Cricket Lecture. His first draft included no mention of the Packer years, until he was persuaded the topic could not be ignored, and he was typically outspoken on India's role in the world game. In October 2012 it was revealed

Greig was suffering from lung cancer; two months later, he died in a Sydney hospital after suffering a heart attack at home. On the Saturday morning when Britain awoke to the news, the honours list was published. Denness had been awarded an OBE. It left Greig as the only England captain without such recognition – an outsider to the end.

HARDMAN, THOMAS RICHARD, was found dead in his bed in student accommodation in Leeds on November 28. He was 21. Initial reports suggested no suspicious circumstances. Tom Hardman was a promising fast bowler from Manchester, who made his debut for the Central Lancashire League club Heywood when he was 12, and a useful batsman who scored a century for Lancashire's Under-17s. He was part of the Leeds/Bradford MCCU side who almost won their initial first-class match, against Surrey at The Oval in April 2012; his first wicket was Tom Maynard. "He was a real hard worker, and a lovely bloke to have around the dressing-room," said Clive Radley, the former England batsman who coaches the combined MCC Universities team. "His leadership qualities were such that I had already earmarked him for the captaincy in 2013."

HILL, GEOFFREY HARRY, died on March 13, aged 77. Geoff Hill was a slow left-armer who took eight for 70 against Gloucestershire at Cheltenham in 1958, his first season for Warwickshire, which he ended with 59 wickets at 20. But his form fell away, and he left the county midway through 1960, remaining a prolific wicket-taker in the Birmingham League.

HOAD, EDWARD LISLE GOLDSWORTHY, died on June 13, aged 86. Ted Hoad was a leg-spinner and tailender although, like his father of the same name, who had a long career for Barbados and played four Tests for West Indies, he occasionally opened the batting. He played nine matches for Barbados between 1944 and 1954, recording his highest score of 74 from the top of the order against Jamaica at Kingston in March 1947.

HOW, EDWARD JOSEPH, died on March 29, aged 37, after a fall while skiing in Val d'Isère, in France. Ed How played 14 first-class matches for Cambridge University in the mid-1990s, appearing twice in the Varsity Match, and also won a football Blue. He went into the City, becoming a vice-president of Deutsche Bank, then abruptly switched careers by moving to Charterhouse School, where he taught chemistry and coached cricket and football with enormous enthusiasm. A left-arm seamer, his overall record was a modest 13 wickets at 88, but he did have one golden day, at Canterbury in June 1997 when he took five for 59. His team-mate Ed Smith remembered: "I never like the phrase 'good club man', but Ed was all the best things about that expression. He was sociable, warm, generous-spirited and fun-loving."

HUEY, SAMUEL SCOTT JOHNSTON, died on March 8, aged 88. Scott Huey was something of a legend in Irish cricket, a teasing slow left-armer who took six for 49 and eight for 48 against MCC in 1954 – and finished top of the first-class averages. In 1965 he claimed five for 68 against the New Zealand tourists. In all, he took 112 wickets for Ireland.

HYAMS, JOHN, died on May 2, aged 92. Jack Hyams claimed to have scored more than 125,000 runs and 170 centuries in a club career that stretched for around 80 years – his last matches were played in Spain in 2010, when he was past 90. His deeds were carefully catalogued at home, and included appearances for MCC and Cross Arrows when over 70, as well as several prominent north London clubs. He was also an inveterate tourist and, on his travels, "a tireless dancer every night into his nineties", according to his friend Michael Blumberg. Hyams had invested in a new bat for the 2012 season, but never got to use it in anger.

HYATT, ROLAND SHANE, died on July 5, aged 50. Roly Hyatt had a fine record in junior and grade cricket, but was unable to translate that into first-class success, despite an extended trial over three seasons for Tasmania from 1983-84. His off-breaks did not spin enough – his career average was over 70 – and an attempt to turn him into a specialist batsman was also unsuccessful, although he did make three fifties against South Australia. After retirement he was beset by financial problems which had legal consequences, compounded by the effect of alcohol on his health.

IFFLA, IRVIN BANCROFT, who died on March 16, aged 88, became a widely admired figure in Scottish cricket after leaving his native Jamaica in 1951 to take up a professional contract with Stirling County. He lived in Scotland for the rest of his life. An off-spinner and useful lower-order batsman, Iffla played four matches for Jamaica before his departure, claiming five for 90 against the 1947-48 MCC tourists. He made an immediate impact in his new country. "He transformed the whole club and the whole of Scottish cricket," said Raymond Bond, Stirling's wicketkeeper at the time. "He was a magician with the ball and brilliant with the bat – and people came flocking to Williamfield, Stirling's home ground, to see him every Saturday." Iffla also had stints at Ayrshire and Stenhousemuir, both of which, like Stirling, won the league title while he was their professional. Mike Denness, the Scot who went on to captain England, was one of many who benefited from Iffla's coaching at Ayrshire: "I learned so much just from watching the man, let alone listening to what he was saying." Iffla continued as an amateur into his sixties, ending his club career with more than 13,000 runs and 1,600 wickets. In 2009, he was granted the Freedom of Stirling; the flag at the city council chambers flew at half-mast for his funeral.

JEGUST, GERTRUDE MARIE, died on February 21, a month short of her 101st birthday. Born in Beckenham in 1911, Marie Jegust was taken to Australia when young: her family helped establish the township of Cowaramup in the south-western corner of Western Australia. In 1930, she became the foundation secretary of the WA Women's Cricket Association, and seven years later returned to the land of her birth with the Australian women's team, although she had a modest tour, and did not play in any of the Tests. Her memoirs, *99 Not Out*, came out shortly before her death.

JORDON, RAYMOND CLARENCE, died on August 13, aged 75. Always known as "Slug", because he had collected a blank bullet in his side during National Service, Ray Jordon was Victoria's wicketkeeper for most of the 1960s. To the seamers, he was safe

Mark Dadswell, Getty Images

A voice "like a chainsaw": Slug Jordon at a reunion of Victoria players, 2003.

and unostentatious but, standing up, his speed and sureness were exceptional: 48 of his 238 dismissals were stumpings, five of them from the fast-medium bowling of Alan Connolly, including Ian and Greg Chappell in the same innings. If batsmen were not intimidated by his withering welcome – in a voice "like a chainsaw", according to Max Walker – they could grow agitated if Jordon decided to lurk in their pocket to a quick bowler. His best match haul was in 1970-71, his final season, when he collected nine catches and a stumping against South Australia. As a batsman, he was a habitual thorn down the list, where he allied a dogged defence to an ability to deal with the loose ones. Jordon's only century came against South Australia in 1963-64.

He was a noted scrapper, but his willingness to push his luck probably cost him a Test cap. He toured India and South Africa in 1969-70, competing for a place with Brian Taber after the retirement of Barry Jarman. Taber was tried first and, when Jordon was given a game against India's South Zone, Ian Chappell was convinced he knowingly let Erapalli Prasanna be given out bowled when the ball had rebounded from his pads. Chappell was adamant he would not play himself if Jordon was selected to replace Taber in a Test.

Jordon was a genuine character, and the stories about him are legion; many are true but few are printable. His vocabulary was not for the faint-hearted: one of his friends announced in the tributes column of a Melbourne paper that "Heaven will make a fortune from the swear-box." Jordon was a dynamic presence in Australian Rules football as an insightful coach of younger players, and was described by Keith Stackpole, a close friend, as "a unique judge of character", despite his abrasiveness. He had a period as a radio commentator on cricket, and his times on air with Richie Benaud gave a new dimension to Puccini's "strange harmony of contrasts". A stroke early in this century saw him draw on his reserves of stoicism, but eventually cancer was too much, even for Slug.

KUNTAL CHANDRA, often known by his nickname "Pappon", was found dead on the side of a road in Daur, not far from Dhaka, on December 3. Police said the 28-year-old was discovered with injury marks on his throat, and his shirt had been used to tie his hands behind his back. No motive was immediately apparent. Chandra, a wicketkeeper-batsman, represented Bangladesh at the Under-19 World Cup early in 2000. Five years later he scored 33 and 71 on first-class debut, for Chittagong against Rajshahi at Bogra, but played only two further matches, both for Sylhet, in 2007.

KYLE, JACK, who died on June 21, aged 82, was president of the Canadian Cricket Association for 15 years until 1993. He played for British Columbia in the 1950s, and in 1955 scored 93 against Manitoba at Brockton Point in Vancouver, the ground rated by Don Bradman as the prettiest he ever saw.

LACHMAN, RUDY, who died on August 19, aged 50, was a left-hand batsman and slow left-armer from Guyana who played for the United States in the ICC Trophy tournaments of 1994, when he made 75 not out against Argentina in Nairobi, and 1997.

LAMASON, JOY GRACE (née Stenberg), who died on February 16, aged 96, was an all-rounder who played four Tests for New Zealand, taking four for 51 against England at Headingley in June 1954. Her brother-in-law Jack, a Wellington stalwart who toured England in 1937 without making the Test side, married Ina Pickering, who also played four Tests for New Zealand.

LEWIS, KEITH, who died on September 12, aged 89, opened the batting for South Australia in 1948-49, making some useful scores, the highest being 73 against Western Australia at Adelaide. Because he turned up to club practice just after the Second World War wearing his army uniform, he was dubbed "The Colonel". His father's sudden death in 1953 forced his retirement from club cricket, and he concentrated on running the family hardware business.

LOMBARD, ELISE, who died on August 9, aged 62, was the only female chief executive in South Africa's provinces, having been in charge of the Northerns Cricket Union, latterly the Titans franchise, for 32 years. "She was an amazing woman who did so much for the Titans," said the South African Test player Faf du Plessis, "and always with a smile on her face."

LOVELL, Sir ALFRED CHARLES BERNARD, OBE, died on August 6, aged 98. Bernard Lovell was one of Britain's greatest scientists, revered worldwide as a pioneer of radio astronomy. His lasting monument is the telescope at Jodrell Bank in Cheshire that now bears his name. It was built in the 1950s thanks chiefly to his drive and determination, although visitors to the site who arrived at lunchtime might have had to wait while he finished his game of cricket with staff and students. Lovell's love of the sport began during his boyhood in Bristol, and continued when he accepted a post in the physics department of Manchester University in 1936. Like Sir Neville Cardus, he relished the fact that the city held the combined attractions of Old Trafford and the Hallé Orchestra. Lovell became a devoted follower of Lancashire – he was club president in 1996 – and could not resist exploring how technology might benefit the game, devising a contraption rather like a clock face that kept spectators informed of the state of the light. Lovell was remarkably far-sighted, writing to John Woodcock – then *Wisden* editor – in 1983 to suggest technology could be used to determine lbws. The TCCB (later the ECB) set up a working party, but the computers involved were too costly and slow. "His wisdom and prescience have been witnessed by the advent of Hawk-Eye," said Woodcock. Lovell also foresaw the possibilities of the snickometer. Jim Cumbes, the former Lancashire chief executive, recalled: "He invented a device that fixed to the top of the bat and would detect a nick, but when we did a test it picked up the frequency of the local taxi company."

LYNCH, RONALD VICTOR, died on June 27, aged 89. Slow left-armer Ron Lynch played three matches for Essex in June 1954 and took his four wickets in one innings – for 54 runs against Northamptonshire at Rushden. His county career might have been brief, but he played club cricket for years, for Ilford and later Chingford; he also represented the Club Cricket Conference and served on their committees.

McGIBBON, LEWIS, who died on September 22, aged 80, was a fast-medium bowler from Newcastle who took 33 wickets in 13 appearances for Northamptonshire in the late 1950s after some success in Minor Counties cricket with Northumberland. His best figures were four for 42 against Somerset in 1958, although he did take seven for 14 for the Second Eleven the following year as Worcestershire were bowled out for 45. An accountant, McGibbon served on Northamptonshire's committee from 1962 to 1980, including a spell as treasurer.

MANGERA, MOOSA, who died on November 15, aged 67, was a useful batsman and fine fielder, often keeping wicket, who played 29 matches now considered first-class for Transvaal's non-white teams in the 1970s and '80s. He scored 98 against Eastern Province at Lenasia in 1973-74. Nicknamed "Monkey" because of his speed and agility, Mangera was also a talented footballer and track athlete.

MANZUR AHMED, who died of a heart attack on January 10, aged 54, was the chief executive of the Bangladesh Cricket Board. A former wicketkeeper, he had a long club career, and was the Brunei association's chief executive before taking up the BCB post in 2010. "The news shocked everyone at the ICC," said their outgoing chief executive Haroon Lorgat. "I worked closely with him during the organising of the 2011 World Cup."

MARSHALL, JOHN CAMPBELL, who died on April 26, aged 83, was a batsman who played 16 matches for Oxford University between 1951 and 1953, winning a Blue in his final year, not long after scoring his only century – 111 against Free Foresters in the Parks. Marshall was better known as a rugby player, winning five caps for Scotland at full-back in 1954. He became a teacher, and soon returned to his old school, Rugby, where he took charge of the cricket.

MARSHALL, WALTER MAXWELL MILNE, died on November 24, 2006, aged 86. Max Marshall was a slow left-armer who played a few matches in Trinidad's Beaumont Cup (not first-class at the time). Later, he was assistant manager on West Indies' tour of Australia in 1960-61 – which started with the Tied Test at Brisbane. When injuries hit the squad mid-trip, he was pressed into service for his only first-class appearance, against Tasmania at Launceston: aged 40, he scored one not out and did not bowl.

MAYNARD, THOMAS LLOYD, died after being electrocuted on a railway line on June 18, aged 23. During the weekend before his death, Tom Maynard was a cheerful presence on television screens, as a guest on Sky's knockabout Saturday show *Cricket AM* and as part of *Finishing School*, a documentary about the England Performance Programme's winter training. There had been a chance to glimpse him in the flesh, too, in Surrey's Sunday afternoon Twenty20 match against Kent at Beckenham. Then, shortly after breakfast time on Monday, came the news that his body had been found on the tracks near Wimbledon Park tube station in south London. Not since the death in 2002 of Ben Hollioake – also of Surrey, also youthful, good-looking and precocious – had English cricket been so numbed by tragedy.

Five weeks earlier, against Worcestershire at New Road, Maynard's talent had been thrillingly laid bare. With Surrey following on, he made a career-best 143, moving to three figures with a six. The watching Kevin Pietersen called Andy Flower that evening to offer an enthusiastic endorsement. Not that this surprised Graham Thorpe, his EPP batting coach: "Tom scored runs when his team needed them, which is crucial for a player who has potential to get to the top."

The innings also underlined a new cricketing maturity acquired in his second season at The Oval. "He had moved to another level," said Dean Conway, the former Glamorgan and England physio who had known him all his life. "Before joining Surrey he had the talent but not the stats." At his funeral, at Llandaff Cathedral in Cardiff, Hugh Morris – the former Glamorgan opening batsman now managing director of England cricket – said Maynard had first toddled into the dressing-room at Sophia Gardens with his father Matthew at the age of two. Thereafter, he was seldom out of it. Conway remembered: "He became like one of the team. We called him 'Bruiser'. Even then, he had massive arms and legs."

Maynard attended Whitchurch High School, a sporting hothouse that also nurtured the talents of Sam Warburton, a future Wales rugby captain, and the Tottenham Hotspur footballer Gareth Bale. From there he went to Millfield where, in his mid-teens, rugby briefly threatened to become his main sport. In June 2007, aged 18, he made a dazzling first senior appearance for Glamorgan, scoring 71 from 75 deliveries against Gloucestershire in the Friends Provident Trophy. At first, his one-day returns were always more eye-catching: in August 2009 came a 57-ball century – one fewer than his father's one-day quickest – against Northamptonshire. But the summer of 2010 ended traumatically, when Glamorgan missed promotion in the Championship on the final day, and Matthew Maynard lost his job as director of cricket. Shocked by the treatment meted out to his father, Tom relocated to Surrey, joining his old Millfield friend Rory Hamilton-Brown. He was energised by the change, and in 2011 played a full part in their promotion in the County Championship and CB40 triumph. There were 1,022 Championship runs at nearly 41, including a seemingly preordained hundred against Glamorgan at Cardiff. His form earned him selection for the EPP in 2011-12, when he impressed Thorpe on a trip to India. "He came across as a caring and kind young man," he said. "I thought he learned a lot from that time away in Asia, and on his return to England he really did look the standout batsman at Surrey."

Matthew Maynard's abundant talent was never successfully transferred to the international stage, but many believed his son had the temperament and ability to prosper there. Morris called him "a player who was surely destined for the highest reaches of the

Nigel French, PA Photos

"Authority and elegance": Tom Maynard en route to a century against Middlesex, July 2011.

game, and whose authority and elegance at the crease reminded so many of his father". Another speaker at Llandaff Cathedral was the Glamorgan captain Mark Wallace. "I will always remember him as the lad who could make me laugh more than anyone else I have ever met," he said. "I just wish he had never made me cry."

MISHRA, SIDDHARTHA, who died of cancer on October 30, aged 41, was a writer with a particular fondness for cricket, and the sports editor of the *New Indian Express*. His last article was about Sachin Tendulkar's century of centuries. He observed: "This number is perhaps the worst measure imaginable for Tendulkar, blessed – and simultaneously cursed – as he is to turn everything he touches into a record-breaking statistic."

MKRAKRA, MASIXOLE, drowned in Bathurst, South Africa, on December 17. "Hassan" Mkrakra was 20, and one of a group of youngsters trying to wash themselves in a disused quarry after a week in the bush that included his circumcision ceremony. They were using empty plastic bottles as buoyancy aids, but Mkrakra gave his to a struggling friend before disappearing under the water. He was a promising cricketer who in March 2012 received a standing ovation at a Sporting Heroes dinner at Lord's, after telling a distinguished audience – including Prince Edward, Derek Underwood and Boris Becker – about the dreams of impoverished youngsters who played for the Tiger Titans cricket team.

MONAGHAN, RUBY, died on June 10, aged 96. Ruby Monaghan (later Lee) grew up playing vigoro, a then-popular blend of cricket and softball for girls, but switched to conventional cricket as a teenager and was selected for New South Wales against the 1934-35 England tourists. In a display of mature concentration and sound defence, she made 25 and 45, adding 84 for the second wicket with Hazel Pritchard. Monaghan, the youngest player in the side, was chosen for the first two internationals of that tour – the inaugural women's Tests – but was dropped after a highest score of 12 in four innings. She had become the second woman, after Pritchard, to face a ball in a Test match.

MOORE, Sir PATRICK ALFRED CALDWELL, CBE, died on December 9, aged 89. Death held no fears for Sir Patrick Moore, who believed that the end of an earthbound life was merely the start of a new existence. "We go on to the next stage," he said. "I shall be interested to see what it is. Who knows? It might be somewhere I can learn to bat decently." Britain's most famous astronomer, who hosted *The Sky at Night* on BBC television for more than 50 years, was a devoted cricket lover who kept his size 12 boots on the hearth in his study, next to his 2001 BAFTA award for services to television, and near the 1908 typewriter on which he wrote more than 100 books. He was cheerfully honest about his hopelessness with the bat in Sussex club cricket, but he was more successful as a leg-spinner; his 14-pace run-up was typically eccentric. In one of his final books, *Can You Play Cricket on Mars?* (2008), he concluded that the contest would be heavily weighted in favour of batsmen, able to hit the ball enormous distances in the thin Martian atmosphere; bowlers would be unable to find any swing, always assuming they could cope with a bulky space suit.

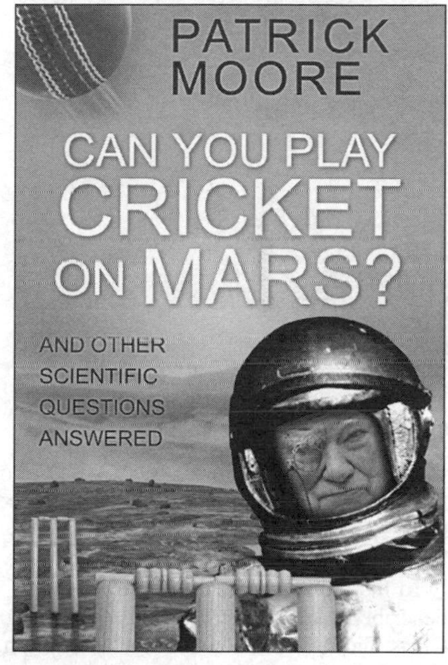

MORTON, RUNAKO SHAKUR, was killed in a car accident on March 4. He was driving home from a club match at the Queen's Park Oval when his car hit a telegraph pole on the Solomon Hochoy Highway in central Trinidad. He was 33.

Morton was originally from Nevis, which has defied its minuscule size and population (around 12,000) to produce six Test players. His promise was recognised as early as 1996, when he was picked for the regional Under-19 team in three matches against their Pakistani counterparts in the Caribbean. A strong and aggressive batsman, if predominantly bottom-handed, he became one of the leading scorers for the Leeward Islands, amassing 4,104 runs at an average of 44 with 11 hundreds, among them successive innings of 210 against Barbados and 231 against the Combined Campuses & Colleges in 2009.

A volatile temperament that repeatedly led him into trouble, allied to technical defects, limited Morton's success at the highest level. Yet, as several of his team-mates attested, his love of the game could not be queried. The first of his widely publicised run-ins with authority led to his expulsion from the West Indian board's initial Academy in 2001. A year later, he left the Champions Trophy early after claiming his grandmother had died. She turned out to be hale and hearty, which – compounded by further indiscretions on an A-team tour – brought him a year-long ban. There were later clashes with the law: a year before his death he and fellow Nevisian Tonito Willett were charged by the T&T police with possession of marijuana, an accusation to which they pleaded not guilty. Friends reported that marriage to a Trinidadian woman, and bringing up their three children, had been a calming influence. After moving to Port-of-Spain, Morton piled up the runs for Queen's Park, Trinidad's oldest and most famous club, where he was a popular mentor to young players; chosen for T&T for what turned out to be his final season in 2011, he became one of the few to represent two territories in the regional first-class tournament.

The first of two strikes by senior players opened the way to his Test debut in Sri Lanka in 2005. Like many of the first-timers, he was embarrassed by the mesmerising spin of Muttiah Muralitharan and the swing of Chaminda Vaas. Still, Morton's breathtaking catching in the slips moved Ian Chappell, commentating on the series, to rate him the best in the position at the time. In 15 Tests up to 2008, going in mostly at No. 3 or 4, Morton averaged just 22. The closest he came to a hundred was at Napier in 2005-06; unbeaten on 70, he was denied by rain. His 67, against Australia at Sabina Park in 2007-08 in a fourth-wicket partnership of 128 with Shivnarine Chanderpaul, was probably his best innings – but the next Test was his last.

Jewel Samad, AFP/Getty Images

True warrior: Runako Morton in one-day mode, where he felt most at home.

Morton was more at home in one-day internationals, in which he averaged 33 despite being shuffled around the order: he was tried in every position from opener to No. 7. He scored centuries against New Zealand and Zimbabwe, although more representative of his belligerence and grit was an unbeaten 90 in Mumbai, in a victory over Australia that helped West Indies to the 2006 Champions Trophy final. Still, the contrasts which made Morton such an enigma had been typified only a few weeks earlier by an innings in a one-day international in Kuala Lumpur – also against Australia, he made a 31-ball duck, a record.

In his eulogy at a service in Trinidad which preceded the burial in Nevis, Brian Lara described Morton as "a fighter [who] worked harder than most, a true team man". And Chris Gayle, Lara's successor as captain, tweeted: "We lost a true warrior… heart of a lion. As captain at the time, I wish I had ten Mortons to lead on a cricket field!"

MUNIR MALIK, who died on November 30, aged 78, was a fast-medium bowler who played three Tests for Pakistan, two of them in 1962 in England, where he took five for 128 in 49 overs at Headingley. One spell from the Kirkstall Lane End lasted from 3pm on the Thursday to 1.30pm on the Friday. Munir had come to prominence with five for 12 and seven for 27 as Rawalpindi beat Peshawar in a Quaid-e-Azam Trophy match in December 1958, despite being bowled out for 53 in the first innings. He made his Test debut against Australia the following season, in a match watched by the American president Dwight Eisenhower. Munir's speciality, according to the Pakistani journalist Qamar Ahmed, was his "vicious leg-cutter, plus a ball which dipped in". His best innings return – eight for 154 – came in what turned out to be the last match of his ten-year career, for Karachi Whites against Punjab University at Lahore in April 1966.

MURRAY, LANCE HAMILTON, who died on October 21, aged 91, was a significant administrator in Trinidad and West Indies cricket. His flighted off-spin earned him three first-class matches, only one for the full Trinidad side – in 1956, the year the Trinidad & Tobago Cricket Board of Control replaced his own Queen's Park club as the sole authority for the sport in the country, a move he strongly supported. He was the new board's first vice-president, and their long-term representative on the West Indian board. He became more widely known as a radio analyst on regional and international matches in Port-of-

Spain – and through the success of his son Deryck Murray, the wicketkeeper who won 62 Test caps between 1963 and 1980. In 1992, Lance was awarded Trinidad and Tobago's second-highest honour, the Chaconia Medal, for his work in sports administration.

NAIDU, TORAM SHESHRAO, who died on April 1, aged 93, was believed to have been the oldest Indian first-class cricketer at the time of his death. Naidu had made his debut for Central Provinces and Berar against Douglas Jardine's 1933-34 MCC tourists, falling to the Kent leg-spinner "Father" Marriott for a duck. He did better in the second innings, making 32 in a useful stand with his captain, C. K. Nayudu. Naidu played six further first-class matches in a career that stretched to 1951-52, scoring 56 against Hyderabad in December 1945. He was a long-time friend of the former Indian board president N. K. P. Salve, who died on the same day.

NEBLETT, CLEMENT EVERTON, died on holiday in St Vincent in March, aged 61. Clem Neblett was a powerful left-hand batsman and right-arm medium-pacer whose heavy scoring for the Police club in his native Guyana merited more than six first-class matches before he emigrated to Toronto in 1978. He soon became one of the leading all-rounders in local club cricket, and captained Canada in the ICC Trophy tournaments in England in 1982 and 1986. At the time of his death, Neblett had been resident in the United States for nearly 20 years.

NIMBALKAR, BHAUSAHEB BABUSAHEB, who died on December 11, the day before his 93rd birthday, will always be remembered for an innings of 443 not out in 1948-49. Nimbalkar was closing in on what was then the world record – Don Bradman's 452 not out for New South Wales against Queensland in 1929-30 – when the opposition refused to play on. Kathiawar had been bowled out for 238 on the opening day at Poona, and when Maharashtra reached 826 for four by tea on the third, the Thakore Saheb of Rajkot – Kathiawar's princely leader – ordered the Maharashtra captain, Raja Gokhale, to declare. If not, his team were going home. Gokhale offered to stop after two more overs, to allow Nimbalkar a chance of the record – but Kathiawar simply packed their bags and left. "Their skipper felt the name of his team would figure in the record books for the wrong reasons," said Nimbalkar. "I was left stranded in the middle of the ground." Only at tea had Nimbalkar been told how close he was: "Had I known, I would have gone for the runs." He had hit 46 fours and a six during more than eight hours at the crease, but there was, though, some consolation. "I got a personal message from Sir Don Bradman," he said. "Even though he had the world record, and I had only the record in India, he still rated my innings as better." Strangely, Nimbalkar never won a Test cap, although he averaged more than 56 in a long Ranji Trophy career that stretched into the 1960s; his only taste of representative cricket was an unofficial Test against a Commonwealth XI in 1949-50, when he batted at No. 9 in both innings. "I don't know why the selectors sidelined me all the time," he said. "What really hurt me was that some less talented players got a chance to represent the country."

NORTON, GERALD IVOR DESMOND, died on July 18, aged 93. Ivor Norton was a talented slow left-armer who captained Malvern College in 1938. He had a long club career, and also played two first-class matches for MCC. In the first, in Dublin in 1958, he took four for 44, then five for 26, as Ireland – needing 97 to win a rain-affected match – hung on for a draw at 82 for nine. Two years later, back in Dublin and now 41 years old, he took six for 57 and two for six, to finish his brief first-class career with 17 wickets at 7.82. Norton's captain in both matches was George Chesterton, another distinguished Malvernian who died in 2012.

PAGARA, THE PIR (Syed Shah Mardan Shah II), who died on January 10, aged 83, was the spiritual leader of the Hurs, a Sufi Muslim community in Pakistan's Sind province. The Pir was also an early patron of Pakistan cricket, embracing the sport despite the fact that the colonial government had hanged his father during an insurrection in 1943. He refounded the Sind Cricket Association, and entered their team in the Quaid-e-Azam

Trophy: in his only first-class appearance he captained Sind against Bahawalpur in November 1953, scoring one and 15. Two seasons later, his own XI took on the touring MCC A-team at Hyderabad. He sponsored several promising cricketers; one of them, the Test fast bowler Mohammad Munaf, once hit him in the groin in the nets, and was dismayed to see a crowd of angry Hurs approaching with raised sticks. The Pir staggered to his feet and restored calm by assuring his followers he was all right. In later years he founded his own political party, the Pakistan Muslim League F (for "functional").

PAGE, GLENYS LYNNE, who died on November 7, aged 72, was a left-arm spinner who played twice for New Zealand in the inaugural women's World Cup, in England in 1973. In her first match, at St Albans, she took six for 20 as West Indies were skittled for 61. In December 1971, Page had taken eight for 54 for Auckland against Canterbury, and a few days later added seven for 55 against Otago.

PARR, FRANCIS DAVID, died on May 8, aged 83. There were some sound judges, Herbert Strudwick among them, who saw Frank Parr keep wicket for Lancashire in the early 1950s and concluded that a rival might be emerging for Godfrey Evans's England place. Instead, Parr's career ended after 49 matches when he became victim of the martinet Cyril Washbrook's promotion to the Lancashire captaincy. Washbrook took vigorous exception to Parr's immersion in jazz music, a world that could hardly have been more different from his captain's view of county cricket.

Parr employed the hands that were so dextrous in the wicketkeeper's gloves to play the trombone and, if his cricket career did not reach the predicted heights, his life as a musician proved more fulfilling. In the late '50s, he was a member of the highly regarded Mick Mulligan Band, with George Melly as lead singer, and also played on stage with Louis Armstrong. Parr was a scruffy bohemian with a relaxed approach to personal hygiene and a penchant for cigarettes and whisky. According to Brian Statham, he "looked what he was: a spare-time musician"; Melly felt he "concealed a formidable, well-read intelligence behind a stylised oafishness".

PA Photos

Always good company: Frank Parr.

He was born in Wallasey, on the Wirral, and made his Lancashire debut at Fenner's in 1951. The following summer, in only his second Championship appearance, he caught the attention of Strudwick at The Oval. And while his keeping to the spinners was a work in progress, he was acrobatic by the standards of the time, especially for a tall man. He was selected for MCC against Yorkshire at Lord's in 1953, and asked whether he might be available to tour the West Indies that winter. But he was not selected, and by July 1954 his first-class career was over.

The reason was simple: the intransigent Washbrook had taken over as captain from the easy-going Nigel Howard. He was enraged when Parr arrived for a House of Commons reception wearing a blue shirt and, when Parr produced an untidy performance at Bristol, it was just the excuse he'd been looking for. As the team prepared to head to Edgbaston, Washbrook told him: "Frank, you're going home." Exiled to the Seconds, Parr began to play better than ever, leading to discussions about a move to Worcestershire. He might have thrived in the relaxed atmosphere of New Road, but Washbrook put paid to those ambitions with a letter to Worcestershire calling him a "grave social risk". Parr was devastated. "It's probably when I took up serious drinking," he said.

He moved to London and joined the Mick Mulligan Band, whose chaotic years on the road are detailed in Melly's book *Owning Up*, which devotes six pages to Parr. He continued to play cricket with a wandering team of jazz musicians called The Ravers, keeping wicket immaculately beyond the age of 60. In his final years, he lived in a council flat not far from Lord's, where the writer Stephen Chalke was a visitor: "He was a good man, intelligent and sensitive, who lived in a state of complete and utter squalor, existing on coffee, whisky and the odd sausage." Parr was a regular at ex-players' evenings at Old Trafford, where Jim Cumbes, the former Lancashire chief executive, recalled: "He used to walk in without fuss, very unobtrusively, looking for the bar. He'd order a large scotch, however early it was. He was always good company."

PATEL, SANTILAL KARA, who died on November 11, aged 90, was a South African administrator, notably as treasurer of the (non-white) Natal Cricket Board for 14 years from 1977-78, after which they united with the "white" association as the integration process cranked into gear. He was involved with Durban's Bharat club for more than 50 years.

PAWSON, HENRY ANTHONY, OBE, died on October 11, aged 91. Tony Pawson was one of the last of the brilliant all-round sportsmen who emerged from the public schools and bestrode English sport in the first half of the 20th century. He had a good war, became a successful cricketer and footballer, and world champion fly-fisherman; he later combined a career in business with journalism for *The Observer* and 14 books. Small and self-effacing almost to vanishing point, he would hardly be noticed amid the bustle of a press box. "Modesty" did not do his demeanour justice: Pawson exuded, if anyone cared to notice, a kind of serenity.

He was the son of Guy Pawson, who captained Oxford in 1910, then joined the Sudan Civil Service: the first fish Tony almost caught was a Nile perch so large it almost caught him. As a 15-year-old at Winchester, he made 237 in a colts match at Lord's, and in 1940 he emerged, said *Wisden*, as school cricket's "batsman of the year" – a cutter and hooker "with a vigilance in defence beyond his years". Thrust into the war, he was commissioned in the Rifle Brigade, attaining the rank of major, saw active service in Italy and North Africa, and was mentioned in despatches. His exploits included taking part in the bloody battle of Fondouk Pass in 1943, a tank attack he compared to the Charge of the Light Brigade. Once, a bullet passed through his forage cap. Having survived all that, he not surprisingly revelled in the joys of post-war cricket. However, his approach to sport, as well as his status, was amateur. Called up by Kent straight after demob in 1946, he made 90 on debut against Hampshire, and was soon given his cap and told by his captain Bryan Valentine he was in for the season. "Sorry, skipper, I'm off fishing," came the reply.

Pawson appeared intermittently, but often successfully, for Kent until 1953. His batting never lost its youthful vigour, and his nifty singles were much appreciated by the spectators (though not by some of the old pros). But his remark to Valentine set the tone: he had too much else to do. At first, this was university: he made 135 in the 1947 Varsity Match, and the following year emulated his father by captaining Oxford to victory at Lord's. Pawson was also a fine footballer – a Blue, an England amateur international, and an Olympian in 1948, before making two appearances for Charlton in the First Division in 1951-52. Asked if he might turn out occasionally, he agreed – assuming that meant the reserves – in return for tickets to the Christmas Day match against Spurs. At the game, the manager, Jimmy Seed, asked him if he fancied turning out on the wing in the return fixture next day. Advised merely to have a pre-match whisky to steady his nerves, he scored the winner. But his main football fame was as the speedy right-winger of the sensational Pegasus team of Oxbridge types that won the Amateur Cup in 1953.

On weekdays, Pawson rose to personnel director of Reed International. In 1968, however, he became cricket and football correspondent of *The Observer*. Although very part-time, he was game enough to head off from a Test and cover a First Division match immediately afterwards. His writing was elegant rather than glittering, but his work could

Patrick Eagar

Still vigorous: Tony Pawson bats for Bertie Joel's XI v Reg Hayter's XI in February 1974. John Murray, of Middlesex and England, keeps wicket.

reveal the competitive steel that underlay his bland persona and apparent dilettantism. For the Cricket Writers' Club collection of essays, *Cricket Heroes*, he chose Douglas Jardine. He explained: "Whatever your attitude to a game, if you play at any level, you should play to win, with every fibre of your being devoted to doing well." And Pawson lived up to his motto in 1984, becoming – at the age of 62 – the first Briton to win the world fly-fishing championship, catching 23 trout in three four-hour sessions on the River Tormes in Spain, the ultimate triumph for his understated skill and determination.

PEART, ERROL, was shot dead in Miami on December 2. He was 59, and had been trying to prevent a robbery at the car wash he owned. Peart, a Jamaican-born opener, was the leading run-scorer for the United States in the 1990 ICC Trophy in the Netherlands with 209, including a century against East and Central Africa.

PERERA, JAYALATHGE BERNARD NIHAL, died on November 9, aged 56. Bernard Perera was one of the Sri Lankan players who took part in an unauthorised tour of apartheid South Africa in 1982, which in effect ended his chances of an international career (the players were originally banned for 25 years, although this was lifted after eight). He went on to coach the national women's team. A hard-hitting batsman and fine fielder, Perera was Sri Lanka's twelfth man in their first official Test, against England in Colombo early in 1982, and toured Pakistan shortly afterwards. But he could not break into the side – despite making 56 not out for the Board President's XI in England's warm-up game – and signed up for the rebel tour later the same year. His only century came on that trip, in his final first-class match: 102 against a strong South African XI, who won by an innings at Cape Town thanks in part to Graeme Pollock, who fell to Perera's off-spin for 197.

PERERA, SOMACHANDRA SARANAPALA, died on October 3, aged around 86. Chandra Perera was a Sri Lankan cricket historian and statistician, dubbed the "Walking Wisden" by friends. He used to collect scraps of information and keep them in cardboard boxes, which came in useful in 1999 for a 600-page collection of trivia and statistics called the *Janashakthi Book of Cricket*, which covered 165 years of the game in Sri Lanka. Perera also produced several books on Sri Lankan schools' cricket, and numerous souvenir programmes for touring teams.

PILLING, HARRY, who died on September 22, aged 69, was 5ft 3in and thought at the time to be the smallest player in county cricket. But his height proved no impediment during the late 1960s and early '70s, when Lancashire were the best one-day side in the country. Pilling's frequent partnerships with Clive Lloyd – more than a foot taller – provided an engaging study in contrasts. Once, the story goes, the two were standing together between overs. "Pilling," said the TV commentator, "is the one in the cap."

Pilling began his cricketing life with Staley in the Saddleworth League and, after leaving school, joined Lancashire in 1959 aged 16. Not that the game brought great security: for much of his career he had to find work when the season finished. He made coffins, was an apprentice butcher, put the handles on umbrellas, and worked in a cotton mill. He even shovelled coal. "I was No. 1 shoveller," he boasted. "Three shovelfuls to a bag – not bad for somebody of my size." When he joined the staff, he was a leg-spinner standing only 4ft 7in and weighing little more than five stone. Jam and bread, he said, had been among his most regular meals. And the Old Trafford he walked into could be unpleasant: the atmosphere was shaped by autocrats such as Cyril Washbrook ("an arrogant professional who wished he was an amateur," reckoned Harry), and it would be nearly another decade until Lancashire's modernisation was led by Jack Bond. "They called them the good old days," said Pilling, "but they weren't always."

Patrick Eagar

"A nicker and a nudger": Harry Pilling, 1971.

For three years he played for the Second Eleven and, when the call came for a first-class match, it was unexpected. "Stand up and give Pierre a round of applause," ordered coach Stan Worthington. Pilling – who had a haircut his team-mates thought made him look like a Frenchman – said: "It were embarrassing. I had to climb off bus past 'em all clapping." Pilling played under three captains before Lancashire settled for Bond in 1968. He created a side, partly by accident, which was ideal for the newish game of one-day cricket. Lloyd and Farokh Engineer arrived, Bond was interested in fielding as an attacking strategy, and young locals such as David Hughes and Jack Simmons were, in Pilling's words, the "kamikaze pilots" who thrashed lower-order runs. The result was Sunday League titles in 1969 and 1970, and a hat-trick of Gillette Cups from 1970. Pilling – now a top-order batsman – was Man of the Match in the first final, despite fearing the format would kill his career. "I was a nicker and a nudger," he said. "I wasn't a big strokeplayer. I thought the one-day stuff was just crash-bang-wallop." As it turned out, his skills of deflection and placement, and his square cut, were perfect attributes: he was the first player to reach 1,000 runs in the Sunday League. "We all adored him in the dressing-room," said the fast bowler Peter Lever. "He was the essence of Lancastrian cricket. It was almost as if he would die for his team-mates."

Pilling scored more than 15,000 first-class runs, but never played for England. He came close twice, in 1970 and 1976, when a pair of hundreds in July looked likely to win him a place against West Indies. He remembered driving with the radio on, listening to the squad being called. "They went past 'P' and I thought: 'That's that, then.' I'd have loved to have played. Just to get one cap and be given the chance. But I wasn't everyone's favourite person." The dressing-room whisper, perhaps apocryphal, was that Washbrook – who had been an England selector – had warned: "Forget it. He's a drunkard." Pilling gladly admitted to liking a few pints, and grinned that he would add a couple of miles to his petrol claims on away trips to pay for them. In truth, he liked too many, and it was after his career ended in 1982 that his drinking became particularly damaging. He described his local pub as "all effin' and blindin' and gum boots". His best mate at Lancashire had been John Sullivan, a former amateur boxing champion, and the pair caused mischief for years. Their dressing-room nicknames of H. Dirt and J. Filth summed up their relationship and pursuits. "We were in a club one night," said Harry, "and some bloke tried to touch John up in t'toilet, so Sully smacked him once and he were flat out on t'stones."

There were many more such tales, some of which Pilling would retell at his bungalow outside Bolton. Speaking with quiet generosity of those he had played with and against, he sipped from a pint mug of tea and drew on a roll-up. His little dog never left his side, knowing there were boiled sweets in the pocket of his tracksuit trousers. "No matter where Harry goes now," said Jack Simmons at his funeral, "he will be loved, because he'll be as popular as he ever was."

RAIT KERR, DIANA MARY, who died on December 18, aged 94, was the first curator of the MCC Collection, principally responsible for the vast array of cricket memorabilia accrued at Lord's over the years. Appointed in 1945, she oversaw the establishment of the MCC museum in 1953; previously, the most interesting items were dotted around the Pavilion. Her father, Colonel R. S. Rait Kerr, was the club's secretary from 1936 to 1952, and "Miss RK" was one of the first women to attend an MCC dinner (in 1964, when the president Dick Twining began the evening with a well-received "Lady and gentlemen"). She was also – 31 years after her retirement – one of the first group of lady members elected in 1999. Rait Kerr co-wrote (with Ian Peebles) *Lord's 1946–70*, a substantial sequel to Sir Pelham Warner's earlier history of MCC and Lord's. Although she had no formal library training, she became an expert on cricket's literary and artistic history, and especially the evolution of players' dress. She was a stickler for convention, and her sucessor Stephen Green for years remained worried that she might make an impromptu visit – or "inspection" – of the museum. "She did present an air of formidability," agreed Trefor Jones, another Lord's colleague. "But actually she was a typical English colonel's daughter of that era, with more good-natured warmth about her than was apparent on first acquaintance." (See also page 41.)

RANA, NARENDRASINH PRATAPSINH, who died of liver failure on May 17, aged 41, was a tall fast bowler who took the new ball for Saurashtra for several seasons in the Ranji Trophy, occasionally with his younger brother Mahendrasinh. Opening the bowling for a weakish team on batsman-friendly pitches at Rajkot meant his overall figures were uninspiring – 46 wickets at 55, with a best of four for 66 against Maharashtra in November 1998 – but team-mates recalled a naturally talented cricketer, from a prominent local family, who was also a handy batsman.

RANDALL, DAVID AARON, who died of bowel cancer on July 6, aged 27, was a fine schoolboy batsman who had been in the running for a place in the England Under-15 team, alongside his friend and club-mate Alastair Cook – they played together for Essex's youth teams, and also for Maldon. Cook attended Randall's funeral, and a few days later scored his 20th Test century against South Africa at The Oval. "It's been an emotional time," he said. "We're lucky enough to play cricket, aren't we? Unfortunately he can't any more."

RAZAULLAH KHAN, who died on November 5, aged 75, played 24 matches for various first-class teams in a long career in Pakistan that stretched from 1957-58 to 1972-73, usually keeping wicket. He made 76, his highest score, opening for Khairpur against Karachi Blues – containing the future Test all-rounder Asif Iqbal, whom he stumped – in Lahore in 1961-62. Later he became president of the Hyderabad Cricket Association and a Pakistan board council member, and managed the national Under-19 side.

REES-MOGG, LORD (William), who died on December 29, aged 84, was editor of *The Times* between 1967 and 1981, and a prominent Establishment figure for many years after that, yet he was best remembered for an editorial written in July 1967 that flew defiantly in the face of Britain's ruling classes. Headlined "Who breaks a butterfly on a wheel?" it criticised the prison sentences handed out to Rolling Stones Mick Jagger and Keith Richards for minor drug offences, sparking an outcry that led to their release.

Rees-Mogg was descended from a line of Somerset squires, and his roots remained planted in the county's soil, even when he held high-profile metropolitan positions. He was an enthusiastic supporter of Somerset cricket, wrote frequently about the game, and had seen hundreds by Hammond and Bradman. When he picked his Somerset dream team for *The Times* in 2007, it drew on decades of first-hand experience. He was also waiting by the phone on the afternoon of September 16, 2010, when Somerset were on the brink of winning the County Championship for the first time. Rees-Mogg was only too willing to write an exultant piece for next day's paper, but Nottinghamshire snatched the title.

At Charterhouse he was a contemporary of Peter May and was taught by Robert Arrowsmith, the obituaries editor of *Wisden*. Rees-Mogg was also the first-team scorer – John Woodcock called him "the keeper of the scorebook and, later, of *The Times*" – and he sometimes introduced cricket into opinion pieces about the great political issues of the day. Writing in *The Sunday Times* in 1964, he called for Alec Douglas-Home's resignation in a piece headlined "A Captain's Innings". In 1994, he wrote a remarkably deft critique of another prime minister's leadership: it did not mention John Major by name, but discussed at length the worthy, unspectacular attributes of the Somerset all-rounder Bertie Buse.

ROBINSON, ALEXANDER WILLIAM, died on June 18, aged 87. His first-class career for Western Australia was confined to two matches in 1952-53, but Alex Robinson had a lasting influence in Perth as a club and school coach, and was one of the first to recognise the potential of the teenage Dennis Lillee. He later gained a master's degree in recreation management from Loughborough University, and moved from teaching to sports administration, eventually being appointed deputy director of WA's Department of Sport and Recreation. Robinson abhorred the sponsorship of sport by tobacco and alcohol companies, both on health and moral grounds, and ultimately resigned from his State coaching positions. His father (also Alex) represented WA against the 1907-08 MCC tourists and was an outstanding Australian Rules footballer, while his older brother, George, played an important role as a batsman when the state won the Sheffield Shield at their first attempt, in 1947-48.

ROBINSON, HENRY BASIL OSWIN, died on December 21, aged 93. A Rhodes Scholar from Canada, Basil Robinson was a sharp-turning off-spinner who won Blues at Oxford in 1947 and 1948. He took six for 55, which remained his best figures, against Worcestershire at New Road in his first season, and added six more in the 1947 Varsity Match, dismissing Trevor Bailey in the first innings and Doug Insole in the second. The following year Robinson took five for 60 against Sussex, but was needed for only three wicketless overs at Lord's as Oxford's seamers wrapped up an innings victory. Robinson went back to Vancouver after that, but returned to England in 1954 as captain of a strong Canadian touring team. He became a diplomat, and later wrote a biography of Canada's prime minister John Diefenbaker, as well as a family history entitled *This Family Robinson.*

ROWLANDS, MEYRICK, collapsed and died shortly after being dismissed in a cricket match in Hook, Pembrokeshire, on July 24. He was 60, and had retired as headmaster of the nearby Pennar Community School only four days earlier. "Cricket was his great passion," said his colleague Martin Cavaney, one of the school's governors.

SAFIULLAH KHAN, who died on March 20, aged 71, was a left-arm seamer who played 42 first-class matches in Pakistan, mainly for Peshawar, between 1957 and 1975. He took nine for 62 against Railways B at Peshawar in March 1972, and later took up umpiring, standing in several first-class matches.

SALVE, NARENDRA KUMAR PRASADRAO, who died on April 1, aged 91, is the man usually credited with moving the World Cup to the subcontinent. He was the Indian board president at the time of India's upset victory over West Indies in the 1983 final and, having had trouble obtaining tickets for the big match at Lord's, hatched the plan over lunch the following day with his Pakistan counterpart, Nur Khan. There was a general assumption that the 1987 tournament, like its three predecessors, would be held in England – but Salve, a long-serving Congress Party MP and minister in Rajiv Gandhi's government, challenged that cosy arrangement, mobilising the support of sympathetic Full and Associate Members of the ICC in a way not seen before, if increasingly familiar since. The 1987 World Cup was indeed staged in India and Pakistan, with the final at Kolkata: "He was responsible for it becoming the global event it is today," said N. Srinivasan, the current BCCI president. Salve was a useful club player in his youth in Nagpur, and also umpired three first-class games in the early 1950s. The annual Challenger Trophy (trial matches for India's one-day side) is named after him.

SARAIYA, SURESH, who died on July 18, aged 76, had been a popular broadcaster on Test cricket since 1969, usually for All India Radio. "Few commentators had his desire and preparation," remembered his colleague Harsha Bhogle. "He was like a child when we broadcast from South Africa in 1992 – he had tears that morning in Durban, when India played South Africa's first home Test since 1970."

SARGENT, MURRAY ALFRED JAMES, died on February 28, aged 83. A late bloomer, Sargent had batted without distinction for the Glenelg club in Adelaide for over a decade from 1947-48. During that time he had two seasons with Leicestershire, where modest success in the Second Eleven was not repeated in the senior side: in 1952, he averaged under 12 from 18 innings. But at the end of the 1950s he suddenly flowered as an opener, and at 32 found himself partnering Les Favell for South Australia for one successful season. Sargent's obdurate methods brought him 164 in nearly nine hours against Queensland. It was then back to grade cricket, where his run-making continued for another decade. He later turned to administration, serving as a South Australian selector for seven seasons from 1984-85, and Glenelg's president for 17.

SATHE, ISHAN SUBODH, was found dead on April 18. He was 20. A promising leg-spinner who had played for Vidarbha's age-group teams and in trials for India's Under-19 side, Sathe was found hanging from the ceiling fan in his room, not long after an argument with his girlfriend. Narendra Hirwani said: "He had that rare ability to turn the ball sharply." Sathe had also caught the eye of Sachin Tendulkar, who arranged for him to train with the Mumbai Indians, his IPL team.

SHARP, PETER ANDREW, who died on February 18, aged 72, played eight first-class matches for Canterbury as an off-spinner in the 1960s, taking 21 wickets, but was better known as a radio commentator. "One of the most famous voices in New Zealand cricket has fallen silent," said his colleague Bruce Russell.

SLACK, JOHN KENNETH EDWARD, DL, who died on May 6, aged 81, scored 135 on his first-class debut, for Cambridge University against Middlesex at Fenner's in 1954, and did enough in the other matches of his final year to win a Blue, although he was out for 12 and nought in the drawn Varsity Match at Lord's. That was the end of his first-class cricket: he turned down an offer to play for Middlesex, preferring to concentrate on his legal career, in which he rose to become a circuit judge known for his expertise in fraud trials. Slack had not finished with cricket, though: a club regular for Beaconsfield, he played for Buckinghamshire, and captained them from 1967 to 1969.

SMITH, ARCHIBALD WILLIAM, died on November 1, aged 89. Archie Smith was a pillar of Cornwall's Minor Counties side for many years, taking 135 wickets, including nine for 49 against Oxfordshire at Penzance in 1953. A headmaster, he founded the Cornwall Schools' Cricket Association in 1956, and was their first secretary (and treasurer until 1977). "He was a real gentleman cricketer," said his friend Michael Williams, a local author. "He never appealed for an lbw unless he was absolutely certain it was necessary."

SNOW, PHILIP ALBERT, OBE, who died on June 5, aged 96, was a first-class cricketer by virtue of five matches, captaining Fiji on a tour of New Zealand in 1947-48. These were given first-class status many years later, almost entirely due to Snow's own lobbying at Lord's. The tour caused considerable interest since the Fijian players (not Snow) wore traditional skirts and no shoes, and entertained the crowds with South Sea songs. The team were competitive too, and beat both Wellington and Auckland. As a cricketer, he failed to get even a trial at Cambridge, but in 1937 and 1938 he captained Leicestershire's Second Eleven, before being appointed an administrator and magistrate in Fiji. He was instantly elected chairman of the Suva Cricket Club, and fell in love with the place. After the war, he founded the Fiji Cricket Association, and set about organising the New Zealand tour. On return to England, he became bursar of Rugby School and, in 1965, Fiji's representative on the International Cricket Conference (later Council), a post he retained for a record 30 years, devotedly championing Fiji's cause. He wrote several books, mainly about the South Seas and his family. He also wrote at least twice in old age to the editor of *Wisden* enclosing his biography for the benefit of his obituarist, in the hope that he would match his older brothers (the novelist C. P. Snow and the Leicestershire cricket historian E. E. Snow) by being included. That he has achieved, but perhaps his greatest wish – the advancement of Fijian cricket – remains unfulfilled.

SPURRIER, MICHAEL CUMBY, who died on July 9, aged 79, was acknowledged as the leading expert on military links with cricket, a subject he covered in some detail in *Wisden Cricket Monthly* in a series on cricketers decorated for gallantry. He had been in the army himself – a major in the Durham Light Infantry – and was apparently once in charge of transport on an exercise in which he started with 400 vehicles, and returned with 401.

SRINIVASAN, KRISHNASWAMI, died on April 27, aged 82. "Balaji" Srinivasan was an attacking batsman and a polished wicketkeeper who played for Mysore (now Karnataka). He scored 106 against Madras in 1952-53, and the following year played twice for India against a strong Commonwealth XI, in what he was later disappointed to discover were unofficial Tests. Opening in the first one at Nagpur after Frank Worrell had stroked 165, Srinivasan made 67. He was a keen student of the game. "I was interested in the poetry and prose of cricket," he said. "It made my modest career colourful and enjoyable."

STOVOLD, MARTIN WILLIS, died on May 11, aged 56. The younger brother of Andy, who had a long career with Gloucestershire, Martin Stovold played for the county too, although his best score in 25 matches was an unbeaten 75 against Oxford University in the Parks in 1980. He managed a solitary half-century in the Championship, 52 against Warwickshire at Nuneaton in 1982, in his penultimate match. After a spell in South Africa, where he coached the young Jacques Kallis in Cape Town, he returned home and took charge of the cricket at Cheltenham College.

SURENDRANATH, RAMAN, who died on May 5, aged 75, was an army officer and hard-working medium-pacer who played 11 Tests for India. He was effective in England in 1959, taking 16 wickets at 26 in a series India lost 5–0, with five-fors at Old Trafford and The Oval. The pick, though, was probably the inswinger that knocked back Peter May's off stump at Lord's. In all, Surendranath took 79 wickets on that tour (only the leg-spinner Subhash Gupte had more, with 95), although *Wisden* was rather sniffy about his tactic of bowling down the leg side to keep the runs down. His Test career was over within 18 months, but he played on for Services until 1968-69. He had taken seven for 14 and six for 62 for them against Railways in Delhi in January 1959, not long after winning his first Test cap, against West Indies, and made 119 against Southern Punjab at Patiala in December 1961.

SWABY, EATON OHIO, who died on February 9, aged 85, was a Jamaican-born fast bowler who made a name for himself in club cricket in south London. He took more than 1,000 first-team wickets for Mitcham – where part of the outfield of their ancient ground became known as "Swabes's Corner" – before joining Sutton CC in his fifties and turning to coaching.

Clint Hughes, Getty Images

"A giant": Heindrich Swanepoel bowls for England's blind team, June 2012.

SWANEPOEL, HEINDRICH, who died of a suspected heart attack while on holiday in Morocco in October, aged 43, was a pillar of England's blind cricket team, almost ever-present since the side were formed in 1996. He played for the Metro club in London, and was part of the team that won the Blind Ashes in 2004 and 2008. He won a bronze medal in the javelin at the 2000 Sydney Paralympics. "Heindrich was a giant," said the ECB's disability cricket manager Ian Martin, "both in physical stature and in terms of his contribution to the blind game as a player and an administrator."

TAYLOR, PHILIP HENRY, who died on December 1, aged 95, had been the oldest surviving England football international: he won three caps in 1947. He was a key member of the Liverpool team that won the first post-war League Championship in 1946-47, and captained them in the 1950 FA Cup final against Arsenal. Taylor, who was born in Bristol, also excelled at cricket, and opened the batting for Gloucestershire Second Eleven in the late 1930s. For his one first-class outing, however, he batted at No. 8, making two and 12 in a ten-wicket defeat by Kent at Gloucester in June 1938. He later managed Liverpool, and his resignation in 1959 paved the way for the arrival of Bill Shankly.

THAKURI, GANESH BAHADUR SHAHI, died on December 13, aged 40. A wicketkeeper-batsman who played in the 2001 ICC Trophy in Canada, he was "the best Nepali wicketkeeper I have seen," according to the former national captain Pawan Agrawal. "More importantly, he was a better human being."

THOMAS, DAVID JAMES, died of multiple sclerosis on July 28, aged 53. There was a time in the early 1980s when David "Teddy" Thomas looked as if he was shaping up to be just the sort of cricketer England were looking for. A left-arm quick bowler who threw everything into his delivery stride following an energetic run-up, he might have added useful variety to the attack, and contributed rapid runs down the order. But he never got the chance to be the new Botham, perhaps because the old Botham was still in full working order. Thomas was named in squads for home Tests, and was twelfth man at Trent Bridge against New Zealand in 1983. It was as close as he came.

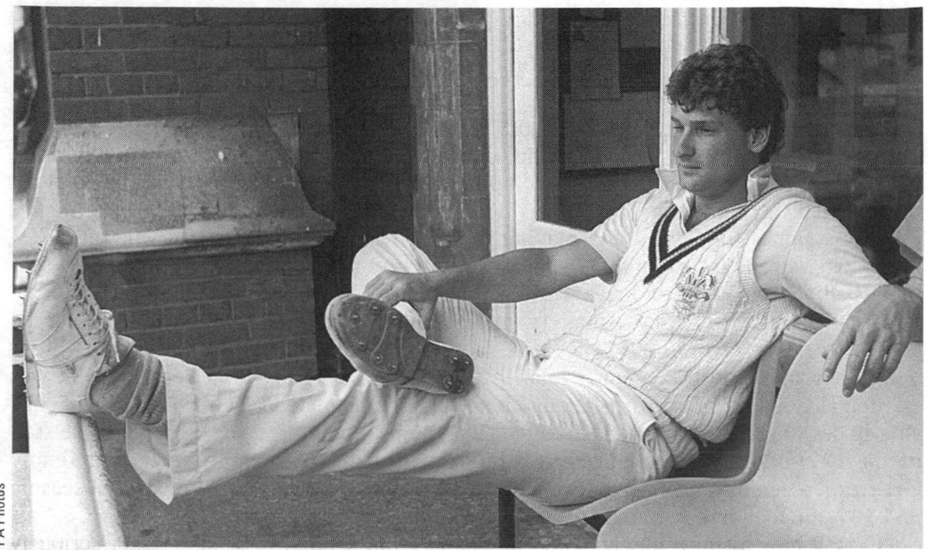

FA Photos

Putting his feet up: David Thomas shows he could also take things slowly.

Not that he was a man to let it spoil his fun. Thomas – the "Teddy" sobriquet was bestowed because of a hairstyle that had echoes of the 1950s – was a valued member of the Surrey team for ten years, not just for his wickets and runs but for his sense of humour. He also spent one season with Gloucestershire, and in South Africa played for Natal and North Transvaal. But his career ended at 29 when he was diagnosed with MS. He spent his final years in a wheelchair, but remained a jocular, upbeat figure who relished reunions with former colleagues. He had been a chairman of Surrey's former players' association.

Thomas came to the attention of Surrey while playing for Beaconsfield, and made his first-class debut in 1977, aged 18. Micky Stewart had captained him in club and ground games, and thought him "hyperactive but a loveble, likeable lad. He couldn't do anything slowly". Stewart also recognised his talent: "He had quick hands with the bat and he could whack it. He was an exciting cricketer." Three appearances for England Under-19s against West Indies in 1978 underlined his potential, but progress for Surrey was no more than steady. Robin Jackman remembered: "He bowled his left-armers at a lively pace and with aggression, but he struggled to swing the ball back into the right hander, which would have produced many more wickets. Against left-handers, bowled and lbw became serious options."

Thomas had two exceptional summers for Surrey. In 1983, he took 57 wickets at 31 and scored 937 runs at 36, including centuries against Nottinghamshire and Sussex. The following season he took 60 wickets at 27, including a career-best six for 36 against Somerset at The Oval. Another great moment came in the 1982 NatWest final, when Surrey at last won a one-day trophy after three successive defeats. Thomas took the match award for his three for 26, including Dennis Amiss and Geoff Humpage for ducks. But after 1984 his returns became more modest as injuries reduced his effectiveness. He moved to Gloucestershire in 1988, but MS was discovered when he was examined for a neck injury sustained in a car accident while he had been at Surrey. He retired after making 150 first-class appearances, in which he took 336 wickets at just under 34, and scored 3,044 runs at 20. He was, however, a cricketer remembered for more than bare statistics. "He brought life and soul into any dressing-room," said Jackman.

THOMAS, MALCOLM CAMPBELL, who died on April 9, aged 82, played four times for Cornwall in the 1951 Minor Counties Championship, scoring 56 at The Oval against Surrey's Second Eleven. But he found greater fame in rugby, as a goal-kicking centre who won 27 caps for Wales (two as captain) and played four times for the British Lions. He scored the decisive try against Ireland as Wales clinched the Triple Crown in 1950, and later that year was the leading points-scorer for the Lions in Australasia.

TINDALL, RONALD ALBERT ERNEST, OAM, who died on September 9, aged 76, was one of that elite band of sportsmen who packed away their bat as the county season came to a close and immediately donned boots to spend the next eight months playing professional football. Ron Tindall was no makeweight at either sport, appearing in 173 first-class games for Surrey and playing 368 Football League games for Chelsea, West Ham, Reading and Portsmouth. "I was busy all year round," he said.

Tindall was a south Londoner, born in Streatham, and came to the attention of Surrey while playing in Camberley. An aggressive batsman, off-spin bowler and agile fielder, he signed on at The Oval in 1952, aged 16, but did not make his first-class debut until four years later, and only became a regular in 1960. Progress in his winter employment was swifter. He joined Chelsea in 1953, and made his first-team debut in November 1955, in a side in decline after winning the League Championship the previous season. At the start of the 1957-58 campaign, he began a productive partnership with 17-year-old Jimmy Greaves ("a genius", said Tindall) that brought them a joint tally of 38 goals that season, and 59 – still a club record – in 1960-61.

He may have been a bigger name in football, but Tindall took his cricket seriously enough to negotiate a contract that allowed him to miss the end of one football season and the start of the next. These were difficult years at Surrey, no longer the dominant force in the domestic game, and they were grateful for Tindall's steady contributions. In 1962, he scored 777 runs and took 66 wickets, which included his best bowling, five for 41 against Cambridge University at The Oval. Next summer he passed 1,000 runs for the only time, making a career-best 109 not out, also at his home ground, against Nottinghamshire.

In truth, though, he was valued in the dressing-room as much for his elaborate jokes, which meandered to a punchline. And, when captain Micky Stewart introduced football as a means of warming up in the mornings, he was especially popular – at least if he was on your side. Tindall foresaw a future in football coaching or management, and retired from cricket in 1966. By this time, he was playing for Portsmouth – a defender now, rather than a forward – before becoming player/coach, then manager in 1970. Later in the decade, he

Patrick Eagar

Surrey reunited: Peter Loader, Ron Tindall, Jim Laker, Tony Lock and Ken Barrington at Perth, 1978.

joined his former Oval team-mates Tony Lock and Peter Loader in Western Australia, where he became director of coaching with the state football federation. Over nearly 30 years he established a considerable reputation, and in 2008 he was awarded the Order of Australia Medal for services to sport.

TOOVEY, ERNEST ALBERT, OAM, MBE, died on July 18, aged 90. The record books would suggest Ernie Toovey had an unspectacular career as a left-hand batsman for Queensland during the first half of the 1950s; his peak was in 1951-52, when he made five half-centuries. He often had to rein in his attacking instincts to shore up his side's fragile batting, and his total of 150 runs in the match against Victoria at the MCG in December 1951 took almost seven hours. During his second-innings 87, he became, according to him, the only batsman to hit mystery spinner Jack Iverson for six in a first-class match, a feat he would recount with relish. Next season, Toovey slipped the leash against the South Africans at Brisbane, hitting 71 in a partnership of 102 in 89 minutes with Ron Archer. In the outfield, he was both brilliant and sure, and his speed across the ground and the bullet-like accuracy of his returns saved countless runs. He was a state selector for 25 years from 1961-62, helping to lay the foundation for Queensland's long-awaited Sheffield Shield title in 1995-96. Toovey was also proud of having captained his club side, Norths, with Ray Lindwall as his bowling spearhead.

As a 19-year-old, Ordinary Seaman Toovey, unlike 353 of his shipmates, survived the sinking of the HMAS *Perth* in the Battle of the Sunda Strait early in 1942. The price of survival, however, was three and a half years as a prisoner of the Japanese, much of it on the Burma railway, where a severely ulcerated leg threatened to turn gangrenous. Toovey dismissed any talk of amputation and underwent excruciating treatment: "Not on your life, I'm going to need that leg to play Sheffield Shield cricket for Queensland." Early in his captivity, he took part in several baseball matches as a member of an Australian team organised by his camp's commandant. When a match was organised against the Japanese guards, Toovey cautioned his side that defeat was the better part of valour. After the war, he gave many years to the Returned Services League and the Australian Prisoners of War Association. Much later, he wrote a privately published book on his experiences as a PoW. David Frith, a long-standing friend, paid tribute to an "archetypal Queenslander of the old school: very friendly and generous. Although his memories of his wartime traumas dogged him until the end, he was an infallibly cheerful bloke".

Toovey subsequently represented Queensland in the Claxton Shield, the national baseball carnival. He was appointed MBE in 1985, and 15 years later received the Medal of the Order of Australia "for service to the welfare of veterans and their families through the RSL, and to cricket and baseball in Australia".

Picture Post, Getty Images

A real bunsen: Barry Trapnell in the lab of the Royal Institution, 1948.

TRAPNELL, BARRY MAURICE WALLER, CBE, DL, who died on August 1, aged 88, was a medium-pacer whose nine first-class matches – all in 1946 – included one for the Gentlemen against the Players at Lord's, in which he opened the bowling and dismissed Cyril Washbrook (although not before he had made 105). Trapnell had also played in the Varsity Match at Lord's a fortnight earlier, when his 41 and four wickets could not prevent an Oxford victory. And just before that, he had taken five for 73 for Cambridge against MCC, also at Lord's. Towards the end of the season he played his only Championship game, Middlesex's top-of-the-table clash with eventual champions Yorkshire at Sheffield in mid-August. After this busy summer Trapnell concentrated on his work, becoming a chemistry don at Cambridge, and later headmaster of Denstone College and Oundle School. He was the national Rugby fives champion in 1949.

TURNER, JOHN BERNARD, who died on September 13, aged 63, was a tall opening batsman who scored a record 7,524 runs for Buckinghamshire in the Minor Counties Championship. He played only one first-class match, for the Minor Counties XI against the Pakistan tourists at Jesmond in 1974 – but made it count, hitting 106 in the second innings against a new-ball attack of Asif Masood and Imran Khan.

VAN HEERDEN, CARL, who died on June 19, aged 78, was president of the Free State Cricket Union from 1994 to 1998. Two of his sons played first-class cricket in South Africa.

VINICOMBE, JOHN BROOKS, who died on October 6, 2011, aged 82, was the main sports writer of the Brighton *Evening Argus* from 1962 to 1994. In a town where the football and cricket teams always produced lively copy in good times and bad, Vinicombe was a well-informed and robust chronicler of their affairs. He greeted visiting journalists at Sussex matches with a warmth tinged by a sardonic humour about the incompetence of the universe, which he would have brought to bear on *Wisden* for being a year late reporting his death.

VORSTER, LOUIS PHILLIPPUS, was shot dead on April 17, aged 45, the victim of an armed robbery at a petrol station in Gauteng. "Another senseless murder," observed his former team-mate Jacques Rudolph, while Albie Morkel, another South African Test player, said he had "lost a great friend". Vorster was a much-travelled left-hander, who made his maiden century for Transvaal against Western Province at Cape Town in January 1988. He entered at 27 for three, against a new-ball attack of Garth le Roux and Steve Jefferies, but went on to score 174, and spent the following summer at Worcester, where he made one first-class appearance, against the touring West Indians, when Graeme Hick scored 172 to complete 1,000 runs before the end of May. Vorster compiled a further five first-class centuries, but never quite made the weight of runs necessary to push for an international place. He became involved in coaching in Namibia, for whom he played in the South African domestic first-class competition as recently as 2009-10.

WADDELL, SIDNEY, who died on August 11, aged 72, was the Arlott of the oche, a man who conferred poetry, literary allusion and a great sweep of history on to the prosaic business of darts commentary. He first brought darts to the small screen in 1972, when he joined Yorkshire Television and created *Indoor League* as a vehicle for Fred Trueman, who was required to affect a caricature of a Yorkshireman while introducing skittles, arm-wrestling, table football and, of course, darts. Trueman was Sid Waddell's sporting hero: he contributed a wonderful paean to him in *The Wisden Cricketer's* My Favourite Cricketer series, and remained a fan of the game. He wrote two series of *Sloggers*, a TV programme about a fictional children's cricket team in Slogthwaite, Lancashire, for which he won a best scriptwriter prize in the Writers' Guild of Great Britain awards in 1994.

WATSON, JOHN MARTIN, died on March 10, aged 90. Jack Watson was an all-rounder who enjoyed a long career in Minor Counties cricket for Durham (for whom he took 394 wickets at 16) and Northumberland. A policeman, he was also prominent in local football, having spells as a scout for Middlesbrough and caretaker manager of Darlington on no fewer than five occasions.

WHITE, COLIN DEREK, who died on February 27, aged 74, was a stylish left-hander who looked likely to win a Blue for Ted Dexter's Cambridge University side in 1958. White had made a bright start to the season, but never quite recovered after being hit in the mouth by New Zealand's Bob Blair. Although he later scored 55 against MCC at Lord's, White was left out of the Varsity Match after averaging only 15. He appeared sporadically over the next two years, scoring 64 against Nottinghamshire at Fenner's in 1960, but never did win that Blue. He later became a banker, and a regular club cricketer in Surrey.

WIGGINS, ANDREA, who died of cancer on September 6, aged 41, was part of the ECB's communications team for nine years, and was a popular figure with colleagues and journalists alike. She was instrumental in devising a lifestyle photography campaign for the England men's team which attracted widespread media interest, and played a pivotal role in establishing the domestic Twenty20 competition. She left Lord's in 2009 to become the International Rugby Board's communications manager.

WILCOCKSON, DAVID, died on June 1, aged 71, having been in a coma for 13 days after being hit by the ball while bowling in a club match in Surrey. "The batsman ran down the pitch and middled it towards him," said a team-mate. "It went straight into his head and he went down." He was airlifted to hospital after the incident, in Old Dorkinians' match against Grafham, but never regained consciousness. Wilcockson had played for the club since 1959, and set himself a target of 3,000 wickets. He finished with 2,899.

WILLIAMS, WENDY, who died on March 3, aged 69, was a Welsh-born bowler with a low slinging action which sometimes endangered the umpire. After narrowly missing selection for England in the first women's World Cup in 1973, she was chosen for the International XI which also played in the tournament, and appeared in all their six matches. Her six wickets included 12–6–20–3 against New Zealand at Chesterfield, to which she later added 18 from No. 8 as her side completed a last-over victory. "She was very popular," recalled the former England captain Rachael Heyhoe-Flint, a West Midlands team-mate, "not only because of her cheerful personality but because she was also a qualified physiotherapist, which meant we could get free treatment!" Williams worked with Bernard Thomas, the long-serving England physio, at his Edgbaston sports clinic.

WILSON, DONALD, died on July 21, aged 74. Don Wilson brought the same unquenchable enthusiasm and broad smile to everything he did in a lifetime dedicated to cricket – bowling his canny slow left-arm for Yorkshire between 1957 and 1974, instilling inner-city youngsters with a love of the game as MCC head coach, or genially cajoling his pupils on the playing fields of Ampleforth College. Wilson was one of the mainstays of the Yorkshire team that won seven Championships between 1959 and 1968, emerging from the giant shadow cast by Johnny Wardle to take more than 1,000 wickets. He also played six Tests for England, but perhaps his greatest legacy was turning Lord's into a centre of coaching excellence. Wilson welcomed them all to the Nursery Ground – goggle-eyed schoolchildren, Test players seeking technical or psychological counselling, and the occasional celebrity. He may be the only cricketer whose autobiography contained a foreword by Peter O'Toole.

His role in Yorkshire's last great era was almost as treasured for his contribution to the team's *esprit de corps* as for his playing efforts. Along with his great friend Phil Sharpe, Wilson was the leader of Yorkshire's very own choir, and led countless rousing sing-songs in sponsors' tents and hotel lounges. In a famously combustible dressing-room, the benefit to morale was incalculable.

Born in Settle in the Dales – not a fertile area of recruitment for Yorkshire – Wilson came to the county's attention in the most startling manner imaginable, bowling Len Hutton in a benefit match between the town club and a Yorkshire XI in 1953. Hutton invited him to a trial and, by 1957, Wilson was taking his initial steps as a first-team player. The following summer, he was the beneficiary of a row between Ronnie Burnet, the new captain, and Wardle. When Wardle was ignominiously sacked, Wilson was handed a frontline spinning role, and in 1959 Burnet's shrewd management of a group of talented Second Eleven graduates bore fruit with Yorkshire's first outright Championship since 1946. Wilson contributed 51 wickets.

Standing a fraction over 6ft 3in, he ran in off five easy paces and, after a prodigious leap, bowled with a classically high action. "He expected to take a wicket with every ball," Sharpe remembered, "and his eyes would nearly pop out." Wilson's line was impeccable and he was an acknowledged master of flight. "He was not a big spinner of the ball, although he could when the pitch was turning," said Sharpe. Now led by the unrelated Vic Wilson, Yorkshire retained the title in 1960, with Don taking 72 wickets, and there were further Championship successes in 1962, 1963 and a hat-trick from 1966 to 1968. Wilson featured prominently in each of these, but his most productive year – 109 wickets at under 14 in all matches – was in the last of those title-winning summers. The Gillette Cup was also won in 1965 and 1969. There were occasional flourishes with the bat, too, notably a one-handed effort with a broken thumb that guided Yorkshire to an unlikely run-chase at New Road in 1961. And in 1967 he won the *Sunday People* trophy for the most sixes in a season. He was also a fine fielder, especially swooping to his left at midwicket – "the Settle windmill," according to Sharpe.

Bob Thomas, Getty Images

Prodigious leap: Don Wilson, 1969.

Wilson's love of the stage was cemented in 1961, when he first encountered the Black and White Minstrels in Scarborough. Already familiar to television audiences, they sang traditional American minstrel songs, backed by a glamorous female dance troupe. Several members were cricket enthusiasts. "They loved cricket and we loved the dancers," said Sharpe. "It was reciprocal trading." Wilson and Sharpe spent the first half of the winter of 1963 on the road with the Minstrels, working as prompters and backstage factotums. They introduced the repertoire to their team-mates, and the evening performances quickly became as much a part of that Yorkshire side as the Championships. Fred Trueman summed up the mood: "This is my type of music, not this bloody rock'n'roll business."

International recognition – for his cricket – came in India in 1963-64, when Wilson played in all five Tests and took nine wickets. He also appeared in the fourth and the fifth matches of the 1970 series against the Rest of the World, claiming four wickets, and was selected for the winter's Ashes tour under Ray Illingworth. With Derek Underwood established, opportunities were limited, and he assumed the role of social secretary, helping to bridge the touring party's north–south divide so successfully that he was retained after a hand injury looked like ending his tour. He was given a chance in the First Test of the series in New Zealand that followed. His Test record was 11 wickets at 42.

The early 1970s were an unhappy time. Too much work in the nets in Australia caused a fault with his bowling (later diagnosed by Fred Titmus from a photograph), and for a while he suffered the yips. The Yorkshire vice-captaincy also brought conflict with the new skipper, Geoff Boycott. Wilson retired from first-class cricket in August 1974, with 1,189 wickets at 21 in 422 matches. He took 100 wickets in a season five times; only three bowlers have taken more wickets for Yorkshire since the war. But his best figures were for MCC: eight for 36 against Ceylon in Colombo in 1969-70. He scored 6,230 runs at 14, his only century coming against South Zone at Hyderabad on that 1963-64 tour.

Wilson was reinvigorated by two years of captaining Lincolnshire, and began a career in coaching that took him to South Africa, where he was head coach at the Wanderers and undertook some pioneering work in the townships. That led, in 1977, to a phone call from E. W. Swanton, offering him the job as head coach at Lord's. He thought Swanton must be mixing him up with a Wilson who had played for Kent, but refrained from saying so. Although Ian Botham had been a recent graduate of the MCC Young Cricketers, the coaching system run by Len Muncer was haphazard. Aided by the opening of the indoor school, Wilson embarked on a revolution, and alumni that included Phil DeFreitas, Phil Tufnell, Norman Cowans, Dermot Reeve and Paul Nixon were testament to his success.

DeFreitas had particular reason to be grateful: "When I went for my trial for the groundstaff, I remember that Phil Tufnell and I were told at the end that we hadn't made it," he recalled. "But Don had seen something in us, and demanded that we were selected. If it hadn't been for Don, we wouldn't have got on the staff." He also quietly looked after their interests. "We were very often excused the usual groundstaff boys' duties when the big matches were on," said DeFreitas. "Don would do his utmost to see that we were somewhere else playing cricket. He told you things straight, in black and white, but we could always have a laugh as well. He was an enormous figure in my life."

Emerging players from overseas were welcomed, too. An 18-year-old Martin Crowe arrived on a scholarship from New Zealand in 1981. "I remember Don's eyeballs popping out and his wild enthusiasm for cricket: 'Now then Crowie, I'm ready for ya, lad,' as he marked out his run-up." Between puffs on his small cigar, Wilson would dispense precious nuggets of advice. "He taught me about hundreds," Crowe recalls. "'No one remembers 60, lad, only big hundreds,' he said."

His house and garden, just behind the Mound Stand, were a popular party venue during Test matches and after one-day finals. Wilson left Lord's at the end of 1990 and took charge of sport at Ampleforth College, back in his native county. He wrote an entertaining autobiography, *Mad Jack* (a nickname first bestowed by Burnet), and to his huge delight became president of the Yorkshire Players' Association. His former spinning colleague Geoff Cope provided perhaps the most fitting epitaph: "I have never found anyone with so much enthusiasm for the game."

WILSON, JOHN STUART, died on July 2, aged 80. Stuart Wilson, a fast-medium bowler from the Brechin and Forfarshire club, played 16 first-class matches for Scotland. A Manchester-born plumber, he made his debut against Lancashire at Old Trafford in 1957, and started well by dismissing the county's openers, Alan Wharton and Jack Dyson. Wilson's best figures of five for 51 came against MCC at The Grange in 1959, while three years later he took four wickets in each innings at Greenock as Scotland won their annual encounter with Ireland.

WIMALADARMA, WELIWITAGODA RAKITHA DILSHAN, died on September 29, aged 27, after watching Sri Lanka's World Twenty20 match against West Indies on television with some friends earlier in the evening. Some reports suggested drugs may have been involved; one of the other party guests also died. Rakitha Wimaladarma was an off-spinner who claimed 53 wickets, mainly for Saracens, in Sri Lanka's domestic first-class competitions in 2009-10, including a career-best eight for 68 against the Army; a few weeks later he took 23 wickets in successive matches against Moors and Tamil Union.

WOODHEAD, DEREK JOHN, died on July 29, 2011, aged 76. After scoring an unbeaten century in only his second Sheffield Shield match for Western Australia in 1958-59, Woodhead looked to have a promising career ahead of him as an opener – but after three failures at the beginning of the next season, he was dropped permanently. His thesis *Fundamentals and Techniques of Batting in Australia* earned him the award of his Teachers' Higher Certificate in 1969, and is held at the J. S. Battye Library of West Australian History in Perth. He coached the Australian fast bowler Mick Malone and, later, Greg Shipperd, who opened the batting for both Western Australia and Tasmania.

WOOLNOUGH, BRIAN CHRISTOPHER, died on September 18, aged 63. When Brian Woolnough was lured away from his job as chief football writer of *The Sun* to become chief sportswriter of the *Daily Star* in 2000, a significant part of the attraction was the chance to write about a wider variety of sports, especially cricket; he also became a familiar face on Sky TV. He was an enthusiastic fast bowler for the Claygate club in Surrey, putting his imposing frame to good use, and retained a love of the game through his years as one of the most high-profile sportswriters in Fleet Street. He was particularly proud of having batted with Rohan Kanhai in a charity match at Lord's. After joining the *Star*, Woolnough became a regular in Test-match press boxes in the summer, especially relishing England's 2005 Ashes triumph. The Oval Test was an annual highlight – on a day with no writing duties, he would join friends and family for a companionable time in the stands.

ZAHIR ALAM, who died of liver failure on May 30, aged 42, was a leading light with the bat for Assam in the Ranji Trophy for several seasons. Against Tripura at Guwahati in 1991-92 he scored 257, and put on 475 with Lalchand Rajput (239) for the second wicket – then a world record, although it has been surpassed three times since.

Wisden *always welcomes information about those who might be included: please send details to almanack@wisden.com, or to John Wisden & Co, 13 Old Aylesfield, Golden Pot, Alton, Hampshire GU34 4BY.*

BRIEFLY NOTED

The following, whose deaths were noted during 2012, played or umpired in 12 or fewer first-class (fc) matches. Further details can be found at www.cricketarchive.co.uk or at www.cricinfo.com (enter the player's name in the search box on the home page).

	Died	*Age*	*Main team(s)*
ANDERSON, Peter Stewart	27.12.2012	62	Northern Districts
Fast bowler; 5-74 and 5-38 as ND beat Canterbury in 1978-79; ten wickets in six other matches.			
CUDDUMBEY, Glenn Winston	15.8.2012	63	Transvaal
Wicketkeeper who played six fc matches for Transvaal's non-white side in the 1970s.			
FORSTER, Frank	23.6.2012	81	Durham
Fast bowler who claimed 1,314 wickets in the Durham Senior League.			
GALLEY, James Martyn	11.10.12	68	Somerset
Long-serving member of Bath's Lansdown club: three fc games in 1969; later played for Wiltshire.			
GHOSH, Lohit Kumar	22.7.2012	75/76	Umpire
Umpire from Bihar who stood in 14 fc matches in India between 1979 and 1992.			
HAYNES, Denis Marshall	26.11.2012	88	Staffordshire
Batsman who played one fc match, for MCC v Oxford University at Lord's in 1956.			
JONES, Bruce Smeath	9.2.2012	84	Cheshire
Batsman who played for Cheshire from 1950 to 1966, captaining them for a time.			
KANE, Terrence Desmond McKibbin	19.10.2012	60	Ireland
Medium-pacer from Ulster who took 5-25 against Canada in 1981.			
KIERNAN, James Andrew	6.1.2012	80	Ireland
Capable Munster batsman; brother of the Ireland and Lions rugby captain Tom.			
LEES, Geoffrey William	17.8.2012	92	Cambridge University
Batsman and leg-spinner who played three fc matches, one for Sussex in 1951.			
LIMAYE, Anil Jagannath	24.12.2011	69	Baroda
Wicketkeeper who played two Ranji Trophy matches in the 1960s, making four stumpings.			

	Died	*Age*	*Main team(s)*
LOWSON, Leonard Edward ("Leo")	21.2.2012	91	Devon
Wicketkeeper – and ex-fighter pilot – who scored prolifically for Plymouth CC.			
McINERNY, James Jeremy	27.5.2012	79	Oxford University
Batsman who played one fc match in both 1955 and 1956.			
MAJEED, Syed Abdul Koran	3.7.2012	71/72	East Pakistan
Batsman who played three fc matches shortly before East Pakistan became Bangladesh.			
MISHRA, Prem	12.2.2012	56/57	Umpire
TV umpire for an ODI in Sharjah in 2000-01.			
NEAL, John Howard	18.4.2012	85	Sussex
Wicketkeeper whose only fc match was an innings defeat at Old Trafford in 1951.			
NORTH, Colin Anthony	5.1.2012	70	Lincolnshire
Wicketkeeper who later filled many administrative posts in Lincolnshire cricket.			
RICHARDSON, Malcolm Henry Hugh	11.8.12	81	Western Province
Scored 132 against Rhodesia in the second of his 12 fc matches, on Boxing Day 1958.			
RINALDI, Keith Richard	6.4.2012	62	Umpire
Perth umpire who stood in seven fc matches, all at the WACA.			
RYAN, Hayccnc Evcrton	22.2.12	60	Leeward Islands
Montserrat left-hander who played two fc matches; bagged a pair against 1980-81 England tourists.			
SUTCLIFFE, Roy Bennett	7.8.2012	84	Eastern Province
Batsman who played four fc matches in 1947-48.			
WEBER, Gary August	7.4.2012	59	Border
Fast bowler who played one fc match (and a one-day game) in 1975-76.			

A LIFE IN NUMBERS

	Runs	*Avge*	*Wkts*	*Avge*
R. G. Abeynaike	412	24.23	9	40.00
S. S. Akbar	1,296	27.00	0	–
R. B. Alaganan	191	21.22	3	6.00
L. J. Alexander	70	8.75	–	–
Raja Ali	4,337	38.38	1	42.00
Alimuddin	7,275	32.77	40	24.00
K. P. Bhikane	147	36.75	6	47.16
P. D. S. Blake	2,067	22.22	0	–
D. J. W. Bridge	55	9.16	5	52.20
E. Burgin	92	13.14	31	25.64
A. H. Carrigan	2,883	35.59	31	47.06
R. G. Carter	635	7.13	243	27.81
G. H. Chesterton	598	8.79	263	22.78
G. C. Cooper	8,134	23.17	100	36.77
L. A. Coury	59	5.90	11	56.36
T. J. Cowley	660	12.94	94	31.51
A. J. Coxon	144	12.00	28	48.21
M. G. Crawford	22	11.00	–	–
K. M. Curran	15,740	36.86	605	27.65
M. M. Dalvi	1,537	48.03	10	35.10
I. R. Dick	27	13.50	–	–
M. A. H. Fuard	406	14.00	51	26.17
R. A. Gaunt	616	10.44	266	26.85
H. Ghosh	2,599	26.79	29	30.68
D. Gibson	3,143	18.93	552	22.22
J. Govender	1,248	19.8	48	20.04
D. M. Gregg	129	6.78	44	29.84
A. W. Greig	16,660	31.19	856	28.85
T. R. Hardman	65	16.25	3	59.66
G. H. Hill	247	5.88	108	29.58
E. L. G. Hoad	303	25.25	15	44.60
E. J. How	7	1.40	13	88.07
S. S. J. Huey	135	5.19	66	18.22
R. S. Hyatt	609	25.37	15	74.26
I. B. Iffla	37	9.25	10	39.00
R. C. Jordon	2,414	25.95	–	–
Kuntal Chandra	132	26.40	–	–
K. Lewis	424	28.26	–	–
R. V. Lynch	7	7.00	4	26.75
L. McGibbon	17	2.83	33	26.00
M. Mangera	952	20.58	40	20.15
J. C. Marshall	710	26.29	–	–
W. M. M. Marshall	1	–	–	–
T. L. Maynard	2,384	32.65	0	–
R. S. Morton	5,980	39.60	8	36.25
Munir Malik	675	11.06	197	21.75
L. H. Murray	55	13.75	11	27.36
T. S. Naidu	212	15.14	–	–
C. E. Neblett	242	34.57	15	28.93
B. B. Nimbalkar	4,841	47.93	58	40.22
G. I. D. Norton	4	4.00	17	7.82
Pir Pagara	16	8.00	–	–
F. D. Parr	507	12.07	–	–
H. A. Pawson	3,807	37.32	7	40.00
J. B. N. Perera	537	38.35	6	46.16
H. Pilling	15,279	32.23	1	195.00
N. P. Rana	403	10.60	46	55.71
Razaullah Khan	525	12.80	1	36.00
A. W. Robinson	24	6.00	–	–
H. B. O. Robinson	325	13.54	53	27.20
Safiullah Khan	364	7.42	145	20.23
M. A. J. Sargent	804	23.64	3	68.00
P. A. Sharp	19	6.33	21	26.90
J. K. E. Slack	434	31.00	–	–

	Runs	Avge	Wkts	Avge
P. A. Snow	121	17.28	4	25.25
K. Srinivasan	769	30.76	–	–
M. W. Stovold	518	16.70	0	–
R. Surendranath	1,351	15.70	278	25.37
P. H. Taylor	14	7.00	–	–
D. J. Thomas	3,044	20.02	336	33.97
R. A. E. Tindall	5,446	24.86	150	32.38
E. A. Toovey	1,346	24.03	0	–
B. M. W. Trapnell	283	16.64	16	38.81
J. B. Turner	127	63.50	–	–
L. P. Vorster	4,786	33.23	1	41.00
C. D. White	606	15.53	0	–
D. Wilson	6,230	14.09	1,189	21.00
J. S. Wilson	66	5.07	44	25.20
W. R. D. Wimaladarma	462	14.43	94	28.77
D. J. Woodhead	269	29.88	–	–
Zahir Alam	1,398	36.78	2	86.00

Alexander made eight catches and five stumpings; Jordon 238 and 45; Kuntal Chandra eight catches and no stumpings; Mangera 24 and one; Parr 71 and 20; Razaullah Khan 29 and 12; and Srinivasan 25 and eight.

Career figures for players who also appeared in Test matches can be found in the Records section (page 1397).

PART FOUR

English International Cricket

NEWBERRY
NEWBERRY
GT 335
SALIX
Prestantia
ICON F2
DXM
GM
ORIGINAL
LIMITED EDITION
QUOTE
WISDEN 2013
FOR A 10%
DISCOUNT
AYRTEK

THE ENGLAND TEAM IN 2012

Out of the rough

STEPHEN BRENKLEY

Redemption took its time. But when it arrived, the satisfaction almost erased the tumultuous 50 weeks that had come before it – almost, but not quite, because the drama surrounding England throughout 2012, both human and sporting, was relentless, intense and compelling.

The wholly unexpected Test victory in India with which they ended their year was a triumph of plotting and redesign. And it had two overwhelming features: the rehabilitation of a team who had grown dangerously accustomed to losing, and the reintegration of a player, Kevin Pietersen, who had come perilously close to the end of his international career.

England's batting was now refreshed in body and mind. The bowling attack, led by the superb Jimmy Anderson and buttressed by the admirable Graeme Swann, appeared to have regained its old verve. Perhaps the most significant aspect of all, however, was the galvanic start provided by the 2–1 win over the Indians to Alastair Cook's tenure as official Test captain. He was exemplary.

ENGLAND IN 2012

	Played	*Won*	*Lost*	*Drawn/No result*
Tests	15	5	7	3
One-day internationals	17	12	2	3
Twenty20 internationals	14	7	6	1

JANUARY – FEBRUARY	3 Tests, 4 ODIs and 3 T20Is (a) (in UAE) v Pakistan	(see page 273)
MARCH – APRIL	2 Tests (a) v Sri Lanka	(page 301)
MAY – JUNE	3 Tests, 3 ODIs and 1 T20I (h) v West Indies	(page 315)
JUNE – JULY	5 ODIs (h) v Australia	(page 337)
JULY – AUGUST – SEPTEMBER	3 Tests, 5 ODIs and 3 T20Is (h) v South Africa	(page 345)
SEPTEMBER – OCTOBER	World Twenty20 (in Sri Lanka)	(page 841)
NOVEMBER – DECEMBER – JANUARY	4 Tests, 5 ODIs and 2 T20Is (a) v India	(page 377)

Appointed formally, all but routinely, after Andrew Strauss's retirement on August 29, Cook scored centuries in each of the first three Tests of the series, tailoring his innings to the demands of the team. His authority burgeoned with his form, and the respect he commanded was clear. Party to the dropping of his vice-captain, Stuart Broad, he demonstrated the ruthless pragmatism required of all leaders.

When England lost the First Test at Ahmedabad, their seventh defeat of an increasingly wretched year, it was merely a continuation of an abysmal inability to adapt to the needs of conditions in Asia. Yet by the time hands were shaken on a draw during the final afternoon of the Fourth Test at Nagpur, Cook had helped deliver a seamless transformation. The series-levelling win at Mumbai already ranked among England's most glorious anywhere, a model example of beating opponents at their own game. To travel then to Kolkata and fashion another comprehensive victory was the mark of a dressing-room genuinely at ease with itself again – if not always with the world outside.

It was Cook's team now. Strauss's decision to quit all cricket, which few had seen coming, suddenly assumed a retrospective air of inevitability, as is often the way of such matters. Not that it should diminish a jot Strauss's contribution as England's captain: an outstanding leader and a man of honour, he will be fondly recalled. In truth, Cook had two teams, since he retained the captaincy of the one-day side he had gained in 2011. England's rapid advance in that sphere – they won their first ten completed one-day internationals, before sharing the home series with South Africa – was as marked as their Test deterioration pre-India. This reunification had barely taken place when it was followed by the separation of senior management duties.

England were restored by the win in Mumbai, which eased considerably the announcement of their decision to divide the role of head coach. Andy Flower retained the official title of team director, but would now oversee the Test squad only. The day-to-day affairs of the two limited-overs sides were put in the hands of Ashley Giles, Test selector, successful director of cricket at Warwickshire, and sometime Ashes hero.

These appointments were devised partly to ensure that Flower, with a wife and three young children, could have some kind of home life again, and would thus stay in the job. It was a sign of a confident management prepared to confront not just the gruelling reality of big-time cricket in the early 21st century, but what it might take to stay a few runs and wickets ahead of the pack. Putting the theory into practice could prove another matter, but formulating it at all had been a bold first step.

Victory in India bordered on the miraculous, for England had been under perpetual siege from the moment they began the year as the world's No. 1 Test side – a ranking reached via the ICC's endearingly arcane points system and officially bestowed by the award of a large mace. But the mace was an albatross by another name. Instead of carrying it aloft like the glorious prize it was supposed to be, England found it throttling the life out of them. In the United Arab Emirates, they batted awfully against Pakistan. Two months later in Sri Lanka, previous mistakes and lapses against slow bowling on slow pitches went initially unheeded, and they escaped with a 1–1 draw thanks to the first

Ian Kington. AFP/Getty Images

That losing feeling: England's players reflect on their series defeat by South Africa, which prompted Andrew Strauss (*centre*) to hand the captaincy to Alastair Cook.

of Pietersen's three breathtaking centuries in the year, plus the wickets of Swann.

Brief respite at home against West Indies was followed by a loss to South Africa, who deservedly claimed the top ranking themselves. South Africa's victory at The Oval (hosting the First Test because Lord's was used for the Olympic archery) was by an innings and 12 runs, yet it was more epic than that: they scored 637 for two and reduced to impotence an attack that imagined themselves the most incisive in the world. The defeat was among England's most shattering.

From late August on – but, for more acute observers, from long before – events in the dressing-room were dominated by the Pietersen saga. The subsequent attempts to draw a line under an unseemly episode, indeed to airbrush it from history, failed to conceal its tawdriness, significance or sheer theatre. That Pietersen was England's stellar cricketer was merely emphasised during the weeks the saga rumbled on. It overshadowed the loss of both the South Africa series and the No. 1 ranking, the insipid defence of the World Twenty20 in Sri Lanka, and the squad announcement for the tour of India, for which he was not originally selected.

It had been clear something was up when Pietersen suddenly announced his retirement from all limited-overs cricket at the end of May. Mutterings abounded that relations between him and Flower were strained – and Flower certainly looked strained. A bleak hiatus was eventually reached at the end of the drawn Second Test with South Africa at Headingley, in which Pietersen had scored the second of those three centuries. Clearly not about to let anything lie, he gave a press conference in which he discussed the difficulties of being him. He also floated the prospect that the Third Test at Lord's could be his last.

Within a few days, it appeared his England career might already be at an end, after claims he had sent text messages disparaging Strauss to members of the South African side. Nothing was ever proven, and much was denied, but Strauss's uncharacteristically bruised reaction told its own story. Relations reached such a low ebb that Pietersen, unwilling – or unable – to deny the allegations, was dropped, and a must-win match became about something else besides: the unity of the squad, the place of the individual in it, and the old mantra that there is no "I" in team. It helped the selectors that Jonny Bairstow, his replacement, made 95 and 54.

England closed ranks, and tried their socks off, but South Africa were simply the better team. It was difficult to tell where Strauss's mind was. But when he shouldered arms to a straight ball from the estimable Vernon Philander at the start of a potentially fascinating run-chase, it was patently not on the proceedings at hand.

The precise nature of the negotiations which ensued between Pietersen and England will be revealed one day (and what different interpretations they may have). But the ECB went into news-management, or rather news-blackout, mode. Perhaps it was a period when they were damned if they did speak and damned if they didn't, but the growing tendency to avoid offering reasoned answers to reasonable questions was one that threatened to sully relations with their faithful public. Throughout, it seemed possible Pietersen's career was over, even while the feeling grew that some senior players might have behaved differently towards him; Flower himself said the strange matter of the fake Twitter account, which poked fun at Pietersen, could have been handled better.

At the end of the Test series, Strauss retired. True to form, he went with the utmost dignity. The Pietersen saga and his retirement were not connected – at least not directly – but it was a huge shame that his announcement should be tarnished. He went, by the way, because he felt he was no longer scoring the necessary runs; two hundreds against West Indies had offered cause for respite, but not genuine rejuvenation.

Pietersen had been signed up to commentate on the World Twenty20 in Sri Lanka and, well though he fulfilled that task, it was clear England were missing him. After their elimination came the beginnings of rapprochement. Giles Clarke, the ECB chairman, and Pietersen gave a surreal press briefing in the bowels of a Colombo hotel, in which Clarke first used the phrase that came to embody the whole shebang: Pietersen was to embark on "a process of reintegration". Clarke was at his most sonorously grave: "In our society we believe that, when an individual transgresses, and when the individual concerns recognises that and apologises, it is important that individual should be given a real opportunity to be reintegrated into our society. This principle is an essential part of having civilised and sensible ethics."

Whatever Pietersen was guilty of, this made it seem somewhat more than a bloke in a cricket team not getting on too well with some of the other blokes in a cricket team. A few days later, he flew back to England from South Africa, where he had been playing in the Champions League with Delhi Daredevils. He had a chat with some of England's other senior players, and it was all done and dusted. He was added to the squad for India, and his limited-overs retirement rescinded.

His presence might have encouraged a semblance of optimism, though it can hardly have infused the team with unbridled confidence. From the first day in Dubai in January, when Pietersen was one of several to fall cheaply to Saeed Ajmal, it had gone too wrong, for too long. Techniques which had coped enviably in Australia and England were suddenly and harshly exposed. England did not know whether to stick or twist: they came out slugging, then tried to retrench. Nearly all the batsmen laboured. Jonathan Trott and Ian Bell, in their different ways, searched vainly for a trusted scoring method. Trott came up with a fighting century in a lost cause at Galle, but was perhaps a victim of the incessant demands made of an international batsman.

From the UAE onwards, Bell rarely made Test runs away from home, which was odd – not only because they had flowed in the previous two years, but because of his renaissance as a one-day opener in Pietersen's absence (and did enough to retain his place in the 50-over side when Pietersen kissed and made up). That both Bell and Trott finished the year with hundreds at Nagpur embodied England's revival.

But neither could have played the innings Pietersen did. The last of his memorable treble came at Mumbai, complementing Cook's wonderfully judged contribution. India's spinners were repelled, while England's – Swann and the recalled Monty Panesar – took 19 wickets in a masterful exhibition of harnessing helpful conditions. This was the first time England seemed properly to have learned from past misdemeanours. The sweep shot, both ally and enemy to them for a decade, yielded 59 runs in 44 balls; for India, it brought only 14 in ten. Yet in Nagpur, where the pitch was slower, England realised it was no longer a judicious option.

The bowlers were magnificent. Their status was seriously challenged by South Africa's hard-nosed batting, but Anderson passed 250 Test wickets early in the year, and Swann 200 at the end, both passing marks set by great forebears: Anderson overhauled his fellow Lancashire seamer Brian Statham; Swann his fellow off-spinner Jim Laker.

In Matt Prior, England still had the best wicketkeeper-batsman in the world, which said much in an accomplished field. His commitment to the team cause could never be doubted, and his telephone call to Pietersen at the height of the shambles was instrumental in bringing the sides together. England finished in good order. Doubts remained over Cook's new long-term opening partner, though Nick Compton – a newcomer with impeccable heritage – acquitted himself with abundant concentration in India. But seven different players were selected to bat at No. 6, and Joe Root of Yorkshire, not yet 22, ended as the man in possession, evoking the thought he might soon be Cook's opening partner.

In the middle of summer, a one-day series of five matches against Australia had gone almost unnoticed. Too much else was happening in cricket and beyond. And two Ashes series loomed in 2013. Such casual disregard was unlikely to recur.

ENGLAND PLAYERS IN 2012

LAWRENCE BOOTH

The following 30 players (there were 33 in 2011 and 27 in 2010) appeared for England in the calendar year 2012, when the team played 15 Tests, 15 one-day internationals and 14 Twenty20 internationals. All statistics refer to the full year, not the 2012 season.

JAMES ANDERSON — Lancashire

No bigger compliment came Anderson's way than Indian captain M. S. Dhoni's assertion in December that he had been the difference between the sides during the Tests. And if that underplayed – deliberately, perhaps – the role of England's spinners, then neither was it idle praise. After a slow start to the series, Anderson undermined India at Kolkata with reverse swing, then kept them subdued at Nagpur, where his spell on the third evening was full of heart, skill and athleticism. By then, he had removed Sachin Tendulkar an unprecedented nine times, and he finished the year with 528 international wickets, equalling Ian Botham's England record. Contrary to the stereotype, the tricky periods had come at home: rested, to his annoyance, for the Edgbaston Test against West Indies, he was comfortably outbowled by Dale Steyn during the defeat by South Africa. But either side of the summer, he got to grips with Asia, taking 30 wickets in nine Tests at under 27 apiece. It was a serious piece of rebranding – more career-redefining even than the 2010-11 Ashes.

14 Tests: 137 runs @ 8.05; 48 wickets @ 29.50.
13 ODI: 5 runs @ 2.50, SR 35.71; 18 wickets @ 26.61, ER 4.71.

JONNY BAIRSTOW — Yorkshire

Questions and answers popped up with indecent haste. The pace of Kemar Roach plainly unsettled him during his debut Test series, against West Indies, yet when Pietersen's absence gave him another chance, against a speedy South African attack at Lord's, he batted with exciting assurance for 95 and 54. Then, in India, England didn't entirely trust him against spin: a stopgap selection with Bell on paternity leave, Bairstow fell on the stroke of a lunch break in his only innings, before slipping behind Root come Nagpur. He managed only one 50-over game all year and, after a promising start in Dubai, his Twenty20 form stalled too: in India in December, he was dropped. Any doubts appeared to surround not his talent, but the best way to harness it.

5 Tests: 196 runs @ 32.66.
1 ODI: 29 runs @ 29.00, SR 55.76.
12 T20I: 142 runs @ 20.28, SR 101.42.

IAN BELL — Warwickshire

Until he helped steer England to safety – and history – at Nagpur, Bell was heading for the worst of his eight full years as a Test batsman. Only at home against West Indies had he flourished; otherwise, he was in danger of reverting to the infuriating pre-2010 model. An integral part of the batting meltdown against Pakistan, he failed to impose himself on South Africa; and, for a while, his mindless first-baller at Ahmedabad, lofting to deep mid-off, looked like the epitome of English ineptitude against spin. But the class that had helped him average 86 over the previous two years reasserted itself in the Fourth Test against India. Oddly, Bell's unbeaten 116 there was more in keeping with his 50-over form. Refreshed by the challenge of opening regularly for the first time in four years following Pietersen's temporary retirement, he had sparkled in all three home series, taking a hundred off West Indies at Southampton, then averaging 47 against Australia and 45 against South Africa. His fluency in blue made his Test travails the harder to fathom.

14 Tests: 672 runs @ 33.60.
11 ODI: 549 runs @ 54.90, SR 82.68.

RAVI BOPARA **Essex**

It had looked as if 2012 would be Bopara's breakthrough, when he followed up a favourable impression in the UAE one-dayers with the most authoritative batting of his career during the 4–0 win against Australia. And his busy medium-pacers were proving England's most economical option. But his return to the Test side, at The Oval against South Africa, was spoiled by two dozy shots, and personal problems ruled him out of the rest of the series. When he came back, for the 50-over matches, he looked like a caught-behind-in-waiting: an average of 91 against Australia now dipped against South Africa to five. His last-ditch selection at the World Twenty20 summed up England's desperation: with the asking-rate mounting against Sri Lanka, he scored one off six balls. It was all rather painful to witness.

1 Test: 22 runs @ 11.00; no wicket for 78.
14 ODI: 339 runs @ 37.66, SR 80.71; 7 wickets @ 25.00, ER 3.43.
6 T20I: 107 runs @ 17.83, SR 108.08; 1 wicket @ 63.00, ER 7.87.

STUART BROAD **Nottinghamshire**

Broad's performances in the UAE built on his splice-jarring excellence against India the previous summer, but a calf strain cut short his tour of Sri Lanka, and after that he shone only sporadically. Eleven wickets against West Indies at Lord's were a reminder that he didn't need to be at his best to cause havoc although, on the final afternoon at Headingley against South Africa, he was genuinely hostile. But two trends were emerging: Broad's pace dropped to the low-80s – he blamed the speedguns, while the management claimed not to be concerned – and he mislaid the fuller length that had served him well in the second half of 2011. A bruised heel early in India hardly helped, and neither did a total of none for 157 at Ahmedabad and Mumbai. Unimpressed, the selectors dropped him from the Test side for the first time in four years, only weeks after he had been confirmed as Cook's vice-captain; soon, the heel meant he was on his way home. His year as Twenty20 leader had to be judged by the surrenders to India and Sri Lanka, and he was dragged into the Pietersen affair when forced to deny involvement in a fake Twitter account that had, it transpired, been started by one of his friends. That indignity felt of a piece with a disjointed year.

11 Tests: 277 runs @ 17.31; 40 wickets @ 31.70.
9 ODI: 23 runs @23.00, SR 135.29; 11 wickets @ 33.45, ER 4.65.
12 T20I: 30 runs @ 10.00, SR 83.33; 11 wickets @ 26.54, ER 6.89.

JOS BUTTLER — Somerset

Philip Brown

England's patience was rewarded at Edgbaston in September, when Buttler put a Twenty20 game beyond South Africa's reach with an awe-inspiring ten-ball unbeaten 32, of which 30 came in a single over from Wayne Parnell. That blast meant a slow start to his international career was forgiven. And 48 undefeated runs off 28 deliveries in the pre-Christmas matches in India, where he replaced Bairstow behind the stumps, confirmed his match-winning potential – especially when his ramp shot was in working order.

1 ODI: 0 runs at 0.00.
14 T20I: 143 runs @ 20.42, SR 133.64; 2 games as wicketkeeper, no dismissals.

NICK COMPTON — Somerset

A prolific season with Somerset and the retirement of Strauss paved the way for Compton's passage to India, where he contentedly played second fiddle to Cook. His value lay not so much in the runs he scored – in that respect he had a middling series – but in the alliance he forged with his captain. If their partnership of 123 in the follow-on at Ahmedabad might have been England's most important of the series, then their 165 at Kolkata was not far behind. Compton's diligence was beyond reproach, and so too his temperament: after two failures in the warm-ups, he forced his way into the Test side with three successive fifties. But it was unclear whether his straitjacket – he scored at 33 runs per 100 balls – had been tailored to circumstance or cut from his natural cloth. On three occasions, he fell between 29 and 37, and a top score of 57 felt, in Indian conditions at least, like a glass ceiling. But a player who was constantly reminded of his dazzling grandfather, and had replaced a modern English great, managed the dual burden with class and composure. Besides, he would always have one over Denis: at Eden Gardens, the Barmy Army honoured Nick with his own song.

4 Tests: 208 runs @ 34.66.

ALASTAIR COOK — Essex

Cook could allow himself a matinee-idol grin when – having just led England to their first Test triumph in India since 1984-85 – it was put to him that his ascent to the captaincy must have seemed like a mixed blessing. In fact, little fazed him, and his haul of 548 runs at Ahmedabad, Mumbai and Kolkata represented one of the feats of an already glittering British sporting year. In Tests, he had endured a quiet time until then, including seven single-figure scores in the defeats by Pakistan and South Africa. But his resilience, refusal to panic, and an enforced sense of responsibility now came together: by the end of the year, only Michael Clarke had scored more Test runs, while Cook – uniquely – could celebrate hundreds in each of his first five Tests as captain (starting with a stand-in stint at Chittagong and Dhaka in 2009-10). As he had done while making the one-day captaincy his own the previous year, Cook added new tricks, leaving the crease to launch straight sixes off India's spinners: in 2012, he hit five in Tests, doubling his career tally. The single-mindedness which was reflected in Cook's desire to take Pietersen to India and pick Root at Nagpur had also been evident in England's one-day fortunes. They won 12 out of 14 completed matches, while none of his team-mates could match his 663 runs, three hundreds or 74 fours. His greatest feat, though, was to assume control so calmly in the post-Strauss era. Famously a non-sweater, Cook had turned a physical oddity into a resounding metaphor.

15 Tests: 1,249 runs @ 48.03.
15 ODI: 663 runs @ 47.35, SR 79.97.

JADE DERNBACH — Surrey

For all the experimentation, an ingredient was still missing: Dernbach could not yet be relied upon to stem the flow. He had his moments, most triumphantly when he gambled on a slower ball from the last delivery of the Twenty20 decider against Pakistan, and deceived Misbah-ul-Haq. He was initially forgiven plenty, bowling more Twenty20 overs than any of his team-mates while conceding more than almost all of them. He celebrated each victim with reassuring intensity, but there was too much anguish in between. And after leaking 7.34 an over in the New Year in India, he was dropped from the one-day side for New Zealand.

5 ODI: 2 runs @ 2.00, SR 33.33; 9 wickets @ 28.33, ER 5.60.
13 T20I: 14 runs @ 14.00, SR 155.55; 13 wickets @ 28.92, ER 8.48.

STEVEN FINN — Middlesex

Menace and promise lurked whenever Finn was handed the ball, but injuries and the seam-bowling hierarchy meant he played in only five of England's 15 Tests – and just once in consecutive games. Eight wickets against South Africa at Lord's were overshadowed by defeat but, when he had finally recovered from a thigh injury in India, his post-lunch spell on the fourth afternoon at Kolkata paved the way for a famous win. A strained disc ruled him out of Nagpur, but there was another troublesome body part: his right knee had a habit of knocking into the stumps at the point of delivery, prompting umpires to call dead ball at the second offence, a ruling that cost him the wicket of Graeme Smith at Headingley. He promised to sort things out, but never quite did, and missed out on another wicket at Mohali in January 2013. In the limited-overs formats, he was outstanding – fast, fiery, frugal. Series figures of 40–3–134–13 had helped demolish Pakistan 4–0, and Finn was also a lone flicker of light during the World Twenty20. Now England just needed to keep him fit.

5 Tests: 16 runs @ 8.00; 20 wickets @ 31.50.
14 ODI: 15 runs without dismissal, SR 187.50; 25 wickets @ 20.00, ER 4.20.
11 T20I: 9 runs without dismissal, SR 69.23; 17 wickets @ 16.70, ER 6.76.

ALEX HALES **Nottinghamshire**

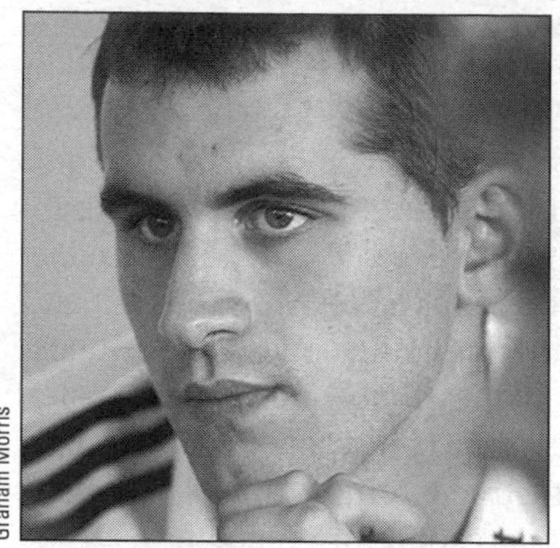
Graham Morris

Less than a year and a half after his England debut, and with Pietersen barely around, Hales could claim to have developed into their leading Twenty20 batsman, finishing 91 runs clear of the pack. His 99 off 68 balls against West Indies at Trent Bridge was a reward for intelligent shot selection, and in the two end-of-year games in India he managed 98 off 68. He even verged on the status of cause célèbre, banned by Nottinghamshire – along with Lumb and Patel – from considering IPL offers. But he knew time was on his side.

10 T20I: 343 runs @ 38.11; SR 137.20.

CRAIG KIESWETTER **Somerset**

It seemed like an identity crisis. Finally demoted in the one-day order to No. 6 after 28 innings as opener had brought him an average of all but 30 and a strike-rate of 94, Kieswetter lost more than he gained. It was slightly curious that England persisted with him at the top of the Twenty20 line-up, where a run a ball and only one score over 35 were barely adequate. Too often, he followed the management's strictures about the preservation of early wickets, but without rotating the strike. And after scoring four off 14 balls in the World Twenty20 against New Zealand, he was dropped. His keeping, on the other hand, improved – not least during the 50-over series against Australia. But it wasn't enough, and after more struggles, in India in early 2013, he was ditched in that format too.

15 ODI: 203 runs @ 33.83, SR 80.55; 26 catches, 5 stumpings.
11 T20I: 180 runs @ 16.36, SR 102.85; 8 catches, 1 stumping.

EOIN MORGAN **Middlesex**

The final act of England's year was Morgan's straight six off Ashok Dinda to seal a last-ball Twenty20 win at Mumbai, but almost all his heroics until then had been confined to the 50-over game. In 12 innings, he was not out six times – and England won the lot. It was no coincidence that he was the only player to appear in all 29 limited-overs internationals in 2012, nor that he was entrusted with the Twenty20 captaincy in India while Broad was at home injured. But his Test career stuttered after both his technique and, more unexpectedly, his temperament deserted him against Pakistan's spinners. By the end of the Indian tour, he had disappeared into the pack, even if he had at least rectified the excessive crouch which had been playing havoc with his balance. Only a return to the Test team, though, would complete the picture.

3 Tests: 82 runs @ 13.66.
15 ODI: 364 runs @ 60.66, SR 98.11.
14 T20I: 243 runs @ 24.30, SR 120.89.

MONTY PANESAR **Sussex**

Here was what Panesar had become: an unaffordable luxury in England, but a potential match-winner in Asia, although even there he was no automatic selection. He missed one Test on each of the three overseas tours, but his performances against Pakistan and India would call the selectors' judgment into question. When he did play, both Strauss and Cook treated him as their No. 1 spinner, partly because he provided more control than Swann: at Nagpur, he bowled 52 overs for 81. But he could be lethal too and – after he was bizarrely overlooked at Ahmedabad – the Wankhede pitch in Mumbai might have been created with his pace and accuracy in mind; he had, he thought, never bowled better. And so the familiar lament: if only Panesar had an all-round game. Two bad drops off Mahela Jayawardene arguably cost England the Galle Test, and he failed to score in five innings out of nine. Such one-dimensionality wouldn't have been a problem for any other team. But England had Swann.

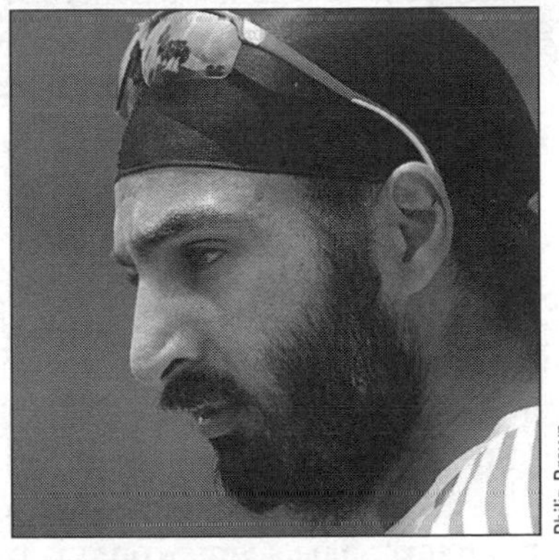
Philip Brown

6 Tests: 26 runs @ 4.33; 33 wickets @ 26.03.

SAMIT PATEL **Nottinghamshire**

The worry was that 2012 spelled the beginning and the end of Patel's Test career. Miscast at No. 7 in Sri Lanka, he was given the chance a place higher against India – but didn't take it. And when Panesar was belatedly selected, for the Second Test, his bonus gig as back-up spinner became redundant; Root's selection for Nagpur was the writing on the wall. Patel's limited-overs performances were not compelling either, save for a skilful 67 off 48 balls in the World Twenty20 against Sri Lanka, when he confirmed himself as one of England's more natural players of spin. But his gifts were glimpsed too rarely, and his slow left-armers too easily milked. In the field, he earned brownie points for his part in the run-out of Virender Sehwag at Kolkata, yet it felt he was no more than a fluff away from riling the coaches.

5 Tests: 109 runs @ 15.57; 4 wickets @ 64.25.
10 ODI: 101 runs @ 50.50, SR 83.47; 5 wickets @ 58.00, ER 5.00.
11 T20I: 133 runs @ 19.00, SR 119.81; 2 wickets @ 87.00, ER 7.90.

KEVIN PIETERSEN **Surrey**

The year ended as it began, with Pietersen getting into a tangle against spin in Asia, but in between he spray-painted English cricket with all the colours of the rainbow. You name it, he did it – and never in half-measures. The early months were either famine (in the Pakistan Tests) or feast (in the subsequent limited-overs matches in the UAE, and during his outrageous 151 in Colombo). Then came fiasco. Emboldened by his new IPL contract with Delhi Daredevils, Pietersen sought to retire from one-day internationals, with apparent disregard for the terms of his central contract: he would have to quit Twenty20 internationals too. A misplaced sense of grievance was not helped by a fake Twitter account in his name. And he became an out-and-out pariah when – a few days after his breathtaking 149 at Headingley and an equally jaw-dropping press conference ("it's tough being me") – it emerged he had been sending "provocative" texts to members of the South African team. For England, enough was enough. Pietersen was dropped for the Third Test at Lord's, then ignored for the World Twenty20 title defence, despite having unretired from the limited-overs formats in August via a YouTube interview. The next episode in the soap opera came during his "reintegration", a designation dreamed up by ECB chairman Giles Clarke during another bizarre press conference, stage-managed in Sri Lanka, where Pietersen was now providing TV punditry. But Cook replaced Strauss, and wanted his best players in India. After a series of meetings with senior players and support staff, Pietersen was welcomed back, and celebrated with his third Test tour de force of the year, a series-turning 186 at Mumbai. Half-centuries at Kolkata and Nagpur – where he knuckled down for the second-slowest score of 50-plus in his Test career – confirmed his return. The scenic route is rarely straightforward.

14 Tests: 1,053 runs @ 43.87; 5 wickets @ 29.40.
4 ODI: 281 runs @ 93.66, SR 84.38; no wicket for 4 runs, ER 4.00.
3 T20I: 112 runs @ 56.00, SR 130.23.

MATT PRIOR — Sussex

It said plenty for Prior's stature that a batting average below 40 felt disappointing. And yet the detail did not tally with the bigger picture, of a supreme counter-attacker forever willing to put team before self – a trait exemplified by his initiative in phoning Pietersen and having it out with him at the height of the texting trouble. In India, he added 157 with Cook during the follow-on at Ahmedabad to help convince colleagues the tour needn't degenerate into a debacle; and he was dismissed for under 40 only once, at Mumbai, when he was run out. Above all, he was Cook's eyes and ears, maintaining standards in the field, and assuming the vice-captaincy when Broad was omitted at Kolkata. Missed chances were mainly limited to stumpings, although Prior was furious after dropping Hashim Amla down the leg side at Lord's; like everyone else, he now expected himself to miss nothing. But he remained the best No. 7 in the game, unfulfilled only in his failure to translate his domestic one-day form into an international recall.

15 Tests: 777 runs @ 38.85; 29 catches, 7 stumpings.

ANDREW STRAUSS — Middlesex

He deserved better than to finish by padding up to a straight one from Vernon Philander – a non-stroke that betrayed a body and mind frazzled by the Pietersen farrago. But Strauss could leave with his pride intact: 100 Tests, and 50 as captain, with 24 wins, only two short of Michael Vaughan's England record. Typically, he wanted no fuss; nor was there any over the easy-to-miss fact that he had ended a difficult summer as his side's leading Test run-scorer. In truth, the hundreds against West Indies at Lord's and Trent Bridge bucked the trend: eight times he reached 20 without going beyond the 30s. And if he never ceded the respect of his players, some of his decision-making at the crease fell short of his own high standards; an ill-conceived sweep off Imran Tahir at The Oval, in particular, rang alarm bells. The wider context, however, was indisputable: an era closed when Strauss retired, and it was one of the greatest in England's history. He concluded it in his own way, quietly writing letters to each of his team-mates – Pietersen excepted. In an understated, English sort of way, you might almost have called them love letters.

11 Tests: 697 runs @ 33.19.

GRAEME SWANN **Nottinghamshire**

If Swann's summer was an extended blip that was hard to ignore, his form in Asia was the work of an off-spinner worthy of inheriting Jim Laker's mantle. All but ten of his 59 Test wickets – second only to Rangana Herath in the calendar year – came in the UAE, Sri Lanka and India, and at a cost of only 24 apiece. He wasn't just hoovering up left-handers either: 15 of his 20 wickets in India were right-handers, and at Ahmedabad he passed Laker's record Test haul for an England off-spinner of 193. Against West Indies in early summer (six wickets at 47) he had been peripheral. But against South Africa (four at 77) he was simply outwitted, both by Graeme Smith, who played him better than any left-hander ever had, and Hashim Amla, who negated him with an off-stump guard; at Headingley, for the first time in 43 Tests under Andy Flower, he was dropped. But Swann's alliance with Panesar at Mumbai, where they shared 19 wickets, was the best day for English spin since the late 1950s, and his removal of Virender Sehwag with the first ball after lunch on the fourth day at Kolkata changed the tone of the match. He was limited to nine one-day internationals by England's rotation policy and an ever-present concern over his right elbow, but in Twenty20s he was mean and incisive. The unspoken worry in his 34th year was how much longer he could keep going.

14 Tests: 376 runs @ 23.50; 59 wickets @ 29.93.
9 ODI: 13 runs @ 13.00, SR 92.85; 8 wickets @ 36.25, ER 4.32.
12 T20I: 56 runs @ 28.00, SR 121.73; 17 wickets @ 14.70, ER 5.68.

JAMES TREDWELL **Kent**

Philip Brown

Unsung and almost certainly underrated, Tredwell quietly established himself as England's No. 2 off-spinner. Typically, he let no one down, although his work went beyond honest yeomanry: at Lord's, three South Africans were lured to their doom, all stumped by Kieswetter. And he was England's least expensive bowler during the drawn Twenty20 series in India.

4 ODI: 7 runs @ 7.00, SR 31.81; 7 wickets @ 19.57, ER 4.41.
2 T20I: 1 run without dismissal, SR 100.00; 1 wicket @ 58.00, ER 7.25.

JONATHAN TROTT Warwickshire

Innings of 87 at Kolkata and 143 at Nagpur provided a gloss to a difficult year in which his only other century came in defeat at Galle, where it merited more. He kept bumping into nemeses: Sri Lanka's Rangana Herath removed him three times; South Africa's Dale Steyn and India's Pragyan Ojha four each. And yet, with the series at stake in India, there was something reassuring about the prospect of Trott batting for as long as he liked on a shirtfront. The instinct to drop anchor was as ingrained as ever and, while his Test average slipped to a shade below 50, it also remained a fraction higher than those of Cook and Pietersen. His one-day form was unfailingly solid – and resolutely unspectacular. A strike-rate of 62 sounded off the pace, but it chimed perfectly with England's tactics, especially at home, of careful accumulation against two new balls. The ends usually justified the means.

15 Tests: 1,005 runs @ 38.65; 1 wicket @ 156.00.
14 ODI: 410 runs @ 41.00, SR 62.31.

LUKE WRIGHT Sussex

The closest thing to a Twenty20 specialist in English cricket, Wright turned himself into a must-have accessory for any self-respecting franchise. Among regulars in the international format, only West Indian Kieron Pollard could better his strike-rate, while his 14 sixes – many of them back over the bowler's head – were four clear of the next England batsman. Two innings stood out, both at the World Twenty20: an unbeaten 99 off 55 balls against Afghanistan, and 76 off 43 against New Zealand. He finished by playing the all-rounder's role, sending down seven overs in two games against India after bowling only three in the year until then. All in all, it seemed a lucrative way of doing business.

9 T20I: 252 runs @ 31.50, SR 151.80; 4 wickets @ 19.50, ER 7.80.

AND THE REST…

James Taylor (Nottinghamshire; 2 Tests) was handed a Test debut against South Africa at Headingley following Bairstow's struggles against the short ball, and Bopara's personal problems, and he was a determined second fiddle in a stand of 147 with Pietersen. But 14 runs at Lord's spelled a temporary halt. **Joe Root** (Yorkshire; 1 Test, 1 T20I) made an instant impression when he ground his way to 73 on a surprise debut at Nagpur, and was rewarded with a place in England's Twenty20 squad and the Lions captaincy. **Chris Tremlett** (Surrey; 1 Test) played in England's opening game of the year, the first of the Dubai Tests, then flew home, wicketless, with a back injury. He never fully recovered. **Graham Onions** (Durham; 1 Test) managed his first Test since January 2010, when the seamers were rotated at Edgbaston, and would have done even better than four for 88 had Tino Best not erupted. **Chris Woakes** (Warwickshire; 2 ODI) was limited to six wicketless overs as South Africa coasted home at Trent Bridge, where only Cook made more than his unbeaten 33. England showed faith in the left-arm spin of **Danny Briggs** (Hampshire; 1 ODI; 3 T20I) by entrusting him with the new ball in the World Twenty20 against New Zealand, although his single over in India was a chastening experience at the hands of Yuvraj Singh. **Michael Lumb** (Nottinghamshire; 3 T20I) was grateful to make 50 off 34 balls in England's final game of the year, the Mumbai Twenty20, after one off ten at Pune had raised question marks. **Stuart Meaker** (Surrey; 2 T20I) hinted at the pros and cons of raw pace, removing Virat Kohli twice while going for nearly nine an over.

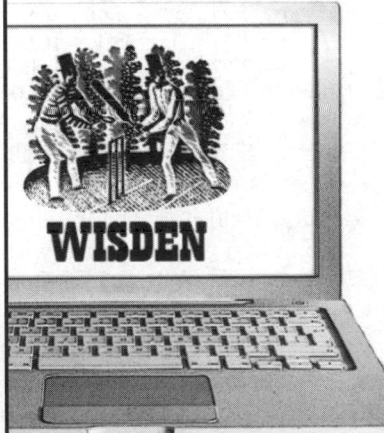

ENGLAND TEST AVERAGES IN CALENDAR YEAR 2012

BATTING AND FIELDING

	T	*I*	*NO*	*R*	*HS*	*100*	*Avge*	*SR*	*Ct/St*
J. E. Root	1	2	1	93	73	0	93.00	32.63	0
†A. N. Cook	15	29	3	1,249	190	4	48.03	41.89	11
K. P. Pietersen	14	25	1	1,053	186	3	43.87	65.12	5
M. J. Prior	15	22	2	777	91	0	38.85	52.64	29/7
I. J. L. Trott	15	28	2	1,005	143	2	38.65	43.67	6
N. R. D. Compton	4	8	2	208	57	0	34.66	33.93	1
I. R. Bell	14	25	5	672	116*	1	33.60	39.71	7
†A. J. Strauss	11	21	0	697	141	2	33.19	43.21	14
J. M. Bairstow	5	7	1	196	95	0	32.66	56.00	5
G. P. Swann	14	20	4	376	56	0	23.50	68.61	12
†S. C. J. Broad	11	18	2	277	58*	0	17.31	68.73	1
T. T. Bresnan	8	9	2	120	39*	0	17.14	32.52	4
J. W. A. Taylor	2	3	0	48	34	0	16.00	31.57	2
S. R. Patel	5	7	0	109	33	0	15.57	42.41	2
†E. J. G. Morgan	3	6	0	82	31	0	13.66	47.67	1
R. S. Bopara	1	2	0	22	22	0	11.00	36.06	0
†J. M. Anderson	14	22	5	137	23*	0	8.05	49.28	13
S. T. Finn	5	6	4	16	10	0	8.00	22.22	1
†M. S. Panesar	6	9	3	26	13	0	4.33	68.42	0
C. T. Tremlett	1	2	0	1	1	0	0.50	5.26	0
G. Onions	1	–	–	–	–	–	–	–	0

BOWLING

	Style	*O*	*M*	*R*	*W*	*BB*	*5I*	*Avge*	*SR*
G. Onions	RFM	29.3	7	88	4	4-88	0	22.00	44.25
M. S. Panesar	SLA	371	105	859	33	6-62	4	26.03	67.45
K. P. Pietersen	OB	36	2	147	5	3-52	0	29.40	43.20
J. M. Anderson	RFM	566.2	141	1,416	48	5-72	1	29.50	70.79
G. P. Swann	OB	634.2	124	1,766	59	6-82	3	29.93	64.50
S. T. Finn	RF	199.5	31	630	20	4-74	0	31.50	59.95
S. C. J. Broad	RFM	418.1	86	1,268	40	7-72	2	31.70	62.72
T. T. Bresnan	RFM	287	59	887	16	4-37	0	55.43	107.62
S. R. Patel	SLA	101	19	257	4	2-27	0	64.25	151.50
I. J. L. Trott	RM	53	5	156	1	1-16	0	156.00	318.00
J. E. Root	OB	1	0	5	0	0-5	–	–	–
C. T. Tremlett	RFM	21	6	53	0	0-53	–	–	–
R. S. Bopara	RM	18	1	78	0	0-78	–	–	–

“When they come to write the textbook of witlessly incompetent coups, they may well find space for the Pietersen Manoeuvre, which involves issuing a ‘back me or sack me’ ultimatum before disappearing on a winter-sun holiday in South Africa.”
It's tough being Kevin, page 70.

ENGLAND ONE-DAY INTERNATIONAL AVERAGES IN CALENDAR YEAR 2012

BATTING AND FIELDING

	M	*I*	*NO*	*R*	*HS*	*100*	*Avge*	*SR*	*Ct/St*
K. P. Pietersen	4	4	1	281	130	2	93.66	84.38	1
†E. J. G. Morgan	15	12	6	364	89*	0	60.66	98.11	4
I. R. Bell	11	11	1	549	126	1	54.90	82.68	3
S. R. Patel	10	5	3	101	45	0	50.50	83.47	2
†A. N. Cook	15	15	1	663	137	3	47.35	79.97	1
I. J. L. Trott	14	12	2	410	71	0	41.00	62.31	4
R. S. Bopara	14	12	3	339	82	0	37.66	80.71	2
C. Kieswetter	15	9	3	203	43	0	33.83	80.55	26/5
J. M. Bairstow	1	1	0	29	29	0	29.00	55.76	0
†S. C. J. Broad	9	2	1	23	22*	0	23.00	135.29	2
G. P. Swann	9	2	1	13	13*	0	13.00	92.85	3
T. T. Bresnan	8	3	1	25	21	0	12.50	108.69	4
†J. C. Tredwell	4	2	1	7	6	0	7.00	31.81	1
†J. M. Anderson	13	2	0	5	5	0	2.50	35.71	2
J. W. Dernbach	5	1	0	2	2	0	2.00	33.33	1
J. C. Buttler	1	1	0	0	0	0	0.00	0.00	0
C. R. Woakes	2	1	1	33	33*	0	–	75.00	0
S. T. Finn	14	1	1	15	15*	0	–	187.50	1
D. R. Briggs	1	–	–	–	–	–	–	–	0

BOWLING

	Style	*O*	*M*	*R*	*W*	*BB*	*4I*	*Avge*	*SR*	*ER*
D. R. Briggs	SLA	10	0	39	2	2-39	0	19.50	30.00	3.90
J. C. Tredwell	OB	31	1	137	7	3-35	0	19.57	26.57	4.41
S. T. Finn	RF	119	6	500	25	4-34	3	20.00	28.56	4.20
R. S. Bopara	RM	51	1	175	7	2-8	0	25.00	43.71	3.43
J. M. Anderson	RFM	101.4	9	479	18	4-44	1	26.61	33.88	4.71
T. T. Bresnan	RFM	61.4	1	346	13	4-34	1	26.61	28.46	5.61
J. W. Dernbach	RFM	45.3	1	255	9	4-45	1	28.33	30.33	5.60
S. C. J. Broad	RFM	79	5	368	11	3-42	0	33.45	43.09	4.65
G. P. Swann	OB	67	4	290	8	2-19	0	36.25	50.25	4.32
S. R. Patel	SLA	58	2	290	5	3-26	0	58.00	69.60	5.00
K. P. Pietersen	OB	1	0	4	0	0-4	0	–	–	4.00
C. R. Woakes	RFM	6	0	35	0	0-35	0	–	–	5.83

"Du Plessis batted almost two full days under acute pressure, like a cowboy with a pair of six-guns backing out of a saloon full of itchy-fingered desperados."

Australia v South Africa, 2012-13, page 907.

ENGLAND TWENTY20 INTERNATIONAL AVERAGES IN CALENDAR YEAR 2012

BATTING AND FIELDING

	M	*I*	*NO*	*R*	*HS*	*50*	*Avge*	*SR*	*4*	*6*	*Ct/St*
K. P. Pietersen	3	3	1	112	62*	1	56.00	130.23	13	2	1
A. D. Hales	10	10	1	343	99	3	38.11	137.20	32	10	3
L. J. Wright	9	9	1	252	99*	2	31.50	151.80	18	14	2
G. P. Swann	12	5	3	56	34	0	28.00	121.73	7	1	3
†E. J. G. Morgan	14	14	4	243	71*	1	24.30	120.89	16	9	8
J. C. Buttler	14	13	6	143	33*	0	20.42	133.64	8	7	1
J. M. Bairstow	12	10	3	142	60*	1	20.28	101.42	11	3	14
S. R. Patel	11	8	1	133	67	1	19.00	119.81	12	4	2
†M. J. Lumb	3	3	0	56	50	1	18.66	116.66	7	2	1
R. S. Bopara	6	6	0	107	59	1	17.83	108.08	6	2	1
C. Kieswetter	11	11	0	180	50	1	16.36	102.85	15	8	8/1
J. W. Dernbach	13	2	1	14	12	0	14.00	155.55	2	0	5
†S. C. J. Broad	12	5	2	30	18*	0	10.00	83.33	1	0	3
T. T. Bresnan	5	3	1	2	1*	0	1.00	20.00	0	0	1
S. T. Finn	11	2	2	9	8*	0	–	69.23	1	0	2
†J. C. Tredwell	2	1	1	1	1*	0	–	100.00	0	0	0
D. R. Briggs	3	–	–	–	–	–	–	–	–	–	0
S. C. Meaker	2	–	–	–	–	–	–	–	–	–	1
J. E. Root	1	–	–	–	–	–	–	–	–	–	2

BOWLING

	Style	*O*	*M*	*R*	*W*	*BB*	*4I*	*Avge*	*SR*	*ER*
G. P. Swann	OB	44	3	250	17	3-13	0	14.70	15.52	5.68
S. T. Finn	RF	42	0	284	17	3-16	0	16.70	14.82	6.76
L. J. Wright	RFM	10	0	78	4	2-38	0	19.50	15.00	7.80
T. T. Bresnan	RFM	17	0	131	5	2-14	0	26.20	20.40	7.70
S. C. J. Broad	RFM	42.2	2	292	11	3-32	0	26.54	23.09	6.89
J. W. Dernbach	RFM	44.2	0	376	13	2-16	0	28.92	20.46	8.48
D. R. Briggs	SLA	7	0	70	2	1-16	0	35.00	21.00	10.00
S. C. Meaker	RF	7.5	0	70	2	1-28	0	35.00	23.50	8.93
J. C. Tredwell	OB	8	0	58	1	1-27	0	58.00	48.00	7.25
R. S. Bopara	RM	8	0	63	1	1-23	0	63.00	48.00	7.87
S. R. Patel	SLA	22	0	174	2	2-6	0	87.00	66.00	7.90

PAKISTAN v ENGLAND IN THE UAE, 2011-12

REVIEW BY JOHN ETHERIDGE

Test matches (3): Pakistan 3, England 0
One-day internationals (4): Pakistan 0, England 4
Twenty20 internationals (3): Pakistan 1, England 2

At the end of a tour of wild fluctuations, two whitewashes and apathy among many locals, England emerged with their win–loss ledger marginally in credit but their spirits decidedly in deficit. If a 4–0 victory in the one-day series came as a pleasant surprise, their 3–0 defeat in the Tests that preceded it was nothing less than calamitous. Based on all previous evidence and any semblance of logic, the results were the wrong way round, although England's 2–1 win in the Twenty20 games at least offered a fleeting adherence to the form guide.

Test cricket was supposedly England's strength. Yet for all three matches their batsmen were teased and tormented by Pakistan's spinners. They had no answer, and produced some of the worst statistics for England in any series they had ever played. Then, as soon as the 50-over contests began, England overwhelmed Pakistan with fast-bowling power and four centuries in four games, all from their openers; the 5–0 defeat in India before Christmas seemed like a bad dream. It was only England's third one-day series whitewash overseas against countries other than Bangladesh and Zimbabwe, and their first in a series of more than three matches. And it was all very confusing.

England's exploits in Test cricket over the previous couple of years had been such that even a 3–0 defeat could not dislodge them from the top of the ICC rankings. Yet they knew they would never achieve their stated aim of becoming an all-time great Test team unless they improved in Asia.

The tone was set on the opening morning of the First Test, when England entered lunch at 52 for five, with Saeed Ajmal already three wickets into an eventual haul of seven. The batsmen looked undercooked and perhaps even complacent. Their warm-up games had not provided opposition of the highest quality; team director Andy Flower later admitted his side's preparation for the tour was not all it might have been. And they were certainly unable to read Ajmal's mixture of off-breaks and doosras. In the manner of Shane Warne, he had made pre-series boasts about another mystery ball – the teesra, or third one. There was little evidence of this new delivery – apart, possibly, from a ball sent down with an almost round-arm action. But his two favourite deliveries proved more than sufficient.

Ajmal finished the three Tests with 24 wickets, although his harvest was not completely unexpected: he had been recognised as the world's premier spin bowler before the start of the series. In many ways, Abdur Rehman's tally of 19 proved more damaging. A journeyman left-arm spinner, whose travels had included four club teams in England, Rehman superbly exploited both the uncertainty created by Ajmal at the other end and the tourists' near-paranoia about the Decision Review System.

TRAVELBAG.co.uk
Your Tailor-Made Australia Experts
To order a brochure or book visit travelbag.co.uk or call 0845 873 8266
Visit your local Travelbag shop: London, Alton, Brighton, Cheltenham, Knutsford, Solihull & Winchester
Photo: Hamilton Lund

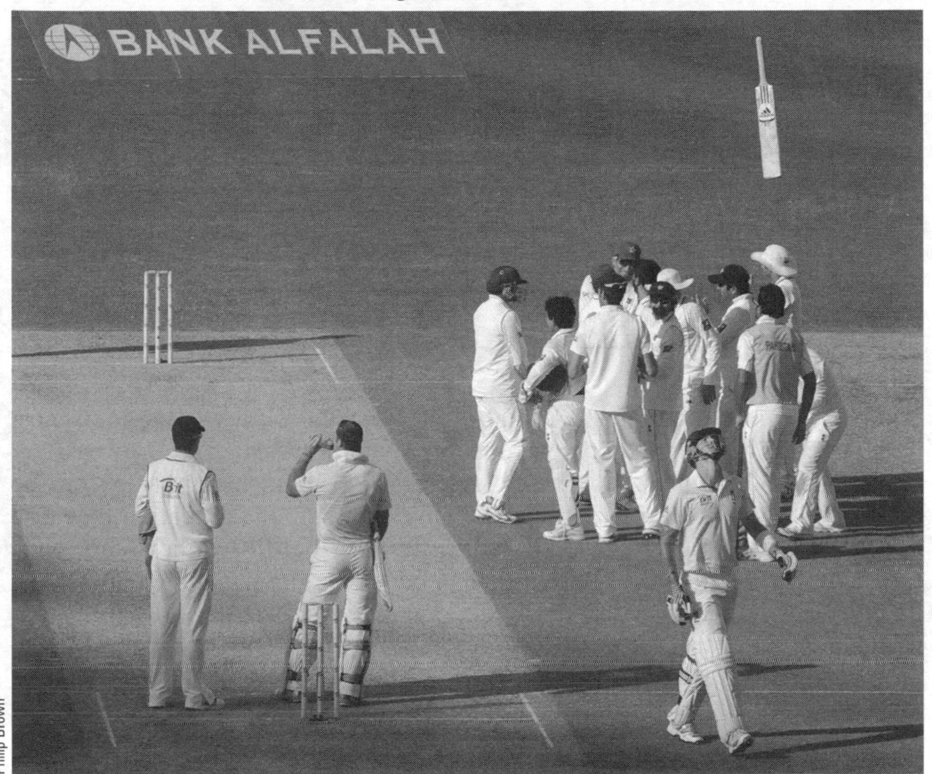

Philip Brown

High dudgeon: Kevin Pietersen finds the combination of left-arm spin, skiddy pitches and the Decision Review System too lethal a cocktail in the Third Test at Dubai.

England's nervous, tentative approach with the bat added up to some horrendous figures. The middle-order engine room of Kevin Pietersen, Ian Bell – utterly flummoxed by Ajmal's doosra – and Eoin Morgan was routinely blown away. Pietersen finished with a total of 67 runs, Bell 51 and Morgan 82, and all three failed to reach 40 in any first-class innings. In all matches on tour, including warm-ups and limited-overs internationals, Morgan had a top score of 31 in 17 attempts. He was dropped for the tour of Sri Lanka soon after.

The top three fared little better. Andrew Strauss extended his sequence to 31 months with only one Test century; like him, Alastair Cook and Jonathan Trott managed only one fifty each. England failed to register an individual century in a Test series for the first time since 1999, when they slumped to the bottom of the Wisden world rankings, and their average of 19 runs per wicket was their lowest in a three-match series since 1888, when Australia's new-ball pair of Charlie "Terror" Turner and J. J. Ferris were in their pomp.

Well though Ajmal and Rehman bowled, England batted as if petrified of a third, even more destructive, opponent. Let's call him Mr DRS. The days of spin bowlers looping the ball, landing it wide of the stumps and hoping for turn – with a bat-pad catch the most likely mode of dismissal – appeared to have changed for ever, at least in Asian conditions. Instead, Ajmal and Rehman aimed at pace for the stumps, and allowed England's inadequacies and the

MOST LBWS IN A TEST SERIES

lbws	*Tests*		
43	**3**	**Pakistan (21) v England (22) in the United Arab Emirates**	**2011-12**
43	5	England (16) v West Indies (27) in England	2000
43	6	England (21) v Australia (22) in England	1981
42	4	West Indies (27) v Australia (15) in the West Indies	1998-99
40	6	England (30) v Australia (10) in England	1989
37	5	England (19) v South Africa (18) in England	1955
37	6	India (19) v West Indies (18) in India	1983-84
35	5	West Indies (18) v Australia (17) in the West Indies	1990-91

The previous record for a three-Test series was 33 for West Indies (16) v Pakistan (17) in 1992-93.

review system to do the rest. A total of 43 batsmen fell lbw – the joint-most for a series of any length, let alone one of only three Tests.

The alarm England's batsmen inevitably felt about being struck on the pads quickly gave way to panic. This was with some justification, because umpires now seemed more prepared to give leg-before verdicts and, once the finger was up, the umpire's-call element of DRS in effect made the wicket four and a half stumps wide. England's concerns infiltrated their techniques and minds. Worried about using their pads, they seemed even more diffident about using their bats: 22 of their batsmen fell lbw, with Ajmal and Rehman claiming 19 between them – Ajmal seven in the First Test alone. The coaching maxim might have been: "You know that stick of wood in your hands? Well, use it!"

Pakistan encountered similar problems, and actually lost more batsmen lbw as the series progressed: three in the First Test, seven in the Second, and 11 in the Third. But while they too struggled against brisk left-arm spin – like Rehman, Monty Panesar won eight lbw appeals – they got into less of a tangle against Graeme Swann's orthodox off-breaks: he removed four batsmen leg-before to Ajmal's 11. Crucially, in the Third Test, Azhar Ali and Younis Khan had the nous to buck the trend, scoring the only centuries of the series in a partnership of 216 during which they deftly kept their pads out of the way.

Thrashed by ten wickets in the First Test, England had good opportunities to win the next two. Indeed, they believed they should have won the series. After three days of disciplined cricket in Abu Dhabi, they faltered to 72 all out in pursuit of 145 for victory. Then, in the Third, England reduced Pakistan to 44 for seven on the first morning on their way to 99 all out, before they fought back to become the first team since 1907 to win a Test after being bowled out for fewer than 100 in the first innings of the game.

Crucial to it all was Ajmal, whose skills did not escape controversy. On the first day of the series – the first day, in fact, on which the teams had played each other since the jailing of three Pakistan players and their agent following the spot-fixing scandal at Lord's in 2010 – his action was called into question. Comments made on television by Bob Willis back in the UK were the catalyst, and there was a flurry of confusion later in the series, when Ajmal appeared to tell the BBC he had been granted permission to bend his arm by 23.5 degrees at the elbow, well outside the permitted 15. The ICC later said

BACK FROM THE DEAD

Teams who won after being dismissed in double figures in the first innings of a Test:

45	England beat Australia by 13 runs at Sydney	1886-87
63	Australia beat England by seven runs at The Oval	1882
75	England beat Australia by 94 runs at Melbourne	1894-95
76	England beat South Africa by 53 runs at Leeds	1907
92	England beat South Africa by 210 runs at Cape Town	1898-99
99	**Pakistan beat England by 71 runs at Dubai (Third Test)**	**2011-12**

the quote had been a product of linguistic confusion, and released the results of scientific tests which showed the extent of Ajmal's flexion was in fact as low as seven degrees.

Although England coach Andy Flower privately harboured suspicions about Ajmal's action, there was a desire on both sides to quell any animosity lingering from the toxic 2010 series. And, in Misbah-ul-Haq – who had been left out of those Tests – Pakistan had a captain anxious not to reopen old wounds. He was calm and considered in everything he did, and apparently managed to unite the Pakistan dressing-room, a task beyond many of his predecessors. Misbah's only skewed judgment came when he was dismissed lbw five times out of five in the Tests, and referred the last four. The technology supported the umpire's verdict on each occasion.

While England's batsmen struggled, their bowlers were superb. Stuart Broad and James Anderson were miserly with new ball and old, drilling an off-stump line and extracting enough movement to trouble the Pakistanis. They had next to no support from other seamers. Chris Tremlett flew home for back surgery after the First Test, while Tim Bresnan – forced to return to the UK because the elbow problem on which he underwent an operation the previous November had not fully healed – missed the whole series, although he was able to come back for the one-day leg.

From the Second Test onwards England fielded two spinners, and Panesar – playing international cricket for the first time since he helped save the Ashes opener at Cardiff with the bat in July 2009 – ended with 14 wickets. He was usually the first spinner called on by Strauss and, in his two games, bowled 141 overs to Swann's 85. Swann ascribed this to the lack of left-handers in Pakistan's line-up. In truth, Panesar outbowled him.

England enjoyed many aspects of the tour – good hotels, top-notch facilities, no internal flights – but the cricket bug has yet to catch on in the UAE. Crowds were poor, with the Emiratis apparently uninterested, and Pakistani immigrants only occasionally willing or able to surrender a day's work to travel to grounds not serviced by public transport.

The Dubai Sports City Stadium was surrounded by half-constructed buildings on which the cranes had not moved for several years. It was like a scene from a post-apocalypse movie set. Abu Dhabi's Sheikh Zayed Stadium was in the middle of the desert, although the building work here, in the wealthiest of the Emirate states, was advancing fast. During the Tests, more than half of the crowd were normally Barmy Army members and assorted other England fans. Relocating matches to the UAE because of security

CRICKET IN THE DESERT

A glimmer of home

MICHAEL PEEL

Not many fans would watch cheerily as their side collapsed to 44 for seven, but Faisal Haroon and the other Pakistani spectators around him were used to remaining upbeat amid upheaval. As his 15-year-old daughter, Maryam, helpfully translated other supporters' undeterred chants – "We're going to win! Yes, we're going to win! Pakistan will win!" – he reflected on the oddness of watching his side play Test cricket against England in Dubai.

"It is strange, but not strange," said Faisal, a car importer and exporter who has lived in the United Arab Emirates for 17 years. "Because we feel this country is home as well."

Displaced to the UAE by long-standing security concerns at home, Pakistan's cricketers have turned their bolt-hole into a Test fortress – if a poorly attended one – and a venue for shorter-form matches as zestfully received by local supporters as any on south Asian soil. In the process, they have raised a set of interesting wider questions, ranging from the UAE's viability as a new centre for the game, to whether cut-price or free admission could be the way for Test cricket to survive.

The sparse attendance of a couple of thousand in Dubai's 25,000-seater stadium for the first day of the Third Test made a stark contrast with the booming crowds who had turned up for the one-day and Twenty20 matches against Sri Lanka in November. Those crowds highlighted the ready market in the Emirates for matches between sides from the subcontinent, whose diaspora is the biggest single group among the expatriates who account for an estimated 85% of the population of Dubai and Abu Dhabi.

For the Third Test, the Dubai stadium – dubbed the "Ring of Fire" for the nocturnal brilliance of its floodlighting – was very much a venue of two halves. Many England supporters opted for the Pizza Express and Foster's lager of the upper-tier tickets, costing 100 dirhams (about £17); some were almost comically bemused by the closure of the bar during Friday lunchtime prayers, the most important weekly act of worship for Muslims. Most Pakistan fans – ranging from middle-class business people to construction workers – went for the 20-dirham lower-tier seats, where biryani and tea were the staple fare.

The Ring of Fire may have a certain relaxed charm on a quiet day, but not everything about it is welcoming. UAE security officials were on hand to seize food and drink, including water bottles, at the entrance. The low winter sun dazzled blindingly off the giant TV screen opposite the English-dominated stand, while a crescent of shadow curled round the outfield and cast a surprisingly British chill on the seats it touched.

The crowd included stalwarts of Pakistani support, such as a trio known as Uncle All-rounder, Uncle T20 – sporting a fine handlebar moustache – and white-bearded Uncle Cricket, who claimed to have seen his country play 500 times and declared: "Barmy Army is my idol." For some spectators, the Dubai experience was proving bittersweet: regret at Pakistan's enforced homelessness salved by pleasure at seeing the team in the flesh and doing well. "So many of these people have been out of the country for such a long time," said Azfar Zaheer. "Anything related to Pakistan – especially when something good is happening to Pakistan – they want to be involved in it."

Philip Brown

That Friday feeling: lured by free entry, migrant Pakistanis throng Abu Dhabi's Sheikh Zayed Stadium.

For Pakistani manual workers, cricket is a rare treat in a life of long days and few social frills. "Normally, we have day off only on Friday," said Sher Zaman, who works for a local car dealership. "We stay at home washing clothes, receiving friends, sometimes we are going to beach" – though workers in this country full of lone men are often barred from Dubai's sands on the grounds that they might harass women sunbathing there.

Paying £3.50 to watch the cricket instead may not seem expensive, but it's still a deterrent: the Dubai crowd was well down on the throng who took advantage of free admission to the Friday of the Second Test in Abu Dhabi. The workers are in the UAE because they earn more than they would in Pakistan, but their wages are still very low by western standards, and they send a good part of them to needy families back home.

Mohammed Riaz, a driver at a construction company, said he earned 1,500 dirhams a month (£260) and immediately wired 850 to his wife and three children in Kashmir. Proportionally, the 20-dirham admission price was the same chunk out of the money he was left with each month as a £60 ticket would be for a Briton earning £24,000 a year. "It's a big amount for me," Mr Riaz said. "But I want to enjoy the cricket."

Also problematic for the mostly carless manual workers was the stadium's location, away from central Dubai: if there was any public transport, no one seemed to know about it. Noor Zardimkhon, a truck driver on 1,600 dirhams a month, said he paid 25 dirhams for a shared taxi.

As the afternoon wore on, a group of increasingly well-oiled England supporters in the loftier seats struck up a ragged chorus of "Jerusalem". Its impact was rather undermined as Ian Bell's dismissal dealt a further blow to his team's chances of a big lead, despite Pakistan having been bowled out for 99. But it was all a bit too much for one middle-aged man, who cast a maudlin eye at the cocky twentysomething Dubai British expats to his left and their long snake of plastic pint glasses. "How come you drink what I'm drinking but you have a lot more fun?" he asked plaintively.

It was not a question being posed in the tier below. As England wickets fell steadily, Pakistan's small but energetic contingent of fans were too busy cheering and drumming their side's latest successful embrace of their curious – but somehow fitting – home from home.

Michael Peel is the Middle East correspondent of the Financial Times.

FIVE STATS YOU MAY HAVE MISSED

BENEDICT BERMANGE

- Saeed Ajmal's figures in the first innings of the First Test were the best in a "neutral" Test:

7-55	**Saeed Ajmal**	**Pakistan v England at Dubai**	**2011-12**
7-94	S. K. Warne	Australia v Pakistan at Colombo (PSS)	2002-03
6-25	**Abdur Rehman**	**Pakistan v England at Abu Dhabi**	**2011-12**
6-33	S. R. Watson	Australia v Pakistan at Leeds	2010
6-55	M. J. North	Australia v Pakistan at Lord's	2010
6-62	**M. S. Panesar**	**England v Pakistan at Abu Dhabi**	**2011-12**
6-105	S. J. Pegler	South Africa v Australia at Manchester	1912

- The First Test was England's 72nd against Pakistan but only the second in which they have fielded a side with a lower average age than their opponents – 29 years 281 days, as against 30 years 318 days. The other occasion was at The Oval in 1996, when the England team had an average age just nine days younger than their Pakistani counterparts. (There is doubt over some Pakistani players' ages; these figures are calculated using the official dates.)

- In the Second Test, Andrew Strauss and Alastair Cook became the fourth pair to open the batting in 100 Test innings. The three other pairs were C. G. Greenidge and D. L. Haynes (West Indies, 148 innings at an average of 47.31), M. S. Atapattu and S. T. Jayasuriya (Sri Lanka, 118 at 40.26) and M. L. Hayden and J. L. Langer (Australia, 113 at 51.88). On Strauss's retirement from international cricket in August 2012, he and Cook had opened in 117 innings at an average of 40.96.

- Misbah-ul-Haq emulated Willie Watson by being dismissed lbw five times in a three-Test series: Watson was lbw five time in six innings for New Zealand against Pakistan in 1990-91 but was not out once; Misbah was lbw in all five of his innings. Kim Hughes was lbw a record seven times (in 12 innings) in the 1981 Ashes series.

- When Azhar Ali scored 157 in the Third Test at Dubai, his strike-rate of 35.52 was the slowest in 480 (now 492) individual Test innings of 150 or more in the 23 years since Shoaib Mohammad's 163 from 516 balls (31.58) for Pakistan against New Zealand at Wellington in 1988-89.

SR			*Balls*		
35.52	**Azhar Ali**	**157**	**442**	**Pakistan v England at Dubai**	**2011-12**
35.90	A. J. Hall	163	454	South Africa v India at Kanpur	2004-05
35.98	T. M. K. Mawoyo	163*	453	Zimbabwe v Pakistan at Bulawayo	2011-12
37.50	M. S. Atapattu	201*	536	Sri Lanka v England at Galle	2000-01
37.60	M. A. Atherton	185*	492	England v South Africa at Johannesburg	1995-96

Benedict Bermange is the cricket statistician for Sky Sports.

concerns seemed an acceptable compromise for the Pakistan Cricket Board, but this was a home series only in the loosest sense.

When the one-day series started, Cook made centuries in the first two games and 80 in the third, while Pietersen reached three figures in the final two. He described his innings of 130, which ensured England's whitewash, as his finest in one-day cricket. The decision to promote him back to the opener's role he performed briefly in the 2011 World Cup – a switch made because of his poor returns at No. 4 and Flower's suspicion that he needed to refire Pietersen's appetite for 50-over cricket – was a huge success, and in

Graham Morris

Look back in anguish: Eoin Morgan falls in the Second Test as England slip towards their first series defeat for three years.

stark contrast to his travails in the Tests. (The story, of course, would later develop a life of its own.)

Just as influential was Steven Finn. He bowled fast and straight to collect 13 wickets in the four matches, including figures of four for 34 in each of the first two. The power of Finn and England's other bowlers was too much for a Pakistan side who had not lost any bilateral one-day series in 2011. England were able to rest a number of senior players for the final match and still win.

Cook advanced his standing as a leader, and his aggressive batting persuaded England to add him to the Twenty20 squad as cover because of minor injuries elsewhere, even if he was never seriously considered for a place in the starting team. Broad became England's third captain of the tour in the Twenty20 matches, and the management seemed happy to continue splitting the job – although the 50-over success under Cook had the unintended consequence of highlighting the Test losses under Strauss. Yet, for the time being at least, Strauss's position was under no serious threat.

England, the reigning world Twenty20 champions, secured the series by winning the final two matches after a careless defeat in the first. Younger players, such as Jonny Bairstow and Jade Dernbach, made useful contributions, although Pietersen and Swann were crucial too. By now, England were more used to the wiles of Pakistan's spin bowlers, and more at ease with fields that were less attacking than in the Tests. If the one-day series had come first, everything might have been different. And maybe even a little more logical.

ENGLAND TOURING PARTY

*A. J. Strauss (Middlesex), J. M. Anderson (Lancashire), I. R. Bell (Warwickshire), R. S. Bopara (Essex), S. C. J. Broad (Nottinghamshire), A. N. Cook (Essex), S. M. Davies (Surrey), S. T. Finn (Middlesex), E. J. G. Morgan (Middlesex), G. Onions (Durham), M. S. Panesar (Sussex), K. P.

Pietersen (Surrey), M. J. Prior (Sussex), G. P. Swann (Nottinghamshire), C. T. Tremlett (Surrey), I. J. L. Trott (Warwickshire).

T. T. Bresnan (Yorkshire) was originally selected, but was replaced by Onions when he withdrew with an elbow problem; he returned for the two limited-overs series. Tremlett withdrew after the First Test for back surgery. For the one-day internationals which followed the Tests, Cook took over the captaincy. J. M. Bairstow (Yorkshire), D. R. Briggs (Hampshire), J. C. Buttler (Somerset), J. W. Dernbach (Surrey), C. Kieswetter (Somerset) and S. R. Patel (Nottinghamshire) replaced Bell, Davies, Onions, Panesar, Prior and Strauss. A. D. Hales (Nottinghamshire) replaced Trott for the Twenty20 series in which Broad resumed the captaincy, and Cook, who was originally scheduled to leave, was kept on.

Coach: A. Flower. *Assistant coach/fielding coach (Tests):* R. G. Halsall; *(limited-overs matches):* A. Hurry. *Batting coach:* G. A. Gooch. *Fast bowling coach:* D. J. Saker. *Spin bowling coach:* Mushtaq Ahmed. *Wicketkeeping coach:* B. N. French. *Strength and conditioning coach:* H. R. Bevan. *Team operations manager:* P. A. Neale. *Physiotherapist:* B. T. Langley. *Team doctor:* Dr M. G. Wotherspoon. *Analyst:* N. A. Leamon. *Sports psychologist:* M. A. K. Bawden. *Massage therapist:* M. E. S. Saxby. *Security manager:* R. C. Dickason. *Media relations manager:* R. C. Evans.

TEST MATCH AVERAGES

PAKISTAN – BATTING AND FIELDING

	T	*I*	*NO*	*R*	*HS*	*100*	*50*	*Avge*	*Ct/St*
Azhar Ali	3	5	0	251	157	1	1	50.20	0
Younis Khan	3	5	0	193	127	1	0	38.60	2
Mohammad Hafeez	3	6	1	190	88	0	1	38.00	4
Misbah-ul-Haq	3	5	0	180	84	0	2	36.00	0
Asad Shafiq	3	5	0	167	58	0	1	33.40	6
Adnan Akmal	3	5	0	89	61	0	1	17.80	9/2
†Taufeeq Umar	3	6	1	87	58	0	1	17.40	1
Umar Gul	3	5	2	27	13	0	0	9.00	1
Saeed Ajmal	3	5	0	42	17	0	0	8.40	0
†Abdur Rehman	3	5	0	16	10	0	0	3.20	3
Aizaz Cheema	2	3	3	0	0*	0	0	–	0

Played in one Test: Junaid Khan 0, 0.

BOWLING

	Style	*O*	*M*	*R*	*W*	*BB*	*5I*	*Avge*
Saeed Ajmal	OB	147	39	353	24	7-55	1	14.70
Mohammad Hafeez	OB	43	12	80	5	3-54	0	16.00
Abdur Rehman	SLA	131.4	34	318	19	6-25	2	16.73
Umar Gul	RFM	74	16	245	11	4-61	0	22.27

Also bowled: Aizaz Cheema (RFM) 27.2–1–70–1; Junaid Khan (LFM) 8–0–33–0.

ENGLAND – BATTING AND FIELDING

	T	*I*	*NO*	*R*	*HS*	*100*	*50*	*Avge*	*Ct/St*
M. J. Prior	3	6	2	150	70*	0	1	37.50	5/1
I. J. L. Trott	3	6	0	161	74	0	1	26.83	0
†A. N. Cook	3	6	0	159	94	0	1	26.50	2
†A. J. Strauss	3	6	0	150	56	0	1	25.00	2
†S. C. J. Broad	3	6	1	105	58*	0	1	21.00	0
G. P. Swann	3	6	0	105	39	0	0	17.50	1
†E. J. G. Morgan	3	6	0	82	31	0	0	13.66	1
K. P. Pietersen	3	6	0	67	32	0	0	11.16	1

	T	I	NO	R	HS	100	50	Avge	Ct/St
†J. M. Anderson	3	6	1	54	15*	0	0	10.80	4
I. R. Bell	3	6	0	51	29	0	0	8.50	0
†M. S. Panesar	2	4	2	8	8	0	0	4.00	0

Played in one Test: C. T. Tremlett 1, 0.

BOWLING

	Style	O	M	R	W	BB	5I	Avge
S. C. J. Broad	RFM	116.4	34	266	13	4-36	0	20.46
M. S. Panesar	SLA	141	44	302	14	6-62	2	21.57
G. P. Swann	OB	114.5	17	326	13	4-107	0	25.07
J. M. Anderson	RFM	107.5	26	249	9	3-35	0	27.66

Also bowled: K. P. Pietersen (OB) 3–0–9–0; C. T. Tremlett (RF) 21–6–53–0; I. J. L. Trott (RM) 12–2–42–1.

ICC COMBINED ASSOCIATE AND AFFILIATE XI v ENGLAND XI

At Dubai (ICC Academy), January 7–9, 2012. England XI won by three wickets. Toss: England XI.

An assortment of Irishmen, Scots, Afghans, Namibians and one Pakistan-born Emirati embarrassed England's batsmen on the second day. Only Cook, fresh from his honeymoon, prospered; no one else reached 20. The bowling looked stronger: in his first game since tearing a shoulder muscle in September, Broad struck in each of his first three overs, and took seven in all. The Combined XI recovered from 90 for six thanks to Viljoen, last out two short of a maiden hundred, and Rankin, appearing as an Irishman, though about to join the England Lions. After Strauss declared behind and the top order collapsed again, Mohammad Shahzad scored a second fifty, to go with five catches, and Porterfield set a target of 261. Strauss got England going, but they slipped to 199 for six against Mohammad Nabi's off-spin. Pietersen fell to slow left-armer Dockrell, a full substitute for Hamid Hassan, who had taken a nasty fall over the boundary fence. But Davies and Broad steered them towards victory with nearly nine overs left.

Close of play: first day, England XI 16-0 (Strauss 8, Cook 8); second day, ICC Combined Associate and Affiliate XI 90-5 (Mohammad Shahzad 34, Mohammad Nabi 9).

ICC Combined Associate and Affiliate XI

*W. T. S. Porterfield c Davies b Broad	1	– c Davies b Anderson	0
P. R. Stirling b Broad	7	– lbw b Broad	0
K. J. Coetzer c Davies b Broad	1	– b Anderson	31
Saqib Ali c Swann b Finn	14	– c Davies b Broad	2
C. G. Williams c Davies b Swann	34	– c Bell b Swann	11
†Mohammad Shahzad c Broad b Anderson	51	– c Broad b Pietersen	74
Mohammad Nabi b Swann	0	– c Cook b Broad	13
C. Viljoen c Anderson b Broad	98	– run out	3
R. M. Haq lbw b Finn	26	– not out	26
W. B. Rankin c Finn b Anderson	43	– b Finn	0
Hamid Hassan not out	0		
L-b 2, w 1, n-b 3	6	L-b 1, n-b 3	4
1/1 (1) 2/10 (2) 3/11 (3) 4/52 (4) (83.3 overs) 5/82 (5) 6/90 (7) 7/122 (6) 8/181 (9) 9/277 (10) 10/281 (8)	281	1/0 (1) (9 wkts dec, 55.3 overs) 2/2 (2) 3/8 (4) 4/31 (5) 5/71 (3) 6/101 (7) 7/119 (8) 8/162 (6) 9/164 (10)	164

G. H. Dockrell replaced Hamid Hassan, who was injured.

Anderson 19–6–46–2; Broad 16.3–6–46–4; Finn 17–3–59–2; Swann 23–0–99–2; Trott 2–0–6–0; Pietersen 6–0–23–0. *Second innings*—Anderson 18–7–62–2; Broad 14–7–22–3; Swann 10–1–33–1; Finn 10.3–4–34–1; Pietersen 3–0–12–1.

England XI

Batsman	First innings		Second innings	
*A. J. Strauss c Haq b Hamid Hassan	17	–	c Williams b Haq	78
A. N. Cook c Mohammad Shahzad b Viljoen	76	–	c Haq b Williams	26
I. J. L. Trott c Mohammad Shahzad b Hamid Hassan	1	–	c Porterfield b Mohammad Nabi	35
K. P. Pietersen c Mohammad Shahzad b Rankin	15	–	c Rankin b Dockrell	1
I. R. Bell c Mohammad Shahzad b Rankin	3	–	c Stirling b Mohammad Nabi	39
E. J. G. Morgan c Stirling b Mohammad Nabi	1	–	c Mohammad Shahzad b Rankin	3
†S. M. Davies lbw b Haq	12	–	not out	37
S. C. J. Broad c Porterfield b Mohammad Nabi	19	–	c Dockrell b Mohammad Nabi	31
G. P. Swann not out	14	–	not out	1
J. M. Anderson not out	12			
B 8, l-b 4, w 1, n-b 2	15		B 8, l-b 1, n-b 1	10
1/44 (1) 2/54 (3) 3/107 (4) 4/121 (5) 5/126 (6) 6/132 (2) 7/159 (7) 8/159 (8) (8 wkts dec, 55 overs)	185		1/63 (2) 2/133 (1) 3/136 (4) 4/180 (3) 5/187 (6) 6/199 (5) 7/260 (8) (7 wkts, 60.1 overs)	261

S. T. Finn did not bat.

Hamid Hassan 11–4–26–2; Viljoen 11–1–42–1; Mohammad Nabi 14–3–42–2; Rankin 16–3–49–2; Haq 3–1–14–1. *Second innings*—Rankin 15–1–58–1; Viljoen 4–0–28–0; Mohammad Nabi 17–1–66–3; Williams 4–1–20–1; Dockrell 6–0–28–1; Haq 12.1–1–42–1; Stirling 2–0–10–0.

Umpires: B. B. Pradhan and Zameer Haider. Referee: G. F. Labrooy.

PAKISTAN CRICKET BOARD XI v ENGLAND XI

At Dubai (ICC Academy), January 11–13, 2012. England XI won by 100 runs. Toss: Pakistan Cricket Board XI.

England completed another warm-up win that lacked conviction. Cook scored a century on the opening day, while Strauss and Trott ran up fifties second time round. But Bell and Morgan failed again, and Pietersen succumbed twice to leg-spinner Yasir Shah. Bresnan had gone home with a bad elbow, so Onions and Panesar were competing for an England comeback with Tremlett, who bowled in dark glasses after a severe infection in his right eye. Panesar's left-arm spin claimed four of the five wickets the PCB XI lost for 28 mid-innings, though a maiden fifty from 19-year-old Raza Hasan at No. 9 gave them some respectability. Strauss and Trott took the lead to 250 by lunch on the final day, before Onions and Tremlett reduced the opposition to 16 for three. Only Fawad Alam put up much resistance; once Pietersen removed him, the remaining five wickets managed only 47. Panesar, like his fellow slow bowler Yasir, finished with eight wickets.

Close of play: first day, Pakistan Cricket Board XI 23-0 (Nasir Jamshed 12, Afaq Raheem 10); second day, England XI 82-0 (Strauss 36, Trott 39).

England XI

Batsman	First innings		Second innings	
*A. J. Strauss c Sarfraz Ahmed b Mohammad Talha	3	–	lbw b Yasir Shah	62
A. N. Cook c Sarfraz Ahmed b Mohammad Talha	133			
I. J. L. Trott lbw b Mohammad Talha	0	–	(2) c Mohammad Khalil b Yasir Shah	93
K. P. Pietersen b Yasir Shah	38	–	(3) c Nasir Jamshed b Yasir Shah	3
I. R. Bell lbw b Yasir Shah	0	–	(4) not out	12
E. J. G. Morgan c Raza Hasan b Yasir Shah	11			
†M. J. Prior c Sarfraz Ahmed b Mohammad Talha	46			
G. P. Swann c Sarfraz Ahmed b Yasir Shah	24			
G. Onions c Mohammad Talha b Yasir Shah	1			
M. S. Panesar not out	0			
L-b 6, w 1, n-b 6	13		B 5, l-b 1, w 1, n-b 4	11
1/13 (1) 2/14 (3) 3/97 (4) 4/101 (5) 5/121 (6) 6/211 (7) 7/257 (8) 8/267 (9) 9/269 (2) (9 wkts dec, 81.1 overs)	269		1/130 (1) 2/140 (3) 3/181 (2) (3 wkts dec, 49.3 overs)	181

C. T. Tremlett did not bat.

Mohammad Talha 15.1–2–42–4; Mohammad Khalil 14–3–46–0; Raza Hasan 26–3–99–0; Yasir Shah 26–1–76–5. *Second innings*—Mohammad Talha 11–2–50–0; Mohammad Khalil 9–2–27–0; Raza Hasan 17–1–57–0; Yasir Shah 11.3–0–38–3; Mohammad Ayub 1–0–3–0.

Pakistan Cricket Board XI

First innings		Second innings	
Nasir Jamshed lbw b Onions	12	– c Prior b Tremlett	0
Afaq Raheem lbw b Tremlett	17	– b Onions	7
Mohammad Ayub c Prior b Panesar	33	– lbw b Onions	0
Usman Salahuddin c Prior b Tremlett	23	– c Swann b Panesar	32
Fawad Alam c Strauss b Panesar	7	– c Trott b Pietersen	51
Haris Sohail lbw b Panesar	6	– lbw b Swann	11
*†Sarfraz Ahmed c Trott b Swann	0	– c Prior b Tremlett	11
Yasir Shah c Swann b Panesar	9	– (9) lbw b Onions	10
Raza Hasan not out	50	– (8) st Prior b Panesar	22
Mohammad Talha c Prior b Panesar	31	– lbw b Panesar	3
Mohammad Khalil not out	1	– not out	0
B 3, l-b 6, w 2	11	N-b 3	3
1/24 (1) 2/40 (2) (9 wkts dec, 79 overs)	200	1/7 (2) 2/7 (1) (52.3 overs)	150
3/78 (4) 4/91 (5) 5/101 (6)		3/16 (3) 4/87 (4)	
6/106 (7) 7/110 (3) 8/119 (8) 9/173 (10)		5/103 (5) 6/114 (7) 7/120 (6)	
		8/134 (9) 9/148 (8) 10/150 (10)	

Onions 13–3–52–1; Tremlett 14–7–30–2; Swann 21–5–49–1; Panesar 29–12–57–5; Pietersen 2–0–3–0. *Second innings*—Tremlett 10–3–32–2; Onions 10–3–38–3; Swann 16–4–24–1; Panesar 14.3–3–46–3; Pietersen 2–0–10–1.

Umpires: Ahsan Raza and Shozab Raza.

PAKISTAN v ENGLAND

First Test Match

DEREK PRINGLE

At Dubai, January 17–19, 2012. Pakistan won by ten wickets. Toss: England.

A little over two months after three Pakistani players were imprisoned for spot-fixing during their previous Test against England, at Lord's in August 2010, the sides met at the neutral venue of the Dubai Sports City Stadium. But the impressive, if sterile, ground did not preside over neutral cricket – at least not from the Pakistanis, who immediately located top gear to despatch England inside three days.

If the meeting of these teams, with their history of volatility, was always likely to be unpredictable, few could have foreseen the drubbing suffered by England in their first Test since officially becoming the world's No. 1 side. To lose by ten wickets was bad enough; to do so after your captain had won the toss, and the pitch offered only moderate assistance to the bowlers, was difficult to credit.

BEST BOWLING IN A MATCH FOR PAKISTAN v ENGLAND

13-101 (9-56, 4-45)	Abdul Qadir at Lahore	1987-88
12-99 (6-53, 6-46)	Fazal Mahmood at The Oval	1954
10-77 (3-37, 7-40)	Imran Khan at Leeds	1987
10-97 (7-55, 3-42)	**Saeed Ajmal at Dubai**	**2011-12**
10-186 (5-88, 5-98)	Abdul Qadir at Karachi	1987-88
10-194 (5-84, 5-110)	Abdul Qadir at Lahore	1983-84
10-211 (7-96, 3-115)	Abdul Qadir at The Oval	1987

The England attack, it's true, performed manfully, but the haplessness of the batsmen, who – for only the third time in a Test since the 2006-07 Ashes – were dismissed twice for under 200, meant their efforts were wasted. And central to the demise was Saeed Ajmal, whose jerky mix of doosras and off-breaks brought him match figures of ten for 97, the best by a Pakistani against England for over 24 years.

During the tea interval on the first day – not long before England were dismissed for 192, itself something of a recovery from 43 for five – Bob Willis, summarising for Sky TV in their London studio, threatened to turn the match into a battle of the bent elbow. It was a prompt the British media took up with glee: no sooner had Ajmal completed career-best figures of seven for 55 than his action became the story.

Willis was a professional cricketer from 1969 to 1984, an age intolerant of bowlers with noticeable snap at the point of delivery. His doubts over the legitimacy of Ajmal's action would have been echoed by many from his era, but the change to the playing conditions in 2005, when the ICC sanctioned flexion of up to 15 degrees, was more significant.

It helped to fan the flames that Ajmal had been reported for a suspect action in 2009 by Billy Bowden, one of the on-field umpires in this Test. Bowden had aired his misgivings during a one-day international against Australia, though Ajmal was cleared on that occasion by experts in human movement at the University of Western Australia. According to their findings, made in controlled laboratory conditions by Professor Bruce Elliott, Ajmal's bowling arm had 23 degrees of flex at the elbow when it was horizontal – but it straightened by only ten degrees when he bowled his off-break, and by seven with his doosra or quicker ball.

Just in case England had been fussing over their protractors, Ajmal and his captain, Misbah-ul-Haq, also planted the possibility of a new mystery delivery, the teesra – or third one. If it did exist, other than as a deliberate distraction in the build-up to the match, Ajmal didn't need to harness it: only Trott and Prior appeared able to pick even the standard variations in his arsenal.

MOST LBWS BY ONE BOWLER IN A TEST

8	†Mohammad Zahid	Pakistan v New Zealand at Rawalpindi	1996-97
8	W. P. U. J. C. Vaas	Sri Lanka v West Indies at Colombo (SSC)	2001-02
7	R. J. Hadlee	New Zealand v West Indies at Dunedin	1979-80
7	Abdul Qadir	Pakistan v England at Lahore	1987-88
7	Waqar Younis	Pakistan v Zimbabwe at Karachi	1993-94
7	I. K. Pathan	India v Bangladesh at Dhaka	2004-05
7	**Saeed Ajmal**	**Pakistan v England at Dubai**	**2011-12**

† *On Test debut.*

The Decision Review System seemed to make England's batsmen doubly jittery. After they were prevented from using their front pads as a reliable line of defence against spin, their techniques unravelled almost as quickly as their confidence. Pietersen, who before the series referred to the DRS as "that bloody machine", looked especially confused. Unable to pick Ajmal, and with a long-standing unease against left-arm spin – purveyed here by the accurate Abdur Rehman – he displayed all the existential angst of Edvard Munch's *The Scream* during his 29-ball innings on the opening day. Ajmal finally put him out of his misery, lbw for two.

None except Prior, who made an unbeaten 70, and Swann, who swung lustily for 34, offered much of a solution. Prior used his feet well – not in the traditional sense of dancing down the pitch, which English batsmen had long avoided, but by stretching well forward or getting right back. When confronted by Ajmal, so many of England's batsmen simply shuffled their feet and hung their bats in submission, a strong indication that they hadn't a clue which way the ball was turning.

Pakistan's retort was an opening stand of 114 between Mohammad Hafeez and Taufeeq Umar, though that belied the stoic efforts of Broad and Anderson. With England opting for just one specialist spinner (Tremlett was preferred to Monty Panesar), they had to rotate their three seamers. As Swann's foils, they ran in bravely and – with a little help from Trott, who trapped Younis Khan with a vicious nip-backer – they managed to dismiss Pakistan for 338. Their lead was 146, but England knew it could have been worse.

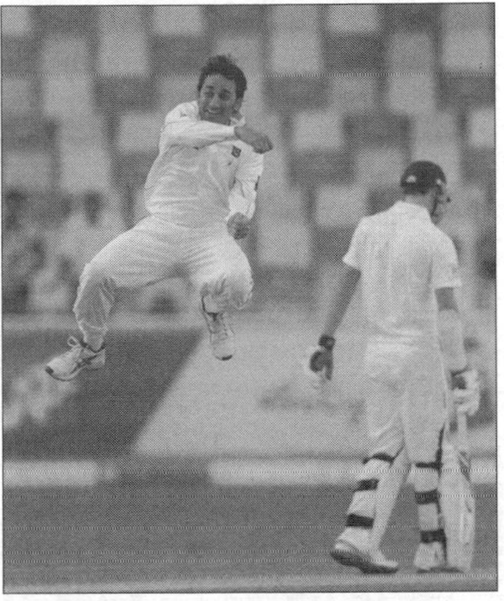

Philip Brown

A giant leap: Saeed Ajmal completes his series-defining ten-wicket haul.

In the event, any vague sense of relief was fleeting. With their second-innings anxieties focused on Ajmal, England appeared to forget that Umar Gul was no slouch either. Charging in from the Southern End, he dismissed Strauss, Cook and Pietersen in his opening spell – though there was enough doubt over Strauss's dismissal, caught down the leg side by Adnan Akmal, for him to review it and, later, for Andy Flower to complain to the match referee.

But Gul's strikes left England's shaky middle order to confront Ajmal and Rehman. And while the pitch held true, resistance – apart from Trott's 49 and another cameo from Swann – was token as the spinners shared six wickets. Trott's efforts at least meant Pakistan needed to bat again, but not for long. Soon after, England were wallowing in their first defeat in ten Tests, since Perth in 2010-11, and their first inside three days since being ambushed by Australia at Headingley in 2009. In those series, England would hold their nerve. Out in the UAE, things were about to get a whole lot worse.

Man of the Match: Saeed Ajmal.

Close of play: first day, Pakistan 42-0 (Mohammad Hafeez 22, Taufeeq Umar 18); second day, Pakistan 288-7 (Adnan Akmal 24).

England

*A. J. Strauss b Saeed Ajmal	19	– c Adnan Akmal b Umar Gul	6
A. N. Cook c Adnan Akmal b Mohammad Hafeez	3	– c Adnan Akmal b Umar Gul	5
I. J. L. Trott c Adnan Akmal b Aizaz Cheema	17	– c Adnan Akmal b Umar Gul	49
K. P. Pietersen lbw b Saeed Ajmal	2	– c Abdur Rehman b Umar Gul	0
I. R. Bell c Adnan Akmal b Saeed Ajmal	0	– lbw b Saeed Ajmal	4
E. J. G. Morgan lbw b Saeed Ajmal	24	– c Adnan Akmal b Abdur Rehman	14
†M. J. Prior not out	70	– lbw b Saeed Ajmal	4
S. C. J. Broad lbw b Saeed Ajmal	8	– c Asad Shafiq b Abdur Rehman	17
G. P. Swann b Abdur Rehman	34	– c Asad Shafiq b Saeed Ajmal	39
C. T. Tremlett lbw b Saeed Ajmal	1	– c Mohammad Hafeez b Abdur Rehman	0
J. M. Anderson lbw b Saeed Ajmal	12	– not out	15
L-b 2	2	B 4, l-b 1, n-b 2	7
1/10 (2) 2/31 (3) 3/42 (1) 4/42 (5) 5/43 (4) 6/82 (6) 7/94 (8) 8/151 (9) 9/168 (10) 10/192 (11) (72.3 overs)	192	1/6 (1) 2/25 (2) 3/25 (4) 4/35 (5) 5/74 (6) 6/87 (3) 7/87 (7) 8/135 (8) 9/135 (10) 10/160 (9) (57.5 overs)	160

Umar Gul 12–4–35–0; Aizaz Cheema 12–0–43–1; Mohammad Hafeez 6–3–5–1; Abdur Rehman 18–5–52–1; Saeed Ajmal 24.3–7–55–7. *Second innings*—Umar Gul 19–5–63–4; Aizaz Cheema 7.2–1–9–0; Mohammad Hafeez 2–0–4–0; Saeed Ajmal 17.3–4–42–3; Abdur Rehman 12–2–37–3.

Pakistan

Mohammad Hafeez lbw b Swann	88	– not out	15
Taufeeq Umar b Broad	58	– not out	0
Azhar Ali c Prior b Broad	1		
Younis Khan lbw b Trott	37		
*Misbah-ul-Haq lbw b Swann	52		
Asad Shafiq c Prior b Anderson	16		
†Adnan Akmal st Prior b Swann	61		
Abdur Rehman b Anderson	4		
Umar Gul c Morgan b Broad	0		
Saeed Ajmal c Cook b Swann	12		
Aizaz Cheema not out	0		
B 2, l-b 5, n-b 2	9		
1/114 (2) 2/128 (3) 3/176 (1) (119.5 overs)	338	(no wkt, 3.4 overs)	15

4/202 (4) 5/231 (6) 6/283 (5)
7/288 (8) 8/289 (9) 9/319 (10) 10/338 (7)

Anderson 30–7–71–2; Tremlett 21–6–53–0; Broad 31–8–84–3; Swann 29.5–3–107–4; Trott 8–2–16–1. *Second innings*—Anderson 2–1–7–0; Broad 1.4–1–8–0.

Umpires: B. F. Bowden and B. N. J. Oxenford. Third umpire: S. J. Davis.
Referee: J. Srinath.

PAKISTAN v ENGLAND

Second Test Match

GEORGE DOBELL

At Abu Dhabi, January 25–28, 2012. Pakistan won by 72 runs. Toss: Pakistan.

Nobody remembers the first 90% of the voyage of the *Titanic*. They forget the prompt departure, excellent catering and swift progress across the north Atlantic. No, all anyone talks about is that unfortunate incident with the iceberg.

So it proved with this Test. By the end, few recalled England's excellent bowling; the dogged 139-run stand between Cook and Trott that seemed to have put them in charge; Broad's counter-attacking half-century; or Panesar's six second-innings wickets, in his first Test since July 2009.

Instead, it was all about England's fourth innings. Set 145 to win, they did not even make it halfway, capitulating for 72 to go 2–0 down with one to play. It was comfortably their lowest total against Pakistan, outdoing 130 at The Oval in 1954, in the first series between these sides, and again at Lahore in 1987-88. It was England's lowest Test score since 51 in Jamaica in February 2009. And it was only the second time in more than a century they had lost chasing a target under 150.

Whichever way you looked at it, this was a shocking reverse for a team playing their first series since whitewashing India to go top of the Test rankings in August 2011. It was the first time they had lost successive Tests since hosting South Africa in 2008, and their first series defeat in ten, dating back to that 2008-09 tour of the West Indies. Records tumbled as quickly as wickets.

Perhaps it should not have come as a huge surprise. England's record in Asia promised little: excluding Bangladesh, and including the game in Dubai, they had won only one of

ENGLAND TEST DEFEATS CHASING UNDER 150

Target	*Total*		
85	77	v Australia at The Oval (lost by seven runs)	1882
124	62	v Australia at Lord's (lost by 61 runs)	1888
124	120	v Australia at Manchester (lost by three runs)	1902
137	64	v New Zealand at Wellington (lost by 72 runs)	1977-78
145	**72**	**v Pakistan at Abu Dhabi (lost by 72 runs)**	**2011-12**

their last 18 Tests there. Meanwhile, Pakistan had won six of their previous eight Tests and were unbeaten in six series – including a one-off Test against Zimbabwe – following the tumultuous summer of 2010. Under the captaincy of Misbah-ul-Haq and the genial guidance of interim coach Mohsin Khan, they had developed into a decent side in any conditions, and an excellent one in the UAE.

Abu Dhabi is the driest Test ground in the world, a fact which, combined with injuries to Chris Tremlett and Tim Bresnan, persuaded England to select two specialist spinners, something they had done only once since July 2009. Even more unusually, those two – Swann and Panesar – formed half of a four-man attack. England had not employed a configuration of two fast and two slow bowlers since Kandy in 2003-04.

From a bowling perspective, the tactic worked. Despite losing an important toss, England used the ball with impressive control on a low surface which snared 29 batsmen bowled or lbw – a record for any Test. Broad, in particular, maintained a wonderfully nagging line and length, and the spinners gained turn from the start as Pakistan slipped to 103 for four. If Anderson, normally so reliable, had held a relatively simple chance at slip off Panesar when Misbah was 30, England might have taken an unassailable advantage.

YOU KNOW THAT STICK OF WOOD? WELL USE IT!

Most batsmen bowled and lbw in a Test:

29	**Pakistan (8 bowled, 7 lbw) v England (5, 9) at Abu Dhabi**	**2011-12**
26	West Indies (2, 9) v Pakistan (4, 11) at Providence	2010-11
25	West Indies (6, 6) v England (9, 4) at Kingston	1953-54
24	England (14, 1) v Australia (9, 0) at Sydney	1886-87
24	England (11, 1) v South Africa (11, 1) at Cape Town	1898-99
24	South Africa (10, 2) v England (9, 3) at Cape Town	1905-06
24	Australia (9, 2) v England (10, 3) at Melbourne	1907-08
24	Australia (6, 4) v India (10, 4) at Adelaide	1947-48
24	Bangladesh (5, 7) v Australia (7, 5) at Fatullah	2005-06

It proved a costly miss. While his colleagues were provoked into errors by England's persistence, Misbah played with discipline and denial, adding 100 with Asad Shafiq. But it was not all grim attrition: when the field was in, Misbah twice lofted Panesar for successive sixes – with his third and fourth scoring shots and, just as improbably, in the last over of the day. Though Shafiq tarnished his innings with a wild sweep, the value of their partnership became apparent when his wicket was the first of six to go for only 54, the final three falling on the second morning at the same score.

Strauss went early but, during the 50 overs in which Cook and Trott were compiling England's highest stand of the series, it seemed they would build a match-defining cushion. Trott, though, was bowled by a beauty from Abdur Rehman that turned past his outside edge, and Cook was defeated by Ajmal's doosra, six runs short of a 20th Test hundred. The middle order flopped again, and it required Broad's belligerence – he faced only 62 balls – to give England a handy lead of 70.

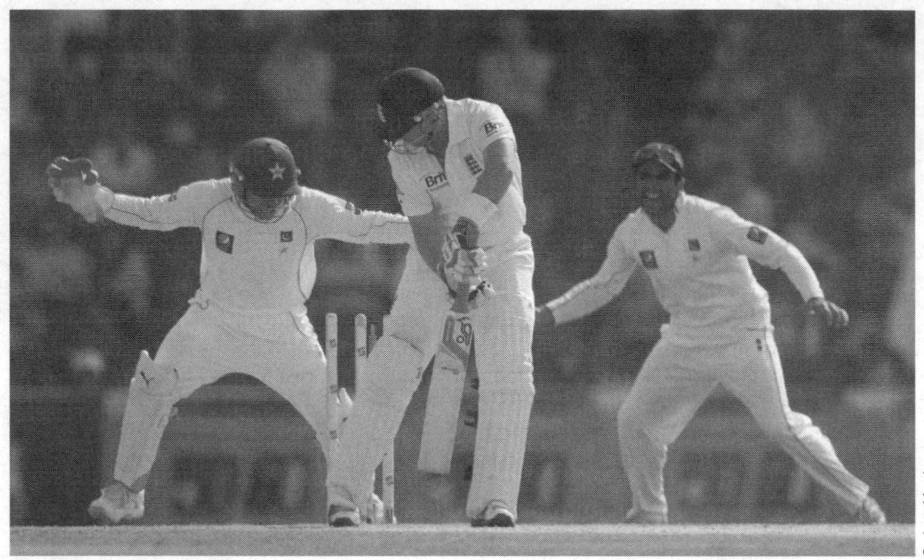

Indecision is final: Ian Bell is flummoxed by Saeed Ajmal's doosra for the third time in four innings.

That looked as if it would be enough when Pakistan slipped to 54 for four second time round. Panesar troubled all the batsmen with sharp turn and, had Pietersen hit with an underarm throw from ten feet and with all three stumps to aim at, Shafiq would have been run out for 26. Instead he and Azhar Ali, two of Pakistan's younger brigade, demonstrated real composure to add 88. The run-rate barely passed two an over, and Azhar's 68 spanned four and a quarter hours, but at least they helped Pakistan eke out a lead of 144: not much to bowl at, but enough to set minds racing – on both sides.

Then came the iceberg. England, paralysed with fear and uncertainty, never gained momentum. Struggling to pick the length because of the remarkable pace of Pakistan's spinners, and wary of missing anything on their stumps on another sluggish pitch, they remained rooted to the crease. Thus encouraged, the bowlers exerted a suffocating grip: Cook's seven occupied 15 overs before he gifted a leading edge back to the off-spin of Mohammad Hafeez, opening the bowling and evidently a specialist against the left-handers; Strauss's 32 took 29 overs. When he was fifth out, at 56, the end was nigh.

Already gone were Bell, deceived for the third time in the series by Ajmal's doosra, plus Pietersen and Morgan, both beaten by Rehman deliveries that skidded on. Trott, batting down the order because of a stomach bug, and Broad were soon defeated by the acute turn of Rehman, who wrapped things up when Anderson swung to deep midwicket. The last five wickets had tumbled in 11 balls, while the waspish, relentless Rehman finished with a career-best six for 25. Only seven men – Charlie Turner, Monty Noble, Aubrey Faulkner, Gerry Hazlitt, Ray Lindwall, Malcolm Marshall and Curtly Ambrose – had taken six or more wickets in a Test innings against England for so few runs. And, with Prior's dismissal, Ajmal became the quickest Pakistan player to 100 Test victims, in his 19th game. Between them, Pakistan's spin trio had claimed 19 wickets.

Seven batsmen failed to score more than a single in England's final collapse, matching the team's humiliation at Kingston in February 2009, their first Test with Strauss and Flower in charge, and only one short of the Test record of eight, when England dismissed New Zealand for 26 at Auckland in 1954-55. No wonder Strauss said it was "a struggle to think of a loss that has hurt more".

Man of the Match: Abdur Rehman.

Close of play: first day, Pakistan 256-7 (Misbah-ul-Haq 83, Saeed Ajmal 0); second day, England 207-5 (Bell 4); third day, Pakistan 125-4 (Azhar Ali 46, Asad Shafiq 35).

Pakistan

Mohammad Hafeez b Panesar	31	– lbw b Panesar	22
Taufeeq Umar b Swann	16	– b Swann	7
Azhar Ali b Broad	24	– c Prior b Anderson	68
Younis Khan b Broad	24	– b Panesar	1
*Misbah-ul-Haq lbw b Broad	84	– lbw b Panesar	12
Asad Shafiq lbw b Swann	58	– c Anderson b Panesar	43
†Adnan Akmal lbw b Broad	9	– c Strauss b Broad	13
Abdur Rehman b Swann	0	– lbw b Swann	10
Saeed Ajmal lbw b Anderson	0	– c Anderson b Panesar	17
Umar Gul not out	0	– not out	10
Junaid Khan c Swann b Anderson	0	– b Panesar	0
B 8, l-b 1, n-b 2	11	B 5, l-b 6	11
1/51 (2) 2/61 (1) 3/98 (4) 4/103 (3) 5/203 (6) 6/216 (7) 7/243 (8) 8/257 (5) 9/257 (9) 10/257 (11) (96.4 overs)	257	1/29 (1) 2/29 (2) 3/36 (4) 4/54 (5) 5/142 (6) 6/170 (3) 7/172 (7) 8/198 (8) 9/208 (9) 10/214 (11) (99.2 overs)	214

Anderson 19.4–5–46–2; Broad 24–4–47–4; Panesar 33–9–91–1; Swann 18–2–52–3; Trott 2–0–12–0. *Second innings*—Anderson 14–3–39–1; Broad 20–9–36–1; Panesar 38.2–18–62–6; Swann 27–5–66–2.

England

*A. J. Strauss c Asad Shafiq b Mohammad Hafeez	11	– lbw b Abdur Rehman	32
A. N. Cook lbw b Saeed Ajmal	94	– c and b Mohammad Hafeez	7
I. J. L. Trott b Abdur Rehman	74	– (7) lbw b Abdur Rehman	1
K. P. Pietersen c Mohammad Hafeez b Saeed Ajmal	14	– lbw b Abdur Rehman	1
I. R. Bell lbw b Umar Gul	29	– (3) b Saeed Ajmal	3
E. J. G. Morgan c Mohammad Hafeez b Saeed Ajmal	3	– (5) b Abdur Rehman	0
†M. J. Prior lbw b Saeed Ajmal	3	– (6) c Asad Shafiq b Saeed Ajmal	18
S. C. J. Broad not out	58	– b Abdur Rehman	0
G. P. Swann lbw b Abdur Rehman	15	– lbw b Saeed Ajmal	0
J. M. Anderson b Mohammad Hafeez	13	– c Umar Gul b Abdur Rehman	1
M. S. Panesar lbw b Mohammad Hafeez	0	– not out	0
B 5, l-b 7, n-b 1	13	L-b 9	9
1/27 (1) 2/166 (3) 3/198 (2) 4/203 (4) 5/207 (6) 6/227 (7) 7/268 (5) 8/291 (9) 9/327 (10) 10/327 (11) (112 overs)	327	1/21 (2) 2/26 (3) 3/33 (4) 4/37 (5) 5/56 (1) 6/68 (7) 7/68 (8) 8/71 (9) 9/72 (6) 10/72 (10) (36.1 overs)	72

Umar Gul 13–1–53–1; Junaid Khan 8–0–33–0; Mohammad Hafeez 22–4–54–3; Saeed Ajmal 40–6–108–4; Abdur Rehman 29–9–67–2. *Second innings*—Mohammad Hafeez 8–3–11–1; Umar Gul 3–0–5–0; Saeed Ajmal 15–7–22–3; Abdur Rehman 10.1–4–25–6.

Umpires: S. J. Davis and B. N. J. Oxenford. Third umpire: B. F. Bowden.
Referee: J. Srinath.

PAKISTAN v ENGLAND

Third Test Match

PAUL NEWMAN

At Dubai, February 3–6, 2012. Pakistan won by 71 runs. Toss: Pakistan.

It seemed appropriate that the Third Test, which produced Pakistan's first clean sweep over England, should end on a referred lbw decision. The DRS, and the way it was implemented by the officials, had been a leitmotif of the Tests – so much so that the

Philip Brown

Taking it in his stride: Younis Khan disarms the spinners in the series' first century.

demise of Panesar was the 43rd lbw in all, an unprecedented number in a three-match series. His forlorn decision to ask for a referral felt like an afterthought, which seemed about right: for the final three days of this game, England had been decidedly off the pace.

Played, like the First Test, at the near-deserted Dubai Sports City Stadium, this one outdid even the previous two for unpredictability. England were left to wonder how they could have dismissed Pakistan for 99 on the first day and still lose. Only twice before – in the Ashes-spawning Oval Test of 1882, and South Africa's first win, at the Old Wanderers in 1905-06 – had they suffered defeat after bowling out a team in their first innings in double figures.

There were two simple reasons for the result. England, their brains now well and truly scrambled by Pakistani spin, mustered only 141 in their reply, when conditions for batting were at their best; and they were unable to separate Azhar Ali and Younis Khan during a second-innings stand of 216 that seemed to mock the loss of 22 wickets for 268 which preceded it. Azhar and Younis might have been playing a different game.

At lunch on the first day, however, which Pakistan took shortly after slipping to 44 for seven, it looked as if England would finish with a consolation win. Led by the excellent Broad, who bowled with Glenn McGrath-like accuracy and hostility for four wickets, they allowed only Asad Shafiq to settle. At the time, his mature 45 out of an eventual total of 99 felt like a futile lone hand. But by the end of the day, with England listing once more at 104 for six, Shafiq's innings was assuming match-winning proportions.

The opening skirmishes were not a triumph for Simon Taufel. Long regarded as one of the best umpires in the world, he saw three of his decisions overturned by the DRS on his first day in the series. While 16 wickets were tumbling, seven of them to spin, it felt as if the old tradition of giving the batsman the benefit of the doubt – a tacit understanding, admittedly, rather than a Law – was being confined to history.

Pietersen certainly thought so. His problems with the spinners had – despite his denials – almost certainly been exacerbated by his concerns about the DRS, and now Taufel adjudged him leg-before to Abdur Rehman when technology showed the ball was barely clipping leg stump. Even the fact that he had fallen once more to a left-arm spinner, for the 22nd time in Tests, was overshadowed by his evident displeasure at the decision. If Pietersen felt it was guesswork, Taufel had been technically vindicated – although Pietersen claimed he later received an apology from the umpire, himself believed to be no great fan of the DRS. The episode did little to dissuade those who thought the technology risked turning batting, especially on slow pitches, into something of a lottery.

With Rehman – bowling wicket to wicket and spearing the ball in – claiming a second successive haul of five or more, England's lead was kept down to a far from formidable 42.

Now, finally, the series was to see a demonstration of proper Test batting, a display of how to nullify spin – and with it the DRS – by using bat rather than pad, both in defence and attack. Suddenly the pace and nature of the game changed perceptibly as Younis, the old master, joined Azhar, who had made only 94 skittish runs in his previous four innings. As if in defiance of this, he now demonstrated infinite patience and application, compiling a monumental 157 off 442 balls in seven minutes short of nine hours.

Younis complemented Azhar's substance with his own elegant style, putting together his 20th Test hundred, after a quiet series. When they were finally parted, Pakistan had gone a considerable way towards completing the whitewash. Their total of 365 left England a target of 324, a damning 132 more than they had managed in four of their five innings thus far.

What followed at least regained a modicum of respectability, as Strauss and Cook began with 48 before Strauss played back to Abdur Rehman. Then Saeed Ajmal struck three times either side of lunch on the fourth day, his victims including Cook, who had been becalmed during a four-hour 49, but became the second-youngest batsman, at 27 years 43 days, to reach 6,000 Test runs; only Sachin Tendulkar (26 years 313 days) had got there earlier.

Then Umar Gul took over, claiming four in 30 deliveries – including the hapless Bell, who slapped a long-hop straight to cover – before Ajmal and Rehman finished things off to end the series with 43 wickets between them. Throw in five for Mohammad Hafeez, and Pakistan's spinners had claimed 48, a national record in any Test series, and only two short of the three-Test record of 50 shared by India and Sri Lanka, both against New Zealand, in 1976-77 and 1997-98 respectively.

While Strauss had arrived talking of Asia as England's final frontier, and left with it resolutely unconquered, Misbah-ul-Haq spoke of a "dream come true". After all that Pakistan cricket had gone through, only the most cold-hearted Englishman could begrudge them their triumph.

Man of the Match: Azhar Ali. *Man of the Series:* Saeed Ajmal.

Close of play: first day, England 104-6 (Strauss 41, Anderson 3); second day, Pakistan 222-2 (Azhar Ali 75, Younis Khan 115); third day, England 36-0 (Strauss 19, Cook 15).

Pakistan

First innings		Second innings	
Mohammad Hafeez lbw b Broad	13	– lbw b Panesar	21
Taufeeq Umar lbw b Anderson	0	– c Strauss b Anderson	6
Azhar Ali c Prior b Broad	1	– c Cook b Swann	157
Younis Khan c Prior b Broad	4	– lbw b Broad	127
*Misbah-ul-Haq lbw b Anderson	1	– lbw b Panesar	31
Asad Shafiq lbw b Panesar	45	– lbw b Panesar	5
†Adnan Akmal lbw b Broad	6	– b Panesar	0
Abdur Rehman c Pietersen b Swann	1	– c Anderson b Swann	1
Saeed Ajmal lbw b Panesar	12	– c Anderson b Swann	1
Umar Gul b Anderson	13	– lbw b Panesar	4
Aizaz Cheema not out	0	– not out	0
L-b 3	3	B 10, l-b 1, n-b 1	12
1/1 (2) 2/8 (3) 3/18 (4) 4/21 (1) 5/21 (5) 6/39 (7) 7/44 (8) 8/78 (9) 9/85 (6) 10/99 (10) (44.1 overs)	99	1/16 (2) 2/28 (1) 3/244 (4) 4/331 (5) 5/339 (6) 6/345 (7) 7/346 (8) 8/350 (9) 9/363 (3) 10/365 (10) (152.4 overs)	365

Anderson 14.1–3–35–3; Broad 16–5–36–4; Panesar 13–4–25–2; Swann 1–1–0–1. *Second innings*—Anderson 28–7–51–1; Broad 24–7–55–1; Panesar 56.4–13–124–5; Swann 39–6–101–3; Trott 2–0–14–0; Pietersen 3–0–9–0.

England

First innings		Second innings	
*A. J. Strauss st Adnan Akmal b Abdur Rehman	56	– lbw b Abdur Rehman	26
A. N. Cook c Adnan Akmal b Umar Gul	1	– c Younis Khan b Saeed Ajmal	49
I. J. L. Trott lbw b Umar Gul	2	– c Abdur Rehman b Saeed Ajmal	18
K. P. Pietersen lbw b Abdur Rehman	32	– b Saeed Ajmal	18
I. R. Bell st Adnan Akmal b Saeed Ajmal	5	– c Asad Shafiq b Umar Gul	10
E. J. G. Morgan lbw b Abdur Rehman	10	– c Adnan Akmal b Umar Gul	31
†M. J. Prior b Abdur Rehman	6	– not out	49
J. M. Anderson b Abdur Rehman	4	– (10) c Younis Khan b Saeed Ajmal	9
S. C. J. Broad lbw b Saeed Ajmal	4	– (8) c Taufeeq Umar b Umar Gul	18
G. P. Swann c Abdur Rehman b Saeed Ajmal	16	– (9) c Asad Shafiq b Umar Gul	1
M. S. Panesar not out	0	– lbw b Abdur Rehman	8
B 1, l-b 4	5	B 4, l-b 8, n-b 3	15
1/5 (2) 2/7 (3) 3/64 (4) 4/75 (5) 5/88 (6) 6/98 (7) 7/106 (8) 8/121 (9) 9/133 (1) 10/141 (10) (55 overs)	141	1/48 (1) 2/85 (3) 3/116 (4) 4/119 (2) 5/156 (5) 6/159 (6) 7/196 (8) 8/203 (9) 9/237 (10) 10/252 (11) (97.3 overs)	252

Umar Gul 7–1–28–2; Aizaz Cheema 4–0–9–0; Saeed Ajmal 23–6–59–3; Abdur Rehman 21–4–40–5. *Second innings*—Umar Gul 20–5–61–4; Aizaz Cheema 4–0–9–0; Mohammad Hafeez 5–2–6–0; Abdur Rehman 41.3–10–97–2; Saeed Ajmal 27–9–67–4.

Umpires: S. J. Davis and S. J. A. Taufel. Third umpire: S. K. Tarapore.
Referee: J. J. Crowe.

At Abu Dhabi, February 10, 2012. **England XI won by nine wickets, but continued to pursue an artificial target of 230. ‡England Lions 96** (28.3 overs) (S. T. Finn 3-28, J. W. Dernbach 3-21); **England XI 231-3** (45.5 overs) (A. N. Cook 68, I. J. L. Trott 75*). *England passed the Lions' total with one wicket down in 20.1 overs but, to extend their batting practice, continued until they had beaten a nominal target of 230.*

LIMITED-OVERS INTERNATIONAL REPORTS BY CHRIS STOCKS

PAKISTAN v ENGLAND

First One-Day International

At Abu Dhabi, February 13, 2012 (day/night). England won by 130 runs. Toss: England.

With their 5–0 one-day whitewash in India in October fresh in the memory, and still stunned by their 3–0 Test defeat here, England entered this series more in hope than expectation. But a career-best 137 from Cook, his third one-day international hundred, set up a victory which instilled the self-belief so far lacking on the tour. Keen to make up for a middling personal return in India, where whispers about his unsuitability for the dual role of captain and opener had resurfaced following a superb summer, Cook displayed aggression and an array of strokes most of his critics had thought beyond him. In all, he faced 142 balls, adding 131 for the third wicket with Bopara. England's 260 for seven proved more than enough to defeat Pakistan, who never recovered from Finn's hostile and penetrative opening spell of four for 20. Only a typically frenetic 22-ball 28 from Shahid Afridi interrupted the procession.

Man of the Match: A. N. Cook.

England

*A. N. Cook b Saeed Ajmal 137	S. C. J. Broad c and b Saeed Ajmal. 1
K. P. Pietersen b Shahid Afridi 14	G. P. Swann not out. 13
I. J. L. Trott b Shahid Afridi 0	L-b 11, w 5, n-b 1 17
R. S. Bopara st Umar Akmal b Saeed Ajmal 50	——
E. J. G. Morgan lbw b Saeed Ajmal 2	1/57 (2) 2/57 (3) (7 wkts, 50 overs) 260
†C. Kieswetter c Wahab Riaz b Saeed Ajmal 9	3/188 (4) 4/196 (5)
S. R. Patel not out 17	5/221 (6) 6/230 (1) 7/232 (8) 10 overs: 48-0

J. M. Anderson and S. T. Finn did not bat.

Umar Gul 8–0–53–0; Mohammad Hafeez 10–1–30–0; Shahid Afridi 10–0–55–2; Saeed Ajmal 10–0–43–5; Wahab Riaz 7–0–47–0; Shoaib Malik 5–0–21–0.

Pakistan

Mohammad Hafeez lbw b Finn 5	Saeed Ajmal c Cook b Broad 5
Imran Farhat c Kieswetter b Finn 10	Wahab Riaz not out. 8
Asad Shafiq lbw b Finn 0	
Younis Khan c Kieswetter b Finn 15	L-b 2, w 7, n-b 5 14
*Misbah-ul-Haq lbw b Patel 14	——
†Umar Akmal st Kieswetter b Swann 22	1/11 (1) 2/11 (3) 3/27 (4) (35 overs) 130
Shoaib Malik c Pietersen b Patel. 7	4/40 (2) 5/53 (5) 6/68 (7)
Shahid Afridi c Swann b Patel. 28	7/96 (6) 8/109 (8) 9/113 (9)
Umar Gul lbw b Swann. 2	10/130 (10) 10 overs: 40-4

Finn 10–1–34–4; Anderson 6–0–24–0; Broad 6–2–21–1; Patel 5–1–26–3; Bopara 1–0–4–0; Swann 7–3–19–2.

Umpires: Ahsan Raza and S. J. A. Taufel. Third umpire: H. D. P. K. Dharmasena.

PAKISTAN v ENGLAND

Second One-Day International

At Abu Dhabi, February 15, 2012 (day/night). England won by 20 runs. Toss: England.

The parallels with the previous game were almost eerie. For the second time in three days, Cook scored a century, Bopara a fifty and – uncannily – Finn repeated his one-day best four for 34. The result may have been closer, but England were now guaranteed at least a share of the four-match series. Cook was again the inspiration, becoming the first England captain – and the tenth Englishman in all – to score back-to-back one-day hundreds. His 102 in 121 balls, an object lesson in timing, was littered with cuts, pulls and sumptuous drives; only on 28, when makeshift wicketkeeper Umar Akmal put down an edged cut off Shahid Afridi, did he put a foot wrong. Bopara once more played

---

BACK-TO-BACK ONE-DAY HUNDREDS FOR ENGLAND

D. I. Gower.	122 and 158	v New Zealand.	1982-83
G. A. Gooch	115 and 117*	v Australia	1985
N. V. Knight.	113 and 125*	v Pakistan.	1996
G. A. Hick.	126* and 109	v Sri Lanka and Australia	1998-99
A. J. Stewart	101 and 100*	v Zimbabwe and West Indies	2000
M. E. Trescothick	109 and 119	v India and Zimbabwe.	2002–2002-03
A. Flintoff.	106 and 123	v New Zealand and West Indies	2004
†K. P. Pietersen.	100* and 116	v South Africa	2004-05
P. D. Collingwood . . .	106 and 120*	v New Zealand and Australia.	2006-07
A. N. Cook	**137 and 102**	**v Pakistan**	**2011-12**
K. P. Pietersen.	**111* and 130**	**v Pakistan**	**2011-12**

† *In three matches; did not bat in the second.*

second fiddle, with 58 in 66 deliveries. In reply, Pakistan stayed in touch, and needed 72 to win off 11 overs with five wickets in hand. But, led by the incisive Finn, England's bowlers rallied. Defeat was inevitable once Misbah-ul-Haq was superbly caught by Kieswetter, running back to pouch a spiralling top edge off Broad, in the 48th over.

Man of the Match: A. N. Cook.

England

*A. N. Cook c and b Shahid Afridi	102
K. P. Pietersen lbw b Saeed Ajmal	26
I. J. L. Trott c Umar Akmal b Aizaz Cheema	23
R. S. Bopara c Umar Akmal b Aizaz Cheema	58
E. J. G. Morgan not out	25
B 1, l-b 5, w 10	16
1/67 (2) 2/116 (3) (4 wkts, 50 overs)	250
3/194 (1) 4/250 (4) 10 overs: 49-0	

†C. Kieswetter, S. R. Patel, S. C. J. Broad, G. P. Swann, J. M. Anderson and S. T. Finn did not bat.

Umar Gul 7–1–43–0; Aizaz Cheema 9–0–49–2; Mohammad Hafeez 4–0–24–0; Abdur Rehman 10–1–36–0; Shahid Afridi 10–1–38–1; Saeed Ajmal 10–0–54–1.

Pakistan

Mohammad Hafeez c Trott b Anderson	26
Imran Farhat run out	47
Azhar Ali b Patel	31
Younis Khan lbw b Patel	5
*Misbah-ul-Haq c Kieswetter b Broad	47
†Umar Akmal c Patel b Finn	21
Shahid Afridi b Anderson	18
Abdur Rehman b Finn	1
Umar Gul lbw b Finn	5
Saeed Ajmal not out	7
Aizaz Cheema b Finn	1
B 1, l-b 11, w 8, n-b 1	21
1/61 (1) 2/92 (2) 3/104 (4) (49 overs)	230
4/142 (3) 5/179 (6) 6/207 (7)	
7/217 (8) 8/217 (5) 9/222 (9)	
10/230 (11) 10 overs: 33-0	

Finn 10–1–34–4; Anderson 9–1–36–2; Broad 10–0–54–1; Swann 8–0–33–0; Bopara 2–0–10–0; Patel 10–0–51–2.

Umpires: Aleem Dar and H. D. P. K. Dharmasena. Third umpire: S. J. A. Taufel.

PAKISTAN v ENGLAND

Third One-Day International

At Dubai, February 18, 2012 (day/night). England won by nine wickets. Toss: Pakistan.

Pietersen's first one-day international century since November 2008 helped England secure the series. His undefeated 111 from 98 balls made a mockery of Pakistan's below-par total, easing England home with 76 deliveries in hand. A huge straight six off Mohammad Hafeez took him past 4,000 one-day international runs and landed in the VVIP section – more important even than the VIP enclosure – in the stadium's second tier. Pietersen's 170-run opening stand with Cook matched England's all-wicket record against Pakistan, by Marcus Trescothick and Owais Shah at Lord's in 2001. Cook fell 20 short of becoming the first England batsman to score three successive one-day hundreds when he edged a defensive push off Saeed Ajmal, but had the consolation of his third six, in his 44th match, pulling Umar Gul over midwicket. Earlier, Finn surpassed himself – if not his figures in the first two games – while Broad, after an opening over that cost 16, produced successive wicket maidens. From 97 for five, Umar Akmal and Shahid Afridi responded with fifties, but a total of 222 never felt enough.

Man of the Match: K. P. Pietersen.

Pakistan

Mohammad Hafeez lbw b Finn	29
Imran Farhat c Kieswetter b Finn	9
Azhar Ali c Kieswetter b Broad	5
Asad Shafiq run out	18
*Misbah-ul-Haq c Swann b Broad	1
Umar Akmal c Patel b Broad	50
Shahid Afridi b Anderson	51
†Adnan Akmal b Finn	9
Umar Gul not out	27
Saeed Ajmal b Anderson	4
Aizaz Cheema run out	5
L-b 11, w 2, n-b 1	14
1/22 (2) 2/49 (3) 3/49 (1) 4/50 (5) 5/97 (4) 6/176 (6) 7/180 (7) 8/204 (8) 9/209 (10) 10/222 (11) (50 overs)	222
10 overs: 50-3	

Anderson 10–0–52–2; Finn 10–1–24–3; Broad 10–2–42–3; Swann 10–0–44–0; Patel 8–1–37–0; Bopara 2–0–12–0.

England

*A. N. Cook c Adnan Akmal b Saeed Ajmal	80
K. P. Pietersen not out	111
E. J. G. Morgan not out	24
L-b 3, w 4, n-b 4	11
1/170 (1) (1 wkt, 37.2 overs)	226
10 overs: 60-0	

I. J. L. Trott, R. S. Bopara, †C. Kieswetter, S. R. Patel, S. C. J. Broad, G. P. Swann, J. M. Anderson and S. T. Finn did not bat.

Umar Gul 7–0–59–0; Aizaz Cheema 6.2–0–40–0; Saeed Ajmal 10–1–40–1; Mohammad Hafeez 6–0–32–0; Shahid Afridi 8–0–52–0.

Umpires: Aleem Dar and S. J. A. Taufel. Third umpire: H. D. P. K. Dharmasena.

PAKISTAN v ENGLAND

Fourth One-Day International

At Dubai, February 21, 2012 (day/night). England won by four wickets. Toss: Pakistan. One-day international debuts: D. R. Briggs, J. C. Buttler.

Trading famine for feast, Pietersen hit his second hundred in four days to propel England to a 4–0 sweep that partially – but only partially – atoned for the Test hammering. He had scored centuries in successive one-day international innings (he did not bat in an intervening match) once before, in South Africa near the start of his England career in 2004-05. This was England's first one-day whitewash against a team other than Zimbabwe or Bangladesh since 1997, when they defeated Australia 3–0. Pietersen faced 153 balls, sharing crucial stands of 109 with Kieswetter and 59 with Patel after England slipped to 68 for four. When he fell, for his highest score in this format, with six balls to go, the job was all but done. Pakistan's total of 237 was disappointing after they had reached 112 for one in the 23rd over. With Anderson and Broad rested, and Swann nursing a calf strain, Dernbach returned a career-best in his first international appearance of the tour, while Hampshire's left-arm spinner Danny Briggs bowled tidily for two wickets on his England debut.

Man of the Match: K. P. Pietersen. *Man of the Series:* A. N. Cook.

Pakistan

Mohammad Hafeez c Kieswetter b Dernbach	1
Azhar Ali c Morgan b Dernbach	58
Asad Shafiq b Bresnan	65
Umar Akmal c Dernbach b Briggs	12
Shoaib Malik lbw b Briggs	23
*Misbah-ul-Haq c Trott b Dernbach	46
Shahid Afridi c Bresnan b Finn	9
†Adnan Akmal run out	2
Abdur Rehman c Trott b Finn	12
Saeed Ajmal b Dernbach	1
Junaid Khan not out	0
B 1, l-b 4, w 3	8
1/1 (1) 2/112 (3) 3/135 (4) 4/144 (2) 5/202 (5) 6/215 (7) 7/220 (8) 8/233 (9) 9/237 (6) 10/237 (10) (50 overs)	237
10 overs: 46-1	

Finn 10–0–42–2; Dernbach 10–0–45–4; Bresnan 9–0–47–1; Briggs 10–0–39–2; Pietersen 1–0–4–0; Patel 10–0–55–0.

England

*A. N. Cook lbw b Junaid Khan	4
K. P. Pietersen c Abdur Rehman b Saeed Ajmal	130
I. J. L. Trott c Mohammad Hafeez b Abdur Rehman	15
E. J. G. Morgan lbw b Saeed Ajmal	15
J. C. Buttler c Azhar Ali b Saeed Ajmal	0
†C. Kieswetter run out	43
S. R. Patel not out	17
T. T. Bresnan not out	4
L-b 3, w 10	13
1/4 (1) 2/50 (3) 3/68 (4) 4/68 (5) 5/177 (6) 6/236 (2) (6 wkts, 49.2 overs)	241
10 overs: 46-1	

D. R. Briggs, S. T. Finn and J. W. Dernbach did not bat.

Junaid Khan 9.2–0–53–1; Abdur Rehman 10–0–31–1; Saeed Ajmal 10–0–62–3; Shahid Afridi 10–0–54–0; Mohammad Hafeez 10–0–38–0.

Umpires: H. D. P. K. Dharmasena and Zameer Haider. Third umpire: S. J. A. Taufel.
Series referee: J. J. Crowe.

PAKISTAN v ENGLAND

First Twenty20 International

At Dubai, February 23, 2012 (floodlit). Pakistan won by eight runs. Toss: England. Twenty20 international debuts: Awais Zia, Hammad Azam.

England were denied by some exquisite death bowling from Umar Gul. Needing 35 from 30 balls with seven wickets in hand, they failed to hit a single boundary as Gul took three for seven in two overs of high-class, full-pitched deliveries. After Pietersen had given them a flying start, Bairstow's struggle was symptomatic: he could not reach the fence once in 21 balls. Swann had kept Pakistan in check as they slipped to 73 for five in the 11th over, only for Shoaib Malik to give them a total to defend. One-day captain Alastair Cook was a late inclusion in England's squad, ostensibly as cover for Bopara, who had missed the final 50-over match with a back injury. Though Cook did not play, his presence raised questions about the authority of Twenty20 captain Broad, who – because of injury – had previously led England only twice in five matches since his appointment in 2011.

Man of the Match: Umar Gul.

Pakistan

		B	*4*	*6*
Mohammad Hafeez *c 5 b 8*	23	22	3	0
Awais Zia *c 9 b 11*	18	12	1	1
Asad Shafiq *run out*	19	17	2	0
Shahid Afridi *c 4 b 8*	7	7	1	0
*Misbah-ul-Haq *not out*	26	26	1	1
†Umar Akmal *c 10 b 8*	0	3	0	0
Shoaib Malik *c 5 b 10*	39	33	4	1
L-b 11, w 1	12			
6 overs: 49-1 (20 overs)	144-6			

1/32 2/65 3/65 4/73 5/73 6/144

Hammad Azam, Umar Gul, Saeed Ajmal and Junaid Khan did not bat.

Finn 4–0–39–1; Dernbach 4–0–31–1; Broad 4–0–19–0; Swann 4–1–13–3; Bopara 1–0–8–0; Patel 3–0–23–0.

England

		B	*4*	*6*
K. P. Pietersen *c 3 b 4*	33	21	4	1
†C. Kieswetter *b 1*	14	18	2	0
R. S. Bopara *b 9*	39	32	2	1
E. J. G. Morgan *b 1*	14	16	1	0
J. M. Bairstow *not out*	22	21	0	0
J. C. Buttler *c 10 b 9*	3	4	0	0
S. R. Patel *lbw b 9*	0	1	0	0
G. P. Swann *not out*	2	7	0	0
B 1, l-b 4, w 4	9			
6 overs: 49-1 (20 overs)	136-6			

1/48 2/51 3/80 4/113 5/121 6/121

*S. C. J. Broad, J. W. Dernbach and S. T. Finn did not bat.

Junaid Khan 4–0–42–0; Umar Gul 4–1–18–3; Saeed Ajmal 4–0–26–0; Shahid Afridi 4–0–27–1; Mohammad Hafeez 4–0–18–2.

Umpires: Ahsan Raza and Shozab Raza. Third umpire: Zameer Haider.

PAKISTAN v ENGLAND

Second Twenty20 International

At Dubai, February 25, 2012 (floodlit). England won by 38 runs. Toss: England.

Bairstow put his tentative innings two days earlier behind him to thrash an unbeaten 60 from 46 balls and set up England's series-squaring victory. His change in approach was highlighted when he hit Umar Gul's slower ball for a towering six over long-on from the penultimate delivery of the innings. It was his first half-century in any game of Twenty20 cricket and, with none of his team-mates passing 31, pivotal to England's total of 150. Pakistan's pursuit looked doomed almost from the outset: two wickets fell in the first eight balls of their reply and, despite some late hitting from Shahid Afridi and Hammad Azam, they never recovered.

Man of the Match: J. M. Bairstow.

England

		B	4	6
K. P. Pietersen *c 9 b 10*	17	13	3	0
†C. Kieswetter *c 9 b 7*	31	24	2	1
R. S. Bopara *lbw b 9*	1	4	0	0
E. J. G. Morgan *lbw b 1*	9	7	2	0
J. M. Bairstow *not out*	60	46	5	2
S. R. Patel *run out*	13	13	1	0
J. C. Buttler *b 9*	7	8	1	0
*S. C. J. Broad *b 11*	2	2	0	0
G. P. Swann *not out*	2	3	0	0
L-b 5, w 3	8			
6 overs: 46-2 (20 overs)	150-7			

1/35 2/38 3/49 4/79 5/118 6/132 7/137

J. W. Dernbach and S. T. Finn did not bat.

Mohammad Hafeez 4–0–25–1; Aizaz Cheema 4–0–31–1; Saeed Ajmal 4–0–20–1; Umar Gul 4–0–31–2; Shahid Afridi 3–0–28–1; Shoaib Malik 1–0–10–0.

Pakistan

		B	4	6
Mohammad Hafeez *c 1 b 11*	0	2	0	0
Awais Zia *c 10 b 8*	6	12	0	1
Asad Shafiq *c and b 10*	1	5	0	0
†Umar Akmal *c 4 b 11*	19	12	2	1
Shoaib Malik *c 5 b 9*	12	11	0	0
*Misbah-ul-Haq *c 5 b 9*	13	24	1	0
Shahid Afridi *c 4 b 8*	25	23	2	1
Hammad Azam *c 7 b 3*	21	15	3	1
Umar Gul *c 2 b 11*	10	4	1	1
Saeed Ajmal *run out*	0	0	0	0
Aizaz Cheema *not out*	0	3	0	0
W 4, n-b 1	5			
6 overs: 33-4 (18.2 overs)	112			

1/0 2/2 3/30 4/32 5/50 6/74 7/98 8/111 9/111

Finn 4–0–30–3; Dernbach 3–0–13–1; Broad 3.2–0–12–2; Swann 4–0–17–2; Bopara 3–0–23–1; Patel 1–0–17–0.

Umpires: Ahsan Raza and Zameer Haider. Third umpire: Shozab Raza.

PAKISTAN v ENGLAND

Third Twenty20 International

At Abu Dhabi, February 27, 2012 (floodlit). England won by five runs. Toss: England.

England ended their two-month odyssey in the desert with a thrilling victory to secure the series 2–1. Misbah-ul-Haq needed to hit the final ball of the match for six, but an audacious slower delivery out of the back of the hand from Dernbach proved too clever, crashing into the stumps as Misbah failed to connect with a leg-side heave. That completed a dramatic late comeback from England's bowlers after Pakistan had reached the last three overs requiring 23 with seven wickets in hand. But Dernbach conceded only six in the 18th over, then Broad went for just four – courtesy of a misfield by Bairstow at long-on – in the 19th, which included the wicket of Umar Akmal. The 13 runs Pakistan thus needed from the last proved too many, rendering Pietersen's unbeaten 62 on a sluggish track the decisive innings.

Man of the Match: K. P. Pietersen. *Man of the Series:* K. P. Pietersen.

Gareth Copley, Getty Images

Sleight of hand: with six needed and the series on the line, Jade Dernbach's slower ball deceives Misbah-ul-Haq.

England

		B	4	6
K. P. Pietersen *not out*	62	52	6	1
†C. Kieswetter *c 8 b 10*	17	17	1	1
R. S. Bopara *c 5 b 11*	1	2	0	0
E. J. G. Morgan *run out*	9	11	0	0
J. M. Bairstow *b 10*	3	8	0	0
J. C. Buttler *lbw b 10*	7	13	0	0
S. R. Patel *st 5 b 10*	16	10	1	1
*S. C. J. Broad *not out*	6	7	0	0
L-b 1, w 7	8			

6 overs: 39-2 (20 overs) 129-6

1/29 2/37 3/62 4/72 5/89 6/109

G. P. Swann, J. W. Dernbach and S. T. Finn did not bat.

Mohammad Hafeez 4–0–22–0; Aizaz Cheema 4–0–25–1; Umar Gul 4–0–39–0; Saeed Ajmal 4–0–23–4; Shahid Afridi 4–0–19–0.

Pakistan

		B	4	6
Awais Zia *lbw b 9*	23	28	1	1
Mohammad Hafeez *c and b 10*	0	1	0	0
Asad Shafiq *run out*	34	32	3	0
*Misbah-ul-Haq *b 10*	28	32	2	0
†Umar Akmal *c 9 b 8*	22	23	1	0
Shahid Afridi *run out*	3	2	0	0
Hammad Azam *not out*	2	2	0	0
L-b 7, w 5	12			

6 overs: 45-1 (20 overs) 124-6

1/8 2/48 3/76 4/113 5/120 6/124

Shoaib Malik, Umar Gul, Saeed Ajmal and Aizaz Cheema did not bat.

Finn 4–0–31–0; Dernbach 4–0–24–2; Broad 4–0–24–1; Patel 4–0–18–0; Swann 4–0–20–1.

Umpires: Shozab Raza and Zameer Haider. Third umpire: Ahsan Raza.
Series referee: J. J. Crowe.

SRI LANKA v ENGLAND, 2011-12

REVIEW BY DEAN WILSON

Test matches (2): Sri Lanka 1, England 1

Noel Coward may have had a point when he wrote about mad dogs, Englishmen and the midday sun – even if he wasn't necessarily thinking of Sri Lanka in April. But in scorching temperatures, England were as heroic in squaring the series in Colombo as they had been flaky while losing at Galle. If the mercury told a relentless tale, England's own gauge fluctuated wildly: few sides could have made Asian conditions look both baffling and straightforward within the space of a week as expertly as they did.

They began this brief tour – just two Tests and no limited-overs matches – still smarting from a 3–0 defeat by Pakistan in the UAE, where their travails against spin had been exposed alarmingly. Despite that trauma, they were still favourites to secure a first series triumph in Sri Lanka for 11 years. On paper, a contest between a Sri Lankan team yet to win a home Test since the retirement of Muttiah Muralitharan, and an England side still ranked No. 1, with a bowling attack in rude health and batsmen who surely couldn't keep failing, would provide only one winner. And yet cricket, as the old pros have it, is played not on paper but on grass – and sometimes on slow turners, where England discovered that Sri Lanka did not need Murali to tie them in knots.

As it was, a 1–1 draw felt about right once the efforts of Mahela Jayawardene, Rangana Herath, Kevin Pietersen and Graeme Swann were stacked up. But, for the third time in the 2011-12 season alone, a high-profile two-Test series was left crying out for a decider. The ECB had wanted a third match, but the hard-up Sri Lankan board had other concerns, so the series was squeezed into a narrow window between the lucrative Asia Cup, whose TV money pleased the administrators, and the IPL, whose contracts placated the players. Test cricket, the sport's so-called jewel in the crown, was once again being treated like a mere bauble.

With equal predictability, it was the arrival of several thousand British tourists that provided Sri Lanka Cricket with their best gate receipts in years. Australian fans the previous September had paid 500 rupees (about £2.50) for their daily tickets. Now, SLC charged travelling supporters ten times as much in the knowledge that – though many had budgeted for far less – enough of them would be prepared, however grudgingly, to fork out. And so it proved: both the Galle International Stadium and the P. Sara Oval in Colombo were packed to the rafters, even if locals – who had access to poorly advertised tickets at 50 rupees each – were disconcertingly hard to spot.

Many England fans, though, voted with their feet, and instead formed a makeshift terrace on the ramparts of the Galle Fort, from where they could watch the First Test at a distance. Access was free – or at least it was until the final day, when a local politician attempted to charge a 1,000-rupee entry fee on the pretext of holding a party which was not due to start until the evening.

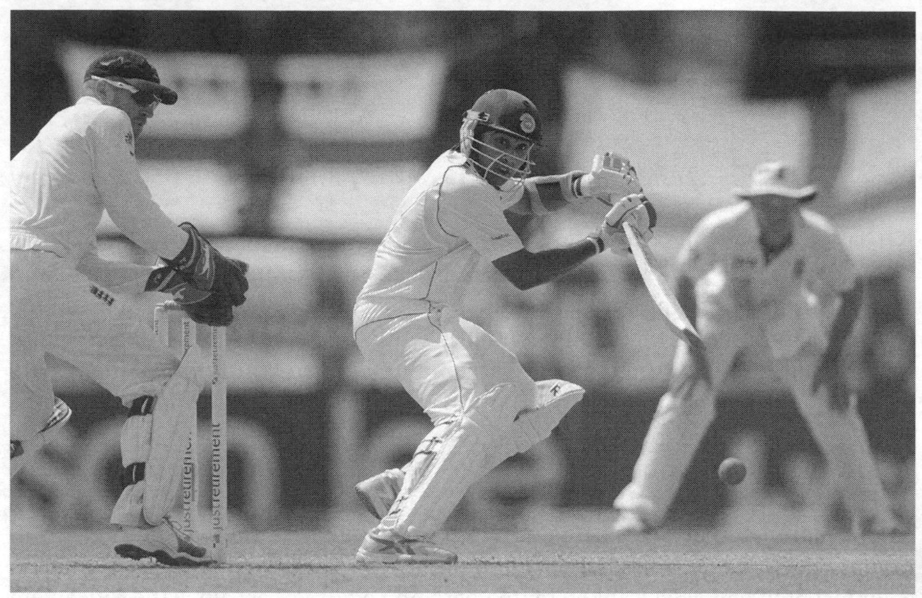

Philip Brown

Deftly does it: Mahela Jayawardene crafted a century in each Test.

The opportunism left a sour taste – as did the litter left behind by spectators on the ramparts – and not everyone made the trip north to Colombo; those who did had no choice but to pay over the odds once more.

The consolation – or possibly the saving grace – came in the form of two absorbing Tests. Central to the plot was Jayawardene, who registered his fifth and sixth hundreds at home against England, a figure bettered only by Don Bradman, with eight. Such was his brilliance in both games that his performance might have been considered career-defining had he not already defined it many times over. Never before, though, had he walked out in successive first innings on a hat-trick. Twice he calmly dealt with an on-song James Anderson – and twice he went on to score centuries. His 180 at Galle may have been an even finer innings than his unbeaten 213 there against England in December 2007, and only when Swann winkled him out on the final morning in Colombo could the tourists feel confident of squaring the series.

Sri Lanka's victory in the First Test owed just as much to the left-arm spin of Herath. With England apparently opting for a policy of sweep or bust – and often both – he needed to do little more than bowl straight: tentative batting and the presence of the Decision Review System did the rest. Herath's 12 wickets surpassed anything Muralitharan had managed in ten home Tests against England, who were spared a greater thrashing only by Jonathan Trott's sensible and unhurried 112.

At Galle, Swann had been accompanied by Monty Panesar and the debutant Samit Patel – the nearest England had come to selecting a trio of front-line spinners since 1987-88, when Nick Cook, John Emburey and Eddie Hemmings all played at Faisalabad. Yet it was Anderson who shone brightest, even though Sri Lanka were allowed to wriggle free from 15 for three in the first innings and 14 for three in the second. For once, England's fielding was ragged.

FIVE STATS YOU MAY HAVE MISSED

BENEDICT BERMANGE

- At Galle, Mahela Jayawardene became the first batsman to score 2,000 runs at two different Test grounds:

		T	*I*	*NO*	*R*	*HS*	*100*	*Avge*
D. P. M. D. Jayawardene (SL)	**Colombo (SSC)**	**25**	**38**	**3**	**2,698**	**374**	**10**	**77.08**
D. P. M. D. Jayawardene (SL)	**Galle**	**20**	**32**	**3**	**2,193**	**237**	**7**	**75.62**
K. C. Sangakkara (SL)	**Colombo (SSC)**	**20**	**30**	**3**	**2,159**	**287**	**8**	**79.96**
J. H. Kallis (SA)	**Cape Town**	**20**	**32**	**5**	**2,098**	**224**	**9**	**77.70**
G. A. Gooch (E)	Lord's	21	39	1	2,015	333	6	53.02

- Six England batsmen fell lbw in the first innings at Galle, which equalled their all-time record:

v South Africa at Leeds	1955
v West Indies at Kingston	1959-60
v Pakistan at Karachi	1977-78
v Sri Lanka at Galle	**2011-12**

The most lbws in any Test innings is seven, by Zimbabwe v England at Chester-le-Street in 2003, and New Zealand v Australia at Christchurch in 2004-05.

- At Galle, Sri Lanka became the first team in which four past or present Test wicketkeepers appeared together in one side – L. D. Chandimal, T. M. Dilshan, H. A. P. W. Jayawardene and K. C. Sangakkara.

- Graeme Swann became only the third non-Asian to take more than one ten-wicket haul in Tests in Asia. Shane Warne (Australia) managed three, and Richard Hadlee (New Zealand) two.

- Rangana Herath joined a select band of bowlers who have taken six or more wickets in at least three successive Test innings:

4	Harbhajan Singh (I)	7-123, 6-73; 7-133, 8-84	v Australia	2000-01
3	G. A. Lohmann (E)	7-38, 8-7; 9-28	v South Africa	1895-96
3	C. V. Grimmett (A)	6-92; 7-116, 7-83	v South Africa	1931-32
3	C. V. Grimmett (A)	7-40; 7-100, 6-73	v South Africa	1935-36
3	J. C. Laker (E)	6-55; 9-37, 10-53	v Australia	1956
3	Imran Khan (P)	8-58, 6-58; 7-52	v Sri Lanka/England	1981-82/1982
3	L. Sivaramakrishnan (I)	6-64, 6-117; 6-99	v England	1984-85
3	D. L. Vettori (NZ)	6-28; 6-70, 6-100	v Bangladesh	2004-05
3	**H. M. R. K. B. Herath (SL)**	**6-74, 6-97; 6-133**	**v England**	**2011-12**

Four Test defeats in a row left Andrew Strauss under pressure before the final match of the winter. Not only were his team losing, but his own form had been patchy; another defeat would cost them their No. 1 status. At the Sara, where England had contested Sri Lanka's inaugural Test 30 years earlier, Strauss's bowlers were thwarted for a while by Jayawardene. But the England captain and his opening partner Alastair Cook left the sweep back in the dressing-room, and proceeded to play as smartly as Trott had done at Galle. Strauss's steady 61 removed some of the heat – metaphorically, at least – and allowed him to sit back and enjoy the batting of Pietersen.

An innings of 151 from 165 balls would have been beyond most of his contemporaries. Throw in a smattering of controversial switch hits, and

Long day at the office... Graeme Swann drags himself off after bowling England to a share of the series in the heat of Colombo.

Pietersen's batting entered the realms of the unique. Swann's second-innings haul of six for 106, to give him ten wickets in the match, ensured he ended the winter as he began it – ahead of Panesar, who had threatened his status as England's go-to spinner with 14 wickets in two Tests in the UAE. Tim Bresnan, meanwhile, the man who replaced Panesar in Colombo, could now celebrate 11 Test wins out of 11.

Above all, the win – only England's second in Asia against a team other than Bangladesh since the 2–1 victory in Sri Lanka in 2000-01 – ensured they would finish a disappointing Test winter still the world's top-ranked team. It had not been easy. But then, for England on the subcontinent, it rarely is.

ENGLAND TOURING PARTY

*A. J. Strauss (Middlesex), J. M. Anderson (Lancashire), I. R. Bell (Warwickshire), R. S. Bopara (Essex), T. T. Bresnan (Yorkshire), S. C. J. Broad (Nottinghamshire), A. N. Cook (Essex), S. M. Davies (Surrey), S. T. Finn (Middlesex), M. S. Panesar (Sussex), S. R. Patel (Nottinghamshire), K. P. Pietersen (Surrey), M. J. Prior (Sussex), G. P. Swann (Nottinghamshire), J. C. Tredwell (Kent), I. J. L. Trott (Warwickshire).

Broad injured his right calf during the First Test and returned home before the Second, but was not replaced.

Coach: A. Flower. *Assistant coach/fielding coach:* R. G. Halsall. *Batting coach:* G. A. Gooch. *Fast bowling coach:* D. J. Saker. *Spin bowling coach:* Mushtaq Ahmed. *Wicketkeeping coach:* B. N. French. *Strength and conditioning coach:* H. R. Bevan. *Team operations manager:* P. A. Neale. *Physiotherapist:* B. T. Langley. *Team doctor:* Dr N. S. Peirce. *Analyst:* N. A. Leamon. *Sports psychologist:* M. A. K. Bawden. *Massage therapist:* M. E. S. Saxby. *Security manager:* R. C. Dickason. *Media relations managers:* A. J. Walpole and R. C. Evans.

SRI LANKA BOARD XI v ENGLAND XI

At Colombo (RPS), March 15–17, 2012. England XI won by an innings and 15 runs. Toss: Sri Lanka Board XI.

England's preparations began with a comfortable victory, although they suffered a scare: Stuart Broad tripped over the boundary rope during fielding practice before the start, damaging his left ankle, and sat out the game as a precaution. In his absence, the other bowlers did a fine job. Anderson took the first four wickets, then Panesar – after failing to strike in 14 overs – produced a spell of five for 14. Cook batted throughout the 100 overs allowed for the first innings, before the bowlers got to work again to complete a convincing victory. It was marred a little by some dissent towards the end, notably when Strauss claimed a slip catch but Dilruwan Perera stood his ground; the umpires said they were unsighted. Swann later upset the locals by claiming – tongue in cheek – that he "wanted to kill" Perera.

Close of play: First day, England XI 6-0 (Strauss 6, Cook 0); Second day, England XI 303-8 (Cook 163, Anderson 12).

Sri Lanka Board XI

W. A. A. M. Silva c Prior b Finn	66	– c Bopara b Anderson	0
F. D. M. Karunaratne c Prior b Anderson	0	– b Swann	31
P. B. B. Rajapaksa c Trott b Anderson	1	– c Swann b Finn	9
A. R. S. Silva b Anderson	21	– c Strauss b Anderson	12
*†H. A. P. W. Jayawardene lbw b Anderson	2	– c Anderson b Finn	0
S. C. Serasinghe c Anderson b Panesar	31	– c Cook b Swann	5
M. D. K. Perera lbw b Panesar	0	– c Prior b Finn	6
K. G. Alwitigala b Panesar	4	– c Prior b Swann	0
H. M. C. M. Bandara c Swann b Panesar	6	not out	28
T. P. Gamage not out	14	– lbw b Panesar	19
W. G. H. N. Premaratne b Panesar	1	– lbw b Anderson	0
B 12, l-b 2, w 5, n-b 4	23	L-b 9	9
1/5 (2) 2/11 (3) 3/65 (4) 4/67 (5) (73.3 overs)	169	1/0 (1) 2/25 (3) (56.4 overs)	119
5/132 (6) 6/134 (7) 7/134 (1)		3/51 (2) 4/51 (5)	
8/138 (8) 9/168 (9) 10/169 (11)		5/62 (6) 6/62 (4) 7/63 (8)	
		8/79 (7) 9/118 (10) 10/119 (11)	

Anderson 11–3–19–4; Finn 16–7–33–1; Bopara 5–0–19–0; Swann 18–4–47–0; Panesar 23.3–11–37–5. *Second Innings*—Anderson 11.4–5–21–3; Finn 13–5–24–3; Panesar 18–8–32–1; Swann 14–5–33–3.

England XI

*A. J. Strauss lbw b Perera	40	S. T. Finn lbw b Bandara	0
A. N. Cook not out	163	J. M. Anderson not out	12
I. J. L. Trott lbw b Bandara	16	L-b 6, w 7, n-b 1	14
K. P. Pietersen lbw b Serasinghe	39		
I. R. Bell b Serasinghe	0	1/89 (1) (8 wkts, 100 overs)	303
R. S. Bopara lbw b Perera	12	2/119 (3) 3/188 (4)	
†M. J. Prior c Jayawardene b Alwitigala	0	4/188 (5) 5/236 (6) 6/237 (7)	
G. P. Swann c Karunaratne b Bandara	7	7/245 (8) 8/247 (9)	

M. S. Panesar did not bat.

Perera 25–2–84–2; Serasinghe 13–2–24–2; Gamage 12–2–24–0; Premaratne 13–0–57–0; Alwitigala 13–1–50–1; Bandara 24–4–58–3.

Umpires: R. A. Kottahachchi and R. R. Wimalasiri. Referee: B. Perera.

"Ramps and Test cricket: it was never really going to work out. Wrong genius, wrong time."

Retirements, page 190.

SRI LANKA CRICKET DEVELOPMENT XI v ENGLAND XI

At Colombo (SSC), March 20–22, 2012. England XI won by four wickets. Toss: Sri Lanka Cricket Development XI.

England's second warm-up game was a closer affair, but they still managed another morale-boosting victory, with just 20 balls to spare. Chamara Silva made a case for a Test recall, passing 10,000 first-class runs during his 163, and sharing stands of 151 with Thilina Kandamby and 93 with Angelo Perera. In reply, Strauss and Trott put on 197 for the first wicket; both retired out on reaching three figures. Perera batted well again in the second innings, biffing six sixes before being stranded ten short of his hundred by a declaration which left England 359 to win from 64 overs. They paced the chase well: after a circumspect start, things hotted up as Prior hit 84 from 60 balls, while Patel – with Eoin Morgan left at home following a traumatic time in the UAE – prepared for a Test debut with 72 from 78.

Close of play: First day, Sri Lanka Cricket Development XI 376-5 (A. K. Perera 61, Lokuarachchi 22); Second day, Sri Lanka Cricket Development XI 44-1 (Munaweera 26, M. D. K. J. Perera 7).

Sri Lanka Cricket Development XI

First innings		Second innings	
E. M. D. Y. Munaweera b Broad	19	– lbw b Bresnan	33
B. S. M. Warnapura c Bopara b Broad	0	– lbw b Broad	4
L. P. C. Silva c Trott b Finn	163		
*S. H. T. Kandamby b Patel	64	– b Swann	13
A. K. Perera c Bresnan b Finn	85	– not out	90
†M. D. K. J. Perera lbw b Broad	35	– (3) c Prior b Finn	9
K. S. Lokuarachchi not out	51	– (6) not out	40
I. Udana not out	0		
L-b 6, w 2, n-b 6	14	B 3, l-b 4, n-b 3	10
1/1 (2) 2/38 (1) 3/189 (4) 4/282 (3) 5/342 (6) 6/427 (5) (6 wkts, 100 overs)	431	1/24 (2) 2/51 (1) 3/53 (3) 4/77 (4) (4 wkts dec, 34 overs)	199

A. B. T. Lakshitha, M. V. T. Fernando and S. Weerakoon did not bat.

Broad 18–3–69–3; Finn 20–2–93–2; Bresnan 18–0–59–0; Swann 21–2–102–0; Bopara 5–1–19–0; Patel 18–2–83–1. *Second Innings*—Broad 5–1–22–1; Bresnan 6–3–16–1; Patel 6–0–44–0; Swann 6–2–30–1; Finn 5–0–17–1; Bell 3–0–34–0; Trott 3–0–29–0.

England XI

First innings		Second innings	
*A. J. Strauss retired out	100		
I. J. L. Trott retired out	101		
K. P. Pietersen st M. D. K. J. Perera b Weerakoon	26	– (1) b Lokuarachchi	52
I. R. Bell c Kandamby b Lakshitha	14	– (2) c M. D. K. J. Perera b Fernando	11
R. S. Bopara not out	12	– (3) c and b Weerakoon	66
S. R. Patel not out	12	– (5) b Lakshitha	72
†M. J. Prior (did not bat)		– (4) b Fernando	84
T. T. Bresnan (did not bat)		– (6) c Udana b Lakshitha	14
S. C. J. Broad (did not bat)		– (7) not out	17
G. P. Swann (did not bat)		– (8) not out	31
L-b 3, w 1, n-b 3	7	B 4, l-b 5, w 3, n-b 1	13
1/197 (1) 2/217 (2) 3/247 (4) 4/247 (3) (4 wkts dec, 66 overs)	272	1/32 (2) 2/101 (1) 3/184 (3) 4/248 (4) 5/270 (6) 6/325 (5) (6 wkts, 60.4 overs)	360

S. T. Finn did not bat.

Lakshitha 12–3–29–1; Fernando 11–0–50–0; Udana 7–1–38–0; Weerakoon 23–2–96–1; Lokuarachchi 13–0–56–0. *Second Innings*—Lakshitha 15–0–89–2; Fernando 13–0–72–2; Weerakoon 17–0–81–1; Udana 7–1–36–0; Lokuarachchi 7.4–0–70–1; Kandamby 1–0–3–0.

Umpires: W. N. de Silva and T. H. Wijewardene. Referee: B. C. M. S. Mendis.

SRI LANKA v ENGLAND

First Test Match

LAWRENCE BOOTH

At Galle, March 26–29, 2012. Sri Lanka won by 75 runs. Toss: Sri Lanka. Test debut: S. R. Patel.

The Union Flag that fluttered on top of Galle's Dutch fort ought to have raised the alarm. It was the wrong way up. Done deliberately, this is supposed to mean SOS; by accident, and it's anyone's guess. For much of a game in which England plunged to their fourth straight Test defeat – their worst sequence since the 2006-07 Ashes whitewash – the batsmen seemed determined to provide their own grim twist: Save Our Sweep.

Five men fell playing a stroke that, as England pointed out with some justification, has its place on Asian pitches. But they played it too often, most perilously to full-length deliveries on the stumps: four of the five departed leg-before, with Prior the exception, creaming one into Thirimanne's midriff at short leg to signal the beginning of the end of England's fourth-innings hopes.

The chief beneficiary was Herath, whose career-best 12 for 171 made him the first slow left-armer to take ten wickets in a Test against England for 50 years. By doing little more than plugging away on a pitch that demanded caution but should not have provoked panic, Herath spun Sri Lanka to their first home win since Muttiah Muralitharan's final Test, also at Galle, in July 2010, and to their second-best match figures against England, behind Murali's 16 for 220 at The Oval in 1998. And if Murali was the more artful, Herath harnessed the zeitgeist: aim for the pads, and leave the rest to scrambled minds and the DRS. Not since Karachi in 1977-78 – when Shakoor Rana was one of the umpires – had England lost six batsmen lbw in a Test innings.

Yet Sri Lanka might have lost had it not been for Mahela Jayawardene, in his first Test as captain for three years and without so much as a fifty in 12 innings. Not long after his

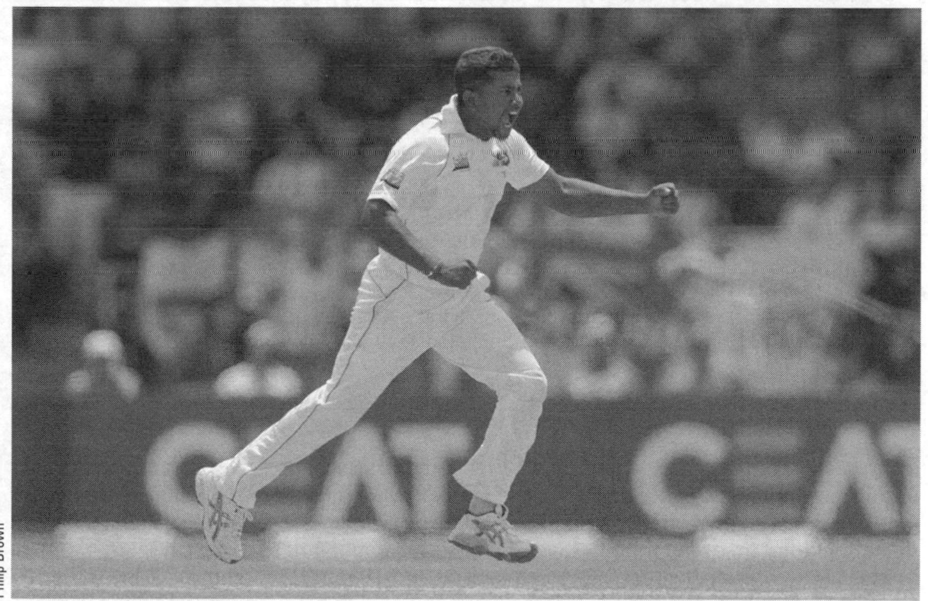

Philip Brown

No Murali, no problem: Rangana Herath's 12 wickets sent England to a fourth straight Test loss.

arrival, Sri Lanka were 15 for three. But he calmly saw off England's new-ball salvo, then found a succession of partners happy to play third fiddle (daylight was second).

Even so, England were generous. With Sri Lanka 138 for five – a recovery of sorts, but still below par after winning a crucial toss – Anderson dropped a half-chance as he back-pedalled from slip after Jayawardene, on 64, had failed to cope with Swann's extra bounce. Then, on 90, he was missed by Anderson again, this time a return catch around his left ear. The next ball was deposited over long-on for six, the shot of a man keen to salt the wound.

HIGHEST PROPORTION OF COMPLETED TOTAL FOR SRI LANKA

%	*Score/total*			
63.41	52*/82	A. P. Gurusinha	v India at Chandigarh	1990-91
58.82	100*/170	K. C. Sangakkara	v New Zealand at Christchurch	2006-07
58.20	156*/268	K. C. Sangakkara	v New Zealand at Wellington	2006-07
57.76	253/438	S. T. Jayasuriya	v Pakistan at Faisalabad	2004-05
56.60	**180/318**	**D. P. M. D. Jayawardene**	**v England at Galle**	**2011-12**
56.19	127/226	P. A. de Silva	v Pakistan at Colombo (PSS)	1994-95

Sangakkara's innings came in successive matches.

For England, it would get worse. Desperate to take the last two wickets, they instead endured a pair of Panesar mishaps. On 147, Jayawardene pulled Anderson's third delivery with the second new ball to long leg, where Panesar, possibly dazzled by the sun, could only parry it over the rope. In the next over, fate inevitably decreed that it was Panesar who should be standing at mid-on under a steepler as Jayawardene – now 152 – miscued a heave off Broad. Down went the chance, and with it English heads, lifting only when the excellent Anderson finally did get Jayawardene to complete his 12th five-wicket haul in Tests and go past his fellow Lancastrian Brian Statham's tally of 252 into fifth place on England's all-time list.

Sri Lanka's last three wickets had added 127, while Jayawardene's 180 was streets ahead of Chandimal, who came next with 27. Not only was it his 30th Test century, but

LEFT REELING

Ten wickets in a Test by a slow left-armer against England:

12-108 (8-55, 4-53)	V. Mankad (India) at Madras	1951-52
12-171 (6-74, 6-97)	**H. M. R. K. B. Herath (Sri Lanka) at Galle**	**2011-12**
11-85 (7-58, 4-27)	C. G. Macartney (Australia) at Leeds	1909
11-204 (8-104, 3-100)	†A. L. Valentine (West Indies) at Manchester	1950
10-160 (4-121, 6-39)	A. L. Valentine (West Indies) at The Oval	1950
10-177 (6-105, 4-72)	S. A. Durani (India) at Madras	1961-62
10-239 (4-129, 6-110)	L. O'B. Fleetwood-Smith (Australia) at Adelaide	1936-37

† *On Test debut.*

his seventh both at Galle and against England. Just as impressive as his occasionally dashing strokeplay was his mastery of the strike: while he faced 315 balls, his ten team-mates faced 268 between them; and he ticked off 51 singles, 23 more than England would manage in total first time round. It was, quite simply, an innings for the ages.

This became even clearer as England subsided to 193, itself a fightback – led by Bell – from 92 for six. Without a carefree last-wicket stand of 36 between Anderson and Panesar, the deficit would have been even greater than 125. Then, when England bowled again,

Philip Brown

Tummy trouble: Matt Prior picks out Lahiru Thirimanne's midriff, and England are heading for defeat.

they kept on fighting. Broad knocked over Dilshan in the second over and, when Swann appeared as early as the seventh, he produced a beauty to bowl the left-handed Thirimanne with his second ball. It was 14 for three when Swann had Jayawardene caught at slip, and Sangakkara quickly followed. In all, 17 wickets fell on the second day, equalling the venue record. By the close, Sri Lanka – five down – led by 209.

Cheered on by a crowd of predominantly white faces on the third day – though some were by now rather red, a combination of the sun and anger at Sri Lanka Cricket's on-the-hoof ticketing policy – England began to believe. And when Swann bowled Herath to pick up his sixth wicket, Sri Lanka were in effect 252 for eight. But Welagedara kept Prasanna Jayawardene company for over an hour before he was caught in the gully off Panesar, and England were further frustrated when – five deliveries later – Broad bounced out Jayawardene, caught at short leg, only for replays to reveal a no-ball. It was one of eight bowled in the match by the usually disciplined Broad; no one else overstepped all game. The 46 runs added thereafter by Jayawardene and Lakmal set England 340, eight more than they had ever made in the fourth innings to win a Test, and 87 more than any side had then managed batting fourth at Galle.

England lost Cook, given out caught behind by third umpire Bruce Oxenford after Rod Tucker had turned down Herath's appeal, and Strauss on the third evening, then Pietersen, chipping carelessly to short midwicket early on the fourth day. When Bell fell on the sweep to Herath, despite claiming a bottom edge, England were 152 for four – and tottering.

But Trott was playing his own game, mixing stoical defence with an unexpected reverse sweep or two, and Prior – batting at No. 6 ahead of the debutant Samit Patel – knuckled down. Sri Lanka went on the defensive; anything seemed possible. But four balls after Trott had reached his seventh Test hundred (it would become his first in defeat), and with England now only 107 short of their target, Prior's slog-sweep somehow lodged in Thirimanne's grasp at short leg. The innings unravelled with indecent haste: the last five tumbled for 12, and England were suddenly one result away from losing their No. 1 ranking. The upside-down flag felt about right.

Man of the Match: H. M. R. K. B. Herath.

Close of play: first day, Sri Lanka 289-8 (D. P. M. D. Jayawardene 168, Welagedara 10); second day, Sri Lanka 84-5 (Chandimal 17, Randiv 2); third day, England 111-2 (Trott 40, Pietersen 29).

Sri Lanka

H. D. R. L. Thirimanne c Swann b Anderson	3	– b Swann	6
T. M. Dilshan c Strauss b Broad	11	– b Broad	0
K. C. Sangakkara c Prior b Anderson	0	– c Bell b Swann	14
*D. P. M. D. Jayawardene c Prior b Anderson	180	– c Anderson b Swann	5
T. T. Samaraweera run out	20	– st Prior b Swann	36
L. D. Chandimal c Bell b Patel	27	– c Pietersen b Panesar	31
†H. A. P. W. Jayawardene lbw b Anderson	23	– (8) not out	61
S. Randiv run out	12	– (7) lbw b Swann	18
H. M. R. K. B. Herath lbw b Patel	5	– b Swann	7
U. W. M. B. C. A. Welagedara b Anderson	19	– c Strauss b Panesar	13
R. A. S. Lakmal not out	0	– run out	13
L-b 14, n-b 4	18	B 1, l-b 4, w 1, n-b 4	10
1/11 (1) 2/11 (3) 3/15 (2) (96.3 overs)	318	1/4 (2) 2/8 (1) (84.3 overs)	214
4/67 (5) 5/128 (6) 6/170 (7)		3/14 (4) 4/41 (3)	
7/191 (8) 8/253 (9) 9/307 (10) 10/318 (4)		5/72 (5) 6/114 (6) 7/115 (7)	
		8/127 (9) 9/167 (10) 10/214 (11)	

Anderson 20.3–5–72–5; Broad 21–3–71–1; Panesar 23–11–42–0; Swann 23–3–92–0; Patel 9–1–27–2. *Second innings*—Anderson 10.3–2–26–0; Broad 11–2–33–1; Swann 30–5–82–6; Panesar 24–6–59–2; Patel 9–4–9–0.

England

*A. J. Strauss lbw b Herath	26	– c Dilshan b Herath	27
A. N. Cook lbw b Lakmal	0	– c H. A. P. W. Jayawardene b Herath	14
I. J. L. Trott st H. A. P. W. Jayawardene b Herath	12	– c Dilshan b Randiv	112
K. P. Pietersen b Welagedara	3	– c D. P. M. D. Jayawardene b Randiv	30
I. R. Bell b Herath	52	– lbw b Herath	13
†M. J. Prior lbw b Herath	7	– c Thirimanne b Herath	41
S. R. Patel lbw b Herath	2	– c Dilshan b Herath	9
S. C. J. Broad lbw b Herath	28	– not out	5
G. P. Swann c Dilshan b Randiv	24	– lbw b Herath	1
J. M. Anderson not out	23	– c H. A. P. W. Jayawardene b Randiv	5
M. S. Panesar lbw b Randiv	13	– c Dilshan b Randiv	0
L-b 2, w 1	3	L-b 6, w 1	7
1/0 (2) 2/40 (3) 3/43 (1) 4/65 (4) (46.4 overs)	193	1/31 (2) 2/48 (1) (99 overs)	264
5/72 (6) 6/92 (7) 7/122 (8)		3/118 (4) 4/152 (5)	
8/157 (9) 9/157 (5) 10/193 (11)		5/233 (6) 6/252 (7) 7/256 (3)	
		8/259 (9) 9/264 (10) 10/264 (11)	

Welagedara 11–2–46–1; Lakmal 9–2–45–1; Herath 19–5–74–6; Randiv 7.4–0–26–2. *Second innings*—Welagedara 13–2–40–0; Lakmal 10–5–22–0; Herath 38–9–97–6; Dilshan 12–1–25–0; Randiv 26–2–74–4.

Umpires: Asad Rauf and R. J. Tucker. Third umpire: B. N. J. Oxenford.

SRI LANKA v ENGLAND

Second Test Match

VIC MARKS

At Colombo (PSS), April 3–7, 2012. England won by eight wickets. Toss: Sri Lanka.

In the last game of a chastening winter, England finally demonstrated they were capable of winning a Test in Asia. Not before time, their batsmen gave proper support to the valiant band of bowlers who had sweated buckets from Dubai to Galle via Abu Dhabi without reward. England romped to victory by eight wickets, having won by seven on

Graham Morris

On–off switch: Tillekeratne Dilshan pulls up after Kevin Pietersen changes to a left-hander's grip.

their previous visit to the cosy Saravanamuttu stadium for Sri Lanka's inaugural Test 30 years earlier. And they clung to their No. 1 ranking, just ahead of South Africa.

It all seemed so simple again. Anderson was incisive with the new ball, Swann gradually asserted himself on a slow, turning pitch and, in unrelenting heat, the commitment in the field never wavered. That had been the pattern of the winter. But now the batsmen also functioned according to the textbook. Cook and Strauss blunted a modest Sri Lankan attack with the help of Trott. Then Pietersen, suddenly free as a bird, shredded the bowlers in an audacious innings of 151 from 165 balls – England's highest Test score in Sri Lanka. This was the Pietersen of old, before the burden of captaincy and the disappointment of losing it. He trusted his instincts, and the ball kept disappearing over the short boundaries. He also unfurled his switch hit, causing delight and controversy in equal measure.

Despite yet more Herculean efforts from Mahela Jayawardene – though there is not a rippling muscle to be seen upon him – England ended up as comfortable victors. If there had been a Third and decisive Test, there was a good chance they would have prevailed, but the impending IPL denied them that luxury. Within three days, Jayawardene and Pietersen were Delhi Daredevils team-mates.

Before the match, Strauss in particular was unusually edgy. He gave what, by his standards, was a brusque press conference, in which – despite many invitations – he declined to speculate on his future. For the first time since he took over from Pietersen in January 2009, there had been rumblings about his hold on the England captaincy, not merely because of the sequence of four defeats, but also because of his own lack of runs.

Strauss also had some ticklish selections to make. With Stuart Broad now back home because of a calf injury, Finn returned for his first Test in ten. More surprisingly, Bresnan replaced Monty Panesar, so ending England's experiment of playing two specialist spinners. Perhaps Strauss was swayed more by the stats than the conditions: in seven Tests together, Swann and Panesar had never experienced victory, while Bresnan could boast wins in all ten previous Test appearances. By mid-afternoon on the fifth day, it was 11 out of 11.

Losing the toss was no great hindrance for Strauss, since Anderson snatched three early wickets, including Sangakkara, out first ball again. Jayawardene, as ever, rescued the situation with another watchful, elegant century, and received dutiful support from

BEYOND TWO MILLION

A notable Test landmark was established on the first morning of the Second Test in Colombo. With Sri Lanka 37 for three, Mahela Jayawardene square-cut James Anderson to the boundary: those four runs included the two millionth in Test history. He sailed on to his eighth century against England, and in the second innings passed 2,000 runs against them. "England's weary bowlers must feel as though most of the two million have been made by Jayawardene," wrote John Etheridge in *The Sun*, after observing that the aggregate statistic must have been worked out by "a man of astonishing geekiness".

Some geeks, however, thought it was Jayawardene's partner, Thilan Samaraweera, who had collected the landmark run in the previous over, from Steven Finn. The confusion arose because of retrospective changes to scorecards (something *Wisden* is opposed to in general, precisely for this sort of reason). South Africa's second-innings total against England in the Second Test at Johannesburg in 1905-06, for example, was given as 34 for one in the record books for the best part of a century – but was revised to 33 for one a few years ago after the scorebook was examined.

The millionth Test run came towards the end of the drawn Third Test between India and Australia at Bombay in October 1986, during a partnership between Dean Jones and Allan Border. The first million Test runs thus took more than 109 years (and 1,054 Tests), while the second million were completed in just over 25 (a further 985 matches). STEVEN LYNCH

Samaraweera and Mathews, back from injury in place of Dinesh Chandimal. Yet when Sri Lanka were all out for 275 before lunch on the second day, England had their chance.

The upper order duly dug in. Their use of the sweep shot was much more sparing and adroit than at Galle, so much so that neither opener dusted off the stroke until the 39th over. Strauss's 61 stopped some of the rumblings, while Cook and Trott gave a reminder of the rewards of self-denial. Then came Pietersen, who would later be almost at a loss to explain such a spectacular return to form (his Test output over the winter had been far worse than his captain's). "When I'm in nick, I like to play like that," he said. "I've never been able to explain how I do it. It's just instinct. If the ball is there to hit, I hit it."

Sometimes Pietersen smashed balls that were *not* there to hit. Straight sixes peppered the boxes of the VIPs, and he could not resist employing his trademark switch hit, which led to an unexpected warning from umpire Asad Rauf. Three times in an over Dilshan, bowling off-breaks from round the wicket to a seven–two leg-side field, declined to release the ball because Pietersen – who began the over on 86 and finished it on 104 – was busy changing into a left-hander. On the third occasion, Pietersen received his warning; another would have added five penalty runs to Sri Lanka's score.

In a rare but justifiable interpretation of the Laws, Pietersen was deemed to be time-wasting because he was causing the impasse that prevented the ball from being delivered. Dilshan was quite entitled to refrain from bowling once he saw Pietersen moving. The only question was whether Pietersen had begun to do so *before* Dilshan had entered his delivery stride; even with the benefit of replays, it was hard to say.

Whatever the precise sequence of events, the brief stand-off was in danger of overshadowing the fact that Pietersen's century separated the teams. This was his 20th in Tests, and his 29th in all international matches, taking him past Graham Gooch's England record; now the batting coach, Gooch was watching with rare contentment from the pavilion. England's lead of 185 was sufficient.

Sri Lanka, who had sent in nightwatchman Prasad to face one over on the third evening, reached a healthy 215 for four on the fourth before Swann snatched two wickets in the penultimate over. They closed with a lead of only 33. Swann would finish with six wickets in the innings – including the prize scalp of Mahela Jayawardene on the final morning – and, for the second time, ten in the match. He also moved past Tony Lock (174 wickets) to become England's third-most-productive Test spinner, finishing the series with 182: only Derek Underwood (297) and Jim Laker (193) remained above him. Curiously, Swann appeared to bowl better without having Panesar at the other end.

England needed 94 to win and – despite the early loss of Strauss for a duck and Trott for five – they did not hang around. Pietersen wrapped things up with 42 from 28 balls and his eighth six of the match, a mighty blow over square leg off his sparring partner Dilshan. It was a gem of a knock, bringing delight both to the England team and Delhi, who were eagerly awaiting his arrival in India.

Man of the Match: K. P. Pietersen. *Man of the Series:* D. P. M. D. Jayawardene.

Close of play: first day, Sri Lanka 238-6 (Mathews 41, Randiv 5); second day, England 154-1 (Cook 77, Trott 15); third day, Sri Lanka 4-0 (Prasad 0, Thirimanne 0); fourth day, Sri Lanka 218-6 (D. P. M. D. Jayawardene 55, Mathews 3).

Sri Lanka

First innings		Second innings	
H. D. R. L. Thirimanne lbw b Anderson	8	– (2) c Strauss b Anderson	11
T. M. Dilshan c Prior b Anderson	14	– (3) c Anderson b Swann	35
K. C. Sangakkara c Strauss b Anderson	0	– (4) c Prior b Swann	21
*D. P. M. D. Jayawardene lbw b Swann	105	– (5) c Cook b Swann	64
T. T. Samaraweera lbw b Bresnan	54	– (6) b Swann	47
A. D. Mathews c Strauss b Swann	57	– (8) c Strauss b Finn	46
†H. A. P. W. Jayawardene c Prior b Finn	7	– (9) b Swann	2
S. Randiv c Pietersen b Swann	12	– (7) b Swann	0
K. T. G. D. Prasad not out	12	– (1) c Bresnan b Finn	34
H. M. R. K. B. Herath c Prior b Bresnan	2	– c Anderson b Patel	2
R. A. S. Lakmal b Swann	0	– not out	4
B 4	4	B 4, l-b 6, w 2	12
1/21 (2) 2/21 (3) 3/30 (1) 4/154 (5) 5/216 (4) 6/227 (7) 7/258 (8) 8/261 (6) 9/270 (10) 10/275 (11) (111.1 overs)	275	1/23 (2) 2/64 (1) 3/104 (3) 4/125 (4) 5/215 (6) 6/215 (7) 7/238 (5) 8/242 (9) 9/251 (10) 10/278 (8) (118.5 overs)	278

Anderson 22–5–62–3; Finn 22–4–51–1; Bresnan 21–3–47–2; Patel 16–3–32–0; Swann 28.1–4–75–4; Pietersen 2–0–4–0. *Second innings*—Anderson 20–6–36–1; Finn 15.5–1–30–2; Swann 40–1–106–6; Bresnan 14–5–24–0; Patel 25–7–54–1; Pietersen 4–0–18–0.

England

First innings		Second innings	
*A. J. Strauss c H. A. P. W. Jayawardene b Dilshan	61	– b Dilshan	0
A. N. Cook c D. P. M. D. Jayawardene b Dilshan	94	– not out	49
I. J. L. Trott c D. P. M. D. Jayawardene b Herath	64	– lbw b Herath	5
K. P. Pietersen lbw b Herath	151	– not out	42
I. R. Bell c Randiv b Prasad	18		
†M. J. Prior c Prasad b Herath	11		
S. R. Patel c Prasad b Randiv	29		
T. T. Bresnan b Herath	5		
G. P. Swann c Dilshan b Herath	17		
J. M. Anderson lbw b Herath	2		
S. T. Finn not out	2		
B 1, l-b 2, w 1, n-b 2	6	L-b 1	1
1/122 (1) 2/213 (2) 3/253 (3) 4/347 (5) 5/380 (6) 6/411 (4) 7/419 (8) 8/454 (9) 9/458 (10) 10/460 (7) (152.3 overs)	460	1/0 (1) 2/31 (3) (2 wkts, 19.4 overs)	97

Lakmal 22–4–81–0; Prasad 23–8–63–1; Herath 53–9–133–6; Dilshan 20–4–73–2; Randiv 34.3–4–107–1. *Second innings*—Dilshan 7.4–1–43–1; Herath 9–0–37–1; Randiv 3–0–16–0.

Umpires: Asad Rauf and B. N. J. Oxenford. Third umpire: R. J. Tucker.
Series referee: J. Srinath.

ENGLAND v WEST INDIES, 2012

REVIEW BY MIKE SELVEY

Test matches (3): England 2, West Indies 0
One-day internationals (3): England 2, West Indies 0
Twenty20 international (1): England 1, West Indies 0

Once upon a time, rather too long ago, the West Indians would roll into town with a swagger, and opponents would obligingly step aside. They had little choice. But if their arrival in England was familiar in one respect – this was their third visit for a Test tour in six summers – the swagger was understandably absent. The decline in their Test fortunes, previously the pride of the Caribbean – indeed the region's only corporate representation, with the possible exception of the University of the West Indies – had been palpable. And, while a testing early-season tour of England had its moments, they never lasted long enough to change the thrust of the narrative.

The side that arrived in May did so almost unnoticed. In fact, it was barely a side at all, for their strength had been plundered by the lure of the Indian Premier League. Absent from the Test series was a string of players, most notably Chris Gayle – still at odds with the West Indies Cricket Board, despite rumours that the stand-off was being sorted out – and all-rounder Dwayne Bravo. The diamond-studded travellers, Gayle included, were back for the limited-overs games that followed the three Tests, but their effect hardly proved dynamic: West Indies did not win an international match in any format.

During the Tests they were outplayed by a much better side, with England captain Andrew Strauss casting aside doubts about his batting – at least until they resurfaced against South Africa – by making hundreds at Lord's, for which he received a memorably affectionate standing ovation, and Trent Bridge. The West Indians, under the virtuous leadership of Darren Sammy, at least gave a spirited account of themselves, which in itself exceeded expectation. It was just that their overall efforts tended to be capsized by the occasional catastrophic session.

Hopes were higher for the one-day internationals and especially the single Twenty20 game, the format best suited to their personnel. But the fizz went flat, and West Indies' only success of the tour came when they thrashed Middlesex in a 50-over warm-up at Lord's. And instead of being fortified by the return of the IPL stars, as he should have been, Sammy seemed to lose some of his authority.

It was a lazy finish to a trip that had hinted at steady improvement, and it allowed England to shrug off the loss of Kevin Pietersen, whose retirement – later rescinded – from international limited-overs cricket would spark an unedifying chain of events. In the one-day internationals, as in the Tests, they ran out comfortable winners, with Ian Bell, promoted to open with Alastair

Philip Brown

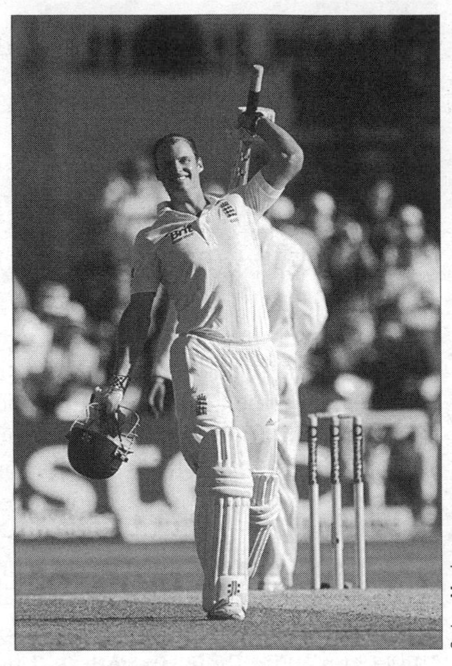

Graham Morris

Grin and bare it: captains Darren Sammy and Andrew Strauss acknowledge the applause after both reached centuries on the second day of the Trent Bridge Test.

Cook in Pietersen's place, scoring a century in the first match, and Cook repeating the dose in the second.

Throughout, however, it was West Indies who faced the greater off-field issues. The impasse between Gayle and the WICB had been the most unwelcome of distractions, disrupting the efforts of coach Ottis Gibson to develop a team in the truest sense of the word, and apparently based on a petty squabble rooted in semantics: two bald men fighting over a comb, as someone put it. The intransigence of the WICB, and Gayle's occasional faux bemusement, did neither credit. So while Gayle roamed the world, hitting sixes for large sums of money, he became a political football back in the Caribbean. His return to the side was worked out only after the involvement of the premiers of St Vincent, Antigua & Barbuda, and Jamaica, his home country.

All the while, criticism was heaped on Gibson, in particular by a number of West Indian greats, including Sir Vivian Richards and Michael Holding. They discerned a blinkered management style that excluded players Gibson regarded as not fully committed to his personal vision. So the experienced batsman Ramnaresh Sarwan, who had enjoyed such a successful series against England in the Caribbean in early 2009, spent the summer playing for Leicestershire; and the claims of Jerome Taylor, whose legendary bowling spell at Sabina Park in that same series had paradoxically been the catalyst for the renaissance of England rather than West Indies, and who was available again after a lengthy spell of injury, were ignored. Neither, it was argued by Gibson, had demonstrated sufficient commitment to replace more dedicated, if less experienced players – and almost certainly less talented ones.

Philip Brown

Skip to it: Alastair Cook takes evasive action as Marlon Samuels finds form at Lord's.

Preparation for the First Test, in matches against Sussex and the England Lions, was scarcely a success. Hampered by appalling weather, West Indies were restricted to 34 overs in three days at Hove. That was followed by the embarrassment of a ten-wicket defeat by the Lions at Northampton, where the promise of Kieran Powell's century was offset by hundreds from James Taylor and, in an unbroken opening stand of 197, Joe Root. With weather conditions expected to suit England's band of seamers, West Indies were given little hope of providing more than token resistance in the Tests.

It was a careless assumption, for at times they played challenging cricket. But they were desperately hampered by the struggles of the top four: Adrian Barath, Powell, Kirk Edwards (who endured a torrid time, was ill during the second innings at Trent Bridge, and dropped for the final Test at Edgbaston), and – most disappointingly of all – Darren Bravo, Dwayne's half-brother.

On the credit side came predictable resistance from Shivnarine Chanderpaul (or "Chanderwall", as he had become known over the years, after so many hours playing a lone hand of resistance). Twice at Lord's he held the line, although he too was absent from the Third Test, for reasons largely unexplained but with speculation ranging from injury to matters of discipline. Despite his runs – he had recently passed 10,000 in Tests – Chanderpaul was no favourite of Gibson's. In the Second Test, Sammy went a considerable way to answering those who doubted his credentials by surviving a nervy spell late in his innings to register a maiden Test hundred, a vibrant affair full of long-levered strokes.

Kemar Roach put the wind up England with some searing pace: had there been another hour's play on the penultimate evening at Lord's, when the ball moved sharply and he had the top order on the rack, there might have been a different result. Roach, unfortunately, was not to last the series because of a shin injury, and neither was the promisingly threatening fast bowler Shannon Gabriel, who made his debut at Lord's but soon flew home because of back spasms.

FIVE STATS YOU MAY HAVE MISSED

BENEDICT BERMANGE

- Stuart Broad's seven first-innings wickets at Lord's were caught by seven different fielders, equalling the feat of England's Jack White during his second-innings eight for 126 against Australia at Adelaide in 1928-29. Both Broad and White took one return catch.

- When Darren Bravo was run out in a mix-up with Shivnarine Chanderpaul on the first day at Lord's, it was the 23rd time Chanderpaul had been involved in a run-out while batting; he had been the victim only three times. Eighty-six batsmen have been involved in at least ten run-outs in their Test careers, but none has a higher survival rate than Chanderpaul:

	Run-outs	*Self out*	*Partner out*	*Partner out %*
S. Chanderpaul (West Indies)	**23**	**3**	**20**	**86.95**
S. R. Waugh (Australia)	27	4	23	85.18
Asif Iqbal (Pakistan)	13	2	11	84.61
S. M. Katich (Australia)	12	2	10	83.33
W. W. Armstrong (Australia)	11	2	9	81.81
A. Flower (Zimbabwe)	11	2	9	81.81
R. B. Richardson (West Indies)	10	2	8	80.00
S. C. Ganguly (India)	17	4	13	76.47
I. V. A. Richards (West Indies)	16	4	12	75.00
I. T. Botham (England)	12	3	9	75.00
P. A. de Silva (Sri Lanka)	12	3	9	75.00
B. C. Lara (West Indies)	12	3	9	75.00
K. D. Walters (Australia)	12	3	9	75.00

- Victory over West Indies at Lord's gave Andrew Strauss his ninth Test win on the ground, breaking the record he held jointly with Fred Trueman:

	Tests	*Won*	*Lost*	*Drawn*
A. J. Strauss	**18**	**9**	**2**	**7**
F. S. Trueman	12	8	2	2
J. M. Anderson	**12**	**7**	**2**	**3**
T. G. Evans	13	7	3	3
A. J. Stewart	20	7	8	5

- Marlon Samuels and Andrew Strauss top-scored in both innings of the Trent Bridge Test. The only previous pair of batsmen to achieve that in an England v West Indies Test was Phil Sharpe and Conrad Hunte, at The Oval in 1963.

- Tino Best's innings of 95 at Edgbaston was the highest in first-class cricket by any No. 11 in England since Graham Stevenson scored 115 not out for Yorkshire against Warwickshire, also at Edgbaston, in 1982.

If Gabriel had not broken down, however, the series would have been deprived of one of its most memorable passages of play. At Edgbaston, a match in which England rested James Anderson and Stuart Broad – to their evident chagrin – and brought in Steven Finn and Graham Onions, Gabriel's own replacement, Tino Best, battered his way to 95, the highest score by a No. 11 in Test history. He and the wicketkeeper, Denesh Ramdin, added 143 for the last wicket, just eight shy of the Test record, with Ramdin celebrating his second Test century in controversial fashion by holding up a sheet of paper on which he had written a colloquial retort to perceived criticism from Viv Richards both before and during the series. This show of impertinence –

bordering on lese-majesty, given Richards's status in the Caribbean – would cost him 20% of his match fee. But at least it showed he cared.

The Third Test also saw the first appearance of Sunil Narine, supposedly a mystery spinner, who had been bamboozling batsmen in the IPL, but singularly failed to make any impact here: across the three formats, he managed one wicket for 199.

The surprise success was Marlon Samuels, whose Test career stretched back to December 2000 and included a two-year ban for alleged misdemeanours in connection with subcontinental bookmakers – charges he denied. What was certain was that this maverick batsman had always fallen short of the level his talent demanded. Now, that changed. At Lord's he made 31 and 86. Then, at Trent Bridge, he scored 117 – his third Test hundred and first for four years, adding 204 for the seventh wicket with Sammy – and an unbeaten 76 out of 165 all out. He batted nearly ten hours in the match, allying the sort of attention span that had previously eluded him with all his customary style. Finally, at rain-sodden Edgbaston, he made another 76. With 386 runs from five innings at an average of 96, there was no question about West Indies' Man of the Series.

Despite losing the Tests 2–0, they could draw considerable encouragement which they were able to carry over into a home series against New Zealand. But their performance in the one-day games was dismal: the two matches that survived the weather were lost by 114 runs and eight wickets. Gayle's differences with the WICB had by then been settled, so he joined the squad, only to miss the first match, at the Rose Bowl, through injury. And of the others returning from their IPL commitments, only Dwayne Bravo had any positive impact on a team that now appeared less close-knit than before.

In the face of this, Sammy – who expected and deserved better – shrank back. There appeared, from the periphery, to be a them-and-us situation. Only in the Twenty20 international, at Trent Bridge, did the West Indians compete, and even then they were undone by an extraordinary batting display from the young Nottinghamshire opener Alex Hales, whose 99 was the highest by an England batsman in the format. That innings alone may have been symptomatic of the difference between the sides: somehow, England always found a way. For all their progress, West Indies were evidently still finding theirs.

WEST INDIAN TOURING PARTY

*D. J. G. Sammy, A. B. Barath, D. M. Bravo, S. Chanderpaul, N. Deonarine, F. H. Edwards, K. A. Edwards, A. B. Fudadin, S. T. Gabriel, K. O. A. Powell, D. Ramdin, R. Rampaul, K. A. J. Roach, M. N. Samuels, S. Shillingford.

Coach: O. D. Gibson. *Team manager:* R. B. Richardson. *Assistant coach:* T. A. Radford. *Selector-on-tour:* R. C. Haynes. *Physiotherapist:* C. J. Clark. *Strength and conditioning co-ordinator:* H. Martinez-Charles. *Massage therapist:* V. A. Browne. *Video and statistical analyst:* R. Berridge. *Security officer:* P. Slowe. *Media manager:* A. J. H. Richard.

Deonarine, Fudadin and Samuels arrived late because of visa problems. Gabriel left after the First Test with a back injury and was replaced by T. L. Best; Roach left after the Second Test with a shin injury and was replaced by S. P. Narine. For the limited-overs games which followed the Tests, D. J. Bravo, J. Charles, C. H. Gayle, K. A. Pollard, A. D. Russell, L. M. P. Simmons and D. R. Smith replaced Barath, Chanderpaul, Deonarine, K. A. Edwards, Fudadin, Powell and Shillingford. D. M. Bravo left after the first one-day international with a groin injury.

TEST MATCH AVERAGES

ENGLAND – BATTING AND FIELDING

	T	I	NO	R	HS	100	50	Avge	Ct
I. R. Bell	3	4	2	222	76*	0	3	111.00	3
†A. J. Strauss	3	5	0	326	141	2	0	65.20	5
K. P. Pietersen	3	4	0	203	80	0	2	50.75	1
†A. N. Cook	3	5	1	176	79	0	1	44.00	0
I. J. L. Trott	3	5	1	140	58	0	1	35.00	1
J. M. Bairstow	3	4	1	38	18	0	0	12.66	1
†J. M. Anderson	2	3	1	6	6	0	0	3.00	5

Played in three Tests: T. T. Bresnan 0, 39* (2 ct); M. J. Prior 19, 16 (4 ct, 1 st); G. P. Swann 30, 1 (4 ct). Played in two Tests: †S. C. J. Broad 10, 25 (1 ct). Played in one Test: S. T. Finn 0* (1 ct); G. Onions did not bat.

BOWLING

	Style	O	M	R	W	BB	5I	Avge
S. C. J. Broad	RFM	102.5	21	304	14	7-72	1	21.71
G. Onions	RFM	29.3	7	88	4	4-88	0	22.00
J. M. Anderson	RFM	111.1	37	242	9	4-43	0	26.88
T. T. Bresnan	RFM	134	36	396	12	4-37	0	33.00
S. T. Finn	RF	32	6	109	3	3-109	0	36.33
G. P. Swann	OB	89.1	20	282	6	3-59	0	47.00

Also bowled: I. J. L. Trott (RM) 21–1–66–0.

WEST INDIES – BATTING AND FIELDING

	T	I	NO	R	HS	100	50	Avge	Ct
M. N. Samuels	3	5	1	386	117	1	3	96.50	0
†S. Chanderpaul	2	4	1	235	91	0	2	78.33	1
D. Ramdin	3	5	1	163	107*	1	0	40.75	8
D. J. G. Sammy	3	5	0	201	106	1	0	40.20	4
A. B. Barath	3	5	0	114	42	0	0	22.80	0
†D. M. Bravo	3	5	0	81	29	0	0	16.20	2
†K. O. A. Powell	3	5	0	71	33	0	0	14.20	2
K. A. J. Roach	2	4	0	31	14	0	0	7.75	0
†R. Rampaul	2	3	1	8	6*	0	0	4.00	0
K. A. Edwards	2	4	0	8	7	0	0	2.00	1

Played in one Test: T. L. Best 95; †N. Deonarine 7; F. H. Edwards 2, 10*; †A. B. Fudadin 28; S. T. Gabriel 0, 13; †S. P. Narine 11; S. Shillingford 16, 0.

BOWLING

	Style	O	M	R	W	BB	5I	Avge
S. T. Gabriel	RFM	26.3	3	86	4	3-60	0	21.50
M. N. Samuels	OB	45.3	5	150	5	2-14	0	30.00
K. A. J. Roach	RF	68	8	274	8	3-60	0	34.25
R. Rampaul	RFM	52	11	142	4	3-75	0	35.50
D. J. G. Sammy	RM	86	6	291	6	2-92	0	48.50

Also bowled: T. L. Best (RF) 12–2–37–2; F. H. Edwards (RF) 33–1–112–1; S. P. Narine (OB) 15–1–70–0; S. Shillingford (OB) 34–5–138–1.

SUSSEX v WEST INDIANS

At Hove, May 5–7. Drawn. Toss: Sussex.

Just 34 overs were possible because of rain and bad light, with no play on the first day when it was colder than the previous Christmas, though more than 2,000 turned up on the second; a beer festival offered a diversion when there was no cricket. The tourists had only 11 players available: Deonarine, Fudadin and Samuels (who had left the IPL early) were held up by visa issues, while Fidel Edwards was sidelined with back spasms. At least their top order got a brief taste of English conditions as the ball nipped around in the two sessions of just over an hour that were possible; Powell played some eye-catching off-side shots – and was attacked by a seagull.

Close of play: first day, no play; second day, West Indians 46-2 (Powell 19, Bravo 1).

West Indians

A. B. Barath b Wernars	16
K. O. A. Powell c Prior b Naved Arif	35
K. A. Edwards c Nash b Liddle	8
D. M. Bravo not out	19
S. Chanderpaul not out	9
N-b 3	3
1/24 (1) 2/45 (3) 3/67 (2) (3 wkts, 34 overs)	90

†D. Ramdin, *D. J. G. Sammy, S. Shillingford, K. A. J. Roach, R. Rampaul and S. T. Gabriel did not bat.

Naved Arif 9–3–17–1; Khan 11–0–42–0; Liddle 6–2–10–1; Wernars 8–3–21–1.

Sussex

*C. D. Nash, L. W. P. Wells, M. W. Machan, †M. J. Prior, J. S. Gatting, B. C. Brown, K. O. Wernars, Naved Arif, A. Khan, M. S. Panesar and C. J. Liddle.

Umpires: P. R. Pollard and G. Sharp.

ENGLAND LIONS v WEST INDIANS

At Northampton, May 10–13. England Lions won by ten wickets. Toss: England Lions.

Not for the last time, one good day could not avert a heavy West Indian defeat. They started the third morning 166 behind, with seven wickets left, before Powell guided them into the lead, sharing century partnerships with Bravo and Chanderpaul. Samuels, newly arrived from India, and Ramdin helped ensure a target of almost 200. But the Lions openers, Root and Carberry, galloped home in 48.5 overs. That was exactly how long the tourists' struggle against the moving ball had lasted on the opening day. Brooks, at his county ground, and Dernbach reduced them to 16 for three, and only Bravo and Samuels averted catastrophe before Meaker struck three times in 14 balls. Next day the Lions limped to 98 for five, with Bell making little of the match practice he had requested. Then Taylor took charge, adding 107 with Bairstow – promoted to the Test squad two days later. Taylor was 86 when the ninth wicket fell, but Dernbach got him past three figures, in a stand of 64 in ten overs. The West Indians lost three men cheaply that evening, and their strong performance on the third day could not make up the lost ground.

Close of play: first day, England Lions 40-1 (Carberry 15, Compton 18); second day, West Indians 28-3 (Powell 8, Bravo 0); third day, West Indians 377-8 (Ramdin 31, Roach 0).

West Indians

	First innings		Second innings	
A. B. Barath c Compton b Brooks	8	–	lbw b Brooks	14
K. O. A. Powell c Bairstow b Dernbach	2	–	b Patel	108
*K. A. Edwards c Bell b Brooks	0	–	lbw b Brooks	4
D. M. Bravo c Brooks b Meaker	51	–	(5) b Brooks	57
S. Chanderpaul c Brooks b Coles	6	–	(6) lbw b Meaker	77
M. N. Samuels c Bairstow b Meaker	32	–	(7) c Brooks b Coles	44
†D. Ramdin c Root b Coles	17	–	(8) c Patel b Coles	33
S. Shillingford b Meaker	2	–	(9) c Bairstow b Meaker	10
K. A. J. Roach lbw b Brooks	13	–	(10) not out	9
R. Rampaul c Bairstow b Dernbach	5	–	(11) c Bairstow b Coles	1
F. H. Edwards not out	0	–	(4) b Coles	0
B 1, l-b 8, w 2	11		B 3, l-b 24, w 6	33
1/12 (1) 2/16 (2) 3/16 (3) 4/29 (5) 5/104 (4) 6/117 (6) 7/123 (8) 8/131 (7) 9/147 (9) 10/147 (10) (48.5 overs)	147		1/21 (1) 2/25 (3) 3/26 (4) 4/134 (5) 5/256 (2) 6/289 (6) 7/354 (7) 8/374 (9) 9/384 (8) 10/390 (11) (120.3 overs)	390

Dernbach 12.5–4–31–2; Brooks 13–7–23–3; Meaker 12–2–42–3; Coles 11–0–42–2. *Second innings*—Meaker 24–5–73–2; Brooks 23–8–46–3; Coles 26.3–5–76–4; Dernbach 17–5–58–0; Patel 20–2–76–1; Root 10–2–34–0.

England Lions

	First innings		Second innings	
M. A. Carberry c Chanderpaul b Rampaul	32	–	not out	72
J. E. Root lbw b F. H. Edwards	3	–	not out	115
N. R. D. Compton b Roach	21			
I. R. Bell b Rampaul	29			
*J. W. A. Taylor c Ramdin b F. H. Edwards	118			
S. R. Patel c and b Shillingford	4			
†J. M. Bairstow c Rampaul b Shillingford	50			
M. T. Coles b Roach	0			
S. C. Meaker b Rampaul	12			
J. A. Brooks c Ramdin b Roach	18			
J. W. Dernbach not out	28			
B 4, l-b 3, w 2, n-b 17	26		B 4, l-b 3, n-b 3	10
1/6 (2) 2/55 (3) 3/92 (1) 4/93 (4) 5/98 (6) 6/205 (7) 7/211 (8) 8/244 (9) 9/277 (10) 10/341 (5) (90 overs)	341		(no wkt, 48.5 overs)	197

F. H. Edwards 21–5–79–2; Rampaul 24–5–79–3; Roach 21–2–90–3; Shillingford 23–5–75–2; Samuels 1–0–11–0. *Second innings*—F. H. Edwards 6–2–21–0; Rampaul 4–1–12–0; Bravo 5–0–19–0; Shillingford 18.5–3–86–0; Samuels 15–1–52–0.

Umpires: N. L. Bainton and S. A. Garratt.

> "Shane Watson combines dominance and vulnerability in equal measure. At least Achilles only had to worry about his heel. Watson is a collection of opposites: tough yet soft, untouchable yet fragile, egotistical yet rueful. Any moment he might bully a ball out of the ground, demolish the stumps – or crumple into a heap."
>
> ICC World Twenty20, 2012-13, page 844

ENGLAND v WEST INDIES

First Investec Test

ANDREW MILLER

At Lord's, May 17–21. England won by five wickets. Toss: England. Test debuts: J. M. Bairstow; S. T. Gabriel.

Lord's is not a happy hunting ground for visiting teams in May. This was the 12th such Test it had hosted since the extension of the international season in 2000, and England had now won eight of them, to go with four draws – plus a sense of ownership that previous generations had been unable to cultivate at their most regular haunt. As with the 1980s West Indians at Bridgetown, or Australia at the Gabba in the 2000s, bearding England in their lair in early-season conditions was becoming one of the toughest challenges in the sport, not least because the opposition tend to be the weaker of the summer's Test visitors. Thanks to Strauss, who produced a timely return to form with his 20th Test century – and his fifth at Lord's – West Indies were never quite close enough to parity to threaten an upset. Nevertheless, with Chanderpaul confirming his world No. 1 ranking by scoring 178 runs for once out, they made England sweat.

Despite the margin, the game was as close as any team has come to challenging them at Lord's, at any stage of the season, since Australia's victory in 2005. Had a pumped-up Roach been able to bowl more than two fearsome overs in the fourth-evening gloom – when he bounced out Strauss for one, had nightwatchman Anderson caught behind down the leg side, and came within an inch or two of trapping Trott leg-before first ball – the result might have been different. At ten for two overnight chasing 191, then at 57 for four the following morning, England were vulnerable. But Cook closed down the crisis with a sheet-anchor 79, and was perfectly complemented by Bell's free-wheeling 63 in a match-clinching stand of 132.

In some ways, it had been a curious contest. England's dominance was at times laughably absolute, not least while Anderson was mocking the West Indian top order with his peerless command of lateral movement. But it was Broad, the less impressive of the two new-ball bowlers, who cashed in on their obvious frailties with a career-best 11 for 165. He joined Gubby Allen, Keith Miller and Ian Botham as the only men to etch their names on to three separate Lord's honours boards: five wickets in an innings, ten in a match and, thanks to his 169 against Pakistan in 2010, a century.

The public perception of the Test was undoubtedly tainted by the absentees in the West Indian ranks, most notably Chris Gayle, who – despite being more than 4,000 miles from St John's Wood – snaffled the limelight on the first evening with an incredible 128 not out from 62 balls in the IPL in Delhi. Yet Gayle's presence hadn't exactly been conducive to team excellence in the same fixture three years earlier, when he arrived in the country 52 hours before leading West Indies to a three-day defeat. This time, under the dedicated leadership of Sammy, they set out to be greater than the sum of their parts. By and large, they succeeded.

There was a stoicism to West Indies' performance that could only really be appreciated in hindsight. Perhaps that says more about Chanderpaul's peculiarly joyless approach to Test batting than anything else but, having spent more than 24 hours at the crease during the 2007 tour, he now loitered for a further ten hours and 25 minutes across 425 balls. With a little more urgency, he could well have become the first visiting batsman since George Headley in 1939 to leave Lord's with a century in both innings. Instead, he ran out of first-innings partners on 87, and was extracted on the sweep for 91 in the second.

Aesthetics never came into the equation but, on the fourth morning, while he and the rehabilitated Samuels were adding 157 for the fifth wicket to turn an apparently routine

Take five: Stuart Broad catches Kemar Roach off his own bowling to secure a first-innings five-for.

defeat into a bid for the spoils, Chanderpaul's effectiveness was self-evident. Unfortunately, too many of West Indies' other moments of resistance were undermined by their own failings – most notably a pair of top-order run-outs, one in each innings, and the brace of loose strokes that ended two promising performances from Barath, the young opener from Trinidad.

The most significant innings of the match, and indeed of the series, came from Strauss, who admitted to having removed a "monkey from my back" in recording his first Test hundred since the start of the 2010-11 Ashes, 18 months and 26 innings earlier. After leading his side to four Test defeats out of five in the winter, and turning 35 in March, he recognised the need to silence those who doubted his continued stomach for the role, even if he was still some way from any votes of no-confidence within his team.

Strauss's home ground – the venue of his century on debut against New Zealand in 2004, and of his most recent hundred on home soil, against Australia in 2009 – was the perfect place to staunch such anxieties. Run-scoring was rarely straightforward against an attack featuring not only Roach but the powerful Shannon Gabriel, who picked up four wickets on debut (followed by a back injury). On 95, Strauss was dropped at slip off a no-ball from Fidel Edwards. But a cathartic cut through backward point off Sammy settled the issue.

From 259 for three overnight, England fell away slightly on the third day as West Indies settled into a disciplined off-stump line – although Bairstow's working-over on Test debut by Roach was immediately noted by video analysts everywhere. But an unruffled 61 from Bell, and Swann's carefree 30 in 25 balls, massaged the lead past 150, and the loss of three West Indian wickets for no runs in nine deliveries immediately before tea reasserted the imbalance.

Strauss was eventually pipped to the match award by Broad, whose haul was the best by any bowler at Lord's since Botham claimed 11 for 140 against New Zealand in 1978. It was, by his admission, a less-than-perfect performance: he was guilty of over-pitching in his early overs, before hauling his length back to cramp West Indies on the drive. But by the end of the first innings he was back in his element, scalping six wickets in his last 50 balls – he claimed the sixth with the first delivery of the second morning – for a Test-best seven for 72.

Despite chasing the game throughout, West Indies found the will to dig in after learning that no tickets had been printed for the fifth day of the match; no one had told them this was standard marketing policy. Trott fell early to Roach on the final morning and, when Pietersen bottom-edged a pull off Gabriel, West Indies were briefly dreaming. Cook's resolve and Bell's elegance soon woke them up.

Man of the Match: S. C. J. Broad. *Attendance:* 108,842.

Close of play: first day, West Indies 243-9 (Chanderpaul 87); second day, England 259-3 (Strauss 121, Bell 5); third day, West Indies 120-4 (Chanderpaul 34, Samuels 26); fourth day, England 10-2 (Cook 0, Trott 0).

West Indies

A. B. Barath c Anderson b Broad	42	– c Prior b Bresnan	24
K. O. A. Powell b Anderson	5	– c Bell b Broad	8
K. A. Edwards lbw b Anderson	1	– run out	0
D. M. Bravo run out	29	b Swann	21
S. Chanderpaul not out	87	– lbw b Swann	91
M. N. Samuels c Bairstow b Broad	31	– c Swann b Broad	86
†D. Ramdin c Strauss b Broad	6	– b Anderson	43
*D. J. G. Sammy c Bresnan b Broad	17	– c Prior b Broad	37
K. A. J. Roach c and b Broad	6	– c Bell b Broad	4
F. H. Edwards c Prior b Broad	2	– not out	10
S. T. Gabriel c Swann b Broad	0	– b Swann	13
B 6, l-b 8, n-b 3	17	L-b 7, n-b 1	8
1/13 (2) 2/32 (3) 3/86 (1) 4/100 (4) 5/181 (6) 6/187 (7) 7/219 (8) 8/231 (9) 9/243 (10) 10/243 (11) (89.5 overs)	243	1/36 (1) 2/36 (2) 3/36 (3) 4/65 (4) 5/222 (6) 6/261 (5) 7/307 (8) 8/313 (9) 9/325 (7) 10/345 (11) (130.5 overs)	345

Anderson 25–8–59–2; Broad 24.5–6–72–7; Bresnan 20–7–39–0; Swann 18–6–52–0; Trott 2–0–7–0. *Second innings*—Anderson 36–11–67–1; Broad 34–6–93–4; Bresnan 36–11–105–1; Swann 18.5–4–59–3; Trott 6–0–14–0.

England

*A. J. Strauss c Ramdin b Roach	122	– c Powell b Roach	1
A. N. Cook b Roach	26	– c K. A. Edwards b Sammy	79
I. J. L. Trott c Ramdin b Sammy	58	– (4) c Sammy b Roach	13
K. P. Pietersen c Ramdin b Samuels	32	– (5) c Ramdin b Gabriel	13
I. R. Bell c Powell b Gabriel	61	– (6) not out	63
J. M. Bairstow lbw b Roach	16	– (7) not out	0
†M. J. Prior b Gabriel	19		
T. T. Bresnan c Ramdin b Sammy	0		
S. C. J. Broad b F. H. Edwards	10		
G. P. Swann b Gabriel	30		
J. M. Anderson not out	0	– (3) c Ramdin b Roach	6
B 9, l-b 3, n-b 12	24	B 4, l-b 3, n-b 11	18
1/47 (2) 2/194 (3) 3/244 (4) 4/266 (1) 5/292 (6) 6/320 (7) 7/323 (8) 8/342 (9) 9/397 (10) 10/398 (5) (113.3 overs)	398	1/1 (1) 2/10 (3) 3/29 (4) 4/57 (5) 5/189 (2) (5 wkts, 46.1 overs)	193

F. H. Edwards 25–1–88–1; Roach 25–3–108–3; Gabriel 21.3–2–60–3; Sammy 28–1–92–2; Samuels 14–3–38–1. *Second innings*—F. H. Edwards 8–0–24–0; Roach 13–2–60–3; Gabriel 5–1–26–1; Sammy 10–1–25–1; Samuels 10.1–0–51–0.

Umpires: Aleem Dar and M. Erasmus. Third umpire: Asad Rauf.

ENGLAND v WEST INDIES

Second Investec Test

JAMES COYNE

At Nottingham, May 25–28. England won by nine wickets. Toss: West Indies.

West Indies came to Nottingham, where they had never lost any of their 22 first-class games – and suffered a few more stinging blows to their regeneration project. The headless rabble that emerged from Caribbean cricket's crumbling empire had at last been succeeded by a united, workaday team fighting for the badge. Unfortunately, they were also fighting against their own limitations: you don't win too many Test matches from positions of 63 for four in the first innings, or 61 for six in the second. The contest between England's four leading bowlers and West Indies' top four batsmen looked like one of the most uneven in Test history.

Following his tenth defeat in 21 Tests as West Indies coach, Ottis Gibson said he had noticed as many mental as technical flaws in his top order. The task of facing Anderson, Broad and Bresnan with their juices flowing would have been taxing for batsmen of experience; for the tourists' callow line-up, it was thoroughly disorientating. There was, of course, no guarantee that Chris Gayle's approach would have served West Indies better. But onlookers could not help wondering what he might have done on the first morning, when they batted in the most amicable conditions imaginable, or on the third evening, when a few crisp blows might have sped them past their first-innings deficit. Instead, a crude collection of swipes and prods left England with only 108 to chase for their record seventh consecutive Test series victory at home.

SEVEN UP – ENGLAND'S INVINCIBLE HOME RUN

2009	2–0 (2) v West Indies.	(*Wisden 2010*, page 463)
	2–1 (5) v Australia	(*Wisden 2010*, page 479)
2010	2–0 (2) v Bangladesh	(*Wisden 2011*, page 283)
	3–1 (4) v Pakistan.	(*Wisden 2011*, page 322)
2011	1–0 (3) v Sri Lanka	(*Wisden 2012*, page 267)
	4–0 (4) v India	(*Wisden 2012*, page 298)
2012	2–0 (3) v West Indies.	

The sequence was topped and tailed by series defeats by South Africa in 2008 and 2012.

Trent Bridge was a blissful sight, filled for the first two days by a near-capacity crowd enticed by glorious sunshine and tickets £10 cheaper than the previous year's Test against India. This beautiful ground will never be the same again: over the 2012-13 winter, the old scoreboard (the first in England to display precise bowling figures upon its completion in 1974) was knocked down to accommodate a second permanent electronic screen, in line with ICC recommendations.

Anderson had a hand in all four early wickets, just one hand in the case of Barath, whose flashing edge lodged in his outstretched left palm at third slip. Even as West Indies were being dismantled, it was clear what a good toss this should have been to win: the ball was doing so little for Anderson that he simply abandoned the outswinger and became a seam bowler for the day.

Bravo drove at Anderson's first ball from round the wicket, to his cost; Chanderpaul was more fortunate when the next, a well-aimed bouncer, brushed his armguard and whirled safely over the cordon. Four decisions made by Asad Rauf in this match were overturned by technology. The second could easily have killed the contest: Chanderpaul

Philip Brown

Stuck in a rut: Kirk Edwards is bowled by James Anderson for seven, his highest Test score in a disastrous tour.

had scuttled to within four of a third successive fifty when he propped forward to Swann and was clipped on the back pad. England's review showed the ball crashing into off stump, and Swann's first Test wicket on his county ground, after 24.2 fruitless overs in three matches, was the world's No. 1 batsman.

At 136 for six, Gibson's critics were sharpening their cleavers. They reckoned without Samuels, now a 31-year-old father of two – and on the brink of fulfilment. His habit of shuffling across his stumps encouraged England to bowl straight, but he played the ball late with a feather's touch, unlike the youngsters before him. He shared some delicious verbal jousting with Anderson, who grew frustrated with both batsman and pitch for yielding nothing. "I haven't found too many bowlers who can bowl and talk," said Samuels later. "I can bat and talk all day." But the fact that it had taken this talent nearly 12 years and 70 innings to achieve three Test hundreds did not reflect well upon him or West Indies cricket.

Sammy diced his way to a century, only his second at first-class level, without quashing the suspicion that he was a one-day cricketer in charge of a Test side; one heave across the line against Trott would have shamed Welbeck Colliery's No. 8. But with a keen eye and strapping forearms, he sent length balls thudding into the boundary boards and kept his team in the match. When Sammy eventually fell to the leg-side trap on the second morning, he and Samuels had put on 204, a seventh-wicket record in Tests on this ground, and for West Indies against England anywhere.

Many blithely assumed that, if West Indies could score 370, England might make 730. It was not that simple. Twice in Roach's opening spell, Cook nicked deliveries slanted across him, only to be saved by no-balls. His continuing uncertainty outside off stump soon drew him to edge Rampaul, who was conjuring more conventional swing than anyone after missing out at Lord's with a stiff neck. But Shillingford, added to the side to bowl long, tidy spells of off-spin, was thwarted by batsmen eager to sweep away nasty memories of Saeed Ajmal in the desert, and started pushing the ball through too quickly.

Strauss had cast off his burden with a drought-breaking 122 at Lord's, and was now climbing into cover-drives as in the glory years. He had passed three figures by the close, only the second instance of opposing Test captains reaching centuries on the same day, after Jackie McGlew, of South Africa, and Peter May at Old Trafford in 1955. It was Strauss's sixth against West Indies and 21st overall, yet he still had an unwanted reputation to shift: morning-after syndrome. Six times Strauss had slept on a hundred, and never added more than six runs the next day. This time he managed another 39, but it took him nearly three hours, with two sweepers posted on the off side to shackle him. It didn't help that he had lost Trott, the rampaging Pietersen and Bell – all when set, all lbw playing across their front pad.

Reinvigorated by the second new ball, Roach unleashed an exhilarating barrage at Bairstow, clearly exposing a weakness against fast, short-pitched bowling of which he had seen little in county cricket. West Indies looked more focused in the field than for many a tour to England, and scooped up the last eight wickets for 161.

But honest professionalism and smart bowling plans could not alter the cold reality: to beat good sides you must win the big sessions. West Indies' recent second-innings performances did not inspire confidence and, when the damage came on the third evening, it felt irreparable – even with Samuels in such sumptuous form. As Kirk Edwards was back at the hotel with flu, Chanderpaul was forced up to No. 4 and out of his comfort zone. He should have known better than to hook Broad's lifter; had the ball been ten overs softer, though, his top edge would probably have landed tamely in no-man's land rather than down fine leg's throat.

At Lord's, Bresnan's inclusion had caused some debate. That looked bewildering now. It was he who had stretched out England's lead and, when it mattered most, he was their canniest bowler, hiding the seam from view and finding reverse swing, apparently from nowhere. Edwards, a quick mover neither to or at the crease, was obliged to trudge out to face Bresnan at 61 for five with eight balls of the third day to see out. No one, least of all Edwards himself, thought he would get that far; two excruciating writhes later, he was crawling back to his bed, poorly, crestfallen and with a first-class tour average of 2.85. For West Indies, so long the sick man of world cricket, the path to full recovery looked steep.

Man of the Match: T. T. Bresnan. *Attendance:* 51,921.

Close of play: first day, West Indies 304-6 (Samuels 107, Sammy 88); second day, England 259-2 (Strauss 102, Pietersen 72); third day, West Indies 61-6 (Samuels 13, Sammy 0).

West Indies

First innings		Second innings	
A. B. Barath c Anderson b Broad	0	lbw b Anderson	7
K. O. A. Powell c Anderson b Broad	33	b Anderson	1
K. A. Edwards b Anderson	7	(7) lbw b Bresnan	0
D. M. Bravo c Swann b Anderson	3	(3) lbw b Bresnan	22
S. Chanderpaul lbw b Swann	46	(4) c Trott b Broad	11
M. N. Samuels c Anderson b Bresnan	117	(5) not out	76
†D. Ramdin b Bresnan	1	(6) lbw b Bresnan	6
*D. J. G. Sammy c Pietersen b Bresnan	106	lbw b Bresnan	25
K. A. J. Roach c Strauss b Bresnan	7	lbw b Anderson	14
S. Shillingford st Prior b Swann	16	c Anderson b Swann	0
R. Rampaul not out	6	c Bresnan b Anderson	0
B 8, l-b 18, w 1, n-b 1	28	B 1, l-b 2	3
1/9 (1) 2/26 (3) 3/42 (4) 4/63 (2) 5/125 (5) 6/136 (7) 7/340 (8) 8/341 (6) 9/360 (9) 10/370 (10) (109.2 overs)	370	1/5 (2) 2/14 (1) 3/31 (4) 4/45 (3) 5/61 (6) 6/61 (7) 7/110 (8) 8/139 (9) 9/148 (10) 10/165 (11) (60.1 overs)	165

Anderson 30–12–73–2; Broad 27–4–81–2; Bresnan 27–4–104–4; Swann 20.2–4–62–2; Trott 5–0–24–0. *Second innings*—Anderson 20.1–6–43–4; Broad 17–5–58–1; Swann 6–1–24–1; Bresnan 17–5–37–4.

England

*A. J. Strauss c Ramdin b Sammy	141	– c Bravo b Samuels	45
A. N. Cook c Ramdin b Rampaul	24	– not out	43
I. J. L. Trott lbw b Rampaul	35	– not out	17
K. P. Pietersen lbw b Rampaul	80		
I. R. Bell lbw b Roach	22		
J. M. Bairstow c Chanderpaul b Roach	4		
†M. J. Prior b Sammy	16		
T. T. Bresnan not out	39		
S. C. J. Broad c Sammy b Shillingford	25		
G. P. Swann c Sammy b Samuels	1		
J. M. Anderson lbw b Samuels	0		
B 9, l-b 10, w 4, n-b 18	41	B 5, n-b 1	6
1/43 (2) 2/123 (3) 3/267 (4) 4/300 (5) 5/308 (6) 6/336 (7) 7/363 (1) 8/416 (9) 9/426 (10) 10/428 (11) (123.4 overs)	428	1/89 (1) (1 wkt, 30.4 overs)	111

Roach 25–1–90–2; Rampaul 32–8–75–3; Sammy 34–3–120–2; Shillingford 26–4–110–1; Samuels 6.4–2–14–2. *Second innings*—Roach 5–2–16–0; Rampaul 6–2–12–0; Sammy 6–0–32–0; Samuels 5.4–0–18–1; Shillingford 8–1–28–0.

Umpires: Aleem Dar and Asad Rauf. Third umpire: M. Erasmus.

At Leicester, June 2–3 (not first-class). **Drawn.** **‡West Indians 150-3** (A. B. Barath 53*, D. M. Bravo 66) **v Leicestershire.** *Rain allowed only 50 overs on the first day, and the second was abandoned before the start. Adrian Barath and Darren Bravo had time to construct a stand of 111 after a spot of bother at 25-2; acting-captain Kirk Edwards was trapped lbw by a full-length delivery from Nadeem Malik without adding to the meagre 20 runs he had managed in his seven first-class innings on tour. Bravo was eventually bowled by left-arm seamer Rob Taylor after hitting ten fours and a six; Barath struck only four fours as he chiselled 53 from 151 deliveries.*

ENGLAND v WEST INDIES

Third Investec Test

JULIAN GUYER

At Birmingham, June 7–11. Drawn. Toss: England. Test debuts: A. B. Fudadin, S. P. Narine.

For a while it seemed the only history this match would make was of the meteorological variety: not since 1964, and Australia's visit to Lord's, had the first two days of a Test in England been washed out. But on the fourth morning, with the game going nowhere, came an unexpected Sunday best – or rather Tino Best, who rescued the match from watery obscurity with an astounding innings of 95, the highest by a Test No. 11.

All series, the talk had been of West Indies missing some illustrious names. Now, they shuffled their existing pack: Sunil Narine – finally part of the tour after helping Kolkata Knight Riders win the IPL – and Assad Fudadin were handed Test debuts, and Deonarine and Best drafted in; Kirk Edwards and Shillingford were dropped, while Roach had been ruled out of the rest of the tour with a shin injury, and Chanderpaul was said to have suffered a side strain. But none performed half as entertainingly as Best. His innings – part of a West Indies record last-wicket stand of 143 with Ramdin – was also used as evidence that England had erred in resting both Anderson, left out of the squad entirely, and Broad, omitted shortly before play eventually started on the third day.

Neither was thrilled by the decision, though it had been defended with some passion by team director Andy Flower, and created room for the recall of Finn and Onions, playing his first Test since January 2010 after recovering from a career-threatening back injury.

THE HIGHEST TEST SCORE BY A No. 11

Oh yeah, Tino!

ALAN TYERS

Tino Best fixes me with an intense, earnest look. "I went out there, and I told myself I'm going to play for Denesh Ramdin to get his century," he says. "I'm going to play sensibly."

We glance over at the hotel-room TV, which is playing a DVD of his 95 in the Third Test. Best is aiming an enormous slog at his third ball, and missing. "Well, it was a beautiful miss," he says. "I think I followed through very well on the shot. Very entertaining for the crowd."

Best laughs heartily. He laughs and smiles a lot, an animated, straightforward face atop a physique of broad-shouldered, gym-dedicated power. "After I got going, Ramdin told me to express myself. I told him if it's close enough to me I'm going to lick it." He chuckles with satisfaction on reviewing a joyous drive on the up through mid-off, complete with a showboating, hold-the-pose flourish for the benefit of the photographers – and the affronted bowler, Steven Finn. His company is as infectious, and as guileless, as his batting.

If part of sport's delight is watching athletically gifted people do incredible things we could never ourselves achieve in a million years, perhaps the most satisfying cricket fantasies have at least a tiny element of plausibility. OK, you definitely wouldn't be able to bowl like Tino Best in a Test but, given a bit of luck, you might have a chance of batting like him. For two hours and 18 minutes at Edgbaston, Best was living the dream of every club slogger and village hopeful: he was giving it some porridge in a Test match – and it was coming off.

"I give thanks and praise to God that I'm not lacking in confidence," he says. "I back myself to play my shots, and I like to look stylish doing it." It was a method both effective and entertaining on a frenetic Sunday morning, when boundaries – many genuine, some slashed – came as quickly as records. First, the highest score by a last man for West Indies against England, beating a mere 19; then a fifty, matching Wes Hall's record for any West Indian No. 11; then passing his own previous first-class high of 51. On 76, he became the highest-scoring No. 11 in Test history. Each was ticked off with a sense of theatre and freedom.

"I was thinking about my uncle Carlisle," says Best of the batsman who played eight Tests up to 1990. "He says to me: 'You're a Best, you're from the Caribbean. You grew up with the legends – show the flair, the determination they played with. This is in your blood.'"

Today's West Indian players have sometimes found the deeds and words of retired legends more of a burden than an inspiration. Indeed, in this innings Ramdin chose to mark his century by holding up a note answering back to Viv Richards.

"I had no idea he was going to do that," says Best. "It's each man to himself. Myself, I feel connected to the past of West Indian cricket. We as a people have come a long way and had a lot of struggles. For us, cricket was something to fight in. People might say I'm over the top, but this is me, a West Indian, playing my cricket the way I live my life."

As Best's score grew, so the good humour of England's bowlers disappeared. There was no mention of the "Mind the windows" incident (when, at Lord's in 2004, he was stumped after being goaded by Andrew Flintoff into trying to slog Ashley Giles into the Pavilion). For this, Best says, was "a much more serious situation".

Graham Morris

Best foot... forward? Tino Best's style was unorthodox – but effective.

With the temperature rising, his former county colleague Tim Bresnan was treated to some smears over midwicket and a straight six. "Bresnan said to me: 'We never saw you bat like that for Yorkshire.' I told him: 'Don't you worry about that – this is the big time now. This is the big stage.'"

As the innings blossomed and England wilted, when did he think a century was a possibility? "I was just playing my shots, trying to have a bit of chat, trying to annoy them," he says. "It wasn't until I was on 88, and Matt Prior said to me: 'I bet you can get there in two hits.' I said, 'All right, then,' and he laughed and said, 'You're something else, mate.'"

Only on 93, he says, did the magnitude of the situation hit him. Best had stoically resisted the temptations of Jonathan Trott's dobbers, and survived the short stuff from Finn. With lunch put back up to half an hour, Andrew Strauss had switched his attack again. "I thought, 'Oh heck, I'm 93 against England in a Test match.' I tried to hit Onions, and it landed short of Bairstow for two. I tried to get a quick single, but I hit it too hard." Ramdin rightly sent him back: it would have been a suicidal run. Nerves were jangling.

"As Onions came in, I said to myself: 'If he pitches this ball close to me, I'm going to lick him back over his head.' I saw him fidget with his hand as he bowled it. I felt my eyes light up! But of course it was the slower ball, and I was through the shot too quickly." He skied it, and was caught by Strauss, running back from slip.

"I can't watch it again," Best says. "It's too sad." But then came another loud laugh. "Still, 95 in a Test match, though! My goal now is to score a hundred. I showed I have the talent. I have been misunderstood but I have a talent and I have something to offer. When people think back to Tino Best, I want them to smile and laugh and say: 'Oh yeah, Tino!'"

Alan Tyers is the author of WG Grace Ate My Pedalo *and* CrickiLeaks – The Secret Ashes Diaries.

Philip Brown

All on a summer's day… the Edgbaston Test lost nine sessions to torrential rain.

But after Strauss won the toss, England were soon missing Anderson, if not necessarily for his bowling. Barath had made only four when he edged Onions to Bell at third slip, Anderson's regular haunt between overs: down went the chance. Then, in the second over after lunch, Bell dropped Barath, on 40, in the same position, this time off Finn.

Onions quickly took Bell out of the equation, trapping Barath leg-before in the next over. England's seamers – headed by Bresnan, soon to surrender his record of winning every Test he had played – belatedly located a better length and began to chip away at the batting. But as at Trent Bridge, Samuels responded well to the bowlers' chatter and completed an elegant fifty by striking Swann for six and four off successive balls, then pointed his bat at Onions in recognition of their ongoing joust. He eventually fell to Bresnan for 76, and the end of the innings appeared nigh when Rampaul was caught behind off the third ball next morning.

But Best promptly cracked Finn through mid-off for four, then held the pose, paving the way for an unreal session in which he drove England to distraction and the ball to the fence in equal measure. Relatively unnoticed at the other end was Ramdin, who had 63 when Best came in, was dropped on 69 by Pietersen in the gully off Finn, and completed a wicketkeeper's hundred, full of cuts and deflections. It was his second in Tests, both against England – and was immediately overshadowed when he produced a piece of paper from his pocket bearing the scrawl: "YEA VIV, TALK NAH".

That followed criticism from Viv Richards during the Second Test, when he had described Ramdin as looking "totally lost". Given that Richards still seemed in the physical shape of his playing days, Ramdin could hardly be said to have chosen a soft target. Unimpressed by his bravado, the ICC fined him 20% of his match fee.

Meanwhile, boundaries flowed from Best: Bresnan was upper-cut for four and driven for a six. England's hope was that, like the Australians here in 2005, the closer Best got to an improbable target, the more nervous he would become. So it proved: on 95, he slashed at a wide, slower ball from Onions, and Strauss ran back from the slips to hold on. The manner in which he threw the ball away told of Strauss's frustration, despite equalling the England record of 120 Test catches, shared by Colin Cowdrey and Ian Botham.

Best had faced only 112 balls, cruising past the highest score by a Test No. 11: Zaheer Khan's 75 for India against Bangladesh at Dhaka in December 2004. His partnership with Ramdin fell eight short of the tenth-wicket Test record of 151, held jointly by Richard Collinge and Brian Hastings, for New Zealand against Pakistan at Auckland in 1972-73, and Azhar Mahmood and Mushtaq Ahmed, for Pakistan against South Africa at Rawalpindi in 1997-98.

MOST VICTORIES AT THE START OF A TEST CAREER

15	A. C. Gilchrist (Australia)	1999-2000–2000-01
13	S. R. Clark (Australia)	2005-06–2007-08
13	**T. T. Bresnan (England)**	**2009–2012**
10*	E. A. E. Baptiste (West Indies)	1983-84–1989-90
10	B. Lee (Australia)	1999-2000–2001
10	T. T. Samaraweera (Sri Lanka)	2001–2002

* *Complete Test career.*

The canny Rampaul quickly removed Cook, before Trott and Strauss – superbly caught by Bravo at first slip off a joyous Best – followed cheaply. At 49 for three, England were in a spot of bother. But Pietersen, in his first innings since announcing his retirement from limited-overs internationals, and Bell batted sublimely, while the only mystery surrounding the Test debut of the feted off-spinner Narine appeared to be why he had failed to live up to the hype. Pietersen looked determined to bring him down to size before, equally unsurprisingly, falling to the less celebrated off-breaks of Samuels.

In the midst of their fluent stand of 137, the umpires twice took the players off for bad light, even though the floodlights were on. At Lord's, the match had carried on under artificial light when it had been far darker, but that was now forgotten. Umpire Tony Hill lamely justified the decision by saying spectators wouldn't wish to bat against Best in such conditions, and that his colleague, Kumar Dharmasena, was struggling to see the ball from square leg. On the final day, however, despite a downpour, the officials didn't call off play until well into the afternoon. To England the series, but to Best imperishable glory.

Man of the Match: T. L. Best. *Attendance:* 54,620.

Men of the Series: England – A. J. Strauss; West Indies – M. N. Samuels.

Close of play: first day, no play; second day, no play; third day, West Indies 280-8 (Ramdin 60, Rampaul 2); fourth day, England 221-5 (Bell 76, Finn 0).

West Indies

A. B. Barath lbw b Onions	41
K. O. A. Powell c Swann b Bresnan	24
A. B. Fudadin c Bell b Bresnan	28
D. M. Bravo c and b Finn	6
M. N. Samuels lbw b Bresnan	76
N. Deonarine c Strauss b Onions	7
†D. Ramdin not out	107
*D. J. G. Sammy c Strauss b Finn	16
S. P. Narine b Onions	11
R. Rampaul c Prior b Finn	2
T. L. Best c Strauss b Onions	95
B 4, l-b 8, w 1	13
1/49 (2) 2/90 (1) 3/99 (4) 4/128 (3) 5/152 (6) 6/208 (5) 7/241 (8) 8/267 (9) 9/283 (10) 10/426 (11) (129.3 overs)	426

Onions 29.3–7–88–4; Bresnan 34–9–111–3; Finn 32–6–109–3; Swann 26–5–85–0; Trott 8–1–21–0.

England

*A. J. Strauss c Bravo b Best	17
A. N. Cook lbw b Rampaul	4
I. J. L. Trott b Sammy	17
K. P. Pietersen c Sammy b Samuels	78
I. R. Bell not out	76
J. M. Bairstow b Best	18
S. T. Finn not out	0
B 1, l-b 7, n-b 3	11
1/13 (2) 2/40 (3) 3/49 (1) 4/186 (4) 5/215 (6) (5 wkts, 58 overs)	221

†M. J. Prior, T. T. Bresnan, G. P. Swann and G. Onions did not bat.

Best 12–2–37–2; Rampaul 14–1–55–1; Sammy 8–1–22–1; Narine 15–1–70–0; Samuels 9–0–29–1.

Umpires: H. D. P. K. Dharmasena and A. L. Hill. Third umpire: Aleem Dar.
Series referee: R. S. Mahanama.

At Lord's, June 13. **West Indians won by 228 runs.** West Indians 335-4 (50 overs) (D. M. Bravo 112*, D. R. Smith 96); ‡**Middlesex 107** (31 overs). *The West Indians massacred Middlesex in their only win of the tour. In his first game for the side since the 2011 World Cup, Gayle hit 34 in 30 balls, with a couple of sixes off Tim Murtagh. But the heart of the innings was a stand of 156 between Darren Bravo and Dwayne Smith, who struck one of his two sixes into the pavilion's top tier; Smith just missed his hundred, Bravo got there in the final over. By then he had been joined by his half-brother, Dwayne, whose 40 came in 21 balls; together they smashed 42 off the last two overs. Middlesex, one man short after Robbie Williams fractured his collarbone in the field, had no answer; no one passed 24, and Gayle ended the game with a double-wicket maiden.*

LIMITED-OVERS INTERNATIONAL REPORTS BY GIDEON BROOKS

ENGLAND v WEST INDIES

First One-Day International

At Southampton, June 16. England won by 114 runs (D/L). Toss: West Indies.

Bell found the shoes vacated by Pietersen at the top of the order a comfortable fit, inspiring England to their biggest win against West Indies. He had opened 27 times in his previous 108 one-day internationals, but this was a thoroughly convincing statement that he intended to make the spot his own – not least because he was batting with ten stitches in his chin after being hit in the nets the day before. Cook fell third ball, but Bell, on 23, brushed aside a plausible shout for caught behind by Rampaul, and finished with 126 from 117 deliveries, equalling his only other century at this level, also at Southampton, against India in 2007. Set a formidable 289, revised to 287 in 48 overs after a rain break, West Indies kept up with the rate, but lost wickets steadily. After Dwayne Smith – a late replacement for Chris Gayle, whose comeback was thwarted by a shin injury – had hurried them to 95 for one, they lost nine for 77 in 18 overs, with Bresnan the pick of the England attack.

Man of the Match: I. R. Bell. *Attendance:* 13,958.

England

Batsman	Runs
*A. N. Cook c Ramdin b Rampaul	0
I. R. Bell c Ramdin b D. J. Bravo	126
I. J. L. Trott c Ramdin b Narine	42
R. S. Bopara c Ramdin b Samuels	8
E. J. G. Morgan b Samuels	21
†C. Kieswetter not out	38
T. T. Bresnan run out	21
S. C. J. Broad not out	22
W 9, n-b 1	10
1/0 (1) 2/108 (3) 3/136 (4) 4/187 (5) 5/216 (2) 6/245 (7) — (6 wkts, 50 overs)	288

10 overs: 49-1

G. P. Swann, S. T. Finn and J. M. Anderson did not bat.

Rampaul 10–0–68–1; Russell 6–0–43–0; Narine 10–0–47–1; Sammy 6–0–32–0; D. J. Bravo 9–0–55–1; Samuels 9–0–43–2.

West Indies

Batsman	Runs
L. M. P. Simmons b Anderson	15
D. R. Smith c Kieswetter b Bresnan	56
†D. Ramdin lbw b Bresnan	22
M. N. Samuels c Swann b Anderson	30
D. J. Bravo lbw b Finn	8
K. A. Pollard c Morgan b Broad	3
*D. J. G. Sammy c Bopara b Swann	11
A. D. Russell c Morgan b Bresnan	7
D. M. Bravo not out	8
R. Rampaul c Trott b Swann	9
S. P. Narine c Kieswetter b Bresnan	0
W 3	3
1/25 (1) 2/95 (2) 3/102 (3) 4/118 (5) 5/127 (6) 6/137 (4) 7/155 (7) 8/157 (8) 9/172 (10) 10/172 (11) — (33.4 overs)	172

10 overs: 59-1

Anderson 8–0–48–2; Finn 6–0–29–1; Bresnan 7.4–0–34–4; Broad 8–0–40–1; Swann 4–0–21–2.

Umpires: H. D. P. K. Dharmasena and R. A. Kettleborough. Third umpire: A. L. Hill.

ENGLAND v WEST INDIES

Second One-Day International

At The Oval, June 19. England won by eight wickets. Toss: England

The death of Surrey cricketer Tom Maynard the previous morning cast a pall over his home ground. A minute's silence was held before the start, black armbands were worn by both teams, and flags flown at half-mast; Cook later admitted the sombre mood had affected some of his players, and Maynard's friend and Surrey team-mate Jade Dernbach accepted the offer of compassionate leave. England won with five overs in hand, clinching the series with a game to spare. Gayle briefly shone on his return to the West Indies side after a 14-month dispute with his board, crashing five sixes in 11 balls, including three in an over from Bresnan, one landing on the roof of the Bedser Stand. His dismissal, however – leg-before to Swann, despite Gayle's belief the ball had struck his bat first – robbed West Indies of momentum. Simmons was run out for a stodgy 12 from 50 deliveries, and it needed Dwayne Bravo's energetic 77 to give them a defendable total. But Cook and Bell began with 122 in 21 overs, and Cook cantered through to his fifth hundred in the format. It was the sixth successive one-day international in which an England opener had scored a century.

Man of the Match: A. N. Cook. *Attendance:* 17,110.

TOP OF THEIR GAME

Most successive one-day internationals in which an opener scored a century for one team:

6	**England**	**A. N. Cook 3, K. P. Pietersen 2, I. R. Bell 1 v Pak, WI**	**2011-12–2012**
4	Pakistan	Inzamam-ul-Haq 2, Ramiz Raja 1, Aamir Sohail 1, v SL, WI, Zim	1991-92
3	Pakistan	Saeed Anwar 3, Asif Mujtaba 1*, v SL, WI	1993-94
3	India	S. C. Ganguly 2, S. R. Tendulkar 1, v SA, NZ, SL	2000-01
3	S. Africa	H. H. Gibbs 3, v Kenya, India, Bang	2002-03
3	Pakistan	Salim Elahi 2, Faisal Iqbal 1, v Zim	2002-03
3	Ireland	J. P. Bray 1, W. T. S. Porterfield 2, v Scot, Bermuda, Kenya	2006-07

* *Saeed Anwar and Asif Mujtaba both scored hundreds in one match.*

West Indies

L. M. P. Simmons run out	12
C. H. Gayle lbw b Swann	53
D. R. Smith c Kieswetter b Broad	0
M. N. Samuels c Bresnan b Broad	13
D. J. Bravo c Bopara b Anderson	77
K. A. Pollard c Anderson b Bresnan	41
*D. J. G. Sammy c Morgan b Finn	21
†D. Ramdin c Kieswetter b Anderson	2
T. L. Best not out	7
S. P. Narine run out	2
R. Rampaul not out	1
L-b 3, w 5, n-b 1	9
1/63 (2) 2/63 (3) 3/79 (1) 4/79 (4) 5/179 (6) 6/220 (7) 7/223 (8) 8/232 (5) 9/237 (10) (9 wkts, 50 overs)	238
10 overs: 48-0	

Anderson 10–2–38–2; Finn 10–1–48–1; Bresnan 10–1–54–1; Swann 10–1–49–1; Broad 9–0–43–2; Bopara 1–0–3–0.

England

*A. N. Cook c Simmons b Sammy	112
I. R. Bell c Gayle b Sammy	53
I. J. L. Trott not out	43
R. S. Bopara not out	19
L-b 3, w 8, n-b 1	12
1/122 (2) 2/203 (1) (2 wkts, 45 overs)	239
10 overs: 60-0	

E. J. G. Morgan, †C. Kieswetter, T. T. Bresnan, S. C. J. Broad, G. P. Swann, S. T. Finn and J. M. Anderson did not bat.

Rampaul 7–0–29–0; Best 7–1–40–0; Bravo 4–0–24–0; Narine 10–1–54–0; Samuels 1–0–11–0; Sammy 10–0–46–2; Smith 3–0–22–0; Pollard 3–0–10–0.

Umpires: R. J. Bailey and A. L. Hill. Third umpire: H. D. P. K. Dharmasena.
Series referee: J. J. Crowe.

ENGLAND v WEST INDIES

Third One-Day International

At Leeds, June 22. Abandoned.

As on West Indies' 2009 tour, the Headingley one-day international was washed out. Three years earlier, controversy had centred on a new drainage system, which failed to cope even though the weather improved. This time, the rain was so heavy that play was never a possibility, and the controversy came beforehand when coach Andy Flower announced he would rest Swann, Broad and local hero Bresnan for the last match of a series they had already won.

Man of the Series: I. R. Bell.

ENGLAND v WEST INDIES

Twenty20 International

At Nottingham, June 24. England won by seven wickets. Toss: West Indies.

Hales smashed England's biggest Twenty20 score, surpassing Morgan's unbeaten 85 at Johannesburg in November 2009, but was distraught to miss their first century. He fell to his haunches after playing round a yorker from Rampaul when he needed one for his hundred and four to win. His high-class innings, on home turf, was full of clever strokes to leg, including each of his four sixes as he sought to harness a strong cross-breeze. Above all, Hales ensured West Indies would head home without an international win on tour. They might have fancied their chances after Smith's early fireworks and a late flourish from Bravo and Pollard, who added 65 in 28 balls. But Hales put on 159 with Bopara for the second wicket – an England all-wicket record, and the third-highest stand in all Twenty20 internationals – to keep up with the rate. Both fell with the end in sight, but Morgan completed England's joint-highest successful Twenty20 run-chase with two balls to spare.

Man of the Match: A. D. Hales. *Attendance:* 16,959.

West Indies

		B	*4*	*6*
D. R. Smith *c 1 b 11*	70	54	5	5
C. H. Gayle *c 6 b 11*	2	8	0	0
L. M. P. Simmons *c 6 b 9*	6	5	1	0
M. N. Samuels *c 1 b 8*	4	4	1	0
D. J. Bravo *not out*	54	36	1	3
K. A. Pollard *not out*	23	13	1	2
B 1, l-b 4, w 8	13			
6 overs: 29-2 (20 overs)	172-4			

1/10 2/24 3/30 4/107

†D. Ramdin, *D. J. G. Sammy, R. Rampaul, S. P. Narine and F. H. Edwards did not bat.

Finn 4–0–22–2; Dernbach 4–0–46–0; Broad 4–0–33–1; Swann 4–0–32–1; Patel 4–0–34–0.

England

		B	*4*	*6*
†C. Kieswetter *c 1 b 9*	3	7	0	0
A. D. Hales *b 9*	99	68	6	4
R. S. Bopara *c 11 b 4*	59	44	4	1
E. J. G. Morgan *not out*	2	1	0	0
J. C. Buttler *not out*	0	0	0	0
L-b 2, w 2, n-b 6	10			
6 overs: 42-1 (19.4 overs)	173-3			

1/10 2/169 3/171

J. M. Bairstow, S. R. Patel, G. P. Swann, *S. C. J. Broad, J. W. Dernbach and S. T. Finn did not bat.

Rampaul 4–0–37–2; Edwards 4–0–33–0; Narine 4–0–28–0; Bravo 2–0–21–0; Sammy 3–0–22–0; Pollard 1–0–15–0; Samuels 1.4–0–15–1.

Umpires: R. K. Illingworth and R. A. Kettleborough. Third umpire: R. J. Bailey.
Referee: J. J. Crowe.

ENGLAND v AUSTRALIA, 2012

RICHARD HOBSON

One day internationals (5): England 4, Australia 0

Australia's players arrived in England with the threat of strike action hanging over negotiations for a new pay deal with their board. As a one-sided NatWest Series unfolded, thoughts of a return home must have seemed increasingly alluring: while the issues concerning terms and conditions were resolved during the trip, questions of a different kind began to emerge – principally, how was it that a side at the top of the ICC rankings could suffer their heaviest defeat in any head-to-head limited-overs campaign?

The scoreline hardly flattered England. If rain had not washed out the third match at Edgbaston, they might easily have completed the 5–0 whitewash required to dislodge Australia and move top of the rankings in all three formats; such dominance would have been unprecedented (even if the Twenty20 listings had been introduced only the previous October). As losses piled up, the tourists did not mince words. Australia's coach, Mickey Arthur, described his team as "submissive", "bullied", and lacking presence, while captain Michael Clarke spoke of "a wake-up call". It could not have been louder had it been rung from the bells of St Paul's.

If this all seemed very un-Australian, then England were very English. Team director Andy Flower built a strategy perfectly suited to home conditions and the personnel available. Batsmen with Test standard techniques were included to combat the two new balls in often tricky conditions, and a bowling attack heavy with specialist pace was threatening throughout. It takes far more than good organisation to overpower Australia so comprehensively, but Flower was entitled to wonder whether his plan could have gone any better. Only the number of dropped catches can have caused any alarm, with the notable exception of Craig Kieswetter's athleticism behind the stumps. By the end, England had extended their sequence of one-day wins to ten (excluding washouts) since the start of the year.

Any lingering concerns about the top three were removed: not even the harshest critic questioned the right of Alastair Cook, Ian Bell and Jonathan Trott to fill those slots. When Bell fell fourth ball in the final game at Old Trafford, it was his first failure since replacing Kevin Pietersen – now retired from the format, at least for the time being – at the start of the previous series, against West Indies. Circumstances allowed Trott to bat at his own pace, and Ravi Bopara grew in confidence to the point where he supervised the chase in Manchester like Eoin Morgan at his calmest. As he also provided some tight contributions with the ball, Bopara was unlucky that Bell pipped him for the Man of the Series award. Morgan himself put a sorry winter behind him to finish unbeaten in his three innings; his 141 runs came at a strike-rate of 130. Australia had wondered in advance whether Tim Bresnan was a potential weakness at No. 7, but in the event he was not required to bat at all, while

Mike Hewitt, Getty Images

Flat-footed: George Bailey at Lord's typified the struggles of the new generation of Australian batsmen in difficult conditions.

Kieswetter at No. 6 faced only 29 balls. In the four games, England lost 14 wickets to Australia's 32.

Those facts speak for the Australian bowling as well as England's batting. Only Clint McKay, persevering and accurate, claimed more than two wickets overall. Pat Cummins was forced to return home with a side strain after the first game, a worrying extension to his run of injuries. Shane Watson and Brett Lee followed after the fourth match, at Chester-le-Street, because of calf problems, though not before Lee – who announced his retirement shortly after the tour – had equalled Glenn McGrath's record of 380 one-day international wickets for Australia. James Pattinson, built up beforehand, did not appear until late in the series – then went wicketless in 16 overs. And Australia lagged even further behind in the spin department, with Graeme Swann outbowling Xavier Doherty before Swann was withdrawn from the squad because of continuing soreness in his right elbow.

Arthur tried to find some comfort, suggesting that England had shown opponents the approach required for the Champions Trophy, which they would be hosting in 2013. The Ashes series later that summer provided another appetising context, with John Inverarity, Australia's chairman of selectors, saying that David Hussey, Peter Forrest and George Bailey represented the next-best batsmen below those in the current Test team. Hussey (who turned 35 shortly after this series) barely needed experience in England, after much success with Nottinghamshire, but he and Bailey, the Twenty20 captain, both proved inconsistent; the only consistent thing about Forrest was his tentative footwork, exposed by the moving ball. A general uncertainty became evident as Australia tried in vain to reshuffle their hand in the absence of Hussey's older brother Mike, at home on paternity leave. By the end, the aces were all England's.

AUSTRALIAN TOURING PARTY

*M. J. Clarke, G. J. Bailey, P. J. Cummins, X. J. Doherty, P. J. Forrest, B. W. Hilfenhaus, D. J. Hussey, M. G. Johnson, B. Lee, C. J. McKay, J. L. Pattinson, S. P. D. Smith, M. S. Wade, D. A. Warner, S. R. Watson. *Coach:* J. M. Arthur.

M. E. K. Hussey was originally selected, but withdrew after the premature birth of his child, and was replaced by Forrest. Cummins injured his side during the first one-day international at Lord's. Before the last match, Lee and Watson both returned home before the final match with calf strains, and M. A. Starc was called into the squad.

At Leicester, June 21. **Australians won by 102 runs** (D/L). **Australians 241-8** (41 overs) (D. A. Warner 74); ‡**Leicestershire 136** (29.4 overs) (C. J. McKay 4-31). *Rain after 26.4 overs of the Australians' innings – at which point Warner retired out, making the score 127-3 – further shortened a match already reduced to 37: Leicestershire's target was eventually revised to 239 from 36. But they never got close in the face of a fine spell from McKay, who sent down some well-disguised slower balls, while Watson took two wickets in his third over and was promptly taken off.*

At Belfast, June 23. IRELAND v AUSTRALIA. No result (see Cricket in Ireland, page 817).

At Chelmsford, June 26 (day/night). **Australians won by 179 runs.** ‡**Australians 313-9** (50 overs) (M. J. Clarke 76, D. J. Hussey 67; R. J. W. Topley 4-46); **Essex 134** (32.4 overs). *MoM:* R. J. W. Topley. *The Australians completed their warm-ups with another thumping victory. Clarke and Hussey put on 137 in 20 overs before Clarke retired, and the eventual total was far beyond Essex's reach. They soon slid to 14-3, and although Ravi Bopara (39) and James Foster (41) resisted for a while, the result was never in doubt. Pat Cummins (3-26) was the tourists' leading wicket-taker.*

ENGLAND v AUSTRALIA

First One-Day International

At Lord's, June 29. England won by 15 runs. Toss: Australia.

Morgan's return to form, on his home ground, gave England an impetus at the end of their innings that Australia only briefly threatened to match. His unbeaten 89 from 63 balls included 34 from the last 11; three of his four sixes came from consecutive deliveries, the pick of them a crouched heave that spectacularly deposited a near-yorker from Lee over wide long-on. Until that flurry, England were heading for around 250, a good effort following a treacherous morning for batting, but slightly below par nonetheless. Rain had stopped play three times in the first six overs, but Cook and Bell did more than ride their luck, and Trott continued smartly in mid-innings. Morgan waited until the 38th over to accelerate, driving Cummins over long-off, and Kieswetter helped him add 83 from 59 balls. Australia then gave themselves a base, only for Anderson, despite a groin strain, to remove Bailey and the more forceful Warner in successive overs. Clarke, neat and busy, rebuilt until a misunderstanding left Wade stranded mid-pitch, then fell in the next over as Bresnan found some reverse swing. Late hitting by Lee merely camouflaged the ease of England's success.

Man of the Match: E. J. G. Morgan.

England

*A. N. Cook c Wade b Cummins	40
I. R. Bell lbw b Lee	41
I. J. L. Trott b Doherty	54
R. S. Bopara c Clarke b McKay	15
E. J. G. Morgan not out	89
†C. Kieswetter c Warner b Watson	25
L-b 4, w 4	8
1/74 (2) 2/89 (1) 3/121 (4) 4/189 (3) 5/272 (6) (5 wkts, 50 overs)	272
10 overs: 37-0	

T. T. Bresnan, S. C. J. Broad, G. P. Swann, S. T. Finn and J. M. Anderson did not bat.

Lee 10–1–57–1; McKay 10–1–43–1; Cummins 10–0–53–1; Doherty 10–0–50–1; Watson 10–0–65–1.

Australia

S. R. Watson c Kieswetter b Finn 12
D. A. Warner c Kieswetter b Anderson. . . . 56
G. J. Bailey b Anderson. 29
*M. J. Clarke lbw b Bresnan 61
D. J. Hussey b Finn 13
S. P. D. Smith c Kieswetter b Bresnan 8
†M. S. Wade run out 27
B. Lee not out 29
C. J. McKay c Kieswetter b Broad 2
P. J. Cummins lbw b Broad. 4
X. J. Doherty not out 6
L-b 3, w 7 10

1/20 (1) 2/96 (3) (9 wkts, 50 overs) 257
3/102 (2) 4/132 (5)
5/147 (6) 6/204 (7) 7/214 (4)
8/226 (9) 9/231 (10) 10 overs: 50-1

Anderson 9–0–55–2; Finn 10–0–47–2; Bresnan 10–0–54–2; Broad 10–0–47–2; Swann 10–0–47–0; Bopara 1–0–4–0.

Umpires: Aleem Dar and R. A. Kettleborough. Third umpire: M. Erasmus.

ENGLAND v AUSTRALIA

Second One-Day International

At The Oval, July 1. England won by six wickets. Toss: Australia.

England needed 81 from 16.3 overs when the Hot Spot cameras detected the faintest of inside edges to spare Morgan a second-ball duck after he had initially been adjudged lbw to Clarke. It proved their final scare, and they finished the game with 26 deliveries in hand; their only disappointment was Bopara's needless dismissal chancing a quick single with two runs needed. But his 82 from 85 balls was an increasingly self-assured effort to back up five overs of medium-pace that had helped strangle the Australian innings. Bailey, in particular, became bogged down against Swann, after Watson had decelerated badly following a run-a-ball fifty: only 24 runs came between the 21st and 30th overs. Bailey eventually raised the tempo, adding 78 with Hussey. Even so, their total of 251 for seven – boosted by four dropped catches of varying difficulty – looked short, and Johnson did not help matters with three no-balls in the first two overs of his recall after more than seven months away, initially with a foot injury. Although he improved in his second spell, an assured innings from Bell all but settled the matter.

Man of the Match: R. S. Bopara.

Australia

S. R. Watson c Finn b Swann 66
D. A. Warner c Bell b Finn 10
P. J. Forrest c Kieswetter b Broad 12
*M. J. Clarke c Kieswetter b Bopara. 10
G. J. Bailey b Bresnan. 65
D. J. Hussey run out 29
†M. S. Wade c Broad b Bresnan 6
B. Lee not out 20
M. G. Johnson not out 8
L-b 15, w 8, n-b 2 25

1/15 (2) 2/66 (3) (7 wkts, 50 overs) 251
3/101 (4) 4/128 (1)
5/206 (6) 6/222 (5) 7/223 (7) 10 overs: 46-1

C. J. McKay and X. J. Doherty did not bat.

Finn 9–0–36–1; Dernbach 10–1–59–0; Bresnan 8–0–50–2; Broad 10–0–48–1; Bopara 5–0–16–1; Swann 8–0–27–1.

England

*A. N. Cook lbw b McKay 18
I. R. Bell b Clarke 75
I. J. L. Trott b Watson 17
R. S. Bopara run out 82
E. J. G. Morgan not out. 43
†C. Kieswetter not out. 0
L-b 4, w 9, n-b 4 17

1/40 (1) 2/81 (3) (4 wkts, 45.4 overs) 252
3/171 (2) 4/250 (4) 10 overs: 53-1

T. T. Bresnan, S. C. J. Broad, G. P. Swann, S. T. Finn and J. W. Dernbach did not bat.

Lee 10–0–58–0; Johnson 7–0–43–0; McKay 10–1–42–1; Doherty 7.4–0–41–0; Watson 6–0–34–1; Hussey 3–0–17–0; Clarke 2–0–13–1.

Umpires: M. Erasmus and R. K. Illingworth. Third umpire: Aleem Dar.

ENGLAND v AUSTRALIA

Third One-Day International

At Birmingham, July 4 (day/night). Abandoned.

The weather denied England the opportunity to press for the 5–0 win they needed to overtake Australia at the top of the one-day rankings. Heavy rain had soaked Birmingham in the 24 hours before the scheduled 2pm start, and a final downpour as the sides prepared for a 28-over match led to abandonment at 6pm. It was the fourth day's international cricket Edgbaston had lost to the elements in 2012, following the truncated Test against West Indies the previous month.

ENGLAND v AUSTRALIA

Fourth One-Day International

At Chester-le-Street, July 7. England won by eight wickets. Toss: England.

Australia's woes continued, with Lee and Watson, two of their most experienced players, pulling up injured with calf strains during an emphatic loss that guaranteed England a seventh successive home series victory. Cook put Australia in on a seam-friendly morning, and his bowlers teased batsmen ill-used to the jagging ball. Survival proved challenging enough: Australia mustered only 15 runs in their first ten overs, and were six down by the time they reached 100 from the last ball of the 33rd. Finn, bowling with pace and hostility, twice found himself on a hat-trick, with Kieswetter's fine catch from an inside edge to remove Wade a highlight. Bopara backed up the specialist bowlers when Patel's spin proved ineffective. Hussey drew upon his time in county cricket to negotiate the movement off the seam, finishing with 70 from 73 balls, and Lee hit out profitably until becoming the 500th victim of Anderson's international career (only Ian Botham, with 528, had taken more for England). In what became his last game for Australia, Lee could not add to his own tally of 718. McKay's control made life awkward for England, but Cook and Bell saw out the early overs, and the techniques of England's top three were an object lesson for the demoralised Australians.

Man of the Match: S. T. Finn.

Australia

S. R. Watson b Bresnan	28
D. A. Warner lbw b Finn	2
P. J. Forrest lbw b Finn	0
*M. J. Clarke b Finn	43
G. J. Bailey b Bopara	9
D. J. Hussey c Anderson b Bresnan	70
†M. S. Wade c Kieswetter b Finn	0
B. Lee c Broad b Anderson	27
C. J. McKay c Bresnan b Anderson	6
J. L. Pattinson not out	8
B. W. Hilfenhaus not out	0
L-b 2, w 4, n-b 1	7
1/6 (2) 2/6 (3) 3/57 (1) 4/68 (5) 5/96 (4) 6/96 (7) 7/166 (8) 8/174 (9) 9/194 (6) (9 wkts, 50 overs)	200
10 overs: 15-2	

Anderson 10–3–34–2; Finn 10–2–37–4; Bresnan 9–0–46–2; Broad 9–1–34–0; Bopara 9–0–29–1; Patel 3–0–18–0.

England

*A. N. Cook c sub (S. P. D. Smith) b McKay	29
I. R. Bell b McKay	69
I. J. L. Trott not out	64
R. S. Bopara not out	33
W 4, n-b 2	6
1/70 (1) 2/136 (2) (2 wkts, 47.5 overs)	201
10 overs: 42-0	

E. J. G. Morgan, †C. Kieswetter, S. R. Patel, T. T. Bresnan, S. C. J. Broad, S. T. Finn and J. M. Anderson did not bat.

Lee 2.2–1–12–0; Hilfenhaus 9.4–0–36–0; McKay 10–1–29–2; Pattinson 10–1–46–0; Watson 1–0–5–0; Clarke 5–0–17–0; Hussey 8.5–0–48–0; Warner 1–0–8–0.

Umpires: M. Erasmus and N. J. Llong. Third umpire: Aleem Dar.

ENGLAND v AUSTRALIA

Fifth One-Day International

At Manchester, July 10 (day/night). England won by seven wickets (D/L method). Toss: England.

A cold, gloomy evening at a ground still under reconstruction proved an appropriately miserable occasion for the end of Australia's tour. Once again they were outplayed, unable to post enough runs in bowler-friendly conditions, then lacking the depth in their own attack to back up a promising start. Rain initially restricted the game to a 32-overs affair, and England soon dismantled a rejigged batting order by taking four wickets in 31 balls. Wade, promoted to open in the absence of Watson, looked particularly unhappy: he ate up 41 deliveries for his dozen runs. Tredwell generated significant turn in his first international appearance since the World Cup quarter-final in Colombo in March 2011, and Bopara again provided a golden arm, strangling Smith down the leg side with his first-ball loosener, then persuading Hussey to nick a shortish delivery. Warner was positive early on, but it needed some late hitting from Bailey, who waited 27 balls for his first boundary, to bring the total even close to respectability; three dropped catches in the opening overs had helped Australia's cause. A short shower reduced England's target to 138 from 29 overs, and they never looked back after Cook, when eight, successfully reviewed a caught-behind decision by umpire Aleem Dar off the bowling of McKay. Working spin neatly, Cook added 92 with Bopara, whose cool, unbeaten 52 from 56 balls included several meaty drives through the off side.

Man of the Match: R. S. Bopara. *Man of the Series:* I. R. Bell.

Australia

†M. S. Wade st Kieswetter b Tredwell	12
D. A. Warner lbw b Tredwell	32
P. J. Forrest run out	3
*M. J. Clarke run out	1
S. P. D. Smith c Kieswetter b Bopara	21
D. J. Hussey c Kieswetter b Bopara	9
G. J. Bailey not out	46
J. L. Pattinson c Kieswetter b Finn	13
C. J. McKay not out	5
L-b 1, w 2	3
1/43 (2) 2/49 (3) 3/49 (1) 4/55 (4) 5/77 (5) 6/86 (6) 7/120 (8) (7 wkts, 32 overs)	145
7 overs: 22-0	

B. W. Hilfenhaus and X. J. Doherty did not bat.

Anderson 5–1–22–0; Finn 6–0–35–1; Broad 7–0–39–0; Tredwell 7–1–23–2; Patel 3–0–17–0; Bopara 4–0–8–2.

England

*A. N. Cook c Clarke b Hilfenhaus	58
I. R. Bell c Bailey b McKay	4
I. J. L. Trott b Clarke	10
R. S. Bopara not out	52
E. J. G. Morgan not out	9
L-b 1, w 4	5
1/5 (2) 2/34 (3) 3/126 (1) (3 wkts, 27.1 overs)	138
6 overs: 25-1	

†C. Kieswetter, S. R. Patel, J. C. Tredwell, S. C. J. Broad, S. T. Finn and J. M. Anderson did not bat.

McKay 6–0–27–1; Hilfenhaus 5.1–0–19–1; Pattinson 6–0–34–0; Clarke 3–0–14–1; Doherty 5–0–34–0; Smith 2–0–9–0.

Umpires: Aleem Dar and I. J. Gould. Third umpire: M. Erasmus.
Series referee: J. Srinath.

ENGLAND v SOUTH AFRICA, 2012

REVIEW BY SIMON WILDE

Test matches (3): England 0, South Africa 2
One-day internationals (5): England 2, South Africa 2
Twenty20 internationals (3): England 1, South Africa 1

South Africa flew home with England grateful they would not be returning for a bilateral series until 2017. This was their third successive visit – each under the leadership of Graeme Smith – to coincide with the resignation of the England captain: for Nasser Hussain in 2003 and Michael Vaughan in 2008, read Andrew Strauss in 2012. It was a summer in which South Africa won the Tests 2–0 to retain the Basil D'Oliveira Trophy and replace England at the top of the ICC rankings; and it left the hosts questioning not only their own carefully established sense of worth, but the team spirit which had helped get them to the top of the world in the first place.

Quite simply, England fell apart: both on the field, where they never truly recovered after Hashim Amla's epic undefeated 311 condemned them to a humiliating loss in the First Test at The Oval; and off it, as a split between Kevin Pietersen and other members of the team sprang into public view. Despite batting brilliantly for 149 in the drawn Second Test at Headingley, Pietersen was dropped for the final game, at Lord's, in part because it emerged he had sent "provocative" BlackBerry messages to South African players (although the ECB later accepted his assurance that the messages had not been derogatory about others within the England camp).

Both teams knew they could not afford to put a foot wrong, but England – defending a record of seven successive Test series wins at home – now found themselves horribly distracted. It was during South Africa's second warm-up game, at Canterbury, that reports surfaced suggesting Pietersen, who had already announced his retirement from the international limited-overs formats, wanted to miss Tests at home to New Zealand in 2013 to spend more time at the IPL. It was hardly likely to endear him to management or team-mates. Then, ahead of the Second Test, Ravi Bopara withdrew, citing domestic problems. He returned for the one-day internationals and Twenty20s, but his meaningful contributions came only with the ball.

As a result, England were obliged to blood James Taylor at Headingley, and recall Jonny Bairstow at Lord's not long after he had been dropped amid concerns about his technique against the short ball. Bairstow played two spirited innings but, despite a late fightback engineered by Matt Prior, England's leading run-scorer in the series, as they chased an improbable 346, he could not prevent defeat. Strauss denied Pietersen was a factor in his resignation, which came after 100 Test appearances, 50 of them in charge. "My race was run," he said. But not everyone was convinced by his claim; at the very least, the Pietersen affair had overshadowed his farewell – a further source of irritation to other team members.

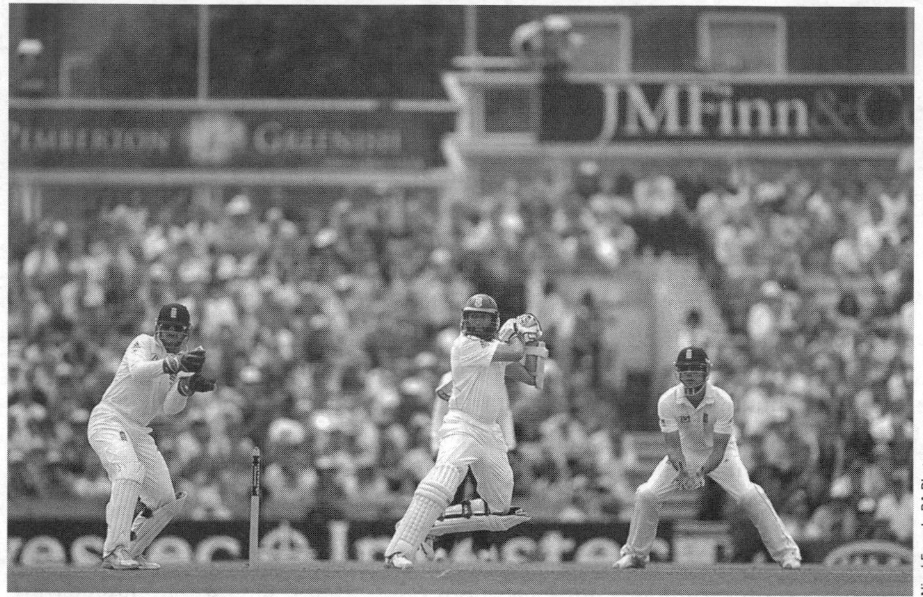

Nigel French, PA Photos

The unbreachable: Hashim Amla begins with a triple-century at The Oval, and seemed never to leave the crease for the rest of the tour.

By contrast, South Africa, who watched the debacle unfold with detached amusement, remained impressively focused, in spite of several potentially destabilising events. Within a week of arriving, Mark Boucher – the veteran wicketkeeper hoping to play his 150th Test at Lord's – sustained a freak injury at Taunton, where a flying bail struck his left eye. It ended not only his tour, but an unflinching career. His distraught team-mates had to regroup quickly.

A. B. de Villiers was pressed into service as batsman-keeper, with J-P. Duminy slotting in at No. 7, a move that actually strengthened the line-up, even though England managed to keep de Villiers relatively quiet. Boucher's misfortune, in fact, appeared only to stiffen the South Africans' resolve. When the series was won, several of them took to the Lord's outfield sporting T-shirts bearing tributes to their absent friend.

The touring party also had to defend themselves against allegations of leaking the Pietersen texts, a charge they denied. Weeks later, following several apologies to his colleagues, Pietersen was preparing for what ECB chairman Giles Clarke called his "reintegration" to the fold, when chief executive David Collier went even further. "The texts were responses to messages from members of the South African team," he told BBC radio. "I certainly think that did provoke the situation. There was definitely a policy. There was a tactic that was used." South Africa, who had maintained all along that the texts were mere banter – a claim undermined by Pietersen himself, with his admission that they were "provocative" – issued strenuous denials, amid talk of legal action; Collier apologised. Whatever the truth, the South Africans never let the matter affect their cricket.

For a team with a reputation for faltering in sight of the big prize, their poise was admirable, and much credit was due to Smith and Gary Kirsten, the coach.

While Strauss appeared exhausted by three and a half years of captaincy, Smith's energy in his tenth year at the helm of the Test side – he, like Strauss, had already ceded the one-day job – seemed undiminished; he even squeezed in a lightning visit home after the Oval Test to attend the birth of his first child. He had, in fact, been talked into staying in charge in 2011 by Kirsten, who may have had personal reasons for wanting to win in England: on each of his three tours as a player, South Africa had blown a 1–0 lead.

Not many rival coaches had got the better of Andy Flower, but Kirsten did. He managed expectation and crises with a sure hand, and it was his idea to take the bulk of the squad to the Swiss Alps for a pre-tour team-building exercise run by polar explorer and mountain climber Mike Horn. They walked and cycled, climbed peaks and plunged into freezing lakes, and arrived in England armed with aphorisms, which were duly aired at every opportunity. Horn must have purred when, with the Tests in the bag, Duminy tweeted: "Getting to the top of the mountain is just the start of the work." Horn, like Boucher, was with the team in spirit every step of the way.

MOST INTERNATIONAL RUNS ON A TOUR OF ENGLAND

Total runs		*Avge*	*Test runs*	*ODI runs*	*T20I runs*
1,045	I. V. A. Richards (WI, 1976)	116.11	829	216	–
974	D. G. Bradman (A, 1930)	139.14	974	–	–
937	G. C. Smith (SA, 2003)	58.56	714	223	–
900	**H. M. Amla (SA, 2012)**	**112.50**	**482**	**335**	**83**
885	B. C. Lara (WI, 1995)	73.75	765	120	–
847	R. Dravid (I, 2002)	77.00	602	245	–
839	M. A. Taylor (A, 1989)	83.90	839	–	–
815	C. H. Gayle (WI, 2004)	50.93	400	415	–
800	Mohammad Yousuf (P, 2006)	72.72	631	149	20
785	A. R. Border (A, 1985)	71.36	597	188	–
758	D. G. Bradman (A, 1934)	94.75	758	–	–

South Africa might have achieved their main goal, but England rallied to earn a share of the one-day and Twenty20 series, preserving their top ranking in one format and regaining it in the other. But these contests felt like an irrelevance, especially after a dramatic final day of the Test series: they were diminished by rain and the absence of some high-profile personnel, and the 20-over games were used by both sides to experiment ahead of the World Twenty20 (a fat lot of good it did either team). In truth, it was a poorly structured tour, partly because of a clash with the London Olympics. Whatever happened to assurances from both boards that England–South Africa would always be a marquee series consisting of at least four matches?

South Africa won most of the tricks that mattered, and England's top three batsmen each had a personal nemesis. Morne Morkel, thrown the new ball on the first morning of the series to general surprise, picked up where he had left off in South Africa on England's tour in 2009-10, tormenting Strauss from round the wicket and removing him with his fourth delivery. Morkel dismissed the England captain only once more, but he was a constant thorn in his side, and Strauss's last act – padding up to Vernon Philander late on the fourth evening at Lord's – was that of a man who had simply become overwhelmed. Only once before, against Sri Lanka in 2011, had he averaged fewer in a series of at least three Tests than the 17 he managed here.

Philander – whose ability to swing the ball received belated reward at Lord's, where he also played two valuable innings – removed Alastair Cook cheaply in each of the three matches after he had begun the series with a century. And Dale Steyn accounted for Jonathan Trott in four of his five completed innings. England's average score at the fall of the second wicket was 67, to South Africa's 124. But even that barely did justice to the gulf in quality between the two batting units.

Smith, who had been sidelined before the tour by an ankle problem, as usual scored heavily, taking his aggregate in 12 Tests in England to 1,355. If his century at The Oval in his 100th Test brought the satisfaction of setting up a crushing win, his fifties at Headingley in two opening stands of 120 were equally valuable. His unorthodox method sent England's bowlers into a predictable tizzy. At Headingley, they came up with all manner of theories, when a simple off-stump line, with a view to an outside edge, was later confirmed as the best policy during the one-day internationals (Steven Finn thought he had removed Smith that way during the Second Test, only for umpire Steve Davis to call dead ball because he had dislodged the bails with his knee).

England presumably spent less time in advance worrying about where to bowl at Alviro Petersen, but he shook off a foot injury to keep them at bay for a nine-hour 182 after they had chosen to field first in the Second Test.

Nothing compared, though, to the majesty and might of Amla who, in going unbeaten for more than 13 hours at The Oval to make South Africa's first Test triple-century, broke not only records but English spirits. His tactic of moving across his stumps to Graeme Swann was instrumental in the off-spinner going wicketless for 52 overs; Swann was immediately dropped by Flower for the first time since being left out of two Tests in the West Indies in 2008-09.

In Swann's absence at Headingley, part-time off-spinner Pietersen took a wicket with his second ball, and finished with four in the game, which only

---

HIGHEST TEST AVERAGE IN ENGLAND

	T	*I*	*NO*	*R*	*HS*	*100*	*Avge*
D. G. Bradman (A)	19	30	4	2,674	334	11	102.84
H. M. Amla (SA)	**7**	**12**	**2**	**757**	**311***	**3**	**75.70**
S. R. Waugh (A)	22	32	10	1,633	177*	7	74.22
D. M. Jones (A)	6	9	1	566	157	2	70.75
R. Dravid (I)	13	23	3	1,376	217	6	68.80
G. C. Smith (SA)	**12**	**22**	**2**	**1,355**	**277**	**5**	**67.75**
S. Chanderpaul (WI)	**15**	**27**	**6**	**1,399**	**136***	**3**	**66.61**
Salim Malik (P)	13	18	4	931	165	3	66.50
S. C. Ganguly (I)	9	15	1	915	136	3	65.35
A. R. Border (A)	25	43	11	2,082	200*	5	65.06
H. Sutcliffe (E)	33	47	7	2,584	161	9	64.60
I. V. A. Richards (WI)	24	34	2	2,057	291	5	64.28

Qualification: 500 runs.

MARK BOUCHER

The tough guy toppled

TELFORD VICE

South African farewells have come in all shapes and sizes. Hansie Cronje left under the darkest of clouds. Shaun Pollock spent an entire one-day series waving goodbye. Makhaya Ntini did so from the back of a golf cart, scuttling around the boundary after a Twenty20 match at a football stadium.

None of the above applies to Mark Boucher, whose 15 years as an international player came to a cruel and sudden end on a grey day in Taunton at the very start of the tour. Imran Tahir bowled Gemaal Hussain. A bail spat from the wicket, as Boucher had seen it do so many times before. Now, though, it hit him in the face and ruptured his left sclera, the white of his eye.

Boucher sank to his knees and put a hand to his head. When he took it away, he was puzzled to see that the fluid on his palm was clear, not red. He took a few unsteady steps towards the dressing-room, but was unable to continue, and lay face down on the outfield. Unbeknown to anyone, parts of his eye lay scattered on the turf beside him. He was unlikely ever to regain full vision.

To see the embodiment of his country's cricket ethos toppled was disturbing. There was some mercy in the fact that almost none of the South Africans who had come to take for granted Boucher's role as the central pillar of that ethos was there to witness his demise. For those who were, the awful memory will live for ever.

It cast a shadow that lingered right up until the dazzling, dying moments of the Lord's Test – which should have been Boucher's 150th – when Graeme Smith attended the press conference wearing a T-shirt proclaiming the handwritten message: "We miss u Bouch".

Even so, this was no sort of climax for a story of talent and temperament welded unusually well into one man. Boucher was what South African cricket likes to think it is, but too often is not: tough, uncompromising, immune to the meltdowns that make mortals out of the rest of us. He was as valuable in the minds of his team-mates and opponents as he was out on the field; slick behind the stumps and solid in front of them. He was also a pain in the backside, which suited South Africa well.

The less celebrated truth was that he was all but a spent force anyway. Boucher had already announced his intention to retire after the Test series, and there was a groundswell of opinion that this would not be a moment too soon. He had long since ceased to be a bulwark of the batting order – his last 19 Test innings yielded only two half-centuries – and there were loud calls for an infusion of young blood from the ranks of South Africa's crop of promising glovemen, which were ignored.

Those cold-hearted sentiments have now, of course, been swiftly silenced. Which is a disservice to Boucher: he could always handle the truth.

highlighted the extent to which England had been thrown off course. For his part, Amla was unfazed by ascending such heights: he crafted runs serenely for the rest of the tour, finishing with 900 in all internationals (including 100 fours and two sixes), and top-scoring in eight innings out of 11.

The series had been billed as a showdown between two experienced and proven pace attacks, and particularly James Anderson and Steyn. It turned out

Graham Morris

Like swallows: South Africa's catching, epitomised by Jacques Kallis holding Jonathan Trott at second slip at Lord's, was streets ahead of England's.

to be a non-event. Anderson's removal of Petersen for a duck in his opening spell sold everyone – not least himself – a huge dummy, and he soon gave way to frustration as the ball stubbornly refused to be as pliant in his hands as in the opposition's. His nine wickets in the series cost 40 apiece.

Stuart Broad was well down on his usual pace – the England camp blithely dismissed these concerns – and was little more than a passenger, except for one vibrant spell on the final afternoon in Leeds. Why, wondered observers, didn't he always bowl like that? Finn, brought in to stir the attack out of somnambulance, looked their most potent weapon, and bowled exceptionally well on the fourth afternoon at Lord's to keep England in the game.

Steyn it was who first stirred South Africa into action. They had laboured largely in vain on the opening day of the series, but he bounded in on the second morning – the skies now handily obscured by grey cloud – to trigger a collapse; South Africa proceeded to win the next ten sessions too. Steyn was a constant threat, although Morkel, thanks to his height and unorthodox angles, posed the most consistently awkward questions.

Jacques Kallis's role as a frontline bowler had appeared to be numbered, but he balanced the attack in impressive fashion. His muscular efforts late on the first day and early on the second at The Oval brought the prized wickets of Pietersen and Ian Bell, and gave Steyn the support he needed in slowing England's advance. And his hard work meant South Africa did not miss Marchant de Lange, who pulled out of the tour in the first week because of a back injury.

As usual, Kallis caught pretty much everything in the field, too, in stark contrast to England's slapdash handling, another area in which their standards had slipped. South Africa benefited from at least eight spilled catches, the most expensive of which reprieved Amla 40 runs into his 311 (admittedly not even a half-chance to Strauss at slip); Petersen 29 runs into his 182; and Amla, again, by the normally immaculate Prior, when he had scored two of his 121 at Lord's. Anderson, England's safest catcher, also put down de Villiers at Lord's, causing a crucial delay in the push for wickets that might have kept the run-chase to more manageable proportions. Overall, South Africa held 33 catches to England's 22, and executed three run-outs to one. As so often, the tension told on the side playing catch-up.

All in all, few better prepared, organised or balanced sides have toured England in modern times. South Africa even coaxed a handy performance out of Imran Tahir, a leg-break and googly bowler born and raised in Pakistan but now qualified by residence. Having sought guidance from Abdul Qadir before the tour, Tahir played a small but vital part – bamboozling Strauss at The Oval and outbowling Swann. This wasn't saying much, but it was enough.

SOUTH AFRICAN TOURING PARTY

*G. C. Smith, H. M. Amla, M. V. Boucher, M. de Lange, A. B. de Villiers, J-P. Duminy, Imran Tahir, J. H. Kallis, M. Morkel, A. N. Petersen, R. J. Peterson, V. D. Philander, J. A. Rudolph, D. W. Steyn, L. L. Tsotsobe.

Coach: G. Kirsten. *Team manager:* M. Moosajee. *Assistant coach:* R. Domingo. *Bowling coach:* A. A. Donald. *Performance director:* P. A. H. Upton. *Physiotherapist:* B. Jackson. *Strength and conditioning coach:* R. Walter. *Video and statistical analyst:* P. Agoram. *Security officer:* Z. Wadee. *Media manager:* L. Malekutu. *Logistics manager:* R. Muller.

Boucher retired from cricket after suffering an eye injury in the opening match; he was replaced in the Test squad by T. L. Tsolekile. De Lange withdrew in the first week with a back injury, and was replaced by J. A. Morkel. F. du Plessis was called up, initially as cover when J. A. Morkel suffered an ankle injury, but was retained for the rest of the tour. De Villiers took over the captaincy for the one-day and Twenty20 series following the Tests. D. Elgar, R. McLaren, J. L. Ontong and W. D. Parnell replaced Kallis, Petersen, Philander and Rudolph in the one-day squad; Kallis returned for the Twenty20 series, in which F. Behardien, J. Botha and R. E. Levi replaced Elgar, Imran Tahir, McLaren and Smith.

TEST MATCH AVERAGES

ENGLAND – BATTING AND FIELDING

	T	*I*	*NO*	*R*	*HS*	*100*	*50*	*Avge*	*Ct/St*
K. P. Pietersen	2	4	0	219	149	1	0	54.75	0
G. P. Swann	2	4	2	100	41	0	0	50.00	1
M. J. Prior	3	6	0	275	73	0	3	45.83	8/3
I. J. L. Trott	3	6	1	217	71	0	2	43.40	0
†A. N. Cook	3	6	0	195	115	1	0	32.50	6
I. R. Bell	3	6	1	144	58	0	2	28.80	1
T. T. Bresnan	2	3	1	37	20*	0	0	18.50	1
†A. J. Strauss	3	6	0	107	37	0	0	17.83	1
J. W. A. Taylor	2	3	0	48	34	0	0	16.00	2
†S. C. J. Broad	3	5	0	70	37	0	0	14.00	0
†J. M. Anderson	3	5	1	30	12	0	0	7.50	1
S. T. Finn	2	3	1	10	10	0	0	5.00	0

Played in one Test: J. M. Bairstow 95, 54 (1 ct); R. S. Bopara 0, 22.

BOWLING

	Style	O	M	R	W	BB	5I	Avge
K. P. Pietersen	OB	19	1	91	4	3-52	0	22.75
S. T. Finn	RF	91	12	322	10	4-74	0	32.20
S. C. J. Broad	RFM	130.4	24	437	11	5-69	1	39.72
J. M. Anderson	RFM	147.4	33	366	9	3-76	0	40.66
G. P. Swann	OB	123.2	30	308	4	2-63	0	77.00

Also bowled: R. S. Bopara (RM) 18–1–78–0; T. T. Bresnan (RFM) 73–8–278–2; I. J. L. Trott (RM) 19–2–46–0.

SOUTH AFRICA – BATTING AND FIELDING

	T	I	NO	R	HS	100	50	Avge	Ct
H. M. Amla	3	5	1	482	311*	2	0	120.50	2
†J-P. Duminy	3	4	2	135	61	0	1	67.50	2
J. H. Kallis	3	5	1	262	182*	1	0	65.50	6
A. N. Petersen	3	5	1	244	182	1	0	61.00	2
†G. C. Smith	3	5	0	272	131	1	2	54.40	6
A. B. de Villiers	3	4	0	161	47	0	0	40.25	9
†J. A. Rudolph	3	4	0	141	69	0	1	35.25	2
V. D. Philander	3	4	0	115	61	0	1	28.75	1
†M. Morkel	3	4	0	63	25	0	0	15.75	0
D. W. Steyn	3	4	0	38	26	0	0	9.50	1
Imran Tahir	3	3	1	3	2*	0	0	1.50	1

BOWLING

	Style	O	M	R	W	BB	5I	Avge
V. D. Philander	RFM	120.5	34	284	12	5-30	1	23.66
D. W. Steyn	RF	131	30	438	15	5-56	1	29.20
M. Morkel	RF	128.2	24	380	11	4-72	0	34.54
J. H. Kallis	RFM	65	18	180	4	2-38	0	45.00
Imran Tahir	LBG	116.4	13	378	8	3-63	0	47.25

Also bowled: J-P. Duminy (OB) 11–2–28–1.

At Taunton, July 9–10 (not first-class). **Drawn.** **‡Somerset 312-8 dec** (J. C. Hildreth 100, P. D. Trego 104, C. A. J. Meschede 50*; L. L. Tsotsobe 3-46) **and 50-1**; **South Africans 282-9 dec** (H. M. Amla 64, J-P. Duminy 53; C. Overton 3-59). *County debut:* M. J. Leach. *Somerset chose from 16 players and the South Africans 13, of whom 11 could bat and 11 field. Mark Boucher suffered a shocking injury when a bail lacerated his left eyeball on the opening afternoon, forcing his immediate retirement from all cricket. He was standing up without the protection of a helmet when the last delivery of the 46th over, a fast googly from Imran Tahir, beat Gemaal Hussain's swipe and sent the off bail flying up into Boucher's face. His team-mates, understandably distracted, did not take another wicket before Somerset declared. Trego's hundred was forgotten in the circumstances, but it was a minor masterpiece, from just 60 balls; he hit Morne Morkel's first six deliveries for four. Coming together at 32-4, Trego and stand-in captain Hildreth added 183 in 24 overs. Amla top-scored for South Africa… not for the last time on the tour.*

Ben Hoskins, Getty Images

Mark Boucher suffers his shocking injury at Taunton when a bail lacerates his left eyeball.

KENT v SOUTH AFRICANS

At Canterbury, July 13–15. Drawn. Toss: South Africans.

Bad weather, and the positive approach of Kent's young homegrown opening pair, restricted the South Africans' scope for batting practice in their second and final warm-up match before the First Test. Northeast, the 22-year-old acting-captain, and Bell-Drummond, not quite 19, started the match with a stand of 81, and ended it with an unbroken 105 to wipe out the deficit. In Kent's first innings, the last seven wickets fell for 86 as Morne Morkel and Imran Tahir, with his best figures for his adopted country, found their range. Rain permitted only 22 overs on the second day, but the South African top seven all spent at least half an hour at the crease.

Close of play: first day, South Africans 31-1 (Petersen 8, Amla 1); second day, South Africans 108-2 (Amla 36, Kallis 23).

Kent

*S. A. Northeast c Smith b Steyn	35	– not out	54
D. J. Bell-Drummond c de Villiers b Morkel	42	– not out	48
B. W. Harmison lbw b Philander	14		
M. J. Powell not out	48		
A. J. Blake lbw b Morkel	9		
†S. W. Billings c Kallis b Duminy	13		
M. T. Coles c Kallis b Imran Tahir	21		
S. J. Cook c de Villiers b Morkel	13		
A. E. N. Riley b Imran Tahir	0		
I. A. A. Thomas b Imran Tahir	0		
C. E. Shreck c Smith b Imran Tahir	2		
B 2, l-b 7, w 1, n-b 3	13	N-b 3	3
1/81 (1) 2/92 (2) 3/105 (3) (74.2 overs)	210	(no wkt, 22 overs)	105

4/124 (5) 5/146 (6) 6/173 (7)
7/191 (8) 8/192 (9) 9/208 (10) 10/210 (11)

Steyn 14–5–42–1; Philander 15–1–52–1; Morkel 18–5–49–3; Imran Tahir 14.2–3–31–4; Kallis 8–4–8–0; Duminy 5–0–19–1. *Second innings*—Morkel 4–1–22–0; Philander 4–0–16–0; Kallis 3–0–25–0; Steyn 4–1–16–0; Duminy 4–0–11–0; Imran Tahir 3–0–15–0.

South Africans

*G. C. Smith c Billings b Shreck	21
A. N. Petersen lbw b Cook	21
H. M. Amla retired out	77
J. H. Kallis retired out	54
†A. B. de Villiers c Bell-Drummond b Coles	14
J. A. Rudolph c and b Riley	50
J-P. Duminy b Thomas	34
V. D. Philander c Riley b Shreck	0
D. W. Steyn lbw b Riley	4
M. Morkel lbw b Shreck	16
Imran Tahir not out	0
B 4, l-b 10, w 8, n-b 1	23
1/29 (1) 2/74 (2) 3/180 (3) 4/180 (4) 5/208 (5) 6/265 (7) 7/266 (8) 8/282 (9) 9/303 (6) 10/314 (10) (93 overs)	314

Shreck 24–2–90–3; Thomas 19–4–59–1; Coles 13–2–51–1; Cook 12–5–19–1; Riley 18–2–70–2; Blake 1–0–1–0; Harmison 6–1–10–0.

Umpires: J. H. Evans and T. E. Jesty.

ENGLAND v SOUTH AFRICA

First Investec Test

HUGH CHEVALLIER

At The Oval, July 19–23. South Africa won by an innings and 12 runs. Toss: England.

On a warm Sunday evening, a beery roar spread across the ground: four blokes in yellow jerseys and fake sideburns were basking in vicarious glory after news arrived from Paris that the real Bradley Wiggins – also sporting a yellow jersey, but more authentic facial hair – had been officially crowned as the first Briton to win the Tour de France.

Spectators were in the mood for applause, since they had seen a tour de force themselves. There are few clearer proofs of a batsman's mental strength or physical adaptability than a Test triple-century, and minutes earlier Hashim Amla had become the first South African to breathe such rarefied air. For at least four reasons it was a genuinely great achievement: with Petersen gone for nought, it was born in adversity; it came away from home against the team rated best in the world; it was an innings of real beauty, with shots played all round the wicket, off front foot and back; and, like only nine of the previous 25 Test triples, it would lead to victory.

VICTORY AFTER LOSING ONLY TWO WICKETS

England (531-2 dec) beat South Africa (273 & 240) by an inns & 18 runs at Lord's	1924
England (267-2 dec) beat New Zealand (67 & 129) by an inns & 71 runs at Leeds	1958
England (459-2 dec) beat India (165 & 216) by an inns & 78 runs at Birmingham	1974
South Africa (470-2 dec) beat Bangladesh (173 & 237) by an inns & 60 runs at Chittagong	2003
South Africa (637-2 dec) beat England (385 & 240) by an inns & 12 runs at The Oval	**2012**

Ian Kingston, AFP, Getty Images

At ease... Hashim Amla's technique in his record-breaking 311 was occasionally divine.

In fact it led to more than that: it led to annihilation. No one was sure when England had been so utterly outflanked, though Hastings in 1066 was a possibility. In losing by an innings, Strauss's team scraped just two wickets, and one of those – Smith bowled via bat and pad – was a touch fluky. Between the dismissal of Ravi Rampaul, West Indies' No. 10, at Edgbaston in June and the end of this Test, England had taken three wickets, once every 260 runs. As the marauding South Africans raced towards their first victory at The Oval, their pack downed batsmen at an average cost of only 31.

After England's eventual marmalising, it was hard to recall the optimism of the first day. The word was that South Africa were undercooked and, without Mark Boucher, had lost their soul. De Villiers, the regular one-day keeper, took the gloves, in his 75th consecutive Test – so equalling Boucher's national record.

The Oval, which was hosting the First Test while Lord's geared up for Olympic archery, had seen endless rain before the game. Another shower delayed the start by 15 minutes, but Strauss, wary of a pitch expected to deteriorate, batted anyway. He immediately faced Morkel (handed the new ball in preference to Steyn) from round the wicket. The fourth delivery struck Strauss – a serial Morkel victim – on the pads, and Smith, utterly convinced of the shout, successfully challenged the not-out decision.

The next breakthrough, though, was a while coming. Philander had bolted to 50 Test wickets from 1,240 balls, quicker than anyone, but now he went wicketless through a whole day for the first time. Steyn, No. 1 in the world rankings, fared no better as the South Africans failed to wake a comatose surface. With the fielding similarly sleepy, imaginary scoreboards whirred inside spectators' heads: England would surely make 500, 600 – perhaps even 700. So it was a shock when Trott drove airily, ending his 170-run stand with Cook, who would go on to his 20th Test century, almost a year after his 19th. Still, Pietersen wouldn't waste such an opportunity, would he? Er, yes. With England in apparent control at 251 for two and the new ball available in moments, he followed an innocuous leg-side bouncer and gloved Kallis to de Villiers.

Next morning, a change in the weather meant England, after sailing serenely through the first day, were suddenly blown on to the rocks. Clouds loured over Kennington, making

the ball as skittish as a kitten. Out went a defensive line wide of off; in came vicious, intimidating swing. First overboard was Cook, dragging a loose drive into his stumps. He had played just one other false stroke: a top-edged hook that brought his first six in his 45 home Tests.

Bopara, replacing Jonny Bairstow in the problematic No. 6 spot, botched his return. Leaving his bat pointing skywards like an abandoned periscope, he was caught in two minds about hooking – and behind for a duck. Bell, though, was beaten by classic Kallis. After two outswingers, he left what he thought was a third. But the ball shaped back in to kiss the off bail: England had nosedived from their overnight 267 for three to 284 for six. Prior counterpunched, but the truth was that six of the top eight fell to soft dismissals, and their total of 385 was more a statement of what might have been than of intent.

When Anderson aped Kallis to despatch Petersen for nought (away + away + in = out), England's failings looked pardonable. But rain that fell just after tea washed more than the players from the field. When cricket resumed at 5.55, it became clear that any scintilla of movement had gone too – at least when England had the ball. Just before the close, Amla, on 40, slashed hard at Bopara. Strauss, the lone slip, fell back to earth with stinging fingertips. As drops go, it was forgivable, but costly.

The left-handed Smith was initially unsettled by Swann, so he eschewed all risk by lunging defensively forward or playing from the crease – a viable option against such sluggish turn. The result was a fifty high on determination and low on aesthetics; at 160 balls, it was his slowest in Tests. (His next fifty, though, came from just 41, as he became the seventh player to mark his 100th Test with a century.) Session merged into session as milestone after milestone slipped by under increasingly blue skies: 200 stand, 100 for Amla, 250 stand…

HUNDRED IN 100TH TEST

M. C. Cowdrey	104	England v Australia at Birmingham	1968
Javed Miandad	145	Pakistan v India at Lahore	1989-90
C. G. Greenidge	149	West Indies v England at St John's	1989-90
A. J. Stewart	105	England v West Indies at Manchester	2000
Inzamam-ul-Haq	184	Pakistan v India at Bangalore	2004-05
R. T. Ponting	120 & 143*	Australia v South Africa at Sydney	2005-06
G. C. Smith	**131**	**South Africa v England at The Oval**	**2012**

On the third afternoon, Smith finally made way for Kallis. Not that it made a ha'p'orth of difference: the England bowlers were as threatening as blancmange – though with distinctly less wobble. Still, Strauss did manage a laugh when his throw smashed the sunglasses that had just slipped from his sunhat, a mishap oddly emblematic of England's plight. More century landmarks peppered play on the fourth day, with the bowlers joining in: 100 for Anderson, 200 for Amla, 100s for Bresnan, Swann and Kallis (his 43rd in Tests), 200 stand…

Amla, who had chosen to defer his Ramadan fast, had an insatiable appetite for runs: on the attack, he was strong, elegant and wristy, while his defence, forward or back, was neat, fluent and commanding. No single shot stood out, but that was testament to his all-round dominance. Against Swann, Amla lingered outside off and played him to leg so effortlessly that the bowler ended with none for 151. And his partner was the Kallis so rarely glimpsed in England – the batsman with oodles of time and every shot in the book… 500 up, 250 for Amla, 250 stand, 300 stand, Amla to 281 (beating de Villiers's national record), 150 for Kallis, 600 up…

Four balls later, in the 184th over, Amla lofted a drive over extra cover. It took him past 300, and from the most exuberant beard in Test cricket there flashed a mile-wide smile. By the time Smith declared at tea, earlier than many expected, Amla had faced 529 balls.

LONGEST TEST INNINGS

Mins	*Balls*			
970	–	Hanif Mohammad (337)	Pakistan v West Indies at Bridgetown	1957-58
878	642	G. Kirsten (275)	South Africa v England at Durban	1999-2000
799	578	S. T. Jayasuriya (340)	Sri Lanka v India at Colombo (RPS)	1997-98
797	847	L. Hutton (364)	England v Australia at The Oval	1938
790	**529**	**H. M. Amla (311*)**	**South Africa v England at The Oval**	**2012**
778	582	B. C. Lara (400*)	West Indies v England at St John's	2003-04
777	548	D. S. B. P. Kuruppu (201*)	Sri Lanka v New Zealand at Colombo (CCC)	1986-87
773	545	A. N. Cook (294)	England v India at Birmingham	2011

Note: Hanif believes he batted 999 minutes. The number of balls he faced is not recorded.

It wasn't quite chanceless – no marathon stretching to 13 hours and ten minutes, the longest undefeated innings in Test history, could possibly be – but it was studded with 35 fours. It was the first triple in England since Graham Gooch's 333 at Lord's in 1990, the first by a visiting batsman since Bobby Simpson's 311 for Australia at Old Trafford in 1964, and unforgettable for its calmness, placement and concentration.

England, trailing by 252, had four sessions in which to save the game. On a pitch that for almost 48 hours had refused bowlers so much as the time of day, it should have been within their compass. Yet the South Africans *did* find movement, and for the third innings in a row an opener fell for a duck. When Pietersen, unsettled by Morkel's aggression, lost his middle stump playing inside a straight one, England were 57 for three. That became 67 for four after a nervy sweep from Strauss looped to backward square leg.

Next morning Bopara, looking to belt the leather off a ball better ignored, dragged on, ending a responsible fifty stand. Bell, however, continued the restraint, and with Prior began to hatch an unlikely escape. He inched his way to 50 from 189 deliveries – like Smith, his slowest in Tests – only to be undermined an hour or so after lunch when Prior could resist the sweep no longer: Kallis snapped up the game's first slip catch as England lost another wicket of their own making. Once Steyn removed Bell with the new ball to leave them 210 for seven, the end was near. With England nine down at 3.40, tea was delayed, and the last wicket came at 3.58. It was a minor inconvenience for South Africa; in truth, England weren't much more trouble.

Man of the Match: H. M. Amla. *Attendance:* 103,387.

Close of play: first day, England 267-3 (Cook 114, Bell 10); second day, South Africa 86-1 (Smith 37, Amla 47); third day, South Africa 403-2 (Amla 183, Kallis 82); fourth day, England 102-4 (Bell 14, Bopara 15).

England

*A. J. Strauss lbw b Morkel	0	– c Philander b Imran Tahir	27
A. N. Cook b Steyn	115	– c de Villiers b Philander	0
I. J. L. Trott c de Villiers b Morkel	71	– c de Villiers b Steyn	10
K. P. Pietersen c de Villiers b Kallis	42	– b Morkel	16
I. R. Bell b Kallis	13	– c Kallis b Steyn	55
R. S. Bopara c de Villiers b Steyn	0	– b Steyn	22
†M. J. Prior c de Villiers b Morkel	60	– c Kallis b Imran Tahir	40
T. T. Bresnan b Imran Tahir	8	– not out	20
S. C. J. Broad b Philander	16	– c de Villiers b Steyn	0
G. P. Swann not out	15	– c Petersen b Steyn	7
J. M. Anderson c de Villiers b Morkel	2	– lbw b Imran Tahir	4
B 2, l-b 24, w 3, n-b 14	43	B 11, l-b 15, w 1, n-b 12	39
1/0 (1) 2/170 (3) 3/251 (4) 4/271 (2) 5/272 (6) 6/284 (5) 7/313 (8) 8/358 (9) 9/383 (7) 10/385 (11) (125.5 overs)	385	1/2 (2) 2/32 (3) 3/57 (4) 4/67 (1) 5/117 (6) 6/203 (7) 7/210 (5) 8/210 (9) 9/218 (10) 10/240 (11) (97 overs)	240

Morkel 24.5–2–72–4; Philander 27–4–79–1; Steyn 30–7–99–2; Kallis 19–7–38–2; Imran Tahir 19–0–61–1; Duminy 6–1–10–0. *Second innings*—Morkel 16–0–41–1; Philander 19–6–29–1; Steyn 21–6–56–5; Imran Tahir 32–7–63–3; Kallis 7–1–22–0; Duminy 2–1–3–0.

South Africa

*G. C. Smith b Bresnan	131
A. N. Petersen lbw b Anderson	0
H. M. Amla not out	311
J. H. Kallis not out	182
B 5, l-b 4, w 2, n-b 2	13
1/1 (2) 2/260 (1) (2 wkts dec, 189 overs)	637

†A. B. de Villiers, J. A. Rudolph, J-P. Duminy, V. D. Philander, D. W. Steyn, M. Morkel and Imran Tahir did not bat.

Anderson 41–7–116–1; Broad 34–6–118–0; Swann 52–10–151–0; Bresnan 37–2–140–1; Bopara 18–1–78–0; Pietersen 3–0–13–0; Trott 4–0–12–0.

Umpires: Asad Rauf and S. J. Davis. Third umpire: H. D. P. K. Dharmasena.

FIVE STATS YOU MAY HAVE MISSED FROM THE OVAL

BENEDICT BERMANGE

- Only once before had a team reached 637 for the loss of two wickets: Sri Lanka lost their third wicket at 638 v South Africa at Colombo (SSC) in 2006, after Kumar Sangakkara and Mahela Jayawardene put on a world-record partnership of 624.
- England scored 31.25 runs per wicket, South Africa 318.50. The difference (287.25) was greater than for any other Test played to a result.
- South Africa's win was their first at The Oval, after six defeats and seven draws. That was the worst record by any Test team at any venue, which then passed to Bangladesh's at the Zahur Ahmed Chowdhury Stadium in Chittagong, where they are without a win in ten matches.
- Jacques Kallis's stand of 377 with Hashim Amla was his 20th involvement in a partnership of 200 or more, more than any other Test batsman:

20	**J. H. Kallis (SA)**	**17**	**R. T. Ponting (A)**	14	D. G. Bradman (A)
18	S. R. Tendulkar (I)	15	R. Dravid (I)	**14**	**G. C. Smith (SA)**

- Graeme Swann's figures were the third-worst for England in a Test innings:

		Style		
49–9–169–0	A. P. Freeman†	LBG	v South Africa at The Oval	1929
57–14–152–0	P. I. Pocock	OB	v West Indies at Kingston	1973-74
52–10–151–0	**G. P. Swann**	**OB**	**v South Africa at The Oval**	**2012**
36–9–146–0	A. R. Caddick	RFM	v Australia at The Oval	2001
29.3–3–143–0	C. M. Old	RFM	v Pakistan at The Oval	1974
61–10–143–0	J. E. Emburey	OB	v Pakistan at The Oval	1987
33–6–142–0	D. E. Malcolm	RF	v West Indies at Bridgetown	1989-90
*36–4–142–0	J. J. Warr‡	RFM	v Australia at Sydney	1950-51
33–1–140–0	C. C. Lewis	RFM	v West Indies at St John's	1993-94

* *Eight-ball overs.* † *Last Test.* ‡ *Test debut.*

At Worcester, July 27–28 (not first-class). **Drawn.** ‡**South Africans 237-9 dec** (A. B. de Villiers 80, J. A. Morkel 50; C. J. Russell 3-40) **and 67-4** (C. J. Russell 3-32); **Worcestershire 245** (M. G. Pardoe 53, A. Kapil 67; R. J. Peterson 4-65). *County debut:* J. Leach. *Each side chose from 12 players, of whom 11 could bat and 11 field. Worcestershire played their part in preventing batsmen who had either failed or been denied an innings in the run-spree at The Oval from getting time at the crease: Rudolph, Petersen and Duminy mustered only 63 between them across both innings. That was mainly due to Chris Russell, a 23-year-old seamer yet to play a first-class match, who twice took three top-order wickets. Worcestershire even claimed a narrow first-innings lead, spurred on by a 44-ball half-century from Aneesh Kapil.*

ENGLAND v SOUTH AFRICA

Second Investec Test

LAWRENCE BOOTH

At Leeds, August 2–6. Drawn. Toss: England. Test debut: J. W. A. Taylor.

An absorbing Test was played out against the weird and not-so-wonderful backdrop of the Kevin Pietersen saga. Or was it the other way round? By the end – as Pietersen followed a typically dazzling 149 on Saturday afternoon with a Monday evening press conference full of cryptic self-pity – it was hard to say: the distinction between plot and subplot had become hopelessly blurred. And with the Olympic athletes down in joyful London resembling one big happy family, the dysfunctional England dressing-room felt depressingly out of kilter.

The facts, though, were these: needing victory to stand a chance of extending their sequence of Test series wins at home to a record eight, England could manage only a draw, despite briefly threatening something extraordinary on the final day, the fifth in succession to be interrupted by rain or bad light. Pietersen then announced that the Third Test at Lord's – on which England's No. 1 ranking now depended – could well be his last, following a breakdown in relations with his team-mates. When it emerged later in the week that he had sent text messages to the South Africans for which he subsequently felt the need to apologise, he was dropped anyway. Really, you couldn't make it up.

So much for the scandal. As if in deference to later events, the opening morning of the game itself had a chaotic air. Graeme Swann was omitted after 43 successive Tests, and Finn brought in as part of an all-pace attack – England's first since they lost here to South Africa in 2003. If selection was made with a poor weather forecast in mind, then Swann's absence obliged Strauss to bowl after winning the toss. And the move might have paid off, had Cook not dropped a straightforward chance at second slip (Swann's usual position) when Petersen had 29. Then, in the next over, Finn had Smith caught at first slip on six, only for umpire Steve Davis to signal dead ball because the bowler had disturbed the non-striker's stumps with his right knee at the point of delivery.

For Finn, it was a familiar problem, though no one could remember an umpire previously denying him – or indeed anyone else – a wicket by invoking Law 23.4(b)(vi), which relates to batsmen "distracted by any noise or movement". Finn had knocked into the stumps at least three times in his first eight deliveries without interesting Davis, but Smith

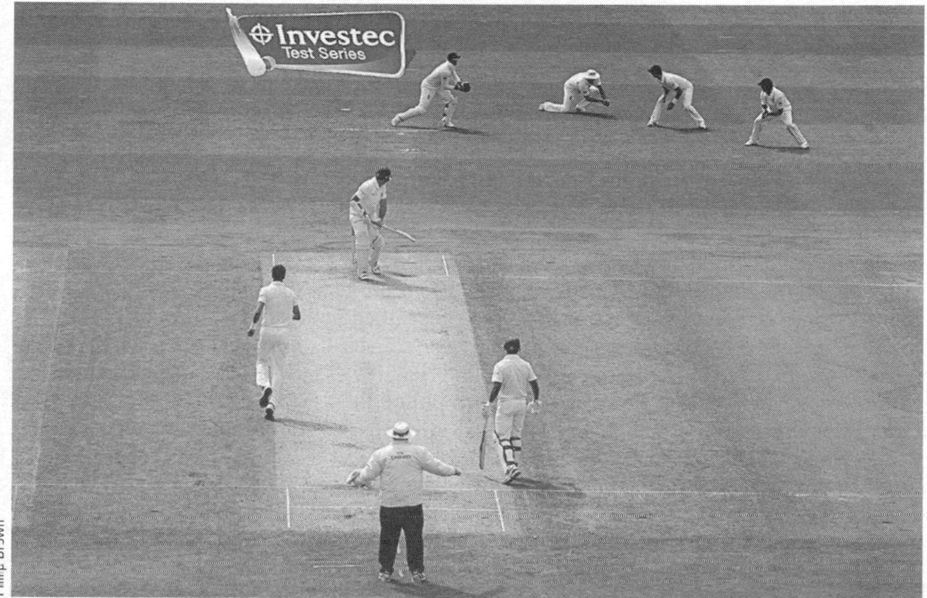

Philip Brown

Steve Davis saves Graeme Smith by signalling dead ball after Steven Finn knocked into the non-striker's stumps; discretion is the better part of valour for the bowler Dale Steyn when Kevin Pietersen cuts loose.

Philip Brown

was now in the umpire's ear, possibly sensing a chance to unsettle his opponent. Obliged to intervene, Davis did so on Finn's ninth ball, a split second before Smith edged it low to Strauss. England were disgruntled, but they might have wondered instead why Finn had not ironed out a long-standing quirk.

Two early wickets could have changed the shape of the game – and the series – but England had to wait until the total reached 120 for their first success: Smith clipped Bresnan to short backward square, where Bell was lurking as part of an elaborate leg-side field. Amla was carelessly run out, going for a third, by Bresnan on the cover boundary, and when Kallis edged Anderson to Cook, who this time held on to a tougher chance,

South Africa were 157 for three and in danger of surrendering the high ground. But Petersen remained resolute, completing a fourth Test hundred that – had it been a piece of rhythmic gymnastics – would have scored more highly for difficulty than artistic merit.

Armed with the second new ball on the first evening, England stayed in touch by striking twice: Broad's first Test wicket in 401 deliveries and nightwatchman Steyn. Pietersen's first contribution was suitably unpredictable as he removed Rudolph with his second ball shortly before lunch on day two, a sharp off-break that immediately called into question the omission of Swann. Petersen, twice reprieved by Hawk-Eye after being given out leg-before on 119 and 124, finally fell for a Test-best 182 after Rod Tucker contrived to miss an edge behind and England asked for a review.

Eventually facing a total of 419 – around 100 more than they might have hoped after South Africa were put in – England survived unscathed until stumps, then slipped to 173 for four moments before tea on the third day. Pietersen had 43 but, when Morkel went round the wicket in the fourth over after the interval, it was as if he had woken the Kraken. Missed on 52 by Amla at short leg, Pietersen pulled the next two balls to the midwicket fence, then drove and carved Steyn for fours. Kallis was pulled for four more, then straight-driven for another. Next over, Pietersen ticked off 7,000 Test runs; six overs after that, he was celebrating his 21st century, pointedly waving his bat in the direction of his wife, Jessica, and only cursorily acknowledging those of his team-mates who had bothered to appear on the dressing-room balcony. His second fifty came from just 52 balls.

He wasn't finished yet. One murderous lofted straight-drive prompted the bowler, Steyn, to take evasive action, à la Lillee to Botham during the other immortal Headingley innings of 149. Soon after, Pietersen dumped him back over his head for six. This was unmissable: for a while, even the West Stand stopped building beer snakes.

Watching from the other end, defending stoutly, was James Taylor, the thimble-sized 22-year-old making his Test debut in place of Ravi Bopara, who had pulled out for personal reasons. In a game-turning stand of 147, Taylor added a compact 34. It was the innings of a high-class stooge, quietly doing his bit while handing the punchlines to Pietersen. The discrepancy in the batsmen's heights, with Pietersen nearly a foot taller, merely emphasised the effect.

Pietersen completed a hundred runs in an elongated final session, but fell second ball on the fourth morning to the persevering Morkel, before Prior helped carve out a six-run lead. With more than five sessions to go, anything seemed possible, only for thunder, lightning and rain to limit South Africa's second innings before stumps to 17 overs.

A draw looked inevitable, even when Pietersen again removed Rudolph – opening because Petersen had a hamstring strain – with his second ball, this time courtesy of a reviewed lbw. After lunch, Pietersen added Smith and Amla, who smacked a full toss to extra cover, at which point Broad took up the baton. Perhaps because he had spent the previous evening watching a DVD of England's miracle win over Sri Lanka at Cardiff in 2011, when the tourists lost eight wickets in a session, and the Test, he was in the mood for a twist: summoning up an extra yard of pace, Broad embarked on a spell of five wickets in 37 balls. Anderson added Steyn and, when Smith made a second successive surprise declaration, England were set 253 in 39 overs: improbable, but maybe not by the standards of an extraordinary week.

Promoted to open, Pietersen managed three fours in seven balls before toe-ending to mid-on, and Strauss – after following him to 7,000 Test runs – hit a full toss back to Duminy. Cook departed for a resourceful 46, and it wasn't until Prior, mysteriously coming in after Strauss and Trott, was run out that England gave up hope of a win. Trott and Bell blocked for an hour before hands were shaken shortly after 7.30pm. Had the weather allowed just one more session, we might have had a thriller. In the event, with Pietersen about to face the press, the fun and games had barely begun.

Man of the Match: K. P. Pietersen. *Attendance:* 54,398.

Close of play: first day, South Africa 262-5 (Petersen 124, Rudolph 1); second day, England 48-0 (Strauss 19, Cook 20); third day, England 351-5 (Pietersen 149, Prior 20); fourth day, South Africa 39-0 (Rudolph 21, Smith 17).

South Africa

First innings		Second innings	
A. N. Petersen c Prior b Broad	182	(8) not out	16
*G. C. Smith c Bell b Bresnan	52	c Taylor b Pietersen	52
H. M. Amla run out	9	c Cook b Pietersen	28
J. H. Kallis c Cook b Anderson	19	(5) c Prior b Broad	27
†A. B. de Villiers b Broad	47	(4) lbw b Broad	44
D. W. Steyn b Finn	0	(9) c and b Anderson	3
J. A. Rudolph st Prior b Pietersen	19	(1) lbw b Pietersen	69
J-P. Duminy not out	48	(6) lbw b Broad	0
V. D. Philander c Bresnan b Finn	13	(7) lbw b Broad	6
M. Morkel c Cook b Broad	19	c Cook b Broad	10
Imran Tahir c Cook b Anderson	0		
B 5, l-b 6	11	L-b 2, w 1	3
1/120 (2) 2/132 (3) 3/157 (4) 4/254 (5) 5/259 (6) 6/318 (7) 7/353 (1) 8/375 (9) 9/414 (10) 10/419 (11) (139.2 overs)	419	1/120 (1) 2/129 (2) 3/182 (3) 4/209 (4) 5/209 (6) 6/223 (7) 7/230 (5) 8/247 (9) 9/258 (10) (9 wkts dec, 67.4 overs)	258

Anderson 33.2–10–61–2; Broad 35–10–96–3; Finn 32–3–118–2; Bresnan 27–4–98–1; Trott 5–1–9–0; Pietersen 7–0–26–1. *Second innings*—Anderson 19–7–40–1; Broad 16.4–2–69–5; Finn 14–2–55–0; Bresnan 9–2–40–0; Pietersen 9–1–52–3.

England

First innings		Second innings	
*A. J. Strauss c de Villiers b Steyn	37	(3) c and b Duminy	22
A. N. Cook lbw b Philander	24	c Rudolph b Steyn	46
I. J. L. Trott c Smith b Steyn	35	(4) not out	30
K. P. Pietersen lbw b Morkel	149	(1) c Imran Tahir b Philander	12
I. R. Bell c Smith b Kallis	11	(6) not out	3
J. W. A. Taylor b Morkel	34		
†M. J. Prior c Steyn b Imran Tahir	68	(5) run out	7
T. T. Bresnan c Smith b Philander	9		
S. C. J. Broad c sub (F. du Plessis) b Imran Tahir	1		
J. M. Anderson b Imran Tahir	8		
S. T. Finn not out	0		
B 7, l-b 17, w 14, n-b 11	49	L-b 8, w 1, n-b 1	10
1/65 (2) 2/85 (1) 3/142 (3) 4/173 (5) 5/320 (6) 6/351 (4) 7/396 (8) 8/407 (9) 9/420 (7) 10/425 (10) (126.4 overs)	425	1/21 (1) 2/75 (3) 3/90 (2) 4/106 (5) (4 wkts, 33 overs)	130

Morkel 32–9–96–2; Philander 30–10–72–2; Steyn 28–8–102–2; Kallis 12–3–34–1; Imran Tahir 23.4–0–92–3; Duminy 1–0–5–0. *Second innings*—Morkel 10–4–33–0; Philander 6–1–26–1; Steyn 7–1–26–1; Imran Tahir 4–0–20–0; Duminy 2–0–10–1; Kallis 4–2–7–0.

Umpires: S. J. Davis and R. J. Tucker. Third umpire: Asad Rauf.

At Derby, August 10–11 (not first-class). **Drawn. South Africans 365-4 dec** (J-P. Duminy 69, A. B. de Villiers 97, F. du Plessis 68*) **and 168-7 dec** (V. D. Philander 68*; M. H. A. Footitt 4-38); **Derbyshire 174-9 dec** (R. A. Whiteley 51*; L. L. Tsotsobe 4-45). *County debut:* A. C. Evans. *Derbyshire chose from 14 players and the South Africans 15, of whom 11 could bat and 11 field. The first day produced 440 runs for five wickets, the second 267 for 16. After the South Africans batted first by mutual agreement, de Villiers hit a fine 97 before tucking his bat under his arm and retiring out – testimony to his superstition that a batsman has only a certain number of hundreds in him, and now was not an occasion to use one up. The South Africans, satisfied with the first innings, shook up their batting order in the second: Philander, despite a blow to the nether regions, hit out for a half-century from No. 7.*

ENGLAND v SOUTH AFRICA

Third Investec Test

STEVEN LYNCH

At Lord's, August 16–20. South Africa won by 51 runs. Toss: South Africa.

When a brainless run-out reduced England to 45 for four on the last morning, still 300 adrift, embarrassment loomed – and with it the tame surrender of the No. 1 ranking in Test cricket. They did lose in the end, but only after a thrilling fightback which briefly persuaded an enthralled, engaged crowd that a miracle was possible.

Jonny Bairstow, playing because Kevin Pietersen had been dropped for textual impropriety, lit the blue touchpaper with a 41-ball fifty, Prior and Broad carried on the fight, and Swann swung freely. After tea, 61 runs cascaded from 41 deliveries, but just as Smith – captaining in a Test for a record 94th time – was beginning to look nervous, Swann was narrowly run out, after lashing five fours and two sixes. And, despite a manic episode when the swashbuckling Prior was caught in the covers, then reprieved just before reaching the Pavilion because replays showed Morkel had overstepped, the frolics were about to end. Shortly afterwards, Prior really was out, and Finn went first ball, both victims of the bouncy Philander, who thus added a five-for to two vital batting contributions.

It had been a spirited retort by England, but victory was always tantalisingly out of reach, mainly because of the sort of self-inflicted wounds – especially run-outs and dropped catches – which typified their performances. The result meant a first home series defeat since the loss to South Africa in 2008, and their sixth in 11 Test matches anywhere since reaching No. 1 themselves a year previously.

The last day provided a fitting conclusion to an absorbing match, conducted on a blameless pitch which, 17 days previously, had been the domain of Olympic archers. Around a third of the outfield had been returfed, after temporary stands were removed, with grass grown near Scunthorpe – an Olympian effort of their own from the groundstaff. Away from Lord's, though, the build-up was dominated by the omission of Pietersen: many wondered how the 149 runs he had scored in the first innings at Headingley could be adequately replaced. Bairstow provided the answer, duly scoring 149 runs in the match, and batting with character and chutzpah.

The imbroglio clearly affected the tight-lipped England camp, however. Strauss, playing in his 100th Test – and captaining for the 50th time – admitted as much afterwards. "It's been a tough week," he said, before reflecting on England's poor run in 2012: "We've lost a lot more than we would have wanted to. Whether it was because of a change of mindset – from being the hunters to the ones that are hunted – I don't know." Nine days later, he announced his retirement.

Controversy was temporarily forgotten, though, as South Africa dipped to 54 for four after choosing to bat on an overcast first morning. Three of them went to Finn, who displayed a Glenn McGrath-like mastery of the Lord's slope to defeat Amla, although the wickets of Petersen and Kallis were less classical, both involving leg-side gloves. Petersen's bottom hand was probably still in contact with the bat handle when it was hit, but third umpire Rod Tucker's decision to overrule his on-field colleague Kumar Dharmasena in the case of Kallis looked like a blooper: *his* bottom hand was indisputably off the handle when Finn's rib-tickler cannoned into it.

South Africa overcame their indignation, regrouping through gritty contributions from Rudolph and Duminy. A maiden half-century from Philander took them past 300, before he became Prior's sixth victim of the innings – and the second for Swann, restored to the side, complete with severe 1950s haircut, in place of Tim Bresnan. There were three wickets for Anderson, but Broad – in his 50th Test – was a little below his usual pace: England might have wished they had opted instead for Graham Onions, who was released from the squad after the toss, drove up to Trent Bridge, and took nine for 67 for Durham).

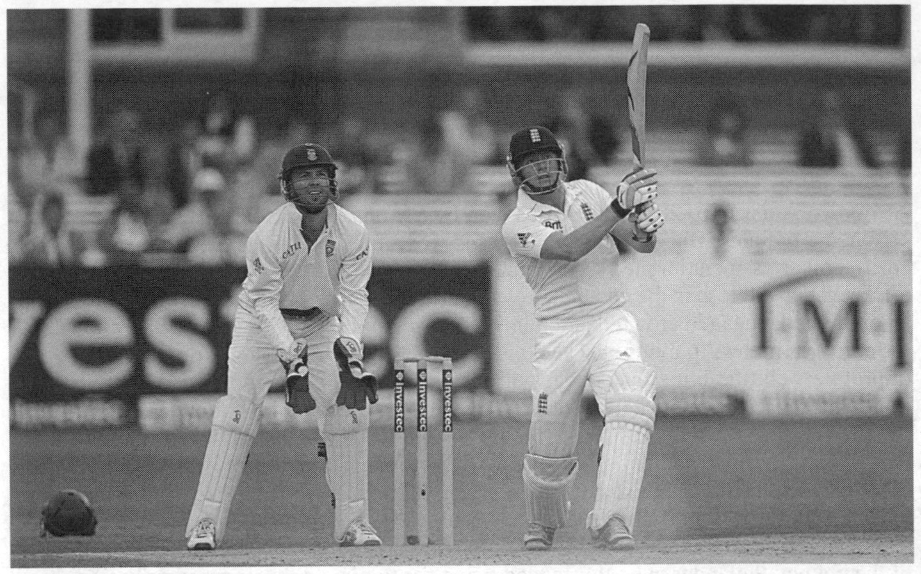

Filling Pietersen's shoes… and his own boots: Jonny Bairstow trusts his instincts during his first-innings 95.

Midway through the second day, England were also 54 for four, before a rescue act of their own. Bairstow had been labelled susceptible to the short ball during the West Indies series, but survived a thorough examination from Steyn and Morkel. Tall and slender, though wide-shouldered, as if he'd left the coat-hanger in place, Bairstow played his natural attacking game, adding 124 with Bell to calm English nerves. Bell was well caught at third slip ten overs before the close, but Bairstow survived, having mixed in the occasional fierce cut with his signature peachy on-drives. Next morning, though, he tried one too many after being tied down for 14 balls on 95, and was bowled by the impressive Morkel. England had been closing in on South Africa's total; they seemed unlikely to get there when Anderson lobbed a catch to gully at 283. But, to wild applause, the last pair inched them level, then just past: as at Headingley, they led by six.

South Africa were quickly back in front, though initial progress was slow. Smith hit only two fours in his first 61 deliveries before cutting Swann to the rope, then was lbw next ball. Shortly afterwards came a match-changing moment: Amla flicked at a leg-side delivery from Broad, Prior covered the ground well but almost overshot the ball, which hit him on the base of the left palm and bounced away. Amla had two at the time and – though Broad was partly mollified when he trapped Petersen in front two deliveries later – he survived to score 119 more.

Batting with the sort of calm, wristy elegance patented by Ranji, Amla did not give another chance. A devout Muslim, he celebrated the festival of Eid with his 16th Test century, and it was a surprise when, halfway through the fourth day, he was again castled by a superb delivery from Finn which this time went up the hill a little. By then de Villiers had also been dropped – on eight, when he chipped a simple chance to Anderson at short midwicket off Swann – and the lead was past 250.

De Villiers advanced to 43 before Strauss clasped his 121st Test catch, to pass the England record previously shared by Colin Cowdrey and Ian Botham. Finn also removed Rudolph during a fine spell of three for 14 in 29 balls. The previous evening he had dismissed Kallis for 31, oddly his highest score in three Tests at Lord's: it remained a statistical curiosity that, of Test cricket's five leading run-scorers, only one (Rahul Dravid in 2011) had scored a century there. Kallis immediately reviewed his lbw decision, but had to walk off, disgusted by the DRS for the second time in the match (the snickometer,

Gareth Copley, Getty Images

Last rites: Vernon Philander removes Steven Finn to complete South Africa's emphatic series win.

not part of the review process, later raised the possibility of a faint nick). Kallis cheered himself up by holding on to a couple of screamers in the slips – including one to end the match – and also took his 50th wicket against England to join an exclusive club.

Finn's spell revived England, but hopes of a swift end – and a more realistic run-chase – were stymied by Philander, who made a forthright 35. Duminy, who survived for 141 minutes, was still there when Anderson, bowling well throughout for little reward, wrapped

JACQUES OF ALL TRADES

1,000 runs and 50 wickets in Tests against England:

	Tests	*Runs*	*Avge*	*Wkts*	*Avge*
W. W. Armstrong (A)	42	2,172	35.03	74	30.91
G. Giffen (A)	31	1,238	23.35	103	27.09
T. L. Goddard (SA)	20	1,193	30.58	63	25.74
J. H. Kallis (SA)	**31**	**2,141**	**44.60**	**50**	**35.50**
Kapil Dev (I)	27	1,355	41.06	85	37.34
K. R. Miller (A)	29	1,511	33.57	87	22.40
M. A. Noble (A)	39	1,905	30.72	115	24.86
G. S. Sobers (WI)	36	3,214	60.64	102	32.57

things up with two late wickets. The first of them was his 50th in Tests at Lord's: only Ian Botham (69) and Fred Trueman (63) had more.

The target of 346 soon looked far distant when Cook was struck in front, then Strauss – possibly betraying the effects of an enervating week – let one go which was destined to flatten middle stump. The overnight 16 for two got worse when Bell was caught, after a juggle, at first slip, and most of the ground groaned when Trott pushed towards wide long-on, but declined a perfectly feasible fourth run: Taylor, in only his second Test, was stranded – "well stuffed by Trott", lamented the watching Michael Vaughan.

There seemed no way back after that – and indeed there wasn't, especially against a side as strong as South Africa, worthy claimants of the ICC Test mace. But England showed enough fight during a classic match, conducted almost throughout in sizzling temperatures, to show why they had been the previous holders.

Man of the Match: V. D. Philander. *Attendance:* 123,555.

Men of the Series: England – M. J. Prior; South Africa – H. M. Amla.

Close of play: first day, South Africa 262-7 (Philander 46, Steyn 21); second day, England 208-5 (Bairstow 72, Prior 22); third day, South Africa 145-3 (Amla 57, Steyn 0); fourth day, England 16-2 (Trott 6, Bell 4).

South Africa

*G. C. Smith c Prior b Anderson	14	– (2) lbw b Swann	23
A. N. Petersen c Prior b Finn	22	– (1) lbw b Broad	24
H. M. Amla b Finn	13	– b Finn	121
J. H. Kallis c Prior b Finn	3	– lbw b Finn	31
†A. B. de Villiers c Cook b Anderson	27	– (6) c Strauss b Finn	43
J. A. Rudolph b Swann	42	– (7) c Prior b Finn	11
J-P. Duminy c Prior b Anderson	61	– (8) not out	26
V. D. Philander st Prior b Swann	61	– (9) c Bairstow b Anderson	35
D. W. Steyn c Swann b Broad	26	– (5) c Taylor b Broad	9
M. Morkel c Prior b Finn	25	– st Prior b Swann	9
Imran Tahir not out	2	– b Anderson	1
B 7, l-b 5, w 1	13	B 6, l-b 8, w 2, n-b 2	18
1/22 (1) 2/49 (2) 3/50 (3) 4/54 (4) 5/105 (5) 6/163 (6) 7/235 (7) 8/270 (9) 9/307 (10) 10/309 (8) (101.2 overs)	309	1/46 (2) 2/50 (1) 3/131 (4) 4/164 (5) 5/259 (3) 6/268 (6) 7/282 (7) 8/336 (9) 9/348 (10) 10/351 (11) (124.2 overs)	351

Anderson 29–5–76–3; Broad 24–4–69–1; Finn 18–2–75–4; Swann 24.2–6–63–2; Trott 6–1–14–0. *Second innings*—Anderson 25.2–4–73–2; Broad 21–2–85–2; Swann 47–14–94–2; Finn 27–5–74–4; Trott 4–0–11–0.

England

*A. J. Strauss b Morkel	20	– lbw b Philander	1
A. N. Cook c Kallis b Steyn	7	– lbw b Philander	3
I. J. L. Trott lbw b Steyn	8	– c Kallis b Steyn	63
I. R. Bell c Petersen b Philander	58	– c Smith b Philander	4
J. W. A. Taylor c Smith b Morkel	10	– run out	4
J. M. Bairstow b Morkel	95	– b Imran Tahir	54
†M. J. Prior c Kallis b Philander	27	– c Smith b Philander	73
S. C. J. Broad c Amla b Steyn	16	– c Amla b Kallis	37
G. P. Swann not out	37	– run out	41
J. M. Anderson c Rudolph b Steyn	12	– not out	4
S. T. Finn c Duminy b Morkel	10	– c Kallis b Philander	0
L-b 10, w 1, n-b 4	15	B 7, w 2, n-b 1	10
1/29 (1) 2/38 (3) 3/39 (2) 4/54 (5) 5/178 (4) 6/221 (7) 7/252 (8) 8/264 (6) 9/283 (10) 10/315 (11) (107.3 overs)	315	1/5 (2) 2/6 (1) 3/34 (4) 4/45 (5) 5/134 (6) 6/146 (3) 7/208 (8) 8/282 (9) 9/294 (7) 10/294 (11) (82.5 overs)	294

Morkel 28.3–6–80–4; Philander 24–9–48–2; Steyn 29–4–94–4; Kallis 12–3–29–0; Imran Tahir 14–3–54–0. *Second innings*—Morkel 17–3–58–0; Philander 14.5–4–30–5; Steyn 16–4–61–1; Kallis 11–2–50–1; Imran Tahir 24–3–88–1.

Umpires: H. D. P. K. Dharmasena and S. J. A. Taufel. Third umpire: R. J. Tucker.
Series referee: J. J. Crowe.

At Bristol, August 22. **South Africans won by three wickets. Gloucestershire 261** (49.5 overs) (D. M. Housego 132; R. McLaren 3-29); ‡**South Africans 262-7** (49 overs) (R. S. Bopara 3-43). *County debut:* R. S. Bopara. *When Gloucestershire issued an appeal for a guest player to spice up this fixture, the ECB volunteered Ravi Bopara – desperate for a score after a miserable run of form and problems in his personal life. He failed again, making three from 14 balls before nicking Ryan McLaren behind, but kept the run-chase interesting by taking three wickets. The South Africans were made to work for victory by a maiden one-day hundred from the confident Dan Housego, who had been discarded by Middlesex over the winter.*

LIMITED-OVERS INTERNATIONAL REPORTS BY SAM PETERS

ENGLAND v SOUTH AFRICA

First One-Day International

At Cardiff, August 24. No result. Toss: South Africa. One-day international debut: D. Elgar.

Fittingly for a series that would never escape the shadow of Kevin Pietersen's will-he-won't-he circus, the absent batsman chose the day of its opening match to announce he would be in Sri Lanka for the upcoming World Twenty20 as a TV pundit. There would have been precious little for him to analyse here as the miserable weather struck again. No fewer than six inspections were made, but play did not get under way until 3pm, by when the game had been reduced to 24 overs a side. Only 5.3 were possible, and Bell played a little gem of an innings, hitting 26 not out in 18 balls, including two sweet sixes off Morkel. Since beating Australia in July, England had reached the top of the ICC's one-day rankings, a fraction ahead of South Africa, following the annual update that cleared out old results from the calculations. The lack of a result maintained that No. 1 ranking – for the time being at least.

Attendance: 13,992.

England

*A. N. Cook not out	10
I. R. Bell not out	26
W 1	1
(no wkt, 5.3 overs)	37
	5 overs: 32-0

I. J. L. Trott, R. S. Bopara, E. J. G. Morgan, †C. Kieswetter, T. T. Bresnan, C. R. Woakes, G. P. Swann, J. M. Anderson and S. T. Finn did not bat.

Morkel 3–0–19–0; Tsotsobe 2.3–0–18–0.

South Africa

G. C. Smith, H. M. Amla, J-P. Duminy, D. Elgar, *†A. B. de Villiers, F. du Plessis, W. D. Parnell, R. McLaren, R. J. Peterson, M. Morkel and L. L. Tsotsobe.

Umpires: H. D. P. K. Dharmasena and R. A. Kettleborough. Third umpire: S. J. A. Taufel.

ENGLAND v SOUTH AFRICA

Second One-Day International

At Southampton, August 28 (day/night). South Africa won by 80 runs. Toss: South Africa.

Amla produced a masterclass of precision strokeplay to ensure South Africa became the first side to top the world rankings in all three formats simultaneously (they had overtaken England in the Twenty20 table in the same annual update that had benefited England in one-day internationals). He continued his superb Test form with a wonderfully crafted 150 from 124 balls. England's display, however, was easily their worst at home during Cook's one-day captaincy; at one stage, it looked as if Pietersen, who was busy making 163 in 168 balls for Surrey in the Championship over at Taunton, might outscore his estranged team-mates all by himself. Yet again they missed a string of chances, including two for Kieswetter, when Amla was on 42 and 92. They had also declined to use the DRS when Patel's lbw appeal, when Amla had 37, was rejected; replays showed he would have been out. In only his 57th one-day innings, Amla comfortably overhauled Viv Richards as the

FASTER THAN THE MASTER BLASTER

Fewest innings to complete 3,000 runs in one-day internationals:

Inns		*ODIs*	*Years*	*Days*	
57	**H. M. Amla (SA)**	**59**	**4**	**172**	**2007-08–2012**
69	I. V. A. Richards (WI)	74	8	355	1975–1984
72	G. Kirsten (SA)	72	3	357	1993-94–1997-98
72	C. G. Greenidge (WI)	72	11	128	1975–1986-87
75	**V. Kohli (I)**	**78**	**3**	**180**	**2008–2011-12**
76	G. A. Gooch (E)	77	13	172	1976–1989-90
78	K. P. Pietersen (E/World)	87	3	364	2004-05–2008-09

fastest batsman to 3,000 runs, and then, on 142, surpassed Graeme Smith's record one-day score for South Africa against England. Cook was yorked second ball by Tsotsobe, and England never recovered once Trott was brilliantly caught by Dean Elgar, diving backwards at fine leg. A bad night got even worse when the players returned to the dressing-room to be greeted with personal letters from Andrew Strauss, informing them he had resigned the Test captaincy. A spectator from Portsmouth, John Guinelly, was spoken to by police after racially insulting three children in the crowd. In January, he was found guilty by Southampton Magistrates' Court and ordered to pay each victim £500.

Man of the Match: H. M. Amla. *Attendance:* 14,722.

South Africa

G. C. Smith c Kieswetter b Bresnan	52
H. M. Amla c Bresnan b Finn	150
J-P. Duminy run out	14
D. Elgar b Swann	15
*†A. B. de Villiers b Swann	28
F. du Plessis not out	22
W. D. Parnell not out	0
B 1, l-b 4, w 1	6
(5 wkts, 50 overs)	287

1/89 (1) 2/121 (3) 3/165 (4) 4/230 (5) 5/285 (2)

10 overs: 49-0

R. McLaren, R. J. Peterson, M. Morkel and L. L. Tsotsobe did not bat.

Anderson 9–0–53–0; Finn 10–0–59–1; Bresnan 8–0–61–1; Swann 10–0–50–2; Patel 10–0–47–0; Bopara 3–0–12–0.

England

*A. N. Cook b Tsotsobe	0
I. R. Bell b Peterson	45
I. J. L. Trott c Elgar b Morkel	23
R. S. Bopara c du Plessis b Peterson	16
E. J. G. Morgan c Elgar b Duminy	27
†C. Kieswetter c Smith b Elgar	20
S. R. Patel c de Villiers b Morkel	45
T. T. Bresnan c de Villiers b Parnell	0
G. P. Swann c de Villiers b Parnell	0
J. M. Anderson run out	5
S. T. Finn not out	15
B 3, l-b 7, w 1	11
(40.4 overs)	207

1/0 (1) 2/64 (3) 3/77 (2) 4/90 (4) 5/118 (6) 6/159 (5) 7/159 (8) 8/159 (9) 9/170 (10) 10/207 (7)

10 overs: 54-1

Tsotsobe 6–0–29–1; McLaren 7–1–31–0; Morkel 5.4–0–29–2; Parnell 7–1–30–2; Peterson 9–0–51–2; Duminy 3–0–16–1; Elgar 3–1–11–1.

Umpires: R. J. Bailey and S. J. A. Taufel. Third umpire: H. D. P. K. Dharmasena.

ENGLAND v SOUTH AFRICA

Third One-Day International

At The Oval, August 31 (day/night). England won by four wickets. Toss: South Africa.

England recorded their first victory of the summer over South Africa and – with onlookers by now losing track and, possibly, interest – reclaimed their No. 1 status. Anderson became the second England bowler after Darren Gough to collect 100 one-day international wickets on home soil, while Dernbach bowled with pace and variation to outfox South Africa's top order, ripping out Amla's leg stump, then bowling Elgar with a back-of-the-hand leg-cutter. Tredwell, playing in place of the rested Graeme Swann, disposed of de Villiers and Duminy, while Bopara got through ten tidy overs before another failure with the bat – he called for a review, which showed nothing on Hot Spot, but was given out on the sound of a nick. It brought Morgan and Trott together at 64 for three, and they played with calm authority to take England to within 40 of victory. Both played to type: Morgan, with an inventive 73 from 67 balls; Trott barely half as quickly.

Man of the Match: E. J. G. Morgan. *Attendance:* 22,382.

South Africa

H. M. Amla b Dernbach	43	M. Morkel b Anderson	7
G. C. Smith b Anderson	18	L. L. Tsotsobe lbw b Anderson	0
D. Elgar b Dernbach	42		
*†A. B. de Villiers c Bell b Tredwell	28	L-b 1, w 1	2
F. du Plessis b Bopara	1		—
J. P. Duminy c Bell b Tredwell	33	1/50 (2) 2/73 (1) (46.4 overs)	211
W. D. Parnell c Kieswetter b Dernbach	13	3/120 (4) 4/122 (5) 5/141 (3)	
R. J. Peterson not out	23	6/155 (7) 7/195 (6) 8/203 (9)	
D. W. Steyn b Anderson	1	9/211 (10) 10/211 (11) 10 overs: 55-1	

Anderson 9.4–0–44–4; Finn 8–0–42–0; Dernbach 9–0–44–3; Bopara 10–1–31–1; Tredwell 10–0–49–2.

England

*A. N. Cook c Elgar b Peterson	20	J. C. Tredwell not out	1
I. R. Bell lbw b Steyn	12		
I. J. L. Trott c de Villiers b Parnell	71	L-b 1, w 6, n-b 1	8
R. S. Bopara c de Villiers b Morkel	0		—
E. J. G. Morgan c and b Peterson	73	1/14 (2) 2/61 (1) (6 wkts, 48 overs)	212
†C. Kieswetter run out	14	3/64 (4) 4/172 (5)	
S. R. Patel not out	13	5/189 (6) 6/207 (3) 10 overs: 45-1	

J. M. Anderson, J. W. Dernbach and S. T. Finn did not bat.

Steyn 7–0–32–1; Tsotsobe 7–0–55–0; Morkel 10–1–41–1; Parnell 10–1–23–1; Peterson 10–0–39–2; Elgar 4–0–21–0.

Umpires: H. D. P. K. Dharmasena and R. A. Kettleborough. Third umpire: S. J. A. Taufel.

ENGLAND v SOUTH AFRICA

Fourth One-Day International

At Lord's, September 2. England won by six wickets. Toss: England.

Smart glovework by Kieswetter and a high-quality innings from Bell gave England a 2–1 lead with one to play, after South Africa's batsmen again failed to achieve a commanding total. Kieswetter became the first England wicketkeeper to make three stumpings in a one-day international, all off the impressive Tredwell, who found unexpected turn and bounce as the tourists got bogged down; only Dernbach conceded more than five an over. Cook fell in the first over for the second time in the series, but Bell sparkled in a stand of 141 with Trott, whose circumspection was partly the result of an early, painful blow on his bottom hand from Steyn; it later emerged he had broken a bone. Bopara failed again, but any hopes of a South African comeback were dashed by Morgan and Kieswetter, who cracked 38 in three overs to seal victory. The result meant England would stay top of the rankings until Christmas at least. But their slip catching and use of the DRS continued to be substandard.

Man of the Match: I. R. Bell. *Attendance:* 26,207.

South Africa

G. C. Smith c Kieswetter b Dernbach	29
H. M. Amla b Bopara	45
J-P. Duminy st Kieswetter b Tredwell	18
*†A. B. de Villiers st Kieswetter b Tredwell	39
F. du Plessis b Bopara	1
D. Elgar c Kieswetter b Finn	35
W. D. Parnell st Kieswetter b Tredwell	5
R. J. Peterson not out	31
R. McLaren run out	1
D. W. Steyn not out	3
L-b 7, w 6	13
1/68 (1) 2/100 (2) 3/106 (3) 4/115 (5) 5/166 (4) 6/174 (7) 7/214 (6) 8/215 (9) (8 wkts, 50 overs)	220
10 overs: 32-0	

L. L. Tsotsobe did not bat.

Finn 10–0–33–1; Anderson 7–0–32–0; Dernbach 9–0–51–1; Bopara 9–0–34–2; Patel 7–0–28–0; Tredwell 8–0–35–3.

England

*A. N. Cook lbw b Steyn	2
I. R. Bell c de Villiers b Steyn	88
I. J. L. Trott lbw b Elgar	48
R. S. Bopara c de Villiers b McLaren	6
E. J. G. Morgan not out	36
†C. Kieswetter not out	21
B 3, l-b 7, w 11, n-b 2	23
1/2 (1) 2/143 (3) 3/156 (4) 4/186 (2) (4 wkts, 46.4 overs)	224
10 overs: 42-1	

S. R. Patel, J. C. Tredwell, J. M. Anderson, J. W. Dernbach and S. T. Finn did not bat.

Steyn 9.4–0–47–2; Tsotsobe 8–0–36–0; McLaren 9–0–52–1; Elgar 5–0–15–1; Parnell 8–0–39–0; Peterson 7–1–25–0.

Umpires: R. K. Illingworth and S. J. A. Taufel. Third umpire: H. D. P. K. Dharmasena.

ENGLAND v SOUTH AFRICA

Fifth One-Day International

At Nottingham, September 5 (day/night). South Africa won by seven wickets. Toss: England.

With team director Andy Flower taking a rare match off, England played like a bunch of naughty schoolboys to allow South Africa a share of the series and provide a disappointing sign-off to an otherwise successful one-day summer. Despite unusually dry and bright conditions, they batted

OVER TO YOU, HASH

Players who top-scored in most consecutive one-day international innings:

6	**H. M. Amla (SA)**	**2011-12–2012**
5	M. D. Crowe (NZ)	1990-91
5	B. C. Lara (WI)	1993-94
5	Salman Butt (P)	2007-08
5	D. F. Watts (Sco)	2010
5	M. E. Waugh (A)	1998-99
5	Zaheer Abbas (P)	1981-82

without any spark: only Cook made a half-century – his first in ten international innings since 115 in the Oval Test – and it needed an unbeaten 33 from Woakes, finally getting into the action, in place of Steven Finn, to avert total disaster. After failing to use 28 of their deliveries, England had to hope South Africa's batsmen would struggle under lights in September and, when Anderson and Dernbach reduced them to 14 for three in the fifth over, they had more than a sniff. But Amla – in the form of his life – calmly compiled a superb unbeaten 97, adding 172 with de Villiers, whose 75 not out was his highest international score of the tour. South Africa romped home with more than 15 overs to spare.

Man of the Match: H. M. Amla. *Attendance:* 16,843.
Man of the Series: H. M. Amla.

England

*A. N. Cook c and b du Plessis	51
I. R. Bell lbw b Peterson	10
R. S. Bopara c de Villiers b Steyn	0
J. M. Bairstow c Ontong b Morkel	29
E. J. G. Morgan c Amla b Duminy	0
†C. Kieswetter c Amla b Morkel	33
S. R. Patel c de Villiers b Steyn	9
C. R. Woakes not out	33
J. C. Tredwell b Peterson	6
J. M. Anderson c Morkel b Peterson	0
J. W. Dernbach c de Villiers b Parnell	2
L-b 3, w 3, n-b 3	9
1/23 (2) 2/24 (3) 3/79 (4) 4/82 (5) 5/99 (1) 6/124 (7) 7/156 (6) 8/175 (9) 9/175 (10) 10/182 (11) (45.2 overs)	182
10 overs: 42-2	

Steyn 9–2–24–2; Peterson 10–0–37–3; Morkel 8–0–41–2; Parnell 8.2–0–38–1; Elgar 4–0–20–0; Duminy 4–0–11–1; du Plessis 2–0–8–1.

South Africa

H. M. Amla not out	97
G. C. Smith c Tredwell b Dernbach	1
F. du Plessis c Kieswetter b Anderson	3
D. Elgar c Kieswetter b Anderson	1
*†A. B. de Villiers not out	75
L-b 1, w 8	9
1/8 (2) 2/11 (3) 3/14 (4) (3 wkts, 34.3 overs)	186
10 overs: 43-3	

J-P. Duminy, J. L. Ontong, W. D. Parnell, R. J. Peterson, D. W. Steyn and M. Morkel did not bat.

Anderson 9–2–41–2; Dernbach 7.3–0–56–1; Woakes 6–0–35–0; Tredwell 6–0–30–0; Patel 2–0–11–0; Bopara 4–0–12–0.

Umpires: H. D. P. K. Dharmasena and R. K. Illingworth. Third umpire: S. J. A. Taufel.
Series referee: A. J. Pycroft.

ENGLAND v SOUTH AFRICA

First Twenty20 International

At Chester-le-Street, September 8. South Africa won by seven wickets. Toss: South Africa. Twenty20 international debut: F. du Plessis.

England delivered another inept batting display. Kieswetter and Hales gave them fleeting hope with a bustling opening stand of 27 before Hales ran himself out, at which point the wheels came off. Bopara's dismal finish to the summer was complete when he was caught at slip off Steyn for six, leaving him with 28 international runs from five innings since returning from his self-imposed sabbatical; he was dropped for the next two games. From 85 for seven, Swann and Broad added a quick 33. And South Africa were tottering a touch at 29 for three, with Hashim Amla rested. But Kallis – back in the side after holidaying in New York during the one-day series – and Duminy calmed nerves in a well-paced, undefeated stand of 90.

Man of the Match: D. W. Steyn. *Attendance:* 8,042.

England

		B	4	6
†C. Kieswetter *lbw b 8*	25	24	3	1
A. D. Hales *run out*	11	6	2	0
R. S. Bopara *c 8 b 10*	6	11	0	0
E. J. G. Morgan *b 8*	10	11	1	0
J. M. Bairstow *c 8 b 7*	15	17	1	0
J. C. Buttler *b 9*	6	9	0	0
S. R. Patel *c 2 b 9*	4	7	0	0
*S. C. J. Broad *not out*	18	22	1	0
G. P. Swann *not out*	18	13	3	0
B 3, l-b 2	5			

6 overs: 40-1 (20 overs) 118-7

1/27 2/40 3/50 4/66 5/76 6/80 7/85

S. T. Finn and J. W. Dernbach did not bat.

Peterson 4–0–27–2; Steyn 4–0–13–1; Tsotsobe 2–0–22–0; Morkel 3–0–12–1; Botha 4–0–19–2; Kallis 3–0–20–0.

South Africa

		B	4	6
R. E. Levi *c 9 b 11*	8	7	2	0
J. H. Kallis *not out*	48	44	7	0
F. du Plessis *lbw b 10*	4	3	0	0
*†A. B. de Villiers *c 1 b 11*	10	6	2	0
J-P. Duminy *not out*	47	54	4	0
L-b 1, w 1	2			

6 overs: 40-3 (19 overs) 119-3

1/9 2/14 3/29

J. L. Ontong, J. A. Morkel, J. Botha, R. J. Peterson, D. W. Steyn and L. L. Tsotsobe did not bat.

Finn 4–0–22–1; Dernbach 4–0–31–2; Broad 4–0–18–0; Bopara 2–0–20–0; Swann 4–0–16–0; Patel 1–0–11–0.

Umpires: R. J. Bailey and R. K. Illingworth. Third umpire: M. A. Gough.

ENGLAND v SOUTH AFRICA

Second Twenty20 International

At Manchester, September 10 (floodlit). No result. Toss: England.

The latest city to have a game of cricket wrecked by rain was Manchester, although another five balls in England's reply would have guaranteed a result in a match already reduced to nine overs a side. England would have needed a further 13 runs, assuming they lost no more wickets. Less surprising than the weather had been another top score from Amla, who hit seven of South Africa's nine fours – and would surely have won his fourth match award of the tour had it been played to a conclusion.

Attendance: 12,348.

South Africa

		B	4	6
R. E. Levi *c 1 b 10*	0	1	0	0
H. M. Amla *not out*	47	30	7	0
*†A. B. de Villiers *c 11 b 10*	1	4	0	0
J. A. Morkel *c 6 b 3*	3	5	0	0
J-P. Duminy *c and b 8*	5	6	0	0
J. L. Ontong *c 1 b 11*	1	2	0	0
J. H. Kallis *not out*	13	7	2	0
L-b 6, n-b 1	7			

3 overs: 32-2 (9 overs) 77-5

1/0 2/20 3/37 4/47 5/49

J. Botha, R. J. Peterson, D. W. Steyn and M. Morkel did not bat.

Finn 2–0–17–2; Broad 2–0–27–0; Swann 2–0–11–1; Wright 1–0–4–1; Dernbach 2–0–12–1.

England

		B	4	6
†C. Kieswetter *c 9 b 10*	1	6	0	0
A. D. Hales *not out*	11	8	0	1
L. J. Wright *c 11 b 4*	14	11	1	0
E. J. G. Morgan *not out*	0	0	0	0
L-b 1, w 2	3			

3 overs: 19-1 (4.1 overs) 29-2

1/3 2/29

J. C. Buttler, J. M. Bairstow, S. R. Patel, G. P. Swann, *S. C. J. Broad, S. T. Finn and J. W. Dernbach did not bat.

M. Morkel 2–0–8–0; Steyn 1–0–10–1; Botha 1–0–10–0; J. A. Morkel 0.1–0–0–1.

Umpires: R. J. Bailey and R. K. Illingworth. Third umpire: R. T. Robinson.

ENGLAND v SOUTH AFRICA

Third Twenty20 International

At Birmingham, September 12 (floodlit). England won by 28 runs. Toss: South Africa. Twenty20 international debut: D. R. Briggs.

On the eve of England's departure for the World Twenty20 in Sri Lanka, Buttler finally came good on the international stage, producing a magnificent exhibition of clean hitting that made Kieswetter's 32-ball 50 appear almost pedestrian. As England looked to accelerate in a match reduced to 11 overs a side, Buttler – whose six previous Twenty20 international innings had yielded a best of 13 – smashed 32 off ten deliveries, including 30 in an eight-ball over from Parnell that cost 32 in all. Only Broad, Buttler's captain, had conceded more runs in a Twenty20 international over – the 36 struck by Yuvraj Singh in the 2007 World Twenty20. Faced with a now-mountainous 118, South Africa never got close, even though the peerless Amla top-scored for his seventh international innings in a row. Earlier, Morne Morkel began with an over costing 16, including a leg-side wide to Kieswetter that outdid even Steve Harmison's Ashes opener at Brisbane in 2006-07 for waywardness. The win meant England began their World Twenty20 defence on top of the ICC's rankings.

Man of the Match: J. C. Buttler *Attendance:* 18,952.

Man of the Series: C. Kieswetter.

England

		B	*4*	*6*
†C. Kieswetter *b 11*	50	32	3	3
M. J. Lumb *b 10*	5	4	1	0
L. J. Wright *c 2 b 8*	6	10	0	0
E. J. G. Morgan *c 6 b 8*	5	9	0	0
J. C. Buttler *not out*	32	10	2	3
J. M. Bairstow *b 11*	4	2	1	0
T. T. Bresnan *not out*	1	1	0	0
L-b 2, w 11, n-b 2	15			
3 overs: 27-1 (11 overs)	118-5			

1/20 2/43 3/64 4/112 5/116

G. P. Swann, *S. C. J. Broad, D. R. Briggs and J. W. Dernbach did not bat.

M. Morkel 2–0–28–2; Parnell 2–0–37–1; J. A. Morkel 1–0–5–0; Peterson 2–0–16–0; Botha 3–0–19–2; Kallis 1–0–11–0.

South Africa

		B	*4*	*6*
R. E. Levi *b 7*	1	4	0	0
H. M. Amla *c 6 b 8*	36	27	6	0
F. du Plessis *c 4 b 10*	8	6	1	0
*†A. B. de Villiers *c 6 b 8*	2	3	0	0
J. A. Morkel *not out*	17	14	0	1
J. L. Ontong *c 4 b 7*	10	7	0	1
J. H. Kallis *not out*	8	5	0	0
B 1, l-b 3, w 4	8			
3 overs: 25-1 (11 overs)	90-5			

1/9 2/34 3/51 4/53 5/69

J. Botha, R. J. Peterson, W. D. Parnell and M. Morkel did not bat.

Briggs 2–0–16–1; Bresnan 2–0–14–2; Broad 2–0–18–0; Swann 3–0–24–2; Dernbach 2–0–14–0.

Umpires: R. J. Bailey and R. K. Illingworth. Third umpire: P. J. Hartley.
Series referee: A. J. Pycroft.

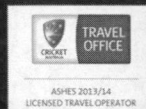

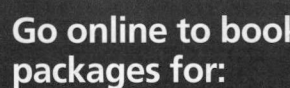

INDIA v ENGLAND, 2012-13

REVIEW BY GEORGE DOBELL

Test matches (4): India 1, England 2
One-day internationals (5): India 3, England 2
Twenty20 internationals (2): India 1, England 1

England left India celebrating a victory for the history books. And yet, in the aftermath of their nine-wicket defeat in the First Test at Ahmedabad, it had been hard to avoid a sense of gloomy inevitability. Ranged against them, apparently, were all their old failings – and some recent ones too: scars from the 3–0 defeat in the UAE by Pakistan and their slow bowlers were still raw. They had not won a series in Asia, Bangladesh excepted, for 12 years; and they had not won in India since 1984-85, when David Gower's side had become the first – and, until now, only – visiting team to beat them in a Test series after falling behind.

There were doubts, too, about the spirit within the squad. Kevin Pietersen had only just returned on a short-term central contract, having been omitted from the final Test of the home series against South Africa and the World Twenty20 squad following revelations about his relationship with his team-mates. And despite Pietersen's return, itself a feather in the cap for the new captain, Alastair Cook, there remained selection issues. With the retirement of Andrew Strauss, England had drafted in as opener Nick Compton, an uncapped 29-year-old accustomed to the No. 3 role in county cricket. The No. 6 slot remained a problem, while an injury in the opening warm-up game to Steven Finn, now a first-choice bowler, especially in these conditions, threatened to disrupt their plans from the start.

Neither could there be any doubting India's determination to avenge their humiliating 4–0 defeat in England in 2011. Talk of payback featured heavily, with the Indian players making it clear England would find life significantly harder in alien conditions. During their three warm-up matches, the tourists were denied exposure to quality opposition. In particular, they faced very little slow bowling, and none of it high-class, before attracting an avalanche of spin in the Tests.

When Andy Flower, England's head coach, acknowledged after Ahmedabad that he had erred in omitting Monty Panesar, and asked for judgment on his team to be suspended until the end of the series, it seemed he was talking more in hope than expectation. Not for the first time, however, Flower was vindicated: by emulating Gower's side and turning deficit into victory, England pulled off one of their least expected series wins. For Flower's opposite number, Duncan Fletcher – who during his time in charge of England had never won a series against India – it was a particularly unpalatable pill.

In the event, India's tactics backfired, as Cook guardedly admitted he hoped they might. While England's top order were warming up almost exclusively against an assortment of seamers and part-time slow bowlers, they were also

Graham Morris

Dancing to his own tune: Alastair Cook used his feet against the spinners, and reaped the rewards.

spending confidence-boosting time at the crease. India's captain M. S. Dhoni kept insisting, to the point of obsession, on turning tracks, designed to capitalise on the two teams' perceived strengths and weaknesses. But it became clear that – once Panesar had been picked – it was England who had the slow bowlers better equipped to exploit the conditions. And while India persisted with the theory that England's batsmen could not play spin, they went into games with poorly balanced attacks, including one seamer and three spinners at Mumbai, then – in a dreadful miscalculation – one and four at Nagpur.

At both Mumbai and Kolkata, Tests were played on recently used pitches, although Dhoni's attempts to put pressure on groundsmen to comply with his demands met with mixed results. Certainly any implied threats from the BCCI about the future of Kolkata's curator fell on deaf ears: Prabir Mukherjee, a fearless octogenarian, was long past the stage where such intimidation offered any concern, and provided a fine Test pitch. Only the deathly slow surface at Nagpur proved unsuitable for a format fighting for space in a crowded marketplace.

As Dhoni's stock fell, despite his face-saving – though not series-salvaging – innings of 99 at Nagpur, Cook's reputation rocketed. Even amid the rubble of England's rout at Ahmedabad, he had sown the seeds of their resurgence with a second-innings century that proved to his colleagues it was possible to prosper against India's spinners. In typically undemonstrative fashion, he went on to score centuries in each of the first three Tests, making him the first man to register hundreds in his first five in charge (he had scored one in each of the two Tests in Bangladesh in 2009-10, when he stood in as captain for the rested Strauss). Cook's air of calm, whether in adversity or triumph, his pragmatic approach to coaxing the best out of the eclectic mix of characters under him,

WINNING IN INDIA

The repeat performance

VIC MARKS

History rarely repeats itself. But cricket correspondents sometimes do. We kept banging on about the similarities between England's 1984-85 tour of India and this one, mainly because there was some justification for doing so.

On both trips phlegmatic, photogenic left-handers captained England teams (David Gower then, Alastair Cook now), and the bookmakers expected defeat. Both sides lost the First Test comfortably, which increased the gloom, only to fight back and take a 2–1 lead. Then, to the infuriation of home captains past and present (Sunil Gavaskar and M. S. Dhoni), India encountered slow, stultifying pitches – at Kanpur in 1984-85, and Nagpur in 2012-13. Thus on both occasions England were able to draw the final Test without too much bother, and win the series.

But first the differences: fortunately, Cook's expedition was not marred by assassinations or environmental catastrophes. On Gower's tour, the Indian Prime Minister, Mrs Gandhi, was shot a few hours after we arrived in Delhi; Percy Norris, Britain's Deputy High Commissioner, was killed 24 hours before the First Test at Bombay; then there was the Bhopal chemical-plant disaster. At various stages, press and players thought they would be going home. By these standards, the BCCI's tiffs with English broadcasters and photographers in 2012-13 were not significant.

The two England captains had contrasting tours with the bat. Cook was inspirational for three Tests, but out of sorts at Nagpur; Gower was practically runless until Kanpur, when he scored 78 and 32 not out. However, both men dealt with so-called troublemakers calmly and to everyone's advantage. Gower was rehabilitating Phil Edmonds, too high-maintenance for previous England captains, and his left-arm spin proved more important than the figures – 14 wickets at 41 – suggest. Cook was rehabilitating Kevin Pietersen, whose 186 in the Second Test at Mumbai was critical to England's resurgence. More broadly, neither captain allowed their squads to retreat into a siege mentality, which can easily be a trap in India.

England's spinners outbowled their opponents on both tours, though Edmonds and Pat Pocock were not as prolific as Graeme Swann and Monty Panesar. Their batsmen were often more patient than the Indians, who in both series seemed seduced by the charms of limited-overs cricket. In 1984-85, India were still basking in their World Cup success in England in 1983; maybe that was also the case in 2012-13, after their World Cup victory the previous year. Moreover, for the modern Indian cricketer there is also the lucrative distraction of the IPL.

In both series, the Indian side was restless and introspective. Gavaskar was having a mini-feud with Kapil Dev, while Dhoni had to lead an ageing team, in which players were constantly looking over their shoulders, and their champion, Sachin Tendulkar, played just one innings of significance. To say the least, this was unsettling.

Cook's England side were almost certainly better than Gower's, who were missing Ian Botham (resting), Graham Gooch and John Emburey (both banned). But before celebrating such an objective assessment from an old-timer, let us end with this thought: since the talents of the 1984-85 side were so relatively modest, perhaps their achievement was the greater.

Vic Marks toured India in 1984-85 as an off-spinner (but didn't play a Test), and in 2012-13 as a journalist for The Guardian, The Observer *and* Test Match Special.

and his desire to succeed meant the post-Strauss transition took place more smoothly than anyone could have dreamed.

Where once he had been an accumulator, satisfied with cutting, pulling and nudging, Cook now showed he had developed a range of strokes to prosper in any conditions. He swept judiciously, a rarity among Englishmen, used his feet precisely, drove sweetly, and demonstrated a willingness to hit over the top. Had umpire Kumar Dharmasena not sawn him off twice at Nagpur – before apologising – Cook would surely have surpassed Ken Barrington's 51-year-old England record for the most runs in a series in India (594), although he was gracious enough to admit he had received the rub of the green a couple of times; he finished instead with 562, though in four Tests to Barrington's five. And at Kolkata he became the first England player to rack up 23 Test centuries, and the only man from any nation to pass 7,000 runs before the age of 28. It was monumental stuff.

But Cook's contribution started long before the team departed for a pre-tour training camp in Dubai. It was partly his determination that helped find a solution to the Pietersen episode after he was left out of the initial touring party, and it was his alliance with Flower that rammed home a no-excuses mindset. Where previous England teams in India had been daunted by the conditions, the travel, the food, the weight of history and just about everything else, this one made a point of embracing the culture and the conditions. Almost without exception – and despite some justification at times – they never breathed a word of complaint. Unsurprisingly, Cook's presence as a tactician grew too, after a shaky start on the first day of the series. By contrast, Dhoni looked one-dimensional, and England privately noted his tendency to change the field in response to the previous ball.

Where Cook led from the front, others gradually followed. At Ahmedabad, only Matt Prior – a beacon of selfless energy and skill throughout – and Swann rallied round their captain. Even at Mumbai, the excellence of a few compensated for the travails of the rest: Pietersen, with an innings of rare genius, turned the tide of the series, before Panesar, with his best match figures in Tests, joined Swann to claim the best analysis – 19 for 323 – by a pair of England spinners in more than 54 years. Panesar and Swann ended up with 37 wickets at 25 apiece, and a combined strike-rate of 60, easily outperforming their Indian counterparts, Pragyan Ojha and the desperately disappointing Ravichandran Ashwin, who between them managed 34 wickets at nearly 40, with a strike-rate of 86. Seldom, if ever, had overseas spinners so dominated in India.

England were fitter and quicker than India in the field; off it, they appeared more united. Ian Bell, who missed the Second Test in a fruitless attempt to get home in time to witness the birth of his first child, struggled with the bat until a final-day hundred at Nagpur. But he had already pulled off a direct hit from midwicket to run out Cheteshwar Pujara, India's prolific No. 3, at Kolkata, then a superb catch at short leg – admittedly off the batsman's elbow – to dismiss him at Nagpur.

Compton, without ever nailing the definitive innings he craved, added solidity, four times in succession putting on 50 or more with Cook; not since

Graham Morris

Ticking over: Cheteshwar Pujara was the engine of the Indian middle order.

Michael Vaughan and Marcus Trescothick in 2002 had the same pair of English openers achieved such a feat. Their overall record – 493 runs at 70 – was 20 better than India's experienced pair of Virender Sehwag and Gautam Gambhir, whose running between the wickets was a liability. Compton, Jonathan Trott and Finn – in his only Test of the series – weighed in at Kolkata. And at Nagpur, Joe Root, who made a composed debut, could also feel satisfied. James Anderson's contribution was telling. After an impotent start, he bowled with greater pace than for some time, gained swing – both reverse and conventional – and extracted movement off unhelpful pitches. He was later described by Dhoni as "the major difference" between the sides; his haul of 12 wickets at 30 apiece barely did him justice.

But the tour was not an unqualified success. Stuart Broad, the new vice-captain, struggled with injury and illness, and was dropped for Kolkata amid suggestions from bowling coach David Saker that he had to "front up". Tim Bresnan, like Broad, finished wicketless, and looked bereft of pace and confidence. Samit Patel's batting failed to compensate for the limitations of his left-arm spin. Dropped for Nagpur after two matches in which Panesar's presence rendered his bowling redundant, he finished with doubts over his Test future.

Philip Brown

My turn: Monty Panesar was a reminder that England's spin threat went beyond Graeme Swann.

However, it was India who had more headaches. Defeated at home for the first time since 2004-05 – and for only the fourth time in 40 bilateral series since losing to Gower's England – this was a result to prick the bubble that had been shielding them from the harsh wind of reality. While whitewashes in England and Australia had been excused – erroneously, in the main – on the grounds that conditions had been manufactured to thwart them, the stain on their proud home record could not be so easily ignored.

There were several issues, not least the paucity of fast-bowling options after the dangerous Umesh Yadav picked up a back injury that ruled him out after Ahmedabad; Zaheer Khan faded, and was dropped, five Test wickets short of 300. The lack of fitness among their leading players was damning; so too the decline of Sachin Tendulkar. Only once before had he averaged under 20 in a series of three Tests or more, while 76 of his 112 runs came in one innings, at Kolkata. Even there, he laboured unedifyingly for almost every one. His announcement soon after the series of his retirement from one-day cricket felt as if it didn't go far enough. Meanwhile, the recall at Mumbai of Harbhajan Singh – who had taken only 18 first-class wickets at 40 each since his previous Test, 16 months earlier – and at Nagpur of Piyush Chawla, a leg-spinner averaging over 40 in his previous three years of first-class cricket, underlined the sense of a nation not boasting strength in depth so much as mediocrity. It had been years since the cupboard looked so bare.

There was some room for optimism. Pujara, unstoppable in the first two Tests, hinted he could yet be a worthy successor to Rahul Dravid, before falling away as umpiring errors and the running of his colleagues conspired

THE INDIAN REACTION

Revenge – and a reality check

ANJALI DOSHI

The Hindi words for "revenge" and "change" are similar, which offered the Indian media an ironic twist and plenty of scope for cheeky puns during the Test series. The rabble-rousing theme of revenge (*badla*) on England's arrival transformed into a mocking lament about how nothing had changed (*kuch nahin badla*) – a reference to India's 8–0 losing streak in England and Australia – followed by a demand for, yes, sweeping changes (*badal dalo*).

Clearly, nobody saw the drubbing coming, least of all the official broadcasters – Rupert Murdoch's Star network – who ran jingoistic promos in colloquial Hindi asking whether India would beat England to a pulp. Once that question had been answered, the promos were pulled off air.

The revenge rhetoric played at full volume when India won the First Test at Ahmedabad, but lost its voice after defeat at Mumbai. M. S. Dhoni's obsession with pitches came in for sharp criticism, as did the listlessness of the Indian spinners. But it was the hopeless surrender at Eden Gardens that culminated in an uproar over the "humiliation at home" on perpetually hyper news networks, such as Times Now, Aaj Tak and Star News, and fever-pitched calls for "heads to roll" in several newspapers, including the *Times of India*.

Just when things could not, it seemed, get any worse, came former selector Mohinder Amarnath's claim on CNN-IBN that Dhoni had managed to hold on to the captaincy earlier in the year only because N. Srinivasan, the BCCI president, had overruled the selectors' decision to sack him. The insinuation was obvious: Srinivasan, vice-chairman of India Cements, the company that owns the Chennai Super Kings IPL team, was out to protect his franchise's brand equity by ensuring their skipper remained India's captain too.

This outburst from Amarnath, who had lost his job after only a year, threatened to overshadow India's worst performance at home since 1999-2000. But it was followed by more quickfire autopsies from former cricketers, including Sunil Gavaskar, who attacked them for "treating Test cricket in a cavalier manner" in the era of Twenty20, and demanded Dhoni's instant removal. Only a couple of pieces really attempted to examine the IPL effect on Indian cricket, and the BCCI's role in the mess. But it was Dhoni himself who came up with the most telling take on India's priorities, saying this crisis was "not even close" to the early exit from the 2007 World Cup.

India's crammed schedule provides little time for introspection. So what could have been a watershed moment prompting serious probing by the media and internal reviews by the board, which reported around £100m in revenue in 2011-12, was soon forgotten. After India won the first Twenty20 game against England, newspaper headlines exclaimed: "Make winning a habit" and "Bashing over, time for bash". When they lost the second at Mumbai, it was already time to preview the limited-overs series against Pakistan.

It was no surprise, perhaps, that the most vociferous critic of India's trouncing was an Englishman. Geoffrey Boycott was the only commentator "free from BCCI shackles", as his Star Cricket colleague Sanjay Manjrekar let slip on Twitter. The tweet disappeared from his timeline within minutes.

Anjali Doshi is a columnist for Wisden India *and a former cricket editor with the Indian TV channel* NDTV 24x7.

against him. Virat Kohli belatedly provided a reminder of his class with a century at Nagpur, while Ojha – despite fading as the series progressed – finished level with Swann as the leading wicket-taker.

But it was telling that, even as Dhoni asked for patience for his team-in-transition, he admitted the pain of defeat was "not even close" to what he had experienced when India were eliminated from the 2007 World Cup. Perhaps their failure to win the two-match Twenty20 series – an unwanted dessert after a satisfying main course, staged just before England returned home for Christmas – stung more. A second-string England side lacking the rested Pietersen and Swann, plus the injured Broad and Finn, came away with a 1–1 draw. Eoin Morgan, captain in Broad's place, hit the last ball of the second match, at the Wankhede, for six to deny India even minor consolation.

The refusal of the BCCI to accept the Decision Review System led, predictably, to renewed scrutiny of umpiring errors and some poor on-field behaviour. Perhaps the absence of technology's safety net played on the officials' minds, with as skilled a judge as Aleem Dar enduring an awful game at Mumbai. While the BCCI's reservations over ball-tracking technology were at least understandable, many of the errors that affected both sides would have been simply corrected by use of the replay facility. The board's stance looked stubborn rather than principled.

The same might have been said for their attitude towards the media. The decision to withhold accreditation from several photo-only agencies, and demand extra funds from the BBC and Sky – both broadcast rights-holders – briefly threatened a partial media blackout. Sky opted to commentate from their base in London and rely on the BCCI's live feed, while most UK publications refused to condone what they saw as an attempt to restrict press freedom, and boycotted live photos entirely; the BBC's extra costs were paid for by a third party, and they covered the series as planned. The BCCI justified their stance on the grounds that providing floor space for broadcasters incurred extra costs; and some photo agencies, they argued, sold their pictures for commercial gain that had little to do with editorial coverage. There was a little truth in both claims, but it was hard to believe that any short-term benefits of the BCCI's policy would not be vastly outweighed by the long-term dilution in the value of media rights.

There were concerns, too, about a national board providing TV coverage and still pictures, and employing commentators. It took 40 minutes for Star Cricket, the host broadcasters, to show a replay of Jonny Bairstow's dismissal at Mumbai after he was wrongly given out caught via the grille of Gambhir's helmet at silly point. Similarly, an unsuccessful appeal against Trott at Nagpur

MOST WICKETS IN A SERIES IN INDIA BY VISITING SPINNERS

49	England (5 Tests)	1961-62	38	England (5 Tests)	1951-52
48	England (5 Tests)	1963-64	37	England (5 Tests)	1972-73
41	Australia (5 Tests)	1969-70	35	Pakistan (5 Tests)	1986-87
39	**England (4 Tests)**	**2012-13**	33	England (3 Tests)	1933-34
39	Australia (5 Tests)	1959-60	32	Australia (3 Tests)	1956-57

FIVE STATS YOU MAY HAVE MISSED

BENEDICT BERMANGE

- Graeme Swann equalled Derek Underwood's record for the most wickets by an England bowler in Tests in Asia:

	T	*Wkts*	*Avge*	*SR*
G. P. Swann	**13**	**73**	**25.97**	**54.82**
D. L. Underwood	22	73	26.65	78.93
A. F. Giles	15	52	34.90	83.44
M. S. Panesar	**14**	**52**	**36.13**	**81.11**
M. J. Hoggard	14	50	28.22	59.24

- Alastair Cook finished as England's leading run-scorer in Tests in Asia:

	T	*I*	*NO*	*Runs*	*HS*	*100*	*50*	*Avge*
A. N. Cook	**18**	**36**	**4**	**1,802**	**190**	**7**	**7**	**56.31**
K. P. Pietersen	**22**	**42**	**3**	**1,573**	**186**	**4**	**6**	**40.33**
I. R. Bell	**21**	**40**	**4**	**1,321**	**138**	**3**	**8**	**36.69**
M. E. Trescothick	17	34	2	1,306	193	3	7	40.81
M. W. Gatting	21	36	4	1,206	207	2	6	37.68

- Cook faced 1,285 deliveries, the most by an England batsman in a series in India, surpassing Dennis Amiss's 1,176 in five Tests in 1976-77.

- At Ahmedabad, Cook made England's highest individual score when following on:

				Result
176	**A. N. Cook**	**v India at Ahmedabad**	**2012-13**	**Lost**
172	K. F. Barrington	v India at Kanpur	1961-62	Drawn
164	A. J. Stewart	v South Africa at Manchester	1998	Drawn
163	D. C. S. Compton	v South Africa at Nottingham	1947	Drawn
157*	D. I. Gower	v India at The Oval	1990	Drawn
154*	K. S. Ranjitsinhji	v Australia at Manchester	1896	Lost
150*	M. W. Gatting	v Pakistan at The Oval	1987	Drawn

- The series included only the third instance of four Tests being played on the same day around the globe:

March 21, 1998 India v Australia at Kolkata (4th day), South Africa v Sri Lanka at Cape Town (3rd), West Indies v England at St John's (2nd), Zimbabwe v Pakistan at Harare (1st).

March 11, 2001 Sri Lanka v England at Kandy (5th), New Zealand v Pakistan at Auckland (4th), West Indies v South Africa at Georgetown (3rd), India v Australia at Kolkata (1st).

November 25, 2012 Bangladesh v West Indies at Khulna (5th), Australia v South Africa at Adelaide (4th), India v England at Mumbai (3rd), Sri Lanka v New Zealand at Colombo (1st).

– arguably the key moment of the fourth day – and the subsequent show of dissent from India's fielders, led by Kohli, was omitted from the first highlights package. Meanwhile, an incident in the First Test, when Trott said he was unsure whether he had taken a slip catch cleanly (replays categorically showed he hadn't) was held against England for the remainder of the series.

While it is true that a tour of India does not present the challenges – in terms of hotels and travel – it once did, the record books underline how difficult it is to win there. Many fine teams have travelled to India in hope, and many have left disappointed. The hosts had lost the likes of Dravid, Anil Kumble and

New generation: England celebrate their first Test series win in India for 28 years. *Standing:* Kevin Pietersen, Joe Root, Tim Bresnan, Graeme Swann, James Anderson, Nick Compton, Monty Panesar, Eoin Morgan. *Crouching:* James Tredwell, Jonny Bairstow, Jonathan Trott, Alastair Cook, Matt Prior, Samit Patel, Ian Bell.

V. V. S. Laxman, but still called on nine of the men who had led them to the top of the world rankings. No visiting team had won back-to-back Tests in India since South Africa early in 2000; England had not done so since 1976-77. By any standards, victory ranked as one of the most impressive feats in their Test history.

Ali Martin writes: England's approach to the one-day series in the New Year was a reflection of their priorities. With the 2013 Champions Trophy being held in England and the 2015 World Cup in Australia and New Zealand, five matches in Asian conditions were always going to sit low on their list. Swann, Anderson and Trott were all rested, while Broad missed the first three games to attend to his sore heel, then the last two when his flight was grounded at Heathrow by snow. Even so, victory in the Tests, and their No. 1 ranking in 50-over cricket, meant England were tipped to fare better than the sides which suffered 5–0 thrashings in India in 2008-09 and 2011-12.

Ashley Giles took on his first assignment as England's limited-overs coach, following team director Andy Flower's workload reduction. There were international bows for new grounds at Rajkot, Ranchi and Dharmasala as the Indian board used second-tier locations rather than the big urban centres. And it worked, with each sold-out venue providing a unique match in a range of conditions. For England, it was also a first look at the new 50-over playing regulations. The fast bowlers could bowl two bouncers per over. No more than four fielders (down from five) were now allowed outside the circle during standard overs, while a solitary five-over batting powerplay was to be started between the 11th and 36th overs following the initial ten; as a result, the batting side tended to opt for wickets in hand followed by a late push.

India's 3–2 victory, built on English collapses in the second and third games, was deserved, even if all five tosses proved match-winning, an advantage most pronounced in the series clincher at Mohali. While weakened of their own volition, England saw two men step up: James Tredwell took 11 wickets at 18, while Root averaged 54 with the bat. But Jade Dernbach went at 7.34 runs an over and was dropped for the New Zealand tour, along with wicketkeeper Craig Kieswetter, who struggled down the order. Pietersen played his first one-day international cricket since coming out of his short-lived retirement, while Bell finished the series as he had the Tests – with a classy unbeaten century.

ENGLAND TOURING PARTY

*A. N. Cook (Essex), J. M. Anderson (Lancashire), J. M. Bairstow (Yorkshire), I. R. Bell (Warwickshire), T. T. Bresnan (Yorkshire), S. C. J. Broad (Nottinghamshire), N. R. D. Compton (Somerset), S. T. Finn (Middlesex), S. C. Meaker (Surrey), E. J. G. Morgan (Middlesex), G. Onions (Durham), M. S. Panesar (Sussex), S. R. Patel (Nottinghamshire), K. P. Pietersen (Surrey), M. J. Prior (Sussex), J. E. Root (Yorkshire), G. P. Swann (Nottinghamshire), I. J. L. Trott (Warwickshire).

J. C. Tredwell (Kent) was added as spin-bowling cover before the Third Test. For the Twenty20 internationals that followed the Tests, D. R. Briggs (Hampshire), J. C. Buttler (Somerset), J. W. Dernbach (Surrey), A. D. Hales (Nottinghamshire), M. J. Lumb (Nottinghamshire) and L. J. Wright (Sussex) replaced Anderson, Bairstow, Bell, Compton, Finn, Onions, Panesar, Pietersen, Prior, Swann and Trott. Broad, originally due to lead the Twenty20 side, injured a heel during the Tests and was replaced by J. A. R. Harris (Middlesex), while Morgan took over as captain. Bell, Cook, Finn and Pietersen returned for the one-day international series, along with C. Kieswetter (Somerset) and C. R. Woakes (Warwickshire); of the Twenty20 squad, Hales, Harris, Lumb and Wright went home. Anderson and Trott were originally selected for the 50-over games, but were rested and replaced by Buttler and Woakes, while Bairstow remained at home for family reasons and was replaced by Root. Broad, having recovered from injury, had been expected to join the squad towards the end of the one-day series, but was prevented from doing so by snow, which disrupted flights from British airports.

Coach: A. Flower (Tests and Twenty20 internationals), A. F. Giles (one-day internationals). *Assistant coach/fielding coach:* R. G. Halsall. *Batting coach:* G. A. Gooch. *Fast bowling coach:* D. J. Saker. *Spin bowling coach:* Mushtaq Ahmed. *Wicketkeeping coach:* B. N. French (one-day internationals only). *Strength and conditioning coach:* H. R. Bevan. *Team operations manager:* P. A. Neale. *Physiotherapist:* B. T. Langley. *Team doctor:* R. H. J. Young (Tests and Twenty20s), M. G. Wotherspoon (one-day internationals). *Analyst:* N. A. Leamon, G. J. Broad. *Sports psychologist:* M. A. K. Bawden. *Massage therapist:* M. E. S. Saxby. *Security manager:* R. C. Dickason. *Security officer:* S. T. Dickason. *Media relations manager:* R. C. Evans.

TEST MATCH AVERAGES

INDIA – BATTING AND FIELDING

	T	*I*	*NO*	*R*	*HS*	*100*	*50*	*Avge*	*Ct/St*
C. A. Pujara	4	7	2	438	206*	2	0	87.60	3
R. Ashwin	4	6	2	243	91*	0	2	60.75	0
†G. Gambhir	4	6	0	251	65	0	2	41.83	2
V. Sehwag	4	7	0	253	117	1	0	36.14	5
M. S. Dhoni	4	6	0	191	99	0	2	31.83	9/1
V. Kohli	4	7	1	188	103	1	0	31.33	4
†Yuvraj Singh	3	5	0	125	74	0	1	25.00	0
S. R. Tendulkar	4	6	0	112	76	0	1	18.66	1
I. Sharma	2	3	1	12	10	0	0	6.00	0
†P. P. Ojha	4	6	4	12	6*	0	0	6.00	2
Zaheer Khan	3	5	0	25	11	0	0	5.00	1

Played in one Test: †P. P. Chawla 1 (1 ct); Harbhajan Singh 21, 6; †R. A. Jadeja 12; U. T. Yadav did not bat (1 ct).

BOWLING

	Style	O	M	R	W	BB	5I	Avge
U. T. Yadav	RFM	30	4	84	4	3-70	0	21.00
P. P. Ojha	SLA	254.2	69	617	20	5-45	2	30.85
P. P. Chawla	LBG	47.5	7	133	4	4-69	0	33.25
R. A. Jadeja	SLA	70	34	117	3	2-58	0	39.00
I. Sharma	RFM	72	20	169	4	3-49	0	42.25
R. Ashwin	OB	236.5	48	737	14	3-80	0	52.64
Zaheer Khan	LFM	88.3	22	213	4	2-59	0	53.25

Also bowled: G. Gambhir (LBG) 2–0–4–0; Harbhajan Singh (OB) 23–1–84–2; V. Sehwag (OB) 1–0–1–0; S. R. Tendulkar (RM/OB/LBG) 1–0–8–0; Yuvraj Singh (SLA) 13–1–46–0.

ENGLAND – BATTING AND FIELDING

	T	I	NO	R	HS	100	50	Avge	Ct/St
†A. N. Cook	4	8	1	562	190	3	0	80.28	2
M. J. Prior	4	5	0	258	91	0	2	51.60	6/1
K. P. Pietersen	4	7	0	338	186	1	2	48.28	1
I. R. Bell	3	6	2	172	116*	1	0	43.00	1
I. J. L. Trott	4	7	0	294	143	1	1	42.00	5
N. R. D. Compton	4	8	2	208	57	0	1	34.66	1
G. P. Swann	4	5	2	98	56	0	1	32.66	5
S. R. Patel	3	4	0	69	33	0	0	17.25	2
T. T. Bresnan	2	3	0	39	20	0	0	13.00	0
†S. C. J. Broad	2	3	0	34	25	0	0	11.33	0
†J. M. Anderson	4	5	1	17	9	0	0	4.25	0
†M. S. Panesar	3	3	1	5	4	0	0	2.50	0

Played in one Test: J. M. Bairstow 9 (3 ct); S. T. Finn 4*; J. E. Root 73, 20*.

BOWLING

	Style	O	M	R	W	BB	5I	Avge
G. P. Swann	OB	185.5	44	495	20	5-144	1	24.75
M. S. Panesar	SLA	183	44	456	17	6-81	2	26.82
S. T. Finn	RF	39	8	118	4	3-45	0	29.50
J. M. Anderson	RFM	126.4	27	363	12	4-81	0	30.25

Also bowled: T. T. Bresnan (RFM) 45–7–142–0; S. C. J. Broad (RFM) 36–2–157–0; S. R. Patel (SLA) 42–4–135–1; K. P. Pietersen (OB) 8–1–25–1; J. E. Root (OB) 1–0–5–0; I. J. L. Trott (RM) 1–0–2–0.

INDIA A v ENGLAND XI

At Mumbai (Brabourne Stadium), October 30–November 1, 2012. Drawn. Toss: India A.

Pietersen's return to England colours for the first time since the Headingley Test in August was overshadowed by an injury to Finn, who limped off with a thigh strain after bowling four overs on the first morning and would not return to the England side until the Kolkata Test. India A recovered from 190 for six – including an innings of 59 from Yuvraj Singh that contained four sixes – thanks to Tiwary, who added 110 with Pathan, and was eighth out, yorked by Bresnan for 93. England lost Compton third ball at the venue where his grandfather, Denis, had made an unbeaten 249 for Holkar in the 1944-45 Ranji Trophy final. Pietersen launched his sixth delivery, off Raina, down the ground for six, but soon provided a lame return catch to his old nemesis Yuvraj, who went on to complete a maiden first-class five-for with his part-time slow left-armers. But from 133 for four, Cook and Patel – cementing a Test spot – added 169, while Prior's 51 off 52 deliveries helped them to a 57-run lead. England's bowlers managed four second-innings wickets before a draw was agreed.

Close of play: first day, India A 369-9 (Vinay Kumar 25, Awana 11); second day, England XI 286-4 (Cook 112, Patel 82).

India A

A. Mukund c Bell b Swann	73	– c Bell b Anderson	3
M. Vijay run out	7	– c Swann b Anderson	32
A. M. Rahane c Pietersen b Bresnan	4	– c Anderson b Patel	54
Yuvraj Singh st Prior b Swann	59	– c Bell b Bresnan	14
*S. K. Raina c Bell b Patel	20	– not out	19
M. K. Tiwary b Bresnan	93	– not out	2
†W. P. Saha lbw b Anderson	20		
I. K. Pathan lbw b Swann	46		
R. Vinay Kumar lbw b Anderson	25		
A. B. Dinda b Bresnan	0		
P. Awana not out	11		
B 1, l-b 9, w 1	11		
1/25 (2) 2/57 (3) 3/113 (1) (90.1 overs) 4/140 (5) 5/168 (4) 6/190 (7) 7/300 (8) 8/347 (6) 9/347 (10) 10/369 (9)	369	1/4 (1) 2/69 (2) (4 wkts, 40 overs) 3/98 (4) 4/118 (3)	124

Anderson 17.1–4–65–2; Finn 4–1–22–0; Bresnan 20–6–59–3; Trott 5–0–21–0; Swann 23–6–90–3; Patel 20–4–95–1; Pietersen 1–0–7–0. *Second innings*—Anderson 7–1–20–2; Bresnan 10–1–37–1; Patel 16–1–40–1; Swann 5–0–19–0; Pietersen 2–0–8–0.

England XI

*A. N. Cook c Saha b Dinda	119
N. R. D. Compton c Saha b Dinda	0
I. J. L. Trott b Raina	56
K. P. Pietersen c and b Yuvraj Singh	23
I. R. Bell c Raina b Yuvraj Singh	5
S. R. Patel c Vijay b Yuvraj Singh	104
†M. J. Prior c Raina b Yuvraj Singh	51
T. T. Bresnan not out	33
G. P. Swann b Vinay Kumar	6
J. M. Anderson c Tiwary b Yuvraj Singh	19
S. T. Finn absent hurt	
B 1, l-b 5, w 2, n-b 2	10
1/2 (2) 2/97 (3) 3/125 (4) (119.5 overs) 4/133 (5) 5/302 (1) 6/367 (6) 7/368 (7) 8/395 (9) 9/426 (10)	426

Pathan 19–4–61–0; Dinda 23–2–86–2; Yuvraj Singh 26.5–1–94–5; Vinay Kumar 17–1–48–1; Awana 12–1–60–0; Tiwary 4–0–23–0; Raina 16–2–43–1; Vijay 2–0–5–0.

Umpires: S. Asnani and S. K. Tarapore. Referee: S. Sharath.

At Mumbai (Dr D. Y. Patil Sports Academy), November 3–5, 2012 (not first-class). **Drawn.** **‡England XI 345-9 dec.** (E. J. G. Morgan 76, J. M. Bairstow 118, S. R. Patel 60; K. M. Waingankar 3-72, S. N. Thakur 3-53) **and 149-2** (N. R. D. Compton 64*); **Mumbai A 286** (C. A. Pujara 87, H. N. Shah 92; M. S. Panesar 3-64, S. R. Patel 3-44). *In a game billed by Cook as a shootout for the second opener's spot in the Tests, Compton moved ahead of Root during a second-innings 64* lasting more than three and a half hours. Cook himself sat out the match against a scratch Mumbai XI, supplemented by Cheteshwar Pujara from Saurashtra and Delhi's Shikhar Dhawan. The England captaincy passed to Broad, who added to their injury worries when he underwent a scan on a bruised left heel on the second evening. They had been rescued on the first day by a century from Bairstow, who added 156 with Morgan and 107 with Patel before becoming the second victim for seamer Javed Khan, playing despite the death of his father the previous evening. Anderson dropped Pujara on 22 at slip off Panesar and, by the time he made amends, Pujara – India's Test No. 3 – had scored 87. But from 210-2, Mumbai A lost eight for 76 to hand England a lead of 59. Compton, who had failed on the opening morning, now knuckled down against a mediocre attack to move into pole position for the First Test after Root misjudged an in-jagger from Shardul Thakur.*

HARYANA v ENGLAND XI

At Ahmedabad (Sardar Patel Stadium B Ground), November 8–11, 2012. Drawn. Toss: England XI.

With Steven Finn and Stuart Broad nursing injuries, and Graeme Swann temporarily back home to be with his ill baby, England gave a workout to their second-string bowlers in the final warm-up match before the First Test. But it was their first-choice batting line-up that cashed in on the flattest

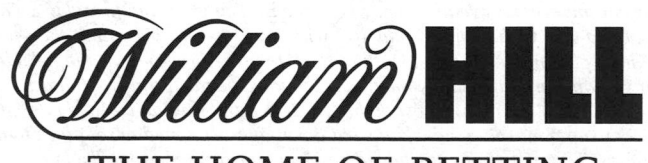

of pitches. Compton shared opening stands of 166 with Cook in the first innings and 162 with Trott in the second, while Pietersen blasted 110 off 94 balls. His second fifty required only 32, and the opening day alone brought 408 runs. Mishra, a leg-spinner with Test experience, did not bring himself on until the 51st over, though he and the 22-year-old Jayant Yadav – who claimed England's aggression betrayed their nerves against spin – shared eight wickets. Rahul Dewan carried his bat in seven hours 41 minutes of unfailing application, before England – armed with a lead of 187 – opted to go in again. Trott made a century, then the bowlers gave Haryana a late scare. On the second day, an unwell Prior was eventually given permission to hand over the gloves to substitute Jonny Bairstow after the BCCI intervened following the umpires' refusal – correct, according to the Laws – to allow Bairstow to take over; later, play was delayed while a langur monkey bounded across the outfield before joining a female companion near the sightscreen.

Close of play: first day, England XI 408-3 (Bell 57, Patel 11); second day, Haryana 172-4 (Dewan 77, Sandeep Singh 2); third day, England XI 118-0 (Compton 54, Trott 61).

England XI

First innings		Second innings	
*A. N. Cook c Sandeep Singh b Yadav	97	– (7) not out	2
N. R. D. Compton lbw b Mishra	74	– (1) c N. Saini b Rana	79
I. J. L. Trott lbw b Mishra	46	– (2) retired hurt	101
K. P. Pietersen retired hurt	110	– (8) c C. Saini b Yadav	0
I. R. Bell c N. Saini b Rana	62	– (3) c Rana b Badhwar	48
S. R. Patel c C. Saini b Yadav	67	– c Sunny Singh b Badhwar	0
†M. J. Prior st Sandeep Singh b Yadav	41	– (4) run out	2
T. T. Bresnan c Dewan b Yadav	3	– (5) c Mishra b Badhwar	14
S. C. Meaker c and b Mishra	0		
G. Onions b Mishra	2		
M. S. Panesar not out	0		
B 11, l-b 1, w 4, n-b 3	19	B 4, l-b 2, w 2	8
1/166 (1) 2/211 (2) 3/247 (3) 4/438 (5) 5/507 (7) 6/517 (8) 7/518 (6) 8/520 (9) 9/521 (10) (118.1 overs)	521	1/162 (1) 2/220 (4) 3/242 (3) 4/242 (6) 5/253 (5) 6/254 (8) (6 wkts dec, 75.2 overs)	254

In the first innings Pietersen retired hurt at 394-3; in the second Trott retired hurt at 213-1.

Badhwar 18–3–83–0; Vashist 26–2–129–0; Rana 24–8–56–1; C. Saini 10–2–64–0; Yadav 23–3–110–4; Mishra 17.1–1–67–4. *Second innings*—Badhwar 20–4–51–3; Vashist 17–3–64–0; Rana 14–1–42–1; C. Saini 13–2–46–0; Khod 3–0–24–0; Yadav 8.2–2–21–1.

Haryana

First innings		Second innings	
†N. Saini c Compton b Bresnan	13	– c Prior b Panesar	50
R. Dewan not out	143	– lbw b Meaker	13
Sunny Singh c Trott b Patel	55	– (4) c Prior b Bresnan	25
A. A. Khod c Trott b Bresnan	3	– (5) c Prior b Bresnan	1
S. Rana lbw b Panesar	6	– (3) lbw b Patel	5
Sandeep Singh c Cook b Bresnan	7	– c Prior b Onions	7
*A. Mishra c Prior b Meaker	17	– not out	19
J. Yadav b Meaker	17	– not out	3
A. Vashist lbw b Patel	16		
C. Saini lbw b Meaker	35		
S. Badhwar c Cook b Pietersen	0		
B 13, l-b 5, w 2, n-b 2	22	B 5, l-b 5	10
1/28 (1) 2/125 (3) 3/136 (4) 4/163 (5) 5/181 (6) 6/211 (7) 7/232 (8) 8/272 (9) 9/332 (10) 10/334 (11) (112.4 overs)	334	1/36 (2) 2/45 (3) 3/88 (4) 4/94 (5) 5/96 (1) 6/110 (6) (6 wkts, 42 overs)	133

Onions 20–2–66–0; Bresnan 21–4–66–3; Meaker 20–1–74–3; Panesar 28–8–52–1; Patel 16–4–39–2; Pietersen 4.4–0–12–1; Trott 3–0–7–0. *Second innings*—Onions 9–2–34–1; Bresnan 7–2–13–2; Meaker 7–2–19–1; Patel 6–0–26–1; Panesar 10–5–18–1; Pietersen 3–1–13–0.

Umpires: A. M. Saheba and C. Shamshuddin. Referee: B. Raghunath.

INDIA v ENGLAND

First Test Match

DEAN WILSON

At Ahmedabad, November 15–19, 2012. India won by nine wickets. Toss: India. Test debut: N. R. D. Compton.

Anything feels possible on the first morning of a Test. Start well, and the game can unroll like a red carpet at a VIP function. Start badly, and you won't get past the bouncer on the door. At the Sardar Patel Stadium, India had a blast, while England's name was not even on the guest list. India's nine-wicket win did not flatter them, and left England pondering whether their repeated claims to have improved in Asian conditions now bordered on the delusional. Cook, in his first Test as permanent captain, was immense – but only after his team had followed on, 330 behind, and India had found a player apparently capable of matching the sangfroid of the retired Rahul Dravid at No. 3. While Pujara was busy scoring 247 runs without being dismissed – 41 of them as opener in the second innings after Gambhir had returned home to Delhi following the death of his grandmother – the debate about a fading batting line-up seemed totally irrelevant.

LONGEST TEST INNINGS BY VISITING BATSMEN IN INDIA

Minutes			
690	Younis Khan (267)	for Pakistan at Bangalore	2004-05
675	H. M. Amla (253*)	for South Africa at Nagpur	2009-10
610	D. P. M. D. Jayawardene (275)	for Sri Lanka at Ahmedabad	2009-10
588	A. J. Hall (163)	for South Africa at Kanpur	2004-05
563	G. Fowler (201)	for England at Madras	1984-85
556	**A. N. Cook (176)**	**for England at Ahmedabad**	**2012-13**
554	C. G. Greenidge (194)	for West Indies at Kanpur	1983-84
548	M. H. Richardson (145)	for New Zealand at Mohali	2003-04
544	A. Flower (232*)	for Zimbabwe at Nagpur	2000-01
543	B. B. McCullum (225)	for New Zealand at Hyderabad	2010-11

Not for the first time in 2012, England's batsmen were flummoxed by quality spin, the absence of which from their three warm-up games had lent those matches an unreal air. To make matters worse, they picked the wrong side, omitting Monty Panesar and opting instead for a three-pronged seam attack that was badly shown up by the home pair of Yadav and Zaheer Khan. Swann admitted the pitch had been even slower and lower than England had feared, though he fought hard, taking six of the nine Indian wickets to fall and moving past Jim Laker (193) as the most prolific English Test off-spinner of all time. But 13 in the match for Ashwin and Ojha, India's slow bowlers, told its own tale.

From the moment Cook lost the toss, England were up against it. More specifically on the opening day, they were up against Sehwag, who hurried India to 120 without loss at lunch and, by the 40th over, had completed his 23rd Test century – though only his second against England – from just 90 balls. It had been two years since his previous hundred, but this was worth the wait, full of languid square-drives and matter-of-fact lofts down the ground. When Sehwag was second out for a run-a-ball 117, missing a mow at Swann, India already had 224, and England – who had been slow to respond to his steers to the unguarded third-man region – were lamenting the absence of Steven Finn, who had failed to recover from a thigh injury. Yet their attack of Anderson, Broad, Bresnan and Swann had been at the heart of the 4–0 win over these opponents in 2011. That, though, had been

Graham Morris

Roaring success: Pragyan Ojha's nine wickets helped India to a resounding victory.

at home. This was Ahmedabad, the city where Gandhi had begun his salt march, and England – as if in homage – were looking distinctly non-aggressive.

Tendulkar came and went quickly, carelessly swatting Swann to deep midwicket, where Patel seemed to be waiting for the miscue, but that merely focused the attention on Pujara, who responded with the kind of remorseless concentration that had once brought him three triple-centuries in all cricket in the space of a month. Fortunate to get away with a leading edge on eight off Bresnan as Anderson misjudged the flight at mid-on, Pujara – from nearby Rajkot – gave his fellow Gujaratis plenty to cheer with an unbeaten double-hundred of stylistic and technical brilliance. In all, he thwarted England for a shade over eight and a half hours, and allowed Yuvraj Singh – returning to Test cricket for the first time in a year, after a battle with cancer – the freedom to settle in. They added 130 for India's fifth wicket.

England's reply to 521 for eight began badly. The debutant Nick Compton crawled to nine before he was gated by a delicious off-break from Ashwin, who thus reached 50 Test wickets in his ninth match, quicker than any other Indian (Anil Kumble got there in ten). With 20 minutes of the second evening still to play, Anderson emerged as nightwatchman, but fell almost immediately to Ojha. And when Ashwin removed Trott, caught at short leg, the crumble was on. It continued next morning. In his first international match since reintegration, Pietersen got into a tangle against Ojha, bowled middle stump as his bat came across the line of the ball in a shot that had become known as the curtain-rail, before Bell fecklessly chipped his first delivery to deepish mid-off. Experienced observers wondered whether it was the worst stroke they had seen from an established Test batsman. Cook edged a drive off Ashwin to slip and, from 97 for seven, only Prior's 48 helped England to as many as 191. Ojha's five-for was the seventh by a spinner against England in 2012, and his control of flight and direction a joy to behold.

Shortly before 2pm on the third day, England were asked to bat again. Things could hardly get worse; in fact, they got rather better. As one of only two batsmen in his side – along with Pietersen – to have scored a Test century in India, Cook took it upon himself to show that playing spin need not necessarily be torture for an Englishman. Compton tucked into his captain's slipstream, and their stand of 123 was not broken until the fourth morning. The demise of Compton, hit in line with leg stump by Zaheer, proved India had more than just slow bowling up their sleeve. And though Trott and the frenetic Pietersen – bowled behind his legs on the sweep as he moved too far across – both fell cheaply to Ojha, the next two blows were struck by Yadav. Almost ignored in the first innings, he now trapped Bell and Patel with successive deliveries to reduce England to 199 for five, still 131 behind. If Patel was unfortunate after appearing to edge the ball, then Yadav's modus operandi was a lesson for England, whose seamers failed to find the same degree of reverse swing. While their trio of quicks would finish the match with combined figures of 72–10–255–1, India's duo managed 72.3–16–166–7 – and they were faster, too.

Once more, England rallied. Cook, grateful for the absence of the DRS when he missed a sweep off Ojha on 41, was at his obdurate best, and Prior a willing ally. At stumps on the fourth day England led by ten, with five wickets in hand and thoughts turning to Johannesburg 1995-96, when Mike Atherton and Jack Russell – another captain/keeper combination – had pulled off their great escape. But Prior chipped a return catch to Ojha in the tenth over of the final morning to fall for 91 – among England wicketkeepers, only Warwickshire's Dick Spooner, with 92 at Calcutta in 1951-52, had scored more in a Test in India – and end a partnership of 157 in more than 60 overs. Soon Cook was gone too, bowled by one from Ojha that spun back and kept slightly low. Another eight minutes and he would have outlasted Graeme Fowler's epic of nine hours 23 minutes at Madras in 1984-85 – still the longest innings played for England in India. The rest followed quickly, leaving Ojha with Test-best match figures of nine for 165.

Dhoni immediately called for the pitch at Mumbai, venue for the Second Test, to spin from the first ball. India were already preparing for the kill. But it was a conviction based on England's first innings rather than their second. And Cook was evidently not in the mood for his side to make the same mistake twice.

Man of the Match: C. A. Pujara.

Close of play: first day, India 323-4 (Pujara 98, Yuvraj Singh 24); second day, England 41-3 (Cook 22, Pietersen 6); third day, England 111-0 (Cook 74, Compton 34); fourth day, England 340-5 (Cook 168, Prior 84).

India

G. Gambhir b Swann	45		
V. Sehwag b Swann	117	– (1) c Pietersen b Swann	25
C. A. Pujara not out	206	– (2) not out	41
S. R. Tendulkar c Patel b Swann	13		
V. Kohli b Swann	19	– (3) not out	14
Yuvraj Singh c Swann b Patel	74		
*†M. S. Dhoni b Swann	5		
R. Ashwin c Prior b Pietersen	23		
Zaheer Khan c Trott b Anderson	7		
P. P. Ojha not out	0		
B 1, l-b 10, n-b 1	12		
1/134 (1) 2/224 (2) (8 wkts dec, 160 overs)	521	1/57 (1) (1 wkt, 15.3 overs)	80
3/250 (4) 4/283 (5) 5/413 (6)			
6/444 (7) 7/510 (8) 8/519 (9)			

U. T. Yadav did not bat.

Anderson 27–7–75–1; Broad 24–1–97–0; Bresnan 19–2–73–0; Swann 51–8–144–5; Patel 31–3–96–1; Pietersen 8–1–25–1. *Second innings*—Anderson 2–0–10–0; Swann 7.3–1–46–1; Patel 6–0–24–0.

England

*A. N. Cook c Sehwag b Ashwin	41	– b Ojha	176
N. R. D. Compton b Ashwin	9	– lbw b Zaheer Khan	37
J. M. Anderson c Gambhir b Ojha	2	– (11) not out	0
I. J. L. Trott c Pujara b Ashwin	0	– (3) c Dhoni b Ojha	17
K. P. Pietersen b Ojha	17	– (4) b Ojha	2
I. R. Bell c Tendulkar b Ojha	0	– (5) lbw b Yadav	22
S. R. Patel lbw b Yadav	10	– (6) lbw b Yadav	0
†M. J. Prior b Ojha	48	– (7) c and b Ojha	91
T. T. Bresnan c Kohli b Ojha	19	– (8) c sub (A. M. Rahane) b Zaheer Khan	20
S. C. J. Broad lbw b Zaheer Khan	25	– (9) c and b Yadav	3
G. P. Swann not out	3	– (10) b Ashwin	17
B 5, l-b 12	17	B 14, l-b 6, w 1	21
1/26 (2) 2/29 (3) 3/30 (4) 4/69 (5) 5/69 (6) 6/80 (1) 7/97 (7) 8/144 (9) 9/187 (10) 10/191 (8) (74.2 overs)	191	1/123 (2) 2/156 (3) 3/160 (4) 4/199 (5) 5/199 (6) 6/356 (7) 7/365 (1) 8/378 (9) 9/406 (10) 10/406 (8) (154.3 overs)	406

Ashwin 27–9–80–3; Zaheer Khan 15–7–23–1; Ojha 22.2–8–45–5; Yuvraj Singh 3–0–12–0; Yadav 7–2–14–1. *Second innings*—Yadav 23–2–70–3; Ojha 55–16–120–4; Ashwin 43–9–111–1; Sehwag 1–0–1–0; Zaheer Khan 27.3–5–59–2; Tendulkar 1–0–8–0; Yuvraj Singh 4–0–17–0.

Umpires: Aleem Dar and A. L. Hill. Third umpire: S. Asnani.
Referee: R. S. Mahanama.

INDIA v ENGLAND

Second Test Match

GIDEON BROOKS

At Mumbai (Wankhede Stadium), November 23–26, 2012. England won by ten wickets. Toss: India.

When Cook lost what looked like a crucial toss, he gazed heavenwards in frustration. And well he might have looked away from the source of his expected chagrin – the roughened red Mumbai soil and a pitch, used for a Ranji Trophy match three weeks earlier, that Dhoni had demanded should spin like a waltzer from ball one. Less than ten sessions later, Cook could have been forgiven for falling jubilantly into the Wankhede's dusty embrace after England had completed a scarcely believable ten-wicket win. It not only dragged them level in the series, but was arguably one of their finest away victories in the 79 years since they had first played Test cricket on the subcontinent, a mile or so away along Marine Drive at the Bombay Gymkhana.

Instead, Cook wrapped his arms round fellow opener Compton, before whipping out three stumps and handing two of them on the dressing-room steps to the pair who had done most to make victory possible – Pietersen, the Man of the Match, and Panesar, a close runner-up. For India, it was only a second home defeat in 24 Tests. Gallingly, they had been trumped in conditions thought to be ideally suited to a three-pronged spin attack, with Harbhajan Singh replacing the injured fast bowler Umesh Yadav; not since India themselves hosted South Africa at Kanpur in 2004-05 had a team entered a Test with only one specialist seamer.

Cook's was a nice touch after his first victory as full-time captain, which arrested an alarming slide in fortunes since the turn of the year. The personal milestones were a bonus: both Cook and Pietersen equalled England's Test record of 22 centuries, while Panesar – who finished with a career-best 11 for 210 – shared 19 wickets with Swann, the best

performance by English spinners in a Test since Tony Lock and Jim Laker, who also took 19, against New Zealand at Headingley in 1958.

The game had sparked into life immediately: Gambhir tucked Anderson's first ball through midwicket, then played fatally round the next. It may just have been the only delivery that swung all match, so it was a shame half the crowd were not there to witness it. Vigilant security is one thing, but an inadequate number of turnstiles, and a list of banned items that appeared to expand and contract on a daily whim, are quite another. Spectators eventually reaching the eye of the needle were told they could not bring in cameras, cigarettes, newspapers, water or food. No wonder Test attendances in India are a cause for concern: you are lucky to get in with the shirt on your back. Latecomers were still settling into their seats when Sehwag departed just over an hour later, bowled in his 100th Test by a full-length delivery from Panesar as he aimed to leg. Included here after England admitted their mistake in leaving him out at Ahmedabad, Panesar struck again before lunch, ripping a left-arm spinner's dream past Tendulkar's forward prod and knocking back his off stump.

Yet if England were encouraged by two further wickets before tea, reducing India to 119 for five, their galloping enthusiasm had to be reined in, as Pujara – who completed his second hundred of the series after Anderson had missed a tough chance in the gully off Panesar when he had 60 – and Ashwin redressed the balance. A close-of-play score of 266 for six left England supporters, here in greater number than at Ahmedabad, fretful about the prospect of chasing too many batting last. And the momentum inched further in India's direction next morning, before Pujara finally ran out of patience and partners, stumped by Prior to exit for 135 – his third century in his seventh Test, and the end of 1,015 unbeaten minutes (nearly 17 hours) and 382 runs in two games; for India, only Tendulkar (1,224 minutes in 2003-04) and Rahul Dravid (1,145 minutes in 2000-01) had batted longer between Test dismissals. Swann had already claimed his 200th Test wicket when Harbhajan walked casually across his stumps, but he was fortunate to add Zaheer Khan: even by the low umpiring standards set in this match by the normally excellent Aleem Dar, the decision to give Zaheer out caught at short leg off pad and chest took some explaining.

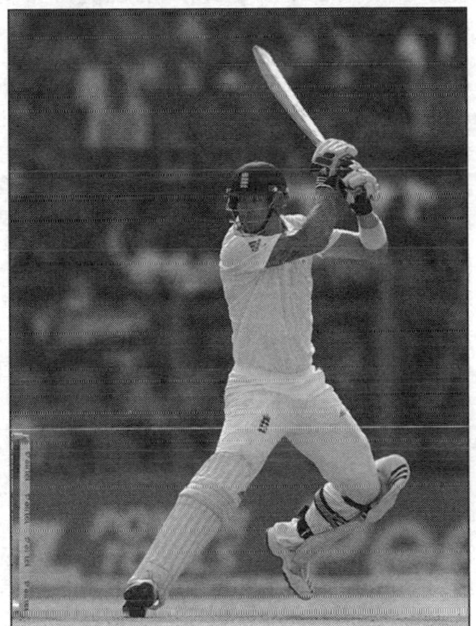

Philip Brown

Mumbai master: Kevin Pietersen forges ahead during a lionhearted 186.

Cook and Compton began the reply to India's 327 with a solid 66, but Compton edged Ojha low to Sehwag at slip and, in Ojha's next over, Trott fell leg-before for a duck. For England, the portents looked ominous – misleadingly so, as Cook and Pietersen came together in a match-winning partnership that would not be broken until eight overs before lunch on the third day. By then, England's captain and their maverick – one steady, the other spectacular – had put on 206, breaking the ground's Test record for the third wicket of 194, set by Tendulkar and Vinod Kambli, a pair of Mumbaikars, against England in 1992-93. It was also the 48th century stand in Tests Cook had been involved in, breaking Geoff Boycott's English record.

This felt apt. A crisp drive wide of mid-off on the third morning had already taken him to his 22nd Test century, where he joined Wally Hammond, Colin Cowdrey and Boycott on England's top step; he also became the first player of any nationality to score hundreds in each of his first four Tests as captain. Twelve balls later, four made room for five as

THE ROAD TO No. 22

Tests required for batsmen to score 22 centuries for England:

Tests	Inns		22nd 100	Tests	Inns		22nd 100
77	127	W. R. Hammond	1939	102	168	M. C. Cowdrey	1968-69
85	**149**	**A. N. Cook**	**2012-13**	107	190	G. Boycott	1981-82
90	**154**	**K. P. Pietersen**	**2012-13**				

Pietersen reverse-swept the ineffectual Harbhajan, reaching three figures in 127 deliveries to Cook's 236. The Mumbai bus system can be even more maddening than London's but, 31 years after Boycott had equalled a record first set in 1939, England were suddenly celebrating two arrivals at once.

Cook eventually perished to the last turn of the old ball, edging Ashwin into Dhoni's gloves. And what ended up as the final delivery before lunch then accounted, in bizarre fashion, for Bairstow, handed his chance while Ian Bell spent time at home with his new son. Bairstow was given out caught at silly point as he pushed forward to Ojha, despite replays that showed the ball sticking briefly under the grille of Gambhir's helmet before dropping into his hands. Law 32.3(e) said this should have been not out, but both Gambhir and Bairstow later admitted they were unaware of it. Not until the local TV coverage replayed the incident less than ten minutes before the restart did England cotton on. In an uneasy echo of the teatime fiasco at Trent Bridge in July 2011, when Bell was given run out, then reprieved, team director Andy Flower quickly made representations to the umpires. Asked on the outfield moments before play resumed whether he wanted to withdraw his appeal, this time Dhoni declined – and he was well within his rights to do so.

Pietersen, meanwhile, batted on, moving to 150 with a cut for four off Ojha, then imperiously slog-sweeping the next ball for six. But, on 186, he deflected Ojha to Dhoni, ending a masterful display of violent intent that had lasted 233 balls. His runs – more than any England batsman had made at the Wankhede, surpassing Graeme Hick's 178 in 1992-93 – came out of 314 while he was at the wicket. He later called it his best innings, even if he had been helped by the tendency of India's spinners to drop short. Prior's careless run-out triggered a collapse which cost England their last four wickets in 13 deliveries, but their lead of 86 felt like decent ammunition for an assault with the ball.

Even so, no one could have predicted what happened next. In the 33 overs that remained on the third evening, India lost seven for 117, five to Panesar, whose extra pace through the air left the batsmen reluctant to commit to the front foot on a surface offering bounce; the demise of Tendulkar, trapped on the crease, was symptomatic. By stumps, India's scorecard resembled a half-decent poker hand: a pair of sixes, a pair of eights and the makings of a low straight flush. But their stakes were as good as lost. The last three fell in 45 minutes the following morning, when Gambhir's hopes of carrying his bat were thwarted by another umpiring error: Tony Hill failed to spot an inside edge.

Panesar, though, had been denied the best Test figures by an English spinner in India when Dar contrived to miss Ojha's thick edge to backward short leg. That record remained with Hedley Verity, a fellow left-arm spinner, and his 11 for 153 at Madras in 1933-34, although Panesar could at least boast England's first ten-wicket haul in India since Neil Foster's 11 for 163, also at Madras, in 1984-85.

Regardless, all 28 wickets to fall to bowlers following Gambhir's removal in the game's first over had now gone to spin. Perhaps determined not to add to the tally, England's openers knocked off the runs in under ten overs. India looked ashen-faced. From nowhere, the series had come alive.

Man of the Match: K. P. Pietersen.

Close of play: first day, India 266-6 (Pujara 114, Ashwin 60); second day, England 178-2 (Cook 87, Pietersen 62); third day, India 117-7 (Gambhir 53, Harbhajan Singh 1).

India

G. Gambhir lbw b Anderson	4	– lbw b Swann	65
V. Sehwag b Panesar	30	– c Swann b Panesar	9
C. A. Pujara st Prior b Swann	135	– c Bairstow b Swann	6
S. R. Tendulkar b Panesar	8	– lbw b Panesar	8
V. Kohli c Compton b Panesar	19	– c sub (J. E. Root) b Swann	7
Yuvraj Singh b Swann	0	– c Bairstow b Panesar	8
*†M. S. Dhoni c Swann b Panesar	29	– c Trott b Panesar	6
R. Ashwin lbw b Panesar	68	– c Patel b Panesar	11
Harbhajan Singh lbw b Swann	21	– c Trott b Swann	6
Zaheer Khan c Bairstow b Swann	11	– c Prior b Panesar	1
P. P. Ojha not out	0	– not out	6
L-b 1, n-b 1	2	B 6, l-b 3	9
1/4 (1) 2/52 (2) 3/60 (4) 4/118 (5) 5/119 (6) 6/169 (7) 7/280 (8) 8/315 (9) 9/316 (3) 10/327 (10) (115.1 overs)	327	1/30 (2) 2/37 (3) 3/52 (4) 4/65 (5) 5/78 (6) 6/92 (7) 7/110 (8) 8/128 (9) 9/131 (10) 10/142 (1) (44.1 overs)	142

Anderson 18–3–61–1; Broad 12–1–60–0; Panesar 47–12–129–5; Swann 34.1–7–70–4; Patel 4–1–6–0. *Second innings*—Anderson 4–1–9–0; Panesar 22–3–81–6; Swann 18.1–6–43–4.

England

*A. N. Cook c Dhoni b Ashwin	122	– not out	18
N. R. D. Compton c Sehwag b Ojha	29	– not out	30
I. J. L. Trott lbw b Ojha	0		
K. P. Pietersen c Dhoni b Ojha	186		
J. M. Bairstow c Gambhir b Ojha	9		
S. R. Patel c Kohli b Ojha	26		
†M. J. Prior run out	21		
S. C. J. Broad c Pujara b Harbhajan Singh	6		
G. P. Swann not out	1		
J. M. Anderson lbw b Harbhajan Singh	2		
M. S. Panesar c Zaheer Khan b Ashwin	4		
B 4, l-b 2, w 1	7	B 8, l-b 2	10
1/66 (2) 2/68 (3) 3/274 (1) 4/298 (5) 5/357 (6) 6/382 (4) 7/406 (7) 8/406 (8) 9/408 (10) 10/413 (11) (121.3 overs)	413	(no wkt, 9.4 overs)	58

Ashwin 42.3–6–145–2; Ojha 40–6–143–5; Zaheer Khan 15–4–37–0; Harbhajan Singh 21–1–74–2; Yuvraj Singh 3–0–8–0. *Second innings*—Ashwin 3.4–0–22–0; Ojha 4–0–16–0; Harbhajan Singh 2–0–10–0.

Umpires: Aleem Dar and A. L. Hill. Third umpire: S. Ravi.
Referee: R. S. Mahanama.

INDIA v ENGLAND

Third Test Match

SURESH MENON

At Kolkata, December 5–9, 2012. England won by seven wickets. Toss: India.

In the days when India merely made up the numbers, their supporters would soften the blow by divorcing team results from individual performances. Gradually, things changed and, by 2009 – when they went top of the Test rankings – there was no longer any need to look for the positives cherished by the losing captain. But after successive 4–0 defeats abroad, India were reverting to type. England, for so long hapless tourists in this part of the world, were doing the opposite. Suddenly, Indian cricket had once more become full

Graham Morris

Brain fade: Alastair Cook realises that, for the first time in his first-class career, he has been run out.

of old-style consolation: Rahul Dravid's three centuries in England, for example, or Kohli's maiden Test hundred at Adelaide. And anyway, went the argument, India were still kings at home. They had the spinners and, in Zaheer Khan, the master of reverse swing, praised during this game by Anderson, who had copied his practice of hiding the ball from the batsman's view until the last minute. And, of course, India had the batting, with Pujara the latest exemplar.

This Test put paid to all such consolation-within-consolations, for it proved Mumbai was no one-off. Anderson reversed the ball better than any Indian and, for the second match running, Swann and Panesar outspun Ashwin and Ojha. Batting with authority and purpose, Cook looked good for a triple-century, but had to settle for 190, in the process extending his own world record to a hundred in each of his first five Tests as captain. Only four other visiting batsmen – Everton Weekes, Garry Sobers, Ken Barrington and Andy Flower – had scored centuries in three successive Tests in India. Cook was batting differently, too, and later gave the game's shorter formats the credit for his extra aggression. At times, as he lofted India's spinners, there were gasps from his countrymen in the crowd.

India had passed 600 in each of the three previous Kolkata Tests, but now squandered an important toss by making only 316. Against an attack that included Sharma, drafted in as a second seamer to balance the line-up in place of Harbhajan Singh, Cook then put on 165 with the adhesive Compton and 173 with Trott. That helped take England to 523, a total bettered at Eden Gardens among visiting teams only by West Indies (twice – in 1958-59 and 1987-88). And when India lost nine second-innings wickets wiping off the deficit, Sehwag sighed: "Only God can save us now." More practical believers wondered whether God wasn't, in fact, biased towards those who helped themselves. Ashwin's imitation of the boy on the burning deck brought him a fine unbeaten 91, but he was in the team as an off-spinner – and, in his main job, he was a let-down.

The public spat between Dhoni and Prabir Mukherjee, the Eden Gardens groundsman who had described the captain's call for a turner as "immoral", kept pre-match discussions

MOST FIRST-CLASS INNINGS BEFORE FIRST RUN-OUT

		Span
393	J. J. Whitaker	1983–1994
317	C. A. Walsh	1981-82–1992-93
311	**A. N. Cook**	**2003–2012-13**
298†	N. V. Radford	1978-79–1995-96
279	B. E. A. Edmeades	1961–1969
272†	T. A. Munton	1986–2001
267	Nawab of Pataudi jun.	1957–1965-66
265	J. Lewis	1995–2009
262	Kapil Dev	1975-76–1985-86
251	M. H. Denness	1959–1967

The following had notable mid-career sequences without a run-out:

543	Hon. F. S. G. Calthorpe	1912–1932
359	R. Howorth	1935–1948

† *Entire career: Radford and Munton were never run out.*

Research: Philip Bailey

---

moored at a low level. The track chosen was brown, unlike the grey pitches which flanked it, and the bowlers' run-ups were still visible from the Ranji Trophy match played on it barely a fortnight earlier. In the end, though, it wasn't the pitch, or its refusal to turn from the start that defeated India, but a better organised England side coming to terms with their own demons in a country where they had not won a series since the days before their captain could even crawl.

India's consolation was no real consolation at all. Tendulkar's first fifty in 11 innings was a scratchy knock, serving to highlight his determination but also his decline. When Panesar had asked him to sign the ball with which he had dismissed him for his first Test wicket in 2005-06, Tendulkar had written on it: "Once in a blue moon, never again". But he had already been proved wrong. And now his struggle against Panesar's left-arm spin, inside-edging and slicing attempted drives, was symbolic. The gap between the two standing ovations Tendulkar was receiving per innings – one walking out to bat, the other returning – had been getting smaller, so his 76 here, which took him past Sunil Gavaskar's Indian record of 2,483 Test runs against England, at least provided temporary respite. Yet he could do nothing about a delivery from Anderson – the first after the drinks break on the first evening – that reversed just enough to take the edge. And for those who see significance in such things, the Indian flag on a building outside the stadium was at half-mast.

That wicket reasserted England's early grip on the match, which had been helped by a terrible piece of running between Gambhir and Sehwag after they had raced to 47 in ten overs on the first morning. England never let go and, at stumps on the second day, were 216 for one, with Cook dominant on 136 – his 23rd Test century, to overtake the national record he had equalled only 11 days earlier in Mumbai. He was not yet 28, prompting many to believe that at least some of Tendulkar's batting records might one day be his. Cook also went past 7,000 runs in his 86th Test, faster than Viv Richards, Ricky Ponting and Greg Chappell. He was also the youngest to reach the mark, at 27 years 347 days; Tendulkar was seven months older. And Cook's fluency allowed Compton to find his form in his own time and with his own methods, though he was unlucky to be given out leg-before on 57: replays showed the ball had brushed his glove as he swept Ojha.

India's big chance had already come and gone when Cook, on 17, edged Zaheer Khan low to first slip, where Pujara couldn't hold on – another area where Dravid was being missed. When Cook finally fell, having batted eight hours 12 minutes and faced 377 balls, it was refreshing to know that the superman who loomed large in the nightmares of Indian bowlers was in fact human after all. He had never been run out in first-class cricket, but now Pietersen turned Zaheer into the leg side to Kohli, the Indian fielder most likely to pull off a direct hit. Backing up, Cook motioned to regain his ground, only to flinch – bat in the air, and still out of his crease – as the throw whizzed past him on to the stumps. He knew instantly he was out, and later called it a "brain fade". Only Arthur Morris, Garry Sobers and Younis Khan had been run out in the 190s in Test cricket before; only Mike Gatting and Graeme Fowler, in the same game at Madras in 1984-85, had scored more for England in a Test innings in India.

The last four wickets fell quickly on the fourth morning, yet there was no hint of the drama to follow when India went to lunch at 86 without loss, 121 behind, with Sehwag in battling form. Swann sneaked the first ball after the break between his bat and pad – and soon, as they struggled for breath, India were reeling at 122 for six. Pujara was run out by a brilliant throw from Bell, before Anderson and Finn, finally recovered from a thigh injury and chosen ahead of Stuart Broad, bowled superbly. It was the session that decided the Test – and, it transpired, the series. Finn bowled with pace, angling the ball in to the batsmen, troubling them with bounce, and inducing edges with the one that held its line. Anderson's control of reverse swing precluded any Cook-like vigil from the Indians. And Tendulkar's brief stay was up when he misread a straight delivery from Swann and edged to slip.

But to the delight of a gratifyingly large crowd, Ashwin kept fighting, driving the new ball and shielding last man Ojha to avert an innings defeat and a four-day finish. Their stand was worth 50 on the final morning before Ojha fell to Anderson – the off bail taking an age to topple after being kissed almost imperceptibly – giving the fast bowlers six wickets to the spinners' three. England needed 41 for a 2–1 lead, but slipped to eight for three, including Cook, who became only the second batsman – after England's Archie MacLaren at Sydney in 1894-95 – to be stumped in the first over of a Test innings. But Bell, back in place of Jonny Bairstow, settled the issue with Compton.

Clearly, India were not handling transition well. Many of those who had helped place them on the pedestal had retired. And those who remained, such as Tendulkar, Harbhajan and Zaheer – who was immediately dropped for the Fourth Test, along with Yuvraj Singh – were floundering. The fielding had also gone backwards, and the many justifications of fielding coach Trevor Penney painted India as a team in denial: "We don't need specialists," he said, loyally backing the stragglers. A banner in the crowd read: "Dhoni, we will stand by you." But India needed more than loyalty.

Man of the Match: A. N. Cook.

Close of play: first day, India 273-7 (Dhoni 22, Zaheer Khan 0); second day, England 216-1 (Cook 136, Trott 21); third day, England 509-6 (Prior 40, Swann 21); fourth day, India 239-9 (Ashwin 83, Ojha 3).

India

G. Gambhir c Trott b Panesar	60	– c Prior b Finn	40
V. Sehwag run out	23	– b Swann	49
C. A. Pujara b Panesar	16	– run out	8
S. R. Tendulkar c Prior b Anderson	76	– c Trott b Swann	5
V. Kohli c Swann b Anderson	6	– c Prior b Finn	20
Yuvraj Singh c Cook b Swann	32	– b Anderson	11
*†M. S. Dhoni c Swann b Finn	52	– c Cook b Anderson	0
R. Ashwin b Anderson	21	– not out	91
Zaheer Khan lbw b Panesar	6	– lbw b Finn	0
I. Sharma b Panesar	0	– b Panesar	10
P. P. Ojha not out	0	– b Anderson	3
B 5, l-b 13, w 5, n-b 1	24	B 8, l-b 2	10
1/47 (2) 2/88 (3) 3/117 (1) (105 overs)	316	1/86 (2) 2/98 (3) (84.4 overs)	247
4/136 (5) 5/215 (6) 6/230 (4)		3/103 (1) 4/107 (4)	
7/268 (8) 8/292 (9) 9/296 (10) 10/316 (7)		5/122 (6) 6/122 (7) 7/155 (5)	
		8/159 (9) 9/197 (10) 10/247 (11)	

Anderson 28–7–89–3; Finn 21–2–73–1; Panesar 40–13–90–4; Swann 16–3–46–1. *Second innings*—Anderson 15.4–4–38–3; Finn 18–6–45–3; Panesar 22–1–75–1; Swann 28–9–70–2; Patel 1–0–9–0.

England

*A. N. Cook run out	190	– st Dhoni b Ashwin	1
N. R. D. Compton lbw b Ojha	57	– not out	9
I. J. L. Trott c Dhoni b Ojha	87	– lbw b Ojha	3
K. P. Pietersen lbw b Ashwin	54	– c Dhoni b Ashwin	0
I. R. Bell c Dhoni b Sharma	5	– not out	28
S. R. Patel c Sehwag b Ojha	33		
†M. J. Prior c Dhoni b Zaheer Khan	41		
G. P. Swann c Sehwag b Ojha	21		
S. T. Finn not out	4		
J. M. Anderson c Sehwag b Ashwin	9		
M. S. Panesar lbw b Ashwin	0		
B 13, l-b 4, n-b 5	22		
1/165 (2) 2/338 (3) 3/359 (1) (167.3 overs)	523	1/4 (1) (3 wkts, 12.1 overs)	41
4/395 (5) 5/420 (4) 6/453 (6)		2/7 (3) 3/8 (4)	
7/510 (8) 8/510 (7) 9/523 (10) 10/523 (11)			

Zaheer Khan 31–6–94–1; Sharma 29–8–78–1; Ashwin 52.3–9–183–3; Ojha 52–10–142–4; Yuvraj Singh 3–1–9–0. *Second innings*—Ashwin 6.1–1–31–2; Ojha 6–3–10–1.

Umpires: H. D. P. K. Dharmasena and R. J. Tucker. Third umpire: V. A. Kulkarni.
Referee: J. J. Crowe.

INDIA v ENGLAND

Fourth Test Match

RICHARD HOBSON

At Nagpur, December 13–17, 2012. Drawn. Toss: England. Test debuts: R. A. Jadeja; J. E. Root.

A Test match that felt like a throwback to a sleepier past produced a series result that was just as unfamiliar to the modern audience: an England win in India. The draw confirmed a 2–1 scoreline, and the sluggish rate of scoring over the five days on a desperately slow pitch mattered not a jot to the victorious Cook, who took the Man of the Series award to boot. The fact that so much rested on the outcome lent a soporific contest a strange kind of tension. Ultimately, though, England batted out their second innings in comfort, and there was something rather low-key – like a County Championship match petering out on a Saturday afternoon – about the conclusion, with hands shaken 50 minutes after tea on the final day. The result had been a formality for several hours as the Warwickshire pair of Trott and Bell stretched their abstemious partnership to 208.

And yet nobody predicted such a dry, dour contest. Following England's win at Kolkata, pundits expected the surface at Nagpur to generate a positive result, perhaps even inside three days. In truth, there was no meaningful precedent. Curator Praveen Hingnikar –

Graham Morris

Grounded: Joe Root makes a level-headed half-century on Test debut.

banned by the BCCI from talking to the media before the game following the outbursts of his Eden Gardens counterpart – had relaid the topsoil earlier in the year; this was the first contest since. Hingnikar was more surprised than anyone that cracks in the new surface refused to widen under sunshine. Dhoni remarked phlegmatically that the game could have continued for another three days and still ended in a draw.

Pietersen described the first-day pitch as the least conducive to strokeplay he had ever encountered. Only towards the end of the match, as fresh grass allowed a little more pace, could batsmen feel confident about playing the odd shot. But by then England had no cause for urgency. Except against the new ball, both captains placed fielders for mistimed drives rather than edges, and it was not unusual for batsmen to shape to duck against deliveries that eventually reached them at hip height. The second day produced the most runs, 218; eight individual fifties were compiled from an average of 127 balls; three hundreds from 271. Timeless Tests of yore must have followed the same tempo.

India did not help themselves with an unbalanced selection. Putting all their snakes in one basket, they chose three specialist slow bowlers, plus Ravindra Jadeja, a left-arm-spinning all-rounder handed a debut in place of Yuvraj Singh. Jadeja proceeded to bowl more overs (70) in the match than either Ashwin or Chawla, the leg-spinner picked in place of Zaheer Khan for his first Test since April 2008; a gap of 49 Tests between appearances was an Indian record. The selectors' error became clear during the game's opening spell, from Sharma, now the lone seamer, which brought two wickets.

With no bite for their spinners, India were at least spared the threat of Steven Finn, missing because of a back injury when his height might have coaxed something from the surface. Bresnan, his replacement, made little impression, yet one England hunch on selection proved inspired, as the 21-year-old Yorkshire opener Joe Root – replacing Samit Patel, and unexpectedly chosen ahead of both Jonny Bairstow and Eoin Morgan – marked his own debut with a display of rare assurance in an unfamiliar slot at No. 6.

Cook himself suffered his only bad match of the series. After winning his first toss in six Tests as captain, he received two questionable decisions from umpire Dharmasena in a contest that left England repeating their support for DRS. Trott, though, could blame only himself, as he left a ball from Jadeja that went straight on, and Bell succumbed to a timid push to short extra cover, having matched Cook in taking 28 balls over a single. When Pietersen flicked to midwicket to end a restrained 73, the England first innings was tottering at 139 for five. But Root showed the temperament and the light footwork that had persuaded the management his technique would hold up against spin. Prior dug in to confirm his maturity as a batsman for all situations and, by stumps, England were an old-fashioned 199 for five from 97 overs, having faced the equivalent of 80 overs of dot-balls. Next day, the pair extended their stand to 103, and a relatively brisk half-century from Swann – his first in Tests for three years – took England beyond 300. Root's 73 came from 229 balls, in 11 minutes short of five hours, and he was furious with himself when a leading edge supplied a return catch to the inoffensive Chawla.

MOST INTERNATIONAL WICKETS FOR ENGLAND

		Test	*ODI*	*T20I*
528	I. T. Botham	383	145	–
528	**J. M. Anderson**	**288**	**222**	**18**
466	D. Gough	229	234	3
405	R. G. D. Willis	325	80	–
392	A. Flintoff	219	168	5
368	**S. C. J. Broad**	**172**	**148**	**48**
361	**G. P. Swann**	**212**	**98**	**51**
329	D. L. Underwood	297	32	–
307	F. S. Trueman	307	–	–
303	A. R. Caddick	234	69	–

Gough also took one wicket (in an ODI), and Flintoff eight (seven in a Test and one in ODIs) for the World XI. S. J. Harmison took 299 international wickets for England (222 in Tests, 76 in ODIs and one in T20Is), plus four in one Test for the World XI.

Figures correct at January 27, 2013.

A total of 330 looked like par, but superb swing bowling by Anderson on the second afternoon defined the middle of the game. The third ball of the innings nipped in to expose Sehwag's leaden footwork. Tendulkar was then bowled via an inside edge by a ball keeping a shade low, a dismissal that stirred, rather than advanced, the debate about his future; it was a record ninth time that he had fallen to Anderson, one clear of Muttiah Muralitharan. A series of inswingers set up the left-handed Gambhir for the one going across, and the wicket of Jadeja was Anderson's 528th in all international cricket, equalling Ian Botham's England record. Pujara, meanwhile, had already fallen to a fine right-handed catch by Bell at short leg off Swann, although replays showed the ball had deviated from forearm rather than glove.

Crucially, Anderson had forced India – 87 for four at the second-day close – to consolidate when the state of the series required them to be positive. Kohli and Dhoni (to some surprise, he had promoted himself above Jadeja who, a fortnight previously, had become the first Indian to score three first-class triple-centuries) responded by taking 507 balls over a stand of 198, watching every one of them like hawks. Neither man had batted for as long in a Test before, with Kohli in particular fighting against poor form as well as his instinct to attack. He eventually departed straight after drinks in the final session of the third day, having completed his third Test hundred from 289 balls. But, excruciatingly, Dhoni fell for 99, run out by a direct hit from Cook at mid-off as he attempted a desperate single. It was his first risk of the innings, an unthinkable liberty had he been on 98 or 100. The pressure of being in the nineties for more than an hour had finally told.

With time of the essence, India's approach on the fourth morning was baffling. Ashwin initially chose to turn down singles to keep Ojha away from strike, and only 29 runs came in the first hour – which suited England – before Dhoni declared four runs behind. England had merely to avoid mishaps, and never allowed themselves to be fazed by their slow progress. Cook had one run to his name from 46 balls by lunch, while Compton hit a single four in 134 deliveries before being adjudged leg-before despite an inside edge (although the ball flew straight to gully, so he was out one way or another).

The afternoon roused passions as Trott, in typically single-minded pursuit of runs, opted to hit a boundary off Jadeja from a ball that had slipped from his hand on to an adjacent strip. Although Trott was within his rights, other batsmen might have allowed the umpire to call dead ball. At the close, Ashwin suggested it had been unsporting. Before then, India had suffered more frustration, when Trott survived a strong (but unproven) appeal for a catch behind off Sharma. Ashwin later threatened to run Trott out at the bowler's end for backing up too far. But Trott remained steadfastly Trott, his self-absorption tailor-made for the situation. By the time he flicked Ashwin to leg slip to depart for 143, made in 405 minutes, England's lead had advanced to an impregnable 306. It proved the only wicket to fall on the final day. Bell ended a 403-minute innings with 116 not out – his first Test hundred in India – tired but satisfied, while the home crowd were generous but resigned. England cracked open the beers, and began to think of Christmas.

Man of the Match: J. M. Anderson. *Man of the Series:* A. N. Cook.

Close of play: first day, England 199-5 (Root 31, Prior 34); second day, India 87-4 (Kohli 11, Dhoni 8); third day, India 297-8 (Ashwin 7); fourth day, England 161-3 (Trott 66, Bell 24).

England

*A. N. Cook lbw b Sharma	1	– c Dhoni b Ashwin	13
N. R. D. Compton c Dhoni b Sharma	3	– lbw b Ojha	34
I. J. L. Trott b Jadeja	44	– c Kohli b Ashwin	143
K. P. Pietersen c Ojha b Jadeja	73	– b Jadeja	6
I. R. Bell c Kohli b Chawla	1	– not out	116
J. E. Root c and b Chawla	73	– not out	20
†M. J. Prior b Ashwin	57		
T. T. Bresnan lbw b Sharma	0		
G. P. Swann lbw b Chawla	56		
J. M. Anderson c Pujara b Chawla	4		
M. S. Panesar not out	1		
B 5, l-b 12	17	B 8, l-b 6, n-b 6	20
1/3 (2) 2/16 (1) 3/102 (3) 4/119 (5) 5/139 (4) 6/242 (7) 7/242 (8) 8/302 (6) 9/325 (9) 10/330 (10) (145.5 overs)	330	1/48 (1) 2/81 (2) 3/94 (4) 4/302 (3) (4 wkts dec, 154 overs)	352

Sharma 28–9–49–3; Ojha 35–12–71–0; Jadeja 37–17–58–2; Chawla 21.5–1–69–4; Ashwin 24–3–66–1. *Second innings*—Sharma 15–3–42–0; Ojha 40–14–70–1; Ashwin 38–11–99–2; Chawla 26–6–64–0; Jadeja 33–17–59–1; Gambhir 2–0–4–0.

India

G. Gambhir c Prior b Anderson	37
V. Sehwag b Anderson	0
C. A. Pujara c Bell b Swann	26
S. R. Tendulkar b Anderson	2
V. Kohli lbw b Swann	103
*†M. S. Dhoni run out	99
R. A. Jadeja lbw b Anderson	12
R. Ashwin not out	29
P. P. Chawla b Swann	1
P. P. Ojha b Panesar	3
I. Sharma not out	2
B 5, l-b 7	12
1/1 (2) 2/59 (3) 3/64 (4) 4/71 (1) 5/269 (5) 6/288 (7) 7/295 (6) 8/297 (9) 9/317 (10) (9 wkts dec, 143 overs)	326

Anderson 32–5–81–4; Bresnan 26–5–69–0; Panesar 52–15–81–1; Swann 31–10–76–3; Trott 1–0–2–0; Root 1–0–5–0.

Umpires: H. D. P. K. Dharmasena and R. J. Tucker. Third umpire: S. Ravi.
Referee: J. J. Crowe.

TWENTY20 INTERNATIONAL REPORTS BY CHRIS STOCKS

INDIA v ENGLAND

First Twenty20 International

At Gahunje, December 20, 2012 (floodlit). India won by five wickets. Toss: India. Twenty20 international debuts: P. Awana; S. C. Meaker, J. C. Tredwell.

Dhoni hit the winning runs with 13 balls to spare, but the night belonged to Yuvraj Singh, whose whirlwind 38 followed career-best Twenty20 international figures. His left-arm spin had applied the brakes after England reached 89 for one in ten overs, thanks to a stand of 68 between Hales and Wright. Dropped from India's Test squad the previous week, Yuvraj removed both plus Morgan, the stand-in captain, in the space of ten balls. It needed an inventive innings from Buttler, taking over wicketkeeping duties after Jonny Bairstow was dropped, to lift England to a respectable total in the first international played at the Subrata Roy Sahara Stadium near Pune. But three wides in Dernbach's opening over set the tone for an ill-disciplined bowling performance and, although Bresnan dismissed both openers in the fifth over, Yuvraj had broken the back of the chase by the time he fell to the last ball of the tenth. Victory against weakened opponents was scant consolation for India after their travails in the Tests, with the injured duo of Stuart Broad – England's Twenty20 captain – and Steven Finn back home, along with the rested Kevin Pietersen and Graeme Swann.

Man of the Match: Yuvraj Singh.

England

		B	4	6
M. J. Lumb *lbw b 8*	1	10	0	0
A. D. Hales *b 4*	56	35	7	2
L. J. Wright *c 2 b 4*	34	21	3	1
*E. J. G. Morgan *c 2 b 4*	5	9	0	0
S. R. Patel *c 2 b 10*	24	22	1	1
†J. C. Buttler *not out*	33	21	0	3
T. T. Bresnan *c 3 b 10*	0	1	0	0
J. C. Tredwell *not out*	1	1	0	0
L-b 2, w 1	3			
6 overs: 51-1 (20 overs)	157-6			

1/21 2/89 3/99 4/100 5/138 6/139

S. C. Meaker, D. R. Briggs and J. W. Dernbach did not bat.

Dinda 3–0–18–2; Ashwin 4–1–33–1; Awana 2–0–29–0; Jadeja 3–0–22–0; Chawla 3–0–24–0; Kohli 1–0–10–0; Yuvraj Singh 4–0–19–3.

India

		B	4	6
G. Gambhir *c 2 b 7*	16	16	3	0
A. M. Rahane *c 5 b 7*	19	13	0	2
V. Kohli *b 9*	21	17	2	0
Yuvraj Singh *c 9 b 3*	38	21	2	3
S. K. Raina *run out*	26	19	1	1
*†M. S. Dhoni *not out*	24	21	2	0
R. A. Jadeja *not out*	0	0	0	0
L-b 4, w 10	14			
6 overs: 52-2 (17.5 overs)	158-5			

1/42 2/44 3/93 4/110 5/148

R. Ashwin, P. P. Chawla, A. B. Dinda and P. Awana did not bat.

Dernbach 3–0–27–0; Bresnan 3–0–26–2; Meaker 3.5–0–28–1; Tredwell 4–0–31–0; Briggs 1–0–18–0; Wright 3–0–24–1.

Umpires: S. Asnani and C. Shamshuddin. Third umpire: V. A. Kulkarni.

INDIA v ENGLAND

Second Twenty20 International

At Mumbai (Wankhede Stadium), December 22, 2012 (floodlit). England won by six wickets. Toss: England. Twenty20 international debut: J. E. Root.

Morgan's huge straight six off Dinda into the second tier of the Wankhede's North Stand sealed a pulsating final-ball victory for England and a share of the series, and rounded off their highest successful Twenty20 run-chase. The target of 178 – more than India had ever failed to defend – had been whittled down to 15 off seven balls, which became nine off six when Buttler launched Parvinder Awana back over his head. The first five deliveries of a protracted final over yielded six of them, leaving England needing three to win off the last, and two to force an eliminator over. But Morgan shaped to play a ramp shot, prompting Dinda to pull out of his delivery, and the ensuing delay cranked up the drama, testing the nerve of both men: Morgan held his, Dinda did not. Dhoni's sixth-wicket stand of 60 with Raina in 27 balls had helped set an imposing target. But Lumb's fifty, his first in Twenty20 internationals, laid the foundations, before he became the first of three victims for Yuvraj Singh, who improved his career-best figures in the format for the second time in three days.

Man of the Match: E. J. G. Morgan. *Man of the Series:* Yuvraj Singh.

India

		B	4	6
G. Gambhir *c 8 b 3*	17	27	1	0
A. M. Rahane *c 7 b 11*	3	5	0	0
V. Kohli *lbw b 10*	38	20	7	0
Yuvraj Singh *c 7 b 3*	4	5	0	0
R. G. Sharma *b 9*	24	19	1	1
S. K. Raina *not out*	35	24	3	1
*†M. S. Dhoni *c 5 b 8*	38	18	3	2
R. Ashwin *c 1 b 11*	1	3	0	0
P. P. Chawla *run out*	0	1	0	0
B 2, l-b 4, w 9, n-b 2	17			
6 overs: 59-1 (20 overs)	177-8			

1/7 2/64 3/71 4/88 5/108 6/168 7/171 8/177

A. B. Dinda and P. Awana did not bat.

Bresnan 4–0–27–1; Dernbach 4–0–37–2; Meaker 4–0–42–1; Wright 4–0–38–2; Tredwell 4–0–27–1.

England

		B	4	6
M. J. Lumb *st 7 b 4*	50	34	6	2
A. D. Hales *c 10 b 4*	42	33	4	1
L. J. Wright *lbw b 4*	5	10	0	0
*E. J. G. Morgan *not out*	49	26	5	2
S. R. Patel *c 1 b 10*	9	10	1	0
†J. C. Buttler *not out*	15	7	1	1
B 1, l-b 8, w 2	11			
6 overs: 62-0 (20 overs)	181-4			

1/80 2/94 3/123 4/149

J. E. Root, T. T. Bresnan, J. C. Tredwell, S. C. Meaker and J. W. Dernbach did not bat.

Dinda 4–0–44–1; Awana 4–0–42–0; Ashwin 4–0–38–0; Chawla 4–0–31–0; Yuvraj Singh 4–0–17–3.

Umpires: V. A. Kulkarni and S. Ravi. Third umpire: S. Asnani.
Series referee: J. J. Crowe.

At Delhi (Palam), January 6, 2013. **India A won by 53 runs** (D/L). **India A 224-4** (39 overs) (A. Mukund 57, M. Vijay 76, K. M. Jadhav 52*); ‡**England XI 175** (36 overs) (I. R. Bell 91; A. L. Menaria 3-43). *After a delayed start, bad light and rain intruded after five overs (India A were 15-0). The match was reduced to 39 overs a side and, after Abhinav Mukund and Murali Vijay put on 118, the England XI were set a revised target of 229. They never got close: apart from Bell, who faced 89 balls, only Pietersen (19) of the top seven reached double figures.*

At Delhi, January 8, 2013 (day/night). **Delhi won by six wickets.** ‡**England XI 294-5** (50 overs) (I. R. Bell 108, E. J. G. Morgan 52; Varun Sood 3-45); **Delhi 295-4** (48.3 overs) (S. Dhawan 110, Milind Kumar 78*). *England's batsmen performed better as Bell continued his good form with 108 from 125 balls. Delhi's captain Shikhar Dhawan started by putting on 98 with Unmukt Chand in 17.4 overs, and went on to a century; but, not long after he was out, Delhi were 192-4, needing another 103 from 13.3 overs. To England's discomfort, they strolled home.*

ONE-DAY INTERNATIONAL REPORTS BY ALI MARTIN

INDIA v ENGLAND

First One-Day International

At Rajkot, January 11, 2013 (day/night). England won by nine runs. Toss: England. One-day international debut: J. E. Root.

On a run-filled pitch for the first one-day international at the Saurashtra C. A. Stadium, England secured their first 50-over win in India in 14 attempts – despite nearly squandering an opening stand of 158 between Cook and Bell. When Pietersen picked out Kohli at long-off in the 44th over, they had slowed to 255 for four, and their eventual 325 – only their second 300-plus score away to India – owed much to Patel, who thrashed 44 off 20 balls; in all, the last 6.1 overs brought 70. But the chase confirmed England's total as little better than par. With lateral movement absent, Rahane and Gambhir raced to 66 in the powerplay, before Cook turned to off-spin from both ends and slowed the run-rate. The debutant Root, unused with the bat, went for just 17 in his first five overs, while his senior partner Tredwell removed the openers. Half-centuries from Yuvraj Singh, from only 38 balls, and Raina kept India in the hunt, but Tredwell returned to claim both and finish with a career-best four for 44. England felt truly safe only when Dernbach had Dhoni caught by Root at long-off for 32, attempting to hit a slower ball for what would have been his fifth six. Dhoni's late salvo may have been in vain, but it hinted at what was to follow.

Man of the Match: J. C. Tredwell.

England

*A. N. Cook c Rahane b Raina	75	S. R. Patel not out	44
I. R. Bell run out	85	W 10, n-b 2	12
K. P. Pietersen c Kohli b Dinda	44		
E. J. G. Morgan c and b Dinda	41	1/158 (2) 2/172 (1) (4 wkts, 50 overs)	325
†C. Kieswetter not out	24	3/248 (4) 4/255 (3)	10 overs: 54-0

J. E. Root, T. T. Bresnan, J. C. Tredwell, S. T. Finn and J. W. Dernbach did not bat.

Bhuvneshwar Kumar 7–0–52–0; Sharma 10–2–86–0; Dinda 8–0–53–2; Ashwin 9–0–61–0; Jadeja 10–0–46–0; Raina 5–0–18–1; Kohli 1–0–9–0.

India

A. M. Rahane c Dernbach b Tredwell	47	A. B. Dinda b Bresnan	3
G. Gambhir c Bell b Tredwell	52	I. Sharma not out	7
V. Kohli c Kieswetter b Bresnan	15		
Yuvraj Singh c Dernbach b Tredwell	61	L-b 1, w 7, n-b 1	9
S. K. Raina c and b Tredwell	50		
*†M. S. Dhoni c Root b Dernbach	32	1/96 (1) 2/102 (2) (9 wkts, 50 overs)	316
R. A. Jadeja b Dernbach	7	3/138 (3) 4/198 (4)	
R. Ashwin c Kieswetter b Finn	13	5/243 (5) 6/271 (6) 7/273 (7)	
Bhuvneshwar Kumar not out	20	8/297 (8) 9/307 (10)	10 overs: 66-0

Finn 10–0–63–1; Dernbach 10–0–69–2; Bresnan 8–0–67–2; Tredwell 10–0–44–4; Root 9–0–51–0; Patel 3–0–21–0.

Umpires: S. J. Davis and S. Ravi. Third umpire: V. A. Kulkarni.

INDIA v ENGLAND

Second One-Day International

At Kochi, January 15, 2013 (day/night). India won by 127 runs. Toss: India.

For the first 40 overs, before a boisterous home crowd in excess of the ground's official capacity of 60,000, England held the aces. India were 177 for five, with Dhoni apparently dormant on 25 from 41 balls and Jadeja fresh to the crease. Then came a brutal assault: 108 in ten overs that seemed to shake the stands. Dhoni, who finished with 72 from 66 deliveries, signalled the charge by smearing Woakes, in for the injured Tim Bresnan, for six over mid-on. Jadeja took his captain's cue, signing off the innings with his second six in a 37-ball 61. At 58 for one after ten overs, England were in touch. But Bhuvneshwar Kumar trapped Cook leg-before, then accounted for Pietersen and Morgan in three deliveries. At 73 for four, England's confidence was ebbing away, and Ashwin and Jadeja cashed in, sharing five wickets to complete a crushing victory. In all, the last nine fell for only 100.

Man of the Match: R. A. Jadeja.

India

A. M. Rahane b Finn	4	R. Ashwin not out	1
G. Gambhir b Dernbach	8		
V. Kohli c Bell b Woakes	37	L-b 5, w 10	15
Yuvraj Singh lbw b Tredwell	32		
S. K. Raina b Finn	55	1/18 (2) 2/18 (1) (6 wkts, 50 overs)	285
*†M. S. Dhoni c Root b Dernbach	72	3/71 (4) 4/119 (3)	
R. A. Jadeja not out	61	5/174 (5) 6/270 (6)	10 overs: 44-2

Bhuvneshwar Kumar, I. Sharma and Shami Ahmed did not bat.

Finn 10–1–51–2; Dernbach 9–0–73–2; Woakes 9–0–60–1; Patel 10–0–43–0; Tredwell 10–0–48–1; Root 2–0–5–0.

England

*A. N. Cook lbw b Bhuvneshwar Kumar	17	J. C. Tredwell lbw b Ashwin	1
I. R. Bell c Dhoni b Shami Ahmed	1	S. T. Finn c Dhoni b Ashwin	0
K. P. Pietersen b Bhuvneshwar Kumar	42	J. W. Dernbach run out	2
J. E. Root b Jadeja	36	B 4, l-b 3, w 4	11
E. J. G. Morgan c Dhoni b Bhuvneshwar Kumar	0	1/4 (2) 2/58 (1) 3/73 (3) (36 overs)	158
†C. Kieswetter c Raina b Ashwin	18	4/73 (5) 5/110 (6) 6/132 (4)	
S. R. Patel not out	30	7/132 (8) 8/135 (9) 9/135 (10)	
C. R. Woakes lbw b Jadeja	0	10/158 (11) 10 overs: 58-1	

Bhuvneshwar Kumar 10–2–29–3; Shami Ahmed 4–1–24–1; Sharma 4–0–28–0; Jadeja 7–1–12–2; Yuvraj Singh 4–0–19–0; Ashwin 7–0–39–3.

Umpires: S. J. Davis and V. A. Kulkarni. Third umpire: S. Asnani.

INDIA v ENGLAND

Third One-Day International

At Ranchi, January 19, 2013 (day/night). India won by seven wickets. Toss: India.

With Ranchi's most famous son returning for the city's maiden international, it seemed inevitable Dhoni would complete a script fit for Bollywood by hitting the winning runs. He later estimated he must have played tennis-ball cricket during his childhood with "at least 15,000" members of the 39,000 crowd, but the reunion nearly wasn't to be: struck on the thumb in the nets the day before the game, he had Jharkhand's capital – which became India's 46th international venue – holding its breath for a few hours before getting the all-clear. England proved obliging guests, crumbling to 155 – three fewer than they had managed in Kochi; amid a raft of injudicious shots, only Pietersen had any cause for complaint, wrongly given out caught behind off Sharma. Dhoni's decision to field had been based on the expectation of dew under lights. Even so, India appeared to be playing on a different surface. Kohli's 79-ball 77 broke the back of the chase, and took him past 4,000 one-day international runs in his 93rd innings, a feat bettered only by Viv Richards (88). England's search for wickets inevitably hastened their demise, but the spectators got what they wanted when Tredwell removed Yuvraj Singh to bring Dhoni to the middle with 12 required. A hooked four behind square off Finn completed a magical night with 131 balls to spare, India's largest cushion in a one-day international against England. This result, and South Africa's defeat by New Zealand later in the day, meant that India rose to first place in the one-day international rankings, recently occupied by England.

Man of the Match: V. Kohli.

England

*A. N. Cook lbw b Shami Ahmed	17	S. T. Finn c Yuvraj Singh b Raina	3
I. R. Bell c Dhoni b Bhuvneshwar Kumar	25	J. W. Dernbach b Jadeja	0
K. P. Pietersen c Dhoni b Sharma	17		
J. E. Root c Dhoni b Sharma	39	L-b 6, w 9	15
E. J. G. Morgan c Yuvraj Singh b Ashwin	10		
†C. Kieswetter b Jadeja	0	1/24 (1) 2/68 (3) 3/68 (2) (42.2 overs)	155
S. R. Patel lbw b Jadeja	0	4/97 (5) 5/98 (6) 6/98 (7)	
T. T. Bresnan b Ashwin	25	7/145 (4) 8/145 (8) 9/155 (10)	
J. C. Tredwell not out	4	10/155 (11) 10 overs: 34-1	

Bhuvneshwar Kumar 10–2–40–1; Shami Ahmed 8–0–23–1; Sharma 7–0–29–2; Jadeja 6.2–0–19–3; Ashwin 10–0–37–2; Raina 1–0–1–1.

India

G. Gambhir c Root b Tredwell	33
A. M. Rahane b Finn	0
V. Kohli not out	77
Yuvraj Singh b Tredwell	30
*†M. S. Dhoni not out	10
B 1, l-b 1, w 5	7
1/11 (2) 2/78 (1) (3 wkts, 28.1 overs)	157
3/144 (4) 10 overs: 48-1	

S. K. Raina, R. A. Jadeja, R. Ashwin, Bhuvneshwar Kumar, I. Sharma and Shami Ahmed did not bat.

Finn 9.1–0–50–1; Dernbach 5–0–45–0; Bresnan 7–2–31–0; Tredwell 7–1–29–2.

Umpires: S. J. Davis and S. Ravi. Third umpire: V. A. Kulkarni.

INDIA v ENGLAND

Fourth One-Day International

At Mohali, January 23, 2013 (day/night). India won by five wickets. Toss: India.

India claimed the series after winning a crucial toss, held in chilly temperatures shortly after heavy fog had lifted. Asked to bat, England planned to take their powerplay in the 36th over, with at least one of the top three still in. Pietersen made it there, but with only 39 from 67 balls, and the total a modest 138 for three – though it might have been better had Cook not fallen to a ball pitching outside leg. Pietersen accelerated to 76, and Root's head-turning 57 not out from 45 balls helped add 100 in ten overs. But afternoon sunshine set up prime conditions for India as Rohit Sharma, recalled in place of Ajinkya Rahane, opened with an expansive 83, before Raina finished the job with an unbeaten 89. Finn had Raina caught at slip on 41, only for umpire Davis – as he had done in the Headingley Test against South Africa – to call dead ball because Finn had disturbed the stumps at the non-striker's end with his knee. England argued that Finn had in previous matches been given one warning before dead ball was called. But it emerged he had been told before that, as a serial offender, he would get no leeway.

Man of the Match: S. K. Raina.

England

*A. N. Cook lbw b Ashwin	76
I. R. Bell c Bhuvneshwar Kumar b I. Sharma	10
K. P. Pietersen b I. Sharma	76
E. J. G. Morgan c Yuvraj Singh b Ashwin	3
S. R. Patel c and b Jadeja	1
J. E. Root not out	57
†J. C. Buttler c Yuvraj Singh b Jadeja	14
T. T. Bresnan c Yuvraj Singh b Jadeja	0
J. C. Tredwell not out	6
B 2, l-b 8, w 4	14
1/37 (2) 2/132 (1) (7 wkts, 50 overs)	257
3/138 (4) 4/142 (5)	
5/220 (3) 6/241 (7) 7/241 (8) 10 overs: 37-1	

S. T. Finn and J. W. Dernbach did not bat.

Bhuvneshwar Kumar 10–2–30–0; Shami Ahmed 8–0–58–0; I. Sharma 10–2–47–2; Ashwin 10–0–63–2; Jadeja 10–2–39–3; Raina 2–0–10–0.

India

G. Gambhir c Buttler b Bresnan	10
R. G. Sharma lbw b Finn	83
V. Kohli c and b Tredwell	26
Yuvraj Singh lbw b Tredwell	3
S. K. Raina not out	89
*†M. S. Dhoni c Morgan b Dernbach	19
R. A. Jadeja not out	21
L-b 2, w 5	7
1/20 (1) 2/72 (3) (5 wkts, 47.3 overs)	258
3/90 (4) 4/158 (2)	
5/213 (6) 10 overs: 35-1	

R. Ashwin, Bhuvneshwar Kumar, I. Sharma and Shami Ahmed did not bat.

Finn 10–1–39–1; Bresnan 10–1–59–1; Dernbach 9.3–0–59–1; Patel 3–0–21–0; Tredwell 10–0–54–2; Root 5–0–24–0.

Umpires: S. Asnani and S. J. Davis. Third umpire: C. Shamshuddin.

INDIA v ENGLAND

Fifth One-Day International

At Dharmasala, January 27, 2013. England won by seven wickets. Toss: England.

Reports of hostile winter weather in the foothills of the Himalayas proved wide of the mark, and Dharmasala turned out to be a stunning addition to the international circuit. The dead-rubber feel added to the sense that the cricket was secondary to the scenery, with the Himachal Pradesh C. A. Stadium, more than 4,000ft above sea level, set against a breathtaking backdrop of snow-capped mountains. A pre-match team outing to McLeod Ganj, home of the Dalai Lama and the Tibetan government-in-exile, seemed to inspire England – or perhaps it was simply that they won another crucial toss. Bresnan, playing his final match before an enforced break to address a recurring elbow problem, took charge: his outswing persuaded Sharma and Kohli to edge consecutive deliveries to Tredwell at second slip in the fourth over. Finn also enjoyed the fresh morning conditions, while the thrifty Tredwell chalked up 11 victims in the series with the wickets of Gambhir and Jadeja, who had helped Raina double the score from 79 for five. But Bell anchored a relatively unthreatened chase with an unbeaten 113, supported first by a watchful 31 from Root, then a muscular run-a-ball unbeaten 40 from Morgan.

Man of the Match: I. R. Bell. *Man of the Series:* S. K. Raina.

India

G. Gambhir c Bell b Tredwell	24
R. G. Sharma c Tredwell b Bresnan	4
V. Kohli c Tredwell b Bresnan	0
Yuvraj Singh c Morgan b Finn	0
S. K. Raina c Bell b Woakes	83
*†M. S. Dhoni lbw b Finn	15
R. A. Jadeja c Bell b Tredwell	39
R. Ashwin c Finn b Patel	19
Bhuvneshwar Kumar c Finn b Bresnan	31
Shami Ahmed c and b Bresnan	1
I. Sharma not out	0
L-b 4, w 6	10
1/13 (2) 2/13 (3) 3/24 (4) (49.4 overs)	226
4/49 (1) 5/79 (6) 6/157 (7)	
7/177 (5) 8/211 (8) 9/225 (9)	
10/226 (10)	10 overs: 35-3

Finn 10–2–27–2; Bresnan 9.4–1–45–4; Woakes 9–1–45–1; Tredwell 10–1–25–2; Root 5–0–34–0; Patel 6–0–46–1.

England

*A. N. Cook b I. Sharma	22
I. R. Bell not out	113
K. P. Pietersen c Jadeja b Shami Ahmed	6
J. E. Root b Jadeja	31
E. J. G. Morgan not out	40
L-b 8, w 7	15
1/53 (1) 2/64 (3) (3 wkts, 47.2 overs)	227
3/143 (4)	10 overs: 42-0

†J. C. Buttler, S. R. Patel, T. T. Bresnan, C. R. Woakes, J. C. Tredwell and S. T. Finn did not bat.

Bhuvneshwar Kumar 9–1–45–0; Shami Ahmed 9–1–46–1; I. Sharma 10–3–37–1; Ashwin 10–0–50–0; Yuvraj Singh 2–0–15–0; Jadeja 7.2–0–26–1.

Umpires: S. Asnani and S. J. Davis. Third umpire: C. Shamshuddin.
Series referee: A. J. Pycroft.

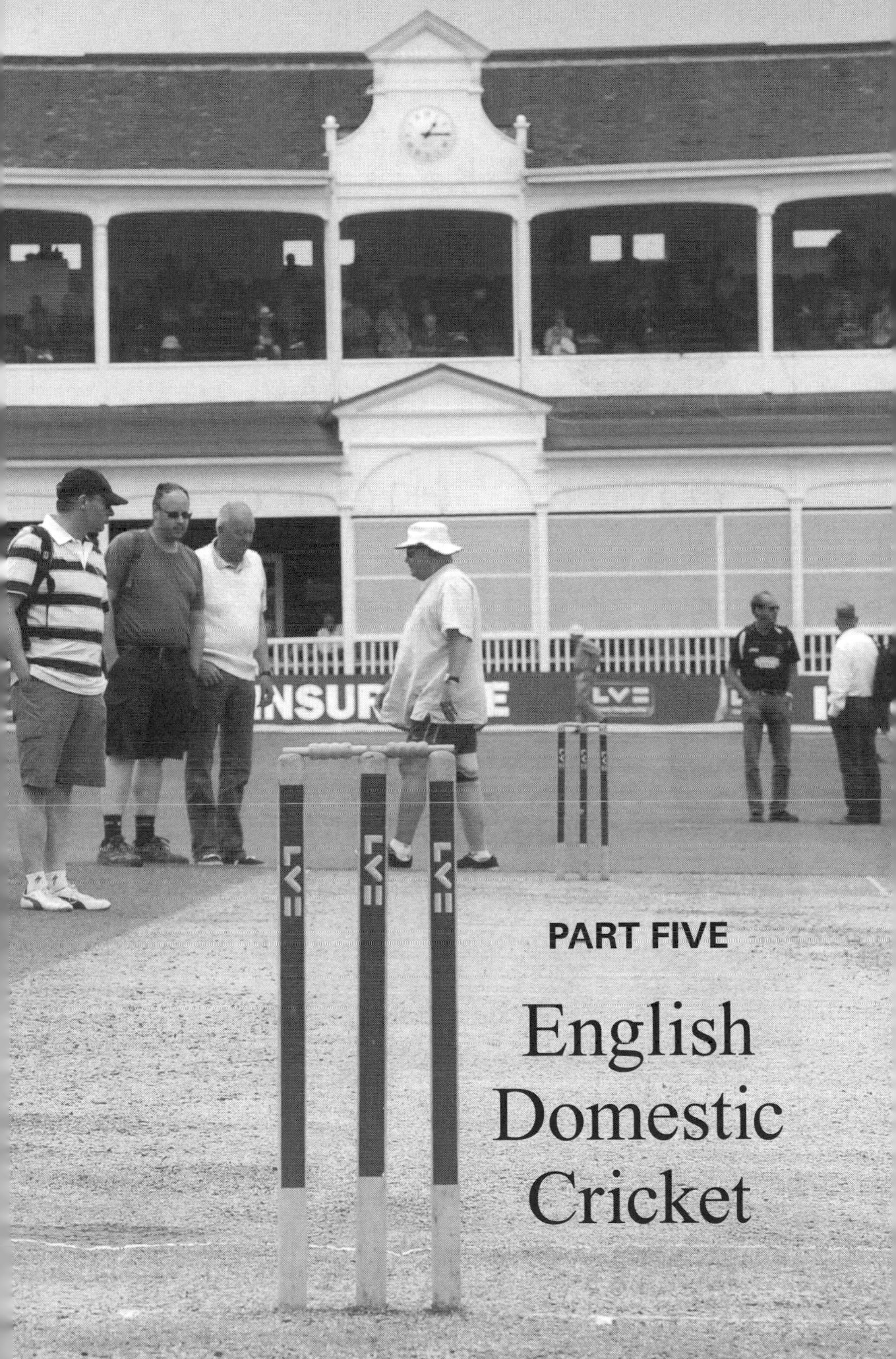

PART FIVE

English Domestic Cricket

FIRST-CLASS AVERAGES, 2012

BATTING AND FIELDING (Qualification: 10 innings)

Note: These averages include MCC v Lancashire at Abu Dhabi.

		M	*I*	*NO*	*R*	*HS*	*100*	*50*	*Avge*	*Ct/St*
1	N. R. D. Compton (*Somerset & Eng. Lions*)	14	21	6	1,494	236	5	7	99.60	0
2	C. R. Woakes (*Warwicks & England Lions*)	10	13	5	588	118*	2	2	73.50	3
3	K. P. Pietersen (*Surrey & England*)	9	15	1	994	234*	3	4	71.00	0
4	S. J. Thakor (*Leics*)	6	10	3	427	85*	0	4	61.00	2
5	C. Kieswetter (*Somerset & England Lions*)	13	20	6	848	152	2	3	60.57	0
6	S. A. Northeast (*Kent*)	12	19	2	969	165	3	6	57.00	6
7	H. T. Waters (*Glam*)	13	14	12	106	39	0	0	53.00	5
8	J. C. Hildreth (*Somerset*)	17	26	3	1,214	268	4	5	52.78	17
9	J. S. Foster (*Essex*)	16	19	4	769	135	2	4	51.26	43/3
10	J. M. Bairstow (*Yorks, Eng. Lions & England*)	15	21	2	972	182	4	4	51.15	0
11	†A. Lyth (*Yorks*)	13	16	1	751	248*	1	5	50.06	13
12	M. J. Guptill (*Derbys*)	8	14	2	594	137	2	2	49.50	13
13	†R. J. Burns (*Surrey*)	10	17	2	741	121	2	4	49.40	7
14	O. A. Shah (*Essex*)	8	13	1	589	161	2	2	49.08	3
15	I. J. L. Trott (*Warwicks & England*)	8	13	2	537	178	1	3	48.81	2
	†U. T. Khawaja (*Derbys*)	8	14	3	537	110*	1	6	48.81	10
17	†J. H. K. Adams (*Hants*)	15	27	6	1,024	149	3	4	48.76	15
18	†B. P. Nash (*Kent*)	16	24	5	908	132*	3	4	47.78	6
19	I. R. Bell (*Warwicks, Eng. Lions & England*)	11	17	4	610	120	1	6	46.92	0
20	†E. J. M. Cowan (*Glos & Australia A*)	7	12	1	513	109	2	2	46.63	0
21	A. McGrath (*Yorks*)	14	17	3	648	106*	2	3	46.28	5
22	C. M. W. Read (*Notts*)	17	26	4	1,014	104*	1	8	46.09	45/1
23	R. Clarke (*Warwicks*)	17	22	4	826	140	3	3	45.88	31
24	R. N. ten Doeschate (*Essex*)	9	12	3	412	69	0	4	45.77	7
25	T. L. Maynard (*Surrey*)	8	16	2	635	143	1	3	45.35	12
26	M. H. Wessels (*Notts*)	13	20	0	905	199	3	1	45.25	8/1
27	†M. J. North (*Glam*)	9	13	0	577	116	1	5	44.38	2
28	†A. J. Strauss (*Middx & England*)	10	18	2	710	141	3	1	44.37	13
29	R. I. Newton (*Northants*)	13	20	3	751	119*	3	2	44.17	3
30	†P. A. Jaques (*Yorks*)	15	19	1	792	160	2	4	44.00	16
	T. R. Ambrose (*Warwicks*)	14	19	4	660	151*	1	3	44.00	46/1
32	†A. G. Prince (*Lancs*)	15	24	1	1,008	144	2	8	43.82	15
33	S. J. Mullaney (*Notts*)	6	10	1	391	94	0	4	43.44	5
34	G. O. Jones (*Kent*)	16	20	4	677	88	0	7	42.31	52
35	J. E. Root (*Yorks & England Lions*)	18	26	3	964	222*	3	3	41.91	0
36	R. R. Sarwan (*Leics*)	14	25	2	941	117	2	5	40.91	7
37	M. J. Powell (*Kent*)	17	21	4	695	134	2	3	40.88	6
38	†M. A. Wallace (*Glam*)	16	24	5	775	122*	3	1	40.78	42/4
39	J. Allenby (*Glam*)	15	22	4	733	125*	2	3	40.72	11
40	†I. J. Westwood (*Warwicks*)	13	20	1	771	120	2	5	40.57	5
41	J. D. Middlebrook (*Northants*)	15	22	4	714	121	2	4	39.66	6
42	†E. C. Joyce (*Sussex*)	14	24	3	829	108*	2	5	39.47	9
43	V. Chopra (*Warwicks & England Lions*)	18	28	1	1,062	195	3	5	39.33	27
44	D. J. Sales (*Northants*)	14	21	3	706	140	2	3	39.22	6
45	†M. E. Trescothick (*Somerset*)	9	13	0	506	146	2	1	38.92	26
46	†M. J. Lumb (*Notts*)	15	25	0	971	171	3	3	38.84	7
47	S. J. Walters (*Glam*)	14	23	2	813	159	1	7	38.71	13
48	†G. S. Ballance (*Yorks*)	17	20	4	617	121*	1	2	38.56	11
49	†D. J. Redfern (*Derbys*)	17	25	3	848	133	2	6	38.54	8
50	†C. J. L. Rogers (*Middx*)	17	31	2	1,108	173	3	6	38.20	7
51	R. W. T. Key (*Kent*)	15	24	3	797	119	1	5	37.95	7
52	C. D. Nash (*Sussex*)	17	28	2	984	162	3	2	37.84	9
53	†L. W. P. Wells (*Sussex*)	15	21	2	713	127	2	3	37.52	12

		M	I	NO	R	HS	100	50	Avge	Ct/St
54	W. L. Madsen (*Derbys*)	17	27	2	928	231*	3	3	37.12	7
55	†A. Harinath (*Surrey*)	6	11	1	368	109	2	0	36.80	0
56	W. J. Durston (*Derbys*)	17	27	3	878	121	2	4	36.58	26
57	J. W. A. Taylor (*Notts, E. Lions & England*)	18	28	4	875	163*	3	1	36.45	0
58	†B. A. Godleman (*Essex*)	8	13	1	437	130	1	2	36.41	5
59	†J. O. Troughton (*Warwicks*)	16	25	3	800	132	2	5	36.36	9
60	†S. M. Ervine (*Hants*)	17	25	4	763	109*	1	4	36.33	10
61	A. G. Wakely (*Northants*)	14	21	2	690	96	0	5	36.31	9
62	H. J. H. Marshall (*MCC & Glos*)	16	27	3	871	117*	1	5	36.29	6
63	†N. J. O'Brien (*MCC & Northants*)	12	19	2	612	182	1	3	36.00	10/1
64	†P. J. Hughes (*Worcs & Australia A*)	10	18	1	611	135*	2	3	35.94	2
65	S. D. Peters (*MCC & Northants*)	16	25	2	823	148	2	3	35.78	11
66	M. Klinger (*Worcs & Australia A*)	11	19	2	606	120	1	4	35.64	10
67	A. J. Wheater (*Essex*)	12	15	2	462	98	0	4	35.53	7
68	†S. M. Katich (*Hants*)	15	23	2	738	196	1	5	35.14	8
69	J. L. Denly (*Middx*)	16	28	4	840	134*	2	4	35.00	7
69	P. D. Trego (*Somerset*)	17	22	4	630	92	0	4	35.00	13
71	†D. J. Willey (*Northants*)	15	18	4	489	76	0	4	34.92	3
72	I. A. Cockbain (*Glos*)	15	24	2	764	112	1	5	34.72	12
73	A. D. Hales (*Notts*)	16	26	1	857	155*	2	4	34.28	18
74	J. J. Cobb (*Leics*)	14	23	1	752	105	1	5	34.18	6
75	T. Westley (*Essex*)	17	25	2	786	185	2	3	34.17	9
76	†N. J. Edwards (*Notts*)	9	16	1	512	195	1	1	34.13	6
77	R. J. Hamilton-Brown (*Surrey*)	9	18	1	577	115	1	4	33.94	4
78	M. L. Pettini (*Essex*)	16	23	4	644	92	0	7	33.89	5
79	P. D. Collingwood (*Durham*)	14	25	3	744	114	1	4	33.81	19
80	†K. W. Hogg (*Lancs*)	14	19	9	336	61*	0	2	33.60	1
81	†T. C. Smith (*Lancs*)	8	13	2	369	91	0	4	33.54	10
82	G. R. Napier (*Essex*)	12	12	2	335	100*	1	0	33.50	4
83	N. J. Dexter (*Middx*)	13	23	2	701	125	2	4	33.38	10
84	†D. J. Malan (*Middx*)	17	27	0	897	140	2	4	33.22	25
85	M. J. Prior (*Sussex & England*)	11	13	0	424	86	0	4	32.61	0
86	†P. J. Franks (*Notts*)	11	19	7	389	86*	0	3	32.41	1
87	P. J. Horton (*Lancs*)	18	29	4	809	137*	2	3	32.36	20
88	M. A. Thornely (*Leics*)	9	16	0	514	131	2	1	32.12	6
89	†M. A. G. Boyce (*Leics*)	14	25	2	733	122	2	4	31.86	9
90	G. M. Smith (*Essex*)	9	10	0	318	160	1	0	31.80	4
91	†I. D. Blackwell (*MCC, Durham & Warwicks*)	12	22	3	596	102*	1	3	31.36	3
92	A. C. Voges (*Notts*)	9	12	2	313	105	1	2	31.30	12
93	A. N. Petersen (*Essex & South Africans*)	11	17	1	500	182	2	0	31.25	0
94	S. J. Croft (*Lancs*)	18	27	2	777	154*	2	3	31.08	15
95	D. I. Stevens (*Kent*)	16	20	0	619	123	2	2	30.95	7
96	E. J. H. Eckersley (*Leics*)	16	28	4	739	137*	1	3	30.79	43/3
97	J. J. Roy (*Surrey*)	13	23	2	644	83	0	3	30.66	11
98	†A. W. Gale (*Yorks*)	15	20	4	487	80	0	2	30.43	4
99	†C. D. J. Dent (*Glos*)	8	15	1	424	114	1	2	30.28	11
100	J. M. Vince (*Hants*)	12	19	1	545	128	2	0	30.27	13
101	T. Poynton (*Derbys*)	14	17	4	393	106	1	2	30.23	42/1
102	S. D. Robson (*Middx*)	16	29	2	814	117	1	4	30.14	12
103	†M. A. Carberry (*Hants & England Lions*)	12	22	3	572	84*	0	4	30.10	4
104	†A. N. Cook (*Essex & England*)	8	14	1	386	115	1	1	29.69	7
105	K. J. Coetzer (*Northants*)	13	19	0	563	120	1	2	29.63	5
106	A. V. Suppiah (*Somerset*)	17	26	0	769	124	2	5	29.57	9
107	†B. A. Stokes (*Durham & England Lions*)	16	28	0	827	121	1	5	29.53	8
108	W. A. White (*Leics*)	16	26	5	616	67	0	4	29.33	1
109	Azeem Rafiq (*Yorks*)	11	11	1	293	75*	0	2	29.30	7
110	†M. J. Di Venuto (*Durham*)	5	10	0	291	96	0	1	29.10	11
111	B. M. Shafayat (*Hants*)	8	10	0	289	93	0	2	28.90	0
112	†J. E. Anyon (*Sussex*)	15	19	8	316	64*	0	2	28.72	6
113	S. P. Crook (*Middx*)	6	10	0	285	67	0	2	28.50	2

		M	I	NO	R	HS	100	50	Avge	Ct/St
114	J. N. Batty (*Glos*)	8	11	2	256	55	0	1	28.44	24/1
115	†R. A. Whiteley (*Derbys*)	15	21	3	509	83	0	3	28.27	5
116	D. M. Housego (*Glos*)	10	16	0	450	62	0	4	28.12	7
117	†J. A. Rudolph (*Surrey & South Africans*)	9	15	0	420	69	0	3	28.00	0
118	†W. R. S. Gidman (*Glos*)	11	17	1	447	72	0	3	27.93	2
119	†L. A. Procter (*Lancs*)	15	23	3	556	77	0	1	27.80	0
120	D. K. H. Mitchell (*Worcs*)	17	32	2	833	133*	2	2	27.76	23
121	J. C. Mickleburgh (*Essex*)	9	14	1	359	126	1	2	27.61	7
	O. P. Rayner (*Middx*)	11	15	2	359	143*	1	1	27.61	12
123	B. J. Wright (*Glam*)	16	27	3	661	104	1	1	27.54	3
124	B. C. Brown (*Sussex*)	14	22	3	521	76*	0	5	27.42	38/3
125	L. J. Wright (*Sussex*)	9	14	1	356	81	0	3	27.38	7
126	L. A. Dawson (*Hants*)	17	27	2	684	134*	1	2	27.36	37
127	J. C. Buttler (*Somerset*)	12	16	1	400	93	0	2	26.66	12/1
128	†J. G. Cameron (*Worcs*)	12	19	4	399	88	0	2	26.60	3
129	†W. T. S. Porterfield (*Warwicks*)	15	23	2	558	84	0	3	26.57	21
130	D. M. Benkenstein (*Durham*)	14	25	3	583	69	0	3	26.50	4
131	†M. D. Stoneman (*Durham*)	14	26	1	661	114	1	2	26.44	9
132	Z. de Bruyn (*Surrey*)	15	27	0	709	125	1	5	26.25	5
133	†T. J. Murtagh (*Middx*)	16	22	7	391	45	0	0	26.06	5
134	†W. D. Bragg (*Glam*)	15	25	0	648	92	0	5	25.92	8
135	A. N. Kervezee (*Worcs*)	7	12	1	283	76	0	3	25.72	7
136	V. S. Solanki (*Worcs*)	14	25	3	556	106	1	3	25.27	18
137	†M. M. Ali (*MCC & Worcs*)	18	32	4	707	94	0	4	25.25	9
138	D. Murphy (*Northants*)	10	11	1	252	54	0	1	25.20	23/2
139	A. P. R. Gidman (*Glos*)	13	22	1	528	129	1	3	25.14	10
140	S. R. Patel (*Notts & England Lions*)	12	18	2	402	69	0	3	25.12	0
141	G. D. Cross (*Lancs*)	17	26	3	577	75*	0	3	25.08	33/3
142	J. Lewis (*Surrey*)	13	19	6	326	42	0	0	25.07	3
143	K. R. Brown (*Lancs*)	18	29	2	675	78	0	3	25.00	5
144	†M. H. Yardy (*Sussex*)	16	25	2	574	110	1	3	24.95	32
145	†Z. S. Ansari (*Cambridge MCCU & Surrey*)	9	15	2	318	83*	0	2	24.46	0
146	D. L. Maddy (*Warwicks*)	15	22	2	478	112	1	0	23.90	12
147	B. A. C. Howell (*Glos*)	13	24	3	497	83*	0	3	23.66	5
148	†K. H. D. Barker (*Warwicks*)	15	17	4	304	46	0	0	23.38	5
149	C. Rushworth (*Durham*)	9	11	7	93	24*	0	0	23.25	1
150	C. P. Wood (*Hants*)	10	15	1	324	105*	1	1	23.14	1
151	M. D. Bates (*Hants*)	17	23	0	530	103	1	2	23.04	56/1
152	G. K. Berg (*Middx*)	16	24	1	526	83	0	3	22.86	13
153	†S. J. Magoffin (*Sussex*)	15	19	3	363	41*	0	0	22.68	4
154	I. D. Saxelby (*Glos*)	11	16	7	200	30	0	0	22.22	4
155	†P. Mustard (*Durham*)	15	25	3	482	80	0	1	21.90	46
156	†S. M. Davies (*Surrey*)	12	20	0	438	104	1	1	21.90	24/1
157	†M. T. Coles (*Kent & England Lions*)	17	19	1	392	103*	1	1	21.77	4
158	W. S. Jones (*Cardiff MCCU & Leics*)	5	10	0	215	48	0	0	21.50	0
159	J. S. Gatting (*Sussex*)	11	16	3	279	72*	0	1	21.46	5
160	P. M. Borrington (*Derbys*)	10	18	3	321	98	0	1	21.40	3
161	†S. G. Borthwick (*Durham*)	14	22	4	380	60	0	2	21.11	21
162	J. L. Clare (*Derbys*)	11	13	1	247	48	0	0	20.58	2
163	†R. J. Sidebottom (*Yorks*)	11	10	2	164	37	0	0	20.50	1
164	T. D. Groenewald (*Derbys*)	14	15	4	225	42	0	0	20.45	3
165	†M. G. Pardoe (*Worcs*)	12	22	2	407	55	0	1	20.35	10
166	†B. W. Harmison (*Kent*)	12	17	1	325	46	0	0	20.31	3
167	G. G. Wagg (*Glam*)	9	13	0	263	60	0	2	20.23	3
168	J. S. Patel (*Warwicks*)	13	14	3	221	76	0	1	20.09	3
169	D. J. Balcombe (*Hants*)	17	22	7	299	73	0	1	19.93	4
170	†M. S. Lineker (*Derbys*)	7	11	0	219	45	0	0	19.90	7
171	C. W. Henderson (*Leics*)	12	19	4	296	57*	0	2	19.73	0
	T. S. Roland-Jones (*Middx*)	15	21	6	296	52	0	1	19.73	3
173	G. Onions (*Durham & England*)	14	18	7	216	36	0	0	19.63	1

		M	I	NO	R	HS	100	50	Avge	Ct/St
174	W. R. Smith (*Durham*)	14	27	1	509	100	1	1	19.57	5
175	†N. A. James (*Glam*)	9	17	0	327	83	0	1	19.23	3
176	A. P. Palladino (*Derbys*)	16	21	3	344	106	1	1	19.11	0
177	A. J. Hall (*Northants*)	12	19	1	343	79	0	3	19.05	4
178	†E. J. G. Morgan (*Middx & England Lions*)	7	10	1	171	71	0	2	19.00	6
179	M. Davies (*Kent*)	15	16	4	227	58	0	1	18.91	4
180	†G. P. Rees (*MCC & Glam*)	13	22	0	416	66	0	1	18.90	11
181	G. P. Smith (*Leics*)	13	23	0	429	77	0	2	18.65	13
182	E. G. C. Young (*Glos*)	8	12	2	186	55*	0	1	18.60	3
183	†D. J. Wainwright (*Derbys*)	17	23	4	350	51*	0	2	18.42	11
184	†Naved Arif (*Sussex*)	8	10	0	184	46	0	0	18.40	2
185	G. Chapple (*Lancs*)	16	24	1	423	46	0	0	18.39	4
186	C. J. C. Wright (*Warwicks*)	16	16	5	201	53	0	1	18.27	2
187	†J. A. Simpson (*Middx*)	14	21	2	343	49*	0	0	18.05	43/5
188	S. A. Patterson (*Yorks*)	16	15	5	180	37	0	0	18.00	1
189	B. J. Phillips (*Notts*)	14	20	4	286	47	0	0	17.87	5
190	J. C. Glover (*Glam*)	7	10	3	125	55	0	1	17.85	3
191	†J. C. Tredwell (*Kent & England Lions*)	15	15	2	232	87	0	1	17.84	16
192	S. C. Meaker (*Surrey & England Lions*)	13	16	4	211	41	0	0	17.58	0
193	D. A. Cosker (*Glam*)	15	17	3	243	49*	0	0	17.35	10
194	G. P. Swann (*Notts & England*)	8	11	2	154	41	0	0	17.11	0
195	C. R. Jones (*Durham MCCU & Somerset*)	7	11	0	185	50	0	1	16.81	4
196	C. J. Jordan (*Surrey*)	8	14	1	213	54	0	1	16.38	4
197	M. W. Goodwin (*Sussex*)	14	23	1	360	77	0	2	16.36	5
198	M. J. Hoggard (*Leics*)	10	12	7	81	28	0	0	16.20	0
199	V. D. Philander (*Somerset & South Africans*)	9	11	0	177	61	0	1	16.09	0
200	S. C. Moore (*Lancs*)	14	24	0	378	47	0	0	15.75	8
201	R. A. Jones (*Worcs*)	10	15	5	151	32	0	0	15.10	5
202	B. J. M. Scott (*Worcs*)	14	21	1	301	106	1	1	15.05	29/5
203	C. E. Shreck (*Kent*)	17	17	11	86	16	0	0	14.33	0
204	D. D. Masters (*Essex*)	14	12	0	165	52	0	1	13.75	3
205	†S. C.J. Broad (*Notts & England*)	7	11	1	135	37	0	0	13.50	2
206	A. Shahzad (*Yorks & Lancs*)	13	18	5	168	28*	0	0	12.92	1
207	L. J. Fletcher (*Notts*)	9	14	5	116	42*	0	0	12.88	2
208	J. du Toit (*Leics*)	6	10	0	127	48	0	0	12.70	4
209	†M. E. Claydon (*Durham*)	8	13	2	139	55	0	1	12.63	0
210	A. W. R. Barrow (*Somerset*)	9	15	0	186	47	0	0	12.40	14
211	J. Leach (*Leeds/Brad MCCU & Worcs*)	7	13	0	159	50	0	1	12.23	0
212	L. M. Daggett (*Northants*)	14	14	5	110	26*	0	0	12.22	5
213	G. J. Batty (*MCC & Surrey*)	15	26	2	293	36	0	0	12.20	16
214	J. K. Fuller (*Glos*)	8	12	1	134	57	0	1	12.18	3
215	G. G. White (*Notts*)	6	11	2	109	30*	0	0	12.11	2
216	C. D. Thorp (*Durham*)	14	21	2	221	36	0	0	11.63	9
217	†G. M. Andrew (*Worcs*)	10	17	3	161	29	0	0	11.50	3
218	A. R. Adams (*Notts*)	12	14	0	151	29	0	0	10.78	8
219	D. A. Payne (*Glos*)	8	10	3	75	16	0	0	10.71	2
220	R. G. Coughtrie (*Glos*)	7	12	0	125	40	0	0	10.41	17
221	C. J. Russell (*Worcs*)	6	10	2	83	22	0	0	10.37	2
222	M. R. Ramprakash (*MCC & Surrey*)	6	12	0	120	37	0	0	10.00	2
223	G. J. Muchall (*Durham*)	7	13	0	125	25	0	0	9.61	5
224	A. C. Thomas (*Somerset*)	9	11	1	96	39*	0	0	9.60	1
225	N. L. Buck (*Leics*)	11	15	2	119	27	0	0	9.15	0
226	J. A. Brooks (*Northants & England Lions*)	11	11	3	72	22	0	0	9.00	0
	G. H. Dockrell (*Somerset*)	11	10	4	54	13*	0	0	9.00	5
228	R. H. Joseph (*Leics*)	9	13	4	79	29	0	0	8.77	2
229	J. W. Dernbach (*Surrey & England Lions*)	8	15	5	83	28*	0	0	8.30	2
230	S. C. Kerrigan (*Lancs & England Lions*)	17	20	8	97	34*	0	0	8.08	0
231	†M. S. Panesar (*Sussex*)	16	16	4	88	31	0	0	7.33	3
232	C. D. Collymore (*Middx*)	7	10	6	29	8	0	0	7.25	0
233	†J. A. Tomlinson (*Hants*)	12	14	7	45	11	0	0	6.42	4

		M	I	NO	R	HS	100	50	Avge	Ct/St
234	T. E. Linley (*Surrey*)	8	11	4	43	15	0	0	6.14	4
235	A. Richardson (*MCC & Worcs*)	15	23	9	84	18	0	0	6.00	3
236	L. C. Norwell (*Glos*)	9	11	4	37	18	0	0	5.28	3
237	T. S. Mills (*Essex*)	8	10	4	30	20*	0	0	5.00	5
238	†J. M. Anderson (*Lancs & England*)	6	10	2	36	12	0	0	4.50	7
239	S. P. Kirby (*Somerset*)	9	11	5	20	6*	0	0	3.33	4
240	S. T. Finn (*Middx & England*)	8	10	6	11	10	0	0	2.75	0

BOWLING (Qualification: 10 wickets in 5 innings)

		Style	O	M	R	W	BB	5I	Avge
1	Abdur Rehman (*Somerset*)	SLA	174	50	383	27	9-65	3	14.18
2	G. Onions (*Durham & England*)	RFM	415.1	114	1,061	72	9-67	5	14.73
3	C. Rushworth (*Durham*)	RFM	210.5	51	623	38	5-38	3	16.39
4	R. D. B. Croft (*Glam*)	OB	141.3	27	403	23	5-31	2	17.52
5	D. D. Masters (*Essex*)	RFM	395.3	119	941	53	7-60	4	17.75
6	C. D. Thorp (*Durham*)	RFM	320.3	90	818	44	5-59	1	18.59
7	J. Leach (*Leeds/Brad MCCU & Worcs*)	RM	68.4	14	226	12	4-73	0	18.83
8	A. R. Adams (*Notts*)	RFM	344.3	63	1,035	54	7-32	4	19.16
9	M. Davies (*Kent*)	RFM	368.3	129	699	36	5-27	1	19.41
10	T. S. Roland-Jones (*Middx*)	RFM	405	87	1,245	64	6-66	4	19.45
11	A. Richardson (*MCC & Worcs*)	RFM	484.3	145	1,157	58	6-47	4	19.94
12	S. J. Magoffin (*Sussex*)	RFM	480.1	161	1,143	57	7-34	2	20.05
13	M. C. Henriques (*Glam*)	RFM	95	18	323	16	4-54	0	20.18
14	H. T. Waters (*Glam*)	RFM	304.2	79	798	39	7-53	2	20.46
15	K. H. D. Barker (*Warwicks*)	LFM	392.1	94	1,166	56	6-40	5	20.82
16	S. A. Patterson (*Yorks*)	RFM	427.2	125	1,115	53	5-77	1	21.03
17	C. D. Nash (*Sussex*)	OB	135.2	23	446	21	3-23	0	21.23
18	J. L. Clare (*Derbys*)	RFM	204.3	40	642	30	6-40	2	21.40
19	W. R. S. Gidman (*Glos*)	RFM	318	58	943	44	5-43	2	21.43
20	R. Clarke (*Warwicks*)	RFM	204	54	569	26	4-46	0	21.88
21	B. A. Stokes (*Durham & England Lions*)	RFM	245.4	50	816	37	4-3	0	22.05
22	M. Kartik (*Surrey*)	SLA	251.1	58	597	27	5-69	1	22.11
23	M. A. Ashraf (*Yorks*)	RFM	117.5	27	376	17	4-36	0	22.11
24	H. Riazuddin (*Hants*)	RFM	92	23	269	12	5-61	1	22.41
25	A. C. Thomas (*Somerset*)	RFM	252.4	50	740	33	6-60	2	22.42
26	M. T. Coles (*Kent & England Lions*)	RFM	400.1	51	1,341	59	6-51	2	22.72
27	J. S. Patel (*Warwicks*)	OB	395.1	87	1,161	51	7-75	4	22.76
28	D. A. Payne (*Glos*)	LFM	147	24	504	22	4-89	0	22.90
29	S. J. Croft (*Lancs*)	RFM/OB	99.4	13	298	13	6-41	1	22.92
30	G. R. Napier (*Essex*)	RFM	317.2	56	1,033	45	5-58	2	22.95
31	G. Chapple (*Lancs*)	RFM	414.5	107	1,061	46	5-47	2	23.06
32	M. S. Panesar (*Sussex*)	SLA	514.1	157	1,227	53	7-60	2	23.15
33	C. J. C. Wright (*Warwicks*)	RFM	471.3	77	1,562	67	5-24	2	23.31
34	V. D. Philander (*Somerset & S. Africans*)	RFM	321	77	843	36	5-30	3	23.41
35	J. Allenby (*Glam*)	RM	359.3	80	992	42	4-39	0	23.61
36	S. T. Finn (*Middx & England*)	RF	293	57	969	41	4-43	0	23.63
37	L. A. Procter (*Lancs*)	RFM	202.1	36	666	28	7-71	2	23.78
38	T. J. Murtagh (*Middx*)	RFM	526.3	127	1,455	61	5-37	2	23.85
39	A. J. Hall (*Northants*)	RM	293.5	73	812	34	5-50	1	23.88
40	D. I. Stevens (*Kent*)	RM	304.3	63	840	35	5-35	1	24.00
41	S. C. Meaker (*Surrey & England Lions*)	RF	355.3	61	1,225	51	8-52	3	24.01
42	G. G. Wagg (*Glam*)	SLA/LM	246.3	45	769	32	6-44	1	24.03
43 {	L. J. Fletcher (*Notts*)	RFM	266.5	77	708	28	4-21	0	25.28
	D. L. Maddy (*Warwicks*)	RM	147	50	354	14	4-39	0	25.28
45	Azeem Rafiq (*Yorks*)	OB	246.5	63	711	28	5-50	1	25.39
46	R. H. Patel (*Middx*)	SLA	104	12	356	14	4-72	0	25.42
47	A. P. Palladino (*Derbys*)	RFM	499.4	107	1,431	56	7-53	3	25.55
48	I. D. Saxelby (*Glos*)	RFM	293.3	58	897	35	6-48	1	25.62
49	I. D. Blackwell (*MCC, Durham & Warks*)	SLA	227.5	50	692	27	7-52	1	25.62

		Style	*O*	*M*	*R*	*W*	*BB*	*5I*	*Avge*
50	A. Khan (*Sussex*)	RFM	167.4	30	564	22	5-25	2	25.63
51	A. McGrath (*Yorks*)	RM	196.1	59	489	19	4-21	0	25.73
52	T. D. Groenewald (*Derbys*)	RFM	399.4	89	1,086	42	5-29	1	25.85
53	T. E. Linley (*Surrey*)	RFM	188.5	39	570	22	5-45	2	25.90
54	J. Harrison (*Durham*)	LFM	68	10	260	10	4-112	0	26.00
55	W. J. Durston (*Derbys*)	OB	177.3	25	574	22	5-34	1	26.09
56	D. J. Balcombe (*Hants*)	RFM	533.1	111	1,671	64	8-71	3	26.10
57	B. J. Phillips (*Notts*)	RFM	345.3	105	841	32	4-33	0	26.28
58	J. A. Tomlinson (*Hants*)	LFM	376.1	82	1,131	43	5-69	2	26.30
59	S. M. Ervine (*Hants*)	RFM	232.2	59	716	27	4-96	0	26.51
60	C. E. Shreck (*Kent*)	RFM	526.3	112	1,544	58	5-41	2	26.62
61	G. J. Batty (*MCC & Surrey*)	OB	327	75	854	32	6-73	2	26.68
62	J. K. Fuller (*Glos*)	RFM	174.2	27	653	24	5-29	1	27.20
63	S. I. Mahmood (*Lancs & Somerset*)	RFM	142	21	550	20	4-38	0	27.50
64	R. A. Jones (*Worcs*)	RFM	200.1	26	857	31	6-32	1	27.64
65	N. J. Dexter (*Middx*)	RM	115	25	332	12	3-23	0	27.66
66	C. P. Wood (*Hants*)	LFM	273.5	73	732	26	5-41	1	28.15
67	J. D. Shantry (*Worcs*)	LFM	135	24	423	15	5-58	1	28.20
68	M. A. Chambers (*Essex*)	RFM	163.1	29	567	20	4-31	0	28.35
69	G. H. Dockrell (*Somerset*)	SLA	340.5	80	996	35	6-27	2	28.45
70	L. C. Norwell (*Glos*)	RFM	194.1	25	632	22	5-51	1	28.72
71	C. R. Woakes (*Warwicks & Eng. Lions*)	RFM	267.5	55	776	27	4-67	0	28.74
72	M. J. Hoggard (*Leics*)	RFM	220.4	42	691	24	4-27	0	28.79
73	G. K. Berg (*Middx*)	RFM	329.4	73	1,014	35	3-25	0	28.97
74	M. M. Ali (*MCC & Worcs*)	OB	304.1	45	986	34	6-29	2	29.00
75	J. W. Dernbach (*Surrey & England Lions*)	RFM	201.5	48	611	21	3-39	0	29.09
76	T. R. Craddock (*Essex*)	LBG	125.5	23	438	15	5-96	1	29.20
77	M. A. Starc (*Yorks & Australia A*)	LFM	97.4	23	351	12	3-50	0	29.25
78	Naved Arif (*Sussex*)	LFM	160	26	528	18	3-34	0	29.33
79	G. M. Hussain (*Somerset*)	RFM	101.4	17	385	13	5-48	1	29.61
80	S. P. Crook (*Middx*)	RFM	158.3	25	534	18	5-48	1	29.66
81	S. G. Borthwick (*Durham*)	LBG	130.4	12	446	15	4-37	0	29.73
82	W. A. White (*Leics*)	RFM	349	41	1,286	43	5-54	3	29.90
83	M. H. A. Footitt (*Derbys*)	LFM	108.2	21	332	11	3-43	0	30.18
84	C. Overton (*Somerset*)	RFM	113.1	23	363	12	4-38	0	30.25
85	S. J. Harmison (*Durham & Yorks*)	RFM	98.2	15	424	14	3-49	0	30.28
86	T. S. Mills (*Essex*)	LFM	129.2	19	425	14	4-25	0	30.35
87	S. C. Kerrigan (*Lancs & England Lions*)	SLA	603.4	102	1,770	58	6-59	1	30.51
88	S. P. Kirby (*Somerset*)	RFM	225.1	47	735	24	3-34	0	30.62
89	J. A. Brooks (*Northants & England Lions*)	RFM	295.4	81	890	29	5-61	2	30.68
90	J. C. Glover (*Glam*)	RM	176.4	40	585	19	4-76	0	30.78
91	D. J. Wainwright (*Derbys*)	SLA	565.5	141	1,542	50	6-33	3	30.84
92	M. E. Claydon (*Durham*)	RFM	126.2	23	495	16	4-84	0	30.93
93	J. M. Anderson (*Lancs & England*)	RFM	295.1	77	713	23	5-82	1	31.00
	D. W. Steyn (*South Africans*)	RF	149	36	496	16	5-56	1	31.00
95	J. Lewis (*Surrey*)	RFM	335	77	980	31	5-41	1	31.61
96	R. H. Joseph (*Leics*)	RFM	202.3	36	762	24	6-47	2	31.75
97	R. J. W. Topley (*Essex*)	LFM	112.1	24	350	11	3-59	0	31.81
98	P. D. Trego (*Somerset*)	RFM	523.5	125	1,609	50	5-53	2	32.18
99	W. B. Rankin (*Warwicks*)	RFM	138.1	15	515	16	5-78	1	32.18
100	L. A. Dawson (*Hants*)	SLA	265.2	62	837	26	5-29	1	32.19
101	M. Morkel (*South Africans*)	RF	150.2	30	451	14	4-72	0	32.21
102	J. A. R. Harris (*Glam & England Lions*)	RFM	173	29	553	17	6-102	2	32.52
103	C. M. Willoughby (*Essex*)	LFM	180	34	621	19	5-70	1	32.68
104	O. P. Rayner (*Middx*)	OB	240.5	38	590	18	4-67	0	32.77
105	A. Shahzad (*Yorks & Lancs*)	RFM	284.4	64	919	28	4-40	0	32.82
106	K. A. J. Roach (*West Indians*)	RF	89	10	364	11	3-60	0	33.09
107	C. J. Russell (*Worcs*)	RFM	134.4	23	563	17	4-43	0	33.11
108	Harbhajan Singh (*Essex*)	OB	176.3	38	431	13	4-91	0	33.15
109	R. J. Sidebottom (*Yorks*)	LFM	297	72	798	24	5-30	1	33.25

		Style	O	M	R	W	BB	5I	Avge
110	S. C. J. Broad (*Notts & England*)	RFM	295.3	53	966	29	7-72	2	33.31
111	H. F. Gurney (*Notts*)	LFM	234.3	52	713	21	4-40	0	33.95
112	D. J. Willey (*Northants*)	LFM	440.1	90	1,474	43	5-39	1	34.27
113	D. A. Griffiths (*Hants*)	RFM	110.3	18	382	11	3-40	0	34.72
114	C. A. J. Meschede (*Somerset*)	RM	119	22	418	12	3-26	0	34.83
115	Kabir Ali (*Hants*)	RFM	216.3	36	769	22	3-42	0	34.95
116	J. C. Tredwell (*Kent & England Lions*)	OB	371	99	912	26	3-35	0	35.07
117	Imran Tahir (*South Africans*)	LBG	134	16	424	12	4-31	0	35.33
118	G. G. White (*Notts*)	SLA	157.4	34	532	15	4-97	0	35.46
119	A. Carter (*Notts*)	RFM	261.2	43	938	26	4-55	0	36.07
120	J. D. Middlebrook (*Northants*)	OB	346.2	100	883	24	5-63	1	36.79
121	R. A. Whiteley (*Derbys*)	LM	177.1	23	736	20	2-6	0	36.80
122	C. W. Henderson (*Leics*)	SLA	390.1	82	1,110	30	5-116	1	37.00
123	T. T. Bresnan (*Yorks & England*)	RFM	337.2	75	1,071	28	5-81	1	38.25
124	D. S. Lucas (*Worcs*)	LFM	239	40	852	22	4-37	0	38.72
125	G. P. Swann (*Notts & England*)	OB	299.5	71	778	20	3-26	0	38.90
126	J. E. Anyon (*Sussex*)	RFM	429.5	73	1,646	42	5-36	2	39.19
127	G. M. Andrew (*Worcs*)	RFM	194	28	745	19	5-86	1	39.21
128	C. J. Jordan (*Surrey*)	RFM	160.3	23	599	15	3-29	0	39.93
129	S. R. Patel (*Notts & England Lions*)	SLA	194.4	35	642	16	4-67	0	40.12
130	R. M. L. Taylor (*Lough MCCU & Leics*)	LM	80	10	408	10	5-91	1	40.80
131	A. U. Rashid (*Yorks*)	LBG	202.5	26	656	16	5-105	1	41.00
132	M. L. Turner (*Derbys*)	RFM	140.5	12	619	15	3-53	0	41.26
133	E. G. C. Young (*Glos*)	SLA	137.5	28	414	10	2-23	0	41.40
134	P. J. Franks (*Notts*)	RFM	204.5	32	667	16	4-47	0	41.68
135	K. W. Hogg (*Lancs*)	RFM	262.4	62	795	19	3-23	0	41.84
136	L. M. Daggett (*Northants*)	RFM	372.1	95	1,218	27	4-76	0	45.11
137	N. L. Buck (*Leics*)	RFM	292	58	955	20	3-50	0	47.75
138	C. D. Collymore (*Middx*)	RFM	187.1	44	540	11	3-66	0	49.09
139	T. Westley (*Essex*)	OB	152.3	24	504	10	3-5	0	50.40
140	D. A. Cosker (*Glam*)	SLA	361.3	83	991	16	4-22	0	61.93

The following bowlers took ten wickets in fewer than five innings:

	Style	O	M	R	W	BB	5I	Avge
S. H. Choudhry (*Worcs*)	SLA	70.4	13	165	10	4-38	0	16.50
L. Evans (*Northants*)	RFM	65	16	214	12	4-38	0	17.83
P. T. Turnbull (*Cambridge MCCU*)	RFM	70	17	237	10	6-108	1	23.70
J. M. Holland (*Australia A*)	SLA	93	19	273	10	3-49	0	27.30

BOWLING STYLES

LBG	Leg-breaks and googlies (4)	**RF**	Right-arm fast (5)
LFM	Left-arm fast medium (16)	**RFM**	Right-arm fast medium (78)
LM	Left-arm medium (3)	**RM**	Right-arm medium (9)
OB	Off-breaks (14)	**SLA**	Slow left-arm (17)

Note: The total comes to 146 because S. J. Croft and G. G. Wagg have two styles of bowling.

INDIVIDUAL SCORES OF 100 AND OVER

There were **204** three-figure innings in 169 first-class matches in 2012, which was 58 fewer than in 2011, when 172 first-class matches were played. Of these, eight were double-hundreds, compared with 17 in 2011. The list includes 169 hundreds in the Championship, compared with 204 in 2011.

N. R. D. Compton (5)
236 Somerset v Cardiff MCCU, Taunton Vale
133 Somerset v Warwicks, Birmingham
204* Somerset v Notts, Nottingham
108 Somerset v Worcs, Worcester
155* Somerset v Worcs, Taunton

J. M. Bairstow (4)
107 Yorks v Kent, Leeds
182 Yorks v Leics, Scarborough
118 Yorks v Leics, Leicester
139 England Lions v Australia A, Manchester

J. C. Hildreth (4)
268 Somerset v Cardiff MCCU, Taunton Vale
102* Somerset v Notts, Nottingham
120 Somerset v Surrey, The Oval
101* Somerset v Sussex, Hove

J. H. K. Adams (3)
122 Hants v Derbys, Southampton
149 Hants v Northants, Southampton
139* Hants v Essex, Southampton

V. Chopra (3)
105 Warwicks v Sussex, Hove
113 Warwicks v Lancs, Birmingham
195 Warwicks v Worcs, Worcester

R. Clarke (3)
140 Warwicks v Lancs, Liverpool
123* Warwicks v Lancs, Birmingham
110* Warwicks v Sussex, Birmingham

M. J. Lumb (3)
131 Notts v Durham, Chester-le-Street
162 Notts v Middx, Nottingham
171 Notts v Sussex, Nottingham

W. L. Madsen (3)
101 Derbys v Glos, Derby
130* Derbys v Glam, Derby
231* Derbys v Northants, Northampton

B. P. Nash (3)
132* Kent v Yorks, Canterbury
114 Kent v Glam, Canterbury
119 Kent v Leics, Leicester

C. D. Nash (3)
128 Sussex v Notts, Hove
162 Sussex v Notts, Nottingham
126 Sussex v Somerset, Hove

R. I. Newton (3)
117 Northants v Glam, Northampton
115 } Northants v Derbys, Northampton
119* }

S. A. Northeast (3)
101* Kent v Glam, Canterbury
140 Kent v Hants, Southampton
165 Kent v Derbys, Canterbury

K. P. Pietersen (3)
234* Surrey v Lancs, Guildford
149 England v South Africa, Leeds
163 Surrey v Somerset, Taunton

C. J. L. Rogers (3)
138* Middx v Lancs, Liverpool
173 Middx v Somerset, Lord's
109 Middx v Warwicks, Birmingham

J. E. Root (3)
115* Eng. Lions v West Indians, Northampton
125 Yorks v Northants, Leeds
222* Yorks v Hants, Southampton

A. J. Strauss (3)
122 England v West Indies, Lord's
141 England v West Indies, Nottingham
127* Middx v Notts, Uxbridge

J. W. A. Taylor (3)
101* Notts v Lough MCCU, Nottingham
118 Eng. Lions v West Indians, Northampton
163* Notts v Sussex, Nottingham

M. A. Wallace (3)
122* Glam v Oxford MCCU, Oxford
118 Glam v Leics, Cardiff
111 Glam v Kent, Canterbury

M. H. Wessels (3)
172 Notts v Lough MCCU, Nottingham
113 Notts v Worcs, Nottingham
199 Notts v Sussex, Hove

J. Allenby (2)
103* Glam v Essex, Colchester
125* Glam v Kent, Cardiff

H. M. Amla (2)
311* South Africa v England, The Oval
121 South Africa v England, Lord's

R. S. Bopara (2)
117* Essex v Yorks, Leeds
174 Essex v Northants, Northampton

M. A. G. Boyce (2)
122 Leics v Yorks, Scarborough
107 Leics v Yorks, Leicester

R. J. Burns (2)
101* Surrey v Leeds/Brad MCCU, The Oval
121 Surrey v Middx, The Oval

E. J. M. Cowan (2)
103 Glos v Essex, Cheltenham
109 Australia A v Derbys, Derby

S. J. Croft (2)
113 Lancs v Somerset, Taunton
154* Lancs v Surrey, Guildford

J. L. Denly (2)
134* Middx v Worcs, Lord's
116* Middx v Somerset, Lord's

N. J. Dexter (2)
101 Middx v Warwicks, Birmingham
125 Middx v Lancs, Lord's

W. J. Durston (2)
121 Derbys v Hants, Southampton
116 Derbys v Essex, Chelmsford

J. S. Foster (2)
114* Essex v Cambridge MCCU, Cambridge
135 Essex v Northants, Northampton

M. J. Guptill (2)
137 Derbys v Northants, Derby
132 Derbys v Glam, Derby

A. D. Hales (2)
101 Notts v Durham, Nottingham
155* Notts v Warwicks, Birmingham

A. Harinath (2)
109 Surrey v Middx, The Oval
105* Surrey v Somerset, Taunton

P. J. Horton (2)
137* Lancs v Warwicks, Birmingham
110 Lancs v Surrey, Guildford

P. J. Hughes (2)
135* Worcs v Warwicks, Birmingham
104 Worcs v Durham, Chester-le-Street

P. A. Jaques (2)
126 Yorks v Essex, Leeds
160 Yorks v Glos, Bristol

E. C. Joyce (2)
108* Sussex v Worcs, Worcester
107 Sussex v Worcs, Hove

C. Kieswetter (2)
152 Somerset v Warwicks, Taunton
112* England Lions v Australia A, Birmingham

A. McGrath (2)
106* Yorks v Hants, Leeds
104 Yorks v Derbys, Leeds

D. J. Malan (2)
106 Middx v Warwicks, Uxbridge
140 Middx v Warwicks, Birmingham

J. D. Middlebrook (2)
121 Northants v Glos, Northampton
100 Northants v Essex, Northampton

D. K. H. Mitchell (2)
102 Worcs v Notts, Nottingham
133* Worcs v Middx, Worcester

S. D. Peters (2)
107 Northants v Yorks, Northampton
148 Northants v Leics, Northampton

A. N. Petersen (2)
145 Essex v Glam, Cardiff
182 South Africa v England, Leeds

M. J. Powell (2)
128* Kent v Northants, Northampton
134 Kent v Leics, Canterbury

A. G. Prince (2)
144 Lancs v Middx, Liverpool
129 Lancs v Somerset, Liverpool

D. J. Redfern (2)
110 Derbys v Northants, Derby
133 Derbys v Hants, Southampton

D. J. Sales (2)
140 Northants v Kent, Canterbury
138* Northants v Glam, Northampton

R. R. Sarwan (2)
105 Leics v Derbys, Derby
117 Leics v Essex, Leicester

O. A. Shah (2)
138 Essex v Glam, Colchester
161 Essex v Hants, Southampton

D. I. Stevens (2)
119 Kent v Essex, Chelmsford
123 Kent v Glam, Canterbury

A. V. Suppiah (2)
124 Somerset v Notts, Nottingham
106 Somerset v Surrey, The Oval

M. A. Thornely (2)
131 Leics v Glam, Cardiff
115 Leics v Essex, Chelmsford

M. E. Trescothick (2)
123 Somerset v Sussex, Taunton
146 Somerset v Worcs, Taunton

J. O. Troughton (2)
132 Warwicks v Somerset, Taunton
119 Warwicks v Surrey, Birmingham

J. M. Vince (2)
128 Hants v Lough MCCU, Southampton
114 Hants v Derbys, Derby

L. W. P. Wells (2)
108 Sussex v Surrey, The Oval
127 Sussex v Surrey, Horsham

T. Westley (2)
125 Essex v Leics, Chelmsford
185 Essex v Glam, Colchester

I. J. Westwood (2)
111 Warwicks v Middx, Uxbridge
120 Warwicks v Middx, Birmingham

K. S. Williamson (2)
128 Glos v Derbys, Derby
111 Glos v Yorks, Bristol

C. R. Woakes (2)
107 Warwicks v Somerset, Taunton
118* Warwicks v Surrey, Birmingham

The following each compiled one three-figure innings:

T. R. Ambrose, 151*, Warwicks v Notts, Birmingham.

G. S. Ballance, 121*, Yorks v Glos, Bristol; M. D. Bates, 103, Hants v Yorks, Leeds; I. R. Bell, 120, Warwicks v Durham, Birmingham; I. D. Blackwell, MCC v Lancs, Abu Dhabi.

J. J. Cobb, 105, Leics v Derbys, Derby; I. A. Cockbain, 112, Glos v Hants, Bristol; K. J. Coetzer, 120, Northants v Leics, Leicester; F. R. J. Coleman, 110, Oxford MCCU v Worcs, Oxford; M. T. Coles, 103*, Kent v Yorks, Leeds; P. D. Collingwood, 114, Durham v Lancs, Liverpool; A. N. Cook, 115, England v South Africa, The Oval.

S. M. Davies, 104, Surrey v Somerset, The Oval; L. A. Dawson, 134*, Hants v Kent, Tunbridge Wells; Z. de Bruyn, 125, Surrey v Lancs, Liverpool; C. D. J. Dent, 114, Glos v Hants, Southampton.

E. J. H. Eckersley, 137*, Leics v Glam, Cardiff; N. J. Edwards, 195, Notts v Loughborough MCCU, Nottingham; Z. Elkin, 138, Cardiff MCCU v Somerset, Taunton Vale; S. M. Ervine, 109*, Hants v Glam, Southampton.

A. P. R. Gidman, 129, Glos v Derbys, Bristol; B. A. Godleman, 130, Essex v Glos, Chelmsford.

R. J. Hamilton-Brown, 115, Surrey v Worcs, Worcester.

J. H. Kallis, 182*, South Africa v England, The Oval; S. M. Katich, 196, Hants v Yorks, Leeds; R. W. T. Key, 119, Kent v Hants, Southampton; U. T. Khawaja, 110*, Derbys v Yorks, Leeds; M. Klinger, 120, Worcs v Oxford MCCU, Oxford.

A. Lyth, 248*, Yorks v Leics, Leicester.

N. D. McKenzie, 139, Hants v Essex, Chelmsford; D. L. Maddy, 112, Warwicks v Lancs, Liverpool; H. J. H. Marshall, 117*, Glos v Northants, Northampton; T. L. Maynard, 143, Surrey v Worcs, Worcester; J. C. Mickleburgh, 126, Essex v Leics, Chelmsford.

G. R. Napier, 100*, Essex v Cambridge MCCU, Cambridge; M. J. North, 116, Glam v Leics, Cardiff.

N. J. O'Brien, 182, Northants v Glam, Cardiff.

A. P. Palladino, 106, Derbys v Australia A, Derby; K. O. A. Powell, 108, West Indians v England Lions, Northampton; T. Poynton, 106, Derbys v Northants, Northampton.

D. Ramdin, 107*, West Indies v England, Birmingham; O. P. Rayner, 143*, Middx v Notts, Nottingham; C. M. W. Read, 104*, Notts v Somerset, Nottingham; S. D. Robson, 117, Middx v Durham MCCU, Northwood.

D. J. G. Sammy, 106, West Indies v England, Nottingham; M. N. Samuels, 117, West Indies v England, Nottingham; B. J. M. Scott, 106, Worcs v Lancs, Manchester; G. C. Smith, 131, South Africa v England, The Oval; G. M. Smith, 160, Essex v Cambridge MCCU, Cambridge; W. R. Smith, 100, Durham v Somerset, Taunton; V. S. Solanki, 106, Worcs v Somerset, Worcester; B. A. Stokes, 121, Durham v Lancs, Chester-le-Street; M. D. Stoneman, 114, Durham v Notts, Nottingham.

I. J. L. Trott, 178, Warwicks v Sussex, Hove.

A. C. Voges, 105, Notts v Middx, Uxbridge.

S. J. Walters, 159, Glam v Essex, Colchester; C. P. Wood, 105*, Hants v Leics, Leicester; B. J. Wright, 104, Glam v Hants, Cardiff.

M. H. Yardy, 110, Sussex v Lancs, Liverpool.

FASTEST HUNDREDS BY BALLS...

Balls	*Mins*		
48	49	G. R. Napier	Essex v Cambridge MCCU at Cambridge.
80	98	C. P. Wood	Hants v Leics at Leicester.
89		M. H. Wessels	Notts v Loughborough MCCU at Nottingham.
93	146	K. P. Pietersen	Surrey v Lancs at Guildford.
97		W. J. Durston	Derbys v Hants at Southampton.
99		S. M. Katich	Hants v Yorks at Leeds.

The time taken in minutes to reach three figures was not always recorded.

...AND THE SLOWEST

Balls	*Mins*		
273	327	D. K. H. Mitchell	Worcs v Middx at Worcester.
270	317	I. J. Westwood	Warwicks v Middx at Uxbridge.
267	328	E. J. M. Cowan	Glos v Essex at Cheltenham.
265	337	N. J. O'Brien	Northants v Glam at Cardiff.
250	328	M. A. G. Boyce	Leics v Yorks v Scarborough.

TEN WICKETS IN A MATCH

There were **17** instances of bowlers taking ten or more wickets in a first-class match in 2012, four fewer than in 2011. All but one were in the County Championship.

G. Onions (3)

10-73, Durham v Middx, Lord's; 11-95, Durham v Lancs, Chester-le-Street; 10-125, Durham v Notts, Nottingham.

The following each took ten wickets in a match on one occasion:

Abdur Rehman, 14-101, Somerset v Worcs, Taunton; A. R. Adams, 10-50, Notts v Lancs, Manchester; M. M. Ali, 12-96, Worcs v Lancs, Manchester.

D. J. Balcombe, 11-119, Hants v Glos, Southampton; K. H. D. Barker, 10-70, Warwicks v Durham, Birmingham; G. J. Batty, 10-142, Surrey v Warwicks, The Oval; S. C. J. Broad, 11-165, England v West Indies, Lord's.

G. Chapple, 10-133, Lancs v Middx, Lord's; J. L. Clare, 11-57, Derbys v Glam, Cardiff.

R. H. Joseph, 12-111, Leics v Glam, Leicester.

S. C. Meaker, 11-167, Surrey v Somerset, The Oval.

M. S. Panesar, 13-137, Sussex v Somerset, Taunton.

A. Richardson, 10-128, Worcs v Surrey, The Oval; T. S. Roland-Jones, 10-118, Middx v Worcs, Worcester.

ECB

LV= COUNTY CHAMPIONSHIP, 2012

NEVILLE SCOTT

There were times last summer when British life seemed so grotesque you thought you were in the pages of a novel by Tom Sharpe or Mervyn Peake. The Leveson inquiry revealed that the prime minister shared gushing emails with the soon-to-be-arrested editor of a tabloid newspaper, who rode the ranges of Oxfordshire alongside him on a charger supplied by the Metropolitan Police, several of whose senior officers faced allegations of corruption. Vince Cable, the government's business secretary, described areas of British banking, so critical to the economy, as "a massive cesspit". And surface-to-air missiles were sited on the roofs of tower blocks up the road from where Graham Gooch first clasped a bat, in innocent days when children still played cricket in London's East End. To top it all, Derbyshire won their first trophy for 19 years.

Yet seeking sanity in the Championship was to find that the heavens had turned more absurd still. Snow preceded the first day of the season, sleet stopped play at Scarborough on May 4 (when temperatures in torrid Hove soared to 5°C), swan-upping in mid-July was cancelled due to floods, and the rain barely relented. Out of the cesspit, into the monsoon.

COUNTY CHAMPIONSHIP TABLE

Division One	Matches	Won	Lost	Drawn	*Bonus points* Batting	*Bonus points* Bowling	Penalty	Points
1 – Warwickshire (**2**)	16	6	1	9	43	45	0	211
2 – Somerset (**4**)	16	5	1	10	32	45	0	187
3 – Middlesex (*1*)	16	5	4	7	33	38	0	172
4 – Sussex (**5**)	16	5	5	6	28	41	0	167
5 – Nottinghamshire (**6**)	16	4	2	10	26	43	0	163
6 – Durham (**3**)	16	5	5	6*	18	45	4	157
7 – Surrey (*2*)	16	3	4	9*	26	40	2	139
8 – Lancashire (**1**)	16	1	5	10	25	35	0	106
9 – Worcestershire (**7**)	16	1	8	7	17	42	0	96

Division Two	Matches	Won	Lost	Drawn	*Bonus points* Batting	*Bonus points* Bowling	Penalty	Points
1 – Derbyshire (*5*)	16	6	2	8	31	43	0	194
2 – Yorkshire (**8**)	16	5	0	11	41	40	0	194
3 – Kent (*8*)	16	4	3	9	39	40	0	170
4 – Hampshire (**9**)	16	4	5	7	28	40	0	153
5 – Essex (*7*)	16	3	3	10	27	40	0	145
6 – Glamorgan (*6*)	16	3	6	7*	28	35	1	131
7 – Leicestershire (*9*)	16	3	3	10	24	33	5	130
8 – Northamptonshire (*3*)	16	2	5	9	37	34	0	130
9 – Gloucestershire (*4*)	16	3	6	7*	22	35	0	126

2011 positions are shown in brackets: Division One in bold, Division Two in italic.

* *Includes one match abandoned.*

Win = 16pts; draw = 3pts; abandoned = 3pts. Penalties were deducted for slow over-rates.

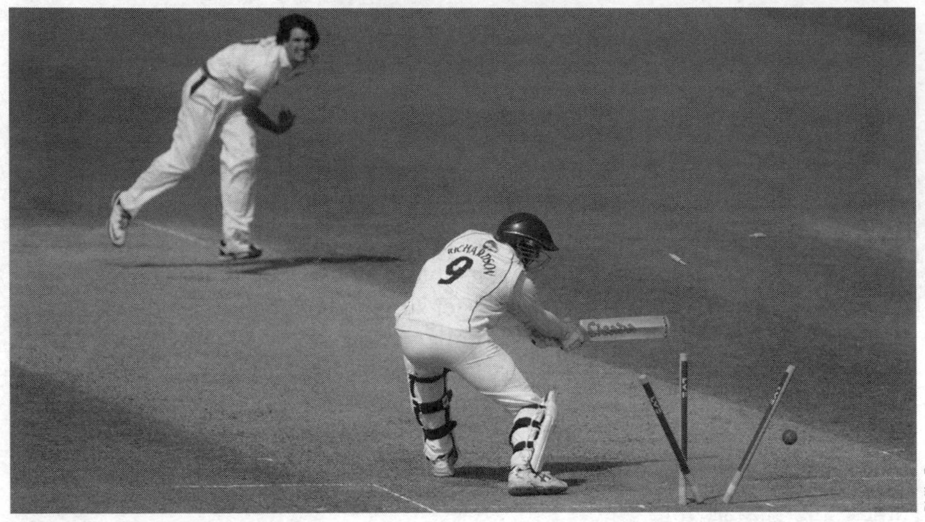

Neck and crop: Chris Wright bowls Alan Richardson... and the Championship title is Warwickshire's with a week to spare.

In the words of Captain Scott, counties "bowed to the will of Providence" and, in the face of the non-stop deluge, just 38% of Division Two matches had produced a result by August 18. The season can be starkly summed up: only 68 (of 144) games were won, and 27 of these wins arrived in the first and last fortnights. In between, summer came and went in late May, during seven days that granted another seven results. Half the victories in 2012 were thus secured in five weeks. The rest was rain and pitch inspections.

Worse, of the 13 results that emerged from 14 games in that frigid first fortnight (all rain-interrupted), several were played on pitches that rendered cricket almost a game of chance. By May 6, when a quarter of the campaign had already passed, the overall average cost of a wicket was 24 runs. Batsmen floundered like airline pilots suddenly having to fly without benefit of onboard computers. There were five counties by that date who, in a combined total of 22 games, had managed three batting points between them from a potential maximum of 110; one of them, Nottinghamshire, held second place in Division One.

But the two sides who seized the early advantage retained it. Tables can mislead, for until the final round some teams have played more games than others; but, on the basis of points per completed match, Derbyshire led the promotion race from their third fixture to the finish, and Warwickshire led the title race from first to last.

Warwickshire were worthy champions. Many who had seen them in 2011 (though not the bookies) tipped them for the crown because they had players with the will and nous to respond when required. Four of their six successes had come by late May, with nine men, including Ian Bell during a rare release by England, contributing at least a match-winning performance. The title arrived five and a half playing days from the close, and Varun Chopra was the sole England-raised batsman to hit 1,000 Championship runs.

HOURS OF PLAYING TIME LOST (HOME AND AWAY)

	2011	*2012*		*2011*	*2012*
Derbyshire	37.75	82.00	Middlesex	51.25	69.75
Durham	41.75	106.25	Northamptonshire	26.50	94.75
Essex	35.75	112.75	Nottinghamshire	44.25	96.75
Glamorgan	33.35	103.00	Somerset	31.75	99.25
Gloucestershire	35.00	115.75	Surrey	21.75	102.75
Hampshire	46.25	110.00	Sussex	12.50	77.50
Kent	23.00	88.75	Warwickshire	21.75	74.00
Lancashire	15.25	117.00	Worcestershire	24.25	91.75
Leicestershire	20.50	99.25	Yorkshire	32.25	138.25

Research: Andrew Hignell

Nottinghamshire, their only real threat until mid-August, had also won four times by May 28, but would not prevail again in the wet. After their first ten games, the remarkable Andre Adams – who had played in nine – had 50 Championship wickets, 12 more than his nearest rival, and it seemed the title would rest on his private battle with the collective excellence of the Warwickshire attack. But Adams lost fitness, playing only three more games for four more wickets, and his side gave six men to England during the final quarter. When Nottinghamshire and Warwickshire met twice in the last three games, both proved to be draws – inevitably rain-affected.

Leapfrogging Nottinghamshire, who slipped back to fifth, **Somerset** won their last two matches in that belatedly bright September to take second place, and **Middlesex**, coming third, achieved their best finish for 17 years. **Sussex**, either side of the Twenty20 hiatus, eluded the showers to win four successive home games, in all of which they inserted their opponents in contests lasting fewer than 270 overs. They finished fourth.

Durham, ageing in 2011, were now simply aged. In each of their first five games, they fielded at least four players who had passed their 33rd birthdays. Half their first ten matches were lost, and another abandoned, before – with ranks refreshed by two young South Africans – they rousingly won five of their last six, thwarting relegation under Paul Collingwood, a new captain at 36. By then, three former Championship-winning stalwarts had either retired or gone out on loan. Of eight matches on questionable pitches in Chester-le-Street, six reached a result. Each came in the overs equivalent of under three days. In all, even discounting matches where declarations attempted to outwit bad weather, 35 victories (51% of the total) were similarly terse.

Having lost to Middlesex in April, Surrey bitterly castigated the Lord's pitch – "awful" was one of the milder comments, but the word gained true weight two months later. Surrey's season was overshadowed by the death of Tom Maynard at 23. It was the club's third such bleak loss in two generations: Graham Kersey, the oldest at 25, had died in 1997, Ben Hollioake in spring 2002. Their bowling, on paper, had looked strong enough to win the title, but on spinning pitches at The Oval, Surrey needed to stir themselves to win their last two home games and stay in the first division.

AVERAGE TEAM TOTALS HOME AND AWAY

Division One

	Home			*Away*			*Home*
	For	*Against*	*Differential*	*For*	*Against*	*Differential*	*advantage*
Middlesex	337	250	+87	271	279	−8	95
Sussex	295	254	+41	272	319	−47	88
Warwickshire	414	275	+139	327	250	+77	62
Surrey	286	283	+3	273	313	−40	43
Durham	217	193	+24	241	244	−3	27
Lancashire	208	287	−79	321	409	−88	9
Somerset	312	269	+43	318	282	+36	7
Worcestershire	238	339	−101	191	284	−93	−8
Nottinghamshire	338	351	−13	277	260	+17	−30

Division Two

	Home			*Away*			*Home*
	For	*Against*	*Differential*	*For*	*Against*	*Differential*	*advantage*
Leicestershire	277	316	−39	265	449	−184	145
Glamorgan	266	253	+13	282	368	−86	99
Gloucestershire	298	251	+47	255	306	−51	98
Northamptonshire	346	327	+19	317	384	−67	86
Yorkshire	391	301	+90	341	282	+59	31
Derbyshire	313	268	+45	293	277	+16	29
Hampshire	317	324	−7	274	299	−25	18
Kent	349	272	+77	329	243	+86	−9
Essex	303	319	−16	313	287	+26	−42

Average team totals = total runs scored divided by total wickets lost multiplied by ten. The "differential" columns represent the average total scored by each team minus the average total they conceded. The final column, home advantage, is calculated by subtracting the away differential from the home differential. A plus figure in the home advantage column indicates that a team did relatively better at home; a minus figure that they did relatively better away. Only five counties – Derbyshire, Kent, Somerset, Warwickshire and Yorkshire – averaged more runs than their opponents both at home and away.

All instances of "joke bowling" are excluded from the figures.

Although one round remained, that second Surrey win condemned **Worcestershire** to relegation. But not for some three hours was **Lancashire's** fate sealed over the river at Lord's; needing victory, they went down blazing, in an impossible attempt to score 304 in 39 overs. They joined Yorkshire in 2002 and Nottinghamshire in 2006 by being demoted the year after taking the title. At least their failure to win any of six games in Liverpool buried the myth that they owed their 2011 triumph to Aigburth: their home and away records that summer were in fact identical. The simpler truth was that a team of largely unspectacular individuals could not again summon the energy to prevail by collective dedication, a reality illustrated by a return of 18 expensive wickets for Kyle Hogg, one of the surprise heroes of the previous season.

If the title race failed to match the drama of the preceding two years, the promotion race was still theoretically alive until the penultimate evening. **Kent**, a revamped side with enough veteran imports to make Durham look callow, remained unbeaten until August 5. They lost their nerve when set for victory at Derby, to be defeated in the division's pivotal result. Shocked, they followed with a home loss to Essex, and humiliation came at Cardiff in the last game. It meant Derbyshire and Yorkshire were safely promoted. Both won on the campaign's final afternoon, and **Derbyshire** became champions shortly before tea. Four of the team had emerged from their Academy.

It would have been a travesty had **Yorkshire** been denied. There is no definitive way of measuring the handicap of rain, but they surrendered a realistic possible maximum of 151 points; Essex, also severely hit, lost 142. By the same criteria, Sussex and Derbyshire missed only 57 points each. Of course there is no way of knowing how many of those points they would actually have collected. Until late on, Yorkshire's attack – on benign home pitches – was statistically among the least penetrative in the country: two of their five wins came after Gloucestershire offered them targets. But with more time, they would clearly have won more matches. The same is true of **Essex**. **Hampshire**, however, squandered a real chance. From second place, ten points clear of Yorkshire, they lost their last three games, their attention perhaps deflected towards limited-overs glory.

The rest were never in it. **Glamorgan** continued to be predictably weaker since boardroom meddling in 2010; **Leicestershire** managed a better season, despite nine former players appearing for other counties in the Championship (and three for England); poachers still prowl at their gates. **Northamptonshire** discarded David Capel in July, with the chief executive's comment that "every coach has his shelf-life in the modern game", before their worst finish for 34 years. And spirited **Gloucestershire**, another club strapped for cash, merited more than a second wooden spoon in five summers.

The Championship itself merited far more. Tempting though it is, we cannot blame the ECB for climate change. But, like Albanian despots arranging re-votes until they receive the mandate they want, the ECB tried to make clubs accept more Twenty20 in a plan already once rejected. They will get their way in 2014 but, crucially, not at the expense of the Championship. The counties refused any dilution of the competition, and also turned down a proposal to start the 2013 campaign on April 3, even though this meant forgoing participation in the Champions League. Yet that loud infant, Twenty20, still dictates too soon a start. In 2012, two matches were entirely abandoned in the same round for the first time in 25 years. They were scheduled to finish on April 29; in 1993, the inaugural season of a purely four-day Championship, that was the day when the first matches began.

More than half the 2012 Championship was over by June 9, part of the reason why patterns of play have become increasingly formulaic. Ignoring joke bowling, first division wickets fell once every 52 balls last year: in not one of the 20 seasons of four-day play has that strike-rate been bettered. Modern seamers have never had it so good. But for spin, a key element in Test cricket, the decline is profound. If three left-armers, Monty Panesar, Simon Kerrigan and David Wainwright, are removed from the equation, England-raised spinners took fewer than one Championship wicket in eight last year. Behind that leading trio, resources are worryingly diminished.

Of course the damp had much to do with this, but certain trends have been growing for years. Every one of the 16 wins for Warwickshire, Somerset and Sussex came after they batted second and, in terms of wins and losses, all but three teams (Lancashire, Nottinghamshire and Essex) had superior records at home to away, often markedly so. Astoundingly, only four of the 35 victories in Division One came after batting first on winning the toss, the historic choice in Tests; two of the four were at Old Trafford, the other two at The Oval. Pitches, tuned to home attacks, are penalising top-order batsmen and promoting seamers without the skill for international success. It is a process arguably encouraged by a points system that, with good motives, has gone marginally too far towards rewarding wins. Creating low-scoring results, even over three days, becomes all.

With the social base of English cricket quite criminally narrowed, a quarter of Championship appearances last year were made by those who learned the game abroad. Keaton Jennings, the South Africa Under-19 captain in 2011, joined Durham last August, suddenly becoming English. His mother is Sunderland-born; father Ray, however, was formerly South Africa's national coach, and is now their Under-19 coach. Nick Compton, who made his Test debut in November, and Gary Ballance, named in the England Performance squad, were natives of South Africa and Zimbabwe who came to Harrow at 16 to complete their cricketing educations. This in the context of government figures conceding that the sale of 31 state-school playing fields had been approved in 27 months since the coalition came to power. Visiting supporters at the Tests last year displayed T-shirts with the message: "Our South Africans are better than yours." They, anyway, could afford to see the joke.

Pre-season betting (best available prices): *Division One* – 9-2 Durham; 11-2 Somerset; 13-2 Lancashire and Nottinghamshire; 7-1 Warwickshire; 8-1 Surrey; 10-1 Sussex; 14-1 Middlesex; 66-1 Worcestershire. *Division Two* – 3-1 Hampshire; 7-2 Yorkshire; 11-2 Essex; 9-1 Glamorgan and Northamptonshire; 12-1 Gloucestershire and Kent; 18-1 Derbyshire; 25-1 Leicestershire.

Prize money

Division One
£550,000 for winners: WARWICKSHIRE.
£235,000 for runners-up: SOMERSET.
£115,000 for third: MIDDLESEX.
£35,000 for fourth: SUSSEX.

Division Two
£135,000 for winners: DERBYSHIRE.
£70,000 for runners-up: YORKSHIRE.

These prizes are divided between players' prize money and a county performance payment. For the winners, players receive £400,000 and the county £150,000; for the runners-up, the split is £185,000/£50,000; for third, £100,000/£15,000; for fourth, £30,000/£5,000. In the second division, the split for the winners is £100,000/£35,000, and for the runners-up £60,000/£10,000.

Winners of each match (both divisions): £1,350.

Leaders: *Division One* – from April 8 Somerset; April 15 Nottinghamshire; April 22 Warwickshire; May 12 Nottinghamshire; May 19 Warwickshire; May 28 Nottinghamshire; July 15 Warwickshire; July 30 Nottinghamshire; August 4 Warwickshire. Warwickshire became champions on September 6. *Division Two* – from April 7 Essex; April 14 Derbyshire; April 29 Kent; May 5 Derbyshire; May 12 Derbyshire and Yorkshire; May 18 Derbyshire. Derbyshire became champions on September 14.

Bottom place: *Division One* – from April 15 Durham, Lancashire and Worcestershire; April 22, Lancashire; April 29 Durham; August 9 Worcestershire.
Division Two – from April 15 Hampshire; April 22 Northamptonshire; April 29 Glamorgan; July 17 Leicestershire; July 30 Glamorgan; August 4 Leicestershire; August 24 Glamorgan; August 31 Gloucestershire; September 6 Glamorgan; September 14 Gloucestershire.

Scoring of Points

(*a*) For a win, 16 points plus any points scored in the first innings.
(*b*) In a tie, each side scores eight points, plus any points scored in the first innings.
(*c*) In a drawn match, each side scores three points, plus any points scored in the first innings.
(*d*) If the scores are equal in a drawn match, the side batting in the fourth innings scores eight points, plus any points scored in the first innings, and the opposing side scores three points plus any points scored in the first innings.
(*e*) First-innings points (awarded only for performances in the first 110 overs of each first innings and retained whatever the result of the match).

(i) A maximum of five batting points to be available: 200 to 249 runs – 1 point; 250 to 299 runs – 2 points; 300 to 349 runs – 3 points; 350 to 399 runs – 4 points; 400 runs or over – 5 points. Penalty runs awarded within the first 110 overs of each first innings count towards the award of bonus points.

(ii) A maximum of three bowling points to be available: 3 to 5 wickets taken – 1 point; 6 to 8 wickets taken – 2 points; 9 to 10 wickets taken – 3 points.

(*f*) If a match is abandoned without a ball being bowled, each side scores three points.
(*g*) The side which has the highest aggregate of points shall be the champion county of their respective division. Should any sides in the Championship table be equal on points, the following tie-breakers will be applied in the order stated: most wins, fewest losses, team achieving most points in head-to-head contests between teams level on points, most wickets taken, most runs scored. At the end of the season, the top two teams from the second division will be promoted and the bottom two teams from the first division will be relegated.
(*h*) The minimum over-rate to be achieved by counties will be 16 overs per hour. Overs will be calculated at the end of the match and penalties applied on a match-by-match basis. For each over (ignoring fractions) that a side has bowled short of the target number, one point will be deducted from their Championship total.
(*i*) A county which is adjudged to have prepared a pitch unfit for four-day first-class cricket will have 24 points deducted. A county adjudged to have prepared a poor pitch will have eight points deducted. This penalty will rise to 12 points if the county has prepared a poor or unfit pitch within the previous 12 months. A county adjudged to have provided a playing area in a condition substantially reducing the possibility of play (subsequent to actions within that county's control) will have eight points deducted.

Under ECB playing conditions, two extras were scored for every no-ball bowled whether scored off or not, and one for every wide. Any runs scored off the bat were credited to the batsman, while byes and leg-byes were counted as no-balls or wides, as appropriate, in accordance with Law 24.13, in addition to the initial penalty.

CONSTITUTION OF COUNTY CHAMPIONSHIP

At least four possible dates have been given for the start of county cricket in England. The first, patchy, references began in 1825. The earliest mention in any cricket publication is in 1864 and eight counties have come to be regarded as first-class from that date, including Cambridgeshire, who dropped out after 1871. For many years, the County Championship was considered to have started in 1873, when regulations governing qualification first applied; indeed, a special commemorative stamp was issued by the Post Office in 1973. However, the Championship was not formally organised until 1890 and before then champions were proclaimed by the press; sometimes publications differed in their views and no definitive list of champions can start before that date. Eight teams contested the 1890 competition – Gloucestershire, Kent, Lancashire, Middlesex, Nottinghamshire, Surrey, Sussex and Yorkshire. Somerset joined in the following year, and in 1895 the Championship began to acquire something of its modern shape when Derbyshire, Essex, Hampshire, Leicestershire and Warwickshire were added. At that point MCC officially recognised the competition's existence. Worcestershire, Northamptonshire and Glamorgan were admitted to the Championship in 1899, 1905 and 1921 respectively and are regarded as first-class from these dates. An invitation in 1921 to Buckinghamshire to enter the Championship was declined, owing to the lack of necessary playing facilities, and an application by Devon in 1948 was unsuccessful. Durham were admitted to the Championship in 1992 and were granted first-class status prior to their pre-season tour of Zimbabwe. In 2000, the Championship was split for the first time into two divisions, on the basis of counties' standings in the 1999 competition. From 2000 onwards, the bottom three teams in Division One were relegated at the end of the season, and the top three teams in Division Two promoted. From 2006, this was changed to two teams relegated and two promoted.

COUNTY CHAMPIONS

The title of champion county is unreliable before 1890. In 1963, *Wisden* formally accepted the list of champions "most generally selected'' by contemporaries, as researched by the late Rowland Bowen (see *Wisden 1959*, pp 91–98). This appears to be the most accurate available list but has no official status. The county champions from 1864 to 1889 were, according to Bowen: 1864 Surrey; 1865 Nottinghamshire; 1866 Middlesex; 1867 Yorkshire; 1868 Nottinghamshire; 1869 Nottinghamshire and Yorkshire; 1870 Yorkshire; 1871 Nottinghamshire; 1872 Nottinghamshire; 1873 Gloucestershire and Nottinghamshire; 1874 Gloucestershire; 1875 Nottinghamshire; 1876 Gloucestershire; 1877 Gloucestershire; 1878 undecided; 1879 Lancashire and Nottinghamshire; 1880 Nottinghamshire; 1881 Lancashire; 1882 Lancashire and Nottinghamshire; 1883 Nottinghamshire; 1884 Nottinghamshire; 1885 Nottinghamshire; 1886 Nottinghamshire; 1887 Surrey; 1888 Surrey; 1889 Lancashire, Nottinghamshire and Surrey.

1890	Surrey
1891	Surrey
1892	Surrey
1893	Yorkshire
1894	Surrey
1895	Surrey
1896	Yorkshire
1897	Lancashire
1898	Yorkshire
1899	Surrey
1900	Yorkshire
1901	Yorkshire
1902	Yorkshire
1903	Middlesex
1904	Lancashire
1905	Yorkshire
1906	Kent
1907	Nottinghamshire
1908	Yorkshire
1909	Kent
1910	Kent
1911	Warwickshire
1912	Yorkshire
1913	Kent
1914	Surrey
1919	Yorkshire
1920	Middlesex
1921	Middlesex
1922	Yorkshire
1923	Yorkshire
1924	Yorkshire
1925	Yorkshire
1926	Lancashire
1927	Lancashire
1928	Lancashire
1929	Nottinghamshire
1930	Lancashire
1931	Yorkshire
1932	Yorkshire
1933	Yorkshire
1934	Lancashire
1935	Yorkshire
1936	Derbyshire
1937	Yorkshire
1938	Yorkshire
1939	Yorkshire
1946	Yorkshire
1947	Middlesex
1948	Glamorgan
1949	Middlesex Yorkshire
1950	Lancashire Surrey
1951	Warwickshire
1952	Surrey
1953	Surrey
1954	Surrey
1955	Surrey
1956	Surrey
1957	Surrey
1958	Surrey
1959	Yorkshire
1960	Yorkshire
1961	Hampshire
1962	Yorkshire
1963	Yorkshire
1964	Worcestershire
1965	Worcestershire
1966	Yorkshire
1967	Yorkshire
1968	Yorkshire
1969	Glamorgan
1970	Kent
1971	Surrey
1972	Warwickshire
1973	Hampshire
1974	Worcestershire
1975	Leicestershire
1976	Middlesex
1977	Middlesex Kent
1978	Kent
1979	Essex
1980	Middlesex
1981	Nottinghamshire
1982	Middlesex
1983	Essex
1984	Essex
1985	Middlesex
1986	Essex
1987	Nottinghamshire
1988	Worcestershire
1989	Worcestershire
1990	Middlesex
1991	Essex
1992	Essex
1993	Middlesex
1994	Warwickshire
1995	Warwickshire
1996	Leicestershire
1997	Glamorgan
1998	Leicestershire
1999	Surrey
2000	Surrey
2001	Yorkshire
2002	Surrey
2003	Sussex
2004	Warwickshire
2005	Nottinghamshire
2006	Sussex
2007	Sussex
2008	Durham
2009	Durham
2010	Nottinghamshire
2011	Lancashire
2012	Warwickshire

Notes: Since the Championship was constituted in 1890 it has been won outright as follows: Yorkshire 30 times, Surrey 18, Middlesex 10, Lancashire 8, Warwickshire 7, Essex, Kent and Nottinghamshire 6, Worcestershire 5, Glamorgan, Leicestershire and Sussex 3, Durham and Hampshire 2, Derbyshire 1. Gloucestershire, Northamptonshire and Somerset have never won.

The title has been shared three times since 1890, involving Middlesex twice, Kent, Lancashire, Surrey and Yorkshire.

Wooden Spoons: Since the major expansion of the Championship from nine teams to 14 in 1895, the counties have finished outright bottom as follows: Derbyshire 15; Somerset 12; Northamptonshire 11; Glamorgan 10; Gloucestershire and Leicestershire 9; Nottinghamshire and Sussex 8; Worcestershire 6; Durham and Hampshire 5; Warwickshire 3; Essex and Kent 2; Yorkshire 1. Lancashire, Middlesex and Surrey have never finished bottom. Leicestershire have also shared bottom place twice, once with Hampshire and once with Somerset.

From 1977 to 1983 the Championship was sponsored by Schweppes, from 1984 to 1998 by Britannic Assurance, from 1999 to 2000 by PPP healthcare, in 2001 by Cricinfo, from 2002 to 2005 by Frizzell and from 2006 by Liverpool Victoria (LV).

COUNTY CHAMPIONSHIP – FINAL POSITIONS, 1890–2012

	Derbyshire	Durham	Essex	Glamorgan	Gloucestershire	Hampshire	Kent	Lancashire	Leicestershire	Middlesex	Northamptonshire	Nottinghamshire	Somerset	Surrey	Sussex	Warwickshire	Worcestershire	Yorkshire
1890	–	–	–	–	6	–	3	2	–	7	–	5	–	1	8	–	–	3
1891	–	–	–	–	9	–	5	2	–	3	–	4	5	1	7	–	–	8
1892	–	–	–	–	7	–	7	4	–	5	–	2	3	1	9	–	–	6
1893	–	–	–	–	9	–	4	2	–	3	–	6	8	5	7	–	–	1
1894	–	–	–	–	9	–	4	4	–	3	–	7	6	1	8	–	–	2
1895	5	–	9	–	4	10	14	2	12	6	–	12	8	1	11	6	–	3
1896	7	–	5	–	10	8	9	2	13	3	–	6	11	4	14	12	–	1
1897	14	–	3	–	5	9	12	1	13	8	–	10	11	2	6	7	–	4
1898	9	–	5	–	3	12	7	6	13	2	–	8	13	4	9	9	–	1
1899	15	–	6	–	9	10	8	4	13	2	–	10	13	1	5	7	12	3
1900	13	–	10	–	7	15	3	2	14	7	–	5	11	7	3	6	12	1
1901	15	–	10	–	14	7	7	3	12	2	–	9	12	6	4	5	11	1
1902	10	–	13	–	14	15	7	5	11	12	–	3	7	4	2	6	9	1
1903	12	–	8	–	13	14	8	4	14	1	–	5	10	11	2	7	6	3
1904	10	–	14	–	9	15	3	1	7	4	–	5	12	11	6	7	13	2
1905	14	–	12	–	8	16	6	2	5	11	13	10	15	4	3	7	8	1
1906	16	–	7	–	9	8	1	4	15	11	11	5	11	3	10	6	14	2
1907	16	–	7	–	10	12	8	6	11	5	15	1	14	4	13	9	2	2
1908	14	–	11	–	10	9	2	7	13	4	15	8	16	3	5	12	6	1
1909	15	–	14	–	16	8	1	2	13	6	7	10	11	5	4	12	8	3
1910	15	–	11	–	12	6	1	4	10	3	9	5	16	2	7	14	13	8
1911	14	–	6	–	12	11	2	4	15	3	10	8	16	5	13	1	9	7
1912	12	–	15	–	11	6	3	4	13	5	2	8	14	7	10	9	16	1
1913	13	–	15	–	9	10	1	8	14	6	4	5	16	3	7	11	12	2
1914	12	–	8	–	16	5	3	11	13	2	9	10	15	1	6	7	14	4
1919	9	–	14	–	8	7	2	5	9	13	12	3	5	4	11	15	–	1
1920	16	–	9	–	8	11	5	2	13	1	14	7	10	3	6	12	15	4
1921	12	–	15	17	7	6	4	5	11	1	13	8	10	2	9	16	14	3
1922	11	–	8	16	13	6	4	5	14	7	15	2	10	3	9	12	17	1
1923	10	–	13	16	11	7	5	3	14	8	17	2	9	4	6	12	15	1
1924	17	–	15	13	6	12	5	4	11	2	16	6	8	3	10	9	14	1
1925	14	–	7	17	10	9	5	3	12	6	11	4	15	2	13	8	16	1
1926	11	–	9	8	15	7	3	1	13	6	16	4	14	5	10	12	17	2
1927	5	–	8	15	12	13	4	1	7	9	16	2	14	6	10	11	17	3
1928	10	–	16	15	5	12	2	1	9	8	13	3	14	6	7	11	17	4
1929	7	–	12	17	4	11	8	2	9	6	13	1	15	10	4	14	16	2
1930	9	–	6	11	2	13	5	1	12	16	17	4	13	8	7	15	10	3
1931	7	–	10	15	2	12	3	6	16	11	17	5	13	8	4	9	14	1
1932	10	–	14	15	13	8	3	6	12	10	16	4	7	5	2	9	17	1
1933	6	–	4	16	10	14	3	5	17	12	13	8	11	9	2	7	15	1
1934	3	–	8	13	7	14	5	1	12	10	17	9	15	11	2	4	16	5

	Derbyshire	Durham	Essex	Glamorgan	Gloucestershire	Hampshire	Kent	Lancashire	Leicestershire	Middlesex	Northamptonshire	Nottinghamshire	Somerset	Surrey	Sussex	Warwickshire	Worcestershire	Yorkshire
1935	2	–	9	13	15	16	10	4	6	3	17	5	14	11	7	8	12	1
1936	1	–	9	16	4	10	8	11	15	2	17	5	7	6	14	13	12	3
1937	3	–	6	7	4	14	12	9	16	2	17	10	13	8	5	11	15	1
1938	5	–	6	16	10	14	9	4	15	2	17	12	7	3	8	13	11	1
1939	9	–	4	13	3	15	5	6	17	2	16	12	14	8	10	11	7	1
1946	15	–	8	6	5	10	6	3	11	2	16	13	4	11	17	14	8	1
1947	5	–	11	9	2	16	4	3	14	1	17	11	11	6	9	15	7	7
1948	6	–	13	1	8	9	15	5	11	3	17	14	12	2	16	7	10	4
1949	15	–	9	8	7	16	13	11	17	1	6	11	9	5	13	4	3	1
1950	5	–	17	11	7	12	9	1	16	14	10	15	7	1	13	4	6	3
1951	11	–	8	5	12	9	16	3	15	7	13	17	14	6	10	1	4	2
1952	4	–	10	7	9	12	15	3	6	5	8	16	17	1	13	10	14	2
1953	6	–	12	10	6	14	16	3	3	5	11	8	17	1	2	9	15	12
1954	3	–	15	4	13	14	11	10	16	7	7	5	17	1	9	6	11	2
1955	8	–	14	16	12	3	13	9	6	5	7	11	17	1	4	9	15	2
1956	12	–	11	13	3	6	16	2	17	5	4	8	15	1	9	14	9	7
1957	4	–	5	9	12	13	14	6	17	7	2	15	8	1	9	11	16	3
1958	5	–	6	15	14	2	8	7	12	10	4	17	3	1	13	16	9	11
1959	7	–	9	6	2	8	13	5	16	10	11	17	12	3	15	4	14	1
1960	5	–	6	11	8	12	10	2	17	3	9	16	14	7	4	15	13	1
1961	7	–	6	14	5	1	11	13	9	3	16	17	10	15	8	12	4	2
1962	7	–	9	14	4	10	11	16	17	13	8	15	6	5	12	3	2	1
1963	17	–	12	2	8	10	13	15	16	6	7	9	3	11	4	4	14	1
1964	12	–	10	11	17	12	7	14	16	6	3	15	8	4	9	2	1	5
1965	9	–	15	3	10	12	5	13	14	6	2	17	7	8	16	11	1	4
1966	9	–	16	14	15	11	4	12	8	12	5	17	3	7	10	6	2	1
1967	6	–	15	14	17	12	2	11	2	7	9	15	8	4	13	10	5	1
1968	8	–	14	3	16	5	2	6	9	10	13	4	12	15	17	11	7	1
1969	16	–	6	1	2	5	10	15	14	11	9	8	17	3	7	4	12	13
1970	7	–	12	2	17	10	1	3	15	16	14	11	13	5	9	7	6	4
1971	17	–	10	16	8	9	4	3	5	6	14	12	7	1	11	2	15	13
1972	17	–	5	13	3	9	2	15	6	8	4	14	11	12	16	1	7	10
1973	16	–	8	11	5	1	4	12	9	13	3	17	10	2	15	7	6	14
1974	17	–	12	16	14	2	10	8	4	6	3	15	5	7	13	9	1	11
1975	15	–	7	9	16	3	5	4	1	11	8	13	12	6	17	14	10	2
1976	15	–	6	17	3	12	14	16	4	1	2	13	7	9	10	5	11	8
1977	7	–	6	14	3	11	1	16	5	1	9	17	4	14	8	10	13	12
1978	14	–	2	13	10	8	1	12	6	3	17	7	5	16	9	11	15	4
1979	16	–	1	17	10	12	5	13	6	14	11	9	8	3	4	15	2	7
1980	9	–	8	13	7	17	16	15	10	1	12	3	5	2	4	14	11	6
1981	12	–	5	14	13	7	9	16	8	4	15	1	3	6	2	17	11	10
1982	11	–	7	16	15	3	13	12	2	1	9	4	6	5	8	17	14	10
1983	9	–	1	15	12	3	7	12	4	2	6	14	10	8	11	5	16	17
1984	12	–	1	13	17	15	5	16	4	3	11	2	7	8	6	9	10	14
1985	13	–	4	12	3	2	9	14	16	1	10	8	17	6	7	15	5	11
1986	11	–	1	17	2	6	8	15	7	12	9	4	16	3	14	12	5	10
1987	6	–	12	13	10	5	14	2	3	16	7	1	11	4	17	15	9	8
1988	14	–	3	17	10	15	2	9	8	7	12	5	11	4	16	6	1	13
1989	6	–	2	17	9	6	15	4	13	3	5	11	14	12	10	8	1	16
1990	12	–	2	8	13	3	16	6	7	1	11	13	15	9	17	5	4	10
1991	3	–	1	12	13	9	6	8	16	15	10	4	17	5	11	2	6	14
1992	5	18	1	14	10	15	2	12	8	11	3	4	9	13	7	6	17	16
1993	15	18	11	3	17	13	8	13	9	1	4	7	5	6	10	16	2	12
1994	17	16	6	18	12	13	9	10	2	4	5	3	11	7	8	1	15	13

	Derbyshire	Durham	Essex	Glamorgan	Gloucestershire	Hampshire	Kent	Lancashire	Leicestershire	Middlesex	Northamptonshire	Nottinghamshire	Somerset	Surrey	Sussex	Warwickshire	Worcestershire	Yorkshire
1995	14	17	5	16	6	13	18	4	7	2	3	11	9	12	15	1	10	8
1996	2	18	5	10	13	14	4	15	1	9	16	17	11	3	12	8	7	6
1997	16	17	8	1	7	14	2	11	10	4	15	13	12	8	18	4	3	6
1998	10	14	18	12	4	6	11	2	1	17	15	16	9	5	7	8	13	3
1999	9	8	12	14	18	7	5	2	3	16	13	17	4	1	11	10	15	6
2000	**9**	**8**	*2*	*3*	*4*	**7**	**6**	**2**	**4**	*8*	*1*	*7*	**5**	**1**	*9*	*6*	*5*	**3**
2001	*9*	*8*	**9**	**8**	*4*	*2*	**3**	**6**	**5**	*5*	**7**	*7*	**2**	**4**	*1*	*3*	*6*	**1**
2002	*6*	*9*	*1*	*5*	*8*	**7**	**3**	**4**	**5**	*2*	*7*	*3*	**8**	**1**	**6**	**2**	*4*	**9**
2003	*9*	*6*	**7**	*5*	*3*	*8*	**4**	**2**	**9**	**6**	*2*	**8**	*7*	**3**	**1**	**5**	*1*	*4*
2004	*8*	*9*	*5*	*3*	**6**	*2*	**2**	**8**	*6*	**4**	**9**	*1*	*4*	**3**	**5**	**1**	**7**	*7*
2005	*9*	*2*	*5*	**9**	**8**	**2**	**5**	*1*	*7*	**6**	*4*	**1**	*8*	**7**	**3**	**4**	*6*	*3*
2006	*5*	**7**	*3*	*8*	*7*	**3**	**5**	**2**	*4*	**9**	*6*	**8**	*9*	*1*	**1**	**4**	*2*	**6**
2007	*6*	**2**	*4*	*9*	*7*	**5**	**7**	**3**	*8*	*3*	*5*	*2*	*1*	**4**	**1**	**8**	**9**	**6**
2008	*6*	**1**	*5*	*8*	*9*	**3**	**8**	**5**	*7*	*3*	*4*	**2**	**4**	**9**	**6**	*1*	*2*	**7**
2009	*6*	**1**	*2*	*5*	*4*	**6**	*1*	**4**	*9*	*8*	*3*	**2**	**3**	*7*	**8**	**5**	**9**	**7**
2010	*9*	**5**	**9**	*3*	*5*	**7**	**8**	**4**	*4*	*8*	*6*	**1**	**2**	*7*	*1*	**6**	*2*	**3**
2011	*5*	**3**	*7*	*6*	*4*	**9**	*8*	**1**	*9*	*1*	*3*	**6**	**4**	*2*	**5**	**2**	**7**	**8**
2012	*1*	**6**	*5*	*6*	*9*	*4*	*3*	**8**	*7*	**3**	*8*	**5**	**2**	**7**	**4**	**1**	**9**	*2*

For the 2000–2012 Championships, Division One placings are in bold, Division Two in italic.

MATCH RESULTS, 1864–2012

County	*Years of Play*	*Played*	*Won*	*Lost*	*Drawn*	*Tied*	*% Won*
Derbyshire	1871–87; 1895–2012	2,483	610	910	962	1	24.56
Durham	1992–2012	346	85	150	111	0	24.56
Essex	1895–2012	2,445	707	713	1,019	6	28.91
Glamorgan	1921–2012	1,976	439	677	860	0	22.21
Gloucestershire	1870–2012	2,718	794	1,005	917	2	29.21
Hampshire	1864–85; 1895–2012	2,554	672	864	1,014	4	26.31
Kent	1864–2012	2,842	1,018	852	967	5	35.81
Lancashire	1865–2012	2,916	1,077	605	1,231	3	36.93
Leicestershire	1895–2012	2,411	547	870	993	1	22.68
Middlesex.	1864–2012	2,622	954	670	993	5	36.38
Northamptonshire . . .	1905–2012	2,180	546	744	887	3	25.04
Nottinghamshire.	1864–2012	2,751	836	743	1,171	1	30.38
Somerset.	1882–85; 1891–2012	2,453	591	955	904	3	24.09
Surrey.	1864–2012	2,996	1,176	665	1,151	4	39.25
Sussex	1864–2012	2,891	822	984	1,079	6	28.43
Warwickshire.	1895–2012	2,425	675	690	1,058	2	27.83
Worcestershire	1899–2012	2,364	602	822	938	2	25.46
Yorkshire	1864–2012	3,020	1,304	536	1,178	2	43.17
Cambridgeshire	1864–69; 1871	19	8	8	3	0	42.10
		22,206	13,463	13,463	8,718	25	

Matches abandoned without a ball bowled are wholly excluded.

Counties participated in the years shown, except that there were no matches in the years 1915–1918 and 1940–1945; Hampshire did not play inter-county matches in 1868–1869, 1871–1874 and 1879; Worcestershire did not take part in the Championship in 1919.

COUNTY CHAMPIONSHIP STATISTICS FOR 2012

	For				Against		
County	*Runs*	*Wickets*	*Avge*	*Runs scored per 100 balls*	*Runs*	*Wickets*	*Avge*
Derbyshire (*1*)	6,355	210	30.26	54.46	6,740	246	27.39
Durham (**6**)	5,670	249	22.77	54.48	5,181	241	21.49
Essex (*5*)	5,678	184	30.85	52.77	6,265	204	30.71
Glamorgan (*6*)	5,863	214	27.39	55.70	6,290	205	30.68
Gloucestershire (*9*)	6,347	225	28.20	51.48	5,559	197	28.21
Hampshire (*4*)	6,498	221	29.40	55.84	7,198	231	31.16
Kent (*3*)	6,609	193	34.24	54.14	5,560	214	25.98
Lancashire (**8**)	5,847	227	25.75	51.43	6,198	184	33.68
Leicestershire (*7*)	6,805	246	27.66	50.09	6,896	183	37.68
Middlesex (**3**)	7,259	242	29.99	54.67	6,999	264	26.51
Northamptonshire (*8*)	6,697	199	33.65	50.89	6,631	188	35.27
Nottinghamshire (**5**)	6,987	228	30.64	55.22	6,580	218	30.18
Somerset (**2**)	6,462	205	31.52	57.54	7,274	263	27.65
Surrey (**7**)	6,815	243	28.04	54.86	5,980	202	29.60
Sussex (**4**)	6,352	225	28.23	52.28	6,711	236	28.43
Warwickshire (**1**)	7,308	199	36.72	54.79	6,841	261	26.21
Worcestershire (**9**)	5,470	258	21.20	47.75	6,406	207	30.94
Yorkshire (*2*)	6,075	165	36.81	56.96	5,788	189	30.62
	115,097	3,933	29.26	53.57	115,097	3,933	29.26

2012 Championship positions are shown in brackets; Division One in bold, Division Two in italic.

ECB PITCHES TABLE OF MERIT, 2012

	First-class	*One-day*		*First-class*	*One-day*
Derbyshire	5.00	5.20	Sussex	4.44	5.08
Durham	4.50	5.21	Warwickshire	5.09	4.56
Essex	5.25	4.85	Worcestershire	4.56	4.70
Glamorgan	4.06	4.27	Yorkshire	5.00	5.41
Gloucestershire	4.86	4.83			
Hampshire	4.89	4.67	Cambridge MCCU	4.60	
Kent	4.56	4.91	Durham MCCU	5.00	
Lancashire	4.44	4.67	Leeds/Bradford MCCU	5.00	
Leicestershire	5.11	5.27	Loughborough MCCU	5.00	
Middlesex	5.14	5.06	Oxford MCCU	4.33	
Northamptonshire	4.67	4.58	Netherlands		4.17
Nottinghamshire	5.20	5.08	Scotland		4.80
Somerset	4.90	4.73	Unicorns		4.17
Surrey	4.67	4.79			

Each umpire in a match marks the pitch on the following scale: 6 – Very good; 5 – Good; 4 – Above average; 3 – Below average; 2 – Poor; 1 – Unfit.

The tables, provided by the ECB, cover major matches, including Tests, Under-19 internationals, women's internationals and MCCU games, played on grounds under the county's or MCCU's jurisdiction. Middlesex pitches at Lord's are the responsibility of MCC. The "First-class" column includes Under-19 and women's Tests, and inter-MCCU games.

Essex had the highest marks for first-class cricket and Yorkshire for one-day cricket, though the ECB points out that the tables of merit are not a direct assessment of the groundsmen's ability. Marks may be affected by many factors, including weather, soil conditions and the resources available.

COUNTY CAPS AWARDED IN 2012

Derbyshire . . . . J. L. Clare, W. J. Durston, M. J. Guptill, A. P. Palladino, D. J. Redfern, D. J. Wainwright.
Glamorgan* . . . . H. T. Waters.
Gloucestershire*. . . . . E. J. M. Cowan, D. M. Housego, B. A. C. Howell, G. J. McCarter, P. J. Muchall, R. J. Nicol.
Hampshire . . . . D. R. Briggs.
Kent . . . . M. T. Coles, S. A. Northeast.
Leicestershire . . . . W. A. White.
Middlesex. . . . . J. L. Denly, T. S. Roland-Jones.
Northamptonshire. . . . J. A. Brooks, A. G. Wakely.
Nottinghamshire. . . . . M. J. Lumb, J. W. A. Taylor.
Surrey. . . . . T. L. Maynard (posthumously), S. C. Meaker.
Warwickshire . . . . V. Chopra, J. S. Patel.
Worcestershire* . . . . . B. L. D'Oliveira, N. L. Harrison, P. J. Hughes, M. Klinger, J. Leach, D. S. Lucas, C. J. Russell.
Yorkshire . . . . G. S. Ballance, S. A. Patterson, J. E. Root.

** Glamorgan's capping system is now based on a player's number of appearances; Gloucestershire now award caps to all first-class players; Worcestershire have replaced caps with colours awarded to all Championship players. Durham abolished their capping system after 2005.*

No caps were awarded by Essex, Lancashire, Somerset or Sussex.

COUNTY BENEFITS AWARDED FOR 2013

Durham	S. J. Harmison.	Nottinghamshire	G. P. Swann.
Essex	D. D. Masters.	Somerset	A. V. Suppiah.
Glamorgan	M. A. Wallace.	Warwickshire	J. O. Troughton.
Northamptonshire	S. D. Peters.		

None of the other 11 counties awarded a benefit for 2013.

DERBYSHIRE

Flying under the radar

MARK EKLID

Few beyond the boundary ropes of the County Ground in April would have backed Derbyshire, the most success-starved of the first-class counties, to finish on top of the pile in Division Two of the Championship. Several within, if truth be told, might have doubted it would happen, too – at least, so soon.

But there had been signs in 2011, when they won five Championship games, that Derbyshire were capable of better days. Galvanised by early victories, they spent most of the 2012 season as table leaders, and defied scepticism over their stamina by clinching the title on the final day, at home to Hampshire. They finished level on points with Yorkshire, but above them on the basis of six wins to Yorkshire's five. For chairman Chris Grant, the former City investment banker who had set out a bold nine-point plan for the club's revitalisation 17 months earlier, it was an unexpectedly swift dividend.

This was Derbyshire's first trophy since the Benson and Hedges Cup in 1993, and the first promotion in their history. Their only previous spell in Division One was in 2000, which had been earned by finishing ninth the year before the Championship was split in two.

They did not, on paper, hold the strongest claim to promotion at the start of the season, when several pundits made them favourites to finish bottom. True, they hold so many wooden spoons – a record 15 – that a kitchen drawer has often seemed more useful than a trophy cabinet. But this side could always set their sights higher than that.

One could see why Derbyshire were able to fly under the radar. The squad was made up of players unwanted or undervalued by their previous counties, supplemented by unproven Academy graduates. Furthermore, they were led by a combination of first-time captain Wayne Madsen, who took the job after Luke Sutton retired in December, and head coach Karl Krikken, the former wicketkeeper promoted from Academy director in May 2011, when John Morris was sacked. It was a young and inexperienced group, with only Wes Durston aged over 30, and only Madsen and Tony Palladino with 60 first-class appearances. Yet this unlikely raw mixture gelled under the calm direction of Krikken, aided by the return of batting coach Dave Houghton, who had resigned as director of cricket in 2007.

Promotion was an achievement of the collective, rather than key individuals, though several of them had very good seasons. Fortune favoured Derbyshire, too, as they avoided serious depletion through injury – which their resources would not have withstood – and endured less disruption than many other counties from the weather. They were, however, deserving champions, winning six matches – equalled only by Division One winners Warwickshire – and taking 20 wickets each time, without any contrivance.

Laurence Griffiths, Getty Images

Wayne Madsen

The strength of their challenge lay in the bowling. Palladino was outstanding. For the second time in two seasons since switching from Essex, he claimed more than 50 first-class victims with his seamers, now including a career-best seven for 53 and a hat-trick. He also scored a maiden first-class century, against Australia A. New-ball partner Tim Groenewald was a consistent gatherer of wickets, finishing with 42, while Jon Clare opened with career-best match figures of 11 for 57 in Cardiff, before injury limited his impact.

Yet it could also be argued that the key figure in Derbyshire's attack was left-arm spinner David Wainwright. He had signed in the close season, activating a release clause in his contract with Yorkshire after becoming frustrated by a lack of first-team opportunities. Wainwright could have no complaints this time: he sent down more Championship overs – 527.5 – than anyone in the country. He took a career-best six for 33 to clinch victory in the opening match, and a 50th first-class wicket as his side closed in on the title-deciding win over Hampshire.

This will not be remembered as a batter's summer, and no Derbyshire batsman came closer to 1,000 first-class runs than Madsen. His 928 included an unbeaten 231 at Northampton, where he and Tom Poynton added 261 to come within 23 of beating the world record for the ninth wicket; given that it was set by another Derbyshire pair, Arnold Warren and John Chapman at Blackwell in 1910, they could not even claim a county record.

Durston continued his admirable first-class renaissance since being discarded by Somerset in 2009, and this was a breakthrough season for the gifted Dan Redfern, who on the opening day of the Championship ended his wait for a maiden century, and grew in stature. New Zealander Martin Guptill and Usman Khawaja of Australia, who shared the role of overseas batsman, combined to contribute 1,131 first-class runs at an average of 49. In January, West Indies veteran Shivnarine Chanderpaul was signed on a two-year contract.

Success in the Championship was not matched in the one-day competitions, where Derbyshire again failed to progress beyond the group stages, but that could not tarnish their achievement. They prepared for the challenges of the top flight by recruiting opening batsman Billy Godleman, released by Essex, and wicketkeeper Richard Johnson, who had already played a handful of games on loan as he sought fresh opportunities away from Warwickshire.

Both are young players eager to improve their game, thus fitting the mould that served Derbyshire so well in 2012. The county may still be considered favourites for an instant return to Division Two, but they now know that pre-season predictions are not always reliable.

Championship attendance: 11,494.

DERBYSHIRE RESULTS

All first-class matches – Played 17: Won 6, Lost 2, Drawn 9.
County Championship matches – Played 16: Won 6, Lost 2, Drawn 8.

LV= County Championship, winners in Division 2;
Friends Life t20, 5th in North Division; Clydesdale Bank 40, 4th in Group C.

COUNTY CHAMPIONSHIP AVERAGES, BATTING AND FIELDING

Cap		*M*	*I*	*NO*	*R*	*HS*	*100*	*50*	*Avge*	*Ct/St*
2012	M. J. Guptill§	8	14	2	594	137	2	2	49.50	13
	U. T. Khawaja§	7	12	2	415	110*	1	4	41.50	7
2011	W. L. Madsen¶	16	25	2	885	231*	3	3	38.47	6
2012	D. J. Redfern	16	24	3	792	133	2	5	37.71	7
2012	W. J. Durston	16	25	2	801	121	2	4	34.82	24
	T. Poynton	14	17	4	393	106	1	2	30.23	42/1
	R. A. Whiteley	14	20	3	498	83	0	3	29.29	5
	P. M. Borrington	10	18	3	321	98	0	1	21.40	3
2012	J. L. Clare	11	13	1	247	48	0	0	20.58	2
2011	T. D. Groenewald¶	14	15	4	225	42	0	0	20.45	3
2012	D. J. Wainwright	16	22	4	332	51*	0	2	18.44	11
	M. S. Lineker†	6	9	0	163	45	0	0	18.11	7
2012	A. P. Palladino	15	19	3	235	58	0	1	14.68	0
	M. L. Turner	6	6	2	42	13	0	0	10.50	6
	M. H. A. Footitt	4	5	2	8	8*	0	0	2.66	2

Also batted: C. F. Hughes¶ (1 match) 28; R. M. Johnson (2 matches) 15*, 1, 4 (4 ct).

† *Born in Derbyshire.* § *Official overseas player.* ¶ *Other non-England-qualified player.*

BOWLING

	Style	*O*	*M*	*R*	*W*	*BB*	*5I*	*Avge*
J. L. Clare	RFM	204.3	40	642	30	6-40	2	21.40
A. P. Palladino	RFM	473.4	100	1,352	56	7-53	3	24.14
T. D. Groenewald	RFM	399.4	89	1,086	42	5-29	1	25.85
W. J. Durston	OB	175.3	25	569	22	5-34	1	25.86
D. J. Wainwright	SLA	527.5	136	1,380	44	6-33	3	31.36
R. A. Whiteley	LM	163.1	23	658	20	2-6	0	32.90
M. L. Turner	RFM	120.5	12	498	13	3-53	0	38.30

Also bowled: P. M. Borrington (OB) 1–0–2–0; M. H. A. Footitt (LFM) 90.2–20–240–9; M. J. Guptill (OB) 3–0–6–0; U. T. Khawaja (RM) 2–0–13–0; M. S. Lineker (SLA) 2–0–2–0; W. L. Madsen (OB) 1–0–1–0; D. J. Redfern (OB) 12–2–47–0.

LEADING CB40 AVERAGES (100 runs/4 wickets)

Batting	*Runs*	*HS*	*Avge*	*SR*	*Ct*
M. J. Guptill	217	125	72.33	112.43	1
W. J. Durston	288	120*	32.00	89.16	7
W. L. Madsen	186	64*	26.57	72.65	5
U. T. Khawaja	124	104	24.80	77.98	2
C. F. Hughes	209	66	20.90	79.16	0
D. J. Redfern	106	49	13.25	72.10	4

Bowling	*W*	*BB*	*Avge*	*ER*
P. I. Burgoyne	5	3-31	12.60	4.50
T. D. Groenewald	15	3-30	21.33	4.57
M. L. Turner	17	4-38	24.00	6.26
W. J. Durston	8	2-30	30.00	5.00
C. F. Hughes	6	5-29	35.83	5.63
D. J. Wainwright	4	1-9	61.50	4.74

LEADING FLT20 AVERAGES (90 runs/16 overs)

Batting	Runs	HS	Avge	SR	Ct
Naved-ul-Hasan	91	40*	30.33	**149.18**	3
C. F. Hughes	160	48	26.66	**129.03**	1
W. J. Durston	201	56	28.71	**127.21**	5
W. L. Madsen	135	33	16.87	**106.29**	2
U. T. Khawaja	131	36	16.37	**94.24**	2

Bowling	W	BB	Avge	ER
D. J. Wainwright	5	2-14	19.00	**5.58**
M. L. Turner	4	2-18	28.25	**7.06**
T. D. Groenewald	6	2-25	28.66	**7.81**
Naved-ul-Hasan	10	3-20	24.50	**8.75**
C. F. Hughes	4	1-14	46.50	**8.85**

FIRST-CLASS COUNTY RECORDS

Highest score for	274	G. A. Davidson v Lancashire at Manchester	1896
Highest score against	343*	P. A. Perrin (Essex) at Chesterfield	1904
Leading run-scorer	23,854	K. J. Barnett (avge 41.12)	1979–1998
Best bowling for	10-40	W. Bestwick v Glamorgan at Cardiff	1921
Best bowling against	10-45	R. L. Johnson (Middlesex) at Derby	1994
Leading wicket-taker	1,670	H. L. Jackson (avge 17.11)	1947–1963
Highest total for	801-8 dec	v Somerset at Taunton	2007
Highest total against	662	by Yorkshire at Chesterfield	1898
Lowest total for	16	v Nottinghamshire at Nottingham	1879
Lowest total against	23	by Hampshire at Burton upon Trent	1958

LIST A COUNTY RECORDS

Highest score for	173*	M. J. Di Venuto v Derbys County Board at Derby	2000
Highest score against	158	R. K. Rao (Sussex) at Derby	1997
Leading run-scorer	12,358	K. J. Barnett (avge 36.67)	1979–1998
Best bowling for	8-21	M. A. Holding v Sussex at Hove	1988
Best bowling against	8-66	S. R. G. Francis (Somerset) at Derby	2004
Leading wicket-taker	246	A. E. Warner (avge 27.13)	1985–1995
Highest total for	366-4	v Combined Universities at Oxford	1991
Highest total against	369-6	by New Zealanders at Derby	1999
Lowest total for	60	v Kent at Canterbury	2008
Lowest total against	42	by Glamorgan at Swansea	1979

TWENTY20 COUNTY RECORDS

Highest score for	111	W. J. Durston v Nottinghamshire at Nottingham	2010
Highest score against	109	I. J. Harvey (Yorkshire) at Leeds	2005
Leading run-scorer	930	G. M. Smith (avge 21.62)	2007–2011
Best bowling for	5-27	T. Lungley v Leicestershire at Leicester	2009
Best bowling against	5-14	P. D. Collingwood (Durham) at Chester-le-Street	2008
Leading wicket-taker	**37**	**T. D. Groenewald (avge 28.27)**	**2009–2012**
Highest total for	222-5	v Yorkshire at Leeds	2010
Highest total against	220-5	by Lancashire at Derby	2009
Lowest total for	81-8	v Lancashire at Manchester	2011
Lowest total against	84	by West Indians at Derby	2007

ADDRESS

County Ground, Grandstand Road, Derby DE21 6AF (01332 388101; **email** info@derbyshireccc.com). **Website** www.derbyshireccc.com

OFFICIALS

Captain W. L. Madsen
Head coach K. M. Krikken
Head of development H. B. Dytham
President D. C. Morgan
Chairman C. I. Grant
Chief executive S. Storey
Head groundsman N. Godrich
Scorer J. M. Brown

DERBYSHIRE v NORTHAMPTONSHIRE

At Derby, April 5–8. Derbyshire won by 202 runs. Derbyshire 20pts, Northamptonshire 5pts. Toss: Northamptonshire. County debut: D. J. Wainwright.

Redfern's long-awaited maiden century and career-best bowling by their new spinner, Wainwright, gave Derbyshire a conclusive victory to launch their campaign – though it might not have been completed without the help of floodlights. Brooks reduced them to 50 for four in the opening session but, on the Championship's earliest starting date yet, Redfern reached its first hundred in mid-afternoon, beating Billy Godleman at Chelmsford by about an hour. He was not yet 22, but this was his sixth season: to reach three figures at last, after 15 half-centuries, was a weight off his shoulders. His 160-run partnership with Whiteley gave Derbyshire a respectable total, but dogged innings for Northamptonshire from Wakely and O'Brien kept the game in the balance until the third day. Then an opening stand of 224 between Guptill and Borrington, who fell two short of a maiden Championship hundred, put Derbyshire on top. Set 337 to win, Northamptonshire were bowled out with 35 minutes remaining. Wainwright, the slow left-armer signed from Yorkshire, struck with his first ball of the innings and collected an outstanding six for 33 – including Middlebrook, caught at cover via silly point's backside.

Close of play: first day, Northamptonshire 28-3 (Sales 8, Wakely 2); second day, Northamptonshire 241-7 (Middlebrook 40, Vaas 5); third day, Derbyshire 213-0 (Guptill 131, Borrington 66).

Derbyshire

M. J. Guptill c Coetzer b Brooks	15	– c Daggett b Brooks	137
P. M. Borrington c Wakely b Brooks	1	– c Sales b Brooks	98
*W. L. Madsen b Daggett	1	– b Willey	19
W. J. Durston lbw b Brooks	17	– not out	12
D. J. Redfern b Willey	110	– not out	26
R. A. Whiteley c Wakely b Brooks	83		
D. J. Wainwright lbw b Middlebrook	11		
†T. Poynton c Wakely b Willey	20		
A. P. Palladino b Willey	8		
T. D. Groenewald c Sales b Brooks	6		
M. H. A. Footitt not out	8		
L-b 6	6	B 3, l-b 14, w 1, n-b 4	22
1/18 (1) 2/19 (3) 3/21 (2) 4/50 (4) (80.3 overs)	286	1/224 (1) (3 wkts dec, 88 overs)	314
5/210 (5) 6/238 (7) 7/252 (6)		2/270 (3) 3/272 (2)	
8/269 (9) 9/272 (8) 10/286 (10)			

Vaas 15–2–49–0; Brooks 19.3–5–61–5; Daggett 16–5–53–1; Willey 13–2–59–3; Middlebrook 17–1–58–1. *Second innings*—Brooks 21–6–76–2; Vaas 16–4–44–0; Daggett 16–4–45–0; Willey 20–3–82–1; Middlebrook 15–1–50–0.

Northamptonshire

S. D. Peters c Wainwright b Groenewald	4	– lbw b Footitt	5
R. I. Newton c Guptill b Palladino	0	– c Borrington b Durston	58
K. J. Coetzer c and b Groenewald	10	– c Redfern b Palladino	3
*D. J. Sales c Redfern b Whiteley	15	– lbw b Wainwright	6
A. G. Wakely lbw b Wainwright	62	– c Guptill b Wainwright	30
†N. J. O'Brien lbw b Whiteley	62	– c Durston b Wainwright	0
J. D. Middlebrook c Poynton b Footitt	45	– c Footitt b Wainwright	11
D. J. Willey lbw b Footitt	7	– (9) lbw b Wainwright	7
W. P. U. J. C. Vaas not out	13	– (8) lbw b Wainwright	5
L. M. Daggett c Guptill b Palladino	4	– b Durston	1
J. A. Brooks c Durston b Palladino	3	– not out	1
B 1, l-b 15, w 11, n-b 12	39	B 4, l-b 1, n-b 2	7
1/3 (2) 2/13 (1) 3/16 (3) (112.3 overs)	264	1/11 (1) 2/22 (3) (66.2 overs)	134
4/69 (4) 5/147 (5) 6/209 (6)		3/41 (4) 4/103 (5)	
7/230 (8) 8/252 (7) 9/259 (10)		5/103 (6) 6/105 (2) 7/116 (8)	
10/264 (11) 110 overs: 258-8		8/127 (7) 9/132 (9) 10/134 (10)	

Palladino 29.3–8–60–3; Groenewald 16–6–25–2; Footitt 23–6–60–2; Wainwright 27–10–50–1; Whiteley 10–3–30–2; Durston 7–1–23–0. *Second innings*—Palladino 8–1–18–1; Footitt 11–3–25–1; Wainwright 26–11–33–6; Whiteley 6–1–21–0; Durston 15.2–6–32–2.

Umpires: D. J. Millns and M. J. Saggers.

At Cardiff, April 12–14. DERBYSHIRE beat GLAMORGAN by 130 runs.

DERBYSHIRE v LEICESTERSHIRE

At Derby, April 19–22. Drawn. Derbyshire 6pts, Leicestershire 9pts. Toss: Derbyshire.

Rain had the final say after the experienced Sarwan and the 21-year-old Cobb had given Leicestershire control. Both emerged from lean times during a fourth-wicket stand of 141, scoring 105 apiece. For Sarwan, leading the side because Hoggard had a broken finger, it was a first century in two years, in which time he had lost his central contract with West Indies, then his international place; for Cobb, it was a second career hundred after two years without a first-class fifty. When White, a former Derbyshire player, took a career-best five for 54 on the third day, Leicestershire led by 144. Only an adventurous 38 from Palladino, top-scoring from No. 10, denied them the option of the follow-on. Instead they pushed on, before Sarwan declared to set Derbyshire 314 in a minimum of 69 overs. But rain, which had already washed out all but 10.5 overs of the first day, spoiled a potentially close finish.

Close of play: first day, Leicestershire 24-1 (Smith 9, du Toit 13); second day, Leicestershire 318-7 (Henderson 1, Joseph 0); third day, Leicestershire 76-1 (Boyce 43, du Toit 25).

Leicestershire

First innings		Second innings	
G. P. Smith b Wainwright	35	– lbw b Footitt	7
M. A. G. Boyce lbw b Palladino	1	– c and b Wainwright	65
J. du Toit c Poynton b Palladino	14	– c Poynton b Clare	48
*R. R. Sarwan c Wainwright b Whiteley	105	– c Guptill b Footitt	24
J. J. Cobb b Footitt	105		
†E. J. H. Eckersley b Clare	14	– (5) not out	10
W. A. White c Poynton b Whiteley	12	– (6) not out	4
C. W. Henderson b Palladino	3		
R. H. Joseph b Footitt	1		
M. N. Malik b Footitt	2		
A. C. F. Wyatt not out	0		
B 5, l-b 13, w 8, n-b 6	32	B 6, l-b 5	11
1/9 (2) 2/25 (3) 3/105 (1) 4/246 (4) 5/277 (6) 6/317 (5) 7/317 (7) 8/320 (9) 9/324 (8) 10/324 (10) (103.3 overs)	324	1/12 (1) 2/121 (3) 3/153 (2) 4/153 (4) (4 wkts dec, 54 overs)	169

Palladino 27–6–66–3; Footitt 22.3–5–43–3; Whiteley 13–3–46–2; Clare 17–2–68–1; Wainwright 21–9–57–1; Durston 3–0–26–0. *Second innings*—Footitt 10–2–36–2; Palladino 14–3–25–0; Clare 10–1–31–1; Whiteley 3–0–20–0; Wainwright 17–2–46–1.

Derbyshire

P. M. Borrington c Eckersley b Joseph	0	– (2) not out	18
*W. L. Madsen c du Toit b White	24		
W. J. Durston c Boyce b Joseph	2		
D. J. Redfern c Sarwan b Malik	30		
M. J. Guptill c du Toit b White	16	– (1) not out	67
R. A. Whiteley c Sarwan b Malik	5		
D. J. Wainwright c Eckersley b Henderson	17		
J. L. Clare b White	13		
†T. Poynton c Eckersley b White	15		
A. P. Palladino c Boyce b White	38		
M. H. A. Footitt not out	0		
B 5, l-b 11, w 2, n-b 2	20	L-b 1, w 1, n-b 4	6
1/0 (1) 2/6 (3) 3/61 (2) 4/70 (4) (60.4 overs)	180	(no wkt, 25 overs)	91
5/84 (6) 6/97 (5) 7/115 (8) 8/135 (7)			
9/151 (9) 10/180 (10)			

Joseph 13–3–37–2; Wyatt 9–1–22–0; Malik 16–3–40–2; White 15.4–1–54–5; Henderson 7–3–11–1. *Second innings*—Joseph 6–2–31–0; Wyatt 8–1–16–0; Henderson 7–1–22–0; White 4–0–21–0.

Umpires: M. J. D. Bodenham and S. J. O'Shaughnessy.

At Derby, April 27–29 (not first-class). **Derbyshire v Cardiff MCCU. Abandoned.** *Heavy rain left prospects of play so remote the match was called off before the scheduled start of the second day.*

DERBYSHIRE v GLOUCESTERSHIRE

At Derby, May 2–5. Drawn. Derbyshire 10pts, Gloucestershire 7pts. Toss: Derbyshire.

A draw seemed unlikely when Gloucestershire were asked to bat again on the third morning, yet they achieved it with extraordinary ease. After a ragged first two days left them facing a deficit of 182, simply avoiding an innings defeat would have been a minor triumph. But a helpful pitch died, and their batsmen, now showing far greater application, wriggled off the hook. Williamson marked his return to the Gloucestershire side with a bolstering 128, supported by Howell, his Northern Districts team-mate Marshall, and Cockbain; all but wicketkeeper Poynton took a turn to bowl as Derbyshire's frustration grew. Earlier, they had reached their best total of the season to date. Madsen and Durston made their first telling contributions of the summer, taking advantage of an erratic, inexperienced attack and poor fielding. Derbyshire's bowlers made far better use of the conditions: five wickets from Palladino allowed them to enforce the follow-on, before Groenewald struck again in his first over. But they managed only one more wicket that day, and just two on the last.

Close of play: first day, Derbyshire 362-9 (Clare 31, Groenewald 0); second day, Gloucestershire 172-9 (Muchall 6, Saxelby 0); third day, Gloucestershire 219-2 (Williamson 106, Marshall 32).

Derbyshire

M. J. Guptill c Coughtrie b Fuller	30
P. M. Borrington c Williamson b Gidman	0
*W. L. Madsen b Fuller	101
W. J. Durston c Gidman b Young	68
D. J. Redfern c Young b Williamson	55
R. A. Whiteley c Fuller b Saxelby	40
D. J. Wainwright c Dent b Howell	9
J. L. Clare b Saxelby	48
†T. Poynton lbw b Saxelby	0
A. P. Palladino b Fuller	16
T. D. Groenewald not out	9
L-b 3, w 1, n-b 8	12
1/6 (2) 2/38 (1) 3/138 (4) (98.1 overs)	388
4/253 (5) 5/282 (3) 6/295 (7)	
7/327 (6) 8/327 (9) 9/355 (10) 10/388 (8)	

Saxelby 24.1–5–79–3; Gidman 20–3–64–1; Fuller 16–2–64–3; Muchall 16–1–98–0; Young 12–2–53–1; Williamson 3–0–14–1; Howell 7–1–13–1.

Gloucestershire

B. A. C. Howell c Poynton b Palladino	0	– b Clare	64
C. D. J. Dent c Guptill b Palladino	55	– b Groenewald	2
K. S. Williamson b Clare	25	– c Poynton b Clare	128
*H. J. H. Marshall b Palladino	10	– lbw b Groenewald	90
I. A. Cockbain c Durston b Groenewald	13	– not out	63
W. R. S. Gidman c Poynton b Clare	21	– not out	33
†R. G. Coughtrie c Poynton b Palladino	17		
E. G. C. Young b Palladino	0		
P. B. Muchall c Durston b Wainwright	21		
J. K. Fuller b Clare	4		
I. D. Saxelby not out	19		
B 9, l-b 1, w 5, n-b 6	21	B 10, l-b 11, w 6, n-b 2	29
1/0 (1) 2/83 (3) 3/97 (4) 4/102 (2) 5/120 (5) 6/159 (7) 7/159 (8) 8/168 (6) 9/172 (10) 10/206 (9) (69.3 overs)	206	1/8 (2) 2/125 (1) 3/291 (3) 4/314 (4) (4 wkts dec, 145 overs)	409

Palladino 18–4–47–5; Groenewald 17–1–64–1; Clare 14–2–48–3; Whiteley 1–0–11–0; Wainwright 19.3–11–26–1. *Second innings*—Palladino 28–5–70–0; Groenewald 25–6–44–2; Clare 13–3–39–2; Whiteley 19–2–77–0; Wainwright 41–13–99–0; Durston 9–2–42–0; Redfern 5–2–8–0; Guptill 3–0–6–0; Borrington 1–0–2–0; Madsen 1–0–1–0.

Umpires: N. G. B. Cook and P. Willey.

At Southampton, May 9–12. DERBYSHIRE drew with HAMPSHIRE.

DERBYSHIRE v GLAMORGAN

At Derby, May 16–18. Derbyshire won by eight wickets. Derbyshire 23pts, Glamorgan 4pts. Toss: Glamorgan.

Derbyshire's second three-day victory over their opponents in five weeks was built on centuries from Guptill and Madsen. Their 170-run partnership underlined Glamorgan's failure to exploit first use of a good surface, though they did pick up their first batting point of the season. Only North, making his Championship debut for a record sixth county, and Wallace made headway against an attack that remained solid, despite the loss of Footitt to a hip injury in the game's eighth over. When Derbyshire replied – with Simon Jones taking the new ball in his first Championship appearance for Glamorgan since 2007 – Guptill was dropped three times on his way to 132, but Madsen remained unbeaten, with his second century in successive home matches. He lost his last five partners quickly on the third morning, which kept the lead down to 119, but only Bragg offered sustained resistance in Glamorgan's second innings as spinners Wainwright and Durston found turn and bounce to take eight wickets between them. Derbyshire cantered home to pull 14 points clear of Yorkshire at the head of the second division.

Close of play: first day, Derbyshire 22-0 (Guptill 13, Borrington 6); second day, Derbyshire 335-5 (Madsen 122, Wainwright 12).

PLAYERS APPEARING FOR FIVE OR MORE COUNTIES

6	**M. J. North**	**Durham 2004, Lancs 2005, Derbys 2006, Glos 2007–08, Hants 2009, Glam 2012**
5	Abdul Razzaq	Middx 2002–03, Worcs 2007, Surrey 2008, *Hants 2010, ‡Leics 2011–12
5	R. P. Davis	Kent 1986–93, Warwicks 1994–95, Glos 1996–97, †Sussex 1998, Leics 2001
5	A. J. Harris	Derbys 1994–99, Notts 2000–08, Glos 2008, Worcs 2008, Leics 2009–10
5	I. J. Harvey	Glos 1999–2006, Yorks 2004–05, Derbys 2007, *Hants 2008, *Northants 2009
5	S. M. Katich	Durham 2000, Yorks 2002, Hants 2003–12, Derbys 2007, Lancs 2010
5	D. G. Wright	Northants 2003–05, Glam 2007, Sussex 2009, Somerset 2010, Worcs 2011

* *Twenty20 matches only.* † *List A matches only.* ‡ *List A and Twenty20 matches only.*

Glamorgan

	First innings		Second innings	
G. P. Rees c Guptill b Whiteley	30	–	lbw b Groenewald	4
N. A. James c Redfern b Clare	7	–	b Groenewald	0
W. D. Bragg c Whiteley b Clare	4	–	c Poynton b Durston	78
M. J. North lbw b Wainwright	79	–	c Guptill b Durston	21
B. J. Wright c Guptill b Groenewald	17	–	c Durston b Wainwright	17
J. Allenby c Wainwright b Whiteley	9	–	lbw b Wainwright	16
*†M. A. Wallace b Groenewald	45	–	c Durston b Wainwright	29
D. A. Cosker b Durston	13	–	b Durston	13
H. T. Waters not out	8	–	b Wainwright	0
M. T. Reed lbw b Groenewald	4	–	not out	5
S. P. Jones c Madsen b Clare	4	–	c Madsen b Wainwright	1
L-b 10, n-b 6	16		L-b 3, w 1	4
1/29 (2) 2/33 (3) 3/59 (1) 4/98 (5) 5/111 (6) 6/188 (7) 7/218 (8) 8/224 (4) 9/231 (10) 10/236 (11) (86 overs)	236		1/5 (1) 2/6 (2) 3/57 (4) 4/123 (5) 5/123 (3) 6/166 (7) 7/175 (6) 8/175 (9) 9/185 (8) 10/188 (11) (67.2 overs)	188

Groenewald 22–8–34–3; Footitt 3.5–0–16–0; Whiteley 18.1–4–62–2; Clare 15–3–45–3; Wainwright 18–6–48–1; Durston 9–2–21–1. *Second innings*—Groenewald 12–3–38–2; Clare 12–2–34–0; Whiteley 5–0–19–0; Wainwright 19.2–7–51–5; Durston 19–2–43–3.

Derbyshire

	First innings		Second innings	
M. J. Guptill lbw b Reed	132	–	c Waters b Reed	30
P. M. Borrington c Wallace b Reed	15	–	not out	21
*W. L. Madsen not out	130	–	lbw b Reed	2
W. J. Durston c Jones b North	30		not out	3
D. J. Redfern c and b North	0			
R. A. Whiteley c Wright b North	9			
D. J. Wainwright c Allenby b Jones	13			
J. L. Clare c Cosker b Waters	1			
†T. Poynton c Wallace b Waters	2			
T. D. Groenewald b Jones	6			
M. H. A. Footitt b Waters	0			
B 9, l-b 5, w 1, n-b 2	17		B 5, l-b 4, n-b 6	15
1/43 (2) 2/213 (1) 3/273 (4) 4/277 (5) 5/305 (6) 6/336 (7) 7/337 (8) 8/341 (9) 9/350 (10) 10/355 (11) (103.5 overs)	355		1/51 (1) 2/59 (3) (2 wkts, 12.3 overs)	71

Waters 26.5–9–78–3; Jones 22–2–70–2; Reed 13–0–66–2; Allenby 8–3–13–0; Cosker 18–1–61–0; North 14–2–40–3; James 2–0–13–0. *Second innings*—Waters 3–0–25–0; Reed 6–0–25–2; Cosker 3.3–1–12–0.

Umpires: N. J. Llong and S. J. O'Shaughnessy.

At Chelmsford, May 23–25. DERBYSHIRE beat ESSEX by ten wickets.

At Bristol, May 30–June 1. DERBYSHIRE lost to GLOUCESTERSHIRE by seven wickets.

At Leicester, June 5–8. DERBYSHIRE drew with LEICESTERSHIRE.

DERBYSHIRE v YORKSHIRE

At Chesterfield, July 18–21. Drawn. Derbyshire 6pts, Yorkshire 6pts. Toss: Yorkshire.

Seventeen wickets on the first day suggested this encounter between the division's top two teams would never last into the fourth; in fact, sustained rain meant there was no more play at all. Yorkshire's hopes of building on a solid stand of 81 between Jaques and Ballance were dashed when their last seven fell for 44. A fiery burst from Turner, whose last first-class game had been in August 2011, brought him three wickets in 12 balls to spark the collapse. Harmison, on loan to Yorkshire from Durham, managed three in 11 when Derbyshire replied, drawing some reckless strokes from the middle order after an erratic first spell.

Close of play: first day, Derbyshire 135-7 (Johnson 15, Palladino 21); second day, no play; third day, no play.

Yorkshire

A. Lyth c Johnson b Groenewald	19
J. E. Root c Lineker b Groenewald	16
*P. A. Jaques c Wainwright b Durston	61
†J. M. Bairstow b Palladino	27
G. S. Ballance c Johnson b Turner	46
A. McGrath c Durston b Turner	0
R. M. Pyrah lbw b Turner	9
Azeem Rafiq c Turner b Durston	0
S. A. Patterson c Durston b Groenewald	11
S. J. Harmison c Madsen b Durston	23
M. A. Ashraf not out	0
L-b 7	7
1/34 (2) 2/43 (1) 3/94 (4) (56.1 overs)	219
4/175 (5) 5/175 (6) 6/185 (7)	
7/185 (3) 8/185 (8) 9/219 (9) 10/219 (10)	

Palladino 11–0–62–1; Groenewald 13–3–38–3; Turner 15–4–53–3; Clare 5–0–27–0; Wainwright 3–1–9–0; Durston 9.1–3–23–3.

Derbyshire

*W. L. Madsen c Azeem Rafiq b Patterson	15
M. S. Lineker b Pyrah	33
U. T. Khawaja b Ashraf	9
W. J. Durston c Lyth b Harmison	16
D. J. Redfern lbw b Ashraf	8
J. L. Clare c Bairstow b Harmison	1
D. J. Wainwright c Ashraf b Harmison	0
†R. M. Johnson not out	15
A. P. Palladino not out	21
L-b 3, w 10, n-b 4	17
1/43 (1) 2/70 (2) (7 wkts, 38 overs)	135
3/70 (3) 4/80 (5)	
5/91 (6) 6/96 (4) 7/105 (7)	

T. D. Groenewald and M. L. Turner did not bat.

Patterson 10–1–49–1; Harmison 9–2–49–3; Ashraf 8–2–13–2; Pyrah 6–2–9–1; McGrath 3–0–7–0; Azeem Rafiq 2–0–5–0.

Umpires: P. J. Hartley and S. Ravi.

At Derby, July 27–29. DERBYSHIRE drew with AUSTRALIA A (see Australia A tour section).

DERBYSHIRE v KENT

At Derby, August 2–5. Derbyshire won by two wickets. Derbyshire 19pts, Kent 5pts. Toss: Derbyshire.

If a season can turn on a single day, then for these sides it was the third here. With a lead of 226, seven wickets in hand, and Key batting splendidly, Kent were well set for a victory that would have lifted them over Derbyshire to the top of the second division. Instead, they wilted as Palladino put everything into a 13-over spell, claiming five wickets in 55 balls to complete a career-best seven for 53. Chasing 295, Derbyshire's top four got them to 197, before Shreck struck three times in nine deliveries to threaten another turnaround. Redfern was dropped on one but advanced to a nerveless 50, sharing an unbroken ninth-wicket stand of 41 with Groenewald that secured the win and put Derbyshire 26 points clear. Earlier, Kent had battled to 265, with fifties from Northeast and Coles at opposite ends of the order, before the hostile Shreck took five wickets; Derbyshire barely avoided the follow-on. Two days later they were celebrating a win which had significant implications for the promotion race.

Close of play: first day, Kent 238-8 (Coles 51, Davies 17); second day, Kent 93-3 (Key 63, Powell 10); third day, Derbyshire 168-2 (Khawaja 43, Durston 37).

Kent

S. A. Northeast b Clare	52	– lbw b Palladino	6
*R. W. T. Key c Durston b Palladino	5	– c Johnson b Palladino	81
B. W. Harmison c Redfern b Turner	5	– lbw b Palladino	5
B. P. Nash c Lineker b Palladino	15	– b Turner	3
M. J. Powell c Johnson b Turner	45	– c Lineker b Groenewald	18
D. I. Stevens b Groenewald	16	– lbw b Palladino	0
†G. O. Jones c Turner b Groenewald	0	– c Durston b Groenewald	2
J. C. Tredwell b Groenewald	2	– c Wainwright b Palladino	1
M. T. Coles c Turner b Durston	57	– c Durston b Palladino	11
M. Davies b Turner	29	– c Wainwright b Palladino	12
C. E. Shreck not out	5	– not out	5
B 10, l-b 13, w 1, n-b 10	34	B 8, l-b 2, w 1, n-b 6	17
1/37 (2) 2/63 (3) 3/69 (1) (75.5 overs)	265	1/16 (1) 2/36 (3) (56.5 overs)	161
4/88 (4) 5/123 (6) 6/127 (7)		3/43 (4) 4/109 (5)	
7/147 (8) 8/174 (5) 9/244 (9) 10/265 (10)		5/110 (6) 6/117 (7) 7/118 (8)	
		8/139 (9) 9/144 (2) 10/161 (10)	

Palladino 20–4–65–2; Groenewald 19–5–41–3; Clare 11–2–45–1; Turner 17.5–1–66–3; Wainwright 5–2–11–0; Durston 3–0–14–1. *Second innings*—Palladino 23.5–5–53–7; Groenewald 17–3–39–2; Turner 11–0–39–1; Clare 1–0–5–0; Wainwright 4–0–15–0.

Derbyshire

*W. L. Madsen c Tredwell b Shreck	0	– c Jones b Coles	30
M. S. Lineker c Powell b Shreck	22	– lbw b Tredwell	45
U. T. Khawaja c Tredwell b Shreck	19	c Jones b Shreck	56
W. J. Durston lbw b Davies	7	– lbw b Shreck	55
D. J. Redfern c Northeast b Coles	0	– not out	50
†R. M. Johnson lbw b Stevens	1	– c Tredwell b Shreck	4
D. J. Wainwright not out	29	– c Northeast b Coles	2
J. L. Clare c Jones b Davies	9	– c sub (A. J. Blake) b Shreck	12
A. P. Palladino c Jones b Stevens	10	– c Coles b Davies	8
T. D. Groenewald c Jones b Shreck	23	– not out	20
M. L. Turner lbw b Shreck	0		
B 4, l-b 4, n-b 4	12	B 1, l-b 13, n-b 2	16
1/1 (1) 2/37 (3) 3/44 (2) 4/47 (5) (47.3 overs)	132	1/83 (1) (8 wkts, 96.2 overs)	298
5/51 (4) 6/51 (6) 7/72 (8) 8/93 (9)		2/95 (2) 3/197 (3)	
9/128 (10) 10/132 (11)		4/200 (4) 5/212 (6) 6/215 (7)	
		7/236 (8) 8/257 (9)	

Davies 12–5–27–2; Shreck 16.3–1–41–5, Coles 8–1–27–1; Stevens 11–4–29–2. *Second innings*—Davies 15.2–1–44–1; Shreck 30–3–99–4; Stevens 10–0–23–0; Tredwell 23–5–47–1; Coles 18–0–71–2.

Umpires: R. J. Bailey and M. A. Gough.

At Derby, August 10–11. DERBYSHIRE drew with SOUTH AFRICANS (see S. African tour section).

At Leeds, August 15–18. DERBYSHIRE drew with YORKSHIRE.

At Northampton, August 21–24. DERBYSHIRE drew with NORTHAMPTONSHIRE.

DERBYSHIRE v ESSEX

At Derby, August 28–31. Drawn. Derbyshire 8pts, Essex 7pts. Toss: Derbyshire.

Essex's hopes of promotion faded as they were left contemplating one that got away. They could do nothing about the loss of the second day, but were too conservative in their declaration on the fourth, when more rain – with 22 minutes remaining and Derbyshire's eighth-wicket pair at the crease – had the final say. Masters, making a brief comeback from a side strain, had helped Essex collect their only batting point, before his outstanding bowling earned five wickets, including his 50th of the summer, and held Derbyshire to a slender first-innings lead. Essex then enjoyed the best conditions of the match, and Westley's 82 was backed up by three middle-order fifties. A target of 274 in 58 overs was unlikely to tempt Derbyshire, but their interest rose while Durston and Redfern were adding 107. The loss of four for five in eight overs soon quashed thoughts of a chase.

Close of play: first day, Derbyshire 28-3 (Borrington 14, Durston 0); second day, no play; third day, Essex 85-1 (Westley 51, Shah 26).

Essex

T. Westley b Groenewald	14	– c Poynton b Turner	82
J. C. Mickleburgh c Poynton b Palladino	5	– c Poynton b Groenewald	4
O. A. Shah b Turner	26	– c Madsen b Palladino	26
M. L. Pettini c Durston b Wainwright	14	– c Turner b Whiteley	50
R. N. ten Doeschate lbw b Wainwright	29	– c Poynton b Turner	52
*†J. S. Foster run out	31	– not out	58
A. J. Wheater lbw b Turner	26	– not out	8
G. R. Napier c Durston b Wainwright	42		
D. D. Masters run out	35		
M. A. Chambers c Turner b Wainwright	2		
T. R. Craddock not out	1		
B 5, l-b 5, w 2, n-b 8	20	B 4, l-b 1, w 9	14
1/5 (2) 2/33 (1) 3/57 (3) 4/74 (4) (78.5 overs)	245	1/24 (2) (5 wkts dec, 55 overs)	294
5/113 (5) 6/144 (6) 7/151 (7)		2/91 (3) 3/133 (1)	
8/225 (8) 9/235 (10) 10/245 (9)		4/189 (4) 5/261 (5)	

Palladino 17–4–52–1; Groenewald 20–3–62–1; Turner 12–0–38–2; Whiteley 5–0–16–0; Wainwright 23.5–5–64–4; Durston 1–0–3–0. *Second innings*—Palladino 9–0–47–1; Groenewald 9–2–48–1; Wainwright 19–1–103–0; Turner 13–1–60–2; Whiteley 5–0–31–1.

Derbyshire

*W. L. Madsen b Masters	2	– lbw b Masters	31
P. M. Borrington lbw b Masters	42	– st Foster b Craddock	13
U. T. Khawaja c Westley b Masters	0	– st Foster b Craddock	6
A. P. Palladino lbw b Napier	5	– (9) not out	1
W. J. Durston c Foster b Masters	1	– (4) b Craddock	60
D. J. Redfern c Westley b Napier	31	– (5) c Shah b Napier	46
R. A. Whiteley b Craddock	56	– (6) not out	11
D. J. Wainwright c Napier b Masters	7	– (7) b Craddock	0
†T. Poynton not out	55	– (8) c Foster b Masters	1
T. D. Groenewald b Napier	18		
M. L. Turner lbw b Craddock	13		
B 8, l-b 10, n-b 18	36	L-b 2, w 2	4
1/12 (1) 2/16 (3) 3/27 (4) 4/32 (5) (89.5 overs)	266	1/42 (1) (7 wkts, 52 overs)	173
5/92 (2) 6/111 (6) 7/120 (8)		2/48 (2) 3/51 (3)	
8/206 (7) 9/240 (10) 10/266 (11)		4/158 (5) 5/160 (4) 6/160 (7) 7/163 (8)	

Masters 30–9–51–5; Chambers 19–1–71–0; Napier 22–4–80–3; ten Doeschate 10–3–22–0; Craddock 8.5–1–24–2. *Second innings*—Masters 14–4–47–2; Chambers 3–0–13–0; Craddock 22–8–66–4; Napier 11–1–35–1; Westley 2–0–10–0.

Umpires: M. R. Benson and J. H. Evans.

At Canterbury, September 4–7. DERBYSHIRE lost to KENT by 222 runs.

DERBYSHIRE v HAMPSHIRE

At Derby, September 11–14. Derbyshire won by six wickets. Derbyshire 21pts, Hampshire 5pts. Toss: Derbyshire.

Shortly after 3pm on the last day of the season, Whiteley swept his fifth six, to confirm Derbyshire as champions of Division Two. It was their first trophy since the Benson and Hedges Cup in 1993.

They had started the final round one point ahead of Yorkshire and six above Kent, and their return to Division One after 12 seasons was assured on the third evening, when Kent lost in Cardiff. But Yorkshire had pulled level on bonus points, and sauntered to victory in Chelmsford at 2pm on the fourth day, so Derbyshire had to beat Hampshire to take the title on the tie-breaker of more wins. Only three runs had separated the teams in the first innings, when Vince struck his first Championship century of the season, before Khawaja led Derbyshire's reply. On the final morning, however, Derbyshire picked up Hampshire's four remaining second innings wickets within 17 overs, which left them needing 196. Khawaja, again, took them there with little fuss and an unbeaten 72, and Whiteley's late hitting prompted scenes of celebration. Attendance, especially on the last two days, was boosted by a scheme run with the *Derby Telegraph* offering some tickets at £1.

Close of play: first day, Derbyshire 50-3 (Khawaja 27, Palladino 0); second day, Derbyshire 167-5 (Khawaja 71, Whiteley 5); third day, Hampshire 142-6 (Shafayat 52, Wood 2).

Hampshire

First innings		Second innings	
M. A. Carberry b Palladino	1	– c Poynton b Palladino	9
*J. H. K. Adams c Khawaja b Whiteley	20	– c Poynton b Groenewald	7
B. M. Shafayat c Redfern b Palladino	8	– run out	81
L. A. Dawson lbw b Palladino	11	– c Poynton b Turner	16
J. M. Vince c Khawaja b Whiteley	114	– c and b Wainwright	26
S. M. Ervine b Wainwright	61	– lbw b Whiteley	20
†M. D. Bates c Khawaja b Durston	29	– c Poynton b Whiteley	2
C. P. Wood c Borrington b Groenewald	3	– c Borrington b Durston	9
D. J. Balcombe not out	20	– lbw b Wainwright	9
D. A. Griffiths c Poynton b Wainwright	0	– c Whiteley b Durston	5
J. A. Tomlinson lbw b Wainwright	0	– not out	0
L-b 3, w 2	5	B 1, l-b 11, n-b 2	14
1/2 (1) 2/14 (3) 3/26 (4) 4/59 (2) 5/195 (6) 6/226 (5) 7/234 (8) 8/271 (7) 9/272 (10) 10/272 (11) (75.4 overs)	272	1/16 (1) 2/16 (2) 3/40 (4) 4/81 (5) 5/126 (6) 6/134 (7) 7/177 (8) 8/186 (3) 9/194 (9) 10/198 (10) (72.3 overs)	198

Palladino 18–7–44–3; Groenewald 18–1–71–1; Turner 9–0–45–0; Whiteley 8–0–37–2; Wainwright 20.4–2–69–3; Durston 2–1–3–1. *Second innings*—Palladino 16–3–36–1; Groenewald 14–2–46–1; Turner 5–2–21–1; Wainwright 20–4–41–2; Durston 12.3–1–36–2; Whiteley 5–2–6–2.

Derbyshire

First innings		Second innings	
*W. L. Madsen c Bates b Tomlinson	8	– b Dawson	24
P. M. Borrington c Carberry b Balcombe	4	– c Adams b Griffiths	21
U. T. Khawaja c Bates b Ervine	71	– not out	72
W. J. Durston c Dawson b Wood	9	– lbw b Griffiths	23
A. P. Palladino c Tomlinson b Ervine	58		
D. J. Redfern c Dawson b Ervine	4	– (5) c Adams b Dawson	11
R. A. Whiteley not out	57	– (6) not out	38
D. J. Wainwright c Adams b Tomlinson	7		
†T. Poynton c Adams b Carberry	24		
T. D. Groenewald c Griffiths b Tomlinson	10		
M. L. Turner c Bates b Balcombe	5		
B 5, l-b 7, n-b 6	18	L-b 2, n-b 6	8
1/12 (1) 2/14 (2) 3/49 (4) 4/137 (5) 5/147 (6) 6/170 (3) 7/191 (8) 8/254 (9) 9/270 (10) 10/275 (11) (86 overs)	275	1/45 (2) 2/45 (1) 3/112 (4) 4/143 (5) (4 wkts, 41.5 overs)	197

Tomlinson 20–6–65–3; Balcombe 20–4–68–2; Wood 12–5–33–1; Griffiths 9–2–29–0; Dawson 13–3–42–0; Ervine 11–2–25–3; Carberry 1–0–1–1. *Second innings*—Tomlinson 4–1–5–0; Balcombe 4–0–19–0; Griffiths 7–0–33–2; Dawson 16.5–1–82–2; Ervine 4–1–25–0; Wood 3–1–13–0; Carberry 3–0–18–0.

Umpires: M. R. Benson and S. C. Gale.

DURHAM

Colly shepherds his side to safety

TIM WELLOCK

Durham's season was an exaggerated reversal of the previous year. In 2011, they had been 23 points clear at the top of Division One after ten games, but finished third; this time, they were 23 adrift at the bottom – and finished sixth. The weather had played a big part in derailing their strokeplayers in 2011, and now they were unable to knuckle down in even more sodden conditions. But the eventual turnaround owed more to leadership than climate: Paul Collingwood replaced Phil Mustard as four-day captain in July, and said he was surprised how much he enjoyed a role he had never coveted.

After failing to win any of their first ten Championship matches, Durham equalled the club record of four successive victories, were denied a fifth by rain, and won the final game. Sixth was their lowest finish for six years, even though only champions Warwickshire had more wins in their division. But Durham gained just 18 batting points, down from 47, and lost four points for a slow over-rate against Lancashire; both shortfalls reflected a lack of discipline under the happy-go-lucky Mustard. Everyone insisted it wasn't his fault, which suggested the blame lay at the door of those who had appointed him.

Durham were expected to challenge for the title, especially if their winter work on rehabilitating Steve Harmison and Liam Plunkett proved successful. It didn't. Harmison spent July on loan to Yorkshire, and Plunkett moved there in October. But there were compensations: the superb form of Graham Onions, the surprising emergence of local seamer Chris Rushworth, and the improved bowling of all-rounder Ben Stokes, who could have been an England contender had he not surrendered his wicket so often.

Stokes was not alone: for the first time in 21 years of first-class cricket, no batsman reached 700 Championship runs. Collingwood led the way, with 697, and was the only one to average over 30. Mustard's average fell from 51 to 20, although he scored three scintillating centuries opening in the CB40. He reached three figures in 66 balls against Nottinghamshire, 74 against Surrey, and 55 against Glamorgan; Durham's previous fastest one-day hundred had come in 72.

All three – and two of Mark Stoneman's three in the same competition – were at Chester-le-Street, where Durham won all five completed CB40 games (they lost all five away) and plundered three totals between 298 and 310. This added to the mystery of how they could bat so abjectly on the same ground in the Championship: in eight first innings there, they were dismissed for under 130 four times.

Durham had planned a serious Twenty20 assault, signing Herschelle Gibbs and Mitchell Johnson, who was then called up by Australia. The South African Johann Myburgh replaced him at the last minute, and was retained for the rest

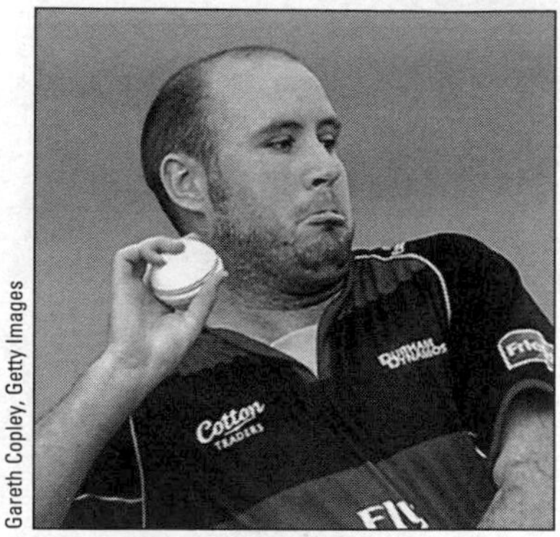

Gareth Copley, Getty Images

Chris Rushworth

of the season, but barely featured. Gibbs just about lived up to his billing; his 83 not out against Derbyshire was a 20-over county record.

Collingwood, who missed the Twenty20 with a broken hand, took the reins in the Championship at Arundel, where his men made Sussex fight all the way when the game seemed hopeless. In a similarly nail-biting finish, at home to Middlesex a week later, Durham somehow squeezed out their first victory. There was more drama at Trent Bridge, where they won by 16 runs with eight balls remaining, after Mark Wood had taken five of the seven wickets to fall in the final session. He came in because Stokes was with England Lions but, amazingly, didn't appear again.

One youngster given a late run was Keaton Jennings, a 6ft 3in left-hander who had led the previous year's South Africa Under-19 tour. Though he was the son of former South African coach Ray Jennings, his Sunderland-born mother gave him a Durham connection, and he had decided to pursue a first-class career in north-east England. His 70 at Liverpool confirmed he could help solve Durham's top-order problems, which were highlighted by the retirement of Michael Di Venuto, the popular Tasmanian, in July. After five and a half seasons of sterling service, he abruptly called it a day, citing the difficulties of staying fit enough to maintain his standards.

Di Venuto's exit roughly coincided with Ian Blackwell's fall from favour, mainly through his own lack of fitness. After missing the seventh Championship match with a back spasm, Blackwell was seen only against Australia A, when he took a career-best seven for 52 with his left-arm spin. Even that didn't atone for his perceived indiscretions, and he loaned to Warwickshire until the end of the season.

The season's highlight came at Trent Bridge, where Onions – judged surplus to England's requirements – arrived from Lord's at lunchtime on the second day, took nine wickets and ran out the other. He missed two Championship games while in the Test squad and one through injury, yet finished with 64 wickets at 14. Rushworth was called up after outstanding one-day bowling against Nottinghamshire, and claimed three five-wicket hauls, each one improving his first-class best, to end with 38 wickets at 16.

Durham were to start the 2013 Championship on minus 2.5 points after breaching the £1.8m salary cap. This resulted from big contracts handed out to, among others, Harmison, who played only three games for the county (in addition to three for Yorkshire). He was awarded a benefit for what was expected to be his final season. Chief executive David Harker announced he would step down in May, after 13 years in which Durham had won two Championships and Chester-le-Street achieved Test status – to be crowned by an Ashes match in August 2013.

Championship attendance: 24,483.

DURHAM RESULTS

All first-class matches – Played 17: Won 7, Lost 5, Drawn 5. Abandoned 1.
County Championship matches – Played 15: Won 5, Lost 5, Drawn 5. Abandoned 1.

LV= County Championship, 6th in Division 1;
Friends Life t20, 3rd in North Division; Clydesdale Bank 40, 5th in Group B.

COUNTY CHAMPIONSHIP AVERAGES, BATTING AND FIELDING

Cap		*M*	*I*	*NO*	*R*	*HS*	*100*	*50*	*Avge*	*Ct*
1998	P. D. Collingwood†	13	24	3	697	114	1	4	33.19	19
	M. J. Di Venuto¶	5	10	0	291	96	0	1	29.10	11
	M. D. Stoneman	13	24	1	636	114	1	2	27.65	8
	B. A. Stokes	13	23	0	625	121	1	3	27.17	6
2005	D. M. Benkenstein	13	23	1	523	69	0	2	23.77	2
	C. Rushworth†	9	11	7	93	24*	0	0	23.25	1
	M. J. Richardson	4	6	0	129	58	0	1	21.50	9
	S. G. Borthwick†	13	21	4	358	60	0	2	21.05	18
	K. K. Jennings¶	5	8	0	168	70	0	1	21.00	0
	P. Mustard†	14	24	2	443	80	0	1	20.13	44
	G. Onions†	12	17	6	193	36	0	0	17.54	1
	I. D. Blackwell	5	10	1	153	38*	0	0	17.00	2
	W. R. Smith	13	25	1	395	100	1	0	16.45	5
	M. E. Claydon	6	10	2	112	55	0	1	14.00	0
	C. D. Thorp	13	20	2	218	36	0	0	12.11	9
	J. Harrison	3	6	1	60	23	0	0	12.00	0
2005	G. J. Muchall	6	11	0	104	25	0	0	9.45	3
1999	S. J. Harmison	3	5	3	6	3*	0	0	3.00	1

Also batted: R. M. R. Brathwaite (1 match) 0, 0*; L. E. Plunkett (1 match) 24, 0; M. A. Wood† (1 match) 34, 30 (1 ct).

† *Born in Durham.* ¶ *Non-England-qualified player. Durham ceased to award caps after 2005.*

BOWLING

	Style	*O*	*M*	*R*	*W*	*BB*	*5I*	*Avge*
G. Onions	RFM	373.4	101	959	64	9-67	5	14.98
C. Rushworth	RFM	210.5	51	623	38	5-38	3	16.39
C. D. Thorp	RFM	301.4	84	789	38	5-59	1	20.76
B. A. Stokes	RFM	219.4	43	718	32	4-40	0	22.43
J. Harrison	LFM	68	10	260	10	4-112	0	26.00
M. E. Claydon	RFM	101.2	15	412	14	4-84	0	29.42
S. G. Borthwick	LBG	125.4	9	443	15	4-37	0	29.53

Also bowled: D. M. Benkenstein (RM/OB) 1–0–2–0; I. D. Blackwell (SLA) 81–20–262–9; R. M. R. Brathwaite (RFM) 5–0–31–1; P. D. Collingwood (RM/OB) 19–3–60–1; S. J. Harmison (RFM) 56.2–11–229–6; K. K. Jennings (RM) 5–2–9–0; L. E. Plunkett (RFM) 12–0–69–0; W. R. Smith (OB) 7.2–1–35–1; M. A. Wood (RFM) 28.4–2–97–5.

LEADING CB40 AVERAGES (100 runs/4 wickets)

Batting	*Runs*	*HS*	*Avge*	*SR*	*Ct/St*
M. D. Stoneman	558	136*	69.75	98.23	2
G. J. Muchall	395	96*	49.37	84.94	5
P. Mustard	475	143	47.50	143.07	11/5
D. M. Benkenstein	141	39*	28.20	100.00	4
P. D. Collingwood	124	32	20.66	80.51	3
B. A. Stokes	155	45	19.37	101.97	3

Bowling	*W*	*BB*	*Avge*	*ER*
B. A. Stokes	8	3-24	15.50	5.27
M. A. Wood	4	3-32	15.75	5.25
C. Rushworth	15	5-31	18.66	5.89
G. R. Breese	10	4-50	20.00	4.76
S. G. Borthwick	13	4-51	27.00	6.23
L. E. Plunkett	7	4-33	27.14	6.12

LEADING FLT20 AVERAGES (100 runs/18 overs)

Batting	Runs	HS	Avge	SR	Ct/St
H. H. Gibbs	277	83*	39.57	**124.21**	2
B. A. Stokes	159	56	22.71	**117.77**	6
P. Mustard	201	51	22.33	**117.54**	7/2
J. G. Myburgh	171	46	24.42	**103.63**	3
G. J. Muchall	111	25*	37.00	**97.36**	3

Bowling	W	BB	Avge	ER
G. R. Breese	6	2-15	21.16	**6.04**
G. Onions	6	2-24	40.00	**6.85**
L. E. Plunkett	3	2-22	60.33	**7.19**
S. G. Borthwick	12	2-19	20.00	**7.74**
M. E. Claydon	9	3-34	16.77	**7.94**
B. A. Stokes	6	2-14	25.50	**8.05**

FIRST-CLASS COUNTY RECORDS

Highest score for	273	M. L. Love v Hampshire at Chester-le-Street	2003
Highest score against	501*	B. C. Lara (Warwickshire) at Birmingham	1994
Leading run-scorer	**8,788**	**D. M. Benkenstein (avge 46.74)**	**2005–2012**
Best bowling for	10-47	O. D. Gibson v Hampshire at Chester-le-Street	2007
Best bowling against	9-36	M. S. Kasprowicz (Glamorgan) at Cardiff	2003
Leading wicket-taker	518	S. J. E. Brown (avge 28.30)	1992–2002
Highest total for	648-5 dec	v Nottinghamshire at Chester-le-Street	2009
Highest total against	810-4 dec	by Warwickshire at Birmingham	1994
Lowest total for	67	v Middlesex at Lord's	1996
Lowest total against	**18**	**by Durham MCCU at Chester-le-Street**	**2012**

LIST A COUNTY RECORDS

Highest score for	150*	B. A. Stokes v Warwickshire at Birmingham	2011
Highest score against	151*	M. P. Maynard (Glamorgan) at Darlington	1991
Leading run-scorer	**4,717**	**P. D. Collingwood (avge 31.65)**	**1995–2012**
Best bowling for	7-32	S. P. Davis v Lancashire at Chester-le-Street	1983
Best bowling against	6-22	A. Dale (Glamorgan) at Colwyn Bay	1993
Leading wicket-taker	298	N. Killeen (avge 23.96)	1995–2010
Highest total for	332-4	v Worcestershire at Chester-le-Street	2007
Highest total against	361-7	by Essex at Chelmsford	1996
Lowest total for	72	v Warwickshire at Birmingham	2002
Lowest total against	63	by Hertfordshire at Darlington	1964

TWENTY20 COUNTY RECORDS

Highest score for	**83***	**H. H. Gibbs v Derbyshire at Chester-le-Street**	**2012**
Highest score against	100	M. B. Loye (Lancashire) at Manchester	2005
Leading run-scorer	**1,938**	**P. Mustard (avge 23.92)**	**2003–2012**
Best bowling for	5-6	P. D. Collingwood v Northants at Chester-le-Street	2011
Best bowling against	5-16	R. M. Pyrah (Yorkshire) at Scarborough	2011
Leading wicket-taker	**73**	**G. R. Breese (avge 21.45)**	**2004–2012**
Highest total for	225-2	v Leicestershire at Chester-le-Street	2010
Highest total against	213-4	by Nottinghamshire at Nottingham	2011
Lowest total for	93	v Kent at Canterbury	2009
Lowest total against	47	by Northamptonshire at Chester-le-Street	2011

ADDRESS

County Ground, Riverside, Chester-le-Street, County Durham DH3 3QR (0191 387 1717; **email** reception@durhamccc.co.uk). **Website** www.durhamccc.co.uk

OFFICIALS

Captain (Championship) P. D. Collingwood
(limited-overs) D. M. Benkenstein
Head coach G. Cook
Academy coach J. B. Windows
Chairman C. W. Leach
Group chief executive D. Harker
Chief operating officer R. Dowson
Head groundsman D. Measor
Scorer B. Hunt

DURHAM v DURHAM MCCU

At Chester-le-Street, April 6–8. Durham won by 373 runs. Toss: Durham MCCU.

The university's last-day total of 18 was the lowest in first-class cricket anywhere in the world since 1983, when Surrey were dismissed for 14 at Chelmsford. Durham had declared overnight to set a target of 392, but bowled out the students in 78 minutes. The previous low against the county was 56 by Somerset in 2003, which had led to their previous biggest win by runs, a mere 318. There was moisture in the pitch, the ball swung and seamed in overcast conditions, and the university batted a man short because Luke Blackaby was injured. They had already sunk to 18 for six in the first innings, recovering to 117 largely through Nat Watkins's unbeaten 38; second time around he hung his bat out to offer the slips practice, reflecting the general malaise. Stokes had figures of four for three, to go with innings of 93 and 65 (including six sixes), made off a combined 115 balls.

LOWEST FIRST-CLASS TOTALS IN ENGLAND SINCE 1945

14	Surrey v Essex at Chelmsford	1983
18	**Durham MCCU v Durham at Chester-le-Street** (*one man absent*)	**2012**
23	Hampshire v Derbyshire at Burton-on-Trent	1958
23	Sussex v Warwickshire at Worthing	1964
23	Yorkshire v Hampshire at Middlesbrough	1965
24	Glamorgan v Leicestershire at Leicester	1971
24	Oxford University v Leicestershire at Oxford	1985
25	Somerset v Gloucestershire at Bristol (Ashley Down)	1947
25	Worcestershire v Surrey at The Oval	1954
25	Worcestershire v Kent at Tunbridge Wells	1960
26	Glamorgan v Lancashire at Cardiff (Arms Park)	1958
27	The Rest v England XI at Bradford	1950
27	Lancashire v Surrey at Manchester	1958
29	Middlesex v Derbyshire at Chesterfield	1957
31	Glamorgan v Surrey at The Oval	1957
31	Hampshire v Worcestershire at Bournemouth	1965
31	Hampshire v Kent at Maidstone	1967
31	Glamorgan v Middlesex at Cardiff	1997

Close of play: first day, Durham 315-4 (Benkenstein 57, Mustard 39); second day, Durham 193-7 (Onions 23, Benkenstein 3).

Durham

Batsman	First innings		Second innings	
W. R. Smith c Salt b Watkins	71	–	c Jones b Salt	43
P. D. Collingwood c Smith b Salt	47			
B. A. Stokes c Wallis b Salt	93	–	(4) st Smith b Watkins	65
D. M. Benkenstein not out	57	–	(9) not out	3
I. D. Blackwell lbw b Sangha	0	–	(3) lbw b Sangha	14
*†P. Mustard not out	39			
S. G. Borthwick (did not bat)		–	(2) c sub (R. D. Cox) b Wallis	22
C. D. Thorp (did not bat)		–	(5) c Wallis b Salt	3
M. E. Claydon (did not bat)		–	(6) c sub (R. D. Cox) b Watkins	9
G. Onions (did not bat)		–	(7) not out	23
R. M. R. Brathwaite (did not bat)		–	(8) c Salt b Watkins	8
B 3, l-b 1, n-b 4	8		L-b 1, w 2	3
1/118 (2) 2/121 (1) 3/246 (3) 4/251 (5) (4 wkts dec, 66 overs)	315		1/36 (2) 2/68 (3) 3/88 (1) 4/108 (5) 5/154 (6) 6/159 (4) 7/180 (8) (7 wkts dec, 40 overs)	193

Wallis 10–1–60–0; Green 11–1–43–0; Blackaby 7–1–30–0; Salt 12–2–47–2; Watkins 13–0–73–1; Sangha 13–0–58–1. *Second innings*—Wallis 7–0–43–1; Green 6–1–24–0; Sangha 9–0–50–1; Salt 7–0–25–2; Watkins 7–0–24–3; Patel 4–0–26–0.

Durham MCCU

First innings		Second innings	
*C. R. Jones c Mustard b Onions	2	c Benkenstein b Thorp	1
S. R. Waters c Benkenstein b Thorp	2	lbw b Onions	2
R. A. C. Shah b Onions	8	lbw b Stokes	7
A. S. Sangha lbw b Thorp	4	c Stokes b Onions	1
L. A. Blackaby c Blackwell b Stokes	24	absent hurt	
L. A. Patel c Borthwick b Thorp	0	(5) c Mustard b Stokes	3
†J. W. G. Smith lbw b Brathwaite	0	(6) c Borthwick b Stokes	0
N. A. T. Watkins not out	38	(7) c Borthwick b Thorp	0
J. D. Salt run out	16	(8) c sub (M. J. Richardson) b Thorp	0
C. A. Wallis c and b Brathwaite	8	(9) b Stokes	0
M. J. E. Green b Brathwaite	0	(10) not out	0
L-b 3, w 2, n-b 10	15	B 1, l-b 1, n-b 2	4
1/2 (2) 2/8 (1) 3/13 (3) 4/18 (4) 5/18 (6) 6/18 (7) 7/69 (5) 8/106 (9) 9/117 (10) 10/117 (11) (52.4 overs)	117	1/3 (2) 2/3 (1) 3/4 (4) 4/15 (5) 5/15 (6) 6/16 (7) 7/16 (3) 8/18 (9) 9/18 (8) (16.5 overs)	18

Onions 6–4–5–2; Thorp 12–3–25–3; Claydon 7–2–16–0; Brathwaite 10.4–2–32–3; Stokes 9–4–27–1; Blackwell 3–0–6–0; Borthwick 5–3–3–0. *Second innings*—Onions 6–2–9–2; Thorp 6.5–3–4–3; Stokes 4–2–3–4.

Umpires: J. H. Evans and G. D. Lloyd.

DURHAM v NOTTINGHAMSHIRE

At Chester-le-Street, April 12–15. Nottinghamshire won by 114 runs. Nottinghamshire 19pts, Durham 3pts. Toss: Durham.

The third day – April 14 – marked the 20th anniversary of Durham's first-class debut, against Oxford in the Parks. This was no sort of celebration: so cold that five of their players wore woolly hats, and by the scheduled close they were 176 for eight, chasing 368. Nottinghamshire claimed the extra half-hour, and Adams soon took his fourth wicket, Mustard falling for 80. But Onions and Claydon survived, and next morning Claydon completed a maiden half-century, contributing 55 to a stand of 73, Durham's biggest of the match. The key moment had come early in Nottinghamshire's second innings, when Lumb got off the mark with a four edged between wicketkeeper and first slip. He went on to 131, blossoming after doggedly supporting Hales's fluent 57; it was his first century since leaving Hampshire. While Durham fielded two spinners, Nottinghamshire picked five seam bowlers, Carter giving them a trio of six-foot-something giants alongside Fletcher and Phillips. But the shorter, skiddier Adams was the most successful, taking two wickets in his first over in Durham's run-chase, then producing an unplayable ball to trim Stokes's off stump.

Close of play: first day, Durham 55-3 (Stokes 18, Benkenstein 6); second day, Nottinghamshire 231-4 (Lumb 104, Read 5); third day, Durham 203-9 (Onions 15, Claydon 18).

Nottinghamshire

First innings		Second innings	
A. D. Hales c Di Venuto b Onions	5	c Stokes b Blackwell	57
N. J. Edwards lbw b Thorp	7	c Stoneman b Onions	5
M. J. Lumb lbw b Stokes	9	c Smith b Thorp	131
S. R. Patel c Mustard b Claydon	13	c Di Venuto b Blackwell	5
J. W. A. Taylor c Thorp b Stokes	32	c Mustard b Stokes	37
*†C. M. W. Read lbw b Claydon	28	b Onions	29
P. J. Franks b Onions	17	c Smith b Claydon	8
B. J. Phillips c and b Onions	17	c Mustard b Claydon	14
A. R. Adams b Claydon	0	b Claydon	22
L. J. Fletcher c Borthwick b Onions	11	not out	0
A. Carter not out	1	c Mustard b Claydon	0
B 2, l-b 6, w 1, n-b 12	21	B 1, l-b 14, n-b 12	27
1/12 (2) 2/16 (1) 3/32 (3) 4/38 (4) 5/104 (5) 6/106 (6) 7/148 (8) 8/148 (9) 9/148 (7) 10/161 (10) (59.3 overs)	161	1/16 (2) 2/101 (1) 3/118 (4) 4/217 (5) 5/289 (6) 6/293 (3) 7/310 (7) 8/332 (9) 9/335 (8) 10/335 (11) (107 overs)	335

Onions 15.3–6–42–4; Thorp 12–4–24–1; Stokes 12–1–42–2; Claydon 14–3–33–3; Benkenstein 1–0–2–0; Blackwell 3–1–8–0; Borthwick 2–0–2–0. *Second innings*—Onions 23–5–59–2; Thorp 23–10–32–1; Claydon 19–2–84–4; Stokes 12–2–57–1; Blackwell 22–9–48–2; Borthwick 8–0–40–0.

Durham

M. J. Di Venuto c Lumb b Phillips	11	– (2) c Franks b Fletcher	6
W. R. Smith c Patel b Adams	11	– (1) lbw b Adams	10
M. D. Stoneman c Edwards b Adams	7	– c Patel b Adams	2
B. A. Stokes b Phillips	33	– b Adams	7
D. M. Benkenstein c Hales b Adams	10	– lbw b Phillips	2
I. D. Blackwell c Edwards b Phillips	0	– c Phillips b Franks	14
*†P. Mustard c Adams b Phillips	7	– c Taylor b Adams	80
S. G. Borthwick b Carter	6	– b Carter	22
C. D. Thorp not out	30	– st Read b Patel	12
G. Onions c Fletcher b Carter	8	– not out	28
M. E. Claydon c Hales b Carter	2	– c Fletcher b Patel	55
L-b 3, w 1	4	L-b 6, w 1, n-b 8	15
1/21 (1) 2/26 (2) 3/33 (3) 4/64 (5) 5/74 (4) 6/77 (6) 7/82 (7) 8/115 (8) 9/125 (10) 10/129 (11) (43.4 overs)	129	1/7 (2) 2/20 (1) 3/21 (3) 4/26 (5) 5/30 (4) 6/54 (6) 7/112 (8) 8/139 (9) 9/180 (7) 10/253 (11) (69.2 overs)	253

Fletcher 8–1–24–0; Phillips 13–3–33–4; Adams 16–6–42–3; Carter 6.4–1–27–3. *Second innings*—Fletcher 7–2–25–1; Phillips 15–6–29–1; Adams 21–0–68–4; Franks 6–1–29–1; Carter 13–2–70–1; Patel 7.2–2–26–2.

Umpires: N. L. Bainton and J. W. Lloyds.

At Lord's, April 19–22. DURHAM drew with MIDDLESEX.

At The Oval, April 26–29. SURREY v DURHAM. Abandoned.

At Birmingham, May 2–4. DURHAM lost to WARWICKSHIRE by nine wickets.

DURHAM v SOMERSET

At Chester-le-Street, May 9–12. Drawn. Durham 6pts, Somerset 8pts. Toss: Somerset.

The loss of two days meant Durham had seen seven washed out of a potential 19. Even so, they might have gone down to defeat had play not started 40 minutes late on the final morning, and had Somerset – with only 11 fit players (average age 23) – not missed three slip catches. Among those let off was former team-mate Blackwell, who managed 38 after totalling 84 in his previous nine innings. And if Barrow at third slip had held a very sharp chance off last man Brathwaite in the 60th over, Somerset would have had nine overs to score 89; as the equation stretched to 93 in seven, and with the last pair still at the crease, they accepted the draw. On the first day, Durham were dismissed for 125, with four wickets for teenager Craig Overton, then reduced Somerset to 65 for four at tea. But the visitors thrashed 155 in the next 29 overs: Meschede raced fearlessly to a 45-ball half-century and recorded career-bests with bat and ball on the same day. Kieswetter played more cautiously in support, but hit two big sixes as he advanced to 96 before being stranded when Dockrell was run out.

Close of play: first day, Somerset 220-8 (Kieswetter 60, Waller 0); second day, no play; third day, no play.

Durham

First innings			Second innings	
M. J. Di Venuto c Kieswetter b Philander	14	–	(2) c Waller b Meschede	38
W. R. Smith c Kieswetter b Meschede	18	–	(1) c Overton b Trego	22
M. D. Stoneman c Overton b Philander	33	–	lbw b Overton	35
P. D. Collingwood c Hildreth b Trego	4	–	lbw b Overton	36
G. J. Muchall lbw b Overton	16	–	c Trego b Meschede	14
I. D. Blackwell c Kieswetter b Overton	14	–	not out	38
*†P. Mustard c Barrow b Meschede	10	–	c Trego b Meschede	2
C. D. Thorp c Philander b Meschede	7	–	c Barrow b Trego	3
M. E. Claydon lbw b Overton	1	–	(10) c Waller b Trego	2
G. Onions not out	0	–	(9) b Philander	20
R. M. R. Brathwaite c Barrow b Overton	0	–	not out	0
L-b 4, n-b 4	8		B 1, l-b 9, w 2, n-b 12	24
1/22 (1) 2/53 (2) 3/62 (4) 4/90 (3) (46 overs) 5/92 (5) 6/117 (7) 7/121 (6) 8/125 (8) 9/125 (9) 10/125 (11)	125		1/61 (1) (9 wkts, 61 overs) 2/85 (2) 3/144 (4) 4/163 (3) 5/165 (5) 6/175 (7) 7/186 (8) 8/213 (9) 9/230 (10)	234

Philander 11–2–41–2; Overton 16–5–38–4; Meschede 9–4–26–3; Trego 10–5–16–1. *Second innings*—Philander 18–1–66–1; Overton 12–3–49–2; Trego 15–2–52–3; Meschede 13–2–38–3; Gregory 3–0–19–0.

Somerset

A. V. Suppiah lbw b Onions	0
L. Gregory c Blackwell b Thorp	18
A. W. R. Barrow lbw b Onions	3
*J. C. Hildreth b Claydon	18
†C. Kieswetter not out	96
P. D. Trego b Brathwaite	40
C. A. J. Meschede c Collingwood b Thorp	62
V. D. Philander c Stoneman b Thorp	8
C. Overton c Di Venuto b Thorp	0
M. T. C. Waller c Mustard b Onions	4
G. H. Dockrell run out	4
B 2, l-b 9, w 1, n-b 2	14
1/0 (1) 2/6 (3) 3/32 (2) (57.2 overs) 4/45 (4) 5/95 (6) 6/202 (7) 7/220 (8) 8/220 (9) 9/227 (10) 10/267 (11)	267

Onions 22–4–73–3; Thorp 19–3–71–4; Claydon 9.2–0–71–1; Brathwaite 5–0–31–1; Blackwell 2–0–10–0.

Umpires: R. K. Illingworth and T. E. Jesty.

At Taunton, May 22–24. DURHAM lost to SOMERSET by five wickets.

DURHAM v LANCASHIRE

At Chester-le-Street, May 30–June 2. Lancashire won by two wickets. Lancashire 19pts, Durham –1pt (after 4pt penalty). Toss: Lancashire.

The respective champions of 2009 and 2011 had started with no wins from a combined 13 matches, but title holders Lancashire finally broke their duck with four balls to spare. Meanwhile an over-rate penalty condemned Durham to a one-point deficit, yet they boasted two outstanding individual performances: Onions claimed 11 for 95, the best match figures of his career, while Stokes made his first century in 12 months, in a game which produced only two other scores of 50-plus. Rain delayed the final day until 2.55, when Lancashire needed a further 144 with nine wickets standing. That had become 32 in 34 balls when No. 10 Hogg came in, but he and Shahzad nervelessly completed the task. The ball had swung lavishly on the opening day, when Procter took five wickets for the first time as Durham succumbed for 102, their lowest total since 90 at Old Trafford in 2008. Onions had Lancashire rocking on 19 for four, but Horton escaped when bowled by a Harrison no-ball with the total on 33 to carry his bat for 49. The last person to do so for Lancashire without reaching 50 was Cyril Washbrook in 1935. Durham had only just cleared their first-innings deficit when Collingwood joined Stokes, but he somehow survived a superb spell by Chapple to contribute 50 to a stand of 132. Horton was trapped by the first ball of the run-chase, and Onions's final-day figures were 16–4–26–5. But Prince's half-century proved crucial.

Close of play: first day, Lancashire 141-8 (Horton 31, Hogg 23); second day, Durham 0-0 (Smith 0, Stoneman 0); third day, Lancashire 56-1 (Moore 23, Brown 30).

Durham

M. D. Stoneman c Kerrigan b Chapple	8	– (2) c Cross b Procter	28
W. R. Smith b Hogg	11	– (1) lbw b Shahzad	22
G. J. Muchall c Cross b Hogg	13	– lbw b Chapple	7
B. A. Stokes c Cross b Hogg	2	– c Hogg b Kerrigan	121
D. M. Benkenstein c Cross b Procter	10	– c Prince b Chapple	2
P. D. Collingwood lbw b Procter	25	– lbw b Hogg	50
*†P. Mustard c Prince b Procter	4	– c Horton b Kerrigan	3
S. G. Borthwick c Horton b Procter	2	– c Prince b Procter	5
G. Onions not out	4	– b Procter	5
J. Harrison b Procter	1	– not out	1
S. J. Harmison b Chapple	1	– lbw b Kerrigan	0
B 5, l-b 13, w 1, n-b 2	21	B 8, l-b 11, w 4	23
1/8 (1) 2/32 (2) 3/33 (3) 4/34 (4) 5/78 (5) 6/82 (7) 7/88 (8) 8/93 (6) 9/99 (10) 10/102 (11) (36.3 overs)	102	1/53 (1) 2/63 (2) 3/65 (3) 4/71 (5) 5/203 (6) 6/216 (7) 7/237 (8) 8/254 (9) 9/266 (4) 10/267 (11) (78.3 overs)	267

Chapple 12.3–2–32–2; Hogg 8–2–23–3; Shahzad 6–3–12–0; Procter 10–4–17–5. *Second innings*—Chapple 18–2–56–2; Hogg 20–5–66–1; Shahzad 13–3–27–1; Procter 17–2–62–3; Kerrigan 10.3–0–37–3.

Lancashire

P. J. Horton not out	49	– lbw b Onions	0
S. C. Moore c Borthwick b Onions	2	– b Onions	28
K. R. Brown lbw b Onions	2	– lbw b Onions	42
A. G. Prince c Collingwood b Onions	6	– c Muchall b Harrison	51
S. J. Croft c Mustard b Onions	4	– c Borthwick b Onions	7
L. A. Procter c Mustard b Stokes	18	– c Mustard b Harrison	15
†G. D. Cross b Harmison	17	– lbw b Onions	3
A. Shahzad lbw b Harrison	1	– (9) not out	19
*G. Chapple lbw b Harrison	13	– (8) c Mustard b Onions	3
K. W. Hogg c Collingwood b Harmison	33	– not out	12
S. C. Kerrigan c Borthwick b Onions	0		
B 1, l-b 13, w 1, n-b 10	25	B 2, l-b 6, w 1, n-b 11	20
1/5 (2) 2/7 (3) 3/13 (4) 4/19 (5) 5/63 (6) 6/80 (7) 7/89 (8) 8/109 (9) 9/155 (10) 10/170 (11) (48.3 overs)	170	1/0 (1) 2/63 (2) 3/80 (3) 4/98 (5) 5/156 (6) 6/159 (4) 7/161 (7) 8/168 (8) (8 wkts, 59.2 overs)	200

Onions 17.3–3–43–5; Harrison 10–2–35–2; Stokes 10–1–40–1; Harmison 11–1–38–2. *Second innings*—Onions 24–5–52–6; Harrison 15–1–60–2; Harmison 14.2–4–60–0; Stokes 6–0–20–0.

Umpires: R. J. Bailey and P. Willey.

DURHAM v WARWICKSHIRE

At Chester-le-Street, June 5–8. Drawn. Durham 8pts, Warwickshire 6pts. Toss: Durham. Championship debut: T. P. Milnes.

After brief interruptions on the first two days, there was no play after 2.30 on the third, and the last was washed out, with Durham leading by 227. They had shown improved application to claim their first home batting points of the season, though Clarke held five catches at second slip, equalling the record against Durham in a first-class innings. With Onions making his Test comeback down at Edgbaston, Mustard's cousin Chris Rushworth came in for only his second Championship appearance since 2010. He had taken a one-day-best five wickets the previous Sunday and followed up with a first-class-best five here, exploiting seamer-friendly conditions superbly: he conceded only one run in his first six overs as second-placed Warwickshire struggled. Chopra led them for the first time, after Jim Troughton pulled out with a back spasm, letting in Tom Milnes, who looked at home in a disciplined seam attack. His maiden Championship wicket was Harrison, who was nightwatchman in both Durham innings and hung around for 75 minutes on the third morning.

Close of play: first day, Durham 228-5 (Collingwood 43, Harrison 0); second day, Durham 28-2 (Muchall 8, Harrison 4); third day, Durham 147-7 (Collingwood 29, Borthwick 15).

Durham

	First innings		Second innings	
M. D. Stoneman c Clarke b Barker	7	–	(2) lbw b Barker	9
W. R. Smith lbw b Wright	47	–	(1) lbw b Woakes	7
G. J. Muchall c Clarke b Woakes	0	–	c Patel b Woakes	17
B. A. Stokes b Wright	66	–	(5) c Ambrose b Barker	14
D. M. Benkenstein c Wright b Woakes	40	–	(6) c Chopra b Woakes	21
P. D. Collingwood lbw b Woakes	43	–	(7) not out	29
J. Harrison c Clarke b Barker	0	–	(4) c Chopra b Milnes	23
*†P. Mustard c Clarke b Barker	25	–	c Chopra b Maddy	5
S. G. Borthwick c Patel b Barker	15	–	not out	15
C. Rushworth c Clarke b Woakes	1			
S. J. Harmison not out	0			
B 4, l-b 15, n-b 14	33		L-b 3, n-b 4	7
1/22 (1) 2/23 (3) 3/132 (4) 4/143 (2) 5/221 (5) 6/228 (6) 7/230 (7) 8/272 (9) 9/277 (8) 10/277 (10) (95.1 overs)	277		1/14 (2) 2/20 (1) 3/41 (3) 4/75 (5) 5/86 (4) 6/106 (6) 7/116 (8) (7 wkts, 52 overs)	147

Barker 23–5–62–4; Woakes 24.1–3–67–4; Maddy 16–8–25–0; Wright 15–2–48–2; Milnes 9–1–38–0; Patel 8–3–18–0. *Second innings*—Woakes 14–3–36–3; Barker 15–2–44–2; Wright 13–4–41–0; Milnes 6–0–14–1; Maddy 4–1–9–1.

Warwickshire

*V. Chopra c Mustard b Harmison	29
I. J. Westwood c Collingwood b Harmison	36
W. T. S. Porterfield c Collingwood b Stokes	5
D. L. Maddy b Rushworth	8
†T. R. Ambrose lbw b Rushworth	23
R. Clarke b Rushworth	0
C. R. Woakes c Mustard b Harrison	29
K. H. D. Barker b Stokes	5
T. P. Milnes c Muchall b Rushworth	24
J. S. Patel c Mustard b Rushworth	0
C. J. C. Wright not out	21
L-b 8, w 1, n-b 8	17
1/61 (2) 2/74 (3) 3/78 (1) 4/86 (4) 5/90 (6) 6/133 (7) 7/140 (8) 8/168 (5) 9/168 (10) 10/197 (9) (67.4 overs)	197

Harrison 16–4–34–1; Rushworth 17.4–6–46–5; Harmison 16–4–49–2; Stokes 16–4–45–2; Borthwick 2–0–15–0.

Umpires: S. A. Garratt and S. J. O'Shaughnessy.

At Worcester, July 10–13. DURHAM drew with WORCESTERSHIRE.

At Arundel, July 18–21. DURHAM lost to SUSSEX by two wickets.

DURHAM v MIDDLESEX

At Chester-le-Street, July 27–29. Durham won by 15 runs. Durham 19pts, Middlesex 3pts. Toss: Middlesex.

Durham's first Championship victory of 2012 came at the 11th attempt. It matched their previous game, at Arundel, for drama: there, Sussex had won by two wickets chasing 94; here, Middlesex needed 118, but failed when their last three fell for four runs. Although the pitch offered seam movement, and 35 wickets tumbled on the first two days, it was clearly a case of the bowling being better than the batting. Middlesex were in control until a rain break on the second afternoon, with Durham 119 for seven, only 36 ahead. Then Borthwick and Thorp went on the attack, plundering 60 in eight overs. Middlesex lost both openers without a run on the board, and resumed on the third morning at 58 for five, which became six when Richardson, deputising for the injured Phil Mustard, caught Simpson. Roland-Jones played sensibly as nightwatchman to steer them to 98, only to fall to Onions, who bowled throughout the 85-minute session, though not at full throttle on his comeback from a hamstring strain. Stokes completed a dramatic win.

Close of play: first day, Middlesex 144-7 (Berg 30); second day, Middlesex 58-5 (Simpson 10, Roland-Jones 15).

Durham

M. D. Stoneman c Simpson b Murtagh	14	– (2) c Simpson b Murtagh	14
W. R. Smith lbw b Murtagh	0	– (1) c Rayner b Finn	7
G. J. Muchall run out	6	– b Finn	4
B. A. Stokes c Morgan b Berg	0	– c Denly b Roland-Jones	23
D. M. Benkenstein c Murtagh b Roland-Jones	18	– c Malan b Murtagh	37
*P. D. Collingwood c Malan b Finn	16	– lbw b Roland-Jones	14
†M. J. Richardson c Simpson b Finn	22	– b Roland-Jones	8
S. G. Borthwick c Simpson b Murtagh	13	– not out	41
C. D. Thorp lbw b Berg	0	– c Simpson b Murtagh	36
G. Onions c Simpson b Berg	0	– b Finn	4
C. Rushworth not out	12	– c Rogers b Finn	5
L-b 1	1	L-b 6, w 1	7
1/3 (2) 2/18 (3) 3/18 (4) 4/24 (1) (41.2 overs) 5/54 (5) 6/54 (6) 7/80 (8) 8/81 (9) 9/83 (10) 10/102 (7)	102	1/12 (1) 2/24 (2) (45.5 overs) 3/32 (3) 4/68 (4) 5/99 (5) 6/114 (6) 7/119 (7) 8/179 (9) 9/186 (10) 10/200 (11)	200

Murtagh 15–3–27–3; Finn 10.2–3–17–2; Berg 11–2–39–3; Roland-Jones 5–0–18–1. *Second innings*—Murtagh 14–3–41–3; Finn 15.5–2–80–4; Roland-Jones 9–1–54–3; Berg 7–2–19–0.

Middlesex

*C. J. L. Rogers c Stokes b Onions	59	– (2) c Smith b Rushworth	0
S. D. Robson lbw b Thorp	7	(1) c Borthwick b Onions	0
J. L. Denly c Collingwood b Stokes	9	– c Borthwick b Thorp	16
D. J. Malan c Collingwood b Thorp	24	– lbw b Rushworth	15
E. J. G. Morgan lbw b Stokes	0	– lbw b Rushworth	2
†J. A. Simpson c Collingwood b Stokes	1	– c Richardson b Onions	10
G. K. Berg c Richardson b Thorp	37	– (8) c Collingwood b Rushworth	5
O. P. Rayner c and b Borthwick	14	– (9) b Stokes	11
T. J. Murtagh c Richardson b Onions	25	– (10) c Richardson b Stokes	3
T. S. Roland-Jones not out	5	– (7) c Richardson b Onions	34
S. T. Finn c Richardson b Onions	0	– not out	0
L-b 2, n-b 2	4	L-b 4, w 2	6
1/34 (2) 2/67 (3) 3/83 (1) 4/84 (5) (68.1 overs) 5/86 (6) 6/112 (4) 7/144 (8) 8/177 (7) 9/185 (9) 10/185 (11)	185	1/0 (1) 2/0 (2) (42.1 overs) 3/26 (4) 4/30 (5) 5/38 (3) 6/58 (6) 7/71 (8) 8/98 (7) 9/98 (9) 10/102 (10)	102

Onions 16.1–4–38–3; Rushworth 14–1–51–0; Thorp 17–4–50–3; Stokes 19–6–44–3; Borthwick 2–2–0–1. *Second innings*—Onions 20–6–38–3; Rushworth 13–2–41–4; Thorp 4–1–10–1; Borthwick 1–0–1–0; Stokes 4.1–1–8–2.

Umpires: R. T. Robinson and P. Willey.

At Chester-le-Street, August 1–3. DURHAM beat AUSTRALIA A by 19 runs (see Australia A tour section).

DURHAM v SURREY

At Chester-le-Street, August 7–9. Durham won by an innings and 38 runs. Durham 22pts, Surrey 2pts (after 1pt penalty). Toss: Surrey. County debut: K. K. Jennings.

Durham rose from the bottom of the division for the first time since April. Following Middlesex's collapse nine days earlier, Surrey did not want to bat last. Instead, they folded on the first afternoon, for 129, and never threatened to make Durham bat twice. Their top-order trio of young left-handers found it tough against a potent seam attack, though Burns held out for three hours second time round. Stokes swung the ball both ways at good pace for match figures of six for 65. After 14 wickets fell in the first 75 overs – including Durham debutant and former South African Under-19 captain Keaton Jennings, who looked accomplished but was brilliantly run out by de Bruyn from deep gully – Benkenstein and Collingwood put on a decisive 132. They used all their experience – and some luck – as both passed their previous season's best. Later that day, umpire Jeff Evans gave Mustard lbw to de Bruyn, then changed his mind; Mustard added only three before Michael Gough gave him lbw to Lewis.

Close of play: first day, Durham 119-4 (Benkenstein 40, Collingwood 17); second day, Surrey 69-5 (Burns 28, Linley 0).

Surrey

R. J. Burns b Stokes	14	– c Mustard b Onions	39
Z. S. Ansari c Mustard b Rushworth	1	– c Collingwood b Onions	6
A. Harinath b Rushworth	28	– lbw b Stokes	5
Z. de Bruyn lbw b Stokes	0	– run out	10
J. J. Roy run out	15	– lbw b Stokes	1
†S. M. Davies c Borthwick b Rushworth	12	– c Mustard b Rushworth	15
M. N. W. Spriegel c Mustard b Onions	1	– (8) c Stokes b Thorp	17
*G. J. Batty c Thorp b Stokes	11	– (9) c Stoneman b Borthwick	22
J. Lewis c Borthwick b Thorp	23	– (10) c Collingwood b Borthwick	10
T. E. Linley c Mustard b Stokes	4	– (7) lbw b Rushworth	0
J. W. Dernbach not out	8	– not out	4
L-b 7, w 1, n-b 4	12	L-b 4, w 8, n-b 2	14
1/6 (2) 2/41 (1) 3/45 (4) 4/67 (5) (48.3 overs) 5/67 (3) 6/80 (7) 7/80 (6) 8/117 (8) 9/117 (9) 10/129 (10)	129	1/17 (2) 2/27 (3) (66.2 overs) 3/47 (4) 4/49 (5) 5/69 (6) 6/69 (7) 7/91 (1) 8/114 (8) 9/138 (10) 10/143 (9)	143

Onions 16–8–23–1; Rushworth 13–5–36–3; Thorp 9–0–23–1; Stokes 10.3–2–40–4. *Second innings*—Onions 18–6–31–2; Rushworth 13–3–35–2; Thorp 14–8–19–1; Stokes 16–5–25–2; Borthwick 5.2–0–29–2.

Durham

M. D. Stoneman c Ansari b Dernbach	6	C. D. Thorp c Batty b Lewis	32
W. R. Smith c Roy b de Bruyn	15	G. Onions c Linley b de Bruyn	0
K. K. Jennings run out	23	C. Rushworth not out	3
B. A. Stokes c Lewis b Linley	6	L-b 12, w 3, n-b 16	31
D. M. Benkenstein b Dernbach	69		
*P. D. Collingwood c Davies b Dernbach	78	1/10 (1) 2/37 (2) 3/56 (3) (105 overs)	310
†P. Mustard lbw b Lewis	46	4/58 (4) 5/190 (5) 6/229 (6)	
S. G. Borthwick c Burns b Linley	1	7/231 (8) 8/303 (7) 9/306 (10) 10/310 (9)	

Dernbach 25–5–88–3; Linley 27–8–71–2; Lewis 26–4–62–2; de Bruyn 22–6–54–2; Batty 3–0–13–0; Ansari 2–0–10–0.

Umpires: J. H. Evans and M. A. Gough.

At Nottingham, August 15–18. DURHAM beat NOTTINGHAMSHIRE by 16 runs.

DURHAM v WORCESTERSHIRE

At Chester-le-Street, August 21–23. Durham won by six wickets. Durham 20pts, Worcestershire 3pts. Toss: Durham.

Another century stand between Benkenstein and Collingwood took Durham to their fourth consecutive Championship win, equalling the club record, and their fifth in a row in all first-class cricket, setting a new one. Another pitch inspector called after 19 wickets fell on the opening day, when swing and seam allowed Rushworth to bag a career-best five for 44, though Stokes and Jennings had few problems adding 72. Next day, Hughes and Mitchell easily wiped out Durham's lead of 114; Hughes cut impressively in a high-class century, but Stokes removed both after an opening stand of 148. That meant only three wickets had fallen on the second day before tea, but after the break Worcestershire batted recklessly, handing five to Thorp, who found some movement, and three to Borthwick's leg-spin. Richardson reduced Durham to 35 for four chasing 151, but once Benkenstein, with only his second Championship fifty of the season, and Collingwood had seen him off, it was plain sailing.

Close of play: first day, Durham 215-9 (Borthwick 23, Rushworth 14); second day, Durham 3-1 (Stoneman 1, Jennings 0).

Worcestershire

*D. K. H. Mitchell c Borthwick b Rushworth	5	– c Thorp b Stokes	45
P. J. Hughes c Stokes b Onions	4	– c Mustard b Stokes	104
M. G. Pardoe lbw b Stokes	36	– c Stoneman b Borthwick	21
M. M. Ali lbw b Onions	4	– c Smith b Borthwick	19
V. S. Solanki b Rushworth	0	– c Mustard b Thorp	11
N. D. Pinner b Rushworth	0	– lbw b Thorp	21
J. Leach lbw b Thorp	11	– c Rushworth b Thorp	0
G. M. Andrew c Stoneman b Rushworth	16	– lbw b Borthwick	5
†B. J. M. Scott c Smith b Rushworth	28	– b Thorp	17
C. J. Russell not out	14	– not out	7
A. Richardson b Onions	0	– c Stoneman b Thorp	5
L-b 2	2	L-b 6, w 1, n-b 2	9
1/9 (1) 2/19 (2) 3/25 (4) 4/26 (5) (34.1 overs) 5/26 (6) 6/52 (7) 7/74 (3) 8/86 (8) 9/120 (9) 10/120 (11)	120	1/148 (2) 2/159 (1) (82.5 overs) 3/195 (3) 4/208 (4) 5/212 (5) 6/212 (7) 7/217 (8) 8/243 (6) 9/254 (9) 10/264 (11)	264

Onions 10.1–3–27–3; Rushworth 10–0–44–5; Thorp 7–1–21–1; Stokes 7–0–26–1. *Second innings*—Onions 15–5–39–0; Rushworth 13–4–36–0; Stokes 13–4–46–2; Thorp 18.5–6–59–5; Borthwick 22–2–76–3; Smith 1–0–2–0.

Durham

M. D. Stoneman lbw b Richardson	0	– (2) lbw b Richardson	22
W. R. Smith c Andrew b Russell	3	– (1) b Russell	2
K. K. Jennings b Russell	30	– b Richardson	3
B. A. Stokes b Andrew	78	– lbw b Richardson	8
D. M. Benkenstein c Scott b Andrew	21	– not out	62
*P. D. Collingwood c Solanki b Richardson	17	– not out	53
†P. Mustard c Solanki b Andrew	4		
S. G. Borthwick lbw b Russell	31		
C. D. Thorp b Andrew	8		
G. Onions c Scott b Andrew	8		
C. Rushworth not out	24		
L-b 8, n-b 2	10	B 3, l-b 1	4
1/0 (1) 2/8 (2) 3/80 (3) 4/131 (4) (63.2 overs) 5/152 (5) 6/160 (7) 7/160 (6) 8/181 (9) 9/193 (10) 10/234 (8)	234	1/3 (1) (4 wkts, 42.4 overs) 2/10 (3) 3/26 (4) 4/35 (2)	154

Richardson 22–4–62–2; Russell 15.2–4–54–3; Andrew 21–2–86–5; Ali 2–0–7–0; Leach 3–0–17–0. *Second innings*—Richardson 14–4–29–3; Russell 11–4–39–1; Andrew 10–2–41–0; Leach 3–0–9–0; Ali 4.4–0–32–0.

Umpires: J. H. Evans and R. T. Robinson.

At Liverpool, August 28–31. DURHAM drew with LANCASHIRE.

DURHAM v SUSSEX

At Chester-le-Street, September 11–13. Durham won by five wickets. Durham 20pts, Sussex 4pts. Toss: Durham.

Batting against the new ball at Chester-le-Street remained hazardous. Brown came in at 67 for five in the first innings and 69 for five in the second, but looked assured during a season's-best 76 on the first day, when it took a run-out to break his century partnership with Wernars. Durham were initially rocked by Magoffin's opening spell of 10–3–19–3, before Mustard and Borthwick put on 83. The game was evenly poised on the third morning: Sussex 96 ahead with five down, but Wells on 51. He failed to advance, becoming the third of the top five to be caught behind off Stokes – the 501st dismissal of Mustard's first-class career. Rushworth wrapped up the innings, improving his career-best for the third time since June, to leave Durham a target of 165. Stokes played his part with the bat, too, finishing with 45 off 49 balls when he lifted Panesar to long-on. Richardson almost saw the job through, with the season's only Championship fifty by a Durham No. 3, but it was Mustard who completed Durham's fifth victory in six matches, after none in the first ten.

Close of play: first day, Durham 131-6 (Mustard 7, Borthwick 4); second day, Sussex 112-5 (Wells 51, Brown 12).

Sussex

First innings		Second innings	
*C. D. Nash c Collingwood b Rushworth	7	(2) lbw b Rushworth	0
L. W. P. Wells c Mustard b Thorp	25	(1) c Mustard b Stokes	51
M. H. Yardy lbw b Rushworth	7	lbw b Thorp	29
J. S. Gatting lbw b Onions	14	c Mustard b Stokes	0
M. W. Machan c Collingwood b Onions	4	c Mustard b Stokes	6
K. O. Wernars run out	50	lbw b Thorp	1
†B. C. Brown not out	76	lbw b Rushworth	30
W. A. Adkin c Mustard b Thorp	9	lbw b Rushworth	6
S. J. Magoffin lbw b Borthwick	0	c Thorp b Rushworth	10
L. J. Hatchett c Borthwick b Thorp	2	not out	18
M. S. Panesar run out	0	c Benkenstein b Rushworth	1
L-b 1, n-b 16	17	B 9, l-b 8, w 3, n-b 8	28
1/9 (1) 2/19 (3) 3/55 (4) 4/61 (5) 5/67 (2) 6/173 (6) 7/198 (8) 8/201 (9) 9/210 (10) 10/211 (11) (56.3 overs)	211	1/6 (2) 2/46 (3) 3/47 (4) 4/68 (5) 5/69 (6) 6/113 (1) 7/140 (8) 8/149 (7) 9/170 (9) 10/180 (11) (57.2 overs)	180

Onions 15–3–58–2; Rushworth 12–3–45–2; Stokes 10–2–39–0; Thorp 13–2–57–3; Borthwick 6.3–0–11–1. *Second innings*—Onions 19–2–54–0; Rushworth 13.2–4–38–5; Stokes 16–4–51–3; Thorp 9–3–20–2.

Durham

First innings		Second innings	
M. D. Stoneman c Yardy b Panesar	52	(2) b Hatchett	26
K. K. Jennings lbw b Hatchett	8	(1) c Yardy b Hatchett	1
M. J. Richardson lbw b Magoffin	0	lbw b Hatchett	58
B. A. Stokes b Magoffin	22	c Adkin b Panesar	45
D. M. Benkenstein b Magoffin	6	b Panesar	11
*P. D. Collingwood c Magoffin b Panesar	19	not out	4
†P. Mustard lbw b Nash	45	not out	16
S. G. Borthwick c Yardy b Wernars	35		
C. D. Thorp b Wernars	1		
G. Onions b Panesar	9		
C. Rushworth not out	14		
B 6, l-b 6, n-b 4	16	B 4, l-b 2	6
1/12 (2) 2/13 (3) 3/47 (4) 4/65 (5) 5/118 (6) 6/119 (1) 7/202 (7) 8/202 (8) 9/203 (9) 10/227 (10) (75.1 overs)	227	1/17 (1) 2/34 (2) 3/101 (4) 4/138 (5) 5/150 (3) (5 wkts, 48.2 overs)	167

Magoffin 23–7–47–3; Hatchett 12–2–53–1; Wernars 12–3–39–2; Adkin 5–1–20–0; Panesar 19.1–9–45–3; Nash 4–0–11–1. *Second innings*—Magoffin 15–2–54–0; Hatchett 13–1–60–3; Panesar 18.2–6–34–2; Wernars 2–0–13–0.

Umpires: N. L. Bainton and D. J. Millns.

ESSEX

Rocked, but not rolling

PAUL HISCOCK

A campaign mired in mediocrity condemned Essex to a summer of disappointment. They never looked like achieving promotion in the Championship, while the failure to make an impact in either the Twenty20 or CB40 underlined their all-round inadequacies. No one threatened 1,000 runs in the Championship – Tom Westley came closest, with 755 – while the old workhorse David Masters was again the leading wicket-taker, with 46.

Their struggles were simply highlighted by the performance of players who had chosen to continue their careers elsewhere: both Varun Chopra and Chris Wright played major roles in Warwickshire's Championship success. To rub more salt into the wounds, Essex's former seamer Tony Palladino proved a key figure at Derbyshire, who topped the second division, collecting 56 wickets as he reaped the benefits of regular first-team cricket.

Bad weather and absences could hardly be blamed, since many sides were similarly hampered. Essex did lose more than 1,800 Championship overs to the elements and, as expected, Alastair Cook and Ravi Bopara missed considerable chunks of the season through international calls. In addition, Owais Shah and Ryan ten Doeschate were at the IPL in the first two months of the summer. The inescapable truth, though, was that Essex lacked strength in depth. They were simply not good enough.

Two new signings failed to meet high expectations. Greg Smith, the South African all-rounder who joined from Derbyshire, managed only 158 runs and six wickets in eight Championship appearances, although he did become an important cog in the one-day side. His compatriot Charl Willoughby, a left-arm seamer with an excellent fitness record, was recruited from Somerset, primarily to support Masters – but sustained an injury shortly before the season began, and continued to suffer niggling setbacks. He seldom looked the bowler who had flourished in the West Country, and eventually announced his retirement.

And yet it had all started so well, with Gloucestershire swept aside in two and a bit days. But there were only two more Championship victories. With only one win from their first seven games in the CB40 – two were washed out – interest in that tournament ended early too. The Twenty20 form was equally patchy, although Essex did at least sneak into the quarter-finals before they were well beaten by Somerset.

None of the overseas players had much success. Alviro Petersen – snatched controversially from Glamorgan, who had expected him to return as a Kolpak player after he captained them in 2011 – promised to be a good signing for the first two months of the season. But his only innings of note was a century against his (fuming) former county; in ten other Championship innings he

Bryn Lennon, Getty Images

Tom Westley

failed to pass 20. The New Zealand all-rounder James Franklin was recruited for the Twenty20, with little effect. And finally Harbhajan Singh – dropped by India – arrived for the last chunk of the summer, but was unable to reignite any flickering hopes of Championship or one-day success. It was left to Masters to carry the attack, supported by Graham Napier in his benefit year. But the batting too often lacked substance. Australian batsman Rob Quiney was signed for the first half of the 2013 season.

Still, there was some optimism, in particular for two left-arm fast bowlers – Reece Topley and the explosive Tymal Mills. Both were products of the Essex Academy, and made advances during 2012. And the likes of Westley, Jaik Mickleburgh and Ben Foakes, among a clutch of younger players who have committed themselves with extended deals at Chelmsford, could yet be the backbone of the batting in the years ahead. Essex also stressed that Adam Wheater – their reserve wicketkeeper, whose opportunities behind the stumps have been limited by the continued good form of captain James Foster – will be staying, at least until his current contract expires at the end of 2013. Wheater played solely as a batsman for much of the time, but in the one game when did keep wicket he nearly conjured an unlikely victory against Hampshire with an attacking 98.

Bopara, after a troubled summer that was interrupted by undisclosed personal problems, also signed another one-year contract. With his international career apparently stalling, he could be more available for the county in 2013.

There are options in the seam department, and Sajid Mahmood joined from Lancashire; while there are hopes the off-breaks of Westley and Tom Craddock's leg-spin could yet flourish, the spin cupboard looks understocked.

Off the field, the spot-fixing scandal that had rocked the club for more than two years – and attracted criticism for its management of the affair – was finally resolved in June, when former Essex and Pakistan leg-spinner Danish Kaneria was banned for life by the ECB for his role in the corruption of fast bowler Mervyn Westfield, who had been released from prison in April.

In October, David East, chief executive since 2000, announced he was taking up a new position with the Emirates Cricket Board in Abu Dhabi. East had spent a lot of time planning the development of the ground at Chelmsford but, by the end of the 2012 season, building work had still not started. He was replaced by Derek Bowden, the former chief executive of Ipswich Town FC.

Essex were one of several parties interested in becoming a tenant of the London Olympic Stadium from 2014, tabling a joint bid with the University of East London to use it as an educational and Academy facility, with the possibility of playing Twenty20 matches inside the running track. In July, however, they pulled out.

Championship attendance: 30,869.

ESSEX RESULTS

All first-class matches – Played 17: Won 3, Lost 3, Drawn 11.
County Championship matches – Played 16: Won 3, Lost 3, Drawn 10.

LV= County Championship, 5th in Division 2;
Friends Life t20, q-f; Clydesdale Bank 40, 5th in Group A.

COUNTY CHAMPIONSHIP AVERAGES, BATTING AND FIELDING

Cap		*M*	*I*	*NO*	*R*	*HS*	*100*	*50*	*Avge*	*Ct/St*
2005	R. S. Bopara‡	5	7	2	331	174	2	0	66.20	0
	O. A. Shah	8	13	1	589	161	2	2	49.08	3
2006	R. N. ten Doeschate¶	9	12	3	412	69	0	4	45.77	7
2001	J. S. Foster†	15	18	3	655	135	1	4	43.66	40/3
2006	M. L. Pettini	15	21	4	624	92	0	7	36.70	5
	T. Westley	16	23	2	755	185	2	3	35.95	9
	A. J. Wheater†	11	13	2	391	98	0	3	35.54	7
	J. C. Mickleburgh	8	12	1	330	126	1	2	30.00	7
	B. A. Godleman	7	11	1	286	130	1	0	28.60	4
	B. T. Foakes†	4	4	0	114	93	0	1	28.50	1
2003	G. R. Napier†	11	11	1	235	43	0	0	23.50	4
	A. N. Petersen§	7	11	0	235	145	1	0	21.36	8
	G. M. Smith¶	8	9	0	158	42	0	0	17.55	3
2008	D. D. Masters	13	11	0	113	35	0	0	10.27	3
	T. R. Craddock	6	8	3	46	16	0	0	9.20	2
	T. S. Mills	8	10	4	30	20*	0	0	5.00	5
	C. M. Willoughby¶	7	6	4	2	1*	0	0	1.00	2
	M. A. Chambers	7	7	1	2	2	0	0	0.33	4
	R. J. W. Topley	3	4	1	1	1	0	0	0.33	0

Also batted: A. N. Cook‡ (cap 2005) (2 matches) 9, 5, 1 (1 ct); Harbhajan Singh§ (5 matches) 40, 5*, 13 (10 ct); T. J. Phillips (cap 2006) (1 match) 7.

† Born in Essex. ‡ ECB contract. § Official overseas player. ¶ Other non-England-qualified player.

BOWLING

	Style	*O*	*M*	*R*	*W*	*BB*	*5I*	*Avge*
D. D. Masters	RFM	371.3	114	873	46	7-60	3	18.97
G. R. Napier	RFM	295.2	49	974	41	5-58	2	23.75
M. A. Chambers	RFM	163.1	29	567	20	4-31	0	28.35
T. R. Craddock	LBG	125.5	23	438	15	5-96	1	29.20
T. S. Mills	LFM	129.2	19	425	14	4-25	0	30.35
R. J. W. Topley	LFM	112.1	24	350	11	3-59	0	31.81
C. M. Willoughby	LFM	174	31	609	19	5-70	1	32.05
Harbhajan Singh	OB	176.3	38	431	13	4-91	0	33.15
T. Westley	OB	143.3	24	470	10	3-5	0	47.00

Also bowled: R. S. Bopara (RM) 2–0–5–0; A. N. Petersen (RM/OB) 1–0–4–0; M. L. Pettini (RM) 3.1–0–72–1; G. M. Smith (RFM/OB) 107–21–353–6; R. N. ten Doeschate (RM) 86–11–332–6; A. J. Wheater 4–0–86–1.

LEADING CB40 AVERAGES (100 runs/4 wickets)

Batting	*Runs*	*HS*	*Avge*	*SR*	*Ct/St*
R. S. Bopara	123	120*	61.50	106.03	0
T. Westley	396	82	44.00	86.27	2
O. A. Shah	209	53	41.80	87.08	7
R. N. ten Doeschate	158	52	39.50	123.43	1
M. L. Pettini	320	111	32.00	86.72	3
J. S. Foster	180	79	30.00	104.65	6/2

Bowling	*W*	*BB*	*Avge*	*ER*
R. S. Bopara	6	3-19	14.83	5.13
Harbhajan Singh	11	5-37	20.18	6.34
D. D. Masters	5	4-41	34.40	5.73
G. R. Napier	9	3-57	34.55	6.45
T. J. Phillips	7	3-34	38.57	5.56
T. S. Mills	5	2-40	48.40	5.43

LEADING FLT20 AVERAGES (100 runs/18 overs)

Batting	Runs	HS	Avge	SR	Ct/St
J. S. Foster	270	65*	33.75	**165.64**	7/4
M. L. Pettini	242	59	24.20	**125.38**	2
R. N. ten Doeschate	175	47	17.50	**121.52**	6
G. R. Napier	111	32	12.33	**118.08**	3
G. M. Smith	142	39	20.28	**110.93**	3
J. E. C. Franklin	248	78	27.55	**110.71**	4

Bowling	W	BB	Avge	ER
G. R. Napier	10	3-16	27.30	**7.21**
T. J. Phillips	10	3-27	22.70	**7.32**
D. D. Masters	6	2-18	39.66	**7.43**
R. N. ten Doeschate	10	2-7	18.10	**7.59**
R. J. W. Topley	17	3-19	14.47	**7.68**
G. M. Smith	10	5-17	14.60	**8.11**

FIRST-CLASS COUNTY RECORDS

Highest score for	343*	P. A. Perrin v Derbyshire at Chesterfield	1904
Highest score against	332	W. H. Ashdown (Kent) at Brentwood	1934
Leading run-scorer	30,701	G. A. Gooch (avge 51.77)	1973–1997
Best bowling for	10-32	H. Pickett v Leicestershire at Leyton	1895
Best bowling against	10-40	E. G. Dennett (Gloucestershire) at Bristol	1906
Leading wicket-taker	1,610	T. P. B. Smith (avge 26.68)	1929–1951
Highest total for	761-6 dec	v Leicestershire at Chelmsford	1990
Highest total against	803-4 dec	by Kent at Brentwood	1934
Lowest total for	30	v Yorkshire at Leyton	1901
Lowest total against	14	by Surrey at Chelmsford	1983

LIST A COUNTY RECORDS

Highest score for	201*	R. S. Bopara v Leicestershire at Leicester	2008
Highest score against	158*	M. W. Goodwin (Sussex) at Chelmsford	2006
Leading run-scorer	16,536	G. A. Gooch (avge 40.93)	1973–1997
Best bowling for	8-26	K. D. Boyce v Lancashire at Manchester	1971
Best bowling against	7-29	D. A. Payne (Gloucestershire) at Chelmsford	2010
Leading wicket-taker	616	J. K. Lever (avge 19.04)	1968–1989
Highest total for	391-5	v Surrey at The Oval	2008
Highest total against	318-8	by Lancashire at Chelmsford	1992
Lowest total for	57	v Lancashire at Lord's	1996
Lowest total against	41	by Middlesex at Westcliff-on-Sea	1972
	41	by Shropshire at Wellington	1974

TWENTY20 COUNTY RECORDS

Highest score for	152*	G. R. Napier v Sussex at Chelmsford	2008
Highest score against	124*	M. J. Lumb (Hampshire) at Southampton	2009
Leading run-scorer	**1,957**	**M. L. Pettini (avge 25.75)**	**2003–2012**
Best bowling for	6-16	T. G. Southee v Glamorgan at Chelmsford	2011
Best bowling against	5-11	Mushtaq Ahmed (Sussex) at Hove	2005
Leading wicket-taker	**70**	**G. R. Napier (avge 22.62)**	**2003–2012**
Highest total for	242-3	v Sussex at Chelmsford	2008
Highest total against	225-2	by Somerset at Chelmsford	2011
Lowest total for	82	v Somerset at Chelmsford	2011
Lowest total against	82	by Gloucestershire at Chelmsford	2011

ADDRESS

County Ground, New Writtle Street, Chelmsford CM2 0PG (01245 252420; **email** administration.essex@ecb.co.uk). **Website** www.essexcricket.org.uk

OFFICIALS

Captain J. S. Foster
First-team coach A. P. Grayson
Academy director J. H. Childs
President D. J. Insole
Chairman N. R. A. Hilliard
Chief executive 2012 – D. E. East
2013 – D. Bowden
Chairman, cricket committee G. J. Saville
Head groundsman S. Kerrison
Scorer A. E. Choat

At Cambridge, March 31–April 2. ESSEX drew with CAMBRIDGE MCCU. *Graham Napier scores a hundred in 48 balls.*

ESSEX v GLOUCESTERSHIRE

At Chelmsford, April 5–7. Essex won by an innings and 38 runs. Essex 23pts, Gloucestershire 3pts. Toss: Gloucestershire. First-class debut: P. B. Muchall. County debuts: A. N. Petersen; D. M. Housego.

It took Essex just two days and 75 minutes to demolish hapless opponents. Petersen launched his brief Essex career by striking his first delivery to the boundary, but it was Godleman who made the telling contribution, playing straight and correctly for almost the whole of the first day to equal his highest score. Gloucestershire were then blown away twice by excellent seam and swing bowling: Chambers showed genuine pace, Masters took three for 17 in nine overs after lunch, and the explosive Mills collected career-best figures; following on 184 behind, Gloucestershire fell victim to Napier. Eight wickets tumbled in the afternoon session on the second day, and five more after tea, with Coughtrie batting for 45 minutes in the second innings before completing a pair. The remaining five wickets fell next morning, although the last pair survived for 11 overs – which at least allowed Essex to rescue their over-rate from minus four to parity.

Close of play: first day, Essex 364; second day, Gloucestershire 55-5 (Cockbain 14, W. R. S. Gidman 5).

Essex

B. A. Godleman b Saxelby	130
A. N. Petersen c A. P. R. Gidman b W. R. S. Gidman	15
T. Westley c Dent b Saxelby	33
M. L. Pettini c Coughtrie b Muchall	9
A. J. Wheater c A. P. R. Gidman b Muchall	56
G. M. Smith c Muchall b Young	34
*†J. S. Foster c Dent b Fuller	46
G. R. Napier c A. P. R. Gidman b Saxelby	27
D. D. Masters c Marshall b Fuller	6
M. A. Chambers c W. R. S. Gidman b Fuller	0
T. S. Mills not out	0
L-b 8	8
1/19 (2) 2/61 (3) 3/76 (4) 4/146 (5) 5/210 (6) 6/304 (7) 7/357 (8) 8/358 (1) 9/359 (10) 10/364 (9) (94.2 overs)	364

W. R. S. Gidman 21–1–73–1; Fuller 19.2–2–86–3; Muchall 11–0–60–2; Saxelby 19–3–76–3; Young 23–4–60–1; Dent 1–0–1–0.

Gloucestershire

C. D. J. Dent b Mills	38	– c Foster b Napier	5
†R. G. Coughtrie c Petersen b Chambers	0	– lbw b Napier	0
D. M. Housego b Masters	39	– c Petersen b Masters	17
*A. P. R. Gidman c Foster b Masters	15	– c Westley b Napier	0
H. J. H. Marshall c Masters b Chambers	1	– lbw b Masters	8
I. A. Cockbain b Chambers	0	– c Foster b Masters	21
W. R. S. Gidman lbw b Mills	14	– lbw b Napier	39
E. G. C. Young c Foster b Masters	13	– c Smith b Mills	23
J. K. Fuller b Mills	17	– c Chambers b Napier	0
P. B. Muchall not out	17	– c Godleman b Smith	2
I. D. Saxelby b Napier	13	– not out	24
L-b 1, n-b 12	13	L-b 5, w 2	7
1/4 (2) 2/66 (1) 3/91 (4) 4/96 (5) 5/102 (6) 6/108 (3) 7/122 (8) 8/148 (9) 9/157 (7) 10/180 (11) (58.4 overs)	180	1/6 (1) 2/19 (2) 3/19 (4) 4/29 (3) 5/42 (5) 6/96 (7) 7/98 (6) 8/103 (9) 9/106 (10) 10/146 (8) (45.2 overs)	146

Masters 20–6–39–3; Chambers 14–3–49–3; Napier 9.4–1–33–1; Smith 6–0–23–0; Mills 9–1–35–3. *Second innings*—Masters 14–7–30–3; Napier 14–1–58–5; Smith 9–2–20–1; Chambers 2–0–6–0; Westley 5–0–22–0; Mills 1.2–0–5–1.

Umpires: M. A. Gough and T. E. Jesty.

At Leeds, April 19–22. ESSEX drew with YORKSHIRE.

ESSEX v NORTHAMPTONSHIRE

At Chelmsford, April 26–29. Drawn. Essex 3pts, Northamptonshire 5pts. Toss: Northamptonshire.

April showers became monsoon-like, permitting play only on the second day – and even that was limited to 27 overs, during which the Essex batsmen endured a torrid time on a damp, seaming pitch. Petersen dabbed a rising delivery to second slip in the seventh over, before Brooks cashed in with four for nine in 18 balls, including Westley and Wheater for ducks, and Bopara, who offered no stroke to a delivery that moved in and clipped his stumps. The match was officially abandoned at 9.30 on the final morning after almost an inch of rain fell in 14 hours.

Close of play: first day, no play; second day, Essex 54-6 (Pettini 16, Foster 8); third day, no play.

Essex

B. A. Godleman b Brooks	9	*†J. S. Foster not out		8
A. N. Petersen c Sales b Vaas	6			
T. Westley lbw b Brooks	0	L-b 4		4
R. S. Bopara b Brooks	6			
A. J. Wheater lbw b Brooks	0	1/15 (2) 2/15 (1)	(6 wkts, 27 overs)	54
M. L. Pettini not out	16	3/16 (3) 4/16 (5)		
G. M. Smith b Willey	5	5/25 (4) 6/40 (7)		

D. D. Masters, T. S. Mills and C. M. Willoughby did not bat.

Vaas 8–3–12–1; Brooks 9–3–22–4; Willey 5–1–14–1; Daggett 5–4–2–0.

Northamptonshire

S. D. Peters, R. I. Newton, K. J. Coetzer, *D. J. Sales, A. G. Wakely, †N. J. O'Brien, J. D. Middlebrook, W. P. U. J. C. Vaas, D. J. Willey, L. M. Daggett and J. A. Brooks.

Umpires: N. G. C. Cowley and S. C. Gale.

At Cardiff, May 2–5. ESSEX drew with GLAMORGAN. *Alviro Petersen hits 145 (in a total of 259) against the county he captained in 2011.*

ESSEX v KENT

At Chelmsford, May 9–12. Drawn. Essex 6pts, Kent 7pts. Toss: Essex. County debut: I. A. A. Thomas.

Play was delayed until after lunch on the opening day when, with conditions offering prolific assistance to the seamers, Kent capitulated sensationally. Newman was caught behind second ball, then Willoughby took four for one in nine deliveries. From the depths of nine for five, Jones and Stevens gradually reclaimed the initiative in a boundary-studded partnership of 194. But Westley wrapped up the tail with his off-spin and, with no one else scoring more than six, the sixth-wicket

---

A TWO-MAN BAND

Highest proportion of team total in one partnership in a completed first-class innings:

%	*Batsmen (wicket)*	*Stand/total*		
91.58	M. R. Hallam/W. Watson (1st)	196/214	Leics v Middlesex at Lord's	1960
90.56	C. P. Davis/P. E. Murray-Willis (1st)	96/106	Northants v Essex at Brentwood	1946
87.21	A. E. Dipper/C. S. Barnett (1st)	116/133	Glos v Glam at Cheltenham	1926
86.22	**D. I. Stevens/G. O. Jones (6th)**	**194/225**	**Kent v Essex at Chelmsford**	**2012**
86.07	J. Vine/R. R. Relf (1st)	204/237	Sussex v Somerset at Hove	1919
85.91	L. A. Shuter/J. Shuter (2nd)	61/71	Surrey v Lancs at Manchester	1880
85.71	Feroze Khan/M. Yusuf Baig (4th)	18/21	Muslims v Europeans at Poona	1915-16
85.25	F. J. Gough/C. D. P. Hansen (5th)	133/156	Qld v S. Africans at Brisbane	1931-32
85.13	R. G. Pollock/A. L. Wilmot (5th)	338/397	E. Prov. v Natal at Port Elizabeth	1975-76

stand constituted more than 86% of the final total. Never before in England – and only six times elsewhere – had a sixth-wicket pair added 100 after coming together with the score still in single figures. The incisive Davies then caused problems and, although Pettini coped well, he was surrounded by confusion. Batting down the order because of injuries sustained while fielding, both Bopara and Petersen used runners and, although Petersen – sensing imminent chaos – soon dispensed with his assistant, Bopara forgot entirely about his. Setting off for a single, he suddenly remembered he didn't need to – and failed by a distance to get back to his crease. But the loss of almost all the first two days prevented any prospect of a result.

Close of play: first day, Kent 17-5 (Stevens 4, Jones 4); second day, Kent 24-5 (Stevens 8, Jones 7); third day, Essex 94-2 (Godleman 27, Pettini 61).

Kent

First innings		Second innings	
S. A. Newman c Foster b Masters	0	c and b Westley	24
*R. W. T. Key lbw b Willoughby	1	not out	40
B. W. Harmison lbw b Willoughby	2	c Westley b Mills	1
B. P. Nash b Willoughby	6	not out	22
M. J. Powell c Foster b Willoughby	0		
D. I. Stevens c Godleman b Willoughby	119		
†G. O. Jones c Willoughby b Masters	88		
J. C. Tredwell lbw b Westley	0		
M. Davies c Masters b Westley	2		
C. E. Shreck c Foster b Westley	0		
I. A. A. Thomas not out	0		
L-b 6, w 1	7	L-b 2, w 1, n-b 2	5
1/0 (1) 2/3 (3) 3/8 (2) 4/8 (5) 5/9 (4) 6/203 (6) 7/204 (8) 8/206 (9) 9/206 (10) 10/225 (7) (68.1 overs)	225	1/54 (1) 2/57 (3) (2 wkts dec, 28 overs)	92

Masters 19.1–3–55–2; Willoughby 20–2–70–5; Smith 14–2–54–0; Mills 10–0–32–0; Bopara 1–0–3–0; Westley 4–2–5–3. *Second innings*—Masters 5–2–9–0; Willoughby 6–1–15–0; Westley 9–0–29–1; Mills 7–0–30–1; Smith 1–0–7–0.

Essex

B. A. Godleman lbw b Davies	27
A. N. Cook lbw b Davies	1
T. Westley c Jones b Davies	0
M. L. Pettini lbw b Thomas	92
G. M. Smith c Tredwell b Shreck	4
*†J. S. Foster c Nash b Thomas	4
A. N. Petersen c Newman b Davies	20
R. S. Bopara run out	19
D. D. Masters c Harmison b Shreck	9
T. S. Mills lbw b Shreck	0
C. M. Willoughby not out	0
L-b 5	5
1/3 (2) 2/3 (3) 3/94 (1) 4/103 (5) 5/133 (6) 6/140 (4) 7/158 (7) 8/181 (9) 9/181 (10) 10/181 (8) (82.4 overs)	181

Davies 24.4–14–20–4; Shreck 20–6–59–3; Thomas 16–7–29–2; Stevens 4–1–24–0; Tredwell 15–5–29–0; Harmison 3–0–15–0.

Umpires: S. J. O'Shaughnessy and G. Sharp.

At Leicester, May 16–19. ESSEX drew with LEICESTERSHIRE.

ESSEX v DERBYSHIRE

At Chelmsford, May 23–25. Derbyshire won by ten wickets. Derbyshire 22pts, Essex 3pts. Toss: Essex.

Derbyshire extended their lead at the top of the table with their fourth win – their first at Chelmsford since 1937 – completing it with more than a day to spare. Pettini batted responsibly, reaching his fourth half-century in four Championship matches, but otherwise the Essex first innings was a mishmash of injudicious shot selection against some fine spin bowling from Wainwright, whose five-for included a wicket with the first ball of three separate spells. Durston showed the merits of good footwork and sensible strokeplay, making his second century of the season before becoming part of a maiden five-wicket haul for leg-spinner Craddock. But Derbyshire still carved out a significant lead, with Poynton hitting freely in a career-best unbeaten 50 from only 35 balls. Essex lost five wickets in clearing the arrears and, although Foster battled hard, he lacked support against well-marshalled opponents. Derbyshire needed only 94, and were hurried home by Guptill, who thrashed three sixes and seven fours in 52 balls.

Close of play: first day, Derbyshire 37-1 (Guptill 19, Madsen 15); second day, Essex 46-2 (Shah 26, Pettini 17).

Essex

First innings		Second innings	
T. Westley b Whiteley	36	– c Durston b Groenewald	1
A. N. Petersen c Guptill b Groenewald	9	– c Guptill b Groenewald	2
O. A. Shah c Poynton b Wainwright	21	– b Durston	75
M. L. Pettini c and b Wainwright	56	– c Durston b Wainwright	27
B. T. Foakes c Poynton b Wainwright	18	– b Wainwright	3
*†J. S. Foster c Durston b Wainwright	0	– lbw b Palladino	96
G. M. Smith c Redfern b Wainwright	19	– lbw b Palladino	17
D. D. Masters c Guptill b Groenewald	13	– c Clare b Wainwright	8
T. R. Craddock not out	7	– run out	0
T. S. Mills lbw b Palladino	0	– c Poynton b Groenewald	0
C. M. Willoughby run out	1	– not out	0
B 1, l-b 1	2	B 2, l-b 3	5
1/20 (2) 2/54 (1) 3/68 (3) 4/101 (5) 5/101 (6) 6/135 (7) 7/166 (8) 8/173 (4) 9/174 (10) 10/182 (11) (79.2 overs)	182	1/2 (2) 2/3 (1) 3/73 (4) 4/77 (5) 5/127 (3) 6/170 (7) 7/183 (8) 8/191 (9) 9/230 (10) 10/234 (6) (84.2 overs)	234

Palladino 16–3–48–1; Groenewald 16–5–26–2; Whiteley 7–2–20–1; Clare 11–3–27–0; Wainwright 22.2–7–51–5; Durston 7–1–8–0. *Second innings*—Palladino 16.2–3–44–2; Groenewald 15–7–26–3; Wainwright 32–10–83–3; Clare 8–2–22–0; Durston 13–1–54–1.

Derbyshire

First innings		Second innings	
M. J. Guptill c Willoughby b Smith	36	– not out	66
P. M. Borrington lbw b Masters	3	– not out	30
*W. L. Madsen c Foster b Masters	50		
W. J. Durston c sub (G. R. Napier) b Craddock	116		
D. J. Redfern c Foster b Willoughby	14		
R. A. Whiteley c Mills b Westley	16		
D. J. Wainwright c Foster b Craddock	5		
J. L. Clare c Petersen b Craddock	1		
†T. Poynton not out	50		
A. P. Palladino lbw b Craddock	0		
T. D. Groenewald st Foster b Craddock	14		
L-b 10, w 6, n-b 2	18		
1/3 (2) 2/84 (1) 3/161 (3) 4/192 (5) 5/232 (6) 6/250 (7) 7/258 (8) 8/263 (4) 9/278 (10) 10/323 (11) (88.5 overs)	323	(no wkt, 18 overs)	96

Masters 20–6–53–2; Willoughby 19–1–69–1; Craddock 18.5–1–96–5; Smith 16–1–49–1; Mills 9–2–28–0; Westley 6–0–18–1. *Second innings*—Masters 5–2–10–0; Willoughby 5–1–24–0; Mills 3–0–14–0; Craddock 3–0–32–0; Smith 2–0–16–0.

Umpires: R. J. Bailey and M. J. D. Bodenham.

At Northampton, June 6–9. ESSEX drew with NORTHAMPTONSHIRE. *Ravi Bopara and James Foster share a fifth-wicket stand of 294, the highest for any wicket in the 2012 Championship.*

At Chelmsford, June 26. ESSEX lost to AUSTRALIANS by 179 runs (see Australian tour section).

At Cheltenham, July 11–14. ESSEX drew with GLOUCESTERSHIRE.

ESSEX v HAMPSHIRE

At Chelmsford, July 19–22. Hampshire won by two runs. Hampshire 19pts, Essex 3pts. Toss: Hampshire.

Two enterprising declarations set up a wonderful finale to make up for the loss of the second day. Mercifully, neither side had to resort to joke bowling, and Essex were eventually set 360 in more than four sessions on a true pitch, which still had some carry for the faster bowlers. All the top six got in, but no one could go on to the significant contribution needed – until the diminutive wicketkeeper Wheater arrived with 161 required and five wickets left, and set about the task with gusto. He put on 68 for the eighth wicket with Harbhajan Singh, but Essex still needed 43 when the ninth fell. Wheater, playing because James Foster was absent for personal reasons, made 40 of them, including successive sixes off Balcombe, while Craddock remained solid but scoreless. Finally, though, attempting to clear the ropes for the fifth time to end the match and bring up his own century, Wheater was caught at long-on. McKenzie batted throughout the first day before he was seventh out when play resumed on the third, and Hampshire's first innings was ended by Harbhajan, whose celebrations at striking for the first time in his 44th over in an Essex sweater were understandable.

Close of play: first day, Hampshire 303-6 (McKenzie 134, Mascarenhas 7); second day, no play; third day, Essex 102-2 (Godleman 37, Pettini 16).

Hampshire

N. D. McKenzie c Wheater b Masters	139	– not out	27
*J. H. K. Adams c Wheater b Napier	2	– not out	23
B. M. Shafayat lbw b ten Doeschate	31		
S. M. Katich c Wheater b ten Doeschate	5		
L. A. Dawson c Napier b Masters	24		
S. M. Ervine b Masters	55		
†M. D. Bates c Wheater b Napier	27		
A. D. Mascarenhas b Napier	7		
D. J. Balcombe b Napier	1		
D. R. Briggs c Smith b Harbhajan Singh	7		
J. A. Tomlinson not out	6		
B 14, l-b 5	19	L-b 3, w 1	4
1/8 (2) 2/64 (3) 3/70 (4) 4/106 (5) 5/216 (6) 6/288 (7) 7/308 (1) 8/308 (8) 9/313 (9) 10/323 (10) (106.3 overs)	323	(no wkt dec, 14.5 overs)	54

Masters 29–10–55–3; Napier 20–4–62–4; Smith 11–1–43–0; Harbhajan Singh 30.3–5–76–1; ten Doeschate 9–0–48–2; Craddock 5–0–17–0; Westley 2–1–3–0. *Second innings*—Smith 3–0–6–0; Napier 2–1–9–0; ten Doeschate 1–0–15–0; Craddock 4.5–2–6–0; Westley 4–0–15–0.

Essex

B. A. Godleman not out	6	– c Bates b Mascarenhas	40
J. C. Mickleburgh not out	11	– b Tomlinson	18
T. Westley (did not bat)		– lbw b Balcombe	26
*M. L. Pettini (did not bat)		– c Dawson b Mascarenhas	25
R. N. ten Doeschate (did not bat)		– c McKenzie b Tomlinson	42
G. M. Smith (did not bat)		– c Adams b Tomlinson	42
†A. J. Wheater (did not bat)		– c Ervine b Tomlinson	98
G. R. Napier (did not bat)		– c Adams b Tomlinson	3
Harbhajan Singh (did not bat)		– st Bates b Briggs	40
D. D. Masters (did not bat)		– lbw b Briggs	6
T. R. Craddock (did not bat)		– not out	0
L-b 1	1	B 7, l-b 8, w 2	17
(no wkt dec, 18 overs)	18	1/25 (2) 2/60 (3) 3/113 (4) 4/132 (1) 5/199 (6) 6/210 (5) 7/222 (8) 8/290 (9) 9/317 (10) 10/357 (7) (123.5 overs)	357

Tomlinson 6–2–10–0; Balcombe 7–6–2–0; Mascarenhas 3–2–1–0; Briggs 2–1–4–0. *Second innings*—Tomlinson 26.5–3–86–5; Balcombe 29–6–80–1; Mascarenhas 31–12–76–2; Ervine 4–0–15–0; Briggs 29–9–79–2; Dawson 4–2–6–0.

Umpires: M. R. Benson and S. A. Garratt.

ESSEX v LEICESTERSHIRE

At Chelmsford, August 1–4. Drawn. Essex 10pts, Leicestershire 7pts. Toss: Essex.

This was another match ruined by the weather, which allowed only six overs on the final day after slicing the first in half. It was almost five and a half hours before Essex lost a wicket, Mickleburgh eventually run out for 126 after he and Westley had put on 248. Full of slick driving on both sides of the wicket and sharp running, it was Essex's first double-century opening stand in eight years, and their sixth-highest overall. Later, Pettini and ten Doeschate raced past 50, adding 120 at six an over to set up a declaration towards the end of the second day. Essex's best hope of victory, given the forecast, was to make Leicestershire follow on. Masters took two quick wickets, and later removed Sarwan cheaply too, but Thornely settled in to put on 178 with Boyce. Masters eventually dismissed them both, and finished with seven wickets. It was the sixth time in eight matches he had taken at least five in an innings against his former county. But the rain returned before Essex had a chance to build on their lead.

Close of play: first day, Essex 161-0 (Westley 75, Mickleburgh 81); second day, Leicestershire 32-2 (Thornely 5, Sarwan 7); third day, Leicestershire 336-9 (Thakor 53, Hoggard 16).

Essex

T. Westley lbw b White	125
J. C. Mickleburgh run out	126
O. A. Shah lbw b Henderson	36
M. L. Pettini not out	72
R. N. ten Doeschate not out	63
L-b 8, n-b 4	12
1/248 (2) 2/272 (1) 3/314 (3) (3 wkts dec, 124 overs) 110 overs: 355-3	434

*†J. S. Foster, A. J. Wheater, G. R. Napier, Harbhajan Singh, D. D. Masters and M. A. Chambers did not bat.

Hoggard 24–4–62–0; Buck 23–3–84–0; White 22–2–70–1; Thakor 9–1–44–0; Henderson 35–3–128–1; Sarwan 3–0–16–0; Thornely 8–0–22–0.

Leicestershire

G. P. Smith c Mickleburgh b Masters 5
M. A. Thornely c Westley b Masters. 115
E. J. H. Eckersley c ten Doeschate b Masters 2
R. R. Sarwan c Harbhajan Singh b Masters 21
M. A. G. Boyce lbw b Masters 77
S. J. Thakor not out 62
W. A. White c Harbhajan Singh b Chambers 5
†P. G. Dixey c ten Doeschate b Harbhajan Singh . 4
C. W. Henderson c Harbhajan Singh b Masters . 4
N. L. Buck lbw b Napier 7
*M. J. Hoggard c Harbhajan Singh b Masters 28
B 12, l-b 10, w 1, n-b 6 29

1/6 (1) 2/8 (3) 3/63 (4) (115.5 overs) 359
4/241 (5) 5/248 (2)
6/263 (7) 7/280 (8) 8/285 (9)
9/303 (10) 10/359 (11) 110 overs: 336-9

Masters 26.5–11–60–7; Napier 15–6–35–1; Chambers 17–5–61–1; Harbhajan Singh 37–7–96–1; ten Doeschate 8–0–31–0; Westley 12–1–54–0.

Umpires: N. L. Bainton and S. J. O'Shaughnessy.

At Canterbury, August 8–10. ESSEX beat KENT by seven wickets.

ESSEX v GLAMORGAN

At Colchester, August 15–18. Drawn. Essex 10pts, Glamorgan 9pts. Toss: Glamorgan.

A benign pitch at Castle Park led to a high-scoring draw, which did little for Essex's fading promotion hopes. First to cash in properly was Walters, who made the most of Masters's absence through a side strain to score his fifth first-class hundred. Wagg hit a half-century to boost Glamorgan to 438, but their bowlers also struggled for penetration. Westley continued his prosperous form, extending a fifth century of his own to a career-best 185 and sharing stands of 179 with Mickleburgh and an entertaining 191 with Shah. Foster's declaration, 82 ahead, arguably came too late, with only six overs left on the third evening. The fourth day was played out to a musical background provided by a festival for the local Filipino community, but Essex failed to add to the party atmosphere. Harbhajan Singh offered some early hope, but a dogged partnership of 180 in 53 overs between Wright and Allenby, helped by some curiously negative field placings, eased Glamorgan to safety.

Close of play: first day, Glamorgan 242-3 (Walters 129, Wright 0); second day, Essex 165-0 (Westley 90, Mickleburgh 72); third day, Glamorgan 16-0 (Bragg 11, James 5).

Glamorgan

W. D. Bragg b Napier	54	– c Foster b Harbhajan Singh	23
N. A. James c Mickleburgh b Chambers	14	– lbw b Harbhajan Singh	32
S. J. Walters c ten Doeschate b Harbhajan Singh	159	– c Foster b Harbhajan Singh	1
M. J. North c Harbhajan Singh b Napier	24	– b Napier	4
B. J. Wright c Wheater b Harbhajan Singh	47	– c Harbhajan Singh b Willoughby	83
J. Allenby c Foster b Napier	5	– not out	103
*†M. A. Wallace c Foster b Harbhajan Singh	36	– (8) not out	7
G. G. Wagg c Westley b Chambers	54	– (7) c Mickleburgh b Willoughby	1
R. D. B. Croft c Harbhajan Singh b Willoughby	16		
D. A. Cosker c ten Doeschate b Harbhajan Singh	4		
H. T. Waters not out	0		
B 2, l-b 17, n-b 6	25	L-b 4, n-b 2	6
1/26 (2) 2/133 (1) 3/236 (4) (115.3 overs)	438	1/48 (1) (6 wkts, 82 overs)	260
4/316 (5) 5/321 (6) 6/349 (3) 7/392 (7)		2/50 (3) 3/55 (4)	
8/417 (9) 9/422 (10) 10/438 (8) 110 overs: 403-7		4/63 (2) 5/243 (5) 6/245 (7)	

Willoughby 23–3–89–1; Chambers 15.3–2–69–2; Napier 29–4–124–3; Harbhajan Singh 35–5–91–4; ten Doeschate 8–1–34–0; Westley 5–1–12–0. *Second innings*—Harbhajan Singh 30–9–62–3; Napier 11–1–38–1; Willoughby 16–2–66–2; Chambers 11–2–36–0; Westley 11–2–38–0; ten Doeschate 3–0–16–0.

Essex

T. Westley lbw b Croft 185
J. C. Mickleburgh c Wallace b Waters 74
O. A. Shah c Allenby b Wagg 138
M. L. Pettini c Bragg b Croft. 3
R. N. ten Doeschate lbw b Wagg 18
*†J. S. Foster c Cosker b Waters 27
A. J. Wheater st Wallace b Croft. 17
G. R. Napier c Waters b Croft. 23
Harbhajan Singh st Wallace b Croft 13
M. A. Chambers not out 0
C. M. Willoughby not out 0

B 5, l-b 5, n-b 12 22

1/179 (2) (9 wkts dec, 130.5 overs) 520
2/370 (1) 3/386 (4)
4/421 (3) 5/427 (5) 6/460 (7) 7/500 (6)
8/512 (8) 9/520 (9) 110 overs: 401-3

Waters 24–7–61–2; Wagg 22–1–117–2; Cosker 18–3–76–0; Allenby 24–6–84–0; Croft 30.5–0–135–5; North 8–1–25–0; Bragg 4–0–12–0.

Umpires: M. R. Benson and M. J. Saggers.

At Derby, August 28–31. ESSEX drew with DERBYSHIRE.

At Southampton, September 4–7. ESSEX beat HAMPSHIRE by 122 runs.

ESSEX v YORKSHIRE

At Chelmsford, September 11–14. Yorkshire won by 239 runs. Yorkshire 22pts, Essex 3pts. Toss: Yorkshire.

Essex were already contemplating another season in the second division, but Yorkshire knew that 19 points would guarantee them a return to the top flight, while results elsewhere could even give them the title. In the event they had to settle for second place, but confirmed their worthiness for promotion with a clinical display. Lyth's forthright 67 set the tone, and later an eighth-wicket partnership of 60 pushed Yorkshire to a total which, surprisingly, proved almost enough to enforce the follow-on. Essex avoided it thanks only to a last-ditch stand of 29 by Craddock and Mills, both born in Yorkshire. It mattered not. Despite Napier's impressive variations of pace and length, which brought him nine wickets in the match, Lyth offered disciplined graft, while McGrath's 68 and a second fifty from 21-year-old Azeem Rafiq at No. 8 swelled the lead. Essex eventually needed an improbable 388, which looked even less likely when two quick wickets went down before the third-day close. Only Shah averted total embarrassment next day as Rafiq capped a splendid all-round match by taking a maiden five-for with his off-spin.

Close of play: first day, Yorkshire 284-8 (Azeem Rafiq 49); second day, Yorkshire 44-3 (Lyth 26, Ballance 1); third day, Essex 28-2 (Shah 4, Craddock 4).

Yorkshire

A. Lyth c Foster b Napier	67	– c Mickleburgh b Westley	51
J. E. Root lbw b Napier	0	– c Pettini b Napier	2
P. A. Jaques c Mills b Napier	38	– c Shah b Napier	6
*A. W. Gale c Mills b Westley	10	– c Pettini b Napier	5
G. S. Ballance c Mickleburgh b Topley	30	– c Craddock b Westley	27
A. McGrath c Foster b Topley	18	– c Wheater b Napier	68
†A. J. Hodd run out	22	– c Foster b Craddock	1
Azeem Rafiq c Foster b Napier	53	– not out	75
R. J. Sidebottom c and b Craddock	37	– (10) not out	9
S. A. Patterson b Napier	17	– (9) b Mills	0
M. A. Ashraf not out	6		
B 3, l-b 6, n-b 5	14	L-b 7, w 1	8

1/4 (2) 2/86 (1) 3/113 (3) (107.2 overs) 312
4/134 (4) 5/165 (5) 6/166 (6)
7/224 (7) 8/284 (9) 9/299 (8) 10/312 (10)

1/14 (2) (8 wkts dec, 97 overs) 252
2/30 (3) 3/36 (4)
4/95 (1) 5/108 (5)
6/111 (7) 7/221 (6) 8/222 (9)

Topley 25–6–85–2; Napier 27.2–3–65–5; Craddock 11–1–37–1; Mills 17–3–44–0; Westley 22–6–50–1; ten Doeschate 5–0–22–0. *Second innings*—Topley 18–4–41–0; Napier 21–6–54–4; ten Doeschate 6–1–16–0; Mills 15–0–52–1; Westley 16–6–37–2; Craddock 21–6–45–1.

Essex

T. Westley lbw b Azeem Rafiq	18	– c Hodd b Patterson	18
J. C. Mickleburgh b Patterson	4	– c Jaques b Azeem Rafiq	2
O. A. Shah c Lyth b Azeem Rafiq	6	– not out	71
M. L. Pettini lbw b Ashraf	1	– (5) c Ballance b Azeem Rafiq	17
R. N. ten Doeschate c Ballance b Azeem Rafiq	62	– (6) c Gale b Ashraf	1
*†J. S. Foster lbw b Patterson	16	– (7) c Jaques b Azeem Rafiq	10
A. J. Wheater c Gale b Sidebottom	16	– (8) c Hodd b Azeem Rafiq	19
G. R. Napier c Lyth b Ashraf	20	– (9) c Jaques b Azeem Rafiq	0
T. R. Craddock c Lyth b Ashraf	8	– (4) c Jaques b Patterson	5
R. J. W. Topley lbw b Ashraf	0	– c Lyth b Patterson	0
T. S. Mills not out	20	– b Patterson	0
B 2, n-b 4	6	L-b 5	5
1/10 (2) 2/25 (1) 3/26 (4) 4/34 (3) 5/97 (6) 6/119 (7) 7/147 (5) 8/148 (8) 9/148 (10) 10/177 (9) (58.5 overs)	177	1/8 (2) 2/22 (1) 3/34 (4) 4/74 (5) 5/75 (6) 6/109 (7) 7/135 (8) 8/135 (9) 9/148 (10) 10/148 (11) (51.5 overs)	148

Sidebottom 13–2–32–1; Patterson 15–2–29–2; Ashraf 11.5–3–36–4; Azeem Rafiq 15–4–65–3; McGrath 4–1–13–0. *Second innings*—Patterson 14.5–2–34–4; Sidebottom 8–3–12–0; Azeem Rafiq 17–3–50–5; Ashraf 11–2–39–1; Root 1–0–8–0.

Umpires: M. J. D. Bodenham and P. Willey.

GLAMORGAN

Tame Dragons fired

EDWARD BEVAN

Glamorgan endured another miserable season. Only a late rally lifted them to sixth in the second division of the Championship, with two fewer wins than in 2011, and they continued their poor one-day form. Jim Allenby, the Player of the Year, admitted: "We were well short of what is expected of us and what we should be doing." Only Scotland finished below them in their CB40 group and, with the weather washing out five of their Twenty20 games, they made sure of non-qualification by winning only two of the other five.

The promised resurgence following the management upheaval at the end of the 2010 campaign has yet to materialise, and reality intruded twice: Robert Croft retired after 24 seasons' service; and the promising young seamer James Harris – who had been with the club since he was 14 – invoked a clause in his contract that allowed him to leave if Glamorgan were not in the first division. He subsequently signed for Middlesex.

There had been another administrative reshuffle before the season, with Colin Metson (previously managing director of cricket) moving to the Cricket Board of Wales, and coach Matthew Mott restyled as head of elite performance. Midway through the season Mott applied for the post of New Zealand's coach; making the short list; even though he did not get the job, it was an unsettling development for the county. Croft has joined the coaching staff, but there is still a need for a batting specialist to complement the work he and Steve Watkin will do with the bowlers. In January 2013, Metson was made redundant.

The dismal weather did not help. Glamorgan lost 11 full days in the Championship, including the entire game at Bristol, and all but 34 overs against Yorkshire at Colwyn Bay; more than 1,600 overs were washed away in first-class cricket alone.

In addition, several of the players were affected by the tragic death of former Glamorgan batsman Tom Maynard; some were among his closest friends. Like those at his new county Surrey, it took them time to adjust to playing cricket again.

Glamorgan had already been on the back foot, losing their first three games. They did not gain a batting point until mid-May, and had lost twice more by the halfway stage of the season. Marcus North, the overseas player, did not arrive until the sixth Championship match because of injury but, although he made an immediate impact in the four-day game, he was anonymous in both limited-overs competitions. The first man to play first-class cricket for six counties, North scored a century and five fifties in just 13 Championship innings – but he also raised hackles among the membership by rejoining Western Australia with two games remaining. He did, however, confirm his availability for the whole of 2013, and was made limited-overs captain.

Jim Allenby

Too often Glamorgan struggled to overcome disappointing first-innings batting performances. Gareth Rees, who at the start of the season had opened for MCC against the champions Lancashire in Abu Dhabi in March, managed just one half-century from 18 innings, and was dropped. North and Allenby were the only two specialist batsmen to average over 40, although Will Bragg eventually found some form after his promotion to open; Stewart Walters was the leading scorer. A mere 28 batting points, compared to 44 the previous summer, reflected the general shortage of runs. Murray Goodwin, who turned 40 at the end of 2012, was signed from Sussex.

Croft appeared in only six Championship matches, but played a significant part in the victories over Gloucestershire and Kent, and ended his final season with the best bowling average in the second division. Dean Cosker, supposedly the frontline spinner, struggled throughout: his 11 wickets cost nearly 86 apiece, and he was dropped for the last game. Croft, arguably Glamorgan's best-ever player, having taken 1,055 wickets for them and scored 12,027 runs, will be succeeded by Cardiff University student Andrew Salter, 19, an off-spinner from Pembrokeshire, who did well in his two one-day appearances.

A promising seam department will be strengthened in 2013 by the addition of Michael Hogan, signed from Western Australia but in possession of a British passport. Huw Waters struck with the first two balls of the Championship season, and was capped after taking 39 first-class wickets at modest cost. John Glover and Mike Reed showed potential: Reed, 6ft 7in tall and with an action not unlike Steve Harmison's, is distinctly lively and an awkward proposition on helpful pitches. But Graham Wagg broke a foot early on, and was absent for three months, including the entire Twenty20 campaign. His combative approach was missed.

Rain also spoiled the international highlight of the summer, allowing only 5.3 overs in the one-dayer against South Africa, although 24 hours later Cardiff did house a capacity crowd for its first Twenty20 finals day.

Glamorgan reported a deficit of £1.7m for 2011, not helped by the £1.2m losses sustained during the rain-affected Test against Sri Lanka. However, the future looks rosier: the ECB have reduced the staging fees, and Cardiff has been allocated 15 days of international cricket over the next four years. Glamorgan also announced that terms had been agreed with existing lenders and new investors for a financial restructuring, promising a firmer footing.

In 2012, Glamorgan had rebranded themselves the Welsh Dragons for limited-overs cricket, supposedly to tap into a national identity. But it didn't catch on, and the county reverted to plain old Glamorgan at the end of the season, with the daffodil reinstated as the club's emblem.

Championship attendance: 12,279.

GLAMORGAN RESULTS

All first-class matches – Played 16: Won 4, Lost 6, Drawn 6. Abandoned 1.
County Championship matches – Played 15: Won 3, Lost 6, Drawn 6. Abandoned 1.

LV= County Championship, 6th in Division 2;
Friends Life t20, 5th in Midlands/Wales/West Division; Clydesdale Bank 40, 6th in Group B.

COUNTY CHAMPIONSHIP AVERAGES, BATTING AND FIELDING

Cap		*M*	*I*	*NO*	*R*	*HS*	*100*	*50*	*Avge*	*Ct/St*
2012	H. T. Waters†	12	14	12	106	39	0	0	53.00	5
	M. J. North§	9	13	0	577	116	1	5	44.38	2
2010	J. Allenby	14	21	4	712	125*	2	3	41.88	11
	S. J. Walters	13	21	1	750	159	1	6	37.50	12
2003	M. A. Wallace†	15	23	4	653	118	2	1	34.36	37/4
2011	B. J. Wright	15	25	2	623	104	1	1	27.08	3
	W. D. Bragg†	15	25	0	648	92	0	5	25.92	8
2009	G. P. Rees†	11	18	0	358	66	0	1	19.88	9
	J. C. Glover†	7	10	3	125	55	0	1	17.85	3
2000	D. A. Cosker	14	17	3	243	49*	0	0	17.35	7
	G. G. Wagg	8	12	0	203	54	0	1	16.91	3
	N. A. James	8	15	0	234	38	0	0	15.60	3
1992	R. D. B. Croft†	6	8	1	79	23	0	0	11.28	2
	M. C. Henriques§	4	7	0	36	16	0	0	5.14	0
	D. L. Lloyd†	2	4	1	11	11*	0	0	3.66	0
	M. T. Reed	4	7	2	18	5*	0	0	3.60	0

Also batted: J. A. R. Harris† (cap 2010) (4 matches) 48, 6, 2; S. P. Jones† (cap 2002) (1 match) 4, 1 (1 ct); W. T. Owen† (3 matches) 0, 7, 13* (2 ct).

† Born in Wales. § Official overseas player. Glamorgan's capping system is based on a player's number of appearances.

BOWLING

	Style	*O*	*M*	*R*	*W*	*BB*	*5I*	*Avge*
R. D. B. Croft	OB	123.2	20	367	21	5-31	2	17.47
H. T. Waters	RFM	280.2	67	770	35	7-53	2	22.00
M. C. Henriques	RFM	85	16	289	13	4-54	0	22.23
G. G. Wagg	SLA/LM	225.3	37	712	31	6-44	1	22.96
J. Allenby	RM	340.3	75	948	38	4-39	0	24.94
J. C. Glover	RM	176.4	40	585	19	4-76	0	30.78
J. A. R. Harris	RFM	129	19	402	10	5-118	1	40.20
D. A. Cosker	SLA	337.3	72	945	11	3-59	0	85.90

Also bowled: W. D. Bragg (SLA) 26.1–2–107–1; N. A. James (SLA) 17–0–68–0; S. P. Jones (RFM) 22–2–70–2; M. J. North (OB) 73–8–223–7; W. T. Owen (RFM) 56.2–5–238–7; M. T. Reed (RFM) 88–10–310–8; G. P. Rees (LM) 4.1–0–22–0; S. J. Walters (RM) 1–0–6–0; B. J. Wright (RM) 13–2–30–0.

LEADING CB40 AVERAGES (100 runs/4 wickets)

Batting	*Runs*	*HS*	*Avge*	*SR*	*Ct/St*
C. B. Cooke	249	137*	31.12	102.04	1
S. J. Walters	183	68	26.14	74.08	4
G. P. Rees	194	60*	24.25	67.12	2
M. A. Wallace	212	105	23.55	95.49	8/2
J. Allenby	130	39*	21.66	73.86	4
M. J. North	125	59	20.83	65.78	5

Bowling	*W*	*BB*	*Avge*	*ER*
J. Allenby	12	3-16	15.25	3.67
W. T. Owen	4	2-38	20.00	4.57
G. G. Wagg	10	4-45	22.90	6.73
D. A. Cosker	9	3-26	32.77	4.33
J. C. Glover	7	3-34	32.85	6.38
S. P. Jones	13	4-23	34.07	6.23

LEADING FLT20 AVERAGES (70 runs/13 overs)

Batting	*Runs*	*HS*	*Avge*	*SR*	*Ct*
S. E. Marsh	209	85	52.25	**129.81**	3
S. J. Walters	75	40*	–	**129.31**	4
J. Allenby	94	33	23.50	**125.33**	0
M. van Jaarsveld	87	36	21.75	**119.17**	0

Bowling	*W*	*BB*	*Avge*	*ER*
S. P. Jones	7	3-29	18.28	**6.73**
R. D. B. Croft	4	2-27	32.75	**7.27**
D. A. Cosker	3	2-23	34.66	**7.89**
J. Allenby	3	1-1	42.00	**8.21**
J. A. R. Harris	4	2-48	36.50	**9.73**

FIRST-CLASS COUNTY RECORDS

Highest score for	309*	S. P. James v Sussex at Colwyn Bay	2000
Highest score against	322*	M. B. Loye (Northamptonshire) at Northampton	1998
Leading run-scorer	34,056	A. Jones (avge 33.03)	1957–1983
Best bowling for	10-51	J. Mercer v Worcestershire at Worcester	1936
Best bowling against	10-18	G. Geary (Leicestershire) at Pontypridd	1929
Leading wicket-taker	2,174	D. J. Shepherd (avge 20.95)	1950–1972
Highest total for	718-3 dec	v Sussex at Colwyn Bay	2000
Highest total against	712	by Northamptonshire at Northampton	1998
Lowest total for	22	v Lancashire at Liverpool	1924
Lowest total against	33	by Leicestershire at Ebbw Vale	1965

LIST A COUNTY RECORDS

Highest score for	162*	I. V. A. Richards v Oxfordshire at Swansea	1993
Highest score against	268	A. D. Brown (Surrey) at The Oval	2002
Leading run-scorer	12,278	M. P. Maynard (avge 37.66)	1985–2005
Best bowling for	7-16	S. D. Thomas v Surrey at Swansea	1998
Best bowling against	7-30	M. P. Bicknell (Surrey) at The Oval	1999
Leading wicket-taker	**356**	**R. D. B. Croft (avge 31.96)**	**1989–2012**
Highest total for	429	v Surrey at The Oval	2002
Highest total against	438-5	by Surrey at The Oval	2002
Lowest total for	42	v Derbyshire at Swansea	1979
Lowest total against	59	by Combined Universities at Cambridge	1983
	59	by Sussex at Hove	1996

TWENTY20 COUNTY RECORDS

Highest score for	116*	I. J. Thomas v Somerset at Taunton	2004
Highest score against	117	M. J. Prior (Sussex) at Hove	2010
Leading run-scorer	991	M. J. Cosgrove (avge 27.52)	2009–2011
Best bowling for	5-16	R. E. Watkins v Gloucestershire at Cardiff	2009
Best bowling against	6-5	A. V. Suppiah (Somerset) at Cardiff	2011
Leading wicket-taker	**87**	**R. D. B. Croft (avge 23.16)**	**2003–2012**
Highest total for	206-6	v Somerset at Taunton	2006
Highest total against	239-5	by Sussex at Hove	2010
Lowest total for	94-9	v Essex at Cardiff	2010
Lowest total against	81	by Gloucestershire at Bristol	2011

ADDRESS

Swalec Stadium, Sophia Gardens, Cardiff CF11 9XR (029 2040 9380; **email** info@glamorgancricket.co.uk). **Website** www.glamorgancricket.com

OFFICIALS

Captain M. A. Wallace (Championship)
M. J. North (limited-overs)
Head of elite performance M. P. Mott
Pathway manager R. V. Almond
President: F. D. Morgan

Chairman B. J. O'Brien
Chief executive A. Hamer
Head groundsman K. W. Exton
Scorer/archivist A. K. Hignell

At Oxford, March 31–April 2. GLAMORGAN beat OXFORD MCCU by 253 runs.

At Leicester, April 5–7. GLAMORGAN lost to LEICESTERSHIRE by 52 runs.

GLAMORGAN v DERBYSHIRE

At Cardiff, April 12–14. Derbyshire won by 130 runs. Derbyshire 19pts, Glamorgan 3pts. Toss: Derbyshire. First-class debut: M. T. Reed.

For the second successive match Glamorgan lost inside three days – and had failed to reach 200 in all four innings, a problem discussed at length at a team meeting after the game. They had needed 233 to win on a pitch that suited the seamers, and were comfortably placed at 59 without loss shortly after lunch on the third day – only to collapse alarmingly. All ten wickets tumbled for 43, including a spell of six for one in 19 balls. It had all started so well when Wagg recorded his best figures for his new county, against his old one, as Derbyshire were restricted to a modest total. But Glamorgan were undone in both innings by the medium-pace of Clare, who completed a stunning match haul of 11 for 57. Clare's batting also helped rescue Derbyshire after they collapsed to 37 for five in the second innings: his robust 43, allied to a more restrained half-century from Wainwright which spanned almost four hours, set up a challenging target.

Close of play: first day, Glamorgan 37-4 (Henriques 4, Cosker 0); second day, Derbyshire 152-6 (Wainwright 30, Clare 40).

Derbyshire

First innings		Second innings	
M. J. Guptill c Cosker b Wagg	4	– lbw b Wagg	0
P. M. Borrington lbw b Wagg	2	– c Wallace b Henriques	9
*W. L. Madsen lbw b Wagg	10	– c Wallace b Henriques	10
W. J. Durston c Wallace b Wagg	18	– lbw b Henriques	15
D. J. Redfern lbw b Allenby	7	– lbw b Allenby	0
R. A. Whiteley b Wagg	28	– run out	39
D. J. Wainwright lbw b Allenby	21	– not out	51
J. L. Clare c Wallace b Wagg	21	– lbw b Allenby	43
†T. Poynton not out	4	– c Wallace b Allenby	0
A. P. Palladino c Walters b Henriques	7	– c Wallace b Henriques	21
M. H. A. Footitt lbw b Henriques	0	– b Wagg	0
B 1, l-b 3, n-b 4	8	L-b 9	9
1/4 (1) 2/16 (3) 3/35 (2) 4/38 (4) 5/44 (5) 6/92 (7) 7/112 (6) 8/121 (8) 9/130 (10) 10/130 (11) (50 overs)	130	1/0 (1) 2/17 (3) 3/30 (2) 4/37 (4) 5/37 (5) 6/97 (6) 7/155 (8) 8/155 (9) 9/196 (10) 10/197 (11) (82.5 overs)	197

Wagg 18–4–44–6; Henriques 11–1–40–2; Allenby 15–7–29–2; Croft 3–0–8–0; Reed 3–0–5–0. *Second innings*—Wagg 14.5–5–21–2; Henriques 24–8–54–4; Allenby 18–5–45–3; Reed 14–4–33–0; Croft 6–3–8–0; Cosker 6–1–27–0.

Glamorgan

G. P. Rees b Palladino	1	– lbw b Clare	41
S. J. Walters b Footitt	9	– b Clare	30
W. D. Bragg lbw b Palladino	8	– c Guptill b Clare	0
B. J. Wright lbw b Clare	8	– c Madsen b Palladino	7
M. C. Henriques b Palladino	16	– lbw b Clare	6
D. A. Cosker b Clare	14	– (9) not out	7
J. Allenby lbw b Clare	14	– (6) lbw b Palladino	1
*†M. A. Wallace b Clare	0	– (7) c Footitt b Clare	0
G. G. Wagg c and b Clare	2	– (8) c Poynton b Clare	0
R. D. B. Croft c Durston b Wainwright	12	– lbw b Palladino	0
M. T. Reed not out	1	– run out	0
L-b 2, n-b 8	10	B 6, l-b 2, n-b 2	10
1/8 (1) 2/16 (2) 3/22 (3) 4/34 (4) (36.1 overs) 5/58 (5) 6/64 (6) 7/64 (8) 8/70 (9) 9/85 (7) 10/95 (10)	95	1/59 (1) 2/59 (3) (31.3 overs) 3/86 (2) 4/92 (5) 5/92 (4) 6/93 (7) 7/93 (8) 8/93 (6) 9/93 (10) 10/102 (11)	102

Palladino 15–4–34–3; Footitt 12–2–39–1; Clare 8–4–17–5; Wainwright 1.1–0–3–1. *Second innings*—Palladino 10–4–29–3; Footitt 8–2–21–0; Clare 12.3–1–40–6; Wainwright 1–0–4–0.

Umpires: M. R. Benson and R. T. Robinson.

GLAMORGAN v HAMPSHIRE

At Cardiff, April 19–22. Hampshire won by two wickets. Hampshire 19pts, Glamorgan 3pts. Toss: Glamorgan.

Another feeble first-innings batting performance contributed to Glamorgan's third successive Championship defeat, but not before they had put up a fight. Balcombe took his haul from seven Championship matches – including five for Kent in 2011 – to 51. Five of them came as Glamorgan dipped to 103 for nine, at which point Wallace declared, reasoning that "with 12 overs remaining at the end of the day we might have picked up a couple of wickets". They did dismiss Adams before the close and, with Waters returning career-best figures next day, Hampshire's lead was restricted to 53. Walters and Wright, who went on to his fifth century, finally found some batting form in Glamorgan's second innings, but a depressingly familiar collapse – the last six wickets fell for only 46 – meant Hampshire's target was less imposing than had seemed likely. They entered the final day needing 92 with six wickets in hand, but rain delayed the start until 4.15. An attacking innings from Ervine took them close, before Riazuddin struck the winning runs from the penultimate ball of the match.

Close of play: first day, Hampshire 29-1 (Dawson 18, Carberry 6); second day, Glamorgan 73-3 (Walters 12, Wright 5); third day, Hampshire 112-4 (Ervine 37, Bates 13).

Glamorgan

G. P. Rees lbw b Wood	12	– b Balcombe	11
S. J. Walters c Dawson b Balcombe	4	– (4) c Bates b Ervine	54
W. D. Bragg c Dawson b Wood	45	– lbw b Riazuddin	10
N. A. James c Bates b Riazuddin	7	– (2) b Ervine	30
B. J. Wright c Vince b Briggs	1	– c Vince b Briggs	104
J. Allenby lbw b Balcombe	6	– c Bates b Riazuddin	11
M. C. Henriques lbw b Balcombe	8	– b Riazuddin	3
*†M. A. Wallace not out	5	– c Vince b Riazuddin	1
G. G. Wagg c Adams b Balcombe	4	– c Balcombe b Riazuddin	1
D. A. Cosker c Bates b Balcombe	0	– b Balcombe	4
H. T. Waters not out	3	– not out	0
L-b 8	8	B 10, l-b 6, w 3, n-b 8	27
1/10 (2) 2/22 (1) (9 wkts dec, 42.3 overs) 3/41 (4) 4/55 (5) 5/68 (6) 6/87 (3) 7/87 (7) 8/95 (9) 9/95 (10)	103	1/18 (1) 2/34 (3) (79.3 overs) 3/64 (2) 4/168 (4) 5/210 (6) 6/222 (7) 7/227 (8) 8/237 (9) 9/256 (5) 10/256 (10)	256

Wood 12.3–4–25–2; Balcombe 14–6–33–5; Riazuddin 7–0–20–1; Ervine 2–0–9–0; Briggs 7–2–8–1. *Second innings*—Wood 15–5–32–0; Balcombe 17.3–4–64–2; Riazuddin 18–3–61–5; Ervine 12–7–27–2; Briggs 17–1–56–1.

Hampshire

*J. H. K. Adams c Wallace b Waters	3	– c Wallace b Wagg	0
L. A. Dawson lbw b Waters	32	– lbw b Wagg	1
M. A. Carberry c Waters b Henriques	27	– (7) b Waters	13
S. M. Katich lbw b Henriques	9	– (3) lbw b Allenby	20
J. M. Vince c Wallace b Waters	26	– (4) lbw b Henriques	28
S. M. Ervine lbw b Waters	9	– (5) c Wallace b Allenby	75
†M. D. Bates c Wallace b Waters	12	– (6) lbw b Waters	13
C. P. Wood lbw b Allenby	3	– c Bragg b Wagg	24
H. Riazuddin c Rees b Waters	11	– not out	12
D. J. Balcombe not out	10	– not out	3
D. R. Briggs c Wright b Waters	9		
L-b 2, w 1, n-b 2	5	B 4, l-b 1, n-b 10	15
1/9 (1) 2/56 (2) 3/70 (4) 4/83 (3) (55.3 overs)	156	1/0 (1) 2/3 (2) (8 wkts, 45.5 overs)	204
5/108 (6) 6/109 (5) 7/112 (8)		3/43 (3) 4/68 (4)	
8/132 (7) 9/137 (9) 10/156 (11)		5/112 (6) 6/134 (7) 7/173 (8) 8/190 (5)	

Wagg 11–0–36–0; Waters 18.3–5–53–7; Henriques 10–2–28–2; Cosker 3–1–8–0; Allenby 13–4–29–1. *Second innings*—Wagg 13–4–43–3; Waters 11–3–45–2; Allenby 14.5–0–62–2; Henriques 6–0–49–1; Cosker 1–1–0–0.

Umpires: N. G. B. Cook and G. Sharp.

At Bristol, April 26–29. GLOUCESTERSHIRE v GLAMORGAN. Abandoned.

GLAMORGAN v ESSEX

At Cardiff, May 2–5. Drawn. Glamorgan 6pts, Essex 8pts. Toss: Glamorgan.

Petersen, Glamorgan's captain in 2011, marked his return to Cardiff after his controversial move to Essex with a chanceless century. Cook, in his first Championship innings for a year, and Bopara both went cheaply; in between, Cosker took his 500th first-class wicket when he removed Godleman. But Petersen rescued his new county with a masterful innings, hitting 16 fours (his team-mates managed three) and a six. In a pre-match interview, Wagg had predicted he would trap his former skipper lbw, and he did – but not before Petersen had dominated a fifth-wicket partnership of 181 with Pettini. The second day was washed out and, after more time was lost to bad light, Glamorgan were eventually set 239 in 50 overs. Essex might have had a better chance of victory had Foster declared earlier, especially as Wagg was unable to bat after breaking a bone in his foot. Glamorgan never looked likely to win, slumping to 37 for four, but an obdurate partnership between Rees and Wallace enabled them to hang on until bad light stopped play eight overs early.

Close of play: first day, Glamorgan 1-0 (Rees 1, James 0); second day, no play; third day, Essex 5-0 (Godleman 1, Cook 4).

Essex

B. A. Godleman c Walters b Cosker	21	–	c Wallace b Wagg	1
A. N. Cook c Wallace b Waters	9	–	b Wagg	5
A. N. Petersen lbw b Wagg	145	–	c Wagg b Waters	4
R. S. Bopara lbw b Henriques	0	–	b Owen	10
T. Westley c Rees b Wagg	3	–	c Rees b Waters	52
M. L. Pettini c Wagg b Waters	56	–	c Rees b Wagg	2
G. M. Smith lbw b Wagg	1	–	c Bragg b Waters	36
*†J. S. Foster b Wagg	0	–	not out	26
D. D. Masters c Owen b Waters	6	–	c Wallace b Waters	13
T. S. Mills not out	3	–	c sub (J. Allenby) b Waters	3
C. M. Willoughby (did not bat)		–	not out	1
B 2, l-b 7, n-b 6	15		B 1, l-b 4, n-b 8	13
1/21 (2) 2/53 (1) (9 wkts dec, 91 overs)	259		1/6 (1) (9 wkts dec, 46 overs)	166
3/60 (4) 4/65 (5) 5/246 (6)			2/11 (3) 3/11 (2)	
6/246 (3) 7/248 (8) 8/251 (7) 9/259 (9)			4/34 (4) 5/37 (6) 6/116 (5)	
			7/119 (7) 8/147 (9) 9/165 (10)	

Waters 20–5–33–3; Wagg 21–4–61–4; Owen 13–2–61–0; Henriques 9–1–34–1; Cosker 23–4–48–1; Bragg 1–0–4–0; James 4–0–9–0. *Second innings*—Wagg 16.5–5–51–3; Waters 16–3–47–5; Owen 7–1–36–1; Cosker 4.1–0–14–0; James 2–0–13–0.

Glamorgan

G. P. Rees b Smith	31	–	c Petersen b Willoughby	33
N. A. James c Mills b Masters	18	–	c Smith b Willoughby	1
W. D. Bragg c Foster b Willoughby	14	–	c Foster b Willoughby	0
S. J. Walters c Pettini b Mills	69	–	b Willoughby	2
B. J. Wright c Cook b Smith	1	–	b Masters	12
*†M. A. Wallace lbw b Masters	13	–	not out	26
G. G. Wagg b Masters	22			
M. C. Henriques b Mills	0			
D. A. Cosker c Petersen b Mills	1			
H. T. Waters not out	1	–	(7) not out	2
W. T. Owen c Foster b Mills	0			
B 1, l-b 14, n-b 2	17		B 12, l-b 11	23
1/23 (2) 2/61 (3) 3/115 (1) (66 overs)	187		1/6 (2) 2/6 (3) (5 wkts, 42 overs)	99
4/119 (5) 5/158 (6) 6/170 (4) 7/176 (8)			3/14 (4) 4/37 (5)	
8/186 (9) 9/186 (7) 10/187 (11)			5/79 (1)	

Masters 25–7–68–3; Willoughby 20–8–41–1; Mills 9–3–25–4; Smith 11–4–36–2; Bopara 1–0–2–0. *Second innings*—Masters 15–5–25–1; Willoughby 14–4–33–4; Mills 6–1–9–0; Smith 7–4–9–0.

Umpires: J. H. Evans and P. J. Hartley.

At Derby, May 16–18. GLAMORGAN lost to DERBYSHIRE by eight wickets. *Marcus North becomes the first to play first-class matches for six different counties.*

At Southampton, May 23–26. GLAMORGAN lost to HAMPSHIRE by 31 runs.

GLAMORGAN v LEICESTERSHIRE

At Cardiff, May 29–June 1. Drawn. Glamorgan 10pts, Leicestershire 6pts. Toss: Leicestershire. County debut: M. A. Thornely.

A placid pitch which offered no encouragement to the bowlers eventually prevented any prospect of a positive result: in the final two innings – during which 19 different bowlers were tried – 874 runs were scored for the loss of 11 wickets. Leicestershire managed just 199 in 96 overs on the first day, although the former Sussex batsman Michael Thornely – playing because Matt Boyce turned his ankle shortly before the start – started his trial period in fine style, missing twin centuries by only three runs. Thornely batted for 11 hours 40 minutes in all, twice improved his previous-best score of 89, and shared stands of 89 and 245 with wicketkeeper Eckersley, who was promoted to No. 3 and made his own career-best. Glamorgan scored at a faster clip, taking the lead in the 61st over: North prospered at the scene of his century for Australia in the 2009 Ashes Test, while Wallace made his first Championship hundred as captain.

Close of play: first day, Leicestershire 199-6 (Mommsen 14, White 10); second day, Glamorgan 302-5 (Allenby 10, Cosker 2); third day, Leicestershire 84-1 (Thornely 36, Eckersley 37).

Leicestershire

G. P. Smith lbw b Allenby	26	– c Wallace b Harris	10
M. A. Thornely c Allenby b Waters	97	– c Rees b Allenby	131
†E. J. H. Eckersley b Harris	41	– not out	137
*R. R. Sarwan c Wallace b Waters	3	– not out	25
J. J. Cobb b Allenby	0		
J. du Toit lbw b Cosker	5		
P. L. Mommsen b Allenby	35		
W. A. White c Waters b Cosker	26		
C. W. Henderson lbw b Allenby	11		
R. H. Joseph not out	18		
N. L. Buck b Cosker	0		
B 2, l-b 7	9	B 9, w 2, n-b 2	13
1/48 (1) 2/137 (3) 3/157 (4) 4/157 (5) 5/170 (6) 6/181 (2) 7/241 (8) 8/241 (7) 9/270 (9) 10/271 (11) (118.5 overs) 110 overs: 245-8	271	1/11 (1) 2/256 (2) (2 wkts dec, 117 overs)	316

Waters 25–8–55–2; Harris 23–3–77–1; Glover 17–7–29–0; Allenby 22–8–39–4; Cosker 30.5–10–59–3; North 1–0–3–0. *Second innings*—Waters 16–2–46–0; Harris 19–5–40–1; Allenby 14–7–15–1; Cosker 28–7–63–0; Glover 16–1–71–0; Bragg 5–1–10–0; North 7–0–26–0; Wright 8–2–17–0; Rees 3–0–13–0; Walters 1–0–6–0.

Glamorgan

G. P. Rees c Mommsen b Joseph	66
W. D. Bragg c Cobb b White	22
S. J. Walters b White	4
M. J. North c Eckersley b Henderson	116
B. J. Wright c Eckersley b Buck	44
J. Allenby lbw b White	61
D. A. Cosker lbw b White	5
*†M. A. Wallace c Mommsen b Henderson	118
J. A. R. Harris c Eckersley b Henderson	48
J. C. Glover not out	6
H. T. Waters not out	7
B 15, l-b 11, w 3, n-b 32	61
1/75 (2) 2/85 (3) 3/188 (1) 4/279 (5) 5/299 (4) 6/309 (7) 7/448 (6) 8/542 (9) 9/547 (8) (9 wkts dec, 129 overs) 110 overs: 473-7	558

Joseph 17–0–105–1; Buck 23–4–75–1; White 24–2–98–4; Thornely 9–1–36–0; du Toit 5–0–19–0; Henderson 33–4–116–3; Cobb 10–0–46–0; Mommsen 2–0–7–0; Sarwan 6–0–30–0.

Umpires: R. K. Illingworth and G. D. Lloyd.

GLAMORGAN v YORKSHIRE

At Colwyn Bay, June 6–9. Drawn. Glamorgan 3pts, Yorkshire 4pts. Toss: Glamorgan.

Only 34 overs were bowled as the weather ruined the annual festival on the North Wales coast, leaving Glamorgan without a Championship victory after nine matches. There was no play after 1.45 on the opening day, and continuous rain brought an abandonment on the fourth morning. The only highlight came when Walters struck Starc, the Australian left-arm fast bowler, for 18 in the first over after lunch, including a six on to the pavilion roof at midwicket.

Close of play: first day, Glamorgan 117-3 (Walters 37, Wright 10); second day, no play; third day, no play.

Glamorgan

G. P. Rees lbw b Starc	35
W. D. Bragg c Brophy b Starc	20
S. J. Walters not out	37
M. J. North c and b Azeem Rafiq	14
B. J. Wright not out	10
L-b 1	1
1/55 (2) 2/58 (1) 3/79 (4) (3 wkts, 34 overs)	117

J. Allenby, *†M. A. Wallace, R. D. B. Croft, D. A. Cosker, H. T. Waters and W. T. Owen did not bat.

Sidebottom 7–2–21–0; Patterson 6–1–22–0; Azeem Rafiq 12–4–29–1; Starc 8–2–39–2; Rashid 1–0–5–0.

Yorkshire

A. Lyth, J. E. Root, P. A. Jaques, *A. W. Gale, G. S. Ballance, †G. L. Brophy, A. U. Rashid, Azeem Rafiq, M. A. Starc, R. J. Sidebottom and S. A. Patterson.

Umpires: P. K. Baldwin and M. R. Benson.

At Northampton, July 14–17. GLAMORGAN beat NORTHAMPTONSHIRE by three wickets. *Glamorgan complete their first Championship win of the season in the final over.*

At Canterbury, July 19–22. GLAMORGAN drew with KENT.

GLAMORGAN v GLOUCESTERSHIRE

At Swansea, August 1–4. Glamorgan won by 26 runs. Glamorgan 20pts, Gloucestershire 3pts. Toss: Glamorgan. Championship debut: R. J. Nicol.

In his last Championship appearance on the ground where he first played at the age of nine, Croft produced a match-winning spell of four wickets in 23 balls to help Glamorgan to only their second victory of the season, and their first at home. Set 248, Gloucestershire started the final hour needing 57, before Croft broke a stubborn seventh-wicket stand of 63 between Cockbain and Taylor. He then wrapped up the match with less than nine overs to spare. Not helped by frequent showers, the pitch remained slow throughout, with predictable consequences. In their first innings, Glamorgan were languishing at 125 for nine before the last pair put on 83 to salvage a batting point. Gloucestershire also struggled, slipping to 42 for six before the last four wickets almost quadrupled the total. Glamorgan's success coincided with the 40th anniversary of the South Wales Balconiers, a group of loyal supporters who have organised the Swansea festival for many years, contributing considerably to the county's coffers.

Close of play: first day, Glamorgan 64-6 (Wright 10, Croft 4); second day, Gloucestershire 91-7 (Cockbain 20, Marshall 3); third day, Glamorgan 167-5 (Wright 31).

Glamorgan

G. P. Rees lbw b Payne	4	–	c Coughtrie b Payne	0
W. D. Bragg lbw b Payne	9	–	lbw b Taylor	13
S. J. Walters c Housego b Taylor	4	–	lbw b Nicol	56
M. J. North c Coughtrie b Taylor	0	–	c Nicol b Saxelby	42
B. J. Wright c Housego b Nicol	33	–	c Payne b Taylor	37
J. Allenby b Saxelby	25	–	c Coughtrie b Saxelby	21
*†M. A. Wallace b Nicol	0	–	c Coughtrie b Saxelby	22
R. D. B. Croft lbw b Saxelby	23	–	not out	3
J. C. Glover c Coughtrie b Nicol	9	–	not out	5
D. A. Cosker not out	49			
H. T. Waters b Nicol	39			
B 8, l-b 4, w 1	13		L-b 4, w 1	5
1/12 (1) 2/19 (3) 3/19 (4) 4/19 (2) 5/57 (6) 6/58 (7) 7/99 (8) 8/118 (9) 9/125 (5) 10/208 (11) (67.5 overs)	208		1/8 (1) 2/26 (2) 3/99 (3) 4/136 (4) 5/167 (6) 6/195 (5) 7/198 (7) (7 wkts dec, 50 overs)	204

Saxelby 20–7–37–2; Payne 15–4–29–2; Taylor 19–3–75–2; Nicol 12.5–0–53–4; Dent 1–0–2–0. *Second innings*—Payne 13–1–55–1; Nicol 6–0–23–1; Saxelby 16–0–77–3; Taylor 9–1–28–2; Howell 6–0–17–0.

Gloucestershire

R. J. Nicol c North b Allenby	9	–	c Walters b Allenby	16
C. D. J. Dent c Walters b Waters	1	–	c Rees b Cosker	2
D. M. Housego b Allenby	17	–	st Wallace b North	47
*A. P. R. Gidman c and b Cosker	7	–	c Wallace b Allenby	0
I. A. Cockbain lbw b Croft	38	–	(6) c Walters b Croft	55
B. A. C. Howell c Walters b Croft	2	–	(7) c Glover b North	7
†R. G. Coughtrie c Walters b Croft	0	–	(9) c Rees b Croft	0
J. M. R. Taylor c Wallace b Allenby	27	–	b Croft	63
H. J. H. Marshall c and b Cosker	31	–	(5) c Waters b Cosker	11
I. D. Saxelby not out	21	–	c Cosker b Croft	3
D. A. Payne c and b Croft	6	–	not out	8
B 4, l-b 2	6		B 5, l-b 4	9
1/5 (2) 2/28 (1) 3/31 (3) 4/37 (4) 5/42 (6) 6/42 (7) 7/83 (8) 8/125 (9) 9/143 (5) 10/165 (11) (90.1 overs)	165		1/15 (2) 2/27 (1) 3/27 (4) 4/48 (5) 5/108 (3) 6/132 (7) 7/195 (6) 8/199 (9) 9/210 (8) 10/221 (10) (61.5 overs)	221

Waters 9–2–26–1; Glover 6–4–5–0; Allenby 21–7–43–3; Cosker 25–10–34–2; Croft 29.1–6–51–4. *Second innings*—Waters 11–2–30–0; Glover 5–1–18–0; Cosker 15–2–47–2; Croft 13.5–3–53–4; Allenby 7–2–25–2; North 10–1–39–2.

Umpires: J. W. Lloyds and R. T. Robinson.

At Colchester, August 15–18. GLAMORGAN drew with ESSEX.

GLAMORGAN v NORTHAMPTONSHIRE

At Cardiff, August 28–31. Drawn. Glamorgan 8pts, Northamptonshire 6pts. Toss: Northamptonshire. First-class debut: R. I. Keogh.

After the second day and the third morning were lost to rain, Hall's refusal to set a target for Glamorgan condemned the game to a dreary draw. He was possibly mindful that a similar agreement had led to defeat at Northampton a few weeks earlier, but the decision was still surprising, as his side had a slim chance of going up if they could win this and their last match. Northamptonshire were in grim mode throughout: they managed only two batting points on a very slow pitch, and showed no inclination to accelerate at any time during their 170-over vigil. O'Brien's career-best 182 lasted more than nine hours and spanned 462 balls, but was out of character, and the Northamptonshire batsmen were slow hand-clapped off the field at tea on the third day. With only bonus points to play for, Glamorgan initially pottered along just as slowly on the final day, with Walters narrowly missing out on a hundred. The game was a poor advertisement for county cricket; even Northamptonshire supporters were critical of their captain's tactics.

Close of play: first day, Northamptonshire 241-4 (O'Brien 114, Hall 17); second day, no play; third day, Glamorgan 10-0 (Bragg 4, James 6).

Northamptonshire

S. D. Peters b Harris 11
N. J. O'Brien c Bragg b North. 182
D. J. Sales c Wallace b Wagg 11
A. G. Wakely b Allenby 75
R. I. Newton lbw b Harris 3
*A. J. Hall b Waters. 21
R. I. Keogh lbw b Cosker 6
†D. Murphy st Wallace b North 54
C. D. de Lange not out 34
L. M. Daggett not out 21
B 3, l-b 5, n-b 6 14

1/22 (1) 2/34 (3) 3/186 (4) 4/196 (5) 5/249 (6) 6/273 (7) 7/357 (2) 8/394 (8) (8 wkts dec, 170 overs) 432
110 overs: 273-6

J. A. Brooks did not bat.

Harris 28–7–75–2; Waters 18–3–42–1; Cosker 42–11–94–1; Wagg 18–4–51–1; Allenby 28–4–69–1; North 24–4–57–2; Wright 4–0–8–0; Bragg 2–0–10–0; James 6–0–18–0.

Glamorgan

W. D. Bragg st Murphy b de Lange 26
N. A. James b Keogh. 36
S. J. Walters b Hall 98
M. J. North c Wakely b Hall 57
B. J. Wright st Murphy b Daggett. 5
J. Allenby not out 46
*†M. A. Wallace not out 21
B 1, l-b 10, n-b 2 13

1/45 (1) 2/73 (2) 3/164 (4) 4/177 (5) 5/278 (3) (5 wkts dec, 100.5 overs) 302

G. G. Wagg, J. A. R. Harris, D. A. Cosker and H. T. Waters did not bat.

Brooks 24–6–70–0; Daggett 22–6–69–1; de Lange 19–8–51–1; Keogh 20–5–69–1; Hall 15.5–5–32–2.

Umpires: S. A. Garratt and N. A. Mallender.

At Leeds, September 4–6. GLAMORGAN lost to YORKSHIRE by eight wickets.

GLAMORGAN v KENT

At Cardiff, September 11–13. Glamorgan won by seven wickets. Glamorgan 23pts, Kent 3pts. Toss: Kent.

Kent arrived in third place and with an outside chance of promotion but, from the moment Key decided to bowl first, they were rarely in contention. Allenby's second century of the season, and his ninth-wicket partnership of 128 with Glover, pushed Glamorgan to a commanding total. Kent then capitulated after a reasonable start, losing their last eight for just 33. Croft, playing his final match after 24 seasons with Glamorgan, took the 51st five-wicket haul of his career. Following on, Kent slumped to 96 for five before a recovery, led by Jones and Powell, at least staved off an innings defeat. But Allenby completed an excellent all-round performance with three wickets in 18 balls before, appropriately enough, Croft applied the *coup de grâce*, to lift his first-class aggregate to 1,175, of which 1,055 were for Glamorgan. The players formed a guard of honour as he left the field for the last time. The modest target of 61 was reached with more than a day to spare, lifting Glamorgan from ninth to sixth, their highest position in 2012. After striking the first six of his career against Glamorgan at Canterbury in July, Shreck tripled his tally here, hitting Croft for one in each innings.

Close of play: first day, Glamorgan 334-8 (Allenby 100, Glover 28); second day, Kent 33-2 (Northeast 15, Nash 15).

Glamorgan

W. D. Bragg lbw b Tredwell	59	– c Nash b Shreck	25
N. A. James c Jones b Stevens	26	– c Jones b Coles	6
S. J. Walters c Powell b Shreck	63	– c Jones b Coles	4
B. J. Wright c Jones b Shreck	26	– not out	15
D. L. Lloyd c Stevens b Tredwell	0	– not out	11
J. Allenby not out	125		
*†M. A. Wallace b Tredwell	16		
G. G. Wagg lbw b Coles	8		
R. D. B. Croft c Jones b Coles	1		
J. C. Glover c Tredwell b Coles	55		
M. T. Reed lbw b Coles	4		
L-b 7	7		
1/55 (2) 2/127 (1) 3/175 (3) 4/178 (5) 5/188 (4) 6/233 (7) 7/248 (8) 8/252 (9) 9/380 (10) 10/390 (11) (112.3 overs) 110 overs: 383-9	390	1/18 (2) 2/28 (3) 3/36 (1) (3 wkts, 14.2 overs)	61

Davies 20–3–66–0; Shreck 28–2–125–2; Stevens 19–4–55–1; Coles 18.3–0–76–4; Tredwell 27–7–61–3. *Second innings*—Shreck 7.2–1–33–1; Coles 7–0–28–2.

Kent

S. A. Northeast lbw b Croft	62	– c Wallace b Glover	40
*R. W. T. Key lbw b Glover	14	– lbw b Wagg	0
D. J. Bell-Drummond lbw b Allenby	33	– c Walters b Wagg	0
B. P. Nash c Allenby b Croft	23	– c Wallace b Glover	50
M. J. Powell c Walters b Reed	2	– c Allenby b Croft	41
D. I. Stevens c Allenby b Reed	3	– lbw b Glover	0
†G. O. Jones c and b Croft	5	– c James b Allenby	81
J. C. Tredwell lbw b Croft	0	– lbw b Allenby	24
M. T. Coles c Allenby b Reed	0	– lbw b Allenby	0
M. Davies not out	2	– not out	18
C. E. Shreck c Glover b Croft	16	– c James b Croft	12
B 4, l-b 2, n-b 4	10	B 2, w 2, n-b 10	14
1/26 (2) 2/96 (3) 3/137 (1) 4/140 (5) 5/140 (4) 6/150 (7) 7/150 (6) 8/150 (9) 9/152 (8) 10/170 (11) (53.5 overs)	170	1/7 (2) 2/7 (3) 3/91 (1) 4/96 (4) 5/96 (6) 6/187 (5) 7/244 (8) 8/244 (9) 9/257 (7) 10/280 (11) (83.4 overs)	280

Wagg 12–2–38–0; Glover 10–1–37–1; Croft 11.5–3–31–5; Reed 12–1–39–3; Allenby 6–0–8–1; James 2–0–11–0. *Second innings*—Wagg 17–1–70–2; Glover 14–4–43–3; Croft 22.4–3–76–2; Allenby 17–3–47–3; Reed 13–2–42–0.

Umpires: S. A. Garratt and T. E. Jesty.

GLOUCESTERSHIRE

Second-season syndrome

ANDY STOCKHAUSEN

A prolonged policy of robbing Peter to pay Paul came home to roost when Gloucestershire finished bottom of the Championship for the second time in five years. Once again, funding previously earmarked for cricket was diverted into ambitious plans to redevelop the club's Nevil Road headquarters with a view to securing regular one-day internationals.

The board argued that the international game was crucial to Gloucestershire's survival, and that not pursuing redevelopment risked squandering over £1m already invested in the scheme, which includes a new media centre and a greatly increased capacity of 17,000. Thus far, the strategy has had mixed fortunes. But in May, Bristol City Council finally gave permission for the four-phase redevelopment, and work started in October. There was, though, a price to pay, and a series of punitive cost-cutting measures rendered it impossible for director of cricket John Bracewell to assemble a squad of his choosing.

Many established players had departed for pastures new, creating a void that was filled mainly by inexperienced youngsters. The changing of the old guard had been completed when Jon Lewis and Chris Taylor, Gloucestershire's leading wicket-taker and run-scorer in 2011, also left – Taylor to become Somerset's fielding coach after reaching an out-of-court settlement with the club following a claim for unfair dismissal.

With little money for recruitment, Bracewell fell back on careful husbandry and a burgeoning scouting network to assemble a squad largely comprising young cricketers starved of opportunities elsewhere. Youthful exuberance had met with some success in 2011, when Gloucestershire flirted with promotion, but now they suffered a bad dose of second-season syndrome.

Opponents had grown wise to players who, 12 months earlier, had been unknown, and Gloucestershire won just three games in the Championship, a disappointing return, even if that was one more than Northamptonshire, who finished eighth. Indeed, there were only five points separating the bottom four teams. All the same, Alex Gidman resigned as captain shortly after the season, saying he was no longer enjoying the job, nor able to rise to the daily challenge of nurturing and encouraging inexperienced players.

It had been clear all was not well when a jaded Gidman ceded the Twenty20 captaincy to Hamish Marshall. Many members saw Marshall as an obvious successor, but he was not willing to take on the full-time role, which became an inducement to land an experienced overseas player. In December, the county plumped for the Australian batsman, Michael Klinger, who is likely to be available for the entire season.

Despite their Championship position, Gloucestershire showed some encouraging signs, recording victories at Southampton in April, and over

Warren Little, Getty Images

Liam Norwell

Derbyshire, the eventual winners of the second division, at Bristol in early June. Dogged by inconsistency, though, they did not win again until Northamptonshire were soundly beaten in September. True, injury played a part, and rain at the Cheltenham Festival frustrated Gidman's side when they were faring well against Essex; against Leicestershire they ended 13 short of victory – and two wickets from defeat.

By that stage, the team had temporarily lost all-rounder Will Gidman, Alex's brother, to a side strain. A pivotal member of the four-day team, he had collected more than 1,000 runs and 50 wickets in 2011; despite his injury, he was still the leading wicket-taker in 2012, and Gloucestershire did not win a Championship match without him. Neither did it help that Kane Williamson was available for only four games, in which he managed two hundreds, before heading to the Caribbean with New Zealand. Opener Chris Dent missed much of the season with finger and shoulder injuries, Dan Housego was unavailable early on with a shoulder problem, and new-ball spearhead Ian Saxelby sat out the last month after aggravating a chronic knee condition.

Others, though, did step up. Former Hampshire batsman Benny Howell arrived on trial and made an immediate impact, especially in limited-overs cricket. The runs dried up after he signed a two-year contract in July, but he looked set for a big future at Bristol. After recovering from injury, Housego also made his mark, and a superb hundred in a losing cause against the South Africans in August suggested rich potential. The 20-year-old seamer Liam Norwell was another to progress, proving his developing frame could cope with the gruelling requirements of an English season.

The most reliable batsmen in an awkward summer were the two ever-presents, Marshall and Ian Cockbain. But in 2013, Gloucestershire will be without another reliable character: Jon Batty retired after three seasons at Bristol (and 13 at The Oval). He began 2012 as second-choice wicketkeeper, but returned to the Championship side when Richard Coughtrie's batting form deserted him. Bracewell described Batty as "the consummate team player".

Bracewell also presided over an improvement in white-ball cricket, with Gloucestershire competitive in both the CB40 and Twenty20. Aided and abetted by overseas hired hands Ed Cowan and Muttiah Muralitharan, the county finished second in their Twenty20 group, reaching the quarter-finals for the first time in five seasons, before losing to Sussex beneath the Hove floodlights. They were also in contention for a semi-final berth in the CB40, only to be let down by an inability to win close matches.

Championship attendance: 16,122.

GLOUCESTERSHIRE RESULTS

All first-class matches – Played 15: Won 3, Lost 6, Drawn 6. Abandoned 1.
County Championship matches – Played 15: Won 3, Lost 6, Drawn 6. Abandoned 1.

LV= County Championship, 9th in Division 2;
Friends Life t20, q-f; Clydesdale Bank 40, 3rd in Group A.

COUNTY CHAMPIONSHIP AVERAGES, BATTING AND FIELDING

Cap		*M*	*I*	*NO*	*R*	*HS*	*100*	*50*	*Avge*	*Ct/St*
2011	K. S. Williamson§	4	7	0	366	128	2	1	52.28	3
2010	J. M. R. Taylor	3	5	1	151	63	0	1	37.75	1
2006	H. J. H. Marshall¶	15	25	3	822	117*	1	5	37.36	6
2011	I. A. Cockbain	15	24	2	764	112	1	5	34.72	12
2010	C. D. J. Dent†	8	15	1	424	114	1	2	30.28	11
2012	E. J. M. Cowan§	3	5	0	147	103	1	0	29.40	0
2010	J. N. Batty	8	11	2	256	55	0	1	28.44	24/1
2012	D. M. Housego	10	16	0	450	62	0	4	28.12	7
2011	W. R. S. Gidman	11	17	1	447	72	0	3	27.93	2
2012	R. J. Nicol§	4	7	2	128	75*	0	1	25.60	6
2004	A. P. R. Gidman	13	22	1	528	129	1	3	25.14	10
2012	B. A. C. Howell	13	24	3	497	83*	0	3	23.66	5
2008	I. D. Saxelby	11	16	7	200	30	0	0	22.22	4
2010	E. G. C. Young	8	12	2	186	55*	0	1	18.60	3
2012	P. B. Muchall	4	7	2	82	23	0	0	16.40	1
2011	J. K. Fuller¶	8	12	1	134	57	0	1	12.18	3
2011	D. A. Payne	8	10	3	75	16	0	0	10.71	2
2011	R. G. Coughtrie	7	12	0	125	40	0	0	10.41	17
2011	L. C. Norwell	9	11	4	37	18	0	0	5.28	3

Also batted: A. J. Ireland¶ (cap 2007) (2 matches) 25*, 22, 0; G. J. McCarter (cap 2012) (1 match) 29* (1 ct).

† *Born in Gloucestershire.* § *Official overseas player.* ¶ *Other non-England-qualified player. Since 2004, Gloucestershire have awarded caps to all players making their first-class debuts.*

BOWLING

	Style	*O*	*M*	*R*	*W*	*BB*	*5I*	*Avge*
W. R. S. Gidman	RFM	318	58	943	44	5-43	2	21.43
D. A. Payne	LFM	147	24	504	22	4-89	0	22.90
I. D. Saxelby	RFM	293.3	58	897	35	6-48	1	25.62
J. K. Fuller	RFM	174.2	27	653	24	5-29	1	27.20
L. C. Norwell	RFM	194.1	25	632	22	5-51	1	28.72
E. G. C. Young	SLA	137.5	28	414	10	2-23	0	41.40

Also bowled: C. D. J. Dent (SLA) 11–0–32–0; A. P. R. Gidman (RM) 14–3–50–2; B. A. C. Howell (RM) 93.4–14–266–6; A. J. Ireland (RFM) 39–2–159–4; G. J. McCarter (RFM) 19–3–67–0; P. B. Muchall (RM) 39.2–3–218–2; R. J. Nicol (OB/RM) 38.5–2–129–7; J. M. R. Taylor (OB) 87–15–277–8; K. S. Williamson (OB) 34.3–4–121–5.

LEADING CB40 AVERAGES (100 runs/4 wickets)

Batting	*Runs*	*HS*	*Avge*	*SR*	*Ct*
K. S. Williamson	232	112	46.40	102.20	2
R. J. Nicol	161	133	40.25	99.38	3
A. P. R. Gidman	304	59	38.00	94.70	5
B. A. C. Howell	286	88	35.75	84.61	5
W. R. S. Gidman	125	76	31.25	73.96	2
I. A. Cockbain	235	58	29.37	104.44	8

Bowling	*W*	*BB*	*Avge*	*ER*
G. J. McCarter	6	3-15	9.33	5.89
L. C. Norwell	8	6-52	16.12	6.78
J. K. Fuller	14	6-35	17.85	5.41
C. D. J. Dent	6	4-43	22.00	4.88
D. A. Payne	8	3-39	23.12	6.41
E. G. C. Young	14	3-25	25.14	4.87

LEADING FLT20 AVERAGES (75 runs/13 overs)

Batting	Runs	HS	Avge	SR	Ct
H. J. H. Marshall	239	72	34.14	**146.62**	8
K. S. Williamson	76	39	38.00	**118.75**	0
D. M. Housego	127	59*	63.50	**125.74**	2
J. K. Fuller	84	36	21.00	**168.00**	1
A. P. R. Gidman	81	44	20.25	**155.76**	0
B. A. C. Howell	77	55*	19.25	**120.31**	2

Bowling	W	BB	Avge	ER
M. Muralitharan	5	2-20	27.00	**5.29**
E. G. C. Young	4	1-16	29.00	**5.80**
I. D. Saxelby	11	4-16	14.54	**7.27**
L. C. Norwell	4	2-41	30.75	**9.46**
J. K. Fuller	8	2-40	33.12	**10.52**

FIRST-CLASS COUNTY RECORDS

Highest score for	341	C. M. Spearman v Middlesex at Gloucester	2004
Highest score against	319	C. J. L. Rogers (Northants) at Northampton	2006
Leading run-scorer	33,664	W. R. Hammond (avge 57.05)	1920–1951
Best bowling for	10-40	E. G. Dennett v Essex at Bristol	1906
Best bowling against	10-66	A. A. Mailey (Australians) at Cheltenham	1921
	10-66	K. Smales (Nottinghamshire) at Stroud	1956
Leading wicket-taker	3,170	C. W. L. Parker (avge 19.43)	1903–1935
Highest total for	695-9 dec	v Middlesex at Gloucester	2004
Highest total against	774-7 dec	by Australians at Bristol	1948
Lowest total for	17	v Australians at Cheltenham	1896
Lowest total against	12	by Northamptonshire at Gloucester	1907

LIST A COUNTY RECORDS

Highest score for	177	A. J. Wright v Scotland at Bristol	1997
Highest score against	189*	J. G. E. Benning (Surrey) at Bristol	2006
Leading run-scorer	7,825	M. W. Alleyne (avge 26.89)	1986–2005
Best bowling for	7-29	D. A. Payne v Essex at Chelmsford	2010
Best bowling against	6-16	Shoaib Akhtar (Worcestershire) at Worcester	2005
Leading wicket-taker	393	M. W. Alleyne (avge 29.88)	1986–2005
Highest total for	401-7	v Buckinghamshire at Wing	2003
Highest total against	496-4	by Surrey at The Oval	2007
Lowest total for	49	v Middlesex at Bristol	1978
Lowest total against	48	by Middlesex at Lydney	1973

TWENTY20 COUNTY RECORDS

Highest score for	119	K. J. O'Brien v Middlesex at Uxbridge	2011
Highest score against	116*	C. L. White (Somerset) at Taunton	2006
Leading run-scorer	**1,592**	**H. J. H. Marshall (avge 28.94)**	**2006–2012**
Best bowling for	4-16	J. M. R. Taylor v Somerset at Bristol	2011
	4-16	**I. D. Saxelby v Northamptonshire at Bristol**	**2012**
Best bowling against	5-16	R. E. Watkins (Glamorgan) at Cardiff	2009
Leading wicket-taker	49	J. Lewis (avge 30.89)	2003–2011
Highest total for	254-3	v Middlesex at Uxbridge	2011
Highest total against	250-3	by Somerset at Taunton	2006
Lowest total for	68	v Hampshire at Bristol	2010
Lowest total against	97	by Surrey at The Oval	2010

ADDRESS

County Ground, Nevil Road, Bristol BS7 9EJ (0117 910 8000; **email** info@glosccc.co.uk).
Website www.glosccc.co.uk

OFFICIALS

Captain 2012 – A. P. R. Gidman
2013 – M. Klinger
Director of cricket J. G. Bracewell
Academy director O. A. Dawkins
President D. A. Allen

Chairman R. Body
Chief executive T. E. M. Richardson
Head groundsman S. Williams
Scorer A. Bull

At Chelmsford, April 5–7. GLOUCESTERSHIRE lost to ESSEX by an innings and 38 runs.

At Southampton, April 12–15. GLOUCESTERSHIRE beat HAMPSHIRE by 33 runs.

At Canterbury, April 19–22. GLOUCESTERSHIRE drew with KENT.

GLOUCESTERSHIRE v GLAMORGAN

At Bristol, April 26–29. Abandoned. Gloucestershire 3pts, Glamorgan 3pts.

This was the first Championship washout at Bristol since Gloucestershire's fixture against Sussex in June 1985.

At Derby, May 2–5. GLOUCESTERSHIRE drew with DERBYSHIRE.

GLOUCESTERSHIRE v YORKSHIRE

At Bristol, May 9–12. Yorkshire won by four wickets. Yorkshire 19pts, Gloucestershire 4pts. Toss: Yorkshire. Championship debut: G. J. McCarter.

Two commanding centuries helped guide Yorkshire home in a rain-affected contest after they had been set 400 from 111 overs. Gloucestershire, without the injured David Payne and James Fuller, reduced the visitors to 117 for three on a slow pitch before Jaques and Ballance, batting in orthodox fashion, added 203. Bresnan weighed in with 38 off 34 deliveries, and Yorkshire completed the second-highest successful run-chase in their history with 20 balls to spare. Rain had prevented any play on the first day and took a chunk out of the next, so Williamson completed his third century in four innings (starting with a Test hundred for New Zealand) on the third morning; he eventually became one of Bresnan's five wickets. Gloucestershire then collapsed from 290 for four to 299 for nine against the new ball, but the captains agreed a contrived target, and so Yorkshire gifted runs (and two bonus points) as Gale and Lyth made life easy for Saxelby and Graeme McCarter, a 19-year-old from Northern Ireland on Championship debut. Yorkshire forfeited their first innings, and Gloucestershire crawled to 48 without loss to set up the chase.

Close of play: first day, no play; second day, Gloucestershire 165-2 (Williamson 89, A. P. R. Gidman 6); third day, Yorkshire 30-1 (Lyth 19, Jaques 8).

Gloucestershire

B. A. C. Howell c Jaques b Bresnan	4	– not out	24
C. D. J. Dent lbw b Patterson	62	– not out	24
K. S. Williamson c Brophy b Bresnan	111		
*A. P. R. Gidman c Brophy b Bresnan	26		
H. J. H. Marshall b Bresnan	47		
I. A. Cockbain c Jaques b Bresnan	38		
W. R. S. Gidman lbw b Patterson	1		
†R. G. Coughtrie c Ballance b Patterson	0		
E. G. C. Young c Bresnan b Patterson	0		
I. D. Saxelby not out	27		
G. J. McCarter not out	29		
L-b 5, w 1	6		
1/9 (1) 2/155 (2) (9 wkts dec, 103.1 overs)	351	(no wkt dec, 27.1 overs)	48

3/203 (4) 4/216 (3)
5/290 (5) 6/293 (6) 7/294 (8) 8/294 (9) 9/299 (7)

Sidebottom 26–8–75–0; Bresnan 32–10–81–5; McGrath 18–7–48–0; Patterson 20–3–77–4; Rashid 4–0–13–0; Lyth 2–0–26–0; Gale 1.1–0–26–0. *Second innings*—McGrath 6–2–12–0; Patterson 5–2–3–0; Rashid 8.1–4–9–0; Lyth 2–1–1–0; Ballance 6–1–23–0.

Yorkshire

Yorkshire forfeited their first innings.

A. Lyth lbw b Saxelby	36
J. J. Sayers c Coughtrie b W. R. S. Gidman	1
P. A. Jaques b W. R. S. Gidman	160
*A. W. Gale c McCarter b Young	21
G. S. Ballance not out	121
A. McGrath c Dent b W. R. S. Gidman	6
T. T. Bresnan b Young	38
†G. L. Brophy not out	2
B 9, l-b 7, w 1	17
1/14 (2) 2/62 (1) 3/117 (4) 4/320 (3) 5/328 (6) 6/383 (7) (6 wkts, 107.4 overs)	402

A. U. Rashid, R. J. Sidebottom and S. A. Patterson did not bat.

Saxelby 28–3–111–1; W. R. S. Gidman 27–5–76–3; Young 24.4–5–99–2; McCarter 19–3–67–0; Howell 5–1–17–0; Williamson 4–0–16–0.

Umpires: M. J. D. Bodenham and R. A. Kettleborough.

At Cambridge, May 18–20. GLOUCESTERSHIRE drew with CAMBRIDGE MCCU.

At Northampton, May 23–26. GLOUCESTERSHIRE lost to NORTHAMPTONSHIRE by 121 runs.

GLOUCESTERSHIRE v DERBYSHIRE

At Bristol, May 30–June 1. Gloucestershire won by seven wickets. Gloucestershire 21pts, Derbyshire 3pts. Toss: Derbyshire.

Once again the Gidman brothers underlined their importance to Gloucestershire, who became the first side to beat the runaway leaders of the second division. Will claimed four for 29, including three for none in seven balls in a devastating burst on the first morning, as Derbyshire collapsed for 95 after choosing to bat on an essentially true pitch. Judging by the reckless manner in which they surrendered their wickets, Derbyshire's batsmen had let their lofty position go to their heads. In contrast, Alex Gidman exercised great patience in compiling 129 – his first hundred in over a year – as Gloucestershire built a first-innings lead of 199. Madsen and Redfern offered sterner resistance second time round, but another incisive spell from Will Gidman, who finished the match with eight wickets, left Gloucestershire needing only 85 for a three-day victory. They could also celebrate Bristol City Council's decision to approve – at the second attempt – their application to redevelop the Nevil Road ground.

Close of play: first day, Gloucestershire 182-5 (A. P. R. Gidman 72, Cockbain 0); second day, Derbyshire 211-5 (Redfern 64, Wainwright 0).

Derbyshire

First innings		Second innings	
M. J. Guptill b Payne	15	c Batty b Saxelby	42
M. S. Lineker c Batty b Payne	4	c Howell b W. R. S. Gidman	8
*W. L. Madsen c Dent b Payne	13	lbw b W. R. S. Gidman	72
W. J. Durston c Dent b W. R. S. Gidman	18	c Batty b W. R. S. Gidman	7
D. J. Redfern c Saxelby b W. R. S. Gidman	13	c Williamson b Payne	77
R. A. Whiteley run out	17	c Batty b W. R. S. Gidman	11
D. J. Wainwright b W. R. S. Gidman	0	c A. P. R. Gidman b Payne	2
J. L. Clare c Batty b Saxelby	7	not out	43
†T. Poynton c Batty b W. R. S. Gidman	1	lbw b Saxelby	8
A. P. Palladino run out	3	lbw b Payne	4
T. D. Groenewald not out	0	lbw b Payne	0
B 1, l-b 1, n-b 2	4	L-b 7, n-b 2	9
1/19 (1) 2/22 (2) 3/45 (3) 4/63 (5) 5/63 (4) 6/63 (7) 7/82 (8) 8/83 (9) 9/93 (6) 10/95 (10) (32.2 overs)	95	1/15 (2) 2/78 (1) 3/91 (4) 4/188 (3) 5/204 (6) 6/215 (7) 7/247 (5) 8/260 (9) 9/283 (10) 10/283 (11) (77.5 overs)	283

Saxelby 10.2–4–13–1; W. R. S. Gidman 8–2–29–4; Payne 8–1–23–3; Norwell 6–1–28–0. *Second innings*—W. R. S. Gidman 21–3–50–4; Saxelby 19–2–62–2; Payne 19.5–2–89–4; Norwell 12–1–42–0; Howell 3–0–18–0; Williamson 3–0–15–0.

Gloucestershire

†J. N. Batty c Poynton b Palladino	2	– lbw b Palladino	0
B. A. C. Howell c Durston b Groenewald	10	– c Lineker b Clare	31
K. S. Williamson c Poynton b Groenewald	56	– c Wainwright b Clare	29
*A. P. R. Gidman lbw b Groenewald	129	– not out	13
H. J. H. Marshall b Whiteley	31	– not out	12
L. C. Norwell c Poynton b Whiteley	1		
I. A. Cockbain c Poynton b Palladino	4		
C. D. J. Dent c Redfern b Clare	7		
W. R. S. Gidman lbw b Palladino	8		
I. D. Saxelby not out	17		
D. A. Payne b Palladino	16		
L-b 4, w 1, n-b 8	13		
1/6 (1) 2/28 (2) 3/109 (3) (92.3 overs)	294	1/0 (1) (3 wkts, 21.2 overs)	85
4/172 (5) 5/174 (6) 6/189 (7)		2/52 (2) 3/63 (3)	
7/214 (8) 8/255 (9) 9/277 (4) 10/294 (11)			

Palladino 25.3–5–84–4; Groenewald 20–5–66–3; Whiteley 12–3–38–2; Clare 15–2–41–1; Wainwright 19–2–59–0; Durston 1–0–2–0. *Second innings*—Palladino 7–1–24–1; Groenewald 6–3–16–0; Clare 4–0–17–2; Whiteley 2–0–10–0; Wainwright 2–0–16–0; Durston 0.2–0–2–0.

Umpires: S. A. Garratt and G. Sharp.

GLOUCESTERSHIRE v ESSEX

At Cheltenham, July 11–14. Drawn. Gloucestershire 5pts, Essex 4pts. Toss: Gloucestershire. County debut: Harbhajan Singh. Championship debut: E. J. M. Cowan.

Two days after his compatriots had been thrashed 4–0 by England in the NatWest Series, Tasmania opener Ed Cowan restored at least a little pride to Australian batsmanship by completing a superb hundred for Gloucestershire. But the weather limited them to 100 overs spread across two soggy days – and wiped out the last two altogether. Cowan batted five and a half hours on a pitch made tricky by the damp, sharing century partnerships with Housego and Marshall. Topley, who found swing, was the only Essex bowler to enjoy much success. Umpire S. Ravi was taking part in an exchange scheme between the ECB and the BCCI, and standing in his first Championship match. In all, six of his nine scheduled days of county cricket were washed out.

Close of play: first day, Gloucestershire 147-2 (Cowan 51, Gidman 6); second day, Gloucestershire 284-4 (Marshall 72, Cockbain 8); third day, no play.

Gloucestershire

B. A. C. Howell lbw b Topley	18
E. J. M. Cowan lbw b Masters	103
D. M. Housego b Topley	60
*A. P. R. Gidman lbw b Topley	8
H. J. H. Marshall not out	72
I. A. Cockbain not out	8
B 4, l-b 9, n-b 2	15
1/23 (1) 2/131 (3) (4 wkts, 100 overs)	284
3/149 (4) 4/253 (2)	

†J. N. Batty, E. G. C. Young, I. D. Saxelby, D. A. Payne and L. C. Norwell did not bat.

Masters 30–7–81–1; Topley 27–5–70–3; Napier 14–0–58–0; Harbhajan Singh 13–4–33–0; ten Doeschate 8–3–20–0; Smith 8–3–9–0.

Essex

T. Westley, M. L. Pettini, J. C. Mickleburgh, B. T. Foakes, *†J. S. Foster, R. N. ten Doeschate, G. M. Smith, G. R. Napier, Harbhajan Singh, D. D. Masters and R. J. W. Topley.

Umpires: S. Ravi and R. T. Robinson.

GLOUCESTERSHIRE v LEICESTERSHIRE

At Cheltenham, July 18–21. Drawn. Gloucestershire 7pts, Leicestershire 6pts. Toss: Leicestershire.

Set 222 in 53 overs, Gloucestershire were on course for a rare victory at 176 for three in the 43rd, only to falter against the pace of Joseph and the steady left-arm spin of Henderson. He bowled unchanged from the Chapel End after tea, as Gloucestershire lost five for 23 in seven overs; with the ninth-wicket pair, Fuller and Payne, shutting up shop for the final three, they finished 13 short. The result was harsh on Saxelby, who appeared to have set them on their way with a career-best six for 48, concluding with a burst of four for two, after the first four sessions had been lost to rain. Fuller's maiden fifty then established a useful lead of 67, before Sarwan dug Leicestershire – captained by the 21-year-old Cobb because Matthew Hoggard had a sore back – out of a hole. Fifties from Housego and Gidman took Gloucestershire close, before the final twist.

Close of play: first day, no play; second day, Gloucestershire 40-2 (Batty 11, Payne 1); third day, Leicestershire 142-5 (Sarwan 30, Boyce 0).

Leicestershire

First innings		Second innings	
G. P. Smith c Batty b Saxelby	0	c Cockbain b Norwell	36
M. A. Thornely b Saxelby	3	lbw b Payne	39
E. J. H. Eckersley c and b Norwell	8	b Young	8
R. R. Sarwan b Payne	50	c Housego b Howell	93
*J. J. Cobb c Young b Fuller	23	c Batty b Fuller	15
M. A. G. Boyce c Batty b Payne	22	(7) run out	23
W. A. White c Cockbain b Saxelby	22	(8) c Cockbain b Saxelby	21
†P. G. Dixey c Batty b Saxelby	13	(9) lbw b Fuller	4
C. W. Henderson not out	1	(10) b Norwell	27
R. H. Joseph c Gidman b Saxelby	0	(6) c Housego b Young	7
N. L. Buck c Batty b Saxelby	0	not out	0
B 3, l-b 11, w 6	20	B 9, l-b 5, w 1	15
1/0 (1) 2/11 (2) 3/13 (3) 4/61 (5) 5/118 (6) 6/127 (4) 7/152 (7) 8/162 (8) 9/162 (10) 10/162 (11) (51.5 overs)	162	1/66 (2) 2/85 (1) 3/89 (3) 4/131 (5) 5/141 (6) 6/214 (7) 7/235 (4) 8/240 (9) 9/288 (8) 10/288 (10) (83.1 overs)	288

Saxelby 13.5–2–48–6; Norwell 13–4–34–1; Fuller 11–5–30–1; Payne 12–3–33–2; Howell 2–1–3–0. *Second innings*—Saxelby 21–5–59–1; Norwell 11.1–0–37–2; Fuller 13–2–50–2; Young 25–3–76–2; Payne 11–1–44–1; Howell 2–1–8–1.

Gloucestershire

First innings		Second innings	
†J. N. Batty lbw b White	26	c Boyce b Henderson	38
B. A. C. Howell c Smith b Buck	7	c Dixey b White	5
D. M. Housego b Henderson	9	c Dixey b Joseph	50
D. A. Payne b White	15	(10) not out	0
*A. P. R. Gidman lbw b White	12	(4) c Eckersley b Henderson	62
H. J. H. Marshall c Cobb b Buck	37	(5) c Smith b Joseph	23
I. A. Cockbain c Smith b Joseph	10	(6) c Dixey b Joseph	2
E. G. C. Young c Smith b Thornely	37	c Eckersley b Henderson	1
J. K. Fuller c Sarwan b Buck	57	(7) not out	18
I. D. Saxelby c and b Thornely	0	(9) c Smith b Henderson	3
L. C. Norwell not out	2		
B 1, l-b 10, n-b 6	17	L-b 2, w 1, n-b 4	7
1/13 (2) 2/36 (3) 3/67 (4) 4/79 (5) 5/90 (1) 6/128 (7) 7/132 (6) 8/227 (8) 9/227 (10) 10/229 (9) (71 overs)	229	1/26 (2) 2/54 (1) 3/148 (4) 4/176 (3) 5/184 (5) 6/193 (6) 7/194 (8) 8/199 (9) (8 wkts, 53 overs)	209

Buck 21–7–50–3; Joseph 14–4–49–1; Henderson 11–2–28–1; White 17–1–62–3; Thornely 8–1–29–2. *Second innings*—Buck 9–5–22–0; Joseph 13–2–36–3; White 6–0–42–1; Cobb 1–0–5–0; Henderson 21–5–80–4; Thornely 3–0–22–0.

Umpires: N. G. C. Cowley and J. H. Evans.

At Swansea, August 1–4. GLOUCESTERSHIRE lost to GLAMORGAN by 26 runs.

GLOUCESTERSHIRE v HAMPSHIRE

At Bristol, August 6–9. Drawn. Gloucestershire 8pts, Hampshire 8pts. Toss: Hampshire.

Cockbain's second century frustrated Hampshire on a final day that promised much before fizzling out. Gloucestershire began on 102 for four, 97 ahead; but, with three seam bowlers carrying injuries, they opted not to set a target, and Cockbain's chanceless 112 allowed them to bat beyond tea. By the time Hampshire – who had lost Mascarenhas to a shoulder problem – dismissed them for 277, the chance of a result had vanished. In trouble in their first innings at 85 for four, Gloucestershire had recovered thanks to a stand of 125 between Marshall and Cockbain. Much of the second day was lost to the weather, yet Hampshire looked set for a telling lead as they advanced to 218 for four just before lunch on the third. However, McKenzie was bowled six shy of a hundred, sparking a collapse in which the last six wickets crashed for 58. It left time for Cockbain to shine, but little else.

Close of play: first day, Gloucestershire 265-8 (Coughtrie 24, Payne 4); second day, Hampshire 104-2 (McKenzie 52, Katich 5); third day, Gloucestershire 102-4 (Housego 24, Cockbain 15).

Gloucestershire

R. J. Nicol c Bates b Balcombe	10	– c Dawson b Balcombe	13
B. A. C. Howell lbw b Kabir Ali	6	– c McKenzie b Ervine	36
D. M. Housego b Mascarenhas	51	– c Bates b Ervine	37
*A. P. R. Gidman run out	2	– b Balcombe	2
H. J. H. Marshall lbw b Dawson	75	– lbw b Balcombe	4
I. A. Cockbain lbw b Balcombe	51	– b Katich	112
P. B. Muchall b Tomlinson	16	– (8) lbw b Tomlinson	0
†R. G. Coughtrie lbw b Tomlinson	26	– (7) lbw b Tomlinson	21
I. D. Saxelby c Dawson b Kabir Ali	7	– lbw b Dawson	10
D. A. Payne c Bates b Kabir Ali	8	– c McKenzie b Adams	7
L. C. Norwell not out	0	– not out	1
B 9, l-b 4, n-b 6	19	B 16, l-b 8, n-b 10	34
1/13 (2) 2/36 (1) 3/49 (4) (99.3 overs)	271	1/51 (1) 2/55 (2) (114 overs)	277
4/85 (3) 5/210 (5) 6/218 (6)		3/68 (4) 4/72 (5)	
7/236 (7) 8/259 (9) 9/267 (8) 10/271 (10)		5/142 (3) 6/229 (7) 7/229 (8)	
		8/269 (9) 9/269 (6) 10/277 (10)	

Kabir Ali 20.3–1–69–3; Tomlinson 21–8–34–2; Balcombe 24–4–55–2; Mascarenhas 12–2–24–1; Shafayat 2–0–15–0; Ervine 7–0–31–0; Dawson 13–2–30–1. *Second innings*—Tomlinson 24–6–73–2; Kabir Ali 16–3–41–0; Ervine 13–2–47–2; Balcombe 24–7–51–3; Dawson 19–8–15–1; Katich 15–4–22–1; Adams 3–2–4–1.

Hampshire

N. D. McKenzie b Payne	94	– (2) not out	0
*J. H. K. Adams c Coughtrie b Saxelby	9	– (1) not out	0
B. M. Shafayat c Nicol b Howell	20		
S. M. Katich run out	31		
L. A. Dawson c Gidman b Nicol	14		
S. M. Ervine c Gidman b Saxelby	44		
†M. D. Bates b Norwell	8		
A. D. Mascarenhas c Gidman b Howell	16		
Kabir Ali c Nicol b Payne	7		
D. J. Balcombe c Marshall b Saxelby	1		
J. A. Tomlinson not out	0		
B 10, l-b 9, w 5, n-b 8	32		
1/9 (2) 2/88 (3) 3/138 (4) (86.3 overs)	276	(no wkt, 2 overs)	0
4/182 (5) 5/218 (1) 6/239 (7)			
7/262 (8) 8/274 (6) 9/276 (10) 10/276 (9)			

Saxelby 16–6–44–3; Norwell 21–5–61–1; Payne 20.3–5–69–2; Muchall 1.2–1–2–0; Howell 17.4–1–44–2; Nicol 10–1–37–1. *Second innings*—Norwell 1–1–0–0; Howell 1–1–0–0.

Umpires: D. J. Millns and M. J. Saggers.

GLOUCESTERSHIRE v KENT

At Bristol, August 15–18. Drawn. Gloucestershire 6pts, Kent 6pts. Toss: Gloucestershire.

This rain-ruined draw ended in blazing sunshine when Gloucestershire closed their first innings after just one ball, so satisfying the regulation that a match cannot be called off before the last hour. Each side finished with six points, which suited neither – especially not Kent, who were looking to make up ground on the three teams above them. The only cricket to escape the rain on the first three days came in 45 minutes on the second morning. When Kent resumed on the last, at 29 for one, their middle order made unspectacular progress in search of bonus points; so too, in a game perhaps better forgotten, did the Gloucestershire bowlers.

Close of play: first day, no play; second day, Kent 29-1 (Northeast 12, Blake 8); third day, no play.

Kent

S. A. Northeast c Nicol b Payne	13
*R. W. T. Key c Batty b Fuller	9
A. J. Blake c Batty b W. R. S. Gidman	73
B. P. Nash c Nicol b Norwell	46
M. J. Powell b Norwell	7
D. I. Stevens c Fuller b Nicol	45
†G. O. Jones not out	65
S. J. Cook c Cockbain b W. R. S. Gidman	15
M. Davies c Nicol b W. R. S. Gidman	4
A. E. N. Riley c Batty b Payne	2
C. E. Shreck not out	4
B 10, l-b 5, w 2	17
(9 wkts dec, 92.4 overs)	300

1/20 (2) 2/33 (1) 3/128 (4) 4/148 (5) 5/160 (3) 6/222 (6) 7/256 (8) 8/270 (9) 9/290 (10)

W. R. S. Gidman 24–3–75–3; Fuller 24–5–77–1; Payne 15–1–57–2; Norwell 17.4–3–50–2; Howell 2–0–10–0; Nicol 10–1–16–1.

Gloucestershire

R. J. Nicol not out	1
B. A. C. Howell not out	0
(no wkt dec, 0.1 overs)	1

D. M. Housego, *A. P. R. Gidman, H. J. H. Marshall, I. A. Cockbain, W. R. S. Gidman, †J. N. Batty, J. K. Fuller, D. A. Payne and L. C. Norwell did not bat.

Davies 0.1–0–1–0.

Umpires: N. L. Bainton and M. J. D. Bodenham.

At Bristol, August 22. GLOUCESTERSHIRE lost to SOUTH AFRICANS by three wickets (see South African tour section).

At Scarborough, August 28–31. GLOUCESTERSHIRE lost to YORKSHIRE by two wickets.

GLOUCESTERSHIRE v NORTHAMPTONSHIRE

At Bristol, September 4–6. Gloucestershire won by 207 runs. Gloucestershire 20pts, Northamptonshire 3pts. Toss: Northamptonshire.

The brisk Norwell claimed eight wickets in the match as Gloucestershire completed a comprehensive victory inside three days. Still only 20, he followed up his three first-innings wickets with five for 51 to ensure that Northamptonshire, despite second-innings resistance from Sales and Hall, ended well adrift of an improbable target of 432. The game had progressed quickly on the opening day, with 17 wickets tumbling, though pitch inspector David Hughes found little untoward. Gloucestershire plummeted from 41 for none to 44 for four as Hall coaxed movement from the pitch, though half-centuries from Alex Gidman and Batty largely righted the ship. Fuller launched into the Northamptonshire reply with a maiden five-for, skittling them for 100 and ensuring a 120-run lead. Hall again made life tricky for the home batsmen, but Cockbain and Will Gidman overcame seamer-friendly conditions to build a commanding position. Norwell then made hay to guide Gloucestershire to their third Championship win of the summer – and briefly off the foot of the table.

Close of play: first day, Northamptonshire 73-7 (Middlebrook 10, Willey 1); second day, Gloucestershire 286-6 (W. R. S. Gidman 52, Batty 23).

Gloucestershire

First innings		Second innings	
E. J. M. Cowan lbw b Hall	8	– (2) c Coetzer b Willey	1
B. A. C. Howell lbw b Evans	29	– (1) run out	1
D. M. Housego b Hall	1	– c Peters b Hall	24
*A. P. R. Gidman lbw b Willey	56	– lbw b Evans	40
H. J. H. Marshall lbw b Hall	0	– c Peters b Evans	30
I. A. Cockbain b Willey	10	– lbw b Hall	99
W. R. S. Gidman c Peters b Brooks	13	– lbw b Willey	52
†J. N. Batty c Newton b Evans	55	– not out	31
J. K. Fuller c Murphy b Evans	3	– b Hall	17
A. J. Ireland c Murphy b Evans	22	– b Hall	0
L. C. Norwell not out	4	– b Hall	0
B 2, l-b 7, n-b 10	19	B 3, l-b 12, w 1	16
1/41 (2) 2/41 (1) 3/44 (3) 4/44 (5) 5/95 (6) 6/128 (4) 7/138 (7) 8/151 (9) 9/209 (10) 10/220 (8) (67 overs)	220	1/2 (1) 2/2 (2) 3/66 (3) 4/70 (4) 5/168 (5) 6/246 (6) 7/288 (7) 8/311 (9) 9/311 (10) 10/311 (11) (91.5 overs)	311

Willey 20–5–64–2; Brooks 16–5–58–1; Hall 13–4–37–3; Evans 13–4–38–4; Middlebrook 4–1–10–0; Coetzer 1–0–4–0. *Second innings*—Willey 19–5–69–2; Brooks 14–4–44–0; Hall 21.5–7–50–5; Evans 16–2–63–2; Middlebrook 14–3–44–0; Coetzer 7–0–26–0.

Northamptonshire

First innings		Second innings	
S. D. Peters b Norwell	35	– lbw b W. R. S. Gidman	0
N. J. O'Brien c Batty b Fuller	10	– c Batty b Norwell	14
D. J. Sales b Norwell	4	– b Norwell	55
K. J. Coetzer c A. P. R. Gidman b Norwell	3	– b Norwell	1
R. I. Newton c Batty b Fuller	1	– c Cockbain b Norwell	44
*A. J. Hall c Batty b Fuller	0	– b Howell	56
J. D. Middlebrook not out	21	– c Norwell b Howell	4
†D. Murphy b Ireland	4	– b Norwell	0
D. J. Willey c Batty b Ireland	6	– not out	23
J. A. Brooks b Fuller	5	– c Howell b Fuller	22
L. Evans c Cockbain b Fuller	5	– c Cockbain b Ireland	0
L-b 2, n-b 4	6	L-b 3, n-b 2	5
1/30 (2) 2/43 (3) 3/49 (4) 4/50 (5) 5/50 (6) 6/56 (1) 7/72 (8) 8/84 (9) 9/92 (10) 10/100 (11) (38.4 overs)	100	1/0 (1) 2/51 (2) 3/53 (4) 4/80 (3) 5/158 (5) 6/167 (7) 7/168 (8) 8/184 (6) 9/223 (10) 10/224 (11) (65 overs)	224

W. R. S. Gidman 12–3–26–0; Ireland 8–1–20–2; Fuller 10.4–3–29–5; Norwell 8–1–23–3. *Second innings*—W. R. S. Gidman 12–2–59–1; Ireland 11–1–34–1; Fuller 15–2–40–1; Norwell 14–2–51–5; Howell 13–2–37–2.

Umpires: S. C. Gale and G. Sharp.

At Leicester, September 11–14. GLOUCESTERSHIRE lost to LEICESTERSHIRE by two wickets.

HAMPSHIRE

Knockouts bring double vision

PAT SYMES

Hampshire can have no complaints about 2012, their two limited-overs triumphs making up for the failure to gain promotion in the Championship. Off the field, work began in September on a 175-bedroom hotel at the Northern End. The £48m joint venure with Eastleigh Borough Council will take the maximum capacity to 25,000, and in the process turn the Ageas Bowl – as the Rose Bowl was officially renamed in spring 2012 – into the first ground in Britain to meet the standards of a "model" Test venue, as defined by the ECB.

But for all the playing success, Hampshire felt the chill wind of financial uncertainty, making the trophy victories at Cardiff and Lord's all the more remarkable. They had decided to remove some of the higher-paid players from the payroll in the wake of relegation at the end of 2011: nine departed, including internationals Dominic Cork, Michael Lumb, Simon Jones and Nic Pothas. In addition, the lease of the ground was sold to the council for £6.5m, and the sale of the stadium naming rights was also timely. Rose Bowl plc accounts for 2011 showed a loss of £3.27m, a figure the company ascribed to redevelopment costs and "exceptionally high" staging fees demanded by the ECB for international matches. The price to be paid for the sale of the lease is that Hampshire's annual rent is now £420,000. At the end of the season, Rod Bransgrove stepped down from the dual role of chairman and chief executive, but retained the less arduous post of chairman; David Mann was promoted from within to become chief executive and group finance director.

Against a straitened background, Hampshire's magnificent limited-overs double was in part a tribute to the youngsters entrusted with the club's future, and to the response of those more experienced players who had been retained. The new captain, Jimmy Adams, pulled both factions together into a cohesive unit in the FLt20 and CB40, though Championship performances were patchy – and the summer ended with an alarming sequence of three defeats, with Hampshire notionally in contention for promotion until the penultimate round of matches. Adams, the leading run-scorer in Division Two, and Sean Ervine were the only players to perform reliably across all formats.

Even with a reduced squad, team manager Giles White and coaches Craig White and Tony Middleton could field differing sides for all competitions. Danny Briggs, well enough regarded to have played 50-over and Twenty20 internationals before he was 22, started only four Championship matches (and took just five wickets at almost 50) because of pitches more suited to seam, and the re-emergence of his fellow left-arm spinner Liam Dawson. In the Championship, the bowling was spearheaded by James Tomlinson and the improved David Balcombe. Tomlinson claimed 43 wickets, while Balcombe – particularly effective on the greener, early-season pitches – took 59. Yet

Mike Hewitt, Getty Images

David Balcombe

neither played a single limited-overs match. Adams had experienced internationals Simon Katich and, later, Neil McKenzie to lean on for advice, but Michael Carberry and Dimitri Mascarenhas were beset by injuries, and made only sporadic contributions: Carberry consistently and brutally in the CB40, and Mascarenhas with his customary parsimony in the 20-over competition.

The road to Twenty20 glory had a bumpy start: Hampshire gained just one point (in an abandoned match) from the first three group games. But the largely unheralded Australian all-rounder Glenn Maxwell proved an inspirational hitter, and helped take them on a run of eight wins (plus two no-results), culminating in triumph at Cardiff. The unexpected finals-day victories over Somerset and Yorkshire were a tribute to the spirit and determination developed under Adams and Mascarenhas.

The CB40 was similar in many respects: Hampshire, without Maxwell but with McKenzie, kept their nerve in tight finishes, before crushing Sussex in the semi-final at Hove where, in a ferocious opening partnership of 129 in 12.4 overs, Carberry and James Vince made light of a target of 220. Warwickshire were favourites for the Lord's final, and felt they should have won. Requiring a single from Kabir Ali's last ball of a high-scoring and pulsating match, Neil Carter missed a full toss – and Hampshire were celebrating their second trophy in three weeks. Soon after, Kabir joined Lancashire.

Championship promotion would have rounded off an exceptional season, but those three defeats scuppered that, and few argued with a fourth-place finish. Hampshire won four matches, twice squeaking home against Glamorgan, once in a skin-of-their-teeth victory at Chelmsford, then mounting a successful run-chase against Northamptonshire after being outplayed for three days. Hampshire's season was mirrored by the talented Vince: outstanding in the one-day game but – until a last-ditch 114 at Derby – averaging only 18 in the Championship. Even so, he, Dawson, Briggs, the highly regarded keeper Michael Bates and left-arm seamer Chris Wood (all Academy products) justified Hampshire's belief that they could create a side capable of further honours; Bates and Wood each recorded maiden first-class centuries. For 2013, the club signed as their overseas player Australian Twenty20 captain George Bailey, and – for August and September – Pakistan off-spinner Saeed Ajmal.

It was too much to expect Hampshire to lift a third limited-overs trophy. Having qualified for the Champions League in South Africa in October, they failed to reproduce the tenacity that had served them so well in domestic competitions, and were swept out in the preliminary round. The compensation for a long and fruitless journey – elimination at the first hurdle brought no prize money – was the invaluable experience of playing high-calibre opposition.

Championship attendance: 20,517.

150 YEARS OF HAMPSHIRE

A South Coast sesquicentenary

PAT SYMES

When Hampshire County Cricket Club was formed during a meeting at the Antelope Inn, Southampton, on September 11, 1863, William Gladstone was chancellor, the American Civil War raging and the Football Association about to be formed. The century and a half that followed has rarely been dull. Here are some of the highlights.

1863 The committee resolve no professional should be paid more than £5. Matches are arranged for the following year against Sussex, Middlesex and Surrey.

1864 Hampshire lose their first match, to Sussex, by ten wickets. The club's first captain and honorary secretary, gentleman jockey G. M. Ede, wins the Grand National on The Lamb in 1868, and dies two years later when his mount falls on him.

1885 The club's headquarters become Northlands Road in Southampton, where Hampshire lose their first three games by an innings.

1895 Hampshire are admitted to the Championship; from 1902 to 1905, they finish last – or joint-last – each year.

1912 Hampshire beat the Australians, led by Syd Gregory, the last county to do so until Surrey prevail in 1956. (They repeat the trick in 2001, against Steve Waugh's tourists.)

1922 At Edgbaston, Hampshire are all out for 15, but still beat Warwickshire by 155 runs. Warwickshire, put in by the Hon. Lionel Tennyson, make 223; Hampshire's first innings lasts 8.5 overs. Following on, they are 177 for six, but go on to make 521 (thanks to centuries by George Brown and Walter Livsey, from No. 10); Warwickshire are bowled out for 158.

1953 Roy Marshall, from Barbados, becomes the club's first modern overseas player. In 1966, he is appointed Hampshire's first professional captain. World-class signings include Barry Richards, Andy Roberts, Malcolm Marshall and Shane Warne, while Gordon Greenidge, who – having attended school in Berkshire – plays for Hampshire before his native Barbados, and is also classified as overseas.

1961 Colin Ingleby-Mackenzie leads Hampshire to their first County Championship title. Derek Shackleton and Roy Marshall are key figures. When they emulate the feat in 1973 – they are yet to win a third title – Richards and Greenidge are the openers, and Richard Gilliat the captain.

1988 Led by Mark Nicholas, Hampshire beat Derbyshire to win the Benson and Hedges Cup (the other 16 counties had all contested a Lord's final before them). They have since added victories in seven other finals, plus three Sunday League titles.

2000 The Rose Bowl stages its first match (a Second Eleven game) three years after work starts on what was previously farmland. Rod Bransgrove is elected to the committee. In 2001, first-class cricket is played at the new stadium; Bransgrove becomes chairman.

2003 Hampshire County Cricket Club become Hampshire Cricket Ltd. The Rose Bowl hosts its first one-day international, between South Africa and Zimbabwe.

2011 Test cricket reaches the South Coast in June, when England play Sri Lanka.

2012 New stands are named after Warne and Ingleby-Mackenzie; the Rose Bowl becomes the Ageas Bowl.

HAMPSHIRE RESULTS

All first-class matches – Played 17: Won 4, Lost 5, Drawn 8.
County Championship matches – Played 16: Won 4, Lost 5, Drawn 7.

LV= County Championship, 4th in Division 2;
Friends Life t20, winners; Clydesdale Bank 40, winners.

COUNTY CHAMPIONSHIP AVERAGES, BATTING AND FIELDING

Cap		*M*	*I*	*NO*	*R*	*HS*	*100*	*50*	*Avge*	*Ct/St*
2010	N. D. McKenzie¶	5	9	3	403	139	1	2	67.16	6
2006	J. H. K. Adams†	14	25	5	987	149	3	4	49.35	15
	S. M. Katich§	15	23	2	738	196	1	5	35.14	8
2005	S. M. Ervine¶	16	23	3	696	109*	1	4	34.80	7
	L. A. Dawson	16	25	2	682	134*	1	2	29.65	35
	B. M. Shafayat	8	10	0	289	93	0	2	28.90	0
2006	M. A. Carberry	10	18	2	414	84*	0	3	25.87	4
	J. M. Vince	11	18	1	417	114	1	0	24.52	13
	C. P. Wood†	9	14	1	318	105*	1	1	24.46	1
	D. J. Balcombe	16	22	7	299	73	0	1	19.93	3
	M. D. Bates	16	22	0	437	103	1	1	19.86	51/1
	Kabir Ali	8	9	1	140	31	0	0	17.50	0
1998	A. D. Mascarenhas	5	5	0	79	27	0	0	15.80	2
	H. Riazuddin	4	6	1	68	28	0	0	13.60	1
2012	D. R. Briggs†	4	6	2	49	20*	0	0	12.25	2
	S. P. Terry†	3	4	0	34	19	0	0	8.50	1
2008	J. A. Tomlinson†	12	14	7	45	11	0	0	6.42	4
	D. A. Griffiths†	4	6	1	27	21	0	0	5.40	2

† *Born in Hampshire.* § *Official overseas player.* ¶ *Other non-England-qualified player.*

BOWLING

	Style	*O*	*M*	*R*	*W*	*BB*	*5I*	*Avge*
H. Riazuddin	RFM	78	17	240	10	5-61	1	24.00
J. A. Tomlinson	LFM	376.1	82	1,131	43	5-69	2	26.30
S. M. Ervine	RFM	220.2	55	689	26	4-96	0	26.50
D. J. Balcombe	RFM	505.1	103	1,589	59	8-71	3	26.93
Kabir Ali	RFM	216.3	36	769	22	3-42	0	34.95
C. P. Wood	LFM	252.5	68	683	19	4-52	0	35.94
L. A. Dawson	SLA	260.5	59	829	23	5-29	1	36.04

Also bowled: J. H. K. Adams (LM) 3–2–4–1; D. R. Briggs (SLA) 82.1–15–249–5; M. A. Carberry (OB) 4–0–19–1; D. A. Griffiths (RFM) 90.4–14–316–9; S. M. Katich (SLC) 33–4–93–2; A. D. Mascarenhas (RM) 104–36–241–7; B. M. Shafayat (RM) 2–0–15–0; J. M. Vince (RM) 3–0–6–0.

LEADING CB40 AVERAGES (100 runs/4 wickets)

Batting	*Runs*	*HS*	*Avge*	*SR*	*Ct*
M. A. Carberry	598	148*	85.42	104.72	2
J. M. Vince	555	102*	55.50	101.64	3
J. H. K. Adams	333	66	33.30	98.23	7
S. M. Katich	213	59*	30.42	86.93	6
N. D. McKenzie	181	88	30.16	79.03	2
S. M. Ervine	218	68	27.25	84.49	4

Bowling	*W*	*BB*	*Avge*	*ER*
D. R. Briggs	19	4-32	21.57	4.88
Kabir Ali	10	3-39	25.60	6.40
D. A. Griffiths	12	3-29	26.50	5.78
S. M. Ervine	11	3-35	26.54	5.40
C. P. Wood	19	5-22	26.89	5.50
A. D. Mascarenhas	6	2-17	28.66	4.52

LEADING FLT20 AVERAGES (100 runs/18 overs)

Batting	*Runs*	*HS*	*Avge*	*SR*	*Ct*
G. J. Maxwell	179	66*	44.75	**175.49**	2
S. M. Katich	165	42*	41.25	**127.90**	3
S. M. Ervine	190	75*	38.00	**125.00**	5
J. M. Vince	254	64*	31.75	**118.69**	7
N. D. McKenzie	140	79*	23.33	**117.64**	0
J. H. K. Adams	195	43	21.66	**114.70**	2

Bowling	*W*	*BB*	*Avge*	*ER*
A. D. Mascarenhas	15	2-11	16.46	**6.50**
L. A. Dawson	9	2-10	24.22	**7.03**
D. R. Briggs	6	2-28	43.50	**7.25**
G. J. Maxwell	7	3-36	26.00	**7.58**
C. P. Wood	9	3-26	31.33	**7.69**
S. M. Ervine	6	2-22	33.50	**8.04**

FIRST-CLASS COUNTY RECORDS

Highest score for	316	R. H. Moore v Warwickshire at Bournemouth	1937
Highest score against	303*	G. A. Hick (Worcestershire) at Southampton	1997
Leading run-scorer	48,892	C. P. Mead (avge 48.84)	1905–1936
Best bowling for	9-25	R. M. H. Cottam v Lancashire at Manchester	1965
Best bowling against	10-46	W. Hickton (Lancashire) at Manchester	1870
Leading wicket-taker	2,669	D. Shackleton (avge 18.23)	1948–1969
Highest total for	714-5 dec	v Nottinghamshire at Southampton	2005
Highest total against	742	by Surrey at The Oval	1909
Lowest total for	15	v Warwickshire at Birmingham	1922
Lowest total against	23	by Yorkshire at Middlesbrough	1965

LIST A COUNTY RECORDS

Highest score for	177	C. G. Greenidge v Glamorgan at Southampton	1975
Highest score against	203	A. D. Brown (Surrey) at Guildford	1997
Leading run-scorer	12,034	R. A. Smith (avge 42.97)	1983–2003
Best bowling for	7-30	P. J. Sainsbury v Norfolk at Southampton	1965
Best bowling against	7-22	J. R. Thomson (Middlesex) at Lord's	1981
Leading wicket-taker	411	C. A. Connor (avge 25.07)	1984–1998
Highest total for	371-4	v Glamorgan at Southampton	1975
Highest total against	358-6	by Surrey at The Oval	2005
Lowest total for	43	v Essex at Basingstoke	1972
Lowest total against	61	by Somerset at Bath	1973
	61	by Derbyshire at Portsmouth	1990

TWENTY20 COUNTY RECORDS

Highest score for	124*	M. J. Lumb v Essex v Southampton	2009
Highest score against	98	L. J. Wright (Sussex) at Hove	2007
Leading run-scorer	**1,626**	**S. M. Ervine (avge 28.03)**	**2005–*2012***
Best bowling for	5-14	A. D. Mascarenhas v Sussex at Hove	2004
Best bowling against	5-21	A. J. Hollioake (Surrey) at Southampton	2003
Leading wicket-taker	**82**	**A. D. Mascarenhas (avge 17.07)**	**2003–*2012***
Highest total for	225-2	v Middlesex at Southampton	2006
Highest total against	220-4	by Somerset at Taunton	2010
Lowest total for	85	v Sussex at Southampton	2008
Lowest total against	67	by Sussex at Hove	2004

ADDRESS

The Ageas Bowl, Botley Road, West End, Southampton SO30 3XH (023 8047 2002; **email** enquiries@ageasbowl.com). **Website** www.ageasbowl.com

OFFICIALS

Captain J. H. K. Adams
A. D. Mascarenhas (Twenty20)
Cricket secretary T. M. Tremlett
Team manager G. W. White
Academy director R. J. Parks
President N. E. J. Pocock

Chairman R. G. Bransgrove
Chief executive D. Mann
Chairman, members committee T. Crump
Head groundsman N. Gray
Scorer A. E. Weld

HAMPSHIRE v LOUGHBOROUGH MCCU

At Southampton, April 6–8. Hampshire won by 274 runs. Toss: Loughborough MCCU. First-class debuts: S. P. Terry; A. J. Morris, A. D. Wilson.

Sam Billings, a wicketkeeper-batsman on Kent's books, twice frustrated Hampshire, but he could not prevent a heavy Loughborough defeat. One of three students to reach double figures in the first innings, and one of only two in the second, Billings made 49 and, with Loughborough facing a notional 391 in two sessions, a defiant 69. He and Will Tavaré added 83 – the only substantial partnership in the students' first innings – as Hampshire exploited the overcast conditions that prevailed throughout. Loughborough wickets fell in clumps on the last day: two on 12, three on 86 and the final four on 116. Earlier, Vince had shown there was little to fear in the early-spring pitch, contributing a classy 128.

Close of play: first day, Hampshire 445-7 (Terry 59, Riazuddin 55); second day, Hampshire 11-1 (Adams 6, Carberry 0).

Hampshire

Batsman	First innings	Runs	Second innings	Runs
*J. H. K. Adams c Billings b Lester		11	– not out	26
L. A. Dawson b Soilleux		1	– lbw b Soilleux	1
M. A. Carberry c Taylor b Soilleux		7	– lbw b Wilson	47
J. M. Vince lbw b Endersby		128		
S. M. Ervine c Endersby b Morris		40	– (4) not out	27
†M. D. Bates b Soilleux		93		
S. P. Terry not out		59		
C. P. Wood run out		6		
H. Riazuddin not out		55		
B 13, l-b 14, w 12, n-b 6		45	L-b 7, w 3	10
1/8 (2) 2/21 (3) 3/25 (1) 4/122 (5) 5/257 (4) 6/363 (6) 7/379 (8)	(7 wkts dec, 100 overs)	445	1/9 (2) 2/81 (3) (2 wkts dec, 34 overs)	111

D. J. Balcombe and D. A. Griffiths did not bat.

Wilson 19–4–73–0; Soilleux 20–5–67–3; Lester 19–2–81–1; Taylor 20–3–101–0; Morris 9–0–47–1; Endersby 10–1–38–1; Evans 3–1–11–0. *Second innings*—Soilleux 9–2–33–1; Taylor 8–1–27–0; Wilson 9–3–24–1; Lester 6–2–18–0; Endersby 2–0–2–0.

Loughborough MCCU

Batsman	First innings	Runs	Second innings	Runs
W. A. Tavaré lbw b Wood		61	– b Wood	7
R. F. Evans c Terry b Riazuddin		17	– b Balcombe	20
N. Patel c Bates b Balcombe		0	– c Dawson b Wood	0
†S. W. Billings b Riazuddin		49	– c Bates b Ervine	69
F. W. Daeche-Marshall b Wood		4	– c Bates b Balcombe	0
*R. M. L. Taylor c Bates b Wood		0	– c Terry b Balcombe	0
D. M. Endersby c Dawson b Balcombe		9	– c Bates b Griffiths	4
A. J. Morris c Ervine b Wood		0	– lbw b Dawson	7
A. C. Soilleux c Ervine b Wood		4	– not out	0
A. D. Wilson c Balcombe b Griffiths		6	– c Ervine b Dawson	0
T. Lester not out		0	– lbw b Dawson	0
B 8, l-b 4, n-b 4		16	B 7, l-b 2	9
1/34 (2) 2/37 (3) 3/120 (4) 4/127 (5) 5/129 (6) 6/152 (1) 7/152 (8) 8/154 (7) 9/158 (9) 10/166 (10)	(49.5 overs)	166	1/12 (1) 2/12 (3) 3/86 (2) 4/86 (5) 5/86 (6) 6/97 (7) 7/116 (4) 8/116 (8) 9/116 (10) 10/116 (11) (51.3 overs)	116

Balcombe 14–4–47–2; Riazuddin 10–4–20–2; Wood 15–3–41–5; Griffiths 7.5–0–31–1; Ervine 3–0–15–0. *Second innings*—Wood 6–2–8–2; Ervine 9–4–12–1; Balcombe 14–4–35–3; Griffiths 12–4–35–1; Riazuddin 4–2–9–0; Dawson 4.3–3–8–3; Carberry 2–2–0–0.

Umpires: M. R. Benson and A. G. Wharf.

HAMPSHIRE v GLOUCESTERSHIRE

At Southampton, April 12–15. Gloucestershire won by 33 runs. Gloucestershire 22pts, Hampshire 3pts. Toss: Hampshire.

Payne bowled Hampshire No. 11 Balcombe to seal victory with 12 balls to spare as Gloucestershire put an innings defeat at Chelmsford behind them. Balcombe was unlucky to be on the losing side after claiming a ground-record eight for 71 in the first innings and 11 for 119 overall – both career-bests. The green-tinged wicket helped all the seamers, with Will Gidman proving almost as penetrative to claim nine for 114. Dent, one of the few batsmen to master the conditions, guided Gloucestershire past 300 with a diligent century. Hampshire trailed by 115, but soon had their opponents 71 for five, only for Cockbain and Gidman to double the score. Set 290, Hampshire were 72 for six before Bates (whose six first-innings catches had equalled another ground record) and Wood added 118, briefly threatening an unlikely win. But Wood fell for a personal-best 65, Gidman took two wickets in four balls, and the last pair could not see out the five remaining overs. Hampshire contributed to their own downfall by conceding 43 more extras than Gloucestershire.

Close of play: first day, Gloucestershire 195-4 (Dent 59, Cockbain 52); second day, Hampshire 182-7 (Wood 21, Riazuddin 3); third day, Gloucestershire 129-5 (Cockbain 27, W. R. S. Gidman 25).

Gloucestershire

First innings		Second innings	
C. D. J. Dent c Bates b Wood	114	c Dawson b Wood	6
†R. G. Coughtrie c Katich b Balcombe	4	lbw b Riazuddin	14
D. M. Housego c Bates b Balcombe	0	c Briggs b Balcombe	14
*A. P. R. Gidman lbw b Ervine	27	c Vince b Riazuddin	3
H. J. H. Marshall lbw b Balcombe	18	c Bates b Riazuddin	16
I. A. Cockbain c Bates b Balcombe	64	run out	47
W. R. S. Gidman c Ervine b Balcombe	0	c Bates b Balcombe	29
E. G. C. Young c Bates b Balcombe	39	c Riazuddin b Balcombe	0
J. K. Fuller c Bates b Balcombe	0	c Briggs b Wood	14
I. D. Saxelby not out	0	lbw b Briggs	5
D. A. Payne c Bates b Balcombe	5	not out	0
B 9, l-b 13, w 1, n-b 20	43	B 10, n-b 16	26
1/8 (2) 2/22 (3) 3/63 (4) 4/87 (5) 5/220 (6) 6/222 (7) 7/302 (8) 8/306 (1) 9/306 (9) 10/314 (11) (96.4 overs)	314	1/12 (1) 2/29 (2) 3/49 (4) 4/67 (5) 5/71 (3) 6/143 (7) 7/143 (8) 8/164 (9) 9/169 (6) 10/174 (10) (54.1 overs)	174

Wood 28–8–79–1; Balcombe 28.4–8–71–8; Riazuddin 19–6–59–0; Ervine 14–2–51–1; Briggs 7–0–32–0. *Second innings*—Wood 15–2–36–2; Balcombe 18–2–48–3; Riazuddin 14–3–51–3; Ervine 6–1–25–0; Briggs 1.1–0–4–1.

Hampshire

First innings		Second innings	
*J. H. K. Adams c Dent b W. R. S. Gidman	8	c Dent b Payne	13
L. A. Dawson c Dent b Saxelby	34	c Saxelby b W. R. S. Gidman	11
M. A. Carberry run out	3	c Coughtrie b W. R. S. Gidman	18
S. M. Katich c Payne b Saxelby	74	c Coughtrie b Saxelby	9
J. M. Vince c A. P. R. Gidman b Saxelby	15	c Cockbain b Saxelby	4
S. M. Ervine lbw b W. R. S. Gidman	11	c Cockbain b Saxelby	0
†M. D. Bates c Dent b W. R. S. Gidman	4	b W. R. S. Gidman	87
C. P. Wood c Dent b W. R. S. Gidman	21	c Marshall b Payne	65
H. Riazuddin b Payne	16	b W. R. S. Gidman	28
D. R. Briggs lbw b W. R. S. Gidman	1	not out	1
D. J. Balcombe not out	0	b Payne	6
B 1, l-b 8, w 1, n-b 2	12	B 1, l-b 11, n-b 2	14
1/14 (1) 2/24 (3) 3/81 (2) 4/101 (5) 5/145 (6) 6/157 (7) 7/160 (4) 8/193 (8) 9/195 (10) 10/199 (9) (63.1 overs)	199	1/23 (2) 2/25 (1) 3/36 (4) 4/54 (5) 5/56 (6) 6/72 (3) 7/190 (8) 8/246 (7) 9/247 (9) 10/256 (11) (78 overs)	256

W. R. S. Gidman 18–7–48–5; Saxelby 18–4–46–3; Fuller 11–1–48–0; Payne 8.1–1–40–1; Young 8–3–8–0. *Second innings*—W. R. S. Gidman 22–4–66–4; Saxelby 17–4–53–3; Payne 19–3–56–3; Young 11–3–29–0; Fuller 9–0–40–0.

Umpires: R. J. Bailey and N. J. Llong.

At Cardiff, April 19–22. HAMPSHIRE beat GLAMORGAN by two wickets.

HAMPSHIRE v LEICESTERSHIRE

At Southampton, April 26–29. Drawn. Hampshire 7pts, Leicestershire 5pts. Toss: Hampshire. Championship debut: S. P. Terry.

Rain washed away the last day, almost all the third and more than 40 overs of the first two. Katich, standing in as captain after Jimmy Adams withdrew because of a family illness, inserted Leicestershire on a wicket expected to favour seam. Hampshire had chosen to omit slow left-armer Danny Briggs to accommodate an extra pace bowler, so it was a surprise when Dawson claimed five for 29 with left-arm spin. He had taken seven for 51 for Mountaineers in Zimbabwe the previous October, but never more than two in the Championship. Greg Smith and Sarwan put on 81 for Leicestershire's third wicket before Dawson removed them both. Sean Terry, son of former Hampshire batsman and coach Paul, began his Championship career with a duck, but Carberry and Katich added 124. Hampshire seemed to be gaining the upper hand when rain intruded.

Close of play: first day, Leicestershire 159-6 (Cobb 4); second day, Hampshire 181-4 (Carberry 73, Ervine 17); third day, Hampshire 217-4 (Carberry 84, Ervine 41).

Leicestershire

G. P. Smith b Dawson 68
M. A. G. Boyce c Bates b Griffiths 10
J. du Toit lbw b Riazuddin 8
*R. R. Sarwan c Ervine b Dawson 46
Kadeer Ali b Wood 8
M. N. Malik lbw b Dawson 1
J. J. Cobb c Griffiths b Dawson 5
†E. J. H. Eckersley c Vince b Balcombe 34
W. A. White lbw b Dawson 21
R. H. Joseph not out 9
A. C. F. Wyatt c Bates b Griffiths 3
B 1, l-b 11, w 1, n-b 8 21

1/34 (2) 2/65 (3) 3/146 (1) (99.2 overs) 234
4/153 (4) 5/155 (5) 6/159 (6)
7/166 (7) 8/217 (8) 9/229 (9) 10/234 (11)

Wood 25–5–44–1; Balcombe 22–4–58–1; Griffiths 20.2–3–56–2; Riazuddin 8–1–22–1; Ervine 4–1–9–0; Dawson 18–4–29–5; Vince 2–0–4–0.

Hampshire

L. A. Dawson c Eckersley b Wyatt 19
S. P. Terry c Smith b Wyatt 0
M. A. Carberry not out 84
*S. M. Katich c Eckersley b Malik 54
J. M. Vince c Sarwan b Wyatt 5
S. M. Ervine not out 41
L-b 6, w 1, n-b 7 14

1/4 (2) 2/25 (1) (4 wkts, 55 overs) 217
3/149 (4) 4/154 (5)

†M. D. Bates, C. P. Wood, H. Riazuddin, D. J. Balcombe and D. A. Griffiths did not bat.

Joseph 9–2–32–0; Wyatt 17–3–63–3; Malik 18–2–64–1; White 4–1–28–0; Kadeer Ali 7–1–24–0.

Umpires: J. H. Evans and D. J. Millns.

At Northampton, May 2–5. HAMPSHIRE lost to NORTHAMPTONSHIRE by 117 runs.

HAMPSHIRE v DERBYSHIRE

At Southampton, May 9–12. Drawn. Hampshire 10pts, Derbyshire 10pts. Toss: Derbyshire. County debut: B. M. Shafayat.

After the first two days were lost to rain, the only hope of a positive outcome lay in forfeitures and a contrived target. But the captains failed to reach agreement, and the match meandered to a draw. Derbyshire had particular cause to regret the caution as they passed Hampshire's total with 22 overs left and seven wickets down. When the covers finally came off, Madsen chose to bowl on another green surface; it proved slow, though Adams and Shafayat added 164 for the second wicket. Shafayat, in his first Championship match since Nottinghamshire released him in 2010 – though he had been playing in the Quaid-e-Azam, Pakistan's domestic first-class competition – justified Hampshire's offer of a contract, falling seven short of a hundred on debut. Durston and Redfern then rebuilt the Derbyshire innings after they had stumbled to 37 for three. Dropped by Dawson in the slips when 37, Durston salted the wound by hitting him for four of his five sixes.

Close of play: first day, no play; second day, no play; third day, Hampshire 352-8 (Kabir Ali 17, Balcombe 7).

Hampshire

L. A. Dawson c Guptill b Palladino	6	Kabir Ali not out	17
*J. H. K. Adams run out	122	D. J. Balcombe not out	7
B. M. Shafayat c Poynton b Clare	93		
S. M. Katich b Wainwright	7	B 4, l-b 15, w 1	20
J. M. Vince c Poynton b Wainwright	36		——
S. M. Ervine c Whiteley b Groenewald	24	1/20 (1) 2/184 (3) (8 wkts dec, 96 overs)	352
S. P. Terry lbw b Palladino	3	3/213 (4) 4/278 (5)	
†M. D. Bates b Clare	17	5/279 (2) 6/292 (7) 7/323 (6) 8/324 (8)	

J. A. Tomlinson did not bat.

Palladino 20–3–71–2; Groenewald 21–4–63–1; Clare 19–5–57–2; Whiteley 5–0–32–0; Wainwright 22–3–61–2; Durston 5–0–25–0; Redfern 4–0–24–0.

Derbyshire

M. J. Guptill c Katich b Tomlinson	4	A. P. Palladino not out	22
P. M. Borrington c Dawson b Kabir Ali	4	T. D. Groenewald not out	20
*W. L. Madsen c Dawson b Kabir Ali	8		
W. J. Durston b Ervine	121	B 1, l-b 6, w 2, n-b 6	15
D. J. Redfern c and b Tomlinson	133		——
R. A. Whiteley c Dawson b Kabir Ali	23	1/9 (2) 2/17 (1) (9 wkts dec, 87.5 overs)	403
D. J. Wainwright c Ervine b Tomlinson	23	3/37 (3) 4/215 (4)	
J. L. Clare c Adams b Balcombe	20	5/266 (6) 6/328 (7)	
†T. Poynton b Balcombe	10	7/333 (5) 8/354 (8) 9/359 (9)	

Kabir Ali 14–3–60–3; Tomlinson 21.5–1–101–3; Balcombe 19–3–69–2; Ervine 8–1–39–1; Dawson 25–1–127–0.

Umpires: J. W. Lloyds and M. J. Saggers.

At Leeds, May 16–19. HAMPSHIRE drew with YORKSHIRE.

HAMPSHIRE v GLAMORGAN

At Southampton, May 23–26. Hampshire won by 31 runs. Hampshire 22pts, Glamorgan 6pts. Toss: Glamorgan.

At 168 for four and with plenty of time left, Glamorgan seemed likely to win in Hampshire for the first time since 1991. They needed another 95, but promptly lost two wickets before recovering to 212 for six, 51 short of victory. Then, on a pitch almost as green as on the first morning, came a collapse of four for 19, handing Hampshire the double over them in five weeks. Crucial had been the 85 runs added by Ervine and Balcombe, Hampshire's last pair, on the first evening. Thanks to Bragg and North, however, Glamorgan gained a modest lead, which they failed to build on. They were hampered by the absence of two injured frontline bowlers, Huw Waters and Graham Wagg, though in his first match of the season Glover exploited a seaming pitch to claim seven wickets. While North was at the crease Glamorgan harboured hopes of victory, but his departure at 119 – bowled by Balcombe for the second time – tipped the balance Hampshire's way.

Close of play: first day, Glamorgan 13-0 (Rees 7, James 6); second day, Hampshire 25-0 (Dawson 19, Adams 6); third day, Glamorgan 53-2 (Rees 17, North 22).

Hampshire

L. A. Dawson lbw b Glover	6 – c Wallace b Owen	23
*J. H. K. Adams b Owen	42 – b Glover	72
M. A. Carberry c Wallace b Glover	0 – c Owen b Allenby	25
S. M. Katich lbw b Owen	36 – c Wallace b Glover	12
J. M. Vince c Wallace b Glover	9 – c Wallace b Allenby	48
S. M. Ervine not out	109 – run out	22
†M. D. Bates b Allenby	41 – b Reed	0
C. P. Wood c Glover b Owen	19 – c James b Allenby	7
Kabir Ali c Bragg b Owen	0 – b Glover	25
J. A. Tomlinson c Bragg b Allenby	4 – (11) not out	0
D. J. Balcombe c Bragg b Glover	39 – (10) b Owen	26
B 4, l-b 2, w 1, n-b 4	11 B 5, l-b 6, n-b 2	13
1/18 (1) 2/22 (3) 3/87 (4) 4/96 (5) (86.4 overs) 5/96 (2) 6/159 (7) 7/204 (8) 8/204 (9) 9/231 (10) 10/316 (11)	316 1/31 (1) 2/102 (3) (86.2 overs) 3/124 (4) 4/141 (2) 5/190 (6) 6/190 (7) 7/210 (8) 8/225 (5) 9/269 (9) 10/273 (10)	273

Glover 18.4–5–76–4; Owen 21–1–87–4; Reed 15–1–66–0; Allenby 19–1–68–2; Cosker 12–4–12–0; North 1–0–1–0. *Second innings*—Glover 20–8–45–3; Allenby 17–2–58–3; Owen 15.2–1–54–2; Reed 12–2–34–1; Cosker 22–6–71–0.

Glamorgan

G. P. Rees c and b Tomlinson	11 – lbw b Tomlinson	21
N. A. James c Bates b Wood	15 – c Adams b Kabir Ali	0
W. D. Bragg c Bates b Balcombe	73 – c Dawson b Tomlinson	8
M. J. North b Balcombe	70 – b Balcombe	69
B. J. Wright c Dawson b Balcombe	28 – c Dawson b Balcombe	32
J. Allenby c Vince b Kabir Ali	8 – c Bates b Tomlinson	23
*†M. A. Wallace c Dawson b Balcombe	27 – c Katich b Kabir Ali	29
J. C. Glover c Bates b Tomlinson	13 – c Katich b Dawson	15
D. A. Cosker not out	40 – lbw b Dawson	0
W. T. Owen b Tomlinson	7 – not out	13
M. T. Reed c Vince b Wood	0 c Vince b Kabir Ali	4
B 12, l-b 5, n-b 18	35 B 3, l-b 12, n-b 2	17
1/19 (1) 2/52 (2) 3/148 (3) (92.2 overs) 4/200 (5) 5/223 (4) 6/234 (6) 7/267 (8) 8/287 (7) 9/326 (10) 10/327 (11)	327 1/1 (2) 2/18 (3) (74.3 overs) 3/59 (1) 4/119 (4) 5/168 (5) 6/168 (6) 7/212 (8) 8/214 (7) 9/214 (9) 10/231 (11)	231

Kabir Ali 20–4–65–1; Tomlinson 22–5–60–3; Balcombe 23–4–91–4; Wood 19.2–8–51–2; Ervine 1–0–6–0; Dawson 7–0–37–0. *Second innings*—Kabir Ali 15.3–0–42–3; Tomlinson 17–4–45–3; Wood 14–2–34–0; Balcombe 17–3–46–2; Dawson 11–3–49–2.

Umpires: M. A. Eggleston and R. K. Illingworth.

At Tunbridge Wells, June 6–9. HAMPSHIRE drew with KENT.

HAMPSHIRE v YORKSHIRE

At Southampton, July 11–14. Drawn. Hampshire 6pts, Yorkshire 7pts. Toss: Hampshire. County debut: S. J. Harmison.

Only Root would have derived any satisfaction from another match ruined by rain. The first and last days were washed out, while 70 overs were lost from the second, and 14 from the third. Even so, Root had time to compile a maiden double-hundred, despite Yorkshire lurching to 108 for six, then 161 for seven. He dominated stands of 121 for the eighth wicket with Patterson (who contributed 37, the next-best score in Yorkshire's innings), and 58 for the tenth with Ashraf (who made four). Until now, Root had hit only one six in first-class matches, but he struck three more as conditions eased. A slow outfield restricted the scoring, and there had been enough movement to justify Adams's decision to bowl. Jaques, in his first match as Yorkshire captain, declared once his team had secured an unexpected fourth batting point. In five overs at the start of a loan spell from Durham, Harmison conceded four wides and 25 runs.

Close of play: first day, no play; second day, Yorkshire 83-3 (Root 46, Ballance 17); third day, Hampshire 39-0 (Adams 20, McKenzie 14).

Yorkshire

A. Lyth lbw b Tomlinson 2
J. E. Root not out 222
*P. A. Jaques c Bates b Kabir Ali 12
†J. M. Bairstow c Bates b Kabir Ali 0
G. S. Ballance c Dawson b Tomlinson 19
A. McGrath c Bates b Mascarenhas 5
R. M. Pyrah c and b Mascarenhas 0
Azeem Rafiq b Kabir Ali 29
S. A. Patterson c Bates b Tomlinson 37
S. J. Harmison c Bates b Tomlinson 2
M. A. Ashraf not out 4

B 8, l-b 9, w 1 18

1/9 (1) 2/28 (3) 3/28 (4) 4/95 (5) 5/103 (6) 6/108 (7) 7/161 (8) 8/282 (9) 9/292 (10) (9 wkts dec, 94 overs) 350

Kabir Ali 24–6–88–3; Tomlinson 25–6–80–4; Balcombe 20–4–62–0; Mascarenhas 15–3–40–2; Ervine 1–0–13–0; Dawson 9–0–50–0.

Hampshire

*J. H. K. Adams not out 20
N. D. McKenzie not out 14
L-b 1, w 4 5

(no wkt, 12 overs) 39

B. M. Shafayat, S. M. Katich, L. A. Dawson, S. M. Ervine, †M. D. Bates, A. D. Mascarenhas, Kabir Ali, D. J. Balcombe and J. A. Tomlinson did not bat.

Harmison 5–1–25–0; Patterson 5–3–8–0; Azeem Rafiq 1–0–1–0; McGrath 1–0–4–0.

Umpires: N. G. C. Cowley and G. Sharp.

At Chelmsford, July 19–22. HAMPSHIRE beat ESSEX by two runs.

HAMPSHIRE v KENT

At Southampton, July 27, 28, 29, 30. Drawn. Hampshire 7pts, Kent 10pts. Toss: Hampshire.

Adams and last man Briggs held out for 20 overs – including a blast with the new ball – to stave off defeat. Needing 175 to make Kent bat again, Hampshire were 144 for nine when Briggs joined his captain. Defying a ring of close fielders and surviving several close lbw decisions, the pair clung on, leaving Kent to rue the loss of more than 60 overs to rain on the third day. After choosing to bat on a pitch that helped the pace bowlers, Adams was obliged to drag his team out of trouble with an innings of 91, arguably as valuable as the 85 not out he made to save the game. Northeast and Key made the best of easier conditions in an opening stand of 252, the basis for Kent's substantial first-innings lead. Hampshire were left a minimum of 89 overs to bat on the last day, but quickly fell to ten for three – and did not stem the bleeding until it was almost too late.

Close of play: first day, Hampshire 292-9 (Briggs 11, Tomlinson 5); second day, Kent 291-5 (Davies 2); third day, Kent 438-8 (Tredwell 21, Coles 19).

Hampshire

*J. H. K. Adams c Jones b Stevens	91	– not out	85
J. M. Vince c Jones b Shreck	4	– b Davies	0
B. M. Shafayat b Davies	0	– lbw b Shreck	2
S. M. Katich lbw b Shreck	32	– c Jones b Shreck	0
L. A. Dawson c Davies b Tredwell	51	– c Northeast b Tredwell	28
S. M. Ervine b Coles	25	– lbw b Nash	31
†M. D. Bates lbw b Tredwell	8	– c and b Tredwell	2
A. D. Mascarenhas c Jones b Davies	27	– c Davies b Tredwell	9
D. J. Balcombe b Shreck	28	– c Stevens b Coles	1
D. R. Briggs c Tredwell b Davies	11	– (11) not out	20
J. A. Tomlinson not out	5	– (10) b Coles	0
B 1, l-b 5, n-b 4	10	L-b 3, w 1, n-b 4	8
1/8 (2) 2/9 (3) 3/67 (4) 4/183 (1) (96.2 overs)	292	1/1 (2) 2/8 (3) (9 wkts, 91 overs)	186
5/189 (5) 6/206 (7) 7/226 (6)		3/10 (4) 4/52 (5)	
8/276 (8) 9/276 (9) 10/292 (10)		5/110 (6) 6/117 (7) 7/143 (8)	
		8/144 (9) 9/144 (10)	

Davies 21.2–6–36–3; Shreck 25–6–85–3; Stevens 19–4–49–1; Coles 14–2–60–1; Tredwell 17–2–56–2. *Second innings*—Davies 14–9–8–1; Shreck 19–5–50–2; Tredwell 33–10–62–3; Coles 15–2–41–2; Stevens 4–1–8–0; Nash 6–0–14–1.

Kent

S. A. Northeast c Bates b Ervine	140
*R. W. T. Key c Bates b Tomlinson	119
B. W. Harmison c Dawson b Balcombe	8
B. P. Nash b Tomlinson	5
M. J. Powell c Bates b Tomlinson	2
M. Davies c Mascarenhas b Tomlinson	17
D. I. Stevens c Tomlinson b Ervine	40
†G. O. Jones b Ervine	36
J. C. Tredwell c Bates b Ervine	31
M. T. Coles c Balcombe b Dawson	29
C. E. Shreck not out	8
B 9, l-b 6, w 1, n-b 16	32
1/252 (1) 2/273 (3) (130.4 overs)	467
3/284 (4) 4/288 (5) 5/291 (2)	
6/324 (6) 7/385 (8) 8/409 (7)	
9/455 (10) 10/467 (9) 110 overs: 366-6	

Tomlinson 28–6–94–4; Mascarenhas 23–10–55–0; Ervine 22.4–1–96–4; Balcombe 26–2–94–1; Briggs 19–2–66–0; Dawson 6–0–25–1; Katich 6–0–22–0.

Umpires: P. J. Hartley and S. J. O'Shaughnessy.

At Bristol, August 6–9. HAMPSHIRE drew with GLOUCESTERSHIRE.

HAMPSHIRE v NORTHAMPTONSHIRE

At Southampton, August 15–18. Hampshire won by eight wickets. Hampshire 21pts, Northamptonshire 7pts. Toss: Hampshire.

With 11 balls to spare, Katich hit the boundary that took Hampshire to victory, after Northamptonshire noses had been in front for three days or more. Hall's declaration late on the fourth morning set Hampshire 326 from 72 overs. Until now, batting had been tricky on a lively pitch, but the surface had flattened out, allowing them to speed towards their fourth win of the season. Adams began the chase by putting on 150 in 39 overs with McKenzie, and then added 127 in 22 with Katich, by which time Northamptonshire had run out of options. Katich and Dawson punished a tiring attack to complete the task. Northamptonshire had built an 80-run first-innings lead on solid contributions down the order – they were 98 for five on a truncated first day – and Evans's career-best four for 38. Wakely's dismissal for 96 was the cue for the declaration. In a summer that, it seemed, could hardly get any wetter, Hampshire fielders were surprised when it did, getting an impromptu shower from the sprinklers after rain had delayed the first-day start.

Close of play: first day, Northamptonshire 170-5 (Newton 46, Middlebrook 26); second day, Hampshire 125-2 (Adams 48, Dawson 19); third day, Northamptonshire 176-5 (Wakely 61, Middlebrook 3).

Northamptonshire

S. D. Peters c Dawson b Wood	47	– c Bates b Kabir Ali	4
N. J. O'Brien c Bates b Tomlinson	8	– c Bates b Tomlinson	15
D. J. Sales b Balcombe	18	– c Vince b Balcombe	24
A. G. Wakely c Ervine b Balcombe	5	– c Dawson b Kabir Ali	96
R. I. Newton c Bates b Balcombe	48	– c Katich b Tomlinson	59
*A. J. Hall c Adams b Tomlinson	2	– c Dawson b Ervine	0
J. D. Middlebrook b Dawson	65	– b Wood	4
†D. Murphy b Tomlinson	43	– c McKenzie b Balcombe	1
D. J. Willey c Katich b Wood	54	– not out	31
L. M. Daggett not out	26		
L. Evans b Dawson	0		
B 16, l-b 6, w 4, n-b 14	40	B 2, l-b 5, n-b 4	11
1/20 (2) 2/59 (3) 3/87 (1) (100.3 overs)	356	1/4 (1) (8 wkts dec, 66.3 overs)	245
4/87 (4) 5/98 (6) 6/172 (5)		2/30 (2) 3/62 (3)	
7/257 (7) 8/301 (8) 9/356 (9) 10/356 (11)		4/161 (5) 5/161 (6)	
		6/181 (7) 7/182 (8) 8/245 (4)	

Kabir Ali 18–1–85–0; Tomlinson 26–8–66–3; Balcombe 24–6–58–3; Wood 18–6–68–2; Ervine 5–0–34–0; Dawson 9.3–2–23–2. *Second innings*—Kabir Ali 12.3–0–72–2; Tomlinson 19–3–60–2; Balcombe 14–2–37–2; Wood 12–2–38–1; Dawson 3–0–23–0; Ervine 6–2–8–1.

Hampshire

*J. H. K. Adams lbw b Willey	73	– (2) c Wakely b Evans	149
N. D. McKenzie c Murphy b Daggett	31	– (1) c Hall b Evans	76
S. M. Katich lbw b Evans	7	– not out	61
L. A. Dawson lbw b Evans	19	– not out	27
J. M. Vince lbw b Evans	4		
S. M. Ervine b Willey	15		
†M. D. Bates c Sales b Hall	28		
C. P. Wood c Willey b Evans	17		
Kabir Ali c Murphy b Hall	31		
D. J. Balcombe c Willey b Hall	15		
J. A. Tomlinson not out	0		
B 12, l-b 13, w 3, n-b 8	36	L-b 3, w 1, n-b 12	16
1/62 (2) 2/85 (3) 3/129 (4) (86.2 overs)	276	1/150 (1) (2 wkts, 70.1 overs)	329
4/135 (5) 5/173 (6) 6/176 (1)		2/277 (2)	
7/212 (8) 8/249 (7) 9/267 (9) 10/276 (10)			

Willey 23–3–103–2; Hall 19.2–6–35–3; Daggett 22–5–75–1; Evans 21–10–38–4; Middlebrook 1–1–0–0. *Second innings*—Willey 12.1–1–54–0; Hall 15–3–61–0; Daggett 12–1–65–0; Evans 15–0–75–2; Middlebrook 16–2–71–0.

Umpires: M. A. Gough and S. J. O'Shaughnessy.

At Leicester, August 21–24. HAMPSHIRE lost to LEICESTERSHIRE by 126 runs. *Chris Wood and David Balcombe add 168 for the tenth wicket in Hampshire's second innings.*

HAMPSHIRE v ESSEX

At Southampton, September 4–7. Essex won by 122 runs. Essex 19pts, Hampshire 4pts. Toss: Hampshire.

Essex emphatically overturned a first-innings deficit of 49 to avenge a two-run defeat at Chelmsford earlier in the summer. The pitch was green, as most were at Southampton in 2012, and the toss appeared crucial. Put in, Essex were dismissed inside 53 overs as Balcombe and Griffiths exploited ideal seam conditions. Hampshire ended the first day only 15 behind with six wickets intact, but next morning Essex fought back as Topley grabbed three. The surface eased during the second half of the match, which was lit up by Shah's 44th century. Mickleburgh helped him add 193 for the second wicket, and there were useful contributions down the order. Hampshire needed a mammoth 425, which looked even less likely once Chambers had reduced them to 23 for three on the third afternoon. Adams, who carried his bat, and Dawson put on 160 for the fourth wicket before the Essex seamers ran through the rest, despite defiance from last man Griffiths. Defeat spelled the end of Hampshire's promotion hopes.

Close of play: first day, Hampshire 165-4 (Shafayat 42, Vince 22); second day, Essex 217-2 (Shah 124, Craddock 2); third day, Hampshire 73-3 (Adams 36, Dawson 25).

Essex

First innings		Second innings	
T. Westley c Adams b Balcombe	4	– c Dawson b Balcombe	15
J. C. Mickleburgh c Dawson b Balcombe	7	– c Dawson b Katich	73
O. A. Shah c Vince b Tomlinson	9	– c Bates b Tomlinson	161
M. L. Pettini c Dawson b Griffiths	58	– (5) c Bates b Dawson	17
R. N. ten Doeschate c Adams b Griffiths	9	– (6) c sub (S. P. Terry) b Dawson	69
*†J. S. Foster c Vince b Balcombe	10	– (7) c Bates b Balcombe	61
A. J. Wheater c Bates b Balcombe	19	– (8) not out	42
G. R. Napier c Bates b Ervine	26	– (9) b Balcombe	2
M. A. Chambers c Bates b Griffiths	0	– (10) b Balcombe	0
T. R. Craddock b Ervine	9	– (4) c Vince b Balcombe	16
R. J. W. Topley not out	0	– c Vince b Dawson	1
B 14, l-b 4, w 1, n-b 10	29	B 3, l-b 5, w 4, n-b 4	16
1/7 (1) 2/25 (2) 3/25 (3) 4/47 (5) 5/86 (6) 6/112 (7) 7/166 (4) 8/166 (8) 9/180 (10) 10/180 (9) (52.2 overs)	180	1/19 (1) 2/212 (2) 3/270 (4) 4/281 (3) 5/318 (5) 6/407 (6) 7/452 (7) 8/460 (9) 9/460 (10) 10/473 (11) (145.4 overs)	473

Tomlinson 13–2–46–1; Balcombe 15–2–57–4; Ervine 11–8–19–2; Griffiths 13.2–2–40–3. *Second innings*—Tomlinson 28–8–68–1; Balcombe 30–7–103–5; Griffiths 22–4–96–0; Ervine 23–11–53–0; Dawson 34.4–8–119–3; Katich 8–0–26–1.

Hampshire

First innings		Second innings	
M. A. Carberry c Napier b Chambers	42	– c Chambers b Topley	6
*J. H. K. Adams c Mickleburgh b Chambers	8	– not out	139
B. M. Shafayat c ten Doeschate b Topley	42	– c Foster b Chambers	3
S. M. Katich c Pettini b ten Doeschate	20	– c Shah b Chambers	0
L. A. Dawson c Foster b Napier	17	– c and b ten Doeschate	90
J. M. Vince c Foster b Topley	26	– c Foster b Topley	15
S. M. Ervine c Pettini b Napier	43	– c Foster b ten Doeschate	4
†M. D. Bates lbw b Topley	6	– b ten Doeschate	0
D. J. Balcombe lbw b Chambers	0	– c Foster b Napier	13
J. A. Tomlinson not out	9	– b Napier	0
D. A. Griffiths b Craddock	1	– b Topley	21
B 4, l-b 7, n-b 4	15	B 8, l-b 1, n-b 2	11
1/21 (2) 2/61 (1) 3/96 (4) 4/128 (5) 5/169 (6) 6/170 (3) 7/184 (8) 8/185 (9) 9/228 (7) 10/229 (11) (64.2 overs)	229	1/18 (1) 2/23 (3) 3/23 (4) 4/183 (5) 5/208 (6) 6/213 (7) 7/213 (8) 8/240 (9) 9/240 (10) 10/302 (11) (84.1 overs)	302

Chambers 19–2–61–3; Topley 21–6–59–3; Napier 14–1–59–2; ten Doeschate 6–0–29–1; Craddock 4.2–1–10–1. *Second innings*—Topley 21.1–3–95–3; Chambers 8.3–1–28–2; Craddock 22–3–85–0; Napier 15–5–33–2; Westley 5.3–0–13–0; ten Doeschate 12–3–39–3.

Umpires: N. G. C. Cowley and J. H. Evans.

At Derby, September 11–14. HAMPSHIRE lost to DERBYSHIRE by six wickets.

KENT

Green shoots in Adams' garden

MARK PENNELL

Kent's main focus in recent years has been refurbishing the St Lawrence Ground. But after finishing the 2011 season one place above the bottom, they turned to an area in even greater need of rebuilding: the squad itself. The close-season departures of director of cricket Paul Farbrace and top-order batsman Martin van Jaarsveld had left big gaps to plug. In fact, they went deeper and wider: Kent had also lost opener Joe Denly and strike bowler Robbie Joseph. The squad was down to the barest bones, low in confidence and experience, and with no firm hand on the tiller.

After scouring the international market, Kent passed over their one-time director of cricket Graham Ford, plumping instead for former West Indies captain Jimmy Adams. Despite a coaching CV that contained little more than batting consultancy for West Indies and his native Jamaica, Adams – cool, calm and utterly deliberate – was installed as head coach in January 2012.

With time short, he set quickly to work, approving the recommendations of high-performance director Simon Willis and captain Rob Key. The seasoned Michael Powell arrived from Glamorgan to boost the batting, while Mark Davies, a highly regarded seamer, and Ben Harmison, a left-handed batsman, travelled south from Durham. Charlie Shreck, from Nottinghamshire, further strengthened the pace attack, and overseas signing Brendan Nash added left-handed grit to the middle order. Nash – born in Australia, but with 21 Tests for West Indies, and links to Jamaica – planned to return in 2013 as a Kolpak.

Adams voiced faith in his new squad: "There is a bigger picture and a desire here at Kent, certainly on my part, to create something strong, something consistently good… All our signings bring character as well as their talent."

How right he was. The new faces were a breath of fresh air, bringing not just character and talent, but a sense of humour and purpose. Results were encouraging from the start: after eight Championship matches, Kent were joint second in the table, with a game in hand on leaders Derbyshire.

In mid-July, an inexperienced side containing several names for the future – Sam Billings, an impish wicketkeeper and improviser in the Alan Knott mould, batsman Daniel Bell-Drummond, off-spinner Adam Riley and seamer Ivan Thomas – held the South African tourists to a heartening draw. But the small core of first-string players was beginning to show signs of fatigue.

The next four Championship fixtures proved crucial. Kent had slightly the better of a high-scoring Canterbury stalemate against Glamorgan, before Hampshire clung on for an unlikely draw at Southampton. Then, on August 5, Derbyshire overcame a deficit of 133 to land a body blow: the Kent batting collapsed in a second-innings heap – Key alone passed 18 – to allow Derbyshire to sneak past. Kent lost by two wickets, their first defeat of the season.

Sam Northeast

The failure in those three games to polish off opponents left the squad bewildered – and things went from bad to worse. Having gone ten Championship matches unbeaten, Kent now lost again, to Essex.

Adams urgently needed to re-energise his troops and, to their credit, they managed emphatic victories over Leicestershire and Derbyshire. That ensured their pursuit of promotion went to the final round, but the drubbing they suffered away to Glamorgan left Kent third in the table – and with nothing to show for their hard work.

Given the atrocious weather, it was no surprise the batsmen struggled. Only Sam Northeast, whose stature grew throughout what felt like a breakthrough season, and Nash approached 1,000 runs. Both hit three centuries, one more than the affable Powell and the versatile Darren Stevens, whose medium-pace claimed 35 victims.

The leading wicket-taker, though, was the frugal Shreck, who picked up 55 in the Championship, while Matt Coles – who also struck a maiden first-class hundred, and played twice for England Lions – took 52. Next, with 36, came Davies, Kent's Player of the Season. He outdid even Shreck for frugality, conceding just 1.89 an over in the Championship. And his accuracy made him an essential member of the one-day team: his economy-rate in the CB40 was a measly 3.69; in the Twenty20 a grudging 5.72.

Kent came within a whisker of making the CB40 semis, but ultimately paid the price for giving the Unicorns their only victory of the summer, at Canterbury. Stevens starred with the ball (20 wickets at 16), while wicketkeeper Geraint Jones, an ever-present in all three competitions, was his indefatigable, irrepressible self, and was awarded a one-year contract extension. Billings, playing as a specialist batsman, was the leading run-scorer in both limited-overs competitions.

There was disappointment in the Twenty20, where Kent's lukewarm showing – four wins and five defeats – mirrored the underperformance of all-rounder Azhar Mahmood, previously their 20-over fulcrum. He and Kent agreed an early end to his contract, allowing him to pursue other Twenty20 interests. Simon Cook, of late mostly restricted to limited-overs appearances, retired after eight wholehearted seasons with the club.

And after seven at the helm, Key – Kent's longest-serving captain since Colin Cowdrey – stood down to concentrate on his batting. He is replaced by England off-spinner James Tredwell. Around the ground, work continues: the club has launched a £4m appeal to redevelop the Frank Woolley Stand.

Championship attendance: 27,541.

KENT RESULTS

All first-class matches – Played 17: Won 4, Lost 3, Drawn 10.
County Championship matches – Played 16: Won 4, Lost 3, Drawn 9.

LV= County Championship, 3rd in Division 2;
Friends Life t20, 4th in South Division; Clydesdale Bank 40, 3rd in Group C.

COUNTY CHAMPIONSHIP AVERAGES, BATTING AND FIELDING

Cap		*M*	*I*	*NO*	*R*	*HS*	*100*	*50*	*Avge*	*Ct*
2012	S. A. Northeast†	11	17	1	880	165	3	5	55.00	6
	B. P. Nash§	16	24	5	908	132*	3	4	47.78	6
2003	G. O. Jones	16	20	4	677	88	0	7	42.31	52
	M. J. Powell	16	20	3	647	134	2	3	38.05	6
2001	R. W. T. Key	15	24	3	797	119	1	5	37.95	7
2005	D. I. Stevens	16	20	0	619	123	2	2	30.95	7
	A. J. Blake†	4	7	1	155	73	0	1	25.83	5
	S. A. Newman	6	9	0	215	64	0	1	23.88	3
2012	M. T. Coles†	14	17	1	371	103*	1	1	23.18	4
	B. W. Harmison	11	16	1	311	46	0	0	20.73	3
2007	J. C. Tredwell†	13	13	2	227	87	0	1	20.63	15
	M. Davies	15	16	4	227	58	0	1	18.91	4
	C. E. Shreck	16	16	11	84	16	0	0	16.80	0
	A. E. N. Riley†	5	5	0	20	8	0	0	4.00	1

Also batted: Azhar Mahmood (1 match) 49, 0 (1 ct); D. J. Bell-Drummond (1 match) 33, 0; S. J. Cook (1 match) 15; I. A. A. Thomas† (1 match) 0*.

† Born in Kent. § Official overseas player.

BOWLING

	Style	*O*	*M*	*R*	*W*	*BB*	*5I*	*Avge*
M. Davies	RFM	368.3	129	699	36	5-27	1	19.41
M. T. Coles	RFM	344.4	44	1,146	52	6-51	2	22.03
D. I. Stevens	RM	304.3	63	840	35	5-35	1	24.00
C. E. Shreck	RFM	502.3	110	1,454	55	5-41	2	26.43
J. C. Tredwell	OB	301	78	752	19	3-38	0	39.57

Also bowled: Azhar Mahmood (RFM) 21–5–71–2; B. W. Harmison (RFM) 13–1–56–0; R. W. T. Key (RM/OB) 4–1–27–0; B. P. Nash (LM) 28.5–1–72–4; S. A. Newman (RM) 6–0–31–0; A. E. N. Riley (OB) 63.4–17–231–5; I. A. A. Thomas (RFM) 16–7–29–2.

LEADING CB40 AVERAGES (100 runs/4 wickets)

Batting	*Runs*	*HS*	*Avge*	*SR*	*Ct/St*
G. O. Jones	152	52*	152.00	117.82	14/2
B. P. Nash	189	70*	94.50	95.45	0
S. W. Billings	315	143	45.00	100.00	3
R. W. T. Key	283	101	35.37	73.50	2
S. A. Northeast	198	69	28.28	71.48	4
D. I. Stevens	197	59	28.14	80.08	7

Bowling	*W*	*BB*	*Avge*	*ER*
D. I. Stevens	20	5-36	16.30	4.39
M. T. Coles	17	6-32	16.52	5.36
J. C. Tredwell	13	4-24	23.07	4.86
M. Davies	10	3-10	25.50	3.69
A. J. Ball	4	2-39	35.50	5.25
S. J. Cook	5	2-30	37.40	4.79

LEADING FLT20 AVERAGES (100 runs/18 overs)

Batting	*Runs*	*HS*	*Avge*	*SR*	*Ct*
D. I. Stevens	207	60	25.87	**135.29**	2
S. A. Northeast	192	60	27.42	**122.29**	2
S. W. Billings	216	59	24.00	**101.88**	4
Azhar Mahmood	110	30	13.75	**98.21**	1
R. W. T. Key	116	51*	16.57	**91.33**	5

Bowling	*W*	*BB*	*Avge*	*ER*
M. Davies	7	2-18	29.42	**5.72**
D. I. Stevens	7	3-13	19.28	**6.13**
J. C. Tredwell	4	2-27	37.25	**6.47**
A. J. Ball	12	2-18	18.08	**7.61**
Azhar Mahmood	10	3-12	21.20	**8.71**

FIRST-CLASS COUNTY RECORDS

Highest score for	332	W. H. Ashdown v Essex at Brentwood	1934
Highest score against	344	W. G. Grace (MCC) at Canterbury	1876
Leading run-scorer	47,868	F. E. Woolley (avge 41.77)	1906–1938
Best bowling for	10-30	C. Blythe v Northamptonshire at Northampton	1907
Best bowling against	10-48	C. H. G. Bland (Sussex) at Tonbridge	1899
Leading wicket-taker	3,340	A. P. Freeman (avge 17.64)	1914–1936
Highest total for	803-4 dec	v Essex at Brentwood	1934
Highest total against	676	by Australians at Canterbury	1921
Lowest total for	18	v Sussex at Gravesend	1867
Lowest total against	16	by Warwickshire at Tonbridge	1913

LIST A COUNTY RECORDS

Highest score for	146	A. Symonds v Lancashire at Tunbridge Wells	2004
Highest score against	167*	P. Johnson (Nottinghamshire) at Nottingham	1993
Leading run-scorer	7,814	M. R. Benson (avge 31.89)	1980–1995
Best bowling for	8-31	D. L. Underwood v Scotland at Edinburgh	1987
Best bowling against	6-5	A. G. Wharf (Glamorgan) at Cardiff	2004
Leading wicket-taker	530	D. L. Underwood (avge 18.93)	1963–1987
Highest total for	384-6	v Berkshire at Finchampstead	1994
Highest total against	344-5	by Somerset at Taunton	2002
Lowest total for	60	v Somerset at Taunton	1979
Lowest total against	60	by Derbyshire at Canterbury	2008

TWENTY20 COUNTY RECORDS

Highest score for	112	A. Symonds v Middlesex at Maidstone	2004
Highest score against	106	A. C. Gilchrist (Middlesex) at Canterbury	2010
Leading run-scorer	**1,982**	**D. I. Stevens (avge 33.03)**	**2005–2012**
Best bowling for	5-17	Wahab Riaz v Gloucestershire at Beckenham	2011
Best bowling against	**5-17**	**G. M. Smith (Essex) at Chelmsford**	**2012**
Leading wicket-taker	**82**	**J. C. Tredwell (avge 25.43)**	**2003–2012**
Highest total for	217	v Gloucestershire at Gloucester	2010
Highest total against	217-4	by Surrey at Canterbury	2006
Lowest total for	72	v Hampshire at Southampton	2011
Lowest total against	82	by Somerset at Taunton	2010

ADDRESS

St Lawrence Ground, Old Dover Road, Canterbury CT1 3NZ (01227 456886; **email** kent@ecb.co.uk). **Website** www.kentccc.com

OFFICIALS

Captain 2012 – R. W. T. Key
2013 – J. C. Tredwell
Head coach J. C. Adams
High-performance director S. C. Willis
President R. Bevan

Chairman G. M. Kennedy
Chief executive J. A. S. Clifford
Chairman, cricket committee G. W. Johnson
Head groundsman A. Peirson
Scorer L. Hart

At Leeds, April 5–8. KENT drew with YORKSHIRE.

At Northampton, April 12–14. KENT beat NORTHAMPTONSHIRE by an innings and 120 runs.

KENT v GLOUCESTERSHIRE

At Canterbury, April 19–22. Drawn. Kent 6pts, Gloucestershire 8pts. Toss: Kent. County debut: B. A. C. Howell.

Played out on a true pitch among squally showers and chill winds, this game ended as a humdrum draw. Gloucestershire generally had the edge, but they lacked the quality and nous – and indeed the time – to enforce victory. They hit four of the game's five half-centuries, and carved out a 105-run lead after Will Gidman's five for 43 helped dismiss Kent for 150. His brother Alex made 70 in the second innings as he and Marshall added 112 for the fourth wicket. Gloucestershire batted into the final day and, when the declaration finally came, set Kent a daunting 363, their caution partly explained by the loss of Payne to a side strain. But Harmison battled against the turning ball for over an hour to make 20, and the pursuit was shelved. The match marked the official retirement of Kent scorer Jack Foley who, after 25 years' service, was made an honorary life member of the county.

Close of play: first day, Gloucestershire 131-6 (W. R. S. Gidman 25, Young 0); second day, Kent 119-6 (Jones 11, Tredwell 7); third day, Gloucestershire 191-3 (A. P. R. Gidman 60, Marshall 55).

Gloucestershire

†R. G. Coughtrie lbw b Davies	3	– c Jones b Tredwell	40
C. D. J. Dent c Jones b Shreck	4	– c Jones b Coles	24
B. A. C. Howell lbw b Coles	44	– lbw b Davies	10
*A. P. R. Gidman c Jones b Coles	13	– lbw b Coles	70
H. J. H. Marshall lbw b Coles	3	– run out	74
I. A. Cockbain c Coles b Davies	32	– lbw b Coles	5
W. R. S. Gidman run out	56	– c Stevens b Tredwell	20
E. G. C. Young not out	55	– not out	8
P. B. Muchall b Davies	23	– not out	3
I. D. Saxelby lbw b Davies	0		
D. A. Payne lbw b Coles	10		
L-b 12	12	L-b 3	3
1/4 (2) 2/14 (1) 3/54 (4) 4/68 (5) (96.2 overs)	255	1/33 (2) (7 wkts dec, 79 overs)	257
5/73 (3) 6/131 (6) 7/174 (7)		2/50 (3) 3/97 (1)	
8/224 (9) 9/224 (10) 10/255 (11)		4/209 (4) 5/219 (6) 6/245 (5) 7/248 (7)	

Davies 25–11–43–4; Shreck 25–7–82–1; Coles 26.2–1–70–4; Stevens 11–0–35–0; Tredwell 9–3–13–0. *Second innings*—Davies 19–2–56–1; Shreck 23–2–76–0; Coles 18–3–55–3; Tredwell 16–2–55–2; Nash 3–0–12–0.

Kent

S. A. Newman b Payne	12	– c Coughtrie b W. R. S. Gidman	17
*R. W. T. Key c Coughtrie b W. R. S. Gidman	5	– not out	32
B. W. Harmison c Coughtrie b W. R. S. Gidman	12	– c sub (J. K. Fuller) b Young	20
B. P. Nash c Coughtrie b Saxelby	12	– not out	5
M. J. Powell c Coughtrie b W. R. S. Gidman	0		
D. I. Stevens b Young	54		
†G. O. Jones c Coughtrie b W. R. S. Gidman	21		
J. C. Tredwell b W. R. S. Gidman	11		
M. T. Coles run out	1		
M. Davies not out	12		
C. E. Shreck c Howell b Young	4		
L-b 3, w 1, n-b 2	6	B 2, l-b 6, n-b 12	20
1/9 (2) 2/26 (1) 3/30 (3) 4/30 (5) (54.5 overs)	150	1/34 (1) (2 wkts, 38.1 overs)	94
5/55 (4) 6/110 (6) 7/132 (8)		2/85 (3)	
8/133 (9) 9/134 (7) 10/150 (11)			

W. R. S. Gidman 16.3–6–43–5; Saxelby 17–3–39–1; Payne 5.3–2–9–1; Muchall 7–1–33–0; Young 8.5–2–23–2. *Second innings*—W. R. S. Gidman 13–5–25–1; Saxelby 9.1–3–18–0; Young 12–4–18–1; Muchall 4–0–25–0.

Umpires: S. A. Garratt and P. J. Hartley.

KENT v YORKSHIRE

At Canterbury, April 26–29. Drawn. Kent 10pts, Yorkshire 7pts. Toss: Kent.

A determined maiden Championship century from Nash assured another rain-ruined game would end in stalemate. Nash, the West Indies Test left-hander, was the only player to pass 50 in a dour match that lost all but 53 balls of the third day and all of the fourth. Coles and rash shot selection had together ushered Yorkshire to 247 in an innings of fits and starts: seven men got to 20, none topped 38. Nash then dominated proceedings, batting almost five hours to finish unbeaten on 132 when the rain arrived in earnest. Jones captained Kent after Key aggravated an ankle injury in the pre-match warm-ups.

Close of play: first day, Kent 4-0 (Newman 2, Northeast 1); second day, Kent 316-6 (Nash 114, Tredwell 28); third day, Kent 350-9 (Nash 132, Shreck 7).

Yorkshire

J. E. Root lbw b Stevens	21
J. J. Sayers b Coles	12
P. A. Jaques lbw b Stevens	30
*A. W. Gale c Jones b Davies	22
†J. M. Bairstow c Northeast b Coles	32
G. S. Ballance b Shreck	38
T. T. Bresnan lbw b Tredwell	33
A. U. Rashid c Jones b Shreck	27
A. Shahzad c Nash b Coles	4
R. J. Sidebottom b Coles	17
S. A. Patterson not out	3
L-b 5, w 1, n-b 2	8
1/23 (2) 2/41 (1) 3/70 (4) (92.3 overs)	247
4/102 (3) 5/120 (5) 6/171 (7)	
7/221 (6) 8/226 (8) 9/228 (9) 10/247 (10)	

Davies 15–4–28–1; Shreck 27–8–65–2; Coles 23.3–4–70–4; Stevens 14–3–39–2; Tredwell 12–2–39–1; Nash 1–0–1–0.

Kent

S. A. Newman c Bairstow b Shahzad	31
S. A. Northeast lbw b Shahzad	26
B. W. Harmison lbw b Patterson	43
B. P. Nash not out	132
M. J. Powell c Bresnan b Sidebottom	3
D. I. Stevens lbw b Bresnan	8
*†G. O. Jones c Ballance b Sidebottom	47
J. C. Tredwell c Jaques b Bresnan	37
M. T. Coles c Bairstow b Bresnan	0
M. Davies b Rashid	0
C. E. Shreck not out	7
L-b 11, w 1, n-b 4	16
1/35 (1) 2/101 (2) (9 wkts, 105.5 overs)	350
3/125 (3) 4/138 (5)	
5/158 (6) 6/235 (7) 7/333 (8)	
8/333 (9) 9/334 (10)	

Bresnan 29.5–8–89–3; Sidebottom 21–2–86–2; Patterson 22–3–61–1; Shahzad 15–0–54–2; Rashid 15–0–44–1; Root 3–2–5–0.

Umpires: T. E. Jesty and P. Willey.

At Oxford, May 2–4. KENT drew with OXFORD MCCU.

At Chelmsford, May 9–12. KENT drew with ESSEX.

KENT v NORTHAMPTONSHIRE

At Canterbury, May 16–19. Drawn. Kent 6pts, Northamptonshire 7pts. Toss: Northamptonshire. Championship debut: C. D. de Lange.

A rain-affected game on a wearing pitch petered out under floodlights. After an interrupted third day, Key declared Kent's first innings at 280 for six – 138 behind – and persuaded Hall, his one-time team-mate, to make a game of it. Key and Newman, both very occasional bowlers, sped up the run-scoring as the Northamptonshire openers registered unbeaten fifties – and set Kent a target of 262 from a minimum of 60 overs. Once Newman had smeared across the line, left-hander Harmison struggled against Middlebrook's off-breaks, prompting Key to bat out time for a pedestrian fifty. Among the bowlers, Brooks caught the eye for Northamptonshire, as did Coles for Kent, though neither gained the return he deserved. On the first day, Newton had his left wrist fractured by Coles, and could take no further part in the game. There was better news for Sales, who made his first hundred for almost two years.

Close of play: first day, Northamptonshire 244-4 (Sales 104, Middlebrook 57); second day, Kent 123-3 (Nash 8, Powell 13); third day, Kent 280-6 (Jones 26, Tredwell 11).

Northamptonshire

S. D. Peters lbw b Stevens	34	–	not out	54
R. I. Newton retired hurt	23			
K. J. Coetzer b Davies	3			
D. J. Sales c Jones b Tredwell	140			
*A. J. Hall c Davies b Shreck	14			
†N. J. O'Brien b Shreck	1			
J. D. Middlebrook lbw b Coles	73	–	(2) not out	64
C. D. de Lange not out	39			
D. J. Willey c Newman b Stevens	64			
L. M. Daggett c Key b Tredwell	1			
J. A. Brooks b Stevens	16			
L-b 3, n-b 2, p 5	10		L-b 1, n-b 4	5
1/55 (3) 2/69 (1) 3/86 (5) 4/87 (6) 5/292 (4) 6/298 (7) 7/398 (9) 8/399 (10) 9/418 (11) — (144.3 overs)	418		(no wkt dec, 36 overs)	123
110 overs: 294-5				

Newton retired hurt at 46-0.

Davies 20–6–55–1; Shreck 33–8–84–2; Coles 24–4–78–1; Tredwell 38–6–112–2; Stevens 24.3–2–63–3; Harmison 1–0–5–0; Nash 3–1–2–0; Key 1–0–11–0. *Second innings*—Davies 3–2–3–0; Shreck 3–2–3–0; Harmison 9–1–36–0; Tredwell 12–1–33–0; Newman 6–0–31–0; Key 3–1–16–0.

Kent

S. A. Newman b Daggett	16	–	lbw b Middlebrook	25
*R. W. T. Key c O'Brien b Hall	48	–	not out	54
B. W. Harmison c Willey b Hall	32	–	not out	26
B. P. Nash c Peters b Brooks	11			
M. J. Powell lbw b Daggett	61			
D. I. Stevens c O'Brien b Hall	57			
†G. O. Jones not out	26			
J. C. Tredwell not out	11			
B 5, l-b 11, n-b 2	18		L-b 5	5
1/38 (1) 2/101 (3) 3/102 (2) 4/130 (4) 5/231 (5) 6/245 (6) — (6 wkts dec, 111 overs)	280		1/45 (1) (1 wkt, 43 overs)	110
110 overs: 280-6				

M. T. Coles, M. Davies and C. E. Shreck did not bat.

Brooks 24–11–47–1; Willey 21–5–55–0; Middlebrook 20–4–48–0; Daggett 23–9–56–2; Hall 19–5–39–3; de Lange 4–0–19–0. *Second innings*—Brooks 6–1–20–0; Willey 5–1–10–0; Middlebrook 10–3–19–1; Daggett 10–2–27–0; de Lange 6–1–13–0; Hall 6–1–16–0.

Umpires: N. G. B. Cook and N. G. C. Cowley.

KENT v LEICESTERSHIRE

At Canterbury, May 23–25. Kent won by an innings and 279 runs. Kent 22pts, Leicestershire 1pt. Toss: Leicestershire. County debut: P. L. Mommsen.

Hoggard made no excuses for an abysmal display in which his Leicestershire side – outwitted and outfought from the off – were crushed inside three days to give Kent their biggest innings win since the war. "There was no fight, no guts and we rolled over far too easily," he said. "Yes, we were a long time in the field, but we are professional athletes and are meant to be able to cope with ten hours in the dirt." Coles took five wickets to help skittle them for 141 on the first afternoon. Then Kent, who lost Northeast first ball, amassed a lead of 392 thanks to a century from Powell, his first at Canterbury, and strong contributions throughout the order. More than 50 overs brought Henderson his first five-for in the Championship for almost two years. Stevens then took four wickets against his former county, and Tredwell three, as Leicestershire succumbed for 113.

LARGEST INNINGS VICTORIES BY KENT

Inns & 314 runs	v Gloucestershire at Catford	1909
Inns & 312 runs	v Somerset at Taunton	1901
Inns & 294 runs	v Warwickshire at Tunbridge Wells	1928
Inns & 294 runs	v Gloucestershire at Folkestone	1933
Inns & 286 runs	v Northamptonshire at Gravesend	1908
Inns & 279 runs	**v Leicestershire at Canterbury**	**2012**
Inns & 243 runs	v Sussex at Hove	1907
Inns & 242 runs	v Gloucestershire at Cheltenham	1910

Close of play: first day, Kent 104-2 (Key 23, Nash 50); second day, Kent 404-6 (Powell 133, Tredwell 29).

Leicestershire

W. I. Jefferson lbw b Shreck	19	– lbw b Shreck	7
G. P. Smith lbw b Shreck	12	– lbw b Stevens	11
J. du Toit c Jones b Shreck	0	– c Jones b Davies	11
R. R. Sarwan c Jones b Coles	17	– b Coles	9
J. J. Cobb c Jones b Coles	5	– c Harmison b Tredwell	12
P. L. Mommsen c Jones b Stevens	9	– c Northeast b Tredwell	5
W. A. White c Jones b Coles	38	– (10) c Powell b Stevens	0
†E. J. H. Eckersley not out	31	– (7) c Jones b Stevens	6
C. W. Henderson c Stevens b Coles	0	– (8) b Tredwell	2
N. L. Buck c Tredwell b Coles	4	– (9) c Jones b Stevens	27
*M. J. Hoggard c Powell b Stevens	0	– not out	18
B 4, n-b 2	6	B 1, n-b 4	5
1/27 (1) 2/27 (3) 3/32 (2) 4/53 (5) (53.5 overs) 5/62 (4) 6/66 (6) 7/122 (7) 8/126 (9) 9/134 (10) 10/141 (11)	141	1/7 (1) 2/20 (3) (46 overs) 3/34 (4) 4/38 (2) 5/53 (6) 6/58 (5) 7/64 (8) 8/72 (7) 9/76 (10) 10/113 (9)	113

Davies 14–5–23–0; Shreck 15–3–51–3; Stevens 13.5–6–22–2; Coles 11–2–41–5. *Second innings*—Davies 7–3–12–1; Shreck 8–2–19–1; Coles 8–2–19–1; Stevens 13–7–24–4; Tredwell 10–2–38–3.

Kent

S. A. Northeast c Smith b Hoggard	0	M. Davies st Eckersley b Henderson	22
*R. W. T. Key b Cobb	85	C. E. Shreck not out	1
B. W. Harmison b Hoggard	30		
B. P. Nash c Smith b White	76	B 10, l-b 1, w 2, n-b 8	21
M. J. Powell c Jefferson b Buck	134		
D. I. Stevens c Cobb b Henderson	23	1/0 (1) 2/36 (3) 3/167 (4) (172.4 overs)	533
†G. O. Jones c du Toit b Henderson	7	4/253 (2) 5/292 (6) 6/312 (7)	
J. C. Tredwell b Henderson	87	7/416 (5) 8/505 (8)	
M. T. Coles c Eckersley b Henderson	47	9/518 (9) 10/533 (10) 110 overs: 311-5	

Hoggard 20–6–67–2; Buck 27–5–77–1; White 30–3–94–1; Henderson 50.4–17–116–5; Mommsen 8–0–36–0; Sarwan 1–0–3–0; du Toit 13–1–35–0; Cobb 23–2–94–1.

Umpires: I. Dawood and T. E. Jesty.

KENT v HAMPSHIRE

At Tunbridge Wells, June 6–9. Drawn. Kent 5pts, Hampshire 6pts. Toss: Kent.

The 100th Tunbridge Wells cricket week was notable for inclement weather, Dawson's unbeaten hundred and a botched run-chase (plus an impromptu homage to Elvis Presley and Andy Williams). After three days punctuated by rain and mopping up, Hampshire's first innings had reached only 229 for six, so Key and Adams agreed a double forfeiture, eventually setting Kent a gettable 304 from a minimum of 70 overs. They enjoyed a decent start, but the decision to stick with the sedate Harmison at No. 3 met with jeers. The required rate ballooned and, when Harmison departed 43 minutes later for 11, the pursuit was practically over: the captains shook hands with 84 still needed. Kent chief executive Jamie Clifford said poor attendance at The Nevill – the next day's CB40 was badly affected, too – cost the club around £50,000. Key lifted spirits and entertained the spectators who did turn up by belting out "Always on my mind" and "Can't take my eyes off you", as well as miming to Luciano Pavarotti singing "Nessun Dorma".

Close of play: first day, Hampshire 50-3 (Katich 21, Dawson 5); second day, Hampshire 90-3 (Katich 43, Dawson 22); third day, Hampshire 229-6 (Dawson 111, Mascarenhas 6).

Hampshire

M. A. Carberry c Jones b Shreck	7	Kabir Ali c Key b Nash	30
*J. H. K. Adams lbw b Davies	8	D. J. Balcombe not out	4
B. M. Shafayat lbw b Davies	9	B 1, l-b 4, w 2	7
S. M. Katich lbw b Tredwell	54		
L. A. Dawson not out	134	1/11 (1) (8 wkts dec, 101.5 overs)	303
S. M. Ervine b Coles	0	2/20 (3) 3/37 (2)	
†M. D. Bates c Tredwell b Shreck	30	4/136 (4) 5/145 (6)	
A. D. Mascarenhas b Coles	20	6/204 (7) 7/251 (8) 8/299 (9)	

J. A. Tomlinson did not bat.

Davies 23–7–40–2; Shreck 23–1–68–2; Stevens 14–3–37–0; Coles 20–1–81–2; Tredwell 21–4–67–1; Nash 0.5–0–5–1.

Hampshire forfeited their second innings.

Kent

Kent forfeited their first innings.

S. A. Northeast c Adams b Balcombe	79	†G. O. Jones not out	12
*R. W. T. Key lbw b Kabir Ali	35		
B. W. Harmison c Adams b Mascarenhas	11	B 1, l-b 6, w 1, n-b 2	10
D. I. Stevens c Carberry b Mascarenhas	28		
M. T. Coles c Carberry b Tomlinson	18	1/75 (2) 2/99 (3) (6 wkts, 68 overs)	220
B. P. Nash c Carberry b Kabir Ali	18	3/147 (4) 4/160 (1)	
M. J. Powell not out	9	5/195 (6) 6/199 (5)	

J. C. Tredwell, M. Davies and C. E. Shreck did not bat.

Kabir Ali 14–2–53–2; Mascarenhas 20–7–45–2; Tomlinson 14–0–51–1; Balcombe 15–3–56–1; Dawson 3–1–6–0; Ervine 2–1–2–0.

Umpires: S. C. Gale and R. K. Illingworth.

At Canterbury, July 13–15. KENT drew with SOUTH AFRICANS (see South African tour section).

KENT v GLAMORGAN

At Canterbury, July 19–22. Drawn. Kent 11pts, Glamorgan 9pts. Toss: Kent.

After three dank days the sun came out and the runs flowed, ensuring Kent's seventh draw in nine Championship games. Harris proved a handful as Kent batted first, but Nash and Stevens (who ticked off 10,000 first-class runs) put on 204 for the fifth wicket, before Waters – off the field with a stomach upset for much of the first day – removed both. Kent gained maximum batting points for the first time in 2012, and declared when play resumed at noon on the third day. Glamorgan dipped to 83 for four before the middle order engineered a recovery: Wallace added 87 with Allenby and a brisk 103 with Cosker to sail past the follow-on target. Wallace also passed Eifion Jones's total of 8,341 to become the leading run-scorer among Glamorgan wicketkeepers. Kent led by 67 and, although there was insufficient time for a result, Northeast managed his first hundred of the summer. Yet the batsman with the broadest smile was not one of the game's four centurions: in his 120th first-class innings, Shreck lofted Cosker for the first six of his career.

Close of play: first day, Kent 310-4 (Nash 110, Stevens 120); second day, Kent 456-9 (Jones 69, Shreck 7); third day, Glamorgan 264-7 (Wallace 46, Glover 1).

Kent

S. A. Northeast lbw b Harris	52	– not out	101
*R. W. T. Key c Wallace b Harris	14	– c Walters b Glover	20
B. W. Harmison c Wallace b Harris	12	– lbw b Glover	13
B. P. Nash c Wallace b Waters	114	– not out	28
M. J. Powell c Wallace b Harris	0		
D. I. Stevens c Cosker b Waters	123		
†G. O. Jones not out	69		
J. C. Tredwell c sub (G. G. Wagg) b Allenby	11		
M. T. Coles c Allenby b Cosker	26		
M. Davies b Harris	24		
C. E. Shreck not out	7		
L-b 4	4	B 1, l-b 5	6
1/27 (2) 2/49 (3) 3/110 (1) 4/110 (5) 5/314 (4) 6/319 (6) 7/343 (8) 8/378 (9) 9/418 (10) (9 wkts dec, 119 overs)	456	1/58 (2) 2/88 (3) (2 wkts dec, 50.1 overs)	168
110 overs: 411-8			

Harris 33–0–118–5; Waters 14–2–49–2; Allenby 28–4–88–1; Glover 16–2–81–0; Cosker 26–3–105–1; Bragg 1–0–6–0; Wright 1–0–5–0. *Second innings*—Harris 3–0–9–0; Cosker 10–1–32–0; Waters 12–1–35–0; Allenby 6–0–21–0; Glover 9–1–16–2; Bragg 9–1–40–0; Rees 1.1–0–9–0.

Glamorgan

G. P. Rees c Stevens b Shreck	20
W. D. Bragg b Coles	22
S. J. Walters c Jones b Stevens	53
M. J. North c Tredwell b Coles	8
B. J. Wright lbw b Stevens	14
J. Allenby c Powell b Nash	86
*†M. A. Wallace c Powell b Stevens	111
J. A. R. Harris lbw b Shreck	2
J. C. Glover lbw b Shreck	1
D. A. Cosker b Stevens	47
H. T. Waters not out	8
B 2, l-b 13, n-b 2	17
1/37 (2) 2/43 (1) 3/56 (4) 4/83 (5) 5/167 (3) 6/254 (6) 7/261 (8) 8/265 (9) 9/368 (10) 10/389 (7) (112.1 overs)	389
110 overs: 380-9	

Davies 17–7–29–0; Shreck 29–2–90–3; Coles 16–1–80–2; Stevens 26.1–2–77–4; Tredwell 22–3–96–0; Nash 2–0–2–1.

Umpires: S. C. Gale and D. J. Millns.

At Southampton, July 27–30. KENT drew with HAMPSHIRE. *Hampshire's last pair bat more than 20 overs to deny Kent victory.*

At Derby, August 2–5. KENT lost to DERBYSHIRE by two wickets.

KENT v ESSEX

At Canterbury, August 8–10. Essex won by seven wickets. Essex 21pts, Kent 4pts.Toss: Kent.

This was comfortably Kent's worst home performance of the season: only on the second morning, when Essex slid to 23 for four, did they ruffle their opponents. Key had opted to bat in testing conditions, and the Essex seamers made the most of the opportunity, dismissing Kent before six o'clock – despite Powell's resolute three-hour 62. It needed an even more dogged innings from Foster, who hit just five of his 226 balls to the fence, to rescue Essex. He and the more forceful Wheater – who managed 12 fours from 109 deliveries – shared a sixth-wicket stand of 126 to give them an initiative they never relinquished. Shreck took a spirited five-for, but the stuffing had been knocked out of Kent and, by the end of the second day, they were nine for three, still 38 behind. They were no better next morning, succumbing lamely to a three-man attack lacking the injured Masters. Essex quickly knocked off the 55 they needed to gain their first victory since the opening round, and so revive their faint promotion hopes.

Close of play: first day, Essex 14-0 (Westley 9, Mickleburgh 5); second day, Kent 9-3 (Blake 0).

Kent

S. A. Northeast c Foster b Chambers	32	– lbw b Harbhajan Singh	3
*R. W. T. Key c and b Chambers	5	– c Foster b Napier	4
A. J. Blake b Napier	19	– (4) c Chambers b Harbhajan Singh	18
B. P. Nash c Harbhajan Singh b Masters	11	– (5) lbw b Chambers	1
M. J. Powell c Harbhajan Singh b Chambers	62	– (6) c Foster b Chambers	5
D. I. Stevens b Napier	20	– (7) lbw b Napier	22
†G. O. Jones lbw b Masters	5	– (8) c ten Doeschate b Harbhajan Singh	13
Azhar Mahmood b Napier	49	– (9) c Mickleburgh b Napier	0
M. T. Coles c Masters b Harbhajan Singh	4	– (10) c Harbhajan Singh b Chambers	17
A. E. N. Riley c Foster b Masters	5	– (3) b Chambers	1
C. E. Shreck not out	2	– not out	4
L-b 8, n-b 4	12	B 4, l-b 5, n-b 4	13
1/12 (2) 2/58 (1) 3/58 (3) (84.3 overs)	226	1/4 (2) 2/9 (3) 3/9 (1) (37 overs)	101
4/82 (4) 5/120 (6) 6/143 (7)		4/12 (5) 5/26 (6) 6/58 (7)	
7/184 (5) 8/193 (9) 9/211 (10) 10/226 (8)		7/64 (4) 8/65 (9) 9/83 (8) 10/101 (10)	

Masters 18.1–6–44–3; Chambers 24–5–65–3; Napier 22.2–5–55–3; Harbhajan Singh 16–5–38–1; ten Doeschate 4–0–16–0. *Second innings*—Chambers 13–5–31–4; Napier 9–1–26–3; Harbhajan Singh 15–3–35–3.

Essex

T. Westley c Key b Coles	10	– b Azhar Mahmood	14
J. C. Mickleburgh c Jones b Shreck	5	– lbw b Azhar Mahmood	1
O. A. Shah lbw b Coles	7	– c Blake b Shreck	13
M. L. Pettini b Shreck	1	– not out	19
R. N. ten Doeschate c Jones b Stevens	33	– not out	8
*†J. S. Foster c Key b Stevens	76		
A. J. Wheater lbw b Riley	82		
G. R. Napier c Jones b Shreck	43		
Harbhajan Singh not out	5		
D. D. Masters c Azhar Mahmood b Shreck	0		
M. A. Chambers c Key b Shreck	0		
B 5, l-b 5, w 1	11		
1/15 (2) 2/22 (3) 3/23 (1) 4/23 (4) 5/76 (5) 6/202 (7) 7/253 (6) 8/269 (8) 9/269 (10) 10/273 (11) (94.4 overs)	273	1/4 (2) 2/19 (1) 3/35 (3) (3 wkts, 18.3 overs)	55

Shreck 25.4–9–51–5; Coles 25–8–71–2; Azhar Mahmood 13–3–46–0; Stevens 20–5–51–2; Riley 11–2–44–1. *Second innings*—Shreck 9–4–19–1; Azhar Mahmood 8–2–25–2; Stevens 1–0–4–0; Riley 0.3–0–7–0.

Umpires: N. J. Llong and J. W. Lloyds.

At Bristol, August 15–18. KENT drew with GLOUCESTERSHIRE.

At Leicester, August 28–31. KENT beat LEICESTERSHIRE by 147 runs.

KENT v DERBYSHIRE

At Canterbury, September 4–7. Kent won by 222 runs. Kent 21 pts, Derbyshire 4pts. Toss: Kent.

With only 43 minutes remaining, Geraint Jones – on his 100th successive Championship appearance – held a tumbling catch to clinch victory for Kent in a controversial and hard-fought game against the Division Two leaders. It boosted Kent's chance of returning to the top flight, and gave the underrated Stevens figures of four for 37. The dramatic climax came at the end of four combative days played out on a slightly grassy pitch that proved perfect for Championship cricket. Batsmen had to concentrate for their runs, and none was more focused than Northeast, whose six-hour 165 (his four-day best) was the difference between the sides. The surface also ensured the seamers remained interested throughout: Davies claimed his first five-wicket haul since leaving Durham. But it was a slow bowler who became the major talking point. Before the match, Kent had nominated Riley, a 20-year-old off-spinner, as the player to make way if the vastly more experienced Tredwell became available. That seemed impossible when, on the second day of this match, Tredwell played in the final one-dayer against South Africa. But Kent claimed that, because England's game had finished 15 overs early, a provision allowing internationals to rejoin counties under "exceptional

MOST CONSECUTIVE CHAMPIONSHIP APPEARANCES FOR KENT

196	J. Seymour	1902–1911	107	A. P. Freeman	1921–1925
183	W. H. Ashdown	1926–1933	106	C. Blythe	1901–1906
154	L. J. Todd	1937–1948	102	C. J. Burnup	1899–1903
151	F. H. Huish	1909–1914	101	H. T. W. Hardinge	1924–1928
136	R. R. Dovey	1949–1953	**101**	**G. O. Jones**	**2006–**
116	L. J. Todd	1933–1937			

Todd missed two successive Championship matches in May 1937, when he was selected for South v North, and for Rest of England v MCC Australian XI. Had he played for Kent, his run of matches would have been 272.

circumstances" should apply – despite the ECB having previously informed the teams and umpires that, if Tredwell played for England, he would be ineligible for Kent. However, the ECB later agreed and, to Derbyshire's wrath, Tredwell took over. There was irony, then, in his failure to take a wicket, though his 33 economical overs ensured Derbyshire's unlikely chase of 404 never gathered momentum.

Close of play: first day, Derbyshire 32-1 (Madsen 21, Durston 11); second day, Kent 59-3 (Northeast 26); third day, Derbyshire 30-1 (Borrington 8, Khawaja 16).

Kent

S. A. Northeast c Groenewald b Whiteley	37	– c Khawaja b Whiteley	165
*R. W. T. Key c Poynton b Turner	9	– b Durston	31
A. J. Blake lbw b Groenewald	1	– (4) c Poynton b Wainwright	0
B. P. Nash lbw b Groenewald	17	– (5) c Poynton b Wainwright	62
M. J. Powell c Groenewald b Whiteley	37	– (6) not out	56
D. I. Stevens c Poynton b Palladino	6	– (7) c Durston b Wainwright	0
†G. O. Jones c Durston b Groenewald	80	– (8) run out	13
M. T. Coles c Khawaja b Durston	24	– (9) run out	0
M. Davies run out	25	– (3) b Durston	0
A. E. N. Riley lbw b Palladino	4		
C. E. Shreck not out	8		
J. C. Tredwell (did not bat)		– (10) not out	2
B 2, l-b 2, w 4, n-b 5	13	B 2, l-b 2, w 3, n-b 6	13
1/19 (2) 2/34 (3) 3/59 (1) 4/73 (4) 5/93 (6) 6/139 (5) 7/196 (8) 8/232 (9) 9/251 (7) 10/261 (10) (82.3 overs)	261	1/58 (2) 2/58 (3) 3/59 (4) 4/196 (5) 5/319 (1) 6/320 (7) 7/338 (8) 8/338 (9) (8 wkts dec, 101.3 overs)	342

Tredwell replaced Riley after returning from playing for England.

Palladino 18.3–3–53–2; Groenewald 19–4–63–3; Turner 14–4–44–1; Whiteley 8–1–22–2; Wainwright 15–2–48–0; Durston 8–1–27–1. *Second innings*—Groenewald 15–3–35–0; Palladino 18–4–55–0; Turner 9–0–49–0; Durston 24.3–3–83–2; Wainwright 28–5–77–3; Whiteley 6–0–33–1; Redfern 1–0–6–0.

Derbyshire

*W. L. Madsen b Davies	64	– c Tredwell b Davies	0
U. T. Khawaja lbw b Davies	0	– (3) lbw b Stevens	53
W. J. Durston c Blake b Davies	14	– (4) lbw b Coles	8
P. M. Borrington c Blake b Riley	23	– (2) lbw b Coles	17
D. J. Redfern c Jones b Coles	0	– c Jones b Stevens	21
R. A. Whiteley c Jones b Davies	6	– run out	0
D. J. Wainwright c Key b Davies	4	– b Davies	21
†T. Poynton b Coles	45	– not out	27
A. P. Palladino c Blake b Stevens	6	– c Tredwell b Stevens	7
T. D. Groenewald c and b Nash	22	– b Stevens	14
M. L. Turner not out	11	– c Jones b Coles	5
L-b 5	5	B 1, l-b 5, n-b 2	8
1/7 (2) 2/37 (3) 3/89 (4) 4/92 (5) 5/106 (6) 6/111 (1) 7/112 (7) 8/130 (9) 9/181 (10) 10/200 (8) (79.2 overs)	200	1/0 (1) 2/57 (2) 3/69 (4) 4/103 (3) 5/103 (6) 6/109 (5) 7/145 (7) 8/158 (9) 9/176 (10) 10/181 (11) (108.2 overs)	181

Davies 18–9–27–5; Shreck 21–8–43–0; Riley 15–3–51–1; Stevens 13–3–42–1; Coles 11.2–0–29–2; Nash 1–0–3–1. *Second innings*—Davies 17–6–31–2; Shreck 20–10–30–0; Tredwell 33–19–34–0; Nash 5–0–14–0; Coles 14.2–5–29–3; Stevens 19–10–37–4.

Umpires: N. G. B. Cook and N. A. Mallender.

At Cardiff, September 11–13. KENT lost to GLAMORGAN by seven wickets.

LANCASHIRE

Hangover downs the champions

MYLES HODGSON

It was perhaps understandable that Lancashire should succumb to a hangover the season after celebrating their first outright Championship title in 77 years: like Yorkshire in 2002 and Nottinghamshire in 2006, the reigning champions suffered relegation. The blunt truth was that a squad which had delivered beyond the sum of its parts for one glorious summer struggled to recreate the magic. Lancashire had been widely written off before their unexpected triumph, and now their ability to strengthen a squad many regarded as already punching above their weight was compromised by the huge cost of redeveloping Old Trafford, which contributed to a £3.96m loss for 2011.

Even without budget restraints, there was a desire to keep faith with the home-grown players who had secured the title. The one major import was Ashwell Prince, the South African back for a third spell with the club, though former England seamer Ajmal Shahzad arrived on loan in May, after falling out with Yorkshire. Prince was a notable success, the only man to score 1,000 first-class runs, but Shahzad made less impact in the Championship: despite claiming two wickets in his first over on debut, he managed just 18 more. He was the country's leading wicket-taker in the CB40, with 21 – all for Lancashire – but moved on to Nottinghamshire in October.

Only Yorkshire were more severely disrupted by the weather: Lancashire lost more than 1,800 Championship overs to rain. But when they did get on to the field, they were unable to force victories from winning positions, as they had done in 2011. The conditions dissuaded them from playing two of the previous season's most potent bowlers in tandem as often as they would have liked: the experienced Gary Keedy and rising star Simon Kerrigan, both left-arm spinners.

They appeared together only four times in the Championship, a factor in Keedy's decision to leave for Surrey after 18 seasons at Old Trafford. His departure saddened many, including his captain, Glen Chapple, who saluted him on Twitter as "an unwavering servant to Lancs and support to me personally!" But few contested the decision to promote Kerrigan, who collected 44 wickets in 15 games.

In 2011, Lancashire had played most of their home games at Aigburth because of the work at Old Trafford, and it became their lucky ground, developing a reputation for its own micro-climate. But the weather there was less helpful this time, and perhaps a second season in exile played its part in unsettling the team. The home Championship fixtures were scheduled to be split four–four between Liverpool and Manchester but, after Lancashire narrowly escaped being docked points for a poor pitch at Old Trafford, in a game lost to fellow strugglers Worcestershire, it was decided to switch the

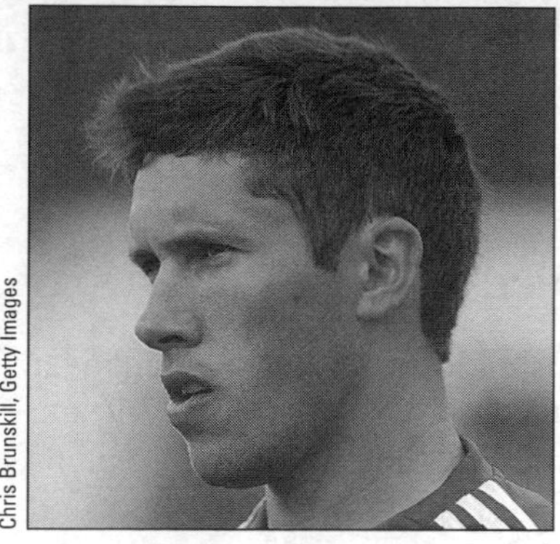
Chris Brunskill, Getty Images

Simon Kerrigan

final two home matches back to Aigburth, to allow more time for the new pitches to bed down.

When there was a consistent spell of dry, but cold, conditions in spring, Lancashire suffered three defeats in their first four games. That set the template. Their only Championship victory did not come until the start of June – halfway through the programme – and their fate was sealed by defeat at Lord's with a match remaining.

"So where did it all go wrong for Lancashire?" asked the *Manchester Evening News*. Statistics suggested the batting was largely responsible. Lancashire were bowled out 15 times for under 300, earned no batting points at all in eight games, and had to wait until their final match, against Surrey, for their first century opening partnership. Their decline was epitomised by Stephen Moore, who had scored 1,000 Championship runs at 40 in their title summer, yet averaged only 17 this time, and was dropped before the season was out. He was by no means alone in failing to maintain standards: none of the batsmen could match their 2011 aggregates. Meanwhile, the attack relied too often on the 38-year-old Chapple, and injuries ruled out Tom Smith for all but six Championship matches. Seam-bowling all-rounder Wayne White was signed from Leicestershire.

Lancashire's poor first-class showing contrasted with some outstanding cricket in the CB40, where they reached the semi-finals before suffering another heart-breaking defeat, their 11th in a semi in 13 seasons, at home to Warwickshire. Their Twenty20 form was less convincing, and they were unable to qualify from their group.

The new year offered Old Trafford a fresh start. Ashes cricket was to return in August 2013, for the first time in eight years, and the Test was already close to selling out ten months ahead. The new players' and media centre, with a fully equipped gym and spa pool (for the cricketers), had opened in September, flanked by two new double-decker stands; the new pavilion, retaining nothing of the old building but the Grade One-listed facade and turrets, was due to be ready in early summer.

As the county planned a swift return to Division One, they signed Simon Katich, now retired from Australian first-class cricket, as their overseas player, and seamer Kabir Ali, both from Hampshire. Ali replaced Sajid Mahmood, who was annoyed at being released after a decade, though he found a new home at Essex.

In December, Daniel Gidney took over as chief executive, joining from the Ricoh Arena (home of Coventry City). He succeeded Jim Cumbes, the popular face of Lancashire cricket administration for 25 years since he returned to the club where he had played in the 1960s.

Championship attendance: 21,956.

LANCASHIRE RESULTS

All first-class matches – Played 18: Won 2, Lost 5, Drawn 11.
County Championship matches – Played 16: Won 1, Lost 5, Drawn 10.

LV= County Championship, 8th in Division 1;
Friends Life t20, 4th in North Division; Clydesdale Bank 40, s-f.

COUNTY CHAMPIONSHIP AVERAGES, BATTING AND FIELDING

Cap		*M*	*I*	*NO*	*R*	*HS*	*100*	*50*	*Avge*	*Ct/St*
2010	A. G. Prince§	15	24	1	1,008	144	2	8	43.82	15
2010	K. W. Hogg	13	18	8	324	61*	0	2	32.40	1
2007	P. J. Horton	16	25	3	654	137*	2	2	29.72	17
2010	T. C. Smith†	6	9	0	267	91	0	3	29.66	4
2010	S. J. Croft†	16	24	1	666	154*	2	2	28.95	15
	K. R. Brown†	16	25	1	594	78	0	3	24.75	5
	L. A. Procter†	13	20	3	414	46	0	0	24.35	0
2007	G. D. Cross†	15	24	2	498	75*	0	3	22.63	28/3
2011	S. C. Moore	12	20	0	348	47	0	0	17.40	7
1994	G. Chapple	15	23	0	381	46	0	0	16.56	3
	A. Shahzad	10	15	5	134	28*	0	0	13.40	1
	S. C. Kerrigan†	15	19	7	96	34*	0	0	8.00	3
2000	G. Keedy	4	4	0	8	5	0	0	2.00	0

Also batted: A. P. Agathangelou¶ (3 matches) 24, 5, 7 (1 ct); J. M. Anderson†‡ (cap 2003) (1 match) 0, 0 (1 ct); T. E. Bailey† (1 match) did not bat; A. L. Davies† (1 match) did not bat (2 ct); S. I. Mahmood† (cap 2007) (3 matches) 0, 1, 3; O. J. Newby† (1 match) did not bat.

† *Born in Lancashire.* ‡ *ECB contract.* § *Official overseas player.* ¶ *Other non-England-qualified player.*

BOWLING

	Style	*O*	*M*	*R*	*W*	*BB*	*5I*	*Avge*
L. A. Procter	RFM	177.1	32	558	25	7-71	2	22.32
G. Chapple	RFM	394.5	101	1,010	42	5-47	2	24.04
S. J. Croft	RFM/OB	96.4	13	289	12	6-41	1	24.08
S. C. Kerrigan	SLA	518.5	85	1,532	44	4-45	0	34.81
A. Shahzad	RFM	216.3	50	709	20	4-40	0	35.45
K. W. Hogg	RFM	242.4	55	746	18	3-23	0	41.44

Also bowled: J. M. Anderson (RFM) 36.2–7–105–5; T. E. Bailey (RFM) 17–2–67–1; K. R. Brown (RM) 3–0–5–0; G. Keedy (SLA) 130.2–17–401–7; S. I. Mahmood (RFM) 36–4–180–4; O. J. Newby (RFM) 13–0–59–1; A. G. Prince (OB) 2–1–5–0; T. C. Smith (RFM) 58–4–236–4.

LEADING CB40 AVERAGES (100 runs/4 wickets)

Batting	*Runs*	*HS*	*Avge*	*SR*	*Ct*
S. J. Croft	513	82	57.00	92.93	13
S. C. Moore	581	113	52.81	103.93	6
K. R. Brown	319	87*	45.57	86.21	3
T. C. Smith	131	106	43.66	179.45	1
P. J. Horton	250	78	31.25	102.88	7
A. G. Prince	317	85	28.81	88.54	5

Bowling	*W*	*BB*	*Avge*	*ER*
O. J. Newby	10	5-35	17.60	5.64
G. Keedy	20	5-55	20.05	5.25
G. Chapple	10	5-26	20.40	4.53
A. Shahzad	21	4-51	20.52	6.08
S. D. Parry	14	4-21	33.85	5.51
S. I. Mahmood	6	2-50	51.50	7.92

LEADING FLT20 AVERAGES (70 runs/13 overs)

Batting	Runs	HS	Avge	SR	Ct/St
S. C. Moore	249	80	31.12	**139.88**	1
S. J. Croft	313	65*	62.60	**129.33**	9
T. C. Smith	227	56	28.37	**122.70**	5
K. R. Brown	145	46	24.16	**117.88**	1
G. D. Cross	74	26	14.80	**105.71**	6/2

Bowling	W	BB	Avge	ER
G. Chapple	9	2-10	13.11	**4.95**
S. D. Parry	6	2-31	31.66	**7.03**
T. C. Smith	1	1-13	92.00	**7.07**
G. Keedy	9	4-25	20.66	**7.75**
Yasir Arafat	10	3-21	22.40	**9.33**

FIRST-CLASS COUNTY RECORDS

Highest score for	424	A. C. MacLaren v Somerset at Taunton	1895
Highest score against	315*	T. W. Hayward (Surrey) at The Oval	1898
Leading run-scorer	34,222	G. E. Tyldesley (avge 45.20)	1909–1936
Best bowling for	10-46	W. Hickton v Hampshire at Manchester	1870
Best bowling against	10-40	G. O. B. Allen (Middlesex) at Lord's	1929
Leading wicket-taker	1,816	J. B. Statham (avge 15.12)	1950–1968
Highest total for	863	v Surrey at The Oval	1990
Highest total against	707-9 dec	by Surrey at The Oval	1990
Lowest total for	25	v Derbyshire at Manchester	1871
Lowest total against	22	by Glamorgan at Liverpool	1924

LIST A COUNTY RECORDS

Highest score for	162*	A. R. Crook v Buckinghamshire at Wormsley	2005
Highest score against	186*	C. G. Greenidge (West Indians) at Liverpool	1984
Leading run-scorer	11,969	N. H. Fairbrother (avge 41.84)	1982–2002
Best bowling for	6-10	C. E. H. Croft v Scotland at Manchester	1982
Best bowling against	8-26	K. D. Boyce (Essex) at Manchester	1971
Leading wicket-taker	480	J. Simmons (avge 25.75)	1969–1989
Highest total for	381-3	v Hertfordshire at Radlett	1999
Highest total against	**350-6**	**by Middlesex at Lord's**	**2012**
Lowest total for	59	v Worcestershire at Worcester	1963
Lowest total against	52	by Minor Counties at Lakenham	1998

TWENTY20 COUNTY RECORDS

Highest score for	102*	L. Vincent v Derbyshire at Manchester	2008
Highest score against	108*	I. J. Harvey (Yorkshire) at Leeds	2004
Leading run-scorer	**1,725**	**S. J. Croft (avge 29.74)**	**2006–2012**
Best bowling for	4-12	A. Flintoff v Durham at Chester-le-Street	2008
Best bowling against	5-21	J. Allenby (Leicestershire) at Manchester	2008
Leading wicket-taker	**72**	**G. Keedy (avge 21.15)**	**2004–2012**
Highest total for	220-5	v Derbyshire at Derby	2009
Highest total against	200-6	by Durham at Chester-le-Street	2011
Lowest total for	91	v Derbyshire at Manchester	2003
Lowest total against	81-8	by Derbyshire at Manchester	2011

ADDRESS

County Cricket Ground, Old Trafford, Manchester M16 0PX (0161 282 4000; **email** enquiries@lccc.co.uk). **Website** www.lccc.co.uk

OFFICIALS

Captain G. Chapple
Director of cricket M. Watkinson
Head coach P. Moores
Academy director J. Stanworth
President J. Livingstone
Chairman M. A. Cairns

Chief executive 2012 – J. Cumbes
2013 – D. Gidney
Chairman, cricket committee P. J. W. Allott
Head groundsman M. Merchant
Scorer A. West

At Abu Dhabi, March 27–30 (day/night). LANCASHIRE beat MCC by six wickets (see MCC section).

At Cambridge, April 6–8. LANCASHIRE drew with CAMBRIDGE MCCU.

LANCASHIRE v SUSSEX

At Liverpool, April 12–14. Sussex won by ten wickets. Sussex 22pts, Lancashire 3pts. Toss: Sussex. County debut: S. J. Magoffin.

Aigburth was Lancashire's stronghold in 2011, but the opening day of their title defence was an anticlimax: there was no Championship pennant flying, and they were dismissed before tea. The pennant's absence, apparently caused by problems with the flagpole and halyard, was rectified by the second morning, but Lancashire never recovered from losing the toss on a sporty pitch. Conditions benefited the taller bowlers, with Anyon taking five wickets to dismiss the champions inside 53 overs. In turn, the home seamers reduced Sussex to 15 for three. But Joyce and Yardy batted with patience and a share of fortune – both were dropped at slip – to add 164 and help secure a 176-run lead. Any prospect of a Lancashire recovery, the hallmark of the previous summer, was removed by the Queenslander, Steve Magoffin. Despite operating in conditions colder than he had ever known, he wrapped up their second innings with seven wickets. Joyce needed only three balls to complete victory on the third afternoon.

Close of play: first day, Sussex 137-3 (Joyce 48, Yardy 70); second day, Lancashire 85-4 (Prince 31, Procter 8).

Lancashire

P. J. Horton c Wells b Anyon	3	– c Wells b Magoffin	24
S. C. Moore b Magoffin	8	– c Yardy b Magoffin	11
K. R. Brown lbw b Anyon	10	– lbw b Magoffin	0
A. G. Prince c Brown b Anyon	4	– c Brown b Magoffin	58
S. J. Croft c Brown b Khan	50	– b Panesar	8
L. A. Procter c Wells b Panesar	9	– c Wells b Panesar	46
†G. D. Cross lbw b Magoffin	0	– not out	18
*G. Chapple c and b Anyon	23	– c Yardy b Magoffin	0
S. I. Mahmood c Brown b Khan	0	– c Yardy b Panesar	1
K. W. Hogg c Gatting b Anyon	6	– b Magoffin	5
S. C. Kerrigan not out	0	– c Brown b Magoffin	0
B 3, l-b 4, n-b 4	11	B 2, l-b 1, n-b 2	5
1/12 (2) 2/12 (1) 3/16 (4) 4/36 (3) 5/67 (6) 6/67 (7) 7/108 (8) 8/109 (9) 9/124 (5) 10/124 (10) (52.2 overs)	124	1/24 (2) 2/24 (3) 3/39 (1) 4/49 (5) 5/137 (6) 6/152 (4) 7/160 (8) 8/161 (9) 9/168 (10) 10/176 (11) (68.5 overs)	176

Anyon 14.2–5–36–5; Magoffin 16–9–21–2; Khan 12–3–28–2; Panesar 9–2–30–1; Nash 1–0–2–0. *Second innings*—Anyon 19–3–63–0; Magoffin 19.5–9–34–7; Khan 5–1–22–0; Panesar 23–5–54–3; Nash 2–2–0–0.

Sussex

	First innings		Second innings	
C. D. Nash c Brown b Hogg	2	–	(2) not out	0
E. C. Joyce c Moore b Procter	64	–	(1) not out	4
L. W. P. Wells lbw b Chapple	1			
M. W. Goodwin b Mahmood	3			
*M. H. Yardy st Cross b Kerrigan	110			
J. S. Gatting c Cross b Kerrigan	18			
†B. C. Brown c Moore b Chapple	12			
S. J. Magoffin c Horton b Chapple	9			
A. Khan b Procter	28			
J. E. Anyon not out	16			
M. S. Panesar c Prince b Procter	0			
B 7, l-b 14, n-b 16	37			
1/3 (1) 2/4 (3) 3/15 (4) 4/179 (2) 5/224 (5) 6/229 (6) 7/244 (8) 8/257 (7) 9/300 (9) 10/300 (11) (104 overs)	300		(no wkt, 0.3 overs)	4

Chapple 26–9–61–3; Hogg 23–5–60–1; Mahmood 19–2–66–1; Kerrigan 19–4–43–2; Procter 16–5–48–3; Croft 1–0–1–0. *Second innings*—Kerrigan 0.3–0–4–0.

Umpires: N. A. Mallender and G. Sharp.

LANCASHIRE v WARWICKSHIRE

At Liverpool, April 19–22. Warwickshire won by five wickets. Warwickshire 22pts, Lancashire 5pts. Toss: Warwickshire.

Warwickshire were 81 for seven on the third morning, still 20 short of saving the follow-on. But Maddy responded with his first century in nearly four years, and Clarke with his highest for the county as they put on 224, four short of Warwickshire's eighth-wicket record, to set up an unlikely lead of 79. Then Lancashire collapsed, with Barker and Patel claiming five apiece. On a pitch now conducive to spin, Warwickshire lost five wickets chasing 70, but edged a welcome victory over the side who had pipped them to the title on the final afternoon of the previous summer. Earlier, Maddy's accurate medium-pace compensated for the loss of Boyd Rankin and Chris Woakes to injuries. Lancashire were reduced to 170 for seven on the second morning, which began with eight maidens and eventually produced 47 runs from 32 overs. An aggressive 44 from Chapple guided them to 250, but it proved insufficient to save Lancashire from losing their opening two Championship matches for the first time since 1965, when they started with four defeats. On the shortened first day, the umpires had to turn off the walkie-talkies they used to speak to the scorers, because they kept hearing messages from a local taxi firm.

Close of play: first day, Lancashire 125-5 (Procter 7, Keedy 2); second day, Warwickshire 68-5 (Maddy 16, Wright 0); third day, Lancashire 44-4 (Prince 5, Keedy 0).

Lancashire

	First innings		Second innings	
P. J. Horton lbw b Clarke	17	–	c Ambrose b Barker	14
S. C. Moore c Clarke b Barker	19	–	c Porterfield b Barker	3
K. R. Brown c Porterfield b Wright	46	–	c Chopra b Barker	9
A. G. Prince c Bell b Maddy	11	–	b Patel	51
S. J. Croft c Clarke b Maddy	10	–	c Carter b Patel	10
L. A. Procter lbw b Maddy	46	–	(7) c Ambrose b Barker	0
G. Keedy c Barker b Wright	2	–	(6) c Carter b Patel	5
†G. D. Cross c Ambrose b Wright	19	–	c Bell b Barker	20
*G. Chapple c Chopra b Maddy	44	–	c sub (I. J. Westwood) b Patel	7
K. W. Hogg not out	15	–	not out	21
S. C. Kerrigan c Ambrose b Patel	2	–	c Porterfield b Patel	0
B 3, l-b 8, w 2, n-b 6	19		L-b 2, n-b 6	8
1/34 (2) 2/77 (1) 3/101 (4) 4/111 (3) 5/123 (5) 6/127 (7) 7/170 (8) 8/230 (9) 9/241 (6) 10/250 (11) (107.2 overs)	250		1/12 (2) 2/25 (1) 3/28 (3) 4/43 (5) 5/58 (6) 6/60 (7) 7/88 (8) 8/107 (9) 9/146 (4) 10/148 (11) (55 overs)	148

Wright 26–9–49–3; Barker 27–7–69–1; Carter 10–3–22–0; Clarke 16–4–44–1; Maddy 18–5–39–4; Patel 10.2–3–16–1. *Second innings*—Wright 8–1–34–0; Barker 19–3–54–5; Patel 25–5–52–5; Clarke 3–1–6–0.

Warwickshire

V. Chopra c Cross b Chapple	0	– lbw b Kerrigan	1
N. M. Carter c Cross b Hogg	8	– b Keedy	15
I. R. Bell c Cross b Chapple	18	– c Prince b Kerrigan	16
W. T. S. Porterfield lbw b Keedy	21	– not out	22
*J. O. Troughton c Croft b Kerrigan	3	– c Croft b Keedy	2
D. L. Maddy c Moore b Hogg	112	– c Moore b Kerrigan	1
C. J. C. Wright lbw b Kerrigan	3		
†T. R. Ambrose c Horton b Kerrigan	0	– (7) not out	11
R. Clarke b Hogg	140		
K. H. D. Barker not out	7		
J. S. Patel c Horton b Kerrigan	1		
B 6, l-b 6, n-b 4	16	B 1, l-b 2	3
1/0 (1) 2/10 (2) 3/35 (3) (102.2 overs)	329	1/3 (1) (5 wkts, 20.2 overs)	71
4/38 (5) 5/64 (4) 6/77 (7) 7/81 (8)		2/23 (3) 3/45 (2)	
8/305 (6) 9/324 (9) 10/329 (11)		4/51 (5) 5/52 (6)	

Chapple 23–5–57–2; Hogg 21–6–68–3; Procter 6–1–18–0; Kerrigan 27.2–2–89–4; Keedy 25–2–85–1. *Second innings*—Chapple 3–1–11–0; Kerrigan 10–1–34–3; Keedy 7.2–2–23–2.

Umpires: T. E. Jesty and R. T. Robinson. M. J. Saggers replaced Robinson after the second day.

At Taunton, April 26–29. LANCASHIRE drew with SOMERSET.

LANCASHIRE v NOTTINGHAMSHIRE

At Manchester, May 2–5. Nottinghamshire won by 185 runs. Nottinghamshire 19pts, Lancashire 3pts. Toss: Nottinghamshire.

The first Championship match at Old Trafford since the square was turned 90 degrees did not change Lancashire's fortunes. Adams, who had clinched the title for Nottinghamshire with a crucial bowling point in the last first-class game played there in 2010, was central again, claiming ten wickets for only 50 runs. Lancashire had seemed to be taking control on the opening day, when they dismissed the visitors for 169 on a slow pitch. Dismal batting was not enhanced by Broad's petulant reaction to being given out caught first ball at short leg by Croft as he tried to sweep Kerrigan; he apologised to the umpires at tea, who chose not to discipline him. But Lancashire themselves abruptly lost their last six for 15 as Adams collected a career-best seven for 32. Nottinghamshire extended their surprise lead to 327, even though Anderson overcame the effects of a thumb injury and tonsillitis to finish with a five-wicket haul. His fellow England bowlers, Broad and Swann, then showed their pedigree as they helped dismiss Lancashire for under 150 again to secure a comfortable victory.

Close of play: first day, Lancashire 48-1 (Moore 23); second day, Nottinghamshire 122-2 (Lumb 40, Patel 21); third day, Lancashire 39-5 (Procter 0, Cross 1).

Nottinghamshire

A. D. Hales lbw b Chapple	9	– b Chapple	5
N. J. Edwards b Chapple	4	– lbw b Kerrigan	40
M. J. Lumb c Prince b Chapple	3	– c Horton b Anderson	62
S. R. Patel c sub (S. I. Mahmood) b Procter	69	– c Cross b Procter	39
J. W. A. Taylor c Prince b Chapple	15	– c Cross b Kerrigan	46
*†C. M. W. Read b Procter	14	– c Cross b Anderson	54
P. J. Franks c Croft b Kerrigan	11	– c Cross b Anderson	4
S. C. J. Broad c Croft b Kerrigan	0	– c Anderson b Kerrigan	12
G. P. Swann lbw b Kerrigan	5	– b Anderson	12
B. J. Phillips not out	19	– not out	0
A. R. Adams st Cross b Kerrigan	9	– b Anderson	0
L-b 3, n-b 8	11	B 9, l-b 9, w 8, n-b 4	30
1/8 (2) 2/15 (1) 3/16 (3) 4/50 (5) (78.4 overs)	169	1/8 (1) 2/87 (2) (108.2 overs)	304
5/83 (6) 6/111 (7) 7/111 (8)		3/163 (4) 4/165 (3)	
8/121 (9) 9/149 (4) 10/169 (11)		5/265 (5) 6/276 (7) 7/290 (6)	
		8/304 (8) 9/304 (9) 10/304 (11)	

Anderson 17–5–23–0; Chapple 19–5–44–4; Smith 3–0–12–0; Procter 17–3–42–2; Kerrigan 22.4–6–45–4. *Second innings*—Chapple 28–5–58–1; Anderson 19.2–2–82–5; Procter 22–5–47–1; Kerrigan 32–7–77–3; Croft 7–0–22–0.

Lancashire

P. J. Horton lbw b Adams	24	– c Swann b Broad	0
S. C. Moore c Read b Adams	43	– b Adams	13
K. R. Brown b Adams	4	– lbw b Broad	7
A. G. Prince c Taylor b Swann	23	– c Hales b Swann	14
S. J. Croft c Read b Adams	20	– c Read b Adams	0
L. A. Procter lbw b Swann	10	– not out	41
†G. D. Cross c Hales b Adams	0	– lbw b Adams	19
T. C. Smith c Lumb b Adams	0	– c Adams b Broad	4
*G. Chapple c Edwards b Adams	9	– b Swann	26
S. C. Kerrigan not out	0	– (11) c Broad b Patel	6
J. M. Anderson b Swann	0	– (10) c Hales b Patel	0
B 5, l-b 6, n-b 2	13	B 3, l-b 1, n-b 8	12
1/48 (1) 2/52 (3) 3/83 (2) (58 overs)	146	1/0 (1) 2/24 (3) (51.2 overs)	142
4/109 (4) 5/131 (5) 6/131 (7) 7/133 (8)		3/36 (2) 4/38 (4)	
8/143 (9) 9/146 (6) 10/146 (11)		5/38 (5) 6/70 (7) 7/88 (8)	
		8/127 (9) 9/132 (10) 10/142 (11)	

Broad 14–1–60–0; Phillips 9–3–15–0; Adams 18–9–32–7; Swann 14–4–26–3; Franks 3–2–2–0. *Second innings*—Broad 17–2–67–3; Phillips 5–3–12–0; Adams 12–4–18–3; Swann 14–5–30–2; Patel 3.2–1–11–2.

Umpires: R. J. Bailey and S. C. Gale.

At Hove, May 9–12. LANCASHIRE drew with SUSSEX.

At Birmingham, May 16–19. LANCASHIRE drew with WARWICKSHIRE.

LANCASHIRE v MIDDLESEX

At Liverpool, May 23–26. Drawn. Lancashire 9pts, Middlesex 5pts. Toss: Lancashire.

Lancashire gave themselves more than a day to bowl out Middlesex, but a six-hour century by Rogers left them still awaiting their first Championship victory, seven matches into their title defence. They did win the toss for only the second time in 13 home games – a club official took the credit for changing the usual £1 coin to a £2 one – and passed 300 at home for the first time since September, thanks to Prince's first century of the summer. But slow scoring meant only three batting points, and once Prince fell the remaining five wickets added just 71. Lancashire still earned a precious 162-run lead, thanks in part to the aggression of Shahzad, on loan from Yorkshire. He removed Denly and Morgan in successive overs, and returned to wrap up Middlesex as their last five went for 48. Lancashire scored briskly on the third afternoon to set an unlikely target of 429. But Rogers's unbeaten 138 ensured only the third draw at Aigburth in 19 Championship matches stretching back to 1997.

Close of play: first day, Lancashire 276-4 (Prince 121, Procter 15); second day, Middlesex 155-5 (Dexter 33, Simpson 28); third day, Middlesex 29-0 (Robson 12, Rogers 16).

Lancashire

P. J. Horton run out	15	– c Morgan b Malan	89
S. C. Moore c Morgan b Berg	25	– c Rayner b Murtagh	19
K. R. Brown c Simpson b Murtagh	1	– c Simpson b Malan	76
A. G. Prince c Rayner b Berg	144	– st Simpson b Malan	26
S. J. Croft c Simpson b Murtagh	78	– c Dexter b Malan	28
L. A. Procter c Denly b Rayner	39	– not out	7
†G. D. Cross c Rogers b Rayner	41	– lbw b Rayner	3
A. Shahzad c Robson b Rayner	3	– c Robson b Malan	3
*G. Chapple c Berg b Murtagh	18	– run out	8
K. W. Hogg run out	2		
S. C. Kerrigan not out	4		
B 4, l-b 8, n-b 10	22	B 7	7
1/36 (1) 2/37 (3) 3/55 (2) 4/231 (5) 5/321 (4) 6/325 (6) 7/337 (8) 8/372 (9) 9/384 (10) 10/392 (7) — (142.1 overs) 110 overs: 315-4	392	1/31 (2) 2/161 (1) 3/206 (4) 4/225 (3) 5/250 (5) 6/254 (7) 7/257 (8) 8/266 (9) — (8 wkts dec, 54 overs)	266

Murtagh 32–8–84–3; Collymore 26–8–71–0; Berg 28–3–90–2; Dexter 9–2–20–0; Rayner 37.1–3–88–3; Denly 10–0–27–0. *Second innings*—Murtagh 10–1–39–1; Collymore 8–1–34–0; Rayner 17–0–66–1; Berg 3–0–21–0; Dexter 5–0–24–0; Denly 2–0–14–0; Malan 9–0–61–5.

Middlesex

*C. J. L. Rogers c Cross b Hogg	1	– (2) not out	138
S. D. Robson lbw b Chapple	19	– (1) c Cross b Hogg	50
J. L. Denly c Brown b Shahzad	32	– not out	61
D. J. Malan c Croft b Kerrigan	24		
E. J. G. Morgan b Shahzad	8		
N. J. Dexter c Cross b Chapple	47		
†J. A. Simpson lbw b Kerrigan	43		
G. K. Berg c Prince b Kerrigan	23		
O. P. Rayner c Prince b Shahzad	2		
T. J. Murtagh not out	7		
C. D. Collymore c Horton b Shahzad	8		
L-b 2, w 2, n-b 12	16	B 5, l-b 4, n-b 7	16
1/1 (1) 2/37 (2) 3/69 (3) 4/79 (5) 5/95 (4) 6/182 (6) 7/188 (7) 8/203 (9) 9/217 (8) 10/230 (11) — (72.5 overs)	230	1/104 (1) — (1 wkt, 96 overs)	265

Chapple 18–3–60–2; Hogg 10–2–33–1; Shahzad 13.5–4–40–4; Kerrigan 30–5–92–3; Croft 1–0–3–0. *Second innings*—Chapple 15–4–40–0; Hogg 11–3–30–1; Shahzad 12–5–19–0; Kerrigan 36–6–86–0; Procter 5–0–15–0; Croft 16–3–61–0; Prince 1–0–5–0.

Umpires: M. A. Gough and R. A. Kettleborough.

At Chester-le-Street, May 30–June 2. LANCASHIRE beat DURHAM by two wickets. *Lancashire's only win of the Championship season.*

At Nottingham, June 6–9. LANCASHIRE drew with NOTTINGHAMSHIRE.

At Guildford, July 11–14. LANCASHIRE drew with SURREY.

LANCASHIRE v WORCESTERSHIRE

At Manchester, July 18–20. Worcestershire won by 205 runs. Worcestershire 21pts, Lancashire 3pts. Toss: Worcestershire.

Counting on a win against relegation rivals, Lancashire suffered a humiliating three-day defeat – and were lucky to escape an eight-point penalty for a poor pitch, which yielded 34 wickets to spin. A panel inspected the strip, one of the new batch created when the square was realigned, but accepted that bad weather had hindered preparations. The omission of slow left-armer Gary Keedy was further evidence there was "no skulduggery", as director of cricket Mike Watkinson put it. Misreading the conditions, however, led to disaster. There was startling turn for Kerrigan and Croft on the opening day, though Pardoe and Scott, who scored his first century for Worcestershire, shared a seventh-wicket stand of 127. Lancashire's own poor technique against spin led to a deficit of 129. Twenty wickets fell on the third day, ten between lunch and tea. Chasing 269, Lancashire folded for 63, their lowest total at Old Trafford since 62 against Somerset in 1963. Off-spinner Moeen Ali improved his career-best twice to finish with 12 for 96.

Close of play: first day, Lancashire 13-0 (Horton 7, Moore 5); second day, Worcestershire 9-0 (Mitchell 8, Hughes 1).

Worcestershire

*D. K. H. Mitchell c Smith b Kerrigan	12	– c Cross b Chapple	23
P. J. Hughes lbw b Croft	32	– c Smith b Kerrigan	12
V. S. Solanki c Prince b Croft	15	– lbw b Croft	50
M. M. Ali c Horton b Croft	2	– c Croft b Kerrigan	5
J. G. Cameron c Croft b Kerrigan	18	– c Prince b Croft	2
M. G. Pardoe run out	55	– lbw b Croft	1
G. M. Andrew c Croft b Kerrigan	0	– c Shahzad b Croft	29
†B. J. M. Scott c Chapple b Kerrigan	106	– c Croft b Kerrigan	0
S. H. Choudhry lbw b Chapple	2	– c and b Croft	6
R. A. Jones lbw b Smith	15	– not out	0
A. Richardson not out	6	– c Brown b Croft	4
B 2, l-b 9, w 1, n-b 16	28	B 4, l-b 3	7
1/40 (1) 2/56 (2) 3/64 (4) 4/69 (3) (97.1 overs) 5/93 (5) 6/93 (7) 7/220 (6) 8/255 (9) 9/279 (10) 10/291 (8)	291	1/36 (1) 2/40 (2) (50.2 overs) 3/50 (4) 4/61 (5) 5/69 (6) 6/116 (7) 7/118 (8) 8/135 (9) 9/135 (3) 10/139 (11)	139

Chapple 15–5–25–1; Hogg 11–3–18–0; Shahzad 13–4–49–0; Kerrigan 36.1–8–117–4; Croft 19–0–64–3; Prince 1–1–0–0; Smith 2–0–7–1. *Second innings*—Chapple 6–2–25–1; Hogg 4–1–11–0; Kerrigan 21–5–55–3; Croft 19.2–4–41–6.

Lancashire

P. J. Horton lbw b Choudhry	34	– lbw b Richardson	0
S. C. Moore c Choudhry b Ali	26	– c Andrew b Richardson	9
K. R. Brown st Scott b Choudhry	9	– c Solanki b Ali	0
A. G. Prince c Scott b Ali	1	– c Scott b Ali	1
S. J. Croft b Choudhry	16	– c Scott b Ali	8
T. C. Smith c Jones b Ali	3	– c Scott b Ali	3
†G. D. Cross c Pardoe b Ali	16	– c Richardson b Ali	20
*G. Chapple c Pardoe b Ali	5	– (9) c Mitchell b Choudhry	9
A. Shahzad c Pardoe b Ali	0	– (10) st Scott b Choudhry	0
K. W. Hogg not out	21	– (8) st Scott b Ali	6
S. C. Kerrigan b Choudhry	20	– not out	2
B 4, l-b 5, n-b 2	11	B 4, l-b 1	5
1/61 (2) 2/65 (1) 3/68 (4) 4/86 (3) (61.2 overs) 5/95 (5) 6/105 (6) 7/118 (7) 8/118 (9) 9/119 (8) 10/162 (11)	162	1/0 (1) 2/13 (2) (31.1 overs) 3/13 (3) 4/21 (5) 5/22 (4) 6/33 (6) 7/50 (7) 8/61 (9) 9/61 (10) 10/63 (8)	63

Richardson 10–1–33–0; Ali 28–10–67–6; Andrew 3–1–15–0; Choudhry 20.2–4–38–4. *Second innings*—Richardson 7–3–7–2; Andrew 3–1–6–0; Ali 12.1–3–29–6; Choudhry 9–2–16–2.

Umpires: G. Sharp and P. Willey.

LANCASHIRE v SOMERSET

At Liverpool, August 1–4. Drawn. Lancashire 6pts, Somerset 6pts. Toss: Somerset. Championship debuts: A. P. Agathangelou; M. J. Leach.

Back in Liverpool, a lunchtime storm on the final day halted the game with Somerset needing another 186 runs and seven wickets left. An outstanding century from Prince had given Lancashire a real chance of victory in a match where no one else passed 45. But his team-mates struggled again in seamer-friendly conditions, losing their last eight for 78 in the first innings and their first six for 50 in the second; in between, they secured a 36-run lead as Somerset found it equally hard going against Chapple's accuracy and Shahzad's pace. Hogg joined Prince before lunch on the third day, at what was in effect 86 for six, and helped add a precious 98. Prince kept the tail going for another two hours, and in return they saw him to his century; he was last out for 129, more than half Lancashire's total, leaving a target of 279. Chapple continued to trouble Somerset with the new ball, again removing both openers, only for heavy rain to thwart a potentially fascinating conclusion.

Close of play: first day, Lancashire 129-5 (Agathangelou 0, Cross 7); second day, Somerset 149; third day, Somerset 22-1 (Trescothick 12, Compton 2).

Lancashire

P. J. Horton lbw b Trego	12	– b Trego	0
S. C. Moore c Trescothick b Trego	2	– run out	1
K. R. Brown b Trego	39	– lbw b Kirby	6
A. G. Prince c Kieswetter b Trego	51	– lbw b Trego	129
S. J. Croft c Trescothick b Thomas	7	– b Thomas	13
A. P. Agathangelou c Trego b Kirby	24	– b Thomas	5
†G. D. Cross lbw b Thomas	7	– run out	3
K. W. Hogg c Compton b Thomas	13	– c Kirby b Leach	38
*G. Chapple c Compton b Thomas	6	– c Trescothick b Leach	14
A. Shahzad not out	11	– lbw b Hussain	5
S. C. Kerrigan c Hildreth b Kirby	1	– not out	9
B 2, l-b 4, n-b 6	12	B 4, l-b 5, n-b 10	19
1/11 (2) 2/28 (1) 3/107 (3) 4/122 (5) 5/122 (4) 6/129 (7) 7/153 (8) 8/161 (9) 9/179 (6) 10/185 (11) (74.3 overs)	185	1/0 (1) 2/7 (2) 3/7 (3) 4/31 (5) 5/41 (6) 6/50 (7) 7/148 (8) 8/180 (9) 9/204 (10) 10/242 (4) (82.2 overs)	242

Trego 23–8–49–4; Kirby 16.3–4–40–2; Thomas 27–8–63–4; Hussain 7–0–25–0; Leach 1–0–2–0. *Second innings*—Trego 17.2–4–60–2; Kirby 12–2–43–1; Thomas 21–4–54–2; Hussain 14–2–39–1; Leach 18–4–37–2.

Somerset

*M. E. Trescothick c Moore b Chapple	1	– lbw b Chapple	27
A. V. Suppiah b Chapple	0	– lbw b Chapple	4
N. R. D. Compton lbw b Kerrigan	22	– not out	27
J. C. Hildreth b Shahzad	45	– c Agathangelou b Hogg	9
†C. Kieswetter c Horton b Kerrigan	16	– not out	21
J. C. Buttler lbw b Hogg	18		
P. D. Trego c Croft b Shahzad	17		
A. C. Thomas lbw b Kerrigan	6		
G. M. Hussain b Hogg	15		
M. J. Leach not out	0		
S. P. Kirby b Chapple	0		
B 5, l-b 2, n-b 2	9	B 1, l-b 2, n-b 2	5
1/1 (2) 2/4 (1) 3/50 (3) 4/89 (5) 5/89 (4) 6/115 (7) 7/124 (8) 8/146 (6) 9/149 (9) 10/149 (11) (63.4 overs)	149	1/13 (2) 2/48 (1) 3/67 (4) (3 wkts, 43 overs)	93

Chapple 15.3–2–38–3; Shahzad 14–5–40–2; Hogg 12.1–7–17–2; Kerrigan 22–4–47–3. *Second innings*—Chapple 14–7–27–2; Shahzad 10–2–26–0; Kerrigan 10–2–14–0; Hogg 7–1–21–1; Croft 2–1–2–0.

Umpires: P. J. Hartley and N. J. Llong.

At Worcester, August 15–18. LANCASHIRE drew with WORCESTERSHIRE.

LANCASHIRE v DURHAM

At Liverpool, August 28–31. Drawn. Lancashire 7pts, Durham 10pts. Toss: Lancashire.

Lancashire desperately needed points to stave off relegation, but top-order failings undermined them once more as Durham dominated a rain-affected encounter. There was no play on the opening morning, and Chapple's decision to bat backfired when Onions, the season's leading wicket-taker, claimed three for two in 18 deliveries to reduce Lancashire to 11 for four. But, the day after a spectacular 44-ball century in a CB40 match at Worcester, Tom Smith showed another side to his game, facing 209 balls for a patient 91, his highest first-class score for two years. Onions finally got him on the third day – the second was washed out – when the last four fell in a hurry. That gave Onions 17 wickets from three Championship innings against Lancashire, and restricted them to two batting points. They managed only two bowling points as well, denied first by Keaton Jennings – a son of former South African coach Ray, and now seeking England qualification – then by Collingwood's first century in a year. When rain intervened, Durham's Division One status was all but secure; Lancashire were left hoping they could win their remaining two matches.

Close of play: first day, Lancashire 221-6 (Smith 86, Hogg 36); second day, no play; third day, Durham 187-4 (Richardson 39, Collingwood 5).

Lancashire

P. J. Horton b Onions	3
L. A. Procter c Borthwick b Onions	6
K. R. Brown c Borthwick b Rushworth	0
A. G. Prince c Stoneman b Stokes	31
S. J. Croft b Onions	0
T. C. Smith c Mustard b Onions	91
†G. D. Cross b Stokes	57
K. W. Hogg not out	60
*G. Chapple b Onions	8
S. C. Kerrigan c Richardson b Stokes	1
G. Keedy c Stokes b Onions	1
N-b 4	4
1/4 (1) 2/7 (3) 3/9 (2) 4/11 (5) 5/58 (4) 6/130 (7) 7/240 (6) 8/250 (9) 9/251 (10) 10/262 (11) (92.1 overs)	262

Onions 26.1–12–41–6; Rushworth 16–2–50–1; Thorp 6–3–9–0; Jennings 5–2–9–0; Stokes 18–3–72–3; Borthwick 16–1–64–0; Collingwood 5–0–17–0.

Durham

M. D. Stoneman c Croft b Kerrigan	44
K. K. Jennings c Croft b Keedy	70
M. J. Richardson c Smith b Kerrigan	41
B. A. Stokes c Prince b Keedy	4
D. M. Benkenstein b Kerrigan	15
*P. D. Collingwood b Croft	114
†P. Mustard c Prince b Kerrigan	5
S. G. Borthwick c Chapple b Keedy	60
C. D. Thorp b Croft	25
G. Onions not out	14
C. Rushworth c Prince b Croft	7
B 4, l-b 7, n-b 6	17
1/90 (1) 2/142 (2) 3/146 (4) 4/180 (5) 5/191 (3) 6/205 (7) 7/353 (8) 8/383 (6) 9/408 (9) 10/416 (11) (124.2 overs)	416
110 overs: 353-7	

Chapple 22–8–47–0; Hogg 12–0–63–0; Smith 7–1–33–0; Kerrigan 44–7–128–4; Keedy 31–2–101–3; Croft 8.2–1–33–3.

Umpires: M. J. D. Bodenham and N. G. C. Cowley.

At Lord's, September 4–7. LANCASHIRE lost to MIDDLESEX by 109 runs. *Lancashire are relegated.*

LANCASHIRE v SURREY

At Liverpool, September 11–14. Drawn. Lancashire 5pts, Surrey 7pts. Toss: Lancashire. First-class debuts: T. E. Bailey, A. L. Davies.

Officially this match had little significance: results the previous week had ensured Lancashire's relegation – a year after their historic Championship – and Surrey's survival. In any case, the first two days were washed out, making a positive result unlikely. But there were opportunities for young players on both sides. Lancashire gave first-class debuts to Tom Bailey, a bustling fast bowler, and wicketkeeper-batsman Alex Davies, an England Under-19 player, while Surrey brought in all-rounder Tom Jewell and seamer Matt Dunn for their first Championship outings of the summer. Jewell scored an impressive 70 and added 177 for the sixth wicket with de Bruyn, who made his first century for 12 months. But the final day belonged to Luke Procter. Swinging it from the River End in his unusual style, which – as with his namesake Mike – looked as if he was delivering the ball off the wrong foot, he claimed Surrey's last five wickets in 17 balls to finish with a career-best seven. He followed up by sharing Lancashire's only century opening partnership of the season, with Tom Smith.

Close of play: first day, no play; second day, no play; third day, Surrey 324-5 (de Bruyn 105, Jewell 57).

Surrey

R. J. Burns c Davies b Smith	73
Z. S. Ansari b Bailey	23
A. Harinath c Horton b Newby	17
Z. de Bruyn lbw b Procter	125
J. J. Roy b Procter	13
†S. M. Davies c Davies b Procter	0
T. M. Jewell c Croft b Procter	70
*G. J. Batty lbw b Procter	0
J. Lewis b Procter	8
T. E. Linley lbw b Procter	1
M. P. Dunn not out	0
B 5, l-b 12, n-b 20	37
1/50 (2) 2/101 (3) (112.1 overs)	367

3/160 (1) 4/178 (5) 5/178 (6) 6/355 (4) 7/355 (8) 8/364 (7) 9/366 (10) 10/367 (9) — 110 overs: 366-8

Newby 13–0–59–1; Bailey 17–2–67–1; Smith 15–1–49–1; Procter 19.1–2–71–7; Kerrigan 30–7–66–0; Keedy 17–4–30–0; Croft 1–0–8–0.

Lancashire

T. C. Smith c Batty b Jewell	83
L. A. Procter b Dunn	36
P. J. Horton not out	10
K. R. Brown not out	1
B 4, l-b 1, w 3, n-b 4	12
1/110 (2) 2/140 (1) (2 wkts dec, 42 overs)	142

*S. J. Croft, A. P. Agathangelou, †A. L. Davies, O. J. Newby, T. E. Bailey, S. C. Kerrigan and G. Keedy did not bat.

Linley 6–0–20–0; Lewis 6–3–9–0; Jewell 11–3–24–1; Ansari 8–2–33–0; Dunn 10–1–50–1; Roy 1–0–1–0.

Umpires: M. A. Gough and J. W. Lloyds.

LEICESTERSHIRE

Occupational therapy

PAUL JONES

After the debacle of the 2011 Championship season, even the slightest improvement was to be welcomed. And if a grand total of three wins – the last of which prevented a second consecutive wooden spoon – was hardly spellbinding, it did at least represent progress. The feeling around Grace Road was that the club had something on which to build.

That optimism was initially strengthened by Ramnaresh Sarwan's decision to commit to Leicestershire for another two years after the collapse of his relationship with the West Indies set-up. But the timing of the subsequent rapprochement – he was picked for the limited-overs tour of Australia in February 2013, which raised the possibility of more international games during the county season – left the club unsure whether to search for a replacement.

Sarwan had immediately made his class count, scoring two centuries and a 94 before West Indies went into the First Test at Lord's with a distinctly callow top order. But in an interview with BBC Radio Leicester, he made clear his unhappiness: "The coach said some negative stuff that hurt me mentally and emotionally," he said. "I was broken down – not from the stress of playing, just certain individuals who drained me. It took a toll on my confidence and the way I play. At one point I didn't know my back foot from my front foot."

Leicestershire proved therapeutic: Sarwan scored 941 runs in 14 Championship games, and only business commitments and a late knee injury denied him the chance of 1,000 – a mark no batsman reached in Division Two. He quickly became an influential member of the squad, particularly in the development of the younger players, and had been awarded the four-day captaincy for 2013.

Josh Cobb batted with a good deal more patience in first-class cricket than he had previously shown, and particularly enjoyed partnering Sarwan: they shared three century stands in April and May. The captaincy, which initially passed to Sarwan when Matthew Hoggard was injured, went the way of Cobb – not yet 22 – from July onwards; the limited-overs part of the job became his permanently, and he also led England in the Hong Kong Sixes in October.

Matt Boyce did well when he moved down the order in mid-season, while Wayne White contributed four fifties, as well as 43 wickets with his seam, more than any other bowler. He was presented with his county cap by Hoggard as he left the field after steering Leicestershire to victory over Gloucestershire on the final day – but in January announced he no longer wished to stay, and signed a three-year deal with Lancashire. In his first full season, Ned Eckersley did a solid job behind the stumps. He has considerable potential as a batsman, but it remains to be seen whether he can continue to bat at No. 3 while also keeping wicket.

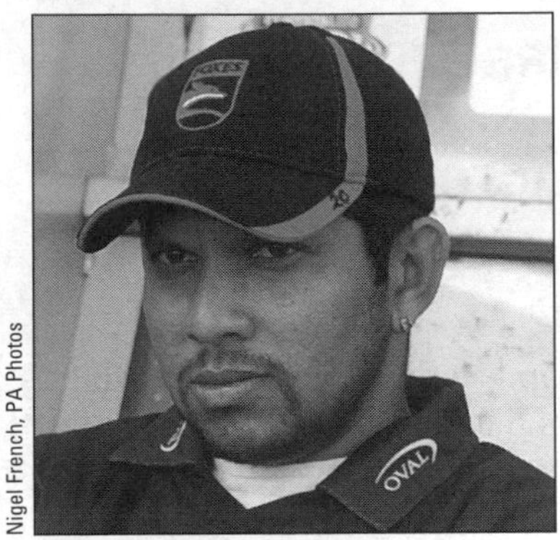
Nigel French, PA Photos

Ramnaresh Sarwan

The real excitement, though, centred on Shiv Thakor. Although still only 18, he was no stranger to Leicestershire supporters, having made a string of record-breaking performances in age-group cricket, then a century on first-class debut, against Loughborough MCCU in 2011. First-team chances had been limited, however, partly because he was still at Uppingham School. But when Thakor was omitted from England's squad for the Under-19 World Cup in Australia, head coach Phil Whitticase slotted him into the Championship side at No. 6 or 7, though no doubt he will move higher. The results augured well. He hit four half-centuries in ten innings, and an unbeaten 39 in two and a half hours saved Leicestershire from defeat at Northampton. His exquisite timing and placement were immediately apparent, as was a steady temperament. There was relief when Thakor signed a two-year contract at the end of the season.

It was a difficult time for opening batsmen everywhere, but too often Leicestershire were forced to recover from dreadful starts, a trend that began immediately: 17 balls into the season, they were one for three. The various opening combinations tried by Whitticase could muster a single half-century stand all season – although Michael Thornely, picked up from the Unicorns, did score two hundreds. Niall O'Brien's arrival from Northamptonshire may help.

The retirement of Will Jefferson, one of the success stories of 2011, was especially sad. He missed the early part of the season with a back problem, and was then diagnosed with a rare hip condition. His best days might have been just around the corner.

Off-spinner Jigar Naik required surgery on ankle ligaments damaged in the opening CB40 game, and missed the bulk of the season. After an encouraging winter with the England Performance Programme, he sent down only 71.2 overs all summer. Robbie Joseph began with 12 for 111 on debut in the opening game, but fell away badly and was released, along with Will Jones, Jacques du Toit and Nadeem Malik. Nathan Buck was disrupted by a back injury, and took only 20 Championship wickets.

There was not even a semblance of a defence of the FLt20 title won so unexpectedly in 2011. That was hardly a surprise: the club were still adapting to the departure of Paul Nixon, Andrew McDonald, James Taylor and Harry Gurney. From players to groundstaff, the entire experience was a struggle.

Cobb scored a memorable maiden List A hundred against Lancashire, before collecting three ducks. His ascent to the one-day captaincy was an attempt to instil some vigour – and Eckersley, Thakor and all-rounder Rob Taylor did produce some eye-catching performances. But there is still some way to go before Leicestershire can contemplate a return to either of the limited-overs finals.

Championship attendance: 11,983.

LEICESTERSHIRE RESULTS

All first-class matches – Played 16: Won 3, Lost 3, Drawn 10.
County Championship matches – Played 16: Won 3, Lost 3, Drawn 10.

LV= County Championship, 7th in Division 2;
Friends Life t20, 6th in North Division; Clydesdale Bank 40, 6th in Group A.

COUNTY CHAMPIONSHIP AVERAGES, BATTING AND FIELDING

Cap		*M*	*I*	*NO*	*R*	*HS*	*100*	*50*	*Avge*	*Ct/St*
	S. J. Thakor†	6	10	3	427	85*	0	4	61.00	2
	R. R. Sarwan§	14	25	2	941	117	2	5	40.91	7
	J. J. Cobb†	14	23	1	752	105	1	5	34.18	6
	M. A. Thornely	9	16	0	514	131	2	1	32.12	6
	M. A. G. Boyce	14	25	2	733	122	2	4	31.86	9
	E. J. H. Eckersley	16	28	4	739	137*	1	3	30.79	43/3
2012	W. A. White	16	26	5	616	67	0	4	29.33	1
	W. S. Jones	3	6	0	138	48	0	0	23.00	2
2004	C. W. Henderson¶	12	19	4	296	57*	0	2	19.73	0
	W. I. Jefferson	2	4	0	75	49	0	0	18.75	1
	G. P. Smith†	13	23	0	429	77	0	2	18.65	13
2010	M. J. Hoggard	10	12	7	81	28	0	0	16.20	0
	Kadeer Ali	3	4	0	63	48	0	0	15.75	1
	J. du Toit¶	6	10	0	127	48	0	0	12.70	4
2011	N. L. Buck†	11	15	2	119	27	0	0	9.15	0
	R. H. Joseph	9	13	4	79	29	0	0	8.77	2
	M. N. Malik	5	7	1	51	21*	0	0	8.50	0
	P. G. Dixey	3	5	1	30	13	0	0	7.50	4/1
	A. C. F. Wyatt	5	6	2	14	8	0	0	3.50	1

Also batted: P. L. Mommsen (2 matches) 9, 5, 35 (2 ct); J. K. H. Naik† (2 matches) 33, 6, 1 (2 ct); R. M. L. Taylor (1 match) 1.

† *Born in Leicestershire.* § *Official overseas player.* ¶ *Other non-England-qualified player.*

BOWLING

	Style	*O*	*M*	*R*	*W*	*BB*	*5I*	*Avge*
M. J. Hoggard	RFM	220.4	42	691	24	4-27	0	28.79
W. A. White	RFM	349	41	1,286	43	5-54	3	29.90
R. H. Joseph	RFM	202.3	36	762	24	6-47	2	31.75
C. W. Henderson	SLA	390.1	82	1,110	30	5-116	1	37.00
N. L. Buck	RFM	292	58	955	20	3-50	0	47.75

Also bowled: M. A. G. Boyce (RM) 2–1–9–0; J. J. Cobb (LBG) 56–4–208–3; J. du Toit (RFM) 18–1–54–0; W. S. Jones (LBG) 26–2–129–5; Kadeer Ali (LBG) 11–2–33–0; M. N. Malik (RFM) 87–10–309–6; P. L. Mommsen (OB) 10–0–43–0; J. K. H. Naik (OB) 56.2–5–205–3; R. R. Sarwan (LBG) 16.1–0–75–0; G. P. Smith (SLA) 1–0–9–0; R. M. L. Taylor (LM) 19–2–91–5; S. J. Thakor (RM) 34–3–159–4; M. A. Thornely (RM) 40–3–150–3; A. C. F. Wyatt (RFM) 100–22–333–9.

LEADING CB40 AVERAGES (100 runs/4 wickets)

Batting	*Runs*	*HS*	*Avge*	*SR*	*Ct/St*
S. J. Thakor	165	83*	55.00	100.00	0
R. R. Sarwan	318	115	35.33	93.52	1
J. J. Cobb	261	137	32.62	108.75	2
M. A. Thornely	226	86	32.28	98.26	0
E. J. H. Eckersley	183	72*	30.50	127.97	7/1
M. A. G. Boyce	214	64	23.77	95.96	1

Bowling	*W*	*BB*	*Avge*	*ER*
J. S. Sykes	6	3-39	24.66	4.77
R. M. L. Taylor	11	2-26	26.45	5.22
M. J. Hoggard	4	3-26	27.25	6.74
W. A. White	6	2-17	41.83	6.78
J. J. Cobb	5	1-35	52.40	6.23
N. L. Buck	5	3-49	60.60	7.12

LEADING FLT20 AVERAGES (100 runs/18 overs)

Batting	Runs	HS	Avge	SR	Ct
J. J. Cobb	187	46	20.77	**135.50**	4
M. A. G. Boyce	175	63*	25.00	**119.04**	2
G. P. Smith	115	23	14.37	**115.00**	1
Abdul Razzaq	266	69	29.55	**112.23**	1
W. A. White	114	22	19.00	**109.61**	2
R. R. Sarwan	138	45	17.25	**103.75**	2

Bowling	W	BB	Avge	ER
R. M. L. Taylor	7	2-7	22.71	**6.91**
C. W. Henderson	2	1-26	76.00	**7.23**
M. J. Hoggard	5	2-25	42.60	**7.60**
J. J. Cobb	2	1-20	76.50	**8.05**
Abdul Razzaq	9	3-20	28.00	**9.00**

FIRST-CLASS COUNTY RECORDS

Highest score for	309*	H. D. Ackerman v Glamorgan at Cardiff	2006
Highest score against	341	G. H. Hirst (Yorkshire) at Leicester	1905
Leading run-scorer	30,143	L. G. Berry (avge 30.32)	1924–1951
Best bowling for	10-18	G. Geary v Glamorgan at Pontypridd	1929
Best bowling against	10-32	H. Pickett (Essex) at Leyton	1895
Leading wicket-taker	2,131	W. E. Astill (avge 23.18)	1906–1939
Highest total for	701-4 dec	v Worcestershire at Worcester	1906
Highest total against	761-6 dec	by Essex at Chelmsford	1990
Lowest total for	25	v Kent at Leicester	1912
Lowest total against	24	by Glamorgan at Leicester	1971
	24	by Oxford University at Oxford	1985

LIST A COUNTY RECORDS

Highest score for	201	V. J. Wells v Berkshire at Leicester	1996
Highest score against	201*	R. S. Bopara (Essex) at Leicester	2008
Leading run-scorer	8,216	N. E. Briers (avge 27.66)	1975–1995
Best bowling for	6-16	C. M. Willoughby v Somerset at Leicester	2005
Best bowling against	6-21	S. M. Pollock (Warwickshire) at Birmingham	1996
Leading wicket-taker	308	K. Higgs (avge 18.80)	1972–1982
Highest total for	406-5	v Berkshire at Leicester	1996
Highest total against	350-5	by Essex at Leicester	2008
Lowest total for	36	v Sussex at Leicester	1973
Lowest total against	62	by Northamptonshire at Leicester	1974
	62	by Middlesex at Leicester	1998

TWENTY20 COUNTY RECORDS

Highest score for	111	D. L. Maddy v Yorkshire at Leeds	2004
Highest score against	92*	S. G. Law (Lancashire) at Manchester	2005
Leading run-scorer	1,455	P. A. Nixon (avge 21.71)	2003–*2011*
Best bowling for	5-13	A. B. McDonald v Nottinghamshire at Nottingham	2010
Best bowling against	5-27	T. Lungley (Derbyshire) at Leicester	2009
Leading wicket-taker	**69**	**C. W. Henderson (avge 26.95)**	**2004–2012**
Highest total for	221-3	v Yorkshire at Leeds	2004
Highest total against	225-2	by Durham at Chester-le-Street	2010
Lowest total for	**96**	**v Nottinghamshire at Leicester**	**2012**
Lowest total against	104-8	by Durham at Chester-le-Street	2006

ADDRESS

County Ground, Grace Road, Leicester LE2 8AD (0116 283 2128; **email** enquiries@leicestershireccc.co.uk). **Website** www.leicestershireccc.co.uk

OFFICIALS

Captain 2012 – M. J. Hoggard
2013 – R. R. Sarwan (Championship)
J. J. Cobb (limited-overs)
Head coach/academy director P. Whitticase
President D. W. Wilson

Chairman P. R. Haywood
Chief executive M. J. Siddall
Operations manager P. Atkinson
Head groundsman A. Ward
Scorer P. J. Rogers

LEICESTERSHIRE v GLAMORGAN

At Leicester, April 5–7. Leicestershire won by 52 runs. Leicestershire 15pts (after 5pt penalty), Glamorgan 2pts (after 1pt penalty). Toss: Glamorgan. County debuts: R. H. Joseph, R. R. Sarwan. Championship debut: M. C. Henriques.

A remarkable county debut by Robbie Joseph helped Leicestershire turn round an atrocious start to beat Glamorgan in the opening fixture for the second year running. With the temperature gauge reading just 6°C, Waters had Smith caught by Rees at short leg, then du Toit lbw, with the first two balls of the season. Boyce followed in Waters's next over, leaving Leicestershire one for three. Sarwan, who faced the hat-trick ball, and Henderson each batted for more than two hours to lead a fine recovery, which Glamorgan could not replicate after they themselves careered to 34 for seven.

BEST MATCH FIGURES ON LEICESTERSHIRE DEBUT

14-89†	A. D. Pougher	v Essex at Leyton	1894
12-111	**R. H. Joseph**	**v Glamorgan at Leicester (Grace Road)**	**2012**
10-118†	G. W. Hillyard	v Yorkshire at Leicester (Grace Road)	1894
9-181	A. R. K. Pierson	v Surrey at Leicester (Grace Road)	1993
8-73	G. J. F. Ferris	v Derbyshire at Derby	1983
8-119	M. N. Malik	v Middlesex at Leicester (Grace Road)	2008
7-47‡	H. M. Bannister	v South Africans at Leicester (Aylestone Road)	1912
7-56	P. M. Such	v Cambridge University at Cambridge	1987
7-88‡	T. Jayes	v Surrey at Leicester (Aylestone Road)	1903
7-161	R. P. Davis	v Northamptonshire at Northampton	2001

† *Pougher and Hillyard achieved it in consecutive matches in May 1894.* ‡ *On first-class debut.*

Wagg at least prevented the follow-on, then played a vital part in dismissing Leicestershire for 110, but a target of 236 was still too much for Glamorgan in difficult conditions. Joseph, playing on a short-term contract after his release by Kent in 2011, troubled the batsmen with his pace; match figures of 12 for 111 were the best for Leicestershire since David Millns in 1991, and their best by a debutant for 118 years. Leicestershire's delight was tempered when they lost five points because of a dismal over-rate; Glamorgan were docked one.

Close of play: first day, Glamorgan 25-5 (Cosker 7, Allenby 0); second day, Glamorgan 21-1 (Walters 11, Bragg 5).

Leicestershire

G. P. Smith c Rees b Waters	0	c Wagg b Waters	4
M. A. G. Boyce c Rees b Waters	0	– lbw b Allenby	11
J. du Toit lbw b Waters	0	– c Wright b Henriques	40
R. R. Sarwan lbw b Wagg	41	– b Wagg	1
J. J. Cobb lbw b Allenby	26	– b Wagg	0
†E. J. H. Eckersley lbw b Allenby	25	– b Henriques	8
W. A. White b Allenby	37	– b Wagg	2
C. W. Henderson not out	57	– c Wallace b Waters	9
R. H. Joseph c Allenby b Croft	29	– b Allenby	9
M. N. Malik c Bragg b Waters	16	– c Allenby b Henriques	4
*M. J. Hoggard b Wagg	0	– not out	4
B 3, l-b 4, w 1, n-b 10	18	B 9, l-b 5, w 2, n-b 2	18
1/0 (1) 2/0 (3) 3/1 (2) 4/29 (5) (83.1 overs)	249	1/14 (1) 2/28 (2) (42.4 overs)	110
5/75 (6) 6/128 (4) 7/140 (7)		3/41 (4) 4/41 (5)	
8/196 (9) 9/244 (10) 10/249 (11)		5/63 (6) 6/72 (7) 7/85 (3)	
		8/87 (8) 9/92 (10) 10/110 (9)	

Waters 19–3–57–4; Wagg 21.1–3–53–2; Allenby 14–2–43–3; Henriques 14–1–59–0; Cosker 9–3–25–0; Croft 6–2–5–1. *Second innings*—Waters 10–4–19–2; Wagg 12–1–29–3; Allenby 8.4–4–21–2; Henriques 11–3–25–3; Cosker 1–0–2–0.

Glamorgan

G. P. Rees lbw b Hoggard	0	– b Joseph	4
S. J. Walters lbw b Joseph	8	– lbw b Joseph	15
W. D. Bragg c Sarwan b Joseph	1	– lbw b Joseph	17
B. J. Wright b Hoggard	1	– lbw b Hoggard	2
M. C. Henriques c Eckersley b Malik	3	– lbw b Hoggard	0
D. A. Cosker c Sarwan b Malik	24	– (10) b White	9
J. Allenby lbw b Joseph	1	– (6) c Joseph b Hoggard	22
*†M. A. Wallace b Joseph	0	– (7) c Eckersley b Joseph	47
G. G. Wagg c Eckersley b Joseph	42	– (8) c Boyce b Joseph	33
R. D. B. Croft b Joseph	20	– (9) lbw b Joseph	4
H. T. Waters not out	5	– not out	17
B 11, l-b 2, w 2, n-b 4	19	L-b 5, n-b 8	13
1/8 (2) 2/8 (1) 3/10 (4) 4/17 (3) 5/25 (5) 6/26 (7) 7/34 (8) 8/79 (6) 9/115 (10) 10/124 (9) (36.1 overs)	124	1/9 (1) 2/30 (2) 3/45 (3) 4/45 (4) 5/46 (5) 6/105 (7) 7/127 (6) 8/139 (9) 9/158 (8) 10/183 (10) (47.2 overs)	183

Hoggard 8–2–21–2; Joseph 14.1–3–47–6; Malik 8–2–22–2; White 6–2–21–0. *Second innings*—Hoggard 16–2–53–3; Joseph 16–3–64–6; White 7.2–0–29–1; Malik 8–0–32–0.

Umpires: S. A. Garratt and P. Willey.

At Loughborough, April 13–15. LEICESTERSHIRE drew with LOUGHBOROUGH MCCU.

At Derby, April 19–22. LEICESTERSHIRE drew with DERBYSHIRE.

At Southampton, April 26–29. LEICESTERSHIRE drew with HAMPSHIRE.

At Scarborough, May 2–5. LEICESTERSHIRE lost to YORKSHIRE by an innings and 22 runs.

LEICESTERSHIRE v NORTHAMPTONSHIRE

At Leicester, May 9–12. Drawn. Leicestershire 5pts, Northamptonshire 7pts. Toss: Leicestershire.

An engrossing run-chase ended with Leicestershire's last pair, White and Hoggard, hanging on grimly for a draw. Northamptonshire tried for 56 balls to dislodge them, but White guarded the strike and saw the job through. Much of the first day and all of the second were lost to rain, but Northamptonshire kept their concentration to pass 300 for the first time in the season, with Coetzer scoring his first hundred for them and Willey striking out decisively for a fourth batting point. Hoggard declared at the start of the last day, giving Northamptonshire eight overs to set up a target of 341 in 86, an equation which took into account the absence of Vaas with a thigh injury. Leicestershire looked in with a chance of claiming their second win of the season while Sarwan and Cobb were dictating matters in the afternoon in a fourth-wicket stand of 103. But they fell either side of tea as Daggett dragged Northamptonshire back into the match to set up a tense finale.

Close of play: first day, Northamptonshire 99-3 (Coetzer 43, Wakely 5); second day, no play; third day, Leicestershire 38-2 (Boyce 15, Sarwan 12).

Northamptonshire

S. D. Peters c Eckersley b Joseph	32	– not out	13
R. I. Newton lbw b Hoggard	0	– not out	10
K. J. Coetzer c Smith b Buck	120		
D. J. Sales c Eckersley b Joseph	9		
A. G. Wakely c and b Cobb	63		
*A. J. Hall c Kadeer Ali b Buck	9		
†N. J. O'Brien c Eckersley b Hoggard	13		
J. D. Middlebrook not out	31		
D. J. Willey not out	45		
B 7, l-b 16, w 1, n-b 6	30	L-b 1, n-b 2	3
1/1 (2) 2/74 (1) 3/88 (4) 4/208 (5) 5/249 (6) 6/254 (3) 7/291 (7) (7 wkts dec, 109 overs)	352	(no wkt dec, 8.1 overs)	26

W. P. U. J. C. Vaas and L. M. Daggett did not bat.

Hoggard 21–5–59–2; Joseph 21–2–79–2; White 10–2–40–0; Buck 22–6–52–2; Henderson 29–4–87–0; Cobb 4–1–5–1; Sarwan 2–0–7–0. *Second innings*—Kadeer Ali 4–1–9–0; Cobb 3–0–7–0; Smith 1–0–9–0; Sarwan 0.1–0–0–0.

Leicestershire

G. P. Smith c O'Brien b Vaas	7	– c O'Brien b Daggett	6
M. A. G. Boyce not out	15	– c Middlebrook b Willey	32
Kadeer Ali c O'Brien b Vaas	0	– c O'Brien b Willey	7
R. R. Sarwan not out	12	– lbw b Middlebrook	94
J. J. Cobb (did not bat)		– b Daggett	59
†E. J. H. Eckersley (did not bat)		– lbw b Hall	35
W. A. White (did not bat)		– not out	29
C. W. Henderson (did not bat)		– run out	6
R. H. Joseph (did not bat)		– lbw b Daggett	1
N. L. Buck (did not bat)		– lbw b Daggett	0
*M. J. Hoggard (did not bat)		– not out	1
L-b 1, w 1, n-b 2	4	B 8, l-b 10, w 1	19
1/8 (1) 2/16 (3) (2 wkts dec, 16 overs)	38	1/10 (1) 2/41 (3) 3/64 (2) 4/167 (5) 5/240 (4) 6/244 (6) 7/267 (8) 8/268 (9) 9/268 (10) (9 wkts, 86 overs)	289

Vaas 7–5–4–2; Willey 6–0–25–0; Hall 2–0–6–0; Daggett 1–0–2–0. *Second innings*—Daggett 25–8–76–4; Willey 22–3–70–2; Hall 21–7–45–1; Middlebrook 18–1–80–1.

Umpires: M. A. Gough and A. G. Wharf.

LEICESTERSHIRE v ESSEX

At Leicester, May 16–19. Drawn. Leicestershire 9pts, Essex 10pts. Toss: Leicestershire. Championship debut: B. T. Foakes.

Jefferson, absent until now with a back injury, edged the first ball of the match to slip, sending Masters on the way to his fifth five-wicket haul against his former county. But Leicestershire still forged a strong position thanks to a free-flowing partnership of 216 between Cobb and Sarwan, whose technical excellence and second century of the season could not persuade West Indies, who were preparing for the next day's opening Test, to bring him back into the fold. A confident 93 from 19-year-old Ben Foakes, making his Championship debut in place of the injured Ravi Bopara, was the highlight of Essex's strong reply. When the final morning was lost to drizzle, the two captains concocted a formula aimed at producing a result: Wheater and Pettini tossed up 7.1 overs of declaration bowling, from which 158 runs were plundered. Sarwan pummelled 37 in 11 balls, Eckersley 70 from 19 and White 50 from 12. In the blink of an eye, Essex were set 270 in 60 overs. But it all came to nothing when the rain returned.

Close of play: first day, Leicestershire 323-5 (White 41, Eckersley 11); second day, Essex 239-5 (Foakes 16); third day, Leicestershire 148-3 (Sarwan 61, Cobb 9).

Leicestershire

W. I. Jefferson c Westley b Masters . . . . 0 – c Foster b Willoughby 49
M. A. G. Boyce b Masters . . . . 4 – c Foster b Willoughby 3
G. P. Smith b Willoughby . . . . 22 – c Foakes b Masters 7
R. R. Sarwan lbw b Masters . . . . 117 – c Mills b Pettini 98
J. J. Cobb c Napier b Masters . . . . 80 – c Westley b Wheater 9
W. A. White c Petersen b Willoughby . . . . 53 – (7) not out 50
†E. J. H. Eckersley c Foster b Masters . . . . 31 – (6) not out 70
C. W. Henderson b Willoughby 0
R. H. Joseph not out 4
N. L. Buck b Napier 6
*M. J. Hoggard b Masters 7
B 13, l-b 9, w 6, n-b 20 48   L-b 15, w 1, n-b 4 20

1/0 (1) 2/25 (2) 3/29 (3) 4/245 (5) (112.2 overs) 372   1/20 (2) (5 wkts dec, 48.1 overs) 306
5/299 (4) 6/351 (6) 7/355 (7)   2/29 (3) 3/126 (1)
8/355 (8) 9/365 (10) 10/372 (11) 110 overs: 367-9   4/149 (5) 5/229 (4)

Masters 33.2–8–82–6; Willoughby 27–5–99–3; Napier 23–4–69–1; Mills 17–5–55–0; Westley 11–1–41–0; Petersen 1–0–4–0. *Second innings*—Masters 11–2–25–1; Willoughby 14–2–60–2; Napier 5–0–22–0; Mills 5–0–19–0; Westley 6–2–7–0; Wheater 4–0–86–1; Pettini 3.1–0–72–1.

Essex

B. A. Godleman lbw b Hoggard . . . . 28 – c Eckersley b Joseph 13
A. N. Petersen lbw b Hoggard . . . . 13 – run out 2
T. Westley lbw b White . . . . 81 – not out 14
M. L. Pettini b White . . . . 57 – not out 0
A. J. Wheater c Eckersley b Buck 8
B. T. Foakes c Eckersley b White 93
*†J. S. Foster c Eckersley b Hoggard 26
G. R. Napier c Eckersley b Henderson 35
D. D. Masters c Eckersley b White 16
T. S. Mills not out 2
C. M. Willoughby b White 0
B 8, l-b 21, w 2, n-b 19 50   L-b 1 1

1/54 (2) 2/55 (1) 3/190 (4) (124 overs) 409   1/10 (2) (2 wkts, 12.2 overs) 30
4/211 (5) 5/239 (3) 6/326 (7)   2/29 (1)
7/369 (6) 8/397 (8) 9/409 (9)
10/409 (11) 110 overs: 363-6

Hoggard 22–3–66–3; Joseph 22–1–76–0; Buck 23–4–89–1; White 30–5–74–5; Henderson 27–6–75–1. *Second innings*—Hoggard 6–1–17–0; Buck 6–3–12–0; Joseph 0.2–0–0–1.

Umpires: J. W. Lloyds and P. Willey.

At Canterbury, May 23–25. LEICESTERSHIRE lost to KENT by an innings and 279 runs.

At Cardiff, May 29–June 1. LEICESTERSHIRE drew with GLAMORGAN.

At Leicester, June 2–3. LEICESTERSHIRE drew with WEST INDIANS (see West Indian tour section).

LEICESTERSHIRE v DERBYSHIRE

At Leicester, June 5–8. Drawn. Leicestershire 4pts, Derbyshire 8pts. Toss: Leicestershire.

A hat-trick from Palladino, which took him to 200 first-class wickets, stood out in another match ravaged by the weather. He removed Thornely and Eckersley, both century-makers in Leicestershire's previous Championship game, at Cardiff, then squared up Sarwan with a yorker. It was the first hat-trick by a Derbyshire bowler since Kevin Dean's on this ground in 2000, and left Leicestershire reeling on seven for three. They never completely recovered, despite a gutsy 48 from Kadeer Ali at No. 8. Derbyshire, responding to their first defeat of the season, at Bristol, and now without their overseas batsman Martin Guptill, breezed past Leicestershire's score, with Redfern contributing a polished unbeaten 81. But he was denied the chance to go on by rain, which washed out 140 overs on the first three days, and all of the last.

Close of play: first day, Derbyshire 5-0 (Lineker 0, Hughes 4); second day, Derbyshire 191-5 (Redfern 40, Wainwright 20); third day, Derbyshire 259-5 (Redfern 81, Wainwright 45).

Leicestershire

M. A. G. Boyce c Madsen b Groenewald . . 50
M. A. Thornely lbw b Palladino 6
†E. J. H. Eckersley c Poynton b Palladino . . 0
R. R. Sarwan b Palladino. 0
J. J. Cobb c Poynton b Clare 30
G. P. Smith c Durston b Groenewald 9
W. A. White c Whiteley b Clare 5
Kadeer Ali c Poynton b Groenewald. 48
N. L. Buck c Durston b Groenewald. 13
M. N. Malik c Durston b Groenewald. 6
*M. J. Hoggard not out 0
B 5, l-b 2, w 1, n-b 2 10

1/7 (2) 2/7 (3) 3/7 (4) (70.4 overs) 177
4/66 (5) 5/95 (1) 6/96 (6)
7/111 (7) 8/169 (9) 9/170 (8) 10/177 (10)

Palladino 16–3–58–3; Groenewald 17.4–5–29–5; Whiteley 3–0–27–0; Clare 12–5–18–2; Wainwright 22–10–38–0.

Derbyshire

M. S. Lineker b Buck 9
C. F. Hughes lbw b Hoggard. 28
*W. L. Madsen c Smith b White 21
W. J. Durston c Thornely b Cobb 44
D. J. Redfern not out 81
R. A. Whiteley b Buck 7
D. J. Wainwright not out. 45
B 4, l-b 9, w 1, n-b 10 24

1/43 (1) 2/51 (2) (5 wkts, 72.4 overs) 259
3/117 (3) 4/123 (4)
5/150 (6)

J. L. Clare, †T. Poynton, A. P. Palladino and T. D. Groenewald did not bat.

Hoggard 15.4–2–47–1; Buck 19–3–72–2; Malik 17–1–60–0; White 15–1–59–1; Cobb 6–1–8–1.

Umpires: R. A. Kettleborough and N. J. Llong.

At Leicester, June 21. LEICESTERSHIRE lost to AUSTRALIANS by 102 runs (D/L) (see Australian tour section).

At Cheltenham, July 18–21. LEICESTERSHIRE drew with GLOUCESTERSHIRE.

LEICESTERSHIRE v YORKSHIRE

At Leicester, July 27–30. Drawn. Leicestershire 8pts, Yorkshire 11pts. Toss: Leicestershire.

Rain again denied Yorkshire a probable victory: the loss of 60 overs on the final day meant more than two-fifths of their Championship programme to date had been wiped out. Azeem Rafiq removed the stubborn pair of White and Eckersley in quick succession, but when time ran out Leicestershire were almost level, with three wickets left. Yorkshire seized the initiative through a magnificent maiden double-century from Lyth, who batted through the innings for eight and a half hours. Oddly, he seemed not to understand his colleagues when they congratulated him for carrying his bat: "I know – I've been carrying it for a day and a half." It was a landmark moment for Lyth, who had been unable to command a first-team place in the early part of the season. He was briefly upstaged by Bairstow, who looked every inch an England player as he stroked 118 from 144 balls in a stand

YOU STILL HERE?

Highest score by an opener carrying his bat through a completed innings in England:

357*	R. Abel	Surrey (811) v Somerset at The Oval	1899
318*	W. G. Grace	Gloucestershire (528) v Yorkshire at Cheltenham	1876
305*	W. H. Ashdown	Kent (560) v Derbyshire at Dover	1935
272*	R. R. Relf	Sussex (433) v Worcestershire at Eastbourne	1909
255*	N. V. Knight	Warwickshire (472) v Hampshire at Birmingham	2002
249*	J. G. Greig	Hampshire (487) v Lancashire at Liverpool	1901
249*	H. T. W. Hardinge	Kent (440) v Leicestershire at Leicester (Aylestone Road)	1922
248*	C. J. L. Rogers	Derbyshire (474) v Warwickshire at Birmingham	2008
248*	**A. Lyth**	**Yorkshire (486) v Leicestershire at Leicester (Grace Road)**	**2012**
245*	N. V. Knight	Warwickshire (493) v Sussex at Birmingham	2002

---

of 197, a much-needed tonic after a difficult debut Test series against West Indies. Leicestershire's first innings was underpinned by Boyce's century – his first since a chilly Scarborough in May – and boosted by 47 extras, 13 of them donated by the on-loan Harmison in an erratic opening spell which included the wicket of Sarwan, surprised by an outswinging yorker; Harmison repeated the trick in the second innings.

Close of play: first day, Leicestershire 318-9 (Boyce 106, Hoggard 1); second day, Yorkshire 336-5 (Lyth 159, McGrath 8); third day, Leicestershire 57-2 (Eckersley 7, Sarwan 2).

Leicestershire

G. P. Smith lbw b Patterson	20	– lbw b McGrath	26
M. A. Thornely c Bairstow b Ashraf	31	– b Harmison	17
E. J. H. Eckersley lbw b Patterson	4	– c Root b Azeem Rafiq	26
R. R. Sarwan b Harmison	8	– b Harmison	6
M. A. G. Boyce c and b Azeem Rafiq	107	– c Root b Harmison	4
S. J. Thakor c Gale b Ashraf	35	– lbw b Patterson	0
W. A. White c Harmison b Azeem Rafiq	28	– c Bairstow b Azeem Rafiq	44
†P. G. Dixey c Jaques b Harmison	6	– not out	3
C. W. Henderson c Root b Patterson	26	– not out	8
N. L. Buck c Ballance b McGrath	6		
*M. J. Hoggard not out	2		
B 5, l-b 10, w 11, n-b 21	47	B 4, l-b 7, w 1, n-b 11	23
1/20 (1) 2/50 (3) 3/59 (4) 4/98 (2) (97.3 overs)	320	1/43 (1) (7 wkts, 59.4 overs)	157
5/166 (6) 6/226 (7) 7/239 (8)		2/49 (2) 3/61 (4)	
8/289 (9) 9/310 (10) 10/320 (5)		4/77 (5) 5/78 (6) 6/145 (7) 7/148 (3)	

Patterson 25–6–56–3; Ashraf 17–4–71–2; Harmison 16–1–69–2; McGrath 14–3–40–1; Azeem Rafiq 23.3–7–64–2; Root 2–1–5–0. *Second innings*—Patterson 20–6–38–1; Ashraf 12–3–25–0; McGrath 8–3–13–1; Harmison 12–0–52–3; Azeem Rafiq 7.4–2–18–2.

Yorkshire

A. Lyth not out	248
J. E. Root b Buck	0
P. A. Jaques c Boyce b Buck	30
*A. W. Gale c Sarwan b Henderson	11
†J. M. Bairstow c Smith b Buck	118
G. S. Ballance lbw b Hoggard	1
A. McGrath c Smith b Hoggard	8
Azeem Rafiq c Dixey b White	23
S. A. Patterson c Eckersley b Henderson	28
S. J. Harmison lbw b Henderson	0
M. A. Ashraf st Dixey b Henderson	0
B 5, l-b 6, w 2, n-b 6	19
1/6 (2) 2/74 (3) 3/112 (4) (127.1 overs)	486
4/309 (5) 5/310 (6)	
6/342 (7) 7/387 (8) 8/460 (9)	
9/474 (10) 10/486 (11) 110 overs: 400-7	

Hoggard 18–0–78–2; Buck 30–2–124–3; White 19–0–78–1; Henderson 47.1–11–126–4; Thornely 3–0–18–0; Sarwan 4–0–19–0; Thakor 6–1–32–0.

Umpires: R. J. Bailey and I. J. Gould.

At Chelmsford, August 1–4. LEICESTERSHIRE drew with ESSEX.

At Northampton, August 10–13. LEICESTERSHIRE drew with NORTHAMPTONSHIRE.

LEICESTERSHIRE v HAMPSHIRE

At Leicester, August 21–24. Leicestershire won by 126 runs. Leicestershire 23pts, Hampshire 3pts. Toss: Hampshire.

Leicestershire's margin of victory was comfortable enough, but they had to endure some distinctly fidgety moments before completing only their third Championship win since September 2010 (the previous two had come at home against Glamorgan). They dominated all except the last 80 minutes against a Hampshire side who were unbeaten in nine games and included four Test batsmen, but barely resembled promotion contenders. Thakor hit a Championship-best unbeaten 85 to resuscitate Leicestershire in the first innings, then took a stunning catch at cover to oust Katich for a duck, as a disciplined attack ran through Hampshire for 181. Hoggard declined a rare opportunity to enforce the follow-on, instead allowing his batsmen to extend the advantage to 440 with four sessions left. For Hampshire to lurch to 146 for nine, against an attack lacking a specialist spinner, was particularly anaemic. But Wood and Balcombe launched an incredible riposte, setting about the bowling in Twenty20 fashion on the eve of the county's appearance in Finals Day. In all, they smashed 168 for the last wicket in 23 overs. Wood raced to a maiden century in 80 balls, while Balcombe lashed 73 from 70 – the highest score by a Hampshire No. 11 – before Buck finally put a stop to their fun.

Close of play: first day, Leicestershire 334-8 (Thakor 71, Hoggard 1); second day, Leicestershire 68-2 (Eckersley 14, Sarwan 29); third day, Hampshire 77-4 (Dawson 16, Tomlinson 0).

Leicestershire

W. S. Jones c Bates b Balcombe	23	–	c Ervine b Balcombe	13
M. A. Thornely lbw b Kabir Ali	0	–	c McKenzie b Tomlinson	9
†E. J. H. Eckersley c McKenzie b Kabir Ali	18	–	b Ervine	39
R. R. Sarwan lbw b Tomlinson	36	–	b Ervine	46
J. J. Cobb b Ervine	82	–	c and b Dawson	42
M. A. G. Boyce c Adams b Ervine	32	–	c Dawson b Ervine	16
S. J. Thakor not out	85	–	c Bates b Kabir Ali	45
W. A. White b Tomlinson	53	–	not out	35
N. L. Buck c Bates b Tomlinson	0	–	c and b Dawson	11
*M. J. Hoggard b Tomlinson	5			
A. C. F. Wyatt c Bates b Tomlinson	3			
B 9, l-b 8, n-b 2	19		B 2, l-b 3, n-b 4	9
1/5 (2) 2/41 (3) 3/43 (1) (101.3 overs)	356		1/20 (2) (8 wkts dec, 85.5 overs)	265
4/118 (4) 5/194 (5) 6/199 (6)			2/23 (1) 3/109 (3)	
7/308 (8) 8/314 (9) 9/344 (10) 10/356 (11)			4/112 (4) 5/166 (6)	
			6/184 (5) 7/246 (7) 8/265 (9)	

Kabir Ali 21–5–76–2; Tomlinson 24.3–6–69–5; Balcombe 22–2–116–1; Wood 12–3–48–0; Ervine 15–4–27–2; Dawson 7–6–3–0. *Second innings*—Kabir Ali 16–4–38–1; Tomlinson 17–3–61–1; Balcombe 12–3–38–1; Ervine 20–7–37–3; Dawson 16.5–3–63–2; Katich 4–0–23–0.

Hampshire

M. A. Carberry lbw b Hoggard	20	– c Boyce b Hoggard	18
*J. H. K. Adams b Hoggard	17	– c Eckersley b Hoggard	22
N. D. McKenzie lbw b Wyatt	16	– b White	6
S. M. Katich c Thakor b Wyatt	0	– c Eckersley b Wyatt	6
L. A. Dawson lbw b Wyatt	23	– st Eckersley b Jones	49
S. M. Ervine not out	58	– (7) b Jones	0
†M. D. Bates b White	0	– (8) b White	0
C. P. Wood lbw b White	0	– (9) not out	105
Kabir Ali b White	7	– (10) run out	4
D. J. Balcombe b Hoggard	31	– (11) b Buck	73
J. A. Tomlinson c Eckersley b Hoggard	0	– (6) c Boyce b Jones	10
B 6, w 3	9	B 8, l-b 4, w 5, n-b 4	21
1/28 (1) 2/45 (3) 3/47 (4) 4/71 (2) 5/99 (5) 6/110 (7) 7/110 (8) 8/131 (9) 9/181 (10) 10/181 (11) (57 overs)	181	1/22 (1) 2/35 (3) 3/42 (4) 4/66 (2) 5/109 (6) 6/109 (7) 7/110 (8) 8/140 (5) 9/146 (10) 10/314 (11) (77.1 overs)	314

Hoggard 14–7–27–4; Buck 12–2–56–0; Wyatt 15–4–35–3; White 13–2–45–3; Jones 2–0–7–0; Cobb 1–0–5–0. *Second innings*—Hoggard 16–5–49–2; Buck 16.1–6–32–1; Wyatt 13–4–62–1; White 18–2–87–2; Jones 13–2–71–3; Cobb 1–0–1–0.

Umpires: S. A. Garratt and G. Sharp.

LEICESTERSHIRE v KENT

At Leicester, August 28–31. Kent won by 147 runs. Kent 21pts, Leicestershire 2pts. Toss: Leicestershire.

Kent moved within four points of the promotion places with a victory that owed much to Leicestershire's willingness to resurrect a damp contest. Nash played skilfully for his third hundred of the season, but the second day was washed out, and 37 overs were lost at the start of the third. Rob Taylor, in his only Championship appearance of the summer, completed a maiden five-wicket haul before the declaration; Boyce, dropped at slip on seven, then steered Leicestershire to 171 for three by the close. In a bizarre start next morning, Boyce and Cobb came out to resume their partnership for just one ball before Hoggard declared 179 behind, having reached an agreement with Key over the equation for a fourth-innings run-chase. Kent batted 23 overs before setting Leicestershire 283 in 68. That was a tough ask against a strong Kent seam attack, and one which became near-impossible at 13 for three. Stevens, a Leicestershire old boy whose outswing was perfectly suited to the conditions, scythed through the middle order with four wickets in four overs.

Close of play: first day, Kent 322-6 (Nash 108); second day, no play; third day, Leicestershire 171-3 (Boyce 78, Cobb 31).

Kent

S. A. Northeast c Eckersley b Wyatt	52	– c Naik b Thornely	20
*R. W. T. Key lbw b Taylor	68	– c Naik b White	14
A. J. Blake c Eckersley b Taylor	9	– not out	35
B. P. Nash c Wyatt b Naik	119	– not out	25
M. J. Powell b Taylor	0		
D. I. Stevens c Thornely b Wyatt	18		
†G. O. Jones c Eckersley b Taylor	52		
M. T. Coles c Eckersley b Taylor	17		
M. Davies not out	0		
B 8, l-b 2, w 1, n-b 4	15	B 4, l-b 1, n-b 4	9
1/110 (1) 2/135 (2) 3/158 (3) 4/158 (5) 5/188 (6) 6/322 (7) 7/350 (8) 8/350 (4) (8 wkts dec, 92.2 overs)	350	1/33 (2) 2/45 (1) (2 wkts dec, 23 overs)	103

A. E. N. Riley and C. E. Shreck did not bat.

Riley replaced J. C. Tredwell after he was called up by England.

Hoggard 21–4–65–0; Wyatt 16–4–44–2; Taylor 19–2–91–5; White 19–3–68–0; Naik 16.2–1–70–1; Jones 1–0–2–0. *Second innings*—Thakor 3–0–19–0; Thornely 6–1–16–1; White 7–0–37–1; Naik 2–0–8–0; Jones 2–0–9–0; Boyce 2–1–9–0; Wyatt 1–1–0–0.

Leicestershire

W. S. Jones c Stevens b Coles	48	– c Jones b Shreck	3
M. A. Thornely c Jones b Shreck	0	– c Jones b Davies	4
†E. J. H. Eckersley c Stevens b Shreck	8	– c Coles b Davies	4
M. A. G. Boyce not out	78	– c Coles b Stevens	23
J. J. Cobb not out	31	– lbw b Stevens	21
S. J. Thakor (did not bat)		– c Northeast b Stevens	22
W. A. White (did not bat)		– b Stevens	2
J. K. H. Naik (did not bat)		– lbw b Davies	33
R. M. L. Taylor (did not bat)		– lbw b Stevens	1
*M. J. Hoggard (did not bat)		– not out	16
A. C. F. Wyatt (did not bat)		– c Blake b Shreck	0
B 2, l-b 4	6	L-b 5, w 1	6
1/2 (2) 2/14 (3) 3/107 (1) (3 wkts dec, 52.1 overs)	171	1/7 (2) 2/7 (1) 3/13 (3) 4/48 (5) 5/78 (6) 6/83 (7) 7/88 (4) 8/94 (9) 9/132 (8) 10/135 (11) (49.5 overs)	135

Davies 13–3–32–0; Shreck 17–3–63–2; Stevens 9–1–40–0; Riley 7.1–4–8–0; Coles 6–0–22–1. *Second innings*—Davies 16–6–24–3; Shreck 10.5–2–30–2; Stevens 14–2–35–5; Coles 7–0–31–0; Riley 2–0–10–0.

Umpires: M. A. Gough and G. Sharp.

LEICESTERSHIRE v GLOUCESTERSHIRE

At Leicester, September 11–14. Leicestershire won by two wickets. Leicestershire 21pts, Gloucestershire 4pts. Toss: Gloucestershire.

Leicestershire held their nerve to scrape home on the last evening and avoid a second consecutive wooden spoon – which now passed to Gloucestershire instead. Needing 236, the hosts were cruising at 205 for four, with Cobb sprinting to 65, until he and Eckersley were out amid a crash of five wickets for 13 runs, blowing the game wide open. White, though, produced a trio of boundaries to haul Leicestershire over the line. There was little to separate the teams throughout a high-tempo encounter. Gloucestershire were only 75 ahead after White took three wickets in an over, all caught behind by Eckersley, who finished with six dismissals in an innings for the second time in 12 months. But Batty, who finished unbeaten on 40 in his last innings before retiring, resisted stoutly with Will Gidman to set Leicestershire a tricky chase. White received his county cap from Hoggard as he left the field after hitting the winning runs, in recognition of his fine all-round work through a frustrating summer.

Close of play: first day, Leicestershire 94-3 (Smith 47, Cobb 10); second day, Leicestershire 220-5 (Thakor 68, White 20); third day, Gloucestershire 254-9 (Batty 16, Norwell 0).

Gloucestershire

	First innings		Second innings	
E. J. M. Cowan b Buck		19	c Eckersley b White	16
B. A. C. Howell b White		7	b Henderson	35
D. M. Housego b Thakor		22	c Eckersley b Hoggard	62
*A. P. R. Gidman lbw b Thakor		11	c Eckersley b White	24
H. J. H. Marshall c Eckersley b Buck		47	c Eckersley b White	0
I. A. Cockbain c Thakor b Henderson		48	c Eckersley b White	0
W. R. S. Gidman lbw b Naik		26	st Eckersley b Henderson	72
†J. N. Batty lbw b Naik		23	(9) not out	40
J. K. Fuller c Eckersley b Henderson		2	(10) lbw b Henderson	1
J. M. R. Taylor not out		5	(8) c White b Hoggard	7
L. C. Norwell c Smith b Henderson		0	b Hoggard	7
B 7, l-b 10, n-b 7		24	B 13, l-b 14, w 1, n-b 4	32
1/31 (1) 2/35 (2) 3/66 (4) 4/71 (3) 5/167 (5) 6/175 (6) 7/225 (7) 8/228 (8) 9/234 (9) 10/234 (11)	(65.5 overs)	234	1/39 (1) 2/79 (2) 3/132 (4) 4/136 (5) 5/136 (6) 6/213 (3) 7/221 (8) 8/252 (7) 9/254 (10) 10/296 (11) (88 overs)	296

Hoggard 10–0–50–0; Buck 14–1–55–2; White 8–3–20–1; Thakor 5–0–24–2; Naik 13–0–36–2; Henderson 15.5–6–32–3. *Second innings*—Buck 11–2–27–0; Hoggard 9–1–30–3; Naik 25–4–91–0; Henderson 28–6–72–3; White 15–3–49–4.

Leicestershire

	First innings		Second innings	
G. P. Smith c Housego b Taylor		77	c Taylor b Norwell	26
M. A. Thornely lbw b W. R. S. Gidman		0	b Fuller	36
†E. J. H. Eckersley b Norwell		25	c Batty b Fuller	63
M. A. G. Boyce lbw b W. R. S. Gidman		10	lbw b Taylor	9
J. J. Cobb b Norwell		11	lbw b W. R. S. Gidman	65
S. J. Thakor c Batty b Fuller		73	lbw b Fuller	5
W. A. White c Housego b Fuller		25	(8) not out	14
J. K. H. Naik c Howell b Fuller		6	(7) lbw b W. R. S. Gidman	1
C. W. Henderson c Howell b Fuller		34	b W. R. S. Gidman	0
N. L. Buck lbw b Norwell		25	not out	6
*M. J. Hoggard not out		0		
B 2, l-b 5, n-b 2		9	B 6, l-b 4, n-b 2	12
1/9 (2) 2/50 (3) 3/80 (4) 4/109 (5) 5/155 (1) 6/225 (7) 7/235 (8) 8/236 (6) 9/273 (10) 10/295 (9)	(91.2 overs)	295	1/45 (1) 2/81 (2) 3/106 (4) 4/205 (5) 5/216 (6) 6/217 (7) 7/217 (3) 8/218 (9) (8 wkts, 58.3 overs)	237

W. R. S. Gidman 20–1–71–2; Fuller 18.2–3–51–4; Taylor 29–4–87–1; Norwell 19–3–62–3; Howell 5–1–17–0. *Second innings*—W. R. S. Gidman 15.3–4–42–3; Fuller 17–2–75–3; Norwell 11–0–54–1; Taylor 11–3–45–1; Howell 4–1–11–0.

Umpires: I. Dawood and G. Sharp.

MIDDLESEX

Staying power

NORMAN DE MESQUITA

After the euphoria of winning the second division in 2011, only one question mattered to Middlesex in 2012: could they justify their place among the elite? The answer was a resounding yes, as five wins led to third place in the table – although Angus Fraser, the director of cricket, admitted his team still had work to do before they could be regarded as serious Championship challengers. As with any relatively young team, there was some inconsistency, most obvious in poor displays away to Durham and Sussex. But those were balanced by a fine victory at Worcester, and a winning position – scuppered by the weather – against the eventual champions Warwickshire at Edgbaston.

The season began with defeat at Taunton, but that was followed by a remarkable three-run win over Surrey at Lord's – an important boost, not just for the points column but for the team's confidence. Three of the first four home matches were won, which meant the players were not constantly worrying about relegation.

Not for the first time, though, Middlesex had leadership issues. Neil Dexter felt the responsibilities were affecting his batting so, while remaining club captain, he handed over to the Australian Chris Rogers in Championship matches. Rogers's powers of persuasion came into play in his second match in charge, when he somehow convinced Worcestershire they had a chance if they declared behind and Middlesex forfeited their second innings. There could be only one winner – and it wasn't Worcestershire.

Dexter's self-imposed return to the ranks produced a moving moment when, on his 28th birthday in August, he scored his first century for 16 months, against Warwickshire at Edgbaston. Dexter dedicated it to his older brother, Keith, who had died suddenly over the winter.

In one respect, Rogers did not bring about any improvement in Middlesex's fortunes: they won the toss in only three of the 16 Championship matches, and just nine times in 38 games all told. Perhaps it was a good year to lose it. Certainly, as long as conditions favoured seam bowling, Middlesex were at their best: the improvement of Toby Roland-Jones, and the emergence of Gareth Berg as an aggressive first change, gave the attack a cutting edge it had lacked even during the previous year's promotion push. The one department with room for improvement was spin: on an Oval pitch that favoured the slow men, Surrey clearly had the upper hand, although some determined tail-end batting almost spirited Middlesex to another unlikely victory.

Overall, there is no danger of complacency, as witnessed by the post-season activity. Rogers accepted a new two-year contract, but Anthony Ireland, Scott Newman, Tom Scollay and Robbie Williams were all released. Newman had in any case spent the spring on loan to Kent.

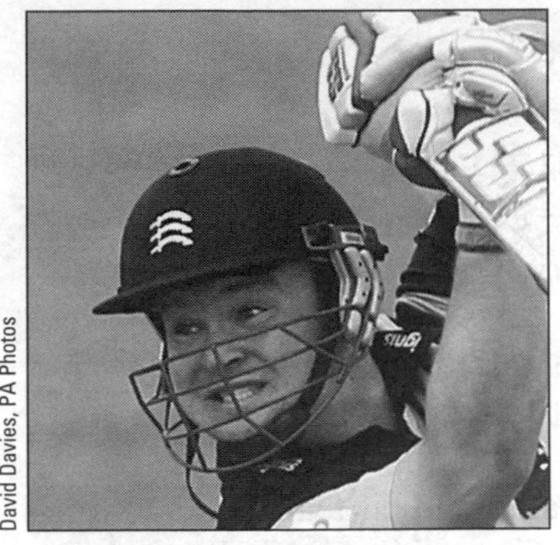
David Davies, PA Photos

Paul Stirling

Four young players joined the staff for 2013, notably James Harris, the highly rated seamer who played for Glamorgan's Second Eleven at 14, and is still only 22. Several counties were interested after he decided to step up a division, but he plumped for Lord's because he relished the chance to work with Fraser, coach Richard Scott and his assistant Richard Johnson. The other new faces are Oli Wilkin, an all-rounder seen as a valuable addition to the one-day squad; the 18-year-old Tom Helm, a fast bowler in the Steven Finn mould; and Nick Gubbins, a prolific scorer at Radley College, Andrew Strauss's alma mater. Strauss himself signed off from Championship cricket with 50 and 127 not out against Nottinghamshire in July, and quit the game in September.

The year was not an unbounded success for everyone. John Simpson continued to look good behind the stumps, but – like Berg – had a disappointing year with the bat. Dexter found runs hard to come by at first, but showed a marked improvement after relinquishing the captaincy. Joe Denly batted superbly for the first half of the season, then fell away. In contrast, Sam Robson and Dawid Malan improved as the year went on, while Steven Crook contributed significantly with both bat and ball in the latter part of the season – but he is returning to Northamptonshire for 2013.

Among the bowlers, Tim Murtagh was once again Mr Reliable, and also made his international debut on account of three Irish grandparents. A total of 61 first-class wickets took his aggregate to 350, at 25 apiece, since joining from Surrey in 2007. And Roland-Jones's excellent season – he was Middlesex's Player of the Year after taking 64 first-class wickets at less than 20 – was rewarded with a place in the England Performance Programme in India.

Form was mixed in the limited-overs competitions. A possible semi-final spot in the CB40 was stymied by the weather, but Twenty20 performances were disappointing, despite some superb displays from Irishman Paul Stirling. Adam Voges from Western Australia was signed for the 2013 competition.

Still, it was a pleasing season, with the progress in Championship cricket a particular cause for pride. It is often said that Middlesex see their principal aim as supplying players to the England team – in which case, with Finn and Eoin Morgan already there, and Roland-Jones making giant strides, there were several reasons to be satisfied. And there was one reason to be intrigued: having retired from the game, Mark Ramprakash returned to the club he had left in acrimony in 2000, to take up the post of batting coach.

Championship attendance: 28,104.

MIDDLESEX RESULTS

All first-class matches – Played 17: Won 5, Lost 4, Drawn 8.
County Championship matches – Played 16: Won 5, Lost 4, Drawn 7.

LV= County Championship, 3rd in Division 1;
Friends Life t20, 5th in South Division; Clydesdale Bank 40, 2nd in Group A.

COUNTY CHAMPIONSHIP AVERAGES, BATTING AND FIELDING

Cap		*M*	*I*	*NO*	*R*	*HS*	*100*	*50*	*Avge*	*Ct/St*
2001	A. J. Strauss‡	4	7	2	277	127*	1	1	55.40	7
2011	C. J. L. Rogers§	16	29	2	1,086	173	3	6	40.22	7
2012	J. L. Denly	16	28	4	840	134*	2	4	35.00	7
2010	N. J. Dexter¶	12	21	2	648	125	2	3	34.10	9
2010	D. J. Malan	16	26	0	827	140	2	3	31.80	23
	S. P. Crook	5	9	0	273	67	0	2	30.33	2
	O. P. Rayner	10	14	2	338	143*	1	1	28.16	12
	S. D. Robson¶	15	28	2	697	72	0	4	26.80	11
2008	T. J. Murtagh	15	21	6	360	45	0	0	24.00	5
2010	G. K. Berg¶	15	23	1	467	83	0	2	21.22	12
2012	T. S. Roland-Jones†	14	20	5	294	52	0	1	19.60	3
2008	E. J. G. Morgan‡	5	7	1	109	71	0	1	18.16	6
2011	J. A. Simpson	13	19	1	279	47	0	0	15.50	42/5
	R. H. Patel†	3	5	2	46	20	0	0	15.33	3
	A. M. Rossington†	3	5	0	62	29	0	0	12.40	9/1
2011	C. D. Collymore¶	7	10	6	29	8	0	0	7.25	0
2009	S. T. Finn‡	5	6	4	1	1*	0	0	0.50	7

Also batted: A. Balbirnie (1 match) 14, 3; T. M. J. Smith (1 match) 31, 0.

† *Born in Middlesex.* ‡ *ECB contract.* § *Official overseas player.* ¶ *Other non-England-qualified player.*

BOWLING

	Style	*O*	*M*	*R*	*W*	*BB*	*5I*	*Avge*
T. S. Roland-Jones	RFM	379	83	1,167	61	6-66	4	19.13
S. T. Finn	RF	170	39	538	28	4-43	0	19.21
T. J. Murtagh	RFM	496.3	117	1,401	59	5-37	2	23.74
R. H. Patel	SLA	104	12	356	14	4-72	0	25.42
N. J. Dexter	RM	102	20	317	12	3-23	0	26.41
G. K. Berg	RFM	329.4	73	1,014	35	3-25	0	28.97
S. P. Crook	RFM	134.4	16	476	14	5-48	1	34.00
O. P. Rayner	OB	205.5	27	529	15	4-67	0	35.26
C. D. Collymore	RFM	187.1	44	540	11	3-66	0	49.09

Also bowled: A. Balbirnie (OB) 8–0–24–0; J. L. Denly (LBG) 27–2–104–1; D. J. Malan (LBG) 47.2–7–199–7; S. D. Robson (LBG) 0.5–0–4–0; T. M. J. Smith (SLA) 27.3–3–71–1.

LEADING CB40 AVERAGES (100 runs/4 wickets)

Batting	*Runs*	*HS*	*Avge*	*SR*	*Ct*
E. J. G. Morgan	263	120*	87.66	146.92	2
C. J. L. Rogers	335	122*	83.75	101.20	4
D. J. Malan	445	134	55.62	104.46	5
J. L. Denly	267	96*	38.14	80.18	2
P. R. Stirling	255	119	36.42	114.34	3
G. K. Berg	165	61	27.50	105.09	5

Bowling	*W*	*BB*	*Avge*	*ER*
T. S. Roland-Jones	11	3-24	12.36	4.68
P. R. Stirling	8	4-27	19.00	5.84
S. P. Crook	14	3-26	21.64	5.61
S. T. Finn	5	3-30	21.80	4.54
T. M. J. Smith	4	3-30	42.25	5.45
N. J. Dexter	6	2-45	49.00	7.00

LEADING FLT20 AVERAGES (90 runs/18 overs)

Batting	Runs	HS	Avge	SR	Ct
S. P. Crook	90	25	15.00	**173.07**	3
P. R. Stirling	271	82*	45.16	**142.63**	1
D. J. Malan	188	46	23.50	**115.33**	3
N. J. Dexter	155	42	22.14	**101.30**	5
J. L. Denly	199	90*	28.42	**101.01**	4
G. K. Berg	98	39	19.60	**97.02**	1

Bowling	W	BB	Avge	ER
O. P. Rayner	3	2-16	64.00	**6.06**
T. M. J. Smith	8	3-24	30.62	**7.20**
S. P. Crook	7	2-21	24.00	**7.63**
G. K. Berg	10	3-17	20.50	**7.88**
T. S. Roland-Jones	11	4-25	20.72	**8.14**
N. J. Dexter	7	3-22	27.85	**8.47**

FIRST-CLASS COUNTY RECORDS

Highest score for	331*	J. D. B. Robertson v Worcestershire at Worcester	1949
Highest score against	341	C. M. Spearman (Gloucestershire) at Gloucester	2004
Leading run-scorer	40,302	E. H. Hendren (avge 48.81)	1907–1937
Best bowling for	10-40	G. O. B. Allen v Lancashire at Lord's	1929
Best bowling against	9-38	R. C. Robertson-Glasgow (Somerset) at Lord's	1924
Leading wicket-taker	2,361	F. J. Titmus (avge 21.27)	1949–1982
Highest total for	642-3 dec	v Hampshire at Southampton	1923
Highest total against	850-7 dec	by Somerset at Taunton	2007
Lowest total for	20	v MCC at Lord's	1864
Lowest total against	31	by Gloucestershire at Bristol	1924
	31	by Glamorgan at Cardiff	1997

LIST A COUNTY RECORDS

Highest score for	163	A. J. Strauss v Surrey at The Oval	2008
Highest score against	163	C. J. Adams (Sussex) at Arundel	1999
Leading run-scorer	12,029	M. W. Gatting (avge 34.96)	1975–1998
Best bowling for	7-12	W. W. Daniel v Minor Counties East at Ipswich	1978
Best bowling against	6-27	J. C. Tredwell (Kent) at Southgate	2009
Leading wicket-taker	491	J. E. Emburey (avge 24.68)	1975–1995
Highest total for	**350-6**	**v Middlesex at Lord's**	**2012**
Highest total against	353-8	by Hampshire at Lord's	2005
Lowest total for	23	v Yorkshire at Leeds	1974
Lowest total against	41	by Northamptonshire at Northampton	1972

TWENTY20 COUNTY RECORDS

Highest score for	106	A. C. Gilchrist v Kent at Canterbury	2010
Highest score against	119	K. J. O'Brien (Gloucestershire) at Uxbridge	2011
Leading run-scorer	1,376	O. A. Shah (avge 34.40)	2003–2010
Best bowling for	5-13	M. Kartik v Essex at Lord's	2007
Best bowling against	6-24	T. J. Murtagh (Surrey) at Lord's	2005
Leading wicket-taker	46	T. Henderson (avge 23.69)	2007–2010
Highest total for	213-4	v Glamorgan at Richmond	2010
Highest total against	254-3	by Gloucestershire at Uxbridge	2011
Lowest total for	102	v Glamorgan at Richmond	2011
Lowest total against	99	by Hampshire at Southampton	2010

ADDRESS

Lord's Cricket Ground, London NW8 8QN (020 7289 1300; **email** enquiries@middlesexccc.com). **Website** www.middlesexccc.com

OFFICIALS

Captain C. J. L. Rogers (Championship)
N. J. Dexter (limited-overs)
Managing director of cricket A. R. C. Fraser
First-team coach R. J. Scott
Academy director A. J. Coleman

President G. W. Norris
Chairman I. N. Lovett
Secretary/chief executive V. J. Codrington
Head groundsman M. J. Hunt
Scorer D. K. Shelley

MIDDLESEX v DURHAM MCCU

At Merchant Taylors' School, Northwood, March 31–April 2. Drawn. Toss: Durham MCCU. First-class debuts: M. J. E. Green, A. S. Sangha, C. A. Wallis.

The season started earlier than it had ever done and, in balmy weather, Sam Robson became the first man to score a first-class century in England in March, reaching three figures shortly before tea on the opening day. When Middlesex bowled, Crook took four cheap wickets, and the students were eventually left to bat out the final day to avoid defeat. Thanks to Rishabh Shah's battling maiden half-century in almost four hours, they did so with some ease. The game had originally been scheduled in Durham, but it was felt that early-season conditions would be preferable in the south of England, so it was switched to Northwood – where it became the inaugural first-class match at Merchant Taylors' School, more than 450 years after it was founded.

Close of play: first day, Durham MCCU 25-2 (Waters 3, Sangha 16); second day, Middlesex 141-2 (Simpson 49, London 10).

Middlesex

A. B. London lbw b Salt	30	– (4) not out	10
S. D. Robson run out	117		
C. J. L. Rogers c Smith b Blackaby	0	– (1) b Salt	22
D. J. Malan c Smith b Blackaby	70		
*N. J. Dexter c Smith b Blackaby	0	– (2) lbw b Watkins	53
†J. A. Simpson c Smith b Green	15	– (3) not out	49
G. K. Berg b Blackaby	59		
O. P. Rayner c Jones b Sangha	21		
S. P. Crook c Shah b Patel	12		
T. J. Murtagh not out	31		
T. S. Roland-Jones not out	2		
L-b 1, w 8, n-b 2	11	B 3, l-b 1, w 3	7
1/86 (1) 2/87 (3) 3/215 (4) 4/217 (5) 5/231 (2) 6/245 (6) 7/292 (8) 8/313 (9) 9/346 (7) (9 wkts dec, 94 overs)	368	1/42 (1) 2/115 (2) (2 wkts dec, 42 overs)	141

Wallis 11–0–56–0; Green 16–1–53–1; Salt 11–2–41–1; Blackaby 17–2–51–4; Watkins 20–1–66–0; Sangha 8–0–36–1; Patel 11–0–64–1. *Second innings*—Wallis 3–0–30–0; Green 9–0–17–0; Salt 6–0–14–1; Sangha 5–0–18–0; Watkins 12–1–36–1; Blackaby 7–3–22–0.

Durham MCCU

*C. R. Jones b Murtagh	0	– c Simpson b Roland-Jones	32
S. R. Waters c Robson b Crook	15	– lbw b Murtagh	30
R. A. C. Shah b Roland-Jones	5	– not out	56
A. S. Sangha c Malan b Roland-Jones	32	– c Malan b Rayner	26
L. A. Blackaby lbw b Rayner	45	– not out	38
L. A. Patel run out	2		
†J. W. G. Smith c Dexter b Rayner	0		
N. A. T. Watkins c Berg b Crook	12		
J. D. Salt b Crook	1		
C. A. Wallis not out	2		
M. J. E. Green b Crook	4		
B 2, l-b 3, w 1	6	B 5, l-b 6, n-b 6	17
1/0 (1) 2/7 (3) 3/51 (4) 4/67 (2) 5/99 (6) 6/103 (5) 7/104 (7) 8/113 (9) 9/118 (8) 10/124 (11) (64.5 overs)	124	1/60 (1) 2/95 (2) 3/124 (4) (3 wkts, 83 overs)	199

Murtagh 18–8–27–1; Roland-Jones 17–3–50–2; Crook 11.5–5–16–4; Dexter 6–2–8–0; Rayner 12–5–18–2. *Second innings*—Murtagh 12–2–27–1; Roland-Jones 9–1–28–1; Crook 12–4–42–0; Rayner 23–6–43–1; Malan 16–6–28–0; Dexter 7–3–7–0; Robson 4–0–13–0.

Umpires: N. A. Mallender and P. R. Pollard. S. J. O'Shaughnessy replaced Mallender on the third day.

At Taunton, April 5–8. MIDDLESEX lost to SOMERSET by six wickets.

MIDDLESEX v SURREY

At Lord's, April 12–15. Middlesex won by three runs. Middlesex 21pts, Surrey 3pts (after 1pt penalty). Toss: Surrey.

When the final day started, Surrey needed just 46 to win with six wickets in hand. But Maynard played around his front pad with only six runs added, Jordan did not last long, and Batty also wafted across the line. Middlesex smelled blood, yet even at nine down, with 11 runs wanted, Surrey still had a chance while Lewis was playing sensibly. But he took a single off the first ball of two overs from Murtagh, leaving Dernbach exposed. On the second occasion, he could not resist temptation, and tried to finish things off with a four over mid-off. Instead, the ball flew high in the air and was well taken by the diving Robson at short extra cover, giving Middlesex an improbable win at the end of a fascinating hour's play. Murtagh, once a Surrey man, disappeared under a heap of whooping team-mates. Chris Adams, Surrey's manager, said the pitch was the worst he had seen at Lord's – but his side did win the toss, and reduced Middlesex to 129 for seven before Malan's five-hour 88 lifted them to a decent total. Surrey failed to match it, despite a good start from Rudolph and Davies. But when Middlesex collapsed again, with only Robson hanging around for long, victory for their London rivals had looked more than likely.

Close of play: first day, Middlesex 225-9 (Malan 62, Collymore 2); second day, Surrey 161-5 (Hamilton-Brown 8, Jordan 1); third day, Surrey 95-4 (Hamilton-Brown 51, Maynard 12).

Middlesex

S. D. Robson b Linley	40	– (2) lbw b Dernbach	43
J. L. Denly c Davies b Lewis	10	– (1) c Batty b de Bruyn	5
C. J. L. Rogers lbw b Dernbach	20	– c Davies b de Bruyn	4
D. J. Malan c Davies b Jordan	88	– b Dernbach	13
*N. J. Dexter b Dernbach	1	– lbw b Lewis	0
†J. A. Simpson c Batty b Dernbach	0	– run out	9
G. K. Berg b Linley	11	– c Batty b Lewis	1
O. P. Rayner b Lewis	2	– c Davies b Lewis	7
T. J. Murtagh lbw b Batty	31	– not out	5
T. S. Roland-Jones c Batty b Jordan	16	– c Rudolph b Lewis	6
C. D. Collymore not out	5	– lbw b Lewis	0
L-b 12, w 6, n-b 14	32	B 4, l-b 5, n-b 4	13
1/33 (2) 2/66 (3) 3/86 (1) 4/91 (5) 5/91 (6) 6/108 (7) 7/129 (8) 8/182 (9) 9/223 (10) 10/256 (4) (93.3 overs)	256	1/21 (1) 2/29 (3) 3/65 (4) 4/76 (2) 5/76 (5) 6/82 (7) 7/90 (6) 8/100 (8) 9/106 (10) 10/106 (11) (34.5 overs)	106

Lewis 15–1–56–2; Linley 19–4–45–2; de Bruyn 5–1–9–0; Jordan 16.3–2–71–2; Dernbach 26–6–48–3; Batty 12–3–15–1. *Second innings*—Lewis 15.5–3–41–5; de Bruyn 6–2–16–2; Dernbach 9–2–25–2; Linley 2–0–11–0; Jordan 1–0–4–0; Batty 1–1–0–0.

Surrey

First innings		Second innings	
J. A. Rudolph st Simpson b Rayner	45	– (2) lbw b Roland-Jones	6
†S. M. Davies c Simpson b Collymore	62	– (1) c Denly b Murtagh	8
M. R. Ramprakash lbw b Dexter	17	– c Malan b Roland-Jones	1
Z. de Bruyn lbw b Roland-Jones	17	– c Rogers b Collymore	15
*R. J. Hamilton-Brown lbw b Roland-Jones	35	– c Simpson b Roland-Jones	63
T. L. Maynard c Berg b Dexter	3	– lbw b Berg	15
C. J. Jordan b Murtagh	8	– b Murtagh	0
G. J. Batty c Denly b Collymore	4	– lbw b Murtagh	0
J. Lewis c Murtagh b Dexter	21	– not out	21
T. E. Linley not out	1	– c Malan b Roland-Jones	2
J. W. Dernbach c Berg b Roland-Jones	0	– c Robson b Murtagh	4
B 6, l-b 1, n-b 2	9	L-b 2	2
1/85 (1) 2/117 (2) 3/148 (3) 4/148 (4) 5/153 (6) 6/184 (7) 7/189 (8) 8/211 (5) 9/221 (9) 10/222 (11) (100 overs)	222	1/14 (2) 2/14 (1) 3/22 (3) 4/68 (4) 5/101 (6) 6/102 (7) 7/104 (8) 8/126 (5) 9/130 (10) 10/137 (11) (40.2 overs)	137

Murtagh 27–9–59–1; Collymore 23–9–43–2; Berg 14–5–41–0; Roland-Jones 19–5–43–3; Rayner 6–1–6–1; Dexter 11–2–23–3. *Second innings*—Murtagh 14.2–2–43–4; Collymore 5–0–25–1; Roland-Jones 10–4–25–4; Berg 8–0–28–1; Dexter 3–0–14–0.

Umpires: S. J. O'Shaughnessy and M. J. Saggers.

MIDDLESEX v DURHAM

At Lord's, April 19–22. Drawn. Middlesex 6pts, Durham 7pts. Toss: Durham.

Before the game Dexter, concerned that the captaincy was affecting his batting, handed over the reins for Championship matches to Rogers, whose first act was to lose the toss. Put in after a blank first day, Middlesex made a terrible start. Strauss and Robson both collected ducks as they lurched to 28 for four, before Dexter, finding some welcome form, clawed back a little ground. Durham should have been out of sight: though eight men made double figures, none passed 45, and they led by only 50. But they still looked certain to win when Middlesex dipped to 91 for eight just after lunch on the final day. The main tormentor was Onions, who bowled excellently throughout and conceded only 73 runs in completing his first ten-wicket match haul. But Simpson and Murtagh counter-attacked boldly in a stand of 82 and, although Durham initially had 45 overs to make 130, more rain trimmed that to 19. Finn's incisive bowling and five catches for Simpson made sure of the draw.

Close of play: first day, no play; second day, Middlesex 132-5 (Dexter 65, Simpson 9); third day, Middlesex 21-1 (Robson 10, Roland-Jones 4).

Middlesex

First innings		Second innings	
A. J. Strauss b Onions	0	– b Onions	6
S. D. Robson c Di Venuto b Thorp	0	– c Di Venuto b Onions	10
J. L. Denly c Collingwood b Onions	1	– (4) c Mustard b Stokes	14
*C. J. L. Rogers c Borthwick b Claydon	9	– (5) lbw b Onions	36
D. J. Malan c Mustard b Onions	35	– (6) c Mustard b Claydon	6
N. J. Dexter c Di Venuto b Stokes	65	– (7) c Mustard b Thorp	1
†J. A. Simpson not out	25	– (8) b Borthwick	47
G. K. Berg c Di Venuto b Thorp	2	– (9) c Di Venuto b Onions	0
T. J. Murtagh c Mustard b Onions	18	– (10) c Mustard b Claydon	45
T. S. Roland-Jones c Blackwell b Onions	17	– (3) c Benkenstein b Stokes	5
S. T. Finn c Collingwood b Onions	0	– not out	0
B 1, l-b 12, w 1, n-b 2	16	B 2, l-b 2, w 1, n-b 4	9
1/0 (1) 2/2 (3) 3/2 (2) 4/28 (4) 5/83 (5) 6/132 (6) 7/137 (8) 8/164 (9) 9/188 (10) 10/188 (11) (57.4 overs)	188	1/12 (1) 2/21 (2) 3/35 (3) 4/43 (4) 5/60 (6) 6/75 (7) 7/91 (5) 8/91 (9) 9/173 (10) 10/179 (8) (60.5 overs)	179

Onions 21.4–7–45–6; Thorp 18–5–43–2; Claydon 11–3–54–1; Stokes 7–0–33–1. *Second innings*—Onions 16–9–28–4; Thorp 16–3–43–1; Blackwell 4–0–9–0; Stokes 7–1–22–2; Claydon 12–2–51–2; Collingwood 3–0–15–0; Borthwick 2.5–0–7–1.

Durham

M. J. Di Venuto b Finn	30	– (2) c Simpson b Finn	29
W. R. Smith c Malan b Murtagh	29	– (1) c Simpson b Murtagh	4
P. D. Collingwood c Strauss b Roland-Jones	19	– lbw b Finn	4
B. A. Stokes c Strauss b Finn	45	– c Simpson b Finn	5
D. M. Benkenstein c Simpson b Berg	24	– (6) c Simpson b Roland-Jones	1
I. D. Blackwell lbw b Finn	12	– (7) c Simpson b Finn	2
*†P. Mustard c Simpson b Berg	5	– (5) not out	25
S. G. Borthwick not out	33	– not out	1
C. D. Thorp lbw b Berg	0		
M. E. Claydon c Finn b Murtagh	8		
G. Onions c Finn b Roland-Jones	20		
L-b 13	13	B 4, l-b 5, n-b 2	11
1/59 (1) 2/63 (2) 3/109 (3) (58.2 overs)	238	1/16 (1) (6 wkts, 18.3 overs)	82
4/142 (4) 5/164 (5) 6/164 (6)		2/21 (3) 3/31 (4)	
7/181 (7) 8/181 (9) 9/194 (10) 10/238 (11)		4/64 (2) 5/67 (6) 6/72 (7)	

Murtagh 17–3–66–2; Finn 15–4–55–3; Roland-Jones 7.2–0–26–2; Berg 14–4–56–3; Dexter 5–1–22–0. *Second innings*—Murtagh 5–1–21–1; Finn 9–1–43–4; Roland-Jones 4.3–0–9–1.

Umpires: N. A. Mallender and D. J. Millns.

MIDDLESEX v WORCESTERSHIRE

At Lord's, May 3–6. Middlesex won by 132 runs. Middlesex 19pts, Worcestershire 2pts. Toss: Worcestershire.

Once again Middlesex were put in – and once again the weather ensured there was no play on the first day. Almost half the overs were lost on the second and third, too, although in that time Middlesex took advantage of some poor bowling, the exception being their former team-mate Richardson, who claimed five of the seven wickets to fall. Strauss and Robson put on 80, then Denly took over, completing his first century since joining from Kent. Worcestershire declared 282 behind, and set about chasing that down after a forfeit. But with all four Middlesex pacemen bowling well, they were never in the hunt. Klinger padded up to a straight one and, with the ball seaming around, the score declined to 96 for eight before Kapil and Jones put on a plucky 54. That was ended by a fine left-handed diving catch by Dexter in the gully, and later in the same over Finn wrapped up the match. The victory, completed midway through the last afternoon, pushed Middlesex up to third in the table.

Close of play: first day, no play; second day, Middlesex 148-2 (Denly 34, Rogers 3); third day, Worcestershire 45-2 (Solanki 4, Ali 0).

Middlesex

A. J. Strauss lbw b Kapil	49
S. D. Robson c Klinger b Richardson	59
J. L. Denly not out	134
*C. J. L. Rogers c Scott b Lucas	9
D. J. Malan c Solanki b Richardson	0
N. J. Dexter b Richardson	0
†J. A. Simpson c Scott b Richardson	14
G. K. Berg c Scott b Richardson	36
T. J. Murtagh not out	8
B 5, l-b 6, w 1, n-b 6	18
1/80 (1) 2/125 (2) (7 wkts dec, 86 overs)	327
3/166 (4) 4/172 (5)	
5/172 (6) 6/210 (7) 7/298 (8)	

T. S. Roland-Jones and S. T. Finn did not bat.

Richardson 33–12–89–5; Lucas 30–4–101–1; Jones 11–0–65–0; Kapil 8–1–43–1; Ali 2–0–7–0; Cameron 2–0–11–0.

Middlesex forfeited their second innings.

Worcestershire

*D. K. H. Mitchell c Dexter b Murtagh	14	– c Malan b Murtagh	9
M. Klinger c Robson b Roland-Jones	17	– lbw b Murtagh	12
V. S. Solanki not out	4	– c Strauss b Berg	11
M. M. Ali not out	0	– c Strauss b Roland-Jones	1
J. G. Cameron (did not bat)		– lbw b Roland-Jones	30
M. G. Pardoe (did not bat)		– c Simpson b Berg	14
†B. J. M. Scott (did not bat)		– b Murtagh	13
A. Kapil (did not bat)		– not out	21
D. S. Lucas (did not bat)		– c Malan b Roland-Jones	3
R. A. Jones (did not bat)		– c Dexter b Finn	32
A. Richardson (did not bat)		– b Finn	0
L-b 10	10	B 1, l-b 2, w 1	4
1/39 (1) 2/45 (2) (2 wkts dec, 16.4 overs)	45	1/21 (2) 2/26 (1) 3/35 (3) 4/35 (4) 5/70 (6) 6/89 (5) 7/93 (7) 8/96 (9) 9/150 (10) 10/150 (11) (47.5 overs)	150

Finn 6–3–7–0; Murtagh 8–2–26–1; Roland-Jones 2.4–0–2–1. *Second innings*—Murtagh 15–6–39–3; Finn 13.5–6–30–2; Berg 7–4–20–2; Roland-Jones 9–2–29–3; Malan 3–0–29–0.

Umpires: N. G. C. Cowley and J. W. Lloyds.

At Nottingham, May 9–12. MIDDLESEX drew with NOTTINGHAMSHIRE.

At Liverpool, May 23–26. MIDDLESEX drew with LANCASHIRE.

MIDDLESEX v SUSSEX

At Lord's, May 30–June 2. Middlesex won by ten wickets. Middlesex 23pts, Sussex 4pts. Toss: Sussex.

Sussex failed to exploit a good pitch after choosing to bat, declining to 33 for four as Murtagh steamed in; only Joyce and Brown made significant contributions. In contrast, only Robson and Malan failed for Middlesex. Rogers fell two short of his hundred and, just when it looked as if Sussex might limit the deficit to manageable proportions, the last two wickets put on 92: Rayner tormented his former county with 69, and Roland-Jones biffed a maiden half-century. Sussex needed to survive for most of the final day to avoid defeat, but again batted unimpressively, slipping to 101 for six shortly before lunch. Brown, with his second sensible innings of the match, helped ensure Middlesex would have to bat again – but the game was over not long after tea.

Close of play: first day, Sussex 242-8 (Magoffin 11, Anyon 11); second day, Middlesex 229-3 (Rogers 93, Morgan 52); third day, Sussex 34-1 (Nash 18, Gatting 4).

Sussex

C. D. Nash c Simpson b Murtagh	0	– (2) b Finn	40
E. C. Joyce c Simpson b Finn	77	– (1) c Berg b Finn	8
J. S. Gatting c Rayner b Murtagh	6	– lbw b Berg	18
M. W. Goodwin c Malan b Murtagh	0	– c Rayner b Finn	5
*M. H. Yardy c Finn b Berg	8	– c Morgan b Roland-Jones	10
L. J. Wright c Simpson b Finn	14	– c Finn b Berg	13
†B. C. Brown c Rayner b Finn	70	– c Berg b Rayner	53
Naved Arif c Berg b Murtagh	38	– c Malan b Berg	15
S. J. Magoffin not out	18	– c Roland-Jones b Malan	37
J. E. Anyon b Murtagh	24	– not out	18
M. S. Panesar c Rayner b Berg	15	– c Finn b Malan	0
B 3, l-b 5, w 1, n-b 4	13	L-b 6, n-b 2	8
1/0 (1) 2/16 (3) 3/16 (4) 4/33 (5) 5/66 (6) 6/147 (2) 7/210 (7) 8/228 (8) 9/264 (10) 10/283 (11) (109.3 overs)	283	1/27 (1) 2/58 (2) 3/64 (4) 4/83 (3) 5/101 (6) 6/101 (5) 7/164 (8) 8/170 (7) 9/223 (9) 10/225 (11) (74.4 overs)	225

Murtagh 27–7–55–5; Finn 29–6–76–3; Berg 20.3–3–62–2; Roland-Jones 12–1–37–0; Rayner 17–2–29–0; Malan 4–0–16–0. *Second innings*—Murtagh 16–8–35–0; Finn 20–5–66–3; Roland-Jones 13–4–34–1; Berg 16–2–53–3; Rayner 6–2–12–1; Malan 3.4–0–19–2.

Middlesex

*C. J. L. Rogers lbw b Wright	98	– (2) not out	7
S. D. Robson lbw b Magoffin	0	– (1) not out	10
J. L. Denly lbw b Panesar	67		
D. J. Malan c Joyce b Anyon	1		
E. J. G. Morgan c Brown b Magoffin	71		
†J. A. Simpson b Naved Arif	34		
G. K. Berg st Brown b Nash	45		
O. P. Rayner c Wright b Nash	69		
T. J. Murtagh c Brown b Anyon	13		
T. S. Roland-Jones c Gatting b Nash	52		
S. T. Finn not out	1		
B 14, l-b 9, w 1, n-b 16	40	W 2	2
1/6 (2) 2/151 (3) 3/152 (4) (140.3 overs)	491	(no wkt, 3.5 overs)	19
4/249 (1) 5/287 (5) 6/324 (6) 7/376 (7)			
8/399 (9) 9/475 (8) 10/491 (10) 110 overs: 360-6			

Anyon 31–6–124–2; Magoffin 27–5–64–2; Wright 13–2–36–1; Naved Arif 23–6–70–1; Panesar 34–7–104–1; Nash 10.3–2–45–3; Yardy 2–0–25–0. *Second innings*—Gatting 2–0–12–0; Nash 1.5–0–7–0.

Umpires: M. A. Gough and N. J. Llong.

MIDDLESEX v SOMERSET

At Lord's, June 5–8. Drawn. Middlesex 10pts, Somerset 4pts. Toss: Middlesex.

Given the perceived strength of Somerset's batting, Rogers's decision to bowl might have seemed risky – but Middlesex's in-form seamers backed him up. After nearly half the first day was washed out, they did not take long to wrap up the remaining six wickets on the second morning, then sat back to enjoy the sight of both Rogers and Denly (dropped at second slip before he had scored) making centuries. Three times Rogers cleared a short leg-side boundary on the Tavern side during a second-wicket partnership of 245. Malan helped swell the lead to 191 by the end of a third day on which the weather allowed only 18 overs, and Middlesex declared next morning. Although both openers fell cheaply, with Barrow bagging a pair, the rest of Somerset's batsmen showed more resolution second time round. Compton dug in for four and a half hours, but was lucky to survive at 43 when – with 46 overs remaining – Rayner dropped a straightforward chance at second slip off Collymore. When Trego and Overton departed in the 54th over Somerset were 176 for seven, still 15 adrift, and a home win was still possible – but Compton and Thomas survived.

Close of play: first day, Somerset 130-4 (Kieswetter 48, Buttler 0); second day, Middlesex 321-2 (Denly 105, Malan 24); third day, Middlesex 364-3 (Denly 116, Morgan 2).

Somerset

Batsman	First innings		Second innings	
A. V. Suppiah	b Roland-Jones	15	(2) c Malan b Collymore	4
A. W. R. Barrow	c Simpson b Collymore	0	(1) lbw b Murtagh	0
N. R. D. Compton	b Murtagh	1	not out	69
J. C. Hildreth	c Simpson b Berg	58	c Morgan b Roland-Jones	38
†C. Kieswetter	c Simpson b Berg	48	c Malan b Roland-Jones	6
J. C. Buttler	b Murtagh	0	c Malan b Berg	16
P. D. Trego	c Morgan b Roland-Jones	38	b Murtagh	50
C. Overton	c Simpson b Murtagh	0	c Simpson b Murtagh	0
*A. C. Thomas	b Berg	0	not out	39
G. H. Dockrell	c Simpson b Roland-Jones	5		
G. M. Hussain	not out	0		
	L-b 4, n-b 4	8	B 1, l-b 2, n-b 2	5
	(67.5 overs)	173	(7 wkts dec, 68.5 overs)	227

1/0 (2) 2/1 (3) 3/45 (1) 4/125 (4) 5/130 (5) 6/130 (6) 7/130 (8) 8/133 (9) 9/164 (10) 10/173 (7)

1/4 (2) 2/4 (1) 3/81 (4) 4/90 (5) 5/113 (6) 6/176 (7) 7/176 (8)

Murtagh 20–6–42–3; Collymore 11.1–3–21–1; Roland-Jones 15.5–2–47–3; Berg 20.5–4–59–3. *Second innings*—Murtagh 14–5–36–3; Collymore 13–2–47–1; Rayner 3–1–4–0; Berg 15–4–43–1; Roland-Jones 17–2–74–2; Malan 4–1–10–0; Denly 2–0–6–0; Robson 0.5–0–4–0.

Middlesex

*C. J. L. Rogers	c Suppiah b Trego	173
S. D. Robson	lbw b Thomas	9
J. L. Denly	not out	116
D. J. Malan	c Barrow b Overton	51
E. J. G. Morgan	not out	2
	L-b 9, w 2, n-b 2	13
	(3 wkts dec, 86.5 overs)	364

1/40 (2) 2/285 (1) 3/359 (4)

†J. A. Simpson, G. K. Berg, O. P. Rayner, T. J. Murtagh, T. S. Roland-Jones and C. D. Collymore did not bat.

Trego 17.5–1–84–1; Hussain 16–3–86–0; Thomas 22–0–72–1; Overton 19–2–45–1; Dockrell 10–1–44–0; Suppiah 2–0–24–0.

Umpires: N. L. Bainton and N. A. Mallender.

At Lord's, June 13. MIDDLESEX lost to WEST INDIANS by 228 runs (see West Indian tour section).

MIDDLESEX v NOTTINGHAMSHIRE

At Uxbridge, July 11–14. Drawn. Middlesex 6pts, Nottinghamshire 9pts. Toss: Nottinghamshire.

Thirty years previously, Mike Brearley had inserted Leicestershire at Uxbridge and watched Brian Davison score a hundred before lunch. But times, and pitches, have changed: now Middlesex themselves were put in – and skittled for 98, which would have been even more embarrassing without 50 from Strauss and 32 from Berg, both victims of the superb Adams. No one else managed more than six. Nottinghamshire lost their fourth wicket when they led by only four, but Middlesex's hopes of keeping the deficit to manageable proportions were ended by a sixth-wicket stand of 143 between Voges, who made his third Championship hundred, and Read. The eventual lead was an imposing 231, but Middlesex put up more resistance second time around. Strauss compiled his 46th (and, as it turned out, last) first-class century, and added 143 with Rogers. Middlesex were just in front with only two wickets down by the end of the third day but, with a new ball almost due, Nottinghamshire felt they still had a chance. Rain, however, washed out the final day.

Close of play: first day, Nottinghamshire 114-4 (Lumb 35, Voges 8); second day, Nottinghamshire 329; third day, Middlesex 239-2 (Strauss 127, Denly 15).

Middlesex

A. J. Strauss b Adams	50	– not out	127
S. D. Robson c Read b Phillips	2	– c Read b Carter	26
*C. J. L. Rogers c Voges b Gurney	5	– lbw b Gurney	59
J. L. Denly c Voges b Gurney	0	– not out	15
D. J. Malan c Hales b Adams	6		
†J. A. Simpson b Adams	0		
G. K. Berg lbw b Adams	32		
O. P. Rayner c Read b Adams	0		
T. J. Murtagh c Hales b Carter	0		
T. S. Roland-Jones not out	0		
C. D. Collymore c Patel b Adams	0		
L-b 1, n-b 2	3	B 4, l-b 7, w 1	12
1/5 (2) 2/10 (3) 3/24 (4) 4/34 (5) 5/34 (6) 6/97 (1) 7/97 (8) 8/98 (9) 9/98 (7) 10/98 (11) (35.4 overs)	98	1/55 (2) 2/198 (3) (2 wkts, 70 overs)	239

Phillips 7–1–20–1; Gurney 10–3–23–2; Adams 11.4–2–32–6; Carter 7–0–22–1. *Second innings*—Phillips 13–2–47–0; Gurney 14–2–38–1; Adams 16–3–51–0; Carter 11–1–36–1; Patel 16–1–56–0.

Nottinghamshire

M. H. Wessels c Simpson b Berg	34
A. D. Hales lbw b Collymore	14
M. J. Lumb c Simpson b Murtagh	50
S. R. Patel lbw b Murtagh	18
J. W. A. Taylor c Simpson b Murtagh	3
A. C. Voges c Simpson b Murtagh	105
*†C. M. W. Read c and b Roland-Jones	71
B. J. Phillips c Rayner b Roland-Jones	6
A. R. Adams b Roland-Jones	10
A. Carter not out	10
H. F. Gurney lbw b Roland-Jones	4
L-b 2, n-b 2	4
1/24 (2) 2/73 (1) 3/98 (4) 4/102 (5) 5/145 (3) 6/288 (7) 7/304 (8) 8/314 (9) 9/316 (6) 10/329 (11) (96 overs)	329

Murtagh 29–3–87–4; Collymore 15–0–61–1; Roland-Jones 24–4–102–4; Berg 17–6–39–1; Rayner 9–0–34–0; Malan 2–0–4–0.

Umpires: M. J. D. Bodenham and J. W. Lloyds.

At Chester-le-Street, July 27–29. MIDDLESEX lost to DURHAM by 15 runs.

MIDDLESEX v WARWICKSHIRE

At Uxbridge, August 1–4. Drawn. Middlesex 8pts, Warwickshire 8pts. Toss: Warwickshire.

With Lord's still off-limits because of the Olympic archery, this was Middlesex's second successive home game at Uxbridge, and again they were put in to bat. But this time they prospered: Malan made his seventh Championship hundred (an eighth would follow in the return match three weeks later), and put on 135 with Denly, who just missed a century of his own. The incisive Woakes removed Simpson and Berg in two balls for ducks, but the tail wagged, lifting the total past 400. Warwickshire lost two early wickets, but Westwood's century propped them up. Against some tight bowling they continued well into the third day, scoring at less than two and a half an over. Middlesex eventually claimed a lead of 78, but there was not enough time to manufacture a result, especially once rain allowed only 50 overs on the last day.

Close of play: first day, Middlesex 324-7 (Rayner 16, Roland-Jones 13); second day, Warwickshire 178-2 (Westwood 89, Troughton 60); third day, Middlesex 104-3 (Dexter 45, Morgan 7).

Middlesex

First innings		Second innings	
*C. J. L. Rogers c Ambrose b Wright	16	– lbw b Maddy	13
J. L. Denly lbw b Maddy	95	– c Ambrose b Wright	16
N. J. Dexter lbw b Clarke	26	– not out	84
D. J. Malan b Wright	106	– c Porterfield b Patel	15
E. J. G. Morgan c Ambrose b Wright	19	– c Ambrose b Wright	7
†J. A. Simpson c Ambrose b Woakes	0	– c Rankin b Wright	18
G. K. Berg c Clarke b Woakes	0	– c Rankin b Patel	1
O. P. Rayner c Ambrose b Woakes	18	– not out	14
T. S. Roland-Jones c Ambrose b Woakes	17		
S. P. Crook c Maddy b Wright	30		
T. J. Murtagh not out	36		
B 7, l-b 13, w 7, n-b 12	39	B 6, l-b 3, n-b 4	13
1/41 (1) 2/97 (3) 3/232 (2) (115.4 overs)	402	1/24 (2) (6 wkts dec, 57 overs)	181
4/285 (4) 5/286 (6) 6/286 (7) 7/290 (5)		2/51 (1) 3/93 (4)	
8/327 (8) 9/330 (9) 10/402 (10) 110 overs: 367-9		4/105 (5) 5/133 (6) 6/147 (7)	

Woakes 28–6–84–4; Wright 29.4–5–92–4; Clarke 11–2–43–1; Rankin 15–0–89–0; Maddy 23–7–47–1; Patel 9–2–27–0. *Second innings*—Woakes 14–2–39–0; Wright 16–1–68–3; Maddy 5–2–17–1; Rankin 9–1–22–0; Patel 13–4–26–2.

Warwickshire

First innings		Second innings	
V. Chopra lbw b Murtagh	3	– not out	38
I. J. Westwood c Malan b Murtagh	111		
W. T. S. Porterfield c Dexter b Murtagh	12	– (2) c Berg b Rayner	23
*J. O. Troughton c Simpson b Berg	60	– (3) not out	10
D. L. Maddy c Berg b Crook	21		
†T. R. Ambrose c Malan b Murtagh	40		
R. Clarke c Rayner b Dexter	11		
C. R. Woakes not out	27		
J. S. Patel c Simpson b Dexter	6		
C. J. C. Wright b Berg	13		
W. B. Rankin c Malan b Rayner	0		
B 4, l-b 10, n-b 6	20	B 3, l-b 1, w 1, n-b 2	7
1/6 (1) 2/26 (3) 3/187 (4) (134.5 overs)	324	1/47 (2) (1 wkt, 27 overs)	78
4/209 (2) 5/239 (5) 6/271 (6) 7/276 (7)			
8/290 (9) 9/319 (10) 10/324 (11) 110 overs: 267-5			

Murtagh 28–6–77–4; Roland-Jones 27–8–71–0; Berg 27–9–56–2; Crook 18–2–45–1; Rayner 20.5–5–39–1; Dexter 12–4–16–2; Malan 2–0–6–0. *Second innings*—Murtagh 5–1–12–0; Roland-Jones 4–0–18–0; Crook 5–0–20–0; Rayner 9–3–13–1; Malan 4–1–11–0.

Umpires: S. A. Garratt and I. J. Gould.

At Hove, August 10–12. MIDDLESEX lost to SUSSEX by eight wickets.

At The Oval, August 15–18. MIDDLESEX lost to SURREY by eight runs.

At Birmingham, August 21–24. MIDDLESEX drew with WARWICKSHIRE.

At Worcester, August 28–31. MIDDLESEX beat WORCESTERSHIRE by five wickets.

MIDDLESEX v LANCASHIRE

At Lord's, September 4–7. Middlesex won by 109 runs. Middlesex 23pts, Lancashire 7pts. Toss: Lancashire.

In their first Championship match at Lord's for almost three months, Middlesex rounded off a fine season with a victory that confirmed Lancashire's relegation, a year after they had lifted the title.

They knew nothing less than a win would do, and quickly reduced Middlesex to 39 for three. But as the conditions became less bowler-friendly, the batsmen cashed in: Dexter made his second hundred in three Championship games, sharing a stand of 148 with Berg as the score hurtled to 389 for six by the first-day close. In the absence of Murtagh – rested by agreement with Cricket Ireland ahead of the World Twenty20 – Middlesex's attack also struggled: five batsmen made half-centuries as Lancashire stole a lead of two. By the end of the third day, Middlesex were 127 in front, and they patiently extended that on the fourth. When Berg was out, making it 289 for eight, Roland-Jones followed him off, believing a declaration had been signalled. In fact it was the twelfth man offering him a drink, and, once the umpires had accepted it was an error, the players trooped back out... whereupon Patel fell first ball to give Chapple ten in the match. A few overs later, there really was a declaration, which set Lancashire 304 in 39 overs: they went for it, as they had to, only for Crook – a former Lancashire player – to take four wickets in 11 balls on the way to career-best figures.

Close of play: first day, Middlesex 389-6 (Dexter 123, Crook 45); second day, Lancashire 236-3 (Prince 57, Brown 5); third day, Middlesex 129-2 (Rogers 57, Malan 37).

Middlesex

First innings		Second innings	
*C. J. L. Rogers lbw b Chapple	0	– c Cross b Kerrigan	86
S. D. Robson lbw b Kerrigan	49	– lbw b Chapple	3
J. L. Denly c Cross b Chapple	4	– b Shahzad	16
D. J. Malan b Shahzad	12	– c Cross b Chapple	95
N. J. Dexter c Cross b Chapple	125	– c Croft b Smith	9
†J. A. Simpson c Cross b Hogg	29	– b Shahzad	27
G. K. Berg c Cross b Hogg	83	– lbw b Chapple	5
S. P. Crook c Horton b Shahzad	66	– c Horton b Chapple	12
T. S. Roland-Jones b Chapple	10	– not out	18
R. H. Patel b Chapple	20	– b Chapple	0
C. D. Collymore not out	4	– not out	4
B 10, l-b 11, w 1, n-b 22	44	B 15, l-b 13, n-b 2	30
1/0 (1) 2/4 (3) 3/39 (4) 4/102 (2) 5/164 (6) 6/312 (7) 7/391 (5) 8/417 (8) 9/427 (9) 10/446 (10) (112.5 overs) 110 overs: 439-9	446	1/5 (2) 2/44 (3) 3/178 (1) 4/207 (5) 5/265 (4) 6/265 (6) 7/282 (8) 8/289 (7) 9/289 (10) (9 wkts dec, 94 overs)	305

Chapple 27.5–5–86–5; Hogg 18–1–81–2; Shahzad 26–5–90–2; Smith 10–1–41–0; Kerrigan 24–2–81–1; Procter 6–0–38–0; Croft 1–0–8–0. *Second innings*—Chapple 19–4–47–5; Hogg 11–1–39–0; Kerrigan 28–5–82–1; Shahzad 17–0–61–2; Croft 11–2–22–0; Smith 8–0–26–1.

Lancashire

First innings		Second innings	
T. C. Smith st Simpson b Patel	55	– (2) st Simpson b Patel	21
L. A. Procter c Robson b Crook	30	– (9) lbw b Patel	26
P. J. Horton c Simpson b Crook	64	– (5) b Crook	6
A. G. Prince c Malan b Roland-Jones	71	– (1) c Patel b Collymore	20
K. R. Brown b Berg	78	– (4) b Crook	33
S. J. Croft b Roland-Jones	3	– (3) b Crook	30
†G. D. Cross c Simpson b Berg	59	– (6) lbw b Crook	0
K. W. Hogg c Malan b Patel	10	– b Patel	2
*G. Chapple st Simpson b Patel	29	– (7) b Crook	19
A. Shahzad lbw b Patel	10	– not out	26
S. C. Kerrigan not out	3	– c Berg b Patel	0
B 5, l-b 14, n-b 17	36	B 6, l-b 3, n-b 2	11
1/95 (2) 2/95 (1) 3/225 (3) 4/266 (4) 5/270 (6) 6/347 (7) 7/375 (8) 8/426 (9) 9/438 (10) 10/448 (5) (135.2 overs) 110 overs: 355-6	448	1/30 (1) 2/50 (2) 3/107 (4) 4/112 (3) 5/112 (6) 6/125 (5) 7/134 (8) 8/146 (7) 9/178 (9) 10/194 (11) (32 overs)	194

Collymore 29–11–75–0; Roland-Jones 27–10–67–2; Patel 35–2–126–4; Berg 18.2–2–57–2; Crook 22–4–88–2; Dexter 2–0–11–0; Malan 2–0–5–0. *Second innings*—Collymore 6–0–23–1; Roland-Jones 4–0–32–0; Patel 12–0–72–4; Crook 8–1–48–5; Berg 2–0–10–0.

Umpires: M. R. Benson and S. J. O'Shaughnessy.

NORTHAMPTONSHIRE

Austerity blues

ANDREW RADD

Rarely since the grim days of the 1930s have the Northamptonshire faithful needed to draw so deeply on their famed reserves of resilience and patience. As if the weather wasn't bad enough – docking more than 1,500 overs (the equivalent of 15 days' play) from the Championship programme – only four matches were won in all competitions, the club's worst tally since the advent of the Sunday League in 1969. Their eighth-place finish in Division Two was in effect their lowest since 1978.

This conspicuous lack of success, particularly in the financially crucial white-ball formats, prompted the mid-season sacking of head coach David Capel. Another long-time stalwart, David Ripley, replaced him for the remainder of the summer and was reappointed for 2013, with Phil Rowe – never a first-class cricketer, but with a burgeoning reputation as an insightful and engaging coach of young players – taking on Ripley's role in charge of the Second Eleven and Academy.

The manner of Capel's departure on July 3 – called in for an early-morning meeting with chief executive David Smith, in his first season at Northampton, and members of the committee ahead of a public announcement – was a sad way for his 33-year involvement with his home county to end. But, in the wake of such depressing results, it hardly came as a surprise.

Stuck in the second tier for eight seasons, Northamptonshire managed only two Championship wins in 2012, both before the end of May; on several occasions, their overburdened bowlers were unable to finish sides off on the last day. Even before the end of the summer – by when Northamptonshire had lost 30 of their last 35 completed limited-overs games – Smith was convinced of the need for change, both on and off the field.

James Middlebrook won the club's Player of the Year award for a Championship return of 714 runs (including two centuries as a makeshift opener) and 24 wickets, plus some miserly limited-overs bowling. A committed and level-headed presence – "the kind of senior player every dressing-room wants", said Ripley – the 35-year-old Middlebrook was rewarded with a new two-year deal.

Two hundreds in August salvaged Stephen Peters's summer, while David Sales also offered glimpses of his best form, and agreed terms for 2013 after initially being given permission to talk to other clubs.

But it was the younger brigade who did most to sustain morale through a difficult few months, and now represent Northamptonshire's best chance of escaping the doldrums. Rob Newton, a richly talented strokemaker, appeared to benefit most from the coaching personnel changes and – having recovered from a fractured wrist – blossomed in the second half of the season when

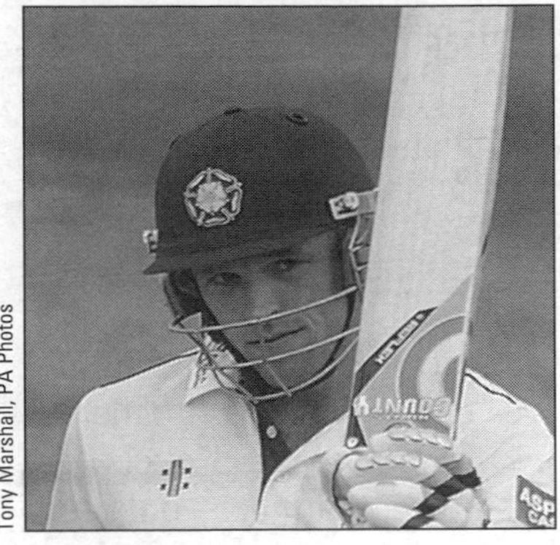

Tony Marshall, PA Photos

David Willey

pushed down to No. 5. Against Derbyshire, he joined the select group of Northamptonshire batsmen to have scored two centuries in a match.

David Willey continued to develop as an exciting all-round cricketer. Strong, aggressive and quick, he claimed 43 Championship wickets – more than anyone – but was often bowled into the ground. Supporters named him their top player; in the same week he was forced to apologise for making disparaging comments about Northampton, his home town, in the club's own short-lived Twitter furore.

Alex Wakely earned praise for his wholehearted approach to the captaincy during Andrew Hall's absences through injury, and cemented his status as leader-in-waiting. He was appointed captain for limited-overs cricket in 2013, with Peters taking over in the Championship. Wakely was again the leading one-day batsman, and made the only fifty by a homegrown player in the Twenty20; Championship hundreds, however, remained elusive.

The rising generation includes seamer Oli Stone, wicketkeeper-batsman Ben Duckett and all-rounder Christian Davis. Smith insisted: "We have got to get these talented young lads playing – it's the right thing to do."

But there were some sizeable holes to fill. The opening attack that served Northamptonshire so well in the short-lived era of the Tiflex ball – with its pronounced seam – had run out of puff. Jack Brooks, given his chance in the first-class game by Capel in 2009, opted to leave for Yorkshire and first division cricket, but "with a heavy heart". The club's disappointment at losing one of their most exciting and identifiable players was tempered by the reality that fitness problems had ruled him out of more than half the matches in 2012. And it proved a season too far for the 38-year-old Sri Lankan Chaminda Vaas, who battled injuries and was let go in August. Australian seamer Trent Copeland was eventually signed as overseas player for the first half of the 2013 season.

Also released was Rob White, who had burst on the scene in 2002 with 277 against Gloucestershire, but struggled for consistency. Niall O'Brien left for Leicestershire after Northamptonshire made it clear they would prefer to reallocate his salary to keep younger players at the club, while Matthew Spriegel and Steven Crook – both deemed to be the kind of multidimensional cricketers required to revive limited-overs fortunes – were signed from Surrey and Middlesex respectively, Crook for a second spell at the county.

In May, officials fulfilled a long-held ambition by purchasing the freehold of the County Ground from the Cockerill Trust (who had leased it to Northamptonshire under a 1,000-year agreement in 1923) for £150,000. This was considered an important step towards long-term financial security. It goes without saying that improved performances on the field would help too.

Championship attendance: 4,173.

NORTHAMPTONSHIRE RESULTS

All first-class matches – Played 16: Won 2, Lost 5, Drawn 9.
County Championship matches – Played 16: Won 2, Lost 5, Drawn 9.

LV= County Championship, 8th in Division 2;
Friends Life t20, 6th in Midlands/Wales/West Division; Clydesdale Bank 40, 6th in Group C.

COUNTY CHAMPIONSHIP AVERAGES, BATTING AND FIELDING

Cap		*M*	*I*	*NO*	*R*	*HS*	*100*	*50*	*Avge*	*Ct/St*
	C. D. de Lange¶	4	5	4	156	40*	0	0	156.00	0
	R. I. Newton	13	20	3	751	119*	3	2	44.17	3
2011	J. D. Middlebrook	15	22	4	714	121	2	4	39.66	6
1999	D. J. Sales	14	21	3	706	140	2	3	39.22	6
2011	N. J. O'Brien	11	17	2	580	182	1	3	38.66	8/1
2007	S. D. Peters	15	23	2	763	148	2	3	36.33	10
2012	A. G. Wakely	14	21	2	690	96	0	5	36.31	9
	D. J. Willey†	15	18	4	489	76	0	4	34.92	3
	K. J. Coetzer	13	19	0	563	120	1	2	29.63	5
	D. Murphy	10	11	1	252	54	0	1	25.20	23/2
2009	A. J. Hall¶	12	19	1	343	79	0	3	19.05	4
	L. M. Daggett	14	14	5	110	26*	0	0	12.22	5
2012	J. A. Brooks	10	10	3	54	22	0	0	7.71	0
2011	W. P. U. J. C. Vaas§	6	4	1	19	13*	0	0	6.33	0

Also batted: D. A. Burton (1 match) 11; L. Evans (2 matches) 0, 5, 0; B. H. N. Howgego (1 match) 1; R. I. Keogh (1 match) 6; O. P. Stone (3 matches) 13, 26*, 8 (3 ct); R. A. White (2 matches) 12, 42, 8*.

† *Born in Northamptonshire.* § *Official overseas player.* ¶ *Other non-England-qualified player.*

BOWLING

	Style	*O*	*M*	*R*	*W*	*BB*	*5I*	*Avge*
L. Evans	RFM	65	16	214	12	4-38	0	17.83
A. J. Hall	RM	293.5	73	812	34	5-50	1	23.88
D. J. Willey	LFM	440.1	90	1,474	43	5-39	1	34.27
J. A. Brooks	RFM	259.4	66	821	23	5-61	2	35.69
J. D. Middlebrook	OB	346.2	100	883	24	5-63	1	36.79
L. M. Daggett	RFM	372.1	95	1,218	27	4-76	0	45.11

Also bowled: D. A. Burton (RFM) 13–1–52–1; K. J. Coetzer (RFM) 19–1–74–1; C. D. de Lange (SLA) 54–11–176–3; R. I. Keogh (OB) 20–5–69–1; N. J. O'Brien (LM) 1 0 3 0; O. P. Stone (RFM) 64–13–202–5; W. P. U. J. C. Vaas (LFM) 107–28–280–6; A. G. Wakely (OB) 7–0–35–0.

LEADING CB40 AVERAGES (100 runs/4 wickets)

Batting	*Runs*	*HS*	*Avge*	*SR*	*Ct*
A. G. Wakely	366	85	45.75	81.87	1
D. J. Sales	313	74	44.71	91.25	1
A. J. Hall	102	52*	34.00	79.06	0
R. I. Newton	160	45	22.85	99.37	1
K. J. Coetzer	190	68	21.11	89.62	2
N. J. O'Brien	115	46	19.16	61.49	3

Bowling	*W*	*BB*	*Avge*	*ER*
L. M. Daggett	12	4-31	11.33	4.85
C. D. de Lange	12	3-31	15.91	4.34
J. D. Middlebrook	7	3-14	26.00	4.33

LEADING FLT20 AVERAGES (100 runs/12 overs)

Batting	Runs	HS	Avge	SR	Ct
C. L. White	228	62*	57.00	**131.03**	2
R. I. Newton	107	38	17.83	**127.38**	0
K. J. Coetzer	198	44	28.28	**117.85**	4
D. J. Willey	105	30*	21.00	**100.96**	1
A. G. Wakely	121	54*	17.28	**93.07**	2

Bowling	W	BB	Avge	ER
C. D. de Lange	8	3-15	18.75	**6.20**
W. P. U. J. C. Vaas	7	2-15	18.71	**6.23**
J. D. Middlebrook	8	3-16	25.75	**7.72**
J. A. Brooks	5	2-23	19.40	**8.08**
D. J. Willey	5	1-5	39.00	**8.18**

FIRST-CLASS COUNTY RECORDS

Highest score for	331*	M. E. K. Hussey v Somerset at Taunton	2003
Highest score against	333	K. S. Duleepsinhji (Sussex) at Hove	1930
Leading run-scorer	28,980	D. Brookes (avge 36.13)	1934–1959
Best bowling for	10-127	V. W. C. Jupp v Kent at Tunbridge Wells	1932
Best bowling against	10-30	C. Blythe (Kent) at Northampton	1907
Leading wicket-taker	1,102	E. W. Clark (avge 21.26)	1922–1947
Highest total for	781-7 dec	v Nottinghamshire at Northampton	1995
Highest total against	673-8 dec	by Yorkshire at Leeds	2003
Lowest total for	12	v Gloucestershire at Gloucester	1907
Lowest total against	33	by Lancashire at Northampton	1977

LIST A COUNTY RECORDS

Highest score for	172*	W. Larkins v Warwickshire at Luton	1983
Highest score against	175*	I. T. Botham (Somerset) at Wellingborough	1986
Leading run-scorer	11,010	R. J. Bailey (avge 39.46)	1983–1999
Best bowling for	7-10	C. Pietersen v Denmark at Brøndby	2005
Best bowling against	7-35	D. E. Malcolm (Derbyshire) at Derby	1997
Leading wicket-taker	251	A. L. Penberthy (avge 30.45)	1989–2003
Highest total for	360-2	v Staffordshire at Northampton	1990
Highest total against	344-6	by Gloucestershire at Cheltenham	2001
Lowest total for	41	v Middlesex at Northampton	1972
Lowest total against	56	by Leicestershire at Leicester	1964
	56	by Denmark at Brøndby	2005

TWENTY20 COUNTY RECORDS

Highest score for	111*	L. Klusener v Worcestershire at Kidderminster	2007
Highest score against	116*	G. A. Hick (Worcestershire) at Luton	2004
Leading run-scorer	**1,340**	**R. A. White (avge 21.61)**	**2003–2012**
Best bowling for	6-21	A. J. Hall v Worcestershire at Northampton	2008
Best bowling against	5-6	P. D. Collingwood (Durham) at Chester-le-Street	2011
Leading wicket-taker	**64**	**A. J. Hall (avge 19.18)**	**2008–2012**
Highest total for	224-5	v Gloucestershire at Milton Keynes	2005
Highest total against	227-6	by Worcestershire at Kidderminster	2007
Lowest total for	47	v Durham at Chester-le-Street	2011
Lowest total against	86	by Worcestershire at Worcester	2006

ADDRESS

County Ground, Wantage Road, Northampton NN1 4TJ (01604 514455; **email** reception@nccc.co.uk). **Website** www.northantscricket.com

OFFICIALS

Captain 2012 – A. J. Hall
2013 – S. D. Peters (Championship)
A. G. Wakely (limited-overs)
First-team coach D. Ripley
Academy coach P. Rowe

President Lord Naseby
Chairman M. Lawrence
Chief executive K. D. Smith
Head groundsman P. Marshall
Scorer A. C. Kingston

At Derby, April 5–8. NORTHAMPTONSHIRE lost to DERBYSHIRE by 202 runs.

NORTHAMPTONSHIRE v KENT

At Northampton, April 12–14. Kent won by an innings and 120 runs. Kent 23pts, Northamptonshire 2pts. Toss: Northamptonshire.

Coles and Powell were the principal architects of Kent's emphatic win, completed inside seven sessions. Fresh from scoring his maiden century against Yorkshire, Coles bowled with impressive pace and control for six for 51 in the second innings and nine for 83 overall, both career-bests. But Northamptonshire's irresolute approach – and the curious decision by Sales to bat first – made Kent's task easier. It was perhaps best summed up by Coetzer's perplexing effort on the first morning: 11 off 59 balls before driving loosely to cover. Brooks reduced Kent to 127 for five, only for Powell – with his first century since July 2009, on his second appearance after leaving Glamorgan – and Jones to bat Northamptonshire out of contention by adding 165 in 51 overs. Jones then held a splendid diving catch to remove Newton, and claimed four more as Northamptonshire crumbled to their second heavy defeat in a row.

Close of play: first day, Kent 127-3 (Nash 40, Davies 2); second day, Northamptonshire 50-4 (Sales 31, O'Brien 5).

Northamptonshire

	First innings		Second innings	
S. D. Peters lbw b Coles	15	–	c Tredwell b Shreck	1
R. I. Newton c Tredwell b Davies	7	–	c Jones b Coles	9
K. J. Coetzer c Nash b Shreck	11	–	lbw b Coles	1
*D. J. Sales c Tredwell b Shreck	13	–	b Coles	42
A. G. Wakely lbw b Stevens	33	–	c Key b Shreck	3
†N. J. O'Brien lbw b Shreck	12	–	not out	25
J. D. Middlebrook c Nash b Coles	3	–	c Jones b Davies	9
W. P. U. J. C. Vaas c Jones b Stevens	0	–	lbw b Tredwell	1
D. J. Willey c Davies b Coles	24	–	c Jones b Coles	8
L. M. Daggett b Stevens	0	–	(11) c Jones b Coles	15
J. A. Brooks not out	3	–	(10) c Jones b Coles	0
L-b 2, w 7, n-b 2	11		L-b 2	2
1/9 (2) 2/26 (1) 3/46 (3) 4/55 (4) (58.1 overs)	132		1/5 (1) 2/11 (2) (55.3 overs)	116
5/76 (6) 6/103 (7) 7/103 (8)			3/12 (3) 4/25 (5)	
8/106 (5) 9/106 (10) 10/132 (9)			5/69 (4) 6/84 (7) 7/85 (8)	
			8/98 (9) 9/98 (10) 10/116 (11)	

Davies 14–9–18–1; Shreck 16–5–42–3; Coles 14.1–4–32–3; Stevens 14–2–38–3. *Second innings*—Davies 10–3–15–1; Shreck 15–5–34–2; Coles 16.3–1–51–6; Stevens 1–0–4–0; Tredwell 13–7–10–1.

Kent

S. A. Newman c Middlebrook b Brooks	26
*R. W. T. Key lbw b Brooks	7
B. W. Harmison run out	46
B. P. Nash b Brooks	40
M. Davies run out	2
M. J. Powell not out	128
D. I. Stevens lbw b Vaas	8
†G. O. Jones b Willey	53
J. C. Tredwell b Brooks	10
M. T. Coles st O'Brien b Middlebrook	17
C. E. Shreck b Brooks	1
B 9, l-b 16, w 1, n-b 4	30
1/32 (2) 2/35 (1) (112.5 overs)	368
3/118 (3) 4/127 (5)	
5/127 (4) 6/158 (7) 7/323 (8) 8/343 (9)	
9/367 (10) 10/368 (11) 110 overs: 365-8	

Vaas 23–7–55–1; Brooks 27.5–4–98–5; Willey 22–1–78–1; Daggett 23–5–84–0; Middlebrook 17–6–28–1.

Umpires: P. K. Baldwin and R. K. Illingworth.

At Durham, April 20–22. NORTHAMPTONSHIRE drew with DURHAM MCCU.

At Chelmsford, April 26–29. NORTHAMPTONSHIRE drew with ESSEX.

NORTHAMPTONSHIRE v HAMPSHIRE

At Northampton, May 2–5. Northamptonshire won by 117 runs. Northamptonshire 20pts, Hampshire 3pts. Toss: Hampshire.

A keenly fought scrap in seamer-friendly conditions ended in a rush, with Hampshire losing their last four wickets in five overs in the final session to give Northamptonshire a morale-boosting first win of the season. Challenged to score 297 in 71 overs, Hampshire were left with only a draw to play for when Willey – bowling with an extra yard of pace – and Daggett reduced them to 106 for five. Keen not to forfeit the initiative completely, Carberry continued to bat positively, but his dismissal in the last over before tea left Willey scenting blood, and he and Brooks finished the job. The absence of an individual half-century until deep into the third day, when Sales scored his first in ten innings, reflected the movement on offer for the seamers. Coetzer took more than three hours to make 41, but his effort looked priceless when Hall struck twice in his first over of the Championship season. The second day was washed out, and Hall's declaration on the last morning was tricky to judge, but the result vindicated what some regarded as excessive caution.

Close of play: first day, Hampshire 42-3 (Dawson 14, Katich 4); second day, no play; third day, Northamptonshire 176-5 (Hall 29, O'Brien 3).

Northamptonshire

S. D. Peters c Katich b Griffiths	44	–	lbw b Ervine	22
R. I. Newton c Dawson b Balcombe	39	–	c Dawson b Balcombe	14
K. J. Coetzer b Wood	41	–	c Dawson b Balcombe	25
D. J. Sales c Ervine b Griffiths	9	–	lbw b Dawson	58
A. G. Wakely b Wood	27	–	c Dawson b Wood	15
*A. J. Hall c Dawson b Ervine	8	–	c Dawson b Wood	41
†N. J. O'Brien b Ervine	10	–	not out	27
J. D. Middlebrook b Wood	1	–	run out	2
D. J. Willey c Terry b Wood	13	–	b Wood	2
L. M. Daggett not out	0	–	c Bates b Balcombe	9
J. A. Brooks c Dawson b Ervine	0	–	not out	3
B 10, l-b 5, w 1, n-b 10	26		B 4, l-b 6, n-b 4	14
1/68 (2) 2/95 (1) 3/109 (4) 4/152 (5) 5/173 (6) 6/197 (3) 7/205 (7) 8/205 (8) 9/218 (9) 10/218 (11) (76.4 overs)	218		1/26 (2) 2/50 (1) 3/74 (3) 4/113 (5) 5/166 (4) 6/192 (6) 7/205 (8) 8/209 (9) 9/223 (10) (9 wkts dec, 80 overs)	232

Wood 21–6–52–4; Balcombe 16–3–62–1; Riazuddin 7–3–18–0; Griffiths 11–1–28–2; Dawson 11–5–9–0; Ervine 9.4–2–32–3; Vince 1–0–2–0. *Second innings*—Wood 24–6–58–3; Balcombe 20–5–70–3; Ervine 8–1–21–1; Griffiths 8–2–34–0; Riazuddin 5–1–9–0; Dawson 15–6–30–1.

Hampshire

L. A. Dawson b Willey	35	– b Willey	4
S. P. Terry b Hall	12	– c Sales b Willey	19
H. Riazuddin b Hall	0	– (9) b Willey	1
M. A. Carberry c Middlebrook b Brooks	4	– (3) lbw b Willey	61
*S. M. Katich c Daggett b Hall	13	– (4) c O'Brien b Daggett	31
J. M. Vince not out	46	– (5) c Hall b Daggett	0
S. M. Ervine c Daggett b Hall	0	– (6) c Middlebrook b Daggett	5
†M. D. Bates c Peters b Daggett	0	– (7) b Brooks	20
C. P. Wood lbw b Willey	26	– (8) c O'Brien b Willey	11
D. J. Balcombe b Brooks	2	– c Daggett b Brooks	8
D. A. Griffiths b Willey	0	– not out	0
B 11, l-b 4, w 1	16	B 16, l-b 3	19
1/27 (2) 2/28 (3) 3/37 (4) 4/70 (1) 5/77 (5) 6/77 (7) 7/84 (8) 8/142 (9) 9/145 (10) 10/154 (11) (54 overs)	154	1/5 (1) 2/46 (2) 3/92 (4) 4/92 (5) 5/106 (6) 6/135 (3) 7/165 (7) 8/168 (9) 9/175 (8) 10/179 (10) (40.2 overs)	179

Brooks 20–8–39–2; Willey 17–3–53–3; Daggett 8–2–23–1; Hall 9–4–24–4. *Second innings*—Brooks 16.2–5–53–2; Willey 11–5–39–5; Hall 4–0–24–0; Daggett 9–2–44–3.

Umpires: M. J. D. Bodenham and N. J. Llong.

At Leicester, May 9–12. NORTHAMPTONSHIRE drew with LEICESTERSHIRE.

At Canterbury, May 16–19. NORTHAMPTONSHIRE drew with KENT.

NORTHAMPTONSHIRE v GLOUCESTERSHIRE

At Northampton, May 23–26. Northamptonshire won by 121 runs. Northamptonshire 22pts, Gloucestershire 4pts. Toss: Northamptonshire.

Middlebrook bowled Northamptonshire to a thrilling victory in the penultimate over, but that was considerably less surprising than the century he scored as an opening batsman at the start of the game. By his own admission, he had pestered head coach David Capel for a couple of seasons for a chance to go in first with Peters. With other contenders either injured or out of favour, that chance had finally arisen, and Middlebrook batted for most of the first day, leaving and cutting like a seasoned opener before falling six short of his career-best. Coetzer should also have hit a hundred, but pulled to deep midwicket searching for the crucial boundary. Both men benefited when Young, the left-arm spinner, temporarily lost his action and served up a series of long-hops. Gloucestershire then plunged to 163 for eight with, apparently, little chance of avoiding the follow-on. But Marshall found a doughty partner in Saxelby, who helped add 90. Sales retired hurt with a torn hamstring, but a fluent innings from Coetzer helped set Gloucestershire 390 on the final day. After a promising start they shed wickets regularly, but the last pair clung on for 70 balls before Middlebrook trapped Norwell in front with four minutes remaining to complete his five-wicket haul and a personal triumph.

Close of play: first day, Northamptonshire 302-4 (Coetzer 81); second day, Gloucestershire 156-6 (Marshall 49, Batty 9); third day, Northamptonshire 246-5 (Hall 9).

Northamptonshire

S. D. Peters b Saxelby	44	– c Marshall b Williamson	58
J. D. Middlebrook c Marshall b A. P. R. Gidman	121	– c Saxelby b W. R. S. Gidman	19
K. J. Coetzer c Young b A. P. R. Gidman	96	– c Williamson b Saxelby	86
D. J. Sales c Cockbain b W. R. S. Gidman	17	– retired hurt	33
A. G. Wakely b W. R. S. Gidman	24	– st Batty b Williamson	22
*A. J. Hall lbw b Saxelby	1	– (7) not out	9
†D. Murphy lbw b Norwell	8		
C. D. de Lange not out	40		
D. J. Willey b Norwell	18	– (6) c Saxelby b Williamson	2
L. M. Daggett b Williamson	15		
D. A. Burton b Young	11		
B 2, l-b 6, w 2, n-b 6	16	L-b 14, w 1, n-b 2	17
1/79 (1) 2/213 (2) 3/253 (4) (147.2 overs)	411	1/42 (2) (5 wkts dec, 63.3 overs)	246
4/302 (5) 5/309 (6) 6/322 (7)		2/119 (1) 3/208 (3)	
7/326 (3) 8/345 (9) 9/391 (10)		4/233 (5) 5/246 (6)	
10/411 (11) 110 overs: 335-7			

In the second innings Sales retired hurt at 230-3.

W. R. S. Gidman 29–5–75–2; Saxelby 32–7–89–2; Norwell 31–3–89–2; A. P. R. Gidman 14–3–50–2; Young 13.2–2–48–1; Howell 15–3–30–0; Dent 2–0–4–0; Williamson 11–4–18–1. *Second innings*—W. R. S. Gidman 11–0–39–1; Saxelby 13–0–46–1; Norwell 8–0–23–0; Howell 11–1–41–0; Williamson 13.3–0–58–3; Dent 7–0–25–0.

Gloucestershire

B. A. C. Howell b Burton	4	– c Murphy b Willey	70
C. D. J. Dent c Peters b Daggett	42	– c Murphy b de Lange	38
K. S. Williamson b Willey	7	– c Coetzer b Middlebrook	10
*A. P. R. Gidman c Hall b Willey	4	– b Middlebrook	4
H. J. H. Marshall not out	117	– lbw b Middlebrook	61
I. A. Cockbain c Peters b Hall	8	– lbw b Hall	6
W. R. S. Gidman b Hall	0	– b Willey	16
†J. N. Batty c Murphy b Daggett	9	– lbw b Hall	7
E. G. C. Young lbw b Willey	0	– b Middlebrook	10
I. D. Saxelby lbw b de Lange	30	– not out	21
L. C. Norwell c Hall b Middlebrook	0	– lbw b Middlebrook	4
B 14, l-b 15, n-b 18	47	B 9, l-b 10, n-b 2	21
1/13 (1) 2/30 (3) 3/38 (4) 4/110 (2) (74 overs)	268	1/101 (2) 2/120 (3) (103.2 overs)	268
5/129 (6) 6/133 (7) 7/162 (8) 8/163 (9)		3/124 (1) 4/142 (4)	
9/253 (10) 10/268 (11)		5/157 (6) 6/201 (7) 7/223 (8)	
		8/225 (5) 9/248 (9) 10/268 (11)	

Willey 15–5–44–3; Burton 10–0–44–1; Middlebrook 12–2–47–1; Daggett 15–4–37–2; Hall 16–3–56–2; de Lange 6–0–11–1. *Second innings*—Willey 19–4–45–2; Daggett 4–0–18–0; Hall 16–4–40–2; Burton 3–1–8–0; de Lange 17–2–75–1; Middlebrook 44.2–23–63–5.

Umpires: N. J. Llong and G. D. Lloyd.

At Leeds, May 30–June 2. NORTHAMPTONSHIRE drew with YORKSHIRE.

NORTHAMPTONSHIRE v ESSEX

At Northampton, June 6–9. Drawn. Northamptonshire 6pts, Essex 9pts. Toss: Essex.

Bopara, anxious to make a point to the England selectors after missing the early-summer Test series through injury, achieved one of the season's more unusual batting feats in this weather-ruined match. He arrived at the crease in the fourth over of the first morning – replacing Shah, beaten by Howgego's throw as he attempted a chancy first-ball single – and was still batting on the fourth afternoon, when he finally holed out for 174 from 290 deliveries. Bopara's 294-run stand with Foster – it would have been 64 for five had he been held at slip on nought – set an Essex record for the fifth wicket against Northamptonshire, and was particularly laudable given the number of times they were forced to restart their partnership. When rain finally relented to allow a full day's play on the fourth, Foster declared with maximum batting points. Northamptonshire had time to claim one of their own, with Middlebrook scoring his second century in three games as opener, following a finger injury to Peters in the field.

Close of play: first day, Essex 138-4 (Bopara 65, Foster 25); second day, Essex 195-4 (Bopara 87, Foster 60); third day, no play.

Essex

T. Westley c Middlebrook b Vaas	12
M. L. Pettini c Murphy b Willey	32
O. A. Shah run out	0
R. S. Bopara c Coetzer b Daggett	174
B. T. Foakes b Willey	0
*†J. S. Foster c sub (R. I. Keogh) b Willey	135
R. N. ten Doeschate not out	26
G. R. Napier not out	14
B 2, l-b 3, n-b 2	7
1/15 (1) 2/15 (3) 3/55 (2) 4/57 (5) 5/351 (6) 6/372 (4) (6 wkts dec, 108.5 overs)	400

D. D. Masters, T. R. Craddock and C. M. Willoughby did not bat.

Brooks 24–5–76–0; Vaas 27–5–68–1; Daggett 30.5–5–136–1; Willey 23–5–74–3; Middlebrook 4–0–41–0.

Northamptonshire

B. H. N. Howgego b Napier	1
J. D. Middlebrook b Craddock	100
K. J. Coetzer b Napier	39
*A. G. Wakely not out	43
R. A. White not out	8
B 4, l-b 2, w 3	9
1/26 (1) 2/116 (3) 3/181 (2) (3 wkts, 47 overs)	200

S. D. Peters, †D. Murphy, D. J. Willey, W. P. U. J. C. Vaas, L. M. Daggett and J. A. Brooks did not bat.

Masters 11–4–29–0; Willoughby 10–2–43–0; Napier 11–1–59–2; Westley 4–0–19–0; ten Doeschate 6–0–24–0; Craddock 5–0–20–1.

Umpires: T. E. Jesty and R. T. Robinson.

NORTHAMPTONSHIRE v GLAMORGAN

At Northampton, July 14–17. Glamorgan won by three wickets. Glamorgan 17pts, Northamptonshire 4pts. Toss: Glamorgan.

Both teams were willing to risk defeat to revive another rain-affected match, and Glamorgan were rewarded with their first Championship win of the season, with five balls to spare. No play was possible on the first and third days and, once Northamptonshire had secured their fourth batting point, a double forfeiture set Glamorgan 351 in 90 overs. That appeared out of reach when North's stumps were rearranged by Willey to make it 192 for five shortly after tea. But Allenby and Wallace took up the challenge with gusto and, though Wallace picked out cover to leave 45 needed from 51 balls, Glover helped Allenby finish the job. Neither opening bowler looked fit, and Vaas was released from his injury-hit season not long afterwards. Northamptonshire had built their total around two contrasting hundreds: Newton unveiled his full range of attacking strokes in 117 from 113 balls, while Sales – with whom he added 187 – was altogether more circumspect in a six-and-a-half hour innings which coincided with the club giving him permission to speak to other counties. An agreement was eventually reached for him to stay.

Close of play: first day, no play; second day, Northamptonshire 336-5 (Sales 129, Middlebrook 17); third day, no play.

Northamptonshire

S. D. Peters c Allenby b Harris	0
K. J. Coetzer b Glover	22
D. J. Sales not out	138
A. G. Wakely c Walters b Glover	30
R. I. Newton c sub (A. J. Norman) b Bragg	117
*A. J. Hall c Wallace b Waters	8
J. D. Middlebrook not out	22
B 4, l-b 9	13
1/0 (1) 2/38 (2) 3/97 (4) 4/284 (5) 5/305 (6) (5 wkts dec, 100 overs)	350

†D. Murphy, D. J. Willey, W. P. U. J. C. Vaas and J. A. Brooks did not bat.

Harris 23–4–83–1; Waters 18–7–35–1; Glover 15–1–51–2; Allenby 15–2–60–0; Cosker 20–3–66–0; North 8–0–32–0; Bragg 1–0–10–1.

Northamptonshire forfeited their second innings.

Glamorgan

Glamorgan forfeited their first innings.

G. P. Rees c Peters b Middlebrook	34
W. D. Bragg c Murphy b Vaas	0
S. J. Walters b Hall	29
M. J. North b Willey	73
B. J. Wright c Murphy b Willey	34
J. Allenby not out	67
*†M. A. Wallace c Newton b Coetzer	54
J. A. R. Harris run out	6
J. C. Glover not out	21
L-b 15, n-b 18	33
1/1 (2) 2/52 (3) 3/100 (1) 4/181 (5) 5/192 (4) 6/306 (7) 7/319 (8) (7 wkts, 89.1 overs)	351

D. A. Cosker and H. T. Waters did not bat.

Vaas 11–2–48–1; Brooks 13–2–48–0; Willey 26–3–103–2; Hall 16.1–4–47–1; Middlebrook 20–2–81–1; Coetzer 3–0–9–1.

Umpires: M. R. Benson and N. G. B. Cook.

NORTHAMPTONSHIRE v YORKSHIRE

At Northampton, August 1–4. Drawn. Northamptonshire 10pts, Yorkshire 7pts. Toss: Yorkshire.

Northamptonshire held the upper hand for most of their 1,000th first-class match at Wantage Road, although Yorkshire's difficulties were largely of their own making – most notably during a shocking first-innings batting display. Jaques looked in ominous touch as he moved to 75 against one of his former counties, but he was late responding to Gale's call for a sharp single and beaten by Daggett's direct hit from mid-off. He was the first of eight wickets to go for 101, almost all to reckless shots. Northamptonshire then forged a lead of 103 over two interrupted days: Peters was in workmanlike mood as he made his first century of the season; Willey more brazen in his career-best 76. Rashid's confidence started to return after two months out of the Championship side, and he ended up with his first five-wicket haul since the opening match of 2011. Yorkshire's batting problems returned on the final day before an afternoon storm rolled in.

Close of play: first day, Yorkshire 249; second day, Northamptonshire 175-3 (Peters 74, Newton 40); third day, Yorkshire 5-0 (Lyth 3, Root 2).

Yorkshire

A. Lyth c Middlebrook b Willey	6	– c Coetzer b Stone	15
J. E. Root c Murphy b Stone	25	– c Peters b Willey	38
P. A. Jaques run out	75	– b Middlebrook	7
*A. W. Gale c and b Daggett	38	– not out	11
†J. M. Bairstow lbw b Daggett	17	– not out	1
G. S. Ballance c Stone b Middlebrook	24		
R. M. Pyrah c Newton b Daggett	0		
A. U. Rashid c Wakely b Middlebrook	15		
Azeem Rafiq c Wakely b Willey	15		
S. A. Patterson not out	25		
M. A. Ashraf lbw b Hall	4		
L-b 3, n-b 2	5	L-b 2	2
1/14 (1) 2/44 (2) 3/148 (3) 4/148 (4) 5/175 (5) 6/185 (7) 7/201 (6) 8/211 (8) 9/223 (9) 10/249 (11) (93.3 overs)	249	1/28 (1) 2/55 (3) 3/67 (2) (3 wkts, 39 overs)	74

Willey 22–6–71–2; Daggett 24–8–64–3; Stone 14–3–35–1; Hall 14.3–3–33–1; Middlebrook 19–7–43–2. *Second innings*—Willey 10–5–10–1; Daggett 5–2–12–0; Middlebrook 14–6–29–1; Stone 5–2–6–1; Hall 5–2–15–0.

Northamptonshire

S. D. Peters c Root b Rashid	107
K. J. Coetzer c Jaques b Azeem Rafiq	31
D. J. Sales c Lyth b Pyrah	11
A. G. Wakely c Jaques b Rashid	12
R. I. Newton c Ballance b Ashraf	43
*A. J. Hall lbw b Ashraf	0
J. D. Middlebrook lbw b Rashid	10
†D. Murphy lbw b Rashid	20
D. J. Willey b Rashid	76
O. P. Stone not out	26
L. M. Daggett c Lyth b Azeem Rafiq	1
B 6, l-b 5, n-b 4	15
1/66 (2) 2/89 (3) 3/106 (4) 4/191 (5) 5/191 (6) 6/212 (7) 7/231 (1) 8/304 (8) 9/347 (9) 10/352 (11) (110.5 overs) 110 overs: 352-9	352

Patterson 24–8–58–0; Ashraf 16–3–55–2; Pyrah 13–3–38–1; Azeem Rafiq 25.5–5–78–2; Rashid 31–2–105–5; Root 1–0–7–0.

Umpires: J. H. Evans and N. A. Mallender.

NORTHAMPTONSHIRE v LEICESTERSHIRE

At Northampton, August 10–13. Drawn. Northamptonshire 9pts, Leicestershire 8pts. Toss: Leicestershire.

An accomplished performance from Shiv Thakor – apparently unfazed by the imminent arrival of his A-level results – denied Northamptonshire the win they needed to stand a realistic chance of promotion. Thakor's omission from the Under-19 World Cup, then taking place in Australia, was described as a "blip" in his career by head coach Phil Whitticase, and he demonstrated judgment and skill to see out the last 40 overs after Leicestershire, set an unlikely 353 from 88, slumped to 130 for five. Thakor had also batted for four and a half hours while repairing Leicestershire's first innings, and taken two important wickets with his medium-pace. Both captains made curious decisions crucial to the outcome: Cobb, in charge because Hoggard chose to leave himself out, was seduced into bowling first on a green pitch, only to watch Peters and O'Brien share the first of their two century opening stands; and Hall erred on the side of caution by delaying his declaration until 25 minutes into the final day. Despite the diligence of Thakor, who was well supported by Henderson, a few extra overs for Northamptonshire's bowlers might have made the difference.

Close of play: first day, Northamptonshire 300-5 (Peters 137); second day, Leicestershire 187-6 (Thakor 30, White 4); third day, Northamptonshire 211-3 (Wakely 20, Newton 26).

Northamptonshire

S. D. Peters b Buck	148	– c and b Jones	56
N. J. O'Brien c Eckersley b White	70	– c Joseph b Jones	79
D. J. Sales c Thornely b White	0	– c Jones b Henderson	24
A. G. Wakely c Thornely b Thakor	8	– not out	38
R. I. Newton lbw b Thakor	5	– b Joseph	37
*A. J. Hall c Eckersley b Buck	59	– c Cobb b Buck	9
J. D. Middlebrook b Buck	20		
†D. Murphy c Cobb b Henderson	31		
D. J. Willey c Thornely b White	10		
O. P. Stone b White	8		
L. M. Daggett not out	11		
B 8, l-b 3, w 2, n-b 16	29	B 5, l-b 2, n-b 2	9
1/126 (2) 2/126 (3) 3/155 (4) (114.3 overs)	399	1/139 (1) (5 wkts dec, 52.5 overs)	252
4/161 (5) 5/300 (6) 6/332 (1) 7/339 (7)		2/146 (2) 3/175 (3)	
8/363 (9) 9/373 (10) 10/399 (8) 110 overs: 388-9		4/243 (5) 5/252 (6)	

Buck 25–4–82–3; Joseph 20–3–90–0; White 27–4–94–4; Thakor 11–1–40–2; Henderson 24.3–8–53–1; Cobb 3–0–13–0; Thornely 3–0–7–0; Jones 1–0–9–0. *Second innings*—Buck 10.5–1–46–1; Joseph 8–0–48–1; Henderson 18–1–70–1; White 5–0–26–0; Cobb 4–0–24–0; Jones 7–0–31–2.

Leicestershire

W. S. Jones b Hall	37	– c Sales b Willey	14
M. A. Thornely lbw b Stone	22	– c Stone b Hall	4
†E. J. H. Eckersley b Middlebrook	27	– lbw b Hall	57
R. R. Sarwan run out	59	– b Willey	14
M. A. G. Boyce lbw b Willey	0	– c Murphy b Stone	19
*J. J. Cobb c Murphy b Willey	5	– c Murphy b Willey	28
S. J. Thakor c Stone b Middlebrook	61	– not out	39
W. A. White c Murphy b Hall	8	– b Middlebrook	9
C. W. Henderson not out	56	– b Middlebrook	20
R. H. Joseph c Murphy b Middlebrook	0	– not out	1
N. L. Buck lbw b Daggett	14		
B 2, l-b 6, n-b 2	10	B 4, l-b 5, w 5, n-b 8	22
1/47 (2) 2/79 (1) 3/93 (3) (121.4 overs)	299	1/8 (2) 2/18 (1) (8 wkts, 88 overs)	227
4/102 (5) 5/108 (6) 6/183 (4) 7/192 (8)		3/45 (4) 4/87 (5)	
8/272 (7) 9/274 (10) 10/299 (11) 110 overs: 269-7		5/130 (3) 6/157 (6) 7/174 (8) 8/226 (9)	

Willey 26–7–71–2; Daggett 23.4–4–69–1; Middlebrook 29–15–36–3; Stone 18–3–61–1; Hall 24–7–51–2; Wakely 1–0–3–0. *Second innings*—Willey 21–5–66–3; Hall 18–1–61–2; Stone 11–3–24–1; Daggett 7–4–16–0; Middlebrook 31–13–51–2.

Umpires: R. T. Robinson and G. Sharp.

At Southampton, August 15–18. NORTHAMPTONSHIRE lost to HAMPSHIRE by eight wickets.

NORTHAMPTONSHIRE v DERBYSHIRE

At Northampton, August 21–24. Drawn. Northamptonshire 9pts, Derbyshire 9pts. Toss: Northants.

A staggering transformation in Derbyshire's fortunes carried them from the brink of following on to a chance of victory. Madsen, appearing at No. 5 after he bruised a rib falling on the ball in the field, had inched his side to 253 for eight when he was joined by Poynton, a 22-year-old wicketkeeper with just one first-class fifty to his name. They added 261 in 73 overs, and were not separated until the eighth ball of the last morning, as a pitch which started green lost all venom. Their stand was the third-highest for the ninth wicket in first-class cricket, just 22 short of the record, set by another Derbyshire pair – Arnold Warren and John Chapman, against Warwickshire in the small mining town of Blackwell in 1910. Madsen faced exactly 400 balls, and helped put on 405 for the last four wickets. Understandably shell-shocked, Northamptonshire collapsed to 37 for four, still 132

MOST RUNS ADDED BY LAST FOUR IN CHAMPIONSHIP

521	Northamptonshire	58-6 to 579	v Essex at Northampton	1999
482	Yorkshire	405-6 to 887	v Warwickshire at Birmingham	1896
476	Essex	224-6 to 700-9 dec	v Nottinghamshire at Chelmsford	2007
430	Sussex	107-6 to 537	v Middlesex at Hove	2003
428	Sussex	92-6 to 520	v Essex at Leyton	1902
405	**Derbyshire**	**164-6 to 569**	**v Northamptonshire at Northampton**	**2012**

behind,with 68 overs left. But Newton, who became their 11th batsman to make two hundreds in a match, and Sales, who scored fifty with a broken finger, buckled down. Willey had to apologise for calling his home town a "dive" on Twitter. "I popped into Northampton town centre to get barged by one guy who didn't apologise, held the door open for a family who didn't say 'thank you', and flashed a car at a junction and didn't get a thank you," he later explained.

Close of play: first day, Northamptonshire 311-6 (Middlebrook 50, Murphy 16); second day, Derbyshire 163-5 (Madsen 37, Whiteley 0); third day, Derbyshire 512-8 (Madsen 223, Poynton 105).

Northamptonshire

K. J. Coetzer b Palladino	5	– c Poynton b Groenewald	15
N. J. O'Brien c Durston b Wainwright	41	– lbw b Wainwright	11
D. J. Sales lbw b Wainwright	26	– (6) not out	53
A. G. Wakely c Lineker b Clare	37	– (3) c Khawaja b Palladino	1
R. I. Newton c Poynton b Palladino	115	– (4) not out	119
*A. J. Hall c Poynton b Whiteley	15	– (5) c Poynton b Palladino	5
J. D. Middlebrook b Wainwright	71		
†D. Murphy c Poynton b Palladino	20		
D. J. Willey not out	60		
L. M. Daggett c Poynton b Palladino	2		
J. A. Brooks lbw b Palladino	1		
L-b 7	7	L-b 4, w 2, n-b 2	8
1/6 (1) 2/42 (3) 3/93 (2) 4/147 (4) (123 overs)	400	1/25 (1) (4 wkts dec, 69 overs)	212
5/206 (6) 6/277 (5) 7/323 (8)		2/26 (3) 3/32 (2)	
8/383 (7) 9/398 (10) 10/400 (11) 110 overs: 350-7		4/37 (5)	

Palladino 30–5–82–5; Groenewald 27–4–71–0; Clare 15–2–60–1; Wainwright 33–6–99–3; Durston 10–0–46–0; Whiteley 8–0–35–1. *Second innings*—Palladino 15–4–43–2; Groenewald 14–1–48–1; Wainwright 20–4–45–1; Clare 2–1–1–0; Whiteley 4–0–25–0; Durston 8–1–22–0; Khawaja 2–0–13–0; Lineker 2–0–2–0; Redfern 2–0–9–0.

Derbyshire

M. S. Lineker b Willey	20
U. T. Khawaja lbw b Daggett	16
W. J. Durston lbw b Hall	14
D. J. Redfern c Murphy b Middlebrook	70
*W. L. Madsen not out	231
A. P. Palladino c Murphy b Middlebrook	0
R. A. Whiteley c Murphy b Willey	0
D. J. Wainwright lbw b Middlebrook	14
J. L. Clare c Murphy b Daggett	28
†T. Poynton b Brooks	106
T. D. Groenewald c Wakely b Daggett	42
B 15, l-b 9, n-b 4	28
1/36 (2) 2/40 (1) 3/79 (3) (163.5 overs)	569
4/155 (4) 5/157 (6) 6/164 (7)	
7/207 (8) 8/253 (9)	
9/514 (10) 10/569 (11) 110 overs: 363-8	

Willey 31–6–104–2; Brooks 25–1–109–1; Daggett 39.5–10–136–3; Middlebrook 30–8–43–3; Hall 23–3–83–1; Coetzer 8–1–35–0; Wakely 6–0–32–0; O'Brien 1–0–3–0.

Umpires: S. C. Gale and T. E. Jesty.

At Cardiff, August 28–31. NORTHAMPTONSHIRE drew with GLAMORGAN.

At Bristol, September 4–6. NORTHAMPTONSHIRE lost to GLOUCESTERSHIRE by 207 runs.

NOTTINGHAMSHIRE

High hopes drain away

SIMON CLEAVES

The 2012 season will be remembered by many as a summer of covers rather than cover-drives: in the Championship, Nottinghamshire lost a quarter of their potential playing time, at home and on the road. Though many counties suffered more, it came as a shock: since the Trent Bridge drainage and outfield were replaced at the end of 2008, the time lost to showers had been measured in minutes, not sessions.

Nottinghamshire were left wondering where they might have finished in more favourable conditions. Fifth place seemed an unfair reflection of their season, even though they failed to win again after beating Sussex at Hove in late May – a victory which director of cricket Mick Newell described as the highlight of the summer. The off-field event of the year had already taken place when, in March, Lisa Pursehouse became the first female chief executive at a first-class county, having worked at the club since 2000.

Newell and captain Chris Read were phlegmatic. Once again, Nottinghamshire had flourished early on, exploiting seamer-friendly pitches: they were top of the table with four wins going into the Twenty20 break in June. As surfaces became more docile, however, they struggled for penetration. At the end of July, they could not finish off Sussex at Trent Bridge, despite a 349-run first-innings lead and more than five sessions to bowl them out. That put extra pressure on the next home fixture, against Durham: asked to chase 366 in 90 overs, Nottinghamshire made a flying start thanks to Alex Hales and Riki Wessels, but ended up losing by 16 runs, their first defeat of the season. With the wind taken from their sails, and injuries and England call-ups biting, they gathered only 19 points from their last three matches, as Warwickshire streaked away to the title.

The burden of taking wickets fell too heavily on Andre Adams, who remained outstanding, with 54 victims. But his advancing years began to show, and he missed four Championship games through injury; relying on a 37-year-old as the attack spearhead is unlikely to win trophies. Back-up seamers Luke Fletcher, Harry Gurney and Andy Carter were all willing, and had their moments, with 70 wickets between them, but at times their lack of experience told. They could learn much from Ben Phillips's work ethic.

Spin seemed unlikely to win many games: Graeme Swann, awarded a benefit in 2013, was England's first-choice slow bowler in all formats, while left-arm spinner Graeme White was still learning his trade, and Samit Patel remained more of a containing bowler.

Ajmal Shahzad signed in October, following his well-publicised departure from Yorkshire and a loan spell at Lancashire. A first-class record of only three five-wicket returns in 59 matches was not encouraging, but

Nottinghamshire hoped new surroundings would rejuvenate him, as they had done Ryan Sidebottom, the last Yorkshireman to make the short move south. If Shahzad's pace, combative attitude and ability to find reverse-swing could be channelled in the right direction, he would give Read a game-changing bowler to call upon when pitches go flat.

Eranga Jayawardena, AP/PA

Michael Lumb

Another import, Michael Lumb, successfully resurrected his career after arriving from Hampshire. He was a revelation at No. 3, with three centuries, as well as and some explosive innings opening in limited-overs cricket. Meanwhile, Read continued to better himself, finishing just short of 1,000 Championship runs, with nine fifties. These two aside, however, batting performances fluctuated. Wessels impressed in bursts and always scored quickly, but James Taylor – recruited from Leicestershire – and Patel often found the going tough, though Taylor made a stunning unbeaten hundred against Hampshire in the CB40. Like Hales, they needed to aim for 1,000-run seasons to push their England claims.

In the CB40, rain-affected defeats in Edinburgh and Swansea cost Nottinghamshire dear, while the Twenty20 campaign ended at the quarter-finals for the second year running. But in 2013 the fearsome top three of Hales, Lumb and Wessels, backed up by an in-form Taylor, Patel and Read, plus a strong bowling attack, could finally make the breakthrough in the frustrating pursuit of a first limited-overs trophy since the 1991 Sunday League.

Injuries took their toll on Darren Pattinson's fitness: he missed the entire Championship programme, although he remained a strong competitor with the white ball. His contract was not renewed after he registered as a domestic player for Australia's Twenty20 Big Bash League.

Also released were Scott Elstone, and openers Neil Edwards and Karl Turner, who joined the growing list of batsmen to fail against the new ball at Trent Bridge. In December, Nottinghamshire signed Australian opener Ed Cowan to play in the months preceding the Ashes; he was due to be replaced by David Hussey, who is returning for an eighth stint at the club. In the meantime Sam Kelsall and Sam Wood – who have graduated from the England Under-19 side – were available to fill any gaps left by senior call-ups.

Read and Newell were determined to get Nottinghamshire over the line. In December, the club announced they would not allow Hales, Lumb or Patel to take part in the 2013 IPL, to ensure they did not miss the start of the Championship season. That was greeted by a warning from the PCA about Nottinghamshire's attractiveness to potential future players, but the trio did not complain – and it underlined the county's determination to start the summer with a bang. The pattern of faltering in the second half of the season had to be overcome, however, if they were to challenge on all fronts.

Championship attendance: 28,432.

NOTTINGHAMSHIRE RESULTS

All first-class matches – Played 17: Won 4, Lost 2, Drawn 11.
County Championship matches – Played 16: Won 4, Lost 2, Drawn 10.

LV= County Championship, 5th in Division 1;
Friends Life t20, q-f; Clydesdale Bank 40, 4th in Group B.

COUNTY CHAMPIONSHIP AVERAGES, BATTING AND FIELDING

Cap		*M*	*I*	*NO*	*R*	*HS*	*100*	*50*	*Avge*	*Ct/St*
1999	C. M. W. Read	16	24	4	975	104*	1	8	48.75	43/1
	S. J. Mullaney	6	10	1	391	94	0	4	43.44	5
2012	M. J. Lumb	14	23	0	910	171	3	3	39.56	7
	M. H. Wessels	12	19	0	733	199	2	1	38.57	7/1
1999	P. J. Franks†	10	17	7	354	86*	0	3	35.40	1
2011	A. D. Hales	15	24	1	797	155*	2	4	34.65	16
2012	J. W. A. Taylor†	14	22	3	608	163*	1	1	32.00	8
2008	A. C. Voges§	9	12	2	313	105	1	2	31.30	12
2008	S. R. Patel	9	14	2	329	69	0	2	27.41	7
	N. J. Edwards	8	15	1	317	53	0	1	22.64	5
	B. J. Phillips	13	18	4	257	47	0	0	18.35	5
	L. J. Fletcher†	8	13	5	93	42*	0	0	11.62	2
2007	A. R. Adams¶	12	14	0	151	29	0	0	10.78	8
2008	S. C. J. Broad†‡	2	4	1	30	12	0	0	10.00	1
	A. Carter	9	8	4	32	17*	0	0	8.00	2
	G. G. White	5	9	0	60	14	0	0	6.66	2
2005	G. P. Swann‡	3	5	0	23	12	0	0	4.60	1
	H. F. Gurney†	10	9	1	10	6	0	0	1.25	0

Also batted: S. Kelsall (1 match) 0, 35; S. K. W. Wood† (1 match) 45, 2.

† Born in Nottinghamshire. ‡ ECB contract. § Official overseas player. ¶ Other non-England-qualified player.

BOWLING

	Style	*O*	*M*	*R*	*W*	*BB*	*5I*	*Avge*
G. P. Swann	OB	87.2	21	188	10	3-26	0	18.80
A. R. Adams	RFM	344.3	63	1,035	54	7-32	4	19.16
B. J. Phillips	RFM	328.3	97	813	30	4-33	0	27.10
L. J. Fletcher	RFM	247.5	70	671	24	4-53	0	27.95
H. F. Gurney	LFM	234.3	52	713	21	4-40	0	33.95
A. Carter	RFM	251.2	40	900	25	4-55	0	36.00
S. R. Patel	SLA	164.4	30	536	14	4-67	0	38.28
P. J. Franks	RFM	187.5	27	618	16	4-47	0	38.62
G. G. White	SLA	144.1	26	519	13	4-97	0	39.92

Also bowled: S. C. J. Broad (RFM) 62–8–225–4; M. J. Lumb (RM) 2–0–13–0; S. J. Mullaney (RM) 16–2–41–0; J. W. A. Taylor (LBG) 2–0–16–0; A. C. Voges (SLC) 7–2–6–1; M. H. Wessels (OB) 15–3–43–1; S. K. W. Wood (OB) 28–2–84–3.

LEADING CB40 AVERAGES (100 runs/4 wickets)

Batting	*Runs*	*HS*	*Avge*	*SR*	*Ct/St*
J. W. A. Taylor	385	115*	64.16	91.88	1
C. M. W. Read	236	71*	59.00	98.33	9/3
A. C. Voges	232	74	38.66	90.27	9
S. R. Patel	340	82	30.90	77.80	2
A. D. Hales	356	94	29.66	92.46	1
M. H. Wessels	312	55	26.00	113.45	10

Bowling	*W*	*BB*	*Avge*	*ER*
G. G. White	12	3-28	19.33	5.09
D. J. Pattinson	12	3-27	19.91	6.51
A. Carter	12	4-45	25.58	6.60
S. R. Patel	15	3-47	28.53	5.35
H. F. Gurney	7	4-22	30.57	4.86
J. T. Ball	5	3-38	31.20	4.77

LEADING FLT20 AVERAGES (100 runs/18 overs)

Batting	Runs	HS	Avge	SR	Ct
M. H. Wessels	150	53	21.42	**153.06**	3
S. R. Patel	109	60	36.33	**149.31**	4
A. D. Hales	127	88	25.40	**139.56**	1
M. J. Lumb	252	62	36.00	**138.46**	1
J. W. A. Taylor	127	45	42.33	**129.59**	1
A. C. Voges	209	70	52.25	**120.11**	7

Bowling	W	BB	Avge	ER
S. R. Patel	7	3-26	24.28	**7.08**
H. F. Gurney	6	2-26	29.83	**7.16**
S. J. Mullaney	9	4-19	21.55	**7.46**
A. Carter	9	3-12	19.22	**7.52**
D. J. Pattinson	6	2-21	27.83	**7.59**

FIRST-CLASS COUNTY RECORDS

Highest score for	312*	W. W. Keeton v Middlesex at The Oval	1939
Highest score against	345	C. G. Macartney (Australians) at Nottingham	1921
Leading run-scorer	31,592	G. Gunn (avge 35.69)	1902–1932
Best bowling for	10-66	K. Smales v Gloucestershire at Stroud	1956
Best bowling against	10-10	H. Verity (Yorkshire) at Leeds	1932
Leading wicket-taker	1,653	T. G. Wass (avge 20.34)	1896–1920
Highest total for	791	v Essex at Chelmsford	2007
Highest total against	781-7 dec	by Northamptonshire at Northampton	1995
Lowest total for	13	v Yorkshire at Nottingham	1901
Lowest total against	16	by Derbyshire at Nottingham	1879
	16	by Surrey at The Oval	1880

LIST A COUNTY RECORDS

Highest score for	167*	P. Johnson v Kent at Nottingham	1993
Highest score against	191	D. S. Lehmann (Yorkshire) at Scarborough	2001
Leading run-scorer	11,237	R. T. Robinson (avge 35.33)	1978–1999
Best bowling for	6-10	K. P. Evans v Northumberland at Jesmond	1994
Best bowling against	7-41	A. N. Jones (Sussex) at Nottingham	1986
Leading wicket-taker	291	C. E. B. Rice (avge 22.60)	1975–1987
Highest total for	346-9	v Ireland at Nottingham	2009
Highest total against	361-8	by Surrey at The Oval	2001
Lowest total for	57	v Gloucestershire at Nottingham	2009
Lowest total against	43	by Northamptonshire at Northampton	1977

TWENTY20 COUNTY RECORDS

Highest score for	91	M. A. Ealham v Yorkshire at Nottingham	2004
Highest score against	111	W. J. Durston (Derbyshire) at Nottingham	2010
Leading run-scorer	**1,755**	**S. R. Patel (avge 26.19)**	**2003–2012**
Best bowling for	5-25	D. J. Pattinson v Warwickshire at Birmingham	2011
Best bowling against	5-13	A. B. McDonald (Leicestershire) at Nottingham	2010
Leading wicket-taker	**71**	**S. R. Patel (avge 24.91)**	**2003–2012**
Highest total for	215-6	v Yorkshire at Nottingham	2011
Highest total against	207-7	by Yorkshire at Nottingham	2004
Lowest total for	91	v Lancashire at Manchester	2006
Lowest total against	**96**	**by Leicestershire at Leicester**	**2012**

ADDRESS

County Cricket Ground, Trent Bridge, Nottingham NG2 6AG (0115 982 3000; **email** administration@nottsccc.co.uk). **Website** www.nottsccc.co.uk

OFFICIALS

Captain C. M. W. Read
Director of cricket M. Newell
Academy director C. M. Tolley
President J. P. Brydon
Chairman P. G. Wright
Chief executive L. J. Pursehouse
Chairman, cricket committee W. Taylor
Head groundsman S. Birks
Scorer R. Marshall

NOTTINGHAMSHIRE v LOUGHBOROUGH MCCU

At Nottingham, April 1–3. Drawn. Toss: Nottinghamshire. First-class debuts: F. W. Daeche-Marshall, D. M. Endersby, T. Lester. County debuts: M. J. Lumb, J. W. A. Taylor.

In an otherwise satisfying start to their season, rain denied Nottinghamshire victory over the Loughborough students. Following the loss of three early wickets, including Hales in the first over – after hitting three fours – Edwards and Wessels showed excellent touch in adding 303, the sixth-highest for Nottinghamshire's fourth wicket, both scoring their first hundreds for the county. Wessels reached his century in 89 balls and raced on to 150 in a further 24; for the more sedate Edwards it was only the fourth of his career, and his first since 2007. Fletcher maintained a disciplined line and length, then Reed, waiving the follow-on, gave James Taylor a second chance of batting practice. He moved smoothly to three figures on the final morning, becoming the tenth player to score a century on debut for Nottinghamshire.

Close of play: first day, Loughborough MCCU 4-0 (Tavaré 4, Evans 0); second day, Nottinghamshire 183-2 (Taylor 61, Read 14).

Nottinghamshire

A. D. Hales c Endersby b Soilleux	12	– c Billings b Sturmer	48
N. J. Edwards lbw b Riley	195		
M. J. Lumb c Endersby b Soilleux	17	– b Endersby	44
J. W. A. Taylor c Riley b Taylor	0	– (2) not out	101
M. H. Wessels c Sturmer b Endersby	172		
*†C. M. W. Read b Taylor	11	– (4) c Endersby b Taylor	28
P. J. Franks b Soilleux	19	– (5) c Billings b Taylor	16
B. J. Phillips c and b Sturmer	14	– (6) b Taylor	15
G. G. White not out	30	– (7) not out	19
L. J. Fletcher b Riley	23		
A. Carter b Lester	4		
B 10, l-b 18, w 1, n-b 2	31	B 9, l-b 3, w 7	19
1/14 (1) 2/44 (3) 3/45 (4) 4/348 (5) 5/369 (6) 6/423 (7) 7/467 (8) 8/481 (2) 9/515 (10) 10/528 (11) (102.1 overs)	528	1/66 (1) 2/167 (3) 3/199 (4) 4/225 (5) 5/241 (6) (5 wkts dec, 49 overs)	290

Soilleux 20–2–97–3; Taylor 19–3–107–2; Sturmer 17–2–83–1; Lester 10.1–0–59–1; Riley 25–2–112–2; Endersby 10–0–41–1; Evans 1–0–1–0. *Second innings*—Soilleux 8–0–66–0; Taylor 14–1–82–3; Sturmer 6–1–35–1; Lester 14–2–55–0; Endersby 7–1–40–1.

Loughborough MCCU

W. A. Tavaré c Edwards b Phillips	9	– not out	13
R. F. Evans c Wessels b Fletcher	5	– not out	14
N. Patel c Hales b Phillips	46		
†S. W. Billings c Read b Fletcher	0		
F. W. Daeche-Marshall lbw b White	32		
R. M. L. Taylor b White	1		
D. M. Endersby c Read b Fletcher	0		
*A. E. N. Riley run out	18		
A. C. Soilleux b Carter	22		
I. W. Sturmer c Hales b Fletcher	5		
T. Lester not out	0		
B 2, l-b 8	10	L-b 1	1
1/14 (1) 2/20 (2) 3/24 (4) 4/76 (5) 5/86 (6) 6/93 (7) 7/102 (3) 8/128 (9) 9/144 (10) 10/148 (8) (63.3 overs)	148	(no wkt, 13 overs)	28

White 13.3–8–13–2; Fletcher 14–6–21–4; Phillips 13–5–23–2; Carter 10–3–38–1; Franks 13–3–43–0. *Second innings*—Fletcher 5–1–16–0; Phillips 4–3–5–0; Franks 4–2–6–0.

Umpires: R. T. Robinson and B. V. Taylor.

NOTTINGHAMSHIRE v WORCESTERSHIRE

At Nottingham, April 5–8. Nottinghamshire won by 92 runs. Nottinghamshire 19pts, Worcestershire 3pts. Toss: Worcestershire. County debuts: M. Klinger, D. S. Lucas.

Nottinghamshire extended their run of winning the opening Championship fixture to six years, though less comfortably than the margin of victory, completed an hour into a drizzly final morning, suggested. With Samit Patel playing for England in Sri Lanka, and Darren Pattinson recovering from a back injury, they must have feared the worst after being bundled out inside 42 overs. Poor shot selection was largely to blame as Jones claimed six for 32. Worcestershire – introducing Michael Klinger as a stand-in for fellow Australian Phil Hughes, still at a national training camp – were equally ring-rusty. Before the first day was out, they too had been dismissed, just 12 ahead. Both sides made a better stab of it next time around, but Wessels's second hundred in six days, backed up by Read, put Nottinghamshire in the box seat. Chasing 392, Worcestershire limped to 61 for two, before a poised stand of 174 between Mitchell (reprieved on nine, when umpire Sharp backtracked on an lbw decision) and Ali reinvigorated them. But Ali's exit just before the second new ball, and two wickets in two deliveries from Fletcher, swung the game Nottinghamshire's way.

Close of play: first day, Worcestershire 130; second day, Nottinghamshire 355-7 (Wessels 104); third day, Worcestershire 258-6 (Cameron 8, Choudhry 1).

Nottinghamshire

First innings		Second innings	
A. D. Hales c Solanki b Richardson	4	– c Jones b Cameron	46
N. J. Edwards lbw b Ali	21	– lbw b Richardson	48
M. J. Lumb c Scott b Lucas	3	– c Scott b Choudhry	40
J. W. A. Taylor c Kervezee b Jones	4	– lbw b Richardson	13
M. H. Wessels c Klinger b Jones	0	– lbw b Richardson	113
*†C. M. W. Read c Mitchell b Jones	4	– lbw b Lucas	68
P. J. Franks not out	51	– lbw b Richardson	6
B. J. Phillips c Solanki b Richardson	2	– lbw b Lucas	16
G. G. White c Kervezee b Jones	14	– c Klinger b Lucas	4
A. R. Adams c Kervezee b Jones	0	– b Richardson	25
L. J. Fletcher c Solanki b Jones	0	– not out	9
B 9, l-b 1, w 1, n-b 4	15	B 1, l-b 7, w 1, n-b 6	15
1/4 (1) 2/17 (3) 3/26 (4) 4/26 (5) (41.4 overs)	118	1/94 (1) 2/103 (2) (105 overs)	403
5/34 (6) 6/74 (2) 7/83 (8) 8/115 (9)		3/137 (4) 4/183 (3)	
9/115 (10) 10/118 (11)		5/317 (6) 6/324 (7) 7/355 (8)	
		8/361 (9) 9/389 (5) 10/403 (10)	

Richardson 15–4–28–2; Lucas 11–3–36–1; Jones 10.4–4–32–6; Cameron 3–0–9–0; Ali 2–1–3–1. *Second innings*—Richardson 32–6–95–5; Lucas 29–5–127–3; Jones 16–0–79–0; Ali 12–0–44–0; Cameron 4–0–21–1; Choudhry 12–3–29–1.

Worcestershire

First innings		Second innings	
*D. K. H. Mitchell lbw b Phillips	8	– b Fletcher	102
M. Klinger c Read b Fletcher	29	– c Read b Phillips	22
V. S. Solanki b Phillips	5	– c White b Adams	22
M. M. Ali c Read b Adams	1	– c Read b Adams	94
A. N. Kervezee b Fletcher	18	– b Phillips	4
J. G. Cameron c Read b Adams	1	– not out	27
†B. J. M. Scott lbw b Phillips	12	– b Fletcher	0
S. H. Choudhry lbw b Franks	20	– lbw b Fletcher	1
D. S. Lucas c Hales b Fletcher	17	– b Adams	12
R. A. Jones not out	10	– c and b Adams	3
A. Richardson c Read b Franks	4	– lbw b Fletcher	0
L-b 3, n-b 2	5	L-b 10, n-b 2	12
1/15 (1) 2/33 (3) 3/38 (4) 4/44 (2) (49.4 overs)	130	1/26 (2) 2/61 (3) (101.5 overs)	299
5/45 (6) 6/67 (5) 7/82 (7) 8/107 (8)		3/235 (4) 4/241 (5)	
9/119 (9) 10/130 (11)		5/253 (1) 6/253 (7) 7/261 (8)	
		8/294 (9) 9/298 (10) 10/299 (11)	

Fletcher 14–3–45–3; Phillips 13–6–29–3; Adams 14–2–30–2; Franks 8.4–0–23–2. *Second innings*—Fletcher 25.5–9–53–4; Phillips 22–4–63–2; Adams 32–6–90–4; Franks 15–1–52–0; White 7–2–31–0.

Umpires: R. T. Robinson and G. Sharp.

At Chester-le-Street, April 12–15. NOTTINGHAMSHIRE beat DURHAM by 114 runs.

NOTTINGHAMSHIRE v SOMERSET

At Nottingham, April 19–22. Drawn. Nottinghamshire 3pts, Somerset 11pts. Toss: Somerset. County debut: H. F. Gurney.

Both counties were deprived of a big name, but Somerset seemed inspired while Nottinghamshire faltered. The home team, whose attack leader Adams had succumbed to flu, failed to collect a single bonus point. Somerset, already resting Philander because of a minor back injury, lost Trescothick when he turned his right ankle chasing a ball in the field (he was out for three months), but still dominated the game. Against bowling that looked sadly inadequate, Compton piled up his second double-hundred of the summer, sharing double-century partnerships with Suppiah and Hildreth. That

SCORING A CENTURY WHEN NO TEAM-MATE PASSED TEN

		Next HS		
G. Gunn	109*	8*	Notts (129-3) v Yorks at Nottingham	1913
G. M. Turner	141*	7	Worcs (169) v Glam at Swansea	1977
C. E. B. Rice	105*	10	Notts (143) v Hants at Bournemouth	1981
Mohammad Ramzan	102*	9	Faisalabad (128-1) v Sargodha at Faisalabad	2000-01
C. M. W. Read	**104***	**10**	**Notts (162) v Somerset at Nottingham**	**2012**

Note: Gunn and Mohammad Ramzan achieved the feat in uncompleted innings.

highlighted the brittleness of Nottinghamshire's first-innings 162, in which Read became only the third player to score a century in an all-out total when no other batsman passed ten; the highest stand was 56 for the last wicket with former Leicestershire seamer Harry Gurney. Making light of Philander's absence, Trego claimed five for 53. But rain plagued most of the match, enabling Read and Taylor to deny Somerset the victory they deserved.

Close of play: first day, Nottinghamshire 93-6 (Read 52, Franks 0); second day, Somerset 78-1 (Suppiah 50, Compton 19); third day, Nottinghamshire 47-0 (Hales 22, Edwards 22).

Nottinghamshire

First innings		Second innings	
A. D. Hales c Kieswetter b Meschede	9	c Hildreth b Meschede	29
N. J. Edwards lbw b Trego	3	c Kieswetter b Trego	26
M. J. Lumb lbw b Trego	0	b Dockrell	23
S. R. Patel c Suppiah b Trego	4	lbw b Trego	11
J. W. A. Taylor c Kieswetter b Kirby	2	not out	38
*†C. M. W. Read not out	104	not out	33
S. J. Mullaney b Gregory	10		
P. J. Franks lbw b Trego	2		
B. J. Phillips c Kieswetter b Trego	4		
L. J. Fletcher c Trescothick b Kirby	1		
H. F. Gurney b Kirby	6		
B 6, l-b 7, n-b 4	17	B 5, l-b 1, w 3	9
1/14 (2) 2/14 (3) 3/20 (1) 4/20 (4) 5/34 (5) 6/89 (7) 7/97 (8) 8/101 (9) 9/106 (10) 10/162 (11) (56.4 overs)	162	1/58 (2) 2/62 (1) 3/85 (4) 4/109 (3) (4 wkts, 58 overs)	169

Kirby 20.4–5–52–3; Trego 20–6–53–5; Meschede 7–1–19–1; Gregory 8–1–23–1; Dockrell 1–0–2–0. *Second innings*—Kirby 4–0–17–0; Trego 21–5–62–2; Meschede 14–2–45–1; Dockrell 16–8–25–1; Gregory 3–0–14–0.

Somerset

A. V. Suppiah c Hales b Franks 124
L. Gregory b Phillips 6
N. R. D. Compton not out 204
J. C. Hildreth not out 102
L-b 5, w 2, n-b 2 9

1/12 (2) (2 wkts dec, 111.4 overs) 445
2/228 (1) 110 overs: 427-2

*M. E. Trescothick, †C. Kieswetter, J. C. Buttler, P. D. Trego, C. A. J. Meschede, G. H. Dockrell and S. P. Kirby did not bat.

Fletcher 24–6–99–0; Phillips 20–7–42–1; Gurney 25–5–89–0; Franks 21–3–84–1; Patel 21.4–1–126–0.

Umpires: N. G. C. Cowley and P. Willey.

At Worcester, April 26–29. NOTTINGHAMSHIRE drew with WORCESTERSHIRE.

At Manchester, May 2–5. NOTTINGHAMSHIRE beat LANCASHIRE by 185 runs.

NOTTINGHAMSHIRE v MIDDLESEX

At Nottingham, May 9–12. Drawn. Nottinghamshire 11pts, Middlesex 8pts. Toss: Nottinghamshire.

Rayner had expected to spend the third day of this match as best man at his cousin's wedding, but instead scored a maiden Championship century. He got a late call-up after Trent Bridge produced a dry pitch for Swann, making a rare domestic appearance. Rayner's off-spin had little impact as Nottinghamshire built their biggest Championship total yet in 2012, with Lumb making the most of three dropped catches (two by Strauss) to score his second hundred of the season. Later, Strauss played a loose defensive shot and was caught behind for his third single-figure score in four innings leading up to the summer's first Test. With Middlesex struggling at 50 for three, Rayner came in as nightwatchman and saw Denly fall early next morning. But he displayed a straight bat and solid technique, prospering for 327 minutes to stave off the follow-on, then took two wickets in two overs by the close. Nottinghamshire declared on the final afternoon, setting a target of 298 in 51 overs. Middlesex opted for caution on a slow pitch with uneven bounce, though Strauss found some form. Hales was fined a week's wages after oversleeping and reporting late for the final day.

Close of play: first day, Nottinghamshire 132-1 (Hales 71, Lumb 51); second day, Middlesex 51-3 (Denly 32, Rayner 0); third day, Nottinghamshire 22-3 (Lumb 0, Wessels 5).

Nottinghamshire

A. D. Hales c Strauss b Murtagh . . . . 79 – b Rayner 12
N. J. Edwards b Finn . . . . 0 – c Strauss b Finn 4
M. J. Lumb c Murtagh b Berg . . . . 162 – (4) c Finn b Rayner 55
M. H. Wessels run out . . . . 41 – (5) lbw b Finn 5
S. J. Mullaney c Berg b Finn . . . . 60 – (6) c Berg b Rayner 73
*†C. M. W. Read c Finn b Dexter . . . . 13 – (7) b Finn 5
S. C. J. Broad c Strauss b Finn . . . . 12 – (9) not out 6
P. J. Franks not out . . . . 10 – not out 12
G. P. Swann lbw b Dexter . . . . 1 – (3) c Denly b Rayner 0
A. R. Adams c Dexter b Finn 29
H. F. Gurney c Rogers b Rayner 0
B 7, l-b 7, n-b 2 . . . . 16 B 2 2

1/0 (2) 2/150 (1) 3/233 (4) (113.2 overs) 423 1/17 (1) (7 wkts dec, 53 overs) 174
4/328 (3) 5/365 (5) 6/382 (7) 7/382 (6) 2/17 (2) 3/17 (3)
8/384 (9) 9/417 (10) 10/423 (11) 110 overs: 403-8 4/22 (5) 5/132 (4) 6/142 (7) 7/166 (6)

Murtagh 28–5–96–1; Finn 35–7–117–4; Berg 18–3–78–1; Dexter 11–2–55–2; Rayner 21.2–0–63–1. *Second innings*—Murtagh 6–1–20–0; Finn 16–2–47–3; Rayner 24–5–67–4; Berg 1–0–6–0; Denly 6–0–32–0.

Middlesex

A. J. Strauss c Read b Gurney	2	– not out	43
S. D. Robson c Read b Adams	9	– not out	39
J. L. Denly c Hales b Adams	35		
*C. J. L. Rogers c Mullaney b Adams	6		
O. P. Rayner not out	143		
D. J. Malan lbw b Gurney	46		
N. J. Dexter c Adams b Swann	17		
†J. A. Simpson b Gurney	1		
G. K. Berg b Broad	16		
T. J. Murtagh b Swann	14		
S. T. Finn not out	0		
B 4, l-b 3, w 2, n-b 2	11	L-b 1, n-b 4	5
1/3 (1) 2/32 (2) (9 wkts dec, 105.1 overs)	300	(no wkt, 35 overs)	87

3/50 (4) 4/63 (3) 5/182 (6)
6/225 (7) 7/236 (8) 8/271 (9) 9/298 (10)

Broad 21–2–79–1; Gurney 24–7–47–3; Adams 26.1–9–75–3; Swann 23–5–55–2; Franks 11–1–37–0. *Second innings*—Broad 10–3–19–0; Gurney 7–0–33–0; Swann 10–2–15–0; Adams 7–3–18–0; Mullaney 1–0–1–0.

Umpires: D. J. Millns and R. T. Robinson.

At Hove, May 25–28. NOTTINGHAMSHIRE beat SUSSEX by seven wickets.

NOTTINGHAMSHIRE v LANCASHIRE

At Nottingham, June 6–9. Drawn. Nottinghamshire 6pts, Lancashire 7pts. Toss: Nottinghamshire.

The captains did their best to contrive a result, but rain and bad light prevailed, with play limited to 59 overs on day one, 21 on day two and 12.5 on day three. During that time, Lancashire accrued runs steadily. Prince scored his seventh half-century of the summer before providing a 600th first-class wicket for Adams, who was the pick of the bowlers until his ankle gave way on the third day. An unbeaten last-wicket stand of 99 between Hogg and Kerrigan allowed the visitors to collect a fourth batting point and declare on the final morning, when forfeited innings set up an intriguing run-chase of 351 in 90 overs. At 95 for four, Nottinghamshire were in trouble, before the pendulum swung again as Taylor and Voges added 99. But when Taylor and Adams fell to successive Shahzad deliveries, the chase was abandoned, with Read standing firm to secure the draw.

Close of play: first day, Lancashire 203-6 (Prince 63, Chapple 0); second day, Lancashire 272-9 (Hogg 9, Kerrigan 9); third day, Lancashire 321-9 (Hogg 44, Kerrigan 22).

Lancashire

P. J. Horton c Voges b Carter	3
S. C. Moore b Adams	24
K. R. Brown c Patel b Adams	34
A. G. Prince c Hales b Adams	80
S. J. Croft c Read b Carter	29
L. A. Procter c Patel b Adams	7
†G. D. Cross c Taylor b Adams	35
*G. Chapple b Franks	24
A. Shahzad c Read b Gurney	3
K. W. Hogg not out	61
S. C. Kerrigan not out	34
B 4, l-b 8, n-b 4	16
1/11 (1) 2/64 (3) (9 wkts dec, 97 overs)	350

3/69 (2) 4/129 (5)
5/151 (6) 6/203 (7) 7/243 (4)
8/247 (8) 9/251 (9)

Gurney 19–5–42–1; Carter 27–6–86–2; Adams 26.4–1–108–5; Franks 18.2–1–67–1; Patel 2–1–6–0; Taylor 2–0–16–0; Lumb 2–0–13–0.

Lancashire forfeited their second innings.

Nottinghamshire

Nottinghamshire forfeited their first innings.

M. H. Wessels lbw b Hogg 15
A. D. Hales c Cross b Chapple 0
M. J. Lumb lbw b Chapple 35
S. R. Patel c Horton b Kerrigan. 24
J. W. A. Taylor lbw b Shahzad 67
A. C. Voges st Cross b Kerrigan 55
*†C. M. W. Read not out 56
A. R. Adams c Chapple b Shahzad 0
P. J. Franks not out 13
B 10, l-b 10, n-b 8 28

1/1 (2) 2/23 (1) (7 wkts, 89.4 overs) 293
3/87 (4) 4/95 (3)
5/194 (6) 6/255 (5) 7/255 (8)

A. Carter and H. F. Gurney did not bat.

Chapple 25–5–62–2; Hogg 17–4–45–1; Shahzad 17–3–58–2; Procter 11–1–45–0; Kerrigan 19.4–1–63–2.

Umpires: J. H. Evans and M. A. Gough.

At Uxbridge, July 11–14. NOTTINGHAMSHIRE drew with MIDDLESEX.

NOTTINGHAMSHIRE v SURREY

At Nottingham, July 18–21. Drawn. Nottinghamshire 8pts, Surrey 8pts. Toss: Surrey.

Only 42 overs were possible on day one, and the next two were called off because of muddy patches on the bowlers' run-ups and vulnerable parts of the square. Nottinghamshire were 84 for five on the first morning, before Read launched another of his rescue acts, with Voges. They extended their stand to 145 on the last day, when Read missed his hundred, bowled by one from Meaker that kept low. He was keen to set up a run-chase, but could not agree a target with Surrey, who opted to accumulate bonus points in their struggle against relegation rather than risk defeat. Wessels took over the wicketkeeping gloves in the final session after Read suffered a blow to his left index finger, and dismissed de Bruyn and Roy, who had entertained the crowd with five breezy sixes on his 22nd birthday. Adams became the first to take 50 first-class wickets for the summer, all in the Championship.

Close of play: first day, Nottinghamshire 178-5 (Voges 38, Read 49); second day, no play; third day, no play.

Nottinghamshire

M. H. Wessels c Jordan b Linley. 23
A. D. Hales b Lewis 14
M. J. Lumb lbw b Jordan. 12
S. R. Patel c Davies b Meaker. 9
J. W. A. Taylor c Davies b Meaker. 16
A. C. Voges lbw b Lewis 59
*†C. M. W. Read b Meaker 98
B. J. Phillips c Burns b Meaker. 47
A. R. Adams c Roy b Meaker 14
A. Carter not out 0
H. F. Gurney c Roy b Kartik 0
B 12, l-b 10, w 4, n-b 10 36

1/35 (1) 2/49 (2) 3/53 (3) (78.4 overs) 328
4/59 (4) 5/84 (5) 6/229 (6)
7/304 (7) 8/328 (9) 9/328 (8) 10/328 (11)

Lewis 18–3–64–2; Linley 16–3–77–1; Jordan 16–5–58–1; Meaker 20–2–78–5; Kartik 8.4–0–29–1.

Surrey

R. J. Burns b Adams 79
Z. S. Ansari b Carter 31
J. J. Roy st Wessels b Patel 83
*Z. de Bruyn c Wessels b Adams 0
†S. M. Davies c Voges b Adams. 3
M. N. W. Spriegel b Adams 17
C. J. Jordan not out 8
S. C. Meaker not out 29
N-b 2 2

1/85 (2) 2/167 (1) (6 wkts, 56.4 overs) 252
3/167 (4) 4/177 (5)
5/215 (3) 6/215 (6)

M. Kartik, J. Lewis and T. E. Linley did not bat.

Phillips 5–1–29–0; Gurney 11–2–54–0; Patel 13–0–67–1; Adams 15–2–51–4; Carter 12.4–0–51–1.

Umpires: R. J. Bailey and N. L. Bainton.

NOTTINGHAMSHIRE v SUSSEX

At Nottingham, July 27–30. Drawn. Nottinghamshire 11pts, Sussex 4pts. Toss: Sussex.

One point behind leaders Warwickshire, who had a game in hand, Nottinghamshire badly wanted a victory. After two days they held all the cards, having bundled out Sussex for 171, and reached 443 for four themselves. Lumb had made the most of being dropped at point, on his overnight 28, to hit his third century of the season – exactly matching the Sussex total – while Taylor registered his first Championship hundred for Nottinghamshire, who eventually declared 349 ahead. But Nash and Joyce fought back in an opening stand of 216. With the pitch flattening and Nottinghamshire lacking a frontline spinner, Nash took his aggregate in his last ten first-class innings against them to 786, which now included three hundreds. Joyce, too, looked set for three figures until Lumb held a flying one-handed catch at midwicket. The result represented an opportunity missed to overtake Warwickshire, who were drawing with Surrey. To make matters worse, Nottinghamshire expected their batting to be weakened by England calls for the rest of the campaign.

Close of play: first day, Nottinghamshire 88-1 (Wessels 38, Lumb 28); second day, Nottinghamshire 443-4 (Taylor 106, Voges 32); third day, Sussex 146-0 (Joyce 63, Nash 79).

Sussex

C. D. Nash c Read b Phillips	15	– (2) c Taylor b Carter	162
E. C. Joyce lbw b Adams	7	– (1) c Lumb b Patel	98
L. W. P. Wells c Read b Gurney	54	– c and b Wessels	59
M. W. Goodwin c Hales b Phillips	19	– b Patel	31
*M. H. Yardy run out	0	– c Adams b Gurney	3
L. J. Wright c Voges b Adams	7	– not out	12
†B. C. Brown lbw b Carter	37	– not out	0
S. J. Magoffin c Read b Gurney	8		
J. E. Anyon c Taylor b Carter	3		
A. Khan b Carter	9		
M. S. Panesar not out	4		
L-b 4, n-b 4	8	B 1, l-b 5, w 4, n-b 10	20
1/22 (2) 2/26 (1) 3/74 (4) 4/74 (5) (70.1 overs)	171	1/216 (1) (5 wkts, 134 overs)	385
5/89 (6) 6/130 (3) 7/144 (8)		2/314 (2) 3/352 (3)	
8/157 (7) 9/166 (9) 10/171 (10)		4/355 (5) 5/380 (4)	

Phillips 16–8–32–2; Gurney 15–7–38–2; Adams 18–4–36–2; Carter 12.1–3–41–3; Patel 9–2–20–0. *Second innings*—Phillips 15–4–29–0; Gurney 24–6–67–1; Adams 25–2–99–0; Patel 32–13–70–2; Carter 22–3–72–1; Wessels 13–3–40–1; Voges 3–1–2–0.

Nottinghamshire

M. H. Wessels b Khan	43	A. C. Voges not out	44
A. D. Hales lbw b Khan	8	B 3, l-b 5, w 7, n-b 33	48
M. J. Lumb b Magoffin	171		
S. R. Patel c Yardy b Nash	43	1/33 (2) 2/94 (1) (4 wkts dec, 137 overs)	520
J. W. A. Taylor not out	163	3/184 (4) 4/372 (3) 110 overs:	406-4

*†C. M. W. Read, B. J. Phillips, A. R. Adams, A. Carter and H. F. Gurney did not bat.

Anyon 17–1–102–0; Magoffin 22–4–71–1; Khan 28–2–124–2; Panesar 35–9–89–0; Wright 16–1–63–0; Nash 18–4–52–1; Wells 1–0–11–0.

Umpires: J. H. Evans and M. A. Gough.

At Taunton, August 7–10. NOTTINGHAMSHIRE drew with SOMERSET.

NOTTINGHAMSHIRE v DURHAM

At Nottingham, August 15–18. Durham won by 16 runs. Durham 19pts, Nottinghamshire 3pts. Toss: Nottinghamshire.

Seeking the win they needed to stay in the title race, Nottinghamshire prepared a seamer-friendly track. But it proved perfect for Onions's pacy, nagging length, and his nine wickets on the second day – seven bowled or lbw – led to their first defeat of 2012, and Durham's third successive win. Despite the loss of two first-day sessions, the strategy had seemed justified when Durham folded for 194. Onions, however, drove straight up from the Lord's Test after England released him on the second morning of this game. He missed lunch, but arrived in time to take the new ball: wreaking havoc in two spells, he looked set to follow former team-mate Ottis Gibson by claiming all ten wickets – and in a sense he did, running out Fletcher, the ninth to fall, with a direct hit from square leg. Stoneman's first century for a year maintained Durham's momentum, and Collingwood set a target of 366. Nottinghamshire gave it their all on an enthralling final day, launched by a belligerent 168-run opening partnership between Hales, also reaching his first hundred of the summer, and Wessels. But they came up just short in the penultimate over, as Mark Wood completed a maiden five-wicket haul. The defeat left them, in all probability, needing three wins from three matches – two of them against leaders Warwickshire – to pinch the title.

BEST BOWLING FOR DURHAM

10-47	O. D. Gibson	v Hampshire at Chester-le-Street	2007
9-64	M. M. Betts	v Northamptonshire at Northampton	1997
9-67	**G. Onions**	**v Nottinghamshire at Nottingham**	**2012**
8-24	M. Davies	v Hampshire at Basingstoke	2008
8-68	O. D. Gibson	v Lancashire at Blackpool	2007
8-101	G. Onions	v Warwickshire at Birmingham	2007
8-118	A. Walker	v Essex at Chelmsford	1995

Close of play: first day, Durham 85-4 (Benkenstein 16, Collingwood 9); second day, Durham 27-0 (Smith 5, Stoneman 19); third day, Durham 301-7 (Collingwood 51, Thorp 0).

Durham

First innings		Second innings	
M. D. Stoneman c Read b Fletcher	46	– (2) lbw b Phillips	114
W. R. Smith b Fletcher	3	– (1) c Read b Fletcher	15
K. K. Jennings lbw b Phillips	2	– lbw b Phillips	31
†P. Mustard c Read b Carter	9	– c Read b Carter	21
D. M. Benkenstein c Voges b Phillips	26	– c Lumb b Fletcher	19
*P. D. Collingwood c Lumb b Fletcher	21	– b White	59
S. G. Borthwick c Wessels b Carter	6	– b White	4
M. A. Wood c Read b White	34	– c Read b Fletcher	30
C. D. Thorp c Carter b Phillips	1	– not out	4
M. E. Claydon c Wessels b Carter	17		
C. Rushworth not out	24		
G. Onions (did not bat)		– (10) not out	11
L-b 2, w 1, n-b 2	5	B 2, l-b 8, w 1, n-b 6	17
1/14 (2) 2/33 (3) 3/48 (4) 4/75 (1) (68.2 overs)	194	1/62 (1) (8 wkts dec, 102 overs)	325
5/103 (6) 6/107 (5) 7/120 (7)		2/136 (3) 3/185 (2)	
8/123 (9) 9/144 (10) 10/194 (8)		4/193 (4) 5/225 (5)	
		6/236 (7) 7/297 (8) 8/314 (6)	

Onions replaced Claydon after being released from the England squad.

Phillips 18–6–39–3; Fletcher 18–4–57–3; Carter 13–3–40–3; Franks 11–3–37–0; Mullaney 4–1–9–0; White 4.2–1–10–1. *Second innings*—Phillips 22–7–48–2; Fletcher 20–8–47–3; Carter 24–5–76–1; Mullaney 2–1–2–0; Franks 13–1–41–0; White 21–3–101–2.

Nottinghamshire

M. H. Wessels b Onions	22	– c Thorp b Rushworth	98
A. D. Hales lbw b Onions	0	– lbw b Wood	101
M. J. Lumb lbw b Onions	12	– c Wood b Borthwick	16
A. C. Voges b Onions	9	– c Mustard b Onions	2
S. J. Mullaney lbw b Onions	23	– not out	60
*†C. M. W. Read c Mustard b Onions	0	– b Wood	8
P. J. Franks lbw b Onions	53	– c Thorp b Borthwick	13
G. G. White c Collingwood b Onions	13	– c Stoneman b Borthwick	8
B. J. Phillips not out	17	– c Borthwick b Wood	22
L. J. Fletcher run out	0	– b Wood	5
A. Carter b Onions	0	– lbw b Wood	0
B 1, l-b 4	5	B 6, l-b 5, w 1, n-b 4	16
1/3 (2) 2/31 (3) 3/41 (4) 4/50 (1) 5/50 (6) 6/115 (5) 7/132 (7) 8/153 (8) 9/154 (10) 10/154 (11) (42.3 overs)	154	1/168 (1) 2/199 (3) 3/212 (4) 4/248 (2) 5/258 (6) 6/288 (7) 7/303 (8) 8/330 (9) 9/349 (10) 10/349 (11) (88.4 overs)	349

Onions 16.3–2–67–9; Rushworth 6–3–10–0; Thorp 5–0–25–0; Wood 5–0–19–0; Borthwick 10–0–28–0. *Second innings*—Onions 17–3–58–1; Rushworth 17–2–61–1; Wood 23.4–2–78–5; Thorp 9–1–47–0; Borthwick 22–1–94–3.

Umpires: S. C. Gale and R. A. Kettleborough.

At Birmingham, August 28–31. NOTTINGHAMSHIRE drew with WARWICKSHIRE.

At The Oval, September 4–7. NOTTINGHAMSHIRE lost to SURREY by 195 runs.

NOTTINGHAMSHIRE v WARWICKSHIRE

At Nottingham, September 11–14. Drawn. Nottinghamshire 6pts, Warwickshire 7pts. Toss: Warwickshire.

Nottinghamshire could still claim the prize money for finishing second or third if they beat Warwickshire, who had won the title in the previous round, and they came close on the final evening, only to be defied for 13 overs by the ninth-wicket pair; in the end they had to settle for fifth. Shorn of four front-rank batsmen, Nottinghamshire had managed just 155 first time round, with England Under-19 player Sam Kelsall, on his home Championship debut, playing on to the game's third ball. But Carter claimed three in ten deliveries to keep them in touch, before their batsmen rolled up their sleeves on the third day when Barker was missing with an ankle injury. Edwards recorded only his third Championship half-century in three seasons, then learned he was being released, and Mullaney and Franks made hefty contributions. Read challenged Warwickshire to score 421 in 90 overs, and held three catches as Fletcher reduced them to 32 for three. But Woakes's defiant 80 helped the new champions hang on for the draw. Franks, who had been told he was free to find another county, collected four for 47, his best return since 2004, and a sign he would stay and fight for his place.

Close of play: first day, Warwickshire 139-6 (Clarke 21, Blackwell 28); second day, Nottinghamshire 49-0 (Kelsall 25, Edwards 16); third day, Nottinghamshire 444-8 (Franks 76, Fletcher 27).

Nottinghamshire

S. Kelsall b Woakes	0	– c Clarke b Patel	35
N. J. Edwards lbw b Barker	3	– lbw b Patel	53
M. H. Wessels lbw b Woakes	13	– lbw b Clarke	38
J. W. A. Taylor lbw b Clarke	17	– c Troughton b Patel	14
S. J. Mullaney c Chopra b Barker	14	– c Troughton b Patel	94
*†C. M. W. Read b Wright	18	– run out	36
P. J. Franks b Wright	44	– not out	86
G. G. White c Clarke b Patel	6	– lbw b Blackwell	1
B. J. Phillips c Johnson b Wright	13	– c Johnson b Maddy	38
L. J. Fletcher not out	11	– not out	42
A. Carter c Westwood b Wright	4		
L-b 8, n-b 4	12	B 14, l-b 11, w 5, n-b 2	32
1/0 (1) 2/16 (2) 3/18 (3) (49.4 overs)	155	1/88 (1) (8 wkts dec, 116 overs)	469
4/41 (5) 5/68 (6) 6/83 (4)		2/137 (3) 3/141 (2)	
7/92 (8) 8/130 (9) 9/143 (7) 10/155 (11)		4/168 (4) 5/287 (6)	
		6/296 (5) 7/297 (8) 8/388 (9)	

Woakes 10–2–27–2; Barker 15–2–53–2; Wright 10.4–3–28–4; Clarke 11–2–33–1; Patel 3–0–6–1. *Second innings*—Woakes 19–4–71–0; Barker 4–0–15–0; Wright 17–2–78–0; Patel 34–7–142–4; Clarke 10–1–44–1; Blackwell 25–5–72–1; Maddy 7–1–22–1.

Warwickshire

V. Chopra b Phillips	16	– c Read b Fletcher	8
I. J. Westwood lbw b Phillips	1	– c Mullaney b White	46
D. L. Maddy b Carter	41	– c Read b Fletcher	5
*J. O. Troughton c Read b Fletcher	10	– c Read b Fletcher	2
†R. M. Johnson b Carter	22	– (8) lbw b Franks	0
R. Clarke b Carter	37	– (5) b Franks	31
C. R. Woakes c Read b Carter	0	– (6) c Edwards b Franks	80
I. D. Blackwell c Mullaney b Phillips	37	– (7) c Mullaney b Franks	44
K. H. D. Barker not out	22	– not out	44
C. J. C. Wright c Read b Franks	3	– not out	19
J. S. Patel c Edwards b Franks	14		
L-b 1	1	L-b 8, w 1, n-b 2	11
1/5 (2) 2/30 (1) 3/45 (4) (65.5 overs)	204	1/14 (1) (8 wkts, 89.5 overs)	290
4/85 (3) 5/90 (5) 6/90 (7) 7/162 (8)		2/30 (3) 3/32 (4)	
8/173 (6) 9/178 (10) 10/204 (11)		4/78 (5) 5/135 (2)	
		6/224 (7) 7/224 (8) 8/235 (6)	

Phillips 19–6–60–3; Fletcher 19–3–45–1; Carter 11–2–55–4; Franks 16.5–1–43–2. *Second innings*—Phillips 16–4–45–0; Fletcher 21–5–58–3; Carter 18.5–2–87–0; Franks 14–4–47–4; White 18–6–42–1; Wessels 2–0–3–0.

Umpires: J. H. Evans and N. A. Mallender.

SOMERSET

So near, so far – so often

RICHARD LATHAM

Somerset came second yet again, this time in their quest for a maiden Championship title, taking their tally of runners-up finishes in domestic competitions to eight in four seasons – and without a single trophy to show for it. This time, however, there was pride rather than frustration in their narrow failure: a season dogged by injury problems – described by outgoing director of cricket Brian Rose as the worst he had known in his long association with the county – ended with an epic chase of 396 at Hove and a thumping innings victory over Worcestershire at Taunton to claim a final position Somerset had previously achieved only in 2001 and 2010.

In the third Championship match, captain Marcus Trescothick injured his ankle, and required surgery, which ruled him out of the next seven fixtures, as well as the entire Twenty20 group stage and the first six CB40 games. A catalogue of fitness issues meant 24 players featured in the Championship, with only Arul Suppiah, James Hildreth and Peter Trego ever-present. At times, the queue for the treatment room was so long that Somerset – also affected by international call-ups for Craig Kieswetter, Jos Buttler, Nick Compton and George Dockrell – fielded the only 11 available, and relied on promising youngsters like the Overton twins, 18-year-olds Jamie and Craig from Barnstaple, to mature quickly. Sajid Mahmood was brought in on loan from Lancashire in August, but did not make enough of an impression to secure a permanent move, and was later signed by Essex instead.

Compton and Hildreth played themselves into form with a county-record partnership of 450 before a ball was bowled in the Championship, both scoring double-centuries against Cardiff MCCU in a game that started on the final day of March. Five and a half months later, the pair occupied the top two places in the country's scoring charts: Compton led the way with 1,494 first-class runs at an average of 99; Hildreth was next, with 1,214 at 52. Kieswetter averaged 60 in 13 appearances.

In one of the wettest seasons on record, with legions of batsmen struggling against the seaming ball, the defensive technique Compton had honed over countless hours of net practice set him apart. An unbeaten 204 at Trent Bridge was the highlight, and he failed by one day to become the first man since Graeme Hick to reach 1,000 runs by the end of May. His selection for England Lions and the Test tour of India was fully deserved.

Trego weighed in with 600 runs, and shouldered a much heavier workload as a seamer than before, sending down more than 500 overs and taking 50 wickets for the first time in his career – many with the new ball. The 50th, that of Worcestershire's Phillip Hughes on the last day of the last match, prompted his team-mates to engulf him soccer-style – testimony to his popularity. Next

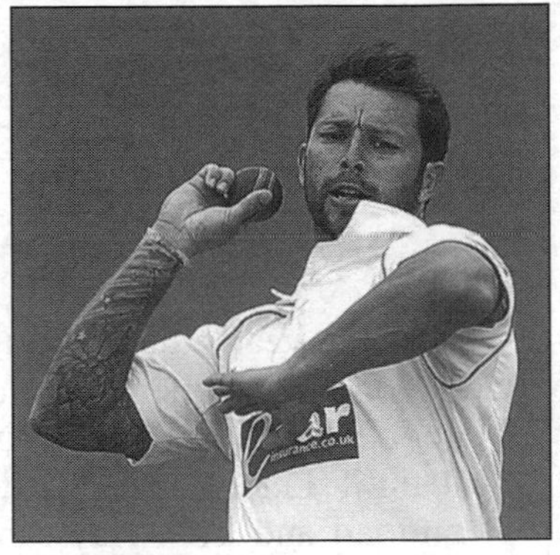
David Davies, PA Photos

Peter Trego

best, with 34 wickets, was Dockrell, the club's leading spinner following the departure of Murali Kartik – who returned to Taunton in August with Surrey, and caused uproar by running out Alex Barrow for backing up too far.

Vernon Philander, Kartik's initial replacement as overseas player, claimed 23 wickets at the beginning of the season – seven of them to inspire a county notorious for their slow starts to victory against Middlesex in the opening game – before returning to help South Africa dismantle England. The likeable Abdur Rehman's 27 wickets in four Championship appearances as the summer drew to a close were tainted when it emerged he had tested positive for cannabis on debut against Nottinghamshire at Taunton. His 12-week ban for recreational drug use was fully supported by the county, but he was re-engaged for the second part of the 2013 summer, when he was due to replace Alviro Petersen, the South African Test opener, who will be at his third county in three seasons.

If Somerset overachieved in Championship cricket, they failed to reach previous standards in the one-day formats. Four straight defeats at the start of the CB40, when the squad was ravaged by injuries, proved so damaging that not even six consecutive victories could earn a semi-final place.

Buttler again showed his liking for 40-over cricket, with 289 runs, but only Kieswetter scored a century, and Somerset's batting lacked its customary intimidation. In this competition, above all, the club relied on its Academy and schoolboy development programme, with the Overtons, Barrow, Craig Meschede, Chris Jones, Lewis Gregory and Jack Leach all given opportunities, sometimes more out of necessity than choice.

Hopes were high for the Twenty20, despite a frustrating build-up in which Somerset missed out on signing Chris Gayle and Faf du Plessis. The club eventually recruited South African power-hitters Richard Levi and Albie Morkel, who both missed games through international duty. Even with Trescothick absent, Somerset looked certainties to reach the knockout stages, until unexpected home defeats by Gloucestershire and Worcestershire. They recovered to qualify as group winners, then beat Essex in the quarter-finals to reach finals day for the fourth consecutive season. With Trescothick fit again, it was assumed the cidermen would at last quaff some celebration scrumpy. Instead, a feeble semi-final batting display handed victory to Hampshire.

It was one marquee defeat too many for Rose, whose eight-year spell as director of cricket, in which he helped transform Somerset from Championship also-rans into the country's strongest all-round team, was ended by mutual consent soon afterwards. He was succeeded by the South African Dave Nosworthy, formerly coach of Highveld Lions.

Championship attendance: 36,815.

THE RACE FOR 1,000

Spring fever

PATRICK KIDD

Of all last year's damp squibs, perhaps the most agonising was Nick Compton's rain-foiled pursuit of 1,000 first-class runs by the end of May. Marooned 50 short by the Worcester weather on May 31, Compton had to wait until June 1 instead. It was his 13th innings, as many as Wally Hammond and Tom Hayward had taken, and fewer than Bill Edrich or Glenn Turner – four of the eight men who have achieved the feat (see page 1264). But because he got there a day late, history records only that Compton made 1,000 runs earlier than anyone since Graeme Hick, in 1988.

The first to do it was W. G. Grace in 1895 – and he needed the fewest days, 22. Some members of the 1,000 club cut things fine. Hick went into his final match in May needing 153 against the touring West Indians; he hit 172. Hayward got there with 92 for Surrey on May 31, 1900. Charlie Hallows of Lancashire needed every run of the 232 he made in his last innings in May 1928.

Others had luck on their side. Don Bradman was thankful when Clarrie Grimmett skittled Hampshire for 151 on May 31, 1930. Needing 46 that afternoon, Bradman opened and made 47 before rain intervened. Eight years later – and four days after he had become the only man to join the club twice – he generously declared Australia's innings against Middlesex to allow Edrich to make the ten runs he required.

Compton, though, leads a gang of nearly men (see page 665). Of the three who got to four figures two days late, Jim Parks was on 927 by May 31, 1937. He batted twice on June 2, after Sussex and Essex were both dismissed cheaply, reaching 1,000 in his second innings. John Langridge, another Sussex man, who began the 1949 season with four hundreds in five innings, was still 221 short by the end of May – but then made 234 in four hours. Rob Key also came close, completing the landmark on June 2, 2004, midway through his innings of 180 for Kent against Lancashire. It was his fifth century in seven innings.

Maurice Hallam was once named with Langridge in John Arlott's list of the best XI never to earn a Test cap for England. Hallam had made 632 by the end of May 30, 1959. After a rest day in Leicestershire's match against Glamorgan, he scored another 194 on June 1, then 157 on June 2. He passed 1,000 two days later with 63 against Nottinghamshire. Don Kenyon got there on June 5, 1954 – but in his fourth innings of the month. Pakistan's Zaheer Abbas did so on the 1971 tour on June 4, five runs from the end of his 274 in the Edgbaston Test. Brian Lara nearly joins the list of nearly men. He reached 1,000 in 1994 on June 6 in his seventh first-class innings of the season, the same number Bradman had needed in 1938.

SOMERSET RESULTS

All first-class matches – Played 17: Won 5, Lost 1, Drawn 11.
County Championship matches – Played 16: Won 5, Lost 1, Drawn 10.

LV= County Championship, 2nd in Division 1;
Friends Life t20, s-f; Clydesdale Bank 40, 3rd in Group B.

COUNTY CHAMPIONSHIP AVERAGES, BATTING AND FIELDING

Cap		*M*	*I*	*NO*	*R*	*HS*	*100*	*50*	*Avge*	*Ct/St*
2011	N. R. D. Compton	11	18	6	1,191	204*	4	7	99.25	7
2009	C. Kieswetter‡	11	17	4	654	152	1	2	50.30	28/1
2007	J. C. Hildreth	16	25	3	946	120	3	5	43.00	16
1999	M. E. Trescothick†	9	13	0	506	146	2	1	38.92	26
2007	P. D. Trego†	16	21	3	600	92	0	4	33.33	12
2009	A. V. Suppiah	16	25	0	728	124	2	5	29.12	9
	J. Overton	3	4	2	55	34*	0	0	27.50	1
	J. C. Buttler†	12	16	1	400	93	0	2	26.66	12/1
	C. A. J. Meschede¶	6	6	0	135	62	0	1	22.50	2
	C. R. Jones	5	7	0	150	50	0	1	21.42	2
	G. M. Hussain	5	7	4	55	29	0	0	18.33	0
	A. W. R. Barrow†	9	15	0	186	47	0	0	12.40	14
	C. Overton	7	8	1	75	50	0	1	10.71	4
	V. D. Philander§	5	6	0	62	38	0	0	10.33	2
	L. Gregory	4	4	0	40	18	0	0	10.00	0
2008	A. C. Thomas¶	9	11	1	96	39*	0	0	9.60	1
	G. H. Dockrell	10	10	4	54	13*	0	0	9.00	5
	Abdur Rehman§	4	5	0	43	17	0	0	8.60	2
	S. I. Mahmood	3	4	1	25	13	0	0	8.33	1
	S. P. Kirby	9	11	5	20	6*	0	0	3.33	4

Also batted: A. J. Dibble (1 match) 1, 43; M. J. Leach† (2 matches) 0*; S. D. Snell (2 matches) 8, 10 (8 ct); M. T. C. Waller (2 matches) 4, 17, 3 (4 ct).

† *Born in Somerset.* ‡ *ECB contract.* § *Official overseas player.* ¶ *Other non-England-qualified player.*

BOWLING

	Style	*O*	*M*	*R*	*W*	*BB*	*5I*	*Avge*
Abdur Rehman	SLA	174	50	383	27	9-65	3	14.18
V. D. Philander	RFM	181.1	42	491	23	5-43	2	21.34
A. C. Thomas	RFM	252.4	50	740	33	6-60	2	22.42
G. H. Dockrell	SLA	309.5	67	950	34	6-27	2	27.94
G. M. Hussain	RFM	92.4	17	353	12	5-48	1	29.41
C. Overton	RFM	113.1	23	363	12	4-38	0	30.25
S. P. Kirby	RFM	225.1	47	735	24	3-34	0	30.62
P. D. Trego	RFM	508.5	123	1,554	50	5-53	2	31.08
C. A. J. Meschede	RM	98	18	350	10	3-26	0	35.00

Also bowled: J. C. Buttler (RM) 2–0–11–0; A. J. Dibble (RFM) 13–2–42–3; L. Gregory (RM) 24–2–127–4; J. C. Hildreth (RM) 2–0–30–0; C. R. Jones (RM) 2–0–17–1; C. Kieswetter (OB) 3–0–3–2; M. J. Leach (SLA) 20–4–43–2; S. I. Mahmood (RFM) 66.1–10–241–8; J. Overton (RFM) 66–7–229–6; A. V. Suppiah (SLA) 73–18–211–3; M. T. C. Waller (LBG) 19–2–83–1.

LEADING CB40 AVERAGES (100 runs/4 wickets)

Batting	*Runs*	*HS*	*Avge*	*SR*	*Ct*
A. W. R. Barrow	108	72	54.00	87.09	2
N. R. D. Compton	237	81	47.40	77.45	1
J. C. Buttler	289	71	41.28	90.59	4
M. E. Trescothick	118	87*	39.33	108.25	5
C. Kieswetter	236	103	33.71	122.91	7
P. D. Trego	245	81	27.22	130.31	3

Bowling	*W*	*BB*	*Avge*	*ER*
Abdur Rehman	9	6-16	8.11	3.50
J. Overton	6	4-42	16.66	5.88
S. P. Kirby	8	3-19	21.87	4.32
C. A. J. Meschede	9	4-27	22.00	5.65
A. C. Thomas	5	2-13	22.40	4.14
P. D. Trego	15	3-26	24.80	6.03

LEADING FLT20 AVERAGES (100 runs/17 overs)

Batting	Runs	HS	Avge	SR	Ct/St
R. E. Levi	179	69	25.57	**161.26**	3
J. C. Hildreth	223	107*	44.60	**133.53**	3
C. Kieswetter	134	63*	44.66	**120.72**	0/3
J. C. Buttler	195	58*	27.85	**116.07**	4/1
N. R. D. Compton	120	42*	24.00	**97.56**	2

Bowling	W	BB	Avge	ER
S. P. Kirby	8	3-37	21.37	**6.41**
G. H. Dockrell	9	2-17	18.77	**6.50**
L. Gregory	6	4-39	20.00	**6.85**
M. T. C. Waller	7	4-16	21.14	**7.04**
A. C. Thomas	8	3-17	35.25	**8.54**

FIRST-CLASS COUNTY RECORDS

Highest score for	342	J. L. Langer v Surrey at Guildford	2006
Highest score against	424	A. C. MacLaren (Lancashire) at Taunton	1895
Leading run-scorer	21,142	H. Gimblett (avge 36.96)	1935–1954
Best bowling for	10-49	E. J. Tyler v Surrey at Taunton	1895
Best bowling against	10-35	A. Drake (Yorkshire) at Weston-super-Mare	1914
Leading wicket-taker	2,165	J. C. White (avge 18.03)	1909–1937
Highest total for	850-7 dec	v Middlesex at Taunton	2007
Highest total against	811	by Surrey at The Oval	1899
Lowest total for	25	v Gloucestershire at Bristol	1947
Lowest total against	22	by Gloucestershire at Bristol	1920

LIST A COUNTY RECORDS

Highest score for	184	M. E. Trescothick v Gloucestershire at Taunton	2008
Highest score against	167*	A. J. Stewart (Surrey) at The Oval	1994
Leading run-scorer	7,349	I. V. A. Richards (avge 39.94)	1974–1986
Best bowling for	8-66	S. R. G. Francis v Derbyshire at Derby	2004
Best bowling against	7-39	A. Hodgson (Northamptonshire) at Northampton	1976
Leading wicket-taker	309	H. R. Moseley (avge 20.03)	1971–1982
Highest total for	413-4	v Devon at Torquay	1990
Highest total against	357-3	by Warwickshire at Birmingham	1995
Lowest total for	58	v Essex at Chelmsford	1977
	58	v Middlesex at Southgate	2000
Lowest total against	60	by Kent at Taunton	1979

TWENTY20 COUNTY RECORDS

Highest score for	141*	C. L. White v Worcestershire at Worcester	2006
Highest score against	116*	I. J. Thomas (Glamorgan) at Taunton	2004
Leading run-scorer	**2,056**	**J. C. Hildreth (avge 23.90)**	**2004–2012**
Best bowling for	6-5	A. V. Suppiah v Glamorgan at Cardiff	2011
Best bowling against	5-18	O. P. Rayner (Sussex) at Hove	2011
Leading wicket-taker	**94**	**A. C. Thomas (avge 18.37)**	**2008–2012**
Highest total for	250-3	v Gloucestershire at Taunton	2006
Highest total against	227-4	by Gloucestershire at Bristol	2006
Lowest total for	82	v Kent at Taunton	2010
Lowest total against	82	by Essex at Chelmsford	2011

ADDRESS

County Ground, St James's Street, Taunton TA1 1JT (0845 337 1875; **email** enquiries@somersetcountycc.co.uk). **Website** www.somersetcountycc.co.uk

OFFICIALS

Captain M. E. Trescothick
Director of cricket 2012 – B. C. Rose
2013 – D. O. Nosworthy
Head coach A. Hurry
Academy director J. I. D. Kerr
President R. C. Kerslake

Chairman A. J. Nash
Chief executive G. W. Lavender
Chairman, cricket committee V. J. Marks
Head groundsman S. Lee
Scorer G. A. Stickley

SOMERSET v CARDIFF MCCU

At Taunton Vale, March 31–April 2. Drawn. Toss: Somerset. First-class debuts: J. E. Burke, J. A. Regan, A. P. Sutton; A. Balbirnie, S. L. Davies, Z. Elkin, T. Friend, P. G. Harris, M. E. Hobden, M. J. Leach, U. A. Qureshi, A. G. Salter, H. G. Siddique.

Both Cardiff MCCU and the Taunton Vale ground made their first-class debuts in what had become a regular warm-up fixture: Compton and Hildreth marked the occasion by rewriting Somerset's batting records. They put on 450, surpassing by 104 the previous Somerset all-wicket record partnership, between Lionel Palairet and Herbert Hewett, made a mile away at the County Ground against Yorkshire in 1892. Zac Elkin had given an early indication of the docile surface by defying an inexperienced attack for six and a half hours, as he and Cardiff batted through the first day.

Close of play: first day, Cardiff MCCU 308-5 (Elkin 127, Friend 35); second day, Somerset 447-1 (Compton 180, Hildreth 200).

Cardiff MCCU

W. S. Jones c Compton b Hussain	5	– c Meschede b Sutton	34
†Z. Elkin lbw b Meschede	138	– c Trego b Dockrell	14
H. G. Siddique lbw b Burke	11	– b Waller	1
*A. Balbirnie b Meschede	19		
U. A. Qureshi run out	47	– (4) lbw b Waller	15
S. L. Davies lbw b Burke	42	– (5) lbw b Waller	14
T. Friend c Hildreth b Sutton	48	– (6) not out	32
A. G. Salter not out	7	– (7) not out	7
P. G. Harris not out	3		
B 1, l-b 9, w 4, n-b 8	22	B 1, l-b 6, n-b 2	9
1/8 (1) 2/32 (3) 3/61 (4) 4/157 (5) 5/244 (6) 6/332 (7) 7/332 (2) (7 wkts dec, 109 overs)	342	1/45 (1) 2/46 (3) 3/54 (2) 4/81 (5) 5/84 (4) (5 wkts, 55 overs)	126

M. J. Leach and M. E. Hobden did not bat

Hussain 9–0–32–1; Sutton 24–5–68–1; Burke 14–2–51–2; Trego 11–1–37–0; Meschede 21–4–68–2; Dockrell 11–3–26–0; Waller 12–3–29–0; Suppiah 7–0–21–0. *Second innings*—Trego 4–1–18–0; Sutton 6–1–31–1; Waller 21–9–33–3; Dockrell 20–10–20–1; Burke 4–1–17–0.

Somerset

N. R. D. Compton c Friend b Salter	236
A. V. Suppiah c Jones b Salter	41
*J. C. Hildreth c Davies b Salter	268
P. D. Trego not out	30
C. A. J. Meschede not out	37
B 10, l-b 4, w 4, n-b 12	30
1/121 (2) 2/571 (1) 3/578 (3) (3 wkts dec, 141 overs)	642

J. E. Burke, †J. A. Regan, M. T. C. Waller, G. M. Hussain, G. H. Dockrell and A. P. Sutton did not bat.

Friend 20–2–91–0; Hobden 24–0–133–0; Harris 16–0–74–0; Salter 33–2–134–3; Leach 41–1–151–0; Jones 7–0–45–0.

Umpires: M. Burns and J. W. Lloyds.

SOMERSET v MIDDLESEX

At Taunton, April 5–8. Somerset won by six wickets. Somerset 22pts, Middlesex 3pts. Toss: Somerset. County debuts: V. D. Philander; J. L. Denly.

Somerset's decision to beef up their pre-season preparations – they had lost their opening two Championship games in the previous two seasons – bore fruit with a positive display led by new overseas signing Vernon Philander. Despite describing the truncated first day as the coldest he had experienced as a cricketer, Philander – a different proposition from the 22-year-old who spent an unremarkable month with Middlesex in 2008 – had Robson caught behind with his third ball and claimed four more victims in the innings, though Denly resisted with 73 on debut for his new county. Compton, also playing against his former side, took six and a half hours to make 99 before pulling to midwicket, though he and Kieswetter earned a lead of 104. Middlesex overtook that on the last morning only one wicket down, and were in a strong position to avoid defeat in their first top-flight match since 2006. But they suffered a shocking collapse, losing their last seven for 40 as Dockrell found surprising turn and bounce from the River End in a destructive career-best spell.

Close of play: first day, Middlesex 118-4 (Denly 64, Simpson 2); second day, Somerset 202-3 (Compton 58, Kieswetter 50); third day, Middlesex 38-1 (Robson 24, Rogers 5).

Middlesex

S. D. Robson c Kieswetter b Philander	0	– (2) lbw b Dockrell	43
J. L. Denly c and b Kirby	73	– (1) lbw b Kirby	9
C. J. L. Rogers c Dockrell b Meschede	17	– c Kieswetter b Dockrell	50
D. J. Malan lbw b Philander	12	– c Kieswetter b Philander	23
*N. J. Dexter b Philander	8	– c Kieswetter b Philander	6
†J. A. Simpson c Dockrell b Philander	15	– c Trescothick b Dockrell	2
G. K. Berg lbw b Philander	7	– lbw b Dockrell	1
O. P. Rayner lbw b Dockrell	14	– st Kieswetter b Dockrell	3
T. J. Murtagh run out	45	– c Compton b Kirby	10
T. S. Roland-Jones not out	23	– c Buttler b Dockrell	10
C. D. Collymore lbw b Dockrell	1	– not out	0
B 8, l-b 9, n-b 14	31	B 4, l-b 8, n-b 6	18
1/0 (1) 2/51 (3) 3/90 (4) 4/114 (5) 5/130 (2) 6/143 (7) 7/150 (6) 8/193 (8) 9/228 (9) 10/246 (11) (68.4 overs)	246	1/27 (1) 2/105 (2) 3/118 (3) 4/135 (5) 5/138 (6) 6/148 (4) 7/150 (7) 8/157 (8) 9/175 (9) 10/175 (10) (72.1 overs)	175

Philander 20–6–43–5; Kirby 20–2–79–1; Meschede 5–1–29–1; Trego 13–3–43–0; Dockrell 10.4–3–35–2. *Second innings*—Philander 18–3–38–2; Kirby 19–4–50–2; Trego 7–2–27–0; Meschede 7–3–20–0; Dockrell 20.1–8–27–6; Suppiah 1–0–1–0.

Somerset

*M. E. Trescothick c Dexter b Rayner	47	– c Rayner b Berg	0
A. V. Suppiah c Simpson b Berg	35	– c Simpson b Berg	12
N. R. D. Compton c Rogers b Roland-Jones	99	– c Malan b Denly	8
J. C. Hildreth b Berg	1	– not out	37
†C. Kieswetter c Malan b Collymore	83	– b Berg	0
J. C. Buttler b Murtagh	14	– not out	16
P. D. Trego b Murtagh	12		
C. A. J. Meschede c Malan b Roland-Jones	37		
V. D. Philander b Collymore	2		
G. H. Dockrell c Rayner b Collymore	0		
S. P. Kirby not out	0		
B 5, l-b 11, n-b 4	20		
1/55 (2) 2/102 (1) 3/103 (4) 4/255 (5) 5/274 (6) 6/298 (7) 7/333 (3) 8/342 (9) 9/342 (10) 10/350 (8) (115 overs) 110 overs: 333-6	350	1/0 (1) 2/13 (2) 3/43 (3) 4/44 (5) (4 wkts, 16 overs)	73

Collymore 23–7–66–3; Murtagh 27–5–88–2; Berg 23–8–60–2; Roland-Jones 25–4–76–2; Rayner 16–5–36–1; Malan 1–0–8–0. *Second innings*—Berg 8–3–25–3; Rayner 5–0–30–0; Denly 3–0–18–1.

Umpires: R. J. Bailey and M. J. D. Bodenham.

At Birmingham, April 12–15. SOMERSET lost to WARWICKSHIRE by two wickets.

At Nottingham, April 19–22. SOMERSET drew with NOTTINGHAMSHIRE.

SOMERSET v LANCASHIRE

At Taunton, April 26–29. Drawn. Somerset 6pts, Lancashire 9pts. Toss: Lancashire. First-class debut: C. Overton.

Croft's 153-ball hundred, on the ground where he had clinched Lancashire's long-awaited Championship title seven months earlier, proved the highlight of a match ruined by rain on days two and three and a washout on the last. Lancashire had lost the first two fixtures of their title defence, and so were grateful to run into a largely inexperienced Somerset attack, which improved on the second morning but offered the batsmen easy relief from Philander and Trego. With Steve Kirby, Gemaal Hussain and Adam Dibble missing through injury, and Alfonso Thomas at the IPL, Somerset gave a debut to 18-year-old Craig Overton from North Devon CC, selected just ahead of twin brother Jamie. He claimed his maiden wicket when Prince pulled to midwicket, but by then Prince had scored 96 and shared a fluent fourth-wicket stand of 208 with Croft. Last man Kerrigan helped secure the fifth batting point before completing Philander's second five-wicket haul for Somerset.

Close of play: first day, Lancashire 363-4 (Croft 113, Cross 20); second day, Lancashire 395-9 (Hogg 3, Kerrigan 1); third day, Somerset 87-3 (Compton 30, Kieswetter 4).

Lancashire

P. J. Horton lbw b Philander	2
S. C. Moore lbw b Trego	47
K. R. Brown lbw b Gregory	50
A. G. Prince c Compton b Overton	96
S. J. Croft c Kieswetter b Philander	113
†G. D. Cross c Kieswetter b Philander	21
L. A. Procter c Kieswetter b Trego	1
*G. Chapple c Hildreth b Dockrell	20
S. I. Mahmood b Philander	3
K. W. Hogg not out	4
S. C. Kerrigan c Suppiah b Philander	1
B 8, l-b 8, n-b 26	42
1/2 (1) 2/97 (3) (108.3 overs)	400
3/118 (2) 4/326 (4) 5/364 (6)	
6/365 (7) 7/365 (5) 8/371 (9)	
9/391 (8) 10/400 (11)	

Philander 24.3–8–71–5; Trego 32–7–76–2; Meschede 13–1–54–0; Overton 14–1–59–1; Gregory 5–0–49–1; Dockrell 20–2–75–1.

Somerset

A. V. Suppiah b Chapple	5
L. Gregory c Horton b Chapple	15
N. R. D. Compton not out	30
*J. C. Hildreth lbw b Procter	30
†C. Kieswetter not out	4
L-b 1, n-b 2	3
1/17 (2) 2/28 (1) (3 wkts, 38 overs)	87
3/81 (4)	

J. C. Buttler, P. D. Trego, C. A. J. Meschede, V. D. Philander, C. Overton and G. H. Dockrell did not bat.

Chapple 11–5–15–2; Hogg 8–4–14–0; Mahmood 7–2–34–0; Procter 7–2–12–1; Kerrigan 5–2–11–0.

Umpires: N. L. Bainton and M. J. Saggers.

At Chester-le-Street, May 9–12. SOMERSET drew with DURHAM.

At The Oval, May 16–19. SOMERSET drew with SURREY.

SOMERSET v DURHAM

At Taunton, May 22–24. Somerset won by five wickets. Somerset 24pts, Durham 7pts. Toss: Durham. First-class debut: J. Harrison.

A Somerset team including the 18-year-old Overton twins, 19-year-old Dockrell, 20-year-old Barrow, and Buttler, a comparative veteran at 21, were too good for Durham, who looked distinctly long in the tooth. That didn't seem to matter while their opening pair were putting on 158: Di Venuto rattled along to the first Championship fifty of the season from Durham's top six, and Will Smith followed with a chanceless century. But from a teatime score of 262 for two they carelessly surrendered wickets and failed to achieve maximum batting points. Somerset did not make the same mistake: Trego played with unusual discretion, while Craig Overton, in a maiden fifty from only 53 balls, dealt harshly with Harmison and Plunkett, who went for a combined one for 129 in their first 23 overs of the Championship season. Collingwood and Blackwell appeared to restore calm, until Blackwell chipped a return catch to Dockrell to spark an astonishing downturn. Dockrell struck four times as Durham writhed on 131, and swept up the last six wickets in 35 balls. Somerset knocked off their modest target, but Compton still emerged with a sense of frustration: a second soft dismissal in the match to Blackwell meant he needed to find 59 from the first two days at Worcester to achieve 1,000 runs before the end of May.

Close of play: first day, Durham 353-8 (Plunkett 7, Harrison 3); second day, Somerset 357-8 (Trego 67, Dockrell 3).

Durham

First innings		Second innings	
M. J. Di Venuto c Kieswetter b Thomas	96	– (2) c Hildreth b J. Overton	26
W. R. Smith c Thomas b J. Overton	100	– (1) c Trego b Thomas	22
M. D. Stoneman run out	27	– c Hildreth b C. Overton	13
B. A. Stokes run out	60	– c Barrow b C. Overton	0
P. D. Collingwood c Suppiah b Dockrell	12	– c Hildreth b Dockrell	32
I. D. Blackwell c Compton b J. Overton	7	– c and b Dockrell	38
*†P. Mustard c Dockrell b Trego	21	– c Barrow b Dockrell	0
L. E. Plunkett c Kieswetter b Thomas	24	– c C. Overton b Dockrell	0
C. D. Thorp c Barrow b Trego	0	– c J. Overton b Dockrell	0
J. Harrison c Barrow b Trego	15	– c Buttler b Dockrell	20
S. J. Harmison not out	2	– not out	3
B 5, l-b 12, w 1, n-b 2	20	B 4, l-b 8, w 1	13
1/158 (1) 2/232 (3) 3/265 (2) 4/284 (5) 5/295 (6) 6/326 (4) 7/350 (7) 8/350 (9) 9/366 (10) 10/384 (8) (105.2 overs)	384	1/36 (2) 2/69 (3) 3/69 (4) 4/69 (1) 5/131 (6) 6/131 (7) 7/131 (8) 8/131 (9) 9/158 (5) 10/167 (10) (50.4 overs)	167

Trego 25–5–90–3; J. Overton 14–0–61–2; Thomas 19.2–3–68–2; C. Overton 18–7–51–0; Dockrell 21–6–63–1; Suppiah 8–2–34–0. *Second innings*—Trego 10–3–34–0; J. Overton 11–2–45–1; Thomas 11–4–22–1; C. Overton 7–3–25–2; Dockrell 11.4–4–29–6.

Somerset

First innings		Second innings	
A. V. Suppiah lbw b Harrison	4	– (2) lbw b Smith	73
A. W. R. Barrow c Mustard b Harmison	25	– (1) lbw b Harrison	0
N. R. D. Compton c Thorp b Blackwell	64	– c Collingwood b Blackwell	8
*J. C. Hildreth b Harrison	53	– c Thorp b Harmison	31
†C. Kieswetter lbw b Thorp	42	– not out	22
J. C. Buttler c Mustard b Blackwell	0	– c Harmison b Blackwell	7
P. D. Trego b Harrison	89	– not out	4
C. Overton c Mustard b Harrison	50		
A. C. Thomas c Stokes b Blackwell	18		
G. H. Dockrell not out	11		
J. Overton not out	9		
B 4, l-b 4, w 1, n-b 26	35	B 4, l-b 1, n-b 2	7
1/6 (1) 2/66 (2) 3/138 (4) 4/199 (3) 5/203 (6) 6/209 (5) 7/308 (8) 8/338 (9) 9/389 (7) (9 wkts dec, 91.5 overs)	400	1/0 (1) 2/17 (3) 3/100 (4) 4/129 (2) 5/138 (6) (5 wkts, 33.4 overs)	152

Harrison 22–3–112–4; Thorp 21.5–4–77–1; Plunkett 12–0–69–0; Harmison 11–2–60–1; Blackwell 25–7–74–3. *Second innings*—Harrison 5–0–19–1; Blackwell 13–0–68–2; Thorp 6–3–6–0; Harmison 4–0–22–1; Smith 5.4–1–32–1.

Umpires: J. W. Lloyds and M. J. Saggers.

At Worcester, May 30–June 2. SOMERSET drew with WORCESTERSHIRE. *Nick Compton reaches 1,000 first-class runs on June 1.*

At Lord's, June 5–8. SOMERSET drew with MIDDLESEX.

At Taunton, July 9–10. SOMERSET drew with SOUTH AFRICANS (see South African tour section).

SOMERSET v WARWICKSHIRE

At Taunton, July 18–21. Somerset won by one wicket. Somerset 21pts, Warwickshire 8pts. Toss: Somerset.

In one of the competition's best matches for years, Kieswetter's stunning 152, from 170 balls, powered Somerset to a memorable victory over the Championship leaders. Entering at 15 for three in a pursuit of 271, Kieswetter went on the rampage against Patel's off-spin, hauling him over the leg-side ropes three times in an over to bring up his hundred; another six off Wright had seven Warwickshire fielders despatched to the boundary in his next over. Somerset were 12 away when Kieswetter was sixth out, hooking to long leg, before Barker – suddenly scenting blood – had three others caught in the slips for the addition of only ten runs. In a thrilling finish, No. 11 Hussain had to see him out for five balls, before Trego clipped the first delivery of Patel's next over through midwicket for the winning runs. That meant Barker's career-best six wickets went unrewarded, as did centuries for Troughton and Woakes in a seventh-wicket stand of 204. Patel claimed career-best figures too, of seven for 75 with the help of secure close catching, but Warwickshire were prevented from enforcing the follow-on by Compton, who resisted for nearly four hours. His cussedness made all the difference when Warwickshire imploded, losing all ten for 92 amid an array of poor strokes to give Hussain five wickets and Thomas nine for 108 in the match.

Close of play: first day, Warwickshire 27-1 (Chopra 17, Evans 0); second day, Warwickshire 387-7 (Troughton 132, Barker 6); third day, Warwickshire 66-3 (Chopra 27, Maddy 2).

Warwickshire

V. Chopra c Kieswetter b Thomas	93	– lbw b Hussain	32
I. J. Westwood c Buttler b Trego	10	– lbw b Hussain	22
L. J. Evans c Trego b Thomas	4	– c Buttler b Suppiah	9
*J. O. Troughton c Kieswetter b Thomas	132	– run out	1
D. L. Maddy c Kieswetter b Thomas	0	– not out	17
†T. R. Ambrose c Trego b Meschede	18	– c Waller b Thomas	1
R. Clarke c and b Waller	1	– c Barrow b Hussain	5
C. R. Woakes c Compton b Suppiah	107	– lbw b Hussain	0
K. H. D. Barker b Thomas	12	– c Kieswetter b Thomas	1
J. S. Patel c Compton b Thomas	6	– c Hildreth b Thomas	21
C. J. C. Wright not out	0	– lbw b Hussain	4
B 6, l-b 5, w 2, n-b 4	17	L-b 4, n-b 7	11
1/27 (2) 2/50 (3) 3/135 (1) 4/135 (5) 5/161 (6) 6/162 (7) 7/366 (8) 8/388 (4) 9/400 (10) 10/400 (9) (109.5 overs)	400	1/32 (2) 2/55 (3) 3/60 (4) 4/74 (1) 5/75 (6) 6/82 (7) 7/82 (8) 8/87 (9) 9/119 (10) 10/124 (11) (37.4 overs)	124

Trego 25–5–84–1; Hussain 20–3–70–0; Thomas 19.5–4–60–6; Meschede 16–3–64–1; Waller 17–2–78–1; Suppiah 12–3–33–1. *Second innings*—Thomas 11–0–48–3; Trego 3–0–11–0; Suppiah 8–4–8–1; Hussain 13.4–3–48–5; Waller 2–0–5–0.

Somerset

A. V. Suppiah c Ambrose b Patel	54	– (2) b Barker	2
A. W. R. Barrow run out	2	– (1) c Maddy b Woakes	0
N. R. D. Compton not out	73	– c Ambrose b Woakes	52
J. C. Hildreth c Chopra b Clarke	7	– c Ambrose b Woakes	8
†C. Kieswetter c Evans b Patel	44	– c Woakes b Barker	152
J. C. Buttler c Woakes b Patel	20	– c Chopra b Barker	24
P. D. Trego c Clarke b Patel	3	– not out	14
C. A. J. Meschede c Clarke b Patel	9	– c Chopra b Barker	4
*A. C. Thomas c Chopra b Clarke	1	– c Clarke b Barker	0
M. T. C. Waller c Westwood b Patel	17	– c Chopra b Barker	3
G. M. Hussain b Patel	0	– not out	0
B 16, l-b 2, n-b 6	24	B 9, l-b 3, n-b 2	14
1/19 (2) 2/87 (1) 3/102 (4) (66.5 overs)	254	1/0 (1) (9 wkts, 69.1 overs)	273
4/155 (5) 5/195 (6) 6/206 (7)		2/2 (2) 3/15 (4)	
7/226 (8) 8/227 (9) 9/254 (10) 10/254 (11)		4/181 (3) 5/236 (6) 6/259 (5)	
		7/263 (8) 8/263 (9) 9/269 (10)	

Woakes 9–2–26–0; Barker 11–2–42–0; Wright 12–1–49–0; Patel 24.5–4–75–7; Clarke 10–1–44–2. *Second innings*—Woakes 16–5–37–3; Barker 15–4–40–6; Patel 23.1–3–96–0; Wright 10–0–57–0; Clarke 5–0–31–0.

Umpires: R. T. Robinson and M. J. Saggers.

At Liverpool, August 1–4. SOMERSET drew with LANCASHIRE.

SOMERSET v NOTTINGHAMSHIRE

At Taunton, August 7–10. Drawn. Somerset 7pts, Nottinghamshire 6pts. Toss: Somerset. County debut: Abdur Rehman.

Less than 24 overs were bowled on the first two days, condemning a potentially key match in the title race to a draw. On the third day, Trescothick equalled a Somerset record he already had two shares in by taking his fifth catch of the innings as an outfielder – all at second slip. After Read's battling half-century, Nottinghamshire's last five wickets went down for 14, with Hussain returning for a spell of 6–4–6–4. Hildreth punished a Nottinghamshire attack weakened by injuries to Adams and Gurney, but there was insufficient time for Somerset to consider victory. Abdur Rehman, the Pakistan left-arm spinner who had tormented England's Test batsmen in the UAE at the start of the year, struck with his second ball in county cricket, pinning Taylor on the paddle-sweep. It later emerged that Rehman had tested positive for cannabis during this game; he was banned for 12 weeks by the ECB for recreational drug use, so missing the Champions League with Sialkot Stallions.

Close of play: first day, Nottinghamshire 18-1 (Hales 7); second day, Nottinghamshire 48-3 (Taylor 3, Voges 5); third day, Somerset 187-6 (Hildreth 63, Abdur Rehman 12).

Nottinghamshire

M. H. Wessels c Trescothick b Trego	6	– (2) c Trescothick b Kirby	22
A. D. Hales c Trescothick b Thomas	12	– (1) lbw b Trego	54
M. J. Lumb lbw b Thomas	16	– c Buttler b Trego	17
J. W. A. Taylor lbw b Abdur Rehman	21	– lbw b Gregory	46
A. C. Voges c Trescothick b Thomas	5	– not out	8
*†C. M. W. Read c Trescothick b Hussain	52	– c Abdur Rehman b Gregory	8
P. J. Franks not out	11	– not out	4
B. J. Phillips c Trego b Hussain	0		
G. P. Swann c Trescothick b Hussain	5		
A. R. Adams c Kirby b Hussain	0		
H. F. Gurney b Kirby	0		
B 8, l-b 8, n-b 12	28	B 4, l-b 2, w 1, n-b 10	17
1/18 (1) 2/39 (3) 3/42 (2) 4/48 (5) (54.4 overs)	156	1/30 (2) (5 wkts, 57 overs)	176
5/120 (4) 6/142 (6) 7/142 (8)		2/85 (3) 3/118 (1)	
8/148 (9) 9/154 (10) 10/156 (11)		4/155 (4) 5/167 (6)	

Trego 17–6–35–1; Kirby 12.1–4–36–1; Thomas 10.3–2–25–3; Hussain 9–4–29–4; Abdur Rehman 6–2–15–1. *Second innings*—Trego 14–2–45–2; Kirby 6–0–20–1; Abdur Rehman 22–6–43–0; Hussain 6–0–29–0; Suppiah 4–1–11–0; Gregory 5–1–22–2.

Somerset

*M. E. Trescothick c Adams b Phillips	0
A. V. Suppiah lbw b Adams	35
C. R. Jones c Phillips b Adams	28
J. C. Hildreth c Wessels b Voges	83
†J. C. Buttler c Hales b Franks	39
L. Gregory c Read b Franks	1
P. D. Trego c Read b Swann	8
Abdur Rehman c Phillips b Swann	17
G. M. Hussain c Voges b Swann	29
A. C. Thomas c Hales b Phillips	1
S. P. Kirby not out	6
B 1, l-b 1	2
1/0 (1) 2/63 (2) 3/64 (3) 4/155 (5) 5/161 (6) 6/175 (7) 7/199 (8) 8/225 (4) 9/233 (10) 10/249 (9) (87.2 overs)	249

Phillips 18–4–44–2; Gurney 6–2–19–0; Adams 14–2–53–2; Franks 21–3–67–2; Swann 26.2–5–62–3; Voges 2–0–2–1.

Umpires: I. J. Gould and S. J. O'Shaughnessy.

SOMERSET v SUSSEX

At Taunton, August 21–24. Drawn. Somerset 7pts, Sussex 8pts. Toss: Somerset. County debut: S. I. Mahmood.

Sussex were robbed of the chance to go top of the table when rain set in on the final afternoon, leaving them 49 short of victory with five wickets in hand. They owed their position to Panesar, who varied his flight and pace expertly on a responsive surface – at times bowling as quickly as Derek Underwood – and was rewarded with career-best figures of seven for 60 in the first innings, and 13 for 137 in the match. He enjoyed a fascinating contest with Trescothick who, in his fourth Championship innings since ankle surgery, made his 50th first-class hundred. Yet Trescothick still felt he had underachieved. "At this stage of my career I am 25 or 30 centuries short," he said. "It puts into context the achievements of Graeme Hick and Mark Ramprakash." Abdur Rehman's left-arm spin proved less effective than Panesar's, but he still took five wickets as Sussex, boosted by Khan's brazen fifty, opened a slim lead. Panesar then sparked Somerset's collapse from 84 without loss with a superb quicker ball to the advancing Trescothick, who steered to slip. Sussex returned on the last morning needing 133, and took some risks with rain in the air – but the dreadful summer would reward neither side.

Close of play: first day, Somerset 175-3 (Trescothick 89, Buttler 17); second day, Sussex 161-6 (Brown 20, Magoffin 7); third day, Sussex 31-0 (Joyce 19, Nash 12).

Somerset

First innings		Second innings	
*M. E. Trescothick c Brown b Nash	123	– c Yardy b Panesar	38
A. V. Suppiah b Magoffin	2	– c Yardy b Anyon	59
C. R. Jones c sub (K. O. Wernars) b Panesar	26	– b Nash	14
J. C. Hildreth c Brown b Panesar	23	– c Wright b Panesar	18
†J. C. Buttler c Magoffin b Panesar	25	– c Brown b Nash	11
A. W. R. Barrow c Wells b Panesar	7	– lbw b Panesar	10
P. D. Trego b Panesar	13	– lbw b Panesar	1
Abdur Rehman lbw b Nash	4	– b Nash	15
S. I. Mahmood c Wells b Panesar	0	– b Panesar	13
G. M. Hussain not out	0	– not out	11
S. P. Kirby c Brown b Panesar	0	– lbw b Panesar	4
B 8, l-b 14, n-b 2	24	L-b 1	1
1/14 (2) 2/75 (3) 3/131 (4) 4/199 (5) 5/213 (6) 6/241 (1) 7/245 (7) 8/247 (8) 9/247 (9) 10/247 (11) (86.5 overs)	247	1/84 (1) 2/106 (2) 3/117 (3) 4/131 (5) 5/144 (6) 6/148 (7) 7/165 (4) 8/178 (9) 9/184 (8) 10/195 (11) (58.5 overs)	195

Anyon 18–4–70–0; Magoffin 22–12–29–1; Wright 2–0–26–0; Panesar 31.5–8–60–7; Khan 4–1–18–0; Nash 9–1–22–2. *Second innings*—Anyon 11–4–38–1; Magoffin 6–2–30–0; Panesar 26.5–6–77–6; Nash 14–2–45–3; Wright 1–0–4–0.

Sussex

C. D. Nash c Suppiah b Hussain	31	– (2) b Trego 26
*E. C. Joyce c Buttler b Trego	12	– (1) c Buttler b Trego 24
L. W. P. Wells c Suppiah b Abdur Rehman	28	– (6) not out 22
M. W. Goodwin c Trescothick b Abdur Rehman	17	– c Mahmood b Abdur Rehman 0
M. H. Yardy lbw b Kirby	18	– c Trescothick b Abdur Rehman 9
L. J. Wright lbw b Hussain	22	– (3) b Trego 22
†B. C. Brown c Trescothick b Abdur Rehman	52	– not out 10
S. J. Magoffin c Suppiah b Trego	11	
A. Khan not out	57	
J. E. Anyon b Abdur Rehman	0	
M. S. Panesar b Abdur Rehman	20	
B 4, l-b 3, n-b 4	11	L-b 2 2
1/45 (1) 2/45 (2) 3/68 (4) (84.3 overs)	279	1/44 (1) (5 wkts, 36.3 overs) 115
4/106 (5) 5/122 (3) 6/146 (6)		2/71 (2) 3/72 (4)
7/178 (8) 8/235 (7) 9/247 (10) 10/279 (11)		4/72 (3) 5/96 (5)

Trego 25–11–59–2; Kirby 11–1–66–1; Hussain 7–2–27–2; Abdur Rehman 30.3–11–70–5; Mahmood 11–1–50–0. *Second innings*—Trego 13–3–60–3; Abdur Rehman 18–3–46–2; Suppiah 1–1–0–0; Kirby 4.3–1–7–0.

Umpires: R. J. Bailey and N. G. B. Cook.

SOMERSET v SURREY

At Taunton, August 28–31. Drawn. Somerset 8pts, Surrey 9pts. Toss: Surrey.

Kartik's decision to run out Barrow for backing up too far caused angry scenes during the tea interval on the third day, with supporters of both teams gathering under the Surrey dressing-room balcony to voice their displeasure. He had warned Barrow earlier in the over for leaving his ground early, and felt he had nothing to apologise for. But on a visit to the press box that evening, Surrey's team director Chris Adams admitted the spirit of cricket had been "challenged" – even if the action itself was within the Laws. In a prolonged conversation with umpire Peter Hartley, Batty was asked three times if he wished to withdraw the appeal; he did not, though he later said sorry for a decision made "in the heat of battle". The mood, already stirred up by Kartik's impassioned reaction to winning three lbw appeals against his former team-mates, soured further, and the umpires had to halt play to warn Batty about excessive chat from Surrey's close fielders. Trego, never one to duck a fight, had 14 when Barrow was dismissed, and clubbed 78 of Somerset's last 103. But with the second day washed out, a draw was always likely. Trescothick tried to engineer a run-chase by deploying four overs of joke bowling, but nothing came of it – save Pietersen becoming Chris Jones's maiden first-class wicket – and Harinath was allowed to complete his second hundred in consecutive matches, after which wicketkeeper Buttler came on to bowl the first two overs of his first-class career. Earlier, all eyes had been on Pietersen, cast out by England after the texts furore. He responded with an effortless 163 from 168 balls.

Close of play: first day, Somerset 42-2 (Jones 15, Hildreth 15); second day, no play; third day, Surrey 58-0 (Burns 37, Ansari 21).

Surrey

R. J. Burns b Mahmood	23	– c Barrow b Dockrell	60
Z. S. Ansari lbw b Kirby	3	– c Trescothick b Mahmood	39
A. Harinath c Trescothick b Dockrell	21	– not out	105
K. P. Pietersen c Buttler b Mahmood	163	– c Barrow b Jones	58
Z. de Bruyn c Buttler b Kirby	34	– c Trescothick b Dockrell	18
J. J. Roy c Buttler b Kirby	0	– b Mahmood	28
†G. C. Wilson st Buttler b Dockrell	27	– not out	30
*G. J. Batty c Hildreth b Mahmood	5		
S. C. Meaker b Mahmood	0		
J. Lewis c Trescothick b Dockrell	3		
M. Kartik not out	23		
B 1, l-b 4, n-b 10	15	B 8, l-b 10, n-b 4	22
1/12 (2) 2/44 (1) 3/73 (3) (79.1 overs)	317	1/102 (1) (5 wkts dec, 95.4 overs)	360
4/164 (5) 5/164 (6) 6/261 (7)		2/118 (2) 3/195 (4)	
7/268 (8) 8/268 (9) 9/285 (10) 10/317 (4)		4/232 (5) 5/287 (6)	

Trego 12–4–50–0; Kirby 13–3–34–3; Mahmood 14.1–1–62–4; Thomas 13–4–52–0; Dockrell 22–2–99–3; Suppiah 5–0–15–0. *Second innings*—Trego 16.4–4–59–0; Kirby 12–2–33–0; Dockrell 37–6–129–2; Mahmood 17–4–45–2; Suppiah 1–0–2–0; Thomas 6–1–16–0; Hildreth 2–0–30–0; Jones 2–0–17–1; Buttler 2–0–11–0.

Somerset

*M. E. Trescothick c and b Meaker	3
A. V. Suppiah c Wilson b Lewis	0
C. R. Jones lbw b Kartik	50
J. C. Hildreth lbw b Kartik	85
†J. C. Buttler lbw b Kartik	14
A. W. R. Barrow run out	12
P. D. Trego b Meaker	92
A. C. Thomas lbw b Kartik	8
G. H. Dockrell c Wilson b Meaker	1
S. I. Mahmood not out	7
S. P. Kirby c Wilson b Meaker	2
B 8, l-b 3, w 1, n-b 8	20
1/5 (2) 2/16 (1) 3/151 (4) (85.3 overs)	294
4/160 (3) 5/167 (5) 6/191 (6)	
7/250 (8) 8/279 (9) 9/284 (7) 10/294 (11)	

Lewis 19–3–86–1; Meaker 21.3–2–75–4; Kartik 25–6–70–4; de Bruyn 14–2–37–0; Batty 6–1–15–0.

Umpires: S. C. Gale and P. J. Hartley.

At Hove, September 4–7. SOMERSET beat SUSSEX by five wickets.

SOMERSET v WORCESTERSHIRE

At Taunton, September 11–13. Somerset won by an innings and 148 runs. Somerset 23pts, Worcestershire 2pts. Toss: Worcestershire.

Nine wickets for Abdur Rehman on the opening day attracted the attention of ECB pitch inspector Bill Hughes, who was spotted peering at the surface between innings. Rehman came on with Worcestershire 70 without loss, and gradually picked his way through a lightweight line-up, though he was denied a chance of all ten when Trego removed Russell at No. 9. Ali briefly caused him some bother: he survived a drop at slip, then hit him for six and seven (courtesy of four overthrows) with his first two scoring shots, before eventually turning him to short leg. Hughes stayed on to watch the second day, but any doubts about a flat, dry pitch were quelled by skilful and patient centuries from Trescothick and Compton, who gave Worcestershire a lesson in how to play the turning ball. Presumably unaware of the stats, Trescothick declared with Compton on 155, when six more runs would have given him 1,500 for the first-class season at an average of 100. Worcestershire, relegated the week before, caved in before the third day was out, allowing Rehman to complete match figures of 14 for 101; both those, and his first-innings haul, were the best figures of the English season – and his career. He took his tally from four Championship matches to 27, and helped Somerset finish runners-up for only the third time in their history.

Close of play: first day, Somerset 142-0 (Trescothick 66, Suppiah 73); second day, Somerset 451-7 (Compton 114, Thomas 9).

Worcestershire

First innings		Second innings	
*D. K. H. Mitchell c Hildreth b Abdur Rehman	28	– c Hildreth b Abdur Rehman	18
P. J. Hughes c Trescothick b Abdur Rehman	42	– c Snell b Trego	4
N. D. Pinner c and b Abdur Rehman	6	– lbw b Thomas	14
M. M. Ali c Jones b Abdur Rehman	24	– c Trescothick b Overton	24
A. N. Kervezee lbw b Abdur Rehman	40	– c Trescothick b Abdur Rehman	76
A. Kapil b Abdur Rehman	22	– b Abdur Rehman	2
B. L. D'Oliveira lbw b Abdur Rehman	2	– b Abdur Rehman	3
†O. B. Cox not out	25	– c Suppiah b Kirby	4
C. J. Russell c Snell b Trego	2	– c Trego b Abdur Rehman	1
N. L. Harrison lbw b Abdur Rehman	10	– b Thomas	0
A. Richardson lbw b Abdur Rehman	0	– not out	0
L-b 5, n-b 6	11	B 1, l-b 1, n-b 4	6
1/74 (2) 2/75 (1) 3/94 (3) (65 overs)	212	1/13 (2) 2/31 (1) (45.4 overs)	152
4/119 (4) 5/165 (5) 6/173 (7)		3/50 (3) 4/78 (4)	
7/174 (6) 8/179 (9) 9/204 (10) 10/212 (11)		5/81 (6) 6/93 (7) 7/124 (8)	
		8/129 (9) 9/152 (10) 10/152 (5)	

Trego 15–2–69–1; Kirby 7–1–21–0; Thomas 11–2–32–0; Abdur Rehman 24–8–65–9; Suppiah 8–1–20–0. *Second innings*—Trego 7–2–18–1; Kirby 7–0–37–1; Abdur Rehman 16.4–6–36–5; Suppiah 1–0–6–0; Thomas 9–0–29–2; Overton 5–0–24–1.

Somerset

*M. E. Trescothick c Mitchell b Richardson	146
A. V. Suppiah c and b Ali	75
N. R. D. Compton not out	155
J. C. Hildreth lbw b Richardson	19
C. R. Jones lbw b Richardson	1
P. D. Trego b Russell	45
C. Overton c Pinner b Ali	4
†S. D. Snell b Ali	10
A. C. Thomas lbw b Richardson	17
Abdur Rehman c Kervezee b Ali	7
S. P. Kirby not out	1
B 21, l-b 3, w 8	32
1/153 (2) (9 wkts dec, 140 overs)	512
2/307 (1) 3/341 (4)	
4/343 (5) 5/417 (6) 6/422 (7) 7/434 (8)	
8/488 (9) 9/503 (10) 110 overs: 359-4	

Richardson 41–14–100–4; Russell 14–1–88–1; Harrison 8–1–36–0; Ali 48–7–143–4; D'Oliveira 18–1–88–0; Kapil 5–0–13–0; Pinner 4–0–13–0; Mitchell 2–0–7–0.

Umpires: S. J. O'Shaughnessy and M. J. Saggers.

SURREY

The saddest of summers

RICHARD SPILLER

The death of Tom Maynard cast a pall over Surrey's season. To lose such a talent, seemingly destined for the international stage, devastated his adopted county as well as his old one, Glamorgan. Maynard, 23, was found dead on the line near Wimbledon Park tube station early on June 18. The tragedy provoked intense grief among team-mates and staff at a club shattered by losing a third player in 15 years, following Graham Kersey and Ben Hollioake.

Rory Hamilton-Brown, Maynard's close friend and housemate, was given extended compassionate leave and eventually relinquished the captaincy. He was still badly out of sorts when he returned and, after the season, no objections were raised to his departure for Sussex, from where he had been signed in 2010. The following year, he had led Surrey to promotion in the Championship and success in the CB40.

Maynard had already been disciplined after a late-night incident during the match against Sussex at Horsham – he suffered a mysterious shoulder injury and a black eye – while Oval officials admitted Hamilton-Brown's lifestyle had been causing concern for some time. Both episodes prompted questions about the discipline of a small but influential group within the squad. In the circumstances, avoiding relegation and only narrowly missing out on the CB40 semi-finals were considerable achievements – for which acting-captain Gareth Batty, who welded together a disconsolate squad, deserved immense credit.

Surrey were less affected by the weather than some, but still lost 11 complete days in the Championship. Runs were scarce, and no one found the going harder than Mark Ramprakash, who at 42 lacked form and fortune. A decline had been hinted at in 2011 and, after 107 runs in ten innings and once more sitting out the Twenty20, he was informed by team director Chris Adams that he would not have his contract renewed, nor would he be considered for the first team again. Since moving to The Oval in 2001, Ramprakash had amassed 15,837 – always watchable – first-class runs at nearly 68, including 61 of his 114 hundreds. He could be excused if he felt the manner of his departure was a clumsy and thoughtless way to treat a great servant.

That added fuel to the fire for critics of Adams, who had invested much credibility in appointing Hamilton-Brown at the age of 22. More opprobrium followed when he went on holiday to Portugal and missed his beleaguered side's Championship match at Edgbaston.

Even before the Maynard tragedy, Surrey were struggling in the four-day game: victory over Sussex was followed by a series of profligate displays which led to three defeats and three draws. The initial lack of an established opening pair didn't help, and the sticking-plaster solution of Jacques Rudolph for the early matches was not a success.

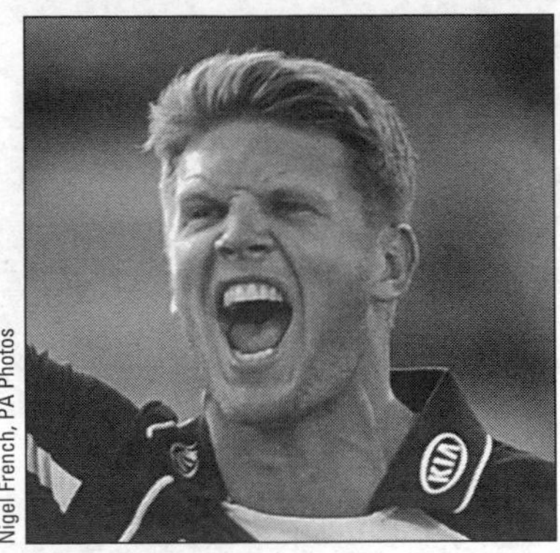
Nigel French, PA Photos

Stuart Meaker

Maynard and Hamilton-Brown flourished early on. But without them and Ramprakash, and with Steve Davies, Zander de Bruyn and Jason Roy in fitful form, the onus fell on a trio of home-grown left-handers. Rory Burns, Arun Harinath and Zafar Ansari all chipped in as Surrey somehow mustered enough points to survive, losing only once more and winning twice.

Kevin Pietersen's awe-inspiring centuries at Guildford and Taunton raised spirits, but it was a 217-run stand between Burns and Harinath which proved pivotal in the crucial win over Middlesex in August; to the warmest of receptions, they reached their maiden Championship centuries within four balls. Ansari continued to do well in one-day cricket and, if opening in the Championship proved demanding, he showed ability and resolve to bat out the final day at Edgbaston. Harinath, all but ignored the previous year, quickly added a second hundred, while Burns opened with aplomb and finished as the club's leading first-class run-scorer. Even so, no one reached 1,000, for the first time since 2001.

Stuart Meaker matched pace with movement to be the outstanding bowler in the Championship, but the veteran Jon Lewis, signed from Gloucestershire, declined sharply. Chris Tremlett appeared only briefly between back and knee problems, while Jade Dernbach was restricted by England calls and injury. After 73 second division scalps in 2011, Tim Linley found himself behind Lewis in the pecking order at first but, characteristically, fought back.

Batty relished some turning pitches at The Oval, claiming 24 of his 30 Championship wickets there, and received help when Murali Kartik was finally free of IPL commitments. But after Kartik ran out Somerset's Alex Barrow for backing up too far at Taunton, and Batty enforced the appeal, Surrey felt obliged to apologise for breaching the game's spirit.

Retention of the CB40 trophy was made harder when two home games were rained off, before defeat at Southampton rendered qualification virtually impossible. The Twenty20 proved a write-off amid the mourning for Maynard. Matthew Spriegel was the outstanding one-day contributor, but a shortage of Championship opportunities saw him leave for Northamptonshire. All-rounder Chris Jordan and batsman Tom Lancefield were also released.

A pre-tax profit of £805,000, after a large deficit the previous year, left Surrey in a stronger position financially, although they all but admitted the scheme to build a hotel at The Oval was defunct.

More reconstruction work was required on the field. Adams turned to two old pros, Worcestershire batsman Vikram Solanki and Lancashire slow left-armer Gary Keedy, to plug gaps, then landed the big fish he wanted when South Africa's Graeme Smith agreed a three-year contract as captain.

Championship attendance: 33,021.

SURREY RESULTS

All first-class matches – Played 16: Won 4, Lost 4, Drawn 8. Abandoned 1.
County Championship matches – Played 15: Won 3, Lost 4, Drawn 8. Abandoned 1.

LV= County Championship, 7th in Division 1;
Friends Life t20, 6th in South Division; Clydesdale Bank 40, 2nd in Group B.

COUNTY CHAMPIONSHIP AVERAGES, BATTING AND FIELDING

Cap		*M*	*I*	*NO*	*R*	*HS*	*100*	*50*	*Avge*	*Ct/St*
	K. P. Pietersen‡	4	7	1	572	234*	2	2	95.33	1
	G. C. Wilson	3	4	1	182	68	0	2	60.66	4
	R. J. Burns†	9	15	0	640	121	1	4	42.66	6
2012	T. L. Maynard	7	14	1	525	143	1	2	40.38	10
2011	R. J. Hamilton-Brown	8	16	1	555	115	1	4	37.00	4
	A. Harinath†	6	11	1	368	109	2	0	36.80	0
	J. J. Roy	12	21	2	612	83	0	3	32.21	11
	Z. de Bruyn¶	15	27	0	709	125	1	5	26.25	5
	J. Lewis	13	19	6	326	42	0	0	25.07	3
	J. A. Rudolph§	5	10	0	229	68	0	1	22.90	2
2011	S. M. Davies	12	20	0	438	104	1	1	21.90	24/1
	Z. S. Ansari	8	13	1	234	83*	0	1	19.50	3
	M. Kartik§	7	8	2	113	23*	0	0	18.83	3
2012	S. C. Meaker	10	14	4	177	41	0	0	17.70	1
2011	G. J. Batty	14	24	2	287	36	0	0	13.04	15
	C. J. Jordan	7	12	1	141	40	0	0	12.81	3
2002	M. R. Ramprakash	5	10	0	107	37	0	0	10.70	2
2011	J. W. Dernbach‡	7	14	4	55	22	0	0	5.50	2
	T. E. Linley	7	10	4	28	14	0	0	4.66	2

Also batted: M. P. Dunn† (1 match) 0*; G. A. Edwards† (2 matches) 17, 10*; T. M. Jewell (1 match) 70; M. N. W. Spriegel† (2 matches) 17, 1, 17; C. T. Tremlett‡ (1 match) did not bat.

† *Born in Surrey.* ‡ *ECB contract.* § *Official overseas player.* ¶ *Other non-England-qualified player.*

BOWLING

	Style	*O*	*M*	*R*	*W*	*BB*	*5I*	*Avge*
M. Kartik	SLA	251.1	58	597	27	5-69	1	22.11
S. C. Meaker	RF	284.3	50	993	44	8-52	3	22.56
G. J. Batty	OB	305	71	789	30	6-73	2	26.30
J. W. Dernbach	RFM	172	39	522	19	3-39	0	27.47
T. E. Linley	RFM	150.3	34	464	16	5-62	1	29.00
J. Lewis	RFM	335	77	980	31	5-41	1	31.61
C. J. Jordan	RFM	125.3	16	517	10	3-29	0	51.70

Also bowled: Z. S. Ansari (SLA) 16–2–55–0; Z. de Bruyn (RM) 130–24–383–6; M. P. Dunn (RFM) 10–1–50–1; G. A. Edwards (RFM) 44.5–6–184–5; R. J. Hamilton-Brown (OB) 13–0–38–1; T. M. Jewell (RFM) 11–3–24–1; K. P. Pietersen (OB) 11–3–27–2; J. J. Roy (RM) 1–0–1–0; C. T. Tremlett (RF) 27–6–82–1.

LEADING CB40 AVERAGES (100 runs/4 wickets)

Batting

	Runs	*HS*	*Avge*	*SR*	*Ct/St*
Z. S. Ansari	160	60*	40.00	90.90	5
T. L. Maynard	118	77	39.33	77.63	1
M. N. W. Spriegel	220	51	27.50	58.82	3
R. J. Hamilton-Brown	204	101	25.50	106.80	2
S. M. Davies	260	72	23.63	97.37	9/8
Z. de Bruyn	210	57	23.33	65.62	3

Bowling

	W	*BB*	*Avge*	*ER*
Z. de Bruyn	5	5-46	9.60	6.26
G. J. Batty	14	3-4	17.64	4.49
M. Kartik	11	4-27	19.27	4.55
S. C. Meaker	9	3-24	21.00	4.74
M. N. W. Spriegel	9	2-14	21.11	4.05
J. W. Dernbach	13	3-39	23.00	5.32

LEADING FLT20 AVERAGES (100 runs/16 overs)

Batting	Runs	HS	Avge	SR	Ct/St
S. M. Davies	184	37	18.40	**143.75**	3/6
J. J. Roy	120	40	12.00	**122.44**	6
G. C. Wilson	182	54*	60.66	**118.95**	0
Z. S. Ansari	144	38*	24.00	**102.85**	0
M. N. W. Spriegel	130	53*	21.66	**88.43**	2

Bowling	W	BB	Avge	ER
G. J. Batty	11	4-13	14.72	**5.22**
M. Kartik	7	3-16	25.57	**5.77**
C. T. Tremlett	7	3-19	16.14	**7.06**
Z. S. Ansari	6	2-26	28.50	**8.55**
D. P. Nannes	4	2-23	51.25	**9.60**

FIRST-CLASS COUNTY RECORDS

Highest score for	357*	R. Abel v Somerset at The Oval	1899
Highest score against	366	N. H. Fairbrother (Lancashire) at The Oval	1990
Leading run-scorer	43,554	J. B. Hobbs (avge 49.72)	1905–1934
Best bowling for	10-43	T. Rushby v Somerset at Taunton	1921
Best bowling against	10-28	W. P. Howell (Australians) at The Oval	1899
Leading wicket-taker	1,775	T. Richardson (avge 17.87)	1892–1904
Highest total for	811	v Somerset at The Oval	1899
Highest total against	863	by Lancashire at The Oval	1990
Lowest total for	14	v Essex at Chelmsford	1983
Lowest total against	16	by MCC at Lord's	1872

LIST A COUNTY RECORDS

Highest score for	268	A. D. Brown v Glamorgan at The Oval	2002
Highest score against	180*	T. M. Moody (Worcestershire) at The Oval	1994
Leading run-scorer	10,358	A. D. Brown (avge 32.16)	1990–2008
Best bowling for	7-30	M. P. Bicknell v Glamorgan at The Oval	1999
Best bowling against	7-15	A. L. Dixon (Kent) at The Oval	1967
Leading wicket-taker	409	M. P. Bicknell (avge 25.21)	1986–2005
Highest total for	496-4	v Gloucestershire at The Oval	2007
Highest total against	429	by Glamorgan at The Oval	2002
Lowest total for	64	v Worcestershire at Worcester	1978
Lowest total against	44	by Glamorgan at The Oval	1999

TWENTY20 COUNTY RECORDS

Highest score for	101*	J. J. Roy v Kent at Beckenham	2010
Highest score against	106*	S. B. Styris (Essex) at Chelmsford	2010
Leading run-scorer	1,719	M. R. Ramprakash (avge 32.43)	2003–2010
Best bowling for	6-24	T. J. Murtagh v Middlesex at Lord's	2005
Best bowling against	4-21	Yasir Arafat (Sussex) at Hove	2006
Leading wicket-taker	53	N. D. Doshi (avge 14.66)	2004–2007
	53	C. P. Schofield (avge 22.62)	2007–2011
Highest total for	224-5	v Gloucestershire at Bristol	2006
Highest total against	217-4	by Lancashire at The Oval	2005
Lowest total for	**88**	**v Kent at The Oval**	**2012**
Lowest total against	68	by Sussex at Hove	2007

ADDRESS

The Oval, Kennington, London SE11 5SS (0207 820 5700; **email** enquiries@surreycricket.com). **Website** www.surreycricket.com

OFFICIALS

Captain 2012 – R. J. Hamilton-Brown
2013 – G. C. Smith
Team director C. J. Adams
First-team coach I. D. K. Salisbury
Academy director G. T. J. Townsend

President Sir Trevor McDonald
Chairman R. W. Thompson
Chief executive R. A. Gould
Head groundsman L. E. Fortis
Scorer K. R. Booth

SURREY v LEEDS/BRADFORD MCCU

At The Oval, March 31–April 2. Surrey won by two runs. Toss: Leeds/Bradford MCCU. First-class debuts: H. Bush, T. R. Hardman, M. Higginbottom, D. M. Hodgson, J. Leach, R. A. L. Moore, L. M. Reece, B. T. Slater, I. A. A. Thomas, J. P. Webb.

This was Leeds/Bradford's first first-class match, and they went agonisingly close to repeating Cambridge's victory over Surrey the previous year. Hamilton-Brown's enterprise in waiving the follow-on and setting 315 on the final day almost backfired, but the persevering Linley rescued him – just. Leeds/Bradford reached 268 for five before Jewell took a superb low return catch to remove Richard Moore, but Dan Hodgson continued the fight until he was caught in the deep, and the last pair were undone deep into a tense final hour. Earlier, Burns aided Maynard's recovery work, then produced deft strokes all around the wicket himself. Los Angeles-born Harry Bush's staunch four-hour 70 prevented the reply from caving in after a burst of three wickets in eight balls from Jordan, who had just become the first man since Jack Hobbs in 1924 to open both the batting and bowling in the first innings of the same match for Surrey (excluding nightwatchmen or very short innings).

Close of play: first day, Leeds/Bradford MCCU 20-1 (Webb 9, Bush 3); second day, Surrey 134-5 (Maynard 19, Burns 0).

Surrey

M. N. W. Spriegel lbw b Thomas	13	– (5) c Hodgson b Higginbottom	25
C. J. Jordan b Reece	54	– c Hodgson b Hardman	18
†G. C. Wilson lbw b Reece	6	– c Hodgson b Hardman	18
*R. J. Hamilton-Brown c Hodgson b Leach	22	– (1) lbw b Thomas	0
T. L. Maynard lbw b Hardman	91	– (6) not out	19
J. J. Roy lbw b Leach	0	– (4) c Leach b Higginbottom	32
R. J. Burns not out	101	– not out	0
T. M. Jewell lbw b Leach	18		
T. E. Linley c Hardman b Leach	15		
F. O. E. van den Bergh not out	16		
B 9, l-b 21, w 7, n-b 12	49	B 4, l-b 4, n-b 14	22
1/49 (1) 2/91 (3) 3/104 (2) 4/136 (4) 5/136 (6) 6/282 (5) 7/314 (8) 8/346 (9) (8 wkts dec, 82.3 overs)	385	1/0 (1) 2/45 (3) 3/58 (2) 4/85 (4) 5/128 (5) (5 wkts dec, 34 overs)	134

M. P. Dunn did not bat.

Thomas 16.3–8–33–1; Higginbottom 4–0–31–0; Hardman 19–2–91–1; Reece 10–0–43–2; Moore 13–3–56–0; Leach 13–0–73–4; Bush 7–0–28–0. *Second innings*—Thomas 9–3–22–1; Hardman 8–1–51–2; Higginbottom 9–3–22–2; Reece 6–1–26–0; Leach 2–0–5–0.

Leeds/Bradford MCCU

B. T. Slater c Wilson b Linley	4	– c Wilson b Jewell	6
J. P. Webb c Jordan b Dunn	38	– c Linley b Jordan	18
H. Bush lbw b Dunn	70	– lbw b van den Bergh	41
J. Leach lbw b Jewell	0	– c Maynard b Linley	50
L. M. Reece c Maynard b Jewell	6	– c Burns b Linley	28
†D. M. Hodgson c Wilson b Jordan	13	– c Linley b Jordan	64
*R. A. L. Moore lbw b Jordan	0	– c and b Jewell	37
C. G. Roebuck b Jordan	0	– lbw b Linley	0
T. R. Hardman c Wilson b Jewell	16	– c Jewell b Linley	5
M. Higginbottom b Dunn	6	– not out	12
I. A. A. Thomas not out	7	– lbw b Linley	10
B 16, l-b 10, w 9, n-b 10	45	B 6, l-b 11, w 4, n-b 15, p 5	41
1/4 (1) 2/75 (2) 3/87 (4) 4/111 (5) 5/150 (6) 6/150 (7) 7/156 (8) 8/192 (9) 9/192 (3) 10/205 (10) (57.1 overs)	205	1/33 (1) 2/39 (2) 3/130 (3) 4/146 (4) 5/184 (5) 6/268 (7) 7/269 (8) 8/279 (9) 9/285 (6) 10/312 (11) (93.2 overs)	312

Linley 19–2–61–1; Jordan 16–5–32–3; Dunn 9.1–0–41–3; Spriegel 1–0–6–0; Jewell 12–4–39–3. *Second innings*—Linley 19.2–3–45–5; Jordan 19–2–50–2; Jewell 16–4–51–2; Dunn 5–0–45–0; Spriegel 11–2–30–0; van den Bergh 23–5–69–1.

Umpires: N. J. Llong and M. J. Saggers.

SURREY v SUSSEX

At The Oval, April 5–8. Surrey won by 86 runs. Surrey 21pts, Sussex 3pts. Toss: Sussex. County debuts: J. Lewis, J. A. Rudolph. Championship debut: R. J. Burns.

Surrey's first victory in the top division since September 2007 was completed 43 minutes into the final day after being delayed by a patient century from Wells, who had resisted nearly six hours. The new regulation allowing the floodlights to be switched on was applied for part or all of each day. After Rudolph started his Surrey career with a duck, Maynard led the fightback with a typically aggressive innings on a murky and cold opening day during which an elderly spectator suffered a fatal heart attack. Surrey's total looked more impressive when Sussex toiled, at least until Gatting – helped by Hamilton-Brown's fruitless attempts to manipulate the strike – harnessed the tail. Anyon's best figures since joining Sussex threatened to wrest control, but Hamilton-Brown batted with characteristic gusto: 68 of his 89 runs came in boundaries. In the run-chase, Nash played on, becoming the 800th first-class victim for Jon Lewis, signed from Gloucestershire, but it was the speed of Meaker which did for Sussex.

Close of play: first day, Sussex 105-5 (Gatting 15); second day, Surrey 250-8 (Meaker 16, Lewis 13); third day, Sussex 240-8 (Wells 96, Anyon 11).

Surrey

J. A. Rudolph c Joyce b Naved Arif	0	– (2) c Gatting b Anyon	21
C. J. Jordan b Khan	7	– (1) st Brown b Yardy	20
M. R. Ramprakash lbw b Hatchett	24	– run out	9
Z. de Bruyn c Brown b Naved Arif	52	– c Yardy b Anyon	1
*R. J. Hamilton-Brown c Brown b Naved Arif	18	– c Goodwin b Naved Arif	89
T. L. Maynard not out	86	– b Anyon	47
†R. J. Burns c Brown b Anyon	23	– c Wells b Naved Arif	16
G. J. Batty b Khan	10	– c Yardy b Anyon	0
S. C. Meaker c Nash b Khan	0	– c Yardy b Naved Arif	27
J. Lewis c Yardy b Khan	1	– c Naved Arif b Anyon	24
J. W. Dernbach c Brown b Khan	5	– not out	1
B 9, l-b 15, w 6, n-b 8	38	B 4, l-b 12, n-b 2	18
1/9 (1) 2/11 (2) 3/79 (3) 4/119 (4) (68.1 overs) 5/124 (5) 6/206 (7) 7/223 (8) 8/229 (9) 9/235 (10) 10/264 (11)	264	1/28 (2) 2/52 (3) 3/53 (1) 4/55 (4) 5/191 (5) 6/206 (6) 7/206 (8) 8/210 (7) 9/267 (9) 10/273 (10) (70 overs)	273

Anyon 18–4–69–1; Naved Arif 16–2–56–3; Khan 19.1–5–57–5; Hatchett 12–3–43–1; Gatting 3–0–15–0. *Second innings*—Naved Arif 18–2–60–3; Anyon 24–5–79–5; Khan 9–0–37–0; Yardy 7–1–31–1; Nash 8–3–20–0; Hatchett 4–0–30–0.

Sussex

C. D. Nash c Hamilton-Brown b Meaker	28 – (2) b Lewis	20
E. C. Joyce lbw b Lewis	0 – (1) b Meaker	12
L. W. P. Wells b Dernbach	32 – c and b Lewis	108
M. W. Goodwin b Dernbach	4 – lbw b Meaker	0
*M. H. Yardy c Rudolph b Jordan	14 – lbw b Dernbach	16
J. S. Gatting not out	72 – c Dernbach b Batty	25
†B. C. Brown c Ramprakash b Jordan	3 – lbw b Meaker	23
Naved Arif c Burns b Jordan	0 – c sub (J. J. Roy) b Dernbach	0
A. Khan c Maynard b Meaker	3 – c Lewis b Batty	15
J. E. Anyon c Jordan b Dernbach	20 – c sub (J. J. Roy) b Lewis	12
L. J. Hatchett run out	1 – not out	0
B 3, l-b 9, w 1, n-b 6	19 B 5, l-b 5, w 2, n-b 12	24
1/3 (2) 2/63 (3) 3/67 (1) 4/73 (4) (49 overs)	196 1/29 (2) 2/36 (1) (94.2 overs)	255
5/105 (5) 6/111 (7) 7/113 (8) 8/122 (9)	3/40 (4) 4/81 (5)	
9/167 (10) 10/196 (11)	5/133 (6) 6/162 (7) 7/173 (8)	
	8/213 (9) 9/244 (10) 10/255 (3)	

Lewis 8–1–30–1; Meaker 13–1–58–2; Dernbach 12–2–39–3; Jordan 11–2–29–3; Batty 5–0–28–0. *Second innings*—Lewis 17.2–7–40–3; de Bruyn 4–3–8–0; Meaker 21–2–75–3; Batty 22–6–47–2; Dernbach 18–3–40–2; Jordan 12–0–35–0.

Umpires: N. G. B. Cook and R. K. Illingworth.

At Lord's, April 12–15. SURREY lost to MIDDLESEX by three runs.

SURREY v WORCESTERSHIRE

At The Oval, April 19–22. Drawn. Surrey 6pts, Worcestershire 6pts. Toss: Worcestershire.

Batting had rarely been as hazardous in recent times at The Oval. Although six of the 12 sessions were lost to rain, the vagaries of a dry and grassy surface which provided lateral movement and inconsistent bounce gave bowlers the upper hand. The second ten-wicket haul of Richardson's career came on a ground where he had enjoyed little previous success, but his height and persistence were ideal. All of the first day was lost and only 35 overs were possible on the second, but the fast-forward button was hit on the third, when 19 wickets tumbled: Richardson's efforts were trumped by Meaker's best first-class figures, as only the left-hander Cameron hung around. At times, batting verged on a lottery: nasty shooters accounted for Ramprakash (whose reaction earned him three disciplinary points) and de Bruyn. Hamilton-Brown proved runs were possible, mixing judicious strokeplay, hard running and occasional good fortune. Worcestershire, set 246 in 70 overs, had Klinger's crisp driving to thank for an excellent start before rain, almost inevitably, had the final say.

Close of play: first day, no play; second day, Surrey 123-7 (Batty 0, Meaker 0); third day, Surrey 131-6 (Hamilton-Brown 55, Batty 15).

Surrey

J. J. Roy lbw b Richardson	38 – c Mitchell b Richardson	14
†S. M. Davies c Scott b Richardson	15 – b Lucas	8
M. R. Ramprakash c Solanki b Jones	1 – lbw b Richardson	10
Z. de Bruyn c Mitchell b Richardson	6 – lbw b Richardson	3
*R. J. Hamilton-Brown c Scott b Jones	3 – c Choudhry b Richardson	76
T. L. Maynard lbw b Richardson	34 – c Lucas b Jones	9
C. J. Jordan b Richardson	20 – c Scott b Jones	9
G. J. Batty c Solanki b Lucas	9 – c Cameron b Lucas	19
S. C. Meaker c Scott b Richardson	4 – c Solanki b Jones	19
J. Lewis not out	3 – not out	24
J. W. Dernbach c Scott b Lucas	0 – c Choudhry b Lucas	22
L-b 2, w 1, n-b 4	7 B 2, l-b 3, w 2, n-b 4	11
1/48 (1) 2/55 (2) 3/55 (3) 4/59 (5) (44 overs)	140 1/20 (1) 2/26 (2) (60.5 overs)	224
5/69 (4) 6/122 (6) 7/123 (7) 8/132 (9)	3/33 (4) 4/50 (3)	
9/140 (8) 10/140 (11)	5/59 (6) 6/103 (7) 7/142 (8)	
	8/164 (5) 9/199 (9) 10/224 (11)	

Richardson 20–7–47–6; Lucas 13–0–51–2; Jones 9–1–33–2; Cameron 2–0–7–0. *Second innings*—Richardson 25–5–81–4; Lucas 17.5–1–66–3; Jones 15–0–62–3; Cameron 3–0–10–0.

Worcestershire

*D. K. H. Mitchell c Maynard b Meaker	14	– b Jordan	20
M. Klinger c Maynard b Lewis	5	– not out	69
V. S. Solanki c Jordan b Lewis	10	– not out	0
M. M. Ali lbw b Meaker	3		
A. N. Kervezee c Maynard b Lewis	3		
J. G. Cameron c Davies b Meaker	41		
†B. J. M. Scott c Davies b Meaker	1		
S. H. Choudhry c Maynard b Meaker	0		
D. S. Lucas b Meaker	10		
R. A. Jones c Batty b Dernbach	22		
A. Richardson not out	0		
B 7, l-b 1, n-b 2	10	B 1, l-b 2, n-b 2	5
1/5 (2) 2/25 (3) 3/28 (4) 4/33 (1) 5/39 (5) 6/46 (7) 7/56 (8) 8/74 (9) 9/115 (10) 10/119 (6) (47.5 overs)	119	1/94 (1) (1 wkt, 31 overs)	94

Lewis 12–6–18–3; de Bruyn 4–0–15–0; Meaker 15.5–4–39–6; Dernbach 12–5–19–1; Jordan 4–0–20–0. *Second innings*—Lewis 8–3–12–0; Dernbach 8–2–30–0; Meaker 8–2–21–0; Batty 3–0–13–0; de Bruyn 2–0–11–0; Jordan 2–1–4–1.

Umpires: J. H. Evans and N. J. Llong.

SURREY v DURHAM

At The Oval, April 26–29. Abandoned. Surrey 3pts, Durham 3pts.

This was the first complete washout at The Oval since August 2007, when Sussex were the visitors. A flooded outfield before the match was augmented by persistent rain in the wettest April on record. The players found various ways to entertain themselves: on the scheduled third day, some of the Durham team visited Sandown Park racecourse where they watched the feature race being won, appropriately enough, by Tidal Bay.

At Worcester, May 9–12. SURREY drew with WORCESTERSHIRE.

SURREY v SOMERSET

At The Oval, May 16–19. Drawn. Surrey 10pts, Somerset 11pts. Toss: Somerset. First-class debut: J. Overton.

Somerset's highest total at The Oval was not enough for victory, although their badly depleted side did not give up hope until two balls before the end. Suppiah and Hildreth took advantage of a more characteristically benign Oval pitch; Jordan's waywardness was compounded by a collision with umpire Jesty on the first day, which left both needing running repairs. The 18-year-old fast bowler Jamie Overton joined his twin brother in the Somerset side and, after outshining Craig with the bat, yorked Rudolph with his fifth ball in first-class cricket. Davies hit his first century of the season but, after some rough early treatment, Philander responded with three wickets in 18 balls. The inventive Maynard, helped by 42 from Lewis, saved the follow-on, before Meaker's late swing at express pace threatened to turn the match: he improved his best first-class figures for the second time in successive home games, and finished with his first haul of ten or more. Surrey – lacking Ramprakash, who had been dropped – needed 305 in 85 overs, but another middle-order slide stalled the chase and left Somerset favourites again. However, in contrast to the brave souls who abseiled off the OCS Stand for charity, the task proved too steep a requirement.

Close of play: first day, Somerset 441-5 (Trego 17, Dockrell 0); second day, Surrey 286-6 (Maynard 63, Batty 18); third day, Somerset 154-7 (Philander 3, C. Overton 2).

Somerset

Batsman	First innings		Second innings	
A. V. Suppiah	run out	106	c Davies b Lewis	10
A. W. R. Barrow	c Maynard b Meaker	47	c Batty b Meaker	9
N. R. D. Compton	lbw b de Bruyn	83	c Maynard b Jordan	50
*J. C. Hildreth	lbw b de Bruyn	120	c Davies b Meaker	4
†C. Kieswetter	lbw b Lewis	49	c Hamilton-Brown b Meaker	43
P. D. Trego	c Maynard b Meaker	21	c Hamilton-Brown b Meaker	4
G. H. Dockrell	c Davies b Lewis	11	(10) not out	5
C. A. J. Meschede	c Batty b Lewis	13	(7) b Meaker	10
V. D. Philander	c Davies b Meaker	1	(8) c de Bruyn b Meaker	5
C. Overton	not out	4	(9) b Meaker	12
J. Overton	not out	34	b Meaker	0
	L-b 11, n-b 12	23	B 2, l-b 7, w 1, n-b 18	28
	(9 wkts dec, 120 overs)	512	(58 overs)	180

1/63 (2) 2/206 (1) 3/290 (3) 4/398 (5) 5/437 (4) 6/445 (6) 7/471 (7) 8/474 (8) 9/474 (9) 110 overs: 474-9

1/18 (1) 2/24 (2) 3/30 (4) 4/122 (5) 5/130 (6) 6/147 (7) 7/147 (3) 8/171 (8) 9/180 (9) 10/180 (11)

Lewis 24–6–97–3; Jordan 14–1–77–0; Meaker 29–4–115–3; Edwards 14–1–74–0; Batty 26–2–89–0; de Bruyn 13–1–49–2. *Second innings*—Lewis 15–4–34–1; de Bruyn 4–1–8–0; Meaker 21–6–52–8; Edwards 2–0–18–0; Jordan 12–0–44–1; Batty 4–0–15–0.

Surrey

Batsman	First innings		Second innings	
J. A. Rudolph	b J. Overton	1	(3) c Suppiah b Dockrell	45
†S. M. Davies	c Barrow b Dockrell	104	b Philander	4
J. J. Roy	c Meschede b Philander	28	(1) c Barrow b Dockrell	41
Z. de Bruyn	c Hildreth b Philander	52	c Meschede b Dockrell	1
*R. J. Hamilton-Brown	lbw b Philander	0	not out	70
T. L. Maynard	c C. Overton b Trego	89	lbw b Trego	13
C. J. Jordan	c Philander b Trego	8	lbw b Trego	6
G. J. Batty	lbw b J. Overton	36	b Dockrell	33
S. C. Meaker	c Hildreth b Philander	2		
J. Lewis	b Dockrell	42	(9) not out	12
G. A. Edwards	not out	10		
	B 4, l-b 8, n-b 4	16	B 8, l-b 4, n-b 2	14
	(104.3 overs)	388	(7 wkts, 84.4 overs)	239

1/5 (1) 2/66 (3) 3/188 (2) 4/188 (4) 5/193 (5) 6/227 (7) 7/319 (8) 8/330 (9) 9/356 (6) 10/388 (10)

1/7 (2) 2/96 (1) 3/103 (3) 4/103 (4) 5/136 (6) 6/148 (7) 7/219 (8)

Philander 20–1–88–4; J. Overton 15–1–62–2; Trego 16–1–61–2; Meschede 11–1–40–0; Dockrell 32.3–3–103–2; C. Overton 5–0–12–0; Suppiah 5–1–10–0. *Second innings*—Philander 21.4–7–42–1; J. Overton 5–1–18–0; Trego 20–5–54–2; Meschede 3–0–15–0; Dockrell 32–8–89–4; Suppiah 3–0–9–0.

Umpires: I. J. Gould and T. E. Jesty.

SURREY v WARWICKSHIRE

At The Oval, May 23–26. Warwickshire won by five wickets. Warwickshire 20pts, Surrey 4pts. Toss: Surrey.

The first Championship match between these sides for five years emphasised Warwickshire's title credentials and punished Surrey's sloppiness on a slow and dry pitch of increasing turn. In a match that was never less than absorbing – around 3,000 invited schoolchildren learned that Championship cricket could be every bit as watchable as the instant variety – Warwickshire's hopes of a large total were thwarted by Batty's off-breaks. Roy then batted with familiar freedom to head the next counter-attack, before Patel became the second off-spinner to flourish, confining Warwickshire's eventual target to 222 from five sessions. Batty struck three times in four overs on his way to the second ten-wicket haul of his career. But Porterfield took charge, before Ambrose – who survived a stumping chance off Hamilton-Brown when 37 – and Clarke calmly knocked off the runs, completing victory 33 minutes into the final day of a game coinciding with the overdue arrival of summer.

Close of play: first day, Warwickshire 106-1 (Chopra 59, Porterfield 32); second day, Surrey 144-4 (Rudolph 17, Maynard 21); third day, Warwickshire 181-5 (Ambrose 74, Clarke 18).

Surrey

J. J. Roy lbw b Barker	21	– c Maddy b Clarke	71
†S. M. Davies run out	34	– c Ambrose b Barker	14
Z. de Bruyn c Porterfield b Clarke	16	– lbw b Maddy	16
J. A. Rudolph c Ambrose b Wright	19	– b Patel	22
*R. J. Hamilton-Brown run out	34	– c Ambrose b Patel	1
T. L. Maynard c Ambrose b Barker	39	– c Chopra b Patel	25
C. J. Jordan c Chopra b Woakes	0	– lbw b Patel	40
G. J. Batty lbw b Woakes	6	– c Woakes b Patel	0
J. Lewis c Ambrose b Wright	37	– c Porterfield b Patel	31
S. C. Meaker not out	5	– not out	9
J. W. Dernbach c Ambrose b Wright	0	– b Woakes	7
B 4, l-b 4, n-b 4	12	L-b 9	9
1/41 (1) 2/79 (3) 3/84 (2) (60.1 overs)	223	1/36 (2) 2/88 (3) (73.4 overs)	245
4/134 (4) 5/137 (5) 6/142 (7)		3/107 (1) 4/108 (5)	
7/164 (8) 8/203 (6) 9/221 (9) 10/223 (11)		5/148 (6) 6/161 (4) 7/165 (8)	
		8/219 (9) 9/234 (7) 10/245 (11)	

Wright 13.1–0–42–3; Barker 13–4–52–2; Clarke 11–2–34–1; Woakes 14–4–53–2; Patel 9–0–34–0. *Second innings*—Wright 16–2–47–0; Barker 5–0–17–1; Woakes 7.4–0–38–1; Patel 32–4–95–6; Maddy 5–0–19–1; Clarke 8–1–20–1.

Warwickshire

V. Chopra b Batty	78	– lbw b Dernbach	0
I. J. Westwood c Batty b Dernbach	5	– c Maynard b Batty	8
W. T. S. Porterfield c Maynard b Batty	46	– lbw b Batty	66
*J. O. Troughton b Meaker	3	– lbw b Batty	0
D. L. Maddy lbw b Meaker	15	– c and b Batty	1
†T. R. Ambrose b Hamilton-Brown	33	– not out	89
R. Clarke lbw b Batty	8	– not out	40
C. R. Woakes not out	15		
K. H. D. Barker st Davies b Batty	2		
J. S. Patel c and b Batty	0		
C. J. C. Wright c Roy b Batty	15		
B 6, l-b 13, n-b 8	27	B 2, l-b 6, n-b 10	18
1/17 (2) 2/131 (3) 3/138 (4) (92.4 overs)	247	1/0 (1) (5 wkts, 70 overs)	222
4/144 (1) 5/186 (5) 6/207 (6)		2/27 (2) 3/33 (4)	
7/207 (7) 8/213 (9) 9/213 (10) 10/247 (11)		4/37 (5) 5/148 (3)	

Dernbach 14–4–54–1; Meaker 16–5–39–2; Lewis 12–3–32–0; Batty 34.4–10–73–6; Jordan 9–4–16–0; Hamilton-Brown 7–0–14–1. *Second innings*—Dernbach 8–2–30–1; Lewis 12–4–28–0; Batty 30–9–69–4; Meaker 11–2–43–0; Jordan 3–0–20–0; Hamilton-Brown 6–0–24–0.

Umpires: J. H. Evans and D. J. Millns.

At Horsham, June 6–9. SURREY lost to SUSSEX by ten wickets.

SURREY v LANCASHIRE

At Guildford, July 11–14. Drawn. Surrey 10pts, Lancashire 8pts. Toss: Surrey.

Pietersen ensured the champions retreated from their first visit to Guildford with bruised hands and dented bowling figures. Lancashire had been grateful to be given first use of a slow but amiable pitch, although Tremlett found occasional bounce in his only first-class appearance of the season, and Meaker's speed was impressive. Horton batted solidly on the first day, then Croft increased the pace on a second deprived of 49 overs by rain in one of the chilliest festivals Woodbridge Road regulars could recall. Pietersen warmed up the third, though, with a display of stupendous strokeplay, taking a particular liking to the left-arm spinner Kerrigan: he hit him for seven of his eight sixes, to go with the 30 fours that flew across the short boundaries. His maiden first-class century for Surrey included 106 between lunch and tea, then another 124 before the close. Pietersen's eventual 234 not out, from 190 balls, was Surrey's highest individual score at Guildford (previously 228 not out by local boy Darren Bicknell against Nottinghamshire in 1995; Justin Langer made 342 for Somerset in 2006). The third day's 490 runs were also a ground record. Pietersen then told reporters he would be willing to return to all three international formats, providing he did so on a reduced schedule. Heavy overnight rain and showers saturated an already soggy square, ensuring the final day was blank.

Close of play: first day, Lancashire 245-3 (Prince 32, Croft 5); second day, Lancashire 425-7 (Croft 104, Shahzad 2); third day, Surrey 430-5 (Pietersen 234, Batty 4).

Lancashire

P. J. Horton c Batty b Tremlett	110	A. Shahzad not out	12
S. C. Moore lbw b Meaker	24		
K. R. Brown c Davies b Meaker	49	B 10, l-b 8, w 2, n-b 16	36
A. G. Prince c de Bruyn b Kartik	34		——
S. J. Croft not out	154	1/47 (2) (7 wkts dec, 137 overs)	485
T. C. Smith run out	7	2/169 (3) 3/233 (1)	
†G. D. Cross c Ansari b Meaker	13	4/252 (4) 5/279 (6) 6/298 (7)	
*G. Chapple lbw b Lewis	46	7/419 (8) 110 overs: 355-6	

K. W. Hogg and S. C. Kerrigan did not bat.

Tremlett 27–6–82–1; Lewis 34–4–101–1; Meaker 28–5–138–3; Kartik 20–3–56–1; de Bruyn 14–0–54–0; Batty 14–1–36–0.

Surrey

R. J. Burns b Chapple	0	*G. J. Batty not out	4
Z. S. Ansari c Smith b Shahzad	21	B 7, l-b 4, n-b 6	17
Z. de Bruyn lbw b Kerrigan	94		——
K. P. Pietersen not out	234	1/0 (1) 2/49 (2) (5 wkts, 85 overs)	430
†S. M. Davies c Cross b Smith	22	3/230 (3) 4/302 (5)	
J. J. Roy c Kerrigan b Shahzad	38	5/391 (6)	

M. Kartik, S. C. Meaker, J. Lewis and C. T. Tremlett did not bat.

Chapple 16–5–46–1; Hogg 15–1–57–0; Shahzad 18–1–96–2; Kerrigan 23–0–152–1; Smith 13–1–68–1.

Umpires: P. J. Hartley and N. A. Mallender.

At Nottingham, July 18–21. SURREY drew with NOTTINGHAMSHIRE.

> "Players were going down with food poisoning during camps, so I wanted to offer them something better than a fried egg sandwich. I was told I couldn't, as that was all the budget could afford."
>
> **Bangladesh Cricket, 2012, page 947**

At Birmingham, July 27–30. SURREY drew with WARWICKSHIRE.

At Chester-le-Street, August 7–9. SURREY lost to DURHAM by an innings and 38 runs.

SURREY v MIDDLESEX

At The Oval, August 15–18. Surrey won by eight runs. Surrey 19pts, Middlesex 4pts. Toss: Surrey. County debut: A. Balbirnie. Championship debut: A. M. Rossington.

Surrey's first victory for four months fuelled their hopes of avoiding relegation, yet they almost fell foul of an adhesive final pair, who had doubled Middlesex's lead in the first innings and were only separated at the climax by Batty's heartfelt appeal for leg-before. Murtagh and Roland-Jones, who both started with Surrey clubs, had also claimed 14 wickets between them, yet it was the spin of Kartik and Batty which proved decisive on a pitch tailored to their needs. Murtagh relished the overhead conditions on the first day, although Roy's fighting response kept Surrey afloat. But once Rogers departed for 56, Middlesex frittered away their advantage in the face of Kartik's artistry. Burns and Harinath delivered a lesson in patience, placement and good running, and within four balls reached their maiden Championship centuries, the first time two Surrey players had done so in the same innings since Arthur McIntyre and Geoff Whittaker in 1946, against Kent at The Oval. Their stand of 217 more than wiped out Middlesex's advantage, only for Roland-Jones to trigger a collapse of nine for 111. Middlesex needed 254, and made a useful start before Rogers – visibly angry at umpire Nigel Cowley's lbw decision – was cut off in full flow. With Kartik wheeling down 47 overs unchanged, as well as grabbing two sharp chances at leg slip, Batty squeezed Surrey home, finishing with six for 83 after the final pair had added 48. Their win made up for the three-run loss to Middlesex at Lord's in April.

Close of play: first day, Middlesex 99-1 (Robson 29, Smith 1); second day, Surrey 86-1 (Burns 40, Harinath 39); third day, Middlesex 45-1 (Robson 22, Smith 0).

Surrey

R. J. Burns c Malan b Murtagh	6	– lbw b Roland-Jones	121
Z. S. Ansari c Rossington b Roland-Jones	10	– c Robson b Roland-Jones	0
A. Harinath lbw b Roland-Jones	14	– c Rogers b Crook	109
Z. de Bruyn lbw b Roland-Jones	0	– c Rogers b Roland-Jones	23
R. J. Hamilton-Brown b Murtagh	2	– lbw b Roland-Jones	2
J. J. Roy not out	55	– lbw b Crook	17
†S. M. Davies c Rossington b Dexter	16	– c Crook b Murtagh	44
*G. J. Batty lbw b Dexter	9	– b Roland-Jones	3
M. Kartik b Murtagh	23	– lbw b Crook	2
T. E. Linley c Robson b Murtagh	0	– not out	1
J. W. Dernbach lbw b Murtagh	0	– c Denly b Smith	0
L-b 5, n-b 4	9	B 5, l-b 3, w 5, n-b 6	19
1/10 (1) 2/28 (2) 3/28 (4) 4/33 (5) 5/41 (3) 6/73 (7) 7/97 (8) 8/138 (9) 9/144 (10) 10/144 (11) (44.4 overs)	144	1/13 (2) 2/230 (3) 3/264 (1) 4/267 (4) 5/278 (5) 6/292 (6) 7/307 (8) 8/318 (9) 9/341 (7) 10/341 (11) (111.3 overs)	341

Murtagh 16.4–5–37–5; Roland-Jones 12–6–38–3; Dexter 10–1–35–2; Crook 6–0–29–0. *Second innings*—Murtagh 17–3–71–1; Roland-Jones 24–9–39–5; Balbirnie 8–0–24–0; Dexter 5–0–14–0; Smith 27.3–3–71–1; Crook 25–3–93–3; Malan 3–1–14–0; Denly 2–0–7–0.

Middlesex

*C. J. L. Rogers b Dernbach	56	– lbw b Batty	19
S. D. Robson lbw b Dernbach	29	– c Roy b Kartik	22
T. M. J. Smith b Kartik	31	– c Kartik b Batty	0
J. L. Denly c Davies b Linley	17	– lbw b Batty	12
D. J. Malan c Burns b Kartik	22	– c Roy b Batty	33
N. J. Dexter c Roy b Kartik	5	– c Kartik b Batty	2
A. Balbirnie lbw b Batty	14	– lbw b Kartik	3
†A. M. Rossington c Batty b Kartik	0	– c Roy b Kartik	25
S. P. Crook lbw b Batty	0	– b Dernbach	67
T. S. Roland-Jones not out	17	– lbw b Batty	17
T. J. Murtagh c Hamilton-Brown b Kartik	26	– not out	25
B 4, l-b 3, n-b 8	15	B 1, l-b 17, n-b 2	20
1/98 (1) 2/99 (2) 3/128 (4) 4/164 (3) 5/171 (5) 6/186 (6) 7/188 (7) 8/188 (9) 9/188 (8) 10/232 (11) (80.4 overs)	232	1/43 (1) 2/45 (2) 3/45 (3) 4/88 (4) 5/92 (6) 6/101 (7) 7/101 (5) 8/197 (9) 9/197 (8) 10/245 (10) (99.3 overs)	245

Dernbach 16–5–37–2; Linley 12–0–46–1; de Bruyn 7–2–21–0; Kartik 28.4–10–69–5; Batty 17–6–52–2. *Second innings*—Dernbach 10–1–42–1; Linley 4–0–8–0; Kartik 47–14–91–3; Batty 36.3–8–83–6; Ansari 2–0–3–0.

Umpires: N. G. C. Cowley and N. J. Llong.

At Taunton, August 28–31. SURREY drew with SOMERSET.

SURREY v NOTTINGHAMSHIRE

At The Oval, September 4–7. Surrey won by 195 runs. Surrey 21pts, Nottinghamshire 4pts. Toss: Surrey.

Surrey's first win over Nottinghamshire for nine years confirmed their first division survival. Against a makeshift side beset by international calls and all but out of the title race, they possessed a better attack – principally spinners Kartik and Batty on a slow, turning pitch – and greater middle-order resilience. De Bruyn and Wilson steadied them on the opening day, then Meaker celebrated his county cap by ensuring an extra batting point, before trapping Wessels and ripping out Voges's off stump. Read's sterling response found few allies, other than the 19-year-old left-hander Sam Wood, who made a patient 45 in a stand of 92 in only his second Championship match. Read mounted a late assault on Linley, but could not prevent him from wrapping up the innings with his fifth wicket. Left-arm spinner White benefited from increasing assistance from the pitch, before de Bruyn and Wilson again showed what patience could achieve. The target of 347 on the final day (plus an over) was never more than notional, especially as Hales had departed after the second day to join up with England's Twenty20 squad, and Batty relished conditions few spinners had experienced in a soggy summer.

Close of play: first day, Surrey 242-9 (Meaker 12, Linley 4); second day, Nottinghamshire 227; third day, Nottinghamshire 0-0 (Gurney 0, Edwards 0).

Surrey

R. J. Burns c White b Gurney	23	– b White	44
Z. S. Ansari c Mullaney b Phillips	3	– c Read b Fletcher	4
A. Harinath b Gurney	11	– b White	14
K. P. Pietersen c Read b Gurney	15	– c Phillips b White	22
Z. de Bruyn lbw b White	71	– lbw b White	78
J. J. Roy b White	20	– c Voges b Wood	41
†G. C. Wilson lbw b Fletcher	68	– c Taylor b Wood	57
*G. J. Batty c Read b Phillips	8	– c Read b Fletcher	17
S. C. Meaker not out	29	– c Read b Wood	1
M. Kartik c Hales b Phillips	0	– c Taylor b Phillips	18
T. E. Linley b Gurney	14	– not out	4
L-b 5, n-b 2	7	L-b 4	4
1/19 (2) 2/30 (1) 3/47 (3) 4/52 (4) 5/83 (6) 6/206 (5) 7/219 (7) 8/231 (8) 9/231 (10) 10/269 (11) (106.2 overs)	269	1/10 (2) 2/50 (3) 3/75 (1) 4/92 (4) 5/164 (6) 6/254 (5) 7/264 (7) 8/268 (9) 9/298 (8) 10/304 (10) (92.3 overs)	304

Phillips 23–8–49–3; Fletcher 23–10–49–1; Gurney 17.2–5–47–4; White 28–4–78–2; Wood 8–0–20–0; Mullaney 7–0–21–0. *Second innings*—Phillips 12.3–3–52–1; Fletcher 13–2–33–2; Gurney 12–1–46–0; White 33–6–97–4; Wood 20–2–64–3; Mullaney 2–0–8–0.

Nottinghamshire

M. H. Wessels lbw b Meaker	5	– (3) lbw b Batty	16
A. D. Hales c Roy b Linley	19		
A. C. Voges b Meaker	2	– (4) c de Bruyn b Pietersen	9
J. W. A. Taylor lbw b Linley	12	– (5) lbw b Batty	6
S. J. Mullaney lbw b Kartik	15	– (6) lbw b Meaker	18
*†C. M. W. Read not out	85	– (7) c Ansari b Kartik	17
S. K. W. Wood c Burns b Kartik	45	– (8) lbw b Batty	2
G. G. White b Linley	1	– (9) b Batty	4
B. J. Phillips b Kartik	14	– (10) not out	20
L. J. Fletcher lbw b Linley	6	– (11) lbw b Kartik	4
H. F. Gurney lbw b Linley	0	– (1) c Pietersen b Linley	0
N. J. Edwards (did not bat)		– (2) c Wilson b Pietersen	31
B 12, l-b 5, n-b 6	23	B 4, l-b 2, w 10, n-b 8	24
1/17 (1) 2/27 (3) 3/41 (2) 4/56 (4) 5/60 (5) 6/152 (7) 7/157 (8) 8/186 (9) 9/209 (10) 10/227 (11) (82.5 overs)	227	1/3 (1) 2/54 (3) 3/66 (4) 4/75 (5) 5/75 (2) 6/100 (7) 7/113 (8) 8/113 (6) 9/146 (9) 10/151 (11) (64.5 overs)	151

Edwards replaced Hales after he was called up by England.

Linley 22.5–6–62–5; Meaker 13–0–50–2; Kartik 29–11–43–3; Batty 8–1–23–0; de Bruyn 8–1–28–0; Ansari 2–0–4–0. *Second innings*—Kartik 15.5–5–21–2; Linley 7–1–28–1; Meaker 9–1–37–1; Batty 21–12–30–4; Ansari 2–0–5–0; Pietersen 10–3–24–2.

Umpires: R. T. Robinson and M. J. Saggers.

At Liverpool, September 11–14. SURREY drew with LANCASHIRE.

SUSSEX

That was the week that wasn't

BRUCE TALBOT

One week scuppered Sussex's season. On August 24, they had an eye on three trophies. Had they completed victory over Somerset that day, they would have moved ahead of Warwickshire in the Championship by a single point, though from a game more. But rain denied Sussex, and the time spent waiting anxiously in the Taunton dressing-room apparently did little for their state of mind.

Yorkshire thrashed them in the Twenty20 semi-final at Cardiff the following day and, although Sussex regrouped at Canterbury 48 hours later to secure a home semi-final in the CB40, they were then overpowered by Hampshire in front of a stunned Hove crowd. Second place in the Championship would have been some compensation, but they lost their last two games and finished fourth – not bad for a side tipped to go down, but an anticlimax nevertheless.

Sussex had gone into their eighth game with only one victory, but beat Surrey at Horsham with a few minutes to spare, and went on to win their next three home matches: a nailbiter at Arundel against Durham, plus two at Hove, where the fast, bouncy, relaid wickets were heaven-sent for their attack – in particular Steve Magoffin and Monty Panesar. But not every venue provided the same assistance. "It was on flat pitches where we let ourselves down," said Sussex coach Mark Robinson.

This wasn't a summer for batsmen to dip their bread. Even so, with the exception of openers Chris Nash and Ed Joyce, the Sussex line-up still underperformed. Nash came closest to 1,000 runs, and took 21 wickets with his underrated off-breaks; Joyce, who assumed the captaincy when Mike Yardy stepped down at the end of July, topped the averages, despite missing two games because of Ireland commitments.

Sussex passed 350 on only three occasions, never claimed maximum batting points and, after a decade of unerring reliability, could not count on Murray Goodwin to get them out of trouble. Goodwin continued to play some sparkling limited-overs innings, but was dropped in the Championship for the first time. A total of 360 runs at 16 was a sad way to finish a magnificent Sussex career in which he scored almost 15,000 in first-class cricket, including 48 hundreds. Goodwin made clear his desire to stay, but he was turning 40 in December, and Sussex felt his race was run. He joined Glamorgan on a one-year contract. At least he departed to a standing ovation from a sun-drenched Hove crowd with his two sons alongside him, having made his highest score of the season.

Luke Wells compiled two classy hundreds against Surrey, but none of the younger batsmen caught the eye, and no one reached three figures in the Second Eleven Championship – as damning a statistic as any. Yardy hit a match-winning 110 at Liverpool, but struggled through much of the summer,

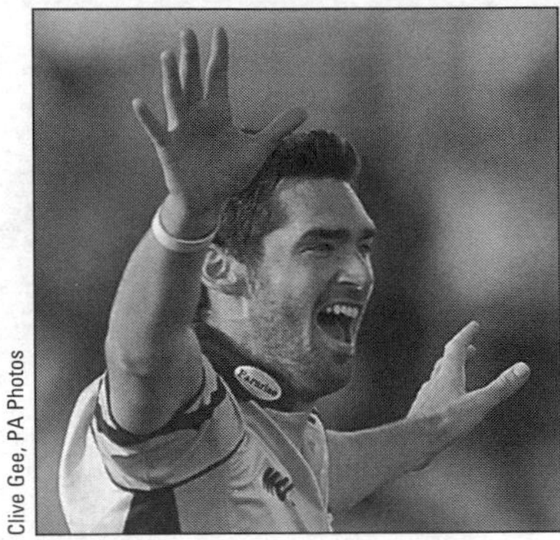
Clive Gee, PA Photos

Chris Liddle

although he was peerless as a slip catcher. Without the pressures of captaincy, he spent the winter tweaking his technique and working on his fitness.

Replacing Goodwin was hardly straightforward, but Sussex were delighted to welcome back Rory Hamilton-Brown, who had spent three years captaining Surrey. After a troubled summer in which Hamilton-Brown lost his friend and team-mate Tom Maynard, Robinson believed he was capable of getting consistent middle-order runs and achieving his England ambitions.

There were few better bowling attacks in the country. In an era of ego-driven overseas locums, the Australian seamer Magoffin was something of a throwback. Utterly dependable and a great team man, he benefited from Robinson's decision to use him sparingly in one-day cricket. Panesar located his mojo in the second half of the summer, when he slowed his pace. James Anyon was not quite as prolific as in 2011, but still took 42 wickets and bowled quickly at times, notably in the win over Surrey that changed Sussex's season. Amjad Khan got better as the summer wore on, before he had to undergo knee surgery again. No bowler in the land took more wickets in the two limited-overs competitions than the 31 collected by the unheralded Chris Liddle. Their stocks were strengthened by the acquisition of Chris Jordan from Surrey.

The single biggest disappointment was the manner of the Twenty20 exit. Fortified by the muscular hitting of Luke Wright, Scott Styris and Matt Prior, Sussex lost just once on their way to the semi-final, and were favourites to lift the trophy for the second time. But, Nash aside, the batting malfunctioned completely on finals day against Yorkshire. Only Derbyshire beat them in the CB40 before Michael Carberry and James Vince exposed their lack of an out-and-out strike bowler in the semi-final.

The format continued to be popular with Sussex supporters, despite miserable weather. Outgoing chief executive Dave Brooks argued that, commercially, a return to 50-over domestic cricket was a mistake. Brooks had been an enlightened and popular figurehead in four years at Hove, and left the county well placed to continue the upward trajectory of the past decade. He was replaced by Zac Toumazi, who had commercial experience at Surrey and Hampshire.

In November, a betting journalist, Ed Hawkins, published a book in which it was claimed Sussex's home CB40 match against Kent in 2011 had been fixed. It attracted almost £14m of turnover on Betfair, around double the figure for an average televised county game. Sussex confirmed some players had been approached, and passed their concerns on to club officials immediately after the match, when the ECB were informed. But a joint ECB–ICC investigation revealed nothing untoward.

Championship attendance: 33,141.

SUSSEX RESULTS

All first-class matches – Played 17: Won 5, Lost 5, Drawn 7.
County Championship matches – Played 16: Won 5, Lost 5, Drawn 6.

LV= County Championship, 4th in Division 1;
Friends Life t20, s-f; Clydesdale Bank 40, s-f.

COUNTY CHAMPIONSHIP AVERAGES, BATTING AND FIELDING

Cap		*M*	*I*	*NO*	*R*	*HS*	*100*	*50*	*Avge*	*Ct/St*
2009	E. C. Joyce	14	24	3	829	108*	2	5	39.47	9
2008	C. D. Nash†	16	28	2	984	162	3	2	37.84	8
	L. W. P. Wells†	14	21	2	713	127	2	3	37.52	12
	A. Khan	7	7	3	142	57*	0	1	35.50	0
2011	J. E. Anyon	15	19	8	316	64*	0	2	28.72	6
	B. C. Brown†	13	22	3	521	76*	0	5	27.42	38/3
2007	L. J. Wright	9	14	1	356	81	0	3	27.38	7
2005	M. H. Yardy	16	25	2	574	110	1	3	24.95	32
2003	M. J. Prior‡	4	5	0	114	86	0	1	22.80	7
	S. J. Magoffin§	15	19	3	363	41*	0	0	22.68	4
	J. S. Gatting†	10	16	3	279	72*	0	1	21.46	5
	Naved Arif¶	7	10	0	184	46	0	0	18.40	2
2001	M. W. Goodwin¶	14	23	1	360	77	0	2	16.36	5
	K. O. Wernars¶	2	4	0	65	50	0	1	16.25	1
	L. J. Hatchett†	3	6	3	32	18*	0	0	10.66	1
2010	M. S. Panesar	15	16	4	88	31	0	0	7.33	3

Also batted: W. A. Adkin (1 match) 9, 6 (1 ct); M. W. Machan† (1 match) 4, 6.

† *Born in Sussex.* ‡ *ECB contract.* § *Official overseas player.* ¶ *Other non-England-qualified player.*

BOWLING

	Style	*O*	*M*	*R*	*W*	*BB*	*5I*	*Avge*
S. J. Magoffin	RFM	480.1	161	1,143	57	7-34	2	20.05
C. D. Nash	OB	135.2	23	446	21	3-23	0	21.23
M. S. Panesar	SLA	514.1	157	1,227	53	7-60	2	23.15
A. Khan	RFM	156.4	30	522	22	5-25	2	23.72
Naved Arif	LFM	151	23	511	17	3-34	0	30.05
J. E. Anyon	RFM	429.5	73	1,646	42	5-36	2	39.19

Also bowled: W. A. Adkin (RM) 5–1–20–0; J. S. Gatting (OB) 12–0–56–0; L. J. Hatchett (LFM) 64.5–12–280–8; L. W. P. Wells (OB) 10–4–37–1; K. O. Wernars (RFM) 36–11–100–4; L. J. Wright (RFM) 79–6–327–5; M. H. Yardy (LM/SLA) 12–1–68–2.

LEADING CB40 AVERAGES (100 runs/4 wickets)

Batting	*Runs*	*HS*	*Avge*	*SR*	*Ct*
M. J. Prior	106	78*	106.00	87.60	1
L. J. Wright	418	122	59.71	106.90	0
M. W. Machan	161	126*	53.66	107.33	1
M. H. Yardy	158	61	31.60	75.59	0
E. C. Joyce	249	102	31.12	81.37	5
C. D. Nash	240	53	26.66	102.12	2

Bowling	*W*	*BB*	*Avge*	*ER*
C. D. Nash	10	3-27	18.70	4.71
C. J. Liddle	14	4-21	23.57	5.33
W. A. T. Beer	9	3-27	23.66	5.07
A. Khan	10	3-51	23.80	4.49
M. H. Yardy	5	2-20	45.40	4.31

LEADING FLT20 AVERAGES (100 runs/16 overs)

Batting	Runs	HS	Avge	SR	Ct
M. J. Prior	249	81	41.50	**196.06**	1
S. B. Styris	204	100*	51.00	**190.65**	2
L. J. Wright	312	91	34.66	**160.00**	3
J. S. Gatting	131	45*	32.75	**139.36**	8
C. D. Nash	319	80*	39.87	**131.27**	5
M. W. Goodwin	262	68*	32.75	**129.70**	3

Bowling	W	BB	Avge	ER
M. H. Yardy	7	2-15	29.85	**6.53**
S. B. Styris	7	3-22	15.85	**6.59**
C. J. Liddle	17	5-17	11.94	**7.33**
A. Khan	8	2-32	23.50	**8.05**
W. A. T. Beer	8	2-26	27.75	**8.53**

FIRST-CLASS COUNTY RECORDS

Highest score for	344*	M. W. Goodwin v Somerset at Taunton	2009
Highest score against	322	E. Paynter (Lancashire) at Hove	1937
Leading run-scorer	34,150	J. G. Langridge (avge 37.69)	1928–1955
Best bowling for	10-48	C. H. G. Bland v Kent at Tonbridge	1899
Best bowling against	9-11	A. P. Freeman (Kent) at Hove	1922
Leading wicket-taker	2,211	M. W. Tate (avge 17.41)	1912–1937
Highest total for	742-5 dec	v Somerset at Taunton	2009
Highest total against	726	by Nottinghamshire at Nottingham	1895
Lowest total for	19	v Surrey at Godalming	1830
	19	v Nottinghamshire at Hove	1873
Lowest total against	18	by Kent at Gravesend	1867

LIST A COUNTY RECORDS

Highest score for	163	C. J. Adams v Middlesex at Arundel	1999
Highest score against	198*	G. A. Gooch (Essex) at Hove	1982
Leading run-scorer	7,969	A. P. Wells (avge 31.62)	1981–1996
Best bowling for	7-41	A. N. Jones v Nottinghamshire at Nottingham	1986
Best bowling against	8-21	M. A. Holding (Derbyshire) at Hove	1988
Leading wicket-taker	370	R. J. Kirtley (avge 22.35)	1995–2010
Highest total for	399-4	v Worcestershire at Horsham	2011
Highest total against	377-9	by Somerset at Hove	2003
Lowest total for	49	v Derbyshire at Chesterfield	1969
Lowest total against	36	by Leicestershire at Leicester	1973

TWENTY20 COUNTY RECORDS

Highest score for	117	M. J. Prior v Glamorgan at Hove	2010
Highest score against	152*	G. R. Napier (Essex) at Chelmsford	2008
Leading run-scorer	**2,200**	**M. W. Goodwin (avge 29.33)**	**2003–2012**
Best bowling for	5-11	Mushtaq Ahmed v Essex at Hove	2005
Best bowling against	5-14	A. D. Mascarenhas (Hampshire) at Hove	2004
Leading wicket-taker	64	R. J. Kirtley (avge 25.89)	2003–2010
Highest total for	239-5	v Glamorgan at Hove	2010
Highest total against	242-3	by Essex at Chelmsford	2008
Lowest total for	67	v Hampshire at Hove	2004
Lowest total against	85	by Hampshire at Southampton	2008

ADDRESS

County Ground, Eaton Road, Hove BN3 3AN (0844 264 0202; **email** info@sussexcricket.co.uk). **Website** www.sussexcricket.co.uk

OFFICIALS

Captain 2012 – M. H. Yardy
2013 – E. C. Joyce
Professional cricket manager M. A. Robinson
Cricket performance manager K. Greenfield
President B. Bedson
Chairman J. R. May
Chief executive 2012 – D. Brooks
2013 – Z. Toumazi
Chairman, cricket committee J. R. T. Barclay
Head groundsman A. Mackay
Scorer M. J. Charman

At The Oval, April 5–8. SUSSEX lost to SURREY by 86 runs.

At Liverpool, April 12–14. SUSSEX beat LANCASHIRE by ten wickets.

SUSSEX v WARWICKSHIRE

At Hove, April 26–29. Drawn. Sussex 5pts, Warwickshire 8pts. Toss: Sussex.

The Sussex groundstaff spent much of the abandoned fourth day repairing the Sea End sightscreen, which blew over when the steel rope and three of the six posts tethering it to the ground were uprooted during overnight gale-force winds. Sussex's morale needed repairing as well. On a surprisingly dry pitch, their seamers – Magoffin excepted – bowled too short and were pummelled by Trott, whose first outing of the season was a near-seven-hour masterclass containing one half-chance. He put on 219 with Chopra, who confirmed his aptitude for early-season conditions following his two double-hundreds in April 2011. Neither were Ambrose and Clarke troubled by an impotent attack, and Warwickshire indulged their policy of extending the punishment until they were bowled out: their last four wickets added 261. Sussex were glad to come off after losing three wickets during the 8.1 overs possible on the third day. Soon the ground was flooded, and the flattened sightscreen was being pecked by sodden seagulls.

Close of play: first day, Warwickshire 281-5 (Trott 132, Wright 13); second day, Sussex 57-2 (Wells 5, Goodwin 8); third day, Sussex 80-5 (Yardy 8, Gatting 4).

Warwickshire

V. Chopra lbw b Wells	105
W. T. S. Porterfield c Joyce b Magoffin	4
I. R. Bell b Anyon	0
I. J. L. Trott c Yardy b Nash	178
*J. O. Troughton c Yardy b Panesar	12
D. L. Maddy lbw b Magoffin	1
C. J. C. Wright b Anyon	15
†T. R. Ambrose c Yardy b Panesar	75
R. Clarke not out	78
K. H. D. Barker lbw b Nash	33
J. S. Patel c Goodwin b Nash	16
B 8, l-b 11, w 1, n-b 8	28
1/8 (2) 2/13 (3) 3/232 (1) 4/257 (5) 5/263 (6) 6/284 (7) 7/394 (4) 8/444 (8) 9/513 (10) 10/545 (11) (152.5 overs)	545
110 overs: 359-6	

Anyon 28–3–132–2; Magoffin 33–8–90–2; Khan 23–3–106–0; Panesar 43–13–111–2; Gatting 5–0–19–0; Wells 6–2–24–1; Nash 14.5–0–44–3.

Sussex

C. D. Nash c Chopra b Barker	18
E. C. Joyce lbw b Patel	14
L. W. P. Wells lbw b Barker	5
M. W. Goodwin lbw b Barker	16
†M. J. Prior b Wright	0
*M. H. Yardy not out	8
J. S. Gatting not out	4
B 4, l-b 7, n-b 4	15
1/39 (1) 2/46 (2) 3/65 (3) 4/66 (5) 5/70 (4) (5 wkts, 38.1 overs)	80

S. J. Magoffin, A. Khan, J. E. Anyon and M. S. Panesar did not bat.

Wright 14.1–3–32–1; Barker 12–4–28–3; Clarke 5–3–7–0; Patel 7–5–2–1.

Umpires: R. J. Bailey and J. W. Lloyds.

At Weetwood, Leeds, May 1–3. SUSSEX lost to LEEDS/BRADFORD MCCU by 79 runs. *Sussex's first three-day defeat by a university side in 22 years.*

At Hove, May 5–7. SUSSEX drew with WEST INDIANS (see West Indian tour section).

SUSSEX v LANCASHIRE

At Hove, May 9–12. Drawn. Sussex 8pts, Lancashire 5pts. Toss: Lancashire. County debut: A. Shahzad.

No play was possible until the final day, but patient spectators – and Sky Sports subscribers – were rewarded with 444 runs and 16 wickets. The champions had yet to win a game of their title defence, and gained little from this exercise, except when Shahzad – beginning a loan spell after falling out with Yorkshire – became the first Lancashire bowler to take two wickets in his first over for the county; he had earlier experienced a 12-ball duck. But Shahzad's figures were spoiled by Prior and Yardy, who flayed some wayward bowling as Sussex raced to a third batting point with two balls to spare. The umpires received catcalls for abandoning the third day in bright sunshine at 3pm; the run-ups were a concern, but both captains were keen to start.

Close of play: first day, no play; second day, no play; third day, no play.

ONE-WAY TRAFFIC OVER THE PENNINES

Players who have represented both Lancashire and Yorkshire in the Championship:

	Birthplace	*Yorkshire*	*Lancashire*
H. J. Tinsley	Malton	1890	1895–1896
C. H. Parkin	Eaglescliffe, Co. Durham	1906	1914–1926
B. Wood	Ossett	1964	1966–1979
S. D. Fletcher	Keighley	1983–91	1992
D. Byas	Kilham	1986–2001	2002
G. Keedy	Sandal	1994	1995–2012
S. M. Katich	Middle Swan, Western Australia	2002	2010
A. Shahzad	**Huddersfield**	**2006–2012**	**2012**

All the above were born in Yorkshire unless otherwise stated.
No Lancashire player has gone on to play for Yorkshire.

Lancashire

P. J. Horton c and b Anyon	16
S. C. Moore c Anyon b Naved Arif	18
K. R. Brown run out	41
A. G. Prince c Prior b Naved Arif	9
S. J. Croft c Joyce b Magoffin	27
L. A. Procter not out	19
†G. D. Cross c Prior b Magoffin	2
A. Shahzad c Prior b Anyon	0
*G. Chapple c Panesar b Naved Arif	9
K. W. Hogg not out	1
L-b 2	2
1/26 (2) 2/45 (1) 3/74 (4) 4/112 (5) 5/116 (3) 6/118 (7) 7/127 (8) 8/140 (9) (8 wkts dec, 45.4 overs)	144

S. I. Mahmood did not bat.

Magoffin 16–4–53–2; Naved Arif 9.4–1–34–3; Anyon 13–3–35–2; Panesar 7–2–20–0.

Sussex

C. D. Nash lbw b Shahzad	33
E. C. Joyce lbw b Shahzad	32
L. W. P. Wells lbw b Shahzad	2
M. W. Goodwin c Cross b Mahmood	8
†M. J. Prior c Brown b Mahmood	86
*M. H. Yardy c Moore b Mahmood	63
J. S. Gatting not out	42
Naved Arif c Cross b Procter	4
S. J. Magoffin c Horton b Procter	6
J. E. Anyon not out	0
L-b 11, w 1, n-b 12	24
1/58 (2) 2/60 (3) 3/71 (4) 4/85 (1) 5/227 (6) 6/246 (5) 7/279 (8) 8/293 (9) (8 wkts, 47.4 overs)	300

M. S. Panesar did not bat.

Chapple 12–3–71–0; Hogg 5–0–25–0; Shahzad 12.4–1–71–3; Mahmood 10–0–80–3; Procter 8–0–42–2.

Umpires: M. R. Benson and N. G. B. Cook.

At Worcester, May 16–19. SUSSEX drew with WORCESTERSHIRE.

SUSSEX v NOTTINGHAMSHIRE

At Hove, May 25–28. Nottinghamshire won by seven wickets. Nottinghamshire 23pts, Sussex 5pts. Toss: Sussex.

On the ground where his father Kepler played his county cricket, Riki Wessels made the difference with a sublime career-best 199. A relaid pitch, used for a CB40 match on the eve of this game, had alarming cracks by the final day, but Nottinghamshire eased past a ticklish target to record their first win at Hove since 1983. Nash made up for two near misses at Worcester by scoring a hundred, and Wright made the first of two half-centuries on his return to the Championship following 11 months beset by injury, tonsillitis and dengue fever; he was fortunate to escape on 25, when a delivery from Carter brushed leg stump only for the bail to stay put. The Sussex bowlers struggled to cope with buffeting crosswinds and Wessels's effervescent strokeplay on the second day, when he and Hales finally put on Nottinghamshire's first century opening partnership in 100 Championship innings that had seen 21 different combinations: they had gone through 19 different opening pairs since Will Jefferson and Bilal Shafayat shared 157 here in August 2008. Sussex lost four wickets clearing their arrears before Goodwin, battling against the worst form of his county career, and Wright gave them false hope in a stand of 107. Adams was unable to bowl on the third day due to a shoulder problem, but Patel filled the breach by varying his pace and flight, then rode his luck in the run-chase.

Close of play: first day, Sussex 305-9 (Naved Arif 24); second day, Nottinghamshire 320-4 (Wessels 184, Voges 5); third day, Sussex 177-4 (Goodwin 52, Wright 37).

Sussex

C. D. Nash b Gurney	128	– (2) lbw b Carter	21
E. C. Joyce c Wessels b Phillips	5	– (1) b Patel	39
J. S. Gatting c Lumb b Patel	19	– b Carter	1
M. W. Goodwin c Voges b Adams	1	– c Lumb b Adams	74
*M. H. Yardy run out	10	– lbw b Carter	17
L. J. Wright c Adams b Patel	81	c Read b Adams	55
†B. C. Brown c Voges b Patel	9	– c Voges b Patel	0
Naved Arif c Phillips b Patel	28	– c Wessels b Carter	19
S. J. Magoffin c Patel b Gurney	19	– b Patel	0
J. E. Anyon c Taylor b Adams	4	– not out	22
M. S. Panesar not out	0	– c Read b Gurney	2
B 2, l-b 1, w 2	5	B 1, l-b 9, w 3	13
1/35 (2) 2/79 (3) 3/83 (4) 4/97 (5) (98.2 overs)	309	1/64 (2) 2/66 (1) (101.2 overs)	263
5/242 (1) 6/248 (6) 7/257 (7)		3/68 (3) 4/99 (5)	
8/285 (9) 9/305 (10) 10/309 (8)		5/206 (6) 6/217 (7) 7/221 (4)	
		8/226 (9) 9/258 (8) 10/263 (11)	

Phillips 18–6–46–1; Gurney 18–4–79–2; Adams 21–1–59–2; Carter 17–5–55–0; Patel 24.2–3–67–4. *Second innings*—Phillips 10–1–20–0; Gurney 17.2–1–51–1; Carter 25–3–64–4; Patel 36–6–87–3; Voges 2–1–2–0; Adams 11–2–29–2.

Nottinghamshire

M. H. Wessels c Brown b Magoffin	199	– c Goodwin b Nash	30
A. D. Hales b Panesar	80	– c Joyce b Yardy	24
M. J. Lumb c Gatting b Naved Arif	23	– lbw b Panesar	25
S. R. Patel c Brown b Nash	11	– not out	50
J. W. A. Taylor c Gatting b Nash	5	– not out	12
A. C. Voges c Panesar b Anyon	7		
*†C. M. W. Read c Anyon b Nash	45		
B. J. Phillips c Panesar b Anyon	6		
A. R. Adams c Magoffin b Anyon	17		
A. Carter not out	17		
H. F. Gurney b Naved Arif	0		
B 1, l-b 5, w 2, n-b 10	18	B 4, l-b 1, w 1	6
1/171 (2) 2/266 (3) 3/289 (4) 4/303 (5) 5/322 (6) 6/349 (1) 7/356 (8) 8/389 (9) 9/428 (7) 10/428 (11) (119.2 overs)	428	1/48 (1) 2/59 (2) 3/90 (3) (3 wkts, 44.3 overs)	147
110 overs: 390-8			

Anyon 28–0–132–3; Magoffin 23–6–66–1; Panesar 34–9–88–1; Naved Arif 17.2–1–76–2; Wright 5–0–27–0; Gatting 2–0–10–0; Nash 10–2–23–3. *Second innings*—Anyon 3–0–16–0; Magoffin 3–1–11–0; Nash 9.3–0–39–1; Panesar 18–6–28–1; Yardy 3–0–12–1; Naved Arif 8–2–36–0.

Umpires: N. G. C. Cowley and S. J. O'Shaughnessy.

At Lord's, May 30–June 2. SUSSEX lost to MIDDLESEX by ten wickets.

SUSSEX v SURREY

At Horsham, June 6–9. Sussex won by ten wickets. Sussex 22pts, Surrey 3pts. Toss: Sussex.

This match would become a footnote to the tragic death of Tom Maynard on June 18. After the second day was all but washed away, Maynard went to Brighton on a night out, and was hit by a car in the early hours. A bruised shoulder and a black eye forced him to sit out the third day's play; he was disciplined by Surrey for the incident. Sussex's display was one of their best since winning their last Championship, in 2007. They achieved it without Goodwin, dropped for the first time in his Sussex career, aged 39, following one fifty in 11 innings. The toss was crucial, and under sullen skies Sussex made the most of it, with Magoffin outstanding. Ramprakash, recalled to open the batting following a trough comparable to Goodwin's, struggled at the start of both innings, and missed a sweep at Panesar in the second to fall for 37 from 101 balls. He was not picked again, and announced his retirement a month later. On the second day, Meaker ran in fearsomely to take three wickets in the six overs that were possible, but Wells survived the melee and took the game away from Surrey with a patient hundred, his second of the season against them. The tail joined in – even Panesar, who struck Kartik for six into the adjacent tennis courts, a shot applauded by the bowler. At one point on the gusty third day, an advertising hoarding blew 40 yards into the middle, causing a terrified Dernbach to run for cover. Sussex chipped away at brittle opponents: Panesar kept one end closed down, Nash struck twice, and Anyon tore in, removing Hamilton-Brown in enough time to allow the openers six overs to knock off the small target.

Close of play: first day, Sussex 81-2 (Wells 33, Yardy 1); second day, Sussex 90-6 (Wells 38, Naved Arif 0); third day, Surrey 39-1 (Ramprakash 3, Meaker 1).

Surrey

J. J. Roy c Anyon b Magoffin	11	– c Wright b Magoffin	35
M. R. Ramprakash c Brown b Magoffin	8	– lbw b Panesar	37
Z. de Bruyn c Yardy b Anyon	5	– (4) lbw b Panesar	21
†S. M. Davies c Wells b Magoffin	6	– (5) c Yardy b Panesar	35
*R. J. Hamilton-Brown c Brown b Anyon	0	– (6) b Anyon	47
T. L. Maynard c Yardy b Anyon	17	– (7) lbw b Nash	5
G. J. Batty c Joyce b Naved Arif	32	– (8) run out	2
J. Lewis c Joyce b Naved Arif	14	– (10) c Brown b Nash	12
M. Kartik not out	23	– b Anyon	11
S. C. Meaker c Brown b Magoffin	3	– (3) b Magoffin	8
J. W. Dernbach b Anyon	0	– not out	4
B 1, l-b 2, n-b 2	5	B 17, l-b 6, w 1, n-b 2, p 5	31
1/19 (1) 2/22 (2) 3/32 (3) 4/32 (5) 5/32 (4) 6/52 (6) 7/96 (7) 8/97 (8) 9/121 (10) 10/124 (11) (40.2 overs)	124	1/38 (1) 2/61 (3) 3/96 (2) 4/145 (4) 5/162 (5) 6/178 (7) 7/181 (8) 8/197 (9) 9/229 (10) 10/248 (6) (106.4 overs)	248

G. C. Wilson briefly replaced Davies, who was called up by England after the first day, but returned later on the second.

Anyon 17.2–4–63–4; Magoffin 14–4–27–4; Wright 2–0–11–0; Panesar 1–1–0–0; Naved Arif 6–1–20–2. *Second innings*—Anyon 27.4–6–71–2; Magoffin 27–6–72–2; Naved Arif 12–3–42–0; Panesar 32–21–33–3; Wells 2–2–0–0; Nash 6–4–2–2.

Sussex

C. D. Nash c Roy b Kartik	38	– (2) not out	1
E. C. Joyce c Davies b Lewis	8	– (1) not out	19
L. W. P. Wells c Davies b Kartik	127		
*M. H. Yardy c Ramprakash b Meaker	1		
J. S. Gatting b Meaker	2		
L. J. Wright c Davies b Kartik	1		
†B. C. Brown lbw b Meaker	1		
Naved Arif c Batty b Kartik	34		
S. J. Magoffin c Roy b Lewis	34		
J. E. Anyon not out	64		
M. S. Panesar c Dernbach b Batty	31		
B 6, l-b 3, w 1	10	N-b 2	2
1/11 (2) 2/80 (1) 3/81 (4) 4/85 (5) 5/86 (6) 6/87 (7) 7/172 (8) 8/236 (9) 9/271 (3) 10/351 (11) (111.5 overs) 110 overs: 330-9	351	(no wkt, 1.5 overs)	22

Lewis 22–8–43–2; Dernbach 14–2–70–0; Meaker 26–8–65–3; de Bruyn 2–0–9–0; Kartik 36–4–102–4; Batty 11.5–0–53–1. *Second innings*—Meaker 1–0–8–0; Lewis 0.5–0–14–0.

Umpires: P. J. Hartley and P. Willey.

At Birmingham, July 12–15. SUSSEX drew with WARWICKSHIRE.

SUSSEX v DURHAM

At Arundel, July 18–21. Sussex won by two wickets. Sussex 20pts, Durham 4pts. Toss: Sussex.

After apparently bowling Sussex to the brink of victory with match figures of nine for 50, Magoffin was then called upon to complete the job with the bat on the final afternoon. On a pitch offering pronounced seam movement throughout and uneven bounce later in the game, neither set of batsmen covered themselves in glory, but Sussex should never have been troubled by a target of 94. Instead, they collapsed to 73 for eight, but the tide turned again when Stokes replaced the tiring Rushworth, and conceded eight from an over. Durham had been almost entirely reliant on Rushworth and Thorp, who took 15 of the 18 Sussex wickets to fall, and limited them to first-innings parity after dogged work from Yardy and Brown. But Durham's batsmen surrendered any momentum on the third afternoon by lurching to 38 for six. Collingwood, in his first match as their permanent captain, held Magoffin up for a while, but not long enough – and his assessment that a chase of 120 would have proved beyond Sussex looked spot on.

Close of play: first day, Durham 92-4 (Benkenstein 11, Collingwood 4); second day, Sussex 100-3 (Goodwin 14, Yardy 29); third day, Durham 80-7 (Collingwood 29, Thorp 8).

Durham

First innings		Second innings	
M. D. Stoneman lbw b Panesar	50	– (2) lbw b Magoffin	0
W. R. Smith c Yardy b Anyon	1	– (1) c Wells b Anyon	12
G. J. Muchall b Anyon	0	– lbw b Magoffin	2
B. A. Stokes c Yardy b Magoffin	20	– c Wright b Magoffin	0
D. M. Benkenstein c Wernars b Magoffin	43	– c Brown b Magoffin	14
*P. D. Collingwood c Brown b Magoffin	9	– lbw b Wernars	29
†P. Mustard c Nash b Panesar	27	– c Nash b Wernars	6
S. G. Borthwick lbw b Nash	50	– c Brown b Wright	3
C. D. Thorp c Goodwin b Wright	4	– lbw b Magoffin	12
M. E. Claydon c Wells b Nash	15	– b Magoffin	4
C. Rushworth not out	1	– not out	2
L-b 9, n-b 2	11	B 4, l-b 4, w 1	9
1/1 (2) 2/1 (3) 3/34 (4) 4/84 (1) 5/97 (6) 6/157 (7) 7/170 (5) 8/175 (9) 9/230 (8) 10/231 (10) (79.4 overs)	231	1/4 (2) 2/6 (3) 3/10 (4) 4/29 (1) 5/29 (5) 6/38 (7) 7/62 (8) 8/80 (6) 9/84 (9) 10/93 (10) (31.4 overs)	93

Anyon 17–3–71–2; Magoffin 22–9–28–3; Wernars 13–5–32–0; Wright 12–1–47–1; Panesar 14–4–39–2; Nash 1.4–0–5–2. *Second innings*—Anyon 7–3–33–1; Magoffin 12.4–5–22–6; Wernars 9–3–16–2; Wright 3–0–14–1.

Sussex

First innings		Second innings	
C. D. Nash lbw b Rushworth	3	– (2) b Thorp	13
L. W. P. Wells b Thorp	41	– (1) lbw b Rushworth	0
J. S. Gatting lbw b Thorp	11	– c Borthwick b Thorp	6
M. W. Goodwin lbw b Rushworth	18	– c Borthwick b Thorp	15
*M. H. Yardy lbw b Collingwood	66	– run out	4
L. J. Wright c Collingwood b Stokes	4	– b Rushworth	1
†B. C. Brown b Rushworth	51	– lbw b Rushworth	8
K. O. Wernars lbw b Thorp	10	– c Mustard b Thorp	4
S. J. Magoffin lbw b Thorp	0	– not out	23
J. E. Anyon not out	0	– not out	15
M. S. Panesar c Muchall b Rushworth	10		
B 1, l-b 13, w 3	17	B 1, l-b 4	5
1/4 (1) 2/42 (3) 3/59 (2) 4/110 (4) 5/119 (6) 6/188 (5) 7/221 (8) 8/221 (9) 9/221 (7) 10/231 (11) (90.4 overs)	231	1/0 (1) 2/13 (3) 3/22 (2) 4/27 (5) 5/36 (6) 6/50 (7) 7/50 (4) 8/73 (8) (8 wkts, 37 overs)	94

Rushworth 23.4–9–52–4; Thorp 22–7–35–4; Claydon 14–1–40–0; Stokes 17–1–54–1; Borthwick 8–2–28–0; Collingwood 6–2–8–1. *Second innings*—Rushworth 15–4–35–3; Thorp 17–3–38–4; Stokes 5–1–16–0.

Umpires: N. J. Llong and N. A. Mallender.

At Nottingham, July 27–30. SUSSEX drew with NOTTINGHAMSHIRE.

SUSSEX v WORCESTERSHIRE

At Hove, August 1–3. Sussex won by an innings and 117 runs. Sussex 23pts, Worcestershire 2pts. Toss: Sussex.

Sussex required just seven sessions to dismantle Worcestershire on a relaid pitch tailor-made for their attack. Joyce considered it a gamble to bowl in his first match since replacing Yardy as captain, but his seamers backed him up admirably. Magoffin likened the bouncy surface to his former home at the WACA and, even with the start delayed until after lunch, Worcestershire could not make it through the day. In the second innings, Cameron was hit on the head by Magoffin; two balls later he retired hurt. Panesar also relished the conditions, which offered a modicum of turn, taking four for seven in eight overs as Sussex closed in. Joyce's captaincy was authoritative, as was his batting: a diligent, high-quality hundred – which began under floodlights on the first evening – was just what Sussex needed to build an unassailable lead. Their catching was flawless, and when Panesar was bowling with expectant fielders clustered around the bat, it was reminiscent of Mushtaq Ahmed in his pomp.

Close of play: first day, Sussex 22-0 (Nash 15, Joyce 7); second day, Sussex 325-7 (Magoffin 29, Anyon 4).

Worcestershire

*D. K. H. Mitchell c Joyce b Khan	8	– b Panesar	48
P. J. Hughes c Yardy b Magoffin	11	– c Brown b Anyon	9
V. S. Solanki b Magoffin	1	– b Magoffin	2
M. M. Ali c Wright b Magoffin	43	– c Yardy b Magoffin	27
J. G. Cameron b Anyon	11	– retired hurt	2
M. G. Pardoe c Yardy b Anyon	4	– c Yardy b Panesar	14
G. M. Andrew c Brown b Khan	11	– b Panesar	0
†B. J. M. Scott c Anyon b Magoffin	0	– c sub (A. J. Hodd) b Panesar	6
R. A. Jones not out	30	– lbw b Khan	1
J. D. Shantry c Brown b Khan	10	– c Wells b Khan	8
A. Richardson b Panesar	4	– not out	1
B 5, l-b 10, n-b 14	29	B 10, l-b 6, w 1, n-b 6	23
1/16 (2) 2/18 (3) 3/32 (1) 4/68 (5) 5/74 (6) 6/106 (7) 7/107 (8) 8/122 (4) 9/145 (10) 10/162 (11) (53.4 overs)	162	1/19 (2) 2/32 (3) 3/87 (4) 4/118 (6) 5/120 (7) 6/129 (1) 7//130 (9) 8/136 (8) 9/141 (10) (62.3 overs)	141

In the second innings Cameron retired hurt at 89-3.

Anyon 13–0–39–2; Magoffin 17–8–34–4; Khan 14–3–36–3; Wright 4–1–17–0; Panesar 5.4–0–21–1. *Second innings*—Anyon 12–1–40–1; Magoffin 14–4–32–2; Khan 13.3–5–30–2; Panesar 23–13–23–4.

Sussex

C. D. Nash b Richardson	18
*E. C. Joyce lbw b Richardson	107
L. W. P. Wells c Mitchell b Richardson	4
M. W. Goodwin lbw b Jones	9
M. H. Yardy c Scott b Richardson	33
L. J. Wright c Mitchell b Andrew	78
†B. C. Brown c Solanki b Ali	28
S. J. Magoffin b Richardson	41
J. E. Anyon not out	56
A. Khan not out	27
B 6, l-b 13	19
1/26 (1) 2/36 (3) 3/65 (4) 4/126 (5) 5/249 (2) 6/275 (6) 7/320 (7) 8/360 (8) (8 wkts dec, 121 overs)	420
110 overs: 357-7	

M. S. Panesar did not bat.

Richardson 37–8–90–5; Andrew 35–3–130–1; Jones 16–2–84–1; Shantry 17–0–52–0; Ali 12–2–33–1; Mitchell 4–0–12–0.

Umpires: M. J. D. Bodenham and N. G. C. Cowley.

SUSSEX v MIDDLESEX

At Hove, August 10–12. Sussex won by eight wickets. Sussex 21pts, Middlesex 3pts. Toss: Sussex.

Sussex's fourth successive home win encouraged the belief they might still challenge Warwickshire for the title – even if their coach, Mark Robinson, did not share that optimism. Roland-Jones had taken a career-best six for 66 for Middlesex, extracting as much out of a lively wicket as the home bowlers, but he was left to carry the burden alone as Joyce and Yardy – captains present and past –

ground out a lead for Sussex. Khan, who had tended to save his best for away games, claimed eight for 64, his finest match figures since leaving Kent, including three wickets in four overs to break the back of the Middlesex second innings. Anyon wrapped it up with three in 12 balls, while Brown's six catches as wicketkeeper equalled the county record held by, among others, Rupert Webb – Sussex's oldest living player, and in the ground for his 90th birthday lunch. Middlesex were only 25 behind with eight wickets left at the start of the third day, but Khan's hostile burst kept the run-chase down to 95 – and Sussex avoided a repeat of their wobble against Durham at Arundel.

Close of play: first day, Sussex 106-3 (Joyce 49, Yardy 24); second day, Middlesex 92-2 (Robson 24, Roland-Jones 5).

Middlesex

*C. J. L. Rogers c Wright b Magoffin	5	– (2) c Brown b Panesar	48
S. D. Robson c Yardy b Khan	24	– (1) c Brown b Khan	36
J. L. Denly c Wright b Magoffin	4	– b Magoffin	8
D. J. Malan c Joyce b Khan	19	– (5) c Nash b Panesar	18
N. J. Dexter c Brown b Khan	4	– (6) c Brown b Anyon	40
O. P. Rayner c Brown b Khan	32	– (9) c Brown b Anyon	9
†J. A. Simpson c Yardy b Wright	1	– c Yardy b Khan	3
G. K. Berg c Yardy b Khan	19	– c Brown b Khan	1
T. S. Roland-Jones lbw b Panesar	9	– (4) c Brown b Magoffin	20
T. J. Murtagh b Magoffin	34	– b Anyon	1
C. D. Collymore not out	6	– not out	1
B 4, l-b 3, n-b 6	13	B 16, l-b 6, n-b 4	26
1/9 (1) 2/17 (3) 3/56 (4) 4/59 (2) 5/62 (5) 6/65 (7) 7/119 (6) 8/128 (8) 9/140 (9) 10/170 (10) (57 overs)	170	1/72 (2) 2/81 (3) 3/111 (4) 4/132 (1) 5/148 (5) 6/151 (7) 7/153 (8) 8/197 (9) 9/208 (6) 10/211 (10) (68.3 overs)	211

Anyon 13–2–37–0; Magoffin 15–5–45–3; Khan 14–4–25–5; Wright 11–1–39–1; Panesar 4–0–17–1. *Second innings*—Anyon 10.3–1–45–3; Magoffin 19–6–56–2; Khan 15–3–39–3; Panesar 24–7–49–2.

Sussex

C. D. Nash c Simpson b Berg	11	– (2) c Dexter b Murtagh	5
*E. C. Joyce c Simpson b Roland-Jones	68	– (1) c and b Rayner	35
L. W. P. Wells c Dexter b Berg	12	– not out	29
M. W. Goodwin lbw b Roland-Jones	1	– not out	19
M. H. Yardy c Murtagh b Roland-Jones	89		
L. J. Wright c Malan b Murtagh	10		
†B. C. Brown c Simpson b Roland-Jones	12		
S. J. Magoffin c Simpson b Collymore	35		
J. E. Anyon b Roland-Jones	29		
A. Khan not out	3		
M. S. Panesar lbw b Roland-Jones	0		
B 8, l-b 7, w 2	17	B 8, l-b 2	10
1/37 (1) 2/63 (3) 3/64 (4) 4/142 (2) 5/166 (6) 6/206 (7) 7/238 (5) 8/281 (8) 9/287 (9) 10/287 (11) (104.4 overs)	287	1/9 (2) 2/67 (1) (2 wkts, 25.3 overs)	98

Murtagh 28–9–63–1; Collymore 24–2–64–1; Berg 19–2–57–2; Roland-Jones 21.4–4–66–6; Dexter 4–1–12–0; Rayner 8–0–10–0. *Second innings*—Murtagh 5–2–16–1; Roland-Jones 6–2–24–0; Berg 4–2–6–0; Rayner 6.3–0–32–1; Collymore 4–1–10–0.

Umpires: S. C. Gale and T. E. Jesty.

At Taunton, August 21–24. SUSSEX drew with SOMERSET.

SUSSEX v SOMERSET

At Hove, September 4–7. Somerset won by five wickets. Somerset 19pts, Sussex 4pts. Toss: Somerset.

Unlike most Championship pitches at Hove in 2012, this one got easier and, despite the loss of four quick wickets before the close on the third day, Somerset cantered to a target of 396 with more than a session to spare. It capped a bad fortnight for Sussex, who had also lost two limited-overs semi-finals. Warwickshire's win at Worcester extinguished both these sides' title hopes on the third day, but at least home supporters had the consolation of seeing Goodwin end his 12-year Sussex career with his highest first-class score of the season, though he was denied the century

MOST FIRST-CLASS CENTURIES FOR SUSSEX

76	J. G. Langridge	1928–1955	**48**	**M. W. Goodwin**	**2001–2012**
68	C. B. Fry	1894–1908	46	E. H. Bowley	1912–1934
58	K. S. Ranjitsinhji	1895–1920	42	H. W. Parks	1926–1948
50	G. Cox	1931–1960	42	J. M. Parks	1949–1972
49	K. G. Suttle	1949–1971	40	A. P. Wells	1981–1996

he craved by the excellent Thomas. Goodwin departed to a standing ovation from a large crowd, accompanied by his two sons; his parents, flown in by the club from Australia, were also in attendance. Sussex's first innings was below par, but Somerset lost nine for 66 once Trescothick – who had earlier held five catches for the second time in a month – shuffled across his stumps soon after reaching 20,000 career runs (only the eighth current player to reach the mark; Goodwin was another). Nash's third hundred of the season appeared to put Sussex in charge but – Magoffin apart – their attack looked toothless as the pitch flattened. Hildreth, missed by Brown on 28, and Trego, typically belligerent, took Somerset home in a stand of 166 in 25.3 overs. Abdur Rehman arrived before lunch on the first day, replaced Jack Leach at 2pm, then knocked over Somerset's tail, having flown through the night from Dubai to Gatwick after Pakistan's one-day international against Australia, which finished at 2.09am Sharjah time. He was believed to be the first professional cricketer to play in two matches in two different continents on the same day.

Close of play: first day, Somerset 30-1 (Trescothick 17, Jones 11); second day, Sussex 186-2 (Nash 106, Goodwin 51); third day, Somerset 155-4 (Hildreth 1, Barrow 4).

Sussex

C. D. Nash c Snell b Kirby	23	– (2) c Snell b Thomas	126
*E. C. Joyce c Snell b Thomas	65	– (1) c Trego b Kirby	7
L. W. P. Wells c Jones b Kirby	28	– c Snell b Thomas	20
M. W. Goodwin c Trescothick b Mahmood	16	– c Snell b Thomas	77
M. J. Prior b Thomas	17	– run out	10
M. H. Yardy c Trescothick b Abdur Rehman	19	– b Thomas	3
†B. C. Brown c Trescothick b Thomas	2	– lbw b Thomas	1
S. J. Magoffin c Trescothick b Mahmood	24	– lbw b Abdur Rehman	18
J. E. Anyon c Trescothick b Abdur Rehman	0	– c Snell b Kirby	16
L. J. Hatchett b Abdur Rehman	0	– not out	11
M. S. Panesar not out	0	– b Abdur Rehman	4
B 5, l-b 8, w 2, n-b 12	27	B 5, l-b 1, w 5, n-b 4	15
1/31 (1) 2/96 (3) 3/130 (4) 4/168 (5) 5/177 (2) 6/179 (7) 7/217 (6) 8/221 (9) 9/221 (8) 10/221 (10) (81.4 overs)	221	1/13 (1) 2/47 (3) 3/230 (2) 4/240 (5) 5/245 (4) 6/247 (7) 7/254 (6) 8/270 (8) 9/303 (9) 10/308 (11) (102.1 overs)	308

Trego 16–5–56–0; Kirby 13–3–38–2; Thomas 19–3–49–3; Mahmood 15–3–31–2; Leach 1–0–4–0; Abdur Rehman 17.4–2–30–3. *Second innings*—Trego 17–0–68–0; Kirby 13–3–35–2; Thomas 24–5–68–5; Mahmood 9–1–53–0; Abdur Rehman 39.1–12–78–2.

Somerset

*M. E. Trescothick lbw b Magoffin	31	– b Panesar	71
A. V. Suppiah lbw b Magoffin	1	– c Prior b Magoffin	70
C. R. Jones c Yardy b Magoffin	30	– b Magoffin	1
J. C. Hildreth c Prior b Panesar	1	– (5) not out	101
A. W. R. Barrow c Brown b Hatchett	21	– (6) c Prior b Magoffin	40
P. D. Trego c Nash b Anyon	22	– (7) not out	89
†S. D. Snell c Hatchett b Panesar	8		
A. C. Thomas c Prior b Hatchett	0		
Abdur Rehman c Goodwin b Panesar	0		
S. I. Mahmood b Hatchett	5		
S. P. Kirby not out	1	– (4) c Nash b Magoffin	2
L-b 8, n-b 6	14	B 17, l-b 2, n-b 4	23
1/6 (2) 2/68 (1) 3/71 (3) 4/71 (4) (46.5 overs)	134	1/147 (1) (5 wkts, 106.2 overs)	397
5/106 (6) 6/122 (7) 7/123 (8)		2/147 (2) 3/150 (3)	
8/124 (9) 9/133 (10) 10/134 (5)		4/151 (4) 5/231 (6)	

Abdur Rehman replaced M. J. Leach after arriving from the UAE, where he had been playing for Pakistan.

Anyon 11–1–43–1; Magoffin 14–6–42–3; Nash 1–0–1–0; Hatchett 7.5–1–25–3; Panesar 13–3–15–3. *Second innings*—Anyon 15–1–93–0; Magoffin 29.2–13–73–4; Panesar 33–11–88–1; Hatchett 16–5–69–0; Nash 13–2–55–0.

Umpires: S. A. Garratt and D. J. Millns.

At Chester-le-Street, September 11–13. SUSSEX lost to DURHAM by five wickets.

WARWICKSHIRE

Champions as good as their word

PAUL BOLTON

Warwickshire kept a promise made by their captain, Jim Troughton – that they would win the County Championship with a round of matches to spare. Troughton's pledge was made in September 2011, shortly after Warwickshire had run out of steam on the final day at Southampton and been pipped to the title by Lancashire. Now, they used that memory of utter dejection as motivation to ensure there would be no repeat.

During a winter of meticulous planning, Warwickshire identified moments when they had allowed match-winning situations to slip; they were determined to become more ruthless. Sure enough, they lost only once, at Taunton, where a brilliant 152 from Craig Kieswetter was required for Somerset to chase down 271. Otherwise, Warwickshire remained calm, from a nerve-jangling opening win over Somerset to the demolition of Worcestershire that clinched the crown. Troughton and Ashley Giles, the director of cricket, dedicated the title to Neal Abberley, a long-standing member of the coaching staff, who had died in August 2011 and was a significant influence on both.

Troughton's understated captaincy hid a ruthless streak. He demonstrated his character by recovering from a total of 50 runs in his first nine innings to finish with 733. Giles, meanwhile, set his players high standards. Both admitted to sleepless nights towards the end of the season; Giles also revealed personal anguish as his wife, Stine, had been treated for two brain tumours, a recurrence of the illness she had suffered five years earlier.

Giles's role in masterminding the seventh Championship title in Warwickshire's history – and their second CB40 final appearance in the tournament's three seasons – did not go unnoticed at the ECB; he had, after all, been a national selector for four years. When Andy Flower concluded in November that he needed more time with his family, Giles left to join England as limited-overs coach, beginning with the 50-over series in India in January. Dougie Brown, previously assistant coach, stepped up to replace him.

The void left by Abberley was filled by bowling coach Graeme Welch, who became increasingly influential as a shrewd judge of a cricketer and a confidant to Giles and the players. It was Welch who persuaded Giles to sign Chris Wright when Essex told him to look for a new county in 2011. Wright repaid Welch's faith with 62 Championship wickets, and at times bowled with genuine pace and hostility, securing a place on the England Performance Programme.

Welch was also responsible for the transformation in Keith Barker's bowling. Barker took 50 wickets for the first time after spending the winter working with Welch to remodel his action so he could swing the ball both ways. Wright and Barker – who all but secured the title by combining to skittle Worcestershire

Nick Potts, PA Photos

Ashley Giles and Jim Troughton

for 60 at New Road – missed only two matches between them, and came to share a heavy workload after Chris Woakes and Boyd Rankin sustained injuries before the season. Rikki Clarke's effectiveness was reduced in the final month by a side strain, but he still scored three centuries and held 29 catches, most of them at second slip. Wright was often the only player in the side without a first-class hundred.

Varun Chopra was Warwickshire's only batsman to top 1,000 runs, and his consistency was recognised with an England Lions debut. Little was seen of Ian Bell and Jonathan Trott because of international commitments, but they contributed a century apiece, with Bell's made in demanding conditions at Edgbaston to set up victory over Durham.

William Porterfield and Darren Maddy were the weak links in the batting, yet Maddy's only century helped defeat Lancashire at Liverpool, and Porterfield turned matches with some brilliant reflex catches at gully. Tim Ambrose, who revealed that depression almost forced him to quit cricket in 2010, and Ian Westwood both played valuable match-shaping innings. Richard Johnson, Ambrose's wicketkeeping understudy, opted to join Derbyshire after a loan spell, which meant he collected medals for winning the first and second division in the same season.

Jeetan Patel proved a popular and productive overseas player, and was the third bowler to take 50 wickets, despite missing a month when he was recalled for New Zealand's tour of India. Chris Metters was out for the entire season with a shoulder problem, so Warwickshire brought in Ian Blackwell, another slow left-armer, on loan from Durham to provide experienced spin cover.

Warwickshire were one run away from adding the CB40 trophy to the Championship, but Hampshire lost fewer wickets in a tied finish at Lord's. Neil Carter was unable to connect with Kabir Ali's last ball, ensuring there was no fairytale ending to his county career. Carter had got Warwickshire to the final with four wickets in the last group match – his first appearance in the competition for a year – and four more in the semi-final against Lancashire; aged 37, he sought an international career with Scotland. The Twenty20 campaign never got off the ground due to foul weather: only two of Warwickshire's five home matches were completed.

It was a difficult first year for Gary Barwell as head groundsman at Edgbaston, but he still consistently produced pitches of high quality. The outfield struggled to cope with the wettest summer for a century, and four out of seven days' international cricket at the ground were washed out. Because of the postponement of the ICC World Test Championship in 2013, Warwickshire will not stage another Test until the 2015 Ashes, and expect to take a hefty financial hit.

Championship attendance: 37,164.

WARWICKSHIRE RESULTS

All first-class matches – Played 17: Won 6, Lost 1, Drawn 10.
County Championship matches – Played 16: Won 6, Lost 1, Drawn 9.

LV= County Championship, winners in Division 1;
Friends Life t20, 4th in Midlands/Wales/West Division; Clydesdale Bank 40, finalists.

COUNTY CHAMPIONSHIP AVERAGES, BATTING AND FIELDING

Cap		*M*	*I*	*NO*	*R*	*HS*	*100*	*50*	*Avge*	*Ct/St*
2009	C. R. Woakes†	8	10	4	431	118*	2	1	71.83	3
	I. D. Blackwell	4	6	1	265	84	0	2	53.00	0
2011	R. Clarke	16	21	4	760	140	3	2	44.70	29
2007	T. R. Ambrose	13	18	4	623	151*	1	3	44.50	42/1
2001	I. R. Bell†‡	4	6	1	215	120	1	1	43.00	6
2008	I. J. Westwood†	12	19	1	771	120	2	5	42.83	5
2012	V. Chopra	16	26	1	1,028	195	3	5	41.12	26
2002	J. O. Troughton	15	24	3	733	132	2	4	34.90	9
2007	D. L. Maddy	14	21	2	473	112	1	0	24.89	10
	W. T. S. Porterfield	14	22	2	482	84	0	2	24.10	20
	K. H. D. Barker	15	17	4	304	46	0	0	23.38	5
2012	J. S. Patel§	13	14	3	221	76	0	1	20.09	3
	C. J. C. Wright	15	15	5	194	53	0	1	19.40	2
	R. M. Johnson†	3	4	0	72	49	0	0	18.00	6
2005	N. M. Carter	2	4	0	51	26	0	0	12.75	2
	W. B. Rankin	6	4	2	9	5	0	0	4.50	2

Also batted: L. J. Evans (1 match) 4, 9 (1 ct); T. P. Milnes (3 matches) 24, 7*; I. J. L. Trott‡ (cap 2005) (2 matches) 178, 2 (1 ct).

† *Born in Warwickshire.* ‡ *ECB contract.* § *Official overseas player.*

BOWLING

	Style	*O*	*M*	*R*	*W*	*BB*	*5I*	*Avge*
K. H. D. Barker	LFM	392.1	94	1,166	56	6-40	5	20.82
J. S. Patel	OB	395.1	87	1,161	51	7-75	4	22.76
C. J. C. Wright	RFM	450.3	74	1,492	62	5-24	2	24.06
C. R. Woakes	RFM	225.5	47	681	27	4-67	0	25.22
R. Clarke	RFM	189	45	554	20	4-46	0	27.70
D. L. Maddy	RM	139	44	344	12	4-39	0	28.66
W. B. Rankin	RFM	138.1	15	515	16	5-78	1	32.18

Also bowled: I. D. Blackwell (SLA) 90.2–15–279–6; N. M. Carter (LFM) 36–4–149–2; V. Chopra (LBG) 2–0–5–0; T. P. Milnes (RFM) 32–1–142–2; I. J. Westwood (OB) 9–4–26–0.

LEADING CB40 AVERAGES (100 runs/4 wickets)

Batting	*Runs*	*HS*	*Avge*	*SR*	*Ct/St*
I. R. Bell	163	82*	163.00	98.78	1
T. R. Ambrose	321	87*	53.50	91.45	8/1
V. Chopra	472	110	52.44	78.27	4
W. T. S. Porterfield	395	100*	39.50	95.18	6
D. L. Maddy	258	79*	32.25	99.61	4
R. Clarke	225	54*	32.14	90.72	12

Bowling	*W*	*BB*	*Avge*	*ER*
N. M. Carter	9	4-16	13.00	5.31
R. Clarke	4	3-22	18.00	4.50
C. R. Woakes	14	4-24	19.92	4.98
C. J. C. Wright	20	3-43	20.80	5.07
K. H. D. Barker	12	3-27	21.50	4.70
J. S. Patel	11	4-27	21.90	3.76

LEADING FLT20 AVERAGES (80 runs/17 overs)

Batting	Runs	HS	Avge	SR	Ct
L. J. Evans	146	68*	73.00	**171.76**	2
J. O. Troughton	123	68*	41.00	**119.41**	1
D. L. Maddy	125	49	20.83	**109.64**	2
V. Chopra	240	56*	48.00	**107.62**	1
R. Clarke	86	48	12.28	**122.85**	2

Bowling	W	BB	Avge	ER
S. A. Piolet	3	2-21	46.66	**6.08**
C. R. Woakes	9	3-27	18.88	**7.39**
K. H. D. Barker	4	1-17	54.25	**7.48**
J. S. Patel	5	1-15	35.20	**7.59**
C. J. C. Wright	4	2-43	36.75	**8.64**

FIRST-CLASS COUNTY RECORDS

Highest score for	501*	B. C. Lara v Durham at Birmingham	1994
Highest score against	322	I. V. A. Richards (Somerset) at Taunton	1985
Leading run-scorer	35,146	D. L. Amiss (avge 41.64)	1960–1987
Best bowling for	10-41	J. D. Bannister v Combined Services at Birmingham	1959
Best bowling against	10-36	H. Verity (Yorkshire) at Leeds	1931
Leading wicket-taker	2,201	W. E. Hollies (avge 20.45)	1932–1957
Highest total for	810-4 dec	v Durham at Birmingham	1994
Highest total against	887	by Yorkshire at Birmingham	1896
Lowest total for	16	v Kent at Tonbridge	1913
Lowest total against	15	by Hampshire at Birmingham	1922

LIST A COUNTY RECORDS

Highest score for	206	A. I. Kallicharran v Oxfordshire at Birmingham	1984
Highest score against	172*	W. Larkins (Northamptonshire) at Luton	1983
Leading run-scorer	11,254	D. L. Amiss (avge 33.79)	1963–1987
Best bowling for	7-32	R. G. D. Willis v Yorkshire at Birmingham	1981
Best bowling against	6-27	M. H. Yardy (Sussex) at Birmingham	2005
Leading wicket-taker	396	G. C. Small (avge 25.48)	1980–1999
Highest total for	392-5	v Oxfordshire at Birmingham	1984
Highest total against	341-6	by Hampshire at Birmingham	2010
Lowest total for	59	v Yorkshire at Leeds	2001
Lowest total against	56	by Yorkshire at Birmingham	1995

TWENTY20 COUNTY RECORDS

Highest score for	89	N. V. Knight v Worcestershire at Worcester	2003
Highest score against	100*	I. J. Harvey (Gloucestershire) at Birmingham	2003
Leading run-scorer	1,871	I. J. L. Trott (avge 40.67)	2003–2011
Best bowling for	5-19	N. M. Carter v Worcestershire at Birmingham	2005
Best bowling against	5-25	D. J. Pattinson (Nottinghamshire) at Birmingham	2011
Leading wicket-taker	**81**	**N. M. Carter (avge 26.65)**	**2003–2012**
Highest total for	205-2	v Northamptonshire at Birmingham	2005
	205-7	v Glamorgan at Swansea	2005
Highest total against	215-6	by Durham at Birmingham	2010
Lowest total for	106-8	v Worcestershire at Worcester	2011
Lowest total against	96	by Northamptonshire at Northampton	2011

ADDRESS

County Ground, Edgbaston, Birmingham B5 7QU (0870 062 1902; **email** info@edgbaston.com). **Website** www.edgbaston.com

OFFICIALS

Captain J. O. Troughton
Director of cricket 2012 – A. F. Giles
2013 – D. R. Brown
Academy director I. G. S. Steer
President Earl of Aylesford

Chairman N. Gascoigne
Chief executive C. Povey
Chairman, cricket committee J. Dodge
Head groundsman G. Barwell
Scorer M. Smith

WARWICKSHIRE v CARDIFF MCCU

At Birmingham, April 6–8. Drawn. Toss: Cardiff MCCU. First-class debuts: D. S. Bendon, A. J. Miles.

Matthew Hobden, a seamer on Sussex's books, exploited a drying pitch to take Cardiff MCCU's maiden five-wicket haul in first-class cricket. Hobden's wickets were spread over three chilly and changeable days, as Warwickshire accelerated after a cautious start. The students struggled against Warwickshire's five seamers, and required a chipper last-wicket partnership between Hobden and Phil Harris to take them into three figures in the first innings. Will Jones, on a summer contract with Leicestershire, and Hamza Siddique, with second-team experience for Derbyshire, also applied themselves, but the umpires halted play after Tom Milnes bounced Adam Miles in fading light.

Close of play: first day, Warwickshire 82-3 (Porterfield 27, Troughton 9); second day, Warwickshire 261-6 (Clarke 25, Javid 4).

Cardiff MCCU

W. S. Jones c Chopra b Wright	15	– c Ambrose b Wright	23
Z. Elkin c Clarke b Miller	10	– c Ambrose b Wright	7
H. G. Siddique lbw b Clarke	4	– c Ambrose b Clarke	37
*A. Balbirnie c Clarke b Wright	2	– b Wright	0
U. A. Qureshi c Porterfield b Clarke	8	– lbw b Clarke	9
T. Friend c Maddy b Milnes	5	– lbw b Clarke	0
A. G. Salter lbw b Maddy	21	– not out	6
D. S. Bendon c Ambrose b Milnes	0	– c Maddy b Milnes	5
†A. J. Miles b Maddy	6	– not out	0
P. G. Harris c Miller b Clarke	20		
M. E. Hobden not out	15		
B 4, l-b 3, n-b 6	13	L-b 2, w 2	4
1/20 (2) 2/34 (1) 3/38 (4) 4/49 (3) 5/54 (6) 6/54 (5) 7/55 (8) 8/83 (7) 9/90 (9) 10/119 (10) (45 overs)	119	1/28 (2) 2/37 (1) 3/37 (4) 4/65 (5) 5/79 (6) 6/80 (3) 7/85 (8) (7 wkts, 32 overs)	91

Wright 13–3–40–2; Miller 8–2–24–1; Milnes 9–2–31–2; Clarke 7–4–7–3; Maddy 8–6–10–2. *Second innings*—Wright 8–0–30–3; Miller 8–1–22–0; Clarke 8–5–8–3; Milnes 8–2–29–1.

Warwickshire

V. Chopra b Harris	24
I. J. Westwood lbw b Hobden	0
W. T. S. Porterfield c Jones b Salter	76
D. L. Maddy c Jones b Hobden	5
*J. O. Troughton c Siddique b Bendon	67
†T. R. Ambrose c Elkin b Hobden	37
R. Clarke c Friend b Hobden	66
A. Javid b Friend	31
T. P. Milnes b Hobden	9
C. J. C. Wright c Salter b Friend	7
A. S. Miller not out	0
B 8, l-b 10, w 3, n-b 6	27
1/11 (2) 2/44 (1) 3/63 (4) 4/165 (3) 5/228 (6) 6/232 (5) 7/326 (7) 8/333 (8) 9/345 (10) 10/349 (9) (90.3 overs)	349

Hobden 25.3–5–62–5; Friend 18–1–96–2; Harris 22–7–63–1; Salter 19–3–77–1; Bendon 6–1–33–1.

Umpires: N. G. C. Cowley and S. C. Gale.

WARWICKSHIRE v SOMERSET

At Birmingham, April 12–15. Warwickshire won by two wickets. Warwickshire 20pts, Somerset 3pts. Toss: Somerset.

Warwickshire scrambled home on the last afternoon, much to the relief of their captain Troughton. He had dropped the simplest of chances at mid-off on the third morning to reprieve Buttler on seven, allowing Buttler and Compton to extend their sixth-wicket stand from 12 to 167, which eventually left Warwickshire a nerve-racking chase of 259. Troughton admitted he had been unable to eat or sleep that night, and was determined to make amends with the bat, but it was Patel, clobbering 15 in four deliveries from Dockrell, who hastened victory before Somerset could take the second new ball.

"It was like a season's worth of play in four days," said a weary Troughton. Somerset struggled against the movement of Wright and Barker, who twice snared Trescothick cheaply, but rallied through the persistence of their own seamers and Compton's unflustered century. Warwickshire faltered with victory in sight, losing five for 17 against a fired-up Trego, but Patel and Troughton regrouped after Trescothick – under a new playing regulation – requested lunch be delayed for four overs with Warwickshire eight wickets down.

Close of play: first day, Warwickshire 111-3 (Chopra 40, Maddy 24); second day, Somerset 127-4 (Compton 61, Dockrell 0); third day, Warwickshire 123-2 (Westwood 17, Porterfield 57).

Somerset

*M. E. Trescothick c Clarke b Barker	9	– lbw b Barker	10
A. V. Suppiah c Clarke b Wright	4	– run out	33
N. R. D. Compton lbw b Wright	5	– b Wright	133
J. C. Hildreth b Barker	0	– b Carter	3
†C. Kieswetter c Maddy b Wright	20	– b Patel	8
J. C. Buttler c Ambrose b Clarke	18	– (7) lbw b Wright	93
P. D. Trego c Maddy b Clarke	27	– (8) b Carter	4
A. J. Dibble run out	1	– (9) b Clarke	43
V. D. Philander c Chopra b Maddy	38	– (10) c Troughton b Clarke	8
G. H. Dockrell not out	13	– (6) c Porterfield b Wright	2
S. P. Kirby c Maddy b Wright	4	– not out	0
B 2, l-b 1, w 3, n-b 2	8	B 6, l-b 4, w 1, n-b 6	17
1/4 (2) 2/14 (1) 3/14 (4) 4/41 (5) (39.5 overs)	147	1/18 (1) 2/104 (2) (105 overs)	354
5/44 (3) 6/83 (6) 7/88 (7) 8/95 (8)		3/108 (4) 4/127 (5)	
9/142 (9) 10/147 (11)		5/131 (6) 6/298 (7) 7/303 (8)	
		8/303 (3) 9/354 (10) 10/354 (9)	

Barker 12–4–34–2; Wright 14.5–0–47–4; Carter 6–0–41–0; Clarke 5–2–13–2; Maddy 2–1–9–1. *Second innings*—Barker 23–7–61–1; Wright 26–7–71–3; Maddy 4–1–8–0; Patel 24–5–87–1; Clarke 8–1–31–2; Carter 20–1–86–2.

Warwickshire

V. Chopra c Hildreth b Kirby	43	– c Kieswetter b Kirby	10
I. J. Westwood lbw b Philander	8	– (3) lbw b Philander	32
W. T. S. Porterfield c Kieswetter b Dibble	7	– (4) c Kieswetter b Trego	84
*J. O. Troughton b Dibble	7	– (6) not out	15
D. L. Maddy lbw b Philander	42	– lbw b Trego	23
†T. R. Ambrose c Buttler b Dibble	10	– (7) c and b Trego	0
R. Clarke b Trego	27	– (8) c and b Kirby	4
K. H. D. Barker b Kirby	46	– (9) hit wkt b Trego	1
N. M. Carter c and b Dockrell	2	– (2) c Buttler b Dockrell	26
J. S. Patel c and b Trego	0	– not out	43
C. J. C. Wright not out	18		
B 17, l-b 10, n-b 6	33	B 2, l-b 12, n-b 10	24
1/19 (2) 2/44 (3) 3/58 (4) (85.2 overs)	243	1/40 (2) (8 wkts, 77.5 overs)	262
4/125 (1) 5/141 (5) 6/171 (6)		2/43 (1) 3/145 (3)	
7/192 (7) 8/195 (9) 9/196 (10) 10/243 (8)		4/190 (5) 5/197 (4)	
		6/197 (7) 7/204 (8) 8/207 (9)	

Philander 24–6–47–2; Kirby 21.2–10–51–2; Dibble 13–2–42–3; Trego 14–3–39–2; Dockrell 12–4–36–1; Suppiah 1–0–1–0. *Second innings*—Philander 24–8–55–1; Kirby 13–2–76–2; Dockrell 21.5–2–80–1; Trego 17–7–37–4; Suppiah 2–2–0–0.

Umpires: S. A. Garratt and M. A. Gough.

At Liverpool, April 19–22. WARWICKSHIRE beat LANCASHIRE by five wickets.

At Hove, April 26–29. WARWICKSHIRE drew with SUSSEX.

WARWICKSHIRE v DURHAM

At Birmingham, May 2–4. Warwickshire won by nine wickets. Warwickshire 21pts, Durham 3pts. Toss: Warwickshire.

Barker's maiden ten-wicket match haul and a restorative century for Bell swept Warwickshire to their first Championship victory over Durham for six years, in the equivalent of two days' play. Barker, swinging the ball both ways with a remodelled action, dismantled Durham's first innings with a triple-wicket maiden, and would have had five for one in 14 balls had Porterfield clung on to Blackwell at slip. Warwickshire in turn slipped to 14 for four but, with the exception of Onions, Durham bowled a shade too short at Bell, who pressed on to his first hundred in 20 innings on a truncated second day to help salve his winter wounds ahead of the Test series against West Indies. Durham lacked Bell's application, and Barker preyed on batsmen low on confidence to finish with figures of ten for 70. Collingwood suffered the indignity of being run out when his partner Benkenstein refused a leg-bye and he slipped scrambling back. Durham's frustration was evident when Thorp kicked a stump out of the ground shortly before Warwickshire completed their easy win; he was reprimanded by the ECB.

Close of play: first day, Warwickshire 116-5 (Bell 59, Ambrose 9); second day, Warwickshire 195-7 (Bell 106, Barker 1).

Durham

M. J. Di Venuto lbw b Wright	29	– (2) b Barker	12
W. R. Smith c Ambrose b Wright	2	– (1) b Barker	1
P. D. Collingwood lbw b Barker	4	– run out	6
B. A. Stokes c Ambrose b Barker	35	– c Porterfield b Barker	9
D. M. Benkenstein lbw b Patel	11	– c Bell b Patel	31
I. D. Blackwell b Wright	19	– lbw b Maddy	9
*†P. Mustard c Clarke b Barker	0	– c Troughton b Patel	45
S. G. Borthwick c Bell b Barker	0	– c Ambrose b Barker	5
C. D. Thorp c Bell b Barker	2	– c Trott b Patel	11
G. Onions c Ambrose b Wright	36	– b Barker	1
M. E. Claydon not out	6	– not out	2
B 8, l-b 11	19	B 1, l-b 4, w 2	7
1/12 (2) 2/17 (3) 3/50 (1) 4/76 (5) 5/99 (4) 6/99 (7) 7/99 (8) 8/103 (9) 9/152 (6) 10/163 (10) (50.3 overs)	163	1/9 (1) 2/16 (2) 3/33 (4) 4/41 (3) 5/58 (6) 6/117 (7) 7/124 (8) 8/132 (5) 9/137 (9) 10/139 (10) (50.2 overs)	139

Barker 17–8–33–5; Wright 13.3–0–41–4; Maddy 2–0–15–0; Clarke 7–3–21–0; Patel 11–1–34–1. *Second innings*—Wright 15–6–31–0; Barker 13.2–2–37–5; Clarke 8–4–21–0; Maddy 7–1–18–1; Patel 7–1–27–3.

Warwickshire

V. Chopra c Collingwood b Onions	0	– hit wkt b Thorp	22
W. T. S. Porterfield b Thorp	2	– not out	9
I. R. Bell c Mustard b Claydon	120	– not out	4
I. J. L. Trott c Di Venuto b Onions	2		
*J. O. Troughton lbw b Claydon	1		
D. L. Maddy c Di Venuto b Onions	35		
†T. R. Ambrose c Di Venuto b Blackwell	39		
R. Clarke lbw b Blackwell	0		
K. H. D. Barker c Mustard b Claydon	14		
J. S. Patel not out	30		
C. J. C. Wright c Mustard b Onions	14		
L-b 6, n-b 4	10	L-b 1	1
1/0 (1) 2/2 (2) 3/5 (4) 4/14 (5) 5/99 (6) 6/186 (7) 7/186 (8) 8/220 (9) 9/234 (3) 10/267 (11) (83 overs)	267	1/31 (1) (1 wkt, 7.4 overs)	36

Onions 26–7–74–4; Thorp 16–8–34–1; Claydon 22–4–79–3; Collingwood 5–1–20–0; Blackwell 12–3–45–2; Borthwick 2–0–9–0. *Second innings*—Onions 3–0–13–0; Thorp 3–0–19–1; Borthwick 1–0–2–0; Smith 0.4–0–1–0.

Umpires: N. L. Bainton and R. A. Kettleborough.

WARWICKSHIRE v LANCASHIRE

At Birmingham, May 16–19. Drawn. Warwickshire 9pts, Lancashire 4pts. Toss: Warwickshire.

Horton's first Championship century since April 2010 saved Lancashire from their fourth defeat in six matches. Dismissed in the nineties four times during the 2011 title-winning campaign, he now batted seven and a half hours, through several periods of poor light, for his unbeaten 137, to blunt Warwickshire's victory push on a flat pitch. Lancashire had been outplayed for most of the first three days. Warwickshire passed their previous highest total in the fixture – 532 for four at Edgbaston in 1901 – thanks to Chopra's elegant 113 and Clarke's powerful and disciplined century, his second of the season against them; Ambrose chipped to short midwicket four short of a hundred. Keedy and Kerrigan were forced to shoulder a heavy workload in the absence of Chapple, who was restricted to one over on the second day by a side strain. Lancashire then folded against a disciplined attack featuring – for the first time this Championship season – Woakes, who slipped back in seamlessly following an ankle injury. Prince alone knuckled down, though his example was emulated by Horton and Cross when they followed on 360 in arrears.

Close of play: first day, Warwickshire 289-4 (Maddy 29, Ambrose 22); second day, Lancashire 61-5 (Prince 14, Cross 4); third day, Lancashire 122-3 (Horton 56, Croft 4).

Warwickshire

V. Chopra c Brown b Kerrigan	113
I. J. Westwood c Horton b Procter	70
W. T. S. Porterfield c Horton b Kerrigan	34
*J. O. Troughton b Shahzad	7
D. L. Maddy c Prince b Keedy	44
†T. R. Ambrose c Moore b Kerrigan	96
R. Clarke not out	123
C. R. Woakes not out	43
B 6, l-b 20, w 1	27
1/168 (2) 2/224 (3) 3/235 (1) 4/246 (4) 5/322 (5) 6/469 (6) (6 wkts dec, 167 overs)	557
110 overs: 335-5	

K. H. D. Barker, J. S. Patel and C. J. C. Wright did not bat.

Chapple 18–4–42–0; Shahzad 29–8–86–1; Procter 21–5–63–1; Kerrigan 49–4–178–3; Keedy 50–7–162–1.

Lancashire

P. J. Horton lbw b Barker	7	– not out	137
S. C. Moore b Wright	17	– c Chopra b Woakes	9
K. R. Brown c Ambrose b Woakes	0	– c Ambrose b Wright	45
A. G. Prince not out	87	– c Clarke b Patel	1
S. J. Croft c Ambrose b Wright	2	– c Clarke b Wright	21
L. A. Procter lbw b Woakes	8	– lbw b Maddy	34
†G. D. Cross c Porterfield b Woakes	11	– not out	75
A. Shahzad c Troughton b Patel	13		
*G. Chapple c Ambrose b Wright	14		
S. C. Kerrigan c Ambrose b Patel	5		
G. Keedy lbw b Patel	0		
B 7, l-b 14, n-b 12	33	B 15, l-b 4, n-b 2	21
1/31 (1) 2/32 (3) 3/36 (2) 4/40 (5) 5/54 (6) 6/99 (7) 7/124 (8) 8/162 (9) 9/197 (10) 10/197 (11) (67.5 overs)	197	1/13 (2) 2/102 (3) 3/103 (4) 4/143 (5) 5/204 (6) (5 wkts, 127 overs)	343

Wright 21–3–58–3; Barker 11–5–31–1; Woakes 11–4–20–3; Patel 17.5–3–53–3; Clarke 7–2–14–0. *Second innings*—Woakes 18–2–63–1; Barker 11–4–36–0; Wright 17–2–64–2; Patel 41–14–88–1; Maddy 16–9–18–1; Clarke 14–7–27–0; Westwood 8–4–23–0; Chopra 2–0–5–0.

Umpires: M. J. D. Bodenham and M. A. Gough.

At The Oval, May 23–26. WARWICKSHIRE beat SURREY by five wickets.

At Chester-le-Street, June 5–8. WARWICKSHIRE drew with DURHAM.

WARWICKSHIRE v SUSSEX

At Birmingham, July 12–15. Drawn. Warwickshire 11pts, Sussex 5pts. Toss: Warwickshire.

Warwickshire took important strides towards the title by claiming all eight bonus points on the final day of a rain-blighted contest. The loss of the middle two days meant nine of the last scheduled 16 at Edgbaston, including internationals, had been washed out. Warwickshire's sharp cricket was typified by their acceleration from 350 to maximum batting points in four overs, thanks to Clarke's run-a-ball century, his third hundred of the season. Clarke then combined with Patel to secure three bowling points against timid Sussex batting. "It feels like a win," said Troughton, whose side displaced Nottinghamshire as leaders. On the opening day, Bell's decision to return to first-class cricket after his superb one-day series against Australia was rewarded with a smooth half-century. He was not in the ground when play began at noon, instead accompanying his pregnant wife Chantal to hospital for routine antenatal scans.

Close of play: first day, Warwickshire 175-3 (Troughton 42, Maddy 5); second day, no play; third day, no play.

Warwickshire

V. Chopra lbw b Panesar	26	K. H. D. Barker c Magoffin b Anyon	34
W. T. S. Porterfield lbw b Panesar	43	J. S. Patel not out	5
I. R. Bell c Nash b Magoffin	57	B 2, l-b 9	11
*J. O. Troughton c Wells b Anyon	81		
D. L. Maddy lbw b Panesar	21	1/66 (2) (8 wkts dec, 109.2 overs)	400
†T. R. Ambrose c Yardy b Panesar	0	2/77 (1) 3/157 (3)	
R. Clarke not out	110	4/208 (5) 5/208 (6)	
C. R. Woakes lbw b Wright	12	6/265 (4) 7/298 (8) 8/394 (9)	

C. J. C. Wright did not bat.

Anyon 22–2–93–2; Magoffin 27.2–11–53–1; Panesar 28–6–95–4; Naved Arif 15–1–53–0; Nash 7–0–52–0; Wright 10–0–43–1.

Sussex

C. D. Nash c Clarke b Patel	33	S. J. Magoffin lbw b Patel	29
E. C. Joyce c Ambrose b Woakes	10	J. E. Anyon lbw b Patel	0
L. W. P. Wells c Bell b Clarke	26	M. S. Panesar not out	1
M. W. Goodwin c Porterfield b Clarke	20	L-b 8, n-b 6	14
†M. J. Prior c Troughton b Patel	1		
*M. H. Yardy c Maddy b Clarke	21	1/31 (2) 2/50 (1) 3/87 (4) (46.1 overs)	191
L. J. Wright c Patel b Wright	36	4/88 (5) 5/102 (3) 6/135 (6)	
Naved Arif c Maddy b Patel	0	7/136 (8) 8/178 (7) 9/182 (10) 10/191 (9)	

Woakes 8–0–49–1; Barker 4–0–20–0; Wright 10–3–18–1; Patel 18.1–2–77–5; Clarke 6–0–19–3.

Umpires: S. C. Gale and I. J. Gould.

At Taunton, July 18–21. WARWICKSHIRE lost to SOMERSET by one wicket. *Warwickshire suffer their only defeat of the Championship season.*

WARWICKSHIRE v SURREY

At Birmingham, July 27–30. Drawn. Warwickshire 10pts, Surrey 7pts. Toss: Warwickshire.

Warwickshire piled up the highest Championship total of the season and their second-highest against Surrey, but were denied victory by the obdurate Ansari, who batted through a rain-interrupted final day for a career-best unbeaten 83. However, Warwickshire's players pointedly refused to applaud when he reached 50: they felt he should have taken Porterfield's word that he had held a clean catch at second slip off Patel on the third evening. Instead, Ansari stood his ground, and was given not out after the umpires conferred. Warwickshire owed much to Troughton and Woakes, who made centuries in the same innings for the second successive match, and to the 127 Woakes added with Patel for the ninth wicket. But they were also indebted to Surrey's profligate bowlers, who gave away 34 in no-balls. Johnson, recalled from a loan spell at Derbyshire after Ambrose was injured, dropped a simple chance off Burns from the first ball of the innings, which caused Warwickshire to sweat a little longer before enforcing the follow-on. While Ansari scrapped to save the match, Rory Hamilton-Brown batted in the Edgbaston nets to prepare for his comeback in a second-team fixture after extended compassionate leave following the death of Tom Maynard; Surrey's team director, Chris Adams, missed the game too, as he holidayed in Portugal.

Close of play: first day, Warwickshire 322-6 (Troughton 74, Woakes 12); second day, Surrey 109-1 (Burns 53, Harinath 44); third day, Surrey 38-0 (Burns 12, Ansari 19).

Warwickshire

V. Chopra b Jordan	60
I. J. Westwood lbw b Batty	67
W. T. S. Porterfield c Davies b Jordan	8
*J. O. Troughton c Davies b Kartik	119
D. L. Maddy lbw b Kartik	4
†R. M. Johnson c de Bruyn b Meaker	49
R. Clarke c Burns b Meaker	5
C. R. Woakes not out	118
K. H. D. Barker c Davies b Kartik	0
J. S. Patel c and b Kartik	76
W. B. Rankin run out	5
B 8, l-b 14, w 4, n-b 34	60
1/130 (1) 2/152 (3) 3/188 (2) 4/197 (5) 5/295 (6) 6/307 (7) 7/429 (4) 8/429 (9) 9/556 (10) 10/571 (11) (157.1 overs)	571

110 overs: 374-6

Lewis 24–5–86–0; Meaker 31.1–6–100–2; Kartik 41–5–116–4; Jordan 25–1–139–2; de Bruyn 13–1–42–0; Batty 23–2–66–1.

Surrey

R. J. Burns c Johnson b Clarke	77	– b Rankin	42
Z. S. Ansari lbw b Woakes	10	– not out	83
A. Harinath c Johnson b Barker	44	– c Johnson b Patel	0
Z. de Bruyn lbw b Woakes	3	– c Barker b Patel	12
J. J. Roy c Troughton b Woakes	0	– not out	42
†S. M. Davies c Porterfield b Clarke	12		
C. J. Jordan lbw b Clarke	15		
*G. J. Batty lbw b Barker	28		
S. C. Meaker c Porterfield b Clarke	41		
J. Lewis not out	33		
M. Kartik c Porterfield b Rankin	13		
B 2, l-b 4, n-b 4	10	B 9, l-b 1, n-b 13	23
1/26 (2) 2/109 (3) 3/122 (4) 4/128 (5) 5/145 (6) 6/158 (1) 7/167 (7) 8/224 (8) 9/269 (9) 10/286 (11) (95.1 overs)	286	1/74 (1) 2/83 (3) 3/113 (4) (3 wkts, 88 overs)	202

Barker 21–5–85–2; Woakes 22–8–49–3; Clarke 19–5–46–4; Rankin 17.1–1–68–1; Patel 12–4–28–0; Maddy 4–3–4–0. *Second innings*—Barker 12–5–27–0; Woakes 11–2–22–0; Clarke 11–2–28–0; Patel 33–13–64–2; Rankin 15–6–26–1; Maddy 6–1–25–0.

Umpires: N. G. C. Cowley and G. Sharp.

At Uxbridge, August 1–4. WARWICKSHIRE drew with MIDDLESEX.

WARWICKSHIRE v WORCESTERSHIRE

At Birmingham, August 8–10. Warwickshire won by seven wickets. Warwickshire 19pts, Worcestershire 4pts. Toss: Worcestershire. First-class debuts: B. L. D'Oliveira, C. J. Russell. Championship debut: J. Leach.

Worcestershire spectacularly surrendered the initiative earned by Hughes's century when they collapsed twice against Patel – losing their last five wickets for seven runs in the first innings, and six in 11 overs in the second. In doing so, they handed Warwickshire their first win since May. Hughes had unhappy memories of Edgbaston, where he had been dropped by Australia during the 2009 Ashes (and told everyone so on Twitter), but became the first Worcestershire batsman in four seasons to carry his bat. Worcestershire crumbled after Solanki, having added 124 with Hughes for the fourth wicket, holed out to deep square leg. Their decision to freshen up their side with three Championship debutants – including Brett D'Oliveira, grandson of Basil – left them sorely lacking experience in the lower order. But one of them, the pacy Chris Russell, then helped dismiss Warwickshire for 132 – their lowest first-innings score in two years – on a dry pitch used for the previous evening's CB40 match. Clarke, the only batsman to cope, was aggrieved to be given out caught at short leg – and his dissent continued when he took the field, earning him a ticking-off from the umpires and a penalty from the ECB. But Warwickshire's bowlers fought back, before Chopra and Westwood batted with greater composure in a chase of 260.

Close of play: first day, Warwickshire 19-3 (Maddy 6, Wright 3); second day, Warwickshire 79-0 (Chopra 46, Westwood 32).

Worcestershire

*D. K. H. Mitchell lbw b Wright	11	– c Clarke b Wright	4
P. J. Hughes not out	135	– lbw b Barker	0
M. G. Pardoe c Ambrose b Barker	9	– c Chopra b Patel	30
M. M. Ali c Ambrose b Rankin	1	– c Chopra b Barker	10
V. S. Solanki c Barker b Patel	57	– c Porterfield b Rankin	33
J. Leach c Chopra b Wright	0	– lbw b Wright	20
B. L. D'Oliveira c Clarke b Wright	19	– lbw b Barker	7
G. M. Andrew c Ambrose b Patel	1	– lbw b Patel	4
†B. J. M. Scott b Rankin	1	– lbw b Patel	11
C. J. Russell c Ambrose b Patel	3	– c Barker b Patel	5
A. Richardson c Clarke b Patel	0	– not out	8
B 4, l-b 4, w 1	9	B 4, l-b 8, w 1	13
1/46 (1) 2/59 (3) 3/73 (4) 4/197 (5) 5/197 (6) 6/239 (7) 7/242 (8) 8/243 (9) 9/246 (10) 10/246 (11) (75 overs)	246	1/4 (2) 2/4 (1) 3/23 (4) 4/70 (5) 5/108 (6) 6/110 (3) 7/114 (8) 8/130 (7) 9/132 (9) 10/145 (10) (46.5 overs)	145

Wright 20–4–63–3; Barker 16–4–47–1; Maddy 6–2–12–0; Rankin 14–2–44–2; Patel 19–3–72–4. *Second innings*—Wright 13–4–40–2; Barker 12–5–21–3; Maddy 1–0–4–0; Rankin 7–0–26–1; Patel 13.5–1–42–4.

Warwickshire

V. Chopra lbw b Richardson	0	– lbw b Russell	58
I. J. Westwood lbw b Russell	0	– c and b Russell	83
W. T. S. Porterfield c Mitchell b Richardson	5	– c Solanki b Ali	37
D. L. Maddy c Mitchell b Russell	11	– (5) not out	45
C. J. C. Wright c Solanki b Russell	3		
R. Clarke c Pardoe b Ali	61		
*J. O. Troughton lbw b Russell	13	– (4) not out	34
†T. R. Ambrose lbw b Andrew	4		
K. H. D. Barker c Richardson b Ali	17		
J. S. Patel c Andrew b Richardson	3		
W. B. Rankin not out	0		
B 8, l-b 7	15	L-b 6	6
1/4 (1) 2/4 (2) 3/10 (3) 4/19 (5) 5/34 (4) 6/72 (7) 7/77 (8) 8/118 (6) 9/127 (10) 10/132 (9) (42.3 overs)	132	1/100 (1) 2/177 (2) 3/193 (3) (3 wkts, 79.5 overs)	263

Richardson 16–5–36–3; Russell 16–5–43–4; Ali 6.3–2–17–2; Andrew 4–0–21–1. *Second innings*—Richardson 19–4–56–0; Russell 14–1–74–2; Ali 33.5–7–80–1; D'Oliveira 9–0–36–0; Andrew 3–0–11–0; Leach 1–1–0–0.

Umpires: N. L. Bainton and M. R. Benson.

WARWICKSHIRE v MIDDLESEX

At Birmingham, August 21–24. Drawn. Warwickshire 9pts, Middlesex 8pts. Toss: Warwickshire. Championship debut: R. H. Patel.

Warwickshire increased their lead at the top by a point, despite enduring what Ashley Giles called their "worst week in the Championship this season". They were grateful for the arrival of rain over at Taunton, which denied Sussex a likely victory, and bad light in the final hour here, which halted play when they were seven wickets down and 215 short of a theoretical target. Middlesex were prevented from bowling their seamers in the gloaming, but Warwickshire still ran into trouble against Ravi Patel, a 21-year-old slow left-armer from Harrow, before the umpires took the players off. Dexter's belligerent century was a poignant one: it came on his 28th birthday, and was his first since the sudden death of his elder brother, Keith, over the winter. "It's almost his birthday gift to me," said Dexter. Warwickshire failed to build on Westwood's second hundred of the season against Middlesex, shedding four for 18 against the second new ball. Middlesex dominated from there on, with Rogers and Malan stroking fluent centuries in adding 203. Wright, who shared all ten with Rankin, reached 50 first-class wickets for the summer.

Close of play: first day, Warwickshire 21-0 (Chopra 8, Westwood 13); second day, Warwickshire 293-8 (Barker 1, Wright 1); third day, Middlesex 351-5 (Malan 138, Berg 53).

Middlesex

First innings		Second innings	
S. D. Robson c Ambrose b Rankin	60	– c Ambrose b Wright	1
*C. J. L. Rogers c Clarke b Barker	6	– c Chopra b Rankin	109
J. L. Denly c Ambrose b Wright	4	– c Clarke b Wright	15
D. J. Malan c Ambrose b Wright	1	– c Ambrose b Wright	140
N. J. Dexter lbw b Rankin	101	– c Porterfield b Rankin	2
†A. M. Rossington c Chopra b Blackwell	29	– c Maddy b Rankin	2
G. K. Berg c Porterfield b Blackwell	8	– c Maddy b Wright	78
S. P. Crook c Porterfield b Blackwell	27	– c Ambrose b Rankin	19
T. S. Roland-Jones c Clarke b Rankin	0	– c Barker b Wright	12
T. J. Murtagh not out	8	– c Clarke b Rankin	0
R. H. Patel c Wright b Blackwell	7	– not out	0
B 6, l-b 6, w 2, n-b 22	36	B 1, l-b 4, w 3, n-b 26	34
1/39 (2) 2/46 (3) 3/48 (4) 4/121 (1) 5/216 (6) 6/229 (7) 7/267 (8) 8/267 (5) 9/268 (9) 10/287 (11) (71.2 overs)	287	1/1 (1) 2/25 (3) 3/228 (2) 4/238 (5) 5/252 (6) 6/357 (4) 7/399 (8) 8/401 (7) 9/404 (10) 10/412 (9) (91 overs)	412

Barker 16–0–50–1; Wright 18–2–79–2; Maddy 7–2–27–0; Rankin 14–1–72–3; Blackwell 16.2–4–47–4. *Second innings*—Barker 17–0–83–0; Wright 21–0–119–5; Rankin 20–1–78–5; Blackwell 26–2–98–0; Maddy 6–0–26–0; Westwood 1–0–3–0.

Warwickshire

First innings		Second innings	
V. Chopra c Robson b Berg	56	– c Murtagh b Roland-Jones	4
I. J. Westwood c sub (T. E. Scollay) b Dexter	120	– c Rossington b Murtagh	0
W. T. S. Porterfield c Dexter b Patel	13	– st Rossington b Patel	12
*J. O. Troughton c Robson b Murtagh	50	– c Rossington b Patel	42
D. L. Maddy c Crook b Dexter	16	– lbw b Berg	10
R. Clarke c Rossington b Roland-Jones	6	– lbw b Roland-Jones	15
†T. R. Ambrose c Rossington b Roland-Jones	0	– not out	33
I. D. Blackwell lbw b Roland-Jones	8	– c and b Patel	23
K. H. D. Barker c Rossington b Murtagh	23	– not out	3
C. J. C. Wright b Murtagh	13		
W. B. Rankin not out	4		
B 1, l-b 14, w 1, n-b 8	24	L-b 6, n-b 4	10
1/175 (1) 2/194 (3) 3/223 (2) 4/247 (5) 5/273 (6) 6/275 (7) 7/289 (8) 8/291 (4) 9/328 (9) 10/333 (10) (101 overs)	333	1/7 (2) 2/11 (1) 3/30 (3) 4/54 (5) 5/86 (6) 6/100 (4) 7/134 (8) (7 wkts, 58.4 overs)	152

Murtagh 27–5–68–3; Roland-Jones 23–0–96–3; Berg 12–2–45–1; Crook 13–0–37–0; Patel 16–2–42–1; Dexter 10–1–30–2. *Second innings*—Murtagh 5–1–14–1; Roland-Jones 10–3–22–2; Crook 7–1–19–0; Patel 18–4–60–3; Berg 5–1–13–1; Dexter 2–1–2–0; Malan 9.4–4–16–0; Denly 2–2–0–0.

Umpires: J. W. Lloyds and M. J. Saggers.

WARWICKSHIRE v NOTTINGHAMSHIRE

At Birmingham, August 28–31. Drawn. Warwickshire 10pts, Notts 9pts. Toss: Warwickshire.

This keenly anticipated contest proved more title eliminator than title decider after rain washed out the second day. Nottinghamshire emerged from the game 28 points behind Warwickshire, one worse off than at the start. They had gambled on the fitness of Adams, recently turned 37, but he laboured through 18 overs before hobbling off with a recurrence of a calf injury. Ambrose, pushed up in the order to replace the dropped Darren Maddy, responded with his first century in three years. Westwood had already made his fifth score above 50 in seven innings, and aggressive half-centuries from nightwatchman Wright, his first for Warwickshire, and Blackwell allowed them to plunder 206 in 37 overs on the third day. Nottinghamshire slipped to 69 for four, but Hales and Read insured against defeat with a stand of 222. Read declared the moment the follow-on was saved to deny Warwickshire a third bowling point, but the gesture had no impact on the title race.

Close of play: first day, Warwickshire 298-5 (Ambrose 64, Wright 6); second day, no play; third day, Nottinghamshire 188-4 (Hales 80, Read 54).

Warwickshire

V. Chopra c Hales b Fletcher	11	– lbw b Fletcher	27
I. J. Westwood lbw b Franks	81	– not out	17
W. T. S. Porterfield b Franks	26	– lbw b White	3
*J. O. Troughton c Read b Franks	40	– c Voges b White	35
†T. R. Ambrose not out	151		
R. Clarke c Read b Fletcher	47		
C. J. C. Wright c Carter b White	53		
I. D. Blackwell not out	69		
B 5, l-b 14, w 1, n-b 6	26	L-b 4	4
1/40 (1) 2/92 (3) (6 wkts dec, 125 overs)	504	1/33 (1) (3 wkts dec, 28.5 overs)	86
3/175 (4) 4/178 (2)		2/44 (3) 3/86 (4)	
5/280 (6) 6/377 (7) 110 overs: 415-6			

K. H. D. Barker, T. P. Milnes and W. B. Rankin did not bat.

Fletcher 37–13–102–2; Carter 22–3–89–0; Adams 18–0–82–0; Franks 23–4–77–3; White 25–1–135–1. *Second innings*—Fletcher 6–0–16–1; Franks 6–2–12–0; Carter 9–1–29–0; White 7.5–3–25–2.

Nottinghamshire

M. H. Wessels c Westwood b Wright	10
A. D. Hales not out	155
M. J. Lumb c Chopra b Barker	12
J. W. A. Taylor hit wkt b Wright	1
A. C. Voges c Porterfield b Milnes	8
*†C. M. W. Read st Ambrose b Blackwell	95
P. J. Franks c Troughton b Rankin	9
G. G. White b Wright	9
A. R. Adams c Porterfield b Wright	4
L. J. Fletcher not out	4
B 6, l-b 13, n-b 30	49
1/24 (1) (8 wkts dec, 89.5 overs)	356
2/45 (3) 3/48 (4)	
4/69 (5) 5/291 (6) 6/302 (7)	
7/342 (8) 8/348 (9)	

A. Carter did not bat.

Wright 27–3–107–4; Barker 15.5–4–50–1; Rankin 19–1–71–1; Milnes 15–0–78–1; Blackwell 13–4–31–1.

Umpires: N. G. B. Cook and T. E. Jesty.

At Worcester, September 4–6. WARWICKSHIRE beat WORCESTERSHIRE by an innings and 202 runs. *Warwickshire win the title with a game to spare.*

At Nottingham, September 11–14. WARWICKSHIRE drew with NOTTINGHAMSHIRE.

WORCESTERSHIRE

Bobbing up and down

JOHN CURTIS

After two years of overachievement, Worcestershire endured a truly dismal summer, finishing bottom of both Division One of the Championship and their CB40 group. The challenge now is to match the stoical response to a difficult 2009, after they had been relegated without a win, and five senior players left the club. Back then, they immediately punched above their weight by gaining promotion in 2010, then avoiding instant relegation for the first time the following season.

But the attributes which served Worcestershire well two seasons ago now deserted them, and too many senior players underperformed, placing responsibility on youngsters yet to prove they are good enough.

The club had been competitive in the majority of their Division One games in 2011, even when losing their opening six matches. This time, however, it was often men against boys. That was never more obvious than when a side containing eight players younger than 24 collapsed to 60 all out – the lowest score of the Championship season – to hand Warwickshire the title at New Road.

Only the excellent Alan Richardson – fresh from being named one of *Wisden*'s Five Cricketers of the Year – reached the required standard, taking 57 Championship wickets at just under 20, and earning a new two-year contract at the age of 37. Worcestershire had Richardson to thank for maintaining a perfect record of bowling bonus points at home, until Warwickshire's batsmen punished them in the last match.

The cosmopolitan make-up of the playing staff in 2011 – when Damien Wright, Shakib Al Hasan, Saeed Ajmal and Kemar Roach all prospered in stints as overseas players – meant Richardson had previously received strong support. But there was no sign of that in 2012, as Worcestershire opted instead for two Australian opening batsmen, Michael Klinger and Phillip Hughes; hopes that Ajmal would return for a second spell in the Twenty20 competition were dashed when Pakistan arranged a series in Sri Lanka for June and July. Gareth Andrew also failed to contribute until late on, as he took time to recover sharpness after a winter knee operation.

Moeen Ali was adequate as a containing spinner, and continues to improve, but he is far from a frontline bowler – though his 12 wickets on a turning pitch at Old Trafford did earn Worcestershire their solitary Championship win.

Yet for all the concern about the bowling department, it was the batting which at times proved woefully inadequate, yielding only 17 bonus points – the lowest by any side since two divisions were introduced in 2000.

Hughes was the exception. His arrival was delayed for seven weeks as he attended an Australian training camp, then his stay interrupted by a call-up to the touring Australia A side. But, when available, he showed plenty of determination to master bowler-friendly pitches – and rebuild his international reputation. Hughes averaged 35 in nine Championship matches, and scored 900 runs at precisely 90 in the shorter formats. The FLt20 was the one competition to provide a ray of sunshine for Worcestershire: four wins put them into the quarter-finals for only the third time, before they lost to Yorkshire at Headingley, when Hughes again stood out, with an unbeaten 80 from 53 balls.

Chris Brunskill, Getty Images

Chris Russell

But none of the other Championship regulars averaged more than 27. Vikram Solanki's decade and a half with the club ended in disappointing fashion when he opted to follow Gareth Batty and Steven Davies to affluent Surrey. Though he is a fluent strokemaker when in full flow, Solanki's weight of runs in 2012 did not live up to his record, and he was left out for the last three games.

Alexei Kervezee suffered a complete loss of form, and looked a shadow of the batsman who had scored a brilliant 128 at Trent Bridge the previous year. He was dropped from the Championship side in May, and a broken finger meant he did not return until the dying embers of the season when he reeled off three fifties in three games. Nor was there much help from the lower order. Ben Scott's century in the win over Lancashire was his only real contribution, and he eventually lost his place as wicketkeeper to 20-year-old Ben Cox.

Worcestershire remained determined to give their Academy graduates a chance. But the returns were underwhelming: Matthew Pardoe and Neil Pinner made just one fifty each, and Brett D'Oliveira's leg-spin was expensive. The most encouraging developer was 23-year-old quick bowler Chris Russell, who took three wickets in each innings against the South Africans, then cemented his place in the Championship side.

With Solanki moving on and Scott and James Cameron – at the age of 26 – both retiring, there was an urgent need for recruitment for 2013 if Worcestershire were to gain a fourth promotion in eight seasons. They moved quickly to sign up Combined Services seamer Graeme Cessford, 29, who agreed to take a year out of his career as an RAF corporal, and later secured the services of the experienced Sri Lankan batsman Thilan Samaraweera.

In such a wet summer, it was inevitable New Road would flood, but only a solitary CB40 match in May had to be moved to Kidderminster. The waters returned with interest in November, by which time work had begun on a £10m hotel and conference complex – crucial to the club's financial future – due to open in October 2013.

Championship attendance: 20,827.

WORCESTERSHIRE RESULTS

All first-class matches – Played 17: Won 1, Lost 8, Drawn 8.
County Championship matches – Played 16: Won 1, Lost 8, Drawn 7.

LV= County Championship, 9th in Division 1;
Friends Life t20, q-f; Clydesdale Bank 40, 7th in Group A.

COUNTY CHAMPIONSHIP AVERAGES, BATTING AND FIELDING

Colours		*M*	*I*	*NO*	*R*	*HS*	*100*	*50*	*Avge*	*Ct/St*
2012	P. J. Hughes§	9	17	1	560	135*	2	2	35.00	2
2009	A. N. Kervezee¶	6	10	1	283	76	0	3	31.44	7
2012	M. Klinger§	6	11	1	293	69*	0	2	29.30	7
2005	D. K. H. Mitchell†	16	30	2	766	133*	2	1	27.35	22
2007	M. M. Ali	16	28	3	652	94	0	4	26.08	5
1998	V. S. Solanki	13	23	3	472	106	1	2	23.60	18
2009	J. D. Shantry	4	5	2	67	22*	0	0	22.33	1
2010	J. G. Cameron	11	17	3	300	52	0	1	21.42	3
2011	M. G. Pardoe†	12	22	2	407	55	0	1	20.35	10
2011	N. D. Pinner†	4	7	0	132	82	0	1	18.85	1
2011	A. Kapil	4	6	1	93	41	0	0	18.60	0
2007	R. A. Jones†	10	15	5	151	32	0	0	15.10	5
2009	O. B. Cox†	3	6	1	67	25*	0	0	13.40	5
2010	B. J. M. Scott	13	20	1	228	106	1	0	12.00	28/5
2008	G. M. Andrew	9	16	2	159	29	0	0	11.35	3
2012	C. J. Russell	6	10	2	83	22	0	0	10.37	2
2012	J. Leach	5	9	0	93	46	0	0	10.33	0
2012	B. L. D'Oliveira†	3	6	0	62	19	0	0	10.33	0
2012	D. S. Lucas	7	9	0	74	19	0	0	8.22	2
2010	A. Richardson	14	21	9	79	18	0	0	6.58	3
2010	S. H. Choudhry	3	5	0	29	20	0	0	5.80	3
2012	N. L. Harrison	2	4	0	12	10	0	0	3.00	0

† Born in Worcestershire. § Official overseas player. ¶ Other non-England-qualified player. Since 2002, Worcestershire have awarded colours to all on Championship debut.

BOWLING

	Style	*O*	*M*	*R*	*W*	*BB*	*5I*	*Avge*
A. Richardson	RFM	461.3	137	1,113	57	6-47	4	19.52
M. M. Ali	OB	284.1	40	901	33	6-29	2	27.30
R. A. Jones	RFM	200.1	26	857	31	6-32	1	27.64
J. D. Shantry	LFM	100	19	321	11	5-58	1	29.18
C. J. Russell	RFM	134.4	23	563	17	4-43	0	33.11
G. M. Andrew	RFM	179	27	685	18	5-86	1	38.05
D. S. Lucas	LFM	239	40	852	22	4-37	0	38.72

Also bowled: J. G. Cameron (RM) 37–1–160–2; S. H. Choudhry (SLA) 41.2–9–83–7; B. L. D'Oliveira (LBG) 43–2–198–0; N. L. Harrison (RFM) 23–3–98–1; A. Kapil (RFM) 35–4–136–4; J. Leach (RM) 40–8–127–4; D. K. H. Mitchell (RM) 8–0–24–0; N. D. Pinner (OB) 4–0–13–0.

LEADING CB40 AVERAGES (100 runs/4 wickets)

Batting	*Runs*	*HS*	*Avge*	*SR*	*Ct*
P. J. Hughes	498	111	83.00	84.98	4
V. S. Solanki	401	121	40.10	82.85	8
M. M. Ali	259	99	23.54	88.09	2
D. K. H. Mitchell	182	48	22.75	93.33	4
G. M. Andrew	157	42	19.62	106.80	5
J. G. Cameron	134	38	19.14	78.82	1

Bowling	*W*	*BB*	*Avge*	*ER*
J. D. Shantry	20	4-32	24.50	6.24
M. M. Ali	12	3-33	31.16	5.75
D. K. H. Mitchell	7	2-10	35.42	5.39
N. L. Harrison	5	2-54	36.80	8.36
G. M. Andrew	5	3-9	42.00	5.36
D. S. Lucas	7	2-11	42.14	5.95

LEADING FLT20 AVERAGES (100 runs/18 overs)

Batting	*Runs*	*HS*	*Avge*	*SR*	*Ct*
G. M. Andrew	148	43	24.66	**154.16**	1
D. K. H. Mitchell	102	31	17.00	**143.66**	3
M. M. Ali	195	82	24.37	**142.33**	4
P. J. Hughes	402	87*	100.50	**126.81**	1
J. G. Cameron	166	57	23.71	**114.48**	5
V. S. Solanki	123	33	15.37	**89.13**	4

Bowling	*W*	*BB*	*Avge*	*ER*
D. S. Lucas	6	2-9	28.83	**6.44**
D. K. H. Mitchell	11	3-13	15.54	**6.84**
M. M. Ali	5	2-14	40.20	**7.01**
J. D. Shantry	9	4-33	27.55	**8.00**
G. M. Andrew	7	3-20	30.14	**8.16**

FIRST-CLASS COUNTY RECORDS

Highest score for	405*	G. A. Hick v Somerset at Taunton	1988
Highest score against	331*	J. D. B. Robertson (Middlesex) at Worcester	1949
Leading run-scorer	34,490	D. Kenyon (avge 34.18)	1946–1967
Best bowling for	9-23	C. F. Root v Lancashire at Worcester	1931
Best bowling against	10-51	J. Mercer (Glamorgan) at Worcester	1936
Leading wicket-taker	2,143	R. T. D. Perks (avge 23.73)	1930–1955
Highest total for	701-6 dec	v Surrey at Worcester	2007
Highest total against	701-4 dec	by Leicestershire at Worcester	1906
Lowest total for	24	v Yorkshire at Huddersfield	1903
Lowest total against	30	by Hampshire at Worcester	1903

LIST A COUNTY RECORDS

Highest score for	180*	T. M. Moody v Surrey at The Oval	1994
Highest score against	158	W. Larkins (Northamptonshire) at Luton	1982
	158	R. A. Smith (Hampshire) at Worcester	1996
Leading run-scorer	16,416	G. A. Hick (avge 41.60)	1985–2008
Best bowling for	7-19	N. V. Radford v Bedfordshire at Bedford	1991
Best bowling against	7-15	R. A. Hutton (Yorkshire) at Leeds	1969
Leading wicket-taker	370	S. R. Lampitt (avge 24.52)	1987–2002
Highest total for	404-3	v Devon at Worcester	1987
Highest total against	399-4	by Sussex at Horsham	2011
Lowest total for	58	v Ireland v Worcester	2009
Lowest total against	45	by Hampshire at Worcester	1988

TWENTY20 COUNTY RECORDS

Highest score for	116*	G. A. Hick v Northamptonshire at Luton	2004
Highest score against	141*	C. L. White (Somerset) at Worcester	2006
Leading run-scorer	**1,472**	**V. S. Solanki (avge 24.13)**	**2004–2012**
Best bowling for	4-11	D. K. H. Mitchell v Gloucestershire at Bristol	2008
Best bowling against	6-21	A. J. Hall (Northamptonshire) at Northampton	2008
Leading wicket-taker	**50**	**G. M. Andrew (avge 26.92)**	**2008–2012**
Highest total for	227-6	v Northamptonshire at Kidderminster	2007
Highest total against	222-3	by Northamptonshire at Kidderminster	2007
Lowest total for	86	v Northamptonshire at Worcester	2006
Lowest total against	93	by Gloucestershire at Bristol	2008

ADDRESS

County Ground, New Road, Worcester WR2 4QQ (01905 748474; **email** info@wccc.co.uk). **Website** www.wccc.co.uk

OFFICIALS

Captain D. K. H. Mitchell
Director of cricket S. J. Rhodes
Academy director D. B. D'Oliveira
President C. D. Fearnley
Chairman J. M. Price
Chief executive D. A. Leatherdale
Head groundsman T. R. Packwood
Scorer D. E. Pugh

At Nottingham, April 5–8. WORCESTERSHIRE lost to NOTTINGHAMSHIRE by 92 runs.

At Oxford, April 13–15. WORCESTERSHIRE drew with OXFORD MCCU.

At The Oval, April 19–22. WORCESTERSHIRE drew with SURREY.

WORCESTERSHIRE v NOTTINGHAMSHIRE

At Worcester, April 26–29. Drawn. Worcestershire 6pts, Nottinghamshire 7pts. Toss: Worcestershire.

Torrential overnight rain washed out the final day and put New Road on flood alert. In the play that was possible, Nottinghamshire registered their first batting point of the season – they had not previously passed 162 in the first innings, despite winning twice – but could not make the most of a rare half-century opening partnership. Kapil's spell of three for two in four overs pegged them back, and Jones mopped up the tail. Worcestershire failed in their own quest for a first batting point, and were in danger of following on when they lurched to 66 for six on a second day shortened to 27.3 overs by bad light. Adams exploited some inconsistent bounce with an exemplary line, claiming four of the seven lbw decisions. But Kapil demonstrated his all-round abilities by resisting for two hours, ensuring Nottinghamshire would have to bat next. Richardson was off the field with a side strain while Edwards extended the lead to 174 before the forecast deluge arrived.

Close of play: first day, Worcestershire 5-0 (Mitchell 0, Klinger 5); second day, Worcestershire 72-6 (Cameron 9, Kapil 3); third day, Nottinghamshire 88-2 (Edwards 49, Patel 7).

Nottinghamshire

A. D. Hales c Mitchell b Jones	49	– c Cameron b Jones	12
N. J. Edwards c Cameron b Richardson	23	– not out	49
M. J. Lumb b Cameron	17	– lbw b Lucas	16
S. R. Patel c Klinger b Richardson	26	– not out	7
J. W. A. Taylor c Scott b Kapil	38		
*†C. M. W. Read c Klinger b Kapil	34		
S. J. Mullaney c Kervezee b Jones	24		
B. J. Phillips c Mitchell b Kapil	2		
A. R. Adams c Kervezee b Jones	21		
L. J. Fletcher b Jones	0		
H. F. Gurney not out	0		
L-b 4, w 1, n-b 4	9	L-b 2, n-b 2	4
1/70 (2) 2/82 (1) 3/109 (3) (88.1 overs)	243	1/23 (1) (2 wkts, 28.1 overs)	88
4/137 (4) 5/193 (6) 6/194 (5)		2/68 (3)	
7/202 (8) 8/232 (9) 9/236 (10) 10/243 (7)			

Richardson 22–11–23–2; Lucas 23–4–86–0; Jones 20.1–5–76–4; Kapil 9–3–17–3; Cameron 8–1–19–1; Ali 6–0–18–0. *Second innings*—Lucas 10.1–1–37–1; Jones 13–2–34–1; Kapil 3–0–11–0; Cameron 1–0–2–0; Ali 1–0–2–0.

Worcestershire

*D. K. H. Mitchell lbw b Adams	24
M. Klinger c Patel b Adams	22
V. S. Solanki lbw b Phillips	1
M. M. Ali lbw b Adams	11
A. N. Kervezee lbw b Adams	0
J. G. Cameron c Read b Gurney	25
†B. J. M. Scott lbw b Gurney	1
A. Kapil lbw b Adams	41
D. S. Lucas lbw b Gurney	2
R. A. Jones c Adams b Gurney	21
A. Richardson not out	2
L-b 7	7
1/35 (2) 2/42 (3) 3/56 (1) (67.5 overs)	157
4/56 (5) 5/63 (4) 6/66 (7)	
7/105 (6) 8/111 (9) 9/135 (8) 10/157 (10)	

Fletcher 12–4–18–0; Phillips 19–4–30–1; Adams 22–5–62–5; Gurney 14.5–2–40–4.

Umpires: N. G. B. Cook and M. A. Gough.

ALL THE STARS ALIGNED

On May 12, these former Millfield School pupils scored first-class hundreds, all in away fixtures:

108 Kieran Powell, West Indies v England Lions at Northampton (see page 321)
121 Wes Durston, Derbyshire v Hampshire at Southampton (see page 513)
115 Rory Hamilton-Brown, Surrey v Worcestershire at Worcester
143 Tom Maynard, Surrey v Worcestershire at Worcester

Another was left a boundary short of a hundred after his team were bowled out:

96* Craig Kieswetter, Somerset v Durham at Chester-le-Street (see page 461)

Research: Andrew Bunbury

At Lord's, May 3–6. WORCESTERSHIRE lost to MIDDLESEX by 132 runs.

WORCESTERSHIRE v SURREY

At Worcester, May 9–12. Drawn. Worcestershire 8pts, Surrey 6pts. Toss: Worcestershire. Championship debut: G. A. Edwards.

Worcestershire's eighth and ninth wickets held out for 18 overs to deny Surrey their second Championship win after following on. The match was switched back to New Road from Kidderminster after the floods receded in time, but Worcestershire's first innings still spanned two rain-hit days, as they notched up their first two batting points of the campaign. Rudolph aside, Surrey's techniques looked iffy in overcast conditions: their deficit of 172 would have been greater had he not been dropped twice by Mitchell off Lucas in single figures; instead, he was last out for 68, having added 60 for the ninth wicket with Southwark-born newcomer George Edwards. However, when Surrey followed on, the sun came out and Richardson was forced off by a shoulder injury. Ramprakash walked after gloving behind for only the third pair of his career, leaving Surrey 11 for two – then Pietersen turned the match on its head. In just his fourth Championship appearance for Surrey, he tore into the change bowlers for a 49-ball fifty. Hamilton-Brown and Maynard, with the highest score of his career, put first-innings ducks behind them in a spectacular fifth-wicket partnership of 225 in 44.3 overs, and any hopes Worcestershire had of chasing 260 in 52 overs were ended by two early strikes for the speedy Edwards. But Pardoe showed great resolve to shepherd Lucas and Jones, and save the match.

Close of play: first day, Worcestershire 58-0 (Mitchell 30, Klinger 16); second day, Worcestershire 285; third day, Surrey 216-4 (Hamilton-Brown 50, Maynard 63).

Worcestershire

*D. K. H. Mitchell b Linley	31	– lbw b Lewis	6
M. Klinger lbw b Linley	20	– c sub (C. J. Jordan) b Edwards	15
V. S. Solanki b Lewis	42	– lbw b Edwards	0
M. M. Ali c Davies b Edwards	61	– b Batty	5
J. G. Cameron c de Bruyn b Linley	52	– b Batty	28
M. G. Pardoe lbw b Batty	12	– not out	38
†B. J. M. Scott run out	12	– b Edwards	0
A. Kapil c Davies b Lewis	5	– c Linley b Edwards	2
D. S. Lucas b Lewis	3	– c Davies b Lewis	19
R. A. Jones lbw b Linley	1	– not out	0
A. Richardson not out	13		
B 4, l-b 10, w 1, n-b 18	33	B 3, l-b 9, w 5, n-b 20	37
1/65 (1) 2/66 (2) 3/168 (3) (97.4 overs)	285	1/29 (2) (8 wkts, 51.5 overs)	150
4/199 (4) 5/220 (6) 6/244 (7)		2/29 (3) 3/29 (1)	
7/249 (8) 8/253 (9) 9/254 (10) 10/285 (5)		4/49 (4) 5/93 (5)	
		6/98 (7) 7/100 (8) 8/135 (9)	

Lewis 28–4–79–3; Linley 28.4–10–78–4; Edwards 16–2–48–1; de Bruyn 12–4–22–0; Batty 12–2–41–1; Pietersen 1–0–3–0. *Second innings*—Lewis 18–5–48–2; Linley 6–2–18–0; Edwards 12.5–3–44–4; Batty 15–7–28–2.

Surrey

J. A. Rudolph b Richardson	68	– (2) b Jones	2
†S. M. Davies c Klinger b Lucas	0	– (1) c Scott b Jones	24
M. R. Ramprakash lbw b Lucas	0	– c Scott b Jones	0
K. P. Pietersen c Scott b Jones	11	– c Mitchell b Jones	69
*R. J. Hamilton-Brown c Mitchell b Jones	0	– c Lucas b Ali	115
T. L. Maynard b Lucas	0	– c Solanki b Lucas	143
Z. de Bruyn lbw b Jones	2	– c Mitchell b Lucas	34
G. J. Batty lbw b Richardson	2	– not out	27
J. Lewis lbw b Jones	5	– not out	2
G. A. Edwards c Scott b Lucas	17		
T. E. Linley not out	1		
B 2, l-b 2, w 1, n-b 2	7	B 7, l-b 3, w 5	15
1/4 (2) 2/8 (3) 3/23 (4) 4/25 (5) (44.1 overs)	113	1/7 (2) (7 wkts dec, 91 overs)	431
5/32 (6) 6/35 (7) 7/38 (8) 8/43 (9)		2/11 (3) 3/98 (1)	
9/103 (10) 10/113 (1)		4/125 (4) 5/350 (5) 6/390 (6) 7/418 (7)	

Richardson 14.1–6–22–2; Lucas 20–4–37–4; Jones 10–1–50–4. *Second innings*—Richardson 1.3–0–4–0; Lucas 25–3–110–2; Jones 23.3–2–121–4; Kapil 10–0–52–0; Ali 17–0–61–1; Cameron 12–0–68–0; Mitchell 2–0–5–0.

Umpires: R. J. Bailey and P. Willey.

WORCESTERSHIRE v SUSSEX

At Worcester, May 16–19. Drawn. Worcestershire 8pts, Sussex 9pts. Toss: Sussex.

Klinger's half-century in his final game before being replaced by fellow Australian Phillip Hughes, plus intervention from the weather, helped Worcestershire to another draw. Sussex tried to compensate for the loss of 44 overs on the third day, and no play before lunch on the fourth, by plundering 115 from ten overs, setting Worcestershire 315 in 60. In the space of 12 balls Panesar broke through twice and Cameron had to retire hurt after being struck in the face by Anyon, but Solanki and Andrew dug in until a draw was agreed with 12 overs remaining. Nash returned to form, giving Sussex early momentum with 84 out of 109 against an attack shorn of the injured Richardson. Shantry took three for five in four overs, but the last four wickets added 148. Magoffin deserved better than two wickets from 30 hostile and accurate overs against his former county, as Sussex claimed a lead of 56. Nash was again in fine touch as he and Joyce compiled their first century partnership in a year, but he fell two short of a hundred in his 100th first-class match.

Close of play: first day, Sussex 283-8 (Magoffin 24, Anyon 2); second day, Worcestershire 231-7 (Shantry 8, Scott 2); third day, Sussex 143-0 (Joyce 70, Nash 69).

Sussex

C. D. Nash c Mitchell b Andrew	84	– (2) lbw b Ali	98
E. C. Joyce c Scott b Jones	6	– (1) not out	108
L. W. P. Wells lbw b Shantry	39		
M. W. Goodwin lbw b Lucas	1	– c Klinger b Lucas	6
*M. H. Yardy lbw b Shantry	15	– (6) not out	1
J. S. Gatting c Pardoe b Shantry	5	– (3) c Pardoe b Ali	36
†B. C. Brown c Solanki b Lucas	42	– (5) c and b Shantry	1
Naved Arif c Scott b Jones	46		
S. J. Magoffin not out	41		
J. E. Anyon c Jones b Andrew	17		
M. S. Panesar b Jones	0		
B 10, l-b 9	19	B 4, l-b 4	8
1/57 (2) 2/109 (1) 3/110 (4) (101.4 overs)	315	1/189 (2) (4 wkts dec, 44 overs)	258
4/153 (5) 5/166 (3) 6/167 (6)		2/239 (3) 3/253 (4)	
7/251 (7) 8/256 (8) 9/315 (10) 10/315 (11)		4/257 (5)	

Lucas 25–6–75–2; Jones 26.4–5–79–3; Shantry 22–5–72–3; Andrew 22–3–57–2; Ali 6–0–13–0. *Second innings*—Lucas 9–2–52–1; Jones 4–1–22–0; Shantry 14–0–70–1; Ali 9–1–50–2; Andrew 8–0–56–0.

Worcestershire

First innings		Second innings	
*D. K. H. Mitchell lbw b Anyon	17	– lbw b Naved Arif	5
M. Klinger c Yardy b Magoffin	15	– c Brown b Anyon	67
V. S. Solanki b Panesar	34	– not out	44
M. M. Ali lbw b Naved Arif	85	– st Brown b Panesar	19
J. G. Cameron c Nash b Panesar	13	– retired hurt	1
M. G. Pardoe c Brown b Naved Arif	28	– lbw b Panesar	1
G. M. Andrew lbw b Magoffin	10	– not out	27
J. D. Shantry not out	22		
†B. J. M. Scott lbw b Anyon	5		
D. S. Lucas run out	8		
R. A. Jones c Naved Arif b Panesar	0		
B 4, l-b 16, n-b 2	22	L-b 8, n-b 2	10
1/31 (1) 2/45 (2) 3/92 (3) (104 overs)	259	1/21 (1) (4 wkts, 47.2 overs)	174
4/110 (5) 5/206 (4) 6/217 (7)		2/97 (2) 3/126 (4)	
7/217 (6) 8/241 (9) 9/257 (10) 10/259 (11)		4/128 (6)	

In the second innings Cameron retired hurt at 127-3.

Anyon 26–8–68–2; Magoffin 30–15–35–2; Naved Arif 21–4–50–2; Panesar 23–5–65–3; Nash 4–1–21–0. *Second innings*—Anyon 14–3–54–1; Magoffin 13–0–54–0; Naved Arif 5–0–14–1; Panesar 14.2–4–42–2; Wells 1–0–2–0.

Umpires: S. A. Garratt and P. J. Hartley.

WORCESTERSHIRE v SOMERSET

At Worcester, May 30–June 2. Drawn. Worcestershire 9pts, Somerset 7pts. Toss: Worcestershire.

Rain denied Compton the chance to become the first player in 24 years to score 1,000 first-class runs before the end of May, on the ground where Graeme Hick was the last to achieve the feat. Compton began his innings on the second afternoon needing 59 runs to join a band of eight men, but had made only nine when persistent drizzle ended proceedings. He brought up the milestone the next day, in front of parents Richard and Glynis, who were visiting from South Africa. Compton, who admitted to sleepless nights as he pursued the target, blamed himself for managing only 72 against Durham the previous week. His cause was not helped when Worcestershire chose to bat. Their innings was underpinned by Solanki's first hundred of the season, though he was dropped on 19 and 20. Trego, manfully carrying the attack for an injury-laden Somerset, was belatedly rewarded when the last seven wickets fell for 38. Compton's innings was a stop–start affair. He went 76 balls without a boundary, needed 130 to reach 50, but only another 87 to reach his fourth century in 13 innings.

THE NEARLY MEN

1,000 first-class runs achieved in the first few days of June:

		Innings	*First match*
June 1	**N. R. D. Compton (Somerset, England Lions)**	**13**	**March 31, 2012**
June 2	J. H. Parks (Sussex, The Rest)	18	May 1, 1937
June 2	J. G. Langridge (Sussex)	12	May 4, 1949
June 2	R. W. T. Key (MCC, Kent)	12	April 9, 2004
June 4	M. R. Hallam (Leicestershire)	15	May 9, 1959
June 4	Zaheer Abbas (Pakistanis)	17	May 1, 1971
June 5	D. Kenyon (Worcestershire)	15	May 8, 1954

A list of the eight players to have achieved 1,000 runs before the end of May appears on page 1264.

Shantry earned Worcestershire a slender lead, but they had an uncomfortable time on the final day against Dockrell. However, the game was safe by the time Kieswetter (right-arm slow) took off his keeping pads and – to considerable amusement – claimed his first two wickets in first-class cricket.

Close of play: first day, Worcestershire 270-3 (Solanki 82, Cameron 14); second day, Somerset 27-2 (Compton 9, Hildreth 5); third day, Somerset 277-7 (C. Overton 4, Thomas 0).

Worcestershire

*D. K. H. Mitchell c Kieswetter b Suppiah	80	– c Barrow b Dockrell	16
P. J. Hughes c Kieswetter b Trego	53	– c Kieswetter b Dockrell	22
V. S. Solanki b Trego	106	– b Trego	7
M. M. Ali lbw b Trego	20	– not out	47
J. G. Cameron c Trego b Thomas	19	– c Hildreth b Dockrell	0
M. G. Pardoe lbw b Trego	5	– b Kieswetter	28
G. M. Andrew c Hildreth b Dockrell	6	– (8) lbw b Kieswetter	0
†B. J. M. Scott lbw b J. Overton	1	– (7) run out	0
D. S. Lucas b Trego	0		
R. A. Jones c Kieswetter b C. Overton	12	– (9) not out	0
J. D. Shantry not out	10		
B 8, l-b 16, w 2, n-b 2	28	L-b 3, n-b 6	9
1/100 (2) 2/180 (1) 3/237 (4) (124.1 overs)	340	1/35 (2) (7 wkts dec, 49 overs)	129
4/302 (5) 5/302 (3) 6/309 (6)		2/48 (3) 3/60 (1)	
7/310 (8) 8/311 (9) 9/324 (7)		4/60 (5) 5/123 (6)	
10/340 (10) 110 overs: 309-6		6/125 (7) 7/128 (8)	

Trego 37–11–75–5; J. Overton 21–3–43–1; Thomas 25–10–63–1; C. Overton 17.1–2–60–1; Dockrell 21–3–58–1; Suppiah 3–0–17–1. *Second innings*—Trego 13–1–28–1; Thomas 4–0–19–0; Dockrell 21–7–56–3; Suppiah 8–3–20–0; Kieswetter 3–0–3–2.

Somerset

A. V. Suppiah c Pardoe b Jones	1
A. W. R. Barrow c Scott b Lucas	10
N. R. D. Compton b Shantry	108
J. C. Hildreth lbw b Shantry	52
†C. Kieswetter c Scott b Shantry	0
J. C. Buttler c Pardoe b Ali	85
P. D. Trego c Pardoe b Shantry	7
C. Overton c Jones b Shantry	5
*A. C. Thomas c Jones b Lucas	6
G. H. Dockrell not out	2
J. Overton c Solanki b Jones	12
B 2, l-b 5, w 1, n-b 2	10
1/11 (2) 2/11 (1) 3/86 (4) (94.1 overs)	298
4/86 (5) 5/253 (6) 6/268 (7)	
7/277 (3) 8/278 (8) 9/286 (9) 10/298 (11)	

Lucas 26–7–74–2; Jones 13.1–2–56–2; Andrew 10–3–38–0; Shantry 28–11–58–5; Ali 15–1–52–1; Cameron 2–0–13–0.

Umpires: M. J. D. Bodenham and T. E. Jesty.

WORCESTERSHIRE v DURHAM

At Worcester, July 10–13. Drawn. Worcestershire 7pts, Durham 7pts. Toss: Worcestershire.

The loss of 213 overs to rain and bad light, including the final four sessions, denied Durham the chance to press for a desperately needed win, despite Worcestershire's latest batting collapse. Paul Collingwood, appointed to replace Mustard as captain in a bid to turn around Durham's joyless campaign, had to delay his coronation as he recovered from a broken hand. Richardson, though, marked his return from a shoulder injury with a typically accomplished performance; seven Durham players reached 22, but none could go beyond 38. Hughes carried over his outstanding Twenty20 form to make 87 out of 145, but his dismissal triggered an all-too-familiar decline, as Worcestershire surrendered their last eight wickets for 60; Jones briefly retired hurt after a fly lodged in his eye. Durham's openers then feasted on wayward bowling – Richardson excepted – in extending the lead to 105, but rain began falling at tea on the third day and did not relent.

Close of play: first day, Durham 127-4 (Benkenstein 16, Richardson 0); second day, Worcestershire 100-2 (Hughes 52, Ali 7); third day, Durham 67-0 (Smith 20, Stoneman 41).

Durham

M. D. Stoneman c Solanki b Richardson	38	– (2) not out	41
W. R. Smith c Ali b Richardson	11	– (1) not out	20
G. J. Muchall c Mitchell b Shantry	25		
B. A. Stokes b Shantry	22		
*D. M. Benkenstein b Andrew	30		
M. J. Richardson c Mitchell b Andrew	0		
†P. Mustard c Hughes b Jones	32		
S. G. Borthwick b Andrew	10		
C. D. Thorp c Ali b Richardson	30		
G. Onions not out	25		
C. Rushworth c Solanki b Richardson	0		
B 8, l-b 11, w 1	20	B 2, l-b 4	6
1/26 (2) 2/89 (1) 3/94 (3) (70.5 overs)	243	(no wkt, 20 overs)	67
4/125 (4) 5/127 (6) 6/150 (5)			
7/166 (8) 8/193 (7) 9/235 (9) 10/243 (11)			

Richardson 24.5–7–52–4; Jones 8–1–43–1; Andrew 20–3–73–3; Shantry 17–3–52–2; Ali 1–0–4–0. *Second innings*—Richardson 8–5–7–0; Jones 4–0–21–0; Andrew 2–0–10–0; Ali 4–2–6–0; Shantry 2–0–17–0.

Worcestershire

*D. K. H. Mitchell c Mustard b Stokes	24
P. J. Hughes lbw b Borthwick	87
V. S. Solanki lbw b Stokes	13
M. M. Ali c Richardson b Borthwick	18
J. G. Cameron c and b Borthwick	24
M. G. Pardoe c Richardson b Borthwick	2
G. M. Andrew c Thorp b Rushworth	6
†B. J. M. Scott c Mustard b Thorp	0
R. A. Jones c Mustard b Rushworth	4
J. D. Shantry c Mustard b Rushworth	17
A. Richardson not out	4
L-b 4, w 2	6
1/63 (1) 2/77 (3) 3/145 (2) (75.1 overs)	205
4/162 (4) 5/169 (6) 6/177 (5)	
7/178 (8) 8/187 (7) 9/196 (9) 10/205 (10)	

Jones, when 0, retired hurt at 179-7 and resumed at 187-8.

Onions 16–1–56–0; Rushworth 14.1–3–43–3; Thorp 16–5–27–1; Stokes 14–5–38–2; Borthwick 15–1–37–4.

Umpires: S. J. O'Shaughnessy and M. J. Saggers.

At Manchester, July 18–20. WORCESTERSHIRE beat LANCASHIRE by 205 runs.

At Worcester, July 27–28. WORCESTERSHIRE drew with SOUTH AFRICANS (see South African tour section).

At Hove, August 1–3. WORCESTERSHIRE lost to SUSSEX by an innings and 117 runs.

At Birmingham, August 8–10. WORCESTERSHIRE lost to WARWICKSHIRE by seven wickets.

WORCESTERSHIRE v LANCASHIRE

At Worcester, August 15–18. Drawn. Worcestershire 8pts, Lancashire 6pts. Toss: Lancashire.

With only 113 overs bowled on the first three days and the captains unable to set up a run-chase, this meeting of the bottom two was reduced to a battle for bonus points. Worcestershire, missing Phillip Hughes to a call-up from Australia A, struggled to 108 for five on a pitch of exaggerated bounce exploited by Chapple, who benefited from two superb diving catches from Cross, but beat the bat often enough to deserve even better figures. The recovery was led by Neil Pinner and Joe Leach, two 21-year-olds who had made ducks on their only previous Championship appearance: they eked out 111 for the sixth wicket until Leach was bowled by a grubber from Shahzad in fading light. Pinner dug in for 190 balls in scoring 82, having waited since May 2011 for a second chance. Worcestershire prevailed in the final day's phoney war, bowling Lancashire out in 64 overs for the concession of only one batting point.

Close of play: first day, no play; second day, Worcestershire 219-6 (Pinner 79, Andrew 0); third day, Lancashire 10-0 (Horton 1, Procter 9).

Worcestershire

*D. K. H. Mitchell c Kerrigan b Chapple	0	– not out	16
M. G. Pardoe c Cross b Chapple	37	– not out	4
J. G. Cameron lbw b Hogg	6		
M. M. Ali lbw b Hogg	35		
V. S. Solanki c Cross b Chapple	4		
N. D. Pinner lbw b Chapple	82		
J. Leach b Shahzad	46		
G. M. Andrew not out	12		
†B. J. M. Scott not out	14		
B 1, l-b 6, n-b 8	15	B 9, l-b 1, w 1, n-b 2	13
1/2 (1) 2/17 (3) 3/62 (2) 4/68 (5) 5/108 (4) 6/219 (7) 7/223 (6) (7 wkts dec, 105.3 overs)	251	(no wkt, 14 overs)	33

C. J. Russell and A. Richardson did not bat.

Chapple 31–10–60–4; Hogg 23.3–7–63–2; Shahzad 15–6–34–1; Procter 12–2–38–0; Kerrigan 18–6–31–0; Croft 6–0–18–0. *Second innings*—Hogg 6–2–12–0; Croft 4–2–6–0; Brown 3–0–5–0; Kerrigan 1–1–0–0.

Lancashire

P. J. Horton c Mitchell b Andrew	15
L. A. Procter b Richardson	16
K. R. Brown lbw b Andrew	12
A. G. Prince c Mitchell b Andrew	9
S. J. Croft c Scott b Andrew	28
A. P. Agathangelou c Scott b Richardson	7
†G. D. Cross b Leach	39
K. W. Hogg c Mitchell b Ali	14
*G. Chapple st Scott b Ali	27
A. Shahzad not out	28
S. C. Kerrigan st Scott b Ali	8
B 8, l-b 4, w 1	13
1/31 (1) 2/35 (2) 3/47 (3) 4/60 (4) 5/89 (6) 6/93 (5) 7/151 (8) 8/151 (7) 9/187 (9) 10/216 (11) (64 overs)	216

Richardson 23–7–53–2; Russell 11–1–48–0; Andrew 15–5–42–4; Leach 5–1–15–1; Ali 10–1–46–3.

Umpires: T. E. Jesty and D. J. Millns.

At Chester-le-Street, August 21–23. WORCESTERSHIRE lost to DURHAM by six wickets.

WORCESTERSHIRE v MIDDLESEX

At Worcester, August 28–31. Middlesex won by five wickets. Middlesex 22pts, Worcestershire 6pts. Toss: Middlesex.

Inspired by a career-best ten for 118 from the unrelenting Roland-Jones, Middlesex chased down 204 with 11 balls to spare, guaranteeing their top-flight status. Worcestershire axed Surrey-bound Vikram Solanki after two decades at the club, and the soon-to-be-released wicketkeeper Ben Scott, but caved in again in their second innings – with the exception of Kervezee, who passed 50 for the second time in his comeback match after four months out of the Championship side. Crucially, they had lost their three most experienced batsmen – Mitchell, Hughes and Ali – on the third evening. Denly, who top-scored in the run-chase, was given a life on 35, when Kervezee missed a skier off Richardson. Earlier, Mitchell emulated Hughes at Edgbaston three weeks previously by carrying his bat, and shepherded Worcestershire past 300 for only the second time in the Championship season. They then kept up their perfect record of bowling points at New Road, led by the tireless Richardson, whose return catch off Malan gave him 50 wickets for the third successive summer. With this sixth defeat, however, he looked destined to be spending the next one in Division Two.

Close of play: first day, Worcestershire 295-8 (Mitchell 129, Russell 8); second day, Middlesex 49-0 (Rogers 17, Robson 27); third day, Worcestershire 44-3 (Pardoe 22, Russell 0).

Worcestershire

First innings		Second innings	
*D. K. H. Mitchell not out	133	– lbw b Murtagh	1
P. J. Hughes c Patel b Roland-Jones	34	– lbw b Roland-Jones	1
M. G. Pardoe lbw b Roland-Jones	5	– lbw b Roland-Jones	28
M. M. Ali c Rossington b Roland-Jones	0	– c Rossington b Roland-Jones	20
A. N. Kervezee c Roland-Jones b Dexter	55	– (6) not out	64
N. D. Pinner c Robson b Patel	7	– (7) b Roland-Jones	2
J. Leach b Crook	10	– (8) c Denly b Roland-Jones	4
†O. B. Cox lbw b Murtagh	18	– (9) lbw b Crook	12
G. M. Andrew c Robson b Roland-Jones	6	– (10) c Berg b Crook	26
C. J. Russell c Malan b Roland-Jones	14	– (5) b Patel	22
A. Richardson b Murtagh	18	– run out	0
B 10, l-b 13	23	B 5, l-b 1	6
1/40 (2) 2/50 (3) 3/52 (4) (102.3 overs)	323	1/2 (2) 2/6 (1) (62.4 overs)	186
4/166 (5) 5/181 (6) 6/219 (7)		3/44 (4) 4/63 (3)	
7/243 (8) 8/262 (9) 9/302 (10) 10/323 (11)		5/95 (5) 6/100 (7) 7/106 (8)	
		8/143 (9) 9/186 (10) 10/186 (11)	

Murtagh 24.3–6–87–2; Berg 11–2–31–0; Roland-Jones 27–7–72–5; Crook 16–3–50–1; Dexter 13–5–39–1; Patel 11–3–21–1. *Second innings*—Murtagh 16–1–52–1; Roland-Jones 20–5–46–5; Crook 14.4–2–47–2; Patel 12–1–35–1.

Middlesex

First innings		Second innings	
*C. J. L. Rogers c Cox b Richardson	22	– (2) lbw b Richardson	15
S. D. Robson c Pardoe b Ali	72	– (1) c Ali b Andrew	35
J. L. Denly b Richardson	4	– c Cox b Ali	48
D. J. Malan c and b Richardson	0	– (5) c Hughes b Ali	22
N. J. Dexter b Leach	90	– (7) not out	15
†A. M. Rossington lbw b Andrew	6		
G. K. Berg c Ali b Russell	30	– (6) not out	26
S. P. Crook b Russell	22	– (4) c Kervezee b Russell	30
T. S. Roland-Jones b Richardson	6		
T. J. Murtagh c and b Russell	6		
R. H. Patel not out	19		
B 19, l-b 8, n-b 2	29	B 4, l-b 6, n-b 4	14
1/55 (1) 2/59 (3) 3/61 (4) (90.1 overs)	306	1/21 (2) (5 wkts, 45.1 overs)	205
4/167 (2) 5/181 (6) 6/241 (7)		2/98 (1) 3/102 (3)	
7/249 (5) 8/265 (9) 9/281 (8) 10/306 (10)		4/152 (5) 5/172 (4)	

Richardson 27–9–62–4; Russell 21.1–3–86–3; Andrew 18–4–65–1; Leach 10–3–28–1; Ali 14–1–38–1. *Second innings*—Richardson 18–4–64–1; Russell 10.1–2–39–1; Ali 10–0–49–2; Andrew 5–0–34–1; Leach 2–0–9–0.

Umpires: N. L. Bainton and P. Willey.

WORCESTERSHIRE v WARWICKSHIRE

At Worcester, September 4–6. Warwickshire won by an innings and 202 runs. Warwickshire 23pts, Worcestershire 1pt. Toss: Worcestershire. Championship debut: N. L. Harrison.

Warwickshire secured their first Championship title in eight years in the most emphatic manner imaginable, crushing Worcestershire's feeble resistance by 1.35pm on the third day and condemning their local rivals to relegation. There was no repeat of the uncertainty or anguish of a year earlier, when Lancashire had pipped them to the trophy on the final day. Director of cricket Ashley Giles dedicated Warwickshire's seventh Championship pennant to Neal Abberley, who served for five decades as player and coach before his death in August 2011. The outcome was never in doubt once Worcestershire folded on the first morning, on a blameless pitch, for 60 – the lowest total by any county all season, their worst since 1971, and their worst ever against Warwickshire. It was an abject display, even from a side containing four players with only nine previous Championship appearances between them. "If I had played like that as a youngster in the Bradford League, I'd have had my backside kicked," said director of cricket Steve Rhodes. Barker and Wright bowled unchanged in the extended opening session to share all ten wickets, each passing 50 in the Championship for the first time. Warwickshire were harsh on a toothless attack, and Chopra – watched by national selector Geoff Miller a week after Andrew Strauss's Test retirement – came within five runs of repeating his double-hundred in this fixture the previous season. He shared his fifth century opening stand of the campaign with Westwood, a third-wicket partnership of 131 with Troughton, and passed 1,000 runs for the second successive summer. Blackwell's quick 84 helped Warwickshire to the fourth batting point that virtually ensured them the title, but it was not enough to earn him a permanent move from Durham. Worcestershire bowled three seven-ball overs late in the innings, due to mistakes by the umpires. Troughton was able to declare with a lead of 411 as early as tea on the second day. A little over two sessions later, he was celebrating the title with a mixture of joy and relief.

Close of play: first day, Warwickshire 215-2 (Chopra 115, Troughton 29); second day, Worcestershire 100-2 (Mitchell 42, Ali 15).

Worcestershire

Batsman	First innings		Second innings	
*D. K. H. Mitchell lbw b Wright	2	–	b Barker	42
P. J. Hughes c Clarke b Barker	10	–	c Porterfield b Barker	0
M. G. Pardoe c Chopra b Wright	0	–	c Westwood b Clarke	35
M. M. Ali c Johnson b Barker	1	–	not out	72
A. N. Kervezee c Clarke b Wright	4	–	lbw b Barker	19
J. Leach lbw b Barker	0	–	b Wright	2
B. L. D'Oliveira c Chopra b Barker	18	–	c Chopra b Rankin	13
†O. B. Cox c Westwood b Wright	4	–	c Clarke b Rankin	4
C. J. Russell c Chopra b Wright	15	–	b Wright	0
N. L. Harrison c Troughton b Barker	0	–	b Wright	2
A. Richardson not out	6	–	b Wright	4
			B 3, l-b 12, w 1	16
1/2 (1) 2/12 (3) 3/12 (2) 4/17 (4) 5/17 (5) 6/21 (6) 7/32 (8) 8/46 (7) 9/46 (10) 10/60 (9) (28.4 overs)	60		1/0 (2) 2/76 (3) 3/104 (1) 4/128 (5) 5/141 (6) 6/178 (7) 7/192 (8) 8/197 (9) 9/201 (10) 10/209 (11) (70.5 overs)	209

Wright 14.4–5–24–5; Barker 14–4–36–5. *Second innings*—Wright 18.5–2–65–4; Barker 18–4–39–3; Milnes 2–0–12–0; Blackwell 10–0–31–0; Clarke 14–2–28–1; Rankin 8–2–19–2.

Warwickshire

V. Chopra b Leach	195
I. J. Westwood c Mitchell b Ali	54
W. T. S. Porterfield c Mitchell b Ali	0
*J. O. Troughton c Cox b Russell	54
†R. M. Johnson c Cox b Harrison	1
R. Clarke lbw b Leach	11
I. D. Blackwell c Cox b Russell	84
K. H. D. Barker b Richardson	40
T. P. Milnes not out	7
C. J. C. Wright not out	0
B 8, l-b 13, w 4	25
1/136 (2) 2/148 (3) 3/279 (4) 4/303 (5) 5/324 (6) 6/380 (1) 7/460 (7) 8/464 (8) (8 wkts dec, 129 overs)	471

110 overs: 355-5

W. B. Rankin did not bat.

Richardson 32–11–73–1; Russell 22–2–92–2; Harrison 15–2–62–1; Leach 16–3–49–2; Ali 28–2–100–2; D'Oliveira 16–1–74–0.

Umpires: M. J. D. Bodenham and J. W. Lloyds.

At Taunton, September 11–13. WORCESTERSHIRE lost to SOMERSET by an innings and 148 runs.

YORKSHIRE

Command performance

DAVID WARNER

Geoffrey Boycott did not mince his words upon being elected Yorkshire president in March 2012. The only thing that really mattered to members was four-day cricket, he said, and the team had to gain immediate promotion to have a chance of becoming county champions in 2013, the club's 150th anniversary. They obeyed the command, having already exceeded their brief, reaching Twenty20 finals day for the first time, and qualifying for the Champions League in South Africa.

Yorkshire were hit harder than any other county by the monsoons: two-fifths of Championship playing time between April and the end of August was lost. It was not until late summer that the rain relented sufficiently for them to win their last three matches and claim the second promotion spot; level on points with Derbyshire, they missed the divisional title on a tie-breaker.

The players' air of commitment suggested the president's remarks had hit home, but captain Andrew Gale also took two gambles which would probably never have been considered when Boycott was in charge. In both matches against Gloucestershire, Gale threw caution – and the certainty of a handful of points from games badly affected by rain – to the wind. At Bristol, Yorkshire forfeited an innings to chase down 400, thanks to centuries from Phil Jaques and Gary Ballance; then, at Scarborough, with time running out, Gloucestershire proved to be once bitten but not twice shy, agreeing to set up a target of 314 off 84 overs, which Yorkshire narrowly achieved.

These successes kept Yorkshire in the hunt. But it was only in September that they could show their true worth, by taking 20 wickets against both Glamorgan and Essex. With the help of 11 draws, they ended unbeaten in first-class cricket for the first time since 1928.

The arrival of Australian Jason Gillespie as first-team coach, while Martyn Moxon remained director of cricket, was rewarding. Gillespie bubbled with enthusiasm, constantly declaring his faith in the side, even when bowling resources were worryingly thin.

Yet two early decisions had been open to question. After a strong pre-season tour in the Caribbean, Joe Sayers was appointed vice-captain and given a run at the expense of Adam Lyth; and Iain Wardlaw, a seamer from the Bradford League, was preferred to Steve Patterson for the first game. Once the experiment ended, Patterson was consistently the best bowler, finishing well ahead of the pack, with 48 wickets at 20. Lyth, too, worked his way back as Sayers faded, and in the second half was the brightest light by far, closing with four consecutive half-centuries and 751 runs from 12 matches, topped only by Jaques. Lyth's pinnacle had come at Leicester, where an unbeaten 248 made him the first Yorkshire player to carry his bat for a double-hundred.

Harry Engels, Getty Images

Azeem Rafiq

Remarkably, in such a soggy season, Joe Root might have beaten him to it. He had already hit an unbeaten 222 against Hampshire, when Yorkshire declared with nine down. Root's star remained in the ascendancy: his technical ability and calm temperament earned him a Test debut at Nagpur in December, where he shone with a patient 73. He leapfrogged Jonny Bairstow, who had already attracted England's eye with early centuries. Although he struggled against West Indies, his recall for the Lord's Test against South Africa was a resounding success as he withstood the pressure of replacing Kevin Pietersen by making 95 and 54.

Supporters were taken aback to learn in May that Ajmal Shahzad would not play for Yorkshire again because of irreconcilable differences over how he was expected to bowl, quickly followed by news that he was joining Lancashire for the remainder of the season. His long-term departure to Nottinghamshire made the fast-bowling resources even thinner; Steve Harmison was signed on loan from Durham. Often erratic during his three matches, Harmison still impressed Gillespie with his pace and the occasional explosive delivery, and would have stayed longer but for a calf injury.

Moin Ashraf improved as time went on, and Ryan Sidebottom could be relied upon when fit, but promotion made strengthening the attack an even greater priority. In the close season, Yorkshire recruited Jack Brooks from Northamptonshire, and Harmison's team-mate Liam Plunkett. The abrupt departure of wicketkeeper Gerard Brophy, who left in August, after the club chose not to renew his contract, led to the loan from Sussex of Andrew Hodd, who nailed a two-year deal with 18 catches in four games. In February 2013, Anthony McGrath announced his retirement after 18 seasons at the club. He planned to stay on in a coaching capacity.

Though they had a mediocre CB40 campaign, Yorkshire had their best year yet in Twenty20. After losing the opening match by two runs to Durham, they won nine on the bounce – excluding two no-results – until defeat by Hampshire in the final. The signings, chiefly for this competition, of Australian pace bowler Mitchell Starc and South African batsman David Miller paid off handsomely; so did the captaincy of 21-year-old Azeem Rafiq, handed the reins for six games while Gale was injured. A former England Under-19 captain, Rafiq emerged with a 100% record in the five matches completed under his leadership, and supplanted Adil Rashid as first-choice spinner in all formats.

Overall, Yorkshire made the best of a bad summer, aided in no small measure by the splendid batting of Ballance and the return to form of Anthony McGrath, who made it impossible to nudge him out of contention. But the real challenge would come in the 150th anniversary season, when they have their chance to fulfil the second part of Boycott's plan.

Championship attendance: 36,802.

YORKSHIRE RESULTS

All first-class matches – Played 17: Won 5, Lost 0, Drawn 12.
County Championship matches – Played 16: Won 5, Lost 0, Drawn 11.

LV= County Championship, 2nd in Division 2;
Friends Life t20, finalists; Clydesdale Bank 40, 5th in Group C.

COUNTY CHAMPIONSHIP AVERAGES, BATTING AND FIELDING

Cap		*M*	*I*	*NO*	*R*	*HS*	*100*	*50*	*Avge*	*Ct*
2010	A. Lyth†	12	15	1	751	248*	1	5	53.64	12
2011	J. M. Bairstow†	9	12	1	588	182	3	1	53.45	14
1999	A. McGrath†	13	15	3	584	106*	2	3	48.66	4
2005	P. A. Jaques¶	15	19	1	792	160	2	4	44.00	16
2012	J. E. Root†	14	19	2	738	222*	2	2	43.41	8
2012	G. S. Ballance	16	19	4	613	121*	1	2	40.86	10
2008	A. W. Gale†	14	18	3	481	80	0	2	32.06	4
	Azeem Rafiq	10	10	1	265	75*	0	2	29.44	5
2007	J. J. Sayers†	5	7	0	165	45	0	0	23.57	2
2000	R. J. Sidebottom†	11	10	2	164	37	0	0	20.50	1
2012	S. A. Patterson†	15	14	5	174	37	0	0	19.33	1
2006	T. T. Bresnan†‡	4	4	0	73	38	0	0	18.25	2
	A. J. Hodd	4	5	0	91	58	0	1	18.20	18
2008	A. U. Rashid†	10	8	0	129	58	0	1	16.12	0
	M. A. Ashraf†	8	6	4	14	6*	0	0	7.00	1
2010	R. M. Pyrah†	4	4	0	9	9	0	0	2.25	0

Also batted: G. L. Brophy (3 matches) 2*, 22 (6 ct); S. J. Harmison (3 matches) 2, 23, 0 (1 ct); A. Shahzad† (3 matches) 25, 5, 4; M. A. Starc§ (2 matches) 28*; I. Wardlaw† (2 matches) 13*, 17* (1 ct).

† Born in Yorkshire. ‡ ECB contract. § Official overseas player. ¶ Other non-England-qualified player.

BOWLING

	Style	*O*	*M*	*R*	*W*	*BB*	*5I*	*Avge*
S. A. Patterson	RFM	389.2	116	999	48	5-77	1	20.81
M. A. Ashraf	RFM	117.5	27	376	17	4-36	0	22.11
Azeem Rafiq	OB	222.5	58	633	26	5-50	1	24.34
T. T. Bresnan	RFM	130.2	31	397	14	5-81	1	28.35
R. J. Sidebottom	LFM	297	72	798	24	5-30	1	33.25
A. McGrath	RM	171.1	50	424	12	4-21	0	35.33
A. U. Rashid	LBG	202.5	26	656	16	5-105	1	41.00

Also bowled: G. S. Ballance (LBG) 6–1–23–0; A. W. Gale (LBG) 6.1–0–97–0; S. J. Harmison (RFM) 42–4–195–8; A. Lyth (RM) 12–3–116–0; R. M. Pyrah (RM) 38–9–128–2; J. E. Root (OB) 48–14–130–1; A. Shahzad (RFM) 68.1–14–210–8; M. A. Starc (LFM) 42.1–13–153–7; I. Wardlaw (RFM) 52–1–225–2.

LEADING CB40 AVERAGES (100 runs/4 wickets)

Batting	*Runs*	*HS*	*Avge*	*SR*	*Ct*
G. S. Ballance	469	103*	58.62	105.15	6
A. W. Gale	393	76	39.30	73.45	3
J. E. Root	208	49	34.66	108.90	5
A. Lyth	260	69	32.50	93.52	1
P. A. Jaques	299	87	29.90	93.73	3

Bowling	*W*	*BB*	*Avge*	*ER*
M. A. Starc	8	3-28	22.62	5.71
J. E. Root	5	2-14	23.00	6.05
A. U. Rashid	12	4-38	25.16	5.39
S. A. Patterson	5	3-25	28.60	4.93
R. J. Sidebottom	6	3-44	29.00	6.21
M. A. Ashraf	11	2-36	32.90	5.24

LEADING FLT20 AVERAGES (100 runs/18 overs)

Batting	Runs	HS	Avge	SR	Ct
D. A. Miller	390	74*	48.75	**153.54**	4
A. W. Gale	165	70	27.50	**144.73**	0
A. Lyth	154	78	30.80	**141.28**	2
J. E. Root	241	65	26.77	**128.87**	6
G. S. Ballance	209	47*	26.12	**128.22**	13
P. A. Jaques	263	64	26.30	**114.84**	2

Bowling	W	BB	Avge	ER
M. A. Starc	21	3-24	10.38	**5.91**
Azeem Rafiq	11	2-28	28.18	**6.73**
R. J. Sidebottom	11	4-25	16.09	**7.08**
M. A. Ashraf	15	4-18	23.93	**7.63**
R. M. Pyrah	15	3-21	23.93	**7.97**

FIRST-CLASS COUNTY RECORDS

Highest score for	341	G. H. Hirst v Leicestershire at Leicester	1905
Highest score against	318*	W. G. Grace (Gloucestershire) at Cheltenham	1876
Leading run-scorer	38,558	H. Sutcliffe (avge 50.20)	1919–1945
Best bowling for	10-10	H. Verity v Nottinghamshire at Leeds	1932
Best bowling against	10-37	C. V. Grimmett (Australians) at Sheffield	1930
Leading wicket-taker	3,597	W. Rhodes (avge 16.02)	1898–1930
Highest total for	887	v Warwickshire at Birmingham	1896
Highest total against	681-7 dec	by Leicestershire at Bradford	1996
Lowest total for	23	v Hampshire at Middlesbrough	1965
Lowest total against	13	by Nottinghamshire at Nottingham	1901

LIST A COUNTY RECORDS

Highest score for	191	D. S. Lehmann v Nottinghamshire at Scarborough	2001
Highest score against	177	S. A. Newman (Surrey) at The Oval	2009
Leading run-scorer	8,699	G. Boycott (avge 40.08)	1963–1986
Best bowling for	7-15	R. A. Hutton v Worcestershire at Leeds	1969
Best bowling against	7-32	R. G. D. Willis (Warwickshire) at Birmingham	1981
Leading wicket-taker	308	C. M. Old (avge 18.96)	1967–1982
Highest total for	411-6	v Devon at Exmouth	2004
Highest total against	375-4	by Surrey at Scarborough	1994
Lowest total for	54	v Essex at Leeds	2003
Lowest total against	23	by Middlesex at Leeds	1974

TWENTY20 COUNTY RECORDS

Highest score for	109	I. J. Harvey v Derbyshire at Leeds	2005
Highest score against	111	D. L. Maddy (Leicestershire) at Leeds	2004
Leading run-scorer	**1,780**	**A. W. Gale (avge 27.38)**	**2004–*2012***
Best bowling for	5-16	R. M. Pyrah v Durham at Scarborough	2011
Best bowling against	4-9	C. K. Langeveldt (Derbyshire) at Leeds	2008
Leading wicket-taker	**79**	**R. M. Pyrah (avge 20.50)**	**2005–2012**
Highest total for	213-7	v Worcestershire at Leeds	2010
Highest total against	222-5	by Derbyshire at Leeds	2010
Lowest total for	90-9	v Durham at Chester-le-Street	2009
Lowest total against	98	by Durham at Chester-le-Street	2006

ADDRESS

Headingley Cricket Ground, Leeds LS6 3BU (0871 971 1222; **email** cricket@yorkshireccc.com). **Website** www.yorkshireccc.com

OFFICIALS

Captain A. W. Gale
Director of professional cricket M. D. Moxon
First-team coach J. N. Gillespie
Director of cricket development I. Dews
President G. Boycott
Executive chairman C. Graves
Head groundsman A. W. Fogarty
Scorer J. T. Potter

YORKSHIRE v KENT

At Leeds, April 5–8. Drawn. Yorkshire 9pts, Kent 10pts. Toss: Kent. County debuts: M. Davies, B. W. Harmison, B. P. Nash, S. A. Newman, M. J. Powell.

Yorkshire had won a Twenty20 trophy on their pre-season tour of Barbados, but found the second division of the Championship harder work. Kent never relinquished the advantage gained through first use of a good pitch: their openers began with 141, and they were well served by five and a half experienced newcomers (Shreck had played once on loan in 2011), though tight bowling from Sidebottom and Shahzad denied them a fifth batting point. But 21-year-old Coles, a seamer from Maidstone, and Davies – with only his second fifty in 108 first-class innings, but on his Kent debut – were rarely troubled in a stand of 153, one short of Headingley's ninth-wicket record, set by Pyrah and Sidebottom against Lancashire the previous season. Coles raised a maiden hundred with his third six, which was some recompense after Key ran himself out three short of a century. Bairstow's delightful 107 raised hopes of averting the follow-on and, when Yorkshire's ninth wicket fell with 32 still needed, Pyrah entered with his left arm in a plaster-cast, having broken his hand fielding. It was brave but futile: he was out to his first ball, providing Shreck with a fourth wicket in 18 deliveries. A century opening stand between Root and Sayers calmed Yorkshire's nerves, and bad light ended the game 26 overs early; weather denied Kent's bowlers 76 overs in all.

Close of play: first day, Kent 345-5 (Stevens 22, Riley 0); second day, Yorkshire 32-0 (Root 13, Sayers 19); third day, Yorkshire 316-6 (Rashid 40, Shahzad 17).

Kent

S. A. Newman b Sidebottom	64
*R. W. T. Key run out	97
B. W. Harmison c Ballance b Rashid	45
B. P. Nash c McGrath b Shahzad	67
M. J. Powell lbw b Rashid	37
D. I. Stevens c Sayers b Shahzad	29
A. E. N. Riley b Rashid	8
†G. O. Jones b Shahzad	2
M. T. Coles not out	103
M. Davies c Ballance b McGrath	58
C. E. Shreck not out	0
B 8, l-b 15, n-b 4	27
(9 wkts dec, 148.3 overs)	537

1/141 (1) 2/201 (2) 3/239 (3) 4/310 (4) 5/344 (5) 6/358 (6) 7/366 (8) 8/374 (7) 9/527 (10) 110 overs: 371-7

Sidebottom 28–6–74–1; Shahzad 31–7–86–3; Pyrah 19–4–81–0; Wardlaw 24–1–106–0; Rashid 40.3–7–141–3; McGrath 5–0–13–1; Root 1–0–13–0.

Yorkshire

J. E. Root c Jones b Coles	25	– b Riley 76
J. J. Sayers c Riley b Davies	24	– lbw b Riley 43
A. McGrath lbw b Davies	0	– not out 16
*A. W. Gale lbw b Davies	44	– c Jones b Shreck 0
†J. M. Bairstow c Jones b Stevens	107	– c Newman b Shreck 8
G. S. Ballance lbw b Riley	45	– not out 0
A. U. Rashid c Jones b Shreck	58	
A. Shahzad lbw b Shreck	25	
R. J. Sidebottom c Harmison b Shreck	2	
I. Wardlaw not out	13	
R. M. Pyrah b Shreck	0	
B 3, l-b 16, n-b 2	21	W 1, n-b 2 3
(101.1 overs)	364	(4 wkts, 53 overs) 146

1/37 (2) 2/37 (3) 3/79 (1) 4/111 (4) 5/226 (6) 6/290 (5) 7/347 (8) 8/351 (9) 9/356 (7) 10/364 (11)

1/115 (1) 2/124 (2) 3/125 (4) 4/145 (5)

Davies 23–7–48–3; Shreck 26.1–1–90–4; Stevens 23–3–72–1; Coles 11–0–49–1; Riley 12–2–68–1; Nash 6–0–18–0. *Second innings*—Davies 7–1–13–0; Shreck 10–4–22–2; Stevens 7–0–32–0; Riley 16–6–43–2; Nash 1–0–1–0; Coles 12–3–35–0.

Umpires: M. A. Eggleston and N. A. Mallender.

YORKSHIRE v LEEDS/BRADFORD MCCU

At Leeds, April 13–15. Drawn. Toss: Leeds/Bradford MCCU. First-class debut: A. MacQueen.

With his place at risk, McGrath needed to show he was worth retaining as an all-rounder, but Yorkshire hardly expected him to end up with more wickets than any of the frontline bowlers. The students, who had fallen only three runs short of beating Surrey a fortnight earlier, also dominated much of this game, despite being 50 for five in their first innings and 56 for six in their second. Luis Reece came to their rescue, while debutant Alex MacQueen's late flourish of ten fours and a six – his ninth-wicket stand of 95 with Matt Higginbottom was the match's highest – carried his side past 200. That looked highly competitive when they led by 76 on first innings, thanks to persistently accurate bowling. Another admirable knock from Reece enabled Leeds/Bradford to set a target of 266, but a hailstorm put paid to an intriguing finish.

Close of play: first day, Yorkshire 80-6 (Azeem Rafiq 8, Brophy 0); second day, Leeds/Bradford MCCU 127-6 (Reece 58, Hardman 28).

Leeds/Bradford MCCU

B. T. Slater run out	14	– lbw b McGrath	15
J. P. Webb c McGrath b Patterson	5	– lbw b Patterson	1
H. Bush c Ballance b Hannon-Dalby	0	– lbw b Patterson	7
J. Leach lbw b McGrath	11	– c Hannon-Dalby b McGrath	5
L. M. Reece c Sayers b Patterson	40	– c Wardlaw b Azeem Rafiq	60
†D. M. Hodgson c Brophy b Wardlaw	0	– lbw b McGrath	0
*R. A. L. Moore lbw b McGrath	29	– lbw b McGrath	10
T. R. Hardman c Lyth b McGrath	0	– lbw b Patterson	44
A. MacQueen c Azeem Rafiq b Hannon-Dalby	69	– c Root b Azeem Rafiq	3
M. Higginbottom not out	31	– not out	30
I. A. A. Thomas c Azeem Rafiq b Hannon-Dalby	2	– c Brophy b Hannon-Dalby	11
B 1, l-b 8, w 1	10	L-b 3	3
1/23 (1) 2/23 (3) 3/31 (2) 4/45 (4) 5/50 (6) 6/97 (7) 7/99 (8) 8/114 (5) 9/209 (9) 10/211 (11) (61 overs)	211	1/1 (2) 2/9 (3) 3/24 (4) 4/38 (1) 5/38 (6) 6/56 (7) 7/129 (5) 8/133 (9) 9/159 (8) 10/189 (11) (64.1 overs)	189

Patterson 15–4–45–2; Hannon-Dalby 15–2–36–3; McGrath 12–5–28–3; Wardlaw 8–1–45–1; Azeem Rafiq 11–0–48–0. *Second innings*—Patterson 23–5–71–3; Hannon-Dalby 10.1–2–18–1; McGrath 13–4–37–4; Wardlaw 5–0–30–0; Azeem Rafiq 13–5–30–2.

Yorkshire

J. E. Root lbw b Thomas	8	– lbw b Thomas	0
J. J. Sayers c Webb b Reece	35	– not out	41
A. McGrath b Higginbottom	21	– lbw b Leach	43
*A. W. Gale b Higginbottom	2	– not out	4
A. Lyth c Hodgson b Reece	0		
G. S. Ballance lbw b Reece	4		
Azeem Rafiq c Hodgson b Leach	28		
†G. L. Brophy c Moore b Thomas	23		
S. A. Patterson c and b Leach	6		
I. Wardlaw c Reece b Leach	1		
O. J. Hannon-Dalby not out	5		
N-b 2	2	W 1, n-b 2	3
1/18 (1) 2/66 (3) 3/66 (2) 4/66 (5) 5/72 (4) 6/80 (6) 7/109 (7) 8/129 (9) 9/129 (8) 10/135 (10) (51.1 overs)	135	1/0 (1) 2/86 (3) (2 wkts, 31.3 overs)	91

Thomas 14–5–24–2; Hardman 6–0–25–0; Reece 12–4–25–3; Higginbottom 12–4–46–2; Leach 7.1–2–15–3. *Second innings*—Thomas 11–5–21–1; Hardman 3–0–12–0; Reece 6–1–26–0; Higginbottom 4–0–21–0; Leach 6.3–4–6–1; MacQueen 1–0–5–0.

Umpires: I. Dawood and P. J. Hartley.

YORKSHIRE v ESSEX

At Leeds, April 19–22. Drawn. Yorkshire 7pts, Essex 6pts. Toss: Yorkshire.

The first two innings produced a pair of centuries but only one batting point, which reflected the class of Jaques and Bopara. Returning to Yorkshire after seven years, Jaques demonstrated why he had averaged nearly 62 over two seasons for them, while Bopara batted with all the determination the England selectors could have asked for. At 203 for three, Yorkshire seemed on course for maximum batting points, but Dewsbury-born left-armer Tymal Mills struck three times in 20 deliveries, and the last seven fell for 43. Two in two balls for Sidebottom and a three-wicket maiden for Patterson reduced Essex to 42 for five. But Bopara remained unruffled, reaching his hundred during a last-wicket stand of 48 with Mills. Root and Sayers opened Yorkshire's second innings with 106, the foundation for a generous declaration which set Essex 262 in 74 overs. Shahzad struck twice before lunch, but rain – which washed out day one – had the final say.

Close of play: first day, no play; second day, Essex 72-5 (Bopara 26, Foster 9); third day, Yorkshire 144-2 (Sayers 45, Gale 6).

Yorkshire

J. E. Root c Godleman b Masters	2	– c Foster b Smith	67
J. J. Sayers c Foster b Mills	32	– c Foster b Masters	45
P. A. Jaques c Petersen b Chambers	126	– lbw b Westley	18
*A. W. Gale c Godleman b Westley	35	– not out	48
†J. M. Bairstow c Petersen b Mills	4	– c Wheater b Smith	24
G. S. Ballance c sub (C. M. Willoughby) b Mills	20	– not out	3
A. McGrath lbw b Mills	1		
A. U. Rashid c sub (C. M. Willoughby) b Masters	0		
A. Shahzad c Foster b Masters	5		
R. J. Sidebottom not out	4		
S. A. Patterson lbw b Chambers	0		
B 4, l-b 7, n-b 6	17	B 2, l-b 5, n-b 2	9
1/2 (1) 2/98 (2) 3/184 (4) (64.1 overs)	246	1/106 (1) (4 wkts dec, 57 overs)	214
4/203 (5) 5/225 (6) 6/230 (7)		2/134 (3) 3/144 (2)	
7/231 (8) 8/241 (3) 9/241 (9) 10/246 (11)		4/193 (5)	

Masters 25–10–65–3; Chambers 10.1–3–40–2; Smith 10–2–50–0; Mills 13–3–62–4; Westley 6–0–18–1. *Second innings*—Masters 20–5–45–1; Chambers 7–0–37–0; Mills 8–1–15–0; Westley 13–2–79–1; Smith 9–2–31–2.

Essex

B. A. Godleman lbw b Sidebottom	9	– lbw b Shahzad	2
A. N. Petersen lbw b Patterson	16	– lbw b Shahzad	3
T. Westley c Bairstow b Sidebottom	0	– not out	12
R. S. Bopara not out	117	– not out	5
A. J. Wheater c Bairstow b Patterson	0		
G. M. Smith lbw b Patterson	0		
*†J. S. Foster c McGrath b Sidebottom	25		
D. D. Masters b Shahzad	1		
T. J. Phillips c Root b Sidebottom	7		
M. A. Chambers lbw b Sidebottom	0		
T. S. Mills run out	2		
B 16, l-b 4, n-b 2	22	L-b 4	4
1/18 (1) 2/24 (3) 3/42 (2) 4/42 (5) (79.5 overs)	199	1/4 (2) 2/7 (1) (2 wkts, 11.1 overs)	26
5/42 (6) 6/107 (7) 7/119 (8)			
8/149 (9) 9/151 (10) 10/199 (11)			

Sidebottom 24–10–30–5; Shahzad 17–4–63–1; Patterson 20–8–54–3; McGrath 9.5–2–22–0; Rashid 7–3–8–0; Root 2–0–2–0. *Second innings*—Sidebottom 6–0–15–0; Shahzad 5.1–3–7–2.

Umpires: R. J. Bailey and A. G. Wharf.

At Canterbury, April 26–29. YORKSHIRE drew with KENT.

YORKSHIRE v LEICESTERSHIRE

At Scarborough, May 2–5. Yorkshire won by an innings and 22 runs. Yorkshire 23pts, Leicestershire 1pt. Toss: Leicestershire.

North Marine Road is probably the only ground in the world that could attract daily four-figure crowds in temperatures hovering around 6°C. In cruel wind, two spectators of indeterminate gender even watched from their sleeping bags; meanwhile Yorkshire were attempting to freeze out questions about Shahzad's abrupt departure. The home fans' stoicism was rewarded with a first win. Although emphatic, it would have arrived sooner but for the weather and Boyce, who dug in for six hours and a career-best 122. But it was Bairstow's 182 which shaped the game. He added 160 with Gale and 159 with McGrath, who then created havoc with his wobbly medium-pacers after Leicestershire lost their top three during a run of seven maidens. Following on, they looked just as spineless, until Boyce and Cobb joined forces. Rain and sleet scattered their second innings over three days, and White also knuckled down in the closing stages; it was almost tea when Patterson disposed of Henderson to register career-best match figures of eight for 94.

Close of play: first day, Yorkshire 329-5 (Bairstow 141, McGrath 49); second day, Leicestershire 3-1 (Boyce 0); third day, Leicestershire 102-3 (Boyce 46, Cobb 45).

Yorkshire

J. E. Root c Boyce b White	19
J. J. Sayers lbw b Joseph	8
P. A. Jaques lbw b Henderson	1
*A. W. Gale c Eckersley b White	80
†J. M. Bairstow c du Toit b White	182
G. S. Ballance c Boyce b Malik	10
A. McGrath c Eckersley b Henderson	90
T. T. Bresnan run out	1
A. U. Rashid b White	4
R. J. Sidebottom c Eckersley b White	20
S. A. Patterson not out	8
B 2, l-b 11, w 3, n-b 8	24
1/28 (2) 2/33 (3) 3/33 (1) 4/193 (4) 5/217 (6) 6/376 (5) 7/390 (8) 8/407 (9) 9/427 (7) 10/447 (10) (133 overs)	447

110 overs: 375-5

Joseph 29–11–68–1; Wyatt 21–4–91–0; Henderson 36–5–94–2; White 27–4–90–5; Malik 20–2–91–1.

Leicestershire

G. P. Smith c Bairstow b Patterson	12	– lbw b Patterson	3
M. A. G. Boyce lbw b Sidebottom	0	– b Sidebottom	122
J. du Toit c Bairstow b Sidebottom	0	– c Sayers b Patterson	1
*R. R. Sarwan lbw b McGrath	11	– lbw b Patterson	5
J. J. Cobb c Bairstow b McGrath	29	– lbw b Patterson	69
†E. J. H. Eckersley lbw b McGrath	4	– b Bresnan	4
W. A. White lbw b Patterson	6	– c and b McGrath	67
C. W. Henderson c Jaques b Bresnan	15	– c Ballance b Patterson	17
R. H. Joseph c Bairstow b Patterson	0	– lbw b Sidebottom	0
M. N. Malik not out	21	– lbw b Rashid	1
A. C. F. Wyatt c Jaques b McGrath	8	– not out	0
B 1, l-b 9	10	B 11, l-b 7, n-b 2	20
1/12 (2) 2/12 (3) 3/12 (1) 4/33 (4) 5/43 (6) 6/64 (5) 7/64 (7) 8/68 (9) 9/104 (8) 10/116 (11) (52.2 overs)	116	1/3 (1) 2/8 (3) 3/14 (4) 4/142 (5) 5/149 (6) 6/282 (7) 7/284 (2) 8/284 (9) 9/299 (10) 10/309 (8) (103.2 overs)	309

Bresnan 12–4–37–1; Sidebottom 13–6–31–2; Patterson 15–8–17–3; McGrath 12.2–4–21–4. *Second innings*—McGrath 21–7–33–1; Patterson 25.2–10–77–5; Sidebottom 19–2–52–2; Bresnan 15–1–57–1; Rashid 18–3–58–1; Root 5–2–14–0.

Umpires: N. A. Mallender and M. J. Saggers.

At Bristol, May 9–12. YORKSHIRE beat GLOUCESTERSHIRE by four wickets.

YORKSHIRE v HAMPSHIRE

At Leeds, May 16–19. Drawn. Yorkshire 9pts, Hampshire 10pts. Toss: Hampshire.

Mitchell Starc – nicknamed Terminal by his new team-mates after enduring 14 long-distance flights in 12 days since Australia's tour of the West Indies – was allowed to delay his debut. And with Bresnan on England duty, Yorkshire's pace attack looked paper-thin. Lengthy hold-ups for bad weather, plus an unresponsive pitch, meant a drab draw was always likely; instead, interest centred on centuries from Katich and McGrath. When Katich appeared briefly for Yorkshire in 2002, he was run out first ball on debut, in a one-day match at Headingley. Now he batted with graceful ease, helped early on by innocuous bowling from McGrath, and reached his hundred in 99 deliveries. In reply, McGrath scored a sturdy century on the third day, exactly 17 years since his debut, at Bradford, where he too had fallen without scoring. On the way he averted the follow-on, and was given a life on 61 – by Katich at first slip. The game's third hundred was a maiden one for Bates, who put on 170 with Katich. Together, they equalled Hampshire's sixth-wicket record against Yorkshire, by Philip Mead and Gerald Harrison at Southampton in 1914.

Close of play: first day, Hampshire 352-5 (Katich 180, Bates 88); second day, Yorkshire 100-3 (Jaques 59, Ballance 26); third day, Hampshire 21-1 (Adams 7, Carberry 1).

Hampshire

L. A. Dawson c Brophy b Sidebottom	0	– c Jaques b Rashid	8
*J. H. K. Adams lbw b Patterson	5	– c Brophy b Wardlaw	49
M. A. Carberry c Ballance b Wardlaw	15	– not out	61
S. M. Katich c Root b Rashid	196	– not out	61
J. M. Vince c Brophy b Patterson	11		
S. M. Ervine c Patterson b Root	44		
†M. D. Bates run out	103		
C. P. Wood c Root b Patterson	8		
Kabir Ali c Wardlaw b Rashid	19		
J. A. Tomlinson c McGrath b Rashid	11		
D. J. Balcombe not out	2		
B 4, l-b 9	13	B 1, l-b 9, n-b 2	12
1/2 (1) 2/6 (2) 3/55 (3) 4/83 (5) (119 overs)	427	1/18 (1) (2 wkts dec, 61 overs)	191
5/207 (6) 6/377 (7) 7/391 (4)		2/88 (2)	
8/395 (8) 9/417 (9) 10/427 (10) 110 overs: 404-8			

Sidebottom 24–5–78–1; Patterson 27–3–87–3; McGrath 7–0–42–0; Wardlaw 21–0–82–1; Rashid 24–1–86–3; Root 16–4–39–1. *Second innings*—Sidebottom 8–4–16–0; Patterson 12–6–17–0; Rashid 16–1–82–1; Wardlaw 7–0–37–1; McGrath 6–2–8–0; Root 9–1–20–0; Lyth 3–2–1–0.

Yorkshire

A. Lyth lbw b Kabir Ali	4
J. E. Root c Dawson b Balcombe	8
P. A. Jaques c Balcombe b Dawson	93
*A. W. Gale run out	0
G. S. Ballance c Bates b Ervine	76
A. McGrath not out	106
†G. L. Brophy c Wood b Dawson	22
A. U. Rashid b Balcombe	3
R. J. Sidebottom c Bates b Kabir Ali	34
S. A. Patterson c Katich b Dawson	12
I. Wardlaw not out	17
B 8, l-b 2, n-b 14	24
1/4 (1) 2/32 (2) (9 wkts dec, 120 overs)	399
3/32 (4) 4/181 (3)	
5/193 (5) 6/232 (7) 7/237 (8)	
8/321 (9) 9/360 (10) 110 overs: 360-8	

Kabir Ali 25–7–80–2; Tomlinson 19–4–57–0; Wood 22–5–72–0; Balcombe 24–3–81–2; Dawson 19–4–61–3; Ervine 11–1–38–1.

Umpires: N. L. Bainton and S. C. Gale.

YORKSHIRE v NORTHAMPTONSHIRE

At Leeds, May 30–June 2. Drawn. Yorkshire 11pts, Northamptonshire 8pts. Toss: Northamptonshire. First-class debut: O. P. Stone. Championship debut: M. A. Starc.

More grim weather removed the equivalent of a day's play but, even with that handicap, Yorkshire should have fared better. Starc, finally making his competition debut, helped reduce Northamptonshire to 45 for five, but they were let off the hook, and Hall steered them past 200 before the second new ball finished off the innings. Root responded with an immaculate 125, but Yorkshire unaccountably slowed down, despite Hall retiring from an already weakened attack with a calf niggle. Thanks in part to Starc, they still acquired maximum batting points for the first time since the Roses match of June 2010. Northamptonshire showed commendable spirit in erasing a deficit of 163, and led by 87 when bad light ended the match.

Close of play: first day, Yorkshire 27-0 (Lyth 14, Root 7); second day, Yorkshire 190-3 (Root 98, Bairstow 36); third day, Northamptonshire 43-1 (Peters 20, Coetzer 12).

Northamptonshire

First innings		Second innings	
S. D. Peters c Jaques b Patterson	7	– b Patterson	22
J. D. Middlebrook lbw b Patterson	9	– lbw b Starc	9
K. J. Coetzer c Bairstow b Sidebottom	12	– c Root b Azeem Rafiq	39
A. G. Wakely b Starc	0	– b Starc	66
R. A. White lbw b Starc	12	– b Patterson	42
*A. J. Hall b Patterson	79	– c Bairstow b Starc	7
†D. Murphy c Bairstow b Sidebottom	40	– not out	31
C. D. de Lange lbw b McGrath	23	– not out	20
D. J. Willey lbw b Sidebottom	39		
O. P. Stone b Azeem Rafiq	13		
L. M. Daggett not out	4		
B 4, l-b 5, n-b 6	15	B 7, l-b 5, n-b 2	14
1/11 (1) 2/20 (2) 3/21 (4) 4/39 (5) (88.4 overs)	253	1/15 (2) (6 wkts, 89 overs)	250
5/45 (3) 6/121 (7) 7/163 (8)		2/47 (1) 3/95 (3)	
8/232 (6) 9/232 (9) 10/253 (10)		4/160 (5) 5/187 (6) 6/198 (4)	

Sidebottom 18–4–37–3; Patterson 18.5–3–61–3; Starc 18.1–7–64–2; McGrath 11–4–30–1; Azeem Rafiq 18.4–5–41–1; Root 4–2–11–0. *Second innings*—Sidebottom 18–5–51–0; Patterson 24–11–46–2; Azeem Rafiq 23–6–66–1; Starc 16–4–50–3; McGrath 5–1–19–0; Root 3–1–6–0.

Yorkshire

A. Lyth c Murphy b Daggett	25
J. E. Root c Murphy b Hall	125
P. A. Jaques lbw b Daggett	3
*A. W. Gale lbw b Stone	17
†J. M. Bairstow b Hall	68
G. S. Ballance c Wakely b Middlebrook	24
A. McGrath lbw b Willey	47
Azeem Rafiq c Murphy b Daggett	37
M. A. Starc not out	28
R. J. Sidebottom c Peters b Daggett	2
S. A. Patterson b Middlebrook	10
B 8, l-b 7, w 1, n-b 14	30
1/42 (1) 2/54 (3) 3/96 (4) (106 overs)	416
4/243 (2) 5/268 (5) 6/300 (6)	
7/368 (8) 8/370 (7) 9/379 (10) 10/416 (11)	

Willey 31–6–111–1; Daggett 30.5–5–109–4; Hall 15.1–4–57–2; Stone 16–2–76–1; Middlebrook 11–1–41–2; de Lange 2–0–7–0.

Umpires: P. J. Hartley and M. J. Saggers.

At Colwyn Bay, June 6–9. YORKSHIRE drew with GLAMORGAN.

At Southampton, July 11–14. YORKSHIRE drew with HAMPSHIRE.

At Chesterfield, July 18–21. YORKSHIRE drew with DERBYSHIRE.

At Leicester, July 27–30. YORKSHIRE drew with LEICESTERSHIRE.

At Northampton, August 1–4. YORKSHIRE drew with NORTHAMPTONSHIRE.

YORKSHIRE v DERBYSHIRE

At Leeds, August 15–18. Drawn. Yorkshire 11pts, Derbyshire 6pts. Toss: Derbyshire. County debut: A. J. Hodd.

Yorkshire returned to Headingley after 73 days without home Championship cricket. In a thrilling start to the final day, they enforced the follow-on with three runs to spare; gallingly for Derbyshire, the ninth wicket had fallen when Wainwright was run out off the ball which brought up his fifty against his former county. Bresnan, not needed by England at Lord's, replaced Ashraf on the second day, then dismissed both openers. But Khawaja epitomised Derbyshire's new-found confidence in a calm century, and Yorkshire conceded their eighth successive draw with 14 overs remaining. Two days before the game, they had released Gerard Brophy and acquired Hodd on loan from Sussex. He proved a more than adequate stand-in for the Test-tied Bairstow, scoring 58 and pouching all five catches in Derbyshire's first innings. Earlier, Lyth just missed a scintillating hundred; McGrath, fighting for his place, made no such mistake and ensured maximum batting points. Durston enjoyed a splendid match, scoring 84 and 39 to follow a career-best five wickets, assisted by Yorkshire sacrificing their last five in 15 balls. The 90 overs lost to weather cost the home side; despite gaining ground on table-toppers Derbyshire, they slipped ten points behind second-placed Hampshire.

Close of play: first day, Yorkshire 127-2 (Lyth 60, Ballance 11); second day, Derbyshire 28-1 (Lineker 12); third day, Derbyshire 233-8 (Wainwright 45, Groenewald 0).

Yorkshire

A. Lyth c Lineker b Whiteley	93
P. A. Jaques b Groenewald	3
*A. W. Gale c Turner b Whiteley	47
G. S. Ballance c Poynton b Groenewald	79
A. McGrath c Wainwright b Durston	104
A. U. Rashid b Durston	12
†A. J. Hodd c Lineker b Durston	58
T. T. Bresnan c Khawaja b Wainwright	1
Azeem Rafiq st Poynton b Durston	1
R. J. Sidebottom c Whiteley b Durston	4
S. A. Patterson not out	1
L-b 14, w 3	17
1/8 (2) 2/95 (3) 3/211 (1) 4/256 (4) 5/280 (6) 6/411 (5) 7/412 (7) 8/415 (8) 9/415 (9) 10/420 (10) (113.4 overs)	420
110 overs: 406-5	

Bresnan replaced M. A. Ashraf after being released from the England squad.

Palladino 27–8–82–0; Groenewald 27–5–93–2; Durston 8.4–0–34–5; Turner 15–0–83–0; Whiteley 10–2–40–2; Wainwright 26–3–74–1.

Derbyshire

*W. L. Madsen lbw b Bresnan	14	– c Azeem Rafiq b Bresnan	5
M. S. Lineker c Hodd b Sidebottom	14	– b Bresnan	8
U. T. Khawaja c Hodd b Sidebottom	3	– not out	110
W. J. Durston b Azeem Rafiq	84	– lbw b Patterson	39
D. J. Redfern c Hodd b Sidebottom	3	– c Hodd b Sidebottom	2
R. A. Whiteley c Hodd b Patterson	35	– c Gale b Azeem Rafiq	17
D. J. Wainwright run out	50	– not out	1
†T. Poynton lbw b Azeem Rafiq	25		
A. P. Palladino lbw b Rashid	0		
T. D. Groenewald c Hodd b Bresnan	21		
M. L. Turner not out	8		
L-b 9, n-b 2	11	B 4, l-b 3, w 1	8
1/28 (1) 2/33 (3) 3/34 (2) 4/42 (5) 5/154 (4) 6/174 (6) 7/225 (8) 8/226 (9) 9/260 (7) 10/268 (10) (90.3 overs)	268	1/9 (1) 2/18 (2) 3/108 (4) 4/111 (5) 5/177 (6) (5 wkts, 72 overs)	190

Bresnan 23.3–5–78–2; Sidebottom 14–3–38–3; Patterson 11–2–50–1; McGrath 5–3–7–0; Rashid 21–5–44–1; Azeem Rafiq 16–6–42–2. *Second innings*—Sidebottom 18–4–45–1; Bresnan 18–3–55–2; Azeem Rafiq 9–4–15–1; Patterson 12–7–24–1; Rashid 11–0–39–0; McGrath 4–2–5–0.

Umpires: S. A. Garratt and J. W. Lloyds.

YORKSHIRE v GLOUCESTERSHIRE

At Scarborough, August 28–31. Yorkshire won by two wickets. Yorkshire 19pts, Gloucestershire 1pt. Toss: Gloucestershire.

Yorkshire re-entered the promotion zone, courtesy of a generous deal which set them 314 in 84 overs after two days were wiped out by rain. It was a case of once bitten but not twice shy for Gloucestershire, who had provided Yorkshire with their previous Championship win, back in May, when they cantered to a 400-run target in a similar arrangement at Bristol. Purists watched in stony silence as Nicol and Howell were fed 159 runs in ten overs to set things up. The chase was given a good start by Lyth and Root, who was capped along with Ballance before the game, only for wickets to fall to poor shots. But the experience of Jaques and McGrath told in the end, with a little late help from Azeem Rafiq's 22-ball cameo. Though Sidebottom (back spasms) and Pyrah (broken hand) were absent, Patterson and Ashraf reduced the visitors to nine for four. Gidman had a fine all-round match for Gloucestershire, who might have taken the spoils had they negotiated a little more boldly.

Close of play: first day, Yorkshire 61-2 (Root 24, Gale 23); second day, no play; third day, no play.

Gloucestershire

R. J. Nicol c Hodd b Ashraf	4	– not out	75
B. A. C. Howell b Patterson	0	– not out	83
D. M. Housego c Lyth b Patterson	0		
*H. J. H. Marshall lbw b Patterson	4		
I. A. Cockbain c Jaques b Azeem Rafiq	30		
W. R. S. Gidman c Lyth b Ashraf	47		
†J. N. Batty b Ashraf	25		
J. K. Fuller lbw b Azeem Rafiq	1		
J. M. R. Taylor c and b Azeem Rafiq	49		
A. J. Ireland not out	25		
L. C. Norwell c Hodd b Rashid	18		
L-b 4, n-b 8	12	W 1	1
1/1 (2) 2/5 (3) 3/9 (4) 4/9 (1) 5/74 (5) 6/102 (6) 7/107 (8) 8/163 (9) 9/179 (7) 10/215 (11) (76.1 overs)	215	(no wkt dec, 10 overs)	159

Patterson 17–7–35–3; Ashraf 18–4–44–3; McGrath 6–0–25–0; Azeem Rafiq 28–6–85–3; Rashid 6.1–0–22–1; Root 1–1–0–0. *Second innings*—Gale 5–0–71–0; Lyth 5–0–88–0.

Yorkshire

A. Lyth c Batty b Gidman	0	– c Norwell b Ireland	40
J. E. Root not out	24	– c Housego b Norwell	43
P. A. Jaques c Batty b Gidman	9	– c Cockbain b Fuller	79
*A. W. Gale not out	23	– c Marshall b Taylor	14
G. S. Ballance (did not bat)		– c Cockbain b Taylor	5
A. McGrath (did not bat)		– not out	76
†A. J. Hodd (did not bat)		– lbw b Gidman	8
A. U. Rashid (did not bat)		– c Batty b Gidman	10
Azeem Rafiq (did not bat)		– c Fuller b Norwell	24
S. A. Patterson (did not bat)		– not out	0
L-b 2, w 1, n-b 2	5	L-b 5, w 2, n-b 10	17
1/0 (1) 2/16 (3) (2 wkts dec, 17 overs)	61	1/72 (1) 2/119 (2) 3/159 (4) 4/183 (5) 5/205 (3) 6/245 (7) 7/267 (8) 8/312 (9) (8 wkts, 81.2 overs)	316

M. A. Ashraf did not bat.

Gidman 6–2–12–2; Norwell 6–1–15–0; Ireland 4–0–28–0; Taylor 1–0–4–0. *Second innings*—Gidman 22–2–70–2; Norwell 15.2–0–63–2; Ireland 16–0–77–1; Fuller 10–0–63–1; Taylor 18–4–38–2.

Umpires: D. J. Millns and S. J. O'Shaughnessy.

YORKSHIRE v GLAMORGAN

At Leeds, September 4–6. Yorkshire won by eight wickets. Yorkshire 22pts, Glamorgan 5pts. Toss: Yorkshire. First-class debut: D. L. Lloyd.

As in 2011, Yorkshire waited until their last home Championship match to win at Headingley. This time it left them well-placed for promotion, rather than powerless to avoid the drop. Gale thought he had made "a massive mistake" bowling first when Bragg and James raised Glamorgan's first century opening stand of the season before lunch. But, once they were parted, Yorkshire had the best of events on a pitch of variable bounce, though Glamorgan were handicapped when the pacy Waters slid into the boundary wall and twisted his ankle. Patterson had a fine game, adding 54 with Sidebottom and taking four wickets in each innings – including 20-year-old David Lloyd twice as he bagged the first pair on debut for Glamorgan since 1976. But it was Ashraf's burst on the third morning, when he removed Bragg and Walters in five deliveries, which opened the floodgates.

Close of play: first day, Yorkshire 20-0 (Lyth 5, Root 9); second day, Glamorgan 27-2 (Bragg 14, Walters 5).

Glamorgan

W. D. Bragg c Hodd b Patterson	92	–	b Ashraf	25
N. A. James c Hodd b Sidebottom	38	–	c Hodd b Patterson	4
S. J. Walters c Lyth b Azeem Rafiq	42	–	(4) c Hodd b Ashraf	9
D. L. Lloyd c Hodd b Patterson	0	–	(5) c Hodd b Patterson	0
B. J. Wright lbw b Sidebottom	24	–	(6) lbw b McGrath	21
J. Allenby c Lyth b McGrath	14	–	(7) b Ashraf	48
*†M. A. Wallace c Jaques b Azeem Rafiq	29	–	(8) lbw b Sidebottom	17
G. G. Wagg b McGrath	0	–	(9) c Hodd b Azeem Rafiq	36
J. C. Glover b Patterson	0	–	(3) c Lyth b Patterson	0
D. A. Cosker c Hodd b Patterson	11	–	c Sidebottom b Patterson	2
H. T. Waters not out	5	–	not out	11
B 5, l-b 10, n-b 2	17		L-b 9	9
1/124 (2) 2/140 (1) 3/156 (4) 4/198 (3) 5/221 (5) 6/223 (6) 7/223 (8) 8/236 (9) 9/257 (7) 10/272 (10) (87.2 overs)	272		1/17 (2) 2/17 (3) 3/45 (1) 4/46 (4) 5/46 (5) 6/101 (6) 7/125 (7) 8/144 (8) 9/149 (10) 10/182 (9) (58.1 overs)	182

Sidebottom 19–5–66–2; Patterson 19.2–6–49–4; Ashraf 12–2–51–0; Azeem Rafiq 18–6–57–2; McGrath 19–8–34–2. *Second innings*—Patterson 21–8–47–4; Sidebottom 13–1–39–1; McGrath 6–1–28–1; Ashraf 12–4–42–3; Azeem Rafiq 6.1–0–17–1.

Yorkshire

A. Lyth lbw b Glover	95	–	lbw b Cosker	50
J. E. Root lbw b Wagg	14	–	lbw b Glover	11
P. A. Jaques lbw b Allenby	13		not out	28
*A. W. Gale b Wagg	55			
G. S. Ballance b Allenby	26	–	(4) not out	19
A. McGrath lbw b Glover	39			
†A. J. Hodd c Walters b Allenby	2			
Azeem Rafiq c Wallace b Glover	8			
R. J. Sidebottom c Wallace b Wagg	35			
S. A. Patterson b Allenby	22			
M. A. Ashraf not out	0			
B 4, l-b 15, n-b 16	35		L-b 2, w 1	3
1/39 (2) 2/70 (3) 3/190 (1) 4/200 (4) 5/261 (5) 6/267 (7) 7/283 (8) 8/286 (6) 9/340 (10) 10/344 (9) (88.4 overs)	344		1/63 (2) 2/63 (1) (2 wkts, 28.1 overs)	111

Wagg 24.4–3–87–3; Waters 9–1–34–0; Glover 22–4–78–3; Allenby 18–2–61–4; Cosker 14–0–63–0; Bragg 1–0–2–0. *Second innings*—Allenby 7–2–20–0; Glover 8–1–35–1; Wagg 4–0–11–0; Cosker 6–0–26–1; Bragg 2.1–0–13–0; James 1–0–4–0.

Umpires: N. L. Bainton and T. E. Jesty.

At Chelmsford, September 11–14. YORKSHIRE beat ESSEX by 239 runs. *Yorkshire promoted.*

FRIENDS LIFE t20, 2012

REVIEW BY ALAN GARDNER

Nostalgia may not be what it was, but neither is cricket's youngest format – at least in the country of its birth. This was the year in which concerns about the structure, presentation and economics of domestic Twenty20 in England came to the boil, as players, administrators and fans (if you listened hard enough) pondered the direction taken by an innovation that has been cast as saviour and envoy of the game, as well as its bête noire.

In its tenth year, and now branded as the Friends Life t20, the competition reverted from a two-season embonpoint to a leaner, ten-game group stage, divided into three regions. During a summer that was wetter than Jacques Cousteau's shower cap, the rain clouds cast a long shadow over the tournament. But the scheduling was a further source of disgruntlement; four home matches in five days for Surrey was just one example of a problematic fixture list.

Poor weather bedevilled the four-week block for the group stage to the extent that several counties called for the tournament to be spread across the season, with matches on specific days of the week to encourage a sense of familiarity with the fixture list among the general public. This echoed the "appointment to view" mantra for Twenty20 espoused by the Morgan Review.

At the same time, the likes of Muttiah Muralitharan, representing Gloucestershire, and Eoin Morgan urged the creation of a franchise system in the mould of Twenty20's prize peacock, the Indian Premier League, as well as the newly minted Big Bash League in Australia. Cricket's format wars have never been as simple as Betamax v VHS, and now a significant split had emerged about the way forward for English Twenty20.

A PCA survey reinforced the players' preference for a dedicated window in which to attract big-name signings and focus broadcaster interest (at a time of disdain for bankers' bonuses, cynics noted the line that argued for "a significant increase in the prize money at stake", including £1m for the winners rather than the current £200,000). But "appointment-to-view" would end up winning the day: once again the county game was characterised as being out of touch with the modern world. The move from forward-thinking pioneers to outdated protectorate in only nine years was quite something.

The IPL is cricket's Lolita, a seductive "trip of three steps down the palate" bewitching those old enough to know better, and by any measure England's Twenty20 tournament appeared to have faded badly. However, while the competitions do not bear much comparison, it was with a baleful synchronicity that the title sponsors of both – Friends Life and DLF – announced on the same day in August that they would not be renewing their contracts.

In all, 16 of the 90 group games were abandoned without a ball bowled, along with four no-results and ten fixtures shortened by rain. On Friday July 6, seven matches out of nine were washed out, a tidal-wave effect that began with Derbyshire's game against Nottinghamshire being called off at 10.21am – more than eight and a half hours before the scheduled start – and finally

TEN SEASONS OF ENGLISH TWENTY20

MOST RUNS

	M	*I*	*NO*	*R*	*HS*	*100*	*50*	*Avge*	*SR*
D. I. Stevens (*Leics, Kent*)	103	97	26	2,209	77	0	11	31.11	135.52
M. W. Goodwin (*Sussex*)	93	86	11	2,200	102*	2	12	29.33	122.90
D. L. Maddy (*Leics, Warwicks*)	81	79	9	2,083	111	1	12	29.75	130.67
S. C. Moore (*Worcs, Lancs*)	87	81	10	1,981	83*	0	13	27.90	130.32
M. E. Trescothick (*Somerset*)	64	63	5	1,968	108*	2	15	33.93	161.04
M. L. Pettini (*Essex*)	84	80	5	1,956	87	0	13	26.08	128.17
P. Mustard (*Durham*)	90	85	4	1,938	75	0	11	23.92	124.63
I. J. L. Trott (*Warwicks*)	65	60	14	1,871	86*	0	12	40.67	118.19
M. van Jaarsveld (*Nhants, Kent, Glam*)	87	79	12	1,829	82	0	13	27.29	131.48
J. L. Denly (*Kent, Middx*)	75	72	5	1,822	91	0	12	27.19	111.23
M. J. Lumb (*Yorks, Hants, Notts*)	81	81	6	1,795	124*	1	11	23.93	144.75
O. A. Shah (*Middx, Essex*)	69	67	12	1,793	80	0	10	32.60	129.45
Azhar Mahmood (*Surrey, Kent*)	96	86	22	1,793	106*	1	6	28.01	142.07

MOST WICKETS

	M	*O*	*R*	*W*	*BB*	*4I*	*Avge*	*SR*	*ER*
Azhar Mahmood (*Surrey, Kent*)	96	325	2,457	103	4-20	1	23.85	18.93	7.56
Yasir Arafat (*Sussex, Kent, Surrey, Lancs*)	74	246	1,953	101	4-17	5	19.33	14.61	7.93
A. J. Hall (*Worcs, Kent, Northants*)	75	241.4	1,870	95	6-21	4	19.68	15.26	7.73
R. D. B. Croft (*Glam*)	88	288.3	2,015	87	3-9	0	23.16	19.89	6.98
S. J. Cook (*Middx, Kent*)	73	255.1	1,919	85	3-13	0	22.57	18.01	7.52
A. D. Mascarenhas (*Hants*)	62	204.5	1,378	82	5-14	2	16.80	14.98	6.72
N. M. Carter (*Warwicks*)	91	298.5	2,159	81	5-19	1	26.65	22.13	7.22
J. C. Tredwell (*Kent*)	92	288	2,068	80	4-21	1	25.85	21.60	7.18
R. M. Pyrah (*Yorks*)	74	214	1,620	79	5-16	3	20.50	16.25	7.57
T. J. Murtagh (*Surrey, Middx*)	75	245	2,097	79	6-24	1	26.54	18.60	8.55
G. M. Andrew (*Somerset, Worcs*)	83	245.2	2,081	76	4-22	1	27.38	19.36	8.48
A. C. Thomas (*Warwicks, Somerset*)	54	191.2	1,382	75	4-27	1	18.42	15.30	7.22

MOST DISMISSALS BY A WICKETKEEPER

	Dis		*M*
J. S. Foster (*Essex*)	74	(39 ct, 35 st)	94
G. D. Cross (*Lancs*)	70	(48 ct, 22 st)	76
P. A. Nixon (*Leics*)	69	(49 ct, 20 st)	90
P. Mustard (*Durham*)	68	(47 ct, 21 st)	90
B. J. M. Scott (*Mx, Worcs*)	65	(34 ct, 31 st)	88
G. O. Jones (*Kent*)	64	(44 ct, 20 st)	83
J. N. Batty (*Surrey, Glos*)	59	(38 ct, 21 st)	64
C. M. W. Read (*Notts*)	58	(40 ct, 18 st)	82
M. A. Wallace (*Glam*)	58	(37 ct, 21 st)	89
S. M. Davies (*Worcs, Sy*)	55	(40 ct, 15 st)	72

MOST CATCHES BY A FIELDER

	Ct	*M*
S. J. Croft (*Lancs*)	46	76
R. Clarke (*Surrey, Warwicks*)	42	87
M. van Jaarsveld (*Nhants, Kent, Glam*)	42	87
A. D. Brown (*Surrey, Notts*)	41	79
D. L. Maddy (*Leics, Warwicks*)	39	81
J. C. Hildreth (*Somerset*)	37	92
H. J. H. Marshall (*Glos*)	37	59
G. R. Breese (*Durham*)	36	84
J. O. Troughton (*Warwicks*)	36	88
W. R. Smith (*Notts, Durham*)	35	59

claimed Hampshire v Sussex as it neared the innings break some 11 hours later.

With a third of the group matches affected by rain, debate was rife about the tournament's structure. Since the availability of England players was almost non-existent, and numerous marquee overseas signings – including Chris Gayle, Lasith Malinga, Saeed Ajmal and Shahid Afridi – had pulled out of deals to play, some of the arguments against spreading the tournament throughout the season were undoubtedly weakened.

Surrey's chief executive Richard Gould was the most vocal advocate of change, championing the ideas of "scheduling and local heroes" in an attempt to turn casual consumers into engaged fans. His county had already been dealt a difficult hand, with a fixture list that included three games at The Oval between July 3 and July 6, but the death of Tom Maynard meant the rearrangement of another home match, against Hampshire, to July 2. That sequence followed a seven-day gap at the height of the tournament in which Surrey didn't play a game at all, home or away.

In tough economic times, it was difficult to market multiple home matches so close together, and Gould argued that fixtures in the early part of the week were a hard sell anyway: most counties preferred to play on Friday evenings (and, in London, Thursdays too, a good night for corporate clients) and at the weekend. A league structure played over a few months would be less likely to fall victim to a concentrated period of rainfall, as well as being easier for the punters to understand.

Glamorgan – who, with five of their ten group games washed out, suffered most – and Somerset expressed similar views, although there remained a group of chief executives convinced that a one-hit, short-burst focus on sixes and celebrity was still the way to go. Spectators, meanwhile, quietly questioned ticket prices and the wide variety of start times – 15 of them in the group stage. And all this was without the added headache of having to factor in hosting the ICC Champions Trophy, as 2013 would demand.

In the end, the reformists had their way. After further horse-trading with the counties on the future of the Championship and domestic one-day cricket, and following the results of a fan survey conducted by market researchers Populus, the ECB announced that from 2014 the Twenty20 competition would be played mostly on Fridays.

With the reduction in 2012 from 16 group games per team to ten, a fall in overall gates was to be expected. But the number of rain-affected matches made it difficult to assess the theory that sharpening up the fixture list would create more demand. Competing with football's European Championship, and advance claims for money and attention from the Olympics, clearly did not help either.

The overall attendance was 313,215 from 90 games, compared with 633,957 from 144 in 2011 – but the average crowd (excluding abandonments) of around 4,500 remained roughly the same. A more useful contrast was with the last time the competition was played in the same structure, during the drier summer of 2009: the overall figure from the group stage that year (with only three abandoned games) was 450,172, and the average attendance 5,000.

Stu Forster, Getty Images

Hogging the limelight: Dimitri Mascarenhas and his Hampshire team celebrate a second Twenty20 triumph in three years.

Counties such as Essex and Somerset were still able to pack out smaller grounds, and spin atmosphere as well as money, while Nottinghamshire continued to make a success of staging Twenty20 at a Test venue. Trent Bridge has been recognised for providing one of the best spectator experiences on the circuit; the club's strategy focused on finding the extra 1% off the field wherever they could, with free entry for members, family ticketing packages, live entertainment and imaginative use of their video replay screen. But the word most commonly used by county chairmen to describe attendances was "disappointing".

The cricket that was played proved solid and competitive, if not spectacular. The average first-innings score (when all 20 overs were available) was a scratchy 151, not aided by slow and often damp pitches. But tension compensated to a degree for a lack of flair: around a third of all completed matches, including the final, were still realistically up for grabs in the last over.

Sussex, led by a gunslinging top order of Chris Nash, Luke Wright and Matt Prior, were the only team to score 200 more than once (they did so four times, including the group match at Hampshire, which was abandoned after 17.4 overs). Nottinghamshire and Yorkshire – who twice broke their own records for opening stands – also piled on the runs. The Midlands/Wales/West Group was the most keenly contested: none of its three quarter-finalists was guaranteed progression until the final round.

There were surprises too. Leicestershire, the defending champions, finished a sorry last in the North Group; Hampshire, the eventual winners, picked up one point (from an abandonment) from their first three South Group games, before going unbeaten through the rest of the competition; Gloucestershire, also-rans in the previous two seasons, reached the last eight, as did Worcestershire, for the first time since 2007; Yorkshire won their first Twenty20 semi-final – beating Sussex, one of the favourites – then lost their first final. More predictably, Northamptonshire won just once, to go with their two victories in 2011.

Tactically, it was a good year for southpaws. The three leading wicket-takers – Yorkshire's Mitchell Starc, Chris Liddle of Sussex, and Essex's Reece Topley – were left-arm seamers, as spinners generally struggled on tracks that weren't for turning (although that didn't stop Surrey from regularly fielding four). A lack of pace was still useful, however, as the success of Dimitri Mascarenhas, Rich Pyrah and Daryl Mitchell showed. Left-handers also led the way with the bat, with Phillip Hughes (who averaged 100 from eight innings) and David Miller (the sixiest hitter of the tournament, with 21) topping the run charts by some distance.

County culture has always been more underneath the mainstream than against it, so it was perhaps fitting that the majority of the overseas recruits who did end up making an impact were of the low-fi variety. Starc and Miller, both young and exciting but hardly names plucked from the firmament, were central to Yorkshire's campaign, while Hampshire were inspired in going for the Australian Glenn Maxwell – then playing for South Wilts in the Southern Premier League – as cover for Shahid Afridi. Scott Styris, a nomad of the format, scored the joint-third-fastest hundred in Twenty20 history in Sussex's quarter-final win over Gloucestershire. His 37-ball century was only the second of the tournament (the lowest number since the inaugural 2003 edition), but was all the more eye-catching for coming at the knockout stage. James Fuller suffered most, conceding 38 runs in one over to equal the record in professional cricket.

In general, the runs flowed during the quarter-finals, with Sussex and Yorkshire passing 200, though three out of four went to form: only Nottinghamshire could not capitalise on home advantage. Hampshire were their nuggety conquerors and, a month later at Cardiff, on another slow, low pitch, Mascarenhas's side ensured that Somerset's fourth consecutive finals day would be another unhappy experience. In the other semi-final, a Jonny Bairstow blast was enough for Yorkshire to see off Sussex.

The final was a tale of innocence and experience, not necessarily in diametric opposition. Yorkshire had seasoned traditional grit with young talent in the form of Bairstow, Joe Root, Gary Ballance, Azeem Rafiq and Moin Ashraf; Hampshire, the 2010 winners and semi-finalists in 2011, relied on five players over the age of 30, but still required mature performances from Danny Briggs, 21, and Chris Wood, 22. Miller's belligerence hauled Yorkshire close, but they could barely touch Wood in the final over as Hampshire claimed a second Twenty20 title.

For both finalists, the Champions League beckoned in South Africa in October. What started out as a summer fling ten years earlier had become a throw-the-kitchen-sink-at-it drama. There may be more angst to come.

Prize money (unchanged from 2011)

£200,000 for winners: HAMPSHIRE.
£84,000 for runners-up: YORKSHIRE.
£27,000 for losing semi-finalists: SOMERSET, SUSSEX.
£5,000 for losing quarter-finalists: ESSEX, GLOUCESTERSHIRE, NOTTINGHAMSHIRE, WORCESTERSHIRE.

Match-award winners received £2,000 in the final, £1,000 in the semi-finals, £500 in the quarter-finals and £250 in group games.

FINAL GROUP TABLES

Midland/Wales/West Group	*Played*	*Won*	*Lost*	*Tied*	*No result*	*Points*	*NRR*
SOMERSET	10	5	2	0	3	13	0.27
GLOUCESTERSHIRE	10	4	2	0	4	12	0.24
WORCESTERSHIRE	10	4	3	0	3	11	0.57
Warwickshire	10	4	3	0	3	11	–0.56
Glamorgan	10	2	3	0	5	9	–0.70
Northamptonshire	10	1	7	0	2	4	–0.61

North Group	*Played*	*Won*	*Lost*	*Tied*	*No result*	*Points*	*NRR*
YORKSHIRE	10	7	1	0	2	16	0.86
NOTTINGHAMSHIRE	10	5	1	0	4	14	1.87
Durham	10	4	4	1	1	10	–0.25
Lancashire	10	3	4	1	2	9	0.10
Derbyshire	10	2	6	0	2	6	–0.56
Leicestershire	10	2	7	0	1	5	–1.35

South Group	*Played*	*Won*	*Lost*	*Tied*	*No result*	*Points*	*NRR*
SUSSEX	10	6	1	0	3	15	1.38
HAMPSHIRE	10	5	2	0	3	13	0.69
ESSEX	10	5	4	0	1	11	–0.03
Kent	10	4	5	0	1	9	–0.46
Middlesex	10	3	7	0	0	6	–0.21
Surrey	10	3	7	0	0	6	–0.70

Where two or more counties finished with an equal number of points, the positions were decided by (a) most points in head-to-head matches, (b) net run-rate (runs scored per over minus runs conceded per over), and (c) most wickets taken per balls bowled in matches achieving a result.

FRIENDS LIFE t20 AVERAGES, 2012

BATTING (200 runs, average 25.00)

		M	*I*	*NO*	*R*	*HS*	*100*	*50*	*Avge*	*SR*	*4*	*6*
1	†P. J. Hughes (*Worcs*)	8	8	4	402	87*	0	4	100.50	126.81	37	7
2	S. J. Croft (*Lancs*)	8	8	3	313	65*	0	2	62.60	129.33	17	11
3	C. L. White (*Northants*)	9	8	4	228	62*	0	2	57.00	131.03	11	10
4	A. C. Voges (*Notts*)	8	8	4	209	70	0	1	52.25	120.11	20	0
5	†S. E. Marsh (*Glam*)	6	5	1	209	85	0	2	52.25	129.81	21	8
6	S. B. Styris (*Sussex*)	8	7	3	204	100*	1	0	51.00	190.65	10	13
7	†D. A. Miller (*Yorks*)	12	11	3	390	74*	0	4	48.75	153.54	30	21
8	V. Chopra (*Warwicks*)	8	7	2	240	56*	0	2	48.00	107.62	20	5
9	P. R. Stirling (*Middx*)	7	7	1	271	82*	0	3	45.16	142.63	32	8
10	J. C. Hildreth (*Somerset*)	9	8	3	223	107*	1	1	44.60	133.53	30	2
11	M. J. Prior (*Sussex*)	7	6	0	249	81	0	2	41.50	196.06	28	11
12	C. D. Nash (*Sussex*)	10	10	2	319	80*	0	3	39.87	131.27	32	8
13	H. H. Gibbs (*Durham*)	9	9	2	277	83*	0	2	39.57	124.21	31	8
14	†M. J. Lumb (*Notts*)	8	8	1	252	62	0	1	36.00	138.46	25	11
15	L. J. Wright (*Sussex*)	10	10	1	312	91	0	2	34.66	160.00	32	11

		M	*I*	*NO*	*R*	*HS*	*100*	*50*	*Avge*	*SR*	*4*	*6*
16	H. J. H. Marshall (*Glos*)...	7	7	0	239	72	0	2	34.14	146.62	26	6
17	J. S. Foster (*Essex*).......	10	10	2	270	65*	0	2	33.75	165.64	18	15
18	M. W. Goodwin (*Sussex*)..	10	9	1	262	68*	0	2	32.75	129.70	31	3
19	J. M. Vince (*Hants*)......	11	10	2	254	64*	0	1	31.75	118.69	28	3
20	S. C. Moore (*Lancs*)......	8	8	0	249	80	0	3	31.12	139.88	26	7
21	Abdul Razzaq (*Leics*).....	9	9	0	266	69	0	2	29.55	112.23	28	7
22	W. J. Durston (*Derbys*)...	8	8	1	201	56	0	2	28.71	127.21	25	4
23	†T. C. Smith (*Lancs*)......	8	8	0	227	56	0	1	28.37	122.70	20	10
24	†J. E. C. Franklin (*Essex*)...	10	10	1	248	78	0	2	27.55	110.71	20	8
25	J. E. Root (*Yorks*)........	12	11	2	241	65	0	1	26.77	128.87	36	1
26	†P. A. Jaques (*Yorks*)......	12	11	1	263	64	0	2	26.30	114.84	29	3
27	†G. S. Ballance (*Yorks*)....	12	11	3	209	47*	0	0	26.12	128.22	14	11
28	D. I. Stevens (*Kent*)......	9	9	1	207	60	0	1	25.87	135.29	11	12

BOWLING (10 wickets)

		Style	*O*	*M*	*R*	*W*	*BB*	*4I*	*Avge*	*SR*	*ER*
1	M. A. Starc (*Yorks*)........	LFM	37	0	218	21	3-24	0	10.38	10.50	5.91
2	C. J. Liddle (*Sussex*).......	LFM	27	0	203	17	5-17	0	11.94	9.70	7.33
3	R. J. W. Topley (*Essex*)....	LFM	32	0	246	17	3-19	0	14.47	11.20	7.68
4	I. D. Saxelby (*Glos*).......	RFM	22	0	160	11	4-16	1	14.54	12.00	7.27
5	G. M. Smith (*Essex*).......	RM/OB	18	0	146	10	5-17	0	14.60	10.80	8.11
6	G. J. Batty (*Surrey*)........	OB	31	0	162	11	4-13	1	14.72	16.90	5.22
7	D. K. H. Mitchell (*Worcs*)..	RM	25	0	171	11	3-13	0	15.54	13.60	6.84
8	R. J. Sidebottom (*Yorks*)....	LFM	25	0	177	11	4-25	1	16.09	13.60	7.08
9	A. D. Mascarenhas (*Hants*).	RM	38	1	247	15	2-11	0	16.46	15.20	6.50
10	A. J. Ball (*Kent*)..........	LFM	28	0	217	12	2-18	0	18.08	14.20	7.61
11	R. N. ten Doeschate (*Essex*).	RM	24	0	181	10	2-7	0	18.10	14.30	7.59
12	S. G. Borthwick (*Durham*)..	LBG	31	0	240	12	2-19	0	20.00	15.50	7.74
13	G. K. Berg (*Middx*)........	RFM	26	0	205	10	3-17	0	20.50	15.60	7.88
14	T. S. Roland-Jones (*Middx*).	RFM	28	0	228	11	4-25	1	20.72	15.20	8.14
15	Azhar Mahmood (*Kent*)....	RFM	24	0	212	10	3-12	0	21.20	14.60	8.71
16	Yasir Arafat (*Lancs*).......	RFM	24	0	224	10	3-21	0	22.40	14.40	9.33
17	T. J. Phillips (*Essex*).......	SLA	31	0	227	10	3-27	0	22.70	18.60	7.32
18	M. A. Ashraf (*Yorks*)......	RFM	47	0	359	15	4-18	1	23.93	18.80	7.63
19	R. M. Pyrah (*Yorks*).......	RM	45	0	359	15	3-21	0	23.93	18.00	7.97
20	Naved-ul-Hasan (*Derbys*)...	RFM	28	0	245	10	3-20	0	24.50	16.80	8.75
21	G. R. Napier (*Essex*).......	RFM	38	0	273	10	3-16	0	27.30	22.70	7.21
22	Azeem Rafiq (*Yorks*).......	OB	46	0	310	11	2-28	0	28.18	25.00	6.73

LEADING WICKETKEEPERS

Dismissals	*M*	
11 (7 ct, 4 st)	10	J. S. Foster (*Essex*)
9 (6 ct, 3 st)	7	T. Poynton (*Derbys*)
9 (6 ct, 3 st)	9	G. O. Jones (*Kent*)
9 (7 ct, 2 st)	9	P. Mustard (*Durham*)
9 (3 ct, 6 st)	10	S. M. Davies (*Surrey*)
8 (6 ct, 2 st)	8	G. D. Cross (*Lancs*)
7 (5 ct, 2 st)	8	B. J. M. Scott (*Worcs*)
6 (5 ct, 1 st)	6	M. A. Wallace (*Glam*)
6 (5 ct, 1 st)	7	J. N. Batty (*Glos*)

LEADING FIELDERS

Ct	*M*	
13	12	G. S. Ballance (*Yorks*)
9	8	S. J. Croft (*Lancs*)
8	7	H. J. H. Marshall (*Glos*)
8	10	J. S. Gatting (*Sussex*)
7	8	A. C. Voges (*Notts*)
7	11	J. M. Vince (*Hants*)

MIDLAND/WALES/WEST GROUP

GLAMORGAN

At Cardiff, June 17, 2012. **Glamorgan won by five runs** (D/L). ‡**Warwickshire 141-5** (18 overs) (V. Chopra 53, D. L. Maddy 49); **Glamorgan 62-1** (8 overs) (S. E. Marsh 30*). *MoM:* V. Chopra. *Attendance:* 6,032. *Varun Chopra and Darren Maddy had added 91 for the third wicket before rain curtailed the Warwickshire innings. Glamorgan's target was revised to 146 in 18 overs, but the weather intruded again: Shaun Marsh and Jim Allenby ensured they stayed ahead of Duckworth/Lewis.*

At Cardiff, June 23, 2012 (floodlit). **Glamorgan v Gloucestershire. Abandoned.**

At Cardiff, June 30, 2012 (floodlit). **Northamptonshire won by nine wickets. Glamorgan 110-9** (20 overs) (S. J. Walters 34*; C. D. de Lange 3-15, J. D. Middlebrook 3-16); ‡**Northamptonshire 111-1** (13.1 overs) (A. G. Wakely 54*). *MoM:* A. G. Wakely. *Attendance:* 2,105. *Northamptonshire's performance suggested they should have won more than this solitary game. With the possible exception of Stewart Walters, the Glamorgan batsmen struggled against spin – Con de Lange and James Middlebrook tied them in knots – on a sluggish pitch. Not that it caused many worries for the visitors: Alex Wakely struck 54* from 40 balls.*

At Cardiff, July 3, 2012. **Glamorgan v Worcestershire. Abandoned.** *This game, originally scheduled for June 20, was rearranged following the death of Tom Maynard.*

At Cardiff, July 6, 2012. **Glamorgan v Somerset. Abandoned.** *Another home abandonment meant that, of Glamorgan's nine games thus far, only four had reached a result.*

Glamorgan away matches

June 14: no result v Northamptonshire.
June 22: lost to Somerset by four wickets.
June 29: lost to Worcestershire by 19 runs.
July 2: abandoned v Gloucestershire.
July 8: beat Warwickshire by 22 runs (D/L).

GLOUCESTERSHIRE

At Bristol, June 14, 2012. **Gloucestershire v Somerset. Abandoned.** *Torrential rain put paid to the local derby expected to attract Bristol's largest gate of the season.*

At Bristol, June 22, 2012. **Gloucestershire won by eight runs. Gloucestershire 139-9** (20 overs) (K. S. Williamson 39, I. A. Cockbain 36); ‡**Northamptonshire 131-8** (20 overs) (K. J. Coetzer 44; I. D. Saxelby 4-16). *MoM:* I. D. Saxelby. *Attendance:* 1,541. *Gloucestershire reduced Northamptonshire to 18-4, and never let them off the leash. Ian Saxelby led the way with 4-16, while Muttiah Muralitharan removed top-scorer Kyle Coetzer in an equally miserly spell. Earlier, Kane Williamson – about to join New Zealand's tour of the Caribbean – hit five fours as Gloucestershire laboured to what seemed a smallish total.*

At Bristol, June 27, 2012. **Warwickshire won by seven wickets.** ‡**Gloucestershire 122-7** (20 overs) (D. M. Housego 59*; P. M. Best 3-19); **Warwickshire 125-3** (18.1 overs) (V. Chopra 56*, J. O. Troughton 30). *MoM:* V. Chopra. *Attendance:* 860. *Left-arm spinner Paul Best claimed 3-19 (plus a catch and a run-out) in only his second T20 game to help limit Gloucestershire to 122. The result was not in doubt once Varun Chopra and Jim Troughton added 69 in 11 overs for the second wicket.*

At Bristol, July 2, 2012. **Gloucestershire v Glamorgan. Abandoned.**

At Bristol, July 5, 2012. **Gloucestershire won by seven wickets.** ‡**Worcestershire 159-6** (20 overs) (J. G. Cameron 32, G. M. Andrew 43, D. K. H. Mitchell 31); **Gloucestershire 160-3** (18 overs) (H. J. H. Marshall 72, E. J. M. Cowan 70). *MoM:* D. K. H. Mitchell. *Attendance:* 1,558. *County debut:* E. J. M. Cowan. *Hamish Marshall smashed 72 off 49 balls and shared a second-wicket stand of 142 in 15 overs with Australian debutant Ed Cowan as Gloucestershire easily overhauled their target. Gareth Andrew had top-scored for Worcestershire, while Daryl Mitchell smote 31 off 13 balls. Spinners Ed Young and Muralitharan had combined figures of 8–0–43–1.*

Gloucestershire away matches

June 17: lost to Worcestershire by 47 runs.
June 23: abandoned v Glamorgan.
June 29: beat Somerset by nine wickets.
July 6: abandoned v Warwickshire.
July 8: beat Northamptonshire by eight wickets (D/L).

NORTHAMPTONSHIRE

At Northampton, June 14, 2012 (floodlit). **No result. Northamptonshire 70-3** (9.3 overs) (K. J. Coetzer 41) v ‡**Glamorgan.** *County debuts:* C. L. White (Northamptonshire); S. E. Marsh (Glamorgan). *Kyle Coetzer struck eight fours in his 29 balls on competition debut for Northamptonshire. Glamorgan had not long disposed of him when rain swept in.*

At Northampton, June 23, 2012. **Worcestershire won by 14 runs.** ‡**Worcestershire 142-5** (20 overs) (P. J. Hughes 52, J. G. Cameron 57); **Northamptonshire 128-5** (20 overs) (K. J. Coetzer 33, C. L. White 62*). *MoM:* M. M. Ali. *Attendance:* 1,483. *A third-wicket stand of 101 in 11 overs between Phillip Hughes and James Cameron (who crashed 57 off 38 balls) gave Worcestershire a solid total. Despite a forthright fifty by Cameron White, Moeen Ali's accurate off-spin (4–0–14–0) helped inflict a fourth straight defeat on Northamptonshire, for whom Chaminda Vaas had claimed 4–0–15–2.*

At Northampton, June 26, 2012 (floodlit). **Somerset won by seven wickets. Northamptonshire 115-6** (20 overs) (A. G. Wakely 34); ‡**Somerset 116-3** (13.4 overs) (C. Kieswetter 51, R. E. Levi 35; C. D. de Lange 3-22). *MoM:* C. Kieswetter. *Attendance:* 1,403. *Unbeaten Somerset, little stretched with bat or ball, despatched winless Northamptonshire. Openers Craig Kieswetter and Richard Levi responded to Northamptonshire's below-par 115 with a spectacular stand of 61 inside six overs. Steve Kirby had taken two for 14 from his four.*

At Northampton, June 29, 2012 (floodlit). **Warwickshire won by seven wickets.** ‡**Northamptonshire 153-7** (20 overs) (C. L. White 39, R. I. Newton 38; C. R. Woakes 3-27); **Warwickshire 154-3** (16.1 overs) (R. Clarke 48, J. O. Troughton 68*, L. J. Evans 33*). *MoM:* J. O. Troughton. *Attendance:* 2,105. *Robust hitting from Rob Newton and Cameron White gave Northamptonshire a chance. But apart from losing Varun Chopra in the first over, it was a cruise for Warwickshire, thanks to Jim Troughton's unbeaten 49-ball 68* and three sixes in a final flourish from Laurie Evans.*

At Northampton, July 8, 2012. **Gloucestershire won by eight wickets** (D/L). **Northamptonshire 31-4** (8.3 overs); ‡**Gloucestershire 23-2** (2.2 overs). *MoM:* I. D. Saxelby. *Attendance:* 884. *County debut:* B. M. Duckett (Northamptonshire). *Victory in a rain-scarred game gained Gloucestershire a quarter-final place. Northamptonshire's innings had been interrupted before the weather brought it to a premature end. A target of 23 in five overs was little obstacle, despite the first-ball loss of Hamish Marshall. Northamptonshire, with David Ripley interim coach following the sacking of David Capel, had now endured 14 home defeats since last winning at Wantage Road, in July 2010.*

Northamptonshire away matches

June 17: lost to Somerset by five wickets.
June 19: lost to Warwickshire by six wickets.
June 22: lost to Gloucestershire by eight runs.
June 30: beat Glamorgan by nine wickets.
July 6: abandoned v Worcestershire.

SOMERSET

At Taunton, June 13, 2012. **Somerset won by 63 runs. Somerset 191-6** (20 overs) (R. E. Levi 69, J. A. Morkel 38); ‡**Warwickshire 128** (18.5 overs) (V. Chopra 37; A. C. Thomas 3-17, M. T. C. Waller 4-16). *MoM:* M. T. C. Waller. *Attendance:* 5,062. *County debuts:* R. E. Levi, J. A. Morkel, K. J. O'Brien (Somerset). *Richard Levi lived up to his reputation as a big-hitting opener, striking four sixes and six fours on his Somerset debut. Leg-spinner Max Waller then demolished Warwickshire's middle order.*

At Taunton, June 17, 2012. **Somerset won by five wickets.** ‡**Northamptonshire 137-5** (20 overs) (C. L. White 47*, D. J. Willey 30*); **Somerset 141-5** (19.5 overs) (J. C. Buttler 58*). *MoM:* J. C. Buttler. *Attendance:* 6,465. *Somerset recruit Kevin O'Brien earned bragging rights over brother*

Niall, catching him off George Dockrell for an all-Irish wicket in Northamptonshire's modest total. Jos Buttler twice scooped Chaminda Vaas to the boundary in the 19th over to help Somerset home.

At Taunton, June 22, 2012. **Somerset won by four wickets.** **‡Glamorgan 178-5** (20 overs) (S. E. Marsh 85, J. Allenby 33, M. van Jaarsveld 36); **Somerset 182-6** (19.5 overs) (J. C. Hildreth 107*). *MoM:* J. C. Hildreth. *Attendance:* 5,845. *Making liberal use of the sweep and reverse sweep, James Hildreth dominated Somerset's reply from the moment he arrived at 24-3, reaching his hundred – the only one of the tournament's group stages – from 53 balls; no one else passed 22. Earlier, Shaun Marsh had batted brilliantly for Glamorgan, striking 85 from 52 deliveries. Both teams wore black armbands in memory of Tom Maynard.*

At Taunton, June 29, 2012. **Gloucestershire won by nine wickets.** **‡Somerset 140-8** (20 overs) (J. A. Morkel 33); **Gloucestershire 141-1** (14.4 overs) (H. J. H. Marshall 66, B. A. C. Howell 55*). *MoM:* H. J. H. Marshall. *Attendance:* 7,731. *Hamish Marshall and Benny Howell's opening stand of 115 in 12 overs enabled Gloucestershire to make light work of a modest target. In front of a full house, Somerset's big hitters had self-destructed on a slow pitch.*

At Taunton, July 1, 2012. **Worcestershire won by 54 runs.** **Worcestershire 173-7** (20 overs) (M. M. Ali 47, V. S. Solanki 33, P. J. Hughes 41; S. P. Kirby 3-37); **‡Somerset 119** (19.1 overs) (D. K. H. Mitchell 3-13, B. L. D'Oliveira 3-20). *MoM:* M. M. Ali. *Attendance:* 7,168. *Moeen Ali, who faced just 23 balls, gave early impetus to a Worcestershire innings later boosted by six penalty runs for a tardy over-rate. Somerset were then stifled by their opponents' lack of pace: Daryl Mitchell's slow-medium and Brett D'Oliveira's leg-spin each claimed three wickets.*

Somerset away matches

June 14: abandoned v Gloucestershire.
June 21: no result v Warwickshire.
June 26: beat Northamptonshire by seven wickets.
July 6: abandoned v Glamorgan.
July 8: beat Worcestershire by seven wickets.

WARWICKSHIRE

At Birmingham, June 15, 2012 (floodlit). **Warwickshire v Worcestershire. Abandoned.** *This was the fourth washout in six scheduled days of cricket at Edgbaston after three blanks in the England v West Indies Test. Warwickshire were expecting a 25,000 crowd, since all tickets had been distributed free as part of a sponsorship deal.*

At Birmingham, June 19, 2012 (floodlit). **Warwickshire won by six wickets.** **‡Northamptonshire 149-4** (20 overs) (R. I. Newton 31, N. J. O'Brien 38, C. L. White 60*); **Warwickshire 152-4** (19 overs) (L. J. Evans 68*). *MoM:* L. J. Evans. *Attendance:* 2,154. *Laurie Evans, who reached his maiden Twenty20 half-century from 34 balls and shared a fifth-wicket stand of 67* in six overs with Chris Woakes, swept Warwickshire to victory. Northamptonshire had been squeezed by Steffan Piolet and Jeetan Patel – their eight overs cost 43 – and Cameron White's counter-attack was not enough.*

At Birmingham, June 21, 2012 (floodlit). **No result.** **Somerset 59-1** (7.1 overs) v **‡Warwickshire.** *Rain continued to blight cricket at Birmingham.*

At Birmingham, July 6, 2012 (floodlit). **Warwickshire v Gloucestershire. Abandoned.**

At Birmingham, July 8, 2012. **Glamorgan won by 22 runs** (D/L). **Glamorgan 173-5** (20 overs) (S. E. Marsh 68, M. van Jaarsveld 36); **‡Warwickshire 61-4** (9 overs). *MoM:* S. E. Marsh. *Attendance:* 3,621. *Victory would have given Warwickshire a quarter-final place, but they stuttered in pursuit of a challenging target, and were well short of par when rain ended proceedings early. Chris Woakes, released from England's one-day squad, had taken heavy punishment from Shaun Marsh, who added 76 in ten overs for the third wicket with Martin van Jaarsveld.*

Warwickshire away matches

June 13: lost to Somerset by 63 runs.
June 17: lost to Glamorgan by five runs (D/L).
June 22: beat Worcestershire by eight wickets.
June 27: beat Gloucestershire by seven wickets.
June 29: beat Northamptonshire by seven wickets.

WORCESTERSHIRE

At Worcester, June 17, 2012. **Worcestershire won by 47 runs.** ‡**Worcestershire 213-2** (20 overs) (M. M. Ali 82, P. J. Hughes 78*, G. M. Andrew 32*); **Gloucestershire 166** (18.5 overs) (H. J. H. Marshall 43, K. S. Williamson 37, J. K. Fuller 36; J. D. Shantry 4-33, G. M. Andrew 3-20). *MoM:* M. M. Ali. *Attendance:* 1,336. A *competition-best 82 off 44 balls by Moeen Ali, plus Phillip Hughes's slightly slower 78* – they added 100 in less than ten overs – ensured Worcestershire began on a winning note. Hamish Marshall hit a lightning 43 in his first match as Gloucestershire's Twenty20 captain, but they were never in contention.*

At Worcester, June 22, 2012. **Warwickshire won by eight wickets.** ‡**Worcestershire 120-7** (20 overs) (V. S. Solanki 32); **Warwickshire 123-2** (16.3 overs) (V. Chopra 49*, D. L. Maddy 39*). *MoM:* V. Chopra. *Attendance:* 2,918. *Despite a solid base, Worcestershire never came to terms with a sluggish pitch. Warwickshire off-spinner Jeetan Patel (4–0–15–1) and medium-pacer Steffan Piolet (4–0–21–2) exercised most control. Varun Chopra and Darren Maddy added 83* in 11 overs as Warwickshire eased home.*

At Worcester, June 29, 2012. **Worcestershire won by 19 runs. Worcestershire 164-5** (20 overs) (P. J. Hughes 87*, J. G. Cameron 31; S. P. Jones 3-29); ‡**Glamorgan 145-6** (20 overs) (S. J. Walters 40*, C. B. Cooke 32). *MoM:* P. J. Hughes. *Attendance:* 1,813. *Hughes's highest Twenty20 score – 87* from 57 balls – included four sixes, all off Will Owen. Glamorgan lurched to 57-5 in the 12th over, before Chris Cooke briefly made hay, striking three sixes in one over from Moeen Ali.*

At Worcester, July 6, 2012. **Worcestershire v Northamptonshire. Abandoned.**

At Worcester, July 8, 2012. **Somerset won by seven wickets. Worcestershire 119-7** (20 overs) (P. J. Hughes 45*; J. A. Morkel 3-30); ‡**Somerset 120-3** (18.5 overs) (N. R. D. Compton 42*, J. C. Hildreth 35*). *MoM:* N. R. D. Compton. *Attendance:* 2,179. *A straightforward win meant Somerset topped the group, but Worcestershire – despite their lowest total of the tournament – squeezed into the quarter-finals too, as one of the two best third-placed teams. Hughes provided their only real resistance with 45* from 50 balls. An unhurried stand of 59* in ten overs between Nick Compton and James Hildreth steered Somerset to victory.*

Worcestershire away matches

June 15: abandoned v Warwickshire.
June 23: beat Northamptonshire by 14 runs.
July 1: beat Somerset by 54 runs.
July 3: abandoned v Glamorgan.
July 5: lost to Gloucestershire by seven wickets.

NORTH GROUP

DERBYSHIRE

At Derby, June 14 (floodlit). **Derbyshire won by 17 runs** (D/L). **Lancashire 168-6** (20 overs) (S. C. Moore 34, S. J. Croft 46); ‡**Derbyshire 118-5** (11.3 overs) (W. J. Durston 31). *MoM:* W. J. Durston. *Attendance:* 1,270. *County debut:* Yasir Arafat (Lancashire). *Naved-ul-Hasan, recruited to bolster an inexperienced bowling attack, suffered the second-worst bowling analysis (4–0–56–0) for Derbyshire in Twenty20 (after Graeme Welch's 4–0–58–0 at Headingley in 2003). But he atoned by striking what proved to be the winning runs off Sajid Mahmood, who suffered a complete disintegration in the pivotal 12th over. He went for 17 off three legitimate deliveries – including wides and a no-ball – before rain became too heavy halfway through the over, terminating the match with Lancashire way behind on Duckworth/Lewis. To make matters worse, Mahmood was issued a penalty by the ECB for bad language.*

At Derby, June 18 (floodlit). **Yorkshire won by 41 runs.** ‡**Yorkshire 150-5** (20 overs) (A. W. Gale 39, J. E. Root 36, G. S. Ballance 47*); **Derbyshire 109** (20 overs) (R. M. Pyrah 3-21, M. A. Ashraf 4-18). *MoM:* G. S. Ballance. *Attendance:* 1,360. *Moin Ashraf and Rich Pyrah took the steam out of Derbyshire's challenge, but it was Gary Ballance's 47* off 35 balls, as Yorkshire added 28 in their last two overs, which changed the contest.*

At Derby, June 20 (floodlit). **Durham won by five wickets.** ‡**Derbyshire 141-6** (20 overs) (U. T. Khawaja 36); **Durham 142-5** (18.5 overs) (H. H. Gibbs 38, J. G. Myburgh 46). *MoM:* S. G.

Borthwick (Durham). *Attendance:* 2,186. *Johann Myburgh's unorthodox 46 got Durham home easily. Scott Borthwick removed Usman Khawaja in the first over of an eye-catching spell of 2-22.*

At Derby, June 29 (floodlit). **Leicestershire won by four wickets. ‡Derbyshire 171-3** (20 overs) (W. J. Durston 55*, C. F. Hughes 48, W. L. Madsen 33); **Leicestershire 173-6** (20 overs) (J. J. Cobb 42). *MoM:* R. M. L. Taylor (Leicestershire). *Attendance:* 1,977. *With Leicestershire needing 34 off 12 balls, Rob Taylor hit two sixes in Alex Hughes's penultimate over, before Wayne White, born in Derby, struck Naved's final delivery for four to complete an astonishing victory.*

At Derby, July 6 (floodlit). **Derbyshire v Nottinghamshire. Abandoned.**

Derbyshire away matches

June 15: no result v Nottinghamshire.
June 22: lost to Leicestershire by eight runs.
June 27: lost to Durham by eight wickets.
July 1: beat Lancashire by three wickets.
July 8: lost to Yorkshire by 21 runs.

DURHAM

At Chester-le-Street, June 17. **Nottinghamshire won by seven wickets. Durham 114-5** (20 overs) (J. G. Myburgh 45); **‡Nottinghamshire 117-3** (16.2 overs) (M. J. Lumb 46, A. D. Hales 30). *MoM:* M. J. Lumb. *Attendance:* 3,259. *Wet weather had not helped pitch preparation, and Durham slipped to 30-4. Johann Myburgh, signed three days earlier, made 45 off 41 balls. But an opening stand of 62 between Alex Hales and Michael Lumb allowed Nottinghamshire to canter home.*

At Chester-le-Street, June 22. **Yorkshire won by 12 runs. Yorkshire 171-6** (20 overs) (A. Lyth 30, J. E. Root 41, D. A. Miller 74*); **‡Durham 159** (19.5 overs) (H. H. Gibbs 76; R. J. Sidebottom 4-25, M. A. Starc 3-33). *MoM:* D. A. Miller. *Attendance:* 3,914. *Two big-hitting South Africans tormented their former counties: David Miller struck six sixes in 74* from 35 balls against his 2011 team-mates; thanks to him, Yorkshire scored 33 off their last two overs, including 19 off the last from Scott Borthwick. Durham were 113-2 in the 12th over but crumbled after Herschelle Gibbs – who played for Yorkshire in 2010 – drove to extra cover. Sidebottom's figures were his best in the format.*

At Chester-le-Street, June 27. **Durham won by eight wickets. ‡Derbyshire 131-7** (20 overs) (U. T. Khawaja 33); **Durham 132-2** (17.1 overs) (P. Mustard 35, H. H. Gibbs 83*). *MoM:* H. H. Gibbs. *Attendance:* 2,765. *Gibbs's 83* off 58 balls was Durham's record Twenty20 score, beating 80 by Ross Taylor here against Leicestershire in 2010. His three sixes towards the end brought some sparkle to an otherwise drab affair.*

At Chester-le-Street, July 1. **Durham won by nine wickets. Leicestershire 114-7** (20 overs) (Abdul Razzaq 47); **‡Durham 117-1** (13.2 overs) (P. Mustard 51, H. H. Gibbs 49*). *MoM:* P. Mustard. *Attendance:* 2,972. *Chris Rushworth opened the match with a maiden to Abdul Razzaq, then three more dots before the Pakistani hit him for four, six and four. Razzaq batted for all but three balls of Leicestershire's underwhelming innings.*

At Chester-le-Street, July 8. **Tied. Lancashire 133-8** (20 overs); **‡Durham 133-7** (20 overs) (P. Mustard 33). *MoM:* G. Chapple (Lancashire). *Attendance:* 3,027. *Both teams went into the final group game knowing a win would take them through as long as Essex lost to Hampshire. But by the time that match at Southampton was washed out, Durham had little chance of overhauling Essex on net run-rate, and Lancashire were out of it anyway. Glen Chapple equalled his most economical Twenty20 spell with 4–0–10–1 off the reel. Durham needed two to win off Ajmal Shahzad's last three balls, but Dale Benkenstein was caught by Paul Horton at short cover off a miscued hook and, after a scampered bye to the wicketkeeper, Gareth Breese pushed to Horton and was run out by a direct hit.*

Durham away matches

June 15: beat Yorkshire by two runs.
June 20: beat Derbyshire by five wickets.
June 25: lost to Lancashire by eight wickets.
June 29: lost to Nottinghamshire by 41 runs.
July 6: no result v Leicestershire.

LANCASHIRE

At Manchester, June 20. **Lancashire won by eight wickets.** ‡**Leicestershire 179-4** (20 overs) (Abdul Razzaq 61, M. A. G. Boyce 63*); **Lancashire 180-2** (19 overs) (S. C. Moore 54, T. C. Smith 42, S. J. Croft 41*, K. R. Brown 39*). *MoM:* G. Chapple (Lancashire). *Attendance:* 2,856. *Glen Chapple produced 2-10, the most economical performance for Lancashire from a full quota, but the other bowlers were taken apart by Matthew Boyce in 63* from 38 balls, his maiden Twenty20 fifty. Lancashire's powerful top four still reeled off the joint-highest run-chase by the county.*

At Manchester, June 22 (floodlit). **Lancashire v Nottinghamshire. Abandoned.**

At Manchester, June 25 (floodlit). **Lancashire won by eight wickets.** ‡**Durham 121** (19.2 overs) (G. R. Breese 33; Yasir Arafat 3-21, G. Keedy 4-25); **Lancashire 122-2** (14 overs) (T. C. Smith 40, S. J. Croft 65*). *MoM:* S. J. Croft. *Attendance:* 2,463. *Yasir Arafat, playing for his fourth county, helped Gary Keedy dismantle Durham on a turning surface.*

At Manchester, July 1. **Derbyshire won by three wickets. Lancashire 122-8** (20 overs) (S. J. Croft 48; Naved-ul-Hasan 3-20); ‡**Derbyshire 124-7** (18.5 overs) (W. J. Durston 56). *MoM:* W. J. Durston. *Attendance:* 3,982. *Wes Durston put a serious dent in Lancashire's knockout hopes. Opening both bowling and batting on a slow pitch, he had Stephen Moore stumped in the first over, and finished with 2-16; then he hit three sixes in the third over of the reply off Steven Croft – whose fourth consecutive score of 40-plus had given Lancashire a chance. But Derbyshire could even afford a late collapse.*

At Manchester, July 6 (floodlit). **Lancashire v Yorkshire. Abandoned.**

Lancashire away matches

June 14: lost to Derbyshire by 17 runs (D/L).
June 15: beat Leicestershire by 11 runs.
June 29: lost to Yorkshire by 19 runs.
July 3: lost to Nottinghamshire by eight wickets (D/L).
July 8: tied with Durham.

LEICESTERSHIRE

At Leicester, June 12. **Nottinghamshire won by six wickets. Leicestershire 96** (17.3 overs) (S. J. Mullaney 4-19); ‡**Nottinghamshire 98-4** (13 overs). *MoM:* S. J. Mullaney. *Attendance:* 1,535. *Leicestershire began their title defence with a lame 96, their lowest total in a competition they had won three times. Steven Mullaney did much of the damage with a wicket in each of his four overs.*

At Leicester, June 15. **Lancashire won by 11 runs. Lancashire 154-6** (20 overs) (S. C. Moore 58); ‡**Leicestershire 143-8** (20 overs) (J. J. Cobb 32, Abdul Razzaq 36). *MoM:* S. C. Moore. *Attendance:* 782. *Despite the best efforts of Abdul Razzaq, who took 2-19, then dealt some blows from No. 7, Leicestershire were outgunned by Stephen Moore's 58 from 44 balls.*

At Leicester, June 22. **Leicestershire won by eight runs.** Reduced to 8 overs a side. **Leicestershire 80-3** (8 overs); ‡**Derbyshire 72-6** (8 overs) (Abdul Razzaq 3-20). *MoM:* R. M. L. Taylor (Leicestershire). *Attendance:* 945. *Rain reduced the game to a short thrash, in which Rob Taylor had the decisive say with 2-7 in his two overs – ending Leicestershire's four-game losing streak.*

At Leicester, June 27. **Yorkshire won by four runs. Yorkshire 151-9** (20 overs) (D. A. Miller 37, R. M. Pyrah 35; N. L. Buck 3-28, Abdul Razzaq 3-37); ‡**Leicestershire 147-9** (20 overs) (R. R. Sarwan 39). *MoM:* R. M. Pyrah. *Attendance:* 1,535. *After a disciplined bowling display kept Yorkshire in check, Leicestershire required nine from the final over. But they were thwarted by Mitchell Starc, who bowled Wayne White (22) and Nathan Buck with the last two balls.*

At Leicester, July 6. **Leicestershire v Durham. Abandoned.**

Leicestershire away matches

June 17: lost to Yorkshire by 22 runs.
June 20: lost to Lancashire by eight wickets.
June 29: beat Derbyshire by four wickets.
July 1: lost to Durham by nine wickets.
July 8: lost to Nottinghamshire by 69 runs.

NOTTINGHAMSHIRE

At Nottingham, June 15. **Nottinghamshire v Derbyshire. Abandoned.**

At Nottingham, June 29. **Nottinghamshire won by 41 runs. ‡Nottinghamshire 210-3** (20 overs) (M. J. Lumb 36, A. D. Hales 88, M. H. Wessels 53; M. E. Claydon 3-34); **Durham 169-7** (20 overs) (B. A. Stokes 56). *MoM:* A. D. Hales. *Attendance:* 7,799. *A county-record second-wicket partnership of 142 between Alex Hales – who had scored 99 for England against West Indies here the previous weekend – and Riki Wessels proved far too much for Durham. Liam Plunkett was banned from the attack for bowling two head-high beamers; Wessels managed to pull both for four.*

At Nottingham, July 3. **Nottinghamshire won by eight wickets** (D/L). **Lancashire 178-4** (20 overs) (S. C. Moore 80, T. C. Smith 56, S. J. Croft 31*); **‡Nottinghamshire 52-2** (4.4 overs). *MoM:* S. C. Moore. *Attendance:* 2,706. *Lancashire's record 119-run opening stand between Stephen Moore and Tom Smith counted for little once rain intervened. Nottinghamshire were set a revised target of 49 off five overs and, after Yasir Arafat conceded 18 off the third to Michael Lumb (22) and Wessels (21*), they strolled it.*

At Nottingham, July 5 (floodlit). **Yorkshire won by six wickets. ‡Nottinghamshire 148-6** (20 overs) (A. C. Voges 70); **Yorkshire 150-4** (17.4 overs) (A. Lyth 33, P. A. Jaques 58*). *MoM:* P. A. Jaques. *Attendance:* 6,962. *After Joe Root removed Wessels with the game's opening ball, exemplary bowling from Mitchell Starc and Rich Pyrah under leaden skies kept Nottinghamshire grounded; Adam Voges was the only batsman to adjust to conditions. Yorkshire proved more adaptable, using the reverse sweep on several occasions. Victory carried them into the quarter-finals for the first time since 2007; it was Nottinghamshire's first home defeat in a group match for two years.*

At Nottingham, July 8. **Nottinghamshire won by 69 runs. Nottinghamshire 196-3** (20 overs) (M. J. Lumb 62, J. W. A. Taylor 45, M. H. Wessels 32); **‡Leicestershire 127-9** (20 overs) (Abdul Razzaq 69; A. Carter 3-12). *MoM:* M. J. Lumb. *Attendance:* 5,810. *Nottinghamshire, needing a win to confirm a home quarter-final, swatted Leicestershire aside with a rash of boundaries. Lumb faced only 26 balls, and hit five fours and six sixes. Abdul Razzaq received no support in the chase.*

Nottinghamshire away matches

June 12: beat Leicestershire by six wickets.
June 17: beat Durham by seven wickets.
June 22: no result v Lancashire.
June 24: no result v Yorkshire.
July 6: no result v Derbyshire.

YORKSHIRE

At Leeds, June 15. **Durham won by two runs. Durham 142-6** (20 overs) (B. A. Stokes 36); **‡Yorkshire 140-8** (20 overs) (R. M. Pyrah 34, G. L. Brophy 32). *MoM:* G. J. Muchall (Durham). *Attendance:* 2,441. *County debuts:* H. H. Gibbs, J. G. Myburgh (Durham). *A six by Azeem Rafiq off the first ball of the final over from Scott Borthwick left Yorkshire requiring ten to win. But the next was controversially saved on the boundary by Ben Stokes and, to the fifth, Rafiq let one go outside off-stump: no wide was signalled by umpire David Millns. Rafiq needed a four off the last ball but could manage only a single. His captain, Andrew Gale, was reprimanded by the ECB for strongly expressing his belief that both a four and wide should have been credited to Yorkshire's score. Two early wickets each for Chris Rushworth and Graham Onions had left Yorkshire 42-5, before Gerard Brophy and Rich Pyrah – in his first appearance since breaking his hand in the opening Championship game – staged a revival of 57 in seven overs.*

At Leeds, June 17. **Yorkshire won by 22 runs. ‡Yorkshire 170-4** (20 overs) (A. W. Gale 70, P. A. Jaques 48, D. A. Miller 30*); **Leicestershire 148** (20 overs) (J. J. Cobb 46, R. R. Sarwan 45; M. A. Starc 3-26). *MoM:* A. W. Gale. *Attendance:* 3,014. *Gale and Phil Jaques began with a Yorkshire-record opening stand of 116, and Mitchell Starc grabbed the last three Leicestershire wickets in the final over.*

At Scarborough, June 24. **No result. Nottinghamshire 105-3** (14 overs) (J. W. A. Taylor 41*) v **‡Yorkshire.** *A dismal afternoon was made worse by the failure of both electronic scoreboards due to the damp. James Taylor gave Nottinghamshire the edge before a third burst of rain ended proceedings.*

At Leeds, June 29. **Yorkshire won by 19 runs. Yorkshire 180-6** (20 overs) (P. A. Jaques 40, D. A. Miller 54, G. S. Ballance 42); ‡**Lancashire 161-5** (20 overs) (T. C. Smith 33, S. J. Croft 56, K. R. Brown 46). *MoM:* D. A. Miller. *Attendance:* 9,569. *Batsmen were kept in check until David Miller and Gary Ballance came together in a fifth-wicket stand of 91, a record for Yorkshire. Yasir Arafat became the first bowler to reach 100 wickets in English Twenty20, but also recorded Lancashire's most expensive figures (4–0–55–1). Their batsmen lacked sufficient firepower late on.*

At Leeds, July 8. **Yorkshire won by 21 runs. Yorkshire 180-5** (20 overs) (A. Lyth 78, P. A. Jaques 64); ‡**Derbyshire 159-9** (20 overs) (C. F. Hughes 30, Naved-ul-Hasan 40*; M. A. Ashraf 3-24). *MoM:* A. Lyth. *Attendance:* 3,034. *County debut:* C. M. Durham (Derbyshire). *Yorkshire's seventh consecutive win – excluding two no-results – meant they topped the group in their most successful Twenty20 season. For the second time in three weeks, they broke their first-wicket record, this time with 131 between Adam Lyth and Jaques. Naved-ul-Hasan, once of Yorkshire, blasted Pyrah for three consecutive sixes, followed by three twos, in the 16th over, but could not retain the strike enough to inflict more harm.*

Yorkshire away matches

June 18: beat Derbyshire by 41 runs.
June 22: beat Durham by 12 runs.
June 27: beat Leicestershire by four runs.
July 5: beat Nottinghamshire by six wickets.
July 6: no result v Lancashire.

SOUTH GROUP

ESSEX

At Chelmsford, June 20 (floodlit). **Essex won by three runs. Essex 158-6** (20 overs) (J. E. C. Franklin 39, J. S. Foster 51); ‡**Kent 155** (20 overs) (S. W. Billings 59; G. M. Smith 5-17). *MoM:* J. S. Foster. *Attendance:* 4,116. *Kent seemed likely winners at 118-3 at the start of the 16th over, but lost seven for 37. There was controversy in the 19th, when Matt Coles was dropped at midwicket and ran two. But the scorers entered a dot-ball instead, apparently distracted by dealing with a six-run penalty for Essex's slow over-rate which the umpires had just levied. Coles was out soon afterwards for six, and insisted he had actually scored eight. However, the ECB ruled the scores as recorded had to stand, and Essex edged home when Mark Davies, needing a four from Graham Napier's last delivery, was bowled. James Foster's earlier 51 from 27 balls, with four sixes, proved crucial.*

At Chelmsford, June 22 (floodlit). **Essex won by three wickets.** ‡**Surrey 144-9** (20 overs) (J. J. Roy 36, M. N. W. Spriegel 35; R. J. W. Topley 3-28); **Essex 145-7** (20 overs) (J. E. C. Franklin 63*; C. T. Tremlett 3-19). *MoM:* J. E. C. Franklin. *Attendance:* 5,747. *Essex's recent overseas signing James Franklin made a telling contribution in front of a packed house, batting through the innings – but it was Tim Phillips (15*) who rounded things off, scoring 13 of the 15 required from the final over.*

At Chelmsford, June 28 (floodlit). **Sussex won by four wickets.** ‡**Essex 177-4** (20 overs) (G. R. Napier 32, R. N. ten Doeschate 39, J. S. Foster 65*); **Sussex 181-6** (19.5 overs) (C. D. Nash 31, L. J. Wright 46, M. J. Prior 35). *MoM:* L. J. Wright. *Attendance:* 4,257. *Sussex's victory was set up by an opening stand of 77 in nine overs between Chris Nash and Luke Wright. It countered James Foster's flourish of 65* from 31 deliveries.*

At Chelmsford, June 29 (floodlit). **Hampshire won by six wickets. Essex 176-4** (20 overs) (J. E. C. Franklin 78, M. L. Pettini 38, J. S. Foster 30*); ‡**Hampshire 177-4** (18 overs) (J. M. Vince 32, S. M. Katich 42*, G. J. Maxwell 60*). *MoM:* G. J. Maxwell. *Attendance:* 5,672. *Hampshire's new signing, the Victoria all-rounder Glenn Maxwell, decided the match with a remarkable onslaught: he faced only 24 balls, but hit four sixes and six fours; 30 came in one over from Phillips – the leading Twenty20 wicket-taker of 2011 – and the winning six in the next. Franklin had underpinned the Essex innings with five fours and five sixes.*

At Chelmsford, July 5 (floodlit). **Essex won by two wickets.** ‡**Middlesex 109** (19.5 overs) (J. L. Denly 53); **Essex 110-8** (17.4 overs) (M. L. Pettini 50; T. M. J. Smith 3-24, O. Wilkin 3-12). *MoM:* M. L. Pettini. *Attendance:* 4,511. *County debut:* O. Wilkin (Middlesex). *Apart from Joe Denly, only Gareth Berg (12) made double figures for Middlesex. Essex made hard work of a modest target:*

Mark Pettini reached 50 from 38 balls, but of the others only Greg Smith (27) managed more than eight.

Essex away matches

June 13: lost to Surrey by 17 runs.
June 21: beat Middlesex by six runs.
June 24: lost to Sussex by 19 runs.
July 6: beat Kent by 23 runs.
July 8: abandoned v Hampshire.

HAMPSHIRE

At Southampton, June 18 (floodlit). **Middlesex won by six wickets.** **‡Hampshire 157-6** (20 overs) (J. M. Vince 64*; T. S. Roland-Jones 4-25); **Middlesex 161-4** (19.2 overs) (P. R. Stirling 71, D. J. Malan 46). *MoM:* P. R. Stirling. *Attendance:* 3,408. *County debut:* G. J. Maxwell (Hampshire). *Middlesex slipped to 18-2, but were rescued by Paul Stirling and Dawid Malan, who put on 107 for the third wicket. Hampshire's defeat was their first at home in 11 matches stretching back to July 2010.*

At Southampton, June 22 (floodlit). **Kent won by three runs.** **Kent 151-5** (20 overs) (S. A. Northeast 46*); **‡Hampshire 148-6** (20 overs) (J. M. Vince 31). *MoM:* S. A. Northeast. *Attendance:* 4,024. *Sam Northeast and Matt Coles plundered 36 from the final two overs of Kent's innings. Hampshire required 37 from their last two, but 18 from Coles's last of the match proved just beyond them once Dimitri Mascarenhas fell to the first ball.*

At Southampton, June 30. **Hampshire won by seven wickets.** **‡Surrey 94-6** (20 overs) (Z. S. Ansari 38*); **Hampshire 95-3** (15.3 overs) (M. Kartik 3-16). *MoM:* A. D. Mascarenhas. *Attendance:* 4,718. *Surrey were 9-4 after three overs, and 42-6 after 12, before Zafar Ansari and Gareth Batty prevented a rout with a stand of 52*. Murali Kartik took three wickets, reducing Hampshire to 53-3, but Glenn Maxwell (22*) took them home.*

At Southampton, July 6 (floodlit). **No result.** **Sussex 203-5** (17.4 overs) (L. J. Wright 38, M. J. Prior 81) v **‡Hampshire.** *Sussex were 84-1 after the six-over powerplay and, in all, Luke Wright and Matt Prior piled on 114 for the second wicket in 51 balls; Chris Wood's first two overs cost 35. However, rain prevented Sussex from cashing in on what was shaping up to be a huge total.*

At Southampton, July 8. **Hampshire v Essex. Abandoned.**

Hampshire away matches

June 14: abandoned v Sussex.
June 24: beat Kent by six wickets.
June 27: beat Middlesex by four wickets.
June 29: beat Essex by six wickets.
July 2: beat Surrey by 19 runs (D/L).

KENT

At Canterbury, June 12 (day/night). **Kent v Sussex. Abandoned.** *Originally scheduled for Tunbridge Wells, this match was shifted to the St Lawrence Ground after heavy rain – to no avail.*

At Beckenham, June 17. **Kent won by eight wickets.** **‡Surrey 116-7** (20 overs) (S. M. Davies 31, G. C. Wilson 53*); **Kent 120-2** (16.2 overs) (R. W. T. Key 51*, D. I. Stevens 43*). *MoM:* R. W. T. Key. *Attendance:* 3,086. *The match will be remembered as Tom Maynard's last for Surrey – he died on a railway line in south London only a few hours after the game.*

At Canterbury, June 24 (day/night). **Hampshire won by six wickets.** **‡Kent 135-6** (20 overs) (D. I. Stevens 60); **Hampshire 138-4** (18.2 overs) (J. H. K. Adams 31, G. J. Maxwell 66*). *MoM:* G. J. Maxwell. *Attendance:* 2,007. *Glenn Maxwell's dazzling 66* from 32 balls, which included six sixes, proved the match-defining knock as Hampshire romped to victory with ten deliveries to spare.*

At Canterbury, June 26 (day/night). **Middlesex won by 48 runs.** **‡Middlesex 207-2** (20 overs) (J. L. Denly 90*, P. R. Stirling 63, E. J. G. Morgan 36); **Kent 159-7** (20 overs) (S. A. Northeast 60, S. W. Billings 43; N. J. Dexter 3-22). *MoM:* J. L. Denly. *Attendance:* 2,891. *Middlesex recorded only their* *second win of the tournament – in some style, too. Joe Denly, returning to his old haunt, collected exactly 50 in boundaries and shared an excellent opening stand of 127 with Paul Stirling, who hit 63 from 37 balls. Azhar Mahmood later admitted on Twitter he had checked the internet to discover whether his 4–0–61–1 were the worst figures in domestic Twenty20 history. They weren't: James Kirtley returned 4–0–67–0 for Sussex v Essex at Chelmsford in 2008.*

At Canterbury, July 6 (day/night). **Essex won by 23 runs. Essex 149-5** (20 overs) (M. L. Pettini 59, G. M. Smith 32; D. I. Stevens 3-13); ‡**Kent 126-9** (20 overs) (R. J. W. Topley 3-19). *MoM:* M. L. Pettini. *Attendance:* 4,060. *A third successive home defeat confirmed Kent's failure to qualify for the knockout stages. Top-scorer Mark Pettini shared a second-wicket stand of 98 with Greg Smith to set up Essex's handy total, then two early run-outs, coupled with Reece Topley's fine stint, ensured Kent were never in the hunt.*

Kent away matches

June 20: lost to Essex by three runs.
June 22: beat Hampshire by three runs.
June 29: lost to Sussex by 83 runs.
July 5: beat Surrey by 48 runs.
July 8: beat Middlesex by three wickets.

MIDDLESEX

At Lord's, June 14 (day/night). **Surrey won by 28 runs** (D/L). ‡**Surrey 149-4** (20 overs) (M. N. W. Spriegel 53*, G. C. Wilson 54*); **Middlesex 99-8** (16 overs) (P. R. Stirling 36; G. J. Batty 4-13). *MoM:* G. J. Batty. *Attendance:* 13,993. *Irrespective of form, Middlesex often seem to struggle against their local rivals in Twenty20 cricket, and this fixture confirmed that trend: it was the 17th match between the two, and Surrey had now won 12. In fact, they had made a poor start – 34-4 after 37 balls – before Matthew Spriegel and Gary Wilson took them to a competitive total with a stand of 117*. Middlesex lurched from 64-1 in the eighth over to 86-8 in the 14th, and were well adrift of the par score when it rained.*

At Lord's, June 17. **Sussex won by 11 runs.** ‡**Sussex 143-8** (20 overs) (M. W. Goodwin 43, S. B. Styris 48; G. K. Berg 3-17); **Middlesex 132-8** (20 overs) (D. J. Malan 38, N. J. Dexter 36; C. J. Liddle 5-17). *MoM:* C. J. Liddle. *Attendance:* 11,179. *County debut:* J. Theron (Sussex). *Scott Styris, an important member of the Middlesex side who won the Twenty20 Cup in 2008, now top-scored for Sussex, with 48 from 30 balls. Left-arm seamer Chris Liddle then claimed a career-best 5-17.*

At Lord's, June 21 (day/night). **Essex won by six runs.** ‡**Essex 155-6** (20 overs) (R. N. ten Doeschate 38); **Middlesex 149-9** (20 overs) (G. K. Berg 39, O. P. Rayner 39*; T. J. Phillips 3-27). *MoM:* G. R. Napier. *Attendance:* 15,161. *Middlesex remained without a home win, despite a fine all-round performance from Ollie Rayner, who followed 2-16 with 39* from 21 balls. But, with slow left-armer Tim Phillips taking three wickets, Essex's total – boosted by 28 from 12 deliveries by Graham Napier, then later by Ryan ten Doeschate, who clubbed three sixes – was enough.*

At Richmond, June 27. **Hampshire won by four wickets. Middlesex 156-2** (20 overs) (P. R. Stirling 82*, D. J. Malan 30*); ‡**Hampshire 160-6** (19.2 overs) (S. M. Katich 40, S. M. Ervine 75*). *MoM:* S. M. Ervine. *Attendance:* 2,446. *Paul Stirling batted through the innings for a career-best 82* from 64 balls, but Middlesex became bogged down, particularly against the off-spin of Glenn Maxwell (4–1–18–0). Hampshire stumbled to 41-3, but Sean Ervine took them home with 75* from 51 deliveries.*

At Uxbridge, July 8. **Kent won by three wickets. Middlesex 124-9** (20 overs) (N. J. Dexter 42; D. I. Stevens 3-23); ‡**Kent 125-7** (19 overs) (Azhar Mahmood 30). *MoM:* D. I. Stevens. *Attendance:* 1,063. *Middlesex changed their batting order – Neil Dexter opened, and made 42 from 38 balls – but the result, on a slow pitch, was the same: they ended the Twenty20 season without a home win. The crowd were lucky to see any play at all after a lot of rain: the outfield was wet, and the ball often plugged on landing.*

Middlesex away matches

June 18: beat Hampshire by six wickets.
June 22: lost to Sussex by 21 runs.
June 26: beat Kent by 48 runs.
July 5: lost to Essex by two wickets.
July 6: beat Surrey by one wicket.

SURREY

At The Oval, June 13 (floodlit). **Surrey won by 17 runs.** ‡**Surrey 128-8** (20 overs) (G. C. Wilson 33; G. R. Napier 3-16); **Essex 111-9** (20 overs) (G. J. Batty 3-20). *MoM:* G. J. Batty. *Attendance:* 8,956. *County debut:* J. E. C. Franklin (Essex). *Surrey's slender total on a slow pitch owed much to Gary Wilson's run-a-ball innings and his stand of 40 with Zafar Ansari, but it seemed unlikely to be enough when Ravi Bopara and Mark Pettini put on 44 in 5.5 overs. However, Gareth Batty removed Owais Shah and Bopara in successive overs, and wickets continued to tumble regularly.*

At The Oval, July 2 (floodlit). **Hampshire won by 19 runs** (D/L). Reduced to 10 overs a side. ‡**Surrey 84-4** (10 overs) (S. M. Davies 30, Z. S. Ansari 35*); **Hampshire 63-0** (5.4 overs). *MoM:* L. A. Dawson. *Attendance:* 5,851. *This game was postponed from June 20 as a mark of respect following the death of Tom Maynard. It was a soggy and sombre affair. Once Steven Davies was out after hitting six of his 11 balls for four, only Ansari's late burst offered Surrey much hope as Liam Dawson (2-10) squeezed hard. James Vince and Jimmy Adams were particularly severe on the pacemen, before the rain returned with Hampshire well ahead of their required score.*

At The Oval, July 3 (floodlit). **Sussex won by six wickets** (D/L). **Surrey 106-6** (16.2 overs) (Z. de Bruyn 30*); ‡**Sussex 110-4** (11.4 overs) (L. J. Wright 32; G. J. Batty 3-11). *MoM:* L. J. Wright. *Attendance:* 11,714. *Sussex cemented their quarter-final place, and ended Surrey's own hopes. Surrey never really got going, and lost the last chunk of their innings to rain. Sussex's target was increased slightly to 109 in 15 overs, and they never looked troubled as Chris Nash crashed 22 from the first two, before Luke Wright (32 from 21 balls) and Matt Prior (25 from ten) waded in.*

At The Oval, July 5 (floodlit). **Kent won by 48 runs. Kent 136-8** (20 overs) (R. W. T. Key 35, A. J. Blake 35); ‡**Surrey 88** (17.3 overs) (Azhar Mahmood 3-12). *MoM:* A. J. Blake. *Attendance:* 15,735. *Rob Key's early work was backed up by the inventive Alex Blake, who reverse-swept liberally. Surrey lurched to 18-4 and, on a turning pitch, crumbled to their lowest Twenty20 total.*

At The Oval, July 6 (floodlit). **Middlesex won by one wicket.** ‡**Surrey 154-4** (20 overs) (K. P. Pietersen 42, S. M. Davies 37, J. J. Roy 40); **Middlesex 157-9** (19.5 overs) (N. J. Dexter 41). *MoM:* N. J. Dexter. *Attendance:* 16,226. *The biggest crowd of any of the qualifying games – even though neither side could make the quarter-finals – saw Surrey follow their lowest T20 total with their highest of the season, based on an opening stand of 76 between Davies and Kevin Pietersen. It looked more than enough when Middlesex dipped to 106-7, but the two Ollies, Rayner (14) and Wilkin (28), gleaned 46 from five overs, and they scraped home.*

Surrey away matches

June 14: beat Middlesex by 28 runs (D/L).
June 17: lost to Kent by eight wickets.
June 22: beat Essex by three wickets.
June 30: lost to Hampshire by seven wickets.
July 8: beat Sussex by seven wickets (D/L).

SUSSEX

At Hove, June 14 (floodlit). **Sussex v Hampshire. Abandoned.**

At Hove, June 22 (floodlit). **Sussex won by 21 runs.** ‡**Sussex 161-4** (20 overs) (L. J. Wright 91); **Middlesex 140-6** (20 overs) (J. L. Denly 36, J. A. Simpson 32). *MoM:* L. J. Wright. *Attendance:* 4,705. *Not even a sluggish pitch could inhibit Luke Wright, who produced some brutal hitting down the ground and to leg. Joe Denly and John Simpson gave Middlesex a good start, and it was only when Dawid Malan fell in the penultimate over that Sussex could feel comfortable. Thirty corporate guests went down with food poisoning; chicken parfait was the suspected culprit.*

At Hove, June 24. **Sussex won by 19 runs.** ‡**Sussex 209-6** (20 overs) (C. D. Nash 52, L. J. Wright 40, S. B. Styris 36, J. S. Gatting 45*; R. J. W. Topley 3-43); **Essex 190** (20 overs) (M. L. Pettini 44, G. M. Smith 39, J. S. Foster 47; C. J. Liddle 3-35). *MoM:* S. B. Styris. *Attendance:* 4,206. *Sussex took control of the group after Wright and Chris Nash plundered 74 in the powerplay. Joe Gatting took them past 200 with his best score in the competition and, although James Foster hit four sixes in a row, 25 off the final over proved far beyond Essex.*

At Hove, June 29 (floodlit). **Sussex won by 83 runs.** ‡**Sussex 212-6** (20 overs) (C. D. Nash 54, M. J. Prior 46, M. W. Goodwin 68*; S. J. Cook 3-41); **Kent 129** (19.4 overs) (S. W. Billings 38; M. J.

Rippon 4-23). *MoM:* M. W. Goodwin. *Attendance:* 6,111. *County debut:* M. J. Rippon. *On the day he signed an 18-month contract, the South African Michael Rippon enjoyed an outstanding debut for Sussex. After Amjad Khan had undermined his former county's reply with two key wickets, Rippon's slow left-arm chinamen proved unfathomable to Kent's middle order. Sussex had once again piled up the runs, helped by Nash's second successive half-century and Goodwin's 31-ball assault, which included 11 fours and two sixes.*

At Hove, July 8. **Surrey won by seven wickets** (D/L). ‡**Sussex 104-0** (9 overs) (C. D. Nash 41*, L. J. Wright 54*); **Surrey 64-3** (4.4 overs) (K. P. Pietersen 36*). *MoM:* L. J. Wright. *Attendance:* 4,946. *After lengthy rain delays, a patient crowd were rewarded with a cameo from Kevin Pietersen, which took Surrey – chasing a revised target of 62 in five overs – to victory. It was Sussex's only defeat of the group stages. Afterwards, their coach Mark Robinson called for an overhaul of the D/L regulations for Twenty20 matches, claiming his side deserved better after they had looked well on course for another 200-plus total before the first rain interruption.*

Sussex away matches

June 12: abandoned v Kent.
June 17: beat Middlesex by 11 runs.
June 28: beat Essex by four wickets.
July 3: beat Surrey by six wickets (D/L).
July 6: no result v Hampshire.

QUARTER-FINALS

At Taunton, July 24, 2012. **Somerset won by 27 runs. Somerset 175-6** (20 overs) (J. C. Buttler 33, J. C. Hildreth 58; R. J. W. Topley 3-27); ‡**Essex 148** (18.3 overs) (R. N. ten Doeschate 47; L. Gregory 4-39). *MoM:* J. C. Hildreth. *Attendance:* 6,678. *Somerset lost Craig Kieswetter to the first delivery of the game, but James Hildreth's 36-ball fifty ensured a competitive score in front of another substantial Taunton crowd. In reply, Essex slumped to 93-7 in the 14th over. Lewis Gregory claimed his fourth wicket when he ended a defiant late blitz from Ryan ten Doeschate – and the match.*

At Hove, July 24, 2012. **Sussex won by 39 runs. Sussex 230-4** (20 overs) (M. J. Prior 60, M. W. Goodwin 55, S. B. Styris 100*); ‡**Gloucestershire 191-8** (20 overs) (H. J. H. Marshall 42, D. M. Housego 47, A. P. R. Gidman 44). *MoM:* S. B. Styris. *Attendance:* 6,458. *Scott Styris, who came to the crease at 101-3 in the 12th over, catapulted Sussex to their third finals day with an electric 37-ball 100 – that won him the Walter Lawrence Trophy for the season's quickest century. Had Gloucestershire not fluffed a straightforward chance to run him out on seven, the match might have followed a different course. But Styris began a brutal assault all round the wicket that brought the second hundred of his Twenty20 career – and the joint-third-quickest in this format. Sussex plundered 115 from the last six overs as Styris cleared the ropes nine times. The frenzy reached its height in the 18th, from James Fuller. The first delivery was a beamer that sped to the fence for six no-balls; the second a front-foot no-ball that Styris belted for four; and the third – a free hit – he lofted for six. One legitimate ball had yielded 18 runs. The remaining five (including a dot) produced another 20, making it the most expensive over in Twenty20 history. Sussex had been 7-2 after two overs before Prior and Goodwin began the recovery. Gloucestershire lacked a batsman of sufficient power to threaten the summer's highest T20 total.*

At Nottingham, July 25, 2012. **Hampshire won by four wickets. Nottinghamshire 178-7** (20 overs) (M. J. Lumb 39, A. C. Voges 33, S. R. Patel 60; G. J. Maxwell 3-36); ‡**Hampshire 182-6** (20 overs) (N. D. McKenzie 79*, L. A. Dawson 30; S. R. Patel 3-26). *MoM:* N. D. McKenzie. *Attendance:* 11,127. *A partisan home crowd was left disappointed when Neil McKenzie showed all his experience to blast Hampshire to victory – and a third successive appearance on finals day. Hampshire required 12 as the last over, bowled by Andy Carter, began. Dimitri Mascarenhas failed to score from the first ball and stole a bye from the second. But McKenzie, now needing a runner, showed the coolest of heads to strike 14 off the last four. Had Nottinghamshire prevailed, the match award might perhaps have gone to Samit Patel for a rapid 60 and three wickets.*

At Leeds, July 25, 2012. **Yorkshire won by 29 runs.** ‡**Yorkshire 212-5** (20 overs) (A. W. Gale 30, J. E. Root 65, D. A. Miller 50, G. S. Ballance 46*); **Worcestershire 183-6** (20 overs) (P. J. Hughes 80*; M. A. Starc 3-24). *MoM:* J. E. Root. *Attendance:* 7,532. *Powerful hitting brought Yorkshire their second-highest Twenty20 total, before three wickets for Mitchell Starc – taking his total to 21, the most in the 2012 competition – marched them to their first finals day. Joe Root and David Miller* *followed up fifties with a stunning piece of fielding: Root caught Cameron on the deep midwicket boundary and, before his momentum took him over the rope, tossed the ball to Miller. Cameron and Hughes had added 75 for the third wicket and, although Hughes finished with 80* from 53 balls, Yorkshire were never in danger.*

FINALS DAY REPORTS BY HUGH CHEVALLIER

SEMI-FINALS

SUSSEX v YORKSHIRE

At Cardiff, August 25. Yorkshire won by 36 runs. Toss: Yorkshire.

Yorkshire, on their first trip to finals day, sauntered past Sussex to take their Twenty20 winning streak to nine. All but one of those victories had come batting first, though once the canny medium-pace of Styris reduced them to 36 for three in the sixth over, the strategy looked questionable. Not a bit of it: Bairstow, showing the coolness and clean hitting that had just brought two Test fifties at Lord's, put on 82 in ten overs with Miller, before accelerating his side to 172, the highest Twenty20 total at Cardiff for 15 months. At 55 for two in the ninth over, Sussex might have had the platform on which to build if only they had possessed more than one batsman in any sort of touch. Nash perfected the Dilscoop – scoring 24 in boundaries over his left shoulder – but hare-brained batting at the other end nullified his inventiveness. Their last hope vanished with Styris, the conjuror of a miraculous hundred in their quarter-final.

Man of the Match: J. M. Bairstow.

Attendance (for all three matches on finals day): 14,848.

Yorkshire

		B	*4*	*6*
*A. W. Gale *c 1 b 6*	11	7	2	0
P. A. Jaques *b 6*	2	9	0	0
J. E. Root *lbw b 6*	11	12	2	0
†J. M. Bairstow *not out*	68	45	2	3
D. A. Miller *c 5 b 1*	47	35	4	2
G. S. Ballance *c 8 b 11*	7	6	0	0
T. T. Bresnan *c 4 b 11*	6	3	1	0
R. M. Pyrah *not out*	3	4	0	0
L-b 15, n-b 2	17			
6 overs: 40-3 (20 overs)	172-6			

1/13 2/19 3/36 4/118 5/147 6/153

Azeem Rafiq, R. J. Sidebottom and M. A. Ashraf did not bat.

Yardy 4–0–23–0; Styris 4–1–22–3; Liddle 3–0–26–2; Beer 3–0–30–0; Khan 3–0–24–0; Nash 2–0–20–1; Wright 1–0–12–0.

Sussex

		B	*4*	*6*
C. D. Nash *not out*	80	58	8	2
L. J. Wright *b 10*	3	4	0	0
†M. J. Prior *c 6 b 7*	2	3	0	0
M. W. Goodwin *c 6 b 8*	15	17	1	0
J. S. Gatting *b 8*	3	6	0	0
S. B. Styris *c 6 b 9*	8	8	0	0
M. W. Machan *c 4 b 7*	7	8	1	0
*M. H. Yardy *run out*	2	7	0	0
W. A. T. Beer *run out*	3	4	0	0
A. Khan *not out*	5	5	0	0
B 1, w 7	8			
6 overs: 39-2 (20 overs)	136-8			

1/12 2/15 3/55 4/62 5/81 6/93 7/101 8/123

C. J. Liddle did not bat.

Root 1–0–3–0; Sidebottom 3–0–28–1; Bresnan 4–0–22–2; Pyrah 4–0–30–2; Ashraf 4–0–31–0; Azeem Rafiq 4–0–21–1.

Umpires: M. A. Gough and J. W. Lloyds. Third umpire: R. J. Bailey.

HAMPSHIRE v SOMERSET

At Cardiff, August 25. Hampshire won by six wickets. Toss: Hampshire.

For the third summer running, these teams squared up on county cricket's big day out. But unlike the electric encounters of the past two years – both had required tie-breakers – this was a one-sided affair decided by the control of the Hampshire bowlers in general, and of their wily captain in particular. By the end of the eighth over, Mascarenhas had pilfered two for 11 from 24 balls of niggling medium-pace, and Somerset had limped to 35 for the loss of three heavyweights. Kieswetter rode his luck to cling on, steering his side past three figures, if not beyond the previous lowest 20-over score on finals day. Trescothick, who had batted at No. 3 in a Somerset team overflowing with openers, needed discipline from his attack, but Thomas – so often the man for the task – was out of sorts. So too was Carberry, who never did find the centre of his bat, despite making a helpful 33. Hampshire briefly looked vulnerable at 72 for four, before the experience of Katich and Ervine guided them to a modest target with few alarums or excursions. It ended Somerset's run of reaching (and losing) five successive limited-overs finals.

Man of the Match: S. M. Ervine.

Somerset

		B	*4*	*6*
†C. Kieswetter *not out*	63	58	5	1
R. E. Levi *c 5 b 8*	1	4	0	0
*M. E. Trescothick *b 8*	12	9	1	1
J. C. Hildreth *b 11*	1	8	0	0
J. C. Buttler *b 6*	16	15	1	1
P. D. Trego *lbw b 6*	1	7	0	0
L. Gregory *run out*	9	10	1	0
A. V. Suppiah *not out*	12	9	0	0
B 1, l-b 7, w 2	10			
6 overs: 29-2 (20 overs)	125-6			

1/6 2/22 3/30 4/54 5/58 6/90

A. C. Thomas, M. T. C. Waller and S. P. Kirby did not bat.

Dawson 4–0–30–0; Mascarenhas 4–0–11–2; Briggs 4–0–29–1; Wood 4–0–25–0; Ervine 4–0–22–2.

Hampshire

		B	*4*	*6*
M. A. Carberry *run out*	33	27	5	0
J. H. K. Adams *c 5 b 11*	8	11	1	0
J. M. Vince *b 10*	7	10	1	0
N. D. McKenzie *lbw b 7*	10	13	0	0
S. M. Katich *not out*	32	30	2	0
S. M. Ervine *not out*	34	23	5	0
W 2	2			
6 overs: 40-1 (19 overs)	126-4			

1/33 2/44 3/52 4/72

L. A. Dawson, *A. D. Mascarenhas, C. P. Wood, †M. D. Bates and D. R. Briggs did not bat.

Thomas 4–0–40–0; Trego 4–0–22–0; Kirby 3–0–16–1; Waller 4–0–27–1; Gregory 2–0–9–1; Suppiah 2–0–12–0.

Umpires: R. J. Bailey and N. G. B. Cook. Third umpire: J. W. Lloyds.

FINAL

HAMPSHIRE v YORKSHIRE

At Cardiff, August 25 (floodlit). Hampshire won by ten runs. Toss: Hampshire.

An astonishing display of brutal strokeplay abruptly transformed a humdrum game into a minor classic. Eleven overs into their pursuit of 151, Yorkshire were languishing at 53 for four, bereft of momentum or confidence. Bairstow, the morning's star, had barely shone, and Miller had maundered to nine from 18 balls. Their last hope was an innings of comic-strip heroism, which was pretty much what happened.

Miller, it turned out, was simply getting his eye in. Yorkshire had taken two runs from Ervine's first over, but from his next four balls Miller middled three sixes, all in the V and increasingly humungous. Anyone walking between the ground and the River Taff risked injury as white balls rained down. The volley of maximums put a dent in both the public footpath and the asking-rate and, after 15 runs came from the 18th over, Miller had zipped to 65 from 40 balls with five sixes and five fours. Momentum? Confidence? You bet!

Yorkshire now needed a gettable 21 from 12 deliveries. In fact, since they were ahead on the six-over score, they needed 20 (provided they lost no more than one wicket), and it was Hampshire searching for answers. Left-arm spinner Briggs came up with some, pitching shorter to Miller to limit his potential for straight hitting, and yielding just seven to leave the game delicately poised: 14 (maybe 13) off the last over.

The trouble for Yorkshire was that Bresnan was on strike – though not for long: he skied Wood's first ball to point, which did at least get Miller to the business end. Wood's next ball was full, and it was all Miller could do to scrape a single; momentum and confidence were ebbing away. Wood kept his length sensibly full, and as the runs dried up so Yorkshire hopes vanished in a flurry of wickets.

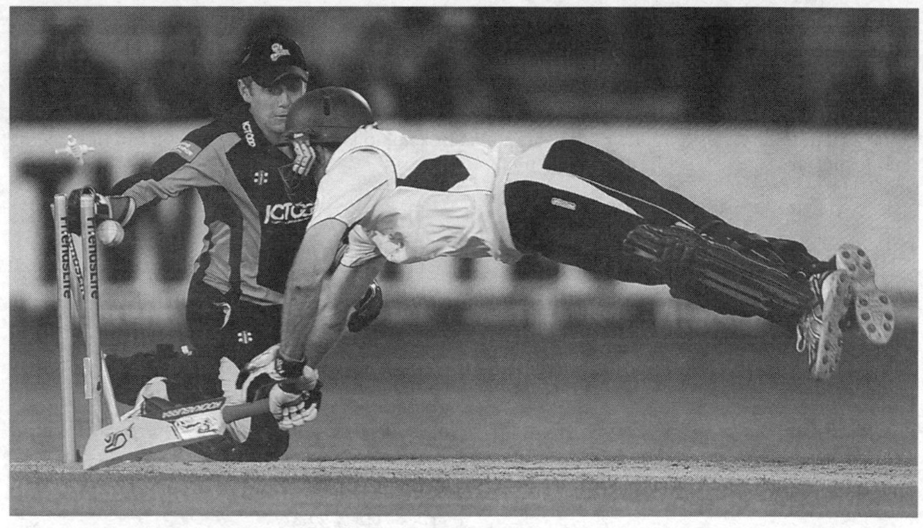

Stu Forster, Getty Images

Incoming flight: Simon Katich's dive is too late, but his 25 runs gave Hampshire a defendable total.

Mascarenhas, keen to scupper his opponents' successful strategy of setting a target, had chosen to bat – despite Hampshire's habitual preference for chasing. Progress was tricky on an increasingly slow pitch, and both Adams and Vince fell just as they seemed to be getting its measure. McKenzie, who had endured a poor tournament, was fined for dissent after protesting he had edged a full toss from the combative Rafiq on to his pads. Impatience then did for Ervine, and Hampshire needed the nous of Katich to drag them to 150. That seemed about par until Yorkshire's top order played a series of panicky strokes. Once again Mascarenhas proved himself the master of cheese-paring medium-pace. Hampshire thought they had removed Miller on seven when he flicked Dawson to McKenzie at midwicket, but the replays – as so often – failed to prove whether the ball had carried. Miller survived to light up the closing stages, and few complained about that.

Man of the Match: D. A. Miller.

Hampshire

		B	*4*	*6*
M. A. Carberry *b 10*	8	10	1	0
J. H. K. Adams *c 6 b 8*	43	37	3	1
J. M. Vince *b 11*	36	33	3	0
N. D. McKenzie *lbw b 9*	4	4	0	0
S. M. Ervine *c 3 b 10*	21	15	0	1
S. M. Katich *run out*	25	16	3	0
L. A. Dawson *not out*	8	5	0	0
L-b 1, w 4	5			
6 overs: 36-1 (20 overs)	150-6			

1/23 2/70 3/76 4/113 5/131 6/150

*A. D. Mascarenhas, C. P. Wood, †M. D. Bates and D. R. Briggs did not bat.

Root 1–0–9–0; Sidebottom 4–0–20–2; Bresnan 3–0–18–0; Pyrah 4–0–37–1; Ashraf 4–0–43–1; Azeem Rafiq 4–0–22–1.

Yorkshire

		B	*4*	*6*
*A. W. Gale *b 8*	15	14	3	0
P. A. Jaques *b 7*	11	13	1	0
J. E. Root *b 8*	7	9	0	0
†J. M. Bairstow *c 10 b 11*	3	5	0	0
D. A. Miller *not out*	72	46	5	5
G. S. Ballance *c 11 b 5*	7	16	0	0
T. T. Bresnan *c 5 b 9*	18	14	2	0
R. M. Pyrah *b 9*	1	2	0	0
Azeem Rafiq *c 5 b 9*	0	1	0	0
B 1, l-b 3, w 2	6			
6 overs: 37-2 (20 overs)	140-8			

1/24 2/34 3/38 4/47 5/87 6/137 7/140 8/140

R. J. Sidebottom and M. A. Ashraf did not bat.

Dawson 4–0–21–1; Mascarenhas 4–0–20–2; Wood 4–0–26–3; Briggs 4–0–27–1; Ervine 4–0–42–1.

Umpires: R. J. Bailey and M. A. Gough. Third umpire: N. G. B. Cook.

A list of winners of the Twenty20 competition 2003–2011 can be found on page 643 of Wisden 2012.

CLYDESDALE BANK 40, 2012

REVIEW BY JON CULLEY

A playing format familiar to domestic audiences in England since the debut of the Sunday League in 1969 does not endure so long without a strong body of followers. As 40-over cricket receives the last rites, there is evidence its passing will sadden more than a few hearts.

The attendance at Lord's for the Clydesdale Bank 40 final was relatively modest: 17,808, compared to the 25,000 who regularly flocked to the old 50- or 60-over showpieces. But around the country, core support remained steady. For most counties, the average turnout varied from about 1,500 to 3,000 – not spectacular, but at least respectable in a damp summer with 14 outright abandonments.

It remains to be seen whether the reversion to 50 overs in 2014 will have any serious impact on gates. When the Morgan Review – published in January 2012 – recommended English cricket fall back into line with the one-day international format, the counter-argument put forward by many county chief executives was that Sunday afternoon matches, of a slightly shorter duration, were more attractive to young families. The ECB decided they needed a wider range of feedback, and commissioned a survey into the entire domestic structure. Results from 25,000 cricket followers expressed "no compelling preference" for the 40-over format – sealing its fate.

Scotland were resigned to being excluded from the new structure, for the first time in 25 years, and went in search of more fixtures against ICC Full Members and their A-teams. They were right to do so: the ECB's plans for 2014 included a streamlined 18-county group stage, with Scotland, the Netherlands and the Unicorns all elbowed out. The return of quarter-finals should cut down on the meaningless raft of games at the tail-end of the CB40, which many fear are ripe for spot-fixing when shown on television – something the ECB belatedly recognised by appointing an anti-corruption team to monitor the later rounds in 2012.

Hampshire's thrilling last-ball triumph over Warwickshire at Lord's was unusual in a season with few tickertape finishes, and completed a double for them in the limited-overs competitions – the first by a county since Adam Hollioake's Surrey won the Twenty20 Cup and National League in 2003.

With his innings of 35 in the final, Hampshire opener Michael Carberry nudged ahead of Lancashire's Stephen Moore as the CB40's leading run-scorer, despite missing two months of the season with a knee injury. Only twice did Carberry fail to make a half-century, and six of his seven fifties were in a winning cause. He converted two to hundreds, of which his unbeaten 148 against Scotland was the highest by anyone. Carberry's tally of 16 sixes was bettered only by Eoin Morgan of Middlesex and Yorkshire's Gary Ballance. And his average over nine innings was a remarkable 85, to go with a strike-rate of 104.

Carberry did not win the title on his own, of course. His opening partner James Vince, with whom he shared two century stands, had his worst summer in first-class cricket, but his best in the CB40. Hampshire's two most exciting young bowlers, Chris Wood and Danny Briggs, took 19 wickets each, two fewer than the competition's leading wicket-taker, Ajmal Shahzad, who played all his games on loan at Lancashire. Like Briggs, Gary Keedy, who finished with 20 wickets, was often overlooked for selection in the Championship, but remained vital to his county's one-day success.

Given that Lancashire won more matches than anyone in the qualifying stage, topped Group A by four points, and had two batsmen – Moore and Steven Croft – scoring over 500 runs, their disappointment at losing to Warwickshire in the semi-final was acute. If any county needed consolation, it was Lancashire: six days after that defeat, they were relegated in the Championship, having won it so memorably in 2011.

A Lancashire player also produced the fastest century, although Tom Smith's phenomenal 44-ball destruction of Worcestershire came in an abandoned game. Morgan needed just five more balls to make his hundred against Lancashire at Lord's. His strike-rate over four innings was nearly 147.

FASTEST HUNDREDS IN ENGLISH LIST A CRICKET

Balls			
36	G. D. Rose	Somerset v Devon at Torquay	1990
43	R. R. Watson	Scotland v Somerset at Edinburgh	2003
44	M. A. Ealham	Kent v Derbyshire at Maidstone	1995
44	**T. C. Smith**	**Lancashire v Worcestershire at Worcester**	**2012**
46	G. D. Rose	Somerset v Glamorgan at Neath	1990
47	M. P. Speight	Sussex v Somerset at Taunton	1993
48	A. J. Lamb	Northamptonshire v Sussex at Northampton	1992
49	**E. J. G. Morgan**	**Middlesex v Lancashire at Lord's**	**2012**

Balls faced are not available for many matches.

Lancashire's wicket count of 100 was more than any other county, yet it was Warwickshire who possessed arguably the most efficient bowling unit. They took all ten wickets five times in the group stage, and repeated the trick in the semi-final, with three Lancashire batsmen falling to Chris Wright, who supplemented his 62 Championship victims with 20 in this competition.

Luke Wright, of beaten semi-finalists Sussex, scored three hundreds, as did Durham's opening pair of Phil Mustard – who had a strike-rate of 143 – and Mark Stoneman, who shared three 150-plus stands at home; their team could not win away. Defending champions Surrey lost a crucial game at Southampton in August, a result overshadowed by a first-ball duck for Kevin Pietersen in his first match since being dropped from England's Test side for the texts saga.

Kent had most reason to grumble about the absence of quarter-finals. They beat Warwickshire home and away, and had a superior run-rate, yet were denied the last semi-final spot on fewer wins – punishment for being the only team to lose to the semi-professional Unicorns. Darren Stevens, now aged 36, took 20 wickets, while Matt Coles began with six for 32 against Yorkshire. That remained the best analysis of the competition, until Abdur Rehman claimed six for 16 for Somerset against Nottinghamshire in August.

For a while, it looked as if the real story would be the Netherlands. They won five of their first seven matches, including victories by one run over Gloucestershire and one wicket over Lancashire. There was also a handsome win at Leicester, where Australian all-rounder Michael Swart scored a century and took three wickets.

His opening partner, Stephan Myburgh, began the competition with 77, 74 not out and 66. But after his hand was broken by Nathan Buck in the return match against Leicestershire, the Netherlands fell away dramatically, losing their last five games – and were bowled out for 57 by Worcestershire and 68 by Lancashire. Their final points haul was worse than they managed in 2011. Despite that, their record over three seasons in the CB40 was superior to four of the counties.

Prize money

£150,000 (no change from 2011) for winners: HAMPSHIRE.
£75,000 (no change) for runners-up: WARWICKSHIRE.
£25,000 (no change) for losing semi-finalists: LANCASHIRE, SUSSEX.
In 2012, there was no financial reward for winning individual matches.

Attendance figures supplied by the ECB and the counties. Approximate figures are given for the home matches of Scotland, Netherlands and Unicorns.

FINAL GROUP TABLES

Group A	*Played*	*Won*	*Lost*	*Tied*	*No result*	*Points*	*NRR*
LANCASHIRE	12	9	2	0	1	19	0.05
Middlesex	12	6	3	1	2	15	0.77
Gloucestershire	12	5	5	0	2	12	0.99
Netherlands	12	5	6	0	1	11	−0.91
Essex	12	4	6	0	2	10	−0.18
Leicestershire	12	3	6	0	3	9	−0.73
Worcestershire	12	3	7	1	1	8	−0.01

Group B	*Played*	*Won*	*Lost*	*Tied*	*No result*	*Points*	*NRR*
HAMPSHIRE	12	7	3	0	2	16	0.75
Surrey	12	6	3	0	3	15	0.46
Somerset	12	6	4	0	2	14	0.38
Nottinghamshire	12	6	5	0	1	13	0.10
Durham	12	5	5	0	2	12	0.26
Glamorgan	12	3	6	0	3	9	−0.97
Scotland	12	1	8	0	3	5	−1.35

Group C	*Played*	*Won*	*Lost*	*Tied*	*No result*	*Points*	*NRR*
SUSSEX	12	7	1	0	4	18	1.01
WARWICKSHIRE	12	8	3	0	1	17	0.66
Kent	12	7	2	0	3	17	0.87
Derbyshire	12	4	5	0	3	11	−0.43
Yorkshire	12	4	7	0	1	9	0.00
Northamptonshire	12	1	6	0	5	7	−0.56
Unicorns	12	1	8	0	3	5	−1.54

Where two or more counties finished with an equal number of points, the positions were decided by (a) most wins (b) net run-rate (runs scored per over minus runs conceded per over) (c) most points in head-to-head matches (d) drawing lots.

CLYDESDALE BANK 40 AVERAGES

BATTING (250 runs at 45.00)

		M	I	NO	R	HS	100	50	Avge	SR	4	6
1	†E. J. G. Morgan (*Middx*)	6	4	1	263	120*	2	0	87.66	146.92	19	17
2	†M. A. Carberry (*Hants*)	10	9	2	598	148*	2	5	85.42	104.72	68	16
3	†C. J. L. Rogers (*Middx*)	8	8	4	335	122*	1	2	83.75	101.20	35	3
4	†P. J. Hughes (*Worcs*)	10	9	3	498	111	2	4	83.00	84.98	40	6
5	†M. D. Stoneman (*Durham*)	11	10	2	558	136*	3	2	69.75	98.23	62	4
6	J. W. A. Taylor (*Notts*)	8	8	2	385	115*	1	2	64.16	91.88	30	7
7	L. J. Wright (*Sussex*)	8	8	1	418	122	3	1	59.71	106.90	52	6
8	†G. S. Ballance (*Yorks*)	11	11	3	469	103*	1	3	58.62	105.15	38	17
9	S. J. Croft (*Lancs*)	13	13	4	513	82	0	6	57.00	92.63	35	10
10	†D. J. Malan (*Middx*)	10	10	2	445	134	1	2	55.62	104.46	41	11
11	J. M. Vince (*Hants*)	14	13	3	554	102*	1	3	55.40	101.64	69	3
12	T. R. Ambrose (*Warwicks*)	11	9	3	321	87*	0	3	53.50	91.45	32	1
13	S. C. Moore (*Lancs*)	13	13	2	581	113	1	6	52.81	103.93	70	5
14	V. Chopra (*Warwicks*)	11	11	2	472	110	1	3	52.44	78.27	45	4
15	†S. J. Myburgh (*Neth*)	9	9	2	346	77	0	3	49.42	109.84	42	11
16	G. J. Muchall (*Durham*)	11	10	2	395	96*	0	3	49.37	84.94	27	4
17	†P. Mustard (*Durham*)	11	10	0	475	143	3	1	47.50	143.07	49	14
18	A. G. Wakely (*Northants*)	10	9	1	366	85	0	4	45.75	81.87	27	6
19	K. R. Brown (*Lancs*)	13	11	4	319	87*	0	2	45.57	86.21	26	7
20	S. W. Billings (*Kent*)	11	11	4	315	143	1	1	45.00	100.00	44	1

BOWLING (12 wickets at 25.00)

		Style	O	M	R	W	BB	4I	Avge	SR	ER
1	L. M. Daggett (*Northants*)	RFM	28	1	136	12	4-31	3	11.33	14.00	4.85
2	J. Allenby (*Glam*)	RM	49.5	5	183	12	3-16	0	15.25	24.91	3.67
3	C. D. de Lange (*Northants*)	SLA	44	1	191	12	3-31	0	15.91	22.00	4.34
4	D. I. Stevens (*Kent*)	RM	74.1	2	326	20	5-36	2	16.30	22.25	4.39
5	M. T. Coles (*Kent*)	RFM	52.2	3	281	17	6-32	1	16.52	18.47	5.36
6	G. J. Batty (*Surrey*)	OB	55	0	247	14	3-4	0	17.64	23.57	4.49
7	J. K. Fuller (*Glos*)	RFM	46.1	1	250	14	6-35	1	17.85	19.78	5.41
8	C. Rushworth (*Durham*)	RFM	47.3	1	280	15	5-31	1	18.66	19.00	5.89
9	G. G. White (*Notts*)	SLA	45.3	2	232	12	3-28	0	19.33	22.75	5.09
10	D. J. Pattinson (*Notts*)	RFM	36.4	1	239	12	3-27	0	19.91	18.33	6.51
11	C. R. Woakes (*Warwicks*)	RFM	56	4	279	14	4-24	1	19.92	24.00	4.98
12	G. Keedy (*Lancs*)	SLA	76.2	1	401	20	5-55	1	20.05	22.90	5.25
13	A. Shahzad (*Lancs*)	RFM	70.5	1	431	21	4-51	1	20.52	20.23	6.08
14	C. J. C. Wright (*Warwicks*)	RFM	82	3	416	20	3-43	0	20.80	24.60	5.07
15	T. D. Groenewald (*Derby*)	RFM	70	7	320	15	3-30	0	21.33	28.00	4.57
16	K. H. D. Barker (*Warwicks*)	LFM	54.5	1	258	12	3-27	0	21.50	27.41	4.70
17	D. R. Briggs (*Hants*)	SLA	84	1	410	19	4-32	1	21.57	26.52	4.88
18	S. P. Crook (*Middx*)	RFM	54	0	303	14	3-26	0	21.64	23.14	5.61
19	J. W. Dernbach (*Surrey*)	RFM	56.1	3	299	13	3-39	0	23.00	25.92	5.32
20	J. C. Tredwell (*Kent*)	OB	61.4	1	300	13	4-24	1	23.07	28.46	4.86
21	C. J. Liddle (*Sussex*)	LFM	61.5	1	330	14	4-21	1	23.57	26.50	5.33
22	M. L. Turner (*Derby*)	RFM	65.1	0	408	17	4-38	2	24.00	23.00	6.26
23	J. D. Shantry (*Worcs*)	LFM	78.3	3	490	20	4-32	2	24.50	23.55	6.24
24	R. M. Haq (*Scotland*)	OB	67.5	0	320	13	3-42	0	24.61	31.30	4.71
25	P. D. Trego (*Somerset*)	RFM	61.4	2	372	15	3-26	0	24.80	24.66	6.03
26	P. M. Seelaar (*Neth*)	SLA	64	0	298	12	4-42	1	24.83	32.00	4.65

GROUP A

ESSEX

At Chelmsford, May 13. **Worcestershire won by seven wickets. Essex 190-9** (40 overs) (M. L. Pettini 64, A. N. Cook 47); ‡**Worcestershire 191-3** (33.5 overs) (M. M. Ali 99, V. S. Solanki 48). *Attendance:* 2,208. *Moeen Ali missed a century when he pulled Alviro Petersen to deep midwicket attempting a fourth six. Essex had lost their way after Mark Pettini and Alastair Cook opened with 84 in 17 overs.*

At Chelmsford, June 4. **Essex won by eight wickets. Gloucestershire 224-5** (40 overs) (K. S. Williamson 77, I. A. Cockbain 52*); ‡**Essex 225-2** (36.5 overs) (R. S. Bopara 120*, T. Westley 82). *Attendance:* 2,644. *Ravi Bopara, forced out of the Test series against West Indies by a thigh injury, returned to action with a sumptuous 120* from 100 balls, including an entertaining second-wicket stand of 185 with Tom Westley.*

At Chelmsford, July 18 (day/night). **Middlesex won by nine wickets.** Reduced to 25 overs a side. **Essex 146-7** (25 overs) (M. L. Pettini 44; T. S. Roland-Jones 3-25); ‡**Middlesex 148-1** (22.3 overs) (C. J. L. Rogers 64, D. J. Malan 76*). *Attendance:* 2,621. *An early double-wicket maiden for Toby Roland-Jones put Middlesex on course in a rain-reduced match, despite 44 from Pettini, captain for the day as James Foster was with his expectant wife. Adam Wheater's explosive 33 included a six through the window of an ice cream van. Chris Rogers and Dawid Malan gathered runs with embarrassing ease in the chase.*

At Chelmsford, August 5. **Essex won by seven wickets.** Reduced to 25 overs a side. **Leicestershire 151-7** (25 overs) (M. A. Thornely 55; Harbhajan Singh 3-29); ‡**Essex 154-3** (23.3 overs) (O. A. Shah 45*). *Attendance:* 3,278. *Essex's batsmen were barely extended after Leicestershire added only 57 while losing six wickets in their last nine overs.*

At Colchester, August 19. **Essex won by 117 runs.** ‡**Essex 314-8** (40 overs) (T. Westley 59, O. A. Shah 44, R. N. ten Doeschate 52, J. S. Foster 79; Mudassar Bukhari 3-80); **Netherlands 197** (32.2 overs) (M. R. Swart 50; Harbhajan Singh 5-37, R. S. Bopara 3-19). *Attendance:* 3,242. *Netherlands debut:* L. V. van Beek. *The Dutch campaign ended in a dispiriting fifth consecutive defeat, following their first concession of 300 or more in the CB40. Westley thumped 38 from his first 18 balls to set the tone for Essex's highest total in 40-over cricket, though Bopara was a notable failure: he laboured over one from 11, nicking behind in his first match after four weeks out for personal reasons.*

At Chelmsford, August 23 (day/night). **Lancashire won by eight wickets.** ‡**Essex 186** (38.1 overs) (O. J. Newby 5-35); **Lancashire 187-2** (36.3 overs) (S. J. Croft 66*, K. R. Brown 87*). *Attendance:* 3,357. *Lancashire swept to their sixth straight win and a home semi-final. Oliver Newby struck in his first three overs on the way to career-best figures, before Steven Croft and Karl Brown flourished in a stand of 160.*

Essex away matches

May 7: no result v Leicestershire.
May 20: lost to Lancashire by 28 runs.
May 29: lost to Netherlands by five wickets.
July 15: no result v Gloucestershire.
July 29: beat Worcestershire by 25 runs.
August 27: lost to Middlesex by 54 runs (D/L).

GLOUCESTERSHIRE

At Bristol, May 6. **Netherlands won by one run. Netherlands 239-6** (40 overs) (S. J. Myburgh 77); ‡**Gloucestershire 238-8** (40 overs) (A. P. R. Gidman 41, B. A. C. Howell 72*; P. M. Seelaar 4-42). *Attendance:* 944. *Netherlands debut:* C. J. Borgas. *Gloucestershire timed their assault marginally too late – and lost on the last ball. Benny Howell, making his one-day debut for them as a triallist, saw three partners fall in four balls, and needed to hit Mudassar Bukhari's final delivery for three; he could manage only a leg-bye. Stephan Myburgh's brazen 77, which began with a second-ball six off Will Gidman, gave the Netherlands early impetus.*

At Bristol, May 13. **Gloucestershire won by 164 runs. Gloucestershire 294-6** (40 overs) (B. A. C. Howell 88, K. S. Williamson 112); ‡**Leicestershire 130** (30.3 overs) (G. J. McCarter 3-15, C. D. J.

Dent 4-43). *Attendance:* 749. *Kane Williamson's sixth and highest one-day hundred set up a resounding Gloucestershire victory, with energetic support from Howell in a third-wicket stand of 152. Leicestershire's middle order caved in to Chris Dent's occasional left-arm spin.*

At Cheltenham, July 15. **Gloucestershire v Essex. Abandoned.**

At Cheltenham, July 17. **Gloucestershire won by four wickets. Worcestershire 144-7** (40 overs) (P. J. Hughes 64*; A. P. R. Gidman 3-20); ‡**Gloucestershire 145-6** (27.1 overs) (M. M. Ali 3-33). *Attendance:* 3,164. *Moeen Ali edged the opening ball behind, and Worcestershire limped along, allowing Alex Gidman to get through eight cheap overs; even Phillip Hughes took 108 deliveries to make 64*. Ali came on in the ninth over and snapped up three wickets in 12 balls for no cost, but Gidman (33*) banished Gloucestershire's butterflies.*

At Cheltenham, July 22. **Middlesex won by ten wickets. Gloucestershire 214-9** (40 overs) (D. M. Housego 68; T. S. Roland-Jones 3-24); ‡**Middlesex 218-0** (30.3 overs) (C. J. L. Rogers 122*, D. J. Malan 89*). *Attendance:* 4,430. *County debut:* R. J. Nicol (Gloucestershire). *Gloucestershire were in with a chance at halfway, after Dan Housego – who began in their Academy but spent several years on the Middlesex staff – propped them up on a competitive wicket. But Chris Rogers and Dawid Malan responded with an unbroken 218, Middlesex's highest first-wicket partnership, surpassing the 210 by Paul Weekes and Ed Smith against Northumberland at Jesmond in the 2005 C&G Trophy.*

At Bristol, August 19. **Lancashire won by 18 runs.** ‡**Lancashire 182-9** (40 overs) (D. A. Payne 3-48, E. G. C. Young 3-25); **Gloucestershire 164** (35.1 overs) (J. K. Fuller 43; G. Chapple 5-26). *Attendance:* 1,508. *Lancashire won the group with two games to spare. Oliver Newby chiselled out a career-best 36* to resuscitate them from 117-7, then removed Alex Gidman for 36. Glen Chapple had Gloucestershire in tatters at 16-4, and returned to knock over the tail for his best one-day figures in 14 years.*

Gloucestershire away matches

May 7: beat Middlesex by five wickets.
June 4: lost to Essex by eight wickets.
June 10: beat Worcestershire by 109 runs.
July 27: beat Netherlands by 90 runs (D/L).
July 30: lost to Lancashire by four wickets.
August 27: no result v Leicestershire.

LANCASHIRE

At Manchester, May 6. **Lancashire won by five runs.** ‡**Lancashire 296-3** (40 overs) (S. C. Moore 74, A. G. Prince 79, S. J. Croft 82, K. R. Brown 44*); **Leicestershire 291-7** (40 overs) (J. J. Cobb 137, M. A. G. Boyce 64; S. C. Kerrigan 3-44). *Attendance:* 1,118. *County debut:* N. S. Tahir (Lancashire). *Stephen Moore dropped Josh Cobb at slip from the first ball of Leicestershire's reply. Cobb responded with six sixes in 99 balls in his maiden one-day century, but lacked the support to overhaul Lancashire's highest 40-over total, set up by Moore and Ashwell Prince in an opening stand of 135. Jigar Naik damaged ankle ligaments in the field and later required surgery.*

At Manchester, May 20. **Lancashire won by 28 runs.** ‡**Lancashire 258-9** (40 overs) (S. C. Moore 62, S. J. Croft 53, P. J. Horton 54; D. D. Masters 4-41); **Essex 230** (37.3 overs) (J. S. Foster 41, G. M. Smith 44, G. R. Napier 51; G. Keedy 3-49). *Attendance:* 1,780. *Moore and Steven Croft again overpowered the opposition on a good pitch, putting on 111 for the second wicket. Essex looked dead at 139-6, although a powerful 23-ball fifty from Graham Napier at least helped their run-rate.*

At Manchester, June 5. **Lancashire won by 12 runs** (D/L). **Worcestershire 259-9** (40 overs) (V. S. Solanki 121, P. J. Hughes 104; A. Shahzad 4-51); ‡**Lancashire 95-1** (14.1 overs) (S. C. Moore 60*). *Attendance:* 1,706. *Initially chasing 260, then 131 in 19 overs, Lancashire were indebted to Moore's fourth successive half-century, which was enough to secure victory when a third stoppage for rain proved terminal. Vikram Solanki and Phillip Hughes put on a county-record second-wicket stand of 208, but no one else passed five, as Worcestershire surrendered eight for 47.*

At Manchester, July 16 (day/night). **Lancashire won by seven wickets** (D/L). Reduced to 32 overs a side. **Middlesex 97-8** (16 overs) (D. J. Malan 48; S. D. Parry 4-21); ‡**Lancashire 97-3** (13.2 overs) (S. J. Croft 45). *Attendance:* 1,267. *Middlesex were denied the services of Eoin Morgan, who chose to travel separately by train and got caught in severe delays on the London–Manchester line. He found an alternative route via York, and arrived at the ground shortly after the scheduled 4.40pm* *start – but by then he had missed the toss and been replaced in the side by Ollie Rayner. Middlesex did not discipline him. When a 16-over game finally began at 6pm, Morgan watched from the dressing-room as Middlesex were restricted by Stephen Parry. Though a further over was trimmed, Lancashire reached their revised target of 97 with ten balls to spare – stealing a march on Middlesex in the race for qualification.*

At Manchester, July 30 (day/night). **Lancashire won by four wickets.** ‡**Gloucestershire 184-7** (40 overs) (D. M. Housego 43, I. A. Cockbain 58); **Lancashire 187-6** (39.1 overs) (K. R. Brown 60, P. J. Horton 46; D. A. Payne 3-39). *Attendance:* 2,180. *Lancashire withstood a half-century from the Liverpool-born Ian Cockbain, a former Second Eleven player of theirs, and son of a former Lancashire player of the same name. Karl Brown and Paul Horton knuckled down in the middle overs for a crucial partnership of 82.*

At Manchester, August 12. **Lancashire won by nine wickets.** Reduced to 27 overs a side. **Netherlands 68** (20.5 overs) (S. D. Parry 3-13, G. Keedy 3-15); ‡**Lancashire 69-1** (16.3 overs) (S. C. Moore 50*). *Attendance:* 2,759. *Netherlands debut:* W. L. Coetsee. *Already missing four injured or unavailable players, the Netherlands were then denied visas for two more by the UK Border Agency. Werner Coetsee was drafted in from Lancashire League side Enfield at the last minute, but contributed little as they were hustled out for 68 by Ajmal Shahzad (2-7), Gary Keedy and Parry on a responsive pitch.*

Lancashire away matches

May 28: lost to Netherlands by one run.
June 10: lost to Middlesex by 167 runs.
July 22: beat Leicestershire by six wickets.
August 19: beat Gloucestershire by 18 runs.
August 23: beat Essex by eight wickets.
August 27: no result v Worcestershire.

LEICESTERSHIRE

At Leicester, May 7. **Leicestershire v Essex. Abandoned.**

At Leicester, May 20. **Middlesex won by 31 runs. Middlesex 241-5** (40 overs) (D. J. Malan 43, N. J. Dexter 54*, G. K. Berg 43); ‡**Leicestershire 210** (38.4 overs) (E. J. H. Eckersley 46; S. T. Finn 3-30). *Attendance:* 517. *Steven Finn, left out of the First Test at Lord's, took out his frustration on Leicestershire with three wickets in seven balls; the first came when Ramnaresh Sarwan missed an intemperate swipe.*

At Leicester, June 4. **Netherlands won by 43 runs. Netherlands 304-3** (40 overs) (M. R. Swart 102, T. L. W. Cooper 68, C. J. Borgas 61*); ‡**Leicestershire 261-9** (40 overs) (R. R. Sarwan 115, J. du Toit 48; M. R. Swart 3-55). *Attendance:* 322. *Tom Cooper's run-out of Sarwan from side on tilted the contest the way of the Dutch, before Michael Swart mopped up the lower order with his off-spin. Earlier, Swart scored his maiden one-day century, supported by two other Australians, Cooper and Cameron Borgas, as the Netherlands made their highest CB40 total. A fifth win in seven matches sent them six points clear at the top – though they had played two more games than anyone.*

At Leicester, July 14. **Leicestershire won by four wickets.** Reduced to 31 overs a side. **Worcestershire 214-5** (31 overs) (M. M. Ali 40, P. J. Hughes 57*, D. K. H. Mitchell 44); ‡**Leicestershire 217-6** (31 overs) (R. R. Sarwan 100). *Attendance:* 575. *Rob Taylor and Will Jones fashioned a thrilling last-ball win, clubbing 29 from the last two overs. Leicestershire seemed to have slipped out of contention when David Lucas bowled Sarwan immediately after he had brought up his 85-ball hundred with a six, then added Ned Eckersley; Matt Boyce was run out in between. But Taylor flashed 22* off ten deliveries, helped by a Lucas no-ball.*

At Leicester, July 22. **Lancashire won by six wickets. Leicestershire 218-8** (40 overs) (M. A. G. Boyce 53, S. J. Thakor 83*; G. Chapple 4-46); ‡**Lancashire 220-4** (35.4 overs) (S. C. Moore 60, A. G. Prince 85, S. J. Croft 57*). *Attendance:* 736. *Well though Shiv Thakor played for his maiden one-day half-century, Leicestershire's total was unlikely to test such powerful opponents.*

At Leicester, August 27. **No result. Leicestershire 264** (38 overs) (J. J. Cobb 42, W. S. Jones 44, S. J. Thakor 52, M. A. G. Boyce 51; L. C. Norwell 6-52); ‡**Gloucestershire 19-1** (4 overs). *Attendance:* 586. *Liam Norwell took four wickets in three overs to end with career-best figures, before rain swept in.*

Leicestershire away matches

May 6: lost to Lancashire by five runs.
May 13: lost to Gloucestershire by 164 runs.
July 11: beat Netherlands by 33 runs.
July 15: no result v Middlesex.
August 5: lost to Essex by seven wickets.
August 19: beat Worcestershire by two wickets.

MIDDLESEX

At Lord's, May 7. **Gloucestershire won by five wickets.** Reduced to 26 overs a side. **Middlesex 157-8** (26 overs) (G. J. McCarter 3-41, E. G. C. Young 3-26); ‡**Gloucestershire 161-5** (22.2 overs) (B. A. C. Howell 45*). *County debut:* G. J. McCarter. *Attendance:* 1,361. *It was a familiar story for Middlesex, as five batsmen got out in the 20s, gifting the 19-year-old Ulsterman Graeme McCarter three wickets on his List A debut.*

At Lord's, June 3. **Middlesex v Netherlands. Abandoned.**

At Lord's, June 10. **Middlesex won by 167 runs. Middlesex 350-6** (40 overs) (J. L. Denly 58, P. R. Stirling 119, E. J. G. Morgan 116; G. Keedy 5-55); ‡**Lancashire 183** (35 overs) (P. J. Horton 49; S. P. Crook 3-26, T. M. J. Smith 3-30). *Attendance:* 2,125. *Lancashire's winning streak came to an abrupt end, as they fell victim to a frightening fusillade from the Irish-born pair Paul Stirling and Eoin Morgan. Stirling had already put on 142 with Joe Denly when Morgan arrived. He reverse-swept Gary Keedy first ball, and began peppering the stands as he sprinted to 50 in 27 deliveries, and 100 in 49 – thrashing 11 sixes in all. They shared 126 in 11 overs before both were out to Keedy, who claimed his 100th List A wicket and second five-for. Middlesex's total was their best in one-day cricket – and the worst conceded by Lancashire, who promptly slumped to 55-5.*

At Uxbridge, July 15. **Middlesex v Leicestershire. Abandoned.**

At Uxbridge, August 5. **Tied.** Reduced to 36 overs a side. **Middlesex 229-4** (36 overs) (E. J. G. Morgan 120*, J. H. Davey 53*); ‡**Worcestershire 229-7** (36 overs) (P. J. Hughes 69, G. M. Andrew 42; T. S. Roland-Jones 3-39). *Attendance:*1,283. *Morgan was again in sumptuous form as he carved 120* from 80 balls in a reduced match, adding an unbroken 162 at eight an over with Josh Davey. Worcestershire put up a spirited response, and Ben Scott, a former Middlesex wicketkeeper, hit 23 from the last over to salvage a tie.*

At Lord's, August 27. **Middlesex won by 54 runs** (D/L). **Middlesex 288** (40 overs) (D. J. Malan 134, G. K. Berg 61; R. S. Bopara 3-55); ‡**Essex 198-7** (35.1 overs) (T. Westley 68, O. A. Shah 53; G. S. Sandhu 3-28). *Attendance:* 3,609. *Middlesex, playing at Lord's for the first time in nine weeks following the Olympics and the South Africa Test, were comfortable winners when rain arrived. Dawid Malan anchored their innings with a second List A hundred. Ravi Bopara, released by England to find some form a day before playing in the one-day international against South Africa in Southampton, could again deliver with the ball but not the bat: three wickets, before getting out in single figures, top-edging a lifter from 20-year-old left-arm seamer Gurjit Sandhu.*

Middlesex away matches

May 14: beat Netherlands by eight wickets.
May 20: beat Leicestershire by 31 runs.
May 27: beat Worcestershire by 56 runs.
July 16: lost to Lancashire by seven wickets (D/L).
July 18: beat Essex by nine wickets.
July 22: beat Gloucestershire by ten wickets.

NETHERLANDS

At Voorburg, May 14. **Middlesex won by eight wickets. Netherlands 212-9** (40 overs) (S. J. Myburgh 66; P. R. Stirling 4-27); ‡**Middlesex 213-2** (37.2 overs) (J. L. Denly 96*, C. J. L. Rogers 83*). *Attendance:* 600. *After two away wins, the Dutch fell back to earth in the first CB40 match held at Voorburg, not far from The Hague. Stephan Myburgh made his fourth consecutive half-century in county matches, but Paul Stirling took four wickets with his occasional off-spin, as he had done for Ireland at Amstelveen two years previously. Joe Denly ended four short of a first one-day hundred for Middlesex when Chris Rogers hit the winning boundary to round off their partnership of 166.*

At Schiedam, May 28. **Netherlands won by one wicket.** ‡**Lancashire 236** (39.4 overs) (S. C. Moore 77, S. J. Croft 55, K. R. Brown 41; M. R. Swart 4-40, M. A. A. Jamil 4-24); **Netherlands 237-9** (39.4 overs) (M. R. Swart 41; S. D. Parry 4-29). *Attendance:* 1,800. *A large Whit Monday crowd witnessed a thriller that went to the final over. From 199-3, Lancashire's last seven batsmen managed only 16 runs between them. Steven Croft dropped Mudassar Bukhari (36 from 26 balls) on the midwicket boundary at a crucial moment, and the final pair – Timm van der Gugten and Ahsan Malik Jamil – scrambled the last nine.*

At Schiedam, May 29. **Netherlands won by five wickets.** Reduced to 36 overs a side. ‡**Essex 112** (33.3 overs) (T. van der Gugten 3-29); **Netherlands 113-5** (22.1 overs) (M. R. Swart 40; T. J. Phillips 3-34). *Attendance:* 1,500. *Essex were 0-2 three balls into van der Gugten's opening over – and never recovered. Five of their batsmen were lbw on a wicket slower and lower than the day before.*

At Voorburg, June 8. **Worcestershire won by nine wickets** (D/L). **Netherlands 57** (23.2 overs) (J. D. Shantry 3-26, G. M. Andrew 3-9); ‡**Worcestershire 61-1** (13.1 overs). *Attendance:* 200. *Four days after plundering their highest CB40 total, the Netherlands slumped to their lowest in one-day cricket. All the batsman were troubled by left-arm seamers David Lucas (5–1–11–2) and Jack Shantry, but Vikram Solanki showed what was possible with 39*. The match was over in two hours.*

At Amstelveen, July 11. **Leicestershire won by 33 runs.** Reduced to 36 overs a side. **Leicestershire 208-7** (36 overs) (M. A. Thornely 86); ‡**Netherlands 175** (32.1 overs) (C. J. Borgas 40; M. J. Hoggard 3-26, J. S. Sykes 3-39). *Attendance:* 750. *Netherlands debut:* Shahbaz Bashir. *Peter Borren gashed a finger trying to hold a return chance from Michael Thornely, who hit five sixes in 77 balls. Myburgh leapt to 21 in 12, but had his thumb broken by a lifter from Nathan Buck, and had to retire hurt, sapping the life from the Dutch challenge.*

At Amstelveen, July 27. **Gloucestershire won by 90 runs** (D/L). ‡**Gloucestershire 290-6** (40 overs) (R. J. Nicol 133, H. J. H. Marshall 47, J. K. Fuller 40); **Netherlands 146** (22 overs) (T. L. W. Cooper 51; J. K. Fuller 6-35). *Attendance:* 1,500. *The first live broadcast of a Dutch home game on Sky Sports was an anticlimax. It began with van der Gugten limping off in his opening over with a sprained ankle; as a result Borren used five different bowlers in the first five, and the New Zealand opening pair Rob Nicol and Hamish Marshall took advantage in a century stand. After the Dutch lost 12 overs to rain, Tom Cooper and Cameron Borgas briefly pushed them ahead on Duckworth/Lewis, until Borgas was bowled in the 15th. With quick runs needed, James Fuller swooped for five wickets in four overs.*

Netherlands away matches

May 6: beat Gloucestershire by one run.
May 7: beat Worcestershire by nine wickets (D/L).
June 3: no result v Middlesex.
June 4: beat Leicestershire by 43 runs.
August 12: lost to Lancashire by nine wickets.
August 19: lost to Essex by 117 runs.

WORCESTERSHIRE

At Kidderminster, May 7. **Netherlands won by nine wickets** (D/L). **Worcestershire 172-4** (27 overs) (V. S. Solanki 63; Mudassar Bukhari 3-29); ‡**Netherlands 139-1** (16.5 overs) (S. J. Myburgh 74*, C. J. Borgas 55*). *Attendance:* 223. *Flooding at New Road meant this fixture was moved to Kidderminster, but it was still interrupted four times by rain as the Netherlands – following Duckworth/Lewis recalculations – completed an opening-weekend double for the second successive season. Stephan Myburgh followed his 77 at Bristol with 74* off 50 balls as he and Cameron Borgas reached the revised target with 13 deliveries to spare.*

At Worcester, May 27. **Worcestershire won by 56 runs.** ‡**Worcestershire 235-5** (40 overs) (P. J. Hughes 111, D. K. H. Mitchell 48); **Middlesex 179** (34.3 overs) (C. J. L. Rogers 44; J. D. Shantry 4-32, M. M. Ali 3-34). *Attendance:* 1,518. *County debut:* P. J. Hughes. *Phillip Hughes marked his Worcestershire debut with a century against his county of 2009. His second 50 came in only 35 balls. Middlesex lost wickets in three consecutive overs to Moeen Ali, and were further eroded by Jack Shantry, who returned one-day best figures.*

At Worcester, June 10. **Gloucestershire won by 109 runs.** ‡**Gloucestershire 238-6** (40 overs) (W. R. S. Gidman 76, A. P. R. Gidman 59; J. D. Shantry 4-37); **Worcestershire 129** (39.1 overs). *Attendance:* 1,013. *Will Gidman compiled 76 from 98 balls – his first limited-overs fifty – before* *brother Alex lifted the momentum with a 6446 sequence off Gareth Andrew. At 25-5, with Will striking twice, Worcestershire briefly endangered their nadir of 58.*

At Worcester, July 29. **Essex won by 25 runs. Essex 269-4** (40 overs) (M. L. Pettini 111, T. Westley 62, R. N. ten Doeschate 50*); ‡**Worcestershire 244-8** (40 overs) (M. M. Ali 42, P. J. Hughes 68; G. R. Napier 3-57). *Attendance:* 668. *Building on a superb 111 from Mark Pettini, Ryan ten Doeschate plundered 50* off 24 deliveries. Worcestershire's challenge dissolved completely when Andrew (32) and Hughes succumbed in consecutive balls from Harbhajan Singh.*

At Worcester, August 19. **Leicestershire won by two wickets. Worcestershire 223-9** (40 overs) (V. S. Solanki 41; N. L. Buck 3-49); ‡**Leicestershire 224-8** (39 overs) (J. J. Cobb 51, E. J. H. Eckersley 72*). *Attendance:* 1,474. *A sudden barrage from No. 8 Ned Eckersley transformed an otherwise sedate contest. Leicestershire slumped to 107-6, and required 92 from the final ten overs, when Eckersley hammered seven sixes in 72* off 44 balls – his maiden List A half-century. Nick Harrison dropped him off his own bowling, and disintegrated in the 39th over, conceding two no-balls and the last 20 runs.*

At Worcester, August 27. **No result.** Reduced to 38 overs a side. **Lancashire 324-4** (37 overs) (S. C. Moore 113, T. C. Smith 106, S. J. Croft 67) v ‡**Worcestershire.** *Attendance:* 311. *County debut:* A. M. Lilley (Lancashire). *Tom Smith struck the joint-fifth-fastest century in one-day cricket, off just 44 balls, on his return from five weeks out with a thigh injury. He smashed 106, including ten sixes, of an opening stand of 150 with Stephen Moore in the first 15 overs, as Lancashire improved their highest 40-over score, despite losing three to rain. Harrison gave away just 11 in his first three overs, but 72 in his next four, including 30 in one as Smith hit him for a sequence of 466446, to finish with the most expensive analysis of the summer: 7–0–83–2. Shantry went for 80 in eight, and was later penalised by the ECB for a show of petulance. Rain denied Vikram Solanki a bat in what turned out to be his last match for Worcestershire.*

Worcestershire away matches

May 13: beat Essex by seven wickets.
June 5: lost to Lancashire by 12 runs (D/L).
June 8: beat Netherlands by nine wickets (D/L).
July 14: lost to Leicestershire by four wickets.
July 17: lost to Gloucestershire by four wickets.
August 5: tied with Middlesex.

GROUP B

DURHAM

At Chester-le-Street, May 13. **Durham won by 14 runs. Durham 222-9** (40 overs) (G. J. Muchall 75, W. R. Smith 55; J. Overton 4-42); ‡**Somerset 208** (39.3 overs) (A. W. R. Barrow 72; L. E. Plunkett 4-33). *County debut:* J. Harrison (Durham). *Attendance:* 1,246. *When Graham Onions was named in England's squad for the First Test against West Indies, Durham called up Jamie Harrison, a 21-year-old left-arm seamer, who had Craig Kieswetter and Peter Trego lbw with his fourth and seventh legitimate balls. Audacious strokeplay from Alex Barrow, one of six in Somerset's team aged 20 or under, kept the result close.*

At Chester-le-Street, May 27. **Durham won by eight wickets. Scotland 258-4** (40 overs) (C. S. MacLeod 48, J. Symes 110); ‡**Durham 259-2** (33.3 overs) (M. D. Stoneman 136*, P. Mustard 91). *Attendance:* 1,634. *Jean Symes hit strongly to leg for 110 from 94 balls, as Scotland made their second-highest 40-over total, but it never looked like enough on a flat pitch. Their modest attack was torn apart in a 207-run opening stand between Phil Mustard and Mark Stoneman, whose maiden one-day century arrived off 87 deliveries.*

At Chester-le-Street, June 3. **Durham won by 91 runs. Durham 310-4** (40 overs) (M. D. Stoneman 72, P. Mustard 100); ‡**Nottinghamshire 219** (37.5 overs) (A. C. Voges 74, P. J. Franks 57; C. Rushworth 5-31). *Attendance:* 1,564. *Mustard's 66-ball century was Durham's fastest in one-day cricket, beating the 72 needed by Paul Collingwood at Worcester in 2004. Chris Rushworth, Mustard's cousin, showed Nottinghamshire's bowlers there was something in the pitch by regularly hitting the seam, single-handedly reducing them to 43-5.*

At Chester-le-Street, August 11. **Durham won by 142 runs.** ‡**Durham 298-9** (40 overs) (P. Mustard 143, M. D. Stoneman 50, B. A. Stokes 45; Z. de Bruyn 5-46); **Surrey 156** (29.1 overs) (J. J. Roy 43;

M. A. Wood 3-32, G. R. Breese 3-18). *Attendance:* 1,519. *Mustard was almost out on one, two and 16, but went on to surpass his career-best with 143 from 91 balls, after which Durham slowed down markedly. He also took two catches and made two stumpings.*

At Chester-le-Street, August 12. **Durham won by 59 runs.** **‡Durham 307-2** (40 overs) (M. D. Stoneman 112*, P. Mustard 107, G. J. Muchall 75); **Glamorgan 248** (36.2 overs) (M. A. Wallace 105, M. J. North 59; G. R. Breese 4-50). *Attendance:* 1,353. *County debut:* A. G. Salter (Glamorgan). *Mustard scored his second century of the weekend, and broke the record for Durham's fastest hundred for the second time in the season, reaching it off 55 balls in the 16th over. Stoneman batted through the innings and shared partnerships of 157 with Mustard and 150 with Gordon Muchall, who was out to the last ball.*

At Chester-le-Street, August 27. **No result.** Reduced to 18 overs a side. **Hampshire 51-1** (5.4 overs) v **‡Durham.** *County debut:* R. D. Pringle (Durham). *After their Twenty20 triumph at Cardiff two days earlier, Hampshire flew up to the North-East, only for the game to be washed out inside six overs. The only wicket to fall was Michael Carberry, who went into the match with six successive scores of 50-plus, but nicked his third ball from Ben Stokes for a duck. With the day's other group games also abandoned, one point was enough to carry Hampshire into the semi-finals.*

Durham away matches

May 20: lost to Surrey by 60 runs.
June 10: lost to Glamorgan by 15 runs.
July 15: lost to Hampshire by four wickets.
July 22: lost to Somerset by eight wickets.
August 5: no result v Scotland.
August 19: lost to Nottinghamshire by 43 runs.

GLAMORGAN

At Cardiff, June 2. **Surrey won by 57 runs** (D/L). **Surrey 173-9** (40 overs) (S. M. Davies 58, Z. de Bruyn 52; J. C. Glover 3-53); **‡Glamorgan 107-9** (26 overs) (M. Kartik 4-27). *Attendance:* 941. *County debuts:* M. van Jaarsveld (Glamorgan); M. Kartik. *Murali Kartik had Gareth Rees lbw with his second ball for Surrey, but rain robbed him of a possible five-for. Zander de Bruyn was dropped early on in his fifty, and had to withdraw four balls into his spell when he hurt a finger blocking a drive from Marcus North; Matthew Spriegel completed the over, and bowled North with the sixth delivery.*

At Colwyn Bay, June 10. **Glamorgan won by 15 runs.** **‡Glamorgan 163** (34.3 overs) (B. A. Stokes 3-24); **Durham 148** (37.5 overs) (M. J. Richardson 45; S. P. Jones 4-23). *Attendance:* 1,088. *The groundstaff brought the boundaries in, having worked through the previous day to dry the surface after days of rain – and were rewarded with Glamorgan's first victory of the season in any competition. Simon Jones was a handful, reducing Durham to 36-3 and returning for the decisive wicket of Michael Richardson when 44 were needed.*

At Cardiff, July 12 (day/night). **Glamorgan v Somerset. Abandoned.**

At Cardiff, July 29. **Glamorgan won by eight wickets.** **‡Scotland 151-9** (40 overs) (P. L. Mommsen 41; J. C. Glover 3-34, J. Allenby 3-16); **Glamorgan 154-2** (28 overs) (G. P. Rees 60*). *Attendance:* 960. *Scotland had thumped Bangladesh in a Twenty20 international five days earlier, but found Glamorgan tougher to crack on a grudging pitch. Jim Allenby went for just two an over, then added an unbeaten 63 with Rees.*

At Swansea, August 5. **Glamorgan won by two runs** (D/L). **‡Glamorgan 181-8** (40 overs) (B. J. Wright 62; S. R. Patel 3-47, G. G. White 3-28); **Nottinghamshire 107-5** (21 overs) (D. A. Cosker 3-26). *Attendance:* 1,317. *The players went off for rain with Nottinghamshire 77-4 in the 18th over. When they returned, the requirement was another 33 from three, then 14 from the last, bowled by Allenby; Chris Read and Scott Elstone managed 11. Robert Croft, playing on his home club ground in his 408th and last one-day match, claimed Riki Wessels as his 411th wicket.*

At Cardiff, August 10 (day/night). **Hampshire won by 107 runs.** **Hampshire 227** (40 overs) (J. M. Vince 48, N. D. McKenzie 88); **‡Glamorgan 120** (32.5 overs) (C. P. Wood 5-22, D. R. Briggs 4-32). *Attendance:* 1,369. *Neil McKenzie delivered a one-day masterclass of 88 in 89 balls. Glamorgan were unable to counter the swing of Chris Wood or the control of Danny Briggs, bowling in tandem at the death and each recording their career-best figures.*

Glamorgan away matches

May 7: lost to Hampshire by 48 runs (D/L).
May 13: no result v Scotland.
July 28: lost to Somerset by three wickets.
August 12: lost to Durham by 59 runs.
August 21: lost to Surrey by 93 runs.
August 27: no result v Nottinghamshire.

HAMPSHIRE

At Southampton, May 7. **Hampshire won by 48 runs** (D/L). ‡**Glamorgan 173-7** (34 overs) (S. J. Walters 68; K. Ali 3-44); **Hampshire 151-2** (23.5 overs) (M. A. Carberry 60, J. M. Vince 83). *Attendance:* 1,684. *Nothing went right for Simon Jones on his return to Southampton, as he was pummelled for 54 in five overs by James Vince and Michael Carberry, who opened with 142. Hampshire were well ahead on Duckworth/Lewis when rain intruded.*

At Southampton, May 31 (day/night). **Nottinghamshire won by 12 runs.** ‡**Nottinghamshire 277-4** (40 overs) (S. R. Patel 66, J. W. A. Taylor 115*); **Hampshire 265** (39.5 overs) (M. A. Carberry 54, J. H. K. Adams 51, S. M. Ervine 68, A. D. Mascarenhas 48; D. J. Pattinson 3-66, S. R. Patel 3-47). *Attendance:* 2,058. *It was another unhappy homecoming for a Hampshire old boy: Nottinghamshire lost Michael Lumb in the first over, but plundered 130 from the final ten; the last 90 of James Taylor's career-best 115* came in 32 balls, including all his seven fours and seven sixes. It was still a close-run thing: Hampshire needed 15 from the final over, but Darren Pattinson removed Kabir Ali and Dimitri Mascarenhas, and kept them to two.*

At Southampton, June 4. **Hampshire won by six wickets.** ‡**Scotland 230-9** (40 overs) (P. L. Mommsen 48, R. M. Haq 53*; D. R. Briggs 3-35); **Hampshire 234-4** (36.1 overs) (M. A. Carberry 148*, S. M. Katich 41). *Attendance:* 2,068. *Carberry's third six settled the match at the start of the 37th over. His 148*, in stands of 106 with Simon Katich and 103 with Liam Dawson, was the highest of his four one-day hundreds, and left Scotland ruing two let-offs.*

At Southampton, July 15. **Hampshire won by four wickets. Durham 200-7** (40 overs) (G. J. Muchall 96*; K. Ali 3-39); ‡**Hampshire 201-6** (38.2 overs) (J. M. Vince 40, S. M. Katich 59*; S. G. Borthwick 4-51). *Attendance:* 2,306. *Simon Katich, pushed up to No. 3 with Carberry injured, calmly charted Hampshire's path to victory.*

At Southampton, August 14 (day/night). **Somerset won by 50 runs. Somerset 228-8** (40 overs) (P. D. Trego 61, J. C. Buttler 51; S. M. Ervine 3-35); ‡**Hampshire 178** (36 overs) (J. M. Vince 95; S. P. Kirby 3-19). *Attendance:* 3,083. *Marcus Trescothick survived a hat-trick ball of sorts from Chris Wood (carried over from Hampshire's game at Cardiff, four days earlier) but drove the fourth delivery of the over to cover. Peter Trego's 61 from 31 included 54 in boundaries. He then chipped in with the ball as five Hampshire batsmen collected ducks, before Vince was last out five short of a century.*

At Southampton, August 19. **Hampshire won by four wickets.** ‡**Surrey 175-9** (40 overs) (M. N. W. Spriegel 47, Z. de Bruyn 57; D. A. Griffiths 3-29); **Hampshire 179-6** (38.1 overs) (M. A. Carberry 54). *Attendance:* 6,376. *Kevin Pietersen, dropped by England for disciplinary reasons, was out first ball on his return to his old club – the second time left-arm spinner Liam Dawson had dismissed him for a golden duck in 2012. Pietersen walked out to applause and a few isolated boos, then back again a minute later to a chorus of jeers from a bumper home crowd. In his first innings after two months out with a knee injury, Carberry passed 50 for the sixth time out of six in the competition to seal a crucial win.*

Hampshire away matches

May 20: beat Scotland by 89 runs.
May 27: beat Somerset by nine wickets.
June 3: no result v Surrey.
July 17: lost to Nottinghamshire by six wickets.
August 10: beat Glamorgan by 107 runs.
August 27: no result v Durham.

NOTTINGHAMSHIRE

At Nottingham, June 4. **Nottinghamshire won by five wickets. Somerset 205-8** (40 overs) (P. D. Trego 47; D. J. Pattinson 3-37, J. T. Ball 3-38); ‡**Nottinghamshire 209-5** (36.4 overs) (M. J. Lumb 65, M. H. Wessels 55). *Attendance:* 2,985. *Darren Pattinson and Jake Ball – the nephew of former*

Nottinghamshire and England wicketkeeper Bruce French, condemned Somerset to their fourth defeat in four.

At Nottingham, July 17 (day/night). **Nottinghamshire won by six wickets. Hampshire 230-7** (40 overs) (J. M. Vince 102*); ‡**Nottinghamshire 231-4** (37.1 overs) (A. D. Hales 70, J. W. A. Taylor 74). *Attendance:* 2,895. *Nottinghamshire crushed the foundations built by James Vince's second List A hundred; Alex Hales and Riki Wessels (38) got their chase off to a flier with 89 inside ten overs.*

At Nottingham, July 22. **Nottinghamshire won by 88 runs.** ‡**Nottinghamshire 265-5** (40 overs) (J. W. A. Taylor 68, S. R. Patel 82, A. C. Voges 64*; G. Goudie 3-44); **Scotland 177** (36 overs) (A. C. Voges 3-37, G. G. White 3-42). *Attendance:* 2,542. *Michael Lumb was lbw first ball to Gordon Goudie – but that was as good as it got for the Scots. James Taylor hit his third fifty of the competition, with support from Samit Patel and the manic Adam Voges (64* in 39). Pattinson limped off with a groin strain two balls into his spell.*

At Nottingham, August 1 (day/night). **Surrey won by four wickets. Nottinghamshire 149** (38 overs) (J. W. Dernbach 3-39); ‡**Surrey 151-6** (36.1 overs) (M. N. W. Spriegel 47). *Attendance:* 1,919. *In a pivotal match, Nottinghamshire were hustled to defeat on a used pitch turning so sharply that Surrey opened with two spinners and chose not to use the pace of Stuart Meaker. Rory Hamilton-Brown was out for two on his return from compassionate leave following the death of Tom Maynard.*

At Nottingham, August 19. **Nottinghamshire won by 43 runs. Nottinghamshire 294-8** (40 overs) (M. J. Lumb 84, M. H. Wessels 43, C. M. W. Read 71*; M. E. Claydon 3-76); ‡**Durham 251** (38.3 overs) (M. D. Stoneman 102; A. Carter 4-45, S. J. Mullaney 3-44). *Attendance:* 4,466. *Nottinghamshire were propelled to their highest 40-over score by stunning strokeplay from Lumb and later Chris Read, as 69 runs came off the last six overs. Mark Stoneman achieved his third century of the competition, but it could not stop them dropping out of semi-final contention.*

At Nottingham, August 27. **No result. Nottinghamshire 264-6** (40 overs) (A. D. Hales 94, N. J. Edwards 58, J. W. A. Taylor 40); ‡**Glamorgan 20-0** (5.3 overs). *Attendance:* 1,311. *Nottinghamshire feasted on wayward bowling, though Neil Edwards's fifty was not enough to save his contract. Rain extended the interval and returned for good in the sixth over.*

Nottinghamshire away matches

May 7: lost to Scotland by 18 runs (D/L).
May 31: beat Hampshire by 12 runs.
June 3: lost to Durham by 91 runs.
July 15: beat Surrey by five wickets.
August 5: lost to Glamorgan by two runs (D/L).
August 12: lost to Somerset by five wickets.

SCOTLAND

At Edinburgh, May 6. **Surrey won by 18 runs** (D/L). **Surrey 187-7** (40 overs) (J. A. Rudolph 69); ‡**Scotland 118-6** (29 overs) (R. D. Berrington 43*). *Attendance:* 300. *Scotland debut:* J. Symes. *A disciplined display in the field from Scotland kept Surrey on a leash: Jacques Rudolph's 69 contained only a single boundary. But the Scots got bogged down themselves, and a second rain break arrived just as Richie Berrington was looking to up the tempo.*

At Edinburgh, May 7. **Scotland won by 18 runs** (D/L). **Nottinghamshire 219-7** (40 overs) (C. M. W. Read 59); ‡**Scotland 108-0** (23 overs) (J. H. Davey 44*, C. S. MacLeod 58*). *Attendance:* 320. *This time rain was to Scotland's advantage. A maiden fifty for Calum MacLeod – who had held four catches – ensured Scotland were ahead of the rate when drizzle became too heavy. It was their only win of the summer against a county.*

At Uddingston, May 13. **No result. Scotland 25-1** (6.5 overs) v ‡**Glamorgan.** *Attendance:* 100. *County debut:* M. J. North (Glamorgan). *The Bothwell Castle Policies ground in Uddingston – a town better known as the home of Tunnock's Caramel Wafers – made a damp debut in county cricket. It was handed the fixture after the square at Aberdeen's Mannofield Park was vandalised with weedkiller in 2011.*

At Uddingston, May 20. **Hampshire won by 89 runs.** ‡**Hampshire 220** (39.4 overs) (M. A. Carberry 76; R. M. Haq 3-42); **Scotland 131** (33 overs). *Attendance:* 250. *In the first uninterrupted match of Scotland's campaign, Michael Carberry and Jimmy Adams (33) flew out of the traps. Majid Haq pegged Hampshire back with three wickets in ten balls, but the Scottish batsmen never came to terms with the conditions.*

At Uddingston, August 5. **Scotland v Durham. Abandoned.** *This match was moved from Edinburgh due to flood damage, but Uddingston also proved unplayable.*

At Uddingston, August 19. **Somerset won by 53 runs** (D/L). ‡**Scotland 163** (37.5 overs) (P. L. Mommsen 67); **Somerset 133-3** (22.4 overs) (A. V. Suppiah 56). *Attendance:* 300. *County debut:* R. G. Mutch (Somerset). *Somerset's sixth consecutive win – confirmed when the heavens opened – kept alive their outside chance of reaching the semi-finals. Berrington played his 100th match for Scotland, aged 25, but made just 12 as his side dipped to 75-6 before a belligerent hand from Preston Mommsen, who was last out.*

Scotland away matches

May 27: lost to Durham by eight wickets.
June 4: lost to Hampshire by six wickets.
June 5: no result v Surrey.
July 15: lost to Somerset by 60 runs.
July 22: lost to Nottinghamshire by 88 runs.
July 29: lost to Glamorgan by eight wickets.

SOMERSET

At Taunton, May 27. **Hampshire won by nine wickets. Somerset 212-9** (40 overs) (N. R. D. Compton 81, J. C. Buttler 71); ‡**Hampshire 216-1** (28.2 overs) (M. A. Carberry 103*, J. H. K. Adams 56, J. M. Vince 44*). *Attendance:* 3,952. *This was Somerset's third consecutive defeat. Michael Carberry won the game with a six that also brought up his 83-ball century.*

At Taunton, July 15. **Somerset won by 60 runs.** ‡**Somerset 206** (38.4 overs) (C. Kieswetter 56; J. H. Davey 3-22, J. Symes 3-31); **Scotland 146** (31.4 overs) (R. D. Berrington 40; C. A. J. Meschede 4-27). *Attendance:* 2,410. *After scoring 56 from 53 balls, Craig Kieswetter handed the wicketkeeping gear to Jos Buttler and took a wicket with his right-arm slow. In between, a spell of three in 20 deliveries for Craig Meschede hastened Somerset's first win. A handful of rowdy Scotland players were reported to have upset guests at the team hotel in Taunton; Cricket Scotland offered to compensate Holiday Inn for a mattress soaked with a jug of iced water.*

At Taunton, July 22. **Somerset won by eight wickets.** ‡**Durham 147** (34 overs) (P. D. Trego 3-26); **Somerset 149-2** (20.2 overs) (C. Kieswetter 103). *Attendance:* 3,859. *Marcus Trescothick made 15 on his return from ankle surgery, but it was Kieswetter who provided the fireworks with 103 in 61 balls – the day after scoring an equally brutal 152 to beat Warwickshire in the Championship. The match was moved from Bath weeks in advance due to prolonged poor weather.*

At Taunton, July 28. **Somerset won by three wickets.** ‡**Glamorgan 250-9** (40 overs) (C. B. Cooke 137*; P. D. Trego 3-45, S. P. Kirby 3-42); **Somerset 251-7** (37.5 overs) (P. D. Trego 81, N. R. D. Compton 53). *Attendance:* 3,951. *Trego compared his one-day batting form to "a rusty gate", but swung smoothly enough for 81 off 43 balls; Trescothick contributed 14 to their opening stand of 92. Glamorgan reserve wicketkeeper Chris Cooke, born in Johannesburg and yet to play a first-class match for the county, finished on the losing side, despite a brilliant 137* from No. 3, while two Somerset players ended up in hospital: Meschede with a damaged finger; and his replacement Alex Barrow, left momentarily concussed when he dived into an advertising hoarding trying to save a four.*

BEST LIST A FIGURES FOR SOMERSET

9.5–0–66–8	S. R. G. Francis	v Derbyshire at Derby	2004
9.3–6–15–7	R. P. Lefebvre	v Devon at Torquay	1990
9.2–2–24–7	Mushtaq Ahmed	v Ireland at Taunton	1997
8–1–16–6	**Abdur Rehman**	**v Nottinghamshire at Taunton**	**2012**
8–0–24–6	I. V. A. Richards	v Lancashire at Manchester	1983
6.4–1–25–6	G. I. Burgess	v Glamorgan at Glastonbury	1972
10.3–3–29–6	J. Garner	v Northamptonshire at Lord's	1979
12–2–30–6	A. R. Caddick	v Gloucestershire at Taunton	1992
8–0–34–6	A. A. Jones	v Essex at Westcliff	1971
8–0–40–6	K. P. Dutch	v Northamptonshire at Northampton	2001
8.3–0–43–6	C. M. Willoughby	v Sri Lankans at Taunton	2006

At Taunton, August 12. **Somerset won by five wickets. Nottinghamshire 206-9** (40 overs) (M. J. Lumb 41, M. H. Wessels 53; Abdur Rehman 6-16); ‡**Somerset 209-5** (29.2 overs) (M. E. Trescothick 87*, C. Kieswetter 44; A. Carter 3-48). *Attendance:* 3,701. *Abdur Rehman took the new ball on a turning pitch, switched ends twice, and finished with 6-16 on his CB40 debut, the best figures for Somerset in 40-over cricket. Trescothick then regained form with 87*.*

At Taunton, August 27. **No result.** Reduced to 39 overs a side. **Surrey 29-1** (4.3 overs) v ‡**Somerset.** *Rain washed away either side's chances of overtaking group leaders Hampshire.*

Somerset away matches

May 4: lost to Surrey by 105 runs.
May 13: lost to Durham by 14 runs.
June 4: lost to Nottinghamshire by five wickets.
July 12: no result v Glamorgan.
August 14: beat Hampshire by 50 runs.
August 19: beat Scotland by 53 runs (D/L).

SURREY

At The Oval, May 4 (day/night). **Surrey won by 105 runs. Surrey 295-6** (40 overs) (R. J. Hamilton-Brown 101, S. M. Davies 72); ‡**Somerset 190** (37.1 overs) (N. R. D. Compton 53; S. C. Meaker 3-24, G. J. Batty 3-37, Z. S. Ansari 3-28). *Attendance:* 3,566. *County debut:* J. Overton (Somerset). *Surrey opened the new competition by repeating their victory over Somerset in the 2011 final – only more emphatically. The tone was set in an opening stand of 163 in 22.4 overs, with Rory Hamilton-Brown pressing on to his second one-day hundred. Stuart Meaker's speed and Surrey's phalanx of spinners did the rest.*

At The Oval, May 20. **Surrey won by 60 runs.** ‡**Surrey 221-7** (40 overs) (T. L. Maynard 77, Z. S. Ansari 60*; M. E. Claydon 3-58); **Durham 161** (35.4 overs) (G. J. Muchall 41). *Attendance:* 1,600. *Once Tom Maynard had seen off Mitch Claydon's initial burst, his stand of 85 in 15.3 overs with Zafar Ansari made light work of a slow pitch. Durham found it stickier, but had no one to unglue Surrey's accurate attack; Gareth Breese was forced to retire hurt on eight when he tore a calf muscle.*

At The Oval, June 3. **No result.** Reduced to 29 overs a side. **Surrey 76-1** (8 overs) v ‡**Hampshire.** *Rain halted Surrey, after Hamilton-Brown crashed 27 out of 35 from the first three overs. As the Diamond Jubilee flotilla made its way down the Thames, The Oval almost turned into a lake.*

At The Oval, June 5. **No result.** ‡**Scotland 124-4** (23 overs) (J. Symes 58*) v **Surrey.** *Scotland's South African-born pair, Jean Symes and Preston Mommsen, fought back after Jade Dernbach reduced them to 46-4, only for more miserable Bank Holiday weather to intervene.*

At Guildford, July 15. **Nottinghamshire won by five wickets.** ‡**Surrey 123** (33.4 overs) (D. J. Pattinson 3-27, H. F. Gurney 4-22); **Nottinghamshire 124-5** (30.3 overs) (J. W. A. Taylor 41*). *Attendance:* 2,251. *A catastrophic start of 8-5 meant Surrey were out of the match inside 19 balls, as Darren Pattinson and Harry Gurney delighted in seam and swing on the wicket used for the Championship game against Lancashire. Surrey could not protect such small boundaries against James Taylor's strokeplay.*

At The Oval, August 21 (day/night). **Surrey won by 93 runs.** ‡**Surrey 219-9** (40 overs) (K. P. Pietersen 43, M. N. W. Spriegel 51; G. G. Wagg 4-45); **Glamorgan 126** (26.3 overs) (G. J. Batty 3-4). Attendance: 10,262. *This match was dedicated to Tom Maynard, a player for both counties, who died on June 18. Before play, his father Matthew led a group of 30 charity cyclists on a lap around the outfield at the finish of a 170-mile ride from Cardiff, which by the end of the year had raised nearly £30,000 for the newly established Tom Maynard Trust. Around 7,000 complimentary tickets were handed out to the local community. Glamorgan captain Mark Wallace admitted he was deeply affected by the occasion: "I certainly wasn't really at the races for about five or ten overs, and a few of the lads were in pieces".*

Surrey away matches

May 6: beat Scotland by 18 runs (D/L).
June 2: beat Glamorgan by 57 runs (D/L).
August 1: beat Nottinghamshire by four wickets.
August 11: lost to Durham by 142 runs.
August 19: lost to Hampshire by four wickets.
August 27: no result v Somerset.

THOMAS LLOYD MAYNARD, 1989–2012

United in grief

STEVE JAMES

After turning left at Oval underground station, we looked desperately for the Hobbs Gate and the end of a bike ride that had begun in Cardiff the previous day at dawn. The sight that greeted us was wholly unexpected: hundreds of people cheering and clapping. A gap opened. We cycled through the car park and out on to the Oval turf. Around the ground we went, led by Matthew Maynard, on a tide of emotion.

I'd never expected to be on that outfield again, and I wish I'd not had to return. But on August 21 we were there in tribute to Matthew's son, Tom, who had been tragically killed on June 18. The match was a CB40 encounter between Tom's two former counties, Surrey and Glamorgan. And our 170-mile journey, organised by Ian Williams – a friend of the Maynard family for over 20 years – was the first event to raise money for the Tom Maynard Trust, set up "to help the development of aspiring disadvantaged cricketers and other sportspeople who require support with different aspects of their career development".

The 30-strong peloton featured Andrew Flintoff and many past and current Glamorgan players – including Will Bragg, David Brown, Jamie Dalrymple, Andrew Davies, Darren Thomas and Ryan Watkins – as well as Jason Ratcliffe and Paul Prichard, two former county players who now work for the PCA. As it reached the pavilion, both teams filed down the steps, united in their grief.

A video montage celebrating Tom's career was played on the big screen, then Richard Thompson – the Surrey chairman who had taken part in the ride alongside his chief executive Richard Gould – presented Matthew with Tom's posthumous county cap and a Surrey shirt, with his number (55) on it. The Surrey players all bore it on their shirts, just as the Glamorgan team wore 33, Tom's number during his time with them.

There was a presentation of cheques from the Trust to David Lloyd of Glamorgan, and Matthew Dunn and George Edwards of Surrey (who were represented by cricket manager Chris Adams). Next came a minute's applause for Tom. It was heartbreakingly emotional.

Seeing up close the effect it had, I have no idea how the two teams managed to play the game that followed so soon afterwards. That Surrey won was irrelevant: this was about helping a family come to terms with the unimaginably premature loss of their son. I know that the ride helped Matthew enormously in giving him a focus.

On his forearms, he now has two tattoos. On one is the first line of the poem *Lend Me A Child* by Edgar Guest, which was read by Matthew's brother Charlie at Tom's funeral at Llandaff Cathedral on July 4: "I'll lend you for a little time…" On the other it says: "Forever in our hearts. Thomas Lloyd."

The cycle ride and the creation of the Trust will hopefully ensure that young Tom Maynard, a cricketer of as much natural talent as his father, remains in all of our minds.

For details of the Tom Maynard Trust, please visit www.tommaynardtrust.com

GROUP C

DERBYSHIRE

At Derby, June 4. **Warwickshire won by 105 runs. Warwickshire 242-6** (40 overs) (T. R. Ambrose 77*, D. L. Maddy 40, R. Clarke 48; M. L. Turner 3-40); ‡**Derbyshire 137** (32.1 overs) (J. L. Clare 57; C. R. Woakes 3-46, S. A. Piolet 4-31). *Attendance:* 1,729. *Chris Woakes struck with the second and third legitimate deliveries of the Derbyshire innings, and again at the start of the fifth over to leave them no way back at 25-4.*

At Chesterfield, July 15. **Derbyshire won by 35 runs. Derbyshire 235-7** (40 overs) (Usman Khawaja 104, C. F. Hughes 66, W. J. Durston 44); ‡**Unicorns 200** (38.5 overs) (L. M. Reece 59; M. L. Turner 4-54). *Attendance:* 680. *County debut:* R. M. Johnson (Derbyshire). *Unicorns debut:* R. J. J. Woolley. *Usman Khawaja made a fluent first one-day century for Derbyshire on a surface slowed by rain, following a first-wicket partnership of 138 with Chesney Hughes. The Unicorns reached 200 for the first time in the campaign, but never threatened the target.*

At Chesterfield, July 22. **Derbyshire won by three wickets. Yorkshire 238-7** (40 overs) (A. W. Gale 51, G. S. Ballance 47, R. M. Pyrah 44); ‡**Derbyshire 239-7** (37.4 overs) (W. L. Madsen 40, R. M. Johnson 79; I. Wardlaw 3-60). *Attendance:* 1,554. *Richard Johnson, loaned by Warwickshire to provide wicketkeeping cover, proved a surprise match-winner with the bat. He was twice dropped by Azeem Rafiq in single figures, and went on to add 80 for the seventh wicket with 20-year-old Alex Hughes (37*), as both put in career-best performances. The teams observed a minute's silence for the former Yorkshire and England spinner Don Wilson, who died the day before, aged 74.*

At Derby, July 31 (day/night). **Kent won by nine wickets** (D/L). **Derbyshire 62-5** (14 overs); ‡**Kent 68-1** (10.5 overs). *Attendance:* 1,618. *Derbyshire were given just six more deliveries to boost their total when play resumed at 9.15pm after a four-hour rain delay. Kent, set 67 in 14 overs against bowlers struggling with a damp ball, took full advantage.*

At Derby, August 8 (day/night). **Derbyshire won by six wickets. Sussex 167** (37.2 overs) (M. W. Goodwin 40; T. D. Groenewald 3-32); ‡**Derbyshire 170-4** (37.4 overs) (W. L. Madsen 64*, D. J. Redfern 49). *Attendance:* 1,183. *Sussex arrived unbeaten, but lost their way in mid-innings when four wickets tumbled in three overs, with Murray Goodwin involved in two run-outs. From 55-3, Wayne Madsen and Dan Redfern, who received his county cap before the game, steadied the response.*

At Derby, August 27. **No result. Northamptonshire 232-8** (40 overs) (K. J. Coetzer 68, D. J. Sales 58; P. I. Burgoyne 3-31) v ‡**Derbyshire.** *Attendance:* 433. *Both teams fielded second-string attacks, which Kyle Coetzer and David Sales exploited for Northamptonshire. Rain arrived between innings to deny Derbyshire the opportunity to do likewise.*

Derbyshire away matches

May 6: beat Unicorns by 129 runs.
May 13: lost to Warwickshire by nine wickets.
May 20: lost to Yorkshire by seven wickets.
June 10: no result v Sussex.
July 13: no result v Northamptonshire.
August 12: lost to Kent by 111 runs.

KENT

At Canterbury, May 20. **Unicorns won by four wickets.** ‡**Kent 165** (39.5 overs) (S. A. Northeast 69; R. G. Querl 4-41); **Unicorns 166-6** (39 overs) (K. A. Parsons 46*; J. C. Tredwell 4-24). *Attendance:* 1,056. *Glenn Querl, having equalled his career-best figures, survived a hat-trick ball from James Tredwell on 128-6, and went on to hit four fours in seven deliveries to inflict Kent's first competitive defeat of the season. It was the Unicorns' fifth win in the CB40, but their only one of 2012.*

At Canterbury, June 1 (day/night). **Kent won by ten wickets** (D/L). ‡**Warwickshire 94-7** (26.3 overs) (M. Davies 3-10); **Kent 96-0** (16.3 overs) (S. W. Billings 58*). *Attendance:* 1,716. *Warwickshire were cut to ribbons by the wily Mark Davies, who had them 9-4 in the seventh over. Rain set Kent a revised target of 96 from 26; it was no test for Rob Key and Sam Billings, who drove and pulled with authority in a maiden fifty two weeks short of his 21st birthday.*

At Tunbridge Wells, June 10. **No result. Northamptonshire 168-5** (32 overs) (A. G. Wakely 42, N. J. O'Brien 46); ‡**Kent 6-0** (1 over). *Attendance:* 1,070. *Rain blighted the 100th Tunbridge Wells cricket week.*

At Canterbury, August 12. **Kent won by 111 runs. Kent 248-6** (40 overs) (S. W. Billings 143, D. I. Stevens 40, G. O. Jones 41*); ‡**Derbyshire 137** (31.4 overs) (M. Davies 3-25, D. I. Stevens 5-36). *Attendance:* 2,918. *Billings's superb 143 from 113 balls was the highest one-day score by a Kent player at Canterbury. He swept and chipped impudently, despite losing Key and Northeast for ducks, and was finally bowled attempting a last-over Dilscoop. Darren Stevens enjoyed a 19-ball purple patch of 5-7 to snuff out Derbyshire's resistance.*

At Canterbury, August 22 (day/night). **Kent won by 30 runs. Kent 226-5** (40 overs) (R. W. T. Key 101, D. I. Stevens 43); ‡**Yorkshire 196** (38.2 overs) (A. W. Gale 57; M. T. Coles 3-25, J. C. Tredwell 3-31). *Attendance:* 3,239. *Key played responsibly on a tricky pitch to make his first one-day hundred for four years. Yorkshire's challenge declined from 160-4, as Andrew Gale and Gary Ballance fell in successive balls.*

At Canterbury, August 27. **Sussex won by nine wickets.** ‡**Kent 210-5** (40 overs) (R. W. T. Key 40, B. P. Nash 51*); **Sussex 211-1** (30 overs) (L. J. Wright 101*, M. J. Prior 78*). *Attendance:* 3,698. *With a semi-final place at stake, Kent adopted a cautious approach on a two-paced pitch – and were made to pay. Steve Magoffin, appearing for Sussex in limited-overs cricket for the first time, tied them down, before Luke Wright and Matt Prior cantered along at seven an over in an unbroken stand of 152. Sussex won the group; Kent slipped behind Warwickshire into third on number of wins.*

Kent away matches

May 6: beat Yorkshire by four wickets.
June 5: no result v Unicorns.
July 16: no result v Sussex.
July 31: beat Derbyshire by nine wickets (D/L).
August 13: beat Warwickshire by six wickets.
August 19: beat Northamptonshire by five wickets.

NORTHAMPTONSHIRE

At Northampton, May 7. **No result.** Reduced to 10 overs a side. ‡**Unicorns 79-3** (10 overs); **Northamptonshire 16-1** (1.4 overs). *Luis Reece and Keith Parsons gave Unicorns a chance by adding 52 in 5.3 overs before rain.*

At Northampton, May 20. **Sussex won by 12 runs.** ‡**Sussex 180** (35.4 overs) (L. J. Wright 59; L. M. Daggett 4-31, C. D. de Lange 3-31); **Northamptonshire 168-7** (40 overs) (D. J. Sales 51). *Attendance:* 164. *Luke Wright's first appearance of the season, after falling ill with dengue fever at the IPL, brought him the match's highest score. It turned Sussex's way when Stephen Peters (39) holed out off Monty Panesar to end a stand of 58 with David Sales.*

At Northampton, May 27. **Warwickshire won by eight wickets.** ‡**Northamptonshire 148** (36.2 overs) (A. G. Wakely 62; K. H. D. Barker 3-27, J. S. Patel 4-27); **Warwickshire 149-2** (32.4 overs) (V. Chopra 87*). *Attendance:* 400. *Varun Chopra eased Warwickshire home in an utterly one-sided affair. Northamptonshire lost their last seven for 46.*

At Northampton, July 13 (day/night). **No result. Northamptonshire 220-8** (40 overs) (A. G. Wakely 85, D. J. Sales 74; M. L. Turner 4-38); ‡**Derbyshire 19-2** (6.1 overs). *Attendance:* 431. *Northamptonshire were favourites to record their first win of the competition until a torrential storm broke over the ground. Alex Wakely and Sales had batted carefully to add 152.*

At Northampton, August 9 (day/night). **Yorkshire won by 69 runs. Yorkshire 262-8** (40 overs) (P. A. Jaques 87, D. A. Miller 44; L. M. Daggett 4-54); ‡**Northamptonshire 193** (40 overs) (D. J. Sales 55; A. U. Rashid 4-38). *Attendance:* 385. *Yorkshire, superior in every department, were set on course by Phil Jaques's bruising 87 from 83 balls, and never slackened their grip. Adil Rashid gave the innings late momentum with 25 from 16 deliveries, before settling the issue with his first four-wicket haul in one-day cricket.*

At Northampton, August 19. **Kent won by five wickets.** ‡**Northamptonshire 232-9** (40 overs) (R. I. Newton 45, A. G. Wakely 74, C. A. L. Davis 54; M. T. Coles 3-45); **Kent 233-5** (38.4 overs) (S. A. Northeast 44, B. P. Nash 70*, G. O. Jones 52*; C. D. de Lange 3-35). *Attendance:* 936. *Brendan Nash (70* from 52 balls) and Geraint Jones (52* from 45) staged a superb recovery from 126-5 to* *take Kent home in the penultimate over and deny Northamptonshire a single home win. It had looked as if Wakely's fourth fifty of the competition, and Christian Davis's first at this level, would be enough.*

Northamptonshire away matches

May 6: lost to Warwickshire by six wickets.
June 3: no result v Yorkshire.
June 10: no result v Kent.
July 22: lost to Sussex by eight wickets.
July 29: beat Unicorns by eight wickets.
August 27: no result v Derbyshire.

SUSSEX

At Hove, May 13. **Sussex won by 144 runs.** ‡**Sussex 291-3** (40 overs) (E. C. Joyce 102, M. W. Machan 126*); **Unicorns 147-9** (40 overs) (C. D. Nash 3-29). *Attendance:* 1,372. *Matthew Machan, twice let off when a catcher stepped over the boundary, hit a maiden hundred in only his third one-day game. His second 50 came in only 21 balls; Ed Joyce's 102 was more prosaic. The Unicorns never threatened a stiff target on a dry pitch suited to Sussex's spinners.*

At Hove, May 24 (day/night). **Sussex won by four wickets.** ‡**Yorkshire 238-9** (40 overs) (A. W. Gale 42, G. S. Ballance 40, J. E. Root 46; A. Khan 3-51); **Sussex 240-6** (33.5 overs) (C. D. Nash 44, L. J. Wright 103, J. S. Gatting 45). *Attendance:* 2,884. *Luke Wright was back to his ebullient best as he scored his second List A hundred, in his first appearance at Hove for ten months. Yorkshire were perhaps 20 runs short on a good pitch, and Mitchell Starc's first over, costing 21, set the tone for a messy bowling performance.*

At Horsham, June 10. **No result. Sussex 111-5** (24 overs) (T. D. Groenewald 3-30) v ‡**Derbyshire.** *County debuts:* S. B. Styris (Sussex); Naved-ul-Hasan (Derbyshire). *Attendance:* 1,139. *Sussex struggled to cope with an accurate eight-over opening spell from Tim Groenewald. Persistent drizzle gradually got too heavy.*

At Arundel, July 16. **Sussex v Kent. Abandoned.**

At Arundel, July 22. **Sussex won by eight wickets. Northamptonshire 129** (39.5 overs) (C. J. Liddle 4-21); ‡**Sussex 130-2** (30.3 overs) (M. W. Goodwin 67*). *Attendance:* 4,667. *The accuracy of Sussex's seam quartet was too much for Northamptonshire. Murray Goodwin cut loose in what turned out to be his last one-day fifty for Sussex.*

At Hove, August 15 (day/night). **Sussex won by 17 runs.** ‡**Sussex 199-9** (40 overs) (M. H. Yardy 61; C. J. C. Wright 3-43, K. H. D. Barker 3-48); **Warwickshire 182** (39.4 overs) (W. A. T. Beer 3-27, C. D. Nash 3-27). *Attendance:* 3,766. *Sussex claimed a vital win over their main group rivals. On a pitch lacking pace, spin was the key: Mike Yardy bowled superbly with the new ball, then Will Beer removed Warwickshire's rump for a career-best 3-27. Yardy was characteristically gritty in compiling the game's only half-century.*

Sussex away matches

May 20: beat Northamptonshire by 12 runs.
June 3: no result v Unicorns.
July 11: no result v Warwickshire.
August 8: lost to Derbyshire by six wickets.
August 19: beat Yorkshire by three wickets (D/L).
August 27: beat Kent by nine wickets.

UNICORNS

At Wormsley, May 6. **Derbyshire won by 129 runs. Derbyshire 287-3** (40 overs) (M. J. Guptill 125, W. J. Durston 120*); ‡**Unicorns 158-9** (40 overs) (C. F. Hughes 5-29). *Attendance:* 650. *Unicorns debuts:* S. P. Cheetham, W. W. Lee, T. J. New, M. D. T. Roberts. *Martin Guptill and Wes Durston put on 222 for the second wicket – the highest partnership in this year's CB40; Durston's 120* was a career-best, surpassing the 117 he made for the Unicorns at Arundel in 2010, the innings which alerted Derbyshire. The Unicorns crumpled against the left-arm spin of Chesney Hughes, who took five wickets for the first time.*

At Scarborough, May 27. **Yorkshire won by eight wickets. Unicorns 184** (40 overs) (T. J. New 83*; R. J. Sidebottom 3-44, M. A. Starc 3-36); ‡**Yorkshire 186-2** (32.2 overs) (A. Lyth 60*, G. S.

Ballance 103*). *This was a Unicorns home fixture, though played in Yorkshire, but the turnout was poor by Scarborough standards. Two wickets for Mitchell Starc in his second spell snuffed out any help for Tom New. Gary Ballance's hundred, achieved in 88 balls, was his first in county one-day cricket, following three in his native Zimbabwe.*

At Southend, June 3. **Unicorns v Sussex. Abandoned.**

At Southend, June 5. **No result. Unicorns 177-8** (40 overs) (J. E. Ord 52); ‡**Kent 9-0** (3 overs). *Unicorns debut:* V. Tripathi. *The Unicorns crept along at a snail's pace on a difficult wicket, before a late flourish by Luis Reece (36* from 35 balls).*

At Wormsley, July 29. **Northamptonshire won by eight wickets.** Reduced to 34 overs a side. ‡**Unicorns 163-8** (34 overs) (B. L. Wadlan 41; L. M. Daggett 4-39, J. D. Middlebrook 3-14); **Northamptonshire 167-2** (26.2 overs) (R. I. Newton 45, A. G. Wakely 52*, D. J. Sales 47*). *Attendance:* 700. *Unicorns debut:* L. J. Hill. *Northamptonshire climbed off the bottom with their only win, set up by James Middlebrook and Lee Daggett, who was twice on a hat-trick.*

At Wormsley, August 19. **Warwickshire won by ten wickets. Unicorns 185** (38.5 overs) (R. G. Querl 44, P. R. Hindmarch 50; C. R. Woakes 4-24); ‡**Warwickshire 186-0** (29.2 overs) (W. T. S. Porterfield 100*, V. Chopra 73*). *Attendance:* 1,020. *County debut:* I. D. Blackwell (Warwickshire). *The Unicorns sunk to 45-7 before Glenn Querl (44 from 27 balls) and No. 11 Paul Hindmarch (50 from 49) hit out. But they could do nothing to stop William Porterfield and Varun Chopra inflating their averages.*

Unicorns away matches

May 7: no result v Northamptonshire.
May 13: lost to Sussex by 144 runs.
May 20: beat Kent by four wickets.
July 15: lost to Derbyshire by 35 runs.
July 22: lost to Warwickshire by 60 runs.
August 12: lost to Yorkshire by five wickets (D/L).

WARWICKSHIRE

At Birmingham, May 6. **Warwickshire won by six wickets.** ‡**Northamptonshire 209-7** (40 overs) (K. J. Coetzer 44, A. J. Hall 52*; K. H. D. Barker 3-41); **Warwickshire 212-4** (37.3 overs) (I. R. Bell 82*, R. Clarke 54*). *Attendance:* 2,124. *Ian Bell followed his Championship century against Durham with a composed 82* on the same pitch, cashing in against the seamers to add an unbroken 103 with Rikki Clarke. It was only Bell's third CB40 appearance – all against Northamptonshire – since winning Warwickshire the 2010 final.*

At Birmingham, May 13. **Warwickshire won by nine wickets. Derbyshire 122** (31.1 overs) (W. J. Durston 44; R. Clarke 3-22, J. S. Patel 3-22); ‡**Warwickshire 125-1** (24.3 overs) (I. J. L. Trott 41*, W. T. S. Porterfield 81*). *Attendance:* 2,154. *Warwickshire held catches off consecutive deliveries without taking a wicket: Dan Redfern pulled a Keith Barker no-ball to deep midwicket; the batsmen crossed, and Wes Durston drove the free hit to mid-off. Derbyshire were still fired out quickly, with Clarke taking three wickets and two catches against his former county. Jonathan Trott eschewed all risk in his final innings before the international summer.*

At Birmingham, July 11 (day/night). **Warwickshire v Sussex. Abandoned.**

At Birmingham, July 22. **Warwickshire won by 60 runs.** ‡**Warwickshire 228-9** (40 overs) (V. Chopra 69, D. L. Maddy 79*; W. W. Lee 3-50); **Unicorns 168-7** (40 overs) (K. A. Parsons 58; C. R. Woakes 3-30). *Attendance:* 2,250. *Darren Maddy's first CB40 half-century for two years provided Warwickshire with welcome acceleration. Chris Woakes took three wickets in four balls; before Keith Parsons, dropped twice, could only delay the inevitable.*

At Birmingham, August 7 (day/night). **Warwickshire won by three wickets** (D/L). **Yorkshire 213-8** (34 overs) (A. W. Gale 76, A. Lyth 69; P. M. Best 3-43); ‡**Warwickshire 239-7** (33.2 overs) (J. O. Troughton 61, T. R. Ambrose 64). *Attendance:* 2,135. *Warwickshire stumbled from 197-4 to 199-7 in four balls before fringe players Steffan Piolet (23* from nine), batting with a runner due to a hamstring injury, and Paul Best (16* from nine) plundered 40 from 17 deliveries to bring victory in the final over. Yorkshire could not build on Adam Lyth's freewheeling 69, which featured three sixes in a row off Chris Wright either side of an hour-long stoppage; Yorkshire lost five wickets in 19 balls upon the resumption.*

At Birmingham, August 13 (day/night). **Kent won by six wickets. Warwickshire 92** (30.4 overs) (D. I. Stevens 4-25); ‡**Kent 93-4** (20.2 overs). *Attendance:* 2,197. *A grassy pitch suited Kent's seam attack, who rolled Warwickshire over for their third-lowest one-day score at Edgbaston.*

Warwickshire away matches

May 27: beat Northamptonshire by eight wickets.
June 1: lost to Kent by ten wickets (D/L).
June 4: beat Derbyshire by 105 runs.
August 15: lost to Sussex by 17 runs.
August 19: beat Unicorns by ten wickets.
August 27: beat Yorkshire by 55 runs (D/L).

YORKSHIRE

At Leeds, May 6. **Kent won by four wickets.** ‡**Yorkshire 175-9** (40 overs) (A. W. Gale 44, J. E. Root 49; M. T. Coles 6-32); **Kent 176-6** (39.2 overs) (R. W. T. Key 40, D. I. Stevens 59; Azeem Rafiq 3-22). *Attendance:* 1,964. *Coles again burned too bright for Yorkshire. Following his maiden century in the Championship meeting at Headingley, and four wickets in the return match at Canterbury, he opened the one-day season with Kent's eighth-best figures. Darren Stevens's no-nonsense fifty kept them in charge, and a clatter of late wickets gave the false impression of a close contest.*

At Leeds, May 20. **Yorkshire won by seven wickets. Derbyshire 219-8** (40 overs) (C. F. Hughes 50, M. J. Guptill 89; M. A. Starc 3-28); ‡**Yorkshire 223-3** (37.4 overs) (P. A. Jaques 47, G. S. Ballance 77*). *Attendance:* 1,851. *County debut:* M. A. Starc. *A powerful opening by Chesney Hughes and Martin Guptill denied Mitchell Starc a wicket in his first spell for Yorkshire – after a tortuous delay for visa clearance – but he came back strongly with 3-11 in his last three overs.*

At Leeds, June 3. **Yorkshire v Northamptonshire. Abandoned.**

At Leeds, August 12. **Yorkshire won by five wickets** (D/L). **Unicorns 150-6** (37 overs) (K. A. Parsons 48*; A. U. Rashid 3-24); ‡**Yorkshire 162-5** (34 overs) (G. S. Ballance 69*). *County debut:* D. M. Hodgson (Yorkshire). *Attendance:* 2,007. *Unicorns debut:* P. R. Hindmarch. *The Unicorns were stifled by Ryan Sidebottom, on his first appearance in six weeks following injury, and the continuing resurgence of Adil Rashid. At 78-5 when rain arrived in the 19th over, Yorkshire would have lost comfortably had the break proved permanent. On the resumption, Gary Ballance, a centurion against the same opponents earlier in the season, hurried Yorkshire to their revised target of 162 from 37 overs.*

At Leeds, August 19. **Sussex won by three wickets** (D/L). **Yorkshire 200-8** (28 overs) (A. W. Gale 43, J. E. Root 41; C. J. Liddle 3-44); ‡**Sussex 207-7** (28 overs) (C. D. Nash 53, E. C. Joyce 54; Azeem Rafiq 3-46). *Attendance:* 1,909. *Azeem Rafiq bowled with discipline until the final over, when he conceded 16: Amjad Khan struck 15 of them, including the two scampered through wide gully that saw Sussex home off the last ball. Brisk half-centuries from Chris Nash and Ed Joyce kept Sussex on top, but Rashid and Rafiq applied pressure to set up a tense finish. The result pushed Sussex top and Yorkshire out of semi-final contention.*

At Scarborough, August 27. **Warwickshire won by 55 runs** (D/L). **Warwickshire 211-6** (29 overs) (W. T. S. Porterfield 43, T. R. Ambrose 87*, D. L. Maddy 44; S. A. Patterson 3-25); ‡**Yorkshire 158** (25.1 overs) (G. S. Ballance 68; N. M. Carter 4-16). *Attendance:* 4,047. *County debut:* J. A. Leaning (Yorkshire). *Yorkshire rested several players between Twenty20 finals day and a Championship match, but Scarborough's festival-goers turned up in good numbers, despite showers and occasional semi-darkness. Rich Pyrah broke his hand intercepting a blow at backward point, before Neil Carter, who had spent much of the season playing for Smethwick in the Birmingham & District League, put the result beyond doubt with the first three wickets. Ballance, captaining Yorkshire for the first time, at least went down fighting, with five sixes. Warwickshire leapfrogged Kent to claim the last semi-final spot.*

Yorkshire away matches

May 24: lost to Sussex by four wickets.
May 27: beat Unicorns by eight wickets.
July 22: lost to Derbyshire by three wickets.
August 7: lost to Warwickshire by three wickets (D/L).
August 9: beat Northamptonshire by 69 runs.
August 22: lost to Kent by 30 runs.

SEMI-FINALS

LANCASHIRE v WARWICKSHIRE

At Manchester, September 1. Warwickshire won by 23 runs. Toss: Warwickshire.

Chopra anchored Warwickshire's innings with a skilful, unhurried century. Still, Lancashire were content to be chasing 251, as they had reined Warwickshire in from 126 without loss, and had in their ranks two of the competition's leading scorers, Moore and Croft, and a 44-ball centurion, Tom Smith. But all three threw away their wickets, and Lancashire were beaten in a limited-overs semi-final for the 11th time in 13 since 2000. Warwickshire executed their bowling plans perfectly, peppering Prince with the short ball and, from 90 for five, Horton – barely needed in the group stage – was left to fight alone. Troughton snapped up four catches, and his only frustration was losing Ambrose to a bizarre thigh strain, picked up when – from the comfort of his chair as he waited to bat – he extended his leg on the dressing-room balcony; Chapple allowed Warwickshire to summon Johnson from Knowle & Dorridge's game at Walsall to stand in as wicketkeeper. It was not Lancashire's only act of generosity: the club made attendance free for all members and under-16s on a glorious Saturday, yet Old Trafford was barely a third full.

Man of the Match: V. Chopra. *Attendance:* 3,554.

Warwickshire

W. T. S. Porterfield c Moore b Keedy 67
V. Chopra c Croft b Shahzad. 110
*J. O. Troughton c Moore b Keedy 11
D. L. Maddy c Brown b Shahzad 18
R. Clarke c Moore b Smith 17
C. R. Woakes c Cross b Shahzad 8
I. D. Blackwell not out 2
P. M. Best not out 8
L-b 3, w 6 9

1/126 (1) 2/150 (3) (6 wkts, 40 overs) 250
3/186 (4) 4/217 (5)
5/240 (6) 6/240 (2) 8 overs: 33-0

†T. R. Ambrose, N. M. Carter and C. J. C. Wright did not bat.

Chapple 8–1–37–0; Shahzad 8–0–52–3; Smith 4–0–38–1; Parry 7–0–49–0; Keedy 8–1–44–2; Croft 5–0–27–0.

Lancashire

S. C. Moore c sub (R. M. Johnson) b Carter 17
T. C. Smith c Troughton b Carter 6
A. G. Prince c Troughton b Blackwell 26
S. J. Croft b Wright 18
K. R. Brown c Maddy b Wright 9
P. J. Horton c Troughton b Carter 78
†G. D. Cross lbw b Blackwell. 19
A. Shahzad c Blackwell b Best 10
*G. Chapple c Troughton b Carter 13
S. D. Parry c Best b Wright. 17
G. Keedy not out 3
B 1, l-b 3, w 7 11

1/18 (2) 2/29 (1) 3/50 (4) (39.4 overs) 227
4/77 (5) 5/90 (3) 6/125 (7)
7/147 (8) 8/184 (9) 9/218 (6)
10/227 (10) 8 overs: 35-2

Carter 8–0–38–4; Woakes 8–0–48–0; Wright 7.4–0–48–3; Blackwell 8–0–36–2; Best 4–0–24–1; Maddy 4–0–29–0.

Umpires: J. H. Evans and J. W. Lloyds. Third umpire: M. A. Gough.

SUSSEX v HAMPSHIRE

At Hove, September 1. Hampshire won by eight wickets. Toss: Sussex.

Carberry and Vince, sensing it was wise to cash in against the hard ball on a slow pitch, laid waste to the Sussex bowling with 129 inside 13 overs; after that, the rest had only to work it around to confirm Hampshire's fourth limited-overs final in four seasons. Carberry showed crushing upper-body strength in thumping five leg-side sixes, raising his seventh fifty in eight innings from 25 balls in a 6444 sequence off Liddle. His performance overshadowed Wright's superb 122 from 100 deliveries, his third century of the competition, which reserved particular punishment for Griffiths. Hampshire should have been made to pay for missing Wright on 35, when Shafayat (who lost his place for the final) put down a chance at deep square leg, but Sussex did not kick on. Prior was cramped on his pads, and failed to hit a boundary in his 52 balls – evidence for those who suspected his game was not suited to high-end one-day cricket. Goodwin, Wright and Brown fell to consecutive deliveries as Sussex mustered only 22 from the last six overs.

Man of the Match: M. A. Carberry. *Attendance:* 3,887.

Sussex

C. D. Nash c Ervine b Briggs	26
L. J. Wright c Briggs b Ervine	122
M. J. Prior b Wood	28
*E. C. Joyce c Dawson b Briggs	0
M. W. Goodwin c Adams b Griffiths	10
M. H. Yardy b Griffiths	1
†B. C. Brown c Bates b Ervine	0
K. O. Wernars c Adams b Ervine	1
W. A. T. Beer not out	10
S. J. Magoffin not out	9
B 1, l-b 2, w 7, n-b 2	12
1/71 (1) 2/159 (3) 3/164 (4) 4/195 (5) 5/195 (2) 6/195 (7) 7/197 (8) 8/199 (6) (8 wkts, 40 overs)	219
8 overs: 46-0	

C. J. Liddle did not bat.

Dawson 8–1–35–0; Wood 8–0–46–1; Griffiths 8–1–67–2; Briggs 8–0–32–2; Ervine 8–1–36–3.

Hampshire

M. A. Carberry c Liddle b Beer	68
J. M. Vince b Beer	58
*J. H. K. Adams not out	44
S. M. Katich not out	47
L-b 1, w 4	5
1/129 (1) 2/130 (2) (2 wkts, 33 overs)	222
8 overs: 75-0	

S. M. Ervine, L. A. Dawson, B. M. Shafayat, †M. D. Bates, C. P. Wood, D. R. Briggs and D. A. Griffiths did not bat.

Wernars 1–0–11–0; Magoffin 5–0–47–0; Yardy 5–0–29–0; Liddle 6–0–43–0; Nash 8–0–43–0; Beer 8–0–48–2.

Umpires: P. J. Hartley and T. E. Jesty. Third umpire: N. G. B. Cook.

FINAL

HAMPSHIRE v WARWICKSHIRE

JAMES COYNE

At Lord's, September 15. Tied. Hampshire won by virtue of losing fewer wickets. Toss: Warwickshire.

The Lord's final, now in its 50th year, was stuck in a midlife crisis – but this game was uncommonly blessed. Contested by two teams in search of a double, it crackled with past, present, or aspiring international cricketers, and was played in an autumnal glow out of step with a miserable summer. For a few hours at least, the imperfections of England's one-day competition could be forgotten.

Warwickshire required five to win off three balls. Blackwell had lost his head, and his stumps, possibly trying to achieve it in one blow, which brought Carter out to face Kabir Ali – selected ahead

Shaun Botterill, Getty Images

Point made: Kabir Ali, a late inclusion for Hampshire, seals their last-ball victory as Neil Carter begins the lonely walk back.

of Hamza Riazuddin only at the last minute. Ali, unerringly full, almost had him lbw first ball, then overpitched with the next and was driven past the groping cover fielder for four. One to win off the last: Carter needed only to make contact and Woakes – like Geoff Miller of Derbyshire in the 1981 NatWest Trophy final – would have been up his end in a flash.

Crucially, however, Hampshire's superb young wicketkeeper Bates was standing up, which minimised the chance of a stolen run. Carter prodded at a dipping full toss – which arrived a bit wider than he thought – and missed; Bates gathered cleanly and quickly destroyed the stumps. Carter hadn't even left his ground; so distraught was he at this fresh-air shot that he simply turned round and marched back to the Pavilion. Hampshire had tied a match, again. But unlike Twenty20 finals day in 2010 and 2011, there was no need for confusion or super overs: they had won because they lost only five wickets to Warwickshire's seven.

Carter, now 37 and still hoping for a final fling with Scotland, had come painfully close to signing off as a hero. And yet, a few balls into the match, he was looking dangerously like a sympathy pick, as his gentle swingers were swatted away by batsmen eager to advance on a slow track. Warwickshire's two spinners stemmed the flow, inadvertently helped by McKenzie who, after a fortnight back home in South Africa, dawdled for 36 balls over 19. Ervine and Katich cut loose in the closing overs, but Warwickshire, conspicuously ragged in the field, were content to chase 245.

The match, as so often when graced by a player of such obvious supremacy, appeared to rest with Bell. He did not open – as he had been doing so successfully for England's one-day team – but instead appeared at 53 for one. By the 26th over, Bell had advanced that to 137 for two, and the options for Adams – who had earlier held Hampshire together – were dwindling fast. His first-choice spinner, Danny Briggs, was away at the World Twenty20, and Dawson was already bowled out. Wood pleaded with his captain to return to the attack, and with his second ball unleashed a rising leg-cutter which was top-edged by Ambrose, playing the day after he went public with his battle against depression; Bates, by now standing up to everyone bar Griffiths, clung on.

When Clarke was bowled by Wood to make it 193 for five, Bell knew it really was up to him. Reading the length masterfully, he converted four of his next six deliveries into boundaries. But when Griffiths served up a full toss on his pads, this most feline of players caressed when he should have clobbered – and the ball flew to Carberry, the best fielder in English cricket, waiting in the shade beneath the Mound Stand. Warwickshire still needed 27. And without Bell, that was one too many.

Man of the Match: J. H. K. Adams. *Attendance:* 17,808.

Hampshire

M. A. Carberry c Patel b Wright	35	L. A. Dawson not out	2
J. M. Vince c Patel b Carter	18	B 1, l-b 2, w 7, n-b 2	12
*J. H. K. Adams b Woakes	66		——
N. D. McKenzie b Blackwell	19	1/48 (2) 2/70 (1) (5 wkts, 40 overs)	244
S. M. Ervine c Ambrose b Maddy	57	3/127 (4) 4/171 (3)	
S. M. Katich not out	35	5/240 (5) 8 overs: 57-1	

†M. D. Bates, C. P. Wood, Kabir Ali and D. A. Griffiths did not bat.

Carter 8–0–63–1; Woakes 8–0–59–1; Blackwell 8–0–42–1; Wright 3–0–14–1; Patel 8–0–32–0; Maddy 5–0–31–1.

Warwickshire

D. L. Maddy c Wood b Dawson	35	I. D. Blackwell b Kabir Ali	2
V. Chopra c Adams b Wood	26	N. M. Carter not out	4
I. R. Bell c Carberry b Griffiths	81	B 1, l-b 6, w 7, n-b 3	17
†T. R. Ambrose c Bates b Wood	26		——
*J. O. Troughton c Adams b Ervine	5	1/53 (2) 2/89 (1) (7 wkts, 40 overs)	244
R. Clarke b Wood	24	3/137 (4) 4/144 (5)	
C. R. Woakes not out	24	5/193 (6) 6/218 (3) 7/240 (8) 8 overs: 41-0	

J. S. Patel and C. J. C. Wright did not bat.

Dawson 8–0–39–1; Kabir Ali 8–0–50–1; Wood 8–0–39–3; Ervine 6–0–46–1; Griffiths 8–0–43–1; Katich 2–0–20–0.

Umpires: R. K. Illingworth and N. A. Mallender. Third umpire: J. H. Evans.

WINNERS 2010–12

		Man of the Match
2010	WARWICKSHIRE‡ beat Somerset by three wickets.	I. R. Bell
2011	SURREY beat Somerset‡ by five wickets.	J. W. Dernbach
2012	HAMPSHIRE beat WARWICKSHIRE† by virtue of losing fewer wickets.	J. H. K. Adams

A full list of past winners of the knockout competition can be found on pages 841–2 of *Wisden 2010*. Winners of the National League can be found on page 855 of *Wisden 2009*. Winners of the Benson and Hedges Cup (1972–2002) can be found on page 857 of *Wisden 2006*.

Past winners of all competitions can be found at www.wisden.com

AUSTRALIA A IN ENGLAND, 2012

REVIEW BY PAUL EDWARDS

The first Australia A tour of England since 1995 was a curious affair. Even a cursory glance would suggest it was ruined by injury, unavailability and rain. Three members of the original squad played no games at all, and three others were flown home early ahead of the World Twenty20 to play in practice matches in Darwin, where another "Australia A" team took the field against an Australia XI. All the while, Ed Cowan was preparing a weakened side to take on England Lions at Edgbaston.

Although the weather left the first unofficial Test at Old Trafford relatively unharmed, only 149 overs were possible in the second. Both were drawn – an unsatisfactory climax to a tour which began with exciting finishes in the two county games. It fulfilled many of the purposes intended by Cricket Australia, who were keen to sort the wheat from the chaff ahead of Ashes series in England in 2013 and 2015.

Cowan, who played for Gloucestershire before and after the tour, scored 366 runs and failed by a single to reach a century at the building site masquerading as Old Trafford. Two other Australians with reputations to restore made important progress: Tim Paine proved he had finally shaken off the serious finger injury which had wrecked 18 months of his career; and in the first innings at Manchester, Mitchell Johnson suggested his bowling could recover some of the accuracy and penetration he possessed in his pomp.

History may show that, for others, this was as close to international cricket as they would get, but Jackson Bird's new-ball bowling was a serious proposition, and Michael Klinger's tight technique and cool temperament served his side well in Manchester. No one was claiming it was a full Australia A-team that took the field at Edgbaston, but it was considerably stronger than the Australia C or D mocked by some critics.

The England selectors found the unofficial Tests useful too, although Ravi Bopara remained a concern. Without any cricket for two and a half weeks after he withdrew from the Second Test against South Africa for personal reasons, he was added to the Lions squad, attended training at Old Trafford, but pulled out at the 11th hour, confessing he still did not feel ready to return.

Nick Compton and Joe Root offered evidence that they were ready for the step up to Test cricket, and both were selected for the senior tour of India. Jonny Bairstow's 139 at Old Trafford earned him a place in the final Test of the summer when Kevin Pietersen paid the price for the text-messaging saga. James Harris and Simon Kerrigan each collected six-wicket hauls, but Chris Woakes – who somehow went wicketless in 42 overs – and James Tredwell bowled every bit as well. On this evidence, Tredwell was unlucky to miss out on initial selection for the India tour, though he was called up as cover ahead of the Third Test at Kolkata.

After some thought, Cowan named Woakes as the outstanding Lions player, but there was less doubt about Australia's star performer. Cowan was an astute skipper and a courteous, intelligent ambassador. Such qualities were particularly laudable given that his wife, the broadcaster Virginia Lette, was about to give birth to a daughter, Romy, who was delivered two days after the tour finished.

AUSTRALIA A TOURING PARTY

*E. J. M. Cowan, G. J. Bailey, J. M. Bird, J. A. Burns, T. L. W. Cooper, N. M. Coulter-Nile, B. C. J. Cutting, L. M. Davis, P. J. Forrest, J. M. Holland, M. G. Johnson, M. Klinger, N. M. Lyon, T. D. Paine, J. L. Pattinson, S. P. D. Smith, M. A. Starc. *Coach:* T. J. Cooley.

P. J. Cummins was originally selected, but suffered an abdominal niggle during Australia's one-day international series against England, and was replaced by Coulter-Nile. Pattinson withdrew with a side strain during the pre-tour training camp in Hampshire, and was replaced by A. C. McDermott. Cutting was diagnosed with a back problem after the Derbyshire game. Bailey, Smith and Starc flew home after the county fixtures to play in practice matches for the World Twenty20. Forrest strained his side in the match at Old Trafford; he was replaced by P. J. Hughes, called up from Worcestershire.

DERBYSHIRE v AUSTRALIA A

At Derby, July 27–29. Drawn. Toss: Australia A. First-class debut: C. M. Durham.

Australia A's opening fixture remained highly entertaining all the way to the last ball. Cowan set a positive tone with his 15th first-class century, and the tourists sprinted along at five an over, allowing their bowlers 16 overs at Derbyshire that evening. But they were stymied next morning by nightwatchman Palladino. Hit in the ribs by Starc in a fearsome opening spell, he shrugged it off to drive, cut and pull his way to a maiden first-class hundred, from 113 balls, against an attack comprising three Test players plus Bird, the leading wicket-taker in the 2011-12 Sheffield Shield. Set 315 from 73 overs, Derbyshire were kept in touch by Khawaja's second half-century of the game against his countrymen but, when four wickets tumbled in 25 balls, they almost paid for maintaining their commitment to the chase. Last pair Chris Durham, on his first-class debut, and Footitt survived the final six overs to see out the draw.

Close of play: first day, Derbyshire 57-1 (Madsen 25, Palladino 4); second day, Australia A 141-6 (Cowan 1, Starc 1).

Australia A

	First innings		Second innings	
*E. J. M. Cowan st Durham b Wainwright	109	–	(7) not out	32
M. Klinger c Khawaja b Turner	25	–	(1) c Durston b Footitt	10
P. J. Forrest c Durston b Wainwright	52	–	(4) c Khawaja b Turner	8
G. J. Bailey c Turner b Wainwright	81	–	(6) c Khawaja b Wainwright	2
J. A. Burns not out	74			
S. P. D. Smith not out	6	–	(3) c Madsen b Redfern	78
†T. D. Paine (did not bat)		–	(2) c Durham b Footitt	9
M. G. Johnson (did not bat)		–	(5) b Wainwright	21
M. A. Starc (did not bat)		–	(8) c Redfern b Wainwright	36
N. M. Lyon (did not bat)		–	(9) not out	8
B 5, l-b 4, w 2, n-b 4	15		B 10, w 5, n-b 2	17
1/35 (2) 2/144 (3) 3/229 (1) 4/340 (4) (4 wkts dec, 72 overs)	362		1/10 (1) 2/30 (2) 3/58 (4) 4/130 (5) 5/136 (3) 6/137 (6) 7/210 (8) (7 wkts dec, 55 overs)	221

J. M. Bird did not bat.

Palladino 14–3–52–0; Turner 11–0–60–1; Footitt 7–0–40–0; Wainwright 28–3–133–3; Whiteley 10–0–63–0; Durston 2–0–5–0. *Second innings*—Footitt 11–1–52–2; Palladino 12–4–27–0; Turner 9–0–61–1; Whiteley 4–0–15–0; Redfern 7–1–25–1; Wainwright 10–2–29–3; Khawaja 2–1–2–0.

Derbyshire

Batter	First innings		Second innings	
*W. L. Madsen	c Klinger b Lyon	34	c Smith b Johnson	9
M. S. Lineker	c Forrest b Starc	22	c and b Lyon	34
A. P. Palladino	b Bird	106	(8) c Paine b Johnson	3
U. T. Khawaja	not out	56	(3) c Smith b Johnson	66
W. J. Durston	not out	37	(7) c Bailey b Lyon	40
D. J. Redfern	(did not bat)		(4) c Paine b Starc	56
R. A. Whiteley	(did not bat)		(5) lbw b Bird	11
D. J. Wainwright	(did not bat)		(6) st Paine b Lyon	18
†C. M. Durham	(did not bat)		not out	12
M. L. Turner	(did not bat)		c Smith b Lyon	1
M. H. A. Footitt	(did not bat)		not out	3
	B 1, l-b 5, n-b 8	14	B 8, l-b 7, n-b 2	17
	1/48 (2) 2/97 (1) 3/200 (3) (3 wkts dec, 66 overs)	269	1/17 (1) 2/109 (2) 3/127 (3) 4/171 (5) 5/196 (4) 6/235 (6) 7/252 (8) 8/256 (7) 9/259 (10) (9 wkts, 73 overs)	270

Johnson 14–1–52–0; Bird 21–1–84–1; Starc 17–2–62–1; Lyon 14–2–65–1. *Second innings*—Bird 14–1–44–1; Johnson 17–2–47–3; Lyon 30–4–115–4; Starc 12–2–49–1.

Umpires: N. G. B. Cook and A. G. Wharf.

DURHAM v AUSTRALIA A

At Chester-le-Street, August 1–3. Durham won by 19 runs. Toss: Durham. First-class debuts: P. Coughlin, R. Singh.

Durham fielded only four of the side that beat Middlesex the previous week, yet managed to overcome an unimpressive touring team. Australia A finally seemed to be showing some class when their opening pair reached 99 in pursuit of 224, but they surrendered headlong to Blackwell's left-arm spin. After being overlooked for more than two months, largely for being unfit, he produced a sequence of seven for 22 in 11 overs to finish with career-best figures. Cowan, who played him comfortably, and Starc were the only two left-handers; the rest struggled against the ball turning away from them. Blackwell had followed a ludicrous dismissal in the first innings – when he ran down the pitch to his fourth ball, and left-arm spinner Holland's second, and nicked it behind – with a forthright 62, reaching 50 with three successive leg-side sixes off Starc in an over which cost 28. Durham still saw fit to send him out on loan to Warwickshire two weeks later.

Close of play: first day, Australia A 111-6 (Paine 19, Coulter-Nile 10); second day, Australia A 56-0 (Davis 38, Cowan 18).

Durham

Batter	First innings		Second innings	
*M. D. Stoneman	c Bailey b McDermott	25	c Paine b Starc	0
R. Singh	lbw b McDermott	22	b McDermott	12
G. J. Muchall	c Paine b Coulter-Nile	11	c Forrest b Coulter-Nile	10
B. A. Stokes	c Starc b McDermott	8	c Paine b McDermott	10
J. G. Myburgh	c Davis b Coulter-Nile	34	c Paine b Coulter-Nile	8
I. D. Blackwell	c Paine b Holland	0	c Bailey b Holland	62
†M. J. Richardson	lbw b Holland	21	lbw b Holland	34
M. A. Wood	b Holland	0	lbw b Coulter-Nile	12
P. Coughlin	not out	29	lbw b Holland	3
M. E. Claydon	c Klinger b McDermott	5	b Starc	13
R. M. R. Brathwaite	lbw b Starc	16	not out	5
	B 13, l-b 8, n-b 5	26	B 2, l-b 13, n-b 1	16
	1/38 (2) 2/61 (3) 3/65 (1) 4/75 (4) 5/75 (6) 6/132 (7) 7/136 (5) 8/136 (8) 9/151 (10) 10/197 (11) (60.5 overs)	197	1/0 (1) 2/22 (2) 3/38 (4) 4/38 (3) 5/49 (5) 6/135 (6) 7/153 (8) 8/162 (9) 9/167 (7) 10/185 (10) (44.4 overs)	185

Starc 14.5–4–36–1; McDermott 15–3–38–4; Coulter-Nile 12–2–43–2; Holland 19–6–59–3. *Second innings*—Starc 11.4–2–51–2; McDermott 13–3–38–2; Coulter-Nile 9–3–32–3; Holland 11–0–49–3.

Australia A

*E. J. M. Cowan lbw b Brathwaite	4	– (2) c Wood b Brathwaite	40
L. M. Davis c Muchall b Wood	40	– (1) lbw b Blackwell	62
M. Klinger lbw b Coughlin	21	– c Richardson b Brathwaite	0
P. J. Forrest c and b Wood	2	– c Muchall b Blackwell	1
G. J. Bailey lbw b Wood	6	– c Stokes b Blackwell	36
T. L. W. Cooper c Richardson b Wood	3	– c Richardson b Blackwell	0
†T. D. Paine c Richardson b Brathwaite	40	– not out	26
N. M. Coulter-Nile b Claydon	10	– c Singh b Blackwell	0
M. A. Starc c Coughlin b Brathwaite	24	– b Blackwell	4
J. M. Holland lbw b Blackwell	2	– c Stoneman b Blackwell	14
A. C. McDermott not out	0	– c Wood b Claydon	12
L-b 4, w 3	7	B 2, l-b 5, w 2	9
1/21 (1) 2/69 (3) 3/72 (2) (42.5 overs) 4/73 (4) 5/77 (6) 6/94 (5) 7/111 (8) 8/152 (9) 9/155 (10) 10/159 (7)	159	1/99 (2) 2/99 (3) (53 overs) 3/110 (4) 4/111 (1) 5/123 (6) 6/160 (5) 7/160 (8) 8/168 (9) 9/188 (10) 10/204 (11)	204

Claydon 11–3–31–1; Brathwaite 6.5–0–32–3; Coughlin 6–0–26–1; Wood 13–3–36–4; Stokes 3–0–19–0; Blackwell 3–0–11–1. *Second innings*—Claydon 7–3–36–1; Brathwaite 11–2–42–2; Wood 5–1–14–0; Blackwell 20–6–52–7; Stokes 6–0–33–0; Coughlin 4–0–20–0.

Umpires: P. R. Pollard and G. Sharp.

ENGLAND LIONS v AUSTRALIA A

At Manchester, August 7–10. Drawn. Toss: England Lions.

An engrossing match ended tamely when Morgan's late declaration prompted Australia A to bat out time rather than attempt a target. They did so easily, thanks to Klinger, whose uncompromising obduracy on a turning pitch would have pleased the watching Australian selector Rod Marsh. The best cricket came in a duel between the rejuvenated Johnson and the English batsmen on the first day, which began at 2.30 because of rain. Compton and Morgan – up at No. 3 following Ravi Bopara's last-minute withdrawal – battled hard and, though Woakes played more freely for 92 next day, he became Johnson's fourth victim. Australia A looked set for a lead, but lost their last nine wickets for 111, six to Kerrigan, who bowled well in tandem with Tredwell. With Compton sidelined by back spasms, Root and Bairstow then produced magnificent strokeplay in the evening sunshine; Johnson was as wayward in the second innings as he had been accurate in the first. Bairstow completed his century on the final morning in savage fashion, and Kieswetter plundered 66 by lunch – when Morgan finally declared, setting the Australians 354 in 64 overs. They declined. Marsh, the eminence grizzled, approved. Probably gruffly.

Close of play: first day, England Lions 140-4 (Patel 13, Kieswetter 15); second day, Australia A 127-1 (Cowan 77, Klinger 36); third day, England Lions 158-3 (Bairstow 73, Tredwell 2).

England Lions

First innings		Second innings	
J. E. Root c Paine b Johnson	6	– c Davis b Holland	70
N. R. D. Compton c and b Lyon	46		
*E. J. G. Morgan c Holland b Johnson	50	– (2) c Davis b Bird	0
J. M. Bairstow c Paine b Lyon	8	– (3) c Paine b Forrest	139
S. R. Patel c Forrest b Bird	55	– (4) c Forrest b Lyon	12
†C. Kieswetter lbw b Holland	16	– not out	66
C. R. Woakes c Bird b Johnson	92	– st Paine b Holland	17
J. A. R. Harris lbw b Bird	1	– not out	1
J. C. Tredwell b Johnson	3	– (5) c Paine b Holland	2
S. C. Meaker c Forrest b Cooper	22		
S. C. Kerrigan not out	1		
L-b 9, n-b 1, p 5	15	B 6, l-b 1, w 1	8
1/7 (1) 2/86 (2) 3/112 (4) 4/114 (3) 5/142 (6) 6/217 (5) 7/223 (8) 8/242 (9) 9/306 (10) 10/315 (7) (133.1 overs)	315	1/5 (2) 2/133 (1) 3/152 (4) 4/163 (5) 5/259 (3) 6/312 (7) (6 wkts dec, 76 overs)	315

Bird 30–12–75–2; Johnson 26.1–8–47–4; Holland 37–10–76–1; Lyon 38–10–101–2; Cooper 2–0–2–1. *Second innings*—Bird 16–5–45–1; Johnson 11–0–75–0; Holland 26–3–89–3; Lyon 14–2–62–1; Forrest 3–1–7–1; Cooper 6–0–30–0.

Australia A

First innings		Second innings	
*E. J. M. Cowan c Kieswetter b Tredwell	99	– (2) c Patel b Harris	9
L. M. Davis lbw b Meaker	4	– (1) c Bairstow b Patel	43
M. Klinger c Root b Tredwell	66	– not out	65
P. J. Forrest lbw b Kerrigan	24		
†T. D. Paine c Bairstow b Kerrigan	19	– c Tredwell b Meaker	17
J. A. Burns b Tredwell	7	– not out	3
T. L. W. Cooper not out	26	– (4) c Patel b Tredwell	4
M. G. Johnson c Root b Kerrigan	1		
N. M. Lyon lbw b Kerrigan	0		
J. M. Holland st Kieswetter b Kerrigan	17		
J. M. Bird c Bairstow b Kerrigan	4		
B 4, l-b 5, w 1	10	L-b 3	3
1/16 (2) 2/166 (1) 3/191 (3) 4/214 (5) 5/229 (6) 6/229 (4) 7/231 (8) 8/231 (9) 9/261 (10) 10/277 (11) (98.3 overs)	277	1/22 (2) 2/82 (1) 3/101 (4) 4/139 (5) (4 wkts, 62 overs)	144

Woakes 10–0–28–0; Meaker 12–0–54–1; Tredwell 37–10–93–3; Harris 14–5–34–0; Kerrigan 25.3–7–59–6. *Second innings*—Woakes 10–4–15–0; Harris 7–1–15–1; Meaker 8–3–13–1; Kerrigan 17–3–53–0; Tredwell 14–4–32–1; Patel 6–2–13–1.

Umpires: R. J. Bailey and P. J. Hartley.

ENGLAND LIONS v AUSTRALIA A

At Birmingham, August 14–17. Drawn. Toss: Australia A.

The loss of more than two days to rain made for a certain draw, but there was still plenty for a sparse crowd to enjoy. Yet again, Cowan led the Australian effort, crafting 73 before he was unfortunate to be given lbw to Tredwell, who went at less than two an over on a surface offering him little. Hughes, drafted in from Worcestershire, helped his captain add 93, and Paine chipped in with a fine half-century – all the more admirable after the insertion of a plate and eight pins in his right index finger had forced him to change the way he gripped the bat. Harris admitted he was a trifle fortunate to end with six wickets when Woakes had none. Cowan's bowlers began to make clever use of reverse swing in reducing the Lions to 99 for five, until their plans was kyboshed by Kieswetter, who straight-drove Lyon into a puddle beyond the rope, soaking the diligently prepared ball; the replacement did not do half as much. It was the cue for Kieswetter and Woakes to launch an uninhibited onslaught of 141 in 23 overs. Rain stopped their fun, and made a prompt resumption impossible on the final day, although the decision to abandon the game felt premature.

Close of play: first day, Australia A 308-9 (Lyon 15, Bird 4); second day, no play; third day, England Lions 240-5 (Kieswetter 112, Woakes 48).

Australia A

*E. J. M. Cowan lbw b Tredwell	73
L. M. Davis lbw b Harris	24
M. Klinger lbw b Harris	6
P. J. Hughes c Root b Harris	51
J. A. Burns b Harris	29
T. L. W. Cooper c Kieswetter b Tredwell	5
†T. D. Paine c Kieswetter b Harris	59
M. G. Johnson c Kieswetter b Tredwell	5
N. M. Coulter-Nile b Harris	24
N. M. Lyon not out	15
J. M. Bird not out	4
B 4, l-b 6, n-b 3	13
1/34 (2) 2/42 (3) 3/135 (4) 4/186 (1) 5/198 (6) 6/207 (5) 7/230 (8) 8/281 (9) 9/292 (7) (9 wkts dec, 92 overs)	308

Woakes 22–4–52–0; Harris 23–4–102–6; Meaker 15–1–50–0; Coles 5–0–26–0; Stokes 4–1–16–0; Tredwell 19–7–35–3; Patel 4–1–17–0.

England Lions

J. E. Root c Paine b Johnson	24
V. Chopra c Davis b Coulter-Nile	10
*E. J. G. Morgan b Coulter-Nile	12
S. R. Patel lbw b Bird	2
†C. Kieswetter not out	112
B. A. Stokes c Paine b Bird	26
C. R. Woakes not out	48
L-b 3, n-b 3	6
1/30 (2) 2/38 (1) 3/46 (4) 4/53 (3) 5/99 (6) (5 wkts, 57 overs)	240

J. A. R. Harris, M. T. Coles, J. C. Tredwell and S. C. Meaker did not bat.

Johnson 14–2–55–1; Bird 16–2–65–2; Coulter-Nile 19–4–70–2; Lyon 8–0–47–0.

Umpires: N. A. Mallender and R. T. Robinson.

THE UNIVERSITIES, 2012

In order to avoid a clash with the World Twenty20 in mid-September, the English first-class season began on March 31, earlier than ever before. In the eyes of many – especially put-upon groundsmen expected to produce pitches in spring – that was obscenely early. But the schedulers appeared to have got away with it when March was blessed with pleasant sunshine and temperatures climbing to 20°C – and Sam Robson, Greg Smith, James Foster, Graham Napier, Mark Wallace, Rory Burns and Cardiff MCCU's Zac Elkin all scored centuries in university fixtures on the final day of the month.

It did not, however, take long for the weather to turn, and the scores to come tumbling down. On April 8, Durham MCCU were bowled out by their parent county for 18 – the lowest first-class total anywhere in the world for 30 years. Graeme Fowler, Durham MCCU coach, admitted he thought they should not have been given first-class status in 2001, as it was unfair to judge students' abilities against those of professional cricketers.

The ECB seemed not to agree, as they had already extended first-class status to Cardiff and Leeds/Bradford MCCUs from 2012 onwards – in return for assurances from MCC that they would continue to fund the Academies with around £75,000 a year. Many will continue to argue – persuasively – that university matches do not come up to first-class standard, but this did at least constitute a sound investment in young cricketers from around the country.

Less understandable was the ECB's decision to confine first-class status to the first two of each university's three fixtures – even though there was no change in the match conditions of the third. Confusingly, Oxford and Leeds/Bradford played first-class matches at exactly the same time as Loughborough played a non-first-class game. And the counties tended to field marginally stronger sides in the first-class games. Sussex rested their entire Championship team against Leeds/Bradford at Weetwood, and were bowled out for 58. But, unless there is a retrospective change of heart, Luis Reece's match figures of ten for 68 for the students will never count in the first-class annals.

REPORTS BY RALPH DELLOR AND STEPHEN LAMB

CAMBRIDGE MCCU v ESSEX

At Cambridge, March 31–April 2. Drawn. Toss: Essex. First-class debuts: T. C. Elliott, J. A. M. Johnson, M. E. T. Salisbury. County debuts: G. M. Smith, C. M. Willoughby.

English first-class cricket was being played in March for the first time – but Essex sprinted along as if it were Chelmsford in August. Student hopes were highest shortly after lunch, when Godleman was bowled by Matt Salisbury to leave Essex 141 for five after 44 overs. But in the next 44 they racked up a further 365, with centuries for Greg Smith (on debut), Foster and Napier – who prompted the declaration by racing from 55 to 100 in ten deliveries, six of them hit for six off Salisbury and Paul Best. In total, 532 runs were scored in the day. The experienced Masters then unsettled Cambridge's batsmen, as only James Johnson, with 61 in his maiden first-class innings, put up prolonged resistance. Essex chose to bat a second time, before Craig Park (the younger brother of Derbyshire's Garry) and Akbar Ansari (older brother of Surrey's Zafar) ended the match with an unbroken partnership of 110 against an attack missing Willoughby, who had pulled up with a groin strain six overs into his Essex debut.

Close of play: first day, Cambridge MCCU 26-1 (Ackland 5, Poysden 1); second day, Essex 113-3 (Godleman 68, Wheater 10).

Essex

T. Westley lbw b Salisbury	30	– (2) lbw b Turnbull	1
B. A. Godleman b Salisbury	57	– (1) c Bell b Salisbury	94
J. C. Mickleburgh c Best b Turnbull	9	– b Salisbury	20
M. L. Pettini c Bell b Turnbull	6	– b Best	14
A. J. Wheater c Bell b Woolley	0	– c Park b Best	71
G. M. Smith c Salisbury b Poysden	160		
*†J. S. Foster not out	114		
G. R. Napier not out	100		
T. J. Phillips (did not bat)		– (6) not out	73
D. D. Masters (did not bat)		– (7) c Park b Woolley	52
B 6, l-b 4, w 1, n-b 19	30	B 3, l-b 2, n-b 4	9
1/62 (1) 2/77 (3) 3/85 (4) 4/91 (5) 5/141 (2) 6/365 (6) (6 wkts dec, 88 overs)	506	1/7 (2) 2/62 (3) 3/93 (4) 4/193 (1) 5/219 (5) 6/334 (7) (6 wkts dec, 79.1 overs)	334

C. M. Willoughby did not bat.

Turnbull 20–4–73–2; Woolley 19–3–75–1; Salisbury 16–2–104–2; Best 22–0–148–0; Poysden 11–0–96–1. *Second innings*—Turnbull 13–4–42–1; Salisbury 14–3–54–2; Best 30–4–143–2; Poysden 14–1–51–0; Woolley 8.1–0–39–1.

Cambridge MCCU

B. J. Ackland lbw b Masters	13	– c Phillips b Masters	7
†D. W. Bell lbw b Masters	10	– c Foster b Napier	7
J. E. Poysden lbw b Napier	7		
J. A. M. Johnson c Foster b Masters	61		
C. M. Park b Masters	9	– (3) not out	71
A. S. Ansari c Foster b Masters	0	– (4) not out	48
*R. J. J. Woolley lbw b Napier	0		
P. M. Best c Godleman b Masters	36		
T. C. Elliott c Smith b Phillips	30		
P. T. Turnbull b Napier	20		
M. E. T. Salisbury not out	0		
B 5, l-b 25, w 1, n-b 2	33	L-b 1	1
1/25 (2) 2/38 (1) 3/52 (3) 4/74 (5) 5/78 (6) 6/85 (7) 7/167 (4) 8/178 (8) 9/205 (10) 10/219 (9) (62.4 overs)	219	1/10 (1) 2/24 (2) (2 wkts, 33 overs)	134

Masters 19–5–52–6; Willoughby 6–3–12–0; Napier 16–6–33–3; Smith 12–1–43–0; Phillips 9.4–0–49–1. *Second innings*—Masters 5–0–16–1; Napier 6–1–26–1; Westley 9–0–34–0; Phillips 10–0–46–0; Smith 3–0–11–0.

Umpires: N. L. Bainton and P. K. Baldwin.

OXFORD MCCU v GLAMORGAN

At Oxford, March 31–April 2. Glamorgan won by 253 runs. Toss: Oxford MCCU. First-class debuts: F. R. H. John, C. A. J. Morris, J. S. Thompson. County debut: M. C. Henriques.

When the students had Glamorgan 162 for six on the first afternoon, Ben Williams's decision to put them in was looking sound. But the seventh-wicket pair responded with a brisk 152, during which Wallace brought up a 125-ball hundred. Oxford then found the Glamorgan bowlers difficult to get away, and Waters recorded the astonishing figures of 18–10–12–4 to help dismiss them for 123. Walters and James played their way into form as Glamorgan stretched their lead to 390 by the third morning. But, after an opening stand of 70 between Sam Agarwal and Ben Stebbings, Oxford lost all ten for 67. Australia all-rounder Moises Henriques, who took three wickets, was the second

Portugal-born cricketer to play in a first-class game in England – after Cyril Wright, who played for Cambridge University before the First World War.

Close of play: first day, Oxford MCCU 6-0 (Agarwal 5, Stebbings 1); second day, Glamorgan 105-1 (Walters 32, James 59).

Glamorgan

G. P. Rees lbw b Conway	46	– b Agarwal	9
S. J. Walters c and b Morris	4	– not out	59
N. A. James lbw b Conway	10	– b Conway	83
B. J. Wright c John b Thompson	27	– not out	11
J. Allenby c Stebbings b Conway	21		
M. C. Henriques b Pascoe	28		
*†M. A. Wallace not out	122		
G. G. Wagg c Stebbings b Agarwal	60		
R. D. B. Croft not out	10		
B 11, l-b 5, n-b 2	18	B 4, l-b 1	5
1/5 (2) 2/41 (3) 3/80 (1) 4/100 (4) 5/132 (5) 6/162 (6) 7/314 (8) (7 wkts dec, 85.5 overs)	346	1/13 (1) 2/130 (3) (2 wkts dec, 58 overs)	167

D. A. Cosker and H. T. Waters did not bat

Morris 18.5–1–99–1; Agarwal 22–4–79–1; Thompson 9–6–13–1; Conway 22–6–67–3; Pascoe 8–0–45–1; Walker 6–0–27–0. *Second innings*—Morris 12–3–43–0; Conway 13–2–58–1; Agarwal 9–3–15–1; Pascoe 17–6–23–0; Williams 3–0–15–0; Walker 4–0–8–0.

Oxford MCCU

S. S. Agarwal lbw b Allenby	18	– run out	51
B. R. W. Stebbings b Allenby	13	– lbw b Henriques	24
J. D. Fleming c Wallace b Waters	0	– c Rees b Croft	7
*B. Williams lbw b Allenby	0	– b Cosker	0
C. A. M. Walker c Cosker b Waters	1	– lbw b Cosker	8
B. A. Jeffery c Wallace b Waters	39	– c Wallace b Henriques	11
†F. R. H. John c Wallace b Waters	27	– lbw b Cosker	2
D. C. Pascoe c Walters b Wagg	0	– c Cosker b Allenby	19
C. A. J. Morris c Wallace b Croft	0	– c Henriques b Cosker	1
J. Thompson c and b Cosker	9	– b Henriques	0
D. O. Conway not out	0	– not out	9
B 7, l-b 3, n-b 6	16	B 5	5
1/38 (1) 2/39 (3) 3/39 (2) 4/40 (4) 5/40 (5) 6/107 (7) 7/110 (8) 8/114 (6) 9/123 (10) 10/123 (9) (64.1 overs)	123	1/70 (2) 2/81 (1) 3/83 (4) 4/91 (3) 5/93 (5) 6/95 (7) 7/123 (8) 8/123 (6) 9/127 (10) 10/137 (9) (52 overs)	137

Waters 18–10–12–4; Wagg 16–7–37–1; Cosker 13–7–24–1; Croft 6.1–2–13–1; Allenby 11–3–27–3. *Second innings*—Waters 6–2–16–0; Wagg 5–1–20–0; Henriques 10–2–34–3; Allenby 8–2–17–1; Croft 12–5–23–1; Cosker 11–4–22–4.

Umpires: B. J. Debenham and T. E. Jesty.

At Merchant Taylor's School, Northwood, March 31–April 2. DURHAM MCCU drew with MIDDLESEX.

At Taunton Vale, March 31–April 2. CARDIFF MCCU drew with SOMERSET.

At The Oval, March 31–April 2. LEEDS/BRADFORD MCCU lost to SURREY by two runs.

At Nottingham, April 1–3. LOUGHBOROUGH MCCU drew with NOTTINGHAMSHIRE.

CAMBRIDGE MCCU v LANCASHIRE

At Cambridge, April 6–8. Drawn. Toss: Lancashire.

Peter Turnbull's nagging accuracy was a stiff early proposition for Lancashire, playing their first first-class match in England since winning the 2011 Championship. But Procter and Croft fought back with a fourth-wicket stand of 150, before Cambridge subsided to 123; all Lancashire's seamers caused problems, though Procter struggled with his run-up and contributed 24 no-balls. Horton and Tom Smith, who was forced to retire hurt with a hamstring injury on 83, extended the advantage to 359. Despite frequent interruptions, Ben Ackland and Zafar Ansari rattled up 50 inside the first eight overs of Cambridge's run-chase, but a heavy downpour just before tea denied Ansari the chance to make a more emphatic statement before he joined Surrey for the summer.

Close of play: first day, Lancashire 277-5 (Croft 80, Cross 7); second day, Lancashire 134-1 (Horton 48, Brown 0).

Lancashire

P. J. Horton b Turnbull	40	– not out	48
S. C. Moore b Turnbull	14	– c Sadler b Turnbull	1
K. R. Brown lbw b Turnbull	42	– (4) not out	0
L. A. Procter lbw b Woolley	77		
*S. J. Croft c Park b Turnbull	83		
T. C. Smith lbw b Turnbull	2	– (3) retired hurt	83
†G. D. Cross not out	49		
S. I. Mahmood c Z. S. Ansari b Turnbull	14		
K. W. Hogg not out	12		
L-b 10, w 5	15	B 2	2
1/23 (2) 2/87 (1) (7 wkts dec, 109 overs)	348	1/5 (2) (1 wkt dec, 35 overs)	134
3/104 (3) 4/254 (4)			
5/262 (6) 6/291 (5) 7/313 (8)			

S. C. Kerrigan and G. Keedy did not bat.

In the second innings Smith retired hurt at 132-1.

Turnbull 30–5–108–6; Woolley 28–7–75–1; Sadler 16–4–44–0; Salisbury 13–2–38–0; Z. S. Ansari 15–1–46–0; Best 7–0–27–0. *Second innings*—Turnbull 7–4–14–1; Woolley 3–1–13–0; Salisbury 4–0–29–0; Sadler 11–2–27–0; Z. S. Ansari 10–3–49–0.

Cambridge MCCU

B. J. Ackland c Cross b Mahmood	0	– c Kerrigan b Keedy	52
Z. S. Ansari c Cross b Smith	25	– not out	59
J. A. M. Johnson b Procter	20	– not out	12
C. M. Park c Cross b Smith	1		
A. S. Ansari lbw b Procter	11		
*R. J. J. Woolley c Smith b Procter	1		
P. M. Best c Smith b Mahmood	18		
†D. W. Bell lbw b Hogg	9		
P. T. Turnbull b Mahmood	0		
M. E. T. Salisbury not out	1		
P. T. Sadler c Horton b Mahmood	2		
L-b 3, n-b 32	35	B 7, l-b 5, n-b 8	20
1/0 (1) 2/44 (3) 3/51 (4) 4/74 (5) (37.4 overs)	123	1/112 (1) (1 wkt, 42.3 overs)	143
5/84 (2) 6/86 (6) 7/112 (7) 8/112 (9)			
9/120 (8) 10/123 (11)			

Mahmood 11.4–2–38–4; Hogg 10–4–18–1; Smith 8–3–12–2; Kerrigan 1–1–0–0; Procter 7–0–52–3. *Second innings*—Mahmood 6–1–29–0; Hogg 10–3–31–0; Procter 6–1–21–0; Kerrigan 11–2–30–0; Keedy 9.3–1–20–1.

Umpires: R. J. Evans and S. J. O'Shaughnessy.

At Chester-le-Street, April 6–8. DURHAM MCCU lost to DURHAM by 373 runs. *The students are bowled out for 18 in their second innings.*

At Southampton, April 6–8. LOUGHBOROUGH MCCU lost to HAMPSHIRE by 274 runs.

At Birmingham, April 6–8. CARDIFF MCCU drew with WARWICKSHIRE.

At Loughborough, April 13–15 (not first-class). **Drawn. Leicestershire 320** (G. P. Smith 85; A. C. Soilleux 6-60) **and 141-6 dec**; **‡Loughborough MCCU 158** (N. Patel 50; T. J. Wells 4-46) **and 122-3**. *County debuts:* J. S. Sykes, T. J. Wells. *As this was the third of Loughborough's fixtures, it did not carry first-class status – and Leicestershire treated it as such by resting four bowlers from the win over Glamorgan; Ramnaresh Sarwan captained in his second game for the county. Adam Soilleux, a seamer attached to Essex, had figures of 25–7–60–6, so had particular reason to feel aggrieved at the ECB's new regulations. Loughborough did well to recover from 22-5 to 158, and a downpour late on the second day prevented Leicestershire from pushing for victory. They declared with a lead of 303, but time ran out on their youthful attack, with Nitesh Patel adding 38 to his first-innings 50.*

OXFORD MCCU v WORCESTERSHIRE

At Oxford, April 13–15. Drawn. Toss: Worcestershire. First-class debuts: O. J. Jones, B. W. Kemp; N. L. Harrison.

Worcestershire made 323 for five on the first day, with Klinger scoring his only century of a short stint as overseas player, but Mitchell defied convention by batting on for another 37 overs next morning. When given the opportunity, the Oxford batsmen scored at a faster lick; the 20-year-old Scotland international Freddie Coleman was the cornerstone of the innings, with 110. Winner of the Walter Lawrence MCCU award for his 141 against Durham MCCU the previous week, Coleman featured in a partnership of 183 with Ben Williams, which took Oxford to an impregnable 349 for three. Without Alan Richardson, Worcestershire's attack looked painfully thin: they turned to seven bowlers before dismissing the students for a lead of just 29. Their batsmen then ran into trouble briefly on the last afternoon.

Close of play: first day, Worcestershire 323-5 (Cameron 13, Scott 10); second day, Oxford MCCU 213-3 (Coleman 19, Williams 30).

Worcestershire

*D. K. H. Mitchell c John b Kemp	60	– (5) lbw b Jones	7
M. Klinger lbw b Ellison	120		
V. S. Solanki c Stebbings b Ellison	83	– b Morris	1
M. M. Ali c Kemp b Morris	9	– not out	11
A. N. Kervezee c John b Ellison	0	– (1) b Morris	0
J. G. Cameron c Jeffery b Agarwal	88	– not out	11
†B. J. M. Scott c Stebbings b Pascoe	73		
S. H. Choudhry not out	1	– (2) run out	1
G. M. Andrew not out	2		
B 19, l-b 8, w 1	28	L-b 1, n-b 2	3
1/124 (1) 2/279 (2) (7 wkts dec, 139 overs) 3/298 (3) 4/298 (4) 5/298 (5) 6/454 (7) 7/461 (6)	464	1/0 (1) 2/2 (3) (4 wkts, 14 overs) 3/4 (2) 4/13 (5)	34

J. D. Shantry and N. L. Harrison did not bat

Morris 26–13–57–1; Ellison 26–9–82–3; Jones 13–1–58–0; Kemp 19–3–71–1; Pascoe 22–4–74–1; Agarwal 33–1–95–1. *Second innings*—Morris 5–2–7–2; Ellison 5–3–6–0; Jones 2–0–7–1; Kemp 1–0–10–0; Stebbings 1–0–3–0.

Oxford MCCU

S. S. Agarwal c Harrison b Choudhry	76	C. A. J. Morris c Ali b Harrison	7
B. R. W. Stebbings c Klinger b Andrew	2	B. W. Kemp b Choudhry	3
O. J. Jones lbw b Shantry	79		
F. R. J. Coleman c and b Shantry	110	B 10, l-b 12, w 1	23
*B. Williams lbw b Choudhry	92		
B. A. Jeffery c Mitchell b Shantry	10	1/11 (2) 2/156 (1) (126.2 overs)	435
†F. R. H. John not out	26	3/166 (3) 4/349 (5)	
D. C. Pascoe c Scott b Harrison	6	5/374 (6) 6/389 (4) 7/408 (8)	
C. P. Ellison c Ali b Shantry	1	8/411 (9) 9/428 (10) 10/435 (11)	

Andrew 15–1–60–1; Shantry 35–5–102–4; Harrison 23–5–78–2; Cameron 11–2–32–0; Choudhry 29.2–4–82–3; Ali 12–2–56–0; Mitchell 1–0–3–0.

Umpires: M. J. D. Bodenham and P. Willey.

At Leeds, April 13–15. LEEDS/BRADFORD MCCU drew with YORKSHIRE.

At Durham, April 20–22 (not first-class). **Northamptonshire 248** (C. D. de Lange 53; B. W. Blackwell 4-83) **and 5-0; ‡Durham MCCU 166** (L. A. Blackaby 51). *County debut:* C. D. de Lange. *Northamptonshire, bereft of confidence after losing their opening two Championship games, did not find the going much easier against Bertie Blackwell and Jonathan Salt, who reduced them to 137-7 before a doughty fifty on debut from Con de Lange, a South African left-arm spinner with a British passport. Durham MCCU took 78 overs to score 166, as Andrew Hall claimed two wickets on his comeback from a calf injury. The third day was washed away.*

At Derby, April 27–29. DERBYSHIRE v CARDIFF MCCU. Abandoned.

At Weetwood, Leeds, May 1–3 (not first-class). **Leeds/Bradford MCCU won by 79 runs. Leeds/Bradford MCCU 164** (W. A. Adkin 3-31, K. O. Wernars 4-28) **and 149-9 dec** (L. J. Hatchett 3-34); **‡Sussex 58** (L. M. Reece 7-21) **and 176** (M. W. Machan 76; I. A. A. Thomas 6-21, L. M. Reece 3-47). *County debuts:* H. Z. Finch, C. F. Jackson. *Sussex paid the price for picking a Second Eleven in all but name, including none of the team that played in the Championship at Edgbaston two days earlier. They had, though, made a good start, as Naved Arif removed Ben Slater lbw with the first ball of the match, and Leeds/Bradford were all out in the afternoon. But on a pitch freshened by a week of steady rain, they met their demise against Luis Reece, a 21-year-old left-arm seamer from Lancashire, who came on for the ninth over, began with a double-wicket maiden, and bowled unchanged for 10.3–6–21–7 as Sussex were dismissed for 58 – their lowest score in two-innings cricket for 15 years. A three-hour 46 by Harry Bush was vital in stretching Leeds/Bradford's advantage to 255 by the third morning. Machan and Wernars put on 96 in 16 overs for Sussex's fourth wicket, but the pursuit was derailed in four balls of the 42nd over, when Ivan Thomas – contracted to Kent – had Machan caught, then bowled Arif and debutant Callum Jackson, to leave Sussex 147-7, and heading for an emphatic defeat.*

At Oxford, May 2–4 (not first-class). **Drawn. ‡Kent 251-8 dec** (S. A. Newman 89, A. J. Blake 97; S. S. Agarwal 4-49); **Oxford MCCU 192-7 dec** (B. Williams 63, C. A. M. Walker 64; A. J. Blake 3-10). *County debuts:* F. K. Cowdrey, D. Masters. *Alex Blake was in sumptuous form as he made 97 from 148 balls, before becoming one of three wickets in four overs for off-spinner Sam Agarwal; Scott Newman offered firm support in the highest score of his loan spell from Middlesex. Adam Ball removed both Oxford openers before the close, but rain washed out the second day and, after a third-wicket partnership of 109 between Ben Williams and Charlie Walker, an early close was agreed on the last. Fabian Cowdrey, 20, son of Chris and grandson of Colin, scored one, and bowled 11 wicketless overs of left-arm spin on his Kent debut.*

At Cambridge, May 18–20 (not first-class). **Drawn. ‡Gloucestershire 227** (D. M. Housego 68; R. J. J. Woolley 5-48) **and 234-3 dec** (H. J. H. Marshall 102*, I. A. Cockbain 55*); **Cambridge MCCU 209** (P. M. Best 62; L. C. Norwell 3-47) **and 189-5** (S. A. Satbhai 66). *Dan Housego, returning from a shoulder problem, averted embarrassment for Gloucestershire, as regular wickets fell to Cambridge captain Rob Woolley. Hamish Marshall and Ian Cockbain added 146* to set up the declaration, as they found conditions easier in the second innings. Chasing 253 in 64 overs, Cambridge were never at risk of losing, and Satyajit Satbhai, a 31-year-old from Pune with first-class experience for Maharashtra, followed a golden duck by hitting out for 66 in 57 balls.*

THE UNIVERSITY MATCHES, 2012

At Oxford, May 25. **Oxford University won by six wickets.** ‡**Cambridge University 151-5** (20 overs) (T. C. Elliott 37); **Oxford University 155-4** (19.4 overs) (S. S. Agarwal 61, B. Williams 49). *Jonno Evans and Matt Hickey lifted Cambridge to 151-5 with a stand of 44 in 26 balls. Sam Agarwal, who scored 88 in the 2010 fixture and 52 in 2011, this time led the reply with 61 from 54 balls, in a second-wicket stand of 91 with Ben Williams. Agarwal was out to Hickey in the last over, but Ben Jeffery hit the next ball for six to win the match.*

At Lord's, June 16. **Cambridge University won by 17 runs. Cambridge University 269-9** (R. T. Timms 84, N. K. S. Senaratne 57, A. S. Ansari 63; S. S. Agarwal 5-53); ‡**Oxford University 252** (49 overs) (D. C. Pascoe 67; J. A. Lodwick 4-39). *Agarwal took three wickets in a frenzied last over as Cambridge batted first, and completed a run-out, but by then they were almost out of sight. Richard Timms and Nipuna Senaratne put in early graft, before the Ansari brothers cut loose with some daring shots: they added 70 in nine overs, and Akbar hit five sixes. Dan Pascoe, in his fourth year of university cricket, kept the game alive, but Oxford were always behind the rate. It was Cambridge's third successive one-day Varsity title.*

OXFORD UNIVERSITY v CAMBRIDGE UNIVERSITY

At Oxford, June 24–27. Drawn. Toss: Cambridge. First-class debuts: J. M. Davies, F. F. J. Johnson; J. J. Evans.

The 167th Varsity Match differed from others in recent years in that only three players were making their first-class debuts. The weather interrupted proceedings often enough to prevent a positive result, and a derisory scoring rate hardly helped. Left-hander Owain Jones, who entered at 46 for three, lent substance to Oxford's middle order alongside the more experienced Raj Sharma. The pick of the Cambridge bowlers was seamer Jonathon Lodwick, who had played in the fixture for Oxford in 2010. Cambridge captain Richard Timms, aged 27, demonstrated the value of eight seasons' first-class experience with a steady fifty. But Cambridge collapsed from 119 for one to 200 for seven, as the spin pairing of Dan Pascoe, winning his fourth Blue, and Sam Agarwal, his third, forged an iron grip. Lodwick struck twice more as Oxford's lead crept up to 35, before an impressive recovery. The game was drifting to a draw when rain intervened for the final time.

Close of play: first day, Oxford University 171-4 (Jones 77, Westaway 13); second day, Cambridge University 129-3 (Ansari 7, Best 3); third day, Oxford University 42-3 (Williams 7, Sharma 12).

Oxford University

S. S. Agarwal lbw b Probert	3	– b Best	19
B. A. Jeffery c Kennedy b Sadler	30	– c Ansari b Lodwick	3
*B. Williams lbw b Probert	1	– c Probert b Lodwick	70
R. Sharma lbw b Best	39	– (5) b Probert	34
O. J. Jones c Kennedy b Lodwick	83	– (6) not out	54
†S. A. Westaway c Evans b Best	14	– (7) not out	26
D. C. Pascoe b Lodwick	38		
J. M. Davies lbw b Probert	31		
T. R. Chadwick c Kennedy b Lodwick	21		
A. J. D. Scott not out	11	– (4) b Lodwick	0
F. F. J. Johnson lbw b Lodwick	0		
B 1, l-b 7, w 1	9	L-b 6, w 1, n-b 2	9
1/10 (1) 2/20 (3) 3/46 (2) (106.5 overs)	280	1/22 (1) (5 wkts dec, 91 overs)	215
4/130 (4) 5/174 (6) 6/180 (5)		2/22 (2) 3/22 (4)	
7/230 (8) 8/267 (7) 9/272 (9) 10/280 (11)		4/119 (5) 5/161 (3)	

Probert 24–8–68–3; Sadler 21–9–50–1; Lodwick 20.5–5–55–4; Best 38–7–86–2; Hickey 3–0–13–0. *Second innings*—Probert 26–5–77–1; Lodwick 26–7–44–3; Best 17–9–35–1; Sadler 12–5–21–0; Hickey 1–0–4–0; Ansari 7–2–15–0; Timms 2–0–13–0.

Cambridge University

*R. T. Timms b Scott	52	P. T. Sadler c and b Pascoe	9
P. H. Hughes c Westaway b Sharma	13	T. J. W. Probert b Agarwal	0
T. C. Elliott c Williams b Pascoe	44		
A. S. Ansari lbw b Pascoe	30	B 8, l-b 9, w 2, n-b 3	22
P. M. Best c Westaway b Agarwal	19		
J. J. Evans c Jeffery b Agarwal	12	1/40 (2) 2/119 (3) (108.5 overs)	267
†A. D. J. Kennedy lbw b Johnson	15	3/120 (1) 4/168 (5)	
M. R. Hickey not out	19	5/178 (4) 6/192 (6) 7/200 (7)	
J. A. Lodwick c Westaway b Jones	32	8/245 (9) 9/266 (10) 10/267 (11)	

Sharma 26–9–62–1; Johnson 11–3–42–1; Jones 15–2–42–1; Pascoe 32–11–53–3; Agarwal 20.5–5–46–3; Scott 4–1–5–1.

Umpires: N. A. Mallender and M. J. Saggers.

This was the 167th University Match, a first-class fixture dating back to 1827. Cambridge have won 58 and Oxford 54, with 55 drawn. It was played at Lord's until 2000.

MCC UNIVERSITIES CHAMPIONSHIP

	Played	*Won*	*Lost*	*1st-inns wins*	*1st-inns losses*	*Drawn/ no result*	*Bonus Points*	*Points*
Cambridge	5	0	0	4	0	1	26	71
Durham	5	0	0	2	1	2	23	53
Loughborough	5	1	0	0	2	2	21	48
Leeds/Bradford	5	0	0	1	1	3	15	40
Oxford	5	0	1	0	2	2	18	28
Cardiff	5	0	0	0	1	4	5	25

Outright win = 17pts; 1st-innings win in a drawn match = 10pts; no result on 1st innings = 5pts; abandoned = 5pts. Up to six bonus points for batting were available (four in 1st innings and two in 2nd).

WINNERS

2001 Loughborough
2002 Loughborough
2003 Loughborough
2004 Oxford
2005 Loughborough
2006 Oxford
2007 Cardiff/Glamorgan
2008 Loughborough
2009 Leeds/Bradford
2010 Durham
2011 Cardiff
2012 Cambridge

MCC UNIVERSITIES CHALLENGE FINAL

At Lord's, June 22. **Durham MCCU won by 74 runs** (D/L). **Durham MCCU 316-6** (48 overs) (C. R. Jones 107, S. R. Waters 70); ‡**Cambridge MCCU 245** (43.5 overs) (D. W. Bell 66, A. S. Ansari 57; A. S. Sangha 4-39). *The class of Somerset batsman Chris Jones and Kenya international Seren Waters propelled Durham to 204-1 in the 39th over, when Jones eventually fell for 107 from 116 balls. Quick runs came from Rishabh Shah (49 from 23) and Ajay Sangha (27 from 12). Akbar Ansari propped up Cambridge's attempt at a revised target of 320 from 48 overs, but Sangha ran out Tom Elliott with 112 needed from ten, and mopped up the rest with his off-spin.*

MCC IN 2012

STEVEN LYNCH

After some years in which animated discussions about the redevelopment plans for Lord's had tended to dominate events, MCC's committee-room was a slightly quieter place in 2012, which was probably a relief for the new secretary and chief executive, Derek Brewer, who took up office in May after joining from Nottinghamshire. Discussions about the redevelopment of the ground continued during the year, and remained a priority. However, more time was spent preparing a petition to the Privy Council for MCC to become incorporated by Royal Charter.

The application was approved in December, and will come into effect on July 1, 2013. The new status enables MCC to hold assets in its own name, rather than them being assigned to a custodian trustee, and also removes any potential liability for individual members in the unlikely event of the club running into severe financial difficulties. MCC had made two previous applications, in 1864 and 1929, which were turned down.

The president for 2012-13, Mike Griffith – who lived in a house adjacent to the ground when his father, S. C. "Billy" Griffith, was the secretary – explained: "This charter means we can better protect our members' rights and assets, and strengthens our ability to work for the good of the game in the UK and abroad."

MCC's World Cricket Committee, chaired by the former England captain Mike Brearley, continued to act as an influential think-tank for the international game. The committee welcomed its first female member during 2012 – the England captain Charlotte Edwards – while Jimmy Adams, Rod Marsh and Michael Vaughan also joined.

There was a six-week period in midsummer in which no cricket was played at Lord's, in the lead-up to the London Olympics. The archery competitions were staged on the ground, to general acclaim. Afterwards, it was necessary to returf around a third of the outfield, on which temporary grandstands had been erected; much to the credit of the groundstaff, the playing area was almost back to its best by the time the exciting Test against South Africa got under way little more than a fortnight later. It was fitting that Mick Hunt won the prestigious annual IOG Groundsman of the Year award.

MCC's out-match fixture list continued to grow. In 2012, no fewer than 457 matches were arranged, mainly against schools and clubs, although 185 had to be abandoned (and five cancelled). Of the rest, 137 were won, 54 drawn, 75 lost, and one tied. The wet summer also affected the MCC women's teams: of 29 matches arranged, 15 were abandoned. Eleven were won, two lost and one drawn, while one ended in a tie.

The year ended on a sad note, with the news of the death of the former England captain Tony Greig – who had delivered the MCC Spirit of Cricket Cowdrey Lecture at Lord's in 2012 – being followed a few days later, on January 1, 2013, by the passing of Christopher Martin-Jenkins, the journalist and broadcaster who was the club's president in 2010-11.

MCC v LANCASHIRE

At Abu Dhabi, March 27–29, 2012 (day/night). Lancashire won by six wickets. Toss: MCC.

Kerrigan enhanced his growing reputation with four wicket in both innings as Lancashire secured a notable win against MCC in the annual champion county fixture. He had played a crucial role in Lancashire's Championship title win in 2011, with nine for 51 against Hampshire in the penultimate round. While his contribution here, with a pink ball under the lights of the Sheikh Zayed Stadium, was less spectacular, it was still crucial. MCC gained a first-innings lead of 67, as Blackwell reached a century and picked up a couple of wickets when Lancashire were bowled out for 199. But Kerrigan helped skittle MCC for 84 second time round, leaving a target of 152. Reduced to 11 for two in the tenth over of their pursuit, Lancashire were put back on course by a calm 98-run partnership between Horton and Procter, which took them in sight of victory; a rapid innings from Croft completed the job with four and a half sessions left. GRAHAM HARDCASTLE

Close of play: First day, Lancashire 38-2 (Brown 12, Keedy 4); Second day, MCC 81-8 (Gregory 0, Naved-ul-Hasan 1).

MCC

First innings		Second innings	
G. P. Rees c Cross b Chapple	3	(2) lbw b Mahmood	0
S. D. Peters c Smith b Kerrigan	32	(1) c Horton b Kerrigan	28
*M. R. Ramprakash b Kerrigan	7	c Chapple b Mahmood	6
H. J. H. Marshall b Smith	18	lbw b Chapple	31
M. M. Ali b Chapple	33	b Smith	2
I. D. Blackwell not out	102	c Moore b Smith	0
†N. J. O'Brien c Smith b Mahmood	28	c Smith b Kerrigan	4
L. Gregory c Cross b Croft	0	not out	3
G. J. Batty c Horton b Kerrigan	6	c Smith b Kerrigan	0
Naved-ul-Hasan b Kerrigan	10	b Chapple	1
A. Richardson b Mahmood	5	c Keedy b Kerrigan	0
B 2, l-b 1, w 1, n-b 18	22	B 8, l-b 1	9
1/8 (1) 2/28 (3) 3/69 (2) 4/73 (4) 5/168 (5) 6/226 (7) 7/227 (8) 8/245 (9) 9/259 (10) 10/266 (11) (75.1 overs)	266	1/2 (2) 2/10 (3) 3/56 (4) 4/67 (5) 5/69 (6) 6/79 (7) 7/80 (1) 8/80 (9) 9/81 (10) 10/84 (11) (40.2 overs)	84

Chapple 12–3–37–2; Mahmood 15.1–3–43–2; Procter 9–2–33–0; Kerrigan 18–1–65–4; Smith 9–0–38–1; Keedy 9–1–38–0; Croft 3–0–9–1. *Second Innings*—Chapple 8–3–14–2; Mahmood 7–1–19–2; Kerrigan 12.2–3–31–4; Smith 6–4–5–2; Keedy 4–1–4–0; Procter 3–1–2–0.

Lancashire

First innings		Second innings	
P. J. Horton c O'Brien b Naved-ul-Hasan	9	c Batty b Ali	58
S. C. Moore lbw b Blackwell	11	c Ali b Blackwell	4
K. R. Brown lbw b Naved-ul-Hasan	39	b Gregory	0
G. Keedy c Naved-ul-Hasan b Richardson	4		
L. A. Procter c O'Brien b Gregory	18	(4) c Rees b Blackwell	47
S. J. Croft b Gregory	4	(5) not out	24
T. C. Smith b Batty	10	(6) not out	7
†G. D. Cross c Peters b Blackwell	30		
*G. Chapple not out	42		
S. I. Mahmood c Ali b Batty	8		
S. C. Kerrigan b Naved-ul-Hasan	8		
L-b 6, n-b 10	16	B 4, l-b 4, n-b 4	12
1/13 (1) 2/25 (2) 3/38 (4) 4/81 (3) 5/87 (6) 6/104 (5) 7/106 (7) 8/160 (8) 9/171 (10) 10/199 (11) (76.5 overs)	199	1/11 (2) 2/11 (3) 3/109 (1) 4/140 (4) (4 wkts, 44.3 overs)	152

Richardson 15–3–34–1; Naved-ul-Hasan 14.5–3–31–3; Gregory 7–2–29–2; Blackwell 22–8–51–2; Batty 18–4–48–2. *Second Innings*—Richardson 8–5–10–0; Naved-ul-Hasan 8–1–23–0; Blackwell 8.3–1–31–2; Gregory 8–0–34–1; Batty 4–0–17–0; Ali 8–3–29–1.

Umpires: M. R. Benson and J. H. Evans.

THE MINOR COUNTIES, 2012

PHILIP AUGUST

Like everyone else, the Minor Counties suffered in a dreadful summer. Twenty of the 40 zonal games in the MCCA Knockout Trophy were lost to the weather, 16 of them without a ball bowled; and 44 days of Championship cricket had no play at all. Only Buckinghamshire seamer Simon Stanway sent down more than 200 overs, and 68 of those were in the Championship final at Truro; in 2011, ten others had bowled as many. Just two batsmen, Khalid Sawas of Cheshire and Suffolk's Martyn Cull, exceeded 500 runs, against 11 the year before.

The competition winners came from the farther-flung outposts of English cricket. **Cumberland** deserved the unofficial title of team of the year. Their last two Championship matches were both severely curtailed by rain, which denied them a chance of challenging for the Eastern Division title. Their one-day form was similarly excellent: they lost only once, by a single run to Cheshire when chasing 313, and thrashed Wiltshire in the final. Cumberland also unearthed the bowler of the year: 21-year-old slow left-armer Toby Bulcock of Northern Premier League club Carnforth, who took 36 Championship wickets, more than anyone. They are likely to lose him to first-class cricket in 2013, but that reflects one of the main functions of the Minor Counties. Gary Pratt captained a fine all-round side, with Josh Tolley and James Lowe providing useful runs.

Cornwall won the Western Division the hard way. In their penultimate match they faced an innings defeat against rivals Oxfordshire at Great Tew, but last pair Robert Harrison and Sam Hockin held out for eight overs to secure a valuable draw, with the help of rain. Two weeks later, Oxfordshire beat Wiltshire, but Cornwall brushed Wales aside in the equivalent of under four sessions to progress to the final on home soil at Truro. The majority of their side were local cricketers playing in the Cornwall Premier League: 20-year-old Jake Libby was their leading scorer, while Hockin took 30 wickets, Tom Sharp 20 and Alex Smeeth 15.

Cornwall's masterstroke, though, was to unearth Shakeel Ahmed, a 46-year-old left-arm spinner born in Kuwait, who removed the Waugh twins in his only Test, for Pakistan, against Australia at Karachi in 1998-99. Shakeel was a former professional for Cornish side St Buryan, but most recently had been coaching at an academy in Slough and playing for Dinton CC, of Buckinghamshire, in the Home Counties Premier League. He took four for 29 on debut at Abergavenny, then ten wickets on a turning pitch in the final against Buckinghamshire, to bowl Cornwall to their maiden Championship title; Buckinghamshire were a little peeved that a player had been pinched from under their nose. Cornwall's win left Northumberland and Wales as the only counties yet to lift the title.

The individual accolades went to Northumberland's 21-year-old opening batsman Daniel Young, who won the Wilfred Rhodes Trophy after 404 runs at

67, and Ashur Morrison, who won the Frank Edwards Trophy for his bowling average of 11, despite not being a frontline seamer for Wiltshire. He took 11 of his 15 wickets in a single match against Wales.

Buckinghamshire had drawn their last game, at Jesmond, to secure the Eastern Division. They had soundly thrashed neighbours Bedfordshire before that, with the former England one-day batsman Mal Loye scoring 179. Losing finalists in 2011, **Cambridgeshire** were runners-up, with off-spinners Paul McMahon and Lewis Bruce crucial to their success. For **Norfolk**, Carl Rogers retired after 23 seasons and 10,176 Championship runs.

Matt Hunn, an 18-year-old seamer, took 14 wickets in four games for **Suffolk**. **Staffordshire** started off by beating Cumberland, but then had to watch as their next two games were abandoned. A total of only seven batting points highlighted their frailties. **Northumberland** lost six and a half of their nine home days' Championship cricket. They drew five games, with the other abandoned; Phil Nicholson, a respected cricketer, decided to retire after 22 years, 13 of them as captain. **Hertfordshire**, **Bedfordshire** and **Lincolnshire** also failed to record a win.

Oxfordshire came close to winning the Western Division. Though rain denied them a vital win against Cornwall, it saved them from certain defeat to Berkshire in their opening match. **Wiltshire** had their best season for years, finishing runners-up in the MCCA Trophy and third in the Championship. They earned more bonus points than anyone, with their South African skipper Joe Breet scoring two centuries in his 480 runs.

Shropshire's fourth-place finish was their highest since 2007. Their batting lacked consistency, with the No. 3 spot managing just 70 runs at an average of ten, but a number of young cricketers were introduced. In between Hampshire commitments, Bilal Shafayat's seldom-aired seamers claimed ten for 76 against Cheshire. **Dorset** endured two abandonments, which inevitably ruined their challenge. Chris Jones, the Somerset batsman, made one appearance for his home county, but it was unforgettable: he helped break Dorset's 83-year-old record for their third wicket when he put on 240 with Aaron Williams (124 not out) against Shropshire at Bournemouth; Jones returned in the second innings to stroke 188 from 185 balls.

Berkshire's captain of six years, Bjorn Mordt, retired at the age of 34, having transformed himself from a wicketkeeper to a wicket-taker, claiming 19 in 2012 with the new ball. Though languishing near the bottom, **Cheshire** produced some outstanding individual performances: slow left-armer Danny Woods took 34 wickets, including nine for 74 in Shropshire's second innings, but ended up on the losing side. Sawas scored 164 against Herefordshire, which helped Cheshire to their record total of 476 for eight declared.

Devon lost more than 50% of playing time in the Championship, which made team building and player development difficult. Their one victory came against Wales at Exmouth, chasing 125 in a match reduced to one innings a side. For the third season running **Wales** failed to win; with two ECB Premier Leagues in the country, it remained surprising their selection was not more balanced towards experienced cricketers. They avoided the wooden spoon because **Herefordshire** had suffered an over-rate penalty.

MINOR COUNTIES CHAMPIONSHIP, 2012

Eastern Division	P	W	L	D	A	Bonus points Batting	Bonus points Bowling	Total points
BUCKINGHAMSHIRE	6	3	0	2	1	10	16	90
Cambridgeshire	6	3	1	2	0	7	21	82¶
Norfolk	6	1	0	5	0	15	21	72
Cumberland	6	2	1	3	0	6	19	69
Suffolk	6	1	1	4	0	14	21	65¶
Staffordshire	6	1	1	2	2	7	11	58
Northumberland	6	0	0	5	1	8	14	50
Hertfordshire	6	0	1	5	0	9	17	46
Bedfordshire	6	0	2	4	0	9	18	37§
Lincolnshire	6	0	4	2	0	5	18	31

Western Division	P	W	L	D	A	Bonus points Batting	Bonus points Bowling	Total points
CORNWALL	6	3	0	3	0	7	21	88
Oxfordshire	6	2	0	3	1	8	19	79
Wiltshire	6	2	2	2	0	15	23	78
Shropshire	6	2	1	3‡	0	10	14	70
Dorset	6	1	1	2	2	12	13	65
Berkshire	6	1	1	4	0	11	18	61
Cheshire	6	1	2	2	1	8	20	60
Devon	6	1*	0	4	1	7	11	54
Wales	6	0	4†	1	1	4	15	35
Herefordshire	6	0	2	4‡	0	3	15	34¶

Final: Cornwall beat Buckinghamshire by 150 runs.

Win = 16pts; draw = 4pts; abandoned = 8pts.

* *Devon received 12 points for winning a match reduced to a single innings.*
† *Wales received four points for losing a match reduced to a single innings.*
‡ *Shropshire and Herefordshire received six points for drawing a match reduced to a single innings.*
¶ *Two-point penalties incurred for slow over-rate.*
§ *Bedfordshire deducted six points for three slow over-rate penalties.*

LEADING AVERAGES, 2012

BATTING (250 runs in 6 completed innings, average 40.00)

	M	I	NO	R	HS	100	50	Avge
D. R. Young (*Northumberland*)	5	8	2	404	123*	2	1	67.33
R. K. Oliver (*Shropshire*)	5	7	1	378	175	1	1	63.00
K. Sawas (*Cheshire*)	6	9	0	518	164	2	3	57.56
M. G. Cull (*Suffolk*)	6	9	0	503	147	1	4	55.89
R. I. Kaufman (*Oxfordshire*)	5	8	0	442	168	2	0	55.25
M. Jones (*Berkshire*)	6	10	1	468	107*	1	3	52.00
F. I. Qureshi (*Buckinghamshire*)	6	11	3	414	110	1	1	51.75
J. R. Tolley (*Cumberland*)	6	9	3	310	90	0	3	51.67
J. A. Lowe (*Cumberland*)	5	6	0	294	134	1	1	49.00
J. J. Breet (*Wiltshire*)	6	11	1	480	126	2	2	48.00
C. L. Park (*Dorset*)	4	6	0	266	61	0	3	44.33
J. M. Spelman (*Norfolk*)	5	8	2	262	63	0	2	43.67
S. D. Stubbings (*Bedfordshire*)	6	10	1	389	125*	1	2	43.22
J. D. Libby (*Cornwall*)	7	11	1	432	139	1	2	43.20
E. J. Foster (*Shropshire*)	6	9	1	344	89	0	3	43.00
T. Williams (*Cornwall*)	7	11	4	298	125*	1	0	42.57
M. B. Loye (*Buckinghamshire*)	5	9	0	372	179	1	1	41.33
D. J. Birch (*Lincolnshire*)	6	11	0	443	87	0	4	40.27
Hassan Adnan (*Suffolk*)	6	9	0	361	119	2	0	40.11

BOWLING (15 wickets at 25.00)

	O	*M*	*R*	*W*	*BB*	*Avge*	*5WI*
A. A. Morrison (*Wiltshire*)	58	15	177	15	6-24	11.80	2
P. J. McMahon (*Cambridgeshire*)	190.3	60	385	31	6-56	12.41	5
T. Bulcock (*Cumberland*)	197.2	55	485	36	6-41	13.47	3
G. R. Willott (*Staffordshire*)	130	49	289	21	7-20	13.76	1
B. W. Houston (*Lincolnshire*)	170.2	43	427	30	8-53	14.23	2
D. A. Woods (*Cheshire*)	191.5	56	550	34	9-74	16.17	3
P. A. Byrne (*Staffordshire*)	128.5	47	276	16	6-13	17.25	2
A. G. Smeeth (*Cornwall*)	82	17	260	15	5-20	17.33	1
C. Brown (*Norfolk*)	160	48	348	20	7-83	17.40	1
L. R. Bruce (*Cambridgeshire*)	127.1	30	350	20	4-38	17.50	0
C. B. Keegan (*Oxfordshire*)	126	35	348	19	5-30	18.31	2
V. Banerjee (*Buckinghamshire*)	114.4	32	280	15	5-69	18.66	1
B. H. D. Mordt (*Berkshire*)	101.2	18	360	19	5-49	18.94	1
S. C. Hockin (*Cornwall*)	162	35	578	30	7-54	19.26	2
T. G. Sharp (*Cornwall*)	193	65	392	20	5-25	19.60	2
Faisal Ali (*Buckinghamshire*)	120.1	26	420	21	4-33	20.00	0
R. I. Kaufman (*Oxfordshire*)	82	10	301	15	5-81	20.06	1
T. B. Huggins (*Suffolk*)	125	28	364	17	4-49	21.41	0
Tahir Afridi (*Wiltshire*)	181.1	43	630	29	6-35	21.72	1
M. R. Bhatt (*Wiltshire*)	147.3	33	422	19	5-48	22.21	1
A. B. Shepherd (*Lincolnshire*)	108.2	23	475	21	5-57	22.61	1
D. King (*Buckinghamshire*)	122.3	34	371	16	6-49	23.18	1
I. J. S. Tait (*Cheshire*)	163.4	37	525	22	6-52	23.86	3

CHAMPIONSHIP FINAL

At Truro, September 9–12. **Cornwall won by 150 runs. Cornwall 257** (90 overs) (C. A. Hunkin 77; S. F. Stanway 4-73, S. A. Khalid 3-77) **and 209** (94.1 overs) (N. S. Curnow 53; Faisal Ali 3-41, S. A. Khalid 3-52); ‡**Buckinghamshire 205-9** (90 overs) (T. G. Sharp 5-76, Shakeel Ahmed 3-73) **and 111** (68.4 overs) (Shakeel Ahmed 7-36). *MoM:* Shakeel Ahmed. *Cornwall were crowned Minor Counties champions for the first time since their admission to the Championship in 1904. They were surprisingly asked to bat on their home ground, and the middle order took control on a slow-turning surface, with Chris Hunkin and Tom Hughes putting on 110 for the seventh wicket. Buckinghamshire, featuring former England batsman Mal Loye, found the going even tougher against spinners Tom Sharp and Shakeel Ahmed – a one-time Pakistan Test slow left-armer – who between them bowled 73 of the 90 overs permitted in the first innings. A man named Cornwall, Neil Curnow, then ground out 53 from 208 balls, and Buckinghamshire inadvertently increased their target to 261 due to a 12 run penalty for a slow over rate. Heading into the fourth (and extra) day, Buckinghamshire needed 169 more with seven wickets intact, but collapsed to Shakeel in just over an hour. Sharp, captain since 2002, took the final catch off Shakeel, who completed match figures of 56.4–19–109–10.*

RECENT MINOR COUNTIES CHAMPIONS

1986	Cumberland	1997	Devon	2005	Cheshire / Suffolk
1987	Buckinghamshire	1998	Staffordshire	2006	Devon
1988	Cheshire	1999	Cumberland	2007	Cheshire
1989	Oxfordshire	2000	Dorset	2008	Berkshire
1990	Hertfordshire	2001	Cheshire / Lincolnshire	2009	Buckinghamshire
1991	Staffordshire	2002	Herefordshire / Norfolk	2010	Dorset
1992	Staffordshire	2003	Lincolnshire	2011	Devon
1993	Staffordshire	2004	Bedfordshire / Devon	2012	Cornwall
1994	Devon				
1995	Devon				
1996	Devon				

A list of previous champions can be found on page 915 of Wisden 2008.

MCCA KNOCKOUT TROPHY FINAL

At Wormsley, August 29, 30. **Cumberland won by seven wickets. Wiltshire 184** (45.4 overs) (A. A. Morrison 59); ‡**Cumberland 186-3** (32.4 overs) (J. R. Tolley 67). *MoM:* C. A. Thompson (Cumberland). *With Lord's unavailable due to the Olympic archery, the 50-over final was staged at Wormsley for the first time, but the weather pushed the game into a reserve day. Heavy rain led to a 4.30pm start on the first day, when only a handful of overs were possible in one of that day's nine County Championship games – testament to the quality of Wormsley's drainage, and the diligence of the groundstaff. Wiltshire limped to 142-8 in 36 overs by the close, with medium-pacer Chris Thompson taking a hat-trick and stand-in wicketkeeper Gary Pratt four catches. Ashur Morrison, 26* overnight, pushed on to 59 from 74 balls, but Wiltshire's total was woefully short of par in sunny conditions. A second-wicket stand of 112 between Josh Tolley and Jonathan Miles (41) made the run-chase easy. Cumberland had travelled hundreds of miles to Cornwall for their quarter-final, and to Dorset for the semi, so fully deserved their crown.*

A list of previous MCCA Knockout Trophy champions can be found on page 905 of Wisden 2010.

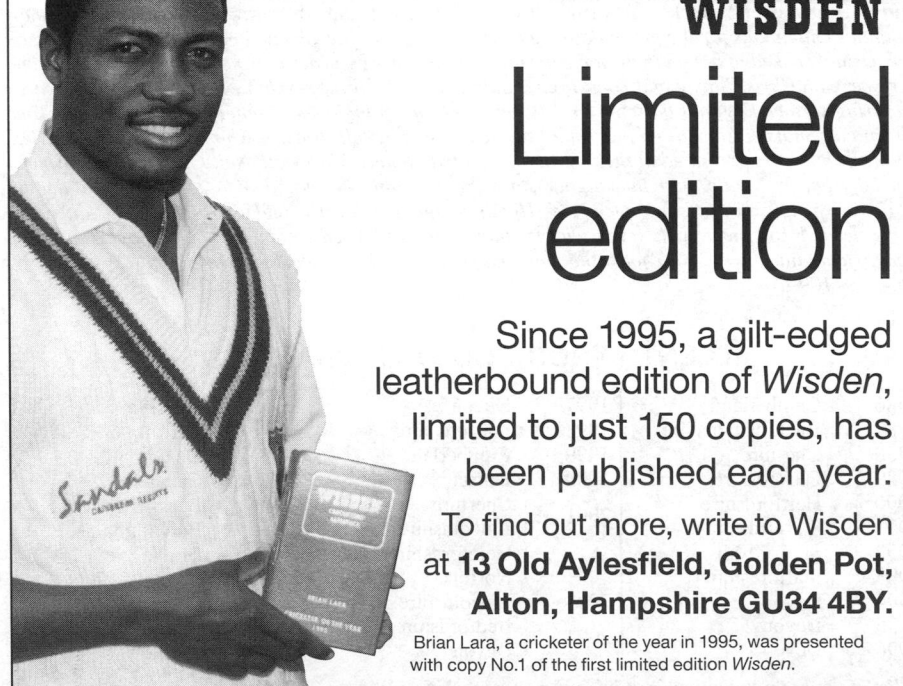

SECOND ELEVEN CHAMPIONSHIP, 2012

	North Division	P	W	L	D	A	Bonus points Bat	Bowl	Pen	Total points
1	Leicestershire (2)	9	3	0	5	1	16	27	0	109
2	Durham (4)	9	2	0	7	0	19	24	0	96
3	Lancashire (3)	9	2	1	6	0	19	24	0	93
4	Northamptonshire (8)	9	1	0	7	1	20	22	0	82
5	Worcestershire (6)	9	1	1	5	2	16	23	0	76
6	MCC Universities (9)	9	1	4	4	0	17	30	0	75
7	Derbyshire (7)	9	1	2	5	1	14	22	1	69
8	Warwickshire (1)	9	0	1	8	0	17	26	0	67
9	Yorkshire (10)	9	1	2	4	2	15	17	0	66
10	Nottinghamshire (5)	9	0	1	7	1	16	20	0	60

	South Division	P	W	L	D	A	Bonus points Bat	Bowl	Pen	Total points
1	Kent (9)	9	3	2	3	1	18	28	1.5	104.5
2	Surrey (7)	9	3	2	3	1	17	28	2	103
3	Glamorgan (1)	9	3	0	3	3	20	15	0	101
4	Middlesex (2)	9	3	2	3	1	14	25	0	99
5	Hampshire (4)	9	3	4	1	1	19	25	0	98
6	Essex (3)	9	2	0	5	2	19	20	0	92
7	Sussex (6)	9	2	2	3	2	17	21	2	83
8	MCC Young Cricketers (8)	9	1	2	3	3	18	14	2.5	63.5
9	Somerset (5)	9	0	3	5	1	9	26	0	53
10	Gloucestershire (10)	9	0	3	3	3	15	17	0	50

2011 positions in brackets.

Win = 16pts; draw/abandoned = 3pts.

Derbyshire, Kent, Surrey, Sussex and MCC Young Cricketers were deducted points for a slow over-rate.

LEADING AVERAGES, 2012

BATTING (360 runs)

		M	I	NO	R	HS	100	Avge
1	A. McGrath (*Yorks*)	3	5	1	373	200*	1	93.25
2	M. S. Lineker (*Derbys*)	5	6	1	404	145	3	80.80
3	W. S. Jones (*Leics*)	4	7	1	471	169	1	78.50
4	B. M. Shafayat (*Hants*)	4	7	1	466	164	1	77.66
5	B. T. Foakes (*Essex*)	3	5	0	374	186	1	74.80
6	K. Turner (*Notts*)	8	12	5	453	105*	1	64.71
7	L. J. Evans (*Warwicks*)	6	8	1	452	140	2	64.57
8	J. C. Mickleburgh (*Essex*)	6	10	1	506	162	3	56.22
9	R. I. Keogh (*Northants*)	6	9	1	435	128	1	54.37
10	M. J. Richardson (*Durham*)	7	7	0	369	118	2	52.71
11	M. D. T. Roberts (*Hants*)	7	14	2	610	110	2	50.83
12	M. A. Comber (*Essex*)	7	10	1	447	119	2	49.66
13	F. K. Cowdrey (*Kent*)	8	13	3	442	83*	0	44.20
14	A. Patel (*Kent, Northants*)	6	9	0	393	106	1	43.66
15	J. M. Lawrence (*Somerset*)	8	12	3	392	125	1	43.55
16	N. R. T. Gubbins (*Middx*)	5	9	0	380	134	1	42.22
17	D. L. Lloyd (*Glam*)	6	10	1	379	182	1	42.11
18	T. P. Lewis (*MCC YC*)	6	11	1	419	96	0	41.90
19	D. J. Bell-Drummond (*Kent*)	5	9	0	366	124	1	40.66
20	A. B. London (*Middx*)	7	12	2	405	196	1	40.50

		M	I	NO	R	HS	100	Avge
21	A. J. Blake (*Kent*)	6	9	0	360	92	0	40.00
22	N. Patel (*MCCU*)	7	13	1	427	98	0	35.58
23	H. Bush (Durham, *MCCU*)	9	14	2	413	56*	0	34.41
24	A. P. Rouse (*Hants*)	8	14	3	377	77	0	34.27
25	L. A. Blackaby (*MCCU*)	9	15	2	431	78	0	33.15

BOWLING (15 wickets)

		O	M	R	W	BB	5I	Avge
1	O. J. Newby (*Lancs*)	98.1	40	195	16	5-20	2	12.18
2	J. A. Tomlinson (*Hants*)	69.4	20	224	16	7-20	1	14.00
3	C. J. Russell (*Worcs*)	101.3	20	334	21	6-75	2	15.90
4	I. A. A. Thomas (*Kent*)	130	39	336	20	5-47	1	16.80
5	R. G. Mutch (*Somerset*)	120.2	29	345	19	5-37	1	18.15
6	T. E. Linley (*Surrey*)	149.2	29	416	22	5-40	1	18.90
7	C. A. J. Morris (*Kent, MCCU, Worcs*)	106	24	333	17	5-27	1	19.58
8	M. A. Chambers (*Essex*)	168.2	38	478	24	4-63	0	19.91
9	G. A. Edwards (*Surrey*)	93	22	305	15	5-20	1	20.33
10	L. J. Hatchett (*Sussex*)	111.1	22	353	16	4-8	0	22.06
11	G. S. Sandhu (*Middx*)	143	32	453	20	5-32	1	22.65
12	C. P. Ashling (*Glam*)	91.2	15	342	15	5-43	1	22.80
13	H. Riazuddin (*Hants*)	142	36	372	16	3-48	0	23.25
14	J. S. Sykes (*Leics*)	210.4	49	622	24	5-55	1	25.91
15	R. H. Patel (*Middx*)	163.3	27	475	18	5-29	1	26.38
16	S. P. Cheetham (*Essex, Yorks*)	120.3	21	396	15	4-45	0	26.40
17	T. P. Milnes (*Warwicks*)	157	35	537	20	5-48	1	26.85
18	J. A. Porter (*MCC YC*)	136	22	458	17	4-1	0	26.94
19	J. D. Sheppard (*Hants*)	121.4	28	433	16	5-63	1	27.06
20	A. MacQueen (*MCCU*)	283.3	49	1,033	38	7-122	1	27.18
21	W. A. Adkin (*Sussex*)	147.4	32	435	16	5-69	1	27.18
22	A. Javid (*Warwicks*)	143.1	20	499	18	5-83	1	27.72
23	G. S. Randhawa (*Yorks*)	126.4	19	440	15	5-42	1	29.33
24	A. S. Miller (*Warwicks*)	189.2	33	572	19	6-71	1	30.10

CHAMPIONSHIP FINAL

At Leicester, September 4–7. **Kent won by one wicket.** **‡Leicestershire 360** (92.5 overs) (N. P. Hawkes 75) **and 219** (69.5 overs) (G. P. Smith 118*; I. A. A. Thomas 3-36, C. J. Haggett 4-50); **Kent 355** (108 overs) (D. J. Bell-Drummond 88, F. K. Cowdrey 60, C. D. Piesley 52; J. K. H. Naik 4-51) **and 225-9** (79.4 overs) (C. J. Haggett 62*; J. S. Sykes 5-55). *Each side chose 12 players, of whom 11 could bat and 11 field. Kent seemed unlikely to win after being 119-7 in their second innings, but Calum Haggett and Simon Cook (35) put on 95.*

SECOND ELEVEN TROPHY FINAL, 2012

At Great Crosby, September 13. **Lancashire won by 76 runs.** **‡Lancashire 190** (39 overs) (L. M. Reece 75; M. E. Claydon 4-35); **Durham 114** (33.3 overs) (G. J. Muchall 31; K. W. Hogg 5-23).

SECOND ELEVEN TWENTY20 FINAL, 2012

At Arundel, June 30. **England Under-19s won by eight wickets.** **‡Sussex 156-6** (20 overs) (L. W. P. Wells 53; B. F. Collins 3-33); **England Under-19s 159-2** (17.4 overs) (S. Kelsall 56, B. M. Duckett 73*).

LEAGUE CRICKET, 2012

GEOFFREY DEAN

Without any doubt, the team of the year was York, who not only secured their sixth consecutive Yorkshire League title, but also won the National Club Championship after beating Wanstead & Snaresbrook of Essex in the final. Not that York ran away with the league, for in the last round of matches they faced second-placed Harrogate in a winner-takes-all decider. Two players produced heroic all-round performances just when their side needed them. Ryan McKendry hit his first hundred at this level, reaching a disciplined fifty off 100 balls before charging to three figures off a further 38. Nick Kay, who thumped 57 off 41 deliveries, helped him add 125 to propel York to 289 for five, then claimed four for 37 as Harrogate were bundled out for 149, with McKendry picking up the last three wickets.

At the other end of the country, Bridgwater sealed their first Premier League title when they won the West of England League on a dramatic last day. At its start they were level with Bath, who were top by virtue of more wins, but Bridgwater secured maximum points after running up 257 for five against bottom club Gloucester City Winget, then skittled them for 100. Bath were unfortunate that they faced relegation-threatened Frocester, who knew a draw might keep them up if Taunton Deane lost to Corsham. Set 234, Frocester saved the match after finishing on 185 for seven and, with Taunton Deane losing, avoided the drop. Bridgwater pipped Bath by a single point.

In the West Midlands, Walsall celebrated 100 years of cricket at their Gorway ground with a 20th Birmingham & District League title in that time, and their 22nd overall. Former Surrey cricketer James Benning combined 815 runs at 67 with 27 wickets at 20 to help High Wycombe retain their Home Counties League crown. Matt Eyles contributed 716 runs at 59.

The bowling performance of the season came in the Essex League in mid-May, when Gareth Fisher, a 22-year-old seamer, returned the astonishing figures of nine for four, winning six lbw decisions, as Woodford Wells were shot out for 24 by Colchester & East Essex at Castle Park. Left-arm seamer Lewis Hatchett claimed nine for 22 (the other was a run-out) for East Grinstead against Brighton & Hove in the Sussex League, where Preston Nomads claimed the title.

Another collapse took place in mid-July in the Swalec League, when Llandudno, having bowled St Asaph out for 91, were themselves dismissed for only 18. Matthew Hulse, who took five for four, said: "When the wickets started falling, we were having a laugh. When you're defending 91, you just say to each other 'well done', and try to hold the batters up. Then, with the fifth and sixth wickets, it was more like 'we can do this'. It's the first time I've returned figures like that." David North helped him out with five for 14.

Llandudno's Duncan Midgley made up for the indignity in the last two games of the season by hammering 171 against Brymbo and 173 against Mold. Llandudno won both games to clinch the title. Gordon Kerr and Sam

Rimmington played important parts, sharing over 100 wickets. At the other end of the table, Ynysygerwn avoided their first-ever relegation, thanks to the weather. Fewer than the required 60% of games were played in the Glamorgan & Monmouthshire feeder league, which meant there could be no promotion to (or relegation from) the Swalec League.

In the South, Wimbledon – half of whose team were of South African origin – retained their Surrey Championship crown and won the National Club Twenty20 final. North of the Thames, Winchmore Hill ended Ealing's hegemony of the Middlesex League by winning their first Premier League title. Fittingly, their triumph was confirmed at Ealing, champions for the previous seven years, in the penultimate game, which they won by 29 runs thanks to left-arm seamer Jamie Thorpe's five-for. Mark Ramprakash turned out several times for Stanmore, helping them narrowly avoid the drop. But another fortysomething ex-England player, Ed Giddins, was not so successful in his quest to preserve his team's top-flight status. Despite his match-winning seven for 27 against Bexhill in July, Eastbourne were relegated from the Sussex League after being pipped by two points by Worthing; in August, they had been docked five after their former Pakistan Test seamer Mohammad Akram was found guilty of dissent against Hastings & St Leonards Priory.

Chris Aspin writes: The Lancashire League championship was decided in the final minutes of the season, when Lowerhouse, in their 150th year, edged six points ahead of Accrington to retain the title. They had already beaten Church by 15 runs to take the Worsley Cup for only the second time.

In a summer in which 23 matches were lost to rain and the Ramsbottom field was flooded twice, Enfield and East Lancashire had to wait until their 12th meeting to complete their Worsley Cup quarter-final. East Lancashire finally won by 11 runs, thanks to a late hat-trick by their South African pro Ockert Erasmus, 33 days after the game had first been scheduled to take place. On the final day of the season the Rishton pro, Daniel Salpietro, a club cricketer from Melbourne who had represented Adelaide Strikers in the Big Bash League, took ten for 34 against wooden-spoonists Rawtenstall, who were dismissed for 78, their 11th total below 100. The last player to take all ten was Nelson's Anton Ferreira, against Accrington in 1988.

The leading run-scorers were Ramsbottom's South African pro Pieter Malan (947 at 63) and the Haslingden skipper Graham Knowles (829 at 43). Both hit three centuries, with Knowles making 156 at Rawtenstall in a total of 306 for five to set up a 224-run win – all three were season's bests. In a game reduced by rain to 41 overs, Enfield made 301 for five against Colne, with Adam Bracewell hammering an unbeaten 151. In May, Malan had smashed an unbeaten 165 off 72 balls against Rawtenstall, as Ramsbottom made 210 for four, before winning by 122 runs.

Two Pakistanis excelled with the ball. Todmorden's slow left-armer Qaiser Abbas, who won one Test cap, against England at Lahore in 2000-01, took 96 wickets, while Burnley off-spinner Adnan Rasool managed 95; both averaged 12. Among the amateurs, left-arm spinner Jon Fielding of Ramsbottom took most wickets, with 89 at 13.

Gary Holder turned out for Rawtenstall against Rishton, nearly 22 years after his last first-team appearance, and scored a single in a total of 56 and a ten-wicket defeat. Police halted play in Burnley's home game with Bacup for half an hour to allow an air ambulance to land on the outfield and take a heart attack victim at a house beside the ground to a Blackpool hospital.

After 48 years, Walsden won the Central Lancashire League outright for the second time – they had also been joint-champions in 1962 – thanks mainly to their Sri Lankan professional, left-arm spinner Ranil Dhammika. The league's most successful bowler with 119 wickets at 7.91, and a best of nine for 69 against Middleton, Dhammika also scored 589 runs at 34. Middleton retained the Lees Wood Cup, beating Norden in the final.

Babar Naeem, the Milnrow professional, claimed 113 wickets at ten and scored 931 runs at 38. But Middleton's pro Michael Smith made most runs (1,260 at 57) and the highest score – 182 not out against Royton. Other pros to top four figures were Norden's Michael Price (1,250 at 56), Littleborough's Clinton Perren (1,050 at 95) and Paul Green of Monton & Weaste (1,027 at 48). For runners-up Heywood, captain Bobby Cross scored three centuries, including an unbeaten 154 against Oldham, and finished the season with 916 runs at 48. Greg Butterworth (Rochdale) picked up 75 wickets at 12, and Dale Highton (Middleton) 75 at 16.

Sixty games were lost to the weather, 45 without a ball being bowled. Heywood's game against Milnrow lasted just 123 legitimate deliveries: seven players failed to score as Milnrow, having elected to bat, were shot out for 24 in 15.1 overs, before Heywood knocked off the runs in 32 balls. In 2013, the league will have two divisions, with promotion and relegation for two clubs. The teams will play each other four times, but all will take part in the knockout cup. The experiment will be reviewed after two seasons.

ECB PREMIER LEAGUE TABLES, 2012

Birmingham & District League

	P	*W*	*L*	*Pts*
Walsall	**22**	**12**	**1**	**310**
Himley	22	7	4	276*
Wolverhampton	22	8	3	273
Berkswell	22	9	4	270
Kidderminster Victoria	22	7	5	251
Shrewsbury	22	4	4	236
Brockhampton	22	5	5	233
Barnt Green	22	6	8	232
W. Bromwich Dartmouth	22	3	7	202
Knowle & Dorridge	22	5	5	200
Leamington Spa	22	2	12	135*
Wellington	22	1	11	100†

* *One-point penalty for slow over-rate.*
† *Ten-point penalty for slow over-rate.*

Cheshire County League

	P	*W*	*L*	*Pts*
Nantwich	**22**	**11**	**4**	**344**
Hyde	22	9	5	332
Chester Boughton Hall	22	10	8	314
Macclesfield	22	10	8	304
Marple	22	8	3	297
Oxton	22	8	7	292
Alderley Edge	22	6	6	262
Didsbury	22	5	9	231
Neston	22	6	10	229
Toft	22	6	10	227
Urmston	22	5	10	227
Widnes	22	6	10	224

Cornwall Premier League

	P	W	L	Pts
Werrington	**18**	**9**	**0**	**248***
St Just	18	8	2	235
Callington	18	6	3	211*
Truro	18	5	6	187
St Austell	18	6	4	184
Falmouth	18	5	6	184*
Grampound Road	18	4	6	180
Camborne	18	4	6	175
Paul	18	3	9	146†
Troon	18	1	9	118

* *One-point penalty for slow over-rate.*
† *Two-point penalty for slow over-rate.*

Derbyshire Premier League

	P	W	L	Pts
Sandiacre Town	**22**	**13**	**2**	**384**
Swarkestone	22	12	2	375
Ockbrook & Borrowash	22	6	3	310
Ticknall	22	6	6	299
Chesterfield	22	8	5	291
Denby	22	7	6	271*
Lullington Park	22	6	6	241
Dunstall	22	3	4	234
Spondon	22	4	7	228
Alvaston & Boulton	22	2	8	225
Quarndon	22	1	5	214
Rolls Royce	22	1	15	126†

* *One-point penalty for slow over-rate.*
† *Twelve-point penalty for slow over-rate.*

Devon League

	P	W	L	Pts
Sidmouth	**18**	**9**	**5**	**222***
Exmouth	18	9	5	219†
Plymouth	18	9	5	214
Bovey Tracey	18	10	5	212‡
North Devon	18	7	7	191
Bradninch	18	6	7	168¶
Budleigh Salterton	18	5	7	158§
Torquay	18	5	9	158
Heathcoat	18	5	9	145†
Sandford	18	4	10	143

* *Five-point penalty for slow over-rate.*
† *One-point penalty for slow over-rate.*
‡ *Four-point penalty for slow over-rate.*
¶ *Two-point penalty for slow over-rate.*
§ *Twelve-point penalty for slow over-rate.*

East Anglian Premier League

	P	W	L	Pts
Swardeston	**22**	**11**	**3**	**369**
Vauxhall Mallards	22	10	2	365
Horsford	22	8	1	356
Clacton-on-Sea	22	9	3	328
Great Witchingham	22	5	4	286
Copdock & Old Ipswichian	22	6	8	283
Bury St Edmunds	22	6	7	267*
Saffron Walden	22	5	5	261
Sudbury	22	5	7	260
Burwell	22	5	8	259
Cambridge Granta	22	3	9	196†
Halstead	22	0	16	76

* *One-point penalty for slow over-rate.*
† *Six-point penalty for slow over-rate.*

Essex Premier League

	P	W	L	Pts
Wanstead & Snaresbrook	**17**	**12**	**2**	**268**
Chelmsford	17	9	4	252
Brentwood	17	7	3	222
Shenfield	17	7	3	211
Colchester & East Essex	17	6	7	193*
Buckhurst Hill	17	5	5	190
Ilford	17	6	9	184
South Woodford	17	5	6	171†
Woodford Wells	17	3	10	127*
Ardleigh Green	17	1	12	83†

* *One-point penalty for slow over-rate.*
† *One-point penalty for failure to notify league of result.*

Home Counties Premier League

	P	W	L	Pts
High Wycombe	**18**	**11**	**1**	**346**
Banbury	18	9	3	309
Tring Park	18	8	5	274
Henley	18	7	2	260
Welwyn Garden City	18	5	5	208*
Burnham	18	4	9	201
Harpenden	18	4	6	188†
Potters Bar	18	3	7	173
Bishop's Stortford	18	2	8	171
Oxford	18	1	8	156

* *Two-point penalty for slow over-rate.*
† *One-point penalty for slow over-rate.*

Kent League

	P	W	L	Pts
Hartley	**18**	**12**	**1**	**252**
Blackheath	18	8	6	215*
Sevenoaks Vine	18	8	6	212
Bromley	18	6	6	183
Beckenham	18	7	7	182
Lordswood	18	6	8	173
Bexley	18	5	6	173*
Bickley Park	18	4	8	160
Canterbury	18	5	10	157
Tunbridge Wells	18	4	8	148

* *One-point penalty for slow over-rate.*

Leicestershire County League

	P	W	L	Pts
Loughborough Town	**22**	**14**	**0**	**385**
Market Harborough	22	11	4	330
Syston Town	22	8	6	300
Kibworth	22	4*	8	254
Sileby Town	22	2*	6	241
Ashby Hastings	22	2	7	239
Broomleys	22	6	6	238
Kegworth Town	22	5	7	216†
Leicester Ivanhoe	22	10	2	196
Stoughton & Thurnby	22	4	9	195
Thorpe Arnold	22	1	9	182
Lutterworth	22	4	7	–47

** Plus one tie.*

† Three-point penalty for slow over-rate.

The following points were deducted for the fielding of unregistered players: Lutterworth 310, Leicester Ivanhoe 141.

The following points were added after the opposition fielded unregistered players: Thorpe Arnold 44, Syston Town 43, Ashby Hastings 33, Sileby Town 18, Loughborough 14, Kibworth 5, Market Harborough 1.

Lincolnshire Cricket Board Premier League

	P	W	L	Pts
Haxey	**21**	**12**	**4**	**271**
Bracebridge Heath	21	8	1	250
Skegness	21	10	7	242
Sleaford	21	8	6	232
Woodhall Spa	21	6	5	215
Lindum	21	8	5	211
Bourne	21	4	5	200
Grimsby Town	21	4	8	190
Hartsholme	21	6	10	179
Louth	21	5	7	171
Market Deeping	21	3	8	149
Boston	21	3	11	133

Liverpool & District Competition

	P	W	L	Pts
Lytham	**22**	**17**	**2**	**422**
Ormskirk	22	11	4	327
Northern	22	10	7	314
Leigh	22	10	8	305
Bootle	22	10	4	291
Highfield	22	9	6	278
Southport & Birkdale	22	9	11	259
New Brighton	22	7	6	247
Maghull	22	5	10	195
Hightown	22	4	12	167
Colwyn Bay	22	2	11	147*
Rainford	22	1	14	136

** One-point penalty for slow over-rate.*

Middlesex County League

	P	W	L	Pts
Winchmore Hill	**18**	**13**	**2**	**136**
Teddington	18	10	4	110
Ealing	18	9	5	100
Eastcote	18	8	4	92
Hornsey	18	7	6	78
Hampstead	18	6	7	69*
Finchley	18	5	7	61
Stanmore	18	4	8	46
Brondesbury	18	3	9	45
Southgate	18	0	13	5

** One-point penalty for slow over-rate.*

Northamptonshire League

	P	W	L	Pts
Peterborough Town	**22**	**18**	**2**	**496**
Northampton Saints	22	12	4	402
Finedon Dolben	22	11	6	380
Old Northamptonians	22	12	4	377
Rushton	22	8	7	302
Brixworth	22	6	5	293
Stony Stratford	22	5	12	260
Wellingborough Town	22	7	7	251
Nhants Cricket Academy	22	3	9	247
Wollaston	22	4	8	239*
Burton Latimer	22	2	13	184
Horton House	22	2	13	180

** Four-point penalty for fielding an unregistered player.*

North East Premier League

	P	W	L	Pts
South Northumberland	**22**	**10**	**1**	**372***
Blaydon	22	11	1	366
Chester-le-Street	22	9	2	347
Sunderland	22	9	3	310
Durham Academy	22	6	4	259
Stockton	22	6	7	239
Hetton Lyons	22	5	8	216
South Shields	22	5	8	208
Tynemouth	22	4	9	199
Newcastle	22	3	7	188¶
Benwell Hill	22	2	10	145
Gateshead Fell	22	2	12	127

** One-point penalty for slow over-rate.*

† Two-point penalty for slow over-rate.

Northern Premier Cricket League

	P	*W*	*L*	*Pts*
Fleetwood	**25**	**15**	**2**	**236**
Barrow	25	15	5	230
Leyland	25	11	4	215
Kendal	25	11	6	215
Netherfield	25	9	5	204
Preston	25	6	10	157
Darwen	25	5	9	154
Morecambe	25	7	7	153
Blackpool	25	7	6	151
Lancashire Cricket Board	13	3	5	136*
Lancaster	25	5	10	122
St Annes	25	4	9	119
Chorley	25	4	13	110
Carnforth	25	2	13	97

** Played only 13 games; their final position was obtained by multiplying their 71 points by 25 and dividing by 13.*

N. Yorkshire & S. Durham Premier League

	P	*W*	*L*	*Pts*
Richmondshire	**26**	**10**	**0**	**371**
Darlington	26	12	5	357
Great Ayton	26	9	2	326
Middlesbrough	26	6	6	296
Marton	26	9	5	293
Stokesley	26	8	10	286
Guisborough	26	7	8	266
Barnard Castle	26	7	8	256
Hartlepool	26	4	8	247
Normanby Hall	26	4	7	242
Thornaby	26	5	12	227
Sedgefield	26	4	5	227
Marske	26	6	8	223
Billingham Synthonia	26	3	10	213

North Staffs & South Cheshire League

	P	*W*	*L*	*Pts*
Leek	**22**	**13**	**4**	**320**
Longton	22	11	3	304*
Wood Lane	22	11	4	281†
Knypersley	22	9	5	272‡
Porthill Park	22	7	5	261
Stone	22	6	5	235‡
Audley	22	6	10	207
Hem Heath	22	4	11	199
Checkley	22	5	10	195
Burslem	22	5	9	168
Little Stoke	22	3	11	165
Cheadle	22	5	8	119¶

** Four-point penalty for slow over-rate.*
† 11-pt penalty for slow over-rate.
‡ One-point penalty for slow over-rate.
¶ 76-pt for fielding ineligible players.

Notts Cricket Board Premier League

	P	*W*	*L*	*Pts*
Cuckney	**22**	**11**	**2**	**313**
Nottinghamshire Cricket Board Academy	22	7	1	290
West Indian Cavaliers	22	8	1	258
Caythorpe	22	6	2	251
Kimberley Institute	22	5	5	247
Mansfield Hosiery Mills	22	6	4	245‡
Clifton Village	22	7	5	243
Plumtree	22	5	5	222
Welbeck Colliery	22	5	9	181
Papplewick & Linby	22	3	8	172
Wollaton	22	2*	11	157
Worksop	22	1*	13	92†

** Plus one tie.*
† Five-point penalty for late notification of result.
‡ Three-point penalty for non-return of umpire report forms.

North Wales Premier League

	P	*W*	*L*	*Pts*
Llandudno	**22**	**13**	**3**	**397**
Menai Bridge	22	12	2	378
Mochdre	22	10	2	332
Connah's Quay	22	6	6	277
St Asaph	22	7	8	247
Pontblyddyn	22	5	3	236
Northop	22	5	10	203
Denbigh	22	5	10	200
Mold	22	4	9	191
Brymbo	22	3	5	187*
Bangor	22	4	8	184
Llay Welfare	22	2	10	139

** Four-point penalty for slow over-rate.*

Southern Premier League

	P	*W*	*L*	*Pts*	*Avge*
South Wilts	**14**	**9**	**2**	**243**	**17.36**
Bashley Rydal	12	7	3	181	15.08
Havant	13	7	4	187	14.38
St Cross Symondians	13	7	3	180	13.85
Alton	11	5	5	129	11.73
Totton & Eling	13	5	7	150	11.54
Lymington	12	5	7	138	11.50
Ventnor	13	4	8	141	10.85
Hampshire Academy	15	4	10	154	10.27
Bournemouth	12	3	6	124*	8.66

** Twenty-point penalty for administrative error.*

Surrey Championship

	P	W	L	Pts
Wimbledon	**18**	**11**	**2**	**137**
Sunbury	18	9	3	106*
Reigate Priory	18	8	6	104
Banstead	18	8	2	96
Guildford	18	7	5	86
Malden Wanderers	18	7	7	84
Sutton	18	6	7	72
Weybridge	18	5	11	64
Normandy	18	3	11	40
Camberley	18	2	12	24

** Nine-point penalty for fielding an unregistered player.*

Sussex League

	P	W	L	Pts
Preston Nomads	**19**	**13**	**2**	**433**
Horsham	19	10	5	388
Hastings & St Leonards Priory	19	7	5	324
East Grinstead	19	8	6	306
Roffey	19	6	5	283†
Brighton & Hove	19	5	9	278
Chichester Priory Park	19	6	7	275‡
Worthing	19	4	8	258
Eastbourne	19	5	8	256‡
Bexhill	19	4	9	237
Sussex Cricket Board	10	1	5	182*

** Played only ten games; their actual points total was multiplied by 1.9.*
† Three-point penalty for slow over-rate.
‡ Five-point penalty for disciplinary reasons.

Swalec Premier League

	P	W	L	Pts
Ammanford	**18**	**8**	**2**	**254**
Mumbles	18	5	3	228
Cardiff	18	7	4	208
Bridgend Town	18	7	2	207
Sully Centurion	18	5	5	204
Port Talbot Town	18	3	7	194
Pontarddulais	18	5	5	183
Newport	18	3	5	181
Ynysygerwn	18	3	6	173
Usk	18	2	9	145

West of England Premier League

	P	W	L	Pts
Bridgwater	**18**	**12**	**3**	**292¶**
Bath	18	12	1	291
Corsham	18	7	3	225
Downend	18	8	4	225
Taunton St Andrews	18	8	5	214
Bristol	18	6	6	190
Ilminster	18	4	8	160
Frocester	18	2*	9	147
Taunton Deane	18	2*	11	143‡§
Gloucester City Winget	18	1	12	102†

** Plus one tie.*
† Ten-point penalty for fielding unregistered players.
‡ Five-point penalty for non-compliance with required actions.
¶ Two-point penalty for slow over-rate.
§ Four-point penalty for slow over-rate.

Yorkshire ECB Premier League

	P	W	L	Pts
York	**26**	**15**	**1**	**159**
Harrogate	26	11	2	139
Barnsley	26	8	2	132
Yorkshire Academy	26	7	2	117
Rotherham Town	26	6	4	112
Driffield Town	26	6	7	100
Scarborough	26	6	5	94
Cleethorpes	26	7	4	90
Hull	26	3	9	66
Sheffield United	26	4	7	63
Doncaster Town	26	3	8	61
Castleford	26	4	12	58
Appleby Frodingham	26	2	10	53
Sheffield Collegiate	26	1	10	49

"Once, as I passed a bibulous lunch in the Harris Garden at Lord's, I heard an elderly member assert that Pietersen was 'the closest thing to Jessop I've ever seen'. Since the Croucher played his last Test in 1912, the claim seemed a touch implausible, yet heads nodded approvingly."

It's tough being Kevin, page 67.

The following leagues do not have ECB Premier League status:

LANCASHIRE LEAGUES, 2012

Lancashire League

	P	W	L	Pts
Lowerhouse	**26**	**17**	**5**	**217**
Accrington	26	17	6	211
Church	26	15	8	195
Enfield	26	15	8	195
Todmorden	26	15*	7	188
Haslingden	26	13	8	179†
Ramsbottom	26	12	10	171
Burnley	26	11*	12	171
Rishton	26	11	12	163
Nelson	26	10	13	143
East Lancashire	26	8	12	133
Colne	26	5	18	99‡
Bacup	26	5	20	98
Rawtenstall	26	4	19	73

* *Plus one tie.*
† *Two-point penalty for slow over-rate.*
‡ *One-point penalty for slow over-rate.*

Central Lancashire League

	P	W	L	Pts
Walsden	**30**	**21**	**2**	**118**
Heywood	30	19	4	110
Milnrow	30	17*	6	98
Norden	30	15	9	91
Rochdale	30	14	6	90
Middleton	30	14	9	81
Clifton	30	13	8	81
Littleborough	30	10*	8	74
Monton & Weaste	30	11	12	71
Royton	30	10	11	69
Crompton	30	8	14	57
Unsworth	30	6	14	56
Werneth	30	4	17	42
Radcliffe	30	6	15	39†
Oldham	30	3	20	32
Ashton	30	2	18	32

* *Plus one tie.*
† *Ten-point penalty for breach of rules.*

OTHER LEAGUE WINNERS, 2012

Airedale & Wharfedale	Collingham
Bolton Association	Spring View
Bolton League	Farnworth
Bradford	Woodlands
Cambridgeshire & Huntingdonshire	Foxton
Central Yorkshire	Wrenthorpe
Durham County	Esh Winning
Durham Senior	Burnmoor
Hertfordshire	Chorleywood
Huddersfield	Hoylandswaine
Lancashire County	Prestwich
Merseyside	Moorfield
Norfolk Alliance	Norwich
North Essex	Frinton-on-Sea
North Lancs & Cumbria	Cockermouth
Northumberland & Tyneside Senior	Swalwell
Pembrokeshire	Carew
Quaid-e-Azam	Keighley RZM
Ribblesdale	Barnoldswick
Saddleworth	Bamford
Shropshire	Quatt
South Wales Association	Swansea
South Yorkshire	Treeton
Thames Valley	Reading
Two Counties	Woolpit
Warwickshire	Kings Heath
Worcestershire	Worcester Nomads
York Senior	Dunnington

KINGFISHER CUP AND NATIONAL CLUB t20, 2012

PAUL EDWARDS

The success of the ECB's two major recreational competitions in 2012 owed much to the flexibility of the clubs and the tolerance of the governing body. Although the weather did its best to wreck the schedules for both the 45-over Kingfisher Cup and the Twenty20 tournament, teams were willing to rearrange games whenever possible, and only three of the 255 matches in the Kingfisher Cup had to be decided by the toss of a coin. Rather than advance to the next round by adhering rigidly to the rubric, cricketers preferred to play cricket – even if this meant that a lucrative game scheduled for a Sunday had to be settled instead by a 20-over contest on a Wednesday evening after work. The ECB responded by extending deadlines whenever possible.

The slight air of chaos did not prevent some of the best clubs in the country reaching the two finals days in September. Three of the teams – Chester-le-Street, Cuckney and Wimbledon – contesting the televised ECB National Club t20 at Edgbaston on September 6 were no strangers to the occasion, while the fourth – Northern, from the Liverpool Competition – have come close in both formats in recent years.

In the Kingfisher Cup, Wanstead & Snaresbrook from the Essex Premier League made their first appearance in a national final but were overpowered by York, the team of the year, who added club cricket's most prestigious trophy to their sixth successive Yorkshire Premier League title. No one who watched them go through their drills on the day before the game could doubt the thoroughness of their preparation, and their approach was in complete contrast to the occasionally bibulous image of club cricket. It also became a little easier to understand how Daniel Woods's side had beaten such powerful and professional teams as South Northumberland and Bamford Fieldhouse on their way to the final at Derby. York's eventual victory in the national knockout was their first since 1975; it will be a surprise if they have to wait another 37 years for their next triumph.

Northern were unfazed by Edgbaston's wide expanses when they beat a battle-hardened Chester-le-Street, of the North East Premier League, by 11 runs in the first of the ECB National Club t20 semi-finals. (One Chester-le-Street player, RAF Corporal Graeme Cessford, may become accustomed to playing in such arenas: he signed a one-year contract with Worcestershire for 2013.) In the final, though, Northern were well beaten by Wimbledon, who added the national short-form title to their second successive Surrey Championship.

The ECB are actively seeking new sponsors for both competitions in 2013, but their tried-and-tested structures will be left unchanged. Logistics suggest that the final of the 45-over tournament should be held in the Midlands, although the availability of a Test ground elsewhere may prompt a rethink. The date and venue of the Twenty20 finals day may be determined by the presence of the television cameras.

ECB NATIONAL CLUB CHAMPIONSHIP FINAL

WANSTEAD & SNARESBROOK v YORK

At Derby, September 16. York won by eight wickets. Toss: Wanstead & Snaresbrook.

York completed victory with more than 15 overs to spare in the most one-sided final of recent years. More dramatic, perhaps, were the preparations of eventual Man of the Match Tom Pringle, who needed a cortisone injection in his right shoulder two days before the game. The decision proved justified: his leg-spin claimed four prime wickets, and he clung on to a fine diving catch, as Wanstead and Snaresbrook slipped to 162, about 60 short of par on a good pitch. The pick of their batsmen was 18-year-old Kishen Velani, whose classy 65-ball 50 illustrated why he had already played for England Under-19s. For York, Oli Hairs made an unbeaten 68 off 45 balls to ease his side home; Pringle thanked his doctors, but declared adrenaline was "the best pain-killer in the world".

Man of the Match: T. Pringle.

Wanstead & Snaresbrook

J. Chambers c and b Woods	21
*Arfan Akram c and b Richmond	8
R. Hassan lbw b Snell	0
K. S. Velani c Hairs b Pringle	50
Adnan Akram c Crossley b Pringle	1
P. Hattingh c Crossley b Pringle	12
†J. Das c Lambert b Pringle	10
S. Saeed b Hairs	3
D. Richardson c Pringle b Woods	10
Z. Shahzad not out	10
J. S. E. Ellis-Grewal not out	12
B 6, l-b 5, w 14	25
1/15 (2) 2/18 (3) 3/71 (1) 4/92 (5) 5/103 (4) 6/123 (7) 7/123 (6) 8/131 (8) 9/140 (9) (9 wkts, 45 overs)	162

Snell 9–2–26–1; Richmond 7–0–26–1; Kay 2–0–12–0; Pringle 9–3–22–4; Woods 9–2–26–2; R. McKendry 5–1–22–0; Hairs 4–0–17–1.

York

L. J. McKendry b Ellis-Grewal	47
D. G. H. Snell c Hattingh b Velani	30
O. J. Hairs not out	68
A. Collins not out	6
B 1, l-b 2, w 9	12
1/62 (2) 2/118 (1) (2 wkts, 29.5 overs)	163

R. McKendry, N. J. C. Kay, S. Lambert, †S. Crossley, T. Pringle, *D. Woods and G. Richmond did not bat.

Shahzad 6–0–23–0; Saeed 3–0–19–0; Velani 6–0–26–1; Ellis-Grewal 9–1–42–1; Richardson 4–0–24–0; Chambers 1–0–8–0; Adnan Akram 0.5–0–18–0.

Umpires: P. W. Joy and J. G. Reed.

A full list of winners from the start of the competition in 1969 appears in *Wisden 2005*, page 941.

ECB CLUB t20 FINALS DAY

At Birmingham, September 6. **First semi-final: Northern won by 11 runs**. ‡**Northern 157-4** (20 overs) (S. Lucas 61, M. Walling 52); **Chester-le-Street 146-8** (20 overs) (J. W. Coxon 32, G. M. Scott 31).

At Birmingham, September 6. **Second semi-final: Wimbledon won by 17 runs.** ‡**Wimbledon 161-4** (20 overs) (G. V. Grace 68, G. Penford 61*); **Cuckney 144** (20 overs) (N. G. Langford 55; S. J. Franke-Matthecka 4-19).

At Birmingham, September 6. **Final: Wimbledon won by seven wickets.** ‡**Northern 90** (19.1 overs) (D. Hooey 3-28) **Wimbledon 91-3** (16.2 overs) (N. R. K. Turk 30, G. V. Grace 32*).

YORKSHIRE TEA VILLAGE CUP, 2012

BENJ MOOREHEAD

After the first Village Championship final in 1972, one national newspaper lamented "the absence of a blacksmith, braces, agricultural hoicks, half-mast flannels and a strolling vicar or two". Did they really expect a competition which dangles the prospect of playing at Lord's to produce cricketers whose success came about by accident as much as design? Such fantasies were exposed by Reed Cricket Club, the 2012 champions from Hertfordshire who pursued their trophy like a pack of hounds after a fox.

Their spearhead was Lee Johnson, who tore in and hurled out a roar with each delivery; spectators squinting over their Sunday papers might have wondered what Peter Siddle – the voluble Australian fast bowler – was doing on their village green. Johnson, the only player in his side not to have been nurtured in the Reed Colts, was supported by a cast of steady seamers, off-spinner Tom Greaves, the competition's leading wicket-taker, with 18, and a web of vociferous fielders. The calm at the centre was 29-year-old captain James Heslam. Foxton, of Cambridgeshire, were the only side to pass 200 against them, during a tense fifth-round tie.

Stuart Smith was Reed's sole centurion in the competition, smashing 100 runs off 56 balls (an even mix of hoicks and authentic shots) during the semi-final against two-time winners Goatacre in Wiltshire. Some of Smith's seven sixes ended up in the garden of Kevin Iles, the well-set 49-year-old Goatacre stalwart, who had made the fastest Village Cup hundred at Lord's – from 39 deliveries – when his club triumphed in 1990. Iles had a good 2012 too, this time as a canny spinner, taking 15 wickets at 15 each – though the highlight was a one-handed catch over his head while diving backwards at mid-on in the quarter-final against Wraysbury, from Surrey.

Of the other heavyweights, Woodhouse Grange made it to Lord's for the fifth time after a semi-final victory over Cropston from Leicestershire. Shipton-under-Wychwood, two-time winners from Oxfordshire, were dumped out in the first round by Cumnor. It was Shipton's first home defeat in the Village Cup since 1996.

Cornwall side Stithians, the most southerly of the 292 entrants, were also the most successful of 52 Village Cup debutants. They were bowled out for 96 in their opening match by Perranarworthal, then dismissed their opponents for 51, before going on to win their group. Some 550 miles north in Stirling, Doune suffered the reverse fate, losing to Torrance Community by 11 runs after restricting them to 59.

In a wet summer, Tattenhall derived at least some benefit during their match against Halkyn in Flintshire. "The bowlers could check their grouping at the end of each over by looking at the bits of the pitch they had taken out," said Tattenhall all-rounder Robin Mulvihill. "We had a built-in pitchmap." In the village game, there's normally an upside.

FINAL

REED v WOODHOUSE GRANGE

At Lord's, September 9. Reed won by six wickets. Toss: Reed.

The match included six pairs of brothers – three on each side – but the game-changer was a cheeky round-faced cricketer who would suit the lead role in a production of *Just William*. Tom Greaves accounted for one of the Biltons, Chris, with his first ball and for the other, Andrew, soon after, and strangled the Woodhouse Grange innings with a nine-over spell of crafty off-spin. Later, coming in at No. 3 after James Heslam had been cut off in full flow, Greaves repelled the Woodhouse attack with the 17-year-old William Heslam, then feasted upon it with an array of full-blooded drives and pulls for a 49-ball 51. It was a performance which belied his 21 years. But Reed still needed the experience of Chris Jackson (33) and Stuart Smith (29) to bring Hertfordshire their first Village Cup. Earlier, a ninth title for Yorkshire appeared more likely when the Woodhouse openers put on 55 inside 11 overs. But the introduction of Greaves and the economical seamer Mitchell Cooper broke the back of the innings; the next 54 runs took 15 overs and cost six wickets, including Nick Hadfield, the competition's most prolific batsman. Nineteen-year-old Tom Young showed great touch to revive his team, until Smith took a dizzying catch running towards his supporters at the long-off boundary.

Man of the Match: T. D. Greaves.

Woodhouse Grange

M. D. Hattee c S. W. Tidey b Johnson	19	A. Horner not out	1
N. G. Hadfield lbw b Cooper	29	D. A. Suddaby not out	3
C. R. Bilton c Jackson b Greaves	4		
†M. N. Burdett lbw b Cooper	1	B 1, l-b 6, w 23	30
A. J. Bilton c S. W. Tidey b Greaves	9		
T. S. Young c Smith b Johnson	42	1/55 (1) 2/60 (3) (9 wkts, 40 overs)	184
*S. D. Burdett lbw b Cooper	11	3/66 (4) 4/75 (5)	
C. J. Suddaby b K. J. Ward	32	5/87 (2) 6/109 (7) 7/152 (6) 8/172 (9)	
T. S. Quinn b J. P. Tidey	3	9/180 (8)	

Johnson 9–1–45–2; J. P. Tidey 6–0–29–1; Cooper 9–2–39–3; Greaves 9–3–22–2; K. L. Ward 5–0–36–0; K. J. Ward 2–0–6–1.

Reed

*J. A. Heslam c and b Quinn	28	M. D. Cooper not out	6
W. J. Heslam c C. J. Suddaby b Hadfield	17	B 1, l-b 4, w 19	24
T. D. Greaves b Horner	51		
C. M. Jackson c sub b Horner	37	1/42 (1) 2/84 (2) (4 wkts, 37.2 overs)	185
S. G. Smith not out	22	3/126 (3) 4/169 (4)	

K. L. Ward, K. J. Ward, J. P. Tidey, †S. W. Tidey and L. A. Johnson did not bat.

Quinn 7–0–14–1; S. D. Burdett 5–0–37–0; Hadfield 7–0–34–1; D. A. Suddaby 7–0–35–0; Horner 8.2–1–41–21; Young 3–0–19–0.

Umpires: T. L. Burstow and L. G. Clemenson.

DISABILITY CRICKET, 2012

PAUL EDWARDS

London's success in staging the Paralympic Games, and the exploits of Team GB during those heady late summer days, ensured 2012 will go down as the most significant year in the history of disabled sport in the UK. Yet if disability cricket did not attain the profile reached by Sarah Storey, David Weir and their medal-winning Paralympic colleagues, it still made huge strides.

Sport England confirmed in December that the disabled game was in a robust state when they endorsed the ECB's four-year development programme for deaf, visually impaired, and learning and physical disability cricketers. Grassroots participation will benefit to the tune of £2m, while £650,000 will be devoted to the Player Pathway, which allows the most gifted to take advantage of their talent.

If young players were looking for a role model as they sought to make use of their unparalleled opportunities, they could do no better than study England Deaf captain Umesh Valjee. The summer was relatively uneventful for the 43-year-old Valjee – high-profile series are not an annual occurrence for disabled cricketers – but in November he received the Deaf Sports Personality of the Year award, and also won the Achievement Through Adversity award at the GG2 Asian Leadership presentation evening. "Umesh has never let his disability get the better of him," said Ian Martin, ECB head of disability cricket. "He is deaf, but his talent, determination and sheer skill have seen him become captain of England and he has led the national side with huge distinction since 1995."

Other players and coaches received deserved accolades: Jeff Levick, 74, a disability cricket volunteer in Hampshire, received an MBE in the 2012 New Year's honours list; England Deaf head coach Bobby Denning was named coach of the year at the Deaf Sports Personality of the Year awards; and Shropshire's Callum Rigby, a member of the victorious England Learning Disability side in the tri-nation series against Australia and South Africa in November 2011, was named Disabled Player of the Year in May.

In the summer, England's Visually Impaired team lost the 40-over Ashes 3–0, before winning both Twenty20 games to survive the weather. The loss of the urn was hard on Hampshire's Andy Powers, who had made two successive centuries. In October the team were devastated by the sudden death of veteran all-rounder Heindrich Swanepoel, who suffered a suspected heart attack, aged 43, while on holiday in Morocco. He had been due to play for England at the inaugural Visually Impaired Twenty20 World Cup in Bangalore in December. Luke Sugg's team were bitterly disappointed to lose by nine wickets to Pakistan in the semi-final, but their achievement in reaching the last four was roughly in line with expectations. India beat Pakistan by 29 runs in a final attended by a crowd of 4,000. There was a brief scare when Pakistan captain Zeeshan Abbasi accidentally sipped from a bottle of phenyl, intended for cleaning purposes, in his hotel room; he was discharged from hospital in time to play in the final.

Each team had to field four cricketers graded as B1 (indicating complete blindness), and seven who are either B2 (moderately affected vision) or B3 (lesser-affected vision). Such sophisticated regulations are the consequence of disabled cricket's determination to be taken seriously, and to run events of the stature of the one in Bangalore.

But global co-operation is made difficult by the fact that no board offers anywhere near the investment in disability cricket as the ECB. In England at least, young disabled cricketers energised by Storey and Weir discovered their skills could be fostered and coached to a level barely thinkable even a decade ago. Many also found their local clubs willing to welcome them and judge them on their ability alone. Heady days, indeed.

YOUTH CRICKET, 2012

PATRICK KIDD

Footwork may be crucial to batsmen, but no one in the England development programme's Under-17 squad expected to be tested on their rumba and cha-cha-cha when they assembled for an out-of-season training session in October. They were greeted by Michael Vaughan, the former England captain, and Natalie Lowe, his partner on BBC's *Strictly Come Dancing*, who showed the youngsters that the pathway from age-group cricket to the senior squad need not be a heavy-footed grind.

"Dancing requires very similar skills to cricket," Vaughan told them. "You need dedication and concentration. Your foot movement and timing have to be spot on." The unusual coaching session, in which some boys reluctantly played the girls' role and were led, proved popular. "I would have hated doing that when I was that age," said Vaughan. "But they bought into it and you could tell they were desperate to impress."

The Under-17s also had a summer training camp at Loughborough, at which they were meant to play two matches against Sussex Second Eleven, but both were rained off. They did manage to get in a 35-over game against the Minor Counties South West Under-21s at Millfield School, losing by two runs.

The Under-19s went to Australia twice: for a quadrangular series in April (see page 935), then for the World Cup in August (see page 879). Both their one-day matches in between against Ireland Under-19 succumbed to the weather – though 43 overs were possible at Leicester, with Ireland skittled for 94. England did, however, win the county Second Eleven Twenty20 competition at the first attempt. They won six out of eight in the group stage, then beat Worcestershire by four wickets in the semi-final. In the final against Sussex, who were playing on home turf at Arundel, England chased down 157 inside 18 overs, helped by a second-wicket stand of 116 between Ben Duckett of Northamptonshire, who made 73 not out from 48 balls, and Nottinghamshire's Sam Kelsall, with 56. "The victory was even more impressive because any England Under-19 players who were, or could have been, playing in county First Elevens were not considered for selection," said Tim Boon, the ECB development programme head coach.

Brighton College has long been the crucible of England women's cricket, and the school held a series of matches in early June between members of the Under-15 development squad. In the first Twenty20, Kelly Castle from Southend had figures of 4–3–3–3, while in a 40-over match Georgia Hennessy of Worcestershire made 96. Eight Sussex players were named in a 39-strong England Under-19 development squad, including Georgia Adams, the daughter of Surrey cricket manager Chris. A side were selected under the captaincy of Essex's Beth MacGregor to play two Twenty20 matches against the full Pakistan women's team on September 1 (see page 810).

The national finals of the annual ASDA Kwik Cricket competition was affected by bad weather at Grace Road, but the organisers were able to move most of the matches indoors. Schools from Nottinghamshire, Wales, Yorkshire and Herefordshire contested the women's semi-finals, with Oaktree Primary coming out on top; Upton Priory Junior School beat teams from Essex, Yorkshire and Shropshire to win the mixed event, with prizes presented by Eoin Morgan.

Winners of county age-group competitions: Under-17 County Championship Nottinghamshire. **Under-17 County Cup:** Surrey. **Under-17 B County Cup:** Norfolk. **Under-17 Women's County Championship:** Lancashire. **Under-15 County Cup:** Lancashire. **Under-15 Bunbury Festival:** The North. **Under-14 County Cup:** Essex and Yorkshire (final abandoned). **Under-13 County Cup:** Derbyshire. **Asda Kwik Cricket: Mixed –** Upton Priory, Cheshire. **Girls –** Oaktree Primary, Nottinghamshire.

SCHOOLS CRICKET, 2012

REVIEW BY DOUGLAS HENDERSON

The weather rendered the 2012 season the most appalling in living memory: 1,075 fixtures were abandoned without a ball bowled, while many of the 242 draws were doubtless ruined by rain too. Such was the constant deluge, it is surprising that as many as 1,883 games reached some form of conclusion.

In recent years the schools season has tended to be drier than the summer as a whole. That was emphatically not the case in 2012. In late March, the ECB sent schools advice on how to cope with drought conditions. Fate was well and truly tempted. On April 6, the day after widespread hosepipe bans were announced, the rain started. By the last day of the state-school term in late July, it had barely stopped – with just a brief but glorious lull in late May. Durham School abandoned all but four of their 18 fixtures. Oddly, though, Barnard Castle, 25 miles away, had at least some play in all of their 13 matches – and gained a result in ten. Further south, St Benedict's School, Ealing, fared even better: all 22 scheduled games got under way, and they won 15.

The Barnards and Benedicts were of course the exceptions. Quite how masters and coaches maintained enthusiasm was a mystery – and they were not helped by an exam system seemingly designed to frustrate the building of a cricket team rather than reveal a student's academic abilities.

Merchiston Castle of Edinburgh won all their matches that survived the weather, which is to say they won two (nine were rained off). Seven other schools achieved a win-rate of more than 80% (see page 774), while four waded through the summer unbeaten. One was Cheltenham, whose season was also marked by sadness: Martin Stovold, their master in charge of cricket, died in May after enduring poor health for some years (see obituary on page 241). Among those offering tributes was Jacques Kallis, whom Stovold had coached in South Africa.

There have been few greater servants of schools cricket than David Kirby of St Peter's, York, who retired in 2012. He played for the school for five years in the 1950s (appearing within these pages in four successive editions), went on to captain Cambridge University and Leicestershire, then returned to St Peter's in 1968 to take charge of their cricket for the next 44 years. One of his most celebrated alumni is Jonny Bairstow, the first recipient of the *Wisden* Schools Cricketer of the Year award, in 2007.

There is no question about the 2012 winner. Thomas Abell's record was astonishing: despite the damp, he made seven centuries from 11 innings for Taunton School, amassing 1,156 runs at 192. A couple of times he dropped down to No. 11 to give opportunities to his team-mates. Simon Hogg, master in charge of cricket at Taunton, described a modest, hugely talented and elegant batsman who hit the ball along the ground. The son of an economics teacher at the school, he also took 19 wickets at 15 with his right-arm seam, plus several catches close to the wicket and in the outfield. He becomes the sixth *Wisden* Schools Cricketer of the Year.

Scott Nelmes, Imagination Photography

Thomas Abell of Taunton School, the sixth *Wisden* Schools Cricketer of the Year.

Abell was alone in reaching four figures, though Ben Duckett of Stowe, who did so last year (and has another chance in 2013), came close. He and Oakham's Tom Fell were the only others to average over 100 from more than one completed innings. Duckett went one better than his peers, though, by scoring the season's only double: 213 not out against Wellingborough.

The 2012 averages had their quirks, often because a batsman was dismissed only once or, like Andrew Umeed (High School of Glasgow) and Jonty Leggett (Ryde), not at all. Most remarkable, though, were the bowling figures of 17-year-old seamer Gavin Main, a team-mate of Umeed. Because of commitments with Durham Academy or Scotland Under-19, he had time to deliver only eight overs for the school. However, his average of 1.62 reflected a return of eight wickets for four runs (all wides) against Kelvinside Academy.

Conditions may have favoured bowlers, but there were fewer chances to exploit them. So only two reached 40 wickets for the season: off-spinner Tom Whitehouse secured 41 for Lancaster Royal Grammar School, while off-spinner Ben Chippendale of St Benedict's, Ealing, who was in Year 9, took 40. No fewer than 66 bowlers averaged under ten.

The rain aside, the summer's most striking feature was the growth in electronic scoring. Many scorers are wary of the notion, but safeguards prevent the horror of losing an entire match (or season) to the ether. The three available systems have an automatic backup system after each ball, and the plan is that all schools will link to the ECB's online cricket network (www.play-cricket.com) which provides a live feed – allowing you to see from your desk how the Junior Colts are faring at that moment – and stores all the data. This should be a godsend for schools who in the past have lost their scorebook or, as documented in *Wisden* a few years ago, had it torn up by disgruntled opponents. Electronic scoring is particularly suited to the humbler games played on a remote outfield; www.schoolscricketonline.co.uk/electronic-scoring/ has more information.

The ECB, concerned that many schools have turned almost entirely to limited-overs cricket, believe young players should experience the game in its various forms and, where practicable, as it is played at the highest levels. This, for example, means that, in an overs game, the lunch interval should fall between innings. Essentially, the ECB believe young cricketers should be taught the game in four formats: two-day (if possible), declaration, overs (both can be all-day or afternoon) and Twenty20. It is clear many young players do not understand the intricacies of declaration cricket, and the fear is that future audiences for Test and first-class matches will dwindle, as has happened elsewhere.

On-field discipline remains a concern, and the last couple of years have seen serious abuse of umpires, even involving adult coaches. David Graveney, the former chairman of selectors and now national performance manager at the ECB, has expressed surprise that umpires (especially in league cricket) are prepared to stand at all. An initiative by the Headmasters' Conference (an association of leading independent schools) instructing umpires to invoke the provisions of Law 42 – Fair and Unfair Play – seems to have had some success.

However, as Paul Bedford of the ECB observes: "Behaviour on the field is often exemplary, but it is noticeable that, if an incident does happen, masters in charge and coaches are less inclined to act than in the past. To ensure cricket retains its special place in British culture, masters and coaches must act decisively if behaviour falls short of the provisions of the Spirit of Cricket. It should not be left to umpires to intervene." No one is advocating a return to a Victorian ideal that frowned upon applause for one's own side (and welcomed it solely for the opposition). Yet the game retains traditions of considerate behaviour and sportsmanship – and to lose them would be sad indeed.

Douglas Henderson is the current editor of Schools Cricket Online (www.schoolscricketonline.co.uk).

WISDEN SCHOOLS CRICKETERS OF THE YEAR

2007	Jonny Bairstow	St Peter's School, York
2008	James Taylor	Shrewsbury School
2009	Jos Buttler	King's College, Taunton
2010	Will Vanderspar	Eton College
2011	Daniel Bell-Drummond	Millfield School
2012	**Thomas Abell**	**Taunton School**

MCC Schools v English Schools Cricket Association

At Lord's, August 24. **MCC Schools won by 28 runs** (D/L). **ESCA 223-5** (50 overs) (K. C. B. Smith 49, D. P. Sibley 39, T. P. Alsop 41); ‡**MCC Schools 212-6** (44 overs) (D. J. Gomersall 49, J. A. L. Scriven 71, R. F. Higgins 35).

MCC Schools *R. F. Higgins (*Bradfield*), G. T. G. Cork (*Denstone*), R. G. Craze (*Kimbolton*), F. J. B. Fairhead (*Radley*), D. J. Gomersall (*Sedbergh*), †J. D. S. Martin (*Thomas Whitham SFC*), J. A. Regan (*King's College, Taunton*), G. F. B. Scott (*St Albans*), J. A. L. Scriven (*Cranleigh*), C. O. Thurston (*Bedford*), S. G. Whittingham (*Christ's Hospital*).

ESCA *D. P. Sibley (*Whitgift*), T. P. Alsop (*Lavington School*), E. G. Barnard (*Meole Brace School*), A. K. Dal (*Nottingham HS*), †H. R. Hosein (*Denstone*), B. P. Gibson (*Crawshaw School*), F. J. Hudson-Prentice (*St Bede's*), R. P. Jones (*Bridgewater HS*), H. J. D. Levy (*Brentwood*), J. Shaw (*Crofton Academy*), K. C. B. Smith (*Marling School*).

Full coverage of the 2012 Eton v Harrow match can be found at wisden.com/almanacklinks.

Schools who wish to be considered for inclusion should email *Wisden* on almanack@wisden.com. State schools and girls' schools are especially welcome.

Note: The following tables cover only those schools listed in the Schools A–Z section.

BEST BATTING AVERAGE (5 completed innings)

	I	*NO*	*Runs*	*HS*	*100s*	*Avge*
T. B. Abell (*Taunton School*)	11	5	1,156	162*	7	192.66
T. C. Fell (*Oakham School*)	13	7	723	103*	2	120.50
B. M. Duckett (*Stowe School*)	11	2	942	213*	4	104.66
R. A. Heywood (*Lord Wandsworth College*)	9	2	645	153	4	92.14
C. Purchase (*Wycliffe College*)	10	3	632	171	3	90.28
T. Kohler-Cadmore (*Malvern College*)	10	3	614	147*	1	87.71
R. Hassan (*Felsted School*)	13	4	787	161*	3	87.44
W. A. Bryan (*Norwich School*)	10	2	626	130	2	78.25
W. W. J. Marriott (*Radley College*)	11	1	776	138*	4	77.60
C. O. Thurston (*Bedford School*)	11	3	606	93	0	75.75
R. Bridgstock (*Framlingham College*)	12	2	732	151*	4	73.20
W. A. R. Fraine (*Silcoates School*)	7	2	364	134*	1	72.80
H. Z. Finch (*Eastbourne College*)	12	3	611	152	1	67.88
M. J. Winter (*Cheadle Hulme School*)	12	3	609	118	1	67.66
A. N. Goodchild (*RGS Guildford*)	8	1	473	67	0	67.57
B. J. Marsden (*King's School, Macclesfield*)	9	3	404	111*	1	67.33
L. H. Hill (*Glasgow Academy*)	6	0	402	179	1	67.00
C. E. Stewart (*Haileybury*)	12	4	529	109*	1	66.12
A. J. S. Redmayne (*Reed's School*)	12	5	445	99*	0	63.57
F. H. Davies (*City of London Freemen's School*)	12	3	571	118*	1	63.44
S. Iyer (*Reading Blue Coat School*)	6	1	316	73*	0	63.20
J. A. Beaumont (*Culford School*)	10	3	438	138*	1	62.57
J. A. L. Scriven (*Cranleigh School*)	12	5	438	101*	1	62.57
C. S. Speller (*Eltham College*)	7	2	304	90	0	60.80
N. C. Jarman (*Wells Cathedral School*)	11	3	485	91*	0	60.62
S. G. Leach (*Shrewsbury School*)	12	4	485	106*	1	60.62

Note: Three other batsmen averaged over 100, all from three innings (twice not out): M. Ackerman (*Forest School*) 187.00; S. A. Burt (*Simon Langton GS*) 173.00; and A. A. Dyson (*St John's, Leatherhead*) 111.00. Two others were not dismissed at all and so did not gain an average: A. R. I. Umeed (*Glasgow HS*) hit 241 runs from two unbeaten innings; J. C. A. Leggett (*Ryde School*) 154 from six.

MOST RUNS

	I	NO	Runs	HS	100s	Avge
T. B. Abell (*Taunton School*)	11	5	1,156	162*	7	192.66
B. M. Duckett (*Stowe School*)	11	2	942	213*	4	104.66
R. Hassan (*Felsted School*)	13	4	787	161*	3	87.44
W. W. J. Marriott (*Radley College*)	11	1	776	138*	4	77.60
R. Bridgstock (*Framlingham College*)	12	2	732	151*	4	73.20
T. C. Fell (*Oakham School*)	13	7	723	103*	2	120.50
D. P. Sibley (*Whitgift School*)	18	4	697	106	1	49.78
B. J. Ringrose (*Cheltenham College*)	14	3	655	117*	1	59.54
R. A. Heywood (*Lord Wandsworth College*)	9	2	645	153	4	92.14
C. Purchase (*Wycliffe College*)	10	3	632	171	3	90.28
L. J. Millman (*St Benedict's School, Ealing*)	21	5	630	84*	0	39.37
W. A. Bryan (*Norwich School*)	10	2	626	130	2	78.25
H. Britt (*St Benedict's School, Ealing*)	20	2	623	93	0	34.61
T. Kohler-Cadmore (*Malvern College*)	10	3	614	147*	1	87.71
H. Z. Finch (*Eastbourne College*)	12	3	611	152	1	67.88
M. J. Winter (*Cheadle Hulme School*)	12	3	609	118	1	67.66
C. O. Thurston (*Bedford School*)	11	3	606	93	0	75.75
L. Bose (*Harrow School*)	13	0	595	118	2	45.76
M. E. Cousens (*Harrow School*)	16	3	593	111*	1	45.61
J. H. Barrett (*St Edward's, Oxford*)	19	1	582	152	1	32.33
T. M. Gallyer (*Charterhouse*)	16	3	575	115*	1	44.23
F. H. Davies (*City of London Freemen's School*)	12	3	571	118*	1	63.44
N. R. T. Gubbins (*Radley College*)	11	1	568	124	2	56.80
J. A. Wells (*Felsted School*)	13	0	567	130	1	43.61
M. A. H. Hammond (*St Edward's, Oxford*)	18	4	532	79*	0	38.00
C. E. Stewart (*Haileybury*)	12	4	529	109*	1	66.12
J. A. Olley (*Stowe School*)	13	1	524	101	1	43.66
J. B. Abbott (*Eton College*)	14	0	516	92	0	36.85
J. A. Regan (*King's College, Taunton*)	12	3	511	116*	2	56.77
G. J. Brothwood (*Cheltenham College*)	14	3	509	119	1	46.27

BEST BOWLING AVERAGE (7 wickets)

	O	M	R	W	BB	Avge
G. T. Main (*Glasgow High School*)	8	1	13	8	8-4	1.62
B. J. Keeler (*Newcastle-under-Lyme School*)	11	2	26	7	4-9	3.71
H. S. Axon (*Harvey Grammar School*)	10	4	27	7	5-10	3.85
S. A. Letcher (*Lancaster RGS*)	30	10	64	13	3-4	4.92
J. Crace (*Oakham School*)	16	7	36	7	6-24	5.14
C. E. Glanville (*St John's, Leatherhead*)	36	10	83	14	5-14	5.92
C. D. Coutts (*Glasgow Academy*)	12	2	42	7	3-14	6.00
T. Roberts (*Kirkham Grammar School*)	30	8	62	10	4-34	6.20
B. G. F. Green (*Exeter School*)	24	3	63	10	4-10	6.30
P. D. Kilpatrick (*Forest School*)	16.4	3	59	9	3-8	6.55
J. L. Atkinson (*Lancaster RGS*)	30	7	86	13	3-6	6.61
C. H. O'Brien (*Hampton School*)	30	4	115	17	3-8	6.76
I. Nagra (*King Henry VIII School*)	15	3	50	7	3-3	7.14
D. L. Petrides (*Alleyn's School*)	28	9	65	9	5-14	7.22
L. C. Williams (*Rossall School*)	35.5	12	94	13	8-24	7.23
B. A. Bhatti (*Tiffin School*)	14.2	1	52	7	3-35	7.42
O. Jump (*Kirkham Grammar School*)	77	14	209	28	7-26	7.46
S. R. Redmayne (*Alleyn's School*)	20	7	53	7	4-38	7.57
J. E. Furnival (*Newcastle-under-Lyme School*)	32.2	7	92	12	7-17	7.66
J. A. Hatton (*Shebbear College*)	31	10	92	12	3-34	7.66
V. Menon (*King Henry VIII School*)	24	7	55	7	4-21	7.85
H. A. M. Dingwall (*Fettes College*)	17	3	55	7	3-28	7.85
W. A. Gent (*Ratcliffe College*)	13.5	1	63	8	3-15	7.87

	O	M	R	W	BB	Avge
S. W. F. Goodwill (*Hampton School*)	65	11	113	14	3-16	8.07
J. A. Loft (*Simon Langton Grammar School*)	26.4	11	73	9	4-42	8.11
A. Khanna (*Tiffin School*)	12.4	3	57	7	6-29	8.14
R. H. Evans (*Victoria College, Jersey*)	18	1	57	7	5-21	8.14
L. H. I. Tyrrell (*Aldenham School*)	39	4	133	16	5-9	8.31
J. L. Deverson (*Dover College*)	53	16	167	20	4-5	8.35
J. Aldous-Fountain (*Monmouth School*)	46.3	8	118	14	5-14	8.42
L. Hyde (*Silcoates School*)	31	12	59	7	5-16	8.42
J. Ellis (*Mill Hill School*)	24	3	76	9	6-9	8.44
I. S. Bhatia (*Ellesmere College*)	39.4	10	127	15	6-15	8.46
T. M. Nugent (*Oratory School*)	60	14	170	20	6-28	8.50

MOST WICKETS

	O	M	R	W	BB	Avge
T. I. Whitehouse (*Lancaster RGS*)	164	41	357	41	6-56	8.70
B. D. P. Chippendale (*St Benedict's School, Ealing*)	125.3	5	550	40	5-11	13.75
L. V. Hadcock (*St Benedict's School, Ealing*)	119.2	26	380	32	7-17	11.87
A. R. Hughes (*King's College School, Wimbledon*)	103.1	21	319	31	4-25	10.29
K. D. Amin (*Westminster School*)	71.2	8	325	30	5-17	10.83
N. J. Shaikh (*St Benedict's School, Ealing*)	113.1	9	420	30	4-12	14.00
M. S. Crane (*Lancing College*)	122	12	464	30	8-11	15.46
A. F. Duncliffe-Vines (*Cheltenham College*)	124	7	506	29	7-28	17.44
O. Jump (*Kirkham Grammar School*)	77	14	209	28	7-26	7.46
J. R. Winslade (*Whitgift School*)	101.5	11	414	28	5-37	14.78
E. J. Duckworth (*Dauntsey's School*)	97.1	17	392	27	6-40	14.51
A. Shinwari (*Whitgift School*)	81	6	313	26	5-36	12.03
F. H. Davies (*City of London Freemen's School*)	101	16	321	26	3-10	12.34
O. C. Thornley (*Cheltenham College*)	118	28	359	26	5-16	13.80
W. J. L. Rollings (*Cranleigh School*)	79.1	10	242	25	4-19	9.68
S. J. Thakor (*Uppingham School*)	82	6	271	25	5-12	10.84
B. J. Ringrose (*Cheltenham College*)	142	27	409	25	4-20	16.36
D. Chohan (*Dulwich College*)	133.4	19	425	25	4-20	17.00
J. B. Kings (*Rugby School*)	163	38	457	25	4-14	18.28
R. G. Wickham (*Cranbrook School*)	64	19	205	24	4-1	8.54
D. R. Pryke (*St Joseph's College, Ipswich*)	87.5	9	407	24	5-44	16.95
F. Baig (*St Edward's, Oxford*)	131	16	467	24	6-33	19.45
G. Brookes (*Kirkham Grammar School*)	84	11	274	23	3-17	11.91
M. B. P. Hart (*Abingdon School*)	73	11	278	23	5-21	12.08
R. Ishtiaq (*Bradford Grammar School*)	99.5	21	305	23	4-31	13.26
F. P. A. Simon (*St Edward's, Oxford*)	95	21	309	23	5-7	13.43
G. N. Wisdom (*Hurstpierpoint College*)	70.2	3	326	23	7-11	14.17
A. D. P. Barras (*Abingdon School*)	101	13	353	23	4-8	15.34
N. J. Couzens (*Warwick School*)	93.5	10	358	23	3-8	15.56
C. G. Roberts (*Stowe School*)	104.4	15	383	23	4-43	16.65
R. J. O'Grady (*Tonbridge School*)	93	6	404	23	4-21	17.56
J. Hughes (*Solihull School*)	88	4	405	23	5-16	17.60
J. R. Lloyd (*Whitgift School*)	131.5	13	476	23	2-14	20.69
M. A. H. Hammond (*St Edward's, Oxford*)	164	31	552	23	3-11	24.00

OUTSTANDING SEASONS (minimum 6 matches)

	P	W	L	D	A	%W
King's College, Taunton	11	10	1	0	8	90.90
Forest School	9	8	0	1	8	88.88
Stowe School	16	14	1	1	4	87.50
Cheltenham College	14	12	0	2	0	85.71
Alleyn's School	7	6	1	0	7	85.71
Brentwood School	7	6	1	0	11	85.71

	P	*W*	*L*	*D*	*A*	*%W*
Ryde School	6	5	0	1	4	83.33
Abingdon School	14	11	2	1	0	78.57
Shrewsbury School	14	11	1	2	5	78.57
Leys School	9	7	1	1	5	77.77
Taunton School	13	10	1	2	4	76.92
Bedford School	13	10	2	1	3	76.92
Haberdashers' Aske's Boys' School	12	9	2	1	9	75.00
Kimbolton School	12	9	1	2	5	75.00
Denstone College	8	6	2	0	6	75.00
Radley College	11	8	1	2	6	72.72
Silcoates School	7	5	1	1	6	71.42
Hymers College	10	7	1	2	2	70.00
King's School, Worcester	10	7	2	1	10	70.00
Norwich School	10	7	1	2	3	70.00
St Albans School	10	7	3	0	8	70.00

Note: Merchiston Castle won both their completed fixtures.

SCHOOLS A–Z

In the results line, A = abandoned without a ball bowled. An asterisk next to a name indicates captain. Schools provide their own reports and averages. The qualification for the averages is usually 150 runs or ten wickets, but in the light of the atrocious weather prevailing for much of the 2012 season, these criteria have been lowered to 100 runs and seven wickets – for this edition only. Twenty20 games are excluded from results and averages.

Abingdon School P14 W11 L2 D1

Master i/c D. C. Shirazi

A young Abingdon side often found ways to win from sticky situations. Gregor Hearn and Dan Matthews were the leading batsmen, while spinners Alex Davies and Sasha Barras were a real threat. With the majority returning next year, the future seems encouraging.

Batting G. C. Hearn 371 at 33.72; D. S. Matthews 350 at 26.92; M. B. P. Hart 169 at 21.12; H. J. Sensecall 227 at 17.46; A. J. Davies 151 at 15.10.

Bowling M. B. P. Hart 23 at 12.08; A. D. P. Barras* 23 at 15.34; L. M. Bethell 12 at 17.33; A. J. Davies 17 at 21.35.

Aldenham School P12 W7 L4 D1 A11

Master i/c M. I. Yeabsley **Coaches** D. J. Goodchild/M. S. W. Hughes

This was an excellent season with wins in seven of the 12 matches. The outstanding performer with bat and ball was Lee Tyrrell (Year 10). He scored a maiden century (100* v UCS) and took five for nine against Mill Hill, including a hat-trick. Other notable contributions came from Jack Gibbins and the captain Rishi Batra.

Batting L. R. W. Paice 100 at 33.33; J. S. Gibbins 307 at 27.90; J. L. Haftel 118 at 23.60; L. H. I. Tyrrell 185 at 23.12; H. A. H. Copley 156 at 19.50; G. P. Uttley 110 at 15.71; R. Batra* 151 at 13.72.

Bowling L. H. I. Tyrrell 16 at 8.31; J. R. Bryer 8 at 9.50; J. S. Gibbins 12 at 14.33; N. Patel 7 at 18.57; H. A. H. Copley 7 at 24.57; D. Patel 10 at 25.90.

Alleyn's School P7 W6 L1 A7

Master i/c R. N. Ody **Coach** P. E. Edwards

A successful second half of the season resulted in six wins and only one defeat. The team were superbly steered by Adam Senn, and the season's highlight was victory against MCC.

Batting A. M. A. Senn* 247 at 61.75; C. W. Handy 118 at 59.00; C. M. Glen 181 at 36.20.

Bowling D. L. Petrides 9 at 7.22; S. R. Redmayne 7 at 7.57; J. L. C. Savage 8 at 8.87; A. M. A. Senn 11 at 10.36; D. J. King 8 at 14.50.

Ampleforth College

P8 W3 L4 D1 A9

Master i/c G. D. Thurman **Coach** A. Rowsell

Edward Robinson showed form with the bat, while Joseph Ainscough, Joshua Reid and Joshua Prest bowled well with little luck. Fergus Black marshalled a happy and united side – though one that failed to develop as the awful weather claimed nine fixtures.

Batting E. J. Robinson 294 at 42.00; R. T. Pratt 210 at 30.00; C. Douglas 151 at 25.16; J. E. Ainscough 148 at 24.66; F. G. G. Black* 148 at 18.50.

Bowling J. A. T. Reid 13 at 17.61; F. C. Rex 9 at 18.66; J. E. Ainscough 12 at 21.16.

Bancroft's School

P12 W2 L9 D1 A5

Master i/c J. K. Lever

With the exception of opener Tom Hartington, the batting struggled to give consistent support to the bowlers. Good players are coming through, however, so there is potential for the future.

Batting V. Handa 210 at 26.25; M. J. Tann 183 at 20.33; T. J. Hartington 226 at 18.83; S. S. Sadra 160 at 17.77; N. E. Jacob* 164 at 14.90.

Bowling M. R. Reid-Evans 20 at 16.85; N. E. Jacob 15 at 17.46; S. S. Sadra 15 at 17.66; M. J. Tann 7 at 25.14; Y. Sohoye 7 at 36.85.

Barnard Castle School

P13 W4 L6 D3

Master i/c M. T. Pepper **Coach** J. Lister

A young team performed well in dreadful conditions. Bret Upton, solidly assisted by Neil Stanwix and Mathew Brown, led with bat and ball. With twins Guy and Jonny Coser, Kit Wilson and Alex Finkill all available for two more seasons, there is optimism about what lies ahead.

Batting B. P. Upton* 332 at 33.20; R. E. G. Barrett 221 at 27.62; N. D. Stanwix 209 at 23.22; G. F. Coser 182 at 20.22; M. P. H. Brown 197 at 17.90; R. D. Newman 213 at 17.75.

Bowling K. S. Wilson 11 at 9.72; W. W. F. Prior 14 at 10.07; B. P. Upton 14 at 19.50; J. W. Coser 10 at 22.80; A. J. Finkill 7 at 37.85; R. E. G. Barrett 7 at 42.57.

Bedford Modern School

P10 W5 L5 A7

Master i/c P. J. Woodroffe

In a bowler-friendly campaign, winning the toss was often decisive. Joe Mitford captained superbly, but the highlight was a century on debut for Kyle Cunningham.

Batting J. Parish 177 at 29.50; K. S. Cunningham 203 at 25.37; H. P. Thurstance 179 at 19.88; W. J. T. Lowerson 103 at 14.71; T. H. J. Burman 107 at 13.37; S. K. Mahendran 106 at 13.25; J. S. Mitford* 101 at 12.62.

Bowling H. K. Waqar 15 at 15.86; J. S. Mitford 12 at 19.75; R. T. Kraus 7 at 34.85.

Bedford School

P13 W10 L2 D1 A3

Master i/c P. Sherwin **Coach** D. W. Randall

Comprehensive wins over Harrow and Oundle were high points in an outstanding season. Sixteen-year-old Charlie Thurston, with seven fifties in 11 innings, was the standout batsman. Big-hitting all-rounder Ed Wharton was the leading wicket-taker.

Batting C. O. Thurston 606 at 75.75; J. H. T. McDuell 338 at 37.55; V. V. S. Sohal* 232 at 33.14; E. C. W. Wharton 255 at 28.33; P. R. J. McDuell 244 at 27.11; T. J. O. Graham 144 at 20.57; G. G. H. Humphreys 132 at 18.85.

Bowling E. C. W. Wharton 19 at 15.89; W. F. P. Wright 11 at 17.72; C. O. Thurston 10 at 18.40; V. V. S. Sohal 16 at 18.87; G. G. H. Humphreys 11 at 25.45; H. W. Morecroft 10 at 27.50; T. J. O. Graham 13 at 31.07.

Berkhamsted School

P12 W5 L7 A6

Master i/c D. J. Gibson **Coach** B. R. Mahoney

In a season ruined by poor weather there were good wins against RGS High Wycombe and MCC, when Xavier Owen took five for 17 on debut. A thrilling run-chase against Haileybury, including a century from Max Maciver, lingered in the memory.

Batting A. G. Leighton 291 at 26.45; J. M. Hawkes* 205 at 25.62; H. D. J. Sambrook 203 at 22.55; S. C. Masters 195 at 17.72; M. T. Maciver 170 at 15.45; J. T. Harrison 107 at 11.88.

Bowling A. R. MacInnes-Poole 16 at 14.68; J. Q. Davies 7 at 17.42; S. C. Masters 14 at 18.42; J. P. Ryan 14 at 21.00; M. T. Maciver 10 at 32.70.

Lee Tyrrell, an outstanding all-rounder from Aldenham, took five for nine against Mill Hill, including a hat-trick. Framlingham's Robbie Bridgstock scored exactly half his 732 runs in four days in June.

Birkenhead School
P10 W3 L5 D2 A6

Master i/c P. N. Lindberg **Coach** G. J. Rickman

With only a handful of the 2011 squad remaining, this was always going to be a difficult season. Several senior players failed to score the expected runs until late in the term, and there was insufficient back-up for Daniel Quinn's strike bowling.

Batting H. D. Sturgess 257 at 32.12; O. A. N. Hearn* 209 at 23.22; D. Quinn 194 at 21.55; A. R. Watkins 207 at 20.70; W. Brewster 138 at 17.25.

Bowling D. Quinn 16 at 10.93.

Bishop's Stortford College
P10 W3 L7 A4

Master i/c M. Drury **Coach** N. D. Hughes

After a good pre-season tour to Cape Town, rain meant any momentum was soon lost. However, there were excellent wins against Felsted and Chigwell.

Batting S. J. Franks 147 at 49.00; A. S. Palmer* 336 at 42.00; T. J. E. Weeks 146 at 20.85; A. D. Cleaves 100 at 12.50.

Bowling T. E. Foot 16 at 16.06; A. Mozumdar 7 at 18.28; J. W. N. Malyon 7 at 23.28; A. S. Palmer 10 at 24.40; T. A. Shepherd 9 at 33.22.

Bloxham School
P9 W2 L7 A5

Master i/c R. W. F. Hastings **Coach** M. Walton

Tom Gurney skippered valiantly through a difficult campaign. With only one player scoring significant runs, the batting was fragile. Six of the team have left, leaving opportunities for those from junior sides.

Batting S. A. De Weymarn 382 at 47.75.

Bowling G. W. Adams 15 at 16.26.

Blundell's School
P6 W3 L3 A9

Master i/c R. J. Turner **Coach** C. L. L. Gabbitass

Jack Dart was selected for Devon; he and Sam Wyatt-Haines represented Devon Under-21s. Jack Maunder and Dominic Bess (Year 10) were chosen for the Bunbury Festival. Alistair Chilcott showed great potential as an opening batsman.

Batting S. J. R. Wyatt-Haines 269 at 44.83; J. F. S. Dart 183 at 30.50; A. E. Chilcott 128 at 25.60.
Bowling D. M. Bess 11 at 17.45; J. F. S. Dart 7 at 21.14; H. N. Folland* 7 at 22.42.

Bradfield College P10 W5 L5 A9

Master i/c M. S. Hill **Coach** J. R. Wood

An excellent pre-season tour to Dubai suggested a talented and experienced squad would enjoy a memorable summer. But, apart from seven-wicket hauls for Ryan Higgins and David Butler, performances rarely matched potential.
Batting C. N. Gaur 327 at 40.87; R. F. Higgins 350 at 35.00; N. M. G. Farr 164 at 32.80; L. D. Glover 227 at 32.42; J. A. J. Rishton 280 at 31.11; J. W. J. Bransgrove 156 at 22.28; H. R. H. Darby 128 at 21.33; B. Piper 126 at 21.00.
Bowling D. T. Butler 15 at 13.73; R. F. Higgins 18 at 18.61; G. W. Simpson* 19 at 21.89; J. W. J. Bransgrove 7 at 35.57.

Bradford Grammar School P11 W5 L3 D3 A8

Master i/c A. G. Smith **Coach** S. A. Kellett

Miserable weather ruined the fixture list – especially disappointing given the team's real promise. All three defeats occurred in the final over, while two wins came off the last ball of even closer contests.
Batting W. R. Johnston 197 at 24.62; R. R. Misra 147 at 24.50; M. A. Thornton 206 at 22.88; N. Devesher 154 at 22.00; G. D. Gill 144 at 18.00; M. Green 101 at 16.83.
Bowling R. Ishtiaq 23 at 13.26; R. R. Misra 13 at 15.15; R. A. Prasad 16 at 19.25; R. Butt 11 at 20.54.

Brentwood School P7 W6 L1 A11

Master i/c B. R. Hardie

Brentwood had a strong side, but little chance to show their talents: 11 games were washed away. Kishen Velani (England's Under-19 World Cup team) and Harry Levy (England Under-17 development programme) worked their way into national squads.
Batting K. Ali 178 at 59.33; G. W. C. Balmford* 264 at 44.00; H. J. D. Levy 188 at 37.60; R. Hussain 111 at 37.00; J. S. Welham 104 at 20.80.
Bowling K. S. Velani 8 at 13.00; H. J. D. Levy 8 at 13.37; G. W. C. Balmford 7 at 14.42; J. Mowll 7 at 16.42.

Brighton College P17 W6 L9 D2 A3

Master i/c Miss A. L. Walker **Coach** M. A. Thornely

The term began well with wins against Eastbourne and Ardingly. One of the highlights was the school's first hat-trick in over 20 years, by Sam Grant against Repton.
Batting H. Richards* 478 at 31.86; J. N. Thornely 226 at 17.38; B. P. Hornby 191 at 13.64; S. E. Grant 189 at 11.81; B. J. A. Meboroh-Collinson 114 at 8.76; E. Kalidasan 104 at 6.93.
Bowling B. J. A. Meboroh-Collinson 16 at 16.62; H. J. O. Klus 16 at 18.87; D. A. Glynne-Jones 21 at 20.42; J. N. Thornely 17 at 22.35; S. E. Grant 12 at 33.50; E. Kalidasan 8 at 37.62.

Bristol Grammar School P9 W1 L7 D1 A8

Master i/c K. R. Blackburn

Charlie Killick guided the side for the third year running, but was let down by inconsistent batting. The bowling, led by the experienced George Bacon and Jack Fairs, made the opposition work hard for their runs.
Batting D. H. Tailor 196 at 32.66; C. R. Killick* 223 at 27.87; G. F. J. Bacon 158 at 19.75; M. R. Tavaré 105 at 17.50; A. R. Patel 118 at 16.85; H. M. Thompson 117 at 16.71.
Bowling L. J. Collingwood 8 at 11.12; G. F. J. Bacon 9 at 21.22; J. H. Fairs 10 at 21.30.

Bromsgrove School P9 W1 L8 A9

Master i/c D. J. Fallows

After a successful pre-season trip to Dubai, the term was a real disappointment: nine games fell to the weather. After scoring over 1,000 runs in 2011, Brett Huxley was again top-scorer, but with many fewer. Oliver Strong (Year 10) was the leading wicket-taker. The junior teams prospered, giving hope for the years to come.
Batting B. Huxley* 201 at 25.12; W. Bowen 192 at 24.00; H. J. Eastgate 153 at 19.12.
Bowling W. Bowen 9 at 14.66; O. E. Strong 11 at 19.00; J. Turner 7 at 23.85; B. Huxley 8 at 42.50.

Bryanston School P10 W2 L6 D2 A8

Master i/c B. J. Lawes **Coach** P. J. Norton

A youthful Bryanston team performed well. The side's only Year 13 player, Ben Ladd-Gibbon, bowled with great skill, and was well supported by all-rounders Oli Weld and Alex Jones. Paddy Oakshott looks an exciting prospect.

Batting A. G. Jones 197 at 28.14; P. C. Oakshott 130 at 26.00; O. L. C. Weld 185 at 23.12; J. A. Horsham 157 at 19.62; S. A. E. Carter 111 at 15.85; R. B. d'Erlanger-Bertrand 110 at 15.71.

Bowling O. L. C. Weld 19 at 14.47; B. I. W. Ladd-Gibbon 17 at 15.11; A. G. Jones 9 at 22.77; O. S. Drew 7 at 31.57.

Canford School P8 W3 L3 D2 A3

Master i/c B. C. Edgell **Coach** M. Keech

Canford enjoyed an exciting and encouraging season. There is talent in depth, and real scope for improvement in a young squad.

Batting B. S. Rogers 261 at 43.50; B. J. Boon 252 at 36.00; O. M. Downey 206 at 29.42; R. C. Triniman* 158 at 26.33; J. Roberts 137 at 22.83.

Bowling A. J. Maher 9 at 15.00; B. S. Rogers 12 at 21.50.

Charterhouse P17 W9 L7 D1 A3

Master i/c M. P. Bicknell

Stalwarts Tom Gallyer, Charlie Kimmins and Jonny Gonszor closed their careers in impressive style. In their three years in the side (four in the case of Kimmins) they amassed over 3,500 runs and 150 wickets. Gallyer captained the side to 18 victories in two years, a school record.

Batting T. M. Gallyer* 575 at 44.23; A. J. Beddows 206 at 34.33; C. E. R. Kimmins 368 at 30.66; O. R. Batchelor 419 at 29.92; R. L. Hughes 328 at 29.81; J. C. Gonszor 364 at 28.00; B. A. E. Phillips 241 at 20.08; T. P. Gordon-Martin 155 at 17.22.

Bowling R. L. Hughes 10 at 18.10; C. E. R. Kimmins 20 at 22.30; T. M. Gallyer 17 at 23.88; J. C. Gonszor 17 at 25.11; T. E. W. Hurley 19 at 26.89; R. A. Carnegie-Brown 11 at 28.09; H. Q. Don 10 at 31.70; M. Mohammad 7 at 46.57.

Cheadle Hulme School P13 W7 L5 D1 A5

Master i/c S. Burnage **Coach** G. Colebourn

The captain Matthew Winter was top run-scorer for the third year in a row. Thirteen-year-old Prithvi Shaw displayed great all-round skill, taking 15 wickets and scoring 230 runs. A successful term, hampered by grim weather, hinted at good times ahead.

Batting M. J. Winter* 609 at 67.66; A. J. Jackson 334 at 55.66; D. Carswell 172 at 34.40; P. Shaw 230 at 32.85.

Bowling P. Shaw 15 at 15.53; J. M. Ridler 12 at 15.75; D. Carswell 16 at 19.18; A. J. Jackson 11 at 24.63.

Cheltenham College P14 W12 D2

Master i/c M. K. Coley **Coach** M. P. Briers

Another very strong season for Cheltenham: 12 wins and two draws were fine achievements on a difficult circuit. Tight bowling and athletic fielding backed up excellent top-order batting. Guy Brothwood led the side superbly; Ben Ringrose gathered 655 runs and 25 wickets.

Batting B. J. Ringrose 655 at 59.54; J. S. Dymoke 195 at 48.75; G. J. Brothwood* 509 at 46.27; B. J. Morton 451 at 45.10; O. C. Soames 338 at 42.25.

Bowling O. C. Thornley 26 at 13.80; B. J. Ringrose 25 at 16.36; A. F. Duncliffe-Vines 29 at 17.44; G. J. Brothwood 20 at 20.75; B. Wyatt 11 at 32.18.

Chigwell School P5 W2 L2 D1 A13

Master i/c F. A. Griffith

Waterlogged pitches prevented Chigwell from playing a single home match. Gabriel Inch captained wonderfully, particularly during the triumph over Mill Hill. The highlight, though, was the victory over Enfield GS by 147 runs. Notable contributions came from Josh Banfield, Edward Sibley and Andrew MacGregor.

Batting J. L. N. Banfield 120 at 60.00.

Bowling E. H. S. Sibley 7 at 16.14; A. J. MacGregor 7 at 19.00.

Chislehurst & Sidcup Grammar School P6 W2 L4 A4

Master i/c R. Wallbridge **Coach** D. L. Pask

Mark Handley captained the team maturely, but a lack of net and match practice, due to poor weather and exams, hindered progress. The MCC match survived, but the visitors ran out comfortable winners.

Batting No one scored 100 runs. The leading batsman was M. A. Handley*, who hit 59 at 11.80.

Bowling T. Francis 8 at 15.75.

Christ College, Brecon P8 W2 L6 A5

Master i/c T. J. Trumper **Coach** A. J. Copp

After an early win at Queen's Taunton, inspired by skipper Tom Trumper and Iolo Morgan, a bright start ebbed away. However, Josef Conway had a good first season, and 15-year-old Iain Mitchell showed promise. Despite 75 from James Mitchell, the school lost an exciting encounter with the Old Boys by two runs.

Batting J. Conway 194 at 27.71; T. M. G. Trumper* 165 at 23.57; J. P. Mitchell 129 at 18.42.

Bowling J. Conway 7 at 28.14.

Christ's Hospital P12 W5 L5 D2 A6

Master i/c H. P. Holdsworth **Coach** T. E. Jesty

The side were guided for a second year by wicketkeeper-batsman Calvin Williams. Strike bowler Stuart Whittingham, selected for Sussex Seconds, was again the top performer. All but one of the defeats were by narrow margins: two runs, four runs, two wickets, and off the last ball.

Batting L. W. Hansford 375 at 41.66; S. G. Whittingham 278 at 34.75; C. P. Williams* 324 at 32.40; A. G. Elmes 196 at 21.77; F. J. C. Wordsworth 103 at 11.44.

Bowling O. W. Koronka 13 at 13.38; J. S. Heath 13 at 15.07; S. G. Whittingham 17 at 15.47; L. W. Hansford 8 at 19.62; M. H. O'Boyle 10 at 23.80; H. F. Ziegler 9 at 26.88.

City of London Freemen's School P12 W6 L5 D1 A8

Master i/c J. G. Moore **Coach** N. M. Stewart

Despite atrocious weather, the school completed 12 games. With inspirational batting, bowling and fielding, captain Fred Davies could do no more. Other players chipped in, but a lack of experience was reflected in mixed results.

Batting F. H. Davies* 571 at 63.44; M. E. Dawes 217 at 24.11; J. A. T. Turton 199 at 19.90; G. MacDonald 218 at 18.16; E. Walton 111 at 12.33.

Bowling F. H. Davies 26 at 12.34; M. E. Dawes 18 at 16.22; A. F. A. Culhane 12 at 17.41.

Clayesmore School P4 L4 A4

Master i/c D. I. Rimmer **Coach** T. O. Flowers

In the few games that survived the dreary weather, the school were unable to do themselves justice. Despite some fair performances, they lacked the touch to finish opponents off.

Batting No one scored 100 runs. The leading batsman was H. G. Clarke, who hit 55 at 13.75.

Bowling No one claimed seven wickets. The leading bowler was H. J. Beardsley*, who took 5 at 20.60.

Clifton College P7 W3 L3 D1 A8

Master i/c J. C. Bobby **Coach** P. W. Romaines

This was the most frustrating and disappointing season for many years, with only six games completed. Tom Smith's brilliant 143 against Westminster College, Adelaide, was the individual performance of the summer.

Batting T. F. Smith 313 at 44.71; G. A. Harris 111 at 27.75; B. J. McGeoch 154 at 25.66; H. M. Matthews 161 at 23.00; J. H. Ellison 131 at 21.83.

Bowling J. S. Probert 13 at 18.00; T. F. Smith 11 at 19.09; L. R. Watson 8 at 25.37.

Colfe's School P12 W8 L3 D1 A10

Master i/c G. S. Clinton

Nearly half the fixtures were abandoned, and the best side Colfe's have had for a few years were denied a proper chance to prove it.

Batting A. W. Graham 261 at 87.00; M. E. Stiddard* 358 at 59.66; E. Johnson 133 at 19.00.

Bowling H. G. Furze 14 at 9.07; E. Johnson 11 at 12.09; S. G. Packard 9 at 12.44; H. R. Graham 8 at 17.12.

Cranbrook School
P12 W8 L4 A13

Master i/c A. J. Presnell **Coach** C. Pohio

A very young team played some aggressive and exciting cricket. The highlight was retaining the Kent Under-19 league title. Finn Hulbert took six wickets in eight balls in the semi-final, while Ali Smallwood smashed 62 from 32 in the final.

Batting F. W. Hulbert 278 at 30.88; A. Smallwood 170 at 28.33; J. E. Schindler* 159 at 19.87; J. Clark 159 at 19.87; R. G. Wickham 115 at 19.16; D. R. Gordon 180 at 16.36.

Bowling R. G. Wickham 24 at 8.54; F. W. Hulbert 18 at 12.11; A. T. Lloyd-Dyke 13 at 19.07; O. P. Dearn 10 at 25.00.

Cranleigh School
P13 W8 L3 T1 D1 A4

Master i/c J. S. Ross **Coach** S. D. Welch

Cranleigh enjoyed a pleasing season, recording a number of impressive wins, notably against Tonbridge, Dulwich and Wellington on successive weekends. With just four leavers, 2013 has the makings of another good campaign.

Batting B. R. M. Scriven 273 at 68.25; J. A. L. Scriven 438 at 62.57; B. M. Broughton 138 at 34.50; M. G. K. Burgess* 148 at 29.60; N. J. Thorpe 148 at 29.60; W. J. L. Rollings 109 at 21.80; E. P. H. Croker 116 at 19.33; P. G. Westcott 120 at 12.00.

Bowling W. J. L. Rollings 25 at 9.68; J. A. L. Scriven 15 at 20.00; B. J. Wilson 8 at 20.25; B. M. Broughton 11 at 24.45; S. R. Thomson 8 at 30.75.

Culford School
P11 W7 L1 D3 A2

Master i/c A. H. Marsh

Culford prospered in the damp conditions. The highlights were wins against Gresham's, Wisbech, Woodbridge and Kimbolton.

Batting J. A. Beaumont 438 at 62.57; F. S. Preston* 308 at 38.50; M. J. St John 194 at 21.55; H. J. Youngson 155 at 19.37.

Bowling F. S. Preston 19 at 13.31; J. A. Beaumont 15 at 13.86; H. J. Youngson 11 at 19.54; J. A. C. Rawcliffe 12 at 28.41.

Dame Allan's School
P4 W2 L2 A7

Master i/c J. A. Benn

Two good wins and two defeats (one narrow) reflected the strength of the team. The captain Xav Taylor concluded a successful career by averaging 75; it has been a pleasure to watch him bat.

Batting X. Taylor* 151 at 75.50.

Bowling T. Hutton 7 at 12.57.

Dauntsey's School
P13 W9 L4 A4

Master i/c A. J. Palmer **Coach** J. R. Ayling

A quick-drying ground, good covers and excellent groundstaff ensured the loss of only four games to the weather. Kit Patrick started the season with wickets and finished with runs, including a match-winning 135 against Kingswood to clinch the Peak Sports League. Max Romer-Lee, a Year 10, showed promise, and nine players return for 2013.

Batting J. M. A. Mynott 348 at 43.50; K. Patrick 386 at 42.88; M. H. Romer-Lee 121 at 40.33; L. B. Hannaford 367 at 36.70; W. J. Christofi 125 at 25.00; E. J. Duckworth* 121 at 12.10.

Bowling K. Patrick 21 at 12.85; E. J. Duckworth 27 at 14.51; J. M. A. Mynott 12 at 17.33; L. B. Hannaford 12 at 21.75.

Dean Close School
P7 W4 L2 D1 A1

Master i/c D. R. Evans **Coach** D. G. Trist

A truncated season contained four victories. Thomas Warren captained ably and carried the batting, helped by Lloyd Evans. Jack Evans, an off-spinner, proved the most effective bowler. The win against MCC – chasing 252 – was the main talking point.

Batting L. A. E. Evans 226 at 45.20; C. Hunte 112 at 37.33; M. Abbley 178 at 29.66; T. Warren* 200 at 28.57; R. McInnes-Gibbons 127 at 21.16.

Bowling J. W. M. Evans 12 at 19.91; C. M. Wheatley 7 at 22.57; J. R. C. Hobbs 8 at 29.37; T. Warren 7 at 30.42.

Denstone College
P8 W6 L2 A6

Master i/c Miss J. R. Morris

Appalling weather curtailed a potentially outstanding season for a young side. The skipper, Alex Thomson, topped both averages, while Dom Burnett was the pick of the seamers.

Batting A. T. Thomson* 414 at 59.14; H. R. Hosein 101 at 25.25; G. T. G. Cork 168 at 21.00.

Bowling A. T. Thomson 9 at 11.88; D. D. Burnett 20 at 11.95; G. T. G. Cork 9 at 14.55; A. S. Crump 8 at 17.37.

Dr Challoner's Grammar School
P6 W4 L2 A8

Master i/c R. S. Ambrose

A season of high promise was hampered by the weather. However, a victory over MCC, for the third year in succession, saw spinners Robin Collins and Izhan Khan share eight wickets. Alex Morgan's unbeaten century against Hampton also drew praise.

Batting A. D. Morgan* 214 at 42.80; H. R. White 131 at 32.75; G. S. Shiel 143 at 28.60; R. P. J. Collins 112 at 28.00; M. C. Yeabsley 118 at 19.66.

Bowling A. T. Watson 10 at 9.80; R. P. J. Collins 9 at 14.22; I. S. Khan 10 at 14.40.

Dollar Academy
P9 W4 L4 D1 A5

Master i/c J. G. A. Frost

Hamish Tester, top batsman and bowler, led the team to some notable wins. His squad improved during the term, but were impeded by the rain.

Batting H. L. Tester* 211 at 30.14; A. J. Mackie 134 at 22.33.

Bowling H. L. Tester 14 at 13.64; A. D. Knapman 9 at 15.33.

Dover College
P11 W4 L5 D2 A4

Master i/c G. R. Hill **Coach** T. L. N. Root

Positive leadership from James Whybrow could not always disguise the fact that the college's bowling was much stronger than their batting; results were uneven. Nevertheless, there are some exciting young batsmen in the junior side who should blossom in 2013.

Batting J. P. Whybrow* 169 at 21.12; M. J. Walsh 179 at 17.90; H. T. Richardson 160 at 17.77.

Bowling J. L. Deverson 20 at 8.35; J. P. Whybrow 19 at 11.10; C. W. Gaete von Wersebe 16 at 15.56; M. J. Walsh 16 at 15.62.

Dulwich College
P12 W7 L4 D1 A3

Master i/c K. G. Shaw **Coach** C. W. J. Athey

Dulwich enjoyed a winning season. Dominic Fraser provided the cutting edge with the new ball, and Darshan Chohan bowled his left-arm spin with great control. Anthony Alleyne said farewell to Dulwich with a magnificent 145 against Harrow. He has the potential for a long career with West Indies.

Batting A. T. Alleyne 402 at 44.66; P. T. W. Stuff 160 at 26.66; A. D. Greenidge 263 at 26.30; S. D. Mirchandani 192 at 21.33; H. E. J. Austin 171 at 19.00; T. T. Gwyther 157 at 17.44; D. Chohan 116 at 16.57.

Bowling D. J. Fraser 13 at 10.92; D. Chohan 25 at 17.00; A. T. Alleyne 18 at 18.16; T. G. Purwar 13 at 24.84.

Durham School
P4 W1 L1 D2 A14

Master i/c B. Mason **Coach** M. B. Fishwick

Prolonged flooding prevented any play in 14 games, leaving a talented squad frustrated. The highlight of a reduced programme was the nine-wicket win over Australian touring side St Paul's, Brisbane, who were dismissed for 56. The Hirsch Award for the best cricketer was won by Adil Arif. For the most improved cricketer, the Bell Award was given to Jacob Bushnell.

Batting J. M. Bushnell 129 at 43.00; A. T. Arif 166 at 41.50; M. J. Bittlestone 106 at 26.50.

Bowling A. T. Arif 7 at 13.85; B. P. Simpson 7 at 20.28.

Eastbourne College
P15 W10 L5 A4

Master i/c M. J. Banes **Coach** A. C. Waller

Ben Green combined opening, keeping and leadership duties. Strong all-round contributions came from Harry Finch, who played for Sussex Seconds, and Francis Wynter. Both scored a century and were consistent wicket-takers.

Batting H. Z. Finch 611 at 67.88; F. Wynter 393 at 35.72; S. H. W. Hyne 260 at 32.50; J. W. Skinner 195 at 27.85; B. M. Green* 336 at 22.40; J. E. Smith 198 at 19.80; F. H. Voorspuy 111 at 12.33.
Bowling H. Z. Finch 19 at 14.94; F. Wynter 22 at 16.63; A. N. Goble 19 at 20.10; H. J. B. Smith 11 at 20.63; G. Cole 12 at 23.66.

The Edinburgh Academy P10 W5 L4 D1 A4

Master i/c M. J. D. Allingham
Performances greatly improved as the season advanced, and Zander Muir, the captain, scored centuries in the last two games. Several matches were played on artificial pitches because of soggy conditions.
Batting A. R. M. Muir* 342 at 57.00; C. J. R. W. Simpson 180 at 25.71; C. G. D. Carmichael 151 at 18.87; A. Rive 188 at 18.80; R. A. Orr 153 at 17.00; G. M. Brown 154 at 15.40; G. Currie 113 at 14.12; R. A. W. Simpson 110 at 13.75.
Bowling C. P. Huntington 9 at 14.55; G. Currie 10 at 19.00; A. Rive 12 at 20.66; C. G. D. Carmichael 10 at 23.20; R. A. W. Simpson 9 at 25.44.

Ellesmere College P9 W5 L3 D1 A6

Master i/c P. J. Hayes **Coach** C. C. Cawcutt
Of the first ten fixtures, five were won and five abandoned. Seamers Dewi Jones and Ishwaraj Bhatia prospered in the damp, each taking 15 wickets. Ishwaraj twice claimed a five-for (with a best of six for 15). Opener Sam Owen scored the only century.
Batting S. L. Owen 232 at 46.40; D. P. Jones 178 at 25.42; H. Malik 129 at 18.42; S. Mahotra 114 at 14.25.
Bowling I. S. Bhatia 15 at 8.46; D. P. Jones 15 at 9.20; A. Bowyer 8 at 18.50; H. Malik 9 at 20.44.

Eltham College P8 W5 L3 A11

Master i/c E. T. Thorogood **Coach** D. DeBeer
Victories against Felsted, King's Canterbury, Bancroft's, the XL Club and MCC marked a successful, if shortened, summer. The captain, Charlie Speller, directed the side well, supported by Freddie Foster's 20 wickets. A tour of South Africa should be sound preparation for 2013.
Batting C. S. Speller* 304 at 60.80; J. A. C. Robertson 282 at 47.00; D. R. Giles 191 at 38.20; G. P. R. Haley 169 at 33.80.
Bowling F. J. H. Foster 20 at 14.15.

Emanuel School P6 W2 L3 T1 A9

Master i/c P. A. King **Coaches** M. J. Roberts/M. G. Stear
After another successful training camp to La Manga, Emanuel endured a disrupted season of predominantly low-scoring matches. Sultaan Mufid's side were particularly sharp in the field.
Batting H. K. Purnell 112 at 22.40.
Bowling M. S. Patel 10 at 10.80.

Enfield Grammar School P7 W1 L6 A4

Master i/c T. M. Price
Despite disrupted training and abandoned fixtures, Enfield made it through to the semi-final of the Middlesex Cup, losing to the eventual winners Mill Hill. Skipper Ewart Thompson held the batting together, but the side never gained momentum.
Batting E. D. Thompson* 234 at 78.00.
Bowling J. Royall 8 at 17.00.

Epsom College P8 W3 L4 D1 A3

Master i/c N. R. Taylor
A disappointing start slowly improved. A hard-fought draw against MCC and a resounding ten-wicket victory over the Old Epsomians were the highlights of a rain-sodden campaign. Harry Allen led the way with the bat, and Tom Williams with the ball.
Batting H. A. Allen 299 at 59.80; M. T. Pittam 193 at 38.60.
Bowling C. J. Bolton 8 at 14.75; T. J. Williams 14 at 14.85; C. J. Du Toit 7 at 19.85; S. T. R. Sander 7 at 20.28.

Eton College

P14 W1 L11 D2 A7

Master i/c R. R. Montgomerie **Coach** J. M. Rice

The highlights of what injuries and miserable weather made a frustrating summer were a magnificent match against Harrow, tight bowling from Rory MacDonagh, and James Abbott's improved batting at the top of the innings.

Batting J. B. Abbott 516 at 36.85; H. L. Hayes* 393 at 35.72; J. S. D. Gnodde 285 at 31.66; E. W. R. James 386 at 27.57; M. J. Roy 192 at 21.33; J. A. Langen 168 at 15.27; J. M. Hubbard 148 at 14.80.

Bowling M. H. P. Carleton-Smith 7 at 23.42; H. L. Hayes 11 at 25.18; R. N. MacDonagh 9 at 34.88; T. K. M. Eckett 8 at 38.00; J. O. Tugwell 9 at 49.00; M. J. Roy 8 at 53.12.

Exeter School

P6 W3 L3 A10

Master i/c J. W. Fawkes

A young side benefited from increased first-team experience. They should continue to improve and, given dry weather, achieve greater success.

Batting T. M. Poustie 119 at 23.80.

Bowling B. G. F. Green 10 at 6.30; M. J. Hoddinott 12 at 8.58.

Felsted School

P14 W7 L4 D3 A5

Master i/c J. E. R. Gallian **Coaches** C. S. Knightley/N. J. Lockhart

Felsted enjoyed a positive season despite trying conditions. There were victories against King's Canterbury, Ipswich and Framlingham. The high spot was reaching the last eight of the National Twenty20 Knockout. Joshua Wells proved a fine leader.

Batting R. Hassan 787 at 87.44; J. A. Wells* 567 at 43.61; J. E. P. Hebron 304 at 25.33; J. Hunter-Jordan 243 at 20.25; C. J. Lewis 175 at 17.50.

Bowling R. W. Burns 13 at 16.76; C. M. Price 14 at 18.42; J. E. P. Hebron 13 at 18.84; R. Hassan 10 at 28.50.

Fettes College

P10 W5 L2 D3 A6

Master i/c C. S. Thomson **Coach** A. B. Russell

Five excellent victories illuminated a damp term. Jack Dingwall, the captain, claimed his 50th wicket for the team, while opener Jack Collister notched 413 runs, including a marvellous 151 against Edinburgh Academy.

Batting J. A. Collister 413 at 45.88; H. P. A. MacLeod 274 at 30.44; W. A. Edwards 119 at 29.75; H. A. Dalgarno 230 at 28.75; S. J. E. Robertson 172 at 24.57.

Bowling H. A. M. Dingwall 7 at 7.85; R. A. Martin 12 at 16.08; J. A. Collister 8 at 24.25; J. P. M. Dingwall* 8 at 26.50; T. S. Darling 7 at 27.28.

Forest School

P9 W8 D1 A8

Master i/c S. J. Foulds **Coach** J. J. Kay

An exceptional side enjoyed a most rewarding season, though games against several strong schools were abandoned. There were significant contributions throughout the team, with Peter Kilpatrick the best of many all-round talents.

Batting M. Ackerman 187 at 187.00; P. D. Kilpatrick 374 at 53.42; P. F. McDermott 173 at 34.60; J. J. Das* 239 at 34.14; N. A. Knight 133 at 22.16; J. D. Poulter 110 at 18.33.

Bowling P. D. Kilpatrick 9 at 6.55; P. F. McDermott 12 at 8.66; A. G. Gilbert 19 at 9.31; G. N. Summers 15 at 10.00; R. I. Ritchie 7 at 19.57.

Framlingham College

P12 W6 L4 D2 A4

Master i/c M. J. Marvell **Coach** B. J. France

The captain Robbie Bridgstock provided a welcome distraction from the weather, compiling 366 runs – precisely half his total for the season – in four days in late June. Meanwhile, Tim Alexander emerged as a genuine all-rounder; Kristian Williman and Lewis Gooderham are names to watch.

Batting R. Bridgstock* 732 at 73.20; K. N. Williman 329 at 54.83; L. S. Gooderham 374 at 41.55; T. D. Alexander 267 at 38.14; O. J. R. Jones 123 at 20.50; T. L. Brown 115 at 14.37.

Bowling S. R. Keshwani 11 at 20.09; T. D. Alexander 18 at 21.61; R. Bridgstock 12 at 26.75; T. J. C. Rider 13 at 27.30; J. R. Carr 7 at 43.00.

George Watson's College P8 W3 L3 T1 D1 A14

Master i/c M. J. Leonard **Coach** A. D. W. Patterson

Despite the cancellation of numerous games, a young squad made progress. Chris Cash captained well, finishing as leading run-scorer and wicket-taker. Among the highlights were James Bedford's aggressive batting and Euan McKay's last-ball six to secure the team's first win.

Batting C. A. Cash* 215 at 30.71; W. A. Brown 107 at 26.75; J. W. T. Bedford 100 at 25.00; F. K. Hutchison 101 at 16.83.

Bowling J. W. T. Bedford 7 at 10.85; C. A. Cash 14 at 13.50; I. R. Hay 7 at 23.28; A. R. Hastings 7 at 25.57.

Giggleswick School P7 W1 L4 D2 A4

Master i/c D. H. Morris **Coach** K. Sharp

Miserable playing conditions and a very young side resulted in a disappointing season. In the school's 500th year, the most memorable moment was a match and dinner with MCC, whose president, Phillip Hodson, was guest speaker.

Batting C. J. Lockett 190 at 27.14.

Bowling J. E. Raper 12 at 19.66.

The Glasgow Academy P10 W5 L4 D1 A2

Master i/c G. S. Wood **Coach** V. Hariharan

The team played well and trained hard, but results did scant justice to their efforts. It was gratifying to win the TGA Sixes tournament, and also the MCC Spirit of Cricket cap, awarded to skipper Suhaib Siddiqui for the manner in which his team conducted themselves.

Batting L. H. Hill 402 at 67.00; S. A. Siddiqui* 107 at 17.83; B. Mazzucco 102 at 12.75.

Bowling C. D. Coutts 7 at 6.00; S. A. Siddiqui 9 at 16.66; B. Mazzucco 11 at 18.00.

The High School of Glasgow P11 W6 L5 A3

Master i/c D. N. Barrett **Coaches** N. R. Clarke/K. J. A. Robertson

A successful season saw most games played to a finish. High points were Andrew Umeed's unbeaten 151 against Stewart's Melville and the first win at Gordonstoun. Gavin Main played for Scotland Under-19 and Durham Academy; Umeed turned out for Scotland Under-19 and Scotland A. Both participated in the Under-19 World Cup in Australia.

Batting A. R. I. Umeed 241 without dismissal; A. W. Galloway* 215 at 23.88; D. N. Satpute 200 at 22.22; N. Majhu 150 at 18.75.

Bowling G. T. Main 8 at 1.62; I. A. Wheel 9 at 15.22; E. C. Clarke 8 at 17.62; A. W. Galloway 11 at 18.90; D. N. Satpute 11 at 19.81; F. J. Godsman 10 at 20.60.

Glenalmond College P2 L2 A10

Master i/c M. J. Davies

The one (unwanted) record of a dreich summer was the fewest games in Glenalmond's cricketing history.

Batting No one scored 100 runs. The leading batsman was R. A. M. Davies*, who hit 36 at 18.00.

Bowling No one claimed seven wickets. The leading bowler was A. G. Porter, who took 3 at 11.33.

Gordonstoun School P8 W3 L4 D1 A5

Master i/c C. J. Barton **Coach** R. Denyer

A very young side performed encouragingly: Archie Houldsworth, Jack Congdon and Edward Gledson underlined their considerable potential. The squad for the next three seasons should be settled – only three are likely to leave – and they will be desperately hoping for better weather.

Batting D. Singh 219 at 31.28; B. L. Laurie 136 at 17.00; A. J. I. Houldsworth 110 at 15.71.

Bowling T. R. Finch Noyes 8 at 11.25; D. Singh 7 at 29.71.

Gresham's School P11 W3 L7 D1 A6

Master i/c P. J. Watson

The bowling was strong: spinners Ben Stromberg, Frankie Sutton and Oliver Sutton gained good support from seamers Jonny Park, Hugo Knapp and Nathan Lomax. However, only Frankie Sutton batted soundly, as Gresham's failed to make the most of their impressive attack.

Batting F. C. Sutton 362 at 32.90; O. Sutton 241 at 24.10; H. G. Blackiston* 200 at 22.22; B. E. Stromberg 130 at 16.25.

Bowling B. E. Stromberg 16 at 10.87; H. J. M. P. Knapp 7 at 15.57; N. Lomax 7 at 18.57; F. C. Sutton 11 at 21.00; J. P. J. Park 10 at 24.20; O. Sutton 9 at 27.00.

Haberdashers' Aske's Boys' School P12 W9 L2 D1 A9

Master i/c S. D. Charlwood **Coaches** D. H. Kerry/D. I. Yeabsley

In a summer of unprecedented rainfall and increasingly tricky team selection – exams kept getting in the way – a return of nine wins in 12 games was commendable. Victories over St Albans and Brighton GS, from Melbourne, were high points. The captain, Nishanth Selvakumar, completed five years in the team, opening the batting and keeping wicket with authority and skill.

Batting T. G. L. Colverd 231 at 38.50; T. K. Malde 294 at 36.75; N. N. Selvakumar* 335 at 33.50; S. Agarwal 221 at 27.62; A. S. Kadiwar 153 at 25.50; K. Setia 194 at 24.25.

Bowling K. Setia 14 at 18.50; A. S. Kadiwar 9 at 20.22; P. A. Sivarajah 18 at 22.38; I. Patel 15 at 22.60; R. Shah 7 at 30.00.

Haileybury P11 W5 L4 D2 A5

Master i/c H. T. B. Baxendale **Coaches** M. J. Cawdron/G. P. Howarth

Haileybury often played excellent cricket: all five victories were by large margins. Caleb Stewart prospered despite the pressures of captaincy, keeping and opening, while a raw attack learned much. Joel Stewart's six for 24 v Hutchins, Tasmania, was a main talking point.

Batting C. E. Stewart* 529 at 66.12; B. Spencer 222 at 37.00; G. N. Horwood 118 at 29.50; W. J. Stanyard 288 at 28.80; J. S. Carter 133 at 14.77.

Bowling R. C. Grigg 8 at 13.12; R. D. Toms 11 at 16.36; R. C. Lane 7 at 24.28; J. B. Howe 10 at 29.90; J. R. Stewart 11 at 32.54.

Hampton School P15 W7 L7 D1 A3

Master i/c A. M. Banerjee **Coach** C. P. Harrison

Mixed results reflected a team in transition – and the soggiest of summers. Nevertheless, the school won the 50/40 League Cup for a fourth consecutive year.

Batting C. H. O'Brien 333 at 41.62; D. J. Fryer 374 at 41.55; G. C. Harper 268 at 26.80; S. W. F. Goodwill 314 at 24.15; J. Madoc-Jones* 266 at 22.16; M. R. Main 197 at 21.88; G. T. E. King 204 at 17.00; M. R. O'Brien 126 at 10.50.

Bowling C. H. O'Brien 17 at 6.76; S. W. F. Goodwill 14 at 8.07; G. T. E. King 9 at 9.66; H. W. Comerford 18 at 11.27; J. J. Goodwill 7 at 14.71; M. R. O'Brien 19 at 16.31; G. A. Tunnacliffe 13 at 19.53; D. J. Fryer 7 at 21.00.

Harrow School P17 W9 L6 D2 A3

Master i/c S. J. Halliday **Coach** S. A. Jones

Second in the Cowdrey Cup was encouraging, but the highlight of a successful season was the thrilling win over Eton at Lord's. Lalit Bose was a powerful opening batsman, while Nick Castleman guided the side superbly.

Batting L. Bose 595 at 45.76; M. E. Cousens 593 at 45.61; R. G. White 474 at 33.85; A. W. Boyd 384 at 32.00; H. W. D. Whitrow 243 at 30.37; N. M. T. Castleman* 245 at 16.33.

Bowling V. M. Patel 10 at 17.00; L. Bose 17 at 19.52; H. D. L. Macintyre 20 at 22.55; T. C. R. Morgan 10 at 22.90; A. R. G. Turner 17 at 23.00; A. W. Boyd 13 at 23.53; M. P. Ward 12 at 25.75.

The Harvey Grammar School P6 W4 L1 D1 A8

Master i/c P. M. Castle

A youthful and promising team completed just six games. Year 10 pupil Henry Axon showed great potential with the ball.

Batting J. S. D. Andersson-Laing 183 at 45.75; B. R. Goodsell* 160 at 40.00.

Bowling H. S. Axon 7 at 3.85.

Highgate School P5 W3 L2 A5

Master i/c A. G. Tapp **Coach** S. Patel

Jamie Powe batted with confidence, and captain Charlie Yorke-Starkey bowled with pace and accuracy. No key players are leaving, so summer 2013 should – weather permitting – be more successful.

Batting J. D. Powe 140 at 46.66; F. L. Mills 151 at 37.75.

Bowling M. W. Boyle 7 at 11.57; C. T. S. Yorke-Starkey* 8 at 13.25; N. Friend 7 at 14.85.

Hurstpierpoint College P15 W10 L4 D1

Master i/c N. J. K. Creed **Coach** R. S. C. Martin-Jenkins

Several strong performances saw the side win ten fixtures. Brad Gayler did well with the bat and gloves, Greg Wisdom was leading wicket-taker and, for the third year running, Jay Barclay scored most runs. The team also reached the final of the Langdale Trophy.

Batting J. H. Ludlow 278 at 55.60; B. J. Gayler 307 at 34.11; J. R. C. Barclay* 374 at 26.71; G. N. Wisdom 345 at 26.53; M. Campopiano 201 at 18.27.

Bowling J. Newland 17 at 13.64; J. R. C. Barclay 18 at 14.00; G. N. Wisdom 23 at 14.17; T. H. Moses 14 at 20.21; J. P. M. Hutchings 14 at 23.78; E. I. P. Blake 9 at 29.33.

Hymers College P10 W7 L1 D2 A2

Master i/c G. Tipping

Hymers won the Bradford GS six-a-side competition and the Pocklington cricket festival, and reached the Yorkshire T20 regional final. Mahir Yousuff made his maiden century, against MCC.

Batting M. Yousuff 447 at 44.70.

Bowling T. B. Jones 10 at 16.80.

Ipswich School P7 W3 L3 D1 A4

Master i/c M. P. Smethurst **Coach** R. E. East

Ipswich had a mixed set of results, but noteworthy performances came from Ashwin Bhatt (five for eight against Brentwood) and Steffan Osman-Wiggan, in Year 10, who grabbed five for 21 on debut against The Perse.

Batting M. R. Burch 219 at 43.80; S. Webb-Snowling 125 at 31.25; J. M. Hodgkinson 106 at 26.50.

Bowling No one claimed seven wickets. The leading bowler was T. W. Watson, who took 6 at 25.50.

The John Fisher School P12 W3 L7 D2 A9

Master i/c T. L. Vandoros

A young, budding squad took advantage of any opportunity the rain allowed to develop their talents. Although the results look disappointing, the team were pitted against some tough opposition; their efforts and determination should bear fruit.

Batting A. J. Dombrandt 340 at 30.90; C. M. Cody 223 at 18.58; S. T. Chmielinski* 183 at 16.63; I. M. Etheridge 140 at 12.72.

Bowling C. M. Cody 15 at 14.53; P. J. Arthur 9 at 16.77; S. J. Smith 11 at 20.36; S. T. Chmielinski 7 at 23.42; I. M. Etheridge 12 at 26.25.

The John Lyon School P7 W4 L3 A7

Master i/c A. S. Ling **Coach** C. T. Peploe

Only seven fixtures survived the deluge, but they included notable victories over Westminster – when Ahsan Jamil hit a superb unbeaten 92 – and, by eight runs, Reading Blue Coats. The captain, Ben Marsh, topped the bowling; Scott Wilsher was the pick of the batsmen.

Batting A. Jamil 137 at 27.40; S. M. Wilsher 160 at 26.66.

Bowling B. H. B. Marsh* 12 at 14.16.

The Judd School P11 W4 L7 A4

Master i/c D. W. Joseph

By the end of term, the team had been largely rebuilt; the core of the new side should return in 2013. George Willis, the skipper, marshalled the team well and also scored most runs. Ross Pilkington and Ed Jenden shared 30 wickets.

Batting G. I. G. Willis* 245 at 22.27; M. W. T. Barnes 101 at 20.20; C. Bryce-Borthwick 163 at 18.11; M. W. Dowding 104 at 14.85; E. M. F. Jenden 100 at 12.50.

Bowling E. M. F. Jenden 15 at 8.86; W. M. Canniford 7 at 9.71; J. E. Thompson 9 at 12.66; M. J. Smith 8 at 14.00; R. D. Pilkington 15 at 16.60; C. S. J. Barkhan 11 at 16.72.

Kimbolton School P12 W9 L1 D2 A5

Master i/c T. Webley **Coach** D. H. J. Griggs

The school achieved outstanding victories against Bishop's Stortford College, Highgate, Eton and Wellingborough. Robert Craze, in his final season, was an excellent captain, and Luke Eddon was the team's leading bowler.

Batting C. G. Gingell 419 at 46.55; R. G. Craze* 357 at 35.70; R. J. Lowin 153 at 19.12; A. J. Masters 191 at 17.36.

Bowling L. T. Eddon 21 at 11.09; M. H. E. Lane 13 at 12.84; R. G. Craze 21 at 14.04; R. J. Lowin 14 at 17.85; J. D. Kenmir 14 at 18.21; J. A. Blindt 12 at 19.50.

King Edward VI School, Southampton P9 W6 L3 A4

Batting J. J. Weatherley 178 at 59.33; T. J. Edwards 309 at 44.14; S. J. McCormick-Cox* 305 at 33.88; R. J. E. Adamson 264 at 33.00; J. Evans 120 at 24.00; J. C. Stanley 100 at 20.00.
Bowling S. J. McCormick-Cox 15 at 11.20; R. G. M. Amos 12 at 15.83; A. J. Berryman 8 at 17.62; A. G. Sharpe 11 at 18.63; W. J. H. Tsang 12 at 21.66.

King Edward VII & Queen Mary's School, Lytham P9 W3 L3 D3 A4

Master i/c S. A. Clarke **Coach** Atiq-uz-Zaman

A youthful team developed rapidly and, in their last game before KEQMS merged with Arnold School, defeated UCS; captain Matthew Cartmell scored 81 and younger brother Chris took six for 13. Other wins came against Merchant Taylors', Crosby – and Arnold.
Batting M. P. Cartmell* 396 at 56.57; M. P. McLaughlin 209 at 23.22; B. P. Saunders 138 at 19.71.
Bowling M. P. Cartmell 18 at 15.05; C. D. Cartmell 9 at 22.33; A. Gregson 9 at 26.77; B. P. Saunders 9 at 28.77.

King Edward's School, Bath P4 L4 A7

Master i/c M. Hawker **Coach** G. Brown

After an unbeaten tour of Antigua the side stuttered in the rain. Some encouraging efforts from younger players included the debut of Year 8 pupil Benedict Gundry.
Batting No one scored 100 runs. The leading batsman was J. R. Weare*, who hit 75 at 25.00.
Bowling No one claimed seven wickets. The leading bowler was R. J. Morgan, who took 6 at 8.50.

King Edward's School, Birmingham P12 W5 L6 D1 A10

Master i/c L. M. Roll **Coach** D. Collins

The team achieved five wins, but failed to trouble their stronger opponents. Nathan Roberts led the side admirably, and Girish Murali claimed 15 wickets.
Batting S. J. Mubarik 244 at 40.66; N. C. Roberts* 383 at 38.30; S. J. White 198 at 24.75; J. J. Jheeta 189 at 17.18; M. T. Galla 147 at 16.33.
Bowling N. M. H. Kumararatne 9 at 11.88; G. S. Murali 15 at 13.40; R. J. Wigley 7 at 17.85; S. J. White 7 at 28.28; J. I. Claughton 9 at 31.55.

King Henry VIII School P6 W3 L1 D2 A8

Master i/c A. M. Parker

Fielding perhaps the most experienced and talented side for almost 20 years, King Henry's looked forward to 2012 with optimism. But by the end of term less than a third of matches had reached a positive conclusion. When play was possible, skipper Steven Abbey and Kunal Sharma, both in their fourth season, led the way.
Batting S. D. Abbey* 137 at 45.66; S. R. Lucas 168 at 42.00.
Bowling I. Nagra 7 at 7.14; V. Menon 7 at 7.85; K. K. Sharma 7 at 9.42; T. L. Brammer 7 at 12.71.

King's College, Taunton P11 W10 L1 A8

Master i/c P. D. Lewis **Coach** D. Breakwell

In testing conditions, the team executed game plans superbly, showing a consistently high level of performance throughout a short, rain-affected season.
Batting J. A. Regan* 511 at 56.77; R. W. Davies 443 at 40.27; P. M. R. Smith 274 at 34.25; N. Brand 192 at 32.00; T. Barrett 314 at 31.40; S. Underdown 161 at 26.83.
Bowling N. Brand 20 at 12.90; J. C. W. Jennings 14 at 18.07; T. Barrett 12 at 22.75.

King's College School, Wimbledon P15 W10 L5 A1

Master i/c T. P. Howland **Coach** S. G. Davies

All but one of the abandoned games were rearranged. This was a very good side, well led by Adil Sheikh, with most of the squad returning for at least one more year.
Batting J. E. Huxtable 363 at 27.92; J. R. T. Churchman 355 at 25.35; M. C. Clifford 228 at 19.00; N. M. Rawlinson 176 at 16.00; M. A. Sheikh* 166 at 15.09; A. R. Hughes 117 at 11.70; B. J. Oates 131 at 10.91; R. J. Crichard 139 at 10.69.
Bowling A. R. Hughes 31 at 10.29; M. A. Sheikh 22 at 11.36; J. J. Whittaker 9 at 15.00; M. P. Neat 18 at 15.88; N. M. Rawlinson 13 at 15.92; R. J. Crichard 15 at 16.00.

King's School, Bruton
P9 W5 L1 D3 A3

Master i/c R. S. Hamilton **Coach** B. Dudley

This was one of the school's best seasons in recent years. A team of good all-rounders bowled and batted well in tough conditions. Harry Best was an outstanding captain on and off the field.

Batting M. Collett 298 at 33.11; O. G. H. Oulton 215 at 30.71; M. H. Dell-White 116 at 23.20; J. E. G. Cadbury 181 at 22.62; G. I. Edgar 107 at 17.83.

Bowling J. E. G. Cadbury 10 at 15.40; M. H. Dell-White 9 at 15.44; M. Collett 9 at 16.33; O. G. H. Oulton 15 at 18.80; H. D. Best* 11 at 23.45.

The King's School, Canterbury
P14 W5 L8 T1 A2

Master i/c R. A. L. Singfield **Coach** M. A. Ealham

Development was the key: an inexperienced side learned rapidly and should come back stronger in 2013. Harry Mann and James Meddings were the pick of the bowlers, with George Baker White scoring well towards the end of term.

Batting H. G. Woodward 133 at 44.33; W. G. J. Baker White 334 at 25.69; G. A. Stacey 294 at 22.61; R. W. D. Macleod* 279 at 21.46; J. H. R Meddings 251 at 17.92; W. J. W. Fabbro 166 at 16.60; E. J. S. Gilmore 143 at 13.00.

Bowling H. J. B. Mann 17 at 16.29; S. N. Leggett 13 at 25.69; B. L. I. Methven 12 at 27.66; J. H. Godden 7 at 27.85; W. J. W. Fabbro 13 at 29.61; J. H. R. Meddings 17 at 30.94.

The King's School, Chester
P13 W4 L6 D3 A7

Masters i/c S. Neal/T. R. Hughes **Coach** N. R. Walker

Spin bowling was the strength, with Peter Boothroyd's six for 18 the best return of the season. Guy Dunbavand's hundred was the batting highlight. In a season of rebuilding, a young side showed glimpses of real promise.

Batting G. T. Dunbavand 411 at 37.36; H. H. W. Makings 205 at 25.62; M. E. R. Williams 203 at 22.55; R. C. Benson* 172 at 21.50; P. E. Boothroyd 145 at 20.71; E. J. Peel 100 at 12.50.

Bowling P. E. Boothroyd 8 at 17.50; A. F. Williams 10 at 22.00; O. W. Dawson 9 at 30.00; J. Kurukkal 7 at 31.28; E. J. Peel 7 at 36.85.

The King's School in Macclesfield
P11 W5 L4 D2 A9

Master i/c S. Moores **Coach** A. Kennedy

A last-ball victory against MCC was the most memorable moment of a rain-ruined summer. The school have lost two fine players in Tom Foreman and Andrew Hodgson; both played four full seasons.

Batting B. J. Marsden 404 at 67.33; A. J. Hodgson 376 at 47.00; T. S. Foreman* 238 at 34.00; W. J. Hodgson 129 at 21.50.

Bowling A. U. Khan 8 at 12.75; T. S. Foreman 9 at 15.88; A. J. Hodgson 15 at 19.40; J. E. R. Egar 8 at 27.87; G. Eyre 7 at 28.28.

King's School, Rochester
P11 W2 L9 A4

Master i/c W. E. Smith **Coach** C. H. Page

This was a difficult and disappointing year, but a dedicated and committed team gave their best. Alistair Saunders, in his fourth year in the first team, made a fine job of the captaincy.

Batting A. C. Saunders* 281 at 28.10; J. A. S. McDonald 151 at 15.10.

Bowling A. J. Wilson 16 at 20.87; D. G. E. Colville 15 at 21.73; A. C. Saunders 13 at 26.61.

King's School, Tynemouth
P7 W2 L4 D1 A5

Masters i/c W. Ryan/P. J. Nicholson **Coach** N. J. Jones

Seam-bowling all-rounder Mark Fearon and opening bat James Brown were the outstanding players, but often weather had the last word. The school's first match against MCC was a notable casualty.

Batting M. W. Fearon 142 at 47.33; J. W. Brown 196 at 39.20; C. J. Brown* 103 at 17.16.

Bowling No one claimed seven wickets. The leading bowler was M. W. Fearon, who took 5 at 13.40.

King's School, Worcester
P10 W7 L2 D1 A10

Master i/c D. P. Iddon **Coach** A. A. D. Gillgrass

A short but pleasing campaign, expertly directed by Joe Fowles, saw the team regularly field five Under-15s. Fourteen-year-olds Nick Hammond (100 against MCC) and Josh Tongue (five for two against RGS Worcester) showed immense promise.

Batting J. G. B. Park 418 at 59.71; N. A. Hammond 298 at 37.25; A. D. Spring 101 at 20.20; A. D. J. Hunt 119 at 19.83; J. C. Tongue 112 at 16.00.

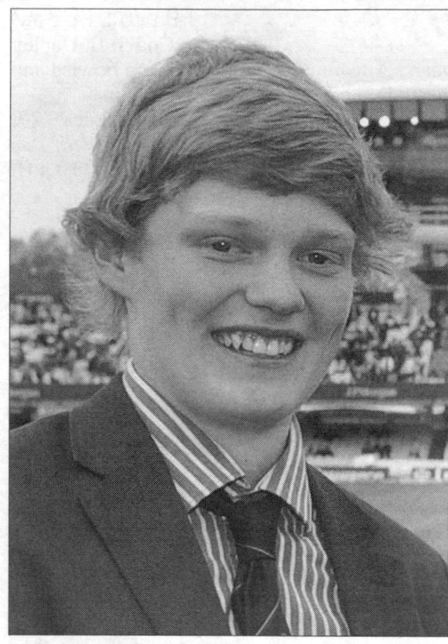

Tom Whitehouse, of Lancaster RGS, was the country's leading wicket-taker, with 41 at 8.70 each. Lord Wandsworth's Robbie Heywood scored four centuries in eight days.

Bowling J. C. Tongue 14 at 11.92; J. Fowles* 19 at 13.47; J. L. Salter 7 at 14.00; J. G. B. Park 9 at 22.88; A. D. J. Hunt 8 at 30.00.

Kingswood School, Bath — P9 W6 L2 D1 A4

Master i/c J. O. Brown

Kingswood won three-quarters of games played to a finish, with brothers Tim and Harry Rouse averaging 89 and 91 respectively. Sam Morris scored his first hundred, while Finn Barnard-Weston and Ollie Meyer claimed maiden five-fors.

Batting H. P. Rouse* 274 at 91.33; T. D. Rouse 356 at 89.00; S. A. Morris 322 at 35.77; F. P. Barnard-Weston 189 at 31.50; F. A. Barnard-Weston 116 at 14.50.

Bowling O. F. Meyer 16 at 10.68; F. A. Barnard-Weston 16 at 13.31; T. D. Rouse 15 at 14.13; R. S. Blackburn 9 at 19.44.

Kirkham Grammar School — P11 W7 L2 D2 A4

Master i/c M. A. Whalley — **Coach** N. S. Passenger

Kirkham had a most successful year, typified by strong victories over Merchant Taylors', Crosby, and the XL Club. George Brookes and Oliver Jump displayed all-round skills, as did keeper James Seward, in Year 9, who contributed 341 runs and 28 dismissals.

Batting J. Seward 341 at 37.88; G. Brookes 359 at 35.90; O. Jump 224 at 22.40; F. Burnie 100 at 16.66; A. Galley* 181 at 15.08; H. Moulding 132 at 13.20.

Bowling T. Roberts 10 at 6.20; O. Jump 28 at 7.46; G. Brookes 23 at 11.91; F. Burnie 8 at 12.62; A. Galley 14 at 16.14; R. Lavelle 7 at 27.28.

Lancaster Royal Grammar School — P17 W11 D6 A2

Master i/c I. W. Ledward — **Coaches** I. Perryman/I. D. Whitehouse

This was a splendid season, thanks largely to a team loaded with all-rounders. Memorable matches included wins against MCC, Bolton, and Manchester GS. The captain, Sam Moorby, excelled as wicketkeeper and batsman. Off-spinner Tom Whitehouse took 41 wickets.

Batting S. J. Moorby* 467 at 35.92; T. I. Whitehouse 209 at 23.22; J. L. Atkinson 252 at 22.90; D. I. Chambers 228 at 22.80; J. W. Roberts 234 at 18.00; K. J. Parekh 144 at 18.00; T. A. Deakin 204 at 17.00.

Bowling S. A. Letcher 13 at 4.92; J. L. Atkinson 13 at 6.61; T. I. Whitehouse 41 at 8.70; D. I. Chambers 16 at 15.62; M. B. Liver 10 at 16.40; J. C. Wells 11 at 17.81; J. W. Roberts 11 at 21.27; T. R. Williamson 15 at 25.73.

Lancing College P13 W5 L7 D1 A3

Master i/c R. J. Maru

For a team with only two regular Year 13s and several youngsters, this was an encouraging term. Mason Crane claimed eight for 11 against the XL Club, while Hector Loughton and Nick Ballamy hit centuries.

Batting N. M. Ballamy 335 at 41.87; H. A. Loughton 415 at 34.58; E. H. D. Clarke 193 at 19.30; N. A. Cook 203 at 16.91; A. J. Wood 117 at 10.63.

Bowling M. S. Crane 30 at 15.46; H. E. Hewitson 20 at 17.75; N. M. Ballamy 16 at 19.25; O. M. Bland 11 at 20.45; H. A. Loughton 12 at 23.58.

Latymer Upper School P9 W3 L6 A1

Master i/c M. P. Sweeney **Coach** B. F. Taylor

The summer started with the first victory over Ibstock Place School, but momentum was lost as rain and exams caused disruption. Excellent all-round performances from Zachir Tunda, Sahil Patel and Joe Jones could not prevent a string of defeats.

Batting Z. Tunda 112 at 18.66.

Bowling S. V. Patel* 14 at 11.35; J. D. Jones 9 at 15.33; Z. Tunda 14 at 15.71.

The Grammar School at Leeds P4 W2 L1 D1 A12

Master i/c S. H. Dunn

Dreadful conditions wrecked the season: only three games reached a result, while a fourth ended as a rain-affected draw. Mike Wren-Kirkham grabbed a hat-trick at St Peter's, York.

Batting R. S. Patel 147 at 49.00.

Bowling No one claimed seven wickets. The leading bowler was B. Morley*, who took 5 at 16.40.

Leicester Grammar School P7 W3 L3 D1 A3

Master i/c L. Potter

Despite the elements, the side performed extremely well, gaining a first victory against Oakham in the Twenty20 Cup, and contesting the Leicestershire County Cup final.

Batting T. Smith 110 at 22.00; W. O. Hunt 109 at 18.16.

Bowling A. Patel* 8 at 14.50.

The Leys School P9 W7 L1 D1 A5

Master i/c R. I. Kaufman **Coach** R. J. Darkins

Oliver Lawson guided a fledgling squad to seven wins in eight all-day fixtures to ensure a fine season. Thomas Wilson topped both averages. A tour of Sri Lanka early in 2013 should see lasting benefits.

Batting T. A. Wilson 243 at 48.60; J. P. Albery 219 at 43.80; O. D. J. Feast 149 at 37.25; O. H. Lawson* 209 at 34.83; A. Salvesen 147 at 29.40; C. J. Tapping 179 at 22.37.

Bowling T. A. Wilson 14 at 17.42; T. P. J. Elmslie 11 at 18.45; O. H. Lawson* 12 at 20.58; D. L. A. Harris 11 at 24.54.

Lord Wandsworth College P9 W5 L3 D1 A6

Master i/c E. J. Coetzer **Coaches** C. C. Hicks/D. Beven

The notable scalps of RGS Guildford, St Paul's and Reed's marked a rewarding term. Talented captain Robbie Heywood scored 645 runs at 92; in one eight-day stretch he hit 551, including four consecutive centuries.

Batting R. A. Heywood* 645 at 92.14; J. O. T. Wilson 324 at 46.28; A. T. S. Hammond 226 at 37.66; T. P. D. Ward 193 at 24.12.

Bowling D. M. Wade 12 at 13.25; R. A. Heywood 11 at 19.45; A. T. S. Hammond 9 at 21.11; J. W. Hopkin 8 at 28.37.

Loughborough Grammar School P7 W2 L5 A10

Master i/c H. T. Tunnicliffe **Coach** M. I. Gidley

The team were capably led by Alex Nathanson, but they never quite hit their stride. Despite winning only twice, there were signs of promise for 2013.

Batting D. P. Tew 139 at 23.16.
Bowling R. R. Gokani 10 at 12.20; G. Foster 9 at 16.44.

Magdalen College School, Oxford P10 W2 L8 A7

Master i/c J. P. Crawley
An appallingly frustrating season meant everyone struggled for momentum. Jai-Hin Patel, who captained the side with skill and panache, was well supported by Charlie Beeson and Jordan Brodley.
Batting C. Beeson 297 at 37.12; J-H. Patel* 260 at 32.50; A. P. Tolson 155 at 22.14; C. J. Nourse 112 at 16.00.
Bowling J. J. Brodley 11 at 22.18; A. P. Tolson 7 at 23.14.

Malvern College P9 W6 L2 D1 A6

Master i/c M. A. Hardinges **Coach** N. A. Brett
Tom Kohler-Cadmore continued where he left off in 2011, averaging over 85 with the bat and leading the team astutely. The crowning moment was the inaugural two-day game against Bradfield: Malvern won a thrilling encounter.
Batting T. Kohler-Cadmore* 614 at 87.71; F. P. A. Martin 241 at 26.77; A. G. Milton 185 at 26.42; C. W. F. Lacey 164 at 23.42; M. G. Drury 129 at 21.50.
Bowling L. Smith 7 at 15.57; C. S. Harwood 17 at 16.70; A. G. T. Jones 9 at 22.88; A. Shah 13 at 24.61.

The Manchester Grammar School P12 W5 L5 D2 A5

Master i/c D. Moss **Coach** M. J. Chilton
Notable victories came in run-chases against Cheadle Hulme and King's Macclesfield. Endless abandonments and interruptions meant it was difficult for batsmen or bowlers to get going.
Batting A. A. Qasim 269 at 26.90; J. Hinds 128 at 25.60; J. T. Cheetham 268 at 24.36; J. E. Lowe 172 at 21.50; M. R. Tully* 192 at 21.33.
Bowling J. A. Smith-Butler 15 at 18.73; J. Hinds 14 at 19.35; M. R. Tully 16 at 20.75; A. T. S. Gill 7 at 23.57; A. T. Read 9 at 38.66; R. Vaish 7 at 41.42.

Marlborough College P7 W2 L4 D1 A7

Master i/c N. E. Briers **Coach** J. H. Beckett
The season finished encouragingly with a hard-fought draw against Rugby in the two-day Colours match (Rugby 268-8 dec and 95-6 dec; Marlborough 180 and 125-3). Wicketkeeper Stuart Swift skilfully captained a side who had grown in stature after touring Cape Town in early 2012.
Batting W. D. N. von Behr 313 at 44.71; A. J. Turner 180 at 36.00; J. C. Sennett 164 at 23.42; J. A. Butler 130 at 21.66; A. J. Combe 114 at 14.25.
Bowling F. E. L. Campbell 9 at 13.22; M. J. B. Koe 12 at 21.83; W. D. N. von Behr 13 at 22.38.

Merchant Taylors' School, Crosby P12 W3 L7 D2 A9

Master i/c S. P. Sutcliffe
This was a season of frustration, both with performances and the weather. The bright spots were a win over MCC (thanks to a fine century by Steven Lucas) and a hundred from Matthew Burridge in a rain-affected draw against Manchester GS.
Batting S. W. Lucas 159 at 53.00; J. D. Snaylam 229 at 25.44; M. S. Burridge 205 at 22.77; M. J. Barton 135 at 16.87; T. S. Sutcliffe 164 at 16.40; J. K. Reade* 108 at 12.00; C. A. Bell 109 at 10.90.
Bowling M. S. Burridge 15 at 12.80; T. S. Sutcliffe 12 at 20.75; M. J. Barton 7 at 25.28.

Merchant Taylors' School, Northwood P11 W5 L3 D3 A4

Master i/c A. J. Booth **Coach** H. C. Latchman
Some outstanding performances with the ball, especially Ashil Shah's eight for four against UCS, won several matches, but batting frailties squandered other winning positions. Harry Latchman retired after coaching the team for 24 years.
Batting A. K. Shah 308 at 38.50; K. A. Vedd 143 at 28.60; J. T. Phillips* 229 at 25.44; A. N. Damani 137 at 19.57; R. Malde 122 at 17.42.
Bowling M. A. Patel 16 at 10.56; A. K. Shah 20 at 13.50; J. T. Phillips 14 at 13.78; T. J. Woods 9 at 15.55; J. N. Jeffrie 10 at 24.20.

Merchiston Castle School P2 W2 A9

Master i/c S. D. Gilmour **Coach** P. J. Deakin

This was an exasperating season, with 13 of 19 days' play washed out. Fine wins over Dollar and Loretto were the only completed Saturday fixtures. Defeat by Stewart's Melville from the last ball in the East final of the Twenty20 Cup was a disappointing end to a soggy summer.

Batting No one scored 100 runs. The leading batsman was C. B. Sole, who hit 66 at 33.00.

Bowling No one claimed seven wickets. The leading bowler was T. B. Sole, who took 6 at 7.50.

Mill Hill School P8 W3 L5 A4

Master i/c I. J. F. Hutchinson

An inexperienced team matured as the season dried out – and won the Middlesex Cup. The captain, Joseph Wray, bowled with energy to claim most victims, but Jonathan Ellis's exceptional spell in the win against Merchant Taylors', Northwood, was the highlight. Benedict Relf was the key contributor with the bat.

Batting B. B. Relf 178 at 35.60; W. G. Harley 100 at 20.00.

Bowling J. Ellis 9 at 8.44; J. Wray* 15 at 15.00.

Millfield School P16 W8 L3 D5 A2

Master i/c R. M. Ellison **Coach** M. A. Garaway

The National Twenty20 title was the highlight of a maddeningly wet season. Will Jenkins led with the bat; Dan Williams bowled with great control.

Batting W. Soczak 291 at 41.57; W. H. Jenkins 324 at 36.00; D. R. Lewis-Williams 162 at 32.40; C. F. Hartley 219 at 24.33; A. J. Easton 176 at 22.00; M. K. Hopper* 156 at 15.60.

Bowling C. F. Hartley 9 at 9.44; D. R. Lewis-Williams 11 at 14.09; D. R. Williams 15 at 14.13; A. J. Davis 9 at 17.33; S. D. Weller 9 at 24.22; A. J. Easton 9 at 24.22.

Monkton Combe School P12 W4 L7 D1 A4

Master i/c M. B. Abington **Coach** S. P. J. Palmer/P. Burke

Skipper and all-rounder James Arney intelligently led a young side. Joe Jenkins, a promising batsman, and Barney Rocke, a quick bowler, regularly caused problems for the opposition.

Batting J. C. W. Arney* 360 at 45.00; J. C. Jenkins 216 at 24.00; D. T. B. Salmon 113 at 14.12; J. S. Lloyd 110 at 13.75.

Bowling G. F. B. Rocke 18 at 11.66; J. C. W. Arney 13 at 15.07; J. P. L. Farley 11 at 15.45; J. S. Lloyd 11 at 17.45.

Monmouth School P9 W6 L2 D1 A8

Master i/c A. J. Jones **Coach** G. I. Burgess

Wet conditions ensured progress was slow, despite good results. The side were brilliantly captained by Jack Scarr, who received solid support from Adarsh Aji; James Lewis had no luck with the ball. Andrew Leering claimed the match award in the Old Boys game.

Batting J. Lawlor 154 at 38.50; G. D. M. R. Warwick 266 at 38.00; A. Aji 248 at 35.42; J. M. O. Scarr* 183 at 20.33; T. M. Vickers 159 at 19.87; D. Monk 124 at 17.71.

Bowling J. Aldous-Fountain 14 at 8.42; G. D. M. R. Warwick 15 at 18.73; G. Wetherall 10 at 22.70.

Newcastle-under-Lyme School P7 W2 L4 D1 A8

Master i/c G. M. Breen

The school regularly produce good bowlers and fielders but, without talented batsmen, continue to lose more matches than they win. Jack Furnival (Year 9) grabbed an all-bowled hat-trick against Castilians.

Batting No one scored 100 runs. The leading batsman was U. Ojha, who hit 81 at 13.50.

Bowling B. J. Keeler 7 at 3.71; J. E. Furnival 12 at 7.66; U. Ojha 8 at 14.25; G. T. P. Mellor 8 at 18.87.

Norwich School P10 W7 L1 D2 A3

Master i/c E. D. Hopkins **Coach** R. W. Sims

Given the side's youth, this was an impressive season. Run-scoring relied heavily on the sublime skills of Will Bryan, while the Year 11 bowling quintet took two-thirds of the wickets; dynamic fielding was a particular strength.

Batting W. A. Bryan 626 at 78.25; H. G. Parkinson 114 at 38.00; M. J. Plater 187 at 26.71; W. R. Catchpole* 161 at 23.00; H. L. D. Windridge 124 at 12.40.

Bowling J. Chatland 7 at 10.28; T. D. M. Chamberlain 13 at 12.15; R. W. Pearson 10 at 17.70; A. R. Pett 10 at 17.80; Y. Kulkarni 8 at 18.87; J. H. Nolan 13 at 20.46; L. P. Ranasinghe 10 at 29.30.

Nottingham High School

P9 W6 L3 A4

Master i/c M. Baker

The most memorable moments of a successful summer were strong team performances against Worksop, Uppingham and Trent College. Sam Johnson and Ben Carr registered two centuries each, while others made useful all-round contributions.

Batting S. J. Johnson* 456 at 57.00; A. K. Dal 241 at 40.16; B. F. D. Carr 346 at 38.44; F. G. Sail 183 at 26.14; R. Sood 141 at 20.14.

Bowling S. J. Johnson 18 at 15.50; A. K. Dal 11 at 16.45; D. R. McCarthy 15 at 17.06; J. C. McElhone 11 at 21.36.

Oakham School

P14 W9 L1 D4 A7

Master i/c F. C. Hayes **Coach** D. S. Steele

Bowler-friendly conditions allowed a useful five-man attack to be competitive throughout, but the batting lost rhythm through lack of opportunity. The exception was Tom Fell, whose 3,463 aggregate runs at over 60 were a school record.

Batting T. C. Fell* 723 at 120.50; W. R. E. Edwards 466 at 42.36; J. Kendall 149 at 37.25; L. M. D. Spears 183 at 30.50; C. W. J. Hurley 333 at 27.75.

Bowling J. Crace 7 at 5.14; O. J. Elson 22 at 13.40; M. M. R. Stark 21 at 15.47; J. Ilott 21 at 17.19; H. G. Foster 18 at 18.72; G. Maybury 9 at 35.11.

The Oratory School

P9 W4 L5 A5

Master i/c S. C. B. Tomlinson **Coach** C. B. Keegan

The squad continued to show promise and, with eight likely to return for two more years, prospects are encouraging. Tom Nugent, captaining in his fifth year in the team, made his debut for Oxfordshire against Wales, and took five wickets.

Batting T. M. Nugent* 324 at 36.00; C. E. Jacobsen 246 at 27.33; E. R. Howlett 186 at 20.66; R. F. Huysinga 146 at 16.22.

Bowling T. M. Nugent 20 at 8.50; J. R. F. Doe 13 at 17.69; C. E. Jacobsen 16 at 17.87.

Oundle School

P13 W4 L7 D2 A5

Master i/c J. R. Wake **Coaches** R. Swann/C. J. Wake

Oundle suffered their poorest results in living memory as they struggled in the wet. But there were heartening signs in the performances of captain-elect Sam Olver, and Ben Graves, an Under-15 all-rounder. Luca Illien delivered a devastating spell of pace bowling against Gresham's, taking six for seven, including four in five balls.

Batting S. T. Olver 463 at 46.30; G. A. Salisbury 189 at 37.80; B. W. M. Graves 261 at 32.62; G. H. Hodgkinson* 190 at 23.75.

Bowling L. M. Illien 13 at 14.46; C. D. F. Field 7 at 23.14; A. G. Titcomb 14 at 26.07; J. P. C. Farquhar 9 at 30.11; B. W. M. Graves 11 at 38.72.

Pate's Grammar School

P9 W2 L5 D2 A4

Master i/c S. J. Dandy **Coach** R. M. May

High expectations were dashed by the weather and a crucial lack of runs. Only Callum Carson and Matthew Williams contributed significantly with the bat. However, a successful cricket week made up for the disappointments, ending with a close draw against MCC.

Batting M. A. Williams 225 at 28.12; M. D. Morris 136 at 27.20; C. E. Carson* 194 at 24.25; J. W. Sherrington 122 at 20.33; M. S. Popli 114 at 19.00; T. P. Grew 108 at 15.42.

Bowling T. P. Grew 14 at 11.07; M. A. Williams 7 at 26.00; C. E. Carson 10 at 26.10; J. J. Savidge 9 at 29.77.

The Perse School

P7 W2 L3 D2 A3

Master i/c D. G. Roots

Wins against Ipswich and Oundle stood out in a wet, fragmented season. Fourteen-year-old Mihir Chandraker's six for 48 on debut, Tom Picton-Turbervill's 78 not out against Oundle, and Thomas Sherwin's unbeaten 79 against Ipswich were highlights.

Batting C. A. Pepper 143 at 47.66; T. J. Picton-Turbervill 155 at 31.00; T. P. H. Sherwin 178 at 29.66; W. J. M. Wright 148 at 24.66.

Bowling M. Chandraker 12 at 23.41.

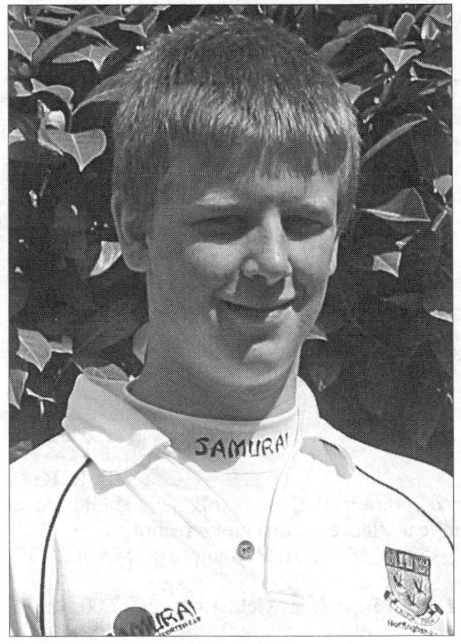

Nottingham High School's Sam Johnson averaged 57 in testing conditions. Alex Redmayne left Reed's with a career aggregate of over 2,500 runs.

Plymouth College P5 W1 L3 D1 A8

Master i/c J. R. Mears **Coach** A. Summons

A fixture card reduced to five matches gave scant opportunity for players to shine. When cricket was possible, Matt Kidd proved an excellent captain and all-rounder. He was well supported by Pasi Mawalage, Callum Cload and several able tyros.

Batting P. M. Mawalage 150 at 30.00; M. J. L. Kidd* 149 at 29.80.

Bowling D. Ackford 8 at 14.37.

Pocklington School P10 W4 L5 D1 A7

Master i/c D. Byas

Tom Sowersby, bolstered by James Hanley's 309 runs, was a capable captain. His brother Jack Sowersby and Frankie Beal chipped in with important wickets.

Batting J. R. Hanley 309 at 44.14.

Bowling J. E. Sowersby 15 at 9.66; T. A. Benthall 9 at 12.11; J. R. Hanley 7 at 19.57; T. M. Sowersby* 8 at 19.62.

Portsmouth Grammar School P9 W4 L4 D1 A7

Master i/c S. J. Curwood **Coach** S. Lavery

Jamie Rood, the skipper, Dom Humphrey and Joe Collings-Wells leave after outstanding contributions. They hand over to bowlers Seth Jackson, James Hammond and Rory Prentice, and to batsmen Andy Gorvin, Jack Marston and Sam Collings-Wells.

Batting H. R. Farrant 103 at 51.50; S. R. Collings-Wells 125 at 41.66; J. T. Marston 109 at 36.33; J. A. Collings-Wells 215 at 35.83; S. A. Jackson 101 at 16.83.

Bowling A. G. Marston 8 at 15.75; S. A. Jackson 11 at 16.18.

Prior Park College P10 W4 L5 D1 A3

Master i/c M. E. Knights **Coach** R. D. Staunton

An encouraging term saw notable contributions from a youthful squad with excellent commitment. Performances under the capable captaincy of Peter Borton improved during the summer.

Batting K. M. Kelly 219 at 24.33; W. W. Neville 188 at 23.50; P. G. S. Borton* 196 at 21.77; J. L. Tapsfield 181 at 18.10.

Bowling K. M. Kelly 9 at 21.22; S. J. Stubbs 13 at 22.61; P. G. S. Borton 9 at 25.66; H. Pearson 9 at 27.77.

Queen Elizabeth Grammar School, Wakefield P6 W3 L3 A6

Master i/c I. A. Wolfenden **Coach** C. Lawson

Downpours, hailstorms and six abandoned fixtures prevented any momentum, but the team still put together several encouraging performances. The school are indebted to five stalwarts who have now left: Nick Busby, Ben James, Chris Hoyle, George Hulme and Tom Cadzow.

Batting H. W. Booth 112 at 22.40; G. H. T. Hulme 106 at 17.66.

Bowling N. G. Busby* 7 at 12.28.

Queen Elizabeth's Hospital P6 L4 D2 A7

Master i/c P. E. Joslin **Coach** D. Forder

When play was possible, Will Pearce proved a thoughtful captain.

Batting No one scored 100 runs. The leading batsman was J. E. D. Young, who hit 52 at 17.33.

Bowling J. E. D. Young 7 at 19.71.

Queen's College, Taunton P9 W2 L4 D3 A5

Master i/c A. S. Free **Coach** D. R. Bates

Although the team bowled and fielded with control and determination, they struggled to build decent totals. Merrick Steward captained well and, after four years, leaves with a proud record.

Batting B. S. Brown 178 at 29.66; M. J. Steward* 153 at 25.50; M. P. Shawcross 165 at 23.57; E. J. N. Hayes 103 at 17.16.

Bowling M. J. Steward 16 at 13.00; B. S. Brown 14 at 13.14; J. A. Geldard 19 at 17.00; T. W. Ziegler-Evans 9 at 19.66; A. J. Benham 7 at 29.57.

Radley College P11 W8 L1 D2 A6

Master i/c J. R. W. Beasley **Coach** A. R. Wagner

A strong Radley played ruthless cricket throughout, winning both the Cowdrey and John Harvey Cups. Wilf Marriott – captain and chief run-scorer – was outstandingly supported by long-serving batsmen Nick Gubbins, who joined Middlesex, and Alex Hearne.

Batting W. W. J. Marriott* 776 at 77.60; N. R. T. Gubbins 568 at 56.80; F. J. B. Fairhead 291 at 41.57; A. G. Hearne 263 at 32.87.

Bowling P. J. B. Wright 15 at 13.73; C. J. E. Hollingworth 11 at 15.72; A. J. Lindsell 10 at 21.30; F. J. B. Fairhead 14 at 21.42; G. H. M. Bibby 10 at 22.40.

Ratcliffe College P6 W3 L2 D1 A8

Master i/c E. O. Woodcock

Joseph Hesketh shepherded the team expertly in the matches that survived near-incessant rainfall. Samuel Nightingale batted well in his first season, and Frederik Notman bowled with aggression.

Batting S. C. Nightingale 222 at 55.50; F. R. Notman 122 at 24.40.

Bowling W. A. Gent 8 at 7.87; F. R. Notman 9 at 12.33; O. W. James 8 at 14.25.

Reading Blue Coat School P7 W3 L2 D2 A6

Master i/c G. C. Turner **Coach** P. D. C. Wise

Just five matches reached a definite conclusion, including victory over Merchant Taylors', Northwood, in the inaugural fixture. James Halson hit a sparkling 132 against MCC, while Shashank Iyer passed 300 runs.

Batting J. J. Halson 212 at 70.66; S. Iyer 316 at 63.20; P. J. Castleden* 145 at 24.16.

Bowling W. J. Stone 9 at 9.55; J. W. Andrews 7 at 12.42; P. J. Castleden 12 at 15.33; J. Pajwani 7 at 17.71.

Reed's School P12 W5 L5 D2 A6

Master i/c M. R. Dunn **Coach** K. T. Medlycott

Alex Redmayne dodged the rain to hit three unbeaten nineties in his final season and pass 2,500 first-team runs. The skipper, Harry Coates, led the bowling, with support from Ben Sandwith, Kieran Corbett and Stephen Hobson.

Batting A. J. S. Redmayne 445 at 63.57; M. A. Macpherson 394 at 49.25; S. K. Stewart-Taylor 124 at 31.00; O. M. D. Kolk 246 at 30.75; P. D. Salt 119 at 23.80; J. A. Malthouse 130 at 21.66.

Bowling H. J. H. Coates* 21 at 13.19; B. M. Sandwith 19 at 15.52; K. M. Corbett 16 at 21.37; S. Hobson 13 at 23.30; R. J. Woolston 7 at 35.71; J. A. Hitchcock 7 at 51.00.

Reigate Grammar School
P6 W1 L5 A9

Master i/c P. R. Mann **Coach** J. E. Benjamin

Nine abandoned fixtures left the team struggling to find form, and results were disappointing. Nevertheless, Luke Drage was a fine captain on and off the field.

Batting L. M. Drage* 138 at 27.60; W. P. Saward 106 at 21.20.

Bowling L. M. Drage 8 at 15.12; D. M. P. Drage 11 at 19.09.

Repton School
P14 W7 L6 D1 A3

Master i/c I. M. Pollock **Coaches** H. B. Dytham/J. A. Afford

Repton completed a good proportion of games considering the rain. A team that had a blend of experience and youth fared less well than they would have liked, although results were perfectly respectable. Canadian international Nitish Kumar was the only centurion.

Batting N. R. Kumar 406 at 33.83; M. R. Fletcher* 301 at 33.44; M. G. I. Goodacre 315 at 31.50; L. P. Cosford 156 at 31.20; H. J. White 176 at 22.00; H. M. Eldred 218 at 21.80; A. T. Hibell 168 at 21.00.

Bowling H. J. White 10 at 16.90; H. M. Eldred 19 at 17.52; S. P. Cotter 17 at 21.11; N. R. Kumar 12 at 24.66; J. M. McDonald 9 at 25.77; O. H. West 7 at 32.42.

Rossall School
P8 W5 L2 D1 A4

Master i/c N. P. James **Coach** D. Jones

Luke Williams's eight for 24 against Merchant Taylors', Crosby, was the star turn of a disrupted summer. Given better weather, a young side developing mature skills should prosper.

Batting J. Morrison 125 at 31.25; J. Wilson 123 at 30.75; L. C. Williams 152 at 25.33; H. Southern 123 at 17.57.

Bowling L. C. Williams 13 at 7.23; J. Landmann 13 at 9.15; W. J. Parker 7 at 11.71; F. J. Forster 7 at 21.42; J. Williams 7 at 21.57.

The Royal Grammar School, Guildford
P10 W6 L3 D1

Master i/c S. B. R. Shore

Steve Shore relinquished responsibility for cricket after 34 years, and the gods sent rain in response: the RGS festival at Lancaster was completely washed out. The captain, Andy Goodchild, batted really well between the deluges to average over 67, and the seamers were tight. The team did enjoy some sun in the Caribbean, with five win and four defeats in St Kitts.

Batting A. N. Goodchild* 473 at 67.57.

Bowling S. J. Jelly 10 at 14.20; A. N. Goodchild 13 at 14.30; A. C. Waghorn 14 at 17.35.

The Royal Grammar School, Worcester
P12 W5 L6 D1 A7

Master i/c M. D. Wilkinson **Coach** P. J. Newport

A good bowling attack was let down by a lack of runs from the top order. Year 10 off-spinner Elliot Bartlett had a fine match against MCC, taking six for 45, including a hat-trick, before hitting 53 not out to win the game.

Batting D. B. Goodyear 308 at 28.00; C. D. Tonks 148 at 21.14; W. G. French* 213 at 17.75; C. E. J. Lawton 164 at 14.90.

Bowling E. A. Bartlett 21 at 13.38; H. L. Bates 16 at 14.87; W. J. E. Bury 11 at 14.90; W. G. French 15 at 17.13; H. M. Selvey 7 at 29.00.

Royal Hospital School
P6 W2 L2 D2 A9

Master i/c T. D. Topley **Coach** D. W. Hawkley

Of the six games not lost to the rain, two – against Woodbridge and the XL Club – were won. Nandish Patel led the side purposefully and, with Ben and Joshua Allday, was responsible for the bulk of runs. Opening bowler Charlie Stuart was the leading seamer.

Batting J. E. Allday 144 at 72.00; B. Allday 201 at 50.25; N. Patel* 181 at 36.20.

Bowling C. Stuart 10 at 21.80.

Rugby School
P13 W5 L3 D5 A10

Master i/c M. J. Semmence **Coach** T. W. Roberts

An eight-wicket win over Oundle was the highlight of a pretty dreadful term. Jake Kings left with aggregates of 2,156 runs and 117 wickets.

Batting W. J. Briggs 245 at 40.83; H. P. Wilson 270 at 33.75; P. G. Clarke 229 at 25.44; J. B. Kings* 278 at 23.16; C. R. D. Goodfellow 156 at 22.28; J. D. Gilder 175 at 21.87; T. P. McKibbin 103 at 14.71.

Bowling A. G. Bennett-Jones 11 at 16.72; J. B. Kings 25 at 18.28; H. J. Mallinder 13 at 18.30; G. E. O. Terry 10 at 20.30; P. G. Clarke 9 at 24.11; J. D. Gilder 10 at 29.80.

Rydal Penrhos School — P9 W1 L7 D1 A4

Master i/c M. T. Leach — **Coach** M. H. Bennett

Despite the loss of three top players from 2011 – and a serious lack of cricket – Rydal remained motivated and enthusiastic. Andrew Welden developed in the art of leadership, and made important all-round contributions.

Batting S. T. Kitchen 253 at 31.62; A. M. Welden* 203 at 22.55; H. W. Holmes 130 at 16.25.

Bowling A. M. Welden 11 at 18.63; H. W. Holmes 7 at 24.42; J. P. Maguire 7 at 27.42.

Ryde School — P6 W5 D1 A4

Master i/c C. Sutton — **Coach** M. J. Jones

Ryde had another excellent campaign, winning five games and drawing with MCC in the sixth. Jonty Leggett and Samuel Starkins, playing with flair and consistency, gave the side backbone. Eight of the squad should return, so prospects seem good.

Batting J. C. A. Leggett* 154 without dismissal; S. Starkins 322 at 80.50; J. C. Asher 174 at 29.00.

Bowling S. Starkins 12 at 16.16; J. C. A. Leggett 11 at 23.00; J. Jayerajah 13 at 29.61.

St Albans School — P10 W7 L3 A8

Master i/c C. C. Hudson — **Coach** M. C. Ilott

This was a strange season: no cricket in the first three weeks, then five matches in three days, followed by another blank three weeks. Centurion, the touring South African team, were St Albans' toughest opponents.

Batting G. F. B. Scott 263 at 37.57; J. E. Scott* 216 at 30.85; P. Scott 128 at 21.33; R. E. Goldstone 149 at 21.28; D. E. Watt 141 at 17.62; A. J. Goldstone 105 at 11.66.

Bowling N. S. Parkash 19 at 8.73; P. Scott 12 at 9.33; A. J. Goldstone 9 at 11.88; G. F. B. Scott 10 at 16.30; A. S. Kulkarni 11 at 17.36; J. E. Scott 9 at 19.66.

St Benedict's School, Ealing — P22 W15 L5 D2

Master i/c J. P. Thisanayagam

A young and dynamic squad enjoyed a highly successful summer. There were strong contributions from all-rounders Leo Hadcock and Nabel Shaikh. Batsmen Louie Millman and Harry Britt also shone. Spinner Ben Chippendale grabbed 40 wickets.

Batting L. J. Millman 630 at 39.37; H. Britt 623 at 34.61; L. V. Hadcock 379 at 27.07; N. J. Shaikh 356 at 20.94; M. A. J. Codrington* 212 at 14.13; J. J. Spanswick 122 at 13.55; M. G. Cassidy 143 at 13.00.

Bowling J. Somerville 7 at 10.57; L. V. Hadcock 32 at 11.87; B. D. P. Chippendale 40 at 13.75; N. J. Shaikh 30 at 14.00; N. Lyndon 14 at 17.21; D. F. L. Howe 11 at 23.63; M. A. J. Codrington 8 at 24.37.

St Edmund's School, Canterbury — P8 W3 L5 A5

Master i/c A. R. Jones — **Coach** S. Buckingham

With Tom Phillis and captain Dominic Barrett alone in showing the skill and aptitude to stay at the crease, the shallowness of the batting proved decisive. Deveena Pithia was outstanding with the ball and, given better fielding, would have taken many more wickets.

Batting T. J. W. Phillis 256 at 36.57; E. Lawlor 117 at 23.40; D. J. Barrett* 170 at 21.25.

Bowling D. Pithia 9 at 23.77; D. J. Barrett 7 at 28.42.

St Edward's School, Oxford — P20 W11 L3 D6 A4

Master i/c S. J. O. Roche — **Coaches** R. W. J. Howitt/R. C. Hooton

Ollie Smith shrewdly led a young side that came of age, gaining 11 victories and suffering just one defeat by another school. Joe Barrett's innings of 152 and Feroz Baig's six for 33 were stand-out performances; George Chaffer made telling all-round contributions.

Batting M. A. H. Hammond 532 at 38.00; J. H. Barrett 582 at 32.33; G. E. J. Chaffer 421 at 26.31; R. T. L. Willis 363 at 25.92; F. Baig 383 at 25.53; C. M. Dickinson 135 at 15.00; O. P. H. Smith* 230 at 13.52; F. J. Kerr-Dineen 120 at 10.90.

Bowling J. M. Morland 11 at 13.27; F. P. A. Simon 23 at 13.43; G. E. J. Chaffer 14 at 15.57; F. Baig 24 at 19.45; A. S. Hargreaves 19 at 23.84; M. A. H. Hammond 23 at 24.00; R. T. L. Willis 11 at 26.18.

Ben Chippendale, from St Benedict's, Ealing, took 40 wickets at 13.75 with his off-spin. Rory Snowball played 60 matches for St George's, Weybridge, over five years.

St George's College, Weybridge

P12 W5 L6 D1 A4

Master i/c M. T. Harrison **Coach** J. R. P. Heath

Three wins to close the season were just reward for Jamie Mann, an outstanding captain. All-rounder Rory Snowball leaves after 60 matches spanning five years. Fourteen-year-old James Smith was the top wicket-taker.

Batting J. P. C. Clark 211 at 42.20; T. C. Rowland 185 at 37.00; R. O. Mainwaring 184 at 36.80; R. G. F. Snowball 316 at 35.11; F. H. Annandale 208 at 26.00; T. H. Wrigley 196 at 21.77; J. D. C. Wright 118 at 14.75; J. E. V. Mann* 129 at 14.33.

Bowling J. E. V. Mann* 13 at 19.92; T. H. Wrigley 10 at 21.70; R. G. F. Snowball 13 at 22.00; J. A. Smith 16 at 27.50; A. C. Hackett 11 at 30.27; J. C. Dominy 7 at 30.57.

St John's School, Leatherhead

P6 W2 L2 D2 A2

Master i/c J. M. A. Ashton **Coach** I. S. Trott

Challenging conditions and miserable weather did not prevent Robbie Heald from leading the side with distinction. Charlie Glanville bowled well with the new ball, and both James Lander and Josh Howe showed their versatility.

Batting A. A. Dyson 111 at 111.00; J. W. Howe 140 at 28.00; J. T. Lander 130 at 26.00; S. R. Roberts 144 at 24.00.

Bowling C. E. Glanville 14 at 5.92; J. W. Howe 8 at 13.50; J. T. Lander 9 at 19.33.

St Joseph's College, Ipswich

P18 W8 L8 D2 A7

Master i/c R. Jones **Coach** M. W. Patterson

Both skipper Ethan Wright and wicketkeeper Ryan Clark prospered with the bat in a dank season. Medium-pacer Daniel Pryke took most wickets, but fellow seamer Matthew Hunn missed much of the summer with Essex Seconds. The best victory came against Framlingham's strong batting side.

Batting E. J. Wright* 492 at 28.94; R. D. Clark 382 at 22.47; M. D. Hunn 167 at 18.55; A. J. Wilkinson 197 at 17.90; J. J. Sayer 125 at 12.50; A. J. Sayer 123 at 10.25.

Bowling M. D. Hunn 16 at 11.93; A. Kingdon 20 at 15.40; D. R. Pryke 24 at 16.95; J. De Cosimo 19 at 19.94; A. Moon 9 at 21.44; A. J. Sayer 9 at 22.11; E. J. Wright 12 at 41.25.

St Lawrence College P10 W2 L6 D2 A3

Master i/c T. Moulton

The batsmen struggled on difficult pitches, and several matches were lost when 20 or 30 more runs might have brought victory. The bowlers enjoyed themselves more, with Connor Bluemel outstanding. Eight of the squad should return, so there is optimism for 2013.

Batting T. J. A. Collins* 239 at 29.87; R. A. Keeley 115 at 12.77.

Bowling J. O. Greenslade 7 at 12.85; C. E. Bluemel 12 at 13.41; T. J. A. Collins 9 at 22.44; A. T. Cape 8 at 26.75.

St Paul's School P16 W5 L9 D2 A3

Master i/c M. G. Howat **Coach** A. G. J. Fraser

Slow left-armer Oscar Dewhurst and medium-pacer Oliver Quarry bowled well. There were good wins in the 50/40 League against RGS Guildford, St George's and Reed's. Fragile batting was the Achilles heel.

Batting S. R. G. Howard 323 at 26.91; L. C. Hardingham 280 at 21.53; G. J. Brown* 296 at 21.14; J. K. R. Fothergill 150 at 18.75; T. B. Edmonds 266 at 17.73.

Bowling O. R. B. Dewhurst 17 at 16.76; O. R. J. Quarry 21 at 20.76; T. R. D. Parker 14 at 28.14; H. Adnan 12 at 29.25.

St Peter's School, York P12 W3 L5 D4 A5

Master i/c D. Kirby **Coach** G. J. Sharp

St Peter's suffered a disappointing season. Although Will Booth and Hamish Lynde fared well, an ostensibly strong batting unit rarely fired. Bowlers were more successful: an opening attack of Charlie Elliot and Hamish Lynde were well supported by spinners Angus Shaw and Jonnie Eleanor.

Batting H. D. Lynde 264 at 37.71; W. A. Booth 308 at 34.22; F. J. Adams 243 at 27.00; S. A. McCullagh 176 at 17.60; C. R. Elliot 163 at 16.30; M. R. Chan 138 at 13.80.

Bowling J. E. A. Eleanor 13 at 12.84; C. R. Elliot 14 at 16.78; H. D. Lynde 18 at 17.00; M. R. Chan 9 at 17.22; A. R. I. Shaw* 17 at 21.11.

Sedbergh School P11 W5 L3 D3 A8

Master i/c C. P. Mahon **Coach** M. P. Speight

A strong side never gathered much momentum, though highlights included back-to-back hundreds for Daniel Gomersall and a nine-wicket win over MCC. The team reached the National Twenty20 semi-final and had an excellent tour of Barbados, where they were unlucky to lose in the semi-final of the Sir Garfield Sobers Festival.

Batting D. J. Gomersall 327 at 46.71; G. A. M. Francis 322 at 40.25; T. D. Raglan* 171 at 34.20; J. H. Jessop 264 at 26.40; M. D. Lloyd 129 at 18.42; J. A. Davis 104 at 17.33.

Bowling G. F. Nicholson 15 at 15.53; T. D. Raglan 15 at 16.20; J. A. Davis 7 at 16.28; H. J. A. Watson 8 at 20.87; C. R. Parker 10 at 22.80.

Sevenoaks School P13 W5 L7 D1 A3

Master i/c C. J. Tavaré **Coach** P. J. Hulston

Stronger at bowling than batting, an inexperienced team came good in the second half of the season. The best win came by 136 runs against Dover College: Jack Hulston made 89 not out, and Rex Boulter 66. Leading wicket-taker Natasha Farrant was called up to the senior Kent Ladies' team.

Batting J. P. Hulston* 338 at 33.80; R. R. C. Boulter 189 at 21.00; N. M. Makepeace 189 at 14.53; L. A. F. Ashe-Jepson 110 at 11.00.

Bowling N. E. Farrant 21 at 8.76; W. P. Gill 8 at 13.62; J. P. Hulston 14 at 17.14; E. C. Thomas 10 at 17.40; K. G. Davey 12 at 21.83; R. W. J. Harris 12 at 22.25.

Shebbear College P6 W3 L3 A4

Master i/c A. B. Bryan

After losing more than half the 2011 side, the team achieved reasonable success. Jack Hatton, the captain, finished top of both averages.

Batting J. A. Hatton* 199 at 66.33; D. Buckland 117 at 29.25; J. Reader 102 at 20.40.

Bowling J. A. Hatton 12 at 7.66; M. Davey 9 at 9.77.

Sherborne School P8 W5 L2 D1 A11

Master i/c J. R. Preston **Coach** A. Willows

Grabbing what cricket they could between the cloudbursts, Sherborne beat Millfield, Marlborough, Bryanston, Blundell's and Somerset College (from Western Cape). Tim Pope led well throughout, while Ed Coulson's 108 against Marlborough was the innings of the season.

Batting T. S. Pope* 275 at 68.75; E. C. Coulson 264 at 44.00; D. S. Buck 251 at 35.85; O. R. T. Sale 175 at 29.16; D. L. Scaglioni 161 at 26.83.

Bowling D. S. Buck 11 at 18.18; O. R. T. Sale 14 at 18.71; A. T. Merritt 12 at 20.25.

Shiplake College P9 W3 L5 T1 A8

Master i/c J. H. Howorth **Coach** S. D. Cane-Hardy

Skipper and wicketkeeper-batsmen Ben Francis directed a decent bowling attack led by Zac Jones and spinner Ollie Maclaurin. For runs, the team relied on Francis, Jones and Henry Breckenridge. Most of the bowlers should return for 2013, but the batting could be thin.

Batting B. Francis* 293 at 36.62; Z. D. A. Jones 246 at 30.75; H. D. Breckenridge 161 at 23.00.

Bowling O. Maclaurin 10 at 9.40; Z. D. A. Jones 15 at 13.13; T. F. Stevens 10 at 17.80; I. A. S. Brown 10 at 18.40.

Shrewsbury School P14 W11 L1 D2 A5

Master i/c A. S. Barnard **Coach** A. P. Pridgeon

With ten of the squad who had won the 2011 National Schools Twenty20 still available, expectations for 2012 were high. Results were excellent, but Millfield proved too strong in the T20. The Upper Sixth group have been outstanding in winning two national T20 awards, beating ten overseas schools and losing only seven games in their first-team careers.

Batting S. G. Leach 485 at 60.62; J. G. Hudson-Williams 273 at 54.60; E. J. Pollock 427 at 53.37; H. G. Lewis* 356 at 39.55; A. W. Pollock 161 at 32.20; J. F. Bailey 149 at 29.80; M. R. J. Prescott 101 at 25.25; R. A. J. Smith 128 at 18.28.

Bowling R. A. J. Smith 20 at 9.15; H. G. Lewis 9 at 14.88; E. J. Pollock 9 at 17.44; J. N. Aston 15 at 18.00; H. C. Blofield 14 at 19.21; M. R. J. Prescott 8 at 20.87; A. W. Pollock 9 at 28.22.

Silcoates School P7 W5 L1 D1 A6

Master i/c G. M. Roberts **Coach** J. F. C. Leathley

This was an excellent season for a young team, who won five games and lost just once. Openers Charlie Mitchell and Will Fraine batted with great maturity. Leg-spinner Liam Hyde (Year 9) made his Yorkshire Academy debut.

Batting W. A. R. Fraine 364 at 72.80; C. H. Mitchell 262 at 65.50; W. M. Simpson 191 at 38.20.

Bowling L. Hyde 7 at 8.42; W. M. Simpson 8 at 21.12; W. A. R. Fraine 8 at 22.75; M. Khan 8 at 28.25.

Simon Langton Grammar School P5 W2 L2 D1 A4

Master i/c R. H. Green

The school's pre-season tour to St Lucia proved the pinnacle of the season, with three victories in five matches. At home, the weather put paid to nearly half the fixtures.

Batting S. A. Burt 173 at 173.00; M. P. Brady 108 at 36.00.

Bowling J. A. Loft 9 at 8.11.

Solihull School P12 W6 L5 D1 A11

Master i/c D. L. Hemp

Given that the weather stymied so much, 2012 was a reasonable season. Darryl Brotherhood was a strong leader, while Jamie Hughes again bowled with accuracy and control.

Batting J. Hughes 357 at 29.75; S. Montieri 131 at 26.20; D. Brotherhood* 293 at 24.41; O. J. Haley 239 at 23.90; C. J. Walker 171 at 21.37; J. W. B. Allen 188 at 20.88; T. G. Starkey 171 at 17.10.

Bowling J. Hughes 23 at 17.60; C. J. Walker 17 at 24.47; D. Brotherhood 9 at 26.33; M. Davis 8 at 29.62; D. J. Wigley 7 at 41.85.

Stamford School P11 W6 L2 T1 D2 A10

Master i/c D. N. Jackson **Coaches** D. G. Colley/D. W. Headley

Between the puddles, a young side matured under the guidance of Jonathan Williams and Alex Emerson. Nine of the squad are expected to return, and prospects seem sound for 2013.

Batting J. A. Richardson 390 at 48.75; T. H. Charlton 275 at 39.28; C. Page-Morris 171 at 28.50; B. E. Groom 241 at 26.77; G. Martin 125 at 15.62.

Bowling J. Corder 12 at 20.00; T. H. Charlton 11 at 20.45; A. Emerson 11 at 28.09; J. P. Harrington 9 at 28.88; C. Page-Morris 7 at 44.42.

Stewart's Melville College, Edinburgh P14 W7 L6 D1 A3

Master i/c A. Ranson

The school were delighted to win the Scottish Schools' Cricketers Cup for the first time.

Batting M. Ahmed* 360 at 30.00; M. D. Angelini 247 at 24.70; M. Miller 303 at 23.30; S. C. Doherty 231 at 19.25; J. J. Sohail 235 at 18.07.

Bowling M. Ahmed 22 at 9.09; J. J. Sohail 18 at 9.88; M. Bunker 12 at 20.25; C. L. Sloman 11 at 25.27.

Stonyhurst College P5 W2 L2 D1 A4

Master i/c G. Thomas

A truncated season saw a young side break even. Senior all-rounder Tim Le Breton led the team outstandingly, almost defeating Giggleswick on his own: he took five for 20, then hit 62* of the 74 needed for victory. Tom Morgan, in Year 11, showed promise with the ball.

Batting T. W. A. Le Breton* 101 at 25.25.

Bowling T. R. C. Morgan 10 at 10.70; T. W. Fogden 9 at 19.33; T. W. A. Le Breton 11 at 22.27.

Stowe School P16 W14 L1 D1 A4

Master i/c J. A. Knott **Coach** P. A. Arnold

With 14 wins in 16 games, this was one of the best seasons in the school's history. The defeats of Bedford (by 140 runs) and Oakham (seven wickets) were exceptional. Against Wellingborough there was a school-record opening stand of 337*, containing centuries from Ben Duckett (213*) and Jake Olley (101*). Success rested on an all-round team performance.

Batting B. M. Duckett* 942 at 104.66; B. T. Paine 298 at 59.60; J. A. Olley 524 at 43.66; R. D. R. White 333 at 37.00; G. L. Jackman 355 at 32.27.

Bowling H. W. H. Woodward 21 at 11.00; H. J. R. Martin 16 at 15.43; C. G. Roberts 23 at 16.65; B. T. Paine 17 at 17.88; R. D. R. White 14 at 19.00; J. R. Chaplin 10 at 24.00.

Strathallan School P6 W1 L2 D3 A9

Master i/c G. S. R. Robertson **Coach** I. L. Philip

Continuity was hard to achieve with so many matches abandoned. Captain and Scotland Under-19 player Nick Farrar had solid batting support from Sam Culham. The team were runners-up in the first year of the Scottish Schools Twenty20 Cup.

Batting N. A. G. Farrar* 177 at 44.25; S. D. Culham 186 at 31.00.

Bowling N. Everett 7 at 22.42.

Sutton Valence School P9 W5 L2 D2 A4

Master i/c V. J. Wells

Taking advantage of the damp conditions, seamers Harry Bee, Harrison Wells and Miles Henslow enjoyed themselves. Of the batsmen, Bobby Harris did well to average 51.

Batting R. C. Harris 409 at 51.12; H. J. Wells 161 at 23.00; W. P. Cook 155 at 22.14; B. D. Cooke 106 at 15.14.

Bowling H. J. Wells 13 at 11.00; M. T. Henslow* 8 at 15.00; H. L. Bee 15 at 17.60; A. J. Dooley 7 at 33.42; R. E. Dooley 7 at 37.85.

Taunton School P13 W10 L1 D2 A4

Master i/c S. T. Hogg **Coach** H. K. C. Todd

Another fine season was dominated by the classy batting of the captain, Thomas Abell. In four seasons he scored over 3,600 runs, including 17 centuries. Abell and George Cook were an effective opening attack, well supported by slow-bowling all-rounders Charlie Miles and Josh Kelly.

Batting T. B. Abell* 1,156 at 192.66; C. L. Miles 347 at 34.70; M. P. Kelly 259 at 32.37; G. P. Hallas 261 at 29.00; C. T. Solanki 229 at 19.08; J. F. Kelly 181 at 16.45.

Bowling G. A. Cook 18 at 14.50; T. B. Abell 19 at 15.68; J. F. Kelly 22 at 18.18; C. L. Miles 17 at 23.76; J. R. Pilcher 7 at 26.57.

Tiffin School P13 W3 L7 D3 A5

Master i/c M. J. Williams

Results were disappointing, with the experienced players struggling to find fluency. However, the younger boys performed well in both disciplines, showing tremendous promise for 2013.

Batting M. J. Dilworth 337 at 33.70; P. G. Chamberlain 168 at 24.00; S. P. Krishnan 212 at 19.27; K. S. Toor* 239 at 18.38; R. S. J. Forster 173 at 17.30.
Bowling B. A. Bhatti 7 at 7.42; A. Khanna 7 at 8.14; A. J. Watkins 18 at 14.05; A. R. Garner 17 at 20.88; E. S. Carter 10 at 21.90; J. A. Baugh 8 at 23.75.

Tonbridge School P16 W8 L6 D2 A2

Master i/c A. R. Whittall **Coach** I. Baldock

Tonbridge had a mixed season, though there were some special performances. Highlights included a ten-wicket victory over Eton and the Twenty20 defeat of Millfield. Tom Coldman showed excellent leadership; all-rounder Richard O'Grady and Oscar King also chipped in.
Batting J. J. C. Smallwood 208 at 41.60; T. F. J. Coldman* 282 at 25.63; R. J. O'Grady 305 at 25.41; O. B. King 374 at 24.93; B. J. Brandt 178 at 17.80; A. H. Ward 172 at 17.20; A. J. O'Neill 188 at 15.66.
Bowling C. R. S. Perera-Slater 19 at 15.63; R. J. O'Grady 23 at 17.56; D. Patel 11 at 22.90; T. F. J. Coldman 22 at 23.13; A. W. Hume 15 at 25.46; M. F. Eliet 10 at 35.30.

Trent College P14 W5 L4 T1 D4 A8

Master i/c S. A. J. Boswell **Coach** D. R. Hartley

The college had a difficult and challenging season with the bat, rarely able to forge winning positions. Connor Marshall was the leading run-scorer, while Ross Carnelley, the top wicket-taker, had best figures of six for six.
Batting C. R. Marshall 303 at 43.28; B. Trembling 151 at 25.16; J. A. Leuenberger 228 at 22.80; A. J. Britton 183 at 18.30; R. T. Carnelley 180 at 18.00.
Bowling R. T. Carnelley 21 at 15.38; C. R. Marshall 14 at 17.64; J. M. A. Fisher 18 at 19.72.

Truro School P5 W2 L1 D2 A11

Master i/c A. D. Lawrence

Week in week out, the summer put paid to any cricketing ambitions. With arguably the strongest squad for over 15 years, Truro managed to play just three games to a decisive finish.
Batting No one scored 100 runs. The leading batsman was T. S. Burford, who hit 70 at 70.00.
Bowling J. Vanstone 9 at 8.66.

University College School P7 W2 L5 A8

Master i/c S. M. Bloomfield **Coach** W. G. Jones

UCS possessed a better side than results suggest. David Franklin led both the team and the batting in upbeat fashion, while Carl Diebitsch was the principal all-rounder; everyone suffered, though, from a lack of practice and match time. Wins against Latymer and Old Gowers showed what was possible.
Batting D. J. Franklin* 188 at 26.85; C. D. Diebitsch 147 at 24.50.
Bowling R. Anzsar 9 at 11.55; M. Z. Chapman 10 at 17.30; C. D. Diebitsch 9 at 17.55.

Uppingham School P12 W2 L6 T1 D3 A2

Master i/c Q. H. Sayed **Coaches** T. R. Ward/T. Makhzangi

The batsmen's fragile temperaments prevented a more impressive win–loss ratio. The bowlers were in better heart, with Rupert Clark, Devesh Patel, Otto Esse and Shiv Thakor providing moments to remember. However, the lasting memory was the team spirit engendered by Thakor's captaincy.
Batting S. J. Thakor* 349 at 49.85; S. C. R. Snoxall 156 at 19.50; L. S. W. Blakey 115 at 19.16; H. A. Glatman 122 at 15.25.
Bowling S. J. Thakor 25 at 10.84; O. T. H. Esse 15 at 23.80; R. H. M. Clark 7 at 28.14.

Victoria College, Jersey P15 W2 L11 D2 A5

Master i/c M. D. Smith **Coach** C. E. Minty

This was a year in which the younger players grabbed their opportunities, with Jack Ingle and James Duckett finishing as leading wicket-takers. Luke Gallichan had an excellent term, scoring 436 runs, including 91 not out against Elizabeth College.
Batting L. E. W. Gallichan 436 at 39.63; A. F. Cooke 222 at 18.50; M. M. O. Watkins 186 at 16.90; O. M. H. Johnson 174 at 15.81; C. J. Bodenstein* 140 at 15.55; E. C. Corbel 152 at 15.20.
Bowling R. H. Evans 7 at 8.14; J. N. Duckett 14 at 13.64; J. R. Ingle 15 at 18.66; W. P. Harris 8 at 20.50; O. M. H. Johnson 9 at 21.55; C. J. Bodenstein 7 at 23.00; A. F. Cooke 9 at 39.33; L. E. W. Gallichan 7 at 39.42.

Left-armer Natasha Farrant took most wickets for Sevenoaks, and played for Kent Ladies. Silcoates' openers Will Fraine and Charlie Mitchell put on an unbroken 261 in 45 overs against Hymers.

Warwick School

P14 W8 L4 D2 A8

Master i/c G. A. Tedstone **Coach** S. R. G. Francis

The school gained success not through individual performances but through team unity, and Jonathan Byrd's exceptional leadership played a pivotal part. A much-improved away record, plus solid home form, made the most of an abysmal summer.

Batting T. J. M. Glanfield 284 at 31.55; G. Tedstone 285 at 28.50; J. E. Salmon 248 at 27.55; J. R. Byrd* 256 at 25.60; T. R. Pigott 156 at 22.28; H. J. Philpot 199 at 18.09.

Bowling N. J. Couzens 23 at 15.56; J. Hickman 14 at 20.78; G. F. A. Sutcliffe 10 at 23.00.

Wellingborough School

P8 W3 L4 D1 A4

Master i/c G. E. Houghton **Coach** M. B. Loye

An inexperienced group produced some fair cricket in poor conditions and showed distinct promise. Charlie Macdonell, a youthful captain, was the stand-out all-rounder. Fourteen-year-old Ben Wall had best figures of six for 15.

Batting C. M. Macdonell* 322 at 53.66; J. W. R. Bowers 169 at 33.80; M. J. Bell 155 at 22.14.

Bowling B. T. Wall 7 at 11.42; C. M. Macdonell 8 at 23.75.

Wellington College

P14 W9 L3 T1 D1 A3

Master i/c D. M. Pratt **Coach** G. D. Franklin

Revelling in the damp conditions, Jack Wood and Virain Kanwar spearheaded the attack; Pete Melhuish and JJ Dewes gave useful assistance. Captain and left-hander Connor Nurse provided the bulk of the runs.

Batting C. J. Nurse* 401 at 30.84; O. W. Rendell 169 at 28.16; J. C. H. Hersh 337 at 22.46; J. M. Wood 144 at 13.09; C. G. J. Leith 123 at 8.78.

Bowling A. J. Newson 7 at 10.28; J. M. Wood 15 at 14.06; P. R. Melhuish 19 at 14.73; C. J. Nurse 15 at 16.73; J. J. N. Dewes 19 at 18.94; V. Kanwar 11 at 19.36; C. G. J. Leith 13 at 22.53; T. D. S. McClean 9 at 22.66.

Wellington School

P9 W2 L5 D2 A4

Master i/c M. H. Richards **Coach** P. S. Jones

James Carson, the skipper, was comfortably the leading batsman, and often cleared the ropes; the spinners offered good control, and the fielding was energetic. An optimist might say the squad gained

valuable experience coping with difficult conditions. Several matches were played in the Twenty20 format.
Batting J. C. Carson* 327 at 40.87.
Bowling W. H. Mellor 10 at 23.40.

Wells Cathedral School P11 W6 L4 D1 A2

Master i/c R. J. Newman **Coach** C. R. Keast

The side finished the season with some encouraging victories. Nick Jarman was especially consistent, and there were strong individual performance from other senior players.
Batting N. C. Jarman* 485 at 60.62; D. G. Nancekievil 368 at 36.80; G. E. Killen 150 at 18.75.
Bowling G. N. Day 16 at 18.37; M. A. Strachan-Stephens 10 at 21.00; N. C. Jarman 11 at 22.36.

West Buckland School P11 W6 L3 D2 A3

Master i/c D. R. Ford

Deprived of the services of the twins Jamie and Craig Overton, who were regularly on duty either for Somerset or England Under-19, the team nevertheless adapted well. A committed squad recorded some excellent results without any individual standing out.
Batting N. M. Shervington 229 at 25.44; H. Platts-Martin 210 at 23.33; H. D. Booker* 178 at 22.25; G. H. Laing 192 at 17.45; S. P. Witheridge 117 at 16.71.
Bowling H. D. Booker 16 at 11.43; P. G. Treweeke 17 at 14.00; P. J. R. Crane 10 at 16.10; F. P. O'Donnell 15 at 16.86; S. P. Witheridge 11 at 18.72.

Westminster School P11 W5 L5 D1 A7

Master i/c J. D. Kershen **Coaches** P. N. Weekes/F. S. M. Barrett

The batting highlights were two centuries from Milo Johnson and one from Kit Winder; George Bustin added reliability. Spinner Kavi Amin claimed four five-fors, and only one first-team regular has left.
Batting M. A. Johnson 429 at 42.90; K. J. Winder 255 at 42.50; G. D. Bustin 285 at 35.62; L. R. Nelson-Jones* 110 at 15.71.
Bowling K. D. Amin 30 at 10.83; B. J. Graff 7 at 18.57; K. J. Winder 9 at 27.11; L. R. Nelson-Jones 10 at 27.40.

Whitgift School P19 W11 L5 T1 D2 A6

Master i/c D. M. Ward **Coach** S. J. Woodward

The 16-year-old captain, Dominic Sibley, led the side intelligently and batted with maturity to average almost 50. Aman Shinwari and Jack Winslade, who picked up 54 wickets between them, headed the bowling attack, as well as hitting useful runs. Whitgift beat Harrow for the first time, and reached the quarter-final of the National Twenty20.
Batting D. P. Sibley* 697 at 49.78; T. Walters 178 at 29.66; A. Shinwari 323 at 29.36; G. J. Dann 316 at 21.06; J. R. Winslade 357 at 19.83; J. R. Lloyd 325 at 19.11; H. Patel 100 at 14.28; H. A. Hanford 110 at 13.75.
Bowling A. Shinwari 26 at 12.03; J. R. Winslade 28 at 14.78; H. Patel 18 at 18.38; J. R. Lloyd 23 at 20.69; D. P. Sibley 18 at 24.88.

Winchester College P12 W4 L8 A7

Master i/c G. J. Watson **Coaches** B. L. Reed/P. N. Gover

The 2012 season was memorable for atrocious weather and the team's fighting spirit: of the eight defeats, four were by tantalisingly small margins. Ollie Mills again proved an efficient captain; a catch here or a decision there could have made a significant difference to a hard-working side.
Batting O. C. H. Mills* 472 at 42.90; D. A. Escott 321 at 40.12; E. A. Wylde 211 at 23.44; A. J. Sachak 102 at 17.00; L. J. Gregory 164 at 14.90; P. S. Rathod 119 at 14.87.
Bowling P. S. Rathod 20 at 16.95; E. A. Wylde 10 at 18.60; D. A. Escott 13 at 24.61; J. P. Truell 12 at 26.08; O. C. H. Mills 14 at 30.92; A. J. Sachak 7 at 33.71.

Wolverhampton Grammar School P8 W2 L3 D3 A7

Master i/c T. King **Coach** N. H. Crust

With the school celebrating their 500th anniversary, it was a shame so few games survived the cloudbursts. Captain Will Nield hit a century against Solihull – a bright spot in a dismal summer.
Batting W. F. Nield* 352 at 58.66; T. G. Weston 186 at 31.00.
Bowling E. R. Hopkin 10 at 17.90.

Woodbridge School

P7 W2 L5 A5

Master i/c D. A. Brous **Coach** M. R. Fernley

Woodbridge narrowly lost several games, perhaps because of a lack of experience. Building partnerships will be the key to success in 2013, when the core of the team will have tasted success after winning the Suffolk Under-15 Cup.

Batting J. A. Rowett* 273 at 54.60; C. G. S. Robson 150 at 50.00; E. J. Eastlake 100 at 20.00.

Bowling C. L. Elmer 7 at 10.71.

Woodhouse Grove School

P7 W3 L2 D2 A8

Master i/c R. I. Frost **Coach** A. Sidebottom

Tom Cummins captained Yorkshire Schools at Under-19 level; Ryan Sharrocks and Jack Hartley were also selected. Woodhouse Grove were runners-up in the North region of the National Twenty20 competition. Alex Fox scored a century in the first match against Ashville College, and Dylan Budge hit 264 at an average of 132 in the 20-over format.

Batting A. T. Fox 207 at 51.75; A. J. Baldwin 231 at 38.50; T. J. Cummins* 223 at 37.16; R. C. Sharrocks 165 at 27.50; D. E. Budge 114 at 19.00.

Bowling A. T. Fox 12 at 12.83; T. J. Cummins 10 at 14.10; R. C. Sharrocks 7 at 21.14.

Worth School

P3 L3 A12

Master i/c R. Chaudhuri

This was a thoroughly dispiriting summer, with 12 of the 15 fixtures called off before a ball was bowled – and all three that were played resulted in defeat. Almost all the squad should return, and so have the opportunity to make the experience count.

Batting No one scored 100 runs. The leading batsman was L. D. P. Donegan, who hit 94 at 31.33.

Bowling No one took seven wickets. The leading bowler was O. F. Rivers, who took 4 at 11.75.

Wrekin College

P10 W5 L3 D2 A4

Master i/c M. de Weymarn **Coach** N. P. Benwell

Despite the dire weather, Wrekin – with an average age of under 16 – did remarkably well, winning five of their six matches against other schools. James Shaw shepherded his flock maturely, while youngsters James Flynn, Harry Gaughan and, in particular, Jake Tanser-Harvey have real potential.

Batting H. van der Berg 240 at 40.00; J. Shaw* 160 at 26.66; J. M. Flynn 135 at 16.87.

Bowling H. van der Berg 20 at 11.45; J. A. J. Tanser-Harvey 21 at 13.04; J. Shaw 20 at 13.50.

Wycliffe College

P12 W8 L2 D2 A3

Master i/c M. J. Kimber

The captain, Christian Purchase, might just be a name to follow. He is a hard-hitting right-hand batsman whose 171 (containing 102 in sixes and 44 in fours) against Dean Close was a school record. Second place in the Peak Sports League was some consolation for the wretched weather.

Batting C. Purchase* 632 at 90.28; J. Wingfield 247 at 49.40; T. W. Shrewsbury 298 at 37.25; L. C. McKissick 182 at 30.33.

Bowling J. Osborne 11 at 10.54; S. N. Young 14 at 13.50; J. Wingfield 16 at 17.25; T. W. Shrewsbury 12 at 21.08; C. Purchase 9 at 36.11.

WOMEN'S CRICKET, 2012

Proof of the subtle, but palpable, transformation in the standing of women's cricket came when England's Sarah Taylor walked out to face Stafanie Taylor of West Indies in the penultimate Twenty20 international of the summer at Hove. Sarah made a typically inventive 43 before Stafanie stopped her in her tracks but, as they were sparring out on the field, an email dropped, announcing the two Taylors had cleaned up the women's one-day and Twenty20 Player of the Year prizes at the ICC awards in Colombo – the first time women had been recognised in both limited-overs formats. Stafanie, who collected the 50-over award, had also been the sole woman among nine longlisted for the ICC Cricketer of the Year.

But no one was disputing it was Sarah's summer. Still only 23, she dominated the English international season, scoring 510 runs at 36; her Twenty20 strike-rate was a phenomenal 127. Taylor's almost unique ability was to waltz down and loft the ball over mid-off, or inside out through extra cover; if a female batsman has an aggressive go-to shot, it tends to be over mid-on or across the line. The one area she really needed to work on was the sweep.

"Hopefully in a few years we won't need to say this about women players, but Sarah bats like a man," said Clare Connor, the ECB head of women's cricket, who had watched Taylor's development from a teenager at Brighton College. It was this uncommon power and placement that encouraged Mark Lane, the England head coach, to explore the idea of Taylor trying her hand at men's Second Eleven cricket with Sussex in 2013. The news, via an in-depth interview with *The Guardian* ahead of the Women's World Cup, caused a minor media frenzy, though it was not immediately obvious which format she might be best suited to.

In November 2011, the ECB had introduced incentivised appearance fees for the women – which rewarded the players three times as much for every match won. By a cute coincidence, England went through the 2011-12 winter unbeaten, then won 12 of 15 matches over the summer. Remarkably, given the bad weather around, all their international fixtures were played to a result.

India were the senior touring side, and gave England a real fright in the one-day series. Since playing the last of their Tests in 2006, India have preferred 50-over cricket, even if their tactics seemed to revolve around letting Mithali Raj bat for long enough to make up for lazy running and errors in the field. Raj, a classically trained Bharatanatyam dancer, had rarely shown the same twinkle-toed nimbleness at the crease, but her powers of occupation were undiminished in her 14th year of international cricket. She was needed more than ever, after Anjum Chopra, the previous captain, was dropped following two series defeats in the West Indies. India's women could be forgiven for feeling the IPL riches had yet to trickle down to them. In March, the BCCI made one-off payments, totalling $13m, to 16 former men's players as retrospective reward for staying loyal in the poor old days of Indian cricket; Raj implored them to extend the generosity to women too.

Raj's unbeaten 94 led India to a first win at Lord's, in the last over; but the flipside of the strategy was seen at Taunton, where she ground out an unbeaten 92 from 138 balls, and India made an inadequate 173 for five. She scored 58 at Truro, where England came close to surrendering the series, but Jenny Gunn rescued them, and they went on to win the decider at Wormsley.

Pakistan arrived in September – from Dublin, where they had beaten Bangladesh and Ireland in two triangular tournaments – for several Twenty20 matches at the ECB Academy, including their first bilateral series against England. Lane was pleasantly surprised by the physical and technical improvements they had made since the Pakistan Cricket Board introduced central contracts in 2011. But they were still no match for England.

For the first time since their 1979 tour, West Indies were awarded a lengthy international series against England, as preparation for the World Twenty20 later in September. Under their coach, the former Test opener Sherwin Campbell, West Indies had penetrated the top bracket of women's teams, but their overreliance on a few players was exposed by England's all-round professionalism. Stafanie Taylor's arrival from Jamaica was delayed as she completed forensic science exams, and the hard-hitting Deandra Dottin came off only in the last game, when she exploded with a barrage of 80-metre sixes at Arundel to end England's 19-match winning streak (excluding one no-result and one abandonment) in Twenty20 internationals.

INDIA TOURING PARTY

*M. Raj, E. Bisht, A. Das, J. Goswami, H. Kaur, V. Krishnamurthy, R. Malhotra, M. R. Meshram, S. Naik, N. Niranjana, P. G. Raut, A. Sharma, S. Sharma, G. Sultana, N. Sunitha. *Coach:* A. Jain.

IRELAND TOURING PARTY

*I. M. H. C. Joyce, L. F. M. Cullen, L. Delany, E. L. C. Flanagan, K. J. Garth, C. N. I. M. Joyce, S. M. Kavanagh, L. N. McCarthy, R. A. Rolfe, M. E. M. O. Scott-Hayward, C. M. A. Shillington, E. J. Tice, M. V. Waldron. *Coach:* J. P. Bray.

PAKISTAN TOURING PARTY

*Sana Mir, Asmavia Iqbal, Batool Fatima, Bismah Maroof, Elizebath Khan, Javeria Khan, Marina Iqbal, Masooma Junaid, Nahida Khan, Nain Abidi, Nida Dar, Qanita Jalil, Rabiya Shah, Sadia Yousuf. *Coach:* Mohtashim Rashid.

WEST INDIES TOURING PARTY

*M. R. Aguilleira, S. A. Campbelle, B. Cooper, S. F. Daley, D. J. S. Dottin, S-A. C-A. King, Kycia A. Knight, A. Mohammed, S. L. Munroe, J. B. Nero, S. L. Quintyne, S. C. Selman, T. D. Smartt, S. R. Taylor. *Coach:* S. L. Campbell.

Taylor joined the tour midway through the England series, upon completing exams in Jamaica.

ENGLAND v IRELAND

At Loughborough (Haslegrave), June 22. **England Academy Women v Ireland XI. Abandoned.**

At Loughborough (Haslegrave), June 23. **Twenty20 international: England won by 51 runs. England 136-4** (20 overs) (C. M. Edwards 72*); ‡**Ireland 85-5** (20 overs). *PoM:* C. M. Edwards. *Charlotte Edwards weathered an accurate new-ball attack, then accelerated to 72* from 61 balls. Ireland lacked the invention to manoeuvre England's three spinners, who all went at less than four an over.*

INDIA v IRELAND

At Loughborough (Haslegrave), June 24. **One-day international: India won by nine wickets.** Reduced to 20 overs a side. **Ireland 107-6** (20 overs) (C. N. I. M. Joyce 35, I. M. H. C. Joyce 32); ‡**India 109-1** (16.4 overs) (P. G. Raut 51*, M. Raj 43*). *One-day international debut:* M. R. Meshram (India). *Originally scheduled as a Twenty20 and, though the teams decided to play a one-day international instead, rain reduced it back to 20 overs. Twins Cecelia and Isobel Joyce both fell with the score on 86, having added 67 for the second wicket. Ireland were unable to part Poonam Raut and Mithali Raj, who put on 102*.*

ENGLAND v INDIA

One-day internationals (5): England 3, India 2
Twenty20 internationals (2): England 2, India 0

At Loughborough (Brockington), June 23. **England Academy Women won by four wickets. India XI 116-6** (20 overs) (M. Raj 41); ‡**England Academy Women 117-6** (20 overs) (H. C. Knight 57). *As in the next game, England Academy Women chose from 12 players and the Indians 15, of whom 11 could bat and 11 field.*

At Loughborough (Brockington), June 23. **India XI won by six wickets. England Academy Women 107-8** (20 overs) (C. M. G. Atkins 31, H. C. Knight 30; N. Niranjana 3-13, S. Sharma 3-23); **India XI 109-4** (19 overs) (M. Raj 50*).

At Canterbury, June 26. **First Twenty20 international: England won by 33 runs. England 137-5** (20 overs) (L. A. Marsh 41, S. J. Taylor 69); ‡**India 104-8** (20 overs). *PoM:* S. J. Taylor. *Twenty20 international debuts:* M. R. Meshram, N. Niranjana (India). *India did not concede a single extra, but a 104-run alliance between Laura Marsh and Sarah Taylor, who faced just 49 balls in a dazzling display, proved damaging enough. Lydia Greenway took a superb diving catch at backward point to remove Poonam Raut in the third over.*

At Chelmsford, June 28. **Second Twenty20 international: England won by eight wickets.** ‡**India 114** (20 overs) (H. Kaur 34; K. H. Brunt 3-18); **England 117-2** (17.1 overs) (S. J. Taylor 67*, L. S. Greenway 30*). *PoM:* S. J. Taylor. *PoS:* S. J. Taylor. *Essex supporters and Sky Sports viewers were treated to a vintage performance from England. They punished India's sloppiness with five run-outs – three in the final over – and the ever-excellent Greenway pulled off a stupendous stop to prevent Harmanpreet Kaur hitting a second six. Taylor's strength down the ground was in full evidence as she struck 67* from 48 balls, assisted by Greenway, who was dropped on nought by wicketkeeper Sulakshana Naik.*

At Lord's, July 1. **First one-day international: India won by five wickets.** ‡**England 229** (49.1 overs) (S. J. Taylor 38, A. Brindle 58; N. Niranjana 3-28, A. Das 4-61); **India 230-5** (49.3 overs) (P. G. Raut 60, M. Raj 94*, H. Kaur 50). *PoM:* M. Raj. *England's unbeaten run in international cricket – stretching back 18 matches over 12 months – was ended by a characteristic show of defiance from India's captain Mithali Raj, who put on 106 with Raut and 89 with Kaur. With their first victory at Lord's at stake, India suffered a wobble of three wickets in 11 balls, before Raj scampered the winning two in the last over.*

At Taunton, July 4. **Second one-day international: India won by 14 runs. India 129** (47.5 overs) (A. Sharma 42*; K. H. Brunt 4-20); ‡**England 115** (47.2 overs) (T. T. Beaumont 31; J. Goswami 4-17). *PoM:* A. Sharma. *India pulled off a remarkable victory to take a 2–0 lead. They looked dead at 71-9, flummoxed by seam movement on a damp, brown pitch – but last pair Amita Sharma and Gouher Sultana dug in for 15 overs to add 58. Jhulan Goswami removed Edwards and Taylor for ducks in the seventh over, before spinners Sultana (10–2–30–2) and Veda Krishnamurthy (10–5–14–2) dried up the runs. Goswami won the match by yorking Georgia Elwiss.*

At Taunton, July 5. **Third one-day international: England won by three wickets. India 173-5** (50 overs) (M. Raj 92*); ‡**England 177-7** (47.2 overs) (T. T. Beaumont 44, S. J. Taylor 34, A. Brindle 40*; G. Sultana 3-26). *PoM:* M. Raj. *Raj struck another ninety, her fourth against England in one-day internationals, but managed only four fours in 138 balls. Arran Brindle kept her head to make a crucial 40* from 52 deliveries.*

At Truro, July 8. **Fourth one-day international: England won by three wickets. India 173-9** (50 overs) (M. Raj 58, H. Kaur 55; A. Brindle 3-20); ‡**England 177-7** (49 overs) (S. J. Taylor 43, J. L. Gunn 36*; N. Niranjana 3-24). *PoM:* J. L. Gunn. *England scrapped to keep the series alive in the first international match played at Boscawen Park, on the banks of the Malpas estuary. They were heading for disaster when Nagarajan Niranjana reduced them to 146-6 in the 44th over, but Raj declined to return to strike bowler Goswami at the death, even though she had two overs left.*

At Wormsley, July 11. **Fifth one-day international: England won by 29 runs** (D/L). **India 152-8** (50 overs) (H. Kaur 40, R. Malhotra 36*; G. A. Elwiss 3-17); ‡**England 124-4** (36 overs) (L. S. Greenway 37*). *PoM:* J. L. Gunn. *PoS:* G. A. Elwiss. *Taylor snapped up all three catches as India lurched to 2-3 against an excellent opening from Katherine Brunt and Elwiss – all but ending their chances of a series win. England were on course to chase down 153 when rain halted the match, and they could even afford another failure from Edwards, who had mustered only 44 from seven innings. Swing bowler Elwiss had eye-catching figures of 10–4–17–3, and finished the one-day series with a grudging economy-rate of 1.93.*

ENGLAND v PAKISTAN

Twenty20 internationals (2): England 2, Pakistan 0

At Loughborough (Brockington), September 1. **Pakistan XI won by 35 runs. Pakistan XI 109-8** (20 overs) (Nain Abidi 36; B. A. Langston 3-18); ‡**England Under-19 Women 74** (17.5 overs) (A. Jones 36; Qanita Jalil 3-9, Nida Dar 3-13). *As in the next two games, each side chose from 12 players, of whom 11 could bat and 11 field.*

At Loughborough (Brockington), September 1. **England Under-19 Women won by three wickets. Pakistan XI 105-8** (20 overs) (N. Farrant 3-28, F. M. K. Morris 3-12); ‡**England Under-19 Women 107-7** (19.5 overs) (Sana Mir 3-12).

At Loughborough (Haslegrave), September 4. **England Academy Women won by 39 runs.** ‡**England Academy Women 121** (20 overs) (N. Sciver 40; Nida Dar 4-17); **Pakistan XI 82** (18.5 overs).

At Loughborough (Haslegrave), September 4. **First Twenty20 international: England won by seven wickets.** ‡**Pakistan 87-7** (20 overs) (A. Shrubsole 4-12); **England 91-3** (15.5 overs) (S. J. Taylor 31, A. Brindle 31*). *PoM:* A. Shrubsole. *Anya Shrubsole, who missed the India series through injury, added bite to England's attack with wickets in each of her first three overs. Pakistan lacked bowlers of her quality, and Sarah Taylor and Arran Brindle comfortably added 60 for the third wicket.*

At Loughborough (Haslegrave), September 5. **Second Twenty20 international: England won by 81 runs.** ‡**England 162-7** (20 overs) (S. J. Taylor 35, D. N. Wyatt 41; Asmavia Iqbal 4-36); **Pakistan 81-5** (20 overs). *PoM:* D. N. Wyatt. *Medium-pacer Asmavia Iqbal took the prize wicket of Taylor, lbw, then Brindle, chopping on, next ball – but was removed from the attack until the final over, when she had Danielle Wyatt caught in the deep to complete a hat-trick. Susie Rowe (29* from 15 balls) responded by thumping Iqbal for two sixes and a four in the last five deliveries, as England galloped to an impregnable score.*

At Loughborough (Haslegrave), September 6. **Pakistan XI won by 42 runs.** ‡**Pakistan XI 150-6** (20 overs) (Qanita Jalil 55, Nain Abidi 33*); **England Academy Women 108** (19 overs). *Each side chose from 12 players, of whom 11 could bat and 11 field.*

PAKISTAN v WEST INDIES

At Loughborough (Haslegrave), September 5. **Twenty20 international: West Indies won by eight wickets.** ‡**Pakistan 98-8** (20 overs) (Bismah Maroof 36, Javeria Khan 37; S. A. Campbelle 3-20); **West Indies 102-2** (19.5 overs) (Kycia A. Knight 50*). *West Indies crept over the line with one ball to spare, following Knight's doughty fifty and two late boundaries from Deandra Dottin.*

ENGLAND v WEST INDIES

Twenty20 internationals (5): England 4, West Indies 1

At Loughborough (Brockington), September 4. **England Academy Women won by three wickets. West Indies XI 94** (20 overs) (G. A. Elwiss 4-12); ‡**England Academy Women 95-7** (19.4 overs) (B. L. Morgan 40*; A. Mohammed 3-8). *Each side chose from 12 players, of whom 11 could bat and 11 field.*

At Chester-le-Street, September 8. **First Twenty20 international: England won by eight wickets.** ‡**West Indies 71-8** (20 overs); **England 72-2** (9.4 overs) (L. A. Marsh 31). *PoM:* L. A. Marsh. *West Indies paid the price for heaving across the line to the swinging new ball: they were 7-3 after ten deliveries, with four of those runs overthrows. That gave Holly Colvin the platform to get through 2-5 in four overs. Charlotte Edwards made a partial return to form with 27*, putting on 59 in the first seven overs with the free-flowing Laura Marsh.*

MOST ECONOMICAL SPELLS IN WOMEN'S T20 INTERNATIONALS

4–2–3–3	**M. Kapp**	**South Africa v West Indies at Gros Islet, St Lucia**	**2012-13**
4–2–4–2	I. T. Guha	England v Sri Lanka at Taunton	2009
4–2–4–2	R. Dhar	India v Sri Lanka at Taunton	2009
4–1–4–1	**S. Ismail**	**South Africa v Bangladesh at Mirpur**	**2012-13**
4–0–5–4	S. J. Coyte	Australia v India at Billericay	2011
4–1–5–2	**H. L. Colvin**	**England v West Indies at Chester-le-Street**	**2012**
4–2–5–1	**Panna Ghosh**	**Bangladesh v Sri Lanka at Guangzhou**	**2012-13**

At Manchester, September 10. **Second Twenty20 international: England won by 28 runs. England 150-3** (20 overs) (S. J. Taylor 53, A. Brindle 42*); ‡**West Indies 122-6** (20 overs) (M. R. Aguilleira 37). *PoM:* S. J. Taylor. *Rain in the evening reduced the men's Twenty20 between England and South Africa to a nine-over thrash, but those who came early witnessed an exciting (and complete) contest. The difference was Sarah Taylor's 53 from 37 balls. Edwards was unhappy at England's sloppy ground-fielding, but Anya Shrubsole produced a one-handed dive at mid-off to remove Deandra Dottin, and Susie Rowe took a sliding catch running back from midwicket. Rowe fractured her thumb during the match, ruling her out of the rest of the series and the World Twenty20.*

At Northampton, September 13. **Third Twenty20 international: England won by ten runs.** ‡**England 103-7** (20 overs); **West Indies 93** (19.2 overs) (A. Brindle 3-16, H. L. Colvin 3-13). *PoM:* A. Brindle. *Both sets of batsmen struggled for fluency on a green pitch, but Arran Brindle, surprisingly handed the new ball ahead of Shrubsole, removed West Indies' openers.*

At Hove, September 15. **Fourth Twenty20 international: England won by 84 runs.** ‡**England 154-3** (20 overs) (S. J. Taylor 43, L. S. Greenway 61*); **West Indies 70-8** (20 overs) (S. R. Taylor 40*; D. Hazell 4-12). *PoM:* L. S. Greenway. *Sarah Taylor celebrated the title of ICC Women's Twenty20 Player of the Year with a typically jaunty 43 from 36 balls, putting on 98 in 11 overs with Lydia Greenway. West Indies' reliance on their own award-winner, one-day Player of the Year Stafanie Taylor, was clear to see, as she ground out 40* from 56 balls, with eight wickets falling around her to England's slower bowlers.*

At Arundel, September 16. **Fifth Twenty20 international: West Indies won by three wickets. England 139-7** (20 overs) (S. J. Taylor 34, K. H. Brunt 35); ‡**West Indies 140-7** (20 overs) (D. J. S. Dottin 62). *PoM:* D. J. S. Dottin. *PoS:* S. J. Taylor. *After a record 20 games without defeat, stretching back to their closing match on the tour of Australia in January 2011, England finally lost a Twenty20 international – and off the final ball. Edwards shook up the batting order and dropped herself to No. 11, but most of England's problems came in the field, where Dottin blasted 62 from 24 balls, with five sixes over Arundel's short boundaries.*

ENGLISH WOMEN'S CRICKET, 2012

A new format for the County Championship was barely visible through the rain. Almost half the matches were lost – only 78 of 138 were completed over four months. The last time the competition was so severely affected was in 2002, when it was still staged over a single week. Since then it had expanded to embrace 37 teams, and in 2012 they were reorganised in four divisions instead of five; the top three divisions each featured nine teams meeting each other once, providing (in drier years, at least) a wider range of opponents than the old divisions of six playing home and away. Finals and promotion–relegation play-offs were introduced to add another level of pressure.

With placings decided on average points from completed games, reigning champions Kent were joined in the final by Essex, the previous year's second division winners, who had played only two of their eight matches because of rain, but whose average points put them a fraction ahead of Sussex, who played five. England captain Charlotte Edwards steered Kent to their fifth Championship title in seven years once Essex collapsed from 59 for one to 99 all out.

Sarah Taylor, who was to hit the headlines in January 2013 when it was suggested that she might turn out for Sussex men's Seconds, scored 345 at 115 in her five games, including two centuries. But she was not needed to bat on the day Sussex claimed the Twenty20 Cup, rolling over Berkshire – in their third successive final – for 52. Izzy Noakes took three for five in 24 deliveries before Sussex strolled to victory in 31 balls.

Warwickshire won the Championship's second division, thanks to off-spinner Isobelle Watson's 18 wickets, and were promoted after a play-off against Somerset, while the Joyce twins pulled Ireland A out of division three. Lancashire won the Under-17 and Under-13 Championship finals, against Yorkshire and Hampshire respectively, while Yorkshire Under-15 beat Kent.

The Super Fours for the leading players were staged in May. No 50-over winner was declared, though Edwards led Diamonds to victory in both their matches and scored 147 as they gave Sapphires a 211-run pasting. Jenny Gunn's Rubies lost both 50-over games but claimed the Twenty20 title.

The traditional season-closer, a final between the champion clubs of the North and South Premier Leagues, disappeared, along with those two leagues, after a competition review by the ECB. Their 12 clubs joined four existing autonomous regional leagues – North, Midlands, South and Southwest – now financially supported by the ECB. This allowed the best players to be spread across 36 clubs, and to compete against each other rather than as team-mates.

SUPER FOURS TWENTY20, 2012

At Loughborough, May 12. **Rubies won by six wickets. Sapphires 110-6** (20 overs) (H. C. Knight 37); ‡**Rubies 113-4** (19.2 overs) (L. S. Greenway 50, J. L. Gunn 37*).

LV= COUNTY CHAMPIONSHIP, 2012

50-over league

Division One

						Bonus points			
	P	*W*	*L*	*NR*	*A*	*Batting*	*Bowling*	*Points*	*Avge pts*
Kent	8	3	0	0	5	12	12	54	18.00
Essex	8	2	0	0	6	8	8	36	18.00
Sussex	8	5	0	0	3	18	19	87	17.40
Middlesex	8	1	2	1	4	10	8	28	9.33
Berkshire	8	1	2	0	5	10	7	27	9.00
Nottinghamshire	8	1	2	0	5	7	8	25	8.33
Surrey	8	1	2	0	5	9	3	22	7.33
Yorkshire	8	0	2	1	5	6	5	11	5.50
Somerset	8	0	4	0	4	12	9	21	5.25

Division Two

						Bonus points			
	P	*W*	*L*	*NR*	*A*	*Batting*	*Bowling*	*Points*	*Avge pts*
Warwickshire	8	6	0	0	2	20	23	103	17.16
Worcestershire	8	4	1	0	3	15	16	71	14.20
Devon	8	4	3	0	1	22	22	84	12.00
Lancashire	8	4	3	0	1	15	24	79	11.28
Cheshire	8	3	3	0	2	15	20	65	10.83
Staffordshire	8	2	3	0	3	11	14	45	9.00
Wales	8	2	4	0	2	14	15	49	8.16
Netherlands	8	2	5	0	1	16	15	51	7.28
Durham	8	0	5	0	3	9	6	15	3.00

Division Three

						Bonus points			
	P	*W*	*L*	*NR*	*A*	*Batting*	*Bowling*	*Points*	*Avge pts*
Ireland A	8	4	0	0	4	16	14	70	17.50
Gloucestershire	8	2	0	1	5	7	8	35	17.50
Leicestershire	8	2	0	1	5	6	8	34	17.00
Hertfordshire	8	3	2	0	3	15	16	61	12.20
Derbyshire	8	1	2	1	4	11	9	30	10.00
Scotland	8	1	3	0	4	10	8	28	7.00
Northamptonshire	8	1	3	0	4	10	8	28	7.00
Cambs & Hunts	8	1	3	1	3	8	7	25	6.25
Hampshire	8	0	2	0	6	3	0	3	1.50

Win – 10pts, tie = 5pts. Up to four batting and four bowling points are available to each team in each match. Final points are divided by the number of matches played (excluding no results) to calculate the average number of points.

Division Four

North and East: Suffolk avge pts 18.00, Buckinghamshire 17.00, Northumberland 7.33, Cumbria 5.75, Norfolk 4.25.
South and West: Oxfordshire avge pts 16.66, Shropshire 13.00, Cornwall 10.50, Dorset 5.00, Wiltshire 4.00.
Division Four Final: Oxfordshire beat Suffolk by four wickets.

Division One Final

At Wokingham, September 2. **Kent won by seven wickets.** ‡**Essex 99** (43.1 overs) (L. R. F. Askew 3-20); **Kent 100-3** (28.1 overs) (C. M. Edwards 32). *Kent retained their county title with nearly 22 overs to spare after grabbing Essex's last nine wickets for 40 runs.*

Division Two Final

At Solihull, August 26. **Warwickshire won by six wickets. Worcestershire 164-8** (45 overs) (G. M. Hennessy 42, C. L. Holtom 53; K. Alsop 3-21); ‡**Warwickshire 166-4** (42.3 overs) (H. V. Shipman 89, E. V. Smart 32). *Amy Jones made four stumpings in Worcestershire's innings before Helen Shipman took her side to the brink of victory.*

Division Three Final

At Alveston, August 26. **Ireland A won by 58 runs. Ireland A 170-3** (28 overs) (C. N. I. M. Joyce 48, I. M. H. C. Joyce 70); ‡**Gloucestershire 112-7** (28 overs) (F. M. K. Morris 31, A. McDonald 42). *Isobel Joyce hit 70 in 57 balls and added 105 for Ireland A's second wicket with her twin, Cecelia.*

Relegation and promotion play-offs

Division One relegation play-off: Yorkshire v Somerset abandoned; Yorkshire stayed up on better league record. **Division One/Division Two play-off:** Warwickshire beat Somerset by one wicket and were promoted. **Division Two relegation play-off:** Durham beat Netherlands on a walkover. **Division Two/Division Three play-off:** Ireland A beat Netherlands by 133 runs and were promoted. **Division Three relegation play-off:** Hampshire beat Cambs & Hunts by 57 runs. **Division Three/Division Four play-off:** Oxfordshire beat Cambs & Hunts by eight wickets and were promoted.

ECB TWENTY20 CUP, 2012

Semi-finals

At Wokingham, August 27. **Berkshire won by four runs. Berkshire 117-9** (20 overs) (A. C. Smith 47; C. M. Edwards 3-29); ‡**Kent 113-9** (20 overs) (C. M. Edwards 37; H. C. Knight 3-19).

At Wokingham, August 27. **Sussex won by 17 runs. Sussex 130-6** (20 overs) (S. J. Taylor 58); ‡**Yorkshire 113-8** (20 overs) (L. Winfield 33; A. L. Walker 3-29, G. A. Elwiss 3-9).

Third-place play-off

At Wokingham, August 27. **Kent won by seven runs. Kent 133-7** (20 overs) (S. E. Rowe 67); ‡**Yorkshire 126-7** (20 overs) (L. Winfield 34, E. C. Perry 45*).

Final

At Wokingham, August 27. **Sussex won by ten wickets. Berkshire 52** (18.3 overs) (I. B. P. Noakes 3-5, G. A. Elwiss 3-15); ‡**Sussex 54-0** (5.1 overs) (A. L. Walker 39*). *Berkshire's third successive final ended in humiliation; only Linsey Smith and Extras managed double figures as they crashed for 52, before Alexia Walker saw Sussex to the title with nearly 15 overs in hand.*

CRICKET IN IRELAND, 2012

Rain on their parade

IAN CALLENDER

It was ultimately a year of frustration for Ireland, who confirmed their status as the leading Associate team but made no impression on the Full Member countries. In a bid to change that, Cricket Ireland produced a new Strategic Plan, with the aim of becoming a Test nation by 2020.

As part of the preparation, the inter-provincial championship returns in 2013 after eight years, and a first-class structure – a requirement of Full Membership – is projected for 2015. The ICC's new Targeted Assistance and Performance Programme, which assigned Ireland an extra $1.5m until then, should help. Ireland, Scotland and Netherlands also began discussions about a European 50-over and Twenty20 League – which may also include Denmark and the Channel Islands.

Across all formats Ireland played 33 matches in 2012 – a further five did not get started – and two-thirds of them were 20-over games. A ten-match winning streak in the World Twenty20 Qualifier took Ireland to their fifth successive global event. In Sri Lanka in September, they lost to Australia, then went out when their second group game, against eventual champions West Indies, was rained off at the halfway stage.

The weather was a constant spoilsport, with the game against Australia at Stormont abandoned after 10.4 overs. The other supposed highlight, a tour by South Africa A, was so badly affected that they went home a week early. Ireland lost 3–0 in a home Twenty20 series against Bangladesh, but beat them in the warm-ups for the World Twenty20 in Colombo, where they also upset Zimbabwe.

Qualification hopes for the 50-over World Cup in 2015 remained high, despite a shock defeat to Kenya. With 13 points out of a possible 16, and six matches remaining Ireland expected to confirm their place in Australasia without the need of the qualification tournament early in 2014.

But they can no longer call on seam bowler Boyd Rankin who, under pressure from Warwickshire coach Ashley Giles (also an England selector), announced he would no longer be available for Ireland after the World Twenty20. At the age of 28, and following 82 matches and 112 wickets for his country, he will be a big loss. There is no sign of an immediate replacement, despite recalls for Peter Connell and Andrew Britton, and a debut for Max Sorensen, a 26-year-old South African who plays for The Hills in Dublin.

Sorensen, who took 31 wickets, was one of five debutants in 2012. The others were John Anderson, an Australian-born batsman who also bowls leg-spin; Stuart Thompson, 20, an all-rounder from Limavady who followed his father Nigel into the Ireland side; Belfast batsman James Shannon; and Tim Murtagh, the Middlesex seamer who qualified through Irish grandparents.

Ireland's year started in Mombasa, where they beat Kenya inside two days in a supposedly four-day Intercontinental Cup match. Only ten runs separated the teams after a match aggregate of just 444; spinners Albert van der Merwe and George Dockrell took all the Kenyan wickets. Ireland struggled in the first of two 50-over World Cricket League games, which Kenya won comfortably, but revenge was swift: Ed Joyce scored 88, and Kenya were rolled for 120. Ireland won all three Twenty20 matches (the last by two runs as they defended 107) to send them to Dubai for the qualifying tournament in good heart.

Niall O'Brien missed the Kenya trip to play in the Bangladesh Premier League, in breach of his national contract. His punishment was to be left out of the Dubai trip, where Ireland made their customary slow start, losing to surprise packages Namibia. But an emphatic ten-wicket victory over Kenya put them back on track, and their only scare en route to the final was against Italy when, chasing 100, they lost eight wickets before scraping home with two balls to spare. The final highlighted everything good about Associate cricket. Afghanistan made 152 for seven but, despite losing captain William Porterfield first ball, Ireland got home by five wickets thanks to Paul Stirling's 79 from 55 deliveries.

It was three months before they returned to action, with the one-off game against Australia at Stormont. It was to the credit of groundsman Philip McCormick that there was any play at all after persistent rain the previous day: Ireland were 36 for three, something of a recovery after losing two wickets in the first three balls, before it returned.

Rain ruined the first of two WCL games against Afghanistan, but Ireland won the second by 59 runs. The first seven sessions of their Intercontinental Cup match were then washed out, although Ireland's first-innings advantage meant they collected 13 points. After four rounds, their lead of 21 meant they could afford to lose one of their last three matches and still progress to the five-day final at the end of 2013.

The first game in the Twenty20 series against Bangladesh was Ireland's 800th in all, but celebrations were muted after a heavy defeat. They performed better in the other two, but lost one by one run, and the other by two wickets off the last ball. The truncated South Africa A tour started with two four-day matches, both ruined by rain, but the tourists easily won two one-dayers before the weather (and a terrible forecast) sent them home early.

For the first time in a calendar year since 2005, no Ireland batsman scored a century. Porterfield endured a miserable season, falling first ball five times and averaging 17. Dockrell, the slow left-armer, was the leading wicket-taker with 37, and picked up the ICC Player of the Year award, as well as the Irish one. Domestically, it was a year of firsts: The Hills lifted the Irish Cup, and CIYMS the NCU Premier League title for the first time, while Donemana became the first club to win the North West double since Limavady in 2000.

Winners of Irish Leagues and Cups

Bob Kerr Irish Senior Cup The Hills. **Leinster League** Leinster. **Leinster Cup** Clontarf. **Munster League** Cork Harlequins. **Munster Cup** Cork County. **Northern Union League** CIYMS. **Northern Union Cup** Instonians. **North West League** Donemana. **North West Cup** Donemana.

OTHER INTERNATIONAL MATCHES IN IRELAND IN 2012

IRELAND v AUSTRALIA

One-Day International

At Belfast, June 23, 2012. No result. Toss: Australia. One-day international debut: T. J. Murtagh.

The Australians were denied much-needed practice before their one-day series against England. After the start was delayed by 45 minutes, Porterfield (first ball) and Joyce (his second) had their stumps demolished by Lee's pace and movement, before Stirling hit four classy boundaries. It would have been five, but for a superb one-handed catch at slip by Clarke. The crowd of over 5,000 were the big losers: had the rain arrived five balls earlier, they would have received a full refund. They got nothing – apart from the offer of free admission to one of Ireland's later games, against Afghanistan or Bangladesh.

Ireland

*W. T. S. Porterfield b Lee	0
P. R. Stirling c Clarke b Cummins	24
E. C. Joyce b Lee	0
N. J. O'Brien not out	11
†G. C. Wilson not out	0
W 1	1
1/0 (1) 2/0 (3) (3 wkts, 10.4 overs)	36
3/35 (2)	10 overs: 35-3

K. J. O'Brien, A. R. Cusack, D. T. Johnston, J. F. Mooney, G. H. Dockrell and T. J. Murtagh did not bat.

Lee 3–1–10–2; Hilfenhaus 4.4–1–15–0; Cummins 3–0–11–1.

Australia

D. A. Warner, S. R. Watson, *M. J. Clarke, †M. S. Wade, X. J. Doherty, B. Lee, D. J. Hussey, P. J. Forrest, S. P. D. Smith, P. J. Cummins, B. W. Hilfenhaus did not bat.

Umpires: M. Hawthorne and R. A. Kettleborough. Third umpire: M. A. Eggleston.
Referee: B. C. Broad.

Ireland v Bangladesh

At Belfast, July 18, 2012. **First Twenty20 international: Bangladesh won by 71 runs. Bangladesh 190-5** (20 overs) (Shakib Al Hasan 57); ‡**Ireland 119-8** (20 overs) (Elias Sunny 5-13). *MoM:* Elias Sunny. *Twenty20 international debuts:* Abul Hasan, Elias Sunny, Ziaur Rahman (Bangladesh). *Slow left-armer Elias Sunny took Bangladesh's first five-wicket haul in this format and set up their biggest victory by runs after their highest total.*

At Belfast, July 20, 2012. **Second Twenty20 international: Bangladesh won by one run.** ‡**Bangladesh 146-6** (20 overs) (Nasir Hossain 50*); **Ireland 145-6** (20 overs). *MoM:* Nasir Hossain. *Ireland, 124-4 after 17 overs, eventually needed ten off Mahmudullah's last over. But they lost Andrew Poynter and Ed Joyce in two deliveries, meaning Trent Johnston's last-ball six was in vain.*

At Belfast, July 21, 2012. **Third Twenty20 international: Bangladesh won by two wickets.** ‡**Ireland 140-8** (20 overs) (Mashrafe bin Mortaza 4-19); **Bangladesh 141-8** (20 overs). *MoM:* Mashrafe bin Mortaza. *Twenty20 international debut:* T. J. Murtagh (Ireland). *Bangladesh swept the series 3–0 after a second tight finish. They needed five from the final over, but Johnston conceded only four from the first five legal deliveries (including a wide). Elias Sunny then pinched the winning run: had Kevin O'Brien hit the stumps from midwicket, it would have been a tie.*

For reports of Ireland's matches in the World Twenty20 Qualifier, see page 1202; in the World Twenty20 see page 841; and for the Intercontinental Cup and World Cricket League, see page 1208.

CRICKET IN SCOTLAND, 2012

Wet weekends

WILLIAM DICK

An air of negativity hung over Scottish cricket through much of 2012 as the national side failed to reach the levels of performance demanded by coach Peter Steindl. The cancellation of the one-day international against England was a major blow, although at least they were given plenty of notice that they would not be required in Edinburgh: the storm and flood damage to the Grange was so severe that the fixture, scheduled for August 12, was called off three weeks in advance. Efforts to find a suitable replacement venue on either side of the border met with no success. England will not return until 2014 at the earliest, so Scotland must hope for better weather when Pakistan and Australia pitch up in 2013. In all, five of Scotland's games had to be moved to Uddingston and Ayr, because of bad weather in Edinburgh and the continuing after-effects of vandalism to the pitch at Aberdeen's Mannofield Park (see *Wisden 2012*, page 763).

For all these complications, Scotland finished the year handily placed in the one-day and four-day tournaments that formed the bread and butter of their international competition. In the 50-over World Cricket League Championship, they bounced back from two defeats in the UAE in March to beat Canada at home in the one match that survived the weather, enough to occupy second place overall behind Ireland. When the competition ends in October 2013, the top two will qualify for the 2015 World Cup; the rest will attend a standalone World Cup qualifier event, which Scotland were long expected to host, but eventually ceded to New Zealand as part of an ICC boardroom compromise.

All four days of the home Intercontinental Cup match against Canada at Uddingston's Bothwell Castle Policies ground were lost to the weather. But a seven-wicket win in the UAE, inspired by 25-year-old Richie Berrington, who scored 110 and 42 not out, helped Scotland finish the year second in that competition too. They still had plenty of work to do to reach their third final in six tournaments, including away matches against Afghanistan and Ireland.

The highlight, though, came in Twenty20 cricket – traditionally Scotland's weakest suit. Sure enough, they lost to Namibia, Ireland, USA and the Netherlands at the 2012 World Twenty20 qualifying tournament. (The qualification process for the next competition should give them a better chance: at the time of writing, six spots were open to non-Full Members.) But in July, Scotland beat Bangladesh in the Netherlands, their first win over a Test-playing nation. Berrington became the first Associate cricketer to score a century in an official Twenty20 international, from 57 balls. The result did not persuade any Bangladesh Premier League franchises to pick up Scottish players for their 2013 event.

The CB40, by contrast, was relentlessly miserable. There was one slightly fortuitous victory over Nottinghamshire, helped by rain, and Scotland's other points came from no-results. Mention of the tournament cannot pass without noting the ECB's decision to exclude Scotland (and the Netherlands) from their new 50-over competition in 2014 – meaning 2013 will be Scotland's last season in county cricket after 34 years. The announcement was accepted with diplomatic resignation – at least publicly – by Cricket Scotland; a less-guarded response might have been that the ECB missed a golden opportunity to continue assisting Associate cricket. It is difficult to see how Scotland can adequately replace 12 fixtures against quality opposition, but they promised they would try. A European league featuring regional sides from Scotland, Ireland, the Netherlands and elsewhere came under discussion, but would surely help bridge the gap between club and Associate cricket only. More useful would be a fuller programme of matches against the Test nations and their A-teams.

Scotland did, however, benefit from ICC largesse. They and Ireland were the first two Associates to receive $500,000 of funding from the new Targeted Assistance and Performance Programme, and were delighted when the ICC eased their eligibility rules following sustained lobbying from Cricket Scotland. They had watched with envy at Dutch and Irish passports being acquired by talented cricketers bearing tenuous links with those countries, but now British passport holders with Scottish parentage will be eligible to pull on the Saltire. Four English-born county players – Richard Coughtrie, Matt Machan, David Murphy and Rob Taylor – represented a Scotland XI on an autumn tour of South Africa; and they will soon be followed by Iain Wardlaw and Neil Carter, the veteran South African all-rounder who left Warwickshire at the end of the summer.

Cricket Scotland were delighted at this perceived levelling of the playing field, but stressed their commitment to producing home-grown talent. There were signs that one or two youngsters may be ready to graduate from the Under-19 team, who finished 11th at the 2012 World Cup in Australia. Ross McLean scored half-centuries against Afghanistan and Pakistan, while Freddie Coleman made 65 against New Zealand, having achieved his maiden first-class hundred for Oxford MCCU against Worcestershire in April.

Given just how badly the weather ruined the domestic game, the jury remained out on the new regional Cricket Scotland League, which replaced the old National League. Dumfries, promoted in 2011, won the Western Premier Division at their first attempt, but lost the new Grand Final against Eastern champions Watsonians. The former international seamer John Blain was the leading wicket-taker, for West of Scotland, months after being removed from his coaching role at Yorkshire.

Winners of Scottish Leagues and Cups

Eastern Premier Division Watsonians. **Western Premier Division** Dumfries. **Eastern First Division** SMRH. **Western First Division** Renfrew. **Scottish Cup** Heriot's. **Murgitroyd Twenty20 Cup** Carlton. **Regional Tri-Series** Western Warriors.

For reports of Scotland's matches in the CB40, see page 719; their Twenty20 against Bangladesh in the Netherlands see page 822; the World Twenty20 Qualifier, see page 1202; and for the Intercontinental Cup and World Cricket League Championship, see page 1208.

CRICKET IN THE NETHERLANDS, 2012

Out of the cage

DAVID HARDY

It felt like a watershed year in Dutch cricket, one in which the game finally began to take on a wider appeal. A major new initiative, the Youth Plan, was launched by the Netherlands Cricket Board (KNCB) at the beginning of 2012, with the aim of doubling player numbers in four years. There is an imperative to spread cricket beyond the densely populated cities in the west: only 18 clubs exist elsewhere in the Netherlands; and only two of them have youth sections.

More and more schools offer a dual Dutch–English curriculum – and what could be a better example of English-language culture than cricket? Around 1,000 children in 28 schools – roughly the same number of juniors that currently play the game – were introduced to it for the first time in a Bilingual Schools Cricket Challenge, culminating with a finals day in Deventer.

A second breakthrough came with an exhibition of Cage Cricket – the brainchild of former Hampshire batsman Lawrence Prittipaul – to primary school pupils in Nijmegen, in October. All over inner-city neighbourhoods, where many immigrant communities live, there are Cruyff Courts, sponsored by the legendary footballer Johan Cruyff to encourage youngsters to play street soccer. These cages are ready-made for street cricket too.

The Netherlands Under-15 team retained the European Championship, and the Under-17s beat Ireland twice. Like the senior team, they reaped the benefit of a few imports, notably Daniel Doram, a two-metre-tall, 14-year-old left-arm spinner, and Shaquille O'Neal Martina, 16, an off-spinning all-rounder – both resident in the Dutch Caribbean territory of Sint Maarten.

The standard of domestic youth cricket was boosted by the creation of a new regional league at Under-19 level, but there is still some way to go before indigenous Dutch cricketers can make a meaningful impact on the senior team again. It was only ten years ago that the overwhelming majority of players were Dutch. Ten years later, it is mainly cricketers who have learned the game elsewhere.

Sydney-born seamer Timm van der Gugten was the latest player to be plucked from Australasia, while South African Stephan Myburgh and Pakistani Shahbaz Bashir, both 29, qualified by residency. Bashir became the first Netherlands player to make a century on first-class debut, in the Intercontinental Cup against the United Arab Emirates; Myburgh was the leading Dutch run-scorer at both the World Twenty20 Qualifier and the Clydesdale Bank 40. He made 77, 74 not out and 66 in consecutive innings, to add to his 55 in the last CB40 match of 2011.

Halfway through the CB40 campaign there were dreams of a home semi-final. The Netherlands stood proudly on top of Group A, with five wins, including a memorable double over Lancashire and Essex on Whitsun weekend in Schiedam. The foundation of the early success was the top-order batting of Myburgh and Australians Michael Swart, Tom Cooper and Cameron Borgas, and the lower-order hitting of Mudassar Bukhari. In a bizarre week in June, the Netherlands posted their highest 40-over total (304 for three v Leicestershire) and their lowest (57 v Worcestershire). Another highlight was Sky Sports' first live broadcast from the Netherlands, for Gloucestershire's visit to Amstelveen in July.

From then on, it was all downhill; perhaps the intensive schedule took its toll. At one stage in July, the national team were in action for nine days out of 12 in four different formats. But in the penultimate match, the second of two Twenty20s against Bangladesh, they managed their third win over a Test country, off the last ball.

In October, the ECB announced 2013 would be the Netherlands' last season in its one-day competition. It was all the more reason for the KNCB to redouble their efforts to play more against Test nations and establish a European regional limited-overs competition.

The Netherlands' last-over defeat by Afghanistan in the group stage of the World Twenty20 Qualifier proved crucial. In the prolonged qualifying tournament for the 2015 World Cup, they ended 2012 in third place, after two home wins against the UAE, but still out of the qualifying spots.

Six young uncapped players – including Doram – were named in a party to tour the UAE and India in November and December, which included intensive coaching at the ICC Global Cricket Academy in Dubai and fixtures against the UAE Academy, Mumbai Academy and the England Performance Programme. Alexei Kervezee was the architect of a surprise 2–1 triumph over the EPP, scoring 96 and 80 in the two victories.

Excelsior 20 Schiedam lifted their ninth national championship in 22 seasons, winning all three play-off matches after finishing fourth in the league. Daan van Bunge, the captain, was in prime form; only Wesley Barresi and New Zealand professional Greg Todd scored more runs in the season. It was the ninth title for veterans Luuk van Troost and Marcel Schewe, the only men to play more than 400 matches in the *Topklasse* (Premier League) over the past 25 years. In a local derby against Excelsior, Todd made 120 and took five for 19 (including a hat-trick) for Hermes DVS.

The leading wicket-taker was a Dutchman, HCC left-arm seamer Reinier Bijloos, with 29. But the story of the year was that of Dosti, the newly promoted Amsterdam club formed in 1978. This team, made up almost entirely of cricketers from a non-Dutch background, made good use of the rule permitting three professionals. It was introduced a couple of seasons ago following more than 30 years of only one official professional player-coach, after Dosti themselves were found guilty of fielding unregistered players. Now they boasted a powerful trio: former Pakistan Test batsman Mohammad Wasim, IPL all-rounder Amit Uniyal, and David Wiese from South African franchise Titans. Dosti finished top after the initial round, then made it to the play-off final, where they lost to Excelsior.

VOC of Rotterdam were relegated after 42 years in the *Topklasse*. This meant that, in 2013, three of the six clubs with grass squares (VOC, Voorburg and Kampong) will be playing in the *Hoofdklasse* (Second Division), leaving only two in the top flight. VRA won the Twenty20 Cup for the third season running; 18-year-old left-arm spinner Victor Lubbers's four for 11 earned him the match award in the final. ACC, their Amstelveen neighbours, regularly featured a father/triplet combination: former Dutch international Ahmed Zulfiqar and his three 15-year-old sons.

KNCB signed the most lucrative sponsorship deal in their history, with the Dutch bank ABN AMRO, who are keen to expand their horizons in the Indian subcontinent. The four-year arrangement involves the Netherlands making more trips to Asia, which began with the first invitation in 16 years to the Hong Kong Sixes (where a strong Netherlands team beat England).

An award of $1.5m over three years from the ICC's new Targeted Assistance Performance Programme is intended to provide more tournaments, expand development initiatives, and support the national side as they build towards the 2015 World Cup. Unfortunately, there was no mention of women's and girls' cricket, an area of great concern in the Netherlands. The national team finished seventh in the 2011 World Cup Qualifier in Bangladesh – losing their one-day international status – and were relegated to Division Three of the ECB's County Championship after losing a play-off to Ireland A.

OTHER INTERNATIONAL MATCHES IN THE NETHERLANDS IN 2012

Bangladesh v Scotland

At Voorburg, July 24. **Twenty20 international: Scotland won by 34 runs.** **‡Scotland 162-7** (20 overs) (R. D. Berrington 100); **Bangladesh 128** (18 overs) (Shakib Al Hasan 31; J. H. Davey 3-23, R. M. Haq 3-27). *MoM:* R. D. Berrington. *Twenty20 international debut:* J. H. Davey. *A phenomenal hundred by Richie Berrington, the seventh in Twenty20 international matches, gave Scotland their first win over a Test-playing nation in any format. Fellow opener Calum MacLeod's 19 was the next-highest score. Preston Mommsen contributed only 11 to a fourth-wicket stand of 64, before sacrificing his wicket in a run-out the delivery after Berrington reached a 57-ball century with a six. Shakib Al Hasan's departure at 102-7 spelled the end for Bangladesh, who dropped back from fourth in the ICC Twenty20 rankings.*

Netherlands v Bangladesh

At Voorburg, July 25. **First Twenty20 international: Bangladesh won by eight wickets.** **‡Netherlands 144-7** (20 overs) (M. R. Swart 57); **Bangladesh 145-2** (18 overs) (Tamim Iqbal 69*, Mushfiqur Rahim 37*). *The Netherlands regretted a bad miss in the first over of Bangladesh's chase, when Tom Cooper grassed Tamim Iqbal at extra cover. Tamim went on to hit two sixes in an over off Pieter Seelaar; Mushfiqur Rahim hit four more. Mashrafe bin Mortaza had the Netherlands 14-3, but opener Michael Swart held the innings together with 57 from 41 balls.*

At Voorburg, July 26. **Second Twenty20 international: Netherlands won by one wicket.** **‡Bangladesh 128** (20 overs) (Tamim Iqbal 50, Mahmudullah 41; T. van der Gugten 3-18); **Netherlands 131-9** (20 overs) (M. R. Swart 61). *Bangladesh collapsed to 8-3, then lost five wickets in the last nine balls. Mushfiqur's stumping of Swart left the Netherlands needing 17 from 13 deliveries, and seemed to tilt the game Bangladesh's way. Eight were needed from Abdur Razzak's last three: Timm van der Gugten hit the first for six, but then fell lbw, before No. 11 Ahsan Malik cut his first ball powerfully through backward point for the winning four. It was Bangladesh's eighth defeat to an Associate since they were elevated to Full Member status in 2000.*

For reports of the Netherlands' matches in the World Twenty20 Qualifier, see page 1202; for the Intercontinental Cup and World Cricket League, see page 1208; and the CB40, see page 714.

PART SIX

Overseas Cricket

WORLD CRICKET IN 2012

Superb South Africa

SIMON WILDE

South Africa were indisputably the team of the year. Unbeaten in every bilateral series across all three formats, they were the only team not to lose a single Test. It was testimony to their talent, tenacity and organisation, and only another poor performance at a major tournament – they lost all their Super Eight games at the World Twenty20 in Sri Lanka – removed any gloss.

The South Africans found most satisfaction in the Test arena, under the leadership of the evergreen Graeme Smith, winning five and drawing five. It was the more impressive for playing only one game at home, beating Sri Lanka in January to clinch a series that had begun in late 2011. On the road for much of the time thereafter, they claimed victories in New Zealand (1–0), England (2–0) and Australia (1–0). By winning in England, they displaced their opponents as the No. 1 Test team, finally regaining a position they had held for four months in 2009; by winning in Australia, they avoided the defeat that would have ceded the top ranking to their hosts. In short, Smith's team had won two away series which doubled up as showdowns for the world Test title.

To succeed in England and Australia within the space of a few months was a rare feat. The South Africans themselves had managed it four years earlier, and so had the great West Indies sides of 1984 and 1988. Yet their deeds could be placed in a more immediate context, too: the only other teams to win Test series away from home in 2012 were Australia, in the West Indies; West Indies themselves, in Bangladesh; and – unexpectedly – England in India, a result that ended a 28-year drought. Few doubted that South Africa merited the No. 1 position: by the end of 2012, they had extended their record to one series defeat out of 21, dating back to 2006. To crown a memorable year, Smith recorded two notable personal milestones, scoring a century in his 100th Test, and beating Allan Border's record of 93 Tests as captain.

South Africa did have to dig themselves out of a couple of holes. At Brisbane in November, they allowed Australia to recover from 40 for three to make 565 for five. Then, at Adelaide, the Australians tore their bowling to shreds to reach a stratospheric 482 for five at stumps on the first day. Left more than four sessions to score 430, or bat out time, South Africa looked beaten at 77 for four going into the final day, but the debutant Faf du Plessis played one of the great match-saving innings, finishing unbeaten on 110 after almost eight hours. Well supported by A. B. de Villiers (33 in four hours) and Jacques Kallis (46 in two and a half), du Plessis was instrumental in his side losing only three wickets on the final day. (This was one of only two Tests in 2012 which were drawn without interference from the weather; the other came at Nagpur between India and England, on a pitch more devoid of life than the average corpse.) South Africa took the deciding Test in Perth by 309 runs to clinch the

TEST MATCHES IN 2012

	Tests	*Won*	*Lost*	*Drawn*	*% won*	*% lost*	*% drawn*
Australia	11	7	1	3	**63.63**	9.09	27.27
South Africa	10	5	0	5	**50.00**	0.00	50.00
Pakistan	6	3	1	2	**50.00**	16.66	33.33
West Indies	10	4	4	2	**40.00**	40.00	20.00
England	15	5	7	3	**33.33**	46.66	20.00
India	9	3	5	1	**33.33**	55.55	11.11
Sri Lanka	10	3	5	2	**30.00**	50.00	20.00
New Zealand	10	2	6	2	**20.00**	60.00	20.00
Zimbabwe	1	0	1	0	**0.00**	100.00	0.00
Bangladesh	2	0	2	0	**0.00**	100.00	0.00

series, although even there the final margin masked the trouble they had been in on the first day, at 75 for six.

South Africa's series with England also produced some dramatic cricket, though there was no doubt which was the stronger team. It was just a shame that neither series was longer than three matches. Even so, both served as excellent adverts for Test cricket.

The key to South Africa's on-field success was the settled nature of the team (off it, however, Gerald Majola, the chief executive of Cricket South Africa, was sacked after being found guilty of misconduct). They called on only 17 players in Tests, of whom six played in all ten matches, and another three missed only one. Smith, Kallis and – either side of the England tour – de Villiers all scored heavily, while Hashim Amla, already acknowledged as a batsman of class and culture, took his game to another level, making almost 2,000 runs in all formats, including a national Test record 311 not out at The Oval. Of these, a record 1,712 came away from home.

The pace attack – led by Dale Steyn, Morne Morkel and Vernon Philander – was the most potent in the world, and leg-spinner Imran Tahir had his moments, before failing spectacularly in Australia and losing his place. A measure of their bowling was that South Africa dismissed Sri Lanka for 43 in a one-day international at Paarl and, in the New Year Test at Cape Town in 2013, bundled New Zealand out for 45.

The only disruptive blow was the loss of veteran wicketkeeper-batsman Mark Boucher to a freak injury at the start of the England tour. De Villiers was pressed into service as a replacement and, although he performed capably, his batting suffered. To lessen the strain, he handed the Twenty20 captaincy to du Plessis for a series against New Zealand in December; de Villiers later withdrew as a player, citing exhaustion.

Managing the workloads of the top players became something of a fad. **Australia**'s anxiety over the inability of their seamers to stay fit led them to pull Mitchell Starc out of the Melbourne Test, only days after he had bowled them to victory over Sri Lanka at Hobart. This ultra-cautious approach – itself a function, perhaps, of a well-stocked fast-bowling cupboard – did not extend to batsmen: Michael Clarke, the captain, played at Melbourne with a hamstring strain, and scored another century to crown a sublime 12 months during which he, like Amla, had never played better.

AP/PA

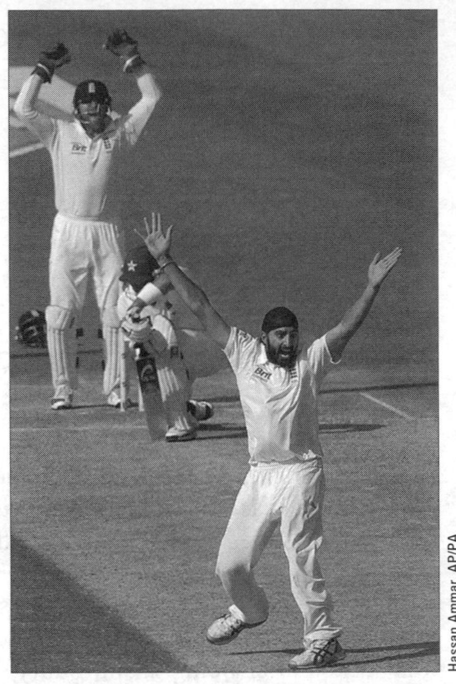

Hassan Ammar, AP/PA

Future of the left: Sri Lanka's Rangana Herath and England's Monty Panesar, both left-arm spinners, took on added importance as batsmen struggled to adapt to the Decision Review System.

Clarke became the first to score four Test double-centuries in a year, the first of which he had converted into an unbeaten 329, against India on his home ground at Sydney. And, at Melbourne, he claimed an Australian record for runs in a calendar year (the previous holder, Ricky Ponting, had retired three weeks earlier). Of Clarke's tally of 1,595, he made 1,407 in Australia, a record for one country in one year. Despite the juggling of bowling personnel, Australia won seven Tests in 2012, more than any other side.

The most radical response to the fixture list was adopted by **England**, who in November announced they were embarking on a "step-change" in the schedules of players and coaches. Andy Flower was to remain overall team director, but the day-to-day running of the 50-over and Twenty20 teams would be handled by Ashley Giles, who had coached Warwickshire to the 2012 Championship and was already an England selector. The move, mainly aimed at keeping Flower fresh, motivated, and in the job, was also a response to a troubled year, in which England had failed to build on their rise to the top of the Test rankings in 2011, and followed the retirement of Andrew Strauss, one of England's most successful Test captains, after the defeat by South Africa. Sport can be unsentimental, and there was no time – and little need – to mourn Strauss's departure, as the team rallied under Alastair Cook to record their first series win in India since 1984-85. Soon after, South Africa announced they were also dividing up the coaching duties, with Russell Domingo, Gary Kirsten's assistant, taking over the Twenty20 side.

MOST TEST RUNS IN ONE COUNTRY IN A CALENDAR YEAR

	Country	*Year*	*M*	*Runs*	*Avge*	*HS*	*100*
M. J. Clarke (A)	**Australia**	**2012**	**8**	**1,407**	**156.33**	**329***	**5**
Mohammad Yousuf (P)	Pakistan	2006	6	1,126	112.60	192	6
G. A. Gooch (E)	England	1990	6	1,058	96.18	333	4
G. R. Viswanath (I)	India	1979	13	1,047	61.58	179	4
S. M. Gavaskar (I)	India	1979	14	1,013	53.31	148*	4
J. L. Langer (A)	Australia	2004	7	1,012	77.84	215	4
R. T. Ponting (A)	Australia	2003	8	980	89.09	257	3
D. G. Bradman (A)	England	1930	5	974	139.14	334	4
D. P. M. D. Jayawardene (SL)	Sri Lanka	2001	11	968	64.53	150	4
M. L. Hayden (A)	Australia	2003	8	933	84.81	380	3

England's bowling attack remained strong, but the batting, which had touched rare heights in 2011, was often unconvincing. Strauss's decline was one issue; another was the turmoil generated by Kevin Pietersen, whose gripes with the management included scheduling and time off to play in the IPL. His temporary exile hurt England's defence of the World Twenty20 title but, even though he didn't appear in the one-day side after February, they won 12 of their 14 completed matches, and remained No. 1 in the rankings until the end of the year. Pietersen was less consistent than Amla or Clarke, but scored three breathtaking Test hundreds, in Colombo, Leeds and Mumbai.

Others also suffered disruption from internal disputes, none more so than **New Zealand**. Ross Taylor quit as captain after being invited to stay on only as head of the Test side; Mike Hesson, appointed coach in succession to John Wright – who himself had resigned, citing differences with director of cricket John Buchanan – had proposed the one-day and Twenty20 teams be passed over to Brendon McCullum. Results had been poor for much of the year, but the timing of the suggested change was odd: Taylor had just masterminded a series-squaring Test victory over Sri Lanka in Colombo, where his double of 142 and 74 was among the finest by a New Zealand captain. The board later apologised to Taylor for his treatment, but he opted out of the end-of-year tour of South Africa. To make matters worse, Jesse Ryder didn't play at all after February, for personal and disciplinary reasons.

Mahela Jayawardene ended his second spell as **Sri Lanka**'s captain after his country's tour of Australia in January 2013, keeping a promise that he

MOST RUNS AWAY FROM HOME IN A CALENDAR YEAR

(All international matches, excluding neutral venues)

	Year	*M*	*Runs*	*Avge*	*HS*	*100*
H. M. Amla (South Africa)	**2012**	**23**	**1,712**	**68.48**	**311***	**5**
K. C. Sangakkara (Sri Lanka)	2006	32	1,609	48.75	156*	3
T. M. Dilshan (Sri Lanka)	2009	17	1,455	72.75	162	9
G. C. Smith (South Africa)	2008	16	1,441	68.61	232	5
R. T. Ponting (Australia)	2005	24	1,418	54.53	156	4
Mohammad Hafeez (Pakistan)	2011	32	1,401	40.02	143	5
R. Dravid (India)	2002	21	1,392	60.52	217	4
I. V. A. Richards (West Indies)	1976	10	1,370	91.33	291	5

ONE-DAY INTERNATIONALS IN 2012

(Full Members only)

	ODIs	Won	Lost	Tied	NR	% won	% lost
England	15	12	2	0	1	**85.71**	14.28
South Africa	13	8	4	0	1	**66.66**	33.33
India	17	9	7	1	0	**55.88**	44.11
Bangladesh	9	5	4	0	0	**55.55**	44.44
West Indies	17	8	8	1	0	**50.00**	50.00
Sri Lanka	33	14	16	1	2	**46.77**	53.22
Australia	23	10	12	1	0	**45.65**	54.34
Pakistan	17	6	10	0	1	**37.50**	62.50
New Zealand	15	4	10	0	1	**28.57**	71.42
Zimbabwe	3	0	3	0	0	**0.00**	100.00

The following teams also played official one-day internationals in 2012, some against Full Members (not included in the table above): Scotland (P1 W1); Ireland (P4 W2 L1 NR1); Kenya (P2 W1 L1); Netherlands (P2 W1 L1); Afghanistan (P5 W1 L4); Canada (P1 L1). Australia and Pakistan both beat Afghanistan, and Australia had a no-result against Ireland.

The % won and lost excludes no-results; ties are counted as half a win.

---

would stay only for 12 months. Then, within days, he said he had lost all confidence in Sri Lanka Cricket, after a confidential request – that the players' guarantee fee from the World Twenty20 staged in Sri Lanka be shared with the support staff and groundsmen – was made public. SLC, whose financial husbandry has often infuriated their players, would not accede to the proposal.

India also experienced turbulence in the wake of whitewashes in England and Australia. Mohinder Amarnath revealed that the selection panel of which he had formerly been a member had recommended the removal of M. S. Dhoni as captain during the tour of Australia, only for the proposal to be blocked by the Indian board president, N. Srinivasan – who is also owner of the Chennai IPL franchise, which is captained by Dhoni. Amarnath renewed calls for Dhoni to step down during the home defeat by England. There was no halting the transition in the ranks, though: Rahul Dravid and V. V. S. Laxman both retired, and Sachin Tendulkar quit one-day internationals. Virat Kohli carried the flag for the next generation, scoring eight international centuries, more than anyone.

In the **West Indies**, Ramnaresh Sarwan successfully sued the board over comments about his fitness, and was awarded $US161,000 in damages, though he was picked for the one-day tour of Australia early in 2013. There was a more conciliatory resolution to Chris Gayle's long-running dispute. Gayle, who had earned fortunes playing in the IPL and other domestic Twenty20 tournaments, returned to West Indies colours for the first time in more than a year after a peace brokered at prime-ministerial level. Crowds flocked to witness his first international appearances in the Caribbean for two years and, on his Test return, he scored 150 and 64 not out against New Zealand in the first Test played at the Sir Vivian Richards Stadium in Antigua since the embarrassing 2008-09 abandonment against England.

Gayle's comeback helped provide his team with the self-belief to win the World Twenty20 in September, secured in fairytale fashion after they had

TWENTY20 INTERNATIONALS IN 2012

	T20Is	*Won*	*Lost*	*No result*	*% won*	*% lost*
Ireland	13	8	4	1	**66.66**	33.33
West Indies	13	8*	4	1	**66.00**	33.33
Sri Lanka	11	6*	4	1	**60.00**	40.00
Scotland	5	3	2	0	**60.00**	40.00
India	14	8	6	0	**57.14**	42.85
South Africa	15	8	6	1	**57.14**	42.85
Pakistan	16	9*	7	0	**56.25**	43.75
Australia	13	7	6*	0	**53.84**	46.15
England	14	7	6	1	**53.84**	46.15
Netherlands	6	3	3	0	**50.00**	50.00
Bangladesh	9	4	5	0	**44.44**	55.55
Afghanistan	5	2	3	0	**40.00**	60.00
New Zealand	17	6	10*	1	**37.50**	62.50
Canada	4	0	4	0	**0.00**	100.00
Zimbabwe	4	0	4	0	**0.00**	100.00
Kenya	5	0	5	0	**0.00**	100.00

Pakistan beat Australia, and Sri Lanka and West Indies both beat New Zealand, in tied matches resolved by one-over eliminators.

come within one run of elimination during the Super Eights against New Zealand. Gayle was Man of the Match in the semi-final against Australia, but the triumph was a fine collective effort under Darren Sammy. Gayle did little in a final against Sri Lanka that ebbed and flowed in a way many thought impossible of a 20-over game. Instead, the hero was the hugely improved Marlon Samuels, who hit half his 78 from 56 balls in just 11 deliveries from Lasith Malinga, a notoriously difficult bowler to face. It was Sri Lanka's fourth defeat in a major final since their World Cup triumph of 1996.

Pakistan began the year strongly, with a 3–0 whitewash of England in the United Arab Emirates, but there was little chance to build on that outstanding result: because of the security situation at home, they played only one more Test series in 2012, losing 1–0 in Sri Lanka. Plans for Bangladesh to visit were twice scrapped, amid suspicions the tour had only ever been mooted as a quid pro quo for Pakistan backing the nomination of Mustafa Kamal, president of the Bangladesh Cricket Board, for the role of ICC vice-president. But, much to Pakistan's delight, an International XI travelled to Karachi in October to play two Twenty20 games. As a second home, the UAE was not ideal for Australia's visit in August: the 50-over matches started at 6pm to avoid the worst of the heat – and even then, the thermometer hovered around 36°C. Pakistan also resumed bilateral relations with India after a four-year hiatus, tying a Twenty20 series that started on Christmas Day, before winning the 50-over matches 2–1.

For the second year running, Pakistan's Saeed Ajmal finished as the leading wicket-taker in all internationals, claiming 95, after picking up 89 in 2011. Next, with 84, came another off-spinner, Graeme Swann of England, who had topped the list in 2010. But one of the features of the year was the rise of orthodox left-arm spin. Rangana Herath of Sri Lanka was the leading Test bowler, with 60 wickets (one more than Swann), including seven five-fors, three more than the next best, fellow slow-left armer Monty Panesar of England. Two others of the breed, Pakistan's Abdur Rehman and India's Pragyan Ojha, also had good years. In all, left-arm spinners claimed 172 Test wickets at a combined average of 27, seven fewer than any other type of bowling; their haul of 15% of available wickets was their highest for 25 years. Spin held less sway in one-day internationals, where the use of two balls per innings may have had an effect, but it remained a potent weapon in the Twenty20 format.

Bangladesh and **Zimbabwe** both felt the impact of the ICC's decision to revise the frequency with which they met the major teams. Across all formats, Zimbabwe featured in just eight matches (and lost the lot), and Bangladesh in 20 – tallies as low as in any year since Zimbabwe entered the Test ranks in 1992, and Bangladesh in 2000. It was also revealed that the Zimbabwean board had debts of $US18m. Bangladesh at least showed spirit at home to West Indies: after conceding 527 in the First Test at Dhaka, they lost by only 77 runs; and in the Second, the debutant Abul Hasan made the highest score (113) by a Test No. 10 for 128 years. One of the West Indies bowlers, Tino Best, had himself set an unlikely record five months earlier, with an exuberant 95 – the highest by a Test No. 11 – against England at Edgbaston. Bangladesh's other consolation was to take the one-day series against West Indies 3–2 to move above New Zealand in the rankings.

It was not necessary to be a close follower of the careers of Gayle and Pietersen to grasp that the shadow cast by the 20-over format was growing. Although no window was formally declared for the IPL, most international teams preferred to clear their diaries rather than risk upsetting – or even losing – their talent. During the eight weeks of the tournament, six Tests were staged in Sri Lanka, the West Indies and England, but the one-day and Twenty20 international formats went into total shutdown. Bangladesh and Sri Lanka both launched new domestic Twenty20 events, and Pakistan unveiled plans to follow suit in March 2013, only to postpone them. International cricket's primacy was being paid lip-service only.

> "India's scorecard resembled a half-decent poker hand: a pair of sixes, a pair of eights and the makings of a low straight flush."
>
> **India v England, 2012-13, Second Test, page 398.**

RELIANCE MOBILE ICC TEAM RANKINGS

ICC TEST CHAMPIONSHIP

(As at January 14, 2013)

		Matches	Points	Rating
1	South Africa	32	3,965	124
2	England	41	4,825	118
3	Australia	42	4,916	117
4	Pakistan	29	3,148	109
5	India	37	3,879	105
6	Sri Lanka	36	3,318	92
7	West Indies	31	2,809	91
8	New Zealand	30	2,333	78
9	Bangladesh	15	0	0

Zimbabwe are excluded as they have played insufficient matches in the qualifying period, but would have a rating of 42.

ICC ONE-DAY CHAMPIONSHIP

(As at January 6, 2013)

		Matches	Points	Rating
1	England	25	3,016	121
2	South Africa	18	2,170	121
3	India	33	3,866	117
4	Australia	28	3,164	113
5	Sri Lanka	35	3,839	110
6	Pakistan	31	3,311	107
7	West Indies	25	2,206	88
8	Bangladesh	21	1,636	78
9	New Zealand	20	1,434	72
10	Zimbabwe	14	700	50
11	Ireland	6	207	35
12	Netherlands	4	63	16
13	Kenya	4	45	11

ICC TWENTY20 CHAMPIONSHIP

(As at December 31, 2012)

		Matches	Qualifying	Points	Rating
1	Sri Lanka	12	15	1,524	127
2	West Indies	13	17	1,585	122
3	India	15	18	1,789	119
4	England	16	22	1,891	118
5	South Africa	16	21	1,868	117
6	Pakistan	20	28	2,324	116
7	Australia	15	20	1,615	108
8	New Zealand	16	21	1,563	98
9	Bangladesh	8	11	668	84
10	Ireland	8	12	659	82
11	Zimbabwe	7	10	306	44

Only teams who have completed at least eight Twenty20 international matches since August 1, 2010, are ranked.

RELIANCE MOBILE ICC PLAYER RANKINGS

Introduced in 1987, the rankings have been backed by various sponsors, but were taken over by the International Cricket Council in January 2005. They rank cricketers on a scale up to 1,000 on their performances in Tests. The rankings take into account playing conditions, the quality of the opposition and the result of the matches. In August 1998, a similar set of rankings for one-day internationals was launched, and Twenty20 rankings were added in October 2011.

The leading players in the Test rankings on January 14, 2013, were:

Rank	*Batsmen*	*Points*	*Rank*	*Bowlers*	*Points*
1	M. J. Clarke (*Australia*)	887	1	D. W. Steyn (*South Africa*)	895
2	H. M. Amla (*South Africa*)	886	2	V. D. Philander (*South Africa*)	850
3	S. Chanderpaul (*West Indies*)	879	3	Saeed Ajmal (*Pakistan*)	832
4	K. C. Sangakkara (*Sri Lanka*)	842	4	H. M. R. K. B. Herath (*SL*)	809
5	A. N. Cook (*England*)	836	5	P. M. Siddle (*Australia*)	800
6	A. B. de Villiers (*South Africa*)	812	6	J. M. Anderson (*England*)	759
7	J. H. Kallis (*South Africa*)	809	7	G. P. Swann (*England*)	755
8	L. R. P. L. Taylor (*New Zealand*)	769	8	M. Morkel (*South Africa*)	746
9	Younis Khan (*Pakistan*)	761	9	P. P. Ojha (*India*)	739
10	K. P. Pietersen (*England*)	759	10	B. W. Hilfenhaus (*Australia*)	721

The leading players in the one-day international rankings on January 6, 2013, were:

Rank	*Batsmen*	*Points*	*Rank*	*Bowlers*	*Points*
1	H. M. Amla (*South Africa*)	901	1	Saeed Ajmal (*Pakistan*)	801
2	A. B. de Villiers (*South Africa*)	852	2	Mohammad Hafeez (*Pakistan*)	753
3	V. Kohli (*India*)	824	3	S. P. Narine (*West Indies*)	724
4	M. S. Dhoni (*India*)	789	4	L. L. Tsotsobe (*South Africa*)	690
5	I. J. L. Trott (*England*)	749	5	M. Morkel (*South Africa*)	676
6	K. C. Sangakkara (*Sri Lanka*)	746	6	S. T. Finn (*England*)	668
7	M. J. Clarke (*Australia*)	718	7	R. Ashwin (*India*)	661
8	A. N. Cook (*England*)	707		G. P. Swann (*England*)	661
9	M. E. K. Hussey (*Australia*)	688	9	Abdur Razzak (*Bangladesh*)	657
10	T. M. Dilshan (*Sri Lanka*)	682	10	D. W. Steyn (*South Africa*)	644

The leading players in the Twenty20 international rankings on December 31, 2012, were:

Rank	*Batsmen*	*Points*	*Rank*	*Bowlers*	*Points*
1	S. R. Watson (*Australia*)	799	1	Saeed Ajmal (*Pakistan*)	756
2	B. B. McCullum (*NZ*)	794	2	B. A. W. Mendis (*Sri Lanka*)	747
3	C. H. Gayle (*West Indies*)	792	3	G. P. Swann (*England*)	720
4	D. P. M. D. Jayawardene (*SL*)	760	4	N. L. McCullum (*N. Zealand*)	669
5	V. Kohli (*India*)	731	5	S. R. Watson (*Australia*)	665
6	M. N. Samuels (*West Indies*)	723	6	K. M. D. N. Kulasekara (*SL*)	660
7	M. J. Guptill (*New Zealand*)	721	7	Abdur Razzak (*Bangladesh*)	644
8	E. J. G. Morgan (*England*)	719	8	Shahid Afridi (*Pakistan*)	643
	S. K. Raina (*India*)	719	9	A. D. Mathews (*Sri Lanka*)	639
10	D. A. Warner (*Australia*)	714	10	S. P. Narine (*West Indies*)	638
				D. W. Steyn (*South Africa*)	638

In October 2008, the ICC launched a set of rankings for women cricketers, based on one-day international performances because of the paucity of women's Test cricket. The ICC said they hoped to raise the profile of the women's game by identifying where the leading players stood, and to give it further competition and context. Twenty20 rankings were added in September 2012.

The leading players in the women's one-day international rankings on December 31, 2012, were:

Rank	*Batsmen*	*Points*	*Rank*	*Bowlers*	*Points*
1	M. Raj (*India*)	767	1	K. H. Brunt (*England*)	777
2	S. R. Taylor (*West Indies*)	737	2	L. C. Sthalekar (*Australia*)	764
3	S. J. Taylor (*England*)	660	3	J. Goswami (*India*)	695
4	L. S. Greenway (*England*)	640	4	E. A. Perry (*Australia*)	685
5	A. E. Satterthwaite (*NZ*)	637	5	L. A. Marsh (*England*)	642
6	M. M. Lanning (*Australia*)	635	6	A. Mohammed (*West Indies*)	634
7	S. W. Bates (*New Zealand*)	611	7	S. R. Taylor (*West Indies*)	601
8	A. J. Blackwell (*Australia*)	581	8	G. Sultana (*India*)	568
	C. M. Edwards (*England*)	581	9	J. L. Gunn (*England*)	548
10	J. E. Cameron (*Australia*)	575	10	S. F. Daley (*West Indies*)	525

The leading players in the women's Twenty20 international rankings on December 31, 2012, were:

Rank	*Batsmen*	*Points*	*Rank*	*Bowlers*	*Points*
1	S. J. Taylor (*England*)	705	1	L. C. Sthalekar (*Australia*)	675
2	C. M. Edwards (*England*)	694	2	H. L. Colvin (*England*)	652
3	M. Raj (*India*)	651	3	S. F. Daley (*West Indies*)	651
4	J. E. Cameron (*Australia*)	610	4	J. L. Hunter (*Australia*)	636
5	D. J. S. Dottin (*West Indies*)	601	5	E. A. Perry (*Australia*)	632
6	S. R. Taylor (*West Indies*)	594	6	A. Mohammed (*West Indies*)	630
7	M. M. Lanning (*Australia*)	574	7	K. H. Brunt (*England*)	628
8	S. W. Bates (*New Zealand*)	572	8	J. Goswami (*India*)	625
9	H. Kaur (*India*)	569	9	S. E. A. Ruck (*New Zealand*)	614
10	L. C. Sthalekar (*Australia*)	557	10	Sana Mir (*Pakistan*)	602

TEST AVERAGES IN CALENDAR YEAR 2012

BATTING (300 runs, average 25.00)

	T	I	NO	R	HS	100	Avge	SR	Ct/St
M. J. Clarke (A)	11	18	3	1,595	329*	5	106.33	65.96	18
†S. Chanderpaul (WI)	9	15	5	987	203*	3	98.70	47.04	6
M. N. Samuels (WI)	7	11	1	866	260	3	86.60	53.75	0
C. A. Pujara (I)	6	10	2	654	206*	3	81.75	47.94	3
H. M. Amla (SA)	10	17	2	1,064	311*	4	70.93	58.94	6
J. H. Kallis (SA)	9	15	1	944	224	4	67.42	55.75	18
†M. E. K. Hussey (A)	11	18	3	898	150*	4	59.86	54.78	15
A. B. de Villiers (SA)	10	16	2	815	169	2	58.21	56.59	19/1
Azhar Ali (P)	6	10	0	551	157	3	55.10	41.08	1
L. R. P. L. Taylor (NZ)	10	18	3	819	142	3	54.60	54.96	8
†C. H. Gayle (WI)	4	8	2	318	150	1	53.00	75.53	3
R. Ashwin (I)	8	12	4	414	91*	0	51.75	60.00	2
†K. C. Sangakkara (SL)	10	19	4	767	199*	2	51.13	47.08	2
V. Kohli (I)	9	16	2	689	116	3	49.21	46.74	9
†G. C. Smith (SA)	10	19	2	825	131	3	48.52	54.20	23
†A. N. Cook (E)	15	29	3	1,249	190	4	48.03	41.89	11
A. N. Petersen (SA)	10	19	2	815	182	3	47.94	49.93	5
Asad Shafiq (P)	6	10	1	424	100*	1	47.11	45.98	8
Mohammad Hafeez (P)	6	12	1	505	196	1	45.90	55.01	5
K. P. Pietersen (E)	14	25	1	1,053	186	3	43.87	65.12	5
†D. A. Warner (A)	11	18	0	788	180	2	43.77	74.83	9
D. Ramdin (WI)	7	10	2	343	126*	2	42.87	47.63	25
R. T. Ponting (A)	9	15	1	600	221	2	42.85	52.77	8
A. D. Mathews (SL)	9	16	2	585	84	0	41.78	43.30	4
M. S. Dhoni (I)	8	13	2	447	99	0	40.63	49.22	13/3
T. M. Dilshan (SL)	8	16	0	637	147	3	39.81	64.67	11
†J. A. Rudolph (SA)	9	13	2	435	105*	1	39.54	47.33	5
M. J. Prior (E)	15	22	2	777	91	0	38.85	52.64	29/7
I. J. L. Trott (E)	15	28	2	1,005	143	2	38.65	43.67	6
†D. M. Bravo (WI)	8	14	1	482	127	1	37.07	43.18	11
†K. O. A. Powell (WI)	9	17	1	587	134	3	36.68	52.22	8
†M. S. Wade (A)	8	14	3	399	106	1	36.27	50.12	25/2
Younis Khan (P)	6	10	0	360	127	1	36.00	45.05	4
D. P. M. D. Jayawardene (SL)	10	19	1	630	180	2	35.00	44.64	12
B. B. McCullum (NZ)	10	19	1	621	84	0	34.50	53.07	5
†E. J. M. Cowan (A)	11	18	0	606	136	1	33.66	43.78	16
I. R. Bell (E)	14	25	5	672	116*	1	33.60	39.71	7
†A. J. Strauss (E)	11	21	0	697	141	2	33.19	43.21	14
K. S. Williamson (NZ)	10	18	1	559	135	2	32.88	37.92	11
T. T. Samaraweera (SL)	10	18	1	554	115*	1	32.58	39.85	4
D. J. G. Sammy (WI)	10	15	1	456	106	1	32.57	72.03	20
†G. Gambhir (I)	9	15	0	474	83	0	31.60	44.80	6
V. Sehwag (I)	9	16	0	505	117	1	31.56	87.67	12
S. R. Watson (A)	6	11	0	346	83	0	31.45	44.41	1
M. J. Guptill (NZ)	10	19	0	567	97	0	29.84	42.66	13
†D. R. Flynn (NZ)	6	12	0	327	53	0	27.25	40.22	3
H. A. P. W. Jayawardene (SL)	9	14	2	306	61*	0	25.50	49.43	16/6

BOWLING (10 wickets, average 50.00)

	Style	O	M	R	W	BB	5I	Avge	SR
T. L. Best (WI)	RF	98.4	14	293	18	6-40	2	16.27	32.88
N. Deonarine (WI)	OB	111	26	285	15	4-37	0	19.00	44.40
M. G. Johnson (A)	LFM	64	6	243	12	4-63	0	20.25	32.00
Saeed Ajmal (P)	OB	302	64	802	39	7-55	2	20.56	46.46

	Style	*O*	*M*	*R*	*W*	*BB*	*5I*	*Avge*	*SR*
V. D. Philander (SA)	RFM	328.2	75	908	43	6-44	3	21.11	45.81
B. W. Hilfenhaus (A)	RFM	338.3	106	802	37	5-106	1	21.67	54.89
K. A. J. Roach (WI)	RF	266.3	49	868	39	5-41	3	22.25	41.00
T. G. Southee (NZ)	RFM	182.5	38	566	25	7-64	2	22.64	43.88
Abdur Rehman (P)	SLA	215.2	48	566	25	6-25	2	22.64	51.68
M. R. Gillespie (NZ)	RFM	58.4	9	251	11	6-113	2	22.81	32.00
P. M. Siddle (A)	RFM	323.3	92	947	41	5-49	2	23.09	47.34
H. M. R. K. B. Herath (SL)	SLA	537.2	91	1,417	60	6-43	7	23.61	53.73
Junaid Khan (P)	LFM	109.2	16	338	14	5-70	2	24.14	46.85
M. A. Starc (A)	LFM	142.5	29	501	20	6-154	2	25.05	42.85
P. P. Ojha (I)	SLA	352.3	100	857	33	5-45	3	25.96	64.09
M. S. Panesar (E)	SLA	371	105	859	33	6-62	4	26.03	67.45
J. H. Kallis (SA)	RFM	122.2	34	311	11	3-35	0	28.27	66.72
C. S. Martin (NZ)	RFM	173.3	36	578	20	6-26	1	28.90	52.05
J. M. Anderson (E)	RFM	566.2	141	1,416	48	5-72	1	29.50	70.79
D. W. Steyn (SA)	RF	380.5	93	1,159	39	5-56	1	29.71	58.58
G. P. Swann (E)	OB	634.2	124	1,766	59	6-82	3	29.93	64.50
R. J. Harris (A)	RFM	140.4	33	363	12	3-31	0	30.25	70.33
M. Morkel (SA)	RF	360.5	80	1,151	38	6-23	2	30.28	56.97
T. A. Boult (NZ)	LFM	207	41	677	22	4-42	0	30.77	56.45
S. T. Finn (E)	RF	199.5	31	630	20	4-74	0	31.50	59.95
S. C. J. Broad (E)	RFM	418.1	86	1,268	40	7-72	2	31.70	62.72
S. Randiv (SL)	OB	226.5	16	711	22	4-13	0	32.31	61.86
Sohag Gazi (B)	OB	128.5	13	394	12	6-74	1	32.83	64.41
N. M. Lyon (A)	OB	446.5	118	1,195	36	5-68	1	33.19	74.47
S. Shillingford (WI)	OB	188.4	42	504	15	6-119	1	33.60	75.46
J. L. Pattinson (A)	RFM	110.1	18	381	11	4-43	0	34.63	60.09
R. Rampaul (WI)	RFM	168.1	33	490	14	3-75	0	35.00	72.07
J. S. Patel (NZ)	OB	141.2	35	390	11	4-100	0	35.45	77.09
D. A. J. Bracewell (NZ)	RFM	281.4	45	972	26	3-26	0	37.38	65.00
R. Ashwin (I)	OB	443.1	81	1,397	37	6-31	3	37.75	71.86
K. M. D. N. Kulasekara (SL)	RFM	216.5	52	577	15	3-48	0	38.46	86.73
Umar Gul (P)	RFM	136	29	465	12	4-61	0	38.75	68.00
U. T. Yadav (I)	RFM	151	11	673	16	5-93	1	42.06	56.62
F. H. Edwards (WI)	RF	138.1	20	481	11	6-90	1	43.72	75.36
R. M. S. Eranga (SL)	RFM	115	15	443	10	3-51	0	44.30	69.00
S. P. Narine (WI)	OB	216.3	37	721	15	5-132	1	48.06	86.60
D. J. G. Sammy (WI)	RM	287	57	835	17	3-74	0	49.11	101.29
Zaheer Khan (I)	LFM	244.5	47	739	15	3-122	0	49.26	97.93

MOST DISMISSALS BY A WICKETKEEPER

Dis		*T*	
36	(29ct, 7st)	15	M. J. Prior (E)
27	(25ct, 2st)	8	M. S. Wade (A)
25	(25ct)	7	D. Ramdin (WI)
24	(23ct, 1st)	9	C. F. K. van Wyk (NZ)
22	(16ct, 6st)	9	H. A. P. W. Jayawardene (SL)
18	(17ct, 1st)	6	A. B. de Villiers (SA)
17	(13ct, 4st)	6	Adnan Akmal (P)
16	(13ct, 3st)	8	M. S. Dhoni (I)
15	(14ct, 1st)	4	M. V. Boucher (SA)

A. B. de Villiers held two more catches in four matches when not keeping wicket.

MOST CATCHES IN THE FIELD

Ct	*T*	
23	10	G. C. Smith (SA)
20	10	D. J. G. Sammy (WI)
18	9	J. H. Kallis (SA)
18	11	M. J. Clarke (A)
16	11	E. J. M. Cowan (A)
15	11	M. E. K. Hussey (A)
14	11	A. J. Strauss (E)
13	10	M. J. Guptill (NZ)
13	14	J. M. Anderson (E)

ONE-DAY INTERNATIONAL AVERAGES IN CALENDAR YEAR 2012

BATTING (500 runs, average 32.00)

	M	*I*	*NO*	*R*	*HS*	*100*	*50*	*Avge*	*SR*	*4*	*6*
A. B. de Villiers (SA)	13	12	6	645	125*	2	3	107.50	108.58	51	12
H. M. Amla (SA)	10	9	1	678	150	2	4	84.75	90.76	66	4
B-J. Watling (NZ)	7	6	2	338	96*	0	4	84.50	83.04	32	3
V. Kohli (I)	17	17	2	1,026	183	5	3	68.40	93.78	92	5
†Nasir Jamshed (P)	8	8	1	462	112	2	2	66.00	86.19	45	5
M. S. Dhoni (I)	16	14	6	524	113*	1	3	65.50	87.62	37	9
†E. J. G. Morgan (E)	15	12	6	364	89*	0	2	60.66	98.11	29	8
I. R. Bell (E)	11	11	1	549	126	1	4	54.90	82.68	59	5
†A. N. Cook (E)	15	15	1	663	137	3	3	47.35	79.97	74	2
M. J. Clarke (A)	15	14	0	656	117	1	5	46.85	82.00	50	9
Azhar Ali (P)	12	12	3	411	96	0	4	45.66	66.07	35	1
†K. C. Sangakkara (SL)	31	29	2	1,184	133	3	6	43.85	79.14	94	11
†G. Gambhir (I)	16	16	0	685	102	2	5	42.81	81.93	55	0
B. B. McCullum (NZ)	11	10	0	416	119	1	2	41.60	92.03	37	11
T. M. Dilshan (SL)	31	30	3	1,119	160*	4	3	41.44	84.64	118	10
†S. K. Raina (I)	17	17	5	492	65*	0	4	41.00	96.85	36	10
I. J. L. Trott (E)	14	12	2	410	71	0	3	41.00	62.31	28	0
G. J. Bailey (A)	13	13	2	441	65	0	3	40.09	77.50	31	6
†Tamim Iqbal (B)	9	9	0	347	70	0	5	38.55	82.81	43	3
A. D. Mathews (SL)	27	23	9	534	80*	0	4	38.14	92.22	36	6
Misbah-ul-Haq (P)	18	18	5	493	72*	0	2	37.92	68.56	34	4
R. S. Bopara (E)	14	12	3	339	82	0	4	37.66	80.71	30	0
M. J. Guptill (NZ)	11	11	0	400	85	0	5	36.36	83.50	43	9
L. D. Chandimal (SL)	30	29	5	845	92*	0	7	35.20	74.38	61	4
†D. A. Warner (A)	25	24	0	840	163	2	3	35.00	82.84	87	10
†J-P. Duminy (SA)	13	11	2	312	66*	0	1	34.66	75.36	22	1
D. J. Hussey (A)	25	24	3	728	74	0	7	34.66	91.11	51	10
†C. H. Gayle (WI)	11	11	1	345	125	1	2	34.50	89.84	27	24
Umar Akmal (P)	17	14	2	407	77	0	4	33.91	78.72	30	7
†G. C. Smith (SA)	11	10	0	338	125	1	2	33.80	72.53	28	5
†M. E. K. Hussey (A)	19	19	1	580	67	0	4	32.22	82.50	39	12
M. N. Samuels (WI)	17	16	1	482	126	2	0	32.13	70.36	50	8
R. J. Nicol (NZ)	15	14	0	449	146	1	2	32.07	77.01	38	13
K. A. Pollard (WI)	17	16	1	481	102	1	2	32.06	86.35	29	26

BOWLING (10 wickets, average 40.00)

	Style	*O*	*M*	*R*	*W*	*BB*	*4I*	*Avge*	*SR*	*ER*
S. P. Narine (WI)	OB	163.5	11	600	34	5-27	3	17.64	28.91	3.66
Junaid Khan (P)	LFM	33.2	1	190	10	4-43	1	19.00	20.00	5.70
K. A. J. Roach (WI)	RF	70.3	4	358	18	5-56	1	19.88	23.50	5.07
S. T. Finn (E)	RF	119	6	500	25	4-34	3	20.00	28.56	4.20
Abdur Razzak (B)	SLA	84	6	332	16	3-19	0	20.75	31.50	3.95
Saeed Ajmal (P)	OB	151.4	8	655	31	5-43	2	21.12	29.35	4.31
M. Morkel (SA)	RF	86.2	5	423	20	5-38	2	21.15	25.90	4.89
M. A. Starc (A)	LFM	72.4	3	383	18	5-42	3	21.27	24.22	5.27
S. R. Watson (A)	RFM	91.4	9	392	17	3-30	0	23.05	32.35	4.27
C. J. McKay (A)	RFM	142.3	11	645	27	5-28	2	23.88	31.66	4.52
K. D. Mills (NZ)	RFM	80.3	9	369	15	3-26	0	24.60	32.20	4.58
L. L. Tsotsobe (SA)	LFM	95.3	6	465	18	3-19	0	25.83	31.83	4.86
J. M. Anderson (E)	RFM	101.4	9	479	18	4-44	1	26.61	33.88	4.71
T. T. Bresnan (E)	RFM	61.4	1	346	13	4-34	1	26.61	28.46	5.61
R. J. Peterson (SA)	SLA	100	3	455	17	3-37	0	26.76	35.29	4.55

	Style	O	M	R	W	BB	4I	Avge	SR	ER
N. L. T. C. Perera (SL)	RFM	144.1	5	859	32	6-44	3	26.84	27.03	5.95
R. Vinay Kumar (I)	RFM	64	4	344	12	3-21	0	28.66	32.00	5.37
I. K. Pathan (I)	LFM	101.1	3	554	19	5-61	2	29.15	31.94	5.47
Mashrafe bin Mortaza (B)	RFM	70.5	4	330	11	2-34	0	30.00	38.63	4.65
T. G. Southee (NZ)	RFM	102.2	7	514	17	3-18	0	30.23	36.11	5.02
B. Lee (A)	RF	128.2	11	704	23	3-42	0	30.60	33.47	5.48
D. T. Christian (A)	RFM	109.1	4	528	17	5-31	1	31.05	38.52	4.83
A. D. Russell (WI)	RFM	101	1	565	18	4-45	3	31.38	33.66	5.59
S. L. Malinga (SL)	RF	266	11	1,508	47	5-54	2	32.08	33.95	5.66
D. W. Steyn (SA)	RF	73.4	6	321	10	2-24	0	32.10	44.20	4.35
Aizaz Cheema (P)	RFM	55.4	0	323	10	4-43	1	32.30	33.40	5.80
J. L. Pattinson (A)	RFM	75.1	4	388	12	4-51	1	32.33	37.58	5.16
B. W. Hilfenhaus (A)	RFM	76.2	5	358	11	5-33	1	32.54	41.63	4.68
R. Rampaul (WI)	RFM	67.2	1	359	11	5-49	1	32.63	36.72	5.33
S. C. J. Broad (E)	RFM	79	5	368	11	3-42	0	33.45	43.09	4.65
M. F. Maharoof (SL)	RFM	83	2	432	12	3-40	0	36.00	41.50	5.20
D. J. G. Sammy (WI)	RM	125.1	4	545	15	3-28	0	36.33	50.06	4.35
X. J. Doherty (A)	SLA	166.2	7	811	22	4-49	1	36.86	45.36	4.87

MOST DISMISSALS BY A WICKETKEEPER

Dis		M	
34	(30ct, 4st)	25	M. S. Wade (A)
33	(30ct, 3st)	31	K. C. Sangakkara (SL)
31	(26ct, 5st)	15	C. Kieswetter (E)
24	(23ct, 1st)	13	A. B. de Villiers (SA)
17	(12ct, 5st)	16	M. S. Dhoni (I)
14	(11ct, 3st)	9	Mushfiqur Rahim (B)
10	(7ct, 3st)	7	D. C. Thomas (WI)

B. B. McCullum made nine catches and one stumping in 11 matches, but held three of those catches in five matches when not keeping wicket.

MOST CATCHES IN THE FIELD

Ct	M	
15	17	K. A. Pollard (WI)
14	17	V. Kohli (I)
14	17	D. J. G. Sammy (WI)
11	19	M. E. K. Hussey (A)
11	25	D. J. Hussey (A)
11	28	H. D. R. L. Thirimanne (SL)
10	13	G. J. Bailey (A)
10	23	N. L. T. C. Perera (SL)
10	30	D. P. M. D. Jayawardene (SL)

TWENTY20 INTERNATIONAL AVERAGES IN CALENDAR YEAR 2012

BATTING (200 runs, average 25.00)

	M	I	NO	R	HS	100	50	Avge	SR	4	6
M. S. Dhoni (I)	14	12	7	268	48*	0	0	53.60	125.82	24	6
M. J. Guptill (NZ)	13	13	3	472	101*	1	2	47.20	130.74	45	21
†Tamim Iqbal (B)	9	9	2	327	88*	0	3	46.71	119.34	33	5
†C. H. Gayle (WI)	11	10	2	368	85*	0	5	46.00	144.88	30	25
†M. E. K. Hussey (A)	11	10	4	264	59*	0	2	44.00	117.33	18	8
D. J. Bravo (WI)	10	9	3	260	54*	0	1	43.33	133.33	11	14
R. D. Berrington (Sco)	5	5	0	212	100	1	0	42.40	153.62	26	6
M. N. Samuels (WI)	12	10	2	325	85*	0	4	40.62	143.17	18	24
S. R. Watson (A)	11	11	1	406	72	0	4	40.60	143.97	28	28
†J-P. Duminy (SA)	10	8	2	237	48	0	0	39.50	113.94	16	5
V. Kohli (I)	14	13	1	471	78*	0	4	39.25	132.67	57	7
A. D. Hales (E)	10	10	1	343	99	0	3	38.11	137.20	32	10

	M	*I*	*NO*	*R*	*HS*	*100*	*50*	*Avge*	*SR*	*4*	*6*
†E. C. Joyce (Ire)	11	9	2	261	78*	0	1	37.28	95.25	22	3
†S. K. Raina (I)	14	11	4	257	45	0	0	36.71	127.22	26	4
D. P. M. D. Jayawardene (SL)	9	9	1	271	65*	0	1	33.87	117.31	34	5
P. R. Stirling (Ire)	13	13	3	338	79	0	3	33.80	135.20	45	7
L. J. Wright (E)	9	9	1	252	99*	0	2	31.50	151.80	18	14
B. B. McCullum (NZ)	15	15	0	459	123	1	1	30.60	135.79	46	17
G. C. Wilson (Ire)	12	10	2	238	41*	0	0	29.75	98.75	21	4
K. A. Pollard (WI)	12	11	3	236	63*	0	2	29.50	168.57	16	17
G. J. Bailey (A)	13	10	3	203	63	0	1	29.00	134.43	17	8
†Yuvraj Singh (I)	10	9	1	224	72	0	1	28.00	141.77	11	16
†D. A. Warner (A)	13	13	1	334	63*	0	3	27.83	133.06	28	18
Shoaib Malik (P)	16	13	5	215	57*	0	1	26.87	97.28	16	4
†Nasir Jamshed (P)	11	11	1	263	56	0	2	26.30	121.19	20	10
†Shakib Al Hasan (B)	8	8	0	209	84	0	2	26.12	137.50	27	3
H. M. Amla (SA)	10	10	2	208	47*	0	0	26.00	128.39	27	3
†G. Gambhir (I)	14	14	2	311	56*	0	1	25.91	109.89	35	2
J. Charles (WI)	11	10	0	251	84	0	1	25.10	117.28	35	6

BOWLING (12 wickets)

	Style	*O*	*M*	*R*	*W*	*BB*	*4I*	*Avge*	*SR*	*ER*
B. A. W. Mendis (SL)	OB/LBG	24	3	147	15	6-8	2	9.80	9.60	6.12
R. M. Haq (Scot)	OB	20	0	119	12	3-22	0	9.91	10.00	5.95
Yuvraj Singh (I)	SLA	28.4	0	179	15	3-17	0	11.93	11.46	6.24
M. A. Starc (A)	LFM	31.1	0	192	14	3-11	0	13.71	13.35	6.16
A. B. Dinda (I)	RFM	20	1	169	12	4-19	1	14.08	10.00	8.45
G. P. Swann (E)	OB	44	3	250	17	3-13	0	14.70	15.52	5.68
Saeed Ajmal (P)	OB	64	1	391	25	4-23	2	15.64	15.36	6.10
S. R. Watson (A)	RFM	41.5	0	269	17	3-26	0	15.82	14.76	6.43
G. H. Dockrell (Ire)	SLA	40.1	1	240	15	3-15	0	16.00	16.06	5.97
S. T. Finn (E)	RF	42	0	284	17	3-16	0	16.70	14.82	6.76
M. C. Sorensen (Ire)	RFM	27	1	208	12	3-20	0	17.33	13.50	7.70
S. P. Narine (WI)	OB	47.4	0	294	16	4-12	1	18.37	17.87	6.16
I. K. Pathan (I)	LFM	26	0	223	12	3-27	0	18.58	13.00	8.57
R. J. Peterson (SA)	SLA	33	1	226	12	2-8	0	18.83	16.50	6.84
Abdur Razzak (B)	SLA	35	1	248	12	2-9	0	20.66	17.50	7.08
Umar Gul (P)	RFM	52	1	436	19	4-37	1	22.94	16.42	8.38
T. G. Southee (NZ)	RFM	42	1	347	14	3-16	0	24.78	18.00	8.26
D. A. J. Bracewell (NZ)	RFM	32.5	0	340	12	3-31	0	28.33	16.41	10.35
J. W. Dernbach (E)	RFM	44.2	0	376	13	2-16	0	28.92	20.46	8.48

MOST DISMISSALS BY A WICKETKEEPER

Dis		*M*	
14	(10ct, 4st)	14	M. S. Dhoni (I)
12	(10ct, 2st)	11	A. B. de Villiers (SA)
11	(5ct, 6st)	10	K. C. Sangakkara (SL)

MOST CATCHES IN THE FIELD

Ct	*M*	
13	11	J. M. Bairstow (E)
10	14	S. K. Raina (I)
10	16	Shoaib Malik (P)
9	13	D. A. Warner (A)
8	11	T. M. Dilshan (SL)
8	14	E. J. G. Morgan (E)
8	15	Umar Gul (P)

J. M. Bairstow held another catch in one match when keeping wicket.

INDEX OF TEST MATCHES

Twelve earlier 2011-12 Test series – Zimbabwe v Bangladesh, Sri Lanka v Australia, Zimbabwe v Pakistan, Pakistan v Sri Lanka, Bangladesh v West Indies, Zimbabwe v New Zealand, India v West Indies, South Africa v Australia, Australia v New Zealand, Bangladesh v Pakistan, South Africa v Sri Lanka, and Australia v India – appeared in *Wisden 2012*.

WEST INDIES v NEW ZEALAND, 2012

July 25	North Sound, Antigua	West Indies won by nine wickets	1181
August 2	Kingston	West Indies won by five wickets	1183

INDIA v NEW ZEALAND, 2012-13

August 23	Hyderabad	India won by an innings and 115 runs	981
August 31	Bangalore	India won by five wickets	982

AUSTRALIA v SOUTH AFRICA, 2012-13

November 9	Brisbane	Drawn	911
November 22	Adelaide	Drawn	913
November 30	Perth	South Africa won by 309 runs	916

BANGLADESH v WEST INDIES, 2012-13

November 13	Mirpur	West Indies won by 77 runs	958
November 21	Khulna	West Indies won by ten wickets	960

INDIA v ENGLAND, 2012-13

November 15	Ahmedabad	India won by nine wickets	392
November 23	Mumbai	England won by ten wickets	395
December 5	Kolkata	England won by seven wickets	399
December 13	Nagpur	Drawn	403

SRI LANKA v NEW ZEALAND, 2012-13

November 17	Galle	Sri Lanka won by ten wickets	1136
November 25	Colombo (PSS)	New Zealand won by 167 runs	1138

AUSTRALIA v SRI LANKA, 2012-13

December 14	Hobart	Australia won by 137 runs	922
December 26	Melbourne	Australia won by an innings and 201 runs	924
January 3	Sydney	Australia won by five wickets	926

SOUTH AFRICA v NEW ZEALAND, 2012-13

January 2	Cape Town	South Africa won by an innings and 27 runs	1079
January 11	Port Elizabeth	South Africa won by an innings and 193 runs	1082

ICC WORLD TWENTY20, 2012-13

REVIEW BY DAVID HOPPS

1. West Indies 2. Sri Lanka 3= Australia and Pakistan

When the World Twenty20 drew to a close in Colombo, with the monsoon rains kindly delaying their arrival, even those most resistant to the charms of cricket's shortest format struggled to deny it had done the game a huge service. For around 20 years, West Indies cricket had seemed in permanent decline. Yet here they were, triumphant in maroon and gold, dancing on the outfield at the Premadasa Stadium, winners once more.

Tipped by many from the outset as potential victors, they had revealed their credentials only in fits and starts. Indeed, had Australia taken three more balls to chase down Ireland's total in the group stages, West Indies would have fallen at the first hurdle on net run-rate. And, during an extraordinary final, they needed to recover a game against the hosts Sri Lanka that had seemed beyond them – a result forged largely by one man, Marlon Samuels, his career at last flowering.

West Indies' uncertainty made their achievement all the more appealing, while the unfailing decency and optimism of their captain, Darren Sammy, were all the more striking for rising above his own limitations. Sammy, a St Lucian, personified their slogan of "One Team, One People, One Goal", and his unbeaten 26 off 15 balls in the final – to follow Samuels's 78 off 56 – dragged West Indies out of inertia and towards what proved a match-winning total of 137 for six.

As they confirmed their status as many neutrals' favourite, there came persuasive evidence that Twenty20 was a game that a new wave of cricketers and fans could embrace throughout the Caribbean. This encouraged the belief that their victory was not just a brief interlude in a story of decline, but the start of a genuine renaissance. In the London Olympics back in August, the medal-winning sprinters Usain Bolt and Yohan Blake had proclaimed themselves Jamaicans, but were quick to stress they were also representatives of the wider West Indian community. Having reasserted a Caribbean identity, whose existence many in cricket had grown to doubt, Bolt and Blake also revealed themselves as lovers of the game. Publicity as good as that does not come along often.

Two months later, Chris Gayle – another high-profile Jamaican – frolicked round the outfield with Sammy and the World Twenty20 trophy, and offered up one last rendition of the Gangnam Style dance that, in cricket circles at least, he had made his own. He, too, could now claim to represent not just Jamaica but also a region that sport had again insisted was more connected than politicians and activists would have you believe. There was even a Blake to Gayle's Bolt, another Jamaican understudy in the form of Samuels – a player of stature in 2012, first in the Test matches of a miserable English spring, now in the tropical heat and Twenty20 of Sri Lanka.

Gareth Copley, Getty Images

Cricket's coolest man? Chris Gayle celebrates Gangnam Style, as West Indies soak in their first global success since the 2004 Champions Trophy.

These West Indians were far removed from their illustrious predecessors, for they had none of their fearsome fast bowling. In fact, with the exception of Ravi Rampaul – chugging along skilfully at around 80mph – they had no fast bowler of impact at all. But they did have batsmen who could slug the ball hard and long: Gayle hit 16 sixes, more than anyone, and Samuels 15. And, in Sunil Narine, they possessed a spinner of genuine mystique.

As the excellent early-tournament pitches, at Pallekele in particular, gave way to tired, powdery surfaces, their lack of pace suited **West Indies** perfectly. They pummelled the ball over the boundary ropes in a manner few could match, and fiddled through their overs as best they could. It was odd to see a West Indian bowling attack succeed that way. But it worked.

Somewhere, looking on in the Caribbean, there must have been young athletes yearning to grab a share of the adulation. Is it too much to hope we have heard the last of the basketball generation; the conclusion that other sports, more favoured in the United States and beamed in on satellite television, have taken hold; and that West Indies' decline is not cyclical, but an irreversible malaise? The rejection of colonialism which had first identified itself in their determination to dominate the cricketing world had been replaced by a rejection of cricket itself. And the issue was even broader than that: not merely that Caribbean youth was enthralled by American sport, as much as the fact that their interest in *all* sport was not quite what it was.

Perhaps the impact of the competition went even wider. But as the World Twenty20 gained a hold on the consciousness, international cricket had an instant format with which it could fight back, so much so that even in the States there was ambitious talk of a professional league. Those who claimed there was no place for Twenty20 beyond the lucrative domestic tournaments were left re-examining their conviction.

So appealing was the story of this competition that it was hard for anybody to contend that it did not matter, that it was an inferior game unworthy of attention, that it demanded no intellect, created no tension, bared no souls. Like its three predecessors, it was a rare thing: a well-run, condensed tournament that, once it got over the preliminary stage, maintained interest.

Sri Lanka Cricket, which had blundered into financial trouble by building two new stadiums and upgrading another for the 2011 World Cup, now staged a slick event. The smart new venue at Pallekele was particularly impressive, with a welcoming feel and a beautiful mountain backdrop. Its pitches were true and, initially at least, possessed surprising pace. It promised to enhance Sri Lankan cricket for years to come.

The early overs in the final, as Gayle of all people made just three in 16 balls, possessed Test-match tension, and there can be no finer accolade than that. If it is not a worthy addition to the game, how then to explain the despair felt by Mahela Jayawardene and Kumar Sangakkara, two players who have offered **Sri Lanka** wise counsel and stirring deeds for the past decade, but who had failed yet again to win a major one-day trophy? Or the hurt of Lasith Malinga, who bowled four overs for 54, then turned off his mobile phone for a couple of days as he faced up to the most painful moment of his career? Sri Lanka had surely never entered a tournament with more vigour since their breakthrough win in the 50-over World Cup 16 years earlier. Yet, for the fourth time in a row, all they had to show was a losing final.

Malinga bowled four overs for 54 – then turned off his mobile

Even those who continued to argue that Twenty20 demanded more luck than skill had to concede that the right four sides contested the semi-finals: West Indies, Sri Lanka and Pakistan had played the best cricket (Pakistan, needless to say, intermittently); and **Australia** deserved to be there because of a heroic tournament from Shane Watson, an all-rounder who combines dominance and vulnerability in equal measure. At least Achilles only had to worry about his heel. Watson is a collection of opposites: tough yet soft, untouchable yet fragile, egotistical yet rueful. Any moment he might bully a ball out of the ground, demolish the stumps – or crumple into a heap.

As he continually stoked Australia's challenge – top-scoring with 249 runs, launching 15 sixes, and taking 11 wickets, second only to Ajantha Mendis – Watson revealed a greater truth about Twenty20: that it is not, as many ex-professionals insist, so much influenced by fortune as potentially settled by a single outstanding performance. That was certainly true in the final, when Samuels secured the match virtually by himself. In an age where individual achievement is so often valued above communal good, that is not about to hold the format back.

England had their own star name – except that Kevin Pietersen, ostracised over the texting saga, was not there (or rather, he was, but as a pundit in a TV studio). Their title defence suffered as a result. Paul Collingwood, who had captained them to a surprise win in the Caribbean in 2010, hailed Stuart Broad's vintage as a more skilful bunch than his own but, with a 19-run defeat by Sri Lanka, England's involvement predictably petered out in the Super Eights.

There may have been an England side that could have reached the semi-finals, but it was not the one which lost three matches out of five. Their nadir came against India's second-string spinners in Colombo, where they careered to 80 all out and a 90-run defeat, and convinced the Indians that slow bowling would be the way to overcome them in the Test series at home that followed soon after (well, it made sense at the time).

Statistical studies informed England's strategy of preserving top-order wickets when batting, and taking them when bowling. Luke Wright, his standing already bolstered by experience of domestic Twenty20 in five countries, responded gamely to the challenge. He averaged 48, with a strike-rate of 169 – the highest of any of the 24 batsmen who topped 100 runs – and hit 13 sixes. His most bitter-sweet episode came with an unbeaten 99 against a capricious Afghanistan side in Colombo, while his best innings was a 43-ball 76 against New Zealand in Pallekele.

Alex Hales had his moments, but the feeling grew that Craig Kieswetter was unsuited to a top-order role, especially if preserving wickets was the mantra. He attacked, failed, blocked, failed once more – and was finally dropped for the game against Sri Lanka, in which Malinga took three wickets in four balls, as good as ending England's pursuit of 170 before it had begun.

An alternative team might have included Ian Bell alongside Hales and Wright at the top; married Pietersen and Eoin Morgan in the middle order (allowing Pietersen to make spectators' hair stand on end, rather than gelling his own to the same effect for the benefit of TV viewers); and recognised Samit Patel's ability against spin, a skill that was belatedly underlined with a 48-ball 67 against Sri Lanka. Kieswetter and Jonny Bairstow could then have contested the keeping position at No. 7. Jos Buttler, exciting and innovative, but naive and far from battle-hardened, would have been a standby batsman able to observe his trade.

The side England *actually* selected, young and untutored in Asian conditions, put excessive onus on setting up the game for Morgan. Yet there were weaknesses with the ball, too. Danny Briggs, whose graceful left-arm spin had been a key component in Hampshire's domestic success, played only one match, opening against New Zealand, and was a less appealing selection under lights, when the ball was more likely to zip around. Steven Finn led the attack with pace and purpose, but Tim Bresnan had a mediocre tournament, and Jade Dernbach's variations did not prevent him from being England's most expensive bowler. Any ambitions for Ravi Bopara's fiddly medium-pace on pitches which grew slower had to be abandoned because his batting was in such parlous shape. His last-gasp inclusion for the Sri Lanka match smacked of desperation; he made one from six balls.

There was criticism of the qualifying stage, which never sparked into life. But it lasted only eight days, and any ennui was as much the fault of the quality of the sides contesting it. **Ireland's** long-serving seamer, Trent Johnston, railed against the habitual description of his team as "minnows", and demanded they be judged by the standards of a Full Member one-day nation – in which case it

Philip Brown

Switching roles: Kevin Pietersen unfurls his trademark stroke in Colombo... unfortunately for England, it was in a TV studio.

is fair to observe that they remain light on quality and will struggle as long as England pilfer their best cricketers.

Bangladesh's fielding was at times abysmal, and **Zimbabwe** were knocked out before five teams had even started their first match. Among the lesser sides, **Afghanistan** alone performed above expectations, playing with flair and aggression, even if it seemed Ten10 might be more their game. India beat them only after considerable discomfort, a reminder in these high-tech days that raw talent cannot be entirely discounted.

The same message came from Akila Dananjaya, a young off-spinner – with lots of variations – who was fast-tracked into the Sri Lanka side after being spotted in the nets by Jayawardene. He suffered a fractured cheekbone missing a fierce return catch on debut against New Zealand, but performed admirably when he had the chance.

There were grumbles that all four preliminary group winners ended up in the same pool, but an element of pre-seeding had logic on its side. A large number of travelling supporters cannot book accommodation in a couple of days, and it was entirely sensible to plan for a scenario in which, say, as long as Afghanistan were eliminated, England would play in Pallekele and India in Colombo in the next stage, whatever their final group positions. To determine Super Eight venues by group results would have risked reducing the number of overseas supporters.

In the Super Eights, India (on net run-rate), New Zealand and **South Africa** – a disappointment once more at a major tournament – succumbed along with England. **India** had the most romantic story – the return of Yuvraj Singh after treatment in the USA for cancer. Yuvraj had a solid tournament, although there were times when his inclusion appeared to add to the confusion of India's selections. Only Virat Kohli, looking ever more likely to succeed Sachin Tendulkar as his country's cricket idol, possessed authority with the bat. With Zaheer Khan on the wane, their pace attack rarely looked competitive.

Quite what it all said about the IPL was hard to judge, for India actually won four games out of five, only to do their run-rate irreparable damage when they were thrashed by Australia in the match that mattered most. It is one thing having the most successful domestic Twenty20 tournament in the world; quite another for that to lead to a successful national side. There was little evidence Indian players were benefiting any more from the IPL than the assortment of international players who descend annually upon their shores. This is no surprise in England, where the glitz and glamour of football's Premier League, awash with foreign players, has not translated into international glory.

New Zealand had an extraordinary tournament. They were involved in two eliminator-over deciders in the Super Eights, against Sri Lanka and West Indies – and lost both, leaving their captain Ross Taylor struggling for words. Their new coach, Mike Hesson, understandably questioned the rationale of using these one-over tie-breakers in group matches, when it ought to have been perfectly possible for the teams to share the spoils. That would not have saved New Zealand from elimination, but Hesson had a case. An American-style aversion to tied matches seems to have crept into cricket without much debate.

Pakistan's semi-final qualification ahead of India owed much to a remarkable recovery against South Africa, when Umar Gul and Umar Akmal put on 49 in 27 balls for the eighth wicket to pull off an unexpected win. But Pakistan's interest ended when, on a crumbling pitch at the Premadasa, Jayawardene produced a delicate gem of an innings to guide Sri Lanka into the final.

West Indies saw off Australia in the other semi as the mighty Watson failed to deliver; Australia were lucky to keep the margin down to 74 runs as their batting line-up, at last exposed, plunged to 43 for six. Nevertheless, a team that had briefly been ranked tenth, just below Ireland, a few weeks before the tournament, had at least silenced the sniggers.

A team of the tournament might have gone something like this: Shane Watson, Chris Gayle, Mahela Jayawardene (captain), Virat Kohli, Marlon Samuels, Eoin Morgan, M. S. Dhoni (wicketkeeper), Mitchell Starc, Sunil Narine, Saeed Ajmal and Dale Steyn. Here were 11 players who had performed excellently in a short, sharp, engrossing tournament. If only the ICC would apply the lesson elsewhere.

> "Sir Home Gordon insisted he once heard a Yorkshireman triumph in a cricketing debate over a Lancastrian with the finality of this declaration: 'I know more than you anyhow, for I've shook 'ands with Lord 'Awke and that's more than you ever did."
>
> **150 Years of Yorkshire, page 94.**

ICC WORLD TWENTY20 STATISTICS

Leading run-scorers

	M	I	NO	R	HS	50	Avge	SR	4	6
S. R. Watson (A)	6	6	1	249	72	3	49.80	150.00	19	15
D. P. M. D. Jayawardene (SL)	7	7	1	243	65*	1	40.50	116.26	29	5
M. N. Samuels (WI)	7	6	0	230	78	3	38.33	132.94	14	15
†C. H. Gayle (WI)	7	6	1	222	75*	3	44.40	150.00	19	16
B. B. McCullum (NZ)	5	5	0	212	123	1	42.40	159.39	20	10
L. J. Wright (E)	5	5	1	193	99*	2	48.25	169.29	14	13
V. Kohli (I)	5	5	1	185	78*	2	46.25	122.51	20	4
T. M. Dilshan (SL)	7	7	0	179	76	1	25.57	120.94	17	4
†K. C. Sangakkara (SL)	7	7	1	170	44	0	28.33	126.86	18	1
Mohammad Hafeez (P)	6	6	0	164	45	0	27.33	98.20	15	4
†M. E. K. Hussey (A)	6	5	3	155	54*	1	77.50	123.01	12	4
Imran Nazir (P)	6	6	0	153	72	1	25.50	150.00	24	3

The only century was B. B. McCullum's 123 for New Zealand v Bangladesh at Pallekele.

Best strike-rates – most runs scored per 100 balls

	SR	Runs		SR	Runs
G. J. Bailey (A)	171.42	84	C. H. Gayle (WI)	150.00	222
L. J. Wright (E)	169.29	193	Imran Nazir (P)	150.00	153
B. B. McCullum (NZ)	159.39	212	L. R. P. L. Taylor (NZ)	145.54	147
F. du Plessis (SA)	159.18	78	Nasir Jamshed (P)	134.54	148
Shakib Al Hasan (B)	153.22	95	K. A. Pollard (WI)	133.33	80
S. R. Watson (A)	150.00	249	M. N. Samuels (WI)	132.94	230

Minimum 75 runs.

Leading wicket-takers

	Style	O	M	R	W	BB	4I	Avge	SR	ER
B. A. W. Mendis (SL)	OB	24	3	147	15	6-8	2	9.80	9.60	6.12
S. R. Watson (A)	RFM	24	0	176	11	3-26	0	16.00	13.09	7.33
M. A. Starc (A)	LFM	24	0	164	10	3-20	0	16.40	14.40	6.83
L. Balaji (I)	RFM	12	0	88	9	3-19	0	9.77	8.00	7.33
S. P. Narine (WI)	OB	24.4	0	139	9	3-9	0	15.44	16.44	5.63
Saeed Ajmal (P)	OB	24	1	163	9	4-30	1	18.11	16.00	6.79
R. Rampaul (WI)	RFM	23.5	1	189	9	3-16	0	21.00	15.88	7.93
Yuvraj Singh (I)	SLA	13.4	0	81	8	3-24	0	10.12	10.25	5.92
S. T. Finn (E)	RF	20	0	123	8	3-16	0	15.37	15.00	6.15
T. G. Southee (NZ)	RFM	18	1	144	8	3-16	0	18.00	13.50	8.00
S. L. Malinga (SL)	RF	24.3	0	207	8	5-31	1	25.87	18.37	8.44

Most economical bowlers – runs per over

	ER	Overs		ER	Overs
D. W. Steyn (SA)	4.82	17	A. D. Mathews (SL)	5.95	20
Raza Hasan (P)	4.93	15	R. Ashwin (I)	6.00	15.5
S. Badree (WI)	5.56	16	N. L. McCullum (NZ)	6.11	17
S. P. Narine (WI)	5.63	24.4	B. A. W. Mendis (SL)	6.12	24
Yuvraj Singh (I)	5.92	13.4	S. T. Finn (E)	6.15	20
Mohammad Hafeez (P)	5.94	18	G. P. Swann (E)	6.15	19

Minimum 10 overs. There were 21 maidens: three by B. A. W. Mendis (SL), two each by S. C. J. Broad (E), Harbhajan Singh (I) and G. P. Swann (E), and one by J. Botha (SA), P. P. Chawla (I), P. J. Cummins (A), J. H. Kallis (SA), A. D. Mathews (SL), R. J. Peterson (SA), R. Rampaul (WI), Raza Hasan (P), Saeed Ajmal (P), Shapoor Zadran (Afg), T. G. Southee (NZ) and D. W. Steyn (SA).

Leading wicketkeepers

	Dis	M		Dis	M
A. B. de Villiers (SA)	9 (7 ct, 2 st)	5	M. S. Wade (A)	5 (4 ct, 1 st)	6
K. C. Sangakkara (SL)	7 (1 ct, 6 st)	7	Kamran Akmal (P)	3 (1 ct, 2 st)	6
M. S. Dhoni (I)	6 (5 ct, 1 st)	5	C. Kieswetter (E)	3 (2 ct, 1 st)	4
D. Ramdin (WI)	6 (4 ct, 2 st)	7			

Leading fielders – most catches

	Ct	M		Ct	M
S. K. Raina (I)	6	5	T. M. Dilshan (SL)	4	7
D. A. Warner (A)	5	6	G. Gambhir (I)	4	5
G. J. Bailey (A)	4	6	L. R. P. L. Taylor (NZ)	4	5
J. M. Bairstow (E)	4	4	K. S. Williamson (NZ)	4	4

Bairstow also kept wicket in one match, when he took another catch.

NATIONAL SQUADS

* *Captain.* ‡ *Did not play in ICC World Twenty20.*

Afghanistan *Nawroz Mangal, Asghar Stanikzai, Dawlat Zadran, Gulbadeen Naib, ‡Hamid Hassan, Izatullah Dawlatzai, ‡Javed Ahmadi, Karim Sadiq, Mohammad Nabi, Mohammad Shahzad, Najibullah Zadran, ‡Nasim Baras, Samiullah Shenwari, Shafiqullah Shinwari, Shapoor Zadran. *Coach:* Kabir Khan.

Australia *G. J. Bailey, D. T. Christian, P. J. Cummins, X. J. Doherty, ‡B. W. Hilfenhaus, G. B. Hogg, D. J. Hussey, M. E. K. Hussey, ‡C. J. McKay, G. J. Maxwell, M. A. Starc, M. S. Wade, D. A. Warner, S. R. Watson, C. L. White. *Coach:* J. M. Arthur.

Bangladesh *Mushfiqur Rahim, Abdur Razzak, Abul Hasan, Elias Sunny, ‡Farhad Reza, ‡Jahurul Islam, ‡Junaid Siddique, Mahmudullah, Mashrafe bin Mortaza, Mohammad Ashraful, Nasir Hossain, Shafiul Islam, Shakib Al Hasan, Tamim Iqbal, Ziaur Rahman. *Coach:* R. A. Pybus.

England *S. C. J. Broad, J. M. Bairstow, R. S. Bopara, T. T. Bresnan, D. R. Briggs, J. C. Buttler, J. W. Dernbach, S. T. Finn, A. D. Hales, C. Kieswetter, ‡M. J. Lumb, E. J. G. Morgan, S. R. Patel, G. P. Swann, L. J. Wright. *Coach:* A. Flower.

India *M. S. Dhoni, R. Ashwin, L. Balaji, P. P. Chawla, A. B. Dinda, G. Gambhir, Harbhajan Singh, V. Kohli, I. K. Pathan, S. K. Raina, V. Sehwag, R. G. Sharma, ‡M. K. Tiwary, Yuvraj Singh, Zaheer Khan. *Coach:* D. A. G. Fletcher.

Ireland *W. T. S. Porterfield, A. R. Cusack, G. H. Dockrell, D. T. Johnston, N. G. Jones, E. C. Joyce, ‡T. J. Murtagh, K. J. O'Brien, N. J. O'Brien, W. B. Rankin, M. C. Sorensen, P. R. Stirling, ‡S. R. Thompson, ‡A. R. White, G. C. Wilson. *Coach:* P. V. Simmons.

New Zealand *L. R. P. L. Taylor, D. A. J. Bracewell, J. E. C. Franklin, M. J. Guptill, R. M. Hira, B. B. McCullum, N. L. McCullum, K. D. Mills, A. F. Milne, R. J. Nicol, J. D. P. Oram, T. G. Southee, D. L. Vettori, ‡B-J. Watling, K. S. Williamson. *Coach:* M. J. Hesson.

Pakistan *Mohammad Hafeez, Abdul Razzaq, ‡Asad Shafiq, Imran Nazir, Kamran Akmal, ‡Mohammad Sami, Nasir Jamshed, Raza Hasan, Saeed Ajmal, Shahid Afridi, Shoaib Malik, Sohail Tanvir, Umar Akmal, Umar Gul, Yasir Arafat. *Coach:* D. F. Whatmore.

South Africa *A. B. de Villiers, H. M. Amla, F. Behardien, J. Botha, J-P. Duminy, F. du Plessis, J. H. Kallis, R. E. Levi, J. A. Morkel, M. Morkel, ‡J. L. Ontong, W. D. Parnell, R. J. Peterson, D. W. Steyn, ‡L. L. Tsotsobe. *Coach:* G. Kirsten.

Sri Lanka *D. P. M. D. Jayawardene, ‡L. D. Chandimal, A. Dananjaya, T. M. Dilshan, ‡R. M. S. Eranga, H. M. R. K. B. Herath, K. M. D. N. Kulasekara, S. L. Malinga, A. D. Mathews, B. A. W. Mendis, B. M. A. J. Mendis, E. M. D. Y. Munaweera, N. L. T. C. Perera, K. C. Sangakkara, H. D. R. L. Thirimanne. *Coach:* G. X. Ford.

West Indies *D. J. G. Sammy, S. Badree, D. J. Bravo, D. M. Bravo, J. Charles, F. H. Edwards, C. H. Gayle, S. P. Narine, K. A. Pollard, D. Ramdin, R. Rampaul, A. D. Russell, M. N. Samuels, ‡L. M. P. Simmons, D. R. Smith. *Coach:* O. D. Gibson.

Zimbabwe *B. R. M. Taylor, E. Chigumbura, A. G. Cremer, C. R. Ervine, K. M. Jarvis, H. Masakadza, S. Matsikenyeri, C. B. Mpofu, ‡F. Mutizwa, ‡R. Muzhange, R. W. Price, V. Sibanda, P. Utseya, B. V. Vitori, M. N. Waller. *Coach:* A. R. Butcher.

All matches were played partially or entirely under floodlights.

MATCH REPORTS BY IAN CALLENDER, SHAHID HASHMI, RICHARD HOBSON, NEIL MANTHORP, CHLOE SALTAU, OSMAN SAMIUDDIN, UTPAL SHUVRO, SA'ADI THAWFEEQ AND ANDY WILSON

GROUP A

AFGHANISTAN v INDIA

At Colombo (RPS), September 19, 2012. India won by 23 runs. Toss: Afghanistan. Twenty20 international debut: Najibullah Zadran.

Afghanistan paid for three dropped catches, which left them with too stiff a chase in a tale of two mid-innings. They missed Raina (when two) and Kohli (33) in successive overs – Samiullah Shenwari at long-on palmed the second chance over the rope for six – and Raina escaped again at 19. Left-armer Shapoor Zadran had removed both openers, but 14 wides testified to a general inconsistency. Kohli hit straight and profitably, and Dhoni struck the last two balls for four and six as Mohammad Nabi failed to find the yorker length for his off-breaks. Afghanistan stumbled after making a good start. They were a run ahead at the halfway mark, at 69 for two, and later needed 85 from 53 deliveries with eight wickets in hand – but then three went down in six balls from Yuvraj Singh and Ashwin. In the 17th over, Ashwin flummoxed Nabi by checking in his delivery stride: the resultant skyer to mid-off ended a spirited counter-attack, and Afghanistan's lack of depth was exposed.

Man of the Match: V. Kohli.

India

		B	4	6
G. Gambhir *b 11*	10	8	1	0
V. Sehwag *c 1 b 11*	8	10	1	0
V. Kohli *c 5 b 10*	50	39	4	2
Yuvraj Singh *c 11 b 3*	18	20	0	1
S. K. Raina *b 5*	38	33	6	0
*†M. S. Dhoni *not out*	18	9	2	1
R. G. Sharma *not out*	1	1	0	0
L-b 2, w 14	16			
6 overs: 34-2 (20 overs)	159-5			

1/15 2/22 3/68 4/114 5/148

I. K. Pathan, R. Ashwin, Zaheer Khan and L. Balaji did not bat.

Shapoor Zadran 4–0–33–2; Dawlat Zadran 4–0–25–1; Gulbadeen Naib 2–0–15–0; Karim Sadiq 4–0–33–1; Mohammad Nabi 4–0–35–1; Samiullah Shenwari 2–0–16–0.

Afghanistan

		B	4	6
†Mohammad Shahzad *c 4 b 11*	18	16	3	0
*Nawroz Mangal *lbw b 4*	22	18	1	1
Karim Sadiq *c 1 b 4*	26	26	3	0
Asghar Stanikzai *c 6 b 4*	6	9	0	0
Mohammad Nabi *c 7 b 9*	31	17	2	2
Samiullah Shenwari *c and b 9*	1	2	0	0
Shafiqullah Shinwari *lbw b 8*	8	9	0	1
Gulbadeen Naib *c 5 b 11*	5	14	0	0
Najibullah Zadran *run out*	5	2	1	0
Dawlat Zadran *b 11*	8	5	2	0
Shapoor Zadran *not out*	0	0	0	0
L-b 2, w 3, n-b 1	6			
6 overs: 42-1 (19.3 overs)	136			

1/26 2/52 3/75 4/75 5/76 6/100 7/119 8/125 9/136

Khan 3–0–32–0; Pathan 4–0–29–1; Balaji 3.3–0–19–3; Sharma 1–0–10–0; Yuvraj Singh 4–0–24–3; Ashwin 4–0–20–2.

Umpires: Asad Rauf and S. J. A. Taufel. Third umpire: Aleem Dar.
Referee: R. S. Madugalle.

AFGHANISTAN v ENGLAND

At Colombo (RPS), September 21, 2012. England won by 116 runs. Toss: Afghanistan.

For one over this threatened to be a contest, maybe even an upset. Kieswetter failed to score from the first five deliveries from Shapoor Zadran, the tall left-arm seamer who had also troubled India, and was bowled by the sixth. After four overs England were still struggling, at 15 for one, but 23 came off the next as Hales and Wright began to cut loose. Hales was run out when Karim Sadiq finger-tipped a straight-drive into the stumps after a stand of 69, but Wright powered on to equal England's highest Twenty20 score, set by Hales in the victory over West Indies at Trent Bridge three months previously; Wright's six sixes were an outright England record, beating Morgan's five against South Africa in 2009-10. England plundered 122 from the last ten overs, including 32 off the 19th, bowled by Izatullah Dawlatzai, which included two no-balls and three successive sixes by Wright. Afghanistan lost wickets to the sixth and seventh balls of their reply, and were soon 26 for eight, with any romance in this fixture – played out in front of a sparse crowd – long gone. They did, though, manage to pass the lowest World Twenty20 total (Ireland's 68 against West Indies at Providence in 2010), with Gulbadeen Naib equalling the highest score by a No. 8 in this format.

Man of the Match: L. J. Wright.

England

		B	4	6
†C. Kieswetter *b 10*	0	6	0	0
A. D. Hales *run out*	31	27	5	0
L. J. Wright *not out*	99	55	8	6
E. J. G. Morgan *c 2 b 11*	27	23	1	1
J. C. Buttler *lbw b 11*	15	7	3	0
J. M. Bairstow *c 4 b 9*	12	5	1	1
S. R. Patel *not out*	0	0	0	0
B 4, l-b 2, w 3, n-b 3	12			
6 overs: 52-1 (20 overs)	196-5			

1/0 2/69 3/141 4/159 5/194

*S. C. J. Broad, G. P. Swann, S. T. Finn and J. W. Dernbach did not bat.

Shapoor Zadran 3–1–24–1; Dawlat Zadran 4–0–22–1; Izatullah Dawlatzai 3–0–56–2; Samiullah Shenwari 4–0–33–0; Karim Sadiq 2–0–9–0; Mohammad Nabi 4–0–46–0.

12th man: R. S. Bopara.

Afghanistan

		B	4	6
†Mohammad Shahzad *c 8 b 10*	1	5	0	0
*Nawroz Mangal *c and b 8*	8	9	1	0
Shafiqullah Shinwari *c 12 b 11*	0	1	0	0
Karim Sadiq *run out*	5	8	0	0
Asghar Stanikzai *c 6 b 8*	4	11	0	0
Mohammad Nabi *b 7*	1	6	0	0
Samiullah Shenwari *c 10 b 9*	2	9	0	0
Gulbadeen Naib *c 4 b 11*	44	32	5	3
Dawlat Zadran *st 1 b 7*	0	3	0	0
Shapoor Zadran *lbw b 9*	9	17	0	1
Izatullah Dawlatzai *not out*	0	3	0	0
L-b 1, w 5	6			
6 overs: 22-5 (17.2 overs)	80			

1/2 2/2 3/14 4/22 5/22 6/25 7/26 8/26 9/70

Finn 4–0–24–1; Dernbach 2.2–0–16–2; Broad 3–1–10–2; Patel 3–0–6–2; Swann 4–2–22–2; Wright 1–0–1–0.

Umpires: H. D. P. K. Dharmasena and S. J. A. Taufel. Third umpire: Asad Rauf.
Referee: R. S. Madugalle.

ENGLAND v INDIA

At Colombo (RPS), September 23, 2012. India won by 90 runs. Toss: England.

Harbhajan Singh justified his recall, more than a year after the disastrous tour of England, by recording India's best Twenty20 figures. He might not have played had India – already qualified – not rested Ashwin. But he entered the contest for the sixth over, with England still in contention at 39 for two, and fizzed an arm-ball past Morgan's attempted cut with his second delivery, before Bairstow fell in the following over, from Chawla, another spinner who feasted on England's incompetence; Kieswetter edged his next ball to slip. Bresnan swept Harbhajan desperately to deep square leg, and Buttler and Swann were snaffled in his last over. England thus slid to their lowest Twenty20 total – matching Afghanistan two days earlier – and their heaviest defeat. Broad insisted it was the loss of two early wickets to Pathan's seam which had undone his side, and defended the decision to select Swann as the sole spinner.

Man of the Match: Harbhajan Singh.

India

		B	4	6
G. Gambhir *c 1 b 10*	45	38	5	0
I. K. Pathan *b 10*	8	8	1	0
V. Kohli *c 5 b 9*	40	32	6	0
R. G. Sharma *not out*	55	33	5	1
*†M. S. Dhoni *c 2 b 11*	9	8	1	0
S. K. Raina *not out*	1	1	0	0
B 1, l-b 3, w 8	12			
6 overs: 52-1 (20 overs)	170-4			

1/24 2/81 3/119 4/166

Yuvraj Singh, Harbhajan Singh, P. P. Chawla, A. B. Dinda and L. Balaji did not bat.

England

		B	4	6
†C. Kieswetter *c 3 b 9*	35	25	4	2
A. D. Hales *b 2*	0	2	0	0
L. J. Wright *lbw b 2*	6	4	0	1
E. J. G. Morgan *b 8*	2	6	0	0
J. M. Bairstow *b 9*	1	8	0	0
J. C. Buttler *b 8*	11	12	1	0
T. T. Bresnan *c 1 b 8*	1	8	0	0
*S. C. J. Broad *c 1 b 10*	3	3	0	0
G. P. Swann *st 5 b 8*	0	3	0	0
S. T. Finn *not out*	8	10	1	0
J. W. Dernbach *run out*	12	7	2	0
W 1	1			
6 overs: 39-3 (14.4 overs)	80			

1/2 2/18 3/39 4/42 5/51 6/54 7/60 8/60 9/60

Finn 4–0–33–2; Dernbach 4–0–45–1; Broad 4–0–36–0; Bresnan 4–0–35–0; Swann 4–0–17–1.

Pathan 3–0–17–2; Balaji 1–0–10–0; Dinda 2–0–26–1; Harbhajan Singh 4–2–12–4; Chawla 4–1–13–2; Yuvraj Singh 0.4–0–2–0.

Umpires: Aleem Dar and S. J. A. Taufel. Third umpire: H. D. P. K. Dharmasena. Referee: R. S. Madugalle.

GROUP B

AUSTRALIA v IRELAND

At Colombo (RPS), September 19, 2012. Australia won by seven wickets. Toss: Ireland.

Australia, beaten finalists in 2010, enjoyed the perfect start with a decisive victory over an Ireland side whose captain admitted they let themselves down. The Australians won the first six overs of each innings, reducing Ireland to 29 for three, then scoring 53 without loss themselves. Although Dockrell had Warner caught at deep midwicket in the eighth over, Watson ensured there would be no upset. Watson had also dismissed Porterfield with the first ball of the match – just as Lee had done in the Belfast one-day international three months earlier – and then disposed of the O'Brien brothers, in the space of four deliveries after a partnership of 52, to end the fightback. Australia's fast start in effect settled things, even though Wollongong-born Johnston, belying his 38 years, ran Watson out with a direct hit from short third man, and Kevin O'Brien dismissed Mike Hussey five balls later.

Man of the Match: S. R. Watson.

Ireland

		B	*4*	*6*
*W. T. S. Porterfield *c 11 b 2*	0	1	0	0
P. R. Stirling *c 2 b 11*	7	12	1	0
E. C. Joyce *c 1 b 6*	16	18	3	0
N. J. O'Brien *b 2*	20	24	2	0
†G. C. Wilson *lbw b 9*	5	5	1	0
K. J. O'Brien *c 7 b 2*	35	29	5	0
A. R. Cusack *not out*	15	14	1	0
D. T. Johnston *b 11*	7	7	1	0
N. G. Jones *not out*	14	10	0	1
L-b 3, w 1	4			
6 overs: 29-3 (20 overs)	123-7			

1/0 2/15 3/25 4/33 5/85 6/86 7/101

G. H. Dockrell and W. B. Rankin did not bat.

Watson 4–0–26–3; Starc 4–0–20–2; Cummins 4–0–29–0; Maxwell 2–0–12–1; Christian 2–0–11–0; Hogg 4–0–22–1.

Australia

		B	*4*	*6*
D. A. Warner *c 6 b 10*	26	23	4	0
S. R. Watson *run out*	51	30	5	3
M. E. K. Hussey *lbw b 6*	10	11	0	0
C. L. White *not out*	22	19	3	0
*G. J. Bailey *not out*	6	8	1	0
L-b 4, w 6	10			
6 overs: 53-0 (15.1 overs)	125-3			

1/60 2/91 3/95

G. J. Maxwell, †M. S. Wade, D. T. Christian, G. B. Hogg, P. J. Cummins and M. A. Starc did not bat.

Rankin 4–0–28–0; Johnston 2–0–21–0; Cusack 2–0–10–0; Dockrell 3.1–0–31–1; Stirling 1–0–13–0; K. J. O'Brien 3–0–18–1.

Umpires: Aleem Dar and H. D. P. K. Dharmasena. Third umpire: Asad Rauf. Referee: R. S. Madugalle.

AUSTRALIA v WEST INDIES

At Colombo (RPS), September 22, 2012. Australia won by 17 runs (D/L). Toss: West Indies.

Watson defeated two forces of nature to push Australia into the next phase with a commanding all-round performance. First, he made some amends for dropping Gayle when four, holding on to a return catch to end his rampage. Substantial damage had been done – by the time Gayle fell, West Indies were 93 for three in the 11th over – but it could have been worse. Then Watson teamed up with Warner to keep Australia ahead of the rate before the monsoon deprived a spirited crowd of a potentially gripping finish. Watson had grassed a difficult chance at third man in the fourth over, allowing Gayle to pounce on some bouncers that failed to get up; he took 18 from Cummins's second over (his first was a maiden), before succumbing to a leading edge. Samuels added a well-timed half-century, but the Australian openers launched another sizzling response. Warner fell to a speculative caught-behind decision in the third over, but his departure did not lessen the tempo, and Mike Hussey helped Watson ensure Australia were on the right side of the Duckworth/Lewis equation when the rain came with the par score 83.

Man of the Match: S. R. Watson.

West Indies

		B	*4*	*6*
D. R. Smith *b 11*	2	5	0	0
C. H. Gayle *c and b 2*	54	33	5	4
J. Charles *b 8*	16	12	2	1
M. N. Samuels *c 1 b 9*	50	32	3	4
D. J. Bravo *b 10*	27	21	1	1
K. A. Pollard *c 3 b 2*	10	8	2	0
*D. J. G. Sammy *c 1 b 11*	12	7	1	1
†D. Ramdin *b 11*	3	2	0	0
R. Rampaul *not out*	0	0	0	0
S. P. Narine *not out*	4	1	1	0
L-b 10, w 2, n-b 1	13			
6 overs: 53-2 (20 overs)	191-8			

1/8 2/47 3/93 4/140 5/162 6/171 7/187 8/187

F. H. Edwards did not bat.

Watson 4–0–29–2; Starc 4–0–35–3; Cummins 4–1–41–1; Christian 3–0–29–1; Hogg 4–0–30–1; Maxwell 1–0–17–0.

Australia

		B	*4*	*6*
D. A. Warner *c 8 b 11*	28	14	3	2
S. R. Watson *not out*	41	24	2	3
M. E. K. Hussey *not out*	28	19	3	1
W 1, n-b 2	3			
6 overs: 62-1 (9.1 overs)	100-1			

1/30

C. L. White, *G. J. Bailey, G. J. Maxwell, †M. S. Wade, D. T. Christian, G. B. Hogg, P. J. Cummins and M. A. Starc did not bat.

Edwards 2–0–16–1; Rampaul 1.1–0–23–0; Narine 2–0–16–0; Sammy 2–0–15–0; Samuels 1–0–22–0; Bravo 1–0–8–0.

Umpires: Aleem Dar and Asad Rauf. Third umpire: H. D. P. K. Dharmasena.
Referee: R. S. Madugalle.

IRELAND v WEST INDIES

At Colombo (RPS), September 24, 2012. No result. Toss: West Indies.

For the second successive World Twenty20, rain ended Ireland's interest. In the Caribbean in 2010 they had been on the verge of an upset against England, but this time – again facing the eventual champions – they could hardly claim to be favourites. Porterfield was dismissed first ball (his fourth golden duck of 2012), but Stirling and Joyce were building momentum, taking ten off Sammy's first over, when a shower interrupted their progress. The innings was reduced by just one over, but Joyce was dismissed third ball after the break, and Ireland never really recovered. Gayle had Wilson caught behind in his first over, and later removed Niall O'Brien. Sammy's men were confident of chasing 130, but more rain got in the way. Despite not winning either of their matches, West Indies went through on run-rate. They finished marginally ahead of Ireland, who would have qualified instead had Australia taken three more balls to beat them five days earlier.

Ireland

		B	4	6
*W. T. S. Porterfield *b 11*	0	1	0	0
P. R. Stirling *c 2 b 7*	19	16	3	0
E. C. Joyce *b 9*	17	19	3	0
N. J. O'Brien *b 2*	25	21	0	1
†G. C. Wilson *c 8 b 2*	21	22	3	0
K. J. O'Brien *b 10*	13	15	0	1
D. T. Johnston *not out*	15	10	0	1
N. G. Jones *not out*	14	11	0	1
L-b 2, w 2, n-b 1	5			
6 overs: 35-2 (19 overs)	129-6			

1/0 2/33 3/37 4/70 5/96 6/107

A. R. Cusack, M. C. Sorensen and G. H. Dockrell did not bat.

Edwards 3–0–23–1; Rampaul 4–0–20–1; Sammy 3–0–23–1; Narine 4–0–21–1; Russell 2–0–19–0; Gayle 3–0–21–2.

West Indies

J. Charles, C. H. Gayle, D. M. Bravo, M. N. Samuels, K. A. Pollard, A. D. Russell, *D. J. G. Sammy, †D. Ramdin, S. P. Narine, R. Rampaul and F. H. Edwards.

Umpires: Asad Rauf and H. D. P. K. Dharmasena. Third umpire: S. J. A. Taufel. Referee: R. S. Madugalle.

GROUP C

SRI LANKA v ZIMBABWE

At Hambantota, September 18, 2012. Sri Lanka won by 82 runs. Toss: Zimbabwe. Twenty20 international debuts: E. M. D. Y. Munaweera; B. V. Vitori.

Ajantha Mendis marked his return to Sri Lankan colours after eight months out injured by improving his own record for the best bowling figures in Twenty20 internationals. He had taken six for 16 against Australia at Pallekele in August 2011, but bettered that against utterly flummoxed opponents. Three wickets came in his first spell to spoil any hopes Zimbabwe might have had of making a game of it, and he completed the demolition in his second with three more, finishing with an eye-popping six for eight. As if one Mendis wasn't enough, a second one – Jeewan – took three wickets himself with his leg-breaks, after earlier putting on 94 with Sangakkara. Zimbabwe's own slow men had performed tidily enough, but their seam bowling was much less impressive as Sri Lanka cantered to an imposing total.

Man of the Match: B. A. W. Mendis.

Sri Lanka

		B	4	6
E. M. D. Y. Munaweera *run out*	17	19	3	0
T. M. Dilshan *c 3 b 7*	39	28	5	0
*D. P. M. D. Jayawardene *run out*	13	18	1	0
†K. C. Sangakkara *run out*	44	26	2	1
B. M. A. J. Mendis *not out*	43	30	4	1
N. L. T. C. Perera *not out*	6	2	0	1
B 4, l-b 6, w 7, n-b 3	20			
6 overs: 53-0 (20 overs)	182-4			

1/54 2/75 3/82 4/176

A. D. Mathews, H. D. R. L. Thirimanne, K. M. D. N. Kulasekara, B. A. W. Mendis and S. L. Malinga did not bat.

12th man: L. D. Chandimal.

Zimbabwe

		B	4	6
H. Masakadza *b 10*	20	23	3	0
V. Sibanda *b 10*	11	16	1	0
*†B. R. M. Taylor *st 4 b 10*	0	1	0	0
E. Chigumbura *b 10*	19	19	1	1
C. R. Ervine *st 4 b 5*	10	13	0	1
M. N. Waller *lbw b 5*	0	2	0	0
A. G. Cremer *b 5*	17	20	2	0
P. Utseya *c 3 b 10*	1	2	0	0
K. M. Jarvis *lbw b 10*	0	3	0	0
B. V. Vitori *not out*	7	4	0	0
C. B. Mpofu *c 12 b 11*	0	2	0	0
L-b 9, w 6	15			
6 overs: 39-2 (17.3 overs)	100			

1/37 2/37 3/43 4/58 5/58 6/80 7/87 8/87 9/93

Jarvis 4–0–31–0; Vitori 3–0–27–0; Utseya 4–0–25–0; Mpofu 4–0–49–0; Cremer 4–0–27–1; Chigumbura 1–0–13–0.

Kulasekara 3–0–16–0; Malinga 2.3–0–20–1; B. A. W. Mendis 4–2–8–6; Mathews 2–0–7–0; Perera 2–0–16–0; B. M. A. J. Mendis 4–0–24–3.

Umpires: I. J. Gould and R. J. Tucker. Third umpire: R. A. Kettleborough.
Referee: J. J. Crowe.

SOUTH AFRICA v ZIMBABWE

At Hambantota, September 20, 2012. South Africa won by ten wickets. Toss: S. Africa.

Zimbabwe had been tipped as the likeliest of the unfancied nations to cause an upset – but they were never in the match, and departed before one group had even begun. Their batsmen struggled on a pitch with pace and bounce: they managed just four runs in the first three overs, amid much playing and missing, before the guileful Kallis read their minds and intentions as easily as a comic book. Every plan worked, from slower-ball bouncers to wide away-swingers, as he produced his best Twenty20 figures. Ervine provided a dash of respectability with an innings of immense determination, but Levi and Amla were as untroubled in knocking off the runs as the bowlers had been in restricting them.

Man of the Match: J. H. Kallis.

Zimbabwe

		B	4	6
H. Masakadza *c 1 b 7*	6	17	1	0
V. Sibanda *b 11*	0	3	0	0
*†B. R. M. Taylor *c 4 b 11*	4	4	0	0
C. R. Ervine *c 4 b 3*	37	40	4	0
S. Matsikenyeri *c 8 b 3*	11	18	0	0
E. Chigumbura *lbw b 3*	0	1	0	0
A. G. Cremer *c 4 b 3*	6	11	0	0
P. Utseya *c 4 b 10*	5	9	0	0
R. W. Price *not out*	7	6	1	0
K. M. Jarvis *not out*	9	11	0	0
L-b 3, w 5	8			
6 overs: 21-3 (20 overs)	93-8			

1/2 2/6 3/16 4/51 5/51 6/60 7/75 8/77

B. V. Vitori did not bat.

Steyn 4–0–9–1; M. Morkel 4–0–16–2; J. A. Morkel 4–0–26–1; Botha 3–0–16–0; Peterson 1–0–8–0; Kallis 4–1–15–4.

South Africa

		B	4	6
R. E. Levi *not out*	50	44	6	0
H. M. Amla *not out*	32	33	3	0
B 3, l-b 5, w 3, n-b 1	12			
6 overs: 56-0 (12.4 overs)	94-0			

J. H. Kallis, *†A. B. de Villiers, J-P. Duminy, F. Behardien, J. A. Morkel, R. J. Peterson, J. Botha, D. W. Steyn and M. Morkel did not bat.

Jarvis 3–0–20–0; Vitori 2–0–21–0; Price 3–0–19–0; Utseya 2–0–13–0; Cremer 2–0–10–0; Matsikenyeri 0.4–0–3–0.

Umpires: S. J. Davis and R. A. Kettleborough. Third umpire: I. J. Gould.
Referee: J. J. Crowe.

SRI LANKA v SOUTH AFRICA

At Hambantota, September 22, 2012. South Africa won by 32 runs. Toss: Sri Lanka.

A capacity crowd had travelled from far and wide to one of the least accessible venues in the world – and, after heavy monsoon rains, it was a tribute to the groundstaff that they were able to watch any cricket at all. The game was reduced to a seven-over thrash, which went entirely South Africa's way, summed up when Malinga adjusted his field, de Villiers deciphered the clues, then hammered a slower-ball bouncer almost 100 metres over deep midwicket. "It was probably a game-changing moment," said de Villiers. Dilshan was run out without facing, and Steyn and Morkel again bowled superbly in helpful conditions. The victory margin was remarkable in a match of only 42 balls per side.

Man of the Match: A. B. de Villiers.

South Africa

		B	4	6
R. E. Levi *c 3 b 9*	4	4	0	0
H. M. Amla *st 4 b 10*	16	9	3	0
F. du Plessis *c 6 b 5*	13	11	0	0
*†A. B. de Villiers *c 6 b 11*	30	13	1	2
J-P. Duminy *not out*	12	5	1	1
J. A. Morkel *not out*	0	0	0	0
L-b 1, w 2	3			
2 overs: 21-1 (7 overs)	78-4			

1/4 2/27 3/65 4/68

J. H. Kallis, F. Behardien, J. Botha, D. W. Steyn and M. Morkel did not bat.

Kulasekara 1–0–9–1; Malinga 2–0–27–1; Herath 2–0–21–1; Mathews 1–0–8–0; Perera 1–0–12–1.

Sri Lanka

		B	4	6
*D. P. M. D. Jayawardene *c 8 b 10*	4	6	1	0
T. M. Dilshan *run out*	0	0	0	0
E. M. D. Y. Munaweera *c 8 b 6*	13	14	1	0
†K. C. Sangakkara *c 4 b 7*	13	11	1	0
N. L. T. C. Perera *c 5 b 10*	1	3	0	0
B. M. A. J. Mendis *not out*	7	5	1	0
H. D. R. L. Thirimanne *not out*	5	3	0	0
L-b 1, w 2	3			
2 overs: 8-2 (7 overs)	46-5			

1/4 2/8 3/30 4/32 5/40

A. D. Mathews, K. M. D. N. Kulasekara, H. M. R. K. B. Herath and S. L. Malinga did not bat.

M. Morkel 2–0–9–0; Steyn 2–0–10–2; Botha 1–0–9–0; Kallis 1–0–9–1; J. A. Morkel 1–0–8–1.

Umpires: R. A. Kettleborough and R. J. Tucker. Third umpire: S. J. Davis. Referee: J. J. Crowe.

GROUP D

BANGLADESH v NEW ZEALAND

At Pallekele, September 21, 2012. New Zealand won by 59 runs. Toss: Bangladesh.

This was the Brendon McCullum show: the leading run-scorer in Twenty20 international cricket now smashed its highest individual innings too. He entered in the fourth over after Abdur Razzak bowled Guptill with his second delivery, and was caught at deep cover off the last ball of the innings. In between he pulverised the bowling, becoming the first to score two centuries in the format. His 18 boundaries included several audacious shots, none more so than a flat-batted six off Mashrafe bin Mortaza over long-off, which resembled a Roger Federer forehand. Mortaza himself later dropped McCullum on 92 off Elias Sunny at extra cover; he hit his next three balls for four, four and six. The result was never in doubt, especially once Bangladesh dipped to 37 for four in the seventh over; Nasir Hossain's half-century delayed the inevitable.

Man of the Match: B. B. McCullum.

New Zealand

		B	4	6
M. J. Guptill *b 10*	11	14	0	1
J. E. C. Franklin *c 9 b 8*	35	36	2	1
†B. B. McCullum *c 1 b 10*	123	58	11	7
*L. R. P. L. Taylor *not out*	14	12	2	0
L-b 2, w 6	8			
6 overs: 34-1 (20 overs)	191-3			

1/19 2/113 3/191

R. J. Nicol, K. S. Williamson, J. D. P. Oram, D. L. Vettori, N. L. McCullum, T. G. Southee and K. D. Mills did not bat.

Bangladesh

		B	4	6
Tamim Iqbal *c 1 b 11*	0	3	0	0
Mohammad Ashraful *lbw b 10*	21	21	3	0
Shakib Al Hasan *c 6 b 11*	11	8	2	0
*†Mushfiqur Rahim *c 6 b 11*	4	6	0	0
Mahmudullah *c 6 b 9*	15	19	0	1
Nasir Hossain *c 1 b 10*	50	39	6	1
Ziaur Rahman *not out*	14	16	0	1
Mashrafe bin Mortaza *c 2 b 7*	5	3	1	0
Elias Sunny *c 7 b 10*	5	3	1	0
Abdur Razzak *not out*	0	2	0	0
L-b 3, w 4	7			
6 overs: 37-3 (20 overs)	132-8			

1/0 2/19 3/33 4/37 5/87 6/115 7/123 8/128

Shafiul Islam did not bat.

Mashrafe bin Mortaza 4–0–26–1; Shafiul Islam 3–0–34–0; Abdur Razzak 4–0–28–2; Shakib Al Hasan 4–0–40–0; Mahmudullah 1–0–13–0; Elias Sunny 3–0–36–0; Ziaur Rahman 1–0–12–0.

Mills 4–0–33–3; Southee 4–1–16–3; Oram 4–0–34–1; Vettori 4–0–31–0; N. L. McCullum 4–0–15–1.

Umpires: M. Erasmus and N. J. Llong. Third umpire: B. N. J. Oxenford.
Referee: G. F. Labrooy.

NEW ZEALAND v PAKISTAN

At Pallekele, September 23, 2012. Pakistan won by 13 runs. Toss: Pakistan.

Pakistan's varied attack helped them pull off a hard-fought win. After their batsmen had raised a challenging total, Nicol made 33 of a confident opening stand of 53, but Pakistan's three spinners clawed back the initiative, crucially keeping Brendon McCullum to a run a ball before he was bowled by an Umar Gul yorker that dribbled on to the stumps via his back foot. Taylor gave them a fright, collecting three boundaries in the 19th over, from Gul, before he was run out. Saeed Ajmal was given the task of defending 19 from the last six balls, and rounded off another fine display to finish with four for 30. New Zealand were unusually sloppy in the field: Taylor dropped Mohammad Hafeez at slip before he had scored, while Nicol at deep square spilled a skimmer from Nasir Jamshed over the boundary for six, both chances coming off the unamused Mills.

Man of the Match: Nasir Jamshed.

Pakistan

		B	*4*	*6*
*Mohammad Hafeez *b 7*	43	38	2	2
Imran Nazir *c and b 9*	25	16	5	0
Nasir Jamshed *c 8 b 4*	56	35	2	4
†Kamran Akmal *c 1 b 5*	3	3	0	0
Umar Akmal *c 8 b 5*	23	15	3	1
Shoaib Malik *not out*	9	7	1	0
Shahid Afridi *c 2 b 9*	12	6	2	0
L-b 2, w 4	6			
6 overs: 51-1 (20 overs)	177-6			

1/47 2/123 3/129 4/134 5/159 6/177

Yasir Arafat, Sohail Tanvir, Umar Gul and Saeed Ajmal did not bat.

Mills 4–0–35–0; Vettori 4–0–23–1; Southee 4–0–31–2; Oram 4–0–44–2; N. L. McCullum 2–0–23–0; Milne 1–0–12–0; Franklin 1–0–7–1.

New Zealand

		B	*4*	*6*
R. J. Nicol *b 7*	33	28	3	1
K. S. Williamson *run out*	15	13	2	0
†B. B. McCullum *b 10*	32	31	4	1
D. L. Vettori *c 3 b 11*	18	16	1	0
J. D. P. Oram *b 11*	11	7	2	0
*L. R. P. L. Taylor *run out*	26	11	3	1
J. E. C. Franklin *c 3 b 9*	13	6	1	1
N. L. McCullum *c 6 b 11*	5	4	1	0
T. G. Southee *c 10 b 11*	1	3	0	0
K. D. Mills *not out*	0	1	0	0
A. F. Milne *not out*	0	0	0	0
L-b 5, w 5	10			
6 overs: 47-0 (20 overs)	164-9			

1/53 2/54 3/102 4/108 5/122 6/143 7/157 8/160 9/164

Mohammad Hafeez 4–0–15–0; Sohail Tanvir 3–0–33–1; Umar Gul 4–0–39–1; Yasir Arafat 1–0–12–0; Shahid Afridi 4–0–30–1; Saeed Ajmal 4–0–30–4.

Umpires: M. Erasmus and B. N. J. Oxenford. Third umpire: N. J. Llong.
Referee: G. F. Labrooy.

BANGLADESH v PAKISTAN

At Pallekele, September 25, 2012. Pakistan won by eight wickets. Toss: Bangladesh.

Inspired by Imran Nazir's blistering 72 at two a ball, Pakistan romped into the Super Eights. It was not looking so rosy when Shakib Al Hasan was hitting to all parts, lifting Bangladesh to their highest Twenty20 total against a Test nation and setting Pakistan more than they had ever scored in the second innings. There was a subplot, too: to qualify at Pakistan's expense, Bangladesh needed to win by at least 36 runs. And they started well. Tamim Iqbal blazed away before he was run out, and Shakib took the fight to Pakistan; his eventual 84 was Bangladesh's highest in Twenty20 matches. He also bowled superbly, without any luck – a quality Nazir had in spades. He was badly dropped at mid-on by Abul Hasan off Shafiul Islam on one, then survived a confident lbw appeal from Shakib's first ball. He went on to dominate an opening stand of 124 with Mohammad Hafeez and, although both fell in the space of four deliveries, by then the result was all but settled.

Man of the Match: Imran Nazir.

Bangladesh

		B	4	6
Tamim Iqbal *run out*	24	12	5	0
Mohammad Ashraful *b 9*	14	13	3	0
Shakib Al Hasan *c 6 b 8*	84	54	11	2
*†Mushfiqur Rahim *c 2 b 8*	25	26	1	1
Mahmudullah *c 6 b 7*	0	2	0	0
Nasir Hossain *b 8*	16	13	2	0
Ziaur Rahman *not out*	1	1	0	0
L-b 2, w 8, n-b 1	11			
6 overs: 61-2 (20 overs)	175-6			

1/34 2/61 3/129 4/133 5/170 6/175

Abul Hasan, Mashrafe bin Mortaza, Abdur Razzak and Shafiul Islam did not bat.

Mohammad Hafeez 3–0–28–0; Sohail Tanvir 3–0–25–1; Umar Gul 3–0–43–0; Shahid Afridi 4–0–20–1; Saeed Ajmal 4–0–32–0; Yasir Arafat 3–0–25–3.

12th man: Farhad Reza.

Pakistan

		B	4	6
*Mohammad Hafeez *c 4 b 8*	45	47	6	0
Imran Nazir *c 12 b 8*	72	36	9	3
Nasir Jamshed *not out*	29	14	2	2
†Kamran Akmal *not out*	22	15	4	0
B 1, l-b 2, w 7	10			
6 overs: 64-0 (18.4 overs)	178-2			

1/124 2/126

Shoaib Malik, Umar Akmal, Shahid Afridi, Yasir Arafat, Sohail Tanvir, Umar Gul and Saeed Ajmal did not bat.

Mashrafe bin Mortaza 3–0–30–0; Shafiul Islam 2.4–0–35–0; Abdur Razzak 4–0–30–0; Shakib Al Hasan 4–0–23–0; Abul Hasan 3–0–33–2; Mahmudullah 2–0–24–0.

Umpires: S. J. Davis and I. J. Gould. Third umpire: R. J. Tucker.
Referee: J. J. Crowe.

FINAL GROUP TABLES

Group A	*Played*	*Won*	*Lost*	*No result*	*Points*	*Net run-rate*
INDIA	2	2	0	0	4	2.82
ENGLAND	2	1	1	0	2	0.65
Afghanistan	2	0	2	0	0	–3.47

Group B	*Played*	*Won*	*Lost*	*No result*	*Points*	*Net run-rate*
AUSTRALIA	2	2	0	0	4	2.18
WEST INDIES	2	0	1	1	1	–1.85
Ireland	2	0	1	1	1	–2.09

Group C	*Played*	*Won*	*Lost*	*No result*	*Points*	*Net run-rate*
SOUTH AFRICA	2	2	0	0	4	3.59
SRI LANKA	2	1	1	0	2	1.85
Zimbabwe	2	0	2	0	0	–3.62

Group D	*Played*	*Won*	*Lost*	*No result*	*Points*	*Net run-rate*
PAKISTAN	2	2	0	0	4	0.70
NEW ZEALAND	2	1	1	0	2	1.15
Bangladesh	2	0	2	0	0	–1.86

SUPER EIGHT STAGE

GROUP ONE

SRI LANKA v NEW ZEALAND

At Pallekele, September 27, 2012. Sri Lanka won after an eliminator over, following a tie. Toss: New Zealand. Twenty20 international debut: A. Dananjaya.

Just when Sri Lanka looked to have wrapped things up, they allowed New Zealand to grab a lifeline, before finally prevailing in the super over. Sri Lanka had started their chase with a superb opening stand of 80 in 44 balls between Jayawardene and Dilshan, and looked set for victory at 160 for three, needing 15 off 11 deliveries to overhaul a spirited New Zealand total. But two run-outs helped bring about only the second tie in World Twenty20 cricket, following the India–Pakistan encounter in 2007-08. The hero in the extra over was Dilshan – top-scorer in the match proper, with 76 – who plucked a catch at long-off after Guptill seemed to have wafted Malinga for six. Had that crossed the rope, New Zealand would have needed two off the last ball. The 19-year-old unorthodox off-spinner Akila Dananjaya made his debut for Sri Lanka before he had appeared in first-class or List A cricket – his only senior experience was a handful of Twenty20 games for Wayamba. He had a painful introduction: his cheekbone was fractured by a fierce straight-drive from Nicol, although he continued to bowl. Jayawardene, who had pressed for Dananjaya's inclusion in the squad after facing him in the nets, said: "When he got hit I went to him thinking he was gone for the game. He said, 'Shit, I missed that catch.' And he was bleeding from his nose. That's his attitude."

Man of the Match: T. M. Dilshan.

New Zealand

		B	*4*	*6*
R. J. Nicol *c 7 b 11*	58	40	3	4
M. J. Guptill *c 6 b 11*	38	30	6	0
†B. B. McCullum *c 6 b 10*	25	16	0	2
*L. R. P. L. Taylor *b 8*	23	15	2	0
J. D. P. Oram *c 2 b 8*	6	6	1	0
N. L. McCullum *b 9*	3	4	0	0
J. E. C. Franklin *not out*	8	5	1	0
K. S. Williamson *run out*	4	4	0	0
L-b 4, w 5	9			
6 overs: 43-0 (20 overs)	174-7			

1/57 2/99 3/137 4/154 5/159 6/164 7/174

D. L. Vettori, T. G. Southee and K. D. Mills did not bat.

Kulasekara 4–0–33–2; Mathews 2–0–14–0; Malinga 4–0–30–1; B. A. W. Mendis 4–0–48–1; Dananjaya 4–0–32–2; B. M. A. J. Mendis 2–0–13–0.

Sri Lanka

		B	*4*	*6*
*D. P. M. D. Jayawardene *c 9 b 5*	44	26	3	3
T. M. Dilshan *run out*	76	53	5	3
†K. C. Sangakkara *run out*	21	14	4	0
B. M. A. J. Mendis *c 4 b 7*	8	9	1	0
A. D. Mathews *not out*	12	11	0	0
N. L. T. C. Perera *b 7*	5	3	1	0
H. D. R. L. Thirimanne *run out*	5	4	1	0
L-b 1, w 2	3			
6 overs: 68-0 (20 overs)	174-6			

1/80 2/119 3/131 4/161 5/167 6/174

K. M. D. N. Kulasekara, S. L. Malinga, B. A. W. Mendis and A. Dananjaya did not bat.

N. L. McCullum 3–0–25–0; Mills 2–0–15–0; Southee 4–0–44–0; Oram 3–0–26–1; Vettori 4–0–29–0; Franklin 4–0–34–2.

Eliminator over: **Sri Lanka 13-1** (1 over) (Jayawardene 4, Perera 5*, Dilshan 0*, Extras 4; Southee 1–0–12–1); **New Zealand 7-1** (1 over) (Guptill 3, B. B. McCullum 1*, Taylor 0*, Extras 3; Malinga 1–0–4–1).

Umpires: Aleem Dar and S. J. A. Taufel. Third umpire: S. J. Davis.
Referee: J. Srinath.

ENGLAND v WEST INDIES

At Pallekele, September 27, 2012. West Indies won by 15 runs. Toss: West Indies.

A limp start to their chase left England overstretched, and they duly fell short – despite an exhilarating recovery by Morgan, whose 36-ball 71 included five sixes. West Indies were heading for a huge victory when Rampaul punished Kieswetter and Wright for rash swings across the line with the second and third balls of the reply. Bairstow struggled to justify his promotion above Morgan, and England were left needing 125 from ten overs. But the fourth wicket added 107 in 58 balls, before a visibly tiring Hales was stumped off Samuels with 18 required from three. That was that, although the partnership did at least limit the damage to England's net run-rate. West Indies could not have begun in more contrasting fashion: Gayle and Johnson Charles, from St Lucia, blasted 103 in 11 overs, including 37 in successive overs from Patel and Swann. Finn dropped Charles on 39 and, if it seemed more than adequate compensation when he caught Gayle next ball, such thoughts were dispelled as Charles raced to 84, a career-best in any format.

Man of the Match: J. Charles.

West Indies

		B	*4*	*6*
J. Charles *c 4 b 11*	84	56	10	3
C. H. Gayle *c 10 b 9*	58	35	6	4
M. N. Samuels *c 5 b 8*	2	8	0	0
K. A. Pollard *c 3 b 10*	1	5	0	0
D. J. Bravo *not out*	11	8	2	0
*D. J. G. Sammy *b 8*	4	3	0	0
A. D. Russell *not out*	10	5	2	0
B 1, l-b 7, w 1	9			
6 overs: 47-0 (20 overs)	179-5			

1/103 2/118 3/128 4/154 5/158

†D. Ramdin, S. P. Narine, R. Rampaul and S. Badree did not bat.

Finn 4–0–26–1; Dernbach 4–0–38–1; Broad 4–1–26–2; Swann 3–0–32–1; Patel 4–0–38–0; Wright 1–0–11–0.

England

		B	*4*	*6*
†C. Kieswetter *c 4 b 10*	0	2	0	0
A. D. Hales *st 8 b 3*	68	51	5	2
L. J. Wright *c 2 b 10*	0	1	0	0
J. M. Bairstow *c 4 b 2*	18	29	2	0
E. J. G. Morgan *not out*	71	36	4	5
J. C. Buttler *not out*	1	1	0	0
B 1, l-b 1, w 4	6			
6 overs: 29-2 (20 overs)	164-4			

1/0 2/0 3/55 4/162

S. R. Patel, *S. C. J. Broad, G. P. Swann, S. T. Finn and J. W. Dernbach did not bat.

Rampaul 4–1–37–2; Badree 4–0–20–0; Narine 4–0–33–0; Sammy 1–0–13–0; Gayle 4–0–27–1; Samuels 3–0–32–1.

Umpires: Asad Rauf and S. J. Davis. Third umpire: Aleem Dar.
Referee: J. Srinath.

ENGLAND v NEW ZEALAND

At Pallekele, September 29, 2012. England won by six wickets. Toss: New Zealand.

Finn was the centre of attention in more ways than one, disrupting New Zealand with some hostile bowling, but also leaving them frustrated with his habit of hitting the stumps with his right knee in the delivery stride. The umpires had been told to warn offenders for the first transgression, then call dead ball thereafter, which they did three times. Taylor complained the calls had cost his side runs and wickets: Brendon McCullum had sliced to third man the ball after what would have been a wide. England's only punishment was a fine for a slow over-rate. But it was not just Finn who choked the runs. Swann also took a grip, and only 41 came in the eight overs following the powerplay, before Franklin attacked Briggs in the 15th to spark a late surge. After a careful start, England needed 89 from ten overs, and Wright reprised his success against Afghanistan, smearing between long-on and deep midwicket. Morgan played second fiddle in a stand of 89; four of Wright's five sixes came in six legitimate balls from Southee and Nicol.

Man of the Match: L. J. Wright.

New Zealand

		B	4	6
M. J. Guptill *lbw b 11*	5	6	1	0
R. J. Nicol *c 6 b 9*	11	15	1	0
†B. B. McCullum *c 3 b 11*	10	10	2	0
K. S. Williamson *c 1 b 10*	17	23	1	0
*L. R. P. L. Taylor *c 2 b 11*	22	23	2	0
J. E. C. Franklin *run out*	50	33	4	2
N. L. McCullum *not out*	16	10	0	2
D. A. J. Bracewell *not out*	2	1	0	0
B 3, l-b 7, w 4, n-b 1	15			

6 overs: 39-2 (20 overs) 148-6

1/7 2/20 3/42 4/67 5/107 6/146

D. L. Vettori, T. G. Southee and K. D. Mills did not bat.

Briggs 4–0–36–1; Finn 4–0–16–3; Bresnan 4–0–29–0; Swann 4–0–20–1; Broad 4–0–37–0.

England

		B	4	6
†C. Kieswetter *b 9*	4	14	0	0
A. D. Hales *b 7*	22	15	3	0
L. J. Wright *c 5 b 8*	76	43	5	5
E. J. G. Morgan *c 8 b 11*	30	31	1	1
J. C. Buttler *not out*	5	8	0	0
J. M. Bairstow *not out*	5	2	1	0
L-b 3, w 4	7			

6 overs: 37-1 (18.5 overs) 149-4

1/21 2/38 3/127 4/142

T. T. Bresnan, *S. C. J. Broad, G. P. Swann, D. R. Briggs and S. T. Finn did not bat.

Mills 4–0–23–1; Southee 2–0–32–0; Vettori 4–0–20–1; N. L. McCullum 4–0–22–1; Nicol 3–0–29–0; Franklin 1–0–12–0; Bracewell 0.5–0–8–1.

Umpires: Asad Rauf and S. J. A. Taufel. Third umpire: S. J. Davis.
Referee: J. Srinath.

SRI LANKA v WEST INDIES

At Pallekele, September 29, 2012. Sri Lanka won by nine wickets. Toss: West Indies.

In what proved a dress rehearsal for the final, West Indies' big guns were spiked by a disciplined Sri Lanka. Apart from a stand of 65 between Samuels and Dwayne Bravo, West Indies were kept in check. Gayle was in for 26 minutes for two, and none of the six bowlers went for more than eight an over. Sri Lanka's fielding was also impeccable, other than a difficult chance when Sangakkara missed stumping Samuels off Herath. Dilshan began the run-chase as if he had a train to catch, sending Edwards's first three balls to the boundary, before Rampaul stopped his fun. But Jayawardene and Sangakkara made sure of a comfortable victory, adding an unbroken 108 from 12.3 overs to give a significant boost to Sri Lanka's net run-rate.

Man of the Match: D. P. M. D. Jayawardene.

West Indies

		B	4	6
J. Charles *st 3 b 11*	12	21	2	0
C. H. Gayle *c 3 b 8*	2	9	0	0
M. N. Samuels *c 2 b 4*	50	35	4	2
D. J. Bravo *c 2 b 5*	40	34	4	2
K. A. Pollard *b 11*	1	6	0	0
A. D. Russell *not out*	19	14	0	1
*D. J. G. Sammy *not out*	1	1	0	0
B 1, l-b 3	4			

6 overs: 20-2 (20 overs) 129-5

1/16 2/16 3/81 4/90 5/123

†D. Ramdin, S. P. Narine, R. Rampaul and F. H. Edwards did not bat.

Mathews 4–0–31–1; Kulasekara 4–0–28–1; Malinga 4–0–26–0; B. A. W. Mendis 4–1–12–2; Herath 2–0–16–0; B. M. A. J. Mendis 2–0–12–1.

Sri Lanka

		B	4	6
*D. P. M. D. Jayawardene *not out*	65	49	10	1
T. M. Dilshan *c 8 b 10*	13	9	3	0
†K. C. Sangakkara *not out*	39	34	5	0
B 2, l-b 1, w 10	13			

6 overs: 55-1 (15.2 overs) 130-1

1/22

A. D. Mathews, B. M. A. J. Mendis, H. D. R. L. Thirimanne, N. L. T. C. Perera, K. M. D. N. Kulasekara, S. L. Malinga, H. M. R. K. B. Herath and B. A. W. Mendis did not bat.

Rampaul 4–0–39–1; Edwards 2–0–24–0; Narine 4–0–23–0; Sammy 4–0–28–0; Russell 1–0–11–0; Gayle 0.2–0–2–0.

Umpires: Aleem Dar and S. J. Davis. Third umpire: S. J. A. Taufel.
Referee: J. Srinath.

NEW ZEALAND v WEST INDIES

At Pallekele, October 1, 2012. West Indies won after an eliminator over, following a tie. Toss: New Zealand.

New Zealand were knocked out in cruel fashion, losing in a super over for the second time in five days. They were left to regret squandered opportunities – first when they needed 55 from 43 balls with seven wickets in hand, then after making 17 in the six-ball tie-breaker. But Southee, who had earlier bowled superbly, began with a front-foot no-ball, which Gayle fired over long-off, and Samuels smashed the fifth legitimate delivery for another six to give West Indies the points. In the match itself, New Zealand had recovered well to restrict West Indies to 139. Southee ended a typically brisk start from Gayle with one that bounced and seamed away and, although 60 runs came in the powerplay, the regular loss of wickets slowed things down. When they batted, New Zealand were in control until Narine flustered them. With nine needed from three balls, Taylor brilliantly flipped a Samuels full toss over short fine leg for six. But from the last delivery the substitute Dwayne Smith ran out Bracewell, who was attempting a winning second run. Afterwards Mike Hesson, New Zealand's coach, queried the need for the eliminator over in non-knockout matches.

Man of the Match: S. P. Narine.

West Indies

		B	*4*	*6*
J. Charles *c and b 8*	8	9	2	0
C. H. Gayle *c 3 b 10*	30	14	3	2
A. D. Russell *c 5 b 8*	6	6	0	1
M. N. Samuels *c 10 b 7*	24	22	2	1
D. M. Bravo *b 7*	16	21	0	1
K. A. Pollard *c 4 b 8*	28	22	3	0
†D. Ramdin *c 4 b 9*	1	2	0	0
*D. J. G. Sammy *c 5 b 10*	11	12	1	0
S. P. Narine *b 10*	3	4	0	0
S. Badree *b 6*	1	4	0	0
R. Rampaul *not out*	1	3	0	0
L-b 2, w 6, n-b 2	10			

6 overs: 60-2 (19.3 overs) 139

1/14 2/36 3/61 4/87 5/98 6/102 7/123 8/133 9/136

Mills 2–0–25–0; Bracewell 4–0–31–3; Southee 4–0–21–3; Oram 1.3–0–17–1; Hira 4–0–24–1; N. L. McCullum 4–0–19–2.

New Zealand

		B	*4*	*6*
R. J. Nicol *lbw b 11*	3	5	0	0
M. J. Guptill *c 4 b 8*	21	27	2	0
†B. B. McCullum *b 10*	22	18	3	0
*L. R. P. L. Taylor *not out*	62	40	3	3
J. E. C. Franklin *c 2 b 9*	14	14	1	0
J. D. P. Oram *lbw b 9*	6	9	0	0
N. L. McCullum *c 1 b 9*	5	7	0	0
D. A. J. Bracewell *run out*	1	1	0	0
L-b 2, w 2, n-b 1	5			

6 overs: 34-1 (20 overs) 139-7

1/8 2/41 3/52 4/85 5/115 6/125 7/139

R. M. Hira, T. G. Southee and K. D. Mills did not bat.

Rampaul 4–0–23–1; Badree 4–0–18–1; Narine 4–0–20–3; Sammy 4–0–35–1; Pollard 2–0–13–0; Gayle 1–0–15–0; Samuels 1–0–13–0.

Eliminator over: **New Zealand 17-0** (1 over) (Taylor 14*, B. B. McCullum 1*, Extras 2; Samuels 1–0–16–0); **West Indies 19-0** (0.5 over) (Gayle 8*, Samuels 9*, Extras 2; Southee 0.5–0–19–0).

Umpires: Aleem Dar and Asad Rauf. Third umpire: S. J. A. Taufel. Referee: J. Srinath.

SRI LANKA v ENGLAND

At Pallekele, October 1, 2012. Sri Lanka won by 19 runs. Toss: England.

In an attempt to keep their trophy defence alive, England reshuffled their batting, but the rejigged order still provided easy pickings for Malinga, who struck three times in his first over, the third of the innings. Patel responded gamely with some emphatic shots over extra cover, to call into question his previous position at No. 7, but the loss of Morgan –

reverse-sweeping – heralded another collapse, this time to spin; some late hitting from Swann was not enough. A stiff target of 170 on a slow, tricky pitch had owed much to the composed Jayawardene, and to several short but sweet contributions after Swann and Broad had both struck with successive balls. The ICC promised to re-examine its regulations after Jayawardene continued to lead on the field, having stepped down as titular captain at the toss in favour of Sangakkara, as both he and the official vice-captain Mathews wanted to avoid risking a possible ban for a second over-rate offence in the year.

Man of the Match: S. L. Malinga.

Sri Lanka

		B	*4*	*6*
D. P. M. D. Jayawardene *c 5 b 9*	42	38	5	1
T. M. Dilshan *lbw b 10*	16	12	1	1
*†K. C. Sangakkara *c 3 b 9*	13	12	1	0
A. D. Mathews *b 8*	28	19	3	1
B. M. A. J. Mendis *c 6 b 8*	18	13	2	1
H. D. R. L. Thirimanne *b 8*	13	7	1	1
N. L. T. C. Perera *not out*	26	16	0	2
K. M. D. N. Kulasekara *not out*	1	3	0	0
B 4, l-b 2, w 6	12			
6 overs: 44-1 (20 overs)	169-6			

1/35 2/74 3/74 4/126 5/126 6/162

S. L. Malinga, B. A. W. Mendis and A. Dananjaya did not bat.

Finn 4–0–24–1; Dernbach 4–0–42–0; Broad 4–0–32–3; Swann 4–0–26–2; Bopara 2–0–12–0; Patel 2–0–27–0.

England

		B	*4*	*6*
L. J. Wright *c 2 b 9*	12	11	1	1
A. D. Hales *lbw b 9*	3	5	0	0
†J. M. Bairstow *c 8 b 9*	2	2	0	0
S. R. Patel *b 9*	67	48	8	2
E. J. G. Morgan *lbw b 11*	10	15	1	0
R. S. Bopara *b 5*	1	6	0	0
J. C. Buttler *c 10 b 9*	8	7	0	0
*S. C. J. Broad *c 1 b 11*	1	2	0	0
G. P. Swann *b 8*	34	20	4	1
S. T. Finn *not out*	1	3	0	0
J. W. Dernbach *not out*	2	2	0	0
B 1, l-b 4, w 3, n-b 1	9			
6 overs: 36-3 (20 overs)	150-9			

1/16 2/18 3/18 4/73 5/76 6/91 7/93 8/144 9/147

Mathews 3–0–21–0; Kulasekara 4–0–22–1; Malinga 4–0–31–5; B. A. W. Mendis 4–0–40–0; Dananjaya 4–0–26–2; B. M. A. J. Mendis 1–0–5–1.

Umpires: S. J. Davis and S. J. A. Taufel. Third umpire: Asad Rauf.
Referee: J. Srinath.

GROUP TWO

PAKISTAN v SOUTH AFRICA

At Colombo (RPS), September 28, 2012. Pakistan won by two wickets. Toss: South Africa.

Both sides had their chances in this madcap contest, but it was Umar Gul, an unlikely batting hero, who ultimately swung it Pakistan's way. In an ode to old-school tail-end slogging, Gul carted three leg-side sixes, two in successive deliveries from Kallis, another off Albie Morkel. And though he fell to the final ball of the 19th over, Umar Akmal and Saeed Ajmal made short work of the nine required from the last, bowled by Morne Morkel. Pakistan had looked in charge when they reduced South Africa to 28 for three. In his first game of the tournament – and opening the bowling ahead of several senior colleagues – the 20-year-old Raza Hasan had set the tone with his darted left-arm spin, and the slow men conceded only 87 in 15 overs as the total hiccoughed to 133. But led by Peterson – whose maiden in the sixth over was immediately followed by a wicket maiden from Botha – South Africa's own spinners helped reduce Pakistan to 76 for seven. Then came Gul's match-changing onslaught.

Man of the Match: Umar Gul.

South Africa

		B	4	6
R. E. Levi *b 10*	8	9	1	0
H. M. Amla *c 5 b 8*	6	6	1	0
J. H. Kallis *c 7 b 1*	12	18	0	1
J-P. Duminy *c 4 b 8*	48	38	2	2
F. Behardien *st 4 b 1*	18	21	2	0
*†A. B. de Villiers *c 2 b 9*	25	18	2	1
J. A. Morkel *not out*	9	6	1	0
R. J. Peterson *not out*	3	4	0	0
L-b 2, w 2	4			

6 overs: 28-2 (20 overs) 133-6

1/8 2/28 3/28 4/66 5/110 6/123

J. Botha, D. W. Steyn and M. Morkel did not bat.

Raza Hasan 3–1–12–0; Yasir Arafat 3–0–25–2; Saeed Ajmal 4–1–26–1; Mohammad Hafeez 4–0–23–2; Shahid Afridi 4–0–26–0; Umar Gul 2–0–19–1.

Pakistan

		B	4	6
*Mohammad Hafeez *st 6 b 8*	15	9	2	1
Imran Nazir *c 6 b 10*	14	11	3	0
Nasir Jamshed *st 6 b 8*	0	2	0	0
†Kamran Akmal *b 9*	1	6	0	0
Shoaib Malik *c 10 b 3*	12	26	1	0
Umar Akmal *not out*	43	41	4	1
Shahid Afridi *c 7 b 4*	0	1	0	0
Yasir Arafat *c 4 b 10*	3	5	0	0
Umar Gul *c 8 b 10*	32	17	2	3
Saeed Ajmal *not out*	4	1	1	0
B 2, l-b 6, w 3, n-b 1	12			

6 overs: 37-3 (19.4 overs) 136-8

1/24 2/30 3/31 4/37 5/63 6/63 7/76 8/125

Raza Hasan did not bat.

Steyn 4–0–22–3; M. Morkel 3.4–0–33–0; Peterson 4–1–15–2; J. A. Morkel 2–0–26–0; Botha 2–1–10–1; Duminy 2–0–5–1; Kallis 2–0–17–1.

Umpires: I. J. Gould and R. J. Tucker. Third umpire: R. A. Kettleborough.
Referee: R. S. Madugalle.

AUSTRALIA v INDIA

At Colombo (RPS), September 28, 2012. Australia won by nine wickets. Toss: India.

After the thrills and spills of Pakistan's win against South Africa, the second part of this Colombo double-header lapsed into a disappointing rout. India thought they might have scrambled to a competitive total, despite struggling during four intelligent overs from Cummins, and losing wickets regularly to Watson. But he and Warner then blasted the Indian attack to all corners of the Premadasa, breaking their own national Twenty20 all-wicket partnership record with 133, inside 14 overs. They became the first pair to put on more than 1,000 runs together in the format; victory was completed with more than five overs to spare. Watson hit seven of Australia's ten sixes, and secured his third consecutive match award. "I think he's set himself to be the Man of the Tournament," said Bailey, his captain. Watson smiled diplomatically at Dhoni's suggestion that India's controversial selection of three spinners – and the exclusion of Virender Sehwag – had been scuppered by a heavy shower that forced them to use a wet ball.

Man of the Match: S. R. Watson.

India

		B	4	6
G. Gambhir *run out*	17	12	3	0
I. K. Pathan *c 5 b 1*	31	30	2	1
V. Kohli *c 8 b 10*	15	13	2	0
Yuvraj Singh *c 3 b 1*	8	10	1	0
R. G. Sharma *b 11*	1	2	0	0
S. K. Raina *c 3 b 1*	26	19	4	0
*†M. S. Dhoni *c 6 b 10*	15	21	2	0
R. Ashwin *not out*	16	12	1	1
Harbhajan Singh *not out*	1	1	0	0
B 2, l-b 2, w 6	10			

6 overs: 50-1 (20 overs) 140-7

1/21 2/56 3/70 4/74 5/74 6/104 7/137

P. P. Chawla and Zaheer Khan did not bat.

12th man: M. K. Tiwary.

Australia

		B	4	6
S. R. Watson *c 12 b 4*	72	42	2	7
D. A. Warner *not out*	63	41	7	3
G. J. Maxwell *not out*	4	6	0	0
W 2	2			

6 overs: 47-0 (14.5 overs) 141-1

1/133

M. E. K. Hussey, C. L. White, *G. J. Bailey, †M. S. Wade, D. T. Christian, G. B. Hogg, P. J. Cummins and M. A. Starc did not bat.

Maxwell 2–0–11–0; Starc 4–0–27–1; Cummins 4–0–16–2; Watson 4–0–34–3; Christian 2–0–19–0; Hogg 4–0–29–0.

Ashwin 3.5–0–32–0; Zaheer Khan 3–0–18–0; Harbhajan Singh 2–0–20–0; Chawla 1–0–14–0; Pathan 1–0–19–0; Kohli 1–0–10–0; Yuvraj Singh 2–0–16–1; Sharma 1–0–12–0.

Umpires: H. D. P. K. Dharmasena and R. A. Kettleborough. Third umpire: I. J. Gould. Referee: R. S. Madugalle.

AUSTRALIA v SOUTH AFRICA

At Colombo (RPS), September 30, 2012. Australia won by eight wickets. Toss: Australia.

Another crushing win for Australia, another major tournament disappointment for South Africa, and another match award for Watson – his fourth in four games, and his eighth in 34 Twenty20 internationals. On this occasion his contribution was 70 from 47 balls, and it came after an unusually slow start: when Morkel bowled Warner in the fourth over, Australia were ten for one. But by the time Watson was dismissed, they were 109 for two in the 14th, and cruised home with 14 balls to spare. South Africa fielded sloppily, dropping Watson on 52, and missing the chance to stump Mike Hussey, although by then the game had gone. They never really recovered after slipping to eight for two in the third over: slow left-armer Doherty relished the new ball in his first appearance of the tournament, bowling the hapless Levi, then claiming the higher-calibre scalp of Kallis, caught behind off a beauty.

Man of the Match: S. R. Watson.

Matthew Lewis, Getty Images

Bully beef: Shane Watson all but knocks South Africa out of another major tournament on his way to a fourth consecutive match award.

South Africa

		B	4	6
R. E. Levi *b 11*	0	3	0	0
H. M. Amla *c 7 b 2*	17	15	1	1
J. H. Kallis *c 7 b 11*	6	7	1	0
J-P. Duminy *st 7 b 11*	30	25	4	0
*†A. B. de Villiers *c 5 b 2*	21	24	0	0
F. Behardien *not out*	31	27	2	1
R. J. Peterson *not out*	32	19	6	0
B 1, w 8	9			
6 overs: 34-3 (20 overs)	146-5			

1/0 2/8 3/33 4/64 5/86

W. D. Parnell, J. Botha, D. W. Steyn and M. Morkel did not bat.

Doherty 4–0–20–3; Starc 4–0–30–0; Cummins 4–0–33–0; Watson 4–0–29–2; Hogg 3–0–26–0; Maxwell 1–0–7–0.

Australia

		B	4	6
D. A. Warner *b 11*	5	9	0	0
S. R. Watson *c 8 b 7*	70	47	8	2
M. E. K. Hussey *not out*	45	37	2	2
C. L. White *not out*	21	13	3	1
B 1, w 5	6			
6 overs: 38-1 (17.4 overs)	147-2			

1/10 2/109

*G. J. Bailey, G. J. Maxwell, †M. S. Wade, G. B. Hogg, P. J. Cummins, M. A. Starc and X. J. Doherty did not bat.

Steyn 3–0–15–0; Morkel 3–0–23–1; Kallis 1–0–8–0; Botha 3.4–0–31–0; Peterson 4–0–41–1; Parnell 2–0–24–0; Duminy 1–0–4–0.

Umpires: H. D. P. K. Dharmasena and I. J. Gould. Third umpire: R. A. Kettleborough. Referee: J. J. Crowe.

INDIA v PAKISTAN

At Colombo (RPS), September 30, 2012. India won by eight wickets. Toss: Pakistan.

Back in the 1980s, Pakistan would routinely thump India, but in recent years that trend had changed: on the biggest stages, India had become the bullies, and Pakistan the cowed. Here was further proof. Despite winning the toss, Pakistan were a nervous wreck of a batting side – some feat given how tentatively India themselves had begun with the ball. Pakistan dangled uneasily between bluster and circumspection, and once Yuvraj Singh took two crucial wickets in successive overs they were effectively gone; Ashwin and Balaji helped hustle them out for 128. India never sweated over their target, even after losing Gambhir in the first over. Kohli, Pakistan's new bête noire, was monstrously good during his 78 and, fittingly, Yuvraj was at the crease at the end. India thus maintained their unbeaten record against Pakistan in global tournaments – five wins out of five in the World Cup, and two in the World Twenty20 (plus a tie in 2007-08, and even then they won the bowl-out).

Man of the Match: V. Kohli.

Pakistan

		B	4	6
*Mohammad Hafeez *b 3*	15	28	1	0
Imran Nazir *lbw b 8*	8	5	2	0
Shahid Afridi *c 5 b 11*	14	12	2	0
Nasir Jamshed *c 7 b 4*	4	5	0	0
†Kamran Akmal *c 7 b 4*	5	6	0	0
Shoaib Malik *c 6 b 9*	28	22	3	0
Umar Akmal *c 5 b 9*	21	18	0	1
Yasir Arafat *run out*	8	11	1	0
Umar Gul *c 7 b 11*	12	10	1	1
Saeed Ajmal *c 7 b 11*	1	2	0	0
Raza Hasan *not out*	0	0	0	0
L-b 1, w 10, n-b 1	12			
6 overs: 42-2 (19.4 overs)	128			

1/17 2/35 3/43 4/49 5/59 6/106 7/115 8/115 9/128

India

		B	4	6
G. Gambhir *c and b 11*	0	2	0	0
V. Sehwag *c 9 b 3*	29	24	4	0
V. Kohli *not out*	78	61	8	2
Yuvraj Singh *not out*	19	16	2	0
W 2, n-b 1	3			
6 overs: 36-1 (17 overs)	129-2			

1/1 2/75

S. K. Raina, R. G. Sharma, *†M. S. Dhoni, I. K. Pathan, R. Ashwin, Zaheer Khan and L. Balaji did not bat.

Zaheer Khan 3–0–22–0; Pathan 3–0–30–1; Balaji 3.4–0–22–3; Ashwin 4–0–16–2; Yuvraj Singh 3–0–16–2; Kohli 3–0–21–1.

Raza Hasan 4–0–22–1; Umar Gul 3–0–30–0; Saeed Ajmal 4–0–25–0; Shahid Afridi 4–0–34–1; Yasir Arafat 1–0–11–0; Mohammad Hafeez 1–0–7–0.

Umpires: R. A. Kettleborough and R. J. Tucker. Third umpire: H. D. P. K. Dharmasena.
Referee: J. J. Crowe.

AUSTRALIA v PAKISTAN

At Colombo (RPS), October 2, 2012. Pakistan won by 32 runs. Toss: Australia.

All four sides in the group had a theoretical chance of making the semi-finals when the day began, but Pakistan's comprehensive win here ultimately meant both these teams went through. First, the increasingly impressive Nasir Jamshed and Kamran Akmal lifted them towards their highest score in the Super Eights, then the spinners removed from the equation Watson and Warner, who until now had been magnificent in Australia's unbeaten surge. But they had occasionally struggled against spin when these teams met in the UAE a few weeks earlier, and did again here. In Pakistan's six-man attack, only Umar Gul was not a slow bowler, and he sent down only two overs as fourth change. After their poor start, Australia were always up against it, and a feeble total of 117 relied almost exclusively on Mike Hussey's typically calculated fifty. That, at least, meant they went through on net run-rate.

Man of the Match: Raza Hasan.

Pakistan

		B	*4*	*6*
*Mohammad Hafeez *lbw b 9*	4	5	0	0
Imran Nazir *c 4 b 1*	14	13	2	0
Nasir Jamshed *c 2 b 11*	55	46	4	2
†Kamran Akmal *c 5 b 9*	32	26	1	1
Umar Akmal *not out*	9	8	1	0
Abdul Razzaq *c 1 b 8*	22	17	2	1
Shahid Afridi *b 9*	4	2	1	0
Shoaib Malik *not out*	4	3	0	0
L-b 2, w 3	5			
6 overs: 31-2 (20 overs)	149-6			

1/5 2/29 3/108 4/108 5/136 6/144

Umar Gul, Saeed Ajmal and Raza Hasan did not bat.

Doherty 4–0–27–1; Starc 4–0–20–3; Watson 4–0–23–1; Cummins 4–0–42–1; Maxwell 1–0–6–0; Hogg 3–0–29–0.

Australia

		B	*4*	*6*
S. R. Watson *lbw b 11*	8	14	1	0
D. A. Warner *lbw b 1*	8	13	1	0
M. E. K. Hussey *not out*	54	47	4	1
*G. J. Bailey *lbw b 10*	15	12	1	1
C. L. White *c 2 b 1*	12	11	0	1
G. J. Maxwell *c 1 b 11*	4	5	0	0
†M. S. Wade *b 10*	13	14	1	0
P. J. Cummins *lbw b 10*	0	1	0	0
M. A. Starc *not out*	1	3	0	0
B 1, w 1	2			
6 overs: 21-2 (20 overs)	117-7			

1/15 2/19 3/44 4/58 5/65 6/110 7/110

G. B. Hogg and X. J. Doherty did not bat.

Mohammad Hafeez 4–0–22–2; Raza Hasan 4–0–14–2; Saeed Ajmal 4–0–17–3; Shahid Afridi 4–0–33–0; Shoaib Malik 2–0–19–0; Umar Gul 2–0–11–0.

Umpires: I. J. Gould and R. A. Kettleborough. Third umpire: H. D. P. K. Dharmasena.
Referee: J. J. Crowe.

INDIA v SOUTH AFRICA

At Colombo (RPS), October 2, 2012. India won by one run. Toss: South Africa.

South Africa's slim chances of reaching the last four had been kyboshed by Pakistan's victory over Australia, and now they ended India's own hopes, despite suffering a third straight defeat: du Plessis hit a swashbuckling 65 to ensure they would score the 122 required to prevent India from surpassing Pakistan's net run-rate. There were loud cheers from the thousands of Pakistan supporters in the ground – and even from a few in the press box – when that target was reached in the 17th over. It was to India's credit that they continued to scrap to win the game, claiming the last five wickets in 16 balls: in a knockabout 20th over, Balaji dismissed the Morkel brothers immediately after each had launched him for six. This could hardly be described as another South African choke, as the pressure was already off, but de Villiers conceded that the "c" word did sum up the earlier loss to Pakistan. For coach Gary Kirsten, this was a ninth consecutive Super Eight defeat: he had been in charge of India when they had lost each of their three games in the previous two tournaments.

Man of the Match: Yuvraj Singh.

India

		B	*4*	*6*
G. Gambhir *b 11*	8	12	1	0
V. Sehwag *b 7*	17	14	1	1
V. Kohli *c 3 b 2*	2	6	0	0
R. G. Sharma *lbw b 7*	25	27	2	0
Yuvraj Singh *b 11*	21	15	1	2
S. K. Raina *run out*	45	34	5	0
*†M. S. Dhoni *not out*	23	13	3	0
L-b 10, n-b 1	11			
6 overs: 36-3 (20 overs)	152-6			

1/23 2/30 3/36 4/68 5/112 6/152

I. K. Pathan, R. Ashwin, L. Balaji and Zaheer Khan did not bat.

Steyn 4–1–26–0; M. Morkel 4–0–28–2; Kallis 3–0–24–1; Peterson 4–0–25–2; Botha 3–0–30–0; du Plessis 1–0–3–0; Duminy 1–0–6–0.

South Africa

		B	*4*	*6*
H. M. Amla *c 2 b 11*	0	2	0	0
J. H. Kallis *c 4 b 8*	6	8	1	0
*†A. B. de Villiers *b 5*	13	13	2	0
F. du Plessis *c 6 b 5*	65	38	6	2
J-P. Duminy *c 1 b 10*	16	23	0	0
F. Behardien *c 6 b 11*	13	12	1	0
R. J. Peterson *b 11*	10	10	1	0
J. A. Morkel *b 10*	10	6	0	1
J. Botha *c 6 b 9*	8	5	0	1
D. W. Steyn *not out*	0	0	0	0
M. Morkel *b 10*	6	3	0	1
L-b 3, n-b 1	4			
6 overs: 46-2 (19.5 overs)	151			

1/0 2/16 3/46 4/95 5/107 6/127 7/127 8/138 9/145

Zaheer Khan 4–0–22–3; Pathan 3–0–26–1; Yuvraj Singh 4–0–23–2; Sharma 1–0–13–0; Ashwin 4–0–27–1; Balaji 3.5–0–37–3.

Umpires: H. D. P. K. Dharmasena and R. J. Tucker. Third umpire: I. J. Gould. Referee: J. J. Crowe.

FINAL SUPER EIGHT TABLES

Group One	*Played*	*Won*	*Lost*	*No result*	*Points*	*Net run-rate*
SRI LANKA	3	3	0	0	6	0.99
WEST INDIES	3	2	1	0	4	–0.37
England	3	1	2	0	2	–0.39
New Zealand	3	0	3	0	0	–0.16

Group Two	*Played*	*Won*	*Lost*	*No result*	*Points*	*Net run-rate*
AUSTRALIA	3	2	1	0	4	0.46
PAKISTAN	3	2	1	0	4	0.27
India	3	2	1	0	4	–0.27
South Africa	3	0	3	0	0	–0.42

SEMI-FINALS

SRI LANKA v PAKISTAN

At Colombo (RPS), October 4, 2012. Sri Lanka won by 16 runs. Toss: Sri Lanka.

A turning pitch, slow and low, shaped a nerve-ridden and largely unmemorable contest which Sri Lanka won by restricting Pakistan to 22 runs in the last four overs when 39 were needed. Batting was a hazardous proposition throughout: various players managed to swipe the odd one successfully, but only Jayawardene looked comfortable, while Dilshan took 43 balls across almost 18 overs for his 35. Playing late, largely square and striving for timing rather than power, Jayawardene oozed class, until a mis-paddle against Shahid Afridi. In the end, the 16 runs taken by Perera and Mathews off the last over of Sri Lanka's innings, from Umar Gul, represented the eventual winning margin. After a slow start to Pakistan's reply, Mohammad Hafeez began to open his shoulders and, at 55 for one in nine overs, they had a decent base. But Mathews returned to check things with variations of pace, before Herath – who had been in and out of the side – delivered the decisive spell. He spun one past Shoaib Malik's defensive push, then removed Hafeez and Afridi with successive balls at the beginning of the 15th over. Hafeez had been reprieved by a dreadful miss by Malinga at long-on when 24, but was undone by some sharp keeping as Sangakkara reacted quickly to the low bounce to complete a stumping. Malinga and Kulasekara proved so effective in the closing stages that Umar Akmal, after a fierce start, contrived to score from only four of the last eight balls he faced. He was later fined half his match fee for changing his batting gloves against the umpires' instructions late in the innings.

Man of the Match: D. P. M. D. Jayawardene.

Sri Lanka

		B	*4*	*6*
*D. P. M. D. Jayawardene *c 11 b 7*	42	36	7	0
T. M. Dilshan *lbw b 9*	35	43	3	0
†K. C. Sangakkara *c 5 b 1*	18	11	3	0
B. M. A. J. Mendis *st 4 b 10*	15	18	1	0
N. L. T. C. Perera *not out*	11	7	2	0
A. D. Mathews *not out*	10	6	1	0
B 3, w 4, n-b 1	8			
6 overs: 34-0 (20 overs)	139-4			

1/63 2/84 3/117 4/118

H. D. R. L. Thirimanne, K. M. D. N. Kulasekara, S. L. Malinga, H. M. R. K. B. Herath and B. A. W. Mendis did not bat.

Sohail Tanvir 3–0–11–0; Raza Hasan 4–0–26–0; Saeed Ajmal 4–0–33–1; Shahid Afridi 4–0–28–1; Mohammad Hafeez 2–0–12–1; Umar Gul 3–0–26–1.

Pakistan

		B	*4*	*6*
*Mohammad Hafeez *st 3 b 10*	42	40	4	1
Imran Nazir *b 11*	20	21	3	0
Nasir Jamshed *lbw b 6*	4	8	0	0
†Kamran Akmal *c 1 b 6*	1	2	0	0
Shoaib Malik *b 10*	6	7	0	0
Umar Akmal *not out*	29	22	3	0
Shahid Afridi *b 10*	0	1	0	0
Sohail Tanvir *st 3 b 11*	8	13	1	0
Umar Gul *not out*	2	6	0	0
L-b 2, w 9	11			
6 overs: 31-1 (20 overs)	123-7			

1/31 2/55 3/57 4/64 5/91 6/91 7/113

Saeed Ajmal and Raza Hasan did not bat.

Mathews 4–0–27–2; Kulasekara 3–0–15–0; Malinga 4–0–19–0; B. A. W. Mendis 4–0–27–2; Perera 1–0–8–0; Herath 4–0–25–3.

Umpires: S. J. A. Taufel and R. J. Tucker. Third umpire: I. J. Gould.
Referee: J. J. Crowe.

AUSTRALIA v WEST INDIES

At Colombo (RPS), October 5, 2012. West Indies won by 74 runs. Toss: West Indies.

All the old clichés about Caribbean flair held true as West Indies smiled, danced, but most of all powered their way into the final. Even though Gayle faced only 41 of the 120 balls in batting through the innings, West Indies piled up 205 for four, the highest score of the tournament, and were on course for a massive victory when they reduced a shell-shocked Australia to 43 for six in the eighth over. Bailey responded by clouting a quickfire 63, but his effort had more impact as an answer to those questioning his place in the team than on the result. Gayle had remained a constant throughout a West Indian innings that accelerated via Samuels and Dwayne Bravo, before exploding as Pollard helped add 65 from the last 25 balls. There were more sixes (14) than fours (13) in the 20 overs, the last eight of which produced 114 runs. Bailey had bowled out his seamers in the forlorn hope of breaking through, leaving Pollard and Gayle to take on Doherty, in a final over that produced four sixes, as though they were practising range hitting. Sammy remained undeterred by this assault against spin, and used a pair of his own – Badree and Samuels – through the six-over powerplay. Between them, they removed Australia's feted top three and, when Sammy switched to pace, Rampaul accounted for White and David Hussey in his first three balls.

Man of the Match: C. H. Gayle.

West Indies

		B	*4*	*6*
J. Charles *c 7 b 9*	10	13	2	0
C. H. Gayle *not out*	75	41	5	6
M. N. Samuels *b 8*	26	20	2	2
D. J. Bravo *c 5 b 8*	37	31	1	3
K. A. Pollard *c 1 b 11*	38	15	3	3
B 6, l-b 5, w 8	19			
6 overs: 46-1 (20 overs)	205-4			

1/16 2/57 3/140 4/205

A. D. Russell, †D. Ramdin, *D. J. G. Sammy, S. P. Narine, R. Rampaul and S. Badree did not bat.

Starc 4–0–32–1; Watson 4–0–35–0; Cummins 4–0–36–2; Doherty 3–0–48–1; Hogg 3–0–21–0; D. J. Hussey 2–0–22–0.

Australia

		B	*4*	*6*
D. A. Warner *b 11*	1	3	0	0
S. R. Watson *b 11*	7	9	1	0
M. E. K. Hussey *c and b 3*	18	12	3	0
C. L. White *c 7 b 10*	5	6	0	0
*G. J. Bailey *c 6 b 5*	63	29	6	4
D. J. Hussey *c and b 10*	0	2	0	0
†M. S. Wade *c 11 b 9*	1	5	0	0
P. J. Cummins *c 1 b 5*	13	15	1	0
M. A. Starc *b 10*	2	5	0	0
G. B. Hogg *st 7 b 9*	7	7	0	0
X. J. Doherty *not out*	9	7	1	0
L-b 3, w 2	5			
6 overs: 42-3 (16.4 overs)	131			

1/2 2/22 3/29 4/42 5/42 6/43 7/111 8/111 9/121

Badree 4–0–27–2; Samuels 3–0–26–1; Rampaul 3.4–0–16–3; Narine 3–0–17–2; Russell 1–0–25–0; Sammy 1–0–11–0; Pollard 1–0–6–2.

Umpires: Aleem Dar and H. D. P. K. Dharmasena. Third umpire: R. A. Kettleborough. Referee: R. S. Madugalle.

FINAL

SRI LANKA v WEST INDIES

VIC MARKS

At Colombo (RPS), October 7, 2012. West Indies won by 36 runs. Toss: West Indies.

West Indies won the World Twenty20 for the first time, sparking more cricketing optimism in the Caribbean than it has known for a decade or more. The margin of victory seemed mammoth for a Twenty20 game, yet there were moments when West Indies seemed doomed to failure – a situation familiar to Darren Sammy's side on their route to the final.

Earlier in the tournament they had looked destined for an early return home. They managed to qualify for the Super Eights without actually winning either of their group games, like previous champions England in 2010. Then, six days before the final, they looked certain to lose to New Zealand, but fought back to tie, against the odds, before prevailing in the super over by smashing the 18 runs required. These scrapes seemed to forge a wonderful, joyous spirit within the West Indian camp, as well as the belief that this would be their trophy.

Gemunu Amarasinghe, AP/PA

Swinging from the hip: whether slower ball, length or yorker, Marlon Samuels puts Lasith Malinga out of the Premadasa.

Even in the final, a West Indies victory seemed out of the question after the first ten overs, at which point they were an unfathomable 32 for two. Their champion, Gayle, had been dismissed for three, and Jayawardene was controlling affairs like a master puppeteer. But Samuels played an astonishing innings. After a cagey start he cracked 78 from 56 balls, smashing six sixes along the way.

His assault on Malinga was breathtaking. While Mathews and Ajantha Mendis bowled their eight overs for 23 runs and five wickets, Malinga – probably the most experienced, and feared, fast bowler in the world in this format – was carted for 54, including five of those sixes. Somehow Samuels differentiated between the slower and quicker balls before depositing them over the leg-side boundary. This was an enthralling display of brutal, calculated hitting. Bravo and Sammy offered handy assistance, and the total advanced to 137 – far more than expected, and enough to generate hope.

Sri Lanka's chase was badly hindered when Dilshan was bowled by Rampaul's first delivery. Then the wise old men, Jayawardene and Sangakkara, set about knocking off the target as sensibly as possible – but they could not score quickly enough on a pitch that offered increasing encouragement to the spinners. Sangakkara was well caught by Pollard at deep midwicket, Jayawardene felt compelled to reverse-sweep and lobbed a catch to point, then panic set in. There were run-outs, as West Indies displayed an athleticism in the outfield that few international sides can match, and the unorthodox spinner Narine, a potential Caribbean star for the next decade, tormented everyone.

There was a little scare when Rampaul conceded 22 in the 16th over, as Kulasekara regularly found the boundary. But soon the game was up, and the cricketers of the Caribbean, as united as they have ever been since the golden days, began to celebrate as only they know how.

It was a proud moment for Sammy. "Today we were down and out, but our never-say-die attitude came out," he said. No one had a smile broader than Gayle, until recently a so-called mercenary, but now the heartbeat of the side.

Man of the Match: M. N. Samuels. *Man of the Tournament:* S. R. Watson.

West Indies

		B	4	6
J. Charles *c 8 b 4*	0	5	0	0
C. H. Gayle *lbw b 10*	3	16	0	0
M. N. Samuels *c 5 b 11*	78	56	3	6
D. J. Bravo *lbw b 10*	19	19	0	1
K. A. Pollard *c 11 b 10*	2	4	0	0
A. D. Russell *lbw b 10*	0	1	0	0
*D. J. G. Sammy *not out*	26	15	3	0
†D. Ramdin *not out*	4	4	0	0
L-b 2, w 3	5			
6 overers: 14-2 (20 overs)	137-6			

1/0 2/14 3/73 4/87 5/87 6/108

S. P. Narine, R. Rampaul and S. Badree did not bat.

Mathews 4–1–11–1; Kulasekara 3–0–22–0; Malinga 4–0–54–0; B. A. W. Mendis 4–0–12–4; Dananjaya 3–0–16–1; B. M. A. J. Mendis 2–0–20–0.

Sri Lanka

		B	4	6
*D. P. M. D. Jayawardene *c 7 b 9*	33	36	2	0
T. M. Dilshan *b 10*	0	3	0	0
†K. C. Sangakkara *c 5 b 11*	22	26	2	0
A. D. Mathews *b 7*	1	5	0	0
B. M. A. J. Mendis *run out*	3	3	0	0
N. L. T. C. Perera *run out*	3	5	0	0
H. D. R. L. Thirimanne *c 1 b 7*	4	7	0	0
K. M. D. N. Kulasekara *c 11 b 9*	26	13	3	1
S. L. Malinga *c 4 b 9*	5	13	0	0
B. A. W. Mendis *c 4 b 3*	1	2	0	0
A. Dananjaya *not out*	0	0	0	0
L-b 2, n-b 1	3			
6 overs: 30-1 (18.4 overs)	101			

1/6 2/48 3/51 4/60 5/61 6/64 7/69 8/96 9/100

Badree 4–0–24–1; Rampaul 3–0–31–1; Samuels 4–0–15–1; Gayle 2–0–14–0; Narine 3.4–0–9–3; Sammy 2–0–6–2.

Umpires: Aleem Dar and S. J. A. Taufel. Third umpire: R. J. Tucker.
Referee: J. J. Crowe.

ICC WORLD TWENTY20 FINALS

		Man of the Match
2007-08	INDIA‡ beat Pakistan by five runs at Johannesburg.	I. K. Pathan
2009	PAKISTAN beat Sri Lanka‡ by eight wickets at Lord's.	Shahid Afridi
2010	ENGLAND‡ beat Australia by seven wickets at Bridgetown.	C. Kieswetter
2012-13	WEST INDIES‡ beat Sri Lanka by 36 runs at Colombo.	M. N. Samuels

ICC WOMEN'S WORLD TWENTY20, 2012-13

ALISON MITCHELL

1. Australia 2. England 3= New Zealand and West Indies

The third Women's World Twenty20 ended with the thriller the tournament was crying out for, as Australia beat England by four runs in Colombo to become the first team – male or female – to retain the title.

England were heavily fancied to repeat their triumph of 2009, in the first tournament, having only recently been halted on a run of 19 Twenty20 international victories (excluding abandonments). They picked the same XI throughout the competition, including four spin bowlers – Holly Colvin, Danielle Hazell, Laura Marsh and Danielle Wyatt. Australia's openers came out firing, however, and they clinched victory off the last ball of a tense final. "I'm disappointed we lost," said England captain Charlotte Edwards. "But I'd rather play in a final which was a great spectacle for the women's game. I'm very proud of that."

For the third time, the women's event ran parallel to the men's. The group games were hosted in Galle, where crowds were small, despite the efforts of ICC marketeers to raise enthusiasm by erecting life-size cardboard cut-outs of the leading players next to their male counterparts on roundabouts across the city and in Colombo. The semi-finals and final were staged as double-headers at Colombo's Premadasa Stadium before the equivalent men's matches, and broadcast worldwide by ESPN STAR Sports.

The semi-finals were a perfect illustration of why the pace of the pitch is so important to women's cricket, which is determined more by canny deflections and careful placement than brute force. A painfully slow turner led to a turgid game between England and New Zealand, but a truer surface the next day made for far more engaging cricket, even though Australia's win over West Indies was similarly one-sided.

England had swept through Group A unbeaten, with their batsmen rarely tested. Against India, Edwards became the first woman to pass 1,500 runs in Twenty20 internationals, and she finished as the tournament's leading scorer, with 172 at 43.

India, long regarded as one of the big four of the women's game, lost every group match, prompting concerns that Australia and England were pulling away from the rest of the world – a theory strengthened by the ease of England's semi-final win over two-time runners-up New Zealand, the other member of the quartet. India's nadir was confirmed when, in an unattractive, low-scoring game, they were unable to chase down 99 in a dead rubber against Pakistan.

It was their first defeat by their arch-rivals, and the first time since 1988, when they did not even send a team, that they had failed to reach the last four of a global tournament. Their captain, the experienced and respected Mithali Raj, said the loss ought to be a jolt for the women's game in her country.

Philip Brown

Rubbing it in: the England players mull over their defeat in the final by Australia, who huddle in ecstasy on the giant screen behind them.

Meanwhile, Pakistan captain Sana Mir renewed her call for more fixtures against the top countries in order for them to improve.

Group B was thrown wide open by the inconsistency of West Indies and New Zealand. West Indies imploded in a rain-affected game against the hosts Sri Lanka, but bounced back with their first win over New Zealand in a competitive match. The quartet eliminated at the group stage went into play-off matches to qualify for the 2014 tournament in Bangladesh. India beat Sri Lanka to avoid the ignominy of having to go to Ireland for the qualifying competition; South Africa also secured their place, with victory over Pakistan off the penultimate ball.

Before the tournament, a media furore had erupted when the scale of the pay gap between the genders became apparent. The ICC granted women players a daily allowance of \$60, compared to \$100 for the men; the women had flown economy class, the men in business; most glaringly of all, prize money of \$60,000 for the victorious Australian women was dwarfed by the \$1m picked up by Darren Sammy's West Indians. Despite all that, and a smaller overall budget for the women's game, an ICC spokesman said it was aiming for "equal everything".

Women's cricket falls under the development arm of the ICC, so staging international events is not a profit-making venture, and it may never reach economic parity with the men's game. But the ICC must ensure the cricket remains attractive. The standards displayed by Australia and England need to be more frequently matched by the countries behind them. Quicker pitches would help too.

Group A

At Galle, September 27, 2012. **England won by 43 runs. England 133-6** (20 overs) (C. M. Edwards 45, L. A. Marsh 54); **‡Pakistan 90** (19.4 overs) (H. L. Colvin 4-9). *Twenty20 international debut:* Sumaiya Siddiqi (Pakistan). *PoM:* L. A. Marsh. *England were in command once Charlotte Edwards and Laura Marsh opened with 102 in 13 overs – both were eventually run out. Holly Colvin then took three wickets in six balls to finish with career-best Twenty20 figures.*

At Galle, September 27, 2012. **Australia won by eight wickets. ‡India 104-8** (20 overs) (E. A. Osborne 3-13); **Australia 105-2** (17.2 overs) (M. M. Lanning 39, J. E. Cameron 36*). *PoM:* E. A. Osborne. *India, well placed at 63-2 after ten overs, collapsed after the run-out of Mithali Raj for 18. Meg Lanning and Alyssa Healy (21) raced out of the blocks with 43 in six overs.*

At Galle, September 29, 2012. **Australia won by 25 runs** (D/L). **‡Australia 146-5** (20 overs) (A. J. Healy 36, J. E. Cameron 42); **Pakistan 38-3** (9 overs). *PoM:* J. E. Cameron. *Australia were on course for an emphatic victory when rain arrived. Jess Cameron thumped two of her 28 balls for six.*

At Galle, September 29, 2012. **England won by nine wickets. ‡India 116-6** (20 overs) (P. G. Raut 51, M. Raj 35); **England 118-1** (17.1 overs) (C. M. Edwards 50*, L. A. Marsh 39). *Twenty20 international debut:* A. A. Patil (India). *PoM:* C. M. Edwards. *Raj and Poonam Raut took 12.4 overs to add 75, on a pitch slowed by morning rain. India's bowlers were then blown away by Edwards, Marsh and Sarah Taylor (25*). Edwards became the second player of either gender – after New Zealand's Brendon McCullum – to pass 1,500 Twenty20 international runs.*

At Galle, October 1, 2012. **Pakistan won by one run. ‡Pakistan 98-9** (20 overs); **India 97-8** (20 overs) (Nida Dar 3-12). *Twenty20 international debut:* R. K. Parwin (India). *PoM:* Nida Dar. *Defeats by England and Australia could be excused, but India's failure to chase 99 against their closest rivals – who had never before beaten one of the big four – was a serious wake-up call. India were sitting pretty at 44-1 in the tenth over, before off-spinner Nida Dar took three wickets in six balls to turn the match. Nagarajan Niranjana made a brave attempt to score 16 off Sana Mir's last over, but was run out returning for a third that would have tied the match.*

At Galle, October 1, 2012. **England won by seven wickets. ‡Australia 144-5** (20 overs) (M. M. Lanning 39, L. C. Sthalekar 38); **England 146-3** (18.1 overs) (S. J. Taylor 65*, D. N. Wyatt 33*). *PoM:* S. J. Taylor. *Taylor underpinned England's ruthless run-chase with 65 from 53 balls, the highest score of the tournament; 62 were still needed from 7.2 overs when Danielle Wyatt came in and hit Ellyse Perry off her length.*

Group B

At Galle, September 26, 2012. **South Africa won by six wickets. Sri Lanka 79** (20 overs); **‡South Africa 80-4** (17.2 overs) (T. Chetty 33). *Twenty20 international debut:* I. Ranaweera (Sri Lanka). *PoM:* T. Chetty. *South Africa wicketkeeper Trisha Chetty was involved in six dismissals – one catch, one stumping and four run-outs – then led the chase with 33 from 40 balls.*

At Galle, September 26, 2012. **West Indies won by seven wickets. New Zealand 117-9** (20 overs) (S. W. Bates 32); **‡West Indies 118-3** (18 overs) (S. R. Taylor 35, D. J. S. Dottin 58*). *PoM:* D. J. S. Dottin. *New Zealand surrendered eight for 47, squandering the chance of a commanding score. West Indies were 5-2 when Deandra Dottin came in; she underlined her status as the most powerful hitter in the game, clearing the ropes twice in 58* from 42 balls.*

At Galle, September 28, 2012. **New Zealand won by 22 runs. New Zealand 151-5** (20 overs) (S. F. M. Devine 59, F. L. Mackay 49); **‡South Africa 129-9** (20 overs) (A. L. Hodgkinson 31, D. van Niekerk 34*; N. J. Browne 3-13). *PoM:* S. F. M. Devine. *Susan Benade (2-15) removed both New Zealand openers, but sustained power from Sophie Devine (59 from 46 balls) and Frances Mackay (49 from 40) left South Africa too much to do.*

At Galle, September 28, 2012. **Sri Lanka won by five runs** (D/L). Reduced to 17 overs a side. **Sri Lanka 50-3** (10.3 overs); **‡West Indies 42-8** (8 overs). *PoM:* C. R. Seneviratne (Sri Lanka). *In a match shortened three times by rain, West Indies were eventually required to score 48 in eight overs.*

They were forced to take several risks, leading to four run-outs, and two stumpings off Chamani Seneviratne's medium-pace – giving Sri Lanka the first upset of the tournament.

At Galle, September 30, 2012. **West Indies won by ten wickets. South Africa 70-8** (20 overs) (S. R. Taylor 3-10); ‡**West Indies 71-0** (9.4 overs) (S. R. Taylor 33*, J. B. Nero 30*). *PoM:* S. R. Taylor. *Knowing the South Africans preferred batting against pace, off-spinner Stafanie Taylor took the new ball and had them reeling at 19-6 halfway through their innings; West Indies sauntered through to the last four.*

At Galle, September 30, 2012. **New Zealand won by eight wickets.** ‡**Sri Lanka 89** (17.4 overs); **New Zealand 90-2** (15.4 overs) (A. E. Satterthwaite 32*). *PoM:* S. J. McGlashan (New Zealand). *Sri Lanka collapsed from 69-3 in the 12th over; 19 extras was their top score.*

GROUP TABLES

Group A

	Played	*Won*	*Lost*	*No result*	*Points*	*Net run-rate*
ENGLAND	3	3	0	0	6	1.34
AUSTRALIA	3	2	1	0	4	0.62
Pakistan	3	1	2	0	2	–1.36
India	3	0	3	0	0	–0.60

Group B

	Played	*Won*	*Lost*	*No result*	*Points*	*Net run-rate*
WEST INDIES	3	2	1	0	4	1.60
NEW ZEALAND	3	2	1	0	4	0.63
Sri Lanka	3	1	2	0	2	–0.69
South Africa	3	1	2	0	2	–1.19

World Twenty20 2014 play-offs

At Colombo (Moors), October 3, 2012. **South Africa won by five wickets.** ‡**Pakistan 87-8** (20 overs) (Bismah Maroof 32; S. Ismail 3-19); **South Africa 88-5** (19.5 overs). *Twenty20 international debut:* Javeria Rauf (Pakistan). *PoM:* S. Ismail. *Sana Mir issued a stern critique of Pakistan's batsmen after they fell short of 100 for the fourth time. South Africa took an age to chase down the runs, scrambling the six they needed from the last over with a ball to spare. They qualified automatically for the 2014 World Twenty20 in Bangladesh, while Pakistan now had to take part in a qualifying tournament in Ireland in 2013.*

At Colombo (NCC), October 3, 2012. **India won by nine wickets.** ‡**Sri Lanka 100-8** (20 overs) (E. Bisht 3-16); **India 102-1** (14.4 overs) (P. G. Raut 45*). *PoM:* E. Bisht. *India's left-arm spinner Ekta Bisht took a hat-trick in the final over, then ran out Sadamali Dolowatte. It was the second hat-trick inside a month in women's Twenty20 internationals, after Asmavia Iqbal for Pakistan against England at Loughborough on September 5 (see page 810).*

Semi-finals

At Colombo (RPS), October 4, 2012. **England won by seven wickets. New Zealand 93-8** (20 overs) (A. E. Satterthwaite 30); ‡**England 94-3** (17.2 overs) (C. M. Edwards 33). *PoM:* C. M. Edwards. *England put in a typically superb fielding display to earn their 23rd win from 24 completed Twenty20 internationals, and deny New Zealand a third consecutive World Twenty20 final appearance. Suzie Bates lamented her side's struggle to sweep square of the wicket – which proved especially costly against England's four-pronged spin attack. Edwards fell with 41 still needed, but Taylor (21*) and Lydia Greenway (22) finished the job.*

At Colombo (RPS), October 5, 2012. **Australia won by 28 runs.** ‡**Australia 115-7** (20 overs); **West Indies 87** (19.2 overs) (J. B. Nero 31; J. L. Hunter 5-22). *PoM:* E. A. Perry (Australia). *Perry, the fastest bowler in women's cricket, castled Taylor and Dottin, both playing across the line, to reduce West Indies to 23-3; she also inadvertently ran out Shemaine Campbelle at the non-striker's end when deflecting a return catch on to the stumps. Julie Hunter took advantage of West Indies' desperation to claim the tournament's only five-wicket haul, and the best figures by an Australian in women's Twenty20 internationals.*

FINAL

AUSTRALIA v ENGLAND

At Colombo (RPS), October 7, 2012. Australia won by four runs. Toss: England.

Australia's women defended their World Twenty20 title. Although England took the match down to the last ball, they were always playing catch-up after their successful formula – bowl first, suffocate the batsmen with spin – was thrown off course by Australia's aggressive openers, Meg Lanning and Alyssa Healy. They harnessed the pace of the ball, and any deviation from the required line and length by Katherine Brunt seemed to result in a boundary. Jess Cameron rattled up 45 off 34 deliveries, including a six over midwicket off Anya Shrubsole in an over that cost 17 as she insisted on bowling full. After that, Charlotte Edwards wisely kept her spinners on until the end. Australia bowled with greater discipline, and England immediately fell behind the rate. But Australian nerves began to fray: four catches went down in the second half of the innings, and Jenny Gunn diluted the equation to 16 from the last over. When Erin Osborne delivered a beamer second ball, England had a sniff. Danielle Hazell needed to hit Osborne's last ball for six, but she mistimed it to midwicket, and Australian celebrations began.

Player of the Match: J. E. Cameron. *Player of the Tournament:* C. M. Edwards.

Australia Women

		B	*4*	*6*
M. M. Lanning *c and b 10*	25	24	4	0
A. J. Healy *b 9*	26	25	3	0
J. E. Cameron *c 7 b 10*	45	34	5	1
L. C. Sthalekar *not out*	23	26	1	0
A. J. Blackwell *run out*	13	12	1	0
L-b 1, w 8, n-b 1	10			
6 overs: 47-0 (20 overs)	142-4			

1/51 2/68 3/119 4/142

*†J. M. Fields, R. L. Haynes, E. A. Osborne, J. L. Hunter, E. A. Perry and J. L. Jonassen did not bat.

Brunt 2–0–20–0; Hazell 4–0–23–1; Wyatt 3–0–20–0; Shrubsole 3–0–31–0; Colvin 4–0–21–2; Marsh 4–0–26–0.

England Women

		B	*4*	*6*
*C. M. Edwards *c 10 b 4*	28	23	4	1
L. A. Marsh *c and b 9*	8	14	2	0
†S. J. Taylor *c 6 b 10*	19	16	2	0
L. S. Greenway *c 10 b 11*	4	10	0	0
A. Brindle *b 4*	13	12	2	0
D. N. Wyatt *c 5 b 11*	9	10	0	0
J. L. Gunn *c 11 b 9*	19	14	1	1
K. H. Brunt *b 11*	3	4	0	0
D. Hazell *not out*	16	13	1	0
H. L. Colvin *run out*	8	5	1	0
A. Shrubsole *not out*	0	0	0	0
B 2, l-b 2, w 6, n-b 1	11			
6 overs: 34-1 (20 overs)	138-9			

1/20 2/44 3/61 4/63 5/86 6/90 7/101 8/120 9/137

Perry 4–0–24–1; Sthalekar 4–0–16–2; Hunter 4–0–36–2; Osborne 4–0–33–0; Jonassen 4–0–25–3.

Umpires: B. F. Bowden and M. Erasmus. Third umpire: A. L. Hill.
Referee: G. F. Labrooy.

WOMEN'S WORLD TWENTY20 FINALS

		Player of the Match
2009	ENGLAND‡ beat New Zealand by six wickets at Lord's.	K. H. Brunt
2010	AUSTRALIA‡ beat New Zealand by three runs at Bridgetown.	E. A. Perry
2012-13	AUSTRALIA beat England‡ by four runs at Colombo.	J. E. Cameron

ICC UNDER-19 WORLD CUP, 2012

REVIEW BY GEORGE BINOY

1. India 2. Australia 3. South Africa 4. New Zealand

The ninth Under-19 World Cup felt like a bowlers' tournament from the moment Reece Topley broke Jimmy Peirson's middle stump in half during the Australia–England match on the opening day. August isn't cricket season in Queensland, so it was no surprise that lively pitches assisted swing and seam movement. What *was* a surprise was that – in these conditions – it was India who eventually triumphed.

Topley would finish as the tournament's leading wicket-taker – with 19 – and the highlight of England's misfiring campaign. Australia and West Indies, whose attack was led by the promising Ronsford Beaton from Montserrat, also possessed seamers capable of approaching 90mph. But while India's weren't as fast, Sandeep Sharma swung it in both directions and was the most dangerous new-ball bowler on show. He was a vital cog in India's title win – their third at this level, equalling Australia's record.

Spin bowlers joined in too: Ireland's slow left-armer George Dockrell was devilishly difficult to get away, with a staggering economy-rate of 2.05, as were Harmeet Singh, a left-arm spinner, and the off-breaks of his Indian team-mate Baba Apparajith. Ashton Turner, another off-spinner, was Australia's leading wicket-taker, and Nepal's slow left-armer Rahul Vishvakarma took six for three against Papua New Guinea.

It's true that 15 centuries were scored in all, compared with five in New Zealand in 2010, and only three in Malaysia in 2008. But the overall run-rate was nothing special. Perhaps it felt like a bowlers' tournament simply because expectations of batsmen have sky-rocketed in an age of 300-plus totals in senior one-day internationals.

Bangladesh captain Anamul Haque, in his fourth and final year as an Under-19 cricketer, was the leading run-scorer, with 365. His Australian counterpart William Bosisto was dismissed only once in six innings – to a run-out – and finished with an astronomical average of 276. Their teams were involved in the tournament's most controversial incident, when in the quarter-final Soumya Sarkar ran out Peirson backing up, without prior warning. The matter-of-fact response from the Australia camp showed how attitudes had moved on in many parts of the world, if not necessarily England.

India's highly impressive captain, Unmukt Chand, delivered when it mattered, scoring 111 not out to win the final. In the previous five months, he had also compiled title-winning hundreds in a quadrangular practice tournament in Queensland (see page 935), and at the Under-19 Asia Cup. Few cricketers could claim to be so decorated at his age; it seemed natural that he graduated immediately to the India A team.

South Africa could boast the highest run-rate (5.39), the highest total (359 for six), and the lowest economy-rate and bowling average (3.62 and 15.80).

They did not concede more than 200 in an innings and were the only team with a 200-run partnership. But several mistakes in the field contributed to their semi-final defeat by Australia.

Most quarter-finalists had prepared by going on tours, or holding training camps, although New Zealand were limited to the quadrangular in Australia in April. Their fourth-place finish, ahead of better-prepared England, Pakistan, Bangladesh and West Indies, was testament to their spirit. In the lengthy Plate competition, Zimbabwe – the weakest Full Member at Under-19 level – lost to Scotland and PNG, two of the Associates, to finish beneath them in the final reckoning. The closest the tournament came to a bona fide upset was when Afghanistan only narrowly lost to New Zealand.

Group A

At Townsville (Tony Ireland Stadium), August 11, 2012. **Australia won by six wickets. England 143** (38.3 overs); ‡**Australia 147-4** (35.1 overs) (T. M. Head 57*). *MoM:* T. M. Head. *On a quick and bouncy pitch, both top orders struggled, but William Bosisto (35*) and Travis Head knuckled down to add the 93 that ensured Australia made a winning start to their title defence.*

At Townsville (Endeavour Park), August 12, 2012. **England won by seven wickets. Ireland 109** (42.2 overs); ‡**England 113-3** (36.2 overs). *MoM:* R. J. W. Topley. *Ireland found Reece Topley (9–4–14–3) impossible to handle.*

At Townsville (Tony Ireland Stadium), August 13, 2012. **Australia won by 212 runs. Australia 294-7** (50 overs) (C. T. Bancroft 125, K. R. Patterson 86); ‡**Nepal 82** (23.5 overs) (A. J. Turner 4-28). *MoM:* C. T. Bancroft. *Nepal had no answer to Cameron Bancroft's canny century – eight of his nine boundaries came from his last 32 balls – or the pace of 6ft 5in Harry Conway (3-15), who hit off stump three times for a hat-trick.*

At Townsville (Endeavour Park No. 2), August 14, 2012. **Australia won by six wickets.** ‡**Ireland 129** (42.5 overs); **Australia 133-4** (40.3 overs). *MoM:* S. Cassel (Australia).

At Townsville (Endeavour Park), August 15, 2012. **Ireland won by 14 runs.** ‡**Ireland 185-8** (50 overs); **Nepal 171** (49.3 overs) (G. H. Dockrell 4-22). *MoM:* G. H. Dockrell. *George Dockrell won lbw appeals from two consecutive balls to turn the contest Ireland's way.*

At Townsville (Tony Ireland Stadium), August 16, 2012. **England won by 127 runs.** ‡**England 274-7** (50 overs) (B. T. Foakes 92, B. M. Duckett 55); **Nepal 147** (46 overs) (S. P. Khakurel 55; S. A. Ali 4-37). *MoM:* B. T. Foakes. *Nepal's challenge ended at 9-4.*

Australia 6pts, England 4pts, Ireland 2pts, Nepal 0pts.

Group B

At Buderim (John Blanck Oval), August 11, 2012. **Pakistan won by 109 runs. Pakistan 253-6** (50 overs) (Babar Azam 75, Mohammad Nawaz 66); ‡**Afghanistan 144** (45.1 overs) (Hashmatullah Sahidi 50; Zia-ul-Haq 4-30). *MoM:* Babar Azam. *No. 7 Mohammad Nawaz pushed the contest beyond Afghanistan with 66 from 50 balls.*

At Buderim (John Blanck Oval), August 12, 2012. **New Zealand won by 39 runs. New Zealand 247-9** (50 overs) (W. A. Young 115, R. R. O'Donnell 50); ‡**Scotland 208** (46.5 overs) (F. R. J. Coleman 65). *MoM:* W. A. Young.

At Buderim (Kev Hackney Oval), August 13, 2012. **Pakistan won by nine wickets.** ‡**Scotland 200** (49.5 overs) (R. E. McLean 59; Mohammad Nawaz 4-20); **Pakistan 204-1** (36.2 overs) (Sami Aslam 78, Babar Azam 106*). *MoM:* Babar Azam. *Scotland were 168-4 before losing four in 16 balls to left-arm spinner Mohammad Nawaz. Sami Aslam, aged 16, and Babar Azam, 17, then opened with 163.*

At Buderim (Kev Hackney Oval), August 14, 2012. **New Zealand won by eight runs.** ‡**New Zealand 198** (50 overs) (R. R. O'Donnell 69, H. A. Walsh 52; Sayed Shirzad 4-34, Yamin Ahmadzai 4-35); **Afghanistan 190-9** (50 overs) (Najibullah Zadran 69; J. A. Duffy 4-40, M. R. Quinn 4-26). *MoM:* M. R. Quinn. *Afghanistan collapsed to 26-5, with Jacob Duffy and Matthew Quinn rampant, although Najibullah Zadran and Afsar Khan (42) gave New Zealand a scare.*

At Buderim (John Blanck Oval), August 15, 2012. **Afghanistan won by ten runs.** †**Afghanistan 191** (48.3 overs) (Javed Ahmadi 71; R. A. J. Smith 4-45, G. T. Main 4-26); **Scotland 181** (49.2 overs) (R. E. McLean 67). *MoM:* Javed Ahmadi. *From 120-2 in the 32nd over, Scotland's challenge waned after the demise of Freddie Coleman (30).*

At Buderim (John Blanck Oval), August 16, 2012. **Pakistan won by five wickets.** ‡**New Zealand 152-8** (50 overs); **Pakistan 153-5** (31.2 overs). *MoM:* Mohammad Nawaz (Pakistan).

Pakistan 6pts, New Zealand 4pts, Afghanistan 2pts, Scotland 0pts.

Group C

At Townsville (Endeavour Park), August 11, 2012. **Zimbabwe won by 104 runs. Zimbabwe 249** (50 overs) (K. T. Kasuza 97; C. N. Kent 5-45); ‡**Papua New Guinea 145** (38.1 overs). *MoM:* K. T. Kasuza.

At Townsville (Tony Ireland Stadium), August 12, 2012. **West Indies won by four wickets. India 166-8** (50 overs) (S. K. Patel 51); ‡**West Indies 167-6** (47.1 overs) (A. T. Alleyne 52). *MoM:* K. R. Mayers (West Indies). *India were bombarded by the pace of Ronsford Beaton (3-33) and Jerome Jones (2-23) on a cracked pitch.*

At Townsville (Endeavour Park No. 2), August 13, 2012. **West Indies won by nine wickets.** ‡**Papua New Guinea 116** (41 overs); **West Indies 117-1** (11.4 overs) (S. W. Ambris 91). *MoM:* S. W. Ambris. *Sunil Ambris, from St Vincent, thrashed 91 of West Indies' 117, from just 43 balls; opening partner Kraigg Brathwaite – the only Test player in the tournament – finished on 17* from 25.*

At Townsville (Tony Ireland Stadium), August 14, 2012. **India won by 63 runs. India 261-6** (50 overs) (P. Chopra 57, U. Chand 78); ‡**Zimbabwe 198** (44.1 overs) (M. B. Lake 118; K. Passi 6-23). *MoM:* K. Passi. *India withstood a solo assault from Malcolm Lake, who thrashed 118 from 107 balls after Kamal Passi had reduced Zimbabwe to 30-4. Lake's medium-pace had earlier gone for just 19 in seven overs, but he was not asked to complete his quota. Instead, Cuthbert Musoko was pummelled for 24 from the last five balls of the innings by Passi.*

At Townsville (Endeavour Park), August 16, 2012. **India won by 107 runs.** ‡**India 204** (45.1 overs) (P. Chopra 58, V. H. Zol 72; C. A. Soper 5-32); **Papua New Guinea 97** (31.5 overs) (Ravikant Singh 5-21). *MoM:* Ravikant Singh.

At Townsville (Endeavour Park No. 2), August 16, 2012. **West Indies won by six wickets. Zimbabwe 148-8** (50 overs); ‡**West Indies 150-4** (35.1 overs) (K. C. Brathwaite 70*). *MoM:* K. C. Brathwaite. *Beaton collected figures of 9–4–9–1.*

West Indies 6pts, India 4pts, Zimbabwe 2pts, Papua New Guinea 0pts.

Group D

At Brisbane (Allan Border Field), August 11, 2012. **Bangladesh won by 25 runs. Bangladesh 249-7** (50 overs) (Anamul Haque 101, Asif Ahmed 84); ‡**Sri Lanka 224** (48.4 overs) (A. J. A. D. D. L. A. Jayasinghe 83). *MoM:* Anamul Haque. *Bangladesh struck first blood in the "group of death", driven on by a third-wicket stand of 141 between Anamul Haque and Asif Ahmed.*

At Brisbane (Allan Border Field), August 12, 2012. **South Africa won by 133 runs. South Africa 294-8** (50 overs) (Q. de Kock 95, T. B. de Bruyn 63); ‡**Bangladesh 161** (34.3 overs). *MoM:* Q. de Kock.

At Brisbane (Allan Border Field), August 13, 2012. **Sri Lanka won by 195 runs.** ‡**Sri Lanka 298-9** (50 overs) (W. L. J. O. S. Perera 69, D. S. Weerakkody 50); **Namibia 103** (35 overs) (L. D. Madushanka 4-15). *MoM:* W. L. J. O. S. Perera.

At Brisbane (Peter Burge Oval), August 14, 2012. **South Africa won by 209 runs.** ‡**South Africa 359-6** (50 overs) (Q. de Kock 126, C. J. Bowes 115); **Namibia 150** (46 overs) (T. B. de Bruyn 4-20). *MoM:* Q. de Kock. *South Africa crushed their neighbours with the tournament's highest score and its highest partnership – 212 between their openers, who each scored hundreds.*

At Brisbane (Peter Burge Oval), August 15, 2012. **South Africa won by four wickets. Sri Lanka 150** (37.4 overs) (D. H. A. P. Tharanga 50*; C. A. Dry 4-16); ‡**South Africa 153-6** (33 overs). *MoM:* C. A. Dry. *Sri Lanka, in desperate need of a win, lost Sebastian Perera lbw to Corné Dry off the first ball of the match, and never truly recovered.*

At Brisbane (Peter Burge Oval), August 16, 2012. **Bangladesh won by seven wickets.** ‡**Namibia 151** (49.4 overs); **Bangladesh 155-3** (37 overs) (Liton Das 70*). *MoM:* Liton Das. *Bangladesh denied Sri Lanka a quarter-final place.*

South Africa 6pts, Bangladesh 4pts, Sri Lanka 2pts, Namibia 0pts.

Quarter-Finals

At Townsville (Endeavour Park No. 2), August 19, 2012. **Australia won by five wickets. Bangladesh 171** (43 overs) (Soumya Sarkar 73); ‡**Australia 172-5** (45.5 overs) (W. G. Bosisto 71*). *MoM:* W. G. Bosisto. *At 33-4 – after Soumya Sarkar ran out Jimmy Peirson without warning for backing up too far – Australia appeared to be crashing out of their own tournament. Bosisto and the umpires spoke to Bangladesh captain Anamul Haque to check if he wanted the appeal to stand: he did. "We certainly won't be getting out like that again," said Bosisto. "It was disappointing from our perspective, but it's within the Laws of the game and I think our boys will learn a lesson." The incident clearly motivated him to grind out a match-winning 71* from 134 balls, while Head (44 from 49) played aggressor.*

At Townsville (Tony Ireland Stadium), August 19, 2012. **South Africa won by 103 runs. South Africa 244** (50 overs) (T. B. de Bruyn 54, M. G. Coetzee 67); ‡**England 141** (40.3 overs) (A. L. Davies 54, B. T. Foakes 54; P. Subrayen 4-24). *MoM:* P. Subrayen. *South Africa coach Ray Jennings predicted his side would score 240, and bowl England out for 180. They surpassed his estimation. Alex Davies and Ben Foakes put on 100 for England's second wicket, before a shocking collapse of nine for 39, principally to off-spinner Prenalan Subrayen. Craig Overton was reprimanded for causing damage to a wall on his way back to the dressing-room after being run out for one.*

At Townsville (Tony Ireland Stadium), August 20, 2012. **India won by one wicket.** ‡**Pakistan 136** (45.1 overs) (Babar Azam 50); **India 137-9** (48 overs) (R. N. B. Apparajith 51). *MoM:* R. N. B. Apparajith. *Pakistan had beaten India by one run in a recent Under-19 Asia Cup group match, then tied the final – and once again the teams could barely be separated. India's last pair, Harmeet Singh and Sandeep Sharma, came together with ten needed, and clung on through seven overs to reach 137. Babar Azam, who had chosen to bat despite cloud cover and overnight rain, had to prop up an ailing Pakistan innings.*

At Townsville (Endeavour Park), August 20, 2012. **New Zealand won by three wickets. West Indies 237** (50 overs) (K. C. Brathwaite 53, A. J. Hosein 54); ‡**New Zealand 238-7** (50 overs) (B. J. Horne 59). *MoM:* I. S. Sodhi (New Zealand). *New Zealand lost their set batsman, Cam Fletcher, for 49, caught off the final ball of the penultimate over, leaving an improbable 18 needed from the last. But Ish Sodhi managed it, hitting a low full-toss from Justin Greaves to the midwicket fence for the winning four.*

Semi-Finals

At Townsville (Tony Ireland Stadium), August 21, 2012. **Australia won by four wickets. South Africa 191-8** (50 overs) (M. G. Coetzee 50); ‡**Australia 193-6** (48.3 overs) (C. T. Bancroft 66). *MoM:* C. T. Bancroft. *Both teams took the batting powerplay at 124-3 after 35 overs – but while South Africa lost 3-10 in theirs, Bancroft and Bosisto added 27 for Australia. The run-out of Bosisto for 40, four short of victory, was his only dismissal of the competition. Most crucially, South Africa dropped Bancroft and Kurtis Patterson (49) three times, all off Colin Savage.*

At Townsville (Tony Ireland Stadium), August 23, 2012. **India won by nine runs. India 209-9** (50 overs) (P. Chopra 52); ‡**New Zealand 200-9** (50 overs) (C. D. Fletcher 53). *MoM:* R. N. B. Apparajith (India). *New Zealand required 18 off the last over, as they had in the quarter-final, but could manage only eight against Sandeep Sharma.*

FINAL

AUSTRALIA v INDIA

GEORGE BINOY

At Townsville (Tony Ireland Stadium), August 26, 2012. India won by six wickets. Toss: India.

The final was a promoter's dream: the host nation against the cash cow. Sandeep Sharma had Australia eight for two, and they slipped to 38 for four before their inspirational captain, William Bosisto, embarked on another unflustered innings. His 87 straddled partnerships of 65 and 93, split only by a run-out, and confirmed him as the player of the tournament. India needed to chase more than any other side on this ground, and Unmukt Chand and Baba Apparajith gave a masterclass in cover-driving, before so nearly wobbling at four wickets down. Chand and Smit Patel each escaped tough chances to wicketkeeper Jimmy Peirson, and Bosisto dropped a much simpler catch at midwicket off Chand with 49 still needed. Chand cut loose to hit three tremendous sixes towards the end – one bringing up his third century in three Under-19 tournament finals in 2012.

Man of the Match: U. Chand. *Man of the Tournament:* W. G. Bosisto.

Australia Under-19

C. T. Bancroft lbw b Sharma	2	J. S. Paris run out	0
†J. J. Peirson b Sharma	0	G. S. Sandhu not out	10
M. J. Buchanan c Patel b Ravikant Singh	12	B 1, l-b 5, w 6, n-b 2	14
K. R. Patterson b Apparajith	16		
*W. G. Bosisto not out	87	1/2 (2) 2/8 (1) (8 wkts, 50 overs)	225
T. M. Head run out	37	3/38 (4) 4/38 (3)	
A. J. Turner c Chand b Sharma	43	5/103 (6) 6/196 (7)	
A. J. Gregory c Nath b Sharma	4	7/204 (8) 8/206 (9) 10 overs: 37-2	

M. T. Steketee did not bat.

Sharma 10–2–54–4; Passi 9–0–44–0; Ravikant Singh 9–0–41–1; Apparajith 10–0–31–1; Baddhan 10–1–36–0; Chand 2–0–13–0.

India Under-19

P. Chopra c Peirson b Steketee	0	†S. K. Patel not out	62
*U. Chand not out	111	L-b 5, w 11	16
R. N. B. Apparajith c Turner b Sandhu	33		
G. H. Vihari c and b Turner	4	1/2 (1) 2/75 (3) (4 wkts, 47.4 overs)	227
V. H. Zol c Peirson b Paris	1	3/82 (4) 4/97 (5) 10 overs: 60-1	

A. D. Nath, H. S. Baddhan, K. Passi, Ravikant Singh and S. Sharma did not bat.

Paris 10–2–33–1; Steketee 9–1–47–1; Sandhu 10–0–43–1; Turner 8.4–1–42–1; Gregory 6–0–40–0; Head 4–0–17–0.

Umpires: R. K. Illingworth and R. E. J. Martinesz.
Third umpire: J. D. Cloete. Referee: R. S. Mahanama.

UNDER-19 WORLD CUP WINNERS

1987-88	AUSTRALIA beat Pakistan by five wickets at Adelaide.
1997-98	ENGLAND beat New Zealand by seven wickets at Johannesburg.
1999-2000	INDIA beat Sri Lanka by six wickets at Colombo (SSC).
2001-02	AUSTRALIA beat South Africa by seven wickets at Lincoln (Bert Sutcliffe Oval).
2003-04	PAKISTAN beat West Indies by 25 runs at Dhaka.
2005-06	PAKISTAN beat India by 38 runs at Colombo (RPS).
2007-08	INDIA beat South Africa by 12 runs (D/L) at Kuala Lumpur.
2009-10	AUSTRALIA beat Pakistan by 25 runs at Lincoln (Bert Sutcliffe Oval).
2012	INDIA beat Australia by six wickets at Townsville (Tony Ireland Stadium).

Third-place Play-off

At Townsville (Endeavour Park), August 25, 2012. **South Africa won by eight wickets.** ‡**New Zealand 90** (36.5 overs) (D. A. Rhoda 4-26); **South Africa 94-2** (14.4 overs) (Q. de Kock 50). *MoM:* C. P. Savage (South Africa). *Savage's 3-14 made up for the disappointment of the semi-final drops off his bowling.*

Fifth-place Play-offs

Semi-finals: At Townsville (Endeavour Park No. 2), August 21, 2012. **England won by four wickets. Bangladesh 217-7** (50 overs) (Liton Das 102, Anamul Haque 56; R. J. W. Topley 5-32); ‡**England 218-6** (48.2 overs). *MoM:* R. J. W. Topley. *Adam Ball (34*) and Aneesh Kapil (33*) knocked off the last 60 to trump Liton Das, whose team-mates were all at sea against Topley.*

At Townsville (Endeavour Park), August 22, 2012. **West Indies won by 16 runs. West Indies 182** (49 overs); ‡**Pakistan 166** (48.3 overs). *MoM:* D. Y. A. Davis (West Indies). *Left-arm spinner Derone Davis took 3-20 in the middle overs.*

Final: At Townsville (Endeavour Park), August 24, 2012. **England won by 13 runs. England 241-9** (50 overs) (S. K. W. Wood 104); ‡**West Indies 228** (48.3 overs) (J. D. Campbell 105). *MoM:* S. K. W. Wood. *Though both Sam Wood – who hit seven sixes – and John Campbell made centuries, it was the unbeaten 49 added for England's last wicket by Tom Knight and Topley which made the difference.*

Seventh-place Play-off

At Townsville (Endeavour Park No. 2), August 24, 2012. **Bangladesh won by five wickets. Pakistan 235-8** (50 overs) (Mohammad Nawaz 82); ‡**Bangladesh 239-5** (46.2 overs) (Liton Das 53, Anamul Haque 128). *MoM:* Anamul Haque. *Anamul Haque signed off from Under-19 cricket with his third one-day century, featuring eight sixes in 112 balls.*

Ninth-place Play-offs

Quarter-finals: At Brisbane (Allan Border Field), August 19, 2012. **Afghanistan won by four wickets.** ‡**Papua New Guinea 239-5** (50 overs) (C. N. Kent 105*, N. Boge 55*); **Afghanistan 244-6** (49 overs) (Mohibullah Paak 58*). *MoM:* C. N. Kent. *Chris Kent, a 20-year-old with experience for PNG's senior team, scored his country's maiden hundred in Under-19 one-day internationals.*

At Brisbane (Peter Burge Oval), August 19, 2012. **Scotland won by 41 runs. Scotland 241-7** (50 overs) (N. A. G. Farrar 58); ‡**Zimbabwe 200-9** (50 overs) (R. P. Burl 52). *MoM:* N. A. G. Farrar. *Scotland's win was the first by an Associate over a Full Member in this tournament.*

At Brisbane (W. E. P. Harris Oval), August 20, 2012. **Ireland won by four wickets.** ‡**Namibia 128-9** (50 overs) (G. J. McCarter 4-32); **Ireland 129-6** (24.3 overs). *MoM:* G. J. McCarter.

At Brisbane (Peter Burge Oval), August 20, 2012. **Sri Lanka won by eight wickets.** ‡**Nepal 79** (27.3 overs); **Sri Lanka 80-2** (20.4 overs). *MoM:* S. I. Fernando (Sri Lanka).

Semi-finals: At Brisbane (Allan Border Field), August 21, 2012. **Afghanistan won by 126 runs.** ‡**Afghanistan 336-7** (50 overs) (Javed Ahmadi 134, Najibullah Zadran 83); **Scotland 210** (39.4 overs). *MoM:* Javed Ahmadi. *Javed Ahmadi's 134, from only 111 balls, was the highest score of the tournament.*

At Brisbane (Allan Border Field), August 22, 2012. **Sri Lanka won by 109 runs.** ‡**Sri Lanka 258** (49.3 overs) (A. J. A. D. D. L. A. Jayasinghe 55, D. S. Weerakkody 112*); **Ireland 149** (37.5 overs) (L. D. Madushanka 6-24). *MoM:* L. D. Madushanka.

Final: At Brisbane (Allan Border Field), August 24, 2012. **Sri Lanka won by seven wickets.** ‡**Afghanistan 194-9** (50 overs); **Sri Lanka 196-3** (39 overs) (D. P. D. N. Dickwella 76*). *MoM:* D. P. D. N. Dickwella. *Javed Ahmadi and Najibullah Zadran played in this match, then flew to the UAE in time to represent the full Afghanistan side in their one-day international against Australia the next day (see page 1215).*

Eleventh-place Play-off

At Brisbane (W. E. P. Harris Oval), August 24, 2012. **Scotland won by five wickets.** ‡**Ireland 182** (49.4 overs) (T. E. Kane 78); **Scotland 185-5** (41.4 overs). *MoM:* R. A. J. Smith (Scotland).

The India Today Group

Bouquets and booty: Unmukt Chand returns to India a decorated captain.

Thirteenth-place Play-offs

Semi-finals: At Brisbane (Peter Burge Oval), August 21, 2012. **Nepal won by 39 runs.** ‡**Nepal 219-7** (50 overs) (P. S. Airee 98*); **Namibia 180** (46.3 overs) (S. J. Baard 56, Z. Groenewald 54; B. Karki 5-21). *MoM:* B. Karki. *Nepal prospered at the death in both innings: Pradeep Airee thumped 98* from 76 balls; left-arm spinner Bikash Karki then took Namibia's last five wickets in 19.*

At Brisbane (W. E. P. Harris Oval), August 21, 2012. **Papua New Guinea won by 12 runs.** ‡**Papua New Guinea 235** (50 overs) (L. Siaka 50, C. J. A. Amini 63); **Zimbabwe 223** (49.1 overs) (L. Masasire 68). *MoM:* C. J. A. Amini.

Final: At Brisbane (Peter Burge Oval), August 23, 2012. **Nepal won by six wickets.** ‡**Papua New Guinea 89** (33.2 overs) (R. K. Vishvakarma 6-3); **Nepal 90-4** (18.5 overs). *MoM:* R. K. Vishvakarma. *In the meeting between two of Associate cricket's most ambitious countries, slow left-armer Rahul Vishvakarma took the best figures of the competition: 6.2–4–3–6.*

Fifteenth-place Play-off

At Brisbane (W. E. P. Harris Oval), August 23, 2012. **Zimbabwe won by 70 runs.** ‡**Zimbabwe 236-9** (50 overs) (M. S. M. Bentley 67, R. P. Burl 78); **Namibia 166** (40.5 overs). *MoM:* R. P. Burl.

Final rankings

1. India 2. Australia 3. South Africa 4. New Zealand 5. England 6. West Indies 7. Bangladesh 8. Pakistan 9. Sri Lanka 10. Afghanistan 11. Scotland 12. Ireland 13. Nepal 14. Papua New Guinea 15. Zimbabwe 16. Namibia.

AUSTRALIAN CRICKET, 2012

Clarke... then the rest

DANIEL BRETTIG

Michael Clarke and James Pattinson, captain and fast bowler. Their fortunes during the Sydney Test against India in the first week of January 2012 were at once contrasting and for Australia, defining. Clarke epitomised all that was strong about his side, erecting a monumental unbeaten 329 and going on to deliver the most prolific year of all by an Australian batsman. He also led his men with intelligence and aggression, guiding them to three Test series victories out of four. But Pattinson personified all that was uncertain: the transition and tribulation of a team that wrestled with the husbanding of resources and the loss of Ricky Ponting and Mike Hussey. Though he removed four of India's top five on the first day, Pattinson ended the match with a foot stress fracture, having been selected against the advice of medical staff who

AUSTRALIA IN 2012

	Played	*Won*	*Lost*	*Drawn/No result*
Tests	11	7	1	3
One-day internationals	26	11	12	3
Twenty20 internationals	13	7	6	–

DECEMBER / JANUARY / FEBRUARY	4 Tests and 2 T20Is (h) v India	(see *Wisden 2012*, page 868, and *Wisden 2013*, page 890)
FEBRUARY / MARCH	Triangular ODI tournament (h) v India and Sri Lanka	(page 892)
MARCH / APRIL	3 Tests, 5 ODIs and 2 T20Is (a) v West Indies	(page 1157)
MAY		
JUNE	1 ODI (a) v Ireland	(page 817)
JUNE / JULY	5 ODIs (a) v England	(page 337)
AUGUST	1 ODI (a) (in UAE) v Afghanistan	(page 1215)
AUGUST / SEPTEMBER	3 ODIs and 3 T20Is (a) (in UAE) v Pakistan	(page 1050)
SEPTEMBER / OCTOBER	World Twenty20 (in Sri Lanka)	(page 841)
NOVEMBER / DECEMBER	3 Tests (h) v South Africa	(page 907)
DECEMBER / JANUARY	3 Tests, 5 ODIs and 2 T20Is (h) v Sri Lanka	(page 919)

For a review of Australian domestic cricket from the 2011-12 season, see page 937.

held data suggesting his workload had entered a zone of high risk. The rest of his year was a tale of recovery, inconsistency, further injury, frustration and back-room battles over his availability, as Cricket Australia tried to implement a rotation and management policy that had yet to produce the hoped-for fruit.

If 2011 had been the year of introspection, recrimination and change, 2012 was a time for Australian cricket to bed down, and possibly mark time. The Argus Review was largely reinforced but occasionally undermined, while the conclusions of a governance review pushed the CA board into a new structure that was both slimmer and better rounded. The AGM witnessed the appointment of the first three independent directors, including the first woman, Jacquie Hey. Elsewhere, the team-performance and commercial arms of CA haggled over players who were expected to build towards sustained success in the international game on the one hand, and act as billboards for the Big Bash League on the other. It was not an easy balance to strike.

Overall, a sense pervaded that much of the sparring on and off the field was a primer for the confrontations of 2013 – from the Test team's tilt at returning the Ashes, to the board's pursuit of a better broadcast-rights deal, which for the first time since World Series Cricket was genuinely open to offers beyond those of Channel Nine. CA had been reinforced for this task, but the team was weakened by retirements. Ponting's exit was hastened by the pained concession he could no longer bat the way he and the team desired; Hussey's departure arrived at a moment when he was arguably more valuable than ever. The selectors were thus forced into a hurried reassessment of the modest batting at their disposal, and players into a rapid assumption of greater seniority.

Such uncertainty seemed distant when India were being coshed every which way, but there were hints of difficulty when the team ventured to the Caribbean in March. Clarke did not go with the limited-overs party as he recovered from a hamstring strain, and in his absence Shane Watson found the going difficult, as West Indies shared both the one-day and Twenty20 series on pitches that were often slow and low. Sunil Narine's variations were a source of puzzlement, and there was as much relief at his exit to the IPL as there was at Clarke's arrival for the Tests.

West Indies were beaten by performances more artisan than artful, though the conclusion to the Barbados Test was genuinely rousing. The most telling contribution of the series belonged to Matthew Wade, who replaced Brad Haddin as wicketkeeper after Haddin had rushed home to be with his 17-month-old daughter Mia, who was gravely ill with cancer. Wade showed a compelling ability to learn from early tremors during the one-day internationals, and punched Australia's only century of the series, in Dominica, to ensure they took the series 2–0. It meant Australia retained the Frank Worrell Trophy they had held since 1994-95.

Less comfortable was a visit to the British Isles for one-day cricket. A rained-off fixture at Edgbaston was the only thing that separated Australia from a 5–0 defeat by England. Hussey absented himself from the trip for family reasons and, as rainy days and injuries to Watson, Pat Cummins and Brett Lee compounded the sting of results, others were forgiven for wishing they had joined him. Lee retired from international cricket after the tour, and

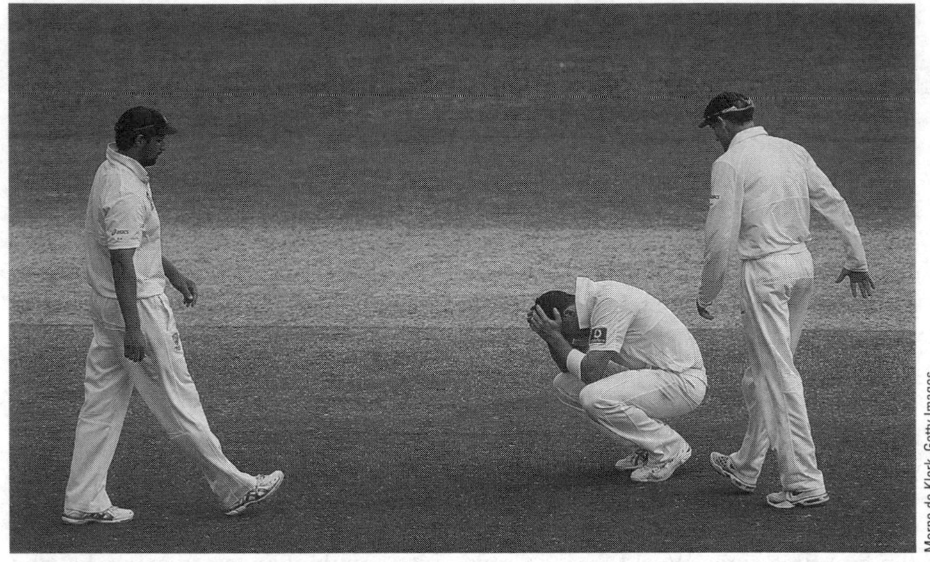

Morne de Klerk, Getty Images

In need of a hug: Peter Siddle is an exhausted man after South Africa escape with a draw at Adelaide; neither he nor Ben Hilfenhaus (*left*) recovered for the decider at Perth.

only Clint McKay and George Bailey improved their reputations. The coach Mickey Arthur surmised after a hiding at Chester-le-Street: "We've allowed ourselves to be bullied, and we're better than that."

Unified by a training camp in Darwin, a more cohesive team performed creditably in the UAE against Pakistan, winning the one-day series and losing the Twenty20s narrowly. In a Twenty20 against India in February, Bailey had made history as Australia's first captain since the very first Test in 1876-77 to be appointed without having played an international match; later in the year he led Australia to the semi-finals of the World Twenty20, when Chris Gayle, Kieron Pollard and Ravi Rampaul ended the campaign. Shortly before the tournament, Australia had been ranked tenth in the Twenty20 world rankings – below Bangladesh and Ireland – but that was more a reflection of the ICC's criteria than any slump. Another long separation from his family during the competition had Hussey resolving privately to quit at the end of the summer.

Clarke prepared for the home Test season by captaining New South Wales in the earliest start to a domestic season, shoved into September by the dual disruptions of the World Twenty20 and the Champions League. Sydney Sixers added that tournament to their inaugural Big Bash title, but at some cost: Watson lacked a first-class prelude to the Test summer, and promptly suffered another calf strain, while Cummins complained of back soreness, which was later revealed to be a stress fracture, to the horror of the CA team-performance manager Pat Howard and the selectors. Later, Howard noted ruefully that "no one owns the players now".

The arrival of South Africa coincided with a quirk in the ICC's Test rankings: by vanquishing England in their previous series, Graeme Smith's team offered Clarke's the chance to pinch No. 1 with a win. Led by another duo of landmark innings by Clarke, double-centuries in Brisbane and Adelaide, Australia came within two wickets of taking the lead. Injury and fatigue were to bite at the most pivotal moments, however. Debutant Faf du Plessis defied Australia's bowlers in the Second Test, helped by the loss of Pattinson to a side injury in the first innings.

South Africa's final-day exertions meant neither Peter Siddle nor Ben Hilfenhaus could be considered for the last Test, at Perth. The selectors' response was to pick a bowling attack hopeful on paper but unbalanced in practice, leaving Smith and Hashim Amla to carry off the match and the series with two hours of breathless batting after Clarke, for once, failed to make a significant score.

Amid rumblings his place was no longer secure, Ponting made the Third Test his last, moving Clarke to tears before the match. South Africa afforded Ponting a guard of honour for his final innings that befitted a king. The reality was less regal: he was pouched at slip off Robin Peterson after an insubstantial stay. It was definitely time to go.

Chastened by their only Test defeat of the year, albeit in the match more pivotal than any other, they collected a 3–0 sweep of Sri Lanka in the showpiece weeks of the season, which had been spurned by South Africa due to their board's preference for a home Twenty20 on Boxing Day. Overlooked when Australia's attack was at their thinnest at Perth, Jackson Bird was called up for the Second Test against Sri Lanka when Hilfenhaus fell injured, and showed himself to be an accomplished seamer in the mould of Stuart Clark. Phillip Hughes returned in Ponting's stead, and David Warner played with a consistency that could make his brazen batting a genuine threat.

Clarke shrugged off a hamstring strain to make his fifth century of the year, but his deputy Watson hobbled to 83, then informed Arthur he no longer wished to be considered an all-rounder. As he processed that revelation, Arthur was doubly shocked to be tapped on the shoulder by Hussey, who told him and Clarke he would be saying goodbye to Test cricket at Sydney. Another XI somewhat odd in composition slogged their way to victory in a manner far less comprehensive than against India 12 months before. Hussey was in the middle when the winning runs were scored, a fitting conclusion to a career that was truly selfless until, perhaps, the moment he chose to end it.

Hussey was deemed surplus to the one-day series that followed the Tests, and found himself donning a Perth Scorchers shirt as the second edition of the BBL limped to Christmas, then found better returns in January. A leaked CA report revealed that $A10m was expected to be lost over the first two seasons in an effort to make the BBL look attractive for broadcasters as well as spectators. That kind of money was also being distributed among the players under a new Memorandum of Understanding that contained performance-based weighting as per the dictates of Argus. Given the battles ahead on the pitch and in the negotiation-room, remuneration may yet fluctuate wildly.

AUSTRALIA v INDIA, 2011-12

Twenty20 internationals (2): Australia 1, India 1

After their commitment came into question during a 4–0 Test pummelling (see *Wisden 2012*, page 868), this short series gave India the chance to let their hair down. But Twenty20 internationals, often a lonely adjunct to an international tour, were now serious business in Australia. Nearly 60,000 flocked to the first match at Stadium Australia – built for the 2000 Olympics – beating the SCG's record for a single day's attendance at cricket in Sydney. James Sutherland, chief executive of Cricket Australia, floated the possibility of an extended Twenty20 series in future, touring the country. His optimism was fuelled by the success of the revamped KFC T20 Big Bash League, which had finished days earlier. Sutherland pledged that if the idea came to pass it would be one-day cricket, and not Tests, which would be scaled back.

Australia picked a squad almost unrecognisable from the Tests, with only David Warner and Shaun Marsh retained; Sutherland's stated intention for a completely separate Twenty20 side had moved a step closer. They were led by Tasmania's George Bailey, 29, who became the first man to captain Australia on debut since Dave Gregory in the inaugural 1876-77 Test. Bailey shuffled his bowling resources intelligently in the first match. But his decision to move Matthew Wade down the order at Melbourne – after 72 as an opener at Sydney – was less successful, and India ended up sharing the series.

INDIAN TOURING PARTY

*M. S. Dhoni, R. Ashwin, G. Gambhir, R. A. Jadeja, V. Kohli, P. Kumar, P. A. Patel, I. K. Pathan, S. K. Raina, V. Sehwag, R. Sharma, R. G. Sharma, S. R. Tendulkar, M. K. Tiwary, R. Vinay Kumar, U. T. Yadav, Zaheer Khan. *Coach:* D. A. G. Fletcher.

Note: Reports of the preceding Test series appeared in *Wisden 2012*, page 868.

MATCH REPORTS BY JESSE HOGAN

AUSTRALIA v INDIA

First Twenty20 International

At Sydney (Stadium Australia), February 1, 2012 (floodlit). Australia won by 31 runs. Toss: India. Twenty20 international debuts: G. J. Bailey, X. J. Doherty, J. P. Faulkner; R. Sharma.

There were talking points aplenty – Bailey becoming only the second player to captain Australia on international debut, the pivotal opening explosion by Wade, and Hogg returning five days short of his 41st birthday. But it was a single six from Warner that stole the attention. The left-hander's switch-hit – or possibly switch-punch – off Ashwin, over what he changed from cover into midwicket, was so crisply struck that most full-time right-handers would have been chuffed, although its legitimacy was questioned by former Australian captain Mark Taylor. Sehwag's third-ball dismissal was a blow for India; even more significant were the meek dismissals of Gambhir and Kohli after promising starts. The record crowd for a cricket match in Sydney – beating the 58,446 who witnessed Wally Hammond begin his double-century on the Saturday of the 1928-29 Ashes Test at the SCG – never had reason to believe a comeback was realistic.

Man of the Match: M. S. Wade. *Attendance:* 59,659.

Australia

		B	4	6
D. A. Warner *c 4 b 11*	25	14	1	2
†M. S. Wade *b 4*	72	43	5	3
T. R. Birt *c 4 b 8*	17	21	1	1
D. J. Hussey *b 9*	42	30	1	3
*G. J. Bailey *not out*	12	11	1	0
M. R. Marsh *not out*	0	1	0	0
L-b 1, w 2	3			

6 overs: 55-1 (20 overs) 171-4

1/38 2/79 3/135 4/170

D. T. Christian, J. P. Faulkner, B. Lee, G. B. Hogg and X. J. Doherty did not bat.

Ashwin 4–0–34–1; P. Kumar 3–0–34–0; Vinay Kumar 4–0–28–1; Raina 3–0–22–1; R. Sharma 3.4–0–27–1; R. G. Sharma 0.2–0–2–0; Jadeja 2–0–23–0.

India

		B	4	6
G. Gambhir *c 6 b 4*	20	14	3	0
V. Sehwag *c 4 b 9*	4	3	1	0
V. Kohli *c 1 b 10*	22	21	0	1
S. K. Raina *b 7*	14	15	1	0
R. G. Sharma *b 4*	0	1	0	0
*†M. S. Dhoni *not out*	48	43	1	3
R. A. Jadeja *c 1 b 7*	7	8	1	0
R. Ashwin *not out*	15	16	1	0
L-b 3, w 6, n-b 1	10			

6 overs: 49-2 (20 overs) 140-6

1/6 2/47 3/53 4/53 5/72 6/81

R. Sharma, P. Kumar and R. Vinay Kumar did not bat.

Lee 4–0–36–1; Doherty 4–0–23–0; Faulkner 2–0–18–0; Christian 4–0–35–2; Hussey 2–0–4–2; Hogg 4–0–21–1.

Umpires: B. N. J. Oxenford and P. R. Reiffel. Third umpire: S. D. Fry.

AUSTRALIA v INDIA

Second Twenty20 International

At Melbourne, February 3, 2012 (floodlit). India won by eight wickets. Toss: Australia.

India finally outplayed their hosts, producing a fielding performance so clinical it gained grudging admiration even from the Australians. Gambhir's nerveless pouching of Warner's towering pull set the tone, and the extension of Shaun Marsh's miserable summer was rightly overshadowed by India snaring four run-outs and a stumping. Jadeja's slick work at backward point did for Finch and Bailey. Next day, Jadeja, who also bowled smartly, was bought for $2m by Chennai Super Kings at the IPL auction. It was only Australia's third defeat in 15 home Twenty20 internationals.

Man of the Match: R. A. Jadeja. *Attendance:* 62,275.

Australia

		B	4	6
D. A. Warner *c 1 b 10*	8	8	1	0
A. J. Finch *run out*	36	23	6	0
S. E. Marsh *c 4 b 10*	0	2	0	0
D. J. Hussey *c and b 7*	24	29	1	1
*G. J. Bailey *run out*	3	4	0	0
†M. S. Wade *run out*	32	29	1	1
M. R. Marsh *st 4 b 9*	13	13	2	0
B. Lee *not out*	6	4	1	0
C. J. McKay *c 4 b 11*	0	1	0	0
G. B. Hogg *lbw b 9*	4	4	1	0
X. J. Doherty *run out*	1	1	0	0
W 4	4			

6 overs: 42-2 (19.4 overs) 131

1/19 2/20 3/49 4/54 5/93 6/119 7/121 8/121 9/130

P. Kumar 3–0–21–2; Vinay Kumar 4–0–25–1; Kohli 1–0–7–0; Jadeja 3–0–16–1; R. Sharma 3.4–0–29–2; Raina 1–0–10–0; Ashwin 4–0–23–0.

India

		B	4	6
G. Gambhir *not out*	56	60	4	0
V. Sehwag *c 3 b 10*	23	16	2	1
V. Kohli *c 6 b 7*	31	24	3	0
*†M. S. Dhoni *not out*	21	18	2	0
W 4	4			

6 overs: 42-0 (19.4 overs) 135-2

1/43 2/97

S. K. Raina, R. G. Sharma, R. A. Jadeja, R. Ashwin, R. Sharma, P. Kumar and R. Vinay Kumar did not bat.

Lee 4–0–24–0; McKay 3.4–0–25–0; Doherty 3–0–29–0; Hogg 3–0–19–1; M. R. Marsh 4–0–30–1; Hussey 2–0–8–0.

Umpires: S. D. Fry and B. N. J. Oxenford. Third umpire: P. R. Reiffel. Series referee: A. J. Pycroft.

COMMONWEALTH BANK SERIES, 2011-12

JESSE HOGAN

1. Australia 2. Sri Lanka 3. India

It was a mark of the quality of this series that, by the time Australia won the third, deciding final against Sri Lanka, the axing of Ricky Ponting was little more than a footnote. This is not to denigrate Ponting's achievements in one-day internationals – merely to acknowledge how Sri Lanka and, very occasionally, India played their part in making the first triangular series in Australia for four years such a success. Perhaps it was no surprise: the teams occupied three of the top four slots in the ICC one-day international standings (South Africa held the other), and six of the world's top ten batsmen came from their ranks.

India kept most of their underperforming batting line-up from the Test whitewash, with Suresh Raina the only significant addition. Sri Lanka, whose players had gone largely unpaid in the ten months since the World Cup, had a new (or newish) captain in Mahela Jayawardene, back for a second stint after replacing Tillekeratne Dilshan. They also had a new coach in Graham Ford, after Geoff Marsh was sacked four months into a two-year contract with little explanation. Four wins in their last five group games earned them a place in the finals.

Australia's most significant change at the start of the series – the elevation of Victoria wicketkeeper Matthew Wade – was initially downplayed by the selectors, who insisted Brad Haddin was merely being rested after a gruelling summer. Within a fortnight, Wade's displays on both sides of the stumps were assured enough to bring an end to the facade: he was now officially the preferred one-day keeper.

Ponting's demise came, awkwardly, after a surging return to form in Tests. His single-figure failures in Australia's first two matches could be ignored, until the trend continued in the third, fourth and fifth. The last innings was the most illustrative: Ponting, now 37 years old, needed 13 balls to get off the mark before tamely holing out for a scratchy seven from 26. He did not retire after being left out, but conceded there was no chance of a one-day recall. To confuse matters, he was dropped while captain, having twice been asked to stand in for the injured Michael Clarke. Even though David Warner was the nominated vice-captain, it was Ponting and Shane Watson who led in Clarke's stead. The response to Ponting's fate was almost universally sympathetic to both sides, with few accusing the selectors of heresy.

India did little to redeem themselves after the Test debacle. Rumours of team divisions festered once Mahendra Singh Dhoni's policy of not selecting Sachin Tendulkar, Virender Sehwag and Gautam Gambhir in the same team – because no more than two of them could be carried in the field – became clear during a press conference. Sehwag claimed to have been unaware that Dhoni believed the presence of all three might cost 20 runs a game, and the strategy had to be abandoned when Dhoni picked up a one-match ban for a slow over-rate at Brisbane: Sehwag briefly assumed the captaincy, and the trio duly played together in India's last three matches. They were still eliminated, but able to return home with a skerrick of satisfaction following an incredible chase of 321 in their final game. As in the Tests, most of India's best work was inspired by the marvellously driven Virat Kohli.

The unusually late finish to the Australian summer meant the series had to compete with the new seasons of the local football codes. This led to below-average crowds of about 20,000 for matches involving the home team. But television ratings – Cricket Australia's new priority – were robust (unsurprisingly, given the decision to ditch the previous bilateral format and include India). So a series judged by the learned to be the best triangular held in Australia got at least some of the recognition it deserved.

NATIONAL SQUADS

Australia *M. J. Clarke, D. T. Christian, X. J. Doherty, P. J. Forrest, R. J. Harris, B. W. Hilfenhaus, D. J. Hussey, M. E. K. Hussey, B. Lee, C. J. McKay, M. R. Marsh, R. T. Ponting, M. A. Starc, M. S. Wade, D. A. Warner. *Coach:* J. M. Arthur.

Lee initially withdrew with a toe injury and was replaced by Hilfenhaus, but returned two weeks later. Marsh dropped out after suffering a stress fracture. J. M. Holland was briefly added to the squad as cover for Doherty, and G. J. Bailey for Clarke. S. R. Watson and J. L. Pattinson replaced Ponting and Harris, who were dropped. Bailey and N. M. Lyon were called up for the third final after Clarke strained a hamstring.

India *M. S. Dhoni, R. Ashwin, G. Gambhir, R. A. Jadeja, V. Kohli, P. Kumar, P. A. Patel, I. K. Pathan, S. K. Raina, V. Sehwag, R. Sharma, R. G. Sharma, S. R. Tendulkar, M. K. Tiwary, R. Vinay Kumar, U. T. Yadav, Zaheer Khan. *Coach:* D. A. G. Fletcher.

Sri Lanka *D. P. M. D. Jayawardene, L. D. Chandimal, T. M. Dilshan, H. M. R. K. B. Herath, K. M. D. N. Kulasekara, M. F. Maharoof, S. L. Malinga, A. D. Mathews, N. L. T. C. Perera, K. T. G. D. Prasad, K. C. Sangakkara, S. M. S. M. Senanayake, W. U. Tharanga, H. D. R. L. Thirimanne, U. W. M. B. C. A. Welagedara. *Coach:* G. X. Ford.

Perera suffered a back injury in the last qualifying match, and was replaced for the finals by C. K. Kapugedera.

AUSTRALIA v INDIA

At Melbourne, February 5, 2012 (day/night). Australia won by 65 runs (D/L). Australia 5pts. Toss: India. One-day international debuts: D. T. Christian, M. S. Wade.

Two days after outfielding Australia to share the Twenty20 series, India regressed. They started well, confining the hosts to 35 for two from 11 overs, before a three-hour downpour cut the match to 32 overs each. Having taken 90 balls to reach 50, Australia made the next 100 in only 62, primarily due to Matthew Wade and the Hussey brothers. Wade's performance on debut added intrigue to the selectors' stated plan to reinstate wicketkeeper Brad Haddin, supposedly rested, later in the series. David Hussey justified his recall with an electric unbeaten 61 from 30 deliveries, but was helped by India's reliance on spin in unfriendly conditions: the adjustment meant the seamers had already bowled most of their reduced allocation before the interruption. Leg-spinner Rahul Sharma sent down two balls of his seventh over, the last of the innings, before the umpires realised only two bowlers were now allowed more than six; Jadeja completed it, but went for 17. Ponting's two catches at backward point, diving forward to dismiss Tendulkar and grasping a rocket from Kohli, were pivotal.

Man of the Match: M. S. Wade. *Attendance:* 29,959.

Australia

†M. S. Wade b R. Sharma	67	D. T. Christian not out	17
D. A. Warner b Vinay Kumar	6	L-b 2, w 4, n-b 2	8
R. T. Ponting c Raina b Vinay Kumar	2		
*M. J. Clarke c R. Sharma b R. G. Sharma	10	1/15 (2) 2/19 (3) (5 wkts, 32 overs)	216
M. E. K. Hussey c Kohli b Vinay Kumar	45	3/49 (4) 4/122 (1)	
D. J. Hussey not out	61	5/154 (5) 10 overs: 25-2	

R. J. Harris, C. J. McKay, M. A. Starc and X. J. Doherty did not bat.

P. Kumar 7–0–35–0; Vinay Kumar 7–0–21–3; Kohli 1–0–4–0; Raina 1–0–4–0; Ashwin 5–0–48–0; R. G. Sharma 2–0–17–1; R. Sharma 6.2–0–44–1; Jadeja 2.4–0–41–0.

India

G. Gambhir c Wade b Starc	5	P. Kumar c Harris b McKay	15
S. R. Tendulkar c Ponting b Starc	2	R. Vinay Kumar not out	12
V. Kohli c Ponting b McKay	31		
R. G. Sharma c Wade b McKay	21	L-b 2, w 5	7
S. K. Raina c D. J. Hussey b Christian	4		
*†M. S. Dhoni c Warner b Doherty	29	1/9 (2) 2/13 (1) 3/64 (3) (29.4 overs)	151
R. A. Jadeja c M. E. K. Hussey b McKay	19	4/65 (4) 5/77 (5) 6/114 (7)	
R. Ashwin run out	5	7/120 (8) 8/123 (9) 9/128 (6)	
R. Sharma b Doherty	1	10/151 (10) 7 overs: 32-2	

Harris 5–0–28–0; Starc 6–0–33–2; Christian 5–0–21–1; McKay 4.4–0–20–4; Doherty 7–0–36–2; Clarke 2–0–11–0.

Umpires: N. J. Llong and B. N. J. Oxenford. Third umpire: P. R. Reiffel.
Referee: A. J. Pycroft.

INDIA v SRI LANKA

At Perth, February 8, 2012 (day/night). India won by four wickets. India 4pts. Toss: Sri Lanka.

Kohli's stature in Australia grew even loftier when he made sure India didn't squander a helpful start. Zaheer Khan reinforced his own importance to India by claiming Tharanga early, then drawing an edge from Sangakkara that was brilliantly taken by Dhoni. Chandimal adeptly played the anchor role for Sri Lanka, but among the other batsmen only Mathews showed sufficient urgency. When Tendulkar fell in the 19th over, India's greatest concern appeared to be his continuing failure to notch his 100th international hundred. But as Rohit Sharma, Raina and Dhoni followed, with 67 still to get, the result looked in the balance. Sri Lanka's chances improved further when Kohli, stoically coping with cramp, was run out by Malinga's direct hit from mid-on. Jayawardene, knowing another wicket would expose India's tail, relentlessly rotated his bowlers, but none was able to threaten Jadeja or Ashwin.

Man of the Match: R. Ashwin. *Attendance:* 6,685.

Sri Lanka

W. U. Tharanga c Tendulkar b Zaheer Khan	4	K. M. D. N. Kulasekara c Sharma b Vinay Kumar	7
T. M. Dilshan c Kohli b Jadeja	48	S. L. Malinga not out	1
†K. C. Sangakkara c Dhoni b Zaheer Khan	26	L-b 6, w 7	13
L. D. Chandimal st Dhoni b Ashwin	64		
*D. P. M. D. Jayawardene c Sharma b Ashwin	23		
N. L. T. C. Perera st Dhoni b Ashwin	7	1/12 (1) 2/74 (3) (8 wkts, 50 overs)	233
A. D. Mathews not out	33	3/100 (2) 4/152 (5) 5/172 (6)	
H. D. R. L. Thirimanne run out	7	6/189 (4) 7/204 (8) 8/228 (9) 10 overs: 46-1	

K. T. G. D. Prasad did not bat.

Zaheer Khan 10–1–44–2; P. Kumar 10–0–54–0; Vinay Kumar 10–1–56–1; Jadeja 10–0–41–1; Ashwin 10–1–32–3.

India

V. Sehwag c Kulasekara b Malinga 10
S. R. Tendulkar b Mathews 48
V. Kohli run out 77
R. G. Sharma c Dilshan b Perera 10
S. K. Raina c sub (S. M. S. M. Senanayake) b Mathews . 24
*†M. S. Dhoni c Malinga b Prasad 4
R. A. Jadeja not out 24
R. Ashwin not out 30
L-b 5, w 2 7

1/14 (1) 2/89 (2) (6 wkts, 46.4 overs) 234
3/122 (4) 4/157 (5)
5/167 (6) 6/181 (3) 10 overs: 47-1

P. Kumar, R. Vinay Khan and Zaheer Khan did not bat.

Malinga 9–0–49–1; Kulasekara 8–0–38–0; Prasad 10–0–47–1; Mathews 9.4–1–31–2; Perera 5–0–37–1; Dilshan 5–0–27–0.

Umpires: N. J. Llong and P. R. Reiffel. Third umpire: B. N. J. Oxenford.
Referee: A. J. Pycroft.

AUSTRALIA v SRI LANKA

At Perth, February 10, 2012 (day/night). Australia won by five runs. Australia 4pts. Toss: Sri Lanka.

A year earlier Clarke had been booed by Australian fans for batting too slowly in the one day series against England. Now, in a game full of wasted starts, his careful 57 off 88 deliveries allowed Australia – boosted by McKay's run-a-ball 25 – to cobble together a total they just about managed to defend. Chasing 232, Sri Lanka lost wickets regularly and looked out of it at 180 for nine, only for Mathews to find a deft balance between scoring runs and occasionally trusting last man Prasad with the strike. When Starc began the final over, Sri Lanka needed 18. Mathews hit the first two balls for four and six to spread panic among the crowd, if not necessarily the Australian players. Two singles followed but, with six needed, Mathews was unable to clear Christian at long-on – a failure which made Clarke's innings look perfectly judged rather than a candidate for more catcalls.

Man of the Match: M. J. Clarke. *Attendance:* 13,085.

Australia

D. A. Warner b Mathews 34
†M. S. Wade c Sangakkara b Kulasekara . . . 1
R. T. Ponting lbw b Malinga 1
*M. J. Clarke c Jayawardene b Mathews . . . 57
M. E. K. Hussey c and b Kulasekara 23
D. J. Hussey c Thirimanne b Malinga 27
D. T. Christian st Sangakkara b Senanayake 33
R. J. Harris c Kulasekara b Senanayake . . . 3
C. J. McKay c Thirimanne b Prasad 25
M. A. Starc c Tharanga b Prasad 14
X. J. Doherty not out 2
L-b 6, w 5 11

1/22 (2) 2/26 (3) 3/50 (1) (49.1 overs) 231
4/81 (5) 5/130 (6) 6/186 (7)
7/190 (4) 8/192 (8) 9/224 (10)
10/231 (9) 10 overs: 51-3

Malinga 10–0–48–2; Kulasekara 10–0–39–2; Mathews 9–0–37–2; Prasad 9.1–0–55–2; Senanayake 10–0–45–2; Dilshan 1–0–1–0.

Sri Lanka

W. U. Tharanga c Clarke b Starc 5
T. M. Dilshan c Wade b Harris 40
†K. C. Sangakkara run out 22
L. D. Chandimal lbw b Clarke 37
*D. P. M. D. Jayawardene c Wade b Christian 13
H. D. R. L. Thirimanne b Doherty 3
A. D. Mathews c Christian b Starc 64
K. M. D. N. Kulasekara c Wade b Christian 8
S. M. S. M. Senanayake st Wade b Doherty 9
S. L. Malinga c Wade b McKay 1
K. T. G. D. Prasad not out 15
L-b 3, w 6 9

1/11 (1) 2/61 (3) 3/88 (2) (49.5 overs) 226
4/110 (5) 5/119 (6) 6/129 (4)
7/143 (8) 8/175 (9) 9/180 (10)
10/226 (7) 10 overs: 31-1

Harris 10–0–43–1; Starc 9.5–0–50–2; McKay 10–0–50–1; Christian 8–1–47–2; Doherty 10–0–24–2; Clarke 2–0–9–1.

Umpires: N. J. Llong and B. N. J. Oxenford. Third umpire: P. R. Reiffel.
Referee: A. J. Pycroft.

AUSTRALIA v INDIA

At Adelaide, February 12, 2012 (day/night). India won by four wickets. India 4pts. Toss: Australia. One-day international debut: P. J. Forrest.

With 12 needed off four balls, Dhoni produced possibly the shot of the tournament, playing back to a half-volley from McKay and pummelling it over long-on for six. It went further than many incredulous locals could recall seeing at the Adelaide Oval; even allowing for his remarkable forearm strength, it was a stupendous blow. The next delivery, a waist-high no-ball, produced three runs – two for the leg-side heave, which was caught at deep square leg, and one for the transgression – before Dhoni pulled McKay for three more to complete a breathless win with two balls to spare. It was a good thing too: at one stage, his typically unhurried approach seemed to presage another loss. Arriving at the crease with India seemingly coasting – despite the loss of Gambhir, harshly ruled leg-before to make it 178 for four in the 35th over – Dhoni scored only two from his first 16 balls. But he was merely biding his time, adding 61 with Raina and shrugging off the loss of Jadeja before the final assault. Australia's challenging total revolved around an energetic fourth-wicket stand of 98 between debutant Peter Forrest and David Hussey, but they were unable to capitalise.

Man of the Match: G. Gambhir. *Attendance:* 22,728.

Australia

D. A. Warner run out	18	C. J. McKay run out	3
R. T. Ponting c Kohli b Vinay Kumar	6		
*M. J. Clarke b Yadav	38	L-b 4, w 4, n-b 1	9
P. J. Forrest c Vinay Kumar b Yadav	66		
D. J. Hussey c Sehwag b Zaheer Khan	72	1/14 (2) 2/53 (1) (8 wkts, 50 overs)	269
D. T. Christian run out	39	3/81 (3) 4/179 (4)	
†M. S. Wade b Vinay Kumar	16	5/235 (5) 6/254 (6)	
R. J. Harris not out	2	7/265 (7) 8/269 (9) 10 overs: 53-2	

M. A. Starc and X. J. Doherty did not bat.

Zaheer Khan 10–0–46–1; Vinay Kumar 10–1–58–2; Jadeja 10–0–50–0; Yadav 10–1–49–2; Ashwin 8–0–47–0; Sharma 2–0–15–0.

India

G. Gambhir lbw b McKay	92	R. Ashwin not out	1
V. Sehwag c Hussey b McKay	20		
V. Kohli c Forrest b McKay	18	L-b 2, w 9, n-b 1	12
R. G. Sharma c Starc b Harris	33		
S. K. Raina b Doherty	38	1/52 (2) 2/90 (3) (6 wkts, 49.4 overs)	270
*†M. S. Dhoni not out	44	3/166 (4) 4/178 (1)	
R. A. Jadeja c Ponting b Doherty	12	5/239 (5) 6/257 (7) 10 overs: 52-1	

R. Vinay Kumar, Zaheer Khan and U. T. Yadav did not bat.

Harris 10–0–57–1; Starc 8–0–49–0; McKay 9.4–1–53–3; Christian 10–0–45–0; Hussey 3–0–13–0; Doherty 9–0–51–2.

Umpires: N. J. Llong and P. R. Reiffel. Third umpire: B. N. J. Oxenford.
Referee: A. J. Pycroft.

INDIA v SRI LANKA

At Adelaide, February 14, 2012 (day/night). Tied. India 2pts, Sri Lanka 2pts. Toss: Sri Lanka.

For the second time in three days Dhoni was saddled with the task of rescuing India at the death. The required boundary off the last ball proved a task too great when Malinga speared it in wide on a full length. Instead, Dhoni flayed it over extra cover's head, and scampered three with Yadav to produce the first tie in 131 one-day internationals between the teams. The result heaped scrutiny on umpire Nigel Llong, who had inadvertently ended the 30th over of India's innings after five deliveries. Sri Lanka had looked poised for more than 250 until three wickets fell in the batting powerplay, and only 64 were scored in the last 14 overs. Gambhir was then one of four Indians to be run out, though his second successive score in the nineties ensured he left them well placed. Jayawardene's strangling fields meant India needed 24 from two overs, but Mathews's uncharacteristic lack of composure with the ball reduced that to nine from the last – when the scene was set once more for Dhoni.

Man of the Match: M. S. Dhoni. *Attendance:* 5,739.

Sri Lanka

W. U. Tharanga c Dhoni b Vinay Kumar	0
T. M. Dilshan c Dhoni b Pathan	16
†K. C. Sangakkara c Gambhir b Ashwin	31
L. D. Chandimal run out	81
*D. P. M. D. Jayawardene lbw b Vinay Kumar	43
A. D. Mathews run out	17
N. L. T. C. Perera c Kohli b Ashwin	5
K. M. D. N. Kulasekara c Gambhir b Vinay Kumar	12
S. M. S. M. Senanayake not out	22
S. L. Malinga run out	0
H. M. R. K. B. Herath not out	1
L-b 3, w 5	8
1/0 (1) 2/28 (2) 3/79 (3) 4/173 (5) 5/178 (4) 6/184 (7) 7/210 (6) 8/232 (8) 9/235 (10) (9 wkts, 50 overs)	236
10 overs: 32-2	

Vinay Kumar 10–1–46–3; Pathan 9–0–38–1; Yadav 9–0–51–0; Ashwin 10–1–30–2; Jadeja 10–0–58–0; Sharma 2–0–10–0.

India

G. Gambhir run out	91
S. R. Tendulkar c Sangakkara b Kulasekara	15
V. Kohli lbw b Perera	15
R. G. Sharma run out	15
S. K. Raina c Sangakkara b Malinga	8
*†M. S. Dhoni not out	58
R. A. Jadeja c Jayawardene b Perera	3
R. Ashwin c Senanayake b Malinga	14
I. K. Pathan run out	8
R. Vinay Kumar run out	1
U. T. Yadav not out	0
L-b 1, w 6, n-b 1	8
1/24 (2) 2/61 (3) 3/94 (4) 4/118 (5) 5/178 (1) 6/184 (7) 7/212 (8) 8/223 (9) 9/233 (10) (9 wkts, 50 overs)	236
10 overs: 44-1	

Malinga 10–1–53–2; Kulasekara 10–0–39–1; Mathews 5–0–35–0; Perera 9–0–45–2; Herath 10–1–33–0; Senanayake 6–0–30–0.

Umpires: S. D. Fry and N. J. Llong. Third umpire: B. N. J. Oxenford.
Referee: A. J. Pycroft.

AUSTRALIA v SRI LANKA

At Sydney, February 17, 2012 (day/night). Sri Lanka won by eight wickets (D/L). Sri Lanka 5pts. Toss: Australia.

By any measure this was a thrashing for Australia – and it might have been worse had Malinga pouched a simple chance at third man when David Hussey had eight and his team were 74 for five. Malinga did his job with the ball, notably an off-cutter that bamboozled Warner, but was outshone by the slower seamers, who thrived in overcast conditions. Among their victims was Ponting, whose temporary return as captain after Clarke strained a hamstring did nothing to reinvigorate his batting. Following a rain delay, which cut nine overs from each innings, a stand of 49 between David Hussey and Starc lifted Australia's score from downright embarrassing to merely poor. Their lack of fluency contrasted with the aggression of Dilshan, who brutally pulled Starc for six, then despatched Lee (returning from a toe injury) for three consecutive fours. Jayawardene scored only two boundaries in the first 17 overs, yet was completely at ease as he went to his first fifty in seven one-day internationals. Sangakkara became the tenth batsman to reach 10,000 runs in the format.

Man of the Match: N. L. T. C. Perera. *Attendance:* 22,365.

Australia

D. A. Warner c Maharoof b Malinga	13	M. A. Starc run out	17
†M. S. Wade run out	15	X. J. Doherty not out	2
*R. T. Ponting c and b Maharoof	2		
P. J. Forrest c Mathews b Maharoof	16	L-b 2, w 11	13
M. E. K. Hussey c Sangakkara b Mathews	13		
D. J. Hussey c Thirimanne b Perera	58	1/21 (1) 2/37 (3) 3/37 (2) (40.5 overs)	158
D. T. Christian lbw b Perera	6	4/60 (5) 5/74 (4) 6/81 (7)	
C. J. McKay lbw b Herath	3	7/95 (8) 8/104 (9) 9/153 (6)	
B. Lee run out	0	10/158 (10) 10 overs: 36-1	

Malinga 8.5–0–42–1; Kulasekara 8–1–29–0; Maharoof 8–1–18–2; Mathews 4–0–26–1; Perera 7–1–29–2; Herath 5–1–12–1.

Sri Lanka

*D. P. M. D. Jayawardene not out	61
T. M. Dilshan c D. J. Hussey b McKay	45
†K. C. Sangakkara c Doherty b Lee	30
L. D. Chandimal not out	6
L-b 5, w 5	10
1/74 (2) 2/133 (3) (2 wkts, 24.1 overs)	152
8 overs: 53-0	

H. D. R. L. Thirimanne, A. D. Mathews, N. L. T. C. Perera, M. F. Maharoof, K. M. D. N. Kulasekara, S. L. Malinga and H. M. R. K. B. Herath did not bat.

Lee 7–0–42–1; Starc 4–0–32–0; McKay 6–1–23–1; Christian 5.1–0–32–0; Doherty 2–0–18–0.

Umpires: B. F. Bowden and S. D. Fry. Third umpire: B. N. J. Oxenford.
Referee: A. J. Pycroft.

AUSTRALIA v INDIA

At Brisbane, February 19, 2012 (day/night). Australia won by 110 runs. Australia 5pts. Toss: Australia.

The game will be remembered as Ponting's 375th and final one-day international. He played it as Australia's acting-captain, but an innings of seven in 26 balls – ended by an anticlimactic paddle to deep square leg – took his series tally to 18 runs in five matches. The following day, he was axed from the squad; the day after that, he announced he did not expect to play one-day international cricket again. His career aggregate of 13,704 runs was second only to Tendulkar. Australia, though, were able to complete an ultimately simple victory, despite looking set for a modest score at 169 for three after 38 overs. But David Hussey and Christian put on 65 in the final six, then Hilfenhaus – in his first one-day international since November 2009 – continued his career-reviving season with one-day-best figures. To compound India's dudgeon, Dhoni was later banned for a match after presiding over a slow over-rate, itself a partial consequence of his bizarre decision not to use the spin of Jadeja.

Man of the Match: B. W. Hilfenhaus. *Attendance:* 32,063.

Australia

†M. S. Wade c and b Sharma	45	D. T. Christian not out	30
D. A. Warner c Tendulkar b Pathan	43	B 2, l-b 12, w 12	26
*R. T. Ponting c Pathan b Zaheer Khan	7		
P. J. Forrest c Kohli b Pathan	52	1/70 (2) 2/83 (3) (5 wkts, 50 overs)	288
M. E. K. Hussey c Raina b Pathan	59	3/117 (1) 4/217 (5)	
D. J. Hussey not out	26	5/223 (4) 10 overs: 51-0	

B. Lee, M. A. Starc, X. J. Doherty and B. W. Hilfenhaus did not bat.

Zaheer Khan 10–0–46–1; Vinay Kumar 10–0–60–0; Pathan 10–0–61–3; Raina 10–0–44–0; Yadav 7–0–46–0; Sharma 3–0–17–1.

India

G. Gambhir c Wade b Lee	5	Zaheer Khan c Wade b Hilfenhaus	9
S. R. Tendulkar c Doherty b Hilfenhaus	3	U. T. Yadav not out	6
V. Kohli c D. J. Hussey b Hilfenhaus	12		
R. G. Sharma c Wade b Lee	0	L-b 4, w 10, n-b 2	16
S. K. Raina c Wade b Christian	28		
*†M. S. Dhoni c Christian b Hilfenhaus	56	1/8 (1) 2/15 (2) 3/16 (4) (43.3 overs)	178
R. A. Jadeja c Forrest b Starc	18	4/36 (3) 5/82 (5) 6/114 (7)	
I. K. Pathan c Wade b Hilfenhaus	19	7/149 (6) 8/162 (9) 9/168 (8)	
R. Vinay Kumar b Lee	6	10/178 (10)	10 overs: 33-3

Hilfenhaus 9.3–1–33–5; Lee 10–0–49–3; Christian 6–0–27–1; Starc 8–0–36–1; Doherty 10–0–29–0.

Umpires: B. F. Bowden and S. J. Davis. Third umpire: B. N. J. Oxenford.
Referee: A. J. Pycroft.

INDIA v SRI LANKA

At Brisbane, February 21, 2012 (day/night). Sri Lanka won by 51 runs. Sri Lanka 4pts. Toss: Sri Lanka.

India had a claim to the moral high ground, but not victory, after they withdrew their appeal following the bowler Ashwin's run-out of Thirimanne at the non-striker's end. It happened in Sri Lanka's 40th over, with Thirimanne – whose repeated encroachment down the pitch as the bowlers entered their delivery stride prompted Ashwin's move – on 44. The appeal was withdrawn after discussion, yet Thirimanne could consider himself fortunate, especially in light of a recent ICC regulation change permitting the bowler to run out the non-striker up to the point of releasing the ball. Stand-in captain Sehwag said: "If we appealed and the umpire gave him out, then somebody will criticise that it was not [in the] spirit of the game. It's soft, but that's the way we are." With Dhoni serving his ban for a slow over-rate, India shelved their rotation policy and played all three senior batsmen, with Gambhir pushed down to No. 3. But Kulasekara removed both him and Tendulkar after Sehwag had fallen second ball, and India – set a daunting 290 – needed 118 when they lost their last specialist, Kohli, in the first over of the batting powerplay. Pathan shone, clubbing seven fours, but ran out of partners. In two matches, India had gone from first position in the competition to last.

Man of the Match: K. M. D. N. Kulasekara. *Attendance:* 5,406.

Sri Lanka

*D. P. M. D. Jayawardene c Sehwag b Pathan	45	M. F. Maharoof not out	4
T. M. Dilshan c Patel b Ashwin	51		
†K. C. Sangakkara c Tendulkar b Yadav	8	B 1, l-b 2, w 18, n-b 1	22
L. D. Chandimal b Pathan	38		
H. D. R. L. Thirimanne c Raina b Ashwin	62	1/95 (1) 2/104 (2) (6 wkts, 50 overs)	289
A. D. Mathews not out	49	3/124 (3) 4/195 (4)	
N. L. T. C. Perera b Raina	10	5/244 (5) 6/265 (7)	10 overs: 53-0

K. M. D. N. Kulasekara, S. L. Malinga and H. M. R. K. B. Herath did not bat.

Vinay Kumar 8–1–48–0; Pathan 10–0–54–2; Yadav 8–0–58–1; Jadeja 10–0–43–0; Ashwin 10–0–50–2; Sehwag 2–0–9–0; Raina 1–0–10–1; Kohli 1–0–14–0.

India

*V. Sehwag c Kulasekara b Malinga	0	R. Vinay Kumar c sub (S. M. S. M. Senanayake) b Perera	0
S. R. Tendulkar b Kulasekara	22	U. T. Yadav not out	0
G. Gambhir c Perera b Kulasekara	29	L-b 7, w 9	16
V. Kohli c Kulasekara b Perera	66		
S. K. Raina c Thirimanne b Maharoof	32		
R. A. Jadeja b Kulasekara	17	1/0 (1) 2/38 (2) 3/54 (3) (45.1 overs)	238
I. K. Pathan c and b Perera	47	4/146 (5) 5/172 (4) 6/191 (6)	
†P. A. Patel c Malinga b Perera	4	7/215 (8) 8/232 (9) 9/233 (10)	
R. Ashwin c Sangakkara b Malinga	5	10/238 (7)	10 overs: 45-2

Malinga 8–0–55–2; Kulasekara 9–0–40–3; Maharoof 10–1–52–1; Mathews 4–0–12–0; Perera 7.1–0–37–4; Herath 7–0–35–0.

Umpires: B. F. Bowden and P. R. Reiffel. Third umpire: S. J. Davis.
Referee: B. C. Broad.

AUSTRALIA v SRI LANKA

At Hobart, February 24, 2012 (day/night). Sri Lanka won by three wickets. Sri Lanka 4pts. Toss: Australia.

A maiden century by Forrest, his first in List A cricket and the first by anyone in the series, went unrewarded as Sri Lanka clinically exploited the slightest complacency. While Forrest justified his surprise selection – before moving to Queensland in 2011, he had been a fringe player for New South Wales – he and Clarke should have scored more briskly than under five an over when they spent more than 30 together; Australia were again grateful for David Hussey's late gloss. Sri Lanka catapulted to 68 for one after ten overs, with Lee and Harris punished for some off-key bowling. Doherty was typically economical but atypically dangerous: his sharp turn removed the excellent Jayawardene, who faced only 81 deliveries. Three late wickets in 26 balls gave Australia a chance, with Sri Lanka needing 14 from nine after Mathews holed out. But Christian's lack of composure was seized upon by Perera, who hit him for four and six off the next two balls to make the last over a breeze.

Man of the Match: D. P. M. D. Jayawardene. *Attendance:* 9,158.

Australia

†M. S. Wade c Jayawardene b Kulasekara . . 5	B. Lee not out 20
D. A. Warner c Sangakkara b Maharoof . . . 7	
P. J. Forrest c Maharoof b Mathews 104	B 1, l-b 1, w 3 5
*M. J. Clarke c Perera b Mathews 72	—
M. E. K. Hussey b Malinga 21	1/5 (1) 2/27 (2) (6 wkts, 50 overs) 280
D. J. Hussey not out 40	3/181 (4) 4/201 (3)
D. T. Christian st Sangakkara b Herath 6	5/243 (5) 6/250 (7) 10 overs: 44-2

R. J. Harris, X. J. Doherty and B. W. Hilfenhaus did not bat.

Malinga 10–0–56–1; Kulasekara 10–0–59–1; Maharoof 10–0–40–1; Herath 9–0–45–1; Mathews 7–0–43–2; Perera 4–0–35–0.

Sri Lanka

*D. P. M. D. Jayawardene st Wade b Doherty 85	N. L. T. C. Perera not out 21
T. M. Dilshan c Forrest b Hilfenhaus 3	K. M. D. N. Kulasekara not out. 4
†K. C. Sangakkara c Warner b Christian. . . . 22	
L. D. Chandimal lbw b Harris 80	B 1, l-b 6, w 8 15
H. D. R. L. Thirimanne c Hilfenhaus	—
b Christian . 24	1/55 (2) 2/90 (3) (7 wkts, 49.2 overs) 283
A. D. Mathews c Warner b Christian 24	3/153 (1) 4/202 (5)
M. F. Maharoof c Harris b Hilfenhaus 5	5/243 (4) 6/250 (7) 7/267 (6) 10 overs: 68-1

S. L. Malinga and H. M. R. K. B. Herath did not bat.

Lee 9.2–0–63–0; Hilfenhaus 10–0–51–2; Harris 6–0–43–1; Christian 8–0–53–3; Doherty 10–1–35–1; Clarke 5–0–27–0; D. J. Hussey 1–0–4–0.

Umpires: B. F. Bowden and B. N. J. Oxenford. Third umpire: S. D. Fry.
Referee: B. C. Broad.

AUSTRALIA v INDIA

At Sydney, February 26, 2012 (day/night). Australia won by 87 runs. Australia 5pts. Toss: Australia.

Another SCG clash between Australia and India was mired in controversy. If this was not quite the Bollyline Test of 2007-08, then two incidents involving batsmen trying to complete a run left a sour taste. David Hussey could have been given out on 17, but India's appeal for handled the ball (or possibly obstructing the field) was rejected in the belief that he had blocked Raina's throw to protect his body rather than his wicket. Dhoni later complained that Hussey should have been given out "plain and simple", although he was going to reach his ground easily in any case. Later, Tendulkar was exasperated when an accidental collision with Lee, the bowler, led to his own run-out – and more displeasure from Dhoni. With Clarke sidelined by a stiff back, Watson's first appearance of the Australian summer after a nagging calf injury was also his first captaining his country. Central to their total were Warner's solid 66-ball innings and a 94-run partnership between Hussey and Wade. Dhoni was again called upon to rescue India, but his usual early caution did not pay off, and his demise – without a boundary after 49 balls – signalled the end. Australia's win sealed their place in the finals, and left India needing Sri Lanka to lose their last two games to stand a chance of qualification.

Man of the Match: D. A. Warner. *Attendance:* 33,639.

Australia

D. A. Warner c Raina b Jadeja	68	B. Lee c Kohli b Sehwag	4
*S. R. Watson c Yadav b Kumar	1	X. J. Doherty not out	13
P. J. Forrest b Kumar	7	L-b 9, w 5	14
M. E. K. Hussey run out	10		——
D. J. Hussey c Dhoni b Yadav	54	1/5 (2) 2/26 (3) (9 wkts, 50 overs)	252
†M. S. Wade c Dhoni b Yadav	56	3/57 (4) 4/107 (1)	
D. T. Christian c Jadeja b Sehwag	24	5/201 (6) 6/212 (5) 7/217 (8)	
C. J. McKay st Dhoni b Sehwag	1	8/232 (9) 9/252 (7)	10 overs: 41-2

B. W. Hilfenhaus did not bat.

Kumar 10–1–37–2; Pathan 5–1–28–0; Ashwin 10–0–45–0; Yadav 6–0–39–2; Jadeja 10–0–51–1; Sehwag 9–0–43–3.

India

V. Sehwag c and b Hilfenhaus	5	P. Kumar b Doherty	1
S. R. Tendulkar run out	14	U. T. Yadav not out	0
G. Gambhir b McKay	23		
V. Kohli c Christian b Watson	21	B 4, l-b 8, w 8, n-b 3	23
S. K. Raina c Wade b Watson	8		——
*†M. S. Dhoni lbw b Hilfenhaus	14	1/7 (1) 2/35 (2) 3/79 (4) (39.3 overs)	165
R. A. Jadeja c Watson b Christian	8	4/83 (3) 5/89 (5) 6/104 (7)	
R. Ashwin c Watson b Doherty	26	7/126 (6) 8/156 (8) 9/163 (9)	
I. K. Pathan c M. E. K. Hussey b Lee	22	10/165 (10)	10 overs: 60-2

Lee 8–0–26–1; Hilfenhaus 8–1–50–2; McKay 6–0–27–1; D. J. Hussey 2–0–7–0; Christian 3–0–8–1; Watson 5–2–9–2; Doherty 7.3–0–26–2.

Umpires: B. F. Bowden and S. J. A. Taufel. Third umpire: S. D. Fry.
Referee: B. C. Broad.

INDIA v SRI LANKA

At Hobart, February 28, 2012 (day/night). India won by seven wickets. India 5pts. Toss: India.

After nine weeks of scorn for their lack of resolve, India finally produced a performance that demanded universal respect. And it was Kohli, not one of the old guard, who stood tallest. To mount the second-highest successful chase in Australia was challenging enough. But India also had to do it within 40 overs to claim a bonus point and thus stay in contention for the finals. Centuries from Dilshan and Sangakkara – in a Sri Lankan record second-wicket stand of 200 – were ultimately

HIGHEST RUN-RATE FOR A CENTURY PARTNERSHIP IN ODIs

Wkt	*RPO*	*Runs*	*Overs*			
7th	15.28	107	7	Abdul Razzaq/Shahid Afridi	Pakistan v Zimbabwe at Multan	2004-05
4th	**13.09**	**120***	**9.1**	**V. Kohli/S. K. Raina**	**India v Sri Lanka at Hobart**	**2011-12**
5th	12.38	128	10.2	J. H. Kallis/M. V. Boucher	SA v Pakistan at Centurion	2006-07
2nd	11.90	121	10.1	L. Vincent/C. D. McMillan	NZ v Zimbabwe at Bulawayo	2005-06
4th	11.89	109	9.1	B. C. Lara/M. N. Samuels	WI v Sri Lanka at Bridgetown	2003
4th	11.43	101*	8.5	S. R. Tendulkar/M. S. Dhoni	India v SA at Gwalior	2009-10

Matches between ICC Full Member nations only.

---

made to appear ordinary; in Dilshan's case it was a second futile 160 against India, following Rajkot in 2009-10. Still, at the change of innings India's hopes looked so fanciful they already had one foot on the airport tarmac. Kohli started patiently, yet overhauled the well-set Gambhir, and was chiefly responsible for Malinga's extraordinary figures, taking 24 from the 35th over. Repeated flicks off his toes against the bowler reputed to possess the world's best yorker took the breath away. Kohli's unbeaten 133 from 86 balls was his ninth one-day international century, six of them in pursuits, all successful. He was already poised to leave Australia with an enhanced reputation, yet this innings – of the type that transcends loyalties – was on another level entirely.

Man of the Match: V. Kohli. *Attendance:* 3,467.

Sri Lanka

*D. P. M. D. Jayawardene c Sehwag b Jadeja	22
T. M. Dilshan not out	160
†K. C. Sangakkara b Kumar	105
N. L. T. C. Perera run out	3
A. D. Mathews c Ashwin b Zaheer Khan	14
L. D. Chandimal not out	2
L-b 3, w 11	14
1/49 (1) 2/249 (3) (4 wkts, 50 overs)	320
3/279 (4) 4/309 (5)	10 overs: 41-0

H. D. R. L. Thirimanne, M. F. Maharoof, K. M. D. N. Kulasekara, S. L. Malinga and H. M. R. K. B. Herath did not bat.

Zaheer Khan 9–0–61–1; Kumar 9–0–64–1; Yadav 8–0–56–0; Jadeja 9–0–43–1; Ashwin 10–0–52–0; Sehwag 3–0–24–0; Raina 2–0–17–0.

India

V. Sehwag c Dilshan b Maharoof	30
S. R. Tendulkar lbw b Malinga	39
G. Gambhir run out	63
V. Kohli not out	133
S. K. Raina not out	40
B 4, l-b 6, w 6	16
1/54 (1) 2/86 (2) (3 wkts, 36.4 overs)	321
3/201 (3)	10 overs: 97-2

*†M. S. Dhoni, R. A. Jadeja, R. Ashwin, P. Kumar, Zaheer Khan and U. T. Yadav did not bat.

Malinga 7.4–0–96–1; Kulasekara 8–0–71–0; Maharoof 3–0–21–1; Perera 7–0–59–0; Mathews 7–0–44–0; Herath 4–0–20–0.

Umpires: Asad Rauf and S. J. A. Taufel. Third umpire: S. D. Fry.
Referee: B. C. Broad.

AUSTRALIA v SRI LANKA

At Melbourne, March 2, 2012 (day/night). Sri Lanka won by nine runs. Sri Lanka 4pts. Toss: Sri Lanka.

Were it not for the telltale cavernous surrounds of the Melbourne Cricket Ground, television viewers could have been forgiven for thinking this was a Sri Lankan home match, such was the vociferous support from the local expat population. Had Australia won, Sri Lanka would have been eliminated and India would have progressed to the finals instead. This looked likely when Jayawardene and Dilshan perished in the first five overs, but Sangakkara and Chandimal fought back, only for the last seven wickets to tumble for 52. In the process, Christian – on the way to his best figures in the format – became the fourth Australian to take a one-day international hat-trick, although he later joked he owed umpire Rod Tucker a beer for his doubtful leg-before decision against Kulasekara: it would probably have missed leg stump, but India's presence in the tournament meant there was no Decision Review System. Watson could not rely on his usual timing and power, but it took a brilliant Malinga yorker to end his stubborn 83-ball innings. David Hussey, with his fifth fifty of the series, kept his composure while tailenders fell around him; but in the final over he holed out looking for the ten runs needed.

Man of the Match: L. D. Chandimal. *Attendance:* 28,091.

Sri Lanka

*D. P. M. D. Jayawardene run out	5
T. M. Dilshan c Wade b Pattinson	9
†K. C. Sangakkara c Forrest b Pattinson	64
L. D. Chandimal c McKay b Pattinson	75
H. D. R. L. Thirimanne b Pattinson	51
A. D. Mathews c Doherty b Christian	5
N. L. T. C. Perera c M. E. K. Hussey b Christian	5
S. M. S. M. Senanayake lbw b Christian	0
K. M. D. N. Kulasekara lbw b Christian	0
H. M. R. K. B. Herath not out	14
S. L. Malinga b Christian	2
B 2, l-b 4, w 2	8
1/10 (1) 2/17 (2) 3/140 (3) 4/186 (4) 5/195 (6) 6/206 (7) 7/206 (8) 8/206 (9) 9/235 (5) 10/238 (11) (50 overs)	238
10 overs: 36-2	

Pattinson 10–0–51–4; Hilfenhaus 7–0–29–0; McKay 8–0–39–0; D. J. Hussey 1–0–6–0; Christian 9–0–31–5; Watson 7–0–28–0; Doherty 8–0–48–0.

Australia

†M. S. Wade lbw b Kulasekara	9
D. A. Warner c Perera b Malinga	6
*S. R. Watson b Malinga	65
P. J. Forrest c Sangakkara b Malinga	2
M. E. K. Hussey c Sangakkara b Thirimanne	29
D. J. Hussey c Dilshan b Kulasekara	74
D. T. Christian c and b Senanayake	3
J. L. Pattinson c Dilshan b Herath	12
C. J. McKay run out	6
X. J. Doherty c Dilshan b Malinga	7
B. W. Hilfenhaus not out	0
W 15, n-b 1	16
1/16 (2) 2/18 (1) 3/26 (4) 4/113 (5) 5/140 (3) 6/151 (7) 7/178 (8) 8/187 (9) 9/226 (10) 10/229 (6) (49.1 overs)	229
10 overs: 41-3	

Malinga 10–0–49–4; Kulasekara 9.1–1–38–2; Mathews 4–0–8–0; Senanayake 10–0–50–1; Perera 0.5–0–8–0; Thirimanne 4.1–0–25–1; Herath 10–0–43–1; Dilshan 1–0–8–0.

Umpires: Asad Rauf and R. J. Tucker. Third umpire: S. D. Fry.
Referee: B. C. Broad.

QUALIFYING TABLE

	Played	*Won*	*Lost*	*Tied*	*Bonus Points*	*Points*	*Net run-rate*
SRI LANKA	8	4	3	1	1	19	0.16
AUSTRALIA	8	4	4	0	3	19	0.45
India	8	3	4	1	1	15	–0.59

Win = 4pts; tie = 2pts. One bonus point awarded for achieving victory with a run-rate 1.25 times that of the opposition. Net run-rate is calculated by subtracting runs conceded per over from runs scored per over. Sri Lanka finished above Australia on head-to-head results.

AUSTRALIA v SRI LANKA

First Final Match

At Brisbane, March 4, 2012 (day/night). Australia won by 15 runs. Toss: Australia.

It was a mark of Warner's powers that, in his own words, he "didn't really hit one off the middle" as he compiled his first fifty – and was still able to plunder 163, from only 157 balls. Warner's exploits in Twenty20 and Tests had set the bar high, to the extent that notching the third-highest one-day international score in Australia seemed almost passé. But he took guard with an average of 22 from 18 one-day matches, and could easily have made way instead of Forrest for the returning Clarke. Wade had been in a hurry too, until he succumbed to a stunning outfield catch from Herath, left arm outstretched behind his shoulder as he tumbled back inside the long-on boundary. When Sri Lanka slumped to 144 for six in the 31st over, a thrashing loomed. Suddenly Kulasekara, without an international fifty in two and a half years, embarrassed Australia's bowlers, smashing 73 in 43 balls and adding 104 with Tharanga, a stand which included a 68-run batting powerplay. In the end, the result was too close for Australia's comfort.

Man of the Match: D. A. Warner. *Attendance:* 12,196.

Australia

D. A. Warner b Prasad	163	M. E. K. Hussey not out	19
†M. S. Wade c Herath b Kulasekara	64	L-b 1, w 5	6
S. R. Watson c Thirimanne b Maharoof	21		
D. T. Christian c Sangakkara b Prasad	10	1/136 (2) 2/186 (3) (6 wkts, 50 overs)	321
D. J. Hussey c and b Herath	1	3/223 (4) 4/224 (5)	
*M. J. Clarke c Jayawardene b Malinga	37	5/288 (6) 6/321 (1) 10 overs: 68-0	

B. Lee, J. L. Pattinson, X. J. Doherty and B. W. Hilfenhaus did not bat.

Malinga 8–0–74–1; Kulasekara 10–0–60–1; Maharoof 9–0–64–1; Dilshan 9–0–35–0; Prasad 7–0–51–2; Herath 7–0–36–1.

Sri Lanka

*D. P. M. D. Jayawardene c Wade b Lee	14	K. T. G. D. Prasad not out	31
T. M. Dilshan b Lee	27	H. M. R. K. B. Herath c Doherty b Watson	5
†K. C. Sangakkara c Watson b Lee	42	S. L. Malinga c M. E. K. Hussey b Watson	1
L. D. Chandimal c Pattinson b D. J. Hussey	14		
H. D. R. L. Thirimanne c Wade b D. J. Hussey	14	B 1, l-b 3, w 11, n-b 2	17
W. U. Tharanga c D. J. Hussey b Watson	60	1/39 (1) 2/52 (2) 3/93 (4) (49.2 overs)	306
M. F. Maharoof c Christian b D. J. Hussey	8	4/115 (3) 5/125 (5) 6/144 (7)	
K. M. D. N. Kulasekara c Doherty b D. J. Hussey	73	7/248 (8) 8/285 (6) 9/301 (10)	
		10/306 (11) 10 overs: 69-2	

Lee 9–1–59–3; Hilfenhaus 4–0–46–0; Pattinson 5–0–49–0; Watson 9.2–0–33–3; Doherty 10–0–39–0; D. J. Hussey 8–0–43–4; Christian 4–0–33–0.

Umpires: Asad Rauf and P. R. Reiffel. Third umpire: B. N. J. Oxenford.
Referee: B. C. Broad.

AUSTRALIA v SRI LANKA

Second Final Match

At Adelaide, March 6, 2012 (day/night). Sri Lanka won by eight wickets. Toss: Australia.

Warner became the eighth Australian to score consecutive one-day international centuries (Ponting did it twice). Yet by the end his innings almost felt like a liability as Sri Lanka ruthlessly forced a third final. Clarke produced a gem of a hundred, at 81 balls easily the fastest of his seven in the format, but picked up a hamstring twinge which ruled him out of the decider. Two days after his

Brisbane heroics, though, Warner surprisingly ate up 140 balls and, after Jayawardene and Dilshan brought up Sri Lanka's 100 in the 16th over, they never lost control. Dilshan became only the second player (after Neil Johnson, for Zimbabwe v Pakistan at Sheikhupura in 1998-99) to open both bowling and batting, deliver ten overs and score a century, his 12th in one-day internationals. Jayawardene's quick thinking was not limited to his batting and field placings. When the topic of his angry confrontation with the umpires – over a very belated no-ball call at the height of Clarke's innings – and the resulting fine of 10% of his match fee was raised in a post-match interview, he quipped he would pay the ICC only when Sri Lanka's board paid him and the rest of his team-mates what they were owed for much of the past year.

Man of the Match: T. M. Dilshan. *Attendance:* 15,309.

Australia

†M. S. Wade b Dilshan	14
D. A. Warner c Dilshan b Malinga	100
S. R. Watson run out	15
*M. J. Clarke run out	117
M. E. K. Hussey b Malinga	6
D. J. Hussey b Malinga	7
D. T. Christian not out	4
B 2, l-b 3, w 2, n-b 1	8
1/22 (1) 2/56 (3) 3/240 (2) 4/256 (5) 5/266 (4) 6/271 (6) (6 wkts, 50 overs)	271
10 overs: 39-1	

C. J. McKay, B. Lee, J. L. Pattinson and X. J. Doherty did not bat.

Dilshan 10–0–40–1; Kulasekara 10–0–57–0; Malinga 10–1–40–3; Maharoof 10–0–71–0; Herath 10–0–58–0.

Sri Lanka

*D. P. M. D. Jayawardene lbw b Pattinson	80
T. M. Dilshan c M. E. K. Hussey b Lee	106
†K. C. Sangakkara not out	51
L. D. Chandimal not out	17
B 4, l-b 4, w 9, n-b 3	20
1/179 (1) 2/234 (2) (2 wkts, 44.2 overs)	274
10 overs: 74-0	

H. D. R. L. Thirimanne, W. U. Tharanga, C. K. Kapugedera, M. F. Maharoof, K. M. D. N. Kulasekara, H. M. R. K. B. Herath and S. L. Malinga did not bat.

Lee 8–1–41–1; McKay 9–0–51–0; Pattinson 8–1–47–1; Doherty 9–0–55–0; Christian 4–0–29–0; D. J. Hussey 1–0–8–0; Watson 5.2–0–35–0.

Umpires: Asad Rauf and B. N. J. Oxenford. Third umpire: P. R. Reiffel.
Referee: B. C. Broad.

AUSTRALIA v SRI LANKA

Third Final Match

At Adelaide, March 8, 2012 (day/night). Australia won by 16 runs. Toss: Sri Lanka. One-day international debut: N. M. Lyon.

Australia handed a one-day debut to Nathan Lyon, playing a second spinner alongside Doherty in an attempt to take advantage of the same pitch used two days earlier, but it was seamers McKay and Lee who inspired them to a tournament-clinching victory. First they added 40 for the eighth wicket to dig their side out of trouble, then combined to take eight wickets and expose what Australian coach Mickey Arthur had described before the game as Sri Lanka's "softer underbelly" – a jibe aimed at the batting below the big three. Tharanga alone threatened to make him eat his words, reducing the target to a run a ball from the last five overs. But a dogged 122-ball innings was ended by Watson's belated decision to return to the attack after an excellent start; McKay knocked over the last two to claim career-best figures. Earlier, Australia's promising beginning – 112 for one after 20 overs – descended into mediocrity when they lost five for 36, only for Lee and McKay to carry out the first stage of their two-part rescue act.

Man of the Match: C. J. McKay. *Attendance:* 11,216.

Man of the Series: T. M. Dilshan.

Australia

†M. S. Wade c Sangakkara b Herath	49
D. A. Warner c Sangakkara b Maharoof	48
*S. R. Watson c Herath b Dilshan	19
M. E. K. Hussey run out	1
D. J. Hussey lbw b Maharoof	19
P. J. Forrest b Herath	3
D. T. Christian c Jayawardene b Maharoof	19
B. Lee b Kulasekara	32
C. J. McKay c Maharoof b Herath	28
X. J. Doherty not out	5
N. M. Lyon c sub (S. M. S. M. Senanayake) b Kulasekara	0
B 2, l-b 3, w 3	8
1/75 (2) 2/115 (3) (49.3 overs)	231

3/119 (4) 4/123 (1) 5/135 (6) 6/151 (5) 7/177 (7) 8/217 (9) 9/231 (8) 10/231 (11) 10 overs: 56-0

Dilshan 10–1–41–1; Kulasekara 9.3–0–40–2; Malinga 10–0–69–0; Maharoof 10–0–40–3; Herath 10–0–36–3.

Sri Lanka

*D. P. M. D. Jayawardene b McKay	15
T. M. Dilshan c D. J. Hussey b Lee	8
†K. C. Sangakkara c Watson b Lee	19
L. D. Chandimal lbw b McKay	5
H. D. R. L. Thirimanne c Warner b Watson	30
W. U. Tharanga c Wade b Watson	71
C. K. Kapugedera c Wade b McKay	7
K. M. D. N. Kulasekara c Lyon b Lee	15
M. F. Maharoof not out	18
H. M. R. K. B. Herath b McKay	0
S. L. Malinga b McKay	6
L-b 9, w 12	21
1/23 (2) 2/47 (3) 3/52 (4) (48.5 overs)	215

4/53 (1) 5/113 (5) 6/142 (7) 7/172 (8) 8/204 (6) 9/205 (10) 10/215 (11) 10 overs: 55-4

Lee 8–0–59–3; Doherty 8–0–49–0; McKay 9.5–1–28–5; Watson 7–1–13–2; Lyon 8–0–36–0; Christian 8–1–21–0.

Umpires: Asad Rauf and B. N. J. Oxenford. Third umpire: S. D. Fry.
Referee: B. C. Broad.

A full list of past winners of the Australian triangular one-day international series appears on page 994 of Wisden 2009.

Reports on the preceding Twenty20 series between Australia and India appear on page 890. Reports of the Test series appear in Wisden 2012, *page 868.*

AUSTRALIA v SOUTH AFRICA, 2012-13

GIDEON HAIGH

Test matches (3): Australia 0, South Africa 1

Graeme Smith's South Africans took the field at the Gabba for the First Test in unprecedented circumstances: it was the first time since the introduction of the ICC rankings in 2003 that they had begun a Test as the world's No. 1 team. During a fleeting previous stint at the top in 2009 they had not played a single game. Now, Smith's men had ceased to be the hunter, and become the hunted. In fact, had Australia taken the series, they would have replaced South Africa – and, for long periods of this three-Test series, this was the outcome that appeared likeliest. In the way they came through difficult phases at Brisbane and Adelaide, and finally asserted pre-eminence at Perth, the South Africans proved themselves worthy holders of the ICC mace.

As often happens now, the blind giant of injury cleaved a path through the series and shaped its outcome. The Australians' loss of James Pattinson in his tenth over at Adelaide had long-term repercussions: not only were they a bowler short as they tried to prise loose the last remaining batsmen on the final day, but the workloads shouldered by Peter Siddle and Ben Hilfenhaus invalided them out of the Test at the WACA soon after, where a callow replacement attack was put to the sword.

South Africa's most serious injury, by contrast, turned out to be a happy accident. It befell J-P. Duminy as he performed a fitness circuit on the Gabba outfield at the end of the first day, and ruptured an Achilles tendon. That provided an opportunity for Faf du Plessis, hitherto regarded as a one-day workhorse, and so inconspicuous that Mark Nicholas wrote a column for ESPNcricinfo saying South Africa had "no specialist batsman in reserve". In fact, there can hardly have been a more impressive Test debut in history: du Plessis batted almost two full days under acute pressure, like a cowboy with a pair of six-guns backing out of a saloon full of itchy-fingered desperados. It was thanks chiefly to his 78 and 101 not out from a total of 535 balls that South Africa were able to go to Perth all square. There, after a shared first day, they flicked on the afterburners, and it was only because of a hearty last-wicket stand that Australia reduced the margin of defeat to 309 runs. Following their successful tour four years earlier, Smith's team had become the first to win consecutive Test series in Australia since West Indies, in 1988-89 and 1992-93.

On a man-for-man basis, 1–0 was a fair reflection, especially of the sides' respective top threes. For South Africa, Smith batted and led well; Alviro Petersen wasted several starts, but was a fluent partner; Hashim Amla made contrasting centuries, both exquisite. For Australia, Ed Cowan and David Warner both made hundreds, but also exhibited frailties; the Victorian Rob Quiney, who usually opens the batting, was drafted in at No. 3 as a kind of crash-test dummy – the selectors were loath to recall Phillip Hughes too soon – and perhaps inevitably failed. Shane Watson resumed in Perth after one of

Mark Kolbe, Getty Images

Holding off the posse: Faf du Plessis stonewalls an exasperated Nathan Lyon in an incredible Test debut at Adelaide.

his many injuries, but to little avail, and the contrast with Jacques Kallis was telling: unlike Watson, who seems to exist in terror of his body's susceptibilities, Kallis ploughed on regardless of an injury in Adelaide that prevented him from bowling; he batted and caught superbly.

South Africa's bowlers had some wretched days. They did not take a wicket for 120 overs at Brisbane, and gave up almost a run a ball on the first day at Adelaide. Imran Tahir's one appearance was calamitous; Rory Kleinveldt's two gradually improved, but from a low base; Dale Steyn, Morne Morkel and Vernon Philander went through merely steady phases. But at Perth the last three were explosive, and the slow left-armers of Robin Peterson benefited from batsmen trying to escape the general encirclement. They also caught well, ten chances settling in Smith's hands like birds descending on a nest. A. B. de Villiers' keeping was sure, though it meant his athleticism was missed in the field, and his batting form returned with a vengeance at Perth, where his 169 reversed over bowlers already flattened by Smith and Amla.

For Australia, Michael Clarke, who emulated Don Bradman and Wally Hammond by scoring two double-hundreds in a series for a second time, was superb, his neatness and composure at the crease augmented by an amazing weight of shot in such a slight figure. He took five fours off an over from Morkel at Adelaide, including one – on the up and down the ground – he could not have played two years ago; he was untiring at the crease, and often seemed to walk straight from a long entrenchment into a boundary-side interview with Channel Nine, pausing only to swap his baggy green for a sponsors' cap, like the model modern professional. Hussey was reliability personified, and made two free-flowing hundreds as Clarke's escort. There was also a feeling, however, that Australia's leadership came from behind, with the most reliable components of their batting hidden at Nos 5 and 6.

KEEPING UP THE PUNISHMENT

Teams who maintained a scoring rate of more than five an over, in an innings of 80 overs or more:

Runs/over			
5.36	Sri Lanka (555-5 dec/103.3 overs)	v Bangladesh at Colombo (SSC)	2001-02
5.12	**Australia (550/107.2)**	**v South Africa at Adelaide**	**2012-13**
5.08	**South Africa (569/111.5)**	**v Australia at Perth**	**2012-13**
5.07	New Zealand (452-9 dec/89)	v Zimbabwe at Harare	2005
5.07	West Indies (450/88.4)	v England at Leeds	1976
5.01	Australia (735-6 dec/146.3)	v Zimbabwe at Perth	2003-04

That was exacerbated by the precipitous decline of Ricky Ponting, who made only 32 runs in five innings – after a prolific beginning to the first-class season for Tasmania. Having nicked off at the Gabba, he was twice bowled at Adelaide, stumbling over a full ball from Kallis, then dragging on an innocuous delivery from Kleinveldt, whereupon he found he no longer had the reserves of resilience to continue. He made the Test at Perth his last, in the course of which he saw up close the growing gap between South Africa and their competition, and witnessed the final interment of the remains of Australia's great period of dominance – of which he had been a personification. He was welcomed to the crease by a guard of honour formed by Smith, then in the WACA's ersatz gymnasium hosted a final press conference that was moving in its understatement and modesty. Ponting explained he had been full of hope for the series, down to the final innings: "I just felt there was one last big push from me, and the game and the day was set up for it, and it didn't last long enough." He could have been speaking for the entire team.

SOUTH AFRICAN TOURING PARTY

*G. C. Smith, H. M. Amla, A. B. de Villiers, J-P. Duminy, F. du Plessis, Imran Tahir, J. H. Kallis, R. K. Kleinveldt, R. McLaren, M. Morkel, A. N. Petersen, R. J. Peterson, V. D. Philander, J. A. Rudolph, D. W. Steyn, T. L. Tsolekile. *Coach:* G. Kirsten.

Duminy ruptured his Achilles tendon during the First Test, and was replaced by D. Elgar.

TEST MATCH AVERAGES

AUSTRALIA – BATTING AND FIELDING

	T	*I*	*NO*	*R*	*HS*	*100*	*50*	*Avge*	*Ct/St*
M. J. Clarke	3	5	1	576	259*	2	0	144.00	7
†M. E. K. Hussey	3	5	0	295	103	2	1	59.00	3
†E. J. M. Cowan	3	5	0	228	136	1	1	45.60	2
†D. A. Warner	3	5	0	206	119	1	0	41.20	1
†M. S. Wade	3	5	1	121	68	0	1	30.25	8/1
N. M. Lyon	3	3	1	45	31	0	0	22.50	1
R. T. Ponting	3	5	0	32	16	0	0	6.40	2
†R. J. Quiney	2	3	0	9	9	0	0	3.00	5

Played in two Tests: B. W. Hilfenhaus 0, 18*; †J. L. Pattinson 42, 29*; P. M. Siddle 6, 1 (1 ct). Played in one Test: J. W. Hastings 32, 20 (1 ct); †M. G. Johnson 7, 3 (4 ct); †M. A. Starc 0*, 68*; S. R. Watson 10, 25.

BOWLING

	Style	*O*	*M*	*R*	*W*	*BB*	*5I*	*Avge*
M. A. Starc	LFM	44.5	6	209	8	6-154	1	26.12
M. G. Johnson	LFM	42	4	164	6	4-110	0	27.33
B. W. Hilfenhaus	RFM	101.1	34	213	6	3-49	0	35.50
P. M. Siddle	RFM	116.5	31	342	9	4-65	0	38.00
J. L. Pattinson	RFM	62.1	9	192	5	3-93	0	38.40
N. M. Lyon	OB	178	50	486	12	3-41	0	40.50

Also bowled: M. J. Clarke (SLA) 26–6–60–1; J. W. Hastings (RFM) 39–3–153–1; M. E. K. Hussey (RM) 9–0–54–0; R. T. Ponting (OB/RM) 2–1–3–0; R. J. Quiney (RM) 25–12–29–0; D. A. Warner (LBG) 14–0–70–1; S. R. Watson (RFM) 18–5–46–1.

SOUTH AFRICA – BATTING AND FIELDING

	T	*I*	*NO*	*R*	*HS*	*100*	*50*	*Avge*	*Ct/St*
F. du Plessis	2	4	2	293	110*	1	2	146.50	2
H. M. Amla	3	6	0	377	196	2	0	62.83	0
J. H. Kallis	3	6	0	339	147	1	1	56.50	5
A. B. de Villiers	3	6	1	276	169	1	0	55.20	8/1
†G. C. Smith	3	6	0	255	122	1	1	42.50	10
A. N. Petersen	3	6	0	200	64	0	2	33.33	1
V. D. Philander	2	4	2	56	30	0	0	28.00	0
†J. A. Rudolph	2	4	0	74	31	0	0	18.50	0
R. K. Kleinveldt	2	3	1	20	17*	0	0	10.00	1
†M. Morkel	3	5	1	31	17	0	0	7.75	0
D. W. Steyn	3	5	0	26	15	0	0	5.20	2

Played in one Test: †J-P. Duminy did not bat; †D. Elgar 0, 0 (1 ct); Imran Tahir 10*; †R. J. Peterson 31, 0.

BOWLING

	Style	*O*	*M*	*R*	*W*	*BB*	*5I*	*Avge*
M. Morkel	RF	109	23	399	14	5-146	1	28.50
R. J. Peterson	SLA	28.1	3	171	6	3-44	0	28.50
D. W. Steyn	RF	109.3	22	370	12	4-40	0	30.83
V. D. Philander	RFM	67	11	199	4	2-41	0	49.75
R. K. Kleinveldt	RFM	60.1	7	243	4	3-65	0	60.75

Also bowled: H. M. Amla (RM) 2–0–9–0; F. du Plessis (LBG) 10–0–60–0; D. Elgar (SLA) 1–0–4–0; Imran Tahir (LBG) 37–1–260–0; J. H. Kallis (RFM) 15.3–4–49–2; A. N. Petersen (RM) 3–0–20–0; G. C. Smith (OB) 9–0–36–0.

At Sydney, November 2–4, 2012. **Drawn. ‡Australia A 480-7 dec** (R. J. Quiney 85, S. P. D. Smith 67, A. J. Doolan 161*, G. J. Maxwell 64, T. D. Paine 60*; D. W. Steyn 3-54) **and 13-1 dec; South Africans 277-6 dec** (G. C. Smith 60, H. M. Amla 53). *Australia A were 185-6 before Tasmania's Alex Doolan extended his fifth first-class century to his highest score, and shared partnerships of 133 with Glenn Maxwell and 162* with Tim Paine. However, the Test place up for grabs went to Rob Quiney, who survived a probing spell from Steyn to make 85. The South African reply was constructed at a sedate 2.63 per over; both Smith and Amla retired out shortly after reaching their half-centuries.*

AUSTRALIA v SOUTH AFRICA

First Test Match

At Brisbane, November 9–13, 2012. Drawn. Toss: South Africa. Test debuts: R. J. Quiney; R. K. Kleinveldt.

Rain that fell for one day, and a pitch that stayed slow for five, condemned the First Test to incompletion after South African, then Australian, batsmen enjoyed themselves – although a late thrust by the hosts pushed the game into the last hour, and the cycle of events drew in the best crowds seen at a Gabba Test outside the Ashes. Five individual centuries were compiled (and five conceded by bowlers), and Clarke, the Man of the Match, stayed the longest and made the most, not offering a chance in an unbeaten 259. It was the highest individual Test score at the ground, passing Alastair Cook's undefeated 235 for England two years earlier, and the first Australian double-century at Brisbane since Greg Chappell made 201 against Pakistan in 1981-82. New caps were given to Rob Quiney and Rory Kleinveldt, though neither had matches to remember.

With only one warm-up match, on a very different pitch at Sydney, the South Africans began a little rustily after winning the toss but, by the afternoon, the Australians were looking rustier still. As so often, it was Amla and Kallis who secured South Africa's ramparts, with their 11th century stand in Tests after Petersen had squandered a solid start by holing out to mid-on. Amla, who passed 5,000 Test runs, offered Siddle a return catch when he was 74; Kallis miscued a pull from Siddle to mid-off when he had 43, only for the retroactive detection of a no-ball. Rarely expansive, sometimes subdued, especially after tea, they added 165 at three an over, to become South Africa's most productive Test pairing, beating the 3,592 runs put on by Kallis himself with Gary Kirsten, now the coach. Their circumspection was justified when Duminy, not long after stumps, strained an Achilles tendon during a fitness circuit on the outfield, reducing South Africa to ten men and depriving their attack of useful variation.

The Australians regrouped while rain blanketed the second day – the first full day's washout in a Brisbane Test since 1983-84 – and their attack huffed and puffed back into calculations on the third, quickly removing the overnight batsmen, and working steadily through the remnants. Hilfenhaus remained a little below par, but Siddle and Pattinson were reformed characters, bowling to fuller lengths and at improved speeds. Australia then lost three wickets in the first ten overs of their reply, including Ponting, pushing Morkel into the slips for a duck, before Cowan and Clarke stabilised things. In fact, Cowan belied his reputation as a quiet accumulator by scoring freely square of the wicket with cuts and pulls, and lost little in comparison with his prolific captain. Both were caught behind from Morkel no-balls – Cowan at 47, Clarke at 135 – and fended and bunted into untenanted space; one of Clarke's early boundaries sheered from the back of an upraised bat as he took evasive action. Otherwise, the sense of cohesion and composure boded well for Australia's summer.

Their partnership expanded to 259 from 75 overs on what was now the penultimate day, and was broken only by a run-out deflection from Steyn's hand. Cowan was the victim – Australia's only one on the fourth day – after extending his maiden Test hundred to an innings lasting almost six and a half hours. But, having dominated Australia's previous home season, Clarke was simply taking up where he had left off, and Hussey did likewise, achieving fluency and momentum instantly. South Africa felt the want of spin so badly that Smith bowled himself and Amla in order to spare his pace attack for the Tests ahead. Neither was a pretty sight with ball in hand, and Amla's action might have recalled Ian Meckiff's in the previous Gabba Test involving these countries, back in 1963-64; Meckiff was no-balled for chucking.

There was no respite for South Africa on the final day, as Clarke and Hussey extended their stand to 228 at five an over, timing crisply, running expertly. Hussey escaped an lbw appeal when 99 by the thinnest of edges, and became the first wicket to fall to a bowler for

120 overs, thanks to a fine catch at short cover by substitute Faf du Plessis soon after completing his 18th Test century.

But the pitch never showed enough signs of deterioration, apart from some variable bounce, to raise the serious prospect of a result. So when Clarke finally contented himself with a lead of 115, the afternoon was spent shadow boxing, with the occasional blow landing, especially during a fiery and vocal spell by Pattinson, in which Smith was beaten several times and Amla bowled – only to become the third batsman reprieved by retrospective surveillance of the front line. Apart from two overs before tea in which Lyon was clubbed for 26, the South Africans kept their noses to the grindstone.

The Australians sensed an opening when Kallis nicked Lyon to slip from round the wicket, and his back-spinner accounted for Rudolph just before the last hour was due to commence, encouraging Clarke to push on. But the near-empty ground at the end reflected the sense of détente about the match, which left the No. 1 spot in the Test rankings to be decided over two games – hardly an ideal arrangement.

Man of the Match: M. J. Clarke.

Close of play: first day, South Africa 255-2 (Amla 90, Kallis 84); second day, no play; third day, Australia 111-3 (Cowan 49, Clarke 34); fourth day, Australia 487-4 (Clarke 218, Hussey 86).

South Africa

*G. C. Smith lbw b Pattinson	10	– (2) c Quiney b Pattinson	23
A. N. Petersen c Hussey b Lyon	64	– (1) c Wade b Pattinson	5
H. M. Amla lbw b Siddle	104	– c Hussey b Siddle	38
J. H. Kallis c Quiney b Pattinson	147	– c Clarke b Lyon	49
†A. B. de Villiers c Warner b Pattinson	40	– not out	29
J. A. Rudolph c Quiney b Lyon	31	– lbw b Lyon	11
V. D. Philander c Clarke b Siddle	11	– not out	1
D. W. Steyn c Wade b Hilfenhaus	15		
R. K. Kleinveldt not out	17		
M. Morkel c Siddle b Hilfenhaus	0		
J-P. Duminy absent hurt			
B 1, l-b 1, w 3, n-b 6	11	B 2, w 4, n-b 4	10
1/29 (1) 2/119 (2) 3/284 (3) 4/374 (4) 5/377 (5) 6/403 (7) 7/426 (6) 8/446 (8) 9/450 (10) (151.4 overs)	450	1/6 (1) 2/55 (2) 3/102 (3) 4/129 (4) 5/165 (6) (5 wkts, 68 overs)	166

Hilfenhaus 32.4–9–73–2; Pattinson 34–6–93–3; Siddle 36–6–111–2; Lyon 37–4–136–2; Hussey 4–0–21–0; Quiney 7–3–10–0; Clarke 1–0–4–0. *Second innings*—Hilfenhaus 15–3–26–0; Pattinson 19–3–58–2; Siddle 17–4–36–1; Lyon 13–5–41–2; Quiney 4–3–3–0.

Australia

E. J. M. Cowan run out	136
D. A. Warner c Kallis b Steyn	4
R. J. Quiney c Steyn b Morkel	9
R. T. Ponting c Kallis b Morkel	0
*M. J. Clarke not out	259
M. E. K. Hussey c sub (F. du Plessis) b Morkel	100
†M. S. Wade not out	19
L-b 14, w 1, n-b 23	38
1/13 (2) 2/30 (3) 3/40 (4) 4/299 (1) 5/527 (6) (5 wkts dec, 138 overs)	565

P. M. Siddle, J. L. Pattinson, B. W. Hilfenhaus and N. M. Lyon did not bat.

Steyn 30–3–129–1; Philander 30–3–103–0; Morkel 31–6–127–3; Kleinveldt 21–1–97–0; Kallis 12–3–30–0; Smith 9–0–36–0; Amla 2–0–9–0; Petersen 3–0–20–0.

Umpires: Asad Rauf and B. F. Bowden. Third umpire: R. A. Kettleborough.

AUSTRALIA v SOUTH AFRICA

Second Test Match

At Adelaide, November 22–26, 2012. Drawn. Toss: Australia. Test debut: F. du Plessis.

In pitiless heat, and at a ground in the throes of extensive rebuilding, South Africa staged a four-day retreat after a disastrous start, and had just enough in reserve to keep the series at 0–0. In effect, it was Duminy's injury that saved them, for it provided a first Test cap for 28-year-old Faf du Plessis, who had 26 one-day internationals already behind him, but looked ready-made for Test cricket: calm, collected, compact and versatile. He batted a total of 11 hours 11 minutes in the game, including the entirety of the last day, falling in the first innings only in the act of hitting out with the No. 11 at the crease, and unconquerable in the second as South Africa stumbled towards sanctuary.

Another injury was also crucial, as Pattinson sustained a side strain in his tenth over, raising the suspicion he would have been wiser to skip the game; as it was, he had to be scratched from the rest of the Test summer. Siddle and Hilfenhaus toiled so manfully in his stead that they bowled themselves to a standstill and out of the Third Test.

But all that lay ahead when the Australians dominated the game's opening stanzas. Warner responded to the loss of three early wickets – including Quiney and Ponting, squared up by a beauty from Kallis – in the only way he knows, with powerful, crazy-brave strokes, enjoying the reshaping of both the arena (21 metres had been trimmed from the straight boundaries, six from the already modest square ones) and South Africa's attack. They were without Vernon Philander, who woke up on the first morning with a sore neck, and included Imran Tahir, who might have ended the day with a sore neck after following the sixes that greeted his inconsistent leg-breaks. They also lost Kallis, who pulled up with hamstring trouble in his fourth over. Warner reached his third Test century shortly after lunch, from 93 balls, with a straight six and a cover-driven four off Tahir. It was an impressive retort from a batsman who had endured a thin time of it since his fine hundred against New Zealand a year earlier.

This assault, however, was merely a prelude, for Clarke and Hussey rampaged through the afternoon as if accelerating towards a declaration. In reaching his fourth Test double-century of the year – a world record – Clarke was particularly harsh on Tahir (whom he hit for 79 off 69 balls) and Morkel (70 off 56), and took Morkel's 18th over for five imperious boundaries. Hussey, as ever, provided industry and enthusiasm, although he too meted out heavy punishment to Tahir (51 from 48). Tahir went at nearly eight an over while taking none for 180; his final match analysis of none for 260 would be the most expensive wicketless performance in all Tests, just beating Khan Mohammad's none for 259 for Pakistan in West Indies' only innings at Kingston in 1957-58, when Garry Sobers made 365 not out.

After adding 272 with Clarke, Australia's highest stand for the fifth wicket in Tests at Adelaide, Hussey was bowled by the last ball of a shortened day to leave his side 482 for five, including 202 in the final session, with 66 fours and nine sixes in all. Only once

---

WORST ECONOMY RATE IN A TEST INNINGS

R/o			
7.82	**Imran Tahir (23–0–180–0)**	**South Africa v Australia at Adelaide**	**2012-13**
6.45	J. H. Sinclair (20–1–129–4)	South Africa v Australia at Johannesburg	1902-03
6.35	R. J. Peterson (20–2–127–3)	South Africa v Australia at Perth	2012-13
6.23	Sohail Khan(21–2–131–0)	Pakistan v Sri Lanka at Karachi	2008-09
6.09	M. G. Johnson (21.4–2–132–3)	Australia v England at Lord's	2009
6.00	Syed Rasel (21.3–2–129–4)	Bangladesh v Sri Lanka at Colombo (PSS)	2005-06

Qualification: 20 overs.

Scott Barbour, Getty Images

Delicate destruction: Michael Clarke tears into Imran Tahir in another double-century.

before had a team scored more on the first day of a Test: Australia hit 494 for six against South Africa at Sydney in 1910-11.

From this point, South Africa could do no better than draw, and set out to do just that, dismissing Clarke soon after the restart on the second morning for 230 off 257 balls, and winnowing away the rest of the Australian innings. They batted patiently after lunch, with Smith shielding his stumps and country for nearly five hours. Petersen helped put on 138, then ran himself out in lackadaisical fashion when Hussey's direct hit from mid-on punished a failure to ground the bat. Otherwise it was a fine effort, ended only by a mysterious caught-behind decision, which Smith reviewed immediately. He was bemused by the merest heat signature on the outside edge; it is conceivable he did not feel it.

The staged withdrawal continued into the third day, as the poised du Plessis was joined at the fall of the seventh wicket by Kallis who, with the minimum of footwork and running between wickets, added 93 with him in 30 overs. Australia's bowlers were now starting to feel the pinch in the enervating heat, and Clarke did his best to spread the wear, then let them put their feet up for 70 overs as his batsmen set up a target of 430. After Quiney

MOST RUNS IN A DAY IN A TEST

588	2nd day	England (398) v India (190) at Manchester	1936
522	2nd	England (503) v South Africa (19) at Lord's	1924
509	2nd	Sri Lanka (509) v Bangladesh at Colombo (PSS)	2002
508	3rd	England (221) v South Africa (287) at The Oval	1935
496	2nd	England (437) v Pakistan (59) at Nottingham	1954
494	1st	Australia (494) v South Africa at Sydney	1910-11
492	2nd	England (179) v South Africa (313) at The Oval	1935
491	3rd	England (267) v New Zealand (224) at Leeds	1949
482	3rd	Australia (221) v India (261) at Sydney	1999-2000
482	**1st**	**Australia (482) v South Africa at Adelaide**	**2012-13**

completed a pair, Hussey played with alacrity, and Ponting with uncertainty, dragging on for his third failure of the summer: little did the crowd know as he traipsed off, but Australia's greatest Test run-scorer was running down his own clock.

Clarke gave his depleted attack about 150 overs to polish off the South Africans, although they made such early inroads this appeared ample: when Petersen was bowled by Siddle in the 21st over, it was 45 for four. But former schoolmates de Villiers and du Plessis painstakingly saw out the rest of the day, adding 32 in 29 overs with the deadest of bats, and resumed next morning with similar deliberation.

South Africa now demonstrated that their No. 1 Test ranking was a function not only of winning, but of not losing too. At first it appeared that batsmen operating so defensively must eventually err through negativity, but the pitch was now playing truly: the challenge was concentration and endurance rather than deceitful deliveries. The pair batted deep into the day, before de Villiers finally nicked the second new ball from Siddle after an innings of 220 deliveries, from only 23 of which he scored; he did not hit a single boundary.

The bowler who caused du Plessis most trouble was actually Clarke, who had him given out by Billy Bowden at 33 and 37, lbw both times, only to be reprieved on review. Du Plessis also caused the Australians to use up their final review, when on 49 he offered no shot to a turning delivery from Lyon; and to waste their one chance in the over before tea, when on 94 he nicked Hilfenhaus to Wade, who missed it standing up. After 41 balls in the nineties, du Plessis became South Africa's fourth Test-debut centurion.

Kallis remained with du Plessis for a further two and a half hours, marginally less mobile than in the first innings, though immobility somehow became him under the circumstances. This time they added 99 from 235 balls, before Lyon at last had Kallis caught at bat-pad. The tail provided further passive resistance, as Siddle hurled himself into the fray during a last, puffing, panting, red-faced, valiant spell, yorking Kleinveldt with four overs to go and two wickets required. But the game ended with Morkel blocking out the last over, then – touchingly – lifting the diminutive Cowan off his feet at short leg from the sheer emotion of it all.

Man of the Match: F. du Plessis.

Close of play: first day, Australia 482-5 (Clarke 224); second day, South Africa 217-2 (Smith 111, Rudolph 25); third day, Australia 111-5 (Clarke 9, Hussey 5); fourth day, South Africa 77-4 (de Villiers 12, du Plessis 19).

Australia

D. A. Warner c Smith b Morkel	119	– (2) c du Plessis b Kleinveldt	41
E. J. M. Cowan c and b Kallis	10	– (1) b Kleinveldt	29
R. J. Quiney c Smith b Morkel	0	– c de Villiers b Kleinveldt	0
R. T. Ponting b Kallis	4	– b Steyn	16
*M. J. Clarke b Morkel	230	– lbw b Steyn	38
M. E. K. Hussey b Steyn	103	– (7) c Steyn b Morkel	54
†M. S. Wade c de Villiers b Morkel	6	– (8) c de Villiers b Morkel	18
P. M. Siddle c Smith b Kleinveldt	6	– (6) c de Villiers b Morkel	1
J. L. Pattinson c Smith b Steyn	42	– not out	29
B. W. Hilfenhaus c Kleinveldt b Morkel	0	– not out	18
N. M. Lyon not out	7		
L-b 11, w 1, n-b 11	23	B 4, l-b 10, n-b 9	23
1/43 (2) 2/44 (3) 3/55 (4) (107.2 overs)	550	1/77 (2) (8 wkts dec, 70 overs)	267
4/210 (1) 5/482 (6) 6/494 (5)		2/77 (3) 3/91 (1)	
7/501 (7) 8/503 (8) 9/504 (10) 10/550 (9)		4/98 (4) 5/103 (6) 6/173 (5)	
		7/206 (7) 8/220 (8)	

Steyn 23.4–4–79–2; Morkel 30–5–146–5; Kallis 3.3–1–19–2; Kleinveldt 20.1–4–81–1; Imran Tahir 23–0–180–0; du Plessis 7–0–34–0. *Second innings*—Steyn 17–5–50–2; Morkel 19–4–50–3; Imran Tahir 14–1–80–0; Kleinveldt 19–2–65–3; du Plessis 1–0–8–0.

South Africa

*G. C. Smith c Wade b Siddle	122	– (2) c Ponting b Hilfenhaus	0
A. N. Petersen run out	54	– (1) b Siddle	24
H. M. Amla st Wade b Warner	11	– c Clarke b Lyon	17
J. A. Rudolph c Quiney b Lyon	29	– c Cowan b Lyon	3
†A. B. de Villiers lbw b Siddle	1	– b Siddle	33
F. du Plessis c Clarke b Hilfenhaus	78	– not out	110
D. W. Steyn c Ponting b Hilfenhaus	1	– (8) c Quiney b Siddle	0
R. K. Kleinveldt b Hilfenhaus	0	– (9) b Siddle	3
J. H. Kallis c Wade b Clarke	58	– (7) c Cowan b Lyon	46
M. Morkel b Lyon	6	– not out	8
Imran Tahir not out	10		
B 7, l-b 2, w 3, n-b 6	18	B 1, l-b 1, w 1, n-b 1	4
1/138 (2) 2/169 (3) 3/233 (4) 4/233 (1) 5/240 (5) 6/246 (7) 7/250 (8) 8/343 (9) 9/352 (10) 10/388 (6) (124.3 overs)	388	1/3 (2) 2/36 (3) 3/45 (4) 4/45 (1) 5/134 (5) 6/233 (7) 7/234 (8) 8/240 (9) (8 wkts, 148 overs)	248

Hilfenhaus 19.3–6–49–3; Pattinson 9.1–0–41–0; Lyon 44–7–91–2; Siddle 30.5–6–130–2; Clarke 7–1–22–1; Hussey 1–0–7–0; Warner 5–0–27–1; Quiney 8–3–12–0. *Second innings*—Hilfenhaus 34–16–65–1; Siddle 33–15–65–4; Clarke 18–5–34–0; Lyon 50–31–49–3; Warner 6–0–29–0; Quiney 6–3–4–0; Ponting 1–1–0–0.

Umpires: B. F. Bowden and R. A. Kettleborough. Third umpire: Asad Rauf.

AUSTRALIA v SOUTH AFRICA

Third Test Match

At Perth, November 30–December 3, 2012. South Africa won by 309 runs. Toss: South Africa. Test debuts: J. W. Hastings; D. Elgar.

South Africa consolidated their grip on top spot in the rankings with an overwhelming victory on a ground where they had drawn and won their only previous Tests – and looked very much at home. It made a poignant backdrop for the farewell of Ricky Ponting, who had done so much to establish the period of Australian dominance, then over the last three years seen it chipped away. At a press conference after training on the eve of the game, he announced his 168th Test – equalling Steve Waugh's Australian record – would be his last: there was little notice, little fanfare and no theatre, as Ponting characteristically deferred all questions about his career until after the match, lest he disrupt the team's preparation. Many in the audience who had been urging him to go sat there faintly stunned that he was now in fact going – and at the venue where he had made his Test debut 17 years earlier. But going he was, and for much of the first day it appeared as though it would be on a high.

The Australians fielded a wholly new pace attack. Siddle and Hilfenhaus had bowled themselves into the ground at Adelaide, while the young back-up seamer Josh Hazlewood was discovered during his preamble to the Test to have stress fractures of the foot. That led to the selection of Victorian debutant John Hastings as an upwind complement to the recalled left-arm duo of Mitchell Starc and Mitchell Johnson, back for his first Test in a year. And this attack actually appeared more than up to the task when it quickly reduced the South Africans, for whom Peterson and the debutant Dean Elgar had replaced Imran Tahir and Jacques Rudolph, to 75 for six soon after lunch. The openers had been separated after an hour by Watson, fit again and displacing the unlucky Rob Quiney, and no further resistance was encountered until du Plessis once more draped himself across the pitch like an iron curtain, remaining undefeated for 195 minutes. The tail's resilience, and two early wickets, gave South Africa a little share of the spoils before the close.

The second day was of a character almost unique in the memory: Australia were outclassed and overwhelmed in every category of the game. Their batsmen were cowed by Steyn, Morkel and Philander, their tail sucked in by Peterson, and their bowlers towelled up by Smith and Amla, who piled Pelion on Ossa with a partnership of 178 in 153 balls. Only a spectacular catch by Lyon at backward square leg to remove Smith curbed the mayhem.

The dismissal of Warner, playing a wild slash, began the Australian capitulation; equally wild and demoralised bowling without a semblance of plan completed it. Ponting saw events for what they were: South Africa were trying on the mantle earned in England, a champion team choosing to play like it. "That was them trying to impose themselves on the series, and they did it better than I have seen any team take a game away from the opposition before," he said later. "A lot of the other teams we have played over the years who have been in that position have been too scared to do that." Smith agreed, calling it "one of the highlights of South African cricket".

On the third day, they were nearly as dominant again. Amla produced his finest innings of the tour, superbly organised and paced as always, but audacious too, manufacturing strokes, manipulating fields and generally running the show. He came down the wicket to the seamers, worked Lyon to leg from outside off, and found unguarded areas square and fine. He was four runs from a double-century after 220 balls when – startlingly – he offered Johnson a return catch, and it was brilliantly taken.

With de Villiers, Amla had gone into harness for a serene stand of 149; de Villiers then knocked up a helter-skelter 102 in 85 deliveries with du Plessis, moving to a 14th Test century – his first as South Africa's keeper – with three exquisite consecutive reverse sweeps from Lyon. He finished with 169 from 184 balls, 36 fewer than it had taken him to score 33 at Adelaide a week earlier. Starc and Johnson shared the wickets, rewards for perseverance and pace respectively; Johnson twice overwhelmed Elgar with sheer speed, inflicting on him an ignominious pair. It was the first time two bowlers with the same first name had ever taken all ten wickets in a Test innings.

Set a monstrous 632, Australia negotiated a gruelling final hour, in which outside edges were singed and arms flung about in arrested celebration as South Africa's quicks again found bounce and sideways movement. But Warner was gone first thing on the fourth morning, and only Cowan set a real price on his wicket, before falling to the hook. The moment everyone had waited for, Ponting's final Test innings, commenced with his welcome by a guard of honour formed by Smith. He hit a pull and an on-drive, both for four, then nicked off to slip, pausing just before the players' entrance to swivel 360 degrees and take in the whole ground. The last pair showed how little was wrong with the conditions by putting together 87 in 75 balls, slightly spoiling the figures of Peterson, whose match analysis of six for 171 was useful given the venue's reputation for being inimical to slow bowling.

So ended the Australian push to recapture the No. 1 spot in Test cricket. So ended the first home series since 2001-02 in which Australia had not won a Test. So ended one of the most distinguished of all Australian cricket careers. In a dignified press conference after the close, Ponting confessed he had been "more nervous this game than any other game I've played", but that he "just felt there was one last big push from me", and that it "would've been nice to have a few next to my name coming off". He confessed the guard of honour had taken him by surprise: "Graeme's gesture and the South African team's gesture, that sort of stuff will remain with me for ever, and I told him that on the field today." There should have been no surprise, and Smith spoke for many when he said: "Having played against Ricky so much over the years, he's certainly the player I respect most."

Man of the Match: H. M. Amla. *Man of the Series:* M. J. Clarke.

Close of play: first day, Australia 33-2 (Warner 12, Lyon 7); second day, South Africa 230-2 (Amla 99, Kallis 17); third day, Australia 40-0 (Cowan 9, Warner 29).

South Africa

*G. C. Smith c Clarke b Watson	16	– (2) c Lyon b Starc	84
A. N. Petersen b Starc	30	– (1) c and b Johnson	23
H. M. Amla run out	11	– c and b Johnson	196
J. H. Kallis b Starc	2	– c Johnson b Starc	37
†A. B. de Villiers c Clarke b Hastings	4	– c Wade b Starc	169
D. Elgar c Wade b Johnson	0	– lbw b Johnson	0
F. du Plessis not out	78	– c Clarke b Johnson	27
R. J. Peterson c Wade b Lyon	31	– c Johnson b Starc	0
V. D. Philander c Hussey b Lyon	30	– not out	14
D. W. Steyn b Johnson	2	– c Wade b Starc	8
M. Morkel c Hastings b Lyon	17	– b Starc	0
L-b 2, w 2	4	B 4, l-b 4, w 3	11
1/38 (1) 2/61 (2) 3/63 (4) 4/67 (3) 5/67 (5) 6/75 (6) 7/132 (8) 8/196 (9) 9/206 (10) 10/225 (11) (74 overs)	225	1/28 (1) 2/206 (2) 3/287 (4) 4/436 (3) 5/436 (6) 6/538 (7) 7/539 (8) 8/557 (5) 9/569 (10) 10/569 (11) (111.5 overs)	569

Starc 16–3–55–2; Hastings 20–2–51–1; Watson 9–2–22–1; Johnson 17–3–54–2; Lyon 12–1–41–3. *Second innings*—Starc 28.5–3–154–6; Watson 9–3–24–0; Johnson 25–1–110–4; Hastings 19–1–102–0; Lyon 22–2–128–0; Hussey 4–0–26–0; Warner 3–0–14–0; Ponting 1–0–3–0.

Australia

D. A. Warner c de Villiers b Steyn	13	– (2) c Smith b Philander	29
E. J. M. Cowan c Kallis b Steyn	0	– (1) c Elgar b Steyn	53
S. R. Watson lbw b Philander	10	– c Smith b Morkel	25
N. M. Lyon c du Plessis b Steyn	7	– (11) c Smith b Steyn	31
R. T. Ponting lbw b Philander	4	– (4) c Kallis b Peterson	8
*M. J. Clarke c de Villiers b Steyn	5	– (5) st de Villiers b Peterson	44
M. E. K. Hussey c Smith b Morkel	12	– (6) c de Villiers b Steyn	26
†M. S. Wade b Peterson	68	– (7) c Smith b Peterson	10
J. W. Hastings c Petersen b Peterson	32	– (8) c Smith b Morkel	20
M. G. Johnson b Peterson	7	– (9) c de Villiers b Philander	3
M. A. Starc not out	0	– (10) not out	68
L-b 5	5	L-b 3, w 2	5
1/3 (2) 2/18 (3) 3/34 (1) 4/35 (4) 5/43 (5) 6/45 (6) 7/100 (7) 8/140 (8) 9/162 (10) 10/163 (9) (53.1 overs)	163	1/40 (2) 2/81 (3) 3/102 (4) 4/130 (1) 5/188 (5) 6/198 (6) 7/198 (7) 8/204 (9) 9/235 (8) 10/322 (11) (82.5 overs)	322

Steyn 16–4–40–4; Philander 16–0–55–2; Morkel 13–6–19–1; Peterson 8.1–1–44–3. *Second innings*—Steyn 22.5–6–72–3; Philander 21–8–41–2; Morkel 16–2–57–2; Peterson 20–2–127–3; Elgar 1–0–4–0; du Plessis 2–0–18–0.

Umpires: Asad Rauf and R. A. Kettleborough. Third umpire: B. F. Bowden.
Series referee: R. S. Madugalle.

AUSTRALIA v SRI LANKA, 2012-13

DANIEL BRETTIG

Test matches (3): Australia 3, Sri Lanka 0
One-day internationals (5): Australia 2, Sri Lanka 2
Twenty20 internationals (2): Australia 0, Sri Lanka 2

Chastened by a home loss to South Africa that might easily have ended in a draw, if not an Australian win, Michael Clarke's team vented their frustration by dismantling an injury-blighted and occasionally distracted Sri Lanka either side of Christmas. Seventeen years after they were last invited to play Tests in Australia during the showpiece weeks of the summer, Sri Lanka would suffer the same deflating 3–0 scoreline. They were unable to grind out a draw at Hobart, surrendered meekly at Melbourne, then wasted chances to put Australia under pressure at Sydney.

The Australians' success came despite issues swirling round the team. Chief among these was the rotation policy aimed at preventing injuries to their fast bowlers. While it had been in place for some time, and was focused on ensuring that young bowlers such as Mitchell Starc and James Pattinson did not fall prey to injury too often before their bodies matured, it was the subject of much discussion, especially after the Hobart Test. Starc had bowled erratically for much of that match, but finished it off with a hostile spell of speed and reverse swing – so he was unhappy to be told he would be left out of the Boxing Day Test because of his workload. Matters were complicated further when Ben Hilfenhaus also missed the game through injury.

Mickey Arthur, the coach, remarked that Australia had begun the summer with a list of fast bowlers in mind, "and we're well down it now". But the policy provided a chance for Jackson Bird to show off his considerable skills of swing and seam. A 26-year-old raised in New South Wales before moving to Tasmania in search of greater opportunities, Bird swiftly demonstrated a method as mean and threatening as it was simple, a methodology recalling Stuart Clark. Bird was Australia's most significant find of the summer.

Less assuring were the various trials of the batting order. Shane Watson finally seemed to have lost his long fight to push his problematic body into service as a Test all-rounder. Long spells to cover Hilfenhaus at Hobart led to a calf strain in Melbourne, after which a meeting with Clarke, Arthur and national selector John Inverarity in Sydney persuaded him to return as a batsman alone. Mike Hussey's decision to retire from international cricket while still at the top of his game was a surprise to all but his closest confidants. The announcement came after the Melbourne Test, and left a considerable hole. Matthew Wade's increasing poise with the bat contrasted with some occasionally scruffy work behind the stumps.

Sri Lanka's board had shown a dispiriting lack of interest in Test cricket for a while, and it was difficult not to fear for their team in the game's longest form. While they showed some fight at Hobart, including a provocative

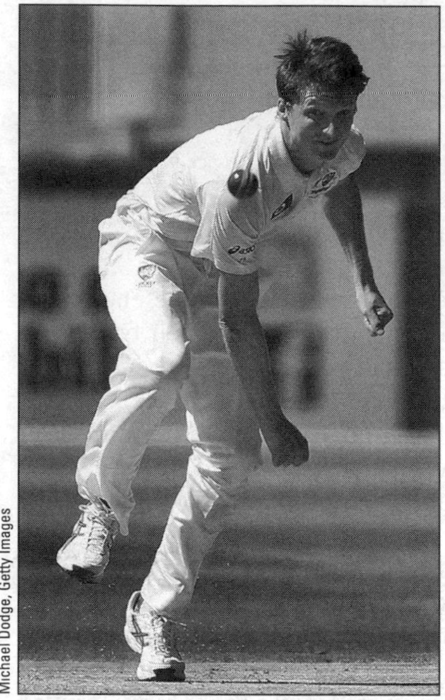

Michael Dodge, Getty Images

Mean and threatening: Jackson Bird reminded onlookers of Stuart Clark.

complaint of ball-tampering against Peter Siddle and Ed Cowan, the collapse at Melbourne was indicative of a side struggling to deal with the physical and mental demands of five-day matches away from home. Thilan Samaraweera, in particular, was guilty of several shots not becoming a batsman of his seniority or skill.

Injuries – especially the broken hand suffered by Kumar Sangakkara in the Second Test – only heightened the feeling of displacement and, after slogging through a public row with Sri Lanka Cricket in Colombo newspapers early in the tour, Mahela Jayawardene looked relieved that his second captaincy stint was about to end. The question of who could adequately replace him did not have an immediate answer, and only the scantest consolation could be found in the bowling of Rangana Herath, plus the runs of Lahiru Thirimanne, Dimuth Karunaratne and Dinesh Chandimal in Sydney. As though the rigours of an Australian tour were not enough, Herath spent one fitful night of the Sydney Test reassuring friends and family back home that a scurrilous rumour propagated on Twitter about his death in a car accident was untrue. If only he had been able to say the same of the series result.

Sri Lanka did have more success in the limited-overs games, in which – to start with at least – they faced a largely experimental Australian side. But they were denied a probable series victory in the one-day internationals by the weather at Sydney, where the umpires decided no resumption was possible, much to the tourists' irritation. They also won both Twenty20 games, the second in conditions similar to those at the SCG.

SRI LANKAN TOURING PARTY

*D. P. M. D. Jayawardene, L. D. Chandimal, T. M. Dilshan, R. M. S. Eranga, A. N. P. R. Fernando, H. M. R. K. B. Herath, H. A. P. W. Jayawardene, F. D. M. Karunaratne, K. M. D. N. Kulasekara, A. D. Mathews, N. T. Paranavitana, K. T. G. D. Prasad, S. Randiv, T. T. Samaraweera, K. C. Sangakkara, U. W. M. B. C. A. Welagedara. *Coach:* G. X. Ford.

During the Second Test, Sangakkara broke his left hand and Welagedara tore a hamstring; they were replaced by H. D. R. L. Thirimanne and R. A. S. Lakmal. For the one-day internationals that followed the Tests, Thirimanne, A. Dananjaya, S. L. Malinga, B. A. W. Mendis, B. M. A. J. Mendis, N. L. T. C. Perera and W. U. Tharanga replaced Fernando, H. A. P. W. Jayawardene, Karunaratne, Paranavitana, Prasad, Randiv and Samaraweera, while M. D. K. J. Perera and Lakmal came in for Sangakkara and Welagedara, who were originally selected. Mathews took over the captaincy for the Twenty20 internationals.

TEST MATCH AVERAGES

AUSTRALIA – BATTING AND FIELDING

	T	*I*	*NO*	*R*	*HS*	*100*	*50*	*Avge*	*Ct*
†M. E. K. Hussey	3	5	3	232	115*	1	0	116.00	9
†M. G. Johnson	2	3	2	106	92*	0	1	106.00	0
M. J. Clarke	3	5	1	316	106	1	3	79.00	3
†M. S. Wade	3	5	2	191	102*	1	1	63.66	14
†D. A. Warner	3	5	0	272	85	0	4	54.40	2
†P. J. Hughes	3	5	0	233	87	0	2	46.60	3
S. R. Watson	2	3	0	118	83	0	1	39.33	0
†E. J. M. Cowan	3	5	0	136	56	0	1	27.20	3
P. M. Siddle	3	3	0	55	38	0	0	18.33	1
N. M. Lyon	3	3	0	16	11	0	0	5.33	0

Played in two Tests: J. M. Bird 0, 6* (1 ct); †M. A. Starc 5, 2 (1 ct). Played in one Test: B. W. Hilfenhaus 0.

BOWLING

	Style	*O*	*M*	*R*	*W*	*BB*	*5I*	*Avge*
J. M. Bird	RFM	63	21	178	11	4-41	0	16.18
P. M. Siddle	RFM	96.5	30	254	15	5-54	1	16.93
M. G. Johnson	LFM	50	6	171	9	4-63	0	19.00
M. A. Starc	LFM	83.2	11	287	10	5-63	1	28.70
N. M. Lyon	OB	98.4	23	307	7	2-23	0	43.85

Also bowled: M. J. Clarke (SLA) 2–0–9–0; B. W. Hilfenhaus (RFM) 12.2–3–30–1; M. E. K. Hussey (RM) 4–1–12–0; M. S. Wade (RFM) S1–1–0–0; D. A. Warner (LBG) 4–0–8–0; S. R. Watson (RFM) 50.4–13–112–2.

SRI LANKA – BATTING AND FIELDING

	T	*I*	*NO*	*R*	*HS*	*100*	*50*	*Avge*	*Ct/St*
†K. C. Sangakkara	2	4	1	152	63	0	2	50.66	1
T. M. Dilshan	3	6	0	208	147	1	0	34.66	0
A. D. Mathews	3	6	0	175	75	0	1	29.16	0
H. A. P. W. Jayawardene	2	3	0	85	40	0	0	28.33	2/1
D. P. M. D. Jayawardene	3	6	0	166	72	0	2	27.66	5
†F. D. M. Karunaratne	3	6	0	140	85	0	1	23.33	1
T. T. Samaraweera	3	6	0	79	49	0	0	13.16	1
†H. M. R. K. B. Herath	3	6	1	48	14	0	0	9.60	1
K. T. G. D. Prasad	2	4	0	34	17	0	0	8.50	2
R. M. S. Eranga	2	4	2	15	6	0	0	7.50	2
U. W. M. B. C. A. Welagedara	2	3	1	0	0*	0	0	0.00	0

Played in one Test: L. D. Chandimal 24, 62* (3 ct); A. N. P. R. Fernando 17*, 9; K. M. D. N. Kulasekara 23, 9 (1 ct); R. A. S. Lakmal 5, 0; †H. D. R. L. Thirimanne 91, 7 (1 ct).

BOWLING

	Style	*O*	*M*	*R*	*W*	*BB*	*5I*	*Avge*
H. M. R. K. B. Herath	SLA	134.4	16	407	12	5-95	1	33.91
U. W. M. B. C. A. Welagedara	LFM	62.4	10	257	6	3-89	0	42.83
R. M. S. Eranga	RFM	63	7	252	5	3-109	0	50.40
K. T. G. D. Prasad	RFM	37	2	159	3	3-106	0	53.00
T. M. Dilshan	OB	58	5	185	3	1-38	0	61.66

Also bowled: A. N. P. R. Fernando (RFM) 22–1–128–2; K. M. D. N. Kulasekara (RFM) 44–5–104–0; R. A. S. Lakmal (RFM) 30–5–113–1; A. D. Mathews (RFM) 38–8–117–2.

At Canberra, December 6–8, 2012 (not first-class). **Drawn.** ‡**Cricket Australia Chairman's XI 439-6 dec** (S. O. Henry 207*, U. T. Khawaja 56, G. J. Maxwell 91); **Sri Lankans 396-6** (T. M. Dilshan 101, K. C. Sangakkara 55, H. A. P. W. Jayawardene 71, L. D. Chandimal 57). *Scott Henry, a 23-year-old opener from New South Wales, batted through his side's 100-over innings. But, since the teams chose from 12 players, 11 of whom could bat and 11 field, he was denied a maiden first-class century. The Sri Lankans also enjoyed a benign pitch, with Dilshan retiring out after reaching his hundred. Only 31 overs were bowled on the third day before the game ended by mutual agreement.*

AUSTRALIA v SRI LANKA

First Test Match

GEOFFREY DEAN

At Hobart, December 14–18, 2012. Australia won by 137 runs. Toss: Australia.

Australia secured a dramatic win at 6.05pm on the final evening with only 10.4 overs remaining, after Sri Lanka – with six wickets in hand at tea – had seemed likely to escape with a draw. Two down at the start of the last day, they lost only one batsman in each of the first two sessions but, with 19 overs remaining, and four wickets still required by Australia, they subsided to some hostile left-arm pace bowling from Starc.

Victory for Australia was temporarily tarnished when news broke of Sri Lanka's request for the umpires to examine the ball for alleged tampering by Siddle and Cowan on the third day. The Sri Lankans did not make an official complaint, but match referee Chris Broad sent TV footage of the incidents to the ICC's headquarters in Dubai. No doubt influenced by the fact that the umpires had found no incriminating evidence themselves, the ICC cleared both players of wrongdoing. Siddle could thus properly enjoy the credit that came his way after a career-best return of nine for 104, achieved largely thanks to a full length and reverse swing; only Shane Warne, with ten-fors at Kandy and Galle in March 2004, had secured better figures for Australia against Sri Lanka.

The basis for success had been laid on the first two days, when Australia's batsmen flourished against some insipid bowling on a sluggish, flat pitch, before their own attack made early inroads. Hughes marked his return after more than a year with his first Test fifty on home soil, at the 13th attempt, although he had to graft: at one point he went 80 balls without a boundary. Clarke continued his golden form, while Hussey completed his third hundred in four Tests when, on 96, he miscued a pull off Eranga to deep midwicket, where Mathews dropped the chance and the ball dribbled over the ropes for four. Hussey's unbroken stand of 146 in 39 overs with Wade set up a positive declaration shortly before tea on a rain-affected second day.

Sri Lanka lost four wickets before stumps, with Mahela Jayawardene and Samaraweera both falling to poor shots. From then on, it was always going to be a battle for them to get anything out of the match. Even so, Dilshan played the innings of the Test, an outstanding 147 full of classical off-side strokes, ended only by a Starc yorker; it was his 15th Test hundred. Mathews batted serenely to make 75 and help Dilshan add 161, a Sri Lankan fifth-wicket record against Australia. But it was not always fluent: Siddle was especially economical, before going on to complete his sixth Test five-for.

Australia were fortunate at the start of their second innings, when Cowan was struck in front by Kulasekara; Sri Lanka did not ask for a review of the not-out decision, but Hawk-Eye suggested it was plumb. By the time the opening partnership was finally broken, Cowan and Warner had put on 132, in effect ensuring Sri Lanka's target would be unattainable on a pitch of increasingly uneven bounce; their coach, Graham Ford, later called it a "minefield", though Jayawardene preferred to describe it as "challenging".

Warner completed his second fifty of the match, slog-sweeping Herath for a huge six that carried 93 metres, and switch-hitting him for four. Clarke charged to 57 off 46 balls before retiring with a hamstring strain, whereupon Herath mopped up the tail to complete his seventh Test five-for of 2012, and inch ahead of England's Graeme Swann as the year's leading wicket-taker, with 60.

Sri Lanka never made any pretence of chasing down a target of 393 in 130 overs. Their chances of surviving for a draw were hit when both openers fell before stumps on the fourth evening, Dilshan to Watson's first delivery. But Hilfenhaus was unable to bowl, having broken down in the first innings with a side strain and, with Lyon unthreatening on a surface that offered some turn, Australia found it difficult to prise out a stubborn middle order. In desperation, Clarke gave an over to Wade, the first Australian wicketkeeper to bowl in a Test since Rod Marsh in December 1983; in his first over in all first-class cricket – a maiden – he managed to clock 82mph with his right-arm seamers.

Mahela Jayawardene resisted for 19 before being well caught low by Clarke, the solitary slip, from his 77th ball. Sangakkara, dropped early on, finally fell to his 226th delivery, when Siddle beat him with movement off a full length. And it was Siddle who claimed two more important wickets, ending Samaraweera's cussed 198-minute stay to expose the tail. Starc now produced a fine spell, surprising Prasanna Jayawardene with bounce from round the wicket to have him caught at second slip. Kulasekara edged a beauty that reversed, before Herath was bowled off his boot by a fast yorker. To palpable Australian relief, Eranga gloved a nasty lifter with time running out.

Man of the Match: P. M. Siddle.

Close of play: first day, Australia 299-4 (Clarke 70, Hussey 37); second day, Sri Lanka 87-4 (Dilshan 50); third day, Australia 27-0 (Cowan 16, Warner 8); fourth day, Sri Lanka 65-2 (Sangakkara 18, D. P. M. D. Jayawardene 5).

Australia

First innings		Second innings	
D. A. Warner run out	57	– (2) c H. A. P. W. Jayawardene b Herath	68
E. J. M. Cowan c Eranga b Welagedara	4	– (1) b Welagedara	56
P. J. Hughes b Welagedara	86	– b Eranga	16
S. R. Watson c D. P. M. D. Jayawardene b Welagedara	30	– st H. A. P. W. Jayawardene b Herath	5
*M. J. Clarke c Sangakkara b Eranga	74	– (6) retired hurt	57
M. E. K. Hussey not out	115	– (7) not out	31
†M. S. Wade not out	68	– (5) c Kulasekara b Herath	11
P. M. Siddle (did not bat)		– c H. A. P. W. Jayawardene b Welagedara	4
M. A. Starc (did not bat)		– lbw b Welagedara	5
N. M. Lyon (did not bat)		– b Herath	11
B. W. Hilfenhaus (did not bat)		– lbw b Herath	0
B 1, l-b 3, w 1, n-b 11	16	L-b 10, n-b 4	14
1/18 (2) 2/97 (1) 3/183 (4) 4/198 (3) 5/304 (5) (5 wkts dec, 131 overs)	450	1/132 (2) 2/140 (1) 3/153 (4) 4/165 (3) 5/181 (5) 6/250 (8) 7/256 (9) 8/271 (10) 9/278 (11) (73.5 overs)	278

In the second innings Clarke retired hurt at 238-5.

Kulasekara 32–2–80–0; Welagedara 26–1–130–3; Eranga 25–5–90–1; Mathews 15–3–41–0; Dilshan 7–0–30–0; Herath 26–4–75–0. *Second innings*—Kulasekara 12–3–24–0; Welagedara 22–3–89–3; Dilshan 2–0–2–0; Eranga 11–0–53–1; Mathews 5–2–5–0; Herath 21.5–2–95–5.

Sri Lanka

F. D. M. Karunaratne c Wade b Hilfenhaus	14 – b Starc	30
T. M. Dilshan b Starc	147 – c Wade b Watson	11
K. C. Sangakkara c Hussey b Siddle	4 – lbw b Siddle	63
*D. P. M. D. Jayawardene lbw b Watson	12 – c Clarke b Siddle	19
T. T. Samaraweera c Wade b Lyon	7 – lbw b Siddle	49
A. D. Mathews lbw b Siddle	75 – c Wade b Siddle	19
†H. A. P. W. Jayawardene lbw b Siddle	40 – c Hussey b Starc	21
K. M. D. N. Kulasekara c sub (J. C. Silk) b Lyon	23 – c Wade b Starc	9
H. M. R. K. B. Herath lbw b Siddle	0 – b Starc	8
R. M. S. Eranga not out	5 – c Wade b Starc	6
U. W. M. B. C. A. Welagedara c Hussey b Siddle	0 – not out	0
B 2, l-b 6, n-b 1	9 B 10, l-b 8, w 1, n-b 1	20
1/25 (1) 2/42 (3) 3/70 (4) 4/87 (5) 5/248 (6) 6/289 (2) 7/316 (7) 8/320 (9) 9/336 (8) 10/336 (11) (109.3 overs)	336 1/26 (2) 2/47 (1) 3/112 (4) 4/151 (3) 5/201 (6) 6/218 (5) 7/235 (7) 8/247 (8) 9/250 (9) 10/255 (10) (119.2 overs)	255

Starc 24–3–104–1; Hilfenhaus 12.2–3–30–1; Lyon 25–8–76–2; Siddle 25.3–11–54–5; Watson 20.4–5–55–1; Clarke 2–0–9–0. *Second innings*—Starc 28.2–7–63–5; Siddle 26–11–50–4; Watson 27–6–54–1; Lyon 32–12–57–0; Hussey 1–0–5–0; Warner 4–0–8–0; Wade 1–1–0–0.

Umpires: A. L. Hill and N. J. Llong. Third umpire: Aleem Dar.

AUSTRALIA v SRI LANKA

Second Test Match

At Melbourne, December 26–28, 2012. Australia won by an innings and 201 runs. Toss: Sri Lanka. Test debut: J. M. Bird.

It may have been Boxing Day nerves. It may have been a feeling of foreboding on their return, 17 years to the day, to the ground where Muttiah Muralitharan was famously no-balled by Darrell Hair. It may also have been lingering disappointment at losing the First Test on the final evening. Whatever the reason, Sri Lanka's opening-day performance was so abject it ended the series in the space of a few hours, setting them on the path to the third-heaviest defeat in their history.

Australia's dramatically recast attack could scarcely believe their good fortune at a string of wrong-headed strokes on a pitch offering bounce but no great lateral movement. The result was further soured for Sri Lanka by injuries that ended the tours of wicketkeeper Prasanna Jayawardene, left-arm seamer Welagedara and, most critically, Sangakkara, the only batsman to make a fight of it on Boxing Day.

Mahela Jayawardene had made a sound enough call at the toss, batting first against opponents who had lost Ben Hilfenhaus to injury and Mitchell Starc to injury-prevention. In their places came the Tasmania debutant Jackson Bird and the recalled Johnson, who carried out their commissions handsomely. Well though Australia bowled, the only blameless Sri Lankan batsman was the first out – the left-hander Karunaratne, who was first cornered by Bird's swing into him, then edged a nicely pitched cutter going across. The rest were guilty of anything from looseness outside off stump (Mahela Jayawardene and Mathews), to hare-brained swats at deliveries that required greater respect (Dilshan and Samaraweera).

Sangakkara alone fought the tide, punching some admirable drives down the ground off Johnson, and raised his bat to a crowd of 67,138 when he became the second Sri Lankan, after Mahela Jayawardene, and the 11th in all, to pass 10,000 Test runs; like Brian Lara and Sachin Tendulkar before him, he got there in his 195th innings (no one has done it more quickly). But he could only look on as Johnson broke Prasanna Jayawardene's thumb with a snorter that was pouched in the slips, then bounced out Prasad next ball. Sangakkara was soon to follow, when he miscued a hook, and Wade sprinted from behind the stumps to dive near the boundary and claim a rousing catch.

By tea, Australia were batting. Warner was soon taking advantage of the absence of the tidy Nuwan Kulasekara, unfit owing to a rib not merely tickled but cracked by Siddle at Hobart: in little more than an hour, Warner had hurried Australia into a dominant position. He miscalculated at 62, pulling Mathews into the deep, before Hughes was wastefully run out, and Cowan – perhaps still distracted by his part in Hughes's demise six balls earlier – nicked to slip. But then Watson and Clarke settled in. Helped by a couple of difficult dropped chances on the first evening, they were not parted until they had added 194. Clarke, who had shrugged off a hamstring niggle to play, reached his fifth century of 2012 – though unlike the other four, this one did not become a double or triple. Watson again fell short of three figures, but it later emerged he had batted with a calf strain suffered while bowling. Johnson ensured a lead of over 300 with a measured innings against a team wounded further by the loss of Welagedara to a hamstring tear, and missed out on a chance of a second Test century only because Bird demonstrated a modesty with the bat to rival Glenn McGrath.

Batting again on the third morning, Sri Lanka were all but ruined inside the first over. From the third ball, Karunaratne saw two runs where Dilshan glimpsed only one, and was wretchedly run out. Johnson's next delivery leapt at Dilshan and lobbed off glove and thigh to short leg. Mahela Jayawardene and Samaraweera were undone by Bird's immaculate line and seam movement, and Sri Lankan misery was complete when Johnson whirred down a ball that fractured Sangakkara's left hand so badly it would require surgery.

A casualty ward of three meant the match concluded when the seventh wicket fell. Only once before, when five Indians were absent hurt in Jamaica in 1975-76, had a Test innings ended with fewer wickets down. Technically, it was Sri Lanka's shortest completed innings, beating by two balls the 24.4 overs they had lasted at Cardiff in 2011. "It feels like the worst Test match I've been involved in," said their coach Graham Ford. Much like England's mauling of Australia here two years earlier, the knockout blow had been landed on Boxing Day.

Man of the Match: M. G. Johnson.

Close of play: first day, Australia 150-3 (Watson 13, Clarke 20); second day, Australia 440-8 (Johnson 73, Lyon 0).

Sri Lanka

F. D. M. Karunaratne c Wade b Bird	5	– run out	1
T. M. Dilshan b Johnson	11	– c Cowan b Johnson	0
K. C. Sangakkara c Wade b Johnson	58	– retired hurt	27
*D. P. M. D. Jayawardene c Wade b Siddle	3	– b Bird	0
T. T. Samaraweera c Warner b Bird	10	– lbw b Bird	1
A. D. Mathews c Hussey b Siddle	15	– b Johnson	35
†H. A. P. W. Jayawardene c Hughes b Johnson	24	– absent hurt	
K. T. G. D. Prasad c Wade b Johnson	0	– (7) c Hughes b Lyon	17
H. M. R. K. B. Herath c Cowan b Lyon	14	– (8) not out	11
R. M. S. Eranga not out	4	– (9) c Cowan b Siddle	0
U. W. M. B. C. A. Welagedara c Hussey b Lyon	0	– absent hurt	
L-b 5, n-b 7	12	L-b 10, n-b 1	11
1/13 (1) 2/19 (2) 3/37 (4) 4/79 (5) 5/99 (6) 6/134 (7) 7/134 (8) 8/147 (3) 9/156 (9) 10/156 (11) (43.4 overs)	156	1/1 (1) 2/1 (2) 3/3 (4) 4/13 (5) 5/74 (6) 6/102 (7) 7/103 (9) (24.2 overs)	103

In the second innings Sangakkara retired hurt at 62-4.

Johnson 14–2–63–4; Bird 13–5–32–2; Siddle 8–1–30–2; Watson 3–2–3–0; Lyon 5.4–0–23–2. *Second innings*—Johnson 8–0–16–2; Bird 9–1–29–2; Siddle 5.2–0–32–1; Lyon 2–0–16–1.

Australia

E. J. M. Cowan c D. P. M. D. Jayawardene b Prasad	36		N. M. Lyon c sub (L. D. Chandimal) b Mathews	1
D. A. Warner c Prasad b Mathews	62		J. M. Bird b Eranga	0
P. J. Hughes run out	10			
S. R. Watson c Samaraweera b Prasad	83			
*M. J. Clarke c D. P. M. D. Jayawardene b Eranga	106		B 9, l-b 5, w 6, n-b 2	22
M. E. K. Hussey c Herath b Dilshan	34			
†M. S. Wade c Eranga b Prasad	1		1/95 (2) 2/117 (3) (134.4 overs)	460
M. G. Johnson not out	92		3/117 (1) 4/311 (5)	
P. M. Siddle c D. P. M. D. Jayawardene b Eranga	13		5/313 (4) 6/315 (7) 7/376 (6) 8/434 (9) 9/451 (10) 10/460 (11)	

Welagedara 14.4–6–38–0; Eranga 27–2–109–3; Prasad 26–2–106–3; Mathews 16–3–60–2; Herath 39–7–95–0; Dilshan 12–1–38–1.

Umpires: Aleem Dar and N. J. Llong. Third umpire: A. L. Hill.

AUSTRALIA v SRI LANKA

Third Test Match

At Sydney, January 3–6, 2013. Australia won by five wickets. Toss: Australia.

Australia completed a 3–0 sweep in Mike Hussey's 79th and last Test, despite complicating the task with curious decisions at the selection table and the toss. The occasion was given a still greater sense of pathos by the death of Tony Greig the day after the Melbourne Test had ended. Greig's family and his ex-colleagues in the Channel Nine commentary box joined the teams for a moment's silence on the first morning, and many in the crowd wore his trademark wide-brimmed sunhat in homage.

Hussey had stunned his team-mates during the Second Test when he informed them of his intention to quit international cricket, so his selection here felt odd, a chance missed to build for the future with the series won. Four seamers were picked on a pitch drier than it had appeared two days earlier, so a debut for the spin-bowling all-rounder Glenn Maxwell was deferred. Wade was promoted to No. 6, and Johnson to No. 7.

With the fast-bowling resources at his disposal, Clarke was obliged to bowl after winning the toss, and he was grateful for Bird's consistency as the rest strained for effect on an ideal day to bat. Jayawardene made his first half-century away from home since November 2009, while Thirimanne, in for the injured Kumar Sangakkara, showed promise

---

HIGHEST TEST AVERAGE FOR AUSTRALIA AT HOME

Avge		*M*	*Runs*	*HS*	*100s*
98.22	D. G. Bradman	33	4,322	299*	18
75.78	R. M. Cowper	9	1,061	307	3
64.93	**M. J. Clarke**	**47**	**4,156**	**329***	**14**
61.19	**M. E. K. Hussey**	**45**	**3,794**	**195**	**14**
57.88	M. L. Hayden	56	5,210	380	21
57.83	K. D. Walters	37	3,065	242	10
56.97	**R. T. Ponting**	**92**	**7,578**	**257**	**23**
56.36	W. M. Lawry	30	2,818	205	8
54.39	G. S. Chappell	55	4,515	204	16
53.80	B. C. Booth	13	1,076	169	4
52.62	M. J. Slater	33	2,842	219	9
52.29	A. L. Hassett	23	1,778	198*	5

Qualification: 1,000 runs.

Rick Rycroft, AP/PA

Way to go: Mike Hussey is run out following an optimistic call by his captain, but his last act as an Australia player was to guide them to victory in the second innings.

and application. He was stopped short of a maiden century by Lyon's flight and a fine diving catch from Warner, while Starc's swerving yorker to Chandimal with the second new ball ensured the total would fall short of 300.

Hughes and Warner led Australia's reply with panache, after Cowan ran himself out – but the failure of either to go on to a century after a stand of 130 left Australia momentarily vulnerable. To the dismay of the crowd, Hussey became the fourth home batsman to be run out in the series, done in by his captain's optimistic call, and Clarke's own dismissal seven overs later gave Sri Lanka the chance to limit the lead. But Wade reprised his fine century against West Indies in Dominica the previous April, and guided Siddle and Bird in damaging partnerships. Bird faced only 11 balls while Wade streaked from 70 to his second Test hundred, reaching three figures with a crunching square-drive that left the deep fielders motionless. After he was dropped at fine leg two balls later, trying to hook Lakmal into the Victor Trumper Stand, Clarke declared.

Dilshan did not linger, before a century stand between Karunaratne and Jayawardene all but erased the deficit of 138. At 155 for two, Sri Lanka were almost on level terms, but a patch of brainless batting to rival the first-day meltdown at Melbourne tilted the match decisively towards Australia. Thirimanne hooked to fine leg, Samaraweera ran heedlessly down to Lyon and skied a catch, and Mathews was run out in a moment of confusion with Jayawardene, who then snicked a dejected drive at Siddle. Those four wickets for 23 meant Australia's chase would never be truly threatening, despite Chandimal's laudable efforts on the fourth morning and a surface by now taking plenty of turn.

Warner fell first ball as Australia set off in pursuit of 141, but Cowan dug in for more than two hours and Hussey was there at the end, although the crowd would have preferred him, rather than Johnson, to have hit the winning run. Clarke expressed mild satisfaction, and Jayawardene profound regret, while Hussey signed off happily from Test matches, passing the honour of singing the team victory song, *Under the Southern Cross*, to Lyon.

Man of the Match: J. M. Bird. *Man of the Series:* M. J. Clarke.

Close of play: first day, Sri Lanka 294; second day, Australia 342-6 (Wade 47, Siddle 16); third day, Sri Lanka 225-7 (Chandimal 22, Herath 9).

Sri Lanka

F. D. M. Karunaratne c Hussey b Bird	5	– c Wade b Bird	85
T. M. Dilshan c Wade b Bird	34	– c Hughes b Johnson	5
*D. P. M. D. Jayawardene c Clarke b Starc	72	– c Clarke b Siddle	60
H. D. R. L. Thirimanne c Warner b Lyon	91	– c Bird b Johnson	7
T. T. Samaraweera lbw b Siddle	12	– c Hussey b Lyon	0
A. D. Mathews c Hussey b Starc	15	– run out	16
†L. D. Chandimal b Starc	24	– not out	62
K. T. G. D. Prasad c Starc b Siddle	2	– c Wade b Starc	15
H. M. R. K. B. Herath c Siddle b Bird	5	– b Bird	10
R. A. S. Lakmal c Hussey b Bird	5	– b Johnson	0
A. N. P. R. Fernando not out	17	– c Wade b Bird	9
L-b 8, w 3, n-b 1	12	B 1, l-b 4, w 1, n-b 3	9
1/26 (1) 2/72 (2) 3/134 (3) 4/167 (5) 5/222 (6) 6/250 (4) 7/256 (8) 8/271 (7) 9/273 (9) 10/294 (10) (87.4 overs)	294	1/24 (2) 2/132 (1) 3/155 (4) 4/158 (5) 5/178 (6) 6/178 (3) 7/202 (8) 8/235 (9) 9/237 (10) 10/278 (11) (81.2 overs)	278

Starc 19–0–71–3; Bird 19.4–10–41–4; Siddle 15–3–46–2; Johnson 13–1–58–0; Lyon 19–2–69–1; Hussey 2–1–1–0. *Second innings*—Starc 12–1–49–1; Bird 21.2–5–76–3; Johnson 15–3–34–3; Siddle 17–4–42–1; Lyon 15–1–66–1; Hussey 1–0–6–0.

Australia

D. A. Warner c Prasad b Dilshan	85	– (2) c Jayawardene b Lakmal	0
E. J. M. Cowan run out	4	– (1) lbw b Herath	36
P. J. Hughes c Chandimal b Herath	87	– lbw b Herath	34
*M. J. Clarke c Karunaratne b Herath	50	– c Thirimanne b Dilshan	29
M. E. K. Hussey run out	25	– not out	27
†M. S. Wade not out	102	– b Herath	9
M. G. Johnson c Chandimal b Fernando	13	– not out	1
P. M. Siddle c Chandimal b Fernando	38		
M. A. Starc lbw b Herath	2		
N. M. Lyon b Herath	4		
J. M. Bird not out	6		
L-b 6, w 7, n-b 3	16	L-b 5	5
1/36 (2) 2/166 (1) 3/195 (3) 4/251 (5) 5/271 (4) 6/307 (7) 7/384 (8) 8/387 (9) 9/393 (10) (9 wkts dec, 107 overs)	432	1/0 (2) 2/45 (3) 3/104 (4) 4/108 (1) 5/132 (6) (5 wkts, 42.5 overs)	141

Lakmal 24–4–95–0; Fernando 20–1–114–2; Prasad 11–0–53–0; Mathews 2–0–11–0; Dilshan 19–2–58–1; Herath 31–3–95–4. *Second innings*—Dilshan 18–2–57–1; Lakmal 6–1–18–1; Herath 16.5–0–47–3; Fernando 2–0–14–0.

Umpires: Aleem Dar and A. L. Hill. Third umpire: N. J. Llong.
Series referee: B. C. Broad.

AUSTRALIA v SRI LANKA

First One-Day International

At Melbourne, January 11, 2013 (day/night). Australia won by 107 runs. Toss: Australia. One-day international debuts: A. J. Finch, P. J. Hughes, U. T. Khawaja.

On the sort of pitch most batsmen would gladly roll up and carry around, a refreshed and hungry – if less familiar – Australian side recorded a thumping victory. Hughes belatedly won his first cap in the 50-over format, and duly advanced to a century from 123 balls. But his fellow first-timers Aaron Finch and Usman Khawaja fell cheaply. The only other occasion a Test-playing nation had given debuts to the top three in the same one-day international was when Australia pitted Graeme Wood, Rick Darling and Graham Yallop against West Indies in Antigua in February 1978 in the absence of the World Series Cricket signings. Bailey captained here while Clarke nursed a hamstring, and his own innings was brimful of crisp shots, including the one that led to his demise on the midwicket boundary. Swift between the wickets and assertive with the bat, David Hussey (whose brother had been denied a farewell series by the selectors after announcing his imminent retirement) rounded off an imposing total with 60 from 34 balls. Sri Lanka never threatened to match the required rate, despite neat innings by Dilshan and Chandimal. McKay collected four wickets, while three were run out.

Man of the Match: P. J. Hughes.

Australia

A. J. Finch c Chandimal b B. A. W. Mendis	16
P. J. Hughes c Chandimal b Malinga	112
U. T. Khawaja run out	3
*G. J. Bailey c B. M. A. J. Mendis b Mathews	89
D. J. Hussey not out	60
G. J. Maxwell c B. A. W. Mendis b Kulasekara	5
†B. J. Haddin not out	10
B 2, l-b 3, w 5	10
1/53 (1) 2/72 (3) 3/212 (2) 4/241 (4) 5/248 (6) (5 wkts, 50 overs)	305
10 overs: 52-0	

M. G. Johnson, M. A. Starc, C. J. McKay and X. J. Doherty did not bat.

Kulasekara 10–0–53–1; Malinga 10–1–61–1; Mathews 8–0–46–1; B. A. W. Mendis 10–0–62–1; Dilshan 4–0–17–0; Perera 4–0–28–0; B. M. A. J. Mendis 4–0–33–0.

Sri Lanka

W. U. Tharanga c Haddin b Starc	1
T. M. Dilshan run out	51
*D. P. M. D. Jayawardene c Finch b McKay	5
†L. D. Chandimal c Haddin b McKay	73
A. D. Mathews run out	12
H. D. R. L. Thirimanne run out	0
B. M. A. J. Mendis c Bailey b Johnson	20
N. L. T. C. Perera c Bailey b Johnson	4
K. M. D. N. Kulasekara c Bailey b McKay	18
S. L. Malinga not out	1
B. A. W. Mendis c Haddin b McKay	0
B 2, l-b 2, w 9	13
1/8 (1) 2/17 (3) 3/111 (2) 4/128 (5) 5/128 (6) 6/167 (7) 7/169 (4) 8/194 (8) 9/198 (9) 10/198 (11) (40 overs)	198
10 overs: 33-2	

Starc 6–0–25–1; McKay 8–0–33–4; Johnson 9–1–43–2; Doherty 8–0–41–0; Maxwell 4–0–28–0; Hussey 5–0–24–0.

Umpires: R. A. Kettleborough and P. R. Reiffel. Third umpire: M. Erasmus.

AUSTRALIA v SRI LANKA

Second One-Day International

At Adelaide, January 13, 2013 (day/night). Sri Lanka won by eight wickets. Toss: Sri Lanka. One-day international debuts: B. C. J. Cutting, K. W. Richardson; M. D. K. J. Perera.

Until now, Sri Lanka's tour had been winless and largely joyless, but they managed to draw renewed life from an Adelaide Oval pitch that aided their swing and seam bowlers while exposing Australia's weakness on surfaces less concrete than the one at Melbourne. Australia also complicated matters by shuffling in Smith for only one match, a decision many found baffling. Sri Lanka's quicks all moved the ball just enough to find edges, while Australia's recognition that this was not a pitch on which bowling could be bullied was so slow that it took Nos. 7 and 8, Haddin and the debutant Queensland all-rounder Ben Cutting, to establish the only meaningful stand of the innings. Chasing a modest target, Sri Lanka lost Tharanga to McKay's angle, before Dilshan and Thirimanne embarked on a composed partnership of 137. Thirimanne was not always fluent, but completed victory – and his maiden international century – by cutting Maxwell for his 12th four.

Man of the Match: H. D. R. L. Thirimanne.

Australia

A. J. Finch c B. M. A. J. Mendis b Mathews . . . 4
P. J. Hughes lbw b Kulasekara 3
*G. J. Bailey c Thirimanne b Malinga. 26
D. J. Hussey run out 29
S. P. D. Smith c M. D. K. J. Perera b N. L. T. C. Perera . 8
G. J. Maxwell c M. D. K. J. Perera b Mathews . 8
†B. J. Haddin c Thirimanne b B. A. W. Mendis . 50
B. C. J. Cutting c M. D. K. J. Perera b Malinga . 27
K. W. Richardson lbw b Malinga 0
C. J. McKay c M. D. K. J. Perera b N. L. T. C. Perera . 4
X. J. Doherty not out 5
B 1, l-b 1, w 4 6

1/7 (1) 2/12 (2) 3/51 (3) 4/60 (5) 5/82 (4) 6/83 (6) 7/140 (8) 8/140 (9) 9/146 (10) 10/170 (7) (46.5 overs) 170
10 overs: 21-2

Kulasekara 9–0–24–1; Mathews 10–1–24–2; N. L. T. C. Perera 9–0–40–2; Malinga 9–0–32–3; B. A. W. Mendis 7.5–0–41–1; B. M. A. J. Mendis 2–0–7–0.

Sri Lanka

W. U. Tharanga c Haddin b McKay 0
T. M. Dilshan c Maxwell b Cutting. 51
H. D. R. L. Thirimanne not out 102
†M. D. K. J. Perera not out 14
L-b 3, w 2 5

1/0 (1) 2/137 (2) (2 wkts, 40.1 overs) 172
10 overs: 32-1

*D. P. M. D. Jayawardene, A. D. Mathews, B. M. A. J. Mendis, N. L. T. C. Perera, K. M. D. N. Kulasekara, S. L. Malinga and B. A. W. Mendis did not bat.

McKay 10–0–43–1; Richardson 6–3–15–0; Cutting 10–0–42–1; Doherty 7–0–34–0; Smith 4–0–16–0; Maxwell 3.1–0–19–0.

Umpires: M. Erasmus and S. D. Fry. Third umpire: R. A. Kettleborough.

AUSTRALIA v SRI LANKA

Third One-Day International

At Brisbane, January 18, 2013 (day/night). Sri Lanka won by four wickets. Toss: Australia.

Bowing to public pressure for the return of more recognisable names, Australia's selectors recalled Clarke, Warner and Wade. If the promoter's billboard was strengthened, the scoreboard was not: the prodigious inswing of Kulasekara razed Australia for 74, their third-lowest total in one-day internationals behind a pair of 70s, against England at Edgbaston in 1977 and New Zealand at Adelaide in 1985-86. Bending the ball unerringly into the right-handers on a warm Brisbane afternoon, Kulasekara scooped five of the first six wickets as Australia nosedived to 40 for nine, before the last pair almost doubled the score. Sri Lanka's pursuit was not plain sailing – Johnson grabbed three wickets in six deliveries – but Kushal Perera held his nerve to ensure one batting calamity would not be followed by another. The entire match lasted just 280 balls, one in the eye for those who had argued that bigger-name players offered greater value for spectators' money.

Man of the Match: K. M. D. N. Kulasekara.

Australia

D. A. Warner c Eranga b Mathews	4	M. A. Starc not out	22
P. J. Hughes c Jayawardene b Kulasekara	3	C. J. McKay c M. D. K. J. Perera b Malinga	0
*M. J. Clarke b Kulasekara	9	X. J. Doherty c Mendis b Eranga	15
D. J. Hussey c M. D. K. J. Perera b Kulasekara	4	L-b 2, w 3	5
G. J. Bailey lbw b Kulasekara	0	1/4 (1) 2/13 (2) (26.4 overs)	74
†M. S. Wade c Dilshan b Malinga	8	3/21 (4) 4/21 (5) 5/28 (3)	
M. C. Henriques b Kulasekara	2	6/30 (7) 7/35 (8) 8/38 (6)	
M. G. Johnson b Malinga	2	9/40 (10) 10/74 (11)	10 overs: 26-4

Mathews 4–0–10–1; Kulasekara 10–2–22–5; Malinga 7–2–14–3; N. L. T. C. Perera 3–0–14–0; Eranga 2.4–0–12–1.

Sri Lanka

*D. P. M. D. Jayawardene c Warner b McKay	1	N. L. T. C. Perera not out	4
T. M. Dilshan c Clarke b Johnson	22		
H. D. R. L. Thirimanne c Warner b Johnson	7	L-b 1, w 3, n-b 1	5
†M. D. K. J. Perera not out	22		
A. D. Mathews c Starc b Johnson	0	1/4 (1) 2/33 (2) (6 wkts, 20 overs)	75
W. U. Tharanga c Clarke b Starc	12	3/37 (3) 4/37 (5)	
B. M. A. J. Mendis c McKay b Starc	2	5/63 (6) 6/71 (7)	10 overs: 33-2

K. M. D. N. Kulasekara, S. L. Malinga and R. M. S. Eranga did not bat.

McKay 8–0–31–1; Starc 7–0–25–2; Johnson 3–0–11–3; Henriques 2–0–7–0.

Umpires: R. A. Kettleborough and P. R. Reiffel. Third umpire: M. Erasmus.

AUSTRALIA v SRI LANKA

Fourth One-Day International

At Sydney, January 20, 2013 (day/night). No result. Toss: Australia.

Sri Lanka were well placed to seal the series after restricting Australia to 222. But rain interrupted their pursuit after 3.2 overs and, to the enormous frustration of the visitors – and a crowd that had stayed on optimistically through the showers – the umpires eventually decided the after-effects of light showers would not dry in time to permit a restart. This was a relief for Australia's batsmen, who had again been exposed by the moving ball: they slipped to 182 for nine before Starc's late hitting spared some more blushes. Hussey's skittish stay raised eyebrows, and he was dropped after the next match. Cricket Australia later wrote to the ICC, asking for a more "fan-centric" approach to decisions about the resumption of play.

Australia

D. A. Warner lbw b N. L. T. C. Perera	60	C. J. McKay b Kulasekara	2
P. J. Hughes c Chandimal b Kulasekara	1	X. J. Doherty not out	10
*M. J. Clarke lbw b Kulasekara	20		
D. J. Hussey c Thirimanne b Malinga	1	B 1, l-b 7, w 2	10
G. J. Bailey c N. L. T. C. Perera b Herath	22		
†M. S. Wade c Kulasekara b N. L. T. C. Perera	31	1/4 (2) 2/50 (3) (9 wkts, 50 overs)	222
M. C. Henriques lbw b Herath	3	3/53 (4) 4/93 (5)	
M. G. Johnson lbw b Malinga	10	5/125 (1) 6/130 (7) 7/145 (8)	
M. A. Starc not out	52	8/166 (6) 9/182 (10)	10 overs: 50-2

Mathews 10–1–50–0; Kulasekara 10–2–30–3; Malinga 10–2–33–2; N. L. T. C. Perera 10–0–64–2; Herath 10–0–37–2.

Sri Lanka

*D. P. M. D. Jayawardene not out	4
T. M. Dilshan not out	9
W 1	1
(no wkt, 3.2 overs)	14

H. D. R. L. Thirimanne, †L. D. Chandimal, M. D. K. J. Perera, A. D. Mathews, B. M. A. J. Mendis, N. L. T. C. Perera, K. M. D. N. Kulasekara, H. M. R. K. B. Herath and S. L. Malinga did not bat.

McKay 2–0–13–0; Starc 1.2–0–1–0.

Umpires: M. Erasmus and P. R. Reiffel. Third umpire: R. A. Kettleborough.

AUSTRALIA v SRI LANKA

Fifth One-Day International

At Hobart, January 23, 2013 (day/night). Australia won by 32 runs. Toss: Sri Lanka.

Australia ended the series as they began it, with a Hughes century and a sturdy victory, thus denying Sri Lanka the series win that had seemed theirs for the taking at Sydney. Hughes's innings, which spanned 154 balls, was nicely modulated: he worked through a difficult early patch of accurate bowling and some scratchy timing before blooming in the closing overs. Even so, Sri Lanka's target was far from unreachable, and it took some diligence from the Australian attack to prevent them from getting there. The most strident defenders were Doherty, who had barely bowled in the series but wheeled away intelligently on his home ground, and Henriques, who showed his medium-pace had developed to the point where it could be relied upon at international level. Soon afterwards, they were both chosen for the Test tour of India.

Man of the Match: P. J. Hughes. *Man of the Series:* K. M. D. N. Kulasekara.

Australia

†M. S. Wade lbw b Kulasekara	23	M. C. Henriques not out	9
D. A. Warner b Dilshan	10	L-b 2, w 5	7
P. J. Hughes not out	138		
*G. J. Bailey c and b N. L. T. C. Perera	17	1/31 (2) 2/37 (1) (5 wkts, 50 overs)	247
D. J. Hussey run out	34	3/97 (4) 4/195 (5)	
G. J. Maxwell c Thirimanne b Malinga	9	5/218 (6) 10 overs: 37-2	

M. G. Johnson, M. A. Starc, C. J. McKay and X. J. Doherty did not bat.

Dilshan 7–3–22–1; Kulasekara 10–1–57–1; Mathews 7–0–44–0; Malinga 10–1–49–1; Herath 10–2–34–0; N. L. T. C. Perera 6–0–39–1.

Sri Lanka

*D. P. M. D. Jayawardene c Starc b Doherty	38	H. M. R. K. B. Herath c Henriques b McKay	2
T. M. Dilshan c Wade b Henriques	19	S. L. Malinga c Johnson b McKay	2
H. D. R. L. Thirimanne c Hussey b Doherty	1		
†L. D. Chandimal b Doherty	6	L-b 12, w 6, n-b 1	19
A. D. Mathews c Bailey b Johnson	67		
M. D. K. J. Perera c Warner b Johnson	14	1/57 (1) 2/62 (3) (48.3 overs)	215
B. M. A. J. Mendis b Henriques	26	3/71 (2) 4/77 (4) 5/108 (6)	
N. L. T. C. Perera b Henriques	7	6/187 (7) 7/187 (5) 8/195 (8)	
K. M. D. N. Kulasekara not out	14	9/200 (10) 10/215 (11) 10 overs: 50-0	

McKay 9.3–0–51–2; Starc 9–0–48–0; Johnson 10–0–45–2; Doherty 8–1–21–3; Henriques 10–1–32–3; Maxwell 2–0–6–0.

Umpires: S. D. Fry and R. A. Kettleborough. Third umpire: M. Erasmus.
Series referee: J. Srinath.

AUSTRALIA v SRI LANKA

First Twenty20 International

At Sydney (Stadium Australia), January 26, 2013 (floodlit). Sri Lanka won by five wickets. Toss: Australia. Twenty20 international debuts: B. C. J. Cutting; M. D. K. J. Perera.

Fine bowling and fielding at the top and tail of Australia's innings presented Sri Lanka with a modest chase, and eventually a comfortable victory on a slow surface at Sydney's Olympic Stadium. The Australian batting was carried almost entirely by Warner, who made a fine 90 but lacked support, with the recalled Marsh particularly tardy in the early overs. Sri Lanka's successful pursuit contained a series of cameos, while Australia's fielding and late-innings bowling failed to match their opponents'.

Man of the Match: D. A. Warner.

Australia

		B	*4*	*6*
D. A. Warner *not out*	90	62	5	3
A. J. Finch *c 1 b 9*	1	3	0	0
S. E. Marsh *run out*	6	17	0	0
*G. J. Bailey *c 2 b 7*	11	9	0	1
A. C. Voges *not out*	25	29	0	0
B 1, l-b 2, w 1	4			
6 overs: 31-1 (20 overs)	137-3			

1/8 2/31 3/53

†M. S. Wade, G. J. Maxwell, B. C. J. Cutting, M. A. Starc, X. J. Doherty and B. Laughlin did not bat.

Mathews 4–0–39–0; Kulasekara 4–0–21–1; Malinga 4–0–19–0; N. L. T. C. Perera 4–0–29–1; B. A. W. Mendis 4–0–26–0.

Sri Lanka

		B	*4*	*6*
M. D. K. J. Perera *c 6 b 7*	33	22	2	1
T. M. Dilshan *c 11 b 10*	16	21	0	1
D. P. M. D. Jayawardene *b 10*	8	10	1	0
†L. D. Chandimal *c 8 b 7*	5	6	0	0
*A. D. Mathews *not out*	35	27	3	1
H. D. R. L. Thirimanne *c 5 b 9*	20	15	2	0
N. L. T. C. Perera *not out*	19	12	0	2
L-b 2, w 1	3			
6 overs: 45-0 (18.5 overs)	139-5			

1/46 2/53 3/61 4/69 5/104

B. M. A. J. Mendis, K. M. D. N. Kulasekara, B. A. W. Mendis and S. L. Malinga did not bat.

Doherty 4–0–21–2; Starc 4–0–19–1; Cutting 3–0–27–0; Laughlin 3.5–0–46–0; Maxwell 3–0–15–2; Finch 1–0–9–0.

Umpires: S. D. Fry and P. R. Reiffel. Third umpire: J. D. Ward.

AUSTRALIA v SRI LANKA

Second Twenty20 International

At Melbourne, January 28, 2013 (floodlit). Sri Lanka won by two runs (D/L). Toss: Australia.

Another rain-interrupted contest ended in a narrow Sri Lankan victory, soothing their initial irritation when the match resumed in conditions similar to those in which the Sydney one-dayer had been abandoned. Jayawardene and Tissara Perera took heavy toll of Laughlin at the death after the bowlers had seemed in control for much of the innings. The rain meant Australia's target was revised to 122 from 15 overs, but they always looked slightly off the pace. Finally, after striking his first two balls to the boundary, the aggressive Maxwell swung at the last delivery of the match – and found only thin air. The game concluded in acrimony as Maxwell, Warner and Wade clashed with Tissara Perera and Jayawardene, the trouble flaring after the batsmen told the Sri Lankans to get a move on during a long discussion about fielding positions before the final ball. The unsavoury scenes – dismissed by both captains as "heat of the moment stuff" – were reminiscent of some of the Big Bash League's excesses.

Man of the Match: N. L. T. C. Perera.

Sri Lanka

		B	4	6
T. M. Dilshan *b 8*	6	10	0	0
M. D. K. J. Perera *c 4 b 5*	15	17	3	0
†L. D. Chandimal *c 4 b 11*	5	9	1	0
D. P. M. D. Jayawardene *not out*	61	45	5	2
B. M. A. J. Mendis *c 8 b 10*	25	24	3	0
N. L. T. C. Perera *not out*	35	15	3	2
B 1, l-b 8, w 5	14			

6 overs: 36-2 (20 overs) 161-4

1/15 2/33 3/39 4/102

*A. D. Mathews, K. M. D. N. Kulasekara, B. A. W. Mendis, S. L. Malinga and A. Dananjaya did not bat.

Maxwell 4–0–23–1; Starc 4–0–35–0; Faulkner 4–0–24–1; Laughlin 4–0–40–1; Doherty 4–0–30–1.

Australia

		B	4	6
A. J. Finch *lbw b 9*	7	6	1	0
D. A. Warner *c 6 b 8*	7	6	1	0
S. E. Marsh *not out*	47	40	2	2
*G. J. Bailey *c 2 b 6*	45	36	4	0
G. J. Maxwell *not out*	8	3	2	0
B 1, l-b 2, w 1, n-b 1	5			

6 overs: 28-2 (15 overs) 119-3

1/10 2/20 3/106

A. C. Voges, †M. S. Wade, J. P. Faulkner, M. A. Starc, X. J. Doherty and B. Laughlin did not bat.

Dilshan 2–0–10–0; Kulasekara 3–0–18–1; B. A. W. Mendis 3–0–25–1; Malinga 3–0–26–0; Dananjaya 1–0–12–0; N. L. T. C. Perera 3–0–25–1.

Umpires: S. D. Fry and J. D. Ward. Third umpire: P. R. Reiffel.
Series referee: J. Srinath.

QUADRANGULAR UNDER-19 SERIES, 2011-12

1. India. 2. Australia 3. England 4. New Zealand

Any tournament in which a team can finish bottom in the group stage yet win overall is liable to cause head-scratching. But this quadrangular series was deliberately designed to allow these four countries a long look at conditions in Queensland ahead of the 2012 Under-19 World Cup, to be held here four months later in August (see page 879).

After losing all three group games, India bounced back with two superb bowling displays against England and Australia in the semi-final and final to carry off the trophy. And their captain, Unmukt Chand, showed a dazzling sense of the big occasion, scoring 94 and 112 not out.

England had an off-day in the semi, but chased successfully in their other four matches. They had two of the competition's three leading scorers – Daniel Bell-Drummond, with 287, and Ben Foakes, with 227; and two of the three top wicket-takers – Adam Ball and Aneesh Kapil, with nine apiece.

ENGLAND UNDER-19 SQUAD

*A. J. Ball (Kent), M. Abid (Lancashire), S. A. Ali (Warwickshire), D. J. Bell-Drummond (Kent), B. T. Foakes (Essex), B. A. Hutton (Nottinghamshire), A. Kapil (Worcestershire), S. Kelsall (Nottinghamshire), J. A. Leaning (Yorkshire), C. Overton (Somerset), J. Overton (Somerset), R. Singh (Durham), S. J. Thakor (Leicestershire), R. J. W. Topley (Essex), S. K. W. Wood (Nottinghamshire). *Coach:* T. J. Boon. *Manager:* J. Abrahams.

Throughout the tournament, each side chose from 12 players, of whom 11 could bat and 11 field.

Group stage

At Townsville (Tony Ireland Stadium), April 5, 2012. **England won by three wickets.** ‡**Australia 203-8** (50 overs) (N. G. Stevens 76*); **England 209-7** (46.3 overs) (D. J. Bell-Drummond 103*). *MoM:* D. J. Bell-Drummond. *England 4pts. Daniel Bell-Drummond scored his maiden hundred at this level after ten fifties, and became the highest run-scorer for England in Under-19 one-day internationals, overtaking Billy Godleman (711). His runs were needed after Nick Stevens rescued Australia from 129-7.*

At Townsville (Endeavour Park), April 5, 2012. **New Zealand won by six wickets. India 123** (47 overs); ‡**New Zealand 127-4** (33.4 overs) (N. F. Kelly 62*; K. Passi 4-25). *MoM:* N. F. Kelly. *New Zealand 5pts. India were caught cold, stumbling to 8-4 – and never really recovered.*

At Townsville (Tony Ireland Stadium), April 7, 2012. **Australia won by four wickets. India 260** (50 overs); ‡**Australia 263-6** (49.1 overs) (K. R. Patterson 99, T. M. Head 54, M. J. Buchanan 51). *MoM:* K. R. Patterson. *Australia 4pts. Six Indians passed 20, but none went beyond 45. Kurtis Patterson shared stands of 103 with Travis Head and 98 with Meyrick Buchanan.*

At Townsville (Endeavour Park), April 7, 2012. **England won by nine wickets. New Zealand 78** (32.4 overs) (A. Kapil 4-6); ‡**England 80-1** (18.1 overs). *MoM:* B. T. Foakes (England). *England 5pts. Keeper Ben Foakes caught five and hit the winning runs as England demolished meek opponents.*

At Townsville (Tony Ireland Stadium), April 9, 2012. **Australia won by six wickets.** ‡**New Zealand 146** (48.4 overs) (J. A. McClelland 4-28); **Australia 147-4** (35.2 overs) (W. G. Bosisto 67*). *MoM:* J. A. McClelland. *Australia 5pts. Pat Cummins – still 18, but with one Test and five one-day* *international caps – made his comeback after five months out with a foot injury, bowling six overs and taking two wickets to help limit New Zealand for another substandard total.*

At Townsville (Endeavour Park), April 9, 2012. **England won by four wickets. India 268-9** (50 overs) (M. Vohra 52, V. H. Zol 60, A. D. Nath 62*); ‡**England 272-6** (49.4 overs) (D. J. Bell-Drummond 55, B. T. Foakes 93, C. Overton 68*). *MoM:* B. T. Foakes. *England 4pts. Another 260-plus score was insufficient for India, who leaked runs to Foakes and Craig Overton in a decisive fourth-wicket stand of 91. England's win ensured the teams would meet again in the semi-finals.*

England 13pts, Australia 9pts, New Zealand 5pts, India 0pts.

Semi-finals

At Townsville (Endeavour Park), April 13, 2012. **Australia won by four runs. Australia 285-9** (50 overs) (J. J. Peirson 54, K. R. Patterson 76, P. J. Cummins 50*, I. S. Sodhi 4-41); ‡**New Zealand 281-9** (50 overs) (J. F. Carter 77, W. A. Young 59). *MoM:* K. R. Patterson. *Cummins's no-nonsense 50* in 24 balls at No. 9 took Australia to an imposing total. He then played a part in the crucial dismissals of Joe Carter and Will Young as New Zealand fell just short.*

At Townsville (Tony Ireland Stadium), April 13, 2012. **India won by 63 runs. India 239** (49.1 overs) (U. Chand 94, S. K. Patel 53); ‡**England 176** (44.5 overs) (M. M. Sayyed 4-31). *MoM:* U. Chand. *India turned the form book on its head. A target of 240 should have been within England's reach, but Sandeep Sharma wiped out the top three, and 16-year-old left-arm seamer Mohsin Sayyed wrecked the middle order.*

Final

At Townsville (Endeavour Park), April 15, 2012. **India won by seven wickets. Australia 194-9** (50 overs) (M. J. Buchanan 59; S. Sharma 4-51); ‡**India 198-3** (42.4 overs) (U. Chand 112*). *MoM:* U. Chand. *India, winless in the group stage, produced a terrific performance. The spinners – Harmeet Singh, Vikas Mishra and Baba Apparajith – all went at less than 3.3 an over, and Sam Hain at No. 7 found it impossible to break free: although he made 41*, he did not once find the boundary in 87 balls. Chand reeled off nine fours and six sixes to seal India's title.*

Third-place Play-off

At Townsville (Tony Ireland Stadium), April 15, 2012. **England won by six wickets. New Zealand 271-9** (50 overs) (B. J. Horne 81, H. A. Walsh 61*); ‡**England 272-4** (44.2 overs) (D. J. Bell-Drummond 63, B. T. Foakes 105*). *MoM:* B. T. Foakes. *MoS:* B. T. Foakes. *England chased successfully for the fourth time out of five, with Foakes scoring his second century of the winter in this format, following 111 v Bangladesh at Chittagong in January.*

DOMESTIC CRICKET IN AUSTRALIA, 2011-12

PETER ENGLISH

Queensland recovered from an unhappy campaign in 2010-11 to lift the Sheffield Shield for the seventh time and regain their reputation as one of the country's most dangerous sides. Following a season filled with player discontent, the exit of local hero Trevor Barsby as coach, and an epidemic of inconsistency, the state rebuilt immediately under Darren Lehmann, the former Test batsman from South Australia.

The summer started with five consecutive outright Shield wins and they had to wait until the last round to secure the home final – although it ended in gutsy fashion with a nerve-shredding victory. Requiring only 133 to beat Tasmania, Queensland turned a comfortable chase into an almost impossible one, slumping from 67 for one to 88 for seven. But Chris Hartley and Steve Magoffin remained immovable, sealing the title on the fourth evening.

It was a season of desperate near-misses for **Tasmania**, who experienced more heartbreak in the 50-over final against South Australia. Wanting two from the last delivery, all-rounder James Faulkner managed only a bye. That tied the game but gave South Australia the Ryobi Cup, as they had finished one point ahead in the group stage. Tasmania's envious eye for interstate talent had paid off again, with New South Wales junior Jackson Bird, a right-arm seamer in his maiden first-class season, capturing 53 wickets in eight Shield games, including a hat-trick against Western Australia. Ed Cowan, also enjoying a second wind after leaving New South Wales, led the competition run-list with 948 at 59, and earned a Test debut against India.

Victoria tied on points with Queensland and Tasmania, but missed out on the final on run-quotient. Versatile left-hander Rob Quiney collected 938 Shield runs and was also prolific in the 50-over arena, winning Australia's State Player of the Year award, and paving the way for Test selection in November 2012. The other highlight of Victoria's season was the emergence of fast bowler Jayde Herrick, a former quarry machinery driver, who mined 45 Shield wickets.

Western Australia challenged for a while but finished fourth in the Shield. Liam Davis peaked with an unbeaten 303 against New South Wales, on the way to 921 runs, while Michael Hogan was second only to Bird, with 46 Shield wickets.

New South Wales, who also underachieved, said goodbye to two former Test players – Phil Jaques and Beau Casson, the left-arm wrist-spinner, who retired because of a long-standing heart condition.

Despite their one-day success, **South Australia** continued to falter in the first-class game, finishing last for the third summer in a row after managing only two points. Michael Klinger, the captain, stood out in all forms, with 835 Shield runs and 498 in the one-day competition, but he could not cover all the deficiencies.

Twenty20's surge led to a major break in Australia's summer tradition. The Big Bash League created eight city-based franchises to replace the six state teams, and operated in a six-week window free of other domestic distractions. **Sydney Sixers**, a squad relying predominantly on local talent, eased past **Perth Scorchers** at the WACA with a seven-wicket victory set up by all-rounder Moises Henriques and Brett Lee.

While crowd records and pay-television viewing figures were broken, the competition at times resembled a retirement-village open day. Shane Warne (42), Brad Hogg, Stuart MacGill and Matthew Hayden (all 40) not only rejoined the circus, but justified their promotion as the competition's stars. Hogg's 13 wickets for Perth came at 14, with an economy-rate of 5.61, and won him a recall to the national Twenty20 team almost four years after he last played for his country. Everything old was new again.

FIRST-CLASS AVERAGES, 2011-12

BATTING (400 runs, average 30.00)

	M	*I*	*NO*	*R*	*HS*	*100*	*Avge*	*Ct/St*
M. J. Clarke (*Australia*)	6	9	1	787	329*	3	98.37	11
R. T. Ponting (*Tas. & Australia*)	10	15	1	1,011	221	4	72.21	12
L. M. Davis (*Western Australia*)	8	15	1	921	303*	3	65.78	7
†D. A. Warner (*NSW, Aus. & Aus. A*)	8	12	2	632	180	3	63.20	9
D. T. Christian (*South Australia*)	5	9	1	475	131*	2	59.37	4
P. J. Forrest (*Queensland*)	6	11	1	581	132*	3	58.10	10
†E. J. M. Cowan (*Tas., Aus. & Aus. A*)	15	26	3	1,299	145*	4	56.47	18
G. J. Bailey (*Tas. & Australia A*)	9	15	2	724	117	3	55.69	8
D. J. Hussey (*Victoria*)	5	9	1	436	130	1	54.50	16
A. C. Voges (*Western Australia*)	9	16	2	757	178	2	54.07	18
P. M. Nevill (*New South Wales*)	9	16	5	570	112*	1	51.81	22
†R. J. Quiney (*Victoria*)	10	19	0	938	119	3	49.36	8
M. Klinger (*South Australia*)	10	19	1	835	219*	1	46.38	6
T. L. W. Cooper (*South Australia*)	10	19	2	756	203*	1	44.47	9
†S. M. Katich (*New South Wales*)	8	12	1	483	125	2	43.90	6
J. A. Burns (*Queensland*)	11	19	0	781	130	2	41.10	6
†C. J. L. Rogers (*Victoria*)	10	19	0	781	124	3	41.10	3
S. P. D. Smith (*NSW & Australia A*)	8	13	0	500	106	1	38.46	12
A. B. McDonald (*Victoria*)	8	14	3	408	76	0	37.09	4
G. J. Maxwell (*Victoria*)	8	14	1	467	92	0	35.92	6
†W. J. Townsend (*Queensland*)	11	19	1	644	166*	1	35.77	11
†S. J. Cazzulino (*Tasmania*)	8	16	1	524	118*	1	34.93	6
P. S. P. Handscomb (*Victoria*)	7	13	1	408	113	1	34.00	6/1
C. J. Ferguson (*South Australia*)	8	15	0	486	126	1	32.40	2
†C. D. Hartley (*Queensland*)	11	18	1	544	111	1	32.00	56/2
†B. J. Rohrer (*New South Wales*)	9	17	1	488	114	1	30.50	2

BOWLING (20 wickets)

	Style	*O*	*M*	*R*	*W*	*BB*	*5I*	*Avge*
A. C. McDermott (*Queensland*)	RFM	160.3	46	447	28	7-24	2	15.96
J. M. Bird (*Tasmania*)	RFM	307.4	84	848	53	6-62	5	16.00
S. J. Magoffin (*Queensland*)	RFM	199.1	69	382	23	6-44	1	16.60
P. M. Siddle (*Victoria & Australia*)	RFM	350.4	103	1,005	54	6-43	3	18.61
N. J. Rimmington (*Western Australia*)	RFM	256.5	77	665	34	5-46	1	19.55
R. J. Harris (*Queensland & Australia*)	RFM	232.1	74	538	26	7-60	1	20.69
J. L. Pattinson (*Vic., Aus. & Aus. A*)	RFM	248	62	796	38	5-27	2	20.94
B. C. J. Cutting (*Qland & Aus. A*)	RFM	237.4	48	825	39	5-43	2	21.15
A. B. McDonald (*Victoria*)	RFM	220.4	77	462	20	5-21	1	23.10
L. R. Butterworth (*Tasmania*)	RM	304.2	99	722	31	4-34	0	23.29
B. W. Hilfenhaus (*Tas., Aus. & Aus. A*)	RFM	406.3	102	1,145	49	5-44	3	23.36
M. G. Hogan (*Western Australia*)	RFM	387.3	103	1,082	46	5-24	2	23.52
J. P. Faulkner (*Tasmania*)	LFM	313.3	85	982	39	4-22	0	25.17
J. M. Mennie (*South Australia*)	RM	200	45	604	23	7-96	2	26.26
J. M. Holland (*Victoria*)	SLA	232.4	39	707	24	4-74	0	29.45
N. M. Coulter-Nile (*Western Australia*)	RF	209.4	51	657	22	4-20	0	29.86
N. M. Lyon (*South Australia & Australia*)	OB	233.3	41	679	22	4-63	0	30.86
J. M. Herrick (*Victoria*)	RFM	366.5	57	1,394	45	5-79	1	30.97
M. A. Beer (*Western Aus. & Aus. A*)	SLA	323.1	91	861	27	7-46	1	31.88
M. A. Starc (*NSW, Aus. & Aus. A*)	LFM	246.2	42	920	27	5-66	1	34.07
C. J. Boyce (*Queensland*)	LBG	170.1	22	688	20	5-110	1	34.40
P. R. George (*South Australia*)	RFM	324.1	62	1,148	31	5-36	1	37.03

SHEFFIELD SHIELD, 2011-12

	Played	*Won*	*Lost*	*Drawn*	*1st-inns points*	*Points*	*Quotient*
Queensland	10	6	2	2	0	36	1.167
Tasmania	10	5	3	2	6	36	1.198
Victoria	10	5	3	2	6	36	1.164
Western Australia	10	5	4	1	4	34	1.176
New South Wales	10	1	4	5	6	12	0.773
South Australia	10	0	6	4	2	2	0.624

Final: Queensland beat Tasmania by three wickets.

Outright win = 6pts; lead on first-innings in a drawn or lost game = 2pts. Teams tied on points were separated on quotient (runs per wicket scored divided by runs per wicket conceded).

At Brisbane, October 11–14, 2011. **Queensland won by 66 runs. Queensland 355 and 243-9 dec** (P. J. Forrest 101); **‡Victoria 298 and 234** (R. J. Quiney 109). *Queensland 6pts. Slip fielder Andrew Robinson held five catches in Victoria's second innings and seven in the match, a record for Queensland, who won with three overs to spare.*

At Perth, October 11–14, 2011. **Western Australia won by 25 runs. Western Australia 176 and 437-4 dec** (L. M. Davis 135, A. C. Voges 150*); **‡Tasmania 206** (M. G. Hogan 5-30) **and 382** (G. J. Bailey 116; M. G. Johnson 5-69). *Western Australia 6pts, Tasmania 2pts. In his first Shield game for 11 months, Ricky Ponting contributed 87 as Tasmania fell not far short of a target of 408.*

At Adelaide, October 17–20, 2011. **Drawn. ‡South Australia 478-9 dec** (D. T. Christian 131*); **New South Wales 217** (P. R. George 5-36) **and 402-5** (U. T. Khawaja 101). *South Australia 2pts. On the opening day, New South Wales spinner Beau Casson was taken to hospital for tests on a congenital heart condition; he took no further part in the match, which proved to be his last.*

At Sydney, October 25–28, 2011. **Drawn. ‡New South Wales 201** (J. M. Herrick 5-79) **and 433-7 dec** (S. M. Katich 110, B. J. Rohrer 114); **Victoria 427** (C. J. L. Rogers 106). *Victoria 2pts. Simon Katich and Ben Rohrer added 216 for New South Wales's fifth wicket to deny Victoria.*

At Brisbane, October 25–27, 2011. **Queensland won by an innings and 28 runs. ‡Queensland 287; Tasmania 129 and 130** (R. J. Harris 7-60). *Queensland 6pts. Queensland claimed 15 wickets on the second day, and won barely an hour into the third.*

At Adelaide, October 25–28, 2011. **Drawn. ‡Western Australia 335** (M. J. North 119; G. D. Putland 5-71) **and 242-7 dec; South Australia 225 and 119-9.** *Western Australia 2pts. South Australia's last-wicket pair Cullen Bailey and Peter George survived 22 overs, the last ten of them maidens, to save the game.*

At Perth, November 1–4, 2011. **Queensland won by 192 runs. Queensland 273** (M. R. Marsh 6-84) **and 341-9 dec** (R. A. Broad 135, P. J. Forrest 132*); **‡Western Australia 221 and 201** (B. C. J. Cutting 5-43). *Queensland 6pts. Marcus Harris, still 19, carried his bat for 91* through Western Australia's second innings, but could not prevent Queensland's third win in three.*

At Hobart, November 4–7, 2011. **Victoria won by 55 runs. ‡Victoria 362** (M. S. Wade 108) **and 190** (B. W. Hilfenhaus 5-44); **Tasmania 235 and 262.** *Victoria 6pts. Bowled out with 16 balls to go, Tasmania suffered their third defeat in their first three games – and their last before the final.*

At Sydney (Bankstown Oval), November 6–9, 2011. **Drawn. ‡New South Wales 474-6 dec** (D. A. Warner 148, S. P. D. Smith 106); **South Australia 266 and 373-5** (T. L. W. Cooper 203*). *New South Wales 2pts. Nic Maddinson (92) and David Warner put on 233 for New South Wales's first wicket. When South Australia followed on, Tom Cooper converted his maiden hundred into a double, and added 260 with Dan Christian (96).*

At Melbourne, November 11–14, 2011. **Western Australia won by five wickets. Victoria 301 and 278; ‡Western Australia 218 and 363-5** (L. M. Davis 108). *Western Australia 6pts, Victoria 2pts. Set 362 in a day plus six overs, Western Australia got there with 11 overs to spare.*

At Brisbane, November 15–18, 2011. **Queensland won by 14 runs. ‡Queensland 282** (M. A. Starc 5-66) **and 218; New South Wales 277 and 209.** *Queensland 6pts. Chasing 224, New South Wales's top six fell for single figures – but captain Steve O'Keefe (82) took them within touching distance of their first win. He was last out as Queensland preserved their 100% record after four matches.*

At Hobart, November 15–18, 2011. **Tasmania won by 182 runs. Tasmania 361 and 300-2 dec** (E. J. M. Cowan 134*, G. J. Bailey 114*); **‡South Australia 260 and 219**. *Tasmania 6pts. Ed Cowan and George Bailey added 204* for the third wicket in Tasmania's second innings to set a target of 402, enough to secure their first win of the season.*

At Melbourne, November 22–25, 2011. **Tasmania won by 93 runs. ‡Tasmania 217** (C. J. McKay 6-40) **and 288**; **Victoria 94** (J. M. Bird 5-35) **and 318** (C. J. L. Rogers 118; J. M. Bird 5-61). *Tasmania 6pts. Jackson Bird took 10-96 in his second first-class match. He started with three in four balls on the first evening, and six of his victims were caught behind by Tom Triffitt, who held nine in the game.*

At Sydney, November 25–28, 2011. **New South Wales won by six wickets. Western Australia 150 and 365** (N. J. Rimmington 102*); **‡New South Wales 441-6 dec** (S. M. Katich 125, K. R. Patterson 157) **and 78-4**. *New South Wales 6pts. Kurtis Patterson scored 157 in 189 balls and added 221 with Simon Katich for New South Wales's fifth wicket. At 18 years 236 days, he was the youngest to reach a Shield century on first-class debut. But it was his only senior appearance of the season; he turned down a Big Bash League contract and returned to Under-19 cricket. Later, No. 9 Nathan Rimmington's maiden century held up New South Wales's progress to their only victory of the season, which they completed with four balls to spare.*

At Adelaide, November 25–28, 2011. **Queensland won by four wickets. ‡South Australia 349-9 dec** (D. T. Christian 108; M. G. Gale 5-81) **and 260-9 dec** (C. J. Boyce 5-110); **Queensland 350-3 dec** (W. J. Townsend 166*) **and 260-6**. *Queensland 6pts. Queensland's fifth win in five matches.*

At Melbourne, December 2–5, 2011. **Drawn. ‡Victoria 498-7 dec** (D. J. Hussey 130) **and 196-3 dec**; **Queensland 295** (C. L. White 5-59) **and 399-9** (J. A. Burns 123, P. J. Forrest 115). *Victoria 2pts. Chasing 400 for a sixth successive win, Queensland reached 385-5, then lost four for 13; the last pair needed two off the final ball but could only level the scores. The draw gave Victoria two points for a first-innings lead. Had the batsmen gone for a second run and been run out, it would have been a tie, worth three points to each side, but they were suspicious of Victorian captain Cameron White's pleas for them to keep running. At the end of the season, an extra point would have put Victoria in the final with Queensland, ahead of Tasmania.*

At Perth, December 5–8, 2011. **Western Australia won by ten wickets. ‡South Australia 93** (M. G. Hogan 5-24) **and 289** (C. J. Ferguson 126); **Western Australia 368** (J. M. Mennie 7-96) **and 16-0**. *Western Australia 6pts. Western Australian wicketkeeper Luke Ronchi held six catches in the first innings and ten in the match.*

At Canberra, December 6–9, 2011. **Drawn. ‡Tasmania 392** (J. K. Lalor 5-97) **and 272-0 dec** (S. J. Cazzulino 118*, E. J. M. Cowan 145*); **New South Wales 264** (P. M. Nevill 112*) **and 292-8**. *Tasmania 2pts. Left-handed openers Steve Cazzulino, with a maiden hundred, and Cowan, with his third in three first-class matches, put on 272* in 54 overs. But New South Wales's ninth-wicket pair held out for 21.2 to ensure the draw.*

At Adelaide, February 2–5, 2012. **Victoria won by 186 runs. ‡Victoria 437** (R. J. Quiney 114, P. S. P. Handscomb 113) **and 231-4 dec** (R. J. Quiney 119); **South Australia 224 and 258**. *Victoria 6pts. Rob Quiney scored a century in each innings, and added 225 with Peter Handscomb for the second wicket in Victoria's first.*

At Brisbane, February 6–9, 2012. **Western Australia won by one wicket. ‡Queensland 251 and 175**; **Western Australia 359** (B. C. J. Cutting 5-99) **and 68-9** (A. C. McDermott 7-24). *Western Australia 6pts. Western Australia needed only 68 to win, but were nearly stopped in their tracks by Alister McDermott's 7-24, the best figures of his career and the Australian season. They were 64-9 before last man Michael Hogan hit his second ball for four, inflicting Queensland's first defeat.*

At Hobart, February 6–9, 2012. **Tasmania won by six wickets. New South Wales 341-7 dec and 150-9 dec**; **‡Tasmania 345-7 dec** (G. J. Bailey 117) **and 150-4**. *Tasmania 6pts. On the first day, New South Wales batsman Simon Katich was concussed when he top-edged a ball from Luke Butterworth into his face; he missed the rest of this match and the next one.*

At Melbourne, February 13–15, 2012. **Victoria won by 34 runs. ‡Victoria 220** (J. M. Mennie 5-43) **and 181** (C. J. Sayers 5-57); **South Australia 100** (A. B. McDonald 5-21) **and 267** (P. M. Siddle 6-43). *Victoria 6pts. White passed Bill Lawry's record of leading Victoria in 56 Shield matches, and extended his own record to 28 wins as South Australia went down to their fifth defeat in a row.*

At Hobart, February 17–20, 2012. **Tasmania won by eight wickets. Queensland 205** (J. M. Bird 6-62) **and 215; ‡Tasmania 260 and 163-2.** *Tasmania 6pts. Cowan passed 1,000 first-class runs for the season during his second-innings 77*, which secured Tasmania's fourth victory.*

At Perth, February 17–19, 2012. **Western Australia won by an innings and 323 runs. ‡New South Wales 91 and 146** (M. A. Beer 7-46); **Western Australia 560-3 dec** (L. M. Davis 303*, A. C. Voges 178). *Western Australia 6pts. This match featured the lowest and highest totals of the 2011-12 Shield, as well as the highest individual score. Liam Davis converted his third century of the season into a maiden treble, only the second for Western Australia, after Geoff Marsh's 355* v South Australia at Perth in 1989-90. Davis batted for ten hours 29 minutes and 524 balls, and struck 41 fours and six sixes; he comfortably out-scored both New South Wales totals added together. Davis and Voges put on 379 for the third wicket to set up Western Australia's biggest victory, which lifted them to the top of the table; but they lost captain Marcus North for the rest of the season after he ruptured tendons in a finger while fielding.*

At Adelaide, February 29–March 3, 2012. **Drawn. ‡South Australia 126 and 421-2** (M. Klinger 219*); **Tasmania 399** (R. T. Ponting 130). *Tasmania 2pts. Michael Klinger scored his third double-hundred, putting on 219 with Tom Stray and 177 with Travis Head, who each scored 90. Six Tasmanians subsequently suffered food poisoning.*

At Sydney, March 1–4, 2012. **Drawn. New South Wales 269** (S. J. Magoffin 6-44) **and 15-0; ‡Queensland 236.** *New South Wales 2pts. Queensland wicketkeeper Chris Hartley completed his 50th first-class dismissal of the season.*

At Perth, March 1–4, 2012. **Victoria won by 212 runs. Victoria 277** (N. J. Rimmington 5-46) **and 390-8 dec** (C. J. L. Rogers 124); **‡Western Australia 301** (P. M. Siddle 5-64) **and 154** (W. D. Sheridan 5-15). *Victoria 6pts, Western Australia 2pts. Peter Siddle's 5-64 took him to 50 first-class wickets in the season and helped Victoria pull level with Queensland and Tasmania on 30 points, four behind Western Australia, going into the final round.*

At Brisbane, March 8–10, 2012. **Queensland won by an innings and 91 runs. South Australia 162 and 103; ‡Queensland 356** (J. A. Burns 130; G. D. Putland 6-72). *Queensland 6pts. Ryan Harris and James Hopes strangled South Australia's second innings, conceding 29 runs in 31 overs between them; only two men managed double figures. Queensland's sixth victory, but their first since November, ensured they headed the table and had home advantage in the final. South Australia were the first state to finish without a Shield win since Victoria in 1992-93.*

At Hobart, March 8–10, 2012. **Tasmania won by eight wickets. Western Australia 142** (J. M. Bird 5-32) **and 241** (J. M. Bird 6-63); **‡Tasmania 363** (E. J. M. Cowan 143, R. T. Ponting 111) **and 21-2.** *Tasmania 6pts. Ricky Ponting, assuming Tasmania's captaincy after George Bailey left with Australia's touring squad, scored his fourth century in five first-class games including the Tests against India, and passed 1,000 runs for the season; he added 205 for Tasmania's third wicket with Cowan. Bird claimed a hat-trick in Western Australia's second innings to finish with 11-95. Victory left Tasmania tied on points with Queensland and Victoria at the top of the table; they qualified for the final ahead of Victoria on run-quotient.*

At Melbourne, March 8–10, 2012. **Victoria won by five wickets. ‡New South Wales 208 and 212; Victoria 185 and 236-5.** *Victoria 6pts, New South Wales 2pts. Andrew McDonald returned figures of 14–9–8–2 in New South Wales's first innings, then batted Victoria to their fourth successive win – but it was not quite enough to see them into the final.*

FINAL

QUEENSLAND v TASMANIA

At Brisbane, March 16–19, 2012. Queensland won by three wickets. Toss: Tasmania.

Queensland collected their seventh first-class trophy, and first since 2005-06, after Chris Hartley and Steve Magoffin twice rescued them from severe wobbles. Both players were feeling wobbly themselves: Hartley was suffering from a virus, Magoffin was on painkillers for a back injury. But

Hartley made the game's only century, having joined his captain, James Hopes, when Queensland were 55 for five in reply to Tasmania's 241. After Hopes provided the 50th wicket of Jackson Bird's debut season, Hartley added 97 with Magoffin to claim the lead. Hopes then picked up five in Tasmania's second innings, leaving a target of 133. Queensland got halfway with one wicket down before crumbling to 88 for seven. Once again, Hartley and Magoffin held firm, clocking up the 45 needed to secure the Shield on the fourth evening. It was a disappointment for Ricky Ponting, whose only previous final had been Tasmania's first, in 1993-94. He managed only seven runs; in the first innings he was one of six victims for Alister McDermott, the spit of his father Craig, whose last Test series, in 1995-96, had been Ponting's first.

Man of the Match: C. D. Hartley. *Attendance:* 6,619.

Close of play: first day, Tasmania 208-6 (Butterworth 11, Triffitt 17); second day, Queensland 139-5 (Hopes 54, Hartley 30); third day, Tasmania 136-6 (Cowan 59, Butterworth 11).

Tasmania

First innings		Second innings	
E. J. M. Cowan c Hartley b Boyce	33	– (2) c Harris b Hopes	71
S. J. Cazzulino c Hartley b McDermott	68	– (1) c Kemp b Magoffin	4
A. J. Doolan c Harris b McDermott	43	– (7) c Magoffin b McDermott	15
*R. T. Ponting c Burns b McDermott	1	– b Hopes	6
N. J. Kruger c Kemp b McDermott	1	– (3) c Robinson b Harris	0
J. P. Faulkner lbw b Hopes	21	– (5) c Robinson b Hopes	3
L. R. Butterworth c Lynn b Magoffin	25	– (8) c Robinson b Hopes	23
†T. I. F. Triffitt c Harris b Magoffin	17	– (6) c Robinson b Harris	35
J. J. Krejza c Harris b McDermott	5	– b Hopes	3
B. G. Drew not out	12	– c McDermott b Harris	4
J. M. Bird b McDermott	0	– not out	0
L-b 8, n-b 7	15	L-b 2, n-b 1	3
1/67 (1) 2/138 (3) 3/140 (4) 4/144 (5) 5/178 (6) 6/178 (2) 7/208 (8) 8/226 (7) 9/241 (9) 10/241 (11) (107.5 overs)	241	1/7 (1) 2/12 (3) 3/32 (4) 4/36 (5) 5/87 (6) 6/105 (7) 7/159 (8) 8/160 (2) 9/167 (9) 10/167 (10) (64 overs)	167

Harris 30–11–71–0; Magoffin 22–10–31–2; Hopes 23–8–42–1; McDermott 24.5–8–54–6; Boyce 8–0–35–1. *Second innings*—Harris 22–5–52–3; Magoffin 12–4–13–1; McDermott 8–3–36–1; Hopes 20–5–61–5; Boyce 2–1–3–0.

Queensland

First innings		Second innings	
W. J. Townsend c Triffitt b Butterworth	5	– (2) c Triffitt b Faulkner	36
A. R. Kemp c Triffitt b Butterworth	0	– (1) c Kruger b Bird	6
A. W. Robinson c Ponting b Faulkner	16	– c Cazzulino b Krejza	31
J. A. Burns c Triffitt b Faulkner	28	– c Kruger b Faulkner	8
C. A. Lynn c Faulkner b Bird	0	– c Kruger b Butterworth	4
*J. R. Hopes lbw b Bird	58	– c Ponting b Faulkner	0
†C. D. Hartley lbw b Bird	111	– not out	19
R. J. Harris c Triffitt b Butterworth	18	– b Butterworth	0
S. J. Magoffin c Triffitt b Butterworth	31	– not out	26
C. J. Boyce c Triffitt b Bird	0		
A. C. McDermott not out	0		
L-b 4, w 5	9	L-b 3	3
1/0 (2) 2/5 (1) 3/48 (4) 4/55 (3) 5/55 (5) 6/144 (6) 7/171 (8) 8/268 (9) 9/273 (10) 10/276 (7) (83.1 overs)	276	1/6 (1) 2/67 (3) 3/83 (4) 4/88 (2) 5/88 (6) 6/88 (5) 7/88 (8) (7 wkts, 62.1 overs)	133

Bird 22.1–5–56–4; Butterworth 24–8–54–4; Drew 7–0–56–0; Faulkner 18–4–64–2; Krejza 12–2–42–0. *Second innings*—Bird 16–4–36–1; Butterworth 16–5–38–2; Faulkner 18–8–27–3; Krejza 12.1–4–29–1.

Umpires: S. D. Fry and B. N. J. Oxenford. Third umpire: J. D. Ward.
Referee: P. L. Marshall.

CHAMPIONS

Sheffield Shield

1892-93	Victoria
1893-94	South Australia
1894-95	Victoria
1895-96	New South Wales
1896-97	New South Wales
1897-98	Victoria
1898-99	Victoria
1899-1900	New South Wales
1900-01	Victoria
1901-02	New South Wales
1902-03	New South Wales
1903-04	New South Wales
1904-05	New South Wales
1905-06	New South Wales
1906-07	New South Wales
1907-08	Victoria
1908-09	New South Wales
1909-10	South Australia
1910-11	New South Wales
1911-12	New South Wales
1912-13	South Australia
1913-14	New South Wales
1914-15	Victoria
1915–19	No competition
1919-20	New South Wales
1920-21	New South Wales
1921-22	Victoria
1922-23	New South Wales
1923-24	Victoria
1924-25	Victoria
1925-26	New South Wales
1926-27	South Australia
1927-28	Victoria
1928-29	New South Wales
1929-30	Victoria
1930-31	Victoria
1931-32	New South Wales
1932-33	New South Wales
1933-34	Victoria
1934-35	Victoria
1935-36	South Australia
1936-37	Victoria
1937-38	New South Wales
1938-39	South Australia
1939-40	New South Wales
1940–46	No competition
1946-47	Victoria
1947-48	Western Australia
1948-49	New South Wales
1949-50	New South Wales
1950-51	Victoria
1951-52	New South Wales
1952-53	South Australia
1953-54	New South Wales
1954-55	New South Wales
1955-56	New South Wales
1956-57	New South Wales
1957-58	New South Wales
1958-59	New South Wales
1959-60	New South Wales
1960-61	New South Wales
1961-62	New South Wales
1962-63	Victoria
1963-64	South Australia
1964-65	New South Wales
1965-66	New South Wales
1966-67	Victoria
1967-68	Western Australia
1968-69	South Australia
1969-70	Victoria
1970-71	South Australia
1971-72	Western Australia
1972-73	Western Australia
1973-74	Victoria
1974-75	Western Australia
1975-76	South Australia
1976-77	Western Australia
1977-78	Western Australia
1978-79	Victoria
1979-80	Victoria
1980-81	Western Australia
1981-82	South Australia
1982-83	New South Wales*
1983-84	Western Australia
1984-85	New South Wales
1985-86	New South Wales
1986-87	Western Australia
1987-88	Western Australia
1988-89	Western Australia
1989-90	New South Wales
1990-91	Victoria
1991-92	Western Australia
1992-93	New South Wales
1993-94	New South Wales
1994-95	Queensland
1995-96	South Australia
1996-97	Queensland*
1997-98	Western Australia
1998-99	Western Australia*

Pura Milk Cup

1999-2000	Queensland

Pura Cup

2000-01	Queensland
2001-02	Queensland
2002-03	New South Wales*
2003-04	Victoria
2004-05	New South Wales*
2005-06	Queensland
2006-07	Tasmania
2007-08	New South Wales

Sheffield Shield

2008-09	Victoria
2009-10	Victoria
2010-11	Tasmania
2011-12	Queensland

New South Wales have won the title 45 times, Victoria 28, Western Australia 15, South Australia 13, Queensland 7, Tasmania 2.

* *Second in table but won final. Finals were introduced in 1982-83.*

RYOBI CUP, 2011-12

50-over league plus final

	Played	*Won*	*Lost*	*Bonus points*	*Points*	*Net run-rate*
South Australia	8	6	2	3	27	0.47
Tasmania	8	6	2	2	26	0.21
New South Wales	8	4	4	1	17	0.17
Queensland	8	4	4	1	17	0.01
Victoria	8	3	5	1	13	–0.14
Western Australia	8	1	7	0	4	–0.74

Win = 4pts; 1 bonus pt awarded for achieving victory with a run-rate 1.25 times that of the opposition. Teams tied on points were separated on net run-rate (calculated by subtracting runs conceded per over from runs scored per over).

Final

At Adelaide, February 25, 2012. **Tied.** South Australia won the Ryobi Cup by virtue of heading the preliminary table. ‡**South Australia 285** (49.4 overs); **Tasmania 285-4** (50 overs) (G. J. Bailey 101). *MoM:* G. J. Bailey. *Attendance:* 10,245. *Tasmanian captain George Bailey scored 101 in 105 balls, but was dismissed in the final over, four short of victory. Needing two from the last delivery, all-rounder James Faulkner managed only a bye, and a tie was not enough to deny South Australia.*

KFC T20 BIG BASH LEAGUE, 2011-12

20-over league plus semi-finals and final

	Played	*Won*	*Lost*	*Points*	*Net run-rate*
Perth Scorchers	7	5	2	10	0.62
Hobart Hurricanes	7	5	2	10	0.56
Sydney Sixers	7	5	2	10	0.26
Melbourne Stars	7	4	3	8	0.25
Brisbane Heat	7	3	4	6	0.32
Adelaide Strikers	7	2	5	4	–0.33
Melbourne Renegades	7	2	5	4	–0.58
Sydney Thunder	7	2	5	4	–1.25

Teams tied on points were separated on net run-rate (calculated by subtracting runs conceded per over from runs scored per over).

Semi-finals

At Perth, January 21, 2012 (floodlit). **Perth Scorchers won by 11 runs.** ‡**Perth Scorchers 174-3** (20 overs); **Melbourne Stars 163-8** (20 overs). *MoM:* M. R. Marsh. *Attendance:* 15,225. *Herschelle Gibbs got Perth going with 71 in 46 balls before Mitchell Marsh took over with 41 in 26.*

At Hobart, January 22, 2012 (floodlit). **Sydney Sixers won by seven runs.** ‡**Sydney Sixers 153-6** (20 overs); **Hobart Hurricanes 146-7** (20 overs). *MoM:* N. J. Maddinson. *Attendance:* 14,185. *Nic Maddinson set up Sydney Sixers' victory with a career-best 68 in 51 balls.*

Final

At Perth, January 28, 2012 (floodlit). **Sydney Sixers won by seven wickets.** ‡**Perth Scorchers 156-5** (20 overs); **Sydney Sixers 158-3** (18.5 overs). *MoM:* M. C. Henriques. *Attendance:* 16,255. *Brett Lee grabbed two wickets in the first over of the match before Mitchell Marsh led Perth's recovery, with 77* in 57 balls. But Moises Henriques hit a career-best 70 in 41 deliveries, and put on 110 in 12 overs for Sydney Sixers' first wicket with Steve O'Keefe.*

BANGLADESH CRICKET, 2012

Tearful Tigers

UTPAL SHUVRO

During his time as the No. 1-ranked all-rounder in Test cricket, Shakib Al Hasan would smile ruefully: "I don't know how long I will be there. When I watch Test matches featuring other countries on TV, the thought often comes to my mind, when will I get the chance to play in whites again?" The man Shakib had dethroned, Jacques Kallis, emphatically regained the position in November. Shakib could not mount a fresh challenge, but that was not his fault. Bangladesh played only two Tests in 2012, the fewest in a year since they were handed Test status in 2000, and just nine one-day internationals, the fewest since 2001. Only Zimbabwe played less often.

When Bangladesh took the field against West Indies at Mirpur in November, it was nearly 11 months since they had last played a Test – and Chris Gayle duly hit the first ball for six. Bangladesh did well to take a first-innings lead, with their highest Test score, 556, but they failed to chase 245 in almost two and a half sessions, then barely put up a fight in the Second Test at Khulna.

In 50-over cricket, though, Bangladesh enjoyed one of their most successful years, winning five out of nine matches (all at home). They actually had a

BANGLADESH IN 2012

	Played	*Won*	*Lost*	*Drawn/No result*
Tests	2	–	2	–
One-day internationals	9	5	4	–
Twenty20 internationals	9	4	5	–

JANUARY		
FEBRUARY		
MARCH	Asia Cup (h)	(page 948)
APRIL		
MAY		
JUNE		
JULY	3 T20Is (a) v Ireland 1 T20I v Scotland (in the Netherlands) 2 T20Is (a) v Netherlands	(page 817) (page 822) (page 822)
AUGUST		
SEPTEMBER / OCTOBER	World Twenty20 (in Sri Lanka)	(page 841)
NOVEMBER / DECEMBER	2 Tests, 5 ODIs and 1 T20I (h) v West Indies	(page 957)

For a review of Bangladesh domestic cricket from the 2011-12 season, see page 970.

Safin Ahmed, Demotix/PA Photos

Our heroes: two giant-killings at the Asia Cup brought Bangladesh's adoring fans out in force.

better strike-rate in 2009, when they won 14 of 19, but there was a difference this time: all Bangladesh's victories came against top-class opposition.

In between the Asia Cup in March and a one-day series against West Indies, Bangladesh played a plethora of Twenty20 games, visiting Zimbabwe, Trinidad, Ireland and the Netherlands (where they lost to both the home side and Scotland) in order to prepare for the World Twenty20 in Sri Lanka. It all came to nothing when they exited in the first round, battered to bits by New Zealand's Brendon McCullum and Imran Nazir of Pakistan.

Bangladesh had hosted the Asia Cup for the third time, and it turned out to be a tournament to savour. On the nine previous occasions they had taken part, they failed to beat any of their mightier neighbours. Now they surprised everyone, including themselves, by chasing down targets against India and Sri Lanka to qualify for their first final in the competition. It was only their second appearance in a one-day final of any kind, after a triangular tournament in 2008-09. But the nation was heartbroken when Shahadat Hossain failed to hit the last ball for four, and Bangladesh lost to Pakistan by an agonising two runs. Shakib and Mushfiqur Rahim cried in public, which only endeared them further to their fans. Shakib was named Man of the Tournament.

Emotionally, the Asia Cup had no parallel. But, in the cold light of day, the high point of Bangladesh's 2012 had to be the one-day series victory over West Indies, who had arrived with a raft of imposing big-hitters. Bangladesh were without Shakib, but won the first two games, including a 160-run mauling in the second, their biggest win in one-day internationals: never had they looked so dominant against a Test-playing nation. West Indies brought it back to 2–2, but the Bangladeshis sneaked the last match by two wickets, igniting a street party outside the National Stadium.

The find of the year was 21-year-old off-spinner Sohag Gazi, who came in useful against a West Indies side with their share of left-handers. Gazi took the first over on Test debut, and recovered from being hit for six by Gayle off his first and fourth balls to get him out two overs later. It was the first of 12 wickets in the two Tests; he added nine in the one-day series. Mushfiqur was considered by many to be a passionate and intelligent young captain – and revealed another string to his bow when he completed a master's degree in history from Jahangirnagar University.

Franchise-based Twenty20 arrived in February 2012, with the Bangladesh Premier League. Although Indian players were unavailable, there were several other international stars. However, the event was marred by controversies, from confusion over the tie-breakers to decide the semi-finalists, to non-payment of players months after the event, and match-fixing.

Before the tournament began, Mashrafe bin Mortaza reported a spot-fixing approach from a 36-year-old player, Shariful Haque, who was banned indefinitely from cricket by the Bangladesh Cricket Board in September. Both the ECB and the Federation of International Cricketers' Associations remained concerned about the payment structure and policing of corruption in the BPL. Mushfiqur slammed the league as "disorganised" – and it had clearly been hurried through to fit a gap in the international schedule. The Pakistan Cricket Board threatened to prevent their players from appearing in the 2013 edition, in retaliation for Bangladesh postponing a tour to their country for the second time because of the security situation. Meanwhile, the BCB extended the franchise model to a new four-day competition, which began in December.

Bangladesh finished the year without a head coach, after two resigned from the post for similar reasons. Stuart Law completed nine months in the role just after the Asia Cup, and left expressing a desire to spend more time with his family; he took up a position with Cricket Australia.

Family was also an issue for Richard Pybus, but his stint ended more acrimoniously. When *Prothom Alo*, Bangladesh's leading daily newspaper, broke the story that he was working without having signed a contract, Pybus resigned, accusing the BCB of "breaching privacy and confidentiality" through leaking. Pybus claimed an agreement had been struck by both parties that he could spend time at home in South Africa between tours, but it was not written into the contract presented to him – so he did not sign it. He also complained about a clunky administrative process. "I couldn't even get the board to sign off on providing healthy sandwiches for the players after training," he said. "Players were going down with food poisoning during camps, so I wanted to offer them something better than a fried egg sandwich. I was told I couldn't, because that was all the budget could afford." The episode showed how amateurishly cricket is run by the BCB. Shane Jurgensen, a former Australian first-class cricketer, stood in as interim coach for the West Indies series.

In line with the ICC's rotating presidency, A. H. M. Mustafa Kamal was nominated as ICC vice-president, and had to resign from his position at the BCB. Nazmul Hasan, like Kamal an MP with the ruling Awami League, replaced him as BCB president in October.

ASIA CUP, 2011-12

MOHAMMAD ISAM

1. Pakistan 2. Bangladesh 3. India 4. Sri Lanka

This was the tenth Asia Cup, a tournament that – since its inception in April 1984 – had generally felt like one commitment too far. Rarely had it stirred fans from any of the top sides into chest-thumping jingoism. But this edition – the third held in Bangladesh – was different, lit up by the unexpected success of the home side, and the completion, at long last, of Sachin Tendulkar's 100th international hundred. After 28 years of anonymity, the Asia Cup gave thanks to the rise of the underdog, and the removal of a giant albatross.

To start with, it looked like the same old story, even though India had just completed a gruelling and humiliating two months in Australia, and had only a fortnight to regroup before heading to Dhaka. They were without Zaheer Khan and Virender Sehwag – both rested – and had to contend with the ongoing soap opera surrounding Tendulkar's landmark. Nonetheless, they still appeared to have a team capable of cleansing their woes. They were also the defending Asia Cup champions, having won the previous competition, in Sri Lanka in June 2010.

Sri Lanka, too, also had fatigue to deal with, after playing four intense games in eight days at the climax of the one-day series in Australia; they went into their first match here without so much as a training session.

Bangladesh were mired in their own drama. The original squad had not been approved by the Bangladesh Cricket Board president, A. H. M. Mustafa Kamal, who ordered Tamim Iqbal to prove his fitness after a bout of fever. The chief selector Akram Khan – Tamim's uncle – quit next day, prompting the prime minister to intervene and restore them both. Mushfiqur Rahim was also in trouble: his criticism of the Bangladesh Premier League had not gone down well with the board, who had made him sign a letter of apology before confirming him as captain.

Pakistan, though, arrived in Dhaka relatively fresh and, for once, trouble-free. Perhaps that explained why Misbah-ul-Haq's side – under new coach Dav Whatmore – emerged as winners, but it was close. More surprising was the identity of the team that took them all the way – Bangladesh. They delighted their fans with several fine displays which, for once, owed more to teamwork than individual brilliance. Shakib Al Hasan, the Man of the Series, was the pick of the Bangladeshis, but Tamim passed 50 in each match, and the rest chipped in.

After almost upsetting Pakistan in the opening game, Bangladesh spoiled Tendulkar's big moment: more than a year after he had scored his 99th international century, he carefully completed his 100th – too carefully, for some tastes – only for Bangladesh to sweep to victory, in the process breaking their record for a run-chase against a senior nation.

India soon broke their own record, thanks to Virat Kohli's four-filled 183 against Pakistan, which meant Bangladesh needed to beat Sri Lanka in the last round-robin match to reach the final at India's expense. And they did, despite a barrage of bouncers and yorkers from Lasith Malinga in a rain-interrupted game. Bangladesh were in the final – only their second of note (the first, at home in January 2009, had come at the expense of Zimbabwe in a triangular series).

Bangladesh had narrowly lost that game, to Sri Lanka, and again fell at the last hurdle here, although only after one of the closest and most emotional finals of recent memory. Pakistan nicked it by two runs thanks, unusually, to their fielding: after they stuttered to 236, it was Younis Khan's safe catching to dismiss the top three, coupled with Hammad Azam's athleticism, which proved the difference.

NATIONAL SQUADS

Bangladesh *Mushfiqur Rahim, Abdur Razzak, Anamul Haque, Elias Sunny, Imrul Kayes, Jahurul Islam, Mahmudullah, Mashrafe bin Mortaza, Nasir Hossain, Nazimuddin, Nazmul Hossain, Shafiul Islam, Shahadat Hossain, Shakib Al Hasan, Tamim Iqbal. *Coach:* S. G. Law.

India *M. S. Dhoni, R. Ashwin, A. B. Dinda, G. Gambhir, R. A. Jadeja, V. Kohli, P. Kumar, I. K. Pathan, Y. K. Pathan, S. K. Raina, R. Sharma, R. G. Sharma, S. R. Tendulkar, M. K. Tiwary, R. Vinay Kumar. *Coach:* D. A. G. Fletcher.

Pakistan *Misbah-ul-Haq, Abdur Rehman, Aizaz Cheema, Asad Shafiq, Azhar Ali, Hammad Azam, Mohammad Hafeez, Nasir Jamshed, Saeed Ajmal, Sarfraz Ahmed, Shahid Afridi, Umar Akmal, Umar Gul, Wahab Riaz, Younis Khan. *Coach:* D. F. Whatmore.

Sri Lanka *D. P. M. D. Jayawardene, L. D. Chandimal, T. M. Dilshan, K. M. D. N. Kulasekara, R. A. S. Lakmal, M. F. Maharoof, S. L. Malinga, A. D. Mathews, N. L. T. C. Perera, S. Prasanna, K. C. Sangakkara, S. M. S. M. Senanayake, W. U. Tharanga, H. D. R. L. Thirimanne. *Coach:* G. X. Ford.

Mathews injured a calf muscle early in the tournament and was replaced by R. M. S. Eranga.

BANGLADESH v PAKISTAN

At Mirpur, March 11, 2012 (day/night). Pakistan won by 21 runs. Pakistan 4pts. Toss: Bangladesh.

Shakib Al Hasan's fatal heave, his stumps splattered behind him, summed up the tournament opener: a game lost by Bangladesh rather than won by Pakistan. Tamim Iqbal had provided some solidity at the top with a watchful 64, then Shakib and Nasir Hossain revived the chase after a mid-innings wobble. The Bangladeshis were 224 for five in the 44th over, needing only 39 more, but Umar Gul scissored an inswinger through Nasir's gate to prompt the decisive collapse. Earlier, Pakistan had banked on solidity, initially from Mohammad Hafeez and Nasir Jamshed, who put on 135; at the end of the innings Gul belted 39 from 25 balls. Shahid Afridi poked his first ball back towards the bowler, Shakib, who juggled it, palmed it on to the chest of Misbah-ul-Haq, the non-striker, then somehow pocketed the rebound.

Man of the Match: Mohammad Hafeez.

Pakistan

Mohammad Hafeez c Shafiul Islam b Shahadat Hossain . 89
Nasir Jamshed run out 54
Younis Khan c Abdur Razzak b Shahadat Hossain . 12
Umar Akmal c Abdur Razzak b Shakib Al Hasan . 21
Asad Shafiq c Mashrafe bin Mortaza b Shahadat Hossain . 4
*Misbah-ul-Haq b Abdur Razzak 8
Shahid Afridi c and b Shakib Al Hasan. . . . 0
†Sarfraz Ahmed not out. 19
Umar Gul b Mashrafe bin Mortaza 39
Saeed Ajmal not out 8
L-b 2, w 5, n-b 1 8

1/135 (2) 2/160 (3) (8 wkts, 50 overs) 262
3/169 (1) 4/175 (5)
5/192 (4) 6/193 (7)
7/198 (6) 8/251 (9) 10 overs: 36-0

Aizaz Cheema did not bat.

Mashrafe bin Mortaza 10–0–55–1; Shafiul Islam 8–0–49–0; Shakib Al Hasan 10–0–41–2; Shahadat Hossain 8–0–53–3; Abdur Razzak 10–0–43–1; Mahmudullah 4–0–19–0.

Bangladesh

Tamim Iqbal b Mohammad Hafeez. 64
Nazimuddin c Umar Gul b Aizaz Cheema . 30
Jahurul Islam b Shahid Afridi 23
*†Mushfiqur Rahim b Shahid Afridi 3
Shakib Al Hasan b Umar Gul 64
Mahmudullah lbw b Mohammad Hafeez . . 0
Nasir Hossain b Umar Gul 47
Abdur Razzak b Saeed Ajmal 1
Mashrafe bin Mortaza b Saeed Ajmal. 1
Shafiul Islam lbw b Umar Gul. 1
Shahadat Hossain not out 0
L-b 2, w 5 7

1/45 (2) 2/90 (3) 3/100 (4) (48.1 overs) 241
4/135 (1) 5/135 (6) 6/224 (7)
7/228 (8) 8/230 (9) 9/235 (10)
10/241 (5) 10 overs: 43-0

Mohammad Hafeez 10–1–40–2; Umar Gul 9.1–0–58–3; Saeed Ajmal 10–0–45–2; Aizaz Cheema 9–0–47–1; Shahid Afridi 10–0–49–2.

Umpires: I. J. Gould and P. R. Reiffel. Third umpire: S. Ravi.

INDIA v SRI LANKA

At Mirpur, March 13, 2012 (day/night). India won by 50 runs. India: 4pts. Toss: Sri Lanka.

Two weeks after he had performed heroics against Sri Lanka in Hobart, Kohli took another century off them, although this was far more measured than his Bellerive barnstormer. On a pitch that tested his patience, Kohli held back the big shots as he built a match-winning alliance with Gambhir. They put on 205 – the third time they had shared a stand of 200 or more – and picked up boundaries at will as they both completed their tenth one-day international centuries. Dhoni and Raina provided a hard-running, big-hitting final flourish which took India past 300 against an attack lacking the rested Lasith Malinga. Sri Lanka stayed in the hunt until the final quarter of the match, thanks to the usual suspects, Jayawardene and Sangakkara. But when Sangakkara fell to the first ball of the 36th over, India sensed their chance – and grabbed it. Pathan finished with four wickets, while Ashwin and Vinay Kumar kept things quiet at the other end.

Man of the Match: V. Kohli.

India

G. Gambhir c Tharanga b Maharoof 100
S. R. Tendulkar c Jayawardene b Lakmal . . 6
V. Kohli c Thirimanne b Maharoof. 108
*†M. S. Dhoni not out 46
S. K. Raina not out 30
L-b 7, w 7 14

1/19 (2) 2/224 (1) (3 wkts, 50 overs) 304
3/226 (3) 10 overs: 43-1

R. G. Sharma, R. A. Jadeja, I. K. Pathan, R. Ashwin, P. Kumar and R. Vinay Kumar did not bat.

Kulasekara 10–0–67–0; Lakmal 10–1–67–1; Dilshan 10–0–54–0; Prasanna 9–0–45–0; Maharoof 10–0–57–2; Kapugedera 1–0–7–0.

Sri Lanka

*D. P. M. D. Jayawardene c Dhoni b Pathan 78	S. Prasanna c Tendulkar b Pathan 8
T. M. Dilshan c Kohli b Pathan. 7	R. A. S. Lakmal not out. 0
†K. C. Sangakkara c Jadeja b Ashwin. 65	
L. D. Chandimal b Ashwin 13	L-b 2, w 6 8
H. D. R. L. Thirimanne lbw b Ashwin 29	——
K. M. D. N. Kulasekara b Vinay Kumar. . . 11	1/31 (2) 2/124 (1) (45.1 overs) 254
W. U. Tharanga b Pathan 17	3/152 (4) 4/196 (3) 5/198 (5)
C. K. Kapugedera c Kohli b Vinay Kumar . 0	6/216 (6) 7/216 (8) 8/241 (7)
M. F. Maharoof c Raina b Vinay Kumar. . . 18	9/254 (9) 10/254 (10) 10 overs: 65-1

Pathan 8.1–1–32–4; P. Kumar 7–0–47–0; Vinay Kumar 9–0–55–3; Jadeja 4–0–31–0; Raina 5–0–34–0; Ashwin 9–0–39–3; Sharma 3–0–14–0.

Umpires: S. J. Davis and I. J. Gould. Third umpire: Shozab Raza.

PAKISTAN v SRI LANKA

At Mirpur, March 15, 2012 (day/night). Pakistan won by six wickets. Pakistan 5pts. Toss: Sri Lanka.

Pakistan booked a place in the final after a combination of Aizaz Cheema's luck, Saeed Ajmal's magic and some excellent catching brought them a comfortable victory, with 61 balls to spare – and a bonus point. Cheema took four wickets in a one-day international for the first time, three of them down to poor shot-selection; the other one – Dilshan top-edging a pull to midwicket – owed much to the bowler's shoulder strength on a pitch that otherwise offered little bounce. Ajmal made the crucial breakthrough when he threaded a doosra through Tharanga's defences to break a stand of 96 with Sangakkara and spark a terminal collapse of six for 27. Pakistan made a nervy start, slipping to 33 for three, but Misbah-ul-Haq and Umar Akmal settled down – defying the returning Malinga – in a stand eventually worth 152.

Man of the Match: Aizaz Cheema.

Sri Lanka

*D. P. M. D. Jayawardene c Mohammad Hafeez b Aizaz Cheema . 12	S. Prasanna not out 5
T. M. Dilshan c Saeed Ajmal b Aizaz Cheema . 20	S. L. Malinga b Aizaz Cheema 1
†K. C. Sangakkara b Aizaz Cheema 71	R. A. S. Lakmal c Nasir Jamshed b Saeed Ajmal . 0
L. D. Chandimal c Younis Khan b Umar Gul 0	
H. D. R. L. Thirimanne c Umar Akmal b Hammad Azam . 7	L-b 5, w 4 9
W. U. Tharanga b Saeed Ajmal. 57	——
M. F. Maharoof c Misbah-ul-Haq b Saeed Ajmal . 2	1/33 (1) 2/43 (2) 3/47 (4) (45.4 overs) 188
	4/65 (5) 5/161 (6) 6/165 (7)
K. M. D. N. Kulasekara c Sarfraz Ahmed b Umar Gul . 4	7/172 (8) 8/182 (3) 9/187 (10)
	10/188 (11) 10 overs: 52-3

Umar Gul 8–1–20–2; Aizaz Cheema 9–0–43–4; Mohammad Hafeez 10–0–40–0; Hammad Azam 4–0–21–1; Saeed Ajmal 8.4–1–27–3; Shahid Afridi 6–0–32–0.

Pakistan

Mohammad Hafeez c Chandimal b Prasanna 11	Hammad Azam not out 4
Nasir Jamshed c Tharanga b Lakmal. 18	L-b 1, w 2, n-b 2 5
Younis Khan c Maharoof b Lakmal 2	——
*Misbah-ul-Haq not out. 72	1/29 (2) 2/31 (1) (4 wkts, 39.5 overs) 189
Umar Akmal c Tharanga b Maharoof 77	3/33 (3) 4/185 (5) 10 overs: 31-1

Shahid Afridi, †Sarfraz Ahmed, Umar Gul, Saeed Ajmal and Aizaz Cheema did not bat.

Malinga 8–1–44–0; Kulasekara 7–2–22–0; Lakmal 8–1–37–2; Prasanna 7.5–1–49–1; Maharoof 7–0–23–1; Dilshan 2–0–13–0.

Umpires: S. J. Davis and P. R. Reiffel. Third umpire: Sharfuddoula.

BANGLADESH v INDIA

At Mirpur, March 16, 2012 (day/night). Bangladesh won by five wickets. Bangladesh 4pts. Toss: Bangladesh.

Under the Dhaka sun, Tendulkar reached his much-hyped oasis after a drought lasting a year (and four days). Such was a nation's collective sense of relief and release, it seemed almost incidental that his 100th international hundred came in a match India would contrive to lose. The search for this statistical nirvana – and the ballyhoo which had accompanied almost every innings since the 99th, against South Africa during the 2011 World Cup – slowed Tendulkar down late on and, with the Bangladeshi bowlers keeping the big hitters quiet at the end, India's final total was imposing rather than impossible. Between the 31st and 40th overs, they managed only 49 runs, with Tendulkar moving from 78 to 95 before finally reaching his milestone off the fourth ball of the 44th over; in all he faced 147 deliveries. Bangladesh, by contrast, collected 73 in that ten-over block, which put them in the box seat, and they completed their mammoth chase – their largest to beat a higher-ranked side – in the final over. Shakib Al Hasan clubbed five fours and two sixes, and Mushfiqur Rahim picked up the baton with 46 off 25 balls, fuelled by a cluster of sixes: in the 48th over, he flicked Pathan over midwicket and hammered the subsequent full toss, before climbing into Kumar in the 49th. Teamwork has rarely been Bangladesh's forte but, on a night that should have belonged exclusively to Tendulkar, they ganged up to steal at least some of the headlines.

Man of the Match: Shakib Al Hasan.

MOST INTERNATIONAL HUNDREDS

		Tests	*ODIs*	*T20Is*
100	**S. R. Tendulkar (India)**	**51**	**49**	**0**
71	**R. T. Ponting (Australia/World)**	**41**	**30**	**0**
61	**J. H. Kallis (South Africa/World/Africa)**	**44**	**17**	**0**
53	B. C. Lara (West Indies/World)	34	19	0
48	**R. Dravid (India/World/Asia)**	**36**	**12**	**0**
47	**D. P. M. D. Jayawardene (Sri Lanka/Asia)**	**31**	**15**	**1**
44	**K. C. Sangakkara (Sri Lanka/World/Asia)**	**30**	**14**	**0**
42	S. T. Jayasuriya (Sri Lanka/Asia)	14	28	0
40	M. L. Hayden (Australia/World)	30	10	0

Figures correct at January 14, 2013.

THE LONG AND WINDING ROAD

Sachin Tendulkar's 100th international hundred was – rather surprisingly – his first against Bangladesh in one-day internationals. His highest score in 11 previous games against them had been 82 not out, in July 2004. But he had made up for it in Tests, with five centuries in seven matches, including his career-best 248 not out at Dhaka in December 2004. Overall, 20 of Tendulkar's 100 international centuries had come at Australia's expense, 17 against Sri Lanka, South Africa 12, England and New Zealand nine, Zimbabwe eight, Pakistan and West Indies seven, Bangladesh six, Kenya four and Namibia one.

Fifty-three came in Indian victories (20 in Tests and 33 in one-day internationals), 25 in defeats (11 in Tests, 14 in one-day internationals), 20 in draws (all in Tests), one in a tie (against England in the 2011 World Cup at Bangalore), and one in a no-result (a rain-affected one-dayer against England at Chester-le-Street in 2002).

Munir-uz-Zaman, AFP/Getty Images

Worth the wait? Sachin Tendulkar finally celebrates his 100th hundred – but India go on to lose.

India

G. Gambhir b Shafiul Islam. 11
S. R. Tendulkar c Mushfiqur Rahim
b Mashrafe bin Mortaza. 114
V. Kohli b Abdur Razzak 66
S. K. Raina c Tamim Iqbal
b Mashrafe bin Mortaza. 51
*†M. S. Dhoni not out 21
R. G. Sharma run out. 4
R. A. Jadeja not out 4
L-b 6, w 10, n-b 2 18

1/25 (1) 2/173 (3) (5 wkts, 50 overs) 289
3/259 (4) 4/259 (2)
5/267 (6) 10 overs: 49-1

I. K. Pathan, R. Ashwin, P. Kumar and A. B. Dinda did not bat.

Mashrafe bin Mortaza 10–1–44–2; Shafiul Islam 5–0–24–1; Shahadat Hossain 10–0–81–0; Shakib Al Hasan 10–0–63–0; Abdur Razzak 10–0–41–1; Mahmudullah 4–0–24–0; Nasir Hossain 1–0–6–0.

Bangladesh

Tamim Iqbal c Jadeja b Kumar 70
Nazimuddin c Sharma b Kumar 5
Jahurul Islam c Sharma b Jadeja 53
Nasir Hossain c Raina b Kumar 54
Shakib Al Hasan st Dhoni b Ashwin. 49
*†Mushfiqur Rahim not out 46
Mahmudullah not out 4
L-b 7, w 3, n-b 2 12

1/15 (2) 2/128 (3) (5 wkts, 49.2 overs) 293
3/156 (1) 4/224 (5)
5/288 (4) 10 overs: 38-1

Mashrafe bin Mortaza, Abdur Razzak, Shafiul Islam and Shahadat Hossain did not bat.

Kumar 10–0–56–3; Pathan 9–0–61–0; Dinda 5.2–1–38–0; Raina 7–1–30–0; Sharma 2–0–13–0; Ashwin 10–0–56–1; Jadeja 6–0–32–1.

Umpires: I. J. Gould and P. R. Reiffel. Third umpire: R. S. A. Palliyaguruge.

INDIA v PAKISTAN

At Mirpur, March 18, 2012 (day/night). India won by six wickets. India 4pts. Toss: Pakistan.

Kohli's fourth century at the Shere Bangla Stadium, an innings of 183 laden with 22 fours and a delightful six over long-off, kept India afloat – for two more days at least. He faced the third ball of the innings, after Gambhir fell to off-spinner Mohammad Hafeez, but combined well with Tendulkar, batting without the millstone of *that* 100th hundred for the first time in more than a year. Their stand was worth 133, before Kohli broke loose in concert with Rohit Sharma, adding 172 in 26 overs. Two overs later, India surpassed the 326 they had made against England on a heady day at Lord's in July 2002 to complete their highest successful one-day run-chase. Pakistan looked to have a good bowling attack, but that counted for little against the in-form Kohli, who trumped a stunning first-wicket stand of 224 inside 36 overs between Hafeez and Nasir Jamshed. The only higher one-day international opening stand in a defeat was 235, also against India, by Herschelle Gibbs and Gary Kirsten for South Africa at Kochi in 1999-2000.

Man of the Match: V. Kohli.

Pakistan

Mohammad Hafeez lbw b Dinda	105
Nasir Jamshed c I. K. Pathan b Ashwin	112
†Umar Akmal c Gambhir b Kumar	28
Younis Khan c Raina b Kumar	52
Shahid Afridi c Kohli b I. K. Pathan	9
Hammad Azam c Kohli b Dinda	4
*Misbah-ul-Haq not out	4
Umar Gul not out	0
B 1, l-b 3, w 10, n-b 1	15
1/224 (2) 2/225 (1) 3/273 (3) 4/313 (5) 5/323 (4) 6/326 (6) (6 wkts, 50 overs)	329
10 overs: 51-0	

Wahab Riaz, Saeed Ajmal and Aizaz Cheema did not bat.

Kumar 10–0–77–2; I. K. Pathan 10–0–69–1; Dinda 8–0–47–2; Raina 2.2–0–15–0; Sharma 3–0–19–0; Y. K. Pathan 5–0–30–0; Ashwin 10–0–56–1; Tendulkar 1.4–0–12–0.

India

G. Gambhir lbw b Mohammad Hafeez	0
S. R. Tendulkar c Younis Khan b Saeed Ajmal	52
V. Kohli c Mohammad Hafeez b Umar Gul	183
R. G. Sharma c Shahid Afridi b Umar Gul	68
S. K. Raina not out	12
*†M. S. Dhoni not out	4
B 5, l-b 1, w 4, n-b 1	11
1/0 (1) 2/133 (2) 3/305 (4) 4/318 (3) (4 wkts, 47.5 overs)	330
10 overs: 58-1	

Y. K. Pathan, I. K. Pathan, R. Ashwin, P. Kumar and A. B. Dinda did not bat.

Mohammad Hafeez 9–0–42–1; Umar Gul 8.5–0–65–2; Aizaz Cheema 8–0–60–0; Saeed Ajmal 9–0–49–1; Shahid Afridi 9–0–58–0; Wahab Riaz 4–0–50–0.

Umpires: S. J. Davis and I. J. Gould. Third umpire: Sharfuddoula.

BANGLADESH v SRI LANKA

At Mirpur, March 20, 2012 (day/night). Bangladesh won by five wickets (D/L). Bangladesh 4pts. Toss: Bangladesh.

Very occasionally, a game of cricket changes the mood of a nation: this was one such moment. Bangladesh calmly chased 212 in 40 overs to gift their fervent supporters a major final after years of disappointment. Just as sweetly, Bangladesh's victory edged out India, thanks to the result in their head-to-head encounter. Again it was Shakib Al Hasan who drove them into a position of strength, but his dismissal – four overs after the departure of Tamim Iqbal set the alarm bells ringing, as the revised target was still 77 runs away (there had been a 90-minute rain delay). However, Mahmudullah and Nasir Hossain coolly took Bangladesh over the line in the face of a barrage from Malinga. Senanayake's off-spin also induced a few jitters, but not enough – and Sri Lanka returned home without a win.

Man of the Match: Shakib Al Hasan.

Sri Lanka

*D. P. M. D. Jayawardene b Nazmul Hossain . . . 5
T. M. Dilshan b Nazmul Hossain 19
†K. C. Sangakkara c Nazimuddin b Nazmul Hossain . 6
C. K. Kapugedera c Shakib Al Hasan b Abdur Razzak . 62
H. D. R. L. Thirimanne st Mushfiqur Rahim b Abdur Razzak . 48
W. U. Tharanga c Mushfiqur Rahim b Shahadat Hossain . 48
M. F. Maharoof c Mushfiqur Rahim b Shakib Al Hasan . 3
K. M. D. N. Kulasekara lbw b Shakib Al Hasan . 1
S. M. S. M. Senanayake not out 19
S. L. Malinga b Mashrafe bin Mortaza 10
R. A. S. Lakmal run out 0
L-b 3, w 8 11

1/19 (1) 2/29 (3) 3/32 (2) (49.5 overs) 232
4/120 (5) 5/169 (4) 6/175 (7)
7/183 (8) 8/204 (6) 9/230 (10)
10/232 (11) 10 overs: 32-3

Mashrafe bin Mortaza 9.5–1–30–1; Nazmul Hossain 8–1–32–3; Shahadat Hossain 8–0–51–1; Abdur Razzak 10–0–44–2; Shakib Al Hasan 10–1–56–2; Mahmudullah 4–0–16–0.

Bangladesh

Tamim Iqbal c Thirimanne b Senanayake . 59
Nazimuddin b Kulasekara 6
Jahurul Islam c Kapugedera b Lakmal 2
*†Mushfiqur Rahim b Kulasekara 1
Shakib Al Hasan lbw b Senanayake 56
Nasir Hossain not out 36
Mahmudullah not out 32
L-b 13, w 7 20

1/8 (2) 2/39 (3) (5 wkts, 37.1 overs) 212
3/40 (4) 4/116 (1)
5/135 (5) 8 overs: 41-3

Mashrafe bin Mortaza, Abdur Razzak, Shahadat Hossain and Nazmul Hossain did not bat.

Malinga 8–0–29–0; Kulasekara 6–0–30–2; Lakmal 7.1–0–44–1; Senanayake 8–0–38–2; Maharoof 6–0–46–0; Dilshan 2–0–12–0.

Umpires: S. J. Davis and P. R. Reiffel. Third umpire: S. Ravi.

QUALIFYING TABLE

	Played	*Won*	*Lost*	*Bonus points*	*Points*	*Net run-rate*
PAKISTAN	3	2	1	1	9	0.44
BANGLADESH.	3	2	1	0	8	0.02
India	3	2	1	0	8	0.37
Sri Lanka	3	0	3	0	0	–0.88

Bangladesh were placed ahead of India by virtue of their victory over them in the qualifying match.

FINAL

BANGLADESH v PAKISTAN

At Mirpur, March 22, 2012 (day/night). Pakistan won by two runs. Toss: Bangladesh.

A final worthy of the occasion was edged by Pakistan, who drew on their greater experience and produced one of their best fielding displays in recent memory. Younis Khan's three catches and Hammad Azam's agility (which atoned for a dropped chance) pressed home the advantage won by Pakistan's three spinners. Saeed Ajmal was deadly on a pitch that had slowed to a standstill: what seemed a modest total – rescued from 133 for six by a 22-ball blast by Shahid Afridi and an enterprising innings from wicketkeeper Sarfraz Ahmed – turned out to be defendable. Tamim Iqbal hit his fourth successive fifty, and Shakib Al Hasan produced the goods yet again, but the rest couldn't wriggle out of the jam, and Bangladesh were unable to manage nine from the final over, delivered by Aizaz Cheema. There was controversy off the first ball, when Cheema seemed to impede Mahmudullah as he was looking for a second run, but the umpires decided the obstruction was unintentional; a later, official, complaint predictably came to nothing. Bangladesh's young team shed tears after their narrow defeat, and looked inconsolable, despite their two splendid victories earlier in the tournament.

Man of the Match: Shahid Afridi. *Man of the Series:* Shakib Al Hasan.

Pakistan

Mohammad Hafeez c Nazmul Hossain b Abdur Razzak . 40
Nasir Jamshed c Mahmudullah b Mashrafe bin Mortaza . 9
Younis Khan lbw b Nazmul Hossain 1
*Misbah-ul-Haq run out 13
Umar Akmal c Mushfiqur Rahim b Mahmudullah . 30
Hammad Azam c and b Shakib Al Hasan . . 30
Shahid Afridi c Nasir Hossain b Shakib Al Hasan . 32
†Sarfraz Ahmed not out 46
Umar Gul c Shakib Al Hasan b Mashrafe bin Mortaza . 4
Saeed Ajmal b Abdur Razzak 4
Aizaz Cheema not out 9
B 2, l-b 8, w 4, n-b 4 18

1/16 (2) 2/19 (3) 3/55 (4) 4/70 (1) 5/129 (6) 6/133 (5) 7/178 (7) 8/199 (9) 9/206 (10) (9 wkts, 50 overs) 236
10 overs: 43-2

Mashrafe bin Mortaza 10–0–48–2; Nazmul Hossain 8–1–36–1; Abdur Razzak 10–3–26–2; Shahadat Hossain 9–0–63–0; Shakib Al Hasan 10–1–39–2; Mahmudullah 3–0–14–1.

Bangladesh

Tamim Iqbal c Younis Khan b Umar Gul . . 60
Nazimuddin c Younis Khan b Shahid Afridi 16
Jahurul Islam c Younis Khan b Saeed Ajmal 0
Nasir Hossain c Misbah-ul-Haq b Umar Gul 28
Shakib Al Hasan b Aizaz Cheema. 68
*†Mushfiqur Rahim c Nasir Jamshed b Aizaz Cheema . 10
Mahmudullah not out 17
Mashrafe bin Mortaza c Nasir Jamshed b Saeed Ajmal . 18
Abdur Razzak b Aizaz Cheema. 6
Shahadat Hossain not out 0
L-b 5, w 4, n-b 2 11

1/68 (2) 2/68 (3) 3/81 (1) 4/170 (4) 5/179 (5) 6/190 (6) 7/218 (8) 8/233 (9) (8 wkts, 50 overs) 234
10 overs: 35-0

Nazmul Hossain did not bat.

Mohammad Hafeez 10–0–30–0; Umar Gul 10–2–65–2; Saeed Ajmal 10–2–40–2; Shahid Afridi 10–1–28–1; Aizaz Cheema 7–0–46–3; Hammad Azam 3–0–20–0.

Umpires: S. J. Davis and I. J. Gould. Third umpire: S. Ravi.
Series referee: D. C. Boon.

ASIA CUP WINNERS

1983-84	INDIA beat Pakistan by 54 runs at Sharjah.
1985-86	SRI LANKA beat Pakistan by five wickets at Colombo.
1988-89	INDIA beat Sri Lanka by six wickets at Dhaka.
1990-91	INDIA beat Sri Lanka by seven wickets at Calcutta.
1994-95	INDIA beat Sri Lanka by eight wickets at Sharjah.
1997-98	SRI LANKA beat India by eight wickets at Colombo.
1999-2000	PAKISTAN beat Sri Lanka by 39 runs at Dhaka.
2004	SRI LANKA beat India by 25 runs at Colombo.
2008	SRI LANKA beat India by 100 runs at Karachi.
2010	INDIA beat Sri Lanka by 81 runs at Dambulla.
2011-12	PAKISTAN beat Bangladesh by two runs at Mirpur.

BANGLADESH v WEST INDIES, 2012-13

UTPAL SHUVRO

Test matches (2): Bangladesh 0, West Indies 2
One-day internationals (5): Bangladesh 3, West Indies 2
Twenty20 international (1): Bangladesh 0, West Indies 1

West Indies toured Bangladesh for the second year running, this time with a bit more swagger after carrying off the World Twenty20 title in Sri Lanka two months previously. Chris Gayle was back, and Sunil Narine's reputation boosted by his performances in the IPL. They looked a united and happy bunch under Darren Sammy's relaxed leadership.

Sammy is an exception in modern cricket: there were no airs about him, and he was hardly seen without a smile on his face throughout the tour, though admittedly it had faded by the time Bangladesh took the one-day series 3–2. West Indies had already won both Tests, and finished on a winning note in the only Twenty20 match, but the one-day defeats were hard to take. Before they started, Sammy had outlined the rankings points he hoped to notch up: it didn't seem like arrogance, as his side were studded with big hitters such as Gayle and Kieron Pollard, and that Twenty20 triumph in Sri Lanka was fresh in the memory. Even Sammy's opposite number, Mushfiqur Rahim, said West Indies were the best one-day team in the world. On the field, however, the story unfolded differently, as Bangladesh's spinners strangled the Caribbean clobberers. The hosts won the first two matches – the second by a record margin – and kept their nerve to clinch the decider after West Indies fought back to 2–2.

Bangladesh's performances in the Tests had to be weighed against the fact that they hadn't played one for almost 11 months, whereas West Indies had already contested eight in 2012. In the circumstances, Bangladesh competed well in the First Test at Mirpur, trumping West Indies' 527 with 556, only to slide to a disappointing defeat on the final day. The Second Test – the first to be played at Khulna – was a more comprehensive victory for the visitors.

Bangladesh's newcomers were also their star performers. In the First Test, Sohag Gazi – a 21-year-old from Barisal – became the first specialist off-spinner to be capped by Bangladesh in almost a decade, and took nine wickets, despite being given the new ball and struck for two sixes by Gayle in the opening over, uniquely, including one off the first ball. Then, in the Second Test, 20-year-old seamer Abul Hasan shocked everyone by becoming only the second No. 10 to score a century on Test debut.

For West Indies, Marlon Samuels continued his fine form, but the big names were disappointments: Gayle scored only 88 runs in the two Tests, and his form didn't improve in the one-dayers, where his best score was 35. Narine, meanwhile, managed only three for 343 in the Tests, although he did have better luck once the limited-overs matches got going. The Tests were a triumph for the fast bowler Tino Best, who improved his career-best in both games, bowling intelligently in the Second despite a hamstring twinge.

WEST INDIAN TOURING PARTY

*D. J. G. Sammy, T. L. Best, D. M. Bravo, S. Chanderpaul, N. Deonarine, F. H. Edwards, K. A. Edwards, A. B. Fudadin, C. H. Gayle, S. P. Narine, V. Permaul, K. O. A. Powell, D. Ramdin, R. Rampaul, M. N. Samuels. *Coach:* O. D. Gibson.

K. A. J. Roach was originally selected for the Test leg, but withdrew with a knee injury and was replaced by F. H. Edwards. Roach was fit to take his place in the limited-overs series, for which he, K. A. Pollard, A. D. Russell, L. M. P. Simmons, D. R. Smith and D. C. Thomas replaced Chanderpaul, Deonarine, F. H. Edwards, K. A. Edwards, Fudadin and Ramdin. Best was originally chosen to stay on for the limited-overs matches, but injured a hamstring before they started; he was replaced by J. O. Holder.

At Savar, November 8–10, 2012. **Bangladesh Cricket Board XI v West Indians. Abandoned.**

BANGLADESH v WEST INDIES

First Test Match

At Mirpur, November 13–17, 2012. West Indies won by 77 runs. Toss: West Indies. Test debuts: Sohag Gazi; V. Permaul.

It was a surprise for the early morning crowd. Was that Sohag Gazi, the new kid on the block? And was he really bowling the first over, with the fearsome Chris Gayle on strike? Yes, it was indeed Gazi, the first debutant slow bowler to take the new ball in the first innings of a Test, since the England leg-spinner Douglas Carr at The Oval against Australia in 1909. It took only one ball to add to the history: Gazi's first delivery was deposited over long-on, the first instance of a six off the first ball of a Test. Gayle hit Gazi's fourth ball over the rope too, and 18 (including four leg-byes) came from the over. But Mushfiqur Rahim bravely kept Gazi on, and was rewarded when Gayle holed out at long-off in his third over, aiming for six more.

And a Test which started in such dramatic fashion had an equally exciting finish. After both teams passed 500 in their first innings – Bangladesh's 556 was a new national record – a draw seemed likely until West Indies slid from 209 for one to 273 all out. Gazi rounded off the collapse, taking the last four wickets on the final morning (including Chanderpaul, who was ill and batted at No. 11) to finish with six for 74, the best debut figures for Bangladesh. That left a tempting target of 245 in two and a half sessions for them to complete a rare Test victory – only for the Bangladeshis to crumble to another defeat in depressingly familiar fashion.

Another new cap, slow left-armer Veerasammy Permaul from Guyana, was expected to be the main threat in the West Indian attack, along with the unorthodox spin of Narine – but it was the wholehearted Best, continuing the good form he had displayed since his surprise recall earlier in the year, who tipped the balance on the last day. Tearing in, and typically unafraid to unleash the bouncer, Best took four wickets either side of lunch, which in effect ended Bangladesh's dreams: fittingly, it was Best who ended the match, castling Mahmudullah an hour into the final session to complete his first five-for in Tests.

While the West Indian players celebrated, Bangladesh's looked woebegone. They had, after all, responded to a huge score with one of their own, passing 500 for the first time: only twice previously had a team exceeded their eventual total and gone on to lose.

In a display of old-fashioned Test cricket (at least after the early fireworks from Gayle), West Indies had amassed 527 for four before declaring. After the well-organised Powell made his second Test century, Chanderpaul ground his way to his 26th, and extended it to his second score of 203 not out, in more than seven and a half hours. He put on an unbroken 296 with Ramdin, who completed his third Test hundred.

TWO CENTURIES IN A TEST FOR WEST INDIES

G. A. Headley	114 and 112	v England at Georgetown	1929-30
G. A. Headley	106 and 107	v England at Lord's	1939
E. D. Weekes	162 and 101	v India at Calcutta	1948-49
C. L. Walcott	126 and 110	v Australia at Port-of-Spain	1954-55
C. L. Walcott	155 and 110	v Australia at Kingston	1954-55
G. S. Sobers	125 and 109*	v Pakistan at Georgetown	1957-58
R. B. Kanhai	117 and 115	v Australia at Adelaide	1960-61
L. G. Rowe†	214 and 100*	v New Zealand at Kingston	1971-72
C. G. Greenidge	134 and 101	v England at Manchester	1976
B. C. Lara	221 and 130	v Sri Lanka at Colombo (SSC)	2001-02
K. O. A. Powell	**117 and 110**	**v Bangladesh at Mirpur**	**2012-13**

† *On debut. Walcott's two instances were, uniquely, in the same series.*

Bangladesh's spirited reply was based on Naeem Islam's maiden Test century, a dogged affair *à la* Chanderpaul. He put on 167 with Shakib Al Hasan, a record for their fourth wicket, and Nasir Hossain and Mahmudullah kept up the fight. They went past the country's previous highest total – 488 against Zimbabwe at Chittagong in 2004-05 – before Mahmudullah was caught at bat-pad. Nasir, who hit four sixes, was unlucky to miss a maiden century of his own, edging low to Gayle at slip.

Gayle fell before the arrears were cleared, but Powell made another fine century – only the 11th instance of two in a match by a West Indian – and a draw looked likely as his side cruised past 200 for the loss of one wicket towards the end of the fourth day. Then came one collapse, swiftly followed by another. Bangladesh had taken a first-innings lead for only the ninth time in their 74 Tests – but in the end it was not enough, as they slid to their 64th defeat.

Man of the Match: K. O. A. Powell.

Close of play: first day, West Indies 361-4 (Chanderpaul 123, Ramdin 52); second day, Bangladesh 164-3 (Naeem Islam 27, Shakib Al Hasan 16); third day, Bangladesh 455-6 (Nasir Hossain 33, Mahmudullah 42); fourth day, West Indies 244-6 (Sammy 15).

West Indies

C. H. Gayle c Mahmudullah b Sohag Gazi	24	– c Mushfiqur Rahim b Rubel Hossain	19
K. O. A. Powell b Sohag Gazi	117	– c Mushfiqur Rahim b Shakib Al Hasan	110
D. M. Bravo c Rubel Hossain b Sohag Gazi	14	– c Mushfiqur Rahim b Rubel Hossain	76
M. N. Samuels c Sohag Gazi b Shahadat Hossain	16	– c Shahriar Nafees b Sohag Gazi	1
S. Chanderpaul not out	203	– (11) lbw b Sohag Gazi	1
†D. Ramdin not out	126	– (5) lbw b Shakib Al Hasan	5
*D. J. G. Sammy (did not bat)		– (6) lbw b Sohag Gazi	16
V. Permaul (did not bat)		– (7) b Sohag Gazi	10
S. P. Narine (did not bat)		– (8) not out	22
R. Rampaul (did not bat)		– (9) b Sohag Gazi	5
T. L. Best (did not bat)		– (10) b Sohag Gazi	0
B 4, l-b 13, w 2, n-b 8	27	B 1, l-b 3, n-b 4	8
1/32 (1) 2/74 (3) 3/106 (4) 4/231 (2) (4 wkts dec, 144 overs)	527	1/20 (1) 2/209 (3) 3/212 (4) 4/218 (2) 5/225 (5) 6/244 (7) 7/249 (6) 8/265 (9) 9/265 (10) 10/273 (11) (74.2 overs)	273

Sohag Gazi 47–7–145–3; Shahadat Hossain 21–3–85–1; Rubel Hossain 18–0–89–0; Mahmudullah 14–0–45–0; Shakib Al Hasan 34–4–104–0; Naeem Islam 8–1–24–0; Nasir Hossain 1–0–8–0; Tamim Iqbal 1–0–10–0. *Second innings*—Sohag Gazi 23.2–2–74–6; Rubel Hossain 19–4–53–2; Mahmudullah 3–0–12–0; Shahadat Hossain 7–1–34–0; Shakib Al Hasan 11–2–56–2; Naeem Islam 8–0–22–0; Nasir Hossain 3–0–18–0.

Bangladesh

Tamim Iqbal c Narine b Sammy	72	– c Ramdin b Rampaul	5
Junaid Siddique c Bravo b Rampaul	7	– c Ramdin b Best	20
Shahriar Nafees c Ramdin b Rampaul	31	– c and b Best	23
Naeem Islam c Ramdin b Sammy	108	– lbw b Permaul	26
Shakib Al Hasan c sub (A. B. Fudadin) b Rampaul	89	– c Ramdin b Best	2
*†Mushfiqur Rahim c and b Permaul	43	– lbw b Best	16
Nasir Hossain c Gayle b Best	96	– b Permaul	21
Mahmudullah c Powell b Narine	62	– b Best	29
Sohag Gazi b Narine	4	– c sub (N. Deonarine) b Permaul	19
Shahadat Hossain b Narine	13	– c Powell b Rampaul	4
Rubel Hossain not out	0	– not out	0
B 8, l-b 12, w 3, n-b 8	31	B 1, n-b 1	2
1/25 (2) 2/88 (3) 3/119 (1) (148.3 overs)	556	1/10 (1) 2/44 (2) (54.3 overs)	167
4/286 (5) 5/362 (4) 6/368 (6)		3/51 (3) 4/55 (5)	
7/489 (8) 8/493 (9) 9/554 (7) 10/556 (10)		5/85 (6) 6/106 (4) 7/119 (7)	
		8/155 (9) 9/159 (10) 10/167 (8)	

Rampaul 32–2–118–3; Best 23–3–77–1; Sammy 23–3–83–2; Narine 32.3–5–148–3; Permaul 29–7–75–1; Gayle 3–0–14–0; Samuels 6–0–21–0. *Second innings*—Rampaul 11–1–32–2; Narine 18–1–56–0; Best 12.3–2–24–5; Permaul 8–0–32–3; Sammy 3–0–13–0; Samuels 2–0–9–0.

Umpires: R. K. Illingworth and B. N. J. Oxenford. Third umpire: Enamul Haque.

BANGLADESH v WEST INDIES

Second Test Match

At Khulna, November 21–25, 2012. West Indies won by ten wickets. Toss: Bangladesh. Test debut: Abul Hasan.

Bangladesh had fought valiantly in the First Test, but this time victory came rather more easily for West Indies, who completed a 2–0 sweep. As they had also beaten New Zealand in both Tests in the Caribbean four months previously, it meant they had won four successive matches, something which had proved beyond them since the dying days of their glory years, in 1992-93. Richie Richardson, now the team manager, was captain then: "The signs of decline were there," he said with a rueful smile, "but I never thought it would take so long to win four consecutive Tests again."

The Sheikh Abu Naser Stadium in Khulna became the seventh Test ground in Bangladesh – and the 107th, all told – which was a source of great pride to the locals, who put up lights and special gates in the streets, and gave the teams a royal welcome. People were queuing to get in, a rare sight for a Test on the subcontinent these days.

Those lucky enough to make it inside witnessed a rare feat: 20-year-old Abul Hasan, making his debut primarily as a fast bowler, came in at No. 10 and scored a scintillating century. It took him only 106 balls, even though he slowed up a little in sight of the historic milestone. The frontline batsmen had struggled on a slow, low pitch, and a swift end was expected when Hasan strolled out at 193 for eight – but he dominated a stand of 184 in 33 overs with the more experienced Mahmudullah. Hasan, a right-arm bowler but a left-hand bat, zoomed to fifty with four and six – using his feet and lofting down the ground – off successive balls from Sammy, and swung Permaul away for two more sixes. He reached his century shortly before the close. Only Australia's Reggie Duff, a batsman

AND THE PENULTIMATE SHALL BE FIRST

Test centuries from No. 10:

W. W. Read	117	England v Australia at The Oval	1884
R. A. Duff	104	Australia v England at Melbourne	1901-02
P. L. Symcox	108	South Africa v Pakistan at Johannesburg	1997-98
Abul Hasan	**113**	**Bangladesh v West Indies at Khulna**	**2012-13**

† *On debut. Read and Duff were specialist batsmen who batted down the order for tactical reasons.*

who went in low down for tactical reasons, had previously scored a debut hundred from No. 10, in the 1901-02 Ashes. And only two batsmen had previously made a hundred on debut for Bangladesh – Aminul Islam, in their inaugural Test against India, at Dhaka in 2000-01, and Mohammad Ashraful, against Sri Lanka in Colombo the following season.

The Bangladesh innings was polished off in 31 balls next morning, as Edwards finished with six for 90. Sammy took three, although the so-called mystery man Narine failed to strike. Sadly for Bangladesh, Hasan proved less of a hit with the ball: having scored 113, he now completed a unique double by conceding 113 too – no debut centurion had ever conceded a century of runs with the ball as well. Only the contrasting spin of Sohag Gazi and Shakib Al Hasan bothered the batsmen: West Indies batted for more than seven sessions, and Sammy did not declare until he had a huge lead and a total touching 650. Even then he might have continued, but did not want to risk aggravating last man Best's sore hamstring.

Bangladesh had started brightly enough in the field. Rubel Hossain dismissed Powell, the twin-centurion of the previous Test, then Gazi got Gayle again, nicking an attempted sweep. But it was nearly 100 overs before another wicket went down, as Bravo and Samuels put on 326. Samuels sailed on after Bravo eventually missed Gazi's quicker one, which ended his fourth Test century, all scored on the subcontinent.

At 369 for three, just about the last new batsman a fielding side would want to see was Chanderpaul, who had thrown off the illness that had bothered him in the later stages at Mirpur. He was soon back in limpet mode, and puttered on with Samuels, adding a further 177 in 54 overs: it was a big surprise when, late on the third day, Rubel got a ball to jump at Samuels, who could only fend it to point. By then he had been at the crease for 618 minutes, and his 260 (just one short of Ramnaresh Sarwan's overall Test record against Bangladesh) contained 31 fours and three sixes. At times he exploited the slowness of the pitch by standing almost square-on against the spinners and working them to leg. He was dropped twice – at 117 and 193 – and also had a stroke of luck when a ball from Shakib rolled into the stumps but did not dislodge the bails. At one point Shakib had none for 134 from 48 overs, but then took four wickets in 17 balls, including his 100th in Tests (Sammy, caught at slip). Only Mohammad Rafique, another left-arm spinner, had previously reached the mark for Bangladesh: he finished with exactly 100, so Shakib soon became their leading wicket-taker too.

When Sammy finally called a halt, Chanderpaul was still there with 150 not out – his 27th Test century – and a series average of 354. Seasoned Bangladesh-watchers feared the lead might be enough for an innings victory, and were almost right: they dipped to 82 for five in the 18th over, before Shakib and Nasir Hossain stopped the rot in a stand eventually worth 144. Both fell just short of centuries: Shakib mistimed an ugly slog against Permaul and was caught at mid-off, while Nasir was cleaned up by Best after reaching 90 for the second time in the series. Best was clearly feeling his hamstring niggle, and bowled below his usual pace – but showed his increased maturity by finding some swing to take three wickets in his first 16 balls, including the important scalp of Tamim Iqbal with his first; his eventual six for 40 meant he had improved his Test-best for the second match running. Shakib and Nasir at least forced West Indies to bat again, but they needed only 27, which the openers knocked off in 28 balls.

Man of the Match: M. N. Samuels. *Man of the Series:* S. Chanderpaul.

Close of play: first day, Bangladesh 365-8 (Mahmudullah 72, Abul Hasan 100); second day, West Indies 241-2 (Bravo 85, Samuels 109); third day, West Indies 564-4 (Chanderpaul 109, Ramdin 4); fourth day, Bangladesh 226-6 (Nasir Hossain 64).

Bangladesh

Tamim Iqbal b Sammy	32	– b Best	28
Nazimuddin c Powell b Edwards	4	– lbw b Edwards	0
Shahriar Nafees c Ramdin b Sammy	26	– c Sammy b Best	21
Naeem Islam b Edwards	16	– b Best	2
Shakib Al Hasan c Ramdin b Edwards	17	– c Best b Permaul	97
*†Mushfiqur Rahim c Ramdin b Edwards	38	– b Permaul	10
Nasir Hossain c Edwards b Permaul	52	– b Best	94
Mahmudullah c and b Sammy	76	– c Ramdin b Permaul	2
Sohag Gazi lbw b Edwards	0	– b Best	7
Abul Hasan c Sammy b Edwards	113	– not out	7
Rubel Hossain not out	5	– c Bravo b Best	14
B 4, l-b 3, n-b 1	8	L-b 3, w 1, n-b 1	5
1/5 (2) 2/64 (3) 3/77 (1) 4/93 (4) (91.1 overs)	387	1/1 (2) 2/49 (1) (70.1 overs)	287
5/98 (5) 6/185 (7) 7/193 (6)		3/51 (4) 4/62 (3)	
8/193 (9) 9/377 (8) 10/387 (10)		5/82 (6) 6/226 (5) 7/228 (8)	
		8/254 (9) 9/269 (7) 10/287 (11)	

Edwards 18.1–2–90–6; Best 10–3–31–0; Sammy 23–4–74–3; Narine 19–0–91–0; Permaul 19–2–79–1; Samuels 2–0–15–0. *Second innings*—Edwards 17–0–95–1; Narine 9–0–48–0; Permaul 20–2–67–3; Best 12.1–1–40–6; Gayle 4–0–15–0; Sammy 8–3–19–0.

West Indies

C. H. Gayle c Mushfiqur Rahim b Sohag Gazi	25	– not out	20
K. O. A. Powell c Shakib Al Hasan b Rubel Hossain	13	– not out	9
D. M. Bravo lbw b Sohag Gazi	127		
M. N. Samuels c sub (Elias Sunny) b Rubel Hossain	260		
S. Chanderpaul not out	150		
†D. Ramdin c Mushfiqur Rahim b Shakib Al Hasan	31		
*D. J. G. Sammy c Mahmudullah b Shakib Al Hasan	0		
V. Permaul c Sohag Gazi b Shakib Al Hasan	13		
S. P. Narine c Shahriar Nafees b Shakib Al Hasan	0		
F. H. Edwards c Shakib Al Hasan b Sohag Gazi	2		
B 10, l-b 7, w 2, n-b 8	27	W 1	1
1/37 (2) 2/43 (1) (9 wkts dec, 200.3 overs)	648	(no wkt, 4.4 overs)	30
3/369 (3) 4/546 (4)			
5/621 (6) 6/621 (7) 7/639 (8) 8/639 (9) 9/648 (10)			

T. L. Best did not bat.

Sohag Gazi 57.3–4–167–3; Abul Hasan 24–0–113–0; Rubel Hossain 31–8–86–2; Naeem Islam 14–1–43–0; Shakib Al Hasan 52–11–151–4; Mahmudullah 10–0–42–0; Nasir Hossain 12–1–29–0. *Second innings*—Sohag Gazi 1–0–8–0; Rubel Hossain 2–0–14–0; Naeem Islam 1.4–1–8–0.

Umpires: R. K. Illingworth and B. N. J. Oxenford. Third umpire: Enamul Haque.
Series referee: D. C. Boon.

At Khulna, November 28, 2012. **West Indians won by 118 runs.** ‡**West Indians 361-7** (50 overs) (L. M. P. Simmons 84, D. C. Thomas 61*; Elias Sunny 3-71); **Bangladesh Cricket Board XI 243** (49.1 overs) (S. P. Narine 3-47). *The sides chose from 12 players, of whom 11 could bat and 11 field. Lendl Simmons set up a big West Indian total, hitting 12 fours and two sixes from 81 deliveries; later Kieron Pollard hit 44 from 28, and Devon Thomas 61* from 43. The Board XI were never on terms.*

LIMITED-OVERS MATCH REPORTS BY MOHAMMAD ISAM

At Khulna, November 30, 2012. **First one-day international: Bangladesh won by seven wickets. ‡West Indies 199** (46.5 overs) (C. H. Gayle 35, D. M. Bravo 35, S. P. Narine 36; Sohag Gazi 4-29, Abdur Razzak 3-39); **Bangladesh 201-3** (40.2 overs) (Tamim Iqbal 58, Anamul Haque 41, Naeem Islam 50*). *MoM:* Sohag Gazi. *One-day international debuts:* Abul Hasan, Anamul Haque, Mominul Haque, Sohag Gazi (Bangladesh). *West Indies struggled against a varied spin attack, and had to be rescued from 133-8 by Narine and Ravi Rampaul (25), who put on 57. Still, the target was not an imposing one, especially after Tamim Iqbal clouted 58 from 51 balls, and Bangladesh strolled home with almost ten overs to spare. Sohag Gazi's figures were the best by any off-spinner in their first one-day international, and included the wickets of Gayle and Samuels in successive overs.*

At Khulna, December 2, 2012. **Second one-day international: Bangladesh won by 160 runs. Bangladesh 292-6** (50 overs) (Anamul Haque 120, Mushfiqur Rahim 79, Mominul Haque 31; R. Rampaul 5-49); **‡West Indies 132** (31.1 overs) (Sohag Gazi 3-21, Abdur Razzak 3-19). *MoM:* Anamul Haque. *Bangladesh completed their largest victory in any one-day international, in front of a stunned but appreciative crowd. Anamul Haque, in only his second match, tarried in the nervous nineties, but made up for it after finally reaching 100 by taking 20 from his last seven deliveries. He put on 174 in 30 overs with Mushfiqur Rahim, to rescue Bangladesh from 21-2. West Indies never got going, and subsided to defeat in the 32nd over, with eight of the wickets going to spin.*

At Mirpur, December 5, 2012 (day/night). **Third one-day international: West Indies won by four wickets. Bangladesh 227** (49.1 overs) (Anamul Haque 33, Mushfiqur Rahim 38, Mahmudullah 52, Sohag Gazi 30; S. P. Narine 4-37); **‡West Indies 228-6** (47 overs) (K. O. A. Powell 47, M. N. Samuels 126). *MoM:* M. N. Samuels. *One-day international debut:* V. Permaul (West Indies). *West Indies kept the series alive after including slow left-armer Veerasammy Permaul to bolster their spin attack. Tamim Iqbal and Anamul Haque gave Bangladesh a good start with a stand of 57, but then Narine struck twice in the 13th over. Mahmudullah supervised a recovery from 110-5, but West Indies were always in charge of the chase, after Samuels – who countered the spinners well with some nimble footwork during his fourth one-day hundred – dominated a second-wicket stand of 111 with Powell.*

At Mirpur, December 7, 2012 (day/night). **Fourth one-day international: West Indies won by 75 runs. West Indies 211-9** (50 overs) (D. M. Bravo 34, D. J. G. Sammy 60*; Mahmudullah 3-46); **‡Bangladesh 136** (34.1 overs) (Mahmudullah 56*; D. J. G. Sammy 3-28). *MoM:* D. J. G. Sammy. *A fine all-round performance from Sammy helped West Indies square the series with an emphatic victory. He entered at 102-6, but hit out to lift them past 200, before reducing Bangladesh to 13-5 with the help of Roach. There was no comeback, despite another stubborn innings from Mahmudullah. Bangladesh did not help their cause with five dropped catches, including Sammy, when he had 30 of his eventual 60* from 62 balls.*

BANGLADESH v WEST INDIES

Fifth One-Day International

At Mirpur, December 8, 2012 (day/night). Bangladesh won by two wickets. Toss: Bangladesh.

West Indies' comeback from 0–2 had led most to predict they would pinch the series but, to general delight in the stands, it was Bangladesh who prevailed as their middle order batted with more assurance when it mattered. Put in, West Indies struggled at first: Gayle's poor run continued when he cut Shafiul Islam (a late inclusion after Mashrafe bin Mortaza withdrew with a thigh strain) straight to backward point, which made it 17 for three in the eighth over. But Bravo and Pollard rescued them with a stand of 132: Pollard smote eight sixes in all, twice hitting Elias Sunny for two in a row, before he eventually missed one more big hit against another slow left-armer, Mominul Haque. But the rest struggled against the spinners, before Shafiul returned to wrap things up. Bangladesh also made a poor start, losing both openers in the third over, but Mushfiqur Rahim and Mahmudullah settled nerves with a stand of 91 in 12.4 overs. Both eventually fell to Narine, but Nasir Hossain took over, sharing important partnerships with Mominul and Sohag Gazi. At 214 for six in the 43rd over – just four to win – it looked all over, but Roach removed Gazi and Abdur Razzak with successive legal deliveries. In the next over from Russell, with one run now required, Nasir cut towards the fence and the batsmen raced off to celebrate – only the ball never reached the rope. By the time it was returned, the batsmen had souvenired the stumps and were being congratulated by their team-mates. After a delay, which included some optimistic West Indian appeals for a run-out, the umpires decided no run had actually been completed, so the scores were still level. Nasir duly cut the next delivery away – and this time it did make it to the boundary, to seal Bangladesh's 3–2 series win.

Man of the Match: Mahmudullah. *Man of the Series:* Mushfiqur Rahim.

West Indies

K. O. A. Powell st Mushfiqur Rahim b Sohag Gazi	11
C. H. Gayle c Nasir Hossain b Shafiul Islam	2
M. N. Samuels run out	1
D. M. Bravo c Mominul Haque b Mahmudullah	51
K. A. Pollard b Mominul Haque	85
*D. J. G. Sammy c Jahurul Islam b Mominul Haque	2
†D. C. Thomas c Mushfiqur Rahim b Shafiul Islam	25
A. D. Russell lbw b Mahmudullah	0
V. Permaul run out	10
S. P. Narine not out	7
K. A. J. Roach lbw b Shafiul Islam	0
L-b 5, w 18	23
1/16 (1) 2/17 (3) 3/17 (2) 4/149 (5) 5/151 (6) 6/188 (4) 7/188 (8) 8/204 (9) 9/217 (7) 10/217 (11) (48 overs)	217
10 overs: 26-3	

Sohag Gazi 10–2–32–1; Shafiul Islam 9–4–31–3; Elias Sunny 8–0–58–0; Abdur Razzak 9–1–39–0; Mahmudullah 10–1–38–2; Mominul Haque 2–0–14–2.

Bangladesh

Tamim Iqbal b Roach	8
Anamul Haque c Pollard b Roach	0
Jahurul Islam c Thomas b Roach	10
*†Mushfiqur Rahim b Narine	44
Mahmudullah b Narine	48
Nasir Hossain not out	39
Mominul Haque lbw b Narine	25
Sohag Gazi c Thomas b Roach	19
Abdur Razzak lbw b Roach	0
Elias Sunny not out	1
B 3, l-b 4, w 18, n-b 2	27
1/8 (1) 2/9 (2) 3/30 (3) 4/121 (5) 5/133 (4) 6/186 (7) 7/214 (8) 8/215 (9) (8 wkts, 44 overs)	221
10 overs: 59-3	

Shafiul Islam did not bat.

Roach 9–0–56–5; Sammy 5–1–23–0; Russell 10–0–51–0; Narine 10–1–38–3; Permaul 9–0–39–0; Samuels 1–0–7–0.

Umpires: Enamul Haque and R. E. J. Martinesz. Third umpire: Anisur Rahman.
Series referee: A. J. Pycroft.

At Mirpur, December 10, 2012 (floodlit). **Twenty20 international: West Indies won by 18 runs.** **‡West Indies 197-4** (20 overs) (M. N. Samuels 85*, D. M. Bravo 41); **Bangladesh 179-1** (20 overs) (Tamim Iqbal 88*, Mahmudullah 64*). *MoM:* M. N. Samuels. *Twenty20 international debuts:* Anamul Haque, Mominul Haque, Sohag Gazi (Bangladesh). *The last match of the tour turned into an exhibition bout between two batsmen: Samuels came out on top after smashing 85* from 43 balls with nine sixes – four of them in Rubel Hossain's final over, which cost 29 – to trump Tamim Iqbal's 88* from 61. The difference came in the middle overs, when Bangladesh were kept in check by a tight spell from Gayle (4–0–18–0).*

ENGLAND LIONS IN BANGLADESH, 2011-12

One-day matches (5): Bangladesh A 3, England Lions 2
Twenty20 matches (2): Bangladesh A 1, England Lions 1

It was a winter which did little for the reputation of English batsmanship. But as the Test team plodded and planted their way to 33 lbw dismissals in five matches against Pakistan and Sri Lanka, work was being done to give the next generation of DRS-influenced batsmen the tools to fight back. Before Christmas, Graham Thorpe, the national lead batting coach, held a training camp for the England Performance Programme in Pune, India, during which his young charges were encouraged to read line and length quickly and play the ball in front of the pad, using half-width bats to help them locate the middle once they reverted to full-size versions.

Thorpe was in effect consigning the forward press – a method he and others used so successfully on Nasser Hussain's seminal 2000-01 tours of Pakistan and Sri Lanka – to history. "Mind you, I never thought the forward press should be a forward plant," said Thorpe. "We have to encourage these young players to use their initiative." He called it the "rocking technique".

The Decision Review System was not in operation when the members of the Performance Programme made the trip as England Lions to play limited-overs matches in Bangladesh and then Sri Lanka (see page 1141), but the tour of Bangladesh still held more than enough challenges. Due to disagreements between the national selectors and the Dhaka clubs – who demanded certain players be freed up for their matches in the Dhaka Premier Division – Bangladesh A were not so much a squad as a travelling circus. They used 34 players in seven internationals, including more than a dozen spinners, while the captaincy passed to whichever of their experienced players was available. Akram Khan, the chief national selector, admitted ahead of the one-day series that "the team is not the best possible one".

This confusion did not make life any easier for the tourists, as individual plans to bowlers and batsmen lost their relevance. The Bangladeshis' traditional tactic of playing three or four slow bowlers, all capable of eliciting slightly different responses from grudging pitches, limited the Lions to five fifty partnerships in the seven internationals. A lengthy tail meant the batting often ended with Scott Borthwick at No. 7.

In Thorpe's opinion, Jonny Bairstow made the greatest progress. Having crashed to earth during England's one-day series in India in October 2011, Bairstow was given time to refine the art of manoeuvring the ball in the middle overs, even if he was not quite able to make a defining score.

Bowling fast in Bangladesh has rarely been an enviable pursuit, but the Lions benefited from the introduction of a new ball from each end, reflecting the regulation changes for one-day internationals. Both the Lions' 50-over victories came when Stuart Meaker or Jack Brooks had scattered the top order with the assistance of morning dew and white Kookaburras which swung and stayed harder for longer.

ENGLAND LIONS TOURING PARTY

*J. W. A. Taylor (Nottinghamshire), J. M. Bairstow (Yorkshire), S. G. Borthwick (Durham), D. R. Briggs (Hampshire), J. A. Brooks (Northamptonshire), N. L. Buck (Leicestershire), J. C. Buttler (Somerset), A. D. Hales (Nottinghamshire), S. C. Kerrigan (Lancashire), T. L. Maynard (Surrey), S. C. Meaker (Surrey), T. S. Mills (Essex), W. B. Rankin (Warwickshire), J. E. Root (Yorkshire), J. J. Roy (Surrey), J. M. Vince (Hampshire).

Rankin joined the squad after playing for an ICC Associate and Affiliate XI against England in the UAE, but returned home after one match due to a pre-existing thigh injury.

Coach: D. Parsons. *Manager:* G. A. M. Jackson. *Batting coaches:* G. P. Thorpe, M. D. Moxon. *Bowling coach:* K. J. Shine. *Fielding coach:* C. G. Taylor. *Physiotherapist:* M. Young. *Strength and conditioning:* M. Spivey. *Team analyst:* G. Broad. *Team doctor:* G. Bhogal. *Security manager:* S. Dickason.

At Chittagong, January 6, 2012. **England Lions won by four wickets. ‡Bangladesh Cricket Board XI 186** (43.2 overs) (Rony Talukder 53; D. R. Briggs 4-41); **England Lions 187-6** (36.2 overs). *The BCB XI chose 13 players, of whom 11 could bat and 11 field. The Gazi Tank club declined to release Asif Ahmed and Mominul Haque for this practice match, but Rony Talukder, one of the late replacements, gave them a steady start, only for the last seven wickets to crumble for 54. Joe Root (35) and Jason Roy (40) opened with 76 in 11 overs.*

50-over series

At Chittagong, January 8, 2012. **Bangladesh A won by six wickets. ‡England Lions 139** (39 overs); **Bangladesh A 141-4** (33 overs) (Imrul Kayes 53). *The pacy and accurate Al-Amin Hossain ripped out three of the Lions top order, leaving them 38-4 in the tenth over. Against an attack containing three spinners of varying style, they never recovered, despite a careful 45 in 81 balls from Jos Buttler, more accustomed to the role of finisher.*

At Chittagong, January 10, 2012. **England Lions won by six wickets. ‡Bangladesh A 176** (44 overs) (Nazimuddin 99*; S. C. Meaker 4-47); **England Lions 177-4** (37.3 overs) (J. M. Bairstow 50*). *The Lions' job was made simpler when the BCB released their four match-winners from the first game – Al-Amin Hossain, Noor Hossain, Imrul Kayes and Mahmudullah – back to their Dhaka Premier Division clubs. Nazimuddin was left to carry the load, batting from the fifth ball to the end and dominating an eighth-wicket stand of 81 with Dolar Mahmud (17). But when Meaker bowled Nos 10 and 11 with successive balls, Nazimuddin was left stranded one short of a century – his only List A hundred had been against England A on their 2006-07 tour. Roy fell to the first ball, but Jonny Bairstow and Buttler (41*) provided late acceleration. During the innings break, the teams observed a minute's silence for BCB chief executive officer Manzur Ahmed, who had died of a heart attack during the night.*

At Chittagong, January 13, 2012. **Bangladesh A won by 75 runs. Bangladesh A 218-9** (50 overs) (Nasiruddin Faruque 53); **‡England Lions 143** (34.4 overs) (Suhrawadi Shuvo 4-25). *The Lions challenged themselves to chase, but came up well short. Boyd Rankin, a late arrival, was one of the guiltiest as they let slip 23 extras in the field. Alex Hales struck seven boundaries in his 39 as the Lions took 58 from the opening powerplay, but Bangladesh A's quartet of spinners delivered in helpful conditions.*

At Sylhet, January 16, 2012. **Bangladesh A won by six wickets. England Lions 208** (49.4 overs) (J. E. Root 81); **‡Bangladesh A 211-4** (45.2 overs) (Imrul Kayes 110*). *Root's 81 from 124 balls was his highest one-day score, as others struggled around him. Imrul Kayes, enjoying a renaissance after a lean run at international level, saw off the new ball in a patient opening stand of 72 with Nasiruddin Faruque (21) and hit three sixes in his fifth one-day century to give Bangladesh A an unassailable 3–1 series lead.*

At Sylhet, January 18, 2012. **England Lions won by six wickets. Bangladesh A 152** (44.1 overs); **‡England Lions 158-4** (37.5 overs) (J. W. A. Taylor 65*). *Jack Brooks obliterated the top order with career-best figures of 3-35, and Bangladesh A spiralled to 75-7 until a 28-ball 38 from No. 9 Noor Hossain prevented a complete embarrassment. James Taylor played himself in for the first time in the series and took on the anchor role, hitting only four fours in 110 balls. Buttler blasted all but three of the last 30 runs.*

20-over series

At Mirpur, January 22, 2012. **England Lions won by 32 runs.** **‡England Lions 143-6** (20 overs) (J. J. Roy 40, J. M. Vince 32); **Bangladesh A 111** (20 overs) (Jahurul Islam 37; N. L. Buck 3-16). *Taylor won a good toss on a featherbed, and the Lions romped along at ten an over until Roy and Bairstow fell to left-armer Mosharraf Hossain in the ninth. Bangladesh A then threw away the initiative through poor running, although Shuvagata Hom was a victim of Buttler's superb arm at long-off.*

At Mirpur, January 23, 2012. **Bangladesh A won by 11 runs.** **‡Bangladesh A 166-6** (20 overs) (Imrul Kayes 62; N. L. Buck 3-22); **England Lions 155-7** (20 overs) (T. L. Maynard 68, J. W. A. Taylor 43). *Imrul Kayes made another decisive contribution, as he launched Bangladesh A towards a winning total, rubber-stamped by Sabbir Rahman's 24* from 11 balls. From 14-3, Tom Maynard and Taylor counterpunched with 87 in 11.3 overs, but Buttler was unable to fire in the closing stages this time – and the series was shared.*

For England Lions' subsequent tour of Sri Lanka, see page 1141; for a report of their match against England in the UAE, see page 294.

BANGLADESH UNDER-19 v ENGLAND UNDER-19, 2011-12

One-day internationals (7): Bangladesh 5, England 2

Bangladesh remain something of a pushover at senior level, but for Under-19 cricketers the place is a byword for purgatory. The third England Under-19 team in seven years to play a one-day series in Bangladesh suffered much the same fate as their predecessors: asphyxiation at the crease by enthusiastic young spinners operating on friendly territory. In that respect, the trip fulfilled an important function of the ECB's development programme – perhaps *the* most important, given England's traditional inadequacies in Asia, which were being simultaneously exposed by Pakistan's Test attack in the UAE.

More than ever, cricket at elite age-group level revolves around one-day internationals. Eight 50-over matches in all set a stiff challenge to this group, and formed part of their preparation for August's Under-19 World Cup in Queensland (see page 879). If England could be accused of slightly overdoing the format – 29 of their 35 international fixtures between World Cups had been 50-over games – then they were at least well prepared. To round off this tour under the grand floodlights of the national stadium, rather than with another daytime match at Fatullah, was a welcome innovation: only a handful of England's squad had played at night before; still fewer had encountered a dewy ball in foreign conditions.

England's most successful players were also the most experienced. Daniel Bell-Drummond, Kent's correct, adaptable batsman – and *Wisden's* Schools Cricketer of the Year for 2011 – opened up against the hard ball and found himself anchoring the innings, probably too often. Ben Foakes, a wicketkeeper-batsman behind both James Foster and Adam Wheater in the pecking order at Essex, scored the only century on either side.

The revelation, though, was Sam Wood. An opening batsman from Nottinghamshire who had come close to making twin hundreds in an Under-19 Test in Colombo the previous winter, he now found himself in the middle order and given the role of frontline spinner. Wood's accurate off-breaks were ideally suited to Bangladeshi pitches, and he finished with 13 wickets and a startling economy rate of 3.52, bowling more overs than anyone in the series. But it was a concern that England's major spin weapon was an occasional bowler.

ENGLAND UNDER-19 TOURING PARTY

*A. J. Ball (Kent), M. Abid (Lancashire), S. A. Ali (Warwickshire), D. J. Bell-Drummond (Kent), B. T. Foakes (Essex), G. T. Griffiths (Lancashire), B. A. Hutton (Nottinghamshire), A. Kapil (Worcestershire), S. Kelsall (Nottinghamshire), J. A. Leaning (Yorkshire), C. Overton (Somerset), J. Overton (Somerset), R. Singh (Durham), K. S. Velani (Essex), S. K. W. Wood (Nottinghamshire). *Coach:* T. J. Boon. *Manager:* J. Abrahams.

At Chittagong, January 18, 2012. **Bangladesh Under-19 XI won by ten wickets. England Under-19 XI 85** (38.5 overs); ‡**Bangladesh Under-19 XI 87-0** (14.5 overs). *England suffered a jarring introduction to the tour, losing eight of their last nine wickets to Bangladesh's quartet of spinners.*

50-over series

At Chittagong, January 21, 2012. **Bangladesh Under-19 won by 44 runs. Bangladesh Under-19 265-8** (50 overs) (Mosaddek Hossain 81, Al-Amin 50); ‡**England Under-19 221** (47.2 overs) (D. J. Bell-Drummond 55; Noor Hossain 4-31). *Bangladesh raced into the distance with a 114-run stand in 15 overs between Al-Amin and 16-year-old Mosaddek Hossain. Noor Hossain, a survivor from England's previous tour in 2009-10, then went to work with his leg-breaks.*

At Chittagong, January 23, 2012. **Bangladesh Under-19 won by 19 runs. Bangladesh Under-19 256-9** (50 overs) (Liton Das 53, Salman Hossain 59); ‡**England Under-19 237-7** (50 overs) (D. J. Bell-Drummond 92). *England batted through their 50 overs, but Bangladesh's spinners kept too tight a rein. The captain Asif Ahmed ran out Ben Foakes without delivering the ball when England were well placed at 110-1. Daniel Bell-Drummond later fell to the last ball of the batting powerplay, and England could not make 98 from the last ten overs without him.*

At Chittagong, January 24, 2012. **England Under-19 won by three wickets. Bangladesh Under-19 252-9** (50 overs) (Asif Ahmed 67; A. J. Ball 4-44); ‡**England Under-19 253-7** (49 overs) (B. T. Foakes 111). *Foakes was run out again – this time in more orthodox fashion – but only after hitting a superb 111 from 118 balls. Adam Ball (24*) and Kishen Velani (12*) knocked off the last 35 of a morale-boosting run-chase.*

At Sylhet, January 28, 2012. **Bangladesh Under-19 won by four wickets. England Under-19 168** (45.4 overs) (Taskin Ahmed 4-46, Mosaddek Hossain 4-26); ‡**Bangladesh Under-19 169-6** (37.2 overs) (Salman Hossain 59). *With three players unavailable through illness, England lurched to 68-5. Aneesh Kapil (48), Craig Overton (36) and Adam Ball (21) eked out another 100, but they could not set a challenging target.*

At Sylhet, January 30, 2012. **England Under-19 won by 28 runs. England Under-19 195-8** (50 overs); ‡**Bangladesh Under-19 167** (45.1 overs). *Brett Hutton took three wickets in eight balls in the opening powerplay to leave Bangladesh on 39-3, a position they could not repair.*

At Sylhet, January 31, 2012. **Bangladesh Under-19 won by six wickets. England Under-19 206-8** (50 overs) (D. J. Bell-Drummond 51; Nasum Ahmed 4-34); ‡**Bangladesh Under-19 211-4** (42.5 overs) (Soumya Sarkar 86, Mosaddek Hossain 51*). *Left-arm spinner Nasum Ahmed ousted Bell-Drummond, and took three more wickets in the game's decisive performance. Soumya Sarkar underpinned the chase, rounded off smartly by Mosaddek's 51* from 40 balls, as Bangladesh wrapped up the series with a game to spare.*

At Mirpur, February 4, 2012 (day/night). **Bangladesh Under-19 won by 76 runs. Bangladesh Under-19 237-5** (50 overs) (Mosaddek Hossain 79*, Al-Amin 65); ‡**England Under-19 161** (41.2 overs) (D. J. Bell-Drummond 55; Al-Amin 5-33). *Though the series was already settled in Bangladesh's favour, this match under the floodlights at the national stadium was anything but a dead rubber. England fielded first to avoid later dew, but Mosaddek and Al-Amin accelerated smartly over the second half of Bangladesh's innings, adding 133 for the fifth wicket. Bell-Drummond scored his fourth fifty of the series before England again collapsed to Al-Amin's off-breaks in the middle overs with the ball skidding on.*

DOMESTIC CRICKET IN BANGLADESH, 2011-12

UTPAL SHUVRO

The constant criticism of Bangladesh's first-class tournament, the National Cricket League, is that it lacks intensity; the media often call it "picnic cricket". So when the Bangladesh Cricket Board diluted the competition by increasing the number of teams from six to eight, eyebrows were bound to rise.

The introduction of Rangpur was a political necessity; the NCL is contested by teams representing the country's administrative divisions, and in 2010 Rangpur, previously the northern half of Rajshahi, had become Bangladesh's seventh division. To keep the number of teams even (it was unclear why), Dhaka Metropolis, who had played one first-class season, in 2000-01, reappeared alongside Dhaka's divisional team.

Even the loss of several quality players, who came from districts now in Rangpur, and the retirement of their inspirational captain Khaled Mashud, could not stop **Rajshahi** winning a fourth successive title. They initially faltered as they adjusted to the changes – finishing fourth in the NCL's first phase was just enough to advance to the second – but their youngsters stepped up to help them crush table-toppers **Khulna** in three days in the final. Rajshahi's fifth first-class title in all was a national record; they had been champions or runners-up for eight years running. By contrast **Dhaka**, four-time winners and finalists the previous season, failed to cope with losing players to Dhaka Metropolis. They lost six of their seven matches and finished bottom, whereas **Dhaka Metropolis** won five games and were in second place after the first phase.

As usual, Rajshahi's hallmark was teamwork. Their leading scorer, Mizanur Rahman, was only fifth in the aggregate list, with 622 runs, while left-arm spinner Saqlain Sajib, with 50 wickets, was their lone representative among the top nine wicket-takers. All-rounder Farhad Hossain, who won the match award in the final, was also Player of the Tournament for his consistency in Rajshahi's upper order and for his effective off-spin; he combined 574 runs with 29 wickets.

Overall, the highest run-scorer was Khulna's Anamul Haque, who scored 816, including three centuries, was appointed captain of Bangladesh Under-19, and made his senior international debut in November. Left-arm spinner Enamul Haque, out of favour with the national selectors, claimed 59 wickets for Sylhet and became the first Bangladeshi to take 300 in first-class cricket. He was instrumental in turning round **Sylhet's** fortunes; they won four games, after failing to win any in the previous four seasons, and finished third.

The usual hiccups showed the NCL was not the BCB's priority. The league took six months to complete; though this was two months less than in 2010-11, the last round of the second phase was postponed from December to April to accommodate the Dhaka Premier League (traditionally the main source of income for Bangladeshi cricketers), and the inaugural Bangladesh Premier League in February.

The BPL was generally considered a success, despite match-fixing allegations – a Pakistani citizen in the crowd was arrested on suspicion of trying to corrupt players – delayed payments, and a dispute over who should qualify for the semi-finals. In the final **Dhaka Gladiators**, fielding five Pakistanis, beat **Barisal Burners**, led by Australia's Brad Hodge but missing their star batsman, West Indian Chris Gayle. The BCB decided there was no time for the one-day NCL, but staged a short triangular tournament as a selection trial in September.

The Dhaka Premier League was suspended for two months because of a dispute over the registration of former Pakistan batsman Mohammad Yousuf. He had moved from Mohammedan to Victoria, who said they had a clearance letter, but Mohammedan said it was faked. Another leading club, Abahani, refused to continue a match against Victoria when Yousuf was about to bat. Victoria had the last laugh when they eventually won the trophy (without Yousuf).

FIRST-CLASS AVERAGES, 2011-12

BATTING (500 runs)

	M	*I*	*NO*	*R*	*HS*	*100*	*Avge*	*Ct/St*
Mithun Ali (*Khulna*)	6	11	0	559	109	3	50.81	16/2
Dhiman Ghosh (*Rangpur*)	7	13	1	571	183	1	47.58	14/2
Asif Ahmed (*Dhaka Metropolis*)	10	20	2	801	152	1	44.50	12
Farhad Hossain (*Rajshahi*)	8	14	1	574	216	1	44.15	11
†Junaid Siddique (*Rajshahi*)	7	12	0	522	161	1	43.50	10
Anamul Haque (*Khulna*)	10	20	1	816	193	3	42.94	10/1
†Mehrab Hossain (*Dhaka Metropolis*)	10	17	3	589	104*	2	42.07	2
Shamsur Rahman (*Dhaka Metropolis*)	10	19	2	668	101*	1	39.29	12
Nazimuddin (*Chittagong & Bangladesh*)	9	17	0	665	126	1	39.11	2
Tushar Imran (*Khulna*)	10	19	2	659	112	1	38.76	8
Rajin Saleh (*Sylhet*)	10	18	2	577	132	1	36.06	23
Mizanur Rahman (*Rajshahi*)	11	22	4	622	105	1	34.55	13
Mohammad Ashraful (*Dhaka Met. & Bang.*)	9	17	1	549	119	1	34.31	3
†Soumya Sarkar (*Khulna*)	10	18	2	533	80	0	33.31	12
Tasamul Haque (*Dhaka Metropolis*)	9	17	0	550	125	2	32.35	9

BOWLING (25 wickets)

	Style	*O*	*M*	*R*	*W*	*BB*	*5I*	*Avge*
Farhad Hossain (*Rajshahi*)	OB	97.4	17	351	29	5-33	1	12.10
Al-Amin Hossain (*Khulna*)	RFM	218.1	55	645	39	7-36	4	16.53
Mosharraf Hossain (*Dhaka*)	SLA	200.2	50	549	33	7-64	1	16.63
Abu Jayed (*Sylhet*)	RFM	202	43	590	35	6-25	3	16.85
Dolar Mahmud (*Khulna*)	RFM	211.4	33	724	40	4-34	0	18.10
Mukhtar Ali (*Rajshahi*)	RFM	220.2	66	645	32	4-39	0	20.15
Arafat Sunny (*Dhaka Metropolis*)	SLA	373	102	1,018	50	7-49	4	20.36
Murad Khan (*Khulna*)	SLA	226.1	32	738	35	7-29	1	21.08
Saqlain Sajib (*Rajshahi*)	SLA	369.4	72	1,095	50	5-59	1	21.90
Abdur Razzak (*Khulna*)	SLA	264	45	841	38	8-123	2	22.13
Enamul Haque (*Sylhet*)	SLA	483.5	96	1,329	59	7-64	6	22.52
Kamrul Islam (*Chittagong*)	LFM	220.5	52	656	26	4-80	0	25.23
Sanjamul Islam (*Rajshahi*)	SLA	269	43	859	28	4-84	0	30.67

WALTON NATIONAL CRICKET LEAGUE, 2011-12

First phase	*P*	*W*	*L*	*Pts*	*NRR*
Khulna	7	5	1	80.84	–0.23
Dhaka Metropolis	7	5	2	79.46	0.28
Sylhet	7	4	2	78.28	–0.20
Rajshahi	7	5	2	73.98	0.34
Chittagong	7	3	4	61.06	0.07
Rangpur	7	2	3	55.60	–0.36
Barisal	7	1	5	44.26	0.25
Dhaka	7	0	6	35.52	–0.08

Second phase	*P*	*W*	*L*	*Pts*	*NRR*
Khulna	10	6	1	114.84	–0.10
Rajshahi	10	7	3	109.98	0.28
Sylhet	10	4	3	100.54	–0.23
Dhaka Metropolis	10	5	3	94.72	0.19

In the first phase, each of the eight teams played each other once. In the second phase, the top four teams played each other again, and their results and points from the first phase were carried through to the final table.

Final: Rajshahi beat Khulna by nine wickets.

Win = 8pts; draw = 2pts; first-innings lead in a drawn match = 2pts; no decision on first innings = 1pt. First-innings bonus points were awarded as follows: 1pt for the first 200 runs and then 0.02 for every subsequent run (up to a maximum of 4pts); 1pt for the fifth wicket taken and then 0.5 for each of the next four, with 4pts for ten wickets.

First phase

At Savar, October 17–19, 2011. **Chittagong won by 105 runs.** ‡**Chittagong 187 and 191**; **Barisal 129 and 144**. *Chittagong 12pts, Barisal 4pts.*

At Bogra, October 17–20, 2011. **Drawn. Dhaka 327 and 298-3 dec** (Rony Talukder 121, Abdul Mazid 104*); ‡**Rangpur 251 and 201-7**. *Dhaka 11.52pts, Rangpur 8pts. This was the first first-class match played by new division Rangpur.*

At Rajshahi, October 17–20, 2011. **Dhaka Metropolis won by six wickets. Rajshahi 193 and 182**; ‡**Dhaka Metropolis 223-9 dec and 153-4**. *Dhaka Metropolis 13.46pts, Rajshahi 3pts. In their first first-class match for more than ten years, Dhaka Metropolis beat the defending champions.*

At Sylhet, October 17–20, 2011. **Drawn. Sylhet 478-8 dec** (Ezaz Ahmed 100*) **and 167-6 dec**; ‡**Khulna 273-9 dec** (Anamul Haque 126) **and 121-6**. *Sylhet 11pts, Khulna 6.94pts. Ten Khulna players bowled in Sylhet's first innings, when Ezaz Ahmed scored a century from No. 8.*

At Sylhet, October 23–25, 2011. **Khulna won by eight wickets.** ‡**Barisal 302** (Sohag Gazi 140; Abdur Razzak 8-123) **and 194** (Abdur Razzak 7-70); **Khulna 332 and 167-2**. *Khulna 15.62pts, Barisal 7.02pts. Sohag Gazi reached his maiden hundred in 67 balls; in all, he hit 140 in 99. Slow left-armer Abdur Razzak recorded the best innings figures of the season, and his 15-193 was the best match return by a Bangladeshi bowler.*

At Savar, October 23–26, 2011. **Chittagong won by six wickets.** ‡**Sylhet 270-9 dec and 183**; **Chittagong 425-9 dec** (Nafis Iqbal 104) **and 31-4**. *Chittagong 15pts, Sylhet 5.38pts.*

At Rajshahi, October 23–24, 2011. **Dhaka Metropolis won by seven wickets. Dhaka 132** (Arafat Salahuddin 5-23) **and 140**; ‡**Dhaka Metropolis 108 and 165-3**. *Dhaka Metropolis 12pts, Dhaka 4pts. Dhaka Metropolis beat their local rivals inside two days.*

At Bogra, October 23–25, 2011. **Rajshahi won by 58 runs. Rajshahi 206 and 210** (Mahmudul Hasan 5-39); ‡**Rangpur 230 and 128**. *Rajshahi 13.12pts, Rangpur 5.6pts. Rangpur wicketkeeper Dhiman Ghosh held five catches in his old side Rajshahi's first innings.*

At Barisal, October 30–November 2, 2011. **Dhaka Metropolis won by 237 runs. Dhaka Metropolis 450-8 dec** (Arman Hossain 114, Arafat Salahuddin 100*) **and 185-5 dec**; ‡**Barisal 120** (Arafat Sunny 5-11) **and 278**. *Dhaka Metropolis 16pts, Barisal 2.5pts. Left-arm spinner Arafat Sunny's 15–9–11–5 helped Dhaka Metropolis to their third straight win.*

At Chittagong, October 30–November 2, 2011. **Rajshahi won by eight wickets.** ‡**Chittagong 378** (Nazimuddin 126) **and 155** (Farhad Reza 5-60); **Rajshahi 453-9 dec** (Farhad Hossain 216) **and 83-2**. *Rajshahi 16pts, Chittagong 7pts. Farhad Hossain batted for five minutes short of nine hours to score a maiden double-century, the only one of this tournament; he added 101 for Rajshahi's ninth wicket with Delwar Hossain (29*). Farhad Reza then reduced Chittagong's second innings to 22-5.*

At Jessore, October 30–November 1, 2011. **Khulna won by 91 runs.** ‡**Khulna 224** (Tushar Imran 112) **and 219**; **Dhaka 158 and 194** (Taposh Ghosh 5-51). *Khulna 13.48pts, Dhaka 4pts.*

At Fatullah, October 30–November 1, 2011. **Sylhet won by an innings and 173 runs. Rangpur 138 and 112** (Abu Jayed 5-24); ‡**Sylhet 423-9 dec** (Rajin Saleh 132). *Sylhet 16pts, Rangpur 3pts. Sylhet completed the third-biggest win in the NCL's history.*

At Bogra, November 14–17, 2011. **Drawn. Rangpur 407-7 dec** (Naeem Islam 136); ‡**Barisal 259-4** (Shahriar Nafees 115). *Barisal 7.16pts, Rangpur 7pts.*

At Chittagong, November 14–16, 2011. **Chittagong won by 26 runs. Chittagong 176 and 213** (Mosharraf Hossain 7-64); ‡**Dhaka 175** (Ameer Khan 6-60) **and 188** (Ameer Khan 6-78). *Chittagong 12pts, Dhaka 4pts. Chittagong wicketkeeper Sadid Hossain made four catches and a stumping, and leg-spinner Ameer Khan collected 12-138.*

At Jessore, November 14–17, 2011. **Khulna won by 31 runs.** ‡**Khulna 278-9 dec** (Anamul Haque 107) **and 214**; **Rajshahi 207 and 254**. *Khulna 14.54pts, Rajshahi 4.14pts.*

At Sylhet, November 14–15, 2011. **Sylhet won by eight wickets. Dhaka Metropolis 118-9 dec** (Enamul Haque 5-37) **and 132** (Enamul Haque 5-40); ‡**Sylhet 231 and 20-2**. *Sylhet 12.62pts, Dhaka Metropolis 4pts. After three victories, Dhaka Metropolis succumbed in two days against the left-arm spin of Enamul Haque, who took five in an innings for the first time in four years and immediately did it again.*

At Barisal, November 21–24, 2011. **Barisal won by 159 runs. Barisal 183 and 278**; **‡Dhaka 199 and 103** (Syed Rasel 5-13). *Barisal 12pts, Dhaka 4pts. Mohammad Sharif took a hat-trick in the match's second over. Refatuzzaman had figures of 12–9–4–1 in Dhaka's second innings.*

At Sylhet, November 21–24, 2011. **Dhaka Metropolis won by 169 runs. ‡Dhaka Metropolis 393** (Tasamul Haque 125) **and 296-7 dec** (Mohammad Ashraful 119); **Chittagong 304** (Arafat Sunny 5-76) **and 216**. *Dhaka Metropolis 15pts, Chittagong 7.06pts.*

At Jessore, November 21–23, 2011. **Rangpur won by five wickets. ‡Khulna 139** (Abdur Rahman 5-25) **and 214** (Mahmudul Hasan 5-75); **Rangpur 131** (Murad Khan 7-29) **and 223-5**. *Rangpur 12pts, Khulna 4pts. Rangpur completed their first first-class victory.*

At Bogra, November 21–24, 2011. **Rajshahi won by five wickets. ‡Sylhet 100-9 dec and 298**; **Rajshahi 175** (Enamul Haque 6-42) **and 224-5**. *Rajshahi 11pts, Sylhet 4pts.*

At Chittagong, November 28–December 1, 2011. **Sylhet won by four wickets. Barisal 264** (Iftekhar Nayem 132; Tapash Baisya 5-50, Abu Jayed 5-71) **and 199** (Enamul Haque 7-64); **‡Sylhet 281 and 186-6**. *Sylhet 14.6pts, Barisal 6.26pts. Barisal wicketkeeper Shahin Hossain held five catches in Sylhet's first innings.*

At Rajshahi, November 28–30, 2011. **Khulna won by eight wickets. Chittagong 200** (Al-Amin Hossain 5-53) **and 144** (Al-Amin Hossain 7-36); **‡Khulna 233-9 dec** (Abdullah Al Mamun 5-35) **and 113-2**. *Khulna 13.66pts, Chittagong 4pts. Al-Amin Hossain took 12-89, including a career-best 7-36.*

At Barisal, November 28–30, 2011. **Rajshahi won by nine wickets. ‡Dhaka 131 and 131**; **Rajshahi 214** (Mahbubul Alam 5-49) **and 49-1**. *Rajshahi 13.28pts, Dhaka 4pts.*

At Fatullah, November 28–December 1, 2011. **Dhaka Metropolis won by nine wickets. Rangpur 354 and 193** (Arafat Sunny 6-41); **‡Dhaka Metropolis 518** (Asif Ahmed 152) **and 30-1**. *Dhaka Metropolis 15pts, Rangpur 8pts. Mohammad Ashraful (71) and Asif Ahmed added 225 for Dhaka Metropolis's second wicket.*

At Jessore, December 5–7, 2011. **Rajshahi won by 175 runs. ‡Rajshahi 222** (Sohag Gazi 5-75) **and 313**; **Barisal 216 and 144**. *Rajshahi 13.44pts, Barisal 5.32pts. Farhad Hossain ended the game with a spell of 3.4–1–8–4, ensuring Rajshahi's place in the second phase of the league.*

At Bogra, December 5–8, 2011. **Rangpur won by 241 runs. Rangpur 122** (Noor Hossain 5-40) **and 587** (Dhiman Ghosh 183, Alauddin Babu 180); **‡Chittagong 118 and 350** (Nafis Iqbal 103). *Rangpur 12pts, Chittagong 4pts. Leg-spinner Noor Hossain wound up Rangpur's first innings with a hat-trick. Dhiman Ghosh and Alauddin Babu added 322 for the fifth wicket in their second innings, helping Rangpur reach 587, which was briefly the third-highest total in an NCL match.*

At Rajshahi, December 5–8, 2011. **Khulna won by 175 runs. Khulna 256** (Mithun Ali 101; Arafat Sunny 7-49) **and 250**; **‡Dhaka Metropolis 164-8 dec** (Al-Amin Hossain 5-33) **and 167**. *Khulna 12.6pts, Dhaka Metropolis 4pts. By defeating Dhaka Metropolis, Khulna pulled a point ahead of them at the top of the table.*

At Sylhet, December 5–8, 2011. **Sylhet won by eight wickets. Dhaka 175 and 231**; **‡Sylhet 285 and 125-2**. *Sylhet 14.68pts, Dhaka 4pts. Sylhet reduced Dhaka to 24-5 on the opening day, and made sure of their place in the second phase.*

Second phase

At Fatullah, December 11–12, 2011. **Khulna won by eight wickets. Rajshahi 149 and 129** (Al-Amin Hossain 6-23); **‡Khulna 179 and 102-2**. *Khulna 12pts, Rajshahi 4pts. Khulna beat Rajshahi for the second time in this tournament, seeing them off in two days.*

At Sylhet, December 11–14, 2011. **Drawn. Dhaka Metropolis 129** (Abu Jayed 6-25) **and 480-7 dec** (Mehrab Hossain 104*); **‡Sylhet 263 and 204-4**. *Sylhet 10.24pts, Dhaka Metropolis 6pts.*

At Sylhet, December 18–21, 2011. **Rajshahi won by nine wickets. Dhaka Metropolis 201** (Saqlain Sajib 5-59) **and 274** (Mehrab Hossain 101); **‡Rajshahi 404-5 dec** (Jahurul Islam 167, Junaid Siddique 161) **and 72-1**. *Rajshahi 16pts, Dhaka Metropolis 2.02pts. Jahurul Islam and Junaid Siddique added 345, a national record for the second wicket.*

At Chittagong, December 18–21, 2011. **Drawn.** **‡Khulna 301-9 dec** (Mithun Ali 109) **and 271** (Mithun Ali 100; Enamul Haque 5-95); **Sylhet 251-9 dec and 164-7**. *Khulna 10pts, Sylhet 7pts. Mithun Ali hit 109 in 106 balls, and added a second hundred in the next innings, his third of the season. Enamul Haque reached 50 wickets for the season, and became the first Bangladeshi to take 300 in his first-class career.*

At Fatullah, April 20–24, 2012. **Drawn.** **‡Khulna 618-8 dec** (Anamul Haque 193, Taposh Ghosh 111*) **and 301** (Imrul Kayes 117; Elias Sunny 5-107); **Dhaka Metropolis 288** (Tasamul Haque 100) **and 275-4** (Shamsur Rahman 101*). *Dhaka Metropolis 7.24pts, Khulna 12pts. The round originally scheduled to start on December 24 finally got going four months late, in the heat of April, and there was a further interruption when a general strike forced a rest day on April 22. Khulna advanced to the highest total of this tournament, and the third-highest in any NCL match, thanks largely to Anamul Haque's third century of the season, a career-best. Ten Dhaka Metropolis players bowled in that innings, including Arafat Sunny, who later reached 50 wickets for the season. Shamsur Rahman hit 101* in 88 balls, with 11 fours and five sixes.*

At Mirpur, April 20–24, 2012. **Rajshahi won by 119 runs.** **‡Rajshahi 387-8 dec** (Mizanur Rahman 105; Enamul Haque 6-127) **and 219**; **Sylhet 277 and 210** (Farhad Hossain 5-33). *Rajshahi 16pts, Sylhet 5.02pts. Rajshahi overtook Sylhet to join Khulna in the final, with part-time off-spinner Farhad Hossain taking five in an innings for the first time.*

Final

At Mirpur, April 26–28, 2012. **Rajshahi won by nine wickets.** **‡Khulna 212 and 172; Rajshahi 258 and 129-1.** *Rajshahi had lost their two previous matches to Khulna, but made it third time lucky. Man of the Match Farhad Hossain opened the bowling with his off-breaks and claimed three wickets in each innings, while his team-mate slow left-armer Saqlain Sajib completed 50 for the season. Farhad also scored 77 in Rajshahi's first innings, adding 173 for the third wicket with Junaid Siddique (95), and was there at the end as his side secured their fourth successive title, with two days to spare.*

NATIONAL CRICKET LEAGUE WINNERS

†1999-2000	Chittagong
2000-01	Biman Bangladesh Airlines
2001-02	Dhaka
2002-03	Khulna
2003-04	Dhaka
2004-05	Dhaka
2005-06	Rajshahi
2006-07	Dhaka
2007-08	Khulna
2008-09	Khulna
2009-10	Rajshahi
2010-11	Rajshahi
2011-12	Rajshahi

† *The National Cricket League was not first-class in 1999-2000.*

Rajshahi have won the title five times, Dhaka four times, Khulna twice, Biman Bangladesh Airlines and Chittagong once each.

BANGLADESH CRICKET BOARD CUP, 2011-12

50-over league plus final

	Played	*Won*	*Lost*	*No result*	*Points*	*Net run-rate*
Bangladesh	4	3	0	1	7	2.40
Bangladesh A	4	1	2	1	3	–0.05
Bangladesh Cricket Board Academy	4	0	2	2	2	–1.88

Final

At Mirpur, September 21, 2011 (day/night). **Bangladesh A won by four wickets.** **‡Bangladesh 185** (46 overs); **Dhaka 187-6** (49 overs). *MoM:* Mahmudullah. *Bangladesh A were 6-3 in the seventh over, but their captain Mahmudullah swung the game their way with 78*.*

BANGLADESH PREMIER LEAGUE, 2011-12

20-over league plus knockout

	Played	*Won*	*Lost*	*Points*	*Net run-rate*
Duronto Rajshahi	10	7	3	14	0.11
Khulna Royal Bengals	10	6	4	12	0.60
Dhaka Gladiators	10	5	5	10	0.21
Barisal Burners	10	5	5	10	0.17
Chittagong Kings	10	5	5	10	0.07
Sylhet Royals	10	2	8	4	–1.23

The BPL chairman informed the press that Chittagong would go through to the semi-finals as, of the six head-to-head matches between the three teams tied on ten points, Dhaka had won three, Chittagong two and Barisal one. But the next day the BPL governing council and technical committee said they had re-examined the rules and that, once Dhaka had been placed top, the head-to-head rule should be reapplied to the two remaining teams and their matches against Dhaka discounted. As Barisal and Chittagong had each won one of their two head-to-heads, Barisal were placed ahead on net run-rate.

Semi-finals

At Mirpur, February 28, 2012. **Barisal Burners won by eight wickets. Duronto Rajshahi 184-6** (20 overs); **‡Barisal Burners 189-2** (16 overs) (Ahmed Shehzad 113*). *MoM:* Ahmed Shehzad. *Yasir Arafat dismissed Rajshahi's top three in the first over of the match, though Sean Ervine (82) and Mushfiqur Rahim (58) fought back with 110 in the next 12 overs. But Ahmed Shehzad steered Barisal into the final with 113 in 49 balls, including six sixes and 12 fours.*

At Mirpur, February 28, 2012 (floodlit). **Dhaka Gladiators won by nine runs. ‡Dhaka Gladiators 191-4** (20 overs); **Khulna Royal Bengals 182-7** (20 overs). *MoM:* Azhar Mahmood. *Azhar Mahmood (65) dominated Dhaka's innings, but the top score of the match was Shakib Al Hasan's 86* in 41 balls as Khulna fell just short in the run-chase.*

Final

At Mirpur, February 29, 2012 (floodlit). **Dhaka Gladiators won by eight wickets. Barisal Burners 140-7** (20 overs); **‡Dhaka Gladiators 144-2** (15.4 overs). *MoM:* Imran Nazir. *Australian Brad Hodge batted throughout Barisal's innings for 70 in 51 balls, while three of Dhaka's five Pakistan internationals ran through his team-mates, before another – Imran Nazir – saw them most of the way home with 75 in 43 balls.*

INDIAN CRICKET, 2012

Transition and denial

ANAND VASU

Thirteen is no lucky number. But, for India, 2013 could not come quickly enough after a year that held precious little joy. If 2011 was saccharine-saturated – India began it No. 1 in the Test standings and lifted the World Cup – 2012 was marked by strife and disappointment.

The year began with a 4–0 Test blanking in Australia, a few months after England had administered the same medicine. The problem was, India refused to swallow it. They believed life would return to normal at home. A predictably flaky New Zealand side reinforced that complacency when they were bundled out for 159 and 164, to go down by an innings and 115 runs at Hyderabad, before losing at Bangalore. India appeared to be in possession of a new star:

INDIA IN 2012

	Played	*Won*	*Lost*	*Drawn/No result*
Tests	9	3	5	1
One-day internationals	17	9	7	1
Twenty20 internationals	15	8	6	1

Month	Fixture	Reference
DECEMBER / JANUARY / FEBRUARY	4 Tests and 2 T20Is (a) v Australia	(see *Wisden 2012*, page 868 and *Wisden 2013*, page 890)
MARCH	Triangular ODI tournament (a) (in Australia) v Australia and Sri Lanka	(page 892)
	Asia Cup (in Bangladesh)	(page 948)
	1 T20I (a) v South Africa	(page 1073)
APRIL		
MAY		
JUNE		
JULY / AUGUST	5 ODIs and 1 T20I (a) v Sri Lanka	(page 1125)
SEPTEMBER	2 Tests and 2 T20Is (h) v New Zealand	(page 979)
OCTOBER	World Twenty20 (in Sri Lanka)	(page 841)
NOVEMBER / DECEMBER	4 Tests and 2 T20Is (h) v England	(page 376)
JANUARY	3 ODIs and 2 T20Is (h) v Pakistan	(page 986)
	5 ODIs (h) v England	(page 376)

For a review of Indian domestic cricket from the 2011-12 season, see page 1005.

Ravichandran Ashwin, the off-spinner with a penchant for bowling doosras, carrom balls and much else besides, took 18 wickets in the two Tests.

New Zealand may have been well beaten, but for India life was far from rosy. The BCCI were confronted with a major challenge over the future of Duncan Fletcher, who could not claim one notable result in his 18 months as coach by the end of the England Test series in December. In fairness, he had presided over a period of transition. On March 9, Rahul Dravid announced his retirement; then, in August, V. V. S. Laxman said he'd had enough too. They did not plan it that way, but Dravid and Laxman had both ended their international careers in the Adelaide Test. "The game is lucky to have you and I have been lucky to play before you," Dravid told fans at the Chinnaswamy Stadium in Bangalore. "My approach to cricket has been reasonably simple: it was about giving everything to the team, playing with dignity and upholding the spirit of the game." It even drew an emotional speech from the usually stony-faced BCCI president N. Srinivasan.

When Laxman signed off, accused by some of holding up the inevitable progress of an as yet unidentified young Indian batsman, it was no less seminal a move. "I've always kept the country's success and need ahead of my personal aspirations," he said. "While I'd love to contribute to the team, especially against England and Australia later in the season, I think it's the right time to give the opportunity to a youngster in home conditions before tough overseas tours next year." That he was still good enough to play – and did so for Hyderabad in the Ranji Trophy – was not in doubt. Neither did he deserve the insinuations and barbs that hastened his departure.

Sachin Tendulkar, for the first time in his career, was exposed to well-founded mutterings too. By the end of the year, Tendulkar, now 39, had gone 17 Tests in almost two years without a century. Against New Zealand, his habit of playing across his front pad, without the assurance of old, left him looking extremely mortal. It prompted deep, but usually sympathetic, debate about his place through England's tour late in the year. Even when scoring 76 at Kolkata, he was battling against the fading of the light. Tendulkar made the move to call time on his one-day international career (which, in truth, had been intermittent for a number of years), in the hope of prolonging his Test life.

With Dravid and Laxman gone, a whole new world opened up for Virat Kohli and Cheteshwar Pujara. While Kohli, ordained for greater things, found the going tough in the second half of 2012, Pujara enhanced his reputation as a doer rather than a talker. His reputation as a greedy run-scorer was confirmed in the First Test against England at Ahmedabad, when he made an unbeaten 206 in seven and a half hours, then 41 not out to see India over the finishing line. It looked as though England might never get him out. His 15 first-class centuries leading into the game were all numbers to be reckoned with – including ten scores between 145 and 302 – but it was not until Ahmedabad that he was accepted as a worthy successor to Dravid at No. 3.

England came back fiercely to win a Test series in India for the first time since 1984-85. Kevin Pietersen's masterful 186 on a Mumbai turner showed India up in conditions that should have suited them best. India were forced to drop the ineffectual Zaheer Khan for the final Test, and played four spinners –

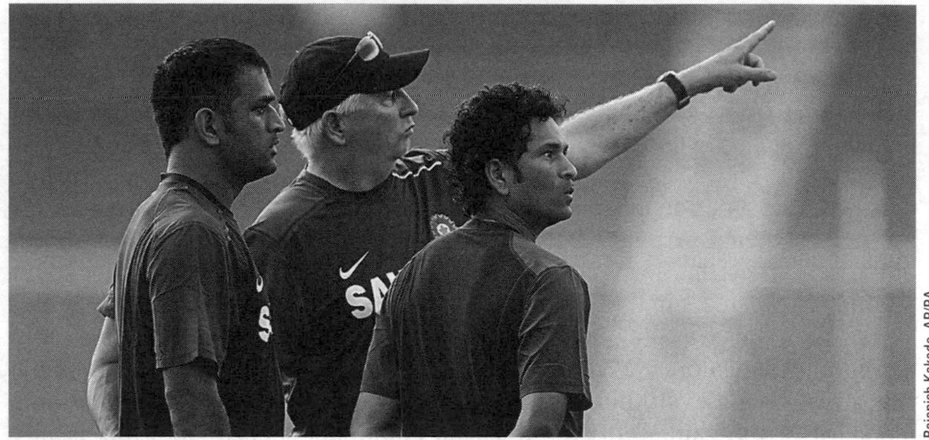

India's three wise men: M. S. Dhoni, Duncan Fletcher and Sachin Tendulkar.

to no avail. As the series turned England's way, it became sullied by a debate about pitches: namely to what extent M. S. Dhoni and Srinivasan could reasonably expect to dictate how they were prepared.

England returned home for Christmas between the Twenty20 and one-day matches, presenting a free window, which was filled by Pakistan, as the countries met for their first bilateral series in five years. But India were overwhelmed by Pakistan's youthful bowlers, and lost the one-day series with a match to spare. A narrow victory over England did at least return India to No. 1 in the ICC one-day rankings. This was the format in which Dhoni was most valuable, but observers were beginning to ask whether he should redefine his role in one or more of the sides to stem the flow of defeats.

Back in March, Kohli had scored superb centuries to beat Sri Lanka and Pakistan, but India were predictably distracted by the spectre of Tendulkar's 100th international hundred and lost the game in which he finally ticked it off, to Bangladesh, costing them a place in the final. India were beaten only once, by Australia, at the World Twenty20, but were so torn apart by Shane Watson in the Super Eights that it left their net run-rate irreparably damaged.

The IPL ran into its share of problems too. Once again, it was left to a media house rather than the authorities to dig up the dirt. From the testimony of several cricketers who bragged about receiving under-the-table cash payments in contravention of the salary caps in place, India TV exposed a culture of lying and a widespread disregard for the rules. The BCCI came down hard on the five players in question – banning T. P. Sudhindra for life for "receiving a consideration to spot-fix in a domestic game" – but they did not censure the franchises allegedly making the illegal payments.

The BCCI maintained their unyielding stance on the Decision Review System, to the frustration of the rest of the cricketing world. The ICC executive board met in Kuala Lumpur in June with a view to enforce the universal application of the DRS. But the BCCI refused to budge. Outgoing ICC president Sharad Pawar chaired the meeting and, without his calling for a vote on the issue, there was no chance of moving forward.

INDIA v NEW ZEALAND, 2012-13

KAUSHIK RAMAKRISHNAN

Test matches (2): India 2, New Zealand 0
Twenty20 internationals (2): India 0, New Zealand 1

India found themselves in a no-win situation going into this brief encounter. Despite the retirement of two of their finest batsmen, they were expected to make short work of a New Zealand side lacking their most experienced and influential player, Daniel Vettori, who missed the Tests with a groin injury. Anything less than their 2–0 sweep would have gone down as a failure, even though India had not played a Test match for seven months following their evisceration in Australia.

For the first time, India hosted a Test in August, towards the end of their monsoon season. The rains generally stayed away, but their preparations were hit instead by the retirement of V. V. S. Laxman only five days before the First Test – and *after* he had been named in the 15-man squad for the series. India were already braced for life without Rahul Dravid, who had bade farewell in March, but Laxman's sudden announcement took the think tank by surprise.

Virender Sehwag, Gautam Gambhir and Sachin Tendulkar were now expected to lead the way and ease the pressure on the new boys. But it was the Young Turks who caught the eye: Virat Kohli made a hundred and two half-centuries in his three innings, while Cheteshwar Pujara celebrated his first Test since January 2011 with a polished, mature 159 under pressure at Hyderabad. M. S. Dhoni pulled his weight at No. 7 as the middle order more than compensated for the fact that Sehwag, Gambhir and Tendulkar failed to pass fifty in nine attempts.

New Zealand had been competitive on Indian soil in recent years – before this series, they had drawn eight of their previous 11 Tests there, dating back to 1995-96 – but they were comprehensively outplayed in the First Test as India's slow men spun a wicked web. Withdrawing into their shells – and their creases – New Zealand's batsmen mustered 159 and 164 as Ravichandran Ashwin and Pragyan Ojha suffocated them on a track providing ample assistance. Ashwin had endured a middling tour of Australia, with only nine wickets in three Tests, but now he befuddled New Zealand, mainly with his stock off-break. Slow left-armer Ojha, a little more defensive but relentlessly accurate, was an admirable second fiddle. Ashwin finished with 18 wickets in the two Tests to Ojha's 13 – fine returns considering that the second game, at the Chinnaswamy Stadium in Bangalore, was played in conditions that were actually more favourable to New Zealand.

Overcast skies and a surface that afforded considerable bounce presented them with their best chance of a first Test win in India since 1988-89. To their credit, they raised their game several notches, with Ross Taylor's brilliant century on the first day a clear indication that the diffidence of Hyderabad had been cast aside. But India – behind for much of the game – managed to keep

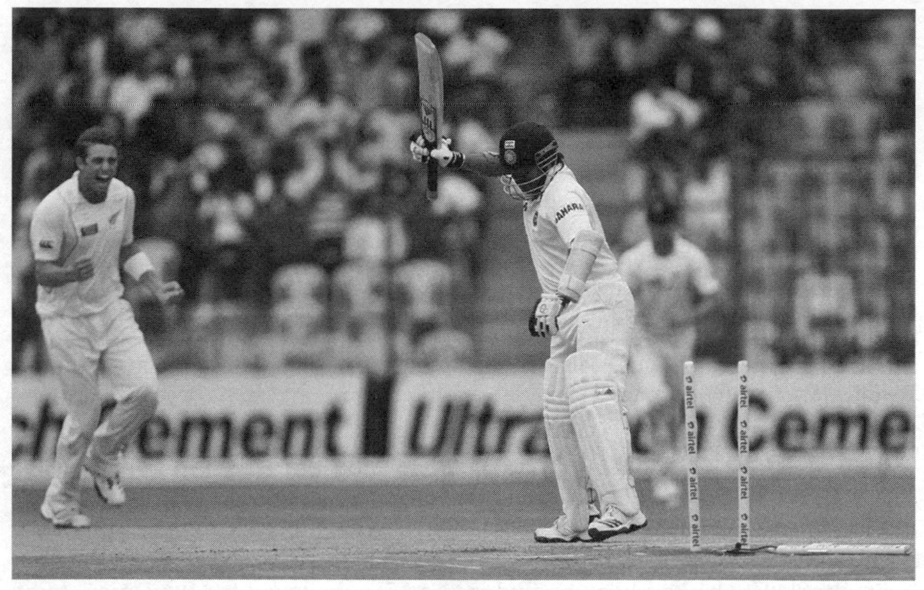

Aijaz Rahi, AP/PA

Missing leg, missing off... Sachin Tendulkar is furious with himself at being bowled for the third time in three innings; Tim Southee is the gleeful conqueror.

themselves in the hunt through sheer grit. Kohli's first-innings century was a particularly fine effort as he countered the marauding Tim Southee, who finished with seven for 64, the best figures by a New Zealander in India. But the batsmen didn't quite build on his exploits, and India were set 261 to complete their expected 2–0 victory.

No Test team had previously made more than 207 to win at Bangalore, but India found their heroes in Kohli and Dhoni, who steadied the ship from 166 for five and took them home without further damage. Even so, the immediate focus was on Tendulkar. For the first time in Tests since the 2002 tour of England, he was bowled three times on the trot, punishment for a propensity to play around his front pad. His future was debated with renewed vigour.

The brief Twenty20 series that followed the Tests was all about Yuvraj Singh, who was making his return to competitive cricket after overcoming a rare germ-cell cancer. His comeback was delayed by incessant rain at Visakhapatnam, but he calmed fears that he had been brought back prematurely with a competent performance in Chennai – even if it wasn't quite enough to prevent New Zealand's only win of the tour.

NEW ZEALAND TOURING PARTY

*L. R. P. L. Taylor, T. A. Boult, D. A. J. Bracewell, D. R. Flynn, J. E. C. Franklin, M. J. Guptill, B. B. McCullum, C. S. Martin, T. S. Nethula, J. S. Patel, T. G. Southee, C. F. K. van Wyk, N. Wagner, B-J. Watling, K. S. Williamson. *Coach:* M. J. Hesson.

For the Twenty20 internationals which followed the Tests, R. M. Hira, K. D. Mills, A. F. Milne, R. J. Nicol, J. D. P. Oram and D. L. Vettori replaced Boult, Flynn, Martin, Nethula, Patel, van Wyk and Wagner.

INDIA v NEW ZEALAND

First Test Match

At Hyderabad (Uppal), August 23–26, 2012. India won by an innings and 115 runs. Toss: India.

India were always heavy favourites, but even they must have been pleasantly surprised at the ease and swiftness of victory with more than a day to spare. New Zealand came unstuck against probing spin, with Ashwin to the fore. He had done well in his debut series, against West Indies in November 2011, but struggled a little in unhelpful conditions in Australia shortly after. Now, though, he was back on home turf, and in his element – teasing and tormenting the batsmen with his control and guile. There was some help for him and his spin partner Ojha, but the pitch was not quite the "real turning track" that Taylor, New Zealand's captain, pronounced it to be.

This was the first Test of the post-Dravid-and-Laxman era, which meant all eyes were on India's relatively inexperienced middle order. Pujara, at No. 3, was playing his first Test for more than 18 months; Raina was recalled after a year-long absence; and Kohli – for all his one-day experience – was winning only his ninth Test cap. If there were worries about whether the young guns could replace the old arsenal, they were to a large extent answered: Pujara compiled a masterful 159, and received excellent support from Kohli after India had found themselves 125 for three on the first day against a New Zealand attack that was more honest than threatening. They doubled the score and, after another mini-stutter, India were hauled out of the woods by Pujara and Dhoni, who added 127 for the sixth wicket to help boost the total past 400.

Flight, loop and dip paid handsome dividends

New Zealand's batting woes began almost immediately. Spin wasn't long in coming, and Ojha struck a massive blow in his first over, when McCullum, their most attacking batsman, skimmed a low catch into the covers. From then on, they waged a losing battle, apparently leaving footwork and soft hands behind in the dressing-room.

Ashwin did away with the over-experimentation that had blighted his tour of Australia and concentrated instead on making the most of his off-break. His ability to test the batsmen with flight, loop and dip paid handsome dividends as he scythed through the order, with only Williamson and Franklin offering much resistance. The parsimonious Ojha produced a genuine beauty which drifted in, then broke away on pitching, to catch Williamson's outside edge. As slip catches go, this one was reasonably straightforward but, throughout the match, Sehwag and Kohli suggested India had found close-in replacements for Dravid and Laxman.

New Zealand were shot out in a shade over four hours and, with the weather closing in, Dhoni had no hesitation in enforcing the follow-on. Trailing by 279, New Zealand showed greater character, but once again they abandoned their natural game and tried to keep wickets intact. With the ball turning and bouncing, and close fielders hovering, it was a tactic fraught with danger.

McCullum and Williamson inched to 98 for one in 45 overs, but the floodgates opened once Yadav won a fortuitous leg-before shout against McCullum, who had got a big edge on to his pads (with no DRS to save him). The last nine wickets clattered for just 66, and Taylor's dismissal – offering no stroke to Ashwin as the ball hit the top of off – epitomised the tourists' uncertainty. Ashwin finished with 12 for 85, match figures bettered against New Zealand only by Courtney Walsh, who took 13 for 55 for West Indies at Wellington in 1994-95.

Man of the Match: R. Ashwin.

Close of play: first day, India 307-5 (Pujara 119, Dhoni 29); second day, New Zealand 106-5 (Franklin 31, van Wyk 0); third day, New Zealand 41-1 (McCullum 16, Williamson 3).

India

G. Gambhir c van Wyk b Boult	22	P. P. Ojha not out	4
V. Sehwag c Guptill b Bracewell	47	U. T. Yadav run out	4
C. A. Pujara c Franklin b Patel	159		
S. R. Tendulkar b Boult	19	B 6, l-b 4, w 2	12
V. Kohli c Guptill b Martin	58		
S. K. Raina c van Wyk b Patel	3	1/49 (1) 2/77 (2) (134.3 overs)	438
*†M. S. Dhoni c Bracewell b Patel	73	3/125 (4) 4/250 (5)	
R. Ashwin st van Wyk b Patel	37	5/260 (6) 6/387 (3) 7/411 (7)	
Zaheer Khan c van Wyk b Boult	0	8/414 (9) 9/430 (8) 10/438 (11)	

Martin 27–4–76–1; Boult 27–4–93–3; Bracewell 19.1–1–88–1; Franklin 13.2–0–40–0; Patel 41–9–100–4; Williamson 7–0–31–0.

New Zealand

B. B. McCullum c Kohli b Ojha	22	– (2) lbw b Yadav	42
M. J. Guptill c Kohli b Ashwin	2	– (1) lbw b Ojha	16
K. S. Williamson c Sehwag b Ojha	32	– c Sehwag b Ojha	52
*L. R. P. L. Taylor c Kohli b Ashwin	2	– b Ashwin	7
D. R. Flynn lbw b Ashwin	16	– lbw b Ashwin	11
J. E. C. Franklin not out	43	– c Sehwag b Ashwin	5
†C. F. K. van Wyk lbw b Yadav	0	– lbw b Ashwin	13
D. A. J. Bracewell st Dhoni b Ojha	17	– c Kohli b Ojha	1
J. S. Patel c and b Ashwin	10	– not out	6
T. A. Boult c Gambhir b Ashwin	4	– c Sehwag b Ashwin	0
C. S. Martin b Ashwin	0	– lbw b Ashwin	0
B 4, l-b 7	11	B 1, l-b 10	11
1/25 (1) 2/29 (2) 3/35 (4) (61.3 overs)	159	1/26 (1) 2/98 (2) (79.5 overs)	164
4/55 (5) 5/99 (3) 6/111 (7)		3/105 (4) 4/138 (3)	
7/141 (8) 8/153 (9) 9/159 (10) 10/159 (11)		5/142 (5) 6/145 (6) 7/148 (8)	
		8/160 (7) 9/164 (10) 10/164 (11)	

Zaheer Khan 11–4–33–0; Yadav 8–0–24–1; Ojha 21–6–44–3; Ashwin 16.3–5–31–6; Sehwag 2–0–4–0; Raina 2–0–6–0; Tendulkar 1–0–6–0. *Second innings*—Ojha 28–9–48–3; Zaheer Khan 13–5–17–0; Yadav 10–1–32–1; Ashwin 26.5–9–54–6; Raina 2–1–2–0.

Umpires: S. J. Davis and I. J. Gould. Third umpire: V. A. Kulkarni.

INDIA v NEW ZEALAND

Second Test Match

DILEEP PREMACHANDRAN

At Bangalore, August 31–September 3, 2012. India won by five wickets. Toss: New Zealand.

After New Zealand's collapse at Hyderabad, where they struggled to match Pujara's 159 in either innings, this was expected to be another Indian procession. That it didn't turn out that way owed much to a tremendous counter-attacking hundred from Taylor, and a superb spell of swing and seam bowling from Southee. The result was no different, though, with Kohli continuing his excellent form, and the spin twins – Ashwin and Ojha – chipping away at New Zealand's resistance. But it needed India's fifth-highest successful run-chase to secure the win, and Taylor was left to rue the absence of a spinner capable of doing more damage than Patel, who took three wickets without ever really giving India the shivers.

In the First Test, New Zealand's batting had been meek and indecisive, with few attempts to upset the spinners' rhythm. Here they opted for Plan B. Dhoni opened the bowling with Ojha but, after some early alarms and the loss of McCullum to Zaheer Khan, the runs came rather more easily. Guptill set the tone with a stroke-filled half-century, before a miscue to midwicket once again trained attention on his poor conversion-rate – in his 26th Test, he had now turned only two of his 14 fifties into hundreds.

Taylor, a crowd favourite after three seasons with Bangalore's Royal Challengers in the IPL, made his intentions clear from the start. The sweep and other cleaves across the line fetched him seven fours off Ojha, and there were also some lovely strokes through cover and straight down the ground. Taylor was not exactly twinkle-toed, and didn't always get to the pitch of the ball, but few scoring opportunities were missed as a barrage of shots left the Indians perplexed.

Emboldened by his captain's methods, Flynn joined in. The session between lunch and tea produced 132 runs, and even the departure of Taylor – who had made 85 of them – shortly after the interval, as he tried to sweep a straight one, didn't staunch the flow. A partnership of 99 between van Wyk and Bracewell, who hit out crisply, allowed New Zealand to reach 365.

India's reply floundered against Southee, who had replaced Chris Martin in the side. Gambhir, in his 50th Test, went cheaply once more, Pujara also failed, and Sehwag squandered another start. When Tendulkar was bowled again, India were staring at embarrassment. But Raina took his cue from Taylor and went for his shots. With Kohli classy and resolute, India gradually redressed the balance. Raina finally departed, tickling one down the leg side, but Kohli's wonderfully paced hundred and bright contributions from Dhoni and Ashwin got India to within 12. Southee's reward was seven for 64, the best figures for New Zealand in India, beating Dion Nash's six for 27 at Mohali in 1999-2000.

On a pitch that never really deteriorated, New Zealand needed to make around 300 to test India. Eight batsmen reached double figures, but the highest score was Franklin's 41; Yadav hit van Wyk on the helmet and, next ball, broke his forearm, but he battled on for another six overs regardless (McCullum kept wicket in the second innings). After Ojha had starred in the first innings, it was now Ashwin's turn to dismantle the middle order following Yadav's early strikes.

India were eventually set 261, and were given a solid base by their openers, before both fell in quick succession. Pujara and Tendulkar rebuilt, only for three quick wickets to give New Zealand a whiff of victory: Tendulkar was bowled yet again – his frustration apparent as he briefly threatened to smash the stumps; Pujara was caught at bat–pad; then Raina harmed his future prospects with a headless-chicken charge.

With 95 still to get, coolness was needed. Kohli took the lead, batting as Dravid and Laxman often did in such situations, and found an unflappable ally in Dhoni, who combined the dead bat and the heavy one to great effect: his second six clinched the series towards the end of the fourth day.

Man of the Match: V. Kohli. *Man of the Series:* R. Ashwin.

Close of play: first day, New Zealand 328-6 (van Wyk 63, Bracewell 30); second day, India 283-5 (Kohli 93, Dhoni 46); third day, New Zealand 232-9 (Patel 10, Boult 0).

> "When Morkel went round the wicket in the fourth over after the interval, it was as if he had woken the Kraken."
>
> England v South Africa 2012, Second Test, page 362.

New Zealand

M. J. Guptill c Gambhir b Ojha	53	– (2) b Yadav	7
B. B. McCullum lbw b Zaheer Khan	0	– (1) c Dhoni b Yadav	23
K. S. Williamson lbw b Ojha	17	– c Sehwag b Ashwin	13
*L. R. P. L. Taylor lbw b Ojha	113	– lbw b Ojha	35
D. R. Flynn lbw b Ashwin	33	– c Sehwag b Ashwin	31
J. E. C. Franklin c Raina b Ojha	8	– st Dhoni b Ashwin	41
†C. F. K. van Wyk c Raina b Zaheer Khan	71	– lbw b Ashwin	31
D. A. J. Bracewell run out	43	– lbw b Ojha	22
T. G. Southee lbw b Ojha	14	– b Ashwin	2
J. S. Patel c Gambhir b Yadav	0	– c Dhoni b Zaheer Khan	22
T. A. Boult not out	2	– not out	4
B 2, l-b 9	11	B 4, l-b 12, w 1	17
1/0 (2) 2/63 (3) 3/89 (1) (90.1 overs)	365	1/30 (2) 2/31 (1) (73.2 overs)	248
4/196 (5) 5/215 (6) 6/246 (4)		3/69 (3) 4/111 (4)	
7/345 (7) 8/353 (8) 9/353 (10) 10/365 (9)		5/140 (5) 6/195 (7) 7/216 (6)	
		8/222 (9) 9/222 (8) 10/248 (10)	

Ojha 28.1–10–99–5; Zaheer Khan 22–2–83–2; Yadav 16–1–90–1; Ashwin 24–5–82–1. *Second innings*—Zaheer Khan 14.2–2–46–1; Yadav 15–0–68–2; Ojha 21–6–49–2; Ashwin 22–1–69–5; Raina 1–1–0–0.

India

G. Gambhir b Southee	2	– c Taylor b Boult	34
V. Sehwag c Flynn b Bracewell	43	– b Patel	38
C. A. Pujara c Boult b Southee	9	– c Flynn b Patel	48
S. R. Tendulkar b Bracewell	17	– b Southee	27
V. Kohli lbw b Southee	103	– not out	51
S. K. Raina c van Wyk b Southee	55	– b Patel	0
*†M. S. Dhoni lbw b Southee	62	– not out	48
R. Ashwin not out	32		
Zaheer Khan c van Wyk b Southee	7		
P. P. Ojha c van Wyk b Southee	0		
U. T. Yadav b Boult	4		
B 11, l-b 2, w 1, n-b 5	19	B 4, l-b 6, w 5, n-b 1	16
1/5 (1) 2/27 (3) 3/67 (2) 4/80 (4) (96.5 overs)	353	1/77 (2) (5 wkts, 63.2 overs)	262
5/179 (6) 6/301 (5) 7/312 (7)		2/83 (1) 3/152 (4)	
8/320 (9) 9/320 (10) 10/353 (11)		4/158 (3) 5/166 (6)	

Boult 23.5–2–90–1; Southee 24–6–64–7; Bracewell 20–4–91–2; Franklin 10–4–17–0; Patel 19–5–78–0. *Second innings*—Boult 16–4–64–1; Southee 18–3–68–1; Bracewell 14–3–52–0; Patel 15.2–3–68–3.

Umpires: S. J. Davis and I. J. Gould. Third umpire: S. Asnani.
Series referee: B. C. Broad.

INDIA v NEW ZEALAND

First Twenty20 International

At Visakhapatnam, September 8, 2012 (floodlit). Abandoned.

This was supposed to have been Yuvraj Singh's comeback to international cricket after his fight against mediastinal seminoma, a rare cancer, but the weather delayed it for three days. Incessant rain and waterlogging rendered the match a non-starter long before it was officially abandoned.

INDIA v NEW ZEALAND

Second Twenty20 International

At Chennai, September 11, 2012 (floodlit). New Zealand won by one run. Toss: India. Twenty20 international debut: L. Balaji.

New Zealand finally had something to celebrate, completing their only victory of a short tour by the narrowest of margins. They had also won all their three previous Twenty20 internationals against India, although at various stages they looked more than likely to lose this one. McCullum rallied his side from two for two with a spectacular 91, from just 55 balls, during which he dismantled Ashwin, India's hero during the Tests. India were well on course while Kohli was replying in kind, then the returning Yuvraj Singh thrilled his fans with a rapid 34. They needed 35 from the last four overs with seven wickets in hand, but Oram and Franklin – who successfully defended 13 in the final over – bowled beautifully.

Man of the Match: B. B. McCullum. *Man of the Series:* B. B. McCullum.

New Zealand

		B	*4*	*6*
R. J. Nicol *b 10*	0	4	0	0
M. J. Guptill *b 8*	1	5	0	0
†B. B. McCullum *b 8*	91	55	11	3
K. S. Williamson *c 9 b 8*	28	26	3	0
*L. R. P. L. Taylor *not out*	25	19	0	1
J. E. C. Franklin *c 4 b 11*	1	2	0	0
J. D. P. Oram *not out*	18	9	3	0
L-b 1, w 2	3			
6 overs: 36-2 (20 overs)	167-5			

1/2 2/2 3/92 4/139 5/142

D. L. Vettori, R. M. Hira, K. D. Mills and A. F. Milne did not bat.

Zaheer Khan 4–0–27–1; Pathan 4–0–31–3; Balaji 4–0–33–1; Yuvraj Singh 2–0–14–0; Ashwin 3–0–34–0; Kohli 3–0–27–0.

India

		B	*4*	*6*
G. Gambhir *c and b 10*	3	6	0	0
V. Kohli *c 12 b 6*	70	41	10	1
S. K. Raina *c 5 b 10*	27	22	2	1
Yuvraj Singh *b 6*	34	26	1	2
*†M. S. Dhoni *not out*	22	23	2	0
R. G. Sharma *not out*	4	2	0	0
L-b 3, w 3	6			
6 overs: 47-1 (20 overs)	166-4			

1/26 2/86 3/120 4/162

M. K. Tiwary, I. K. Pathan, R. Ashwin, Zaheer Khan and L. Balaji did not bat.

Mills 3–0–17–2; Milne 3–0–36–0; Oram 4–0–27–0; Vettori 4–0–37–0; Hira 2–0–20–0; Franklin 4–0–26–2.

12th man T. G. Southee.

Umpires: V. A. Kulkarni and S. Ravi. Third umpire: S. Asnani.
Referee: B. C. Broad.

INDIA v PAKISTAN, 2012-13

DILEEP PREMACHANDRAN

One-day internationals (3): India 1, Pakistan 2
Twenty20 internationals (2): India 1, Pakistan 1

The first bilateral series between India and Pakistan in five years was a big step towards restoring the cross-border cricket connection following the terror atrocities – blamed on Pakistani extremists – in Mumbai in November 2008. Between 2003-04, when India embarked on their first full tour of Pakistan in nearly 15 years, and 2007-08, these old rivals had played each other at every opportunity. Post-Mumbai, the on-field skirmishes had been restricted to global events. An Indian trip to Pakistan had been cancelled in early 2009, and the attack on Sri Lanka's cricketers in Lahore shortly after ensured there would be little talk of rescheduling.

Pakistani players had taken part in the first edition of the IPL in 2008, but been ignored since; no Pakistani team appeared in the Champions League until 2012, and Indian responses to their neighbour's proposals for playing at a neutral venue had been distinctly chilly. But a thaw in governmental relations coincided with a rare window in India's schedule. Five India–Pakistan matches were squeezed in, and the necessary visa hurdles cleared.

The teams had journeyed in different directions since India's World Cup triumph in 2011, when they saw off Pakistan in the semi-final at Mohali. India then relinquished their No. 1 Test ranking after being routed 4–0 in England; six months later, Pakistan beat England 3–0. Pakistan won the 2012 Asia Cup, despite losing to India in the group stages; and, although India won their head-to-head at the World Twenty20 in Sri Lanka, it was Pakistan who made the last four.

Given Indian cricket's state of flux now, it was no real surprise that Pakistan were the better side. Their bowlers bossed the opening Twenty20 match, at Bangalore, before a breathtaking innings from Yuvraj Singh at Ahmedabad gave India a share of the spoils. But there would be no such parity in the 50-over arena, with Pakistan's new-ball bowlers and off-spinner Saeed Ajmal exerting a stranglehold only M. S. Dhoni managed to escape. Halfway through the final game, at Delhi, Pakistan were well on course for a 3–0 clean sweep, but a combination of doughty Indian bowling and the sort of batting implosion that has occasionally bedevilled their opponents gave the vocal crowd a consolation victory to cheer. Even so, India had gone down to their first home defeat in a bilateral one-day series since losing to Australia three years previously.

As well as the Pakistani bowlers performed – India's highest total in the five games was 227 – the star of the show was the 23-year-old Nasir Jamshed. Solidly built and with no pretensions to athleticism, he preyed on India's traditional problems against left-handers, scoring match-winning hundreds at Chennai and Kolkata. He was often watchful early on, but timed the ball beautifully once he settled in.

India's own bowlers did not let them down, with Ishant Sharma, Ravindra Jadeja and Bhuvneshwar Kumar – a seamer from Uttar Pradesh – all catching the eye. But the once-formidable batting had few answers to the seven-footer Mohammad Irfan or the pacy Junaid Khan, who swung his way through the top order in Chennai. Dhoni batted superbly for 203 runs for once out in the 50-over series, but no one else registered a half-century. Pakistan were not as reliant on Jamshed, and found cameos from elsewhere. In a low-scoring series, that was the difference.

PAKISTAN TOURING PARTY

*Misbah-ul-Haq, Anwar Ali, Azhar Ali, Haris Sohail, Imran Farhat, Junaid Khan, Kamran Akmal, Mohammad Hafeez, Mohammad Irfan, Nasir Jamshed, Saeed Ajmal, Shoaib Malik, Umar Akmal, Umar Gul, Wahab Riaz, Younis Khan, Zulfiqar Babar. *Coach:* D. F. Whatmore.

For the Twenty20 internationals which preceded the 50-over matches, Ahmed Shehzad, Asad Ali, Shahid Afridi, Sohail Tanvir and Umar Amin replaced Anwar Ali, Azhar Ali, Haris Sohail, Imran Farhat, Misbah-ul-Haq, Wahab Riaz and Younis Khan; Mohammad Hafeez captained.

INDIA v PAKISTAN

First Twenty20 International

At Bangalore, December 25, 2012 (floodlit). Pakistan won by five wickets. Toss: Pakistan. Twenty20 international debuts: Bhuvneshwar Kumar; Mohammad Irfan.

At 77 without loss in the 11th over, India looked set for a huge total. Then Rahane lofted to deep extra cover, the first of nine wickets to fall for 47 in 46 balls. Apart from him and Gambhir – run out yet again, his 19th such dismissal in all internationals – no one else passed ten; Umar Gul bowled fast and straight, and Saeed Ajmal breached the defences of Dhoni and Raina. The economical Bhuvneshwar Kumar took three wickets in his first two overs on debut to raise Indian hopes, only for Mohammad Hafeez and Shoaib Malik to add 106, a Pakistan fourth-wicket record in this format. But India struck twice to cause some panic, and there was drama when Malik, on 47, was caught off Ishant Sharma, only for the delivery to be ruled a no-ball on height. With tension mounting, Sharma and the non-striker Kamran Akmal became involved in a slanging match, which earned them both a fine. Pakistan were left needing ten from the final over, bowled by Jadeja, and the reprieved Malik sealed their first Twenty20 win over India, at the fourth attempt, with a nonchalant straight six.

Man of the Match: Mohammad Hafeez.

India

		B	*4*	*6*
G. Gambhir *run out*	43	41	2	1
A. M. Rahane *c 4 b 7*	42	31	5	1
V. Kohli *c 6 b 11*	9	11	1	0
Yuvraj Singh *c 4 b 9*	10	9	0	1
*†M. S. Dhoni *b 10*	1	2	0	0
S. K. Raina *b 10*	10	9	1	0
R. G. Sharma *run out*	2	2	0	0
R. A. Jadeja *c 6 b 9*	2	4	0	0
Bhuvneshwar Kumar *not out*	6	6	0	0
I. Sharma *b 9*	0	1	0	0
A. B. Dinda *not out*	3	4	0	0
L-b 2, w 3	5			

6 overs: 37-0 (20 overs) 133-9

1/77 2/90 3/103 4/108 5/115 6/122 7/123 8/124 9/124

Mohammad Irfan 4–0–25–1; Sohail Tanvir 4–0–22–0; Umar Gul 3–0–21–3; Saeed Ajmal 4–0–25–2; Shahid Afridi 3–0–26–1; Mohammad Hafeez 2–0–12–0.

Pakistan

		B	*4*	*6*
Nasir Jamshed *b 9*	2	6	0	0
Ahmed Shehzad *c 5 b 9*	5	7	1	0
*Mohammad Hafeez *c 9 b 10*	61	44	6	2
Umar Akmal *b 9*	0	4	0	0
Shoaib Malik *not out*	57	50	3	3
†Kamran Akmal *c 10 b 11*	1	6	0	0
Shahid Afridi *not out*	3	2	0	0
L-b 1, w 3, n-b 1	5			

6 overs: 22-3 (19.4 overs) 134-5

1/2 2/11 3/12 4/118 5/123

Sohail Tanvir, Umar Gul, Saeed Ajmal and Mohammad Irfan did not bat.

Bhuvneshwar Kumar 4–0–9–3; Dinda 4–0–26–1; I. Sharma 4–0–23–1; Kohli 2–0–21–0; Yuvraj Singh 3–0–25–0; Jadeja 2.4–0–29–0.

Umpires: S. Ravi and C. Shamshuddin. Third umpire: V. A. Kulkarni.

INDIA v PAKISTAN

Second Twenty20 International

At Ahmedabad, December 28, 2012 (floodlit). India won by 11 runs. Toss: Pakistan.

This was a tale of two devastating innings, with India holding their nerve to register a series-levelling victory. Batting first, they had no great impetus for 12 overs before Yuvraj Singh began clearing the rope with the casual disdain of a man swatting flies during his best score in the format, adding 97 in 7.2 overs with Dhoni. Pakistan's usually parsimonious trio of spinners went for 86 in eight wicketless overs, and it was left to Umar Gul to limit the damage. Pakistan were boosted by handy contributions from their top three, but it was the captain, Mohammad Hafeez, who kept India on edge with an innings even more rapid than Yuvraj's. It wasn't until he holed out to the second ball of the penultimate over that the crowd really believed the game was safe. Dinda, with his awkward-looking leap and lively pace, picked up three key wickets.

Man of the Match: Yuvraj Singh. *Man of the Series:* Mohammad Hafeez.

India

		B	*4*	*6*
G. Gambhir *lbw b 8*	21	11	4	0
A. M. Rahane *c and b 8*	28	26	4	0
V. Kohli *run out*	27	22	3	0
Yuvraj Singh *c 7 b 8*	72	36	4	7
*†M. S. Dhoni *b 8*	33	23	4	0
S. K. Raina *not out*	1	1	0	0
R. G. Sharma *not out*	4	2	1	0
L-b 5, n-b 1	6			
6 overs: 48-1 (20 overs)	192-5			

1/44 2/53 3/88 4/185 5/187

Bhuvneshwar Kumar, R. Ashwin, I. Sharma and A. B. Dinda did not bat.

Mohammad Irfan 4–0–20–0; Sohail Tanvir 4–0–44–0; Umar Gul 4–0–37–4; Saeed Ajmal 4–0–42–0; Shahid Afridi 3–0–33–0; Mohammad Hafeez 1–0–11–0.

Pakistan

		B	*4*	*6*
Nasir Jamshed *c 3 b 9*	41	32	4	1
Ahmed Shehzad *st 5 b 4*	31	29	3	1
Umar Akmal *b 11*	24	17	1	1
*Mohammad Hafeez *c 6 b 11*	55	26	6	3
Shahid Afridi *c 7 b 8*	11	5	1	1
†Kamran Akmal *c 3 b 11*	5	3	1	0
Shoaib Malik *not out*	3	3	0	0
Umar Gul *c 2 b 10*	5	5	1	0
L-b 2, w 4	6			
6 overs: 54-0 (20 overs)	181-7			

1/74 2/84 3/146 4/163 5/168 6/172 7/181

Sohail Tanvir, Saeed Ajmal and Mohammad Irfan did not bat.

Bhuvneshwar Kumar 4–0–46–1; I. Sharma 4–0–34–1; Dinda 4–0–36–3; Ashwin 4–0–28–1; Raina 2–0–12–0; Yuvraj Singh 2–0–23–1.

Umpires: S. Asnani and V. A. Kulkarni. Third umpire: C. Shamshuddin.
Series referee: R. S. Mahanama.

INDIA v PAKISTAN

First One-Day International

At Chennai, December 30, 2012. Pakistan won by six wickets. Toss: Pakistan. One-day international debut: Bhuvneshwar Kumar.

This match was settled in the first ten overs, as Pakistan's new-ball pair scythed through India's top order. The lofty Mohammad Irfan jarred bat handles with steep bounce and genuine pace, while Junaid Khan clean-bowled three of one-day cricket's most illustrious performers with a display of swing bowling that brought back memories of Wasim Akram in his pomp. The first five made just 18 runs between them, leaving Raina and Dhoni to conduct a sedate grind to respectability. Dhoni's first fifty took 86 balls, but from his next 39 he bludgeoned 63, limiting Ashwin's doughty contribution to a stand of 125 – India's best for the seventh wicket in one-day internationals – to 31.

It was Dhoni's eighth one-day hundred for India, but his first for nearly three years. The debutant Bhuvneshwar Kumar then bowled Hafeez, shouldering arms, with his first ball, and soon added Azhar Ali, as Pakistan made a hesitant start. Only Sadagoppan Ramesh, a batsman given a rare bowl against West Indies in Singapore in September 1999, had previously struck with his first ball in one-day internationals for India. Nasir Jamshed could have been run out when seven, should have been given out caught off bat and pad at 24, and was badly missed by Yuvraj Singh at point when 68 – lapses India were to rue as he continued through the innings. Younis Khan's sprightly 58 eased run-rate worries, but it was Jamshed, batting with increasing confidence, who was the main man; he reached his second successive one-day century against India – following the Asia Cup in March – just before Shoaib Malik swatted Dinda for the winning boundary with 11 balls to spare.

Man of the Match: M. S. Dhoni.

India

G. Gambhir b Mohammad Irfan	8
V. Sehwag b Junaid Khan	4
V. Kohli b Junaid Khan	0
Yuvraj Singh b Junaid Khan	2
R. G. Sharma c Mohammad Hafeez b Junaid Khan	4
S. K. Raina b Mohammad Hafeez	43
*†M. S. Dhoni not out	113
R. Ashwin not out	31
L-b 11, w 9, n-b 2	22
1/17 (2) 2/17 (1) 3/19 (3) 4/20 (4) 5/29 (5) 6/102 (6) (6 wkts, 50 overs)	227
10 overs: 29-5	

Bhuvneshwar Kumar, I. Sharma and A. B. Dinda did not bat.

Mohammad Irfan 9–2–58–1; Junaid Khan 9–1–43–4; Umar Gul 8–0–38–0; Saeed Ajmal 10–1–42–0; Mohammad Hafeez 10–2–26–1; Shoaib Malik 4–0–9–0.

Pakistan

Mohammad Hafeez b Bhuvneshwar Kumar	0
Nasir Jamshed not out	101
Azhar Ali c R. G. Sharma b Bhuvneshwar Kumar	9
Younis Khan c Ashwin b Dinda	58
*Misbah-ul-Haq b I. Sharma	16
Shoaib Malik not out	34
L-b 6, w 3, n-b 1	10
1/0 (1) 2/21 (3) 3/133 (4) 4/172 (5) (4 wkts, 48.1 overs)	228
10 overs: 21-1	

†Kamran Akmal, Junaid Khan, Umar Gul, Saeed Ajmal and Mohammad Irfan did not bat.

Bhuvneshwar Kumar 9–3–27–2; I. Sharma 10–0–39–1; Dinda 9.1–0–45–1; Ashwin 10–0–34–0; Yuvraj Singh 5–0–33–0; Raina 2.1–0–23–0; Kohli 2.5–0–21–0.

Umpires: B. F. Bowden and S. Ravi. Third umpire: S. Asnani.

INDIA v PAKISTAN

Second One-Day International

At Kolkata, January 3, 2013 (day/night). Pakistan won by 85 runs. Toss: India.

Nasir Jamshed struck his third consecutive hundred against India, then watched Pakistan's bowlers embarrass the home batsmen again in a match as one-sided as the result suggests. Once Junaid Khan and Umar Gul had made early inroads, India's pursuit of 251 was never on. Even Dhoni, so heroic at Chennai, dawdled untypically, consuming 89 balls for his unbeaten 54. India had been just as poor with the ball at first, allowing Jamshed and Mohammad Hafeez to put on 141 at nearly six an over. An ugly heave against Jadeja – recalled in place of Rohit Sharma to strengthen the bowling – cost Hafeez, and Ishant Sharma helped keep the Pakistan total to manageable proportions. But Jamshed's beautifully paced 106 was an effort no Indian came close to emulating in the face of more hostile and accurate bowling. It was Pakistan's fourth one-day international against India at Eden Gardens – and they had won all of them.

Man of the Match: Nasir Jamshed.

Pakistan

Nasir Jamshed st Dhoni b Jadeja	106	Junaid Khan not out	0
Mohammad Hafeez b Jadeja	76	Mohammad Irfan b Sharma	0
Azhar Ali run out	2		
Younis Khan lbw b Raina	10		
*Misbah-ul-Haq lbw b Ashwin	2	W 6	6
Shoaib Malik c Yuvraj Singh b Sharma	24		
†Kamran Akmal c Sehwag b Jadeja	0	1/141 (2) 2/145 (3) (48.3 overs)	250
Umar Gul b Sharma	17	3/177 (4) 4/182 (5) 5/210 (1)	
Saeed Ajmal c Sehwag b Bhuvneshwar Kumar	7	6/210 (7) 7/236 (6) 8/249 (9) 9/250 (8) 10/250 (11)	10 overs: 59-0

Bhuvneshwar Kumar 9–0–61–1; Dinda 7–0–42–0; Sharma 9.3–0–34–3; Ashwin 10–0–49–1; Raina 2–0–13–1; Jadeja 10–1–41–3; Yuvraj Singh 1–0–10–0.

India

G. Gambhir b Junaid Khan	11	Bhuvneshwar Kumar lbw b Saeed Ajmal	0
V. Sehwag lbw b Umar Gul	31	A. B. Dinda lbw b Saeed Ajmal	0
V. Kohli c Kamran Akmal b Junaid Khan	6	I. Sharma b Junaid Khan	2
Yuvraj Singh c Kamran Akmal b Umar Gul	9	L-b 4, w 14	18
S. K. Raina st Kamran Akmal b Mohammad Hafeez	18	1/42 (1) 2/55 (3) 3/59 (2) (48 overs)	165
*†M. S. Dhoni not out	54	4/70 (4) 5/95 (5) 6/103 (7)	
R. Ashwin st Kamran Akmal b Shoaib Malik	3	7/131 (8) 8/131 (9) 9/132 (10)	
R. A. Jadeja c Junaid Khan b Saeed Ajmal	13	10/165 (11)	10 overs: 42-1

Mohammad Irfan 10–0–46–0; Junaid Khan 9–1–39–3; Umar Gul 7–0–24–2; Mohammad Hafeez 10–0–29–1; Saeed Ajmal 10–1–20–3; Shoaib Malik 2–1–3–1.

Umpires: B. F. Bowden and V. A. Kulkarni. Third umpire: S. Ravi.

INDIA v PAKISTAN

Third One-Day International

At Delhi, January 6, 2013 (day/night). India won by ten runs. Toss: India. One-day international debut: Shami Ahmed.

This was a morale-boosting win for India – and a clean sweep spurned by Pakistan. Misbah-ul-Haq's attack had again been too good for a batting line-up lacking form and confidence, but the work was undone by a diffident chase that never gained momentum once the impressive Bhuvneshwar Kumar picked up two early wickets. Misbah's 39 spanned 82 balls, and Shami Ahmed, a debutant seamer from Bengal, hustled through four maidens. But at 113 for three with 16 overs to go, Pakistan were cruising; to lose seven for 44 was shockingly careless. India's modest total owed much to a stand of 48 between Raina and Dhoni, and a late cameo from Jadeja. This time, Mohammad Irfan made the early incisions before Saeed Ajmal bamboozled the rest with his variations, finishing with his best figures in one-day internationals. Dhoni top-scored again, with a steady 36 that included three huge sixes, and later led with sufficient imagination to win the match award. But avoiding India's first home one-day whitewash for 19 years was small consolation at the end of a poor series for his team.

Man of the Match: M. S. Dhoni. *Man of the Series:* Nasir Jamshed.

India

G. Gambhir c Umar Akmal b Mohammad Irfan . 15
A. M. Rahane c Kamran Akmal b Mohammad Irfan . 4
V. Kohli c Younis Khan b Junaid Khan . . . 7
Yuvraj Singh b Mohammad Hafeez 23
S. K. Raina lbw b Saeed Ajmal. 31
*†M. S. Dhoni c Umar Akmal b Umar Gul . . 36
R. Ashwin lbw b Saeed Ajmal 0
R. A. Jadeja c Umar Akmal b Saeed Ajmal 27
Bhuvneshwar Kumar lbw b Saeed Ajmal . . 2
I. Sharma c and b Saeed Ajmal 5
Shami Ahmed not out 0

L-b 4, w 7, n-b 1, p 5. 17

1/19 (2) 2/29 (1) 3/37 (3) (43.4 overs) 167
4/63 (4) 5/111 (5) 6/111 (7)
7/131 (6) 8/141 (9) 9/160 (10)
10/167 (8) 10 overs: 38-3

Mohammad Irfan 7–1–28–2; Junaid Khan 9–1–17–1; Umar Gul 8–1–45–1; Mohammad Hafeez 10–0–44–1; Saeed Ajmal 9.4–1–24–5.

Pakistan

Nasir Jamshed lbw b Ashwin 34
†Kamran Akmal lbw b Bhuvneshwar Kumar 0
Younis Khan b Bhuvneshwar Kumar 6
*Misbah-ul-Haq c Rahane b Ashwin. 39
Umar Akmal st Dhoni b Jadeja 25
Shoaib Malik lbw b Sharma 5
Mohammad Hafeez c Yuvraj Singh b Sharma . 21
Umar Gul c Jadeja b Sharma. 11
Saeed Ajmal c Dhoni b Shami Ahmed 1
Junaid Khan run out 0
Mohammad Irfan not out. 0

L-b 1, w 13, n-b 1 15

1/3 (2) 2/14 (3) 3/61 (1) (48.5 overs) 157
4/113 (4) 5/119 (6)
6/125 (5) 7/144 (8) 8/145 (9)
9/145 (10) 10/157 (7) 10 overs: 22-2

Bhuvneshwar Kumar 10–2–31–2; Shami Ahmed 9–4–23–1; Sharma 9.5–0–36–3; Ashwin 10–1–47–2; Jadeja 10–2–19–1.

Umpires: S. Asnani and B. F. Bowden. Third umpire: V. A. Kulkarni.
Series referee: R. S. Mahanama.

THE INDIAN PREMIER LEAGUE, 2011-12

REVIEW BY NAGRAJ GOLLAPUDI

It was no surprise to see the fifth incarnation of the Indian Premier League continuing to hog media attention. Cricket in India – especially the IPL's potent mixture of glamour, politics, money and sport – is a restless, unpredictable beast, rarely content to remain meekly on the back pages. The first few years had been dominated by the alleged corruption of Lalit Modi, one of the least meek of cricket administrators; now came a slew of controversies ranging from match-fixing to drug abuse and accusations of assault. It was no small mercy that the main cricketing headline – a first IPL triumph for Kolkata Knight Riders – proved strong enough to distract attention from the off-field shenanigans.

The match-fixing bombshell went off on May 14, when the Hindi television channel India TV broadcast footage of a sting operation that appeared to show offers of spot-fixing and attempts to negotiate extra (illegal) pay. "We will not tolerate this nonsense," said N. Srinivasan, president of the Board of Control for Cricket in India. "We have zero tolerance on corruption and you will not be disappointed by the action we take." He commissioned a report from Ravi Sawani, head of the BCCI's anti-corruption unit, which found wrongdoing by five Indian domestic players. T. P. Sudhindra, a fast bowler from Madhya Pradesh and the leading wicket-taker in the 2011-12 Ranji Trophy, was given a life ban for "receiving a consideration to spot-fix" in a domestic match. He played three IPL games for Deccan. A five-year ban was handed to Uttar Pradesh fast bowler Shalabh Srivastava (14 matches for Punjab) for agreeing to negotiate terms to fix a match, although no fixing actually took place.

Three more players – Madhya Pradesh batsman Mohnish Mishra (11 matches for Deccan and seven for Pune), Goa off-spinner Amit Yadav and Himachal Pradesh all-rounder Abhinav Bali (both on Punjab's books) – received one-year bans for "bringing the game into disrepute through loose talk and unsubstantiated bragging". All bar Yadav had played in the short-lived, unofficial Indian Cricket League; none of the alleged misdemeanours related to the IPL.

The next crisis came on May 17, when Australian batsman Luke Pomersbach (contracted to Bangalore, though he never played in IPL5) was detained by Delhi police. A US national alleged he had assaulted her and her fiancé at the team hotel. Pomersbach was granted bail, and the case later settled out of court.

The third controversy took place on May 20, when police raided a party at a plush hotel in suburban Mumbai. Among the 42 revellers to test positive for drugs were Wayne Parnell and Rahul Sharma, who both played for Pune – though news of the positive tests did not emerge until July. The tests were for cannabis and ecstasy, but precisely what had been found remained unclear.

And then there was the banning of Shah Rukh Khan, the Bollywood heart-throb, from Mumbai's Wankhede Stadium. On May 16, after Kolkata – co-owned by Khan – had beaten Mumbai in a group match, ground officials tried to prevent him walking on to the pitch. They claimed he was drunk and had verbally abused them. Khan counterclaimed that the officials' behaviour was "unpardonable" in manhandling children he was collecting from the stadium. The upshot was a five-year ban.

Whatever Khan did or didn't do at Mumbai, he certainly behaved like a deliriously happy fan at the M. A. Chidambaram Stadium on May 27, launching himself into impromptu cartwheels on a humid Chennai evening. He could be easily excused: **Kolkata Knight Riders** had won their first IPL crown in five attempts.

For the first three seasons, they had struggled. But in 2011 their fortunes had changed: with a new captain, the passionate and aggressive Gautam Gambhir, and a new CEO in Venky Mysore, Kolkata bounced back with fresh resolve and hunger, finishing fourth. King Khan, though, would not settle for anything but the crown.

Mysore, whose background was in insurance, hired a company to organise mock auctions, built decision trees, and picked line-ups based more on skill sets than celebrity. The Australian Trevor Bayliss, who took Sri Lanka to the World Cup final, came on board. Mysore even recruited sports psychologist Rudi Webster, who had worked with Clive Lloyd's West Indians in the late 1970s, as a mental skills coach. So when Kolkata bought Sunil Narine, a little-known off-spinner from Trinidad & Tobago for a whopping $700,000, they clearly believed they knew what they were doing. And they did.

The Zen-like Kallis could take a back seat

Narine dazzled fans – and batsmen – with mesmerising finger-spin, especially the ball that, coupled with a smart change of pace, moved away from the bat. He became the go-to man for Gambhir. Though he went wicketless in the final, Narine allied penetration with parsimony, finishing second on the lists of wicket-takers and economy-rates. Of his 24 victims, which came at an average of 13.50, all but six had come in the slog overs (15–20). In a season where pace was dominant, he was the one slow bowler in the top eight wicket-takers.

But Kolkata's biggest strength was getting the best from each player. Gambhir, who claimed his team contained 11 match-winners, was the batting bulwark in nearly every game. And when he did fail, in the final, Kolkata kept going without him. Manvinder Bisla, a tall, sturdy, wicketkeeper-batsman from Himachal Pradesh, played the innings of his life, showing an equilibrium that allowed the Zen-like Jacques Kallis to take a back seat in a crucial stand of 136. Bisla had come in at the last minute after the most economical bowler of IPL5, Lakshmipathy Balaji, pulled a hamstring. In previous seasons, captain and coach had looked in different directions; now Kolkata worked as one. They had no centurion, but were easily the best bowling side: opponents hit just seven fifties, and no team managed more than their 107 wickets.

A headline in the Kolkata *Telegraph* called Khan the "Twelfth Knight": his positive energy rubbed off on his team and, in the run-up to the final, he produced a motivational film thanking players, coaches and their families for their efforts. Gambhir, originally from Delhi, warmed hearts on his team's return home by shouting "*ami Kolkatar chhele*" ("I am the son of Kolkata").

Around 50,000 lined the six-kilometre route as the players' open-top bus toured the city, while 65,000 witnessed further celebrations at Eden Gardens.

But it was **Delhi Daredevils**, with 11 wins, who topped the league, before messing things up in the play-offs – despite two chances to make the final. Their worst act of hara-kiri came in the second qualifier, against defending champions **Chennai Super Kings**, when they left South African fast bowler Morne Morkel on the bench. Dropping the league's highest wicket-taker allowed Chennai to pile on 222, the season's highest total. Delhi never came close, departing at the semi-final stage for the third time in five years.

Not that Chennai had a smooth ride. This was probably their worst IPL season, with the batsmen often failing in the league games. They spent much of the tournament in mid-table obscurity, and scraped into the play-offs. Although they did improve, thanks to inspired performances from Indian Test opener Murali Vijay and IPL debutant Ben Hilfenhaus of Australia, the two-time champions lacked the authority of the previous season.

The traditional powerhouse, **Mumbai Indians**, finished third in the table before losing the elimination final. Mumbai had the best bunch of domestic cricketers, but never settled: they fielded 24 players, and tried eight opening combinations, with only sporadic success. **Royal Challengers Bangalore** came painfully close to qualifying for the second stage, but were pipped on net run-rate. Virat Kohli, who took over the captaincy from Daniel Vettori, showed character, but a lack of bowling firepower increased the pressure on him and Chris Gayle to produce big totals. Gayle duly obliged, again becoming the tournament's highest run-scorer.

For the third time in four years, frequent underachievers **Kings XI Punjab** squandered a decent chance to progress. Defeat by Delhi in their final game meant they finished sixth. Adam Gilchrist missed nine matches with a hamstring injury, but fellow Australian David Hussey took over the leadership as Punjab improved a season that, at the halfway stage, had brought just three wins. Though they finished with eight – the same as Chennai and Bangalore – they had one more defeat. **Rajasthan Royals**, led by the resilient Rahul Dravid, finished seventh after losing their last two matches. Ajinkya Rahane was their stand-out batsman, juggling the roles of stabilising and finishing the innings.

Shikar Dhawan fulfilled a similar function for **Deccan Chargers**, who nevertheless lost 11 matches. He finished second only to Gayle on the run charts, but had little reliable support. Dale Steyn, the world's No. 1 fast bowler, also ploughed a lone furrow: his burst of three for eight cost Bangalore a play-off spot. Later in the year, Deccan's owners, Deccan Chronicle Holdings Ltd, ran into financial trouble, and put the franchise up for sale. But they turned down the only offer, and on September 14 had their IPL contract terminated by the BCCI, pending a court hearing.

Pune Warriors, whose owners had pulled out on the eve of the player auction only to be lured back, propped up the table. They began reasonably, but ended with nine straight defeats, an unwelcome tournament record.

Overall, there was nothing extraordinary about the cricket, though overseas recruits – especially South Africans – pulled more weight: England's Kevin Pietersen played just eight matches, yet was Delhi's third-highest run-maker;

Morkel brought aggression and accuracy, while Steyn was his destructive self; Kallis perfected the role of the all-rounder. And the crowds returned, perhaps drawn back by a series of tight games: seven were won from the last ball by the team batting second, and 11 more in the last over. In November 2012, Pepsi replaced DLF Group as the tournament sponsors in a five-year deal worth over $70m.

IPL STATISTICS

Leading run-scorers

	M	*I*	*NO*	*Runs*	*HS*	*50*	*Avge*	*SR*	*4*	*6*
†C. H. Gayle (*Bangalore*)	15	14	2	733	128*	7	61.08	160.74	46	59
†G. Gambhir (*Kolkata*)	17	17	1	590	93	6	36.87	143.55	64	17
†S. Dhawan (*Deccan*)	15	15	1	569	84	5	40.64	129.61	58	18
A. M. Rahane (*Rajasthan*)	16	16	2	560	103*	3	40.00	129.33	73	10
V. Sehwag (*Delhi*)	16	16	1	495	87*	5	33.00	161.23	57	19
C. L. White (*Deccan*)	13	13	2	479	78	5	43.54	149.68	41	20
R. Dravid (*Rajasthan*)	16	16	0	462	58	2	28.87	112.13	63	4
†S. K. Raina (*Chennai*)	19	18	1	441	73	1	25.94	135.69	36	19
R. G. Sharma (*Mumbai*)	17	16	2	433	109*	3	30.92	126.60	39	18
Mandeep Singh (*Punjab*)	16	16	0	432	75	2	27.00	126.31	53	7
J. H. Kallis (*Kolkata*)	17	17	1	409	79	2	25.56	106.51	34	10
R. V. Uthappa (*Pune*)	16	16	1	405	69	2	27.00	118.07	38	10

There were six centuries: 128 by C. H. Gayle (Bangalore v Delhi); 113 by M. Vijay (Chennai v Delhi); 109* by D. A. Warner (Delhi v Deccan); 109* by R. G. Sharma (Mumbai v Kolkata); 103* by A. M. Rahane (Rajasthan v Bangalore); and 103* by K. P. Pietersen (Delhi v Deccan).*

Leading wicket-takers

	Style	*O*	*M*	*R*	*W*	*BB*	*4I*	*Avge*	*ER*	*SR*
M. Morkel (*Delhi*)	RF	63	1	453	25	4/20	1	18.12	7.19	15.10
S. P. Narine (*Kolkata*)	OB	59.1	1	324	24	5/19	2	13.50	5.47	14.70
S. L. Malinga (*Mumbai*)	RF	55.3	1	350	22	4/16	1	15.90	6.30	15.10
U. T. Yadav (*Delhi*)	RFM	61	2	453	19	3/19	0	23.84	7.42	19.20
R. Vinay Kumar (*Bangalore*)	RFM	55.5	0	480	19	3/22	0	25.26	8.59	17.60
D. W. Steyn (*Deccan*)	RF	46.4	2	285	18	3/8	0	15.83	6.10	15.50
P. Awana (*Punjab*)	RFM	47	0	372	17	4/34	1	21.88	7.91	16.50
Zaheer Khan (*Bangalore*)	LFM	60	1	453	17	3/38	0	26.64	7.55	21.10
K. A. Pollard (*Mumbai*)	RM	43.5	0	350	16	4/44	1	21.87	7.98	16.40
P. P. Chawla (*Punjab*)	LBG	57	1	419	16	3/18	0	26.18	7.35	21.30
M. Muralitharan (*Bangalore*)	OB	40	0	260	15	3/21	0	17.33	6.50	16.00
M. M. Patel (*Mumbai*)	RFM	46.4	2	367	15	4/20	2	24.46	7.86	18.60
J. H. Kallis (*Kolkata*)	RFM	54	0	403	15	2/7	0	26.86	7.46	21.60
D. J. Bravo (*Chennai*)	RFM	57.4	0	462	15	2/10	0	30.80	8.01	23.00

Two other bowlers took five wickets in an innings: R. A. Jadeja (5-16, Chennai v Deccan); and A. D. Mascarenhas (5-25, Punjab v Pune). The best economy-rate by anyone bowling ten overs or more was 5.40 by L. Balaji (for Kolkata).

Leading wicketkeepers

Dis	*M*	
16 (14 ct, 2 st)	18	N. V. Ojha (*Delhi*)
14 (8 ct, 6 st)	12	B. B. McCullum (*Kolkata*)
14 (12 ct, 2 st)	19	M. S. Dhoni (*Chennai*)
11 (9 ct, 2 st)	10	N. Saini (*Punjab*)

Leading fielders – most catches

Ct	*M*		*Ct*	*M*	
13	17	R. G. Sharma (*Mumbai*)	10	15	S. P. D. Smith (*Pune*)
11	16	A. M. Rahane (*Rajasthan*)	10	16	M. K. Tiwary (*Kolkata*)
11	19	S. K. Raina (*Chennai*)			

INDIAN PREMIER LEAGUE, 2011-12

20-over league plus knockout

	Played	*Won*	*Lost*	*No-result*	*Points*	*Net run-rate*
DELHI DAREDEVILS	16	11	5	0	22	0.61
KOLKATA KNIGHT RIDERS	16	10	5	1	21	0.56
MUMBAI INDIANS	16	10	6	0	20	–0.10
CHENNAI SUPER KINGS	16	8	7	1	17	0.10
Royal Challengers Bangalore	16	8	7	1	17	–0.02
Kings XI Punjab	16	8	8	0	16	–0.21
Rajasthan Royals	16	7	9	0	14	0.20
Deccan Chargers	16	4	11	1	9	–0.50
Pune Warriors	16	4	12	0	8	–0.55

All matches were played partially or entirely under floodlights.

The top two teams met for a place in the final. The loser of that game then played the winner of the elimination final between the third- and fourth-placed teams for the other spot in the final.

At Chennai, April 4, 2012. **Mumbai Indians won by eight wickets. Chennai Super Kings 112** (19.5 overs) (S. K. Raina 36); **‡Mumbai Indians 115-2** (16.5 overs) (R. E. Levi 50). *MoM:* R. E. Levi. *Mumbai upset the defending champions, restricting them to 112 before South African Richard Levi hit 50 from 35 balls on his IPL debut. Mumbai had a scare when Sachin Tendulkar (16*) was hit on the hand by Doug Bollinger and retired hurt.*

At Kolkata, April 5, 2012. **Delhi Daredevils won by eight wickets. Kolkata Knight Riders 97-9** (12 overs) (M. Morkel 3-18); **‡Delhi Daredevils 100-2** (11.1 overs) (A. J. Finch 30, I. K. Pathan 42*). *MoM:* I. K. Pathan. *In a match reduced by rain to 12 overs a side, Kolkata slumped, with Jacques Kallis and Manoj Tiwary yorked by successive balls from Morne Morkel. Irfan Pathan hit three sixes as Delhi won at a canter.*

At Mumbai, April 6, 2012. **Pune Warriors won by 28 runs. Pune Warriors 129-9** (20 overs) (R. V. Uthappa 36, S. P. D. Smith 39); **‡Mumbai Indians 101-9** (20 overs) (J. E. C. Franklin 32, K. D. Karthik 32; A. B. Dinda 4-18). *MoM:* S. P. D. Smith. Pune captain *Sourav Ganguly marshalled his spinners cleverly after seamer Ashok Dinda had helped reduce Mumbai – missing Tendulkar with a bruised hand – to 5-3.*

At Jaipur, April 6, 2012. **Rajasthan Royals won by 31 runs. Rajasthan Royals 191-4** (20 overs) (A. M. Rahane 98); **‡Kings XI Punjab 160-9** (20 overs) (Mandeep Singh 34; K. Cooper 4-26). *MoM:* A. M. Rahane. *Ajinkya Rahane was bowled aiming to reach a 66-ball hundred. Trinidadian Kevon Cooper promptly smashed 11 from the last three deliveries before wrecking Punjab with his medium-pace variations.*

At Bangalore, April 7, 2012. **Royal Challengers Bangalore won by 20 runs. Royal Challengers Bangalore 157-8** (20 overs) (A. B. McDonald 30, A. B. de Villiers 64*; D. A. J. Bracewell 3-32); **‡Delhi Daredevils 137-7** (20 overs) (N. V. Ojha 33; M. Muralitharan 3-25). *MoM:* A. B. de Villiers. *Bangalore – lacking Chris Gayle, out with a groin injury – started their campaign with a victory, hastened by Muttiah Muralitharan and Daniel Vettori (1-28), who applied the brakes in the middle overs.*

At Visakhapatnam, April 7, 2012. **Chennai Super Kings won by 74 runs. Chennai Super Kings 193-6** (20 overs) (F. du Plessis 39, R. A. Jadeja 48, D. J. Bravo 43*); **‡Deccan Chargers 119** (17.1 overs) (R. A. Jadeja 5-16). *MoM:* R. A. Jadeja. *Dwayne Bravo thumped five sixes in the last ten balls of Chennai's innings. Ravindra Jadeja, who had trodden on his own stumps, swept through the Deccan tail for the tournament's best figures.*

BEST BOWLING FIGURES IN THE IPL

4–0–14–6	Sohail Tanvir, Rajasthan v Chennai at Jaipur	2007-08
3.1–1–5–5	A. Kumble, Bangalore v Rajasthan at Cape Town	2008-09
3–0–12–5	I. Sharma, Deccan v Kochi at Kochi	2010-11
3.4–1–13–5	S. L. Malinga, Mumbai v Delhi at Delhi	2010-11
4–0–16–5	**R. A. Jadeja, Chennai v Deccan at Visakhapatnam**	**2011-12**
4–0–17–5	A. Mishra, Delhi v Deccan at Delhi	2007-08
4–0–18–5	Harbhajan Singh, Mumbai v Chennai at Mumbai	2010-11
4–0–19–5	**S. P. Narine, Kolkata v Punjab at Kolkata**	**2011-12**

At Jaipur, April 8, 2012. **Rajasthan Royals won by 22 runs. Rajasthan Royals 164-5** (20 overs) (A. L. Menaria 40, B. J. Hodge 44); ‡**Kolkata Knight Riders 142** (20 overs) (M. K. Tiwary 59; K. Cooper 3-28). *MoM:* B. J. Hodge. *Three wickets in three deliveries reduced Kolkata to 8-3 – and they never recovered, despite Tiwary's 49-ball innings. Brad Hodge hit 44 off 29 deliveries to underpin Rajasthan.*

At Gahunje, April 8, 2012. **Pune Warriors won by 22 runs.** ‡**Pune Warriors 166-6** (20 overs) (M. N. Samuels 46, R. V. Uthappa 40; H. S. Bansal 3-24); **Kings XI Punjab 144-8** (20 overs) (B. Sharma 35*). *MoM:* M. N. Samuels. *Pune scored 27 off the 19th over. Bipul Sharma conceded three sixes after Harmeet Singh was removed for bowling two beamers. Marlon Samuels, who had earlier hit 46, stifled Punjab's reply.*

At Visakhapatnam, April 9, 2012. **Mumbai Indians won by five wickets.** ‡**Deccan Chargers 138-9** (20 overs) (S. Dhawan 41, D. T. Christian 39, C. L. White 30*; M. M. Patel 4-20, S. L. Malinga 3-27); **Mumbai Indians 142-5** (20 overs) (R. G. Sharma 73*; D. W. Steyn 3-12). *MoM:* R. G. Sharma. *Mumbai needed 18 off the last over, bowled by Dan Christian, then 11 from three balls. Rohit Sharma carved a six over point, took two to long-off, then clubbed a full-toss over long-on for his fifth six. There was controversy in Deccan's innings when Kumar Sangakkara's inside edge dislodged the bails, but the umpire initially said not out, thinking the ball had rebounded off the wicketkeeper; the decision was eventually corrected.*

At Bangalore, April 10, 2012. **Kolkata Knight Riders won by 42 runs. Kolkata Knight Riders 165-8** (20 overs) (G. Gambhir 64, M. Bisla 46); ‡**Royal Challengers Bangalore 123-9** (20 overs) (L. Balaji 4-18). *MoM:* L. Balaji. *Bangalore took seven wickets and conceded only 50 in the last eight overs, but their star-studded batting line-up failed abjectly.*

At Delhi, April 10, 2012. **Delhi Daredevils won by eight wickets. Chennai Super Kings 110-8** (20 overs); ‡**Delhi Daredevils 111-2** (13.2 overs) (V. Sehwag 33, K. P. Pietersen 43*). *MoM:* M. Morkel (Chennai). *Murali Vijay was run out off the first ball of the match, and three more run-outs followed in Chennai's underwhelming innings. Kevin Pietersen (26 deliveries) helped inflict Chennai's largest IPL defeat in terms of balls remaining (40).*

At Mumbai, April 11, 2012. **Mumbai Indians won by 27 runs. Mumbai Indians 197-6** (20 overs) (A. T. Rayudu 47*, K. A. Pollard 64); ‡**Rajasthan Royals 170** (19.4 overs) (A. M. Rahane 40, O. A. Shah 76; M. M. Patel 4-28, K. A. Pollard 4-44). *MoM*: K. A. Pollard. *Kieron Pollard's breakneck 64 from 33 balls took Mumbai close to 200. He and Munaf Patel grabbed four wickets each, and Lasith Malinga settled matters with 4–0–13–2, including the wicket of the audacious Owais Shah.*

At Chennai, April 12, 2012. **Chennai Super Kings won by five wickets.** ‡**Royal Challengers Bangalore 205-8** (20 overs) (M. A. Agarwal 45, C. H. Gayle 68, V. Kohli 57; D. E. Bollinger 3-24); **Chennai Super Kings 208-5** (20 overs) (F. du Plessis 71, M. S. Dhoni 41; M. Muralitharan 3-21). *MoM:* F. du Plessis. *A Bangalore victory looked inevitable when, with 43 needed, M. S. Dhoni fell to the last ball of the 18th over. But Albie Morkel smashed 28 off the 19th, from Virat Kohli. Chennai then needed 14 off four balls after Morkel hit his seventh ball straight to the sweeper, but the next delivery was a rib-high full-toss (and therefore a no-ball) that Dwayne Bravo top-edged for four; he then slashed a six so that Chennai required three from three. But Bravo managed only a single off the next two, leaving Ravi Jadeja to face the last ball of the innings – his first. An edge to the boundary secured the highest run-chase of IPL5. Earlier, Gayle's share of a first-wicket stand of 53 was just six (from five balls); he then opened up, clearing the ropes six times. Bangalore lost five wickets in six deliveries as they plummeted from 198-3 to 199-8.*

At Mohali, April 12, 2012. **Kings XI Punjab won by seven wickets. Pune Warriors 115** (19 overs) (M. Manhas 31; A. D. Mascarenhas 5-25); **‡Kings XI Punjab 116-3** (17.4 overs) (S. E. Marsh 64*). *MoM:* A. D. Mascarenhas. *Adam Gilchrist had chosen to bowl in Punjab's first two matches with little success, but it was third time lucky as Dimitri Mascarenhas and Harmeet Singh (2-23) exploited a green pitch.*

At Kolkata, April 13, 2012. **Kolkata Knight Riders won by five wickets. ‡Rajasthan Royals 131-5** (20 overs) (O. A. Shah 31; Shakib Al Hasan 3-17); **Kolkata Knight Riders 137-5** (19.2 overs) (J. H. Kallis 31). *MoM:* Shakib Al Hasan. *Left-arm spinner Shakib Al Hasan claimed three wickets on a slow pitch, then biffed 16 in ten balls to help Kolkata home after Rajasthan fell 15 or so short of par.*

At Gahunje, April 14, 2012. **Pune Warriors won by seven wickets. ‡Chennai Super Kings 155-5** (20 overs) (F. du Plessis 43, R. A. Jadeja 44); **Pune Warriors 156-3** (19.2 overs) (J. D. Ryder 73*, S. P. D. Smith 44*). *MoM:* J. D. Ryder. *Unfancied Pune's third win took them top of the table. Tight bowling, especially by leg-spinner Rahul Sharma (3–0–16–2), reined in Chennai before Jesse Ryder and Steve Smith (22 balls) powered them home.*

At Kolkata, April 15, 2012. **Kings XI Punjab won by two runs. Kings XI Punjab 134-9** (20 overs) (Mandeep Singh 38, D. J. Hussey 32; S. P. Narine 5-19); **‡Kolkata Knight Riders 132-7** (20 overs) (D. B. Das 35*; P. P. Chawla 3-18). *MoM:* S. P. Narine. *Kolkata were well placed at 73-2 in the 12th over, but leg-spinners Piyush Chawla and Harmeet Singh (whose last over cost six, when nine were needed) had the edge.*

At Bangalore, April 15, 2012. **Rajasthan Royals won by 59 runs. ‡Rajasthan Royals 195-2** (20 overs) (A. M. Rahane 103*, O. A. Shah 60); **Royal Challengers Bangalore 136** (19.5 overs) (M. A. Agarwal 34; S. K. Trivedi 4-25). *MoM:* A. M. Rahane. *Rahane scored the season's first century, a 60-ball assault which contained six fours in an over off Sreenath Aravind – the IPL's first such instance. Siddarth Trivedi's four victims were all bowled.*

At Mumbai, April 16, 2012. **Delhi Daredevils won by seven wickets. Mumbai Indians 92** (19.2 overs) (Harbhajan Singh 33); **‡Delhi Daredevils 93-3** (14.5 overs) (V. Sehwag 32). *MoM:* S. Nadeem (Delhi). *The lively Umesh Yadav returned figures of 4–0–11–2 as only two Mumbai batsmen reached double figures. Delhi moved top of the table with their third win in four.*

At Jaipur, April 17, 2012. **Rajasthan Royals won by five wickets. ‡Deccan Chargers 196-2** (20 overs) (K. C. Sangakkara 44, S. Dhawan 52, J-P. Duminy 58*); **Rajasthan Royals 197-5** (19.4 overs) (R. Dravid 42, A. M. Rahane 44, B. J. Hodge 48*; A. Mishra 3-32). *MoM:* B. J. Hodge. *Five sixes in 26 deliveries by J-P. Duminy propelled Deccan to their best total of IPL5. Rajasthan, though, were always in the hunt, and a brutal 21-ball 48* from Hodge proved enough.*

At Bangalore, April 17, 2012. **Royal Challengers Bangalore won by six wickets. ‡Pune Warriors 182-6** (20 overs) (R. V. Uthappa 69, J. D. Ryder 34, M. N. Samuels 34); **Royal Challengers Bangalore 186-4** (20 overs) (C. H. Gayle 81, S. S. Tiwary 36*, A. B. de Villiers 33*). *MoM:* C. H. Gayle. *Bangalore were 76-3, requiring 107 from 48 balls, when Gayle hit five successive sixes off Rahul Sharma. Twenty-one were still needed from Ashish Nehra's final over, but de Villiers clouted 4661 before Saurabh Tiwary sent the last ball skimming over long-on. Gayle's fourth six broke the nose of a ten-year-old girl in the crowd. He later visited her in hospital: "She told me to keep hitting sixes and not to worry."*

At Mohali, April 18, 2012. **Kolkata Knight Riders won by eight wickets. ‡Kings XI Punjab 124-7** (20 overs) (A. C. Gilchrist 40*, S. E. Marsh 33); **Kolkata Knight Riders 127-2** (16.3 overs) (G. Gambhir 66*, J. H. Kallis 30*). *MoM:* G. Gambhir. *A pulled hamstring forced Gilchrist to retire hurt for 11 overs. He returned to hit the only six of a miserable Punjab innings, but Gautam Gambhir's 66* made the chase a formality.*

At Delhi, April 19, 2012. **Delhi Daredevils won by five wickets. ‡Deccan Chargers 157-8** (20 overs) (S. Dhawan 44, P. A. Patel 45; M. Morkel 3-23, S. Nadeem 3-16); **Delhi Daredevils 162-5** (19.1 overs) (K. P. Pietersen 103*). *MoM:* K. P. Pietersen. *Pietersen made the most of being dropped three times to smash a Twenty20-best 103* from 64 balls, including nine sixes – the most in an innings in IPL5; Delhi's next-best was Yogesh Nagar's 23*.*

At Chennai, April 19, 2012. **Chennai Super Kings won by 13 runs. Chennai Super Kings 164-5** (20 overs) (F. du Plessis 58, S. Badrinath 57; M. N. Samuels 3-39); **‡Pune Warriors 151-7** (20 overs). *MoM:* K. M. D. N. Kulasekara (Chennai). *Chennai openers Faf du Plessis and Subramaniam Badrinath put on 116 in 15 overs before the bare-headed Dhoni walloped 28 from 12 balls. Tight fielding and sharp catching ensured Pune fell short.*

At Mohali, April 20, 2012. **Royal Challengers Bangalore won by five wickets. Kings XI Punjab 163-6** (20 overs) (D. J. Hussey 41, Azhar Mahmood 33*); ‡**Royal Challengers Bangalore 166-5** (19.3 overs) (C. H. Gayle 87, A. B. de Villiers 52; P. Awana 4-34). *MoM:* C. H. Gayle. *A fourth-wicket stand of 131 between Gayle and de Villiers helped Bangalore home in the final over; no one else reached double figures. Azhar Mahmood, the former Pakistan all-rounder and now owner of a British passport, made his IPL debut.*

At Chennai, April 21, 2012. **Chennai Super Kings won by seven wickets.** ‡**Rajasthan Royals 146-4** (20 overs) (O. A. Shah 52, A. L. Menaria 36); **Chennai Super Kings 147-3** (20 overs) (F. du Plessis 73). *MoM:* F. du Plessis. *Chennai were coasting before du Plessis and Suresh Raina (26) fell to Cooper in three balls. That left them requiring 30 from 21, which they managed when Dhoni and Dwayne Bravo scampered two off the last.*

At Delhi, April 21, 2012. **Pune Warriors won by 20 runs. Pune Warriors 192-3** (20 overs) (J. D. Ryder 86, S. C. Ganguly 41, S. P. D. Smith 34*; M. Morkel 3-50); ‡**Delhi Daredevils 172-7** (20 overs) (V. Sehwag 57, K. P. Pietersen 32; A. C. Thomas 3-22). *MoM:* S. C. Ganguly. *Ryder put the game beyond the in-form hosts with 86 from 58 balls. He added 93 with Ganguly and 67 with Smith. Virender Sehwag's early fireworks were in vain.*

At Mumbai, April 22, 2012. **Kings XI Punjab won by six wickets.** ‡**Mumbai Indians 163-6** (20 overs) (J. E. C. Franklin 79, K. D. Karthik 35); **Kings XI Punjab 164-4** (19.3 overs) (N. Saini 30, S. E. Marsh 68*). *MoM:* S. E. Marsh. *Tendulkar returned after injury, but it was his fellow opener James Franklin who held Mumbai together. Pollard (4–0–14–2) slowed the Punjab reply, but Shaun Marsh bided his time in a match-winning fifty.*

At Cuttack, April 22, 2012. **Kolkata Knight Riders won by five wickets. Deccan Chargers 126-7** (20 overs) (S. Dhawan 50); ‡**Kolkata Knight Riders 127-5** (19 overs) (G. Gambhir 30, M. K. Tiwary 30*). *MoM:* B. Lee (Kolkata). *On a slow pitch, Deccan slipped to their fifth defeat out of five, although Kolkata had to work hard for their fourth victory. Kolkata's Brett Lee had figures of 4–0–15–1.*

At Jaipur, April 23, 2012. **Royal Challengers Bangalore won by 46 runs. Royal Challengers Bangalore 189-3** (20 overs) (T. M. Dilshan 76*, A. B. de Villiers 59*); ‡**Rajasthan Royals 143-7** (20 overs) (R. Dravid 58; K. P. Appanna 4-19). *MoM:* A. B. de Villiers. *Slow left-armer K. P. Appanna removed the top four to undo the steady start given to Rajasthan by Rahul Dravid. With Gayle unwell and failing at No. 4, Dilshan and de Villiers delivered 122 runs in the last 50 balls.*

At Gahunje, April 24, 2012. **Delhi Daredevils won by eight wickets.** ‡**Pune Warriors 146-2** (20 overs) (M. K. Pandey 80*, R. V. Uthappa 60*); **Delhi Daredevils 148-2** (16 overs) (V. Sehwag 87*). *MoM:* V. Sehwag. *Delhi gained instant revenge for their defeat three days earlier as Sehwag cracked 87* from 48 balls. Pune had been 1-2, before Manish Pandey and Robin Uthappa put on 145*, though never quite urgently enough: Uthappa ate up 58 balls.*

At Kolkata, April 24, 2012. **Kolkata Knight Riders v Deccan Chargers. Abandoned.** *A temporary wooden structure for security staff collapsed, injuring three, as high winds and rain prevented play at Eden Gardens – but gave Deccan their first point.*

At Mohali, April 25, 2012. **Mumbai Indians won by four wickets.** ‡**Kings XI Punjab 168-3** (20 overs) (D. J. Hussey 68*, D. A. Miller 34*); **Mumbai Indians 171-6** (19.5 overs) (S. R. Tendulkar 34, R. G. Sharma 50, A. T. Rayudu 34*; P. Awana 3-39). *MoM:* A. T. Rayudu. *When Harbhajan Singh departed for a duck, Mumbai still needed 34 from 14 balls – but the 19th over, from Piyush Chawla, cost 27 (446166), as Ambati Rayudu and Robin Peterson (on IPL debut) took them home.*

At Bangalore, April 25, 2012. ‡**Royal Challengers Bangalore v Chennai Super Kings. Abandoned.**

At Gahunje, April 26, 2012. **Deccan Chargers won by 18 runs.** ‡**Deccan Chargers 177-4** (20 overs) (C. L. White 78); **Pune Warriors 159-7** (20 overs). *MoM:* C. L. White. *Cameron White finally began to justify his $1.1m contract, hitting 78 off 46 balls to give Deccan the edge. Pune never got going, and no one could do better than Uthappa's 29.*

At Delhi, April 27, 2012. **Delhi Daredevils won by 37 runs. Delhi Daredevils 207-5** (20 overs) (D. P. M. D. Jayawardene 55, V. Sehwag 73, K. P. Pietersen 50*; R. J. Peterson 3-37); ‡**Mumbai Indians 170-9** (20 overs) (K. D. Karthik 40, A. T. Rayudu 62). *MoM:* V. Sehwag. *Delhi openers Jayawardene and Sehwag, whose 39-ball 73 was his third consecutive half-century, put on 135 before Pietersen smote 50* from 26. Mumbai never fully recovered from 19-3; leaders Delhi moved three points clear.*

At Chennai, April 28, 2012. **Kings XI Punjab won by seven runs.** ‡**Kings XI Punjab 156-8** (20 overs) (Mandeep Singh 56, S. E. Marsh 32; J. A. Morkel 3-29); **Chennai Super Kings 149-8** (20 overs) (D. J. Bravo 30; Azhar Mahmood 3-25). *MoM:* Mandeep Singh. *A late collapse from 127-2 in the 16th over seemed to have scuppered Punjab. But Chennai also folded, slipping from 71-2 to 98-6, and the task of collecting 17 from Azhar Mahmood's final over proved too much.*

At Kolkata, April 28, 2012. **Kolkata Knight Riders won by 47 runs.** ‡**Kolkata Knight Riders 190-4** (20 overs) (B. B. McCullum 43, G. Gambhir 93, J. H. Kallis 41); **Royal Challengers Bangalore 143-6** (20 overs) (C. H. Gayle 86). *MoM:* G. Gambhir. *Dropped twice, Gambhir underpinned a formidable Kolkata total. Only Gayle offered any resistance.*

At Delhi, April 29, 2012. **Delhi Daredevils won by one run.** ‡**Delhi Daredevils 152-6** (20 overs) (V. Sehwag 63); **Rajasthan Royals 151-3** (20 overs) (R. Dravid 40, A. M. Rahane 84*). *MoM:* V. Sehwag. *A superb penultimate over from Morne Morkel – who produced four yorkers, conceded three singles and took the wicket of Hodge – stunned Rajasthan. Needing 12 off Yadav's final over, they managed only ten, with Shah run out off the last delivery trying to sneak a bye. Sehwag's 39-ball 63 had paved the way for the hosts.*

At Mumbai, April 29, 2012. **Mumbai Indians won by five wickets. Deccan Chargers 100** (18.4 overs) (S. L. Malinga 4-16); ‡**Mumbai Indians 101-5** (18.1 overs) (R. G. Sharma 42). *MoM:* D. W. Steyn (Deccan). *Deccan fell apart on a fresh pitch as Harbhajan Singh took 2-13 and Malinga 4-16. Steyn (4–0–10–2) struck with the first ball of the reply, but had little support.*

At Chennai, April 30, 2012. **Kolkata Knight Riders won by five wickets.** ‡**Chennai Super Kings 139-5** (20 overs) (S. K. Raina 44, M. S. Dhoni 34*); **Kolkata Knight Riders 140-5** (19.4 overs) (G. Gambhir 63). *MoM:* D. B. Das (Kolkata). *Gambhir anchored Kolkata's successful chase on a sluggish pitch with 63 from 52 balls, although there were a few nerves when he was out in the 19th over, with 16 still needed.*

At Cuttack, May 1, 2012. **Deccan Chargers won by 13 runs.** ‡**Deccan Chargers 186-4** (20 overs) (C. L. White 74, K. C. Sangakkara 82); **Pune Warriors 173-5** (20 overs) (M. J. Clarke 41, S. C. Ganguly 45, S. P. D. Smith 47*). *MoM:* K. C. Sangakkara. *For the first time in an IPL match, batsmen – Parthiv Patel and Manish Pandey – were out to the first ball of each innings. Deccan's clincher was a 157-run partnership between White and Sangakkara. Michael Clarke scored 41 on IPL debut.*

At Jaipur, May 1, 2012. **Delhi Daredevils won by six wickets.** ‡**Rajasthan Royals 141-6** (20 overs) (R. Dravid 57, A. M. Rahane 42; P. Negi 4-18); **Delhi Daredevils 144-4** (15.2 overs) (V. Sehwag 73, K. P. Pietersen 36). *MoM:* P. Negi. *A fifth successive fifty from Sehwag (73 off 38 balls) eased Delhi home after left-arm spinner Pawan Negi disturbed the rhythm of Rajasthan's batting. From 71-0 in the ninth over, they slowed down fatally.*

At Bangalore, May 2, 2012. **Kings XI Punjab won by four wickets. Royal Challengers Bangalore 158-5** (20 overs) (C. H. Gayle 71, V. Kohli 45; Azhar Mahmood 3-20); ‡**Kings XI Punjab 163-6** (19.5 overs) (Mandeep Singh 43, N. Saini 50, D. J. Hussey 45). *MoM:* Azhar Mahmood. *With Punjab needing 13 from 24 balls, panic unexpectedly set in, and three run-outs almost derailed their chase. Earlier, Gayle and Kohli added 119 for the second wicket, though no one could score off Praveen Kumar (4–0–8–0).*

At Gahunje, May 3, 2012. **Mumbai Indians won by one run.** ‡**Mumbai Indians 120-9** (20 overs) (S. R. Tendulkar 34); **Pune Warriors 119-6** (20 overs) (M. Manhas 42*). *MoM:* S. L. Malinga (Mumbai). *Pune needed eight off the last two balls, from Munaf Patel – and Praveen Kumar's boundary made it interesting. But he managed only two from the final delivery. It was a fourth straight defeat for Pune, whose captain, Ganguly, was criticised after scoring 16 from 24 balls.*

At Chennai, May 4, 2012. **Chennai Super Kings won by ten runs.** ‡**Chennai Super Kings 160-6** (20 overs) (F. du Plessis 42, S. K. Raina 32, M. S. Dhoni 34); **Deccan Chargers 150-5** (20 overs) (S. Dhawan 36, C. L. White 77). *MoM:* S. K. Raina. *Chennai's solid batting display proved out of White's reach.*

At Kolkata, May 5, 2012. **Kolkata Knight Riders won by seven runs.** ‡**Kolkata Knight Riders 150-5** (20 overs) (G. Gambhir 56, B. B. McCullum 42); **Pune Warriors 143-8** (20 overs) (A. D. Mathews 35, S. C. Ganguly 36; M. de Lange 3-34). *MoM:* S. P. Narine. *The wicket of Ganguly, on his return to Eden Gardens, proved terminal after he and Angelo Mathews had steadied Pune from 55-5. Sunil Narine (4–1–13–1) was unplayable at times, and Kolkata had just enough.*

At Mohali, May 5, 2012. **Rajasthan Royals won by 43 runs. ‡Rajasthan Royals 177-6** (20 overs) (R. Dravid 46, S. R. Watson 36, A. L. Menaria 34, B. J. Hodge 36; R. J. Harris 4-34); **Kings XI Punjab 134-8** (20 overs) (S. E. Marsh 34). *MoM:* S. R. Watson. *Rajasthan comfortably ended a run of four defeats. Consistent scoring down the order brought a competitive total, and Punjab struggled from the first over – a wicket maiden from Shane Watson.*

At Mumbai, May 6, 2012. **Mumbai Indians won by two wickets. Chennai Super Kings 173-8** (20 overs) (M. Vijay 41, S. K. Raina 36, D. J. Bravo 40; R. P. Singh 3-28, S. L. Malinga 3-25); **‡Mumbai Indians 174-8** (20 overs) (S. R. Tendulkar 74, R. G. Sharma 60). *MoM:* D. R. Smith (Mumbai). *Mumbai were cruising while Tendulkar and Rohit Sharma were adding 126, but 147-2 soon became 159-8. With 15 needed off four balls from Ben Hilfenhaus, non-striker Dwayne Smith – in his first match of the season – told R. P. Singh: "Take a single, I'll do the rest." And he did, hammering a six and two fours.*

At Bangalore, May 6, 2012. **Royal Challengers Bangalore won by five wickets. Deccan Chargers 181-2** (20 overs) (D. J. Harris 47, S. Dhawan 73*, C. L. White 45); **‡Royal Challengers Bangalore 185-5** (18.5 overs) (T. M. Dilshan 71, A. B. de Villiers 47*). *MoM:* A. B. de Villiers. *With 39 required from three overs, de Villiers thrashed Steyn for two sixes and two fours, including an astonishing carve over extra cover off a pinpoint yorker. Four more boundaries came from Anand Rajan's next over.*

At Delhi, May 7, 2012. **Kolkata Knight Riders won by six wickets. ‡Delhi Daredevils 153-9** (20 overs) (D. P. M. D. Jayawardene 30, I. K. Pathan 36); **Kolkata Knight Riders 154-4** (18.4 overs) (B. B. McCullum 56, G. Gambhir 36, J. H. Kallis 30). *MoM:* J. H. Kallis. *Kolkata replaced Delhi at the top of the table after Gambhir and Brendon McCullum gave their run-chase a flying start with 68 in seven overs.*

At Gahunje, May 8, 2012. **Rajasthan Royals won by seven wickets. ‡Pune Warriors 125-6** (20 overs) (A. P. Majumdar 30; S. W. Tait 3-13); **Rajasthan Royals 126-3** (16.2 overs) (S. R. Watson 90*). *MoM:* S. R. Watson. *Shaun Tait and Watson controlled this match. Tait bowled with pace and control, before Watson dominated the reply: he hit 64 in boundaries (ten fours and four sixes) from 51 balls; Pune managed just 32 in 20 overs.*

At Hyderabad (Uppal), May 8, 2012. **Kings XI Punjab won by 25 runs. Kings XI Punjab 170-5** (20 overs) (Mandeep Singh 75); **‡Deccan Chargers 145-8** (20 overs) (D. J. Harris 30). *MoM:* Mandeep Singh. *Mandeep Singh's 75 from 48 balls set up a total which Deccan never threatened once David Hussey removed his fellow Australians Daniel Harris and White in his only over (the 11th), and Sangakkara departed a few balls later.*

At Mumbai, May 9, 2012. **Royal Challengers Bangalore won by nine wickets. Mumbai Indians 141-6** (20 overs) (K. D. Karthik 44); **‡Royal Challengers Bangalore 142-1** (18 overs) (C. H. Gayle 82*, V. Kohli 36*). *MoM:* C. H. Gayle. *Mumbai stuttered to 5-2, the lowest score after four overs of an IPL match. In reply, Gayle scored only two off his first ten balls, but three sixes in a Pragyan Ojha over turned the chase around.*

At Hyderabad (Uppal), May 10, 2012. **Delhi Daredevils won by nine wickets. ‡Deccan Chargers 187-4** (20 overs) (S. Dhawan 84, C. L. White 65); **Delhi Daredevils 193-1** (16.4 overs) (D. A. Warner 109*, N. V. Ojha 64*). *MoM:* D. A. Warner. *In only his second game in IPL5, David Warner hit ten fours and seven sixes in his 54-ball 109*, putting on 189* with Naman Ojha. That eclipsed Deccan's third-wicket stand of 126 in 11.4 overs between Shikhar Dhawan and White.*

At Jaipur, May 10, 2012. **Chennai Super Kings won by four wickets. Rajasthan Royals 126-6** (20 overs) (B. J. Hodge 33); **‡Chennai Super Kings 127-6** (18.1 overs). *MoM:* B. W. Hilfenhaus (Chennai). *At 84-6 in the 17th over, Chennai seemed out of it, but Albie Morkel and Srikkanth Anirudha added 43 from 11 legitimate deliveries. Earlier, Hilfenhaus (4–1–8–2) had strangled Rajasthan.*

At Gahunje, May 11, 2012. **Royal Challengers Bangalore won by 35 runs. Royal Challengers Bangalore 173-3** (20 overs) (C. H. Gayle 57, T. M. Dilshan 53, S. S. Tiwary 36*); **‡Pune Warriors 138-9** (20 overs) (R. V. Uthappa 38, A. P. Majumdar 31; R. Vinay Kumar 3-32). *MoM:* C. H. Gayle. *Bangalore moved third after a straightforward victory, set up by Gayle's 57 from 31 balls, with six sixes.*

At Kolkata, May 12, 2012. **Mumbai Indians won by 27 runs. ‡Mumbai Indians 182-1** (20 overs) (H. H. Gibbs 66*, R. G. Sharma 109*); **Kolkata Knight Riders 155-4** (20 overs) (J. H. Kallis 79,

Y. K. Pathan 40*). *MoM:* R. G. Sharma. *Kolkata's seven-match unbeaten run was ended by a maiden IPL century from Rohit Sharma, who shared 167* with Herschelle Gibbs. Kolkata were 3-2 before Kallis steadied the ship.*

At Chennai, May 12, 2012. **Chennai Super Kings won by nine wickets. Delhi Daredevils 114-5** (20 overs) (Y. Nagar 43*; B. W. Hilfenhaus 3-27); **‡Chennai Super Kings 115-1** (15.2 overs) (M. E. K. Hussey 38, M. Vijay 48*). *MoM:* B. W. Hilfenhaus. *Hilfenhaus bowled Sehwag in the first over, and quickly added the equally dangerous Warner. From 24-4 on a lively surface, Delhi never recovered.*

At Jaipur, May 13, 2012. **Rajasthan Royals won by 45 runs. ‡Rajasthan Royals 170-4** (20 overs) (A. M. Rahane 61, S. R. Watson 58; A. Nehra 3-23); **Pune Warriors 125-9** (20 overs) (S. P. D. Smith 37; A. Chandila 4-13). *MoM:* A. Chandila. *Pune lost an eighth successive game thanks largely to off-spinner Ajit Chandila, opening the bowling in his second match for Rajasthan. With the last two balls of the first over and first of the third, he claimed a hat-trick of internationals: Ganguly, Ryder and Uthappa.*

At Mohali, May 13, 2012. **Kings XI Punjab won by four wickets. ‡Deccan Chargers 190-4** (20 overs) (S. Dhawan 71, C. L. White 67*); **Kings XI Punjab 194-6** (20 overs) (Azhar Mahmood 31, D. J. Hussey 65*). *MoM:* D. J. Hussey. *Punjab looked out of it at 149-6 in the 17th over, and again when David Hussey – who hit five sixes – lost the strike after two balls of Manpreet Gony's final over. But Gurkeerat Singh spanked 6424 to keep his side's play-off hopes alive.*

At Bangalore, May 14, 2012. **Mumbai Indians won by five wickets. Royal Challengers Bangalore 171-6** (20 overs) (T. M. Dilshan 47, M. A. Agarwal 64*); **‡Mumbai Indians 173-5** (19.4 overs) (A. T. Rayudu 81*, K. A. Pollard 52*). *MoM:* A. T. Rayudu. *Rayudu and Pollard's partnership of 122* was a sixth-wicket record in Twenty20 cricket. Rayudu, however, lost his match fee for an ugly spat with Harshal Patel at the finish; Harbhajan Singh was fined $20,000 for Mumbai's slow-over rate. They had to win the hard way, after Munaf Patel offered up four free hits in a row, and was later thumped for 24 in Bangalore's final over by 21-year-old Mayank Agarwal.*

At Kolkata, May 14, 2012. **Chennai Super Kings won by five wickets. Kolkata Knight Riders 158-6** (20 overs) (G. Gambhir 62, B. B. McCullum 37); **‡Chennai Super Kings 160-5** (20 overs) (M. E. K. Hussey 56, M. Vijay 36). *MoM:* M. E. K. Hussey. *With five needed off the last ball, Dwayne Bravo hit a Rajat Bhatia full toss over long-on to take Chennai into the top four with a game to go. Narine (4–0–14–2) was again outstanding.*

At Delhi, May 15, 2012. **Delhi Daredevils won by five wickets. ‡Kings XI Punjab 136-8** (20 overs) (D. J. Hussey 40*; U. T. Yadav 3-21); **Delhi Daredevils 140-5** (19 overs) (D. P. M. D. Jayawardene 56*, N. V. Ojha 34; P. Awana 3-22). *MoM:* U. T. Yadav. *Delhi eased into the play-offs, while Punjab's future now depended on others. David Hussey did his best to glue Punjab's innings together, but 136 was a poor total. Jayawardene could take his time with a match-winning 40-ball 56.*

At Mumbai, May 16, 2012. **Kolkata Knight Riders won by 32 runs. Kolkata Knight Riders 140-7** (20 overs) (M. K. Tiwary 41); **‡Mumbai Indians 108** (19.1 overs) (S. P. Narine 4-15). *MoM:* S. P. Narine. *Mumbai failed to fathom Narine, whose 3.1–0–15–4 included top-scorer Tendulkar (27), flummoxed by one that spat back and hit off stump. Kolkata were virtually assured of a play-off spot, but Shah Rukh Khan, their celebrity owner, was slapped with a five-year ban from the Wankhede Stadium after abusing officials who tried to stop him going on to the field after the game.*

At Dharmasala, May 17, 2012. **Kings XI Punjab won by six wickets. Chennai Super Kings 120-7** (20 overs) (D. J. Bravo 48); **‡Kings XI Punjab 123-4** (16.3 overs) (A. C. Gilchrist 64*). *MoM:* A. C. Gilchrist. *Punjab's win kept them in contention for the play-offs; Chennai's defeat left them waiting on other results. Gilchrist, who batted through the innings in his first match back from a month out, was the crucial figure.*

At Delhi, May 17, 2012. **Royal Challengers Bangalore won by 21 runs. Royal Challengers Bangalore 215-1** (20 overs) (C. H. Gayle 128*, V. Kohli 73*); **‡Delhi Daredevils 194-9** (20 overs) (Y. Venugopal Rao 36, L. R. P. L. Taylor 55, A. D. Russell 31; Zaheer Khan 3-38, P. Parameswaran 3-30). *MoM:* C. H. Gayle. *Gayle played out a maiden, and had one off nine balls, before he went berserk. In all, he faced 62 deliveries and hit 13 for six, equalling the IPL record set by Brendon McCullum on the tournament's opening night in 2008. Gayle's second-wicket stand of 204* with Kohli was the second-highest in all Twenty20 cricket as Bangalore stayed on course for the top four.*

At Hyderabad (Uppal), May 18, 2012. **Deccan Chargers won by five wickets. ‡Rajasthan Royals 126-8** (20 overs) (R. Dravid 39); **Deccan Chargers 128-5** (18.4 overs) (P. Akshath Reddy 42). *MoM:* D. W. Steyn. *The contrasting variations of Amit Mishra's leg-spin (2-20) and Steyn's pace (2-16) gave Deccan control. Rajasthan needed to win to have a chance of reaching the play-offs, but the result ensured neither side would do so.*

At Dharmasala, May 19, 2012. **Delhi Daredevils won by six wickets. Kings XI Punjab 141-8** (20 overs) (S. D. Chitnis 38, Azhar Mahmood 36; M. Morkel 4-20, U. T. Yadav 3-19); **‡Delhi Daredevils 145-4** (18.2 overs) (D. A. Warner 79). *MoM:* U. T. Yadav. *After defeat ended Punjab's play-off hopes, their 40-year-old captain/coach Gilchrist admitted: "I would say I've played my last game of cricket just there. There isn't that fire burning in my belly quite like it used to." He bowed out with nine as his side dipped to 20-4 in the sixth over. Warner hit 79 from 44 balls as Delhi cruised to the top of the table.*

At Gahunje, May 19, 2012. **Kolkata Knight Riders won by 34 runs. ‡Kolkata Knight Riders 136-4** (20 overs) (B. B. McCullum 41, Shakib Al Hasan 42); **Pune Warriors 102-8** (20 overs). *MoM:* Shakib Al Hasan. *Kolkata earned a place in the First Qualifying Final back on this ground. Shakib and McCullum batted intelligently on a grudging wicket, and all their bowlers were tidy. Pune had begun the season with three wins in four; they ended it with a ninth straight defeat.*

At Hyderabad (Uppal), May 20, 2012. **Deccan Chargers won by nine runs. Deccan Chargers 132-7** (20 overs) (J-P. Duminy 74; R. Vinay Kumar 3-22); **‡Royal Challengers Bangalore 123-9** (20 overs) (V. Kohli 42, S. S. Tiwary 30; D. W. Steyn 3-8, A. Ashish Reddy 3-25). *MoM:* D. W. Steyn (Deccan). *Bangalore missed out on a play-off place as Steyn (4–0–8–3) inspired Deccan's defence of a modest target following his South African colleague Duminy's lone-hand 74 off 53 balls. Chennai qualified instead.*

At Jaipur, May 20, 2012. **Mumbai Indians won by ten wickets. ‡Rajasthan Royals 162-6** (20 overs) (S. R. Watson 45, S. T. R. Binny 30; D. S. Kulkarni 3-18); **Mumbai Indians 163-0** (18 overs) (S. R. Tendulkar 58*, D. R. Smith 87*). *MoM:* D. R. Smith. *Nothing rode on this game: Mumbai had already made the play-offs, while Rajasthan could not. Seamer Dhawal Kulkarni took three wickets before the openers steered Mumbai home, sharing the highest opening stand in the IPL.*

First Qualifying Final

At Gahunje, May 22, 2012. **Kolkata Knight Riders won by 18 runs. ‡Kolkata Knight Riders 162-4** (20 overs) (B. B. McCullum 31, G. Gambhir 32, J. H. Kallis 30, Y. K. Pathan 40*); **Delhi Daredevils 144-8** (20 overs) (D. P. M. D. Jayawardene 40). *MoM:* Y. K. Pathan. *At 83-2 after ten overs, Delhi looked well placed. But on a slow, turning pitch, Kolkata's spinners kept things tight, and the asking-rate rose inexorably from a seemingly manageable eight an over. Earlier, McCullum had been unusually subdued in making 31 from 36 balls; not so Yusuf Pathan, who slammed 40 from 21. Kolkata reached their first IPL final.*

Elimination Final

At Bangalore, May 23, 2012. **Chennai Super Kings won by 38 runs. Chennai Super Kings 187-5** (20 overs) (M. E. K. Hussey 49, S. Badrinath 47, M. S. Dhoni 51*, D. J. Bravo 33*; D. S. Kulkarni 3-46); **‡Mumbai Indians 149-9** (20 overs) (D. R. Smith 38). *MoM:* M. S. Dhoni. *Chennai had lost seven times in scraping into the play-offs, yet somehow stayed alive. Mike Hussey and Badrinath put on 94; then Dhoni and Bravo, in an astonishing assault, pelted 73 from the last 29 balls. Mumbai lost wickets too regularly to challenge.*

Second Qualifying Final

At Chennai, May 25, 2012. **Chennai Super Kings won by 86 runs. Chennai Super Kings 222-5** (20 overs) (M. Vijay 113, D. J. Bravo 33*); **‡Delhi Daredevils 136** (16.5 overs) (D. P. M. D. Jayawardene 55; R. Ashwin 3-23). *MoM:* M. Vijay. *Earlier in the tournament, Chennai had dropped Vijay, but he made up for lost time with a 58-ball 113 that included 15 fours and four sixes as Delhi rued omitting Morne Morkel, the leading wicket-taker of IPL5. Varun Aaron's four overs cost 63. Jayawardene gained scant support from his team-mates; Delhi had topped the table, but a second play-off defeat meant they missed the final.*

MOST EXPENSIVE BOWLING FIGURES IN THE IPL

4–0–63–2	**V. R. Aaron, Delhi v Chennai at Chennai**	**2011-12**
4–0–59–1	R. P. Singh, Deccan v Kolkata at Hyderabad (Uppal)	2007-08
4–0–59–0	S. K. Trivedi, Rajasthan v Punjab at Mohali	2010-11
4–0–58–0	Mashrafe bin Mortaza, Kolkata v Deccan at Johannesburg	2008-09
4–0–57–1	P. Amarnath, Chennai v Mumbai at Chennai	2007-08
4–0–56–0	V. R. Singh, Punjab v Mumbai at Mumbai	2007-08
4–0–56–2	J. A. Morkel, Chennai v Rajasthan at Chennai	2009-10
4–0–56–1	A. N. Ahmed, Mumbai v Bangalore at Chennai	2010-11
4–0–55–0	M. M. Patel, Rajasthan v Deccan at Hyderabad (Uppal)	2007-08
4–0–55–1	M. M. Patel, Rajasthan v Chennai at Chennai	2007-08
4–0–55–0	**A. Singh, Rajasthan v Deccan at Jaipur**	**2011-12**

FINAL

CHENNAI SUPER KINGS v KOLKATA KNIGHT RIDERS

At Chennai, May 27, 2012. Kolkata Knight Riders won by five wickets. Toss: Chennai Super Kings.

Amid the carnival atmosphere that surrounded the competition climax, the man who sealed Kolkata's first IPL crown was the unheralded Manvinder Bisla, who was not even supposed to be playing. An itinerant 27-year-old wicketkeeper-batsman, Bisla – who had appeared only once in the previous month – was recalled when Lakshmipathy Balaji's hamstring injury led to a reorganisation of the Kolkata team: Lee returned to take the new ball and, with only four foreign players allowed, that meant no place for Brendon McCullum. But Bisla was the perfect replacement, hammering five sixes and eight fours from only 48 deliveries as Kolkata chased down a sizeable target after Raina's 38-ball blitz seemed to have set Chennai up for a third successive title. Bisla and Kallis put on 136 in 14 overs to compensate for the loss of Gambhir, Kolkata's leading batsman in the tournament, in the first over. Victory was sealed when Manoj Tiwary heaved successive fours in Bravo's final over.

Man of the Match: M. S. Bisla. *Man of the Series:* S. P. Narine.

Chennai Super Kings

		B	*4*	*6*
M. E. K. Hussey *b 3*	54	43	4	2
M. Vijay *c 6 b 8*	42	32	4	1
S. K. Raina *c 9 b 6*	73	38	3	5
*†M. S. Dhoni *not out*	14	9	2	0
L-b 3, w 2, n-b 2	7			
6 overs: 54-0 (20 overs)	190-3			

1/87 2/160 3/190

S. Badrinath, D. J. Bravo, R. A. Jadeja, J. A. Morkel, R. Ashwin, S. B. Jakati and B. W. Hilfenhaus did not bat.

Lee 4–0–42–0; Shakib Al Hasan 3–0–25–1; Narine 4–0–37–0; Iqbal Abdulla 1–0–9–0; Kallis 4–0–34–1; Bhatia 3–0–23–1; Pathan 1–0–17–0.

Kolkata Knight Riders

		B	*4*	*6*
†M. Bisla *c 5 b 8*	89	48	8	5
*G. Gambhir *b 11*	2	4	0	0
J. H. Kallis *c 7 b 11*	69	49	7	1
L. R. Shukla *c 1 b 6*	3	6	0	0
Y. K. Pathan *c 5 b 9*	1	2	0	0
Shakib Al Hasan *not out*	11	7	1	0
M. K. Tiwary *not out*	9	3	2	0
L-b 1, w 6, n-b 1	8			
6 overs: 56-1 (19.4 overs)	192-5			

1/3 2/139 3/152 4/164 5/175

R. Bhatia, B. Lee, Iqbal Abdulla and S. P. Narine and did not bat.

Hilfenhaus 4–0–25–2; Morkel 4–0–38–1; Ashwin 4–0–41–1; Bravo 3.4–0–49–1; Jakati 4–0–38–0.

Umpires: B. F. Bowden and S. J. A. Taufel. Third umpire: B. R. Doctrove. Referee: R. S. Madugalle.

DOMESTIC CRICKET IN INDIA, 2011-12

R. MOHAN

The fifth season of the IPL, Indian domestic cricket's biggest attraction, may have been fraught with controversy, but there was no doubting its capacity to pour money into BCCI coffers. As well as lining the pockets of star players, some of the funds were disbursed among 170 cricketers who had appeared for India in earlier days when there was little financial benefit. But while India's best domestic performers plough on in the hope of landing a lucrative IPL contract, first-class cricket may seem dull by comparison.

Rajasthan did not complain. First-time champions in 2010-11, they became only the fifth side to claim back-to-back Ranji Trophy titles, under the captaincy of Hrishikesh Kanitkar. They started slowly, before two wins saw them through to the knockouts, where they marched to victory away to Hyderabad and Haryana. In the final, Rajasthan outbatted Tamil Nadu on a slow pitch at Chennai. Vineet Saxena lasted more than 15 hours, the third-longest innings in all first-class cricket, while the consistent Robin Bist became the 12th man to complete 1,000 runs in a Ranji season. Bist and Saxena were the top run-makers of the tournament, and Rajasthan's leading wicket-taker was Pankaj Singh, with 34 wickets.

The most successful bowler in the competition was T. P. Sudhindra, who took 40 for Madhya Pradesh. But in June the BCCI banned him for life, after he was one of five players implicated in spot-fixing by a television sting during the IPL.

In general, batsmen held sway on benign pitches from the season's opening fixture, the Irani Cup, played for by the Ranji champions and the **Rest of India**. Hosting the match on a flat track, Rajasthan lost the toss and watched left-handed opener Shikhar Dhawan score big hundreds in both innings. With plenty of runs to back him, left-arm spinner Pragyan Ojha earned a bag of nine wickets, and the Rest won by 404. The cooler months of December and January restored a little of the balance between bat and ball, offering assistance for swing, particularly in the north. There was a world record in November when Hyderabad wicketkeeper Ibrahim Khaleel made 14 dismissals against Assam in the Ranji Plate League.

The most successful bowler was later banned for life

In February **East Zone** claimed their first Duleep Trophy, with two outright wins in three games. On an Indore pitch with some life in it, Bengal fast bowler Ashok Dinda used the short pitched ball to good effect. His performance, as well as a classy 170 from Wriddhaman Saha, India's reserve wicketkeeper on the Test tour of Australia, signalled East Zone's belated arrival on the national scene. Dinda took 59 first-class wickets in all, more than any other bowler, and pushed his way back into the Indian one-day team.

Dinda's call-up meant he missed the semi and final of the 50-over Vijay Hazare Trophy, but **Bengal** won anyway, led by former Test captain Sourav Ganguly. **India Reds** and **Greens** shared the Challenger Trophy after a thrilling tie, when Piyush Chawla needed 17 runs from the last over and was last man to go, run out off what he believed to be the last ball – it had been called a wide. **West Zone** won the Deodhar Trophy and **Baroda** took the national Twenty20 title, the Mushtaq Ali Trophy.

At the end of another long season, a sense of discontent over the format of domestic cricket led to much introspection. After considering recommendations from the technical committee, chaired by Ganguly, the BCCI moved the Duleep Trophy to the start of the 2012-13 season, in another attempt to strengthen the competition, while the Ranji Trophy reverted to three groups leading to a knockout, with the promotion and relegation of the Elite and Plate Leagues discarded.

FIRST-CLASS AVERAGES, 2011-12

BATTING (500 runs, average 50.00)

	M	*I*	*NO*	*R*	*HS*	*100*	*Avge*	*Ct/St*
M. K. Tiwary (*Bengal*)	4	4	0	595	267	3	148.75	1
W. P. Saha (*Bengal & East Zone*)	5	7	3	528	170	3	132.00	18/1
R. S. Paradkar (*Vidarbha*)	6	7	2	562	189*	2	112.40	7
†D. S. Jadhav (*Assam & East Zone*)	8	13	5	812	135*	5	101.50	0
†A. M. Nayar (*Mumbai & West Zone*)	7	10	1	693	243	2	77.00	1
A. R. Bawne (*Maharashtra*)	7	9	2	531	166*	2	75.85	5
†A. Mukund (*Tamil Nadu, South Zone & Rest*)	11	18	4	1,057	220	3	75.50	6
Mandeep Singh (*Punjab, North Zone & Rest*)	7	12	4	592	175*	1	74.00	6
R. D. Bist (*Rajasthan & Central Zone*)	13	22	4	1,331	176	5	73.94	9
S. A. Yadav (*Mumbai & West Zone*)	10	13	0	922	200	3	70.92	4
A. L. Menaria (*Rajasthan*)	6	10	2	562	230	1	70.25	1
P. Akshath Reddy (*Hyderabad*)	7	11	1	687	151	4	68.70	2
S. T. R. Binny (*Karnataka & South Zone*)	9	12	0	798	189	3	66.50	2
P. Dogra (*Himachal Pradesh & North Zone*)	7	8	0	512	205	2	64.00	8
V. R. Samant (*Tripura*)	5	10	1	543	200*	1	60.33	13
K. B. Pawan (*Karnataka*)	8	13	2	659	251*	2	59.90	6
C. G. Khurana (*Maharashtra*)	5	9	0	539	123	2	59.88	4
D. B. Ravi Teja (*Hyderabad*)	7	11	2	522	185*	1	58.00	10
M. Sidana (*Punjab & North Zone*)	8	14	2	694	122	1	57.83	2
N. V. Ojha (*Madhya Pradesh & Central Zone*)	9	15	0	861	160	4	57.40	31/1
M. Kaif (*Uttar Pradesh & Central Zone*)	9	13	0	711	152	2	54.69	5
Parvinder Singh (*Uttar Pradesh & C. Zone*)	9	13	1	656	202*	2	54.66	2
†S. Dhawan (*Delhi, North Zone & Rest*)	8	14	1	706	177	2	54.30	9
†A. A. Verma (*Karnataka & South Zone*)	9	13	2	587	173	3	53.36	4
P. Bisht (*Delhi & North Zone*)	7	11	1	510	223*	1	51.00	23

BOWLING (25 wickets, average 35.00)

	Style	*O*	*M*	*R*	*W*	*BB*	*5I*	*Avge*
S. K. Cheruvathur (*Kerala*)	RM	172	46	368	25	6-25	2	14.72
R. R. Singh (*Rajasthan & Central Zone*)	RM	149.3	32	490	27	7-45	3	18.14
S. T. R. Binny (*Karnataka & South Zone*)	RM	165.4	42	487	25	5-49	2	19.48
T. P. Sudhindra (*M. Pradesh & C. Zone*)	RM	354.4	91	861	44	7-48	4	19.56
A. B. Dinda (*Bengal & East Zone*)	RFM	376.1	71	1,177	59	8-123	5	19.94
A. A. Darekar (*Maharashtra & West Zone*)	OB	339	93	856	42	8-20	5	20.38
P. P. Ojha (*Hyderabad, India & Rest*)	SLA	251.1	59	659	31	6-47	3	21.25
A. Lalith Mohan (*Hyderabad*)	SLA	243.2	64	581	25	6-109	3	23.24
J. Kaushik (*Tamil Nadu & South Zone*)	RFM	258	72	709	30	5-56	1	23.63
S. M. Fallah (*Maharashtra & West Zone*)	LM	316.2	88	741	31	4-31	0	23.90
H. V. Patel (*Haryana & North Zone*)	RFM	247	55	741	30	8-34	2	24.70
P. Awana (*Delhi & North Zone*)	RFM	277.1	47	882	35	6-84	3	25.20
Bhuvneshwar Kumar (*U. Pradesh & C. Zone*)	RM	295.3	76	800	30	5-84	1	26.66
J. D. Unadkat (*Saurashtra*)	LFM	249.5	63	703	26	6-87	2	27.03
B. C. Mohanty (*Orissa & East Zone*)	RFM	388.3	116	892	31	4-86	0	28.77
I. C. Pandey (*Madhya Pradesh*)	RFM	243.3	68	725	25	6-31	1	29.00
R. Dhawan (*Himachal Pradesh*)	RM	260.2	53	822	27	5-60	2	30.44
S. O. Mathur (*Rajasthan*)	RFM	296.4	71	897	29	6-33	2	30.93
Pankaj Singh (*Rajasthan & Central Zone*)	RM	388	101	1,084	35	5-64	2	30.97
V. Y. Mahesh (*Tamil Nadu & South Zone*)	RFM	268	66	794	25	6-47	1	31.76
S. M. Maniar (*Saurashtra & West Zone*)	RFM	231.4	38	837	26	5-71	1	32.19
K. P. Appanna (*Karnataka & South Zone*)	SLA	345.5	73	1,049	30	6-68	2	34.96

IRANI CUP, 2011-12

Ranji Trophy Champions (Rajasthan) v Rest of India

At Jaipur (Sawai Mansingh), October 1–5, 2011. **Rest of India won by 404 runs.** ‡**Rest of India 663** (S. Dhawan 177, A. M. Rahane 152) **and 354-2 dec** (A. Mukund 154, S. Dhawan 155); **Rajasthan 400** (P. P. Ojha 5-86) **and 213.** *In the 50th Irani Cup match, Rest of India claimed their biggest victory by runs to win the trophy for the sixth successive year. Since 1999-2000, only Railways (twice) have interrupted their winning streak. Shikhar Dhawan became the first batsman to score twin centuries in the fixture: 177 in 165 balls in the first innings, putting on 190 for the Rest's second wicket with Ajinkya Rahane; and 155 in 126 in the second, while raising 310 in just 45 overs with fellow opener Abhinav Mukund, who scored his third hundred in this fixture in three seasons. Rajasthan fought back from 53-3 in their first innings, but collapsed on the final day.*

RANJI TROPHY, 2011-12

Elite Group A	*P*	*W*	*L*	*D*	*Pts*
Mumbai	7	3	0	4	25
Karnataka	7	2	0	5	22
Rajasthan	7	2	0	5	16
Saurashtra	7	2	1	4	16
Uttar Pradesh	7	0	1	6	16
Punjab	7	1	2	4	15
Railways	7	1	3	3	13
Orissa	7	0	4	3	2

Elite Group B	*P*	*W*	*L*	*D*	*Pts*
Tamil Nadu	6	1	0	5	20
Madhya Pradesh	6	2	1	3	17
Haryana	6	1	0	5	14
Baroda	6	2	2	2	13
Bengal	6	1	1	4	13
Delhi	6	1	2	3	11
Gujarat	6	1	3	2	8

The top three in each group were joined in the quarter-finals by the Plate semi-final winners.

Quarter-finals: Rajasthan drew with Hyderabad; Haryana beat Karnataka by six wickets; Mumbai drew with Madhya Pradesh; Tamil Nadu drew with Maharashtra. Rajasthan, Mumbai and Tamil Nadu joined Haryana in the semi-finals by virtue of their first-innings leads.

Semi-finals: Rajasthan beat Haryana by 64 runs; Tamil Nadu drew with Mumbai but reached the final by virtue of their first-innings lead.

Final: Rajasthan drew with Tamil Nadu but won the Trophy by virtue of their first-innings lead.

Plate Group A	*P*	*W*	*L*	*D*	*Pts*
Vidarbha	5	1	0	4	15
Himachal Pradesh	5	1	1	3	15
Kerala	5	2	0	3	14
Andhra	5	1	1	3	12
Services	5	1	0	4	11
Tripura	5	0	4	1	1

Plate Group B	*P*	*W*	*L*	*D*	*Pts*
Maharashtra	5	3	0	2	22
Hyderabad	5	2	1	2	16
Goa	5	1	2	2	9
Jharkhand	5	1	1	3	9
Jammu and Kashmir	5	0	1	4	8
Assam	5	0	2	3	6

Semi-finals: Maharashtra drew with Himachal Pradesh but advanced by virtue of their first-innings lead; Hyderabad drew with Vidarbha but advanced by virtue of a superior run-rate.

No final was held, as Maharashtra and Hyderabad advanced to the Elite League quarter-finals.

Outright win = 5pts; lead on first innings in a drawn match = 3pts; deficit on first innings in a drawn match = 1pt; abandoned or very little play = 2pts each; win by an innings or ten wickets = 1 bonus pt. Teams tied on points were ranked on most wins, and then on quotient (runs scored per wicket divided by runs conceded per wicket).

Elite League Group A

At Cuttack (Barabati), November 3–6, 2011. **Drawn. Saurashtra 545** (R. A. Jadeja 314); ‡**Orissa 494-7** (N. B. Behera 209). *Ravi Jadeja advanced from his second double-hundred to 314, a Saurashtra record, and the highest score anywhere in first-class cricket in 2011. He batted for nine hours 18 minutes, and hit 29 fours and nine sixes in 375 balls. In reply, Natraj Behera batted even longer – for 12 hours 11 minutes – and reached a maiden double-century. No points were awarded as Orissa's first innings remained uncompleted.*

At Mohali, November 3–6, 2011. **Drawn. ‡Punjab 350** (Mandeep Singh 175*; R. P. Singh 5-72) **and 280-7**; **Uttar Pradesh 596-5 dec** (Parvinder Singh 138, S. K. Raina 204*). *Punjab 1pt, Uttar Pradesh 3pts. Parvinder Singh and Suresh Raina, with his second double-century, added 241 for Uttar Pradesh's fourth wicket.*

At Delhi (Karnail Singh), November 3–6, 2011. **Mumbai won by ten wickets. ‡Mumbai 483** (R. G. Sharma 175; S. N. Khanolkar 5-78) **and 20-0**; **Railways 256 and 244**. *Mumbai 6pts.*

At Udaipur (Field Club), November 3–6, 2011. **Drawn. Karnataka 623-6 dec** (K. B. Pawan 251*, S. T. R. Binny 151); **‡Rajasthan 255 and 317-7**. *Rajasthan 1pt, Karnataka 3pts. Kolar Pawan batted for 11 hours 27 minutes and hit a maiden double-hundred; he put on 237 for Karnataka's sixth wicket with Stuart Binny, who scored twice as quickly to reach a career-best 151 in 141 balls.*

At Mumbai (Brabourne), November 10–13, 2011. **Drawn. ‡Rajasthan 530** (H. H. Kanitkar 141) **and 70-2**; **Mumbai 625** (A. M. Nayar 243, R. G. Sharma 100; Pankaj Singh 5-111). *Mumbai 3pts, Rajasthan 1pt. Despite a large first-innings total, defending champions Rajasthan conceded 600 for the third match running (including the Irani Cup). Abhishek Nayar, who retired with severe cramps on 155, resumed the following day to complete a maiden double-century.*

At Mohali, November 10–12, 2011. **Punjab won by eight wickets. Orissa 251** (S. Sharma 5-53) **and 73** (M. S. Gony 5-13); **‡Punjab 255-9 dec and 70-2**. *Punjab 5pts.*

At Delhi (Karnail Singh), November 10–12, 2011. **Karnataka won by an innings and 51 runs. ‡Karnataka 347** (R. V. Uthappa 117; M. Kartik 5-88); **Railways 134** (K. P. Appanna 5-39) **and 162** (K. P. Appanna 6-68). *Karnataka 6pts.*

At Meerut (Cantonment), November 10–13, 2011. **Drawn. Uttar Pradesh 362** (T. M. Srivastava 175*) **and 317-7 dec** (R. A. Jadeja 5-77); **‡Saurashtra 281** (J. N. Shah 112) **and 85-1**. *Uttar Pradesh 3pts, Saurashtra 1pt. Tanmay Srivastava carried his bat for Uttar Pradesh.*

At Mumbai (Brabourne), November 17–20, 2011. **Drawn. ‡Karnataka 635-9 dec** (M. K. Pandey 200*, A. A. Verma 173) **and 147-3**; **Mumbai 441** (A. M. Nayar 191*). *Mumbai 1pt, Karnataka 3pts. Manish Pandey, who retired suffering from dehydration on 101, resumed next day to reach a maiden double-hundred.*

At Sambalpur, November 17–20, 2011. **Drawn. ‡Orissa 482** (B. B. Samantray 171; P. P. Chawla 5-105); **Uttar Pradesh 590-4** (T. M. Srivastava 115, Parvinder Singh 202*, A. N. Alam 118*). *Orissa 1pt, Uttar Pradesh 3pts. Biplab Samantray and Abhilash Mallick (99) added 212 for Orissa's fourth wicket. Parvinder Singh, with a maiden double-century, and Arish Alam put on 267* for Uttar Pradesh's fifth.*

At Mohali, November 17–20, 2011. **Saurashtra won by an innings and 144 runs. Saurashtra 542** (S. D. Jogiyani 164, S. H. Kotak 166*; M. S. Gony 6-143); **‡Punjab 278** (J. D. Unadkat 6-87) **and 120**. *Saurashtra 6pts. Shitanshu Kotak and Jayesh Odedra (53) put on 171 for Saurashtra's ninth wicket; their last man, Siddharth Trivedi, fell first ball, but took a hat-trick in Punjab's second innings.*

At Delhi (Karnail Singh), November 17–20, 2011. **Drawn. ‡Rajasthan 521-8 dec** (R. D. Bist 167, A. L. Menaria 230; K. Anureet Singh 5-153) **and 21-4**; **Railways 525-8 dec** (M. Rawat 145; V. Yadav 6-134). *Railways 3pts, Rajasthan 1pt. Robin Bist, who batted for ten hours 24 minutes, and Ashok Menaria, nine hours seven minutes, added 398 for the third wicket, an all-wicket record for Rajasthan; but they conceded first-innings points again thanks to Mahesh Rawat's career-best 145.*

At Bangalore (Chinnaswamy), November 29–December 2, 2011. **Drawn. Karnataka 503-7 dec** (K. B. Pawan 118, B. Chipli 159*); **‡Saurashtra 260 and 112-4**. *Karnataka 3pts, Saurashtra 1pt.*

At Cuttack (Dhaneswar Rath), November 29–December 2, 2011. **Mumbai won by an innings and 210 runs. ‡Mumbai 529-8 dec** (K. R. Pawar 127, S. A. Yadav 200); **Orissa 93 and 226** (R. R. Powar 6-57). *Mumbai 6pts. This was the first match at the Dhaneswar Rath Institute of Engineering and Management Sciences in Cuttack, and resulted in a heavy defeat for the hosts after Surya Yadav converted his maiden hundred into a double.*

At Mohali, November 29–December 2, 2011. **Drawn. Punjab 366** (U. Kaul 131; K. Upadhyay 7-76) **and 242-9 dec**; **‡Railways 273** (M. S. Gony 5-91) **and 129-3**. *Punjab 3pts, Railways 1pt. Krishnakant Upadhyay took a hat-trick on the second day, the second against Punjab in two games. Railways were rescued from 98-7 by Sanjay Bangar and Ashish Yadav, who added 113.*

At Jaipur (Sawai Mansingh), November 29–December 2, 2011. **Drawn. Uttar Pradesh 492** (V. Yadav 5-121); ‡**Rajasthan 274 and 349-2** (A. Chopra 135, R. D. Bist 100*). *Rajasthan 1pt, Uttar Pradesh 3pts. Aakash Chopra passed 10,000 first-class runs during his 28th hundred.*

At Bhubaneswar, December 6–9, 2011. **Karnataka won by 139 runs. Karnataka 278 and 277-7 dec** (A. A. Verma 102*); ‡**Orissa 255** (S. T. R. Binny 5-51) **and 161** (S. T. R. Binny 5-49). *Karnataka 5pts.*

At Jaipur (Sawai Mansingh), December 6–9, 2011. **Drawn.** ‡**Punjab 597-8 dec** (R. Inder Singh 133, K. Goel 167, M. Sidana 122, Amitoze Singh 103) **and 94-2**; **Rajasthan 500** (R. D. Bist 176). *Rajasthan 1pt, Punjab 3pts. Rajasthan's bowlers were under the hammer again from Punjab's four centurions. Ravi Inder Singh and Karan Goel put on 219 for the second wicket, before Mayank Sidana and Amitoze Singh added 157 for the sixth; Amitoze hit 103 in 97 balls. Robin Bist put on 221 for the fifth wicket with Rashmi Parida.*

At Rajkot (Khandheri), December 6–9, 2011. **Drawn.** ‡**Saurashtra 580-9 dec** (C. R. Pathak 116, B. M. Chauhan 157); **Mumbai 360** (S. A. Yadav 111, H. N. Shah 113; S. M. Maniar 5-71) **and 276-4** (Wasim Jaffer 110*). *Saurashtra 3pts, Mumbai 1pt. Surya Yadav hit 111 in 92 balls. Wasim Jaffer passed 15,000 first-class runs.*

At Mohan Nagar, December 6–8, 2011. **Railways won by an innings and 94 runs. Railways 374** (N. S. Bhille 123); ‡**Uttar Pradesh 79** (S. B. Bangar 5-20) **and 201** (M. Kartik 5-27). *Railways 6pts. Nitin Bhille added 218 for the second wicket with Shivakant Shukla (98).*

At Bangalore (Chinnaswamy), December 13–16, 2011. **Drawn.** ‡**Punjab 357 and 274-8 dec** (U. Kaul 100*); **Karnataka 281** (S. T. R. Binny 119) **and 157-1.** *Karnataka 1pt, Punjab 3pts.*

At Delhi (Karnail Singh), December 13–16, 2011. **Drawn.** ‡**Railways 379** (M. Rawat 103) **and 113-2**; **Orissa 331**. *Railways 3pts, Orissa 1pt.*

At Jaipur (Sawai Mansingh), December 13–16, 2011. **Rajasthan won by 229 runs. Rajasthan 396** (V. A. Saxena 127, P. R. Yadav 108; J. D. Unadkat 5-71) **and 241-4 dec**; ‡**Saurashtra 265** (Pankaj Singh 5-64) **and 143** (S. O. Mathur 6-33). *Rajasthan 5pts. Vineet Saxena and Puneet Yadav put on 215 for Rajasthan's fifth wicket.*

At Lucknow, December 13–16, 2011. **Drawn.** ‡**Mumbai 414** (S. H. Marathe 102) **and 11-2**; **Uttar Pradesh 312** (R. R. Powar 5-69). *Uttar Pradesh 1pt, Mumbai 3pts.*

At Shimoga, December 21–24, 2011. **Drawn. Karnataka 314** (Bhuvneshwar Kumar 5-84) **and 561-5** (G. Satish 190, A. A. Verma 102, S. T. R. Binny 189); ‡**Uttar Pradesh 419** (M. Kaif 152). *Karnataka 1pt, Uttar Pradesh 3pts. The first first-class match in Shimoga for 32 years attracted 2,000 supporters on the opening day. Ganesh Satish and Binny, who faced 161 balls, added 253 for Karnataka's fourth wicket. A point was enough to see them into the quarter-finals.*

At Mumbai (Wankhede), December 21–24, 2011. **Mumbai won by nine wickets. Punjab 226** (B. S. Sandhu 5-66) **and 330**; ‡**Mumbai 430 and 132-1**. *Mumbai 5pts. Mumbai made sure of heading the group with their third victory, despite losing two players to injury. First-class debutant Balwinder Sandhu took five wickets on the opening day.*

At Delhi (Karnail Singh), December 21–23, 2011. **Saurashtra won by 97 runs.** ‡**Saurashtra 175 and 152**; **Railways 81** (R. A. Jadeja 6-23) **and 149** (K. R. Makwana 5-47). *Saurashtra 5pts. The match ended on the third morning, after 18 wickets fell on each of the first two days; the BCCI's technical committee later banned the Karnail Singh Stadium from hosting Railways' home matches in 2012-13 because of the poor pitch provided.*

At Jaipur (Sawai Mansingh), December 21–23, 2011. **Rajasthan won by an innings and 56 runs. Rajasthan 423** (R. D. Bist 127*); ‡**Orissa 134** (S. O. Mathur 5-30) **and 233** (R. R. Singh 6-75). *Rajasthan 6pts. Rajasthan won their last two matches, tied on 16 points with two other teams, and scraped into the quarter-finals on quotient. Bist hit his fourth hundred in five games.*

Elite League Group B

At Kolkata (Eden Gardens), November 3–6, 2011. **Drawn.** ‡**Bengal 560-6 dec** (M. K. Tiwary 132, W. P. Saha 167*); **Gujarat 495** (P. A. Patel 143, P. K. Panchal 139). *Bengal 3pts, Gujarat 1pt. Parthiv Patel and Priyank Panchal opened Gujarat's innings with 284.*

At Delhi (Roshanara), November 3–6, 2011. **Drawn. Haryana 293** (P. Sangwan 5-67) **and 318-8** (Sunny Singh 157*); **‡Delhi 352** (Milind Kumar 119, R. Bhatia 107). *Delhi 3pts, Haryana 1pt. Milind Kumar, aged 20, scored a century on first-class debut.*

At Chennai (Chidambaram), November 3–6, 2011. **Drawn. ‡Baroda 38-0** v **Tamil Nadu.** *Tamil Nadu 2pts, Baroda 2pts. Rain permitted no play on the first three days, and only 12 overs on the last. Each team received two points as it was a near washout.*

At Vadodara (Moti Bagh), November 10–13, 2011. **Baroda won by eight wickets. Madhya Pradesh 63 and 365** (I. K. Pathan 5-54); **‡Baroda 375** (A. T. Rayudu 119; J. S. Saxena 5-61) **and 54-2.** *Baroda 5pts. Madhya Pradesh crashed to 32-8 on the first morning.*

At Valsad, November 10–13, 2011. **Gujarat won by an innings and 35 runs. ‡Gujarat 520** (P. A. Patel 100, N. K. Patel 228*; V. Mishra 7-116); **Delhi 233 and 252** (M. Manhas 103). *Gujarat 6pts. Niraj Patel hit 32 fours and two sixes in a maiden double-hundred.*

At Chennai (Chidambaram), November 10–13, 2011. **Drawn. ‡Haryana 348 and 200** (V. Y. Mahesh 6-47); **Tamil Nadu 403** (A. Mukund 204) **and 141-8.** *Tamil Nadu 3pts, Haryana 1pt. Abhinav Mukund hit his fourth double-century in four seasons.*

At Vadodara (Moti Bagh), November 17–20, 2011. **Drawn. Haryana 390** (R. Dewan 164, N. Saini 112; M. Y. Vahora 5-78) **and 195** (I. K. Pathan 5-37); **‡Baroda 214 and 228-7.** *Baroda 1pt, Haryana 3pts. Rahul Dewan and Nitin Saini put on 239 for Haryana's first wicket.*

At Kolkata (Jadavpur), November 17–20, 2011. **Drawn. ‡Bengal 496** (A. S. Das 105, M. K. Tiwary 267) **and 114-1; Madhya Pradesh 533** (N. V. Ojha 127, M. D. Mishra 132; Shami Ahmed 5-116). *Bengal 1pt, Madhya Pradesh 3pts. Manoj Tiwary hit his fourth and highest double-hundred, and added 209 for Bengal's third wicket with Arindam Das.*

At Delhi (Feroz Shah Kotla), November 17–20, 2011. **Drawn. ‡Delhi 212 and 311; Tamil Nadu 306 and 129-3.** *Delhi 1pt, Tamil Nadu 3pts.*

At Delhi (Feroz Shah Kotla), November 29–December 2, 2011. **Delhi won by ten wickets. Baroda 318** (R. K. Solanki 113; A. Nehra 6-102) **and 144** (P. Awana 5-52); **‡Delhi 415** (P. Bisht 223*; I. K. Pathan 7-114) **and 48-0.** *Delhi 6pts. Puneet Bisht came in at 74-5 and hit a maiden double-century.*

At Rohtak, November 29–December 2, 2011. **Drawn. ‡Haryana 358** (R. Dewan 115, Sunny Singh 111; A. B. Dinda 5-98) **and 169** (A. B. Dinda 7-44); **Bengal 339** (S. C. Ganguly 135) **and 128-5.** *Haryana 3pts, Bengal 1pt. Ashok Dinda took 12-142 in the match.*

At Indore (Emerald HS), November 29–December 2, 2011. **Madhya Pradesh won by five wickets. Gujarat 130** (I. C. Pandey 6-31) **and 272** (T. P. Sudhindra 6-60); **‡Madhya Pradesh 205** (M. B. Patel 5-54) **and 198-5.** *Madhya Pradesh 5pts. Madhya Pradesh wicketkeeper Naman Ojha held ten catches in the match.*

At Vadodara (Moti Bagh), December 6–9, 2011. **Baroda won by 241 runs. Baroda 203** (I. H. Chaudhary 5-69) **and 330** (A. T. Rayudu 105); **‡Gujarat 169 and 123** (Gagandeep Singh 5-29). *Baroda 5pts.*

At Kolkata (Eden Gardens), December 6–9, 2011. **Tamil Nadu won by ten wickets. Tamil Nadu 391** (K. Vasudevadas 106) **and 34-0; ‡Bengal 176 and 246.** *Tamil Nadu 6pts.*

At Indore (Emerald HS), December 6–9, 2011. **Madhya Pradesh won by two wickets. ‡Delhi 158 and 296** (T. P. Sudhindra 5-65); **Madhya Pradesh 156 and 300-8** (N. V. Ojha 107; P. Awana 5-93). *Madhya Pradesh 5pts. Madhya Pradesh started the last morning needing 59 runs with five wickets; Parvinder Awana took three of those before they got home.*

At Kolkata (Eden Gardens), December 13–16, 2011. **Drawn. Delhi 392** (R. Bhatia 163*) **and 186-3; ‡Bengal 397-9 dec** (M. K. Tiwary 187; P. Sangwan 5-107). *Bengal 3pts, Delhi 1pt. Tiwary hit his third century in successive innings.*

At Ahmedabad (Motera), December 13–16, 2011. **Drawn. ‡Tamil Nadu 698-8 dec** (A. Mukund 220, S. Badrinath 102, K. D. Karthik 135, K. Vasudevadas 105) **and 100-0; Gujarat 539** (M. C. Juneja 201*). *Gujarat 1pt, Tamil Nadu 3pts. Tamil Nadu's total, the highest in this tournament, featured four centuries. Abhinav Mukund struck his second double-hundred of the season, and his fifth in all; he added 223 for the second wicket with Subramaniam Badrinath and 170 for the third with Dinesh Karthik. In reply, 21-year-old debutant Manprit Juneja hit 201*.*

At Rohtak, December 13–16, 2011. **Drawn.** **‡Madhya Pradesh 487** (N. V. Ojha 160, D. Bundela 112); **Haryana 126** (T. P. Sudhindra 7-48) **and 346-7**. *Haryana 1pt, Madhya Pradesh 3pts. T. P. Sudhindra took four wickets in his first five overs on his way to career-best figures, and Haryana had to recover from 21-5.*

At Vadodara (Moti Bagh), December 21–24, 2011. **Bengal won by nine wickets.** **Baroda 284** (A. B. Dinda 5-96) **and 139** (A. B. Dinda 5-66); **‡Bengal 390** (A. P. Majumdar 111; Gagandeep Singh 6-94) **and 36-1**. *Bengal 5pts.*

At Surat, December 21–24, 2011. **Haryana won by 140 runs.** **‡Haryana 207 and 321-5 dec**; **Gujarat 228 and 160**. *Haryana 5pts. Victory took Haryana into the quarter-finals.*

At Chennai (Chidambaram), December 21–24, 2011. **Drawn.** **Tamil Nadu 486** (K. D. Karthik 156) **and 208**; **‡Madhya Pradesh 289**. *Tamil Nadu 3pts, Madhya Pradesh 1pt. First-innings points ensured Tamil Nadu headed the group, three points ahead of Madhya Pradesh.*

Quarter-finals

At Hyderabad (Uppal), January 2–5, 2012. **Drawn.** Rajasthan qualified for the semi-finals by virtue of their first-innings lead. **‡Rajasthan 421** (A. Chopra 142, D. H. Yagnik 101; Mehdi Hasan 5-62) **and 25-0**; **Hyderabad 144 and 431-2 dec** (P. Akshath Reddy 151, D. B. Ravi Teja 185*). *Following on, Hyderabad were given a better start by openers Akshath Reddy and Dharaka Ravi Teja, who put on 275, too late to prevent Rajasthan advancing.*

At Bangalore (Chinnaswamy), January 2–4, 2012. **Haryana won by six wickets.** **‡Karnataka 151** (H. V. Patel 8-40) **and 262**; **Haryana 272** (R. Dewan 101) **and 144-4**. *Harshal Patel, a 21-year-old seamer in his first season, took a career-best 8-40.*

At Indore (Holkar), January 2–5, 2012. **Drawn.** Mumbai qualified for the semi-finals by virtue of their first-innings lead. **Madhya Pradesh 192** (D. S. Kulkarni 5-74) **and 474-3 dec** (M. D. Mishra 174*, D. Bundela 101*); **‡Mumbai 434** (K. R. Pawar 161, A. A. Chavan 102*; T. P. Sudhindra 5-96) **and 113-1**. *Mohnish Mishra and Devendra Bundela added 225* for Madhya Pradesh's fourth wicket, but Mumbai had already taken the crucial lead.*

At Chennai (Chidambaram), January 2–5, 2012. **Drawn.** Tamil Nadu qualified for the semi-finals by virtue of their first-innings lead. **‡Maharashtra 232** (J. Kaushik 5-56) **and 322-4 dec** (H. H. Khadiwale 105, C. G. Khurana 102); **Tamil Nadu 415 and 45-1**. *Harshad Khadiwale and Chirag Khurana opened with 116 in the first innings and 217 in the second, but lacked support.*

Semi-finals

At Rohtak, January 10–12, 2012. **Rajasthan won by 64 runs.** **Rajasthan 89** (H. V. Patel 8-34) **and 192**; **‡Haryana 97** (R. R. Singh 7-45) **and 120** (R. R. Singh 5-37). *For the second match running, Harshal Patel took a career-best eight wickets on the first day, when 18 fell; he finished with 10-39 in the match. Rituraj Singh collected 12-82 to help Rajasthan through to the final, despite their first-innings 89.*

At Mumbai (Wankhede), January 10–13, 2012. **Drawn.** Tamil Nadu qualified for the final by virtue of their first-innings lead. **Tamil Nadu 359** (R. Prasanna 104; B. S. Sandhu 5-88) **and 331-8 dec** (M. Vijay 142; B. S. Sandhu 5-74); **‡Mumbai 157 and 88-3**. *Mumbai's hopes were dashed when they slid to 96-8, though Balwinder Sandhu took ten wickets in his third first-class match.*

Final

At Chennai (Chidambaram), January 19–23, 2012. **Drawn.** Rajasthan won the Ranji Trophy by virtue of their first-innings lead. **‡Rajasthan 621** (V. A. Saxena 257) **and 204-5 dec**; **Tamil Nadu 295** (K. D. Karthik 150) **and 8-2**. *Vineet Saxena batted 907 minutes, the third-longest first-class innings in history, and faced 665 balls in a maiden double-century. Only two wickets fell over the first two days as he put on 236 for Rajasthan's first wicket with Aakash Chopra (94), and also shared hundred stands with captain Hrishikesh Kanitkar and Robin Bist for the next two wickets. Bist passed 1,000 first-class runs for the season in the first innings, and 1,000 Ranji runs in the second; he finished with 1,034, the joint-eighth-highest aggregate in a Ranji tournament. Left-arm spinner*

Aushik Srinivas bowled 85 overs in Rajasthan's first innings, and 113 in the match. Whereas Rajasthan's third wicket fell at 485 in the 207th over, Tamil Nadu's went at 24 in the tenth. They conceded a lead of 326, which guaranteed that Rajasthan would retain their title.

RANJI TROPHY WINNERS

1934-35	Bombay	1960-61	Bombay	1986-87	Hyderabad
1935-36	Bombay	1961-62	Bombay	1987-88	Tamil Nadu
1936-37	Nawanagar	1962-63	Bombay	1988-89	Delhi
1937-38	Hyderabad	1963-64	Bombay	1989-90	Bengal
1938-39	Bengal	1964-65	Bombay	1990-91	Haryana
1939-40	Maharashtra	1965-66	Bombay	1991-92	Delhi
1940-41	Maharashtra	1966-67	Bombay	1992-93	Punjab
1941-42	Bombay	1967-68	Bombay	1993-94	Bombay
1942-43	Baroda	1968-69	Bombay	1994-95	Bombay
1943-44	Western India	1969-70	Bombay	1995-96	Karnataka
1944-45	Bombay	1970-71	Bombay	1996-97	Mumbai
1945-46	Holkar	1971-72	Bombay	1997-98	Karnataka
1946-47	Baroda	1972-73	Bombay	1998-99	Karnataka
1947-48	Holkar	1973-74	Karnataka	1999-2000	Mumbai
1948-49	Bombay	1974-75	Bombay	2000-01	Baroda
1949-50	Baroda	1975-76	Bombay	2001-02	Railways
1950-51	Holkar	1976-77	Bombay	2002-03	Mumbai
1951-52	Bombay	1977-78	Karnataka	2003-04	Mumbai
1952-53	Holkar	1978-79	Delhi	2004-05	Railways
1953-54	Bombay	1979-80	Delhi	2005-06	Uttar Pradesh
1954-55	Madras	1980-81	Bombay	2006-07	Mumbai
1955-56	Bombay	1981-82	Delhi	2007-08	Delhi
1956-57	Bombay	1982-83	Karnataka	2008-09	Mumbai
1957-58	Baroda	1983-84	Bombay	2009-10	Mumbai
1958-59	Bombay	1984-85	Bombay	2010-11	Rajasthan
1959-60	Bombay	1985-86	Delhi	2011-12	Rajasthan

Bombay/Mumbai have won the Ranji Trophy 39 times, Delhi 7, Karnataka 6, Baroda 5, Holkar 4, Bengal, Hyderabad, Madras/Tamil Nadu, Maharashtra, Railways and Rajasthan 2, Haryana, Nawanagar, Punjab, Uttar Pradesh and Western India 1.

Plate League Group A

At Delhi (Palam), November 3–6, 2011. **Drawn. ‡Andhra 219 and 307-9 dec** (G. K. Chiranjeevi 105*); **Services 95** (K. S. Sahabuddin 5-21) **and 229-2** (Jasvir Singh 133). *Services 1pt, Andhra 3pts. Gonnabattula Chiranjeevi, aged 19, scored 105* on first-class debut.*

At Agartala, November 3–6, 2011. **Himachal Pradesh won by an innings and 15 runs. Himachal Pradesh 531** (A. Bali 122, P. Dogra 205; T. K. Chanda 8-133); **‡Tripura 304 and 212** (Gurvinder Singh 5-52). *Himachal Pradesh 6pts. Abhinav Bali and Paras Dogra, with a maiden double-century, put on 241 for Himachal Pradesh's second wicket; both were among Timir Chanda's eight victims.*

At Nagpur, November 3–6, 2011. **Drawn. ‡Vidarbha 572-7 dec** (S. U. Shrivastava 104, R. S. Paradkar 178*; P. Prasanth 5-106) **and 3-0**; **Kerala 431** (S. K. Cheruvathur 104). *Vidarbha 3pts, Kerala 1pt.*

At Visakhapatnam, November 10–13, 2011. **Andhra won by 124 runs. ‡Andhra 235** (M. B. Murasingh 5-74) **and 271-6 dec**; **Tripura 174 and 208**. *Andhra 5pts.*

At Dharmasala, November 10–12, 2011. **Vidarbha won by three wickets. Himachal Pradesh 195** (A. G. Jungade 5-67) **and 200** (S. R. Singh 5-41); **‡Vidarbha 142** (R. Dhawan 5-60) **and 257-7**. *Vidarbha 5pts.*

At Kochi, November 10–13, 2011. **Drawn. ‡Services 253 and 148**; **Kerala 249 and 130-9** (Yashpal Singh 5-37). *Kerala 1pt, Services 3pts. Chasing 153, Kerala were 103-9 – but their Nos 10 and 11 held out for 21 overs to draw.*

At Vijayawada, November 17–20, 2011. **Drawn.** ‡**Andhra 265** (V. Malik 5-58) **and 342** (G. Shankar Rao 148; V. Bhatia 5-76); **Himachal Pradesh 341** (P. Dogra 106, V. Sharma 104*) **and 91-0.** *Andhra 1pt, Himachal Pradesh 3pts.*

At Kochi, November 17–19, 2011. **Kerala won by an innings and 53 runs.** ‡**Tripura 139** (S. K. Cheruvathur 6-40) **and 124**; **Kerala 316** (U. B. Patel 5-75). *Kerala 6pts.*

At Delhi (Harbax Singh), November 17–20, 2011. **Drawn.** ‡**Vidarbha 508-6 dec** (A. P. Chore 157); **Services 240 and 194-7** (Yashpal Singh 124*). *Services 1pt, Vidarbha 3pts.*

At Dharmasala, November 29–December 2, 2011. **Drawn. Himachal Pradesh 364** (Amit Kumar 119*); ‡**Services 202** (R. Dhawan 5-74) **and 394-7** (P. P. Desai 205*). *Himachal Pradesh 3pts, Services 1pt. Debutant Amit Kumar, aged 22, came in at 95-5 on the first day and hit an unbeaten century. Pratik Desai batted throughout Services' follow-on for a maiden double-hundred.*

At Kochi, November 29–December 2, 2011. **Kerala won by two runs.** ‡**Kerala 130** (T. Atchuti Rao 6-43) **and 131**; **Andhra 74** (S. K. Cheruvathur 6-25) **and 185.** *Kerala 5pts. Despite their first-innings 74, Andhra almost stole a low-scoring match. They needed just three runs to win on the final morning, but lost their last wicket to its fourth ball.*

At Agartala, November 29–December 2, 2011. **Drawn. Tripura 281** (S. R. Singh 6-79) **and 433-8 dec** (V. R. Samant 200*); ‡**Vidarbha 368** (S. V. Bahutule 134*) **and 17-0.** *Tripura 1pt, Vidarbha 3pts. Vinayak Samant scored a maiden double-century in 248 balls.*

At Cuddapah, December 6–9, 2011. **Drawn. Vidarbha 382** (R. S. Paradkar 189*); ‡**Andhra 402-8** (D. B. Prasanth Kumar 109, A. G. Pradeep 171). *Andhra 3pts, Vidarbha 1pt. In the first first-class match at the Y. S. Raja Reddy Stadium, Prasanth Kumar and Andimani Pradeep added 223 for home side Andhra's fourth wicket. Vidarbha headed the group on quotient.*

At Thalassery, December 6–9, 2011. **Drawn.** ‡**Himachal Pradesh 452-8 dec** (A. Bali 120); **Kerala 257** (Gurvinder Singh 5-34) **and 209-4.** *Kerala 1pt, Himachal Pradesh 3pts. Himachal Pradesh beat Kerala to the semi-finals.*

At Agartala, December 6–9, 2011. **Services won by six wickets.** ‡**Tripura 242 and 227**; **Services 253** (T. K. Chanda 5-73) **and 217-4.** *Services 5pts.*

Plate League Group B

At Porvorim, November 3–6, 2011. **Drawn. Maharashtra 443** (R. T. D'Souza 5-94) **and 91** (G. D. Narvekar 5-48); ‡**Goa 405** (V. U. Naik 165*) **and 18-1.** *Goa 1pt, Maharashtra 3pts. Vaibhav Naik carried his bat through Goa's first innings for a maiden hundred. Goa later suspended acting-captain Swapnil Asnodkar for two matches after team-mates reported that he told them not to attempt a target of 130 in 19 overs.*

At Hyderabad (Uppal), November 3–6, 2011. **Drawn.** ‡**Hyderabad 416** (S. A. Quadri 105) **and 113-2 dec**; **Jharkhand 280** (A. Lalith Mohan 5-55) **and 74-1.** *Hyderabad 3pts, Jharkhand 1pt.*

At Srinagar, November 3–6, 2011. **Drawn. Assam 297-4 dec** (D. S. Jadhav 135*); ‡**Jammu and Kashmir 232-3** (I. Dev Singh 103). *Jammu and Kashmir 2pts, Assam 2pts.*

At Guwahati (Nehru), November 10–13, 2011. **Drawn.** ‡**Assam 195 and 190-4** (D. S. Jadhav 102*); **Goa 336** (R. J. Pinto 130; A. N. Ahmed 5-97). *Assam 1pt, Goa 3pts. Abu Nachim Ahmed took a hat-trick to reduce Goa's first innings to 85-6.*

At Hyderabad (Uppal), November 10–11, 2011. **Maharashtra won by an innings and six runs.** ‡**Hyderabad 124** (A. A. Darekar 5-48) **and 54** (A. A. Darekar 8-20); **Maharashtra 184** (S. A. Quadri 5-28). *Maharashtra 6pts. Off-spinner Akshay Darekar improved his career-best twice and finished with 13-68 as Maharashtra won inside two days. Half Hyderabad's second-innings total came from opener Akshath Reddy (27). They were later warned about the state of the pitch.*

At Srinagar, November 10–13, 2011. **Drawn. Jammu and Kashmir 270-4 dec** (I. Dev Singh 121); ‡**Jharkhand 105-2.** *Jammu and Kashmir 2pts, Jharkhand 2pts.*

At Guwahati (Nehru), November 17–20, 2011. **Hyderabad won by an innings and 78 runs. Assam 227 and 169** (A. Lalith Mohan 5-42); ‡**Hyderabad 474-6 dec** (P. Akshath Reddy 112, S. A. Quadri 107*). *Hyderabad 6pts. Hyderabad wicketkeeper Ibrahim Khaleel made a world-record 14 dismissals*

– four catches and three stumpings in Assam's first innings, and seven catches in their second. He beat Wayne James's 13, for Matabeleland v Mashonaland Country Districts in 1995-96.

At Jammu (Gandhi), November 17–20, 2011. **Goa won by 177 runs. Goa 281 and 376-9 dec** (S. S. Yadav 118); **‡Jammu and Kashmir 260** (Hardeep Singh 109) **and 220**. *Goa 5pts.*

At Nasik, November 17–20, 2011. **Maharashtra won by nine wickets. Maharashtra 460** (C. G. Khurana 123) **and 106-1**; **‡Jharkhand 283 and 282**. *Maharashtra 5pts. Nineteen-year-old opener Chirag Khurana scored 123 on first-class debut. Jharkhand wicketkeeper Shiv Gautam completed six catches and a stumping in Maharashtra's first innings; when Jharkhand replied, Sangram Atitkar held five catches in the field.*

At Porvorim, November 29–December 1, 2011. **Hyderabad won by an innings and 157 runs. Goa 147 and 104**; **‡Hyderabad 408** (P. Akshath Reddy 118). *Hyderabad 6pts.*

At Dhanbad, November 29–December 2, 2011. **Drawn. ‡Assam 502** (D. S. Jadhav 102, A. S. Sinha 109, G. K. Sharma 115) **and 181-1** (D. S. Jadhav 106*); **Jharkhand 373** (I. R. Jaggi 188; A. N. Ahmed 5-106). *Jharkhand 1pt, Assam 3pts. Dheeraj Jadhav scored a century in each innings. Ishank Jaggi and Shiv Gautam (82) added 217 for Jharkhand's fourth wicket.*

At Ratnagiri, November 29–December 2, 2011. **Drawn. ‡Jammu and Kashmir 388** (A. A. Darekar 5-79) **and 177-7**; **Maharashtra 635-9 dec** (A. R. Bawne 166*). *Maharashtra 3pts, Jammu and Kashmir 1pt.*

At Guwahati (Nehru), December 6–9, 2011. **Maharashtra won by seven wickets. ‡Assam 279** (D. S. Jadhav 105*; A. A. Darekar 5-65) **and 182**; **Maharashtra 244 and 221-3**. *Maharashtra 5pts. Jadhav carried his bat for his fifth century in five matches, but a third victory meant Maharashtra comfortably headed the group.*

At Hyderabad (Uppal), December 6–9, 2011. **Drawn. ‡Hyderabad 311** (B. P. Sandeep 112; R. Dutta 6-79) **and 296-2** (T. L. Suman 160, P. Akshath Reddy 106*); **Jammu and Kashmir 365** (I. Dev Singh 168*; A. Lalith Mohan 6-109). *Hyderabad 1pt, Jammu and Kashmir 3pts. T. L. Suman and Akshath Reddy put on 262 for Hyderabad's second wicket. A point was enough to ensure their progress to the semi-finals.*

At Jamshedpur, December 6–9, 2011. **Jharkhand won by 45 runs. ‡Jharkhand 218 and 204** (A. R. Yadav 5-39); **Goa 189** (S. S. Quadri 5-43) **and 188** (S. Nadeem 5-60). *Jharkhand 5pts.*

Plate League Semi-finals

At Gahunje, December 21–24, 2011. **Drawn.** Maharashtra qualified for the Elite quarter-finals by virtue of their first-innings lead. **‡Maharashtra 415** (A. R. Bawne 137) **and 283-5** (H. H. Khadiwale 139); **Himachal Pradesh 236**. *This was the first first-class match at the Subrata Roy Stadium. Home side Maharashtra made sure of qualification by taking a 179-run first-innings lead.*

At Nagpur, December 21–24, 2011. **Drawn.** Hyderabad qualified for the Elite quarter-finals by virtue of a faster scoring-rate. **‡Vidarbha 531** (A. G. Jungade 115); **Hyderabad 486-8** (A. S. Yadav 128). *Vidarbha were 342-8 but No. 9 Amol Jungade and No. 10 Akshay Wakhare (72) added 166. When Hyderabad's first innings was not completed on the fourth and last day, they qualified on the basis of scoring 2.92 runs an over to Vidarbha's 2.77.*

Maharashtra and Hyderabad advanced to the quarter-finals of the Ranji Elite League.

DULEEP TROPHY, 2011-12

Quarter-final

At Valsad, January 27–30, 2012. **East Zone won by five wickets. West Zone 314** (S. A. Yadav 134) **and 201**; **‡East Zone 343** (N. B. Behera 130, A. P. Majumdar 102*) **and 173-5** (A. A. Darekar 5-87).

Semi-final

At Chennai (Chidambaram), February 4–7, 2012. **Drawn.** Central Zone qualified for the final by virtue of their first-innings lead. ‡**Central Zone 293** (M. Kaif 109) **and 530-8 dec** (N. V. Ojha 104, R. D. Bist 160); **South Zone 183 and 152-2**. *In Central Zone's second innings, Robin Bist reached his fifth century of the season and added 212 for the sixth wicket with Bhuvneshwar Kumar (85).*

At Delhi (Feroz Shah Kotla), February 4–7, 2012. **Drawn.** East Zone qualified for the final by virtue of their first-innings lead. ‡**East Zone 315** (W. P. Saha 124; P. Awana 6-84) **and 319-5 dec** (M. S. Vardhan 125, A. P. Majumdar 144); **North Zone 287** (A. B. Dinda 8-123) **and 126-3**. *Manish Vardhan and Anustup Majumdar put on 251 for East Zone's second wicket. Ashok Dinda's career-best 8-123 included his 50th first-class wicket of the season.*

Final

At Indore (Holkar), February 12–14, 2012. **East Zone won by an innings and 20 runs. Central Zone 133 and 217**; ‡**East Zone 370** (W. P. Saha 170). *East Zone won with more than a day to spare to take the Duleep Trophy for the first time. Wriddhaman Saha scored his second century in successive matches since his return from Australia.*

DEODHAR TROPHY, 2011-12

50-over knockout

Quarter-final

At Mohali, March 16, 2012. **Central Zone won by four wickets. South Zone 224-9** (50 overs); ‡**Central Zone 225-6** (39.3 overs).

Semi-finals

At Mohali, March 17, 2012. **West Zone won by 108 runs. West Zone 342** (50 overs) (K. M. Jadhav 114); ‡**East Zone 234** (40 overs) (S. S. Tiwary 112*; Iqbal Abdulla 6-32). *Kedar Jadhav scored 114 in 69 balls, Saurabh Tiwary 112* in 95.*

At Dharmasala, March 18, 2012. **North Zone won by 22 runs. North Zone 289-8** (50 overs); ‡**Central Zone 267-9** (50 overs) (P. Awana 6-49).

Final

At Dharmasala, March 19, 2012. **West Zone won by 113 runs. West Zone 355-4** (50 overs) (A. M. Rahane 118); ‡**North Zone 242** (42.2 overs). *A year earlier, the same two finalists had scored 208-15 between them; this time, they managed 597-14, set on their way by Ajinkya Rahane's 118 in 122 balls; he shared stands of 131 and 116 with Parthiv Patel and Cheteshwar Pujara for West Zone's first two wickets.*

N. K. P. SALVE CHALLENGER TROPHY, 2011-12

50-over mini-league plus final

Final

At Nagpur, October 13, 2011 (day/night). **Tied. India Green 238-8** (50 overs); ‡**India Red 238** (49.5 overs). *The teams shared the trophy after Piyush Chawla was run out for 92 trying to score the winning run – not realising he had another chance, because what he thought was the final ball was in fact a wide.*

VIJAY HAZARE TROPHY, 2011-12

50-over league plus knockout

Semi-finals

At Delhi (Palam), March 10, 2012. **Bengal won by three wickets.** ‡**Punjab 205-8** (50 overs); **Bengal 208-7** (47.5 overs).

At Delhi (Feroz Shah Kotla), March 10, 2012. **Mumbai won by 140 runs.** ‡**Mumbai 295-5** (50 overs); **Delhi 155** (45 overs).

Final

At Delhi (Feroz Shah Kotla), March 12, 2012. **Bengal won by six wickets.** ‡**Mumbai 248** (49.2 overs); **Bengal 252-4** (46.1 overs) (L. R. Shukla 106*). *Laxmi Shukla took 4-38, including Mumbai's top three, before seeing Bengal home with 106* in 90 balls.*

SYED MUSHTAQ ALI TROPHY, 2011-12

20-over league plus knockout

Semi-finals

At Mumbai (Bandra Kurla), March 26, 2012. **Baroda won by seven wickets. Delhi 169-9** (20 overs); ‡**Baroda 173-3** (17.1 overs). *Kedar Devdhar scored 96 in 40 balls to take Baroda to within 20 runs of victory.*

At Mumbai (Bandra Kurla), March 26, 2012. **Punjab won by five wickets. Mumbai 122-9** (20 overs); ‡**Punjab 124-5** (19 overs).

Final

At Mumbai (Brabourne), March 27, 2012. **Baroda won by eight runs.** ‡**Baroda 149-6** (20 overs); **Punjab 141-8** (20 overs). *Punjab were 136-5, needing 14 runs from 11 balls, but lost three wickets and scored only five.*

NEW ZEALAND CRICKET, 2012

Breakdown in relations

ANDREW ALDERSON

New Zealand are no strangers to cricketing drama, but Hollywood's finest scriptwriters would have marvelled at the turmoil packed into 2012. Fluctuating performances, leadership conflicts and vehement protests from fans and former players made for a compelling but destructive soap opera.

The year was bookended with Test victories over Zimbabwe – by a national-record innings and 301 runs at Napier – and Sri Lanka, a 167-run triumph in Colombo born in adversity. But precious little came in between, with six defeats in eight other Tests. Adding to the malaise were ten losses in 14 completed one-day internationals, and eight in 16 Twenty20 matches (plus two eliminator-over failures at the World Twenty20).

Worse, the goodwill engendered from New Zealand's first Test win in Sri Lanka for more than 14 years evaporated immediately, when – at the instigation of coach Mike Hesson – Ross Taylor was removed from all forms of captaincy, and replaced by Brendon McCullum. A public-relations shambles ensued.

NEW ZEALAND IN 2012

	Played	*Won*	*Lost*	*Drawn/No result*
Tests	10	2	6	2
One-day internationals	16	4	10	2
Twenty20 internationals	18	6	10	2

Month	Tour	Page
JANUARY – FEBRUARY	1 Test, 3 ODIs and 2 T20Is (h) v Zimbabwe	(page 1020)
FEBRUARY – MARCH	3 Tests, 3 ODIs and 3 T20Is (h) v South Africa	(page 1025)
APRIL		
MAY		
JUNE – JULY – AUGUST	2 Tests, 5 ODIs and 2 T20Is (a) v West Indies	(page 1173)
AUGUST – SEPTEMBER	2 Tests and 2 T20Is (a) v India	(page 979)
SEPTEMBER – OCTOBER	World Twenty20 (in Sri Lanka)	(page 841)
OCTOBER – NOVEMBER	2 Tests, 5 ODIs and 1 T20I (a) v Sri Lanka	(page 1131)
DECEMBER – JANUARY	2 Tests, 3 ODIs and 3 T20Is (a) v South Africa	(page 1075)

For a review of New Zealand domestic cricket from the 2011-12 season, see page 1039.

"I knew [working with Hesson] would be tough from the outset," said Taylor. "I gave him as much support as I could, but it wasn't reciprocated." Taylor had batted New Zealand to a series-levelling victory in Colombo with 142 and 74, knowing Hesson would recommend his demotion as captain regardless. Hesson maintained that his intention, articulated in hotel-room meetings the day after the 50-over series defeat earlier on the tour, was to push for a split leadership, in which Taylor would keep the Test captaincy but pass on limited-overs duties to McCullum. Taylor claimed this plan was not made clear at the time, and interpreted it as a move to get rid of him altogether. In his last match in charge, he saved his side from the ignominy of equalling New Zealand's worst losing streak of six Tests, set in the dark days of the mid-1950s. But it did not stop him pulling out of the end-of-year visit to South Africa, saying: "I don't believe I can give 100% to the game at this time."

Some good did emerge from the mess, as anecdotal evidence of apathy towards cricket in New Zealand proved exaggerated. Taylor's treatment unleashed rare passion from fans and past players, who claimed he had not received the traditional Kiwi fair go. It prompted Martin Crowe, arguably the country's greatest batsman and a long-time mentor of Taylor, to tweet that he had burned his New Zealand blazer in protest. He later insisted the burning had been "metaphorical", and would be giving the blazer to charity "very soon". Meanwhile, Hesson's supporters believed he had been forced to make a brave decision in the interests of a dispirited team ranked eighth in Tests and Twenty20s, and ninth in one-day internationals, below Bangladesh.

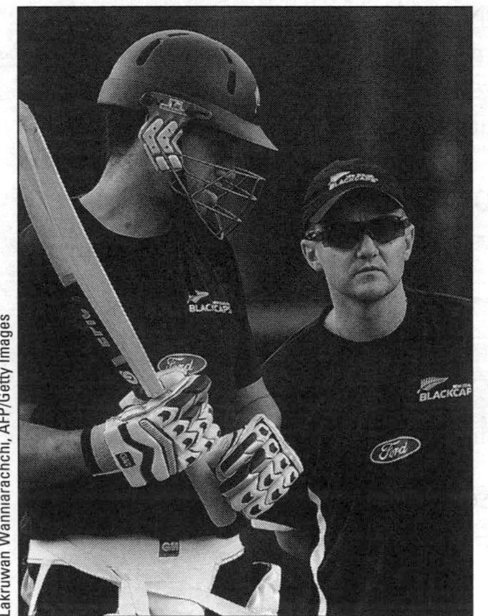

Lakruwan Wanniarachchi, AFP/Getty Images

Men apart: Ross Taylor and Mike Hesson struggled to find common ground.

Hesson's predecessor, John Wright, had completed a 19-month spell at the end of the West Indies tour in August, having signalled his intention to leave in May after struggling to gain the autonomy he wanted from director of cricket John Buchanan. New Zealand lost all but one of in nine internationals in the Caribbean, but the tour was spared in-depth probing by the media because of the concurrent success for the Olympic team in London.

Wright's exit left New Zealand cricket in a melancholic state. A respected former opener, he had helped orchestrate their first Test win over Australia since 1992-93, and their first appearance in the semi-finals of a subcontinental World Cup, and made some bold selections based on form (Mark Gillespie and Dean Brownlie) and potential (Doug Bracewell and, as wicketkeeper, B-J. Watling).

The 38-year-old Hesson, a former Otago coach apparently rated highly by New Zealand Cricket for his man-management skills, succeeded Wright for the India tour in August after curtailing his contract with Kenya in May citing security concerns. New Zealand produced a credible performance under him at the World Twenty20, tying with eventual finalists West Indies and Sri Lanka in the Super Eights, but they lacked killer instinct.

Individual highlights were thin on the ground. Martin Guptill excelled in the Tests against West Indies, and the limited-overs matches against Zimbabwe, and reached a 69-ball century off the last delivery to topple South Africa in a Twenty20 match in East London. He completed a sequence of five consecutive international half-centuries against Zimbabwe and South Africa – a feat previously achieved for New Zealand only by Andrew Jones – but appeared to have developed a mental block converting fifties into hundreds.

Taylor's batting flourished as captain, with three Test centuries, and Kane Williamson's unbeaten 102 to draw the Wellington Test against South Africa was among the gutsiest innings played by a New Zealander, let alone a 21-year-old. The troubled Jesse Ryder opted out of international cricket after an altercation with a member of the public at a Napier hotel in February – the latest in a long line of indiscretions.

Tim Southee showed glimpses of becoming the attack's spearhead, with 25 wickets at 22 in six Tests after struggling to hold his place earlier in the year; the highlight was seven for 64 at Bangalore, New Zealand's best in India. Trent Boult, still only 23, emerged as Southee's new-ball partner and, by the end of the year, his Test record stood at 26 wickets from eight matches.

Bowling coach Damien Wright resigned for family reasons during the India tour, but the pace prospects looked good. Bracewell performed excellently on occasion; Gillespie took two five-fors against South Africa on his Test comeback; Pretoria-born Neil Wagner, the leading Plunket Shield wicket-taker, qualified for New Zealand through residency; and fellow left-armer Mitchell McClenaghan showed zest in December's Twenty20 series defeat by South Africa. At 38, Chris Martin's international days look numbered, despite passing Chris Cairns as the country's third-highest Test wicket-taker.

The man just above him in the list, Daniel Vettori, was hampered by injury, and played only five Tests in 2012. He returned at the World Twenty20, before hobbling away for surgery on his hernia and Achilles tendon. A long-term spin-bowling successor in Test cricket is yet to be found.

The sport's administration had an undulating year. Former Test opener David White became NZC chief executive in December 2011, and relocated the support services (including commercial and marketing) from Christchurch to Auckland. In November, the board reported a better-than-budgeted deficit of $NZ1.87m, thanks mainly to an eight-year deal with Pitch International to sell overseas media rights for home matches.

However, building a market share in the United States through a proposed Twenty20 league (NZC were a shareholder in Cricket Holdings America) remained problematic. Potential franchisees claimed the market justified little more than 10% of the $US40m per franchise put forward by NZC.

NEW ZEALAND v ZIMBABWE, 2011-12

REVIEW BY ANDREW ALDERSON

Test match (1): New Zealand 1, Zimbabwe 0
One-day internationals (3): New Zealand 3, Zimbabwe 0
Twenty20 internationals (2): New Zealand 2, Zimbabwe 0

The teams started with vastly different expectations. Zimbabwe were looking to prove that their performance against New Zealand the previous October – when they won a one-day international and came close to pulling off a surprise Test victory – was no fluke. New Zealand's conundrum, meanwhile, was to blend the need to dominate with the desire to try out new players. In the end, it was all very one-sided: the New Zealanders won all six international matches.

Zimbabwe tried hard, but all their moves were countered by a confident team buoyed by a rare Test victory over Australia, in December. The tourists' calamitous collapse to 51 all out in the one-off Test at Napier presaged a run of defeats which hindered Zimbabwe's quest for credibility after resuming Test cricket in 2011 following a six-year hiatus.

Players such as batsman Malcolm Waller and pace bowler Kyle Jarvis, who had done well for Zimbabwe at home, struggled to reproduce that form on New Zealand pitches which had more pace and bounce. Even the long-serving slow left-armer Ray Price could not conjure up any magic. Just before the tour, Brendan Taylor, Zimbabwe's captain, had gleaned some valuable local experience with Wellington in the domestic Twenty20 competition, and this paid off with some consistent performances in the one-day games. He was given a smattering of support by Elton Chigumbura and Hamilton Masakadza, but the limited penetration of the bowling left Zimbabwe impotent, and their fielding repeatedly let them down.

New Zealand simply flexed their muscles. Martin Guptill, strong on the pull and the drive, crafted 374 runs in five innings across the three formats, becoming the first to make five consecutive international half-centuries for New Zealand since Roger Twose in 2000 (he soon added a sixth, against South Africa, to break the national record). Chris Martin produced the bowling performance of the series with a career-best six for 26 in the second innings of the Test. His final strike put him level with Chris Cairns in third place on New Zealand's all-time list, with 218 Test wickets.

Brendon McCullum stepped in as captain after Ross Taylor sustained a calf injury in the Test and had to miss the limited-overs games. McCullum offered some characteristically aggressive leadership – in the field, catchers regularly outnumbered sweepers – and his bowlers responded.

New Zealand's dominance afforded coach and selector John Wright the chance to try out new ideas and players. Debate surrounded the promotion of part-time wicketkeeper B-J. Watling to take the gloves in the Test, but he responded with a tidy display, holding four catches in the second innings and conceding only four byes; he also made his maiden Test century.

The home side's bench strength was then underlined in the limited-overs matches. Tom Latham from Canterbury, a 19-year-old left-hander (and son of the former international Rod), provided solidity in the middle order; Central Districts' Tarun Nethula, born in India, became the first specialist leg-spinner to play for New Zealand for ten years; and Auckland's Roneel Hira looked a capable slow left-armer in the Twenty20 games.

New Zealand's camaraderie was highlighted by the Test victory, achieved inside three days. Riffs from tunes such as "Why does love do this to me?" – from the local band The Exponents – floated up from the dressing-room, and the team gathered in the middle once the crowds had gone, for their traditional toast and chant.

ZIMBABWEAN TOURING PARTY

*B. R. M. Taylor, R. W. Chakabva, E. Chigumbura, A. G. Cremer, K. M. Jarvis, H. Masakadza, S. W. Masakadza, S. Matsikenyeri, T. M. K. Mawoyo, K. O. Meth, F. Mutizwa, R. W. Price, T. Taibu, B. V. Vitori, M. N. Waller. *Coach:* A. R. Butcher.

For the limited-overs matches which followed the Test, Cremer was replaced by P. Utseya.

At Gisborne, January 21–23, 2012 (not first-class). **Drawn.** **‡New Zealand XI 272-7 dec** (B-J. Watling 84, S. R. Wells 65) **and 274-5** (C. F. K. van Wyk 61, K. S. Williamson 52, L. R. P. L. Taylor 54); **Zimbabweans 329** (T. Taibu 66, M. N. Waller 58, R. W. Chakabva 87*; N. Wagner 3-86). *Both sides chose 13 players, of whom 11 could bat and 11 field. Only one bowler, Graeme Cremer, took a wicket in the NZ XI's second innings; the other four batsmen out all retired*

NEW ZEALAND v ZIMBABWE

Test Match

DON CAMERON

At Napier, January 26–28, 2012. New Zealand won by an innings and 301 runs. Toss: Zimbabwe. Test debuts: S. W. Masakadza, F. Mutizwa.

In advance, there seemed little reason for Zimbabwe to fear their first overseas Test for nearly seven years. Not only had they come within a whisker of claiming the one-off Test at Bulawayo a few months earlier, having already chased down 329 to win one of the one-day internationals. And in the warm-up game before this match, they took a first-innings lead against a strong New Zealand XI. Then reality bit, painfully so: blown away inside a day for 51 and 143, they slumped to their heaviest Test defeat, a result that doubled up as New Zealand's largest win. "They were embarrassed in the dressing-room," said Zimbabwe's coach Alan Butcher, "and they should have been."

Their problems began when Brendan Taylor chose to bowl, perhaps deceived by a pre-match promise from McLean Park's curator, Phil Stoyanoff. Usually a producer of hard, true surfaces of the kind that break bowlers' hearts and gladden batsmen's, Stoyanoff suggested it would be different this time, and gave the pitch an extra watering before it was covered on the eve of the Test. But any local cricketer might have guessed what lay in wait: all it needed was two or three hours of sunshine the next morning, and the batsmen would be smiling once more.

So it proved, as Zimbabwe's seamers bowled a full length for an hour in search of imaginary help, and McCullum and Guptill happily gathered 68 riskless runs. By the time Guptill was caught behind shortly after lunch off Shingi Masakadza – the younger brother of opener Hamilton, and one of two Zimbabwean debutants, along with top-order batsman Forster Mutizwa – New Zealand had 124 on the board, and the game was already feeling beyond Zimbabwe's reach. And after McCullum departed for 83, Ross Taylor rattled along to his sixth Test hundred, against some undemanding bowling: leg-spinner Cremer struggled to settle, one over costing 17.

Rain limited the second day to 15.2 overs, during which Taylor retired with a strained calf muscle that would keep him out of the one-day matches. But once Watling – asked to keep wicket for the first time in Tests – had completed his maiden century on the third morning, New Zealand declared at 495, to allow their bowlers 15 overs at Zimbabwe before lunch. The tourists reached the interval a shell-shocked 20 for five; little more than an hour afterwards they were all out for 51, their lowest total in Tests and the lowest by any team against New Zealand. Only Waller managed double figures.

Armed with a lead of 444, their largest in Tests, stand-in captain McCullum enforced the follow-on. And when Zimbabwe collapsed to 12 for five second time round, most of Napier was hoping they would fail to get past 26, Test cricket's nadir, set 57 years previously by New Zealand. Zimbabwe avoided that ignominy, although their loss of the first five wickets in each innings for a combined total of 31 runs was easily a Test record, beating 45 (scores of 28 for five and 17 for five) by West Indies against Australia at Melbourne in 2000-01.

Regis Chakabva, in just his second Test, fought a lone hand with a half-century, only for the 37-year-old Martin – operating with a smoother run-up that improved his accuracy – to wrap up the innings with two wickets in two balls; his figures of six for 26 were his best in first-class cricket. It was only the third time any Test team had been bowled out twice in a day, following India against England at Old Trafford in July 1952, and Zimbabwe themselves against New Zealand at Harare in August 2005.

If Zimbabwe were dismal, New Zealand were ruthless, letting rip with an aggressive four-man pace attack, and catching brilliantly behind the wicket. At times, they posted two gullies and four slips: of the 13 catches taken in the cordon, five were held at third slip by Brownlie. Remarkably, it was New Zealand's first victory at Napier in all ten Tests there.

Man of the Match: C. S. Martin.

Close of play: first day, New Zealand 331-5 (Taylor 111, Watling 15); second day, New Zealand 392-5 (Watling 52, Bracewell 11).

New Zealand

B. B. McCullum lbw b Jarvis	83
M. J. Guptill c Taibu b S. W. Masakadza	51
K. S. Williamson run out	4
*L. R. P. L. Taylor retired hurt	122
D. G. Brownlie c Taibu b H. Masakadza	0
D. L. Vettori st Taibu b Cremer	38
†B-J. Watling not out	102
D. A. J. Bracewell b Vitori	11
T. G. Southee c Waller b Cremer	44
T. A. Boult not out	5
B 1, l-b 21, w 2, n-b 11	35
1/124 (2) (7 wkts dec, 123.4 overs)	495

2/131 (3) 3/195 (1) 4/196 (5) 5/278 (6) 6/392 (8) 7/466 (9)

C. S. Martin did not bat.

Taylor retired hurt at 365-5.

Jarvis 32.4–7–120–1; Vitori 25–3–94–1; S. W. Masakadza 23–2–102–1; H. Masakadza 21–6–45–1; Cremer 22–2–112–2.

Zimbabwe

	First innings		Second innings	
T. M. K. Mawoyo b Martin	2	–	c Guptill b Martin	2
H. Masakadza c Brownlie b Boult	0	–	c McCullum b Martin	0
F. Mutizwa b Martin	6	–	c Watling b Bracewell	18
*B. R. M. Taylor c Guptill b Bracewell	9	–	c Watling b Martin	2
†T. Taibu c Brownlie b Boult	2	–	c Williamson b Bracewell	4
M. N. Waller c Brownlie b Southee	23	–	lbw b Bracewell	0
R. W. Chakabva lbw b Bracewell	3	–	c Brownlie b Martin	63
A. G. Cremer lbw b Vettori	3	–	c Bracewell b Williamson	26
S. W. Masakadza not out	3	–	c Watling b Martin	21
K. M. Jarvis run out	0	–	not out	0
B. V. Vitori c Brownlie b Southee	0	–	c Watling b Martin	0
			B 4, l-b 3	7
1/2 (1) 2/8 (3) 3/8 (2) 4/19 (4) 5/19 (5) 6/24 (7) 7/46 (8) 8/50 (6) 9/50 (10) 10/51 (11) (28.5 overs)	51		1/2 (1) 2/3 (2) 3/5 (4) 4/12 (5) 5/12 (6) 6/37 (3) 7/100 (8) 8/134 (9) 9/143 (7) 10/143 (11) (48.3 overs)	143

Martin 6–2–5–2; Boult 9–3–24–2; Bracewell 6–2–12–2; Vettori 4–3–2–1; Southee 3.5–0–8–2. *Second innings*—Martin 8.3–3–26–6; Southee 8–2–20–0; Bracewell 10–4–26–3; Vettori 10–1–25–0; Boult 9–4–15–0; Guptill 1–0–12–0; Williamson 2–0–12–1.

Umpires: Enamul Haque and R. J. Tucker. Third umpire: N. J. Llong.
Referee: D. C. Boon.

LIMITED-OVERS INTERNATIONAL REPORTS BY ANDREW ALDERSON

At Dunedin (University Oval), February 3, 2012. **First one-day international: New Zealand won by 90 runs. New Zealand 248** (48.3 overs) (M. J. Guptill 70, K. S. Williamson 35, N. L. McCullum 30, A. M. Ellis 33; S. W. Masakadza 4-46); **‡Zimbabwe 158** (41.1 overs) (B. R. M. Taylor 58; K. D. Mills 3-26, R. J. Nicol 4-19). *MoM:* M. J. Guptill. *One-day international debuts:* D. G. Brownlie, A. M. Ellis, T. W. M. Latham (New Zealand). *New Zealand were reeling at 4-2 in the second over, but Guptill struck nine fours in a crisp innings, putting on 88 with Williamson, then Tom Latham (24) and Andrew Ellis added sound debut knocks. Zimbabwe chased poorly: at 15-3 in the seventh over they were up against it. Nicol gave his off-breaks some loop, and the batsmen could not resist, giving him flattering figures from just 4.1 overs. Brendan Taylor did hit Nicol out of the ground, but misjudged the pace and width of the next delivery and was swallowed at long-off.*

At Whangarei, February 6, 2012. **Second one-day international: New Zealand won by 141 runs. New Zealand 372-6** (50 overs) (R. J. Nicol 146, M. J. Guptill 77, J. D. P. Oram 59, T. W. M. Latham 48; P. Utseya 3-71); **‡Zimbabwe 231-8** (50 overs) (T. Taibu 50, E. Chigumbura 63, S. W. Masakadza 38; J. D. P. Oram 3-29). *MoM:* R. J. Nicol. *One-day international debut:* T. S. Nethula (New Zealand). *Whangarei's Cobham Oval became the 12th ground in New Zealand to host a one-day international, and Simon Harvey, the head groundsman, erred on the side of a batsman's paradise. New Zealand took full advantage: those seated in front of the wicket could not afford to be distracted by conversation, coffee or crossword. Nicol anchored the innings with his second one-day century in five matches – he hit six sixes and ten fours from 134 balls – while Guptill, Oram and Latham blazed around him, even peppering the neighbouring rugby stadium. Oram's promotion to No. 3 was a highlight: his 59 came from just 28 balls. There were 16 sixes in all, and 117 came from the last ten overs. Zimbabwe started poorly again, managed only two fours in the first half of their innings, and toiled for the duration in what became batting practice.*

At Napier, February 9, 2012 (day/night). **Third one-day international: New Zealand won by 202 runs. ‡New Zealand 373-8** (50 overs) (R. J. Nicol 61, M. J. Guptill 85, B. B. McCullum 119, K. S. Williamson 38); **Zimbabwe 171** (44 overs) (B. R. M. Taylor 65). *MoM:* B. B. McCullum. *One-day international debut:* M. D. Bates (New Zealand). *A tarmac-like surface and McLean Park's short square boundaries allowed New Zealand to surpass their Whangarei run-fest by one, again hitting 16 sixes. They had made only two higher scores in one-day internationals: 402-2 v Ireland at Aberdeen in 2008, and 397-5 (in 44 overs) v Zimbabwe at Bulawayo in 2005. Nicol and Guptill put*

MOST RUNS CONCEDED IN A ONE-DAY INTERNATIONAL

10–0–113–1	M. L. Lewis	Australia v South Africa at Johannesburg	2005-06
9–0–105–1	**B. V. Vitori**	**Zimbabwe v New Zealand at Napier**	**2011-12**
10–0–105–0	T. G. Southee	New Zealand v India at Christchurch	2008-09
12–1–105–2	M. C. Snedden	New Zealand v England at The Oval	1983
10–0–99–0	M. Muralitharan	Sri Lanka v Australia at Sydney	2005-06
9–0–97–2	Shafiul Islam	Bangladesh v England at Birmingham	2010
10–0–97–1	A. L. F. de Mel	Sri Lanka v West Indies at Karachi	1987-88
10–0–97–0	S. J. Harmison	England v Sri Lanka at Leeds	2006
7.4–0–96–1	**S. L. Malinga**	**Sri Lanka v India at Hobart**	**2011-12**
9–0–96–2	A. M. Blignaut	Zimbabwe v New Zealand at Bulawayo	2005-06
10–0–96–1	R. D. M. Leverock	Bermuda v India at Port-of-Spain	2006-07

on 153 in 22 overs before falling to successive deliveries (Guptill was stumped off a wide), then Brendon McCullum waded in with 119 from 88 balls. Left-arm fast bowler Brian Vitori finished with 1-105 from nine overs. Chigumbura (10–0–92–1) also conceded more than 90, a unique double. Price became the fourth Zimbabwean to take 100 wickets in ODIs when he had Nathan McCullum caught at cover. Zimbabwe made another shaky start – 14-2 after seven overs – and this time did not manage to bat out their full allocation.

At Auckland, February 11, 2012 (floodlit). **First Twenty20 international: New Zealand won by seven wickets. ‡Zimbabwe 159-8** (20 overs) (H. Masakadza 53, E. Chigumbura 48; M. D. Bates 3-31); **New Zealand 160-3** (16.5 overs) (M. J. Guptill 91*, K. S. Williamson 48). *MoM:* M. J. Guptill. *Twenty20 international debuts:* M. D. Bates, C. de Grandhomme, R. M. Hira (New Zealand); K. O. Meth (Zimbabwe). *Guptill's purple patch continued with his fifth consecutive international half-century: some neat straight shots were the highlight as he eased New Zealand to victory with 19 balls to spare. Spinner Roneel Hira and paceman Michael Bates – left-armers both – made satisfactory debuts: Bates finished with three wickets, while Hira had no qualms about floating the ball up. Zimbabwe demonstrated some of the competitive spirit that makes them a force at home – Hamilton Masakadza's 53 came from 36 balls, while Chigumbura's 24-ball 48 included four sixes – but were again let down by sloppy fielding.*

At Hamilton, February 14 (floodlit). **Second Twenty20 international: New Zealand won by five wickets. ‡Zimbabwe 200-2** (20 overs) (H. Masakadza 62, S. Matsikenyeri 32, B. R. M. Taylor 75*); **New Zealand 202-5** (19.4 overs) (R. J. Nicol 56, J. E. C. Franklin 60, B. B. McCullum 38). *MoM:* J. E. C. Franklin. *Twenty20 international debut:* A. M. Ellis (New Zealand). *In easily the closest match of the tour, New Zealand needed 21 off nine balls after losing the McCullum brothers to consecutive deliveries in the 19th over. But Williamson carved 20 from five (42464) to ensure a clean sweep of the international matches. Earlier, in their best batting effort of the trip, Zimbabwe reached 200 for the first time in a Twenty20 international as Taylor and Hamilton Masakadza took advantage of a well-paced pitch and short boundaries. But although Guptill was rested, they were matched by New Zealand's openers Nicol and James Franklin.*

NEW ZEALAND v SOUTH AFRICA, 2011-12

NEIL MANTHORP

Test matches (3): New Zealand 0, South Africa 1
One-day internationals (3): New Zealand 0, South Africa 3
Twenty20 internationals (3): New Zealand 1, South Africa 2

One-sided contests can deaden even the most ardent enthusiasm, but New Zealand's demolition of Zimbabwe in the month before South Africa arrived had the opposite effect. It may have been a limp appetiser to the main course of the summer, but New Zealand devoured it with such ease and conviction that most believed they would be able to handle the South Africans – and maybe even upset them.

A great deal was made of the random structure of the Future Tours Programme: South Africa had not visited for eight years. The optimistic saw this as an opportunity to prove New Zealand's worthiness of more tours by the major nations, and they looked vindicated when their team won the first Twenty20 international convincingly. But once they handed the third, in barely credible fashion, to their guests, they did not win another day's play until the last of the tour, when they drew the Third Test with pride partially restored.

What made it worse for New Zealand was that they had chances – and plenty of moments when the scorecard suggested they were on top. But the batsmen fell time and again in the no-man's-land between a start and a score, and the bowlers lost discipline when it mattered. Paradoxically, it might even have been less frustrating for them if – like Zimbabwe – they had been demolished.

South African coach Gary Kirsten, who had played the last of his 101 Tests in Wellington on the previous tour, inadvertently upped the ante by admitting that he viewed New Zealand as "very good preparation" for the trip to England later in the year, and suggested he would be looking for "the right combinations across all three formats" It was a comment that invited embarrassment but proved an accurate prediction, particularly with the emergence of Twenty20 debutants Richard Levi and Marchant de Lange, and a fine one-day series from Faf du Plessis.

FEWEST TESTS TO REACH 50 WICKETS

Tests	*Inns*		
6	10	C. T. B. Turner (Australia)	1886-87–1888
7	13	T. Richardson (England)	1893–1896
7	**13**	**V. D. Philander (South Africa)**	**2011-12**
8	14	A. L. Valentine (West Indies)	1950–1951-52
8	15	F. R. Spofforth (Australia)	1876-77–1882-83
8	15	R. M. Hogg (Australia)	1978-79
8	15	T. M. Alderman (Australia)	1981–1981-82

Hogg took the fewest days (116, followed by Philander's 139). The youngest bowler to take 50 Test wickets was Mohammad Aamer (Pakistan), at 18 years 136 days.

Vernon Philander was the main talking point before the Tests, having collected an astonishing 30 wickets in his first four. Nobody doubted he would have some success in New Zealand, but most were expecting some sort of comedown. Instead, Philander nabbed another 21 with his right-arm seam at an average of 15, making him the joint-second-fastest to 50 Test wickets – at the 19th-century average of 14 runs apiece.

New Zealand gambled in batting Daniel Vettori at No. 6 for the first two Tests, but the balance never looked remotely right. It was a brave move and should be remembered as such, but their desire for sufficient bowling resources left them short of batting depth.

Events off the field also gave cause for concern. The tension between the Australian director of cricket, John Buchanan, and the Kiwi head coach John Wright was simmering through the cracks, and later led to Wright's resignation. At least the tour was well attended and comfortably maintained its presence in the public domain, despite the start of the Super Rugby season in a country only too happy to trumpet its sporting priorities.

Had South Africa enjoyed more luck with the weather, meanwhile, they might even have finished the tour ahead of England at the top of the Test rankings: rain deprived them of the chance to win at Dunedin and Wellington, and thus of the necessary 3–0 margin of victory. Their ascent would have to wait.

SOUTH AFRICAN TOURING PARTY

*G. C. Smith, H. M. Amla, M. V. Boucher, M. de Lange, A. B. de Villiers, J-P. Duminy, Imran Tahir, J. H. Kallis, M. Morkel, A. N. Petersen, R. J. Peterson, V. D. Philander, J. A. Rudolph, D. W. Steyn, L. L. Tsotsobe. *Coach:* G. Kirsten.

A. B. de Villiers led the team in the Twenty20 and one-day international series preceding the Tests. The Twenty20 squad included J. Botha, C. A. Ingram, R. E. Levi, J. A. Morkel, J. L. Ontong, W. D. Parnell and J. Theron instead of Smith, Boucher, Imran Tahir, Kallis, Petersen, Philander, Rudolph and Steyn. For the one-day series, F. du Plessis, Kallis, Smith and Steyn replaced Ingram, Levi and Theron.

TEST MATCH AVERAGES

NEW ZEALAND – BATTING AND FIELDING

	T	*I*	*NO*	*R*	*HS*	*100*	*50*	*Avge*	*Ct*
K. S. Williamson	3	5	1	229	102*	1	1	57.25	4
L. R. P. L. Taylor	3	5	2	171	48*	0	0	57.00	4
B. B. McCullum	3	6	1	203	61	0	2	40.60	1
C. F. K. van Wyk	3	5	0	123	39	0	0	24.60	8
M. J. Guptill	3	6	0	122	59	0	1	20.33	2
†D. L. Vettori	3	5	0	97	46	0	0	19.40	0
M. R. Gillespie	2	3	0	51	27	0	0	17.00	1
D. A. J. Bracewell	3	5	1	45	25	0	0	11.25	1
R. J. Nicol	2	4	0	28	19	0	0	7.00	2
C. S. Martin	3	4	2	7	5	0	0	3.50	0

Played in one Test: B. J. Arnel 3, 8*; T. A. Boult 33* (1 ct); D. G. Brownlie 29, 15; †D. R. Flynn 45, 0 (1 ct); T. G. Southee 0 (1 ct).

BOWLING

	Style	O	M	R	W	BB	5I	Avge
M. R. Gillespie	RFM	58.4	9	251	11	6-113	2	22.81
D. A. J. Bracewell	RFM	101	15	339	9	3-70	0	37.66
C. S. Martin	RFM	98	18	325	8	4-56	0	40.62
D. L. Vettori	SLA	117	24	285	3	1-31	0	95.00

Also bowled: B. J. Arnel (RFM) 12–2–64–0; T. A. Boult (LFM) 34–4–151–2; D. G. Brownlie (RM) 2–0–20–0; R. J. Nicol (RM/OB) 2.5–1–13–0; T. G. Southee (RFM) 36–5–140–0; K. S. Williamson (OB) 22.3–5–75–2.

SOUTH AFRICA – BATTING AND FIELDING

	T	I	NO	R	HS	100	50	Avge	Ct
†G. C. Smith	3	6	1	282	115	1	2	56.40	6
†J. A. Rudolph	3	4	1	169	105*	1	1	56.33	3
H. M. Amla	3	5	1	189	63	0	2	47.25	2
A. B. de Villiers	3	5	0	218	83	0	2	43.60	2
A. N. Petersen	3	6	0	261	156	1	0	43.50	1
J. H. Kallis	2	3	0	119	113	1	0	39.66	1
M. V. Boucher	3	4	1	108	46	0	0	36.00	11
V. D. Philander	3	3	0	65	29	0	0	21.66	0
D. W. Steyn	3	3	0	13	9	0	0	4.33	1
†M. Morkel	3	3	3	58	35*	0	0	–	1

Played in two Tests: Imran Tahir 10, 16 (1 ct). Played in one Test: †J-P. Duminy 103, 33*; M. de Lange did not bat.

BOWLING

	Style	O	M	R	W	BB	5I	Avge
V. D. Philander	RFM	101.3	19	325	21	6-44	2	15.47
M. Morkel	RF	90.4	27	230	10	6-23	1	23.00
D. W. Steyn	RF	100.2	33	239	9	3-49	0	26.55
Imran Tahir	LBG	54.2	11	152	4	2-12	0	38.00

Also bowled: M. de Lange (RF) 38.2–5–151–1; J-P. Duminy (OB) 23–2–74–0; J. H. Kallis (RFM) 27–10–47–2.

At Christchurch (Hagley Oval), February 15, 2012. **South Africans won by 20 runs. South Africans 150-6** (20 overs) (R. E. Levi 63; G. H. Worker 3-23); **‡Canterbury 130** (19 overs) (L. L. Tsotsobe 4-18). *In a Twenty20 match to raise funds for the Christchurch earthquake appeal, Richard Levi set up the South African innings with 63 in 32 balls. Lonwabo Tsotsobe removed Canterbury's top three with a hat-trick, and they were 63-7 before Matt McEwan, playing his second senior match, on his 21st birthday, added 59 in five overs with 20-year-old Matt Henry, who hit five sixes in 17 balls.*

NEW ZEALAND v SOUTH AFRICA

First Twenty20 International

At Wellington (Westpac Stadium), February 17, 2012 (floodlit). New Zealand won by six wickets. Toss: New Zealand. Twenty20 international debut: R. E. Levi.

Guptill made light work of a below-par target given some respectability only by Ontong, who hoicked Williamson for four consecutive sixes over midwicket. Southee bowled particularly well at important times, but the South Africans looked and played like jet-lagged tourists. Guptill's innings was smart as well as skilful, mostly calm but occasionally brutal. He launched a delivery from Tsotsobe on to the roof of the stadium, a shot measured by television gadgetry at a staggering 127 metres, one of the biggest recorded. New Zealand were captained by Brendon McCullum in the absence of Ross Taylor, who was suffering from a calf injury.

Man of the Match: M. J. Guptill.

South Africa

		B	4	6
R. E. Levi *c 8 b 10*	13	12	1	1
H. M. Amla *run out*	19	15	2	1
C. A. Ingram *st 3 b 7*	0	2	0	0
*†A. B. de Villiers *c 2 b 11*	8	17	0	0
J-P. Duminy *c 9 b 10*	41	37	3	0
J. L. Ontong *c and b 10*	32	17	0	4
J. A. Morkel *not out*	13	12	1	0
J. Botha *not out*	14	8	1	1
L-b 7	7			
6 overs: 38-3 (20 overs)	147-6			

1/24 2/34 3/38 4/52 5/102 6/127

J. Theron, M. Morkel and L. L. Tsotsobe did not bat.

N. L. McCullum 4–0–16–1; Mills 4–0–44–0; Southee 4–0–28–3; Hira 2–0–12–1; Bracewell 3–0–10–0; Williamson 2–0–27–0; Nicol 1–0–3–0.

New Zealand

		B	4	6
R. J. Nicol *c 2 b 9*	13	18	1	0
M. J. Guptill *not out*	78	55	5	4
*†B. B. McCullum *b 5*	16	17	0	0
K. S. Williamson *run out*	24	21	3	0
C. de Grandhomme *c 1 b 10*	2	3	0	0
J. E. C. Franklin *not out*	8	4	1	0
L-b 3, w 2, n-b 2	7			
6 overs: 44-0 (19.2 overs)	148-4			

1/49 2/90 3/127 4/136

N. L. McCullum, D. A. J. Bracewell, K. D. Mills, T. G. Southee and R. M. Hira did not bat.

J. A. Morkel 3–0–20–0; Tsotsobe 3–0–28–0; M. Morkel 4–1–26–1; Botha 3.2–0–24–0; Theron 4–0–27–1; Duminy 2–0–20–1.

Umpires: G. A. V. Baxter and B. G. Frost. Third umpire: C. B. Gaffaney.

NEW ZEALAND v SOUTH AFRICA

Second Twenty20 International

At Hamilton, February 19, 2012 (floodlit). South Africa won by eight wickets. Toss: South Africa. Twenty20 international debut: M. de Lange.

Richard Levi hit 13 sixes and a 45-ball century, both Twenty20 international records. In search of fireworks, Seddon Park's administrators reduced their already petite playing area to the size of a colts ground by bringing in the ropes – and the powerful Levi, a 24-year-old from Johannesburg, obliged. Mills got off lightly compared to Bracewell, but still saw fit to describe the conditions as "ridiculous", insisting Levi "would have been caught three or four times on a normal ground". The batsman himself had the grace to admit that a couple of the sixes were mishits. That still left at least ten which were not, and a couple carried well over 65 metres on the leg side at barely above head height. Another, a swat over long-off, travelled even further. By the time he switched his phone on after the match, there were messages from three IPL franchises. A month earlier, he had been uncertain of his place in the Cobras team in Cape Town; a week later, he was signed by Mumbai Indians for a life-changing $400,000.

Man of the Match: R. E. Levi.

MOST SIXES IN AN INNINGS IN TWENTY20 MATCHES

16	G. R. Napier (152)	Essex v Sussex at Chelmsford	2008
14	C. G. Williams (116)	Namibia v Scotland at Windhoek	2011-12
13	B. B. McCullum (158)	Kolkata KR v RC Bangalore at Bangalore	2007-08
13	**R. E. Levi (117)**	**South Africa v New Zealand at Hamilton**	**2011-12**
13	**C. H. Gayle (128)**	**RC Bangalore v Delhi Daredevils at Delhi**	**2011-12**
12	L. P. van der Westhuizen (145)	Namibia v Kenya at Windhoek	2011-12

New Zealand

		B	4	6
R. J. Nicol *run out*	23	17	3	1
M. J. Guptill *c 7 b 9*	47	35	7	1
*†B. B. McCullum *c 6 b 8*	35	31	4	1
K. S. Williamson *not out*	28	20	1	2
J. E. C. Franklin *c 4 b 10*	28	10	0	4
C. de Grandhomme *not out*	3	7	0	0
B 1, l-b 3, w 5	9			
6 overs: 49-1 (20 overs)	173-4			

1/37 2/97 3/114 4/159

N. L. McCullum, D. A. J. Bracewell, K. D. Mills, T. G. Southee and R. M. Hira did not bat.

Botha 4–0–22–1; Tsotsobe 3–0–23–0; M. Morkel 4–0–38–1; de Lange 4–0–43–1; Parnell 2–0–15–0; Duminy 3–0–28–0.

South Africa

		B	4	6
R. E. Levi *not out*	117	51	5	13
H. M. Amla *c 5 b 7*	2	3	0	0
W. D. Parnell *st 3 b 1*	4	6	1	0
*†A. B. de Villiers *not out*	39	36	4	0
L-b 2, w 10	12			
6 overs: 63-2 (16 overs)	174-2			

1/25 2/41

J-P. Duminy, J. L. Ontong, J. A. Morkel, J. Botha, M. de Lange, M. Morkel and L. L. Tsotsobe did not bat.

N. L. McCullum 2–0–18–1; Bracewell 2–0–37–0; Southee 4–0–40–0; Nicol 1–0–10–1; Hira 4–0–34–0; Mills 2–0–26–0; Franklin 1–0–7–0.

Umpires: G. A. V. Baxter and C. B. Gaffaney. Third umpire: B. G. Frost.

NEW ZEALAND v SOUTH AFRICA

Third Twenty20 International

At Auckland, February 22, 2012 (floodlit). South Africa won by three runs. Toss: New Zealand.

New Zealand lost an unloseable game – or at least it should have been. They needed 25 runs from the final five overs with seven wickets in hand, and just 17 from four overs with six left. But Ryder became inexplicably becalmed to signal the beginning of the choke. He scored only four from his last 15 balls, admittedly against some skilled bowling from Morne Morkel and, particularly, Botha, who sent down the 17th and 19th overs at a combined cost of five runs. The remaining batsmen lost their heads entirely, swinging wildly at everything. De Lange had seven runs to defend in the final over and claimed two wickets for three, despite bowling a no-ball with his sixth delivery. That meant Southee needed four off the last ball, a free hit, but – in keeping with New Zealand's haplessness – he failed to score.

Man of the Match: J. Botha.

South Africa

		B	4	6
R. E. Levi *c 1 b 6*	11	7	1	1
H. M. Amla *c 4 b 8*	33	22	4	1
J. A. Morkel *c 1 b 9*	10	9	0	1
*†A. B. de Villiers *b 1*	29	23	2	1
J-P. Duminy *run out*	38	20	2	2
J. L. Ontong *lbw b 1*	6	5	1	0
J. Botha *c 2 b 9*	2	7	0	0
W. D. Parnell *not out*	22	17	2	1
R. J. Peterson *not out*	11	10	1	0
L-b 1, w 2	3			
6 overs: 54-2 (20 overs)	165-7			

1/20 2/39 3/59 4/121 5/129 6/130 7/137

M. de Lange and M. Morkel did not bat.

Hira 2–0–20–0; Bates 3–0–29–0; Franklin 2–0–23–1; Southee 4–0–22–2; Bracewell 4–0–28–1; N. L. McCullum 2–0–22–0; Nicol 3–0–20–2.

New Zealand

		B	4	6
R. J. Nicol *c 1 b 11*	33	19	5	1
M. J. Guptill *c 2 b 7*	26	19	3	1
J. D. Ryder *c 11 b 7*	52	42	5	2
*†B. B. McCullum *c 4 b 9*	18	19	1	1
K. S. Williamson *c 3 b 11*	6	9	0	0
J. E. C. Franklin *not out*	9	8	0	0
N. L. McCullum *c 4 b 10*	0	2	0	0
D. A. J. Bracewell *c 2 b 10*	0	2	0	0
T. G. Southee *not out*	0	1	0	0
L-b 5, w 12, n-b 1	18			
6 overs: 65-1 (20 overs)	162-7			

1/65 2/73 3/112 4/142 5/158 6/160 7/160

M. D. Bates and R. M. Hira did not bat.

Peterson 4–0–34–1; de Lange 4–0–36–2; J. A. Morkel 1–0–13–0; M. Morkel 4–0–31–2; Botha 4–0–20–2; Parnell 1–0–14–0; Duminy 2–0–9–0.

Umpires: G. A. V. Baxter and C. B. Gaffaney. Third umpire: B. G. Frost.
Series referee: R. S. Mahanama.

NEW ZEALAND v SOUTH AFRICA

First One-Day International

At Wellington (Westpac Stadium), February 25, 2012 (day/night). South Africa won by six wickets. Toss: New Zealand.

New Zealand squandered a promising start in the face of aggressive bowling by South Africa, who refused to go on the defensive, even when their hosts were 137 for two with 20 overs to go. Kallis suckered Brendon McCullum into thrashing a catch to deep cover and did much the same with Ryder, caught at deep square leg. Those wickets changed the course of the innings, which fizzled out. The game caught alight again, briefly, with three wickets at the start of South Africa's run-chase, but McCullum later admitted he had been guilty of backing off and allowing his fellow captain (and keeper) de Villiers to play himself in without pressure. Dabs to third man were the feature of de Villiers's innings, despite four sixes. His single-taking was as brilliant as it was infuriating. The result was emphatic, with du Plessis clubbing a weary attack in the pressure-free closing overs.

Man of the Match: A. B. de Villiers.

New Zealand

R. J. Nicol c Kallis b Peterson	30	K. D. Mills not out	4
M. J. Guptill c de Villiers b Tsotsobe	7	T. G. Southee not out	4
*†B. B. McCullum c Peterson b Kallis	56		
K. S. Williamson c de Villiers b Tsotsobe	55	B 4, l-b 10, w 7, n-b 3	24
J. D. Ryder c Smith b Kallis	6		
J. E. C. Franklin c Amla b M. Morkel	32	1/25 (2) 2/58 (1) (9 wkts, 50 overs)	253
A. M. Ellis b Steyn	20	3/137 (3) 4/153 (5)	
N. L. McCullum b M. Morkel	15	5/194 (4) 6/211 (6) 7/230 (7)	
D. A. J. Bracewell st de Villiers b Peterson	0	8/234 (9) 9/249 (8)	10 overs: 38-1

Tsotsobe 10–1–41–2; M. Morkel 9–0–49–2; Steyn 9–0–37–1; Peterson 10–1–45–2; Duminy 5–0–22–0; Kallis 7–0–45–2.

South Africa

H. M. Amla b Southee	8	F. du Plessis not out	66
G. C. Smith c Ryder b Mills	9	L-b 1, w 5	6
J. H. Kallis c Williamson b Bracewell	13		
J-P. Duminy c and b Nicol	46	1/17 (1) 2/17 (2) (4 wkts, 45.2 overs)	254
*†A. B. de Villiers not out	106	3/35 (3) 4/125 (4)	10 overs: 36-3

J. A. Morkel, R. J. Peterson, D. W. Steyn, M. Morkel and L. L. Tsotsobe did not bat.

Mills 7–0–27–1; Southee 10–0–64–1; Bracewell 10–1–61–1; N. L. McCullum 7–0–25–0; Nicol 5–0–43–1; Ellis 5–0–26–0; Franklin 1–0–5–0; Williamson 0.2–0–2–0.

Umpires: C. B. Gaffaney and R. K. Illingworth. Third umpire: Aleem Dar.

NEW ZEALAND v SOUTH AFRICA

Second One-Day International

At Napier, February 29, 2012 (day/night). South Africa won by six wickets. Toss: South Africa.

New Zealand were delighted by de Villiers's decision to bowl on a perfect pitch at the country's highest-scoring ground. But their wastefulness four days earlier was nothing compared to this. They were 131 for one in the 25th over; 300 seemed not just possible, but likely. Then the wily Kallis removed Guptill, the skilful Tsotsobe claimed the next two, and the brutal Morne Morkel collected the last five for a career-best. Steyn was just as important; it was a mystery that he dismissed only Ryder – albeit for a second-ball duck. Also instrumental was the captaincy of de Villiers, who held his nerve against the measured, potentially dangerous early batting of Guptill and McCullum. He never opted for containment, deploying at least one strike bowler and at least one extra fielder in the 30-metre circle at all times. Amla was denied a century by a cunning deception from leg-spinner Nethula, who was New Zealand's only bright spot but unflattered by his figures.

Man of the Match: M. Morkel.

New Zealand

R. J. Nicol lbw b Tsotsobe	11
M. J. Guptill c de Villiers b Kallis	58
*†B. B. McCullum c Ontong b Tsotsobe	85
K. S. Williamson c Kallis b Tsotsobe	13
J. D. Ryder c de Villiers b Steyn	0
J. E. C. Franklin b M. Morkel	6
A. M. Ellis c Steyn b M. Morkel	19
K. D. Mills c Peterson b M. Morkel	0
T. G. Southee c Steyn b M. Morkel	28
T. S. Nethula c de Villiers b M. Morkel	0
A. J. McKay not out	0
L-b 5, w 5	10
1/24 (1) 2/131 (2) 3/163 (4) 4/175 (3) 5/179 (5) 6/184 (6) 7/184 (8) 8/221 (9) 9/221 (10) 10/230 (7) — (47.3 overs)	230
10 overs: 47-1	

Tsotsobe 10–0–43–3; Steyn 10–1–37–1; M. Morkel 9.3–1–38–5; J. A. Morkel 3–0–30–0; Peterson 8–0–43–0; Kallis 6–0–32–1; Duminy 1–0–2–0.

South Africa

H. M. Amla c McCullum b Nethula	92
J. H. Kallis c McCullum b Mills	4
F. du Plessis c Guptill b Ellis	34
J-P. Duminy c and b Nethula	43
*†A. B. de Villiers not out	31
J. L. Ontong not out	17
B 2, l-b 2, w 6	10
1/11 (2) 2/80 (3) 3/167 (4) 4/192 (1) — (4 wkts, 38.2 overs)	231
10 overs: 63-1	

J. A. Morkel, R. J. Peterson, D. W. Steyn, M. Morkel and L. L. Tsotsobe did not bat.

Mills 6.2–1–41–1; Southee 8–0–61–0; McKay 10–1–45–0; Ellis 3–0–16–1; Nethula 10–0–60–2; Nicol 1–0–4–0.

Umpires: Aleem Dar and G. A. V. Baxter. Third umpire: R. K. Illingworth.

NEW ZEALAND v SOUTH AFRICA

Third One-Day International

At Auckland, March 3, 2012 (day/night). South Africa won by five wickets. Toss: South Africa. One-day international debuts: C. de Grandhomme; M. de Lange.

South Africa's thumping wins in the previous two games at least contained moments of suspense. Not this time. New Zealand coach John Wright admitted his team were distracted by the banning of Jesse Ryder and Doug Bracewell, who had become involved in an altercation with a man in a bar – though their technical breach of team etiquette had been to drink alcohol while injured. It was the latest disciplinary indiscretion of Ryder's troubled career. New Zealand's batting was anaemic and lacked belief or intent, quite the opposite of Marchant de Lange's bowling, which exploded with youthful ferocity and manful pace. Brendon McCullum, the only senior batsman, seemed overburdened by the responsibility and never managed to break the shackles. In his first 50-over international, the Zimbabwe-born Colin de Grandhomme briefly illustrated his ball-striking ability. Amla made certain there were no wobbles chasing a junior total, and Albie Morkel's aggressive 41 stopped him wondering why he was on the tour. But as a contest, the match never started.

Man of the Match: M. de Lange.

New Zealand

R. J. Nicol c de Villiers b Botha	12
M. J. Guptill c du Plessis b Tsotsobe	7
*†B. B. McCullum c du Plessis b de Lange	47
K. S. Williamson run out	22
J. E. C. Franklin c Amla b de Lange	36
C. de Grandhomme run out	36
N. L. McCullum c Amla b de Lange	10
A. M. Ellis c Amla b de Lange	2
K. D. Mills lbw b Peterson	5
M. D. Bates lbw b Peterson	13
A. J. McKay not out	2
L-b 3, w 10, n-b 1	14
1/13 (2) 2/45 (1) 3/74 (3) 4/105 (4) 5/160 (6) 6/169 (5) 7/171 (8) 8/189 (7) 9/195 (9) 10/206 (10) — (47 overs)	206
10 overs: 29-1	

Tsotsobe 9–2–36–1; Steyn 7–2–28–0; de Lange 9–1–46–4; Peterson 10–1–36–2; Botha 7–0–28–1; Parnell 4–0–18–0; Duminy 1–0–11–0.

South Africa

H. M. Amla c B. B. McCullum b Mills	76	J. Botha not out	5
W. D. Parnell b Ellis	27	L-b 2, w 3, n-b 1	6
J. A. Morkel c de Grandhomme b Bates	41		——
F. du Plessis lbw b Nicol	19	1/80 (2) 2/138 (1) (5 wkts, 43.2 overs)	208
J-P. Duminy b Nicol	25	3/155 (3) 4/188 (4)	
*†A. B. de Villiers not out	9	5/195 (5) 10 overs: 57-0	

R. J. Peterson, D. W. Steyn, M. de Lange and L. L. Tsotsobe did not bat.

Mills 8–1–41–1; Bates 6–0–28–1; N. L. McCullum 10–0–35–0; McKay 8–0–40–0; Ellis 6–0–35–1; Nicol 3.2–0–14–2; de Grandhomme 1–0–9–0; Williamson 1–0–4–0.

Umpires: C. B. Gaffaney and R. K. Illingworth. Third umpire: Aleem Dar.
Series referee: R. S. Mahanama.

NEW ZEALAND v SOUTH AFRICA

First Test Match

At Dunedin (University Oval), March 7–11, 2012. Drawn. Toss: New Zealand. Test debuts: R. J. Nicol, C. F. K. van Wyk.

Rain washed out the final day of a compelling game. Set 401 in well over four sessions, New Zealand concluded the fourth evening on 137 for two with their marquee batsmen, McCullum and Taylor, well set. Talk about the possibilities was bold, but the reality was far less compelling. They required another 264 against a high-class attack. New Zealand deserved at least some hope, because of the apparent ease with which McCullum and Taylor had accumulated 82 in 21 overs. In truth, though, some of that hope stemmed from charity: South Africa had declared their second innings only five down.

On the first day, Martin's tried and trusted seam bowling had knocked the stuffing out of the tourists' first innings: the exalted trio of Smith, Kallis and de Villiers perished in the space of four deliveries from him, with Smith starting the stumble to 90 for four with a loose drive into a glaring trap at cover just after tea. But Rudolph showed the value of genuine class at No. 6, and South Africa scraped something presentable together, although it was at least 100 short of par.

When New Zealand reached 106 for two in reply, McCullum and Taylor should have steered them to something much better, but McCullum nudged a full toss back to leg-spinner Imran Tahir, and Taylor slashed outside off stump against the pace of Morkel. Vettori's elevation to No. 6 was under close scrutiny and, batting with his customary lower-order unorthodoxy, he so nearly made a difference. But Kallis launched a sustained, short-pitched attack, before diving forward to claim a low return catch as Vettori fended a lifter away from his ribcage. It was yet another example of the ageing Kallis's ability to manufacture the odd much-needed wicket, as opposed to the sporadic clumps he took in his youth.

Wicketkeeper Kruger van Wyk, called up two days before the Test because B-J. Watling had a sore hip, showed all the doughty resistance his former countrymen expected. Determined to play international cricket but unlikely to usurp Mark Boucher in South Africa, the diminutive van Wyk – born in maize-farming country in the North West Province – had emigrated six years earlier in search of brighter prospects. Now 32, he became the first to make his Test debut against the country of his birth since the Hollioake brothers, Adam and Ben, against Australia at Trent Bridge in 1997. On one internal flight, van Wyk (presumably because of his name) was inadvertently seated among his South African opponents.

New Zealand closed the second day with a fragile lead of five, and the hapless Martin at one end. Yet he doubled the lead on the third morning with a single stroke – a block-and-run to cover against Steyn, which would have led to his run-out by half the pitch if Petersen's throw had hit; instead it went to the boundary. Boult then delivered a frenzied attack on Philander's first over of the day, which yielded 22 – a trio of sixes and a four. Martin went next over, and the lead was still only 35, but it was a withering slap to South African faces.

Smith and Kallis restored order and dignity with a masterclass of accumulation for most of the third day. There was no special tactic, no bowler specifically targeted, no mistakes made and no chances offered – just patience, unforgiving punishment of the bad balls, and the systematic placing of their team in the ascendancy. Kallis's 42nd Test hundred took him past Ricky Ponting to second on the all-time list.

Rudolph's century, the third of the innings, was built of similar stuff, but owed more than a slice of luck to a let-off just before stumps. He had 12 when Aleem Dar's lbw decision in favour of Bracewell was overturned, after Virtual Eye showed the ball to have pitched fractionally outside leg stump. Rudolph was so convinced he was out that he started walking, but he was persuaded by Kallis to give it a go.

Smith's declaration equation included "strong possibilities of showers in the morning". In fact, it started raining on the fourth evening – and didn't stop.

Man of the Match: G. C. Smith.

Close of play: first day, South Africa 191-7 (Rudolph 46, Philander 4); second day, New Zealand 243-9 (Boult 8, Martin 0); third day, South Africa 268-3 (Kallis 107, Rudolph 13); fourth day, New Zealand 137-2 (McCullum 58, Taylor 48).

South Africa

*G. C. Smith c Nicol b Martin	53	– (2) b Bracewell	115
A. N. Petersen lbw b Boult	11	– (1) c Southee b Bracewell	25
H. M. Amla c Taylor b Vettori	62	– c Guptill b Bracewell	2
J. H. Kallis c Taylor b Martin	0	– c Nicol b Boult	113
A. B. de Villiers lbw b Martin	0	– (6) c McCullum b Williamson	29
J. A. Rudolph c Boult b Bracewell	52	– (5) not out	105
†M. V. Boucher run out	4	– not out	34
D. W. Steyn c Taylor b Bracewell	9		
V. D. Philander c Williamson b Martin	22		
M. Morkel not out	13		
Imran Tahir run out	10		
L-b 1, n-b 1	2	B 2, l-b 6, w 1, n-b 3	12
1/34 (2) 2/86 (1) 3/90 (4) 4/90 (5) (68.2 overs)	238	1/45 (1) (5 wkts dec, 140 overs)	435
5/156 (3) 6/161 (7) 7/179 (8)		2/47 (3) 3/247 (2)	
8/214 (9) 9/222 (6) 10/238 (11)		4/283 (4) 5/353 (6)	

Martin 18–2–56–4; Southee 10–1–40–0; Boult 8–0–58–1; Bracewell 16.2–2–52–2; Vettori 15–4–31–1; Nicol 1–1–0–0. *Second innings*—Martin 23–4–74–0; Boult 26–4–93–1; Bracewell 25–3–70–3; Southee 26–4–100–0; Vettori 32–5–65–0; Nicol 1–0–9–0; Williamson 7–4–16–1.

New Zealand

R. J. Nicol c Smith b Philander	6	– c Smith b Imran Tahir	19
M. J. Guptill b Morkel	16	– c de Villiers b Philander	6
B. B. McCullum c and b Imran Tahir	48	– not out	58
*L. R. P. L. Taylor c Boucher b Morkel	44	– not out	48
K. S. Williamson c Boucher b Philander	11		
D. L. Vettori c and b Kallis	46		
†C. F. K. van Wyk c Smith b Philander	36		
D. A. J. Bracewell b Steyn	25		
T. G. Southee c Smith b Philander	0		
T. A. Boult not out	33		
C. S. Martin c Amla b Steyn	5		
L-b 3	3	L-b 2, w 2, n-b 2	6
1/7 (1) 2/41 (2) 3/106 (3) (88.2 overs)	273	1/16 (2) (2 wkts, 41 overs)	137
4/116 (4) 5/135 (5) 6/188 (6)		2/55 (1)	
7/229 (7) 8/229 (9) 9/239 (8) 10/273 (11)			

Steyn 20.2–4–79–2; Philander 18–1–72–4; Morkel 18–5–52–2; Imran Tahir 24–6–55–1; Kallis 8–2–12–1. *Second innings*—Steyn 8–2–25–0; Philander 12–2–29–1; Morkel 9–2–33–0; Imran Tahir 8–2–33–1; Kallis 4–1–15–0.

Umpires: Aleem Dar and B. R. Doctrove. Third umpire: R. A. Kettleborough.
Referee: R. S. Mahanama.

NEW ZEALAND v SOUTH AFRICA

Second Test Match

At Hamilton, March 15–17, 2012. South Africa won by nine wickets. Toss: South Africa.

Only twice before had five wickets fallen on the same score during a Test innings, in 1945-46 and 1964-65. On those occasions too, the ignominy had belonged to New Zealand. The latest episode, on the first evening of this game, was astonishing by the standards of any era, yet there was nothing freakish or inexplicable about any of the dismissals: all rewarded classic fast bowling by Steyn and Philander. South Africa went on to win in two and a half days, but it was a peculiar contest: despite overwhelming their hosts, they never really landed another memorable punch after the five-for-nothing flurry on the first evening.

Marty Melville, AFP/Getty Images

In his sights: Vernon Philander sizes up the New Zealand batsmen at Hamilton.

McCullum and Taylor had displayed heaps of resilience in nursing their side to 133 for two on a nippy pitch and under overcast skies. There was always the feeling that a wicket could fall… but not five at once! It started with an uncontrolled pull from McCullum – hurried by Steyn's extra pace – to deep square leg. Taylor edged a lifter to slip, and Williamson went the same way seven balls later. Vettori was bowled by a snorting nip-backer from Philander, and Bracewell nicked his third delivery to Boucher. Within the space of 20 balls after tea the innings had collapsed from tentatively promising to utterly derelict. There was a distinct feeling that the result had been decided already.

That view was under serious threat on day two, however, when a magnificent morning spell from Gillespie reduced South Africa to 88 for six (Martin had already removed Smith, for the eighth time in Tests, the previous evening). But where the touring bowlers had attacked like sharks at the first drop of blood, the New Zealanders ran out of steam when confronted by the relentless (though appropriately subdued) skills of de Villiers. His outrageous talent was all but stripped of bells and whistles although, having calmed nerves in a stand of 63 with Boucher, he gently encouraged the tailenders to be themselves. Morkel responded with a notably controlled block–hit–hit–block 35 to give South Africa a lead of 68; it felt at least a hundred more.

Once again, the result seemed a foregone conclusion when Steyn and Philander claimed two each to leave New Zealand still three runs behind with six wickets left by the end of the second day. After 25 balls, at seven for three, a two-day Test had seemed possible.

MOST RUNS IN SUCCESSFUL FOURTH-INNINGS RUN-CHASES

Runs		*Inns*	*HS*	*Avge*
1,085	**G. C. Smith (South Africa)**	**20**	**154***	**90.41**
913	M. L. Hayden (Australia)	27	101*	57.06
911	**R. T. Ponting (Australia)**	**24**	**143***	**82.81**
850	C. G. Greenidge (West Indies)	23	214*	65.38
849	J. L. Langer (Australia)	23	127	49.94
809	D. L. Haynes (West Indies)	30	112*	67.41

In all Test fourth innings, Smith has scored 1,504 runs at 57.84, and is fourth on the list behind S. R. Tendulkar and R. Dravid, who have scored 1,590 and 1,575 in fourth innings for India, and S. Chanderpaul, with 1,518 for West Indies. Figures correct to December 31, 2012.

Shortly before the close, Taylor was lbw to a Steyn delivery which looked likely to miss leg stump, even on replay, yet his appeal to the third umpire was rejected on the evidence of Virtual Eye. The technology system's developer later admitted that poor light had compromised the data gathering, and suggested that the third umpire should use gut instinct in such cases. Taylor was phlegmatic: "Overall we're better with it than without it."

Williamson looked unperturbed, and there was still abstract hope of an extraordinary turnaround when New Zealand reached 141 for five just before lunch on the third day, a lead of 73. But it was very abstract: van Wyk fell an over before the break, and the remaining four wickets lasted just 29 balls after it. The extraordinary Philander claimed six in an innings for the first time in his six Tests, to finish with his second haul of ten in a match. His secret was simple: less is more. Whereas lavish swing and bounteous seam movement draw gasps of appreciation, smaller amounts induce more edges, hit stumps more often and earn more lbws. And when six out of six deliveries (rather than four or five) are asking similar but slightly different questions, batsmen are far more likely to come up with the wrong answers.

With just 101 required for victory, Smith was in his element. The most prolific scorer in the history of successful fourth-innings run-chases, he compiled his tenth such score of fifty-plus (including four hundreds). Whenever the debate surfaces about big-match temperament, this statistic should feature.

Man of the Match: V. D. Philander.

Close of play: first day, South Africa 27-2 (Petersen 8, Amla 2); second day, New Zealand 65-4 (Williamson 41, Vettori 0).

New Zealand

R. J. Nicol c Boucher b Philander	2	– b Philander	1
M. J. Guptill b Steyn	22	– c Amla b Steyn	1
B. B. McCullum c Rudolph b Steyn	61	– lbw b Philander	5
*L. R. P. L. Taylor c Smith b Philander	44	– lbw b Steyn	17
K. S. Williamson c Smith b Steyn	0	– c Boucher b Philander	77
D. L. Vettori b Philander	0	– c Boucher b Kallis	21
†C. F. K. van Wyk lbw b Morkel	21	– b Philander	20
D. A. J. Bracewell c Boucher b Philander	0	– b Morkel	0
M. R. Gillespie c Petersen b Imran Tahir	27	– c Boucher b Philander	14
B. J. Arnel lbw b Imran Tahir	3	– not out	8
C. S. Martin not out	0	– b Philander	0
L-b 3, n-b 2	5	L-b 4	4
1/11 (1) 2/44 (2) 3/133 (3) (61.2 overs)	185	1/1 (1) 2/7 (3) (67.5 overs)	168
4/133 (4) 5/133 (5) 6/133 (6)		3/7 (2) 4/64 (4) 5/99 (6)	
7/133 (8) 8/176 (7) 9/184 (9) 10/185 (10)		6/141 (7) 7/142 (5) 8/142 (8)	
		9/160 (9) 10/168 (11)	

Steyn 18–5–49–3; Philander 15–3–70–4; Kallis 9–4–9–0; Morkel 14–2–42–1; Imran Tahir 5.2–1–12–2. *Second innings*—Steyn 16–5–31–2; Philander 15.5–3–44–6; Morkel 13–5–26–1; Imran Tahir 17–2–52–0; Kallis 6–3–11–1.

South Africa

*G. C. Smith c van Wyk b Martin	13	– (2) not out	55
A. N. Petersen lbw b Gillespie	29	– (1) c van Wyk b Bracewell	1
D. W. Steyn c van Wyk b Martin	4		
H. M. Amla c Williamson b Gillespie	16	– (3) not out	46
J. H. Kallis c van Wyk b Gillespie	6		
A. B. de Villiers b Vettori	83		
J. A. Rudolph c van Wyk b Gillespie	1		
†M. V. Boucher b Gillespie	24		
V. D. Philander b Bracewell	14		
M. Morkel not out	35		
Imran Tahir c Gillespie b Williamson	16		
B 1, l-b 9, w 1, n-b 1	12	N-b 1	1
1/14 (1) 2/18 (3) 3/63 (4) 4/69 (5) 5/84 (2) 6/88 (7) 7/151 (8) 8/185 (9) 9/219 (6) 10/253 (11) (77.3 overs)	253	1/5 (1) (1 wkt, 19.5 overs)	103

Martin 16–6–38–2; Bracewell 18–7–50–1; Gillespie 15–2–59–5; Vettori 19–3–49–1; Arnel 9–2–46–0; Williamson 0.3–0–1–1. *Second innings*—Martin 3–1–18–0; Bracewell 5–0–14–1; Vettori 2–0–2–0; Gillespie 4–0–24–0; Arnel 3–0–18–0; Williamson 2–0–23–0; Nicol 0.5–0–4–0.

Umpires: B. R. Doctrove and R. A. Kettleborough. Third umpire: Aleem Dar.
Referee: R. S. Madugalle.

NEW ZEALAND v SOUTH AFRICA

Third Test Match

At Wellington (Basin Reserve), March 23–27, 2012. Drawn. Toss: New Zealand.

Near-apocalyptic weather in advance led even locals to predict a washout. In the event, the teams played the equivalent of four days – but New Zealand, and particularly Williamson, deserved considerable credit for batting out the final 81 overs for an honourable draw.

Petersen put a miserable two Tests behind him with a solid century and, if he had scored more rapidly, South Africa might even have won. But sodden conditions, grey skies and half a dozen breaks for rain – not to mention his own predicament – made life tricky. In the circumstances, his batting was solidity itself. Meanwhile, Amla suffered a horrendous blow when he edged a ball from Martin into his groin on 33; he was barely able to stagger from the field when, 30 runs later, he finally top-edged a hook. He was taken straight to hospital for emergency surgery on his scrotum.

Duminy seized his late chance after Kallis woke with a stiff neck. He made a century of sublime cover-drives interspersed with much less convincing hooks and pulls, and even those were admirable for his determination to tackle a reputed weakness against the short ball. Gillespie collected four late wickets to finish with burnished figures of six for 113, but they were well deserved, given his stamina and a painful cut on his left big toe. South Africa batted until after tea on the third day, and conventional wisdom suggested the match was doomed to be drawn. Still, there were more than 200 overs to play.

Flynn and Guptill reached 65 by the close with little bother, confirming the view that the contest would meander towards forgettability. But Philander and Steyn worked their way ruthlessly through the batting on day four – in spite of a pitch that was apparently improving rather than deteriorating – and Morkel broke Taylor's left arm; his next game would be as Morkel's team-mate with Delhi Daredevils three weeks later, though he missed the first three IPL matches. Inflicting the follow-on was South Africa's best chance, but at 263 for five – in effect, six – New Zealand required just a dozen runs and the draw seemed more certain than ever. Then three wickets fell at the same score. Gillespie was left with the task of adding 12 in the unlikely company of Martin, who managed to contribute a couple before Gillespie completed the job with consecutive fours, one nicked over first slip's head, the next inside-edged to fine leg.

Philander's extraordinary start to Test cricket had brought his 50th wicket – Bracewell – in his seventh match, the joint-second-fastest ever, behind Charlie Turner's six Tests in the 1880s. Among modern players, only Turner's fellow Australians Terry Alderman and Rodney Hogg had come close, with eight Tests apiece.

Smith and Petersen reached 75 at five an over by the close, and on the final morning the rate was upped to more than six thanks to de Villiers, who Twenty20'd his way to 68 from 49 deliveries, and Duminy. Smith delayed the declaration longer than anyone had predicted, until the lead was 388. The South Africans may have been keen to win 2–0, but not enough to allow New Zealand the tiniest scent of victory. "I didn't think they deserved any more," he said afterwards. "They batted conservatively and used up a lot of time. They didn't make much attempt to force the pace and win the game. I wasn't going to give them a chance."

MOST DISMISSALS IN ALL INTERNATIONAL CRICKET

		Tests	*ODIs*	*T20Is*
999 (953ct*, 46st)	**M. V. Boucher (South Africa/World/Africa)**	**555**	**425**	**19**
905 (813ct, 92st)	A. C. Gilchrist (Australia/World)	416	472	17
637 (519ct*, 118st)	**K. C. Sangakkara (Sri Lanka/World/Asia)**	**189**	**411**	**37**
628 (560ct, 68st)	I. A. Healy (Australia)	395	233	–
538 (430ct, 108st)	**M. S. Dhoni (India/Asia)**	**235**	**274**	**29**
479 (463ct, 16st)	R. W. Marsh (Australia)	355	124	–
477 (443ct*, 34st)	**B. B. McCullum (New Zealand)**	**185**	**251**	**41**
476 (450ct*, 26st)	P. J. L. Dujon (West Indies)	272	204	–
451 (422ct*, 29st)	A. J. Stewart (England)	277	174	–

* Boucher's figures include one catch when not keeping wicket; Sangakkara took 64, Dujon 2, McCullum 35 and Stewart 47 in the field. Figures correct to December 31, 2012.

As it happened, 81 overs should have been more than enough for South Africa to win. But a catch by Petersen at cover off Steyn was controversially denied by TV umpire Billy Doctrove to give Williamson his first life, on seven. He had another, on 22, courtesy of a rare error by de Villiers at second slip. But Williamson made the most of his luck to compile a second Test century, which was good enough even for Smith to note that it could be "career-defining". His fortitude was immense: he withstood relentless verbal intimidation from most of the fielders, while the fast bowlers seemed more interested in attracting the attention of the resident ambulance driver than the umpire.

Morkel, given the new ball by Smith on a hunch, responded with his best spell of the series. Bowling a fuller length than usual, he accounted for McCullum, Brownlie and Vettori with classic yorkers, and went on to become the first South African to claim the first six wickets in a Test innings since Ernie Vogler at Lord's in 1907. When Boucher caught Flynn, it was the 999th catch or stumping he had completed in international cricket (998 as wicketkeeper); but a freak eye injury at Taunton in July, on the first day of the tour of England, would force his retirement – and deprive him of 1,000.

South Africa's final chance was blown with ten overs to go when de Villiers dropped another catch, Bracewell on eight off de Lange. At seven down, with Taylor absent and only Gillespie and Martin to come, it would have been hard to deny the tourists, despite Williamson's obduracy.

Man of the Match: M. Morkel.

Close of play: first day, South Africa 136-2 (Petersen 44, Duminy 23); second day, South Africa 246-2 (Petersen 96, Duminy 76); third day, New Zealand 65-0 (Flynn 35, Guptill 28); fourth day, South Africa 75-0 (Petersen 38, Smith 34).

South Africa

*G. C. Smith c van Wyk b Bracewell	5	– (2) c Bracewell b Vettori	41
A. N. Petersen lbw b Martin	156	– (1) run out	39
H. M. Amla c van Wyk b Gillespie	63		
J-P. Duminy c Taylor b Gillespie	103	– not out	33
A. B. de Villiers b Martin	38	– (3) c Williamson b Bracewell	68
J. A. Rudolph c van Wyk b Gillespie	11		
†M. V. Boucher c Williamson b Gillespie	46		
D. W. Steyn c Guptill b Gillespie	0		
V. D. Philander c Flynn b Gillespie	29		
M. Morkel not out	10		
B 6, l-b 1, w 3, n-b 3	13	L-b 3, w 3, n-b 2	8
1/13 (1) 2/106 (3) (9 wkts dec, 148.4 overs)	474	1/77 (1) (3 wkts dec, 29.4 overs)	189
3/306 (4) 4/362 (2) 5/381 (5)		2/106 (2) 3/189 (3)	
6/388 (6) 7/404 (8) 8/459 (7) 9/474 (9)			

M. de Lange did not bat.

Martin 28–5–95–2; Bracewell 30–3–106–1; Gillespie 33.4–7–113–6; Vettori 42–11–98–0; Brownlie 2–0–20–0; Williamson 13–1–35–0. *Second innings*—Martin 10–0–44–0; Bracewell 6.4–0–47–1; Gillespie 6–0–55–0; Vettori 7–1–40–1.

New Zealand

D. R. Flynn c Boucher b Philander	45	– (2) c Boucher b Morkel	0
M. J. Guptill lbw b Philander	59	– (1) c Rudolph b Morkel	18
B. B. McCullum c Boucher b Steyn	31	– lbw b Morkel	0
*L. R. P. L. Taylor retired hurt	18		
K. S. Williamson c Boucher b Steyn	39	– (4) not out	102
D. G. Brownlie c Steyn b Philander	29	– (5) b Morkel	15
D. L. Vettori c Rudolph b Philander	30	– (6) b Morkel	0
†C. F. K. van Wyk c sub (Imran Tahir) b de Lange	7	– (7) c and b Morkel	39
D. A. J. Bracewell b Philander	0	– (8) not out	20
M. R. Gillespie c de Villiers b Philander	10		
C. S. Martin not out	2		
L-b 2, w 2, n-b 1	5	L-b 6	6
1/86 (1) 2/136 (3) 3/145 (2) (96 overs)	275	1/1 (2) (6 wkts, 80.4 overs)	200
4/219 (6) 5/242 (5) 6/263 (7) 7/263 (9)		2/1 (3) 3/32 (1)	
8/263 (8) 9/275 (10)		4/83 (5) 5/83 (6) 6/163 (7)	

In the first innings Taylor retired hurt at 160-3.

Steyn 23–8–41–2; Philander 22–4–81–6; Morkel 20–6–54–0; de Lange 21–1–74–1; Duminy 10–0–23–0. *Second innings*—Morkel 16.4–7–23–6; Philander 18.4–6–29–0; de Lange 17.2–4–77–0; Steyn 15–9–14–0; Duminy 13–2–51–0.

Umpires: Aleem Dar and R. A. Kettleborough. Third umpire: B. R. Doctrove.
Referee: R. S. Madugalle.

DOMESTIC CRICKET IN NEW ZEALAND, 2011-12

MARK GEENTY

Three of New Zealand's six provincial teams tasted success in 2011-12. The country's best nursery for international players, Northern Districts, claimed the Plunket Shield for the third time in six years; Auckland became the first side to retain the Twenty20 HRV Cup; and Central Districts won the 50-over Ford Trophy as Michael Mason's long career reached a dream ending.

The Plunket Shield points system was reformed, with the reward for an outright victory doubled to 12, and first-innings points replaced by up to eight bonus points for the first 110 overs of each first innings – a maximum of 20 rather than eight. Northern secured four outright wins, the same as Central, but six more batting points, which proved the crucial difference.

Northern Districts had six of New Zealand's 20 centrally contracted players, and plenty of experience beyond them, including the Marshall twins James and Hamish, seamer Brent Arnel and Scott Styris. Coached by former New Zealand all-rounder Grant Bradburn, they appointed three captains. Opening batsman Brad Wilson took the reins for the Plunket Shield, James Marshall for the Ford Trophy (in which they finished last), and Styris, now retired from international cricket and playing only limited-overs, for the Twenty20 side. After demolishing Wellington by an innings and 230 runs in round two of the Plunket Shield – the most emphatic win in their history – Northern never surrendered the lead. That victory, the defining moment of the season, featured two standout performances by Test players preparing to take on Australia: Tim Southee took seven for 37 in Wellington's first innings, and Kane Williamson was 284 when Northern declared at 608 for nine.

Central Districts remained contenders, despite a crippling injury toll among their young pace bowlers in the second half of the season, when Zimbabwean Kyle Jarvis proved a useful addition, collecting 31 wickets. Former Test batsman Mathew Sinclair was the leading run-scorer in the Plunket Shield with 809. Central managed to top the 50-over ladder with three wins and four washouts, and hosted Auckland (who had four wins) in the final at New Plymouth. This provided the feelgood story of the season as former New Zealand seamer Mason retired a winner. After taking three for 52, he blasted 41 off 19 balls to lead Central to their target with one delivery to spare, sparking a pitch invasion by his jubilant team-mates. Central's most notable achievement in the Twenty20 competition was Jamie How's 45-ball century against Wellington, a domestic record.

Auckland were the most consistent team, finishing third in the Plunket Shield and confirming their status as the country's 20-over specialists. They won seven of their ten preliminary matches in the HRV Cup, before beating Canterbury in the final, where New Zealand opener Martin Guptill hit 70 in 41 balls. He amassed 504 runs in all, and Auckland were also boosted by Azhar Mahmood, the Pakistani all-rounder with a British passport.

Canterbury slipped from defending Plunket Shield champions to last place, though they were Twenty20 finalists. George Worker, a tall left-hander, scored 680 first-class runs and contributed heavily in limited-overs cricket too.

Otago's best finish was third in the Ford Trophy. Hamish Rutherford, son of former Test captain Ken, scored three hundreds in his four first-class matches, and South African left-armer Neil Wagner, who qualified for New Zealand in April, was the leading Plunket Shield wicket-taker with 46, though none of his team-mates passed 17.

Wellington underachieved again: fourth in the Plunket Shield, fifth in the Ford Trophy and last in the HRV Cup. But their four-day campaign was solid enough, and they were title contenders until the final round. They lured Muttiah Muralitharan to play in the first half of the Twenty20 competition, but won only two of the five games he played – and none of those he didn't.

FIRST-CLASS AVERAGES, 2011-12

BATTING (500 runs)

	M	*I*	*NO*	*R*	*HS*	*100*	*Avge*	*Ct/St*
K. S. Williamson (*N. Districts & New Zealand*)	5	7	2	517	284*	2	103.40	7
†H. D. Rutherford (*Otago*)	4	7	0	607	239	3	86.71	4
C. de Grandhomme (*Auckland*)	8	12	3	631	125	3	70.11	11
†D. R. Flynn (*N. Districts & New Zealand*)	6	11	2	629	136	3	69.88	5
†L. J. Woodcock (*Wellington*)	9	14	4	641	100*	1	64.10	4
C. F. K. van Wyk (*C. Districts & New Zealand*)	10	16	4	761	131	2	63.41	26
M. S. Sinclair (*Central Districts*)	10	17	2	809	121	3	53.93	13
†J. E. C. Franklin (*Wellington*)	7	12	2	536	162	2	53.60	3
C. Cachopa (*Central Districts*)	10	15	1	667	151	3	47.64	7
G. J. Hopkins (*Auckland*)	9	13	2	523	130	2	47.54	31/1
S. J. Murdoch (*Wellington*)	9	16	1	578	103	2	38.53	5
S. L. Stewart (*Canterbury*)	9	17	2	571	61	0	38.06	2
†J. M. Brodie (*Wellington*)	9	16	1	569	210	2	37.93	8
C. D. Cumming (*Otago*)	10	18	1	638	129	1	37.52	3
†G. H. Worker (*Canterbury*)	10	20	1	680	120*	1	35.78	11
P. G. Fulton (*Canterbury*)	10	20	2	631	88	0	35.05	6
†T. W. M. Latham (*Canterbury*)	9	17	1	541	145	1	33.81	9
†J. A. F. Yovich (*Northern Districts*)	9	16	0	531	103	1	33.18	1
B. S. Wilson (*Northern Districts*)	10	17	0	550	85	0	32.35	7
G. D. Elliott (*Wellington*)	10	17	1	509	188*	1	31.81	8
J. A. H. Marshall (*Northern Districts*)	10	17	0	536	98	0	31.52	3

BOWLING (15 wickets)

	Style	*O*	*M*	*R*	*W*	*BB*	*5I*	*Avge*
V. D. Philander (*South Africa*)	RFM	101.3	19	325	21	6-44	2	15.47
M. J. Henry (*Canterbury*)	RFM	137.1	28	441	19	5-21	1	23.21
K. M. Jarvis (*C. Districts & Zimbabwe*)	RFM	230.2	41	773	32	5-58	2	24.15
B. J. Arnel (*N. Districts & New Zealand*)	RFM	318	77	901	36	5-13	2	25.02
M. D. Bates (*Auckland*)	LFM	186.2	49	453	18	4-37	0	25.16
C. S. Martin (*Auckland & New Zealand*)	RFM	228.3	57	636	25	6-26	1	25.44
G. W. Aldridge (*Northern Districts*)	RFM	247.2	49	726	28	6-41	1	25.92
T. A. Boult (*N. Districts & New Zealand*)	LFM	236.4	56	707	27	5-51	2	26.18
M. R. Gillespie (*Wellington & N. Zealand*)	RFM	300.1	55	1,077	41	6-41	5	26.26
N. Wagner (*Otago*)	LFM	369.3	81	1,211	46	7-46	3	26.32
J. M. McMillan (*Otago*)	RFM	154.3	39	464	17	4-51	0	27.29
K. Noema-Barnett (*Central Districts*)	RM	205	70	515	18	3-20	0	28.61
M. J. McClenaghan (*Auckland*)	LFM	194.1	44	603	21	8-23	2	28.71
W. M. Lonsdale (*Canterbury*)	LFM	291.4	65	930	32	6-53	1	29.06
I. G. Butler (*Otago*)	RFM	164	35	498	17	4-62	0	29.29
T. S. Nethula (*Central Districts*)	LBG	233	27	792	26	6-32	2	30.46
R. F. Badenhorst (*Central Districts*)	RFM	133.4	37	471	15	3-55	0	31.40
D. L. Vettori (*N. Districts & New Zealand*)	SLA	232.1	65	508	16	5-89	1	31.75
J. S. Patel (*Wellington*)	OB	327.4	95	833	24	5-39	1	34.70
Bhupinder Singh (*Auckland*)	OB	207.3	65	576	16	6-50	1	36.00
B. P. Martin (*Auckland*)	SLA	443.5	96	1,369	37	6-38	2	37.00
T. D. Astle (*Canterbury*)	LBG	299.2	30	1,189	31	4-43	0	38.35
S. C. Kuggeleijn (*Wellington*)	RFM	175	28	770	20	4-50	0	38.50
A. J. McKay (*Wellington*)	LFM	213	38	772	20	4-57	0	38.60
A. M. Ellis (*Canterbury*)	RFM	208.2	45	672	17	4-81	0	39.52

PLUNKET SHIELD, 2011-12

	Played	Won	Lost	Drawn	Bonus points Batting	Bonus points Bowling	Points	Net avge runs per wkt
Northern Districts	10	4	2	4	16	32	96	6.24
Central Districts	10	4	2	4	10	31	89	5.78
Auckland.	10	3	2	5	17	29	82	–0.53
Wellington	10	3	2	5	12	29	77	1.75
Otago	10	2	5	3	7	30	61	–5.35
Canterbury	10	1	4	5	15	30	57	–7.62

Outright win = 12pts. Bonus points were awarded as follows for the first 110 overs of each team's first innings: one batting point for the first 250 runs and then for 300, 350 and 400; one bowling point for the third wicket taken and then for the fifth, seventh and ninth. Net average runs per wicket is calculated by subtracting average runs conceded per wicket from average runs scored per wicket.

At Rangiora, November 7–10, 2011. **Otago won by six wickets. ‡Canterbury 420-9 dec** (R. J. Nicol 107) **and 61** (N. Wagner 5-33); **Otago 300-5 dec and 182-4**. *Otago 16pts, Canterbury 4pts. Otago declared behind after a wet third day, then skittled Canterbury for 61, with only Shanan Stewart reaching double figures.*

At Napier (Nelson Park), November 7–10, 2011. **Drawn. Central Districts 253 and 377-4** (J. M. How 187*); **‡Wellington 536-6 dec** (S. J. Murdoch 103, J. E. C. Franklin 162). *Central Districts 3pts, Wellington 7pts. James Franklin and Luke Woodcock (86*) added 198 for Wellington's sixth wicket.*

At Whangarei, November 7–9, 2011. **Auckland won by 19 runs. Auckland 260** (T. A. Boult 5-51) **and 139; ‡Northern Districts 136** (A. R. Adams 6-71) **and 244** (A. R. Adams 5-52). *Auckland 17pts, Northern Districts 4pts. Auckland wicketkeeper Gareth Hopkins held six catches in Northern Districts' first innings. Needing 264 to win, Northern reached 221-6 before Andre Adams took three wickets in five overs, finishing with 11-123.*

At Rangiora, November 14–17, 2011. **Drawn. ‡Canterbury 491-7 dec** (D. G. Brownlie 171) **and 243-9 dec** (G. H. Worker 120*); **Auckland 381** (M. J. Guptill 195*, C. de Grandhomme 117) **and 196-4**. *Canterbury 8pts, Auckland 5pts. Martin Guptill carried his bat through Auckland's first innings and put on 211 for the sixth wicket with Colin de Grandhomme. All four centuries in the game were career-bests.*

At Lincoln (Bert Sutcliffe Oval), November 14–16, 2011. **Central Districts won by an innings and seven runs. Otago 207** (T. S. Nethula 6-32) **and 63** (M. J. Mason 6-20); **‡Central Districts 277**. *Central Districts 17pts, Otago 4pts. Otago's last nine wickets tumbled for 34.*

At Lincoln (No. 3), November 14–16, 2011. **Northern Districts won by an innings and 230 runs. Wellington 162** (T. G. Southee 7-37) **and 216; ‡Northern Districts 608-9 dec** (K. S. Williamson 284*). *Northern Districts 20pts, Wellington 1pt. Tim Southee took Wellington's last six wickets in six overs on the opening day, before Kane Williamson made a maiden double-century and went on to the highest individual score for Northern Districts, in eight minutes under ten hours. He steered his team to their second-highest total, then added three wickets as they completed their biggest victory.*

At Lincoln (Bert Sutcliffe Oval), November 20–23, 2011. **Drawn. Auckland 357-7 dec** (T. G. McIntosh 104) **and 125** (J. S. Patel 5-39); **‡Wellington 233-5 dec** (L. J. Woodcock 100*) **and 86-5**. *Auckland 5pts, Wellington 3pts.*

At Rangiora, November 20–23, 2011. **Drawn. Central Districts 307** (C. F. K. van Wyk 131) **and 288-4 dec** (M. S. Sinclair 118*); **‡Canterbury 251-6 dec and 10-1**. *Canterbury 5pts, Central Districts 4pts.*

At Dunedin (University Oval), November 20–23, 2011. **Drawn. ‡Northern Districts 482-5 dec** (B-J. Watling 150); **Otago 210-7**. *Otago 1pt, Northern Districts 6pts.*

At Auckland (Colin Maiden Park), November 29–December 2, 2011. **Drawn. Central Districts 367** (K. Noema-Barnett 107) **and 367-6 dec** (P. J. Ingram 139, M. S. Sinclair 108*); **‡Auckland 447** (J. A. Raval 164, C. de Grandhomme 120*). *Auckland 7pts, Central Districts 6pts. De Grandhomme scored 120* in 100 balls.*

At Hamilton, November 29–December 2, 2011. **Northern Districts won by 241 runs. Northern Districts 169** (M. J. Henry 5-21) **and 436-9 dec** (H. J. H. Marshall 134); ‡**Canterbury 151** (B. J. Arnel 5-43) **and 213** (G. W. Aldridge 6-41). *Northern Districts 16pts, Canterbury 4pts. The Marshall twins, James (98) and Hamish, added 163 for the third wicket in Northern's second innings. The win put their side 12 points clear at the top of the table at the midsummer break.*

At Wellington, November 29–December 2, 2011. **Wellington won by 286 runs. Wellington 312** (N. Wagner 7-96) **and 371-7 dec** (J. E. C. Franklin 106*); ‡**Otago 242 and 155**. *Wellington 18pts, Otago 4pts. Neil Wagner followed up career-best figures by hitting 66* in 43 balls, with seven sixes and four fours – but finished on the losing side.*

At Rangiora, February 17–20, 2012. **Wellington won by five wickets. Canterbury 334** (R. A. Young 104; H. K. P. Boam 6-51) **and 144** (M. R. Gillespie 6-41); ‡**Wellington 201** (L. V. van Beek 5-42) **and 280-5** (J. M. Brodie 116). *Wellington 16pts, Canterbury 6pts. Canterbury led by 207 with nine second-innings wickets left, then collapsed as Mark Gillespie claimed a career-best, and Josh Brodie's highest score engineered victory.*

At Gisborne, February 17–20, 2012. **Northern Districts won by 65 runs. Northern Districts 309** (K. M. Jarvis 5-58) **and 280**; ‡**Central Districts 183 and 341** (M. S. Sinclair 121, C. F. K. van Wyk 110; T. A. Boult 5-69). *Northern Districts 18pts, Central Districts 4pts. Mathew Sinclair and Kruger van Wyk added 222 for the fifth wicket, but Central ultimately failed in their pursuit of 407.*

At Dunedin (University Oval), February 17–20, 2012. **Auckland won by four wickets. Otago 226** (M. J. McClenaghan 6-87) **and 170**; ‡**Auckland 242** (C. Munro 130) **and 155-6**. *Auckland 16pts, Otago 4pts. Colin Munro, whose previous best was 37, came in at 46-5 and hit 130 in 115 balls, with seven sixes and 12 fours.*

At Auckland (Colin Maiden Park) February 24–27, 2012. **Wellington won by seven wickets. Auckland 320** (M. R. Gillespie 5-67) **and 201** (M. R. Gillespie 5-72); ‡**Wellington 479** (J. M. Brodie 210, M. H. W. Papps 111; B. P. Martin 6-187) **and 43-3**. *Wellington 18pts, Auckland 3pts. Josh Brodie hit his maiden double-hundred and put on 236 for Wellington's first wicket with Michael Papps, while Mark Gillespie took ten in a match for the first time to set them on course for their third consecutive win.*

At Rangiora, February 24–27, 2012. **Northern Districts won by 134 runs. Northern Districts 197** (W. M. Lonsdale 6-53) **and 426-7 dec** (J. A. F. Yovich 103); ‡**Canterbury 121** (B. J. Arnel 5-13) **and 368** (D. L. Vettori 5-89). *Northern Districts 16pts, Canterbury 4pts. In addition to seven wickets, Daniel Vettori held six catches in the match, equalling the record for Northern Districts, who completed their third successive victory.*

At Queenstown, February 24–27, 2012. **Central Districts won by five wickets.** ‡**Otago 281-8 dec** (C. D. Cumming 129) **and 115**; **Central Districts 198-6 dec and 199-5**. *Central Districts 15pts, Otago 3pts.*

At Napier (McLean Park), March 2–5, 2012. **Central Districts won by six wickets. Auckland 234** (G. J. Hopkins 130) **and 248-9 dec** (K. M. Jarvis 5-80); ‡**Central Districts 143** (B. P. Martin 6-38) **and 341-4** (C. Cachopa 108). *Central Districts 16pts, Auckland 4pts.*

At Hamilton, March 2–5, 2012. **Drawn. Northern Districts 300-6 dec** (D. R. Flynn 113*) **and 239**; ‡**Otago 228-3 dec** (H. D. Rutherford 107) **and 308-5** (H. D. Rutherford 118). *Northern Districts 3pts, Otago 2pts. In his first first-class match of the season, Hamish Rutherford scored 107 in 96 balls, his maiden century, and then 118 in 120, but his team finished four runs short of victory.*

At Wellington, March 2–5, 2012. **Drawn. Canterbury 337 and 192-1 dec**; ‡**Wellington 188-1 dec** (S. J. Murdoch 101*) **and 217-7**. *Wellington 3pts, Canterbury 2pts.*

At Auckland (Colin Maiden Park), March 9–12, 2012. **Auckland won by an innings and 34 runs.** ‡**Otago 63** (M. J. McClenaghan 8-23) **and 250** (Bhupinder Singh 6-50); **Auckland 347-8 dec** (G. J. Hopkins 109*). *Auckland 17pts, Otago 3pts. Mitchell McClenaghan's figures of 17–10–23–8 were the best of the season, and the best for Auckland since 1929-30. Gareth Hopkins caught six in that innings, five off McClenaghan, then scored an unbeaten century.*

At Nelson (Saxton Oval), March 9–12, 2012. **Canterbury won by 178 runs.** ‡**Canterbury 420-9 dec** (T. W. M. Latham 145) **and 159-9 dec**; **Central Districts 283-5 dec** (C. Cachopa 151) **and 118**. *Canterbury 17pts, Central Districts 4pts. This was the first first-class match at the Saxton Oval, and gave visitors Canterbury their only win.*

At Wellington, March 9–12, 2012. **Drawn. Northern Districts 309 and 303** (D. R. Flynn 136); **‡Wellington 283 and 241-9**. *Wellington 5pts, Northern Districts 6pts. Bad light ended play with Wellington nine wickets down.*

At Auckland (Colin Maiden Park), March 18–21, 2012. **Drawn. Northern Districts 351-8 dec** (D. R. Flynn 123*); **‡Auckland 43-2 dec and 31-1**. *Auckland 3pts, Northern Districts 3pts.*

At Dunedin (University Oval), March 18–21, 2012. **Drawn. Canterbury 199** (R. A. Young 103*) **and 265-6 dec; ‡Otago 197 and 259-5**. *Otago 4pts, Canterbury 4pts. Otago were thwarted nine short of victory by bad light.*

At Wellington (Karori Park), March 18–21, 2012. **Drawn. ‡Wellington 501-6 dec** (G. D. Elliott 188*, L. Ronchi 111); **Central Districts 1-0**. *Wellington 4pts, Central Districts 2pts. Luke Ronchi hit 111 in 91 balls in the first first-class match at Karori Park.*

At Auckland (Colin Maiden Park), March 26–29, 2012. **Drawn. ‡Auckland 452-7 dec** (C. de Grandhomme 125) **and 271-4 dec** (T. G. McIntosh 142*, A. K. Kitchen 100); **Canterbury 363-6 dec and 189-4**. *Auckland 5pts, Canterbury 3pts. De Grandhomme and Munro (75) added 202 for Auckland's sixth wicket, making sure of maximum batting points, but their bowlers could not keep them in the title race. There was another double-century stand as Tim McIntosh and Anaru Kitchen put on 211 for Auckland's third wicket in their second innings.*

At Napier (Nelson Park), March 26–29, 2012. **Central Districts won by 252 runs. ‡Central Districts 342** (C. Cachopa 111, K. Noema-Barnett 105*) **and 323-4 dec; Northern Districts 244 and 169** (T. S. Nethula 5-57). *Central Districts 18pts, Northern Districts 4pts. Northern Districts lost the match but were already sure of the Plunket Shield after collecting enough bonus points to keep them ahead of Auckland – who were knocked into third place by Central's victory.*

At Dunedin (University Oval), March 26–29, 2012. **Otago won by an innings and 64 runs. Wellington 112** (N. Wagner 7-46) **and 343; ‡Otago 519-8 dec** (H. D. Rutherford 239). *Otago 20pts, Wellington 2pts. Wagner took seven wickets against Wellington for the second time in the season, improving his career-best again. This time he was on the winning side, after Hamish Rutherford scored a maiden double-hundred and put on 216 for Otago's sixth wicket with Derek de Boorder (92).*

CHAMPIONS

Plunket Shield

1921-22	Auckland
1922-23	Canterbury
1923-24	Wellington
1924-25	Otago
1925-26	Wellington
1926-27	Auckland
1927-28	Wellington
1928-29	Auckland
1929-30	Wellington
1930-31	Canterbury
1931-32	Wellington
1932-33	Otago
1933-34	Auckland
1934-35	Canterbury
1935-36	Wellington
1936-37	Auckland
1937-38	Auckland
1938-39	Auckland
1939-40	Auckland
1945-46	Canterbury
1946-47	Auckland
1947-48	Otago
1948-49	Canterbury
1949-50	Wellington
1950-51	Otago
1951-52	Canterbury
1952-53	Otago
1953-54	Central Districts
1954-55	Wellington
1955-56	Canterbury
1956-57	Wellington
1957-58	Otago
1958-59	Auckland
1959-60	Canterbury
1960-61	Wellington
1961-62	Wellington
1962-63	Northern Districts
1963-64	Auckland
1964-65	Canterbury
1965-66	Wellington
1966-67	Central Districts
1967-68	Central Districts
1968-69	Auckland
1969-70	Otago
1970-71	Central Districts
1971-72	Otago
1972-73	Wellington
1973-74	Wellington
1974-75	Otago

Shell Trophy

1975-76	Canterbury
1976-77	Otago
1977-78	Auckland
1978-79	Otago
1979-80	Northern Districts
1980-81	Auckland
1981-82	Wellington
1982-83	Wellington
1983-84	Canterbury
1984-85	Wellington
1985-86	Otago
1986-87	Central Districts
1987-88	Otago
1988-89	Auckland
1989-90	Wellington
1990-91	Auckland
1991-92	Central Districts Northern Districts
1992-93	Northern Districts
1993-94	Canterbury

1994-95	Auckland	*State Championship*		2007-08	Canterbury
1995-96	Auckland	2001-02	Auckland	2008-09	Auckland
1996-97	Canterbury	2002-03	Auckland		
1997-98	Canterbury	2003-04	Wellington	*Plunket Shield*	
1998-99	Central Districts	2004-05	Auckland	2009-10	Northern Districts
1999-2000	Northern Districts	2005-06	Central Districts	2010-11	Canterbury
2000-01	Wellington	2006-07	Northern Districts	2011-12	Northern Districts

Auckland have won the title outright 22 times, Wellington 20, Canterbury 16, Otago 13, Central Districts and Northern Districts 7. Central Districts and Northern Districts also shared the title once.

THE FORD TROPHY, 2011-12

50-over league plus knockout

	Played	*Won*	*Lost*	*No result*	*Bonus points*	*Points*	*Net run-rate*
Central Districts	8	3	1	4	2	22	0.53
Auckland	8	4	3	1	2	20	0.08
Otago	8	3	2	3	1	19	0.39
Canterbury	8	3	3	2	1	17	0.06
Wellington	8	3	4	1	1	15	0.10
Northern Districts	8	2	5	1	0	10	–0.93

Preliminary finals

1st v 2nd: Central Districts v Auckland – no result, but Central Districts qualified for the final by virtue of heading the table. **3rd v 4th:** Otago beat Canterbury by 12 runs. **Final play-off:** Auckland beat Otago by 73 runs.

Final

At New Plymouth, February 12, 2012. **Central Districts won by two wickets.** ‡**Auckland 282-8** (50 overs) (N. R. Parlane 106); **Central Districts 285-8** (49.5 overs) (R. J. Nicol 119). *In his last match before retirement, Michael Mason came in at 225-8 and smashed 41* in 19 deliveries; he and Marty Kain completed the win with one ball to spare. For the second year running, a century had not been enough to give Auckland the one-day trophy. Neal Parlane hit 106, and put on 111 for the fourth wicket with Gareth Hopkins (68* in 51 balls). After Mitchell McClenaghan reduced Central Districts to 35-3, Dean Robinson (63) and Kruger van Wyk (66) added 113. But it took Kain and Mason to secure the victory.*

HRV CUP, 2011-12

20-over league plus knockout

	Played	*Won*	*Lost*	*No result*	*Points*	*Net run-rate*
Auckland	10	7	2	1	30	0.77
Canterbury	10	6	2	2	28	1.13
Northern Districts	10	4	5	1	18	0.07
Otago	10	3	4	3	18	–0.31
Central Districts	10	3	5	2	16	–0.04
Wellington	10	2	7	1	10	–1.50

Final

At Auckland (Colin Maiden Park), January 22, 2012. **Auckland won by 44 runs. Auckland 196-5** (20 overs); ‡**Canterbury 152** (18.3 overs). *Auckland retained their title after Martin Guptill scored 70 in 41 deliveries; in reply, Canterbury slumped to 57-5 before Andrew Ellis gave them some respectability with 41 in 17 balls.*

PAKISTAN CRICKET, 2012

The placebo effect

OSMAN SAMIUDDIN

No death. No corruption scandal. No players banned. No players jailed. No ball-tampering uproar. No terror attack. No captaincy palaver. No bust-ups with the ICC. No major player disputes. No major administrative overhaul. No major catfight with another board. No Ijaz Butt. Could this really have been a year belonging to Pakistan?

For the first time since 2005, their cricket seemed to be at peace with itself. The year wasn't without issues, but it sure felt as if it had emerged from a long, dark tunnel in which Pakistan had seemed content just to be, to play, to survive, to move on. In short, it felt cathartic.

Unsurprisingly for those who see a correlation between stable administration and on-field results – nearly everyone else, in other words – Pakistan began the year with their most significant victory since 2005-06. Then, they had beaten

PAKISTAN IN 2012

	Played	*Won*	*Lost*	*Drawn/No result*
Tests	6	3	1	2
One-day internationals	18	7	10	1
Twenty20 internationals	16	9	7	–

JANUARY – FEBRUARY	3 Tests, 4 ODIs and 3 T20Is (h) (in UAE) v England 1 ODI (h) (in UAE) v Afghanistan	(page 273) (page 1048)
MARCH	Asia Cup (in Bangladesh)	(page 948)
APRIL		
MAY		
JUNE – JULY	3 Tests, 5 ODIs and 2 T20Is (a) v Sri Lanka	(page 1110)
AUGUST – SEPTEMBER	3 ODIs and 3 T20Is (h) (in UAE) v Australia	(page 1050)
SEPTEMBER – OCTOBER	World Twenty20 (in Sri Lanka)	(page 841)
NOVEMBER		
DECEMBER – JANUARY	3 ODIs and 2 T20Is (a) v India	(page 986)

For a review of Pakistan domestic cricket from the 2011-12 season, see page 1056.

an England side fresh from victory in one of the great modern Test series. In 2012, they beat England as Test cricket's top-ranked nation. In fact, they whitewashed them, at their surrogate home in the UAE, though in typically Pakistani fashion: a series won 3–0 could conceivably have been lost 2–1.

But it was fully deserved, a wondrous, fantastical performance and fitting reward for captain Misbah-ul-Haq in particular. Too bland, dull and colourless for many Pakistani tastes, he had calmly moulded players of a similar outlook and made them into a robust team. Saeed Ajmal was confirmed as the best spinner in world cricket, and Azhar Ali – who twice scored 157 – was a class act at first drop.

It was all the more reason to lament what followed. At the time, there were two ways of looking at the win against England: as the last, unexpected hurrah of a fine side; or as the beginning of a new and promising age. It soon became clear it was more likely to be the former. A crucial administrative gaffe had been made over previous years when, in negotiating Future Tours Programme commitments, the Pakistan Cricket Board came up with a 2012 schedule almost devoid of Tests.

After England, Pakistan played only one more Test series, in Sri Lanka – and that, too, nearly five months later. They lost. And then there was nothing, until a series in South Africa in February 2013. Other than 2008, when they famously played no Tests at all, their tally of six Tests was their fewest in a year since 2001. This was an old side at their core, and their tightness was bound to unwind through time and inactivity.

Predictably, they managed many more limited-overs contests, though results were far sketchier. Pakistan lost each of the three bilateral one-day series played entirely in 2012, though they won memorably in India, in a series that spilled into 2013, and lifted the Asia Cup for the first time in four attempts. And they were impressive at the World Twenty20, losing in the last four to hosts Sri Lanka. It was their sixth successive ICC tournament semi-final, a handy statistic, but not far from choking territory: they had won only one of those six tournaments. By this point, Misbah – who turned 38 in May – had already ceded Twenty20 leadership duties to Mohammad Hafeez; it was assumed he would do the same in 50-over cricket some time in 2013.

Off the field, it was tempting to see an Ijaz Butt-free year as a triumph. But in reality, any assessment of Zaka Ashraf, his successor as PCB chairman, required greater nuance. A battle-scarred former board official struck the right mood in likening Ashraf to homeopathic medicine: "You're not sure whether he's done any good or bad, or anything at all. He's like a placebo."

Prime among his gains would appear to be the partial resumption of ties with India. When Pakistan toured there at the end of the year to play two Twenty20s and three one-day internationals, it was the first bilateral engagement between the two in five cold years scarred by the Mumbai terror attacks. It was a real breakthrough, too, given the financial benefits of playing India. But how much was it Ashraf's doing, and how much simply part of a broader thaw between the two countries, compelled by politicians upon the BCCI in particular?

The much-discussed return of international cricket to Pakistan produced fewer results, though again there was little Ashraf could do. He got close with

Asif Hassan, AFP/Getty Images

On guard: the return of full international cricket to Pakistan remained elusive.

Bangladesh, only to be burned twice. The fault lay with the duplicitous approach of Bangladesh officials, not with the final decision or Ashraf's intent.

But when an international XI of retired, cast-off and Associate cricketers travelled to Karachi for two Twenty20s in October, it seemed like a minor triumph – except that the matches were the work of Dr Mohammad Ali Shah, a cricket-mad surgeon, patron and provincial sports minister. The PCB refused to sanction them. But they did allow use of the National Stadium and, once the matches passed by without incident and with huge, throbbing crowds, they pretended they'd been involved. That tour was preceded by six months by the visit of a British Universities side to Lahore (featuring several players of Pakistani descent), but they came without the blessing of either the ECB or MCC.

Soon the financial crunch of no home games (and no full India series in five years) will begin to bite. A senior PCB official believes a new broadcast deal in 2013, and revenues from the 2011 World Cup (which Pakistan didn't host, but for which they received a hosting-rights fee) are enough for two more years. Against this backdrop, the announcement of a fortnight-long Pakistan Super League (scheduled to start on March 26, 2013) took on greater significance. But in February, the PCB postponed the tournament, ostensibly to allow investors more time to buy the five franchises. The Federation of International Cricketers Associations, however, maintained that the PSL would pose "an unmanageable" security risk. The postponement struck a rare note of disruption in a year of relative sanity.

For the time being, at least, craziness has been loaned out to New Zealand Cricket.

PAKISTAN v AFGHANISTAN IN THE UAE, 2011-12

PAUL RADLEY

One-day international (1): Pakistan 1, Afghanistan 0

Two neighbours sharing cultural history and international exile met in Sharjah in February. For Pakistan, it was a warm-up for their one-day series against England; for Afghanistan, a more momentous occasion – their first 50-over international against an ICC Full Member, following 18 against Associates. Each side could claim Sharjah as their surrogate home, but there was little doubt it was the Afghan expats making up the majority of the 15,000 crowd who had flooded in after Friday prayers. They came bearing flags, horns, bagpipes and life-size posters of President Hamid Karzai, and their players initially responded with brio. But Pakistan proved too adept, too experienced and simply too good. The Taliban, who had long since tolerated men's cricket in Afghanistan, sent a message of support to the team on the morning of the game.

PAKISTAN v AFGHANISTAN

One-Day International

At Sharjah, February 10, 2012 (day/night). Pakistan won by seven wickets. Toss: Afghanistan. One-day international debut: Hamza Hotak.

Pakistan found they were no longer the only show in town, as Afghans flocked to the Sharjah Stadium to watch their country's maiden one-day international against a Full Member – but the more polished side brought down the curtain with nearly 13 overs to spare. Karim Sadiq gave Afghanistan a rousing start with 40 off 47 balls, including two sixes, and Mohammad Shahzad, the rambunctious wicketkeeper-batsman, reverse-swept another off Saeed Ajmal's third ball – the same bowler who had tied England in knots in the Test series. Mohammad Nabi, who plays his cricket like a lesser Shahid Afridi, hit the man himself into the top tier of the main stand. But after taking Afghanistan to 147 for five in the 35th over, Nabi was run out from midwicket after backing up too far, in effect ending any hopes of a surprise win. Afridi picked up his third five-for in six one-day internationals, which hastened Afghanistan's capitulation and moved him past Anil Kumble into second among spinners in the list of one-day international wicket-takers, with 338 to Muttiah Muralitharan's 534. Younis Khan put on 99 with Misbah-ul-Haq as Pakistan coasted home.

Man of the Match: Shahid Afridi.

Afghanistan

Karim Sadiq c Umar Akmal b Shahid Afridi	40
Noor Ali Zadran c and b Umar Gul	9
†Mohammad Shahzad c Asad Shafiq b Shahid Afridi	20
*Nawroz Mangal b Shahid Afridi	11
Mohammad Nabi run out	37
Gulbadeen Naib lbw b Shahid Afridi	7
Samiullah Shenwari lbw b Umar Gul	32
Mirwais Ashraf lbw b Shahid Afridi	12
Dawlat Zadran b Wahab Riaz	12
Hamza Hotak c Umar Akmal b Wahab Riaz	0
Shapoor Zadran not out	2
B 4, l-b 5, w 4	13
1/23 (2) 2/54 (3) 3/71 (4) 4/88 (1) 5/101 (6) 6/147 (5) 7/165 (8) 8/193 (9) 9/193 (7) 10/195 (10) (48.3 overs)	195
10 overs: 58-2	

Umar Gul 8–0–30–2; Wahab Riaz 9.3–1–37–2; Saeed Ajmal 10–1–32–0; Shahid Afridi 10–0–36–5; Mohammad Hafeez 7–1–28–0; Shoaib Malik 4–0–23–0.

Pakistan

Mohammad Hafeez b Dawlat Zadran	8
Imran Farhat c and b Samiullah Shenwari	52
Asad Shafiq lbw b Dawlat Zadran	20
Younis Khan not out	70
*Misbah-ul-Haq not out	40
L-b 1, w 5, n-b 2	8
1/9 (1) 2/42 (3) (3 wkts, 37.1 overs)	198
3/99 (2) 10 overs: 42-2	

†Umar Akmal, Shahid Afridi, Shoaib Malik, Saeed Ajmal, Umar Gul and Wahab Riaz did not bat.

Shapoor Zadran 8–1–49–0; Dawlat Zadran 9–2–38–2; Mirwais Ashraf 5–0–27–0; Karim Sadiq 2–0–10–0; Hamza Hotak 4–0–22–0; Mohammad Nabi 5.1–0–29–0; Samiullah Shenwari 4–0–22–1.

Umpires: Shozab Raza and S. J. A. Taufel. Third umpire: Ahsan Raza.
Referee: J. J. Crowe.

PAKISTAN v AUSTRALIA IN THE UAE, 2012-13

OSMAN SAMIUDDIN

One-day internationals (3): Pakistan 1, Australia 2
Twenty20 internationals (3): Pakistan 2, Australia 1

When this limited-overs series was first mooted, three years previously, only one thing seemed clear: it could not possibly be held in the United Arab Emirates in the summer months, when temperatures exceed 40°C, and the oppressive humidity defies analogy. Oh yes it could!

Australia were concerned, with some justification, about playing 50-over games in this heat. But Pakistan had nowhere else to go once Sri Lanka pulled out because the dates clashed with the launch of their Twenty20 league; and Malaysia was ruled out because of an underdeveloped stadium infrastructure.

There were brief suggestions of a tour comprising Twenty20 games only, thus allowing the matches to be played in the cooler evenings. More palatable to broadcasters, though, was the decision to push back the start times of the one-day internationals. Drinks breaks and ice vests were added; Australia's board and players' union sent a fact-finding team. Finally, a month before the start, the plan was confirmed. This, though, left a different concern. A tour made up of three one-day internationals and three Twenty20s – the Test leg was scheduled for 2014 – revealed the paradox of the modern calendar: both jam-packed and unfulfilling.

Yet by the time the final Twenty20 game ended – a dead rubber on a weekday night that almost filled out the stadium in Dubai – the tour had gone better than anyone could have hoped. Primarily this was because the matches were close enough to excite spectators. Four of the six games stayed alive – flirting here, teasing there – before turning on a missed catch, a review not taken, a small misjudgment. It was about right that, while Australia won the one-day series 2–1, Pakistan should prevail by the same margin in the Twenty20s.

Two bowlers shone. Mitchell Starc, Australia's tall left-arm seamer, took nine wickets in the one-day internationals at 15, and conceded less than four an over in his two Twenty20s. And the Pakistan off-spinner Saeed Ajmal continued his love affair with the Middle East, collecting ten one-day wickets at under ten apiece, and six at eight in the Twenty20 matches.

With the games tight, the heat actually garnished the spectacle. Cricket is often derided for not being physically taxing. But here the exertion was clear – in sweaty, kilogram-shedding, high definition. The abiding image was of Mike Hussey, no doubt fit enough to complete a triathlon before play, on his haunches between every delivery during the Abu Dhabi one-dayer, desperately drawing breath.

Because of the 6pm starts, the one-day internationals ended well past 1am, so that they were, technically, two-day games. The match in Abu Dhabi even spanned two months, starting in August and finishing in September.

AUSTRALIAN TOURING PARTY

*M. J. Clarke, G. J. Bailey, D. T. Christian, X. J. Doherty, C. J. Ferguson, D. J. Hussey, M. E. K. Hussey, M. G. Johnson, A. C. McDermott, G. J. Maxwell, J. L. Pattinson, S. P. D. Smith, M. A. Starc, M. S. Wade, D. A. Warner. *Coach:* J. M. Arthur.

C. J. McKay was originally selected, but injured a hamstring shortly before the tour and was replaced by McDermott. For the Twenty20 series that followed the one-day internationals, McKay (fit again), P. J. Cummins, B. W. Hilfenhaus, G. B. Hogg, S. R. Watson and C. L. White replaced Clarke, Ferguson, Johnson, Pattinson and Smith; Bailey took over as captain. S. J. Rixon took charge of coaching for the one-day internationals, while Arthur prepared for the World Twenty20.

Note: For Australia's one-day international against Afghanistan at Sharjah, see page 1215.

PAKISTAN v AUSTRALIA

First One-Day International

At Sharjah, August 28, 2012 (day/night). Australia won by four wickets. Toss: Pakistan.

Australia don't play spin well, went the thinking, something even Clarke agreed with. But the failing had not often proved terminal: coming into this series, they had lost only one bilateral series in Asia since 1992. So it was here. Chasing 199 on an icky-sticky wicket, Australia slipped to 67 for four against the slow men. But they found a way through, thanks mainly to the fluid Clarke. The chase was finished off by Bailey, whose position as Twenty20 captain – and place in the side itself – was under debate. Pakistan needed a few more runs: had they batted with any sense after Umar Akmal and Asad Shafiq put on a sprightly 61, they might have got them. But a spate of unthinking shots, and incisive stuff from the frighteningly good Starc, meant they lost their last six for 38.

Man of the Match: M. A. Starc.

Pakistan

Mohammad Hafeez c D. J. Hussey b Pattinson	4
Nasir Jamshed c Wade b Starc	23
Azhar Ali c Johnson b Pattinson	5
Asad Shafiq b Starc	56
*Misbah-ul-Haq b Christian	26
Umar Akmal c Bailey b Starc	52
†Kamran Akmal c Clarke b Starc	4
Shahid Afridi c Clarke b Starc	0
Sohail Tanvir c D. J. Hussey b Johnson	1
Saeed Ajmal b Pattinson	8
Aizaz Cheema not out	2
L-b 13, w 4	17
1/20 (1) 2/28 (3) 3/40 (2) 4/99 (5) 5/160 (4) 6/174 (7) 7/175 (8) 8/180 (6) 9/184 (9) 10/198 (10) (45.1 overs)	198
10 overs: 40-3	

Pattinson 9.1–0–19–3; Starc 10–2–42–5; Clarke 3–0–8–0; D. J. Hussey 2–0–9–0; Johnson 9–0–43–1; Christian 8–0–37–1; Maxwell 4–0–27–0.

Australia

D. A. Warner b Mohammad Hafeez	5
†M. S. Wade c Misbah-ul-Haq b Shahid Afridi	10
*M. J. Clarke lbw b Mohammad Hafeez	66
M. E. K. Hussey lbw b Saeed Ajmal	5
D. J. Hussey c Misbah-ul-Haq b Saeed Ajmal	3
G. J. Bailey not out	57
G. J. Maxwell lbw b Saeed Ajmal	38
D. T. Christian not out	3
B 1, l-b 5, w 6	12
1/13 (1) 2/42 (2) 3/57 (4) 4/67 (5) 5/121 (3) 6/184 (7) (6 wkts, 48.2 overs)	199
10 overs: 40-1	

M. G. Johnson, J. L. Pattinson and M. A. Starc did not bat.

Sohail Tanvir 8–0–47–0; Mohammad Hafeez 10–1–29–2; Aizaz Cheema 7.2–0–38–0; Shahid Afridi 10–0–37–1; Saeed Ajmal 10–0–30–3; Azhar Ali 3–0–12–0.

Umpires: B. F. Bowden and Zameer Haider. Third umpire: N. J. Llong.
Referee: J. Srinath.

PAKISTAN v AUSTRALIA

Second One-Day International

At Abu Dhabi, August 31, 2012 (day/night). Pakistan won by seven wickets. Toss: Australia.

It had been a long time since Pakistan had a group of young batsmen as promising as their current crop, and two of them ensured a surprisingly comfortable triumph on a ridiculously humid night. Nasir Jamshed and Azhar Ali paved the way with a stand of 101 in 16 overs, with Jamshed going on to a bullying, imposing 97. He had been around the national set-up for four years, but recently had become far more expansive, particularly through the leg side (though he remained prone to injury and fitness issues). Azhar gave considered support, and the target never looked out of reach. Australia's innings had been typically Australian, with every run on offer taken; predictably, Mike Hussey was at its heart. A late flurry from the lower order added some gloss, but Pakistan always had an element of control in the shape of Saeed Ajmal.

Man of the Match: Nasir Jamshed.

Australia

†M. S. Wade b Junaid Khan	7	M. G. Johnson b Junaid Khan	2
D. A. Warner lbw b Saeed Ajmal	24	J. L. Pattinson not out	2
*M. J. Clarke lbw b Mohammad Hafeez	37	M. A. Starc not out	11
M. E. K. Hussey b Saeed Ajmal	61		
D. J. Hussey lbw b Saeed Ajmal	0	L-b 9, w 5, n-b 5	19
G. J. Bailey c and b Abdur Rehman	39		
G. J. Maxwell st Kamran Akmal b Saeed Ajmal	28	1/8 (1) 2/74 (2) 3/86 (3) 4/87 (5) (9 wkts, 50 overs)	248
D. T. Christian c Nasir Jamshed b Junaid Khan	18	5/153 (6) 6/211 (4) 7/214 (7) 8/235 (8) 9/235 (9)	10 overs: 44-1

Sohail Tanvir 9–0–59–0; Junaid Khan 9–0–52–3; Mohammad Hafeez 10–1–28–1; Abdur Rehman 10–0–54–1; Saeed Ajmal 10–0–32–4; Azhar Ali 2–0–14–0.

Pakistan

Mohammad Hafeez c M. E. K. Hussey b Christian	23	*Misbah-ul-Haq not out	35
Nasir Jamshed c Starc b Johnson	97	L-b 6, w 20	26
Azhar Ali not out	59	1/66 (1) 2/167 (2) (3 wkts, 43.4 overs)	249
Asad Shafiq b Pattinson	9	3/190 (4)	10 overs: 53-0

Umar Akmal, †Kamran Akmal, Sohail Tanvir, Abdur Rehman, Saeed Ajmal and Junaid Khan did not bat.

Pattinson 8–0–46–1; Starc 7.5–0–43–0; Johnson 9–0–51–1; Christian 8–0–40–1; Maxwell 4.4–0–37–0; Clarke 3.1–0–12–0; M. E. K. Hussey 1–0–8–0; D. J. Hussey 2–0–6–0.

Umpires: Ahsan Raza and N. J. Llong. Third umpire: B. F. Bowden.
Referee: R. S. Mahanama.

PAKISTAN v AUSTRALIA

Third One-Day International

At Sharjah, September 3, 2012 (day/night). Australia won by three wickets. Toss: Australia.

In years to come the full effects of an untaken review ought to be examined, in terms not only of the result but the impact on the side not taking it. Saeed Ajmal had just claimed the crucial wicket of Clarke in the 18th over of Australia's chase, and in came Mike Hussey. He was trapped plumb in front fourth ball, but Billy Bowden turned down the appeal, and Pakistan – excitable and unreliable with reviews – decided not to challenge his decision. It would cost them, even though Ajmal dismissed David Hussey and Bailey soon after. But the senior Hussey steadied himself and advanced to 65, before a whirlwind innings from Maxwell – 56 not out from 38 balls, ending with the match-clinching six off Junaid Khan – sealed another tight win and the series. Again, Pakistan wondered how they hadn't scored more, especially given the platform laid by Mohammad Hafeez and Nasir Jamshed; again, they had to conclude that their own rashness and Starc's energy had combined to deny them. Abdur Rehman, who had not been picked for the upcoming Twenty20 matches, flew through the night to England to play on what was now the same day for Somerset in a County Championship match at Hove.

Man of the Match: M. E. K. Hussey. *Man of the Series:* M. A. Starc.

Pakistan

Mohammad Hafeez lbw b Clarke	78
Nasir Jamshed c Wade b Johnson	48
Shahid Afridi c Maxwell b Johnson	7
Asad Shafiq c Bailey b Starc	27
*Misbah-ul-Haq c Warner b Starc	25
Umar Akmal c D. J. Hussey b Starc	0
Azhar Ali not out	27
†Kamran Akmal b Starc	2
Abdur Rehman not out	12
B 4, l-b 1, w 13	18
1/129 (2) 2/140 (3) 3/155 (1) 4/185 (4) 5/185 (6) 6/220 (5) 7/223 (8) (7 wkts, 50 overs)	244
10 overs: 36-0	

Saeed Ajmal and Junaid Khan did not bat.

Pattinson 10–1–50–0; Starc 10–0–51–4; Johnson 9–0–33–2; Maxwell 7–0–33–0; Christian 10–0–55–0; D. J. Hussey 2–0–14–0; Clarke 2–0–3–1.

Australia

D. A. Warner c sub (Shoaib Malik) b Abdur Rehman	21
D. J. Hussey c Abdur Rehman b Saeed Ajmal	43
*M. J. Clarke st Kamran Akmal b Saeed Ajmal	32
M. E. K. Hussey b Junaid Khan	65
G. J. Bailey c Kamran Akmal b Saeed Ajmal	1
†M. S. Wade b Abdur Rehman	22
G. J. Maxwell not out	56
D. T. Christian c sub (Imran Farhat) b Junaid Khan	2
M. G. Johnson not out	1
L-b 4, w 3	7
1/44 (1) 2/88 (3) 3/105 (2) 4/108 (5) 5/159 (6) 6/226 (4) 7/238 (8) (7 wkts, 47 overs)	250
10 overs: 51-1	

J. L. Pattinson and M. A. Starc did not bat.

Junaid Khan 6–0–42–2; Mohammad Hafeez 10–0–49–0; Abdur Rehman 9–0–41–2; Shahid Afridi 10–0–62–0; Saeed Ajmal 9–1–37–3; Azhar Ali 3–0–15–0.

Umpires: Ahsan Raza and B. F. Bowden. Third umpire: N. J. Llong.
Referee: R. S. Mahanama.

PAKISTAN v AUSTRALIA

First Twenty20 International

At Dubai, September 5, 2012 (floodlit). Pakistan won by seven wickets. Toss: Pakistan. Twenty20 international debuts: Nasir Jamshed, Raza Hasan; G. J. Maxwell.

This was one of those nights when Pakistan's Twenty20 attack is the best in the world. Umar Gul was right in rhythm and head, Mohammad Hafeez controlling the rate, Saeed Ajmal on song, and slow left-armer Raza Hasan making a debut that left many wondering why it had not come sooner. Gul trapped Watson early, before his team-mates more than compensated for the absence of the injured Shahid Afridi to rip through a shell-shocked Australian line-up. The result was never really in doubt after that, although Pakistan rarely do comprehensive or crushing, especially against Australia: they lost three needless wickets before Kamran Akmal provided the exclamation mark.

Man of the Match: Mohammad Hafeez.

Australia

		B	*4*	*6*
S. R. Watson *lbw b 9*	8	11	1	0
D. A. Warner *c and b 1*	22	25	2	0
M. E. K. Hussey *c 5 b 8*	1	3	0	0
*G. J. Bailey *c 6 b 1*	14	19	0	0
D. J. Hussey *c 10 b 11*	3	4	0	0
C. L. White *b 10*	15	22	0	0
†M. S. Wade *c 2 b 11*	6	13	0	0
G. J. Maxwell *c 3 b 10*	4	7	0	0
P. J. Cummins *c 6 b 8*	1	4	0	0
X. J. Doherty *not out*	6	8	0	0
B. W. Hilfenhaus *c 4 b 8*	0	1	0	0
L-b 6, w 3	9			
6 overs: 82-2 (19.3 overs)	89			

1/12 2/13 3/46 4/51 5/52 6/72 7/81 8/81 9/88

Mohammad Hafeez 4–0–24–2; Sohail Tanvir 2.3–0–13–3; Umar Gul 4–0–17–1; Saeed Ajmal 4–0–13–2; Raza Hasan 4–0–15–2; Shoaib Malik 1–0–1–0.

Pakistan

		B	*4*	*6*
*Mohammad Hafeez *c 5 b 9*	17	15	2	0
Imran Nazir *c 6 b 1*	22	26	3	0
Nasir Jamshed *b 11*	10	10	2	0
†Kamran Akmal *not out*	31	24	3	1
Shoaib Malik *not out*	9	14	1	0
W 1	1			
6 overs: 38-1 (14.5 overs)	90-3			

1/30 2/44 3/68

Umar Akmal, Abdul Razzaq, Sohail Tanvir, Umar Gul, Saeed Ajmal and Raza Hasan did not bat.

Maxwell 2–0–25–0; Hilfenhaus 3–0–18–1; Cummins 3–0–14–1; Doherty 3–0–12–0; Watson 2.5–0–9–1; White 1–0–12–0.

Umpires: Ahsan Raza and Shozab Raza. Third umpire: Zameer Haider.

PAKISTAN v AUSTRALIA

Second Twenty20 International

At Dubai, September 7, 2012 (floodlit). Pakistan won after an eliminator over, following a tie. Toss: Pakistan. Twenty20 international debut: M. A. Starc.

The best match of the tour, watched by the loudest, biggest crowd on a weekend night, ended in one of those unsatisfying one-over eliminators which nobody deserves to lose. In it, Umar Akmal and Abdul Razzaq chased down the 12 runs needed – if chased is the right word. Nasir Jamshed, Mohammad Hafeez and Kamran Akmal had earlier given Pakistan a total they were confident of defending, especially after Australia's performance two nights before. And once Watson and Warner had gone, it looked as if they would indeed defend it. But Bailey played his most captainly innings yet – on his 30th birthday – perishing only to the first ball of the last over (and Abdul Razzaq's first of the tour). The game looked gone, but Cummins struck a monstrous six over long-on to level the scores off the penultimate delivery, only to be caught at mid-off from the last.

Man of the Match: Saeed Ajmal.

Pakistan

		B	*4*	*6*
*Mohammad Hafeez *c 1 b 2*	45	42	6	0
Imran Nazir *b 11*	0	2	0	0
Nasir Jamshed *c 8 b 9*	45	36	4	1
†Kamran Akmal *not out*	43	26	6	0
Umar Akmal *c 4 b 8*	13	12	1	0
Abdul Razzaq *not out*	2	2	0	0
L-b 1, w 2	3			
6 overs: 37-1 (20 overs)	151-4			

1/13 2/89 3/97 4/143

Shoaib Malik, Sohail Tanvir, Umar Gul, Saeed Ajmal and Raza Hasan did not bat.

12th man: Yasir Arafat.

Australia

		B	*4*	*6*
D. A. Warner *b 10*	31	19	3	2
S. R. Watson *lbw b 10*	33	28	2	2
M. E. K. Hussey *c 7 b 9*	23	27	1	1
C. L. White *run out*	5	5	0	0
*G. J. Bailey *c 12 b 6*	42	27	4	2
D. J. Hussey *b 8*	1	2	0	0
†M. S. Wade *run out*	6	6	0	0
D. T. Christian *not out*	2	3	0	0
P. J. Cummins *c 2 b 6*	7	3	0	1
L-b 1	1			
6 overs: 41-1 (20 overs)	151-8			

1/40 2/79 3/84 4/109 5/117 6/142 7/142 8/151

G. B. Hogg and M. A. Starc did not bat.

Cummins 4–0–37–1; Starc 4–0–17–1; Watson 4–0–29–1; D. J. Hussey 1–0–7–0; Christian 3–0–22–1; Hogg 4–0–38–0.

Sohail Tanvir 4–0–30–1; Mohammad Hafeez 3–0–28–0; Umar Gul 4–0–32–1; Saeed Ajmal 4–0–20–2; Raza Hasan 4–0–31–0; Abdul Razzaq 1–0–9–2.

Eliminator over: **Australia 11-1** (1 over) (Warner 5, Watson 5*, Bailey 0*, Extras 1; Umar Gul 1–0–11–1); **Pakistan 12-0** (1 over) (Umar Akmal 6*, Abdul Razzaq 5*, Extras 1; Cummins 1–0–12–0).

Umpires: Shozab Raza and Zameer Haider. Third umpire: Ahsan Raza.
Referee: R. S. Mahanama.

PAKISTAN v AUSTRALIA

Third Twenty20 International

At Dubai, September 10, 2012 (floodlit). Australia won by 94 runs. Toss: Pakistan.

Australia ended a satisfactory tour in good working order for a World Twenty20 on the subcontinent, with Watson, Warner and Starc again combining to set up a thumping victory. The opening stand of 111 was as powerful an exhibition of six-hitting as had been seen at the stadium: in 19 balls from the start of the eighth over, they hit nine of their 11 sixes. It hardly mattered that Australia fell away so sharply after Watson departed, losing seven for 56 (the theme would recur in Sri Lanka at the World Twenty20). Starc and Cummins never allowed Pakistan a sniff, reducing them to 19 for five in the sixth over.

Man of the Match: D. A. Warner. *Man of the Series:* Saeed Ajmal.

Australia

		B	*4*	*6*
D. A. Warner *c 1 b 8*	59	34	1	6
S. R. Watson *c 9 b 8*	47	32	1	5
G. J. Maxwell *c 3 b 11*	27	20	3	1
M. E. K. Hussey *b 10*	12	14	1	0
*G. J. Bailey *b 10*	3	6	0	0
C. L. White *c 6 b 9*	0	4	0	0
D. T. Christian *c 5 b 9*	3	3	0	0
†M. S. Wade *not out*	6	6	0	0
P. J. Cummins *not out*	1	1	0	0
B 4, l-b 2, w 4	10			
6 overs: 42-0 (20 overs)	168-7			

1/111 2/114 3/140 4/145 5/152 6/159 7/167

G. B. Hogg and M. A. Starc did not bat.

Abdul Razzaq 2–0–12–0; Umar Gul 4–0–30–2; Yasir Arafat 3–0–30–2; Saeed Ajmal 4–0–19–2; Raza Hasan 3–0–34–1; Shoaib Malik 1–0–20–0; Mohammad Hafeez 3–0–17–0.

12th man: D. J. Hussey.

Pakistan

		B	*4*	*6*
*Mohammad Hafeez *c 7 b 9*	9	5	1	0
Imran Nazir *lbw b 11*	1	5	0	0
Nasir Jamshed *c 5 b 3*	17	23	2	0
Shoaib Malik *b 9*	0	3	0	0
†Kamran Akmal *c 2 b 11*	0	4	0	0
Umar Akmal *c 4 b 2*	2	6	0	0
Abdul Razzaq *c 12 b 9*	13	27	1	0
Yasir Arafat *c 6 b 10*	15	19	0	1
Umar Gul *run out*	3	6	0	0
Saeed Ajmal *b 11*	1	5	0	0
Raza Hasan *not out*	5	12	1	0
B 4, w 4	8			
6 overs: 21-5 (19.1 overs)	74			

1/7 2/15 3/15 4/16 5/19 6/36 7/56 8/60 9/64

Watson 3–0–13–1; Starc 3.1–0–11–3; Cummins 4–0–15–3; Hogg 4–1–11–1; Maxwell 4–0–12–1; Christian 1–0–8–0.

Umpires: Ahsan Raza and Zameer Haider. Third umpire: Shozab Raza.
Series referee: R. S. Mahanama.

DOMESTIC CRICKET IN PAKISTAN, 2011-12

ABID ALI KAZI

With security concerns preventing any international cricket in Pakistan for the third season running – a Bangladesh court order prevented their national team from visiting in April – the domestic game was the only fare on offer. Unusually, the structure of the domestic tournaments remained unchanged, with the Quaid-e-Azam Trophy again contested by 22 departmental and regional sides split between two first-class divisions. But the Pakistan Cricket Board reverted to type later in the year, announcing that – after five seasons of a combined competition – in 2012-13 the departmental teams would resume playing in a separate first-class tournament, the President's Trophy, preserving the Quaid-e-Azam for the regional teams.

The better-paid departmental sides had dominated the first division in 2011-12, filling five of the top slots. **Pakistan International Airlines** won their seventh Quaid-e-Azam title – more than any team not drawn from Karachi. A year earlier, they had lost the first final to be played under floodlights, to Habib Bank; now, they came from behind to beat **Zarai Taraqiati Bank Limited**. The pace trio of Najaf Shah, Anwar Ali and Ali Imran tore through ZTBL's second innings to dismiss them for 70, leaving a target of 108, which PIA passed with a day and a half to spare. Again, the match was played under lights, but this time it featured the pink ball being tested by the ICC for possible use in day/night Tests, rather than the previous orange one. **Water and Power Development Authority** had dominated Division One for most of the season, but faltered in the closing stages; a tie in the penultimate round cost them a place in the final. **Multan** could be grateful for the latest reform of the competition; after failing to win a match for two years, they were to lose their first-class status, but the new Quaid-e-Azam format retained the same 13 regional sides and added a 14th, Bahawalpur.

Punjab won the final by 511 runs

PIA also won the Division One final in the Faysal Bank One-Day National Cup, defeating the previous year's double champions Habib Bank. A regional team, **Peshawar**, won the Quaid-e-Azam Division Two final against Sui Northern Gas – their ninth win in ten games – while **United Bank** lifted the Division Two one-day trophy.

The other first-class tournament, the Pentangular Cup, remained unaltered, with five provincial teams taking part. **Punjab** were victors for the first time, thrashing the holders, Sind, by 511 runs in the final. **Sialkot Stallions** regained the Faysal Bank Twenty20 title, which they had won from 2005-06 to 2009-10; after missing the previous semis, they returned to win the final against Rawalpindi Rams in October, and followed up in April with the Faysal Bank Super Eight T20 Cup, beating Karachi Dolphins by eight wickets.

Nine batsmen achieved the landmark of 1,000 first-class runs, up from three in 2010-11, with six more in the 900s. Afaq Raheem of Islamabad and Federal Areas was the leading scorer, with 1,420, though his success failed to rub off on either team. Close behind was Usman Salahuddin of Lahore Ravi and Punjab, who scored 1,401 at 77 with seven hundreds, three of them in the Pentangular Cup. Tabish Khan of Karachi Whites and Sind collected 77 wickets at 19 apiece, and 14 further bowlers took 50 wickets or more; all were seamers, apart from former Test leg-spinner Danish Kaneria, who captained Sind. But in June 2012 Kaneria's role in the Mervyn Westfield spot-fixing affair led to a lifetime ban by the ECB, and in July the PCB followed suit by suspending him, though he launched an appeal. Kaneria had also featured in match-fixing allegations concerning a Twenty20 match between Karachi Zebras and Peshawar Panthers in March, but a panel accepted his explanation that he had withdrawn after bowling four balls because of a side strain.

FIRST-CLASS AVERAGES, 2011-12

BATTING (700 runs, average 35.00)

	M	*I*	*NO*	*R*	*HS*	*100*	*Avge*	*Ct/St*
Usman Salahuddin (*Lahore Ravi & Punjab*)	13	22	4	1,401	132*	7	77.83	10
†Fawad Alam (*National Bank & Sind*)	13	21	4	1,062	157*	3	62.47	3
Saeed Bin Nasir (*Karachi Whites & Sind*)	12	17	3	834	251*	3	59.57	12
Afaq Raheem (*Islamabad & Federal Areas*)	15	28	2	1,420	137	4	54.61	12
Mohammad Saad (*Lahore Ravi & Punjab*)	10	18	3	813	188	2	54.20	8/1
Akbar Badshah (*Peshawar & Khy. Pakh.*)	13	21	4	911	113	3	53.58	7
Faisal Iqbal (*PIA & Sind*)	14	22	3	1,013	165*	5	53.31	12
†Aqeel Anjum (*National Bank & Sind*)	13	20	3	880	203*	3	51.76	8
Aamer Sajjad (*WAPDA & Punjab*)	11	19	1	925	252	2	51.38	17
Sarfraz Ahmed (*PIA & Sind*)	12	17	2	742	152	3	49.46	48
†Haris Sohail (*ZTBL & Punjab*)	16	24	0	1,184	151	5	49.33	7
Mohammad Ayub (*Sialkot & Punjab*)	16	28	3	1,224	200	4	48.96	12
†Nasir Jamshed (*National Bank & Punjab*)	13	24	2	1,066	168	2	48.45	12
Kamran Akmal (*National Bank*)	11	17	1	764	146	3	47.75	40/4
Fahad Iqbal (*PIA & Sind*)	17	26	5	987	136	2	47.00	10
Yasir Hameed (*ZTBL & Khyber Pakh.*)	15	25	1	1,124	167	3	46.83	10
Shoaib Khan (*PIA & Khyber Pakh.*)	15	24	5	885	130*	3	46.57	18
Ahmed Shehzad (*Habib Bank & Punjab*)	13	23	1	970	161	2	44.09	16
†Naved Yasin (*Baluchistan & Multan*)	12	19	1	755	138	2	41.94	5
†Mohammad Yasin (*Sialkot & Punjab*)	13	25	3	915	110	1	41.59	5
Shahzaib Hasan (*Karachi Blues & Sind*)	13	23	0	951	144	2	41.34	13
†Kamran Sajid (*PIA*)	12	21	1	823	173	3	41.15	4
Mohammad Fayyaz (*Pesh. & Khy. Pakh.*)	12	21	1	820	243	2	41.00	27
Rafatullah Mohmand (*WAPDA*)	11	21	3	717	117	2	39.83	16
†Umair Khan (*Islamabad & Fed. Areas*)	15	28	2	1,020	96	0	39.23	6
Usman Saeed (*Rawalpindi & Federal Areas*)	13	22	2	714	111*	1	35.70	3

BOWLING (45 wickets)

	Style	*O*	*M*	*R*	*W*	*BB*	*5I*	*Avge*
Fahad Masood (*Habib Bank*)	RFM	285.1	68	841	52	6-28	4	16.17
Mohammad Sami (*Karachi B. & Sind*)	RFM	347	86	931	56	6-62	3	16.62
Ali Imran (*PIA*)	RFM	300.2	57	1,073	60	6-41	5	17.88
Bilawal Bhatti (*Sui N. Gas & Punjab*)	RFM	417.4	69	1,424	76	6-38	5	18.73
Rizwan Haider (*Baluchistan & S. Bank*)	LFM	320.2	82	902	48	7-46	2	18.79
Mohammad Khalil (*ZTBL & Punjab*)	LFM	342.4	56	1,263	67	9-100	6	18.85
Rahat Ali (*KRL & Baluchistan*)	LFM	386.2	75	1,160	61	6-62	5	19.01
Asif Raza (*Lahore Shalimar & Punjab*)	RFM	331.4	59	1,054	54	8-101	4	19.51
Imran Khan (*WAPDA & Khyber Pakh.*)	RFM	310.3	42	1,202	61	9-77	6	19.70
Tabish Khan (*Karachi Whites & Sind*)	RFM	526.4	120	1,537	77	7-38	4	19.96
Sadaf Hussain (*R'pindi & Fed. Areas*)	LFM	362.2	74	1,198	58	9-37	4	20.65
Iftikhar Anjum (*ZBTL & Federal Areas*)	RFM	361.1	83	1,050	47	6-37	3	22.34
Abdur Rauf (*Faisalabad*)	RFM	334.4	67	961	45	5-53	4	21.35
Mohammad Imran (*Sialkot*)	RFM	274	55	963	45	6-34	3	21.40
Anwar Ali (*PIA & Sind*)	RFM	368.1	77	1,211	53	8-16	4	22.84
Waqar Ahmed (*Peshawar & Khy. Pakh.*)	LFM	481.5	71	1,602	67	8-96	4	23.91
Danish Kaneria (*Habib Bank & Sind*)	LBG	553.5	87	1,795	70	7-102	6	25.64
Saad Altaf (*State Bank & Federal Areas*)	LFM	487.4	101	1,598	61	7-59	6	26.19
Prince Abbas (*Sialkot & Punjab*)	RFM	437.2	97	1,500	52	5-79	2	28.84

QUAID-E-AZAM TROPHY, 2011-12

Division One	P	W	L	D	Pts
PIA	11	6	1	4	57
ZTBL	11	6	4	1	57
WAPDA	11	6	3	1†	53
State Bank	11	5	3	3	47
National Bank	11	4	1	6	41
Sialkot	11	4	4	3	39
Rawalpindi	11	4	5	2	36
Karachi Blues	11	4	5	2	36
Habib Bank	11	4	4	2†	35
Abbottabad	11	3	7	1	27
Islamabad	11	2	4	5	27
Faisalabad	11	1	8	2	12

Division Two	P	W	L	D	Pts
Peshawar	9	8	0	1	72
Sui Northern Gas	9	8	1	0	72
Karachi Whites	9	6	2	1	57
KRL	9	5	4	0	42
United Bank	9	4	3	2	36
Lahore Ravi	9	3	3	3	33
Hyderabad	9	2	5	2	18
Quetta	9	1	5	3	15
Lahore Shalimar	9	1	7	1	9
Multan	9	0	8	1	0

† *Plus one tie.*

PIA = Pakistan International Airlines; WAPDA = Water and Power Development Authority; ZTBL = Zarai Taraqiati Bank Limited (formerly ADBP); KRL = Khan Research Laboratories.

Division One Final: PIA beat ZTBL by nine wickets.

Division Two Final: Peshawar beat Sui Northern Gas by six wickets.

Outright win = 6pts; tie = 2pts; lead on first innings in a won, tied or drawn game = 3pts; tie on first innings in a drawn game = 2pts. Teams tied on points were ranked on most wins, then fewest losses, then on net run-rate (runs conceded per over from runs scored per over).

Division One

At Abbottabad, October 6–9, 2011. **WAPDA won by ten wickets. Abbottabad 259 and 125**; **‡WAPDA 325** (Ali Azmat 105) **and 61-0**. *WAPDA 9pts.*

At Faisalabad (Iqbal), October 6–8, 2011. **ZTBL won by an innings and 124 runs. Faisalabad 199** (Zohaib Khan 5-51) **and 140** (Mohammad Khalil 5-20); **‡ZTBL 463** (Sharjeel Khan 154, Yasir Hameed 167; Aqeel Ahmed 5-114). *ZTBL 9pts. Sharjeel Khan and Yasir Hameed added 207 for ZTBL's second wicket.*

At Islamabad (Diamond), October 6–9, 2011. **Drawn. PIA 423-5 dec** (Agha Sabir 171, Shoaib Khan 101*) **and 157-3 dec**; **‡Islamabad 281** (Afaq Raheem 137; Anwar Ali 5-65) **and 99-1**. *PIA 3pts.*

At Karachi (National), October 6–8, 2011. **State Bank won by an innings and 11 runs. ‡Karachi Blues 253** (Hasan Mahmood 6-88) **and 113** (Kashif Siddiq 5-14); **State Bank 377** (Adnan Raees 190). *State Bank 9pts. Leg-spinner Kashif Siddiq took a hat-trick of lbws in Karachi Blues' second innings.*

At Rawalpindi (Cricket), October 6–9, 2011. **Drawn. National Bank 153** (Nasir Malik 7-42) **and 482-8 dec** (Umar Amin 131, Fawad Alam 142, Kamran Akmal 139); **‡Rawalpindi 348 and 52-1**. *Rawalpindi 3pts. Nasir Malik claimed a hat-trick in National Bank's first innings, and Umar Amin and Fawad Alam added 260 for the fourth wicket in their second.*

At Sialkot (Jinnah), October 6–9, 2011. **Sialkot won by 59 runs. Sialkot 397** (Mohammad Ayub 186*; Kamran Hussain 6-105) **and 83** (Danish Kaneria 6-24); **‡Habib Bank 293** (Imran Farhat 105) **and 128**. *Sialkot 9pts.*

At Abbottabad, October 12–15, 2011. **Habib Bank won by three wickets. Abbottabad 272** (Rameez Ahmed 107; Sarmad Anwar 5-57) **and 250** (Danish Kaneria 5-106); **‡Habib Bank 156** (Ikramullah Khan 5-53) **and 369-7** (Ahmed Shehzad 161). *Habib Bank 6pts. Shan Masood (74) and Ahmed Shehzad opened with 234 in Habib Bank's second innings.*

At Sargodha, October 12–15, 2011. **WAPDA won by seven wickets. Faisalabad 217 and 174** (Imran Khan 5-37); **‡WAPDA 133 and 262-3**. *WAPDA 6pts.*

At Islamabad (Diamond), October 12–15, 2011. **Drawn. Islamabad 198 and 315**; **‡National Bank 211** (Nasrullah Khan 5-53) **and 287-8** (Khurram Manzoor 107; Afaq Raheem 6-47). *National Bank 3pts. National Bank captain and wicketkeeper Kamran Akmal made nine dismissals in the match, and also launched his side's first-innings recovery from 39-6.*

At Karachi (National), October 12–15, 2011. **Karachi Blues won by an innings and 12 runs. Karachi Blues 400** (Shahzaib Hasan 144, Javed Mansoor 107; Mohammad Khalil 6-101); **‡ZTBL 192 and 196** (Mohammad Sami 5-37). *Karachi Blues 9pts.*

At Rawalpindi (Cricket), October 12–15, 2011. **Drawn. PIA 348** (Fahad Iqbal 136) **and 229-8 dec** (Nasir Malik 5-80); **‡Rawalpindi 224** (Ali Imran 5-54) **and 336-5** (Naved Malik 139*). *PIA 3pts.*

At Sialkot (Jinnah), October 12–15, 2011. **Drawn. State Bank 341** (Rameez Aziz 121; Prince Abbas 5-106) **and 220** (Prince Abbas 5-79); **‡Sialkot 358** (Waqas Ahmed 5-86) **and 11-1**. *Sialkot 3pts.*

At Abbottabad, October 18–20, 2011. **National Bank won by eight wickets. Abbottabad 222 and 185** (Mohammad Talha 5-69); **‡National Bank 187** (Ahmed Jamal 6-55) **and 221-2** (Khurram Manzoor 105*). *National Bank 6pts.*

At Faisalabad (Iqbal), October 18–21, 2011. **Drawn. PIA 396** (Shoaib Khan 120; Abdur Rauf 5-93) **and 315-6** (Fahad Iqbal 105*, Sarfraz Ahmed 152); **‡Faisalabad 415** (Farrukh Shehzad 128). *Faisalabad 3pts. Fahad Iqbal and Sarfraz Ahmed added 268 for the fifth wicket in PIA's second innings.*

At Islamabad (Diamond), October 18–21, 2011. **Drawn. Islamabad 276** (Afaq Raheem 100; Saad Altaf 5-76) **and 274-2 dec** (Afaq Raheem 129); **‡State Bank 193 and 188-6**. *Islamabad 3pts. Afaq Raheem scored a century in each innings.*

At Karachi (National), October 18–21, 2011. **WAPDA won by six wickets. ‡Karachi Blues 144 and 284; WAPDA 219 and 210-4** (Rafatullah Mohmand 105*). *WAPDA 9pts.*

At Rawalpindi (Cricket), October 18–21, 2011. **Habib Bank won by 131 runs. Habib Bank 114** (Sadaf Hussain 9-37) **and 376** (B. M. Shafayat 104; Sadaf Hussain 6-117); **‡Rawalpindi 161** (Fahad Masood 5-56) **and 198**. *Habib Bank 6pts. Sadaf Hussain's 9-37 (of which three were bowled, and four lbw) was the best innings return in the world in 2012; a 21-year-old left-arm seamer, he finished with 15-154 – but on the losing side.*

At Sialkot (Jinnah), October 18–21, 2011. **ZTBL won by 258 runs. ZTBL 121** (Mohammad Abbas 5-43) **and 502-9 dec** (Sharjeel Khan 205, Haris Sohail 104); **‡Sialkot 97** (Sohail Tanvir 6-19) **and 268** (Mohammad Khalil 9-100). *ZTBL 9pts. Sohail Tanvir had figures of 18.1–9–19–6 in Sialkot's first innings. Sharjeel Khan hit 205, his maiden double-century, in just 186 balls, with 33 fours and five sixes. Mohammad Khalil took the first nine wickets in Sialkot's second innings, only for Iftikhar Anjum to nip in with the match-clincher; Khalil finished with 13-159.*

At Abbottabad, October 25–27, 2011. **State Bank won by eight wickets. Abbottabad 285 and 106** (Saad Altaf 6-36); **‡State Bank 346** (Waqar Orakzai 150; Mohammad Naeem 5-93) **and 48-2**. *State Bank 9pts.*

At Faisalabad (Iqbal), October 25–28, 2011. **Drawn. National Bank 539-4 dec** (Aqeel Anjum 146, Fawad Alam 157*, Qaiser Abbas 101*); **‡Faisalabad 376 and 108-5**. *National Bank 3pts.*

At Islamabad (Diamond), October 25–27, 2011. **Habib Bank won by an innings and 27 runs. Habib Bank 401** (Khaqan Arsal 122; Zohaib Ahmed 7-84); **‡Islamabad 108** (Fahad Masood 5-31) **and 266** (Danish Kaneria 7-102). *Habib Bank 9pts.*

At Karachi (National), October 25–27, 2011. **PIA won by an innings and 49 runs. PIA 450** (Sheharyar Ghani 161, Sarfraz Ahmed 131); **‡Karachi Blues 147 and 254**. *PIA 9pts. Sheharyar Ghani and Sarfraz Ahmed added 252 for PIA's sixth wicket.*

At Rawalpindi (Cricket), October 25–28, 2011. **Rawalpindi won by 25 runs. Rawalpindi 304** (Iftikhar Anjum 5-49) **and 162; ‡ZTBL 212** (Sadaf Hussain 6-55) **and 229** (Sadaf Hussain 6-113). *Rawalpindi 9pts.*

At Sialkot (Jinnah), October 25–28, 2011. **WAPDA won by five wickets. ‡Sialkot 139** (Sarfraz Ahmed 5-36) **and 396** (Mohammad Ayub 200; Sarfraz Ahmed 5-74); **WAPDA 296** (Ali Azmat 101) **and 241-5** (Ali Azmat 106*). *WAPDA 9pts. Mohammad Ayub reached a maiden double-hundred, the only one in this tournament which did not lead to victory, as Ali Azmat's twin hundreds and Sarfraz Ahmed's ten wickets set up WAPDA's fourth straight win.*

At Abbottabad, October 30–November 1, 2011. **PIA won by an innings and two runs. Abbottabad 175** (Ali Imran 6-48) **and 231** (Almar Afridi 102*; Ali Imran 6-41); **‡PIA 408-8 dec** (Shoaib Khan 130*). *PIA 9pts. Ali Imran improved his career-best figures twice in the match and took a hat-trick in Abbottabad's second innings, which reduced them to 6-5.*

At Sargodha, October 30–November 2, 2011. **State Bank won by an innings and 46 runs. State Bank 356** (Naseer Akram 5-71); ‡**Faisalabad 153** (Saad Altaf 5-84, Mohammad Ali 5-52) **and 157**. *State Bank 9pts.*

At Islamabad (Diamond), October 30–November 1, 2011. **ZTBL won by an innings and 28 runs. Islamabad 123** (Junaid Nadir 5-14) **and 218** (Rehan Riaz 5-52); ‡**ZTBL 369** (Imran Nazir 108). *ZTBL 9pts.*

At Karachi (National), October 30–November 2, 2011. **Drawn.** ‡**Habib Bank 376** (Ahmed Shehzad 108; Tanvir Ahmed 5-82, Atif Maqbool 5-174) **and 210-4**; **Karachi Blues 394**. *Karachi Blues 3pts. Shan Masood and Ahmed Shehzad shared opening stands of 195 and 116 for Habib Bank. Shehzad was suspended for the next match after disputing his second-innings dismissal.*

At Rawalpindi (Cricket), October 30–November 1, 2011. **Rawalpindi won by 108 runs. Rawalpindi 159 and 224** (Usman Saeed 111*; Naved-ul-Hasan 6-85); ‡**WAPDA 173** (Mohammad Ayaz 5-64) **and 102**. *Rawalpindi 6pts.*

At Sialkot (Jinnah), October 30–November 2, 2011. **Drawn. National Bank 481** (Kamran Akmal 146, Qaiser Abbas 162*); ‡**Sialkot 314 and 298-6**. *National Bank 3pts. Kamran Akmal and Qaiser Abbas added 234 for National Bank's sixth wicket.*

At Abbottabad, November 12–14, 2011. **ZTBL won by an innings and 206 runs. ZTBL 498-9 dec** (Haris Sohail 151); ‡**Abbottabad 197 and 95**. *ZTBL 9pts. Another second-innings collapse led to Abbottabad's sixth consecutive defeat.*

At Faisalabad (Iqbal), November 12–15, 2011. **Faisalabad won by 139 runs. Faisalabad 247** (Danish Kaneria 6-91) **and 234**; ‡**Habib Bank 156** (Abdur Rauf 5-53) **and 186** (Naseer Akram 5-43). *Faisalabad 9pts.*

At Islamabad (Diamond), November 12–15, 2011. **WAPDA won by nine wickets. Islamabad 232 and 210** (Naved-ul-Hasan 5-74); ‡**WAPDA 388** (Aamer Sajjad 106; Fakhar Hussain 5-89) **and 55-1**. *WAPDA 9pts.*

At Karachi (National), November 12–15, 2011. **National Bank won by nine wickets. Karachi Blues 298** (Asad Baig 102; Wahab Riaz 6-55) **and 318** (Khalid Latif 114); ‡**National Bank 520-3 dec** (Nasir Jamshed 168, Aqeel Anjum 203*, Fawad Alam 100*) **and 99-1**. *National Bank 9pts. Aqeel Anjum scored his second double-century, adding 276 for the third wicket with Nasir Jamshed and 215* for the fourth with Fawad Alam.*

At Rawalpindi (Cricket), November 12–15, 2011. **State Bank won by 93 runs. State Bank 238** (Mohammad Rameez 5-38) **and 215** (Babar Naeem 5-57); ‡**Rawalpindi 121** (Saad Altaf 7-59) **and 239**. *State Bank 9pts. Mohammad Rameez's full figures were 32.4–19–38–5.*

At Sialkot (Jinnah), November 12–15, 2011. **Drawn. PIA 505-4 dec** (Kamran Sajid 173, Faisal Iqbal 165*) **and 153-3**; ‡**Sialkot 407** (Mohammad Yasin 110; Anwar Ali 7-109). *PIA 3pts. Kamran Sajid and Faisal Iqbal added 204 for PIA's third wicket.*

At Swabi, November 18–20, 2011. **Abbottabad won by an innings and 37 runs.** ‡**Faisalabad 74** (Ahmed Jamal 6-25) **and 200**; **Abbottabad 311**. *Abbottabad 9pts. After six defeats by departmental sides, Abbottabad bounced back with an innings win over another regional team. Slow left-armer Khalid Usman had figures of 10.2–6–8–3 in Faisalabad's first-day collapse.*

At Rawalpindi (Cricket), November 18–21, 2011. **ZTBL won by 133 runs. ZTBL 201** (Sarmad Anwar 6-52) **and 330** (Danish Kaneria 5-60); ‡**Habib Bank 156 and 242** (Rehan Riaz 5-48). *ZTBL 9pts.*

At Islamabad (Diamond), November 18–20, 2011. **Islamabad won by three wickets. Islamabad 289** (Rashid Latif 6-84) **and 87-7**; ‡**Rawalpindi 119 and 256** (Fakhar Hussain 5-74). *Islamabad 9pts. Islamabad scraped home after sliding to 76-7 chasing 87.*

At Faisalabad (Iqbal), November 18–21, 2011. **Drawn. National Bank 282 and 313-5 dec**; ‡**State Bank 282** (Mohammad Talha 5-78) **and 183-9**. *National Bank 2pts, State Bank 2pts. State Bank's last pair held out for 27 minutes to save the game.*

At Islamabad (Marghzar), November 18–20, 2011. **PIA won by eight wickets.** ‡**WAPDA 178 and 218** (Ali Imran 5-48); **PIA 186** (Naved-ul-Hasan 5-51) **and 211-2** (Kamran Sajid 104*). *PIA 9pts. PIA reduced divisional leaders WAPDA to 48-5 on the first morning.*

At Sialkot (Jinnah), November 18–21, 2011. **Karachi Blues won by 214 runs. ‡Karachi Blues 166** (Mohammad Imran 5-40) **and 432-9 dec; Sialkot 249 and 135**. *Karachi Blues 6pts.*

At Abbottabad, November 24–27, 2011. **Drawn. Islamabad 337 and 526-8; ‡Abbottabad 288** (Nasrullah Khan 6-95). *Islamabad 3pts. Six batsmen – and Extras – passed 50 in Islamabad's second innings, but none reached 100.*

At Faisalabad (Iqbal), November 24–27, 2011. **Karachi Blues won by 235 runs. ‡Karachi Blues 338 and 248** (Naseer Akram 6-71); **Faisalabad 231 and 120**. *Karachi Blues 9pts.*

At Islamabad (Diamond), November 24–27, 2011. **State Bank won by 12 runs. State Bank 204** (Sajid Shah 6-34) **and 185; ‡Habib Bank 144** (Saad Altaf 5-63) **and 233** (Rizwan Haider 7-46). *State Bank 9pts.*

At Sialkot (Jinnah), November 24–27, 2011. **PIA won by three wickets. National Bank 248 and 248; ‡PIA 238** (Mohammad Talha 7-77) **and 259-7**. *PIA 6pts.*

At Rawalpindi (Cricket), November 24–26, 2011. **Rawalpindi won by an innings and 19 runs. Rawalpindi 404** (Babar Naeem 111); **‡Sialkot 97** (Mohammad Rameez 5-31) **and 288**. *Rawalpindi 9pts.*

At Islamabad (National), November 24–27, 2011. **Drawn. WAPDA 192 and 425-7 dec** (Rafatullah Mohmand 117); **‡ZTBL 315** (Imran Khan 5-61) **and 139-2**. *ZTBL 3pts.*

At Sargodha, November 30–December 2, 2011. **Rawalpindi won by 92 runs. Rawalpindi 179** (Abdur Rauf 5-61) **and 198** (Abdur Rauf 5-78); **‡Faisalabad 104** (Nasir Malik 5-30) **and 181** (Rashid Latif 5-46). *Rawalpindi 9pts. Nasir Malik reduced Faisalabad's first innings to 4-4, and Rashid Latif took a hat-trick of lbws in their second.*

At Faisalabad (Iqbal), November 30–December 3, 2011. **Drawn. ‡National Bank 243** (Fahad Masood 5-40) **and 484-6** (Kamran Akmal 110); **Habib Bank 305**. *Habib Bank 3pts.*

At Islamabad (Diamond), November 30–December 3, 2011. **Sialkot won by six runs. ‡Sialkot 255 and 194** (Zohaib Ahmed 5-82); **Islamabad 140** (Mohammad Abbas 7-58) **and 303** (Afaq Raheem 108). *Sialkot 9pts. Chasing 310, Islamabad reached 282-7, but fell just short.*

At Karachi (National), November 30–December 2, 2011. **Abbottabad won by 188 runs. Abbottabad 216** (Mohammad Sami 5-60) **and 210** (Sohail Khan 5-82); **‡Karachi Blues 142** (Ikramullah Khan 8-51) **and 96** (Khalid Usman 5-36). *Abbottabad 9pts. Ikramullah Khan took 12-93, and left-arm spinner Khalid Usman four in four balls in Karachi Blues' second innings.*

At Lahore (Gaddafi), November 30–December 3, 2011. **PIA won by nine wickets. ZTBL 178 and 223; ‡PIA 390** (Kamran Sajid 136, Faisal Iqbal 125) **and 12-1**. *PIA 9pts. Kamran Sajid and Faisal Iqbal added 211 for PIA's third wicket. The match turned out to be a rehearsal for the final, and had exactly the same result.*

At Islamabad (Marghzar), November 30–December 2, 2011. **WAPDA won by ten wickets. State Bank 94** (Imran Khan 5-26) **and 160; ‡WAPDA 254 and 4-0**. *WAPDA 9pts. Left-arm spinner Zulfiqar Babar took a hat-trick in State Bank's second innings.*

At Swabi, December 8–10, 2011. **Sialkot won by one wicket. Abbottabad 97** (Mohammad Imran 6-34) **and 170** (Mohammad Abbas 5-56); **‡Sialkot 104** (Ahmed Jamal 5-42, Ikramullah Khan 5-35) **and 164-9** (Ahmed Jamal 5-63). *Sialkot 9pts. In a low-scoring game, it was left to Sialkot's last man, Mohammad Abbas, to steal the winning run – their second successive nail-biter.*

At Lahore (Gaddafi), December 8–11, 2011. **Tied. Habib Bank 245** (Imran Khan 5-57) **and 178** (Imran Khan 9-77); **‡WAPDA 233 and 190**. *Habib Bank 5pts, WAPDA 2pts. Imran Khan took 14-134; he was the third bowler to take nine in an innings in this tournament. Chasing 191, WAPDA were 176-6 before losing four for 14, the last two with the scores level. It was the first tied match in Pakistan for 23 years, and the first in all first-class cricket for eight.*

At Islamabad (Diamond), December 8–10, 2011. **Islamabad won by 130 runs. Islamabad 169 and 191; ‡Faisalabad 106 and 124** (Shehzad Azam 5-52). *Islamabad 9pts.*

At Karachi (National), December 8–11, 2011. **Karachi Blues won by 305 runs. ‡Karachi Blues 299** (Nasir Malik 5-70) **and 256-9 dec** (Babar Naeem 5-65); **Rawalpindi 107** (Sohail Khan 5-30) **and 143**. *Karachi Blues 9pts. Haseeb Azam carried his bat for 59* in Rawalpindi's first innings.*

At Lahore (LCCA), December 8–11, 2011. **National Bank won by five wickets. ZTBL 255** (Wahab Riaz 7-74) **and 144** (Umaid Asif 5-39); **‡National Bank 201 and 202-5**. *National Bank 6pts.*

At Islamabad (National), December 8–11, 2011. **PIA won by 189 runs. PIA 137 and 361** (Faisal Iqbal 113, Sarfraz Ahmed 103); **‡State Bank 269** (Anwar Ali 5-69) **and 40** (Anwar Ali 8-16). *PIA 6pts. Anwar Ali bowled straight through State Bank's second innings for figures of 10–4–16–8 (and 13-85 in the match); only one man reached double figures, and a total of 40 was the season's lowest. PIA's sixth win put them four points clear at the top of the division with a round to go.*

At Lahore (LCCA), December 14–16, 2011. **Habib Bank won by 243 runs. Habib Bank 128** (Ali Imran 6-45) **and 361** (Hasan Raza 141*; Akhtar Waheed 6-107); **‡PIA 184 and 62** (Fahad Masood 6-28). *Habib Bank 6pts. Danish Kaneria of Habib Bank took his 1,000th first-class wicket, helping to inflict PIA's only defeat of the season; needing 306, they collapsed for 62.*

At Karachi (National), December 14–17, 2011. **Drawn. Karachi Blues 264 and 303**; **‡Islamabad 398** (Azam Hussain 5-85) **and 78-0**. *Islamabad 3pts.*

At Lahore (Gaddafi), December 14–17, 2011. **National Bank won by 82 runs. ‡National Bank 358** (Qaiser Abbas 103; Imran Khan 5-126) **and 215-6 dec** (Khurram Manzoor 101); **WAPDA 270 and 221**. *National Bank 9pts. Defeat cost WAPDA a place in the final.*

At Rawalpindi (Cricket), December 14–16, 2011. **Abbottabad won by six wickets. ‡Rawalpindi 215 and 251**; **Abbottabad 309** (Mir Azam 133; Ahsan Khan 7-119) **and 158-4**. *Abbottabad 9pts.*

At Sialkot (Jinnah), December 14–17, 2011. **Sialkot won by 185 runs. ‡Sialkot 452** (Mohammad Ayub 118) **and 147-7 dec**; **Faisalabad 173** (Mohammad Imran 6-73) **and 241**. *Sialkot 9pts.*

At Islamabad (Diamond), December 14–16, 2011. **ZTBL won by an innings and 28 runs. ZTBL 263** (Haris Sohail 106; Mohammad Ali 7-59); **‡State Bank 112** (Junaid Zia 5-31) **and 123** (Iftikhar Anjum 6-37). *ZTBL 9pts. ZTBL were the only one of the four teams who started the last round with a chance of reaching the final to win; their sixth victory put them level on points with PIA.*

Division One Final

At Karachi (National), December 20–23, 2011 (day/night). **PIA won by nine wickets. ZTBL 337** (Haris Sohail 112) **and 70**; **‡PIA 300 and 110-1**. *ZTBL took a first-innings lead, thanks to Haris Sohail, whose six-hour innings saw them past 300, but PIA's pace attack dismissed them for 70 second time round. Needing only 108 to win, PIA achieved it with five sessions to spare.*

QUAID-E-AZAM TROPHY WINNERS

1953-54	Bahawalpur	1976-77	United Bank	1994-95	Karachi Blues
1954-55	Karachi	1977-78	Habib Bank	1995-96	Karachi Blues
1956-57	Punjab	1978-79	National Bank	1996-97	Lahore City
1957-58	Bahawalpur	1979-80	PIA	1997-98	Karachi Blues
1958-59	Karachi	1980-81	United Bank	1998-99	Peshawar
1959-60	Karachi	1981-82	National Bank	1999-2000	PIA
1961-62	Karachi Blues	1982-83	United Bank	2000-01	Lahore City Blues
1962-63	Karachi A	1983-84	National Bank	2001-02	Karachi Whites
1963-64	Karachi Blues	1984-85	United Bank	2002-03	PIA
1964-65	Karachi Blues	1985-86	Karachi	2003-04	Faisalabad
1966-67	Karachi	1986-87	National Bank	2004-05	Peshawar
1968-69	Lahore	1987-88	PIA	2005-06	Sialkot
1969-70	PIA	1988-89	ADBP	2006-07	Karachi Urban
1970-71	Karachi Blues	1989-90	PIA	2007-08	Sui Northern Gas
1972-73	Railways	1990-91	Karachi Whites	2008-09	Sialkot
1973-74	Railways	1991-92	Karachi Whites	2009-10	Karachi Blues
1974-75	Punjab A	1992-93	Karachi Whites	2010-11	Habib Bank
1975-76	National Bank	1993-94	Lahore City	2011-12	PIA

The competition has been contested sometimes by regional teams, sometimes by departments, and sometimes by a mixture of the two. Karachi teams have won the Quaid-e-Azam Trophy 19 times, PIA 7, National Bank 5, Lahore teams and United Bank 4, Bahawalpur, Habib Bank, Peshawar, Punjab, Railways and Sialkot 2, ADBP, Faisalabad and Sui Northern Gas 1.

Division Two

At Hyderabad (Niaz), October 6–9, 2011. **Drawn.** **‡Hyderabad 390 and 215-9 dec** (Gohar Faiz 5-52); **Quetta 311 and 163-3** (Bismillah Khan 100*). *Hyderabad 3pts.*

At Rawalpindi (KRL), October 6–9, 2011. **Sui Northern Gas won by 119 runs.** **Sui Northern Gas 223** (Yasir Ali 5-47) **and 242-8 dec**; **‡KRL 192** (Mohammad Hafeez 6-55) **and 154** (Mohammad Hafeez 5-29). *Sui Northern Gas 9pts.*

At Lahore (LCCA), October 6–9, 2011. **Lahore Ravi won by 244 runs.** **Lahore Ravi 276** (Ali Manzoor 6-76) **and 290-3 dec** (Abid Ali 108); **‡Lahore Shalimar 192** (Mohammad Irfan 6-35) **and 130**. *Lahore Ravi 9pts.*

At Peshawar (Arbab Niaz), October 6–8, 2011. **Peshawar won by an innings and 11 runs.** **Multan 67 and 287** (Waqar Ahmed 5-83); **‡Peshawar 365-3 dec** (Sajjad Ahmed 119*, Akbar Badshah 101*). *Peshawar 9pts. A team containing six first-class debutants collapsed for 67 on the opening day; one of them, Mohammad Waris, was the top scorer with 27, the other five made seven runs between them. Peshawar opening bowler Riaz Afridi's figures were 11.3–3–12–4.*

At Karachi (UBL), October 6–8, 2011. **Karachi Whites won by seven wickets.** **United Bank 139** (Tabish Khan 6-48) **and 241** (Faraz Ahmed 5-70); **‡Karachi Whites 204** (Saeed Bin Nasir 109*; Kashif Bhatti 5-65) **and 180-3**. *Karachi Whites 9pts. United Bank crumbled to 28-7 in their first innings, and Murtaza Majeed held five catches in the field in their second.*

At Hyderabad (Niaz), October 12–15, 2011. **United Bank won by nine wickets.** **United Bank 460-8 dec** (Itmad-ul-Haq 102*) **and 15-1**; **‡Hyderabad 274 and 197** (Misbah Khan 5-71). *United Bank 9pts.*

At Karachi (NBP), October 12–14, 2011. **Karachi Whites won by an innings and 61 runs.** **‡Karachi Whites 346**; **Quetta 93 and 192**. *Karachi Whites 9pts.*

At Lahore (LCCA), October 12–15, 2011. **KRL won by eight wickets.** **‡Lahore Shalimar 84** (Nayyer Abbas 5-31) **and 327** (Fahad-ul-Haq 194); **KRL 357-6 dec** (Bazid Khan 103) **and 55-2**. *KRL 9pts.*

At Multan (Cricket), October 12–15, 2011. **Sui Northern Gas won by an innings and 153 runs.** **Sui Northern Gas 510-8 dec** (Ali Waqas 105, Umar Akmal 165); **‡Multan 206 and 151** (Bilawal Bhatti 5-39). *Sui Northern Gas 9pts. Ali Waqas and Umar Akmal added 227 for Sui Northern's third wicket, and their team-mate Azhar Shafiq had figures of 10–5–9–3 in Multan's first innings.*

At Peshawar (Arbab Niaz), October 12–14, 2011. **Peshawar won by 55 runs.** **Peshawar 190 and 214** (Aamer Hayat 7-79); **‡Lahore Ravi 185** (Noor-ul-Amin 5-50) **and 164** (Noor-ul-Amin 6-49). *Peshawar 9pts. Lahore Ravi wicketkeeper Mohammad Zohaib held ten catches in the match.*

At Karachi (NBP), October 18–20, 2011. **Sui Northern Gas won by an innings and 65 runs.** **‡Sui Northern Gas 436** (Ali Waqas 175); **Karachi Whites 181** (Bilawal Bhatti 5-41) **and 190**. *Sui Northern Gas 9pts.*

At Karachi (UBL), October 18–21, 2011. **KRL won by three wickets.** **Hyderabad 270 and 135**; **‡KRL 243** (Zahid Mahmood 5-64) **and 163-7**. *KRL 6pts.*

At Lahore (LCCA), October 18–21, 2011. **Drawn.** **United Bank 218** (Emmad Ali 5-41) **and 300-8 dec**; **‡Lahore Ravi 259 and 169-5**. *Lahore Ravi 3pts.*

At Lahore (Gaddafi), October 18–21, 2011. **Peshawar won by an innings and 45 runs.** **‡Peshawar 556-8 dec** (Mohammad Fayyaz 243); **Lahore Shalimar 376** (Riaz Afridi 5-121) **and 135** (Sajjad Ahmed 5-34). *Peshawar 9pts. Mohammad Fayyaz hit 32 fours and seven sixes in a maiden double-hundred as Peshawar reached the highest total of this tournament.*

At Multan (Cricket), October 18–21, 2011. **Quetta won by an innings and 90 runs.** **Multan 304** (Arun Lal 5-58) **and 82** (Arun Lal 6-36); **‡Quetta 476-5 dec** (Ata-ur-Rehman 104). *Quetta 9pts.*

At Karachi (NBP), October 25–28, 2011. **Karachi Whites won by 111 runs.** **Karachi Whites 251** (Saeed Bin Nasir 109; Rahat Ali 6-62) **and 175**; **‡KRL 122** (Tabish Khan 7-38) **and 193** (Tabish Khan 7-52). *Karachi Whites 9pts. Tabish Khan took 14-90 in the match. Mohammad Wasim of KRL passed 10,000 first-class runs.*

At Lahore (Gaddafi), October 25–28, 2011. **Drawn. Lahore Ravi 383** (Usman Salahuddin 131) **and 253-2** (Mohammad Zohaib 103*, Usman Salahuddin 116*); **‡Multan 356** (Naved Yasin 138). *Lahore Ravi 3pts. Usman Salahuddin scored twin centuries and added 232* with Mohammad Zohaib for the third wicket in Lahore Ravi's second innings.*

At Lahore (LCCA), October 25–28, 2011. **Drawn. Quetta 276** (Asif Raza 5-53) **and 278-4 dec** (Taimur Ali 129*, Abid Ali 100*); **‡Lahore Shalimar 230** (Saeed Khan 6-62) **and 151-3**. *Quetta 3pts. Abid Ali scored a century on first-class debut, adding 232* for Quetta's fifth wicket with his captain, Taimur Ali.*

At Peshawar (Arbab Niaz), October 25–28, 2011. **Peshawar won by 153 runs. Peshawar 260** (Akbar Badshah 103*; Tahir Mughal 5-66) **and 276**; **‡United Bank 173** (Noor-ul-Amin 5-44) **and 210** (Riaz Afridi 6-64). *Peshawar 9pts.*

At Karachi (UBL), October 25–27, 2011. **Sui Northern Gas won by an innings and 66 runs. ‡Hyderabad 97** (Bilawal Bhatti 6-38) **and 298**; **Sui Northern Gas 461-7 dec** (Imran Khalid 101*). *Sui Northern Gas 9pts. Bilawal Bhatti took a hat-trick as Hyderabad's first innings imploded to 29-8.*

At Hyderabad (Niaz), October 30–November 2, 2011. **Karachi Whites won by nine wickets. Karachi Whites 371** (Faraz Ahmed 124) **and 56-1**; **‡Hyderabad 197** (Tabish Khan 5-78) **and 229**. *Karachi Whites 9pts. Faraz Ahmed and Mansoor Ahmed (70) added 150 for Karachi Whites' eighth wicket.*

At Lahore (Gaddafi), October 30–November 1, 2011. **Lahore Ravi won by an innings and 185 runs. Quetta 172 and 130**; **‡Lahore Ravi 487-9 dec** (Mohammad Saad 188; Saeed Khan 5-140). *Lahore Ravi 9pts.*

At Lahore (LCCA), October 30–November 2, 2011. **United Bank won by 146 runs. United Bank 308** (Saad Sukhail 140) **and 272-5 dec** (Mohammad Sami 110*); **‡Lahore Shalimar 196 and 238**. *United Bank 9pts.*

At Peshawar (Arbab Niaz), October 30–November 2, 2011. **Peshawar won by 42 runs. Peshawar 304** (Adil Raza 5-98) **and 196** (Bilawal Bhatti 5-58); **‡Sui Northern Gas 200** (Naeemuddin 101*) **and 258** (Waqar Ahmed 7-118). *Peshawar 9pts. Both sides had won their four previous matches; Peshawar extended their run and ended Sui Northern's.*

At Multan (Cricket), October 31–November 2, 2011. **KRL won by an innings and 61 runs. KRL 304** (Yasir Arafat 170; Shahbaz Hussain 5-40); **‡Multan 129 and 114**. *KRL 9pts. KRL recovered from 9-5 on the first morning, thanks to Mohammad Idrees (86) and Yasir Arafat, who added 192 for the sixth wicket, which eventually led to an innings win.*

At Karachi (NBP), November 12–15, 2011. **Karachi Whites won by an innings and 151 runs. Karachi Whites 440-7 dec** (Saeed Bin Nasir 251*); **‡Multan 210** (Faraz Ahmed 5-49) **and 79**. *Karachi Whites 9pts. Again, Multan lost by an innings after a convincing start. They reduced Karachi Whites to 51-5, but Saeed Bin Nasir scored a maiden double-century, batting four minutes short of nine hours; he added 192* for Karachi Whites' eighth wicket with Mansoor Ahmed (56*).*

At Lahore (Gaddafi), November 12–15, 2011. **Sui Northern Gas won by an innings and 120 runs. ‡Sui Northern Gas 491-8 dec** (Naeemuddin 136, Usman Arshad 158); **Lahore Ravi 242** (Asad Ali 5-52) **and 129** (Asad Ali 5-36). *Sui Northern Gas 9pts.*

At Lahore (LCCA), November 12–15, 2011. **Hyderabad won by four wickets. Lahore Shalimar 348** (Irfan Haider 148) **and 79** (Mir Ali 5-15); **‡Hyderabad 266** (Hasan Dar 6-67) **and 162-6**. *Hyderabad 6pts.*

At Peshawar (Arbab Niaz), November 12–15, 2011. **Peshawar won by five wickets. KRL 164 and 261**; **‡Peshawar 124 and 304-5**. *Peshawar 6pts. Peshawar scored 304 in the fourth innings to complete their sixth successive win.*

At Islamabad (National), November 12–15, 2011. **Drawn. United Bank 273** (Tahir Mughal 130*) **and 200**; **‡Quetta 277** (Shabbir Ahmed 6-47) **and 124-7**. *Quetta 3pts. Tahir Mughal scored his maiden hundred in the 110th match of a 14-year career.*

At Hyderabad (Niaz), November 18–21, 2011. **Drawn. Hyderabad 286** (Rizwan Ahmed 104) **and 236**; **‡Peshawar 308 and 26-0**. *Peshawar 3pts.*

At Rawalpindi (KRL), November 18–20, 2011. **KRL won by an innings and 86 runs. KRL 405** (Zulfiqar Jan 120*; Arun Lal 6-82); **‡Quetta 90** (Yasir Ali 5-27) **and 229**. *KRL 9pts. Zulfiqar Jan and Rahat Ali (32) added 111 for KRL's last wicket – more than Quetta's entire first innings.*

At Lahore (Gaddafi), November 18–21, 2011. **Drawn. Lahore Ravi 280** (Usman Salahuddin 120) **and 217-4** (Mohammad Saad 101*); **‡Karachi Whites 401** (Mohammad Hasan 129). *Karachi Whites 3pts.*

At Lahore (LCCA), November 18–20, 2011. **Sui Northern Gas won by ten wickets. Lahore Shalimar 170 and 157**; **‡Sui Northern Gas 278** (Asif Raza 6-60) **and 50-0**. *Sui Northern Gas 9pts.*

At Multan (Cricket), November 18–20, 2011. **United Bank won by ten wickets. ‡United Bank 387 and 4-0**; **Multan 205 and 183** (Mohammad Irshad 5-37). *United Bank 9pts. United Bank's last two batsmen, Kashif Bhatti (91) and Rumman Raees (42*), added 115.*

At Hyderabad (Niaz), November 24–26, 2011. **Lahore Ravi won by an innings and six runs. Lahore Ravi 333** (Usman Salahuddin 132*); **‡Hyderabad 139 and 188**. *Lahore Ravi 9pts. Usman Salahuddin scored his fourth century in five matches.*

At Karachi (National), November 24–27, 2011. **Peshawar won by an innings and ten runs. Peshawar 440** (Akbar Badshah 113, Mohammad Rizwan 138); **‡Karachi Whites 241** (Riaz Afridi 5-53) **and 189** (Sajjad Ahmed 5-61). *Peshawar 9pts. Akbar Badshah and Mohammad Rizwan added 213 for Peshawar's sixth wicket; victory guaranteed their place in the final.*

At Lahore (LCCA), November 24–26, 2011. **United Bank won by 20 runs. United Bank 121 and 136** (Rahat Ali 5-45); **‡KRL 94** (Tahir Mughal 6-36) **and 143** (Tahir Mughal 5-87). *United Bank 9pts.*

At Multan (Cricket), November 24–27, 2011. **Lahore Shalimar won by three wickets. Multan 110** (Asif Raza 7-40) **and 250** (Asif Raza 8-101); **‡Lahore Shalimar 145** (Mohammad Zahid 5-54) **and 216-7**. *Lahore Shalimar 9pts. Asif Raza improved his career-best twice in the match and finished with 15-141.*

At Lahore (Gaddafi), November 24–27, 2011. **Sui Northern Gas won by seven wickets. Quetta 199** (Yasir Shah 5-48) **and 226** (Asad Ali 6-42); **‡Sui Northern Gas 231** (Bilawal Bhatti 100) **and 198-3** (Khurram Shehzad 101*). *Sui Northern Gas 9pts. Sui Northern Gas ensured their place in the final.*

At Karachi (NBP), November 30–December 3, 2011. **Karachi Whites won by 262 runs. ‡Karachi Whites 551-7 dec** (Behram Khan 175, Mohammad Hasan 251*) **and 21-1 dec**; **Lahore Shalimar 178 and 132**. *Karachi Whites 9pts. Mohammad Hasan was the second Karachi Whites player in four matches to convert a maiden double-century into 251*. He put on 359 for the fifth wicket with Behram Khan, who scored a maiden hundred. Despite leading by 373, Karachi did not enforce the follow-on, but declared after four overs of their second innings.*

At Lahore (LCCA), November 30–December 2, 2011. **KRL won by ten wickets. Lahore Ravi 180 and 175**; **‡KRL 224 and 135-0**. *KRL 9pts.*

At Bahawalpur, November 30–December 3, 2011. **Hyderabad won by an innings and 75 runs. Hyderabad 500-7 dec** (Rizwan Ahmed 200*, Lal Kumar 133); **‡Multan 249** (Naved Yasin 122; Imran Chandio 5-76) **and 176** (Mir Ali 5-29). *Hyderabad 9pts. Rizwan Ahmed batted nine hours for a maiden double-century, and added 251 for Hyderabad's fourth wicket with Lal Kumar. Mir Ali took a hat-trick in Multan's second innings. For the second year running, Multan ended the season with no wins, a single draw and no points.*

At Peshawar (Arbab Niaz), November 30–December 3, 2011. **Peshawar won by 251 runs. ‡Peshawar 239 and 312-8 dec** (Mohammad Fayyaz 178; Shahzaib Ahmed 6-90); **Quetta 145** (Riaz Afridi 5-37) **and 155** (Waqar Ahmed 8-96). *Peshawar 9pts. Waqar Ahmed's career-best 8-96 helped Peshawar to their eighth win in nine games.*

At Sialkot (Jinnah), November 30–December 2, 2011. **Sui Northern Gas won by eight wickets. United Bank 127 and 301**; **‡Sui Northern Gas 393** (Khurram Shehzad 122) **and 36-2**. *Sui Northern Gas 9pts. United Bank's opening bowler, Tahir Mughal, took his 500th first-class wicket. Khurram Shehzad and Ali Waqas (97) added 215 for Sui Northern's fifth wicket; they, too, finished with eight wins in nine matches.*

Division Two Final

At Peshawar (Arbab Niaz), December 8–11, 2011. **Peshawar won by six wickets.** **‡Sui Northern Gas 202 and 301** (Waqar Ahmed 6-92); **Peshawar 351** (Jamaluddin 124) **and 153-4**. *Jamaluddin shared century stands with his captain, Akbar Badshah, in both innings, the second one guiding Peshawar to victory.*

FAYSAL BANK PENTANGULAR CUP, 2011-12

	Played	*Won*	*Lost*	*Drawn*	*1st-inns points*	*Points*	*Net run-rate*
Punjab	4	3	0	1	12	30	–0.18
Sind	4	2	1	1	6	18	0.23
Baluchistan	4	1	2	1	3	9	–0.50
Federal Areas	4	0	1	3	3	3	0.36
Khyber Pakhtunkhwa	4	0	2	2	0	0	0.09

Final: Punjab beat Sind by 511 runs.

Outright win = 6pts; lead on first innings in a won or drawn game = 3pts. Net run-rate is calculated by subtracting runs conceded per over from runs scored per over.

At Islamabad (Diamond), January 19–22, 2012. **Drawn. Federal Areas 223** (Mohammad Khalil 5-53) **and 259-8 dec**; **‡Punjab 226** (Sohail Tanvir 6-75) **and 77-4**. *Punjab 3pts.*

At Karachi (National), January 19–22, 2012. **Sind won by five wickets.** **‡Sind 403** (Aqeel Anjum 126, Faisal Iqbal 100) **and 122-5**; **Khyber Pakhtunkhwa 192 and 331** (Mohammad Sami 6-62). *Sind 9pts.*

At Karachi (National), January 25–27, 2012. **Sind won by an innings and 114 runs. Baluchistan 164 and 209**; **‡Sind 487** (Shahzaib Hasan 119, Faisal Iqbal 112; Rahat Ali 5-106). *Sind 9pts.*

At Lahore (Gaddafi), January 26–29, 2012. **Punjab won by ten wickets.** **‡Khyber Pakhtunkhwa 210** (Raza Hasan 5-80) **and 241** (Raza Hasan 5-68); **Punjab 377** (Shoaib Malik 112, Usman Salahuddin 108*; Khalid Usman 5-89) **and 77-0**. *Punjab 9pts. Nineteen-year-old slow left-armer Raza Hasan completed his first ten-wicket haul.*

At Peshawar (Arbab Niaz), January 31–February 3, 2012. **Drawn.** **‡Khyber Pakhtunkhwa 205** (Saad Altaf 5-65) **and 327-6** (Yasir Hameed 100); **Federal Areas 471** (Shan Masood 127). *Federal Areas 3pts.*

At Lahore (Gaddafi), January 31–February 2, 2012. **Punjab won by an innings and 73 runs. Punjab 440-8 dec** (Usman Salahuddin 114; Rahat Ali 5-138); **‡Baluchistan 107** (Mohammad Khalil 5-38) **and 260**. *Punjab 9pts.*

At Multan (Cricket), February 6–8, 2012. **Baluchistan won by 149 runs. Baluchistan 229 and 226** (Iftikhar Anjum 6-43); **‡Federal Areas 185** (Rizwan Haider 5-35) **and 121** (Rahat Ali 5-36). *Baluchistan 9pts. Baluchistan wicketkeeper Gulraiz Sadaf made ten dismissals in the match.*

At Lahore (Gaddafi), February 6–9, 2012. **Punjab won by seven wickets.** **‡Sind 225** (Bilawal Bhatti 5-58) **and 331** (Raza Hasan 5-73); **Punjab 426** (Nasir Jamshed 131, Usman Salahuddin 102*) **and 133-3**. *Punjab 9pts. Usman Salahuddin scored his third century in successive innings, and his seventh of the season.*

At Rawalpindi (Cricket), February 12–15, 2012. **Drawn.** **‡Federal Areas 221-3 v Sind.** *No play was possible on the first three days, but on the last Afaq Raheem took his aggregate to 1,420 first-class runs, which remained the season's highest.*

At Peshawar (Arbab Niaz), February 12–15, 2012. **Drawn. Khyber Pakhtunkhwa 355** (Yasir Hameed 150; Ahmed Raza 7-132); **‡Baluchistan 252-5** (Saeed Anwar 103*). *After two days were washed out, Ahmed Raza's 7-132 was the best return of the tournament.*

Final

At Lahore (Gaddafi), February 18–22, 2012. **Punjab won by 511 runs. ‡Punjab 496** (Aamer Sajjad 252; Danish Kaneria 6-160) **and 412** (Mohammad Ayub 123, Haris Sohail 150); **Sind 235** (Mohammad Khalil 5-73) **and 162.** *Punjab batted Sind out of the match. In their first innings, Aamer Sajjad occupied the crease for ten hours 35 minutes in his third double-century, and the highest score of the season (more than Sind managed in either innings); in their second, Mohammad Ayub and Haris Sohail added 221 for the fifth wicket, setting up a target of 674. Usman Salahuddin finished with 1,401 runs in the season.*

PENTANGULAR CUP WINNERS

1973-74	PIA	1984-85	United Bank	2006-07	Habib Bank
1974-75	National Bank	1985-86	PACO	2007-08	Sind
1975-76	PIA	1986-87	PIA	2008-09	North West FP
1976-77	PIA	1990-91	United Bank	2009-10	Sui Northern Gas
1980-81	PIA	1994-95	National Bank	2010-11	Sind
1981-82	Habib Bank	1995-96	United Bank	2011-12	Punjab
1982-83	Habib Bank	2005-06	National Bank		

FAYSAL BANK ONE-DAY NATIONAL CUP DIVISION ONE, 2011-12

Two 50-over leagues plus knockout

Semi-finals

At Faisalabad (Iqbal), March 19, 2012. **Habib Bank won by 154 runs. ‡Habib Bank 334-6** (50 overs) (Imran Farhat 125, Taufeeq Umar 100); **Sialkot Stallions 180** (42.1 overs). *Imran Farhat and Taufeeq Umar opened with 220.*

At Lahore (Gaddafi), March 19, 2012. **PIA won by four wickets. Islamabad Leopards 212-7** (50 overs); **‡PIA 214-6** (49.2 overs).

Final

At Lahore (Gaddafi), March 21, 2012. **PIA won by 36 runs. PIA 237** (49.5 overs) (Danish Kaneria 7-39); **‡Habib Bank 201** (47.1 overs). *Danish Kaneria took the last seven wickets of PIA's innings for a career-best, but still finished on the losing side.*

ONE-DAY NATIONAL CUP DIVISION TWO, 2011-12

Two 50-over leagues plus knockout

Semi-finals

At Karachi (National), March 9, 2012. **KRL won by eight wickets. Lahore Eagles 219-9** (50 overs); **‡KRL 220-2** (47 overs) (Zain Abbas 105*).

At Karachi (NBP), March 9, 2012. **United Bank won by nine wickets. ‡Quetta Bears 192** (49.3 overs); **United Bank 193-1** (38.4 overs).

Final

At Karachi (National), March 11, 2012. **United Bank won by 166 runs. United Bank 262** (50 overs); **‡KRL 96** (33.2 overs). *MoM:* Adnan Baig (United Bank).

FAYSAL BANK TWENTY20 CUP, 2011-12

Four 20-over leagues plus knockout

Semi-finals

At Karachi (National), October 1, 2011 (floodlit). **Sialkot Stallions won by six wickets.** ‡**Lahore Eagles 167** (19.3 overs); **Sialkot Stallions 171-4** (18.5 overs). *MoM:* Shoaib Malik (Sialkot Stallions). *Shoaib Malik hit 88* in 49 balls.*

At Karachi (National), October 1, 2011 (floodlit). **Rawalpindi Rams won by 77 runs.** ‡**Rawalpindi Rams 168** (19.5 overs); **Peshawar Panthers 91** (16 overs). *MoM:* Umar Amin (Rawalpindi Rams).

Final

At Karachi (National), October 2, 2011 (floodlit). **Sialkot Stallions won by ten runs.** ‡**Sialkot Stallions 180-6** (20 overs); **Rawalpindi Rams 170-8** (20 overs). *MoM:* Raza Hasan (Sialkot Stallions).

FAYSAL BANK SUPER EIGHT T20 CUP, 2011-12

Two 20-over leagues plus knockout

Semi-finals

At Rawalpindi (Cricket), March 31, 2012. **Karachi Dolphins won by seven wickets.** ‡**Lahore Lions 167-7** (20 overs); **Karachi Dolphins 170-3** (19 overs). *MoM:* Shahzaib Hasan (Karachi Dolphins).

At Rawalpindi (Cricket), March 31, 2012. **Sialkot Stallions won by 40 runs.** ‡**Sialkot Stallions 197-1** (20 overs) (Shakeel Ansar 100*); **Peshawar Panthers 157-8** (20 overs). *MoM:* Shakeel Ansar (Sialkot Stallions).

Final

At Rawalpindi (Cricket), April 1, 2012. **Sialkot Stallions won by eight wickets.** ‡**Karachi Dolphins 167-8** (20 overs); **Sialkot Stallions 170-2** (18.5 overs) (Shakeel Ansar 100*). *MoM:* Shoaib Malik (Sialkot Stallions). *Raza Hasan claimed four wickets and a run-out in the 18th and 20th overs of Karachi Dolphins' innings.*

SOUTH AFRICAN CRICKET, 2012

All bases covered

COLIN BRYDEN

South Africa ignored boardroom uncertainty to put together arguably their best year in Test cricket. Unbeaten in ten matches, they won all four series – three away from home – to finish 2012 as the undisputed No. 1 team in the world. Victories at home against Sri Lanka, followed by wins in New Zealand, England – the team they deposed at the top of the rankings – and Australia vindicated the unorthodox approach of their coach, Gary Kirsten, who placed the emphasis on mental freshness rather than physical preparation.

Although most of the team had not played first-class cricket for more than three months, South Africa had only one two-day match and one first-class three-day fixture before their Test series against England. The main event of their build-up had been a team-building exercise in Switzerland with

SOUTH AFRICA IN 2012

	Played	*Won*	*Lost*	*Drawn/No result*
Tests	10	5	–	5
One-day internationals	13	8	4	1
Twenty20 internationals	15	8	6	1

Month	Fixture	Reference
DECEMBER / JANUARY	3 Tests and 5 ODIs (h) v Sri Lanka	(see *Wisden 2012*, page 1043)
FEBRUARY / MARCH	3 Tests, 3 ODIs and 3 T20Is (a) v New Zealand	(page 1025)
	1 T20I (h) v India	(page 1073)
APRIL		
MAY		
JUNE		
JULY / AUGUST / SEPTEMBER	3 Tests, 5 ODIs and 3 T20Is (a) v England	(page 345)
SEPTEMBER / OCTOBER	World Twenty20 (in Sri Lanka)	(page 841)
NOVEMBER / DECEMBER	3 Tests (a) v Australia	(page 907)
DECEMBER / JANUARY	2 Tests, 3 ODIs and 3 T20Is (h) v New Zealand	(page 1075)

For a review of South African domestic cricket from the 2011-12 season, see page 1093.

the Johannesburg-born mountaineer and adventurer Mike Horn, who had worked with Kirsten before, during his stint as coach of India. The Alpine adventure evidently had the desired effect of energising and motivating the players.

Despite struggling in the field on the first day at The Oval, South Africa then came as close to the perfect Test match against credible opposition as possible, winning by an innings while losing only two wickets, and celebrating Hashim Amla's epic unbeaten 311, the first Test triple-century by a South African. When a hard-earned victory in the Third Test at Lord's settled the series, England handed over the ICC mace.

As in 2008, triumph in England was followed by a tour of Australia – and, once again, South Africa were able to complete a remarkable double. On this occasion, though, there were legitimate grounds to wonder if they had gone into the three-match series with sufficient physical preparation. After a less than convincing warm-up game against Australia A, their bowlers took a pummelling in the First Test at Brisbane, although defeat was never likely after the second day was washed out.

Australia then dominated the Second Test, at Adelaide, with Michael Clarke making his second successive double-century, and seemed set for victory when South Africa, set an improbable 430, ended the fourth day on 77 for four. But Francois du Plessis – "Faf" to almost everyone – led a remarkable rearguard action on Test debut to steer South Africa to safety with two wickets to spare. On the only pitch which gave their fast bowlers any assistance, they then gained a huge win in the decisive Test, at Perth.

Impressively solid batting and a potent fast-bowling attack had been the foundation of their success. A top five of Graeme Smith, Alviro Petersen, Amla, Jacques Kallis and A. B. de Villiers made 4,463 runs between them at an average of nearly 58. Amla headed the list, with 1,064 runs at 70, including four centuries – two each against England and Australia – and Kallis was not far behind, with 944 at 67. Petersen underlined his value as Smith's opening partner, and it was a measure of South Africa's success that his 815 runs at almost 48 made him the least successful of the quintet. Kallis missed one Test because of injury, but the other four played in all ten.

A horrific eye injury which ended the career of long-serving wicketkeeper Mark Boucher had the unintended consequence of strengthening the batting, as de Villiers took the gloves and South Africa were able to field seven batsmen. J-P. Duminy took advantage of his opportunities, first when Kallis was injured in New Zealand, then as the extra batsman in England, and averaged 90 before he ruptured an Achilles tendon while warming down after the opening day of the Test series in Australia. But that simply opened the door for du Plessis. The performances at No. 6 of Jacques Rudolph (435 runs at 39) were relatively modest.

The pace trio of Dale Steyn, Morne Morkel and Vernon Philander took 120 of the 160 wickets claimed by South African bowlers during the year, despite operating mainly on unhelpful pitches. But Imran Tahir's leg-spin proved less effective, and he was dropped for Perth, where slow left-armer Robin Peterson, a perennial tourist but seldom a Test cricketer, made an impressive comeback.

Gareth Copley, Getty Images

On a high: England were swept aside by Graeme Smith's formidable South African machine.

There was concern about the bowling depth, with Marchant de Lange – who had made a sensational debut in the last Test of 2011 – not playing at all after pulling out of the England tour with a stress fracture. Rory Kleinveldt played in two Tests in Australia with mixed success.

Under the new leadership of de Villiers, South Africa won eight one-day internationals and lost four, winning series against Sri Lanka and New Zealand, and sharing the honours in England. Amla top-scored in the last two matches in New Zealand, and in all four innings in England, to set a world record. But an ongoing problem was the lack of an effective bowling combination at the death.

The biggest disappointment came at the World Twenty20 in Sri Lanka. After winning both their group matches, including a rain-shortened encounter against the hosts, South Africa lost all three in the Super Eights, against Pakistan, Australia and India. Poor starts with the bat, and equally poor bowling towards the end of innings, were largely to blame.

The cricket took place against a backdrop of legal wrangling over the dismissal of chief executive Gerald Majola, and controversy over the implementation of a new system of administration. Cricket South Africa's annual general meeting, normally held in August, was postponed twice, the second time until February 2013, by which time the presidency and the chief executive's role had been in the hands of acting-officials for almost a year.

In what should have been an end to a saga that started when South Africa hosted the IPL in 2009, Judge Chris Nicholson's findings after a ministerial enquiry were damning of Majola. He recommended a criminal investigation and disciplinary action by CSA following Majola's pocketing of undeclared bonuses. Majola refused to take part in the hearing, which recommended he be sacked, choosing instead to take the matter to the Labour Court in Johannesburg.

Nicholson recommended an overhaul of the system of governance, with a majority of independent directors. CSA initially opted for an even split, but it was not a universally popular decision. When the annual meeting was finally held on February 2, 2013, a split of seven non-independent and five independent directors was approved. Chris Nenzani, a relative newcomer to administration who had been president of the Border Cricket Board since 2010, was elected president.

Norman Arendse, a former president of CSA, was elected lead independent director. A nomination panel had initially recommended him, but this was vetoed by CSA on the grounds that he had recently been involved in cricket. He challenged the ruling and was eventually accepted as a director. Arendse's tenure as CSA president between 2007 and 2008 was notable for acrimony and alleged interference in selection.

Jacques Faul, the acting-chief executive, made no secret of his frustration with the ongoing wrangling, and announced he would not be available for a full-time role at national level. Instead he was named chief executive of the Northerns Union.

Yet another cloud on the horizon was a row over the non-selection of Thami Tsolekile for the Test series against New Zealand in January 2013. Tsolekile had been told he would probably take over behind the stumps after the Australia series, only for de Villiers to decide he wanted to keep wicket on a long-term basis. With no black African players in the squad, the controversy became a racial issue. Makhaya Ntini, the only black African to have made a major impact in international cricket, claimed Tsolekile would have been picked if he had been white.

In South Africa, cricket is seldom a matter of simply playing the game.

SOUTH AFRICA v INDIA, 2011-12

NEIL MANTHORP

Twenty20 international (1): South Africa 1, India 0

In January 2011, South Africa and India provided the focal point in a night of "cricketainment" at a packed Moses Mabhida Stadium in Durban, built specifically for the 2010 football World Cup. Filled to capacity at 50,000, it was the largest attendance for a cricket match on the African continent. A Bollywood song-and-dance extravaganza starring Kolkata Knight Riders owner Shah Rukh Khan followed the Twenty20 match, and the event was such a success that both boards immediately agreed to a sequel.

A year is a long time in sport, however, and the magic could not be repeated – certainly not away from Durban, home to the world's biggest Indian diaspora. A game at the Wanderers was shoehorned into the schedule eight days after the Asia Cup, three days after South Africa had finished their Test series in New Zealand, and five days before the IPL. To cap it off, the final of South Africa's domestic Twenty20 tournament (to be held on the same ground) was postponed by 24 hours. Without any obvious justification for the fixture, it became a "tribute match" to Jacques Kallis – although it would have made more sense to pay homage to a Cape Town boy at Newlands. The South Africans did not even hold a pre-match training session.

A contribution was made to the Jacques Kallis Scholarship Foundation, which had been helping underprivileged children with schooling and cricketing education for six years, and Kallis made a donation of his own to the recently established Yuvraj Singh Foundation to assist cancer sufferers. Thankfully, much good was done, because as a one-off game of international cricket, it ranked among the most irrelevant of all time.

INDIA SQUAD

*M. S. Dhoni, R. Ashwin, A. B. Dinda, G. Gambhir, R. A. Jadeja, V. Kohli, P. Kumar, I. K. Pathan, Y. K. Pathan, S. K. Raina, R. Sharma, R. G. Sharma, M. K. Tiwary, R. V. Uthappa, R. Vinay Kumar. *Coach:* D. A. G. Fletcher.

SOUTH AFRICA v INDIA

Twenty20 International

At Johannesburg, March 30, 2012 (floodlit). South Africa won by 11 runs (D/L). Toss: India. Twenty20 international debuts: F. Behardien, D. J. Vilas.

"Let's hope it doesn't rain," quipped Dhoni as he left the pre-match press conference. Unfortunately it did. Kallis, one of only two – with Tsotsobe – in South Africa's squad to have made the trip from New Zealand, made light work of jet lag to belt 61 from 42 balls, in a match somewhat crassly dedicated to him. Ingram was even more destructive, forcing Dhoni to persist with part-time spinners for longer than desirable. Gambhir responded with a quick 49 but, with Uthappa struggling to get Tsotsobe away at the other end, India were 12 runs behind on Duckworth/Lewis when a thunderstorm ended play in the eighth over. That meant South Africa achieved the oddity of winning without claiming a wicket. The whole thing was an oddity, to be frank.

Man of the Match: C. A. Ingram.

South Africa

		B	4	6
R. E. Levi *c 4 b 8*	19	7	4	0
J. H. Kallis *c 4 b 9*	61	42	5	2
C. A. Ingram *c 4 b 5*	78	50	8	3
F. Behardien *not out*	20	11	2	0
J. L. Ontong *b 5*	22	7	2	2
J. A. Morkel *not out*	16	3	1	2
L-b 1, w 2	3			
6 overs: 55-1 (20 overs)	219-4			

1/22 2/141 3/168 4/203

*J. Botha, †D. J. Vilas, W. D. Parnell, J. Theron and L. L. Tsotsobe did not bat.

P. Kumar 2–0–22–0; I. K. Pathan 4–0–44–1; Vinay Kumar 3–0–32–0; Ashwin 4–0–33–1; Y. K. Pathan 1–0–9–0; Raina 4–0–49–2; Sharma 1–0–14–0; Kohli 1–0–15–0.

India

		B	4	6
R. V. Uthappa *not out*	18	19	1	0
G. Gambhir *not out*	49	28	7	1
L-b 3, w 1	4			
6 overs: 51-0 (7.5 overs)	71-0			

V. Kohli, R. G. Sharma, S. K. Raina, *†M. S. Dhoni, Y. K. Pathan, I. K. Pathan, R. Ashwin, P. Kumar and R. Vinay Kumar did not bat.

Tsotsobe 3–0–15–0; Morkel 1–0–16–0; Theron 1–0–13–0; Parnell 1.5–0–14–0; Botha 1–0–10–0.

Umpires: J. D. Cloete and S. George. Third umpire: A. T. Holdstock. Referee: B. C. Broad.

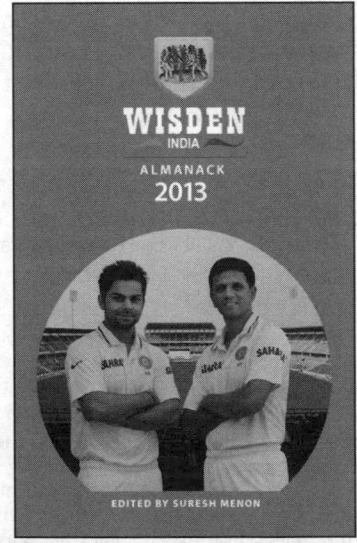

SOUTH AFRICA v NEW ZEALAND, 2012-13

NEIL MANTHORP

Test matches (2): South Africa 2, New Zealand 0
One-day internationals (3): South Africa 1, New Zealand 2
Twenty20 internationals (3): South Africa 2, New Zealand 1

New Zealand were always facing stiff odds against the world's top-ranked Test side, even before injuries ruled out Daniel Vettori and Tim Southee, two of their best bowlers. But when they contrived to lose their single world-class batsman because of inept management on an epic scale, they moved from outsiders to no-hopers. The crass removal of Ross Taylor from the captaincy on the tour of Sri Lanka, and his subsequent decision to sit this one out, hung over the trip like a family imprisonment. Taylor was missed during the Twenty20 series, and outrageously so during the Tests, when his team-mates were bowled out for 45 at Cape Town and reduced to 62 for nine at Port Elizabeth.

So weedy did Cricket South Africa consider New Zealand, that they axed the traditional Boxing Day Test in favour of three Twenty20 internationals. They hoped to raise more TV revenue, but the move backfired when the South African Broadcasting Corporation pulled out of showing the Tests live because of financial problems. For the first time since readmission, South Africa's home Tests were not available on free-to-air state television, though the satellite channel SuperSport did show all the games.

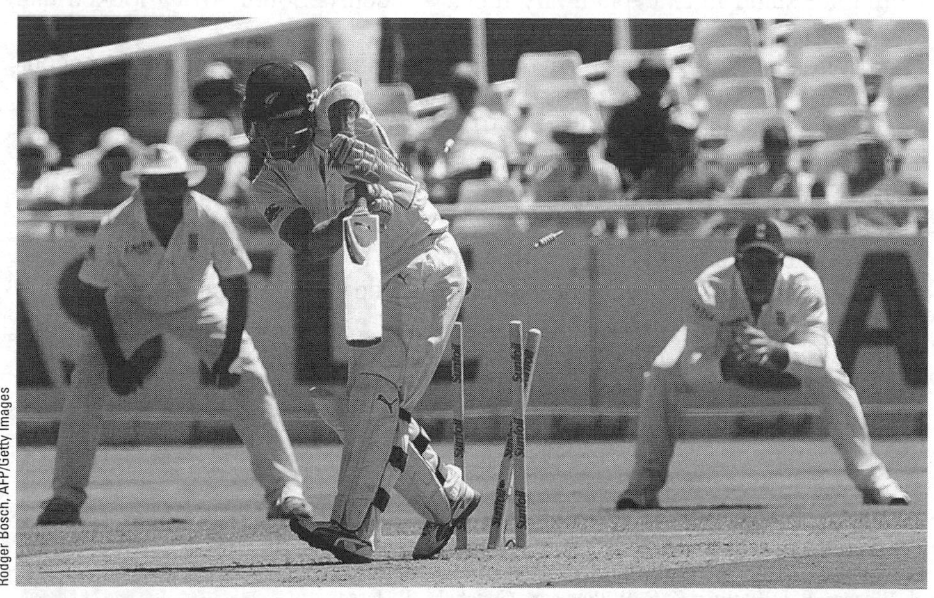

Rodger Bosch, AFP/Getty Images

Welcome to the captaincy: Brendon McCullum is bowled by Vernon Philander as New Zealand slip to 45 on the opening morning of the series at Cape Town.

New Zealand coach Mike Hesson maintained an embarrassed rather than a dignified silence throughout, even when a leaked letter from bowling coach Shane Bond emerged, appearing to back up Taylor's claim that Hesson had lied about wanting to keep him as captain of the Test team. New Zealand Cricket chief executive David White maintained there was "considerable variance" between Bond's account and that of other coaching staff.

Having aspired to the national captaincy for much of his career, Brendon McCullum wasn't about to let the chance slip away. He spoke with candour and – whenever possible – optimism, despite performances that were plainly unacceptable. So perhaps more people should have listened when he insisted before the one-day series that his side would be "far more competitive, because we are far more comfortable in this format and know our games so much better". Comfort and knowledge were one thing; "more competitive" sounded like pure fantasy.

The reversal could not be taken at face value, though, because most of the faces had changed. Seasoned veterans such as Kyle Mills and Grant Elliott came into New Zealand's squad, while South Africa decided to rest many of their key men. They continued to debate the future of A. B. de Villiers as wicketkeeper, in the light of his chronic back problems. He made a late decision to retain the gloves in the Tests, to the annoyance of the long-suffering Thami Tsolekile, who had been told by the selectors he would finally get a go. De Villiers did hand them to 20-year-old Quinton de Kock for the limited-overs matches, allowing him to sit out the Twenty20s and concentrate on captaining in one-day cricket. But then de Villiers was banned for the last two games for falling six overs behind the clock at Paarl; Hashim Amla missed the same matches through injury, having already informed the selectors he would not stand in as captain any more. Suddenly, South Africa looked like an A-team.

Not only did New Zealand win the series, but they came within an outrageous scoop for six – by Ryan McLaren at Potschefstroom – of being the first team to whitewash South Africa in the 50-over format at home. It was truly an astonishing turnaround in fortunes. So low had been the nation's expectations that not a single member of the travelling press contingent stayed on after the Test series.

New Zealand arrived home with Taylor set to return for the series against England, and confront what he admitted would be a "difficult" relationship with Hesson. South Africa, meanwhile, could reflect on a double, emphatic, confirmation of what they already knew. Their Test side was the best in the world and, quite possibly, South Africa's best ever – yet, frustratingly, the limited-overs team remained anything but.

NEW ZEALAND TOURING PARTY

*B. B. McCullum, T. A. Boult, D. A. J. Bracewell, D. G. Brownlie, D. R. Flynn, J. E. C. Franklin, P. G. Fulton, M. J. Guptill, M. J. McClenaghan, B. P. Martin, C. S. Martin, C. Munro, J. S. Patel, N. Wagner, B-J. Watling, K. S. Williamson. *Coach:* M. J. Hesson.

T. G. Southee was originally selected in the Test squad, but injured his thumb in a domestic match, and was replaced by McClenaghan. Fulton withdrew when he aggravated a knee injury during the three-day warm-up match. For the Twenty20 series that preceded the Tests, C. J. Anderson, M. D. Bates, D. C. de Boorder, R. M. Hira, N. L. McCullum, J. D. S. Neesham and R. J. Nicol were selected in place of Brownlie, Flynn, B. P. Martin, C. S. Martin, Patel, Southee, Wagner, Watling and Williamson. A. F. Milne was originally selected in both limited-overs squads, but suffered an Achilles injury before the tour, and was replaced in the Twenty20 squad by M. R. Gillespie, who himself strained a muscle in a Plunket Shield match and was replaced by Bates; Milne was replaced by Wagner in the one-day squad. For that series, Hira, N. L. McCullum, K. D. Mills, Neesham and Nicol replaced Bracewell, Brownlie, Flynn, Fulton, B. P. Martin, C. S. Martin and Patel. Anderson hurt his hand in net practice before the series, and was replaced by G. D. Elliott.

At Pietermaritzburg, December 18, 2012. **New Zealanders won by 24 runs.** ‡**New Zealanders 140-8** (20 overs) (B. B. McCullum 32, C. Munro 39; K. J. Abbott 4-16); **South Africa A 116-9** (20 overs) (V. B. van Jaarsveld 43; M. J. McClenaghan 3-19, R. M. Hira 3-35). *Each side chose from 12 players, of whom 11 could bat and 11 field. In the space of 11 balls, Mitchell McClenaghan, a 26-year-old left-arm pace bowler yet to make his international debut, bowled Davy Jacobs and Stiaan van Zyl, then had Dane Vilas caught behind.*

SOUTH AFRICA v NEW ZEALAND

First Twenty20 International

At Durban, December 21, 2012 (floodlit). South Africa won by eight wickets. Toss: New Zealand. Twenty20 international debuts: H. Davids, Q. de Kock, C. H. Morris; C. J. Anderson, M. J. McClenaghan, C. Munro, J. D. S. Neesham.

Both sides began afresh after disappointing World Twenty20 campaigns, blooding a rush of debutants – South Africa had even appointed a new Twenty20 coach, 37-year-old Russell Domingo, previously their assistant coach. Pre-tour fears that a callow New Zealand would be humiliated came horribly true, yet it was neither lack of ability nor the intimidation factor which undid them. Instead, they backed themselves too heavily. Even Twenty20 requires some degree of planning, yet New Zealand assumed they could bat with complete abandon on an untrustworthy surface. By the time Peterson came on, they were 36 for five, and he proceeded to earn South Africa's most economical four-over analysis. Levi's fifth-ball departure – nicking to slip off debutant Mitchell McClenaghan – was New Zealand's sole moment of hope, before du Plessis and Quinton de Kock, captain and wicketkeeper respectively in the absence of A. B. de Villiers, completed the most routine of victories. South Africa's only sour note came when debutant all-rounder Chris Morris limped off with a hamstring strain.

Man of the Match: R. K. Kleinveldt.

New Zealand

		B	*4*	*6*
R. J. Nicol *c 4 b 11*	3	5	0	0
P. G. Fulton *c 10 b 9*	9	13	2	0
*†B. B. McCullum *c 9 b 11*	6	11	1	0
J. E. C. Franklin *c 4 b 8*	0	3	0	0
C. Munro *c and b 10*	23	18	4	0
C. J. Anderson *c 1 b 10*	5	5	1	0
N. L. McCullum *b 7*	1	7	0	0
J. D. S. Neesham *b 7*	10	7	2	0
D. A. J. Bracewell *not out*	21	25	3	0
R. M. Hira *c 11 b 9*	5	13	0	0
M. J. McClenaghan *c 7 b 11*	0	3	0	0
L-b 1, w 2	3			
6 overs: 27-3 (18.2 overs)	86			

1/9 2/19 3/19 4/27 5/34 6/36 7/54 8/60 9/81

McLaren 4–0–27–1; Steyn 3–0–13–2; Kleinveldt 3.2–1–18–3; Morris 3.4–0–19–2; Peterson 4–0–8–2; du Plessis 0.2–0–0–0.

South Africa

		B	*4*	*6*
R. E. Levi *c 2 b 11*	0	5	0	0
H. Davids *b 10*	20	13	3	1
*F. du Plessis *not out*	38	32	6	0
†Q. de Kock *not out*	28	23	5	0
W 1	1			
6 overs: 46-2 (12.1 overs)	87-2			

1/0 2/45

D. A. Miller, F. Behardien, R. J. Peterson, R. McLaren, D. W. Steyn, C. H. Morris and R. K. Kleinveldt did not bat.

McClenaghan 3–1–20–1; Bracewell 2–0–21–0; Hira 3–0–15–1; Anderson 1–0–11–0; N. L. McCullum 2–0–7–0; Nicol 1–0–11–0; Neesham 0.1–0–2–0.

Umpires: J. D. Cloete and S. George. Third umpire: A. T. Holdstock.

SOUTH AFRICA v NEW ZEALAND

Second Twenty20 International

At East London, December 23, 2012 (floodlit). New Zealand won by eight wickets (D/L). Toss: New Zealand. Twenty20 international debut: A. M. Phangiso.

The oft-quoted line that a single player can win a game of Twenty20 has seldom been better illustrated. Guptill scored an inspired hundred, the third by a New Zealander in Twenty20 internationals, when – with four needed off the last ball – he smeared Kleinveldt's attempted yorker to the cover boundary. It provided Brendon McCullum, owner of the other two centuries, with his first win as New Zealand's full-time captain. Henry Davids and du Plessis had played smartly before Miller added some zip, but three wickets for Bracewell in the final over cost South Africa dearly. The match was reduced to 19 overs a side after a floodlight failure during the first innings, increasing New Zealand's target by three to 169 – more than any team had chased down against South Africa. But Guptill, returning from a stomach bug, played an innings to remember: orthodox in his shots down the ground, relentlessly powerful and perfectly paced.

Man of the Match: M. J. Guptill.

South Africa

		B	*4*	*6*
R. E. Levi *c 7 b 10*	5	13	0	0
H. Davids *c 8 b 11*	55	38	7	1
*F. du Plessis *c 6 b 9*	63	43	8	1
D. A. Miller *c 10 b 9*	33	18	2	2
F. Behardien *not out*	5	2	1	0
R. J. Peterson *c 8 b 9*	0	1	0	0
†Q. de Kock *not out*	0	0	0	0
L-b 2, w 1, n-b 1	4			
6 overs: 37-1 (19 overs)	165-5			

1/13 2/81 3/160 4/160 5/161

R. McLaren, R. K. Kleinveldt, A. M. Phangiso and M. Morkel did not bat.

McClenaghan 4–0–32–1; Hira 4–0–37–1; Bracewell 3–0–33–3; Anderson 2–0–21–0; N. L. McCullum 4–0–23–0; Franklin 1–0–10–0; Nicol 1–0–7–0.

New Zealand

		B	*4*	*6*
M. J. Guptill *not out*	101	69	9	6
R. J. Nicol *c 4 b 6*	25	24	4	0
*†B. B. McCullum *c 4 b 8*	17	15	2	0
C. Munro *not out*	8	7	0	0
L-b 9, w 8, n-b 1	18			
6 overs: 39-0 (19 overs)	169-2			

1/76 2/149

J. E. C. Franklin, C. J. Anderson, N. L. McCullum, J. D. S. Neesham, D. A. J. Bracewell, R. M. Hira and M. J. McClenaghan did not bat.

Peterson 3–0–28–1; Morkel 4–0–29–0; Kleinveldt 4–0–35–0; McLaren 4–0–26–1; Phangiso 4–0–42–0.

Umpires: S. George and A. T. Holdstock. Third umpire: J. D. Cloete.

SOUTH AFRICA v NEW ZEALAND

Third Twenty20 International

At Port Elizabeth, December 26, 2012. South Africa won by 33 runs. Toss: South Africa.

Normal service was resumed. Davids completed a memorable debut series with a confident 68, assisted by the recalled Ontong in a stand of 89, and South Africa's total proved insurmountable on another tricky, two-paced pitch. Both Guptill and Brendon McCullum perished attempting to up the rate, and the contest was all but finished by the tenth over. Fringe players McLaren and Aaron Phangiso, a left-arm spinner from a township near Pretoria, looked every bit potential match-winners, returning identical figures in different circumstances. This was the first year since readmission that South Africa had not played a Test match on Boxing Day.

Man of the Match: H. Davids.

South Africa

		B	4	6
H. Davids *c 8 b 11*	68	51	7	2
*F. du Plessis *b 10*	1	9	0	0
†Q. de Kock *c 8 b 11*	2	4	0	0
J. L. Ontong *c 8 b 5*	48	30	1	3
D. A. Miller *c 8 b 9*	28	15	4	0
F. Behardien *c 11 b 9*	22	11	2	1
R. K. Kleinveldt *not out*	0	0	0	0
L-b 4, w 6	10			
6 overers: 36-2 (20 overs)	179-6			

1/2 2/26 3/115 4/135 5/179 6/179

R. J. Peterson, R. McLaren, A. M. Phangiso and M. Morkel did not bat.

McClenaghan 4–0–24–2; Hira 4–1–24–1; N. L. McCullum 3–0–27–0; Franklin 3–0–30–1; Bracewell 3–0–35–2; Neesham 3–0–35–0.

New Zealand

		B	4	6
R. J. Nicol *lbw b 9*	5	3	1	0
M. J. Guptill *c 8 b 10*	24	20	3	1
*†B. B. McCullum *c 4 b 10*	25	22	3	1
C. Munro *c 3 b 9*	3	10	0	0
J. E. C. Franklin *c 4 b 10*	16	13	1	1
J. D. S. Neesham *c 11 b 8*	12	10	2	0
N. L. McCullum *c 8 b 9*	17	14	2	0
C. J. Anderson *run out*	12	9	1	0
D. A. J. Bracewell *not out*	15	9	2	0
R. M. Hira *c 4 b 7*	12	9	2	0
M. J. McClenaghan *not out*	1	1	0	0
L-b 1, w 3	4			
6 overs: 45-1 (20 overs)	146-9			

1/6 2/53 3/56 4/60 5/84 6/87 7/116 8/116 9/137

McLaren 4–0–25–3; Peterson 3–0–24–1; Morkel 4–0–37–0; Kleinveldt 4–0–25–1; Phangiso 4–0–25–3; Ontong 1–0–9–0.

Umpires: J. D. Cloete and A. T. Holdstock. Third umpire: S. George.
Series referee: A. J. Pycroft.

At Paarl, December 28–30 (not first-class). **Drawn.** **‡New Zealanders 311-6 dec** (K. S. Williamson 59, B. B. McCullum 65; C. N. Ackermann 3-46) **and 117-2 dec** (M. J. Guptill 68*); **South African Invitation XI 359-7 dec** (H. E. van der Dussen 76, M. C. Kleinveldt 78, K. D. Petersen 76*, P. J. N. Jeftha 54*). *The South African Invitation XI chose from 12 players and the New Zealanders 13, of whom 11 could bat and 11 field. New Zealand's bowlers went wicketless for the first 53 overs of the hosts' innings, as Rassie van der Dussen and Matthew Kleinveldt, a 23-year-old cousin of Test bowler Rory, put on 161. To make matters worse, the New Zealanders lost Peter Fulton from the tour with a recurrence of a knee injury.*

SOUTH AFRICA v NEW ZEALAND

First Test Match

At Cape Town, January 2–4, 2013. South Africa won by an innings and 27 runs. Toss: New Zealand.

Fully exploiting generous, but not extravagant, seam movement, Philander single-handedly reduced New Zealand to 27 for five in his first 25 balls – and that, in effect, was the Test match decided. Morkel and Steyn, who claimed his 300th Test wicket with a

CHEAPEST FIVE-FORS IN TESTS

2.3–1–2–5†	E. R. H. Toshack	Australia v India at Brisbane	1947-48
6.5–4–3–6	J. J. C. Lawson	West Indies v Bangladesh at Dhaka	2002-03
7.2–5–6–5	H. Ironmonger	Australia v South Africa at Melbourne	1931-32
9.4–5–7–8‡	G. A. Lohmann	England v South Africa at Port Elizabeth	1895-96
6.3–4–7–6	A. E. R. Gilligan	England v South Africa at Birmingham	1924
6–3–7–5	**V. D. Philander**	**South Africa v New Zealand at Cape Town**	**2012-13**
6.5–3–9–5	T. B. A. May	Australia v West Indies at Adelaide	1992-93
6.2–0–9–6	M. J. Clarke	Australia v India at Mumbai	2004-05

† *Eight-ball overs.* ‡ *Five-ball overs.*

peach of an outswinger to bowl Bracewell, mopped up the tailenders so quickly there was even time for Smith to be dismissed before lunch. All this after poor McCullum had chosen to bat in his first Test since replacing Ross Taylor as captain.

South Africa applied themselves diligently on a surface which seemed to improve as the ball got older, but their task was made spectacularly easy with a total of only 45 in their sights. Brownlie's maiden Test century, and a resolutely dull 42 from Watling helped the follow-on span 102 overs, 83 more than first time around, but did little to diminish New Zealand's humiliation. It was pathetic.

But it had been gripping to watch Philander wobble and nibble the new ball around with such dexterity. Every delivery did something, but not a lot – which was the point. It was almost always just enough. Two edges to the wicketkeeper, one to first slip, one bowled and one lbw: done and dusted. The fastest five-for in Test history (from the start of a match) was not a bad reinforcement of his rare skill, following the sequence of five in 20 balls he claimed against Australia on debut at the same ground 14 months earlier. This from a man described as "provisionally fit" by his captain on the eve of the game.

Williamson provided New Zealand's lone score in double figures, while the five extras that came in the second over as Guptill and McCullum ran a leg-bye that turned into four overthrows accounted for 11% of the eventual total. Flynn did his best to stem the carnage but, joined by Martin, the world's most abject batsman, in the 19th over, he top-edged a pull. New Zealand's 45 all out was a throwback to a different era of low scores – one in which these countries featured prominently. Still, at 116 balls, this was New Zealand's shortest innings ever. It was the lowest Test total by any side in almost 40 years, since Geoff Arnold and Chris Old demolished India for 42 at Lord's in 1974 – and the joint-12th-lowest in all.

Conditions remained the same for New Zealand's bowlers, but the quality of the batsmen was very different, and South Africa needed only 184 balls from the start of the match to take the lead – another Test record. Amla looked as though he could play the seam movement off the pitch during an easy 66 from 74 balls, then Kallis unfurled an array of cuts and pulls which lesser batsmen had eschewed amid the variable bounce. With a thick edge past gully, he became the fourth man to 13,000 Test runs.

BLACK HUMOUR

Shortest completed innings by New Zealand in Tests:

Balls	*Total*	*Runs/over*	*Inns*		
116	**45**	**2.32**	**1**	**v South Africa at Cape Town**	**2012-13**
162	26	0.96	3	v England at Auckland	1954-55
182	73	2.40	2	v Pakistan at Lahore	2001-02
193	110	3.41	3	v Pakistan at Auckland	1993-94
194	54	1.67	3	v Australia at Wellington	1945-46
195	47	1.44	2	v England at Lord's	1958

Petersen, meanwhile, had dug himself a foxhole from which he rarely ventured, having established a game plan of dabbing and pushing until a gift presented itself. It was a fine example of the opening batsman's art of self-denial, particularly from one capable of aggression. The reward was a fifth Test century and, finally, the glue for his place in the XI. De Villiers displayed similar restraint before perishing in the flighty moments before the declaration. Patronising though it may sound, New Zealand's seamers should be credited for never giving up.

Pride and dignity were all they could bat for when they returned to the crease 302 in arrears and with almost 11 sessions to play. There was no hope. When Guptill flicked the last ball of Steyn's first over straight to the most obvious short midwicket, there was even more reason to despair. But a wry smile was the order of the day as the Perth-born Brownlie showed off an impressive selection of attacking back-foot strokes to make 109. It was just what New Zealand needed from the man asked to step into Taylor's shoes at No. 4. Philander, having taken 25 balls to complete his first-innings five-for, had to wait nearly 22 overs for his next wicket (Watling was the victim on both occasions). But New Zealand's belated resistance barely touched the debt of their first innings.

Man of the Match: V. D. Philander.

Close of play: first day, South Africa 252-3 (Petersen 103, de Villiers 19); second day, New Zealand 169-4 (Brownlie 69, Watling 10).

New Zealand

First innings		Second innings	
M. J. Guptill c de Villiers b Philander	1	– c Amla b Steyn	0
*B. B. McCullum b Philander	7	– lbw b Peterson	51
K. S. Williamson lbw b Philander	13	– c Petersen b Kallis	15
D. G. Brownlie c Smith b Philander	0	– c Peterson b Morkel	109
D. R. Flynn c and b Steyn	8	– c de Villiers b Kallis	14
†B-J. Watling c de Villiers b Philander	0	– c Smith b Philander	42
J. E. C. Franklin c Smith b Morkel	1	– b Steyn	22
D. A. J. Bracewell b Steyn	2	– c Petersen b Philander	0
J. S. Patel c Amla b Morkel	5	– b Steyn	8
T. A. Boult c de Villiers b Morkel	1	– not out	2
C. S. Martin not out	0	– run out	0
L-b 6, n-b 1	7	B 1, l-b 8, w 3	12
1/7 (1) 2/14 (2) 3/14 (4) 4/27 (3) 5/27 (6) 6/28 (7) 7/31 (8) 8/38 (9) 9/45 (10) 10/45 (5) (19.2 overs)	45	1/0 (1) 2/29 (3) 3/118 (2) 4/155 (5) 5/229 (4) 6/252 (6) 7/252 (8) 8/265 (9) 9/274 (7) 10/275 (11) (102.1 overs)	275

Steyn 7.2–2–18–2; Philander 6–3–7–5; Morkel 6–2–14–3. *Second innings*—Steyn 30–6–67–3; Philander 24–8–76–2; Morkel 21–6–50–1; Kallis 11.1–3–31–2; Peterson 16–6–42–1.

South Africa

*G. C. Smith lbw b Bracewell	1
A. N. Petersen b Boult	106
H. M. Amla lbw b Franklin	66
J. H. Kallis c Watling b Boult	60
†A. B. de Villiers b Martin	67
F. du Plessis c Williamson b Martin	15
D. Elgar c Watling b Boult	21
R. J. Peterson b Martin	5
V. D. Philander not out	0
B 1, l-b 2, w 2, n-b 1	6
1/1 (1) 2/108 (3) 3/212 (4) 4/255 (2) 5/281 (6) 6/335 (7) 7/342 (5) 8/347 (8) (8 wkts dec, 95.2 overs)	347

D. W. Steyn and M. Morkel did not bat.

Boult 21–2–78–3; Bracewell 24–4–93–1; Martin 19.2–4–63–3; Franklin 14–1–50–1; Patel 17–4–60–0.

Umpires: I. J. Gould and R. J. Tucker. Third umpire: H. D. P. K. Dharmasena.

SOUTH AFRICA v NEW ZEALAND

Second Test Match

At Port Elizabeth, January 11–14, 2013. South Africa won by an innings and 193 runs. Toss: South Africa. Test debut: C. Munro.

It was obvious from the outset that the St George's Park groundstaff – preparing for their first Test in more than five years – had taken South Africa coach Gary Kirsten's request for "lively" pitches seriously. Such was his uncertainty about the right course, Smith admitted he was hoping McCullum would call correctly at the toss. He did not. Smith chose to bat, and contributed a tidy half-century to a total that was at least 200 above par, on a dry and unusually cracked wicket which produced unpredictable bounce from the first morning, then got lower. When South Africa reached 325 for four by the close, there was a universal sense of foreboding for New Zealand and their fragile batting line-up.

Smith declared shortly after tea next day, allowing his fellow left-hander Dean Elgar to complete an aggressive century – a spirited U-turn to a Test career which had begun with a pair on debut two games earlier, at Perth. Thereafter, New Zealand descended towards defeat with the inevitability of a sunset – all that changed was the position from which it was viewed.

Amla assessed conditions brilliantly from early in his innings – and probably before he'd faced a ball. He clinically removed some of the more productive and adventurous shots from his repertoire, notably square of the wicket; the unreliable bounce made them unworthy of the risk. The result was a 19th Test century of exquisite minimalism which, oddly, made it just as compelling as some of his more vivid offerings, though he was missed by Williamson in the gully on 48. Three or four years earlier such a century would have taken him many hours and hundreds of balls. Now the fledgling-great Amla required just 187, while striking only eight fours.

It was pillows against machine guns

Even de Villiers struggled for timing, but New Zealand's three main seamers grew tired and disconsolate as the ball resolutely refused to take the edge; Patel, too, bowled as well as a conventional off-spinner could hope to. By the time du Plessis had settled in with a couple of rasping cover-drives (thanks to Amla's stickability, he could afford to gamble on the bounce), New Zealand shoulders were drooping. The total was already too high, at 286 for four, when they granted du Plessis an outrageous life on 42. After blatantly gloving Boult down the leg side, he snatched his bottom hand off the bat, and his near-miss play-acting proved so convincing that McCullum and his lieutenants eventually decided against a review. Within seconds, the dressing-room alerted them to the clanger they had dropped.

Reasoning that the dog had chosen to lie down of its own accord, du Plessis decided that kicking it was fair enough. All his risks paid off, including a pair of sixes to reach 50 and pass 100. It was impressive and entertaining. Elgar, too, was prepared to leave the crease when facing Patel and the medium-pace of debutant Colin Munro, and landed a series of blows – admittedly into a punch bag.

Vernon Philander's dicky hamstring had ruled him out this time, but Steyn was so overdue a bagful of wickets he would have been induced had he been pregnant. He ripped out the first two via the slip cordon (after Kallis, unusually, had dropped one in the first over), and returned to leave New Zealand 62 for nine and every observer red-faced at the prospect of another two-figure total. But Watling found a decent hitter in Boult, and the last pair came within three of doubling the score.

Guptill would have compiled the lowest two-Test aggregate by an opener in history had the DRS not saved him from a third-ball duck, caught behind off his shoulder rather than the bat's. What would have been a sequence of 1, 0, 1, 0 became 1, 0, 1, 48 – but in the face of a follow-on deficit of 404, it was still insufficient. As at Cape Town, Brownlie and

Watling showed some fight, but it was pillows against machine guns. South Africa wrapped up their biggest win against New Zealand on the fourth morning, surpassing an innings and 180 runs at Wellington 60 years earlier.

Man of the Match: D. W. Steyn.

Close of play: first day, South Africa 325-4 (Amla 106, du Plessis 69); second day, New Zealand 47-6 (Watling 15, Bracewell 3); third day, New Zealand 157-4 (Brownlie 44, Watling 41).

South Africa

A. N. Petersen c Patel b Bracewell	21
*G. C. Smith c Watling b Wagner	54
H. M. Amla c Watling b Boult	110
J. H. Kallis c Watling b Bracewell	8
†A. B. de Villiers c Williamson b Patel	51
F. du Plessis c McCullum b Munro	137
D. Elgar not out	103
R. J. Peterson c Patel b Munro	8
D. W. Steyn c Patel b Bracewell	5
R. K. Kleinveldt not out	7
B 6, l-b 8, w 4, n-b 3	21
1/29 (1) (8 wkts dec, 153.5 overs)	525
2/121 (2) 3/137 (4)	
4/223 (5) 5/336 (3)	
6/467 (6) 7/481 (8) 8/508 (9)	

M. Morkel did not bat.

Boult 32–5–108–1; Bracewell 34–6–94–3; Wagner 33–4–135–1; Patel 36.5–2–134–1; Munro 18–4–40–2.

New Zealand

M. J. Guptill c Petersen b Steyn	1	– b Kleinveldt	48
*B. B. McCullum c Kallis b Peterson	13	– lbw b Peterson	11
K. S. Williamson c Smith b Steyn	4	– b Peterson	11
D. G. Brownlie c de Villiers b Kleinveldt	10	– c de Villiers b Kallis	53
D. R. Flynn lbw b Kleinveldt	0	– c de Villiers b Kleinveldt	0
†B-J. Watling c Smith b Morkel	63	– b Steyn	63
C. Munro c Elgar b Peterson	0	– c Petersen b Morkel	15
D. A. J. Bracewell c de Villiers b Steyn	7	– c Petersen b Steyn	0
N. Wagner lbw b Steyn	0	– c de Villiers b Steyn	4
J. S. Patel b Steyn	0	– (11) not out	0
T. A. Boult not out	17	– (10) c Peterson b Morkel	3
L-b 5, w 1	6	L-b 2, w 1	3
1/2 (1) 2/8 (3) 3/27 (4) (44.4 overs)	121	1/40 (2) 2/64 (3) (86.4 overs)	211
4/27 (5) 5/39 (2) 6/39 (7)		3/84 (1) 4/84 (5)	
7/61 (8) 8/62 (9) 9/62 (10) 10/121 (6)		5/182 (4) 6/203 (7) 7/203 (6)	
		8/204 (8) 9/207 (10) 10/211 (9)	

Steyn 13–5–17–5; Morkel 12.4–6–26–1; Kleinveldt 11–3–53–2; Peterson 7–2–20–2; Kallis 1–1–0–0. *Second innings*—Steyn 15.4–2–48–3; Morkel 16–6–36–2; Kleinveldt 15–8–44–2; Peterson 26–13–47–2; Kallis 9–3–18–1; Smith 1–0–10–0; Petersen 4–0–6–0.

Umpires: H. D. P. K. Dharmasena and I. J. Gould. Third umpire: R. J. Tucker.
Series referee: D. C. Boon.

SOUTH AFRICA v NEW ZEALAND

First One-Day International

At Paarl, January 19, 2013. New Zealand won by one wicket. Toss: New Zealand. One-day international debuts: Q. de Kock, R. K. Kleinveldt; M. J. McClenaghan, J. D. S. Neesham.

New Zealand's victory was little less than heroic, cricket's answer to the *Rocky* movies. They hauled themselves off the canvas while many were heading for the exit, so safe did South Africa seem. New Zealand were 105 for seven halfway through their chase, and aggrieved that Brendon

McCullum had been denied the chance to review his lbw dismissal by a power blackout – triggered when host broadcasters SuperSport lost the use of their generator and apparently tried to plug into the stadium's power supply. Sensing South Africa's desire to get it over with, Franklin tormented the bowlers through exaggerated caution, at times looking like he was trying *not* to score – and his obduracy began to pay off. South Africa conceded 15 in wides, ten from Kleinveldt, who failed dismally to control the reverse swing. Franklin added 35 with Nathan McCullum, 47 with Mills, then an unbroken 22 with McClenaghan, who wasn't even required to score. McClenaghan had led New Zealand's attack smartly in his fourth international appearance, while Williamson enhanced his reputation as a partnership-breaker. The South African innings escaped tedium when Kleinveldt struck Mills for three sixes in the 46th over, but the lack of entertainment extended into the run-chase, when South Africa fell 30 minutes behind on the over-rate; de Villiers was banned for the rest of the series, and his team-mates lost their match fees. Like a funeral, there was drama in this game, but it wasn't much fun.

Man of the Match: J. E. C. Franklin.

South Africa

H. M. Amla lbw b Mills	13
G. C. Smith lbw b McClenaghan	7
C. A. Ingram c N. L. McCullum b Williamson	29
*A. B. de Villiers lbw b McClenaghan	7
F. du Plessis c Nicol b Williamson	57
†Q. de Kock c N. L. McCullum b Franklin	18
R. McLaren c B. B. McCullum b Williamson	33
R. J. Peterson lbw b McClenaghan	0
R. K. Kleinveldt c Mills b Williamson	26
D. W. Steyn b McClenaghan	0
L. L. Tsotsobe not out	0
B 4, l-b 3, w 10, n-b 1	18
(46.2 overs)	208

1/25 (1) 2/27 (2) 3/37 (4) 4/83 (3) 5/119 (6) 6/178 (7) 7/179 (8) 8/182 (5) 9/182 (10) 10/208 (9) 10 overs: 30-2

Mills 8–1–55–1; McClenaghan 10–2–20–4; N. L. McCullum 6–0–34–0; Franklin 10–1–44–1; Williamson 7.2–0–22–4; Neesham 4–0–22–0; Elliott 1–0–4–0.

New Zealand

R. J. Nicol c Smith b Tsotsobe	4
M. J. Guptill run out	0
B-J. Watling b McLaren	45
K. S. Williamson c du Plessis b Tsotsobe	5
*†B. B. McCullum lbw b Kleinveldt	26
G. D. Elliott c Smith b Kleinveldt	1
J. E. C. Franklin not out	47
J. D. S. Neesham lbw b McLaren	0
N. L. McCullum lbw b McLaren	24
K. D. Mills b McLaren	26
M. J. McClenaghan not out	0
L-b 13, w 15, n-b 3	31
(9 wkts, 45.4 overs)	209

1/0 (2) 2/4 (1) 3/21 (4) 4/73 (5) 5/81 (6) 6/105 (3) 7/105 (8) 8/140 (9) 9/187 (10) 10 overs: 35-3

Steyn 10–3–33–0; Tsotsobe 8–2–43–2; Kleinveldt 9–0–37–2; McLaren 8.4–0–46–4; Peterson 10–0–37–0.

Umpires: Enamul Haque and S. George. Third umpire: Aleem Dar.

SOUTH AFRICA v NEW ZEALAND

Second One-Day International

At Kimberley, January 22, 2013 (day/night). New Zealand won by 27 runs. Toss: South Africa. One-day international debuts: F. Behardien; C. Munro.

South Africa's reputation for choking under pressure in one-day cricket resurfaced spectacularly, and cost them their first series defeat at home to New Zealand in any format. Requiring 106 from nearly 19 overs with nine wickets in hand, they gagged so badly that the final margin of defeat flattered them. Hashim Amla injured his leg in the warm-ups and, with A. B. de Villiers suspended, they had lost the world's two top-ranked one-day batsmen. Nonetheless, it was galling to suffer five run-outs – the tenth such instance, but the first by South Africa. Brendon McCullum captained superbly, always with an extra man or two inside the circle, but the opposition was more than pliant. The crash began when Smith – having added 129 with Ingram – unwisely attempted a third run to Franklin's arm in the deep. Du Plessis got too cute with Nathan McCullum at short cover, the in-form Ingram tamely chipped him to mid-off and, when Miller was run out off the same player's fingertips at the bowler's end, the noose had been attached and the trapdoor was creaking. Brendon McCullum rated Williamson's unbeaten 145 from 136 balls "as good as we've seen from a New Zealander". It was also the highest score for them against major one-day opposition. His leg-side improvisation was as effective as it was ungainly, partly because of cramp late on.

Man of the Match: K. S. Williamson.

New Zealand

M. J. Guptill c du Plessis b Kleinveldt	0	N. L. McCullum c Tsotsobe b Morkel	19
B-J. Watling lbw b Morkel	12	K. D. Mills not out	15
K. S. Williamson not out	145	L-b 4, w 5	9
G. D. Elliott c de Kock b Kleinveldt	48		—
*†B. B. McCullum b Morkel	17	1/0 (1) 2/32 (2) (8 wkts, 50 overs)	279
C. Munro c Ingram b Tsotsobe	9	3/159 (4) 4/188 (5)	
J. E. C. Franklin b Tsotsobe	0	5/201 (6) 6/202 (7)	
J. D. S. Neesham run out	5	7/211 (8) 8/245 (9)	10 overs: 19-1

M. J. McClenaghan did not bat.

Kleinveldt 10–2–45–2; Tsotsobe 10–2–38–2; Morkel 10–1–71–3; McLaren 8–0–57–0; Peterson 9–0–45–0; du Plessis 3–0–19–0.

South Africa

†Q. de Kock b Mills	25	M. Morkel not out	19
G. C. Smith run out	66	L. L. Tsotsobe b Neesham	9
C. A. Ingram c Watling b N. L. McCullum	79		
*F. du Plessis run out	2	W 4, n-b 1	5
F. Behardien run out	31		—
D. A. Miller run out	14	1/38 (1) 2/167 (2) (49.1 overs)	252
R. McLaren c Guptill b Franklin	2	3/174 (4) 4/180 (3) 5/211 (6)	
R. K. Kleinveldt run out	0	6/215 (7) 7/216 (8) 8/224 (5)	
R. J. Peterson c N. L. McCullum b Mills	0	9/232 (9) 10/252 (11)	10 overs: 43-1

Mills 9–2–28–2; McClenaghan 10–0–51–0; N. L. McCullum 10–0–56–1; Williamson 3–0–22–0; Franklin 10–0–52–1; Neesham 3.1–0–20–1; Elliott 4–0–23–0.

Umpires: Aleem Dar and J. D. Cloete. Third umpire: Enamul Haque.

SOUTH AFRICA v NEW ZEALAND

Third One-Day International

At Potchefstroom, January 25, 2013 (day/night). South Africa won by one wicket. Toss: New Zealand. One-day international debut: A. M. Phangiso.

McLaren became the sixth man to win a one-day international by hitting the last ball for six. With three needed off Franklin, he assessed his options and chose the one marked "maximum risk, maximum reward" – an audacious lap-sweep to a ball outside off stump, which cleared the fine-leg rope with room to spare. His bravura meant South Africa avoided the ignominy of a home whitewash. Local supporters had looked on in horror as, from 165 for two in the 34th over, their side threatened

MAXIMUM REWARD

One-day internationals won with a six off the last ball:

Batsman	*Bowler*	*Runs required*		
Javed Miandad	C. Sharma	4	Pakistan v India at Sharjah	1985-86
L. Klusener	D. J. Nash	4	South Africa v New Zealand at Napier	1998-99
B. R. M. Taylor	Mashrafe bin Mortaza	5	Zimbabwe v Bangladesh at Harare	2006-07
S. Chanderpaul	W. P. U. J. C. Vaas	6	West Indies v Sri Lanka at Port-of-Spain	2007-08
E. C. Rainsford	K. J. O'Brien	1	Zimbabwe v Ireland at Harare	2010-11
R. McLaren	**J. E. C. Franklin**	**3**	**South Africa v New Zealand at Potchefstroom**	**2012-13**

Research: Andrew Samson

to repeat the choke of three days earlier. Smith appeared certain to bat through the chase, but tried to up the tempo and was caught at long-on after completing his tenth century in the format, and one of his best. McLaren lost Steyn to the penultimate ball of the match, but managed to sprint past him and regain the strike before the catch was taken. South Africa's improved bowling performance was undone by half-centuries from Munro, in his second one-day international, and Franklin, who helped gather 85 from the last ten overs.

Man of the Match: G. C. Smith.

New Zealand

M. J. Guptill c Ingram b Tsotsobe	5
B-J. Watling c du Plessis b McLaren	20
K. S. Williamson c de Kock b Tsotsobe	6
G. D. Elliott c Steyn b Tsotsobe	54
*†B. B. McCullum c Steyn b McLaren	13
C. Munro c de Kock b Tsotsobe	57
J. E. C. Franklin not out	53
N. L. McCullum c de Kock b McLaren	2
J. D. S. Neesham lbw b McLaren	13
K. D. Mills run out	7
M. J. McClenaghan not out	2
B 1, l-b 10, w 17	28
(9 wkts, 50 overs)	260

1/15 (1) 2/27 (3) 3/46 (2) 4/68 (5) 5/129 (4) 6/196 (6) 7/199 (8) 8/216 (9) 9/234 (10) — 10 overs: 27-2

Steyn 10–1–56–0; Tsotsobe 10–2–45–4; Kleinveldt 10–1–44–0; Phangiso 8–0–43–0; McLaren 10–0–52–4; Behardien 2–0–9–0.

South Africa

†Q. de Kock b Franklin	31
G. C. Smith c Watling b Williamson	116
C. A. Ingram c Guptill b N. L. McCullum	25
*F. du Plessis c Guptill b Mills	19
F. Behardien c and b Williamson	4
D. A. Miller b Mills	15
R. McLaren not out	25
R. K. Kleinveldt b McClenaghan	6
A. M. Phangiso c B. B. McCullum b McClenaghan	9
D. W. Steyn c Elliott b Franklin	4
L. L. Tsotsobe not out	0
B 4, l-b 1, w 5	10
(9 wkts, 50 overs)	264

1/83 (1) 2/122 (3) 3/165 (4) 4/174 (5) 5/205 (6) 6/229 (2) 7/237 (8) 8/251 (9) 9/258 (10) — 10 overs: 54-0

Mills 10–0–40–2; McClenaghan 10–0–70–2; Neesham 3–0–22–0; N. L. McCullum 10–1–35–1; Franklin 6–0–38–2; Elliott 3–0–14–0; Williamson 8–0–40–2.

Umpires: Enamul Haque and A. T. Holdstock. Third umpire: Aleem Dar.
Series referee: D. C. Boon.

CHAMPIONS LEAGUE, 2012-13

GRAHAM HARDCASTLE

For the second time in its four-year existence, the Champions League took place in South Africa, because of concerns the competition would clash with the Indian monsoon season and the Durga Puja festival, which celebrates the triumph of good over evil in Hinduism. Local spectators, though, had to be content with the triumph of Sydney Sixers, who deservedly claimed the $2.5m prize after proving themselves comfortably the best of the 14 teams on show.

Properly tested only once in six matches, the Australian franchise dominated a one-sided final at a sold-out Wanderers against home side Lions, who had made a habit of winning matches from positions of weakness. Sydney's squad included five players – plus general manager Stuart Clark – who had won the inaugural title with New South Wales in 2009.

Brad Haddin – Sydney's captain, opening batsman and wicketkeeper – was not averse to springing a surprise, the biggest coming in the final when, having elected to bowl on a batting track, he opened with spinners Steve O'Keefe and Nathan McCullum. They went for just 35 runs in their eight overs, and Lions could not recover from losing their top four batsmen in the first four overs.

Haddin was also blessed with an international-class attack: Pat Cummins, still only 19, Josh Hazlewood, 21, and Mitchell Starc, 22 – the competition's leading wicket-taker, with 14. They also had the top run-scorer, Michael Lumb, with 226 at a strike-rate of 155. After a handful of middling scores, he saved his best for the final. Hampshire and Yorkshire, Lumb's two former counties, could both have done with the impetus he provided at the top.

The tournament did not have as many nailbiting encounters as in 2011 but, even so, there were a number of upsets. Yorkshire overcame the absence of Tim Bresnan, rested by England, and Jonny Bairstow, who had a wrist injury, to emerge from the qualifying phase at the expense of Uva Next, from Sri Lanka, and 2009 finalists Trinidad & Tobago, who arrived with five of West Indies' World Twenty20-winning squad. Auckland's decision to fly to South Africa two weeks before their first match paid off when they qualified from the other pool – the first New Zealand side to do so. Their campaign in the tournament proper began with a seven-wicket win over IPL champions Kolkata Knight Riders, arguably the biggest surprise of the three weeks.

Apart from Delhi Daredevils, who reached the semi-finals – when a lone hand from Kevin Pietersen was unable to save them against Lions – the IPL teams struggled to adapt to the quicker pitches. Crowds were generally poor, boosted only by the presence of the home teams, Lions and Titans, who both reached the last four: Titans gave Sydney their only scare, nearly defending 163, but Starc and Cummins scrambled a bye off the last ball to prevent an all-South African final.

Hampshire, winners of a limited-overs double in the English summer, lost both their qualifying matches, to Auckland and Sialkot Stallions, the five-time winners of Pakistan's Twenty20 tournament but making their Champions

League debut after their previous exclusion for political reasons. Yorkshire's only consolation for losing all three matches in Group B was that no one hit more sixes than Gary Ballance's 11.

Despite the high quality of cricket, the tournament continued to be plagued by criticism on the grounds that it was not a bona fide Champions League. For the second year running there were four IPL teams, including Mumbai Indians, who qualified as reigning champions (but failed to win a game). In 2013, when the competition was expected to revert to a mid-September start, there will be no English representatives, after counties refused to fit their domestic schedule around it. Player and fan fatigue was another obvious issue: the World Twenty20 finished just two days before the qualifying tournament began.

"The view is that over time this competition will grow," said tournament director Naasai Appiah. "Just look at the FIFA World Cup in soccer. That started out at a few teams – now it's 32. We want to expand the competition in a similar way. It's still young and still growing."

QUALIFYING TOURNAMENT

Pool A

At Johannesburg, October 9, 2012 (floodlit). **Auckland won by six wickets.** ‡**Sialkot Stallions 130-9** (20 overs) (Shahid Yousuf 39); **Auckland 136-4** (17.1 overs) (M. J. Guptill 40, A. K. Kitchen 33*). *MoM:* K. D. Mills (Auckland). *Sialkot made their Champions League debut unbeaten in nine Twenty20 matches – but were undone on a bouncy, seaming Wanderers pitch. Miserly bowling from Kyle Mills (4–1–6–2) restricted them, but Anaru Kitchen rubber-stamped the result.*

At Centurion, October 10, 2012. **Auckland won by eight wickets. Hampshire 121-8** (20 overs) (M. A. Carberry 65; Azhar Mahmood 5-24); ‡**Auckland 123-2** (14.3 overs) (M. J. Guptill 38, Azhar Mahmood 55*). *MoM:* Azhar Mahmood. *Hampshire crashed out after just one match. On a sticky pitch, Azhar Mahmood, a familiar foe from years of county cricket, took the best figures in the Champions League's brief history, then hit a blistering 55* from 31 balls to guide Auckland to the main event. Both sides fielded a Michael David Bates, but the Hampshire wicketkeeper – down at No. 11 – did not get a chance to face the New Zealand left-arm seamer.*

At Johannesburg, October 11, 2012 (floodlit). **Sialkot Stallions won by six wickets. Hampshire 143-8** (20 overs) (G. J. Maxwell 42); ‡**Sialkot Stallions 144-4** (19.1 overs) (Haris Sohail 63*, Shoaib Malik 39). *MoM:* Haris Sohail. *Glenn Maxwell and Shahid Afridi fell to successive balls from Umaid Asif in the 17th over to stall Hampshire. Sialkot slipped to 28-3, but Haris Sohail added 96 with captain Shoaib Malik.*

Auckland 8pts, Sialkot Stallions 4pts, Hampshire 0pts.

Pool B

At Johannesburg, October 9, 2012. **Yorkshire won by five wickets. Uva Next 150-7** (20 overs); ‡**Yorkshire 151-5** (19.3 overs) (P. A. Jaques 32, D. A. Miller 39*, A. U. Rashid 36*; E. M. D. Y. Munaweera 3-32). *MoM:* A. U. Rashid. *Umar Gul's bouncer squeezed between the helmet's grille and peak to break David Miller's nose and force him to retire on 22. Yorkshire then stumbled against Dilshan Munaweera's part-time spin but, with 18 needed off ten balls, Miller bravely returned to secure victory, hitting Gul for the winning runs.*

At Centurion, October 10, 2012 (floodlit). **Yorkshire won by six wickets.** ‡**Trinidad & Tobago 148-9** (20 overs) (D. M. Bravo 45, D. Ramdin 59; R. J. Sidebottom 3-13); **Yorkshire 154-4** (18.5 overs) (G. S. Ballance 64*, A. U. Rashid 33*). *MoM:* G. S. Ballance. *Yorkshire stunned the 2009 finalists when, from 51-4, Gary Ballance and Adil Rashid put on 103*. T&T had endured a spell of*

19 balls without a run off the bat as they slipped to 8-3, and were entirely reliant on Darren Bravo and Denesh Ramdin for their recovery. But it was not enough.

At Johannesburg, October 11, 2012. **No result. Trinidad & Tobago 181-3** (20 overs) (L. M. P. Simmons 34, W. K. D. Perkins 32, D. M. Bravo 54*, D. Ramdin 50*); ‡**Uva Next 0-1** (0.1 overs). *Bravo and Ramdin combined again to add 95 for the fourth wicket. Shannon Gabriel had Munaweera caught, upper-cutting to third man, with the only ball of Uva's reply before rain arrived.*

Yorkshire 8pts, Uva Next 2pts, Trinidad & Tobago 2pts.

Group A

At Centurion, October 13, 2012. **Titans won by 39 runs. Titans 163-4** (20 overs) (J. A. Rudolph 83*, H. Davids 54); ‡**Perth Scorchers 124-7** (20 overs) (M. R. Marsh 52*; C. J. D. de Villiers 3-16). *MoM:* C. J. D. de Villiers. *Titans openers Henry Davids and Jacques Rudolph, who scored a career-best 83*, feasted on Perth's overpitched bowling. C. J. de Villiers got his length just right.*

At Centurion, October 13, 2012 (floodlit). **Delhi Daredevils won by 52 runs. Delhi Daredevils 160-8** (20 overs) (U. Chand 40, L. R. P. L. Taylor 36; S. P. Narine 3-21); ‡**Kolkata Knight Riders 108-7** (20 overs) (M. K. Tiwary 33). *MoM:* I. K. Pathan (Delhi). *Fresh from his stint as a studio pundit at the World Twenty20, Kevin Pietersen was put down three times before holing out for 14; Delhi instead relied on the India Under-19 captain Unmukt Chand. Kolkata were 3-3 after seven deliveries – with Irfan Pathan removing the openers – which in effect became 3-4 when Jacques Kallis had to retire hurt after being struck on the right hand by Morne Morkel.*

At Cape Town, October 15, 2012 (floodlit). **Auckland won by seven wickets.** ‡**Kolkata Knight Riders 137-6** (20 overs) (M. Bisla 38, B. B. McCullum 40; Azhar Mahmood 3-16); **Auckland 139-3** (17.4 overs) (L. Vincent 30, Azhar Mahmood 51*). *MoM:* Azhar Mahmood. *Kolkata lurched from 72-1 to 72-4 in the space of six balls from Ronnie Hira and Azhar Mahmood, who then anchored Auckland's response with a controlled half-century, his second in two innings, to secure the shock of the tournament.*

At Durban, October 17, 2012. **Titans won by 59 runs. Titans 172-4** (20 overs) (H. Davids 36, J. A. Rudolph 63, F. Behardien 48*); ‡**Auckland 113** (18.1 overs) (A. R. Adams 30; N. E. Mbhalati 3-26, A. C. Thomas 3-18). *MoM:* F. Behardien. *Rudolph starred again in a routine Titans win, while Farhaan Behardien provided late fireworks. Auckland careered to 68-9 before last pair Andre Adams and Michael Bates (14) had a little fun.*

At Durban, October 17, 2012 (floodlit). **No result. Perth Scorchers 91-2** (14 overs) (S. E. Marsh 38, S. M. Katich 43*) v ‡**Kolkata Knight Riders.** *Shaun Marsh and Simon Katich put on 70 for the second wicket to leave Perth in a healthy state, before rain arrived to knock Kolkata out.*

At Durban, October 19, 2012 (floodlit). **Auckland v Delhi Daredevils. Abandoned.**

At Cape Town, October 21, 2012. **Delhi Daredevils won by three wickets. Perth Scorchers 121-5** (20 overs) (S. E. Marsh 39, S. M. Katich 34; M. Morkel 3-19); ‡**Delhi Daredevils 123-7** (19.3 overs) (V. Sehwag 52). *MoM:* A. B. Agarkar (Delhi). *Both teams struggled on a two-paced Newlands pitch, although an unusually measured fifty from Virender Sehwag pushed Delhi into the semi-finals; Perth, who lost Marsh and Katick to successive balls from Ajit Agarkar (4–0–13–2) were eliminated.*

At Cape Town, October 21, 2012 (floodlit). **Kolkata Knight Riders won by 99 runs. Kolkata Knight Riders 188-5** (20 overs) (G. Gambhir 44, B. B. McCullum 36, D. B. Das 43*); ‡**Titans 89** (16.4 overs) (L. Balaji 4-19). *MoM:* D. B. Das. *Titans slumped to Lakshmipathy Balaji, endangering their semi-final chances.*

At Centurion, October 23, 2012. **Perth Scorchers won by 16 runs.** ‡**Perth Scorchers 140-7** (20 overs) (M. J. North 37, P. D. Collingwood 38; M. D. Bates 4-34); **Auckland 124-8** (20 overs) (M. J. Guptill 36; M. A. Beer 3-13). *MoM:* M. A. Beer. *Auckland's encouraging campaign ended with a whimper, sending Titans through to the last four. Left-arm spinner Michael Beer took the new ball and claimed career-best figures as Perth secured their only win. But it could not mask the discord in their camp, stemming from a breach of team protocol by, among others, the Marsh brothers, who were both dropped for this game. Perth captain Marcus North criticised a group who had "let the team down" before their match against Delhi; they were believed to have stayed out late celebrating Mitchell Marsh's 21st birthday.*

At Centurion, October 23, 2012 (floodlit). **Delhi Daredevils v ‡Titans. Abandoned.**

Group B

At Johannesburg, October 14, 2012. **Sydney Sixers won by 14 runs. Sydney Sixers 185-5** (20 overs) (S. R. Watson 46, M. C. Henriques 49*); ‡**Chennai Super Kings 171-9** (20 overs) (F. du Plessis 43, S. K. Raina 57; M. A. Starc 3-31, M. C. Henriques 3-23). *MoM:* M. C. Henriques. *Shane Watson and Moises Henriques excelled at either end of Sydney's innings; 61 runs came from the last four overs. Henriques then removed Suresh Raina and M. S. Dhoni in the 17th over as Chennai flunked the inevitable slog.*

At Johannesburg, October 14, 2012 (floodlit). **Lions won by eight wickets. Mumbai Indians 157-6** (20 overs) (M. G. Johnson 30); ‡**Lions 158-2** (18.5 overs) (Q. de Kock 51*, N. D. McKenzie 68*). *MoM:* N. D. McKenzie. *Dirk Nannes (1-15) and Aaron Phangiso (1-17) tied Mumbai down to a middling score, knocked off by Quinton de Kock and Neil McKenzie in a clinical stand of 121*.*

At Cape Town, October 16, 2012. **Sydney Sixers won by eight wickets.** ‡**Yorkshire 96-9** (20 overs) (M. A. Starc 3-22); **Sydney Sixers 98-2** (8.5 overs) (M. J. Lumb 43*, B. J. Haddin 41). *MoM:* B. J. Haddin. *Yorkshire were blown away by two old boys: first the threatening Mitchell Starc, and then Michael Lumb, who showed an invention their batsmen had lacked, with eight fours in 24 balls.*

At Cape Town, October 16, 2012 (floodlit). **Lions won by six wickets. Chennai Super Kings 158-6** (20 overs) (M. S. Dhoni 34); ‡**Lions 159-4** (19.3 overs) (G. H. Bodi 64, N. D. McKenzie 32, J. Symes 39*). *MoM:* A. M. Phangiso (Lions). *Lions were 8-2 when Gulam Bodi exploded into action; Jean Symes and Chris Morris then achieved a stiff requirement of 44 from the last 22 balls.*

At Cape Town, October 18, 2012. **Sydney Sixers won by five wickets. Lions 137-9** (20 overs) (G. H. Bodi 61; M. A. Starc 3-19); ‡**Sydney Sixers 141-5** (19 overs) (S. R. Watson 47, B. J. Haddin 32; A. M. Phangiso 3-14). *MoM:* M. A. Starc. *Bodi delivered another assault at the top, with 61 from 44 balls, but his team-mates could muster only 56 off the last 57, as Starc took three wickets for the third match running.*

At Cape Town, October 18, 2012 (floodlit). **No result. Mumbai Indians 156-6** (17.5 overs) (D. R. Smith 37, K. A. Pollard 37*) v ‡**Yorkshire.** *Kieron Pollard batted in a beanie hat against the slower bowlers, but there was nothing woolly about strokeplay which punished an off-key Yorkshire, who may have been grateful for a steady downpour.*

At Johannesburg, October 20, 2012. **Lions won by five wickets. Yorkshire 131-7** (20 overs) (P. A. Jaques 31); ‡**Lions 134-5** (19.2 overs) (Q. de Kock 32). *MoM:* J. Symes (Lions). *An injury-ravaged Yorkshire battled gamely after again underperforming with the bat. With 20 needed off two overs, Lions were struggling to confirm a semi-final berth – but Symes helped take 14 off the penultimate, from Twenty20 debutant Oliver Hannon-Dalby.*

At Johannesburg, October 20, 2012 (floodlit). **Chennai Super Kings won by six runs. Chennai Super Kings 173-8** (20 overs) (M. Vijay 39, F. du Plessis 52, M. S. Dhoni 35; S. L. Malinga 5-32); ‡**Mumbai Indians 167-7** (20 overs) (R. G. Sharma 32, K. D. Karthik 74, K. A. Pollard 31). *MoM:* B. W. Hilfenhaus (Chennai). *Rocked by Ben Hilfenhaus and Albie Morkel, Mumbai were 95-4 in the 14th over, then hauled back to contention by Dinesh Karthik and Pollard until both fell in the last ten balls. Lasith Malinga, thumped for 16 in his first over, returned spectacularly with five wickets in his next three.*

At Durban, October 22, 2012. **Chennai Super Kings won by four wickets. Yorkshire 140-6** (20 overs) (G. S. Ballance 58); ‡**Chennai Super Kings 141-6** (19 overs) (S. K. Raina 31, S. Badrinath 47, M. S. Dhoni 31). *MoM:* S. Badrinath. *With nothing riding on the result, Dhoni passed the captaincy to Suresh Raina and the gloves to Wriddhiman Saha, then experimented with a few back-of-the-hand deliveries and was hit for two sixes by Ballance, who made his second half-century. Dhoni later batted Chennai to within one run of victory.*

At Durban, October 22, 2012 (floodlit). **Sydney Sixers won by 12 runs.** ‡**Sydney Sixers 136-7** (20 overs) (S. P. D. Smith 41); **Mumbai Indians 124-8** (20 overs). *MoM:* S. P. D. Smith. *Sydney underlined their favourites tag with an excellent defence of a gettable 137. Mumbai reached 52-0 in the ninth over, but fell way short.*

CHAMPIONS LEAGUE TWENTY20

Group A	*Played*	*Won*	*Lost*	*Tied*	*No result*	*Points*	*Net run-rate*
DELHI DAREDEVILS	4	2	0	1	1	12	1.44
TITANS	4	2	1	1	0	10	–0.01
Kolkata Knight Riders	4	1	2	0	1	6	0.48
Perth Scorchers	4	1	2	0	1	6	–0.47
Auckland	4	1	2	0	1	6	–0.96

Group B	*Played*	*Won*	*Lost*	*Tied*	*No result*	*Points*	*Net run-rate*
SYDNEY SIXERS	4	4	0	0	0	16	1.65
LIONS	4	3	1	0	0	12	0.14
Chennai Super Kings	4	2	2	0	0	8	–0.04
Mumbai Indians	4	0	3	0	1	2	–0.47
Yorkshire	4	0	3	0	1	2	–1.79

Semi-finals

At Durban, October 25, 2012 (floodlit). **Lions won by 22 runs. Lions 139-5** (20 overs) (G. H. Bodi 50, N. D. McKenzie 46*); ‡**Delhi Daredevils 117-9** (20 overs) (K. P. Pietersen 50). *MoM:* N. D. McKenzie. *From 62-2 in the 12th, Delhi lost wickets in six successive overs to five different bowlers, as Pietersen stood alone on the burning deck. He made the same score as Bodi, the man often preferred to him in the KwaZulu-Natal sides of the late 1990s – a selection sometimes blamed for Pietersen's move to England.*

At Centurion, October 26, 2012 (floodlit). **Sydney Sixers won by two wickets.** ‡**Titans 163-5** (20 overs) (H. Davids 59*, D. Wiese 61*); **Sydney Sixers 164-8** (20 overs) (S. N. J. O'Keefe 32, M. J. Lumb 33). *MoM:* S. N. J. O'Keefe. *Davids batted through the innings, and David Wiese scored the tournament's fastest fifty, from 25 balls. But unlike Delhi 24 hours earlier, Sydney recovered from a mid-innings wobble at 132-7, and Cummins and Starc scrambled a bye off the last ball, with wicketkeeper Heino Kuhn missing his shy at the stumps.*

FINAL

LIONS v SYDNEY SIXERS

At Johannesburg, October 28, 2012 (floodlit). Sydney Sixers won by ten wickets. Toss: Sydney Sixers.

Players and commentators likened the Wanderers pitch to the track used for the famous one-day international in 2006, when South Africa hauled in Australia's 434. This time it was an Australian cakewalk. Haddin heaped pressure on the home side by electing to bowl and giving the new ball to spinners McCullum and O'Keefe – with three international pace bowlers in reserve. The match was all but decided inside four overs, when Lions slumped to nine for four, though Symes fashioned some sort of total by sensibly hitting through the line. Both Sydney openers were dropped, Lumb at long-off by Bodi, whom he soon overtook as the tournament's leading run-scorer. Haddin, batting with a swollen and infected thumb, let Lumb take charge in the city of his birth with five sixes in his highest Twenty20 score since June 2009. Victory came with 45 balls to spare.

Man of the Match: M. J. Lumb. *Man of the Series:* M. A. Starc.

Lions

		B	4	6
*A. N. Petersen *c 7 b 8*	1	6	0	0
G. H. Bodi *c 6 b 7*	6	3	0	1
Q. de Kock *c 8 b 11*	1	7	0	0
N. D. McKenzie *c 6 b 11*	0	4	0	0
Sohail Tanvir *lbw b 7*	11	12	1	0
J. Symes *c 2 b 11*	51	46	8	0
†T. L. Tsolekile *c 8 b 7*	20	19	1	2
D. Pretorius *run out*	21	13	1	2
C. H. Morris *run out*	5	5	0	0
A. M. Phangiso *c 11 b 10*	3	5	0	0
D. P. Nannes *not out*	0	0	0	0
L-b 1, w 1	2			
6 overs: 29-4 (20 overs)	121			

1/7 2/8 3/8 4/9 5/32 6/73 7/111 8/112 9/120

McCullum 4–0–24–3; O'Keefe 4–0–11–1; Hazlewood 4–1–22–3; Starc 4–0–36–1; Cummins 4–0–27–0.

Sydney Sixers

		B	4	6
M. J. Lumb *not out*	82	42	8	5
*†B. J. Haddin *not out*	37	33	4	1
L-b 1, w 4	5			
6 overs: 33-0 (12.3 overs)	124-0			

N. J. Maddinson, S. P. D. Smith, M. C. Henriques, B. J. Rohrer, N. L. McCullum, S. N. J. O'Keefe, P. J. Cummins, M. A. Starc and J. R. Hazlewood did not bat.

Sohail Tanvir 3–0–16–0; Nannes 4–0–28–0; Morris 2–0–25–0; Phangiso 2–0–29–0; Symes 1–0–9–0; Pretorius 0.3–0–16–0.

Umpires: Aleem Dar and S. J. A. Taufel. Third umpire: H. D. P. K. Dharmasena. Referee: R. S. Madugalle.

CHAMPIONS LEAGUE FINALS

2009-10 NEW SOUTH WALES BLUES beat Trinidad & Tobago‡ by 41 runs at Hyderabad.
2010-11 CHENNAI SUPER KINGS beat Warriors‡ by eight wickets at Johannesburg.
2011-12 MUMBAI INDIANS‡ beat Royal Challengers Bangalore by 31 runs at Chennai.
2012-13 SYDNEY SIXERS‡ beat Lions by ten wickets at Johannesburg.

DOMESTIC CRICKET IN SOUTH AFRICA, 2011-12

COLIN BRYDEN

The **Titans** returned to the top of the South African domestic tree after two barren seasons, winning both the first-class SuperSport Series and the financially rewarding MiWay T20 Challenge. They failed only in the Franchise One-Day Cup, won by the Cape Cobras. Under a new coach, former England batsman Matthew Maynard, and a new captain, Martin van Jaarsveld, the Centurion-based Titans franchise lost three of their first six SuperSport matches, including an innings defeat by the Cape Cobras, the defending champions. But they hit form in the New Year, and a tense two-wicket win over the Cobras in Paarl established them as genuine contenders. The Titans clinched the title with an overwhelming innings victory over a substandard Dolphins team in the final round.

Faf du Plessis starred in all three formats, consistently with the bat and occasionally with his leg-spin. It was a tribute to the depth of the Titans squad that their leading batsmen in the first-class averages – du Plessis, Jacques Rudolph and Albie Morkel – made only occasional appearances because of international calls and injury, while no fewer than 11 bowlers took nine or more wickets. Rowan Richards, a left-arm seamer, collected 26 at 20 in six matches.

The Twenty20 competition in March hinged on a dramatic finish to the play-off between the Knights, from Bloemfontein, and the Titans to decide who played in the final against table leaders the Highveld Lions. Alfonso Thomas hit a six off the last ball to earn the Titans a tie, then bowled a tight eliminator over to see his side home. They went on to a comfortable win at the Lions' ground in Johannesburg.

The **Cape Cobras** started well, winning the Franchise One-Day Cup, an early-season tournament with no sponsor – at which point they held all three domestic trophies. They competed in the SuperSport Series until the last week. Vernon Philander's dramatic success in Test cricket robbed them of their leading fast bowler for half the season; he still topped the national SuperSport averages, closely followed by team-mate Rory Kleinveldt, who was suspended during the Twenty20 campaign after testing positive for cannabis. Cobras coach Richard Pybus departed in March, with chief executive Andre Odendaal saying he had lost the support of most of the black players. Former Test spinner Paul Adams took over.

Alviro Petersen – SuperSport's leading scorer with 816 – Neil McKenzie and the promising Temba Bavuma shone with the bat for the **Lions**, though their attack struggled to dismiss teams twice. Chris Morris emerged as a promising fast-bowling all-rounder and played a significant role in the side's run to the Twenty20 final. The **Knights** were the nearly team of the season, finishing third in all three competitions. Dean Elgar scored heavily and was selected for the national one-day side in January, only for a knee injury to delay his debut by eight months. The **Warriors** reached the final of the One-Day Cup, but were otherwise disappointing and disjointed. Captain Davey Jacobs was unfit until late on, and four different players led the side in his absence. In the SuperSport Series, off-spinner Simon Harmer took 44 wickets, more than anyone else, and Colin Ingram averaged 57 with the bat. The **Dolphins** had a miserable time on and off the field. Coach Graham Ford left in mid-season to join Sri Lanka, amid reports of conflict with an interfering board. A seventh team, the **Impi**, joined the Twenty20 tournament. Led by England's World Twenty20-winning captain Paul Collingwood, they featured amateur and fringe franchise cricketers, bolstered by up to four overseas players, but failed to win a match.

Griqualand West won the first-class amateur provincial league, while **Free State** took the one-day title, and **Northerns** the inaugural Twenty20 competition.

FIRST-CLASS AVERAGES, 2011-12

BATTING (700 runs)

	M	*I*	*NO*	*R*	*HS*	*100*	*Avge*	*Ct/St*
R. C. C. Canning (*Western Province*)	9	16	6	717	95	0	71.70	27/2
A. N. Petersen (*Lions, SA & SA A*)	9	17	1	1,029	186	5	64.31	9
H. M. Amla (*Dolphins & SA*)	8	13	1	740	208	3	61.66	8
C. Jonker (*South Western Districts*)	13	21	1	1,189	190	5	59.45	7
N. D. McKenzie (*Lions*)	10	18	4	790	170	4	56.42	10
P. J. Malan (*Northerns*)	13	20	1	1,035	157	4	54.47	9
A. R. Swanepoel (*Knights & G. West*)	9	15	1	760	138	4	54.28	4
†M. Q. Adams (*Western Province*)	11	20	1	1,006	138	3	52.94	7
†J. F. le Clus (*Northerns*)	13	21	2	983	112	3	51.73	22
M. B. A. Smith (*Eastern Province*)	12	22	3	968	205*	2	50.94	17
G. Snyman (*Namibia*)	11	18	1	832	127	2	48.94	3
†J. A. Rudolph (*Titans & SA*)	11	19	1	826	210	2	45.88	8
B. J. Pelser (*North West*)	12	19	2	771	153*	3	45.35	10
M. N. van Wyk (*Knights*)	10	20	3	754	155	2	44.35	32/1
T. Bavuma (*Lions, Gauteng & SA Inv. XI*)	11	20	4	702	147	3	43.87	8
J. T. Smuts (*Warriors*)	9	18	1	742	143*	3	43.64	13
R. S. Second (*Free State*)	12	19	0	824	209	2	43.36	53/2
D. J. van Wyk (*Dolphins & KZNI*)	16	26	1	987	174	2	39.48	16/1
R. R. Hendricks (*Knights & SA Inv. XI*)	11	21	0	814	124	1	38.76	7
T. G. Mokoena (*Gauteng*)	13	23	2	813	120	2	38.71	8
†A. Jacobs (*Warriors & E. Province*)	11	22	1	800	152	1	38.09	26/1
B. Moses (*Easterns*)	13	24	4	747	108	2	37.35	10
S. C. Cook (*Lions & Gauteng*)	15	30	2	885	131	2	31.60	13
M. L. Price (*Warriors & Eastern Prov.*)	14	27	2	788	118	1	31.52	4
T. M. Bodibe (*Titans & Easterns*)	14	27	0	724	148	1	26.81	14

BOWLING (35 wickets)

	Style	*O*	*M*	*R*	*W*	*BB*	*5I*	*Avge*
G. R. Rabie (*Warriors & SW Districts*)	RFM	340.5	89	922	62	8-60	5	14.87
Y. Pangabantu (*Border*)	RFM	216.4	50	621	40	6-46	3	15.52
V. D. Philander (*Cape Cobras, SA & SA A*)	RFM	334.4	90	919	57	7-61	5	16.12
J. Coetzee (*Griqualand West*)	LF	260.4	64	716	44	6-38	3	16.27
S. de Kock (*Border*)	SLA	261.5	49	782	44	5-14	1	17.77
G. I. Hume (*Gauteng*)	RFM	258.4	77	740	41	5-34	1	18.04
S. W. Liebisch (*Easterns*)	RFM	321.2	99	889	48	5-33	4	18.52
G. A. Vries (*Free State*)	RFM	280.2	74	778	40	6-63	1	19.45
J. P. Bothma (*Cape Cobras & W. Province*)	RF	354.2	83	1,165	56	5-31	5	20.80
K. A. Maharaj (*Dolphins & KZ-Natal*)	SLA	302.1	54	943	40	5-56	2	23.57
Q. Friend (*Knights & Free State*)	RFM	300.3	74	975	41	6-45	3	23.78
H. H. Paulse (*Boland*)	RF	264.5	47	1,017	41	7-58	1	24.80
D. D. Carolus (*Griqualand West*)	RFM	328.3	79	1,017	40	4-33	0	25.42
T. Shamsi (*Dolphins & KZN Inland*)	SLC	317.5	50	1,178	45	8-164	3	26.17
G. C. Viljoen (*Titans, Easterns & SA Inv. XI*)	RF	314	53	1,174	43	5-36	1	27.30
E. Leie (*Lions & Gauteng*)	LBG	336.4	33	1,342	49	5-53	3	27.38
S. R. Harmer (*Warriors & E. Prov.*)	OB	486.1	91	1,601	53	8-72	3	30.20
Imran Tahir (*Dolphins & South Africa*)	LBG	424.5	49	1,445	40	5-67	1	36.12

Averages include CSA Provincial Three-Day Challenge matches played in Namibia, and Bangladesh A's tour in April.

SUPERSPORT SERIES, 2011-12

	Played	Won	Lost	Drawn	Bonus points Batting	Bonus points Bowling	Points
Titans	10	5	3	1†	40.28	34	129.28
Cape Cobras	10	4	2	4	44.90	32	116.90
Knights	10	4	1	5	39.52	36	112.52*
Lions	10	3	2	5	39.20	32	101.20
Warriors	10	2	7	0†	28.80	28	81.80
Dolphins	10	1	4	5	31.50	31	72.50

† Plus one match abandoned. ** 1pt deducted for slow over-rate.*

Outright win = 10pts; abandoned = 5pts. Bonus points awarded for the first 100 overs of each team's first innings. One batting point was awarded for the first 150 runs and 0.02 of a point for every subsequent run. One bowling point was awarded for the third wicket taken and for every subsequent two.

At Johannesburg, September 29–October 2, 2011. **Drawn.** ‡**Lions 359** (A. N. Petersen 186; R. Frylinck 6-52) **and 260-5; Dolphins 567-9 dec** (H. M. Amla 208, V. B. van Jaarsveld 103). *Lions 5.22pts, Dolphins 8.2pts. Lions captain Alviro Petersen batted nearly eight hours for 186, before Hashim Amla replied with his third double-hundred, adding 200 for the Dolphins' third wicket with Vaughn van Jaarsveld.*

At Centurion, September 29–October 2, 2011. **Knights won by six wickets.** ‡**Titans 227** (J. J. van der Wath 6-53) **and 270; Knights 400** (R. McLaren 133*) **and 100-4**. *Knights 18.64pts, Titans 5.54pts.*

At Pietermaritzburg, October 6–9, 2011. **Titans won by seven wickets.** ‡**Dolphins 243** (P. L. Harris 5-37) **and 288** (S. von Berg 5-76); **Titans 360** (J. A. Rudolph 118) **and 172-3**. *Titans 18.76pts, Dolphins 6.86pts.*

At Kimberley, October 6–9, 2011. **Drawn.** ‡**Lions 455-9 dec** (S. C. Cook 131, D. R. Deeb 101*) **and 266-4 dec** (N. D. McKenzie 110*, T. Bavuma 100*); **Knights 378-8 dec** (A. J. Pienaar 119) **and 189-6** (W. A. Deacon 5-49). *Knights 7.56pts, Lions 7.14pts. No. 9 Dale Deeb scored a maiden hundred and added 128 for the Lions' ninth wicket with Ethan O'Reilly; in the second innings, Neil McKenzie and Temba Bavuma put on 194* for the fifth wicket.*

At Durban, October 13–16, 2011. **Knights won by four wickets.** ‡**Dolphins 338 and 160; Knights 203 and 298-6** (D. Elgar 114). *Knights 16.06pts, Dolphins 8.76pts.*

At Potchefstroom, October 13–16, 2011. **Titans won by 243 runs. Titans 406** (J. A. Rudolph 210; P. Matshikwe 5-102) **and 375-8 dec** (D. Wiese 124); ‡**Lions 306 and 232**. *Titans 20.04pts, Lions 8.12pts. Jacques Rudolph batted throughout the Titans' first innings in his fourth double-century (his first in South African domestic cricket). He put on 187 for the first wicket with Tumelo Bodibe (58).*

At East London, October 13–15, 2011. **Cape Cobras won by eight wickets. Warriors 216 and 200;** ‡**Cape Cobras 290** (J. L. Ontong 105; A. C. R. Birch 6-75) **and 129-2**. *Cape Cobras 17.8pts, Warriors 6.32pts. The Cape Cobras and the Warriors joined the competition in the third round, after returning from the Champions League in India.*

At Cape Town, October 20–23, 2011. **Drawn.** ‡**Cape Cobras 337 and 163-5; Dolphins 316** (I. Khan 141*). *Cape Cobras 5.06pts, Dolphins 4.3pts. Imraan Khan carried his bat for two minutes short of nine hours, while Cobras captain Justin Kemp returned figures of 13–9–4–1.*

At Johannesburg, October 20–23, 2011. **Lions won by nine wickets.** ‡**Lions 511** (N. D. McKenzie 170) **and 145-1; Warriors 228 and 424** (J. T. Smuts 143). *Lions 18.52pts, Warriors 4.56pts.*

At Kimberley, October 27–30, 2011. **Knights won by 211 runs. Knights 349 and 381-8 dec** (D. Elgar 160); ‡**Warriors 206 and 313** (J. J. van der Wath 5-86). *Knights 18.32pts, Warriors 5.12pts.*

At Benoni, October 27–29, 2011. **Cape Cobras won by an innings and 46 runs. Titans 112** (R. K. Kleinveldt 5-26) **and 236;** ‡**Cape Cobras 394** (D. J. Vilas 161*). *Cape Cobras 19.88pts, Titans 4pts. Cobras wicketkeeper Dane Vilas hit 24 fours and two sixes in 165 balls.*

At Cape Town, December 15–17, 2011. **Cape Cobras won by an innings and 83 runs. Lions 86** (J. Louw 5-37) **and 172** (R. K. Kleinveldt 5-42); ‡**Cape Cobras 341** (J. L. Ontong 146). *Cape*

Cobras 18.82pts, Lions 4pts. The Lions were dismissed for their lowest total as the Cobras resumed after a triumphant one-day campaign with a second innings win.

At Bloemfontein, December 15–18, 2011. **Drawn. Knights 438** (R. R. Rossouw 145, M. N. van Wyk 139; R. R. Richards 5-87) **and 358** (H. H. Dippenaar 112); **‡Titans 461** (F. Behardien 141, F. du Plessis 153; Q. Friend 5-73) **and 303-6** (M. van Jaarsveld 167*). *Knights 9.76pts, Titans 10.4pts. Rilee Rossouw and Morne van Wyk put on 223 for the Knights' sixth wicket, and Farhaan Berhardien and Faf du Plessis 272 for the Titans' fifth. Martin van Jaarsveld hit 167* in 161 balls as Titans attempted to chase down 336 in 64 overs.*

At Port Elizabeth, December 15–18, 2011. **Warriors won by 91 runs. ‡Warriors 295** (C. A. Ingram 121) **and 369-9 dec** (J. T. Smuts 107); **Dolphins 223 and 350** (D. J. van Wyk 102). *Warriors 17.9pts, Dolphins 6.46pts. Colin Ingram and Basheer Walters, who hit a maiden fifty, added 110 for the last wicket in the Warriors' first innings.*

At Paarl, December 27–30, 2011. **Warriors won by 139 runs. ‡Warriors 320** (C. A. Ingram 140) **and 211**; **Cape Cobras 239 and 153** (S. R. Harmer 8-72). *Warriors 17.24pts, Cape Cobras 4.78pts. Off-spinner Simon Harmer's 8-72 was the best return of the season; he was also involved in a run-out, and took 11-149 in the match.*

At Bloemfontein, December 27–30, 2011. **Drawn. Knights 340** (R. Frylinck 5-90, M. Shezi 5-83) **and 218-7 dec**; **‡Dolphins 240** (Q. Friend 5-42) **and 245-7**. *Knights 7.62pts, Dolphins 5.8pts.*

At Benoni, December 27–30, 2011. **Lions won by nine wickets. ‡Titans 354** (E. Leie 5-93) **and 210** (E. Leie 5-53); **Lions 407** (S. C. Cook 109, A. N. Petersen 115) **and 159-1**. *Lions 18.52pts, Titans 8.08pts. Leg-spinner Eddie Leie took ten wickets in a match for the first time.*

At Kimberley, January 5–7, 2012. **Cape Cobras won by an innings and 54 runs. ‡Knights 218** (R. K. Kleinveldt 5-26) **and 160** (J. M. Kemp 5-31); **Cape Cobras 432** (D. J. Vilas 187). *Cape Cobras 20.64pts, Knights 6.36pts. Vilas dominated their third innings win in four games. He held ten catches, and in between scored 187 in 198 balls, with 23 fours and six sixes, adding 257 with Robin Peterson, a national record for the eighth wicket.*

At Benoni, January 5–8, 2012. **Titans won by 202 runs. ‡Titans 393** (F. du Plessis 112, J. A. Morkel 127*) **and 326-6 dec** (H. Davids 105); **Warriors 264 and 253** (J. T. Smuts 143*). *Titans 19.86pts, Warriors 7.28pts.*

At Pietermaritzburg, January 12–15, 2012. **Drawn. ‡Cape Cobras 432** (S. van Zyl 110) **and 160-2 dec**; **Dolphins 192 and 271-6**. *Dolphins 3.84pts, Cape Cobras 8.46pts.*

At Port Elizabeth, January 12–15, 2012. **Lions won by 94 runs. ‡Lions 519-8 dec** (A. N. Petersen 165, T. Bavuma 147) **and 171-8 dec**; **Warriors 340 and 256** (K. R. Smuts 100). *Lions 19.4pts, Warriors 5.8pts. The Warriors collapsed in the second innings, losing their last six wickets for three runs in 12 balls – including a hat-trick for Chris Morris.*

At Paarl, January 26–28, 2012. **Titans won by two wickets. ‡Cape Cobras 199** (R. R. Richards 5-49) **and 165** (H. Davids 5-22); **Titans 207** (R. J. Peterson 5-60) **and 158-8**. *Titans 16.14pts, Cape Cobras 5.98pts. Despite lurching to 68-6 in the final innings, the Titans pulled 1.4pts ahead of the Cobras, thanks to an unbeaten fifty from Albie Morkel.*

At Durban, January 26–29, 2012. **Dolphins won by 227 runs. ‡Dolphins 321** (V. B. van Jaarsveld 106; S. R. Harmer 6-94) **and 275-8 dec**; **Warriors 211** (Imran Tahir 5-67) **and 158** (M. Shezi 5-26). *Dolphins 17.46pts, Warriors 4.22pts. The Dolphins completed their only victory of the season.*

At Johannesburg, January 26–29, 2012. **Drawn. ‡Knights 338 and 264-8 dec**; **Lions 280 and 83-5**. *Lions 6.6pts, Knights 8.28pts.*

At Cape Town, February 2–5, 2012. **Drawn. ‡Knights 345** (R. R. Hendricks 124, R. R. Rossouw 144*; V. D. Philander 7-61) **and 176-7**; **Cape Cobras 529-9 dec** (J-P. Duminy 104, M. V. Boucher 131, J. Louw 108*). *Cape Cobras 7.08pts, Knights 6.12pts. Vernon Philander took his 50th first-class wicket of the season in a career-best 7-61. Johann Louw and Johannes Bothma added 118 for the Cobras' ninth wicket. They moved a fraction ahead of the Titans, whose match was washed out.*

At Durban, February 2–5, 2012. **Drawn. ‡Lions 418** (N. D. McKenzie 108, T. Bavuma 121; K. J. Abbott 5-76) **and 268-6 dec** (N. D. McKenzie 101*); **Dolphins 477-6 dec and 50-1**. *Dolphins 6.82pts, Lions 5.34pts. Neil McKenzie, who scored a century in each innings and passed 16,000 first-class runs, added 228 for the Lions' fourth wicket with Bavuma.*

At East London, February 2–5, 2012. **Warriors v Titans. Abandoned.** *Warriors 5pts, Titans 5pts.*

At Johannesburg, February 9–12, 2012. **Drawn. Lions 410 and 164-4 dec**; **‡Cape Cobras 420** (M. Y. Vallie 167). *Lions 8.34pts, Cape Cobras 8.4pts. Petersen passed 1,000 runs for the season; together with rain and bad light, he ended the Cobras' hopes of retaining the title.*

At Centurion, February 9–11, 2012. **Titans won by an innings and 325 runs. Titans 473-9 dec** (H. G. Kuhn 128, F. du Plessis 157); **‡Dolphins 62 and 86** (N. E. Mbhalati 5-32). *Titans 21.46pts, Dolphins 4pts. The Titans secured the SuperSport title with the biggest win since the franchise system was introduced in 2004, and the eighth-biggest in South African cricket. Du Plessis's 157, from 162 balls proved more than the Dolphins could muster over two innings; 62 was their lowest total, and 86 in the follow-on their third-lowest.*

At Port Elizabeth, February 9–12, 2012. **Knights won by 161 runs. ‡Knights 240 and 373** (M. N. van Wyk 155); **Warriors 318** (A. Jacobs 152; J. J. van der Wath 5-61) **and 134** (Q. Friend 6-45). *Knights 16.8pts, Warriors 8.36pts. Ryan McLaren played a key role in the Knights' victory: in their first innings, he scored 74 and added 135 for the eighth wicket with Johan van der Wath; in their second, coming in at 92-6 when they were just 14 ahead, he made 90 and put on 214 for the seventh with Morne van Wyk.*

CHAMPIONS

Currie Cup

1889-90	Transvaal
1890-91	Kimberley
1892-93	Western Province
1893-94	Western Province
1894-95	Transvaal
1896-97	Western Province
1897-98	Western Province
1902-03	Transvaal
1903-04	Transvaal
1904-05	Transvaal
1906-07	Transvaal
1908-09	Western Province
1910-11	Natal
1912-13	Natal
1920-21	Western Province
1921-22	Transvaal Natal Western Province
1923-24	Transvaal
1925-26	Transvaal
1926-27	Transvaal
1929-30	Transvaal
1931-32	Western Province
1933-34	Natal
1934-35	Transvaal
1936-37	Natal
1937-38	Natal Transvaal
1946-47	Natal
1947-48	Natal
1950-51	Transvaal
1951-52	Natal
1952-53	Western Province
1954-55	Natal
1955-56	Western Province
1958-59	Transvaal
1959-60	Natal
1960-61	Natal
1962-63	Natal
1963-64	Natal
1965-66	Natal Transvaal
1966-67	Natal
1967-68	Natal
1968-69	Transvaal
1969-70	Transvaal Western Province
1970-71	Transvaal
1971-72	Transvaal
1972-73	Transvaal
1973-74	Natal
1974-75	Western Province
1975-76	Natal
1976-77	Natal
1977-78	Western Province
1978-79	Transvaal
1979-80	Transvaal
1980-81	Natal
1981-82	Western Province
1982-83	Transvaal
1983-84	Transvaal
1984-85	Transvaal
1985-86	Western Province
1986-87	Transvaal
1987-88	Transvaal
1988-89	Eastern Province
1989-90	Eastern Province Western Province

Castle Cup

1990-91	Western Province
1991-92	Eastern Province
1992-93	Orange Free State
1993-94	Orange Free State
1994-95	Natal
1995-96	Western Province

SuperSport Series

1996-97	Natal
1997-98	Free State

1998-99	Western Province	2005-06	Dolphins / Titans
1999-2000	Gauteng	2006-07	Titans
2000-01	Western Province	2007-08	Eagles
2001-02	KwaZulu-Natal	2008-09	Titans
2002-03	Easterns	2009-10	Cape Cobras
2003-04	Western Province	2010-11	Cape Cobras
2004-05	Dolphins / Eagles	2011-12	Titans

Transvaal/Gauteng have won the title outright 25 times, Natal/KwaZulu-Natal 21, Western Province 18, Orange Free State/Free State and Titans 3, Cape Cobras and Eastern Province 2, Eagles, Easterns and Kimberley 1. The title has been shared seven times as follows: Transvaal 4, Natal and Western Province 3, Dolphins 2, Eagles, Eastern Province and Titans 1.

From 1971-72 to 1990-91, the non-white South African Cricket Board of Control (later the South African Cricket Board) organised their own three-day tournaments. These are now recognised as first-class (see *Wisden 2006*, pages 79–80). A list of winners appears in *Wisden 2007*, page 1346.

CSA PROVINCIAL THREE-DAY CHALLENGE, 2011-12

					Bonus points		
	Played	*Won*	*Lost*	*Drawn*	*Batting*	*Bowling*	*Points*
Griqualand West	13	6	1	6	47.70	44	151.70
Gauteng	13	6	2	5	35.94	49	144.94
South Western Districts	13	6	2	5	40.58	44	144.58
Easterns	13	4	3	6	47.24	50	137.24
North West	13	5	4	3†	33.08	45	133.08
Border	13	4	4	5	35.14	50	125.14
Western Province	13	3	5	5	35.66	48	113.66
Free State	13	3	3	6†	35.98	42	112.98
Northerns	13	3	1	9	36.00	40	105.00*
KwaZulu-Natal	13	1	3	8†	37.62	43	95.62
Boland	13	3	5	5	20.78	42	92.78
Eastern Province	13	0	4	8†	35.32	44	84.32
KwaZulu-Natal Inland	13	2	4	6†	25.43	33	83.43
Namibia	13	0	5	7†	30.66	37	72.66

† *Plus one match abandoned.* * *1pt deducted for slow over-rate.*

Outright win = 10pts; abandoned = 5pts. Bonus points awarded for the first 100 overs of each team's first innings. One bonus batting point was awarded for the first 150 runs and 0.02 of a point for every subsequent run. One bonus bowling point was awarded for the third wicket taken and for every subsequent two.

At Benoni, September 29–30, 2011. **Easterns won by six wickets. ‡North West 148** (G. C. Viljoen 5-36) **and 159**; **Easterns 177 and 132-4**. *Easterns 15.54pts, North West 4pts.*

At Kimberley, September 29–October 1, 2011. **Drawn. Griqualand West 369** (A. P. McLaren 103) **and 271**; **‡Gauteng 299-8 dec** (Q. de Kock 133*) **and 93-2**. *Griqualand West 8.38pts, Gauteng 7.98pts.*

At Oudtshoorn, September 29–October 1, 2011. **South Western Districts won by 70 runs. South Western Districts 367-5 dec** (B. C. de Wett 103) **and 213-3 dec**; **‡KwaZulu-Natal Inland 297** (G. N. Addicott 115, K. Nipper 112; B. C. de Wett 5-76) **and 213**. *South Western Districts 19.34pts, KwaZulu-Natal Inland 5.94pts. Burton de Wett was the second South African to score a hundred and a fifty and take nine wickets in a first-class match, after Andre van Vuuren for KwaZulu-Natal Inland against Kei at Pietermaritzburg, 2006-07.*

At Cape Town, September 29–October 1, 2011. **KwaZulu-Natal won by eight wickets. KwaZulu-Natal 385** (L. E. Bosman 102, M. M. Hulett 124) **and 66-2**; **‡Western Province 207** (M. Shezi 5-31) **and 243**. *KwaZulu-Natal 19.7pts, Western Province 6.14pts.*

At Paarl, October 6–8, 2011. **Boland won by 25 runs. ‡Boland 177** (A. Gqamane 5-34) **and 231** (A. Gqamane 5-54); **Border 235 and 148** (C. H. Raubenheimer 6-47). *Boland 15.54pts, Border 6.7pts.*

At Windhoek, October 13–15, 2011. **Drawn. ‡Namibia 386** (G. Snyman 109) **and 95-4; Northerns 571-6 dec** (P. J. Malan 146, G. L. van Buuren 109*, E. R. Links 101*). *Namibia 6.3pts, Northerns 6.3pts. Graeme van Buuren and Eden Links scored maiden centuries as they added 190* for Northerns' seventh wicket.*

At Pretoria, October 6–8, 2011. **Drawn. Easterns 414** (D. Wiese 128; M. W. Olivier 5-106) **and 309-7; ‡Northerns 315-9 dec** (C. F. Schoeman 128*). *Northerns 8.3pts, Easterns 10.2pts. David Wiese and Mangaliso Mosehle (99) put on 225 for Easterns' fifth wicket.*

At Paarl, October 13–15, 2011. **Drawn. Eastern Province 393-7 dec** (W. E. Bell 116); **‡Boland 234 and 111-2**. *Boland 3.24pts, Eastern Province 6.86pts.*

At Bloemfontein, October 13–15, 2011. **Free State won by six wickets. ‡North West 144 and 180; Free State 225 and 102-4**. *Free State 16.5pts, North West 4pts. Free State wicketkeeper Rudi Second held eight catches in North West's second innings and 12 in the match, at the time equalling the national records, and only one short of the overall first-class records. North West's left-arm spinner Aaron Phangiso took a hat-trick in Free State's first innings.*

At Pietermaritzburg, October 13–15, 2011. **Western Province won by an innings and 247 runs. ‡KwaZulu-Natal Inland 131 and 68** (S. Simetu 7-21); **Western Province 446** (M. W. Keraan 189*). *Western Province 19.6pts, KwaZulu-Natal Inland 3pts. Weshaam Keraan, already 29, made the second-highest debut score in South African cricket.*

At East London, October 20–22, 2011. **Western Province won by 99 runs. Western Province 186** (Y. Pangabantu 5-31) **and 154; ‡Border 140** (J. P. Bothma 5-35) **and 101**. *Western Province 15.72pts, Border 4pts.*

At Bloemfontein, October 20–22, 2011. **Griqualand West won by ten wickets. Griqualand West 541-9 dec** (W. L. Coetsee 202*, A. R. Swanepoel 109) **and 6-0; ‡Free State 206 and 339**. *Griqualand West 21.28pts, Free State 5.12pts. Werner Coetsee scored a maiden double-hundred in 210 balls and added 177 for Griquas' sixth wicket with Swanepoel.*

At Windhoek, October 20–22, 2011. **Gauteng won by six wickets. ‡Namibia 284 and 291; Gauteng 347** (S. F. Burger 6-60) **and 234-4**. *Gauteng 18.94pts, Namibia 7.68pts. Gauteng wicketkeeper Quinton de Kock took nine catches in the match.*

At Port Elizabeth, October 27–28, 2011. **South Western Districts won by an innings and 67 runs. South Western Districts 390** (C. Jonker 173); **‡Eastern Province 131 and 192**. *South Western Districts 19.8pts, Eastern Province 4pts.*

At Bloemfontein, October 27–29, 2011. **Drawn. ‡Free State 335** (R. S. Second 164) **and 222-3; Easterns 556-9 dec** (J. J. Pienaar 185, M. R. Sekhoto 131). *Free State 7.08pts, Easterns 12.06pts. Cobus Pienaar and Mpho Sekhoto put on 262 for Easterns' fifth wicket.*

At Johannesburg (Witwatersrand University), October 27–29, 2011. **Gauteng won by an innings and 119 runs. ‡North West 189 and 153** (R. Das Neves 7-58); **Gauteng 461** (D. A. Hendricks 121, Q. de Kock 143). *Gauteng 19.56pts, North West 2.78pts.*

At Port Elizabeth, November 3–5, 2011. **Drawn. Eastern Province 355 and 190-8 dec; ‡Western Province 235** (S. R. Harmer 6-55) **and 258-7**. *Eastern Province 9.1pts, Western Province 6.7pts.*

At Kimberley, November 3–5, 2011. **Drawn. Griqualand West 305** (A. R. Swanepoel 138) **and 265** (A. R. Swanepoel 122; L. M. G. Masekela 7-104); **‡Northerns 396-7 dec** (J. F. le Clus 106) **and 101-6**. *Griqualand West 6.1pts, Northerns 7.9pts. Aubrey Swanepoel's twin hundreds gave him three in three first-class innings.*

At Oudtshoorn, November 3–5, 2011. **South Western Districts won by 19 runs. ‡South Western Districts 198 and 139** (Y. Pangabantu 6-46); **Border 150** (G. R. Rabie 6-44) **and 168** (R. D. McMillan 6-47). *South Western Districts 15.96pts, Border 5pts.*

At East London, November 10–12, 2011. **Drawn. ‡Eastern Province 310-7 dec** (S. R. Harmer 100*); **Border 156-3** (B. L. Bennett 100*). *Border 4.12pts, Eastern Province 5.2pts.*

At Chatsworth, November 10–12, 2011. **Drawn. KwaZulu-Natal 257-3 dec; ‡Boland 37-1.** *KwaZulu-Natal 3.14pts, Boland 1pts.*

At Potchefstroom, November 10–12, 2011. **Drawn. Northerns 155** (B. J. Pelser 5-47) **and 372-5 dec** (P. J. Malan 147); **‡North West 199 and 270-7** (B. J. Pelser 106*). *North West 5.98pts, Northerns 5.1pts. Pieter Malan added 235 for the third wicket of Northerns' second innings with Abraham Ndlovu.*

At Benoni, November 17–19, 2011. **Drawn. ‡Griqualand West 234** (J. J. Pienaar 5-62) **and 313-6 dec; Easterns 247 and 107-2.** *Easterns 6.94pts, Griqualand West 6.68pts.*

At Durban, November 17–19, 2011. **Drawn. South Western Districts 238** (C. Jonker 129); **‡KwaZulu-Natal 38-1.** *KwaZulu-Natal 4pts, South Western Districts 2.76pts.*

At Pietermaritzburg, November 17–19, 2011. **Drawn. ‡Eastern Province 331-4 dec** (D. J. White 118) **and 115-2; KwaZulu-Natal Inland 186.** *KwaZulu-Natal Inland 2.72pts, Eastern Province 8.4pts.*

At Windhoek, November 17–19, 2011. **Drawn. ‡Free State 467-9 dec** (R. S. Second 209, P. J. van Biljon 128; B. M. Scholtz 5-91); **Namibia 260 and 292-7.** *Namibia 4.2pts, Free State 10.32pts. Second scored a maiden double-century and put on 282 for Free State's third wicket with Petrus van Biljon.*

At East London, November 24–26, 2011. **Drawn. ‡KwaZulu-Natal 315** (C. Chetty 119) **and 66-3; Border 227.** *Border 6.54pts, KwaZulu-Natal 8.3pts.*

At Pietermaritzburg, December 1–3, 2011. **Drawn. ‡Namibia 435** (T. Shamsi 8-164) **and 2-0; KwaZulu-Natal Inland 466** (D. J. van Wyk 174, D. P. Conway 106; B. M. Scholtz 5-112, N. R. P. Scholtz 5-103). *KwaZulu-Natal Inland 8.32pts, Namibia 6.06pts.*

At Cape Town (Northerns-Goodwood), December 8–10, 2011. **South Western Districts won by 64 runs. ‡South Western Districts 211 and 208; Western Province 115 and 240.** *South Western Districts 16.22pts, Western Province 4pts.*

At Paarl, December 15–17, 2011. **Boland won by 235 runs. Boland 153 and 336-5 dec** (U. K. J. Birkenstock 136*); **‡KwaZulu-Natal Inland 165** (D. B. Childs 5-38) **and 89.** *Boland 15.06pts, KwaZulu-Natal Inland 5.3pts.*

At Johannesburg (ABSA Oval), December 15–16, 2011. **Gauteng won by an innings and 72 runs. Free State 148 and 142; ‡Gauteng 362** (G. A. Vries 6-63). *Gauteng 19.24pts, Free State 4pts.*

At Kimberley, December 15–17, 2011. **Griqualand West won by an innings and 54 runs. Griqualand West 349** (C. Viljoen 5-46); **‡Namibia 137** (W. L. Coetsee 5-28) **and 158** (C. Pietersen 6-68). *Griqualand West 18.98pts, Namibia 4pts.*

At Johannesburg (Witwatersrand University), December 27–28, 2011. **Gauteng won by an innings and 131 runs. Gauteng 338** (G. H. Bodi 134); **‡Easterns 50** (L. Mokoena 5-9) **and 157** (C. J. Dala 5-31). *Gauteng 18.76pts, Easterns 4pts. Hloni Mokoena had figures of 7–2–9–5 – including a hat-trick – and Graham Hume 7–4–8–3 as Easterns collapsed for 50.*

At Port Elizabeth (Nelson Mandela Metropole University), January 5–7, 2012. **Drawn. ‡Eastern Province 164** (B. M. Scullard 5-54) **and 413-3** (M. B. A. Smith 205*, C. N. Ackermann 123*); **KwaZulu-Natal 353.** *Eastern Province 5.28pts, KwaZulu-Natal 8.66pts. Michael Smith, with his first double-hundred, and Colin Ackerman, with his first century, put on 308* for Eastern Province's fourth wicket.*

At Pietermaritzburg, January 5–7, 2012. **Drawn. KwaZulu-Natal Inland 279-9 dec and 83-1; ‡Border 431-9 dec** (R. J. Ramoo 106; T. Shamsi 7-138). *KwaZulu-Natal Inland 5.56pts, Border 8.44pts.*

At Potchefstroom, January 5–7, 2012. **North West won by ten wickets. ‡Namibia 256** (C. J. Alexander 5-55) **and 205; North West 418-9 dec** (N. J. van den Bergh 159) **and 44-0.** *North West 20.36pts, Namibia 7.12pts.*

At Centurion, January 5–7, 2012. **Northerns won by seven wickets. Gauteng 121 and 237** (C. J. D. de Villiers 5-61); **‡Northerns 217 and 143-3.** *Northerns 16.34pts, Gauteng 4pts.*

At Oudtshoorn, January 5–7, 2012. **South Western Districts won by five wickets.** ‡**Boland 163** (G. R. Rabie 5-31) **and 273**; **South Western Districts 360** (R. D. McMillan 111; P. J. N. Jeftha 5-95) **and 77-5**. *South Western Districts 19.2pts, Boland 5.26pts.*

At Benoni, January 12–14, 2012. **Easterns won by seven wickets.** ‡**Namibia 96 and 217**; **Easterns 163-9 dec and 151-3**. *Easterns 15.26pts, Namibia 4pts.*

At Durban, January 12–14, 2012. **KwaZulu-Natal Inland won by nine wickets. KwaZulu-Natal 233** (K. Nipper 6-56) **and 175**; ‡**KwaZulu-Natal Inland 325** (C. W. J. Fortune 5-86) **and 85-1**. *KwaZulu-Natal Inland 18.35pts, KwaZulu-Natal 5.66pts.*

At Potchefstroom, January 12–14, 2012. **Griqualand West won by an innings and 108 runs. Griqualand West 452** (W. L. Coetsee 152*); ‡**North West 212 and 132**. *Griqualand West 21.04pts, North West 6.24pts. Coetsee and Jandre Coetzee put on 159 for Griquas' eight wicket.*

At Pretoria, January 12–14, 2012. **Drawn. Northerns 184 and 226-4** (P. J. Malan 122*); ‡**Free State 361-9 dec** (R. T. Bailey 118). *Northerns 3.68pts, Free State 8.4pts.*

At Bellville, January 12–14, 2012. **Boland won by five wickets.** ‡**Western Province 244** (M. Q. Adams 132; C. H. Raubenheimer 5-84) **and 291-5 dec** (M. Q. Adams 113*); **Boland 231 and 308-5**. *Boland 16.62pts, Western Province 6.88pts. Qaasim Adams scored his maiden hundred – and in the second innings added another.*

At East London (Buffalo Flats), January 26–27, 2012. **Border won by nine wickets.** ‡**Namibia 177 and 94** (S. de Kock 5-14); **Border 190 and 82-1**. *Border 15.8pts, Namibia 5.54pts.*

At Bloemfontein, January 26–27, 2012. **Free State won by an innings and 43 runs.** ‡**Boland 105** (D. du Preez 5-36) **and 124**; **Free State 272**. *Free State 17.44pts, Boland 4pts.*

At Kimberley, January 26–28, 2012. **Griqualand West won by 332 runs. Griqualand West 330** (A. R. Swanepoel 108) **and 285-8 dec** (A. P. McLaren 134); ‡**KwaZulu-Natal 204** (J. Coetzee 5-60) **and 79** (J. Coetzee 6-38). *Griqualand West 18.6pts, KwaZulu-Natal 6.08pts. Adrian McLaren hit 134 in 116 balls.*

At Pretoria, January 26–28, 2012. **Northerns won by ten wickets. Northerns 233** (A. L. Ndlovu 104*) **and 123-0**; ‡**South Western Districts 73 and 282** (L. M. G. Masekela 5-51). *Northerns 16.66pts, South Western Districts 4pts.*

At Cape Town (Northerns-Goodwood), January 26–28, 2012. **Western Province won by 127 runs.** ‡**Western Province 172 and 275** (R. Das Neves 5-79); **Gauteng 193** (J. P. Bothma 5-60) **and 127** (J. P. Bothma 5-42). *Western Province 15.44pts, Gauteng 5.86pts.*

At Paarl, February 2–4, 2012. **Griqualand West won by 87 runs. Griqualand West 180** (H. H. Paulse 7-58) **and 299** (A. P. McLaren 106, G. N. Nieuwoudt 126); ‡**Boland 175** (J. Coetzee 6-39) **and 217**. *Griqualand West 15.6pts, Boland 5.5pts.*

At Port Elizabeth (Nelson Mandela Metropole University), February 2–4, 2012. **Eastern Province v Free State. Abandoned.** *Eastern Province 5pts, Free State 5pts.*

At Johannesburg (ABSA Oval), February 2–4, 2012. **Drawn. KwaZulu-Natal Inland 170 and 307-9 dec**; ‡**Gauteng 205 and 234-3** (R. Cameron 112*). *Gauteng 6.1pts, KwaZulu-Natal Inland 5.4pts.*

At Windhoek, February 2–4, 2012. **Namibia v KwaZulu-Natal. Abandoned.** *Namibia 5pts, KwaZulu-Natal 5pts.*

At Potchefstroom, February 2–3, 2012. **North West won by an innings and 40 runs. North West 380**; ‡**Border 200 and 140** (C. J. Alexander 6-50). *North West 19.6pts, Border 6pts.*

At Paarl, February 9–11, 2012. **North West won by five wickets.** ‡**Boland 181 and 179**; **North West 263 and 100-5**. *North West 17.26pts, Boland 5.62pts.*

At East London, February 9–11, 2012. **Border won by 125 runs. Border 336 and 166-3 dec**; ‡**Northerns 189** (L. L. Mnyanda 6-27) **and 188** (D. Hewitt 103). *Border 17.84pts, Northerns 4.78pts.*

At Benoni, February 9–11, 2012. **Easterns won by 43 runs. Easterns 303-9 dec** (B. M. Dolley 5-73) **and 187-8 dec** (S. S. B. Magala 5-54); ‡**Eastern Province 196** (S. W. Liebisch 5-57) **and 251**. *Easterns 18.06pts, Eastern Province 5.92pts.*

At Pietermaritzburg, February 9–11, 2012. **Drawn. Griqualand West 242-5** v **‡KwaZulu-Natal Inland.** *KwaZulu-Natal Inland 2pts, Griqualand West 2.84pts.*

At Cape Town, February 9–11, 2012. **Drawn. ‡Western Province 292 and 189**; **Free State 294 and 112-5**. *Western Province 7.84pts, Free State 7.88pts.*

At Windhoek, February 9–11, 2012. **Drawn. ‡South Western Districts 352** (C. Jonker 190); **Namibia 164 and 183-4**. *Namibia 5.28pts, South Western Districts 9.04pts. Christiaan Jonker hit nine sixes and 13 fours in 196 balls.*

At Port Elizabeth (Nelson Mandela Metropole University), February 16–18, 2012. **Drawn. Northerns 226 and 268-6 dec**; **‡Eastern Province 241 and 69-3**. *Eastern Province 6.82pts, Northerns 6.52pts. Northerns captain Francois le Clus held five catches in Eastern Province's first innings.*

At Benoni, February 16–18, 2012. **Border won by four wickets. Easterns 266 and 95** (Y. Pangabantu 5-19); **‡Border 244** (A. M. Sodumo 116) **and 121-6** (S. W. Liebisch 5-37). *Border 16.88pts, Easterns 7.32pts. Abongile Sodumo hit 116 in 97 balls.*

At Durban, February 16–18, 2012. **Drawn. KwaZulu-Natal 346-5 dec** (C. J. Bowes 127) **and 42-2 dec**; **‡Gauteng 159 and 153-6**. *KwaZulu-Natal 8.62pts, Gauteng 3.18pts.*

At Oudtshoorn, February 16–18, 2012. **Drawn. ‡South Western Districts 164** (A. F. Erasmus 5-60) **and 378-7 dec** (B. C. de Wett 112, C. Jonker 128); **North West 343** (B. J. Pelser 153*; G. R. Rabie 8-60) **and 109-7**. *South Western Districts 5.28pts, North West 7.86pts. Brett Pelser added 120 for North West's last wicket with Johannes Diseko, who became the eighth victim of Gurshwin Rabie as he returned the best figures of the tournament.*

At Cape Town, February 16–18, 2012. **Drawn. Western Province 351-7 dec** (M. Q. Adams 138) **and 216-9 dec** (C. G. Williams 5-44); **‡Namibia 345** (G. Snyman 127) **and 147-5**. *Western Province 8.02pts, Namibia 5.9pts.*

At East London, February 23–25, 2012. **Border won by an innings and 52 runs. ‡Free State 184** (P. Botha 103*) **and 196**; **Border 432-4 dec** (K. D. Bennett 163*, C. Tshiki 175). *Border 18.46pts, Free State 1.68pts. Kevin Bennett and Cebo Tshiki put on 322 for Border's third wicket.*

At Pietermaritzburg, February 23–25, 2012. **KwaZulu-Natal Inland won by 19 runs. ‡KwaZulu-Natal Inland 226** (D. Stanley 5-53, S. W. Liebisch 5-39) **and 213**; **Easterns 292** (B. Moses 100) **and 128** (T. Shamsi 7-39). *KwaZulu-Natal Inland 16.52pts, Easterns 7.84pts.*

At Windhoek, February 23–25, 2012. **Drawn. Namibia 151** (P. J. N. Jeftha 6-34) **and 22-1**; **‡Boland 103**. *Namibia 5.02pts, Boland 4pts.*

At Potchefstroom, February 23–25, 2012. **North West won by ten wickets. ‡KwaZulu-Natal 108** (D. Klein 7-37) **and 252**; **North West 313** (A. H. Razak 7-49) **and 48-0**. *North West 18.26pts, KwaZulu-Natal 4pts.*

At Oudtshoorn, February 23–24, 2012. **South Western Districts won by ten wickets. Griqualand West 115** (G. R. Rabie 5-48) **and 190** (G. R. Rabie 6-60); **‡South Western Districts 273 and 35-0**. *South Western Districts 17.46pts, Griqualand West 4pts. Christiaan Jonkers of South Western Districts passed 1,000 first-class runs for the season. Rabie took 11-108.*

At Cape Town (Durbanville), February 23–25, 2012. **Northerns won by an innings and 90 runs. ‡Northerns 354-9 dec** (P. J. Malan 157; J. P. Bothma 5-44); **Western Province 158 and 106**. *Northerns 18.74pts, Western Province 3.16pts.*

At Bloemfontein, March 1–3, 2012. **Free State won by an innings and 32 runs. KwaZulu-Natal Inland 166 and 208**; **‡Free State 406-9 dec**. *Free State 18.48pts, KwaZulu-Natal Inland 3.32pts.*

At Johannesburg, March 1–3, 2012. **Gauteng won by 153 runs. Gauteng 176 and 315-6 dec** (T. G. Mokoena 100*); **‡Boland 138 and 200**. *Gauteng 15.52pts, Boland 4pts.*

At Kimberley, March 1–2, 2012. **Griqualand West won by eight wickets. Western Province 148 and 110**; **‡Griqualand West 179** (J. P. Bothma 5-31) **and 81-2**. *Griqualand West 15.58pts, Western Province 4pts.*

At Potchefstroom, March 1–3, 2012. **North West won by eight wickets. ‡Eastern Province 201 and 202** (M. B. A. Smith 128; A. F. Erasmus 6-63); **North West 287** (B. J. Pelser 105) **and 117-2**. *North West 17.74pts, Eastern Province 6.02pts.*

At Oudtshoorn, March 1–3, 2012. **Easterns won by nine wickets. South Western Districts 168** (S. W. Liebisch 5-33) **and 164**; ‡**Easterns 290** (T. M. Bodibe 148) **and 46-1**. *Easterns 17.8pts, South Western Districts 5.36pts.*

At Benoni, March 8–10, 2012. **Drawn. Western Province 351-8 dec** (M. C. Kleinveldt 134, M. G. Pote 119) **and 231-2 dec** (M. G. Pote 100*); ‡**Easterns 273-9 dec and 204-5**. *Easterns 6.46pts, Western Province 9pts. Matthew Kleinveldt and Michael Pote opened with 247 in Western Province's first innings and 174 in their second; Pote contributed a century in both.*

At Kimberley, March 8–10, 2012. **Drawn. Eastern Province 319** (M. L. Price 118) **and 182-6 dec**; ‡**Griqualand West 219 and 256-9**. *Griqualand West 6.38pts, Eastern Province 8.38pts.*

At Durban, March 8–10, 2012. **Drawn. Free State 186 and 216** (L. N. Mosena 100); ‡**KwaZulu-Natal 231 and 143-6**. *KwaZulu-Natal 6.62pts, Free State 5.72pts.*

At Paarl, March 15–17, 2012. **Drawn. Easterns 272** (B. Moses 108; O. J. Erasmus 5-41) **and 316-8**; ‡**Boland 295**. *Boland 7.74pts, Easterns 7.44pts.*

At Port Elizabeth, March 15–17, 2012. **Gauteng won by one wicket.** ‡**Eastern Province 255 and 194-6 dec**; **Gauteng 123** (S. S. B. Magala 5-54, N. D. Howard 5-61) **and 327-9** (R. Das Neves 112*; S. S. B. Magala 6-78). *Gauteng 14pts, Eastern Province 7.1pts.*

At Pretoria, March 15–17, 2012. **Drawn. Northerns 74-5** v ‡**KwaZulu-Natal Inland.** *KwaZulu-Natal Inland 2pts.*

At Johannesburg (Witwatersrand University), March 22–24, 2012. **Drawn.** ‡**South Western Districts 275-8 dec** (W. Lategan 117) **and 271** (E. Leie 5-111); **Gauteng 406** (T. G. Mokoena 120, G. I. Hume 105; R. J. Plaatjies 5-58) **and 52-4**. *Gauteng 7.8pts, South Western Districts 6.5pts. Graham Hume and Eddie Leie put on 154 for Gauteng's ninth wicket.*

At Kimberley, March 22–24, 2012. **Drawn. Border 411** (L. L. Mnyanda 145, K. D. Bennett 132) **and 163-8 dec**; ‡**Griqualand West 262-9 dec and 247-8**. *Griqualand West 6.24pts, Border 10pts. Luthando Mnyanda and Kevin Bennett added 267 for Border's second wicket.*

At Chatsworth, March 22–24, 2012. **Drawn. Northerns 282** (J. F. le Clus 112) **and 190** (K. A. Maharaj 5-56); ‡**KwaZulu-Natal 248 and 178-7**. *KwaZulu-Natal 6.96pts, Northerns 7.64pts. Pieter Malan of Northerns passed 1,000 first-class runs for the season.*

At Pietermaritzburg, March 22–24, 2012. **KwaZulu-Natal Inland v North West. Abandoned.** *KwaZulu-Natal Inland 5pts, North West 5pts.*

At East London, March 29–31, 2012. **Drawn. Gauteng 107 and 52-3**; ‡**Border 168** (G. I. Hume 5-34). *Border 5.36pts, Gauteng 4pts. Gauteng wicketkeeper Ryan Bishop held six catches.*

At Port Elizabeth, March 29–31, 2012. **Drawn. Eastern Province 212 and 94-7**; ‡**Namibia 228** (S. S. B. Magala 5-64). *Eastern Province 6.24pts, Namibia 6.56pts. Namibian wicketkeeper Kobus Delport made nine dismissals (eight catches and a stumping) in the match, while Eastern Province captain Michael Smith held five catches in Namibia's first innings.*

At Benoni, March 29–31, 2012. **Drawn. Easterns 379-9 dec** (K. A. Maharaj 5-130) **and 225-7 dec**; ‡**KwaZulu-Natal 353** (B. T. Kruger 117) **and 36-1**. *Easterns 8.32pts, KwaZulu-Natal 8.88pts.*

At Bloemfontein, March 29–31, 2012. **Drawn. South Western Districts 233** (C. Jonker 103); ‡**Free State 168-4**. *Free State 5.36pts, South Western Districts 3.66pts.*

At Potchefstroom, March 29–31, 2012. **Drawn.** ‡**Western Province 358**; **North West 123-5**. *North West 4pts, Western Province 7.16pts. Western Province's Adams passed 1,000 first-class runs for the season.*

At Pretoria, March 29–31, 2012. **Drawn. Boland 404-7 dec** (T. W. R. Cloete 112, L. van Wyk 110); ‡**Northerns 202-2** (J. F. le Clus 110*). *Northerns 4.04pts, Boland 5.2pts.*

FRANCHISE ONE-DAY CUP, 2011-12

50-over league plus knockout

	Played	*Won*	*Lost*	*No result*	*Bonus points*	*Points*	*Net run-rate*
Cape Cobras	10	7	1	1†	1	33	0.55
Knights	10	6	4	0	3	27	0.61
Warriors	10	5	4	1	3	25	0.76
Dolphins	10	2	4	4	0	16	–1.33
Titans	10	3	6	1	1	15	–0.65
Lions	10	2	6	1†	1	13	–0.92

† *Plus one match abandoned.*

Play-off

At Bloemfontein, December 4, 2011. **Warriors won by four wickets.** ‡**Knights 280-5** (50 overs); **Warriors 282-6** (49 overs) (C. A. Ingram 112). *MoM:* C. A. Ingram. *Warriors captain Colin Ingram hit 112 in 111 balls and added 126 for the second wicket with Arno Jacobs.*

Final

At Cape Town, December 9, 2011 (day/night). **Cape Cobras won by five wickets. Warriors 242-9** (50 overs) (C. K. Langeveldt 5-45); ‡**Cape Cobras 245-5** (48.3 overs). *MoM:* C. K. Langeveldt. *Charl Langeveldt wrecked the Warriors' batting, before Richard Levi and Owais Shah took the Cobras most of the way to the title by adding 122 for the third wicket.*

MiWAY T20 CHALLENGE, 2011-12

	Played	*Won*	*Lost*	*Tied*	*No result*	*Bonus points*	*Points*	*Net run-rate*
Lions	12	7	2	0	2†	3	37	1.43
Titans	12	7	3	0	1†	3	35	0.40
Knights	12	7	3	1	0†	1	34	0.40
Dolphins	12	4	3	0	2‡	0	26	–0.19
Cape Cobras	12	5	6	1	0	1	24	0.03
Warriors	12	4	7	0	0†	3	21	–0.19
Impi	12	0	10	0	1†	0	4	–1.70

† *Plus one match abandoned.* ‡ *Plus three matches abandoned.*

Win = 4pts; tie = 3pts; no result/abandoned = 2pts.

Play-off

At Centurion, March 25, 2012. **Tied.** Titans won an eliminator over. **Knights 144-6** (20 overs); ‡**Titans 144-8** (20 overs). *In the eliminator over, the Titans scored 19-1 and the Knights a mere 6-0.*

Final

At Johannesburg, April 1, 2012. **Titans won by 45 runs. Titans 187-6** (20 overs); ‡**Lions 142** (18.5 overs). *Albie Morkel (3-28) and Faf du Plessis (4-24) bowled the Titans to victory.*

CSA PROVINCIAL ONE-DAY CHALLENGE, 2011-12

50-over league

	Played	*Won*	*Lost*	*No result*	*Bonus points*	*Points*	*Net run-rate*
Free State	7	6	0	1	3	29	1.52
KwaZulu-Natal	7	5	0	1†	2	26	1.17
Northerns	7	5	2	0	2	22	0.47
Eastern Province	7	4	3	0	1	17	–0.10
South Western Districts	7	4	3	0	1	17	–0.33
Border	7	4	3	0	0	16	–0.54
Western Province	7	3	4	0	3	15	–0.14
Griqualand West	7	3	3	0†	1	15	0.23
Boland	7	3	4	0	2	14	–0.16
Gauteng	7	3	4	0	1	13	–0.18
KwaZulu-Natal Inland	7	2	4	0†	2	12	0.17
North West	7	2	5	0	1	9	–0.11
Namibia	7	1	5	0†	1	7	–0.42
Easterns	7	1	6	0	1	5	–1.06

† *Plus one match abandoned.*

CSA PROVINCIAL T20, 2011-12

20-over league plus final

Coastal	*P*	*W*	*L*	*T*	*BP*	*Pts*	*NRR*
E. Province	6	6	0	0	1	25	0.87
W. Province	6	3	2	0†	0	14	0.10
Boland	6	3	3	0	1	13	–0.37
KZ-Natal	6	2	2	1†	1	13	0.14
SWDistricts	6	1	3	1†	1	9	0.35
KZN Inland	6	1	3	0‡	0	8	–0.58
Border	6	1	4	0†	0	6	–0.64

Inland	*P*	*W*	*L*	*BP*	*Pts*	*NRR*
Northerns	6	4	2	2	18	1.08
North West	6	4	2	1	17	0.43
Free State	6	4	2	1	17	0.00
Griqualand W.	6	4	2	0	16	0.28
Gauteng	6	3	3	0	12	0.11
Easterns	6	2	4	0	8	–0.26
Namibia	6	0	6	0	0	–1.81

† *Plus one match abandoned.* ‡ *Plus two matches abandoned.*

Final

At Port Elizabeth, January 21. **Northerns won by 16 runs. Northerns 154-5** (20 overs); ‡**Eastern Province 138-9** (20 overs). *Northerns opener Henry Davids scored 70 in 47 balls, and added 103 in 12.4 overs for their third wicket with Farhaan Behardien.*

SRI LANKA CRICKET, 2012

Taking Haroon's medicine

SA'ADI THAWFEEQ

Sri Lanka moved into 2013 hoping that the lion's share of the independent report submitted by former ICC chief executive Haroon Lorgat would be implemented to streamline administration and make the board more financially viable. Sri Lanka Cricket had hired the services of Lorgat, an accountant, in July in the face of mounting debts and heavy overstaffing. He was given three months to talk to stakeholders, and had access to financial accounts.

His report, delivered in November, was welcomed by sports minister Mahindananda Aluthgamage, who wanted several of the recommendations to be pushed through – chief among them to make cricket exempt from the Sports Law that governs every sporting body in Sri Lanka (which requires the sports minister to approve major selectorial decisions).

SRI LANKA IN 2012

	Played	*Won*	*Lost*	*Drawn/No result*
Tests	10	3	5	2
One-day internationals	34	14	16	4
Twenty20 internationals	11	6	4	1

DECEMBER – JANUARY	3 Tests and 5 ODIs (a) v South Africa	(see *Wisden 2012*, page 1043)
FEBRUARY – MARCH	Triangular ODI tournament (a) (in Australia) v Australia and India	(page 892)
	Asia Cup (in Bangladesh)	
MARCH – APRIL	2 Tests (h) v England	(page 301)
MAY		
JUNE – JULY	3 Tests, 5 ODIs and 2 T20Is (h) v Pakistan	(page 1110)
JULY – AUGUST	5 ODIs and 1 T20I (h) v India	(page 1125)
SEPTEMBER – OCTOBER	World Twenty20 (h)	(page 841)
OCTOBER – NOVEMBER	2 Tests, 5 ODIs and 1 T20I (h) v New Zealand	(page 1131)
DECEMBER – JANUARY	3 Tests, 5 ODIs and 2 T20Is (a) v Australia	(page 919)

For a review of Sri Lankan domestic cricket from the 2011-12 season, see page 1143.

All in all, 2012 turned out to be an uncomfortable year, beginning as it did with the sacking of head coach Geoff Marsh, and ending with a dismal innings defeat in the Boxing Day Test at Melbourne. But the most serious blow came in between, when Sri Lanka failed to win the World Twenty20 in home conditions. Defeat by West Indies in Colombo was the fourth time in five years they had lost a major tournament final.

Like Marsh, who unsuccessfully sought legal redress for his removal, Tillekeratne Dilshan paid with his position as captain after the South Africa tour of 2011-12, having presided over four straight series defeats in both Tests and one-day internationals. Mahela Jayawardene agreed to come back in his place for one year, until the end of the tour of Australia in January 2013. Angelo Mathews took over, with Dinesh Chandimal becoming captain of the Twenty20 team. Changes also came in the selection committee, with Ashantha de Mel returning as chairman in place of Duleep Mendis. Marsh's replacement, the South African Graham Ford, had become the fourth man to coach Sri Lanka since the 2011 World Cup. He fitted in well, and helped turn the players into a more professional unit.

Under the new structure, Sri Lanka were able at least to arrest their run of Test defeats. At home, they drew 1–1 with England, beat Pakistan, then drew – disappointingly, perhaps – with New Zealand. For this, they were indebted to the flourishing of left-arm spinner Rangana Herath at the age of 34. Though a slightly ungainly, round-arm bowler, he took five six-wicket hauls in the home Tests, not always with the help of the DRS. He finished with more Test wickets in the year (60) than anyone, and at a strike-rate of 53, two better than Muttiah Muralitharan's career figure. The rest of Sri Lanka's bowlers took only 79 wickets between them, with Suraj Randiv the next-highest on 22. He could have done with help from elsewhere, but only Kumar Sangakkara and Mathews averaged above 40 with the bat.

After seven years of government-appointed interim committees, SLC finally held an annual general meeting in January 2012. The change of attitude followed an ICC resolution that all member boards should be free of political interference. But amid allegations of voter intimidation, Upali Dharmadasa – SLC president from 1996–98, and interim committee chairman before it was dissolved – won uncontested when his chief rival for the presidency, Thilanga Sumathipala, withdrew. In fact, all the opposition candidates withdrew in protest, and all the main office bearers were elected uncontested, in a process presided over by the sports ministry.

The first task of this new committee was to clear a deficit approaching $70m, mostly a result of constructing new venues at Hambantota and Pallekele, and renovating Colombo's Premadasa Stadium for the 2011 World Cup. "It will be a struggle for about five years," predicted Dharmadasa, whose request for financial assistance from the government was turned down.

SLC had not had enough money to pay the salaries of their employees and 100 contracted cricketers since the World Cup. However, Aluthgamage negotiated with the state-owned Bank of Ceylon to release SLRs600m ($5.07m) to SLC. This, coupled with the 42% of World Cup participation fees which the ICC paid directly to the players' accounts in December 2011, allowed

Gareth Copley, Getty Images

Not again! Mahela Jayawardene and Kumar Sangakkara rue another defeat in a final.

the outstanding dues to be settled. By cutting down on administrative overheads and contracted players, as well as receiving revenues from hosting a one-day tour by India and the World Twenty20, SLC managed to clear some of their deficit.

The inaugural Sri Lankan Premier League was supposed to rake in more money, although it had been in danger of not getting off the ground when SLC ran into a contractual issue with their international players. Somerset Entertainment Ventures, a sporting business company based in Singapore, secured SLPL rights for the next seven years, guaranteeing SLC $4m each year. The timing of the tournament, two months before the World Twenty20 in Sri Lanka, failed to entice the spectators, although several international cricketers – especially Pakistanis ostracised from the IPL – appeared for the seven teams involved. Sri Lanka managed to unearth two new players: opener Dilshan Munaweera and spinner Akila Dananjaya both featured in the World Twenty20.

SLC sacrificed two Tests in the Caribbean and a three-Test home series against South Africa scheduled for 2013 in order to accommodate the IPL and a triangular one-day series. Sri Lanka's Test calendar was looking empty. SLC came in for severe criticism from past players and administrators for undermining Test cricket. The debacle at Melbourne, where Sri Lanka lost inside three days, was cited as evidence that they needed to play more Tests to be rated among the top nations. That was a battle the Dharmadasa administration had to wage against a sagging bank balance.

SRI LANKA v PAKISTAN, 2012

SA'ADI THAWFEEQ

Test matches (3): Sri Lanka 1, Pakistan 0
One-day internationals (5): Sri Lanka 3, Pakistan 1
Twenty20 internationals (2): Sri Lanka 1, Pakistan 1

Sri Lanka's close-run victory arrested a worrying sequence of eight Test series without a win, and blotted the copybook of Misbah-ul-Haq, who had not lost any of the seven in which he had previously captained Pakistan. Perhaps it was no coincidence that the only defeat, in the First Test at Galle, came under the leadership of Mohammad Hafeez while Misbah served a one-match ban for his team's slow over-rate in the final one-day international.

It was the fourth time since February 2009 that these sides had met in a Test series – but still the Decision Review System had not played a part. Pakistan were on the receiving end of several poor umpiring decisions during their 209-run loss, prompting both Hafeez and Sri Lankan captain Mahela Jayawardene to request that the DRS be used in all Test series; Jayawardene renewed his appeal for the ICC to help make up the cost on behalf of poorer boards, such as his own.

Dav Whatmore, Sri Lanka's 1996 World Cup-winning coach, but now working with Pakistan, was especially displeased. "The home board had [the DRS] against England. Why aren't we having it here?" he asked. "It doesn't seem right to me where you have it for one series and not for the other. It's difficult to understand." Sri Lanka Cricket secretary Nishantha Ranatunga hit back: whereas the ECB, he said, had agreed to help foot the bill for the DRS when England visited in March and April, the Pakistan Cricket Board were less willing. It was just as well that Pakistan did not seek to blame their defeat on umpiring decisions: poor fielding, and regular stoppages for rain, were just as crucial.

Sri Lanka could have won 2–0, but Jayawardene was not prepared to risk throwing away a series victory – their first since the retirement of Muttiah Muralitharan – by attempting a target of 270 in 71 overs on the last day of the final Test, at Pallekele. Sri Lanka used up 62 overs in reaching 195 for four, reluctant to chance their arm against Saeed Ajmal, who took 15 wickets, and Junaid Khan, who finished with 14 and an enhanced reputation for prowess with the old ball. He went a long way to compensating for Pakistan's other seamers, who managed only two wickets between them. It was unclear whether the continued absence of a bowling coach – Aqib Javed had left to take charge of the UAE national team in March – was a serious factor. Ajmal was Pakistan's principal threat but, after the Sri Lankan authorities alerted match referee David Boon to their concerns about his bowling action in the opening Test, his menace diminished.

After the heavy defeat at Galle – Pakistan's first in 11 Tests stretching back to May 2011 – their batsmen found their feet. The two junior members, Azhar

Ali and Asad Shafiq, each scored hundreds, and Hafeez bounced back from a dreadful run of form with 196 in the Second Test, in Colombo. This was Pakistan's best chance to level the series, but they were frustrated by the weather and the famously benign pitch at the Sinhalese Sports Club.

Sri Lanka's batting was stitched together by Kumar Sangakkara, who had an outstanding series, scoring 490 runs and propelling his career average against Pakistan to 89. He was in prime form, though he was twice deprived of a ninth Test double-century: stranded on 199 not out at Galle when he ran out of partners, he was caught off a careless shot on 192 at the SSC. Tillekeratne Dilshan also made centuries in the first two Tests, but stepped down from the Third when one of his children was taken ill. His decision came in the early hours before the game, and forced Sri Lanka to bring in Dinesh Chandimal as a stopgap opener, an unfamiliar role to which he adjusted well.

Sri Lanka struggled to settle on a new-ball combination once Chanaka Welagedara was ruled out of the series with a torn shoulder muscle. The onus fell once more on the spinners, principally Rangana Herath, who bowled 171.3 overs across the three Tests and took 15 wickets. But, after taking seven at Galle, Suraj Randiv provided little control in Colombo, and made way for an additional seamer in the lusher conditions at Pallekele.

Pace bowlers were pleasantly surprised by the movement and bounce on offer in the limited-overs matches, especially at Pallekele and Colombo's Premadasa Stadium, a trend partly explained by playing at night in June, and on relaid surfaces.

Sri Lanka won the one-day internationals 3–1. Excluding victory in a triangular tournament with Scotland and Ireland, this was their first win in eight one-day series or competitions since beating West Indies at home in early 2011. The outstanding performer was Tissara Perera, who encouraged the belief that he and Angelo Mathews could provide Sri Lanka with two accomplished all-rounders in all forms of the game – so long as they could stay fit.

As for Pakistan, they had to settle for a share of the Twenty20 series at the start of the tour. But by the end, that had been long forgotten.

PAKISTANI TOURING PARTY

*Misbah-ul-Haq, Abdur Rehman, Adnan Akmal, Afaq Raheem, Aizaz Cheema, Asad Shafiq, Azhar Ali, Faisal Iqbal, Junaid Khan, Mohammad Ayub, Mohammad Hafeez, Mohammad Sami, Saeed Ajmal, Taufeeq Umar, Umar Gul, Younis Khan. *Coach:* D. F. Whatmore.

The Twenty20 squad included only Mohammad Hafeez (as captain), Mohammad Sami, Saeed Ajmal and Umar Gul of the Test squad (above), supplemented by Ahmed Shahzad, Hammad Azam, Haris Sohail, Khalid Latif, Raza Hasan, Shahid Afridi, Shakeel Ansar, Shoaib Malik, Sohail Tanvir, Umar Akmal and Yasir Arafat. Compared with the Test party, the one-day squad included Imran Farhat, Rahat Ali, Sarfraz Ahmed, Shahid Afridi and Umar Akmal in place of Adnan Akmal, Afaq Raheem, Faisal Iqbal, Junaid Khan, Mohammad Ayub and Taufeeq Umar. Nasir Jamshed, named in both limited-overs squads, was ruled out with a broken finger; Sohail Tanvir replaced him in the one-day side.

TEST MATCH AVERAGES

SRI LANKA – BATTING AND FIELDING

	T	*I*	*NO*	*R*	*HS*	*100*	*50*	*Avge*	*Ct*
†K. C. Sangakkara	3	6	3	490	199*	2	1	163.33	1
T. M. Dilshan	2	4	0	306	121	2	1	76.50	2
†N. T. Paranavitana	3	6	0	178	75	0	1	29.66	3
H. A. P. W. Jayawardene	3	4	1	83	48	0	0	27.66	9
A. D. Mathews	3	5	2	64	47	0	0	21.33	0
T. T. Samaraweera	3	5	0	104	73	0	1	20.80	3
D. P. M. D. Jayawardene	3	6	1	100	62	0	1	20.00	3
K. M. D. N. Kulasekara	3	3	0	33	33	0	0	11.00	1
†H. M. R. K. B. Herath	3	3	1	12	10*	0	0	6.00	0

Played in two Tests: A. N. P. R. Fernando 0, 1; S. Randiv 8, 5. Played in one Test: L. D. Chandimal 8, 65; C. R. D. Fernando 0*; †N. L. T. C. Perera 75 (1 ct).

BOWLING

	Style	*O*	*M*	*R*	*W*	*BB*	*5I*	*Avge*
S. Randiv	OB	74.3	5	258	10	4-13	0	25.80
H. M. R. K. B. Herath	SLA	171.3	30	425	15	4-99	0	28.33
K. M. D. N. Kulasekara	RFM	112	34	291	8	3-48	0	36.37
N. L. T. C. Perera	RFM	43	7	151	4	4-63	0	37.75
C. R. D. Fernando	RFM	35	2	122	3	3-74	0	40.66

Also bowled: T. M. Dilshan (OB) 1–0–9–0; A. N. P. R. Fernando (RFM) 56–9–235–1; A. D. Mathews (RM) 41–7–121–2; T. T. Samaraweera (OB) 1–0–2–0.

PAKISTAN – BATTING AND FIELDING

	T	*I*	*NO*	*R*	*HS*	*100*	*50*	*Avge*	*Ct/St*
Asad Shafiq	3	5	1	257	100*	1	2	64.25	2
Azhar Ali	3	5	0	300	157	2	0	60.00	1
Misbah-ul-Haq	2	3	1	111	66*	0	1	55.50	0
Mohammad Hafeez	3	6	0	315	196	1	1	52.50	1
Adnan Akmal	3	6	3	113	40*	0	0	37.66	4/2
Younis Khan	3	5	0	167	87	0	1	33.40	2
†Taufeeq Umar	3	6	1	159	65	0	1	31.80	3
†Abdur Rehman	2	4	1	69	36	0	0	23.00	1
Junaid Khan	3	3	2	13	8	0	0	13.00	0
Saeed Ajmal	3	4	0	23	12	0	0	5.75	2
Umar Gul	2	4	0	13	7	0	0	3.25	0

Played in one Test: Mohammad Ayub 25, 22 (1 ct); Mohammad Sami 9, 3; Aizaz Cheema did not bat.

BOWLING

	Style	*O*	*M*	*R*	*W*	*BB*	*5I*	*Avge*
Junaid Khan	LFM	101.2	16	305	14	5-70	2	21.78
Saeed Ajmal	OB	155	25	449	15	5-146	1	29.93
Mohammad Hafeez	OB	41.2	4	116	3	3-55	0	38.66
Abdur Rehman	SLA	83.4	14	248	6	4-78	0	41.33

Also bowled: Aizaz Cheema (RFM) 26–5–97–0; Azhar Ali (LB) 4–0–10–0; Mohammad Sami (RFM) 25–1–92–1; Umar Gul (RFM) 62–13–220–1; Younis Khan (RM/LB) 5–0–11–0.

LIMITED-OVERS INTERNATIONAL REPORTS BY REX CLEMENTINE

SRI LANKA v PAKISTAN

First Twenty20 International

At Hambantota, June 1, 2012 (floodlit). Sri Lanka won by 37 runs. Toss: Sri Lanka. Twenty20 international debuts: K. S. Lokuarachchi, S. M. S. M. Senanayake, H. D. R. L. Thirimanne; Shakeel Ansar.

Preparations for the World Twenty20 – to be hosted by Sri Lanka in September and October – began in earnest, but neither side could produce appetising cricket on a grudging pitch. Sri Lanka's top order struggled with the awkward angle and movement of Sohail Tanvir, who struck in each of his first three overs. They were 89 for seven by the 17th, but Umar Gul's last two went for 31, mostly to Perera. Pakistan started the reply as favourites, but their prospects nosedived in two balls: new Twenty20 captain Mohammad Hafeez and Shakeel Ansar – their second-oldest debutant in the format, at 33 years 203 days – were unable to get on top of cut shots, and picked out Dilshan at backward point. Ansar's golden duck capped a miserable debut: he had missed a chance to stump Thirimanne on eight. Sri Lanka conceded 17 in wides and were guilty of several misfields, but still fired Pakistan out for what was then their second-lowest Twenty20 total.

Man of the Match: N. L. T. C. Perera.

Sri Lanka

		B	*4*	*6*
*D. P. M. D. Jayawardene *c 5 b 8*	2	3	0	0
T. M. Dilshan *c 9 b 8*	5	8	0	0
†K. C. Sangakkara *b 8*	19	12	3	0
L. D. Chandimal *b 10*	10	15	0	0
A. D. Mathews *b 11*	9	25	0	0
H. D. R. L. Thirimanne *c 9 b 11*	30	25	5	0
K. S. Lokuarachchi *run out*	11	10	1	0
N. L. T. C. Perera *not out*	32	16	2	2
K. M. D. N. Kulasekara *not out*	6	6	1	0
B 1, l-b 3, w 4	8			
6 overs: 36-3 (20 overs)	132-7			

1/2 2/11 3/31 4/39 5/65 6/89 7/89

S. M. S. M. Senanayake and S. L. Malinga did not bat.

Sohail Tanvir 4–0–12–3; Umar Gul 4–0–43–0; Mohammad Sami 2–0–22–1; Shahid Afridi 2–0–9–0; Mohammad Hafeez 4–0–22–0; Saeed Ajmal 4–0–20–2.

Pakistan

		B	*4*	*6*
*Mohammad Hafeez *c 2 b 9*	0	1	0	0
Ahmed Shehzad *b 10*	36	42	3	1
†Shakeel Ansar *c 2 b 9*	0	1	0	0
Khalid Latif *c 3 b 5*	3	12	0	0
Shoaib Malik *c 8 b 5*	9	16	0	0
Umar Akmal *c 9 b 11*	12	10	2	0
Shahid Afridi *c 7 b 10*	1	2	0	0
Sohail Tanvir *run out*	1	1	0	0
Umar Gul *c 6 b 11*	5	10	0	0
Mohammad Sami *not out*	4	7	0	0
Saeed Ajmal *c 3 b 8*	5	4	1	0
L-b 2, w 17	19			
6 overs: 23-3 (17.4 overs)	95			

1/0 2/0 3/12 4/46 5/68 6/70 7/71 8/85 9/87

Kulasekara 3–0–13–2; Malinga 3–0–12–2; Mathews 4–1–8–2; Perera 2.4–0–23–1; Lokuarachchi 2–0–17–0; Senanayake 3–0–20–2.

Umpires: E. A. R. de Silva and R. E. J. Martinesz. Third umpire: R. S. A. Palliyaguruge.

SRI LANKA v PAKISTAN

Second Twenty20 International

At Hambantota, June 3, 2012 (floodlit). Pakistan won by 23 runs. Toss: Pakistan.

Pakistan, lesson learned from their debacle in the first match, adopted a cautious approach and crawled to 40 for three at the halfway mark. Shahid Afridi's late hitting enabled them to reach a defendable score, although he needed two huge strokes of luck to remain unbeaten: Dilshan, of all people, dropped a sitter at deep midwicket when he had 41; then the last ball of the innings, from Kulasekara, brushed leg stump without dislodging a bail. The promotion of Kulasekara to No. 3 failed as Yasir Arafat struck twice in his second over, and Afridi and Saeed Ajmal soon suffocated the middle order. None of the Sri Lankans reached 20, and they missed Mahela Jayawardene, rested as the captaincy passed to Mathews for the first time.

Man of the Match: Shahid Afridi. *Man of the Series:* Sohail Tanvir.

Pakistan

		B	4	6
*Mohammad Hafeez *c 6 b 9*	24	34	3	0
Ahmed Shehzad *lbw b 3*	6	6	1	0
Khalid Latif *run out*	1	6	0	0
Umar Akmal *lbw b 9*	5	12	0	0
Shoaib Malik *c 2 b 8*	27	26	3	0
Shahid Afridi *not out*	52	33	5	1
Yasir Arafat *c 2 b 3*	2	3	0	0
Sohail Tanvir *not out*	0	0	0	0
B 2, l-b 1, w 2	5			
6 overs: 18-2 (20 overs)	122-6			

1/11 2/18 3/29 4/41 5/109 6/119

†Shakeel Ansar, Mohammad Sami and Saeed Ajmal did not bat.

Kulasekara 4–1–13–2; Mathews 2–0–9–0; Perera 4–0–31–1; Udana 4–1–18–0; Lokuarachchi 4–0–31–2; Senanayake 2–0–17–0.

Sri Lanka

		B	4	6
†K. C. Sangakkara *c 5 b 7*	8	9	1	0
T. M. Dilshan *b 6*	18	21	4	0
K. M. D. N. Kulasekara *c 5 b 7*	0	4	0	0
C. K. Kapugedera *b 6*	19	23	2	1
L. D. Chandimal *b 8*	12	18	0	0
H. D. R. L. Thirimanne *c 9 b 10*	18	19	2	0
*A. D. Mathews *c 6 b 7*	11	11	0	0
N. L. T. C. Perera *b 10*	0	2	0	0
K. S. Lokuarachchi *st 9 b 11*	0	3	0	0
S. M. S. M. Senanayake *c 8 b 10*	1	4	0	0
I. Udana *not out*	1	2	0	0
L-b 2, w 9	11			
6 overs: 31-2 (19.2 overs)	99			

1/19 2/19 3/39 4/62 5/76 6/85 7/90 8/91 9/94

Sohail Tanvir 4–0–15–1; Yasir Arafat 3.2–0–18–3; Mohammad Sami 3–0–16–3; Shahid Afridi 4–0–17–2; Saeed Ajmal 4–0–20–1; Mohammad Hafeez 1–0–11–0.

Umpires: R. E. J. Martinesz and R. S. A. Palliyaguruge. Third umpire: E. A. R. de Silva.
Series referee: B. C. Broad.

SRI LANKA v PAKISTAN

First One-Day International

At Pallekele, June 7, 2012 (day/night). Pakistan won by six wickets (D/L). Toss: Sri Lanka.

Fans could hark back to the glory days of Pakistan cricket, when Wasim Akram and Waqar Younis were in their pomp, as Umar Gul and Mohammad Sami – two bowlers with different styles and methods – carved through Sri Lanka's top order. It was a good toss for Misbah-ul-Haq to lose: with the ball nipping and skidding around under cloudy skies, Pakistan did not concede a boundary until the 12th over – and only six in all. Three rain delays further upset Sri Lanka's rhythm, and they limped into the third stoppage on 107 for seven; when play resumed an hour and a half later, they were left with only five more overs. With 42 overs to equal Sri Lanka's total and win on Duckworth/Lewis, Pakistan were kept on course, after two early wickets, by the steady Misbah, who freed up Umar Akmal to play his strokes.

Man of the Match: Umar Gul.

Sri Lanka

*D. P. M. D. Jayawardene lbw b Umar Gul	3
T. M. Dilshan c Saeed Ajmal b Umar Gul	5
†K. C. Sangakkara lbw b Mohammad Sami	9
L. D. Chandimal b Umar Gul	0
W. U. Tharanga b Mohammad Hafeez	10
A. D. Mathews c Misbah-ul-Haq b Mohammad Sami	0
H. D. R. L. Thirimanne not out	42
N. L. T. C. Perera lbw b Mohammad Hafeez	17
K. M. D. N. Kulasekara c Sohail Tanvir b Mohammad Sami	18
H. M. R. K. B. Herath not out	0
L-b 7, w 23, n-b 1	31
1/8 (2) 2/12 (1) (8 wkts, 42 overs)	135

3/23 (4) 4/40 (3) 5/41 (6)
6/56 (5) 7/81 (8) 8/131 (9) 10 overs: 24-3

S. L. Malinga did not bat.

Umar Gul 9–2–24–3; Sohail Tanvir 8–0–30–0; Mohammad Sami 6–2–19–3; Mohammad Hafeez 10–3–20–2; Saeed Ajmal 5–0–23–0; Shahid Afridi 4–2–12–0.

Pakistan

Mohammad Hafeez st Sangakkara b Herath	37	Shahid Afridi not out	2
Azhar Ali c Sangakkara b Malinga	3	B 2, l-b 13, w 6, n-b 1	22
Younis Khan b Kulasekara	5		——
*Misbah-ul-Haq run out	30	1/11 (2) 2/27 (3) (4 wkts, 34.1 overs)	135
Umar Akmal not out	36	3/78 (1) 4/133 (4) 10 overs: 27-2	

†Sarfraz Ahmed, Sohail Tanvir, Umar Gul, Saeed Ajmal and Mohammad Sami did not bat.

Malinga 7–2–24–1; Kulasekara 9–3–29–1; Mathews 6–1–18–0; Perera 6.1–0–31–0; Herath 6–0–18–1.

Umpires: R. E. J. Martinesz and P. R. Reiffel. Third umpire: R. S. A. Palliyaguruge.

SRI LANKA v PAKISTAN

Second One-Day International

At Pallekele, June 9, 2012 (day/night). Sri Lanka won by 76 runs. Toss: Sri Lanka. One-day international debut: Rahat Ali.

Dilshan, who had scored only 28 in three innings, dropped anchor in a reassuring hundred on a batsman-friendly pitch. But it was Perera, emerging as an all-round force, who catapulted Sri Lanka to a comfortable victory. He gave the innings late impetus with 24 off 14 deliveries, prompting his coach Graham Ford to make comparisons with Lance Klusener. Then, brought on as second change after the new ball failed to separate the openers, he instantly set in motion Pakistan's slump with a sharp diving return catch to dismiss Mohammad Hafeez. Each of Perera's next two spells also began with a wicket; figures of six for 44 were his best in one-day cricket, and the best by anyone against Pakistan, beating five for 16 by Carl Rackemann at Adelaide in 1983-84 and Sourav Ganguly at Toronto in 1997-98. Azhar Ali constructed a fluent 96, full of delightful timing, to confound the belief that he was a Test specialist. But when he was yorked by Kulasekara, the chase fizzled out.

Man of the Match: N. L. T. C. Perera.

Sri Lanka

W. U. Tharanga c Sarfraz Ahmed b Sohail Tanvir	18	*D. P. M. D. Jayawardene b Saeed Ajmal	53
T. M. Dilshan not out	119	N. L. T. C. Perera not out	24
†K. C. Sangakkara c and b Mohammad Hafeez	18	B 1, l-b 7, w 7, n-b 1	16
			——
L. D. Chandimal lbw b Shahid Afridi	32	1/37 (1) 2/84 (3) (4 wkts, 50 overs)	280
		3/154 (4) 4/240 (5) 10 overs: 53-1	

A. D. Mathews, H. D. R. L. Thirimanne, K. M. D. N. Kulasekara, H. M. R. K. B. Herath and S. L. Malinga did not bat.

Umar Gul 9–0–58–0; Sohail Tanvir 9–1–51–1; Shahid Afridi 10–0–50–1; Rahat Ali 4–0–34–0; Saeed Ajmal 10–0–49–1; Mohammad Hafeez 8–1–30–1.

Pakistan

Mohammad Hafeez c and b Perera	14	Saeed Ajmal c Sangakkara b Malinga	4
Azhar Ali b Kulasekara	96	Rahat Ali not out	0
Younis Khan c Sangakkara b Perera	4		
*Misbah-ul-Haq lbw b Perera	27	L-b 2	2
Umar Akmal c Sangakkara b Perera	3		——
Shahid Afridi c Sangakkara b Malinga	17	1/48 (1) 2/78 (3) 3/127 (4) (46.2 overs)	204
†Sarfraz Ahmed lbw b Kulasekara	20	4/139 (5) 5/157 (2) 6/165 (6)	
Sohail Tanvir c Tharanga b Perera	3	7/170 (8) 8/197 (9) 9/204 (10)	
Umar Gul lbw b Perera	14	10/204 (7) 10 overs: 48-0	

Kulasekara 8.2–1–33–2; Malinga 8–1–40–2; Mathews 10–0–48–0; Perera 10–0–44–6; Herath 10–1–37–0.

Umpires: R. S. A. Palliyaguruge and P. R. Reiffel. Third umpire: R. E. J. Martinesz.

SRI LANKA v PAKISTAN

Third One-Day International

At Colombo (RPS), June 13, 2012 (day/night). No result. Toss: Pakistan. One-day international debut: S. Weerakoon.

Torrential rain allowed only 38 balls, the fourth of which accounted for Mohammad Hafeez. That came after a 75-minute delay following the very first delivery.

Pakistan

Mohammad Hafeez c Sangakkara b Malinga	0
Azhar Ali lbw b Kulasekara	7
Asad Shafiq not out	5
*Misbah-ul-Haq not out	0
1/0 (1) 2/12 (2) (2 wkts, 6.2 overs)	12

Younis Khan, Umar Akmal, Shahid Afridi, †Sarfraz Ahmed, Sohail Tanvir, Umar Gul and Saeed Ajmal did not bat.

Malinga 3–0–9–1; Kulasekara 3–1–3–1; Mathews 0.2–0–0–0.

Sri Lanka

W. U. Tharanga, T. M. Dilshan, †K. C. Sangakkara, L. D. Chandimal, *D. P. M. D. Jayawardene, N. L. T. C. Perera, A. D. Mathews, H. D. R. L. Thirimanne, K. M. D. N. Kulasekara, S. L. Malinga and S. Weerakoon.

Umpires: E. A. R. de Silva and P. R. Reiffel. Third umpire: R. S. A. Palliyaguruge.

SRI LANKA v PAKISTAN

Fourth One-Day International

At Colombo (RPS), June 16, 2012 (day/night). Sri Lanka won by 44 runs. Toss: Sri Lanka.

Perera's hat-trick turned the match on its head during a passage of play which immediately joined the long list of madcap moments involving Pakistan. With ten overs to go, they were 176 for four, requiring another 68 for a series lead. But Younis Khan was caught behind, Shahid Afridi lobbed feebly to cover, and Sarfraz Ahmed was clasped low down by Jayawardene, who had moved himself to wide slip for the hat-trick ball. From the last delivery of the over, Azhar Ali – who had played superbly until pulling a calf muscle – called Sohail Tanvir for a leg-bye, only to change his mind and leave him stranded. And in the next over, Umar Gul bagged the sixth duck of the innings, equalling the one-day international record. Pakistan had lost five wickets in seven legitimate balls, and

SIX DUCKS IN A ONE-DAY INTERNATIONAL INNINGS

Pakistan (213-9) v England at Birmingham	1987
Pakistan (43) v West Indies at Cape Town	1992-93
South Africa (106) v Australia at Sydney	2001-02
†Zimbabwe (127) v Sri Lanka at Harare	2008-09
Pakistan (199) v Sri Lanka at Colombo (RPS)	**2012**

† *Six consecutive wickets.*

surrendered their last eight for 33, a sorry figure massaged by a tenth-wicket stand of 20. Azhar became only the ninth batsman – and second from Pakistan, after Saeed Anwar – to carry his bat through a completed one-day international innings.

Man of the Match: N. L. T. C. Perera.

Sri Lanka

W. U. Tharanga c Younis Khan b Umar Gul 4
T. M. Dilshan lbw b Mohammad Hafeez . . 24
†K. C. Sangakkara c Azhar Ali b Saeed Ajmal 97
L. D. Chandimal b Mohammad Hafeez. . . . 18
*D. P. M. D. Jayawardene b Sohail Tanvir . . 40
N. L. T. C. Perera c Umar Akmal b Saeed Ajmal . 8
A. D. Mathews not out 10
H. D. R. L. Thirimanne run out 13
K. M. D. N. Kulasekara b Sohail Tanvir . . . 3
S. L. Malinga not out 0
B 5, l-b 10, w 11 26

1/9 (1) 2/64 (2) 3/90 (4) 4/200 (5) 5/204 (3) 6/214 (6) 7/237 (8) 8/243 (9) (8 wkts, 50 overs) 243
10 overs: 35-1

S. Weerakoon did not bat.

Umar Gul 8–1–51–1; Sohail Tanvir 10–2–43–2; Shahid Afridi 10–0–36–0; Younis Khan 2–0–11–0; Saeed Ajmal 10–1–50–2; Mohammad Hafeez 10–0–37–2.

Pakistan

Mohammad Hafeez c Kulasekara b Malinga 0
Azhar Ali not out 81
Asad Shafiq lbw b Weerakoon 25
*Misbah-ul-Haq c Kulasekara b Malinga . . . 57
Umar Akmal c Sangakkara b Kulasekara . . 0
Younis Khan c Sangakkara b Perera 1
Shahid Afridi c Chandimal b Perera 0
†Sarfraz Ahmed c Jayawardene b Perera . . . 0
Sohail Tanvir run out 0
Umar Gul c Sangakkara b Mathews 0
Saeed Ajmal c Thirimanne b Perera 12
L-b 9, w 14 23

1/0 (1) 2/53 (3) 3/166 (4) 4/169 (5) 5/176 (6) 6/176 (7) 7/176 (8) 8/176 (9) 9/179 (10) 10/199 (11) (45 overs) 199
10 overs: 29-1

Malinga 7–0–30–2; Kulasekara 9–0–36–1; Mathews 9–0–33–1; Weerakoon 10–0–49–1; Perera 10–1–42–4.

Umpires: R. E. J. Martinesz and P. R. Reiffel. Third umpire: R. S. A. Palliyaguruge.

SRI LANKA v PAKISTAN

Fifth One-Day International

At Colombo (RPS), June 18, 2012 (day/night). Sri Lanka won by two wickets. Toss: Pakistan.

Fifteen months earlier, Sri Lanka had beaten New Zealand on this ground to reach the World Cup final. But they had not won a one-day series since (excluding a triangular with Scotland and Ireland). They owed the end of the drought to the inspirational Mathews. Set 248, they looked doomed at 138 for six when Perera was run out for a duck. But Mathews added 37 with both Thirimanne and Mendis, then found another ally in Kulasekara. Even so, his task looked too steep when Sohail Tanvir conceded only six in the penultimate over, leaving 15 required from the last. Pakistan, as so often, chose the key moment to disintegrate: Mohammad Sami began with a wide, Umar Akmal blew a run-out chance with both batsmen stranded, and Mathews bunted the next ball for six over long-on. That reduced it to six off four, which he achieved with ease. Misbah-ul-Haq blamed defeat on fielding lapses and the decision to leave out Saeed Ajmal in conditions expected to aid swing. The recall of Imran Farhat was more successful but, after passing 50, he set the tone for a string of lax dismissals. Worse still, Pakistan's regular conferences as the run-chase climaxed put them three overs behind the required rate: the players were fined 40% of their match fees, and Misbah was suspended from the First Test.

Man of the Match: A. D. Mathews. *Man of the Series:* N. L. T. C. Perera.

Pakistan

Imran Farhat c Chandimal b Perera	56
Mohammad Hafeez b Kulasekara	6
Azhar Ali c Thirimanne b Mendis	30
Asad Shafiq run out	38
*Misbah-ul-Haq c Perera b Mendis	32
Umar Akmal not out	55
Shahid Afridi c Jayawardene b Kulasekara	9
Sohail Tanvir c Tharanga b Malinga	11
Umar Gul not out	2
B 2, l-b 3, w 3	8
1/22 (2) 2/82 (1) 3/113 (3) 4/146 (4) 5/207 (5) 6/229 (7) 7/244 (8) (7 wkts, 50 overs)	247
10 overs: 39-1	

†Sarfraz Ahmed and Mohammad Sami did not bat.

Malinga 10–1–52–1; Kulasekara 10–1–53–2; Mathews 10–0–41–0; Dilshan 3–0–12–0; Perera 8–0–54–1; Mendis 9–0–30–2.

Sri Lanka

W. U. Tharanga b Sohail Tanvir	2
T. M. Dilshan b Sohail Tanvir	10
†K. C. Sangakkara st Sarfraz Ahmed b Shahid Afridi	40
L. D. Chandimal c Mohammad Sami b Mohammad Hafeez	54
*D. P. M. D. Jayawardene c and b Shahid Afridi	0
A. D. Mathews not out	80
N. L. T. C. Perera run out	0
H. D. R. L. Thirimanne run out	11
B. M. A. J. Mendis c Asad Shafiq b Sohail Tanvir	19
K. M. D. N. Kulasekara not out	10
L-b 10, w 12	22
1/18 (2) 2/19 (1) 3/97 (3) 4/97 (5) 5/135 (4) 6/138 (7) 7/175 (8) 8/212 (9) (8 wkts, 49.4 overs)	248
10 overs: 36-2	

S. L. Malinga did not bat.

Umar Gul 10–1–43–0; Sohail Tanvir 10–0–42–3; Mohammad Hafeez 10–0–30–1; Mohammad Sami 9.4–0–75–0; Shahid Afridi 10–0–48–2.

Umpires: R. E. J. Martinesz and P. R. Reiffel. Third umpire: R. S. A. Palliyaguruge.
Series referee: B. C. Broad.

SRI LANKA v PAKISTAN

First Test Match

At Galle, June 22–25, 2012. Sri Lanka won by 209 runs. Toss: Sri Lanka. Test debut: Mohammad Ayub.

Sri Lanka had won only two of their previous 19 Tests, but this one they controlled from the start. Mahela Jayawardene was criticised in some quarters for not enforcing the follow-on after they had dismissed Pakistan for 100 but, weighing up the threat of rain against the desire to keep his bowlers fresh, he preferred to bat again. It allowed Sri Lanka to shut Pakistan out of the match once and for all, even if they put up an improved performance in the second innings.

Sri Lanka's two spinners, Herath and Randiv, bore the brunt of what was once Muttiah Muralitharan's workload, taking 12 wickets between them in 102.3 overs, while Kulasekara, coming in at a gentler lick than either the injured Chanaka Welagedara or the retired Chaminda Vaas, helped their cause by providing early breakthroughs.

There had been much discussion beforehand about the quickening pace of Sri Lankan pitches. This one had a helpful covering of grass, but it seemed business as usual as Dilshan and Sangakkara accumulated centuries and rocketed Sri Lanka to 300 for two on the first day. Dilshan produced an unusually refined display to achieve his first Test hundred at home since August 2009.

On the second evening, Sangakkara was the victim of a scoreboard error that deprived him of the chance to join Brian Lara on nine Test double-centuries, behind only Don Bradman. As Sri Lanka went into the 153rd over nine wickets down, the board had Sangakkara on 194; in fact, he had 193. Thinking he was one big hit away, he slogged Saeed Ajmal for six over deep midwicket and began to celebrate, only to be made aware by his team-mates on the balcony that he was still one short. It took a while for Sangakkara to absorb the embarrassment and, when he failed to take a single off the next ball – the last of the over – No. 11 Pradeep Fernando was left to face Mohammad Hafeez. He negotiated one delivery before he was castled, to the mortification of Sangakkara, the second batsman in Test history to be stranded unbeaten on 199, after Zimbabwe's Andy Flower, against South Africa at Harare 11 years earlier. Sangakkara was livid when he returned to the pavilion, and his team-mates left him alone to recover, and he was ten minutes late taking the field.

WHY DID I GIVE HIM THE STRIKE?

Stranded on 199 not out in a first-class match:

G. Ulyett	Yorkshire v Derbyshire at Sheffield	1887
N. F. Druce	†Cambridge University v MCC at Cambridge	1895
N. Claxton	South Australia v Victoria at Melbourne	1905-06
R. J. Hawson	Tasmania v Victoria at Melbourne	1912-13
A. J. Stewart	Surrey v Sussex at The Oval	1989
A. Flower	Zimbabwe v South Africa at Harare	2001-02
K. C. Sangakkara	**Sri Lanka v Pakistan at Galle**	**2012**

† *A 12-a-side match.*

Despite his initial anger, Sangakkara later reflected: "It's strange how you change as a player. When you're young, you're angry and you throw the bat in the dressing-room. Now, when you take a breather, you realise there are bigger things than getting out or not out on 199. As long as you put everything in perspective, you'll be fine." He dedicated the innings to his father, whose birthday it was.

Sangakkara's unnecessary scramble only came about because of a fierce fightback by Pakistan's bowlers on the second day, when they mopped up the last five wickets for 57. Batting against spin had suddenly become a more difficult proposition.

But that good work was quickly forgotten as Pakistan lurched to 48 for five by the close; next day they were routed for 100, thanks to a combination of miserable batting and mediocre umpiring. It was not easy for Steve Davis and Ian Gould, with close fielders thronging the bat for the spinners, and no DRS to fall back on. Younis Khan was especially unfortunate to be given out lbw with an accompanying nick, while both Taufeeq Umar and nightwatchman Ajmal could feel aggrieved at their dismissals. Pakistan's bowlers copped the worst of it, too: at various points, Paranavitana, Mahela Jayawardene and Dilshan were all grateful the DRS was not in operation.

Pakistan could, however, make few excuses for the self-destructive display which cost them the match, and ultimately the series. The man chosen to fill the gap of the suspended Misbah-ul-Haq was Mohammad Ayub – at 32 years 283 days, thought to be Pakistan's fifth-eldest debutant, and the oldest since the 1950s, when they first entered Test cricket. Ayub battled gamely, but before he was out for a two-hour 25, he threw away his goodwill by declining Adnan Akmal's call for a second run. "My call, my call, I said 'yes'!" a furious Adnan shouted at him as he stormed off. Pakistan were in and out so quickly – by lunch on the third day – that Jayawardene could afford to give his batsmen time to push the lead to an impregnable 509.

When Pakistan lurched to stumps at 36 for three, rattled by the persistent Kulasekara, a complete humiliation was on the cards. Then Younis and Asad Shafiq ground it out for nearly two sessions, adding 151 for the fifth wicket, and almost stretched the match into the last day. Pakistan were eight down by the scheduled close, but Jayawardene claimed the extra half-hour, and Randiv struck in successive overs.

Man of the Match: K. C. Sangakkara.

Close of play: first day, Sri Lanka 300-2 (Sangakkara 111, D. P. M. D. Jayawardene 55); second day, Pakistan 48-5 (Younis Khan 15, Mohammad Ayub 1); third day, Pakistan 36-3 (Younis Khan 0, Saeed Ajmal 11).

Sri Lanka

First innings			Second innings	
N. T. Paranavitana st Adnan Akmal b Saeed Ajmal	24	–	lbw b Saeed Ajmal	25
T. M. Dilshan lbw b Saeed Ajmal	101	–	lbw b Junaid Khan	56
K. C. Sangakkara not out	199	–	c Taufeeq Umar b Saeed Ajmal	1
*D. P. M. D. Jayawardene b Saeed Ajmal	62	–	c Adnan Akmal b Junaid Khan	14
T. T. Samaraweera st Adnan Akmal b Saeed Ajmal	6	–	c Younis Khan b Junaid Khan	15
A. D. Mathews c and b Saeed Ajmal	0	–	not out	7
†H. A. P. W. Jayawardene c Adnan Akmal b Mohammad Hafeez	48	–	not out	9
S. Randiv c and b Abdur Rehman	8			
K. M. D. N. Kulasekara c Mohammad Ayub b Mohammad Hafeez	0			
H. M. R. K. B. Herath run out	0			
A. N. P. R. Fernando b Mohammad Hafeez	0			
B 10, l-b 7, w 5, n-b 2	24		B 6, l-b 2, n-b 2	10
1/63 (1) 2/187 (2) 3/315 (4) 4/335 (5) 5/335 (6) 6/415 (7) 7/438 (8) 8/439 (9) 9/455 (10) 10/472 (11) (153.2 overs)	472		1/81 (1) 2/85 (2) 3/93 (3) 4/114 (4) 5/119 (5) (5 wkts dec, 41 overs)	137

Umar Gul 27–8–76–0; Junaid Khan 18–5–52–0; Mohammad Hafeez 19.2–3–55–3; Saeed Ajmal 46–9–146–5; Abdur Rehman 43–7–126–1. *Second innings*—Umar Gul 4–0–11–0; Junaid Khan 13–2–44–3; Abdur Rehman 5–0–25–0; Saeed Ajmal 17–3–47–2; Younis Khan 2–0–2–0.

Pakistan

First innings			Second innings	
*Mohammad Hafeez lbw b Randiv	20	–	c D. P. M. D. Jayawardene b Kulasekara	4
Taufeeq Umar lbw b Kulasekara	9	–	b Kulasekara	10
Azhar Ali c H. A. P. W. Jayawardene b Kulasekara	0	–	c Samaraweera b Herath	7
Younis Khan lbw b Herath	29	–	c H. A. P. W. Jayawardene b Kulasekara	87
Saeed Ajmal c Paranavitana b Randiv	0	–	run out	12
Asad Shafiq c H. A. P. W. Jayawardene b Herath	0	–	c D. P. M. D. Jayawardene b Herath	80
Mohammad Ayub lbw b Herath	25	–	lbw b Fernando	22
†Adnan Akmal run out	9	–	not out	40
Abdur Rehman lbw b Randiv	1	–	c Sangakkara b Randiv	14
Umar Gul c H. A. P. W. Jayawardene b Randiv	2	–	c Samaraweera b Randiv	4
Junaid Khan not out	2	–	c sub (B. M. A. J. Mendis) b Randiv	8
L-b 2, w 1	3		B 9, l-b 2, w 1	12
1/17 (2) 2/17 (3) 3/43 (1) 4/43 (5) 5/44 (6) 6/65 (4) 7/88 (8) 8/94 (9) 9/98 (7) 10/100 (10) (54.3 overs)	100		1/8 (1) 2/21 (3) 3/25 (2) 4/38 (5) 5/189 (6) 6/212 (4) 7/243 (7) 8/266 (9) 9/280 (10) 10/300 (11) (114 overs)	300

Kulasekara 13–7–27–2; Fernando 9–2–28–0; Herath 21–6–30–3; Mathews 2–2–0–0; Randiv 9.3–1–13–4. *Second innings*—Kulasekara 23–8–48–3; Fernando 15–4–56–1; Herath 42–9–91–2; Mathews 4–1–8–0; Randiv 30–4–86–3.

Umpires: S. J. Davis and I. J. Gould. Third umpire: R. E. J. Martinesz.

SRI LANKA v PAKISTAN

Second Test Match

At Colombo (SSC), June 30–July 4, 2012. Drawn. Toss: Sri Lanka.

Sri Lanka nearly paid the price for inviting Pakistan to bat on a placid track, and were lucky to escape with the draw that preserved their series lead. Mahela Jayawardene made no attempt to deny his miscalculation. "It was a gamble in a way, but not a very good one," he admitted. The only mitigation, he argued, was that rain – which skimmed the equivalent of a day and a half – prevented the pitch from taking on a fifth-day complexion.

Jayawardene's generosity was gleefully accepted by Pakistan, desperate for a route back into the series; they went on to compile a massive 551 for six declared. It was not entirely Sri Lanka's fault they conceded so many: the nature of the pitch betrayed them a little. The Sinhalese Sports Club is generally helpful to seamers in the first session, but this wicket offered scarcely any movement or bounce, and after an hour's play Sri Lanka must have known they had a fight on their hands to save the Test.

The only success before lunch on the first day came when Taufeeq Umar edged Mathews to wicketkeeper Prasanna Jayawardene, standing up. There was one other nick, which fell short of second slip; another ball beat the outside edge. The usually sedate Taufeeq had plundered 65 out of an opening stand of 78 with Mohammad Hafeez, and Pakistan went on to score 300 in a day for the first time in 23 Tests stretching back to January 2010.

Hafeez, woefully short on runs, pressed on to a career-best 196 before Herath finally broke through his defence. He was so calm and composed that he barely drew attention to himself during seven hours and seven minutes at the crease. Meanwhile, Azhar Ali, whose 157 equalled his previous best, against England in February, blunted the attack with an array of strokes through an apparently well-set off-side field. Hafeez and Azhar put on 287 – the highest for any visiting team in Sri Lanka – but Pakistan's charge was halted by rain, which allowed only 44.2 overs on the second day. In that time, Younis Khan's rotten luck continued: he was struck outside the line by Herath, but given out by Simon Taufel; for the third time in three innings, the DRS would have reprieved him.

Misbah-ul-Haq, returning as captain after his one-match over-rate ban, passed up the opportunity to declare overnight on 488, choosing another hour of quick runs on the third morning instead. But it was clear Pakistan would be battling the weather to bowl Sri Lanka out twice in the remaining eight and a half sessions. The prospect nosedived further in the course of a 225-run stand for the second wicket between Dilshan and Sangakkara, who each scored centuries between the rain breaks. Either side of their efforts, four others made ducks; Mahela Jayawardene's was his first on the ground where he holds the record for most Test runs at any single venue. Saeed Ajmal found the going tough: no Pakistan bowler had bowled as many as 34 overs in an innings without a maiden before.

Sangakkara again missed out on a double-century, this time by eight runs, when he charged Abdur Rehman and slapped to midwicket. He became the second man in Test cricket, after Mohammad Yousuf, to finish in the 190s on three separate occasions. But by then he had gone past Don Bradman to 30 Test centuries. Nine had come against Pakistan, beating Aravinda de Silva's world record of eight against them; in the same innings, he passed Sunil Gavaskar's 2,089 Test runs against Pakistan, another record.

Dilshan escaped several ungainly slashes and nicks to reach 121, at which point he became the eighth Sri Lankan to 5,000 Test runs. In the next over, he was lbw to Junaid Khan, in the same spirited burst of old-ball bowling which claimed Jayawardene and briefly enlivened the Test. Junaid steamed in from round the wicket and found reverse swing towards the end of the fourth day, but once Sangakkara and Mathews had guided Sri Lanka beyond the follow-on mark, there was little hope of a Pakistan win.

Man of the Match: Junaid Khan.

Close of play: first day, Pakistan 334-1 (Mohammad Hafeez 172, Azhar Ali 92); second day, Pakistan 488-4 (Misbah-ul-Haq 29, Asad Shafiq 1); third day, Sri Lanka 70-1 (Dilshan 46, Sangakkara 22); fourth day, Sri Lanka 278-5 (Sangakkara 144).

Pakistan

Mohammad Hafeez b Herath	196	– c Dilshan b Randiv	21
Taufeeq Umar c H. A. P. W. Jayawardene b Mathews	65	– not out	42
Azhar Ali c Kulasekara b Randiv	157		
Younis Khan lbw b Herath	32		
*Misbah-ul-Haq not out	66		
Asad Shafiq run out	2		
†Adnan Akmal c Dilshan b Herath	5	– (4) not out	0
Abdur Rehman not out	18	– (3) b Randiv	36
L-b 5, w 1, n-b 4	10	N-b 1	1
1/78 (2) 2/365 (1) 3/435 (4) 4/486 (3) 5/491 (6) 6/519 (7) (6 wkts dec, 147 overs)	551	1/51 (1) 2/99 (3) (2 wkts dec, 18 overs)	100

Saeed Ajmal, Aizaz Cheema and Junaid Khan did not bat.

Kulasekara 27–6–84–0; Mathews 15–1–55–1; Fernando 24–3–103–0; Randiv 31–0–131–1; Herath 49–5–164–3; Dilshan 1–0–9–0. *Second innings*—Kulasekara 5–0–23–0; Fernando 8–0–48–0; Randiv 4–0–28–2; Herath 1–0–1–0.

Sri Lanka

N. T. Paranavitana c Azhar Ali b Junaid Khan	0	– lbw b Saeed Ajmal	32
T. M. Dilshan lbw b Junaid Khan	121	– lbw b Abdur Rehman	28
K. C. Sangakkara c Taufeeq Umar b Abdur Rehman	192	– not out	24
*D. P. M. D. Jayawardene lbw b Junaid Khan	0	– not out	1
T. T. Samaraweera lbw b Saeed Ajmal	0		
S. Randiv lbw b Abdur Rehman	5		
A. D. Mathews c Adnan Akmal b Junaid Khan	47		
†H. A. P. W. Jayawardene c Adnan Akmal b Abdur Rehman	6		
K. M. D. N. Kulasekara b Junaid Khan	0		
H. M. R. K. B. Herath not out	10		
A. N. P. R. Fernando c Saeed Ajmal b Abdur Rehman	1		
B 4, l-b 5	9	L-b 1	1
1/11 (1) 2/236 (2) 3/250 (4) 4/259 (5) 5/278 (6) 6/370 (7) 7/378 (3) 8/379 (9) 9/385 (8) 10/391 (11) (124.4 overs)	391	1/48 (2) 2/78 (1) (2 wkts, 22 overs)	86

Aizaz Cheema 24–5–86–0; Junaid Khan 28–6–73–5; Saeed Ajmal 34–0–106–1; Abdur Rehman 26.4–5–78–4; Mohammad Hafeez 8–0–29–0; Azhar Ali 4–0–10–0. *Second innings*—Junaid Khan 4–0–21–0; Aizaz Cheema 2–0–11–0; Abdur Rehman 9–2–19–1; Saeed Ajmal 7–0–34–1.

Umpires: I. J. Gould and S. J. A. Taufel. Third umpire: R. S. A. Palliyaguruge.

> “Unable to pick Saeed Ajmal, and with a long-standing unease against left-arm spin, he displayed all the existential angst of Edvard Munch’s *The Scream* during his 29-ball innings.”
>
> **Pakistan v England 2011-12, First Test, page 286.**

SRI LANKA v PAKISTAN

Third Test Match

At Pallekele, July 8–12, 2012. Drawn. Toss: Sri Lanka.

Hill-country Sri Lanka was lush from months of rain, and offered the opposite to Colombo: a juicy Test pitch for bowlers to sink their teeth into. Mahela Jayawardene's gamble in inserting Pakistan for a second game in a row, after winning his third toss of the series, this time proved the right one, as his bowlers reduced them to 56 for four, then 226 all out. It was hardly the ideal platform for the series-levelling assault Pakistan had in mind.

Sri Lanka fielded four seamers in their line-up for the first time at home since July 2009. Perera, scourge of Pakistan in the one-day series but surprisingly left out of the first two Tests, extended his upward curve with a fine career-best display of swing bowling in favourable conditions that fetched him four of the top five. They included the two big century-makers from Colombo, Mohammad Hafeez and Azhar Ali, plus Misbah-ul-Haq, whose demise ended a pesky fourth-wicket stand of 85 with Asad Shafiq.

Dilhara Fernando, on his 17th comeback to the Test side, bowled too short, but inflicted an important blow by fracturing Adnan Akmal's left ring finger with a sharp delivery. Adnan was unable to keep wicket due to the pain, and had to hand over the gloves to the part-timer Taufeeq Umar, who did a fine job in the circumstances.

Sri Lanka's joy was short-lived, as the whippier pace of Junaid Khan and Mohammad Sami reduced them to 44 for three by stumps. Sangakkara, whose near-double-hundreds in the first two Tests had shut Pakistan out, was this time tormented by Junaid's inward movement: almost lbw to the first two balls, he had his stumps rearranged by the third.

The hosts' recovery, after a blank second day, was prompted by two of the most defensive players in modern cricket, Paranavitana and Samaraweera – both in desperate need of a score. They gritted out 143 in 47 overs, clearing the floor for the carefree pair of Perera and Kulasekara, who had given Pakistan such a headache with the new ball and now indulged in a stand of 84, helping Sri Lanka to a handy lead of 111. Pakistan's catching was shoddy: the usually reliable Younis Khan spilled Samaraweera on 49, and Misbah dropped Perera on 22, both off the luckless Umar Gul.

Pakistan had to do it the hard way if they were to level the series and maintain their unbeaten Test series record under Misbah. They wiped out the deficit with only two wickets down, and steadily built a lead on Azhar Ali's third century against Sri Lanka, and Asad Shafiq's second in all Tests; here, even in a vain effort, was the future of Pakistani batting. On a gently turning pitch, Azhar – in another technically assured innings – was able to step out and drive Herath, who became the third Sri Lankan, after Muralitharan and Vaas, to take 100 Test wickets at home.

Shafiq, though, was the key to averting defeat and setting a target. He was assisted by a brave performance from Adnan, who came out to bat late on the fourth evening, following painkilling injections, and returned next day to defend stoutly for an hour and a half and see Shafiq to his hundred. They added 81 and were helped by a slightly negative approach from Jayawardene, who set spread fields for Shafiq, apparently having given up hope of dismissing him.

Misbah left Sri Lanka a theoretical target of 270 in 71 overs. They set off positively and, when Chandimal and Sangakkara were together, an aggressive tilt looked possible. But the quality of the Pakistani attack, and Sri Lanka's narrow lead in the series, were such that, once the breakthrough was achieved, the shutters came down. The appearance of Samaraweera in his customary position at No. 5, ahead of the strokemakers Mathews and Perera, was the final proof. Hands were shaken nine overs from the scheduled close, confirming Misbah's first Test series defeat as captain.

"No one gave us a chance, even in the one-dayers," said Jayawardene. "I remember in the first press conference someone asked about a 4–1 win for Pakistan. But to come out winning the one-dayers and Test series, we should take a lot of credit."

Man of the Match: Asad Shafiq. *Man of the Series:* K. C. Sangakkara.

Close of play: first day, Sri Lanka 44-3 (Paranavitana 13); second day, no play; third day, Pakistan 27-1 (Mohammad Hafeez 8, Azhar Ali 6); fourth day, Pakistan 299-8 (Asad Shafiq 55, Adnan Akmal 0).

Pakistan

First innings		Second innings	
Mohammad Hafeez b Perera	22	– c Paranavitana b Fernando	52
Taufeeq Umar lbw b Perera	29	– lbw b Kulasekara	4
Azhar Ali c Samaraweera b Perera	0	– c H. A. P. W. Jayawardene b Fernando	136
Younis Khan c H. A. P. W. Jayawardene b Kulasekara	0	– c Paranavitana b Herath	19
*Misbah-ul-Haq c H. A. P. W. Jayawardene b Perera	40	– c D. P. M. D. Jayawardene b Herath	5
Asad Shafiq c H. A. P. W. Jayawardene b Herath	75	– not out	100
†Adnan Akmal b Herath	24	– (10) not out	35
Mohammad Sami c Perera b Mathews	9	– (7) lbw b Fernando	3
Umar Gul b Kulasekara	7	– (8) lbw b Herath	0
Saeed Ajmal lbw b Herath	6	– (9) lbw b Herath	5
Junaid Khan not out	3		
L-b 11	11	B 6, l-b 8, w 7	21
1/35 (1) 2/41 (3) 3/50 (4) 4/56 (2) 5/141 (5) 6/175 (8) 7/198 (7) 8/217 (9) 9/217 (6) 10/226 (10) (72.5 overs)	226	1/16 (2) 2/110 (1) 3/158 (4) 4/176 (5) 5/276 (3) 6/280 (7) 7/281 (8) 8/299 (9) (8 wkts dec, 128.4 overs)	380

In the first innings Adnan Akmal, when 10, retired hurt at 162-5 and resumed at 175-6.

Kulasekara 16–4–44–2; Perera 18–5–63–4; Mathews 8–3–20–1; Herath 18.5–6–40–3; Fernando 12–1–48–0. *Second innings*—Kulasekara 28–9–65–1; Perera 25–2–88–0; Herath 39.4–4–99–4; Fernando 23–1–74–3; Mathews 12–0–38–0; Samaraweera 1–0–2–0.

Sri Lanka

First innings		Second innings	
N. T. Paranavitana b Saeed Ajmal	75	– c Younis Khan b Junaid Khan	22
L. D. Chandimal lbw b Junaid Khan	8	– c Asad Shafiq b Saeed Ajmal	65
K. C. Sangakkara b Junaid Khan	0	– not out	74
*D. P. M. D. Jayawardene lbw b Mohammad Sami	12	– c Mohammad Hafeez b Saeed Ajmal	11
T. T. Samaraweera lbw b Saeed Ajmal	73	– b Saeed Ajmal	10
A. D. Mathews c Asad Shafiq b Junaid Khan	9	– not out	1
†H. A. P. W. Jayawardene lbw b Umar Gul	20		
N. L. T. C. Perera b Junaid Khan	75		
K. M. D. N. Kulasekara c Taufeeq Umar b Junaid Khan	33		
H. M. R. K. B. Herath lbw b Saeed Ajmal	2		
C. R. D. Fernando not out	0		
B 16, l-b 7, w 6, n-b 1	30	B 2, l-b 10	12
1/14 (2) 2/14 (3) 3/44 (4) 4/187 (5) 5/200 (6) 6/204 (1) 7/236 (7) 8/320 (9) 9/337 (10) 10/337 (8) (100.2 overs)	337	1/44 (1) 2/132 (2) 3/150 (4) 4/178 (5) (4 wkts, 62 overs)	195

Umar Gul 22–3–90–1; Junaid Khan 28.2–3–70–5; Mohammad Sami 17–1–69–1; Saeed Ajmal 25–5–66–3; Younis Khan 3–0–9–0; Mohammad Hafeez 5–0–10–0. *Second innings*—Umar Gul 9–2–43–0; Junaid Khan 10–0–45–1; Mohammad Hafeez 9–1–22–0; Saeed Ajmal 26–8–50–3; Mohammad Sami 8–0–23–0.

Umpires: S. J. Davis and S. J. A. Taufel. Third umpire: R. E. J. Martinesz.
Series referee: D. C. Boon.

SRI LANKA v INDIA, 2012

REX CLEMENTINE

One-day internationals (5): Sri Lanka 1, India 4
Twenty20 international (1): Sri Lanka 0, India 1

If familiarity had bred contempt, no one could have blamed Sri Lanka or India. This was their fourth bilateral one-day series since 2008, to go with four triangular tournaments. The main reason for this overkill has been Sri Lanka Cricket's financial problems, which left them heavily dependent on the goodwill of their Indian counterparts.

The inevitable quid pro quo is that SLC have usually felt obliged to toe the BCCI's line: in 2009, for example, Sri Lanka's proposed tour of England was called off so their best cricketers could play throughout the IPL. This encounter, it seemed, allowed India to return the favour. It was originally slated as a Test series, but the Sri Lankan authorities judged that five one-day internationals, and a single game of Twenty20, would be more lucrative – although the first two matches, in rural Hambantota (about 150 miles from Colombo by road), were poorly attended.

The BCCI's implacable opposition to the Decision Review System was a constant source of debate. The Sri Lankans felt they were hard done by on several occasions, and by the fourth match Mahela Jayawardene could hold his tongue no longer: a confident caught-behind appeal against Suresh Raina was turned down when he had made only two; he went on to smash an unbeaten 58 to help India seal the series. "I thought we had Suresh caught behind," grumbled Jayawardene. "I don't know how much I have to say this. I preferred DRS from the beginning."

India's star performer was Virat Kohli, who had hardly looked back since being named vice-captain in March. Here he accumulated 364 runs in the six matches, and was a well-deserved Man of the Series in both the 50- and 20-overs games (the lone Twenty20 game really did have separate match and series awards). Kohli's focus and attitude stood out, and he showed he had become a fine finisher. He scored his 12th and 13th one-day hundreds: only Sachin Tendulkar (14) had made more before turning 24.

But despite the scoreline, it was not all good news for India. Rohit Sharma – only 25, but a veteran of 85 one-day internationals – was a flop, managing 13 runs in five innings. India persisted with him, though, with Gautam Gambhir saying he had batted better in the nets than anyone. It was frustrating for Manoj Tiwary, who sat out the first three matches.

The final one-day international was a sign of things to come in Sri Lanka. Jayawardene was rested, Kumar Sangakkara absent after breaking a finger in the third match, and Tillekeratne Dilshan out for a duck. Angelo Mathews took charge for the first time, and did well with his bowling changes and field placings. He did, however, cop a fine for a slow over-rate. In that match, Sri Lanka's other young guns – Lahiru Thirimanne, Jeewan Mendis and Tissara

Perera – fought tenaciously before coming up just short, but their performances reassured home fans there was hope.

For another old hand, though, there were ominous signs. Lasith Malinga proved expensive and, although he reached 200 one-day wickets in the final match, he was not helped by the new regulation providing two new balls, which did not deteriorate enough for him to find his trademark reverse-swing at the death.

INDIAN TOURING PARTY

*M. S. Dhoni, R. Ashwin, A. B. Dinda, G. Gambhir, V. Kohli, P. P. Ojha, I. K. Pathan, A. M. Rahane, S. K. Raina, V. Sehwag, R. Sharma, R. G. Sharma, M. K. Tiwary, U. T. Yadav, Zaheer Khan. *Coach:* D. A. G. Fletcher.

R. Vinay Kumar was originally selected, but injured a hamstring and was replaced by Pathan.

SRI LANKA v INDIA

First One-Day International

At Hambantota, July 21, 2012 (day/night). India won by 21 runs. Toss: India.

The pitch at the Mahinda Rajapaksa Stadium had proved tough for batsmen during the Pakistan series a few weeks previously, but this time more than 600 runs flowed. Sehwag put on 173 with Kohli, who completed his 12th one-day international century, although there was a mix-up when Kohli signalled to the dressing-room for a cap, and the umpires thought he was asking for the batting powerplay. He and Sehwag didn't change their approach, and later asked for the powerplay – only to be told they had already had it: luckily, the confusion made no difference to the result. Perera took three wickets (and ran Sehwag out just short of his century), but Malinga proved expensive, breaking his own unwanted record for runs conceded (81) by a Sri Lankan on home soil; Kulasekara limped out of the series with a groin injury. Led by Sangakkara, who became the first man to pass 1,000 runs in one-day internationals in 2012, Sri Lanka made a brave effort to chase down their lofty target – but his main support came too late, in a seventh-wicket stand of 78 with Perera, whose 44 came from just 28 balls. Dhoni and the Indian team were fined afterwards for a slow over-rate.

Man of the Match: V. Kohli.

India

G. Gambhir b Kulasekara 3
V. Sehwag run out 96
V. Kohli c sub (S. M. S. M. Senanayake) b Perera . 106
R. G. Sharma b Mathews 5
S. K. Raina c sub (S. M. S. M. Senanayake) b Perera . 50
*†M. S. Dhoni c Thirimanne b Perera 35
I. K. Pathan not out 7
R. Ashwin not out 0
B 1, l-b 2, w 7, n-b 2 12

1/7 (1) 2/180 (2) 3/191 (4) 4/228 (3) 5/307 (5) 6/307 (6) (6 wkts, 50 overs) 314

10 overs: 45-1

Zaheer Khan, P. P. Ojha and U. T. Yadav did not bat.

Kulasekara 5–0–20–1; Malinga 10–0–83–0; Mathews 10–0–58–1; Perera 10–0–70–3; Dilshan 5–0–28–0; Herath 10–0–52–0.

Sri Lanka

W. U. Tharanga c Sehwag b Ashwin	28	S. L. Malinga not out	19
T. M. Dilshan lbw b Pathan	6	K. M. D. N. Kulasekara not out	1
†K. C. Sangakkara b Yadav	133		
L. D. Chandimal c Dhoni b Yadav	13	B 1, l-b 6, w 16	23
*D. P. M. D. Jayawardene lbw b Ojha	12		
A. D. Mathews c Gambhir b Zaheer Khan	7	1/9 (2) 2/86 (1) (9 wkts, 50 overs)	293
H. D. R. L. Thirimanne lbw b Ashwin	7	3/117 (4) 4/132 (5)	
N. L. T. C. Perera c Kohli b Pathan	44	5/172 (6) 6/191 (7)	
H. M. R. K. B. Herath run out	0	7/269 (3) 8/271 (9) 9/275 (8)	10 overs: 41-1

Zaheer Khan 10–0–63–1; Pathan 10–1–37–2; Yadav 10–0–76–2; Ashwin 10–1–46–2; Sehwag 4–0–20–0; Ojha 6–0–44–1.

Umpires: R. E. J. Martinesz and B. N. J. Oxenford. Third umpire: R. S. A. Palliyaguruge.

SRI LANKA v INDIA

Second One-Day International

At Hambantota, July 24, 2012 (day/night). Sri Lanka won by nine wickets. Toss: India. One-day international debut: I. Udana.

India shot out of the blocks with 31 in the first three overs, as debutant left-armer Isuru Udana sent down five wides in an opening over that lasted 11 balls and cost 16. Jayawardene was forced into a double bowling change, and it paid off: Perera began with three wicket maidens – including Sehwag, to a terrific diving return catch – and would have claimed a fourth victim had Mathews not dropped Dhoni at slip. By the eighth over it was 41 for four, and the innings was done and dusted inside 34 overs, with rash shots outnumbering unplayable deliveries. Mathews and Perera took six for 33 between them, and Gambhir was last out for 65. Tharanga and Dilshan made light of the target, putting on 119 in 16.4 overs.

Man of the Match: N. L. T. C. Perera.

India

G. Gambhir c Sangakkara b Malinga	65	P. P. Ojha c Sangakkara b Mathews	5
V. Sehwag c and b Perera	15	U. T. Yadav not out	0
V. Kohli c Sangakkara b Perera	1		
R. G. Sharma b Mathews	0	B 2, l-b 4, w 5	11
S. K. Raina b Perera	1		
*†M. S. Dhoni c Sangakkara b Mathews	11	1/31 (2) 2/33 (3) 3/38 (4) (33.3 overs)	138
I. K. Pathan c Perera b Malinga	6	4/41 (5) 5/60 (6) 6/79 (7)	
R. Ashwin run out	21	7/107 (8) 8/113 (9) 9/132 (10)	
Zaheer Khan lbw b Herath	2	10/138 (1)	10 overs: 47-4

Malinga 7.3–0–36–2; Udana 6–0–42–0; Perera 8–3–19–3; Mathews 7–2–14–3; Herath 5–0–21–1.

Sri Lanka

W. U. Tharanga not out	59
T. M. Dilshan c Dhoni b Ashwin	50
L. D. Chandimal not out	6
L-b 10, w 14	24
1/119 (2) (1 wkt, 19.5 overs)	139
	10 overs: 78-0

†K. C. Sangakkara, *D. P. M. D. Jayawardene, A. D. Mathews, H. D. R. L. Thirimanne, N. L. T. C. Perera, H. M. R. K. B. Herath, I. Udana and S. L. Malinga did not bat.

Zaheer Khan 6–0–39–0; Pathan 4–0–27–0; Yadav 4–0–38–0; Ashwin 5–1–18–1; Ojha 0.5–0–7–0.

Umpires: B. N. J. Oxenford and R. S. A. Palliyaguruge. Third umpire: R. E. J. Martinesz.

SRI LANKA v INDIA

Third One-Day International

At Colombo (RPS), July 28, 2012 (day/night). India won by five wickets. Toss: Sri Lanka.

After poor crowds in Hambantota, the Sri Lankan authorities were relieved to see a packed house at the 35,000-seater Premadasa Stadium. And when their side recovered from a poor start to reach 286, locals thought the game was secure: Sri Lanka had never previously lost a one-day international at home after scoring more than 250 batting first, while chasing under lights here had historically proved difficult. Sehwag fell quickly, but Gambhir's run-a-ball hundred – his 11th in one-day internationals, and sixth against Sri Lanka – kept India in touch. When he departed in the 39th over, Sri Lanka were still favourites, but Raina and Pathan piled on 92 without further loss to complete victory with two balls to spare. Defeat was hard enough to take for the home team, but then came news that Sangakkara's little finger had been broken by a bouncer from Dinda.

Man of the Match: S. K. Raina.

Sri Lanka

W. U. Tharanga c Dhoni b Zaheer Khan	8	B. M. A. J. Mendis not out	45
T. M. Dilshan b Zaheer Khan	4		
†K. C. Sangakkara c Kohli b Dinda	73	B 2, l-b 8, w 9, n-b 1	20
L. D. Chandimal lbw b Pathan	0		
*D. P. M. D. Jayawardene lbw b R. Sharma	65	1/9 (2) 2/19 (1) (5 wkts, 50 overs)	286
A. D. Mathews not out	71	3/20 (4) 4/141 (5) 5/182 (3)	10 overs: 40-3

N. L. T. C. Perera, H. M. R. K. B. Herath, I. Udana and S. L. Malinga did not bat.

Zaheer Khan 10–0–39–2; Pathan 10–0–59–1; Dinda 10–0–76–1; R. Sharma 8–0–45–1; Ashwin 10–0–50–0; Sehwag 1–0–3–0; R. G. Sharma 1–0–4–0.

India

G. Gambhir run out	102	I. K. Pathan not out	34
V. Sehwag c sub (S. M. S. M. Senanayake) b Perera	3	L-b 11, w 4	15
V. Kohli c and b Herath	38		
*†M. S. Dhoni b Malinga	31	1/8 (2) 2/113 (3) (5 wkts, 49.4 overs)	288
R. G. Sharma lbw b Malinga	0	3/180 (4) 4/180 (5)	
S. K. Raina not out	65	5/196 (1)	10 overs: 58-1

R. Ashwin, Zaheer Khan, R. Sharma and A. B. Dinda did not bat.

Malinga 10–0–60–2; Perera 9–0–57–1; Udana 6–0–42–0; Mathews 8.4–0–49–0; Herath 9–0–36–1; Dilshan 3–0–14–0; Mendis 4–0–19–0.

Umpires: H. D. P. K. Dharmasena and B. N. J. Oxenford. Third umpire: R. E. J. Martinesz.

SRI LANKA v INDIA

Fourth One-Day International

At Colombo (RPS), July 31, 2012 (day/night). India won by six wickets. Toss: Sri Lanka. One-day international debut: A. N. P. R. Fernando.

India sealed the series with a game to spare, thanks once more to Kohli, who smashed his fifth hundred – four of them against Sri Lanka – in eight one-day international innings. His 128, from only 119 balls, ushered India past a reasonable target with 46 deliveries unused. India's other star was Tiwary, who had hit his maiden century against West Indies in his last one-day international, in December 2011. Dhoni might have expected an over or two from his occasional leg-spin, but four wickets from a full stint was an unexpected bonus. Later, Tiwary made 21 and, although he departed at 109 for four, Raina – given not out when the Sri Lankans thought he was caught behind off Herath when two, then dropped at slip by Jayawardene on 19 – helped Kohli knock off the runs.

Man of the Match: V. Kohli.

Sri Lanka

W. U. Tharanga st Dhoni b Ashwin	51	H. M. R. K. B. Herath not out	17
T. M. Dilshan c Dhoni b Dinda	42	S. L. Malinga not out	15
H. D. R. L. Thirimanne b Ashwin	47	L-b 2, w 13	15
†L. D. Chandimal c Pathan b Tiwary	28		——
*D. P. M. D. Jayawardene c Dhoni b Sehwag	3	1/91 (2) 2/102 (1) (8 wkts, 50 overs)	251
A. D. Mathews c Kohli b Tiwary	14	3/152 (4) 4/155 (5)	
B. M. A. J. Mendis b Tiwary	17	5/190 (6) 6/213 (7)	
N. L. T. C. Perera c Raina b Tiwary	2	7/218 (8) 8/219 (3) 10 overs: 45-0	

A. N. P. R. Fernando did not bat.

Zaheer Khan 6–0–36–0; Pathan 6–0–27–0; Dinda 6–0–28–1; Kohli 2–0–7–0; Sehwag 8–1–38–1; Ashwin 10–1–46–2; Tiwary 10–1–61–4; Sharma 2–0–6–0.

India

G. Gambhir b Malinga	0	S. K. Raina not out	58
V. Sehwag c sub (S. M. S. M. Senanayake) b Mathews	34	L-b 2, w 6, n-b 2	10
V. Kohli not out	128		——
R. G. Sharma lbw b Fernando	4	1/0 (1) 2/52 (2) (4 wkts, 42.2 overs)	255
M. K. Tiwary lbw b Mendis	21	3/60 (4) 4/109 (5) 10 overs: 52-2	

*†M. S. Dhoni, I. K. Pathan, R. Ashwin, Zaheer Khan and A. B. Dinda did not bat.

Malinga 8–1–41–1; Perera 6–0–51–0; Mathews 6–1–18–1; Fernando 8–0–52–1; Herath 7–0–44–0; Mendis 6–0–37–1; Dilshan 1.2–0–10–0.

Umpires: H. D. P. K. Dharmasena and B. N. J. Oxenford. Third umpire: T. H. Wijewardene.

SRI LANKA v INDIA

Fifth One-Day International

At Pallekele, August 4, 2012 (day/night). India won by 20 runs. Toss: India.

India completed a 4–1 victory, which lifted them to second in the ICC rankings. Gambhir continued his good form, then Tiwary made 65 before he and Raina fell to successive balls from Malinga, who took his 200th one-day wicket when Dhoni nicked an intended pull. Irfan Pathan, a late replacement for the tour, shone with both bat and ball. After an important cameo – he and Dhoni put on 77 in ten overs – Pathan took five wickets for only the second time, in effect ending the contest when he dismissed Perera and Mendis (for a fine 72) in his ninth over, having bagged both openers in his first spell. Sri Lanka were without Jayawardene (rested) and Sangakkara (injured), and never really recovered from the loss of Dilshan in the second over.

Man of the Match: I. K. Pathan. *Man of the Series:* V. Kohli.

India

G. Gambhir c Malinga b Senanayake	88	I. K. Pathan not out	29
A. M. Rahane lbw b Perera	9	R. Ashwin not out	2
V. Kohli lbw b Fernando	23	L-b 10, w 6	16
R. G. Sharma b Fernando	4		——
M. K. Tiwary c Perera b Malinga	65	1/29 (2) 2/77 (3) (7 wkts, 50 overs)	294
S. K. Raina c Thirimanne b Malinga	0	3/87 (4) 4/197 (5)	
*†M. S. Dhoni c Chandimal b Malinga	58	5/197 (6) 6/213 (1) 7/290 (7) 10 overs: 53-1	

Zaheer Khan and A. B. Dinda did not bat.

Malinga 10–0–64–3; Perera 10–0–53–1; Mathews 5–0–29–0; Fernando 10–0–63–2; Senanayake 10–0–50–1; Mendis 5–0–25–0.

Sri Lanka

W. U. Tharanga c Rahane b Pathan	31
T. M. Dilshan c Zaheer Khan b Pathan	0
H. D. R. L. Thirimanne run out	77
†L. D. Chandimal lbw b Dinda	8
*A. D. Mathews run out	13
C. K. Kapugedera lbw b Zaheer Khan	9
B. M. A. J. Mendis c Dhoni b Pathan	72
N. L. T. C. Perera c Kohli b Pathan	18
S. M. S. M. Senanayake b Pathan	7
S. L. Malinga c Raina b Dinda	10
A. N. P. R. Fernando not out	0
B 2, l-b 14, w 13	29
	—
1/13 (2) 2/61 (1) 3/74 (4) (45.4 overs)	274

4/89 (5) 5/102 (6) 6/204 (3)
7/252 (8) 8/256 (7) 9/266 (9)
10/274 (10) 10 overs: 74-2

Zaheer Khan 9–1–53–1; Pathan 10–0–61–5; Dinda 7.4–0–55–2; Kohli 1–0–3–0; Ashwin 9–0–37–0; Sharma 6–0–23–0; Raina 2–0–12–0; Tiwary 1–0–14–0.

Umpires: B. N. J. Oxenford and T. H. Wijewardene. Third umpire: R. S. A. Palliyaguruge.
Series referee: B. C. Broad.

SRI LANKA v INDIA

Twenty20 International

At Pallekele, August 7, 2012 (floodlit). India won by 39 runs. Toss: Sri Lanka. Twenty20 international debuts: R. M. S. Eranga; U. T. Yadav.

For both sides this was a final trial run before the World Twenty20 in Sri Lanka in September, and India ended up with another comfortable victory. They made a power-packed start, as 50 came up from just 30 deliveries, but then the spinners applied the brakes before Kohli smacked 68 from 48 balls. He hit nine of his first 19 deliveries for four, including three in a row off Perera. Medium-pacer Shaminda Eranga, returning after injury, completed a unique hat-trick of first-over dismissals by bowling Gambhir with his fourth ball in Twenty20 internationals: in 2011 he had taken wickets with his first ball in Tests, and his second in one-day internationals. Pathan again derailed Sri Lanka's innings with two wickets in three deliveries, and later removed Jayawardene too. The lively Dinda wrapped things up with three wickets in five balls.

Man of the Match: I. K. Pathan. *Man of the Series:* V. Kohli.

India

		B	4	6
G. Gambhir *b 9*	6	8	1	0
A. M. Rahane *c and b 6*	21	25	0	1
V. Kohli *c 4 b 9*	68	48	11	1
S. K. Raina *not out*	34	25	3	1
*†M. S. Dhoni *not out*	16	14	2	0
L-b 7, w 3	10			
	—			
6 overs: 50-1 (20 overs)	155-3			

1/7 2/81 3/129

R. G. Sharma, M. K. Tiwary, I. K. Pathan, R. Ashwin, U. T. Yadav and A. B. Dinda did not bat.

Mathews 3–0–23–0; Eranga 4–0–30–2; Malinga 4–0–31–0; Perera 4–0–34–0; Herath 3–0–17–0; Mendis 2–0–13–1.

Sri Lanka

		B	4	6
*D. P. M. D. Jayawardene *lbw b 8*	26	19	5	0
T. M. Dilshan *b 8*	0	1	0	0
W. U. Tharanga *c 4 b 8*	5	4	0	0
H. D. R. L. Thirimanne *b 9*	20	15	2	0
A. D. Mathews *c 5 b 11*	31	29	3	0
B. M. A. J. Mendis *c 2 b 10*	11	15	0	0
†L. D. Chandimal *c 3 b 11*	7	11	1	0
N. L. T. C. Perera *run out 7*	1	5	0	0
R. M. S. Eranga *c 9 b 11*	6	7	1	0
S. L. Malinga *c 5 b 11*	0	2	0	0
H. M. R. K. B. Herath *not out*	0	0	0	0
L-b 2, w 7	9			
	—			
6 overs: 52-3 (18 overs)	116			

1/7 2/14 3/35 4/68 5/96 6/100 7/102 8/116 9/116

Pathan 4–0–27–3; Yadav 3–0–24–1; Dinda 3–1–19–4; Kohli 3–0–13–0; Sharma 1–0–9–0; Ashwin 4–0–22–1.

Umpires: H. D. P. K. Dharmasena and T. H. Wijewardene. Third umpire: R. S. A. Palliyaguruge.
Referee: B. C. Broad.

SRI LANKA v NEW ZEALAND, 2012-13

SA'ADI THAWFEEQ

Test matches (2): Sri Lanka 1, New Zealand 1
One-day internationals (5): Sri Lanka 3, New Zealand 0
Twenty20 international (1): Sri Lanka 0, New Zealand 0

The start of New Zealand's tour was blighted by terrible weather, as rain ruined the solitary Twenty20 international, before Sri Lanka took charge of the one-day matches. When the sun finally came out and Sri Lanka claimed the First Test too, it seemed certain New Zealand would go home without a win – only for Ross Taylor to lead from the front to set up a memorable victory in Colombo and square the series.

But the drama wasn't over. It later emerged that Taylor's heroics had come after the new coach, Mike Hesson, had told him early in the tour he wanted a change of leadership: after Taylor scored 142 and 74 in New Zealand's 167-run win, Hesson said he was actually looking for someone to share the load by skippering in the shorter formats. But Taylor quit anyway. It seemed a clumsy way to treat the country's best batsman, and the New Zealand board eventually apologised, which didn't stop Taylor sitting out the tour of South Africa that followed. "After my first meeting with the coach, my dad asked me what I thought," he revealed. "I said 'I don't think I'll be in the job longer than 12 months.' I was wrong, it was six."

The monsoon rains which descended soon after New Zealand's arrival washed out the first two games and interrupted the next two as well, even though they had been shifted to Pallekele when the river next to Colombo's Premadasa Stadium overflowed, causing extensive flooding. Hambantota, usually in a dry zone, was not spared either, and Sri Lanka emerged with a slightly flattering 3–0 victory in the 50-over series. The bad weather had an adverse effect on the tour finances; although admission was cheap for the Tests, only a few thousand took advantage.

There was some good news, though: by the time the Tests began, the sun had appeared. Galle produced a low-scoring match, with Sri Lanka completing a ten-wicket win inside three days, but New Zealand found the Sara Oval more to their liking. Sparked by centuries from Taylor and Kane Williamson, they ran up a big first-innings total, before the seamers – led by Tim Southee – exposed flaws in the Sri Lankans' technique.

The New Zealand management had stolen a march on their counterparts by hiring Chaminda Vaas, Sri Lanka's most successful seamer, with 355 Test wickets, as an adviser. His local knowledge proved useful: New Zealand's pacemen did well in both Tests, with Southee, Trent Boult and Doug Bracewell accounting for 23 of the 29 wickets to fall to bowlers. At Galle, they swept through the top order, and Sri Lanka were tottering at 50 for five before Mahela Jayawardene and Angelo Mathews put on 156; in Colombo, they were 12 for three and 63 for five.

Sri Lanka were caught napping at the Sara Oval and, for the first time since 1999-2000, when they hosted Australia, they failed to register an individual century in a home series. Their only real positive was with the ball, as slow left-armer Rangana Herath continued his good form, taking 11 wickets in the victory at Galle, and nine in Colombo.

The series was meant to help Sri Lanka prepare for their tour of Australia, but they were jolted by the manner of their defeat in the Second Test, which left worrying doubts about the top order's ability against the moving ball. "New Zealand's bowlers kept asking questions and kept the pressure up," admitted Jayawardene.

NEW ZEALAND TOURING PARTY

*L. R. P. L. Taylor, T. D. Astle, T. A. Boult, D. A. J. Bracewell, D. R. Flynn, J. E. C. Franklin, M. J. Guptill, B. B. McCullum, C. S. Martin, R. J. Nicol, J. S. Patel, T. G. Southee, C. F. K. van Wyk, N. Wagner, K. S. Williamson. *Coach:* M. J. Hesson.

For the limited-overs matches that preceded the Tests, A. M. Ellis, R. M. Hira, T. W. M. Latham, N. L. McCullum, A. F. Milne, K. D. Mills, J. D. P. Oram and B-J. Watling replaced Astle, Bracewell, Flynn, Guptill, Martin, Patel, van Wyk and Wagner.

SRI LANKA v NEW ZEALAND

Twenty20 International

At Pallekele, October 30, 2012. No result. Toss: Sri Lanka.

Mathews took the helm for Sri Lanka – Mahela Jayawardene had stepped down from the captaincy in this format after the World Twenty20 final – but was thwarted by rain after New Zealand had collapsed. They were 24 for five in the ninth over when the first shower arrived, then lost a wicket soon after the resumption, with the innings reduced to 14 overs. New Zealand inched to 74, but the heavens opened again only two overs into Sri Lanka's pursuit of 72 from 14.

New Zealand

		B	*4*	*6*
R. J. Nicol *lbw b 11*	1	12	0	0
T. W. M. Latham *b 9*	4	5	1	0
†B. B. McCullum *c 8 b 9*	1	10	0	0
*L. R. P. L. Taylor *c 3 b 8*	4	10	0	0
J. E. C. Franklin *c 3 b 8*	2	7	0	0
B-J. Watling *c 7 b 10*	8	11	1	0
A. M. Ellis *c 6 b 10*	16	10	1	1
J. D. P. Oram *not out*	10	9	1	0
T. G. Southee *not out*	21	10	4	0
L-b 3, w 4	7			
6 overs: 16-3 (14 overs)	74-7			

1/4 2/10 3/15 4/18 5/24 6/28 7/51

R. M. Hira and K. D. Mills did not bat.

Mathews 3–1–4–0; Kulasekara 3–0–13–2; Eranga 3–0–23–1; Perera 3–0–22–2; Dananjaya 2–0–9–2.

Sri Lanka

		B	*4*	*6*
E. M. D. Y. Munaweera *not out*	4	4	0	0
T. M. Dilshan *not out*	2	8	0	0
(2 overs)	6-0			

†K. C. Sangakkara, *A. D. Mathews, B. M. A. J. Mendis, H. D. R. L. Thirimanne, L. D. Chandimal, N. L. T. C. Perera, K. M. D. N. Kulasekara, A. Dananjaya and R. M. S. Eranga did not bat.

Mills 1–0–3–0; Oram 1–0–3–0.

Umpires: R. E. J. Martinesz and R. S. A. Palliyaguruge. Third umpire: T. H. Wijewardene.
Referee: A. J. Pycroft.

SRI LANKA v NEW ZEALAND

First One-Day International

At Pallekele, November 1, 2012 (day/night). Abandoned.

SRI LANKA v NEW ZEALAND

Second One-Day International

At Pallekele, November 4, 2012 (day/night). Sri Lanka won by 14 runs (D/L). Toss: New Zealand.

New Zealand reached their highest one-day total in Sri Lanka, then took three important wickets – so they could feel aggrieved at what ended up as their eighth defeat in nine completed one-day internationals. After Nicol and Watling shared a patient stand of 83 in 20 overs, Taylor cracked 72 from 62 balls, and made the most of the new playing conditions, which allowed only four fielders (rather than five) outside the circle during the non-powerplay overs. But New Zealand were kept quiet in the batting powerplay itself, managing only 31, largely against a barrage of short-pitched bowling from Malinga. The Sri Lankans, knowing rain was expected, kept their noses in front: when the downpour finally arrived, after 22.5 overs, the par score was 104. This match and the next had originally been scheduled for Colombo, but were moved when the Premadasa Stadium was flooded.

Man of the Match: S. L. Malinga.

New Zealand

R. J. Nicol c Sangakkara b Perera	46
T. W. M. Latham b Malinga	2
†B-J. Watling c Jayawardene b Herath	55
*L. R. P. L. Taylor c Mathews b Kulasekara	72
J. E. C. Franklin not out	35
N. L. McCullum c Perera b Mathews	16
A. M. Ellis b Malinga	4
B 1, l-b 8, w 11	20
1/17 (2) 2/100 (1) 3/130 (3) 4/221 (4) 5/242 (6) 6/250 (7) (6 wkts, 50 overs)	250
10 overs: 28-1	

K. S. Williamson, K. D. Mills, T. G. Southee and T. A. Boult did not bat.

Malinga 10–0–39–2; Kulasekara 10–1–50–1; Mathews 7–0–38–1; Perera 7–0–52–1; Herath 10–0–28–1; Mendis 6–0–34–0.

Sri Lanka

W. U. Tharanga c Watling b Mills	6
T. M. Dilshan c Williamson b McCullum	37
†K. C. Sangakkara c Nicol b Boult	11
*D. P. M. D. Jayawardene not out	43
A. D. Mathews not out	7
L-b 8, w 6	14
1/21 (1) 2/39 (3) 3/98 (2) (3 wkts, 22.5 overs)	118
10 overs: 49-2	

H. D. R. L. Thirimanne, B. M. A. J. Mendis, N. L. T. C. Perera, K. M. D. N. Kulasekara, H. M. R. K. B. Herath and S. L. Malinga did not bat.

Mills 5–0–33–1; Boult 6–0–26–1; Southee 4–0–16–0; Franklin 3–0–16–0; McCullum 2.5–0–12–1; Nicol 2–0–7–0.

Umpires: H. D. P. K. Dharmasena and I. J. Gould. Third umpire: R. E. J. Martinesz.

SRI LANKA v NEW ZEALAND

Third One-Day International

At Pallekele, November 6, 2012 (day/night). Sri Lanka won by seven wickets (D/L). Toss: Sri Lanka.

Once again New Zealand were on the receiving end of the weather. After being sent in, they looked on course for a competitive total, thanks almost entirely to Watling, who hit a dozen fours but was left stranded on a career-best 96 – their innings was shortened to 33 overs after two rain interruptions. Sri Lanka's target was increased slightly to 197 and, although three wickets went down inside the first 15 overs, they galloped home with 11 deliveries to spare, as the bowlers struggled to grip the ball in the greasy conditions. Dilshan reached his 14th one-day hundred, despite having pain-killing injections after straining a back muscle in the warm-up; he missed the rest of the one-day series and the First Test.

Man of the Match: T. M. Dilshan.

New Zealand

R. J. Nicol c Jayawardene b Malinga	7
†B-J. Watling not out	96
B. B. McCullum lbw b Mathews	13
*L. R. P. L. Taylor run out	7
J. D. P. Oram lbw b Mendis	2
J. E. C. Franklin b Kulasekara	26
K. S. Williamson c Mathews b Mendis	5
N. L. McCullum not out	22
B 1, l-b 2, w 7	10
1/9 (1) 2/31 (3) 3/43 (4) 4/49 (5) 5/105 (6) 6/117 (7) — (6 wkts, 33 overs)	188
9 overs: 28-1	

K. D. Mills, T. G. Southee and T. A. Boult did not bat.

Malinga 7–0–40–1; Kulasekara 7–1–45–1; Mathews 5–0–15–1; Perera 4–0–22–0; Mendis 5–0–34–2; Dilshan 2–0–9–0; Herath 3–0–20–0.

Sri Lanka

W. U. Tharanga c Oram b Southee	10
T. M. Dilshan not out	102
†K. C. Sangakkara c Taylor b Mills	15
*D. P. M. D. Jayawardene c Oram b N. L. McCullum	5
A. D. Mathews not out	54
L-b 7, w 6, n-b 1	14
1/30 (1) 2/65 (3) 3/73 (4) — (3 wkts, 31.1 overs)	200
7 overs: 43-1	

H. D. R. L. Thirimanne, B. M. A. J. Mendis, N. L. T. C. Perera, K. M. D. N. Kulasekara, H. M. R. K. B. Herath and S. L. Malinga did not bat.

Mills 6.1–0–35–1; Boult 5–0–29–0; Southee 7–0–50–1; Oram 7–1–43–0; N. L. McCullum 5–0–28–1; Franklin 1–0–8–0.

Umpires: H. D. P. K. Dharmasena and I. J. Gould. Third umpire: R. E. J. Martinesz.

SRI LANKA v NEW ZEALAND

Fourth One-Day International

At Hambantota, November 10, 2012 (day/night). Sri Lanka won by seven wickets (D/L). Toss: Sri Lanka. One-day international debut: A. F. Milne.

Rain delayed the start, reducing the match to 42 overs a side, then another downpour trimmed ten more off each team's allocation. By then, though, New Zealand were in deep trouble at 107 for seven in the 30th over after Jeewan Mendis claimed three wickets in five balls with his leg-spin. Sri Lanka's target was 131 in 32 overs, and they eased home to take the series 3–0 after a patient innings from Tillekeratne Dilshan's replacement Chandimal, whose 43 occupied 65 balls.

Man of the Match: B. M. A. J. Mendis.

New Zealand

R. J. Nicol c Tharanga b Kulasekara	11	T. G. Southee not out	7
†B-J. Watling run out	15	A. F. Milne not out	12
B. B. McCullum c Chandimal b Herath	30	L-b 3, w 5	8
*L. R. P. L. Taylor c Sangakkara b Perera	6		——
K. S. Williamson b Mendis	21	1/16 (1) 2/45 (2) (8 wkts, 32 overs)	131
J. E. C. Franklin lbw b Kulasekara	21	3/62 (4) 4/73 (3)	
N. L. McCullum b Mendis	0	5/105 (5) 6/105 (7)	
A. M. Ellis lbw b Mendis	0	7/107 (8) 8/116 (6)	9 overs: 32-1

T. A. Boult did not bat.

Malinga 6–1–38–0; Kulasekara 5–1–17–2; Mathews 6–0–19–0; Perera 5–0–16–1; Herath 6–0–23–1; Mendis 4–0–15–3.

Sri Lanka

W. U. Tharanga c Nicol b Southee	27
L. D. Chandimal b Boult	43
†K. C. Sangakkara not out	42
H. D. R. L. Thirimanne c Watling b Ellis	0
A. D. Mathews not out	2
B 4, l-b 2, w 9, n-b 2	17
	——
1/36 (1) 2/123 (2) (3 wkts, 26.2 overs)	131
3/128 (4)	7 overs: 31-0

*D. P. M. D. Jayawardene, B. M. A. J. Mendis, N. L. T. C. Perera, K. M. D. N. Kulasekara, H. M. R. K. B. Herath and S. L. Malinga did not bat.

Boult 7–0–32–1; Southee 7–0–32–1; Milne 4.2–0–21–0; Ellis 6–0–23–1; N. L. McCullum 2–0–17–0.

Umpires: I. J. Gould and R. S. A. Palliyaguruge. Third umpire: T. H. Wijewardene.

SRI LANKA v NEW ZEALAND

Fifth One-Day International

At Hambantota, November 12, 2012 (day/night). No result. Toss: New Zealand. One-day international debut: A. Dananjaya.

Yet more rain returned to deny New Zealand a probable consolation victory. They had decided to bowl first under sunny skies, which darkened after Southee took two quick wickets, and Boult removed Mathews for a duck. Sri Lanka stumbled to 123 for eight, with only Tharanga – whose 60 consumed 94 balls – putting up much resistance against the seamers. But that was it: rain forced the players off and, although a restart was mooted for 8.30pm, another downpour ended the game just as the covers were being removed. Off-spinner Akila Dananjaya, who had already played for Sri Lanka in the World Twenty20 made his List A debut here.

Man of the Series: B-J. Watling.

Sri Lanka

W. U. Tharanga c Watling b Southee	60	R. M. S. Eranga not out	0
L. D. Chandimal b Southee	0		
H. D. R. L. Thirimanne c Watling b Southee	17	L-b 3, w 3	6
A. D. Mathews c Southee b Boult	0		——
†K. C. Sangakkara c Watling b Milne	5	1/3 (2) 2/33 (3) (8 wkts, 28.3 overs)	123
*D. P. M. D. Jayawardene run out	24	3/34 (4) 4/44 (5)	
B. M. A. J. Mendis c Taylor b Ellis	0	5/91 (6) 6/92 (7)	
N. L. T. C. Perera c Milne b Ellis	11	7/119 (8) 8/123 (1)	10 overs: 40-3

A. Dananjaya and S. L. Malinga did not bat.

Boult 5–0–23–1; Southee 5.3–2–18–3; Milne 5–0–17–1; N. L. McCullum 7–0–28–0; Nicol 2–0–12–0; Ellis 4–0–22–2.

New Zealand

R. J. Nicol, †B-J. Watling, B. B. McCullum, *L. R. P. L. Taylor, K. S. Williamson, J. E. C. Franklin, N. L. McCullum, A. M. Ellis, T. G. Southee, A. F. Milne and T. A. Boult.

Umpires: I. J. Gould and T. H. Wijewardene. Third umpire: R. S. A. Palliyaguruge.
Series referee: A. J. Pycroft.

SRI LANKA v NEW ZEALAND

First Test Match

At Galle, November 17–19, 2012. Sri Lanka won by ten wickets. Toss: New Zealand. Test debut: F. D. M. Karunaratne.

Sri Lanka continued to enjoy Galle, pulling off a sixth win in the last eight Tests there, and a 12th in 21 overall. Herath also maintained his success rate: his 11 wickets took his tally at the ground to 46 at little more than 20 apiece. Still, New Zealand's fifth consecutive Test defeat since July – their worst run since losing six in a row in the mid-1950s – owed more to a lack of confidence on a pitch conducive to spin than it did to Herath's bowling.

New Zealand struggled from the start, managing just 221 after winning the toss. McCullum and Flynn provided the only partnership of substance, putting on 90 for the fourth wicket after Kulasekara and Eranga had made early inroads. Herath broke the stand, deceiving McCullum with a slightly quicker delivery that turned and clipped the top of off, and Franklin soon followed. Flynn eventually thick-edged an attempted drive, and was well caught by wicketkeeper Prasanna Jayawardene.

New Zealand did, though, claim a wicket before the close, when Southee's inswinger trapped the debutant opener Dimuth Karunaratne for a third-ball duck. Karunaratne, who had replaced the injured Tillekeratne Dilshan, received his Test cap before the start from team manager Charith Senanayake – who had also failed to score on his Test debut against New Zealand, 21 years earlier at Wellington.

Next morning, Paranavitana made a duck too, edging into his leg stump as the Sri Lankans were subjected to a severe test against the moving ball by Southee and left-armer Boult. By the end of the 16th over, they were 50 for five, and New Zealand were contemplating a handy lead but, as the ball lost its shine, Mahela Jayawardene and his deputy Mathews took control in a face-saving stand of 156. But once Franklin broke through by inducing Mathews to edge behind – his first Test wicket since April 2009 – the floodgates were open again, and the innings was quickly polished off. Jayawardene looked set for another century but, at 91, gave himself out after an attempt to sweep Patel resulted

---

SPIN ALL THE WAY

Best match figures in Tests at Galle:

13-171	M. Muralitharan	Sri Lanka v South Africa	2000
12-171	H. M. R. K. B. Herath	Sri Lanka v England	2011-12
11-93	M. Muralitharan	Sri Lanka v England	2003-04
11-108	**H. M. R. K. B. Herath**	**Sri Lanka v New Zealand**	**2012-13**
11-170	M. Muralitharan	Sri Lanka v West Indies	2001-02
11-212	M. Muralitharan	Sri Lanka v Australia	2003-04
10-153	Harbhajan Singh	India v Sri Lanka	2008
10-159	S. K. Warne	Australia v Sri Lanka	2003-04
10-209	B. A. W. Mendis	Sri Lanka v India	2008

in the ball popping up off his glove; keeper van Wyk dived forward to take a sharp catch. Sri Lanka had a slender lead of 26, and New Zealand ten overs to survive on the second evening – but they lost McCullum, who took on Herath and was caught in the deep.

After two days of absorbing cricket, the game was evenly poised, but the third brought a dramatic turn of events, as New Zealand collapsed in a heap. By lunch they were languishing at 96 for eight, and Sri Lanka soon completed a comprehensive victory. Kulasekara had begun the day with the wickets of Guptill and Williamson, and the rest of the batting was consumed by Herath, who completed match figures of 11 for 108, the best by a Sri Lankan against New Zealand. Sri Lanka needed only 93 to win and, with Southee missing because of a side strain, the attack lacked the cutting edge of the first innings. The openers, who both started on pairs, had no difficulty in completing the task, scoring at more than five an over. Karunaratne boosted his confidence with a pleasing run-a-ball 60.

Man of the Match: H. M. R. K. B. Herath.

Close of play: first day, Sri Lanka 9-1 (Paranavitana 0, Randiv 3); second day, New Zealand 35-1 (Guptill 13, Williamson 9).

New Zealand

First innings		Second innings	
M. J. Guptill c Mathews b Eranga	11	– b Kulasekara	13
B. B. McCullum b Herath	68	– c Kulasekara b Herath	13
K. S. Williamson c Paranavitana b Eranga	0	– c H. A. P. W. Jayawardene b Kulasekara	10
*L. R. P. L. Taylor b Kulasekara	9	– lbw b Herath	18
D. R. Flynn c H. A. P. W. Jayawardene b Herath	53	– b Herath	20
J. E. C. Franklin lbw b Herath	3	– st H. A. P. W. Jayawardene b Herath	2
†C. F. K. van Wyk b Herath	28	– not out	13
D. A. J. Bracewell c D. P. M. D. Jayawardene b Herath	12	– lbw b Herath	0
T. G. Southee c Mathews b Eranga	16	– st H. A. P. W. Jayawardene b Randiv	16
J. S. Patel not out	12	– c Karunaratne b Herath	0
T. A. Boult b Kulasekara	7	– c D. P. M. D. Jayawardene b Randiv	13
L-b 1, n-b 1	2		
1/29 (1) 2/29 (3) 3/40 (4) 4/130 (2) 5/142 (6) 6/155 (5) 7/181 (8) 8/196 (7) 9/207 (9) 10/221 (11) (82.5 overs)	221	1/18 (2) 2/35 (1) 3/46 (3) 4/60 (4) 5/70 (6) 6/79 (5) 7/79 (8) 8/96 (9) 9/97 (10) 10/118 (11) (44.1 overs)	118

Kulasekara 12.5–5–31–2; Eranga 16–5–51–3; Mathews 3–0–11–0; Herath 30–5–65–5; Randiv 21–1–62–0. *Second innings*—Kulasekara 12–4–28–2; Eranga 4–2–10–0; Herath 18–3–43–6; Randiv 10.1–0–37–2.

Sri Lanka

First innings		Second innings	
N. T. Paranavitana b Southee	0	– not out	31
F. D. M. Karunaratne lbw b Southee	0	– not out	60
S. Randiv c Guptill b Southee	9		
K. C. Sangakkara c McCullum b Boult	5		
*D. P. M. D. Jayawardene c van Wyk b Patel	91		
T. T. Samaraweera lbw b Southee	17		
A. D. Mathews c van Wyk b Franklin	79		
†H. A. P. W. Jayawardene c Bracewell b Patel	4		
K. M. D. N. Kulasekara c and b Patel	8		
H. M. R. K. B. Herath not out	11		
R. M. S. Eranga c Bracewell b Boult	4		
B 9, l-b 8, n-b 2	19	W 2	2
1/2 (2) 2/9 (1) 3/18 (3) 4/20 (4) 5/50 (6) 6/206 (7) 7/215 (8) 8/229 (5) 9/242 (9) 10/247 (11) (80.2 overs)	247	(no wkt, 18.3 overs)	93

Boult 16.2–3–46–2; Southee 18–4–46–4; Bracewell 16–1–67–0; Franklin 7–2–16–1; Patel 23–7–55–3. *Second innings*—Boult 4–1–15–0; Bracewell 5.3–0–35–0; Patel 5–1–22–0; Franklin 3–0–15–0; Williamson 1–0–6–0.

Umpires: M. Erasmus and N. J. Llong. Third umpire: R. E. J. Martinesz.
Referee: J. Srinath.

SRI LANKA v NEW ZEALAND

Second Test Match

At Colombo (PSS), November 25–29, 2012. New Zealand won by 167 runs. Toss: New Zealand. Test debut: T. D. Astle.

New Zealand displayed great resolve to pull off a stunning victory and square this short series. It was their first in Sri Lanka since Stephen Fleming's side won by exactly the same margin in May 1998, and ended a run of five successive defeats. For Sri Lanka, who had expected nothing less than victory against unfancied opponents, it was an unwelcome jolt ahead of their tour of Australia. The team for that trip had to be chosen before this match, as the Australian High Commission in Colombo insisted it would take at least four weeks to obtain visas.

Taylor reserved his best for what he knew was the last match of his stint as New Zealand's captain. It was his determined innings, coupled with Williamson's six-and-a-half-hour stay, which blunted the Sri Lankan attack in a stand of 262 after the early loss of Guptill and McCullum. It would have been 36 for three had Mathews not missed a hard, diving chance at third slip when Taylor had 14. The let-off proved costly: he and Williamson dug in to forge a record for any New Zealand wicket in Sri Lanka, beating the unbroken 246 of Jeff Crowe and Richard Hadlee for the sixth wicket at the Colombo Cricket Club in 1986-87.

Taylor, whose century was his first against Sri Lanka, reined in his usual attacking tendencies, hitting only 11 fours from 306 balls; Williamson, just 22, was equally restrained, with 12 from 305. Herath bowled his heart out to scalp six more victims, four of them leg-before as the batsmen hit across the line and, at 300 for six, Sri Lanka had a chance to limit the damage. But the tail helped Flynn add a further 112 to ensure an imposing total, and the innings did not end until after tea on the second day. Sri Lanka then lost three important wickets before the close, with the impressive Southee removing Dilshan and Sangakkara in three balls.

Paranavitana and Mathews put on 90 but, when three quick wickets went down to leave Sri Lanka 128 for six, it seemed they might have to follow on. Samaraweera dug in to avoid that indignity, despite batting with three stitches in his right hand after splitting the webbing between his fingers as he tried to catch Patel in the slips. He made a staunch 76, and put on 97 with Randiv, who batted spiritedly for three hours.

Still, the new-ball pair of Southee and Boult took nine wickets between them, and Sri Lanka conceded a lead of 168. New Zealand increased that to 362 on the fourth day, with Taylor once more leading the way: again a model of self-denial, he hit only two of the 95 balls he faced to the rope, but still managed 74. His declaration with nine wickets down left Sri Lanka 16 overs to survive on the fourth evening, and the match was all but decided when they made a mess of it. Paranavitana fell to the first ball of the innings, and Dilshan – who had been recalled after his back injury, even though many felt Karunaratne should have been given another chance – soon followed. When Sangakkara and Mahela Jayawardene also fell before the close, Sri Lanka were 46 for four and the game was as good as up.

Any chance they might have had of batting out the final day vanished when Samaraweera ran himself out in the tenth over. He set off for a non-existent single after playing the ball towards short cover, and was almost three-quarters of the way down the pitch before realising Mathews wasn't interested; Patel's return to van Wyk easily beat him back. Mathews fought on, grafting for five hours before he was last out for 84, edging Boult to second slip soon after tea.

Lakruwan Wanniarachchi, AFP/Getty Images

Parting shot: Ross Taylor drove New Zealand on to a notable win in Colombo, all the while knowing his days in charge were numbered.

It was appropriate that one of New Zealand's seamers enjoyed the last word: they had taken 17 wickets between them. Patel had one to add to his run-out, while the Canterbury leg-spinner Todd Astle managed one on his debut. "We got a lot of stick last week for our performance," admitted Taylor. "But we fought hard."

Man of the Match: L. R. P. L. Taylor. *Man of the Series:* H. M. R. K. B. Herath.

Close of play: first day, New Zealand 223-2 (Williamson 95, Taylor 119); second day, Sri Lanka 43-3 (Paranavitana 9, Mathews 20); third day, Sri Lanka 225-6 (Samaraweera 76, Randiv 34); fourth day, Sri Lanka 47-4 (Samaraweera 1, Mathews 1).

New Zealand

M. J. Guptill c Mathews b Kulasekara	4	– c Dilshan b Eranga	11
B. B. McCullum lbw b Eranga	4	– st H. A. P. W. Jayawardene b Herath	35
K. S. Williamson lbw b Herath	135	– c Paranavitana b Kulasekara	18
*L. R. P. L. Taylor lbw b Herath	142	– run out	74
D. R. Flynn lbw b Herath	53	– lbw b Kulasekara	0
†C. F. K. van Wyk b Dilshan	0	– c Paranavitana b Herath	0
T. D. Astle lbw b Herath	3	– c Dilshan b Randiv	35
D. A. J. Bracewell c Herath b Randiv	24	– c Kulasekara b Herath	1
T. G. Southee b Herath	15	– not out	8
J. S. Patel not out	25	– st H. A. P. W. Jayawardene b Randiv	0
T. A. Boult b Herath	1	– not out	6
B 2, l-b 2, n-b 2	6	L-b 4, n-b 2	6
1/4 (1) 2/14 (2) 3/276 (4) 4/290 (3) 5/291 (6) 6/300 (7) 7/346 (8) 8/374 (9) 9/410 (5) 10/412 (11) (153 overs)	412	1/32 (1) 2/56 (2) 3/74 (3) 4/74 (5) 5/75 (6) 6/172 (7) 7/177 (8) 8/180 (4) 9/182 (10) (9 wkts dec, 54 overs)	194

Kulasekara 24–2–76–1; Eranga 22–0–91–1; Mathews 10–1–25–0; Herath 49–10–103–6; Randiv 39–3–94–1; Dilshan 9–2–19–1. *Second innings*—Kulasekara 12–2–47–2; Eranga 10–1–39–1; Herath 21–3–67–3; Randiv 11–1–37–2.

Sri Lanka

N. T. Paranavitana c van Wyk b Southee	40	– lbw b Southee	0
T. M. Dilshan b Southee	5	– c van Wyk b Southee	14
K. C. Sangakkara c Boult b Southee	0	– b Bracewell	16
*D. P. M. D. Jayawardene c Williamson b Boult	4	– c van Wyk b Bracewell	5
A. D. Mathews c Guptill b Southee	47	– (6) c Guptill b Boult	84
T. T. Samaraweera c Guptill b Boult	76	– (5) run out	7
†H. A. P. W. Jayawardene c Williamson b Patel	12	– c van Wyk b Astle	29
S. Randiv lbw b Boult	39	– c Guptill b Boult	0
K. M. D. N. Kulasekara c Taylor b Southee	6	– c Williamson b Boult	18
H. M. R. K. B. Herath c Williamson b Boult	5	– (11) not out	6
R. M. S. Eranga not out	3	– (10) c Williamson b Southee	0
L-b 3, w 1, n-b 3	7	B 4, l-b 11, w 1	16
1/7 (2) 2/7 (3) 3/12 (4) 4/102 (1) 5/103 (5) 6/128 (7) 7/225 (6) 8/232 (8) 9/240 (9) 10/244 (10) (94 overs)	244	1/0 (1) 2/35 (2) 3/41 (3) 4/46 (4) 5/63 (5) 6/119 (7) 7/122 (8) 8/168 (9) 9/169 (10) 10/195 (6) (85.5 overs)	195

Southee 22–4–62–5; Boult 21–7–42–4; Patel 22–3–47–1; Astle 13–2–41–0; Bracewell 13–1–44–0; Williamson 3–1–5–0. *Second innings*—Southee 20–5–58–3; Boult 17.5–6–33–3; Bracewell 13–6–13–2; Patel 16–7–20–0; Astle 18–4–56–1; Flynn 1–1–0–0.

Umpires: M. Erasmus and N. J. Llong. Third umpire: R. S. A. Palliyaguruge.
Series referee: J. Srinath.

ENGLAND LIONS IN SRI LANKA, 2011-12

One-day matches (5): Sri Lanka A 2, England Lions 3

The England Lions arrived in Sri Lanka direct from Bangladesh, where their techniques and temperaments had been tested by spinners queuing up to bowl on comatose wickets (see page 965). Their party was strengthened by four players with one-day international experience – Jade Dernbach, Craig Kieswetter, Samit Patel and Chris Woakes – and the batsmen responded with vim and vigour, racking up an average of 284 a game. The only surprise was that the Lions never set themselves the challenge of batting second.

Kieswetter, with scores of 53 and 112 not out from the middle order, and Patel, who hit a half-century when promoted to open in Colombo, passed important auditions ahead of England's limited-overs series against Pakistan (for which seven of this squad were called up). No one, though, made as big an impact as Jos Buttler, who – in the opening game at Dambulla – produced an astonishing finish: he pummelled 102 in only 56 balls, including 26 from the last over, and followed it four days later with 119, this time tasked with anchoring the innings. Here, patently, was a special talent.

When the fortunes of England's Test batsmen plummeted during the winter, some expected the selectors to turn to James Taylor. But he was going through technical battles of his own: he passed 50 only once in 13 innings in Bangladesh and Sri Lanka, and was discovering that trying to turn the ball to leg off his pads was fraught with danger on these wickets – even without the Decision Review System. However, Graham Thorpe, accompanying the Lions as batting coach, detected in him a developing leader and personality.

ENGLAND LIONS TOURING PARTY

*J. W. A. Taylor (Nottinghamshire), J. M. Bairstow (Yorkshire), S. G. Borthwick (Durham), D. R. Briggs (Hampshire), J. A. Brooks (Northamptonshire), N. L. Buck (Leicestershire), J. C. Buttler (Somerset), J. W. Dernbach (Surrey), A. D. Hales (Nottinghamshire), C. Kieswetter (Somerset), S. C. Meaker (Surrey), S. R. Patel (Nottinghamshire), J. E. Root (Yorkshire), J. M. Vince (Hampshire), C. R. Woakes (Warwickshire).

Meaker was ruled out of the series on February 1 with a back injury, and was replaced by M. T. Coles (Kent).

Coach: D. Parsons. *Manager:* G. A. M. Jackson. *Batting coach:* G. P. Thorpe. *Bowling coach:* K. J. Shine. *Wicketkeeping coach:* B. N. French. *Physiotherapist:* S. McAllister. *Strength and conditioning:* M. Spivey. *Team analyst:* G. Broad. *Team doctor:* G. Bhogal. *Security manager:* S. Dickason.

50-over series

At Dambulla, January 27, 2012. **England Lions won by 68 runs. England Lions 335-5** (50 overs) (A. D. Hales 94, C. Kieswetter 53, J. C. Buttler 102*); ‡**Sri Lanka A 267** (45.3 overs) (S. H. T. Kandamby 54; N. L. Buck 4-39). *Several times in his short career, Jos Buttler had been denied an almost certain hundred by the constraints of the English domestic one-day format, capped at 40 overs. Not so here: he arrived at the fall of Alex Hales at 173-4, with 16 overs left, and struck the ball with prodigious power to make 102* from 56 deliveries, his maiden one-day century. Buttler began the last over on 76, and hit Kanishka Alwitigala for 644444. Samit Patel contributed only five* *to their unbroken partnership of 56 from the last 23 balls – after the powerplays had been taken. Nathan Buck then removed Kosala Kulasekara and Thilina Kandamby in successive overs to kill the chase and take his first List A four-wicket haul.*

At Dambulla, January 29, 2012. **England Lions won by 67 runs.** **‡England Lions 293-9** (50 overs) (C. Kieswetter 112*); **Sri Lanka A 226** (46.1 overs) (M. D. K. J. Perera 59). *Challenged by the selectors to prove himself a credible middle-order international batsman, Craig Kieswetter scored a well-paced century from No. 5, including six fours and six sixes. His 100-run partnership with Patel (43) carried the game away from Sri Lanka A, who began their pursuit briskly, but fell behind the rate against Danny Briggs, who finished with 3-31.*

At Kurunegala, January 31, 2012. **Sri Lanka A won by six wickets.** **‡England Lions 258-9** (50 overs) (J. C. Buttler 119); **Sri Lanka A 263-4** (47.3 overs) (F. D. M. Karunaratne 94, P. B. B. Rajapaksa 72, S. H. T. Kandamby 55*). *When the Lions slipped to 22-2, Buttler knuckled down to make a responsible 119 in 130 balls; unusually for him, though, he struck only one six and was unable to accelerate as he might have wished. Jade Dernbach had Dhanushka Gunathilleke lbw to the first ball of the reply, but Dimuth Karunaratne pulled off a fine chase in stands of 132 with Bhanuka Rajapaksa and 82 with Kandamby.*

At Colombo (RPS), February 3, 2012. **Sri Lanka A won by four wickets.** **England Lions 204** (42.1 overs) (S. R. Patel 50, A. D. Hales 62); **‡Sri Lanka A 206-6** (42.1 overs). *The series moved on to a hotter Colombo, where both middle orders found conditions difficult. The new opening pair of Patel and Hales began with 85 in 14 overs; Karunaratne (45) and Gunathilleke (41) with 84 inside 20. But Hales lost five partners as the spinners descended, and the Lions were bowled out for the only time in the series, setting up a decider.*

At Colombo (RPS), February 6, 2012. **England Lions won by 117 runs.** **‡England Lions 330-6** (50 overs) (J. E. Root 110*, J. C. Buttler 64); **Sri Lanka A 213** (40.2 overs) (M. L. Udawatte 52). *There was only one team in it. Batting first for the fifth time out of five, the Lions produced the textbook one-day innings. Joe Root benefited most from the familiarity, with a maiden List A century, while Buttler (64 from 31 balls) and Jonny Bairstow (27 from 12) delivered crushing late power as 164 came from the last 15 overs. On the same day, England's Test side lost to Pakistan in Dubai – confirming a 3–0 whitewash.*

For England Lions' preceding tour of Bangladesh, see page 965; for a report of their match against England in the UAE, see page 294.

DOMESTIC CRICKET IN SRI LANKA, 2011-12

SA'ADI THAWFEEQ

The much-hyped inaugural Sri Lanka Premier League, postponed from 2011, was expected to be the focus of the domestic season. In fact, it attracted little attention. Staged over three weeks in August, just after visits from Pakistan and India, and just before the World Twenty20, it featured seven privately owned provincial teams, and was frequently played in front of half-empty stands. The weather was poor: one semi-final was completely washed out, and the final was decided on Duckworth/Lewis. **Uva Next** took the title, beating **Nagenahira Nagas** to qualify for the Champions League in South Africa.

There was a sprinkling of stars from other countries, particularly Pakistan, but the Indian authorities refused to allow their players to appear, citing the need to rest them ahead of a heavy international schedule, and also suspecting that the tournament organisers, Somerset Entertainment Ventures of Singapore, were linked to the former IPL mogul Lalit Modi.

Colts won the first-class Premier League's Tier A for the second time in four seasons. They all but made sure of the title in the penultimate round, when they came out on top of a draw with **Sinhalese**, their closest rivals. Sinhalese seemed in charge when they piled up 401, but Colts opener Harsha Vithana and wicketkeeper Kushal Perera added 320 for the second wicket, enabling their side to pick up eight first-innings points. The Colts captain, former Test opener Malinda Warnapura, praised a team effort from a young squad, who rose to the occasion with three senior players absent on international duty. Early leaders **Ragama** finished third, their best position yet, after running up 601, the season's highest total, to beat Tamil Union in their final match.

Army ruled Tier B, winning seven of their nine matches, but only a change in the format of the tournament saved Nondescripts, who were winless, from relegation from Tier A. **Nondescripts** had started the season on a high, beating Sinhalese in the December final of the Premier limited-overs tournament. In April, **Burgher** won the Premier clubs' Twenty20 tournament, revived after five years as the interprovincial Twenty20 competition was abandoned.

Chamara Silva of Bloomfield was the only batsman to top 1,000 first-class runs for the season. Slow bowling maintained its hold, despite Sri Lanka Cricket's requests for grassier pitches: of 32 bowlers claiming 25 wickets, only four were seamers. Navy's Dulanjana Kalhara Mendis led the field with 64, but might easily have been overtaken by his fellow leg-spinner Seekkuge Prasanna, who collected 50 in just five matches for Army before an international call-up.

Several county cricketers took part in the competition, and two enjoyed notable success: Warwickshire opener Varun Chopra carried his bat for 233 in his first game for Tamil Union, and added 192 in his fourth; Worcestershire's Moeen Ali hit 157 in his third and final game for Moors.

SLC planned to reform the next season's Premier League by increasing the number of clubs in Tier A from ten to 14, while removing first-class status from Tier B. This was opposed by most clubs from both Tiers, on the grounds that the strategy of the past three years had been to make the standard more competitive by reducing Tier A from 12 teams to ten through relegating more teams than were promoted. The cricket committee's counterargument was that, because attempts to revive the interprovincial tournament had failed, clubs from the South, Central and North Western provinces should have a chance to join Tier A for the game to survive in the outstations. A compromise was reached for 2012-13: the 20 clubs from Tiers A and B combined in a single first-class competition, consisting of two groups of ten (an even mix of A and B teams); the two group winners would meet in a final, and the bottom three from each group would be relegated, achieving SLC's preferred format of 14 first-class teams in 2013-14.

FIRST-CLASS AVERAGES, 2011-12

BATTING (600 runs)

	M	*I*	*NO*	*R*	*HS*	*100*	*Avge*	*Ct/St*
L. P. C. Silva (*Bloomfield & SLC Dev. XI*)	10	16	1	1,306	216	5	87.06	19
T. T. Samaraweera (*Sinhalese & Sri Lanka*)	9	15	4	808	148	3	73.45	2
A. R. S. Silva (*Colts & SL Board XI*)	9	14	5	638	132*	3	70.88	15
†N. T. Paranavitana (*Sinhalese*)	8	11	0	713	223	2	64.81	4
†W. A. A. M. Silva (*Lankan & SL Board XI*)	9	18	3	915	175	4	61.00	7
G. K. Amarasinghe (*Saracens*)	9	17	3	823	160	4	58.78	0
†W. W. A. G. Maneshan (*Kurunegala Youth*)	9	18	1	983	150	4	57.82	15/5
C. U. Jayasinghe (*Bloomfield*)	9	14	1	740	173*	2	56.92	7
N. H. G. Cooray (*Chilaw Marians*)	9	14	2	663	231	2	55.25	9/2
L. J. P. Gunaratne (*Chilaw Marians*)	9	14	2	633	180	1	52.75	4
A. K. Perera (*Nondescripts & SLC Dev. XI*)	10	18	1	893	138	3	52.52	15
G. I. Daniel (*Ragama*)	9	16	2	734	140	4	52.42	2
†J. Mubarak (*Nondescripts*)	8	15	2	676	131*	3	52.00	15
W. M. B. Perera (*Moors*)	9	15	0	762	152	2	50.80	7
†K. D. K. Vithanage (*Tamil Union*)	9	14	0	651	125	2	46.50	5
J. K. Silva (*Sinhalese*)	9	14	1	600	141	3	46.15	24/2
†M. D. U. S. Jayasundera (*Ragama*)	9	16	0	624	154	2	39.00	9
L. A. C. Ruwansiri (*Army*)	9	17	1	605	116	1	37.81	10
K. P. S. P. Karunanayake (*Badureliya*)	9	18	1	626	123	1	36.82	4
E. M. D. Y. Munaweera (*Bloom./SLC Dev. XI*)	10	17	0	625	101	1	36.76	8

BOWLING (30 wickets, average 30.00)

	Style	*O*	*M*	*R*	*W*	*BB*	*5I*	*Avge*
S. Prasanna (*Army*)	LBG	213.3	27	683	50	7-52	6	13.66
D. K. R. C. Jayatissa (*Army*)	OB	157	19	543	34	6-59	2	15.97
M. A. Liyanapathiranage (*Colombo*)	OB	204.3	40	607	36	7-98	4	16.86
D. M. G. S. Dissanayake (*Ports Authority*)	SLA	334.1	67	843	49	6-59	5	17.20
B. M. D. K. Mendis (*Navy*)	LBG	345.1	57	1,159	64	8-93	5	18.10
A. W. Ekanayake (*Kurunegala Youth*)	SLA	306	60	978	45	6-53	3	21.73
R. M. G. K. Sirisoma (*Lankan*)	SLA	202.2	26	790	36	6-22	3	21.94
W. G. H. N. Premaratne (*Ragama/SL Bd XI*)	LFM	196.5	28	777	35	8-53	3	22.20
M. D. K. Perera (*Colts & SL Board XI*)	OB	288.1	48	918	41	6-39	2	22.39
P. M. Pushpakumara (*Chilaw Marians*)	SLA	347	33	1,272	56	9-46	3	22.71
S. C. D. Boralessa (*Nondescripts*)	SLA	357.4	67	1,115	48	5-48	4	23.22
C. A. M. Madusanka (*Burgher*)	SLA	301.2	46	1,049	45	6-29	2	23.31
M. N. R. Cooray (*Panadura*)	LBG	285.2	59	845	35	6-62	2	24.14
S. Weerakoon (*Colts & SLC Dev. XI*)	SLA	337.1	65	1,103	44	5-61	2	25.06
S. C. Serasinghe (*Tamil Union/SL Bd XI*)	OB	257.2	39	874	34	5-75	2	25.70
D. H. A. Isanka (*Air Force*)	SLA	306.3	46	1,037	40	5-69	3	25.92
S. Randiv (*Bloomfield & Sri Lanka*)	OB	335	41	1,235	44	8-128	2	28.06

PREMIER LEAGUE, 2011-12

Tier A

	P	*W*	*L*	*D*	*Pts*
Colts CC	9	4	0	5	116.590
Sinhalese SC	9	3	0	6	107.070
Ragama CC	9	3	2	4	95.495
Chilaw Marians CC	9	2	1	6	92.170
Bloomfield C & AC	9	3	1	5	89.675
Tamil Union C & AC	9	2	1	6	82.770
Lankan CC	9	0	6	3	54.205
Badureliya SC	9	0	4	5	47.895
Moors SC	9	1	1	7	47.750
Nondescripts CC	9	0	2	7	39.400

Tier B

	P	*W*	*L*	*D*	*Pts*
Army SC	9	7	0	2	131.730
Navy SC	9	3	3	3	95.325
Burgher RC	9	4	3	2	93.715
Ports Authority CC	9	3	1	5	87.455
Saracens SC	9	3	4	2	81.890
Kurunegala Youth CC	9	1	3	5	73.075
Air Force SC	9	1	2	6	68.915
Colombo CC	9	2	2	5	68.575
Panadura SC	9	0	1	8	56.780
Police SC	9	0	5	4	44.695

Police were relegated and replaced by Galle for 2012-13.

Outright win = 12pts; win by an innings = 2pts extra; lead on first innings in a drawn game = 8pts. Bonus points were awarded as follows: 0.1pt for each wicket taken and 0.005pt for each run scored, up to 400 runs per innings.

Tier A

At Colombo (Bloomfield), January 18–20, 2012. **Drawn.** **‡Colts 266** (A. R. S. Silva 105) **and 402-9 dec** (S. A. D. U. Indrasiri 5-111); **Bloomfield 239** (C. U. Jayasinghe 131) **and 169-8**. *Bloomfield 3.94pts, Colts 13.13pts. Chinthaka Jayasinghe galloped to 100 in 55 balls; in all, he hit ten sixes and nine fours in 95 deliveries.*

At Colombo (Colts), January 20–22, 2012. **Ragama won by six wickets.** **‡Lankan 118** (W. G. H. N. Premaratne 8-53) **and 211** (A. M. L. Perera 5-77); **Ragama 141** (R. M. G. K. Sirisoma 6-22) **and 192-4**. *Ragama 15.665pts, Lankan 3.045pts. Left-armer Nilanka Premaratne took a career-best 8-53 on the opening day, when 20 wickets fell.*

At Colombo (Moors), January 20–22, 2012. **Drawn.** **Moors 338** (R. J. M. G. M. Rupasinghe 136; G. A. C. R. Perera 5-62) **and 322** (W. M. B. Perera 152; P. M. Pushpakumara 8-139); **‡Chilaw Marians 441-9 dec** (L. J. P. Gunaratne 180). *Moors 4.2pts, Chilaw Marians 12pts. Slow left-armer Malinda Pushpakumara began the season with a career-best 8-139. Janaka Gunaratne hit 16 fours and eight sixes in 187 balls.*

At Colombo (NCC), January 20–22, 2012. **Drawn.** **Badureliya 349** (K. P. S. P. Karunanayake 123; S. C. D. Boralessa 5-60) **and 251-7**; **‡Nondescripts 347** (A. K. Perera 126; I. A. R. L. Illeperuma 5-61). *Nondescripts 3.435pts, Badureliya 12pts. Shalika Karunanayake and Sahan Wijeratne (98) added 215 for Badureliya's fifth wicket.*

At Colombo (PSS), January 20–22, 2012. **Drawn.** **‡Tamil Union 416** (V. Chopra 233*) **and 89-3**; **Sinhalese 535-6 dec** (N. T. Paranavitana 216, J. K. Silva 120, K. S. Lokuarachchi 100*). *Tamil Union 3.045pts, Sinhalese 11.3pts. Varun Chopra carried his bat for his third and highest double-hundred, following two for Warwickshire the previous April. Tharanga Paranavitana responded with his fourth, all for Sinhalese, and added 241 for their second wicket with Kaushal Silva.*

At Colombo (Bloomfield), January 26–28, 2012. **Drawn.** **‡Bloomfield 260** (P. M. Pushpakumara 5-115) **and 320-7 dec** (L. P. C. Silva 142*); **Chilaw Marians 510-7 dec** (N. H. G. Cooray 231, T. M. U. S. Karunaratne 114*). *Bloomfield 3.6pts, Chilaw Marians 11.7pts. Harsha Cooray scored a maiden double-century and added 216 for Chilaw Marians' seventh wicket with Umesh Karunaratne, who completed his first hundred; Chilaw passed 500 for the first time.*

At Colombo (Moors), January 26–28, 2012. **Drawn.** **‡Moors 319 and 345-4 dec**; **Ragama 408-9 dec** (S. S. Pathirana 117) **and 68-2**. *Moors 4.42pts, Ragama 11.74pts. Batting at No. 8, Sachith Pathirana hit 117 in 93 balls, his maiden century, with eight fours and seven sixes.*

At Colombo (Colts), January 27–29, 2012. **Drawn.** **Colts 406-9 dec** (A. R. S. Silva 110*); **‡Nondescripts 221 and 216-8**. *Colts 11.8pts, Nondescripts 3.085pts.*

At Colombo (SSC), January 27–29, 2012. **Sinhalese won by seven wickets.** **Lankan 118 and 340-6 dec** (W. A. A. M. Silva 113*); **‡Sinhalese 199** (J. K. Silva 100) **and 260-3** (K. S. Lokuarachchi 108*). *Sinhalese 15.895pts, Lankan 3.59pts.*

At Colombo (PSS), January 27–29, 2012. **Tamil Union won by an innings and 70 runs.** **Tamil Union 420-9 dec** (S. C. Serasinghe 154, I. Udana 109*); **‡Badureliya 217** (S. K. C. Randunu 5-61) **and 133**. *Tamil Union 18pts, Badureliya 2.65pts. Isuru Udana scored a maiden century from No. 8, adding 171 for Tamil Union's seventh wicket with Sachithra Serasinghe.*

At Moratuwa, February 5–7, 2012. **Drawn.** **Badureliya 184** (R. M. G. K. Sirisoma 6-54) **and 263** (R. M. G. K. Sirisoma 6-87); **‡Lankan 288** (A. A. S. Silva 5-91) **and 6-0**. *Badureliya 3.235pts, Lankan 11.47pts. Slow left-armer Gayan Sirisoma took 12-141.*

At Colombo (Bloomfield), February 5–7, 2012. **Drawn.** **‡Bloomfield 500-6 dec** (L. P. C. Silva 158, C. U. Jayasinghe 173*); **Nondescripts 213** (S. A. D. U. Indrasiri 5-62) **and 327-6** (K. Y. de Silva 124, C. K. Kapugedera 158). *Bloomfield 11.6pts, Nondescripts 3.3pts. Chamara Silva and Chinthaka Jayasinghe added 302 for Bloomfield's fifth wicket in 51 overs; they hit 31 fours and 11 sixes* *between them. When Nondescripts followed on, Yohan de Silva and Chamara Kapugedera put on 259 for the third wicket to save the game.*

At Colombo (Colts), February 5–7, 2012. **Drawn. Ragama 495** (G. I. Daniel 140); **‡Chilaw Marians 207** (W. G. H. N. Premaratne 5-52) **and 180-3**. *Chilaw Marians 2.935pts, Ragama 11.3pts.*

At Colombo (Moors), February 5–7, 2012. **Drawn. ‡Sinhalese 459-9 dec** (T. T. Samaraweera 148) **and 45-5; Moors 383** (M. M. Ali 157). *Moors 3.315pts, Sinhalese 11.225pts. Moeen Ali of Worcestershire scored 157 on his third and final appearance for Moors.*

At Colombo (PSS), February 5–7, 2012. **Drawn. ‡Colts 308 and 124-4; Tamil Union 441** (G. V. Pushpakumara 6-138). *Tamil Union 11.4pts, Colts 3.16pts.*

At Maggona, February 10–12, 2012. **Drawn. ‡Badureliya 302** (D. Hettiarachchi 5-102) **and 308-9; Moors 299**. *Badureliya 12.05pts, Moors 3.395pts. This was the first first-class match played at Surrey Village, so called because it was built as part of a post-tsunami aid project funded by the Oval Relief Trust, set up by Surrey CCC. Roshan Laksiri Illeperuma (67) and Charith Bandara (39*) added 110 for the last wicket in Badureliya's first innings.*

At Colombo (Bloomfield), February 10–12, 2012. **Bloomfield won by 142 runs. ‡Bloomfield 315** (W. G. H. N. Premaratne 5-98) **and 308-7 dec** (E. M. D. Y. Munaweera 101); **Ragama 191** (T. P. Gamage 5-55) **and 290** (R. S. S. S. de Zoysa 128; M. V. T. Fernando 5-62). *Bloomfield 17.115pts, Ragama 4.105pts.*

At Colombo (Colts), February 10–11, 2012. **Colts won by six wickets. Lankan 78** (S. A. C. Kumara 5-21) **and 196; ‡Colts 207** (P. A. S. S. Jeewantha 5-58) **and 68-4**. *Colts 15.375pts, Lankan 2.77pts. Lankan were bowled out inside 30 overs for the lowest total of the season as 20 wickets fell on the opening day; Colts completed their first win on the second.*

At Colombo (NCC), February 10–12, 2012. **Drawn. ‡Nondescripts 315** (K. Y. de Silva 111; I. Udana 5-65) **and 303-7** (C. K. Kapugedera 114, A. K. Perera 121); **Tamil Union 414** (V. Chopra 192; S. C. D. Boralessa 5-104). *Nondescripts 4.09pts, Tamil Union 11.7pts. Chopra fell only eight runs short of his second double-hundred in four matches.*

At Colombo (SSC), February 10–12, 2012. **Drawn. Chilaw Marians 425** (R. M. S. Eranga 100*) **and 103-4; ‡Sinhalese 542-7 dec** (J. K. Silva 141, W. G. R. K. Alwis 100*). *Sinhalese 11.4pts, Chilaw Marians 3.215pts. Shaminda Eranga and Arosh Janoda (68) added 123 for Chilaw Marians' last wicket.*

At Maggona, February 17–19, 2012. **Drawn. ‡Badureliya 186 and 148-7; Chilaw Marians 346**. *Badureliya 2.67pts, Chilaw Marians 11.43pts.*

At Colombo (Bloomfield), February 17–19, 2012. **Tamil Union won by seven wickets. ‡Bloomfield 178 and 276** (S. K. C. Randunu 5-141); **Tamil Union 332** (K. D. K. Vithanage 121; S. A. D. U. Indrasiri 5-143) **and 123-3**. *Tamil Union 16.275pts, Bloomfield 3.57pts. Kithuruwan Vithanage hit 121 in 83 balls, with eight sixes and nine fours. Test wicketkeeper Prasanna Jayawardene confirmed his recovery from hernia surgery with three catches and two stumpings in Tamil Union's first innings.*

At Colombo (Colts), February 17–19, 2012. **Colts won by eight wickets. ‡Colts 398** (A. R. S. Silva 132*; H. U. K. Madushanka 5-102) **and 51-2; Moors 196 and 252** (M. D. K. Perera 6-78). *Colts 16.245pts, Moors 3.44pts.*

At Colombo (NCC), February 17–19, 2012. **Drawn. Lankan 424** (W. A. A. M. Silva 175) **and 240-5; ‡Nondescripts 292** (J. Mubarak 127*; W. R. S. de Silva 5-58, N. V. R. Perera 5-69). *Nondescripts 2.96pts, Lankan 12.2pts.*

At Colombo (SSC), February 17–19, 2012. **Drawn. Ragama 202 and 292-7** (G. I. Daniel 117*); **‡Sinhalese 425-4 dec** (F. D. M. Karunaratne 210*). *Sinhalese 11.7pts, Ragama 2.87pts. Sinhalese captain and keeper Kaushal Silva held six catches in Ragama's first innings and seven in all. Dimuth Karunaratne scored a maiden double-hundred.*

At Colombo (SSC), February 21–23, 2012. **Sinhalese won by eight wickets. Sinhalese 348** (P. B. B. Rajapaksa 174) **and 36-2; ‡Badureliya 129** (C. Gunasinghe 5-23) **and 254** (K. S. Lokuarachchi 6-73). *Sinhalese 15.92pts, Badureliya 3.115pts.*

At Colombo (Bloomfield), February 23–25, 2012. **Bloomfield won by an innings and 72 runs. Bloomfield 450** (H. A. P. W. Jayawardene 127); **‡Lankan 208 and 170** (S. Randiv 7-66). *Bloomfield 18pts, Lankan 2.89pts.*

At Colombo (PSS), February 23–25, 2012. **Drawn.** ‡**Tamil Union 519-6 dec** (H. G. J. M. Kulatunga 148, S. C. Serasinghe 152*) **and 234-4** (M. Pushpakumara 102*); **Moors 492** (W. M. B. Perera 107). *Tamil Union 12.17pts, Moors 3pts.*

At Colombo (Colts), February 24–25, 2012. **Colts won by an innings and 192 runs.** ‡**Colts 452** (M. D. K. J. Perera 131*); **Ragama 91 and 169** (S. Weerakoon 5-61). *Colts 18pts, Ragama 2.3pts.*

At Colombo (NCC), February 24–26, 2012. **Chilaw Marians won by an innings and 84 runs.** ‡**Nondescripts 98 and 220**; **Chilaw Marians 402-9 dec** (N. H. G. Cooray 106*). *Chilaw Marians 18pts, Nondescripts 2.49pts.*

At Colombo (PSS), February 27–29, 2012. **Drawn.** ‡**Lankan 465-9 dec** (W. A. A. M. Silva 157, D. S. D. Weerasinghe 121*) **and 164** (S. C. Serasinghe 5-75, S. K. C. Randunu 5-63); **Tamil Union 229**. *Tamil Union 3.045pts, Lankan 11.82pts.*

At Colombo (SSC), February 28–March 1, 2012. **Drawn.** ‡**Bloomfield 480** (L. P. C. Silva 216); **Sinhalese 493-4** (N. T. Paranavitana 223). *Sinhalese 11pts, Bloomfield 2.4pts. Chamara Silva scored a maiden double-century; in reply Paranavitana scored his fifth, and second in seven innings.*

At Colombo (Colts), March 1–3, 2012. **Colts won by 43 runs.** ‡**Colts 175 and 223** (L. J. P. Gunaratne 5-51); **Chilaw Marians 247** (T. A. M. Siriwardene 112) **and 108** (M. D. K. Perera 6-39). *Colts 15.99pts, Chilaw Marians 3.775pts. Colts won their fourth successive match, despite collapsing to 80-8 on the first day and leaving a target of only 152.*

At Colombo (Moors), March 2–4, 2012. **Drawn. Nondescripts 180 and 285** (J. Mubarak 121, A. K. Perera 138); ‡**Moors 134** (S. C. D. Boralessa 5-48) **and 299-8** (M. I. Ghouse 154*). *Moors 4.165pts, Nondescripts 12.125pts. Jehan Mubarak and Angelo Perera added 242 for the fourth wicket in Nondescripts' second innings, when no one else passed six, after their team claimed their only first-innings points of the season and came within two wickets of an outright win.*

At Maggona, March 4–6, 2012. **Ragama won by 145 runs. Ragama 320 and 292** (A. A. S. Silva 5-115); ‡**Badureliya 229 and 238**. *Ragama 17.06pts, Badureliya 4.335pts. Ragama captain Kaushalya Weeraratne hit 97 in 67 balls, in their first innings, and then reduced Badureliya to 7-3 with three wickets in nine deliveries.*

At Colombo (Bloomfield), March 9–11, 2012. **Bloomfield won by seven wickets.** ‡**Badureliya 226** (P. K. J. R. N. Nonis 100) **and 379** (S. Randiv 8-128); **Bloomfield 513-8 dec** (N. M. N. P. Nawela 117) **and 94-3**. *Bloomfield 16.47pts, Badureliya 4.125pts.*

At Colombo (Colts), March 9–11, 2012. **Drawn.** ‡**Sinhalese 401** (T. T. Samaraweera 102, S. H. T. Kandamby 124) **and 51-4**; **Colts 435-4 dec** (H. E. Vithana 157, M. D. K. J. Perera 186). *Colts 11.4pts, Sinhalese 2.655pts. Colts effectively settled the title when Harsha Vithana and Kushal Perera, who both reached career-bests, added 320 for their second wicket, putting them on course to overtake Sinhalese's 401 and claim eight points for a first-innings lead.*

At Colombo (Moors), March 9–11, 2012. **Moors won by 186 runs.** ‡**Moors 304 and 272-5 dec** (L. H. D. Dilhara 101*); **Lankan 198** (W. A. A. M. Silva 109; D. S. N. F. G. Jayasuriya 5-56) **and 192** (D. Hettiarachchi 8-55). *Moors 16.88pts, Lankan 3.45pts. Moors' left-arm spinner Dinuka Hettiarachchi took 8-55 on the final day to complete victory.*

At Colombo (NCC), March 9–11, 2012. **Drawn.** ‡**Ragama 217** (M. L. R. Buddika 109) **and 374-8 dec** (M. D. U. S. Jayasundera 154, G. I. Daniel 110); **Nondescripts 184** (H. M. C. M. Bandara 7-56) **and 270-5** (J. Mubarak 131*). *Nondescripts 4.07pts, Ragama 12.455pts. Udara Jayasundera and Ian Daniel opened Ragama's second innings with 217 – equalling their team total in the first innings.*

At Colombo (PSS), March 9–11, 2012. **Drawn.** ‡**Chilaw Marians 373** (S. C. Serasinghe 5-108) **and 261-6 dec**; **Tamil Union 285** (K. D. K. Vithanage 125) **and 134-2**. *Tamil Union 3.695pts, Chilaw Marians 12.37pts.*

At Maggona, March 16–18, 2012. **Drawn. Badureliya 235** (S. Weerakoon 5-73) **and 308-8** (P. K. J. R. N. Nonis 120); ‡**Colts 338**. *Badureliya 3.715pts, Colts 11.49pts.*

At Colombo (Bloomfield), March 16–18, 2012. **Drawn.** ‡**Bloomfield 361** (D. S. N. F. G. Jayasuriya 5-95) **and 295-9 dec** (L. P. C. Silva 108); **Moors 350 and 257-7**. *Bloomfield 12.98pts, Moors 4.935pts. Chamara Silva passed 1,000 runs for the season in Bloomfield's first innings, and scored his fourth century of the season in the second.*

At Colombo (Moors), March 16–18, 2012. **Chilaw Marians won by 255 runs. ‡Chilaw Marians 302 and 247-5 dec; Lankan 150 and 144** (P. M. Pushpakumara 9-46). *Chilaw Marians 16.745pts, Lankan 2.97pts. Slow left-armer Pushpakumara completed victory with the best innings return of the season, which he ended with 56 wickets. He had taken 10-215 in the opening match, and claimed 13-107 here.*

At Colombo (NCC), March 16–18, 2012. **Sinhalese won by 26 runs. ‡Sinhalese 209** (T. T. Samaraweera 102) **and 186** (S. C. D. Boralessa 5-57); **Nondescripts 138 and 231**. *Sinhalese 15.975pts, Nondescripts 3.845pts. Desperately short of players, Nondescripts called up all-rounder Upul Chandana, who would be 40 in May, for his first game in three years; he took four wickets in each innings but could not save his old side from finishing bottom.*

At Colombo (PSS), March 16–18, 2012. **Ragama won by an innings and 93 runs. Ragama 601-9 dec** (M. D. U. S. Jayasundera 120, G. I. Daniel 121; B. M. A. J. Mendis 5-157); **‡Tamil Union 308** (M. R. Jaleel 6-113) **and 200** (M. R. Jaleel 5-51). *Ragama 18pts, Tamil Union 3.44pts. Jayasundera and Daniel shared their second double-century opening partnership in successive matches, raising 252 in the first 49 overs of the game, to set up Ragama's highest total, and the best of the season. Six of their top seven passed 50.*

CHAMPIONS

Lakspray Trophy	
1988-89	Nondescripts CC / Sinhalese SC
1989-90	Sinhalese SC
P. Saravanamuttu Trophy	
1990-91	Sinhalese SC
1991-92	Colts CC
1992-93	Sinhalese SC
1993-94	Nondescripts CC
1994-95	Bloomfield C & AC / Sinhalese SC
1995-96	Colombo CC
1996-97	Bloomfield C & AC
1997-98	Sinhalese SC
Premier League	
1998-99	Bloomfield C & AC
1999-2000	Colts CC
2000-01	Nondescripts CC
2001-02	Colts CC
2002-03	Moors SC
2003-04	Bloomfield C & AC
2004-05	Colts CC
2005-06	Sinhalese SC
2006-07	Colombo CC
2007-08	Sinhalese SC
2008-09	Colts CC
2009-10	Chilaw Marians
2010-11	Bloomfield C & AC
2011-12	Colts CC

Sinhalese and Colts have won the title outright 6 times each, Bloomfield 4, Colombo and Nondescripts 2, Moors 1. Sinhalese have also shared the title twice, and Bloomfield, Chilaw Marians and Nondescripts once each.

Tier B

At Colombo (Air Force), January 20–22, 2012. **Saracens won by seven wickets. ‡Air Force 191 and 135** (Y. A. N. Mendis 7-35); **Saracens 278 and 49-3**. *Saracens 15.635pts, Air Force 2.93pts.*

At Colombo (Burgher), January 20–22, 2012. **Drawn. Panadura 257 and 262-6 dec** (G. S. U. Fernando 118); **‡Burgher 406** (W. T. Abeyratne 137; M. T. P. Fernando 6-111). *Burgher 11.6pts, Panadura 3.595pts.*

At Kurunegala, January 20–22, 2012. **Army won by four wickets. Kurunegala Youth 301** (S. Prasanna 6-84) **and 148** (S. Prasanna 6-73); **‡Army 332** (R. M. N. Ratnayake 5-48) **and 120-6**. *Army 16.26pts, Kurunegala Youth 3.845pts. Leg-spinner Seekkuge Prasanna began the tournament with 12-157.*

At Welisara, January 20–22, 2012. **Drawn. Navy 268 and 264**; **‡Colombo 201 and 271-7** (W. S. Jayantha 110). *Navy 12.36pts, Colombo 4.36pts.*

At Colombo (Police), January 20–22, 2012. **Drawn. ‡Ports Authority 137** (K. K. M. R. Perera 5-37) **and 264** (R. P. Kellepotha 5-66); **Police 168 and 198-6**. *Police 11.83pts, Ports Authority 3.605pts. Police wicketkeeper Eranda Harshaka completed nine dismissals on first-class debut.*

At Panadura, January 26–28, 2012. **Drawn. Panadura 393** (M. M. D. R. Cooray 166); **‡Police 185** (H. D. N. de Silva 6-34) **and 232-7**. *Panadura 11.665pts, Police 3.085pts.*

At Colombo (Air Force), January 27–29, 2012. **Air Force won by three wickets. Ports Authority 379** (D. M. G. S. Dissanayake 131; D. H. A. Isanka 5-127) **and 148** (D. H. A. Isanka 5-69, P. W. B. Sandaruwan 5-62); ‡**Air Force 274 and 256-7**. *Air Force 16.65pts, Ports Authority 4.335pts.*

At Panagoda, January 27–29, 2012. **Army won by six wickets. Burgher 136** (A. J. C. Silva 6-50) **and 263-9 dec** (W. R. Palleguruge 5-59); ‡**Army 246 and 154-4**. *Army 15.9pts, Burgher 3.395pts.*

At Colombo (CCC), January 27–29, 2012. **Colombo won by nine wickets.** ‡**Saracens 169 and 241** (D. G. R. Dhammika 5-45); **Colombo 267 and 144-1**. *Colombo 16.055pts, Saracens 3.15pts. The highest stand in the match was for the ninth wicket in Saracens' second innings, when opener Amila Sandaruwan (52), who had retired hurt, resumed to put on 107 with Mohomad Aslam (81*).*

At Welisara, January 27–29, 2012. **Navy won by 77 runs.** ‡**Navy 188** (A. W. Ekanayake 6-53) **and 199**; **Kurunegala Youth 185** (B. M. D. K. Mendis 6-70) **and 125** (B. M. D. K. Mendis 6-62). *Navy 15.935pts, Kurunegala Youth 3.55pts. Leg-spinner Dulanjana Kalhara Mendis took 12-132.*

At Panagoda, February 5–7, 2012. **Drawn. Army 153 and 263-5**; ‡**Panadura 295** (D. K. R. C. Jayatissa 5-81). *Army 3.08pts, Panadura 10.975pts.*

At Colombo (Burgher), February 5–7, 2012. **Burgher won by seven wickets. Saracens 135** (C. A. M. Madusanka 6-29) **and 285** (G. K. Amarasinghe 103); ‡**Burgher 332** (Y. A. N. Mendis 6-53) **and 91-3**. *Burgher 16.115pts, Saracens 3.4pts.*

At Colombo (CCC), February 5–7, 2012. **Drawn. Colombo 319** (K. R. N. U. Perera 5-67) **and 17-0**; ‡**Ports Authority 379** (K. A. D. M. Fernando 146; G. K. D. B. Gunaratne 5-80). *Colombo 2.68pts, Ports Authority 10.895pts.*

At Kurunegala, February 5–7, 2012. **Drawn. Kurunegala Youth 309** (W. W. A. G. Maneshan 115) **and 268**; ‡**Air Force 271**. *Kurunegala Youth 11.885pts, Air Force 3.355pts.*

At Welisara, February 5–7, 2012. **Navy won by an innings and 12 runs. Police 151 and 146** (B. M. D. K. Mendis 5-41, L. A. C. Ruwansiri 5-17); ‡**Navy 309** (L. A. C. Ruwansiri 116). *Navy 17.545pts, Police 2.485pts.*

At Colombo (Air Force), February 10–12, 2012. **Drawn. Air Force 282 and 303** (W. M. M. W. E. V. Gangoda 5-54); ‡**Burgher 201 and 271-8**. *Air Force 12.725pts, Burgher 4.36pts.*

At Panagoda, February 10–12, 2012. **Drawn. Ports Authority 274 and 57-3**; ‡**Army 401-8 dec** (T. D. T. Soysa 108*). *Army 11.3pts, Ports Authority 2.455pts.*

At Colombo (CCC), February 10–12, 2012. **Drawn.** ‡**Kurunegala Youth 303 and 164-4**; **Colombo 131 and 396-8 dec** (B. A. R. S. Priyadarshana 121, A. V. S. Nikethana 101*). *Colombo 4.035pts, Kurunegala Youth 12.135pts.*

At Welisara, February 10–12, 2012. **Drawn. Navy 326** (K. W. G. Christopher 127; M. N. R. Cooray 6-62) **and 163-8 dec**; ‡**Panadura 233** (B. M. D. K. Mendis 8-93) **and 151-5**. *Navy 11.945pts, Panadura 3.72pts.*

At Colombo (Police), February 12–14, 2012. **Drawn.** ‡**Saracens 432-9 dec** (G. K. Amarasinghe 160) **and 57-1**; **Police 374** (L. A. H. de Silva 5-84). *Police 2.87pts, Saracens 11.285pts. Gamindu Kanishka Amarasinghe and Lahiru Lakmal (85) added 208 for Saracens' fourth wicket.*

At Panagoda, February 17–19, 2012. **Army won by an innings and 25 runs. Army 352-7 dec**; ‡**Navy 119** (S. Prasanna 7-52) **and 208**. *Army 17.76pts, Navy 2.335pts.*

At Colombo (CCC), February 17–19, 2012. **Burgher won by four wickets.** ‡**Colombo 248 and 212**; **Burgher 229 and 234-6**. *Burgher 16.315pts, Colombo 3.9pts.*

At Kurunegala, February 17–19, 2012. **Drawn.** ‡**Kurunegala Youth 270 and 309** (W. W. A. G. Maneshan 127); **Ports Authority 232** (M. D. H. D. Gunathilleke 102) **and 151-3**. *Kurunegala Youth 12.195pts, Ports Authority 3.915pts.*

At Panadura, February 17–19, 2012. **Saracens won by 24 runs. Saracens 204 and 318-8 dec** (G. K. Amarasinghe 135*); ‡**Panadura 158** (W. G. C. D. Ranaweera 5-37) **and 340** (M. T. T. Fernando 131). *Saracens 16.61pts, Panadura 4.29pts.*

At Colombo (Police), February 17–19, 2012. **Drawn.** ‡**Police 298** (R. P. Kellepotha 100*; D. H. A. Isanka 5-83) **and 185**; **Air Force 218 and 171-8**. *Police 12.215pts, Air Force 3.945pts. Prasad Kellepotha and Buddika Sanjeewa (32) put on 120 for Police's tenth wicket.*

At Colombo (Air Force), February 24–26, 2012. **Drawn.** **‡Colombo 175** (S. I. Vithana 5-33) **and 339-6 dec** (M. S. Warnapura 108); **Air Force 234** (B. M. R. N. B. Ratnayake 111; J. M. S. Perera 6-83) **and 136-4**. *Air Force 11.45pts, Colombo 3.97pts. Madawa Warnapura, son of Sri Lanka's first Test captain Bandula Warnapura, scored a maiden century for Colombo.*

At Colombo (Burgher), February 24–26, 2012. **Navy won by 157 runs. Navy 278 and 304-9 dec** (C. A. M. Madusanka 6-88); **‡Burgher 215 and 210** (K. L. Keerthiratne 5-45). *Navy 16.91pts, Burgher 4.025pts.*

At Kurunegala, February 24–26, 2012. **Drawn. ‡Kurunegala Youth 413-8 dec** (W. W. A. G. Maneshan 150; D. E. T. Rathnayake 5-76) **and 226-3** (W. W. A. G. Maneshan 114); **Saracens 423** (G. K. Amarasinghe 103). *Kurunegala Youth 4.13pts, Saracens 11.1pts. Gayan Maneshan scored twin hundreds, making it three in three innings and four in four matches.*

At Panadura, February 24–26, 2012. **Drawn. ‡Panadura 123 and 319**; **Ports Authority 353** (B. M. T. T. Mendis 108; M. N. R. Cooray 5-106) **and 67-4**. *Panadura 3.61pts, Ports Authority 12.1pts.*

At Colombo (Police), February 24–26, 2012. **Army won by ten wickets. ‡Police 317** (S. Prasanna 7-126) **and 136** (S. Prasanna 7-55); **Army 442** (D. A. S. Gunaratne 155*; R. P. Kellepotha 5-126) **and 15-0**. *Army 16.075pts, Police 3.265pts. Leg-spinner Prasanna took 14-181, the best match return of the season, and the third time in this tournament he had claimed ten or more; in between he scored a career-best 79 while helping Asela Gunaratne put on 116 for Army's ninth wicket.*

At Panagoda, March 2–3, 2012. **Army won by an innings and 90 runs. Saracens 114** (N. K. Liyanapathirana 5-35, S. Prasanna 5-58) **and 90**; **‡Army 294** (H. H. M. de Zoysa 100; I. R. Weerasinghe 6-56). *Army 17.47pts, Saracens 2.02pts. Prasanna reached 50 wickets for the season in just five matches.*

At Colombo (Burgher), March 2–4, 2012. **Burgher won by three wickets. Kurunegala Youth 271 and 244**; **‡Burgher 296 and 222-7** (A. W. Ekanayake 5-88). *Burgher 16.59pts, Kurunegala Youth 4.275pts.*

At Colombo (CCC), March 2–4, 2012. **Colombo won by an innings and 17 runs. Police 198** (J. M. S. Perera 5-57) **and 188**; **‡Colombo 403-9 dec** (B. A. R. S. Priyadarshana 113, E. F. M. U. Fernando 110). *Colombo 18pts, Police 2.83pts.*

At Welisara, March 2–4, 2012. **Ports Authority won by seven wickets. ‡Navy 227** (D. M. G. S. Dissanayake 6-60) **and 183** (D. M. G. S. Dissanayake 6-59); **Ports Authority 330 and 81-3**. *Ports Authority 16.055pts, Navy 3.35pts. Slow left-armer Shanuka Dissanayake improved his career-best analysis twice.*

At Panadura, March 2–4, 2012. **Drawn. ‡Air Force 249 and 278**; **Panadura 217 and 55-1**. *Panadura 3.36pts, Air Force 11.735pts.*

At Colombo (CCC), March 8–10, 2012. **Drawn. Panadura 330** (M. A. Liyanapathiranage 7-98) **and 129** (M. A. Liyanapathiranage 5-49); **‡Colombo 379** (E. F. M. U. Fernando 115) **and 10-1**. *Colombo 11.945pts, Panadura 3.395pts. Off-spinner Maduka Liyanapathiranage took 12-147.*

At Panagoda, March 9–11, 2012. **Army won by an innings and 28 runs. Air Force 196 and 113** (W. R. Palleguruge 5-43); **‡Army 337**. *Army 17.685pts, Air Force 2.545pts. Army's sixth win secured the Tier B title with a round to spare.*

At Colombo (Burgher), March 9–11, 2012. **Ports Authority won by seven wickets. Burgher 209** (D. M. G. S. Dissanayake 5-73) **and 208** (D. M. G. S. Dissanayake 5-64); **‡Ports Authority 305 and 114-3**. *Ports Authority 16.095pts, Burgher 3.385pts. Shanuka Dissanayake took 10-137 and scored 101 runs in the match.*

At Welisara, March 9–10, 2012. **Saracens won by one wicket. Navy 196 and 107** (Y. A. N. Mendis 5-44); **‡Saracens 115** (B. M. D. K. Mendis 7-40) **and 189-9** (S. V. Liyanage 5-49). *Saracens 15.52pts, Navy 3.415pts. Twenty-one wickets fell on the first day, when leg-spinner Dulanjana Kalhara Mendis claimed his 50th victim of the season, and 18 on the second. Lahiru Lakmal held five catches in the field in Navy's second innings, to follow a career-best 4-65 and a run-out in the first. But he managed only a duck in the run-chase, when last pair Amila Mendis and Eranga Rathnayake came together with ten runs required; they knocked them off in four balls to complete a two-day win.*

At Colombo (Police), March 9–11, 2012. **Kurunegala Youth won by 288 runs. Kurunegala Youth 317** (W. C. Sisirakumara 111) **and 306-7 dec** (G. S. K. de Silva 108*); ‡**Police 191** (A. W. Ekanayake 5-54) **and 144** (S. D. P. A. Premaratne 7-54). *Kurunegala Youth 17.115pts, Police 3.375pts. Off-spinner Aravinda Premaratne took 10-62 on first-class debut.*

At Colombo (Air Force), March 16–18, 2012. **Drawn. Air Force 150** (N. K. M. Perera 5-48) **and 246** (J. R. G. Namal 134); ‡**Navy 153** (K. L. Rukmal 5-53) **and 153-6.** *Air Force 3.58pts, Navy 11.53pts.*

At Colombo (CCC), March 16–18, 2012. **Army won by 114 runs.** ‡**Army 264** (M. A. Liyanapathiranage 5-109) **and 176** (M. A. Liyanapathiranage 6-57); **Colombo 145** (W. R. Palleguruge 5-38) **and 181** (D. K. R. C. Jayatissa 6-59). *Army 16.2pts, Colombo 3.63pts. Army ended the season with their fifth successive win, and their seventh in all.*

At Panadura, March 16–18, 2012. **Drawn.** ‡**Kurunegala Youth 214 and 335** (G. S. K. de Silva 122; M. T. P. Fernando 5-76); **Panadura 441** (G. A. S. Perera 106) **and 34-2**. *Panadura 12.17pts, Kurunegala Youth 3.945pts. Amila Perera and Danuja Nandana (59*) added 156 for the tenth wicket of Panadura's first innings – the fourth last-wicket century stand of the season.*

At Colombo (Police), March 16–18, 2012. **Burgher won by an innings and 38 runs.** ‡**Police 220 and 128**; **Burgher 386** (A. D. Solomons 166). *Burgher 17.93pts, Police 2.74pts.*

At Panagoda, March 16–18, 2012. **Ports Authority won by an innings and four runs.** ‡**Ports Authority 438** (B. M. T. T. Mendis 111); **Saracens 257** (D. M. G. S. Dissanayake 5-86) **and 177.** *Ports Authority 18pts, Saracens 3.17pts.*

PREMIER LIMITED-OVERS TOURNAMENT, 2011-12

Two tiers of 50-over leagues plus knockouts

Tier A Semi-finals

At Colombo (Colts), December 14, 2011. **Sinhalese won by six wickets. Chilaw Marians 160** (47.2 overs) (S. M. S. M. Senanayake 5-23); ‡**Sinhalese 166-4** (43.1 overs).

At Colombo (Moors), December 14, 2011. **Nondescripts won by four runs** (D/L). **Nondescripts 263-9** (50 overs); ‡**Colts 220-6** (45 overs). *Colts' revised target was 225 in 45 overs.*

Tier A Final

At Colombo (PSS), December 17, 2011. **Nondescripts won by 32 runs. Nondescripts 268** (49.5 overs); ‡**Sinhalese 236** (47.2 overs).

Tier B Final

At Colombo (PSS), December 16, 2011. **Ports Authority won by three wickets. Navy 206** (49.5 overs); ‡**Ports Authority 209-7** (48.1 overs). *Dinusha Fernando (81*) and Ranesh Perera (54) rescued Ports Authority from 85-6 with a stand of 120, which saw them to the brink of victory.*

CSN PREMIER CLUBS T20 TOURNAMENT, 2011-12

20-over league plus knockout

Semi-finals

At Colombo (SSC), April 1, 2012. **Colts won by 64 runs. Colts 190-7** (20 overs); ‡**Nondescripts 126** (15.1 overs). *Colts captain Malinda Warnapura scored a career-best 95 in 46 balls.*

At Colombo (SSC), April 1, 2012. **Burgher won by 37 runs. Burgher 156-8** (20 overs); ‡**Panadura 119** (16.4 overs).

Third-place play-off

At Colombo (SSC), April 2, 2012. **Nondescripts won by 64 runs. Nondescripts 198-5** (20 overs); ‡**Panadura 134-8** (20 overs). *Chamara Kapugedera hit 86* in 39 balls.*

Final

At Colombo (SSC), April 2, 2012. **Burgher won by four runs.** ‡**Burgher 157** (20 overs); **Colts 153-9** (20 overs).

SRI LANKA PREMIER LEAGUE, 2012

	Played	*Won*	*Lost*	*Abandoned*	*Points*	*Net run-rate*
Wayamba United	6	5	1	0	10	1.37
Nagenahira Nagas	6	4	2	0	8	–0.35
Kandurata Warriors	6	3	2	1	7	0.42
Uva Next	6	3	2	1	7	0.08
Ruhuna Royals	6	2	4	0	4	–0.14
Uthura Rudras	6	2	4	0	4	–0.52
Basnahira Cricket Dundee	6	1	5	0	2	–0.88

Semi-finals

At Colombo (RPS), August 28, 2012 (floodlit). **Uva Next won by 20 runs.** ‡**Uva Next 171-6** (20 overs); **Wayamba United 151-8** (20 overs). *MoM:* J. D. P. Oram (Uva Next). *Uva's bowlers, headed by New Zealander Jacob Oram, reduced Wayamba to 27-7. A stand of 120 between Azhar Mahmood (75* in 47 balls) and Isuru Udana (42), though a world record for the eight wicket in Twenty20 cricket, was not enough to turn the match round.*

At Colombo (RPS), August 29, 2012 (floodlit). **Kandurata Warriors v Nagenahira Nagas. Abandoned.** *Nagenahira advanced to the final on their better record in the qualifying rounds.*

Final

At Colombo (RPS), August 31, 2012 (floodlit). **Uva Next won by 19 runs** (D/L). ‡**Nagenahira Nagas 134-4** (15 overs); **Uva Next 63-1** (5.1 overs). *MoM:* E. M. D. Y. Munaweera (Uva Next). *Player of the Tournament:* R. M. S. Eranga (Nagenahira Nagas). *Nagenahira captain Angelo Mathews scored 73* in 27 balls in an innings cut to 15 overs by rain. Uva's original target was 137 in 15; when rain ended play in the sixth, with Dilshan Munaweera on 44 from 23 balls, they were well ahead of a retrospective target of 45.*

WEST INDIES CRICKET, 2012

Peace brings prizes

TONY COZIER

For West Indies Cricket Board president Julian Hunte it was "a watershed year" for the sport in the Caribbean. The region was, he declared in his annual review, "better positioned for the rest of the decade on many fronts". And there certainly was a climate of rare optimism. Hunte's confidence was predicated on victory at the World Twenty20 in Sri Lanka, as well as a lucrative agreement with Taj TV for global rights for the next seven years which, he said, would ensure West Indies' financial viability. Another potentially profitable deal was done with Verus International, a merchant bank based in New York and Barbados, for a license to operate a private, professional Twenty20 league of six city-based franchise teams, to replace the WICB's existing tournament from October 2013.

Ajmal Khan, the chief executive of Verus, proclaimed his intention to make the Caribbean Premier League "one of the most enviable franchises anywhere in the world", and said he would invest "whatever it takes, in the hundreds of

WEST INDIES IN 2012

	Played	*Won*	*Lost*	*Drawn/No result*
Tests	10	4	4	2
One-day internationals	18	8	8	2
Twenty20 internationals	13	8	4	1

Month	Fixtures	Page
JANUARY		
FEBRUARY		
MARCH / APRIL	3 Tests, 5 ODIs and 2 T20Is (h) v Australia	(page 1157)
MAY / JUNE	3 Tests, 3 ODIs and 1 T20I (a) v England	(page 315)
JULY / AUGUST	2 Tests, 5 ODIs and 2 T20Is (h) v New Zealand	(page 1173)
SEPTEMBER / OCTOBER	World Twenty20 (in Sri Lanka)	(page 841)
NOVEMBER / DECEMBER	2 Tests, 5 ODIs and 1 T20I (a) v Bangladesh	(page 957)

For a review of West Indian domestic cricket from the 2011-12 season, see page 1186.

millions" to ensure its success. These were phrases that might have come straight from Allen Stanford's handbook of hyperbole but, following their blessing of Stanford 20/20, which had embarrassingly crashed three years earlier after the fraudulent Texan's arrest and 110-year sentence, the WICB emphasised they had thoroughly verified Verus's credentials.

West Indies cricket, though, was still riddled with weaknesses. The game at regional level remained substandard, hampered by poor pitches and unreliable umpiring. The WICB, meanwhile, were mired in the past: for the second time, they rejected the main proposals of a report commissioned by Hunte himself, which called upon the board to modernise their structure and governance. The successive resignations of the constantly quarrelling chief executives – Dinanath Ramnarine of the West Indies Players' Association, and the WICB's Ernest Hilaire – at least brought a welcome period of détente between the union and the board, but WIPA's two lawsuits against the WICB, one seeking $20m for restraint of trade, carried over into 2013.

More than a year after the Guyanese government had replaced the WICB's affiliate board with an interim management committee, no settlement of the dispute was in sight; the upshot was a moratorium on all regional and international matches in Guyana, a country that had staged their inaugural first-class match in 1865, and the first of their 32 Tests in 1930.

The widespread euphoria at the Twenty20 title was reflected in an editorial in the *Trinidad Express*, which declared it had "lifted the spirit of the entire region as one". The reaction was much the same after West Indies' victory in the 2004 Champions Trophy; but that had quickly dissipated into the distress of disputes and defeat. This time, the victory was straddled by a pair of 2–0 Test wins, over New Zealand and Bangladesh. And a 2–1 home success for West Indies A in unofficial Tests against India A added a little more substance to the excitement. However, a 3–2 one-day loss in Bangladesh brought the year to an unsatisfactory end.

In the more difficult Test assignments, West Indies lost 2–0 both to Australia at home and England away. Still, they took all but one of the six games in those two series to the fifth day – a detail that, in the context of recent history, was confirmation West Indies had grown increasingly competitive; Australia's coach Mickey Arthur said they had "gone toe-to-toe with us". And that was without three key players – Chris Gayle (reinstated midway through the England tour through the intervention of two prime ministers after a lengthy standoff with the WICB), Marlon Samuels and Sunil Narine (both engaged in the IPL, Narine triumphantly so).

Four wins in ten Tests exactly doubled the 2011 ratio, while 14 hundreds were spread among seven different batsmen; only three had scored centuries the previous year. Samuels was the star. His renaissance after a two-year suspension for suspected dealings with an Indian bookmaker was a tribute to his determination, and an example to others. The overdue fulfilment of his dormant class brought an awesome striking power to an uncertain middle order. He amassed 866 runs in seven Tests, including a double-hundred and two singles; his *pièce de résistance* was the breathtaking 78 off 56 balls that stunned Sri Lanka in the World Twenty20 final. But a fracas with Shane Warne

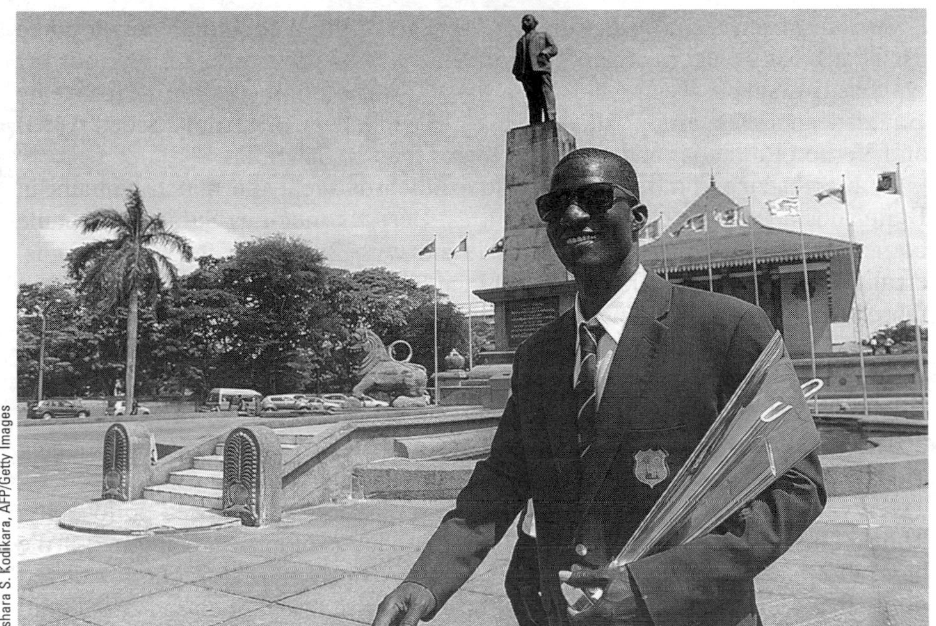

Ishara S. Kodikara, AFP/Getty Images

On the shoulders of giants: Darren Sammy emulated Clive Lloyd by winning a major global title.

in the 2012-13 Big Bash in Australia showed he could still be needled by the opposition.

Shivnarine Chanderpaul kept churning out runs, as he had for most of his 18 years as West Indies' impenetrable wall. No longer burdened with the white-ball game, he gathered 987 runs in nine Tests, regaining his No. 1 spot in the ICC rankings, before yielding to the comet that was Michael Clarke.

Captain Darren Sammy and wicketkeeper Denesh Ramdin, both under constant public scrutiny, produced timely hundreds down the order. Sammy's, at Nottingham, was his first in Tests, and his role as player and leader – especially at the World Twenty20 – earned him new respect. Centuries for Ramdin at Edgbaston and Mirpur settled his tenuous position for the time being.

Chanderpaul, 38 at year's end, was the oldest contemporary Test player bar Sachin Tendulkar. Gayle was 33, Samuels 31, Sammy and Ramdin both in their late twenties. So the development of younger players was of more relevance to the future direction of West Indies cricket. Kieran Powell, a tall, stylish left-handed opener, finally realised the value of scores in three figures rather than two, and was carried along to his maiden Test hundred in the slipstream of Gayle's 150 against New Zealand in Antigua; two matches later in Bangladesh, Powell joined the elite company of Headley, Weekes, Walcott, Sobers, Kanhai, Rowe, Greenidge and Lara as the only West Indians to score hundreds in each innings of a Test. The batting is likely to revolve around him and the equally elegant Darren Bravo, 23, for some time. Ramnaresh Sarwan – alienated under coach Ottis Gibson – was finally chosen again for the one-day series in Australia in February 2013, but not before he had successfully sued the WICB for $161,000 over comments they had made about his fitness.

As it has been from the beginning, the heart of the West Indian bowling – in Tests at least – was pace, and Kemar Roach was its spearhead. He took 39 wickets in seven Tests, before a knee injury eliminated him from the Bangladesh series; among those to take 20 wickets in 2012, only Saeed Ajmal and Vernon Philander had a lower average than Roach's 22.

In his absence, Tino Best and Fidel Edwards were the match-winners in Bangladesh, despite the lifeless surfaces. Best, as much as Samuels, was the comeback story of the year. Aged 31, and with 28 expensive wickets in 14 erratic Tests between 2003 and 2009, he had appeared finished. Still fit and fast, however, he now applied accuracy to claim 18 more in four Tests, though his electrifying 95 at Edgbaston, a record for a Test No. 11, gave him as much satisfaction.

The WICB's decision to replace two home Tests against Sri Lanka in May 2013 with a later triangular tournament also involving India (to accommodate the IPL) was an indication that, like others, they had been seduced by Twenty20. Sammy was among those who regarded it as a flawed philosophy. "The T20 win doesn't mean West Indies is back on top," he cautioned. "We have to beat Australia, England and South Africa [in Tests]. Once we start doing that consistently, the team will be heading in the right direction." For all Hunte's confidence, that still seemed a long way off.

For Tony Cozier's account of 50 years of touring England, see page 100.

WEST INDIES v AUSTRALIA, 2011-12

TONY COZIER

Test matches (3): West Indies 0, Australia 2
One-day internationals (5): West Indies 2, Australia 2
Twenty20 internationals (2): West Indies 1, Australia 1

Australia's captain and coach had encouraging words for West Indies after the most competitive contests between the two teams since the start of the millennium. Michael Clarke described the trip as "really hard-fought", and hoped "West Indies get a lot of credit for the way they played". And, after both limited-overs series were shared, Mickey Arthur conceded that the hosts had "gone toe-to-toe with us".

Yet Clarke's most relevant comment came in explaining how, despite all this, Australia retained the Frank Worrell Trophy they had held since 1994-95. This was their seventh series victory over West Indies in that time, to go with a draw in the Caribbean in 1998-99. Clarke felt the key was that his evolving team "just managed to win the tough battles at times that you need to win Test matches – you can't afford to be off for an hour". As they had been during their 2–0 loss in India before Christmas, West Indies were too often "off for an hour" – and more.

The defining session came on the fourth day of the opening Test. Australia were 250 for seven, responding to 449, with all their big guns already silenced; only the wicketkeeper Matthew Wade remained, plus the bowlers – Ryan Harris, Ben Hilfenhaus and Nathan Lyon, none with a Test batting average above 15. Yet over the next two and a half hours the tail comfortably added 121, changing the course of the match and, ultimately, the series. Their resistance allowed the adventurous Clarke to declare 43 behind against clearly deflated rivals. Almost immediately, West Indies were 17 for four; soon they were dismissed for 148. All that now stood between Australia and their eventual triumph was the fading light.

After a rain-spoiled draw at Port-of-Spain, the Bridgetown narrative was repeated in the final Test, in Dominica. Late on the opening day, Australia were tottering again at 169 for seven, and it was left to Wade – playing only because Brad Haddin had returned home to be with his unwell young daughter – to respond with a commanding 103. With Mitchell Starc, the left-arm fast bowler in his only match of the tour, and Hilfenhaus as partners, Wade carried Australia to 328, on another of the spinning pitches that featured throughout. And against West Indies' brittle, inexperienced line-up, that was just about that.

On such surfaces, batting was never straightforward. There were only two hundreds: Wade's first and, almost inevitably, the calm, calculating, age-defying Shivnarine Chanderpaul's 25th; his 346 runs were 127 more than the next man on either side – and 200 ahead of the other eminent veteran, Ricky Ponting. In Dominica, Chanderpaul joined Brian Lara as the second West

Stan Honda, AFP/Getty Images

Emmanuel Dunand, AFP/Getty Images

Orthodox faith: both sides leant heavily on their off-spinners, with Nathan Lyon and Shane Shillingford taking 27 wickets between them in the Tests.

Indian to pass 10,000 Test runs, and went back to No. 1 in the ICC's batting rankings. In the same game, Ponting ignored Darren Sammy's jibe that the Test might prove his last to move ahead of Rahul Dravid (13,288 runs) and back into second place behind Sachin Tendulkar on the overall list.

Everybody who got a bowl got a wicket – 11 Australians and seven West Indians. Clarke gave his left-arm spin a rare outing in West Indies' second innings in Dominica: it turned out to be his longest spell in 83 Tests, and key to the result. Among his five victims was the entrenched Chanderpaul, to the last ball of the fourth day, just as West Indies were beginning to harbour visions of their record run-chase of 418 in Antigua against Steve Waugh's team nine years earlier.

Both sides' off-spinners thrived. Lyon took time to acclimatise before claiming most wickets for Australia; Shane Shillingford, returning for the first time in over a year after correcting a flawed action, had 14 in two matches, ten of them on his home ground in Roseau, the first such return by a West Indian spinner since Lance Gibbs against England in 1966. Shillingford was immediately appointed Dominica's ambassador for sport by their government, and issued with a diplomatic passport.

Yet undoubtedly the bowler of the series was Kemar Roach. He was relentlessly fast and direct in spite of the unfavourable surfaces, and his 19 wickets came at just under 20 runs each. His dominance over Ponting, which had started in Australia in 2008-09, was extended to five dismissals in six Tests.

Australia's fast-bowling stocks were diminished by injuries that kept Pat Cummins and Mitchell Johnson at home, and restricted Peter Siddle and James

Pattinson to one Test apiece. But West Indies were harder hit by the exodus of five players to the IPL after the limited-overs matches. The most telling absentee was the spinner Sunil Narine, who had proved all but unfathomable to the Australians. Narine, not among the board's contracted players, chose to take up the $700,000 on offer from the Kolkata franchise instead of staying on for the Tests. With Twenty20 tournaments mushrooming hither, thither and yon, it is a dilemma increasingly certain to concern West Indies – and world – cricket.

AUSTRALIAN TOURING PARTY

*M. J. Clarke, M. A. Beer, E. J. M. Cowan, P. J. Forrest, R. J. Harris, B. W. Hilfenhaus, M. E. K. Hussey, N. M. Lyon, P. M. Nevill, J. L. Pattinson, R. T. Ponting, P. M. Siddle, M. A. Starc, M. S. Wade, D. A. Warner, S. R. Watson. *Coach:* J. M. Arthur.

B. J. Haddin was originally selected, but returned home before the first match of the tour for family reasons, and was replaced by Nevill. For the one-day matches that preceded the Tests, G. J. Bailey, D. T. Christian, X. J. Doherty, D. J. Hussey, B. Lee and C. J. McKay replaced Beer, Clarke, Cowan, Harris, Pattinson, Ponting, Siddle and Starc. Clarke was originally selected for the one-day international squad, but injured a hamstring before departure and remained in Australia until shortly before the Tests. Watson captained in the 50-over matches, Bailey in the Twenty20 internationals.

TEST MATCH AVERAGES

WEST INDIES – BATTING AND FIELDING

	T	*I*	*NO*	*R*	*HS*	*100*	*50*	*Avge*	*Ct*
†S. Chanderpaul	3	5	1	346	103*	1	3	86.50	3
†D. M. Bravo	3	6	1	184	51	0	1	36.80	7
D. J. G. Sammy	3	6	1	157	61	0	1	31.40	9
†N. Deonarine	3	5	0	117	55	0	1	23.40	3
†K. O. A. Powell	2	4	0	87	40	0	0	21.75	2
S. Shillingford	2	3	1	35	31*	0	0	17.50	1
C. S. Baugh	3	5	0	83	23	0	0	16.60	6
K. C. Brathwaite	3	5	0	71	57	0	1	14.20	2
K. A. J. Roach	3	5	1	52	25	0	0	13.00	0
A. B. Barath	3	6	0	65	29	0	0	10.83	2
F. H. Edwards	2	3	1	13	10	0	0	6.50	0

Played in one Test: †D. Bishoo 18*, 7* (1 ct); K. A. Edwards 61, 1 (1 ct); †R. Rampaul 31, 11.

BOWLING

	Style	*O*	*M*	*R*	*W*	*BB*	*5I*	*Avge*
K. A. J. Roach	RF	122	24	375	19	5-41	2	19.73
N. Deonarine	OB	70	13	194	9	4-53	0	21.55
S. Shillingford	OB	154.4	37	366	14	6-119	1	26.14
D. J. G. Sammy	RM	86	25	204	5	2-65	0	40.80
F. H. Edwards	RF	70	17	184	3	2-92	0	61.33

Also bowled: D. Bishoo (LBG) 53–10–169–1; R. Rampaul (RFM) 33–7–102–1.

AUSTRALIA – BATTING AND FIELDING

	T	*I*	*NO*	*R*	*HS*	*100*	*50*	*Avge*	*Ct/St*
N. M. Lyon	3	5	4	62	40*	0	0	62.00	0
R. J. Harris	2	4	2	85	68*	0	1	42.50	2
†M. S. Wade	3	6	1	198	106	1	0	39.60	7/1
†M. E. K. Hussey	3	6	0	219	73	0	1	36.50	3
S. R. Watson	3	6	0	193	56	0	2	32.16	1
M. J. Clarke	3	6	0	188	73	0	1	31.33	4
†D. A. Warner	3	6	0	171	50	0	1	28.50	3
†E. J. M. Cowan	3	6	0	152	55	0	1	25.33	6
R. T. Ponting	3	6	0	146	57	0	1	24.33	1
B. W. Hilfenhaus	3	6	1	56	24	0	0	11.20	1

Played in one Test: M. A. Beer 2; †J. L. Pattinson 32; P. M. Siddle 0 (1 ct); †M. A. Starc 35, 21.

BOWLING

	Style	*O*	*M*	*R*	*W*	*BB*	*5I*	*Avge*
B. W. Hilfenhaus	RFM	101	34	208	10	4-27	0	20.80
M. J. Clarke	SLA	30	1	113	5	5-86	1	22.60
N. M. Lyon	OB	133.3	37	337	13	5-68	1	25.92
D. A. Warner	LBG	19	1	81	3	2-45	0	27.00
R. J. Harris	RF	62.4	12	184	6	3-31	0	30.66
P. M. Siddle	RFM	48	12	115	3	2-32	0	38.33
S. R. Watson	RFM	55	14	137	3	1-20	0	45.66

Also bowled: M. A. Beer (SLA) 29.4–10–66–2; M. E. K. Hussey (RM) 8–1–25–1; J. L. Pattinson (RFM) 11–2–40–1; M. A. Starc (LFM) 21.2–6–55–2.

WEST INDIES v AUSTRALIA

First One-Day International

At Arnos Vale, St Vincent, March 16, 2012. Australia won by 64 runs. Toss: Australia. One-day international debuts: J. Charles; G. J. Bailey.

A tense finish was looming in a low-scoring contest as Samuels and Dwayne Bravo repaired West Indies' start of 33 for three with a partnership of 64. But they both fell at 97, as did Baugh: in total, six wickets went down for seven runs, and the contest was all but over. Sammy lashed three sixes, but they were scant consolation for those spectators who had not already headed for the exits. Doherty, launched for three straight sixes by Samuels in his first over, had a satisfying comeback with two wickets in three balls, and quickly added Russell and Narine, effectively settling the outcome. Just a week after Australia's triumph over Sri Lanka in the home tri-series finals, their batsmen had found it difficult to come to terms with a slow, turning pitch that restricted strokeplay against some tight bowling, especially from Roach and Narine. Five passed 20, but none bettered George Bailey's 48 from 67 balls on his one-day debut; it would be the highest score of the match.

Man of the Match: G. J. Bailey.

Australia

*S. R. Watson lbw b D. J. Bravo	21
D. A. Warner c Pollard b Samuels	40
P. J. Forrest st Baugh b Samuels	26
M. E. K. Hussey c Roach b D. J. Bravo	32
D. J. Hussey c Baugh b Roach	0
G. J. Bailey c Narine b Roach	48
†M. S. Wade c D. J. Bravo b Narine	0
D. T. Christian not out	18
B. Lee c Charles b D. J. Bravo	5
C. J. McKay not out	0
B 3, l-b 6, w 5	14
1/31 (1) 2/91 (3) 3/92 (2) 4/99 (5) 5/162 (4) 6/162 (7) 7/195 (6) 8/203 (9) — (8 wkts, 50 overs)	204

10 overs: 51-1

X. J. Doherty did not bat.

Roach 10–1–33–2; D. J. Bravo 10–1–58–3; Russell 4–0–21–0; Sammy 8–0–30–0; Narine 10–0–24–1; Samuels 8–0–29–2.

West Indies

K. O. A. Powell c Bailey b Lee	8	S. P. Narine c Bailey b Doherty	0
J. Charles c M. E. K. Hussey b McKay	13	K. A. J. Roach not out	1
M. N. Samuels c Watson b Doherty	35		
D. M. Bravo run out	4	B 4, w 3	7
D. J. Bravo b Christian	32		
K. A. Pollard c Bailey b Christian	4	1/15 (2) 2/23 (1) 3/33 (4) (32.2 overs)	140
†C. S. Baugh lbw b Doherty	0	4/97 (5) 5/97 (3) 6/97 (7)	
A. D. Russell st Wade b Doherty	1	7/101 (8) 8/103 (6) 9/104 (10)	
*D. J. G. Sammy c Christian b McKay	35	10/140 (9) 10 overs: 32-2	

Lee 7–1–25–1; McKay 5.2–1–22–2; Watson 4–1–13–0; D. J. Hussey 2–0–15–0; Doherty 8–2–49–4; Christian 6–2–12–2.

Umpires: H. D. P. K. Dharmasena and P. J. Nero. Third umpire: S. K. Tarapore.

WEST INDIES v AUSTRALIA

Second One-Day International

At Arnos Vale, St Vincent, March 18, 2012. West Indies won by five wickets (D/L). Toss: West Indies.

A sellout crowd, already buoyed by the presence of Chris Gayle in the stands and (premature) reports that his dispute with the board was about to end, celebrated with typical Caribbean abandon as West Indies completed their first one-day international victory over Australia in 15 attempts since the 2006 Champions Trophy. The pattern of a match reduced to 40 overs a side by morning rain was similar to that of the first game, two days earlier, at the same venue. Sent in, Australia made laboured progress on a slow surface, mainly against Roach and Narine, whose confusing, each-way spin earned him four wickets. Powell fell to the first ball of the reply, and West Indies wobbled until a fifth-wicket partnership of 64. It was ended when Dwayne Bravo became the second run-out victim, 20 short of the revised target of 158, with an unpredictable tail to follow. But Baugh completed the job with a swept six off Doherty, after one of Pollard's four sixes (he hit no fours) finished in the vicinity of the adjoining airport.

Man of the Match: S. P. Narine.

Australia

*S. R. Watson c sub (D. Bishoo) b Sammy	25	C. J. McKay st Baugh b Narine	6
D. A. Warner b Roach	13	X. J. Doherty not out	0
P. J. Forrest c Sammy b Roach	0		
M. E. K. Hussey c Baugh b Narine	24	B 2, l-b 3, w 2, n-b 1	8
D. J. Hussey b Narine	37		
G. J. Bailey c Samuels b D. J. Bravo	21	1/19 (2) 2/19 (3) (9 wkts, 40 overs)	154
D. T. Christian run out	6	3/46 (1) 4/77 (4)	
†M. S. Wade c Roach b Narine	3	5/109 (6) 6/121 (7) 7/136 (8)	
B. Lee not out	11	8/136 (5) 9/154 (10) 8 overs: 26-2	

Roach 8–3–23–2; D. J. Bravo 6–0–30–1; Sammy 4–0–19–1; Russell 6–0–14–0; Narine 8–1–27–4; Pollard 4–0–18–0; Samuels 4–0–18–0.

West Indies

K. O. A. Powell lbw b Lee 0
J. Charles run out 26
M. N. Samuels b Watson 20
D. M. Bravo b Doherty 16
D. J. Bravo run out 30
K. A. Pollard not out 47
†C. S. Baugh not out 18
B 4, w 2 6

1/0 (1) 2/42 (3) (5 wkts, 38.2 overs) 163
3/67 (2) 4/74 (4)
5/138 (5) 8 overs: 30-1

A. D. Russell, *D. J. G. Sammy, S. P. Narine and K. A. J. Roach did not bat.

Lee 8–1–37–1; McKay 8–2–16–0; Watson 7–1–28–1; D. J. Hussey 3–0–13–0; Christian 5–0–26–0; Doherty 7.2–0–39–1.

Umpires: G. O. Brathwaite and S. K. Tarapore. Third umpire: H. D. P. K. Dharmasena.

WEST INDIES v AUSTRALIA

Third One-Day International

At Arnos Vale, St Vincent, March 20, 2012. Tied. Toss: Australia.

The uproar from the packed stands was deafening when Sammy blasted Lee's third ball of the final over to the long-on boundary to bring the scores level. It was followed by stunned silence as Sammy squeezed the next delivery, a yorker, to point, and last man Roach, eager for the winning run, charged down the pitch. He and his captain were next to each other when Lee calmly gathered Bailey's throw to seal the tie. Free scoring had again proved difficult, yet Australia were well-placed at 170 for three in the 40th over. Then Samuels accounted for Bailey and Hussey after a patient stand of 112; Roach, Narine and a run-out did the rest, as the last six wickets tumbled for 18. However, in spite of 45 from the St Lucian Johnson Charles, West Indies were floundering at 78 for five before the later batsmen took them agonisingly close to victory. When Russell had 31, he was bowled by Watson – but the TV replay showed he had overstepped. Thus granted a free hit, Russell was bowled by the next ball too.

Man of the Match: M. E. K. Hussey.

Australia

*S. R. Watson run out 10
D. A. Warner c Pollard b Sammy 37
†M. S. Wade b Narine 2
G. J. Bailey c D. J. Bravo b Samuels 59
M. E. K. Hussey st Baugh b Samuels 67
D. J. Hussey b Roach 15
D. T. Christian lbw b Narine 12
B. Lee b Roach 0
C. J. McKay c Baugh b Narine 0
X. J. Doherty run out 0
N. M. Lyon not out 4
B 4, l-b 6, w 3, n-b 1 14

1/34 (1) 2/38 (3) 3/58 (2) (49.5 overs) 220
4/170 (4) 5/202 (5) 6/202 (6)
7/203 (8) 8/208 (9) 9/208 (10)
10/220 (7) 10 overs: 38-2

Roach 10–0–42–2; D. J. Bravo 8–1–30–0; Narine 9.5–1–32–3; Sammy 5–0–27–1; Russell 5–0–28–0; Samuels 9–0–39–2; Pollard 3–0–12–0.

West Indies

K. O. A. Powell st Wade b Doherty 12
J. Charles c Christian b Watson 45
M. N. Samuels lbw b Watson 2
D. M. Bravo c Bailey b Watson 0
D. J. Bravo c Wade b Doherty 13
K. A. Pollard c Doherty b Lyon 36
†C. S. Baugh c Christian b McKay 33
A. D. Russell c Wade b McKay 37
*D. J. G. Sammy run out 10
S. P. Narine c D. J. Hussey b Lee 10
K. A. J. Roach not out 9
B 1, l-b 5, w 6, n-b 1 13

1/27 (1) 2/52 (3) 3/52 (4) (49.4 overs) 220
4/72 (2) 5/78 (5) 6/117 (6)
7/181 (8) 8/190 (7) 9/204 (10)
10/220 (9) 10 overs: 45-1

Lee 9.4–1–52–1; McKay 10–1–50–2; Doherty 10–2–30–2; Watson 10–4–30–3; Lyon 8–2–41–1; Christian 2–0–11–0.

Umpires: H. D. P. K. Dharmasena and P. J. Nero. Third umpire: S. K. Tarapore.

WEST INDIES v AUSTRALIA

Fourth One-Day International

At Gros Islet, St Lucia, March 23, 2012. West Indies won by 42 runs. Toss: Australia.

Some characteristically robust hitting by Pollard, who powered eight sixes in his 102 from 70 balls, was aided and abetted by Russell and Sammy as West Indies piled on 117 in their last ten overs. In his first match since the tour of India the previous December, Barath had provided a rousing start, hitting nine fours from 31 balls. Australia regained control, restricting the score to 146 for five in the 36th over, before Pollard and Russell ambushed them with a rapid stand of 94. Only Lee could respond in kind: his one-day best 59, from 48 balls, including five sixes, was some payback for the 72 he conceded from his ten overs. He was struck on the arm by a beamer from Roach (who immediately apologised) and, still simmering, cracked 24 from his next over. But by then it was too late, as Australia – now 2–1 down with one to play – had been fatally stalled by the miserly Narine.

Man of the Match: K. A. Pollard.

West Indies

J. Charles c Lee b Doherty	37
A. B. Barath c Wade b McKay	41
M. N. Samuels c Wade b Lee	11
D. M. Bravo c D. J. Hussey b Watson	25
D. J. Bravo lbw b Doherty	0
K. A. Pollard c M. E. K. Hussey b Lee	102
A. D. Russell c Bailey b Watson	34
*D. J. G. Sammy not out	31
†C. S. Baugh not out	0
L b 3, w 10	13
1/56 (2) 2/83 (3) 3/106 (1) 4/106 (5) 5/146 (4) 6/240 (7) 7/278 (6) (7 wkts, 50 overs)	294
10 overs: 56-0	

S. P. Narine and K. A. J. Roach did not bat.

Lee 10–0–72–2; Hilfenhaus 10–1–43–0; McKay 10–1–57–1; Watson 10–0–55–2; Doherty 10–1–64–2.

Australia

*S. R. Watson c Roach b Sammy	28
D. A. Warner c Narine b D. J. Bravo	1
P. J. Forrest c Charles b Sammy	24
G. J. Bailey c Baugh b Russell	25
M. E. K. Hussey c Baugh b Russell	26
D. J. Hussey b Roach	57
†M. S. Wade c Russell b Pollard	15
B. Lee c sub (G. E. Mathurin) b Roach	59
C. J. McKay c Pollard b D. J. Bravo	2
X. J. Doherty c Sammy b Narine	1
B. W. Hilfenhaus not out	0
L-b 1, w 11, n-b 2	14
1/3 (2) 2/56 (1) 3/62 (3) 4/111 (4) 5/112 (5) 6/179 (7) 7/196 (6) 8/235 (9) 9/250 (10) 10/252 (8) (46.3 overs)	252
10 overs: 62-2	

Roach 9.3–0–74–2; D. J. Bravo 6–0–47–2; Narine 10–0–21–1; Sammy 9–0–42–2; Russell 7–0–34–2; Samuels 3–0–17–0; Pollard 2–0–16–1.

Umpires: G. O. Brathwaite and S. K. Tarapore. Third umpire: H. D. P. K. Dharmasena.

WEST INDIES v AUSTRALIA

Fifth One-Day International

At Gros Islet, St Lucia, March 25, 2012. Australia won by 30 runs. Toss: West Indies.

West Indies' task of overhauling 281 to secure the series was beyond them once Pollard was seventh out in the 32nd over at 118. But there was some consolation for the home crowd in local boy Sammy's ferocious hitting: his highest score in one-day internationals came off only 50 deliveries and featured six sixes. The half-century came up in just 20 balls, equalling his own West Indian record, set against South Africa two years earlier, as he dominated a stand of 101 from less than ten overs with Russell. Australia's sizeable innings had been built around an opening partnership of 118 between Watson and Warner, then Peter Forrest's measured 53. In spite of Sammy's late bombardment, Australia ensured they retained their unbeaten record in bilateral series against West Indies since a 4–1 defeat in the Caribbean in 1994-95. Narine finished the five-match series with 11 wickets and at an economy-rate of just 3.32. Pollard topped the run-charts with 222, at a strike-rate of nearly 99.

Man of the Match: D. J. G. Sammy. *Man of the Series:* K. A. Pollard.

Australia

*S. R. Watson c Samuels b Russell	66	X. J. Doherty not out	1
D. A. Warner c D. J. Bravo b Narine	69	B. W. Hilfenhaus not out	0
P. J. Forrest c Roach b Russell	53		
G. J. Bailey c Russell b Roach	19	B 2, l-b 1, w 7	10
B. Lee b Narine	12		—
M. E. K. Hussey c Pollard b Russell	25	1/118 (2) 2/161 (1) (9 wkts, 50 overs)	281
D. J. Hussey c Baugh b Russell	0	3/193 (4) 4/212 (5)	
†M. S. Wade c D. M. Bravo b Roach	26	5/241 (3) 6/241 (7) 7/279 (6)	
C. J. McKay c D. M. Bravo b Roach	0	8/279 (9) 9/279 (8)	10 overs: 51-0

Roach 9–0–53–3; D. J. Bravo 6–0–40–0; Narine 10–0–55–2; Sammy 6–0–29–0; Russell 9–0–61–4; Samuels 10–0–40–0.

West Indies

J. Charles c and b Lee	0	S. P. Narine c Wade b McKay	7
A. B. Barath c Bailey b Doherty	42	K. A. J. Roach not out	2
M. N. Samuels c Wade b Lee	0		
D. M. Bravo c Wade b McKay	3		
D. J. Bravo c Bailey b Watson	19	L-b 1, w 6	7
K. A. Pollard c M. E. K. Hussey b Watson	33		—
†C. S. Baugh c Hilfenhaus b Lee	13	1/0 (1) 2/5 (3) 3/37 (4) (47.2 overs)	251
A. D. Russell lbw b Doherty	41	4/63 (5) 5/76 (2) 6/111 (7)	
*D. J. G. Sammy c M. E. K. Hussey b Hilfenhaus	84	7/118 (6) 8/219 (8) 9/232 (10)	
		10/251 (9)	10 overs: 27-2

Lee 9–3–42–3; Hilfenhaus 8.2–1–36–1; McKay 10–0–68–2; Watson 10–0–44–2; Doherty 10–0–60–2.

Umpires: H. D. P. K. Dharmasena and P. J. Nero. Third umpire: S. K. Tarapore.
Series referee: A. J. Pycroft.

WEST INDIES v AUSTRALIA

First Twenty20 International

At Gros Islet, St Lucia, March 27, 2012. Australia won by eight wickets. Toss: West Indies. Twenty20 international debut: S. P. Narine.

West Indies made a sedate start to reach 66 for three in the 11th over. And though Pollard reached his first fifty in Twenty20 internationals, plundering four sixes and two fours in the 16th and 17th overs alone – including an enormous straight blow off Doherty that ended up on top of the stand – the eventual total was not too daunting. Warner was bowled by the fifth ball of Australia's innings, from the Jamaican left-arm seamer Krishmar Santokie, but there were no further alarms as Watson and Mike Hussey added 108 in 12.5 overs. Bailey, one of Australia's three captains on the tour, supplied the finishing touches.

Man of the Match: S. R. Watson.

West Indies

		B	4	6
J. Charles *lbw b 2*	24	16	4	0
D. R. Smith *c 6 b 8*	10	10	2	0
N. E. Bonner *b 7*	24	33	2	0
D. M. Bravo *c 10 b 7*	12	14	2	0
K. A. Pollard *not out*	54	26	2	5
D. J. Bravo *c 5 b 7*	14	11	1	0
*D. J. G. Sammy *c 5 b 8*	7	8	1	0
†C. S. Baugh *run out*	1	1	0	0
G. E. Mathurin *not out*	1	1	0	0
L-b 1, w 2	3			

6 overs: 38-1 (20 overs) 150-7

1/19 2/38 3/66 4/72 5/134 6/144 7/148

K. Santokie and S. P. Narine did not bat.

Lee 4–0–30–2; Pattinson 3–0–21–0; McKay 3–0–21–0; Watson 4–0–16–1; Doherty 3–0–34–0; Christian 3–0–27–3.

Australia

		B	4	6
D. A. Warner *b 10*	0	5	0	0
S. R. Watson *c 5 b 9*	69	43	5	6
M. E. K. Hussey *not out*	59	45	4	2
*G. J. Bailey *not out*	21	17	2	0
L-b 1, w 2, n-b 1	4			

6 overs: 52-1 (18.1 overs) 153-2

1/0 2/108

D. J. Hussey, †M. S. Wade, D. T. Christian, B. Lee, C. J. McKay, J. L. Pattinson and X. J. Doherty did not bat.

Santokie 3–0–27–1; Mathurin 4–0–33–1; Narine 4–0–21–0; Sammy 2.1–0–22–0; D. J. Bravo 3–0–21–0; Pollard 1–0–16–0; Smith 1–0–12–0.

Umpires: G. O. Brathwaite and P. J. Nero. Third umpire: N. Duguid.

WEST INDIES v AUSTRALIA

Second Twenty20 International

At Bridgetown, Barbados, March 30, 2012. West Indies won by 14 runs. Toss: West Indies.

A West Indian total in excess of 200 looked possible when Dwayne Smith and Charles began with a partnership of 72 off 6.4 overs. Sammy tinkered with the order, promoting Pollard to No. 3 and himself to No. 5; though that particular tactic failed, West Indies still ended up with enough. Australia kept the target in sight, but Dwayne Bravo rightly identified the turning-point as his direct hit from midwicket in the 13th over to run out the threatening Warner. It typified West Indies' electrifying fielding. The pace of Edwards, Bravo's variations and the spin of Samuels did the rest.

Man of the Match: D. R. Smith. *Man of the Series:* S. R. Watson.

West Indies

		B	4	6
D. R. Smith *c 5 b 11*	63	34	6	4
J. Charles *c 7 b 2*	37	21	6	1
K. A. Pollard *c 6 b 8*	1	3	0	0
D. J. Bravo *c 7 b 2*	23	24	0	0
*D. J. G. Sammy *b 9*	5	9	0	0
D. P. Hyatt *c 3 b 9*	6	7	1	0
M. N. Samuels *c 1 b 7*	2	3	0	0
†C. S. Baugh *c 6 b 8*	7	9	1	0
S. P. Narine *run out*	2	4	0	0
G. E. Mathurin *not out*	3	4	0	0
F. H. Edwards *b 8*	0	1	0	0
L-b 1, w 9, n-b 1	11			

6 overs: 65-0 (19.4 overs) 160

1/72 2/80 3/110 4/120 5/134 6/140 7/155 8/155 9/159

Pattinson 2–0–34–0; Lee 3.4–0–23–3; McKay 4–0–24–2; Doherty 3–0–32–1; Watson 4–0–26–2; Christian 3–0–20–1.

Australia

		B	4	6
D. A. Warner *run out*	58	43	5	3
S. R. Watson *c 5 b 11*	0	2	0	0
*G. J. Bailey *c 6 b 7*	24	18	2	1
M. E. K. Hussey *c and b 7*	14	10	0	1
D. J. Hussey *c 3 b 4*	19	15	1	1
†M. S. Wade *c and b 7*	17	20	1	1
D. T. Christian *c 5 b 11*	3	3	0	0
B. Lee *b 11*	0	1	0	0
C. J. McKay *b 4*	7	7	0	1
J. L. Pattinson *not out*	0	0	0	0
X. J. Doherty *not out*	2	1	0	0
W 2	2			

6 overs: 53-1 (20 overs) 146-9

1/1 2/64 3/89 4/98 5/133 6/136 7/136 8/144 9/144

Edwards 4–0–23–3; Narine 4–0–33–0; Mathurin 2–0–23–0; Sammy 1–0–11–0; Bravo 4–0–27–2; Samuels 4–0–23–3; Pollard 1–0–6–0.

Umpires: P. J. Nero and J. S. Wilson. Third umpire: N. Duguid. Series referee: A. J. Pycroft.

At Bridgetown (Three Ws Oval), Barbados, April 2–4, 2012 (not first-class). **Australians won by eight wickets. ‡West Indies Cricket Board President's XI 201** (K. O. A. Powell 42, D. R. Smith 62, J. O. Holder 49; R. J. Harris 4-23, M. A. Beer 4-41) **and 98** (B. W. Hilfenhaus 4-8, N. M. Lyon 4-17); **Australians 214** (S. R. Watson 42, M. J. Clarke 30, P. J. Forrest 53*; R. A. Austin 3-43, N. E. Bonner 3-43) **and 87-2.** *Both sides included 12 players, of whom 11 could bat and 11 field. On the first day the President's XI declined to 78-6, before Dwayne Smith and Jason Holder put on 103 in 20 overs. The Australians also struggled with the bat on a slow, grassless pitch, before demolishing the President's XI again. The highest score in their second innings was Carlton Baugh's 27*; the last four wickets fell for two runs. The tourists needed only 14.5 overs to complete victory on the third morning.*

TEST MATCH REPORTS BY DANIEL BRETTIG

WEST INDIES v AUSTRALIA

First Test Match

At Bridgetown, Barbados, April 7–11, 2012. Australia won by three wickets. Toss: West Indies. Test debut: M. S. Wade.

Australia won a slow-burning, ultimately thrilling, Test because they never stopped believing. West Indies, so unfamiliar with Test wins and the confidence they can instil, showed the fragility that had cost them in India in November, and allowed the Australians – behind for vast tracts of the match – to burst past them at the finish.

West Indies, still without Chris Gayle, had bade farewell to a bevy of their best one-day performers, before they convened in Barbados; Australia's batsmen were especially happy to see the back of Sunil Narine, who was off to the IPL. But in spite of the personnel they had lost, West Indies made a sturdy start. The Barbadian opener Kraigg Brathwaite frustrated the Australians in a stay of over four and a half hours, Kirk Edwards showed plenty of power before becoming the first Test victim of Warner's occasional leg-spin, and Darren Bravo played attractively. The tail then lingered in the company of Chanderpaul, who offered his customary mixture of deflections and dynamism, all wrapped up in a technique as comfortable on the docile Kensington pitch as a tourist on the local beaches. It was his 25th Test hundred.

The innings meandered and, with his pacemen failing to find the right lines or lengths, Clarke tried eight bowlers in 153 overs, before Sammy allowed himself the rare luxury of a declaration, West Indies' first against Australia in 21 years. All 11 batsmen reached double figures – the 12th such instance in Tests, but the first by West Indies. A total of 449 seemed large enough, and accumulated over enough time, at least to insure against defeat; Australia's early struggles did little to quell the notion.

They found it difficult to score at any great pace, a succession of batsmen scraping around before succumbing to the speed of Roach and Fidel Edwards or the parsimony of Sammy. Ponting was chaotically run out, with Watson (in his first innings at No. 3) later admitting his guilt over the mix-up. Bishoo struggled for traction in what turned out to be a poor match for specialist spinners on both sides but, at 285 for eight, Australia were in serious trouble.

Harris, though, had long promised more with the bat than his modest Test record indicated, and found determined partners in Hilfenhaus and Lyon. Between them, they dragged the innings towards 400, helped by an extended morning session on the fourth day: it started half an hour early because of previous delays for bad light, and lunch was then put back by 30 minutes because the last pair were still together. Sammy's bowlers grew weary in the three-hour session, and Harris and Lyon grew in confidence in an unbroken stand of 77. An Australian declaration became West Indies' most likely means of getting off the field. When Clarke called his men in – following Test-bests for both Harris and Lyon – they still trailed by 43. With the exception of the leather-jacket match at Centurion in 1999-2000, with its two blank innings, only one team had ever won a Test after declaring behind: England beat West Indies at this very venue on a rain-affected pitch in 1934-35.

DOUBLES ALL ROUND!

All 11 batsmen reaching double figures in a Test innings:

England (475) v Australia at Melbourne	1894-95
South Africa (385) v England at Johannesburg	1905-06
England (636) v Australia at Sydney	1928-29
South Africa (358) v Australia at Melbourne	1930-31
Australia (575-8 dec†) v India at Melbourne	1947-48
India (397) v Pakistan at Calcutta	1952-53
India (359) v New Zealand at Dunedin	1967-68
India (524-9 dec) v New Zealand at Kanpur	1976-77
Australia (471) v Sri Lanka at Colombo (SSC)	1992-93
England (470) v West Indies at The Oval	2004
India (664) v England at The Oval	2007
West Indies (449-9 dec) v Australia at Bridgetown	**2011-12**

† *One batsman retired hurt.*

The momentum now was Australia's, and Clarke bravely reasoned that, with a shade over four sessions to go, he had little to lose. Things turned out rather better than that. Asked to bat for half an hour before tea, West Indies wilted against Hilfenhaus, who showed he had learned from the first day by pitching full and straight. Barath aimed a drive and lost his leg stump, Brathwaite swished unnecessarily outside off to be taken behind by the debutant Matthew Wade, and Kirk Edwards shuffled across and was lbw in a manner that would become familiar to English observers later in the year.

After the break, Harris collected the most critical scalp of all, angling the ball in from round the wicket and darting it away to send back Chanderpaul; Siddle then snuffed out a brief rally from Bravo before the close, which West Indies reached with a lead of 114 but only five wickets in hand. A series of nuisance-value lower-order stands soaked up time on the final morning, setting Australia 192 from 62 overs. It would test both their ability to score quickly on a wearing surface and the limits of light that had faded early on every day of the Test.

Clarke's plan called for the preservation of wickets up to tea, which was taken at 61 for one from 22 overs, and a headlong pursuit thereafter. Cowan dropped anchor – to the irritation of a section of fans – and Watson played aggressively for a 57-ball 52. He became the first of four quick wickets for Deonarine's gentle off-spin, including Cowan after 100 balls and just one boundary, but Sammy's subsequent field-placings suggested West Indies' priority remained salvaging a draw. Australia, by contrast, stayed focused on victory, and now Hussey and Wade put together a partnership of infinitely greater value than the 37 runs it accrued, steadying the innings while also rushing it forward.

Roach removed Wade with 15 needed, and Hussey with only three to go, but the winning runs came as the sun hid behind the Hall and Griffith Stand. Australia celebrated proudly, and in full view of a disconsolate Sammy, who promised to remember their jubilation. Clarke found parallels with the 2006-07 Adelaide Ashes Test, when Shane Warne had insisted the match would be won from similarly unpromising beginnings. "As a young player I thought: 'Righto, that's my attitude, I'm going to win.' A few years on and I'm in the change-rooms telling the boys we're going to win this Test match," said Clarke. "Hopefully a few of them believed me the way I believed Warnie back then."

Man of the Match: R. J. Harris.

Close of play: First day, West Indies 179-3 (Bravo 20, Chanderpaul 8); Second day, Australia 44-0 (Cowan 13, Warner 27); Third day, Australia 248-5 (Hussey 47, Wade 19); Fourth day, West Indies 71-5 (Deonarine 20, Baugh 2).

West Indies

A. B. Barath c Siddle b Harris	22	– b Hilfenhaus	2
K. C. Brathwaite c Wade b Siddle	57	– c Wade b Hilfenhaus	0
K. A. Edwards c and b Warner	61	– lbw b Hilfenhaus	1
D. M. Bravo c Hussey b Watson	51	– c Wade b Siddle	32
S. Chanderpaul not out	103	– c Wade b Harris	12
N. Deonarine c Wade b Harris	21	– lbw b Harris	21
†C. S. Baugh run out	22	c Harris b Hilfenhaus	23
*D. J. G. Sammy c Cowan b Hilfenhaus	41	– b Watson	14
K. A. J. Roach c Clarke b Lyon	16	– b Harris	25
F. H. Edwards c Hussey b Warner	10	– c Watson b Siddle	3
D. Bishoo not out	18	– not out	7
B 12, l-b 9, w 4, n-b 2	27	B 4, l-b 3, n-b 1	8
1/38 (1) 2/142 (3) 3/167 (2) 4/240 (4) 5/285 (6) 6/316 (7) 7/369 (8) 8/402 (9) 9/421 (10) (9 wkts dec, 153 overs)	449	1/2 (1) 2/3 (2) 3/4 (3) 4/17 (5) 5/67 (4) 6/75 (6) 7/106 (8) 8/116 (7) 9/125 (10) 10/148 (9) (66.4 overs)	148

Harris 29–8–83–2; Hilfenhaus 33–12–67–1; Siddle 31–10–83–1; Lyon 31–11–94–1; Clarke 2–0–4–0; Watson 15–5–46–1; Warner 10–0–45–2; Hussey 2–0–6–0. *Second Innings*—Hilfenhaus 17–7–27–4; Watson 12–1–30–1; Harris 8.4–2–31–3; Siddle 17–2–32–2; Lyon 11–4–19–0; Clarke 1–0–2–0.

Australia

E. J. M. Cowan c Baugh b Sammy	14	– (2) c Chanderpaul b Deonarine	34
D. A. Warner c Bravo b Sammy	42	– (1) c Baugh b Sammy	22
S. R. Watson c Baugh b Roach	39	– c sub (K. O. A. Powell) b Deonarine	52
R. T. Ponting run out	4	– b Deonarine	14
*M. J. Clarke c Deonarine b Bishoo	73	– c and b Deonarine	6
M. E. K. Hussey c Baugh b Roach	48	– b Roach	32
†M. S. Wade c Bravo b F. H. Edwards	28	– c Bishoo b Roach	18
P. M. Siddle c K. A. Edwards b F. H. Edwards	0		
R. J. Harris not out	68	– (8) not out	4
B. W. Hilfenhaus b Roach	24	– (9) not out	2
N. M. Lyon not out	40		
L-b 16, w 5, n-b 5	26	B 1, l-b 3, w 2, n-b 2	8
1/50 (1) 2/65 (2) 3/84 (4) 4/133 (3) 5/215 (5) 6/249 (6) 7/250 (8) 8/285 (7) 9/329 (10) (9 wkts dec, 145 overs)	406	1/31 (1) 2/106 (3) 3/126 (2) 4/131 (4) 5/140 (5) 6/177 (7) 7/189 (6) (7 wkts, 47 overs)	192

F. H. Edwards 31–4–92–2; Roach 29–8–72–3; Bishoo 45–10–125–1; Sammy 21–6–65–2; Deonarine 19–5–36–0. *Second Innings*—Roach 12–0–45–2; F. H. Edwards 6–0–19–0; Sammy 10–2–27–1; Bishoo 8–0–44–0; Deonarine 11–1–53–4.

Umpires: I. J. Gould and A. L. Hill. Third umpire: M. Erasmus.

WEST INDIES v AUSTRALIA

Second Test Match

At Port-of-Spain, Trinidad, April 15–19, 2012. Drawn. Toss: Australia.

Rain had the final say in a contest that was enticingly poised, ensuring Australia retained the Frank Worrell Trophy they had held for 17 years. The Queen's Park Oval pitch was subcontinental in nature, drawing comparisons from Australia's coach Mickey Arthur with Green Park at Kanpur, and turned from the first session. Australia recalled slow left-armer Michael Beer for his second Test, more than 15 months after his first, against England at Sydney, and thus chose two specialist spinners for the first time since Nagpur in 2008-09. They also recalled Pattinson, leaving out Siddle (injured) and Harris, Man of the Match in Barbados but rested by fitness staff concerned about his capacity to survive back-to-back Tests. West Indies lost Kirk Edwards to a knee problem, and drafted in Kieran Powell.

Clarke did not contain his happiness at winning the toss and batting first, but his own struggles – he needed more than two hours to make 45 – typified Australia's approach against an attack that stuck diligently to their task and used the conditions wisely. Shillingford, replacing the out-of-sorts Bishoo, struck in his first over when Warner walked into a drive and snicked an off-break to slip. Roach was all unbridled attack at one end, and did for Ponting with a snorter which Sammy caught at first slip on the rebound from Baugh, while Deonarine again proved an able addition to the bowling ranks. Hussey spent four hours over his 73, and later said he had seldom felt so drained. His seventh-wicket partnership of 89 with Pattinson helped the innings stagger past 300.

Clarke's knack for the lateral was demonstrated again when he handed the new ball to Beer, who became the first Australian spinner to open the bowling in the opposition's first innings since 1938, when leg-spinner Bill O'Reilly partnered Ernie McCormick at Trent Bridge. Charlie Barnett and Len Hutton opened up with 219 that day, but Beer did his unusual commission justice by trapping Barath in his third over, while Hilfenhaus and Pattinson prospered at the other end. Before the second day was out, however, Pattinson wrenched his back while throwing off-balance, and did not bowl again.

The third day's resumption was delayed for 20 minutes, in bright sunshine, when the host broadcaster's two generators cut out at precisely the scheduled start time. The players, umpires and match referee discussed the implications of playing on without any recourse to the DRS (there was also a contractual issue concerning the absence of a live TV feed). But by the time they agreed the show could go on, power had been restored.

Chanderpaul and Deonarine batted deep into the day as West Indies reached 230 for four, and they were just beginning to think in terms of a lead when Lyon got to work. Previously his rhythm had been lacking and his body action out of sync, but now he fizzed out five batsmen in the evening session: suddenly, West Indies trailed by 54. Wade also emerged with credit, claiming a catch and a stumping, and – on a pitch that produced sharp spin and low bounce – conceding only a single bye in 104.4 overs.

Australia's efforts to set a target quickly were then upset by Roach and the rain. Roach's menace on a pitch far from suited to his art was considerable, and his ten-wicket haul was the first by a West Indian against Australia since Curtly Ambrose at Adelaide in 1992-93, a match West Indies won by one run. Roach said he had been inspired by Malcolm Marshall, who would have been 54 on the fourth day of this game, and whose skiddy supremacy had informed Roach's methods.

The weather drained more time from the match, dragging Australia's innings into the final day and reducing the chance of a result. Clarke remained aggressive in pursuit of a win, and ultimately set West Indies a tantalising 215 in 59 overs. Sammy responded to the challenge by promoting himself to No. 3, and was hitting out effectively before the rain closed in for good. Whether he could have sustained the assault for any meaningful length of time was a question which, frustratingly, was left hanging in the damp air.

Man of the Match: K. A. J. Roach.

Close of play: First day, Australia 208-5 (Hussey 26, Wade 11); Second day, West Indies 49-3 (Bravo 16, Chanderpaul 1); Third day, West Indies 252-9 (Baugh 17, Edwards 0); Fourth day, Australia 73-3 (Ponting 32, Clarke 3).

Australia

First innings		Second innings	
D. A. Warner c Sammy b Shillingford	29	– (2) c Bravo b Roach	17
E. J. M. Cowan lbw b Roach	28	– (1) lbw b Roach	20
S. R. Watson c Barath b Shillingford	56	– b Roach	0
R. T. Ponting c Sammy b Roach	7	– c Powell b Edwards	41
*M. J. Clarke c Shillingford b Deonarine	45	– c and b Sammy	15
M. E. K. Hussey c Brathwaite b Deonarine	73	– b Roach	24
†M. S. Wade c Bravo b Roach	11	– not out	31
J. L. Pattinson c Bravo b Shillingford	32		
B. W. Hilfenhaus b Roach	5	– (8) b Roach	0
N. M. Lyon not out	7	– (9) c Sammy b Shillingford	3
M. A. Beer lbw b Roach	2		
B 5, l-b 5, w 1, n-b 5	16	B 4, l-b 1, w 1, n-b 3	9
1/53 (1) 2/65 (2) 3/83 (4) (135 overs)	311	1/26 (2) (8 wkts dec, 61.5 overs)	160
4/167 (5) 5/178 (3) 6/208 (7)		2/26 (3) 3/57 (1)	
7/297 (6) 8/297 (8) 9/309 (9) 10/311 (11)		4/93 (4) 5/95 (5) 6/145 (6)	
		7/149 (8) 8/160 (9)	

Edwards 23–11–45–0; Roach 27–5–105–5; Sammy 16–6–27–0; Shillingford 49–17–92–3; Deonarine 20–6–32–2. *Second Innings*—Edwards 10–2–28–1; Shillingford 23.5–4–55–1; Roach 18–4–41–5; Sammy 8–0–17–1; Deonarine 2–0–14–0.

West Indies

First innings		Second innings	
A. B. Barath lbw b Beer	7	– c Clarke b Hilfenhaus	5
K. C. Brathwaite lbw b Hilfenhaus	0		
K. O. A. Powell lbw b Pattinson	19	– (2) lbw b Hilfenhaus	4
D. M. Bravo lbw b Hussey	38	– not out	8
S. Chanderpaul lbw b Lyon	94		
N. Deonarine st Wade b Lyon	55		
†C. S. Baugh lbw b Beer	21		
*D. J. G. Sammy c Hussey b Lyon	1	– (3) not out	30
S. Shillingford c Cowan b Lyon	4		
K. A. J. Roach c Wade b Lyon	0		
F. H. Edwards not out	0		
B 1, l-b 8, w 1, n-b 8	18	B 6	6
1/0 (2) 2/26 (1) 3/38 (3) (104.4 overs)	257	1/6 (2) 2/13 (1) (2 wkts, 11 overs)	53
4/100 (4) 5/230 (6) 6/231 (5)			
7/237 (8) 8/241 (9) 9/249 (10) 10/257 (7)			

Beer 25.4–9–56–2; Hilfenhaus 16–4–39–1; Lyon 29–9–68–5; Pattinson 11–2–40–1; Hussey 6–1–19–1; Watson 12–5–14–0; Warner 3–1–9–0; Clarke 2–0–3–0. *Second Innings*—Beer 4–1–10–0; Hilfenhaus 4–0–22–2; Watson 3–1–15–0.

Umpires: M. Erasmus and I. J. Gould. Third umpire: A. L. Hill.

WEST INDIES v AUSTRALIA

Third Test Match

At Roseau, Dominica, April 23–27, 2012. Australia won by 75 runs. Toss: Australia.

A match originally scheduled for Guyana, then taken away by the West Indies Cricket Board because of political interference in the country's own board, proved a mixed blessing for the people of Dominica, whose celebrations at their compatriot Shane

Shillingford's ten-wicket haul were cut short by Australia's series-clinching victory. Not since 1966 had a West Indies spinner taken ten or more in a Test, prompting discussion that Shillingford – the first Dominican to play a Test at home – would join former seamer Norbert Phillip and umpire Billy Doctrove in having his name attached to one of Windsor Park's stands. But the main plaudits were Australia's, as they again overcame unfamiliar conditions and a determined opposition to secure a 2–0 triumph.

They owed their win largely to a startling century from Wade, who pushed Australia's first innings to heights West Indies were unable to reach. A total of 328 had looked distant on the first afternoon, as Shillingford found bounce and quick turn to follow up the recalled Rampaul's second-over defeat of Cowan. Hands that had crept lower and lower over several weeks were now stung by off-breaks and top-spinners that leapt on to the gloves, creating chances that Sammy and his fellow close fielders claimed with glee.

Australia were in trouble at 169 for seven after Roach chipped in with the wicket of Harris, but they regathered ground through Starc, who had replaced the injured Pattinson, before Wade converted his overnight 22 into something special on the second morning. His first 50 occupied a sturdy 110 balls, his second – including three sixes, two in

BEST FIGURES IN A TEST BY A WEST INDIES SPINNER

11-152	S. Ramadhin	v England at Lord's	1950
11-157	L. R. Gibbs	v England at Manchester	1963
11-204†	A. L. Valentine	v England at Manchester	1950
11-229	W. Ferguson	v England at Port-of-Spain	1947-48
10-106	L. R. Gibbs	v England at Manchester	1966
10-160	A. L. Valentine	v England at The Oval	1950
10-219	**S. Shillingford**	**v Australia at Roseau**	**2011-12**

† *On Test debut.*

succession off Shillingford – a breakneck 33. Partnerships of 57 with Starc, then 102 for the ninth wicket with Hilfenhaus (who eventually became Shillingford's sixth victim), almost doubled the score, and knocked West Indies near-senseless.

Their reply was immediately unsteadied by the loss of Brathwaite, caught up in a poor run that would cost him a place on the tour of England. After a brief rally by Barath and Powell, Lyon struck twice before Warner produced a perfect leg-break to dispose of Bravo. At 120 for eight, West Indies were in danger of following on and, although Chanderpaul – who batted nearly four hours – added 66 with Rampaul and 32 with Roach, the eventual deficit of 110 still felt decisive.

Cowan and Ponting – Australia's least prolific batsmen of the series – built on the advantage with a pair of blue-collar half-centuries, while Shillingford completed his ten-wicket haul and Roach continued to harry the batsmen. But a target of 370 was well beyond the ambitions of any team on a turning pitch, let alone of a West Indies side prone to collapse.

Sure enough, they made another deflating start. Hilfenhaus nabbed Barath with swing and bounce, before Clarke chose the right moment for the most substantial bowling stint of his captaincy so far. Noting that Lyon was flagging a little, Clarke whirred his slow left-armers into the pitch and was soon spinning it enough to confound Brathwaite, Powell and, pivotally, Chanderpaul, who had earlier become only the tenth batsman – and the second West Indian, after Brian Lara – to pass 10,000 Test runs. But he fell on referral to what became the final ball of the fourth day after initially surviving a shout for leg-before. Australia had used the system far more shrewdly than West Indies throughout, prompting their coach Ottis Gibson to complain in Trinidad about its use by the umpires. An ICC fine swiftly followed.

The final day of the series promised little, but ultimately offered up a microcosm of all the cricket that had preceded it. West Indies fought doughtily, but without ever suggesting they were going to win. Sammy's 51-ball 61 at least provided rich entertainment for another bountiful crowd, before Clarke – with his second Test five-for, more than seven years after the first – and Lyon mopped up. For West Indies there was a sense of recurring themes. They had pushed India in similar fashion in two series the previous year, but seemed not much wiser for having done so.

Man of the Match: M. S. Wade. *Man of the Series:* S. Chanderpaul.

Close of play: First day, Australia 212-7 (Wade 22, Starc 24); Second day, West Indies 165-8 (Chanderpaul 34, Rampaul 24); Third day, Australia 200-6 (Hussey 17, Harris 4); Fourth day, West Indies 173-5 (Deonarine 11).

Australia

First innings		Second innings	
E. J. M. Cowan lbw b Rampaul	1	– (2) c Sammy b Deonarine	55
D. A. Warner c Powell b Shillingford	50	– (1) c Chanderpaul b Roach	11
S. R. Watson c Deonarine b Sammy	41	– c Sammy b Shillingford	5
R. T. Ponting c Sammy b Shillingford	23	– c Chanderpaul b Roach	57
*M. J. Clarke c Barath b Shillingford	24	– c Bravo b Shillingford	25
M. E. K. Hussey c Sammy b Shillingford	10	– c Sammy b Shillingford	32
†M. S. Wade c Bravo b Shillingford	106	– lbw b Deonarine	4
R. J. Harris c Baugh b Roach	4	– c Baugh b Deonarine	9
M. A. Starc run out	35	– b Roach	21
B. W. Hilfenhaus b Shillingford	19	– c Brathwaite b Shillingford	6
N. M. Lyon not out	0	– not out	12
B 4, l-b 6, w 3, n-b 2	15	B 8, l-b 9, w 1, n-b 4	22
1/1 (1) 2/84 (3) 3/105 (2) 4/142 (4) 5/157 (5) 6/164 (6) 7/169 (8) 8/226 (9) 9/328 (7) 10/328 (10) (114.5 overs)	328	1/17 (1) 2/25 (3) 3/112 (2) 4/168 (4) 5/171 (5) 6/196 (7) 7/220 (6) 8/230 (8) 9/237 (10) 10/259 (9) (85 overs)	259

Roach 23–5–72–1; Rampaul 24–6–65–1; Sammy 21–7–48–1; Shillingford 42.5–9–119–6; Deonarine 4–0–14–0. *Second Innings*—Rampaul 9–1–37–0; Roach 13–2–40–3; Shillingford 39–7–100–4; Sammy 10–4–20–0; Deonarine 14–1–45–3.

West Indies

First innings		Second innings	
A. B. Barath c Cowan b Lyon	29	– c Cowan b Hilfenhaus	0
K. C. Brathwaite c Harris b Hilfenhaus	0	– lbw b Clarke	14
K. O. A. Powell b Lyon	40	– b Clarke	24
D. M. Bravo c Cowan b Warner	10	– c Wade b Watson	45
S. Chanderpaul lbw b Starc	68	– lbw b Clarke	69
N. Deonarine lbw b Harris	7	– c and b Clarke	13
†C. S. Baugh c Cowan b Lyon	5	– c Ponting b Lyon	12
*D. J. G. Sammy run out	10	– c Hilfenhaus b Lyon	61
S. Shillingford b Starc	0	– (11) not out	31
R. Rampaul c Warner b Lyon	31	– c Warner b Clarke	11
K. A. J. Roach not out	9	– (9) c Clarke b Lyon	2
B 1, l-b 2, w 1, n-b 5	9	B 3, l-b 9	12
1/1 (2) 2/62 (1) 3/73 (4) 4/85 (3) 5/96 (6) 6/103 (7) 7/120 (8) 8/120 (9) 9/186 (10) 10/218 (5) (87.2 overs)	218	1/0 (1) 2/28 (2) 3/45 (3) 4/155 (4) 5/173 (5) 6/180 (6) 7/206 (7) 8/234 (9) 9/245 (10) 10/294 (8) (96.3 overs)	294

Hilfenhaus 18–6–30–1; Starc 12.2–4–29–2; Harris 13–0–36–1; Watson 4–0–12–0; Lyon 33–7–69–4; Warner 5–0–21–1; Clarke 2–0–18–0. *Second Innings*—Hilfenhaus 13–5–23–1; Starc 9–2–26–0; Lyon 29.3–6–87–3; Harris 12–2–34–0; Clarke 23–1–86–5; Watson 9–2–20–1; Warner 1–0–6–0.

Umpires: M. Erasmus and A. L. Hill. Third umpire: I. J. Gould.
Series referee: J. J. Crowe.

WEST INDIES v NEW ZEALAND, 2012

TONY COZIER

Test matches (2): West Indies 2, New Zealand 0
One-day internationals (5): West Indies 4, New Zealand 1
Twenty20 internationals (2): West Indies 2, New Zealand 0

Even at the peak of their powers in the 1980s, West Indies rarely dominated a team as categorically as this. Hosting New Zealand for the first time in ten years, they won both Tests, four of the five one-day internationals and both Twenty20 internationals (staged on neutral ground in Florida). West Indies had not won a Test series by two clear matches – other than against Zimbabwe or Bangladesh – since 1997-98, when they beat England 3–1 at home. This, then, was heady stuff. But for New Zealand it was nothing short of a disaster: they began the Test and one-day series ahead of West Indies in the respective rankings, and slipped behind them in both.

New Zealand accumulated as many problems off the field as on it, a situation with which West Indies could identify. Before departing for the Caribbean, their former opening batsman John Wright announced it was to be his last tour as coach, following the appointment of John Buchanan as director of cricket and Kim Littlejohn, another Australian, as national selection manager. A personality clash was at the root of the problem; neither did it help when Wright proposed a pre-tour camp for the team, only for Buchanan to knock it back as too costly.

There were signs of rustiness as New Zealand began their first series in three months without playing a warm-up match. As Wright handed over to his successor, Mike Hesson, he attacked an individual lack of responsibility. "You just can't come off and wave a dismissal away with phrases like 'it's the way I play' and 'I didn't quite execute'," he said. "It's a brutal game at international level and you have to be very brutal in your self-analysis."

New Zealand were so badly let down by their batting that their only hundred was captain Ross Taylor's 110 in the fourth one-day game – and they lost even that. And when all they needed in Kingston was a reasonable second-innings effort, to convert a lead of 51 into a series-saving victory, they folded for 154 – the sort of performance usually turned in at that stage of a match by West Indies. Only Martin Guptill, the tall opener, emerged with reputation intact after Test scores of 97, 67, 71 and 42. Their two most experienced bowlers, Daniel Vettori and Chris Martin, made little impression in the First Test; Vettori was eliminated from the Second by a groin injury, while Martin was dropped. Their fielding, historically a strength, let them down. The one plus was their young pace attack, but they never had enough runs to play with.

West Indies were strengthened by Chris Gayle's return at the top of the order, not to mention the peaceful conclusion of his 15-month stand-off with the board. Back after his globetrotting exploits in the IPL and other lucrative franchise tournaments, Gayle smashed 85 not out and 53 in the Twenty20

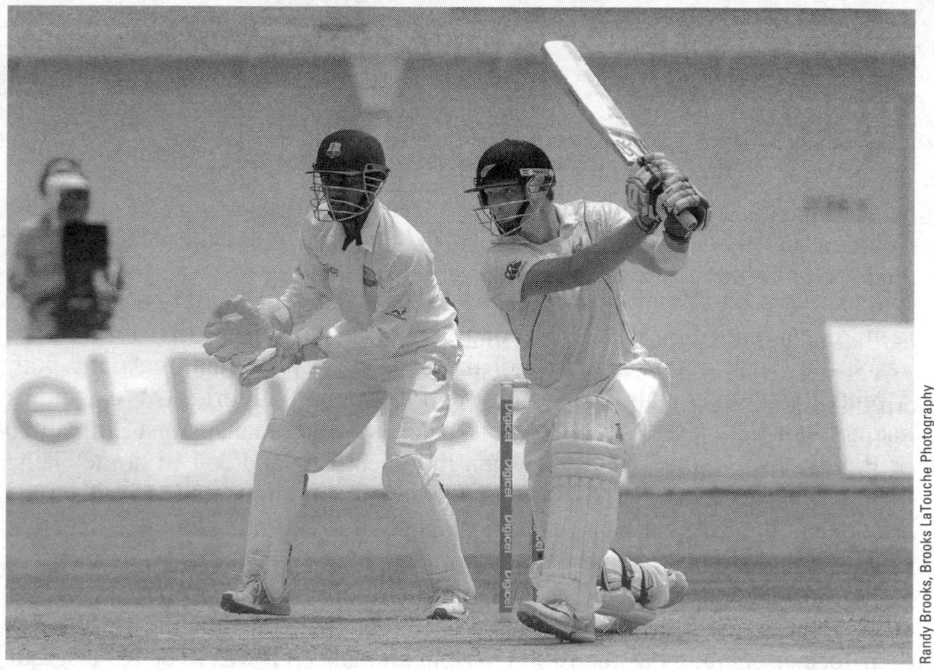

Randy Brooks, Brooks LaTouche Photography

Slim pickings: Martin Guptill gave New Zealand a start in every Test innings, but to no avail.

matches, marked his first international appearance in his native Kingston for three years with 63 not out and 125 in the two 50-over matches there, then compiled 150 and an unbeaten 64 to seal victory in the Antigua Test, his first since December 2010.

The availability of off-spinner Sunil Narine for an entire tour for the first time was also crucial. After a disappointing trip to England, he was as mesmerising in the shorter formats as he had been in the IPL, with seven wickets for 46 in his eight Twenty20 overs, and 13 wickets at 11 and an economy rate of 2.92 in the one-day internationals. He had to work harder in the Tests, but was always a threat.

West Indies' success did not revolve entirely around the IPL superstars. Darren Sammy, the captain, described it as a "one-for-all, all-for-one mission". Marlon Samuels, continuing his sublime form from the Tests in England, stroked two hundreds in front of his fellow Jamaicans at Sabina Park. His 123 out of 209 in the Second Test was especially memorable, and was followed by a nerve-steadying 52 when West Indies were stuttering in their quest for 206.

Kemar Roach, consistently fast and capable of a destructive spell, was Man of the Series for his 12 Test wickets, and would have had a couple more but for recurrent overstepping. When Narine was below-par in Jamaica, Narsingh Deonarine, an underrated off-spinner, took up the slack; with the bat, both he and his fellow Guyanese left-hander Assad Fudadin filled the breach left by Darren Bravo's absence through injury and Shivnarine Chanderpaul's loss of form. Kieran Powell, the 22-year-old opener, followed in Gayle's wake to his first Test hundred, in an opening partnership of 254 in Antigua.

The two Twenty20 internationals at the compact Central Broward Regional Park in Lauderhill were West Indies' first venture into the United States – and, many thought, an overdue one. The 8,000 or so who turned out for each match in sweltering heat were almost exclusively relocated West Indians, sporting more of their team's replica shirts than are usually seen at any home venue. The few conspicuous Americans wore flak jackets marked "sheriff" and kept menacing, if redundant, guns in their holsters. Two comfortable West Indies victories and the 25 sixes they clubbed along the way enhanced the festive mood. Unlike the awkward pitch that had accounted for low-scoring matches between New Zealand and Sri Lanka at Lauderhill in 2010, this surface was hard, true and ideal for the game's shortest format.

Yet not everyone was happy. Donald Ramotar, the president of Guyana, criticised the West Indies Cricket Board for the "abomination" of staging matches in Florida. He complained that "key matches are now being taken out of the region while some of our territories are deliberately deprived" – a reference to the WICB's moving of all international and regional matches out of Guyana following their government's replacement of the Guyana Cricket Board with an interim management committee.

The overall standard of the cricket did little to dispel the media's description of the tour as a bottom-of-the-table clash. But neither that, nor the distraction of the public's gaze by the brilliant Caribbean athletes at the London Olympics, mattered a jot to West Indies. Recent victories had been few and far between, and none as emphatic as this.

NEW ZEALAND TOURING PARTY

*L. R. P. L. Taylor, T. A. Boult, D. A. J. Bracewell, D. G. Brownlie, D. R. Flynn, M. J. Guptill, B. B. McCullum, C. S. Martin, T. S. Nethula, T. G. Southee, C. F. K. van Wyk, D. L. Vettori, N. Wagner, B-J. Watling, K. S. Williamson. *Coach:* J. G. Wright.

The squad for the Twenty20 series in Florida included A. M. Ellis, R. M. Hira, T. W. M. Latham, N. L. McCullum, K. D. Mills, R. J. Nicol and J. D. P. Oram in place of Boult, B. B. McCullum, Martin, Nethula, van Wyk, Vettori and Wagner. Boult and B. B. McCullum, initially named only for the Tests, were drafted in for the one-day internationals, along with Nethula, after the first Twenty20 when Hira dislocated a finger and went home, and Oram strained a knee. Southee, originally chosen for the limited-overs matches only, was added to the Test squad when M. R. Gillespie was ruled out of the tour by an ankle injury.

WEST INDIES v NEW ZEALAND

First Twenty20 International

At Lauderhill, June 30, 2012. West Indies won by 56 runs. Toss: New Zealand. Twenty20 international debuts: S. Badree; T. W. M. Latham.

New Zealand, rusty in all departments in their first fixture for three months, lost not only the match but also their captain Taylor (temporarily) and the left-arm spinner Hira (for the rest of the tour). Taylor fell heavily on his left shoulder when he missed a swirling catch off Pollard and, after cutting two fours in the run-chase, winced and retired hurt. Gayle was inadvertently responsible for two other injuries: Hira dislocated a finger trying to intercept a ferocious straight blow; Oram strained his left knee attempting to prevent the second of Gayle's seven fours, and had trouble running in to bowl or between the wickets. Gayle and Pollard, who hit five sixes each, blazed 108 off the last seven overs as West Indies clocked up their highest total in Twenty20 internationals. New Zealand were never in contention against Narine's befuddling spin and sharp fielding that produced two direct-hit run-outs in the same over.

Man of the Match: C. H. Gayle.

West Indies

		B	4	6
D. R. Smith *b 10*	17	13	1	2
C. H. Gayle *not out*	85	52	7	5
J. Charles *c 7 b 4*	24	29	3	0
K. A. Pollard *not out*	63	29	5	5
B 1, l-b 3, w 13, n-b 3	20			
6 overs: 43-1 (20 overs)	209-2			

1/27 2/101

*D. J. G. Sammy, D. J. Bravo, M. N. Samuels, †D. Ramdin, S. Badree, S. P. Narine and F. H. Edwards did not bat.

McCullum 4–0–30–0; Bracewell 4–0–47–1; Southee 4–0–35–0; Oram 2–0–26–0; Hira 2.2–0–22–0; Williamson 1.4–0–21–1; Nicol 2–0–24–0.

New Zealand

		B	4	6
R. J. Nicol *c 11 b 6*	32	31	5	0
M. J. Guptill *st 8 b 10*	11	9	2	0
*L. R. P. L. Taylor *retired hurt*	10	11	2	0
K. S. Williamson *c and b 5*	10	10	0	0
T. G. Southee *st 8 b 10*	23	18	0	2
†T. W. M. Latham *run out*	15	11	1	0
J. D. P. Oram *c 6 b 11*	27	13	2	2
D. G. Brownlie *run out*	0	2	0	0
N. L. McCullum *lbw b 10*	0	1	0	0
D. A. J. Bracewell *not out*	11	5	0	1
R. M. Hira *absent hurt*				
L-b 8, w 6	14			
6 overs: 51-1 (18.3 overs)	153			

1/38 2/72 3/84 4/114 5/115 6/116 7/124 8/153

Taylor retired hurt at 51-1.

Edwards 3.3–0–25–1; Badree 4–0–33–0; Narine 4–0–34–3; Samuels 2–0–14–0; Sammy 2–0–13–1; Bravo 3–0–26–1.

Umpires: P. J. Nero and J. S. Wilson. Third umpire: G. O. Brathwaite.

WEST INDIES v NEW ZEALAND

Second Twenty20 International

At Lauderhill, July 1, 2012. West Indies won by 61 runs. Toss: West Indies.

Gayle did not face a ball until the third over, then played out a maiden from Mills – but he still went on to top-score again, with 53 from 39 deliveries. Dwayne Bravo was on hand to help raise 53 off West Indies' final four overs. Their total proved well beyond the depleted New Zealanders, who were checked by Narine's variations: he picked up four wickets, including the openers from successive balls. A wide, nine singles and two runs off a leading edge accounted for the 12 he conceded. It was quite an introduction to captaincy for Williamson, standing in for the injured Taylor. At 21 years and 328 days, he was the youngest man to lead New Zealand.

Man of the Match: S. P. Narine. *Man of the Series:* C. H. Gayle.

West Indies

		B	4	6
D. R. Smith *c and b 10*	13	8	0	2
C. H. Gayle *b 8*	53	39	3	4
J. Charles *c 3 b 1*	36	32	4	1
L. M. P. Simmons *c 3 b 8*	18	16	0	2
*D. J. G. Sammy *c 4 b 3*	13	11	1	0
D. J. Bravo *not out*	35	11	1	4
M. N. Samuels *not out*	4	4	0	0
L-b 1, w 3, n-b 1	5			
6 overs: 43-1 (20 overs)	177-5			

1/14 2/86 3/117 4/124 5/161

†D. Ramdin, S. Badree, S. P. Narine and F. H. Edwards did not bat.

Mills 4–1–20–0; Bracewell 3–0–43–1; Southee 4–0–43–1; Ellis 4–0–40–0; McCullum 3–0–19–2; Nicol 2–0–11–1.

New Zealand

		B	4	6
R. J. Nicol *st 8 b 10*	7	12	0	0
M. J. Guptill *c 11 b 10*	18	18	2	1
T. G. Southee *c 3 b 9*	3	5	0	0
*K. S. Williamson *run out*	6	5	1	0
D. R. Flynn *c 2 b 7*	22	19	0	2
D. G. Brownlie *b 10*	1	4	0	0
†T. W. M. Latham *b 7*	19	19	1	0
N. L. McCullum *c and b 6*	14	15	0	0
A. M. Ellis *c 6 b 10*	1	3	0	0
D. A. J. Bracewell *c 1 b 6*	20	11	0	2
K. D. Mills *not out*	1	1	0	0
L-b 2, w 2	4			
6 overs: 33-3 (18.4 overs)	116			

1/26 2/26 3/33 4/39 5/43 6/69 7/85 8/90 9/114

Edwards 3–0–20–0; Badree 4–0–20–1; Narine 4–0–12–4; Sammy 2–0–14–0; Bravo 2.4–0–23–2; Samuels 3–0–25–2.

Umpires: P. J. Nero and J. S. Wilson. Third umpire: N. Duguid.
Series referee: A. J. Pycroft.

WEST INDIES v NEW ZEALAND

First One-Day International

At Kingston, Jamaica, July 5, 2012. West Indies won by nine wickets (D/L). Toss: West Indies.

Russell's opening burst of three for 20 in six overs and Narine's unerring control kept New Zealand down to 117 for six from their first 35. Although Watling, favouring the leg side, gave the innings late impetus, Gayle – appearing for West Indies on his home ground for the first time since June 2009 – and Dwayne Smith made mincemeat of an inadequate target in an unbroken partnership of 130. At 93 for one off 18 overs, they were 12 balls short of the 20 required to constitute a match when a fierce thunderstorm held up play for nearly two hours. On the resumption, the goal was revised to 136 from 33, and West Indies got there easily.

Man of the Match: A. D. Russell.

YOUNGEST CAPTAINS IN ONE-DAY INTERNATIONALS

Years	*Days*			
20	297	Rajin Saleh	Bangladesh v South Africa at Birmingham	2004
20	342	T. Taibu	Zimbabwe v Sri Lanka at Bulawayo	2003-04
21	125	P. Utseya	Zimbabwe v Bangladesh at Harare	2006
21	**332**	**K. S. Williamson**	**New Zealand v West Indies at Kingston**	**2012**

Note: Rajin Saleh and Williamson were standing in for an absent appointed captain.

New Zealand

R. J. Nicol c Simmons b Russell	14
M. J. Guptill c Sammy b Russell	1
D. R. Flynn b Russell	12
*K. S. Williamson c Ramdin b Sammy	24
D. G. Brownlie lbw b Narine	1
†B-J. Watling lbw b Rampaul	60
J. D. P. Oram b Rampaul	32
A. M. Ellis b Narine	14
K. D. Mills c Samuels b Russell	1
T. G. Southee not out	9
T. S. Nethula not out	9
B 1, l-b 1, w 10, n-b 1	13
1/3 (2) 2/30 (3) 3/33 (1) 4/48 (5) 5/71 (4) 6/117 (7) 7/161 (8) 8/164 (9) 9/173 (6) — (9 wkts, 50 overs)	190
10 overs: 36-3	

Rampaul 10–0–42–2; Russell 10–0–45–4; Narine 10–2–26–2; Bravo 7–0–32–0; Samuels 7–1–20–0; Sammy 6–0–23–1.

West Indies

L. M. P. Simmons c Watling b Mills	0
C. H. Gayle not out	63
D. R. Smith not out	65
L-b 6, w 2	8
1/6 (1) — (1 wkt, 24.2 overs)	136
10 overs: 42-1	

M. N. Samuels, K. A. Pollard, D. J. Bravo, †D. Ramdin, *D. J. G. Sammy, S. P. Narine, R. Rampaul and A. D. Russell did not bat.

Mills 5–1–7–1; Southee 7–1–37–0; Oram 5–0–37–0; Nicol 3–0–20–0; Nethula 4–1–27–0; Guptill 0.2–0–2–0.

Umpires: R. A. Kettleborough and P. J. Nero. Third umpire: R. K. Illingworth.

WEST INDIES v NEW ZEALAND

Second One-Day International

At Kingston, Jamaica, July 7, 2012. West Indies won by 55 runs. Toss: New Zealand.

To the delight of the biggest crowd at Sabina Park since Caribbean cricket's heyday in the 1980s, Gayle produced a brilliant display of straight hitting to overtake Brian Lara's West Indies record of 19 one-day international hundreds. Even after Gayle swung a catch to deep midwicket attempting

MOST ONE-DAY INTERNATIONAL HUNDREDS FOR WEST INDIES

100	*ODIs*		*100*	*ODIs*	
20	**231**	**C. H. Gayle**	11	187	I. V. A. Richards
19	295	B. C. Lara	11	128	C. G. Greenidge
17	238	D. L. Haynes	11	268	S. Chanderpaul

his tenth six, Samuels – who had helped him add 129 – retained the Jamaican theme, advancing in the final over to his own century, the third of his one-day international career and the first since his two-year ban ended in May 2010. None of the eight bowlers went for less than 5.5 runs an over as West Indies compiled their highest total against New Zealand. Watling, with an unbeaten 72 off 62 balls to follow his 60 two days earlier, led a decent but unthreatening response.

Man of the Match: M. N. Samuels.

West Indies

L. M. P. Simmons c Watling b Southee	3
C. H. Gayle c Latham b Mills	125
D. R. Smith c McCullum b Nethula	24
M. N. Samuels not out	101
K. A. Pollard lbw b Southee	8
D. J. Bravo b Southee	3
*D. J. G. Sammy not out	31
L-b 5, w 15	20
1/10 (1) 2/98 (3) 3/227 (2) 4/253 (5) 5/272 (6) (5 wkts, 50 overs)	315
10 overs: 58-1	

†D. Ramdin, S. P. Narine, R. Rampaul and A. D. Russell did not bat.

Mills 10–0–55–1; Southee 10–1–55–3; McCullum 6–0–35–0; Oram 10–0–68–0; Nethula 10–1–66–1; Nicol 2–0–14–0; Flynn 1–0–9–0; Williamson 1–0–8–0.

New Zealand

R. J. Nicol c Sammy b Rampaul	15
M. J. Guptill c and b Samuels	51
D. R. Flynn c Bravo b Narine	21
*K. S. Williamson lbw b Rampaul	58
T. W. M. Latham c sub (J. Charles) b Samuels	2
†B-J. Watling not out	72
T. G. Southee run out	2
N. L. McCullum b Narine	1
J. D. P. Oram c Smith b Russell	10
K. D. Mills b Rampaul	6
T. S. Nethula run out	3
L-b 5, w 11, n-b 3	19
1/24 (1) 2/62 (3) 3/121 (2) 4/125 (5) 5/195 (4) 6/200 (7) 7/214 (8) 8/242 (9) 9/253 (10) 10/260 (11) (47 overs)	260
10 overs: 51-1	

Russell 9–0–51–1; Rampaul 9–0–50–3; Bravo 3–0–20–0; Narine 10–0–45–2; Sammy 8–0–43–0; Samuels 8–0–46–2.

Umpires: G. O. Brathwaite and R. K. Illingworth. Third umpire: R. A. Kettleborough.

> "They might as well have tossed him to the saltwater crocs."
> Five Cricketers of the Year, page 125.

WEST INDIES v NEW ZEALAND

Third One-Day International

At Basseterre, St Kitts, July 11, 2012. New Zealand won by 88 runs. Toss: West Indies. One-day international debut: T. A. Boult.

After four successive thrashings, New Zealand emphatically kept the series alive. Williamson discerned "a great shift in momentum", though this proved optimistic. Sent in, they had recovered from 125 for five in the 27th over – when the dominant Nicol tamely tapped a return catch to Samuels – to reach an adequate total on a flat pitch. Watling contributed again, but a thigh strain added him to New Zealand's lengthy injured list; Latham kept wicket in his stead. Gayle's first failure of the series, edging an away-swinger from Southee, reinforced the notion that his early dismissal was crucial. Nervous run-outs and reckless shots left West Indies 103 for eight in the 28th over, and Russell's four sixes were scant consolation for a big crowd. The match was dedicated to the memory of Runako Morton, the West Indies batsman from neighbouring Nevis who was killed in a car crash in March, aged 33.

Man of the Match: R. J. Nicol.

New Zealand

R. J. Nicol c and b Samuels	59
M. J. Guptill lbw b Russell	11
D. R. Flynn c Ramdin b Bravo	28
*K. S. Williamson b Narine	9
T. W. M. Latham c Gayle b Sammy	12
†B-J. Watling c Narine b Russell	40
N. L. McCullum c Bravo b Russell	50
J. D. P. Oram st Ramdin b Narine	7
K. D. Mills c Gayle b Russell	2
T. G. Southee not out	17
T. A. Boult not out	1
L-b 6, w 5, n-b 2	13
1/24 (2) 2/71 (3) 3/97 (4) 4/124 (5) 5/125 (1) 6/191 (6) 7/216 (8) 8/219 (9) 9/239 (7) (9 wkts, 50 overs)	249
10 overs: 59-1	

Rampaul 10–0–61–0; Russell 9–0–57–4; Bravo 7–0–47–1; Narine 10–0–28–2; Sammy 8–1–22–1; Samuels 6–0–28–1.

West Indies

J. Charles lbw b Boult	15
C. H. Gayle c Nicol b Southee	11
D. R. Smith c McCullum b Oram	19
M. N. Samuels run out	11
D. J. Bravo run out	2
K. A. Pollard c sub (D. G. Brownlie) b McCullum	16
†D. Ramdin lbw b Oram	14
*D. J. G. Sammy c and b McCullum	7
A. D. Russell not out	42
S. P. Narine run out	10
R. Rampaul c Southee b Boult	9
L-b 3, w 1, n-b 1	5
1/19 (1) 2/33 (2) 3/50 (3) 4/52 (5) 5/62 (4) 6/85 (6) 7/95 (8) 8/103 (7) 9/133 (10) 10/161 (11) (34.3 overs)	161
10 overs: 42-2	

Mills 7–2–37–0; Boult 8.3–0–45–2; Southee 6–1–14–1; Oram 7–1–22–2; McCullum 6–0–40–2.

Umpires: R. A. Kettleborough and J. S. Wilson. Third umpire: R. K. Illingworth.

WEST INDIES v NEW ZEALAND

Fourth One-Day International

At Basseterre, St Kitts, July 14, 2012. West Indies won by 24 runs. Toss: West Indies.

It was West Indies' turn to fight back from a poor start, then hold their nerve, despite Taylor's masterful hundred. Their resolve earned them their first one-day series victory – excluding those over Zimbabwe, Bangladesh or the Associates – since beating Sri Lanka in April 2008, and their first win at Warner Park in their last five attempts. Gayle was among the first three wickets which fell for 20 and, when Samuels was lbw to Nathan McCullum after hitting him for six and four in the over, West Indies were 105 for five. Pollard steadied the ship with the slowest of his seven half-centuries in the format, from 63 balls, before Sammy and Russell provided the muscle for a meaty finish. New Zealand took 63 from the mandatory powerplay but, except for Taylor – in his first innings since injuring his shoulder in the tour's opening match – the batsmen were badly stalled by Narine. The outcome was settled once Taylor, who hit five sixes, skied to point in Best's fiery final spell.

Man of the Match: S. P. Narine.

West Indies

J. Charles c Williamson b Bracewell	1
C. H. Gayle lbw b Southee	16
D. R. Smith c Taylor b Southee	0
M. N. Samuels lbw b N. L. McCullum	46
D. J. Bravo c Boult b Oram	18
K. A. Pollard c B. B. McCullum b Oram	56
†D. C. Thomas c Taylor b Nicol	37
*D. J. G. Sammy c Guptill b Boult	26
A. D. Russell c Guptill b Oram	29
S. P. Narine not out	6
T. L. Best b Southee	3
L-b 5, w 20, n-b 1	26
1/17 (1) 2/19 (2) 3/20 (3) 4/59 (5) 5/105 (4) 6/190 (7) 7/202 (6) 8/234 (8) 9/258 (9) 10/264 (11) (49.5 overs)	264
10 overs: 26-3	

Bracewell 10–2–58–1; Boult 10–2–47–1; Southee 9.5–1–53–3; Oram 10–1–42–3; N. L. McCullum 4–0–34–1; Nicol 6–1–25–1.

New Zealand

R. J. Nicol c Bravo b Sammy	35
M. J. Guptill lbw b Best	0
B. B. McCullum c Sammy b Russell	10
*L. R. P. L. Taylor c Sammy b Best	110
K. S. Williamson lbw b Narine	3
†T. W. M. Latham c Thomas b Samuels	32
N. L. McCullum c Sammy b Best	11
J. D. P. Oram b Best	6
D. A. J. Bracewell c Pollard b Narine	5
T. G. Southee run out	3
T. A. Boult not out	1
B 5, l-b 10, w 8, n-b 1	24
1/8 (2) 2/50 (3) 3/63 (1) 4/75 (5) 5/146 (6) 6/170 (7) 7/219 (8) 8/234 (9) 9/237 (4) 10/240 (10) (49.3 overs)	240
10 overs: 63-2	

Best 10–1–46–4; Russell 6–0–49–1; Sammy 10–1–41–1; Narine 10–1–20–2; Samuels 10–0–50–1; Bravo 3.3–0–19–0.

Umpires: R. K. Illingworth and P. J. Nero. Third umpire: R. A. Kettleborough.

WEST INDIES v NEW ZEALAND

Fifth One-Day International

At Basseterre, St Kitts, July 16, 2012. West Indies won by 20 runs. Toss: West Indies.

The fifth match followed an almost identical pattern to the fourth: New Zealand again found themselves needing eight an over off the last six with four wickets intact – only to be obliterated by Narine. West Indies had faltered after Gayle's third successive failure, before a careful fifty from Dwayne Bravo and an explosive one from Russell set a competitive, if hardly imposing, total. New Zealand initially struggled in reply, before Williamson – in partnerships of 31 with Latham and 68 with Ellis – carried them to within view. But Narine, attacking from a new line around the wicket, struck three times in nine balls for his best one-day international figures, and the best by any West Indies spinner, surpassing Jimmy Adams's five for 37 against Pakistan at Adelaide in 1996-97. "In our conditions, Narine is unplayable," declared Sammy.

Man of the Match: S. P. Narine. *Man of the Series:* S. P. Narine.

West Indies

J. Charles c Nicol b Southee	15	S. P. Narine c McCullum b Mills	6
C. H. Gayle c Nicol b Mills	5	T. L. Best not out	5
D. R. Smith lbw b Southee	9		
M. N. Samuels c Guptill b Southee	43	L-b 8, w 9	17
D. J. Bravo c McCullum b Ellis	53		
K. A. Pollard c Guptill b Williamson	7	1/23 (2) 2/32 (1) (9 wkts, 50 overs)	241
†D. C. Thomas c Southee b Ellis	20	3/37 (3) 4/97 (4)	
*D. J. G. Sammy c Latham b Mills	2	5/104 (6) 6/157 (7)	
A. D. Russell not out	59	7/160 (8) 8/180 (5) 9/216 (10) 10 overs: 44-3	

Mills 10–1–40–3; Boult 8–0–29–0; Southee 10–1–37–3; Ellis 10–1–54–2; Nicol 5–0–27–0; Flynn 2–0–10–0; Williamson 5–0–36–1.

New Zealand

R. J. Nicol c Bravo b Best	2	T. G. Southee not out	4
M. J. Guptill lbw b Narine	33	T. A. Boult c Pollard b Bravo	5
B. B. McCullum c Sammy b Narine	33		
*L. R. P. L. Taylor st Thomas b Samuels	28	L-b 2, w 5	7
K. S. Williamson c Gayle b Narine	69		
D. R. Flynn c Sammy b Best	0	1/2 (1) 2/64 (3) 3/77 (2) (50 overs)	221
†T. W. M. Latham c Thomas b Bravo	11	4/108 (4) 5/109 (6) 6/140 (7)	
A. M. Ellis b Narine	28	7/208 (5) 8/212 (8) 9/213 (9)	
K. D. Mills b Narine	1	10/221 (11) 10 overs: 55-1	

Best 10–0–58–2; Russell 4–1–25–0; Sammy 10–0–30–0; Narine 10–1–27–5; Samuels 10–0–49–1; Bravo 6–0–30–2.

Umpires: R. A. Kettleborough and J. S. Wilson. Third umpire: R. K. Illingworth.
Series referee: A. J. Pycroft.

At North Sound, Antigua, July 20–22, 2012. **Drawn. New Zealanders 149** (K. S. Williamson 55; K. A. J. Roach 4-34, V. Permaul 3-34) **and 181-8** (B. B. McCullum 51; S. Shillingford 5-77); ‡**West Indies Cricket Board President's XI 326** (S. Chanderpaul 51, N. Deonarine 106; N. Wagner 3-65, D. L. Vettori 6-48). *There was an unusual intensity to this warm-up game, played on a strip close to the Test wicket, and featuring six of West Indies' Test squad plus their reserve spinner, Shillingford. Williamson ground out 55 in close to four hours as the tourists struggled in overcast conditions; Deonarine found run-scoring easier in his 115-ball hundred. Neil Wagner, making his first senior appearance for New Zealand, swung the ball at pace, and clung on for 59 minutes alongside another native South African, Kruger van Wyk (38*), to save the match.*

WEST INDIES v NEW ZEALAND

First Test Match

At North Sound, Antigua, July 25–29, 2012. West Indies won by nine wickets. Toss: New Zealand. Test debut: N. Wagner.

West Indies' first Test victory over New Zealand since April 1996 was built upon Gayle's resounding return 16 months after his contentious exclusion, his crushing opening stand of 254 with Powell, and the contrasting abilities of Narine and Roach to overcome a sluggish pitch.

Twice New Zealand batted themselves into a promising position; twice they gave ground with the loss of two late wickets. On the first evening, 223 for two became 232 for four; on the fourth, they went from 170 for one – a single from clearing the first-innings deficit – to 199 for three. On neither occasion could they recover. For their part, West Indies capitalised on the foundation laid by Gayle and Powell to amass their fifth-highest total against New Zealand, before their bowlers seized on indiscipline in the second innings.

New Zealand had made a fine start: Guptill put on 97 with Flynn, then 90 for the third wicket with Taylor. But with six overs left in the day, Taylor – not for the first time – got himself into a tangle against Narine, and was bowled off the glove. In Narine's next over, Guptill – who had spent 11 overs moving from 90 to 97 – became unsettled by the approach of both the close and what would have been his third Test hundred: in trying to raise it with a six, he top-edged a slog-sweep. He had batted just short of six hours without blemish, and now trudged off like a man who had thrown away a winning lottery ticket. New Zealand failed to reclaim the momentum the following day, and it took Bracewell's robust 39 off 31 balls at No. 10 to carry them past 350.

Gayle immediately delivered an uncompromising riposte, despatching the last four balls of Martin's opening over to the boundary. He should have gone no further than 36, when Flynn misjudged a head-high catch at point off Bracewell; Powell had edged the previous ball from Neil Wagner, the debutant left-arm quick, a foot wide of second slip. Aside from the rarity of a first-ball dismissal for Chanderpaul – only his sixth in 244 Test innings – to a gloved catch off Martin's sharp lifter, there was little subsequent encouragement for New Zealand.

The longer Gayle batted, the more subdued he became, taking 39 balls for his first fifty, 90 for his second, and eventually spending 206 deliveries in making 150, his 14th Test century. Following the trail blazed by his senior partner, the tall, relaxed Powell completed his first, before three successive fours in an over from Wagner enticed him to go for another: instead, he nicked it behind, providing the bowler with his first Test wicket. Fudadin and Deonarine, two of five left-handers in West Indies' top six, comfortably compiled half-centuries, although Fudadin – in his second Test – wasted the chance of going further: like Gayle he was caught at long-off by McCullum off Williamson. Sammy's forthright fifty, with three sixes, sent the total past 500 as New Zealand's bowlers struggled in unfamiliar conditions.

Vettori had taken six for 48 in the practice match against the Board President's XI on the same ground. But now, restricted by the groin strain that would rule him out of the Second Test and, later, the tour of India, he wheeled away for 51 overs for just Sammy's wicket. Martin, meanwhile, travelled at almost four and a half an over. In the circumstances, the younger bowlers took up the slack admirably.

As Guptill and McCullum carried New Zealand to within one run of parity over the last two sessions of the fourth day, there was the prospect of a tricky last innings for West Indies – only for the sundowner effect to take its toll once more. Guptill, who had already escaped being caught off a Roach no-ball on 42, was taken sharply at bat-pad off Narine's bouncing off-break with 15 overs remaining; McCullum, in control for more than three hours, then played on to a delivery from Roach that was too close to cut.

New Zealand's excessive caution on the last day, along with Roach's fast, direct assault, snuffed out any resistance. The 26 overs before lunch yielded 26 runs and two wickets, and it was little wonder that only a few hundred spectators were dotted around a stadium designed to accommodate 20,000. In that session Wagner – nightwatchman for the second time in his first Test – occupied 83 balls for nine, Taylor 30 for ten and Brownlie 47 for five, though no one had an answer to Roach, who dismissed Williamson with an unplayable leg-cutter, and had figures of 10.2–3–16–4 on the day. Requiring 102 off 46 overs, Gayle and Powell were in no mood to delay the inevitable. Although Powell fell to Bracewell at 77, Gayle remained unbeaten on 64 off 49 balls as Fudadin nudged the winning run.

Man of the Match: S. P. Narine.

Close of play: first day, New Zealand 232-4 (Wagner 4, Williamson 2); second day, West Indies 145-0 (Gayle 85, Powell 58); third day, West Indies 442-6 (Deonarine 54, Sammy 8); fourth day, New Zealand 199-3 (Taylor 11, Wagner 4).

New Zealand

D. R. Flynn c Powell b Narine	45	– (2) lbw b Narine	20
M. J. Guptill c Deonarine b Narine	97	– (1) c Fudadin b Narine	67
B. B. McCullum c Deonarine b Roach	25	– b Roach	84
*L. R. P. L. Taylor b Narine	45	– lbw b Roach	21
N. Wagner c Sammy b Narine	4	– c Ramdin b Roach	13
K. S. Williamson b Roach	19	– b Roach	0
D. G. Brownlie c Ramdin b Rampaul	23	– c Gayle b Rampaul	5
†C. F. K. van Wyk c Fudadin b Narine	11	– b Roach	30
D. L. Vettori c Deonarine b Sammy	17	– c Ramdin b Rampaul	13
D. A. J. Bracewell c Chanderpaul b Rampaul	39	– lbw b Narine	0
C. S. Martin not out	4	– not out	0
B 14, l-b 1, w 1, n-b 6	22	B 7, l-b 8, n-b 4	19
1/97 (1) 2/133 (3) 3/223 (4) 4/228 (2) 5/233 (5) 6/273 (6) 7/281 (7) 8/308 (9) 9/309 (8) 10/351 (10) (129.1 overs)	351	1/47 (2) 2/170 (1) 3/194 (3) 4/217 (4) 5/217 (6) 6/225 (5) 7/225 (7) 8/251 (9) 9/258 (10) 10/272 (8) (105.2 overs)	272

Rampaul 23.1–9–44–2; Roach 23–8–55–2; Sammy 26–7–76–1; Narine 43–9–132–5; Samuels 6–2–14–0; Fudadin 5–1–11–0; Deonarine 3–1–4–0. *Second innings*—Rampaul 17–3–52–2; Roach 23.2–4–60–5; Narine 42–13–91–3; Sammy 16 6 25–0; Samuels 3–1–22–0; Deonarine 4–2–7–0.

West Indies

C. H. Gayle c McCullum b Williamson	150	– not out	64
K. O. A. Powell c van Wyk b Wagner	134	– c Brownlie b Bracewell	30
A. B. Fudadin c McCullum b Williamson	55	– not out	7
M. N. Samuels b Martin	28		
S. Chanderpaul c van Wyk b Martin	0		
N. Deonarine b Martin	79		
†D. Ramdin b Bracewell	3		
*D. J. G. Sammy c and b Vettori	50		
S. P. Narine run out	4		
K. A. J. Roach not out	6		
R. Rampaul lbw b Bracewell	1		
L-b 9, n-b 3	12	W 1	1
1/254 (1) 2/304 (2) 3/355 (4) 4/355 (5) 5/410 (3) 6/428 (7) 7/497 (6) 8/502 (9) 9/516 (8) 10/522 (11) (163.3 overs)	522	1/77 (2) (1 wkt, 19.3 overs)	102

Martin 30–9–134–3; Bracewell 29.3–5–96–2; Wagner 33–8–112–1; Vettori 51–14–124–1; Williamson 20–2–47–2. *Second innings*—Bracewell 6–0–25–1; Martin 4–0–12–0; Williamson 3–1–30–0; Wagner 5–0–32–0; Vettori 1.3–0–3–0.

Umpires: R. A. Kettleborough and P. R. Reiffel. Third umpire: M. Erasmus.

WEST INDIES v NEW ZEALAND

Second Test Match

At Kingston, Jamaica, August 2–5, 2012. West Indies won by five wickets. Toss: West Indies.

The sport that first created West Indies' reputation for athletic excellence was so secondary to Jamaican expectation of Olympic medals that provision was made to shift the last drinks break on the final two days to allow players and spectators to watch the women's and men's 100 metres finals on the big screen. They saw Shelly-Ann Fraser-Pryce take the women's race on the Saturday, but by the time Usain Bolt and Yohan Blake mopped up gold and silver, at 3.50pm Jamaica time on Sunday, West Indies had already completed a hard-fought victory.

That completed an emphatic, and timely, thrashing of the New Zealanders in all three formats. Following varying degrees of progress against Australia and England, this was another modest sign of a revival after 20 years in which a disillusioned public had increasingly transferred its attention to other, more successful sports, primarily athletics.

It was also apt that, on the eve of the 50th anniversary of Jamaica's independence from Britain, Marlon Samuels – a Kingston boy – should have led the way, just like Bolt and friends in London. His exceptional 123, out of a first-innings 209, averted the humiliation of a double-digit total and limited the deficit to 51. Only four West Indies batsmen had been responsible for a greater share of a completed innings total than Samuels's 58.85%.

HIGHEST PERCENTAGE OF A WEST INDIES TEST TOTAL

%		*Score*	*Total*		
63.50	C. G. Greenidge	134	211	v England at Manchester	1976
61.87	S. M. Nurse	258	417	v New Zealand at Christchurch	1968-69
60.26	H. A. Gomes	91	151	v India at Madras	1978-79
59.45	B. C. Lara	176	296	v South Africa at Bridgetown	2004-05
58.85	**M. N. Samuels**	**123**	**209**	**v New Zealand at Kingston**	**2012**
58.07	B. F. Butcher	133	229	v England at Lord's	1963

After New Zealand's second-innings meltdown to the spin of Narine and Deonarine, West Indies were left with an awkward 206 to win; Samuels's 52 steadied nerves after the early loss of the openers, and set the course for Chanderpaul, the assertive nightwatchman Roach, and Deonarine to complete the job before lunch on the fourth day.

As in Antigua, New Zealand's first innings turned into a wasted opportunity. After two early wickets rewarded Sammy's decision to bowl first with moisture in the pitch, Guptill and Taylor added 103. But Taylor's edged slash off Best began a steady decline only briefly checked by the lower order. Guptill once more top-scored, with a diligent 71 off 174 balls, but – hampered by a groin twinge – he was sixth out, beaten by Best's direct hit from cover after van Wyk unwisely called for a quick single.

New Zealand's young swing and seam quartet – at 26, Wagner, in his second Test, was the oldest – responded gamely to the burden placed on them by their batsmen. In the absence of the two leading bowlers – Daniel Vettori, out with a groin strain, and Chris Martin, dropped after a poor performance in Antigua – Boult and Wagner (both left-arm) and Bracewell and Southee (both right) seldom varied from the required line and length.

As wickets tumbled around him, Samuels moved on in his effortless way. He was 78 when Southee ended Sammy's breezy stay with a toe-crusher and, with only the tail left, it was a signal for changed tactics. Best was his sole remaining partner when he flat-drove Southee over extra cover for six to raise his first Test hundred in the Caribbean at the 31st attempt. Two more sixes followed off the next two deliveries, and another off Bracewell's first ball of the following over. Going for a fifth, he was caught on the cover boundary. Of the 47 runs added for the last three wickets, all but two came from Samuels.

Guptill and Watling (in for the injured Daniel Flynn) carefully doubled New Zealand's advantage, before Antigua's sunset syndrome returned: Deonarine, the fifth bowler, removed both with back-foot lbw dismissals in the day's final three overs. The recovery never got going next morning. Best accounted for Wagner, again the nightwatchman, and Taylor in the same over, and only Brownlie survived as long as an hour and a half.

New Zealand lost their last eight wickets for 74, but West Indies still faced a target with the potential to induce panic. Gayle and Powell went cheaply again, and the outcome might have been different had Watling not spilled a straightforward catch at gully off Bracewell with Samuels on 20 and the total 56. Bracewell had to wait another 26 overs before he got his man towards the third day's close, by which point Samuels had passed 50 for the sixth time in seven Test innings.

West Indies resumed the following day with 71 more to get, six wickets in hand, and unexpectedly clear skies above – the tropical storm Ernesto, which had swept through the Windward Islands, was nowhere to be seen. Nightwatchman Roach, soon to be named Man of the Series for his bowling, all but settled matters with a calculated aggression that brought him his highest Test score. Another 23 were needed when he drove Williamson to backward point, but Chanderpaul and Deonarine comfortably saw it through, winning before lunch, and a full four and a half hours before the planned break to watch the first of Bolt's three Olympic golds.

Man of the Match: M. N. Samuels. *Man of the Series:* K. A. J. Roach.

Close of play: first day, West Indies 11-0 (Gayle 1, Powell 10); second day, New Zealand 59-2 (Wagner 2, McCullum 1); third day, West Indies 135-4 (Chanderpaul 20, Roach 10).

New Zealand

First innings		Second innings	
B-J. Watling c Gayle b Roach	2	– (2) lbw b Deonarine	11
M. J. Guptill run out	71	– (1) lbw b Deonarine	42
B. B. McCullum c Ramdin b Best	0	– (4) c Fudadin b Deonarine	19
*L. R. P. L. Taylor c Ramdin b Best	60	– (5) c Ramdin b Best	0
K. S. Williamson c Sammy b Deonarine	22	– (6) c Sammy b Deonarine	8
D. G. Brownlie c Ramdin b Roach	0	– (7) c Deonarine b Narine	35
†C. F. K. van Wyk b Deonarine	16	– (8) c Chanderpaul b Narine	5
D. A. J. Bracewell b Narine	14	– (9) c Fudadin b Narine	14
N. Wagner c Best b Roach	23	– (3) c Ramdin b Best	6
T. G. Southee c Sammy b Roach	18	– c Narine b Roach	7
T. A. Boult not out	14	– not out	0
B 6, l-b 2, w 1, n-b 11	20	L-b 1, w 1, n-b 5	7
1/10 (1) 2/11 (3) 3/114 (4) 4/161 (5) 5/162 (6) 6/170 (2) 7/202 (8) 8/202 (7) 9/225 (10) 10/260 (9) (82.5 overs)	260	1/55 (2) 2/56 (1) 3/80 (3) 4/80 (5) 5/85 (4) 6/98 (6) 7/105 (8) 8/142 (9) 9/151 (7) 10/154 (10) (65.2 overs)	154

Roach 17.5–2–70–4; Best 16–1–40–2; Sammy 10–1–31–0; Narine 26–7–66–1; Samuels 1–0–2–0; Deonarine 12–3–43–2. *Second innings*—Roach 12.2–3–34–1; Best 13–2–44–2; Sammy 6–2–19–0; Narine 12–1–19–3; Deonarine 22–7–37–4.

West Indies

First innings		Second innings	
C. H. Gayle c Watling b Wagner	8	– lbw b Boult	8
K. O. A. Powell c Brownlie b Boult	10	– lbw b Southee	6
A. B. Fudadin lbw b Boult	5	– b Wagner	27
M. N. Samuels c Wagner b Bracewell	123	– c Taylor b Bracewell	52
S. Chanderpaul c Taylor b Southee	9	– not out	43
N. Deonarine c van Wyk b Boult	0	– (7) not out	15
†D. Ramdin c Williamson b Wagner	15		
*D. J. G. Sammy lbw b Southee	32		
S. P. Narine c Guptill b Bracewell	1		
K. A. J. Roach c Guptill b Bracewell	0	– (6) c Southee b Williamson	41
T. L. Best not out	0		
L-b 4, w 2	6	B 4, l-b 2, w 8	14
1/11 (2) 2/17 (3) 3/53 (1) 4/82 (5) 5/83 (6) 6/113 (7) 7/162 (8) 8/177 (9) 9/183 (10) 10/209 (4) (64.3 overs)	209	1/20 (1) 2/20 (2) 3/94 (3) 4/113 (4) 5/183 (6) (5 wkts, 63.2 overs)	206

Boult 17–2–58–3; Bracewell 15.3–3–46–3; Southee 19–5–70–2; Wagner 10–3–24–2; Williamson 3–0–7–0. *Second innings*—Boult 12–1–46–1; Bracewell 13–0–38–1; Southee 14–4–30–1; Wagner 12–3–41–1; Williamson 7.2–1–18–1; Guptill 4–0–21–0; Brownlie 1–0–6–0.

Umpires: M. Erasmus and P. R. Reiffel. Third umpire: R. A. Kettleborough.
Series referee: R. S. Madugalle.

DOMESTIC CRICKET IN THE WEST INDIES, 2011-12

HAYDN GILL

Jamaica's name was firmly etched on the Headley–Weekes Trophy currently awarded to the Caribbean's first-class champions. Their stranglehold was confirmed by a fifth successive four-day triumph, a run matched only by Barbados, who shared the 1976 Shell Shield with Trinidad & Tobago before claiming the next four outright. In some ways, this was Jamaica's most commanding performance: they claimed their 12th championship – as the country celebrated 50 years since independence – with an unblemished record of eight victories, four of them completed in three days. But it was also their most nerve-jangling.

Barbados, the once mighty powerhouse with a record 20 titles, had been crushed by 120 runs when they met Jamaica in February. But in the final they threatened to upset their rivals' plans. Their last-wicket pair established a narrow first-innings lead – the first conceded by Jamaica in the competition. That meant Jamaica needed an outright win and, when rain wiped out part of the third afternoon, they had some catching up to do. They ran up 114 in 18 overs on the final morning and then declared, leaving Barbados ample time to chase a generous target of 230. But Dave Bernard tore in with the new ball to grab four wickets, and Barbados took lunch at 36 for five. Jamaican spin twins Nikita Miller and Odean Brown did the rest, though the match award went to the opposing spinner, Sulieman Benn, for his nine wickets.

Jamaica were led by the region's most successful domestic captain, Tamar Lambert, and their standout performers were Miller, the tournament's leading wicket-taker, with 49 at ten apiece, and the consistent Brown, with 36 at 15; Donovan Pagon contributed 569 runs and Lambert himself 450. They also reached both limited-overs finals, winning the Super50 title in October by beating **Trinidad & Tobago**. Trinidad had their revenge in January when they retained the Twenty20 title and qualified again for the Champions League; they also featured in the four-day semi-finals. So did **Guyana**, who had occupied the cellar position for the previous three seasons but improved significantly to finish fourth, despite being forced to play all their matches away from home because of a dispute between their board and the Guyanese government. They had the tournament's two top run-scorers, left-handers Narsingh Deonarine, with 582, and Assad Fudadin, with 576; both were picked for West Indies later in the year.

Only one game ended in a draw

Windward Islands' best moments came in the Twenty20 group stage, where they won all four matches. **Combined Campuses & Colleges** took a nosedive: after heading the four-day round-robin table in 2011, they lost five of their six games and finished next to bottom. But the most disappointing team were **Leeward Islands**, who also lost five matches, and were bowled out for 39, the lowest total in the tournament's history, by Campuses & Colleges. In all they were dismissed for under 150 nine times, never passed 200, and averaged 116.

That was the worst manifestation of the decline of Caribbean batting, but the overall picture ought to have raised serious concerns among the authorities. Of the 24 first-class fixtures, 14 finished inside three days, including three that lasted less than two; only one game ended in a draw. There were ten totals of under 100, and just three over 400. Only four batsmen topped 500 runs, and there were a mere 11 centuries, while eight bowlers claimed ten in a match. All six who collected 30 wickets in the tournament were spinners. Meanwhile the growth of Twenty20 leagues continued to threaten the domestic game, with several star players leaving for the Bangladesh Premier League after a single round of first-class matches.

FIRST-CLASS AVERAGES, 2011-12

BATTING (250 runs)

	M	*I*	*NO*	*R*	*HS*	*100*	*Avge*	*Ct/St*
†S. Chanderpaul (*Guyana & West Indies*)	6	10	4	616	125*	2	102.66	5
†B. P. Nash (*Jamaica*)	5	9	3	381	205*	1	63.50	1
D. Ramdin (*Trinidad & Tobago*)	4	8	2	341	151*	1	56.83	7
†A. B. Fudadin (*Guyana*)	7	13	1	576	108	2	48.00	7
†N. Deonarine (*Guyana & West Indies*)	10	18	0	699	89	0	38.83	10
D. J. Pagon (*Jamaica*)	8	15	0	569	155	1	37.93	7
C. R. Brathwaite (*Barbados & West Indies A*)	5	9	2	254	62	0	36.28	6
T. L. Lambert (*Jamaica*)	8	14	1	450	61	0	34.61	11
K. A. Edwards (*Barbados & West Indies*)	6	12	0	402	99	0	33.50	4
†J. L. Carter (*Barbados & West Indies A*)	10	19	0	608	99	0	32.00	13
N. E. Bonner (*Campuses & Colleges & WI A*)	7	13	0	392	127	1	30.15	5
D. J. G. Sammy (*Windward Islands & WI*)	5	10	1	269	88	0	29.88	11
B. A. Parchment (*Jamaica*)	5	10	1	256	58	0	28.44	6
†D. M. Bravo (*Trinidad & Tobago & WI*)	7	14	1	366	64	0	28.15	13
D. P. Hyatt (*Jamaica & West Indies A*)	8	15	0	411	92	0	27.40	11
C. S. Baugh (*Jamaica & West Indies*)	8	12	0	302	140	1	25.16	13/2
†L. R. Johnson (*Guyana*)	7	13	0	327	72	0	25.15	12
K. Lesporis (*Windward Islands*)	6	12	0	259	84	0	21.58	6
D. E. Bernard (*Jamaica*)	8	14	0	295	70	0	21.07	2
†K. O. A. Powell (*Leeward Islands & WI*)	6	12	0	250	55	0	20.83	2
A. B. Barath (*Trinidad & Tobago & WI*)	7	13	1	250	114	1	20.83	5
K. C. Brathwaite (*Barbados & West Indies*)	10	18	1	351	62	0	20.64	8
†O. J. Phillips (*Barbados*)	8	15	0	299	87	0	19.93	2

BOWLING (15 wickets)

	Style	*O*	*M*	*R*	*W*	*BB*	*5I*	*Avge*
N. O. Miller (*Jamaica*)	SLA	335.1	117	527	49	5-16	3	10.75
S. P. Narine (*Trinidad & Tobago & WI A*)	OB	159.1	44	360	33	8-17	5	10.90
A. D. Russell (*Jamaica & West Indies A*)	RFM	72.1	18	219	17	5-36	1	12.88
J. P. R. Scantlebury-Searles (*Barbados*)	RFM	60.1	16	198	15	6-44	2	13.20
G. C. Tonge (*Leeward Islands*)	RFM	94.1	25	302	21	6-78	2	14.38
S. J. Benn (*Barbados*)	SLA	240.3	61	662	45	5-28	3	14.71
O. V. Brown (*Jamaica*)	LBG	217.5	48	538	36	6-100	3	14.94
D. E. Bernard (*Jamaica*)	RFM	132.3	22	384	24	7-23	1	16.00
K. Kantasingh (*Trinidad & Tobago*)	SLA	163.5	46	400	24	6-77	2	16.66
S. Shillingford (*Windward Islands & WI*)	OB	347.1	76	871	52	8-33	5	16.75
K. A. J. Roach (*Barbados & West Indies*)	RF	202	42	606	34	5-31	3	17.82
A. P. Richardson (*Jamaica*)	RFM	148.2	27	466	26	5-36	2	17.92
J. O. Holder (*Campuses & Colleges*)	RFM	152.3	50	418	23	5-48	1	18.17
R. A. Austin (*Campuses & Colleges*)	OB	231	44	697	38	7-84	4	18.34
N. Deonarine (*Guyana & West Indies*)	OB	220.4	45	532	29	7-26	2	18.34
K. R. McClean (*Campuses & Colleges*)	RF	136.2	37	411	22	4-53	0	18.68
G. E. Mathurin (*Windward Islands*)	SLA	132.5	36	339	18	5-34	1	18.83
Suhrawadi Shuvo (*Bangladesh A*)	SLA	101.1	21	315	16	5-81	1	19.68
T. L. Best (*Barbados*)	RF	87.2	13	351	17	4-33	0	20.64
V. Permaul (*Guyana & West Indies A*)	OB	346.1	94	816	37	6-91	2	22.05
D. Bishoo (*Guyana & West Indies*)	LBG	191.3	28	624	25	5-62	2	24.96
N. T. Pascal (*Windward Islands & WI A*)	RF	198.5	34	707	28	5-50	1	25.25
S. T. Gabriel (*Trinidad & Tobago & WI A*)	RFM	233.3	41	767	30	5-78	1	25.56

Averages include Bangladesh A's tour in November and Australia's tour in April, but not New Zealand's tour in July–August 2012.

HEADLEY–WEEKES TROPHY, 2011-12

	Played	*Won*	*Lost*	*Drawn*	*1st-inns points*	*Points*
Jamaica	6	6	0	0	0	72
Barbados	6	4	2	0	0	48
Trinidad & Tobago	6	3	2	1	7	46
Guyana	6	3	2	1	0	39
Windward Islands	6	2	4	0	4	28
Combined Campuses & Colleges	6	1	5	0	4	16
Leeward Islands	6	1	5	0	0	12

Semi-finals: Jamaica beat Guyana by 133 runs; Barbados beat Trinidad & Tobago by 227 runs.

Final: Jamaica beat Barbados by 139 runs.

Win = 12pts; draw = 3pts; first-innings lead in a drawn match = 3pts; first-innings lead in a lost match = 4pts.

At Bridgetown (Three Ws Oval), Barbados, February 3–5, 2012 (day/night). **Trinidad & Tobago won by 172 runs. ‡Trinidad & Tobago 229** (R. A. Austin 7-84) **and 168** (J. O. Holder 5-48); **Combined Campuses & Colleges 111** (S. P. Narine 5-22) **and 114** (S. P. Narine 8-17). *Trinidad & Tobago 12pts. Sunil Narine's 8-17 in 14.1 overs was the best return of the season; he took 13-39 in all, overshadowing fellow off-spinner Ryan Austin's nine.*

At Roseau, Dominica, February 3–5, 2012. **Guyana won by 234 runs. Guyana 208** (G. C. Tonge 5-53) **and 226**; **‡Leeward Islands 98 and 102**. *Guyana 12pts.*

At Kingston, Jamaica, February 3–5, 2012. **Jamaica won by 81 runs. Jamaica 180** (G. E. Mathurin 5-34) **and 298** (C. H. Gayle 165; S. Shillingford 6-75); **‡Windward Islands 159** (A. P. Richardson 5-36) **and 238** (D. S. Smith 103). *Jamaica 12pts. Chris Gayle played his first first-class match in 14 months, and his last before leaving for the Bangladesh Premier League; he hit 165 in 155 balls, with eight fours and 14 sixes, to set Jamaica on a winning path.*

At Bridgetown (Three Ws Oval), Barbados, February 10–11, 2012. **Combined Campuses & Colleges won by an innings and 15 runs. Leeward Islands 39** (R. A. Austin 5-19) **and 113** (R. A. Austin 5-52); **‡Combined Campuses & Colleges 167**. *Combined Campuses & Colleges 12pts. Leewards were bowled out for the lowest total in the Caribbean since 1942, and the lowest ever in the first-class regional tournament (undercutting Guyana's 41 at Kingston in 1985-86). Ryan Austin took 5-19 in 5.2 overs, and he improved that to 10-71 as Campuses & Colleges won inside two days.*

At Roseau, Dominica, February 10–13, 2012. **Windward Islands won by five wickets. ‡Guyana 138** (N. T. Pascal 5-50) **and 294**; **Windward Islands 252** (V. Permaul 6-91) **and 183-5**. *Windward Islands 12pts. Windwards wicketkeeper Lindon James held six catches in Guyana's first innings.*

At Kingston, Jamaica, February 10–12, 2012. **Jamaica won by 120 runs. ‡Jamaica 287 and 162** (K. A. J. Roach 5-31); **Barbados 157** (N. O. Miller 5-25) **and 172** (N. O. Miller 5-24). *Jamaica 12pts. Slow left-armer Nikita Miller's first-innings figures were 22–8–25–5.*

At Bridgetown (Kensington Oval), Barbados, February 16–19, 2012. **Barbados won by five wickets. Trinidad & Tobago 338** (F. H. Edwards 5-64) **and 119**; **‡Barbados 279** (S. P. Narine 5-78) **and 180-5**. *Barbados 12pts, Trinidad & Tobago 4pts.*

At Basseterre, St Kitts, February 16–19, 2012. **Guyana won by four wickets. ‡Combined Campuses & Colleges 194** (V. Permaul 5-63) **and 342** (C. A. K. Walton 119*; C. D. Barnwell 6-78); **Guyana 320** (A. B. Fudadin 102*) **and 219-6**. *Guyana 12pts.*

At Kingston, Jamaica, February 16–18, 2012. **Jamaica won by an innings and 201 runs. ‡Jamaica 404-8 dec** (D. J. Pagon 155); **Leeward Islands 104** (O. V. Brown 5-6) **and 99** (N. O. Miller 5-16). *Jamaica 12pts.*

At Bridgetown (Kensington Oval), Barbados, February 24–26, 2012 (day/night). **Barbados won by 189 runs. ‡Barbados 237 and 238-4 dec; Combined Campuses & Colleges 145 and 141**. *Barbados 12pts.*

At North Sound, Antigua, February 24–27, 2012 (day/night). **Jamaica won by eight wickets. ‡Guyana 294** (O. V. Brown 6-100) **and 187**; **Jamaica 454-9 dec** (B. P. Nash 205*; D. Bishoo

5-115) **and 30-2**. *Jamaica 12pts. Brendan Nash's second double-hundred was the only one scored in the West Indian season, and Jamaica's 454 the highest total.*

At Port-of-Spain, Trinidad, February 24–27, 2012. **Trinidad & Tobago won by four wickets.** **‡Trinidad & Tobago 364-9 dec** (D. Ramdin 151*) **and 98-6; Windward Islands 203** (S. P. Narine 5-49) **and 258** (S. P. Narine 5-78). *Trinidad & Tobago 12pts. Chasing 98, Trinidad & Tobago stumbled to 84-6 before completing victory.*

At Bridgetown (Kensington Oval), Barbados, March 9–12, 2012. **Guyana won by an innings and 66 runs. Barbados 317 and 58** (N. Deonarine 7-26); **‡Guyana 441** (S. Chanderpaul 125*; C. J. Jordan 5-77). *Guyana 12pts. The first two innings of the match totalled 758, with Guyana's last pair, Shivnarine Chanderpaul and Brandon Bess (33), adding 115; Barbados then crumbled for 58 against off-spinner Narsingh Deonarine's career-best 7-26, while Assad Fudadin held five catches in the field. Pedro Collins of Barbados took his 500th first-class wicket.*

At North Sound, Antigua, March 9–11, 2012 (day/night). **Leeward Islands won by 30 runs. ‡Leeward Islands 121** (K. K. Peters 5-43) **and 177; Windward Islands 178** (G. C. Tonge 6-78) **and 90.** *Leeward Islands 12pts, Windward Islands 4pts. Leewards recorded their only victory of a disastrous season.*

At Port-of-Spain, Trinidad, March 9–12, 2012. **Jamaica won by 192 runs. ‡Jamaica 290** (C. S. Baugh 140; K. Kantasingh 6-94) **and 157; Trinidad & Tobago 143 and 112** (D. E. Bernard 7-23). *Jamaica 12pts. Carlton Baugh's century rescued Jamaica from 84-5 before he joined West Indies' one-day squad against Australia in mid-match.*

At Bridgetown (Kensington Oval), Barbados, March 16–18, 2012. **Barbados won by an innings and seven runs. Leeward Islands 138 and 172** (S. J. Benn 5-53); **‡Barbados 317.** *Barbados 12pts.*

At Port-of-Spain, Trinidad, March 16–19, 2012. **Drawn. Guyana 290 and 208-5** (A. B. Fudadin 108); **‡Trinidad & Tobago 349** (A. B. Barath 114; N. Deonarine 6-71). *Trinidad & Tobago 6pts, Guyana 3pts. This was the only draw of the tournament, and featured its highest stand – 148 for the second wicket between Adrian Barath and Marlon Barclay (58). Fudadin became the only man to score two centuries during the domestic season.*

At St George's (Queen's Park New), Grenada, March 16–18, 2012. **Windward Islands won by 22 runs. Windward Islands 149 and 191; ‡Combined Campuses & Colleges 209 and 109** (S. Shillingford 7-34). *Windward Islands 12pts, Combined Campuses & Colleges 4pts.*

At Bridgetown (Three Ws Oval), Barbados, March 23–26, 2012. **Jamaica won by 154 runs. ‡Jamaica 200 and 257** (R. A. Austin 5-89); **Combined Campuses & Colleges 137 and 166** (O. V. Brown 5-25). *Jamaica 12pts.*

At Basseterre, St Kitts, March 23–24, 2012. **Trinidad & Tobago won by nine wickets. ‡Leeward Islands 81 and 158** (K. Kantasingh 6-77); **Trinidad & Tobago 172 and 68-1.** *Trinidad & Tobago 12pts. Another low-scoring match ended in two days.*

At St George's (Queen's Park New), Grenada, March 23–24, 2012. **Barbados won by 71 runs. ‡Barbados 192** (S. Shillingford 6-77) **and 85** (S. Shillingford 8-33); **Windward Islands 133** (J. P. R. Scantlebury-Searles 6-44) **and 73** (J. P. R. Scantlebury-Searles 5-39). *Barbados 12pts. Off-spinner Shane Shillingford improved his career-best for the second successive match and took 14-110 in all, but ultimately Javon Scantlebury-Searles's 11-83 swung a game completed in two days; each total was lower than the last. Windwards were 0-3 after seven balls of their second innings.*

Semi-finals

At Kingston, Jamaica, March 30–April 1, 2012. **Jamaica won by 133 runs. ‡Jamaica 196 and 189** (D. Bishoo 5-62); **Guyana 126 and 126.**

At Port-of-Spain, Trinidad, March 30–April 1, 2012. **Barbados won by 227 runs. ‡Barbados 223 and 216** (S. T. Gabriel 5-78); **Trinidad & Tobago 84** (S. J. Benn 5-28) **and 128.** *Trinidad & Tobago lost their last seven first-innings wickets for just 21.*

Final

At Kingston, Jamaica, April 13–16, 2012. **Jamaica won by 139 runs.** **‡Jamaica 273** (S. J. Benn 5-90) **and 247-5 dec**; **Barbados 291** (A. P. Richardson 5-71) **and 90**. *Jonathan Carter of Barbados equalled his career-best 99 before their last-wicket pair, Sulieman Benn and Tino Best, added 22 to build a slender lead. But, after Jamaica declared on the final morning to set a 230-run target, Dave Bernard grabbed four wickets before lunch, and Barbados could not fight back from 25-5.*

REGIONAL CHAMPIONS

Shell Shield	
1965-66	Barbados
1966-67	Barbados
1967-68	No competition
1968-69	Jamaica
1969-70	Trinidad
1970-71	Trinidad
1971-72	Barbados
1972-73	Guyana
1973-74	Barbados
1974-75	Guyana
1975-76	Trinidad Barbados
1976-77	Barbados
1977-78	Barbados
1978-79	Barbados
1979-80	Barbados
1980-81	Combined Islands
1981-82	Barbados
1982-83	Guyana
1983-84	Barbados
1984-85	Trinidad & Tobago
1985-86	Barbados
1986-87	Guyana
Red Stripe Cup	
1987-88	Jamaica
1988-89	Jamaica
1989-90	Leeward Islands
1990-91	Barbados
1991-92	Jamaica
1992-93	Guyana
1993-94	Leeward Islands
1994-95	Barbados
1995-96	Leeward Islands
1996-97	Barbados
President's Cup	
1997-98	Leeward Islands Guyana
Busta Cup	
1998-99	Barbados
1999-2000	Jamaica
2000-01	Barbados
2001-02	Jamaica
Carib Beer Cup	
2002-03	Barbados
2003-04	Barbados
2004-05	Jamaica
2005-06	Trinidad & Tobago
2006-07	Barbados
2007-08	Jamaica
2008-09	Jamaica
President's Trophy	
2009-10	Jamaica
2010-11	Jamaica
Hedley–Weekes Trophy	
2011-12	Jamaica

Barbados have won the title outright 19 times, Jamaica 12, Guyana 5, Trinidad/Trinidad & Tobago 4, Leeward Islands 3, Combined Islands 1. Barbados, Guyana, Leeward Islands and Trinidad have also shared the title.

REGIONAL SUPER 50, 2011-12

50-over league plus knockout

Group A	*P*	*W*	*L*	*NR*	*Pts*
Guyana	3	2	0	1	12
Sagicor HP Centre	3	1	0	2	8
Barbados	3	0	1	2	3
Windward Islands	3	0	2	1	–1

Group B	*P*	*W*	*L*	*NR*	*Pts*
Jamaica	3	2	1	0	14
Trinidad & Tobago	3	2	1	0	12
Campuses & Colleges	3	2	1	0	8
Leeward Islands	3	0	3	0	–5

Semi-finals

At Providence, Guyana, October 26, 2011 (day/night). **Trinidad & Tobago won by four wickets.** **‡Guyana 200-9** (50 overs); **Trinidad & Tobago 201-6** (46.1 overs). *MoM:* J. N. Mohammed (T&T). *Jason Mohammed steered Trinidad home with 65* in 74 balls.*

At Providence, Guyana, October 27, 2011 (day/night). **Jamaica won by one wicket.** **‡Sagicor High Performance Centre 176-9** (50 overs); **Jamaica 178-9** (49.5 overs). *MoM:* K. Santokie (Jamaica). *Krishmar Santokie had Sagicor HPC struggling on 23-3 in the seventh over. But the youngsters almost pulled off a shock win before Jamaica's last-wicket pair Santokie and Odean Brown, who came together needing 13 off 13 balls, hit the winning runs with one to spare.*

Final

At Providence, Guyana, October 29, 2011 (day/night). **Jamaica won by five wickets.** ‡**Trinidad & Tobago 118** (46.1 overs); **Jamaica 122-5** (35.5 overs). *MoM:* N. O. Miller (Jamaica). *Andre Russell and slow left-armer Nikita Miller reduced Trinidad to 30-4 in the 15th over, only for Jamaica to stumble to 42-4 in reply; they recovered far better, however, to take the trophy with 14.1 overs in hand.*

CARIBBEAN T20, 2011-12

20-over league plus knockout

Group A	P	W	L	Pts	NRR
Windward Islands	4	4	0	16	0.81
Trinidad & Tobago	4	3	1	12	2.57
Guyana	4	2	2	8	0.10
Leeward Islands	4	1	3	4	–2.02
Canada	4	0	4	0	–1.55

Group B	P	W	L	Pts	NRR
Barbados	4	4	0	16	3.58
Jamaica	4	3	1	12	0.15
Campuses & Colleges	4	1	3	4	–0.94
Sussex	4	1	3	4	–0.98
Netherlands	4	1	3	4	–1.48

Semi-finals

At Bridgetown (Kensington Oval), Barbados, January 21, 2012. **Jamaica won by five wickets.** ‡**Windward Islands 98-8** (20 overs); **Jamaica 99-5** (18 overs). *MoM:* O. V. Brown (Jamaica).

At Bridgetown (Kensington Oval), Barbados, January 21, 2012 (floodlit). **Trinidad & Tobago won by five wickets.** ‡**Barbados 90** (19.5 overs); **Trinidad & Tobago 93-5** (14 overs). *MoM:* S. P. Narine (T&T). *Sunil Narine took two top-order wickets for just ten runs in his four overs.*

Third-place play-off

At Bridgetown (Kensington Oval), Barbados, January 22, 2012. **Windward Islands won by seven wickets.** ‡**Barbados 101** (20 overs) (D. E. Johnson 5-5); **Windward Islands 105-3** (17.5 overs). *MoM:* D. E. Johnson (Windwards). *Delorn Johnson took four wickets in nine balls to leave Barbados reeling on 7-4 in the fourth over.*

Final

At Bridgetown (Kensington Oval), Barbados, January 22, 2012 (floodlit). **Trinidad & Tobago won by 63 runs.** ‡**Trinidad & Tobago 168-6** (20 overs); **Jamaica 105-5** (20 overs). *MoM:* D. J. Bravo (T&T). *MoS:* K. A. Pollard (T&T). *Trinidad & Tobago retained their title thanks to Dwayne Bravo, who steadied them with 49, and Kieron Pollard, who hit 26 runs off the final over of the innings, then pulled off a run-out and two catches.*

ZIMBABWE CRICKET, 2012

A fork in the road

MEHLULI SIBANDA

Zimbabwe cricket was mired in stagnation. Not only did the national team play a paltry eight international matches in all formats, they lost them all too. To demonstrate how far their stock had fallen, they hosted no international fixtures in 2012, except for an unofficial triangular series featuring South Africa and Bangladesh in July, which at least ended in a surprise victory for the home side, spurred on by the batting of Hamilton Masakadza.

Zimbabwe were clearly stuck in limbo between the more powerful Full Members, who were reluctant to engage them in lengthy series, and the Associates, who would provide more frequent opposition – but at a price, both financially and in terms of the quality of cricket. Due to the cost required to set up the domestic franchise system in 2009, Zimbabwe Cricket were believed to have built up debts of around US$18m, which made the $1.5m awarded to them as part of the ICC's Targeted Assistance and Performance Programme over the next three years look like a drop in the ocean.

ZIMBABWE IN 2012

	Played	*Won*	*Lost*	*Drawn/No result*
Tests	1	–	1	–
One-day internationals	3	–	3	–
Twenty20 internationals	4	–	4	–

JANUARY / FEBRUARY	1 Test, 3 ODIs and 2 T20Is (a) v New Zealand	(page 1120)
MARCH		
APRIL		
MAY		
JUNE		
JULY		
AUGUST		
SEPTEMBER / OCTOBER	World Twenty20 (in Sri Lanka)	(page 841)
NOVEMBER		
DECEMBER		

For a review of Zimbabwean domestic cricket from the 2011-12 season, see page 1197.

Tsvangirayi Mukwazhi, AP/PA

Try telling them it's unofficial: cricket-starved Zimbabwe fans mob Hamilton Masakadza after he powered them to a win over South Africa in Harare.

In January, Zimbabwe had undertaken their first tour of New Zealand for 11 years. It was a chastening experience in often cold conditions, and they were beaten in all six internationals by a team not exactly long on confidence themselves. The solitary Test at Napier was a dismemberment: Zimbabwe were underpowered with the ball, then dismissed twice in a day to lose by an innings and 301 runs – the heaviest defeat in their Test history. More bruisings followed in the one-day series, but Zimbabwe did show some fight in the two Twenty20 games, taking the second down to the last over.

With another seven months before the World Twenty20, Zimbabwe were in desperate need of practice in the format, so their board conceived a triangular tournament in Harare, to which Bangladesh and South Africa sent young teams. Each side won two games in the group stage, but Zimbabwe sneaked past Bangladesh on net run-rate, then thumped South Africa in the final. When captain Brendan Taylor pulled the four that confirmed a rare (if unofficial) victory over their neighbours, an exuberant crowd starved of top-class cricket invaded the pitch and mobbed the players. Masakadza, who put on 118 with Taylor in the final, led the scoring charts, with 267 runs in five innings – but, sadly for him, they did not count in the Twenty20 international records.

In June, Ozias Bvute resigned as Zimbabwe Cricket's managing director, and was replaced by his deputy, Wilfred Mukondiwa. The debate will rage on as to whether Bvute was good for the game. Bvute, who took over in 2004, will probably always be remembered as the man whose hardline stance led to the mass exodus of senior players following the sacking that year of captain Heath Streak. That sad episode led to Zimbabwe eventually withdrawing from Test cricket in 2006, after a string of disastrous results. Bvute remained connected to the commercial arm of the board in a consultancy role.

Zimbabwe were too often let down by short-sighted administrative decisions, and the six weeks they spent preparing in Sri Lanka for the World Twenty20 included only two warm-up matches against other nations. With such shoddy arrangements, it was no surprise when they were thrashed by both Sri Lanka and South Africa – bowing out of the tournament before five other teams had even taken the field.

Tatenda Taibu had long been a devout Christian – banning television from his house, and holding Bible sessions with his family – and in July he quit cricket to devote his life to the church. "When I was growing up I used to think that success meant having money, a good wife and family, but that is wrong," he said. "I was the first black captain in the country, the youngest Test captain in the history of the sport, and also the first local player to score two centuries against South Africa, but that was not enough. I have achieved everything in life, but one thing I am trying to achieve is the salvation of my soul."

Taibu walked away from the game at 29, usually the age when batsmen are reaching their prime. It was not the first time he had done so. In 2006, he quit Zimbabwe with the intention of qualifying for South Africa, only to return the following year. But he remained frustrated by the way cricket was being run: on the eve of Zimbabwe's Test return in August 2011, Taibu had spoken out against the ZC leadership for their tardiness in paying players – a practice which persisted into 2012. With age on his side, there was still hope that Taibu might reconsider his decision.

In November, head coach Alan Butcher signalled he would not be seeking a renewal of his contract beyond April 2013, as his family were not prepared to relocate from England. It meant his last assignment would be Zimbabwe's tour of the West Indies in February and March. Butcher was at pains to point out that the Bridgetown Test would be their first for more than a year. He had turned them into a competitive unit at home, but results abroad remained worrying. And though he gave his all to the role, he was often let down by the decision-makers above him.

TRI-NATION T20, 2012

ANT SIMS

1. Zimbabwe 2. South Africa 3. Bangladesh

South Africa wanted warm-up matches and Bangladesh some cricket, but Zimbabwe were keen to show the world they had grown up. And they did so in style, beating South Africa in the final of this unofficial triangular to give the 5,000 or so fans who turned up for each of their last three matches genuine cause for cheer. It provided a reminder that, despite the absence of world-class facilities available to many of their competitors, Zimbabwe were a team filled with potential. But it was one of their more seasoned players who provided the backbone: 28-year-old Hamilton Masakadza made four half-centuries in five games, following a hundred in a warm-up match against the Bangladeshis.

South Africa brought a young team so they could assess their options ahead of the World Twenty20 in September, while Bangladesh brought with them a chunk of sponsors – and a new head coach, Richard Pybus. Both touring sides paid their own way to help the impecunious Zimbabwean board – hosting international cricket for the first time in over seven months – to cover the tournament costs. With Zimbabwe's victory came $3,500 prize money too.

Richard Levi was a powerful presence at the top of South Africa's order but, without Morne Morkel and Dale Steyn, their bowlers struggled to adapt to slower conditions. Bangladesh, who rested leading all-rounder Shakib Al Hasan, showed guts, beating both opponents to stay in the hunt for a place in the final until the very end. As Zimbabwe's chances grew, the support swelled and, by the time they had lifted the trophy, thousands of fans had invaded the pitch to join in the jubilation. Zimbabwe Cricket hoped the tournament would open the door for other Test-playing nations to come knocking more often.

NATIONAL SQUADS

Bangladesh *Mushfiqur Rahim, Abdur Razzak, Abul Hasan, Anamul Haque, Elias Sunny, Farhad Reza, Jahurul Islam, Junaid Siddique, Mahmudullah, Mashrafe bin Mortaza, Mohammad Ashraful, Nasir Hossain, Nazmul Hossain, Tamim Iqbal, Ziaur Rahman. *Coach:* R. A. Pybus.

Shakib Al Hasan was originally selected, but withdrew before the tournament at his own request because of fatigue. He was replaced by Jahurul Islam.

South Africa *H. M. Amla, F. Behardien, M. de Lange, J-P. Duminy, F. du Plessis, C. A. Ingram, R. E. Levi, J. A. Morkel, C. H. Morris, J. L. Ontong, W. D. Parnell, R. J. Peterson, L. L. Tsotsobe, D. J. Vilas. *Coach:* G. Kirsten.

J. Botha was originally selected as captain, but withdrew before the tournament with a knee injury.

Zimbabwe *B. R. M. Taylor, R. W. Chakabva, E. Chigumbura, A. G. Cremer, C. R. Ervine, K. M. Jarvis, H. Masakadza, S. Matsikenyeri, C. B. Mpofu, R. Muzhange, V. Sibanda, P. Utseya, B. V. Vitori, M. N. Waller. *Coach:* A. R. Butcher.

At Harare, June 17, 2012. **Zimbabwe XI won by 11 runs.** ‡**Zimbabwe XI 154-6** (20 overs) (H. Masakadza 62, B. R. M. Taylor 38); **Bangladesh XI 143-5** (20 overs) (Tamim Iqbal 38). *MoM:* H. Masakadza. *Bangladesh looked set to succeed until Chris Mpofu – who had just let a catch slip through his fingers at long-on – returned with two wickets in his second spell, ensuring Hamilton Masakadza's 35-ball 62 did not go to waste.*

At Harare, June 19, 2012. **South Africa XI won by 39 runs.** ‡**South Africa XI 209-3** (20 overs) (R. E. Levi 37, H. M. Amla 88*); **Bangladesh XI 170-8** (20 overs) (Mohammad Ashraful 33, Mushfiqur Rahim 50*, Mahmudullah 34). *MoM*: H. M. Amla. *Hashim Amla hit a career-best 88* from 53 balls. Robin Peterson (4–0–16–2) completed a double-wicket maiden, and South Africa could even afford three dropped catches.*

At Harare, June 20, 2012. **Zimbabwe XI won by 29 runs.** ‡**Zimbabwe XI 176-4** (20 overs) (V. Sibanda 58, H. Masakadza 55, B. R. M. Taylor 38); **South Africa XI 147** (19.2 overs) (R. E. Levi 40, C. A. Ingram 48; C. B. Mpofu 3-20, A. G. Cremer 3-29). *MoM*: C. B. Mpofu. *South Africa struggled to contain openers Masakadza and Vusi Sibanda as they put on 114 in 13.3 overs, as well as Brendan Taylor, who crashed 38 from 21 balls. South Africa's middle order was left exposed, with Dane Vilas and J-P. Duminy defeated by Graeme Cremer's googly.*

At Harare, June 21, 2012. **Bangladesh XI won by six wickets.** ‡**Zimbabwe XI 149-8** (20 overs) (H. Masakadza 56); **Bangladesh XI 153-4** (17.3 overs) (Mushfiqur Rahim 31, Nasir Hossain 41*). *MoM*: Mashrafe bin Mortaza (Bangladesh XI). *Masakadza again propped up the innings, but Zimbabwe lost some of their bite. Only frenetic running between the wickets threatened to derail the Bangladesh chase.*

At Harare, June 22, 2012. **Bangladesh XI won by three wickets.** ‡**South Africa XI 129-7** (20 overs) (J. L. Ontong 41); **Bangladesh XI 132-7** (19.5 overs) (Mohammad Ashraful 40; M. de Lange 3-25). *MoM*: Mahmudullah (Bangladesh XI). *South Africa – having declined to practise the day before – stumbled again. The top order could not get going, and the bowlers missed their lengths. From 84-5, Bangladesh were boosted by a stand of 40 between Mahmudullah (28) and Ziaur Rahman (27*), whose sliced four completed a tense victory with a ball to spare, keeping alive their chance of reaching the final.*

At Harare, June 23, 2012. **South Africa XI won by six wickets.** ‡**Zimbabwe XI 124-6** (20 overs) (H. Masakadza 36; W. D. Parnell 3-16); **South Africa XI 130-4** (17.4 overs) (R. E. Levi 54). *MoM*: W. D. Parnell. *Needing to win to make the final, South Africa were grateful for canny bowling from Peterson and Wayne Parnell, and explosive batting from Levi. But the Zimbabweans managed to delay defeat until the 18th over; had they lost inside 15, Bangladesh would have qualified on net run-rate instead.*

South Africa XI 8pts (net run-rate 0.378), Zimbabwe XI 8pts (–0.08), Bangladesh XI 8pts (–0.28).

Final

At Harare, June 24, 2012. **Zimbabwe XI won by nine wickets.** ‡**South Africa XI 146-6** (20 overs) (F. du Plessis 66, J. A. Morkel 34*); **Zimbabwe XI 150-1** (17.1 overs) (H. Masakadza 58*, B. R. M. Taylor 59*). *MoM*: B. R. M. Taylor. *MoS*: H. Masakadza. *A crowd starved of international cricket invaded the pitch to celebrate Zimbabwe's rare and emphatic victory, delivered by Masakadza and Taylor in a stand of 118* in 13.4 overs. Masakadza was lucky to survive Lonwabo Tsostobe's strong appeal for lbw to the first ball of the innings, but joined forces with Taylor for the crucial assault on Peterson. South Africa themselves lost Levi lbw first ball, before Faf du Plessis and Albie Morkel gave their bowlers something to defend. Zimbabwe's win was their second in four days over the South Africans, having beaten them only twice before in 38 official 50- and 20-over internationals.*

DOMESTIC CRICKET IN ZIMBABWE, 2011-12

JOHN WARD

Zimbabwe's long-awaited return to Test cricket had an unfortunate knock-on effect. Five teams visited between June and November 2011, draining Zimbabwe Cricket's coffers; a sixth tour, by West Indies A, had to be cancelled. All too little cash was left for domestic cricket, and the first-class Logan Cup shrank from 12 matches a side to eight. The B League was cancelled, depriving reserve players of match practice. Squads were pruned, pay was cut. Some promising youngsters turned down new contracts, a few left the country. The rise in standards over the previous two seasons reversed sharply; the batting, in particular, proved fragile against bowling that was rarely challenged.

The Pro50 tournament – increased from 40 overs a side to reflect one-day internationals, and played on Saturdays instead of random weekdays – did better, drawing crowds between 100 and 500, except in Harare, where no marketing was done. In the final, home side Mashonaland Eagles beat Mid West Rhinos in front of fewer than 50 spectators; in earlier matches, it had been hard to find even one. Nearly 4,000 attended the Twenty20 final, also in Harare, where Mountaineers beat Mashonaland, but that was less than half the attendance of previous years.

The recession was least obvious in Bulawayo. **Matabeleland Tuskers** retained the Logan Cup in style. Dave Houghton was an influential coach, and they won the award for the best-run franchise. The batting was strong enough to keep Charles Coventry out of the first-class team, and the seam bowling too much for most, though the spin was weak. Swing bowler Glenn Querl, a regular for the Unicorns in England, took 45 wickets at under 13, but not everyone was convinced by his action, even though it had been cleared after being queried in English club cricket in 2008.

Mashonaland Eagles had failed to win a Cup match the previous season, but started with a remarkable victory at Masvingo, where Southern Rocks seemed to be heading for their first Logan Cup success in three years of the franchise system after setting Mashonaland 339, the highest total of the game. Instead, Forster Mutizwa hit a magnificent unbeaten 164 to snatch victory and give them the confidence for three more wins, despite Matabeleland Tuskers twice crushing them by an innings. A well-balanced team finished runners-up in the Logan Cup, won the Pro50 and were Twenty20 finalists.

Mid West Rhinos had the season's outstanding domestic player, Gary Ballance, born in Harare but now with Yorkshire and qualified for England; he would have been a certainty for the Zimbabwe team had he made himself available. He passed 1,000 runs in eight matches, including six centuries, and topped the batting averages with team-mate Riki Wessels. But a lack of batting depth told against the side, despite an excellent six-man bowling attack led by Edward Rainsford; the best they could achieve was runners-up in the Pro50. Vusi Sibanda refused a central contract from Zimbabwe Cricket, spent six weeks playing grade cricket in Sydney, and was omitted from the New Zealand tour; he appeared for Rhinos when available, but less successfully than usual.

Mountaineers, who had dominated the previous Logan Cup before their surprise defeat in the final, still seemed to be suffering from that reverse. They had a fine seam attack, but their batting often failed. Seven top players left **Southern Rocks** before the season because of problems with local administrators. The controversial Mark Vermeulen signed, but soon retired (only to return for Rhinos a year later). Their morale seemed to be shattered by the opening defeat against Mashonaland; they lost the next six games, before Mountaineers' lackadaisical approach allowed them a scarcely deserved draw at the last.

Mashonaland Eagles correspond to the 2008-09 season's Northerns, Matabeleland Tuskers to Westerns, Midwest Rhinos to Centrals (previously Midlands), Mountaineers to Easterns (previously Manicaland) and Southern Rocks to Southerns (previously Masvingo).

FIRST-CLASS AVERAGES, 2011-12

BATTING (350 runs)

	M	*I*	*NO*	*R*	*HS*	*100*	*Avge*	*Ct/St*
M. H. Wessels (*Mid West Rhinos*)	6	10	3	631	197	2	90.14	17
†G. S. Ballance (*Mid West Rhinos*)	8	15	2	1,093	210	6	84.07	16
B. R. M. Taylor (*Zimbabwe*)	4	8	1	499	117	2	71.28	9
F. Mutizwa (*Mashonaland Eagles*)	4	7	1	409	164*	2	68.16	9/1
M. N. Waller (*Mid West Rhinos & Zimbabwe*)	5	9	3	384	174	1	64.00	1
†T. Duffin (*Matabeleland Tuskers*)	8	14	3	423	104	1	38.45	4
P. J. Horton (*Matabeleland Tuskers*)	7	12	2	374	104	1	37.40	9
V. Sibanda (*Mid West Rhinos & Zimbabwe*)	10	19	0	684	162	1	36.00	12
T. Maruma (*Mountaineers*)	8	12	0	424	149	2	35.33	3
†C. R. Ervine (*Matabeleland Tuskers & Zim.*)	11	18	2	516	82	0	32.25	6
T. M. K. Mawoyo (*Mountaineers & Zim.*)	10	18	1	545	163*	1	32.05	9
H. Masakadza (*Mountaineers & Zimbabwe*)	10	18	0	555	104	1	30.83	7
R. W. Chakabva (*Mashonaland E. & Zim.*)	7	13	0	352	95	0	27.07	13/4

BOWLING (20 wickets, average 25.00)

	Style	*O*	*M*	*R*	*W*	*BB*	*5I*	*Avge*
R. G. Querl (*Matabeleland Tuskers*)	RM	277.2	93	579	45	6-20	5	12.86
S. W. Masakadza (*Mountaineers*)	RFM	181.2	41	453	33	6-54	2	13.72
L. T. Gumunyu-Manatsa (*Mashonaland E.*)	RFM	136.5	25	439	24	5-89	1	18.29
D. T. Tiripano (*Mountaineers*)	RFM	226.4	60	623	32	4-84	0	19.46
E. C. Rainsford (*Mid West Rhinos*)	RFM	206.4	57	470	23	5-35	1	20.43
N. Ncube (*Matabeleland Tuskers & Zim.*)	RFM	229.2	58	602	29	7-35	1	20.75
R. Muzhange (*Mid West Rhinos*)	RM	167	41	441	21	5-30	1	21.00
K. M. Jarvis (*Mashonaland Eagles & Zim.*)	RFM	224.2	44	735	33	5-23	3	22.27
T. L. Chatara (*Mountaineers & Zimbabwe*)	RFM	228.5	51	674	30	5-56	2	22.46
C. B. Mpofu (*Matabeleland Tuskers & Zim.*)	RFM	180.2	36	546	24	5-55	1	22.75
S. M. Mugava (*Mid West Rhinos*)	OB	169.3	40	506	21	6-41	1	24.09
B. V. Vitori (*Southern Rocks & Zimbabwe*)	LFM	165.2	27	597	24	5-26	2	24.87

Includes tours by Australia A, Bangladesh and Pakistan between July and September 2011.

CASTLE LOGAN CUP, 2011-12

	Played	*Won*	*Lost*	*Drawn*	*1st-inns points*	*Points*
Matabeleland Tuskers	8	5	1	2	6	36
Mashonaland Eagles	8	4	2	2	4	28
Mid West Rhinos	8	3	1	4	6	24
Mountaineers	8	2	3	3	3	15
Southern Rocks	8	0	7	1	1	1

Win = 6pts; lead on first innings = 1pt.

At Mutare, September 26–29, 2011. **Matabeleland Tuskers won by 106 runs.** ‡**Matabeleland Tuskers 306** (G. M. Ewing 102; N. Mushangwe 5-110) **and 186**; **Mountaineers 294** (C. B. Mpofu 5-55) **and 92**. *Matabeleland Tuskers 7pts.*

At Masvingo, September 26–29, 2011. **Mashonaland Eagles won by three wickets. Southern Rocks 266** (M. R. H. Mbofana 5-41) **and 219**; ‡**Mashonaland Eagles 147 and 342-7** (F. Mutizwa 164*). *Mashonaland Eagles 6pts, Southern Rocks 1pt.*

At Mutare, October 3–6, 2011. **Mashonaland Eagles won by 132 runs.** ‡**Mashonaland Eagles 267 and 212** (L. A. Dawson 7-51); **Mountaineers 229** (L. A. Dawson 110*) **and 118**. *Mashonaland Eagles 7pts. Hampshire's Liam Dawson followed an unbeaten century with a career-best 7-51, and still finished on the losing side.*

At Masvingo, October 3–5, 2011. **Mid West Rhinos won by an innings and 215 runs. ‡Southern Rocks 150** (M. T. Chinouya 5-26) **and 137; Mid West Rhinos 502-4 dec** (G. S. Ballance 210, M. N. Waller 174). *Mid West Rhinos 7pts. Gary Ballance hit a maiden double-hundred – the highest score of the Zimbabwean season – and added 341 for Mid West Rhinos' third wicket, a national record, with Malcolm Waller, who also reached a career-best.*

At Kwekwe, October 17–20, 2011. **Drawn. Mid West Rhinos 321** (L. T. Gumunyu-Manatsa 5-89) **and 299** (G. S. Ballance 128); **‡Mashonaland Eagles 463** (S. Matsikenyeri 144) **and 154-9.** *Mashonaland Eagles 1pt.*

At Masvingo, October 17–19, 2011. **Matabeleland Tuskers won by nine wickets. Southern Rocks 148** (R. G. Querl 6-38) **and 204** (K. O. Meth 5-53); **‡Matabeleland Tuskers 253 and 100-1.** *Matabeleland Tuskers 7pts.*

At Harare (Sports Club), October 31–November 2, 2011. **Matabeleland Tuskers won by an innings and 228 runs. ‡Matabeleland Tuskers 418** (P. J. Horton 104); **Mashonaland Eagles 52** (R. G. Querl 6-20) **and 138.** *Matabeleland Tuskers 7pts. None of Mashonaland's last six managed a run in their first-innings 52. The only lower total by a Mashonaland team was 47 in 2006-07, when they played as Northerns.*

At Kwekwe, October 31–November 3, 2011. **Mountaineers won by three wickets. Mid West Rhinos 309** (G. S. Ballance 100; S. W. Masakadza 5-47) **and 143** (T. L. Chatara 5-56); **‡Mountaineers 224** (K. T. Kasuza 132*) **and 230-7.** *Mountaineers 6pts, Mid West Rhinos 1pt. Ballance scored his third hundred in three games.*

At Bulawayo (Queens), November 14–17, 2011. **Drawn. ‡Mid West Rhinos 407-9 dec** (M. H. Wessels 197; R. G. Querl 5-132) **and 220-4 dec; Matabeleland Tuskers 320-5 dec and 142-2.** *Mid West Rhinos 1pt. Riki Wessels hit nine sixes and 12 fours, but narrowly missed a maiden double-century.*

At Mutare, November 14–16, 2011. **Mountaineers won by an innings and 114 runs. Southern Rocks 146 and 207; ‡Mountaineers 467-7 dec** (P. Mustard 105, T. Maruma 149). *Mountaineers 7pts. Leg-spinner Natsai Mushangwe had figures of 11–9–2–1 in Southern Rocks' first innings; later, Timycen Maruma and Prosper Utseya added 199 for Mountaineers' sixth wicket.*

At Harare (Sports Club), December 12–13, 2011. **Mashonaland Eagles won by an innings and 89 runs. ‡Mashonaland Eagles 335** (F. Mutizwa 118; B. V. Vitori 5-26); **Southern Rocks 98** (K. M. Jarvis 5-23) **and 148** (K. M. Jarvis 5-30). *Mashonaland Eagles 7pts. Kyle Jarvis claimed the only ten-wicket return of the tournament.*

At Bulawayo (Queens), December 12–15, 2011. **Drawn. Matabeleland Tuskers 236 and 43-4; ‡Mountaineers 129** (R. G. Querl 5-29). *Matabeleland Tuskers 1pt.*

At Harare (Sports Club), January 9–11, 2012. **Mashonaland Eagles won by seven wickets. ‡Mountaineers 219 and 55; Mashonaland Eagles 238** (E. Chigumbura 121; S. W. Masakadza 6-54) **and 39-3.** *Mashonaland Eagles 7pts. Mountaineers were 18-5 in their second innings before making Mashonaland Eagles bat again.*

At Kwekwe, January 9–12, 2012. **Mid West Rhinos won by seven wickets. ‡Southern Rocks 178** (E. C. Rainsford 5-35) **and 313** (A. G. Cremer 5-107); **Mid West Rhinos 444-8 dec** (G. S. Ballance 124, M. H. Wessels 133; B. V. Vitori 5-90) **and 48-3.** *Mid West Rhinos 7pts. Wessels scored 133 in 112 balls.*

At Harare (Sports Club), January 23–26, 2012. **Drawn. ‡Mashonaland Eagles 207 and 165** (M. T. Chinouya 5-45); **Mid West Rhinos 212** (G. S. Ballance 101*) **and 34-1.** *Mid West Rhinos 1pt.*

At Bulawayo (Queens), January 23–24, 2012. **Matabeleland Tuskers won by ten wickets. Southern Rocks 83** (R. G. Querl 5-28) **and 125** (N. Ncube 7-35); **‡Matabeleland Tuskers 177 and 36-0.** *Matabeleland Tuskers 7pts. Southern Rocks suffered their seventh defeat in seven games, after Njabulo Ncube returned the best figures of the season.*

At Harare (Sports Club), February 6–8, 2012. **Matabeleland Tuskers won by an innings and 30 runs. Mashonaland Eagles 181 and 70; ‡Matabeleland Tuskers 281** (T. Duffin 104; C. T. Mutombodzi 5-88). *Matabeleland Tuskers 7pts. Tatenda Gumunyu-Manatsa of Mashonaland Eagles recorded his first run in first-class cricket in his tenth innings, equalling a world record; he finished on 3*. But he added another duck when Matabeleland Tuskers dismissed Mashonaland in double figures for the second time in four months; the result sealed the first-class title.*

At Mutare, February 6–9, 2012. **Drawn. ‡Mid West Rhinos 253** (T. L. Chatara 5-63) **and 421-6 dec** (V. Sibanda 162, G. S. Ballance 116); **Mountaineers 313** (D. K. H. Mitchell 178) **and 85-2.** *Mountaineers 1pt. Ballance scored his third hundred in three matches, and sixth in seven. He added 232 for Mid West Rhinos' second wicket with Vusi Sibanda.*

At Kwekwe, February 13–15, 2012. **Mid West Rhinos won by 154 runs. Mid West Rhinos 116 and 296**; **‡Matabeleland Tuskers 115** (R. Muzhange 5-30) **and 143** (S. M. Mugava 6-41). *Mid West Rhinos 7pts. On first-class debut, Matabeleland wicketkeeper Tonny Mupariwa, brother of the international seamer Tawanda, held seven catches in Mid West Rhinos' first innings, including Ballance, after he had passed 1,000 runs for the season. But the champions went down to their only defeat.*

At Masvingo, February 13–16, 2012. **Drawn. ‡Mountaineers 412-9 dec** (T. Maruma 143, D. T. Tiripano 102*); **Southern Rocks 145 and 114-6**. *Mountaineers 1pt.*

LOGAN CUP WINNERS

1993-94	Mashonaland Under-24	2000-01	Mashonaland	2007-08	Northerns
1994-95	Mashonaland	2001-02	Mashonaland	2008-09	Easterns
1995-96	Matabeleland	2002-03	Mashonaland	2009-10	Mashonaland Eagles
1996-97	Mashonaland	2003-04	Mashonaland	2010-11	Matabeleland Tuskers
1997-98	Mashonaland	2004-05	Mashonaland	2011-12	Matabeleland Tuskers
1998-99	Matabeleland	2005-06	No competition		
1999-2000	Mashonaland	2006-07	Easterns		

Mashonaland/Northerns/Mashonaland Eagles have won the title 11 times, Matabeleland/Matabeleland Tuskers four times, Easterns twice, Mashonaland Under-24 once.

COCA-COLA PRO50 CHAMPIONSHIP, 2011-12

50-over league plus final

	Played	*Won*	*Lost*	*Tied*	*Bonus points*	*Points*	*Net run-rate*
Mashonaland Eagles	8	6	2	0	4	28	1.02
Mid West Rhinos	8	5	2	1	2	24	0.39
Matabeleland Tuskers	8	3	5	0	3	15	0.01
Southern Rocks	8	3	4	1	1	15	–0.47
Mountaineers	8	2	6	0	2	10	–0.75

Final

At Harare (Sports Club), February 25, 2012. **Mashonaland Eagles won by 63 runs. Mashonaland Eagles 220-8** (50 overs) (E. Chigumbura 104*); **‡Mid West Rhinos 157** (42.1 overs). *Mashonaland Eagles slumped to 34-5 in the 11th over before Elton Chigumbura rescued their innings almost singlehandedly; he made 104 in 115 balls, when no one else could pass 26. He followed up with 3-27 as Mid West Rhinos struggled in turn to 55-6; Graeme Cremer hit back with 47 but could not prevent Mashonaland winning with nearly eight overs in hand. Fewer than 50 spectators attended.*

STANBIC BANK TWENTY20, 2011-12

	Played	*Won*	*Lost*	*No result*	*Bonus points*	*Points*	*Net run-rate*
Mountaineers	4	3	1	0	2	14	0.73
Matabeleland Tuskers	4	3	1	0	1	13	0.86
Mid West Rhinos	4	2	1	1	0	10	0.08
Mashonaland Eagles	4	1	3	0	1	5	0.14
Southern Rocks	4	0	3	1	0	2	–2.36

Preliminary finals

1st v 2nd: Mountaineers beat Matabeleland Tuskers by seven wickets and went straight through to the final. **3rd v 4th:** Mashonaland Eagles beat Mid West Rhinos by 53 runs. **Final play-off:** Mashonaland Eagles beat Matabeleland Tuskers by 23 runs (D/L).

Final

At Harare (Sports Club), December 4, 2011. **Mountaineers won by 27 runs. ‡Mountaineers 142-6** (20 overs); **Mashonaland Eagles 115** (18.1 overs). *MoM:* C. Z. Harris. *Player of the Tournament:* P. D. Trego (166 runs at a strike-rate of 118, plus nine wickets and an economy-rate of 7.08 for Mashonaland Eagles). *Durham's Phil Mustard opened for Mountaineers with 56 in 31 balls, and 42-year-old New Zealander Chris Harris followed up with 34* and two wickets; Shingi Masakadza wrapped up Mashonaland Eagles' innings with 3-21.*

ICC WORLD TWENTY20 QUALIFIER, 2011-12

REVIEW BY TIM BROOKS

1. Ireland   2. Afghanistan   3. Namibia   4. Netherlands

The World Twenty20 Qualifier in the United Arab Emirates was the culmination of a process in which 90 Associate and Affiliate sides competed in 13 regional tournaments for the opportunity to play in the global showcase event. It was broadcast to 118 countries, with 16 teams battling for just two places in Sri Lanka six months later: the controversial decision by the ICC in 2011 to reduce the number of qualifiers from the proposed six meant Ireland and Afghanistan – now the most compelling rivalry below Test level – were overwhelming favourites. And so it proved.

While qualification was the main story, there were absorbing sub-plots: for the lesser teams there was the opportunity to close the gap on the better-funded High Performance Programme nations (Afghanistan, Canada, Ireland, Kenya, the Netherlands and Scotland) and press for more resources and exposure; for the players, a shop window for lucrative Twenty20 contracts across the globe. Anticipation was heightened by some eye-catching late selections – notably Michael Di Venuto for Italy and Geraint Jones for Papua New Guinea – that encouraged hopes of the odd upset, and also ensured the familiar argument about reliance on expats was rehearsed with more vigour than ever.

Many games were played in a *shamal*, an Arabian wind that throws swirls of dust into the atmosphere, which made fielding difficult: steepling catches went to ground, and mishits sailed over unsighted fielders. At times, the umpires even considered wearing dust masks. That would not have been the tournament's only sartorial curio: on the first day alone, 14 players – including six Omanis and four Afghans – were reprimanded by the ICC for breaching their stringent clothing and equipment regulations.

The group stages, comprising 56 games in eight days, followed a predictable pattern, as the professionalism of the HPP countries proved too much for the rest, with Namibia the honourable exception. Bermuda, Denmark, Oman and Uganda were outclassed, while Hong Kong and Nepal showed promise before faltering. But Namibia – boosted by opening batsman and Player of the Tournament Raymond van Schoor, who averaged 54 – emerged from the pack with a shock early victory over Ireland, and won their next six games to top Group B. Afghanistan won Group A, and were joined in the knockout stages by Namibia, Ireland, Canada, the Netherlands and – after a nailbiting defeat by the USA – Scotland, who had to endure an hour's wait before the ICC confirmed they had, by 0.007, a superior net run-rate to Kenya.

In a convoluted qualification process for the final itself, Namibia succumbed meekly to Afghanistan, while Ireland saw off Canada, the Netherlands and then Namibia to set up an eagerly awaited climax. A 3,500-strong crowd assembled in the Dubai Sports City Stadium, with Afghan hordes – part of the large Pashtun diaspora of migrant workers in the UAE – heavily outnumbering the Blarney Army. Drums rolled and bagpipes blew; amid the Afghan flags was a banner that read "Cricket = Peace".

Afghanistan set a commanding total, but Paul Stirling hadn't read the script: in the blink of an eye, he struck the second-fastest fifty in Twenty20 internationals, off 17 balls. Frustrated Afghan spectators were then provoked by a fan unfurling a Pakistani flag; some scaled the wall of the stand and charged at him, causing a stoppage in play. Back in the middle, Ireland calmly picked off the remaining runs, before William Porterfield held the trophy aloft to confirm his side's status as the best Twenty20 team outside the Test-playing brethren.

Group A

	Played	*Won*	*Lost*	*Points*	*Net run-rate*
AFGHANISTAN	7	7	0	14	1.88
NETHERLANDS	7	6	1	12	1.67
CANADA	7	5	2	10	0.80
Papua New Guinea	7	3	4	6	0.04
Nepal	7	3	4	6	–0.19
Hong Kong	7	2	5	4	–1.25
Bermuda	7	1	6	2	–0.99
Denmark	7	1	6	2	–2.00

Group B

	Played	*Won*	*Lost*	*Points*	*Net run-rate*
NAMIBIA	7	7	0	14	1.18
IRELAND	7	6	1	12	2.21
SCOTLAND	7	4	3	8	0.34
Kenya	7	4	3	8	0.34
Italy	7	3	4	6	0.00
USA	7	2	5	4	–1.00
Uganda	7	2	5	4	–1.19
Oman	7	0	7	0	–1.80

Scotland were ranked above Kenya on the third decimal point of net run-rate.

Group matches

Of the 56 group games, only the six between HPP sides had official Twenty20 international status; their scores are given below. Full scores from the group and plate matches can be found under Cricket in the United Arab Emirates 2011-12 at cricketarchive.co.uk

Group A

At Dubai (Sports City), March 13, 2012. **Netherlands won by 42 runs.** ‡**Netherlands 135-6** (20 overs) (H. S. Baidwan 3-29); **Canada 93** (16.4 overs) (A. S. Hansra 30; P. M. Seelaar 3-16). *Twenty20 international debuts:* R. Gunasekera, A. S. Hansra, Junaid Siddiqui, N. R. Kumar, Raza-ur-Rehman, Rustam Bhatti, Zahid Hussain (Canada); W. Barresi, T. L. W. Cooper, M. A. A. Jamil, S. J. Myburgh, M. R. Swart, T. van der Gugten (Netherlands). *MoM:* Mudassar Bukhari. *After Tom Cooper and Alexei Kervezee both scored 29, Mudassar Bukhari made 28* from 15 balls at the end of the Netherlands' innings, then took two wickets in his first three deliveries as Canada slumped to 26-5.*

At Dubai (Sports City), March 14, 2012. **Afghanistan won by four wickets.** ‡**Netherlands 149-6** (20 overs) (A. N. Kervezee 58*; Izatullah Dawlatzai 3-33); **Afghanistan 150-6** (19.4 overs) (Mohammad Shahzad 54). *Twenty20 international debuts:* Dawlat Zadran, Gulbadeen Naib, Izatullah Dawlatzai, Javed Ahmadi (Afghanistan). *MoM:* Mohammad Shahzad. *Kervezee hit three sixes – two of them in the last over – to lift the Netherlands to a respectable total, but Afghanistan always had the chase in hand.*

At Dubai (ICC Academy), March 18, 2012. **Afghanistan won by 41 runs.** ‡**Afghanistan 174-8** (20 overs) (Karim Sadiq 36, Samiullah Shenwari 61; Zahid Hussain 3-16); **Canada 133-9** (20 overs) (N. R. Kumar 38; Samiullah Shenwari 4-14). *Twenty20 international debuts:* Shabir Noori, Zamir Khan (Afghanistan); T. G. Gordon (Canada). *MoM:* Samiullah Shenwari. *Afghanistan were 52-0 before slow left-armer Zahid Hussain took three wickets in four balls; Samiullah Shenwari clouted 61 from 34, then took four wickets with his leg-breaks.*

Group B

At Dubai (ICC Academy), March 13, 2012. **Scotland won by 14 runs.** ‡**Scotland 178-7** (20 overs) (C. S. MacLeod 55, K. J. Coetzer 46); **Kenya 164** (20 overs) (A. A. Obanda 35, C. O. Obuya 50; G. D. Drummond 3-20). *Twenty20 international debuts:* R. Flannigan, P. L. Mommsen, S. M. Sharif, C. D. Wallace (Scotland). *MoM:* C. S. MacLeod. *Calum MacLeod hit seven fours from 35 balls and, although Kenya started with an opening stand of 55 in 5.2 overs, they lost regular wickets after that – three to run-outs by Richie Berrington.*

At Dubai (Sports City), March 14, 2012. **Ireland won by ten wickets.** ‡**Kenya 71** (19 overs) (W. B. Rankin 3-20); **Ireland 72-0** (7.2 overs) (W. T. S. Porterfield 56*). *MoM:* W. B. Rankin. *Kenya were shot out for the fourth-lowest total in Twenty20 internationals (the lowest, 67, was also by Kenya v Ireland, at Belfast in 2008). Only Tanmay Mishra (28) reached double figures. Alex Cusack took 2-5 in three overs. Ireland's openers overhauled the target with 76 balls to spare, a record for Twenty20 internationals (previously 74, by New Zealand v Kenya at Durban in September 2007).*

At Dubai (Sports City), March 18, 2012. **Ireland won by 17 runs.** ‡**Ireland 159-5** (20 overs) (E. C. Joyce 78*); **Scotland 142-7** (20 overs) (K. J. Coetzer 62, D F. Watts 33; K. J. O'Brien 3-35). *Twenty20 international debut:* M. A. Parker (Scotland). *MoM:* E. C. Joyce. *Ireland were 8-2 after seven balls, but Ed Joyce anchored them to a total that proved beyond Scotland, who also made a poor start (22-3 in the fourth over).*

Preliminary Finals

The teams heading each group met in the first qualifying final; the winners advanced to the overall final. The teams finishing second in each group met the teams finishing third in the other group; the winners advanced to the preliminary final. The winners of the preliminary final met the losers of the first qualifying final in the second qualifying final; the winners advanced to the overall final. The two finalists qualified for the World Twenty20 tournament in 2012-13.

Second v third. At Dubai (Sports City), March 22, 2012. **Ireland won by ten wickets.** ‡**Canada 106-8** (20 overs) (M. C. Sorensen 3-20, G. H. Dockrell 3-19); **Ireland 109-0** (9.3 overs) (W. T. S. Porterfield 42*, P. R. Stirling 61*). *Twenty20 international debut:* A. D. Poynter (Ireland). *MoM:* P. R. Stirling. *For the fifth match out of eight, Ireland took a wicket in the first over, and Max Sorensen and George Dockrell did not relax their iron grip. Paul Stirling's 21-ball fifty was, at the time, the fastest for Ireland in any format.*

Second v third. At Dubai (ICC Academy), March 22, 2012. **Netherlands won by three wickets.** ‡**Scotland 166-6** (20 overs) (R. D. Berrington 37, C. S. MacLeod 57); **Netherlands 169-7** (19.1 overs) (S. J. Myburgh 36, T. L. W. Cooper 60, R. M. Haq 3-22). *Twenty20 international debuts:* T. G. J. Gruijters (Netherlands); M. M. Iqbal (Scotland). *MoM:* T. L. W. Cooper. *Tom Cooper carried the chase with 60 from 32 balls and, though he chipped a catch with 15 still needed from two overs, Tim Gruijters smashed the second ball he faced for six to ease the Netherlands' passage.*

First qualifying final. At Dubai (Sports City), March 22, 2012. **Afghanistan won by 47 runs.** ‡**Afghanistan 146** (20 overs) (C. Viljoen 3-34, S. F. Burger 3-16); **Namibia 99** (18.1 overs) (Dawlat Zadran 3-5, Aftab Alam 4-25). *MoM:* Dawlat Zadran. *Afghanistan's emphatic win, their eighth in succession, sealed their place in the final – and also the tournament proper in Sri Lanka. Namibia did well to restrict them to 146, but Dawlat Zadran, in a fearsome opening spell, bowled Raymond van Schoor with the first ball of the reply, and had them in tatters at 13-3.*

Preliminary final. At Dubai (Sports City), March 23, 2012. **Ireland won by seven wickets.** **Netherlands 114-7** (20 overs) (A. N. Kervezee 56); ‡**Ireland 115-3** (16.4 overs) (P. R. Stirling 33, K. J. O'Brien 30*). *MoM:* K. J. O'Brien. *Porterfield held a stunning catch, running back 20 metres* *from point, to dismiss Stephan Myburgh and leave the Netherlands 17-2 in the fifth over – a position Kervezee tried in vain to repair. Stirling was playing his 100th game for Ireland in all formats, still aged only 21.*

Second qualifying final. At Dubai (Sports City), March 24, 2012. **Ireland won by nine wickets.** ‡**Namibia 94-6** (20 overs); **Ireland 96-1** (10.1 overs) (P. R. Stirling 59*). *MoM:* M. C. Sorensen (Ireland). *Namibia, who had produced the shock of the tournament to beat Ireland on the opening day, rolled over with barely a whimper when it mattered most – allowing the Irish to saunter into their third successive World Twenty20. Sorensen sent Namibia's innings into reverse, conceding no runs from his first eight balls, and finishing with 4–2–8–2. Stirling then cracked 59* from 32 deliveries.*

FINAL

AFGHANISTAN v IRELAND

At Dubai (Sports City), March 24, 2012. Ireland won by five wickets. Toss: Afghanistan. Twenty20 international debut: Aftab Alam.

Stirling settled a gripping, high-quality final with an astonishing 79 from 38 balls, crowning him as the tournament's leading run-scorer, with 357 from 227. This time he raced to 50 in 17 – only Yuvraj Singh, who took just 12 against England in the inaugural World Twenty20, had made a quicker half-century in Twenty20 internationals. Afghanistan were just as explosive: Karim Sadiq pulled the first ball of the innings, from Boyd Rankin, over the long-on ropes, Gulbadeen Naib struck the last two for six, and Mohammad Shahzad cut loose in between. Then, with the first ball of Ireland's reply, Dawlat Zadran ripped out Porterfield's middle stump with a yorker. But with Stirling in their stable, Ireland had enough to canter home.

Man of the Match: P. R. Stirling. *Man of the Tournament:* R. van Schoor (Namibia).

Afghanistan

		B	4	6
Karim Sadiq *b 10*	16	10	2	1
Javed Ahmadi *c 10 b 8*	6	5	1	0
†Mohammad Shahzad *c 1 b 9*	77	57	7	2
Mirwais Ashraf *c 1 b 5*	9	8	0	1
*Nawroz Mangal *c 9 b 5*	10	15	0	0
Samiullah Shenwari *c 10 b 9*	11	12	0	1
Mohammad Nabi *c 9 b 2*	1	2	0	0
Gulbadeen Naib *not out*	17	8	0	2
Aftab Alam *not out*	1	3	0	0
L-b 2, w 2	4			
6 overs: 55-2 (20 overs)	152-7			

1/18 2/27 3/56 4/78 5/119 6/131 7/137

Dawlat Zadran and Izatullah Dawlatzai did not bat.

Rankin 4–0–22–1; Johnston 4–0–41–1; Sorensen 3–0–26–2; O'Brien 4–0–18–2; Dockrell 3–0–26–0; Stirling 2–0–17–1.

Ireland

		B	4	6
*W. T. S. Porterfield *b 10*	0	1	0	0
P. R. Stirling *c 8 b 10*	79	38	9	3
E. C. Joyce *c 7 b 9*	11	16	2	0
†G. C. Wilson *c 4 b 9*	32	39	2	0
K. J. O'Brien *c 3 b 10*	0	1	0	0
A. D. Poynter *not out*	23	17	2	1
A. R. White *not out*	1	1	0	0
L-b 6, w 4	10			
6 overs: 62-2 (18.5 overs)	156-5			

1/0 2/33 3/113 4/113 5/150

D. T. Johnston, M. C. Sorensen, W. B. Rankin and G. H. Dockrell did not bat.

Dawlat Zadran 4–0–21–3; Mirwais Ashraf 1–0–17–0; Aftab Alam 3.5–0–34–2; Izatullah Dawlatzai 3–0–33–0; Samiullah Shenwari 3–0–15–0; Mohammad Nabi 3–0–25–0; Gulbadeen Naib 1–0–5–0.

Umpires: C. B. Gaffaney and B. B. Pradhan. Referee: D. T. Jukes.

Final rankings

Positions 5–16 were determined by play-offs:

1. Ireland 2. Afghanistan 3. Namibia 4. Netherlands 5. Scotland 6. Canada 7. Nepal 8. Papua New Guinea 9. Kenya 10. Italy 11. Hong Kong 12. USA 13. Bermuda 14. Uganda 15. Oman 16. Denmark.

OTHER FIRST-CLASS TOURS

INDIA A IN WEST INDIES, 2012

India A, captained by Cheteshwar Pujara, toured the Caribbean in June and July 2012, playing three first-class fixtures against West Indies A. The sides also contested a Twenty20 series, which West Indies A won 1–0 (with one tied), and shared a one-day series 1–1 (with one abandoned).

At Bridgetown, Barbados, June 2–5, 2012. **India A won by two wickets. West Indies A 252** (D. C. Thomas 57, V. Permaul 66) **and 210** (L. M. P. Simmons 53, K. C. Brathwaite 50; R. G. Sharma 4-41); **‡India A 277** (C. A. Pujara 50, R. G. Sharma 94, W. P. Saha 56; J. L. Carter 5-63) **and 188-8** (C. A. Pujara 96*; J. O. Holder 5-55). *Pujara, the outstanding batsman on either side, led India A to an exciting win with a defiant 96* from 222 balls. With showers in the air on the final day, they dipped to 95-7 against 20-year-old giant Jason Holder, but Pujara's skill and bravery – he was hit on the hand on 26 – carried them through.*

At Kingstown, St Vincent, June 9–12, 2012. **West Indies A won by 125 runs. ‡West Indies A 217** (K. C. Brathwaite 66; Shami Ahmed 4-48) **and 204** (J. L. Carter 74, D. J. Pagon 67; A. A. Darekar 6-67); **India A 202** (C. A. Pujara 67; V. Permaul 5-58) **and 94** (D. E. Johnson 6-34, V. Permaul 4-22). *Kraigg Brathwaite doted over 66 from 297 balls, and Pujara 67 from 170, as neither side could seize the initiative. The difference proved to be a sixth-wicket stand of 86 between Jonathan Carter and Donovan Pagon in West Indies A's second innings, which lifted the target to 220. That proved too much for the Indians: Delorn Johnson reduced them to 30-4, and captain and slow left-armer Veerasammy Permaul finished with career-best match figures of 9-80.*

At Gros Islet, St Lucia, June 16–19, 2012. **West Indies A won by ten wickets. India A 230** (J. S. Saxena 61) **and 202** (M. K. Tiwary 62, W. P. Saha 52; K. R. McClean 5-57); **‡West Indies A 336** (K. O. A. Powell 139, D. C. Thomas 50) **and 97-0** (K. O. A. Powell 56*). *India A's batsmen misfired again, and Kieran Powell proved a superb addition to the home side, having just completed a difficult Test series in England. He hit three sixes in a career-best 139, and later helped knock off the small target.*

SRI LANKA A IN SOUTH AFRICA, 2012

Sri Lanka A, captained by Dimuth Karunaratne, toured South Africa in June and July 2012, playing two first-class matches against South Africa A.

At Durban, June 30–July 2, 2012. **South Africa A won by an innings and eight runs. Sri Lanka A 170** (C. K. B. Kulasekara 51; R. K. Kleinveldt 4-47) **and 247** (A. R. S. Silva 50; R. McLaren 5-60); **‡South Africa A 425-6 dec** (D. Elgar 171, F. du Plessis 144). *The Sri Lankans had hit five half-centuries in their warm-up game, but found South Africa's second-string Test attack a tougher proposition. Dean Elgar and Faf du Plessis, who would each score Test centuries over the next six months, did so here too, putting on 292 for the third wicket. Imran Tahir, who chose to stay at home rather than head with the rest of South Africa's squad to Switzerland to prepare for the tour of England, took 3-82 in 22.4 overs, as the home side won with a day to spare.*

At Durban, July 6–9, 2012. **Drawn. Sri Lanka A 336** (F. D. M. Karunaratne 83, S. C. Serasinghe 53; R. McLaren 4-51) **and 302-5 dec** (F. D. M. Karunaratne 150*, M. D. K. Perera 51); **‡South Africa A 290** (F. Behardien 66, W. D. Parnell 70) **and 130-2** (F. du Plessis 55*). *Thami Tsolekile held eight catches in the first innings to equal a first-class record shared by ten other wicketkeepers. But Sri Lanka were steered to safety by Karunaratne's 150*.*

SOUTH AFRICA A IN IRELAND, 2012

South Africa A, captained by Justin Ontong, toured Ireland in August 2012, playing two first-class matches against an Ireland XI. The sides also contested a one-day series, which South Africa A won 2–0 (with one no-result). A subsequent four-match Twenty20 series was cancelled, at the behest of the tourists, after the first game at Wicklow was washed out. Cricket South Africa preferred their players to prepare in better climes at home for the upcoming World Twenty20.

At Wicklow, August 6–9, 2012. **Drawn. South Africa A 315-8 dec** (H. G. Kuhn 103*, R. K. Kleinveldt 74); **‡Ireland XI 202** (J. N. K. Shannon 59; W. D. Parnell 7-56) **and 76-0.** *First-class* *debuts:* S. A. Britton, J. N. K. Shannon (Ireland XI). *The first two days of Oak Hill Cricket Club's maiden first-class match were lost to rain, but there was plenty for the South Africans to savour when play did start. Heino Kuhn, one of several wicketkeepers hoping A. B. de Villiers might soon relinquish the gloves at international level, scored 103* from 114 balls, as the tourists rattled along at four an over before the declaration. Wayne Parnell celebrated his selection in South Africa's World Twenty20 squad with a career-best 7-56, as Ireland were made to follow on.*

At Coleraine, August 13–16, 2012. **Drawn. ‡Ireland XI 180** (J. Anderson 68, K. J. O'Brien 58; W. D. Parnell 5-52); **South Africa A 219-6** (H. G. Kuhn 57*). *Rory Kleinveldt took the opening three wickets in four balls, and did not concede a run off the bat in his first seven overs. John Anderson, born in Durban, was on nought for 37 deliveries but, with the help of a few edges, added 109 for the sixth wicket with captain Kevin O'Brien. The first and fourth days were washed out.*

INDIA A IN NEW ZEALAND, 2012-13

India A, captained by Abhinav Mukund, toured New Zealand in September and October 2012, playing two first-class matches against New Zealand A. The sides also contested a one-day series, shared 1–1 (with one tied).

At Lincoln, September 26–29, 2012. **Drawn. India A 339** (U. Chand 54, A. T. Rayudu 105) **and 208-4 dec** (A. P. Majumdar 58); **‡New Zealand A 234-8 dec** (T. W. M. Latham 132, R. A. Young 54) **and 273-8** (G. H. Worker 89, N. T. Broom 72). *After a pair of positive declarations, the match was finely poised: New Zealand A needed 41 runs, and India A two wickets, only for bad light to arrive 20 overs from the finish. Ambati Rayudu gave the tourists the whip hand on a rain-affected opening day, before Tom Latham dominated for New Zealand A with his second first-class hundred.*

At Lincoln, October 3–6, 2012. **Drawn. ‡India A 554-8 dec** (A. P. Majumdar 56, Mandeep Singh 193, A. L. Menaria 173, R. Vinay Kumar 50*) **and 246-4 dec** (A. Mukund 132*); **New Zealand A 424-7 dec** (H. D. Rutherford 99, D. G. Brownlie 106, L. J. Woodcock 58, S. R. Wells 69*) **and 0-0.** *A characteristically flat pitch at the Bert Sutcliffe Oval allowed batsmen to inflate their averages. Little mercy was shown by Mandeep Singh and Ashok Menaria, who put on 318 for the fifth wicket in only 62 overs. George Worker suffered his second golden duck of the series, but Hamish Rutherford (run out on 99) and Dean Brownlie warded off the Indian attack. Mukund scored 76 runs in the 33 overs possible on the last day.*

ICC INTERCONTINENTAL CUP, 2011–13

Ireland continued to lead the pack of non-Test nations, heading both the four-day and one-day tables by the end of 2012. They won their first Intercontinental Cup match, in Mombasa, despite being given a scare by Kenya, who bowled them out for 75 on a hectic first day that featured 22 wickets in all, then had the better of a rain-affected game against Afghanistan in Dublin. The Irish finished the year with a comfortable 21-point cushion over Scotland, and were set to appear in the final towards the end of 2013.

Each round of fixtures now includes two World Cricket League games, as well as the four-day Intercontinental Cup match, and the one-dayers have assumed greater significance since the ICC's decision – confirmed after the competition started in 2011 – to make the WCL the first stage of qualifying for the 2015 World Cup. The top two teams in the table will go through automatically to the final stages in Australasia, while the other six will have to face another qualifying competition, also involving the top two sides from the second division. Despite an early loss to Kenya, Ireland looked on course for a third successive World Cup appearance, although they have to face their three closest challengers in 2013. Crucially, perhaps, they had home advantage for their games against Scotland, who were second at the start of the year.

ICC INTERCONTINENTAL CUP

Remaining matches in this tournament will appear in Wisden 2014.

At Mombasa, February 12–13, 2012. **Ireland won by ten runs.** **‡Ireland 75** (H. A. Varaiya 6-22) **and 152** (H. A. Varaiya 6-51); **Kenya 109** (A. van der Merwe 5-41, G. H. Dockrell 5-37) **and 108** (A. van der Merwe 6-27). *Ireland 14pts, Kenya 6pts. On an extraordinary first day, 22 wickets fell on a pitch helpful to the spinners, all to catches (but only one by the wicketkeeper). Table-toppers Ireland were shot out for 75, but recovered to take a handy lead into the second day. They looked secure at 142-4, only to lose six wickets for ten, and set Kenya 119 to win. They were soon 36-8 (four wickets fell at 31), but Nelson Odhiambo (32) and Hiren Varaiya (27, to go with match figures of 12-73) inched them towards their target with a stand of 58. Last man Shem Ngoche hit out, but finally Varaiya became the 11th wicket of the match for off-spinner Albert van der Merwe, conceding only 68 in the process; slow left-armer George Dockrell took the other nine.*

At Sharjah, February 16–19, 2012. **Scotland won by seven wickets.** **‡United Arab Emirates 100 and 318**; **Scotland 305** (R. D. Berrington 110) **and 117-3**. *Scotland 20pts. The UAE were regretting their decision to bat first after Dunfermline's Huddersfield-born seamer Safyaan Sharif (3-27) helped reduce them to 27-4. Scotland also struggled initially, as 15 wickets went down on the first day, but a century from Richie Berrington, who put on 99 with wicketkeeper Simon Smith (54), set up a big lead. It was enough, even though the UAE batted much better second time round.*

At Sharjah, April 2–4, 2012. **Afghanistan won by three wickets.** **Netherlands 133 and 228** (Izatullah Dawlatzai 5-45); **‡Afghanistan 129** (Mudassar Bukhari 6-43) **and 233-7**. *Afghanistan 14pts, Netherlands 6pts. The trend for wicket-packed opening days continued: 21 went down here. Tom Heggelman was the Netherlands' top-scorer with 29* from No. 10; and, apart from Nawroz Mangal (67), only Mirwais Ashraf reached double figures for Afghanistan. Late runs from Peter Borren and Pieter Seelaar, who both made 43 (from Nos 8 and 10), stretched the Dutch lead to 232. Afghanistan were rocking at 33-3 and 111-6, but wicketkeeper Afsar Khan anchored them to victory with 84*.*

At Windhoek (Wanderers), April 5–8, 2012. **Namibia won by eight wickets.** **Canada 274 and 213** (C. Viljoen 7-61); **‡Namibia 374** (S. F. Burger 135) **and 119-2**. *Namibia 20pts. Zeeshan Siddiqi's 87 set up a decent Canada total, but Namibia trumped it, their captain Sarel Burger facing 261 balls in a responsible innings; he put on 107 for the fifth wicket with Raymond van Schoor (71), and 101* *for the seventh with Ian Opperman (35). Siddiqi, with 73*, was the backbone of Canada's second innings too, but the others could make little of the medium-pace of Christi Viljoen, who returned career-best figures.*

At Aberdeen, July 4–7, 2012. **Scotland v Canada. Abandoned.** *Scotland 10pts, Canada 10pts.*

At Dublin (Rathmines), July 9–12, 2012. **Drawn. Afghanistan 84 and 208-7**; **‡Ireland 251-4 dec**. *Ireland 13pts, Afghanistan 7pts. Rain washed out the first two days, but Ireland still came close to victory, bowling Afghanistan out in 29.1 overs, then reaching 126-2 by the third-day close. But they were thwarted on the fourth by an opening stand of 106 between Karim Sadiq (46) and Javed Ahmadi (59), and Asghar Stanikzai (51*) ensured there would be no late collapse.*

At Deventer, July 16–19, 2012. **Drawn. Netherlands 308** (Shahbaz Bashir 102); **‡United Arab Emirates 74-2**. *Netherlands 7pts, United Arab Emirates 7pts. Only 37.1 overs were possible on the first day, and there was no play at all on the second and fourth. On the third, Shahbaz Bashir hit 12 fours in becoming the first to score a century on first-class debut for the Netherlands.*

At Windhoek (United), September 29–October 2, 2012. **Namibia won by an innings and one run. ‡Kenya 304** (T. Mishra 108) **and 325**; **Namibia 630-7 dec** (C. G. Williams 140, G. Snyman 201*). *Namibia 20pts. Tanmay Mishra stroked 17 fours to set up what looked like a useful Kenyan total – but it was put in perspective as Sarel Burger (85) and Craig Williams added 192, before Gerrie Snyman clouted 22 fours and seven sixes in his unbeaten double-century. It was the second time he had exploded against Kenya in the Intercontinental Cup: at Sharjah in January 2008 he had struck 11 sixes in his 230, in an all-out total of 282.*

ICC Intercontinental Cup four-day table (as at March 1, 2013, after four matches each): Ireland 67pts, Scotland 46pts, Afghanistan 44pts, Namibia 43pts, UAE 30pts, Netherlands 30pts, Kenya 22pts, Canada 10pts.

ICC WORLD CRICKET LEAGUE CHAMPIONSHIP

Remaining matches in this tournament will appear in Wisden 2014.

At Mombasa, February 18, 2012. **Kenya won by seven wickets. ‡Ireland 200** (47.3 overs); **Kenya 201-3** (42.4 overs) (T. Mishra 70*). *Ireland suffered their first defeat of the competition after struggling against Kenya's spinners; Collins Obuya took 3-24 with his leg-breaks. Tanmay Mishra and Rakep Patel (42*) eased Kenya home with a fourth-wicket stand of 100* in 15 overs.*

At Mombasa, February 20, 2012. **Ireland won by 117 runs. ‡Ireland 237-9** (50 overs) (E. C. Joyce 88); **Kenya 120** (35.1 overs). *Ed Joyce, who faced 125 balls, anchored Ireland to a score that proved well beyond Kenya, who never recovered after slipping to 37-5.*

At Sharjah, March 7, 2012. **United Arab Emirates won by four wickets. Scotland 167** (48.5 overs); **‡United Arab Emirates 171-6** (47.5 overs) (Shaiman Anwar 58, S. P. Patil 55*). *The UAE's matches – like Namibia's – did not have official one-day international status, which is restricted to the six Associate teams who played in the 2011 World Cup. But they upset higher-ranked opposition here, restricting Scotland to 167, then recovering from 35-4.*

At Sharjah, March 9, 2012. **United Arab Emirates won by two wickets. ‡Scotland 205-9** (50 overs) (K. J. Coetzer 73); **United Arab Emirates 209-8** (49.5 overs) (Shaiman Anwar 77*). *Scotland had gone through 2011 undefeated, but now lost for the second time in three days. After 36 overs the UAE were 128-6, needing another 78, but scraped home with a ball to spare: Shaiman Anwar, a 33-year-old originally from Sialkot in Pakistan, top-scored for the second match running.*

At Sharjah, March 29, 2012. **Netherlands won by nine wickets. ‡Afghanistan 153** (39.2 overs) (P. W. Borren 4-32); **Netherlands 156-1** (26.2 overs) (A. N. Kervezee 83*). *One-day international debuts:* Zakiullah Zaki (Afghanistan); T. van der Gugten (Netherlands). *Only Mohammad Nabi (41) survived for long, as Afghanistan were bowled out with more than ten overs unused; then Alexei Kervezee hit 83* from 63 balls to power his side home.*

At Sharjah, March 31, 2012. **Afghanistan won by five wickets. Netherlands 256-9** (50 overs) (M. R. Swart 52, T. L. W. Cooper 52, W. Barresi 51; Izatullah Dawlatzai 4-38); **‡Afghanistan 259-5** (46.2 overs) (Karim Sadiq 100). *The Dutch set a stiff target, but Karim Sadiq blasted four sixes and 12 fours in his second one-day international century, before he was the first out, in the 20th over, with the total 141. Mohammad Shahzad (37) and Nawroz Mangal (45*) took up the cudgels, and Afghanistan won with some ease.*

At Windhoek (Wanderers), April 10, 2012. **Canada won by two wickets. Namibia 183** (47.1 overs) (R. van Schoor 90); ‡**Canada 184-8** (48.5 overs). *Raymond van Schoor came in at 16-4 and helped Namibia recover to 183, and his side looked likely winners when Canada dipped to 112-6. But Jimmy Hansra made 49, and the tail did just enough to ensure Canada's first victory of the tournament.*

At Windhoek (Wanderers), April 12, 2012. Namibia won by 21 runs. ‡**Namibia 154** (45.5 overs) (C. Viljoen 50*; Rizwan Cheema 6-34); **Canada 133** (46.5 overs). *Namibia struggled against the military-mediums of Rizwan Cheema, who had never taken more than three wickets in a one-day international innings (and still hadn't, as this was not an official ODI). This time, though, Canada's later batsmen could not save them after another shaky start.*

At Dublin (Castle Avenue), July 3–4, 2012. **Ireland v Afghanistan. Abandoned.**

At Dublin (Castle Avenue), July 5, 2012. **Ireland won by 59 runs. Ireland 163** (47 overs) (E. C. Joyce 67*); ‡**Afghanistan 104** (33.1 overs). *One-day international debut:* Najibullah Zadran. *Ireland made a poor start (33-4) on a sticky pitch, but Ed Joyce, who faced 124 balls, lifted them to a total that proved too much for Afghanistan in unfamiliar conditions, and kept Ireland clear at the top of the table.*

At Ayr, July 9–10, 2012. **Scotland v Canada. Abandoned.** *This match and the next one were moved from Edinburgh after the Grange flooded, but incessant rain meant this game could not start either.*

At Ayr, July 11–12, 2012. **Scotland won by four wickets. Canada 176** (49.1 overs) (R. Gunasekera 53); ‡**Scotland 177-6** (42.1 overs) (C. S. MacLeod 99*). *One-day international debuts:* C. D. Wallace (Scotland); D. Daesrath, J. O. A. Gordon, D. R. Ramsammy, Zeeshan Siddiqi (Canada). *Canada looked well placed at 134-3 in the 38th over, but lost seven for 42. Scotland lost regular wickets too, but opener Calum MacLeod – whose previous-highest score in one-day internationals was 35 – kept his cool. With one run required he had 98*, so needed to hit a boundary – but the winning run came from an overthrow after he had played a defensive stroke, which left him stranded on 99*. It was the 12th such instance in ODIs, but the first for an Associate team.*

At Rotterdam, July 21, 2012. **Netherlands won by seven wickets. United Arab Emirates 96** (31.2 overs) (T. van der Gugten 4-41, Mudassar Bukhari 4-32); ‡**Netherlands 97-3** (21.4 overs). *The UAE stumbled from 25-0 to 26-4, and never recovered.*

At Deventer, July 23, 2012. **Netherlands won by three wickets. United Arab Emirates 221-9** (50 overs) (Khurram Khan 71); ‡**Netherlands 222-7** (48.4 overs). *The Netherlands kept their hopes of automatic World Cup qualification alive by doing the double over the UAE, despite an improved batting effort by the visitors.*

At Windhoek (United), October 2, 2012. **Kenya won by six wickets. Namibia 129** (43.1 overs); ‡**Kenya 132-4** (30.5 overs). *Namibia were 15-3 in the ninth over, and struggled to a total which Kenya had no difficulty in overhauling.*

At Windhoek (United), October 4, 2012. **Namibia won by seven wickets. Kenya 187** (42.1 overs) (A. A. Obanda 71); ‡**Namibia 188-3** (42 overs) (C. G. Williams 59*). *Namibia changed their batting order, and new openers Ian Opperman (45) and Raymond van Schoor (32) gave them a good start in pursuit of Kenya's handy total. From 110-3 in the 27th over, Sarel Burger (41*) and Craig Williams put on 78* to complete only Namibia's second victory of the tournament.*

ICC World Cricket League Championship table (as at March 1, 2013, after eight matches each): Ireland 13pts, Scotland 11pts, Netherlands 10pts, UAE 10pts, Afghanistan 7pts, Kenya 6pts, Namibia 4pts, Canada 3pts.

ICC INTERCONTINENTAL CUP FINALS

2004	SCOTLAND beat Canada by an innings and 84 runs at Sharjah.
2005	IRELAND beat Kenya by six wickets at Windhoek.
2006–07	IRELAND beat Canada by an innings and 115 runs at Leicester.
2007–08	IRELAND beat Namibia by nine wickets at Port Elizabeth.
2009–10	AFGHANISTAN beat Scotland by seven wickets at Dubai.

NEW ZEALAND WOMEN v ENGLAND WOMEN, 2011-12

One-day internationals (3): New Zealand 0, England 3
Twenty20 internationals (5): New Zealand 0, England 4

By the time Sarah Taylor's hundred secured a clean sweep in the one-day series, England's women had won all 12 international matches of their winter to survive the weather (there had been five in South Africa in October 2011). The ease with which they were able to brush aside New Zealand – considered their superiors only a few years earlier – was a matter of concern for lovers of the women's game. The hosts' failings in the first three Twenty20 internationals – curtain-raisers for matches between the men of New Zealand and South Africa at Wellington, Hamilton and Auckland – were beamed across the world on television.

Only in the third and fifth Twenty20s did New Zealand's bowlers make significant inroads, reducing England to 12 for four at Eden Park, and 61 for five at Invercargill – but on both occasions they let the lower order break free. Charlotte Edwards failed in those games, but scored 425 runs overall on the tour; she considered her phenomenal unbeaten 137, made in just 26 overs of a rain-reduced second one-day international, to be the best of her long career.

Arguably the most encouraging development for England was the form of Anya Shrubsole, the Somerset seamer. Shrubsole made her debut in 2008, aged 16, but had been limited to 22 internationals by a catalogue of injuries. She stayed fit this time, leading the pace attack in the absence of the rested Katherine Brunt, and finished with 19 wickets in ten games. Isa Guha figured only in the warm-up matches, and retired after the tour, aged 26, to concentrate on a PhD and her broadcasting career.

England's major inconvenience came in the first one-day international at Lincoln University, when Jenny Gunn was cited for a suspect action by the home umpires. Gunn had twice been reported in Australia in 2008-09, then subsequently cleared by the ECB under the old system of testing by a player's home board. Now, Gunn underwent independent analysis after the tour by the ICC's panel of human-movement specialists in Perth. They ruled in May that her unusual action created an optical illusion caused by hyperextension of the elbow – and that she did not breach the ICC's limit of 15 degrees' bend.

ENGLAND TOURING PARTY

*C. M. Edwards (Kent), T. T. Beaumont (Kent), A. Brindle (Sussex), G. A. Elwiss (Sussex), L. S. Greenway (Kent), I. T. Guha (Berkshire), J. L. Gunn (Yorkshire), D. Hazell (Yorkshire), H. C. Knight (Berkshire), L. A. Marsh (Kent), B. L. Morgan (Middlesex), S. E. Rowe (Kent), A. Shrubsole (Somerset), S. J. Taylor (Sussex), D. N. Wyatt (Staffordshire). *Coach:* M. G. Lane.

At Lincoln, February 11, 2012. **England XI won by 181 runs.** ‡**England XI 292-9** (50 overs) (C. M. Edwards 123 ret out, S. J. Taylor 32, A. Brindle 33, Extras 31; D. M. Doughty 3-49); **New Zealand Emerging Players Women 111** (38.1 overs) (A. M. Peterson 42; A. Shrubsole 5-5). *As in the next two games, each side chose from 12 players, 11 of whom could bat and 11 field. Charlotte Edwards reached her hundred from 91 balls, and retired out with 11 overs to spare. Anya Shrubsole took the last three wickets in seven deliveries.*

At Lincoln, February 13, 2012. **England XI won by eight wickets.** ‡**New Zealand Emerging Players Women 86-6** (20 overs); **England XI 87-2** (12.4 overs) (S. J. Taylor 43*).

At Lincoln, February 14, 2012. **England XI won by 54 runs. England XI 140-8** (20 overs) (L. S. Greenway 46); ‡**New Zealand Emerging Players Women 86-5** (20 overs) (A. M. Peterson 41). *Left-arm seamer Maneka Singh removed England openers Edwards and Laura Marsh in a double-wicket maiden in the fifth over, but did not bowl again. Isa Guha went wicketless in what proved her final match before she retired from international cricket.*

At Wellington (Westpac Stadium), February 17, 2012. **First Twenty20 international: England won by six wickets. New Zealand 80-9** (20 overs) (A. Shrubsole 5-11, D. Hazell 3-15); ‡**England 81-4** (17.4 overs) (S. J. Taylor 31*). *PoM:* A. Shrubsole. *Shrubsole seamed the ball in to the right-handers to bowl three of New Zealand's top four, then returned to complete a five-wicket haul – the first for England Women in Twenty20 internationals. Only two others – New Zealand's Amy Satterthwaite and Anisa Mohammed of West Indies – had recorded better figures in the format. Sarah Taylor and Tammy Beaumont's stand of 37* was comfortably the highest of the match.*

BEST FIGURES FOR ENGLAND IN TWENTY20 INTERNATIONALS

4–0–11–5	**A. Shrubsole**	**v New Zealand at Wellington**	**2011-12**
2–0–9–4	J. L. Gunn	v South Africa at Taunton	2007
3.4–0–9–4	**H. L. Colvin**	**v Pakistan at Galle**	**2012-13**
3–0–11–4	D. N. Wyatt	v South Africa at Basseterre, St Kitts	2009-10
4–0–12–4	**A. Shrubsole**	**v Pakistan at Loughborough**	**2012**
4–1–12–4	**D. Hazell**	**v West Indies at Hove**	**2012**
4–0–27–4	R. A. Birch	v New Zealand at Hove	2004

At Hamilton, February 19, 2012. **Second Twenty20 international: England won by 48 runs. England 166-7** (20 overs) (C. M. Edwards 33, L. A. Marsh 48, S. J. Taylor 45); ‡**New Zealand 118** (19.2 overs) (S. W. Bates 37; D. N. Wyatt 3-24). *PoM:* L. A. Marsh. *The teams wore black armbands to mark the death of Peter Sharp, a commentator and former Canterbury player, the day before. Marsh seized upon a lightning-fast pitch and outfield to hit 11 fours in 29 deliveries, then missed a slower ball from Lea Tahuhu. New Zealand declined badly from 89-2 in the 15th over.*

At Auckland, February 22, 2012. **Third Twenty20 international: England won by ten runs** (D/L). **England 108-6** (20 overs) (J. L. Gunn 30*); ‡**New Zealand 90-7** (18.5 overs). *PoM:* J. L. Gunn. *England showed their mettle in front of a worldwide television audience by coming back from 12-4. They had already lost both openers – Marsh for a golden duck – when two non-strikers were run out in successive balls in the third over: first the bowler Frances Mackay deflected a drive by Lydia Greenway onto Taylor's stumps; then Arran Brindle was too slow in setting off when Greenway called her through for a single. But Jenny Gunn added 48* with Susie Rowe (15*) in the last six overs. New Zealand suffered a loss of nerve in the dying stages – exploited by spinners Danielle Wyatt (2-25) and Danielle Hazell (2-22) – and were ten behind Duckworth/Lewis when rain arrived seven balls from the end.*

At Invercargill, February 25, 2012. **Fourth Twenty20 international. New Zealand v England. Abandoned.**

At Invercargill, February 26, 2012. **Fifth Twenty20 international: England won by five wickets. New Zealand 109-6** (20 overs); ‡**England 110-5** (18.5 overs) (M. J. G. Nielsen 4-10). *PoM:* A. Shrubsole. *Left-armer Morna Nielsen struck twice in the 12th over to leave England 61-5. But Gunn (22*) again took the game away from New Zealand, this time putting on 49* with Brindle (23*).*

At Lincoln, March 1, 2012. **First one-day international: England won by five wickets. New Zealand 233-6** (50 overs) (A. E. Satterthwaite 38, S. J. McGlashan 74, A. M. Peterson 33); ‡**England 234-5** (48.2 overs) (C. M. Edwards 84, L. S. Greenway 36, L. A. Marsh 44). *One-day international debut:* A. M. Peterson. *PoM:* L. A. Marsh. *Edwards's attempt to exploit a damp pitch was stymied by Sara McGlashan, who shared stands of 71 with both Satterthwaite and Anna Peterson. But England's captain made amends by leading the run-chase with 84 from 107 balls. Three winters after Gunn's medium-pace first came under scrutiny in Australia, she was reported for a suspect action by umpires Phil Jones and Derek Walker during a nine-over spell. She continued to bowl on the tour, and her action was cleared by the ICC in May.*

At Lincoln, March 3, 2012. **Second one-day international: England won by 59 runs** (D/L). Reduced to 28 overs a side. **England 219-6** (26 overs) (C. M. Edwards 137*, S. J. Taylor 39); ‡**New Zealand 164** (26 overs) (A. E. Satterthwaite 69; A. Shrubsole 3-28). *PoM:* C. M. Edwards. *It was tempting to wonder what Edwards might have achieved had rain not denied her 24 overs. As it was, she opened and made 137* from 88 balls, including 20 fours. "I don't think I've ever played better than that," she said. Ninety-eight runs flowed in the 10.2 overs she and Taylor spent together for the second wicket. Satterthwaite made 69 from 56, but had no chance of hauling in New Zealand's revised target of 224.*

At Lincoln, March 5, 2012. **Third one-day international: England won by six wickets.** ‡**New Zealand 220** (48.4 overs) (K. J. Martin 33, S. W. Bates 38, A. E. Satterthwaite 58, K. T. Perkins 51; L. A. Marsh 3-28, D. N. Wyatt 3-36); **England 222-4** (42.4 overs) (S. J. Taylor 109*, L. S. Greenway 84). *PoM:* S. J. Taylor. *PoS:* A. Shrubsole (England). *Taylor's fourth hundred in one-day internationals – but her first since taking a sabbatical from international cricket in New Zealand in late 2010 – ensured England remained unbeaten in all fixtures through their winter. Taylor and Greenway put on 201 for the third wicket, the sixth double-century partnership by an England pair.*

CRICKET IN AFGHANISTAN, 2012

Step by step

SHAHID HASHMI

Slowly but surely, Afghanistan's cricketing infrastructure began to catch up with the success of their national team – bringing Associate membership of the ICC into view. Afghanistan have won the hearts of many for their rapid rise through the World Cricket League, culminating in the grant of one-day international status in 2009, so the rubber-stamping of their application – promoted by the Asian Cricket Council – should be a formality at the ICC's annual board meeting in June 2013.

"The most significant decision at this year's ACC AGM was to substantiate the claim of Afghanistan to be an Associate Member of the ICC," said ACC chief executive Ashraful Haque in September. "Afghanistan have been the strongest side among the Affiliate Members, so we are backing them for promotion." Vanuatu were the last country to be elevated from Affiliate to Associate membership, in 2009.

It was a surprise to many that it had taken so long. Privately, the ICC expressed mild irritation over Afghanistan's previous lack of interest, as they had been the second-strongest non-Test nation – certainly in Twenty20 – for a few years. They had been one win away from qualifying for the 2011 World Cup (a tortuous journey memorably documented in the film *Out of the Ashes*), and made it to the 2010 and 2012 World Twenty20 tournaments where, despite losing twice on both occasions, their lively approach suggested they could, in time, become a force with a little more discipline. Defeats by India and England in the 2012 competition betrayed their artlessness against quality spin.

A major prerequisite of Associate status, however, is the active promotion of women's cricket – and the Afghanistan Cricket Board faced accusations of being slow to support those who play and promote the women's game, despite risks to their safety. In January 2013, the Afghan women's team were prevented from travelling to Thailand for what would have been their first official tournament, the ACC Women's T20 Championship, for "political reasons".

In 2012, Pakistan and Australia became the first Full Members to play the men's team in one-day internationals – at Afghanistan's surrogate home in Sharjah. Afghanistan lost both games, but beat Trinidad & Tobago and Barbados to win a quadrangular tournament (also involving a Bangladesh XI) in Port-of-Spain, which acted as practice for the World Twenty20. Afghanistan had serious ground to make up in the race for the 2015 World Cup: failure to finish in the top two of the 50-over World Cricket League Championship in 2013 would leave them having to attend a second qualifying event, in New Zealand in 2014, to try to claim one of the last two spots available.

Although the UAE remained the logical home for Afghanistan's international fixtures, in January 2013 the ACB announced a long-term desire to base their elite training in Pakistan – a country with which they share much more than a border. The national squad underwent a four-week conditioning camp at Lahore's National Academy ahead of matches against Scotland in the UAE in March; the ACB and the Pakistan Cricket Board also announced they had struck a "verbal agreement" over a long-term development programme. An obvious drawback, however, was the continued reluctance of other international teams to tour Pakistan.

"Sharjah gave us basic facilities, but unfortunately we didn't find quality cricket to develop with," said Kabir Khan, the Afghanistan coach and a former Pakistan player. "The cost of being in Sharjah is a lot more than here in Pakistan. We are in the process of building our infrastructure [in Afghanistan] and have two stadiums as well. But while we have academies, we don't have specialised coaches. In Pakistan we can find the quality coaches and quality teams to play against." Meanwhile, the best Afghan players found themselves picked up by franchises in the Bangladesh Premier League.

The ACB made major changes to their set-up in 2012. Shahzada Masoud, previously the board president, took over as chairman from Omar Zakhilwal in October, who was busy as finance minister in Hamid Karzai's government (two months earlier, Zakhilwal had been forced to deny corruption charges linked to Karzai's 2009 re-election campaign). Masoud remains an advisor to the government on tribal affairs.

Thc Afghan government have spent heavily to develop the two existing international-standard stadiums, in Kabul and Jalalabad, while the ACB are determined to complete three more grounds over the next two years, with plans afoot for academies too. They also hope to found a Twenty20 league, possibly in 2014.

AFGHANISTAN v AUSTRALIA

One-Day International

SHAHID HASHMI

At Sharjah, August 25, 2012 (day/night). Australia won by 66 runs. Toss: Australia. One-day international debut: G. J. Maxwell.

Afghanistan were not embarrassed in their first meeting with Australia, who warmed up for their limited-overs encounters against Pakistan with a victory that was comfortable but not overwhelming. It was Afghanistan's 23rd official one-day international, but only their second against a Test-playing country, following one against Pakistan here six months earlier. And after Wade and Clarke braved the stifling heat during battling 75s, the Afghans had their chances, reducing Australia to 210 for five after 44 overs before a late burst inspired by Mike Hussey and Bailey lifted them to 272. Hussey was fortunate to escape on 18 when Javed Ahmadi at mid-off missed a relatively straightforward run-out chance, the ball after his brother really *was* run out, by a fine direct hit from extra cover. Ahmadi was playing in this match the day after captaining Afghanistan in the plate final of the Under-19 World Cup in Brisbane; not surprisingly, perhaps, he and his Under-19 team-mate Najibullah Zadran

WOMEN'S CRICKET IN AFGHANISTAN

Headscarved heroines

TIM WIGMORE

Afghanistan's cricketers have enthralled sporting romantics for a few years now. But the country is host to more than one team: the other team play in scarves, long and baggy trousers and shirts, and yearn for the opportunities afforded to the men.

The story of Afghan women's cricket begins with one family. The four Barakzai sisters learned cricket when they fled Taliban rule in 1999 and became refugees in Pakistan. Returning home ten years later, the sisters – led by Diana, who is now 24 – tried to encourage others to take up the sport. In October 2011, they all completed ICC coaching courses at a camp held jointly by the charity Afghan Connection and the MCC Foundation. They have become mainstays of the fledgling Afghan women's squad. As Diana stresses, none of this would have been possible without her father and brother, "who have always been supportive to us, always teaching us about cricket". It was her father Mohammad Naeem Barakzai's decision to convert a plot of land at his old house near Kabul into a cricket pitch that has provided the women's squad with somewhere safe to play.

"Playing cricket for a girl was not less than suicide, but my spirit, and the strong support of my family, encouraged me not to stop my activities," says Diana, who bemoans "community negative attitudes and lack of fundraising resources". As the Afghanistan Cricket Board's first female development officer, she hopes to improve the situation. Raees Ahmadzai, the former Afghanistan captain and now head of the Afghan Youth Cricket Support Organisation, says there are "no proper venues for women's cricket", and "the girls will not feel happy to play in front of men". As a result, women have used basketball courts and even the old National Stadium, scene of executions under the Taliban.

So, exactly how far has women's cricket come? Official figures show there are almost 4,000 registered female players in Afghanistan, 700 of them disabled. In October 2012, an eight-team tournament was held between school teams. But the majority of registered cricketers have the opportunity to play for only a few days a year, and some do not even tell their families. Women's cricket is a regular occurrence in only four of Afghanistan's 34 provinces, invariably the more westernised areas. Many Afghans who cheered the success of the men's side feel differently about the women.

Unsurprisingly, then, Afghanistan have yet to play an official international women's game, despite several attempts – although they did travel to Tajikistan in July 2012 for an unofficial three-match 25-over series, and won 2–1. Most recently, in January 2013, they were on the verge of taking part in the Asian Cricket Council Women's T20 Championship in Thailand. ACB chief executive Noor Mohammad Murad admitted "political reasons" lay behind the withdrawal, and said: "It needs long-term planning, including clear strategy to convey the message to the community that we will strictly follow up all religious rules for women cricket."

The circumstances of these cancellations have prompted some to question the extent of the board's commitment to women's cricket. One prominent figure in Afghan cricket, speaking anonymously, said the board "were arranging a day or two of cricket camps for the ladies, just to show the media they are working with Afghan girls to learn cricket". The source also claimed the ACB "wanted a women's department just as a symbolic thing to show to the ICC"; the ICC have declined to comment. As the ACB bid for Associate status, a women's set-up is one requirement. As more money is invested in Afghan cricket, it must be supported by deed as well as word.

Shah Marai, AFF/Getty Images

Pioneer spirit: the first generation of Afghan women cricketers practise on a basketball court at a school in Kabul, December 2010.

There is no shortage of willing contributors. UNICEF hosted a camp for 140 in Jalalabad in 2010, and the Swedish Committee for Afghanistan – yes, really – have also helped Afghan Connection and MCC to build cricket pitches in schools.

Afghan Connection have been particularly significant. Working closely with MCC and a range of charities, including Cricket for Change, they have held camps and allowed girls the chance to play at school. In 2012 alone, they were responsible for building pitches for 16,000 children in ten schools although, given the difficulty of finding locations that can provide the necessary security for girls, these will primarily benefit boys. In recognition of her achievements, Afghan Connection founder and chief executive Sarah Fane was elected an honorary life member of MCC.

Fane emphasises the "massive progress" women's cricket has made, and the "incredible talent" of many who play it. Yet she is also realistic about the need for camps to be conducted in "a culturally sensitive way". She says: "We do them only in the big cities. We make sure we get parental consent, and we do them in girls' schools behind a wall so they all feel secure." Above all she wants to guard against repercussions. "If we suddenly did a cricket camp for girls in a conservative area, there'd be such a backlash against them and against us – so we're moving very slowly with girls." Nevertheless, some cricketers have been labelled prostitutes for having the temerity to play the game.

No one can be naive about the challenges facing women's cricket in Afghanistan. But there is a commendable optimism and resolve in those who play it. Let the last word go to Diana Barakzai. "The boys' national team had very good achievements during the last few years, and the reason is the strong support from the government, donors and all other agencies. If we also receive support, I am sure we can have a brilliant women's cricket team in the near future."

Tim Wigmore is a freelance journalist, and writes for ESPNcricinfo, The Independent *and* New Statesman. *For more information about Afghan Connection, visit www.afghanconnection.org*

both made ducks (Najibullah was out first ball, so was dismissed by successive deliveries on successive days roughly 7,500 miles apart). Afghanistan's openers were unsettled by the pace of Starc, who finished with four wickets. But Asghar Stanikzai rebuilt the innings with Mohammad Nabi, who clobbered four towering sixes.

Man of the Match: M. A. Starc.

Australia

†M. S. Wade c and b Mohammad Nabi 75
D. A. Warner c Mohammad Shahzad b Shapoor Zadran . 24
*M. J. Clarke st Mohammad Shahzad b Samiullah Shenwari . 75
G. J. Maxwell c Najibullah Zadran b Mohammad Nabi . 2
M. E. K. Hussey b Karim Sadiq 49
D. J. Hussey run out 13
G. J. Bailey b Shapoor Zadran........... 23
M. G. Johnson not out................. 1
J. L. Pattinson b Karim Sadiq 1
M. A. Starc not out 1

B 1, l-b 4, w 1, n-b 2 8

1/37 (2) 2/168 (1) 3/172 (4) 4/181 (3) 5/210 (6) 6/263 (7) 7/269 (5) 8/271 (9) (8 wkts, 50 overs) 272

10 overs: 47-1

X. J. Doherty did not bat.

Shapoor Zadran 8–0–60–2; Dawlat Zadran 10–0–53–0; Gulbadeen Naib 2–0–18–0; Karim Sadiq 6–0–22–2; Javed Ahmadi 4–0–16–0; Samiullah Shenwari 10–1–48–1; Mohammad Nabi 10–0–50–2.

Afghanistan

Karim Sadiq b Starc.................... 17
Javed Ahmadi b Starc 0
Asghar Stanikzai c Clarke b Starc........ 66
†Mohammad Shahzad c Wade b Pattinson .. 11
*Nawroz Mangal lbw b Pattinson 0
Mohammad Nabi b Johnson 46
Samiullah Shenwari b Starc............. 14
Najibullah Zadran c Wade b Johnson 0
Gulbadeen Naib c Wade b Pattinson...... 22
Dawlat Zadran c M. E. K. Hussey b Doherty 8
Shapoor Zadran not out................ 1

B 1, l-b 9, w 11 21

1/6 (2) 2/26 (1) 3/49 (4) 4/49 (5) 5/135 (6) 6/165 (3) 7/166 (8) 8/171 (7) 9/199 (9) 10/206 (10) (43.5 overs) 206

10 overs: 45-2

Pattinson 9–1–46–3; Starc 9–1–47–4; Johnson 9–1–34–2; Doherty 7.5–1–34–1; Maxwell 5–2–21–0; D. J. Hussey 2–0–8–0; Clarke 2–0–6–0.

Umpires: B. F. Bowden and Shozab Raza. Third umpire: Zameer Haider.
Referee: J. Srinath.

For Australia's one-day and Twenty20 international matches against Pakistan in the UAE which followed this match, see page 1050.

For a report of Afghanistan's one-day international against Pakistan in Sharjah see page 1048; for their matches in the World Twenty20 Qualifier, see page 1202; for their matches in the World Twenty20 itself, see page 841; and for the Intercontinental Cup and World Cricket League Championship, see page 1208.

CRICKET IN CANADA, 2012

All-star fudge

FARAZ SARWAT

Canadian cricket has developed a tendency to start the year on the wrong foot – and 2012 was no exception. In January the national team participated in the Caribbean T20 as preparation for the World Twenty20 qualifying tournament, but went down to heavy defeats in all four matches. The following month, captain Jimmy Hansra stepped down.

The official press release, which quoted Hansra as saying "I am very happy with the organisation and I believe we are definitely heading in the right direction," had a touch of Stockholm syndrome. Rizwan Cheema, surprisingly sidestepped in favour of Hansra once Ashish Bagai had quit the team after the 2011 World Cup, was finally put in charge for the World Twenty20 qualifiers in the UAE, but results hardly picked up. Canada managed to see off lesser teams, but came unstuck against stronger opposition – losing to the Netherlands, Afghanistan, Ireland and Scotland.

Shortly after the tournament, Michael Dighton resigned as coach, only seven months into the job. Gus Logie, Canada's coach during the 2003 World Cup, returned to the role, and David Patterson, the former head of New South Wales' Emerging Players programme for a decade, was hired as High Performance Manager in October. With many players still adjusting to cricket at a high level, Patterson's arrival may have been the highlight of the year.

On April 1, Cricket Canada held elections for president, with Alberta's Ravin Moorthy taking on the incumbent, Ranjit Saini from Ontario. When the votes among delegates ended in a tie, the brains trust of Canadian cricket apparently decided to settle the matter with the toss of a coin, which Moorthy won. The toss took place on April Fool's Day, so it was perhaps sensible that Cricket Canada did not go public with their method of deciding the presidency.

Poor showings in Namibia and Scotland meant Canada finished the year bottom of both the ICC 50-over World Cricket League Championship and the first-class Intercontinental Cup (which were both due to finish in April 2013). These were tournaments Canada once aspired to win. Some success finally came in November, when the team retained the Auty Cup against the even more dysfunctional USA. Canada's modest 196 – against a second-string American attack – proved enough to win on first innings in Florida.

The intended centrepiece of Canada's year, an all-star Twenty20 exhibition match in May, turned into a farce when many advertised players failed to show up – and those who did were not paid on time. The Rogers Centre (formerly the SkyDome), home of Major League Baseball's Toronto Blue Jays, is a marvel of a building. But a drop-in artificial pitch with spring-fitted stumps made the game difficult to take seriously, even with the likes of Sanath Jayasuriya and Jacob Oram doing their best to keep everyone entertained. A crowd generously estimated at 12,000 looked sparse in a stadium that can accommodate more than four times as many.

Match organisers Kat Rose Inc had promised to include Shahid Afridi, Saeed Ajmal, Misbah-ul-Haq and Umar Akmal – among others – in the Asia XI but, with Pakistan about to tour Sri Lanka, it was always unlikely they would be released by their board. Brian Lara also pulled out of captaining the International XI. Kat Rose continued to list the players on their website on the eve of the match. The no-shows hit the promoters hard and, by October, the Federation of International Cricketers' Associations had initiated legal proceedings against the organisers over non-payment to 16 players.

Cricket Canada chief executive Doug Hannum described the event as a "national embarrassment" on a television newscast, which irked many of his colleagues, though his assessment was not far wrong. The board insisted they had carried out due diligence in researching the unknown promotions company before sanctioning the event.

A lack of accountability and cynicism in Cricket Canada continued unabated, with office-bearers holding on to their positions come what may. And so 2012 went down as a year with no international cricket in Canada, no progress on building a national stadium, and disastrous results on the field. Those who follow the sport here had every right to feel aggrieved.

For reports of Canada's matches in the World Twenty20 Qualifier, see page 1202; for the Intercontinental Cup and World Cricket League Championship, see page 1208.

CRICKET IN KENYA, 2012

Heading in one direction

MARTIN WILLIAMSON

The restructuring forced on Cricket Kenya by their dismal performance at the 2011 World Cup continued, but there was no significant upturn on the field – despite the retention of a fully paid squad. Kenya lost their two matches in the Intercontinental Cup, the first-class tournament for the leading Associate countries, to leave them languishing second from bottom. In the one-day World Cricket League Championship, Kenya at least managed wins over Ireland and Namibia, but still finished the year in sixth. With only the top two automatically gaining places for the 2015 World Cup, Kenya will go into a ten-country qualifying tournament in New Zealand to decide the two remaining slots.

Kenya performed as feared at the World Twenty20 qualifiers in Dubai, beating only the real minnows – and missing out on the knockout stages by 0.007 of a run, to Scotland. More heartening were the performances of Alex Obanda, Collins Obuya and Duncan Allan, who all scored more than 250 runs. Kenya's women, meanwhile, made next to no impression, finishing last in the ICC Africa Women's Twenty20 qualifying tournament.

At present, Cricket Kenya are in a sound financial position. But fear is growing inside the country that they will struggle to retain their top-six Associate status at the 2014 World Cup qualifier – and thus miss out on the substantial ICC High Performance funding that goes with it. CK doggedly retained 20 players on professional contracts, but that would almost certainly end without the extra ICC money, as would the ability to attract high-quality administrators and coaches. Tom Sears left the chief executive's post in June to move to Irish rugby union franchise Connacht, and had not been replaced by the end of the year. In May, national coach Mike Hesson returned home to New Zealand citing safety concerns for his family, and was replaced on an interim basis by Robin Brown, a former Zimbabwe player and coach (Hesson became New Zealand coach in July). Security issues in Mombasa, often blamed on the Somali Islamist militant group Al-Shabaab, led to some international matches being shelved and others relocated to Dubai. Ireland did go ahead with their tour in February after some doubts, and won all three Twenty20 internationals.

A senior international administrator privately admitted the Kenyans had squandered a decade of substantial investment. A few years ago, they had been rated the best outside the Test nations, but there are now at least half a dozen ahead of them in the pecking order; even in Africa, Namibia and Uganda are seen as better long-term prospects. At least a successful second edition of the elite domestic tournaments – broadcast on the SuperSport satellite network for the first time – gave the local game a boost.

Board elections should have been held in March 2012, but were delayed because of squabbling within the fractious Nairobi province, then a last-minute court order obtained by Tom Tikolo, the disgraced former CK chief executive. When elections finally took place in November, Jackie Janmohamed – a close associate of Sharad Ghai, the former boss of the old Kenyan Cricket Association forced from office in 2005 – was elected to succeed the internationally respected Samir Inamdar as chairperson. She was the first woman chosen to head a major cricket governing body. Even her supporters recognised Janmohamed faced a hard battle to convince the wider community she was not a throwback to the bad old days, and within weeks she was embroiled in a number of internal disputes. One involved an unofficial tournament – aptly named "Cricket Wars" – backed by Ghai and intended to take place at Nairobi Gymkhana, but CK refused to sanction the event. Janmohamed had a year to turn things round. The odds seemed stacked against her.

It emerged in May that an unnamed Kenyan player was being investigated on suspicion of spot-fixing during the 2011 World Cup game against Pakistan. "The Kenyan Ministry of Sport and Youth Affairs are aware of the allegations," said Sears. The ICC refused to comment.

OTHER INTERNATIONAL MATCHES IN KENYA IN 2012

Kenya v Ireland

At Mombasa, February 22, 2012. **First Twenty20 international: Ireland won by six wickets. Kenya 107** (20 overs) (T. Mishra 34; G. H. Dockrell 3-15); **‡Ireland 109-4** (K. J. O'Brien 30*) (15.3 overs). *MoM:* G. H. Dockrell. *Twenty20 international debuts:* D. I. Allan, J. O. Ngoche, E. Otieno (Kenya); R. D. McCann, M. C. Sorensen (Ireland). *George Dockrell removed the openers in the first and third overs, and Kenya never got going. Ed Joyce took a superb catch back-pedalling on the midwicket boundary, flicking the ball up before going over the rope, to give Max Sorensen his second international wicket. Ireland's run-chase began chaotically, with Shem Ngoche delivering five wides, then another, before William Porterfield was run out off the first legitimate ball. But Kevin O'Brien and Joyce added an important 47 for the fourth wicket. Ireland's victory meant they entered the ICC's Twenty20 rankings in ninth, above Zimbabwe.*

At Mombasa, February 23, 2012. **Second Twenty20 international: Ireland won by eight wickets. ‡Kenya 131-7** (20 overs); **Ireland 132-2** (17.3 overs) (P. R. Stirling 65*). *MoM:* P. R. Stirling. *Paul Stirling was the only player to take two wickets, or score a half-century. Andrew White joined Kyle McCallan in making 200 appearances in all cricket for Ireland, but was not required to bat or bowl.*

At Mombasa, February 24, 2012. **Third Twenty20 international: Ireland won by two runs. ‡Ireland 107-9** (20 overs) (G. C. Wilson 32, E. C. Joyce 38; S. O. Ngoche 4-14); **Kenya 105-7** (20 overs) (C. O. Obuya 42, T. Mishra 37). *MoM:* S. O. Ngoche. *Porterfield was involved in another calamitous start, as Stirling was run out off the first ball without facing, before O'Brien sliced the fourth for a catch. Kenya were well placed after Tanmay Mishra added 53 with Collins Obuya and 35 with Ragheb Aga, and needed seven from the last over, but John Mooney changed his pace cannily and conceded only four.*

For reports of Kenya's matches in the World Twenty20 Qualifier, see page 1202; for the Intercontinental Cup and World Cricket League Championship, see page 1208.

CRICKET ROUND THE WORLD

COMPILED BY JAMES COYNE AND TIMOTHY ABRAHAM

Seven countries and a French overseas territory make their debuts in this year's Cricket Round the World.

ICC WORLD CRICKET LEAGUE

As the World Cricket League – the 50-over pyramid for non-Test nations which began in 2007 – reached the end of its second cycle, it was becoming easier to identify decline and fall. Nepal carried off the Division Four title in September, earning their highest WCL ranking yet. On slow pitches in Kuala Lumpur, their spinners were too canny: Shakti Gauchan returned 9–4–8–1 against Singapore and 10–8–2–3 against Malaysia. A top-two finish in Division Three in May 2013 would earn Nepal a place in the 2015 World Cup qualifying tournament in New Zealand.

Nepal also won the Asian Cricket Council Elite Trophy for the first time, sharing it with the United Arab Emirates after a tie in Sharjah; they lost nine wickets to the UAE's six, so were fortunate the tournament had no tie-breaker. UAE's semi-final thrashing of Afghanistan – remarkably, their seventh win out of seven against them in 50-over cricket – meant they and Nepal were rewarded with inclusion in a one-day tournament against A-teams from India, Pakistan, Sri Lanka and Bangladesh, scheduled for 2013. More such arrangements are needed to avoid the leading Associates being cut adrift.

Argentina, though, were in complete free fall, and finished bottom of Division Five – suffering their fourth consecutive relegation. With Bermuda also slipping back two divisions since 2007 – the year they appeared at the World Cup in the Caribbean – it was clear the cricketing malaise in the Americas went deep. It remains to be seen whether West Indies' World Twenty20 triumph can act as a spark in the region.

Were Argentina to be relegated again in 2013, they would face elimination from global competition, after the ICC Development Committee decided to cut back from eight WCL divisions to six for the next cycle (beginning in 2014). There was a feeling that one-day cricket was not always appropriate at the lower level: some teams struggle to bat out 50 overs, possibly because they do not play the format domestically. But it was primarily a financial decision: in Europe, it costs around £10,000–12,000 to host a WCL event. The cutback was especially bad news for the East Asia Pacific region: Fiji, Vanuatu, Japan and Samoa, all likely to finish the cycle in Divisions Seven and Eight, will be left without global 50-over cricket.

ANDORRA

Sir Ian Botham's next skiing holiday to the Pyrenees won't be just about the slopes if Andorra's emerging cricketers get their way. Botham has been a regular visitor to Hotel Montané, in the village of Arinsal, run by Fiona Dean, also Britain's Honorary Consul in the principality. She was contacted by Dr Michel Bakker from a nomadic Dutch team called Fellowship of Fairly Odd Places Cricket Club, founded in 2005, whose aim, as their name suggests, is to enjoy a game once a year in unconventional locations – hence they were keen to play the first recorded match in Andorra. Though not a player herself, Dean enlisted a "rag tag bunch of expats", including a Swiss national who had never played cricket before, to take on FFOPCC in September on an artificial surface at a football ground in the town of Ordino – 1,298m above sea level. Huib van Walsem scored an unbeaten 110 as the Dutch posted 187 for five from their 30 overs; in reply, the Andorra XI could manage only 105 – giving FFOPCC their first win over international opposition, after previous defeats by Iceland and Vatican City (see *Wisden 2012*, page 1201). Andorra-born teenager Daniel Carrington was the closest the home side got to a native player, although the game generated enough interest to lead the front page of *Diari d'Andorra*. "Sir Ian actually agreed to umpire the game, but unfortunately a clash of commitments prevented him from doing so," said Dean. "A few of the players are planning to coax him into giving them some coaching and advice on his next holiday." Andorra were planning home and away fixtures against teams from over the border in France for 2013.

TIMOTHY ABRAHAM

BULGARIA

Saif Rehman is the pioneering force of Bulgarian cricket, a soap star, semi-finalist in *Bulgaria's Got Talent* – and now symbol of egalitarianism in his adopted country. During the Communist era, Bulgarian disabled children were often hidden from view by their families, or abandoned in state institutions. While there has been undoubted progress, some attitudes have proved hard to shake. A 2008 investigation by Europe's highest social-rights body criticised the Bulgarian government for failing to provide disabled children with an education. Two years later, it was reported that 166 had died from neglect in care homes over the previous decade. Rehman, 39, originally from Pakistan, was deeply upset at what he saw, and vowed to bring cricket to the less fortunate. In January 2012, he introduced a group of children from Sofia to table cricket, a miniature tabletop version of the game for six players. By November, around 100 Bulgarians aged six to 17 with cerebral palsy, Down's Syndrome or other disabilities were playing table cricket, and a national championship was held. "We've had great results," said Rehman. "Doctors have told me that a 16-year-old opened his hand for the first time after he started playing, because he was getting movement in it and was so determined to play." The widespread praise for the initiative inside Bulgaria persuaded Rehman to begin coaching a national squad of blind cricketers, whom he hopes to take on a tour to England in 2013. Germany and Spain are the only other countries in continental Europe to play any official disability cricket. "My ambition is to form a disability cricket league and encourage it in nearby countries," Rehman declared. "This is my duty." TRISTAN LAVALETTE

CAMBODIA

Manish Sharma's mission to spread the gospel was stirred by a chance meeting in a Hong Kong restaurant, when he overheard a lament by schoolboys who were desperate to play but couldn't afford the kit. Sharma, the director of Rudrapriya Sports, a Hong Kong-based retailer, gave the boys a couple of pairs of batting gloves – and embarked on a crusade to help more would-be cricketers. But his offer to provide equipment was rebuffed by the established clubs in Hong Kong, who wanted to allocate his money themselves. Upset but undeterred, he set his sights on Cambodia, a country with next to no heritage in the sport. Sharma's plans were ambitious: bring structure to the disparate expat cricketing culture, and immerse the local population in the game – no easy feat when children attend school from 7am to 5pm, and spend the evening in language classes. The solution was simple: start practice at 5am. Sharma woke up in time, and so did more than 3,500 Cambodian schoolchildren eager to learn – leading in 2012 to the establishment of a youth league, including eight schools, and a girls' team. Sharma, vice-chairman of the Cricket Association of Cambodia, successfully lobbied the Cambodian Olympic Committee to include cricket on the curriculum – opening up the possibility of participation in the Asian Games; the board also won Associate status from the Asian Cricket Council. Next on Sharma's list is Madagascar. The fact that cattle-wrestling is one of the island's most popular spectator sports, and that its sole world champion played pétanque, suggests it could be his biggest challenge yet. TIM BROOKS

CHINA

In May, Jiang Shuyao, a PE student at Shenyang Sports University, became the first cricketer from mainland China to play a league match overseas – for Cleethorpes Academy against Holton-le-Clay Fourth Eleven in the East Lindsey Cricket League. Jiang walked out, took first strike and scored an unbeaten 76 to chase down 121. Paul Hewstone, cricket chairman at Cleethorpes, said "Shu would have got into the first team on his fielding alone. He's one of the best in the club." But the first team already had a South African fast bowler as their registered overseas professional in the Yorkshire Premier League. Instead, Jiang found his level in the seconds, averaging 30 and helping out with the wicket at the first-class ground, where Nottinghamshire used to play the occasional game. The Asian Cricket Council paid for his flights and travel costs, and Jiang's family – by no means members of China's nouveau riche – forked out 50,000 yuan (£5,000) to support him for six months. Cleethorpes players put him up for the entire trip. "He'd only really played Twenty20 before," said Hewstone. "There were a couple of times early on when he'd cream two fours, then slice one up in the air." The student learned fast. As the season wore on, Jiang grew more cautious, and less likely to throw his bat at one on a sticky dog. Armed with a translation device on his smartphone, he gradually got to grips with the language too, with the odd understandable mishap – among them a three-hour wait in a car park in Doncaster after missing his stop on the train. Tactics were less of a problem. "He instinctively understood field positions and strategy – and started to contribute more in the field as he became more confident in English," said Hewstone. But he did well to refrain from using either English or Mandarin in a fractious cup match at Nettleham, when Jiang was last man out for 50, five short of victory, to a questionable lbw decision; he simply put his bat under his arm and walked off. Opportunities to play at such a high standard have been rare for Chinese cricketers, who remain largely excluded from the expat-dominated leagues in Beijing and Shanghai. But in 2012, three of Jiang's national team-mates spent time playing and training in Sydney; three other men and three women came to England as guests of the charity Capital Kids Cricket. Alas, their trip coincided with the wettest June in London in living memory, which obliterated almost all their matches. JAMES COYNE

FRANCE

MCC marked London 2012 by crossing the Channel in June for an Olympic commemoration fixture. It was conceived as a rematch of sorts of the 1900 Paris Olympics, when Devon County Wanderers, representing Great Britain, beat the Union des Sociétés Françaises de Sports Athlétiques (France) by 158 runs in a two-innings game (see *Wisden 2012*, page 108). This time, a Twenty20 game was played at the charming Château de Thoiry, west of Paris. To a soundtrack of roaring lions and other exotic wildlife from the zoo in the grounds, MCC won by 34 runs. That was a far cry from the last time they were in town: in 1989, to mark the bicentenary of the French Revolution, they slipped to a seven-wicket defeat against a France team led by an Irishman, Jack Short, and containing just one Frenchman. It was a hollow victory – cricket hasn't progressed much since, and remains largely the preserve of expats. But that may change. The France Cricket Association has invested heavily in Kwik Cricket, introducing the game into 150 schools in September. The aim is to reach 300 to 500 schools – and 40,000 children – within three years. Around 150 teachers have been trained up in the basics of the game; that figure is expected to reach 800. A full-time project co-ordinator has been hired, along with five regional development officers. The FCA have also forged an Anglo-French relationship with Kent: 18-year-old leg-spinner Zika Ali has spent time at the Academy in Canterbury, and received a leg-spin masterclass from board patron Richie Benaud at Thoiry. If the kids come through, then in 15 years perhaps MCC will be able to play a team of thoroughbred Frenchmen. BARNEY SPENDER

GERMANY

The first summer's cricket on the spectacular Maifeld, beside Berlin's Olympic Stadium, was an almost unmitigated success. Cricketers had been evicted from the nearby Körnerplatz field in 2011, after fears about potential damage caused by flying cricket balls, but a new venue was eventually agreed, with the grant of two new synthetic pitches. Highlights included the emergence of a young Afghan tweaker, and the first schools match at the ground, during which children aged eight to 11 inspired hopes that cricket may yet gain a grassroots footing in the German capital. An incursion by the national polo championships in August was tolerated with good humour, although the cricketers showed less understanding when a local groundsman decided to paint a line down the centre of one pitch to demarcate the viewing area for a fireworks display. But no season in Berlin would be complete without controversy. During one league match involving DSSC Berlin, the eventual champions, the age-old question of ball-tampering raised its head. The umpires, noticing the number of abrasions on one side, confiscated the ball and sent it in for inspection; fines and suspensions ensued. FABIAN MUIR

GUATEMALA

Guatemala, cradle of the Mayan civilisation, but new to the game of cricket, won the regional Easter Cup by whitewashing El Salvador home and away. Cricket's early pioneers were Manuel Farfan, a PE teacher who introduced it into public schools on the advice of British friends, and Asociación Manos Amigas, a non-governmental organisation keen to reduce violence among disadvantaged children. But it took Luke Humphries, a young Christian missionary from Hampshire, to establish the first club, in 2011. It has since morphed into Guatemala City Jaguars and Santiago Sacatepéquez Knights, while the Asociación de Cricket de Guatemala has been set up to entice more Guatemalans to the game. Training takes place on football grounds, with competitive matches at the Democracia Stadium in Guatemala City. Those of us first enchanted by the game on trips overseas were honoured to represent our nation, and have done her proud.

STUARDO MONROY

LIBERIA

William Gabriel Kpoleh, a combative opposition leader and political prisoner, probably had little time for cricket. But long after his passing, the school that bears his name is keeping the game afloat. An enthusiastic headmaster, an expanding group of curious students, and the cricket-mad Indian community have created their own hub on a playground on the outskirts of Monrovia. Hop on a downtown motorbike taxi, cling on for dear life and, 45 minutes later, with occasional stops for barked instructions, you are in New Georgia. On a scorching Sunday morning, a practice match is already under way. The wicket is improvised, lovingly assembled by a Liberian devotee based on pictures downloaded from the internet. Bats are generously shared around. For now, bowlers make do with a tennis ball. There is no Liberian Alf Gover yet, but Anish Panchal has volunteered his services as a coach. He is convinced of cricket's healing power. "Cricket has done a great deal to strengthen unity between Muslims and Hindus in India," he says. "These are strong, fit guys. They have adapted quickly to a new sport, and understand it requires daily practice to become a good player. I regularly screen DVDs from the last World Cup, so the guys can learn about tactics, field placings, how to chase a target." Watching from the side, with visible pride, are Michael Nyanneh, president of the Liberia National Cricket Federation, and the secretary, James Brown III. Nyanneh noticed Asians

KENYA'S MAASAI CRICKETERS

Cornered lions

BARNEY DOUGLAS

It's an awe-inspiring sight – red robes flooding through the air, the crisp chink of beads, eyes wide and homing in on the target. In years gone by, that target would have been a wild animal. Now, it merely has a bat and pads by way of self-defence.

This is the Maasai Warriors cricket team, a side that have developed over the last few years in the village of Ilpolei in Kenya's Rift Valley. Introduced to the sport by Aliya Bauer, a South African volunteer and qualified coach, the Warriors related cricket to their traditional hunting techniques. The ball is the spear, and the bat the shield, while the footwork recalls their nimbleness and stamina built up from herding cattle across rough terrain. After witnessing the game being taught to schoolchildren as a means of communicating HIV/Aids awareness messages, the Maasai came to realise cricket could inspire them. It has brought warring clans together, educated young men, given them a common goal and spirit.

But a darker heart exists in their community, where HIV/Aids is rife, female genital mutilation still practised, and abuse of women a huge social issue. The team are aiming to encourage the Maasai to move away from such behaviour. They feel this is the only way to progress and preserve their future as a people. However, elders fear even this change will herald the end of the Maasai. It is tradition versus progress, identity versus change.

Sonyanga is the captain of the Warriors. Quiet and unassuming, he leads by example – particularly off the field. He has a hunger to learn, and a thirst for education. He is proud of his heritage, but you can see in his eyes the conflict he must overcome to break from the elders' path. He convinced his own father to abandon female genital mutilation, saving his sister from the prospect of pain, physical and mental scarring, and considerable health risks. "Being in cricket gave me the confidence of going against the community," he says. "You know, some of the elders won't take it positively. But you have to tell them it's no good. You have to gain that courage."

The Warriors hope to play a tournament in England in 2013, believing it will energise Maasai youth and usher through changes back home. Even to fly overseas has a large bearing on their status in the community. "Without change," says one player, "we will surely perish." As the Maasai saying goes: "The eye that leaves the village sees further than the eye that stays."

Barney Douglas is a director and producer. His film, Warriors, *is due for release in late 2013. The England bowler James Anderson is an executive producer.*

playing cricket when he was a refugee in neighbouring Ivory Coast during the civil war years. Upon his return to Liberia, he flirted with the idea of setting up a baseball association – perhaps a more logical choice in a country founded by freed African-American slaves. But the sports ministry suggested cricket instead. They were supportive, but had no money to offer, so he turned to the small but prosperous Indian community. And in February 2012, an inaugural tournament was staged at Samuel K. Doe Sports Complex, where an LNCF XI, mixing Liberians with Indians, earned a three-run victory over Monrovia Super Kings, a cash prize of $450 and an unspecified package from the sponsor. *The New Republic*, betraying its American influence, declared the Super Kings had been "whipped 116–113". CHRIS SIMPSON

MALDIVES

In 2010, the American R&B superstar Akon was due to play a concert at Ekuveni Stadium on Malé, the largest island in the Maldives, until it was shelved at the last minute following threats by Islamic groups who objected to his raunchier songs. The building knocked together to house his band's equipment now acts as a cricket pavilion. Space is at a premium in this archipelago of 200 inhabited (and 1,000 uninhabited) islands, so cricketers share the stadium with the nation's athletes: the pitch is contained within the running track on a sand-and-seashell surface. Another ground was built in late 2011, on the southern island of Fuvahmulah, for a tournament between Under-25 teams from the leading cricketing nations in Asia. The competition, won by Pakistan, ran parallel with a South Asian regional political summit hosted by then-president Mohamed Nasheed – famous for hosting a cabinet meeting underwater to highlight what climate change might do to his low-lying nation. Nasheed, who learned the rudiments of the game at Dauntsey's School in Wiltshire, apparently had grand plans to install more grounds, including the country's first turf wicket, but since he was ousted in February 2012 – at gunpoint, he claimed – funding for cricket appears to have decreased. A year of political turmoil did not prevent the Maldives taking part in the ACC Trophy Elite for the first time, after which Maldivian cricket legend Moosa Kaleem retired, aged 37. JAMES COYNE

MONGOLIA

On the outskirts of Ulan Bator, in the brown, barren earth, there is a patch of land that stands out. It is mainly flat and stoneless; most importantly, it is 22 yards long. And every Sunday in summer, it belongs to the only cricket club in Mongolia. Wedged between Siberia and China, and untouched by the British Empire, the country hasn't seen much of the sport. But in 1995, Indian and British expats formed the Mongolian Cricket Club. Five years later, Lord's gave them permission to use the initials MCC (provided there was no clash of interest). By 2005, the game was fading, but it was reborn in a restaurant on the sixth floor of the UB Hotel, run by an Indian, Babu Joseph. After a quiz night, a group of Indians and Australians decided they wanted to play regularly again. They had no real pitch, so they built their own. "It was hard work, but the mining companies helped," said Shiva Velchuri, a 34-year-old from Andhra Pradesh who works in IT. "They have all the toys – excavators, rollers, compactors. We even got staff from the Indian Embassy to help, picking out stones." Three-quarters of the players are Indian, the rest mostly Australian. They've had South Africans and Zimbabweans, and Americans and Canadians who like to practise their baseball. The club play Twenty20 matches among themselves. Mongolians have also tried their hand for the first time. "Every week, locals will walk through the field while we're playing. One even stopped to watch standing right in the middle – can you believe it?" spluttered Velchuri. They've also been visited by the police a couple of times. "They were curious, I think. They asked our local players some questions, and made sure we weren't drinking alcohol, but they let us play." The club have tried, and failed, to find out who owns the land. But no one seems to object to their presence. OWEN AMOS

NEW CALEDONIA

It's 8am on a Saturday morning in September, and two games of traditional cricket are in full swing at Stade de N'Du. From the otherwise empty concrete stand there is a flurry of activity from women wearing brightly coloured, calf-length, loose dresses. Thirteen scattered fielders and four batters make up each game: two to hit, two to run. The umpires are men. There is no protective gear, and bats – flat-faced clubs, really – are one metre long. The bowlers come in off two or three paces. The shots are mostly vigorous leg-side flails. With a loud thud, some middle the heavy, fist-sized ball made from the sap of the banyan; others squirt or balloon it into the off side. If the ball slants down leg, the batter tries to connect by flipping her blade behind her legs – a tricky shot for a quick single, at best (even Eoin Morgan hasn't tried this one). Good hand–eye co-ordination is vital: the ball tends to fall apart, causing dangerously unpredictable bounce. It hurts too. National-team player Noel Sinyeue recalls how supporters once discouraged him from attempting a catch for fear of injury. He held on, and became an instant 16-year-old hero. Cricket was imported to these perfect islands in the south-west Pacific in the mid-19th century by British Protestant missionaries, who tried to convert the naturally competitive Melanesians to the sport as a replacement for more violent pastimes. The game rapidly absorbed indigenous rituals, and the number of registered players has since spiralled to 2,600 in 72 clubs. They field several teams for men, women and youngsters, making cricket one of the most popular New Caledonian sports – popular enough to survive Napoleon III's annexation of "Nouvelle-Calédonie" in 1853, and 160 years of enduring French jurisdiction. The game is so deeply ingrained in the culture that, some years ago, a New Caledonian brewery chose the silhouette of a female cricketer as the logo for its beer, Adele. Sadly, the beer wasn't a success. Neither has been international cricket. Although it has been played in New Caledonia for decades, there is a hard core of only around 30 experienced cricketers. In the 2003 Pacific Games, the men's team suffered one of the heaviest defeats in 50-over cricket, by 468 runs: Papua New Guinea 502 for nine, New Caledonia 34 all out. But the enthusiasts are hopeful that burgeoning partnerships with traditional clubs can help drive New Caledonia to ICC Affiliate status. NEIL GODDEN

OMAN

Oman's capital can claim the title of the driest city in the cricket-playing world, traditionally leading to rough and unsafe surfaces. So perhaps it is no surprise that the country's best-known Arab cricketer, HH Qais bin Khalid Al Said, a cousin of the Sultan, learned the game at Millfield School rather than Muscat. But now Al Emerat, the first fully turf ground in the Sultanate, has been assiduously prepared for the new season. For the first time, fielders will be able to attack the ball, rather than edge in tentatively from the boundary trying to predict bounce and trajectory on scorched-earth ground. Batsmen and bowlers will finally get off matting wickets, and learn to deal with spin and seam. When Oman finished 15th out of 16 at the 2012 World Twenty20 Qualifying tournament, the sports ministry expressed their "deep disappointment", and enquired why more Omani nationals had not been considered for selection. As in many Gulf states, league matches are often subcontinental corporate affairs between expat semi-professionals – with a single token Omani thrown in to satisfy league membership regulations. Yet Oman has the best record in the Middle East for producing indigenous cricketers: around 200 of the 1,100 regular players in the country are Arabs. Oman is the only country in the region to insist upon three nationals in their representative youth sides from 16 upwards. And, as coaches head into schools, more and more Arab boys and girls are discovering, to their surprise, that this peculiar game is their nation's most successful international sport. PAUL BIRD

POLAND

If the players of Warsaw CC are guilty of taking their eye off the ball, it might just be because there's a nudist beach opposite their ground. Founded in 1994, the club play their matches in the plush surroundings of the Panorama Country Club, a former hangout of British Embassy staff which still oozes old-school tie. And that stiff upper lip has been required at times after the Wał Miedzeszyński beach on the banks of the river Wisła became a popular spot for naturists. The last couple of years have been significant for the growth of cricket in Poland, with the formation of a three-team national league: two clubs come from Warsaw, while Lodz CC have acquired their own ground on the outskirts of Poland's third-largest city. Cricket has also sprung up in Lublin, and been revived in Krakow and Wroclaw, with tentative plans elsewhere too. For around a decade, there was minimal contact with the rest of European cricket. But in 2008 an XI made up of players of Polish descent, starring auctioneer Adam Franciszek Partridge from BBC antiques show *Flog It!*, and former Cumberland all-rounder Jimmy Wisniewski, participated in the inaugural Euro Twenty20 tournament at Carmel & District CC in Wales. Four years later, a Poland representative team drawn from the domestic league, including two natives, Szymon Rokicki and Piotr Sochaj, won the 2012 event in Sofia, beating Romania in the final. The presence of Vineet Sinha – who was once clocked at 85mph, and bowled Matt Prior while playing for a Mumbai XI during England's tour of India in 2008-09 – helped their cause. TIMOTHY ABRAHAM

ROMANIA

The 2007 World Cup remains, for most cricket lovers, a competition best forgotten – but it captivated one man so profoundly that the future of the game in Europe may change for ever. Gabriel Marin, 53, is a former Romania Under-19 basketball player who, three years after the fall of Nicolae Ceauşescu in 1989, set up his own IT company with $500 – much to his family's despair. Twenty-one years on, Omnilogic is one of the success stories of the Romanian market economy, and its chief executive the archetypal post-Communist self-made man. Marin could afford to send his son, Radu, to Lyceum Alpinum Zuoz, an exclusive international boarding school in Switzerland, where students play cricket in winter on the frozen lake at St Moritz. One holiday in 2007, Radu returned home with tales of wonder about a peculiar English game, and persuaded his father to buy a Sky Sports subscription so he could follow the World Cup in the Caribbean. They sat up all night, watching match after match. "What drew me to cricket is the unarmed combat," said Gabriel. "The idea that a guy can be batting for six or seven hours, facing a ball every 40 seconds, with no recourse to physical confrontation or arguing with the umpire."

Marin embarked upon a crash-course world tour, taking in England's 2009 Ashes win at Lord's, the 2011 World Cup semi-final in Colombo, and a Rajasthan Royals game at the IPL, where he chinwagged with Lalit Modi: "I can't comment on the mess he got involved with, but I thought his views on cricket development were pretty sound." Shane Warne's shirt from his Test farewell at the SCG hangs proudly on Marin's office wall.

He grew so smitten that he pledged €5m for a sport that had only one club in the entire country before he became involved. When he first met with officials from Transylvania CC in late 2008, they were playing against bibulous touring sides at the national rugby stadium, on a plastic Flickx pitch hammered on top of a wooden board. Marin helped establish an official body, Cricket Romania, which has drawn together the country's cricketing pockets into four clubs in Bucharest, three in Timişoara, and another in Cluj, with more to come in Constanta, Oradea and Iaşi. Most are heavily reliant on expats, often Indian medical students, but Timişoara Titans are entirely Romanian. In 2012, each club was obliged to field two Romanian-born players in league matches, and the board claim 300 Romanian children in 20 schools are now playing regularly – the best of them with a hard ball. Cricket Romania applied for ICC Affiliate membership in 2012, and expected a positive response by June 2013; they are targeting Associate status by 2020.

Their patron insists on a sustainable legacy. "It's pretty obvious the 'Stanford way' is not the way to do it," grinned Marin. "If the main guy disappears for whatever reason, there's nothing left. So we're trying to organise institutional sponsorship and embed it into the local system. I believe the game won't survive in Romania if it's confined to expats. We must create a local tradition." Marin's money and influence have allowed Romania to pursue projects unimaginable for other countries. Moara Vlăsiei, a jaw-dropping ground 30km from Bucharest, is destined to be the envy of all non-Test-playing nations. Three years in the making, it has been lovingly curated by an experienced British groundsman, Alan Lewis, who has trained up a team of local groundstaff to cut, scarify, roll and mark eight strips. There are ambitious – and fully costed – blueprints for a cricket academy and indoor school at the site. Assuming the square survives the harsh Wallachian winter, Moara Vlăsiei will open for play in Easter 2013 – as the only grass wicket between Denmark and Abu Dhabi. JAMES COYNE

CRICKET ON EUROSPORT

Breaking the sound barrier

JAMES COYNE

"Where the English language is unspoken there can be no real cricket, which is to say that Americans have never excelled at the game." It's hard not to chuckle at Neville Cardus's classic put-down, whether you agree with it or not. But even he failed to foresee the impact globalisation would have on his beloved sport.

On a second-floor office above a bank in downtown Belgrade, Cardus's axiom is being spectacularly undermined. England are collapsing to India's spinners at the World Twenty20, and two Eurosport commentators, Predrag Vukanovic and Vladimir Ninkovic, are telling the Balkans about it in Serbian. Their language varies only minimally from Bosnian, Montenegrin and Croatian, something Eurosport takes advantage of by screening its Serbian coverage across the former Yugoslavia. Albania have to make do with the feed from Germany – who knows what might have happened if C. B. Fry had accepted the throne?

On holiday in Sarajevo a few days later, walking past the Catholic cathedral impeccably rebuilt after the siege, I notice something on a TV screen in one of the many indistinguishable café-bars on the main drag – it's England v New Zealand in the Super Eights on Eurosport 2. I ask a waiter (in English) if he can turn the volume up, and what he thinks of the game. "Very weird," he fires back.

This is the third time, after England 2009 and West Indies 2010, that Eurosport has purchased the World Twenty20 feed from ESPN STAR Sports – and given 18 different languages the keys to the kingdom of cricket. It costs Eurosport a pittance by modern broadcasting standards, but then cricket has to compete with snooker and Polish football in the schedule. Cricket aficionados, usually high-ranking officers in the national associations like Ninkovic – general secretary of the Serbian Cricket Federation – are brought in to provide expert analysis, and spread news of their crusade. Ninkovic knows what he's talking about, and proudly shows off an Essex cap collected from Reece Topley on the boundary at Chelmsford. For enthusiasts like him, Eurosport, Facebook and YouTube have been a revelation.

Naturally, there is the odd cautionary tale: in Romania, the lead commentator is a football man, who speaks in terms of points rather than runs, and hollers every time a run is scampered, let alone when a boundary is hit or a wicket taken. The Romanian cricket authorities are lobbying ICC Europe and Eurosport to have him gently moved aside for the next tournament.

Vukanovic, though, is a consummate broadcaster, blessed with a deep, authoritative baritone. He knows who all the players are, and what they do – which, in the case of Irfan Pathan opening the batting, is not very much. As Jade Dernbach is whacked for consecutive fours by Gautam Gambhir, Ninkovic ribs England about the number of South Africans playing for them. Vukanovic has called five tournaments to date, so perhaps a touch of Twenty20-weariness has crept into his commentary. "The Champions League is a nice competition," he tells me later. "I expect a few surprises, because the top cricket stars look like they are on holiday in South Africa."

As England slide to defeat in Colombo, it doesn't take long for the duo to diagnose that young English batsmen struggle to read spin bowling out of the hand. By the time Jonny Bairstow is cleaned up trying to slog Piyush Chawla, foxed by a googly, mild mirth has broken out in the commentary box. It's strangely reassuring that, even in Belgrade, English cricket is capable of being a laughing stock.

ST HELENA

A vast fundraising campaign on St Helena came up with the £24,000 needed to cover the costs of sending the island's cricketers to their maiden international tournament, ICC Africa Division Three in Johannesburg – which meant a five-day voyage to Cape Town on the Royal Mail Ship *St Helena*. The squad filled the time by thrashing the boat's crew in a series of matches played with a rope ball, then huddled around a TV set to watch *Out of the Ashes*, the documentary about the improbable rise of Afghanistan through the global pyramid. At a training session, the players hastily applied some green spraypaint to their pads to match the new one-day pyjama kits. Since they had developed a distinct cricketing philosophy on an isolated island of 4,000 people, it was impossible to know how they would get on. An emotional opening morning answered many questions, as Cameroon were bowled out for 36, with Dane Leo taking a hat-trick in his only over. The win over Gambia was a father-and-son affair: Gavin George, now aged 57, and David George, 33, each scored 48. Heartbreakingly, the team were beaten by Seychelles in a super over, and lost by a single run to Rwanda. Three more runs, and St Helena would have been promoted to Division Two. SIMON GREEN

SPAIN

On September 4, Tariq Ali Awan – a 38-year-old Pakistani expat living in Madrid – emulated the great Sussex stylist Ranjitsinhji by scoring two centuries on the same day. Opening for Spain in the European Championship Division Two Twenty20 tournament in Corfu, Tariq took advantage of short boundaries at the Messonghi beach resort ground to blaze 150 not out from 66 balls, including 16 sixes, in a morning match against Estonia. The game dragged on longer than intended, due to the time spent retrieving balls from the neighbouring boccia and tennis courts, and from a hotel, which suffered a number of broken windows. Tariq returned in the afternoon to take on Portugal, and decided to step up the pace: this time he hit 18 of his 55 balls for six in an innings of 148. Perhaps wisely, Akbar Saiyad, Portugal's 66-year-old captain, had chosen to sit it out. JAMES COYNE

TAJIKISTAN

In 1997, at the end of Tajikistan's messy five-year civil war that followed the break-up of the Soviet Union, Indian students and exiled Afghans began playing tennis-ball cricket in the capital, Dushanbe. Locals noticed the similarities with *suzi musi*, a traditional Tajik bat-and-ball game, and joined in. There are now eight men's and two women's teams affiliated to the Tajikistan Cricket Federation, and a Pakistani tape-ball community pining for entry. The hotbed is Shahrinaw, 50km west of Dushanbe, where cricket is played at municipality grounds and an orphanage. The TCF will have to hurdle several obstacles to expand cricket in Central Asia's poorest country: internet use is rare, with access to social networking sites cut off at the whim of the government. And around a million Tajik men are drawn to Russia every year for work, in order to feed their families and prop up their country's fragile economy. So it may be women that do the heavy lifting. Assadullah Khan, a former Afghanistan player now coaching in Tajikistan, has declared that, in two years, his all-Tajik women's team will be the best in Asia. In July, Tajikistan played Afghanistan in a three-match series in Shahrinaw – the first women's international games in each country's history. The Afghan team made the journey north across the border with the sponsorship of a private NGO, as women's sport was considered too sensitive an issue for Kabul. The Afghans, clad in headscarves, won 2–1. JAMES COYNE

USA

Looking for controversial elections, habitual infighting, breakaway governing bodies and on-field talent that soldiers on in spite of it all? Then look no further. The USA Cricket Association general elections, postponed throughout 2011, finally took place in April, but only after 32 of 47 member leagues were denied the right to vote. USACA presidential candidate Ram Varadarajan's 11th-hour lawsuit couldn't reverse the board's decision to disenfranchise leagues they considered "not of good standing". The only non-incumbent voted on to the board was Kenwyn Williams – who pledged prior to his election to impose a gag order preventing all USACA players and employees from speaking to the media. Six months after he was elected executive secretary, Williams plunged USACA's Facebook page into a social media meltdown (see *Cricket and Blogs*, page 182). Williams was eventually suspended by USACA, before they removed him from the board altogether. Another consequence of the elections was the formation of the American Cricket Federation, a breakaway group attempting to usurp USACA as the official national governing body. The ACF staged their inaugural national championship in Los Angeles in October, with eight former USACA leagues participating. The Southern California Cricket Association won the title, and two of their players were subsequently picked to represent USA against Canada, eliminating fears that anyone playing in ACF events would be ostracised by USACA. The national team experienced mixed fortunes on the field, finishing 12th out of 16 at the ICC World Twenty20 Qualifier, but winning promotion from WCL Division Four. USA's leading scorer in both events was stalwart Sushil Nadkarni. His hard-hitting opening partner Steven Taylor, an 18-year-old from Florida who also took part in a World XI match in Pakistan, showed signs he could become America's first home-grown star since Bart King toured the UK at the start of the 20th century. PETER DELLA PENNA

With special thanks to Mahendra Mapagunaratne.

Wisden *always welcomes engaging tales of cricket from improbable corners of the globe. Please contact* james.coyne@wisden.com

ICC GLOBAL TOURNAMENTS

WORLD CRICKET LEAGUE 2012

Competition	*Date*	*Winner*	*Runner-up*	*Others (in finishing order)*
WCL Division Four	Sep	Nepal	USA	Singapore, Denmark, Malaysia, Tanzania
WCL Division Five	Feb	Singapore	Malaysia	Guernsey, Cayman Islands, Bahrain, Argentina
WCL Division Eight	Sep	Vanuatu	Ghana	Japan, Belgium, Norway, Samoa, Suriname, Bhutan
WCL Division Eight European Qualifier	Jun	Belgium	France	Gibraltar, Austria

REGIONAL ONE-DAY TOURNAMENTS

Competition	*Date*	*Winner*	*Runner-up*	*Others (in finishing order)*
ACC Trophy Elite	Oct	Nepal/UAE (shared title)	–	Afghanistan, Malaysia, Hong Kong, Oman, Kuwait, Maldives, Bhutan, Saudi Arabia
ACC Trophy Challenge	Dec	Singapore	Bahrain	Qatar, Thailand, Iran, China, Myanmar

REGIONAL TWENTY20 TOURNAMENTS

Competition	*Date*	*Winner*	*Runner-up*	*Others (in finishing order)*
Africa Division Two	Oct	Botswana	Tanzania	Zambia, Ghana, Seychelles, Mozambique, Swaziland, Sierra Leone
Africa Division Three	Apr	Zambia	Seychelles	Gambia, Rwanda, St Helena, Morocco, Cameroon, Mali
European Division Two	Sep	Isle of Man	Sweden	Spain, Israel, Greece, Finland, Portugal, Estonia, Luxembourg, Croatia, Cyprus, Malta
European Division Three	June	Estonia	Slovenia	Bulgaria

WOMEN'S TOURNAMENTS

Competition	*Date*	*Winner*	*Runner-up*	*Others (in finishing order)*
Americas Women's T20	Apr	Canada	USA	Argentina, Cayman Islands, Bermuda, Brazil
Women's T20 Asia Cup	Oct	India	Pakistan	Sri Lanka, Bangladesh, China, Thailand, Nepal, Hong Kong
East Asia–Pacific Women's T20	May	Japan	PNG	Samoa, Vanuatu, Fiji, Cook Islands

PART SEVEN

Records and Registers

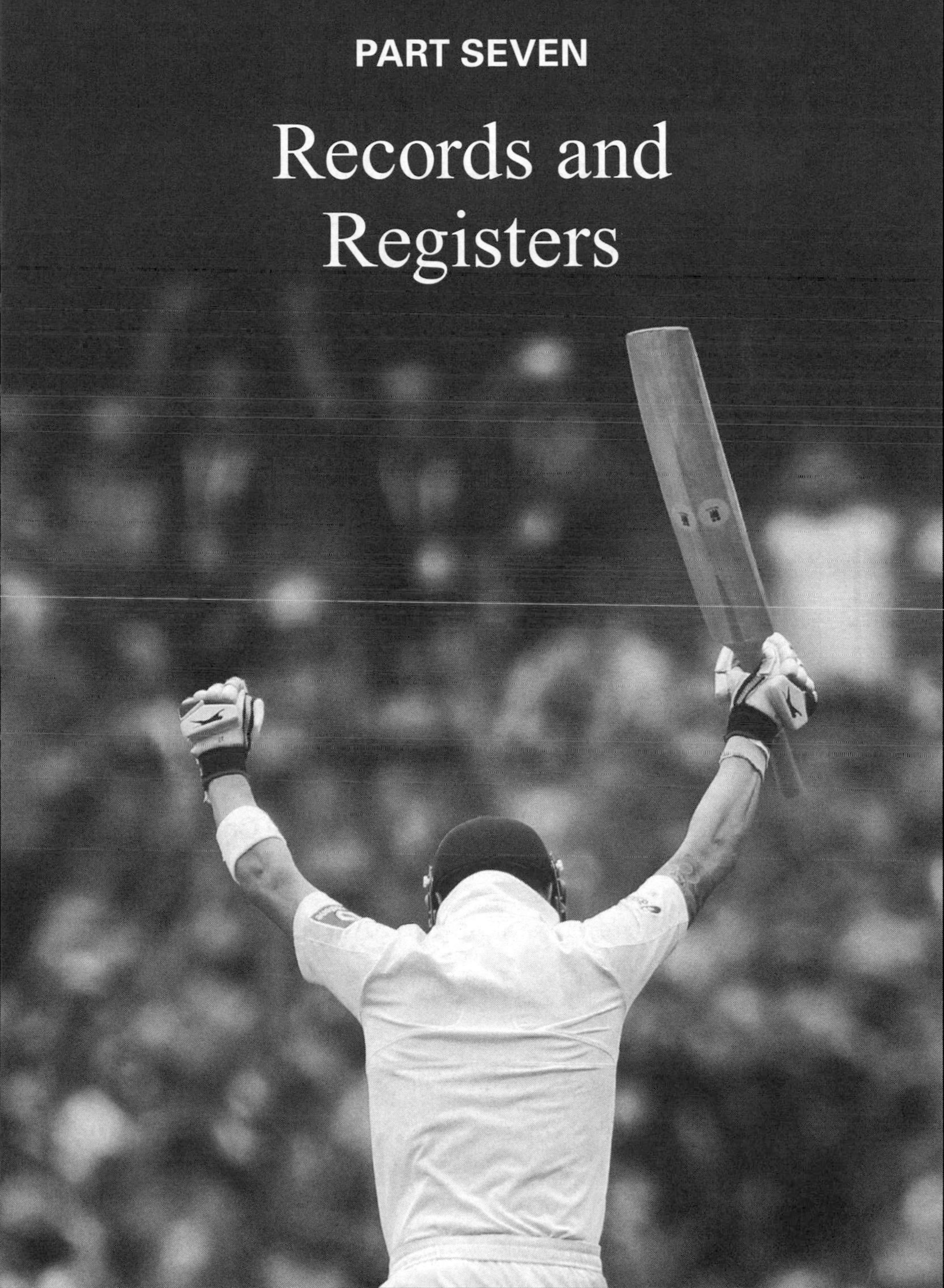

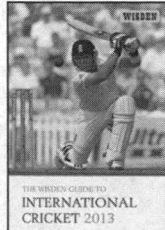

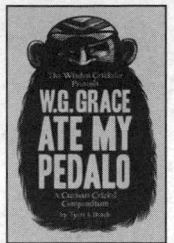

FEATURES OF 2012

In the past, *Wisden* has run separate lists of the statistical features of the English and overseas seasons (eg 2007 and 2006-07). These have now been combined in a single list of statistical features of the calendar year. Because the section now covers the calendar year, some of the features listed occurred in matches reported in *Wisden 2012* and some will be reported in *Wisden 2014*; these items are indicated by [W12] or [W14].

Double-Hundreds (58)

	Mins	*Balls*	*4*	*6*		
331	707	501	29	7	‡R. A. Jadeja	Saurashtra v Railways at Rajkot.[W14]
329*	609	468	39	1	‡M. J. Clarke	Australia v India at Sydney.[W12]
327	524	312	54	2	K. M. Jadhav	Maharashtra v Uttar Pradesh at Gahunje.[W14]
311*	790	529	35	0	H. M. Amla	South Africa v England at The Oval.
303*	629	524	41	6	L. M. Davis	Western Australia v New South Wales at Perth.
303*	561	400	37	4	‡R. A. Jadeja	Saurashtra v Gujarat at Surat.[W14]
282	651	493	35	2	S. D. Jogiyani	Saurashtra v Gujarat at Surat.[W14]
281	596	397	34	2	Umar Amin	Port Qasim Auth. v Habib Bank at Islamabad.[W14]
269*	443	252	27	14	C. Munro	Auckland v Wellington at Auckland.[W14]
268	365	305	35	0	J. C. Hildreth	Somerset v Cardiff MCCU at Taunton.
266	618	394	36	6	M. Vijay	Rest of India v Rajasthan at Bangalore.[W14]
264*	642	464	32	1	‡C. M. Gautam	Karnataka v Maharashtra at Gahunje.[W14]
260	618	455	31	3	M. N. Samuels.	West Indies v Bangladesh at Khulna.
259*	582	398	26	0	‡M. J. Clarke	Australia v South Africa at Brisbane.
257	907	665	26	2	V. A. Saxena	Rajasthan v Tamil Nadu at Chennai.
257	576	394	20	0	‡C. M. Gautam	Karnataka v Vidarbha at Mysore.[W14]
252	635	462	32	0	Aamer Sajjad	Punjab v Sind at Lahore.
250*	528	361	31	5	Yashpal Singh	Services v Tripura at Agartala.[W14]
248*	509	395	28	3	A. Lyth	Yorkshire v Leicestershire at Leicester.
243	635	462	30	1	D. S. Jadhav.	Assam v Tripura at Guwahati.[W14]
239	505	347	36	0	H. D. Rutherford . . .	Otago v Wellington at Dunedin.
236	450	357	20	2	‡N. R. D. Compton . .	Somerset v Cardiff MCCU at Taunton.
234*	286	190	30	8	K. P. Pietersen	Surrey v Lancashire at Guildford.
233*		348	25	1	V. Chopra	Tamil Union v Sinhalese at Colombo.
231*	514	400	31	0	W. L. Madsen	Derbyshire v Northamptonshire at Northampton.
231		421	27	0	N. H. G. Cooray . . .	Chilaw Marians v Bloomfield at Colombo.
230	345	257	40	1	‡M. J. Clarke	Australia v South Africa at Adelaide.
224	433	325	31	1	J. H. Kallis.	South Africa v Sri Lanka at Cape Town.[W12]
223		370	21	4	‡N. T. Paranavitana . .	Sinhalese v Bloomfield at Colombo.
222*	384	270	26	3	J. E. Root	Yorkshire v Hampshire at Southampton.
222	623	417	31	1	A. P. Tare	Mumbai v Saurashtra at Rajkot.[W14]
221	516	404	21	0	R. T. Ponting	Australia v India at Adelaide.[W12]
220	476	310	34	0	R. T. Bailey	Knights v Titans at Kimberley.[W14]
219*	531	422	23	2	M. Klinger	South Australia v Tasmania at Adelaide.
216		375	27	2	‡N. T. Paranavitana . .	Sinhalese v Tamil Union at Colombo.
216		282	24	2	L. P. C. Silva	Bloomfield v Sinhalese at Colombo.
213	496	368	33	0	Jiwanjot Singh	Punjab v Hyderabad at Mohali.[W14]
212*	498	359	17	9	A. P. McLaren	SW Districts v KZ-Natal at Oudtshoorn.[W14]
211	411	306	32	1	Mandeep Singh	Punjab v Mumbai at Mumbai.[W14]
211	451	367	26	0	J. Yadav.	Haryana v Karnataka at Hubli.[W14]
210*		285	25	1	F. D. M. Karunaratne	Sinhalese v Ragama at Colombo.
210	380	275	26	1	‡M. J. Clarke	Australia v India at Adelaide.[W12]
210	507	394	30	0	J. M. Brodie.	Wellington v Auckland at Auckland.
210		334	25	1	P. Dogra.	Himachal Pradesh v Services at Amtar.[W14]
209	507	395	20	1	Marshall Ayub.	Dhaka Metropolis v Chittagong at Bogra.[W14]
208*	493	369	17	4	M. N. Waller	MW Rhinos v Matabele Tuskers at Kwekwe.[W14]
208	333	241	33	3	Yuvraj Singh	North Zone v Central Zone at Hyderabad.[W14]
206*	513	389	21	0	‡C. A. Pujara	India v England at Ahmedabad.
206*	350	313	19	2	M. H. W. Papps	Wellington v Canterbury at Rangiora.[W14]

	Mins	*Balls*	*4*	*6*		
205*	496	389	21	0	M. B. A. Smith	Eastern Province v KZ-Natal at Port Elizabeth.
205*		378	18	1	B. P. Nash	Jamaica v Guyana at North Sound.
204*	406	323	15	3	‡N. R. D. Compton . .	Somerset v Nottinghamshire at Nottingham.
203*	457	372	22	0	S. Chanderpaul	West Indies v Bangladesh at Mirpur.
203*	303	221	30	1	‡C. A. Pujara	Saurashtra v Madhya Pradesh at Rajkot.[W14]
203	452	329	24	3	R. G. Sharma	Mumbai v Punjab at Mumbai.[W14]
202*	567	373	21	1	A. Mishra.	Haryana v Karnataka at Hubli.[W14]
201*		192	22	7	G. Snyman.	Namibia v Kenya at Windhoek.
200*		418	18	1	G. Satish	Karnataka v Tamil Nadu at Chennai.[W14]

‡ *Clarke scored four double-hundreds (all in Tests), and Jadeja two triple-hundreds, while Compton, Gautam, Paranavitana and Pujara each scored two double-hundreds.*

Hundred on First-Class Debut

126 / 112	V. S. Awate	Maharashtra v Vidarbha at Nagpur.[W14]
102*	P. I. Burgoyne.	Southern Rocks v Mashonaland Eagles at Harare.[W14]
138	Z. Elkin.	Cardiff MCCU v Somerset at Taunton.
213	Jiwanjot Singh	Punjab v Hyderabad at Mohali.[W14]
100*	V. Rawal.	Delhi v Tamil Nadu at Delhi.[W14]
102	Shahbaz Bashir.	Netherlands v United Arab Emirates at Deventer.
152	Shoaib Ahmed	KRL v ZTBL at Sialkot.[W14]

Three Hundreds in Successive Innings

P. Dogra (Himachal Pradesh)	121	v Kerala at Amtar.[W14]
	210	v Services at Amtar.[W14]
	122	v Andhra at Amtar.[W14]
W. W. A. G. Maneshan (Kurunegala Y). . . .	127	v Ports Authority at Kurunegala.[W14]
	150 and 114	v Saracens at Kurunegala.[W14]
Tamim Iqbal (Chittagong)	192 and 113*	v Dhaka Metropolis at Bogra.[W14]
	183	v Sylhet at Savar.[W14]
Usman Salahuddin (Punjab)	108*	v Khyber Pakhtunkhwa at Lahore.[W14]
	114	v Baluchistan at Lahore.[W14]
	102*	v Sind at Lahore.[W14]

Hundred in Each Innings of a Match

M. Q. Adams.	132	113*	Western Province v Boland at Bellville.
V. S. Awate.	126	112	Maharashtra v Vidarbha at Nagpur (*on debut*).[W14]
D. Bundela	108	100*	Madhya Pradesh v Punjab at Gwalior.[W14]
P. G. Fulton.	102	108	Canterbury v Otago at Dunedin.[W14]
K. R. Kapoor.	106	100*	Karnataka v Haryana at Hubli.[W14]
N. D. McKenzie	108	101*	Lions v Dolphins at Durban.
W. W. A. G. Maneshan.	150	114	Kurunegala Youth v Saracens at Kurunegala.
A. A. Muzumdar.	101	104	Andhra v Himachal Pradesh at Amtar.[W14]
R. I. Newton	115	119*	Northamptonshire v Derbyshire at Northampton.
M. G. Pote.	119	100*	Western Province v Easterns at Benoni.
K. O. A. Powell.	117	110	West Indies v Bangladesh at Mirpur.
R. J. Quiney	114	119	Victoria v South Australia at Adelaide.
A. J. Redmond	133	123	Otago v Canterbury at Rangiora.[W14]
L. Ronchi	113	108	Wellington v Northern Districts at Wellington.[W14]
H. D. Rutherford	107	118	Otago v Northern Districts at Hamilton.
J. D. Ryder	117*	174	Wellington v Central Districts at Napier.[W14]
Tamim Iqbal	192	113*	Chittagong v Dhaka Metropolis at Bogra.[W14]

Carrying Bat through Completed Innings

J. H. K. Adams	139*	Hampshire (302) v Essex at Southampton.
V. Chopra	233*	Tamil Union (416) v Sinhalese at Colombo.
A. S. Das	98*	Bengal (201) v Mumbai at Mumbai.[W14]
I. Dev Singh	117*	Jammu and Kashmir (215) v Kerala at Perintalmanna.[W14]
R. Dewan	143*	Haryana (334) v England XI at Ahmedabad.
P. J. Horton	49*	Lancashire (170) v Durham at Chester-le-Street.
P. J. Hughes	135*	Worcestershire (246) v Warwickshire at Birmingham.
V. A. Jagadeesh	199*	Kerala (314) v Services at Delhi.[W14]
A. Lyth	248*	Yorkshire (486) v Leicestershire at Leicester.
D. K. H. Mitchell	133*	Worcestershire (323) v Middlesex at Worcester.
K. R. Pawar	111*	Mumbai (304) v Madhya Pradesh at Indore.[W14]

Most Sixes in an Innings

15	Ziaur Rahman (152*)	South Zone v Central Zone at Mirpur.[W14]
14	C. H. Gayle (165)	Jamaica v Windward Islands at Kingston.
14	C. Munro (269*)	Auckland v Wellington at Auckland.[W14]
12	Tamim Iqbal (183)	Chittagong v Sylhet at Savar.[W14]
10	C. U. Jayasinghe (131)	Bloomfield v Colts at Colombo.
9	C. Jonker (190)	South Western Districts v Namibia at Windhoek.
9	A. P. McLaren (212*)	South Western Districts v KZ-Natal at Oudtshoorn.[W14]

Most Runs in Boundaries

	4	*6*		
228	54	2	K. M. Jadhav (327)	Maharashtra v Uttar Pradesh at Gahunje.[W14]
200	41	6	L. M. Davis (303*)	Western Australia v New South Wales at Perth.

Longest Innings

Mins		
907	V. A. Saxena (257)	Rajasthan v Tamil Nadu at Chennai.
790	H. M. Amla (311*)	South Africa v England at The Oval.
707	R. A. Jadeja (331)	Saurashtra v Railways at Rajkot.[W14]
651	S. D. Jogiyani (282)	Saurashtra v Gujarat at Surat.[W14]
642	C. M. Gautam (264*)	Karnataka v Maharashtra at Gahunje.[W14]
635	Aamer Sajjad (252)	Punjab v Sind at Lahore.
635	D. S. Jadhav (243)	Assam v Tripura at Guwahati.[W14]
629	L. M. Davis (303*)	Western Australia v New South Wales at Perth.
623	A. P. Tare (222)	Mumbai v Saurashtra at Rajkot.[W14]
618	M. N. Samuels (260)	West Indies v Bangladesh at Khulna.
618	M. Vijay (266)	Rest of India v Rajasthan at Bangalore.[W14]
609	M. J. Clarke (329*)	Australia v India at Sydney.[W12]

Unusual Dismissals

Handled the Ball

W. S. A. Williams (1) . . . . Canterbury v Otago at Dunedin.[W14]

First-Wicket Partnership of 100 in Each Innings

116 217 H. H. Khadiwale/C. G. Khurana, Maharashtra v Tamil Nadu at Chennai.
247 174 M. C. Kleinveldt/M. G. Pote, Western Province v Easterns at Benoni.
126 139 S. D. Peters/N. J. O'Brien, Northamptonshire v Leicestershire at Northampton.
120 120 A. N. Petersen (1st inns)/J. A. Rudolph (2nd)/G. C. Smith, South Africa v England at Leeds.
166 162 A. N. Cook (1st inns)/N. R. D. Compton/I. J. L. Trott (2nd), England XI v Haryana at Ahmedabad.

Highest Wicket Partnerships

First Wicket
288 Jiwanjot Singh/K. Goel, Punjab v Hyderabad at Mohali.[W14]
275 P. Akshath Reddy/D. B. Ravi Teja, Hyderabad v Rajasthan at Hyderabad.
267 Mizanur Rahman/Junaid Siddique, Rajshahi v Barisal at Rajshahi.[W14]
254 C. H. Gayle/K. O. A. Powell, West Indies v New Zealand at North Sound.
252 M. D. U. S. Jayasundera/G. I. Daniel, Ragama v Tamil Union at Colombo.
252 S. A. Northeast/R. W. T. Key, Kent v Hampshire at Southampton.

Second Wicket
450 N. R. D. Compton/J. C. Hildreth, Somerset v Cardiff MCCU at Taunton.
386 P. Akshath Reddy/G. H. Vihari, Hyderabad v Mumbai at Hyderabad.[W14]
320 H. E. Vithana/M. D. K. J. Perera, Colts v Sinhalese at Colombo.
287 Mohammad Hafeez/Azhar Ali, Pakistan v Sri Lanka at Colombo.
267 L. L. Mnyanda/K. D. Bennett, Border v Griqualand West at Kimberley.
259 G. C. Smith/H. M. Amla, South Africa v England at The Oval.
251 M. S. Vardhan/A. P. Majumdar, East Zone v North Zone at Delhi.

Third Wicket
539‡ S. D. Jogiyani/R. A. Jadeja, Saurashtra v Gujarat at Surat.[W14]
379 L. M. Davis/A. C. Voges, Western Australia v New South Wales at Perth.
377* H. M. Amla/J. H. Kallis, South Africa v England at The Oval.
326 D. M. Bravo/M. N. Samuels, West Indies v Bangladesh at Khulna.
322 K. D. Bennett/C. Tshiki, Border v Free State at East London.
292 D. Elgar/F. du Plessis, South Africa A v Sri Lanka A at Durban.
278 A. P. Tare/R. G. Sharma, Mumbai v Saurashtra at Rajkot.[W14]
276 Tamim Iqbal/Mominul Haque, Chittagong v Dhaka Metropolis at Bogra.[W14]
272 K. L. Rahul/C. M. Gautam, Karnataka v Vidarbha at Mysore.[W14]
270 H. E. van der Dussen/K. M. Vardhan, North West v Northerns at Pretoria.[W14]
262 K. S. Williamson/L. R. P. L. Taylor, New Zealand v Sri Lanka at Colombo.
259 K. Y. de Silva/C. K. Kapugedera, Nondescripts v Bloomfield at Colombo.
256 M. H. W. Papps/J. D. Ryder, Wellington v Central Districts at Wellington.[W14]

Fourth Wicket
386 R. T. Ponting/M. J. Clarke, Australia v India at Adelaide.[W12]
337 Umar Amin/Khalid Latif, Port Qasim Authority v Habib Bank at Islamabad.[W14]
311 Marshall Ayub/Mehrab Hossain, Dhaka Metropolis v Chittagong at Bogra.[W14]
308* M. B. A. Smith/C. N. Ackermann, Eastern Province v KwaZulu-Natal at Port Elizabeth.
303 N. J. Edwards/M. H. Wessels, Nottinghamshire v Loughborough MCCU at Nottingham.
291 A. H. Gupta/Yashpal Singh, Services v Tripura at Agartala.[W14]
288 R. T. Ponting/M. J. Clarke, Australia v India at Sydney.[W12]
283 D. R. Flynn/C. J. Anderson, Northern Districts v Otago at Hamilton.[W14]
259 E. J. M. Cowan/M. J. Clarke, Australia v South Africa at Brisbane.
257 B. R. M. Taylor/M. N. Waller, Mid West Rhinos v Matabeleland Tuskers at Kwekwe.[W14]

Fifth Wicket
340 C. M. Gautam/S. T. R. Binny, Karnataka v Maharashtra at Gahunje.[W14]
334* M. J. Clarke/M. E. K. Hussey, Australia v India at Sydney.[W12]
318 Mandeep Singh/A. L. Menaria, India A v New Zealand A at Lincoln.

314 K. M. Jadhav/R. H. Motwani, Maharashtra v Uttar Pradesh at Gahunje.[W14]
302 L. P. C. Silva/C. U. Jayasinghe, Bloomfield v Nondescripts at Colombo.
296* S. Chanderpaul/D. Ramdin, West Indies v Bangladesh at Mirpur.
294 R. S. Bopara/J. S. Foster, Essex v Northamptonshire at Northampton.
272 M. J. Clarke/M. E. K. Hussey, Australia v South Africa at Adelaide.
259 R. T. Bailey/M. N. van Wyk, Knights v Titans at Kimberley.[W14]
251 Shoaib Khan/Faisal Iqbal, PIA v WAPDA at Mirpur.[W14]

Sixth Wicket
377 C. Munro/C. Cachopa, Auckland v Wellington at Auckland.[W14]
239 M. C. Juneja/R. H. Bhatt, Gujarat v Saurashtra at Surat.[W14]

Seventh Wicket
292 R. A. Jadeja/K. R. Makwana, Saurashtra v Railways at Rajkot.[W14]
216 N. H. G. Cooray/T. M. U. S. Karunaratne, Chilaw Marians v Bloomfield at Colombo.
214 M. N. van Wyk/R. McLaren, Knights v Warriors at Port Elizabeth.
204 M. N. Samuels/D. J. G. Sammy, West Indies v England at Nottingham.
204 J. O. Troughton/C. R. Woakes, Warwickshire v Somerset at Taunton.

Eighth Wicket
392‡ A. Mishra/J. Yadav, Haryana v Karnataka at Hubli.[W14]
257‡ D. J. Vilas/R. J. Peterson, Cape Cobras v Knights at Kimberley.
224 D. L. Maddy/R. Clarke, Warwickshire v Lancashire at Liverpool.
212 N. J. van den Bergh/D. R. Deeb, North West v Free State at Potchefstroom.[W14]
162* A. J. Doolan/T. D. Paine, Australia A v South Africans at Sydney.
159 W. L. Coetsee/J. Coetzee, Griqualand West v North West at Potchefstroom.
159 M. C. Juneja/R. B. Kalaria, Gujarat v Railways at Bhubaneswar.[W14]

Ninth Wicket
261 W. L. Madsen/T. Poynton, Derbyshire v Northamptonshire at Northampton.
184 Mahmudullah/Abul Hasan, Bangladesh v West Indies at Khulna.
154 G. I. Hume/E. Leie, Gauteng v South Western Districts at Johannesburg.
153 M. T. Coles/A. M. Davies, Kent v Yorkshire at Leeds.

Tenth Wicket
168 C. P. Wood/D. J. Balcombe, Hampshire v Leicestershire at Leicester.
156 G. A. S. Perera/H. D. N. de Silva, Panadura v Kurunegala Youth at Panadura.
143 D. Ramdin/T. L. Best, West Indies v England at Birmingham.
127 Bhuvneshwar Kumar/R. R. Singh, Central Zone v North Zone at Hyderabad.[W14]
123 R. M. S. Eranga/J. G. A. Janoda, Chilaw Marians v Sinhalese at Colombo.
120 B. J. Pelser/J. N. Diseko, North West v South Western Districts at Oudtshoorn.
120 R. P. Kellepotha/B. B. Sanjeewa, Police v Air Force at Colombo.
115 S. Chanderpaul/B. J. Bess, Guyana v Barbados at Bridgetown.
113 A. J. McKay/M. R. Gillespie, Wellington v Canterbury at Rangiora.[W14]
110 I. A. R. L. Illeperuma/A. M. C. M. K. Bandara, Badureliya v Moors at Maggona.
104 S. C. van Schalkwyk/M. P. Siboto, Knights v Dolphins at Bloemfontein.[W14]

‡ *National record.*

Most Wickets in an Innings

9-23 A. A. Chavan . . . . Mumbai v Punjab at Mumbai.[W14]
9-46 P. M. Pushpakumara . . . . Chilaw Marians v Lankan at Colombo.
9-65 Abdur Rehman . . . . Somerset v Worcestershire at Taunton.
9-67 G. Onions . . . . Durham v Nottinghamshire at Nottingham.
9-84 Abdur Razzak . . . . Khulna v Chittagong at Bogra.[W14]
8-17 S. P. Narine . . . . Trinidad & Tobago v Comb. Campuses & Colls at Bridgetown.
8-23 M. J. McClenaghan . . . . . Auckland v Otago at Auckland.
8-31 R. V. Dhruve . . . . Gujarat v Rajasthan at Ahmedabad.[W14]
8-33 S. Shillingford . . . . Windward Islands v Barbados at St George's.
8-34 H. V. Patel . . . . Haryana v Rajasthan at Rohtak.

8-35	Talha Jubair.	Dhaka Metropolis v Rangpur at Bogra.[W14]
8-40	H. V. Patel	Haryana v Karnataka at Bangalore.
8-42	E. C. Rainsford	Mid West Rhinos v Mountaineers at Mutare.[W14]
8-44	C. H. Morris.	Lions v Dolphins at Johannesburg.[W14]
8-51	C. P. Shahid.	Kerala v Jammu & Kashmir at Perintalmanna.[W14]
8-52	S. C. Meaker	Surrey v Somerset at The Oval.
8-53	W. G. H. N. Premaratne .	Ragama v Lankan at Colombo.
8-55	D. Hettiarachchi.	Moors v Lankan at Colombo.
8-60	G. R. Rabie	South Western Districts v North West at Oudtshoorn.
8-71	D. J. Balcombe	Hampshire v Gloucestershire at Southampton.
8-93	B. M. D. K. Mendis.	Navy v Panadura at Welisara.
8-97	K. V. Sharma.	Railways v Rajasthan at Bhubaneswar.[W14]
8-123	A. B. Dinda	East Zone v North Zone at Delhi.
8-128	S. Randiv.	Bloomfield v Badureliya at Colombo.
8-139	P. M. Pushpakumara	Chilaw Marians v Moors at Colombo.

Most Wickets in a Match

14-96	R. V. Dhruve	Gujarat v Rajasthan at Ahmedabad.[W14]
14-101	Abdur Rehman	Somerset v Worcestershire at Taunton.
14-110	S. Shillingford	Windward Islands v Barbados at St George's.
14-181	S. Prasanna	Army v Police at Colombo.
13-39	S. P. Narine	Trinidad & Tobago v Comb. Campuses & Colls at Bridgetown.
13-107	P. M. Pushpakumara . . .	Chilaw Marians v Lankan at Colombo.
13-112	Abdur Razzak	Khulna v Chittagong at Bogra.[W14]
13-115	Enamul Haque.	Sylhet v Barisal at Barisal.[W14]
13-137	M. S. Panesar.	Sussex v Somerset at Taunton.
12-73	H. A. Varaiya	Kenya v Ireland at Mombasa.
12-82	R. R. Singh	Rajasthan v Haryana at Rohtak.
12-85	R. Ashwin	India v New Zealand at Hyderabad.
12-92	G. D. Putland.	South Australia v Victoria at Melbourne.[W14]
12-96	M. M. Ali.	Worcestershire v Lancashire at Manchester.
12-101	C. H. Morris	Lions v Dolphins at Johannesburg.[W14]
12-111	R. H. Joseph	Leicestershire v Glamorgan at Leicester.
12-119	D. M. G. S. Dissanayake	Ports Authority v Navy at Welisara.
12-132	B. M. D. K. Mendis. . . .	Navy v Kurunegala Youth at Welisara.
12-141	R. M. G. K. Sirisoma. . .	Lankan v Badureliya at Moratuwa.
12-141	Tanvir Ahmed	Port Qasim Authority v National Bank at Lahore.[W14]
12-147	M. A. Liyanapathiranage	Colombo v Panadura at Colombo.
12-157	S. Prasanna	Army v Kurunegala Youth at Kurunegala.
12-165	A. A. Chavan.	Mumbai v Punjab at Mumbai.[W14]
12-171	H. M. R. K. B. Herath . .	Sri Lanka v England at Galle.

Outstanding Innings Analyses

10–5–6–7 M. N. Piedt SW Districts v Western Province at Oudtshoorn (*on debut*).[W14]

Hat-Tricks (7)

J. M. Bird	Tasmania v Western Australia at Hobart.
D. du Preez	Free State v Griqualand West at Kimberley.[W14]
C. H. Morris	Lions v Warriors at Port Elizabeth.
A. P. Palladino	Derbyshire v Leicestershire at Leicester.
Shami Ahmed	Bengal v Madhya Pradesh at Indore.[W14]
Sohag Gazi	Barisal v Khulna at Khulna.[W14]
Yasin Arafat	Chittagong v Barisal at Sylhet.[W14]

Most Balls Bowled in an Innings

510	85–27–192–4	R. Aushik Srinivas	Tamil Nadu v Rajasthan at Chennai.

Most Balls Bowled in a Match

678	113–37–253–4	R. Aushik Srinivas	Tamil Nadu v Rajasthan at Chennai.

Match Double (100 runs and 10 wickets)

D. M. G. S. Dissanayake	90, 11*; 5-73, 5-64	Ports Authority v Burgher at Colombo.
A. G. Murtaza	106, 10; 7-80, 3-62	Uttar Pradesh v Tamil Nadu at Chennai.[W14]

Most Wicketkeeping Dismissals in an Innings

8 (8ct)	T. L. Tsolekile	South Africa A v Sri Lanka A at Durban.
7 (7ct)	T. T. Mupariwa	Matabeleland Tuskers v MW Rhinos at Kwekwe (*on debut*).
6 (6ct)	M. D. Bates	Hampshire v Gloucestershire at Southampton.
6 (6ct)	A. Bhalaik	Himachal Pradesh v Andhra at Amtar.[W14]
6 (6ct)	R. Bishop	Gauteng v Border at East London.
6 (6ct)	B. C. Brown	Sussex v Middlesex at Hove.
6 (6ct)	D. C. de Boorder	Otago v Northern Districts at Hamilton.[W14]
6 (5ct, 1st)	K. Delport	Namibia v Eastern Province at Port Elizabeth.
6 (5ct, 1st)	E. J. H. Eckersley	Leicestershire v Gloucestershire at Leicester.
6 (6ct)	C. M. Gautam	Karnataka v Orissa at Bangalore.[W14]
6 (6ct)	C. M. Gautam	Karnataka v Delhi at Bangalore.[W14]
6 (4ct, 2st)	K. D. E. Harshaka	Police v Ports Authority at Colombo.
6 (6ct)	G. J. Hopkins	Auckland v Otago at Auckland.
6 (6ct)	L. O. D. James	Windward Islands v Guyana at Roseau.
6 (6ct)	U. Kaul	Punjab v Hyderabad at Mohali.[W14]
6 (5ct, 1st)	Liton Das	Rangpur v Barisal at Rajshahi.[W14]
6 (5ct, 1st)	M. J. Prior	England v South Africa at Lord's.
6 (6ct)	L. Ronchi	Wellington v Northern Districts at Wellington.[W14]
6 (6ct)	J. K. Silva	Sinhalese v Ragama at Colombo.
6 (6ct)	T. I. F. Triffitt	Tasmania v Queensland at Brisbane.
6 (6ct)	D. J. Vilas	Cape Cobras v Knights at Kimberley.
6 (6ct)	L. R. Walters	Eastern Province v KZ-Natal Inland at Port Elizabeth.[W14]
6 (6ct)	L. R. Walters	Eastern Province v KwaZulu-Natal at Chatsworth.[W14]

Most Wicketkeeping Dismissals in a Match

10 (9ct, 1st)	Gulraiz Sadaf	Baluchistan v Federal Areas at Multan.
10 (9ct, 1st)	Liton Das	Rangpur v Barisal at Rajshahi.[W14]
10 (10ct)	D. J. Vilas	Cape Cobras v Knights at Kimberley.
9 (9ct)	A. Bhalaik	Himachal Pradesh v Andhra at Amtar.[W14]
9 (9ct)	D. C. de Boorder	Otago v Northern Districts at Hamilton.[W14]
9 (8ct, 1st)	K. Delport	Namibia v Eastern Province at Port Elizabeth.
9 (7ct, 2st)	K. D. E. Harshaka	Police v Ports Authority at Colombo.
9 (9ct)	T. L. Tsolekile	South Africa A v Sri Lanka A at Durban.
9 (9ct)	R. van Schoor	Namibia v Kenya at Windhoek.[W14]

Most Catches in an Innings in the Field

5 R. N. B. Apparajith . . . . Tamil Nadu v Uttar Pradesh at Chennai.[W14]
5 R. Clarke . . . . Warwickshire v Durham at Chester-le-Street.
5 A. B. Fudadin. . . . . Guyana v Barbados at Bridgetown.
5 M. W. L. S. Lakmal . . . . Saracens v Navy at Welisara.
5 J. F. le Clus. . . . . Northerns v Eastern Province at Port Elizabeth.
5 G. C. Smith . . . . South Africa v Australia at Perth.
5 M. B. A. Smith. . . . . Eastern Province v Namibia at Port Elizabeth.
5 M. E. Trescothick. . . . . Somerset v Nottinghamshire at Taunton.
5 M. E. Trescothick. . . . . Somerset v Sussex at Hove.

Most Catches in a Match in the Field

7 L. A. Dawson . . . . Hampshire v Northamptonshire at Northampton.
6 R. N. B. Apparajith . . . . Tamil Nadu v Uttar Pradesh at Chennai.[W14]
6 Asad Shafiq . . . . Habib Bank v United Bank at Rawalpindi.[W14]
6 V. A. Jagadeesh . . . . Kerala v Andhra at Cuddapah.[W14]
6 J. H. Kallis . . . . South Africa v Sri Lanka at Cape Town.[W12]
6 F. Mutizwa. . . . . Mashonaland Eagles v Mountaineers at Harare.
6 A. K. Perera . . . . Nondescripts v Sinhalese at Colombo.
6 G. C. Smith . . . . South Africa v Australia at Perth.
6 M. E. Trescothick. . . . . Somerset v Nottinghamshire at Taunton.
6 D. L. Vettori. . . . . Northern Districts v Canterbury at Rangiora.

No Byes Conceded in Total of 500 or More

L. D. Chandimal. . . . . Sri Lanka v South Africa (580-4 dec) at Cape Town.[W12]
S. M. Davies. . . . . Surrey v Somerset (512-9 dec) at The Oval.
A. B. de Villiers . . . . South Africa v Australia (565-5 dec) at Brisbane.
A. B. de Villiers . . . . South Africa v Australia (550) at Adelaide.
B. J. Haddin . . . . New South Wales v Western Australia (560-3 dec) at Perth.
H. A. P. W. Jayawardene . . . . Sri Lanka v Pakistan (551-6 dec) at Colombo.
S. D. Jogiyani. . . . . Saurashtra v Gujarat (600-9 dec) at Surat.[W14]
H. G. Kuhn. . . . . Titans v Dolphins (548-6 dec) at Durban.[W14]
P. A. Patel. . . . . Gujarat v Bengal (526-7 dec) at Kolkata.[W14]
M. Rawat . . . . Railways v Mumbai (570) at Mumbai.[W14]
N. Saini . . . . Haryana v Tamil Nadu (571-6 dec) at Chennai.[W14]
A. V. Ubarhande . . . . Vidarbha v Uttar Pradesh (548-8 dec) at Nagpur.[W14]
C. F. K. van Wyk. . . . . New Zealand v West Indies (522) at North Sound.

Highest Innings Totals

764-6 dec Maharashtra v Uttar Pradesh at Gahunje.[W14]
716-3 Saurashtra v Gujarat at Surat.[W14]
699 Hyderabad v Mumbai at Hyderabad.[W14]
675-6 dec Port Qasim Authority v Habib Bank at Islamabad.[W14]
669-7 Uttar Pradesh v Maharashtra at Gahunje.[W14]
659-4 dec Australia v India at Sydney.[W12]
658-9 dec Auckland v Wellington at Auckland.[W14]
648-9 dec West Indies v Bangladesh at Khulna.
643-6 dec ZTBL v United Bank at Islamabad.[W14]
642-3 dec Somerset v Cardiff MCCU at Taunton.
637-2 dec South Africa v England at The Oval.
632-7 dec Dhaka Metropolis v Chittagong at Bogra.[W14]
630-7 dec Namibia v Kenya at Windhoek.[W14]
621 Rajasthan v Tamil Nadu at Chennai.
619-8 dec Karnataka v Vidarbha at Mysore.[W14]
618-8 dec Khulna v Dhaka Metropolis at Fatullah.

607-7 dec Rest of India v Rajasthan at Bangalore.[W14]
606-5 dec Mumbai v Saurashtra at Rajkot.[W14]
604-7 dec Australia v India at Adelaide.[W12]
601-9 dec Ragama v Tamil Union at Colombo.
600-9 dec Gujarat v Saurashtra at Surat.[W14]

Lowest Innings Totals

18‡ Durham MCCU v Durham at Chester-le-Street.
26 Mountaineers v Southern Rocks at Masvingo.[W14]
34 Western Province v South Western Districts at Oudtshoorn.[W14]
39 Leeward Islands v Combined Campuses & Colleges at Bridgetown.
51 Zimbabwe v New Zealand at Napier.
55 Mountaineers v Mashonaland Eagles at Harare.
55 Haryana v Vidarbha at Rohtak.[W14]
58 Barbados v Guyana at Bridgetown.
58 Southern Rocks v Mountaineers at Masvingo.[W14]
59 Punjab v Mumbai at Mumbai.[W14]
59 Lions v Warriors at Johannesburg.[W14]
60 Worcestershire v Warwickshire at Worcester.
60 Namibia v Easterns at Windhoek.[W14]
62 Dolphins v Titans at Centurion.
63 Otago v Auckland at Auckland.
63 Lancashire v Worcestershire at Manchester.
65 Mid West Rhinos v Matabeleland Tuskers at Kwekwe.[W14]
66 Haryana v Orissa at Rohtak.[W14]
66 Border v South Western Districts at Alice.[W14]
67 Western Australia v Tasmania at Hobart.[W14]
70 Mashonaland Eagles v Matabeleland Tuskers at Bulawayo.
72 England v Pakistan at Abu Dhabi.
73 South Western Districts v Northerns at Pretoria.
73 Windward Islands v Barbados at St George's.
74 United Bank v Sui Northern Gas at Rawalpindi.[W14]
75 Ireland v Kenya at Mombasa.

‡ *One batsman absent hurt.*

Highest Fourth-Innings Totals

402-6 Yorkshire v Gloucestershire at Bristol (set 400).

Match Aggregate of 1,500 Runs

1,523 for 34 West Indies (527-4 dec and 273) v Bangladesh (556 and 167) at Mirpur.

Matches Dominated by Batting (1,200 runs at 100 runs per wicket)

1,433-13 (110.23) Maharashtra (764-6 dec) v Uttar Pradesh (669-7) at Gahunje.[W14]
1,316-12 (109.66) Gujarat (600-9 dec) v Saurashtra (716-3) at Surat.[W14]

Four Individual Hundreds in an Innings

Delhi (555-4 dec) v Tamil Nadu at Delhi.[W14]

Six Individual Fifties in an Innings

Ragama (601-9 dec) v Tamil Union at Colombo.
Tamil Nadu (538-4 dec) v Karnataka at Chennai.[W14]
Gujarat (551-8 dec) v Railways at Bhubaneswar.[W14]
Karnataka (475-9 dec) v Delhi at Bangalore.[W14]
Dolphins (548-6 dec) v Titans at Durban.[W14]

Large Margin of Victory

Punjab (496 and 412) beat Sind (235 and 162) at Lahore by 511 runs.

Tied Match

Border (210 and 210) v Boland (219 and 201) at East London.[W14]

Most Extras in an Innings

	b	*l-b*	*w*	*n-b*	
64	22	10	16	16	Port Qasim Authority (675-6 dec) v Habib Bank at Islamabad.[W14]
61	15	11	3	32	Glamorgan (558-9 dec) v Leicestershire at Cardiff.
60	8	14	4	34	Warwickshire (571) v Surrey at Birmingham.
56	19	11	4	22	Cape Cobras (529-9 dec) v Knights at Cape Town.
56	15	14	13	14	Orissa (441) v Maharashtra at Sambalpur.[W14]
53	6	15	6	26	Trinidad & Tobago (229) v Comb. Campuses & Colls at Bridgetown.
52	7	15	23	7	Central Districts (476) v Otago at Napier.[W14]
51	28	17	5	1	Vidarbha (566-8) v Tamil Nadu at Nagpur.[W14]
50	8	21	2	19	Essex (409) v Leicestershire at Leicester.
50	16	6	4	24	Karnataka (562-6) v Tamil Nadu at Chennai.[W14]
50	13	18	16	3	Goa (512-8 dec) v Kerala at Perintalmanna.[W14]
50	13	23	5	9	Kerala (400) v Tripura at Agartala.[W14]

Career Aggregate Milestones

25,000 runs.	M. J. Di Venuto.
20,000 runs.	M. E. Trescothick.
15,000 runs.	K. P. Pietersen.
10,000 runs.	M. J. Clarke, Faisal Iqbal, Imran Farhat, H. H. Kanitkar, H. J. H. Marshall, A. N. Petersen, L. P. C. Silva, D. I. Stevens.
500 wickets	J. M. Anderson, P. T. Collins, D. A. Cosker, P. J. Franks, D. D. Masters, M. S. Panesar, A. Richardson, Tanvir Ahmed.
500 dismissals	B. J. Haddin, P. Mustard, M. A. Wallace, Zulfiqar Jan.

RECORDS

COMPILED BY PHILIP BAILEY

This section covers

- first-class records to December 31, 2012 (page 1253).
- List A one-day records to December 31, 2012 (page 1287).
- List A Twenty20 records to December 31, 2012 (page 1290).
- Test records to January 14, 2013, the end of the South Africa v New Zealand series (page 1292).
- Test records series by series (page 1331).
- one-day international records to January 6, 2013 (page 1372).
- World Cup records (page 1382).
- Twenty20 international records to December 31, 2012 (page 1383).
- miscellaneous other records to December 31, 2012 (page 1387).
- women's Test, one-day international and Twenty20 international records to December 31, 2012 (page 1391).

The sequence

- Test series records begin with those involving England, arranged in the order their opponents entered Test cricket (Australia, South Africa, West Indies, New Zealand, India, Pakistan, Sri Lanka, Zimbabwe, Bangladesh). Next come all remaining series involving Australia, then South Africa – and so on until Zimbabwe v Bangladesh records appear on page 1369.

Notes

- Unless otherwise stated, all records apply only to first-class cricket. This is considered to have started in 1815, after the Napoleonic War.
- mid-year seasons taking place outside England are given simply as 2002, 2003, etc.
- (E), (A), (SA), (WI), (NZ), (I), (P), (SL), (Z) or (B) indicates the nationality of a player or the country in which a record was made.
- in career records, dates in italic indicate seasons embracing two different years (i.e. non-English seasons). In these cases, only the first year is given, e.g. *2008* for 2008-09.

See also

- up-to-date records on www.wisdenrecords.com.
- Features of 2012 (page 1236).

CONTENTS

FIRST-CLASS RECORDS

BATTING RECORDS

BOWLING RECORDS

ALL-ROUND RECORDS

WICKETKEEPING RECORDS

FIELDING RECORDS

TEAM RECORDS

LIST A ONE-DAY RECORDS

LIST A TWENTY20 RECORDS

TEST RECORDS

BATTING RECORDS

BOWLING RECORDS

ALL-ROUND RECORDS

WICKETKEEPING RECORDS

FIELDING RECORDS

TEAM RECORDS

PLAYERS

UMPIRES

TEST SERIES

ONE-DAY INTERNATIONAL RECORDS

TWENTY20 INTERNATIONAL RECORDS

MISCELLANEOUS RECORDS

WOMEN'S TEST AND OTHER INTERNATIONAL RECORDS

FIRST-CLASS RECORDS

Note: Throughout this section, bold type denotes performances in the calendar year 2012 or, in career figures, players who appeared in first-class cricket in that year.

BATTING RECORDS

HIGHEST INDIVIDUAL INNINGS

In the history of first-class cricket, there have been **187** individual scores of 300 or more. The highest are:

501*	B. C. Lara	Warwickshire v Durham at Birmingham	1994
499	Hanif Mohammad	Karachi v Bahawalpur at Karachi	1958-59
452*	D. G. Bradman	NSW v Queensland at Sydney	1929-30
443*	B. B. Nimbalkar	Maharashtra v Kathiawar at Poona	1948-49
437	W. H. Ponsford	Victoria v Queensland at Melbourne	1927-28
429	W. H. Ponsford	Victoria v Tasmania at Melbourne	1922-23
428	Aftab Baloch	Sind v Baluchistan at Karachi	1973-74
424	A. C. MacLaren	Lancashire v Somerset at Taunton	1895
405*	G. A. Hick	Worcestershire v Somerset at Taunton	1988
400*	B. C. Lara	West Indies v England at St John's	2003-04
394	Naved Latif	Sargodha v Gujranwala at Gujranwala	2000-01
390	S. C. Cook	Lions v Warriors at East London	2009-10
385	B. Sutcliffe	Otago v Canterbury at Christchurch	1952-53
383	C. W. Gregory	NSW v Queensland at Brisbane	1906-07
380	M. L. Hayden	Australia v Zimbabwe at Perth	2003-04
377	S. V. Manjrekar	Bombay v Hyderabad at Bombay	1990-91
375	B. C. Lara	West Indies v England at St John's	1993-94
374	D. P. M. D. Jayawardene	Sri Lanka v South Africa at Colombo	2006
369	D. G. Bradman	South Australia v Tasmania at Adelaide	1935-36
366	N. H. Fairbrother	Lancashire v Surrey at The Oval	1990
366	M. V. Sridhar	Hyderabad v Andhra at Secunderabad	1993-94
365*	C. Hill	South Australia v NSW at Adelaide	1900-01
365*	G. S. Sobers	West Indies v Pakistan at Kingston	1957-58
364	L. Hutton	England v Australia at The Oval	1938
359*	V. M. Merchant	Bombay v Maharashtra at Bombay	1943-44
359	R. B. Simpson	NSW v Queensland at Brisbane	1963-64
357*	R. Abel	Surrey v Somerset at The Oval	1899
357	D. G. Bradman	South Australia v Victoria at Melbourne	1935-36
356	B. A. Richards	South Australia v Western Australia at Perth	1970-71
355*	G. R. Marsh	Western Australia v South Australia at Perth	1989-90
355	B. Sutcliffe	Otago v Auckland at Dunedin	1949-50
353	V. V. S. Laxman	Hyderabad v Karnataka at Bangalore	1999-2000
352	W. H. Ponsford	Victoria v NSW at Melbourne	1926-27
350	Rashid Israr	Habib Bank v National Bank at Lahore	1976-77
345	C. G. Macartney	Australians v Nottinghamshire at Nottingham	1921
344*	G. A. Headley	Jamaica v Lord Tennyson's XI at Kingston	1931-32
344*	M. W. Goodwin	Sussex v Somerset at Taunton	2009
344	W. G. Grace	MCC v Kent at Canterbury	1876
343*	P. A. Perrin	Essex v Derbyshire at Chesterfield	1904
342	J. L. Langer	Somerset v Surrey at Guildford	2006
341	G. H. Hirst	Yorkshire v Leicestershire at Leicester	1905
341	C. M. Spearman	Gloucestershire v Middlesex at Gloucester	2004
340*	D. G. Bradman	NSW v Victoria at Sydney	1928-29
340	S. M. Gavaskar	Bombay v Bengal at Bombay	1981-82
340	S. T. Jayasuriya	Sri Lanka v India at Colombo	1997-98
339	D. S. Lehmann	Yorkshire v Durham at Leeds	2006
338*	R. C. Blunt	Otago v Canterbury at Christchurch	1931-32

338	W. W. Read	Surrey v Oxford University at The Oval	1888
337*	Pervez Akhtar	Railways v Dera Ismail Khan at Lahore	1964-65
337*	D. J. Cullinan	Transvaal v Northern Transvaal at Johannesburg	1993-94
337	Hanif Mohammad	Pakistan v West Indies at Bridgetown	1957-58
336*	W. R. Hammond	England v New Zealand at Auckland	1932-33
336	W. H. Ponsford	Victoria v South Australia at Melbourne	1927-28
335*	M. W. Goodwin	Sussex v Leicestershire at Hove	2003
334*	M. A. Taylor	Australia v Pakistan at Peshawar	1998-99
334	D. G. Bradman	Australia v England at Leeds	1930
333	K. S. Duleepsinhji	Sussex v Northamptonshire at Hove	1930
333	G. A. Gooch	England v India at Lord's	1990
333	C. H. Gayle	West Indies v Sri Lanka at Galle	2010-11
332	W. H. Ashdown	Kent v Essex at Brentwood	1934
331*	J. D. Robertson	Middlesex v Worcestershire at Worcester	1949
331*	M. E. K. Hussey	Northamptonshire v Somerset at Taunton	2003
331	**R. A. Jadeja**	**Saurashtra v Railways at Rajkot**	**2012-13**
329*	M. E. K. Hussey	Northamptonshire v Essex at Northampton	2001
329*	**M. J. Clarke**	**Australia v India at Sydney**	**2011-12**
329	Inzamam-ul-Haq	Pakistan v New Zealand at Lahore	2002
327	**K. M. Jadhav**	**Maharashtra v Uttar Pradesh at Gahunje**	**2012-13**
325*	H. L. Hendry	Victoria v New Zealanders at Melbourne	1925-26
325	A. Sandham	England v West Indies at Kingston	1929-30
325	C. L. Badcock	South Australia v Victoria at Adelaide	1935-36

A fuller list can be found in *Wisdens* up to 2011.

DOUBLE-HUNDRED ON DEBUT

227	T. Marsden	Sheffield & Leicester v Nottingham at Sheffield	1826
207	N. F. Callaway†	New South Wales v Queensland at Sydney	1914-15
240	W. F. E. Marx	Transvaal v Griqualand West at Johannesburg	1920-21
200*	A. Maynard	Trinidad v MCC at Port-of-Spain	1934-35
232*	S. J. E. Loxton	Victoria v Queensland at Melbourne	1946-47
215*	G. H. G. Doggart	Cambridge University v Lancashire at Cambridge	1948
202	J. Hallebone	Victoria v Tasmania at Melbourne	1951-52
230	G. R. Viswanath	Mysore v Andhra at Vijayawada	1967-68
260	A. A. Muzumdar	Bombay v Haryana at Faridabad	1993-94
209*	A. Pandey	Madhya Pradesh v Uttar Pradesh at Bhilai	1995-96
210*	D. J. Sales	Northants v Worcestershire at Kidderminster	1996
200*	M. J. Powell	Glamorgan v Oxford University at Oxford	1997
201*	M. C. Juneja	Gujarat v Tamil Nadu at Ahmedabad	2011-12
213	**Jiwanjot Singh**	**Punjab v Hyderabad at Mohali**	**2012-13**

† *In his only first-class innings. He was killed in action in France in 1917.*

TWO SEPARATE HUNDREDS ON DEBUT

148	and 111	A. R. Morris	New South Wales v Queensland at Sydney	1940-41
152	and 102*	N. J. Contractor	Gujarat v Baroda at Baroda	1952-53
132*	and 110	Aamer Malik	Lahore A v Railways at Lahore	1979-80
130	and 100*	Noor Ali	Afghanistan v Zimbabwe XI at Mutare	2009
158	and 103*	K. H. T. Indika	Police v Seeduwa Raddoluwa at Colombo	2010-11
126	**and 112**	**V. S. Awate**	**Maharashtra v Vidarbha at Nagpur**	**2012-13**

TWO DOUBLE-HUNDREDS IN A MATCH

A. E. Fagg	244	202*	Kent v Essex at Colchester	1938

TRIPLE-HUNDRED AND HUNDRED IN A MATCH

G. A. Gooch	333	123	England v India at Lord's	1990

DOUBLE-HUNDRED AND HUNDRED IN A MATCH

In addition to Fagg and Gooch, there have been **57** further instances of a batsman scoring a double-hundred and a hundred in the same first-class match. The most recent are:

B. C. Lara	221	130	West Indies v Sri Lanka at Colombo	2001-02
Minhazul Abedin	210	110	Chittagong v Dhaka at Mymensingh	2001-02
A. T. Rayudu	210	159*	Hyderabad v Andhra at Secunderabad	2002-03
H. H. Kanitkar	112	207*	Maharashtra v Services at Aurangabad	2003-04
M. J. Horne	118	209*	Auckland v Northern Districts at Auckland	2003-04
S. A. Newman	117	219	Surrey v Glamorgan at The Oval	2005
P. A. Jaques	240	117	Australia A v India A at Cairns	2006
C. J. L. Rogers	128	222*	Northamptonshire v Somerset at Taunton	2006
M. W. Goodwin	119	205*	Sussex v Surrey at Hove	2007
Younis Khan	106	202*	Yorkshire v Hampshire at Southampton	2007
V. Sibanda	209	116*	Zimbabwe XI v Kenya at Kwekwe	2009-10
S. M. Ervine	208	160	Southern Rocks v MW Rhinos at Masvingo	2009-10
C. J. L. Rogers	200	140*	Derbyshire v Surrey at The Oval	2010
M. R. Ramprakash	223	103*	Surrey v Middlesex at The Oval	2010

Notes: Zaheer Abbas achieved the feat four times, for Gloucestershire between 1976 and 1981, and was not out in all eight innings. M. R. Hallam did it twice for Leicestershire, in 1959 and 1961; N. R. Taylor twice for Kent, in 1990 and 1991; G. A. Gooch for England in 1990 (see above) and Essex in 1994; M. W. Goodwin twice for Sussex, in 2001 and 2007; and C. J. L. Rogers for Northamptonshire in 2006 and for Derbyshire in 2010.

TWO SEPARATE HUNDREDS IN A MATCH MOST TIMES

R. T. Ponting	8	J. B. Hobbs	6	M. L. Hayden	5
Zaheer Abbas	8	G. M. Turner	6	G. A. Hick	5
W. R. Hammond	7	C. B. Fry	5		
M. R. Ramprakash	7	G. A. Gooch	5		

Current players only:

C. J. L. Rogers	4	M. E. Trescothick	3
A. N. Petersen	3	M. van Jaarsveld	3

Notes: W. Lambert scored 107 and 157 for Sussex v Epsom at Lord's in 1817, and it was not until W. G. Grace made 130 and 102* for South of the Thames v North of the Thames at Canterbury in 1868 that the feat was repeated.

FIVE HUNDREDS OR MORE IN SUCCESSION

D. G. Bradman (1938-39)	6	B. C. Lara (1993-94/1994)	5
C. B. Fry (1901)	6	P. A. Patel (2007/2007-08)	5
M. J. Procter (1970-71)	6	E. D. Weekes (1955-56)	5
M. E. K. Hussey (2003)	5		

Notes: Bradman also scored four hundreds in succession twice, in 1931-32 and 1948/1948-49; W. R. Hammond did it in 1936-37 and 1945/1946, and H. Sutcliffe in 1931 and 1939.

Current players only:

S. Badrinath (2007/2007-08)	4	S. R. Tendulkar (1994-95)	4
Ijaz Ahmed, jun. (1994-95)	4	Yasir Hameed (2002-03/2003)	4
V. Sibanda (2009-10)	4	Younis Khan (1999-2000)	4

Notes: T. W. Hayward (Surrey v Nottinghamshire and Leicestershire), D. W. Hookes (South Australia v Queensland and New South Wales) and V. Sibanda (Zimbabwe XI v Kenya and Mid West v Southern Rocks) are the only players to score two hundreds in each of two successive matches. Hayward scored his in six days, June 4-9, 1906.

The most fifties in consecutive innings is ten – by E. Tyldesley in 1926, by D. G. Bradman in the 1947-48 and 1948 seasons and by R. S. Kaluwitharana in 1994-95.

MOST HUNDREDS IN A SEASON

D. C. S. Compton (1947)	18	W. R. Hammond (1937)	13
J. B. Hobbs (1925)	16	T. W. Hayward (1906)	13
W. R. Hammond (1938)	15	E. H. Hendren (1923)	13
H. Sutcliffe (1932)	14	E. H. Hendren (1927)	13
G. Boycott (1971)	13	E. H. Hendren (1928)	13
D. G. Bradman (1938)	13	C. P. Mead (1928)	13
C. B. Fry (1901)	13	H. Sutcliffe (1928)	13
W. R. Hammond (1933)	13	H. Sutcliffe (1931)	13

Since 1969 (excluding G. Boycott – above)

G. A. Gooch (1990)	12	M. R. Ramprakash (1995)	10
S. J. Cook (1991)	11	M. R. Ramprakash (2007)	10
Zaheer Abbas (1976)	11	G. M. Turner (1970)	10
G. A. Hick (1988)	10	Zaheer Abbas (1981)	10
H. Morris (1990)	10		

Note: The most achieved outside England is nine by V. Sibanda in Zimbabwe (2009-10), followed by eight by D. G. Bradman in Australia (1947-48), D. C. S. Compton (1948-49), R. N. Harvey and A. R. Morris (both 1949-50) all three in South Africa, M. D. Crowe in New Zealand (1986-87), Asif Mujtaba in Pakistan (1995-96), V. V. S. Laxman in India (1999-2000) and M. G. Bevan in Australia (2004-05).

MOST DOUBLE-HUNDREDS IN A SEASON

D. G. Bradman (1930)	6	W. R. Hammond (1933)	4
K. S. Ranjitsinhji (1900)	5	W. R. Hammond (1934)	4
E. D. Weekes (1950)	5	E. H. Hendren (1929-30)	4
Arun Lal (1986-87)	4	V. M. Merchant (1944-45)	4
C. B. Fry (1901)	4	G. M. Turner (1971-72)	4

Current players only:

A. Chopra (2007-08)	3	D. S. Jadhav (2003-04)	3
R. Dravid (2003-04)	3	P. A. Jaques (2006)	3
B. J. Hodge (2004)	3	M. R. Ramprakash (1995)	3
M. E. K. Hussey (2001)	3		

Note: R. Dravid scored his three double-hundreds in three different countries; P. A. Jaques scored his in two.

MOST DOUBLE-HUNDREDS IN A CAREER

D. G. Bradman	37	C. P. Mead	13	**R. Dravid**	**10**
W. R. Hammond	36	W. H. Ponsford	13	M. W. Gatting	10
E. H. Hendren	22	J. T. Tyldesley	13	S. M. Gavaskar	10
M. R. Ramprakash	**17**	P. Holmes	12	J. Hardstaff, jun	10
H. Sutcliffe	17	Javed Miandad	12	V. S. Hazare	10
C. B. Fry	16	J. L. Langer	12	B. J. Hodge	10
G. A. Hick	16	R. B. Simpson	12	I. V. A. Richards	10
J. B. Hobbs	16	J. W. Hearne	11	A. Shrewsbury	10
C. G. Greenidge	14	L. Hutton	11	R. T. Simpson	10
K. S. Ranjitsinhji	14	D. S. Lehmann	11	G. M. Turner	10
G. A. Gooch	13	V. M. Merchant	11	Zaheer Abbas	10
W. G. Grace	13	A. Sandham	11		
B. C. Lara	13	G. Boycott	10		

MOST HUNDREDS IN A CAREER

(100 or more)

		Total	Total Inns	100th 100 Season	Inns	400+	300+	200+
1	J. B. Hobbs	197	1,315	1923	821	0	1	16
2	E. H. Hendren	170	1,300	1928-29	740	0	1	22
3	W. R. Hammond	167	1,005	1935	680	0	4	36
4	C. P. Mead	153	1,340	1927	892	0	0	13
5	G. Boycott	151	1,014	1977	645	0	0	10
6	H. Sutcliffe	149	1,088	1932	700	0	1	17
7	F. E. Woolley	145	1,532	1929	1,031	0	1	9
8	G. A. Hick	136	871	1998	574	1	3	16
9	L. Hutton	129	814	1951	619	0	1	11
10	G. A. Gooch	128	990	1992-93	820	0	1	13
11	W. G. Grace	126	1,493	1895	1,113	0	3	13
12	D. C. S. Compton	123	839	1952	552	0	1	9
13	T. W. Graveney	122	1,223	1964	940	0	0	7
14	D. G. Bradman	117	338	1947-48	295	1	6	37
15	I. V. A. Richards	114	796	1988-89	658	0	1	10
	M. R. Ramprakash	**114**	**764**	**2008**	**676**	**0**	**1**	**17**
17	Zaheer Abbas	108	768	1982-83	658	0	0	10
18	A. Sandham	107	1,000	1935	871	0	1	11
	M. C. Cowdrey	107	1,130	1973	1,035	0	1	3
20	T. W. Hayward	104	1,138	1913	1,076	0	1	8
21	G. M. Turner	103	792	1982	779	0	1	10
	J. H. Edrich	103	979	1977	945	0	1	4
23	L. E. G. Ames	102	951	1950	916	0	0	9
	E. Tyldesley	102	961	1934	919	0	0	7
	D. L. Amiss	102	1,139	1986	1,081	0	0	3

Notes: In the above table, 200+, 300+ and 400+ include all scores above those figures.

E. H. Hendren, D. G. Bradman and I. V. A. Richards scored their 100th hundreds in Australia; G. A. Gooch scored his in India. His record includes his century in South Africa in 1981-82, which is no longer accepted by the ICC. Zaheer Abbas scored his 100th in Pakistan. Zaheer Abbas and G. Boycott did so in Test matches.

Other Current Players

In addition to M. R. Ramprakash, the following who played in 2012 have scored 30 or more hundreds.

S. R. Tendulkar 79
R. T. Ponting 78
R. Dravid 68
M. W. Goodwin 67
S. Chanderpaul 64
M. E. K. Hussey 61
J. H. Kallis 61
M. J. Di Venuto 60
C. J. L. Rogers 56
V. V. S. Laxman 55
S. M. Katich 54
M. van Jaarsveld 52
M. E. Trescothick 51
D. P. M. D. Jayawardene 48
K. P. Pietersen 47
R. W. T. Key 46
N. D. McKenzie 46
J. A. Rudolph 46
A. J. Strauss 46
Wasim Jaffer 45
O. A. Shah 44
A. N. Cook 42
D. J. Hussey 41
I. R. Bell 40
P. A. Jaques 40
Younis Khan 40
K. C. Sangakkara 39
H. M. Amla 38
D. M. Benkenstein 38
M. J. Clarke 38
T. T. Samaraweera 38
V. Sehwag 38
T. M. Dilshan 36
Hasan Raza 36
M. S. Sinclair 36
A. McGrath 35
Misbah-ul-Haq 35
G. C. Smith 35
H. H. Dippenaar 34
M. J. North 34
S. C. Ganguly 33
H. H. Kanitkar 33
A. G. Prince 33
R. R. Sarwan 33
G. Gambhir 32
S. Sriram 32
C. H. Gayle 31
V. S. Solanki 31
I. J. L. Trott 31
A. A. Muzumdar 30

MOST RUNS IN A SEASON

	Season	*I*	*NO*	*R*	*HS*	*100*	*Avge*
D. C. S. Compton	1947	50	8	3,816	246	18	90.85
W. J. Edrich	1947	52	8	3,539	267*	12	80.43
T. W. Hayward	1906	61	8	3,518	219	13	66.37
L. Hutton	1949	56	6	3,429	269*	12	68.58
F. E. Woolley	1928	59	4	3,352	198	12	60.94
H. Sutcliffe	1932	52	7	3,336	313	14	74.13
W. R. Hammond	1933	54	5	3,323	264	13	67.81
E. H. Hendren	1928	54	7	3,311	209*	13	70.44
R. Abel	1901	68	8	3,309	247	7	55.15

Notes: 3,000 in a season has been surpassed on 19 other occasions (a full list can be found in *Wisden* 1999 and earlier editions). W. R. Hammond, E. H. Hendren and H. Sutcliffe are the only players to achieve the feat three times. K. S. Ranjitsinhji was the first batsman to reach 3,000 in a season, with 3,159 in 1899. M. J. K. Smith (3,245 in 1959) and W. E. Alley (3,019 in 1961) are the only players except those listed above to have reached 3,000 since World War II.

W. G. Grace scored 2,739 runs in 1871 – the first batsman to reach 2,000 runs in a season. He made ten hundreds including two double-hundreds, with an average of 78.25 in all first-class matches.

The highest aggregate in a season since the reduction of County Championship matches in 1969 is 2,755 by S. J. Cook (42 innings) in 1991, and the last batsman to achieve 2,000 was M. R. Ramprakash (2,026 in 2007).

2,000 RUNS IN A SEASON MOST TIMES

J. B. Hobbs	17	F. E. Woolley	13	C. P. Mead	11
E. H. Hendren	15	W. R. Hammond	12	T. W. Hayward	10
H. Sutcliffe	15	J. G. Langridge	11		

Note: Since the reduction of County Championship matches in 1969, G. A. Gooch is the only batsman to have reached 2,000 runs in a season five times.

1,000 RUNS IN A SEASON MOST TIMES

Includes overseas tours and seasons

W. G. Grace	28	A. Jones	23	G. Gunn	20
F. E. Woolley	28	T. W. Graveney	22	T. W. Hayward	20
M. C. Cowdrey	27	W. R. Hammond	22	G. A. Hick	20
C. P. Mead	27	D. Denton	21	James Langridge	20
G. Boycott	26	J. H. Edrich	21	J. M. Parks	20
J. B. Hobbs	26	G. A. Gooch	21	**M. R. Ramprakash**	**20**
E. H. Hendren	25	W. Rhodes	21	A. Sandham	20
D. L. Amiss	24	D. B. Close	20	M. J. K. Smith	20
W. G. Quaife	24	K. W. R. Fletcher	20	C. Washbrook	20
H. Sutcliffe	24	M. W. Gatting	20		

Notes: F. E. Woolley reached 1,000 runs in 28 consecutive seasons (1907–1938), C. P. Mead in 27 (1906–1936).

Outside England, 1,000 runs in a season has been reached most times by D. G. Bradman (in 12 seasons in Australia).

Three batsmen have scored 1,000 runs in a season in each of four different countries: G. S. Sobers in West Indies, England, India and Australia; M. C. Cowdrey and G. Boycott in England, South Africa, West Indies and Australia.

HIGHEST AGGREGATES OUTSIDE ENGLAND

In Australia	*Season*	*I*	*NO*	*R*	*HS*	*100*	*Avge*
D. G. Bradman	1928-29	24	6	1,690	340*	7	93.88
In South Africa							
J. R. Reid	1961-62	30	2	1,915	203	7	68.39
In West Indies							
E. H. Hendren	1929-30	18	5	1,765	254*	6	135.76
In New Zealand							
M. D. Crowe	1986-87	21	3	1,676	175*	8	93.11
In India							
C. G. Borde	1964-65	28	3	1,604	168	6	64.16
In Pakistan							
Saadat Ali	1983-84	27	1	1,649	208	4	63.42
In Sri Lanka							
R. P. Arnold	1995-96	24	3	1,475	217*	5	70.23
In Zimbabwe							
V. Sibanda	2009-10	26	4	1,612	215	9	73.27
In Bangladesh							
Minhazul Abedin	2001-02	15	1	1,012	210	3	72.28

Note: In more than one country, the following aggregates of over 2,000 runs have been recorded:

	Season	I	NO	R	HS	100	Avge
M. Amarnath (P/I/WI)	1982-83	34	6	2,234	207	9	79.78
J. R. Reid (SA/A/NZ)	1961-62	40	2	2,188	203	7	57.57
S. M. Gavaskar (I/P)	1978-79	30	6	2,121	205	10	88.37
R. B. Simpson (I/P/A/WI)	1964-65	34	4	2,063	201	8	68.76
M. H. Richardson (Z/SA/NZ)	2000-01	34	3	2,030	306	4	65.48

LEADING BATSMEN IN AN ENGLISH SEASON

(Qualification: 8 completed innings)

Season	*Leading scorer*	*Runs*	*Avge*	*Top of averages*	*Runs*	*Avge*
1946	D. C. S. Compton	2,403	61.61	W. R. Hammond	1,783	84.90
1947	D. C. S. Compton	3,816	90.85	D. C. S. Compton	3,816	90.85
1948	L. Hutton	2,654	64.73	D. G. Bradman	2,428	89.92
1949	L. Hutton	3,429	68.58	J. Hardstaff	2,251	72.61
1950	R. T. Simpson	2,576	62.82	E. D. Weekes	2,310	79.65
1951	J. D. Robertson	2,917	56.09	P. B. H. May	2,339	68.79
1952	L. Hutton	2,567	61.11	D. S. Sheppard	2,262	64.62
1953	W. J. Edrich	2,557	47.35	R. N. Harvey	2,040	65.80
1954	D. Kenyon	2,636	51.68	D. C. S. Compton	1,524	58.61
1955	D. J. Insole	2,427	42.57	D. J. McGlew	1,871	58.46
1956	T. W. Graveney	2,397	49.93	K. D. Mackay	1,103	52.52

Season	*Leading scorer*	*Runs*	*Avge*	*Top of averages*	*Runs*	*Avge*
1957	T. W. Graveney	2,361	49.18	P. B. H. May	2,347	61.76
1958	P. B. H. May	2,231	63.74	P. B. H. May	2,231	63.74
1959	M. J. K. Smith	3,245	57.94	V. L. Manjrekar	755	68.63
1960	M. J. K. Smith	2,551	45.55	R. Subba Row	1,503	55.66
1961	W. E. Alley	3,019	56.96	W. M. Lawry	2,019	61.18
1962	J. H. Edrich	2,482	51.70	R. T. Simpson	867	54.18
1963	J. B. Bolus	2,190	41.32	G. S. Sobers	1,333	47.60
1964	T. W. Graveney	2,385	54.20	K. F. Barrington	1,872	62.40
1965	J. H. Edrich	2,319	62.67	M. C. Cowdrey	2,093	63.42
1966	A. R. Lewis	2,198	41.47	G. S. Sobers	1,349	61.31
1967	C. A. Milton	2,089	46.42	K. F. Barrington	2,059	68.63
1968	B. A. Richards	2,395	47.90	G. Boycott	1,487	64.65
1969	J. H. Edrich	2,238	69.93	J. H. Edrich	2,238	69.93
1970	G. M. Turner	2,379	61.00	G. S. Sobers	1,742	75.73
1971	G. Boycott	2,503	100.12	G. Boycott	2,503	100.12
1972	Majid Khan	2,074	61.00	G. Boycott	1,230	72.35
1973	G. M. Turner	2,416	67.11	G. M. Turner	2,416	67.11
1974	R. T. Virgin	1,936	56.94	C. H. Lloyd	1,458	63.39
1975	G. Boycott	1,915	73.65	R. B. Kanhai	1,073	82.53
1976	Zaheer Abbas	2,554	75.11	Zaheer Abbas	2,554	75.11
1977	I. V. A. Richards	2,161	65.48	G. Boycott	1,701	68.04
1978	D. L. Amiss	2,030	53.42	C. E. B. Rice	1,871	66.82
1979	K. C. Wessels	1,800	52.94	G. Boycott	1,538	102.53
1980	P. N. Kirsten	1,895	63.16	A. J. Lamb	1,797	66.55
1981	Zaheer Abbas	2,306	88.69	Zaheer Abbas	2,306	88.69
1982	A. I. Kallicharran	2,120	66.25	G. M. Turner	1,171	90.07
1983	K. S. McEwan	2,176	64.00	I. V. A. Richards	1,204	75.25
1984	G. A. Gooch	2,559	67.34	C. G. Greenidge	1,069	82.23
1985	G. A. Gooch	2,208	71.22	I. V. A. Richards	1,836	76.50
1986	C. G. Greenidge	2,035	67.83	C. G. Greenidge	2,035	67.83
1987	G. A. Hick	1,879	52.19	M. D. Crowe	1,627	67.79
1988	G. A. Hick	2,713	77.51	R. A. Harper	622	77.75
1989	S. J. Cook	2,241	60.56	D. M. Jones	1,510	88.82
1990	G. A. Gooch	2,746	101.70	G. A. Gooch	2,746	101.70
1991	S. J. Cook	2,755	81.02	C. L. Hooper	1,501	93.81
1992	P. D. Bowler M. A. Roseberry	2,044 2,044	65.93 56.77	Salim Malik	1,184	78.93
1993	G. A. Gooch	2,023	63.21	D. C. Boon	1,437	75.63
1994	B. C. Lara	2,066	89.82	J. D. Carr	1,543	90.76
1995	M. R. Ramprakash	2,258	77.86	M. R. Ramprakash	2,258	77.86
1996	G. A. Gooch	1,944	67.03	S. C. Ganguly	762	95.25
1997	S. P. James	1,775	68.26	G. A. Hick	1,524	69.27
1998	J. P. Crawley	1,851	74.04	J. P. Crawley	1,851	74.04
1999	S. G. Law	1,833	73.32	S. G. Law	1,833	73.32
2000	D. S. Lehmann	1,477	67.13	M. G. Bevan	1,124	74.93
2001	M. E. K. Hussey	2,055	79.03	D. R. Martyn	942	104.66
2002	I. J. Ward	1,759	62.82	R. Dravid	773	96.62
2003	S. G. Law	1,820	91.00	S. G. Law	1,820	91.00
2004	R. W. T. Key	1,896	79.00	R. W. T. Key	1,896	79.00
2005	O. A. Shah	1,728	66.46	M. E. K. Hussey	1,074	76.71
2006	M. R. Ramprakash	2,278	103.54	M. R. Ramprakash	2,278	103.54
2007	M. R. Ramprakash	2,026	101.30	M. R. Ramprakash	2,026	101.30
2008	S. C. Moore	1,451	55.80	T. Frost	1,003	83.58
2009	M. E. Trescothick	1,817	75.70	M. R. Ramprakash	1,350	90.00
2010	M. R. Ramprakash	1,595	61.34	J. C. Hildreth	1,440	65.45
2011	M. E. Trescothick	1,673	79.66	I. R. Bell	1,091	90.91
2012	**N. R. D. Compton**	**1,494**	**99.60**	**N. R. D. Compton**	**1,494**	**99.60**

Notes: The highest average recorded in an English season was 115.66 (2,429 runs, 26 innings) by D. G. Bradman in 1938.

In 1953, W. A. Johnston averaged 102.00 from 17 innings, 16 not out.

MOST RUNS

Dates in italics denote the first half of an overseas season; i.e. *1945* denotes the 1945-46 season.

		Career	*R*	*I*	*NO*	*HS*	*100*	*Avge*
1	J. B. Hobbs.	1905–1934	61,237	1,315	106	316*	197	50.65
2	F. E. Woolley	1906–1938	58,969	1,532	85	305*	145	40.75
3	E. H. Hendren.	1907–1938	57,611	1,300	166	301*	170	50.80
4	C. P. Mead	1905–1936	55,061	1,340	185	280*	153	47.67
5	W. G. Grace	1865–1908	54,896	1,493	105	344	126	39.55
6	W. R. Hammond	1920–1951	50,551	1,005	104	336*	167	56.10
7	H. Sutcliffe.	1919–1945	50,138	1,088	123	313	149	51.95
8	G. Boycott	1962–1986	48,426	1,014	162	261*	151	56.83
9	T. W. Graveney	1948–*1971*	47,793	1,223	159	258	122	44.91
10	G. A. Gooch	1973–2000	44,846	990	75	333	128	49.01
11	T. W. Hayward.	1893–1914	43,551	1,138	96	315*	104	41.79
12	D. L. Amiss	1960–1987	43,423	1,139	126	262*	102	42.86
13	M. C. Cowdrey.	1950–1976	42,719	1,130	134	307	107	42.89
14	A. Sandham	1911–*1937*	41,284	1,000	79	325	107	44.82
15	G. A. Hick	*1983*–2008	41,112	871	84	405*	136	52.23
16	L. Hutton	1934–1960	40,140	814	91	364	129	55.51
17	M. J. K. Smith	1951–1975	39,832	1,091	139	204	69	41.84
18	W. Rhodes	1898–1930	39,802	1,528	237	267*	58	30.83
19	J. H. Edrich.	1956–1978	39,790	979	104	310*	103	45.47
20	R. E. S. Wyatt.	1923–1957	39,405	1,141	157	232	85	40.04
21	D. C. S. Compton. . . .	1936–1964	38,942	839	88	300	123	51.85
22	E. Tyldesley	1909–1936	38,874	961	106	256*	102	45.46
23	J. T. Tyldesley	1895–1923	37,897	994	62	295*	86	40.66
24	K. W. R. Fletcher	1962–1988	37,665	1,167	170	228*	63	37.77
25	C. G. Greenidge	1970–1992	37,354	889	75	273*	92	45.88
26	J. W. Hearne.	1909–1936	37,252	1,025	116	285*	96	40.98
27	L. E. G. Ames.	1926–1951	37,248	951	95	295	102	43.51
28	D. Kenyon	1946–1967	37,002	1,159	59	259	74	33.63
29	W. J. Edrich	1934–1958	36,965	964	92	267*	86	42.39
30	J. M. Parks	1949–1976	36,673	1,227	172	205*	51	34.76
31	M. W. Gatting	1975–1998	36,549	861	123	258	94	49.52
32	D. Denton.	1894–1920	36,479	1,163	70	221	69	33.37
33	G. H. Hirst	1891–1929	36,323	1,215	151	341	60	34.13
34	I. V. A. Richards	*1971*–1993	36,212	796	63	322	114	49.40
35	A. Jones	1957–1983	36,049	1,168	72	204*	56	32.89
36	W. G. Quaife	1894–1928	36,012	1,203	185	255*	72	35.37
37	R. E. Marshall	*1945*–1972	35,725	1,053	59	228*	68	35.94
38	**M. R. Ramprakash. .**	**1987–2012**	**35,659**	**764**	**93**	**301***	**114**	**53.14**
39	G. Gunn	1902–1932	35,208	1,061	82	220	62	35.96
40	D. B. Close.	1949–1986	34,994	1,225	173	198	52	33.26
41	Zaheer Abbas	*1965–1986*	34,843	768	92	274	108	51.54
42	J. G. Langridge.	1928–1955	34,380	984	66	250*	76	37.45
43	G. M. Turner	*1964–1982*	34,346	792	101	311*	103	49.70
44	C. Washbrook.	1933–1964	34,101	906	107	251*	76	42.67
45	M. Leyland.	1920–1948	33,660	932	101	263	80	40.50
46	H. T. W. Hardinge . . .	1902–1933	33,519	1,021	103	263*	75	36.51
47	R. Abel.	1881–1904	33,124	1,007	73	357*	74	35.46
48	A. I. Kallicharran	*1966*–1990	32,650	834	86	243*	87	43.64
49	A. J. Lamb	*1972*–1995	32,502	772	108	294	89	48.94
50	C. A. Milton	1948–1974	32,150	1,078	125	170	56	33.73
51	J. D. Robertson.	1937–1959	31,914	897	46	331*	67	37.50
52	J. Hardstaff, jun	1930–1955	31,847	812	94	266	83	44.35
53	James Langridge.	1924–1953	31,716	1,058	157	167	42	35.20
54	K. F. Barrington	1953–1968	31,714	831	136	256	76	45.63
55	C. H. Lloyd.	*1963*–1986	31,232	730	96	242*	79	49.26
56	Mushtaq Mohammad .	*1956*–1985	31,091	843	104	303*	72	42.07

		Career	*R*	*I*	*NO*	*HS*	*100*	*Avge*
57	C. B. Fry	1892–*1921*	30,886	658	43	258*	94	50.22
58	D. Brookes	1934–1959	30,874	925	70	257	71	36.10
59	P. Holmes	1913–1935	30,573	810	84	315*	67	42.11
60	R. T. Simpson	*1944*–1963	30,546	852	55	259	64	38.32
61	L. G. Berry	1924–1951	30,225	1,056	57	232	45	30.25
61	K. G. Suttle	1949–1971	30,225	1,064	92	204*	49	31.09

Note: Some works of reference provide career figures which differ from those in this list, owing to the exclusion or inclusion of matches recognised or not recognised as first-class by *Wisden.* A fuller list can be found in *Wisdens* up to 2011.

Other Current Players with 20,000 Runs

	Career	*R*	*I*	*NO*	*HS*	*100*	*Avge*
M. J. Di Venuto	*1991*–2012	25,200	591	42	254*	60	45.90
S. R. Tendulkar	*1988–2012*	24,701	474	48	248*	79	57.98
R. Dravid	*1990–2011*	23,794	497	67	270	68	55.33
R. T. Ponting	*1992–2012*	23,101	478	59	257	78	55.13
M. E. K. Hussey	*1994–2012*	22,396	474	47	331*	61	52.44
M. W. Goodwin	*1994*–2012	22,113	513	42	344*	67	46.94
S. Chanderpaul	*1991–2012*	21,686	474	89	303*	64	56.32
M. E. Trescothick	1993–2012	20,221	502	29	284	51	42.75

HIGHEST CAREER AVERAGE

(Qualification: 10,000 runs)

Avge		*Career*	*I*	*NO*	*R*	*HS*	*100*
95.14	D. G. Bradman	*1927–1948*	338	43	28,067	452*	117
71.22	V. M. Merchant	*1929–1951*	229	43	13,248	359*	44
67.46	Ajay Sharma	*1984–2000*	166	16	10,120	259*	38
65.18	W. H. Ponsford	*1920–1934*	235	23	13,819	437	47
64.99	W. M. Woodfull	*1921–1934*	245	39	13,388	284	49
58.24	A. L. Hassett	*1932–1953*	322	32	16,890	232	59
58.19	V. S. Hazare	*1934–1966*	365	45	18,621	316*	60
57.98	**S. R. Tendulkar**	***1988–2012***	**474**	**48**	**24,701**	**248***	**79**
57.83	D. S. Lehmann	1987–2007	479	33	25,795	339	82
57.32	M. G. Bevan	*1989–2006*	400	66	19,147	216	68
57.22	A. F. Kippax	*1918–1935*	256	33	12,762	315*	43
56.83	G. Boycott	1962–1986	1,014	162	48,426	261*	151
56.55	C. L. Walcott	*1941–1963*	238	29	11,820	314*	40
56.37	K. S. Ranjitsinhji	1893–1920	500	62	24,692	285*	72
56.32	**S. Chanderpaul**	***1991–2012***	**474**	**89**	**21,686**	**303***	**64**
56.22	R. B. Simpson	*1952–1977*	436	62	21,029	359	60
56.10	W. R. Hammond	1920–1951	1,005	104	50,551	336*	167
56.02	M. D. Crowe	*1979–1995*	412	62	19,608	299	71
55.51	L. Hutton	1934–1960	814	91	40,140	364	129
55.34	E. D. Weekes	*1944*–1964	241	24	12,010	304*	36
55.33	**R. Dravid**	***1990–2011***	**497**	**67**	**23,794**	**270**	**68**
55.13	**R. T. Ponting**	***1992–2012***	**478**	**59**	**23,101**	**257**	**78**
55.11	S. V. Manjrekar	*1984–1997*	217	31	10,252	377	31
55.07	**J. H. Kallis**	***1993–2012***	**409**	**57**	**19,386**	**224**	**61**
54.87	G. S. Sobers	*1952*–1974	609	93	28,315	365*	86
54.74	B. A. Richards	*1964–1982*	576	58	28,358	356	80
54.67	R. G. Pollock	*1960–1986*	437	54	20,940	274	64
54.24	F. M. M. Worrell	*1941*–1964	326	49	15,025	308*	39
54.05	A. Flower	*1986*–2006	372	69	16,379	271*	49

Note: G. A. Headley (*1927*–1954) scored 9,921 runs, average 69.86.

FASTEST FIFTIES

Minutes			
11	C. I. J. Smith (66)	Middlesex v Gloucestershire at Bristol	1938
13	Khalid Mahmood (56)	Gujranwala v Sargodha at Gujranwala	2000-01
14	S. J. Pegler (50)	South Africans v Tasmania at Launceston	1910-11
14	F. T. Mann (53)	Middlesex v Nottinghamshire at Lord's	1921
14	H. B. Cameron (56)	Transvaal v Orange Free State at Johannesburg	1934-35
14	C. I. J. Smith (52)	Middlesex v Kent at Maidstone	1935

Note: The number of balls taken to achieve fifties was rarely recorded until recently. C. I. J. Smith's two fifties (above) may have taken only 12 balls each. Khalid Mahmood reached his fifty in 15 balls.

Fifties scored in contrived circumstances and with the bowlers' compliance are excluded from the above list, including the fastest of them all, in 8 minutes (13 balls) by C. C. Inman, Leicestershire v Nottinghamshire at Nottingham, 1965, and 10 minutes by G. Chapple, Lancashire v Glamorgan at Manchester, 1993.

FASTEST HUNDREDS

Minutes			
35	P. G. H. Fender (113*)	Surrey v Northamptonshire at Northampton	1920
40	G. L. Jessop (101)	Gloucestershire v Yorkshire at Harrogate	1897
40	Ahsan-ul-Haq (100*)	Muslims v Sikhs at Lahore	1923-24
42	G. L. Jessop (191)	Gentlemen of South v Players of South at Hastings	1907
43	A. H. Hornby (106)	Lancashire v Somerset at Manchester	1905
43	D. W. Hookes (107)	South Australia v Victoria at Adelaide	1982-83
44	R. N. S. Hobbs (100)	Essex v Australians at Chelmsford	1975

Notes: The fastest recorded authentic hundred in terms of balls received was scored off 34 balls by D. W. Hookes (above). Research of the scorebook has shown that P. G. H. Fender scored his hundred from between 40 and 46 balls. He contributed 113 to an unfinished sixth-wicket partnership of 171 in 42 minutes with H. A. Peach.

E. B. Alletson (Nottinghamshire) scored 189 out of 227 runs in 90 minutes against Sussex at Hove in 1911. It has been estimated that his last 139 runs took 37 minutes.

Hundreds scored in contrived circumstances and with the bowlers' compliance are excluded, including the fastest of them all, in 21 minutes (27 balls) by G. Chapple, Lancashire v Glamorgan at Manchester, 1993, 24 minutes (27 balls) by M. L. Pettini, Essex v Leicestershire at Leicester, 2006, and 26 minutes (36 balls) by T. M. Moody, Warwickshire v Glamorgan at Swansea, 1990.

FASTEST DOUBLE-HUNDREDS

Minutes			
113	R. J. Shastri (200*)	Bombay v Baroda at Bombay	1984-85
120	G. L. Jessop (286)	Gloucestershire v Sussex at Hove	1903
120	C. H. Lloyd (201*)	West Indians v Glamorgan at Swansea	1976
130	G. L. Jessop (234)	Gloucestershire v Somerset at Bristol	1905
131	V. T. Trumper (293)	Australians v Canterbury at Christchurch	1913-14

FASTEST TRIPLE-HUNDREDS

Minutes			
181	D. C. S. Compton (300)	MCC v North Eastern Transvaal at Benoni	1948-49
205	F. E. Woolley (305*)	MCC v Tasmania at Hobart	1911-12
205	C. G. Macartney (345)	Australians v Nottinghamshire at Nottingham	1921
213	D. G. Bradman (369)	South Australia v Tasmania at Adelaide	1935-36

MOST RUNS IN A DAY BY ONE BATSMAN

390*	B. C. Lara	Warwickshire v Durham at Birmingham	1994
345	C. G. Macartney	Australians v Nottinghamshire at Nottingham	1921
334	W. H. Ponsford	Victoria v New South Wales at Melbourne	1926-27
333	K. S. Duleepsinhji	Sussex v Northamptonshire at Hove	1930
331*	J. D. Robertson	Middlesex v Worcestershire at Worcester	1949
325*	B. A. Richards	South Australia v Western Australia at Perth	1970-71

Note: These scores do not necessarily represent the complete innings. See pages 1253–54.

There have been another **14** instances of a batsman scoring 300 runs in a day, most recently 319 by R. R. Rossouw, Eagles v Titans at Centurion in 2009-10 (see *Wisden* 2003, pages 278–279, for full list).

LONGEST INNINGS

Hrs	*Mins*			
16	55	R. Nayyar (271)	Himachal Pradesh v Jammu and Kashmir at Chamba	1999-2000
16	10	Hanif Mohammad (337)	Pakistan v West Indies at Bridgetown	1957-58
		Hanif believes he batted 16 hours 39 minutes.		
15	**7**	**V. A. Saxena (257)**	**Rajasthan v Tamil Nadu at Chennai**	**2011-12**
14	38	G. Kirsten (275)	South Africa v England at Durban	1999-2000
13	58	S. C. Cook (390)	Lions v Warriors at East London	2009-10
13	41	S. S. Shukla (178*)	Uttar Pradesh v Tamil Nadu at Nagpur	2008-09
13	32	A. Chopra (301*)	Rajasthan v Maharashtra at Nasik	2010-11
13	19	S. T. Jayasuriya (340)	Sri Lanka v India at Colombo	1997-98
13	17	L. Hutton (364)	England v Australia at The Oval	1938
13	16	S. H. Kotak (168*)	Saurashtra v Mumbai at Mumbai	2007-08
13	**10**	**H. M. Amla (311*)**	**South Africa v England at The Oval**	**2012**
13	5	Bhupinder Singh, jun. (297)	Punjab v Delhi at Delhi	1994-95
13	0	Naved Latif (394)	Sargodha v Gujranwala	2000-01

1,000 RUNS IN MAY

	Runs	*Avge*
W. G. Grace, May 9 to May 30, 1895 (22 days)	1,016	112.88
Grace was 46 years old.		
W. R. Hammond, May 7 to May 31, 1927 (25 days)	1,042	74.42
Hammond scored his 1,000th run on May 28, thus equalling Grace's record of 22 days.		
C. Hallows, May 5 to May 31, 1928 (27 days)	1,000	125.00

1,000 RUNS IN APRIL AND MAY

	Runs	*Avge*
T. W. Hayward, April 16 to May 31, 1900	1,074	97.63
D. G. Bradman, April 30 to May 31, 1930	1,001	143.00
On April 30 Bradman was 75 not out.		
D. G. Bradman, April 30 to May 31, 1938	1,056	150.85
Bradman scored 258 on April 30, and his 1,000th run on May 27.		
W. J. Edrich, April 30 to May 31, 1938	1,010	84.16
Edrich was 21 not out on April 30. All his runs were scored at Lord's.		
G. M. Turner, April 24 to May 31, 1973	1,018	78.30
G. A. Hick, April 17 to May 29, 1988	1,019	101.90
Hick scored a record 410 runs in April, and his 1,000th run on May 28.		

MOST RUNS SCORED OFF AN OVER

(All instances refer to six-ball overs)

36	G. S. Sobers	off M. A. Nash, Nottinghamshire v Glamorgan at Swansea (six sixes)	1968
36	R. J. Shastri	off Tilak Raj, Bombay v Baroda at Bombay (six sixes)	1984-85
34	E. B. Alletson	off E. H. Killick, Nottinghamshire v Sussex at Hove (46604446; including two no-balls)	1911
34	F. C. Hayes	off M. A. Nash, Lancashire v Glamorgan at Swansea (646666)	1977
34†	A. Flintoff	off A. J. Tudor, Lancashire v Surrey at Manchester (64444660; including two no-balls)	1998
34	C. M. Spearman	off S. J. P. Moreton, Gloucestershire v Oxford UCCE at Oxford (666646) *Moreton's first over in first-class cricket.*	2005
32	I. T. Botham	off I. R. Snook, England XI v Central Districts at Palmerston North (466466)	1983-84
32	P. W. G. Parker	off A. I. Kallicharran, Sussex v Warwickshire at Birmingham (466664)	1982
32	I. R. Redpath	off N. Rosendorff, Australians v Orange Free State at Bloemfontein (666644)	1969-70
32	C. C. Smart	off G. Hill, Glamorgan v Hampshire at Cardiff (664664)	1935
32	Khalid Mahmood	off Naved Latif, Gujranwala v Sargodha at Gujranwala (666662)	2000-01

† Altogether 38 runs were scored off this over, the two no-balls counting for two extra runs each under ECB regulations.

Notes: The following instances have been excluded because of the bowlers' compliance: 34 – M. P. Maynard off S. A. Marsh, Glamorgan v Kent at Swansea, 1992; 34 – G. Chapple off P. A. Cottey, Lancashire v Glamorgan at Manchester, 1993; 34 – F. B. Touzel off F. J. J. Viljoen, Western Province B v Griqualand West at Kimberley, 1993-94. Chapple scored a further 32 off Cottey's next over.

There were 35 runs off an over received by A. T. Reinholds off H. T. Davis, Auckland v Wellington at Auckland 1995-96, but this included 16 extras and only 19 off the bat.

In a match against KwaZulu-Natal at Stellenbosch in 2006-07, W. E. September (Boland) conceded 34 in an over: 27 to M. Bekker, six to K. Smit, plus one no-ball.

In a match against Canterbury at Christchurch in 1989-90, R. H. Vance (Wellington) deliberately conceded 77 runs in an over of full tosses which contained 17 no-balls and, owing to the umpire's understandable miscalculation, only five legitimate deliveries.

The greatest number of runs scored off an eight-ball over is 34 (40446664) by R. M. Edwards off M. C. Carew, Governor-General's XI v West Indians at Auckland, 1968-69.

MOST SIXES IN AN INNINGS

16	A. Symonds (254*)	Gloucestershire v Glamorgan at Abergavenny	1995
16	G. R. Napier (196)	Essex v Surrey at Croydon	2011
16	J. D. Ryder (175)	New Zealanders v Australia A at Brisbane	2011-12
15	J. R. Reid (296)	Wellington v Northern Districts at Wellington	1962-63
15	**Ziaur Rahman (152*)**	**South Zone v Central Zone at Mirpur**	**2012-13**
14	Shakti Singh (128)	Himachal Pradesh v Haryana at Dharmsala	1990-91
14	D. J. Hussey (275)	Nottinghamshire v Essex at Nottingham	2007
14	**C. H. Gayle (165)**	**Jamaica v Windward Islands at Kingston**	**2011-12**
14	**C. Munro (269*)**	**Auckland v Wellington at Auckland**	**2012-13**
13	Majid Khan (147*)	Pakistanis v Glamorgan at Swansea	1967
13	C. G. Greenidge (273*)	D. H. Robins' XI v Pakistanis at Eastbourne	1974
13	C. G. Greenidge (259)	Hampshire v Sussex at Southampton	1975
13	G. W. Humpage (254)	Warwickshire v Lancashire at Southport	1982
13	R. J. Shastri (200*)	Bombay v Baroda at Bombay	1984-85
12	Gulfraz Khan (207)	Railways v Universities at Lahore	1976-77
12	I. T. Botham (138*)	Somerset v Warwickshire at Birmingham	1985
12	R. A. Harper (234)	Northamptonshire v Gloucestershire at Northampton	1986
12	D. M. Jones (248)	Australians v Warwickshire at Birmingham	1989

12	U. N. K. Fernando (160)	Sinhalese v Sebastianites at Colombo	1990-91
12	D. N. Patel (204)	Auckland v Northern Districts at Auckland	1991-92
12	W. V. Raman (206)	Tamil Nadu v Kerala at Madras	1991-92
12	G. D. Lloyd (241)	Lancashire v Essex at Chelmsford	1996
12	Wasim Akram (257*)	Pakistan v Zimbabwe at Sheikhupura	1996-97
12	S. I. de Saram (188)	Ragama v Badureliya at Colombo	2007-08
12	K. J. O'Brien (171*)	Ireland v Kenya at Nairobi	2008
12	H. G. J. M. Kulatunga (234)	Colts v Ragama at Colombo	2008-09
12	**Tamim Iqbal (183)**	**Chittagong v Sylhet at Savar**	**2012-13**

Note: F. B. Touzel (128*) hit 13 sixes for Western Province B v Griqualand West in contrived circumstances at Kimberley in 1993-94.

MOST SIXES IN A MATCH

20	A. Symonds (254*, 76)	Gloucestershire v Glamorgan at Abergavenny	1995
17	W. J. Stewart (155, 125)	Warwickshire v Lancashire at Blackpool	1959

MOST SIXES IN A SEASON

80	I. T. Botham	1985	49	I. V. A. Richards	1985
66	A. W. Wellard	1935	48	A. W. Carr	1925
57	A. W. Wellard	1936	48	J. H. Edrich	1965
57	A. W. Wellard	1938	48	A. Symonds	1995
51	A. W. Wellard	1933			

MOST BOUNDARIES IN AN INNINGS

	4s/6s			
72	62/10	B. C. Lara (501*)	Warwickshire v Durham at Birmingham	1994
68	68/–	P. A. Perrin (343*)	Essex v Derbyshire at Chesterfield	1904
65	64/1	A. C. MacLaren (424)	Lancashire v Somerset at Taunton	1895
64	64/–	Hanif Mohammad (499)	Karachi v Bahawalpur at Karachi	1958-59
57	52/5	J. H. Edrich (310*)	England v New Zealand at Leeds	1965
57	52/5	Naved Latif (394)	Sargodha v Gujranwala at Gujranwala	2000-01
56	**54/2**	**K. M. Jadhav (327)**	**Maharashtra v U. Pradesh at Gahunje**	**2012-13**
55	55/–	C. W. Gregory (383)	NSW v Queensland at Brisbane	1906-07
55	53/2	G. R. Marsh (355*)	W. Australia v S. Australia at Perth	1989-90
55	51/3†	S. V. Manjrekar (377)	Bombay v Hyderabad at Bombay	1990-91
55	52/3	D. S. Lehmann (339)	Yorkshire v Durham at Leeds	2006
55	54/1	D. K. H. Mitchell (298)	Worcestershire v Somerset at Taunton	2009
55	54/1	S. C. Cook (390)	Lions v Warriors at East London	2009-10
55	47/8	R. R. Rossouw (319)	Eagles v Titans at Centurion	2009-10
54	53/1	G. H. Hirst (341)	Yorkshire v Leicestershire at Leicester	1905
53	53/–	A. W. Nourse (304*)	Natal v Transvaal at Johannesburg	1919-20
53	45/8	K. R. Rutherford (317)	NZ v D. B. Close's XI at Scarborough	1986
53	51/2	V. V. S. Laxman (353)	Hyderabad v Karnataka at Bangalore	1999-2000
53	52/1	M. W. Goodwin (335*)	Sussex v Leicestershire at Hove	2003
52	47/5	N. H. Fairbrother (366)	Lancashire v Surrey at The Oval	1990
52	50/2	C. J. L. Rogers (319)	Northamptonshire v Glos at Northampton	2006
51	51/–	W. G. Grace (344)	MCC v Kent at Canterbury	1876
51	47/4	C. G. Macartney (345)	Australians v Notts at Nottingham	1921
51	50/1	B. B. Nimbalkar (443*)	Maharashtra v Kathiawar at Poona	1948-49
51	49/2	G. A. Hick (315*)	Worcestershire v Durham at Worcester	2002
51	50/1	Salman Butt (290)	Punjab v Federal Areas at Lahore	2007-08
51	44/7	Sunny Singh (312)	Haryana v Madhya Pradesh at Indore	2009-10
50	47/–‡	A. Ducat (306*)	Surrey v Oxford U. at The Oval	1919
50	46/4	D. G. Bradman (369)	S. Australia v Tasmania at Adelaide	1935-36
50	35/15	J. R. Reid (296)	Wellington v N. Districts at Wellington	1962-63
50	42/8	I. V. A. Richards (322)	Somerset v Warwickshire at Taunton	1985
50	50/–	Shoaib Khan (300*)	Peshawar v Quetta at Peshawar	2003-04

† *Plus one five.* ‡ *Plus three fives.*

PARTNERSHIPS OVER 500

624	for 3rd	K. C. Sangakkara (287)/D. P. M. D. Jayawardene (374), Sri Lanka v South Africa at Colombo	2006
580	for 2nd	Rafatullah Mohmand (302*)/Aamer Sajjad (289), WAPDA v Sui Southern Gas at Sheikhupura	2009-10
577	for 4th	V. S. Hazare (288)/Gul Mahomed (319), Baroda v Holkar at Baroda	1946-47
576	for 2nd	S. T. Jayasuriya (340)/R. S. Mahanama (225), Sri Lanka v India at Colombo	1997-98
574*	for 4th	F. M. M. Worrell (255*)/C. L. Walcott (314*), Barbados v Trinidad at Port-of-Spain	1945-46
561	for 1st	Waheed Mirza (324)/Mansoor Akhtar (224*), Karachi Whites v Quetta at Karachi	1976-77
555	for 1st	P. Holmes (224*)/H. Sutcliffe (313), Yorkshire v Essex at Leyton	1932
554	for 1st	J. T. Brown (300)/J. Tunnicliffe (243), Yorks v Derbys at Chesterfield	1898
539	**for 3rd**	**S. D. Jogiyani (282)/R. A. Jadeja (303*), Saurashtra v Gujarat at Surat**	**2012-13**
523	for 3rd	M. A. Carberry (300*)/N. D. McKenzie (237), Hants v Yorks at Southampton	2011
520*	for 5th	C. A. Pujara (302*)/R. A. Jadeja (232*), Saurashtra v Orissa at Rajkot	2008-09
502*	for 4th	F. M. M. Worrell (308*)/J. D. C. Goddard (218*), Barbados v Trinidad at Bridgetown	1943-44

HIGHEST PARTNERSHIPS FOR EACH WICKET

First Wicket

561	Waheed Mirza/Mansoor Akhtar, Karachi Whites v Quetta at Karachi	1976-77
555	P. Holmes/H. Sutcliffe, Yorkshire v Essex at Leyton	1932
554	J. T. Brown/J. Tunnicliffe, Yorkshire v Derbyshire at Chesterfield	1898
490	E. H. Bowley/J. G. Langridge, Sussex v Middlesex at Hove	1933
464	R. Sehgal/R. Lamba, Delhi v Himachal Pradesh at Delhi	1994-95
462	M. Vijay/A. Mukund, Tamil Nadu v Maharashtra at Nasik	2008-09
459	Wasim Jaffer/S. K. Kulkarni, Mumbai v Saurashtra at Rajkot	1996-97
456	E. R. Mayne/W. H. Ponsford, Victoria v Queensland at Melbourne	1923-24
451*	S. Desai/R. M. H. Binny, Karnataka v Kerala at Chikmagalur	1977-78
431	M. R. J. Veletta/G. R. Marsh, Western Australia v South Australia at Perth	1989-90

Second Wicket

580	Rafatullah Mohmand/Aamer Sajjad, WAPDA v Sui S. Gas at Sheikhupura	2009-10
576	S. T. Jayasuriya/R. S. Mahanama, Sri Lanka v India at Colombo	1997-98
480	D. Elgar/R. R. Rossouw, Eagles v Titans at Centurion	2009-10
475	Zahir Alam/L. S. Rajput, Assam v Tripura at Gauhati	1991-92
465*	J. A. Jameson/R. B. Kanhai, Warwicks v Gloucestershire at Birmingham	1974
455	K. V. Bhandarkar/B. B. Nimbalkar, Maharashtra v Kathiawar at Poona	1948-49
451	W. H. Ponsford/D. G. Bradman, Australia v England at The Oval	1934
450	**N. R. D. Compton/J. C. Hildreth, Somerset v Cardiff MCCU at Taunton**	**2012**
446	C. C. Hunte/G. S. Sobers, West Indies v Pakistan at Kingston	1957-58
441	C. C. Bradfield/J. D. C. Bryant, E. Province v North West at Potchefstroom	2002-03

Third Wicket

624	K. C. Sangakkara/D. P. M. D. Jayawardene, Sri Lanka v SA at Colombo	2006
539	**S. D. Jogiyani/R. A. Jadeja, Saurashtra v Gujarat at Surat**	**2012-13**
523	M. A. Carberry/N. D. McKenzie, Hampshire v Yorks at Southampton	2011
467	A. H. Jones/M. D. Crowe, New Zealand v Sri Lanka at Wellington	1990-91
459	C. J. L. Rogers/M. J. North, Western Australia v Victoria at Perth	2006-07
456	Khalid Irtiza/Aslam Ali, United Bank v Multan at Karachi	1975-76

451	Mudassar Nazar/Javed Miandad, Pakistan v India at Hyderabad	1982-83
445	P. E. Whitelaw/W. N. Carson, Auckland v Otago at Dunedin	1936-37
438*	G. A. Hick/T. M. Moody, Worcestershire v Hampshire at Southampton	1997
436*	D. L. Maddy/B. J. Hodge, Leics v Loughborough UCCE at Leicester	2003
436	S. S. Das/S. S. Raul, Orissa v Bengal at Baripada	2001-02

Fourth Wicket

577	V. S. Hazare/Gul Mahomed, Baroda v Holkar at Baroda	1946-47
574*	C. L. Walcott/F. M. M. Worrell, Barbados v Trinidad at Port-of-Spain	1945-46
502*	F. M. M. Worrell/J. D. C. Goddard, Barbados v Trinidad at Bridgetown	1943-44
470	A. I. Kallicharran/G. W. Humpage, Warwicks v Lancs at Southport	1982
462*	D. W. Hookes/W. B. Phillips, South Australia v Tasmania at Adelaide	1986-87
448	R. Abel/T. W. Hayward, Surrey v Yorkshire at The Oval	1899
437	D. P. M. D. Jayawardene/T. T. Samaraweera, SL v Pakistan at Karachi	2008-09
436	S. Abbas Ali/P. K. Dwevedi, Madhya Pradesh v Railways at Indore	1997-98
425*	A. Dale/I. V. A. Richards, Glamorgan v Middlesex at Cardiff	1993
424	I. S. Lee/S. O. Quin, Victoria v Tasmania at Melbourne	1933-34

Fifth Wicket

520*	C. A. Pujara/R. A. Jadeja, Saurashtra v Orissa at Rajkot	2008-09
479	Misbah-ul-Haq/Usman Arshad, Sui N. Gas v Lahore Shalimar at Lahore	2009-10
464*	M. E. Waugh/S. R. Waugh, New South Wales v Western Australia at Perth	1990-91
420	Mohammad Ashraful/Marshall Ayub, Dhaka v Chittagong at Chittagong	2006-07
410*	A. Chopra/S. Badrinath, India A v South Africa A at Delhi	2007-08
405	S. G. Barnes/D. G. Bradman, Australia v England at Sydney	1946-47
401	M. B. Loye/D. Ripley, Northamptonshire v Glamorgan at Northampton	1998
397	W. Bardsley/C. Kelleway, New South Wales v South Australia at Sydney	1920-21
393	E. G. Arnold/W. B. Burns, Worcestershire v Warwickshire at Birmingham.	1909
391	A. Malhotra/S. Dogra, Delhi v Services at Delhi	1995-96

Sixth Wicket

487*	G. A. Headley/C. C. Passailaigue, Jamaica v Lord Tennyson's XI at Kingston	1931-32
428	W. W. Armstrong/M. A. Noble, Australians v Sussex at Hove	1902
417	W. P. Saha/L. R. Shukla, Bengal v Assam at Kolkata	2010-11
411	R. M. Poore/E. G. Wynyard, Hampshire v Somerset at Taunton	1899
379	S. L. Stewart/C. F. K. van Wyk, Canterbury v C. Dists at New Plymouth	2009-10
377	**C. Munro/C. Cachopa, Auckland v Wellington at Auckland**	**2012-13**
376	R. Subba Row/A. Lightfoot, Northamptonshire v Surrey at The Oval	1958
372*	K. P. Pietersen/J. E. Morris, Nottinghamshire v Derbyshire at Derby	2001
371	V. M. Merchant/R. S. Modi, Bombay v Maharashtra at Bombay	1943-44
365	B. C. Lara/R. D. Jacobs, West Indians v Australia A at Hobart	2000-01
365	S. C. Cook/T. L. Tsolekile, Lions v Warriors at East London	2009-10

Seventh Wicket

460	Bhupinder Singh, jun./P. Dharmani, Punjab v Delhi at Delhi	1994-95
347	D. St E. Atkinson/C. C. Depeiza, West Indies v Australia at Bridgetown	1954-55
344	K. S. Ranjitsinhji/W. Newham, Sussex v Essex at Leyton	1902
340	K. J. Key/H. Philipson, Oxford University v Middlesex at Chiswick Park	1887
336	F. C. W. Newman/C. R. N. Maxwell, Sir Julien Cahn's XI v Leics at Nottingham	1935
335	C. W. Andrews/E. C. Bensted, Queensland v New South Wales at Sydney	1934-35
325	G. Brown/C. H. Abercrombie, Hampshire v Essex at Leyton	1913
323	E. H. Hendren/L. F. Townsend, MCC v Barbados at Bridgetown	1929-30
315	D. M. Benkenstein/O. D. Gibson, Durham v Yorkshire at Leeds	2006
308	Waqar Hassan/Imtiaz Ahmed, Pakistan v New Zealand at Lahore	1955-56

Eighth Wicket

433	A. Sims and V. T. Trumper, A. Sims' Aust. XI v Canterbury at Christchurch	1913-14
392	**A. Mishra/J. Yadav, Haryana v Karnataka at Hubli**	**2012-13**
332	I. J. L. Trott/S. C. J. Broad, England v Pakistan at Lord's	2010
313	Wasim Akram/Saqlain Mushtaq, Pakistan v Zimbabwe at Sheikhupura	1996-97
292	R. Peel/Lord Hawke, Yorkshire v Warwickshire at Birmingham	1896
291	R. S. C. Martin-Jenkins/M. J. G. Davis, Sussex v Somerset at Taunton	2002
270	V. T. Trumper/E. P. Barbour, New South Wales v Victoria at Sydney	1912-13
268	S. Sriram/M. R. Srinivas, Tamil Nadu v Punjab at Mohali	2002-03
263	D. R. Wilcox/R. M. Taylor, Essex v Warwickshire at Southend	1946
257	N. Pothas/A. J. Bichel, Hampshire v Gloucestershire at Cheltenham	2005
257	**D. J. Vilas/R. J. Peterson, Cape Cobras v Knights at Kimberley**	**2011-12**

Ninth Wicket

283	A. Warren/J. Chapman, Derbyshire v Warwickshire at Blackwell	1910
268	J. B. Commins/N. Boje, South Africa A v Mashonaland at Harare	1994-95
261	**W. L. Madsen/T. Poynton, Derbyshire v Northants at Northampton**	**2012**
251	J. W. H. T. Douglas/S. N. Hare, Essex v Derbyshire at Leyton	1921
249*†	A. S. Srivastava/K. Seth, Madhya Pradesh v Vidarbha at Indore	2000-01
246	T. T. Bresnan/J. N. Gillespie, Yorkshire v Surrey at The Oval	2007
245	V. S. Hazare/N. D. Nagarwalla, Maharashtra v Baroda at Poona	1939-40
244*	Arshad Ayub/M. V. Ramanamurthy, Hyderabad v Bihar at Hyderabad	1986-87
239	H. B. Cave/I. B. Leggat, Central Districts v Otago at Dunedin	1952-53
236	Mohammad Sharif/Mosharraf Hossain, Dhaka v Rajshahi at Fatullah	2010-11

† 276 unbeaten runs were scored for this wicket in two separate partnerships; after Srivastava retired hurt, Seth and N. D. Hirwani added 27.

Tenth Wicket

307	A. F. Kippax/J. E. H. Hooker, New South Wales v Victoria at Melbourne	1928-29
249	C. T. Sarwate/S. N. Banerjee, Indians v Surrey at The Oval	1946
239	Aqeel Arshad/Ali Raza, Lahore Whites v Hyderabad at Lahore	2004-05
235	F. E. Woolley/A. Fielder, Kent v Worcestershire at Stourbridge	1909
233	Ajay Sharma/Maninder Singh, Delhi v Bombay at Bombay	1991-92
230	R. W. Nicholls/W. Roche, Middlesex v Kent at Lord's	1899
228	R. Illingworth/K. Higgs, Leicestershire v Northamptonshire at Leicester	1977
219	D. J. Thornely/S. C. G. MacGill, NSW v Western Australia at Sydney	2004-05
218	F. H. Vigar/T. P. B. Smith, Essex v Derbyshire at Chesterfield	1947
214	N. V. Knight/A. Richardson, Warwickshire v Hampshire at Birmingham	2002

Note: There have been only 11 last-wicket stands of 200 or more, the 11th being 211 by M. Ellis and T. J. Hastings for Victoria v South Australia at Melbourne in 1902-03.

UNUSUAL DISMISSALS

Handled the Ball

There have been **57** instances in first-class cricket. The most recent are:

G. A. Gooch	England v Australia at Manchester	1993
A. C. Waller	Mashonaland CD v Mashonaland Under-24 at Harare	1994-95
K. M. Krikken	Derbyshire v Indians at Derby	1996
A. Badenhorst	Eastern Province B v North West at Fochville	1998-99
S. R. Waugh	Australia v India at Chennai	2000-01
M. P. Vaughan	England v India at Bangalore	2001-02
Tushar Imran	Bangladesh A v Jamaica at Spanish Town	2001-02
Al Sahariar	Dhaka v Chittagong at Dhaka	2003-04
Junaid Zia	Rawalpindi v Lahore at Lahore	2003-04
D. J. Watson	Dolphins v Eagles at Bloemfontein	2004-05
M. Zondeki	Cape Cobras v Eagles at Bloemfontein	2006-07
L. N. Mosena	Free State v Limpopo at Bloemfontein	2006-07
W. S. A. Williams	**Canterbury v Otago at Dunedin**	**2012-13**

Obstructing the Field

There have been **23** instances in first-class cricket. T. Straw of Worcestershire was given out for obstruction v Warwickshire in both 1899 and 1901. The most recent are:

Arshad Ali	Sukkur v Quetta at Quetta	1983-84
H. R. Wasu	Vidarbha v Rajasthan at Akola	1984-85
Khalid Javed	Railways v Lahore at Lahore	1985-86
C. Binduhewa	Singha SC v Sinhalese SC at Colombo	1990-91
S. J. Kalyani	Bengal v Orissa at Calcutta	1994-95
R. C. Rupasinghe	Rio v Kurunegala Youth at Colombo	2001-02
K. N. S. Fernando	Lankan v Army at Welisara	2006-07
H. R. Jadhav	Baroda v Uttar Pradesh at Baroda	2006-07
Riaz Kail	Abbottabad v Quetta at Abbottabad	2009-10
M. R. Ramprakash	Surrey v Gloucestershire at Cheltenham	2011
Z. E. Surkari	Canada v Afghanistan at King City	2011

Hit the Ball Twice

There have been **21** instances in first-class cricket. The last occurrence in England involved J. H. King of Leicestershire v Surrey at The Oval in 1906. The most recent are:

Aziz Malik	Lahore Division v Faisalabad at Sialkot	1984-85
Javed Mohammad	Multan v Karachi Whites at Sahiwal	1986-87
Shahid Pervez	Jammu and Kashmir v Punjab at Srinagar	1986-87
Ali Naqvi	PNSC v National Bank at Faisalabad	1998-99
A. George	Tamil Nadu v Maharashtra at Pune	1998-99
Maqsood Raza	Lahore Division v PNSC at Sheikhupura	1999-2000
D. Mahajan	Jammu and Kashmir v Bihar at Jammu	2005-06

Timed Out

There have been **four** instances in first-class cricket:

A. Jordaan	Eastern Province v Transvaal at Port Elizabeth (SACB match)	1987-88
H. Yadav	Tripura v Orissa at Cuttack	1997-98
V. C. Drakes	Border v Free State at East London	2002-03
A. J. Harris	Nottinghamshire v Durham UCCE at Nottingham	2003

BOWLING RECORDS

TEN WICKETS IN AN INNINGS

In the history of first-class cricket, there have been **80** instances of a bowler taking all ten wickets in an innings:

	O	*M*	*R*		
E. Hinkly (Kent)				v England at Lord's	1848
*J. Wisden (North)				v South at Lord's	1850
V. E. Walker (England)	43	17	74	v Surrey at The Oval	1859
V. E. Walker (Middlesex)	44.2	5	104	v Lancashire at Manchester	1865
G. Wootton (All England)	31.3	9	54	v Yorkshire at Sheffield	1865
W. Hickton (Lancashire)	36.2	19	46	v Hampshire at Manchester	1870
S. E. Butler (Oxford)	24.1	11	38	v Cambridge at Lord's	1871
James Lillywhite (South)	60.2	22	129	v North at Canterbury	1872
A. Shaw (MCC)	36.2	8	73	v North at Lord's	1874
E. Barratt (Players)	29	11	43	v Australians at The Oval	1878
G. Giffen (Australian XI)	26	10	66	v The Rest at Sydney	1883-84
W. G. Grace (MCC)	36.2	17	49	v Oxford University at Oxford	1886
G. Burton (Middlesex)	52.3	25	59	v Surrey at The Oval	1888
†A. E. Moss (Canterbury)	21.3	10	28	v Wellington at Christchurch	1889-90
S. M. J. Woods (Cambridge U.)	31	6	69	v Thornton's XI at Cambridge	1890
T. Richardson (Surrey)	15.3	3	45	v Essex at The Oval	1894

	O	M	R		
H. Pickett (Essex)	27	11	32	v Leicestershire at Leyton	1895
E. J. Tyler (Somerset)	34.3	15	49	v Surrey at Taunton	1895
W. P. Howell (Australians)	23.2	14	28	v Surrey at The Oval	1899
C. H. G. Bland (Sussex)	25.2	10	48	v Kent at Tonbridge	1899
J. Briggs (Lancashire)	28.5	7	55	v Worcestershire at Manchester	1900
A. E. Trott (Middlesex)	14.2	5	42	v Somerset at Taunton	1900
A. Fielder (Players)	24.5	1	90	v Gentlemen at Lord's	1906
E. G. Dennett (Gloucestershire)	19.4	7	40	v Essex at Bristol	1906
A. E. E. Vogler (E. Province)	12	2	26	v Griqualand W. at Johannesburg	1906-07
C. Blythe (Kent)	16	7	30	v Northants at Northampton	1907
J. B. King (Philadelphia)	18.1	7	53	v Ireland at Haverford‡	1909
A. Drake (Yorkshire)	8.5	0	35	v Somerset at Weston-s-Mare	1914
W. Bestwick (Derbyshire)	19	2	40	v Glamorgan at Cardiff	1921
A. A. Mailey (Australians)	28.4	5	66	v Gloucestershire at Cheltenham	1921
C. W. L. Parker (Glos.)	40.3	13	79	v Somerset at Bristol	1921
T. Rushby (Surrey)	17.5	4	43	v Somerset at Taunton	1921
J. C. White (Somerset)	42.2	11	76	v Worcestershire at Worcester	1921
G. C. Collins (Kent)	19.3	4	65	v Nottinghamshire at Dover	1922
H. Howell (Warwickshire)	25.1	5	51	v Yorkshire at Birmingham	1923
A. S. Kennedy (Players)	22.4	10	37	v Gentlemen at The Oval	1927
G. O. B. Allen (Middlesex)	25.3	10	40	v Lancashire at Lord's	1929
A. P. Freeman (Kent)	42	9	131	v Lancashire at Maidstone	1929
G. Geary (Leicestershire)	16.2	8	18	v Glamorgan at Pontypridd	1929
C. V. Grimmett (Australians)	22.3	8	37	v Yorkshire at Sheffield	1930
A. P. Freeman (Kent)	30.4	8	53	v Essex at Southend	1930
H. Verity (Yorkshire)	18.4	6	36	v Warwickshire at Leeds	1931
A. P. Freeman (Kent)	36.1	9	79	v Lancashire at Manchester	1931
V. W. C. Jupp (Northants)	39	6	127	v Kent at Tunbridge Wells	1932
H. Verity (Yorkshire)	19.4	16	10	v Nottinghamshire at Leeds	1932
T. W. Wall (South Australia)	12.4	2	36	v New South Wales at Sydney	1932-33
T. B. Mitchell (Derbyshire)	19.1	4	64	v Leicestershire at Leicester	1935
J. Mercer (Glamorgan)	26	10	51	v Worcestershire at Worcester	1936
T. W. J. Goddard (Glos.)	28.4	4	113	v Worcestershire at Cheltenham	1937
T. F. Smailes (Yorkshire)	17.1	5	47	v Derbyshire at Sheffield	1939
E. A. Watts (Surrey)	24.1	8	67	v Warwickshire at Birmingham	1939
*W. E. Hollies (Warwickshire)	20.4	4	49	v Notts at Birmingham	1946
J. M. Sims (East)	18.4	2	90	v West at Kingston	1948
T. E. Bailey (Essex)	39.4	9	90	v Lancashire at Clacton	1949
J. K. Graveney (Glos.)	18.4	2	66	v Derbyshire at Chesterfield	1949
R. Berry (Lancashire)	36.2	9	102	v Worcestershire at Blackpool	1953
S. P. Gupte (President's XI)	24.2	7	78	v Combined XI at Bombay	1954-55
J. C. Laker (Surrey)	46	18	88	v Australians at The Oval	1956
J. C. Laker (England)	51.2	23	53	v Australia at Manchester	1956
G. A. R. Lock (Surrey)	29.1	18	54	v Kent at Blackheath	1956
K. Smales (Nottinghamshire)	41.3	20	66	v Gloucestershire at Stroud	1956
P. M. Chatterjee (Bengal)	19	11	20	v Assam at Jorhat	1956-57
J. D. Bannister (Warwickshire)	23.3	11	41	v Comb. Services at Birmingham§	1959
A. J. G. Pearson (Cambridge U.)	30.3	8	78	v Leics at Loughborough	1961
N. I. Thomson (Sussex)	34.2	19	49	v Warwickshire at Worthing	1964
P. J. Allan (Queensland)	15.6	3	61	v Victoria at Melbourne	1965-66
I. J. Brayshaw (W. Australia)	17.6	4	44	v Victoria at Perth	1967-68
Shahid Mahmood (Karachi Whites)	25	5	58	v Khairpur at Karachi	1969-70
E. E. Hemmings (International XI)	49.3	14	175	v West Indies XI at Kingston	1982-83
P. Sunderam (Rajasthan)	22	5	78	v Vidarbha at Jodhpur	1985-86
S. T. Jefferies (W. Province)	22.5	7	59	v Orange Free State at Cape Town	1987-88
Imran Adil (Bahawalpur)	22.5	3	92	v Faisalabad at Faisalabad	1989-90
G. P. Wickremasinghe (Sinhalese)	19.2	5	41	v Kalutara at Colombo	1991-92
R. L. Johnson (Middlesex)	18.5	6	45	v Derbyshire at Derby	1994
Naeem Akhtar (Rawalpindi B)	21.3	10	28	v Peshawar at Peshawar	1995-96
A. Kumble (India)	26.3	9	74	v Pakistan at Delhi	1998-99

	O	*M*	*R*		
D. S. Mohanty (East Zone)	19	5	46	v South Zone at Agartala	2000-01
O. D. Gibson (Durham)	17.3	1	47	v Hampshire at Chester-le-Street	2007
M. W. Olivier (Warriors)	26.3	4	65	v Eagles at Bloemfontein	2007-08
Zulfiqar Babar (Multan)	39.4	3	143	v Islamabad at Multan	2009-10

Note: In addition, the following instances were achieved in 12-a-side matches:

E. M. Grace (MCC)	32.2	7	69	v Gents of Kent at Canterbury	1862
W. G. Grace (MCC)	46.1	15	92	v Kent at Canterbury	1873
†D. C. S. Hinds (A. B. St Hill's XII)	19.1	6	36	v Trinidad at Port-of-Spain	1900-01

* *J. Wisden and W. E. Hollies achieved the feat without the direct assistance of a fielder. Wisden's ten were all bowled; Hollies bowled seven and had three lbw.*

† *On debut in first-class cricket.* ‡ *Pennsylvania.* § *Mitchells & Butlers Ground.*

OUTSTANDING BOWLING ANALYSES

	O	*M*	*R*	*W*		
H. Verity (Yorkshire)	19.4	16	10	10	v Nottinghamshire at Leeds	1932
G. Elliott (Victoria)	19	17	2	9	v Tasmania at Launceston	1857-58
Ahad Khan (Railways)	6.3	4	7	9	v Dera Ismail Khan at Lahore	1964-65
J. C. Laker (England)	14	12	2	8	v The Rest at Bradford	1950
D. Shackleton (Hampshire)	11.1	7	4	8	v Somerset at Weston-s-Mare	1955
E. Peate (Yorkshire)	16	11	5	8	v Surrey at Holbeck	1883
K. M. Dabengwa (Westerns)	4.4	3	1	7	v Northerns at Harare	2006-07
F. R. Spofforth (Australians)	8.3	6	3	7	v England XI at Birmingham	1884
W. A. Henderson (NE Transvaal)	9.3	7	4	7	v OFS at Bloemfontein	1937-38
Rajinder Goel (Haryana)	7	4	4	7	v Jammu and Kashmir at Chandigarh	1977-78
N. W. Bracken (NSW)	7	5	4	7	v South Australia at Sydney	2004-05
V. I. Smith (South Africans)	4.5	3	1	6	v Derbyshire at Derby	1947
S. Cosstick (Victoria)	21.1	20	1	6	v Tasmania at Melbourne	1868-69
Israr Ali (Bahawalpur)	11	10	1	6	v Dacca U. at Bahawalpur	1957-58
A. D. Pougher (MCC)	3	3	0	5	v Australians at Lord's	1896
G. R. Cox (Sussex)	6	6	0	5	v Somerset at Weston-s-Mare	1921
R. K. Tyldesley (Lancashire)	5	5	0	5	v Leicestershire at Manchester	1924
P. T. Mills (Gloucestershire)	6.4	6	0	5	v Somerset at Bristol	1928

MOST WICKETS IN A MATCH

19-90	J. C. Laker	England v Australia at Manchester	1956
17-48†	C. Blythe	Kent v Northamptonshire at Northampton	1907
17-50	C. T. B. Turner	Australians v England XI at Hastings	1888
17-54	W. P. Howell	Australians v Western Province at Cape Town	1902-03
17-56	C. W. L. Parker	Gloucestershire v Essex at Gloucester	1925
17-67	A. P. Freeman	Kent v Sussex at Hove	1922
17-89	W. G. Grace	Gloucestershire v Nottinghamshire at Cheltenham	1877
17-89	F. C. L. Matthews	Nottinghamshire v Northants at Nottingham	1923
17-91	H. Dean	Lancashire v Yorkshire at Liverpool	1913
17-91†	H. Verity	Yorkshire v Essex at Leyton	1933
17-92	A. P. Freeman	Kent v Warwickshire at Folkestone	1932
17-103	W. Mycroft	Derbyshire v Hampshire at Southampton	1876
17-106	G. R. Cox	Sussex v Warwickshire at Horsham	1926
17-106†	T. W. J. Goddard	Gloucestershire v Kent at Bristol	1939
17-119	W. Mead	Essex v Hampshire at Southampton	1895
17-137	W. Brearley	Lancashire v Somerset at Manchester	1905

17-137	J. M. Davison	Canada v USA at Fort Lauderdale	2004
17-159	S. F. Barnes	England v South Africa at Johannesburg	1913-14
17-201	G. Giffen	South Australia v Victoria at Adelaide	1885-86
17-212	J. C. Clay	Glamorgan v Worcestershire at Swansea	1937

† *Achieved in a single day.*

Note: H. Arkwright took 18-96 for MCC v Gentlemen of Kent in a 12-a-side match at Canterbury in 1861.

There have been **58** instances of a bowler taking 16 wickets in an 11-a-side match, the most recent being 16-100 by J. U. Chaturanga for Singha v Antonians at Gampaha, 2010-11.

FOUR WICKETS WITH CONSECUTIVE BALLS

There have been **39** instances in first-class cricket. R. J. Crisp achieved the feat twice, for Western Province in 1931-32 and 1933-34. A. E. Trott took four in four balls and another hat-trick in the same innings for Middlesex v Somerset in 1907, his benefit match. Occurrences since the Second World War:

F. Ridgway	Kent v Derbyshire at Folkestone	1951
A. K. Walker‡	Nottinghamshire v Leicestershire at Leicester	1956
D. Robins†	South Australia v New South Wales at Adelaide	1965-66
S. N. Mohol	President's XI v Combined XI at Poona	1965-66
P. I. Pocock	Surrey v Sussex at Eastbourne	1972
S. S. Saini†	Delhi v Himachal Pradesh at Delhi	1988-89
D. Dias	W. Province (Suburbs) v Central Province at Colombo	1990-91
Ali Gauhar	Karachi Blues v United Bank at Peshawar	1994-95
K. D. James§	Hampshire v Indians at Southampton	1996
G. P. Butcher	Surrey v Derbyshire at The Oval	2000
Fazl-e-Akbar	PIA v Habib Bank at Lahore	2001-02
C. M. Willoughby	Cape Cobras v Dolphins at Durban	2005-06
Tabish Khan	Karachi Whites v ZTBL at Karachi	2009-10
Kamran Hussain	Habib Bank v Lahore Shalimar at Lahore	2009-10
N. Wagner	Otago v Wellington at Queenstown	2010-11
Khalid Usman	Abbottabad v Karachi Blues at Karachi	2011-12

† *Not all in the same innings.*
‡ *Having bowled Firth with the last ball of the first innings, Walker achieved a unique feat by dismissing Lester, Tompkin and Smithson with the first three balls of the second.*
§ *James also scored a century, a unique double.*

Notes: In their match with England at The Oval in 1863, Surrey lost four wickets in the course of a four-ball over from G. Bennett.

Sussex lost five wickets in the course of the final (six-ball) over of their match with Surrey at Eastbourne in 1972. P. I. Pocock, who had taken three wickets in his previous over, captured four more, taking in all seven wickets with 11 balls, a feat unique in first-class matches. (The eighth wicket fell to a run-out.)

HAT-TRICKS

Double Hat-Trick

Besides Trott's performance, which is mentioned in the preceding section, the following instances are recorded of players having performed the hat-trick twice in the same match, Rao doing so in the same innings.

A. Shaw	Nottinghamshire v Gloucestershire at Nottingham	1884
T. J. Matthews	Australia v South Africa at Manchester	1912
C. W. L. Parker	Gloucestershire v Middlesex at Bristol	1924
R. O. Jenkins	Worcestershire v Surrey at Worcester	1949
J. S. Rao	Services v Northern Punjab at Amritsar	1963-64
Amin Lakhani	Combined XI v Indians at Multan	1978-79

Five Wickets in Six Balls

W. H. Copson	Derbyshire v Warwickshire at Derby	1937
W. A. Henderson	N.E. Transvaal v Orange Free State at Bloemfontein	1937-38
P. I. Pocock	Surrey v Sussex at Eastbourne	1972
Yasir Arafat	Rawalpindi v Faisalabad at Rawalpindi	2004-05
N. Wagner	Otago v Wellington at Queenstown	2010-11

Yasir Arafat's five wickets were spread across two innings and interrupted only by a no-ball. Wagner was the first to take five wickets in a single over.

Most Hat-Tricks

D. V. P. Wright	7	R. G. Barlow	4	T. G. Matthews	4
T. W. J. Goddard	6	Fazl-e-Akbar	4	M. J. Procter	4
C. W. L. Parker	6	A. P. Freeman	4	T. Richardson	4
S. Haigh	5	J. T. Hearne	4	F. R. Spofforth	4
V. W. C. Jupp	5	J. C. Laker	4	F. S. Trueman	4
A. E. G. Rhodes	5	G. A. R. Lock	4		
F. A. Tarrant	5	G. G. Macaulay	4		

Current players only:

M. J. Hoggard	3	Elias Sunny	2	G. J-P. Kruger	2
Abdur Rauf	2	J. E. C. Franklin	2	C. M. Willoughby	2
Asad Ali	2	S. J. Harmison	2		

Hat-Trick on Debut

There have been **18** instances in first-class cricket. Occurrences since the Second World War:

J. C. Treanor	New South Wales v Queensland at Brisbane	1954-55
V. B. Ranjane	Maharashtra v Saurashtra at Poona	1956-57
Arshad Khan	Dacca University v East Pakistan B at Dacca	1957-58
N. Fredrick	Ceylon v Madras at Colombo	1963-64
J. S. Rao	Services v Jammu and Kashmir at Delhi	1963-64
Mehboodullah	Uttar Pradesh v Madhya Pradesh at Lucknow	1971-72
R. O. Estwick	Barbados v Guyana at Bridgetown	1982-83
S. A. Ankola	Maharashtra v Gujarat at Poona	1988-89
J. Srinath	Karnataka v Hyderabad at Secunderabad	1989-90
S. P. Mukherjee	Bengal v Hyderabad at Secunderabad	1989-90
S. M. Harwood	Victoria v Tasmania at Melbourne	2002-03
P. Connell	Ireland v Netherlands at Rotterdam	2008
A. Mithun	Karnataka v Uttar Pradesh at Meerut	2009-10
Zohaib Shera	Karachi Whites v National Bank at Karachi	2009-10

Notes: R. R. Phillips (Border) took a hat-trick in his first over in first-class cricket (v Eastern Province at Port Elizabeth, 1939-40) having previously played in four matches without bowling.

J. S. Rao took two more hat-tricks in his next match.

250 WICKETS IN A SEASON

	Season	*O*	*M*	*R*	*W*	*Avge*
A. P. Freeman	1928	1,976.1	423	5,489	304	18.05
A. P. Freeman	1933	2,039	651	4,549	298	15.26
T. Richardson	1895‡	1,690.1	463	4,170	290	14.37
C. T. B. Turner	1888†	2,427.2	1,127	3,307	283	11.68

A. P. Freeman	1931	1,618	360	4,307	276	15.60
A. P. Freeman	1930	1,914.3	472	4,632	275	16.84
T. Richardson	1897‡	1,603.4	495	3,945	273	14.45
A. P. Freeman	1929	1,670.5	381	4,879	267	18.27
W. Rhodes	1900	1,553	455	3,606	261	13.81
J. T. Hearne	1896‡	2,003.1	818	3,670	257	14.28
A. P. Freeman	1932	1,565.5	404	4,149	253	16.39
W. Rhodes	1901	1,565	505	3,797	251	15.12

† *Indicates 4-ball overs.* ‡ *5-ball overs.*

Notes: In four consecutive seasons (1928-31), A. P. Freeman took 1,122 wickets, and in eight consecutive seasons (1928-35), 2,090 wickets. In each of these eight seasons he took over 200 wickets.

T. Richardson took 1,005 wickets in four consecutive seasons (1894-97).

The earliest date by which any bowler has taken 100 wickets in an English season is June 12, achieved by J. T. Hearne in 1896 and C. W. L. Parker in 1931, when A. P. Freeman did it on June 13.

200 WICKETS IN A SEASON MOST TIMES

A. P. Freeman	8	J. T. Hearne	3	T. Richardson	3
C. W. L. Parker	5	G. A. Lohmann	3	M. W. Tate	3
T. W. J. Goddard	4	W. Rhodes	3	H. Verity	3

Notes: A. P. Freeman reached 200 wickets in eight successive seasons – 1928 to 1935 – including 304 in 1928.

The last bowler to reach 200 wickets in a season was G. A. R. Lock (212 in 1957).

100 WICKETS IN A SEASON MOST TIMES

(Includes overseas tours and seasons)

W. Rhodes	23	C. W. L. Parker	16	G. H. Hirst	15
D. Shackleton	20	R. T. D. Perks	16	A. S. Kennedy	15
A. P. Freeman	17	F. J. Titmus	16		
T. W. J. Goddard	16	J. T. Hearne	15		

Notes: D. Shackleton reached 100 wickets in 20 successive seasons – 1949 to 1968.

Since the reduction of County Championship matches in 1969, D. L. Underwood (five times) and J. K. Lever (four times) are the only bowlers to have reached 100 wickets in a season more than twice. The highest aggregate in a season since 1969 is 134 by M. D. Marshall in 1982.

100 WICKETS IN A SEASON OUTSIDE ENGLAND

W		*Season*	*Country*	*R*	*Avge*
116	M. W. Tate	1926-27	India/Ceylon	1,599	13.78
113	Kabir Khan	1998-99	Pakistan	1,706	15.09
107	Ijaz Faqih	1985-86	Pakistan	1,719	16.06
106	C. T. B. Turner	1887-88	Australia	1,441	13.59
106	R. Benaud	1957-58	South Africa	2,056	19.39
105	Murtaza Hussain	1995-96	Pakistan	1,882	17.92
104	S. F. Barnes	1913-14	South Africa	1,117	10.74
104	Sajjad Akbar	1989-90	Pakistan	2,328	22.38
103	Abdul Qadir	1982-83	Pakistan	2,367	22.98

LEADING BOWLERS IN AN ENGLISH SEASON

(Qualification: 10 wickets in 10 innings)

Season	*Leading wicket-taker*	*Wkts*	*Avge*	*Top of averages*	*Wkts*	*Avge*
1946	W. E. Hollies	184	15.60	A. Booth	111	11.61
1947	T. W. J. Goddard	238	17.30	J. C. Clay	65	16.44
1948	J. E. Walsh	174	19.56	J. C. Clay	41	14.17
1949	R. O. Jenkins	183	21.19	T. W. J. Goddard	160	19.18
1950	R. Tattersall	193	13.59	R. Tattersall	193	13.59
1951	R. Appleyard	200	14.14	R. Appleyard	200	14.14
1952	J. H. Wardle	177	19.54	F. S. Trueman	61	13.78
1953	B. Dooland	172	16.58	C. J. Knott	38	13.71
1954	B. Dooland	196	15.48	J. B. Statham	92	14.13
1955	G. A. R. Lock	216	14.49	R. Appleyard	85	13.01
1956	D. J. Shepherd	177	15.36	G. A. R. Lock	155	12.46
1957	G. A. R. Lock	212	12.02	G. A. R. Lock	212	12.02
1958	G. A. R. Lock	170	12.08	H. L. Jackson	143	10.99
1959	D. Shackleton	148	21.55	J. B. Statham	139	15.01
1960	F. S. Trueman	175	13.98	J. B. Statham	135	12.31
1961	J. A. Flavell	171	17.79	J. A. Flavell	171	17.79
1962	D. Shackleton	172	20.15	C. Cook	58	17.13
1963	D. Shackleton	146	16.75	C. C. Griffith	119	12.83
1964	D. Shackleton	142	20.40	J. A. Standen	64	13.00
1965	D. Shackleton	144	16.08	H. J. Rhodes	119	11.04
1966	D. L. Underwood	157	13.80	D. L. Underwood	157	13.80
1967	T. W. Cartwright	147	15.52	D. L. Underwood	136	12.39
1968	R. Illingworth	131	14.36	O. S. Wheatley	82	12.95
1969	R. M. H. Cottam	109	21.04	A. Ward	69	14.82
1970	D. J. Shepherd	106	19.16	Majid Khan	11	18.81
1971	L. R. Gibbs	131	18.89	G. G. Arnold	83	17.12
1972	T. W. Cartwright B. Stead	98 98	18.64 20.38	I. M. Chappell	10	10.60
1973	B. S. Bedi	105	17.94	T. W. Cartwright	89	15.84
1974	A. M. E. Roberts	119	13.62	A. M. E. Roberts	119	13.62
1975	P. G. Lee	112	18.45	A. M. E. Roberts	57	15.80
1976	G. A. Cope	93	24.13	M. A. Holding	55	14.38
1977	M. J. Procter	109	18.04	R. A. Woolmer	19	15.21
1978	D. L. Underwood	110	14.49	D. L. Underwood	110	14.49
1979	D. L. Underwood J. K. Lever	106 106	14.85 17.30	J. Garner	55	13.83
1980	R. D. Jackman	121	15.40	J. Garner	49	13.93
1981	R. J. Hadlee	105	14.89	R. J. Hadlee	105	14.89
1982	M. D. Marshall	134	15.73	R. J. Hadlee	61	14.57
1983	J. K. Lever D. L. Underwood	106 106	16.28 19.28	Imran Khan	12	7.16
1984	R. J. Hadlee	117	14.05	R. J. Hadlee	117	14.05
1985	N. V. Radford	101	24.68	R. M. Ellison	65	17.20
1986	C. A. Walsh	118	18.17	M. D. Marshall	100	15.08
1987	N. V. Radford	109	20.81	R. J. Hadlee	97	12.64
1988	F. D. Stephenson	125	18.31	M. D. Marshall	42	13.16
1989	D. R. Pringle S. L. Watkin	94 94	18.64 25.09	T. M. Alderman	70	15.64
1990	N. A. Foster	94	26.61	I. R. Bishop	59	19.05
1991	Waqar Younis	113	14.65	Waqar Younis	113	14.65
1992	C. A. Walsh	92	15.96	C. A. Walsh	92	15.96
1993	S. L. Watkin	92	22.80	Wasim Akram	59	19.27
1994	M. M. Patel	90	22.86	C. E. L. Ambrose	77	14.45
1995	A. Kumble	105	20.40	A. A. Donald	89	16.07
1996	C. A. Walsh	85	16.84	C. E. L. Ambrose	43	16.67
1997	A. M. Smith	83	17.63	A. A. Donald	60	15.63

Season	*Leading wicket-taker*	*Wkts*	*Avge*	*Top of averages*	*Wkts*	*Avge*
1998	C. A. Walsh	106	17.31	V. J. Wells	36	14.27
1999	A. Sheriyar	92	24.70	Saqlain Mushtaq	58	11.37
2000	G. D. McGrath	80	13.21	C. A. Walsh	40	11.42
2001	R. J. Kirtley	75	23.32	G. D. McGrath	40	15.60
2002	M. J. Saggers	83	21.51	C. P. Schofield	18	18.38
	K. J. Dean	83	23.50			
2003	Mushtaq Ahmed	103	24.65	Shoaib Akhtar	34	17.05
2004	Mushtaq Ahmed	84	27.59	D. S. Lehmann	15	17.40
2005	S. K. Warne	87	22.50	M. Muralitharan	36	15.00
2006	Mushtaq Ahmed	102	19.91	Naved-ul-Hasan	35	16.71
2007	Mushtaq Ahmed	90	25.66	Harbhajan Singh	37	18.54
2008	J. A. Tomlinson	67	24.76	M. Davies	41	14.63
2009	Danish Kaneria	75	23.69	G. Onions	69	19.95
2010	A. R. Adams	68	22.17	J. K. H. Naik	35	17.68
2011	D. D. Masters	93	18.13	T. T. Bresnan	29	17.68
2012	**G. Onions**	**72**	**14.73**	**G. Onions**	**72**	**14.73**

2,000 WICKETS

Dates in italics denote the first half of an overseas season; i.e. *1970* denotes the 1970-71 season.

		Career	*W*	*R*	*Avge*
1	W. Rhodes	1898–1930	4,187	69,993	16.71
2	A. P. Freeman	1914–1936	3,776	69,577	18.42
3	C. W. L. Parker	1903–1935	3,278	63,817	19.46
4	J. T. Hearne	1888–1923	3,061	54,352	17.75
5	T. W. J. Goddard	1922–1952	2,979	59,116	19.84
6	W. G. Grace	1865–1908	2,876	51,545	17.92
7	A. S. Kennedy	1907–1936	2,874	61,034	21.23
8	D. Shackleton	1948–1969	2,857	53,303	18.65
9	G. A. R. Lock	1946–*1970*	2,844	54,709	19.23
10	F. J. Titmus	1949–1982	2,830	63,313	22.37
11	M. W. Tate	1912–1937	2,784	50,571	18.16
12	G. H. Hirst	1891–1929	2,739	51,282	18.72
13	C. Blythe	1899–1914	2,506	42,136	16.81
14	D. L. Underwood	1963–1987	2,465	49,993	20.28
15	W. E. Astill	1906–1939	2,431	57,783	23.76
16	J. C. White	1909–1937	2,356	43,759	18.57
17	W. E. Hollies	1932–1957	2,323	48,656	20.94
18	F. S. Trueman	1949–1969	2,304	42,154	18.29
19	J. B. Statham	1950–1968	2,260	36,999	16.37
20	R. T. D. Perks	1930–1955	2,233	53,770	24.07
21	J. Briggs	1879–1900	2,221	35,431	15.95
22	D. J. Shepherd	1950–1972	2,218	47,302	21.32
23	E. G. Dennett	1903–1926	2,147	42,571	19.82
24	T. Richardson	1892–1905	2,104	38,794	18.43
25	T. E. Bailey	1945–1967	2,082	48,170	23.13
26	R. Illingworth	1951–1983	2,072	42,023	20.28
27	N. Gifford	1960–1988	2,068	48,731	23.56
	F. E. Woolley	1906–1938	2,068	41,066	19.85
29	G. Geary	1912–1938	2,063	41,339	20.03
30	D. V. P. Wright	1932–1957	2,056	49,307	23.98
31	J. A. Newman	1906–1930	2,032	51,111	25.15
32	†A. Shaw	1864–1897	2,027	24,580	12.12
33	S. Haigh	1895–1913	2,012	32,091	15.94

† *The figures for A. Shaw exclude one wicket for which no analysis is available.*

Note: Some works of reference provide career figures which differ from those in this list, owing to the exclusion or inclusion of matches recognised or not recognised as first-class by *Wisden*. A fuller list can be found in *Wisdens* up to 2011.

Current Players with 1,000 Wickets

	Career	*W*	*R*	*Avge*
R. D. B. Croft	1989–2012	1,175	41,229	35.08
Danish Kaneria	*1998–2011*	1,023	26,791	26.18

ALL-ROUND RECORDS

REMARKABLE ALL-ROUND MATCHES

V. E. Walker	20*	108	10-74	4-17	England v Surrey at The Oval	1859
W. G. Grace	104		2-60	10-49	MCC v Oxford University at Oxford	1886
G. Giffen	271		9-96	7-70	South Australia v Victoria at Adelaide	1891-92
B. J. T. Bosanquet	103	100*	3-75	8-53	Middlesex v Sussex at Lord's	1905
G. H. Hirst	111	117*	6-70	5-45	Yorkshire v Somerset at Bath	1906
F. D. Stephenson	111	117	4-105	7-117	Notts v Yorkshire at Nottingham	1988

Note: E. M. Grace, for MCC v Gentlemen of Kent in a 12-a-side match at Canterbury in 1862, scored 192* and took 5-77 and 10-69.

HUNDRED AND HAT-TRICK

G. Giffen, Australians v Lancashire at Manchester . . . 1884
W. E. Roller, Surrey v Sussex at The Oval. *Unique instance of 200 and hat-trick* . . . 1885
W. B. Burns, Worcestershire v Gloucestershire at Worcester . . . 1913
V. W. C. Jupp, Sussex v Essex at Colchester . . . 1921
R. E. S. Wyatt, MCC v Ceylonese at Colombo . . . 1926-27
L. N. Constantine, West Indians v Northamptonshire at Northampton . . . 1928
D. E. Davies, Glamorgan v Leicestershire at Leicester . . . 1937
V. M. Merchant, Dr C. R. Pereira's XI v Sir Homi Mehta's XI at Bombay . . . 1946-47
M. J. Procter, Gloucestershire v Essex at Westcliff-on-Sea . . . 1972
M. J. Procter, Gloucestershire v Leicestershire at Bristol . . . 1979
K. D. James, Hampshire v Indians at Southampton. *Unique instance of 100 and four wickets in four balls* . . . 1996
J. E. C. Franklin, Gloucestershire v Derbyshire at Cheltenham . . . 2009

THE DOUBLE

The double was traditionally regarded as 1,000 runs and 100 wickets in an English season. The feat became exceptionally rare after the reduction of County Championship matches in 1969.

Remarkable Seasons

	Season	*R*	*W*
G. H. Hirst	1906	2,385	208
J. H. Parks	1937	3,003	101

1,000 Runs and 100 Wickets

W. Rhodes	16	W. G. Grace	8	F. J. Titmus	8
G. H. Hirst	14	M. S. Nichols	8	F. E. Woolley	7
V. W. C. Jupp	10	A. E. Relf	8	G. E. Tribe	7
W. E. Astill	9	F. A. Tarrant	8		
T. E. Bailey	8	M. W. Tate	8†		

† *M. W. Tate also scored 1,193 runs and took 116 wickets on the 1926-27 MCC tour of India and Ceylon.*

Note: R. J. Hadlee (1984) and F. D. Stephenson (1988) are the only players to perform the feat since the reduction of County Championship matches in 1969. A complete list of those performing the feat before then may be found on page 202 of the 1982 *Wisden*. T. E. Bailey (1959) was the last player to achieve 2,000 runs and 100 wickets in a season; M. W. Tate (1925) the last to reach 1,000 runs and 200 wickets. Full lists may be found in *Wisdens* up to 2003.

Wicketkeeper's Double

The only wicketkeepers to achieve 1,000 runs and 100 dismissals in a season were L. E. G. Ames (1928, 1929 and 1932, when he scored 2,482 runs) and J. T. Murray (1957).

WICKETKEEPING RECORDS

MOST DISMISSALS IN AN INNINGS

9 (8ct, 1st)	Tahir Rashid	Habib Bank v PACO at Gujranwala	1992-93
9 (7ct, 2st)	W. R. James*	Matabeleland v Mashonaland CD at Bulawayo	1995-96
8 (all ct)	A. T. W. Grout	Queensland v Western Australia at Brisbane	1959-60
8 (all ct)†	D. E. East	Essex v Somerset at Taunton	1985
8 (all ct)	S. A. Marsh‡	Kent v Middlesex at Lord's	1991
8 (6ct, 2st)	T. J. Zoehrer	Australians v Surrey at The Oval	1993
8 (7ct, 1st)	D. S. Berry	Victoria v South Australia at Melbourne	1996-97
8 (7ct, 1st)	Y. S. S. Mendis	Bloomfield v Kurunegala Youth at Colombo	2000-01
8 (7ct, 1st)	S. Nath§	Assam v Tripura at Guwahati	2001-02
8 (all ct)	J. N. Batty¶	Surrey v Kent at The Oval	2004
8 (all ct)	Golam Mabud	Sylhet v Dhaka at Dhaka	2005-06
8 (all ct)	A. Z. M. Dyili	Eastern Province v Free State at Port Elizabeth	2009-10
8 (all ct)	D. C. de Boorder	Otago v Wellington at Wellington	2009-10
8 (all ct)	R. S. Second	Free State v North West at Bloemfontein	2011-12
8 (all ct)	**T. L. Tsolekile**	**South Africa A v Sri Lanka A at Durban**	**2012**

There have been **91** further instances of seven dismissals in an innings. R. W. Taylor achieved the feat three times, and G. J. Hopkins, Kamran Akmal, S. A. Marsh, K. J. Piper, Shahin Hossain and Wasim Bari twice. One of Marsh's two instances was of eight dismssals – see above. A fuller list can be found in *Wisdens* before 2004.

* *W. R. James also scored 99 and 99 not out.*
† *The first eight wickets to fall.*
‡ *S. A. Marsh also scored 108 not out.*
§ *On his only first-class appearance.*
¶ *J. N. Batty also scored 129.*

WICKETKEEPERS' HAT-TRICKS

W. H. Brain, Gloucestershire v Somerset at Cheltenham, 1893 – three stumpings off successive balls from C. L. Townsend.

G. O. Dawkes, Derbyshire v Worcestershire at Kidderminster, 1958 – three catches off successive balls from H. L. Jackson.

R. C. Russell, Gloucestershire v Surrey at The Oval, 1986 – three catches off successive balls from C. A. Walsh and D. V. Lawrence (2).

MOST DISMISSALS IN A MATCH

14 (11ct, 3st)	I. Khaleel	Hyderabad v Assam at Guwahati	2011-12
13 (11ct, 2st)	W. R. James*	Matabeleland v Mashonaland CD at Bulawayo	1995-96
12 (8ct, 4st)	E. Pooley	Surrey v Sussex at The Oval	1868
12 (9ct, 3st)	D. Tallon	Queensland v New South Wales at Sydney	1938-39
12 (9ct, 3st)	H. B. Taber	New South Wales v South Australia at Adelaide	1968-69
12 (all ct)	P. D. McGlashan	Northern Districts v Central Districts at Whangarei	2009-10
12 (11ct, 1st)	T. L. Tsolekile	Lions v Dolphins at Johannesburg	2010-11
12 (all ct)	Kashif Mahmood	Lahore Shalimar v Abbottabad at Abbottabad	2010-11
12 (all ct)	R. S. Second	Free State v North West at Bloemfontein	2011-12

11 (all ct)	A. Long	Surrey v Sussex at Hove	1964
11 (all ct)	R. W. Marsh	Western Australia v Victoria at Perth	1975-76
11 (all ct)	D. L. Bairstow	Yorkshire v Derbyshire at Scarborough	1982
11 (all ct)	W. K. Hegg	Lancashire v Derbyshire at Chesterfield	1989
11 (all ct)	A. J. Stewart	Surrey v Leicestershire at Leicester	1989
11 (all ct)	T. J. Nielsen	South Australia v Western Australia at Perth	1990-91
11 (10ct, 1st)	I. A. Healy	Australians v N. Transvaal at Verwoerdburg	1993-94
11 (10ct, 1st)	K. J. Piper	Warwickshire v Derbyshire at Chesterfield	1994
11 (all ct)	D. S. Berry	Victoria v Pakistanis at Melbourne	1995-96
11 (10ct, 1st)	W. A. Seccombe	Queensland v Western Australia at Brisbane	1995-96
11 (all ct)	R. C. Russell	England v South Africa (2nd Test) at Johannesburg	1995-96
11 (10ct, 1st)	D. S. Berry	Victoria v South Australia at Melbourne	1996-97
11 (all ct)	Wasim Yousufi	Peshawar v Bahawalpur at Peshawar	1997-98
11 (all ct)	Aamer Iqbal	Pakistan Customs v Karachi Whites at Karachi	1999-2000
11 (10ct, 1st)	S. Nath†	Assam v Tripura at Guwahati	2001-02
11 (all ct)	Wasim Ahmed	Dadu v PWD at Karachi	2002-03
11 (7ct, 4st)	J. N. Batty	Surrey v Lancashire at Manchester	2004
11 (7ct, 4st)	M. S. Dhoni	India A v Zimbabwe Select XI at Harare	2004
11 (all ct)	Adnan Akmal	Lahore Blues v Karachi Blues at Karachi	2004-05
11 (9ct, 2st)	M. S. Bisla	Himachal Pradesh v Saurashtra at Dharmasala	2004-05

* *W. R. James also scored 99 and 99 not out.* † *On his only first-class appearance.*

100 DISMISSALS IN A SEASON

128 (79ct, 49st)	L. E. G. Ames	1929	104 (82ct, 22st)	J. T. Murray	1957
122 (70ct, 52st)	L. E. G. Ames	1928	102 (69ct, 33st)	F. H. Huish	1913
110 (63ct, 47st)	H. Yarnold	1949	102 (95ct, 7st)	J. T. Murray	1960
107 (77ct, 30st)	G. Duckworth	1928	101 (62ct, 39st)	F. H. Huish	1911
107 (96ct, 11st)	J. G. Binks	1960	101 (85ct, 16st)	R. Booth	1960
104 (40ct, 64st)	L. E. G. Ames	1932	100 (91ct, 9st)	R. Booth	1964

Note: L. E. G. Ames achieved the two highest stumping totals in a season: 64 in 1932, and 52 in 1928.

1,000 DISMISSALS

Dates in italics denote the first half of an overseas season; i.e. *1914* denotes the 1914-15 season.

			Career	*M*	*Ct*	*St*
1	R. W. Taylor	1,649	1960–1988	639	1,473	176
2	J. T. Murray	1,527	1952–1975	635	1,270	257
3	H. Strudwick	1,497	1902–1927	675	1,242	255
4	A. P. E. Knott	1,344	1964–1985	511	1,211	133
5	R. C. Russell	1,320	1981–2004	465	1,192	128
6	F. H. Huish	1,310	1895–1914	497	933	377
7	B. Taylor	1,294	1949–1973	572	1,083	211
8	S. J. Rhodes	1,263	1981–2004	440	1,139	124
9	D. Hunter	1,253	1888–1909	548	906	347
10	H. R. Butt	1,228	1890–1912	550	953	275
11	J. H. Board	1,207	1891–*1914*	525	852	355
12	H. Elliott	1,206	1920–1947	532	904	302
13	J. M. Parks	1,181	1949–1976	739	1,088	93
14	R. Booth	1,126	1951–1970	468	948	178
15	L. E. G. Ames	1,121	1926–1951	593	703	418†
16	D. L. Bairstow	1,099	1970–1990	459	961	138
17	G. Duckworth	1,096	1923–1947	504	753	343
18	H. W. Stephenson	1,082	1948–1964	462	748	334
19	J. G. Binks	1,071	1955–1975	502	895	176
20	T. G. Evans	1,066	1939–1969	465	816	250

			Career	M	Ct	St
21	A. Long	1,046	1960–1980	452	922	124
22	G. O. Dawkes	1,043	1937–1961	482	895	148
23	R. W. Tolchard	1,037	1965–1983	483	912	125
24	W. L. Cornford	1,017	1921–1947	496	675	342

† *Record.*

Current Players with 500 Dismissals

		Career	*M*	*Ct*	*St*
849	C. M. W. Read	*1997*–2012	274	804	45
749	M. V. Boucher	*1995–2011*	212	712	37
673	J. N. Batty	1994–2012	220	605	68
664	Kamran Akmal	*1997–2012*	178	612	52
626	J. S. Foster	2000–2012	206	575	51
588	M. J. Prior	2001–*2012*	219	547	41
582	H. A. P. W. Jayawardene	*1997–2012*	217	481	101
575	G. O. Jones	2001–2012	175	540	35
545	M. A. Wallace	1999–2012	199	499	46
507	B. J. Haddin	*1999–2012*	149	476	31
503	P. Mustard	2002–*2012*	148	486	17
502	Zulfiqar Jan	*1999–2012*	138	478	24

Note: Some of these figures include catches taken in the field.

FIELDING RECORDS

excluding wicketkeepers

MOST CATCHES IN AN INNINGS

7	M. J. Stewart	Surrey v Northamptonshire at Northampton	1957
7	A. S. Brown	Gloucestershire v Nottinghamshire at Nottingham	1966
7	R. Clarke	Warwickshire v Lancashire at Liverpool	2011

MOST CATCHES IN A MATCH

10	W. R. Hammond†	Gloucestershire v Surrey at Cheltenham	1928
9	R. Clarke	Warwickshire v Lancashire at Liverpool	2011
8	W. B. Burns	Worcestershire v Yorkshire at Bradford	1907
8	F. G. Travers	Europeans v Parsees at Bombay	1923-24
8	A. H. Bakewell	Northamptonshire v Essex at Leyton	1928
8	W. R. Hammond	Gloucestershire v Worcestershire at Cheltenham	1932
8	K. J. Grieves	Lancashire v Sussex at Manchester	1951
8	C. A. Milton	Gloucestershire v Sussex at Hove	1952
8	G. A. R. Lock	Surrey v Warwickshire at The Oval	1957
8	J. M. Prodger	Kent v Gloucestershire at Cheltenham	1961
8	P. M. Walker	Glamorgan v Derbyshire at Swansea	1970
8	Masood Anwar	Rawalpindi v Lahore Division at Rawalpindi	1983-84
8	M. C. J. Ball	Gloucestershire v Yorkshire at Cheltenham	1994
8	J. D. Carr	Middlesex v Warwickshire at Birmingham	1995
8	G. A. Hick	Worcestershire v Essex at Chelmsford	2005

† *Hammond also scored a hundred in each innings.*

MOST CATCHES IN A SEASON

78	W. R. Hammond	1928	69	P. M. Walker	1960
77	M. J. Stewart	1957	66	J. Tunnicliffe	1895
73	P. M. Walker	1961	65	W. R. Hammond	1925
71	P. J. Sharpe	1962	65	P. M. Walker	1959
70	J. Tunnicliffe	1901	65	D. W. Richardson	1961
69	J. G. Langridge	1955			

Note: The most catches by a fielder since the reduction of County Championship matches in 1969 is 59 by G. R. J. Roope in 1971.

750 CATCHES

Dates in italics denote the first half of an overseas season; i.e. *1970* denotes the 1970-71 season.

		Career	*M*			*Career*	*M*
1,018	F. E. Woolley	1906–1938	979	784	J. G. Langridge	1928–1955	574
887	W. G. Grace	1865–1908	879	764	W. Rhodes	1898–1930	1,107
830	G. A. R. Lock	1946–*1970*	654	758	C. A. Milton	1948–1974	620
819	W. R. Hammond	1920–1951	634	754	E. H. Hendren	1907–1938	833
813	D. B. Close	1949–1986	786				

Note: The most catches by a current player is 417 by M. J. Di Venuto (*1991*–2012).

TEAM RECORDS

HIGHEST INNINGS TOTALS

1,107	Victoria v New South Wales at Melbourne	1926-27
1,059	Victoria v Tasmania at Melbourne	1922-23
952-6 dec	Sri Lanka v India at Colombo	1997-98
951-7 dec	Sind v Baluchistan at Karachi	1973-74
944-6 dec	Hyderabad v Andhra at Secunderabad	1993-94
918	New South Wales v South Australia at Sydney	1900-01
912-8 dec	Holkar v Mysore at Indore	1945-46
912-6 dec†	Tamil Nadu v Goa at Panjim	1988-89
910-6 dec	Railways v Dera Ismail Khan at Lahore	1964-65
903-7 dec	England v Australia at The Oval	1938
900-6 dec	Queensland v Victoria at Brisbane	2005-06
887	Yorkshire v Warwickshire at Birmingham	1896
868†	North Zone v West Zone at Bhilai	1987-88
863	Lancashire v Surrey at The Oval	1990
855-6 dec†	Bombay v Hyderabad at Bombay	1990-91
850-7 dec	Somerset v Middlesex at Taunton	2007
849	England v West Indies at Kingston	1929-30
843	Australians v Oxford & Cambridge U P & P at Portsmouth	1893
839	New South Wales v Tasmania at Sydney	1898-99
826-4	Maharashtra v Kathiawar at Poona	1948-49
824	Lahore Greens v Bahawalpur at Lahore	1965-66
821-7 dec	South Australia v Queensland at Adelaide	1939-40
815	New South Wales v Victoria at Sydney	1908-09
811	Surrey v Somerset at The Oval	1899
810-4 dec	Warwickshire v Durham at Birmingham	1994

807	New South Wales v South Australia at Adelaide	1899-1900
806-8 dec	Victoria v Queensland at Melbourne	2008-09
805	New South Wales v Victoria at Melbourne	1905-06
803-4 dec	Kent v Essex at Brentwood	1934
803	Non-Smokers v Smokers at East Melbourne	1886-87
802-8 dec	Karachi Blues v Lahore City at Peshawar	1994-95
802	New South Wales v South Australia at Sydney	1920-21
801-8 dec	Derbyshire v Somerset at Taunton	2007
801	Lancashire v Somerset at Taunton	1895

† *Tamil Nadu's total of 912-6 dec included 52 penalty runs from their opponents' failure to meet the required bowling rate. North Zone's total of 868 included 68, and Bombay's total of 855-6 dec included 48.*

Note: The highest total in a team's second innings is 770 by New South Wales v South Australia at Adelaide in 1920-21.

HIGHEST FOURTH-INNINGS TOTALS

654-5	England v South Africa at Durban *After being set 696 to win. The match was left drawn on the tenth day.*	1938-39
604	Maharashtra (*set 959 to win*) v Bombay at Poona	1948-49
576-8	Trinidad (*set 672 to win*) v Barbados at Port-of-Spain	1945-46
572	New South Wales (*set 593 to win*) v South Australia at Sydney	1907-08
541-7	West Zone (*won*) v South Zone at Hyderabad	2009-10
529-9	Combined XI (*set 579 to win*) v South Africans at Perth	1963-64
518	Victoria (*set 753 to win*) v Queensland at Brisbane	1926-27
513-9	Central Province (*won*) v Southern Province at Kandy	2003-04
507-7	Cambridge University (*won*) v MCC and Ground at Lord's	1896
506-6	South Australia (*won*) v Queensland at Adelaide	1991-92
503-4	South Zone (*won*) v England A at Gurgaon	2003-04
502-6	Middlesex (*won*) v Nottinghamshire at Nottingham	1925
502-8	Players (*won*) v Gentlemen at Lord's	1900
500-7	South African Universities (*won*) v Western Province at Stellenbosch	1978-79

MOST RUNS IN A DAY (ONE SIDE)

721	Australians (721) v Essex at Southend (1st day)	1948
651	West Indians (651-2) v Leicestershire at Leicester (1st day)	1950
649	New South Wales (649-7) v Otago at Dunedin (2nd day)	1923-24
645	Surrey (645-4) v Hampshire at The Oval (1st day)	1909
644	Oxford U. (644-8) v H. D. G. Leveson Gower's XI at Eastbourne (1st day)	1921
640	Lancashire (640-8) v Sussex at Hove (1st day)	1937
636	Free Foresters (636-7) v Cambridge U. at Cambridge (1st day)	1938
625	Gloucestershire (625-6) v Worcestershire at Dudley (2nd day)	1934

MOST RUNS IN A DAY (BOTH SIDES)

(excluding the above)

685	North (169-8 and 255-7), South (261-8 dec) at Blackpool (2nd day)	1961
666	Surrey (607-4), Northamptonshire (59-2) at Northampton (2nd day)	1920
665	Rest of South Africa (339), Transvaal (326) at Johannesburg (1st day)	1911-12
663	Middlesex (503-4), Leicestershire (160-2) at Leicester (2nd day)	1947
661	Border (201), Griqualand West (460) at Kimberley (1st day)	1920-21
649	Hampshire (570-8), Somerset (79-3) at Taunton (2nd day)	1901

HIGHEST AGGREGATES IN A MATCH

Runs	*Wkts*		
2,376	37	Maharashtra v Bombay at Poona	1948-49
2,078	40	Bombay v Holkar at Bombay	1944-45
1,981	35	South Africa v England at Durban	1938-39
1,945	18	Canterbury v Wellington at Christchurch	1994-95
1,929	39	New South Wales v South Australia at Sydney	1925-26
1,911	34	New South Wales v Victoria at Sydney	1908-09
1,905	40	Otago v Wellington at Dunedin	1923-24

In Britain

Runs	*Wkts*		
1,815	28	Somerset v Surrey at Taunton	2002
1,808	20	Sussex v Essex at Hove	1993
1,795	34	Somerset v Northamptonshire at Taunton	2001
1,723	31	England v Australia at Leeds	1948
1,706	23	Hampshire v Warwickshire at Southampton	1997
1,683	14	Middlesex v Glamorgan at Southgate	2005
1,665	33	Warwickshire v Yorkshire at Birmingham	2002
1,659	13	Somerset v Middlesex at Taunton	2007
1,655	25	Derbyshire v Nottinghamshire at Derby	2001
1,650	19	Surrey v Lancashire at The Oval	1990

LOWEST INNINGS TOTALS

12†	Oxford University v MCC and Ground at Oxford	1877
12	Northamptonshire v Gloucestershire at Gloucester	1907
13	Auckland v Canterbury at Auckland	1877-78
13	Nottinghamshire v Yorkshire at Nottingham	1901
14	Surrey v Essex at Chelmsford	1983
15	MCC v Surrey at Lord's	1839
15†	Victoria v MCC at Melbourne	1903-04
15†	Northamptonshire v Yorkshire at Northampton	1908
15	Hampshire v Warwickshire at Birmingham	1922
	Following on, Hampshire scored 521 and won by 155 runs.	
16	MCC and Ground v Surrey at Lord's	1872
16	Derbyshire v Nottinghamshire at Nottingham	1879
16	Surrey v Nottinghamshire at The Oval	1880
16	Warwickshire v Kent at Tonbridge	1913
16	Trinidad v Barbados at Bridgetown	1942-43
16	Border v Natal at East London (first innings)	1959-60
17	Gentlemen of Kent v Gentlemen of England at Lord's	1850
17	Gloucestershire v Australians at Cheltenham	1896
18	The Bs v England at Lord's	1831
18†	Kent v Sussex at Gravesend	1867
18	Tasmania v Victoria at Melbourne	1868-69
18†	Australians v MCC and Ground at Lord's	1896
18	Border v Natal at East London (second innings)	1959-60
18†	**Durham MCCU v Durham at Chester-le-Street**	**2012**
19	Sussex v Surrey at Godalming	1830
19†	Sussex v Nottinghamshire at Hove	1873
19	MCC and Ground v Australians at Lord's	1878
19	Wellington v Nelson at Nelson	1885-86
19	Matabeleland v Mashonaland at Harare	2000-01

† *One man absent.*

Note: At Lord's in 1810, The Bs, with one man absent, were dismissed by England for 6.

LOWEST TOTALS IN A MATCH

34	(16 and 18) Border v Natal at East London	1959-60
42	(27 and 15) Northamptonshire v Yorkshire at Northampton	1908

Note: Northamptonshire batted one man short in each innings.

LOWEST AGGREGATE IN A COMPLETED MATCH

Runs	*Wkts*		
85	11†	Quetta v Rawalpindi at Islamabad	2008-09
105	31	MCC v Australians at Lord's	1878

† *Both teams forfeited their first innings.*

Note: The lowest aggregate in a match in which the losing team was bowled out twice since 1900 is 157 for 22 wickets, Surrey v Worcestershire at The Oval, 1954.

LARGEST VICTORIES

Largest Innings Victories

Inns and 851 runs	Railways (910-6 dec) v Dera Ismail Khan at Lahore	1964-65
Inns and 666 runs	Victoria (1,059) v Tasmania at Melbourne	1922-23
Inns and 656 runs	Victoria (1,107) v New South Wales at Melbourne	1926-27
Inns and 605 runs	New South Wales (918) v South Australia at Sydney	1900-01
Inns and 579 runs	England (903-7 dec) v Australia at The Oval	1938
Inns and 575 runs	Sind (951-7 dec) v Baluchistan at Karachi	1973-74
Inns and 527 runs	New South Wales (713) v South Australia at Adelaide	1908-09
Inns and 517 runs	Australians (675) v Nottinghamshire at Nottingham	1921

Largest Victories by Runs Margin

685 runs	New South Wales (235 and 761-8 dec) v Queensland at Sydney	1929-30
675 runs	England (521 and 342-8 dec) v Australia at Brisbane	1928-29
638 runs	New South Wales (304 and 770) v South Australia at Adelaide	1920-21
609 runs	Muslim Commercial Bank (575 and 282-0 dec) v WAPDA at Lahore	1977-78
585 runs	Sargodha (336 and 416) v Lahore Municipal Corporation at Faisalabad	1978-79
573 runs	Sinhalese (395-7 dec and 350-2 dec) v Sebastianites at Colombo	1990-91
571 runs	Victoria (304 and 649) v South Australia at Adelaide	1926-27
562 runs	Australia (701 and 327) v England at The Oval	1934
556 runs	Nondescripts (397-8 dec and 313-6 dec) v Matara at Colombo	1998-99
552 runs	South Zone (443 and 504-7 dec) v Central Zone at Hyderabad	2010-11

Victory Without Losing a Wicket

Lancashire (166-0 dec and 66-0) beat Leicestershire by ten wickets at Manchester	1956
Karachi A (277-0 dec) beat Sind A by an innings and 77 runs at Karachi	1957-58
Railways (236-0 dec and 16-0) beat Jammu and Kashmir by ten wickets at Srinagar	1960-61
Karnataka (451-0 dec) beat Kerala by an innings and 186 runs at Chikmagalur	1977-78

Notes: There have been **29** wins by an innings and 400 runs or more, the most recent being an innings and 415 runs by Islamabad v Quetta at Islamabad in 2008-09.

There have been **20** wins by 500 runs or more, the most recent being **511 runs by Punjab v Sind at Lahore in 2011-12**.

There have been **32** wins by a team losing only one wicket, the most recent being by Rawalpindi v Quetta at Islamabad in 2008-09.

TIED MATCHES

Since 1948, a tie has been recognised only when the scores are level with all the wickets down in the fourth innings. There have been **34** instances since then, including two Tests (see Test record section); Sussex have featured in five of those, Essex and Kent in four each.

The most recent instances are:

Bahawalpur v Peshawar at Bahawalpur	1988-89
Wellington v Canterbury at Wellington	1988-89
Sussex v Kent at Hove	1991
Nottinghamshire v Worcestershire at Nottingham	1993
Somerset v West Indies A at Taunton	†2002
Warwickshire v Essex at Birmingham	2003
Worcestershire v Zimbabweans at Worcester	2003
Habib Bank v WAPDA at Lahore	2011-12
Border v Boland at East London	**2012-13**

† *Somerset (453) made the highest total to tie a first-class match.*

MATCHES COMPLETED ON FIRST DAY

(Since 1946)

Derbyshire v Somerset at Chesterfield, June 11	1947
Lancashire v Sussex at Manchester, July 12	1950
Surrey v Warwickshire at The Oval, May 16	1953
Somerset v Lancashire at Bath, June 6 (H. F. T. Buse's benefit)	1953
Kent v Worcestershire at Tunbridge Wells, June 15	1960
Griqualand West v Easterns at Kimberley, March 10	2010-11

SHORTEST COMPLETED MATCHES

Balls		
121	Quetta (forfeit and 41) v Rawalpindi (forfeit and 44-1) at Islamabad	2008-09
350	Somerset (35 and 44) v Middlesex (86) at Lord's	1899
352	Victoria (82 and 57) v Tasmania (104 and 37-7) at Launceston	1850-51
372	Victoria (80 and 50) v Tasmania (97 and 35-2) at Launceston	1853-54
419*	England XI (82 and 26) v Australians (76 and 33-6) at Aston	1884
425	Derbyshire (180-0 dec and forfeit) v Northamptonshire (forfeit and 181-2) at Northampton	1992
432	Victoria (78 and 67) v Tasmania (51 and 25) at Hobart	1857-58
435	Northamptonshire (4-0 dec and 86) v Yorkshire (4-0 dec and 88-5) at Bradford	1931
442*	Wellington (31 and 48) v Nelson (73 and 7-1) at Nelson	1887-88
445	Glamorgan (272-1 dec and forfeit) v Lancashire (forfeit and 51) at Liverpool	1997
450	Bengal Governor's XI (33 and 59) v Maharaja of Cooch-Behar's XI (138) at Calcutta	1917-18

* *Match completed on first day.*

An expanded and regularly updated online version of the Records can be found at www.wisdenrecords.com

LIST A ONE-DAY RECORDS

List A is a concept intended to provide an approximate equivalent in one-day cricket of first-class status. It was introduced by the Association of Cricket Statisticians and Historians and is now recognised by the ICC, with a separate category for Twenty20 cricket. Further details are available at stats.acscricket.com/ListA/Description.html. List A games comprise:

(a) One-day internationals.
(b) Other international matches (e.g. A-team internationals).
(c) Premier domestic one-day tournaments in Test-playing countries.
(d) Official tourist matches against the main first-class teams (e.g. counties, states, provinces and national Board XIs).

The following matches are excluded:

(a) Matches originally scheduled as less than 40 overs per side (e.g. Twenty20 games).
(b) World Cup warm-up games.
(c) Tourist matches against teams outside the major domestic competitions (e.g. universities).
(d) Festival games and pre-season friendlies.

Notes: This section covers one-day cricket to December 31, 2012. Bold type denotes performances in the calendar year 2012 or, in career figures, players who appeared in List A cricket in that year.

BATTING RECORDS

HIGHEST INDIVIDUAL INNINGS

268	A. D. Brown	Surrey v Glamorgan at The Oval	2002
222*	R. G. Pollock	Eastern Province v Border at East London	1974-75
219	V. Sehwag	India v West Indies at Indore	2011-12
207	Mohammad Ali	Pakistan Customs v DHA at Sialkot	2004-05
206	A. I. Kallicharran	Warwickshire v Oxfordshire at Birmingham	1984
204*	Khalid Latif	Karachi Dolphins v Quetta Bears at Karachi	2008-09
203	A. D. Brown	Surrey v Hampshire at Guildford	1997
202*	A. Barrow	Natal v SA African XI at Durban	1975-76
201*	R. S. Bopara	Essex v Leicestershire at Leicester	2008
201	V. J. Wells	Leicestershire v Berkshire at Leicester	1996
200*	S. R. Tendulkar	India v South Africa at Gwalior	2009-10

MOST RUNS

	Career	*M*	*I*	*NO*	*R*	*HS*	*100*	*Avge*
G. A. Gooch	1973–1997	614	601	48	22,211	198*	44	40.16
G. A. Hick	*1983*–2008	651	630	96	22,059	172*	40	41.30
S. R. Tendulkar	***1989–2011***	**551**	**538**	**55**	**21,999**	**200***	**60**	**45.54**
I. V. A. Richards	1973–1993	500	466	61	16,995	189*	26	41.96
C. G. Greenidge	1970–1992	440	436	33	16,349	186*	33	40.56
R. T. Ponting	***1992–2012***	**451**	**441**	**53**	**16,221**	**164**	**34**	**41.80**
S. T. Jayasuriya	*1989–2011*	557	542	25	16,128	189	31	31.19
A. J. Lamb	1972–1995	484	463	63	15,658	132*	19	39.14
D. L. Haynes	1976–1996	419	416	44	15,651	152*	28	42.07
S. C. Ganguly	***1989–2011***	**437**	**421**	**43**	**15,622**	**183**	**31**	**41.32**
K. J. Barnett	1979–2005	527	500	54	15,564	136	17	34.89
R. Dravid	*1992*–2011	449	416	55	15,271	153	21	42.30
M. G. Bevan	*1989–2006*	427	385	124	15,103	157*	13	57.86

HIGHEST PARTNERSHIP FOR EACH WICKET

326*	for 1st	Ghulam Ali and Sohail Jaffer, PIA v ADBP at Sialkot	2000-01
331	for 2nd	S. R. Tendulkar and R. Dravid, India v New Zealand at Hyderabad	1999-2000
309*	for 3rd	T. S. Curtis and T. M. Moody, Worcestershire v Surrey at The Oval	1994
275*	for 4th	M. Azharuddin and A. Jadeja, India v Zimbabwe at Cuttack	1997-98
267*	for 5th	Minhazul Abedin and Khaled Mahmud, Bangladeshis v Bahawalpur at Karachi	1997-98
226	for 6th	N. J. Llong and M. V. Fleming, Kent v Cheshire at Bowdon	1999
203*	for 7th	S. H. T. Kandamby and H. M. R. K. B. Herath, Sri Lanka A v South Africa A at Benoni	2008-09
203	for 8th	Shahid Iqbal and Haaris Ayaz, Karachi Whites v Hyderabad at Karachi	1998-99
155	for 9th	C. M. W. Read and A. J. Harris, Notts v Durham at Nottingham	2006
106*	for 10th	I. V. A. Richards and M. A. Holding, West Indies v England at Manchester	1984

BOWLING RECORDS

BEST BOWLING ANALYSES

8-15	R. L. Sanghvi	Delhi v Himachal Pradesh at Una	1997-98
8-19	W. P. U. J. C. Vaas	Sri Lanka v Zimbabwe at Colombo	2001-02
8-20*	D. T. Kottehewa	Nondescripts v Ragama at Colombo	2007-08
8-21	M. A. Holding	Derbyshire v Sussex at Hove	1988
8-26	K. D. Boyce	Essex v Lancashire at Manchester	1971
8-30	G. D. R. Eranga	Burgher v Army at Colombo	2007-08
8-31	D. L. Underwood	Kent v Scotland at Edinburgh	1987
8-43	S. W. Tait	South Australia v Tasmania at Adelaide	2003-04
8-52	K. A. Stoute	West Indies A v Lancashire at Manchester	2010
8-66	S. R. G. Francis	Somerset v Derbyshire at Derby	2004

* *Including two hat-tricks.*

MOST WICKETS

	Career	*M*	*B*	*R*	*W*	*BB*	*4I*	*Avge*
Wasim Akram	*1984*–2003	594	29,719	19,303	881	5-10	46	21.91
A. A. Donald	*1985–2003*	458	22,856	14,942	684	6-15	38	21.84
M. Muralitharan	*1991–2010*	453	23,734	15,270	682	7-30	29	22.39
Waqar Younis	*1988–2003*	412	19,841	15,098	675	7-36	44	22.36
J. K. Lever	1968–1990	481	23,208	13,278	674	5-8	34	19.70
J. E. Emburey	1975–2000	536	26,399	16,811	647	5-23	26	25.98
I. T. Botham	1973–1993	470	22,899	15,264	612	5-27	18	24.94

WICKETKEEPING AND FIELDING RECORDS

MOST DISMISSALS IN AN INNINGS

8	(all ct)	D. J. S. Taylor	Somerset v Combined Universities at Taunton	1982
8	(5ct, 3st)	S. J. Palframan	Boland v Easterns at Paarl	1997-98
8	(all ct)	D. J. Pipe	Worcestershire v Hertfordshire at Hertford	2001
7	(6ct, 1st)	R. W. Taylor	Derbyshire v Lancashire at Manchester	1975
7	(4ct, 3st)	Rizwan Umar	Sargodha v Bahawalpur at Sargodha	1991-92
7	(all ct)	A. J. Stewart	Surrey v Glamorgan at Swansea	1994
7	(all ct)	I. Mitchell	Border v Western Province at East London	1998-99
7	(6ct, 1st)	M. K. P. B. Kularatne	Galle v Colts at Colombo	2001-02
7	(5ct, 2st)	T. R. Ambrose	Warwickshire v Middlesex at Birmingham	2009
7	(3ct, 4st)	W. A. S. Niroshan	Chilaw Marians v Saracens at Katunayake	2009-10
7	**(all ct)**	**M. Rawat**	**Railways v Madhya Pradesh at Nagpur**	**2011-12**

MOST CATCHES IN AN INNINGS IN THE FIELD

5	V. J. Marks	Combined Universities v Kent at Oxford	1976
5	J. M. Rice	Hampshire v Warwickshire at Southampton	1978
5	A. J. Kourie	Transvaal v Western Province at Johannesburg	1979-80
5	J. N. Rhodes	South Africa v West Indies at Bombay	1993-94
5	J. W. Wilson	Otago v Auckland at Dunedin	1993-94
5	K. C. Jackson	Boland v Natal at Durban	1995-96
5	Mohammad Ramzan	PNSC v PIA at Karachi	1998-99
5	Amit Sharma	Punjab v Jammu and Kashmir at Ludhiana	1999-2000
5	B. E. Young	South Australia v Tasmania at Launceston	2001-02
5	Hasnain Raza	Bahawalpur v Pakistan Customs at Karachi	2002-03
5	D. J. Sales	Northamptonshire v Essex at Northampton	2007
5	L. N. Mosena	Free State v North West at Bloemfontein	2007-08

TEAM RECORDS

HIGHEST INNINGS TOTALS

496-4	(50 overs)	Surrey v Gloucestershire at The Oval	2007
443-9	(50 overs)	Sri Lanka v Netherlands at Amstelveen	2006
438-5	(50 overs)	Surrey v Glamorgan at The Oval	2002
438-9	(49.5 overs)	South Africa v Australia at Johannesburg	2005-06
434-4	(50 overs)	Australia v South Africa at Johannesburg	2005-06
429	(49.5 overs)	Glamorgan v Surrey at The Oval	2002
424-5	(50 overs)	Buckinghamshire v Suffolk at Dinton	2002
418-5	(50 overs)	South Africa v Zimbabwe at Potchefstroom	2006-07
418-5	(50 overs)	India v West Indies at Indore	2011-12
414-7	(50 overs)	India v Sri Lanka at Rajkot	2009-10
413-4	(60 overs)	Somerset v Devon at Torquay	1990
413-5	(50 overs)	India v Bermuda at Port-of-Spain	2006-07
412-4	(50 overs)	United Arab Emirates v Argentina at Windhoek	2007-08
412-6	(50 overs)	Madhya Pradesh v Railways at Indore	2009-10
411-6	(50 overs)	Yorkshire v Devon at Exmouth	2004
411-8	(50 overs)	Sri Lanka v India at Rajkot	2009-10
410-5	(50 overs)	Canterbury v Otago at Timaru	2009-10
409-6	(50 overs)	Trinidad & Tobago v North Windward Islands at Kingston	2001-02
408-4	(50 overs)	KRL v Sialkot at Sialkot	2002-03
406-5	(60 overs)	Leicestershire v Berkshire at Leicester	1996
405-4	(50 overs)	Queensland v Western Australia at Brisbane	2003-04
404-3	(60 overs)	Worcestershire v Devon at Worcester	1987
403-3	(50 overs)	Somerset v Scotland at Taunton	2009
402-2	(50 overs)	New Zealand v Ireland at Aberdeen	2008
401-3	(50 overs)	India v South Africa at Gwalior	2009-10
401-7	(50 overs)	Gloucestershire v Buckinghamshire at Wing	2003

LOWEST INNINGS TOTALS

18	(14.3 overs)	West Indies Under-19 v Barbados at Blairmont	2007-08
19	**(10.5 overs)**	**Saracens v Colts at Colombo**	**2012-13**
23	(19.4 overs)	Middlesex v Yorkshire at Leeds	1974
30	(20.4 overs)	Chittagong v Sylhet at Dhaka	2002-03
31	(13.5 overs)	Border v South Western Districts at East London	2007-08
34	(21.1 overs)	Saurashtra v Mumbai at Mumbai	1999-2000
35	(18 overs)	Zimbabwe v Sri Lanka at Harare	2003-04
36	(25.4 overs)	Leicestershire v Sussex at Leicester	1973
36	(18.4 overs)	Canada v Sri Lanka at Paarl	2002-03
38	(15.4 overs)	Zimbabwe v Sri Lanka at Colombo	2001-02
39	(26.4 overs)	Ireland v Sussex at Hove	1985
39	(15.2 overs)	Cape Cobras v Eagles at Paarl *(one man absent)*	2008-09

LIST A TWENTY20 RECORDS

Notes: This section covers Twenty20 cricket to December 31, 2012. Bold type denotes performances in the calendar year 2012 or, in career figures, players who appeared in Twenty20 cricket in that year.

BATTING RECORDS

HIGHEST INDIVIDUAL INNINGS

158*	B. B. McCullum	Kolkata Knight Riders v RC Bangalore at Bangalore	2007-08
152*	G. R. Napier	Essex v Sussex at Chelmsford	2008
145	L. P. van der Westhuizen	Namibia v Kenya at Windhoek	2011-12
141*	C. L. White	Somerset v Worcestershire at Worcester	2006
135*	D. A. Warner	New South Wales v Chennai Super Kings at Chennai	2011-12
128*	**C. H. Gayle**	**RC Bangalore v Delhi Daredevils at Delhi**	**2011-12**
127	M. Vijay	Chennai Super Kings v Rajasthan Royals at Chennai	2009-10
125	C. G. Williams	Namibia v Kenya at Windhoek	2011-12

MOST RUNS

	Career	*M*	*I*	*NO*	*R*	*HS*	*100*	*Avge*
D. J. Hussey	**2004–*2012***	**195**	**187**	**34**	**4,749**	**100***	**1**	**31.03**
B. J. Hodge	**2003–*2012***	**164**	**159**	**27**	**4,723**	**106**	**2**	**35.78**
B. B. McCullum	***2004–2012***	**157**	**155**	**15**	**4,461**	**158***	**5**	**31.86**
C. H. Gayle	**2005–*2012***	**123**	**120**	**16**	**4,408**	**128***	**8**	**42.38**
O. A. Shah	**2003–*2012***	**161**	**154**	**37**	**4,042**	**80**	**0**	**34.54**
D. A. Warner	***2006–2012***	**139**	**138**	**10**	**3,946**	**135***	**5**	**30.82**
H. H. Gibbs	***2003–2012***	**158**	**155**	**12**	**3,735**	**101***	**1**	**26.11**
S. K. Raina	***2006–2012***	**133**	**126**	**20**	**3,506**	**101**	**1**	**33.07**
L. R. P. L. Taylor	***2005–2012***	**147**	**138**	**29**	**3,427**	**111***	**1**	**31.44**
D. P. M. D. Jayawardene	***2004–2012***	**139**	**134**	**22**	**3,384**	**110***	**2**	**30.21**
R. G. Sharma	***2006–2012***	**140**	**129**	**24**	**3,304**	**109***	**2**	**31.46**
G. Gambhir	***2006–2012***	**126**	**123**	**14**	**3,269**	**93**	**0**	**29.99**
S. B. Styris	***2004–2012***	**157**	**144**	**22**	**3,229**	**106***	**2**	**26.46**
K. A. Pollard	**2006–*2012***	**171**	**149**	**37**	**3,210**	**89***	**0**	**28.66**
J. H. Kallis	***2003–2012***	**118**	**114**	**20**	**3,206**	**89***	**0**	**34.10**
K. C. Sangakkara	***2004–2012***	**123**	**118**	**10**	**3,172**	**94**	**0**	**29.37**
S. E. Marsh	***2005–2012***	**89**	**87**	**12**	**3,123**	**115**	**2**	**41.64**
C. L. White	***2004–2012***	**142**	**133**	**32**	**3,084**	**141***	**2**	**30.53**
J-P. Duminy	***2003–2012***	**128**	**121**	**32**	**3,068**	**99***	**0**	**34.47**

HIGHEST PARTNERSHIP FOR EACH WICKET

201	**for 1st**	**P. J. Ingram and J. M. How, C. Dist. v Wellington at New Plymouth**	**2011-12**
206	for 2nd	A. C. Gilchrist and S. E. Marsh, Kings XI Punjab v Royal Challengers Bangalore at Dharmasala	2010-11
162	for 3rd	Abdul Razzaq and Nasir Jamshed, Lahore Lions v Quetta Bears at Lahore	2009
140*	for 4th	N. L. McCullum and A. D. Mascarenhas, Otago v Canterbury at Dunedin	2008-09
		E. Chigumbura and C. Zhuwawo, Northerns v Centrals at Bulawayo	2009
149	for 5th	Y. V. Takawale and S. V. Bahutule, Maharashtra v Gujarat at Mumbai	2006-07
122*	**for 6th**	**A. T. Rayudu and K. A. Pollard, Mumbai Indians v Royal Challengers Bangalore at Bangalore**	**2011-12**
99*	for 7th	A. Thyagarajan and O. M. Baker, USA v Ireland at Abu Dhabi	2009-10
120	**for 8th**	**Azhar Mahmood and I. Udana, Wayamba v Uva at Colombo**	**2012**
64	**for 9th**	**K. Magage and H. S. M. Zoysa, Burgher v Panadura at Colombo**	**2011-12**
59	for 10th	H. H. Streak and J. E. Anyon, Warwickshire v Worcs at Birmingham	2005

BOWLING RECORDS

BEST BOWLING ANALYSES

6-5	A. V. Suppiah	Somerset v Glamorgan at Cardiff	2011
6-7	**S. L. Malinga**	**Melbourne Stars v Perth Scorchers at Perth**	**2012-13**
6-8	**B. A. W. Mendis**	**Sri Lanka v Zimbabwe at Hambantota**	**2012-13**
6-14	Sohail Tanvir	Rajasthan Royals v Chennai Superstars at Jaipur	2007-08
6-15	S. R. Abeywardene	Panadura v Air Force at Colombo	2005-06
6-16	T. G. Southee	Essex v Glamorgan at Chelmsford	2011
6-16	B. A. W. Mendis	Sri Lanka v Australia at Pallekele	2011
6-16	**S. W. Masakadza**	**Mountaineers v Matabeleland Tuskers at Mutare**	**2012-13**

MOST WICKETS

	Career	*M*	*B*	*R*	*W*	*BB*	*4I*	*Avge*
D. P. Nannes	***2007–2012***	**166**	**3,571**	**4,323**	**201**	**5-40**	**7**	**21.50**
S. L. Malinga	***2004–2012***	**135**	**2,907**	**3,189**	**188**	**6-7**	**9**	**16.96**
A. C. Thomas	***2003–2012***	**156**	**3,113**	**3,784**	**181**	**4-8**	**2**	**20.90**
Yasir Arafat	***2005–2012***	**146**	**2,928**	**3,928**	**177**	**4-17**	**5**	**22.19**
J. A. Morkel	***2003–2012***	**205**	**3,401**	**4,486**	**171**	**4-30**	**2**	**26.23**
Azhar Mahmood	**2003–*2012***	**147**	**2,993**	**3,826**	**158**	**5-24**	**3**	**24.21**
Shahid Afridi	**2004–*2012***	**128**	**2,800**	**3,015**	**155**	**5-20**	**5**	**19.45**
Saeed Ajmal	***2004–2012***	**107**	**2,357**	**2,482**	**154**	**4-14**	**6**	**16.11**
M. Muralitharan	**2005–*2012***	**134**	**3,039**	**3,227**	**150**	**4-16**	**3**	**21.51**
Umar Gul	***2004–2012***	**106**	**2,270**	**2,770**	**149**	**5-6**	**9**	**18.59**
Naved-ul-Hasan	***2004–2012***	**113**	**2,377**	**2,841**	**144**	**5-17**	**3**	**19.72**
K. A. Pollard	**2006–*2012***	**171**	**2,338**	**3,073**	**137**	**4-15**	**3**	**22.43**
Abdul Razzaq	**2003–*2012***	**134**	**2,385**	**3,033**	**133**	**4-13**	**2**	**22.80**

WICKETKEEPING AND FIELDING RECORDS

MOST DISMISSALS IN AN INNINGS

7 (all ct)	E. F. M. U. Fernando	Lankan v Moors at Colombo	2005-06

MOST CATCHES IN AN INNINGS IN THE FIELD

5	Manzoor Ilahi	Jammu and Kashmir v Delhi at Delhi	2010-11
5	J. M. Vince	Hampshire v Leeward Islands at North Sound	2010-11

TEAM RECORDS

HIGHEST INNINGS TOTALS

260-6	(20 overs)	Sri Lanka v Kenya at Johannesburg	2007-08
254-3	(20 overs)	Gloucestershire v Middlesex at Uxbridge	2011
250-3	(20 overs)	Somerset v Gloucestershire at Taunton	2006
246-5	(20 overs)	Chennai Super Kings v Rajasthan Royals at Chennai	2009-10
245-4	(20 overs)	Nondescripts v Air Force at Colombo	2005-06

LOWEST INNINGS TOTALS

30	(11.1 overs)	Tripura v Jharkhand at Dhanbad	2009-10
44	**(12.5 overs)**	**Leeward Islands v Trinidad & Tobago at North Sound**	**2011-12**
47	(14.3 overs)	Titans v Eagles at Centurion	2003-04
47	(12.5 overs)	Northamptonshire v Durham at Chester-le-Street	2011
55	(10.4 overs)	Namibia v Scotland at Windhoek	2011-12

TEST RECORDS

Notes: This section covers all Tests up to January 14, 2013.
Throughout this section, bold type denotes performances since January 1, 2012, or, in career figures, players who have appeared in Test cricket since that date.

BATTING RECORDS

HIGHEST INDIVIDUAL INNINGS

400*	B. C. Lara	West Indies v England at St John's	2003-04
380	M. L. Hayden	Australia v Zimbabwe at Perth	2003-04
375	B. C. Lara	West Indies v England at St John's	1993-94
374	D. P. M. D. Jayawardene	Sri Lanka v South Africa at Colombo (SSC)	2006
365*	G. S. Sobers	West Indies v Pakistan at Kingston	1957-58
364	L. Hutton	England v Australia at The Oval	1938
340	S. T. Jayasuriya	Sri Lanka v India at Colombo (RPS)	1997-98
337	Hanif Mohammad	Pakistan v West Indies at Bridgetown	1957-58
336*	W. R. Hammond	England v New Zealand at Auckland	1932-33
334*	M. A. Taylor	Australia v Pakistan at Peshawar	1998-99
334	D. G. Bradman	Australia v England at Leeds	1930
333	G. A. Gooch	England v India at Lord's	1990
333	C. H. Gayle	West Indies v Sri Lanka at Galle	2010-11
329*	**M. J. Clarke**	**Australia v India at Sydney**	**2011-12**
329	Inzamam-ul-Haq	Pakistan v New Zealand at Lahore	2002
325	A. Sandham	England v West Indies at Kingston	1929-30
319	V. Sehwag	India v South Africa at Chennai	2007-08
317	C. H. Gayle	West Indies v South Africa at St John's	2004-05
313	Younis Khan	Pakistan v Sri Lanka at Karachi	2008-09
311*	**H. M. Amla**	**South Africa v England at The Oval**	**2012**
311	R. B. Simpson	Australia v England at Manchester	1964
310*	J. H. Edrich	England v New Zealand at Leeds	1965
309	V. Sehwag	India v Pakistan at Multan	2003-04
307	R. M. Cowper	Australia v England at Melbourne	1965-66
304	D. G. Bradman	Australia v England at Leeds	1934
302	L. G. Rowe	West Indies v England at Bridgetown	1973-74
299*	D. G. Bradman	Australia v South Africa at Adelaide	1931-32
299	M. D. Crowe	New Zealand v Sri Lanka at Wellington	1990-91
294	A. N. Cook	England v India at Birmingham	2011
293	V. Sehwag	India v Sri Lanka at Mumbai (BS)	2009-10
291	I. V. A. Richards	West Indies v England at The Oval	1976
291	R. R. Sarwan	West Indies v England at Bridgetown	2008-09
287	R. E. Foster	England v Australia at Sydney	1903-04
287	K. C. Sangakkara	Sri Lanka v South Africa at Colombo (SSC)	2006
285*	P. B. H. May	England v West Indies at Birmingham	1957
281	V. V. S. Laxman	India v Australia at Kolkata	2000-01
280*	Javed Miandad	Pakistan v India at Hyderabad	1982-83
278*	A. B. de Villiers	South Africa v Pakistan at Abu Dhabi	2010-11
278	D. C. S. Compton	England v Pakistan at Nottingham	1954
277	B. C. Lara	West Indies v Australia at Sydney	1992-93
277	G. C. Smith	South Africa v England at Birmingham	2003
275*	D. J. Cullinan	South Africa v New Zealand at Auckland	1998-99
275	G. Kirsten	South Africa v England at Durban	1999-2000
275	D. P. M. D. Jayawardene	Sri Lanka v India at Ahmedabad	2009-10

Note: There have been **39** further instances of 250 or more runs in a Test innings.

The highest innings for the countries not mentioned above are:

266	D. L. Houghton	Zimbabwe v Sri Lanka at Bulawayo	1994-95
158*	Mohammad Ashraful	Bangladesh v India at Chittagong	2004-05

HUNDRED ON TEST DEBUT

C. Bannerman (165*)	Australia v England at Melbourne	1876-77
W. G. Grace (152)	England v Australia at The Oval	1880
H. Graham (107)	Australia v England at Lord's	1893
†K. S. Ranjitsinhji (154*)	England v Australia at Manchester	1896
†P. F. Warner (132*)	England v South Africa at Johannesburg	1898-99
†R. A. Duff (104)	Australia v England at Melbourne	1901-02
§R. E. Foster (287)	England v Australia at Sydney	1903-04
G. Gunn (119)	England v Australia at Sydney	1907-08
†R. J. Hartigan (116)	Australia v England at Adelaide	1907-08
†H. L. Collins (104)	Australia v England at Sydney	1920-21
W. H. Ponsford (110)	Australia v England at Sydney	1924-25
A. A. Jackson (164)	Australia v England at Adelaide	1928-29
†G. A. Headley (176)	West Indies v England at Bridgetown	1929-30
J. E. Mills (117)	New Zealand v England at Wellington	1929-30
Nawab of Pataudi sen. (102)	England v Australia at Sydney	1932-33
B. H. Valentine (136)	England v India at Bombay	1933-34
†L. Amarnath (118)	India v England at Bombay	1933-34
†P. A. Gibb (106)	England v South Africa at Johannesburg	1938-39
S. C. Griffith (140)	England v West Indies at Port-of-Spain	1947-48
A. G. Ganteaume (112)	West Indies v England at Port-of-Spain	1947-48
†J. W. Burke (101*)	Australia v England at Adelaide	1950-51
P. B. H. May (138)	England v South Africa at Leeds	1951
R. H. Shodhan (110)	India v Pakistan at Calcutta	1952-53
B. H. Pairaudeau (115)	West Indies v India at Port-of-Spain	1952-53
†O. G. Smith (104)	West Indies v Australia at Kingston	1954-55
A. G. Kripal Singh (100*)	India v New Zealand at Hyderabad	1955-56
C. C. Hunte (142)	West Indies v Pakistan at Bridgetown	1957-58
C. A. Milton (104*)	England v New Zealand at Leeds	1958
†A. A. Baig (112)	India v England at Manchester	1959
Hanumant Singh (105)	India v England at Delhi	1963-64
Khalid Ibadulla (166)	Pakistan v Australia at Karachi	1964-65
B. R. Taylor (105)	New Zealand v India at Calcutta	1964-65
K. D. Walters (155)	Australia v England at Brisbane	1965-66
J. H. Hampshire (107)	England v West Indies at Lord's	1969
†G. R. Viswanath (137)	India v Australia at Kanpur	1969-70
G. S. Chappell (108)	Australia v England at Perth	1970-71
‡§L. G. Rowe (214, 100*)	West Indies v New Zealand at Kingston	1971-72
A. I. Kallicharran (100*)	West Indies v New Zealand at Georgetown	1971-72
R. E. Redmond (107)	New Zealand v Pakistan at Auckland	1972-73
†F. C. Hayes (106*)	England v West Indies at The Oval	1973
†C. G. Greenidge (107)	West Indies v India at Bangalore	1974-75
†L. Baichan (105*)	West Indies v Pakistan at Lahore	1974-75
G. J. Cosier (109)	Australia v West Indies at Melbourne	1975-76
S. Amarnath (124)	India v New Zealand at Auckland	1975-76
Javed Miandad (163)	Pakistan v New Zealand at Lahore	1976-77
†A. B. Williams (100)	West Indies v Australia at Georgetown	1977-78
†D. M. Wellham (103)	Australia v England at The Oval	1981
†Salim Malik (100*)	Pakistan v Sri Lanka at Karachi	1981-82
K. C. Wessels (162)	Australia v England at Brisbane	1982-83
W. B. Phillips (159)	Australia v Pakistan at Perth	1983-84
¶M. Azharuddin (110)	India v England at Calcutta	1984-85
D. S. B. P. Kuruppu (201*)	Sri Lanka v New Zealand at Colombo (CCC)	1986-87
†M. J. Greatbatch (107*)	New Zealand v England at Auckland	1987-88
M. E. Waugh (138)	Australia v England at Adelaide	1990-91
A. C. Hudson (163)	South Africa v West Indies at Bridgetown	1991-92
R. S. Kaluwitharana (132*)	Sri Lanka v Australia at Colombo (SSC)	1992-93
D. L. Houghton (121)	Zimbabwe v India at Harare	1992-93
P. K. Amre (103)	India v South Africa at Durban	1992-93
†G. P. Thorpe (114*)	England v Australia at Nottingham	1993

G. S. Blewett (102*)	Australia v England at Adelaide	1994-95
S. C. Ganguly (131)	India v England at Lord's	1996
†Mohammad Wasim (109*)	Pakistan v New Zealand at Lahore	1996-97
Ali Naqvi (115)	Pakistan v South Africa at Rawalpindi	1997-98
Azhar Mahmood (128*)	Pakistan v South Africa at Rawalpindi	1997-98
M. S. Sinclair (214)	New Zealand v West Indies at Wellington	1999-2000
†Younis Khan (107)	Pakistan v Sri Lanka at Rawalpindi	1999-2000
Aminul Islam (145)	Bangladesh v India at Dhaka	2000-01
†H. Masakadza (119)	Zimbabwe v West Indies at Harare	2001
T. T. Samaraweera (103*)	Sri Lanka v India at Colombo (SSC)	2001
Taufeeq Umar (104)	Pakistan v Bangladesh at Multan	2001-02
†Mohammad Ashraful (114)	Bangladesh v Sri Lanka at Colombo (SSC)	2001-02
V. Sehwag (105)	India v South Africa at Bloemfontein	2001-02
L. Vincent (104)	New Zealand v Australia at Perth	2001-02
S. B. Styris (107)	New Zealand v West Indies at St George's	2002
J. A. Rudolph (222*)	South Africa v Bangladesh at Chittagong	2003
‡Yasir Hameed (170, 105)	Pakistan v Bangladesh at Karachi	2003
†D. R. Smith (105*)	West Indies v South Africa at Cape Town	2003-04
A. J. Strauss (112)	England v New Zealand at Lord's	2004
M. J. Clarke (151)	Australia v India at Bangalore	2004-05
†A. N. Cook (104*)	England v India at Nagpur	2005-06
M. J. Prior (126*)	England v West Indies at Lord's	2007
M. J. North (117)	Australia v South Africa at Johannesburg	2008-09
†Fawad Alam (168)	Pakistan v Sri Lanka at Colombo (PSS)	2009
†I. J. L. Trott (119)	England v Australia at The Oval	2009
Umar Akmal (129)	Pakistan v New Zealand at Dunedin	2009-10
†A. B. Barath (104)	West Indies v Australia at Brisbane	2009-10
A. N. Petersen (100)	South Africa v India at Kolkata	2009-10
S. K. Raina (120)	India v Sri Lanka at Colombo (SSC)	2010
K. S. Williamson (131)	New Zealand v India at Ahmedabad	2010-11
†K. A. Edwards (110)	West Indies v India at Roseau	2011
S. E. Marsh (141)	Australia v Sri Lanka at Pallekele	2011-12
Abul Hasan (113)	**Bangladesh v West Indies at Khulna**	**2012-13**
†F. du Plessis (110*)	**South Africa v Australia at Adelaide**	**2012-13**

† *In his second innings of the match.*
‡ *L. G. Rowe and Yasir Hameed are the only batsmen to score a hundred in each innings on debut.*
§ *R. E. Foster (287, 19) and L. G. Rowe (214, 100*) are the only batsmen to score 300 runs in their debut Tests.*
¶ *M. Azharuddin is the only batsman to score hundreds in each of his first three Tests.*

Notes: L. Amarnath and S. Amarnath were father and son.
Ali Naqvi and Azhar Mahmood achieved the feat in the same innings.
Only Bannerman, Houghton and Aminul Islam scored hundreds in their country's first Test.

TRIPLE-HUNDRED AND HUNDRED IN A TEST

G. A. Gooch (England)	333 and 123 v India at Lord's	1990

The only instance in first-class cricket. M. A. Taylor (Australia) scored 334 and 92 v Pakistan at Peshawar in 1998-99.*

DOUBLE-HUNDRED AND HUNDRED IN A TEST

K. D. Walters (Australia)	242 and 103 v West Indies at Sydney	1968-69
S. M. Gavaskar (India)	124 and 220 v West Indies at Port-of-Spain	1970-71
†L. G. Rowe (West Indies)	214 and 100* v New Zealand at Kingston	1971-72
G. S. Chappell (Australia)	247* and 133 v New Zealand at Wellington	1973-74
B. C. Lara (West Indies)	221 and 130 v Sri Lanka at Colombo (SSC)	2001-02

† *On Test debut.*

TWO SEPARATE HUNDREDS IN A TEST

S. M. Gavaskar (I)	3	G. A. Gooch (E)	1	J. Moroney (A)	1
R. T. Ponting (A)	**3**	C. G. Greenidge (WI)	1	A. R. Morris (A)	1
A. R. Border (A)	2†	A. P. Gurusinha (SL)	1	E. Paynter (E)	1
G. S. Chappell (A)	2	W. R. Hammond (E)	1	**K. O. A. Powell (WI)**	**1**
P. A. de Silva (SL)	2‡	Hanif Mohammad (P)	1	L. G. Rowe (WI)	1¶
R. Dravid (I)	**2**	V. S. Hazare (I)	1	A. C. Russell (E)	1
M. L. Hayden (A)	2	G. P. Howarth (NZ)	1	R. B. Simpson (A)	1
G. A. Headley (WI)	2	**P. J. Hughes (A)**	**1**	G. S. Sobers (WI)	1
J. H. Kallis (SA)	**2**	Inzamam-ul-Haq (P)	1	A. J. Stewart (E)	1
H. Sutcliffe (E)	2	Javed Miandad (P)	1	**A. J. Strauss (E)**	**1**
C. L. Walcott (WI)	2§	A. H. Jones (NZ)	1	M. E. Trescothick (E)	1
H. M. Amla (SA)	**1**	D. M. Jones (A)	1	G. M. Turner (NZ)	1
W. Bardsley (A)	1	R. B. Kanhai (WI)	1	M. P. Vaughan (E)	1
D. G. Bradman (A)	1	G. Kirsten (SA)	1	Wajahatullah Wasti (P)	1
I. M. Chappell (A)	1	B. C. Lara (WI)	1	K. D. Walters (A)	1
D. C. S. Compton (E)	1	A. Melville (SA)	1	S. R. Waugh (A)	1
T. M. Dilshan (SL)	**1**	L. R. D. Mendis (SL)	1	E. D. Weekes (WI)	1
A. Flower (Z)	1	B. Mitchell (SA)	1	Yasir Hameed (P)	1¶
G. W. Flower (Z)	1	Mohammad Yousuf (P)	1		

† *A. R. Border scored 150* and 153 against Pakistan in 1979-80 to become the first to score 150 in each innings of a Test match.*
‡ *P. A. de Silva scored 138* and 103* against Pakistan in 1996-97 to become the first to score two not-out hundreds in a Test match.*
§ *C. L. Walcott scored twin hundreds twice in one series, against Australia in 1954-55.*
¶ *L. G. Rowe's and Yasir Hameed's two hundreds were on Test debut.*

MOST DOUBLE-HUNDREDS

D. G. Bradman (A)	12	**R. T. Ponting (A)**	**6**	C. G. Greenidge (WI)	4
B. C. Lara (WI)	9	**V. Sehwag (I)**	**6**	L. Hutton (E)	4
K. C. Sangakkara (SL)	**8**	**S. R. Tendulkar (I)**	**6**	Mohammad Yousuf (P)	4
W. R. Hammond (E)	7	**R. Dravid (I)**	**5**	**G. C. Smith (SA)**	**4**
M. S. Atapattu (SL)	6	G. S. Chappell (A)	4	Zaheer Abbas (P)	4
Javed Miandad (P)	6	†**M. J. Clarke (A)**	**4**		
D. P. M. D. Jayawardene (SL)	**6**	S. M. Gavaskar (I)	4		

† *All of Clarke's four double-hundreds came in the calendar year 2012.*

MOST HUNDREDS

S. R. Tendulkar (I)	**51**	**G. C. Smith (SA)**	**26**	M. C. Cowdrey (E)	22
J. H. Kallis (SA)	**44**	G. S. Sobers (WI)	26	W. R. Hammond (E)	22
R. T. Ponting (A)	**41**	Inzamam-ul-Haq (P)	25	**K. P. Pietersem (E)**	**22**
R. Dravid (I)	**36**	G. S. Chappell (A)	24	D. C. Boon (A)	21
S. M. Gavaskar (I)	34	Mohammad Yousuf (P)	24	R. N. Harvey (A)	21
B. C. Lara (WI)	34	I. V. A. Richards (WI)	24	G. Kirsten (SA)	21
S. R. Waugh (A)	32	**A. N. Cook (E)**	**23**	**A. J. Strauss (E)**	**21**
D. P. M. D. Jayawardene (SL)	**31**	Javed Miandad (P)	23	K. F. Barrington (E)	20
M. L. Hayden (A)	30	J. L. Langer (A)	23	P. A. de Silva (SL)	20
K. C. Sangakkara (SL)	**30**	**V. Sehwag (I)**	**23**	G. A. Gooch (E)	20
D. G. Bradman (A)	29	M. Azharuddin (I)	22	M. E. Waugh (A)	20
A. R. Border (A)	27	G. Boycott (E)	22	**Younis Khan (P)**	**20**
S. Chanderpaul (WI)	**27**	**M. J. Clarke (A)**	**22**		

Note: The most hundreds for New Zealand is 17 by M. D. Crowe, the most for Zimbabwe is 12 by A. Flower, and the most for Bangladesh is 5 by Mohammad Ashraful.

MOST HUNDREDS AGAINST ONE TEAM

D. G. Bradman	19	Australia v England	**S. R. Tendulkar**	**11**	**India v Australia**
S. M. Gavaskar	13	India v West Indies	G. S. Sobers	10	West Indies v England
J. B. Hobbs	12	England v Australia	S. R. Waugh	10	Australia v England

MOST DUCKS

	0s	*Inns*		*0s*	*Inns*
C. A. Walsh (WI)	43	185	B. S. Chandrasekhar (I)	23	80
C. S. Martin (NZ)	**36**	**104**	M. S. Atapattu (SL)	22	156
G. D. McGrath (A)	35	138	S. R. Waugh (A)	22	260
S. K. Warne (A)	34	199	S. J. Harmison (E)	21	86
M. Muralitharan (SL)	33	164	M. Ntini (SA)	21	116
Zaheer Khan (I)	**27**	**120**	Waqar Younis (P)	21	120
M. Dillon (WI)	26	68	B. S. Bedi (I)	20	101
C. E. L. Ambrose (WI)	26	145	**D. L. Vettori (NZ/World)**	**20**	**173**
Danish Kaneria (P)	25	84	M. A. Atherton (E)	20	212
D. K. Morrison (NZ)	24	71			

CARRYING BAT THROUGH TEST INNINGS

(Figures in brackets show team's total)

A. B. Tancred	26*	(47)	South Africa v England at Cape Town	1888-89
J. E. Barrett	67*	(176)†	Australia v England at Lord's	1890
R. Abel	132*	(307)	England v Australia at Sydney	1891-92
P. F. Warner	132*	(237)†	England v South Africa at Johannesburg	1898-99
W. W. Armstrong	159*	(309)	Australia v South Africa at Johannesburg	1902-03
J. W. Zulch	43*	(103)	South Africa v England at Cape Town	1909-10
W. Bardsley	193*	(383)	Australia v England at Lord's	1926
W. M. Woodfull	30*	(66)§	Australia v England at Brisbane	1928-29
W. M. Woodfull	73*	(193)‡	Australia v England at Adelaide	1932-33
W. A. Brown	206*	(422)	Australia v England at Lord's	1938
L. Hutton	202*	(344)	England v West Indies at The Oval	1950
L. Hutton	156*	(272)	England v Australia at Adelaide	1950-51
Nazar Mohammad¶	124*	(331)	Pakistan v India at Lucknow	1952-53
F. M. M. Worrell	191*	(372)	West Indies v England at Nottingham	1957
T. L. Goddard	56*	(99)	South Africa v Australia at Cape Town	1957-58
D. J. McGlew	127*	(292)	South Africa v New Zealand at Durban	1961-62
C. C. Hunte	60*	(131)	West Indies v Australia at Port-of-Spain	1964-65
G. M. Turner	43*	(131)	New Zealand v England at Lord's	1969
W. M. Lawry	49*	(107)	Australia v India at Delhi	1969-70
W. M. Lawry	60*	(116)‡	Australia v England at Sydney	1970-71
G. M. Turner	223*	(386)	New Zealand v West Indies at Kingston	1971-72
I. R. Redpath	159*	(346)	Australia v New Zealand at Auckland	1973-74
G. Boycott	99*	(215)	England v Australia at Perth	1979-80
S. M. Gavaskar	127*	(286)	India v Pakistan at Faisalabad	1982-83
Mudassar Nazar¶	152*	(323)	Pakistan v India at Lahore	1982-83
S. Wettimuny	63*	(144)	Sri Lanka v New Zealand at Christchurch	1982-83
D. C. Boon	58*	(103)	Australia v New Zealand at Auckland	1985-86
D. L. Haynes	88*	(211)	West Indies v Pakistan at Karachi	1986-87
G. A. Gooch	154*	(252)	England v West Indies at Leeds	1991
D. L. Haynes	75*	(176)	West Indies v England at The Oval	1991
A. J. Stewart	69*	(175)	England v Pakistan at Lord's	1992
D. L. Haynes	143*	(382)	West Indies v Pakistan at Port-of-Spain	1992-93
M. H. Dekker	68*	(187)	Zimbabwe v Pakistan at Rawalpindi	1993-94
M. A. Atherton	94*	(228)	England v New Zealand at Christchurch	1996-97
G. Kirsten	100*	(239)	South Africa v Pakistan at Faisalabad	1997-98
M. A. Taylor	169*	(350)	Australia v South Africa at Adelaide	1997-98
G. W. Flower	156*	(321)	Zimbabwe v Pakistan at Bulawayo	1997-98
Saeed Anwar	188*	(316)	Pakistan v India at Calcutta	1998-99

M. S. Atapattu	216*	(428)	Sri Lanka v Zimbabwe at Bulawayo	1999-2000
R. P. Arnold	104*	(231)	Sri Lanka v Zimbabwe at Harare	1999-2000
Javed Omar	85*	(168)†‡	Bangladesh v Zimbabwe at Bulawayo	2000-01
V. Sehwag	201*	(329)	India v Sri Lanka at Galle	2008
S. M. Katich	131*	(268)	Australia v New Zealand at Brisbane	2008-09
C. H. Gayle	165*	(317)	West Indies v Australia at Adelaide	2009-10
Imran Farhat	117*	(223)	Pakistan v New Zealand at Napier	2009-10
R. Dravid	146*	(300)	India v England at The Oval	2011
T. M. K. Mawoyo	163*	(412)	Zimbabwe v Pakistan at Bulawayo	2011-12
D. A. Warner	123*	(233)	Australia v New Zealand at Hobart	2011-12

† *On debut.* ‡*One man absent.* § *Two men absent.* ¶ *Father and son.*

Notes: G. M. Turner (223*) holds the record for the highest score by a player carrying his bat through a Test innings. He is also the youngest player to do so, being 22 years 63 days old when he first achieved the feat (1969).

D. L. Haynes, who is alone in achieving this feat on three occasions, also opened the batting and was last man out in each innings for West Indies v New Zealand at Dunedin, 1979-80.

750 RUNS IN A SERIES

	T	*I*	*NO*	*R*	*HS*	*100*	*Avge*		
D. G. Bradman	5	7	0	974	334	4	139.14	A v E	1930
W. R. Hammond . . .	5	9	1	905	251	4	113.12	E v A	1928-29
M. A. Taylor	6	11	1	839	219	2	83.90	A v E	1989
R. N. Harvey	5	9	0	834	205	4	92.66	A v SA	1952-53
I. V. A. Richards . . .	4	7	0	829	291	3	118.42	WI v E	1976
C. L. Walcott	5	10	0	827	155	5	82.70	WI v A	1954-55
G. S. Sobers	5	8	2	824	365*	3	137.33	WI v P	1957-58
D. G. Bradman	5	9	0	810	270	3	90.00	A v E	1936-37
D. G. Bradman	5	5	1	806	299*	4	201.50	A v SA	1931-32
B. C. Lara	5	8	0	798	375	2	99.75	WI v E	1993-94
E. D. Weekes	5	7	0	779	194	4	111.28	WI v I	1948-49
†S. M. Gavaskar	4	8	3	774	220	4	154.80	I v WI	1970-71
A. N. Cook	5	7	1	766	235*	3	127.66	E v A	2010-11
B. C. Lara	6	10	1	765	179	3	85.00	WI v E	1995
Mudassar Nazar . . .	6	8	2	761	231	4	126.83	P v I	1982-83
D. G. Bradman	5	8	0	758	304	2	94.75	A v E	1934
D. C. S. Compton . .	5	8	0	753	208	4	94.12	E v SA	1947
‡G. A. Gooch	3	6	0	752	333	3	125.33	E v I	1990

† *Gavaskar's aggregate was achieved in his first Test series.*
‡ *G. A. Gooch is alone in scoring 1,000 runs in Test cricket during an English season with 1,058 runs in 11 innings against New Zealand and India in 1990.*

MOST RUNS IN A CALENDAR YEAR

	T	*I*	*NO*	*R*	*HS*	*100*	*Avge*	*Year*
Mohammad Yousuf (P)	11	19	1	1,788	202	9	99.33	2006
I. V. A. Richards (WI)	11	19	0	1,710	291	7	90.00	1976
G. C. Smith (SA)	15	25	2	1,656	232	6	72.00	2008
M. J. Clarke (A)	**11**	**18**	**3**	**1,595**	**329***	**5**	**106.33**	**2012**
S. R. Tendulkar (I)	14	23	3	1,562	214	7	78.10	2010
S. M. Gavaskar (I)	18	27	1	1,555	221	5	59.80	1979
R. T. Ponting (A)	15	28	5	1,544	207	6	67.13	2005
R. T. Ponting (A)	11	18	3	1,503	257	6	100.20	2003
J. L. Langer (A)	14	27	0	1,481	215	5	54.85	2004
M. P. Vaughan (E)	14	26	2	1,481	197	6	61.70	2002
V. Sehwag (I)	14	27	1	1,462	319	3	56.23	2008

Notes: M. Amarnath reached 1,000 runs in 1983 on May 3.

The only batsman to score 1,000 runs in a year before World War II was C. Hill of Australia: 1,060 in 1902.

M. L. Hayden (Australia) scored 1,000 runs in each year from 2001 to 2005.

MOST RUNS

1	**S. R. Tendulkar (India)**	**15,645**	22	G. Boycott (England)	8,114
2	**R. T. Ponting (Australia)**	**13,378**	23	G. S. Sobers (West Indies)	8,032
3	**R. Dravid (India/World)**	**13,288**	24	M. E. Waugh (Australia)	8,029
4	**J. H. Kallis (South Africa/World)**	**13,048**	25	M. A. Atherton (England)	7,728
5	B. C. Lara (West Indies/World)	11,953	26	J. L. Langer (Australia)	7,696
6	A. R. Border (Australia)	11,174	27	M. C. Cowdrey (England)	7,624
7	S. R. Waugh (Australia)	10,927	28	C. G. Greenidge (West Indies)	7,558
8	**D. P. M. D. Jayawardene (SL)**	**10,806**	29	Mohammad Yousuf (Pakistan)	7,530
9	**S. Chanderpaul (West Indies)**	**10,696**	30	M. A. Taylor (Australia)	7,525
10	S. M. Gavaskar (India)	10,122	31	C. H. Lloyd (West Indies)	7,515
11	**K. C. Sangakkara (Sri Lanka)**	**10,045**	32	D. L. Haynes (West Indies)	7,487
12	G. A. Gooch (England)	8,900	33	D. C. Boon (Australia)	7,422
13	Javed Miandad (Pakistan)	8,832	**34**	**K. P. Pietersen (England)**	**7,414**
14	Inzamam-ul-Haq (Pakistan/World)	8,830	35	G. Kirsten (South Africa)	7,289
15	**V. V. S. Laxman (India)**	**8,781**	36	W. R. Hammond (England)	7,249
16	M. L. Hayden (Australia)	8,625	37	S. C. Ganguly (India)	7,212
17	**G. C. Smith (South Africa/Wld)**	**8,624**	38	S. P. Fleming (New Zealand)	7,172
18	**V. Sehwag (India/World)**	**8,559**	**39**	**A. N. Cook (England)**	**7,117**
19	I. V. A. Richards (West Indies)	8,540	40	G. S. Chappell (Australia)	7,110
20	A. J. Stewart (England)	8,463	**41**	**A. J. Strauss (England)**	**7,037**
21	D. I. Gower (England)	8,231	42	D. G. Bradman (Australia)	6,996

MOST RUNS FOR EACH COUNTRY

ENGLAND

		T	*I*	*NO*	*R*	*HS*	*100*	*Avge*
1	G. A. Gooch	118	215	6	8,900	333	20	42.58
2	A. J. Stewart	133	235	21	8,463	190	15	39.54
3	D. I. Gower	117	204	18	8,231	215	18	44.25
4	G. Boycott	108	193	23	8,114	246*	22	47.72
5	M. A. Atherton	115	212	7	7,728	185*	16	37.69
6	M. C. Cowdrey	114	188	15	7,624	182	22	44.06
7	**K. P. Pietersen**	**92**	**158**	**8**	**7,414**	**227**	**22**	**49.42**
8	W. R. Hammond	85	140	16	7,249	336*	22	58.45
9	**A. N. Cook**	**87**	**154**	**10**	**7,117**	**294**	**23**	**49.42**
10	**A. J. Strauss**	**100**	**178**	**6**	**7,037**	**177**	**21**	**40.91**
11	L. Hutton	79	138	15	6,971	364	19	56.67
12	K. F. Barrington	82	131	15	6,806	256	20	58.67
13	G. P. Thorpe	100	179	28	6,744	200*	16	44.66
14	M. E. Trescothick	76	143	10	5,825	219	14	43.79
15	D. C. S. Compton	78	131	15	5,807	278	17	50.06
16	N. Hussain	96	171	16	5,764	207	14	37.18
17	M. P. Vaughan	82	147	9	5,719	197	18	41.44
18	**I. R. Bell**	**83**	**141**	**19**	**5,699**	**235**	**17**	**46.71**
19	J. B. Hobbs	61	102	7	5,410	211	15	56.94
20	I. T. Botham	102	161	6	5,200	208	14	33.54
21	J. H. Edrich	77	127	9	5,138	310*	12	43.54

AUSTRALIA

		T	*I*	*NO*	*R*	*HS*	*100*	*Avge*
1	**R. T. Ponting**	**168**	**287**	**29**	**13,378**	**257**	**41**	**51.85**
2	A. R. Border	156	265	44	11,174	205	27	50.56
3	S. R. Waugh	168	260	46	10,927	200	32	51.06
4	M. L. Hayden	103	184	14	8,625	380	30	50.73

		T	*I*	*NO*	*R*	*HS*	*100*	*Avge*
5	M. E. Waugh	128	209	17	8,029	153*	20	41.81
6	J. L. Langer	105	182	12	7,696	250	23	45.27
7	M. A. Taylor	104	186	13	7,525	334*	19	43.49
8	D. C. Boon	107	190	20	7,422	200	21	43.65
9	G. S. Chappell	87	151	19	7,110	247*	24	53.86
10	D. G. Bradman	52	80	10	6,996	334	29	99.94
11	**M. J. Clarke**	**89**	**148**	**15**	**6,989**	**329***	**22**	**52.54**
12	**M. E. K. Hussey**	**79**	**137**	**16**	**6,235**	**195**	**19**	**51.52**
13	R. N. Harvey	79	137	10	6,149	205	21	48.41
14	A. C. Gilchrist	96	137	20	5,570	204*	17	47.60
15	K. D. Walters	74	125	14	5,357	250	15	48.26
16	I. M. Chappell	75	136	10	5,345	196	14	42.42
17	M. J. Slater	74	131	7	5,312	219	14	42.83
18	W. M. Lawry	67	123	12	5,234	210	13	47.15

SOUTH AFRICA

		T	*I*	*NO*	*R*	*HS*	*100*	*Avge*
1	**J. H. Kallis**	**159†**	**268**	**39**	**12,965**	**224**	**44**	**56.61**
2	**G. C. Smith**	**106†**	**185**	**12**	**8,612**	**277**	**26**	**49.78**
3	G. Kirsten	101	176	15	7,289	275	21	45.27
4	H. H. Gibbs	90	154	7	6,167	228	14	41.95
5	**A. B. de Villiers**	**82**	**137**	**15**	**6,012**	**278***	**14**	**49.27**
6	**H. M. Amla**	**67**	**116**	**9**	**5,499**	**311***	**19**	**51.39**
7	**M. V. Boucher**	**146†**	**204**	**24**	**5,498**	**125**	**5**	**30.54**

† *J. H. Kallis also scored 44 and 39*, G. C. Smith 12 and 0, and M. V. Boucher 0 and 17 for the ICC World XI v Australia in the Super Series Test of 2005-06.*

WEST INDIES

		T	*I*	*NO*	*R*	*HS*	*100*	*Avge*
1	B. C. Lara	130†	230	6	11,912	400*	34	53.17
2	**S. Chanderpaul**	**146**	**249**	**42**	**10,696**	**203***	**27**	**51.67**
3	I. V. A. Richards	121	182	12	8,540	291	24	50.23
4	G. S. Sobers	93	160	21	8,032	365*	26	57.78
5	C. G. Greenidge	108	185	16	7,558	226	19	44.72
6	C. H. Lloyd	110	175	14	7,515	242*	19	46.67
7	D. L. Haynes	116	202	25	7,487	184	18	42.29
8	**C. H. Gayle**	**95**	**167**	**8**	**6,691**	**333**	**14**	**42.08**
9	R. B. Kanhai	79	137	6	6,227	256	15	47.53
10	R. B. Richardson	86	146	12	5,949	194	16	44.39
11	R. R. Sarwan	87	154	8	5,842	291	15	40.01
12	C. L. Hooper	102	173	15	5,762	233	13	36.46

† *B. C. Lara also scored 5 and 36 for the ICC World XI v Australia in the Super Series Test of 2005-06.*

NEW ZEALAND

		T	*I*	*NO*	*R*	*HS*	*100*	*Avge*
1	S. P. Fleming	111	189	10	7,172	274*	9	40.06
2	M. D. Crowe	77	131	11	5,444	299	17	45.36
3	J. G. Wright	82	148	7	5,334	185	12	37.82

An expanded and regularly updated online version of the Records can be found at www.wisdenrecords.com

INDIA

		T	*I*	*NO*	*R*	*HS*	*100*	*Avge*
1	**S. R. Tendulkar**	**194**	**320**	**32**	**15,645**	**248***	**51**	**54.32**
2	**R. Dravid**	**163†**	**284**	**32**	**13,265**	**270**	**36**	**52.63**
3	S. M. Gavaskar	125	214	16	10,122	236*	34	51.12
4	**V. V. S. Laxman**	**134**	**225**	**34**	**8,781**	**281**	**17**	**45.97**
5	**V. Sehwag**	**101†**	**175**	**6**	**8,476**	**319**	**23**	**50.15**
6	S. C. Ganguly	113	188	17	7,212	239	16	42.17
7	D. B. Vengsarkar	116	185	22	6,868	166	17	42.13
8	M. Azharuddin	99	147	9	6,215	199	22	45.03
9	G. R. Viswanath	91	155	10	6,080	222	14	41.93
10	Kapil Dev	131	184	15	5,248	163	8	31.05

† *R. Dravid also scored 0 and 23, and V. Sehwag also scored 76 and 7, for the ICC World XI v Australia in the Super Series Test of 2005-06.*

PAKISTAN

		T	*I*	*NO*	*R*	*HS*	*100*	*Avge*
1	Javed Miandad	124	189	21	8,832	280*	23	52.57
2	Inzamam-ul-Haq	119†	198	22	8,829	329	25	50.16
3	Mohammad Yousuf	90	156	12	7,530	223	24	52.29
4	**Younis Khan**	**79**	**138**	**11**	**6,565**	**313**	**20**	**51.69**
5	Salim Malik	103	154	22	5,768	237	15	43.69
6	Zaheer Abbas	78	124	11	5,062	274	12	44.79

† *Inzamam-ul-Haq also scored 1 and 0 for the ICC World XI v Australia in the Super Series Test of 2005-06.*

SRI LANKA

		T	*I*	*NO*	*R*	*HS*	*100*	*Avge*
1	**D. P. M. D. Jayawardene**	**138**	**232**	**14**	**10,806**	**374**	**31**	**49.56**
2	**K. C. Sangakkara**	**115**	**196**	**16**	**10,045**	**287**	**30**	**55.80**
3	S. T. Jayasuriya	110	188	14	6,973	340	14	40.07
4	P. A. de Silva	93	159	11	6,361	267	20	42.97
5	M. S. Atapattu	90	156	15	5,502	249	16	39.02
6	**T. T. Samaraweera**	**81**	**132**	**20**	**5,462**	**231**	**14**	**48.76**
7	**T. M. Dilshan**	**85**	**141**	**11**	**5,255**	**193**	**15**	**40.42**
8	A. Ranatunga	93	155	12	5,105	135*	4	35.69

ZIMBABWE

No player has scored 5,000 Test runs for Zimbabwe. The highest total is:

	T	*I*	*NO*	*R*	*HS*	*100*	*Avge*
A. Flower	63	112	19	4,794	232*	12	51.54

BANGLADESH

No player has scored 5,000 Test runs for Bangladesh. The highest total is:

	T	*I*	*NO*	*R*	*HS*	*100*	*Avge*
Habibul Bashar	50	99	1	3,026	113	3	30.87

CAREER AVERAGE OVER 50

(Qualification: 20 innings)

Avge		*T*	*I*	*NO*	*R*	*HS*	*100*
99.94	D. G. Bradman (A)	52	80	10	6,996	334	29
60.97	R. G. Pollock (SA)	23	41	4	2,256	274	7
60.83	G. A. Headley (WI)	22	40	4	2,190	270*	10
60.73	H. Sutcliffe (E)	54	84	9	4,555	194	16
59.23	E. Paynter (E)	20	31	5	1,540	243	4
58.67	K. F. Barrington (E)	82	131	15	6,806	256	20
58.61	E. D. Weekes (WI)	48	81	5	4,455	207	15
58.45	W. R. Hammond (E)	85	140	16	7,249	336*	22
57.78	G. S. Sobers (WI)	93	160	21	8,032	365*	26
56.94	J. B. Hobbs (E)	61	102	7	5,410	211	15
56.73	**J. H. Kallis (SA/World)**	**160**	**270**	**40**	**13,048**	**224**	**44**
56.68	C. L. Walcott (WI)	44	74	7	3,798	220	15
56.67	L. Hutton (E)	79	138	15	6,971	364	19
55.80	**K. C. Sangakkara (SL)**	**115**	**196**	**16**	**10,045**	**287**	**30**
55.00	E. Tyldesley (E)	14	20	2	990	122	3
54.32	**S. R. Tendulkar (I)**	**194**	**320**	**32**	**15,645**	**248***	**51**
54.20	C. A. Davis (WI)	15	29	5	1,301	183	4
54.20	V. G. Kambli (I)	17	21	1	1,084	227	4
53.86	G. S. Chappell (A)	87	151	19	7,110	247*	24
53.81	A. D. Nourse (SA)	34	62	7	2,960	231	9
52.88	B. C. Lara (WI/World)	131	232	6	11,953	400*	34
52.57	Javed Miandad (P)	124	189	21	8,832	280*	23
52.54	**M. J. Clarke (A)**	**89**	**148**	**15**	**6,989**	**329***	**22**
52.31	**R. Dravid (I/World)**	**164**	**286**	**32**	**13,288**	**270**	**36**
52.29	Mohammad Yousuf (P)	90	156	12	7,530	223	24
51.85	**R. T. Ponting (A)**	**168**	**287**	**29**	**13,378**	**257**	**41**
51.69	**Younis Khan (P)**	**79**	**138**	**11**	**6,565**	**313**	**20**
51.67	**S. Chanderpaul (WI)**	**146**	**249**	**42**	**10,696**	**203***	**27**
51.62	J. Ryder (A)	20	32	5	1,394	201*	3
51.54	A. Flower (Z)	63	112	19	4,794	232*	12
51.52	**M. E. K. Hussey (A)**	**79**	**137**	**16**	**6,235**	**195**	**19**
51.39	**H. M. Amla (SA)**	**67**	**116**	**9**	**5,499**	**311***	**19**
51.12	S. M. Gavaskar (I)	125	214	16	10,122	236*	34
51.06	S. R. Waugh (A)	168	260	46	10,927	200	32
50.73	M. L. Hayden (A)	103	184	14	8,625	380	30
50.56	A. R. Border (A)	156	265	44	11,174	205	27
50.23	I. V. A. Richards (WI)	121	182	12	8,540	291	24
50.06	D. C. S. Compton (E)	78	131	15	5,807	278	17
50.05	**V. Sehwag (I/World)**	**102**	**177**	**6**	**8,559**	**319**	**23**

Note: S. G. Barnes (A) scored 1,072 runs at 63.05 from 19 innings.

HIGHEST PERCENTAGE OF TEAM'S RUNS OVER TEST CAREER

(Qualification: 20 Tests)

	Tests	*Runs*	*Team Runs*	*% of Team Runs*
D. G. Bradman (Australia)	52	6,996	28,810	24.28
G. A. Headley (West Indies)	22	2,190	10,239	21.38
B. C. Lara (West Indies)	131	11,953	63,328	18.87
L. Hutton (England)	79	6,971	38,440	18.13
J. B. Hobbs (England)	61	5,410	30,211	17.90
A. D. Nourse (South Africa)	34	2,960	16,659	17.76

	Tests	*Runs*	*Team Runs*	*% of Team Runs*
E. D. Weekes (West Indies)	48	4,455	25,667	17.35
B. Mitchell (South Africa)	42	3,471	20,175	17.20
H. Sutcliffe (England)	54	4,555	26,604	17.12
B. Sutcliffe (New Zealand)	42	2,727	16,158	16.87

The percentage shows the proportion of a team's runs scored by that player in all Tests in which he played, including team runs in innings in which he did not bat.

FASTEST FIFTIES

Minutes			
27	Mohammad Ashraful	Bangladesh v India at Mirpur	2007
28	J. T. Brown	England v Australia at Melbourne	1894-95
29	S. A. Durani	India v England at Kanpur	1963-64
30	E. A. V. Williams	West Indies v England at Bridgetown	1947-48
30	B. R. Taylor	New Zealand v West Indies at Auckland	1968-69

The fastest fifties in terms of balls received (where recorded) are:

Balls			
24	J. H. Kallis	South Africa v Zimbabwe at Cape Town	2004-05
26	Shahid Afridi	Pakistan v India at Bangalore	2004-05
26	Mohammad Ashraful	Bangladesh v India at Mirpur	2007
27	Yousuf Youhana	Pakistan v South Africa at Cape Town	2002-03
28	E. A. V. Williams	West Indies v England at Bridgetown	1947-48
28	I. T. Botham	England v India at Delhi	1981-82
29	B. Yardley	Australia v West Indies at Bridgetown	1977-78
29	T. G. Southee	New Zealand v England at Napier	2007-08
30	Kapil Dev	India v Pakistan at Karachi	1982-83
30	T. M. Dilshan	Sri Lanka v New Zealand at Galle	2009

FASTEST HUNDREDS

Minutes			
70	J. M. Gregory	Australia v South Africa at Johannesburg	1921-22
75	G. L. Jessop	England v Australia at The Oval	1902
78	R. Benaud	Australia v West Indies at Kingston	1954-55
80	J. H. Sinclair	South Africa v Australia at Cape Town	1902-03
81	I. V. A. Richards	West Indies v England at St John's	1985-86
86	B. R. Taylor	New Zealand v West Indies at Auckland	1968-69

The fastest hundreds in terms of balls received (where recorded) are:

Balls			
56	I. V. A. Richards	West Indies v England at St John's	1985-86
57	A. C. Gilchrist	Australia v England at Perth	2006-07
67	J. M. Gregory	Australia v South Africa at Johannesburg	1921-22
69	S. Chanderpaul	West Indies v Australia at Georgetown	2002-03
69	**D. A. Warner**	**Australia v India at Perth**	**2011-12**
70	C. H. Gayle	West Indies v Australia at Perth	2009-10
71	R. C. Fredericks	West Indies v Australia at Perth	1975-76
74	Majid Khan	Pakistan v New Zealand at Karachi	1976-77
74	Kapil Dev	India v Sri Lanka at Kanpur	1986-87
74	M. Azharuddin	India v South Africa at Calcutta	1996-97
75	A. B. de Villiers	South Africa v India at Centurion	2010-11
76	G. L. Jessop	England v Australia at The Oval	1902

FASTEST DOUBLE-HUNDREDS

Minutes			
214	D. G. Bradman	Australia v England at Leeds	1930
217	N. J. Astle	New Zealand v England at Christchurch	2001-02
223	S. J. McCabe	Australia v England at Nottingham	1938
226	V. T. Trumper	Australia v South Africa at Adelaide	1910-11
234	D. G. Bradman	Australia v England at Lord's	1930
240	W. R. Hammond	England v New Zealand at Auckland	1932-33
241	S. E. Gregory	Australia v England at Sydney	1894-95
245	D. C. S. Compton	England v Pakistan at Nottingham	1954

The fastest double-hundreds in terms of balls received (where recorded) are:

Balls			
153	N. J. Astle	New Zealand v England at Christchurch	2001-02
168	V. Sehwag	India v Sri Lanka at Mumbai (BS)	2009-10
182	V. Sehwag	India v Pakistan at Lahore	2005-06
194	V. Sehwag	India v South Africa at Chennai	2007-08
211	H. H. Gibbs	South Africa v Pakistan at Cape Town	2002-03
212	A. C. Gilchrist	Australia v South Africa at Johannesburg	2001-02
220	I. T. Botham	England v India at The Oval	1982
221	C. H. Gayle	West Indies v Sri Lanka at Galle	2010-11
222	V. Sehwag	India v Pakistan at Multan	2003-04
226	**M. J. Clarke**	**Australia v South Africa at Adelaide**	**2012-13**
227	V. Sehwag	India v Sri Lanka at Galle	2008
229	P. A. de Silva	Sri Lanka v Bangladesh at Colombo (PSS)	2002

FASTEST TRIPLE-HUNDREDS

Minutes			
288	W. R. Hammond	England v New Zealand at Auckland	1932-33
336	D. G. Bradman	Australia v England at Leeds	1930

The fastest triple-hundred in terms of balls received (where recorded) is:

Balls			
278	V. Sehwag	India v South Africa at Chennai	2007-08

MOST RUNS SCORED OFF AN OVER

28	B. C. Lara (466444)	off R. J. Peterson	WI v SA at Johannesburg	2003-04
27	Shahid Afridi (666621)	off Harbhajan Singh	P v I at Lahore	2005-06
26	C. D. McMillan (444464)	off Younis Khan	NZ v P at Hamilton	2000-01
26	B. C. Lara (406664)	off Danish Kaneria	WI v P at Multan	2006-07
26	M. G. Johnson (446066)	off P. L. Harris	A v SA at Johannesburg	2009-10

MOST RUNS IN A DAY

309	D. G. Bradman	Australia v England at Leeds	1930
295	W. R. Hammond	England v New Zealand at Auckland	1932-33
284	V. Sehwag	India v Sri Lanka at Mumbai	2009-10
273	D. C. S. Compton	England v Pakistan at Nottingham	1954
271	D. G. Bradman	Australia v England at Leeds	1934

MOST SIXES IN A CAREER

A. C. Gilchrist (A)	100	I. V. A. Richards (WI)	84
J. H. Kallis (SA/World)	**97**	A. Flintoff (E/World)	82
V. Sehwag (I/World)	**91**	M. L. Hayden (A)	82
B. C. Lara (WI)	88	**K. P. Pietersen (E)**	**73**
C. L. Cairns (NZ)	87	**R. T. Ponting (A)**	**73**
C. H. Gayle (WI)	**85**	C. H. Lloyd (WI)	70

SLOWEST INDIVIDUAL BATTING

0	in 101 minutes	G. I. Allott, New Zealand v South Africa at Auckland	1998-99
4*	in 110 minutes	Abdul Razzaq, Pakistan v Australia at Melbourne	2004-05
7	in 123 minutes	G. Miller, England v Australia at Melbourne	1978-79
9*	in 184 minutes	Arshad Khan, Pakistan v Sri Lanka at Colombo (SSC)	2000
18	in 194 minutes	W. R. Playle, New Zealand v England at Leeds	1958
19*	in 217 minutes	M. D. Crowe, New Zealand v Sri Lanka at Colombo (SSC)	1983-84
25	in 242 minutes	D. K. Morrison, New Zealand v Pakistan at Faisalabad	1990-91
28*	in 250 minutes	J. W. Burke, Australia v England at Brisbane	1958-59
29*	in 277 minutes	R. C. Russell, England v South Africa at Johannesburg	1995-96
35	in 332 minutes	C. J. Tavaré, England v India at Madras	1981-82
43	in 340 minutes	Javed Omar, Bangladesh v Zimbabwe at Dhaka	2004-05
55	in 348 minutes	J. G. Wright, New Zealand v England at Wellington	1977-78
60	in 390 minutes	D. N. Sardesai, India v West Indies at Bridgetown	1961-62
62	in 408 minutes	Ramiz Raja, Pakistan v West Indies at Karachi	1986-87
68	in 458 minutes	T. E. Bailey, England v Australia at Brisbane	1958-59
86	in 474 minutes	Shoaib Mohammad, Pakistan v West Indies at Karachi	1990-91
99	in 505 minutes	M. L. Jaisimha, India v Pakistan at Kanpur	1960-61
104	in 529 minutes	S. V. Manjrekar, India v Zimbabwe at Harare	1992-93
105	in 575 minutes	D. J. McGlew, South Africa v Australia at Durban	1957-58
114	in 591 minutes	Mudassar Nazar, Pakistan v England at Lahore	1977-78
120*	in 609 minutes	J. J. Crowe, New Zealand v Sri Lanka at Colombo (CCC)	1986-87
136*	in 675 minutes	S. Chanderpaul, West Indies v India at St John's	2001-02
163	in 720 minutes	Shoaib Mohammad, Pakistan v New Zealand at Wellington	1988-89
201*	in 777 minutes	D. S. B. P. Kuruppu, Sri Lanka v NZ at Colombo (CCC)	1986-87
275	in 878 minutes	G. Kirsten, South Africa v England at Durban	1999-2000
337	in 970 minutes	Hanif Mohammad, Pakistan v West Indies at Bridgetown	1957-58

SLOWEST HUNDREDS

557 minutes	Mudassar Nazar, Pakistan v England at Lahore	1977-78
545 minutes	D. J. McGlew, South Africa v Australia at Durban	1957-58
535 minutes	A. P. Gurusinha, Sri Lanka v Zimbabwe at Harare	1994-95
516 minutes	J. J. Crowe, New Zealand v Sri Lanka at Colombo (CCC)	1986-87
500 minutes	S. V. Manjrekar, India v Zimbabwe at Harare	1992-93
488 minutes	P. E. Richardson, England v South Africa at Johannesburg	1956-57

Notes: The slowest hundred for any Test in England is 458 minutes (329 balls) by K. W. R. Fletcher, England v Pakistan, The Oval, 1974.

The slowest double-hundred in a Test was scored in 777 minutes (548 balls) by D. S. B. P. Kuruppu for Sri Lanka v New Zealand at Colombo (CCC), 1986-87, on his debut.

PARTNERSHIPS OVER 400

624	for 3rd	K. C. Sangakkara (287)/D. P. M. D. Jayawardene (374)	SL v SA	Colombo (SSC)	2006
576	for 2nd	S. T. Jayasuriya (340)/R. S. Mahanama (225)	SL v I	Colombo (RPS)	1997-98
467	for 3rd	A. H. Jones (186)/M. D. Crowe (299)	NZ v SL	Wellington	1990-91
451	for 2nd	W. H. Ponsford (266)/D. G. Bradman (244)	A v E	The Oval	1934
451	for 3rd	Mudassar Nazar (231)/Javed Miandad (280*)	P v I	Hyderabad	1982-83
446	for 2nd	C. C. Hunte (260)/G. S. Sobers (365*)	WI v P	Kingston	1957-58
438	for 2nd	M. S. Atapattu (249)/K. C. Sangakkara (270)	SL v Z	Bulawayo	2003-04
437	for 4th	D. P. M. D. Jayawardene (240)/T. T. Samaraweera (231)	SL v P	Karachi	2008-09
429*	for 3rd	J. A. Rudolph (222*)/H. H. Dippenaar (177*)	SA v B	Chittagong	2003
415	for 1st	N. D. McKenzie (226)/G. C. Smith (232)	SA v B	Chittagong	2007-08
413	for 1st	V. Mankad (231)/Pankaj Roy (173)	I v NZ	Madras	1955-56
411	for 4th	P. B. H. May (285*)/M. C. Cowdrey (154)	E v WI	Birmingham	1957
410	for 1st	V. Sehwag (254)/R. Dravid (128*)	I v P	Lahore	2005-06
405	for 5th	S. G. Barnes (234)/D. G. Bradman (234)	A v E	Sydney	1946-47

Notes: 415 runs were added for the third wicket for India v England at Madras in 1981-82 by D. B. Vengsarkar (retired hurt), G. R. Viswanath and Yashpal Sharma. 408 runs were added for the first wicket for India v Bangladesh at Mirpur in 2007 by K. D. Karthik (retired hurt), Wasim Jaffer (retired hurt), R. Dravid and S. R. Tendulkar.

HIGHEST PARTNERSHIPS FOR EACH WICKET

First Wicket

415	N. D. McKenzie (226)/G. C. Smith (232)	SA v B	Chittagong	2007-08
413	V. Mankad (231)/Pankaj Roy (173)	I v NZ	Madras	1955-56
410	V. Sehwag (254)/R. Dravid (128*)	I v P	Lahore	2005-06
387	G. M. Turner (259)/T. W. Jarvis (182)	NZ v WI	Georgetown	1971-72
382	W. M. Lawry (210)/R. B. Simpson (201)	A v WI	Bridgetown	1964-65
368	G. C. Smith (151)/H. H. Gibbs (228)	SA v P	Cape Town	2002-03
359	L. Hutton (158)/C. Washbrook (195)	E v SA	Johannesburg	1948-49
338	G. C. Smith (277)/H. H. Gibbs (179)	SA v E	Birmingham	2003
335	M. S. Atapattu (207*)/S. T. Jayasuriya (188)	SL v P	Kandy	2000
329	G. R. Marsh (138)/M. A. Taylor (219)	A v E	Nottingham	1989

Second Wicket

576	S. T. Jayasuriya (340)/R. S. Mahanama (225)	SL v I	Colombo (RPS)	1997-98
451	W. H. Ponsford (266)/D. G. Bradman (244)	A v E	The Oval	1934
446	C. C. Hunte (260)/G. S. Sobers (365*)	WI v P	Kingston	1957-58
438	M. S. Atapattu (249)/K. C. Sangakkara (270)	SL v Z	Bulawayo	2003-04
382	L. Hutton (364)/M. Leyland (187)	E v A	The Oval	1938
369	J. H. Edrich (310*)/K. F. Barrington (163)	E v NZ	Leeds	1965
351	G. A. Gooch (196)/D. I. Gower (157)	E v A	The Oval	1985
344*	S. M. Gavaskar (182*)/D. B. Vengsarkar (157*)	I v WI	Calcutta	1978-79
331	R. T. Robinson (148)/D. I. Gower (215)	E v A	Birmingham	1985
331	C. H. Gayle (317)/R. R. Sarwan (127)	WI v SA	St John's	2004-05

Third Wicket

624	K. C. Sangakkara (287)/D. P. M. D. Jayawardene (374)	SL v SA	Colombo (SSC)	2006
467	A. H. Jones (186)/M. D. Crowe (299)	NZ v SL	Wellington	1990-91
451	Mudassar Nazar (231)/Javed Miandad (280*)	P v I	Hyderabad	1982-83
429*	J. A. Rudolph (222*)/H. H. Dippenaar (177*)	SA v B	Chittagong	2003
397	Qasim Omar (206)/Javed Miandad (203*)	P v SL	Faisalabad	1985-86
377*	**H. M. Amla (311*)/J. H. Kallis (182*)**	**SA v E**	**The Oval**	**2012**
370	W. J. Edrich (189)/D. C. S. Compton (208)	E v SA	Lord's	1947
363	Younis Khan (163)/Mohammad Yousuf (192)	P v E	Leeds	2006
352*†	Ijaz Ahmed, sen. (211)/Inzamam-ul-Haq (200*)	P v SL	Dhaka	1998-99
350	I. R. Bell (235)/K. P. Pietersen (175)	E v I	The Oval	2011

† *366 runs were scored for this wicket in two separate partnerships; Inzamam retired ill when he and Ijaz had added 352 runs.*

Fourth Wicket

437	D. P. M. D. Jayawardene (240)/ T. T. Samaraweera (231)	SL v P	Karachi	2008-09
411	P. B. H. May (285*)/M. C. Cowdrey (154)	E v WI	Birmingham	1957
399	G. S. Sobers (226)/F. M. M. Worrell (197*)	WI v E	Bridgetown	1959-60
388	W. H. Ponsford (181)/D. G. Bradman (304)	A v E	Leeds	1934
386	**R. T. Ponting (221)/M. J. Clarke (210)**	**A v I**	**Adelaide**	**2011-12**
353	S. R. Tendulkar (241*)/V. V. S. Laxman (178)	I v A	Sydney	2003-04
352	R. T. Ponting (209)/M. J. Clarke (166)	A v P	Hobart	2009-10
350	Mushtaq Mohammad (201)/Asif Iqbal (175)	P v NZ	Dunedin	1972-73
336	W. M. Lawry (151)/K. D. Walters (242)	A v WI	Sydney	1968-69
322	Javed Miandad (153*)/Salim Malik (165)	P v E	Birmingham	1992

Fifth Wicket

405	S. G. Barnes (234)/D. G. Bradman (234)	A v E	Sydney	1946-47
385	S. R. Waugh (160)/G. S. Blewett (214)	A v SA	Johannesburg	1996-97
376	V. V. S. Laxman (281)/R. Dravid (180)	I v A	Kolkata	2000-01
334*	**M. J. Clarke (329*)/M. E. K. Hussey (150*)**	**A v I**	**Sydney**	**2011-12**
332*	A. R. Border (200*)/S. R. Waugh (157*)	A v E	Leeds	1993
327	J. L. Langer (144)/R. T. Ponting (197)	A v P	Perth	1999-2000
322†	B. C. Lara (213)/J. C. Adams (94)	WI v A	Kingston	1998-99
303	R. Dravid (233)/V. V. S. Laxman (148)	I v A	Adelaide	2003-04
300	S. C. Ganguly (239)/Yuvraj Singh (169)	I v P	Bangalore	2007-08
296*	**S. Chanderpaul (203*)/D. Ramdin (126*)**	**WI v B**	**Mirpur**	**2012-13**

† *344 runs were scored for this wicket in two separate partnerships; P. T. Collins retired hurt when he and Lara had added 22 runs.*

Sixth Wicket

351	D. P. M. D. Jayawardene (275)/ H. A. P. W. Jayawardene (154*)	SL v I	Ahmedabad	2009-10
346	J. H. Fingleton (136)/D. G. Bradman (270)	A v E	Melbourne	1936-37
339	M. J. Guptill (189)/B. B. McCullum (185)	NZ v B	Hamilton	2009-10
317	D. R. Martyn (133)/A. C. Gilchrist (204*)	A v SA	Johannesburg	2001-02
307	M. E. K. Hussey (195)/B. J. Haddin (136)	A v E	Brisbane	2010-11
298*	D. B. Vengsarkar (164*)/R. J. Shastri (121*)	I v A	Bombay	1986-87
282*	B. C. Lara (400*)/R. D. Jacobs (107*)	WI v E	St John's	2003-04

281	G. P. Thorpe (200*)/A. Flintoff (137).	E v NZ	Christchurch	2001-02
279	M. L. Hayden (153)/A. Symonds (156)	A v E	Melbourne	2006-07
274*	G. S. Sobers (163*)/D. A. J. Holford (105*)	WI v E	Lord's	1966

Seventh Wicket

347	D. St E. Atkinson (219)/C. C. Depeiza (122)	WI v A	Bridgetown	1954-55
308	Waqar Hassan (189)/Imtiaz Ahmed (209)	P v NZ	Lahore	1955-56
259*	V. V. S. Laxman (143*)/M. S. Dhoni (132*)	I v SA	Kolkata	2009-10
248	Yousuf Youhana (203)/Saqlain Mushtaq (101*) . . .	P v NZ	Christchurch	2000-01
246	D. J. McGlew (255*)/A. R. A. Murray (109)	SA v NZ	Wellington	1952-53
235	R. J. Shastri (142)/S. M. H. Kirmani (102).	I v E	Bombay	1984-85
225	C. L. Cairns (158)/J. D. P. Oram (90).	NZ v SA	Auckland	2003-04
224	V. V. S. Laxman (176*)/M. S. Dhoni (144)	I v WI	Kolkata	2011-12
223*	H. A. P. W. Jayawardene (120*)/ W. P. U. J. C. Vaas (100*)	SL v B	Colombo (SSC)	2007
221	D. T. Lindsay (182)/P. L. van der Merwe (76)	SA v A	Johannesburg	1966-67

Eighth Wicket

332	I. J. L. Trott (184)/S. C. J. Broad (169).	E v P	Lord's	2010
313	Wasim Akram (257*)/Saqlain Mushtaq (79)	P v Z	Sheikhupura	1996-97
256	S. P. Fleming (262)/J. E. C. Franklin (122*)	NZ v SA	Cape Town	2005-06
253	N. J. Astle (156*)/A. C. Parore (110)	NZ v A	Perth	2001-02
246	L. E. G. Ames (137)/G. O. B. Allen (122)	E v NZ	Lord's	1931
243	R. J. Hartigan (116)/C. Hill (160)	A v E	Adelaide	1907-08
217	T. W. Graveney (165)/J. T. Murray (112).	E v WI	The Oval	1966
173	C. E. Pellew (116)/J. M. Gregory (100)	A v E	Melbourne	1920-21
170	D. P. M. D. Jayawardene (237)/ W. P. U. J. C. Vaas (69)	SL v SA	Galle	2004
168	R. Illingworth (107)/P. Lever (88*)	E v I	Manchester	1971
168	H. H. Streak (127*)/A. M. Blignaut (91)	Z v WI	Harare	2003-04

Ninth Wicket

195	M. V. Boucher (78)/P. L. Symcox (108).	SA v P	Johannesburg	1997-98
190	Asif Iqbal (146)/Intikhab Alam (51)	P v E	The Oval	1967
184	**Mahmudullah (76)/Abul Hasan (113)**	**B v WI**	**Khulna**	**2012-13**
180	J-P. Duminy (166)/D. W. Steyn (76)	SA v A	Melbourne	2008-09
163*	M. C. Cowdrey (128*)/A. C. Smith (69*)	E v NZ	Wellington	1962-63
161	C. H. Lloyd (161*)/A. M. E. Roberts (68)	WI v I	Calcutta	1983-84
161	Zaheer Abbas (82*)/Sarfraz Nawaz (90).	P v E	Lahore	1983-84
154	S. E. Gregory (201)/J. McC. Blackham (74).	A v E	Sydney	1894-95
151	W. H. Scotton (90)/W. W. Read (117)	E v A	The Oval	1884
150	E. A. E. Baptiste (87*)/M. A. Holding (69)	WI v E	Birmingham	1984

Tenth Wicket

151	B. F. Hastings (110)/R. O. Collinge (68*)	NZ v P	Auckland	1972-73
151	Azhar Mahmood (128*)/Mushtaq Ahmed (59)	P v SA	Rawalpindi	1997-98
143	**D. Ramdin (107*)/T. L. Best (95)**.	**WI v E**	**Birmingham**	**2012**
133	Wasim Raja (71)/Wasim Bari (60*)	P v WI	Bridgetown	1976-77
133	S. R. Tendulkar (248*)/Zaheer Khan (75)	I v B	Dhaka	2004-05
130	R. E. Foster (287)/W. Rhodes (40*)	E v A	Sydney	1903-04
128	K. Higgs (63)/J. A. Snow (59*)	E v WI	The Oval	1966
127	J. M. Taylor (108)/A. A. Mailey (46*)	A v E	Sydney	1924-25
124	J. G. Bracewell (83*)/S. L. Boock (37).	NZ v A	Sydney	1985-86
120	R. A. Duff (104)/W. W. Armstrong (45*).	A v E	Melbourne	1901-02

HIGHEST PARTNERSHIPS FOR EACH COUNTRY

ENGLAND

359	for 1st	L. Hutton (158)/C. Washbrook (195)	v SA	Johannesburg	1948-49
382	for 2nd	L. Hutton (364)/M. Leyland (187)	v A	The Oval	1938
370	for 3rd	W. J. Edrich (189)/D. C. S. Compton (208)	v SA	Lord's	1947
411	for 4th	P. B. H. May (285*)/M. C. Cowdrey (154)	v WI	Birmingham	1957
254	for 5th	K. W. R. Fletcher (113)/A. W. Greig (148)	v I	Bombay	1972-73
281	for 6th	G. P. Thorpe (200*)/A. Flintoff (137)	v NZ	Christchurch	2001-02
197	for 7th	M. J. K. Smith (96)/J. M. Parks (101*)	v WI	Port-of-Spain	1959-60
332	for 8th	I. J. L. Trott (184)/S. C. J. Broad (169)	v P	Lord's	2010
163*	for 9th	M. C. Cowdrey (128*)/A. C. Smith (69*)	v NZ	Wellington	1962-63
130	for 10th	R. E. Foster (287)/W. Rhodes (40*)	v A	Sydney	1903-04

AUSTRALIA

382	for 1st	W. M. Lawry (210)/R. B. Simpson (201)	v WI	Bridgetown	1964-65
451	for 2nd	W. H. Ponsford (266)/D. G. Bradman (244)	v E	The Oval	1934
315	for 3rd	R. T. Ponting (206)/D. S. Lehmann (160)	v WI	Port-of-Spain	2002-03
388	for 4th	W. H. Ponsford (181)/D. G. Bradman (304)	v E	Leeds	1934
405	for 5th	S. G. Barnes (234)/D. G. Bradman (234)	v E	Sydney	1946-47
346	for 6th	J. H. Fingleton (136)/D. G. Bradman (270)	v E	Melbourne	1936-37
217	for 7th	K. D. Walters (250)/G. J. Gilmour (101)	v NZ	Christchurch	1976-77
243	for 8th	R. J. Hartigan (116)/C. Hill (160)	v E	Adelaide	1907-08
154	for 9th	S. E. Gregory (201)/J. McC. Blackham (74)	v E	Sydney	1894-95
127	for 10th	J. M. Taylor (108)/A. A. Mailey (46*)	v E	Sydney	1924-25

SOUTH AFRICA

415	for 1st	N. D. McKenzie (226)/G. C. Smith (232)	v B	Chittagong	2007-08
315*	for 2nd	H. H. Gibbs (211*)/J. H. Kallis (148*)	v NZ	Christchurch	1998-99
429*	for 3rd	J. A. Rudolph (222*)/H. H. Dippenaar (177*)	v B	Chittagong	2003
249	for 4th	J. H. Kallis (177)/G. Kirsten (137)	v WI	Durban	2003-04
267	for 5th	J. H. Kallis (147)/A. G. Prince (131)	v WI	St John's	2004-05
271	for 6th	A. G. Prince (162*)/M. V. Boucher (117)	v B	Centurion	2008-09
246	for 7th	D. J. McGlew (255*)/A. R. A. Murray (109)	v NZ	Wellington	1952-53
150	for 8th	N. D. McKenzie (103)/S. M. Pollock (111)	v SL	Centurion	2000-01
		G. Kirsten (130)/M. Zondeki (59)	v E	Leeds	2003
195	for 9th	M. V. Boucher (78)/P. L. Symcox (108)	v P	Johannesburg	1997-98
107*	for 10th	A. B. de Villiers (278*)/M. Morkel (35*)	v P	Abu Dhabi	2010-11

WEST INDIES

298	for 1st	C. G. Greenidge (149)/D. L. Haynes (167)	v E	St John's	1989-90
446	for 2nd	C. C. Hunte (260)/G. S. Sobers (365*)	v P	Kingston	1957-58
338	for 3rd	E. D. Weekes (206)/F. M. M. Worrell (167)	v E	Port-of-Spain	1953-54
399	for 4th	G. S. Sobers (226)/F. M. M. Worrell (197*)	v E	Bridgetown	1959-60
322	for 5th†	B. C. Lara (213)/J. C. Adams (94)	v A	Kingston	1998-99
282*	for 6th	B. C. Lara (400*)/R. D. Jacobs (107*)	v E	St John's	2003-04
347	for 7th	D. St E. Atkinson (219)/C. C. Depeiza (122)	v A	Bridgetown	1954-55
148	for 8th	J. C. Adams (101*)/F. A. Rose (69)	v Z	Kingston	1999-2000
161	for 9th	C. H. Lloyd (161*)/A. M. E. Roberts (68)	v I	Calcutta	1983-84
143	**for 10th**	**D. Ramdin (107*)/T. L. Best (95)**	**v E**	**Birmingham**	**2012**

† 344 runs were added between the fall of the 4th and 5th wickets: P. T. Collins retired hurt when he and Lara had added 22 runs.

NEW ZEALAND

387	for 1st	G. M. Turner (259)/T. W. Jarvis (182)	v WI	Georgetown	1971-72
241	for 2nd	J. G. Wright (116)/A. H. Jones (143)	v E	Wellington	1991-92
467	for 3rd	A. H. Jones (186)/M. D. Crowe (299)	v SL	Wellington	1990-91
271	for 4th	L. R. P. L. Taylor (151)/J. D. Ryder (201)	v I	Napier	2008-09
222	for 5th	N. J. Astle (141)/C. D. McMillan (142)	v Z	Wellington	2000-01
339	for 6th	M. J. Guptill (189)/B. B. McCullum (185)	v B	Hamilton	2009-10
225	for 7th	C. L. Cairns (158)/J. D. P. Oram (90)	v SA	Auckland	2003-04
256	for 8th	S. P. Fleming (262)/J. E. C. Franklin (122*) . .	v SA	Cape Town	2005-06
136	for 9th	I. D. S. Smith (173)/M. C. Snedden (22)	v I	Auckland	1989-90
151	for 10th	B. F. Hastings (110)/R. O. Collinge (68*)	v P	Auckland	1972-73

INDIA

413	for 1st	V. Mankad (231)/Pankaj Roy (173)	v NZ	Madras	1955-56
344*	for 2nd	S. M. Gavaskar (182*)/D. B. Vengsarkar (157*) .	v WI	Calcutta	1978-79
336	for 3rd†	V. Sehwag (309)/S. R. Tendulkar (194*)	v P	Multan	2003-04
353	for 4th	S. R. Tendulkar (241*)/V. V. S. Laxman (178) . .	v A	Sydney	2003-04
376	for 5th	V. V. S. Laxman (281)/R. Dravid (180)	v A	Kolkata	2000-01
298*	for 6th	D. B. Vengsarkar (164*)/R. J. Shastri (121*) . .	v A	Bombay	1986-87
259*	for 7th	V. V. S. Laxman (143*)/M. S. Dhoni (132*) . .	v SA	Kolkata	2009-10
161	for 8th	A. Kumble (88)/M. Azharuddin (109)	v SA	Calcutta	1996-97
149	for 9th	P. G. Joshi (52*)/R. B. Desai (85)	v P	Bombay	1960-61
133	for 10th	S. R. Tendulkar (248*)/Zaheer Khan (75)	v B	Dhaka	2004-05

†415 runs were scored for India's 3rd wicket v England at Madras in 1981-82, in two partnerships: D. B. Vengsarkar and G. R. Viswanath put on 99 before Vengsarkar retired hurt, then Viswanath and Yashpal Sharma added a further 316.

PAKISTAN

298	for 1st	Aamir Sohail (160)/Ijaz Ahmed, sen. (151) . . .	v WI	Karachi	1997-98
291	for 2nd	Zaheer Abbas (274)/Mushtaq Mohammad (100)	v E	Birmingham	1971
451	for 3rd	Mudassar Nazar (231)/Javed Miandad (280*) .	v I	Hyderabad	1982-83
350	for 4th	Mushtaq Mohammad (201)/Asif Iqbal (175) . .	v NZ	Dunedin	1972-73
281	for 5th	Javed Miandad (163)/Asif Iqbal (166)	v NZ	Lahore	1976-77
269	for 6th	Mohammad Yousuf (223)/Kamran Akmal (154)	v E	Lahore	2005-06
308	for 7th	Waqar Hassan (189)/Imtiaz Ahmed (209)	v NZ	Lahore	1955-56
313	for 8th	Wasim Akram (257*)/Saqlain Mushtaq (79) . .	v Z	Sheikhupura	1996-97
190	for 9th	Asif Iqbal (146)/Intikhab Alam (51)	v E	The Oval	1967
151	for 10th	Azhar Mahmood (128*)/Mushtaq Ahmed (59)	v SA	Rawalpindi	1997-98

SRI LANKA

335	for 1st	M. S. Atapattu (207*)/S. T. Jayasuriya (188) . .	v P	Kandy	2000
576	for 2nd	S. T. Jayasuriya (340)/R. S. Mahanama (225) .	v I	Colombo (RPS)	1997-98
624	for 3rd	K. C. Sangakkara (287)/ D. P. M. D. Jayawardene (374)	v SA	Colombo (SSC)	2006
437	for 4th	D. P. M. D. Jayawardene (240)/ T. T. Samaraweera (231)	v P	Karachi	2008-09
280	for 5th	T. T. Samaraweera (138)/T. M. Dilshan (168) .	v B	Colombo (PSS)	2005-06
351	for 6th	D. P. M. D. Jayawardene (275)/ H. A. P. W. Jayawardene (154*)	v I	Ahmedabad	2009-10
223*	for 7th	H. A. P. W. Jayawardene (120*)/ W. P. U. J. C. Vaas (100*)	v B	Colombo (SSC)	2007
170	for 8th	D. P. M. D. Jayawardene (237)/ W. P. U. J. C. Vaas (69)	v SA	Galle	2004
118	for 9th	T. T. Samaraweera (83)/B. A. W. Mendis (78) .	v I	Colombo (PSS)	2010
79	for 10th	W. P. U. J. C. Vaas (68*)/M. Muralitharan (43)	v A	Kandy	2003-04

ZIMBABWE

164	for 1st	D. D. Ebrahim (71)/A. D. R. Campbell (103) .	v WI	Bulawayo	2001
135	for 2nd	M. H. Dekker (68*)/A. D. R. Campbell (75) . .	v P	Rawalpindi	1993-94
194	for 3rd	A. D. R. Campbell (99)/D. L. Houghton (142).	v SL	Harare	1994-95
269	for 4th	G. W. Flower (201*)/A. Flower (156)	v P	Harare	1994-95
277*	for 5th	M. W. Goodwin (166*)/A. Flower (100*)	v P	Bulawayo	1997-98
165	for 6th	D. L. Houghton (121)/A. Flower (59).	v I	Harare	1992-93
154	for 7th	H. H. Streak (83*)/A. M. Blignaut (92)	v WI	Harare	2001
168	for 8th	H. H. Streak (127*)/A. M. Blignaut (91)	v WI	Harare	2003-04
87	for 9th	P. A. Strang (106*)/B. C. Strang (42).	v P	Sheikhupura	1996-97
97*	for 10th	A. Flower (183*)/H. K. Olonga (11)	v I	Delhi	2000-01

BANGLADESH

185	for 1st	Tamim Iqbal (103)/Imrul Kayes (75)	v E	Lord's	2010
200	for 2nd	Tamim Iqbal (151)/Junaid Siddique (55)	v I	Mirpur	2009-10
130	for 3rd	Javed Omar (119)/Mohammad Ashraful (77) .	v P	Peshawar	2003
167	**for 4th**	**Naeem Islam (108)/Shakib Al Hasan (89)** . . .	**v WI**	**Mirpur**	**2012-13**
180	for 5th	Shahriar Nafees (97)/Shakib Al Hasan (144) . .	v P	Mirpur	2011-12
191	for 6th	Mohammad Ashraful (129*)/ Mushfiqur Rahim (80).	v SL	Colombo (PSS)	2007
145	for 7th	Shakib Al Hasan (87)/Mahmudullah (115)	v NZ	Hamilton	2009-10
113	for 8th	Mushfiqur Rahim (79)/Naeem Islam (38).	v E	Chittagong	2009-10
184	**for 9th**	**Mahmudullah (76)/Abul Hasan (113)**.	**v WI**	**Khulna**	**2012-13**
69	for 10th	Mohammad Rafique (65)/Shahadat Hossain (3*)	v A	Chittagong	2005-06

UNUSUAL DISMISSALS

Handled the Ball

W. R. Endean	South Africa v England at Cape Town	1956-57
A. M. J. Hilditch	Australia v Pakistan at Perth	1978-79
Mohsin Khan	Pakistan v Australia at Karachi	1982-83
D. L. Haynes	West Indies v India at Bombay	1983-84
G. A. Gooch	England v Australia at Manchester	1993
S. R. Waugh	Australia v India at Chennai	2000-01
M. P. Vaughan	England v India at Bangalore	2001-02

Obstructing the Field

L. Hutton	England v South Africa at The Oval	1951

Note: There have been no cases of Hit the Ball Twice or Timed Out in Test cricket.

BOWLING RECORDS

MOST WICKETS IN AN INNINGS

10-53	J. C. Laker	England v Australia at Manchester.	1956
10-74	A. Kumble	India v Pakistan at Delhi.	1998-99
9-28	G. A. Lohmann	England v South Africa at Johannesburg	1895-96
9-37	J. C. Laker	England v Australia at Manchester.	1956
9-51	M. Muralitharan.	Sri Lanka v Zimbabwe at Kandy	2001-02
9-52	R. J. Hadlee	New Zealand v Australia at Brisbane	1985-86
9-56	Abdul Qadir.	Pakistan v England at Lahore	1987-88
9-57	D. E. Malcolm	England v South Africa at The Oval.	1994
9-65	M. Muralitharan.	Sri Lanka v England at The Oval	1998
9-69	J. M. Patel	India v Australia at Kanpur.	1959-60

9-83	Kapil Dev	India v West Indies at Ahmedabad	1983-84
9-86	Sarfraz Nawaz	Pakistan v Australia at Melbourne	1978-79
9-95	J. M. Noreiga	West Indies v India at Port-of-Spain	1970-71
9-102	S. P. Gupte	India v West Indies at Kanpur	1958-59
9-103	S. F. Barnes	England v South Africa at Johannesburg	1913-14
9-113	H. J. Tayfield	South Africa v England at Johannesburg	1956-57
9-121	A. A. Mailey	Australia v England at Melbourne	1920-21
8-7	G. A. Lohmann	England v South Africa at Port Elizabeth	1895-96
8-11	J. Briggs	England v South Africa at Cape Town	1888-89
8-24	G. D. McGrath	Australia v Pakistan at Perth	2004-05
8-29	S. F. Barnes	England v South Africa at The Oval	1912
8-29	C. E. H. Croft	West Indies v Pakistan at Port-of-Spain	1976-77
8-31	F. Laver	Australia v England at Manchester	1909
8-31	F. S. Trueman	England v India at Manchester	1952
8-34	I. T. Botham	England v Pakistan at Lord's	1978
8-35	G. A. Lohmann	England v Australia at Sydney	1886-87
8-38	L. R. Gibbs	West Indies v India at Bridgetown	1961-62
8-38	G. D. McGrath	Australia v England at Lord's	1997

Note: There have been **60** further instances of eight wickets in a Test innings.

The best bowling figures for the countries not mentioned above are:

8-109	P. A. Strang	Zimbabwe v New Zealand at Bulawayo	2000-01
7-36	Shakib Al Hasan	Bangladesh v New Zealand at Chittagong	2008-09

OUTSTANDING BOWLING ANALYSES

	O	*M*	*R*	*W*		
J. C. Laker (E)	51.2	23	53	10	v Australia at Manchester	1956
A. Kumble (I)	26.3	9	74	10	v Pakistan at Delhi	1998-99
G. A. Lohmann (E)	14.2	6	28	9	v South Africa at Johannesburg	1895-96
J. C. Laker (E)	16.4	4	37	9	v Australia at Manchester	1956
G. A. Lohmann (E)	9.4	5	7	8	v South Africa at Port Elizabeth	1895-96
J. Briggs (E)	14.2	5	11	8	v South Africa at Cape Town	1888-89
S. J. Harmison (E)	12.3	8	12	7	v West Indies at Kingston	2003-04
J. Briggs (E)	19.1	11	17	7	v South Africa at Cape Town	1888-89
M. A. Noble (A)	7.4	2	17	7	v England at Melbourne	1901-02
W. Rhodes (E)	11	3	17	7	v Australia at Birmingham	1902
J. J. C. Lawson (WI)	6.5	4	3	6	v Bangladesh at Dhaka	2002-03
A. E. R. Gilligan (E)	6.3	4	7	6	v South Africa at Birmingham	1924
M. J. Clarke (A)	6.2	0	9	6	v India at Mumbai	2004-05
S. Haigh (E)	11.4	6	11	6	v South Africa at Cape Town	1898-99
Shoaib Akhtar (P)	8.2	4	11	6	v New Zealand at Lahore	2002
D. L. Underwood (E)	11.6	7	12	6	v New Zealand at Christchurch	1970-71
S. L. V. Raju (I)	17.5	13	12	6	v Sri Lanka at Chandigarh	1990-91
H. J. Tayfield (SA)	14	7	13	6	v New Zealand at Johannesburg	1953-54
C. T. B. Turner (A)	18	11	15	6	v England at Sydney	1886-87
M. H. N. Walker (A)	16	8	15	6	v Pakistan at Sydney	1972-73
E. R. H. Toshack (A)	2.3	1	2	5	v India at Brisbane	1947-48
H. Ironmonger (A)	7.2	5	6	5	v South Africa at Melbourne	1931-32
V. D. Philander (SA)	**6**	**3**	**7**	**5**	**v New Zealand at Cape Town**	**2012-13**
T. B. A. May (A)	6.5	3	9	5	v West Indies at Adelaide	1992-93
Pervez Sajjad (P)	12	8	5	4	v New Zealand at Rawalpindi	1964-65
K. Higgs (E)	9	7	5	4	v New Zealand at Christchurch	1965-66
P. H. Edmonds (E)	8	6	6	4	v Pakistan at Lord's	1978
J. C. White (E)	6.3	2	7	4	v Australia at Brisbane	1928-29
J. H. Wardle (E)	5	2	7	4	v Australia at Manchester	1953
R. Appleyard (E)	6	3	7	4	v New Zealand at Auckland	1954-55
R. Benaud (A)	3.4	3	0	3	v India at Delhi	1959-60

WICKET WITH FIRST BALL IN TEST CRICKET

	Batsman dismissed			
T. P. Horan	W. W. Read	A v E	Sydney	1882-83
A. Coningham	A. C. MacLaren	A v E	Melbourne	1894-95
W. M. Bradley	F. Laver	E v A	Manchester	1899
E. G. Arnold	V. T. Trumper	E v A	Sydney	1903-04
A. E. E. Vogler	E. G. Hayes	SA v E	Johannesburg	1905-06
J. N. Crawford	A. E. E. Vogler	E v SA	Johannesburg	1905-06
G. G. Macaulay	G. A. L. Hearne	E v SA	Cape Town	1922-23
M. W. Tate	M. J. Susskind	E v SA	Birmingham	1924
M. Henderson	E. W. Dawson	NZ v E	Christchurch	1929-30
H. D. Smith	E. Paynter	NZ v E	Christchurch	1932-33
T. F. Johnson	W. W. Keeton	WI v E	The Oval	1939
R. Howorth	D. V. Dyer	E v SA	The Oval	1947
Intikhab Alam	C. C. McDonald	P v A	Karachi	1959-60
R. K. Illingworth	P. V. Simmons	E v WI	Nottingham	1991
N. M. Kulkarni	M. S. Atapattu	I v SL	Colombo (RPS)	1997-98
M. K. G. C. P. Lakshitha	Mohammad Ashraful	SL v B	Colombo (SSC)	2002
N. M. Lyon	K. C. Sangakkara	A v SL	Galle	2011-12
R. M. S. Eranga	S. R. Watson	SL v A	Colombo (SSC)	2011-12

HAT-TRICKS

F. R. Spofforth	Australia v England at Melbourne	1878-79
W. Bates	England v Australia at Melbourne	1882-83
J. Briggs	England v Australia at Sydney	1891-92
G. A. Lohmann	England v South Africa at Port Elizabeth	1895-96
J. T. Hearne	England v Australia at Leeds	1899
H. Trumble	Australia v England at Melbourne	1901-02
H. Trumble	Australia v England at Melbourne	1903-04
T. J. Matthews† T. J. Matthews	Australia v South Africa at Manchester	1912
M. J. C. Allom‡	England v New Zealand at Christchurch	1929-30
T. W. J. Goddard	England v South Africa at Johannesburg	1938-39
P. J. Loader	England v West Indies at Leeds	1957
L. F. Kline	Australia v South Africa at Cape Town	1957-58
W. W. Hall	West Indies v Pakistan at Lahore	1958-59
G. M. Griffin	South Africa v England at Lord's	1960
L. R. Gibbs	West Indies v Australia at Adelaide	1960-61
P. J. Petherick‡	New Zealand v Pakistan at Lahore	1976-77
C. A. Walsh§	West Indies v Australia at Brisbane	1988-89
M. G. Hughes§	Australia v West Indies at Perth	1988-89
D. W. Fleming‡	Australia v Pakistan at Rawalpindi	1994-95
S. K. Warne	Australia v England at Melbourne	1994-95
D. G. Cork	England v West Indies at Manchester	1995
D. Gough	England v Australia at Sydney	1998-99
Wasim Akram¶	Pakistan v Sri Lanka at Lahore	1998-99
Wasim Akram¶	Pakistan v Sri Lanka at Dhaka	1998-99
D. N. T. Zoysa‖	Sri Lanka v Zimbabwe at Harare	1999-2000
Abdul Razzaq	Pakistan v Sri Lanka at Galle	2000
G. D. McGrath	Australia v West Indies at Perth	2000-01
Harbhajan Singh	India v Australia at Kolkata	2000-01
Mohammad Sami	Pakistan v Sri Lanka at Lahore	2001-02
J. J. C. Lawson§	West Indies v Australia at Bridgetown	2002-03
Alok Kapali	Bangladesh v Pakistan at Peshawar	2003
A. M. Blignaut	Zimbabwe v Bangladesh at Harare	2003-04

M. J. Hoggard	England v West Indies at Bridgetown	2003-04
J. E. C. Franklin	New Zealand v Bangladesh at Dhaka	2004-05
I. K. Pathan‖	India v Pakistan at Karachi	2005-06
R. J. Sidebottom	England v New Zealand at Hamilton	2007-08
P. M. Siddle	Australia v England at Brisbane	2010-11
S. C. J. Broad	England v India at Nottingham	2011

† *T. J. Matthews did the hat-trick in each innings of the same match.*
‡ *On Test debut.*
§ *Not all in the same innings.*
¶ *Wasim Akram did the hat-trick in successive matches.*
‖ *D. N. T. Zoysa did the hat-trick in the match's second over; I. K. Pathan in the match's first over.*

FOUR WICKETS IN FIVE BALLS

M. J. C. Allom	England v New Zealand at Christchurch *On debut, in his eighth over: W-WWW*	1929-30
C. M. Old	England v Pakistan at Birmingham *Sequence interrupted by a no-ball: WW-WW*	1978
Wasim Akram	Pakistan v West Indies at Lahore (*WW-WW*)	1990-91

MOST WICKETS IN A TEST

19-90	J. C. Laker	England v Australia at Manchester	1956
17-159	S. F. Barnes	England v South Africa at Johannesburg	1913-14
16-136†	N. D. Hirwani	India v West Indies at Madras	1987-88
16-137†	R. A. L. Massie	Australia v England at Lord's	1972
16-220	M. Muralitharan	Sri Lanka v England at The Oval	1998
15-28	J. Briggs	England v South Africa at Cape Town	1888-89
15-45	G. A. Lohmann	England v South Africa at Port Elizabeth	1895-96
15-99	C. Blythe	England v South Africa at Leeds	1907
15-104	H. Verity	England v Australia at Lord's	1934
15-123	R. J. Hadlee	New Zealand v Australia at Brisbane	1985-86
15-124	W. Rhodes	England v Australia at Melbourne	1903-04
15-217	Harbhajan Singh	India v Australia at Chennai	2000-01

† *On Test debut.*

Note: There have been **ten** further instances of 14 wickets in a Test match.

The best bowling figures for the countries not mentioned above are:

14-116	Imran Khan	Pakistan v Sri Lanka at Lahore	1981-82
14-149	M. A. Holding	West Indies v England at The Oval	1976
13-132	M. Ntini	South Africa v West Indies at Port-of-Spain	2004-05
12-200	Enamul Haque, jun.	Bangladesh v Zimbabwe at Dhaka	2004-05
11-255	A. G. Huckle	Zimbabwe v New Zealand at Bulawayo	1997-98

MOST BALLS BOWLED IN A TEST

S. Ramadhin (West Indies) sent down 774 balls in 129 overs against England at Birmingham, 1957. It was the most delivered by any bowler in a Test, beating H. Verity's 766 for England against South Africa at Durban, 1938-39. In this match Ramadhin also bowled the most balls (588) in a Test or first-class innings, since equalled by Arshad Ayub, Hyderabad v Madhya Pradesh at Secunderabad, 1991-92.

MOST WICKETS IN A SERIES

	T	R	W	Avge		
S. F. Barnes	4	536	49	10.93	England v South Africa	1913-14
J. C. Laker	5	442	46	9.60	England v Australia	1956
C. V. Grimmett	5	642	44	14.59	Australia v South Africa	1935-36
T. M. Alderman	6	893	42	21.26	Australia v England	1981
R. M. Hogg	6	527	41	12.85	Australia v England	1978-79
T. M. Alderman	6	712	41	17.36	Australia v England	1989
Imran Khan	6	558	40	13.95	Pakistan v India	1982-83
S. K. Warne	5	797	40	19.92	Australia v England	2005

Notes: The most for South Africa is 37 by H. J. Tayfield against England in 1956-57, for West Indies 35 by M. D. Marshall against England in 1988, for India 35 by B. S. Chandrasekhar against England in 1972-73 (all in five Tests), for New Zealand 33 by R. J. Hadlee against Australia in 1985-86, for Sri Lanka 30 by M. Muralitharan against Zimbabwe in 2001-02, for Zimbabwe 22 by H. H. Streak against Pakistan in 1994-95 (all in three Tests), and for Bangladesh 18 by Enamul Haque, jun. against Zimbabwe in 2004-05 (two Tests).

75 WICKETS IN A CALENDAR YEAR

	T	R	W	Avge	5I	10M	Year
S. K. Warne (A)	15	2,114	96	22.02	6	2	2005
M. Muralitharan (SL)	11	1,521	90	16.89	9	5	2006
D. K. Lillee (A)	13	1,781	85	20.95	5	2	1981
A. A. Donald (SA)	14	1,571	80	19.63	7	–	1998
M. Muralitharan (SL)	12	1,699	80	21.23	7	4	2001
J. Garner (WI)	15	1,604	77	20.83	4	–	1984
Kapil Dev (I)	18	1,739	75	23.18	5	1	1983
M. Muralitharan (SL)	10	1,463	75	19.50	7	3	2000

MOST WICKETS

1	M. Muralitharan (SL/World)	800
2	S. K. Warne (Australia)	708
3	A. Kumble (India)	619
4	G. D. McGrath (Australia)	563
5	C. A. Walsh (West Indies)	519
6	Kapil Dev (India)	434
7	R. J. Hadlee (New Zealand)	431
8	S. M. Pollock (South Africa)	421
9	Wasim Akram (Pakistan)	414
10	**Harbhajan Singh (India)**	**408**
11	C. E. L. Ambrose (West Indies)	405
12	M. Ntini (South Africa)	390
13	I. T. Botham (England)	383
14	M. D. Marshall (West Indies)	376
15	Waqar Younis (Pakistan)	373
16	Imran Khan (Pakistan)	362
17	**D. L. Vettori (New Zealand/World)**	**360**
18	D. K. Lillee (Australia)	355
	W. P. U. J. C. Vaas (Sri Lanka)	355
20	A. A. Donald (South Africa)	330
21	R. G. D. Willis (England)	325
22	**D. W. Steyn (South Africa)**	**312**
23	B. Lee (Australia)	310
24	L. R. Gibbs (West Indies)	309
25	F. S. Trueman (England)	307
26	D. L. Underwood (England)	297
27	**Zaheer Khan (India)**	**295**
28	C. J. McDermott (Australia)	291
29	**J. H. Kallis (South Africa/World)**	**285**
30	B. S. Bedi (India)	266

MOST WICKETS FOR EACH COUNTRY

ENGLAND

		T	Balls	R	W	Avge	5I	10M
1	I. T. Botham	102	21,815	10,878	383	28.40	27	4
2	R. G. D. Willis	90	17,357	8,190	325	25.20	16	–
3	F. S. Trueman	67	15,178	6,625	307	21.57	17	3
4	D. L. Underwood	86	21,862	7,674	297	25.83	17	6
5	**J. M. Anderson**	**77**	**16,943**	**8,754**	**288**	**30.39**	**12**	**1**
6	J. B. Statham	70	16,056	6,261	252	24.84	9	1
7	M. J. Hoggard	67	13,909	7,564	248	30.50	7	1

		T	*Balls*	*R*	*W*	*Avge*	*5I*	*10M*
8	A. V. Bedser	51	15,918	5,876	236	24.89	15	5
9	A. R. Caddick	62	13,558	6,999	234	29.91	13	1
10	D. Gough	58	11,821	6,503	229	28.39	9	–
11	S. J. Harmison	62†	13,192	7,091	222	31.94	8	1
12	A. Flintoff	78†	14,747	7,303	219	33.34	3	–
13	**G. P. Swann**	**50**	**12,709**	**6,176**	**212**	**29.13**	**14**	**2**
14	J. A. Snow	49	12,021	5,387	202	26.66	8	1

† *A. Flintoff also took 4-59 and 3-48, and S. J. Harmison also took 1-60 and 3-41, for the ICC World XI v Australia in the Super Series Test of 2005-06.*

AUSTRALIA

		T	*Balls*	*R*	*W*	*Avge*	*5I*	*10M*
1	S. K. Warne	145	40,705	17,995	708	25.41	37	10
2	G. D. McGrath	124	29,248	12,186	563	21.64	29	3
3	D. K. Lillee	70	18,467	8,493	355	23.92	23	7
4	B. Lee	76	16,531	9,554	310	30.81	10	–
5	C. J. McDermott	71	16,586	8,332	291	28.63	14	2
6	J. N. Gillespie	71	14,234	6,770	259	26.13	8	–
7	R. Benaud	63	19,108	6,704	248	27.03	16	1
8	G. D. McKenzie	60	17,681	7,328	246	29.78	16	3
9	R. R. Lindwall	61	13,650	5,251	228	23.03	12	–
10	C. V. Grimmett	37	14,513	5,231	216	24.21	21	7
11	M. G. Hughes	53	12,285	6,017	212	28.38	7	1
12	S. C. G. MacGill	44	11,237	6,038	208	29.02	12	2
13	**M. G. Johnson**	**50**	**11,224**	**6,281**	**205**	**30.63**	**7**	**2**
14	J. R. Thomson	51	10,535	5,601	200	28.00	8	–

SOUTH AFRICA

		T	*Balls*	*R*	*W*	*Avge*	*5I*	*10M*
1	S. M. Pollock	108	24,353	9,733	421	23.11	16	1
2	M. Ntini	101	20,834	11,242	390	28.82	18	4
3	A. A. Donald	72	15,519	7,344	330	22.25	20	3
4	**D. W. Steyn**	**62**	**12,974**	**7,265**	**312**	**23.28**	**19**	**4**
5	**J. H. Kallis**	**159†**	**19,504**	**9,197**	**284**	**32.38**	**5**	**–**

† *J. H. Kallis also took 0-35 and 1-3 for the ICC World XI v Australia in the Super Series Test of 2005-06.*

WEST INDIES

		T	*Balls*	*R*	*W*	*Avge*	*5I*	*10M*
1	C. A. Walsh	132	30,019	12,688	519	24.44	22	3
2	C. E. L. Ambrose	98	22,103	8,501	405	20.99	22	3
3	M. D. Marshall	81	17,584	7,876	376	20.94	22	4
4	L. R. Gibbs	79	27,115	8,989	309	29.09	18	2
5	J. Garner	58	13,169	5,433	259	20.97	7	–
6	M. A. Holding	60	12,680	5,898	249	23.68	13	2
7	G. S. Sobers	93	21,599	7,999	235	34.03	6	–
8	A. M. E. Roberts	47	11,135	5,174	202	25.61	11	2

NEW ZEALAND

		T	*Balls*	*R*	*W*	*Avge*	*5I*	*10M*
1	R. J. Hadlee	86	21,918	9,611	431	22.29	36	9
2	**D. L. Vettori**	**111†**	**28,508**	**12,281**	**359**	**34.20**	**20**	**3**
3	**C. S. Martin**	**71**	**14,026**	**7,878**	**233**	**33.81**	**10**	**1**
4	C. L. Cairns	62	11,698	6,410	218	29.40	13	1

† *D. L. Vettori also took 1-73 and 0-38 for the ICC World XI v Australia in the Super Series Test of 2005-06.*

INDIA

		T	*Balls*	*R*	*W*	*Avge*	*5I*	*10M*
1	A. Kumble	132	40,850	18,355	619	29.65	35	8
2	Kapil Dev	131	27,740	12,867	434	29.64	23	2
3	**Harbhajan Singh**	**99**	**27,789**	**13,168**	**408**	**32.27**	**25**	**5**
4	**Zaheer Khan**	**88**	**17,612**	**9,545**	**295**	**32.35**	**10**	**1**
5	B. S. Bedi	67	21,364	7,637	266	28.71	14	1
6	B. S. Chandrasekhar	58	15,963	7,199	242	29.74	16	2
7	J. Srinath	67	15,104	7,196	236	30.49	10	1

PAKISTAN

		T	*Balls*	*R*	*W*	*Avge*	*5I*	*10M*
1	Wasim Akram	104	22,627	9,779	414	23.62	25	5
2	Waqar Younis	87	16,224	8,788	373	23.56	22	5
3	Imran Khan	88	19,458	8,258	362	22.81	23	6
4	Danish Kaneria	61	17,697	9,082	261	34.79	15	2
5	Abdul Qadir	67	17,126	7,742	236	32.80	15	5
6	Saqlain Mushtaq	49	14,070	6,206	208	29.83	13	3

SRI LANKA

		T	*Balls*	*R*	*W*	*Avge*	*5I*	*10M*
1	M. Muralitharan	132†	43,715	18,023	795	22.67	67	22
2	W. P. U. J. C. Vaas	111	23,438	10,501	355	29.58	12	2

† M. Muralitharan also took 2-102 and 3-55 for the ICC World XI v Australia in the Super Series Test of 2005-06.

ZIMBABWE

		T	*Balls*	*R*	*W*	*Avge*	*5I*	*10M*
1	H. H. Streak	65	13,559	6,079	216	28.14	7	–

BANGLADESH

No player has taken 200 Test wickets for Bangladesh. The highest total is:

	T	*Balls*	*R*	*W*	*Avge*	*5I*	*10M*
Shakib Al Hasan	**28**	**6,963**	**3,322**	**102**	**32.56**	**9**	**–**

BEST CAREER AVERAGES

(Qualification: 75 wickets)

Avge		*T*	*W*	*Avge*		*T*	*W*
10.75	G. A. Lohmann (E)	18	112	18.63	C. Blythe (E)	19	100
16.43	S. F. Barnes (E)	27	189	20.39	J. H. Wardle (E)	28	102
16.53	C. T. B. Turner (A)	17	101	20.53	A. K. Davidson (A)	44	186
16.98	R. Peel (E)	20	101	20.94	M. D. Marshall (WI)	81	376
17.75	J. Briggs (E)	33	118	20.97	J. Garner (WI)	58	259
18.41	F. R. Spofforth (A)	18	94	20.99	C. E. L. Ambrose (WI)	98	405
18.56	F. H. Tyson (E)	17	76				

BEST CAREER STRIKE-RATES

(Balls per wicket. Qualification: 75 wickets)

SR		*T*	*W*	*SR*		*T*	*W*
34.19	G. A. Lohmann (E)	18	112	45.42	F. H. Tyson (E)	17	76
38.75	S. E. Bond (NZ)	18	87	45.46	C. Blythe (E)	19	100
41.58	**D. W. Steyn (SA)**	**62**	**312**	45.74	Shoaib Akhtar (P)	46	178
41.65	S. F. Barnes (E)	27	189	46.76	M. D. Marshall (WI)	81	376
43.49	Waqar Younis (P)	87	373	47.02	A. A. Donald (SA)	72	330
44.52	F. R. Spofforth (A)	18	94	48.78	Mohammad Asif (P)	23	106
45.12	J. V. Saunders (A)	14	79	49.32	C. E. H. Croft (WI)	27	125
45.18	J. Briggs (E)	33	118	49.43	F. S. Trueman (E)	67	307

BEST CAREER ECONOMY-RATES

(Runs per six balls. Qualification: 75 wickets)

ER		*T*	*W*	*ER*		*T*	*W*
1.64	T. L. Goddard (SA)	41	123	1.94	W. J. O'Reilly (A)	27	144
1.67	R. G. Nadkarni (I)	41	88	1.94	H. J. Tayfield (SA)	37	170
1.88	H. Verity (E)	40	144	1.95	A. L. Valentine (WI)	36	139
1.88	G. A. Lohmann (E)	18	112	1.95	F. J. Titmus (E)	53	153
1.89	J. H. Wardle (E)	28	102	1.97	S. Ramadhin (WI)	43	158
1.91	R. Illingworth (E)	61	122	1.97	R. Peel (E)	20	101
1.93	C. T. B. Turner (A)	17	101	1.97	A. K. Davidson (A)	44	186
1.94	M. W. Tate (E)	39	155	1.98	L. R. Gibbs (WI)	79	309

HIGHEST PERCENTAGE OF TEAM'S WICKETS OVER TEST CAREER

(Qualification: 20 Tests)

	Tests	*Wkts*	*Team Wkts*	*% of Team Wkts*
M. Muralitharan (Sri Lanka/World)	133	800	2,070	38.64
S. F. Barnes (England)	27	189	494	38.25
R. J. Hadlee (New Zealand)	86	431	1,255	34.34
C. V. Grimmett (Australia)	37	216	636	33.96
Fazal Mahmood (Pakistan)	34	139	410	33.90
W. J. O'Reilly (Australia)	27	144	446	32.28
S. P. Gupte (India)	36	149	470	31.70
Saeed Ajmal (Pakistan)	**23**	**122**	**389**	**31.36**
Mohammad Rafique (Bangladesh)	33	100	328	30.48
A. V. Bedser (England)	51	236	777	30.37
Shakib Al Hasan (Bangladesh)	**28**	**102**	**337**	**30.26**

Note: Excluding the Super Series Test, Muralitharan took 795 out of 2,050 wickets in his 132 Tests for Sri Lanka, a percentage of 38.78.

The percentage shows the proportion of a team's wickets taken by that player in all Tests in which he played, including team wickets in innings in which he did not bowl.

ALL-ROUND RECORDS

HUNDRED AND FIVE WICKETS IN AN INNINGS

England					
A. W. Greig	148	6-164	v West Indies	Bridgetown	1973-74
I. T. Botham	103	5-73	v New Zealand	Christchurch	1977-78
I. T. Botham	108	8-34	v Pakistan	Lord's	1978
I. T. Botham	114	6-58, 7-48	v India	Bombay	1979-80
I. T. Botham	149*	6-95	v Australia	Leeds	1981
I. T. Botham	138	5-59	v New Zealand	Wellington	1983-84
Australia					
C. Kelleway	114	5-33	v South Africa	Manchester	1912
J. M. Gregory	100	7-69	v England	Melbourne	1920-21
K. R. Miller	109	6-107	v West Indies	Kingston	1954-55
R. Benaud	100	5-84	v South Africa	Johannesburg . . .	1957-58
South Africa					
J. H. Sinclair	106	6-26	v England	Cape Town	1898-99
G. A. Faulkner	123	5-120	v England	Johannesburg . . .	1909-10
J. H. Kallis	110	5-90	v West Indies	Cape Town	1998-99
J. H. Kallis	139*	5-21	v Bangladesh	Potchefstroom . . .	2002-03
West Indies					
D. St E. Atkinson	219	5-56	v Australia	Bridgetown	1954-55
O. G. Smith	100	5-90	v India	Delhi	1958-59
G. S. Sobers	104	5-63	v India	Kingston	1961-62
G. S. Sobers	174	5-41	v England	Leeds	1966
New Zealand					
B. R. Taylor†	105	5-86	v India	Calcutta	1964-65
India					
V. Mankad	184	5-196	v England	Lord's	1952
P. R. Umrigar	172*	5-107	v West Indies	Port-of-Spain	1961-62
R. Ashwin	103	5-156	v West Indies	Mumbai	2011-12
Pakistan					
Mushtaq Mohammad	201	5-49	v New Zealand	Dunedin	1972-73
Mushtaq Mohammad	121	5-28	v West Indies	Port-of-Spain	1976-77
Imran Khan	117	6-98, 5-82	v India	Faisalabad	1982-83
Wasim Akram	123	5-100	v Australia	Adelaide	1989-90
Zimbabwe					
P. A. Strang	106*	5-212	v Pakistan	Sheikhupura	1996-97
Bangladesh					
Shakib Al Hasan	144	6-82	v Pakistan	Mirpur	2011-12

† *On debut.*

HUNDRED AND FIVE DISMISSALS IN AN INNINGS

D. T. Lindsay	182	6ct	SA v A	Johannesburg	1966-67
I. D. S. Smith	113*	4ct, 1st	NZ v E	Auckland	1983-84
S. A. R. Silva	111	5ct	SL v I	Colombo (PSS)	1985-86
A. C. Gilchrist	133	4ct, 1st	A v E	Sydney	2002-03
M. J. Prior	118	5ct	E v A	Sydney	2010-11

100 RUNS AND TEN WICKETS IN A TEST

A. K. Davidson	44 80	5-135 6-87	A v WI	Brisbane	1960-61
I. T. Botham	114	6-58 7-48	E v I	Bombay	1979-80
Imran Khan	117	6-98 5-82	P v I	Faisalabad	1982-83

2,000 RUNS AND 200 WICKETS

	Tests	*Runs*	*Wkts*	*Tests for 1,000/100 Double*
R. Benaud (Australia)	63	2,201	248	32
†I. T. Botham (England)	102	5,200	383	21
C. L. Cairns (New Zealand)	62	3,320	218	33
A. Flintoff (England/World)	79	3,845	226	43
R. J. Hadlee (New Zealand)	86	3,124	431	28
Harbhajan Singh (India)	**99**	**2,191**	**408**	**93**
Imran Khan (Pakistan)	88	3,807	362	30
†J. H. Kallis (South Africa/World)	**160**	**13,048**	**285**	**53**
Kapil Dev (India)	131	5,248	434	25
A. Kumble (India)	132	2,506	619	56
S. M. Pollock (South Africa)	108	3,781	421	26
†G. S. Sobers (West Indies)	93	8,032	235	48
W. P. U. J. C. Vaas (Sri Lanka)	111	3,089	355	47
D. L. Vettori (New Zealand/World)	**112**	**4,516**	**360**	**47**
†S. K. Warne (Australia)	145	3,154	708	58
Wasim Akram (Pakistan)	104	2,898	414	45

Note: H. H. Streak scored 1,990 runs and took 216 wickets in 65 Tests for Zimbabwe.

† J. H. Kallis has also taken 192 catches, S. K. Warne 125, I. T. Botham 120 and G. S. Sobers 109. These four and C. L. Hooper (5,762 runs, 114 wickets and 115 catches for West Indies) are the only players to have achieved the treble of 1,000 runs, 100 wickets and 100 catches in Test cricket.

WICKETKEEPING RECORDS

MOST DISMISSALS IN AN INNINGS

7 (all ct)	Wasim Bari	Pakistan v New Zealand at Auckland	1978-79
7 (all ct)	R. W. Taylor	England v India at Bombay	1979-80
7 (all ct)	I. D. S. Smith	New Zealand v Sri Lanka at Hamilton	1990-91
7 (all ct)	R. D. Jacobs	West Indies v Australia at Melbourne	2000-01

Notes: The first instance of seven wicketkeeping dismissals in a Test innings was a joint effort for Pakistan v West Indies at Kingston in 1976-77. Majid Khan made four catches, deputising for the injured wicketkeeper Wasim Bari, who made three more catches on his return.

There have been **23** instances of players making six dismissals in a Test innings, the most recent being **M. J. Prior (5ct, 1st) for England v South Africa at Lord's, 2012.**

MOST STUMPINGS IN AN INNINGS

5	K. S. More	India v West Indies at Madras	1987-88

MOST DISMISSALS IN A TEST

11 (all ct)	R. C. Russell	England v South Africa at Johannesburg	1995-96
10 (all ct)	R. W. Taylor	England v India at Bombay	1979-80
10 (all ct)	A. C. Gilchrist	Australia v New Zealand at Hamilton	1999-2000
9 (8ct, 1st)	G. R. A. Langley	Australia v England at Lord's	1956
9 (all ct)	D. A. Murray	West Indies v Australia at Melbourne	1981-82
9 (all ct)	R. W. Marsh	Australia v England at Brisbane	1982-83
9 (all ct)	S. A. R. Silva	Sri Lanka v India at Colombo (SSC)	1985-86
9 (8ct, 1st)	S. A. R. Silva	Sri Lanka v India at Colombo (PSS)	1985-86
9 (all ct)	D. J. Richardson	South Africa v India at Port Elizabeth	1992-93
9 (all ct)	Rashid Latif	Pakistan v New Zealand at Auckland	1993-94
9 (all ct)	I. A. Healy	Australia v England at Brisbane	1994-95
9 (all ct)	C. O. Browne	West Indies v England at Nottingham	1995
9 (7ct, 2st)	R. C. Russell	England v South Africa at Port Elizabeth	1995-96
9 (8ct, 1st)	M. V. Boucher	South Africa v Pakistan at Port Elizabeth	1997-98
9 (8ct, 1st)	R. D. Jacobs	West Indies v Australia at Melbourne	2000-01
9 (all ct)	Kamran Akmal	Pakistan v West Indies at Kingston	2004-05
9 (all ct)	G. O. Jones	England v Bangladesh at Chester-le-Street	2005
9 (8ct, 1st)	A. C. Gilchrist	Australia v England at Sydney	2006-07
9 (8ct, 1st)	B. B. McCullum	New Zealand v Pakistan at Napier	2009-10
9 (all ct)	B. J. Haddin	Australia v Pakistan at Sydney	2009-10
9 (all ct)	M. V. Boucher	South Africa v India at Durban	2010-11

Notes: S. A. R. Silva made 18 dismissals in two successive Tests.

The most stumpings in a match is 6 by K. S. More for India v West Indies at Madras in 1987-88.

J. J. Kelly (8ct) for Australia v England in 1901-02 and L. E. G. Ames (6ct, 2st) for England v West Indies in 1933 were the only wicketkeepers to make eight dismissals in a Test before World War II.

MOST DISMISSALS IN A SERIES

(Played in 5 Tests unless otherwise stated)

28 (all ct)	R. W. Marsh	Australia v England	1982-83
27 (25ct, 2st)	R. C. Russell	England v South Africa	1995-96
27 (25ct, 2st)	I. A. Healy	Australia v England (6 Tests)	1997
26 (23ct, 3st)	J. H. B. Waite	South Africa v New Zealand	1961-62
26 (all ct)	R. W. Marsh	Australia v West Indies (6 Tests)	1975-76
26 (21ct, 5st)	I. A. Healy	Australia v England (6 Tests)	1993
26 (25ct, 1st)	M. V. Boucher	South Africa v England	1998
26 (24ct, 2st)	A. C. Gilchrist	Australia v England	2001
26 (24ct, 2st)	A. C. Gilchrist	Australia v England	2006-07
25 (23ct, 2st)	I. A. Healy	Australia v England	1994-95
25 (23ct, 2st)	A. C. Gilchrist	Australia v England	2002-03
25 (all ct)	A. C. Gilchrist	Australia v India	2007-08

Notes: S. A. R. Silva made 22 dismissals (21ct, 1st) in three Tests for Sri Lanka v India in 1985-86.

H. Strudwick, with 21 (15ct, 6st) for England v South Africa in 1913-14, was the only wicketkeeper to make as many as 20 dismissals in a series before World War II.

200 DISMISSALS

			T	*Ct*	*St*
1	**M. V. Boucher (South Africa/World)**	**555**	**147**	**532**	**23**
2	A. C. Gilchrist (Australia)	416	96	379	37
3	I. A. Healy (Australia)	395	119	366	29
4	R. W. Marsh (Australia)	355	96	343	12
5	P. J. L. Dujon (West Indies)	270	79	265	5
6	A. P. E. Knott (England)	269	95	250	19
7	A. J. Stewart (England)	241	82	227	14
8	**M. S. Dhoni (India)**	**234**	**73**	**203**	**31**

9	Wasim Bari (Pakistan)	228	81	201	27
10	R. D. Jacobs (West Indies)	219	65	207	12
	T. G. Evans (England)	219	91	173	46
12	Kamran Akmal (Pakistan)	206	53	184	22
13	A. C. Parore (New Zealand)	201	67	194	7

Notes: The record for P. J. L. Dujon excludes two catches taken in two Tests when not keeping wicket; A. J. Stewart's record likewise excludes 36 catches taken in 51 Tests and A. C. Parore's three in 11 Tests.

Excluding the Super Series Test, **M. V. Boucher** has made **553** dismissals (530ct, 23st in 146 Tests) for South Africa, a national record.

W. A. Oldfield made 52 stumpings, a Test record, in 54 Tests for Australia; he also took 78 catches.

The most dismissals by a wicketkeeper playing for the countries not mentioned above are:

		T	*Ct*	*St*
K. C. Sangakkara (Sri Lanka)	151	48	131	20
A. Flower (Zimbabwe)	151	55	142	9
Khaled Mashud (Bangladesh)	87	44	78	9

Note: K. C. Sangakkara's record excludes 38 catches taken in 67 matches when not keeping wicket but includes two catches taken as wicketkeeper in a match where he took over when the designated keeper was injured; A. Flower's record excludes nine catches in eight Tests when not keeping wicket.

FIELDING RECORDS

(Excluding wicketkeepers)

MOST CATCHES IN AN INNINGS

5	V. Y. Richardson	Australia v South Africa at Durban	1935-36
5	Yajurvindra Singh	India v England at Bangalore	1976-77
5	M. Azharuddin	India v Pakistan at Karachi	1989-90
5	K. Srikkanth	India v Australia at Perth	1991-92
5	S. P. Fleming	New Zealand v Zimbabwe at Harare	1997-98
5	**G. C. Smith**	**South Africa v Australia at Perth**	**2012-13**

MOST CATCHES IN A TEST

7	G. S. Chappell	Australia v England at Perth	1974-75
7	Yajurvindra Singh	India v England at Bangalore	1976-77
7	H. P. Tillekeratne	Sri Lanka v New Zealand at Colombo (SSC)	1992-93
7	S. P. Fleming	New Zealand v Zimbabwe at Harare	1997-98
7	M. L. Hayden	Australia v Sri Lanka at Galle	2003-04

Note: There have been **27** instances of players taking six catches in a Test, the most recent being **G. C. Smith for South Africa v Australia at Perth, 2012-13.**

MOST CATCHES IN A SERIES

(Played in 5 Tests unless otherwise stated)

15	J. M. Gregory	Australia v England	1920-21
14	G. S. Chappell	Australia v England (6 Tests)	1974-75
13	R. B. Simpson	Australia v South Africa	1957-58
13	R. B. Simpson	Australia v West Indies	1960-61
13	B. C. Lara	West Indies v England (6 Tests)	1997-98
13	R. Dravid	India v Australia (4 Tests)	2004-05
13	B. C. Lara	West Indies v India (4 Tests)	2005-06

100 CATCHES

Ct	*T*		*Ct*	*T*	
210	**164†**	**R. Dravid (India/World)**	**121**	**100**	**A. J. Strauss (England)**
196	**168**	**R. T. Ponting (Australia)**	120	102	I. T. Botham (England)
194	**138**	**D. P. M. D. Jayawardene (SL)**	120	114	M. C. Cowdrey (England)
193	**160†**	**J. H. Kallis (SA/World)**	115	102	C. L. Hooper (West Indies)
181	128	M. E. Waugh (Australia)	**114**	**194**	**S. R. Tendulkar (India)**
171	111	S. P. Fleming (New Zealand)	112	168	S. R. Waugh (Australia)
164	131†	B. C. Lara (West Indies/World)	110	62	R. B. Simpson (Australia)
157	104	M. A. Taylor (Australia)	110	85	W. R. Hammond (England)
156	156	A. R. Border (Australia)	109	93	G. S. Sobers (West Indies)
152	**107†**	**G. C. Smith (SA/World)**	108	125	S. M. Gavaskar (India)
135	**134**	**V. V. S. Laxman (India)**	105	75	I. M. Chappell (Australia)
128	103	M. L. Hayden (Australia)	105	99	M. Azharuddin (India)
125	145	S. K. Warne (Australia)	105	100	G. P. Thorpe (England)
122	87	G. S. Chappell (Australia)	**103**	**89**	**M. J. Clarke (Australia)**
122	121	I. V. A. Richards (West Indies)	103	118	G. A. Gooch (England)

† *Excluding the Super Series Test, Dravid has made 209 catches in 163 Tests for India, Kallis 189 in 159 Tests for South Africa, and Lara 164 in 130 Tests for West Indies, all national records. G. C. Smith has made 149 catches in 106 Tests for South Africa.*

Note: The most catches in the field for other countries are Pakistan 93 in 124 Tests (Javed Miandad); Zimbabwe 60 in 60 Tests (A. D. R. Campbell); Bangladesh 24 in 57 Tests (Mohammad Ashraful).

TEAM RECORDS

HIGHEST INNINGS TOTALS

952-6 dec	Sri Lanka v India at Colombo (RPS)	1997-98
903-7 dec	England v Australia at The Oval	1938
849	England v West Indies at Kingston	1929-30
790-3 dec	West Indies v Pakistan at Kingston	1957-58
765-6 dec	Pakistan v Sri Lanka at Karachi	2008-09
760-7 dec	Sri Lanka v India at Ahmedabad	2009-10
758-8 dec	Australia v West Indies at Kingston	1954-55
756-5 dec	Sri Lanka v South Africa at Colombo (SSC)	2006
751-5 dec	West Indies v England at St John's	2003-04
749-9 dec	West Indies v England at Bridgetown	2008-09
747	West Indies v South Africa at St John's	2004-05
735-6 dec	Australia v Zimbabwe at Perth	2003-04
729-6 dec	Australia v England at Lord's	1930
726-9 dec	India v Sri Lanka at Mumbai (BS)	2009-10
713-3 dec	Sri Lanka v Zimbabwe at Bulawayo	2003-04
710-7 dec	England v India at Birmingham	2011
708	Pakistan v England at The Oval	1987
707	India v Sri Lanka at Colombo (SSC)	2010
705-7 dec	India v Australia at Sydney	2003-04
701	Australia v England at The Oval	1934

The highest innings for the countries not mentioned above are:

682-6 dec	South Africa v England at Lord's	2003
671-4	New Zealand v Sri Lanka at Wellington	1990-91
563-9 dec	Zimbabwe v West Indies at Harare	2001
556	**Bangladesh v West Indies at Mirpur**	**2012-13**

HIGHEST FOURTH-INNINGS TOTALS

To win

418-7	West Indies (needing 418) v Australia at St John's	2002-03
414-4	South Africa (needing 414) v Australia at Perth	2008-09
406-4	India (needing 403) v West Indies at Port-of-Spain	1975-76
404-3	Australia (needing 404) v England at Leeds	1948
387-4	India (needing 387) v England at Chennai	2008-09
369-6	Australia (needing 369) v Pakistan at Hobart	1999-2000
362-7	Australia (needing 359) v West Indies at Georgetown	1977-78
352-9	Sri Lanka (needing 352) v South Africa at Colombo (PSS)	2006
348-5	West Indies (needing 345) v New Zealand at Auckland	1968-69
344-1	West Indies (needing 342) v England at Lord's	1984

To tie

347	India v Australia at Madras	1986-87

To draw

654-5	England (needing 696 to win) v South Africa at Durban	1938-39
429-8	India (needing 438 to win) v England at The Oval	1979
423-7	South Africa (needing 451 to win) v England at The Oval	1947
408-5	West Indies (needing 836 to win) v England at Kingston	1929-30

To lose

451	New Zealand (lost by 98 runs) v England at Christchurch	2001-02
445	India (lost by 47 runs) v Australia at Adelaide	1977-78
440	New Zealand (lost by 38 runs) v England at Nottingham	1973
431	New Zealand (lost by 121 runs) v England at Napier	2007-08
417	England (lost by 45 runs) v Australia at Melbourne	1976-77
413	Bangladesh (lost by 107 runs) v Sri Lanka at Mirpur	2008-09
411	England (lost by 193 runs) v Australia at Sydney	1924-25
410	Sri Lanka (lost by 96 runs) v Australia at Hobart	2007-08
406	Australia (lost by 115 runs) v England at Lord's	2009
402	Australia (lost by 103 runs) v England at Manchester	1981

MOST RUNS IN A DAY (BOTH SIDES)

588	England (398-6), India (190-0) at Manchester (2nd day)	1936
522	England (503-2), South Africa (19-0) at Lord's (2nd day)	1924
509	Sri Lanka (509-9) v Bangladesh at Colombo (PSS) (2nd day)	2002
508	England (221-2), South Africa (287-6) at The Oval (3rd day)	1935

MOST RUNS IN A DAY (ONE SIDE)

509	Sri Lanka (509-9) v Bangladesh at Colombo (PSS) (2nd day)	2002
503	England (503-2) v South Africa at Lord's (2nd day)	1924
494	Australia (494-6) v South Africa at Sydney (1st day)	1910-11
482	**Australia (482-5) v South Africa at Adelaide (1st day)**	**2012-13**
475	Australia (475-2) v England at The Oval (1st day)	1934
471	England (471-8) v India at The Oval (1st day)	1936
458	Australia (458-3) v England at Leeds (1st day)	1930
455	Australia (455-1) v England at Leeds (2nd day)	1934
452	New Zealand (452-9 dec) v Zimbabwe at Harare (1st day)	2005-06
450	Australia (450) v South Africa at Johannesburg (1st day)	1921-22

MOST WICKETS IN A DAY

27	England (18-3 to 53 all out and 62) v Australia (60) at Lord's (2nd day)	1888
25	Australia (112 and 48-5) v England (61) at Melbourne (1st day)	1901-02

HIGHEST AGGREGATES IN A TEST

Runs	*Wkts*			*Days played*
1,981	35	South Africa v England at Durban	1938-39	10†
1,815	34	West Indies v England at Kingston	1929-30	9‡
1,764	39	Australia v West Indies at Adelaide	1968-69	5
1,753	40	Australia v England at Adelaide	1920-21	6
1,747	25	Australia v India at Sydney	2003-04	5
1,723	31	England v Australia at Leeds	1948	5
1,702	28	Pakistan v India at Faisalabad	2005-06	5

† *No play on one day.* ‡ *No play on two days.*

LOWEST INNINGS TOTALS

26	New Zealand v England at Auckland	1954-55
30	South Africa v England at Port Elizabeth	1895-96
30	South Africa v England at Birmingham	1924
35	South Africa v England at Cape Town	1898-99
36	Australia v England at Birmingham	1902
36	South Africa v Australia at Melbourne	1931-32
42	Australia v England at Sydney	1887-88
42	New Zealand v Australia at Wellington	1945-46
42†	India v England at Lord's	1974
43	South Africa v England at Cape Town	1888-89
44	Australia v England at The Oval	1896
45	England v Australia at Sydney	1886-87
45	South Africa v Australia at Melbourne	1931-32
45	**New Zealand v South Africa at Cape Town**	**2012-13**
46	England v West Indies at Port-of-Spain	1993-94
47	South Africa v England at Cape Town	1888-89
47	New Zealand v England at Lord's	1958
47	West Indies v England at Kingston	2003-04
47	Australia v South Africa at Cape Town	2011-12

The lowest innings for the countries not mentioned above are:

51	**Zimbabwe v New Zealand at Napier**	**2011-12**
53†	Pakistan v Australia at Sharjah	2002-03
62	Bangladesh v Sri Lanka at Colombo (PSS)	2007
71	Sri Lanka v Pakistan at Kandy	1994-95

† *Batted one man short.*

FEWEST RUNS IN A FULL DAY'S PLAY

95	Australia (80), Pakistan (15-2) at Karachi (1st day, 5½ hrs)	1956-57
104	Pakistan (0-0 to 104-5) v Australia at Karachi (4th day, 5½ hrs)	1959-60
106	England (92-2 to 198) v Australia at Brisbane (4th day, 5 hrs). *England were dismissed five minutes before the close of play, leaving no time for Australia to start their second innings.*	1958-59
111	S. Africa (48-2 to 130-6 dec), India (29-1) at Cape Town (5th day, 5½ hrs)	1992-93
112	Australia (138-6 to 187), Pakistan (63-1) at Karachi (4th day, 5½ hrs)	1956-57
115	Australia (116-7 to 165 and 66-5 after following on) v Pakistan at Karachi (4th day, 5½ hrs)	1988-89
117	India (117-5) v Australia at Madras (1st day, 5½ hrs)	1956-57
117	New Zealand (6-0 to 123-4) v Sri Lanka at Colombo (SSC) (5th day, 5¾ hrs)	1983-84

In England

151	England (175-2 to 289), New Zealand (37-7) at Lord's (3rd day, 6 hrs)	1978
158	England (211-2 to 369-9) v South Africa at Manchester (5th day, 6 hrs)	1998
159	Pakistan (208-4 to 350), England (17-1) at Leeds (3rd day, 6 hrs)	1971

LOWEST AGGREGATES IN A COMPLETED TEST

Runs	*Wkts*			*Days played*
234	29	Australia v South Africa at Melbourne	1931-32	3†
291	40	England v Australia at Lord's	1888	2
295	28	New Zealand v Australia at Wellington	1945-46	2
309	29	West Indies v England at Bridgetown	1934-35	3
323	30	England v Australia at Manchester	1888	2

† *No play on one day.*

LARGEST VICTORIES

Largest Innings Victories

Inns & 579 runs	England (903-7 dec) v Australia (201 & 123†) at The Oval	1938
Inns & 360 runs	Australia (652-7 dec) v South Africa (159 & 133) at Johannesburg	2001-02
Inns & 336 runs	West Indies (614-5 dec) v India (124 & 154) at Calcutta	1958-59
Inns & 332 runs	Australia (645) v England (141 & 172) at Brisbane	1946-47
Inns & 324 runs	Pakistan (643) v New Zealand (73 & 246) at Lahore	2002
Inns & 322 runs	West Indies (660-5 dec) v New Zealand (216 & 122) at Wellington	1994-95
Inns & 310 runs	West Indies (536) v Bangladesh (139 & 87) at Dhaka	2002-03
Inns & 301 runs	**New Zealand (495-7 dec) v Zimbabwe (51 & 143) at Napier**	**2011-12**

† *Two men absent in both Australian innings.*

Largest Victories by Runs Margin

675 runs	England (521 & 342-8 dec) v Australia (122 & 66†) at Brisbane	1928-29
562 runs	Australia (701 & 327) v England (321 & 145‡) at The Oval	1934
530 runs	Australia (328 & 578) v South Africa (205 & 171§) at Melbourne	1910-11
491 runs	Australia (381 & 361-5 dec) v Pakistan (179 & 72) at Perth	2004-05
465 runs	Sri Lanka (384 and 447-6 dec) v Bangladesh (208 and 158) at Chittagong	2008-09
425 runs	West Indies (211 & 411-5 dec) v England (71 & 126) at Manchester	1976
409 runs	Australia (350 & 460-7 dec) v England (215 & 186) at Lord's	1948
408 runs	West Indies (328 & 448) v Australia (203 & 165) at Adelaide	1979-80

† *One man absent in Australia's first innings; two men absent in their second.*
‡ *Two men absent in England's first innings; one man absent in their second.*
§ *One man absent in South Africa's second innings.*

TIED TESTS

West Indies (453 & 284) v Australia (505 & 232) at Brisbane	1960-61
Australia (574-7 dec & 170-5 dec) v India (397 & 347) at Madras	1986-87

MOST CONSECUTIVE TEST VICTORIES

16	Australia	1999-2000–2000-01
16	Australia	2005-06–2007-08
11	West Indies	1983-84–1984-85
9	Sri Lanka	2001–2001-02
9	South Africa	2001-02–2003
8	Australia	1920-21–1921
8	England	2004–2004-05

MOST CONSECUTIVE TESTS WITHOUT VICTORY

44	New Zealand	1929-30–1955-56	23	New Zealand	1962-63–1967-68
34	Bangladesh	2000-01–2004-05	22	Pakistan	1958-59–1964-65
31	India	1981-82–1984-85	21	Sri Lanka	1985-86–1992-93
28	South Africa	1935–1949-50	20	West Indies	1968-69–1972-73
24	India	1932–1951-52	20	West Indies	2004-05–2007
24	Bangladesh	2004-05–2008-09			

WHITEWASHES

Teams winning every game in a series of four Tests or more:

Five-Test Series

Australia beat England	1920-21	West Indies beat England	1985-86
Australia beat South Africa	1931-32	South Africa beat West Indies	1998-99
England beat India	1959	Australia beat West Indies	2000-01
West Indies beat India	1961-62	Australia beat England	2006-07
West Indies beat England	1984		

Four-Test Series

Australia beat India	1967-68	England beat India	2011
South Africa beat Australia	1969-70	Australia beat India	2011-12
England beat West Indies	2004		

Note: The winning team in each instance was at home, except for West Indies in England, 1984.

PLAYERS

YOUNGEST TEST PLAYERS

Years	*Days*			
15	124	Mushtaq Mohammad	Pakistan v West Indies at Lahore	1958-59
16	189	Aqib Javed	Pakistan v New Zealand at Wellington	1988-89
16	205	S. R. Tendulkar	India v Pakistan at Karachi	1989-90

The above table should be treated with caution. All birthdates for Bangladesh and Pakistan (after Partition) must be regarded as questionable because of deficiencies in record-keeping. Hasan Raza was claimed to be 14 years 227 days old when he played for Pakistan against Zimbabwe at Faisalabad in 1996-97; this age was rejected by the Pakistan Cricket Board, although no alternative has been offered. Suggestions that Enamul Haque jun. was 16 years 230 days old when he played for Bangladesh against England in Dhaka in 2003-04 have been discounted by well-informed local observers, who believe he was 18.

The youngest Test players for countries not mentioned above are:

17	122	J. E. D. Sealy	West Indies v England at Bridgetown	1929-30
17	128	Mohammad Sharif	Bangladesh v Zimbabwe at Bulawayo	2000-01
17	189	C. D. U. S. Weerasinghe	Sri Lanka v India at Colombo (PSS)	1985-86
17	239	I. D. Craig	Australia v South Africa at Melbourne	1952-53
17	352	H. Masakadza	Zimbabwe v West Indies at Harare	2001
18	10	D. L. Vettori	New Zealand v England at Wellington	1996-97
18	149	D. B. Close	England v New Zealand at Manchester	1949
18	340	P. R. Adams	South Africa v England at Port Elizabeth	1995-96

OLDEST PLAYERS ON TEST DEBUT

Years	*Days*			
49	119	J. Southerton	England v Australia at Melbourne	1876-77
47	284	Miran Bux	Pakistan v India at Lahore	1954-55
46	253	D. D. Blackie	Australia v England at Sydney	1928-29
46	237	H. Ironmonger	Australia v England at Brisbane	1928-29
42	242	N. Betancourt	West Indies v England at Port-of-Spain	1929-30
41	337	E. R. Wilson	England v Australia at Sydney	1920-21
41	27	R. J. D. Jamshedji	India v England at Bombay	1933-34
40	345	C. A. Wiles	West Indies v England at Manchester	1933
40	295	O. Henry	South Africa v India at Durban	1992-93
40	216	S. P. Kinneir	England v Australia at Sydney	1911-12
40	110	H. W. Lee	England v South Africa at Johannesburg	1930-31
40	56	G. W. A. Chubb	South Africa v England at Nottingham	1951
40	37	C. Ramaswami	India v England at Manchester	1936

Note: The oldest Test player on debut for New Zealand was H. M. McGirr, 38 years 101 days, v England at Auckland, 1929-30; for Sri Lanka, D. S. de Silva, 39 years 251 days, v England at Colombo (PSS), 1981-82; for Zimbabwe, A. C. Waller, 37 years 84 days, v England at Bulawayo, 1996-97; for Bangladesh, Enamul Haque, sen. 35 years 58 days, v Zimbabwe at Harare, 2000-01. A. J. Traicos was 45 years 154 days old when he made his debut for Zimbabwe (v India at Harare, 1992-93) having played three Tests for South Africa in 1969-70.

OLDEST TEST PLAYERS

(Age on final day of their last Test match)

Years	*Days*			
52	165	W. Rhodes	England v West Indies at Kingston	1929-30
50	327	H. Ironmonger	Australia v England at Sydney	1932-33
50	320	W. G. Grace	England v Australia at Nottingham	1899
50	303	G. Gunn	England v West Indies at Kingston	1929-30
49	139	J. Southerton	England v Australia at Melbourne	1876-77
47	302	Miran Bux	Pakistan v India at Peshawar	1954-55
47	249	J. B. Hobbs	England v Australia at The Oval	1930
47	87	F. E. Woolley	England v Australia at The Oval	1934
46	309	D. D. Blackie	Australia v England at Adelaide	1928-29
46	206	A. W. Nourse	South Africa v England at The Oval	1924
46	202	H. Strudwick	England v Australia at The Oval	1926
46	41	E. H. Hendren	England v West Indies at Kingston	1934-35
45	304	A. J. Traicos	Zimbabwe v India at Delhi	1992-93
45	245	G. O. B. Allen	England v West Indies at Kingston	1947-48
45	215	P. Holmes	England v India at Lord's	1932
45	140	D. B. Close	England v West Indies at Manchester	1976

MOST TEST APPEARANCES

194	**S. R. Tendulkar (India)**
168	**R. T. Ponting (Australia)**
168	S. R. Waugh (Australia)
164	**R. Dravid (India/World)**
160	**J. H. Kallis (South Africa/World)**
156	A. R. Border (Australia)
147	**M. V. Boucher (South Africa/World)**
146	**S. Chanderpaul (West Indies)**
145	S. K. Warne (Australia)
138	**D. P. M. D. Jayawardene (Sri Lanka)**
134	**V. V. S. Laxman (India)**
133	M. Muralitharan (Sri Lanka/World)
133	A. J. Stewart (England)
132	A. Kumble (India)
132	C. A. Walsh (West Indies)
131	Kapil Dev (India)
131	B. C. Lara (West Indies/World)
128	M. E. Waugh (Australia)
125	S. M. Gavaskar (India)
124	Javed Miandad (Pakistan)
124	G. D. McGrath (Australia)
121	I. V. A. Richards (West Indies)
120	Inzamam-ul-Haq (Pakistan/World)

Note: Excluding the Super Series Test, **J. H. Kallis** has made **159** appearances for South Africa, a national record. The most appearances for New Zealand is 111 by S. P. Fleming; for Zimbabwe, 67 by G. W. Flower; and for Bangladesh 57 by Mohammad Ashraful.

MOST CONSECUTIVE TEST APPEARANCES FOR A COUNTRY

153	A. R. Border (Australia)	March 1979 to March 1994
107	M. E. Waugh (Australia)	June 1993 to October 2002
106	S. M. Gavaskar (India)	January 1975 to February 1987
96†	A. C. Gilchrist (Australia)	November 1999 to January 2008
93	R. Dravid (India)	June 1996 to December 2005
93	**D. P. M. D. Jayawardene (Sri Lanka)**	**November 2002 to January 2013**
87	G. R. Viswanath (India)	March 1971 to February 1983
86	M. L. Hayden (Australia)	March 2000 to January 2008
85	G. S. Sobers (West Indies)	April 1955 to April 1972
85	**A. N. Cook (England)**	**May 2006 to December 2012**
84	S. R. Tendulkar (India)	November 1989 to June 2001
82	**A. B. de Villiers (South Africa)**	**December 2004 to January 2013**
79†	**M. E. K. Hussey (Australia)**	**November 2005 to January 2013**
75	M. V. Boucher (South Africa)	February 1998 to August 2004
73	R. T. Ponting (Australia)	November 2004 to December 2010
72	S. P. Fleming (New Zealand)	July 1999 to March 2008
72	D. L. Haynes (West Indies)	December 1979 to June 1988
72	**B. B. McCullum (New Zealand)**	**March 2004 to January 2013**
71	I. M. Chappell (Australia)	January 1966 to February 1976

The most consecutive Test appearances for the countries not mentioned above are:

56	A. D. R. Campbell (Zimbabwe)	October 1992 to September 2001
53	Javed Miandad (Pakistan)	December 1977 to January 1984
38	Mohammad Ashraful (Bangladesh)	February 2004 to February 2010

† *Complete Test career.*

Bold type denotes sequence which was still in progress after January 1, 2012.

MOST TESTS AS CAPTAIN

	P	*W*	*L*	*D*
G. C. Smith (SA/World)	**99**	**47**	**26†**	**26**
A. R. Border (A)	93	32	22	38*
S. P. Fleming (NZ)	80	28	27	25
R. T. Ponting (A)	77	48	16	13
C. H. Lloyd (WI)	74	36	12	26
S. R. Waugh (A)	57	41	9	7
A. Ranatunga (SL)	56	12	19	25
M. A. Atherton (E)	54	13	21	20
W. J. Cronje (SA)	53	27	11	15
M. P. Vaughan (E)	51	26	11	14
I. V. A. Richards (WI)	50	27	8	15
M. A. Taylor (A)	50	26	13	11
A. J. Strauss (E)	**50**	**24**	**11**	**15**
S. C. Ganguly (I)	49	21	13	15
G. S. Chappell (A)	48	21	13	14
Imran Khan (P)	48	14	8	26
M. Azharuddin (I)	47	14	14	19
B. C. Lara (WI)	47	10	26	11
S. M. Gavaskar (I)	47	9	8	30
N. Hussain (E)	45	17	15	13
M. S. Dhoni (I)	**43**	**20**	**12**	**11**
P. B. H. May (E)	41	20	10	11
Nawab of Pataudi jun. (I)	40	9	19	12

* *One match tied.*

† *Includes defeat as World XI captain in Super Series Test against Australia.*

Most Tests as captain of other countries:

	P	*W*	*L*	*D*
A. D. R. Campbell (Z)	21	2	12	7
Habibul Bashar (B)	18	1	13	4

Notes: A. R. Border captained Australia in 93 consecutive Tests.

W. W. Armstrong (Australia) captained his country in the most Tests without being defeated: ten matches with eight wins and two draws.

Mohammad Ashraful (Bangladesh) captained his country in the most Tests without ever winning: 12 defeats and one draw.

UMPIRES

MOST TESTS

		First Test	*Last Test*
128	S. A. Bucknor (West Indies)	1988-89	2008-09
108	R. E. Koertzen (South Africa)	1992-93	2010
95	D. J. Harper (Australia)	1998-99	2011
92	D. R. Shepherd (England)	1985	2004-05
78	**Aleem Dar (Pakistan)**	**2003-04**	**2012-13**
78	D. B. Hair (Australia)	1991-92	2008
74	**S. J. A. Taufel (Australia)**	**2000-01**	**2012**
73	S. Venkataraghavan (India)	1992-93	2003-04
72	**B. F. Bowden (New Zealand)**	**1999-2000**	**2012-13**
66	H. D. Bird (England)	1973	1996

An expanded and regularly updated online version of the Records can be found at www.wisdenrecords.com

SUMMARY OF TESTS

To January 14, 2013

	Opponents	*Tests*	*Won by* E	A	SA	WI	NZ	I	P	SL	Z	B	Wld	*Tied*	*Drawn*
England	Australia	**326**	102	133	–	–	–	–	–	–	–	–	–	–	91
	South Africa	**141**	56	–	31	–	–	–	–	–	–	–	–	–	54
	West Indies	**148**	45	–	–	53	–	–	–	–	–	–	–	–	50
	New Zealand	**94**	45	–	–	–	8	–	–	–	–	–	–	–	41
	India	**107**	40	–	–	–	–	20	–	–	–	–	–	–	47
	Pakistan	**74**	22	–	–	–	–	–	16	–	–	–	–	–	36
	Sri Lanka	**26**	10	–	–	–	–	–	–	7	–	–	–	–	9
	Zimbabwe	**6**	3	–	–	–	–	–	–	–	0	–	–	–	3
	Bangladesh	**8**	8	–	–	–	–	–	–	–	–	0	–	–	0
Australia	South Africa	**88**	–	48	20	–	–	–	–	–	–	–	–	–	20
	West Indies	**111**	–	54	–	32	–	–	–	–	–	–	–	1	24
	New Zealand	**52**	–	27	–	–	8	–	–	–	–	–	–	–	17
	India	**82**	–	38	–	–	–	20	–	–	–	–	–	1	23
	Pakistan	**57**	–	28	–	–	–	–	12	–	–	–	–	–	17
	Sri Lanka	**26**	–	17	–	–	–	–	–	1	–	–	–	–	8
	Zimbabwe	**3**	–	3	–	–	–	–	–	–	0	–	–	–	0
	Bangladesh	**4**	–	4	–	–	–	–	–	–	–	0	–	–	0
	ICC World XI	**1**	–	1	–	–	–	–	–	–	–	–	0	–	0
South Africa	West Indies	**25**	–	–	16	3	–	–	–	–	–	–	–	–	6
	New Zealand	**40**	–	–	23	–	4	–	–	–	–	–	–	–	13
	India	**27**	–	–	12	–	–	7	–	–	–	–	–	–	8
	Pakistan	**18**	–	–	8	–	–	–	3	–	–	–	–	–	7
	Sri Lanka	**20**	–	–	10	–	–	–	–	5	–	–	–	–	5
	Zimbabwe	**7**	–	–	6	–	–	–	–	–	0	–	–	–	1
	Bangladesh	**8**	–	–	8	–	–	–	–	–	–	0	–	–	0
West Indies	New Zealand	**39**	–	–	–	12	9	–	–	–	–	–	–	–	18
	India	**88**	–	–	–	30	–	14	–	–	–	–	–	–	44
	Pakistan	**46**	–	–	–	15	–	–	16	–	–	–	–	–	15
	Sri Lanka	**15**	–	–	–	3	–	–	–	6	–	–	–	–	6
	Zimbabwe	**6**	–	–	–	4	–	–	–	–	0	–	–	–	2
	Bangladesh	**10**	–	–	–	6	–	–	–	–	–	2	–	–	2
New Zealand	India	**52**	–	–	–	–	9	18	–	–	–	–	–	–	25
	Pakistan	**50**	–	–	–	–	7	–	23	–	–	–	–	–	20
	Sri Lanka	**28**	–	–	–	–	10	–	–	8	–	–	–	–	10
	Zimbabwe	**15**	–	–	–	–	9	–	–	–	0	–	–	–	6
	Bangladesh	**9**	–	–	–	–	8	–	–	–	–	0	–	–	1
India	Pakistan	**59**	–	–	–	–	–	9	12	–	–	–	–	–	38
	Sri Lanka	**35**	–	–	–	–	–	14	–	6	–	–	–	–	15
	Zimbabwe	**11**	–	–	–	–	–	7	–	–	2	–	–	–	2
	Bangladesh	**7**	–	–	–	–	–	6	–	–	–	0	–	–	1
Pakistan	Sri Lanka	**43**	–	–	–	–	–	–	16	10	–	–	–	–	17
	Zimbabwe	**15**	–	–	–	–	–	–	9	–	2	–	–	–	4
	Bangladesh	**8**	–	–	–	–	–	–	8	–	–	0	–	–	0
Sri Lanka	Zimbabwe	**15**	–	–	–	–	–	–	–	10	0	–	–	–	5
	Bangladesh	**12**	–	–	–	–	–	–	–	12	–	0	–	–	0
Zimbabwe	Bangladesh	**9**	–	–	–	–	–	–	–	–	5	1	–	–	3
		2,071	331	353	134	158	72	115	115	65	9	3	0	2	714

	Tests	*Won*	*Lost*	*Drawn*	*Tied*	*% Won*	*Toss Won*
England	930	331	268	331	–	35.59	448
Australia	750†	353†	195	200	2	47.06	379
South Africa	374	134	126	114	–	35.82	181
West Indies	488	158	162	167	1	32.37	252
New Zealand	379	72	156	151	–	18.99	193
India	468	115	149	203	1	24.57	236
Pakistan	370	115	101	154	–	31.08	175
Sri Lanka	220	65	80	75	–	29.54	118
Zimbabwe	87	9	52	26	–	10.34	50
Bangladesh	75	3	65	7	–	4.00	39
ICC World XI	1	0	1	0	–	0.00	0

† *Includes Super Series Test between Australia and ICC World XI.*

ENGLAND v AUSTRALIA

Season	England	*Captains* Australia	T	E	A	D
1876-77	James Lillywhite	D. W. Gregory	2	1	1	0
1878-79	Lord Harris	D. W. Gregory	1	0	1	0
1880	Lord Harris	W. L. Murdoch	1	1	0	0
1881-82	A. Shaw	W. L. Murdoch	4	0	2	2
1882	A. N. Hornby	W. L. Murdoch	1	0	1	0

THE ASHES

Season	England	*Captains* Australia	T	E	A	D	Held by
1882-83	Hon. Ivo Bligh	W. L. Murdoch	4*	2	2	0	E
1884	Lord Harris[1]	W. L. Murdoch	3	1	0	2	E
1884-85	A. Shrewsbury	T. P. Horan[2]	5	3	2	0	E
1886	A. G. Steel	H. J. H. Scott	3	3	0	0	E
1886-87	A. Shrewsbury	P. S. McDonnell	2	2	0	0	E
1887-88	W. W. Read	P. S. McDonnell	1	1	0	0	E
1888	W. G. Grace[3]	P. S. McDonnell	3	2	1	0	E
1890†	W. G. Grace	W. L. Murdoch	2	2	0	0	E
1891-92	W. G. Grace	J. McC. Blackham	3	1	2	0	A
1893	W. G. Grace[4]	J. McC. Blackham	3	1	0	2	E
1894-95	A. E. Stoddart	G. Giffen[5]	5	3	2	0	E
1896	W. G. Grace	G. H. S. Trott	3	2	1	0	E
1897-98	A. E. Stoddart[6]	G. H. S. Trott	5	1	4	0	A
1899	A. C. MacLaren[7]	J. Darling	5	0	1	4	A
1901-02	A. C. MacLaren	J. Darling[8]	5	1	4	0	A
1902	A. C. MacLaren	J. Darling	5	1	2	2	A
1903-04	P. F. Warner	M. A. Noble	5	3	2	0	E
1905	Hon. F. S. Jackson	J. Darling	5	2	0	3	E
1907-08	A. O. Jones[9]	M. A. Noble	5	1	4	0	A
1909	A. C. MacLaren	M. A. Noble	5	1	2	2	A
1911-12	J. W. H. T. Douglas	C. Hill	5	4	1	0	E
1912	C. B. Fry	S. E. Gregory	3	1	0	2	E
1920-21	J. W. H. T. Douglas	W. W. Armstrong	5	0	5	0	A
1921	Hon. L. H. Tennyson[10]	W. W. Armstrong	5	0	3	2	A
1924-25	A. E. R. Gilligan	H. L. Collins	5	1	4	0	A
1926	A. W. Carr[11]	H. L. Collins[12]	5	1	0	4	E
1928-29	A. P. F. Chapman[13]	J. Ryder	5	4	1	0	E
1930	A. P. F. Chapman[14]	W. M. Woodfull	5	1	2	2	A
1932-33	D. R. Jardine	W. M. Woodfull	5	4	1	0	E
1934	R. E. S. Wyatt[15]	W. M. Woodfull	5	1	2	2	A
1936-37	G. O. B. Allen	D. G. Bradman	5	2	3	0	A
1938†	W. R. Hammond	D. G. Bradman	4	1	1	2	A
1946-47	W. R. Hammond[16]	D. G. Bradman	5	0	3	2	A
1948	N. W. D. Yardley	D. G. Bradman	5	0	4	1	A
1950-51	F. R. Brown	A. L. Hassett	5	1	4	0	A
1953	L. Hutton	A. L. Hassett	5	1	0	4	E
1954-55	L. Hutton	I. W. Johnson[17]	5	3	1	1	E
1956	P. B. H. May	I. W. Johnson	5	2	1	2	E
1958-59	P. B. H. May	R. Benaud	5	0	4	1	A
1961	P. B. H. May[18]	R. Benaud[19]	5	1	2	2	A
1962-63	E. R. Dexter	R. Benaud	5	1	1	3	A
1964	E. R. Dexter	R. B. Simpson	5	0	1	4	A
1965-66	M. J. K. Smith	R. B. Simpson[20]	5	1	1	3	A
1968	M. C. Cowdrey[21]	W. M. Lawry[22]	5	1	1	3	A
1970-71†	R. Illingworth	W. M. Lawry[23]	6	2	0	4	E
1972	R. Illingworth	I. M. Chappell	5	2	2	1	E

Season	Captains: England	Captains: Australia	T	E	A	D	Held by
1974-75	M. H. Denness[24]	I. M. Chappell	6	1	4	1	A
1975	A. W. Greig[25]	I. M. Chappell	4	0	1	3	A
1976-77‡	A. W. Greig	G. S. Chappell	1	0	1	0	—
1977	J. M. Brearley	G. S. Chappell	5	3	0	2	E
1978-79	J. M. Brearley	G. N. Yallop	6	5	1	0	E
1979-80‡	J. M. Brearley	G. S. Chappell	3	0	3	0	—
1980‡	I. T. Botham	G. S. Chappell	1	0	0	1	—
1981	J. M. Brearley[26]	K. J. Hughes	6	3	1	2	E
1982-83	R. G. D. Willis	G. S. Chappell	5	1	2	2	A
1985	D. I. Gower	A. R. Border	6	3	1	2	E
1986-87	M. W. Gatting	A. R. Border	5	2	1	2	E
1987-88‡	M. W. Gatting	A. R. Border	1	0	0	1	—
1989	D. I. Gower	A. R. Border	6	0	4	2	A
1990-91	G. A. Gooch[27]	A. R. Border	5	0	3	2	A
1993	G. A. Gooch[28]	A. R. Border	6	1	4	1	A
1994-95	M. A. Atherton	M. A. Taylor	5	1	3	1	A
1997	M. A. Atherton	M. A. Taylor	6	2	3	1	A
1998-99	A. J. Stewart	M. A. Taylor	5	1	3	1	A
2001	N. Hussain[29]	S. R. Waugh[30]	5	1	4	0	A
2002-03	N. Hussain	S. R. Waugh	5	1	4	0	A
2005	M. P. Vaughan	R. T. Ponting	5	2	1	2	E
2006-07	A. Flintoff	R. T. Ponting	5	0	5	0	A
2009	A. J. Strauss	R. T. Ponting	5	2	1	2	E
2010-11	A. J. Strauss	R. T. Ponting[31]	5	3	1	1	E
	In Australia		170	57	86	27	
	In England		156	45	47	64	
	Totals		326	102	133	91	

* *The Ashes were awarded in 1882-83 after a series of three matches which England won 2–1. A fourth match was played and this was won by Australia.*

† *The matches at Manchester in 1890 and 1938 and at Melbourne (Third Test) in 1970-71 were abandoned without a ball being bowled and are excluded.*

‡ *The Ashes were not at stake in these series.*

Notes: The following deputised for the official touring captain or were appointed by the home authority for only a minor proportion of the series:

[1]A. N. Hornby (First). [2]W. L. Murdoch (First), H. H. Massie (Third), J. McC. Blackham (Fourth). [3]A. G. Steel (First). [4]A. E. Stoddart (First). [5]J. McC. Blackham (First). [6]A. C. MacLaren (First, Second and Fifth). [7]W. G. Grace (First). [8]H. Trumble (Fourth and Fifth). [9]F. L. Fane (First, Second and Third). [10]J. W. H. T. Douglas (First and Second). [11]A. P. F. Chapman (Fifth). [12]W. Bardsley (Third and Fourth). [13]J. C. White (Fifth). [14]R. E. S. Wyatt (Fifth). [15]C. F. Walters (First). [16]N. W. D. Yardley (Fifth). [17]A. R. Morris (Second). [18]M. C. Cowdrey (First and Second). [19]R. N. Harvey (Second). [20]B. C. Booth (First and Third). [21]T. W. Graveney (Fourth). [22]B. N. Jarman (Fourth) [23]I. M. Chappell (Seventh). [24]J. H. Edrich (Fourth). [25]M. H. Denness (First). [26]I. T. Botham (First and Second). [27]A. J. Lamb (First). [28]M. A. Atherton (Fifth and Sixth). [29]M. A. Atherton (Second and Third). [30]A. C. Gilchrist (Fourth). [31]M. J. Clarke (Fifth).

HIGHEST INNINGS TOTALS

For England in England: 903-7 dec at The Oval 1938
in Australia: 644 at Sydney 2010-11

For Australia in England: 729-6 dec at Lord's 1930
in Australia: 659-8 dec at Sydney 1946-47

LOWEST INNINGS TOTALS

For England in England: 52 at The Oval . . . 1948
in Australia: 45 at Sydney . . . 1886-87

For Australia in England: 36 at Birmingham . . . 1902
in Australia: 42 at Sydney . . . 1887-88

DOUBLE-HUNDREDS

For England (13)

364	L. Hutton at The Oval	1938
287	R. E. Foster at Sydney	1903-04
256	K. F. Barrington at Manchester	1964
251	W. R. Hammond at Sydney	1928-29
240	W. R. Hammond at Lord's	1938
235*	A. N. Cook at Brisbane	2010-11
231*	W. R. Hammond at Sydney	1936-37
227	K. P. Pietersen at Adelaide	2010-11
216*	E. Paynter at Nottingham	1938
215	D. I. Gower at Birmingham	1985
207	N. Hussain at Birmingham	1997
206	P. D. Collingwood at Adelaide	2006-07
200	W. R. Hammond at Melbourne	1928-29

For Australia (23)

334	D. G. Bradman at Leeds	1930
311	R. B. Simpson at Manchester	1964
307	R. M. Cowper at Melbourne	1965-66
304	D. G. Bradman at Leeds	1934
270	D. G. Bradman at Melbourne	1936-37
266	W. H. Ponsford at The Oval	1934
254	D. G. Bradman at Lord's	1930
250	J. L. Langer at Melbourne	2002-03
244	D. G. Bradman at The Oval	1934
234	S. G. Barnes at Sydney	1946-47
234	D. G. Bradman at Sydney	1946-47
232	D. G. Bradman at The Oval	1930
232	S. J. McCabe at Nottingham	1938
225	R. B. Simpson at Adelaide	1965-66
219	M. A. Taylor at Nottingham	1989
212	D. G. Bradman at Adelaide	1936-37
211	W. L. Murdoch at The Oval	1884
207	K. R. Stackpole at Brisbane	1970-71
206*	W. A. Brown at Lord's	1938
206	A. R. Morris at Adelaide	1950-51
201*	J. Ryder at Adelaide	1924-25
201	S. E. Gregory at Sydney	1894-95
200*	A. R. Border at Leeds	1993

INDIVIDUAL HUNDREDS

For England (231)

12: J. B. Hobbs.
9: D. I. Gower, W. R. Hammond.
8: H. Sutcliffe.
7: G. Boycott, J. H. Edrich, M. Leyland.
5: K. F. Barrington, D. C. S. Compton, M. C. Cowdrey, L. Hutton, F. S. Jackson, A. C. MacLaren.
4: I. T. Botham, B. C. Broad, A. N. Cook, M. W. Gatting, G. A. Gooch, A. J. Strauss, M. P. Vaughan.
3: M. A. Butcher, E. H. Hendren, P. B. H. May, K. P. Pietersen, D. W. Randall, A. C. Russell, A. Shrewsbury, G. P. Thorpe, I. J. L. Trott, J. T. Tyldesley, R. A. Woolmer.
2: C. J. Barnett, L. C. Braund, E. R. Dexter, B. L. D'Oliveira, W. J. Edrich, W. G. Grace, G. Gunn, T. W. Hayward, N. Hussain, A. P. E. Knott, B. W. Luckhurst, K. S. Ranjitsinhji, R. T. Robinson, Rev. D. S. Sheppard, R. A. Smith, A. G. Steel, A. E. Stoddart, R. Subba Row, C. Washbrook, F. E. Woolley.
1: R. Abel, L. E. G. Ames, M. A. Atherton, R. W. Barber, W. Barnes, I. R. Bell, J. Briggs, J. T. Brown, A. P. F. Chapman, P. D. Collingwood, M. H. Denness, K. S. Duleepsinhji, K. W. R. Fletcher, A. Flintoff, R. E. Foster, C. B. Fry, T. W. Graveney, A. W. Greig, W. Gunn, J. Hardstaff, jun., J. W. Hearne, K. L. Hutchings, G. L. Jessop, A. J. Lamb, J. W. H. Makepeace, C. P. Mead, Nawab of Pataudi, sen., E. Paynter, M. J. Prior, M. R. Ramprakash, W. W. Read, W. Rhodes, C. J. Richards, P. E. Richardson, R. C. Russell, J. Sharp, R. T. Simpson, A. J. Stewart, G. Ulyett, A. Ward, W. Watson.

For Australia (287)

19: D. G. Bradman.
10: S. R. Waugh.
9: G. S. Chappell.
8: A. R. Border, A. R. Morris, R. T. Ponting.
7: D. C. Boon, W. M. Lawry, M. J. Slater.
6: R. N. Harvey, M. A. Taylor, V. T. Trumper, M. E. Waugh, W. M. Woodfull.
5: M. L. Hayden, J. L. Langer, C. G. Macartney, W. H. Ponsford.
4: W. W. Armstrong, P. J. Burge, I. M. Chappell, M. J. Clarke, S. E. Gregory, A. L. Hassett, C. Hill, M. E. K. Hussey, S. J. McCabe, K. D. Walters.
3: W. Bardsley, G. S. Blewett, W. A. Brown, H. L. Collins, J. Darling, A. C. Gilchrist, K. J. Hughes, D. M. Jones, P. S. McDonnell, K. R. Miller, K. R. Stackpole, G. M. Wood, G. N. Yallop.
2: S. G. Barnes, B. C. Booth, R. A. Duff, R. Edwards, M. T. G. Elliott, J. H. Fingleton, H. Graham, B. J. Haddin, I. A. Healy, F. A. Iredale, R. B. McCosker, C. C. McDonald, G. R. Marsh, D. R. Martyn, W. L. Murdoch, M. J. North, N. C. O'Neill, C. E. Pellew, I. R. Redpath, J. Ryder, R. B. Simpson.
1: C. L. Badcock, C. Bannerman, G. J. Bonnor, J. W. Burke, R. M. Cowper, J. Dyson, G. Giffen, J. M. Gregory, R. J. Hartigan, H. L. Hendry, A. M. J. Hilditch, T. P. Horan, A. A. Jackson, S. M. Katich, C. Kelleway, A. F. Kippax, R. R. Lindwall, J. J. Lyons, C. L. McCool, C. E. McLeod, R. W. Marsh, G. R. J. Matthews, M. A. Noble, V. S. Ransford, A. J. Richardson, V. Y. Richardson, G. M. Ritchie, H. J. H. Scott, A. Symonds, J. M. Taylor, G. H. S. Trott, D. M. Wellham, K. C. Wessels.

RECORD PARTNERSHIPS FOR EACH WICKET

For England

323 for 1st	J. B. Hobbs and W. Rhodes at Melbourne	1911-12
382 for 2nd†	L. Hutton and M. Leyland at The Oval	1938
262 for 3rd	W. R. Hammond and D. R. Jardine at Adelaide	1928-29
310 for 4th	P. D. Collingwood and K. P. Pietersen at Adelaide	2006-07
206 for 5th	E. Paynter and D. C. S. Compton at Nottingham	1938
215 for 6th	L. Hutton and J. Hardstaff jun. at The Oval	1938
	G. Boycott and A. P. E. Knott at Nottingham	1977
143 for 7th	F. E. Woolley and J. Vine at Sydney	1911-12
124 for 8th	E. H. Hendren and H. Larwood at Brisbane	1928-29
151 for 9th	W. H. Scotton and W. W. Read at The Oval	1884
130 for 10th†	R. E. Foster and W. Rhodes at Sydney	1903-04

For Australia

329 for 1st	G. R. Marsh and M. A. Taylor at Nottingham	1989
451 for 2nd†	W. H. Ponsford and D. G. Bradman at The Oval	1934
276 for 3rd	D. G. Bradman and A. L. Hassett at Brisbane	1946-47
388 for 4th†	W. H. Ponsford and D. G. Bradman at Leeds	1934
405 for 5th†	S. G. Barnes and D. G. Bradman at Sydney	1946-47
346 for 6th†	J. H. Fingleton and D. G. Bradman at Melbourne	1936-37
165 for 7th	C. Hill and H. Trumble at Melbourne	1897-98
243 for 8th†	R. J. Hartigan and C. Hill at Adelaide	1907-08
154 for 9th†	S. E. Gregory and J. McC. Blackham at Sydney	1894-95
127 for 10th†	J. M. Taylor and A. A. Mailey at Sydney	1924-25

† *Record partnership against all countries.*

MOST RUNS IN A SERIES

England in England	732 (average 81.33)	D. I. Gower	1985
England in Australia	905 (average 113.12)	W. R. Hammond	1928-29
Australia in England	974 (average 139.14)	D. G. Bradman	1930
Australia in Australia	810 (average 90.00)	D. G. Bradman	1936-37

TEN WICKETS OR MORE IN A MATCH

For England (38)

13-163 (6-42, 7-121)	S. F. Barnes, Melbourne	1901-02
14-102 (7-28, 7-74)	W. Bates, Melbourne	1882-83
10-105 (5-46, 5-59)	A. V. Bedser, Melbourne	1950-51
14-99 (7-55, 7-44)	A. V. Bedser, Nottingham	1953
11-102 (6-44, 5-58)	C. Blythe, Birmingham	1909
11-176 (6-78, 5-98)	I. T. Botham, Perth	1979-80
10-253 (6-125, 4-128)	I. T. Botham, The Oval	1981
11-74 (5-29, 6-45)	J. Briggs, Lord's	1886
12-136 (6-49, 6-87)	J. Briggs, Adelaide	1891-92
10-148 (5-34, 5-114)	J. Briggs, The Oval	1893
10-215 (3-121, 7-94)	A. R. Caddick, Sydney	2002-03
10-104 (6-77, 4-27)†	R. M. Ellison, Birmingham	1985
10-179 (5-102, 5-77)†	K. Farnes, Nottingham	1934
10-60 (6-41, 4-19)	J. T. Hearne, The Oval	1896
11-113 (5-58, 6-55)	J. C. Laker, Leeds	1956
19-90 (9-37, 10-53)	J. C. Laker, Manchester	1956
10-124 (5-96, 5-28)	H. Larwood, Sydney	1932-33
11-76 (6-48, 5-28)	W. H. Lockwood, Manchester	1902
12-104 (7-36, 5-68)	G. A. Lohmann, The Oval	1886
10-87 (8-35, 2-52)	G. A. Lohmann, Sydney	1886-87
10-142 (8-58, 2-84)	G. A. Lohmann, Sydney	1891-92
12-102 (6-50, 6-52)†	F. Martin, The Oval	1890
11-68 (7-31, 4-37)	R. Peel, Manchester	1888
15-124 (7-56, 8-68)	W. Rhodes, Melbourne	1903-04
10-156 (5-49, 5-107)†	T. Richardson, Manchester	1893
11-173 (6-39, 5-134)	T. Richardson, Lord's	1896
13-244 (7-168, 6-76)	T. Richardson, Manchester	1896
10-204 (8-94, 2-110)	T. Richardson, Sydney	1897-98
11-228 (6-130, 5-98)†	M. W. Tate, Sydney	1924-25
11-88 (5-58, 6-30)	F. S. Trueman, Leeds	1961
11-93 (7-66, 4-27)	P. C. R. Tufnell, The Oval	1997
10-130 (4-45, 6-85)	F. H. Tyson, Sydney	1954-55
10-82 (4-37, 6-45)	D. L. Underwood, Leeds	1972
11-215 (7-113, 4-102)	D. L. Underwood, Adelaide	1974-75
15-104 (7-61, 8-43)	H. Verity, Lord's	1934
10-57 (6-41, 4-16)	W. Voce, Brisbane	1936-37
13-256 (5-130, 8-126)	J. C. White, Adelaide	1928-29
10-49 (5-29, 5-20)	F. E. Woolley, The Oval	1912

For Australia (43)

10-151 (5-107, 5-44)	T. M. Alderman, Leeds	1989
10-239 (4-129, 6-110)	L. O'B. Fleetwood-Smith, Adelaide	1936-37
10-160 (4-88, 6-72)	G. Giffen, Sydney	1891-92
11-82 (5-45, 6-37)†	C. V. Grimmett, Sydney	1924-25
10-201 (5-107, 5-94)	C. V. Grimmett, Nottingham	1930
10-122 (5-65, 5-57)	R. M. Hogg, Perth	1978-79
10-66 (5-30, 5-36)	R. M. Hogg, Melbourne	1978-79
12-175 (5-85, 7-90)†	H. V. Hordern, Sydney	1911-12
10-161 (5-95, 5-66)	H. V. Hordern, Sydney	1911-12
10-164 (7-88, 3-76)	E. Jones, Lord's	1899
11-134 (6-47, 5-87)	G. F. Lawson, Brisbane	1982-83
10-181 (5-58, 5-123)	D. K. Lillee, The Oval	1972
11-165 (6-26, 5-139)	D. K. Lillee, Melbourne	1976-77
11-138 (6-60, 5-78)	D. K. Lillee, Melbourne	1979-80
11-159 (7-89, 4-70)	D. K. Lillee, The Oval	1981
11-85 (7-58, 4-27)	C. G. Macartney, Leeds	1909
11-157 (8-97, 3-60)	C. J. McDermott, Perth	1990-91

12-107 (5-57, 7-50)	S. C. G. MacGill, Sydney	1998-99
10-302 (5-160, 5-142)	A. A. Mailey, Adelaide	1920-21
13-236 (4-115, 9-121)	A. A. Mailey, Melbourne	1920-21
16-137 (8-84, 8-53)†	R. A. L. Massie, Lord's	1972
10-152 (5-72, 5-80)	K. R. Miller, Lord's	1956
13-77 (7-17, 6-60)	M. A. Noble, Melbourne	1901-02
11-103 (5-51, 6-52)	M. A. Noble, Sheffield	1902
10-129 (5-63, 5-66)	W. J. O'Reilly, Melbourne	1932-33
11-129 (4-75, 7-54)	W. J. O'Reilly, Nottingham	1934
10-122 (5-66, 5-56)	W. J. O'Reilly, Leeds	1938
11-165 (7-68, 4-97)	G. E. Palmer, Sydney	1881-82
10-126 (7-65, 3-61)	G. E. Palmer, Melbourne	1882-83
13-148 (6-97, 7-51)	B. A. Reid, Melbourne	1990-91
13-110 (6-48, 7-62)	F. R. Spofforth, Melbourne	1878-79
14-90 (7-46, 7-44)	F. R. Spofforth, The Oval	1882
11-117 (4-73, 7-44)	F. R. Spofforth, Sydney	1882-83
10-144 (4-54, 6-90)	F. R. Spofforth, Sydney	1884-85
12-89 (6-59, 6-30)	H. Trumble, The Oval	1896
10-128 (4-75, 6-53)	H. Trumble, Manchester	1902
12-173 (8-65, 4-108)	H. Trumble, The Oval	1902
12-87 (5-44, 7-43)	C. T. B. Turner, Sydney	1887-88
10-63 (5-27, 5-36)	C. T. B. Turner, Lord's	1888
11-110 (3-39, 8-71)	S. K. Warne, Brisbane	1994-95
11-229 (7-165, 4-64)	S. K. Warne, The Oval	2001
10-162 (4-116, 6-46)	S. K. Warne, Birmingham	2005
12-246 (6-122, 6-124)	S. K. Warne, The Oval	2005

† *On first appearance in England–Australia Tests.*

Note: A. V. Bedser, J. Briggs, J. C. Laker, T. Richardson in 1896, R. M. Hogg, A. A. Mailey, H. Trumble and C. T. B. Turner took ten wickets or more in successive Tests. J. Briggs was omitted, however, from the England team for the first Test match in 1893.

SEVEN WICKETS OR MORE IN AN INNINGS

In addition to those listed above, the following have taken seven wickets or more in an innings:

For England

7-40	R. G. Barlow, Sydney	1882-83
7-44	R. G. Barlow, Manchester	1886
7-60	S. F. Barnes, Sydney	1907-08
8-107	B. J. T. Bosanquet, Nottingham	1905
8-81	L. C. Braund, Melbourne	1903-04
7-78	J. E. Emburey, Sydney	1986-87
7-68	T. Emmett, Melbourne	1878-79
7-109	M. J. Hoggard, Adelaide	2006-07
7-71	W. H. Lockwood, The Oval	1899
7-17	W. Rhodes, Birmingham	1902
7-40	J. A. Snow, Sydney	1970-71
7-57	J. B. Statham, Melbourne	1958-59
7-79	F. J. Titmus, Sydney	1962-63
7-27	F. H. Tyson, Melbourne	1954-55
7-36	G. Ulyett, Lord's	1884
7-50	D. L. Underwood, The Oval	1968
7-78	R. G. D. Willis, Lord's	1977
8-43	R. G. D. Willis, Leeds	1981
7-105	D. V. P. Wright, Sydney	1946-47

For Australia

7-148	A. Cotter, The Oval	1905
7-117	G. Giffen, Sydney	1884-85
7-128	G. Giffen, The Oval	1893
7-37	J. N. Gillespie, Leeds	1997
7-69	J. M. Gregory, Melbourne	1920-21
7-105	N. J. N. Hawke, Sydney	1965-66
7-25	G. R. Hazlitt, The Oval	1912
7-92	P. M. Hornibrook, The Oval	1930
7-36	M. S. Kasprowicz, The Oval	1997
7-55	T. K. Kendall, Melbourne	1876-77
7-64	F. J. Laver, Nottingham	1905
8-31	F. J. Laver, Manchester	1909
7-81	G. F. Lawson, Lord's	1981
7-63	R. R. Lindwall, Sydney	1946-47
8-141	C. J. McDermott, Manchester	1985
8-38	G. D. McGrath, Lord's	1997
7-76	G. D. McGrath, The Oval	1997
7-76	G. D. McGrath, Leeds	2001
7-153	G. D. McKenzie, Manchester	1964
7-60	K. R. Miller, Brisbane	1946-47
7-100	M. A. Noble, Sydney	1903-04
7-189	W. J. O'Reilly, Manchester	1934
8-43	A. E. Trott, Adelaide	1894-95
7-28	H. Trumble, Melbourne	1903-04
8-143	M. H. N. Walker, Melbourne	1974-75

MOST WICKETS IN A SERIES

England in England	46 (average 9.60)	J. C. Laker	1956
England in Australia	38 (average 23.18)	M. W. Tate	1924-25
Australia in England	42 (average 21.26)	T. M. Alderman (6 Tests)	1981
Australia in Australia	41 (average 12.85)	R. M. Hogg (6 Tests)	1978-79

WICKETKEEPING – MOST DISMISSALS

	M	*Ct*	*St*	*Total*
†R. W. Marsh (Australia)	42	141	7	148
I. A. Healy (Australia)	33	123	12	135
A. P. E. Knott (England)	34	97	8	105
A. C. Gilchrist (Australia)	20	89	7	96
†W. A. Oldfield (Australia)	38	59	31	90
A. A. Lilley (England)	32	65	19	84
A. J. Stewart (England)	26	76	2	78
A. T. W. Grout (Australia)	22	69	7	76
T. G. Evans (England)	31	64	12	76

† The number of catches by R. W. Marsh (141) and stumpings by W. A. Oldfield (31) are respective records in England–Australia Tests.

Note: Stewart held a further 6 catches in 7 matches when not keeping wicket.

SCORERS OF OVER 2,000 RUNS

	T	*I*	*NO*	*R*	*HS*	*100s*	*Avge*
D. G. Bradman	37	63	7	5,028	334	19	89.78
J. B. Hobbs	41	71	4	3,636	187	12	54.26
A. R. Border	47	82	19	3,548	200*	8	56.31
D. I. Gower	42	77	4	3,269	215	9	44.78
S. R. Waugh	46	73	18	3,200	177*	10	58.18
G. Boycott	38	71	9	2,945	191	7	47.50
W. R. Hammond	33	58	3	2,852	251	9	51.85
H. Sutcliffe	27	46	5	2,741	194	8	66.85
C. Hill	41	76	1	2,660	188	4	35.46
J. H. Edrich	32	57	3	2,644	175	7	48.96
G. A. Gooch	42	79	0	2,632	196	4	33.31
G. S. Chappell	35	65	8	2,619	144	9	45.94
M. A. Taylor	33	61	2	2,496	219	6	42.30
R. T. Ponting	35	58	2	2,476	196	8	44.21
M. C. Cowdrey	43	75	4	2,433	113	5	34.26
L. Hutton	27	49	6	2,428	364	5	56.46
R. N. Harvey	37	68	5	2,416	167	6	38.34
V. T. Trumper	40	74	5	2,263	185*	6	32.79
D. C. Boon	31	57	8	2,237	184*	7	45.65
W. M. Lawry	29	51	5	2,233	166	7	48.54
M. E. Waugh	29	51	7	2,204	140	6	50.09
S. E. Gregory	52	92	7	2,193	201	4	25.80
W. W. Armstrong	42	71	9	2,172	158	4	35.03
I. M. Chappell	30	56	4	2,138	192	4	41.11
K. F. Barrington	23	39	6	2,111	256	5	63.96
A. R. Morris	24	43	2	2,080	206	8	50.73

BOWLERS WITH 100 WICKETS

	T	*Balls*	*R*	*W*	*5W/i*	*10W/m*	*Avge*
S. K. Warne	36	10,757	4,535	195	11	4	23.25
D. K. Lillee	29	8,516	3,507	167	11	4	21.00
G. D. McGrath	30	7,280	3,286	157	10	0	20.92
I. T. Botham	36	8,479	4,093	148	9	2	27.65
H. Trumble	31	7,895	2,945	141	9	3	20.88
R. G. D. Willis	35	7,294	3,346	128	7	0	26.14
M. A. Noble	39	6,895	2,860	115	9	2	24.86
R. R. Lindwall	29	6,728	2,559	114	6	0	22.44
W. Rhodes	41	5,790	2,616	109	6	1	24.00
S. F. Barnes	20	5,749	2,288	106	12	1	21.58
C. V. Grimmett	22	9,224	3,439	106	11	2	32.44
D. L. Underwood	29	8,000	2,770	105	4	2	26.38
A. V. Bedser	21	7,065	2,859	104	7	2	27.49
G. Giffen	31	6,391	2,791	103	7	1	27.09
W. J. O'Reilly	19	7,864	2,587	102	8	3	25.36
C. T. B. Turner	17	5,179	1,670	101	11	2	16.53
R. Peel	20	5,216	1,715	101	5	1	16.98
T. M. Alderman	17	4,717	2,117	100	11	1	21.17
J. R. Thomson	21	4,951	2,418	100	5	0	24.18

RESULTS ON EACH GROUND

In England

	Matches	*England wins*	*Australia wins*	*Drawn*
The Oval	35	16	6	13
Manchester	28	7	7	14†
Lord's	34	6‡	14	14
Nottingham	20	4	7	9
Leeds	24	7	9	8
Birmingham	13	5	3	5
Sheffield	1	0	1	0
Cardiff	1	0	0	1

† *Excludes two matches abandoned without a ball bowled.*
‡ *England have won only twice (1934 and 2009) since 1896.*

In Australia

	Matches	*England wins*	*Australia wins*	*Drawn*
Melbourne	54	20	27	7†
Sydney	54	22	25	7
Adelaide	30	9	16	5
Brisbane				
Exhibition Ground	1	1	0	0
Woolloongabba	19	4	10	5
Perth	12	1	8	3

† *Excludes one match abandoned without a ball bowled.*

An expanded and regularly updated online version of the Records can be found at www.wisdenrecords.com

ENGLAND v SOUTH AFRICA

	Captains					
Season	*England*	*South Africa*	*T*	*E*	*SA*	*D*
1888-89	C. A. Smith[1]	O. R. Dunell[2]	2	2	0	0
1891-92	W. W. Read	W. H. Milton	1	1	0	0
1895-96	Lord Hawke[3]	E. A. Halliwell[4]	3	3	0	0
1898-99	Lord Hawke	M. Bisset	2	2	0	0
1905-06	P. F. Warner	P. W. Sherwell	5	1	4	0
1907	R. E. Foster	P. W. Sherwell	3	1	0	2
1909-10	H. D. G. Leveson Gower[5]	S. J. Snooke	5	2	3	0
1912	C. B. Fry	F. Mitchell[6]	3	3	0	0
1913-14	J. W. H. T. Douglas	H. W. Taylor	5	4	0	1
1922-23	F. T. Mann	H. W. Taylor	5	2	1	2
1924	A. E. R. Gilligan[7]	H. W. Taylor	5	3	0	2
1927-28	R. T. Stanyforth[8]	H. G. Deane	5	2	2	1
1929	J. C. White[9]	H. G. Deane	5	2	0	3
1930-31	A. P. F. Chapman	H. G. Deane[10]	5	0	1	4
1935	R. E. S. Wyatt	H. F. Wade	5	0	1	4
1938-39	W. R. Hammond	A. Melville	5	1	0	4
1947	N. W. D. Yardley	A. Melville	5	3	0	2
1948-49	F. G. Mann	A. D. Nourse	5	2	0	3
1951	F. R. Brown	A. D. Nourse	5	3	1	1
1955	P. B. H. May	J. E. Cheetham[11]	5	3	2	0
1956-57	P. B. H. May	C. B. van Ryneveld[12]	5	2	2	1
1960	M. C. Cowdrey	D. J. McGlew	5	3	0	2
1964-65	M. J. K. Smith	T. L. Goddard	5	1	0	4
1965	M. J. K. Smith	P. L. van der Merwe	3	0	1	2
1994	M. A. Atherton	K. C. Wessels	3	1	1	1
1995-96	M. A. Atherton	W. J. Cronje	5	0	1	4
1998	A. J. Stewart	W. J. Cronje	5	2	1	2
1999-2000	N. Hussain	W. J. Cronje	5	1	2	2
2003	M. P. Vaughan[13]	G. C. Smith	5	2	2	1

THE BASIL D'OLIVEIRA TROPHY

	Captains						
Season	*England*	*South Africa*	*T*	*E*	*SA*	*D*	*Held by*
2004-05	M. P. Vaughan	G. C. Smith	5	2	1	2	E
2008	M. P. Vaughan[14]	G. C. Smith	4	1	2	1	SA
2009-10	A. J. Strauss	G. C. Smith	4	1	1	2	SA
2012	**A. J. Strauss**	**G. C. Smith**	**3**	**0**	**2**	**1**	**SA**
	In South Africa		77	29	18	30	
	In England		**64**	**27**	**13**	**24**	
	Totals		**141**	**56**	**31**	**54**	

Notes: *The following deputised for the official touring captain or were appointed by the home authority for only a minor proportion of the series:*

[1]M. P. Bowden (Second). [2]W. H. Milton (Second). [3]Sir T. C. O'Brien (First). [4]A. R. Richards (Third). [5]F. L. Fane (Fourth and Fifth). [6]L. J. Tancred (Second and Third). [7]J. W. H. T. Douglas (Fourth). [8]G. T. S. Stevens (Fifth). [9]A. W. Carr (Fourth and Fifth). [10]E. P. Nupen (First), H. B. Cameron (Fourth and Fifth). [11]D. J. McGlew (Third and Fourth). [12]D. J. McGlew (Second). [13]N. Hussain (First). [14]K. P. Pietersen (Fourth).

SERIES RECORDS

Highest score	*E*	243	E. Paynter at Durban	1938-39
	SA	**311***	**H. M. Amla at The Oval**	**2012**
Best bowling	*E*	9-28	G. A. Lohmann at Johannesburg	1895-96
	SA	9-113	H. J. Tayfield at Johannesburg	1956-57

Highest total	*E*	654-5	at Durban	1938-39
	SA	682-6 dec	at Lord's	2003
Lowest total	*E*	76	at Leeds	1907
	SA	30	at Port Elizabeth	1895-96
		30	at Birmingham	1924

ENGLAND v WEST INDIES

Captains

Season	*England*	*West Indies*	*T*	*E*	*WI*	*D*
1928	A. P. F. Chapman	R. K. Nunes	3	3	0	0
1929-30	Hon. F. S. G. Calthorpe	E. L. G. Hoad[1]	4	1	1	2
1933	D. R. Jardine[2]	G. C. Grant	3	2	0	1
1934-35	R. E. S. Wyatt	G. C. Grant	4	1	2	1
1939	W. R. Hammond	R. S. Grant	3	1	0	2
1947-48	G. O. B. Allen[3]	J. D. C. Goddard[4]	4	0	2	2
1950	N. W. D. Yardley[5]	J. D. C. Goddard	4	1	3	0
1953-54	L. Hutton	J. B. Stollmeyer	5	2	2	1
1957	P. B. H. May	J. D. C. Goddard	5	3	0	2
1959-60	P. B. H. May[6]	F. C. M. Alexander	5	1	0	4

THE WISDEN TROPHY

Captains

Season	*England*	*West Indies*	*T*	*E*	*WI*	*D*	*Held by*
1963	E. R. Dexter	F. M. M. Worrell	5	1	3	1	WI
1966	M. C. Cowdrey[7]	G. S. Sobers	5	1	3	1	WI
1967-68	M. C. Cowdrey	G. S. Sobers	5	1	0	4	E
1969	R. Illingworth	G. S. Sobers	3	2	0	1	E
1973	R. Illingworth	R. B. Kanhai	3	0	2	1	WI
1973-74	M. H. Denness	R. B. Kanhai	5	1	1	3	WI
1976	A. W. Greig	C. H. Lloyd	5	0	3	2	WI
1980	I. T. Botham	C. H. Lloyd[8]	5	0	1	4	WI
1980-81†	I. T. Botham	C. H. Lloyd	4	0	2	2	WI
1984	D. I. Gower	C. H. Lloyd	5	0	5	0	WI
1985-86	D. I. Gower	I. V. A. Richards	5	0	5	0	WI
1988	J. E. Emburey[9]	I. V. A. Richards	5	0	4	1	WI
1989-90‡	G. A. Gooch[10]	I. V. A. Richards[11]	4	1	2	1	WI
1991	G. A. Gooch	I. V. A. Richards	5	2	2	1	WI
1993-94	M. A. Atherton	R. B. Richardson[12]	5	1	3	1	WI
1995	M. A. Atherton	R. B. Richardson	6	2	2	2	WI
1997-98§	M. A. Atherton	B. C. Lara	6	1	3	2	WI
2000	N. Hussain[13]	J. C. Adams	5	3	1	1	E
2003-04	M. P. Vaughan	B. C. Lara	4	3	0	1	E
2004	M. P. Vaughan	B. C. Lara	4	4	0	0	E
2007	M. P. Vaughan[14]	R. R. Sarwan[15]	4	3	0	1	E
2008-09§	A. J. Strauss	C. H. Gayle	5	0	1	4	WI
2009	A. J. Strauss	C. H. Gayle	2	2	0	0	E
2012	**A. J. Strauss**	**D. J. G. Sammy**	**3**	**2**	**0**	**1**	**E**
	In England		**83**	**32**	**29**	**22**	
	In West Indies		65	13	24	28	
	Totals		**148**	**45**	**53**	**50**	

† *The Second Test, at Georgetown, was cancelled owing to political pressure and is excluded.*
‡ *The Second Test, at Georgetown, was abandoned without a ball being bowled and is excluded.*
§ *The First Test at Kingston in 1997-98 and the Second Test at North Sound in 2008-09 were called off on their opening days because of unfit pitches and are shown as draws.*

Notes: The following deputised for the official touring captain or were appointed by the home authority for only a minor proportion of the series:

[1]N. Betancourt (Second), M. P. Fernandes (Third), R. K. Nunes (Fourth). [2]R. E. S. Wyatt (Third). [3]K. Cranston (First). [4]G. A. Headley (First), G. E. Gomez (Second). [5]F. R. Brown (Fourth). [6]M. C. Cowdrey (Fourth and Fifth). [7]M. J. K. Smith (First), D. B. Close (Fifth). [8]I. V. A. Richards (Fifth). [9]M. W. Gatting (First), C. S. Cowdrey (Fourth), G. A. Gooch (Fifth). [10]A. J. Lamb (Fourth and Fifth). [11]D. L. Haynes (Third). [12]C. A. Walsh (Fifth). [13]A. J. Stewart (Second). [14]A. J. Strauss (First). [15]D. Ganga (Third and Fourth).

SERIES RECORDS

Highest score	*E*	325	A. Sandham at Kingston	1929-30
	WI	400*	B. C. Lara at St John's	2003-04
Best bowling	*E*	8-53	A. R. C. Fraser at Port-of-Spain	1997-98
	WI	8-45	C. E. L. Ambrose at Bridgetown	1989-90
Highest total	*E*	849	at Kingston	1929-30
	WI	751-5 dec	at St John's	2003-04
Lowest total	*E*	46	at Port-of-Spain	1993-94
	WI	47	at Kingston	2003-04

ENGLAND v NEW ZEALAND

	Captains					
Season	*England*	*New Zealand*	*T*	*E*	*NZ*	*D*
1929-30	A. H. H. Gilligan	T. C. Lowry	4	1	0	3
1931	D. R. Jardine	T. C. Lowry	3	1	0	2
1932-33	D. R. Jardine[1]	M. L. Page	2	0	0	2
1937	R. W. V. Robins	M. L. Page	3	1	0	2
1946-47	W. R. Hammond	W. A. Hadlee	1	0	0	1
1949	F. G. Mann[2]	W. A. Hadlee	4	0	0	4
1950-51	F. R. Brown	W. A. Hadlee	2	1	0	1
1954-55	L. Hutton	G. O. Rabone	2	2	0	0
1958	P. B. H. May	J. R. Reid	5	4	0	1
1958-59	P. B. H. May	J. R. Reid	2	1	0	1
1962-63	E. R. Dexter	J. R. Reid	3	3	0	0
1965	M. J. K. Smith	J. R. Reid	3	3	0	0
1965-66	M. J. K. Smith	B. W. Sinclair[3]	3	0	0	3
1969	R. Illingworth	G. T. Dowling	3	2	0	1
1970-71	R. Illingworth	G. T. Dowling	2	1	0	1
1973	R. Illingworth	B. E. Congdon	3	2	0	1
1974-75	M. H. Denness	B. E. Congdon	2	1	0	1
1977-78	G. Boycott	M. G. Burgess	3	1	1	1
1978	J. M. Brearley	M. G. Burgess	3	3	0	0
1983	R. G. D. Willis	G. P. Howarth	4	3	1	0
1983-84	R. G. D. Willis	G. P. Howarth	3	0	1	2
1986	M. W. Gatting	J. V. Coney	3	0	1	2
1987-88	M. W. Gatting	J. J. Crowe[4]	3	0	0	3
1990	G. A. Gooch	J. G. Wright	3	1	0	2
1991-92	G. A. Gooch	M. D. Crowe	3	2	0	1
1994	M. A. Atherton	K. R. Rutherford	3	1	0	2
1996-97	M. A. Atherton	L. K. Germon[5]	3	2	0	1
1999	N. Hussain[6]	S. P. Fleming	4	1	2	1
2001-02	N. Hussain	S. P. Fleming	3	1	1	1

Season	England	New Zealand	T	E	NZ	D
	Captains					
2004	M. P. Vaughan[7]	S. P. Fleming	3	3	0	0
2007-08	M. P. Vaughan	D. L. Vettori	3	2	1	0
2008	M. P. Vaughan	D. L. Vettori	3	2	0	1
	In New Zealand		44	18	4	22
	In England		50	27	4	19
	Totals		94	45	8	41

Notes: The following deputised for the official touring captain or were appointed by the home authority for only a minor proportion of the series:

[1]R. E. S. Wyatt (Second). [2]F. R. Brown (Third and Fourth). [3]M. E. Chapple (First). [4]J. G. Wright (Third). [5]S. P. Fleming (Third). [6]M. A. Butcher (Third). [7]M. E. Trescothick (First).

SERIES RECORDS

Highest score	*E*	336*	W. R. Hammond at Auckland	1932-33
	NZ	222	N. J. Astle at Christchurch	2001-02
Best bowling	*E*	7-32	D. L. Underwood at Lord's	1969
	NZ	7-74	B. L. Cairns at Leeds	1983
Highest total	*E*	593-6 dec	at Auckland	1974-75
	NZ	551-9 dec	at Lord's	1973
Lowest total	*E*	64	at Wellington	1977-78
	NZ	26	at Auckland	1954-55

ENGLAND v INDIA

Season	England	India	T	E	I	D
	Captains					
1932	D. R. Jardine	C. K. Nayudu	1	1	0	0
1933-34	D. R. Jardine	C. K. Nayudu	3	2	0	1
1936	G. O. B. Allen	Maharaj of Vizianagram	3	2	0	1
1946	W. R. Hammond	Nawab of Pataudi sen.	3	1	0	2
1951-52	N. D. Howard[1]	V. S. Hazare	5	1	1	3
1952	L. Hutton	V. S. Hazare	4	3	0	1
1959	P. B. H. May[2]	D. K. Gaekwad[3]	5	5	0	0
1961-62	E. R. Dexter	N. J. Contractor	5	0	2	3
1963-64	M. J. K. Smith	Nawab of Pataudi jun.	5	0	0	5
1967	D. B. Close	Nawab of Pataudi jun.	3	3	0	0
1971	R. Illingworth	A. L. Wadekar	3	0	1	2
1972-73	A. R. Lewis	A. L. Wadekar	5	1	2	2
1974	M. H. Denness	A. L. Wadekar	3	3	0	0
1976-77	A. W. Greig	B. S. Bedi	5	3	1	1
1979	J. M. Brearley	S. Venkataraghavan	4	1	0	3
1979-80	J. M. Brearley	G. R. Viswanath	1	1	0	0
1981-82	K. W. R. Fletcher	S. M. Gavaskar	6	0	1	5
1982	R. G. D. Willis	S. M. Gavaskar	3	1	0	2
1984-85	D. I. Gower	S. M. Gavaskar	5	2	1	2
1986	M. W. Gatting[4]	Kapil Dev	3	0	2	1
1990	G. A. Gooch	M. Azharuddin	3	1	0	2
1992-93	G. A. Gooch[5]	M. Azharuddin	3	0	3	0
1996	M. A. Atherton	M. Azharuddin	3	1	0	2
2001-02	N. Hussain	S. C. Ganguly	3	0	1	2
2002	N. Hussain	S. C. Ganguly	4	1	1	2
2005-06	A. Flintoff	R. Dravid	3	1	1	1

	Captains					
Season	*England*	*India*	*T*	*E*	*I*	*D*
2007	M. P. Vaughan	R. Dravid	3	0	1	2
2008-09	K. P. Pietersen	M. S. Dhoni	2	0	1	1
2011	A. J. Strauss	M. S. Dhoni	4	4	0	0
2012-13	**A. N. Cook**	**M. S. Dhoni**	**4**	**2**	**1**	**1**
	In England		52	27	5	20
	In India		**55**	**13**	**15**	**27**
	Totals		**107**	**40**	**20**	**47**

Since 1951-52, series in India have been for the De Mello Trophy. Since 2007, series in England have been for the Pataudi Trophy.

Notes: The 1932 Indian touring team was captained by the Maharaj of Porbandar but he did not play in the Test match.

The following deputised for the official touring captain or were appointed by the home authority for only a minor proportion of the series:

[1]D. B. Carr (Fifth). [2]M. C. Cowdrey (Fourth and Fifth). [3]Pankaj Roy (Second). [4]D. I. Gower (First). [5]A. J. Stewart (Second).

SERIES RECORDS

Highest score	*E*	333	G. A. Gooch at Lord's	1990
	I	224	V. G. Kambli at Bombay	1992-93
Best bowling	*E*	8-31	F. S. Trueman at Manchester	1952
	I	8-55	V. Mankad at Madras	1951-52
Highest total	*E*	710-7 dec	at Birmingham	2011
	I	664	at The Oval	2007
Lowest total	*E*	101	at The Oval	1971
	I	42	at Lord's	1974

ENGLAND v PAKISTAN

	Captains					
Season	*England*	*Pakistan*	*T*	*E*	*P*	*D*
1954	L. Hutton[1]	A. H. Kardar	4	1	1	2
1961-62	E. R. Dexter	Imtiaz Ahmed	3	1	0	2
1962	E. R. Dexter[2]	Javed Burki	5	4	0	1
1967	D. B. Close	Hanif Mohammad	3	2	0	1
1968-69	M. C. Cowdrey	Saeed Ahmed	3	0	0	3
1971	R. Illingworth	Intikhab Alam	3	1	0	2
1972-73	A. R. Lewis	Majid Khan	3	0	0	3
1974	M. H. Denness	Intikhab Alam	3	0	0	3
1977-78	J. M. Brearley[3]	Wasim Bari	3	0	0	3
1978	J. M. Brearley	Wasim Bari	3	2	0	1
1982	R. G. D. Willis[4]	Imran Khan	3	2	1	0
1983-84	R. G. D. Willis[5]	Zaheer Abbas	3	0	1	2
1987	M. W. Gatting	Imran Khan	5	0	1	4
1987-88	M. W. Gatting	Javed Miandad	3	0	1	2
1992	G. A. Gooch	Javed Miandad	5	1	2	2
1996	M. A. Atherton	Wasim Akram	3	0	2	1
2000-01	N. Hussain	Moin Khan	3	1	0	2
2001	N. Hussain[6]	Waqar Younis	2	1	1	0
2005-06	M. P. Vaughan[7]	Inzamam-ul-Haq	3	0	2	1

Season	England	*Captains* Pakistan	T	E	P	D
2006†	A. J. Strauss	Inzamam-ul-Haq	4	3	0	1
2010	A. J. Strauss	Salman Butt	4	3	1	0
2011-12*U*	**A. J. Strauss**	**Misbah-ul-Haq**	**3**	**0**	**3**	**0**
	In England		47	20	9	18
	In Pakistan		24	2	4	18
	In United Arab Emirates		**3**	**0**	**3**	**0**
	Totals		**74**	**22**	**16**	**36**

† In 2008, the ICC changed the result of the forfeited Oval Test of 2006 from an England win to a draw, in contravention of the Laws of Cricket, only to rescind their decision in January 2009.

U Played in United Arab Emirates.

Notes: The following deputised for the official touring captain or were appointed by the home authority for only a minor proportion of the series:

[1]D. S. Sheppard (Second and Third). [2]M. C. Cowdrey (Third). [3]G. Boycott (Third). [4]D. I. Gower (Second). [5]D. I. Gower (Second and Third). [6]A. J. Stewart (Second). [7]M. E. Trescothick (First).

SERIES RECORDS

Highest score	*E*	278	D. C. S. Compton at Nottingham	1954
	P	274	Zaheer Abbas at Birmingham	1971
Best bowling	*E*	8-34	I. T. Botham at Lord's	1978
	P	9-56	Abdul Qadir at Lahore	1987-88
Highest total	*E*	558-6 dec	at Nottingham	1954
	P	708	at The Oval	1987
Lowest total	*E*	**72**	**at Abu Dhabi**	**2011-12**
	P	72	at Birmingham	2010

ENGLAND v SRI LANKA

Season	England	*Captains* Sri Lanka	T	E	SL	D
1981-82	K. W. R. Fletcher	B. Warnapura	1	1	0	0
1984	D. I. Gower	L. R. D. Mendis	1	0	0	1
1988	G. A. Gooch	R. S. Madugalle	1	1	0	0
1991	G. A. Gooch	P. A. de Silva	1	1	0	0
1992-93	A. J. Stewart	A. Ranatunga	1	0	1	0
1998	A. J. Stewart	A. Ranatunga	1	0	1	0
2000-01	N. Hussain	S. T. Jayasuriya	3	2	1	0
2002	N. Hussain	S. T. Jayasuriya	3	2	0	1
2003-04	M. P. Vaughan	H. P. Tillekeratne	3	0	1	2
2006	A. Flintoff	D. P. M. D. Jayawardene	3	1	1	1
2007-08	M. P. Vaughan	D. P. M. D. Jayawardene	3	0	1	2
2011	A. J. Strauss	T. M. Dilshan[1]	3	1	0	2
2011-12	**A. J. Strauss**	**D. P. M. D. Jayawardene**	**2**	**1**	**1**	**0**
	In England		13	6	2	5
	In Sri Lanka		**13**	**4**	**5**	**4**
	Totals		**26**	**10**	**7**	**9**

Note: The following deputised for the official touring captain for only a minor proportion of the series:

[1]K. C. Sangakkara (Third).

SERIES RECORDS

Highest score	*E*	203	I. J. L. Trott at Cardiff	2011
	SL	213*	D. P. M. D. Jayawardene at Galle	2007-08
Best bowling	*E*	7-70	P. A. J. DeFreitas at Lord's	1991
	SL	9-65	M. Muralitharan at The Oval	1998
Highest total	*E*	551-6 dec	at Lord's	2006
	SL	628-8 dec	at Colombo (SSC)	2003-04
Lowest total	*E*	81	at Galle	2007-08
	SL	81	at Colombo (SSC)	2000-01

ENGLAND v ZIMBABWE

	Captains					
Season	*England*	*Zimbabwe*	*T*	*E*	*Z*	*D*
1996-97	M. A. Atherton	A. D. R. Campbell	2	0	0	2
2000	N. Hussain	A. Flower	2	1	0	1
2003	N. Hussain	H. H. Streak	2	2	0	0
	In England		4	3	0	1
	In Zimbabwe		2	0	0	2
	Totals		6	3	0	3

SERIES RECORDS

Highest score	*E*	137	M. A. Butcher at Lord's	2003
	Z	148*	M. W. Goodwin at Nottingham	2000
Best bowling	*E*	6-33	R. L. Johnson at Chester-le-Street	2003
	Z	6-87	H. H. Streak at Lord's	2000
Highest total	*E*	472	at Lord's	2003
	Z	376	at Bulawayo	1996-97
Lowest total	*E*	147	at Nottingham	2000
	Z	83	at Lord's	2000

ENGLAND v BANGLADESH

	Captains					
Season	*England*	*Bangladesh*	*T*	*E*	*B*	*D*
2003-04	M. P. Vaughan	Khaled Mahmud	2	2	0	0
2005	M. P. Vaughan	Habibul Bashar	2	2	0	0
2009-10	A. N. Cook	Shakib Al Hasan	2	2	0	0
2010	A. J. Strauss	Shakib Al Hasan	2	2	0	0
	In England		4	4	0	0
	In Bangladesh		4	4	0	0
	Totals		8	8	0	0

SERIES RECORDS

Highest score	*E*	226	I. J. L. Trott at Lord's	2010
	B	108	Tamim Iqbal at Manchester	2010
Best bowling	*E*	5-35	S. J. Harmison at Dhaka	2003-04
	B	5-98	Shahadat Hossain at Lord's	2010
Highest total	*E*	599-6 dec	at Chittagong	2009-10
	B	419	at Mirpur	2009-10
Lowest total	*E*	295	at Dhaka	2003-04
	B	104	at Chester-le-Street	2005

AUSTRALIA v SOUTH AFRICA

Season	Captains: Australia	Captains: South Africa	T	A	SA	D
1902-03*S*	J. Darling	H. M. Taberer[1]	3	2	0	1
1910-11*A*	C. Hill	P. W. Sherwell	5	4	1	0
1912*E*	S. E. Gregory	F. Mitchell[2]	3	2	0	1
1921-22*S*	H. L. Collins	H. W. Taylor	3	1	0	2
1931-32*A*	W. M. Woodfull	H. B. Cameron	5	5	0	0
1935-36*S*	V. Y. Richardson	H. F. Wade	5	4	0	1
1949-50*S*	A. L. Hassett	A. D. Nourse	5	4	0	1
1952-53*A*	A. L. Hassett	J. E. Cheetham	5	2	2	1
1957-58*S*	I. D. Craig	C. B. van Ryneveld[3]	5	3	0	2
1963-64*A*	R. B. Simpson[4]	T. L. Goddard	5	1	1	3
1966-67*S*	R. B. Simpson	P. L. van der Merwe	5	1	3	1
1969-70*S*	W. M. Lawry	A. Bacher	4	0	4	0
1993-94*A*	A. R. Border	K. C. Wessels[5]	3	1	1	1
1993-94*S*	A. R. Border	K. C. Wessels	3	1	1	1
1996-97*S*	M. A. Taylor	W. J. Cronje	3	2	1	0
1997-98*A*	M. A. Taylor	W. J. Cronje	3	1	0	2
2001-02*A*	S. R. Waugh	S. M. Pollock	3	3	0	0
2001-02*S*	S. R. Waugh	M. V. Boucher	3	2	1	0
2005-06*A*	R. T. Ponting	G. C. Smith	3	2	0	1
2005-06*S*	R. T. Ponting	G. C. Smith[6]	3	3	0	0
2008-09*A*	R. T. Ponting	G. C. Smith	3	1	2	0
2008-09*S*	R. T. Ponting	G. C. Smith[7]	3	2	1	0
2011-12*S*	M. J. Clarke	G. C. Smith	2	1	1	0
2012-13*A*	**M. J. Clarke**	**G. C. Smith**	**3**	**0**	**1**	**2**
	In South Africa		47	26	12	9
	In Australia		**38**	**20**	**8**	**10**
	In England		3	2	0	1
	Totals		**88**	**48**	**20**	**20**

S Played in South Africa. A Played in Australia. E Played in England.

Notes: The following deputised for the official touring captain or were appointed by the home authority for only a minor proportion of the series:

[1]J. H. Anderson (Second), E. A. Halliwell (Third). [2]L. J. Tancred (Third). [3]D. J. McGlew (First). [4]R. Benaud (First). [5]W. J. Cronje (Third). [6]J. H. Kallis (Third). [7]J. H. Kallis (Third).

SERIES RECORDS

Highest score	*A*	299*	D. G. Bradman at Adelaide	1931-32
	SA	274	R. G. Pollock at Durban	1969-70
Best bowling	*A*	8-61	M. G. Johnson at Perth	2008-09
	SA	7-23	H. J. Tayfield at Durban	1949-50
Highest total	*A*	652-7 dec	at Johannesburg	2001-02
	SA	651	at Cape Town	2008-09
Lowest total	*A*	47	at Cape Town	2011-12
	SA	36	at Melbourne	1931-32

AUSTRALIA v WEST INDIES

Season	Captains: Australia	Captains: West Indies	T	A	WI	T	D
1930-31*A*	W. M. Woodfull	G. C. Grant	5	4	1	0	0
1951-52*A*	A. L. Hassett[1]	J. D. C. Goddard[2]	5	4	1	0	0
1954-55*W*	I. W. Johnson	D. St E. Atkinson[3]	5	3	0	0	2

THE FRANK WORRELL TROPHY

		Captains						
Season	*Australia*	*West Indies*	*T*	*A*	*WI*	*T*	*D*	*Held by*
1960-61*A*	R. Benaud	F. M. M. Worrell	5	2	1	1	1	A
1964-65*W*	R. B. Simpson	G. S. Sobers	5	1	2	0	2	WI
1968-69*A*	W. M. Lawry	G. S. Sobers	5	3	1	0	1	A
1972-73*W*	I. M. Chappell	R. B. Kanhai	5	2	0	0	3	A
1975-76*A*	G. S. Chappell	C. H. Lloyd	6	5	1	0	0	A
1977-78*W*	R. B. Simpson	A. I. Kallicharran[4]	5	1	3	0	1	WI
1979-80*A*	G. S. Chappell	C. H. Lloyd[5]	3	0	2	0	1	WI
1981-82*A*	G. S. Chappell	C. H. Lloyd	3	1	1	0	1	WI
1983-84*W*	K. J. Hughes	C. H. Lloyd[6]	5	0	3	0	2	WI
1984-85*A*	A. R. Border[7]	C. H. Lloyd	5	1	3	0	1	WI
1988-89*A*	A. R. Border	I. V. A. Richards	5	1	3	0	1	WI
1990-91*W*	A. R. Border	I. V. A. Richards	5	1	2	0	2	WI
1992-93*A*	A. R. Border	R. B. Richardson	5	1	2	0	2	WI
1994-95*W*	M. A. Taylor	R. B. Richardson	4	2	1	0	1	A
1996-97*A*	M. A. Taylor	C. A. Walsh	5	3	2	0	0	A
1998-99*W*	S. R. Waugh	B. C. Lara	4	2	2	0	0	A
2000-01*A*	S. R. Waugh[8]	J. C. Adams	5	5	0	0	0	A
2002-03*W*	S. R. Waugh	B. C. Lara	4	3	1	0	0	A
2005-06*A*	R. T. Ponting	S. Chanderpaul	3	3	0	0	0	A
2007-08*W*	R. T. Ponting	R. R. Sarwan[9]	3	2	0	0	1	A
2009-10*A*	R. T. Ponting	C. H. Gayle	3	2	0	0	1	A
2011-12*W*	**M. J. Clarke**	**D. J. G. Sammy**	**3**	**2**	**0**	**0**	**1**	**A**
	In Australia		63	35	18	1	9	
	In West Indies		**48**	**19**	**14**	**0**	**15**	
	Totals		**111**	**54**	**32**	**1**	**24**	

A Played in Australia. *W Played in West Indies.*

Notes: The following deputised for the official touring captain or were appointed by the home authority for only a minor proportion of the series:

[1]A. R. Morris (Third). [2]J. B. Stollmeyer (Fifth). [3]J. B. Stollmeyer (Second and Third). [4]C. H. Lloyd (First and Second). [5]D. L. Murray (First). [6]I. V. A. Richards (Second). [7]K. J. Hughes (First and Second). [8]A. C. Gilchrist (Third). [9]C. II. Gayle (Third).

SERIES RECORDS

Highest score	*A*	242	K. D. Walters at Sydney	1968-69
	WI	277	B. C. Lara at Sydney	1992-93
Best bowling	*A*	8-71	G. D. McKenzie at Melbourne	1968-69
	WI	7-25	C. E. L. Ambrose at Perth	1992-93
Highest total	*A*	758-8 dec	at Kingston	1954-55
	WI	616	at Adelaide	1968-69
Lowest total	*A*	76	at Perth	1984-85
	WI	51	at Port-of-Spain	1998-99

AUSTRALIA v NEW ZEALAND

		Captains				
Season	*Australia*	*New Zealand*	*T*	*A*	*NZ*	*D*
1945-46*N*	W. A. Brown	W. A. Hadlee	1	1	0	0
1973-74*A*	I. M. Chappell	B. E. Congdon	3	2	0	1
1973-74*N*	I. M. Chappell	B. E. Congdon	3	1	1	1
1976-77*N*	G. S. Chappell	G. M. Turner	2	1	0	1
1980-81*A*	G. S. Chappell	G. P. Howarth[1]	3	2	0	1
1981-82*N*	G. S. Chappell	G. P. Howarth	3	1	1	1

TRANS-TASMAN TROPHY

	Captains						
Season	*Australia*	*New Zealand*	*T*	*A*	*NZ*	*D*	*Held by*
1985-86*A*	A. R. Border	J. V. Coney	3	1	2	0	NZ
1985-86*N*	A. R. Border	J. V. Coney	3	0	1	2	NZ
1987-88*A*	A. R. Border	J. J. Crowe	3	1	0	2	A
1989-90*A*	A. R. Border	J. G. Wright	1	0	0	1	A
1989-90*N*	A. R. Border	J. G. Wright	1	0	1	0	NZ
1992-93*N*	A. R. Border	M. D. Crowe	3	1	1	1	NZ
1993-94*A*	A. R. Border	M. D. Crowe[2]	3	2	0	1	A
1997-98*A*	M. A. Taylor	S. P. Fleming	3	2	0	1	A
1999-2000*N*	S. R. Waugh	S. P. Fleming	3	3	0	0	A
2001-02*A*	S. R. Waugh	S. P. Fleming	3	0	0	3	A
2004-05*A*	R. T. Ponting	S. P. Fleming	2	2	0	0	A
2004-05*N*	R. T. Ponting	S. P. Fleming	3	2	0	1	A
2008-09*A*	R. T. Ponting	D. L. Vettori	2	2	0	0	A
2009-10*N*	R. T. Ponting	D. L. Vettori	2	2	0	0	A
2011-12*A*	M. J. Clarke	L. R. P. L. Taylor	2	1	1	0	A
	In Australia		28	15	3	10	
	In New Zealand		24	12	5	7	
	Totals		52	27	8	17	

A Played in Australia. N Played in New Zealand.

Notes: The following deputised for the official touring captain: [1]M. G. Burgess (Second). [2]K. R. Rutherford (Second and Third).

SERIES RECORDS

Highest score	*A*	250	K. D. Walters at Christchurch	1976-77
	NZ	188	M. D. Crowe at Brisbane	1985-86
Best bowling	*A*	6-31	S. K. Warne at Hobart	1993-94
	NZ	9-52	R. J. Hadlee at Brisbane	1985-86
Highest total	*A*	607-6 dec	at Brisbane	1993-94
	NZ	553-7 dec	at Brisbane	1985-86
Lowest total	*A*	103	at Auckland	1985-86
	NZ	42	at Wellington	1945-46

AUSTRALIA v INDIA

	Captains						
Season	*Australia*	*India*	*T*	*A*	*I*	*T*	*D*
1947-48*A*	D. G. Bradman	L. Amarnath	5	4	0	0	1
1956-57*I*	I. W. Johnson[1]	P. R. Umrigar	3	2	0	0	1
1959-60*I*	R. Benaud	G. S. Ramchand	5	2	1	0	2
1964-65*I*	R. B. Simpson	Nawab of Pataudi jun.	3	1	1	0	1
1967-68*A*	R. B. Simpson[2]	Nawab of Pataudi jun.[3]	4	4	0	0	0
1969-70*I*	W. M. Lawry	Nawab of Pataudi jun.	5	3	1	0	1
1977-78*A*	R. B. Simpson	B. S. Bedi	5	3	2	0	0
1979-80*I*	K. J. Hughes	S. M. Gavaskar	6	0	2	0	4
1980-81*A*	G. S. Chappell	S. M. Gavaskar	3	1	1	0	1
1985-86*A*	A. R. Border	Kapil Dev	3	0	0	0	3
1986-87*I*	A. R. Border	Kapil Dev	3	0	0	1	2
1991-92*A*	A. R. Border	M. Azharuddin	5	4	0	0	1

THE BORDER–GAVASKAR TROPHY

	Captains							
Season	*Australia*	*India*	*T*	*A*	*I*	*T*	*D*	*Held by*
1996-97*I*	M. A. Taylor	S. R. Tendulkar	1	0	1	0	0	I
1997-98*I*	M. A. Taylor	M. Azharuddin	3	1	2	0	0	I
1999-2000*A*	S. R. Waugh	S. R. Tendulkar	3	3	0	0	0	A
2000-01*I*	S. R. Waugh	S. C. Ganguly	3	1	2	0	0	I
2003-04*A*	S. R. Waugh	S. C. Ganguly	4	1	1	0	2	I
2004-05*I*	R. T. Ponting[4]	S. C. Ganguly[5]	4	2	1	0	1	A
2007-08*A*	R. T. Ponting	A. Kumble	4	2	1	0	1	A
2008-09*I*	R. T. Ponting	A. Kumble[6]	4	0	2	0	2	I
2010-11*I*	R. T. Ponting	M. S. Dhoni	2	0	2	0	0	I
2011-12*A*	**M. J. Clarke**	**M. S. Dhoni[7]**	**4**	**4**	**0**	**0**	**0**	**A**
	In Australia		**40**	**26**	**5**	**0**	**9**	
	In India		42	12	15	1	14	
	Totals		**82**	**38**	**20**	**1**	**23**	

A Played in Australia. I Played in India.

Notes: The following deputised for the official touring captain or were appointed by the home authority for only a minor proportion of the series:

[1]R. R. Lindwall (Second). [2]W. M. Lawry (Third and Fourth). [3]C. G. Borde (First). [4]A. C. Gilchrist (First, Second and Third). [5]R. Dravid (Third and Fourth). [6]M. S. Dhoni (Second and Fourth). [7]V. Sehwag (Fourth).

SERIES RECORDS

Highest score	*A*	**329***	**M. J. Clarke at Sydney**	**2011-12**
	I	281	V. V. S. Laxman at Kolkata	2000-01
Best bowling	*A*	8-215	J. J. Krejza at Nagpur	2008-09
	I	9-69	J. M. Patel at Kanpur	1959-60
Highest total	*A*	674	at Adelaide	1947-48
	I	705-7 dec	at Sydney	2003-04
Lowest total	*A*	83	at Melbourne	1980-81
	I	58	at Brisbane	1947-48

AUSTRALIA v PAKISTAN

	Captains					
Season	*Australia*	*Pakistan*	*T*	*A*	*P*	*D*
1956-57*P*	I. W. Johnson	A. H. Kardar	1	0	1	0
1959-60*P*	R. Benaud	Fazal Mahmood[1]	3	2	0	1
1964-65*P*	R. B. Simpson	Hanif Mohammad	1	0	0	1
1964-65*A*	R. B. Simpson	Hanif Mohammad	1	0	0	1
1972-73*A*	I. M. Chappell	Intikhab Alam	3	3	0	0
1976-77*A*	G. S. Chappell	Mushtaq Mohammad	3	1	1	1
1978-79*A*	G. N. Yallop[2]	Mushtaq Mohammad	2	1	1	0
1979-80*P*	G. S. Chappell	Javed Miandad	3	0	1	2
1981-82*A*	G. S. Chappell	Javed Miandad	3	2	1	0
1982-83*P*	K. J. Hughes	Imran Khan	3	0	3	0
1983-84*A*	K. J. Hughes	Imran Khan[3]	5	2	0	3
1988-89*P*	A. R. Border	Javed Miandad	3	0	1	2
1989-90*A*	A. R. Border	Imran Khan	3	1	0	2
1994-95*P*	M. A. Taylor	Salim Malik	3	0	1	2
1995-96*A*	M. A. Taylor	Wasim Akram	3	2	1	0
1998-99*P*	M. A. Taylor	Aamir Sohail	3	1	0	2
1999-2000*A*	S. R. Waugh	Wasim Akram	3	3	0	0
2002-03*S/U*	S. R. Waugh	Waqar Younis	3	3	0	0

	Captains					
Season	*Australia*	*Pakistan*	*T*	*A*	*P*	*D*
2004-05*A*	R. T. Ponting	Inzamam-ul-Haq[4]	3	3	0	0
2009-10*A*	R. T. Ponting	Mohammad Yousuf	3	3	0	0
2010*E*	R. T. Ponting	Shahid Afridi[5]	2	1	1	0
	In Pakistan		20	3	7	10
	In Australia		32	21	4	7
	In Sri Lanka		1	1	0	0
	In United Arab Emirates		2	2	0	0
	In England		2	1	1	0
	Totals		57	28	12	17

P Played in Pakistan. A Played in Australia.
S/U First Test played in Sri Lanka, Second and Third Tests in United Arab Emirates. E Played in England.

Notes: The following deputised for the official touring captain or were appointed by the home authority for only a minor proportion of the series:

[1]Imtiaz Ahmed (Second). [2]K. J. Hughes (Second). [3]Zaheer Abbas (First, Second and Third). [4]Yousuf Youhana *later known as Mohammad Yousuf* (Second and Third). [5]Salman Butt (Second).

SERIES RECORDS

Highest score	*A*	334*	M. A. Taylor at Peshawar	1998-99
	P	237	Salim Malik at Rawalpindi	1994-95
Best bowling	*A*	8-24	G. D. McGrath at Perth	2004-05
	P	9-86	Sarfraz Nawaz at Melbourne	1978-79
Highest total	*A*	617	at Faisalabad	1979-80
	P	624	at Adelaide	1983-84
Lowest total	*A*	80	at Karachi	1956-57
	P	53	at Sharjah	2002-03

AUSTRALIA v SRI LANKA

	Captains					
Season	*Australia*	*Sri Lanka*	*T*	*A*	*SL*	*D*
1982-83*S*	G. S. Chappell	L. R. D. Mendis	1	1	0	0
1987-88*A*	A. R. Border	R. S. Madugalle	1	1	0	0
1989-90*A*	A. R. Border	A. Ranatunga	2	1	0	1
1992-93*S*	A. R. Border	A. Ranatunga	3	1	0	2
1995-96*A*	M. A. Taylor	A. Ranatunga[1]	3	3	0	0
1999-2000*S*	S. R. Waugh	S. T. Jayasuriya	3	0	1	2
2003-04*S*	R. T. Ponting	H. P. Tillekeratne	3	3	0	0
2004*A*	R. T. Ponting[2]	M. S. Atapattu	2	1	0	1

THE WARNE–MURALITHARAN TROPHY

	Captains						
Season	*Australia*	*Sri Lanka*	*T*	*A*	*SL*	*D*	*Held by*
2007-08*A*	R. T. Ponting	D. P. M. D. Jayawardene	2	2	0	0	A
2011-12*S*	M. J. Clarke	T. M. Dilshan	3	1	0	2	A
2012-13A	**M. J. Clarke**	**D. P. M. D. Jayawardene**	**3**	**3**	**0**	**0**	**A**
	In Australia		**13**	**11**	**0**	**2**	
	In Sri Lanka		13	6	1	6	
	Totals		**26**	**17**	**1**	**8**	

A Played in Australia. S Played in Sri Lanka.

Note: The following deputised for the official touring captain:
[1]P. A. de Silva (Third). [2]A. C. Gilchrist (First).

SERIES RECORDS

Highest score	*A*	219	M. J. Slater at Perth	1995-96
	SL	192	K. C. Sangakkara at Hobart	2007-08
Best bowling	*A*	7-39	M. S. Kasprowicz at Darwin	2004
	SL	7-157	H. M. R. K. B. Herath at Colombo (SSC)	2011-12
Highest total	*A*	617-5 dec	at Perth	1995-96
	SL	547-8 dec	at Colombo (SSC)	1992-93
Lowest total	*A*	120	at Kandy	2003-04
	SL	97	at Darwin	2004

AUSTRALIA v ZIMBABWE

Season	*Captains* *Australia*	*Zimbabwe*	*T*	*A*	*Z*	*D*
1999-2000*Z*	S. R. Waugh	A. D. R. Campbell	1	1	0	0
2003-04*A*	S. R. Waugh	H. H. Streak	2	2	0	0
	In Australia		2	2	0	0
	In Zimbabwe		1	1	0	0
	Totals		3	3	0	0

A Played in Australia. Z Played in Zimbabwe.

SERIES RECORDS

Highest score	*A*	380	M. L. Hayden at Perth	2003-04
	Z	118	S. V. Carlisle at Sydney	2003-04
Best bowling	*A*	6-65	S. M. Katich at Sydney	2003-04
	Z	6-121	R. W. Price at Sydney	2003-04
Highest total	*A*	735-6 dec	at Perth	2003-04
	Z	321	at Perth	2003-04
Lowest total	*A*	403	at Sydney	2003-04
	Z	194	at Harare	1999-2000

AUSTRALIA v BANGLADESH

Season	*Captains* *Australia*	*Bangladesh*	*T*	*A*	*B*	*D*
2003*A*	S. R. Waugh	Khaled Mahmud	2	2	0	0
2005-06*B*	R. T. Ponting	Habibul Bashar	2	2	0	0
	In Australia		2	2	0	0
	In Bangladesh		2	2	0	0
	Totals		4	4	0	0

A Played in Australia. B Played in Bangladesh.

SERIES RECORDS

Highest score	*A*	201*	J. N. Gillespie at Chittagong	2005-06
	B	138	Shahriar Nafees at Fatullah	2005-06
Best bowling	*A*	8-108	S. C. G. MacGill at Fatullah	2005-06
	B	5-62	Mohammad Rafique at Fatullah	2005-06
Highest total	*A*	581-4 dec	at Chittagong	2005-06
	B	427	at Fatullah	2005-06
Lowest total	*A*	269	at Fatullah	2005-06
	B	97	at Darwin	2003

AUSTRALIA v ICC WORLD XI

Season	*Australia*	*ICC World XI*	*T*	*A*	*ICC*	*D*
2005-06*A*	R. T. Ponting	G. C. Smith	1	1	0	0

A Played in Australia.

SERIES RECORDS

Highest score	*A*	111	M. L. Hayden at Sydney	2005-06
	Wld	76	V. Sehwag at Sydney	2005-06
Best bowling	*A*	5-43	S. C. G. MacGill at Sydney	2005-06
	Wld	4-59	A. Flintoff at Sydney	2005-06
Highest total	*A*	345	at Sydney	2005-06
	Wld	190	at Sydney	2005-06
Lowest total	*A*	199	at Sydney	2005-06
	Wld	144	at Sydney	2005-06

SOUTH AFRICA v WEST INDIES

	Captains					
Season	*South Africa*	*West Indies*	*T*	*SA*	*WI*	*D*
1991-92*W*	K. C. Wessels	R. B. Richardson	1	0	1	0
1998-99*S*	W. J. Cronje	B. C. Lara	5	5	0	0

SIR VIVIAN RICHARDS TROPHY

	Captains						
Season	*South Africa*	*West Indies*	*T*	*SA*	*WI*	*D*	*Held by*
2000-01*W*	S. M. Pollock	C. L. Hooper	5	2	1	2	SA
2003-04*S*	G. C. Smith	B. C. Lara	4	3	0	1	SA
2004-05*W*	G. C. Smith	S. Chanderpaul	4	2	0	2	SA
2007-08 *S*	G. C. Smith	C. H. Gayle[1]	3	2	1	0	SA
2010*W*	G. C. Smith	C. H. Gayle	3	2	0	1	SA
	In South Africa		12	10	1	1	
	In West Indies		13	6	2	5	
	Totals		25	16	3	6	

S Played in South Africa. W Played in West Indies.

Note: The following deputised for the official touring captain:
[1]D. J. Bravo (Third).

SERIES RECORDS

Highest score	*SA*	192	H. H. Gibbs at Centurion	2003-04
	WI	317	C. H. Gayle at St John's	2004-05
Best bowling	*SA*	7-37	M. Ntini at Port-of-Spain	2004-05
	WI	7-84	F. A. Rose at Durban	1998-99
Highest total	*SA*	658-9 dec	at Durban	2003-04
	WI	747	at St John's	2004-05
Lowest total	*SA*	141	at Kingston	2000-01
	WI	102	at Port-of-Spain	2010

SOUTH AFRICA v NEW ZEALAND

	Captains					
Season	*South Africa*	*New Zealand*	*T*	*SA*	*NZ*	*D*
1931-32*N*	H. B. Cameron	M. L. Page	2	2	0	0
1952-53*N*	J. E. Cheetham	W. M. Wallace	2	1	0	1
1953-54*S*	J. E. Cheetham	G. O. Rabone[1]	5	4	0	1
1961-62*S*	D. J. McGlew	J. R. Reid	5	2	2	1
1963-64*N*	T. L. Goddard	J. R. Reid	3	0	0	3
1994-95*S*	W. J. Cronje	K. R. Rutherford	3	2	1	0
1994-95*N*	W. J. Cronje	K. R. Rutherford	1	1	0	0
1998-99*N*	W. J. Cronje	D. J. Nash	3	1	0	2
2000-01*S*	S. M. Pollock	S. P. Fleming	3	2	0	1
2003-04*N*	G. C. Smith	S. P. Fleming	3	1	1	1
2005-06*S*	G. C. Smith	S. P. Fleming	3	2	0	1
2007-08*S*	G. C. Smith	D. L. Vettori	2	2	0	0
2011-12*N*	**G. C. Smith**	**L. R. P. L. Taylor**	**3**	**1**	**0**	**2**
2012-13*S*	**G. C. Smith**	**B. B. McCullum**	**2**	**2**	**0**	**0**
	In New Zealand		**17**	**7**	**1**	**9**
	In South Africa		**23**	**16**	**3**	**4**
	Totals		**40**	**23**	**4**	**13**

N Played in New Zealand. S Played in South Africa.

Note: The following deputised for the official touring captain:
[1]B. Sutcliffe (Fourth and Fifth).

SERIES RECORDS

Highest score	*SA*	275*	D. J. Cullinan at Auckland	1998-99
	NZ	262	S. P. Fleming at Cape Town	2005-06
Best bowling	*SA*	8-53	G. B. Lawrence at Johannesburg	1961-62
	NZ	6-60	J. R. Reid at Dunedin	1963-64
Highest total	*SA*	621-5 dec	at Auckland	1998-99
	NZ	595	at Auckland	2003-04
Lowest total	*SA*	148	at Johannesburg	1953-54
	NZ	**45**	**at Cape Town**	**2012-13**

SOUTH AFRICA v INDIA

	Captains					
Season	*South Africa*	*India*	*T*	*SA*	*I*	*D*
1992-93*S*	K. C. Wessels	M. Azharuddin	4	1	0	3
1996-97*I*	W. J. Cronje	S. R. Tendulkar	3	1	2	0
1996-97*S*	W. J. Cronje	S. R. Tendulkar	3	2	0	1
1999-2000*I*	W. J. Cronje	S. R. Tendulkar	2	2	0	0
2001-02*S*†	S. M. Pollock	S. C. Ganguly	2	1	0	1
2004-05*I*	G. C. Smith	S. C. Ganguly	2	0	1	1
2006-07*S*	G. C. Smith	R. Dravid	3	2	1	0
2007-08*I*	G. C. Smith	A. Kumble[1]	3	1	1	1
2009-10*I*	G. C. Smith	M. S. Dhoni	2	1	1	0
2010-11*S*	G. C. Smith	M. S. Dhoni	3	1	1	1
	In South Africa		15	7	2	6
	In India		12	5	5	2
	Totals		27	12	7	8

S Played in South Africa. I Played in India.

† *The Third Test at Centurion was stripped of its official status by the ICC after a disciplinary dispute and is excluded.*

Note: The following was appointed by the home authority for only a minor proportion of the series:
[1]M. S. Dhoni (Third).

SERIES RECORDS

Highest score	*SA*	253*	H. M. Amla at Nagpur	2009-10
	I	319	V. Sehwag at Chennai	2007-08
Best bowling	*SA*	8-64	L. Klusener at Calcutta	1996-97
	I	7-87	Harbhajan Singh at Kolkata	2004-05
Highest total	*SA*	620-4 dec	at Centurion	2010-11
	I	643-6 dec	at Kolkata	2009-10
Lowest total	*SA*	84	at Johannesburg	2006-07
	I	66	at Durban	1996-97

SOUTH AFRICA v PAKISTAN

Season	*South Africa* (Captains)	*Pakistan* (Captains)	*T*	*SA*	*P*	*D*
1994-95*S*	W. J. Cronje	Salim Malik	1	1	0	0
1997-98*P*	W. J. Cronje	Saeed Anwar	3	1	0	2
1997-98*S*	W. J. Cronje[1]	Rashid Latif[2]	3	1	1	1
2002-03*S*	S. M. Pollock	Waqar Younis	2	2	0	0
2003-04*P*	G. C. Smith	Inzamam-ul-Haq[3]	2	0	1	1
2006-07*S*	G. C. Smith	Inzamam-ul-Haq	3	2	1	0
2007-08*P*	G. C. Smith	Shoaib Malik	2	1	0	1
2010-11*U*	G. C. Smith	Misbah-ul-Haq	2	0	0	2
	In South Africa		9	6	2	1
	In Pakistan		7	2	1	4
	In United Arab Emirates		2	0	0	2
	Totals		18	8	3	7

S Played in South Africa. P Played in Pakistan. U Played in United Arab Emirates.

Notes: The following deputised for the official touring captain or were appointed by the home authority for only a minor proportion of the series:

[1]G. Kirsten (First). [2]Aamir Sohail (First and Second). [3]Yousuf Youhana *later known as Mohammad Yousuf* (First).

SERIES RECORDS

Highest score	*SA*	278*	A. B. de Villiers at Abu Dhabi	2010-11
	P	136	Azhar Mahmood at Johannesburg	1997-98
Best bowling	*SA*	7-128	P. R. Adams at Lahore	2003-04
	P	6-78	Mushtaq Ahmed at Durban	1997-98
	P	6-78	Waqar Younis at Port Elizabeth	1997-98
Highest total	*SA*	620-7 dec	at Cape Town	2002-03
	P	456	at Rawalpindi	1997-98
Lowest total	*SA*	124	at Port Elizabeth	2006-07
	P	92	at Faisalabad	1997-98

SOUTH AFRICA v SRI LANKA

Season	*South Africa* (Captains)	*Sri Lanka* (Captains)	*T*	*SA*	*SL*	*D*
1993-94*SL*	K. C. Wessels	A. Ranatunga	3	1	0	2
1997-98*SA*	W. J. Cronje	A. Ranatunga	2	2	0	0
2000*SL*	S. M. Pollock	S. T. Jayasuriya	3	1	1	1
2000-01*SA*	S. M. Pollock	S. T. Jayasuriya	3	2	0	1

2002-03*SA*	S. M. Pollock	S. T. Jayasuriya[1]	2	2	0	0
2004*SL*	G. C. Smith	M. S. Atapattu	2	0	1	1
2006*SL*	A. G. Prince	D. P. M. D. Jayawardene	2	0	2	0
2011-12*SA*	**G. C. Smith**	**T. M. Dilshan**	**3**	**2**	**1**	**0**
	In South Africa		**10**	**8**	**1**	**1**
	In Sri Lanka		10	2	4	4
	Totals		**20**	**10**	**5**	**5**

SA Played in South Africa. *SL Played in Sri Lanka.*

Note: The following deputised for the official captain:
[1]M. S. Atapattu (Second).

SERIES RECORDS

Highest score	*SA*	**224**	**J. H. Kallis at Cape Town**	**2011-12**
	SL	374	D. P. M. D. Jayawardene at Colombo (SSC)	2006
Best bowling	*SA*	**7-81**	**M. de Lange at Durban**	**2011-12**
	SL	7-84	M. Muralitharan at Galle	2000
Highest total	*SA*	**580-4 dec**	**at Cape Town**	**2011-12**
	SL	756-5 dec	at Colombo (SSC)	2006
Lowest total	*SA*	**168**	**at Durban**	**2011-12**
	SL	95	at Cape Town	2000-01

SOUTH AFRICA v ZIMBABWE

Captains

Season	*South Africa*	*Zimbabwe*	*T*	*SA*	*Z*	*D*
1995-96*Z*	W. J. Cronje	A. Flower	1	1	0	0
1999-2000*S*	W. J. Cronje	A. D. R. Campbell	1	1	0	0
1999-2000*Z*	W. J. Cronje	A. Flower	1	1	0	0
2001-02*Z*	S. M. Pollock	H. H. Streak	2	1	0	1
2004-05*S*	G. C. Smith	T. Taibu	2	2	0	0
	In Zimbabwe		4	3	0	1
	In South Africa		3	3	0	0
	Totals		7	6	0	1

S Played in South Africa. *Z Played in Zimbabwe.*

SERIES RECORDS

Highest score	*SA*	220	G. Kirsten at Harare	2001-02
	Z	199*	A. Flower at Harare	2001-02
Best bowling	*SA*	8-71	A. A. Donald at Harare	1995-96
	Z	5-101	B. C. Strang at Harare	1995-96
Highest total	*SA*	600-3 dec	at Harare	2001-02
	Z	419-9 dec	at Bulawayo	2001-02
Lowest total	*SA*	346	at Harare	1995-96
	Z	54	at Cape Town	2004-05

SOUTH AFRICA v BANGLADESH

	Captains					
Season	*South Africa*	*Bangladesh*	*T*	*SA*	*B*	*D*
2002-03*S*	S. M. Pollock[1]	Khaled Mashud	2	2	0	0
2003*B*	G. C. Smith	Khaled Mahmud	2	2	0	0
2007-08*B*	G. C. Smith	Mohammad Ashraful	2	2	0	0
2008-09*S*	G. C. Smith	Mohammad Ashraful	2	2	0	0
	In South Africa		4	4	0	0
	In Bangladesh		4	4	0	0
	Totals		8	8	0	0

S Played in South Africa. *B Played in Bangladesh.*

Note: The following deputised for the official captain:
[1]M. V. Boucher (First).

SERIES RECORDS

Highest score	*SA*	232	G. C. Smith at Chittagong	2007-08
	B	75	Habibul Bashar at Chittagong	2003
Best bowling	*SA*	5-19	M. Ntini at East London	2002-03
	B	6-27	Shahadat Hossain at Mirpur	2007-08
Highest total	*SA*	583-7 dec	at Chittagong	2007-08
	B	259	at Chittagong	2007-08
Lowest total	*SA*	170	at Mirpur	2007-08
	B	102	at Dhaka	2003

WEST INDIES v NEW ZEALAND

	Captains					
Season	*West Indies*	*New Zealand*	*T*	*WI*	*NZ*	*D*
1951-52*N*	J. D. C. Goddard	B. Sutcliffe	2	1	0	1
1955-56*N*	D. St E. Atkinson	J. R. Reid[1]	4	3	1	0
1968-69*N*	G. S. Sobers	G. T. Dowling	3	1	1	1
1971-72*W*	G. S. Sobers	G. T. Dowling[2]	5	0	0	5
1979-80*N*	C. H. Lloyd	G. P. Howarth	3	0	1	2
1984-85*W*	I. V. A. Richards	G. P. Howarth	4	2	0	2
1986-87*N*	I. V. A. Richards	J. V. Coney	3	1	1	1
1994-95*N*	C. A. Walsh	K. R. Rutherford	2	1	0	1
1995-96*W*	C. A. Walsh	L. K. Germon	2	1	0	1
1999-2000*N*	B. C. Lara	S. P. Fleming	2	0	2	0
2002*W*	C. L. Hooper	S. P. Fleming	2	0	1	1
2005-06*N*	S. Chanderpaul	S. P. Fleming	3	0	2	1
2008-09*N*	C. H. Gayle	D. L. Vettori	2	0	0	2
2012*W*	**D. J. G. Sammy**	**L. R. P. L. Taylor**	**2**	**2**	**0**	**0**
	In New Zealand		24	7	8	9
	In West Indies		**15**	**5**	**1**	**9**
	Totals		**39**	**12**	**9**	**18**

N Played in New Zealand. *W Played in West Indies.*

Notes: The following deputised for the official touring captain or were appointed by the home authority for only a minor proportion of the series:
[1]H. B. Cave (First). [2]B. E. Congdon (Third, Fourth and Fifth).

SERIES RECORDS

Highest score	*WI*	258	S. M. Nurse at Christchurch	1968-69
	NZ	259	G. M. Turner at Georgetown	1971-72
Best bowling	*WI*	7-37	C. A. Walsh at Wellington	1994-95
	NZ	7-27	C. L. Cairns at Hamilton	1999-2000
Highest total	*WI*	660-5 dec	at Wellington	1994-95
	NZ	543-3 dec	at Georgetown	1971-72
Lowest total	*WI*	77	at Auckland	1955-56
	NZ	74	at Dunedin	1955-56

WEST INDIES v INDIA

	Captains					
Season	*West Indies*	*India*	*T*	*WI*	*I*	*D*
1948-49*I*	J. D. C. Goddard	L. Amarnath	5	1	0	4
1952-53*W*	J. B. Stollmeyer	V. S. Hazare	5	1	0	4
1958-59*I*	F. C. M. Alexander	Ghulam Ahmed[1]	5	3	0	2
1961-62*W*	F. M. M. Worrell	N. J. Contractor[2]	5	5	0	0
1966-67*I*	G. S. Sobers	Nawab of Pataudi jun.	3	2	0	1
1970-71*W*	G. S. Sobers	A. L. Wadekar	5	0	1	4
1974-75*I*	C. H. Lloyd	Nawab of Pataudi jun.[3]	5	3	2	0
1975-76*W*	C. H. Lloyd	B. S. Bedi	4	2	1	1
1978-79*I*	A. I. Kallicharran	S. M. Gavaskar	6	0	1	5
1982-83*W*	C. H. Lloyd	Kapil Dev	5	2	0	3
1983-84*I*	C. H. Lloyd	Kapil Dev	6	3	0	3
1987-88*I*	I. V. A. Richards	D. B. Vengsarkar[4]	4	1	1	2
1988-89*W*	I. V. A. Richards	D. B. Vengsarkar	4	3	0	1
1994-95*I*	C. A. Walsh	M. Azharuddin	3	1	1	1
1996-97*W*	C. A. Walsh[5]	S. R. Tendulkar	5	1	0	4
2001-02*W*	C. L. Hooper	S. C. Ganguly	5	2	1	2
2002-03*I*	C. L. Hooper	S. C. Ganguly	3	0	2	1
2005-06*W*	B. C. Lara	R. Dravid	4	0	1	3
2011*W*	D. J. G. Sammy	M. S. Dhoni	3	0	1	2
2011-12*I*	D. J. G. Sammy	M. S. Dhoni	3	0	2	1
	In India		43	14	9	20
	In West Indies		45	16	5	24
	Totals		88	30	14	44

I Played in India. W Played in West Indies.

Notes: The following deputised for the official touring captain or were appointed by the home authority for only a minor proportion of the series:

[1]P. R. Umrigar (First), V. Mankad (Fourth), H. R. Adhikari (Fifth). [2]Nawab of Pataudi jun. (Third, Fourth and Fifth). [3]S. Venkataraghavan (Second). [4]R. J. Shastri (Fourth). [5]B. C. Lara (Third).

SERIES RECORDS

Highest score	*WI*	256	R. B. Kanhai at Calcutta	1958-59
	I	236*	S. M. Gavaskar at Madras	1983-84
Best bowling	*WI*	9-95	J. M. Noreiga at Port-of-Spain	1970-71
	I	9-83	Kapil Dev at Ahmedabad	1983-84
Highest total	*WI*	644-8 dec	at Delhi	1958-59
	I	644-7 dec	at Kanpur	1978-79
Lowest total	*WI*	103	at Kingston	2005-06
	I	75	at Delhi	1987-88

WEST INDIES v PAKISTAN

	Captains					
Season	*West Indies*	*Pakistan*	*T*	*WI*	*P*	*D*
1957-58*W*	F. C. M. Alexander	A. H. Kardar	5	3	1	1
1958-59*P*	F. C. M. Alexander	Fazal Mahmood	3	1	2	0
1974-75*P*	C. H. Lloyd	Intikhab Alam	2	0	0	2
1976-77*W*	C. H. Lloyd	Mushtaq Mohammad	5	2	1	2
1980-81*P*	C. H. Lloyd	Javed Miandad	4	1	0	3
1986-87*P*	I. V. A. Richards	Imran Khan	3	1	1	1
1987-88*W*	I. V. A. Richards[1]	Imran Khan	3	1	1	1
1990-91*P*	D. L. Haynes	Imran Khan	3	1	1	1
1992-93*W*	R. B. Richardson	Wasim Akram	3	2	0	1
1997-98*P*	C. A. Walsh	Wasim Akram	3	0	3	0
1999-2000*W*	J. C. Adams	Moin Khan	3	1	0	2
2001-02*U*	C. L. Hooper	Waqar Younis	2	0	2	0
2004-05*W*	S. Chanderpaul	Inzamam-ul-Haq[2]	2	1	1	0
2006-07*P*	B. C. Lara	Inzamam-ul-Haq	3	0	2	1
2010-11*W*	D. J. G. Sammy	Misbah-ul-Haq	2	1	1	0
	In West Indies		23	11	5	7
	In Pakistan		21	4	9	8
	In United Arab Emirates		2	0	2	0
	Totals		46	15	16	15

P Played in Pakistan. W Played in West Indies. U Played in United Arab Emirates.

Note: The following were appointed by the home authority or deputised for the official touring captain for a minor proportion of the series:

[1]C. G. Greenidge (First). [2]Younis Khan (First).

SERIES RECORDS

Highest score	*WI*	365*	G. S. Sobers at Kingston	1957-58
	P	337	Hanif Mohammad at Bridgetown	1957-58
Best bowling	*WI*	8-29	C. E. H. Croft at Port-of-Spain	1976-77
	P	7-80	Imran Khan at Georgetown	1987-88
Highest total	*WI*	790-3 dec	at Kingston	1957-58
	P	657-8 dec	at Bridgetown	1957-58
Lowest total	*WI*	53	at Faisalabad	1986-87
	P	77	at Lahore	1986-87

WEST INDIES v SRI LANKA

	Captains					
Season	*West Indies*	*Sri Lanka*	*T*	*WI*	*SL*	*D*
1993-94*S*	R. B. Richardson	A. Ranatunga	1	0	0	1
1996-97*W*	C. A. Walsh	A. Ranatunga	2	1	0	1
2001-02*S*	C. L. Hooper	S. T. Jayasuriya	3	0	3	0
2003*W*	B. C. Lara	H. P. Tillekeratne	2	1	0	1
2005*S*	S. Chanderpaul	M. S. Atapattu	2	0	2	0
2007-08*W*	C. H. Gayle	D. P. M. D. Jayawardene	2	1	1	0
2010-11*S*	D. J. G. Sammy	K. C. Sangakkara	3	0	0	3
	In West Indies		6	3	1	2
	In Sri Lanka		9	0	5	4
	Totals		15	3	6	6

W Played in West Indies. S Played in Sri Lanka.

SERIES RECORDS

Highest score	*WI*	333	C. H. Gayle at Galle	2010-11
	SL	204*	H. P. Tillekeratne at Colombo (SSC)	2001-02
Best bowling	*WI*	7-57	C. D. Collymore at Kingston	2003
	SL	8-46	M. Muralitharan at Kandy	2005
Highest total	*WI*	580-9 dec	at Galle	2010-11
	SL	627-9 dec	at Colombo (SSC)	2001-02
Lowest total	*WI*	113	at Colombo (SSC)	2005
	SL	150	at Kandy	2005

WEST INDIES v ZIMBABWE

	Captains					
Season	*West Indies*	*Zimbabwe*	*T*	*WI*	*Z*	*D*
1999-2000*W*	J. C. Adams	A. Flower	2	2	0	0
2001*Z*	C. L. Hooper	H. H. Streak	2	1	0	1
2003-04*Z*	B. C. Lara	H. H. Streak	2	1	0	1
	In West Indies		2	2	0	0
	In Zimbabwe		4	2	0	2
	Totals		6	4	0	2

W Played in West Indies. *Z Played in Zimbabwe.*

SERIES RECORDS

Highest score	*WI*	191	B. C. Lara at Bulawayo	2003-04
	Z	127*	H. H. Streak at Harare	2003-04
Best bowling	*WI*	5-51	R. D. King at Kingston	1999-2000
	Z	6-73	R. W. Price at Harare	2003-04
Highest total	*WI*	559-6 dec	at Bulawayo	2001
	Z	563-9 dec	at Harare	2001
Lowest total	*WI*	128	at Bulawayo	2003-04
	Z	63	at Port-of-Spain	1999-2000

WEST INDIES v BANGLADESH

	Captains					
Season	*West Indies*	*Bangladesh*	*T*	*WI*	*B*	*D*
2002-03*B*	R. D. Jacobs	Khaled Mashud	2	2	0	0
2003-04*W*	B. C. Lara	Habibul Bashar	2	1	0	1
2009*W*	F. L. Reifer	Mashrafe bin Mortaza[1]	2	0	2	0
2011-12*B*	D. J. G. Sammy	Mushfiqur Rahim	2	1	0	1
2012-13*B*	**D. J. G. Sammy**	**Mushfiqur Rahim**	**2**	**2**	**0**	**0**
	In West Indies		4	1	2	1
	In Bangladesh		**6**	**5**	**0**	**1**
	Totals		**10**	**6**	**2**	**2**

B Played in Bangladesh. *W Played in West Indies.*

Note: The following deputised for the official touring captain for a minor proportion of the series:
[1]Shakib Al Hasan (Second).

SERIES RECORDS

Highest score	*WI*	261*	R. R. Sarwan at Kingston	2003-04
	B	128	Tamim Iqbal at St Vincent	2009
Best bowling	*WI*	6-3	J. J. C. Lawson at Dhaka	2002-03
	B	**6-74**	**Sohag Gazi at Mirpur**	**2012-13**
Highest total	*WI*	**648-9 dec**	**at Khulna**	**2012-13**
	B	**556**	**at Mirpur**	**2012-13**
Lowest total	*WI*	181	at St Vincent	2009
	B	87	at Dhaka	2002-03

NEW ZEALAND v INDIA

	Captains					
Season	*New Zealand*	*India*	*T*	*NZ*	*I*	*D*
1955-56*I*	H. B. Cave	P. R. Umrigar[1]	5	0	2	3
1964-65*I*	J. R. Reid	Nawab of Pataudi jun.	4	0	1	3
1967-68*N*	G. T. Dowling[2]	Nawab of Pataudi jun.	4	1	3	0
1969-70*I*	G. T. Dowling	Nawab of Pataudi jun.	3	1	1	1
1975-76*N*	G. M. Turner	B. S. Bedi[3]	3	1	1	1
1976-77*I*	G. M. Turner	B. S. Bedi	3	0	2	1
1980-81*N*	G. P. Howarth	S. M. Gavaskar	3	1	0	2
1988-89*I*	J. G. Wright	D. B. Vengsarkar	3	1	2	0
1989-90*N*	J. G. Wright	M. Azharuddin	3	1	0	2
1993-94*N*	K. R. Rutherford	M. Azharuddin	1	0	0	1
1995-96*I*	L. K. Germon	M. Azharuddin	3	0	1	2
1998-99*N*†	S. P. Fleming	M. Azharuddin	2	1	0	1
1999-2000*I*	S. P. Fleming	S. R. Tendulkar	3	0	1	2
2002-03*N*	S. P. Fleming	S. C. Ganguly	2	2	0	0
2003-04*I*	S. P. Fleming	S. C. Ganguly[4]	2	0	0	2
2008-09*N*	D. L. Vettori	M. S. Dhoni[5]	3	0	1	2
2010-11*I*	D. L. Vettori	M. S. Dhoni	3	0	1	2
2012-13*I*	**L. R. P. L. Taylor**	**M. S. Dhoni**	**2**	**0**	**2**	**0**
	In India		**31**	**2**	**13**	**16**
	In New Zealand		21	7	5	9
	Totals		**52**	**9**	**18**	**25**

I Played in India. N Played in New Zealand.

† *The First Test at Dunedin was abandoned without a ball being bowled and is excluded.*

Notes: The following deputised for the official touring captain or were appointed by the home authority for a minor proportion of the series:

[1]Ghulam Ahmed (First). [2]B. W. Sinclair (First). [3]S. M. Gavaskar (First). [4]R. Dravid (Second). [5]V. Sehwag (Second).

SERIES RECORDS

Highest score	*NZ*	239	G. T. Dowling at Christchurch	1967-68
	I	231	V. Mankad at Madras	1955-56
Best bowling	*NZ*	7-23	R. J. Hadlee at Wellington	1975-76
	I	8-72	S. Venkataraghavan at Delhi	1964-65
Highest total	*NZ*	630-6 dec	at Mohali	2003-04
	I	583-7 dec	at Ahmedabad	1999-2000
Lowest total	*NZ*	94	at Hamilton	2002-03
	I	81	at Wellington	1975-76

NEW ZEALAND v PAKISTAN

Season	Captains: New Zealand	Pakistan	T	NZ	P	D
1955-56*P*	H. B. Cave	A. H. Kardar	3	0	2	1
1964-65*N*	J. R. Reid	Hanif Mohammad	3	0	0	3
1964-65*P*	J. R. Reid	Hanif Mohammad	3	0	2	1
1969-70*P*	G. T. Dowling	Intikhab Alam	3	1	0	2
1972-73*N*	B. E. Congdon	Intikhab Alam	3	0	1	2
1976-77*P*	G. M. Turner[1]	Mushtaq Mohammad	3	0	2	1
1978-79*N*	M. G. Burgess	Mushtaq Mohammad	3	0	1	2
1984-85*P*	J. V. Coney	Zaheer Abbas	3	0	2	1
1984-85*N*	G. P. Howarth	Javed Miandad	3	2	0	1
1988-89*N*†	J. G. Wright	Imran Khan	2	0	0	2
1990-91*P*	M. D. Crowe	Javed Miandad	3	0	3	0
1992-93*N*	K. R. Rutherford	Javed Miandad	1	0	1	0
1993-94*N*	K. R. Rutherford	Salim Malik	3	1	2	0
1995-96*N*	L. K. Germon	Wasim Akram	1	0	1	0
1996-97*P*	L. K. Germon	Saeed Anwar	2	1	1	0
2000-01*N*	S. P. Fleming	Moin Khan[2]	3	1	1	1
2002*P*‡	S. P. Fleming	Waqar Younis	1	0	1	0
2003-04*N*	S. P. Fleming	Inzamam-ul-Haq	2	0	1	1
2009-10*N*	D. L. Vettori	Mohammad Yousuf	3	1	1	1
2010-11*N*	D. L. Vettori	Misbah-ul-Haq	2	0	1	1
	In Pakistan		21	2	13	6
	In New Zealand		29	5	10	14
	Totals		50	7	23	20

N Played in New Zealand. P Played in Pakistan.

† *The First Test at Dunedin was abandoned without a ball being bowled and is excluded.*
‡ *The Second Test at Karachi was cancelled owing to civil disturbances.*

Note: The following were appointed by the home authority for only a minor proportion of the series or deputised for the official touring captain:
[1]J. M. Parker (Third). [2]Inzamam-ul-Haq (Third).

SERIES RECORDS

Highest score	*NZ*	204*	M. S. Sinclair at Christchurch	2000-01
	P	329	Inzamam-ul-Haq at Lahore	2002
Best bowling	*NZ*	7-52	C. Pringle at Faisalabad	1990-91
	P	7-52	Intikhab Alam at Dunedin	1972-73
Highest total	*NZ*	563	at Hamilton	2003-04
	P	643	at Lahore	2002
Lowest total	*NZ*	70	at Dacca	1955-56
	P	102	at Faisalabad	1990-91

NEW ZEALAND v SRI LANKA

Season	Captains: New Zealand	Sri Lanka	T	NZ	SL	D
1982-83*N*	G. P. Howarth	D. S. de Silva	2	2	0	0
1983-84*S*	G. P. Howarth	L. R. D. Mendis	3	2	0	1
1986-87*S*†	J. J. Crowe	L. R. D. Mendis	1	0	0	1
1990-91*N*	M. D. Crowe[1]	A. Ranatunga	3	0	0	3
1992-93*S*	M. D. Crowe	A. Ranatunga	2	0	1	1
1994-95*N*	K. R. Rutherford	A. Ranatunga	2	0	1	1
1996-97*N*	S. P. Fleming	A. Ranatunga	2	2	0	0

1997-98*S*	S. P. Fleming	A. Ranatunga	3	1	2	0
2003*S*	S. P. Fleming	H. P. Tillekeratne	2	0	0	2
2004-05*N*	S. P. Fleming	M. S. Atapattu	2	1	0	1
2006-07*N*	S. P. Fleming	D. P. M. D. Jayawardene	2	1	1	0
2009*S*	D. L. Vettori	K. C. Sangakkara	2	0	2	0
2012-13*S*	**L. R. P. L. Taylor**	**D. P. M. D. Jayawardene**	**2**	**1**	**1**	**0**
	In New Zealand		13	6	2	5
	In Sri Lanka		**15**	**4**	**6**	**5**
	Totals		**28**	**10**	**8**	**10**

N Played in New Zealand. S Played in Sri Lanka.

† *The Second and Third Tests were cancelled owing to civil disturbances.*

Note: The following was appointed by the home authority for only a minor proportion of the series: [1]I. D. S. Smith (Third).

SERIES RECORDS

Highest score	*NZ*	299	M. D. Crowe at Wellington	1990-91
	SL	267	P. A. de Silva at Wellington	1990-91
Best bowling	*NZ*	7-130	D. L. Vettori at Wellington	2006-07
	SL	**6-43**	**H. M. R. K. B. Herath at Galle**	**2012-13**
Highest total	*NZ*	671-4	at Wellington	1990-91
	SL	498	at Napier	2004-05
Lowest total	*NZ*	102	at Colombo (SSC)	1992-93
	SL	93	at Wellington	1982-83

NEW ZEALAND v ZIMBABWE

	Captains					
Season	*New Zealand*	*Zimbabwe*	*T*	*NZ*	*Z*	*D*
1992-93*Z*	M. D. Crowe	D. L. Houghton	2	1	0	1
1995-96*N*	L. K. Germon	A. Flower	2	0	0	2
1997-98*Z*	S. P. Fleming	A. D. R. Campbell	2	0	0	2
1997-98*N*	S. P. Fleming	A. D. R. Campbell	2	2	0	0
2000-01*Z*	S. P. Fleming	H. H. Streak	2	2	0	0
2000-01*N*	S. P. Fleming	H. H. Streak	1	0	0	1
2005-06*Z*	S. P. Fleming	T. Taibu	2	2	0	0
2011-12*Z*	L. R. P. L. Taylor	B. R. M. Taylor	1	1	0	0
2011-12*N*	**L. R. P. L. Taylor**	**B. R. M. Taylor**	**1**	**1**	**0**	**0**
	In New Zealand		**6**	**3**	**0**	**3**
	In Zimbabwe		9	6	0	3
	Totals		**15**	**9**	**0**	**6**

N Played in New Zealand. Z Played in Zimbabwe.

SERIES RECORDS

Highest score	*NZ*	157	M. J. Horne at Auckland	1997-98
	Z	203*	G. J. Whittall at Bulawayo	1997-98
Best bowling	*NZ*	**6-26**	**C. S. Martin at Napier**	**2011-12**
	Z	8-109	P. A. Strang at Bulawayo	2000-01
Highest total	*NZ*	**495-7 dec**	**at Napier**	**2011-12**
	Z	461	at Bulawayo	1997-98
Lowest total	*NZ*	207	at Harare	1997-98
	Z	**51**	**at Napier**	**2011-12**

NEW ZEALAND v BANGLADESH

Season	*Captains* New Zealand	Bangladesh	*T*	*NZ*	*B*	*D*
2001-02*N*	S. P. Fleming	Khaled Mashud	2	2	0	0
2004-05*B*	S. P. Fleming	Khaled Mashud	2	2	0	0
2007-08*N*	D. L. Vettori	Mohammad Ashraful	2	2	0	0
2008-09*B*	D. L. Vettori	Mohammad Ashraful	2	1	0	1
2009-10*N*	D. L. Vettori	Shakib Al Hasan	1	1	0	0
	In New Zealand		5	5	0	0
	In Bangladesh		4	3	0	1
	Totals		9	8	0	1

B Played in Bangladesh. N Played in New Zealand.

SERIES RECORDS

Highest score	*NZ*	202	S. P. Fleming at Chittagong	2004-05
	B	115	Mahmudullah at Hamilton	2009-10
Best bowling	*NZ*	7-53	C. L. Cairns at Hamilton	2001-02
	B	7-36	Shakib Al Hasan at Chittagong	2008-09
Highest total	*NZ*	553-7 dec	at Hamilton	2009-10
	B	408	at Hamilton	2009-10
Lowest total	*NZ*	171	at Chittagong	2008-09
	B	108	at Hamilton	2001-02

INDIA v PAKISTAN

Season	*Captains* India	Pakistan	*T*	*I*	*P*	*D*
1952-53*I*	L. Amarnath	A. H. Kardar	5	2	1	2
1954-55*P*	V. Mankad	A. H. Kardar	5	0	0	5
1960-61*I*	N. J. Contractor	Fazal Mahmood	5	0	0	5
1978-79*P*	B. S. Bedi	Mushtaq Mohammad	3	0	2	1
1979-80*I*	S. M. Gavaskar[1]	Asif Iqbal	6	2	0	4
1982-83*P*	S. M. Gavaskar	Imran Khan	6	0	3	3
1983-84*I*	Kapil Dev	Zaheer Abbas	3	0	0	3
1984-85*P*	S. M. Gavaskar	Zaheer Abbas	2	0	0	2
1986-87*I*	Kapil Dev	Imran Khan	5	0	1	4
1989-90*P*	K. Srikkanth	Imran Khan	4	0	0	4
1998-99*I*	M. Azharuddin	Wasim Akram	2	1	1	0
1998-99*I*†	M. Azharuddin	Wasim Akram	1	0	1	0
2003-04*P*	S. C. Ganguly[2]	Inzamam-ul-Haq	3	2	1	0
2004-05*I*	S. C. Ganguly	Inzamam-ul-Haq	3	1	1	1
2005-06*P*	R. Dravid	Inzamam-ul-Haq[3]	3	0	1	2
2007-08*I*	A. Kumble	Shoaib Malik[4]	3	1	0	2
	In India		33	7	5	21
	In Pakistan		26	2	7	17
	Totals		59	9	12	38

I Played in India. P Played in Pakistan.

† This Test was part of the Asian Test Championship and was not counted as part of the preceding bilateral series.

Note: The following were appointed by the home authority for only a minor proportion of the series or deputised for the official touring captain:

[1]G. R. Viswanath (Sixth). [2]R. Dravid (First and Second). [3]Younis Khan (Third). [4]Younis Khan (Second and Third).

SERIES RECORDS

Highest score	*I*	309	V. Sehwag at Multan	2003-04
	P	280*	Javed Miandad at Hyderabad	1982-83
Best bowling	*I*	10-74	A. Kumble at Delhi	1998-99
	P	8-60	Imran Khan at Karachi	1982-83
Highest total	*I*	675-5 dec	at Multan	2003-04
	P	699-5	at Lahore	1989-90
Lowest total	*I*	106	at Lucknow	1952-53
	P	116	at Bangalore	1986-87

INDIA v SRI LANKA

Captains

Season	*India*	*Sri Lanka*	*T*	*I*	*SL*	*D*
1982-83*I*	S. M. Gavaskar	B. Warnapura	1	0	0	1
1985-86*S*	Kapil Dev	L. R. D. Mendis	3	0	1	2
1986-87*I*	Kapil Dev	L. R. D. Mendis	3	2	0	1
1990-91*I*	M. Azharuddin	A. Ranatunga	1	1	0	0
1993-94*S*	M. Azharuddin	A. Ranatunga	3	1	0	2
1993-94*I*	M. Azharuddin	A. Ranatunga	3	3	0	0
1997-98*S*	S. R. Tendulkar	A. Ranatunga	2	0	0	2
1997-98*I*	S. R. Tendulkar	A. Ranatunga	3	0	0	3
1998-99*S*†	M. Azharuddin	A. Ranatunga	1	0	0	1
2001*S*	S. C. Ganguly	S. T. Jayasuriya	3	1	2	0
2005-06*I*	R. Dravid[1]	M. S. Atapattu	3	2	0	1
2008*S*	A. Kumble	D. P. M. D. Jayawardene	3	1	2	0
2009-10*I*	M. S. Dhoni	K. C. Sangakkara	3	2	0	1
2010*S*	M. S. Dhoni	K. C. Sangakkara	3	1	1	1
	In India		17	10	0	7
	In Sri Lanka		18	4	6	8
	Totals		35	14	6	15

I Played in India. S Played in Sri Lanka.

† *This Test was part of the Asian Test Championship.*

Note: The following was appointed by the home authority for only a minor proportion of the series:
[1]V. Sehwag (Third).

SERIES RECORDS

Highest score	*I*	293	V. Sehwag at Mumbai (BS)	2009-10
	SL	340	S. T. Jayasuriya at Colombo (RPS)	1997-98
Best bowling	*I*	7-51	Maninder Singh at Nagpur	1986-87
	SL	8-87	M. Muralitharan at Colombo (SSC)	2001
Highest total	*I*	726-9 dec	at Mumbai (BS)	2009-10
	SL	952-6 dec	at Colombo (RPS)	1997-98
Lowest total	*I*	138	at Colombo (SSC)	2008
	SL	82	at Chandigarh	1990-91

INDIA v ZIMBABWE

Season	Captains India	Captains Zimbabwe	T	I	Z	D
1992-93*Z*	M. Azharuddin	D. L. Houghton	1	0	0	1
1992-93*I*	M. Azharuddin	D. L. Houghton	1	1	0	0
1998-99*Z*	M. Azharuddin	A. D. R. Campbell	1	0	1	0
2000-01*I*	S. C. Ganguly	H. H. Streak	2	1	0	1
2001*Z*	S. C. Ganguly	H. H. Streak	2	1	1	0
2001-02*I*	S. C. Ganguly	S. V. Carlisle	2	2	0	0
2005-06*Z*	S. C. Ganguly	T. Taibu	2	2	0	0
	In India		5	4	0	1
	In Zimbabwe		6	3	2	1
	Totals		11	7	2	2

I Played in India. Z Played in Zimbabwe.

SERIES RECORDS

Highest score	*I*	227	V. G. Kambli at Delhi	1992-93
	Z	232*	A. Flower at Nagpur	2000-01
Best bowling	*I*	7-59	I. K. Pathan at Harare	2005-06
	Z	6-73	H. H. Streak at Harare	2005-06
Highest total	*I*	609-6 dec	at Nagpur	2000-01
	Z	503 6	at Nagpur	2000-01
Lowest total	*I*	173	at Harare	1998-99
	Z	146	at Delhi	2001-02

INDIA v BANGLADESH

Season	Captains India	Captains Bangladesh	T	I	B	D
2000-01*B*	S. C. Ganguly	Naimur Rahman	1	1	0	0
2004-05*B*	S. C. Ganguly	Habibul Bashar	2	2	0	0
2007*B*	R. Dravid	Habibul Bashar	2	1	0	1
2009-10*B*	M. S. Dhoni[1]	Shakib Al Hasan	2	2	0	0
	In Bangladesh		7	6	0	1

B Played in Bangladesh.

Note: The following deputised for the official touring captain for a minor proportion of the series:
[1]V. Sehwag (First).

SERIES RECORDS

Highest score	*I*	248*	S. R. Tendulkar at Dhaka	2004-05
	B	158*	Mohammad Ashraful at Chittagong	2004-05
Best bowling	*I*	7-87	Zaheer Khan at Mirpur	2009-10
	B	6-132	Naimur Rahman at Dhaka	2000-01
Highest total	*I*	610-3 dec	at Mirpur	2007
	B	400	at Dhaka	2000-01
Lowest total	*I*	243	at Chittagong	2009-10
	B	91	at Dhaka	2000-01

PAKISTAN v SRI LANKA

	Captains					
Season	*Pakistan*	*Sri Lanka*	*T*	*P*	*SL*	*D*
1981-82*P*	Javed Miandad	B. Warnapura[1]	3	2	0	1
1985-86*P*	Javed Miandad	L. R. D. Mendis	3	2	0	1
1985-86*S*	Imran Khan	L. R. D. Mendis	3	1	1	1
1991-92*P*	Imran Khan	P. A. de Silva	3	1	0	2
1994-95*S*†	Salim Malik	A. Ranatunga	2	2	0	0
1995-96*P*	Ramiz Raja	A. Ranatunga	3	1	2	0
1996-97*S*	Ramiz Raja	A. Ranatunga	2	0	0	2
1998-99*P*‡	Wasim Akram	H. P. Tillekeratne	1	0	0	1
1998-99*B*‡	Wasim Akram	P. A. de Silva	1	1	0	0
1999-2000*P*	Saeed Anwar[2]	S. T. Jayasuriya	3	1	2	0
2000*S*	Moin Khan	S. T. Jayasuriya	3	2	0	1
2001-02*P*‡	Waqar Younis	S. T. Jayasuriya	1	0	1	0
2004-05*P*	Inzamam-ul-Haq	M. S. Atapattu	2	1	1	0
2005-06*S*	Inzamam-ul-Haq	D. P. M. D. Jayawardene	2	1	0	1
2008-09*P*§	Younis Khan	D. P. M. D. Jayawardene	2	0	0	2
2009*S*	Younis Khan	K. C. Sangakkara	3	0	2	1
2011-12*U*	Misbah-ul-Haq	T. M. Dilshan	3	1	0	2
2012*S*	**Misbah-ul-Haq[3]**	**D. P. M. D. Jayawardene**	**3**	**0**	**1**	**2**
	In Pakistan		21	8	6	7
	In Sri Lanka		**18**	**6**	**4**	**8**
	In Bangladesh		1	1	0	0
	In United Arab Emirates		3	1	0	2
	Totals		**43**	**16**	**10**	**17**

P Played in Pakistan. S Played in Sri Lanka. B Played in Bangladesh.
U Played in United Arab Emirates.

† *One Test was cancelled owing to the threat of civil disturbances following a general election.*
‡ *These Tests were part of the Asian Test Championship.*
§ *The Second Test ended after a terrorist attack on the Sri Lankan team bus on the third day.*

Note: The following deputised for the official touring captain or were appointed by the home authority for only a minor proportion of the series:
[1]L. R. D. Mendis (Second). [2]Moin Khan (Third). [3]Mohammad Hafeez (First).

SERIES RECORDS

Highest score	*P*	313	Younis Khan at Karachi	2008-09
	SL	253	S. T. Jayasuriya at Faisalabad	2004-05
Best bowling	*P*	8-58	Imran Khan at Lahore	1981-82
	SL	8-83	J. R. Ratnayeke at Sialkot	1985-86
Highest total	*P*	765-6 dec	at Karachi	2008-09
	SL	644-7 dec	at Karachi	2008-09
Lowest total	*P*	90	at Colombo (PSS)	2009
	SL	71	at Kandy	1994-95

PAKISTAN v ZIMBABWE

	Captains					
Season	*Pakistan*	*Zimbabwe*	*T*	*P*	*Z*	*D*
1993-94*P*	Wasim Akram[1]	A. Flower	3	2	0	1
1994-95*Z*	Salim Malik	A. Flower	3	2	1	0
1996-97*P*	Wasim Akram	A. D. R. Campbell	2	1	0	1
1997-98*Z*	Rashid Latif	A. D. R. Campbell	2	1	0	1

1998-99*P*†	Aamir Sohail[2]	A. D. R. Campbell	2	0	1	1
2002-03*Z*	Waqar Younis	A. D. R. Campbell	2	2	0	0
2011-12*Z*	B. R. M. Taylor	Misbah-ul-Haq	1	1	0	0
	In Pakistan		7	3	1	3
	In Zimbabwe		8	6	1	1
	Totals		15	9	2	4

P Played in Pakistan. Z Played in Zimbabwe.

† *The Third Test at Faisalabad was abandoned without a ball being bowled and is excluded.*

Notes: The following were appointed by the home authority for only a minor proportion of the series:
[1]Waqar Younis (First). [2]Moin Khan (Second).

SERIES RECORDS

Highest score	*P*	257*	Wasim Akram at Sheikhupura	1996-97
	Z	201*	G. W. Flower at Harare	1994-95
Best bowling	*P*	7-66	Saqlain Mushtaq at Bulawayo	2002-03
	Z	6-90	H. H. Streak at Harare	1994-95
Highest total	*P*	553	at Sheikhupura	1996-97
	Z	544-4 dec	at Harare	1994-95
Lowest total	*P*	103	at Peshawar	1998-99
	Z	133	at Faisalabad	1996-97

PAKISTAN v BANGLADESH

	Captains					
Season	*Pakistan*	*Bangladesh*	*T*	*P*	*B*	*D*
2001-02*P*†	Waqar Younis	Naimur Rahman	1	1	0	0
2001-02*B*	Waqar Younis	Khaled Mashud	2	2	0	0
2003-04*P*	Rashid Latif	Khaled Mahmud	3	3	0	0
2011-12*B*	Misbah-ul-Haq	Mushfiqur Rahim	2	2	0	0
	In Pakistan		4	4	0	0
	In Bangladesh		4	4	0	0
	Totals		8	8	0	0

P Played in Pakistan. B Played in Bangladesh.

† *This Test was part of the Asian Test Championship.*

SERIES RECORDS

Highest score	*P*	204*	Yousuf Youhana at Chittagong	2001-02
	B	144	Shakib Al Hasan at Mirpur	2011-12
Best bowling	*P*	7-77	Danish Kaneria at Dhaka	2001-02
	B	6-82	Shakib Al Hasan at Mirpur	2011-12
Highest total	*P*	594-5 dec	at Chittagong	2011-12
	B	361	at Peshawar	2003-04
Lowest total	*P*	175	at Multan	2003-04
	B	96	at Peshawar	2003-04

SRI LANKA v ZIMBABWE

	Captains					
Season	*Sri Lanka*	*Zimbabwe*	*T*	*SL*	*Z*	*D*
1994-95*Z*	A. Ranatunga	A. Flower	3	0	0	3
1996-97*S*	A. Ranatunga	A. D. R. Campbell	2	2	0	0
1997-98*S*	A. Ranatunga	A. D. R. Campbell	2	2	0	0
1999-2000*Z*	S. T. Jayasuriya	A. Flower	3	1	0	2
2001-02*S*	S. T. Jayasuriya	S. V. Carlisle	3	3	0	0
2003-04*Z*	M. S. Atapattu	T. Taibu	2	2	0	0
	In Sri Lanka		7	7	0	0
	In Zimbabwe		8	3	0	5
	Totals		15	10	0	5

S Played in Sri Lanka. Z Played in Zimbabwe.

SERIES RECORDS

Highest score	*SL*	270	K. C. Sangakkara at Bulawayo	2003-04
	Z	266	D. L. Houghton at Bulawayo	1994-95
Best bowling	*SL*	9-51	M. Muralitharan at Kandy	2001-02
	Z	5-106	P. A. Strang at Colombo (RPS)	1996-97
Highest total	*SL*	713-3 dec	at Bulawayo	2003-04
	Z	462-9 dec	at Bulawayo	1994-95
Lowest total	*SL*	218	at Bulawayo	1994-95
	Z	79	at Galle	2001-02

SRI LANKA v BANGLADESH

	Captains					
Season	*Sri Lanka*	*Bangladesh*	*T*	*SL*	*B*	*D*
2001-02*S*†	S. T. Jayasuriya	Naimur Rahman	1	1	0	0
2002*S*	S. T. Jayasuriya	Khaled Mashud	2	2	0	0
2005-06*S*	M. S. Atapattu	Habibul Bashar	2	2	0	0
2005-06*B*	D. P. M. D. Jayawardene	Habibul Bashar	2	2	0	0
2007*S*	D. P. M. D. Jayawardene	Mohammad Ashraful	3	3	0	0
2008-09*B*	D. P. M. D. Jayawardene	Mohammad Ashraful	2	2	0	0
	In Sri Lanka		8	8	0	0
	In Bangladesh		4	4	0	0
	Totals		12	12	0	0

S Played in Sri Lanka. B Played in Bangladesh.

† This Test was part of the Asian Test Championship.

SERIES RECORDS

Highest score	*SL*	222*	K. C. Sangakkara at Kandy	2007
	B	136	Mohammad Ashraful at Chittagong	2005-06
Best bowling	*SL*	6-18	M. Muralitharan at Colombo (RPS)	2005-06
	B	5-70	Shakib Al Hasan at Mirpur	2008-09
Highest total	*SL*	577-6 dec	at Colombo (SSC)	2007
	B	413	at Mirpur	2008-09
Lowest total	*SL*	293	at Mirpur	2008-09
	B	62	at Colombo (PSS)	2007

ZIMBABWE v BANGLADESH

Season	*Captains* *Zimbabwe*	*Bangladesh*	*T*	*Z*	*B*	*D*
2000-01*Z*	H. H. Streak	Naimur Rahman	2	2	0	0
2001-02*B*	B. A. Murphy[1]	Naimur Rahman	2	1	0	1
2003-04*Z*	H. H. Streak	Habibul Bashar	2	1	0	1
2004-05*B*	T. Taibu	Habibul Bashar	2	0	1	1
2011-12*Z*	B. R. M. Taylor	Shakib Al Hasan	1	1	0	0
	In Zimbabwe		5	4	0	1
	In Bangladesh		4	1	1	2
	Totals		9	5	1	3

Z Played in Zimbabwe. B Played in Bangladesh.

Note: The following deputised for the official touring captain:

[1]S. V. Carlisle (Second).

SERIES RECORDS

Highest score	*Z*	153	T. Taibu at Dhaka	2004-05
	B	121	Nafis Iqbal at Dhaka	2004-05
Best bowling	*Z*	6-59	D. T. Hondo at Dhaka	2004-05
	B	7-95	Enamul Haque, jun. at Dhaka	2004-05
Highest total	*Z*	542-7 dec	at Chittagong	2001-02
	B	488	at Chittagong	2004-05
Lowest total	*Z*	154	at Chittagong	2004-05
	B	107	at Dhaka	2001-02

TEST GROUNDS

in chronological order

	City and Ground	*First Test Match*		*Tests*
1	**Melbourne, Melbourne Cricket Ground**	**March 15, 1877**	**A v E**	**105**
2	**London, Kennington Oval**	**September 6, 1880**	**E v A**	**95**
3	**Sydney, Sydney Cricket Ground (No. 1)**	**February 17, 1882**	**A v E**	**101**
4	Manchester, Old Trafford	July 11, 1884	E v A	74
5	**London, Lord's**	**July 21, 1884**	**E v A**	**125**
6	**Adelaide, Adelaide Oval**	**December 12, 1884**	**A v E**	**71**
7	**Port Elizabeth, St George's Park**	**March 12, 1889**	**SA v E**	**24**
8	**Cape Town, Newlands**	**March 25, 1889**	**SA v E**	**49**
9	Johannesburg, Old Wanderers	March 2, 1896	SA v E	22
	Now the site of Johannesburg Railway Station.			
10	**Nottingham, Trent Bridge**	**June 1, 1899**	**E v A**	**58**
11	**Leeds, Headingley**	**June 29, 1899**	**E v A**	**71**
12	**Birmingham, Edgbaston**	**May 29, 1902**	**E v A**	**47**
13	Sheffield, Bramall Lane	July 3, 1902	E v A	1
	Sheffield United Football Club have built a stand over the cricket pitch.			
14	Durban, Lord's	January 21, 1910	SA v E	4
	Ground destroyed and built on.			
15	Durban, Kingsmead	January 18, 1923	SA v E	39
16	Brisbane, Exhibition Ground	November 30, 1928	A v E	2
	No longer used for cricket.			
17	Christchurch, Lancaster Park	January 10, 1930	NZ v E	40
	Ground also known under sponsors' names.			
18	**Bridgetown, Kensington Oval**	**January 11, 1930**	**WI v E**	**48**
19	**Wellington, Basin Reserve**	**January 24, 1930**	**NZ v E**	**53**

	City and Ground	*First Test Match*		*Tests*
20	**Port-of-Spain, Queen's Park Oval**	**February 1, 1930**	**WI v E**	**58**
21	Auckland, Eden Park	February 17, 1930	NZ v E	47
22	Georgetown, Bourda	February 21, 1930	WI v E	30
23	**Kingston, Sabina Park**	**April 3, 1930**	**WI v E**	**46**
24	**Brisbane, Woolloongabba**	**November 27, 1931**	**A v SA**	**55**
25	Bombay, Gymkhana Ground	December 15, 1933	I v E	1
	No longer used for first-class cricket.			
26	**Calcutta (*now Kolkata*), Eden Gardens**	**January 5, 1934**	**I v E**	**38**
27	Madras (*now Chennai*), Chepauk (Chidambaram Stadium)	February 10, 1934	I v E	30
28	Delhi, Feroz Shah Kotla	November 10, 1948	I v WI	31
29	Bombay (*now Mumbai*), Brabourne Stadium	December 9, 1948	I v WI	18
	Rarely used for first-class cricket.			
30	Johannesburg, Ellis Park	December 27, 1948	SA v E	6
	Mainly a football and rugby stadium, no longer used for cricket.			
31	Kanpur, Green Park (Modi Stadium)	January 12, 1952	I v E	21
32	Lucknow, University Ground	October 25, 1952	I v P	1
	Ground destroyed, now partly under a river bed.			
33	Dacca (*now Dhaka*), Dacca (*now Bangabandhu*) Stadium	January 1, 1955	P v I	17
	Originally in East Pakistan, now Bangladesh, no longer used for cricket.			
34	Bahawalpur, Dring (*now Bahawal*) Stadium	January 15, 1955	P v I	1
	Still used for first-class cricket.			
35	Lahore, Lawrence Gardens (Bagh-e-Jinnah)	January 29, 1955	P v I	3
	Still used for club and occasional first-class matches.			
36	Peshawar, Services Ground	February 13, 1955	P v I	1
	Superseded by new stadium.			
37	Karachi, National Stadium	February 26, 1955	P v I	41
38	Dunedin, Carisbrook	March 11, 1955	NZ v E	10
39	Hyderabad, Fateh Maidan (Lal Bahadur Stadium)	November 19, 1955	I v NZ	3
40	Madras, Corporation Stadium	January 6, 1956	I v NZ	9
	Superseded by rebuilt Chepauk Stadium.			
41	Johannesburg, Wanderers	December 24, 1956	SA v E	33
42	Lahore, Gaddafi Stadium	November 21, 1959	P v A	40
43	Rawalpindi, Pindi Club Ground	March 27, 1965	P v NZ	1
	Superseded by new stadium.			
44	Nagpur, Vidarbha C.A. Ground	October 3, 1969	I v NZ	9
	Superseded by new stadium.			
45	**Perth, Western Australian C.A. Ground**	**December 11, 1970**	**A v E**	**40**
46	Hyderabad, Niaz Stadium	March 16, 1973	P v E	5
47	**Bangalore, Karnataka State C.A. Ground (Chinnaswamy Stadium)**	**November 22, 1974**	**I v WI**	**20**
48	**Bombay (*now Mumbai*), Wankhede Stadium**	**January 23, 1975**	**I v WI**	**23**
49	Faisalabad, Iqbal Stadium	October 16, 1978	P v I	24
50	**Napier, McLean Park**	**February 16, 1979**	**NZ v P**	**10**
51	Multan, Ibn-e-Qasim Bagh Stadium	December 30, 1980	P v WI	1
	Superseded by new stadium.			
52	St John's (Antigua), Recreation Ground	March 27, 1981	WI v E	22
53	**Colombo, P. Saravanamuttu (Sara) Stadium**	**February 17, 1982**	**SL v E**	**17**
54	Kandy, Asgiriya Stadium	April 22, 1983	SL v A	21
55	Jullundur, Burlton Park	September 24, 1983	I v P	1
56	**Ahmedabad, Sardar Patel (Gujarat) Stadium**	**November 12, 1983**	**I v WI**	**12**
57	**Colombo, Sinhalese Sports Club Ground**	**March 16, 1984**	**SL v NZ**	**36**
58	Colombo, Colombo Cricket Club Ground	March 24, 1984	SL v NZ	3
59	Sialkot, Jinnah Stadium	October 27, 1985	P v SL	4
60	Cuttack, Barabati Stadium	January 4, 1987	I v SL	2
61	Jaipur, Sawai Mansingh Stadium	February 21, 1987	I v P	1
62	**Hobart, Bellerive Oval**	**December 16, 1989**	**A v SL**	**11**
63	Chandigarh, Sector 16 Stadium	November 23, 1990	I v SL	1
	Superseded by Mohali ground.			

	City and Ground	*First Test Match*		*Tests*
64	**Hamilton, Seddon Park**	**February 22, 1991**	**NZ v SL**	**19**
	Ground also known under various sponsors' names.			
65	Gujranwala, Municipal Stadium	December 20, 1991	P v SL	1
66	Colombo, R. Premadasa (Khettarama) Stadium	August 28, 1992	SL v A	7
67	Moratuwa, Tyronne Fernando Stadium	September 8, 1992	SL v A	4
68	**Harare, Harare Sports Club**	**October 18, 1992**	**Z v I**	**27**
69	Bulawayo, Bulawayo Athletic Club	November 1, 1992	Z v NZ	1
	Superseded by Queens Sports Club ground.			
70	Karachi, Defence Stadium	December 1, 1993	P v Z	1
71	Rawalpindi, Rawalpindi Cricket Stadium	December 9, 1993	P v Z	8
72	Lucknow, K. D. "Babu" Singh Stadium	January 18, 1994	I v SL	1
73	**Bulawayo, Queens Sports Club**	**October 20, 1994**	**Z v SL**	**19**
74	Mohali, Punjab Cricket Association Stadium	December 10, 1994	I v WI	10
75	Peshawar, Arbab Niaz Stadium	September 8, 1995	P v SL	6
76	Centurion (*formerly Verwoerdburg*), Centurion Park	November 16, 1995	SA v E	17
77	Sheikhupura, Municipal Stadium	October 17, 1996	P v Z	2
78	St Vincent, Arnos Vale	June 20, 1997	WI v SL	2
79	**Galle, International Stadium**	**June 3, 1998**	**SL v NZ**	**21**
80	Bloemfontein, Springbok Park	October 29, 1999	SA v Z	4
	Ground also known under various sponsors' names.			
81	Multan, Multan Cricket Stadium	August 29, 2001	P v B	5
82	Chittagong, Chittagong Stadium	November 15, 2001	B v Z	8
	Ground also known as M. A. Aziz Stadium.			
83	Sharjah, Sharjah Cricket Association Stadium	January 31, 2002	P v WI	5
84	St George's, Grenada, Queen's Park New Stadium	June 28, 2002	WI v NZ	2
85	East London, Buffalo Park	October 18, 2002	SA v B	1
86	Potchefstroom, North West Cricket Stadium	October 25, 2002	SA v B	1
	Ground now known under sponsor's name.			
87	Chester-le-Street, Riverside Ground	June 5, 2003	E v Z	4
88	Gros Islet, St Lucia, Beausejour Stadium	June 20, 2003	WI v SL	3
89	Darwin, Marrara Cricket Ground	July 18, 2003	A v B	2
90	Cairns, Cazaly's Football Park	July 25, 2003	A v B	2
	Ground also known under sponsor's name.			
91	Chittagong, Chittagong Divisional Stadium	February 28, 2006	B v SL	10
	Ground also known as Bir Shrestha Shahid Ruhul Amin Stadium and Zohur Ahmed Chowdhury Stadium.			
92	Bogra, Shaheed Chandu Stadium	March 8, 2006	B v SL	1
93	Fatullah, Narayanganj Osmani Stadium	April 9, 2006	B v A	1
94	Basseterre, St Kitts, Warner Park	June 22, 2006	WI v I	3
95	**Mirpur (Dhaka), Shere Bangla National Stadium**	**May 25, 2007**	**B v I**	**9**
96	**Dunedin, University Oval**	**January 4, 2008**	**NZ v B**	**4**
97	Providence Stadium, Guyana	March 22, 2008	WI v SL	2
98	**North Sound, Antigua, Sir Vivian Richards Stadium**	**May 30, 2008**	**WI v A**	**3**
99	**Nagpur, Vidarbha C. A. Stadium, Jamtha**	**November 6, 2008**	**I v A**	**4**
100	Cardiff, Sophia Gardens	July 8, 2009	E v A	2
	Ground now known under sponsor's name.			
101	**Hyderabad, Rajiv Gandhi International Stadium**	**November 12, 2010**	**I v NZ**	**2**
102	**Dubai, Dubai Sports City Stadium**	**November 12, 2010**	**P v SA**	**4**
103	**Abu Dhabi, Sheikh Zayed Stadium**	**November 20, 2010**	**P v SA**	**3**
104	**Pallekele, Muttiah Muralitharan Stadium**	**December 1, 2010**	**SL v WI**	**3**
105	Southampton, Rose Bowl	June 16, 2011	E v SL	1
106	**Roseau, Dominica, Windsor Park**	**July 6, 2011**	**WI v I**	**2**
107	**Khulna, Khulna Division Stadium**	**November 21, 2012**	**B v WI**	**1**
	Ground also known as Bir Shrestha Shahid Flight Lieutenant Motiur Rahman Stadium and Shaikh Abu Naser Stadium.			

Bold type denotes grounds used for Test cricket since January 1, 2012.

ONE-DAY INTERNATIONAL RECORDS

Matches in this section do not have first-class status.

Note: Throughout this section, bold type denotes performances in the calendar year 2012 or, in career figures, players who appeared in one-day internationals in that year.

SUMMARY OF ONE-DAY INTERNATIONALS

1970-71 to January 6, 2013

	Opponents	*Matches*	*Won by*															
			E	*A*	*SA*	*WI*	*NZ*	*I*	*P*	*SL*	*Z*	*B*	*Ass*	*Asia*	*Wld*	*Afr*	*Tied*	*NR*
England	Australia	**117**	46	67	–	–	–	–	–	–	–	–	–	–	–	–	2	2
	South Africa	**50**	21	–	25	–	–	–	–	–	–	–	–	–	–	–	1	3
	West Indies	**85**	40	–	–	41	–	–	–	–	–	–	–	–	–	–	–	4
	New Zealand	**70**	29	–	–	–	35	–	–	–	–	–	–	–	–	–	2	4
	India	**81**	33	–	–	–	–	43	–	–	–	–	–	–	–	–	2	3
	Pakistan	**72**	42	–	–	–	–	–	28	–	–	–	–	–	–	–	–	2
	Sri Lanka	**50**	26	–	–	–	–	–	–	24	–	–	–	–	–	–	–	–
	Zimbabwe	**30**	21	–	–	–	–	–	–	–	8	–	–	–	–	–	–	1
	Bangladesh	**15**	13	–	–	–	–	–	–	–	–	2	–	–	–	–	–	–
	Associates	**17**	15	–	–	–	–	–	–	–	–	–	1	–	–	–	–	1
Australia	South Africa	**80**	–	41	36	–	–	–	–	–	–	–	–	–	–	–	3	–
	West Indies	**130**	–	65	–	59	–	–	–	–	–	–	–	–	–	–	3	3
	New Zealand	**124**	–	85	–	–	34	–	–	–	–	–	–	–	–	–	–	5
	India	**109**	–	64	–	–	–	37	–	–	–	–	–	–	–	–	–	8
	Pakistan	**89**	–	54	–	–	–	–	31	–	–	–	–	–	–	–	1	3
	Sri Lanka	**84**	–	53	–	–	–	–	–	28	–	–	–	–	–	–	–	3
	Zimbabwe	**28**	–	26	–	–	–	–	–	–	1	–	–	–	–	–	–	1
	Bangladesh	**19**	–	18	–	–	–	–	–	–	–	1	–	–	–	–	–	–
	Associates	**18**	–	17	–	–	–	–	–	–	–	–	0	–	–	–	–	1
	ICC World XI	**3**	–	3	–	–	–	–	–	–	–	–	–	–	0	–	–	–
South Africa	West Indies	**51**	–	–	38	12	–	–	–	–	–	–	–	–	–	–	–	1
	New Zealand	**55**	–	–	33	–	18	–	–	–	–	–	–	–	–	–	–	4
	India	**66**	–	–	40	–	–	24	–	–	–	–	–	–	–	–	–	2
	Pakistan	**57**	–	–	38	–	–	–	18	–	–	–	–	–	–	–	–	1
	Sri Lanka	**51**	–	–	25	–	–	–	–	24	–	–	–	–	–	–	1	1
	Zimbabwe	**32**	–	–	29	–	–	–	–	–	2	–	–	–	–	–	–	1
	Bangladesh	**14**	–	–	13	–	–	–	–	–	–	1	–	–	–	–	–	–
	Associates	**19**	–	–	19	–	–	–	–	–	–	–	0	–	–	–	–	–
West Indies	New Zealand	**56**	–	–	–	28	21	–	–	–	–	–	–	–	–	–	–	7
	India	**106**	–	–	–	57	–	46	–	–	–	–	–	–	–	–	1	2
	Pakistan	**120**	–	–	–	66	–	–	52	–	–	–	–	–	–	–	2	–
	Sri Lanka	**49**	–	–	–	26	–	–	–	20	–	–	–	–	–	–	–	3
	Zimbabwe	**41**	–	–	–	31	–	–	–	–	9	–	–	–	–	–	–	1
	Bangladesh	**25**	–	–	–	16	–	–	–	–	–	7	–	–	–	–	–	2
	Associates	**19**	–	–	–	17	–	–	–	–	–	–	1	–	–	–	–	1
New Zealand	India	**88**	–	–	–	–	37	46	–	–	–	–	–	–	–	–	–	5
	Pakistan	**89**	–	–	–	–	35	–	51	–	–	–	–	–	–	–	1	2
	Sri Lanka	**78**	–	–	–	–	35	–	–	37	–	–	–	–	–	–	1	5
	Zimbabwe	**35**	–	–	–	–	25	–	–	–	8	–	–	–	–	–	1	1
	Bangladesh	**21**	–	–	–	–	16	–	–	–	–	5	–	–	–	–	–	–
	Associates	**13**	–	–	–	–	13	–	–	–	–	–	0	–	–	–	–	–
India	Pakistan	**124**	–	–	–	–	–	49	71	–	–	–	–	–	–	–	–	4
	Sri Lanka	**139**	–	–	–	–	–	75	–	52	–	–	–	–	–	–	1	11
	Zimbabwe	**51**	–	–	–	–	–	39	–	–	10	–	–	–	–	–	2	–
	Bangladesh	**24**	–	–	–	–	–	21	–	–	–	3	–	–	–	–	–	–
	Associates	**24**	–	–	–	–	–	22	–	–	–	–	2	–	–	–	–	–
Pakistan	Sri Lanka	**132**	–	–	–	–	–	–	77	50	–	–	–	–	–	–	1	4
	Zimbabwe	**44**	–	–	–	–	–	–	40	–	2	–	–	–	–	–	1	1
	Bangladesh	**31**	–	–	–	–	–	–	30	–	–	1	–	–	–	–	–	–
	Associates	**22**	–	–	–	–	–	–	21	–	–	–	1	–	–	–	–	–
Sri Lanka	Zimbabwe	**47**	–	–	–	–	–	–	–	39	7	–	–	–	–	–	–	1
	Bangladesh	**30**	–	–	–	–	–	–	–	27	–	3	–	–	–	–	–	–
	Associates	**16**	–	–	–	–	–	–	–	15	–	–	1	–	–	–	–	–
Zimbabwe	Bangladesh	**56**	–	–	–	–	–	–	–	–	26	30	–	–	–	–	–	–
	Associates	**43**	–	–	–	–	–	–	–	–	34	–	6	–	–	–	1	2
Bangladesh	Associates	**32**	–	–	–	–	–	–	–	–	–	22	10	–	–	–	–	–

	Opponents	*Matches*	*Won by*															
			E	*A*	*SA*	*WI*	*NZ*	*I*	*P*	*SL*	*Z*	*B*	*Ass*	*Asia*	*Wld*	*Afr*	*Tied*	*NR*
Associates	Associates	**138**	–	–	–	–	–	–	–	–	–	–	133	–	–	–	–	5
Asian CC XI	ICC World XI	**1**	–	–	–	–	–	–	–	–	–	–	–	0	1	–	–	–
	African XI	**6**	–	–	–	–	–	–	–	–	–	–	–	4	–	1	–	1
		3,316	286	493	296	353	269	402	419	316	107	75	155	4	1	1	27	112

Note: Associate and Affiliate Members of ICC who have played one-day internationals are Afghanistan, Bermuda, Canada, East Africa, Hong Kong, Ireland, Kenya, Namibia, Netherlands, Scotland, United Arab Emirates and USA. Sri Lanka, Zimbabwe and Bangladesh also played one-day internationals before being given Test status; these are not included among the Associates' results.

RESULTS SUMMARY OF ONE-DAY INTERNATIONALS

1970-71 to January 6, 2013 (3,316 matches)

	Matches	*Won*	*Lost*	*Tied*	*No Result*	*% Won (excl. NR)*
South Africa	475	296	161	5	13	64.61
Australia	801	493	273	9	26	64.19
Pakistan	780	419	338	6	17	55.30
West Indies	682	353	299	6	24	54.10
India	812	402	369	6	35	52.12
England	587	286	274	7	20	51.05
Sri Lanka	676	316	328	4	28	49.07
New Zealand	629	269	322	5	33	45.55
Bangladesh	267	75	190	–	2	28.30
Zimbabwe	407	107	286	5	9	27.51
Asian Cricket Council XI	7	4	2	–	1	66.66
Afghanistan	23	12	11	–	–	52.17
Ireland	74	34	35	1	4	49.28
Netherlands	69	26	41	–	2	38.80
Scotland	55	19	33	–	3	36.53
Kenya	146	39	102	–	5	27.65
ICC World XI	4	1	3	–	–	25.00
Canada	71	17	53	–	1	24.28
Bermuda	35	7	28	–	–	20.00
African XI	6	1	4	–	1	20.00
United Arab Emirates	11	1	10	–	–	9.09
USA	2	–	2	–	–	0.00
East Africa	3	–	3	–	–	0.00
Hong Kong	4	–	4	–	–	0.00
Namibia	6	–	6	–	–	0.00

Note: Matches abandoned without a ball bowled are not included except (from 2004) where the toss took place, in accordance with an ICC ruling. Such matches, like those called off after play began, are now counted as official internationals in their own right, even when replayed on another day. In the percentages of matches won, ties are counted as half a win.

BATTING RECORDS

HIGHEST INDIVIDUAL INNINGS

219	V. Sehwag	India v West Indies at Indore	2011-12
200*	S. R. Tendulkar	India v South Africa at Gwalior	2009-10
194*	C. K. Coventry	Zimbabwe v Bangladesh at Bulawayo	2009
194	Saeed Anwar	Pakistan v India at Chennai	1997-97
189*	I. V. A. Richards	West Indies v England at Manchester	1984
189	S. T. Jayasuriya	Sri Lanka v India at Sharjah	2000-01
188*	G. Kirsten	South Africa v UAE at Rawalpindi	1995-96

186*	S. R. Tendulkar	India v New Zealand at Hyderabad	1999-2000
185*	S. R. Watson	Australia v Bangladesh at Mirpur	2010-11
183*	M. S. Dhoni	India v Sri Lanka at Jaipur	2005-06
183	S. C. Ganguly	India v Sri Lanka at Taunton	1999
183	**V. Kohli**	**India v Pakistan at Mirpur**	**2011-12**
181*	M. L. Hayden	Australia v New Zealand at Hamilton	2006-07
181	I. V. A. Richards	West Indies v Sri Lanka at Karachi	1987-88
178*	H. Masakadza	Zimbabwe v Kenya at Harare	2009-10
177	P. R. Stirling	Ireland v Canada at Toronto	2010
175*	Kapil Dev	India v Zimbabwe at Tunbridge Wells	1983
175	H. H. Gibbs	South Africa v Australia at Johannesburg	2005-06
175	S. R. Tendulkar	India v Australia at Hyderabad	2009-10
175	V. Sehwag	India v Bangladesh at Mirpur	2010-11

Note: The highest individual scores for other Test countries are:

172	L. Vincent	New Zealand v Zimbabwe at Bulawayo	2005-06
167*	R. A. Smith	England v Australia at Birmingham	1993
154	Tamim Iqbal	Bangladesh v Zimbabwe at Bulawayo	2009

MOST HUNDREDS

S. R. Tendulkar (I)	**49**
R. T. Ponting (A/World)	**30**
S. T. Jayasuriya (SL/Asia)	28
S. C. Ganguly (I/Asia)	22
H. H. Gibbs (SA)	21
C. H. Gayle (WI/World)	**20**
Saeed Anwar (P)	20
B. C. Lara (WI/World)	19
M. E. Waugh (A)	18
D. L. Haynes (WI)	17
J. H. Kallis (SA/Wld/Af)	**17**
N. J. Astle (NZ)	16
A. C. Gilchrist (A/World)	16
D. P. M. D. Jayawardene (SL/Asia)	**15**
Mohammad Yousuf (P/As)	15
V. Sehwag (I/Wld/Asia)	**15**
T. M. Dilshan (SL)	**14**
K. C. Sangakkara (SL/World/Asia)	**14**
A. B. de Villiers (SA)	**13**
G. Kirsten (SA)	13
V. Kohli (I)	**13**
Yuvraj Singh (I/Asia)	**13**
R. Dravid (I/World/Asia)	12
W. U. Tharanga (SL)	**12**
M. E. Trescothick (E)	12
M. S. Atapattu (SL)	11
S. Chanderpaul (WI)	11
P. A. de Silva (SL)	11
G. Gambhir (I)	**11**
C. G. Greenidge (WI)	11
I. V. A. Richards (WI)	11
H. M. Amla (SA)	**10**
M. L. Hayden (A/World)	10
Ijaz Ahmed, sen. (P)	10
Inzamam-ul-Haq (P/Asia)	10

Most hundreds for other countries:

A. D. R. Campbell (Z)	7
Shakib Al Hasan (B)	**5**

Note: Ponting's hundreds include one for the World XI; no other player reached three figures for a combined team.

MOST RUNS

		M	*I*	*NO*	*R*	*HS*	*100*	*Avge*
1	**S. R. Tendulkar (India)**	**463**	**452**	**41**	**18,426**	**200***	**49**	**44.83**
2	**R. T. Ponting (Australia/World)**	**375**	**365**	**39**	**13,704**	**164**	**30**	**42.03**
3	S. T. Jayasuriya (Sri Lanka/Asia)	445	433	18	13,430	189	28	32.36
4	Inzamam-ul-Haq (Pakistan/Asia)	378	350	53	11,739	137*	10	39.52
5	**J. H. Kallis (S. Africa/World/Africa)**	**321**	**307**	**53**	**11,498**	**139**	**17**	**45.26**
6	S. C. Ganguly (India/Asia)	311	300	23	11,363	183	22	41.02
7	**K. C. Sangakkara (SL/Asia/World)**	**337**	**316**	**33**	**10,915**	**138***	**14**	**38.56**
8	R. Dravid (India/World/Asia)	344	318	40	10,889	153	12	39.16
9	**D. P. M. D. Jayawardene (SL/Asia)**	**386**	**361**	**36**	**10,844**	**144**	**15**	**33.36**
10	B. C. Lara (West Indies/World)	299	289	32	10,405	169	19	40.48
11	Mohammad Yousuf (Pakistan/Asia)	288	273	40	9,720	141*	15	41.71
12	A. C. Gilchrist (Australia/World)	287	279	11	9,619	172	16	35.89
13	M. Azharuddin (India)	334	308	54	9,378	153*	7	36.92
14	P. A. de Silva (Sri Lanka)	308	296	30	9,284	145	11	34.90
15	Saeed Anwar (Pakistan)	247	244	19	8,824	194	20	39.21
16	S. Chanderpaul (West Indies)	268	251	40	8,778	150	11	41.60
17	D. L. Haynes (West Indies)	238	237	28	8,648	152*	17	41.37
18	M. S. Atapattu (Sri Lanka)	268	259	32	8,529	132*	11	37.57

		M	I	NO	R	HS	100	Avge
19	M. E. Waugh (Australia)	244	236	20	8,500	173	18	39.35
20	**C. H. Gayle (West Indies)**	**239**	**234**	**17**	**8,432**	**153***	**20**	**38.85**
21	**V. Sehwag (India/Asia/World)**	**251**	**245**	**9**	**8,273**	**219**	**15**	**35.05**
22	H. H. Gibbs (South Africa)	248	240	16	8,094	175	21	36.13
23	**Yuvraj Singh (India/Asia)**	**277**	**255**	**38**	**8,085**	**139**	**13**	**37.25**
24	S. P. Fleming (New Zealand/World)	280	269	21	8,037	134*	8	32.40

Notes: The leading aggregates for players who have appeared for other Test countries are:

	M	I	NO	R	HS	100	Avge
A. Flower (Zimbabwe)	213	208	16	6,786	145	4	35.34
P. D. Collingwood (England)	197	181	37	5,092	120*	5	35.36
Shakib Al Hasan (Bangladesh)	**126**	**121**	**19**	**3,635**	**134***	**5**	**35.63**

Excluding runs scored for combined teams, the record aggregate for Australia is **13,589** in 374 matches by **R. T. Ponting**; for Sri Lanka, 13,364 in 441 matches by S. T. Jayasuriya; for Pakistan, 11,701 in 375 matches by Inzamam-ul-Haq; for South Africa, **11,469** in 316 matches by **J. H. Kallis**; for West Indies, 10,348 in 295 matches by B. C. Lara; and for New Zealand, 8,007 in 279 matches by S. P. Fleming.

BEST CAREER STRIKE-RATES BY BATSMEN

(Runs per 100 balls. Qualification: 700 runs)

SR		Position	M	I	R	Avge
114.95	Rizwan Cheema (Canada)	2/6	31	30	707	24.37
113.78	**Shahid Afridi (P/World/Asia)**	**2/7**	**349**	**323**	**7,075**	**23.24**
113.60	**Y. K. Pathan (India)**	**7**	**57**	**41**	**810**	**27.00**
105.22	B. L. Cairns (NZ)	9/8	78	65	987	16.72
104.33	**V. Sehwag (I/World/Asia)**	**1/2**	**251**	**245**	**8,273**	**35.05**
104.17	J. M. Davison (Canada)	1/2	32	32	799	26.63
101.72	**D. J. G. Sammy (WI)**	**7/8**	**87**	**69**	**1,063**	**21.69**
100.25	**J. A. Morkel (SA)**	**7/8**	**58**	**43**	**782**	**23.69**
99.43	I. D. S. Smith (NZ)	8	98	77	1,055	17.29
96.94	A. C. Gilchrist (A/World)	1/2	287	279	9,619	35.89
96.68	**K. A. Pollard (WI)**	**6/7**	**68**	**62**	**1,547**	**25.78**
96.66	R. L. Powell (WI)	6	109	100	2,085	24.82
96.16	Kapil Dev (I)	7/6	225	198	3,783	23.79
96.14	**P. R. Stirling (Ireland)**	**2**	**38**	**38**	**1,448**	**39.13**
96.12	**M. G. Johnson (A)**	**8/9**	**112**	**64**	**720**	**17.56**

Note: Position means a batsman's most usual position in the batting order.

FASTEST ONE-DAY INTERNATIONAL FIFTIES

Balls			
17	S. T. Jayasuriya	Sri Lanka v Pakistan at Singapore	1995-96
18	S. P. O'Donnell	Australia v Sri Lanka at Sharjah	1989-90
18	Shahid Afridi	Pakistan v Sri Lanka at Nairobi	1996-97
18	Shahid Afridi	Pakistan v Netherlands at Colombo (SSC)	2002
19	M. V. Boucher	South Africa v Kenya at Cape Town	2001-02
19	J. M. Kemp	South Africa v Zimbabwe at Durban	2004-05
19	B. B. McCullum	New Zealand v Bangladesh at Queenstown	2007-08
19	D. J. Hussey	Australia v West Indies at Basseterre	2008
20	Shahid Afridi	Pakistan v India at Kanpur	2004-05
20	Shahid Afridi	Pakistan v South Africa at Durban	2006-07
20	B. B. McCullum	New Zealand v Canada at Gros Islet	2006-07
20	D. J. G. Sammy	West Indies v South Africa at North Sound	2010
20	R. D. Berrington	Scotland v Ireland at Edinburgh	2011
20	**D. J. G. Sammy**	**West Indies v Australia at Gros Islet**	**2011-12**

FASTEST ONE-DAY INTERNATIONAL HUNDREDS

Balls			
37	Shahid Afridi	Pakistan v Sri Lanka at Nairobi	1996-97
44	M. V. Boucher	South Africa v Zimbabwe at Potchefstroom	2006-07
45	B. C. Lara	West Indies v Bangladesh at Dhaka	1999-2000
45	Shahid Afridi	Pakistan v India at Kanpur	2004-05
48	S. T. Jayasuriya	Sri Lanka v Pakistan at Singapore	1995-96
50	K. J. O'Brien	Ireland v England at Bangalore	2010-11

HIGHEST PARTNERSHIP FOR EACH WICKET

286	for 1st	W. U. Tharanga and S. T. Jayasuriya	SL v E	Leeds	2006
331	for 2nd	S. R. Tendulkar and R. Dravid	I v NZ	Hyderabad	1999-2000
237*	for 3rd	R. Dravid and S. R. Tendulkar	I v K	Bristol	1999
275*	for 4th	M. Azharuddin and A. Jadeja	I v Z	Cuttack	1997-98
223	for 5th	M. Azharuddin and A. Jadeja	I v SL	Colombo (RPS)	1997-98
218	for 6th	D. P. M. D. Jayawardene and M. S. Dhoni	As v Af	Chennai	2007
130	for 7th	A. Flower and H. H. Streak	Z v E	Harare	2001-02
138*	for 8th	J. M. Kemp and A. J. Hall	SA v I	Cape Town	2006-07
132	for 9th	A. D. Mathews and S. L. Malinga	SL v A	Melbourne	2010-11
106*	for 10th	I. V. A. Richards and M. A. Holding	WI v E	Manchester	1984

BOWLING RECORDS

BEST BOWLING ANALYSES

8-19	W. P. U. J. C. Vaas	Sri Lanka v Zimbabwe at Colombo (SSC)	2001-02
7-15	G. D. McGrath	Australia v Namibia at Potchefstroom	2002-03
7-20	A. J. Bichel	Australia v England at Port Elizabeth	2002-03
7-30	M. Muralitharan	Sri Lanka v India at Sharjah	2000-01
7-36	Waqar Younis	Pakistan v England at Leeds	2001
7-37	Aqib Javed	Pakistan v India at Sharjah	1991-92
7-51	W. W. Davis	West Indies v Australia at Leeds	1983

Note: The best analyses for other countries are:

6-12	A. Kumble	India v West Indies at Calcutta	1993-94
6-19	S. E. Bond	New Zealand v India at Bulawayo	2005-06
6-19	H. K. Olonga	Zimbabwe v England at Cape Town	1999-2000
6-22	M. Ntini	South Africa v Australia at Cape Town	2005-06
6-26	Mashrafe bin Mortaza	Bangladesh v Kenya at Nairobi	2006
6-31	P. D. Collingwood	England v Bangladesh at Nottingham	2005

HAT-TRICKS

Jalal-ud-Din	Pakistan v Australia at Hyderabad	1982-83
B. A. Reid	Australia v New Zealand at Sydney	1985-86
Chetan Sharma	India v New Zealand at Nagpur	1987-88
Wasim Akram	Pakistan v West Indies at Sharjah	1989-90
Wasim Akram	Pakistan v Australia at Sharjah	1989-90
Kapil Dev	India v Sri Lanka at Calcutta	1990-91
Aqib Javed	Pakistan v India at Sharjah	1991-92
D. K. Morrison	New Zealand v India at Napier	1993-94
Waqar Younis	Pakistan v New Zealand at East London	1994-95
Saqlain Mushtaq‡	Pakistan v Zimbabwe at Peshawar	1996-97
E. A. Brandes	Zimbabwe v England at Harare	1996-97
A. M. Stuart	Australia v Pakistan at Melbourne	1996-97
Saqlain Mushtaq	Pakistan v Zimbabwe at The Oval	1999
W. P. U. J. C. Vaas	Sri Lanka v Zimbabwe at Colombo (SSC)	2001-02
Mohammad Sami	Pakistan v West Indies at Sharjah	2001-02

W. P. U. J. C. Vaas§	Sri Lanka v Bangladesh at Pietermaritzburg	2002-03
B. Lee	Australia v Kenya at Durban	2002-03
J. M. Anderson	England v Pakistan at The Oval	2003
S. J. Harmison	England v India at Nottingham	2004
C. K. Langeveldt	South Africa v West Indies at Bridgetown	2004-05
Shahadat Hossain	Bangladesh v Zimbabwe at Harare	2006
J. E. Taylor	West Indies v Australia at Mumbai	2006-07
S. E. Bond	New Zealand v Australia at Hobart	2006-07
S. L. Malinga†	Sri Lanka v South Africa at Providence	2006-07
A. Flintoff	England v West Indies at Gros Islet, St Lucia	2008-09
M. F. Maharoof	Sri Lanka v India at Dambulla	2010
K. A. J. Roach	West Indies v Netherlands at Delhi	2010-11
S. L. Malinga	Sri Lanka v Kenya at Colombo (RPS)	2010-11
S. L. Malinga	Sri Lanka v Australia at Colombo (RPS)	2011-12
D. T. Christian	**Australia v Sri Lanka at Melbourne**	**2011-12**
N. L. T. C. Perera	**Sri Lanka v Pakistan at Colombo (RPS)**	**2012**

† *Four wickets in four balls.* ‡ *Four wickets in five balls.* § *The first three balls of the match*

MOST WICKETS

		M	*Balls*	*R*	*W*	*BB*	*4I*	*Avge*
1	M. Muralitharan (SL/World/Asia)	350	18,811	12,326	534	7-30	25	23.08
2	Wasim Akram (Pakistan)	356	18,186	11,812	502	5-15	23	23.52
3	Waqar Younis (Pakistan)	262	12,698	9,919	416	7-36	27	23.84
4	W. P. U. J. C. Vaas (SL/Asia)	322	15,775	11,014	400	8-19	13	27.53
5	S. M. Pollock (SA/World/Africa)	303	15,712	9,631	393	6-35	17	24.50
6	G. D. McGrath (Australia/World)	250	12,970	8,391	381	7-15	16	22.02
7	**B. Lee (Australia)**	**221**	**11,185**	**8,877**	**380**	**5-22**	**23**	**23.36**
8	**Shahid Afridi (Pakistan/World/Asia)**	**349**	**15,276**	**11,730**	**348**	**6-38**	**12**	**33.70**
9	A. Kumble (India/Asia)	271	14,496	10,412	337	6-12	10	30.89
10	S. T. Jayasuriya (Sri Lanka/Asia)	445	14,874	11,871	323	6-29	12	36.75
11	J. Srinath (India)	229	11,935	8,847	315	5-23	10	28.08
12	S. K. Warne (Australia/World)	194	10,642	7,541	293	5-33	13	25.73
13	Saqlain Mushtaq (Pakistan)	169	8,770	6,275	288	5-20	17	21.78
	A. B. Agarkar (India)	191	9,484	8,021	288	6-42	12	27.85
15	**Zaheer Khan (India/Asia)**	**200**	**10,097**	**8,301**	**282**	**5-42**	**8**	**29.43**
	D. L. Vettori (New Zealand/World)	272	12,903	8,880	282	5-7	9	31.48
17	A. A. Donald (South Africa)	164	8,561	5,926	272	6-23	13	21.78
18	**J. H. Kallis (S. Africa/World/Asia)**	**321**	**10,636**	**8,558**	**270**	**5-30**	**4**	**31.69**
19	Abdul Razzaq (Pakistan/Asia)	265	10,941	8,564	269	6-35	11	31.83
20	M. Ntini (South Africa/World)	173	8,687	6,559	266	6-22	12	24.65
21	Harbhajan Singh (India/Asia)	229	12,059	8,651	259	5-31	5	33.40
22	Kapil Dev (India)	225	11,202	6,945	253	5-43	4	27.45
23	Shoaib Akhtar (Pakistan/Wld/Asia)	163	7,764	6,168	247	6-16	10	24.97
24	H. H. Streak (Zimbabwe)	189	9,468	7,129	239	5-32	8	29.82
25	D. Gough (England/World)	159	8,470	6,209	235	5-44	12	26.42
26	C. A. Walsh (West Indies)	205	10,822	6,918	227	5-1	7	30.47
27	C. E. L. Ambrose (West Indies)	176	9,353	5,429	225	5-17	10	24.12

Notes: The leading aggregates for players who have appeared for other countries are:

	M	Balls	R	W	BB	4I	Avge
Abdur Razzak (Bangladesh)	**138**	**7,227**	**5,382**	**195**	**5-29**	**8**	**27.60**

Excluding wickets taken for combined teams, the record aggregate for Sri Lanka is 523 in 343 matches by M. Muralitharan; for South Africa, 387 in 294 matches by S. M. Pollock; for Australia, 380 in 249 matches by G. D. McGrath; for India, 334 in 269 matches by A. Kumble; for New Zealand, 274 in 268 matches by D. L. Vettori; for Zimbabwe, 237 in 187 matches by H. H. Streak; and for England, 234 in 158 matches by D. Gough.

BEST CAREER STRIKE-RATES BY BOWLERS

(Balls per wicket. Qualification: 1,500 balls)

SR		*M*	*W*
27.22	S. W. Tait (A)	35	62
27.46	**N. L. T. C. Perera (SL)**	**48**	**69**
28.28	**L. L. Tsotsobe (SA)**	**35**	**59**
28.68	**C. J. McKay (A)**	**32**	**57**
28.70	**B. A. W. Mendis (SL)**	**59**	**96**
28.72	**M. Morkel (SA/Africa)**	**58**	**99**
28.72	R. N. ten Doeschate (Netherlands)	33	55
29.21	S. E. Bond (NZ)	82	147
29.38	G. I. Allott (NZ)	31	52
29.43	**B. Lee (A)**	**221**	**380**
29.58	L. S. Pascoe (A)	29	53

BEST CAREER ECONOMY-RATES

(Runs conceded per six balls. Qualification: 50 wickets)

ER		*M*	*W*
3.09	J. Garner (WI)	98	146
3.28	R. G. D. Willis (E)	64	80
3.30	R. J. Hadlee (NZ)	115	158
3.32	M. A. Holding (WI)	102	142
3.40	A. M. E. Roberts (WI)	56	87
3.48	C. E. L. Ambrose (WI)	176	225

WICKETKEEPING AND FIELDING RECORDS

MOST DISMISSALS IN AN INNINGS

6 (all ct)	A. C. Gilchrist	Australia v South Africa at Cape Town	1999-2000
6 (all ct)	A. J. Stewart	England v Zimbabwe at Manchester	2000
6 (5ct, 1st)	R. D. Jacobs	West Indies v Sri Lanka at Colombo (RPS)	2001-02
6 (5ct, 1st)	A. C. Gilchrist	Australia v England at Sydney	2002-03
6 (all ct)	A. C. Gilchrist	Australia v Namibia at Potchefstroom	2002-03
6 (all ct)	A. C. Gilchrist	Australia v Sri Lanka at Colombo (RPS)	2003-04
6 (all ct)	M. V. Boucher	South Africa v Pakistan at Cape Town	2006-07
6 (5ct, 1st)	M. S. Dhoni	India v England at Leeds	2007
6 (all ct)	A. C. Gilchrist	Australia v India at Vadodara	2007-08
6 (5ct, 1st)	A. C. Gilchrist	Australia v India at Sydney	2007-08
6 (all ct)	M. J. Prior	England v South Africa at Nottingham	2008

MOST DISMISSALS

			M	*Ct*	*St*
1	472	A. C. Gilchrist (Australia/World)	282	417	55
2	424	M. V. Boucher (South Africa/Africa)	294	402	22
3	**392**	**K. C. Sangakkara (Sri Lanka/World/Asia)**	**293**	**312**	**80**
4	287	Moin Khan (Pakistan)	219	214	73
5	**268**	**M. S. Dhoni (India/Asia)**	**214**	**200**	**68**
6	234	I. A. Healy (Australia)	168	195	39
7	**233**	**B. B. McCullum (New Zealand)**	**178**	**218**	**15**
8	220	Rashid Latif (Pakistan)	166	182	38
9	206	R. S. Kaluwitharana (Sri Lanka)	186	131	75
10	204	P. J. L. Dujon (West Indies)	169	183	21
11	189	R. D. Jacobs (West Indies)	147	160	29

			M	*Ct*	*St*
12	**169**	**Kamran Akmal (Pakistan)**	**143**	**140**	**29**
13	165	D. J. Richardson (South Africa)	122	148	17
	165	A. Flower (Zimbabwe)	186	133	32
15	163	A. J. Stewart (England)	138	148	15
16	154	N. R. Mongia (India)	140	110	44
17	**145**	**T. Taibu (Zimbabwe)**	**143**	**112**	**33**
18	136	B. J. Haddin (Australia)	84	127	9
	136	A. C. Parore (New Zealand)	150	111	25
20	**131**	**D. Ramdin (West Indies)**	**94**	**125**	**6**
21	126	Khaled Mashud (Bangladesh)	126	91	35
22	124	R. W. Marsh (Australia)	92	120	4
23	**115**	**Mushfiqur Rahim (Bangladesh)**	**111**	**82**	**33**
24	103	Salim Yousuf (Pakistan)	86	81	22

Notes: Excluding dismissals for combined teams, the most for Australia is 470 (416ct, 54st) in 281 matches by A. C. Gilchrist; for South Africa, 415 (394ct, 21st) in 289 matches by M. V. Boucher; for Sri Lanka, **383** (306ct, 77st) in 286 matches by **K. C. Sangakkara**; and for India, **262** (197ct, 65st) in 211 matches by **M. S. Dhoni**.

M. V. Boucher's list excludes 1 catch taken in 1 one-day international when not keeping wicket; K. C. Sangakkara's record excludes 19 in 44; B. B. McCullum's excludes 13 in 28; R. S. Kaluwitharana's 1 in 3; A. Flower's 8 in 27; A. J. Stewart's 11 in 32; T. Taibu's 2 in 7; and A. C. Parore's 5 in 29. A. C. Gilchrist played five one-day internationals without keeping wicket, B. J. Haddin in nine and Mushfiqur Rahim in two, but none of the three made any catches in those games. R. Dravid (India) has made 210 dismissals (196ct, 14st) in 344 one-day internationals but only 86 (72ct, 14st) in 74 as wicketkeeper (including one where he took over during the match).

MOST CATCHES IN AN INNINGS IN THE FIELD

5	J. N. Rhodes	South Africa v West Indies at Bombay	1993-94

Note: There have been **27** instances of four catches in an innings.

MOST CATCHES

Ct	*M*		*Ct*	*M*	
194	**386**	**D. P. M. D. Jayawardene (SL/Asia)**	109	213	R. S. Mahanama (Sri Lanka)
160	**375**	**R. T. Ponting (Australia/World)**	108	197	P. D. Collingwood (England)
156	334	M. Azharuddin (India)	108	244	M. E. Waugh (Australia)
140	**463**	**S. R. Tendulkar (India)**	108	248	H. H. Gibbs (South Africa)
133	280	S. P. Fleming (New Zealand/World)	108	303	S. M. Pollock (SA/Wld/Africa)
130	350	M. Muralitharan (SL/World/Asia)	**105**	**185**	**M. E. K. Hussey (Australia)**
127	273	A. R. Border (Australia)	**105**	**239**	**C. H. Gayle (West Indies)**
125	**321**	**J. H. Kallis (SA/World/Africa)**	105	245	J. N. Rhodes (South Africa)
124	271	R. Dravid (India/World/Asia)	100	187	I. V. A. Richards (West Indies)
123	**245**	**Younis Khan (Pakistan)**	100	311	S. C. Ganguly (India/Asia)
123	445	S. T. Jayasuriya (Sri Lanka/Asia)			
120	227	C. L. Hooper (West Indies)			
120	299	B. C. Lara (West Indies/World)	*Most catches for other countries:*		
113	378	Inzamam-ul-Haq (Pakistan/Asia)	*Ct*	*M*	
112	**349**	**Shahid Afridi (Pak/World/Asia)**	86	221	G. W. Flower (Zimbabwe)
111	325	S. R. Waugh (Australia)	**38**	**126**	**Mashrafe bin Mortaza (Bang)**

Notes: Excluding catches taken for combined teams, the record aggregate for Sri Lanka is **189** in 380 matches by **D. P. M. D. Jayawardene**; for Australia, **158** in 374 by **R. T. Ponting**; for New Zealand, 132 in 279 by S. P. Fleming; and for South Africa, **125** in 316 by **J. H. Kallis**.

R. Dravid's record excludes 72 catches and 14 stumpings made in 74 one-day internationals as wicketkeeper (including one where he took over during the match); Younis Khan's excludes 5 in 3.

TEAM RECORDS

HIGHEST INNINGS TOTALS

443-9	(50 overs)	Sri Lanka v Netherlands at Amstelveen	2006
438-9	(49.5 overs)	South Africa v Australia at Johannesburg	2005-06
434-4	(50 overs)	Australia v South Africa at Johannesburg	2005-06
418-5	(50 overs)	South Africa v Zimbabwe at Potchefstroom	2006-07
418-5	(50 overs)	India v West Indies at Indore	2011-12
414-7	(50 overs)	India v Sri Lanka at Rajkot	2009-10
413-5	(50 overs)	India v Bermuda at Port-of-Spain	2006-07
411-8	(50 overs)	Sri Lanka v India at Rajkot	2009-10
402-2	(50 overs)	New Zealand v Ireland at Aberdeen	2008
401-3	(50 overs)	India v South Africa at Gwalior	2009-10
399-6	(50 overs)	South Africa v Zimbabwe at Benoni	2010-11
398-5	(50 overs)	Sri Lanka v Kenya at Kandy	1995-96
397-5	(44 overs)	New Zealand v Zimbabwe at Bulawayo	2005-06
392-4	(50 overs)	India v New Zealand at Christchurch	2008-09
392-6	(50 overs)	South Africa v Pakistan at Centurion	2006-07
391-4	(50 overs)	England v Bangladesh at Nottingham	2005
387-5	(50 overs)	India v England at Rajkot	2008-09
385-7	(50 overs)	Pakistan v Bangladesh at Dambulla	2010

Note: The highest totals by other countries are:

360-4	(50 overs)	West Indies v Sri Lanka at Karachi	1987-88
351-7	(50 overs)	Zimbabwe v Kenya at Mombasa	2008-09
320-8	(50 overs)	Bangladesh v Zimbabwe at Bulawayo	2009

HIGHEST TOTALS BATTING SECOND

438-9	(49.5 overs)	South Africa v Australia at Johannesburg (*Won by 1 wicket*)	2005-06
411-8	(50 overs)	Sri Lanka v India at Rajkot (*Lost by 3 runs*)	2009-10
350-9	(49.3 overs)	New Zealand v Australia at Hamilton (*Won by 1 wicket*)	2006-07
347	(49.4 overs)	India v Australia at Hyderabad (*Lost by 3 runs*)	2009-10
344-8	(50 overs)	Pakistan v India at Karachi (*Lost by 5 runs*)	2003-04
340-5	(48.4 overs)	New Zealand v Australia at Auckland (*Won by 5 wickets*)	2006-07
340-7	(50 overs)	New Zealand v England at Napier (*Tied*)	2007-08
338-8	(50 overs)	England v India at Bangalore (*Tied*)	2010-11
335-5	(50 overs)	New Zealand v Australia at Perth (*Lost by 8 runs*)	2006-07

HIGHEST MATCH AGGREGATES

872-13	(99.5 overs)	South Africa v Australia at Johannesburg	2005-06
825-15	(100 overs)	India v Sri Lanka at Rajkot	2009-10
726-14	(95.1 overs)	New Zealand v India at Christchurch	2008-09
697-14	(99.4 overs)	India v Australia at Hyderabad	2009-10
696-14	(99.3 overs)	New Zealand v Australia at Hamilton	2006-07
693-15	(100 overs)	Pakistan v India at Karachi	2003-04
691-19	(98.3 overs)	Netherlands v Sri Lanka at Amstelveen	2006
683-15	(99.2 overs)	India v West Indies at Indore	2011-12
680-13	(100 overs)	New Zealand v England at Napier	2007-08

LOWEST INNINGS TOTALS

35	(18 overs)	Zimbabwe v Sri Lanka at Harare	2003-04
36	(18.4 overs)	Canada v Sri Lanka at Paarl	2002-03
38	(15.4 overs)	Zimbabwe v Sri Lanka at Colombo (SSC)	2001-02
43	(19.5 overs)	Pakistan v West Indies at Cape Town	1992-93
43	**(20.1 overs)**	**Sri Lanka v South Africa at Paarl**	**2011-12**
44	(24.5 overs)	Zimbabwe v Bangladesh at Chittagong	2009-10
45	(40.3 overs)	Canada v England at Manchester	1979
45	(14 overs)	Namibia v Australia at Potchefstroom	2002-03
54	(26.3 overs)	India v Sri Lanka at Sharjah	2000-01
54	(23.2 overs)	West Indies v South Africa at Cape Town	2003-04
55	(28.3 overs)	Sri Lanka v West Indies at Sharjah	1986-87
58	(18.5 overs)	Bangladesh v West Indies at Mirpur	2010-11
61	(22 overs)	West Indies v Bangladesh at Chittagong	2011-12
63	(25.5 overs)	India v Australia at Sydney	1980-81
64	(35.5 overs)	New Zealand v Pakistan at Sharjah	1985-86
65	(24 overs)	USA v Australia at Southampton	2004
65	(24.3 overs)	Zimbabwe v India at Harare	2005-06

The lowest totals by other Test-playing countries are:

69	(28 overs)	South Africa v Australia at Sydney	1993-94
70	(25.2 overs)	Australia v England at Birmingham	1977
70	(26.3 overs)	Australia v New Zealand at Adelaide	1985-86
86	(32.4 overs)	England v Australia at Manchester	2001

LARGEST VICTORIES

290 runs	New Zealand (402-2 in 50 overs) v Ireland (112 in 28.4 ov) at Aberdeen	2008
272 runs	South Africa (399-6 in 50 overs) v Zimbabwe (127 in 29 overs) at Benoni	2010-11
258 runs	**South Africa (301-8 in 50 overs) v Sri Lanka (43 in 20.1 overs) at Paarl**	**2011-12**
257 runs	India (413-5 in 50 overs) v Bermuda (156 in 43.1 overs) at Port-of-Spain	2006-07
256 runs	Australia (301-6 in 50 overs) v Namibia (45 in 14 overs) at Potchefstroom	2002-03
256 runs	India (374-4 in 50 overs) v Hong Kong (118 in 36.5 overs) at Karachi	2008
245 runs	Sri Lanka (299-5 in 50 overs) v India (54 in 26.3 overs) at Sharjah	2000-01
243 runs	Sri Lanka (321-6 in 50 overs) v Bermuda (78 in 24.4 overs) at P-of-Spain	2006-07
234 runs	Sri Lanka (309-5 in 50 overs) v Pakistan (75 in 22.5 overs) at Lahore	2008-09
233 runs	Pakistan (320-3 in 50 overs) v Bangladesh (87 in 34.2 overs) at Dhaka	1999-2000
232 runs	Australia (323-2 in 50 overs) v Sri Lanka (91 in 35.5 overs) at Adelaide	1984-85
231 runs	S. Africa (351-5 in 50 overs) v Netherlands (120 in 34.5 overs) at Mohali	2010-11

There have been **45** instances of victory by ten wickets.

TIED MATCHES

There have been **27** tied one-day internationals. Australia have tied eight matches; Bangladesh are the only Test-playing country never to have tied. The most recent ties are:

Australia (196 in 48.5 overs) v England (196-9 in 50 overs) at Lord's	2005
Ireland (221-9 in 50 overs) v Zimbabwe (221 in 50 overs) at Kingston	2006-07
England (340-6 in 50 overs) v New Zealand (340-7 in 50 overs) at Napier	2007-08
India (338 in 49.5 overs) v England (338-8 in 50 overs) at Bangalore	2010-11
India (280-5 in 50 overs) v England (270-8 in 48.5 overs) at Lord's (D/L)	2011
Australia (220 in 49.5 overs) v West Indies (220 in 49.4 overs) at St Vincent	**2011-12**
Sri Lanka (236-9 in 50 overs) v India (236-9 in 50 overs) at Adelaide	**2011-12**

OTHER RECORDS

MOST APPEARANCES

463	**S. R. Tendulkar (I)**	311	S. C. Ganguly (I/Asia)
445	S. T. Jayasuriya (SL/Asia)	308	P. A. de Silva (SL)
386	**D. P. M. D. Jayawardene (SL/Asia)**	303	S. M. Pollock (SA/World/Africa)
378	Inzamam-ul-Haq (P/Asia)	299	B. C. Lara (WI/World)
375	**R. T. Ponting (A/World)**	295	M. V. Boucher (SA/Africa)
356	Wasim Akram (P)	288	Mohammad Yousuf (P/Asia)
350	M. Muralitharan (SL/World/Asia)	287	A. C. Gilchrist (A/World)
349	**Shahid Afridi (P/World/Asia)**	283	Salim Malik (P)
344	R. Dravid (I/World/Asia)	280	S. P. Fleming (NZ/World)
337	**K. C. Sangakkara (SL/World/Asia))**	**277**	**Yuvraj Singh (I/Asia)**
334	M. Azharuddin (I)	273	A. R. Border (A)
325	S. R. Waugh (A)	272	D. L. Vettori (NZ/World)
322	W. P. U. J. C. Vaas (SL/Asia)	271	A. Kumble (I/Asia)
321	**J. H. Kallis (SA/World/Africa)**		

Notes: The most appearances for other countries are 221 by G. W. Flower (Z), 197 by P. D. Collingwood (E), and 169 by Mohammad Ashraful (B). Excluding appearances for combined teams, the record for Sri Lanka is 441 appearances by S. T. Jayasuriya; for Pakistan, 375 by Inzamam-ul-Haq; for Australia, **374** by **R. T. Ponting**; for South Africa, **316** by **J. H. Kallis**; for West Indies, 295 by B. C. Lara; and for New Zealand, 279 by S. P. Fleming.

MOST MATCHES AS CAPTAIN

	P	*W*	*L*	*T*	*NR*
R. T. Ponting (A/World)	**230**	**165**	**51**	**2**	**12**
S. P. Fleming (NZ)....	218	98	106	1	13
A. Ranatunga (SL)....	193	89	95	1	8
A. R. Border (A).....	178	107	67	1	3
M. Azharuddin (I)....	174	90	76	2	6
G. C. Smith (SA/Af)..	150	92	51	1	6
S. C. Ganguly (I/Asia).	147	76	66	0	5
Imran Khan (P).......	139	75	59	1	4
W. J. Cronje (SA).....	138	99	35	1	3
M. S. Dhoni (I)	**130**	**74**	**45**	**3**	**8**
B. C. Lara (WI)......	125	59	59	0	7
D. P. M. D. Jayawardene (SL/As) .	**124**	**69**	**47**	**1**	**7**
S. T. Jayasuriya (SL)..	118	66	47	2	3
Wasim Akram (P)....	109	66	41	2	0
S. R. Waugh (A)).....	106	67	35	3	1
I. V. A. Richards (WI).	105	67	36	0	2

WORLD CUP FINALS

1975	WEST INDIES (291-8) beat Australia (274) by 17 runs	Lord's
1979	WEST INDIES (286-9) beat England (194) by 92 runs	Lord's
1983	INDIA (183) beat West Indies (140) by 43 runs	Lord's
1987	AUSTRALIA (253-5) beat England (246-8) by seven runs	Calcutta
1992	PAKISTAN (249-6) beat England (227) by 22 runs	Melbourne
1996	SRI LANKA (245-3) beat Australia (241-7) by seven wickets	Lahore
1999	AUSTRALIA (133-2) beat Pakistan (132) by eight wickets	Lord's
2003	AUSTRALIA (359-2) beat India (234) by 125 runs	Johannesburg
2007	AUSTRALIA (281-4) beat Sri Lanka (215-8) by 53 runs (D/L method)	Bridgetown
2011	INDIA (277-4) beat Sri Lanka (274-6) by six wickets	Mumbai

An expanded and regularly updated online version of the Records can be found at www.wisdenrecords.com

TWENTY20 INTERNATIONAL RECORDS

Matches in this section do not have first-class status.

Note: Throughout this section, bold type denotes performances in the calendar year 2012 or, in career figures, players who appeared in Twenty20 internationals in that year.

RESULTS SUMMARY OF TWENTY20 INTERNATIONALS

2004-05 to December 31, 2012 (298 matches)

	Matches	*Won*	*Lost*	*No Result*	*% Won (excl. NR)*
South Africa	55	34	20	1	62.96
Pakistan	66	40*	26*	0	60.60
Sri Lanka	49	29*	19	1	60.41
India	45	25*	19	1	56.81
England	55	28	24	3	53.84
Australia	58	30	27†	1	52.63
West Indies	46	22†	23*	1	48.88
New Zealand	62	29†	32‡	1	47.54
Bangladesh	27	8	19	0	29.62
Zimbabwe	22	4*	18	0	18.18
Netherlands	16	9	6	1	60.00
Ireland	30	15	12	3	55.55
Afghanistan	13	6	7	0	46.15
Scotland	17	5	11	1	31.25
Kenya	17	4	13	0	23.52
Canada	15	3	12*	0	20.00
Bermuda	3	0	3	0	0.00

* *Includes one game settled by a tie-break.* † *Includes two settled by a tie-break.*
‡ *Includes three settled by a tie-break. Ties were decided by bowling contests or one-over eliminators.*

Note: Matches abandoned without a ball bowled are not included except where the toss took place, when they are shown as no result.

BATTING RECORDS

HUNDREDS

123	**B. B. McCullum**	**New Zealand v Bangladesh at Pallekele**	**2012-13**
117*	**R. E. Levi**	**South Africa v New Zealand at Hamilton**	**2011-12**
117	C. H. Gayle	West Indies v South Africa at Johannesburg	2007-08
116*	B. B. McCullum	New Zealand v Australia at Christchurch	2009-10
104*	T. M. Dilshan	Sri Lanka v Australia at Pallekele	2011-12
101*	**M. J. Guptill**	**New Zealand v South Africa at East London**	**2012-13**
101	S. K. Raina	India v South Africa at Gros Islet, St Lucia	2010
100	D. P. M. D. Jayawardene	Sri Lanka v Zimbabwe at Providence	2010
100	**R. D. Berrington**	**Scotland v Bangladesh at Voorburg**	**2012**

MOST RUNS

		M	*I*	*NO*	*R*	*HS*	*100*	*Avge*
1	**B. B. McCullum (New Zealand)**	**57**	**57**	**8**	**1,704**	**123**	**2**	**34.77**
2	**D. P. M. D. Jayawardene (Sri Lanka)**	**44**	**44**	**6**	**1,224**	**100**	**1**	**32.21**
3	**K. P. Pietersen (England)**	**36**	**36**	**5**	**1,176**	**79**	**0**	**37.93**
4	**D. A. Warner (Australia)**	**42**	**42**	**1**	**1,109**	**89**	**0**	**27.04**
5	**T. M. Dilshan (Sri Lanka)**	**46**	**45**	**7**	**1,098**	**104***	**1**	**28.89**

		M	I	NO	R	HS	100	Avge
6	**K. C. Sangakkara (Sri Lanka)**	**43**	**41**	**5**	**1,080**	**78**	**0**	**30.00**
7	**M. J. Guptill (New Zealand)**	**38**	**36**	**6**	**1,018**	**101***	**1**	**33.93**
8	**C. H. Gayle (West Indies)**	**31**	**30**	**3**	**985**	**117**	**1**	**36.48**
9	**G. C. Smith (South Africa)**	**33**	**33**	**2**	**982**	**89***	**0**	**31.67**
10	**S. R. Watson (Australia)**	**36**	**35**	**3**	**980**	**81**	**0**	**30.62**
11	**J-P. Duminy (South Africa)**	**42**	**39**	**10**	**952**	**96***	**0**	**32.82**
12	**G. Gambhir (India)**	**37**	**36**	**2**	**932**	**75**	**0**	**27.41**
13	**Mohammad Hafeez (Pakistan)**	**42**	**40**	**0**	**927**	**71**	**0**	**23.17**

HIGHEST PARTNERSHIP FOR EACH WICKET

170	for 1st	G. C. Smith and L. L. Bosman	SA v E	Centurion	2009-10
166	for 2nd	D. P. M. D. Jayawardene and K. C. Sangakkara	SL v WI	Bridgetown	2010
120*	for 3rd	H. H. Gibbs and J. M. Kemp	SA v WI	Johannesburg	2005-06
112	for 4th	K. P. Pietersen and E. J. G. Morgan	E v P	Dubai	2009-10
119*	for 5th	Shoaib Malik and Misbah-ul-Haq	P v A	Johannesburg	2007-08
101*	for 6th	M. E. K. Hussey and C. L. White	A v SL	Bridgetown	2010
91	for 7th	P. D. Collingwood and M. H. Yardy	E v WI	The Oval	2007
64*	for 8th	W. D. Parnell and J. Theron	SA v A	Johannesburg	2011-12
44	for 9th	S. L. Malinga and C. R. D. Fernando	SL v NZ	Auckland	2006-07
31*	for 10th	Wahab Riaz and Shoaib Akhtar	P v NZ	Auckland	2010-11

BOWLING RECORDS

BEST BOWLING ANALYSES

6-8	**B. A. W. Mendis**	**Sri Lanka v Zimbabwe at Hambantota**	**2012-13**
6-16	B. A. W. Mendis	Sri Lanka v Australia at Pallekele	2011-12
5-6	Umar Gul	Pakistan v New Zealand at The Oval	2009
5-13	**Elias Sunny**	**Bangladesh v Ireland at Belfast**	**2012**
5-18	T. G. Southee	New Zealand v Pakistan at Auckland	2010-11
5-19	R. McLaren	South Africa v West Indies at North Sound	2010
5-20	N. N. Odhiambo	Kenya v Scotland at Nairobi	2009-10
5-26	D. J. G. Sammy	West Indies v Zimbabwe at Port-of-Spain	2009-10
5-31	**S. L. Malinga**	**Sri Lanka v England at Pallekele**	**2012-13**

HAT-TRICKS

B. Lee	Australia v Bangladesh at Cape Town	2007-08
J. D. P. Oram	New Zealand v Sri Lanka at Colombo	2009
T. G. Southee	New Zealand v Pakistan at Auckland	2010-11

MOST WICKETS

		M	B	R	W	BB	4I	Avge
1	**Saeed Ajmal (Pakistan)**	**50**	**1,116**	**1,159**	**71**	**4-19**	**4**	**16.32**
2	**Umar Gul (Pakistan)**	**51**	**1,036**	**1,211**	**69**	**5-6**	**5**	**17.55**
3	**Shahid Afridi (Pakistan)**	**58**	**1,301**	**1,371**	**63**	**4-11**	**3**	**21.76**
4	**B. A. W. Mendis (Sri Lanka)**	**27**	**618**	**592**	**55**	**6-8**	**5**	**10.76**
5	**G. P. Swann (England)**	**39**	**810**	**859**	**51**	**3-13**	**0**	**16.84**
6	**S. L. Malinga (Sri Lanka)**	**40**	**822**	**1,025**	**48**	**5-31**	**1**	**21.35**
	S. C. J. Broad (England)	**43**	**909**	**1,113**	**48**	**3-17**	**0**	**23.18**
8	**N. L. McCullum (New Zealand)**	**42**	**704**	**758**	**40**	**4-16**	**1**	**18.95**
9	**D. W. Steyn (South Africa)**	**29**	**618**	**649**	**39**	**4-9**	**1**	**16.64**
	M. Morkel (South Africa)	**31**	**669**	**762**	**39**	**4-17**	**2**	**19.53**
11	**D. L. Vettori (New Zealand)**	**33**	**769**	**720**	**37**	**4-20**	**1**	**19.45**
	J. Botha (South Africa)	**40**	**774**	**823**	**37**	**3-16**	**0**	**22.24**

		M	B	R	W	BB	4I	Avge
13	**M. G. Johnson (Australia)**	**28**	**608**	**724**	**36**	**3-15**	**0**	**20.11**
	T. G. Southee (New Zealand)	**31**	**654**	**917**	**36**	**5-18**	**1**	**25.47**
15	**Abdur Razzak (Bangladesh)**	**24**	**552**	**628**	**35**	**4-16**	**1**	**17.94**
	D. J. G. Sammy (West Indies	**37**	**616**	**703**	**35**	**5-26**	**2**	**20.08**
	S. R. Watson (Australia)	**36**	**596**	**715**	**35**	**4-15**	**1**	**20.42**
	K. D. Mills (New Zealand)	**35**	**742**	**1,029**	**35**	**3-33**	**0**	**29.40**

WICKETKEEPING AND FIELDING RECORDS

MOST DISMISSALS IN AN INNINGS

4 (all ct)	A. C. Gilchrist	Australia v Zimbabwe at Cape Town	2007-08
4 (all ct)	M. J. Prior	England v South Africa at Cape Town	2007-08
4 (all ct)	A. C. Gilchrist	Australia v New Zealand at Perth	2007-08
4 (all st)	Kamran Akmal	Pakistan v Netherlands at Lord's	2009
4 (3ct, 1st)	N. J. O'Brien	Ireland v Sri Lanka at Lord's	2009
4 (2ct, 2st)	A. B. de Villiers	South Africa v West Indies at North Sound	2010
4 (all ct)	M. S. Dhoni	India v Afghanistan at Gros Islet, St Lucia	2010
4 (3ct, 1st)	**G. C. Wilson**	**Ireland v Kenya at Dubai**	**2011-12**
4 (all ct)	**A. B. de Villiers**	**South Africa v Zimbabwe at Hambantota**	**2012-13**
4 (all ct)	**M. S. Dhoni**	**India v Pakistan at Colombo (RPS)**	**2012-13**

MOST DISMISSALS

			M	Ct	St
1	**52**	**Kamran Akmal (Pakistan)**	**48**	**22**	**30**
2	**37**	**K. C. Sangakkara (Sri Lanka)**	**43**	**20**	**17**
3	**32**	**D. Ramdin (West Indies)**	**33**	**25**	**7**
4	**29**	**B. B. McCullum (New Zealand)**	**39**	**22**	**7**
	29	**M. S. Dhoni (India)**	**42**	**21**	**8**
6	**26**	**A. B. de Villiers (South Africa)**	**21**	**20**	**6**
	26	**Mushfiqur Rahim (Bangladesh)**	**26**	**11**	**15**

Note: B. B. McCullum's record excludes nine catches taken in 18 Twenty20 internationals when not keeping wicket, and A. B. de Villiers's record excludes 22 in 23. Kamran Akmal played one Twenty20 international in which he did not keep wicket and did not take a catch.

MOST CATCHES IN AN INNINGS IN THE FIELD

4 D. J. G. Sammy .... West Indies v Ireland at Providence 2010

MOST CATCHES

Ct	M		Ct	M	
31	**47**	**L. R. P. L. Taylor (New Zealand)**	**22**	**23**	**A. B. de Villiers (South Africa)**
25	**45**	**D. A. Warner (Australia)**	**22**	**32**	**Umar Akmal (Pakistan)**
24	**39**	**D. J. Hussey (Australia)**	**21**	**38**	**C. L. White (Australia)**
24	**52**	**Shoaib Malik (Pakistan)**	**20**	**38**	**M. E. K. Hussey (Australia)**

Note: A. B. de Villiers's record excludes 26 dismissals (20ct, 6st) in 21 Twenty20 internationals when keeping wicket, and Umar Akmal's record excludes ten (8ct, 2st) in ten.

TEAM RECORDS

HIGHEST INNINGS TOTALS

260-6	(20 overs)	Sri Lanka v Kenya at Johannesburg	2007-08
241-6	(20 overs)	South Africa v England at Centurion	2009-10
221-5	(20 overs)	Australia v England at Sydney	2006-07
219-4	**(20 overs)**	**South Africa v India at Johannesburg**	**2011-12**
218-4	(20 overs)	India v England at Durban	2007-08
215-5	(20 overs)	Sri Lanka v India at Nagpur	2009-10
214-4	(20 overs)	Australia v New Zealand at Christchurch	2009-10
214-5	(20 overs)	Australia v New Zealand at Auckland	2004-05
214-6	(20 overs)	New Zealand v Australia at Christchurch	2009-10

LOWEST INNINGS TOTALS

67	(17.2 overs)	Kenya v Ireland at Belfast	2008
68	(16.4 overs)	Ireland v West Indies at Providence	2010
70	(20 overs)	Bermuda v Canada at Belfast	2008
71	**(19 overs)**	**Kenya v Ireland at Dubai**	**2011-12**
73	(16.5 overs)	Kenya v New Zealand at Durban	2007-08
74	(17.3 overs)	India v Australia at Melbourne	2007-08
74	**(19.1 overs)**	**Pakistan v Australia at Dubai**	**2012**
75	(19.2 overs)	Canada v Zimbabwe at King City	2007-08

OTHER RECORDS

MOST APPEARANCES

58	**Shahid Afridi (Pakistan)**	**50**	**Saeed Ajmal (Pakistan)**
57	**B. B. McCullum (New Zealand)**	**49**	**Kamran Akmal (Pakistan)**
52	**Shoaib Malik (Pakistan)**	**47**	**L. R. P. L. Taylor (New Zealand)**
51	**Umar Gul (Pakistan)**	**46**	**T. M. Dilshan (Sri Lanka)**

WORLD TWENTY20 FINALS

2007-08	INDIA (157-5) beat Pakistan (152) by five runs	Johannesburg
2009	PAKISTAN (139-2) beat Sri Lanka (138-6) by eight wickets	Lord's
2010	ENGLAND (148-3) beat Australia (147-6) by seven wickets	Bridgetown
2012-13	WEST INDIES (137-6) beat Sri Lanka (101) by 36 runs	Colombo (RPS)

MISCELLANEOUS RECORDS

LARGE ATTENDANCES

Test Series

943,000	Australia v England (5 Tests)	1936-37
In England		
549,650	England v Australia (5 Tests)	1953

Test Matches

†‡465,000	India v Pakistan, Calcutta	1998-99
350,534	Australia v England, Melbourne (Third Test)	1936-37

Note: Attendance at India v England at Calcutta in 1981-82 may have exceeded 350,000.

In England		
158,000+	England v Australia, Leeds	1948
137,915	England v Australia, Lord's	1953

Test Match Day

‡100,000	India v Pakistan, Calcutta (first four days)	1998-99
90,800	Australia v West Indies, Melbourne (Fifth Test, second day)	1960-61
89,155	Australia v England, Melbourne (Fourth Test, first day)	2006-07

Other First-Class Matches in England

93,000	England v Australia, Lord's (Fourth Victory Match, 3 days)	1945
80,000+	Surrey v Yorkshire, The Oval (3 days)	1906
78,792	Yorkshire v Lancashire, Leeds (3 days)	1904
76,617	Lancashire v Yorkshire, Manchester (3 days)	1926

One-Day Internationals

‡100,000	India v South Africa, Calcutta	1993-94
‡100,000	India v West Indies, Calcutta	1993-94
‡100,000	India v West Indies, Calcutta	1994-95
‡100,000	India v Sri Lanka, Calcutta (World Cup semi-final)	1995-96
‡100,000	India v Australia, Kolkata	2003-04
‡90,000	India v Pakistan, Calcutta	1986-87
‡90,000	India v South Africa, Calcutta	1991-92
87,182	England v Pakistan, Melbourne (World Cup final)	1991-92
86,133	Australia v West Indies, Melbourne	1983-84

Twenty20 International

84,041	Australia v India, Melbourne	2007-08

† *Estimated.*
‡ *No official attendance figures were issued for these games, but capacity at Calcutta (now Kolkata) is believed to have reached 100,000 following rebuilding in 1993.*

LORD'S CRICKET GROUND

Lord's and the Marylebone Cricket Club were founded in London in 1787. The Club has enjoyed an uninterrupted career since that date, but there have been three grounds known as Lord's. The first (1787–1810) was situated where Dorset Square now is; the second (1809–13), at North Bank, had to be abandoned owing to the cutting of the Regent's Canal; and the third, opened in 1814, is the present one at St John's Wood. It was not until 1866 that the freehold of Lord's was secured by MCC. The present pavilion was erected in 1890 at a cost of £21,000.

HIGHEST INDIVIDUAL SCORES MADE AT LORD'S

333	G. A. Gooch	England v India	1990
316*	J. B. Hobbs	Surrey v Middlesex	1926
315*	P. Holmes	Yorkshire v Middlesex	1925
315	M. A. Wagh	Warwickshire v Middlesex	2001
303*	N. V. Knight	Warwickshire v Middlesex	2004

Note: The longest innings in a first-class match at Lord's was N. V. Knight's, which lasted 644 minutes.

HIGHEST TOTALS AT LORD'S

First-Class Matches

729-6 dec	Australia v England	1930
682-6 dec	South Africa v England	2003
665	West Indians v Middlesex	1939
653-4 dec	England v India	1990
652-8 dec	West Indies v England	1973

Minor Matches

735-9 dec	MCC and Ground v Wiltshire	1888

BIGGEST HIT AT LORD'S

The only known instance of a batsman hitting a ball over the present pavilion at Lord's occurred when A. E. Trott, appearing for MCC against Australians on July 31, August 1, 2, 1899, drove M. A. Noble so far and high that the ball struck a chimney pot and fell behind the building.

MINOR CRICKET

HIGHEST INDIVIDUAL SCORES

628*	A. E. J. Collins, Clark's House v North Town at Clifton College. *A junior house match. His innings of 6 hours 50 minutes was spread over four afternoons*	1899
566	C. J. Eady, Break-o'-Day v Wellington at Hobart	1901-02
515	D. R. Havewalla, B. B. and C. I. Railways v St Xavier's at Bombay	1933-34
506*	J. C. Sharp, Melbourne GS v Geelong College at Melbourne	1914-15
502*	Chaman Lal, Mehandra Coll., Patiala v Government Coll., Rupar at Patiala	1956-57
498	Arman Jaffer, Rizvi Springfield School v IES Raja Shivaji School at Mumbai	2010-11
485	A. E. Stoddart, Hampstead v Stoics at Hampstead	1886
475*	Mohammad Iqbal, Muslim Model HS v Islamia HS, Sialkot at Lahore	1958-59
466*	G. T. S. Stevens, Beta v Lambda (University College School house match) at Neasden. *Stevens scored his 466 and took 14 wickets on one day*	1919
459	J. A. Prout, Wesley College v Geelong College at Geelong	1908-09
451*	**V. H. Mol, Maharashtra Under-19 v Assam Under-19 at Nasik**	**2011-12**

Note: The highest score in a Minor County match is 323* by F. E. Lacey for Hampshire v Norfolk at Southampton in 1887; the highest in the Minor Counties Championship is 282 by E. Garnett for Berkshire v Wiltshire at Reading in 1908.

HIGHEST PARTNERSHIPS

721* for 1st	B. Manoj Kumar and M. S. Tumbi, St Peter's High School v St Philip's High School at Secunderabad	2006-07
664* for 3rd	V. G. Kambli and S. R. Tendulkar, Sharadashram Vidyamandir School v St Xavier's High School at Bombay	1987-88

Notes: Manoj Kumar and Tumbi scored 721 in 40 overs in an Under-13 inter-school match; they hit 103 fours between them, but no sixes. Their opponents were all out for 21 in seven overs.

Kambli was 16 years old, Tendulkar 14. Tendulkar made his Test debut 21 months later.

MOST WICKETS WITH CONSECUTIVE BALLS

There are **two** recorded instances of a bowler taking nine wickets with consecutive balls. Both came in school games: Paul Hugo, for Smithfield School v Aliwal North at Smithfield, South Africa, in 1930-31, and Stephen Fleming (not the future Test captain), for Marlborough College A v Bohally School at Blenheim, New Zealand, in 1967-68. There are five further verified instances of eight wickets in eight balls, the most recent by Mike Walters for the Royal Army Educational Corps v Joint Air Transport Establishment at Beaconsfield in 1979.

TEN WICKETS FOR NO RUNS

There are **24** recorded instances of a bowler taking all ten wickets in an innings for no runs, the most recent by David Morton, for Bayside Muddies v Ranatungas in Brisbane in 1998-99. The previous instance was also in Australia, by the schoolgirl Emma Liddell, for Metropolitan East v West at Penrith (Sydney) in 1995-96. When Jennings Tune did it, for the Yorkshire club Cliffe v Eastrington at Cliffe in 1923, all ten of his victims were bowled.

NOUGHT ALL OUT

In minor matches, this is more common than might be imagined. The historian Peter Wynne-Thomas says the first recorded example was in Norfolk, where an Eleven of Fakenham, Walsingham and Hempton were dismissed for nought by an Eleven of Licham, Dunham and Brisley in July 1815.

MOST DISMISSALS IN AN INNINGS

The only recorded instance of a wicketkeeper being involved in all ten dismissals in an innings was by Welihinda Badalge Bennett, for Mahinda College against Richmond College in Ceylon (now Sri Lanka) in 1952-53. His feat comprised six catches and four stumpings. There are three other known instances of nine dismissals in the same innings, one of which – by H. W. P. Middleton for Priory v Mitre in a Repton School house match in 1930 – included eight stumpings. Young Rangers' innings against Bohran Gymkhana in Karachi in 1969-70 included nine run-outs.

The widespread nature – and differing levels of supervision – of minor cricket matches mean that record claims have to be treated with caution. Additions and corrections to the above records for minor cricket will only be considered for inclusion in Wisden *if they are corroborated by independent evidence of the achievement.*

Research: Steven Lynch

RECORD HIT

The Rev. W. Fellows, while at practice on the Christ Church ground at Oxford in 1856, drove a ball bowled by Charles Rogers 175 yards from hit to pitch.

THROWING THE CRICKET BALL

140 yards 2 feet, Robert Percival, on the Durham Sands racecourse, Co. Durham. c1882
140 yards 9 inches, Ross Mackenzie, at Toronto 1872
140 yards, "King Billy" the Aborigine, at Clermont, Queensland 1872

Note: Extensive research by David Rayvern Allen has shown that these traditional records are probably authentic, if not necessarily wholly accurate. Modern competitions have failed to produce similar distances although Ian Pont, the Essex all-rounder who also played baseball, was reported to have thrown 138 yards in Cape Town in 1981. There have been speculative reports attributing throws of 150 yards or more to figures as diverse as the South African Test player Colin Bland, the Latvian javelin thrower Janis Lusis, who won a gold medal for the Soviet Union in the 1968 Olympics, and the British sprinter Charley Ransome. The definitive record is still awaited.

COUNTY CHAMPIONSHIP

MOST APPEARANCES

762	W. Rhodes	Yorkshire	1898–1930
707	F. E. Woolley	Kent	1906–1938
668	C. P. Mead	Hampshire	1906–1936
617	N. Gifford	Worcestershire (484), Warwickshire (133)	1960–1988
611	W. G. Quaife	Warwickshire	1895–1928
601	G. H. Hirst	Yorkshire	1891–1921

MOST CONSECUTIVE APPEARANCES

423	K. G. Suttle	Sussex	1954–1969
412	J. G. Binks	Yorkshire	1955–1969

Notes: J. Vine made 417 consecutive appearances for Sussex in all first-class matches (399 of them in the Championship) between July 1900 and September 1914.

J. G. Binks did not miss a Championship match for Yorkshire between making his debut in June 1955 and retiring at the end of the 1969 season.

UMPIRES

MOST COUNTY CHAMPIONSHIP APPEARANCES

570	T. W. Spencer	1950–1980
531	F. Chester	1922–1955
523	D. J. Constant	1969–2006
517	H. G. Baldwin	1932–1962
511	A. G. T. Whitehead	1970–2005

MOST SEASONS ON ENGLISH FIRST-CLASS LIST

38	D. J. Constant	1969–2006
36	A. G. T. Whitehead	1970–2005
31	K. E. Palmer	1972–2002
31	T. W. Spencer	1950–1980
30	R. Julian	1972–2001
30	P. B. Wight	1966–1995
29	H. D. Bird	1970–1998
28	F. Chester	1922–1955
28	B. Leadbeater	1981–2008
28	R. Palmer	1980–2007
27	B. Dudleston	1984–2010
27	J. W. Holder	1983–2009
27	J. Moss	1899–1929
26	W. A. J. West	1896–1925
25	H. G. Baldwin	1932–1962
25	A. Jepson	1960–1984
25	J. G. Langridge	1956–1980
25	B. J. Meyer	1973–1997
25	D. R. Shepherd	1981–2005

WOMEN'S TEST RECORDS

Amended to December 31, 2012

Note: No women's Tests were played in the calendar year 2012.

BATTING RECORDS

HIGHEST INDIVIDUAL INNINGS

242	Kiran Baluch	Pakistan v West Indies at Karachi	2003-04
214	M. Raj	India v England at Taunton	2002
209*	K. L. Rolton	Australia v England at Leeds	2001
204	K. E. Flavell	New Zealand v England at Scarborough	1996
204	M. A. J. Goszko	Australia v England at Shenley Park	2001
200	J. Broadbent	Australia v England at Guildford	1998
193	D. A. Annetts	Australia v England at Collingham	1987
190	S. Agarwal	India v England at Worcester	1986
189	E. A. Snowball	England v New Zealand at Christchurch	1934-35
179	R. Heyhoe-Flint	England v Australia at The Oval	1976
177	S. C. Taylor	England v South Africa at Shenley Park	2003
176*	K. L. Rolton	Australia v England at Worcester	1998

1,000 RUNS IN A CAREER

R	*T*		*R*	*T*	
1,935	27	J. A. Brittin (England)	1,110	13	S. Agarwal (India)
1,594	22	R. Heyhoe-Flint (England)	1,078	12	E. Bakewell (England)
1,522	19	C. M. Edwards (England)	1,030	15	S. C. Taylor (England)
1,301	19	D. A. Hockley (New Zealand)	1,007	14	M. E. Maclagan (England)
1,164	18	C. A. Hodges (England)	1,002	14	K. L. Rolton (Australia)

BOWLING RECORDS

BEST BOWLING ANALYSES

8-53	N. David	India v England at Jamshedpur	1995-96
7-6	M. B. Duggan	England v Australia at Melbourne	1957-58
7-7	E. R. Wilson	Australia v England at Melbourne	1957-58
7-10	M. E. Maclagan	England v Australia at Brisbane	1934-35
7-18	A. Palmer	Australia v England at Brisbane	1934-35
7-24	L. Johnston	Australia v New Zealand at Melbourne	1971-72
7-34	G. E. McConway	England v India at Worcester	1986
7-41	J. A. Burley	New Zealand v England at The Oval	1966
7-51	L. C. Pearson	England v Australia at Sydney	2002-03
7-59	Shaiza Khan	Pakistan v West Indies at Karachi	2003-04
7-61	E. Bakewell	England v West Indies at Birmingham	1979

MOST WICKETS IN A MATCH

13-226	Shaiza Khan	Pakistan v West Indies at Karachi	2003-04

50 WICKETS IN A CAREER

W	*T*		*W*	*T*	
77	17	M. B. Duggan (England)	60	19	S. Kulkarni (India)
68	11	E. R. Wilson (Australia)	57	16	R. H. Thompson (Australia)
63	20	D. F. Edulji (India)	55	15	J. Lord (New Zealand)
60	13	C. L. Fitzpatrick (Australia)	50	12	E. Bakewell (England)
60	14	M. E. Maclagan (England)			

WICKETKEEPING RECORDS

SIX DISMISSALS IN AN INNINGS

8 (6ct, 2st)	L. Nye	England v New Zealand at New Plymouth	1991-92
6 (2ct, 4st)	B. A. Brentnall	New Zealand v South Africa at Johannesburg	1971-72

25 DISMISSALS IN A CAREER

		T	*Ct*	*St*
58	C. Matthews (Australia)	20	46	12
43	J. Smit (England)	21	39	4
36	S. A. Hodges (England)	11	19	17
28	B. A. Brentnall (New Zealand)	10	16	12

TEAM RECORDS

HIGHEST INNINGS TOTALS

569-6 dec	Australia v England at Guildford	1998
525	Australia v India at Ahmedabad	1983-84
517-8	New Zealand v England at Scarborough	1996
503-5 dec	England v New Zealand at Christchurch	1934-35

LOWEST INNINGS TOTALS

35	England v Australia at Melbourne	1957-58
38	Australia v England at Melbourne	1957-58
44	New Zealand v England at Christchurch	1934-35
47	Australia v England at Brisbane	1934-35
50	Netherlands v South Africa at Rotterdam	2007

WOMEN'S ONE-DAY INTERNATIONAL RECORDS

Amended to December 31, 2012

Note: Throughout this section, bold type denotes performances in the calendar year 2012 or, in career figures, players who appeared in women's one-day internationals in that year.

BATTING RECORDS

HIGHEST INDIVIDUAL INNINGS

229*	B. J. Clark	Australia v Denmark at Mumbai	1997-98
173*	C. M. Edwards	England v Ireland at Pune	1997-98
168	S. W. Bates	New Zealand v Pakistan at Sydney	2008-09
156*	L. M. Keightley	Australia v Pakistan at Melbourne	1996-97

156*	S. C. Taylor	England v India at Lord's	2006
154*	K. L. Rolton	Australia v Sri Lanka at Christchurch	2000-01
153*	J. Logtenberg	South Africa v Netherlands at Deventer	2007
151	K. L. Rolton	Australia v Ireland at Dublin	2005

MOST RUNS IN A CAREER

R	*M*		*R*	*M*	
4,844	118	B. J. Clark (Australia)	**4,490**	**141**	**M. Raj (India)**
4,814	141	K. L. Rolton (Australia)	4,101	126	S. C. Taylor (England)
4,783	**160**	**C. M. Edwards (England)**	4,064	118	D. A. Hockley (New Zealand)

BOWLING RECORDS

BEST BOWLING ANALYSES

7-4	Sajjida Shah	Pakistan v Japan at Amsterdam	2003
7-8	J. M. Chamberlain	England v Denmark at Haarlem	1991
7-14	A. Mohammed	West Indies v Pakistan at Mirpur	2011-12
7-24	S. Nitschke	Australia v England at Kidderminster	2005
6-10	J. Lord	New Zealand v India at Auckland	1981-82
6-10	M. Maben	India v Sri Lanka at Kandy	2003-04
6-10	S. Ismail	South Africa v Netherlands at Savar	2011-12
6-20	G. L. Page	New Zealand v Trinidad & Tobago at St Albans	1973
6-31	J. Goswami	India v England at Southgate	2011
6-32	B. H. McNeill	New Zealand v England at Lincoln	2007-08

MOST WICKETS IN A CAREER

W	*M*		*W*	*M*	
180	109	C. L. Fitzpatrick (Australia)	102	105	C. E. Taylor (England)
145	**126**	**J. Goswami (India)**	101	83	I. T. Guha (England)
141	97	N. David (India)	**100**	**78**	**N. Al Khader (India)**
137	**118**	**L. C. Sthalekar (Australia)**			

WICKETKEEPING RECORDS

MOST DISMISSALS IN AN INNINGS

6 (4ct, 2st)	S. L. Illingworth	New Zealand v Australia at Beckenham	1993
6 (1ct, 5st)	V. Kalpana	India v Denmark at Slough	1993
6 (2ct, 4st)	Batool Fatima	Pakistan v West Indies at Karachi	2003-04
6 (4ct, 2st)	Batool Fatima	Pakistan v Sri Lanka at Colombo	2010-11

MOST DISMISSALS IN A CAREER

		M	*Ct*	*St*
133	R. J. Rolls (New Zealand)	104	90	43
114	J. Smit (England)	109	69	45
100	J. C. Price (Australia)	84	70	30

TEAM RECORDS

HIGHEST INNINGS TOTALS

455-5	New Zealand v Pakistan at Christchurch	1996-97
412-3	Australia v Denmark at Mumbai	1997-98
397-4	Australia v Pakistan at Melbourne	1996-97
376-2	England v Pakistan at Vijayawada	1997-98
375-5	Netherlands v Japan at Schiedam	2003
373-7	New Zealand v Pakistan at Sydney	2008-09

LOWEST INNINGS TOTALS

22	Netherlands v West Indies at Deventer	2008
23	Pakistan v Australia at Melbourne	1996-97
24	Scotland v England at Reading	2001
26	India v New Zealand as St Saviour	2002
27	Pakistan v Australia at Hyderabad (India)	1997-98
28	Japan v Pakistan at Amsterdam	2003
29	Netherlands v Australia at Perth	1988-89

WOMEN'S WORLD CUP WINNERS

1973	England	1988-89	Australia	2000-01	New Zealand
1977-78	Australia	1993	England	2004-05	Australia
1981-82	Australia	1997-98	Australia	2008-09	England

WOMEN'S TWENTY20 INTERNATIONAL RECORDS

Amended to December 31, 2012

Note: Throughout this section, bold type denotes performances in the calendar year 2012 or, in career figures, players who appeared in women's Twenty20 internationals in that year.

BATTING RECORDS

HIGHEST INDIVIDUAL INNINGS

116*	S. A. Fritz	South Africa v Netherlands at Potchefstroom	2010-11
112*	D. J. S. Dottin	West Indies v South Africa at Basseterre	2010
96*	K. L. Rolton	Australia v England at Taunton	2005
90	S. R. Taylor	West Indies v Ireland at Dublin	2008
90	**A. J. Healy**	**Australia v India at Visakhapatnam**	**2011-12**

MOST RUNS IN A CAREER

R	*M*		*R*	*M*	
1,599	**61**	**C. M. Edwards (England)**	**821**	**49**	**D. J. S. Dottin (West Indies)**
1,219	**36**	**S. J. Taylor (England)**	**794**	**50**	**S. J. McGlashan (New Zealand)**
1,008	**40**	**S. R. Taylor (West Indies)**	**784**	**40**	**L. J. Poulton (Australia)**
949	**47**	**S. W. Bates (New Zealand)**	776	36	S. Nitschke (Australia)
885	**37**	**M. Raj (India)**	772	36	A. L. Watkins (New Zealand)
837	**54**	**L. S. Greenway (England)**	**771**	**50**	**A. J. Blackwell (Australia)**

BOWLING RECORDS

BEST BOWLING ANALYSES

6-17	A. E. Satterthwaite	New Zealand v England at Taunton	2007
5-10	A. Mohammed	West Indies v South Africa at Cape Town	2009-10
5-11	**J. Goswami**	**India v Australia at Visakhapatnam**	**2011-12**
5-11	**A. Shrubsole**	**England v New Zealand at Wellington**	**2011-12**
5-16	P. Roy	India v Pakistan at Taunton	2009
5-22	**J. L. Hunter**	**Australia v West Indies at Colombo (RPS)**	**2012-13**

MOST WICKETS IN A CAREER

W	*M*		*W*	*M*	
64	**47**	**A. Mohammed (West Indies)**	43	36	S. Nitschke (Australia)
59	**43**	**H. L. Colvin (England)**	**43**	**41**	**E. A. Perry (Australia)**
59	**51**	**L. C. Sthalekar (Australia)**	**43**	**43**	**S. F. Daley (West Indies)**
51	**55**	**L. A. Marsh (England)**	**42**	**36**	**S. R. Taylor (West Indies)**
43	**35**	**D. Hazell (England)**			

WICKETKEEPING RECORDS

MOST DISMISSALS IN AN INNINGS

4 (3ct, 1st)	J. M. Fields	Australia v New Zealand at Brisbane (ABF)	2009
4 (1ct, 3st)	S. Naik	India v England at Mumbai (BKC)	2009-10
4 (all st)	S. A. Campbelle	West Indies v Sri Lanka at Cayon	2010
4 (2ct, 2st)	**S. Naik**	**India v Pakistan at Guanggong**	**2012-13**

MOST DISMISSALS IN A CAREER

		M	*Ct*	*St*
42	**S. J. Taylor (England)**	**46**	**14**	**28**
42	***J. L. Gunn (England)**	**61**	**42**	
37	**J. M. Fields (Australia)**	**31**	**23**	**14**
31	**S. Naik (India)**	**31**	**10**	**21**
29	***L. S. Greenway (England)**	**54**	**29**	
26	R. H. Priest (New Zealand)	28	13	13
26†	**M. R. Aguilleira (West Indies)**	**42**	**11**	**15**

* *Catches made by non-wicketkeepers in the field.* † *Aguilleira's total includes one catch in the field in eight matches not keeping wicket.*

TEAM RECORDS

HIGHEST INNINGS TOTALS

205-1	South Africa v Netherlands at Potchefstroom	2010-11
191-4	West Indies v Netherlands at Potchefstroom	2010-11
186-7	New Zealand v South Africa at Taunton	2007
184-4	West Indies v Ireland at Dublin	2008
180-5	England v South Africa at Taunton	2007
180-5	New Zealand v West Indies at Gros Islet, St Lucia	2010

LOWEST INNINGS TOTALS

57	**Sri Lanka v Bangladesh at Guanggong**	**2012-13**
60	Pakistan v England at Taunton	2009
62	India v Australia at Billericay	2011
62	**Bangladesh v Sri Lanka at Guanggong**	**2012-13**
63	**Pakistan v India at Guanggong**	**2012-13**
65	Pakistan v West Indies at St Andrew's, Grenada.	2011-12
69	**New Zealand v Australia at Sydney**	**2011-12**

WOMEN'S WORLD TWENTY20 WINNERS

2009	England	2010	Australia	2012-13	Australia

BIRTHS AND DEATHS

TEST CRICKETERS

Full list from 1876-77 to January 14, 2013

In the Test career column, dates in italics indicate seasons embracing two different years (i.e. non-English seasons). In these cases, only the first year is given, e.g. *1876* for 1876-77. Some non-English series taking place outside the host country's normal season are dated by a single year.

The Test career figures are complete up to January 14, 2013; the one-day international totals are complete up to January 6, 2013; and the Twenty20 international totals up to December 31, 2012. Career figures are for one national team only; those players who have appeared for more than one Test team are listed on page 1447, and for more than one one-day international team on page 1479.

The forename by which a player is known is underlined if it is not his first name.

Family relationships are indicated by superscript numbers; where the relationship is not immediately apparent from a shared name, see the notes at the end of this section. (*CY 1889*) signifies that the player was a Wisden Cricketer of the Year in the 1889 Almanack. The 5/10 column indicates instances of a player taking five wickets in a Test innings and ten wickets in a match. O/T signifies number of one-day and Twenty20 internationals played.

[1] *Father and son(s).* [2] *Brothers.* [3] *Grandfather, father and son.* [4] *Grandfather and grandson.* [5] *Great-grandfather and great-grandson.*
† *Excludes matches for another Test team.* ‡ *Excludes matches for another ODI team.*

ENGLAND (655 players)

	Born	*Died*	*Tests*	*Test Career*	*Runs*	*HS*	*100s*	*Avge*	*Wkts*	*BB*	*5/10*	*Avge*	*Ct/St*	*O/T*
Abel Robert (*CY 1890*)	30.11.1857	10.12.1936	13	1888–1902	744	132*	2	37.20	–	–	–/–	–	13	
Absolom Charles Alfred	7.6.1846	30.7.1889	1	*1878*	58	52	0	29.00	–	–	–/–	–	0	
Adams Christopher John (*CY 2004*)	6.5.1970		5	*1999*	104	31	0	13.00	1	1-42	0/0	59.00	6	5
Afzaal Usman	9.6.1977		3	2001	83	54	0	16.60	1	1-49	0/0	49.00	0	
Agnew Jonathan Philip (*CY 1988*)	4.4.1960		3	1984–1985	10	5	0	10.00	4	2-51	0/0	93.25	0	3
Ali Kabir	24.11.1980		1	2003	10	9	0	5.00	5	3-80	0/0	27.20	0	14
Allen David Arthur	29.10.1935		39	*1959–1966*	918	88	0	25.50	122	5-30	4/0	30.97	10	
Allen *Sir* George Oswald Browning ("Gubby")	31.7.1902	29.11.1989	25	1930–*1947*	750	122	1	24.19	81	7-80	5/1	29.37	20	
Allom Maurice James Carrick	23.3.1906	8.4.1995	5	*1929–1930*	14	8*	0	14.00	14	5-38	1/0	18.92	0	
Allott Paul John Walter	14.9.1956		13	1981–1985	213	52*	0	14.20	26	6-61	1/0	41.69	4	13
Ambrose Timothy Raymond	1.12.1982		11	*2007–2008*	447	102	1	29.80	–	–	–/–	–	31	5/1
Ames Leslie Ethelbert George CBE (*CY 1929*)	3.12.1905	27.2.1990	47	1929–*1938*	2,434	149	8	40.56	–	–	–/–	–	74/23	
Amiss Dennis Leslie MBE (*CY 1975*)	7.4.1943		50	1966–1977	3,612	262*	11	46.30	–	–	–/–	–	24	18

	Born	*Died*	*Tests*	*Test Career*	*Runs*	*HS*	*100s*	*Avge*	*Wkts*	*BB*	*5/10*	*Avge*	*Ct/St*	*O/T*
Anderson James Michael (*CY 2009*)	30.7.1982		77	2003–*2012*	709	34	0	10.90	288	7-43	12/1	30.39	43	164/19
Andrew Keith Vincent	15.12.1929	27.12.2010	2	*1954*–1963	29	15	0	9.66	–	–	–/–	–	1	
Appleyard Robert MBE (*CY 1952*)	27.6.1924		9	1954–1956	51	19*	0	17.00	31	5-51	1/0	17.87	4	
Archer Alfred German	6.12.1871	15.7.1935	1	*1898*	31	24*	0	31.00	–	–	–/–	–	0	
Armitage Thomas	25.4.1848	21.9.1922	2	*1876*	33	21	0	11.00	0	0-15	0/0	–	0	
Arnold Edward George	7.11.1876	25.10.1942	10	*1903*–1907	160	40	0	13.33	31	5-37	1/0	25.41	8	
Arnold Geoffrey Graham (*CY 1972*)	3.9.1944		34	1967–1975	421	59	0	12.02	115	6-45	6/0	28.29	9	14
Arnold John	30.11.1907	4.4.1984	1	1931	34	34	0	17.00	–	–	–/–	–	0	
Astill William Ewart (*CY 1933*)	1.3.1888	10.2.1948	9	*1927–1929*	190	40	0	12.66	25	4-58	0/0	34.24	7	
Atherton Michael Andrew OBE (*CY 1991*)	23.3.1968		115	1989–2001	7,728	185*	16	37.69	2	1-20	0/0	151.00	83	54
Athey Charles William Jeffrey	27.9.1957		23	1980–1988	919	123	1	22.97	–	–	–/–	–	13	31
Attewell William (*CY 1892*)	12.6.1861	11.6.1927	10	*1884–1891*	150	43*	0	16.66	28	4-42	0/0	22.35	9	
Bailey Robert John	28.10.1963		4	1988–*1989*	119	43	0	14.87	–	–	–/–	–	0	4
Bailey Trevor Edward CBE (*CY 1950*)	3.12.1923	10.2.2011	61	1949–*1958*	2,290	134*	1	29.74	132	7-34	5/1	29.21	32	
[1] **Bairstow** David Leslie	1.9.1951	5.1.1998	4	1979–*1980*	125	59	0	20.83	–	–	–/–	–	12/1	21
[1] **Bairstow** Jonathan Marc	26.9.1989		5	2012–*2012*	196	95	0	32.66	–	–	–/–	–	5	7/15
Bakewell Alfred Harry (*CY 1934*)	2.11.1908	23.1.1983	6	1931–1935	409	107	1	45.44	0	0-8	0/0	–	3	
Balderstone John Christopher	16.11.1940	6.3.2000	2	1976	39	35	0	9.75	1	1-80	0/0	80.00	1	
Barber Robert William (*1967*)	26.9.1935		28	1960–1968	1,495	185	1	35.59	42	4-132	0/0	43.00	21	
Barber Wilfred	18.4.1901	10.9.1968	2	1935	83	44	0	20.75	1	1-0	0/0	0.00	1	
Barlow Graham Derek	26.3.1950		3	*1976*–1977	17	7*	0	4.25	–	–	–/–	–	0	6
Barlow Richard Gorton	28.5.1851	31.7.1919	17	*1881–1886*	591	62	0	22.73	34	7-40	3/0	22.55	14	
Barnes Sydney Francis (*CY 1910*)	19.4.1873	26.12.1967	27	*1901–1913*	242	38*	0	8.06	189	9-103	24/7	16.43	12	
Barnes William (*CY 1890*)	27.5.1852	24.3.1899	21	1880–1890	725	134	1	23.38	51	6-28	3/0	15.54	19	
Barnett Charles John (*CY 1937*)	3.7.1910	28.5.1993	20	1933–1948	1,098	129	2	35.41	0	0-1	0/0	–	14	
Barnett Kim John (*CY 1989*)	17.7.1960		4	1988–1989	207	80	0	29.57	0	0-32	0/0	–	1	1
Barratt Fred	12.4.1894	29.1.1947	5	1929–*1929*	28	17	0	9.33	5	1-8	0/0	47.00	2	
Barrington Kenneth Frank (*CY 1960*)	24.11.1930	14.3.1981	82	1955–1968	6,806	256	20	58.67	29	3-4	0/0	44.82	58	
Barton Victor Alexander	6.10.1867	23.3.1906	1	*1891*	23	23	0	23.00	–	–	–/–	–	0	
Bates Willie	19.11.1855	8.1.1900	15	*1881–1886*	656	64	0	27.33	50	7-28	4/1	16.42	9	
Batty Gareth Jon	13.10.1977		7	*2003*–2005	144	38	0	20.57	11	3-55	0/0	66.63	3	10/1
Bean George	7.3.1864	16.3.1923	3	*1891*	92	50	0	18.40	–	–	–/–	–	4	
Bedser *Sir* Alec Victor CBE (*CY 1947*)	4.7.1918	4.4.2010	51	1946–1955	714	79	0	12.75	236	7-44	15/5	24.89	26	
Bell Ian Ronald MBE (*CY 2008*)	11.4.1982		83	2004–*2012*	5,699	235	17	46.71	1	1-33	0/0	76.00	64	119/7
Benjamin Joseph Emmanuel	2.2.1961		1	1994	0	0	0	0.00	4	4-42	0/0	20.00	0	2
Benson Mark Richard	6.7.1958		1	1986	51	30	0	25.50	–	–	–/–	–	0	1

	Born	Died	Tests	Test Career	Runs	HS	100s	Avge	Wkts	BB	5/10	Avge	Ct/St	O/T
Berry Robert	29.1.1926	2.12.2006	2	1950	6	4*	0	3.00	9	5-63	1/0	25.33	2	
Bicknell Martin Paul (*CY 2001*)	14.1.1969		4	1993–2003	45	15	0	6.42	14	4-84	0/0	38.78	2	7
Binks James Graham (*CY 1969*)	5.10.1935		2	*1963*	91	55	0	22.75	–	–	–/–	–	8	
Bird Morice Carlos	25.3.1888	9.12.1933	10	*1909–1913*	280	61	0	18.66	8	3-11	0/0	15.00	5	
Birkenshaw Jack MBE	13.11.1940		5	*1972–1973*	148	64	0	21.14	13	5-57	1/0	36.07	3	
Blackwell Ian David	10.6.1978		1	*2005*	4	4	0	4.00	0	0-28	0/0	–	0	34
Blakey Richard John	15.1.1967		2	*1992*	7	6	0	1.75	–	–	–/–	–	2	3
Bligh *Hon.* Ivo Francis Walter	13.3.1859	10.4.1927	4	*1882*	62	19	0	10.33	–	–	–/–	–	7	
Blythe Colin (*CY 1904*)	30.5.1879	8.11.1917	19	*1901–1909*	183	27	0	9.63	100	8-59	9/4	18.63	6	
Board John Henry	23.2.1867	15.4.1924	6	*1898–1905*	108	29	0	10.80	–	–	–/–	–	8/3	
Bolus John Brian	31.1.1934		7	1963–*1963*	496	88	0	41.33	0	0-16	0/0	–	2	
Booth Major William (*CY 1914*)	10.12.1886	1.7.1916	2	*1913*	46	32	0	23.00	7	4-49	0/0	18.57	0	
Bopara Ravinder Singh	4.5.1985		13	*2007*–2012	575	143	3	31.94	1	1-39	0/0	290.00	6	83/22
Bosanquet Bernard James Tindal (*CY 1905*)	13.10.1877	12.10.1936	7	*1903*–1905	147	27	0	13.36	25	8-107	2/0	24.16	9	
Botham *Sir* Ian Terence OBE (*CY 1978*)	24.11.1955		102	1977–1992	5,200	208	14	33.54	383	8-34	27/4	28.40	120	116
Bowden Montague Parker	1.11.1865	19.2.1892	2	*1888*	25	25	0	12.50	–	–	–/–	–	1	
Bowes William Eric (*CY 1932*)	25.7.1908	4.9.1987	15	1932–1946	28	10*	0	4.66	68	6-33	6/0	22.33	2	
Bowley Edward Henry (*CY 1930*)	6.6.1890	9.7.1974	5	1929–*1929*	252	109	1	36.00	0	0-7	0/0	–	2	
Boycott Geoffrey OBE (*CY 1965*)	21.10.1940		108	1964–*1981*	8,114	246*	22	47.72	7	3-47	0/0	54.57	33	36
Bradley Walter Morris	2.1.1875	19.6.1944	2	1899	23	23*	0	23.00	6	5-67	1/0	38.83	0	
Braund Leonard Charles (*CY 1902*)	18.10.1875	23.12.1955	23	*1901–1907*	987	104	3	25.97	47	8-81	3/0	38.51	39	
Brearley John Michael OBE (*CY 1977*)	28.4.1942		39	1976–1981	1,442	91	0	22.88	–	–	–/–	–	52	25
Brearley Walter (*CY 1909*)	11.3.1876	30.1.1937	4	1905–1912	21	11*	0	7.00	17	5-110	1/0	21.11	0	
Brennan Donald Vincent	10.2.1920	9.1.1985	2	1951	16	16	0	8.00	–	–	–/–	–	0/1	
Bresnan Timothy Thomas (*CY 2012*)	28.2.1985		18	2009–*2012*	438	91	0	31.28	57	5-48	1/0	32.54	7	65/25
Briggs John (*CY 1889*)	3.10.1862	11.1.1902	33	*1884*–1899	815	121	1	18.11	118	8-11	9/4	17.75	12	
[1] **Broad** Brian Christopher	29.9.1957		25	1984–1989	1,661	162	6	39.54	0	0-4	0/0	–	10	34
[1] **Broad** Stuart Christopher John (*CY 2010*)	24.6.1986		52	*2007–2012*	1,612	169	1	26.00	172	7-72	6/1	31.93	14	93/43
Brockwell William (*CY 1895*)	21.1.1865	30.6.1935	7	1893–1899	202	49	0	16.83	5	3-33	0/0	61.80	6	
Bromley-Davenport Hugh Richard	18.8.1870	23.5.1954	4	*1895–1898*	128	84	0	21.33	4	2-46	0/0	24.50	1	
Brookes Dennis (*CY 1957*)	29.10.1915	9.3.2006	1	*1947*	17	10	0	8.50	–	–	–/–	–	1	
Brown Alan	17.10.1935		2	*1961*	3	3*	0	–	3	3-27	0/0	50.00	1	
Brown David John	30.1.1942		26	1965–1969	342	44*	0	11.79	79	5-42	2/0	28.31	7	
Brown Frederick Richard MBE (*CY 1933*)	16.12.1910	24.7.1991	22	1931–1953	734	79	0	25.31	45	5-49	1/0	31.06	22	
Brown George	6.10.1887	3.12.1964	7	1921–*1922*	299	84	0	29.90	–	–	–/–	–	9/3	
Brown John Thomas (*CY 1895*)	20.8.1869	4.11.1904	8	*1894*–1899	470	140	1	36.15	0	0-22	0/0	–	7	

	Born	Died	Tests	Test Career	Runs	HS	100s	Avge	Wkts	BB	5/10	Avge	Ct/St	O/T
Brown Simon John Emmerson	29.6.1969		1	1996	11	10*	0	11.00	2	1-60	0/0	69.00	1	
Buckenham Claude Percival	16.1.1876	23.2.1937	4	*1909*	43	17	0	6.14	21	5-115	1/0	28.23	2	
[1] **Butcher** Alan Raymond (*CY 1991*)	7.1.1954		1	1979	34	20	0	17.00	0	0-9	0/0	–	0	1
[1] **Butcher** Mark Alan	23.8.1972		71	1997–*2004*	4,288	173*	8	34.58	15	4-42	0/0	36.06	61	
Butcher Roland Orlando	14.10.1953		3	*1980*	71	32	0	14.20	–	–	–/–	–	3	3
Butler Harold James	12.3.1913	17.7.1991	2	1947–*1947*	15	15*	0	15.00	12	4-34	0/0	17.91	1	
Butt Henry Rigden	27.12.1865	21.12.1928	3	*1895*	22	13	0	7.33	–	–	–/–	–	1/1	
Caddick Andrew Richard (*CY 2001*)	21.11.1968		62	1993–*2002*	861	49*	0	10.37	234	7-46	13/1	29.91	21	54
Calthorpe *Hon.* Frederick Somerset Gough-	27.5.1892	19.11.1935	4	*1929*	129	49	0	18.42	1	1-38	0/0	91.00	3	
Capel David John	6.2.1963		15	1987–*1989*	374	98	0	15.58	21	3-88	0/0	50.66	6	23
Carberry Michael Alexander	29.9.1980		1	*2009*	64	34	0	32.00	–	–	–/–	–	1	
Carr Arthur William (*CY 1923*)	21.5.1893	7.2.1963	11	*1922*–1929	237	63	0	19.75	–	–	–/–	–	3	
Carr Donald Bryce OBE (*CY 1960*)	28.12.1926		2	*1951*	135	76	0	33.75	2	2-84	0/0	70.00	0	
Carr Douglas Ward (*CY 1910*)	17.3.1872	23.3.1950	1	1909	0	0	0	0.00	7	5-146	1/0	40.28	0	
Cartwright Thomas William MBE	22.7.1935	30.4.2007	5	1964–1965	26	9	0	5.20	15	6-94	1/0	36.26	2	
Chapman Arthur Percy Frank (*CY 1919*)	3.9.1900	16.9.1961	26	1924–*1930*	925	121	1	28.90	0	0-10	0/0	–	32	
Charlwood Henry Rupert James	19.12.1846	6.6.1888	2	*1876*	63	36	0	15.75	–	–	–/–	–	0	
Chatterton William	27.12.1861	19.3.1913	1	*1891*	48	48	0	48.00	–	–	–/–	–	0	
Childs John Henry (*CY 1987*)	15.8.1951		2	1988	2	2*	0	–	3	1-13	0/0	61.00	1	
Christopherson Stanley	11.11.1861	6.4.1949	1	1884	17	17	0	17.00	1	1-52	0/0	69.00	0	
Clark Edward Winchester	9.8.1902	28.4.1982	8	1929–1934	36	10	0	9.00	32	5-98	1/0	28.09	0	
Clarke Rikki	29.9.1981		2	*2003*	96	55	0	32.00	4	2-7	0/0	15.00	1	20
Clay John Charles	18.3.1898	11.8.1973	1	1935	–	–	–	–	0	0-30	0/0	–	1	
Close Dennis Brian CBE (*CY 1964*)	24.2.1931		22	1949–1976	887	70	0	25.34	18	4-35	0/0	29.55	24	3
Coldwell Leonard John	10.1.1933	6.8.1996	7	1962–1964	9	6*	0	4.50	22	6-85	1/0	27.72	1	
Collingwood Paul David MBE (*CY 2007*)	26.5.1976		68	*2003–2010*	4,259	206	10	40.56	17	3-23	0/0	59.88	96	197/35
[4] **Compton** Denis Charles Scott CBE (*CY 1939*)	23.5.1918	23.4.1997	78	1937–*1956*	5,807	278	17	50.06	25	5-70	1/0	56.40	49	
[4] **Compton** Nicholas Richard Denis (*CY 2013*)	26.6.1983		4	*2012*	208	57	0	34.66	–	–	–/–	–	1	
Cook Alastair Nathan MBE (*CY 2012*)	25.12.1984		87	*2005–2012*	7,117	294	23	49.42	0	0-1	0/0	–	75	56/4
Cook Cecil ("Sam")	23.8.1921	5.9.1996	1	1947	4	4	0	2.00	0	0-40	0/0	–	0	
Cook Geoffrey	9.10.1951		7	*1981–1982*	203	66	0	15.61	0	0-4	0/0	–	9	6
Cook Nicholas Grant Billson	17.6.1956		15	1983–1989	179	31	0	8.52	52	6-65	4/1	32.48	5	3
Cope Geoffrey Alan	23.2.1947		3	*1977*	40	22	0	13.33	8	3-102	0/0	34.62	1	2
Copson William Henry (*CY 1937*)	27.4.1908	13.9.1971	3	1939–1947	6	6	0	6.00	15	5-85	1/0	19.80	1	
Cork Dominic Gerald (*CY 1996*)	7.8.1971		37	1995–2002	864	59	0	18.00	131	7-43	5/0	29.81	18	32
Cornford Walter Latter	25.12.1900	6.2.1964	4	*1929*	36	18	0	9.00	–	–	–/–	–	5/3	

	Born	Died	Tests	Test Career	Runs	HS	100s	Avge	Wkts	BB	5/10	Avge	Ct/St	O/T
Cottam Robert Michael Henry	16.10.1944		4	*1968–1972*	27	13	0	6.75	14	4-50	0/0	23.35	2	
Coventry *Hon.* Charles John	26.2.1867	2.6.1929	2	*1888*	13	12	0	13.00	–	–	–/–	–	0	
Cowans Norman George	17.4.1961		19	*1982*–1985	175	36	0	7.95	51	6-77	2/0	39.27	9	23
[1] **Cowdrey** Christopher Stuart	20.10.1957		6	*1984*–1988	101	38	0	14.42	4	2-65	0/0	77.25	5	3
[1] **Cowdrey** *Lord* [Michael <u>Colin</u>] CBE (*CY 1956*)	24.12.1932	4.12.2000	114	*1954–1974*	7,624	182	22	44.06	0	0-1	0/0	–	120	1
Coxon Alexander	18.1.1916	22.1.2006	1	1948	19	19	0	9.50	3	2-90	0/0	57.33	0	
Cranston James	9.1.1859	10.12.1904	1	1890	31	16	0	15.50	–	–	–/–	–	1	
Cranston Kenneth	20.10.1917	8.1.2007	8	1947–1948	209	45	0	14.92	18	4-12	0/0	25.61	3	
Crapp John Frederick	14.10.1912	13.2.1981	7	1948–*1948*	319	56	0	29.00	–	–	–/–	–	7	
Crawford John Neville (*CY 1907*)	1.12.1886	2.5.1963	12	*1905–1907*	469	74	0	22.33	39	5-48	3/0	29.48	13	
Crawley John Paul	21.9.1971		37	1994–*2002*	1,800	156*	4	34.61	–	–	–/–	–	29	13
Croft Robert Damien Bale MBE	25.5.1970		21	1996–2001	421	37*	0	16.19	49	5-95	1/0	37.24	10	50
Curtis Timothy Stephen	15.1.1960		5	1988–1989	140	41	0	15.55	0	0-7	0/0	–	3	
Cuttell Willis Robert (*CY 1898*)	13.9.1863	9.12.1929	2	*1898*	65	21	0	16.25	6	3-17	0/0	12.16	2	
Dawson Edward William	13.2.1904	4.6.1979	5	*1927–1929*	175	55	0	19.44	–	–	–/–	–	0	
Dawson Richard Kevin James	4.8.1980		7	*2001–2002*	114	19*	0	11.40	11	4-134	0/0	61.54	3	
Dean Harry	13.8.1884	12.3.1957	3	1912	10	8	0	5.00	11	4-19	0/0	13.90	2	
DeFreitas Phillip Anthony Jason (*CY 1992*)	18.2.1966		44	*1986*–1995	934	88	0	14.82	140	7-70	4/0	33.57	14	103
Denness Michael Henry OBE (*CY 1975*)	1.12.1940		28	1969–1975	1,667	188	4	39.69	–	–	–/–	–	28	12
Denton David (*CY 1906*)	4.7.1874	16.2.1950	11	1905–*1909*	424	104	1	20.19	–	–	–/–	–	8	
Dewes John Gordon	11.10.1926		5	1948–*1950*	121	67	0	12.10	–	–	–/–	–	0	
Dexter Edward Ralph CBE (*CY 1961*)	15.5.1935		62	1958–1968	4,502	205	9	47.89	66	4-10	0/0	34.93	29	
Dilley Graham Roy	18.5.1959	5.10.2011	41	*1979*–1989	521	56	0	13.35	138	6-38	6/0	29.76	10	36
Dipper Alfred Ernest	9.11.1885	7.11.1945	1	1921	51	40	0	25.50	–	–	–/–	–	0	
Doggart George <u>Hubert</u> Graham OBE	18.7.1925		2	1950	76	29	0	19.00	–	–	–/–	–	3	
D'Oliveira Basil Lewis CBE (*CY 1967*)	4.10.1931	18.11.2011	44	1966–1972	2,484	158	5	40.06	47	3-46	0/0	39.55	29	4
Dollery Horace Edgar ("Tom") (*CY 1952*)	14.10.1914	20.1.1987	4	1947–1950	72	37	0	10.28	–	–	–/–	–	1	
Dolphin Arthur	24.12.1885	23.10.1942	1	*1920*	1	1	0	0.50	–	–	–/–	–	1	
Douglas John William Henry Tyler (*CY 1915*)	3.9.1882	19.12.1930	23	*1911–1924*	962	119	1	29.15	45	5-46	1/0	33.02	9	
Downton Paul Rupert	4.4.1957		30	*1980*–1988	785	74	0	19.62	–	–	–/–	–	70/5	28
Druce Norman <u>Frank</u> (*CY 1898*)	1.1.1875	27.10.1954	5	*1897*	252	64	0	28.00	–	–	–/–	–	5	
Ducat Andrew (*CY 1920*)	16.2.1886	23.7.1942	1	1921	5	3	0	2.50	–	–	–/–	–	1	
Duckworth George (*CY 1929*)	9.5.1901	5.1.1966	24	1924–1936	234	39*	0	14.62	–	–	–/–	–	45/15	
Duleepsinhji Kumar Shri (*CY 1930*)	13.6.1905	5.12.1959	12	1929–1931	995	173	3	58.52	0	0-7	0/0	–	10	
Durston Frederick <u>John</u>	11.7.1893	8.4.1965	1	1921	8	6*	0	8.00	5	4-102	0/0	27.20	0	
Ealham Mark Alan	27.8.1969		8	1996–1998	210	53*	0	21.00	17	4-21	0/0	28.70	4	64

	Born	*Died*	*Tests*	*Test Career*	*Runs*	*HS*	*100s*	*Avge*	*Wkts*	*BB*	*5/10*	*Avge*	*Ct/St*	*O/T*
Edmonds Philippe-Henri	8.3.1951		51	1975–1987	875	64	0	17.50	125	7-66	2/0	34.18	42	29
Edrich John Hugh MBE (*CY 1966*)	21.6.1937		77	1963–1976	5,138	310*	12	43.54	0	0-6	0/0	–	43	7
Edrich William John (*CY 1940*)	26.3.1916	24.4.1986	39	1938–*1954*	2,440	219	6	40.00	41	4-68	0/0	41.29	39	
Elliott Harry	2.11.1891	2.2.1976	4	*1927–1933*	61	37*	0	15.25	–	–	–/–	–	8/3	
Ellison Richard Mark (*CY 1986*)	21.9.1959		11	1984–1986	202	41	0	13.46	35	6-77	3/1	29.94	2	14
Emburey John Ernest (*CY 1984*)	20.8.1952		64	1978–1995	1,713	75	0	22.53	147	7-78	6/0	38.40	34	61
Emmett George Malcolm	2.12.1912	18.12.1976	1	1948	10	10	0	5.00	–	–	–/–	–	0	
Emmett Thomas	3.9.1841	29.6.1904	7	*1876–1881*	160	48	0	13.33	9	7-68	1/0	31.55	9	
Evans Alfred John	1.5.1889	18.9.1960	1	1921	18	14	0	9.00	–	–	–/–	–	0	
Evans Thomas Godfrey CBE (*CY 1951*)	18.8.1920	3.5.1999	91	1946–1959	2,439	104	2	20.49	–	–	–/–	–	173/46	
Fagg Arthur Edward	18.6.1915	13.9.1977	5	1936–1939	150	39	0	18.75	–	–	–/–	–	5	
Fairbrother Neil Harvey	9.9.1963		10	1987–*1992*	219	83	0	15.64	0	0-9	0/0	–	4	75
Fane Frederick Luther	27.4.1875	27.11.1960	14	*1905–1909*	682	143	1	26.23	–	–	–/–	–	6	
Farnes Kenneth (*CY 1939*)	8.7.1911	20.10.1941	15	1934–*1938*	58	20	0	4.83	60	6-96	3/1	28.65	1	
Farrimond William	23.5.1903	15.11.1979	4	*1930*–1935	116	35	0	16.57	–	–	–/–	–	5/2	
Fender Percy George Herbert (*CY 1915*)	22.8.1892	15.6.1985	13	*1920*–1929	380	60	0	19.00	29	5-90	2/0	40.86	14	
Ferris John James	21.5.1867	17.11.1900	1†	*1891*	16	16	0	16.00	13	7-37	2/1	7.00	0	
Fielder Arthur (*CY 1907*)	19.7.1877	30.8.1949	6	*1903–1907*	78	20	0	11.14	26	6-82	1/0	27.34	4	
Finn Steven Thomas	4.4.1989		17	*2009–2012*	51	19	0	8.50	70	6-125	3/0	28.22	4	25/13
Fishlock Laurence Barnard (*CY 1947*)	2.1.1907	25.6.1986	4	1936–*1946*	47	19*	0	11.75	–	–	–/–	–	1	
Flavell John Alfred (*CY 1965*)	15.5.1929	25.2.2004	4	1961–1964	31	14	0	7.75	7	2-65	0/0	52.42	0	
Fletcher Keith William Robert OBE (*CY 1974*)	20.5.1944		59	1968–*1981*	3,272	216	7	39.90	2	1-6	0/0	96.50	54	24
Flintoff Andrew MBE (*CY 2004*)	6.12.1977		78§	1998–2009	3,795	167	5	31.89	219	5-58	3/0	33.34	52	138‡/7
Flowers Wilfred	7.12.1856	1.11.1926	8	*1884*–1893	254	56	0	18.14	14	5-46	1/0	21.14	2	
Ford Francis Gilbertson Justice	14.12.1866	7.2.1940	5	*1894*	168	48	0	18.66	1	1-47	0/0	129.00	5	
Foster Frank Rowbotham (*CY 1912*)	31.1.1889	3.5.1958	11	*1911*–1912	330	71	0	23.57	45	6-91	4/0	20.57	11	
Foster James Savin	15.4.1980		7	*2001–2002*	226	48	0	25.11	–	–	–/–	–	17/1	11/5
Foster Neil Alan (*CY 1988*)	6.5.1962		29	1983–1993	446	39	0	11.73	88	8-107	5/1	32.85	7	48
Foster Reginald Erskine ("Tip") (*CY 1900*)	16.4.1878	13.5.1914	8	*1903*–1907	602	287	1	46.30	–	–	–/–	–	13	
Fothergill Arnold James	26.8.1854	1.8.1932	2	*1888*	33	32	0	16.50	8	4-19	0/0	11.25	0	
Fowler Graeme	20.4.1957		21	1982–*1984*	1,307	201	3	35.32	0	0-0	0/0	–	10	26
Fraser Angus Robert Charles MBE (*CY 1996*)	8.8.1965		46	1989–*1998*	388	32	0	7.46	177	8-53	13/2	27.32	9	42
Freeman Alfred Percy ("Tich") (*CY 1923*)	17.5.1888	28.1.1965	12	*1924*–1929	154	50*	0	14.00	66	7-71	5/3	25.86	4	
French Bruce Nicholas	13.8.1959		16	1986–*1987*	308	59	0	18.11	–	–	–/–	–	38/1	13
Fry Charles Burgess (*CY 1895*)	25.4.1872	7.9.1956	26	*1895*–1912	1,223	144	2	32.18	0	0-3	0/0	–	17	

§ *Flintoff's figures exclude 50 runs and seven wickets for the ICC World XI v Australia in the Super Series Test in 2005-06.*

	Born	Died	Tests	Test Career	Runs	HS	100s	Avge	Wkts	BB	5/10	Avge	Ct/St	O/T
Gallian Jason Edward Riche	25.6.1971		3	1995–*1995*	74	28	0	12.33	0	0-6	0/0	–	1	
Gatting Michael William OBE (*CY 1984*)	6.6.1957		79	*1977–1994*	4,409	207	10	35.55	4	1-14	0/0	79.25	59	92
Gay Leslie Hewitt	24.3.1871	1.11.1949	1	*1894*	37	33	0	18.50	–	–	–/–	–	3/1	
Geary George (*CY 1927*)	9.7.1893	6.3.1981	14	1924–1934	249	66	0	15.56	46	7-70	4/1	29.41	13	
Gibb Paul Antony	11.7.1913	7.12.1977	8	*1938–1946*	581	120	2	44.69	–	–	–/–	–	3/1	
Giddins Edward Simon Hunter	20.7.1971		4	1999–2000	10	7	0	2.50	12	5-15	1/0	20.00	0	
Gifford Norman MBE (*CY 1975*)	30.3.1940		15	1964–1973	179	25*	0	16.27	33	5-55	1/0	31.09	8	2
Giles Ashley Fraser MBE (*CY 2005*)	19.3.1973		54	1998–*2006*	1,421	59	0	20.89	143	5-57	5/0	40.60	33	62
[2]**Gilligan** Alfred Herbert Harold	29.6.1896	5.5.1978	4	*1929*	71	32	0	17.75	–	–	–/–	–	0	
[2]**Gilligan** Arthur Edward Robert (*CY 1924*)	23.12.1894	5.9.1976	11	*1922–1924*	209	39*	0	16.07	36	6-7	2/1	29.05	3	
Gimblett Harold (*CY 1953*)	19.10.1914	30.3.1978	3	1936–1939	129	67*	0	32.25	–	–	–/–	–	1	
Gladwin Clifford	3.4.1916	9.4.1988	8	1947–1949	170	51*	0	28.33	15	3-21	0/0	38.06	2	
Goddard Thomas William John (*CY 1938*)	1.10.1900	22.5.1966	8	1930–1939	13	8	0	6.50	22	6-29	1/0	26.72	3	
Gooch Graham Alan OBE (*CY 1980*)	23.7.1953		118	1975–*1994*	8,900	333	20	42.58	23	3-39	0/0	46.47	103	125
Gough Darren (*CY 1999*)	18.9.1970		58	1994–2003	855	65	0	12.57	229	6-42	9/0	28.39	13	158‡/2
Gover Alfred Richard MBE (*CY 1937*)	29.2.1908	7.10.2001	4	1936–1946	2	2*	0	–	8	3-85	0/0	44.87	1	
Gower David Ivon OBE (*CY 1979*)	1.4.1957		117	1978–1992	8,231	215	18	44.25	1	1-1	0/0	20.00	74	114
[2]**Grace** Edward Mills	28.11.1841	20.5.1911	1	1880	36	36	0	18.00	–	–	–/–	–	1	
[2]**Grace** George Frederick	13.12.1850	22.9.1880	1	1880	0	0	0	0.00	–	–	–/–	–	2	
[2]**Grace** William Gilbert (*CY 1896*)	18.7.1848	23.10.1915	22	1880–1899	1,098	170	2	32.29	9	2-12	0/0	26.22	39	
Graveney Thomas William OBE (*CY 1953*)	16.6.1927		79	1951–1969	4,882	258	11	44.38	1	1-34	0/0	167.00	80	
Greenhough Thomas	9.11.1931	15.9.2009	4	1959–1960	4	2	0	1.33	16	5-35	1/0	22.31	1	
Greenwood Andrew	20.8.1847	12.2.1889	2	*1876*	77	49	0	19.25	–	–	–/–	–	2	
[2]**Greig** Anthony William (*CY 1975*)	6.10.1946	29.12.2012	58	1972–1977	3,599	148	8	40.43	141	8-86	6/2	32.20	87	22
[2]**Greig** Ian Alexander	8.12.1955		2	1982	26	14	0	6.50	4	4-53	0/0	28.50	0	
Grieve Basil Arthur Firebrace	28.5.1864	19.11.1917	2	*1888*	40	14*	0	40.00	–	–	–/–	–	0	
Griffith Stewart Cathie CBE ("Billy")	16.6.1914	7.4.1993	3	*1947–1948*	157	140	1	31.40	–	–	–/–	–	5	
[2]**Gunn** George (*CY 1914*)	13.6.1879	29.6.1958	15	*1907–1929*	1,120	122*	2	40.00	0	0-8	0/0	–	15	
[2]**Gunn** John Richmond (*CY 1904*)	19.7.1876	21.8.1963	6	*1901*–1905	85	24	0	10.62	18	5-76	1/0	21.50	3	
Gunn William (*CY 1890*)	4.12.1858	29.1.1921	11	*1886*–1899	392	102*	1	21.77	–	–	–/–	–	5	
Habib Aftab	7.2.1972		2	1999	26	19	0	8.66	–	–	–/–	–	0	
Haig Nigel Esmé	12.12.1887	27.10.1966	5	1921–*1929*	126	47	0	14.00	13	3-73	0/0	34.46	4	
Haigh Schofield (*CY 1901*)	19.3.1871	27.2.1921	11	*1898*–1912	113	25	0	7.53	24	6-11	1/0	25.91	8	
Hallows Charles (*CY 1928*)	4.4.1895	10.11.1972	2	1921–1928	42	26	0	42.00	–	–	–/–	–	0	
Hamilton Gavin Mark	16.9.1974		1	*1999*	0	0	0	0.00	0	0-63	0/0	–	0	0‡
Hammond Walter Reginald (*CY 1928*)	19.6.1903	1.7.1965	85	*1927–1946*	7,249	336*	22	58.45	83	5-36	2/0	37.80	110	

	Born	*Died*	*Tests*	*Test Career*	*Runs*	*HS*	*100s*	*Avge*	*Wkts*	*BB*	*5/10*	*Avge*	*Ct/St*	*O/T*
Hampshire John Harry	10.2.1941		8	1969–1975	403	107	1	26.86	–	–	–/–	–	9	3
Hardinge Harold Thomas William ("Wally") (*CY 1915*)	25.2.1886	8.5.1965	1	1921	30	25	0	15.00	–	–	–/–	–	0	
[1] **Hardstaff** Joseph, sen	9.11.1882	2.4.1947	5	*1907*	311	72	0	31.10	–	–	–/–	–	1	
[1] **Hardstaff** Joseph, jun (*CY 1938*)	3.7.1911	1.1.1990	23	1935–1948	1,636	205*	4	46.74	–	–	–/–	–	9	
Harmison Stephen James MBE (*CY 2005*)	23.10.1978		62§	2002–2009	742	49*	0	12.16	222	7-12	8/1	31.94	7	58/2
Harris *Lord* [George Robert Canning]	3.2.1851	24.3.1932	4	*1878*–1884	145	52	0	29.00	0	0-14	0/0	–	2	
Hartley John Cabourn	15.11.1874	8.3.1963	2	*1905*	15	9	0	3.75	1	1-62	0/0	115.00	2	
Hawke *Lord* [Martin Bladen] (*CY 1909*)	16.8.1860	10.10.1938	5	*1895–1898*	55	30	0	7.85	–	–	–/–	–	3	
Hayes Ernest George (*CY 1907*)	6.11.1876	2.12.1953	5	*1905*–1912	86	35	0	10.75	1	1-28	0/0	52.00	2	
Hayes Frank Charles	6.12.1946		9	1973–1976	244	106*	1	15.25	–	–	–/–	–	7	6
Hayward Thomas Walter (*CY 1895*)	29.3.1871	19.7.1939	35	*1895*–1909	1,999	137	3	34.46	14	4-22	0/0	36.71	19	
[3] **Headley** Dean Warren	27.1.1970		15	1997–1999	186	31	0	8.45	60	6-60	1/0	27.85	7	13
[2] **Hearne** Alec (*CY 1894*)	22.7.1863	16.5.1952	1	*1891*	9	9	0	9.00	–	–	–/–	–	1	
[1, 2] **Hearne** Frank	23.11.1858	14.7.1949	2†	*1888*	47	27	0	23.50	–	–	–/–	–	1	
[2] **Hearne** George Gibbons	7.7.1856	13.2.1932	1	*1891*	0	0	0	0.00	–	–	–/–	–	0	
Hearne John Thomas (*CY 1892*)	3.5.1867	17.4.1944	12	*1891*–1899	126	40	0	9.00	49	6-41	4/1	22.08	4	
Hearne John William (*CY 1912*)	11.2.1891	14.9.1965	24	*1911*–1926	806	114	1	26.00	30	5-49	1/0	48.73	13	
Hegg Warren Kevin	23.2.1968		2	*1998*	30	15	0	7.50	–	–	–/–	–	8	
Hemmings Edward Ernest	20.2.1949		16	1982–*1990*	383	95	0	22.52	43	6-58	1/0	42.44	5	33
Hendren Elias Henry ("Patsy") (*CY 1920*)	5.2.1889	4.10.1962	51	*1920–1934*	3,525	205*	7	47.63	1	1-27	0/0	31.00	33	
Hendrick Michael (*CY 1978*)	22.10.1948		30	1974–1981	128	15	0	6.40	87	4-28	0/0	25.83	25	22
Heseltine Christopher	26.11.1869	13.6.1944	2	*1895*	18	18	0	9.00	5	5-38	1/0	16.80	3	
Hick Graeme Ashley MBE (*CY 1987*)	23.5.1966		65	1991–*2000*	3,383	178	6	31.32	23	4-126	0/0	56.78	90	120
Higgs Kenneth (*CY 1968*)	14.1.1937		15	1965–1968	185	63	0	11.56	71	6-91	2/0	20.74	4	
Hill Allen	14.11.1843	28.8.1910	2	*1876*	101	49	0	50.50	7	4-27	0/0	18.57	1	
Hill Arthur James Ledger	26.7.1871	6.9.1950	3	*1895*	251	124	1	62.75	4	4-8	0/0	2.00	1	
Hilton Malcolm Jameson (*CY 1957*)	2.8.1928	8.7.1990	4	1950–*1951*	37	15	0	7.40	14	5-61	1/0	34.07	1	
Hirst George Herbert (*CY 1901*)	7.9.1871	10.5.1954	24	*1897*–1909	790	85	0	22.57	59	5-48	3/0	30.00	18	
Hitch John William (*CY 1914*)	7.5.1886	7.7.1965	7	*1911*–1921	103	51*	0	14.71	7	2-31	0/0	46.42	4	
Hobbs *Sir* John Berry (*CY 1909*)	16.12.1882	21.12.1963	61	*1907*–1930	5,410	211	15	56.94	1	1-19	0/0	165.00	17	
Hobbs Robin Nicholas Stuart	8.5.1942		7	1967–1971	34	15*	0	6.80	12	3-25	0/0	40.08	8	
Hoggard Matthew James MBE (*CY 2006*)	31.12.1976		67	2000–*2007*	473	38	0	7.27	248	7-61	7/1	30.50	24	26
Hollies William Eric (*CY 1955*)	5.6.1912	16.4.1981	13	*1934*–1950	37	18*	0	5.28	44	7-50	5/0	30.27	2	
[2] **Hollioake** Adam John (*CY 2003*)	5.9.1971		4	1997–*1997*	65	45	0	10.83	2	2-31	0/0	33.50	4	35

§ *Harmison's figures exclude one run and four wickets for the ICC World XI v Australia in the Super Series Test in 2005-06.*

	Born	*Died*	*Tests*	*Test Career*	*Runs*	*HS*	*100s*	*Avge*	*Wkts*	*BB*	*5/10*	*Avge*	*Ct/St*	*O/T*
[2] **Hollioake** Benjamin Caine	11.11.1977	23.3.2002	2	1997–1998	44	28	0	11.00	4	2-105	0/0	49.75	2	20
Holmes Errol Reginald Thorold (*CY 1936*)	21.8.1905	16.8.1960	5	*1934*–1935	114	85*	0	16.28	2	1-10	0/0	38.00	4	
Holmes Percy (*CY 1920*)	25.11.1886	3.9.1971	7	1921–1932	357	88	0	27.46	–	–	–/–	–	3	
Hone Leland	30.1.1853	31.12.1896	1	*1878*	13	7	0	6.50	–	–	–/–	–	2	
Hopwood John Leonard	30.10.1903	15.6.1985	2	1934	12	8	0	6.00	0	0-16	0/0	–	0	
Hornby Albert Neilson ("Monkey")	10.2.1847	17.12.1925	3	*1878*–1884	21	9	0	3.50	1	1-0	0/0	0.00	0	
Horton Martin John	21.4.1934	3.4.2011	2	1959	60	58	0	30.00	2	2-24	0/0	29.50	2	
Howard Nigel David	18.5.1925	31.5.1979	4	*1951*	86	23	0	17.20	–	–	–/–	–	4	
Howell Henry	29.11.1890	9.7.1932	5	*1920*–1924	15	5	0	7.50	7	4-115	0/0	79.85	0	
Howorth Richard	26.4.1909	2.4.1980	5	1947–*1947*	145	45*	0	18.12	19	6-124	1/0	33.42	2	
Humphries Joseph	19.5.1876	7.5.1946	3	*1907*	44	16	0	8.80	–	–	–/–	–	7	
Hunter Joseph	3.8.1855	4.1.1891	5	*1884*	93	39*	0	18.60	–	–	–/–	–	8/3	
Hussain Nasser OBE (*CY 2003*)	28.3.1968		96	*1989*–2004	5,764	207	14	37.18	0	0-15	0/0	–	67	88
Hutchings Kenneth Lotherington (*CY 1907*)	7.12.1882	3.9.1916	7	*1907*–1909	341	126	1	28.41	1	1-5	0/0	81.00	9	
[1] **Hutton** *Sir* Leonard (*CY 1938*)	23.6.1916	6.9.1990	79	1937–*1954*	6,971	364	19	56.67	3	1-2	0/0	77.33	57	
[1] **Hutton** Richard Anthony	6.9.1942		5	1971	219	81	0	36.50	9	3-72	0/0	28.55	9	
Iddon John	8.1.1902	17.4.1946	5	*1934*–1935	170	73	0	28.33	0	0-3	0/0	–	0	
Igglesden Alan Paul	8.10.1964		3	1989–*1993*	6	3*	0	3.00	6	2-91	0/0	54.83	1	4
Ikin John Thomas	7.3.1918	15.9.1984	18	1946–1955	606	60	0	20.89	3	1-38	0/0	118.00	31	
Illingworth Raymond CBE (*CY 1960*)	8.6.1932		61	1958–1973	1,836	113	2	23.24	122	6-29	3/0	31.20	45	3
Illingworth Richard Keith	23.8.1963		9	1991–*1995*	128	28	0	18.28	19	4-96	0/0	32.36	5	25
Ilott Mark Christopher	27.8.1970		5	1993–*1995*	28	15	0	7.00	12	3-48	0/0	45.16	0	
Insole Douglas John CBE (*CY 1956*)	18.4.1926		9	1950–1957	408	110*	1	27.20	–	–	–/–	–	8	
Irani Ronald Charles	26.10.1971		3	1996–1999	86	41	0	17.20	3	1-22	0/0	37.33	2	31
Jackman Robin David (*CY 1981*)	13.8.1945		4	*1980*–1982	42	17	0	7.00	14	4-110	0/0	31.78	0	15
Jackson *Sir* Francis Stanley (*CY 1894*)	21.11.1870	9.3.1947	20	1893–1905	1,415	144*	5	48.79	24	5-52	1/0	33.29	10	
Jackson Herbert Leslie (*CY 1959*)	5.4.1921	25.4.2007	2	1949–1961	15	8	0	15.00	7	2-26	0/0	22.14	1	
James Stephen Peter	7.9.1967		2	1998	71	36	0	17.75	–	–	–/–	–	0	
Jameson John Alexander	30.6.1941		4	1971–*1973*	214	82	0	26.75	1	1-17	0/0	17.00	0	3
Jardine Douglas Robert (*CY 1928*)	23.10.1900	18.6.1958	22	1928–*1933*	1,296	127	1	48.00	0	0-10	0/0	–	26	
Jarvis Paul William	29.6.1965		9	*1987–1992*	132	29*	0	10.15	21	4-107	0/0	45.95	2	16
Jenkins Roland Oliver (*CY 1950*)	24.11.1918	22.7.1995	9	*1948*–1952	198	39	0	18.00	32	5-116	1/0	34.31	4	
Jessop Gilbert Laird (*CY 1898*)	19.5.1874	11.5.1955	18	1899–1912	569	104	1	21.88	10	4-68	0/0	35.40	11	
Johnson Richard Leonard	29.12.1974		3	2003–*2003*	59	26	0	14.75	16	6-33	2/0	17.18	0	10
Jones Arthur Owen	16.8.1872	21.12.1914	12	1899–1909	291	34	0	13.85	3	3-73	0/0	44.33	15	
Jones Geraint Owen MBE	14.7.1976		34	*2003–2006*	1,172	100	1	23.91	–	–	–/–	–	128/5	49/2

	Born	*Died*	*Tests*	*Test Career*	*Runs*	*HS*	*100s*	*Avge*	*Wkts*	*BB*	*5/10*	*Avge*	*Ct/St*	*O/T*
[1] **Jones** Ivor Jeffrey	10.12.1941		15	*1963–1967*	38	16	0	4.75	44	6-118	1/0	40.20	4	
[1] **Jones** Simon Philip MBE (*CY 2006*)	25.12.1978		18	2002–2005	205	44	0	15.76	59	6-53	3/0	28.23	4	8
Jupp Henry	19.11.1841	8.4.1889	2	*1876*	68	63	0	17.00	–	–	–/–	–	2	
Jupp Vallance William Crisp (*CY 1928*)	27.3.1891	9.7.1960	8	1921–1928	208	38	0	17.33	28	4-37	0/0	22.00	5	
Keeton William Walter (*CY 1940*)	30.4.1905	10.10.1980	2	1934–1939	57	25	0	14.25	–	–	–/–	–	0	
Kennedy Alexander Stuart (*CY 1933*)	24.1.1891	15.11.1959	5	*1922*	93	41*	0	15.50	31	5-76	2/0	19.32	5	
Kenyon Donald	15.5.1924	12.11.1996	8	*1951*–1955	192	87	0	12.80	–	–	–/–	–	5	
Key Robert William Trevor (*CY 2005*)	12.5.1979		15	2002–*2004*	775	221	1	31.00	–	–	–/–	–	11	5/1
Khan Amjad	14.10.1980		1	*2008*	–	–	–	–	1	1-111	0/0	122.00	0	0/1
Killick *Rev.* Edgar Thomas	9.5.1907	18.5.1953	2	1929	81	31	0	20.25	–	–	–/–	–	2	
Kilner Roy (*CY 1924*)	17.10.1890	5.4.1928	9	1924–1926	233	74	0	33.28	24	4-51	0/0	30.58	6	
King John Herbert	16.4.1871	18.11.1946	1	1909	64	60	0	32.00	1	1-99	0/0	99.00	0	
Kinneir Septimus Paul (*CY 1912*)	13.5.1871	16.10.1928	1	*1911*	52	30	0	26.00	–	–	–/–	–	0	
Kirtley Robert James	10.1.1975		4	2003–*2003*	32	12	0	5.33	19	6-34	1/0	29.52	3	11/1
Knight Albert Ernest (*CY 1904*)	8.10.1872	25.4.1946	3	*1903*	81	70*	0	16.20	–	–	–/–	–	1	
Knight Barry Rolfe	18.2.1938		29	*1961*–1969	812	127	2	26.19	70	4-38	0/0	31.75	14	
Knight Donald John (*CY 1915*)	12.5.1894	5.1.1960	2	1921	54	38	0	13.50	–	–	–/–	–	1	
Knight Nicholas Verity	28.11.1969		17	1995–2001	719	113	1	23.96	–	–	–/–	–	26	100
Knott Alan Philip Eric (*CY 1970*)	9.4.1946		95	1967–1981	4,389	135	5	32.75	–	–	–/–	–	250/19	20
Knox Neville Alexander (*CY 1907*)	10.10.1884	3.3.1935	2	1907	24	8*	0	8.00	3	2-39	0/0	35.00	0	
Laker James Charles (*CY 1952*)	9.2.1922	23.4.1986	46	*1947–1958*	676	63	0	14.08	193	10-53	9/3	21.24	12	
Lamb Allan Joseph (*CY 1981*)	20.6.1954		79	1982–1992	4,656	142	14	36.09	1	1-6	0/0	23.00	75	122
Langridge James (*CY 1932*)	10.7.1906	10.9.1966	8	1933–1946	242	70	0	26.88	19	7-56	2/0	21.73	6	
Larkins Wayne	22.11.1953		13	*1979–1990*	493	64	0	20.54	–	–	–/–	–	8	25
Larter John David Frederick	24.4.1940		10	1962–1965	16	10	0	3.20	37	5-57	2/0	25.43	5	
Larwood Harold MBE (*CY 1927*)	14.11.1904	22.7.1995	21	1926–*1932*	485	98	0	19.40	78	6-32	4/1	28.35	15	
Lathwell Mark Nicholas	26.12.1971		2	1993	78	33	0	19.50	–	–	–/–	–	0	
Lawrence David Valentine ("Syd")	28.1.1964		5	1988–*1991*	60	34	0	10.00	18	5-106	1/0	37.55	0	1
Leadbeater Edric	15.8.1927	17.4.2011	2	*1951*	40	38	0	20.00	2	1-38	0/0	109.00	3	
Lee Henry William	26.10.1890	21.4.1981	1	*1930*	19	18	0	9.50	–	–	–/–	–	0	
Lees Walter Scott (*CY 1906*)	25.12.1875	10.9.1924	5	*1905*	66	25*	0	11.00	26	6-78	2/0	17.96	2	
Legge Geoffrey Bevington	26.1.1903	21.11.1940	5	*1927–1929*	299	196	1	49.83	0	0-34	0/0	–	1	
Leslie Charles Frederick Henry	8.12.1861	12.2.1921	4	*1882*	106	54	0	15.14	4	3-31	0/0	11.00	1	
Lever John Kenneth MBE (*CY 1979*)	24.2.1949		21	*1976*–1986	306	53	0	11.76	73	7-46	3/1	26.72	11	22
Lever Peter	17.9.1940		17	*1970*–1975	350	88*	0	21.87	41	6-38	2/0	36.80	11	10
Leveson Gower *Sir* Henry Dudley Gresham	8.5.1873	1.2.1954	3	*1909*	95	31	0	23.75	–	–	–/–	–	1	

	Born	*Died*	*Tests*	*Test Career*	*Runs*	*HS*	*100s*	*Avge*	*Wkts*	*BB*	*5/10*	*Avge*	*Ct/St*	*O/T*
Levett William Howard Vincent ("Hopper")	25.1.1908	1.12.1995	1	*1933*	7	5	0	7.00	–	–	–/–	–	3	
Lewis Anthony Robert CBE	6.7.1938		9	*1972*–1973	457	125	1	32.64	–	–	–/–	–	0	
Lewis Clairmonte Christopher	14.2.1968		32	1990–1996	1,105	117	1	23.02	93	6-111	3/0	37.52	25	53
Lewis Jonathan	26.8.1975		1	2006	27	20	0	13.50	3	3-68	0/0	40.66	0	13/2
Leyland Maurice (*CY 1929*)	20.7.1900	1.1.1967	41	1928–1938	2,764	187	9	46.06	6	3-91	0/0	97.50	13	
Lilley Arthur Frederick Augustus ("Dick") (*CY 1897*)	28.11.1866	17.11.1929	35	1896–1909	903	84	0	20.52	1	1-23	0/0	23.00	70/22	
Lillywhite James	23.2.1842	25.10.1929	2	*1876*	16	10	0	8.00	8	4-70	0/0	15.75	1	
Lloyd David	18.3.1947		9	1974–*1974*	552	214*	1	42.46	0	0-4	0/0	–	11	8
Lloyd Timothy Andrew	5.11.1956		1	1984	10	10*	0	–	–	–	–/–	–	0	3
Loader Peter James (*CY 1958*)	25.10.1929	15.3.2011	13	1954–*1958*	76	17	0	5.84	39	6-36	1/0	22.51	2	
Lock Graham Anthony Richard (*CY 1954*)	5.7.1929	30.3.1995	49	1952–*1967*	742	89	0	13.74	174	7-35	9/3	25.58	59	
Lockwood William Henry (*CY 1899*)	25.3.1868	26.4.1932	12	1893–1902	231	52*	0	17.76	43	7-71	5/1	20.53	4	
Lohmann George Alfred (*CY 1889*)	2.6.1865	1.12.1901	18	1886–1896	213	62*	0	8.87	112	9-28	9/5	10.75	28	
Lowson Frank Anderson	1.7.1925	8.9.1984	7	1951–1955	245	68	0	18.84	–	–	–/–	–	5	
Lucas Alfred Perry	20.2.1857	12.10.1923	5	*1878*–1884	157	55	0	19.62	0	0-23	0/0	–	1	
Luckhurst Brian William (*CY 1971*)	5.2.1939	1.3.2005	21	*1970–1974*	1,298	131	4	36.05	1	1-9	0/0	32.00	14	3
Lyttelton *Hon.* Alfred	7.2.1857	5.7.1913	4	1880–1884	94	31	0	15.66	4	4-19	0/0	4.75	2	
Macaulay George Gibson (*CY 1924*)	7.12.1897	13.12.1940	8	*1922*–1933	112	76	0	18.66	24	5-64	1/0	27.58	5	
MacBryan John Crawford William (*CY 1925*)	22.7.1892	14.7.1983	1	1924	–	–	–	–	–	–	–/–	–	0	
McCague Martin John	24.5.1969		3	1993–*1994*	21	11	0	4.20	6	4-121	0/0	65.00	1	
McConnon James Edward	21.6.1922	26.1.2003	2	1954	18	11	0	9.00	4	3-19	0/0	18.50	4	
McGahey Charles Percy (*CY 1902*)	12.2.1871	10.1.1935	2	*1901*	38	18	0	9.50	–	–	–/–	–	1	
McGrath Anthony	6.10.1975		4	2003	201	81	0	40.20	4	3-16	0/0	14.00	3	14
MacGregor Gregor (*CY 1891*)	31.8.1869	20.8.1919	8	1890–1893	96	31	0	12.00	–	–	–/–	–	14/3	
McIntyre Arthur John William (*CY 1958*)	14.5.1918	26.12.2009	3	1950–1955	19	7	0	3.16	–	–	–/–	–	8	
MacKinnon Francis Alexander	9.4.1848	27.2.1947	1	*1878*	5	5	0	2.50	–	–	–/–	–	0	
MacLaren Archibald Campbell (*CY 1895*)	1.12.1871	17.11.1944	35	*1894*–1909	1,931	140	5	33.87	–	–	–/–	–	29	
McMaster Joseph Emile Patrick	16.3.1861	7.6.1929	1	*1888*	0	0	0	0.00	–	–	–/–	–	0	
Maddy Darren Lee	23.5.1974		3	1999–*1999*	46	24	0	11.50	0	0-40	0/0	–	4	8/4
Mahmood Sajid Iqbal	21.12.1981		8	2006–*2006*	81	34	0	8.10	20	4-22	0/0	38.10	0	26/4
Makepeace Joseph William Henry	22.8.1881	19.12.1952	4	*1920*	279	117	1	34.87	–	–	–/–	–	0	
Malcolm Devon Eugene (*CY 1995*)	22.2.1963		40	1989–1997	236	29	0	6.05	128	9-57	5/2	37.09	7	10
Mallender Neil Alan	13.8.1961		2	1992	8	4	0	2.66	10	5-50	1/0	21.50	0	
[1] **Mann** Francis George CBE	6.9.1917	8.8.2001	7	*1948*–1949	376	136*	1	37.60	–	–	–/–	–	3	
[1] **Mann** Francis Thomas	3.3.1888	6.10.1964	5	*1922*	281	84	0	35.12	–	–	–/–	–	4	

	Born	Died	Tests	Test Career	Runs	HS	100s	Avge	Wkts	BB	5/10	Avge	Ct/St	O/T
Marks Victor James	25.6.1955		6	1982–*1983*	249	83	0	27.66	11	3-78	0/0	44.00	0	34
Marriott Charles Stowell ("Father")	14.9.1895	13.10.1966	1	1933	0	0	0	0.00	11	6-59	2/1	8.72	1	
Martin Frederick (*CY 1892*)	12.10.1861	13.12.1921	2	1890–*1891*	14	13	0	7.00	14	6-50	2/1	10.07	2	
Martin John William	16.2.1917	4.1.1987	1	1947	26	26	0	13.00	1	1-111	0/0	129.00	0	
Martin Peter James	15.11.1968		8	1995–1997	115	29	0	8.84	17	4-60	0/0	34.11	6	20
Mason John Richard (*CY 1898*)	26.3.1874	15.10.1958	5	*1897*	129	32	0	12.90	2	1-8	0/0	74.50	3	
Matthews Austin David George	3.5.1904	29.7.1977	1	1937	2	2*	0	–	2	1-13	0/0	32.50	1	
May Peter Barker Howard CBE (*CY 1952*)	31.12.1929	27.12.1994	66	1951–1961	4,537	285*	13	46.77	–	–	–/–	–	42	
Maynard Matthew Peter (*CY 1998*)	21.3.1966		4	1988–*1993*	87	35	0	10.87	–	–	–/–	–	3	14
Mead Charles Philip (*CY 1912*)	9.3.1887	26.3.1958	17	*1911–1928*	1,185	182*	4	49.37	–	–	–/–	–	4	
Mead Walter (*CY 1904*)	1.4.1868	18.3.1954	1	1899	7	7	0	3.50	1	1-91	0/0	91.00	1	
Midwinter William Evans	19.6.1851	3.12.1890	4†	*1881*	95	36	0	13.57	10	4-81	0/0	27.20	5	
Milburn Colin (*CY 1967*)	23.10.1941	28.2.1990	9	1966–*1968*	654	139	2	46.71	–	–	–/–	–	7	
Miller Audley Montague	19.10.1869	26.6.1959	1	*1895*	24	20*	0	–	–	–	–/–	–	0	
Miller Geoffrey	8.9.1952		34	1976–1984	1,213	98*	0	25.80	60	5-44	1/0	30.98	17	25
Milligan Frank William	19.3.1870	31.3.1900	2	*1898*	58	38	0	14.50	0	0-0	0/0	–	1	
Millman Geoffrey	2.10.1934	6.4.2005	6	*1961*–1962	60	32*	0	12.00	–	–	–/–	–	13/2	
Milton Clement Arthur (*CY 1959*)	10.3.1928	25.4.2007	6	1958–1959	204	104*	1	25.50	0	0-12	0/0	–	5	
Mitchell Arthur	13.9.1902	25.12.1976	6	*1933*–1936	298	72	0	29.80	0	0-4	0/0	–	9	
Mitchell Frank (*CY 1902*)	13.8.1872	11.10.1935	2†	*1898*	88	41	0	22.00	–	–	–/–	–	2	
Mitchell Thomas Bignall	4.9.1902	27.1.1996	5	*1932*–1935	20	9	0	5.00	8	2-49	0/0	62.25	1	
Mitchell-Innes Norman Stewart ("Mandy")	7.9.1914	28.12.2006	1	1935	5	5	0	5.00	–	–	–/–	–	0	
Mold Arthur Webb (*CY 1892*)	27.5.1863	29.4.1921	3	1893	0	0*	0	0.00	7	3-44	0/0	33.42	1	
Moon Leonard James	9.2.1878	23.11.1916	4	*1905*	182	36	0	22.75	–	–	–/–	–	4	
Morgan Eoin Joseph Gerard (*CY 2011*)	10.9.1986		16	2010–*2011*	700	130	2	30.43	–	–	–/–	–	11	63/32
Morley Frederick	16.12.1850	28.9.1884	4	1880–*1882*	6	2*	0	1.50	16	5-56	1/0	18.50	4	
Morris Hugh	5.10.1963		3	1991	115	44	0	19.16	–	–	–/–	–	3	
Morris John Edward	1.4.1964		3	1990	71	32	0	23.66	–	–	–/–	–	3	8
Mortimore John Brian	14.5.1933		9	*1958*–1964	243	73*	0	24.30	13	3-36	0/0	56.38	3	
Moss Alan Edward	14.11.1930		9	*1953*–1960	61	26	0	10.16	21	4-35	0/0	29.80	1	
Moxon Martyn Douglas (*CY 1993*)	4.5.1960		10	1986–1989	455	99	0	28.43	0	0-3	0/0	–	10	8
Mullally Alan David	12.7.1969		19	1996–2001	127	24	0	5.52	58	5-105	1/0	31.24	6	50
Munton Timothy Alan (*CY 1995*)	30.7.1965		2	1992	25	25*	0	25.00	4	2-22	0/0	50.00	0	
Murdoch William Lloyd	18.10.1854	18.2.1911	1†	*1891*	12	12	0	12.00	–	–	–/–	–	0/1	
Murray John Thomas MBE (*CY 1967*)	1.4.1935		21	1961–1967	506	112	1	22.00	–	–	–/–	–	52/3	
Newham William	12.12.1860	26.6.1944	1	*1887*	26	17	0	13.00	–	–	–/–	–	0	

	Born	Died	Tests	Test Career	Runs	HS	100s	Avge	Wkts	BB	5/10	Avge	Ct/St	O/T
Newport Philip John	11.10.1962		3	1988–*1990*	110	40*	0	27.50	10	4-87	0/0	41.70	1	
Nichols Morris Stanley (*CY 1934*)	6.10.1900	26.1.1961	14	*1929*–1939	355	78*	0	29.58	41	6-35	2/0	28.09	11	
Oakman Alan Stanley Myles	20.4.1930		2	1956	14	10	0	7.00	0	0-21	0/0	–	7	
O'Brien *Sir* Timothy Carew	5.11.1861	9.12.1948	5	1884–*1895*	59	20	0	7.37	–	–	–/–	–	4	
O'Connor Jack	6.11.1897	22.2.1977	4	1929–*1929*	153	51	0	21.85	1	1-31	0/0	72.00	2	
Old Christopher Middleton (*CY 1979*)	22.12.1948		46	*1972*–1981	845	65	0	14.82	143	7-50	4/0	28.11	22	32
Oldfield Norman	5.5.1911	19.4.1996	1	1939	99	80	0	49.50	–	–	–/–	–	0	
Onions Graham (*CY 2010*)	9.9.1982		9	2009–2012	30	17*	0	10.00	32	5-38	1/0	29.90	0	4
Ormond James	20.8.1977		2	2001–*2001*	38	18	0	12.66	2	1-70	0/0	92.50	0	
Padgett Douglas Ernest Vernon	20.7.1934		2	1960	51	31	0	12.75	0	0-8	0/0	–	0	
Paine George Alfred Edward (*CY 1935*)	11.6.1908	30.3.1978	4	*1934*	97	49	0	16.16	17	5-168	1/0	27.47	5	
Palairet Lionel Charles Hamilton (*CY 1893*)	27.5.1870	27.3.1933	2	1902	49	20	0	12.25	–	–	–/–	–	2	
Palmer Charles Henry CBE	15.5.1919	31.3.2005	1	*1953*	22	22	0	11.00	0	0-15	0/0	–	0	
Palmer Kenneth Ernest MBE	22.4.1937		1	*1964*	10	10	0	10.00	1	1-113	0/0	189.00	0	
Panesar Mudhsuden Singh ("Monty") (*CY 2007*)	25.4.1982		45	*2005–2012*	213	26	0	5.32	159	6-37	12/2	32.64	9	26/1
Parfitt Peter Howard (*CY 1963*)	8.12.1936		37	*1961*–1972	1,882	131*	7	40.91	12	2-5	0/0	47.83	42	
Parker Charles Warrington Leonard (*CY 1923*)	14.10.1882	11.7.1959	1	1921	3	3*	0	–	2	2-32	0/0	16.00	0	
Parker Paul William Giles	15.1.1956		1	1981	13	13	0	6.50	–	–	–/–	–	0	
Parkhouse William Gilbert Anthony	12.10.1925	10.8.2000	7	1950–1959	373	78	0	28.69	–	–	–/–	–	3	
Parkin Cecil Harry (*CY 1924*)	18.2.1886	15.6.1943	10	*1920*–1924	160	36	0	12.30	32	5-38	2/0	35.25	3	
[1] **Parks** James Horace (*CY 1938*)	12.5.1903	21.11.1980	1	1937	29	22	0	14.50	3	2-26	0/0	12.00	0	
[1] **Parks** James Michael (*CY 1968*)	21.10.1931		46	1954–*1967*	1,962	108*	2	32.16	1	1-43	0/0	51.00	103/11	
[1] **Pataudi** Iftikhar Ali Khan, Nawab of (*CY 1932*)	16.3.1910	5.1.1952	3†	*1932*–1934	144	102	1	28.80	–	–	–/–	–	0	
Patel Minal Mahesh	7.7.1970		2	1996	45	27	0	22.50	1	1-101	0/0	180.00	2	
Patel Samit Rohit	30.11.1984		5	*2011–2012*	109	33	0	15.57	4	2.27	0/0	64.25	2	31/16
[2] **Pattinson** Darren John	2.8.1979		1	2008	21	13	0	10.50	2	2-95	0/0	48.00	0	
Paynter Edward (*CY 1938*)	5.11.1901	5.2.1979	20	*1931–1939*	1,540	243	4	59.23	–	–	–/–	–	7	
Peate Edmund	2.3.1855	11.3.1900	9	*1881*–1886	70	13	0	11.66	31	6-85	2/0	22.03	2	
Peebles Ian Alexander Ross (*CY 1931*)	20.1.1908	27.2.1980	13	*1927*–1931	98	26	0	10.88	45	6-63	3/0	30.91	5	
Peel Robert (*CY 1889*)	12.2.1857	12.8.1941	20	*1884*–1896	427	83	0	14.72	101	7-31	5/1	16.98	17	
Penn Frank	7.3.1851	26.12.1916	1	1880	50	27*	0	50.00	0	0-2	0/0	–	0	
Perks Reginald Thomas David	4.10.1911	22.11.1977	2	*1938*–1939	3	2*	0	–	11	5-100	2/0	32.27	1	
Philipson Hylton	8.6.1866	4.12.1935	5	*1891–1894*	63	30	0	9.00	–	–	–/–	–	8/3	
Pietersen Kevin Peter MBE (*CY 2006*)	27.6.1980		92	2005–*2012*	7,414	227	22	49.42	10	3-52	0/0	86.90	54	125‡/36
Pigott Anthony Charles Shackleton	4.6.1958		1	*1983*	12	8*	0	12.00	2	2-75	0/0	37.50	0	
Pilling Richard (*CY 1891*)	11.8.1855	28.3.1891	8	*1881*–1888	91	23	0	7.58	–	–	–/–	–	10/4	

	Born	Died	Tests	Test Career	Runs	HS	100s	Avge	Wkts	BB	5/10	Avge	Ct/St	O/T
Place Winston	7.12.1914	25.1.2002	3	*1947*	144	107	1	28.80	–	–	–/–	–	0	
Plunkett Liam Edward	6.4.1985		9	*2005*–2007	126	44*	0	11.45	23	3-17	0/0	39.82	3	29/1
Pocock Patrick Ian	24.9.1946		25	*1967–1984*	206	33	0	6.24	67	6-79	3/0	44.41	15	1
Pollard Richard	19.6.1912	16.12.1985	4	1946–1948	13	10*	0	13.00	15	5-24	1/0	25.20	3	
Poole Cyril John	13.3.1921	11.2.1996	3	*1951*	161	69*	0	40.25	0	0-9	0/0	–	1	
Pope George Henry	27.1.1911	29.10.1993	1	1947	8	8*	0	–	1	1-49	0/0	85.00	0	
Pougher Arthur Dick	19.4.1865	20.5.1926	1	*1891*	17	17	0	17.00	3	3-26	0/0	8.66	2	
Price John Sidney Ernest	22.7.1937		15	*1963*–1972	66	32	0	7.33	40	5-73	1/0	35.02	7	
Price Wilfred Frederick Frank	25.4.1902	13.1.1969	1	1938	6	6	0	3.00	–	–	–/–	–	2	
Prideaux Roger Malcolm	31.7.1939		3	1968–*1968*	102	64	0	20.40	0	0-0	0/0	–	0	
Pringle Derek Raymond	18.9.1958		30	1982–1992	695	63	0	15.10	70	5-95	3/0	35.97	10	44
Prior Matthew James (*CY 2010*)	26.2.1982		62	2007–*2012*	3,326	131*	6	43.19	–	–	–/–	–	173/13	68/10
Pullar Geoffrey (*CY 1960*)	1.8.1935		28	1959–*1962*	1,974	175	4	43.86	1	1-1	0/0	37.00	2	
Quaife William George (*CY 1902*)	17.3.1872	13.10.1951	7	1899–*1901*	228	68	0	19.00	0	0-6	0/0	–	4	
Radford Neal Victor (*CY 1986*)	7.6.1957		3	1986–*1987*	21	12*	0	7.00	4	2-131	0/0	87.75	0	6
Radley Clive Thornton MBE (*CY 1979*)	13.5.1944		8	*1977*–1978	481	158	2	48.10	–	–	–/–	–	4	4
Ramprakash Mark Ravin MBE (*CY 2007*)	5.9.1969		52	1991–*2001*	2,350	154	2	27.32	4	1-2	0/0	119.25	39	18
Randall Derek William (*CY 1980*)	24.2.1951		47	*1976*–1984	2,470	174	7	33.37	0	0-1	0/0	–	31	49
Ranjitsinhji Kumar Shri (*CY 1897*)	10.9.1872	2.4.1933	15	1896–1902	989	175	2	44.95	1	1-23	0/0	39.00	13	
Read Christopher Mark Wells (*CY 2011*)	10.8.1978		15	1999–*2006*	360	55	0	18.94	–	–	–/–	–	48/6	36/1
Read Holcombe Douglas ("Hopper")	28.1.1910	5.1.2000	1	1935	–	–	–	–	6	4-136	0/0	33.33	0	
Read John Maurice (*CY 1890*)	9.2.1859	17.2.1929	17	1882–1893	461	57	0	17.07	–	–	–/–	–	8	
Read Walter William (*CY 1893*)	23.11.1855	6.1.1907	18	*1882*–1893	720	117	1	27.69	0	0-27	0/0	–	16	
Reeve Dermot Alexander OBE (*CY 1996*)	2.4.1963		3	*1991*	124	59	0	24.80	2	1-4	0/0	30.00	1	29
Relf Albert Edward (*CY 1914*)	26.6.1874	26.3.1937	13	*1903–1913*	416	63	0	23.11	25	5-85	1/0	24.96	14	
Rhodes Harold James	22.7.1936		2	1959	0	0*	0	–	9	4-50	0/0	27.11	0	
Rhodes Steven John (*CY 1995*)	17.6.1964		11	1994–*1994*	294	65*	0	24.50	–	–	–/–	–	46/3	9
Rhodes Wilfred (*CY 1899*)	29.10.1877	8.7.1973	58	1899–*1929*	2,325	179	2	30.19	127	8-68	6/1	26.96	60	
Richards Clifton James ("Jack")	10.8.1958		8	*1986*–1988	285	133	1	21.92	–	–	–/–	–	20/1	22
[2] **Richardson** Derek Walter ("Dick")	3.11.1934		1	1957	33	33	0	33.00	–	–	–/–	–	1	
[2] **Richardson** Peter Edward (*CY 1957*)	4.7.1931		34	1956–1963	2,061	126	5	37.47	3	2-10	0/0	16.00	6	
Richardson Thomas (*CY 1897*)	11.8.1870	2.7.1912	14	1893–*1897*	177	25*	0	11.06	88	8-94	11/4	25.22	5	
Richmond Thomas Leonard	23.6.1890	29.12.1957	1	1921	6	4	0	3.00	2	2-69	0/0	43.00	0	
Ridgway Frederick	10.8.1923		5	*1951*	49	24	0	8.16	7	4-83	0/0	54.14	3	
Robertson John David Benbow (*CY 1948*)	22.2.1917	12.10.1996	11	1947–*1951*	881	133	2	46.36	2	2-17	0/0	29.00	6	
Robins Robert Walter Vivian (*CY 1930*)	3.6.1906	12.12.1968	19	1929–1937	612	108	1	26.60	64	6-32	1/0	27.46	12	

	Born	*Died*	*Tests*	*Test Career*	*Runs*	*HS*	*100s*	*Avge*	*Wkts*	*BB*	*5/10*	*Avge*	*Ct/St*	*O/T*
Robinson Robert Timothy (*CY 1986*)	21.11.1958		29	*1984*–1989	1,601	175	4	36.38	0	0-0	0/0	–	8	26
Roope Graham Richard James	12.7.1946	26.11.2006	21	*1972–1978*	860	77	0	30.71	0	0-2	0/0	–	35	8
Root Charles Frederick	16.4.1890	20.1.1954	3	1926	–	–	–	–	8	4-84	0/0	24.25	1	
Root Joseph Edward	30.12.1990		1	*2012*	93	73	0	93.00	0	0-5	0/0	–	0	0/1
Rose Brian Charles (*CY 1980*)	4.6.1950		9	*1977–1980*	358	70	0	25.57	–	–	–/–	–	4	2
Royle Vernon Peter Fanshawe Archer	29.1.1854	21.5.1929	1	*1878*	21	18	0	10.50	0	0-6	0/0	–	2	
Rumsey Frederick Edward	4.12.1935		5	1964–1965	30	21*	0	15.00	17	4-25	0/0	27.11	0	
Russell Albert Charles ("Jack") (*CY 1923*)	7.10.1887	23.3.1961	10	*1920–1922*	910	140	5	56.87	–	–	–/–	–	8	
Russell Robert Charles ("Jack") (*CY 1990*)	15.8.1963		54	1988–*1997*	1,897	128*	2	27.10	–	–	–/–	–	153/12	40
Russell William Eric	3.7.1936		10	*1961*–1967	362	70	0	21.29	0	0-19	0/0	–	4	
Saggers Martin John	23.5.1972		3	*2003*–2004	1	1	0	0.33	7	2-29	0/0	35.28	1	
Salisbury Ian David Kenneth (*CY 1993*)	21.1.1970		15	1992–*2000*	368	50	0	16.72	20	4-163	0/0	76.95	5	4
Sandham Andrew (*CY 1923*)	6.7.1890	20.4.1982	14	1921–*1929*	879	325	2	38.21	–	–	–/–	–	4	
Schofield Christopher Paul	6.10.1978		2	2000	67	57	0	22.33	0	0-73	0/0	–	0	0/4
Schultz Sandford Spence	29.8.1857	18.12.1937	1	*1878*	20	20	0	20.00	1	1-16	0/0	26.00	0	
Scotton William Henry	15.1.1856	9.7.1893	15	*1881–1886*	510	90	0	22.17	0	0-20	0/0	–	4	
Selby John	1.7.1849	11.3.1894	6	*1876–1881*	256	70	0	23.27	–	–	–/–	–	1	
Selvey Michael Walter William	25.4.1948		3	1976–*1976*	15	5*	0	7.50	6	4-41	0/0	57.16	1	
Shackleton Derek (*CY 1959*)	12.8.1924	28.9.2007	7	1950–1963	113	42	0	18.83	18	4-72	0/0	42.66	1	
Shah Owais Alam	22.10.1978		6	*2005–2008*	269	88	0	26.90	0	0-12	0/0	–	2	71/17
Shahzad Ajmal	27.7.1985		1	2010	5	5	0	5.00	4	3-45	0/0	15.75	2	11/3
Sharp John	15.2.1878	28.1.1938	3	1909	188	105	1	47.00	3	3-67	0/0	37.00	1	
Sharpe John William (*CY 1892*)	9.12.1866	19.6.1936	3	1890–*1891*	44	26	0	22.00	11	6-84	1/0	27.72	2	
Sharpe Philip John (*CY 1963*)	27.12.1936		12	1963–1969	786	111	1	46.23	–	–	–/–	–	17	
Shaw Alfred	29.8.1842	16.1.1907	7	*1876–1881*	111	40	0	10.09	12	5-38	1/0	23.75	4	
Sheppard *Rt Rev. Lord* [David Stuart] (*CY 1953*)	6.3.1929	5.3.2005	22	1950–*1962*	1,172	119	3	37.80	–	–	–/–	–	12	
Sherwin Mordecai (*CY 1891*)	26.2.1851	3.7.1910	3	*1886*–1888	30	21*	0	15.00	–	–	–/–	–	5/2	
Shrewsbury Arthur (*CY 1890*)	11.4.1856	19.5.1903	23	*1881*–1893	1,277	164	3	35.47	0	0-2	0/0	–	29	
Shuter John	9.2.1855	5.7.1920	1	1888	28	28	0	28.00	–	–	–/–	–	0	
Shuttleworth Kenneth	13.11.1944		5	*1970*–1971	46	21	0	7.66	12	5-47	1/0	35.58	1	
[1] **Sidebottom** Arnold	1.4.1954		1	1985	2	2	0	2.00	1	1-65	0/0	65.00	0	
[1] **Sidebottom** Ryan Jay (*CY 2008*)	15.1.1978		22	2001–*2009*	313	31	0	15.65	79	7-47	5/1	28.24	5	25/18
Silverwood Christopher Eric Wilfred	5.3.1975		6	*1996–2002*	29	10	0	7.25	11	5-91	1/0	40.36	2	7
Simpson Reginald Thomas (*CY 1950*)	27.2.1920		27	*1948–1954*	1,401	156*	4	33.35	2	2-4	0/0	11.00	5	
Simpson-Hayward George Hayward Thomas	7.6.1875	2.10.1936	5	*1909*	105	29*	0	15.00	23	6-43	2/0	18.26	1	
Sims James Morton	13.5.1903	27.4.1973	4	1935–*1936*	16	12	0	4.00	11	5-73	1/0	43.63	6	

	Born	Died	Tests	Test Career	Runs	HS	100s	Avge	Wkts	BB	5/10	Avge	Ct/St	O/T
Sinfield Reginald Albert	24.12.1900	17.3.1988	1	1938	6	6	0	6.00	2	1-51	0/0	61.50	0	
Slack Wilfred Norris	12.12.1954	15.1.1989	3	*1985*–1986	81	52	0	13.50	–	–	–/–	–	3	2
Smailes Thomas Francis	27.3.1910	1.12.1970	1	1946	25	25	0	25.00	3	3-44	0/0	20.66	0	
Small Gladstone Cleophas	18.10.1961		17	1986–*1990*	263	59	0	15.47	55	5-48	2/0	34.01	9	53
Smith Alan Christopher CBE	25.10.1936		6	*1962*	118	69*	0	29.50	–	–	–/–	–	20	
Smith Andrew Michael	1.10.1967		1	1997	4	4*	0	4.00	0	0-89	0/0	–	0	
Smith Cedric Ivan James (*CY 1935*)	25.8.1906	8.2.1979	5	*1934*–1937	102	27	0	10.20	15	5-16	1/0	26.20	1	
Smith *Sir* Charles Aubrey	21.7.1863	20.12.1948	1	*1888*	3	3	0	3.00	7	5-19	1/0	8.71	0	
[2] **Smith** Christopher Lyall (*CY 1984*)	15.10.1958		8	1983–1986	392	91	0	30.15	3	2-31	0/0	13.00	5	4
Smith David Mark	9.1.1956		2	*1985*	80	47	0	20.00	–	–	–/–	–	0	2
Smith David Robert	5.10.1934	17.12.2003	5	*1961*	38	34	0	9.50	6	2-60	0/0	59.83	2	
Smith Denis (*CY 1935*)	24.1.1907	12.9.1979	2	1935	128	57	0	32.00	–	–	–/–	–	1	
Smith Donald Victor	14.6.1923		3	1957	25	16*	0	8.33	1	1-12	0/0	97.00	0	
Smith Edward Thomas	19.7.1977		3	2003	87	64	0	17.40	–	–	–/–	–	5	
Smith Ernest James ("Tiger")	6.2.1886	31.8.1979	11	*1911–1913*	113	22	0	8.69	–	–	–/–	–	17/3	
Smith Harry	21.5.1891	12.11.1937	1	1928	7	7	0	7.00	–	–	–/–	–	1	
Smith Michael John Knight OBE (*CY 1960*)	30.6.1933		50	1958–1972	2,278	121	3	31.63	1	1-10	0/0	128.00	53	
[2] **Smith** Robin Arnold (*CY 1990*)	13.9.1963		62	1988–*1995*	4,236	175	9	43.67	0	0-6	0/0	–	39	71
Smith Thomas Peter Bromley (*CY 1947*)	30.10.1908	4.8.1967	4	1946–*1946*	33	24	0	6.60	3	2-172	0/0	106.33	1	
Smithson Gerald Arthur	1.11.1926	6.9.1970	2	*1947*	70	35	0	23.33	–	–	–/–	–	0	
Snow John Augustine (*CY 1973*)	13.10.1941		49	1965–1976	772	73	0	13.54	202	7-40	8/1	26.66	16	9
Southerton James	16.11.1827	16.6.1880	2	*1876*	7	6	0	3.50	7	4-46	0/0	15.28	2	
Spooner Reginald Herbert (*CY 1905*)	21.10.1880	2.10.1961	10	1905–1912	481	119	1	32.06	–	–	–/–	–	4	
Spooner Richard Thompson	30.12.1919	20.12.1997	7	*1951*–1955	354	92	0	27.23	–	–	–/–	–	10/2	
Stanyforth Ronald Thomas	30.5.1892	20.2.1964	4	*1927*	13	6*	0	2.60	–	–	–/–	–	7/2	
Staples Samuel James (*CY 1929*)	18.9.1892	4.6.1950	3	*1927*	65	39	0	13.00	15	3-50	0/0	29.00	0	
Statham John Brian CBE (*CY 1955*)	17.6.1930	10.6.2000	70	*1950*–1965	675	38	0	11.44	252	7-39	9/1	24.84	28	
Steel Allan Gibson	24.9.1858	15.6.1914	13	1880–1888	600	148	2	35.29	29	3-27	0/0	20.86	5	
Steele David Stanley OBE (*CY 1976*)	29.9.1941		8	1975–1976	673	106	1	42.06	2	1-1	0/0	19.50	7	1
Stephenson John Patrick	14.3.1965		1	1989	36	25	0	18.00	–	–	–/–	–	0	
Stevens Greville Thomas Scott (*CY 1918*)	7.1.1901	19.9.1970	10	*1922–1929*	263	69	0	15.47	20	5-90	2/1	32.40	9	
Stevenson Graham Barry	16.12.1955		2	*1979–1980*	28	27*	0	28.00	5	3-111	0/0	36.60	0	4
[1] **Stewart** Alec James OBE (*CY 1993*)	8.4.1963		133	*1989*–2003	8,463	190	15	39.54	0	0-5	0/0	–	263/14	170
[1] **Stewart** Michael James OBE (*CY 1958*)	16.9.1932		8	1962–*1963*	385	87	0	35.00	–	–	–/–	–	6	
Stoddart Andrew Ernest (*CY 1893*)	11.3.1863	3.4.1915	16	*1887–1897*	996	173	2	35.57	2	1-10	0/0	47.00	6	
Storer William (*CY 1899*)	25.1.1867	28.2.1912	6	*1897*–1899	215	51	0	19.54	2	1-24	0/0	54.00	11	

	Born	Died	Tests	Test Career	Runs	HS	100s	Avge	Wkts	BB	5/10	Avge	Ct/St	O/T
Strauss Andrew John OBE (*CY 2005*)	2.3.1977		100	2004–2012	7,037	177	21	40.91	–	–	–/–	–	121	127/4
Street George Benjamin	6.12.1889	24.4.1924	1	*1922*	11	7*	0	11.00	–	–	–/–	–	0/1	
Strudwick Herbert (*CY 1912*)	28.1.1880	14.2.1970	28	*1909*–1926	230	24	0	7.93	–	–	–/–	–	61/12	
[2] **Studd** Charles Thomas	2.12.1860	16.7.1931	5	1882–*1882*	160	48	0	20.00	3	2-35	0/0	32.66	5	
[2] **Studd** George Brown	20.10.1859	13.2.1945	4	*1882*	31	9	0	4.42	–	–	–/–	–	8	
Subba Row Raman CBE (*CY 1961*)	29.1.1932		13	1958–1961	984	137	3	46.85	0	0-2	0/0	–	5	
Such Peter Mark	12.6.1964		11	1993–1999	67	14*	0	6.09	37	6-67	2/0	33.56	4	
Sugg Frank Howe (*CY 1890*)	11.1.1862	29.5.1933	2	1888	55	31	0	27.50	–	–	–/–	–	0	
Sutcliffe Herbert (*CY 1920*)	24.11.1894	22.1.1978	54	1924–1935	4,555	194	16	60.73	–	–	–/–	–	23	
Swann Graeme Peter (*CY 2010*)	24.3.1979		50	*2008–2012*	1,176	85	0	23.52	212	6-65	14/2	29.13	44	73/39
Swetman Roy	25.10.1933		11	*1958–1959*	254	65	0	16.93	–	–	–/–	–	24/2	
[1] **Tate** Frederick William	24.7.1867	24.2.1943	1	1902	9	5*	0	9.00	2	2-7	0/0	25.50	2	
[1] **Tate** Maurice William (*CY 1924*)	30.5.1895	18.5.1956	39	1924–1935	1,198	100*	1	25.48	155	6-42	7/1	26.16	11	
Tattersall Roy	17.8.1922	9.12.2011	16	*1950*–1954	50	10*	0	5.00	58	7-52	4/1	26.08	8	
Tavaré Christopher James	27.10.1954		31	1980–1989	1,755	149	2	32.50	0	0-0	0/0	–	20	29
Taylor James William Arthur	6.1.1990		2	2012	48	34	0	16.00	–	–	–/–	–	2	1
Taylor Jonathan Paul	8.8.1964		2	*1992*–1994	34	17*	0	17.00	3	1-18	0/0	52.00	0	1
Taylor Kenneth	21.8.1935		3	1959–1964	57	24	0	11.40	0	0-6	0/0	–	1	
Taylor Leslie Brian	25.10.1953		2	1985	1	1*	0	–	4	2-34	0/0	44.50	1	2
Taylor Robert William MBE (*CY 1977*)	17.7.1941		57	*1970–1983*	1,156	97	0	16.28	0	0-6	0/0	–	167/7	27
Tennyson *Lord* Lionel Hallam (*CY 1914*)	7.11.1889	6.6.1951	9	*1913*–1921	345	74*	0	31.36	0	0-1	0/0	–	6	
Terry Vivian Paul	14.1.1959		2	1984	16	8	0	5.33	–	–	–/–	–	2	
Thomas John Gregory	12.8.1960		5	*1985*–1986	83	31*	0	13.83	10	4-70	0/0	50.40	0	3
Thompson George Joseph (*CY 1906*)	27.10.1877	3.3.1943	6	1909–*1909*	273	63	0	30.33	23	4-50	0/0	27.73	5	
Thomson Norman Ian	23.1.1929		5	*1964*	69	39	0	23.00	9	2-55	0/0	63.11	3	
Thorpe Graham Paul MBE (*CY 1998*)	1.8.1969		100	1993–2005	6,744	200*	16	44.66	0	0-0	0/0	–	105	82
Titmus Frederick John MBE (*CY 1963*)	24.11.1932	23.3.2011	53	1955–*1974*	1,449	84*	0	22.29	153	7-79	7/0	32.22	35	2
Tolchard Roger William	15.6.1946		4	*1976*	129	67	0	25.80	–	–	–/–	–	5	1
[1] **Townsend** Charles Lucas (*CY 1899*)	7.11.1876	17.10.1958	2	1899	51	38	0	17.00	3	3-50	0/0	25.00	0	
[1] **Townsend** David Charles Humphery	20.4.1912	27.1.1997	3	*1934*	77	36	0	12.83	0	0-9	0/0	–	1	
Townsend Leslie Fletcher (*CY 1934*)	8.6.1903	17.2.1993	4	*1929–1933*	97	40	0	16.16	6	2-22	0/0	34.16	2	
Tredwell James Cullum	27.2.1982		1	*2009*	37	37	0	37.00	6	4-82	0/0	30.16	1	9/2
[4] **Tremlett** Christopher Timothy	2.9.1981		11	2007–*2011*	98	25*	0	10.88	49	6-48	2/0	26.75	4	15/1
[4] **Tremlett** Maurice Fletcher	5.7.1923	30.7.1984	3	*1947*	20	18*	0	6.66	4	2-98	0/0	56.50	0	
Trescothick Marcus Edward MBE (*CY 2005*)	25.12.1975		76	2000–2006	5,825	219	14	43.79	1	1-34	0/0	155.00	95	123/3
[2] **Trott** Albert Edwin (*CY 1899*)	6.2.1873	30.7.1914	2†	*1898*	23	16	0	5.75	17	5-49	1/0	11.64	0	

	Born	*Died*	*Tests*	*Test Career*	*Runs*	*HS*	*100s*	*Avge*	*Wkts*	*BB*	*5/10*	*Avge*	*Ct/St*	*O/T*
Trott Ian Jonathan Leonard (*CY 2011*)	22.4.1981		38	2009–*2012*	2,970	226	8	49.50	3	1-5	0/0	113.66	17	54/7
Trueman Frederick Sewards OBE (*CY 1953*)	6.2.1931	1.7.2006	67	1952–1965	981	39*	0	13.81	307	8-31	17/3	21.57	64	
Tudor Alex Jeremy	23.10.1977		10	*1998–2002*	229	99*	0	19.08	28	5-44	1/0	34.39	3	3
Tufnell Neville Charsley	13.6.1887	3.8.1951	1	*1909*	14	14	0	14.00	–	–	–/–	–	0/1	
Tufnell Philip Clive Roderick	29.4.1966		42	*1990*–2001	153	22*	0	5.10	121	7-47	5/2	37.68	12	20
Turnbull Maurice Joseph Lawson (*CY 1931*)	16.3.1906	5.8.1944	9	*1929*–1936	224	61	0	20.36	–	–	–/–	–	1	
[2] **Tyldesley** [George] Ernest (*CY 1920*)	5.2.1889	5.5.1962	14	1921–*1928*	990	122	3	55.00	0	0-2	0/0	–	2	
[2] **Tyldesley** John Thomas (*CY 1902*)	22.11.1873	27.11.1930	31	*1898*–1909	1,661	138	4	30.75	–	–	–/–	–	16	
Tyldesley Richard Knowles (*CY 1925*)	11.3.1897	17.9.1943	7	1924–1930	47	29	0	7.83	19	3-50	0/0	32.57	1	
Tylecote Edward Ferdinando Sutton	23.6.1849	15.3.1938	6	*1882*–1886	152	66	0	19.00	–	–	–/–	–	5/5	
Tyler Edwin James	13.10.1864	25.1.1917	1	*1895*	0	0	0	0.00	4	3-49	0/0	16.25	0	
Tyson Frank Holmes (*CY 1956*)	6.6.1930		17	1954–*1958*	230	37*	0	10.95	76	7-27	4/1	18.56	4	
Udal Shaun David	18.3.1969		4	*2005*	109	33*	0	18.16	8	4-14	0/0	43.00	1	11
Ulyett George	21.10.1851	18.6.1898	25	*1876*–1890	949	149	1	24.33	50	7-36	1/0	20.40	19	
Underwood Derek Leslie MBE (*CY 1969*)	8.6.1945		86	1966–*1981*	937	45*	0	11.56	297	8-51	17/6	25.83	44	26
Valentine Bryan Herbert	17.1.1908	2.2.1983	7	*1933–1938*	454	136	2	64.85	–	–	–/–	–	2	
Vaughan Michael Paul OBE (*CY 2003*)	29.10.1974		82	*1999*–2008	5,719	197	18	41.44	6	2-71	0/0	93.50	44	86/2
Verity Hedley (*CY 1932*)	18.5.1905	31.7.1943	40	1931–1939	669	66*	0	20.90	144	8-43	5/2	24.37	30	
Vernon George Frederick	20.6.1856	10.8.1902	1	*1882*	14	11*	0	14.00	–	–	–/–	–	0	
Vine Joseph (*CY 1906*)	15.5.1875	25.4.1946	2	*1911*	46	36	0	46.00	–	–	–/–	–	0	
Voce William (*CY 1933*)	8.8.1909	6.6.1984	27	*1929–1946*	308	66	0	13.39	98	7-70	3/2	27.88	15	
Waddington Abraham	4.2.1893	28.10.1959	2	*1920*	16	7	0	4.00	1	1-35	0/0	119.00	1	
Wainwright Edward (*CY 1894*)	8.4.1865	28.10.1919	5	1893–*1897*	132	49	0	14.66	0	0-11	0/0	–	2	
Walker Peter Michael	17.2.1936		3	1960	128	52	0	32.00	0	0-8	0/0	–	5	
Walters Cyril Frederick (*CY 1934*)	28.8.1905	23.12.1992	11	1933–1934	784	102	1	52.26	–	–	–/–	–	6	
Ward Alan	10.8.1947		5	1969–1976	40	21	0	8.00	14	4-61	0/0	32.35	3	
Ward Albert (*CY 1890*)	21.11.1865	6.1.1939	7	1893–*1894*	487	117	1	37.46	–	–	–/–	–	1	
Ward Ian James	30.9.1972		5	2001	129	39	0	16.12	–	–	–/–	–	1	
Wardle John Henry (*CY 1954*)	8.1.1923	23.7.1985	28	*1947*–1957	653	66	0	19.78	102	7-36	5/1	20.39	12	
Warner *Sir* Pelham Francis (*CY 1904*)	2.10.1873	30.1.1963	15	*1898*–1912	622	132*	1	23.92	–	–	–/–	–	3	
Warr John James	16.7.1927		2	*1950*	4	4	0	1.00	1	1-76	0/0	281.00	0	
Warren Arnold	2.4.1875	3.9.1951	1	1905	7	7	0	7.00	6	5-57	1/0	18.83	1	
Washbrook Cyril CBE (*CY 1947*)	6.12.1914	27.4.1999	37	1937–1956	2,569	195	6	42.81	1	1-25	0/0	33.00	12	
Watkin Steven Llewellyn (*CY 1994*)	15.9.1964		3	1991–1993	25	13	0	5.00	11	4-65	0/0	27.72	1	4
Watkins Albert John ("Allan")	21.4.1922	3.8.2011	15	1948–1952	810	137*	2	40.50	11	3-20	0/0	50.36	17	
Watkinson Michael	1.8.1961		4	1995–*1995*	167	82*	0	33.40	10	3-64	0/0	34.80	1	1

	Born	*Died*	*Tests*	*Test Career*	*Runs*	*HS*	*100s*	*Avge*	*Wkts*	*BB*	*5/10*	*Avge*	*Ct/St*	*O/T*
Watson Willie (*CY 1954*)	7.3.1920	23.4.2004	23	1951–*1958*	879	116	2	25.85	–	–	–/–	–	8	
Webbe Alexander Josiah	16.1.1855	19.2.1941	1	*1878*	4	4	0	2.00	–	–	–/–	–	2	
Wellard Arthur William (*CY 1936*)	8.4.1902	31.12.1980	2	1937–1938	47	38	0	11.75	7	4-81	0/0	33.85	2	
Wells Alan Peter	2.10.1961		1	1995	3	3*	0	3.00	–	–	–/–	–	0	1
Wharton Alan	30.4.1923	26.8.1993	1	1949	20	13	0	10.00	–	–	–/–	–	0	
Whitaker John James (*CY 1987*)	5.5.1962		1	*1986*	11	11	0	11.00	–	–	–/–	–	1	2
White Craig	16.12.1969		30	1994–*2002*	1,052	121	1	24.46	59	5-32	3/0	37.62	14	51
White David William ("Butch")	14.12.1935	1.8.2008	2	*1961*	0	0	0	0.00	4	3-65	0/0	29.75	0	
White John Cornish (*CY 1929*)	19.2.1891	2.5.1961	15	1921–*1930*	239	29	0	18.38	49	8-126	3/1	32.26	6	
Whysall William Wilfrid (*CY 1925*)	31.10.1887	11.11.1930	4	*1924*–1930	209	76	0	29.85	0	0-9	0/0	–	7	
Wilkinson Leonard Litton	5.11.1916	3.9.2002	3	*1938*	3	2	0	3.00	7	2-12	0/0	38.71	0	
Willey Peter	6.12.1949		26	1976–1986	1,184	102*	2	26.90	7	2-73	0/0	65.14	3	26
Williams Neil FitzGerald	2.7.1962	27.3.2006	1	1990	38	38	0	38.00	2	2-148	0/0	74.00	0	
Willis Robert George Dylan MBE (*CY 1978*)	30.5.1949		90	*1970*–1984	840	28*	0	11.50	325	8-43	16/0	25.20	39	64
[2] **Wilson** Clement Eustace Macro	15.5.1875	8.2.1944	2	*1898*	42	18	0	14.00	–	–	–/–	–	0	
Wilson Donald	7.8.1937	21.7.2012	6	*1963–1970*	75	42	0	12.50	11	2-17	0/0	42.36	1	
[2] **Wilson** Evelyn Rockley	25.3.1879	21.7.1957	1	*1920*	10	5	0	5.00	3	2-28	0/0	12.00	0	
Wood Arthur (*CY 1939*)	25.8.1898	1.4.1973	4	1938–1939	80	53	0	20.00	–	–	–/–	–	10/1	
Wood Barry	26.12.1942		12	1972–1978	454	90	0	21.61	0	0-2	0/0	–	6	13
Wood George Edward Charles	22.8.1893	18.3.1971	3	1924	7	6	0	3.50	–	–	–/–	–	5/1	
Wood Henry (*CY 1891*)	14.12.1853	30.4.1919	4	1888–*1891*	204	134*	1	68.00	–	–	–/–	–	2/1	
Wood Reginald	7.3.1860	6.1.1915	1	*1886*	6	6	0	3.00	–	–	–/–	–	0	
Woods Samuel Moses James (*CY 1889*)	13.4.1867	30.4.1931	3†	*1895*	122	53	0	30.50	5	3-28	0/0	25.80	4	
Woolley Frank Edward (*CY 1911*)	27.5.1887	18.10.1978	64	1909–1934	3,283	154	5	36.07	83	7-76	4/1	33.91	64	
Woolmer Robert Andrew (*CY 1976*)	14.5.1948	18.3.2007	19	1975–1981	1,059	149	3	33.09	4	1-8	0/0	74.75	10	6
Worthington Thomas Stanley (*CY 1937*)	21.8.1905	31.8.1973	9	*1929–1936*	321	128	1	29.18	8	2-19	0/0	39.50	8	
Wright Charles William	27.5.1863	10.1.1936	3	*1895*	125	71	0	31.25	–	–	–/–	–	0	
Wright Douglas Vivian Parson (*CY 1940*)	21.8.1914	13.11.1998	34	1938–*1950*	289	45	0	11.11	108	7-105	6/1	39.11	10	
Wyatt Robert Elliott Storey (*CY 1930*)	2.5.1901	20.4.1995	40	*1927–1936*	1,839	149	2	31.70	18	3-4	0/0	35.66	16	
Wynyard Edward George	1.4.1861	30.10.1936	3	1896–*1905*	72	30	0	12.00	0	0-2	0/0	–	0	
Yardley Norman Walter Dransfield (*CY 1948*)	19.3.1915	3.10.1989	20	*1938*–1950	812	99	0	25.37	21	3-67	0/0	33.66	14	
Young Harding Isaac ("Sailor")	5.2.1876	12.12.1964	2	1899	43	43	0	21.50	12	4-30	0/0	21.83	1	
Young John Albert	14.10.1912	5.2.1993	8	1947–1949	28	10*	0	5.60	17	3-65	0/0	44.52	5	
Young Richard Alfred	16.9.1885	1.7.1968	2	*1907*	27	13	0	6.75	–	–	–/–	–	6	

AUSTRALIA (431 players)

	Born	*Died*	*Tests*	*Test Career*	*Runs*	*HS*	*100s*	*Avge*	*Wkts*	*BB*	*5/10*	*Avge*	*Ct/St*	*O/T*
a'Beckett Edward Lambert	11.8.1907	2.6.1989	4	*1928–1931*	143	41	0	20.42	3	1-41	0/0	105.66	4	
Alderman Terence Michael (*CY 1982*)	12.6.1956		41	1981–*1990*	203	26*	0	6.54	170	6-47	14/1	27.15	27	65
Alexander George	22.4.1851	6.11.1930	2	*1880–1884*	52	33	0	13.00	2	2-69	0/0	46.50	2	
Alexander Harry Houston	9.6.1905	15.4.1993	1	*1932*	17	17*	0	17.00	1	1-129	0/0	154.00	0	
Allan Francis Erskine	2.12.1849	9.2.1917	1	*1878*	5	5	0	5.00	4	2-30	0/0	20.00	0	
Allan Peter John	31.12.1935		1	*1965*	–	–	–	–	2	2-58	0/0	41.50	0	
Allen Reginald Charles	2.7.1858	2.5.1952	1	*1886*	44	30	0	22.00	–	–	–/–	–	2	
Andrews Thomas James Edwin	26.8.1890	28.1.1970	16	1921–1926	592	94	0	26.90	1	1-23	0/0	116.00	12	
Angel Jo	22.4.1968		4	*1992–1994*	35	11	0	5.83	10	3-54	0/0	46.30	1	3
[2] **Archer** Kenneth Alan	17.1.1928		5	*1950–1951*	234	48	0	26.00	–	–	–/–	–	0	
[2] **Archer** Ronald Graham	25.10.1933	27.5.2007	19	*1952–1956*	713	128	1	24.58	48	5-53	1/0	27.45	20	
Armstrong Warwick Windridge (*CY 1903*)	22.5.1879	13.7.1947	50	*1901*–1921	2,863	159*	6	38.68	87	6-35	3/0	33.59	44	
Badcock Clayvel Lindsay ("Jack")	10.4.1914	13.12.1982	7	*1936*–1938	160	118	1	14.54	–	–	–/–	–	3	
[2] **Bannerman** Alexander Chalmers	21.3.1854	19.9.1924	28	*1878*–1893	1,108	94	0	23.08	4	3-111	0/0	40.75	21	
[2] **Bannerman** Charles	23.7.1851	20.8.1930	3	*1876–1878*	239	165*	1	59.75	–	–	–/–	–	0	
Bardsley Warren (*CY 1910*)	6.12.1882	20.1.1954	41	1909–1926	2,469	193*	6	40.47	–	–	–/–	–	12	
Barnes Sidney George	5.6.1916	16.12.1973	13	1938–1948	1,072	234	3	63.05	4	2-25	0/0	54.50	14	
Barnett Benjamin Arthur	23.3.1908	29.6.1979	4	1938	195	57	0	27.85	–	–	–/–	–	3/2	
Barrett John Edward	15.10.1866	6.2.1916	2	1890	80	67*	0	26.66	–	–	–/–	–	1	
Beard Graeme Robert	19.8.1950		3	*1979*	114	49	0	22.80	1	1-26	0/0	109.00	0	2
Beer Michael Anthony	9.6.1984		2	*2010–2011*	6	2*	0	3.00	3	2-56	0/0	59.33	1	
[2] **Benaud** John	11.5.1944		3	*1972*	223	142	1	44.60	2	2-12	0/0	6.00	0	
[2] **Benaud** Richard OBE (*CY 1962*)	6.10.1930		63	*1951–1963*	2,201	122	3	24.45	248	7-72	16/1	27.03	65	
Bennett Murray John	6.10.1956		3	*1984*–1985	71	23	0	23.66	6	3-79	0/0	54.16	5	8
Bevan Michael Gwyl	8.5.1970		18	*1994–1997*	785	91	0	29.07	29	6-82	1/1	24.24	8	232
Bichel Andrew John	27.8.1970		19	*1996–2003*	355	71	0	16.90	58	5-60	1/0	32.24	16	67
Bird Jackson Munro	11.12.1986		2	*2012*	6	6*	0	6.00	11	4-41	0/0	16.18	1	
Blackham John McCarthy (*CY 1891*)	11.5.1854	28.12.1932	35	*1876–1894*	800	74	0	15.68	–	–	–/–	–	37/24	
Blackie Donald Dearness	5.4.1882	18.4.1955	3	*1928*	24	11*	0	8.00	14	6-94	1/0	31.71	2	
Blewett Gregory Scott	28.10.1971		46	*1994–1999*	2,552	214	4	34.02	14	2-9	0/0	51.42	45	32
Bollinger Douglas Erwin	24.7.1981		12	*2008–2010*	54	21	0	7.71	50	5-28	2/0	25.92	2	39/2
Bonnor George John	25.2.1855	27.6.1912	17	1880–1888	512	128	1	17.06	2	1-5	0/0	42.00	16	
Boon David Clarence MBE (*CY 1994*)	29.12.1960		107	*1984–1995*	7,422	200	21	43.65	0	0-0	0/0	–	99	181

	Born	Died	Tests	Test Career	Runs	HS	100s	Avge	Wkts	BB	5/10	Avge	Ct/St	O/T
Booth Brian Charles MBE	19.10.1933		29	1961–*1965*	1,773	169	5	42.21	3	2-33	0/0	48.66	17	
Border Allan Robert (*CY 1982*)	27.7.1955		156	*1978–1993*	11,174	205	27	50.56	39	7-46	2/1	39.10	156	273
Boyle Henry Frederick	10.12.1847	21.11.1907	12	*1878–1884*	153	36*	0	12.75	32	6-42	1/0	20.03	10	
Bracken Nathan Wade	12.9.1977		5	*2003–2005*	70	37	0	17.50	12	4-48	0/0	42.08	2	116/19
Bradman *Sir* Donald George AC (*CY 1931*)	27.8.1908	25.2.2001	52	*1928*–1948	6,996	334	29	99.94	2	1-8	0/0	36.00	32	
Bright Raymond James	13.7.1954		25	1977–*1986*	445	33	0	14.35	53	7-87	4/1	41.13	13	11
Bromley Ernest Harvey	2.9.1912	1.2.1967	2	*1932*–1934	38	26	0	9.50	0	0-19	0/0	–	2	
Brown William Alfred (*CY 1939*)	31.7.1912	16.3.2008	22	1934–1948	1,592	206*	4	46.82	–	–	–/–	–	14	
Bruce William	22.5.1864	3.8.1925	14	*1884–1894*	702	80	0	29.25	12	3-88	0/0	36.66	12	
Burge Peter John Parnell (*CY 1965*)	17.5.1932	5.10.2001	42	*1954–1965*	2,290	181	4	38.16	–	–	–/–	–	23	
Burke James Wallace (*CY 1957*)	12.6.1930	2.2.1979	24	*1950–1958*	1,280	189	3	34.59	8	4-37	0/0	28.75	18	
Burn Edwin James <u>Kenneth</u> (K. E.)	17.9.1862	20.7.1956	2	1890	41	19	0	10.25	–	–	–/–	–	0	
Burton Frederick John	2.11.1865	25.8.1929	2	*1886–1887*	4	2*	0	2.00	–	–	–/–	–	1/1	
Callaway Sydney Thomas	6.2.1868	25.11.1923	3	*1891–1894*	87	41	0	17.40	6	5-37	1/0	23.66	0	
Callen Ian Wayne	2.5.1955		1	*1977*	26	22*	0	–	6	3-83	0/0	31.83	1	5
Campbell Gregory Dale	10.3.1964		4	1989–*1989*	10	6	0	2.50	13	3-79	0/0	38.69	1	12
Carkeek William ("Barlow")	17.10.1878	20.2.1937	6	1912	16	6*	0	5.33	–	–	–/–	–	6	
Carlson Phillip Henry	8.8.1951		2	*1978*	23	21	0	5.75	2	2-41	0/0	49.50	2	4
Carter Hanson	15.3.1878	8.6.1948	28	*1907–1921*	873	72	0	22.97	–	–	–/–	–	44/21	
Casson Beau	7.12.1982		1	*2007*	10	10	0	10.00	3	3-86	0/0	43.00	2	
2, 4 **Chappell** Gregory Stephen MBE (*CY 1973*)	7.8.1948		87	*1970–1983*	7,110	247*	24	53.86	47	5-61	1/0	40.70	122	74
2, 4 **Chappell** Ian Michael (*CY 1976*)	26.9.1943		75	*1964–1979*	5,345	196	14	42.42	20	2-21	0/0	65.80	105	16
2, 4 **Chappell** Trevor Martin	21.10.1952		3	1981	79	27	0	15.80	–	–	–/–	–	2	20
Charlton Percie Chater	9.4.1867	30.9.1954	2	1890	29	11	0	7.25	3	3-18	0/0	8.00	0	
Chipperfield Arthur Gordon	17.11.1905	29.7.1987	14	1934–1938	552	109	1	32.47	5	3-91	0/0	87.40	15	
Clark Stuart Rupert	28.9.1975		24	*2005*–2009	248	39	0	13.05	94	5-32	2/0	23.86	4	39/9
Clark Wayne Maxwell	19.9.1953		10	*1977–1978*	98	33	0	5.76	44	4-46	0/0	28.75	6	2
Clarke Michael John (*CY 2010*)	2.4.1981		89§	*2004–2012*	6,989	329*	22	52.54	30	6-9	2/0	36.60	103	221/34
Colley David John	15.3.1947		3	1972	84	54	0	21.00	6	3-83	0/0	52.00	1	1
Collins Herbert Leslie	21.1.1888	28.5.1959	19	*1920*–1926	1,352	203	4	45.06	4	2-47	0/0	63.00	13	
Coningham Arthur	14.7.1863	13.6.1939	1	*1894*	13	10	0	6.50	2	2-17	0/0	38.00	0	
Connolly Alan Norman	29.6.1939		29	*1963–1970*	260	37	0	10.40	102	6-47	4/0	29.22	17	1
Cook Simon Hewitt	29.1.1972		2	*1997*	3	3*	0	–	7	5-39	1/0	20.28	0	
Cooper Bransby Beauchamp	15.3.1844	7.8.1914	1	*1876*	18	15	0	9.00	–	–	–/–	–	2	
5 **Cooper** William Henry	11.9.1849	5.4.1939	2	*1881–1884*	13	7	0	6.50	9	6-120	1/0	25.11	1	

§ Clarke's figures include 44 runs and one catch for Australia v the ICC World XI in the Super Series Test in 2005-06.

	Born	*Died*	*Tests*	*Test Career*	*Runs*	*HS*	*100s*	*Avge*	*Wkts*	*BB*	*5/10*	*Avge*	*Ct/St*	*O/T*
Copeland Trent Aaron	14.3.1986		3	*2011*	39	23*	0	13.00	6	2-24	0/0	37.83	2	
Corling Grahame Edward	13.7.1941		5	1964	5	3	0	1.66	12	4-60	0/0	37.25	0	
Cosier Gary John	25.4.1953		18	*1975–1978*	897	168	2	28.93	5	2-26	0/0	68.20	14	9
Cottam John Thomas	5.9.1867	30.1.1897	1	*1886*	4	3	0	2.00	–	–	–/–	–	1	
Cotter Albert ("Tibby")	3.12.1883	31.10.1917	21	*1903–1911*	457	45	0	13.05	89	7-148	7/0	28.64	8	
Coulthard George	1.8.1856	22.10.1883	1	*1881*	6	6*	0	–	–	–	–/–	–	0	
Cowan Edward James McKenzie	16.6.1982		13	*2011–2012*	722	136	1	32.81	–	–	–/–	–	19	
Cowper Robert Maskew	5.10.1940		27	1964–1968	2,061	307	5	46.84	36	4-48	0/0	31.63	21	
Craig Ian David	12.6.1935		11	*1952–1957*	358	53	0	19.88	–	–	–/–	–	2	
Crawford William Patrick Anthony	3.8.1933	21.1.2009	4	1956–*1956*	53	34	0	17.66	7	3-28	0/0	15.28	1	
Cullen Daniel James	10.4.1984		1	*2005*	–	–	–	–	1	1-25	0/0	54.00	0	5
Cummins Patrick James	8.5.1993		1	*2011*	15	13*	0	15.00	7	6-79	1/0	16.71	1	5/11
Dale Adam Craig	30.12.1968		2	*1997–1998*	6	5	0	2.00	6	3-71	0/0	31.16	0	30
Darling Joseph (*CY 1900*)	21.11.1870	2.1.1946	34	*1894*–1905	1,657	178	3	28.56	–	–	–/–	–	27	
Darling Leonard Stuart	14.8.1909	24.6.1992	12	*1932–1936*	474	85	0	27.88	0	0-3	0/0	–	8	
Darling Warrick Maxwell	1.5.1957		14	*1977–1979*	697	91	0	26.80	–	–	–/–	–	5	18
Davidson Alan Keith MBE (*CY 1962*)	14.6.1929		44	1953–*1962*	1,328	80	0	24.59	186	7-93	14/2	20.53	42	
Davis Ian Charles	25.6.1953		15	*1973*–1977	692	105	1	26.61	–	–	–/–	–	9	3
Davis Simon Peter	8.11.1959		1	*1985*	0	0	0	0.00	0	0-70	0/0	–	0	39
De Courcy James Harry	18.4.1927	20.6.2000	3	1953	81	41	0	16.20	–	–	–/–	–	3	
Dell Anthony Ross	6.8.1947		2	*1970–1973*	6	3*	0	–	6	3-65	0/0	26.66	0	
Dodemaide Anthony Ian Christopher	5.10.1963		10	*1987–1992*	202	50	0	22.44	34	6-58	1/0	28.02	6	24
Doherty Xavier John	22.12.1982		2	*2010*	27	16	0	9.00	3	2-41	0/0	102.00	0	37/8
Donnan Henry	12.11.1864	13.8.1956	5	*1891*–1896	75	15	0	8.33	0	0-22	0/0	–	2	
Dooland Bruce (*CY 1955*)	1.11.1923	8.9.1980	3	*1946–1947*	76	29	0	19.00	9	4-69	0/0	46.55	3	
Duff Reginald Alexander	17.8.1878	13.12.1911	22	*1901*–1905	1,317	146	2	35.59	4	2-43	0/0	21.25	14	
Duncan John Ross Frederick	25.3.1944		1	*1970*	3	3	0	3.00	0	0-30	0/0	–	0	
Dyer Gregory Charles	16.3.1959		6	*1986–1987*	131	60	0	21.83	–	–	–/–	–	22/2	23
Dymock Geoffrey	21.7.1945		21	*1973–1979*	236	31*	0	9.44	78	7-67	5/1	27.12	1	15
Dyson John	11.6.1954		30	*1977–1984*	1,359	127*	2	26.64	–	–	–/–	–	10	29
Eady Charles John	29.10.1870	20.12.1945	2	1896–*1901*	20	10*	0	6.66	7	3-30	0/0	16.00	2	
Eastwood Kenneth Humphrey	23.11.1935		1	*1970*	5	5	0	2.50	1	1-21	0/0	21.00	0	
Ebeling Hans Irvine	1.1.1905	12.1.1980	1	1934	43	41	0	21.50	3	3-74	0/0	29.66	0	
Edwards John Dunlop	12.6.1860	31.7.1911	3	1888	48	26	0	9.60	–	–	–/–	–	1	
Edwards Ross	1.12.1942		20	1972–1975	1,171	170*	2	40.37	0	0-20	0/0	–	7	9
Edwards Walter John	23.12.1949		3	*1974*	68	30	0	11.33	–	–	–/–	–	0	1

	Born	*Died*	*Tests*	*Test Career*	*Runs*	*HS*	*100s*	*Avge*	*Wkts*	*BB*	*5/10*	*Avge*	*Ct/St*	*O/T*
Elliott Matthew Thomas Gray (*CY 1998*)	28.9.1971		21	*1996–2004*	1,172	199	3	33.48	0	0-0	0/0	–	14	1
Emery Philip Allen	25.6.1964		1	*1994*	8	8*	0	–	–	–	–/–	–	5/1	1
Emery Sidney Hand	15.10.1885	7.1.1967	4	1912	6	5	0	3.00	5	2-46	0/0	49.80	2	
Evans Edwin	26.3.1849	2.7.1921	6	*1881*–1886	82	33	0	10.25	7	3-64	0/0	47.42	5	
Fairfax Alan George	16.6.1906	17.5.1955	10	*1928–1930*	410	65	0	51.25	21	4-31	0/0	30.71	15	
Favell Leslie Ernest MBE	6.10.1929	14.6.1987	19	*1954–1960*	757	101	1	27.03	–	–	–/–	–	9	
Ferris John James (*CY 1889*)	21.5.1867	17.11.1900	8†	*1886*–1890	98	20*	0	8.16	48	5-26	4/0	14.25	4	
Fingleton John Henry Webb OBE	28.4.1908	22.11.1981	18	*1931*–1938	1,189	136	5	42.46	–	–	–/–	–	13	
Fleetwood-Smith Leslie O'Brien ("Chuck")	30.3.1908	16.3.1971	10	*1935*–1938	54	16*	0	9.00	42	6-110	2/1	37.38	0	
Fleming Damien William	24.4.1970		20	*1994–2000*	305	71*	0	19.06	75	5-30	3/0	25.89	9	88
Francis Bruce Colin	18.2.1948		3	1972	52	27	0	10.40	–	–	–/–	–	1	
Freeman Eric Walter	13.7.1944		11	*1967–1969*	345	76	0	19.16	34	4-52	0/0	33.17	5	
Freer Frederick Alfred William	4.12.1915	2.11.1998	1	*1946*	28	28*	0	–	3	2-49	0/0	24.66	0	
Gannon John Bryant ("Sam")	8.2.1947		3	*1977*	3	3*	0	3.00	11	4-77	0/0	32.81	3	
Garrett Thomas William	26.7.1858	6.8.1943	19	*1876–1887*	339	51*	0	12.55	36	6-78	2/0	26.94	7	
Gaunt Ronald Arthur	26.2.1934	30.3.2012	3	*1957–1963*	6	3	0	3.00	7	3-53	0/0	44.28	1	
Gehrs Donald Raeburn Algernon	29.11.1880	25.6.1953	6	*1903–1910*	221	67	0	20.09	0	0-4	0/0	–	6	
George Peter Robert	16.10.1986		1	*2010*	2	2	0	1.00	2	2-48	0/0	38.50	0	
[2] **Giffen** George (*CY 1894*)	27.3.1859	29.11.1927	31	*1881*–1896	1,238	161	1	23.35	103	7-117	7/1	27.09	24	
[2] **Giffen** Walter Frank	20.9.1861	28.6.1949	3	*1886–1891*	11	3	0	1.83	–	–	–/–	–	1	
Gilbert David Robert	29.12.1960		9	1985–*1986*	57	15	0	7.12	16	3-48	0/0	52.68	0	14
Gilchrist Adam Craig (*CY 2002*)	14.11.1971		96§	*1999–2007*	5,570	204*	17	47.60	–	–	–/–	–	379/37	286‡/13
Gillespie Jason Neil (*CY 2002*)	19.4.1975		71	*1996–2005*	1,218	201*	1	18.73	259	7-37	8/0	26.13	27	97/1
Gilmour Gary John	26.6.1951		15	*1973–1976*	483	101	1	23.00	54	6-85	3/0	26.03	8	5
Gleeson John William	14.3.1938		29	*1967*–1972	395	45	0	10.39	93	5-61	3/0	36.20	17	
Graham Henry	22.11.1870	7.2.1911	6	1893–1896	301	107	2	30.10	–	–	–/–	–	3	
[2] **Gregory** David William	15.4.1845	4.8.1919	3	*1876–1878*	60	43	0	20.00	0	0-9	0/0	–	0	
[1,2] **Gregory** Edward James	29.5.1839	22.4.1899	1	*1876*	11	11	0	5.50	–	–	–/–	–	1	
Gregory Jack Morrison (*CY 1922*)	14.8.1895	7.8.1973	24	*1920–1928*	1,146	119	2	36.96	85	7-69	4/0	31.15	37	
Gregory Ross Gerald	28.2.1916	10.6.1942	2	*1936*	153	80	0	51.00	0	0-14	0/0	–	1	
[1] **Gregory** Sydney Edward (*CY 1897*)	14.4.1870	31.7.1929	58	1890–1912	2,282	201	4	24.53	0	0-4	0/0	–	25	
Grimmett Clarence Victor (*CY 1931*)	25.12.1891	2.5.1980	37	*1924–1935*	557	50	0	13.92	216	7-40	21/7	24.21	17	
Groube Thomas Underwood	2.9.1857	5.8.1927	1	1880	11	11	0	5.50	–	–	–/–	–	0	
Grout Arthur Theodore Wallace	30.3.1927	9.11.1968	51	*1957–1965*	890	74	0	15.08	–	–	–/–	–	163/24	
Guest Colin Ernest John	7.10.1937		1	*1962*	11	11	0	11.00	0	0-8	0/0	–	0	

§ Gilchrist's figures include 95 runs, five catches and two stumpings for Australia v the ICC World XI in the Super Series Test in 2005-06.

	Born	Died	Tests	Test Career	Runs	HS	100s	Avge	Wkts	BB	5/10	Avge	Ct/St	O/T
Haddin Bradley James	23.10.1977		43	2007–2011	2,256	169	3	35.80	–	–	–/–	–	160/4	93/25
Hamence Ronald Arthur	25.11.1915	24.3.2010	3	1946–1947	81	30*	0	27.00	–	–	–/–	–	1	
Hammond Jeffrey Roy	19.4.1950		5	1972	28	19	0	9.33	15	4-38	0/0	32.53	2	1
Harris Ryan James	11.10.1979		12	2009–2011	212	68*	0	17.66	47	6-47	2/0	23.63	4	21/3
Harry John	1.8.1857	27.10.1919	1	1894	8	6	0	4.00	–	–	–/–	–	1	
Hartigan Roger Joseph	12.12.1879	7.6.1958	2	1907	170	116	1	42.50	0	0-7	0/0	–	1	
Hartkopf Albert Ernst Victor	28.12.1889	20.5.1968	1	1924	80	80	0	40.00	1	1-120	0/0	134.00	0	
[2] **Harvey** Mervyn Roye	29.4.1918	18.3.1995	1	1946	43	31	0	21.50	–	–	–/–	–	0	
[2] **Harvey** Robert Neil MBE (*CY 1954*)	8.10.1928		79	1947–1962	6,149	205	21	48.41	3	1-8	0/0	40.00	64	
Hassett Arthur Lindsay MBE (*CY 1949*)	28.8.1913	16.6.1993	43	1938–1953	3,073	198*	10	46.56	0	0-1	0/0	–	30	
Hastings John Wayne	4.11.1985		1	2012	52	32	0	26.00	1	1-51	0/0	153.00	1	11/3
Hauritz Nathan Michael	18.10.1981		17	2004–2010	426	75	0	25.05	63	5-53	2/0	34.98	3	58/3
Hawke Neil James Napier	27.6.1939	25.12.2000	27	1962–1968	365	45*	0	16.59	91	7-105	6/1	29.41	9	
Hayden Matthew Lawrence (*CY 2003*)	29.10.1971		103§	1993–2008	8,625	380	30	50.73	0	0-7	0/0	–	128	160‡/9
Hazlitt Gervys Rignold	4.9.1888	30.10.1915	9	1907–1912	89	34*	0	11.12	23	7-25	1/0	27.08	4	
Healy Ian Andrew (*CY 1994*)	30.4.1964		119	1988–1999	4,356	161*	4	27.39	–	–	–/–	–	366/29	168
Hendry Hunter Scott Thomas Laurie ("Stork")	24.5.1895	16.12.1988	11	1921–1928	335	112	1	20.93	16	3-36	0/0	40.00	10	
Hibbert Paul Anthony	23.7.1952	27.11.2008	1	1977	15	13	0	7.50	–	–	–/–	–	1	
Higgs James Donald	11.7.1950		22	1977–1980	111	16	0	5.55	66	7-143	2/0	31.16	3	
Hilditch Andrew Mark Jefferson	20.5.1956		18	1978–1985	1,073	119	2	31.55	–	–	–/–	–	13	8
Hilfenhaus Benjamin William	15.3.1983		27	2008–2012	355	56*	0	13.65	99	5-75	2/0	28.50	7	25/7
Hill Clement (*CY 1900*)	18.3.1877	5.9.1945	49	1896–1911	3,412	191	7	39.21	–	–	–/–	–	33	
Hill John Charles	25.6.1923	11.8.1974	3	1953–1954	21	8*	0	7.00	8	3-35	0/0	34.12	2	
Hoare Desmond Edward	19.10.1934		1	1960	35	35	0	17.50	2	2-68	0/0	78.00	2	
Hodge Bradley John	29.12.1974		6	2005–2007	503	203*	1	55.88	0	0-8	0/0	–	9	25/8
Hodges John Robart	11.8.1855	d unknown	2	1876	10	8	0	3.33	6	2-7	0/0	14.00	0	
Hogan Tom George	23.9.1956		7	1982–1983	205	42*	0	18.63	15	5-66	1/0	47.06	2	16
Hogg George Bradley	6.2.1971		7	1996–2007	186	79	0	26.57	17	2-40	0/0	54.88	1	123/12
Hogg Rodney Malcolm	5.3.1951		38	1978–1984	439	52	0	9.75	123	6-74	6/2	28.47	7	71
Hohns Trevor Victor	23.1.1954		7	1988–1989	136	40	0	22.66	17	3-59	0/0	34.11	3	
Hole Graeme Blake	6.1.1931	14.2.1990	18	1950–1954	789	66	0	25.45	3	1-9	0/0	42.00	21	
Holland Robert George	19.10.1946		11	1984–1985	35	10	0	3.18	34	6-54	3/2	39.76	5	2
Hookes David William	3.5.1955	19.1.2004	23	1976–1985	1,306	143*	1	34.36	1	1-4	0/0	41.00	12	39
Hopkins Albert John Young	3.5.1874	25.4.1931	20	1901–1909	509	43	0	16.41	26	4-81	0/0	26.76	11	
Horan Thomas Patrick	8.3.1854	16.4.1916	15	1876–1884	471	124	1	18.84	11	6-40	1/0	13.00	6	

§ *Hayden's figures include 188 runs and three catches for Australia v the ICC World XI in the Super Series Test in 2005-06.*

	Born	Died	Tests	Test Career	Runs	HS	100s	Avge	Wkts	BB	5/10	Avge	Ct/St	O/T
Hordern Herbert Vivian MBE	10.2.1883	17.6.1938	7	*1910–1911*	254	50	0	23.09	46	7-90	5/2	23.36	6	
Hornibrook Percival Mitchell	27.7.1899	25.8.1976	6	*1928*–1930	60	26	0	10.00	17	7-92	1/0	39.05	7	
Howell William Peter	29.12.1869	14.7.1940	18	*1897–1903*	158	35	0	7.52	49	5-81	1/0	28.71	12	
Hughes Kimberley John (*CY 1981*)	26.1.1954		70	1977–*1984*	4,415	213	9	37.41	0	0-0	0/0	–	50	97
Hughes Mervyn Gregory (*CY 1994*)	23.11.1961		53	*1985–1993*	1,032	72*	0	16.64	212	8-87	7/1	28.38	23	33
Hughes Phillip Joel	30.11.1988		20	*2008–2012*	1,305	160	3	36.25	–	–	–/–	–	10	
Hunt William Alfred	26.8.1908	30.12.1983	1	*1931*	0	0	0	0.00	0	0-14	0/0	–	1	
Hurst Alan George	15.7.1950		12	*1973–1979*	102	26	0	6.00	43	5-28	2/0	27.90	3	8
Hurwood Alexander	17.6.1902	26.9.1982	2	*1930*	5	5	0	2.50	11	4-22	0/0	15.45	2	
Hussey Michael Edward Killeen	27.5.1975		79	*2005–2012*	6,235	195	19	51.52	7	1-0	0/0	43.71	85	185/38
Inverarity Robert John	31.1.1944		6	1968–1972	174	56	0	17.40	4	3-26	0/0	23.25	4	
Iredale Francis Adams	19.6.1867	15.4.1926	14	*1894*–1899	807	140	2	36.68	0	0-3	0/0	–	16	
Ironmonger Herbert	7.4.1882	31.5.1971	14	*1928–1932*	42	12	0	2.62	74	7-23	4/2	17.97	3	
Iverson John Brian	27.7.1915	24.10.1973	5	*1950*	3	1*	0	0.75	21	6-27	1/0	15.23	2	
Jackson Archibald Alexander	5.9.1909	16.2.1933	8	*1928–1930*	474	164	1	47.40	–	–	–/–	–	7	
Jaques Philip Anthony	3.5.1979		11	*2005–2007*	902	150	3	47.47	–	–	–/–	–	7	6
Jarman Barrington Noel	17.2.1936		19	*1959–1968*	400	78	0	14.81	–	–	–/–	–	50/4	
Jarvis Arthur Harwood	19.10.1860	15.11.1933	11	*1884–1894*	303	82	0	16.83	–	–	–/–	–	9/9	
Jenner Terrence James	8.9.1944	24.5.2011	9	*1970–1975*	208	74	0	23.11	24	5-90	1/0	31.20	5	1
Jennings Claude Burrows	5.6.1884	20.6.1950	6	1912	107	32	0	17.83	–	–	–/–	–	5	
Johnson Ian William Geddes CBE	8.12.1917	9.10.1998	45	*1945–1956*	1,000	77	0	18.51	109	7-44	3/0	29.19	30	
Johnson Leonard Joseph	18.3.1919	20.4.1977	1	*1947*	25	25*	0	–	6	3-8	0/0	12.33	2	
Johnson Mitchell Guy	2.11.1981		50	*2007–2012*	1,403	123*	1	22.62	205	8-61	7/2	30.63	17	112/28
Johnston William Arras (*CY 1949*)	26.2.1922	25.5.2007	40	*1947–1954*	273	29	0	11.37	160	6-44	7/0	23.91	16	
Jones Dean Mervyn (*CY 1990*)	24.3.1961		52	*1983–1992*	3,631	216	11	46.55	1	1-5	0/0	64.00	34	164
Jones Ernest	30.9.1869	23.11.1943	19	*1894–1902*	126	20	0	5.04	64	7-88	3/1	29.01	21	
Jones Samuel Percy	1.8.1861	14.7.1951	12	*1881–1887*	428	87	0	21.40	6	4-47	0/0	18.66	12	
Joslin Leslie Ronald	13.12.1947		1	*1967*	9	7	0	4.50	–	–	–/–	–	0	
Julian Brendon Paul	10.8.1970		7	1993–*1995*	128	56*	0	16.00	15	4-36	0/0	39.93	4	25
Kasprowicz Michael Scott	10.2.1972		38	*1996–2005*	445	25	0	10.59	113	7-36	4/0	32.88	16	43/2
Katich Simon Mathew	21.8.1975		56§	2001–*2010*	4,188	157	10	45.03	21	6-65	1/0	30.23	39	45/3
Kelleway Charles	25.4.1886	16.11.1944	26	*1910–1928*	1,422	147	3	37.42	52	5-33	1/0	32.36	24	
Kelly James Joseph (*CY 1903*)	10.5.1867	14.8.1938	36	1896–1905	664	46*	0	17.02	–	–	–/–	–	43/20	
Kelly Thomas Joseph Dart	3.5.1844	20.7.1893	2	*1876–1878*	64	35	0	21.33	–	–	–/–	–	1	
Kendall Thomas Kingston	24.8.1851	17.8.1924	2	*1876*	39	17*	0	13.00	14	7-55	1/0	15.35	2	

§ Katich's figures include two runs and one catch for Australia v the ICC World XI in the Super Series Test in 2005-06.

	Born	*Died*	*Tests*	*Test Career*	*Runs*	*HS*	*100s*	*Avge*	*Wkts*	*BB*	*5/10*	*Avge*	*Ct/St*	*O/T*
Kent Martin Francis	23.11.1953		3	1981	171	54	0	28.50	–	–	–/–	–	6	5
Kerr Robert Byers	16.6.1961		2	*1985*	31	17	0	7.75	–	–	–/–	–	1	4
Khawaja Usman Tariq	18.12.1986		6	*2010–2011*	263	65	0	29.22	–	–	–/–	–	3	
Kippax Alan Falconer	25.5.1897	5.9.1972	22	*1924*–1934	1,192	146	2	36.12	0	0-2	0/0	–	13	
Kline Lindsay Francis	29.9.1934		13	*1957–1960*	58	15*	0	8.28	34	7-75	1/0	22.82	9	
Krejza Jason John	14.1.1983		2	*2008*	71	32	0	23.66	13	8-215	1/1	43.23	4	8
Laird Bruce Malcolm	21.11.1950		21	*1979–1982*	1,341	92	0	35.28	0	0-3	0/0	–	16	23
Langer Justin Lee (*CY 2001*)	21.11.1970		105§	*1992–2006*	7,696	250	23	45.27	0	0-3	0/0	–	73	8
Langley Gilbert Roche Andrews (*CY 1957*)	14.9.1919	14.5.2001	26	*1951–1956*	374	53	0	14.96	–	–	–/–	–	83/15	
Laughlin Trevor John	30.1.1951		3	*1977–1978*	87	35	0	17.40	6	5-101	1/0	43.66	3	6
Laver Frank Jonas	7.12.1869	24.9.1919	15	1899–1909	196	45	0	11.52	37	8-31	2/0	26.05	8	
Law Stuart Grant (*CY 1998*)	18.10.1968		1	*1995*	54	54*	0	–	0	0-9	0/0	–	1	54
Lawry William Morris (*CY 1962*)	11.2.1937		67	1961–*1970*	5,234	210	13	47.15	0	0-0	0/0	–	30	1
Lawson Geoffrey Francis	7.12.1957		46	*1980–1989*	894	74	0	15.96	180	8-112	11/2	30.56	10	79
Lee Brett (*CY 2006*)	8.11.1976		76§	*1999–2008*	1,451	64	0	20.15	310	5-30	10/0	30.81	23	221/25
Lee Philip Keith	15.9.1904	9.8.1980	2	*1931–1932*	57	42	0	19.00	5	4-111	0/0	42.40	1	
Lehmann Darren Scott (*CY 2001*)	5.2.1970		27	*1997–2004*	1,798	177	5	44.95	15	3-42	0/0	27.46	11	117
Lillee Dennis Keith MBE (*CY 1973*)	18.7.1949		70	*1970–1983*	905	73*	0	13.71	355	7-83	23/7	23.92	23	63
Lindwall Raymond Russell MBE (*CY 1949*)	3.10.1921	23.6.1996	61	*1945–1959*	1,502	118	2	21.15	228	7-38	12/0	23.03	26	
Love Hampden Stanley Bray	10.8.1895	22.7.1969	1	*1932*	8	5	0	4.00	–	–	–/–	–	3	
Love Martin Lloyd	30.3.1974		5	*2002–2003*	233	100*	1	46.60	–	–	–/–	–	7	
Loxton Samuel John Everett OBE	29.3.1921	3.12.2011	12	*1947–1950*	554	101	1	36.93	8	3-55	0/0	43.62	7	
Lyon Nathan Michael	20.11.1987		19	*2011–2012*	178	40*	0	13.69	61	5-34	2/0	32.16	5	2
Lyons John James	21.5.1863	21.7.1927	14	*1886–1897*	731	134	1	27.07	6	5-30	1/0	24.83	3	
McAlister Peter Alexander	11.7.1869	10.5.1938	8	*1903*–1909	252	41	0	16.80	–	–	–/–	–	10	
Macartney Charles George (*CY 1922*)	27.6.1886	9.9.1958	35	*1907*–1926	2,131	170	7	41.78	45	7-58	2/1	27.55	17	
McCabe Stanley Joseph (*CY 1935*)	16.7.1910	25.8.1968	39	1930–1938	2,748	232	6	48.21	36	4-13	0/0	42.86	41	
McCool Colin Leslie	9.12.1916	5.4.1986	14	*1945–1949*	459	104*	1	35.30	36	5-41	3/0	26.61	14	
McCormick Ernest Leslie	16.5.1906	28.6.1991	12	*1935*–1938	54	17*	0	6.00	36	4-101	0/0	29.97	8	
McCosker Richard Bede (*CY 1976*)	11.12.1946		25	*1974–1979*	1,622	127	4	39.56	–	–	–/–	–	21	14
McDermott Craig John (*CY 1986*)	14.4.1965		71	*1984–1995*	940	42*	0	12.20	291	8-97	14/2	28.63	19	138
McDonald Andrew Barry	15.6.1981		4	*2008*	107	68	0	21.40	9	3-25	0/0	33.33	2	
McDonald Colin Campbell	17.11.1928		47	*1951*–1961	3,107	170	5	39.32	0	0-3	0/0	–	14	
McDonald Edgar Arthur (*CY 1922*)	6.1.1891	22.7.1937	11	*1920–1921*	116	36	0	16.57	43	5-32	2/0	33.27	3	
McDonnell Percy Stanislaus	13.11.1858	24.9.1896	19	1880–1888	955	147	3	28.93	0	0-11	0/0	–	6	

§ *Langer's figures include 22 runs and one catch and Lee's four runs, two wickets and one catch for Australia v the ICC World XI in the Super Series Test in 2005-06.*

	Born	Died	Tests	Test Career	Runs	HS	100s	Avge	Wkts	BB	5/10	Avge	Ct/St	O/T
McGain Bryce Edward	25.3.1972		1	2008	2	2	0	1.00	0	0-149	0/0	–	0	
MacGill Stuart Charles Glyndwr	25.2.1971		44§	1997–2007	349	43	0	9.69	208	8-108	12/2	29.02	16	3
McGrath Glenn Donald (*CY 1998*)	9.2.1970		124§	1993–2006	641	61	0	7.36	563	8-24	29/3	21.64	38	249‡/2
McIlwraith John	7.9.1857	5.7.1938	1	1886	9	7	0	4.50	–	–	–/–	–	1	
McIntyre Peter Edward	27.4.1966		2	1994–1996	22	16	0	7.33	5	3-103	0/0	38.80	0	
McKay Clinton James	22.2.1983		1	2009	10	10	0	10.00	1	1-56	0/0	101.00	1	32/4
Mackay Kenneth Donald MBE	24.10.1925	13.6.1982	37	1956–1962	1,507	89	0	33.48	50	6-42	2/0	34.42	16	
McKenzie Graham Douglas (*CY 1965*)	24.6.1941		60	1961–1970	945	76	0	12.27	246	8-71	16/3	29.78	34	1
McKibbin Thomas Robert	10.12.1870	15.12.1939	5	1894–1897	88	28*	0	14.66	17	3-35	0/0	29.17	4	
McLaren John William	22.12.1886	17.11.1921	1	1911	0	0*	0	–	1	1-23	0/0	70.00	0	
Maclean John Alexander	27.4.1946		4	1978	79	33*	0	11.28	–	–	–/–	–	18	2
[2] **McLeod** Charles Edward	24.10.1869	26.11.1918	17	1894–1905	573	112	1	23.87	33	5-65	2/0	40.15	9	
[2] **McLeod** Robert William	19.1.1868	14.6.1907	6	1891–1893	146	31	0	13.27	12	5-53	1/0	31.83	3	
McShane Patrick George	18.4.1858	11.12.1903	3	1884–1887	26	12*	0	5.20	1	1-39	0/0	48.00	2	
Maddocks Leonard Victor	24.5.1926		7	1954–1956	177	69	0	17.70	–	–	–/–	–	19/1	
Maguire John Norman	15.9.1956		3	1983	28	15*	0	7.00	10	4-57	0/0	32.30	2	23
Mailey Arthur Alfred	3.1.1886	31.12.1967	21	1920–1926	222	46*	0	11.10	99	9-121	6/2	33.91	14	
Mallett Ashley Alexander	13.7.1945		38	1968–1980	430	43*	0	11.62	132	8-59	6/1	29.84	30	9
Malone Michael Francis	9.10.1950		1	1977	46	46	0	46.00	6	5-63	1/0	12.83	0	10
Mann Anthony Longford	8.11.1945		4	1977	189	105	1	23.62	4	3-12	0/0	79.00	2	
Manou Graham Allan	23.4.1979		1	2009	21	13*	0	21.00	–	–	–/–	–	3	4
Marr Alfred Percy	28.3.1862	15.3.1940	1	1884	5	5	0	2.50	0	0-3	0/0	–	0	
[1] **Marsh** Geoffrey Robert	31.12.1958		50	1985–1991	2,854	138	4	33.18	–	–	–/–	–	38	117
Marsh Rodney William MBE (*CY 1982*)	4.11.1947		96	1970–1983	3,633	132	3	26.51	0	0-3	0/0	–	343/12	92
[1] **Marsh** Shaun Edward	9.7.1983		7	2011	301	141	1	27.36	–	–	–/–	–	4	36/8
Martin John Wesley	28.7.1931	16.7.1992	8	1960–1966	214	55	0	17.83	17	3-56	0/0	48.94	5	
Martyn Damien Richard (*CY 2002*)	21.10.1971		67	1992–2006	4,406	165	13	46.37	2	1-0	0/0	84.00	36	208/4
Massie Hugh Hamon	11.4.1854	12.10.1938	9	1881–1884	249	55	0	15.56	–	–	–/–	–	5	
Massie Robert Arnold Lockyer (*CY 1973*)	14.4.1947		6	1972–1972	78	42	0	11.14	31	8-53	2/1	20.87	1	3
Matthews Christopher Darrell	22.9.1962		3	1986–1988	54	32	0	10.80	6	3-95	0/0	52.16	1	
Matthews Gregory Richard John	15.12.1959		33	1983–1992	1,849	130	4	41.08	61	5-103	2/1	48.22	17	59
Matthews Thomas James	3.4.1884	14.10.1943	8	1911–1912	153	53	0	17.00	16	4-29	0/0	26.18	7	
May Timothy Brian Alexander	26.1.1962		24	1987–1994	225	42*	0	14.06	75	5-9	3/0	34.74	6	47
Mayne Edgar Richard	2.7.1882	26.10.1961	4	1912–1921	64	25*	0	21.33	0	0-1	0/0	–	2	
Mayne Lawrence Charles	23.1.1942		6	1964–1969	76	13	0	9.50	19	4-43	0/0	33.05	3	

§ MacGill's figures include no runs and nine wickets and McGrath's two runs and three wickets for Australia v the ICC World XI in the Super Series Test in 2005-06.

	Born	Died	Tests	Test Career	Runs	HS	100s	Avge	Wkts	BB	5/10	Avge	Ct/St	O/T
Meckiff Ian	6.1.1935		18	*1957–1963*	154	45*	0	11.84	45	6-38	2/0	31.62	9	
Meuleman Kenneth Douglas	5.9.1923	10.9.2004	1	*1945*	0	0	0	0.00	–	–	–/–	–	1	
Midwinter William Evans	19.6.1851	3.12.1890	8†	*1876–1886*	174	37	0	13.38	14	5-78	1/0	23.78	5	
Miller Colin Reid	6.2.1964		18	*1998–2000*	174	43	0	8.28	69	5-32	3/1	26.15	6	
Miller Keith Ross MBE (*CY 1954*)	28.11.1919	11.10.2004	55	*1945–1956*	2,958	147	7	36.97	170	7-60	7/1	22.97	38	
Minnett Roy Baldwin	13.6.1888	21.10.1955	9	*1911*–1912	391	90	0	26.06	11	4-34	0/0	26.36	0	
Misson Francis Michael	19.11.1938		5	*1960*–1961	38	25*	0	19.00	16	4-58	0/0	38.50	6	
Moody Thomas Masson (*CY 2000*)	2.10.1965		8	*1989–1992*	456	106	2	32.57	2	1-17	0/0	73.50	9	76
Moroney John	24.7.1917	1.7.1999	7	*1949–1951*	383	118	2	34.81	–	–	–/–	–	0	
Morris Arthur Robert MBE (*CY 1949*)	19.1.1922		46	*1946–1954*	3,533	206	12	46.48	2	1-5	0/0	25.00	15	
Morris Samuel	22.6.1855	20.9.1931	1	*1884*	14	10*	0	14.00	2	2-73	0/0	36.50	0	
Moses Henry	13.2.1858	7.12.1938	6	*1886–1894*	198	33	0	19.80	–	–	–/–	–	1	
Moss Jeffrey Kenneth	29.6.1947		1	*1978*	60	38*	0	60.00	–	–	–/–	–	0	1
Moule William Henry	31.1.1858	24.8.1939	1	1880	40	34	0	20.00	3	3-23	0/0	7.66	1	
Muller Scott Andrew	11.7.1971		2	*1999*	6	6*	0	–	7	3-68	0/0	36.85	2	
Murdoch William Lloyd	18.10.1854	18.2.1911	18†	*1876*–1890	896	211	2	32.00	–	–	–/–	–	14	
Musgrove Henry Alfred	27.11.1858	2.11.1931	1	*1884*	13	9	0	6.50	–	–	–/–	–	0	
Nagel Lisle Ernest	6.3.1905	23.11.1971	1	*1932*	21	21*	0	21.00	2	2-110	0/0	55.00	0	
Nash Laurence John	2.5.1910	24.7.1986	2	*1931–1936*	30	17	0	15.00	10	4-18	0/0	12.60	6	
Nicholson Matthew James	2.10.1974		1	*1998*	14	9	0	7.00	4	3-56	0/0	28.75	0	
Nitschke Homesdale Carl ("Jack")	14.4.1905	29.9.1982	2	*1931*	53	47	0	26.50	–	–	–/–	–	3	
Noble Montague Alfred (*CY 1900*)	28.1.1873	22.6.1940	42	*1897*–1909	1,997	133	1	30.25	121	7-17	9/2	25.00	26	
Noblet Geffery	14.9.1916	16.8.2006	3	*1949–1952*	22	13*	0	7.33	7	3-21	0/0	26.14	1	
North Marcus James	28.7.1979		21	*2008–2010*	1,171	128	5	35.48	14	6-55	1/0	42.21	17	2/1
Nothling Otto Ernest	1.8.1900	26.9.1965	1	*1928*	52	44	0	26.00	0	0-12	0/0	–	0	
O'Brien Leo Patrick Joseph	2.7.1907	13.3.1997	5	*1932–1936*	211	61	0	26.37	–	–	–/–	–	3	
O'Connor John Denis Alphonsus	9.9.1875	23.8.1941	4	*1907*–1909	86	20	0	12.28	13	5-40	1/0	26.15	3	
O'Donnell Simon Patrick	26.1.1963		6	1985–*1985*	206	48	0	29.42	6	3-37	0/0	84.00	4	87
Ogilvie Alan David	3.6.1951		5	*1977*	178	47	0	17.80	–	–	–/–	–	5	
O'Keeffe Kerry James	25.11.1949		24	*1970*–1977	644	85	0	25.76	53	5-101	1/0	38.07	15	2
Oldfield William Albert Stanley MBE (*CY 1927*)	9.9.1894	10.8.1976	54	*1920–1936*	1,427	65*	0	22.65	–	–	–/–	–	78/52	
O'Neill Norman Clifford Louis (*CY 1962*)	19.2.1937	3.3.2008	42	*1958–1964*	2,779	181	6	45.55	17	4-41	0/0	39.23	21	
O'Reilly William Joseph OBE (*CY 1935*)	20.12.1905	6.10.1992	27	*1931–1945*	410	56*	0	12.81	144	7-54	11/3	22.59	7	
Oxenham Ronald Keven	28.7.1891	16.8.1939	7	*1928–1931*	151	48	0	15.10	14	4-39	0/0	37.28	4	
Paine Timothy David	8.12.1984		4	2010–*2010*	287	92	0	35.87	–	–	–/–	–	16/1	26/5
Palmer George Eugene ("Joey")	22.2.1859	22.8.1910	17	1880–1886	296	48	0	14.09	78	7-65	6/2	21.51	13	

	Born	Died	Tests	Test Career	Runs	HS	100s	Avge	Wkts	BB	5/10	Avge	Ct/St	O/T
Park Roy Lindsay	30.7.1892	23.1.1947	1	1920	0	0	0	0.00	0	0-9	0/0	–	0	
Pascoe Leonard Stephen	13.2.1950		14	1977–1981	106	30*	0	10.60	64	5-59	1/0	26.06	2	29
2 **Pattinson** James Lee	3.5.1990		7	2011–2012	191	42	0	38.20	31	5-27	2/0	22.09	0	11/4
Pellew Clarence Everard ("Nip")	21.9.1893	9.5.1981	10	1920–1921	484	116	2	37.23	0	0-3	0/0	–	4	
Phillips Wayne Bentley	1.3.1958		27	1983–1985	1,485	159	2	32.28	–	–	–/–	–	52	48
Phillips Wayne Norman	7.11.1962		1	1991	22	14	0	11.00	–	–	–/–	–	0	
Philpott Peter Ian	21.11.1934		8	1964–1965	93	22	0	10.33	26	5-90	1/0	38.46	5	
Ponsford William Harold MBE (*CY 1935*)	19.10.1900	6.4.1991	29	1924–1934	2,122	266	7	48.22	–	–	–/–	–	21	
Ponting Ricky Thomas (*CY 2006*)	19.12.1974		168§	1995–2012	13,378	257	41	51.85	5	1-0	0/0	55.20	196	374‡/17
Pope Roland James	18.2.1864	27.7.1952	1	1884	3	3	0	1.50	–	–	–/–	–	0	
Quiney Robert John	20.8.1982		2	2012	9	9	0	3.00	0	0-3	0/0	–	5	
Rackemann Carl Gray	3.6.1960		12	1982–1990	53	15*	0	5.30	39	6-86	3/1	29.15	2	52
Ransford Vernon Seymour (*CY 1910*)	20.3.1885	19.3.1958	20	1907–1911	1,211	143*	1	37.84	1	1-9	0/0	28.00	10	
Redpath Ian Ritchie MBE	11.5.1941		66	1963–1975	4,737	171	8	43.45	0	0-0	0/0	–	83	5
Reedman John Cole	9.10.1865	25.3.1924	1	1894	21	17	0	10.50	1	1-12	0/0	24.00	1	
Reid Bruce Anthony	14.3.1963		27	1985–1992	93	13	0	4.65	113	7-51	5/2	24.63	5	61
Reiffel Paul Ronald	19.4.1966		35	1991–1997	955	79*	0	26.52	104	6-71	5/0	26.96	15	92
Renneberg David Alexander	23.9.1942		8	1966–1967	22	9	0	3.66	23	5-39	2/0	36.08	2	
Richardson Arthur John	24.7.1888	23.12.1973	9	1924–1926	403	100	1	31.00	12	2-20	0/0	43.41	1	
4 **Richardson** Victor York OBE	7.9.1894	30.10.1969	19	1924–1935	706	138	1	23.53	–	–	–/–	–	24	
Rigg Keith Edward	21.5.1906	28.2.1995	8	1930–1936	401	127	1	33.41	–	–	–/–	–	5	
Ring Douglas Thomas	14.10.1918	23.6.2003	13	1947–1953	426	67	0	22.42	35	6-72	2/0	37.28	5	
Ritchie Gregory Michael	23.1.1960		30	1982–1986	1,690	146	3	35.20	0	0-10	0/0	–	14	44
Rixon Stephen John	25.2.1954		13	1977–1984	394	54	0	18.76	–	–	–/–	–	42/5	6
Robertson Gavin Ron	28.5.1966		4	1997–1998	140	57	0	20.00	13	4-72	0/0	39.61	1	13
Robertson William Roderick	6.10.1861	24.6.1938	1	1884	2	2	0	1.00	0	0-24	0/0	–	0	
Robinson Richard Daryl	8.6.1946		3	1977	100	34	0	16.66	–	–	–/–	–	4	2
Robinson Rayford Harold	26.3.1914	10.8.1965	1	1936	5	3	0	2.50	–	–	–/–	–	1	
Rogers Christopher John Llewellyn	31.8.1977		1	2007	19	15	0	9.50	–	–	–/–	–	1	
Rorke Gordon Frederick	27.6.1938		4	1958–1959	9	7	0	4.50	10	3-23	0/0	20.30	1	
Rutherford John Walter	25.9.1929		1	1956	30	30	0	30.00	1	1-11	0/0	15.00	0	
Ryder John	8.8.1889	3.4.1977	20	1920–1928	1,394	201*	3	51.62	17	2-20	0/0	43.70	17	
Saggers Ronald Arthur	15.5.1917	17.3.1987	6	1948–1949	30	14	0	10.00	–	–	–/–	–	16/8	
Saunders John Victor	21.3.1876	21.12.1927	14	1901–1907	39	11*	0	2.29	79	7-34	6/0	22.73	5	
Scott Henry James Herbert	26.12.1858	23.9.1910	8	1884–1886	359	102	1	27.61	0	0-9	0/0	–	8	

§ Ponting's figures include 100 runs and one catch for Australia v the ICC World XI in the Super Series Test in 2005-06.

	Born	*Died*	*Tests*	*Test Career*	*Runs*	*HS*	*100s*	*Avge*	*Wkts*	*BB*	*5/10*	*Avge*	*Ct/St*	*O/T*
Sellers Reginald Hugh Durning	20.8.1940		1	*1964*	0	0	0	0.00	0	0-17	0/0	–	1	
Serjeant Craig Stanton	1.11.1951		12	1977–*1977*	522	124	1	23.72	–	–	–/–	–	13	3
[5] **Sheahan** Andrew Paul	30.9.1946		31	*1967–1973*	1,594	127	2	33.91	–	–	–/–	–	17	3
Shepherd Barry Kenneth	23.4.1937	17.9.2001	9	*1962–1964*	502	96	0	41.83	0	0-3	0/0	–	2	
Siddle Peter Matthew	25.11.1984		37	*2008–2012*	649	43	0	15.45	141	6-54	6/0	28.51	16	17/2
Sievers Morris William	13.4.1912	10.5.1968	3	*1936*	67	25*	0	13.40	9	5-21	1/0	17.88	4	
Simpson Robert Baddeley (*CY 1965*)	3.2.1936		62	*1957–1977*	4,869	311	10	46.81	71	5-57	2/0	42.26	110	2
Sincock David John	1.2.1942		3	*1964–1965*	80	29	0	26.66	8	3-67	0/0	51.25	2	
Slater Keith Nichol	12.3.1936		1	*1958*	1	1*	0	–	2	2-40	0/0	50.50	0	
Slater Michael Jonathon	21.2.1970		74	1993–2001	5,312	219	14	42.83	1	1-4	0/0	10.00	33	42
Sleep Peter Raymond	4.5.1957		14	*1978–1989*	483	90	0	24.15	31	5-72	1/0	45.06	4	
Slight James	20.10.1855	9.12.1930	1	1880	11	11	0	5.50	–	–	–/–	–	0	
Smith David Bertram Miller	14.9.1884	29.7.1963	2	1912	30	24*	0	15.00	–	–	–/–	–	0	
Smith Steven Barry	18.10.1961		3	*1983*	41	12	0	8.20	–	–	–/–	–	1	28
Smith Steven Peter Devereux	2.6.1989		5	2010–*2010*	259	77	0	28.77	3	3-51	0/0	73.33	3	32/20
Spofforth Frederick Robert	9.9.1853	4.6.1926	18	*1876–1886*	217	50	0	9.43	94	7-44	7/4	18.41	11	
Stackpole Keith Raymond MBE (*CY 1973*)	10.7.1940		43	*1965–1973*	2,807	207	7	37.42	15	2-33	0/0	66.73	47	6
Starc Mitchell Aaron	13.1.1990		7	*2011–2012*	182	68*	0	30.33	28	6-154	2/0	29.32	2	11/8
Stevens Gavin Byron	29.2.1932		4	*1959*	112	28	0	16.00	–	–	–/–	–	2	
Symonds Andrew	9.6.1975		26	*2003–2008*	1,462	162*	2	40.61	24	3-50	0/0	37.33	22	198/14
Taber Hedley Brian	29.4.1940		16	*1966–1969*	353	48	0	16.04	–	–	–/–	–	56/4	
Tait Shaun William	22.2.1983		3	2005–*2007*	20	8	0	6.66	5	3-97	0/0	60.40	1	35/19
Tallon Donald (*CY 1949*)	17.2.1916	7.9.1984	21	*1945*–1953	394	92	0	17.13	–	–	–/–	–	50/8	
Taylor John Morris	10.10.1895	12.5.1971	20	*1920*–1926	997	108	1	35.60	1	1-25	0/0	45.00	11	
Taylor Mark Anthony (*CY 1990*)	27.10.1964		104	*1988–1998*	7,525	334*	19	43.49	1	1-11	0/0	26.00	157	113
Taylor Peter Laurence	22.8.1956		13	*1986–1991*	431	87	0	26.93	27	6-78	1/0	39.55	10	83
Thomas Grahame	21.3.1938		8	*1964–1965*	325	61	0	29.54	–	–	–/–	–	3	
Thoms George Ronald	22.3.1927	29.8.2003	1	*1951*	44	28	0	22.00	–	–	–/–	–	0	
Thomson Alan Lloyd ("Froggy")	2.12.1945		4	*1970*	22	12*	0	22.00	12	3-79	0/0	54.50	0	1
Thomson Jeffrey Robert	16.8.1950		51	*1972*–1985	679	49	0	12.81	200	6-46	8/0	28.00	20	50
Thomson Nathaniel Frampton Davis	29.5.1839	2.9.1896	2	*1876*	67	41	0	16.75	1	1-14	0/0	31.00	3	
Thurlow Hugh Motley ("Pud")	10.1.1903	3.12.1975	1	*1931*	0	0	0	0.00	0	0-33	0/0	–	0	
Toohey Peter Michael	20.4.1954		15	*1977–1979*	893	122	1	31.89	0	0-4	0/0	–	9	5
Toshack Ernest Raymond Herbert	8.12.1914	11.5.2003	12	*1945*–1948	73	20*	0	14.60	47	6-29	4/1	21.04	4	
Travers Joseph Patrick Francis	10.1.1871	15.9.1942	1	*1901*	10	9	0	5.00	1	1-14	0/0	14.00	1	
Tribe George Edward (*CY 1955*)	4.10.1920	5.4.2009	3	*1946*	35	25*	0	17.50	2	2-48	0/0	165.00	0	

	Born	Died	Tests	Test Career	Runs	HS	100s	Avge	Wkts	BB	5/10	Avge	Ct/St	O/T
[2]**Trott** Albert Edwin (*CY 1899*)	6.2.1873	30.7.1914	3†	*1894*	205	85*	0	102.50	9	8-43	1/0	21.33	4	
[2]**Trott** George Henry Stevens (*CY 1894*)	5.8.1866	10.11.1917	24	1888–*1897*	921	143	1	21.92	29	4-71	0/0	35.13	21	
[2]**Trumble** Hugh (*CY 1897*)	12.5.1867	14.8.1938	32	1890–*1903*	851	70	0	19.79	141	8-65	9/3	21.78	45	
[2]**Trumble** John William	16.9.1863	17.8.1944	7	*1884*–1886	243	59	0	20.25	10	3-29	0/0	22.20	3	
Trumper Victor Thomas (*CY 1903*)	2.11.1877	28.6.1915	48	1899–*1911*	3,163	214*	8	39.04	8	3-60	0/0	39.62	31	
Turner Alan	23.7.1950		14	1975–*1976*	768	136	1	29.53	–	–	–/–	–	15	6
Turner Charles Thomas Biass (*CY 1889*)	16.11.1862	1.1.1944	17	*1886–1894*	323	29	0	11.53	101	7-43	11/2	16.53	8	
Veivers Thomas Robert	6.4.1937		21	*1963–1966*	813	88	0	31.26	33	4-68	0/0	41.66	7	
Veletta Michael Robert John	30.10.1963		8	*1987–1989*	207	39	0	18.81	–	–	–/–	–	12	20
Wade Matthew Scott	26.12.1987		9	*2011–2012*	510	106	2	42.50	0	0-0	0/0	–	29/2	25/15
Waite Mervyn George	7.1.1911	16.12.1985	2	1938	11	8	0	3.66	1	1-150	0/0	190.00	1	
Walker Maxwell Henry Norman	12.9.1948		34	*1972*–1977	586	78*	0	19.53	138	8-143	6/0	27.47	12	17
Wall Thomas Welbourn ("Tim")	13.5.1904	26.3.1981	18	*1928*–1934	121	20	0	6.36	56	5-14	3/0	35.89	11	
Walters Francis Henry	9.2.1860	1.6.1922	1	*1884*	12	7	0	6.00	–	–	–/–	–	2	
Walters Kevin Douglas MBE	21.12.1945		74	*1965–1980*	5,357	250	15	48.26	49	5-66	1/0	29.08	43	28
Ward Francis Anthony	23.2.1906	25.3.1974	4	*1936*–1938	36	18	0	6.00	11	6-102	1/0	52.18	1	
Warne Shane Keith (*CY 1994*)	13.9.1969		145§	*1991–2006*	3,154	99	0	17.32	708	8-71	37/10	25.41	125	193‡
Warner David Andrew	27.10.1986		15	*2011–2012*	1,068	180	3	44.50	4	2-45	0/0	43.00	15	35/42
Watkins John Russell	16.4.1943		1	*1972*	39	36	0	39.00	0	0-21	0/0	–	1	
Watson Graeme Donald	8.3.1945		5	*1966*–1972	97	50	0	10.77	6	2-67	0/0	42.33	1	2
Watson Shane Robert	17.6.1981		38§	*2004–2012*	2,481	126	2	37.02	62	6-33	3/0	30.06	25	154/36
Watson William James	31.1.1931		4	*1954*	106	30	0	17.66	0	0-5	0/0	–	2	
[2]**Waugh** Mark Edward (*CY 1991*)	2.6.1965		128	*1990–2002*	8,029	153*	20	41.81	59	5-40	1/0	41.16	181	244
[2]**Waugh** Stephen Rodger (*CY 1989*)	2.6.1965		168	*1985–2003*	10,927	200	32	51.06	92	5-28	3/0	37.44	112	325
Wellham Dirk Macdonald	13.3.1959		6	1981–*1986*	257	103	1	23.36	–	–	–/–	–	5	17
Wessels Kepler Christoffel (*CY 1995*)	14.9.1957		24†	*1982–1985*	1,761	179	4	42.95	0	0-2	0/0	–	18	54‡
Whatmore Davenell Frederick	16.3.1954		7	*1978–1979*	293	77	0	22.53	0	0-11	0/0	–	13	1
White Cameron Leon	18.8.1983		4	*2008*	146	46	0	29.20	5	2-71	0/0	68.40	1	87/38
Whitney Michael Roy	24.2.1959		12	1981–*1992*	68	13	0	6.18	39	7-27	2/1	33.97	2	38
Whitty William James	15.8.1886	30.1.1974	14	1909–1912	161	39*	0	13.41	65	6-17	3/0	21.12	4	
Wiener Julien Mark	1.5.1955		6	*1979*	281	93	0	25.54	0	0-19	0/0	–	4	7
Williams Brad Andrew	20.11.1974		4	*2003*	23	10*	0	7.66	9	4-53	0/0	45.11	4	25
Wilson John William	20.8.1921	13.10.1985	1	*1956*	–	–	–	–	1	1-25	0/0	64.00	0	
Wilson Paul	12.1.1972		1	*1997*	0	0*	0	–	0	0-50	0/0	–	0	11
Wood Graeme Malcolm	6.11.1956		59	*1977–1988*	3,374	172	9	31.83	–	–	–/–	–	41	83

§ Warne's figures include 12 runs and six wickets and Watson's 34 runs and no wicket for Australia v the ICC World XI in the Super Series Test in 2005-06.

	Born	Died	Tests	Test Career	Runs	HS	100s	Avge	Wkts	BB	5/10	Avge	Ct/St	O/T
Woodcock Ashley James	27.2.1947		1	1973	27	27	0	27.00	–	–	–/–	–	1	1
Woodfull William Maldon OBE (*CY 1927*)	22.8.1897	11.8.1965	35	1926–1934	2,300	161	7	46.00	–	–	–/–	–	7	
Woods Samuel Moses James (*CY 1889*)	13.4.1867	30.4.1931	3†	1888	32	18	0	5.33	5	2-35	0/0	24.20	1	
Woolley Roger Douglas	16.9.1954		2	1982–1983	21	13	0	10.50	–	–	–/–	–	7	4
Worrall John	20.6.1860	17.11.1937	11	1884–1899	478	76	0	25.15	1	1-97	0/0	127.00	13	
Wright Kevin John	27.12.1953		10	1978–1979	219	55*	0	16.84	–	–	–/–	–	31/4	5
Yallop Graham Neil	7.10.1952		39	1975–1984	2,756	268	8	41.13	1	1-21	0/0	116.00	23	30
Yardley Bruce	5.9.1947		33	1977–1982	978	74	0	19.56	126	7-98	6/1	31.63	31	7
Young Shaun	13.6.1970		1	1997	4	4*	0	4.00	0	0-5	0/0	–	0	
Zoehrer Timothy Joseph	25.9.1961		10	1985–1986	246	52*	0	20.50	–	–	–/–	–	18/1	22

SOUTH AFRICA (315 players)

	Born	Died	Tests	Test Career	Runs	HS	100s	Avge	Wkts	BB	5/10	Avge	Ct/St	O/T
Ackerman Hylton Deon	14.2.1973		4	1997	161	57	0	20.12	–	–	–/–	–	1	
Adams Paul Regan	20.1.1977		45	1995–2003	360	35	0	9.00	134	7-128	4/1	32.87	29	24
Adcock Neil Amwin Treharne (*CY 1961*)	8.3.1931	6.1.2013	26	1953–1961	146	24	0	5.40	104	6-43	5/0	21.10	4	
Amla Hashim Mahomed (*CY 2013*)	31.3.1983		67	2004–2012	5,499	311*	19	51.39	0	0-4	0/0	–	58	62/15
Anderson James Henry	26.4.1874	11.3.1926	1	1902	43	32	0	21.50	–	–	–/–	–	1	
Ashley William Hare	10.2.1862	14.7.1930	1	1888	1	1	0	0.50	7	7-95	1/0	13.57	0	
Bacher Adam Marc	29.10.1973		19	1996–1999	833	96	0	26.03	0	0-4	0/0	–	11	13
Bacher Aron ("Ali")	24.5.1942		12	1965–1969	679	73	0	32.33	–	–	–/–	–	10	
Balaskas Xenophon Constantine	15.10.1910	12.5.1994	9	1930–1938	174	122*	1	14.50	22	5-49	1/0	36.63	5	
Barlow Edgar John	12.8.1940	30.12.2005	30	1961–1969	2,516	201	6	45.74	40	5-85	1/0	34.05	35	
Baumgartner Harold Vane	17.11.1883	8.4.1938	1	1913	19	16	0	9.50	2	2-99	0/0	49.50	1	
Beaumont Rolland	4.2.1884	25.5.1958	5	1912–1913	70	31	0	7.77	0	0-0	0/0	–	2	
Begbie Denis Warburton	12.12.1914	10.3.2009	5	1948–1949	138	48	0	19.71	1	1-38	0/0	130.00	2	
Bell Alexander John	15.4.1906	1.8.1985	16	1929–1935	69	26*	0	6.27	48	6-99	4/0	32.64	6	
Bisset *Sir* Murray	14.4.1876	24.10.1931	3	1898–1909	103	35	0	25.75	–	–	–/–	–	2/1	
Bissett George Finlay	5.11.1905	14.11.1965	4	1927	38	23	0	19.00	25	7-29	2/0	18.76	0	
Blanckenberg James Manuel	31.12.1892	d unknown	18	1913–1924	455	59	0	19.78	60	6-76	4/0	30.28	9	
Bland Kenneth Colin (*CY 1966*)	5.4.1938		21	1961–1966	1,669	144*	3	49.08	2	2-16	0/0	62.50	10	
Bock Ernest George	17.9.1908	5.9.1961	1	1935	11	9*	0	–	0	0-42	0/0	–	0	
Boje Nico	20.3.1973		43	1999–2006	1,312	85	0	25.23	100	5-62	3/0	42.65	18	113‡/1
Bond Gerald Edward	5.4.1909	27.8.1965	1	1938	0	0	0	0.00	0	0-16	0/0	–	0	

	Born	*Died*	*Tests*	*Test Career*	*Runs*	*HS*	*100s*	*Avge*	*Wkts*	*BB*	*5/10*	*Avge*	*Ct/St*	*O/T*
Bosch Tertius	14.3.1966	14.2.2000	1	*1991*	5	5*	0	–	3	2-61	0/0	34.66	0	2
Botha Johan	2.5.1982		5	*2005–2010*	83	25	0	20.75	17	4-56	0/0	33.70	3	76‡/40
Botten James Thomas ("Jackie")	21.6.1938	14.5.2006	3	1965	65	33	0	10.83	8	2-56	0/0	42.12	1	
Boucher Mark Verdon (*CY 2009*)	3.12.1976		146§	*1997–2011*	5,498	125	5	30.54	1	1-6	0/0	6.00	530/23	290‡/25
Brann William Henry	4.4.1899	22.9.1953	3	*1922*	71	50	0	14.20	–	–	–/–	–	2	
Briscoe Arthur Wellesley ("Dooley")	6.2.1911	22.4.1941	2	*1935–1938*	33	16	0	11.00	–	–	–/–	–	1	
Bromfield Harry Dudley	26.6.1932		9	*1961*–1965	59	21	0	11.80	17	5-88	1/0	35.23	13	
Brown Lennox Sidney	24.11.1910	1.9.1983	2	*1931*	17	8	0	5.66	3	1-30	0/0	63.00	0	
Burger Christopher George de Villiers	12.7.1935		2	*1957*	62	37*	0	20.66	–	–	–/–	–	1	
Burke Sydney Frank	11.3.1934		2	*1961–1964*	42	20	0	14.00	11	6-128	2/1	23.36	0	
Buys Isaac Daniel	4.2.1895	d unknown	1	*1922*	4	4*	0	4.00	0	0-20	0/0	–	0	
Cameron Horace Brakenridge ("Jock") (*CY 1936*)	5.7.1905	2.11.1935	26	*1927*–1935	1,239	90	0	30.21	–	–	–/–	–	39/12	
Campbell Thomas	9.2.1882	5.10.1924	5	*1909*–1912	90	48	0	15.00	–	–	–/–	–	7/1	
Carlstein Peter Rudolph	28.10.1938		8	*1957–1963*	190	42	0	14.61	–	–	–/–	–	3	
Carter Claude Pagdett	23.4.1881	8.11.1952	10	1912–1924	181	45	0	18.10	28	6-50	2/0	24.78	2	
Catterall Robert Hector (*CY 1925*)	10.7.1900	3.1.1961	24	*1922–1930*	1,555	120	3	37.92	7	3-15	0/0	23.14	12	
Chapman Horace William	30.6.1890	1.12.1941	2	*1913–1921*	39	17	0	13.00	1	1-51	0/0	104.00	1	
Cheetham John Erskine	26.5.1920	21.8.1980	24	*1948*–1955	883	89	0	23.86	0	0-2	0/0	–	13	
Chevalier Grahame Anton	9.3.1937		1	*1969*	0	0*	0	0.00	5	3-68	0/0	20.00	1	
Christy James Alexander Joseph	12.12.1904	1.2.1971	10	1929–*1931*	618	103	1	34.33	2	1-15	0/0	46.00	3	
Chubb Geoffrey Walter Ashton	12.4.1911	28.8.1982	5	1951	63	15*	0	10.50	21	6-51	2/0	27.47	0	
Cochran John Alexander Kennedy	15.7.1909	15.6.1987	1	*1930*	4	4	0	4.00	0	0-47	0/0	–	0	
Coen Stanley Keppel ("Shunter")	14.10.1902	29.1.1967	2	*1927*	101	41*	0	50.50	0	0-7	0/0	–	1	
Commaille John McIllwaine Moore ("Mick")	21.2.1883	28.7.1956	12	*1909–1927*	355	47	0	16.90	–	–	–/–	–	1	
Commins John Brian	19.2.1965		3	*1994*	125	45	0	25.00	–	–	–/–	–	2	
Conyngham Dalton Parry	10.5.1897	7.7.1979	1	*1922*	6	3*	0	–	2	1-40	0/0	51.50	1	
Cook Frederick James	1870	30.11.1915	1	*1895*	7	7	0	3.50	–	–	–/–	–	0	
Cook Stephen James (*CY 1990*)	31.7.1953		3	*1992–1993*	107	43	0	17.83	–	–	–/–	–	0	4
Cooper Alfred Henry Cecil	2.9.1893	18.7.1963	1	*1913*	6	6	0	3.00	–	–	–/–	–	1	
Cox Joseph Lovell	28.6.1886	4.7.1971	3	*1913*	17	12*	0	3.40	4	2-74	0/0	61.25	1	
Cripps Godfrey	19.10.1865	27.7.1943	1	*1891*	21	18	0	10.50	0	0-23	0/0	–	0	
Crisp Robert James	28.5.1911	2.3.1994	9	1935–*1935*	123	35	0	10.25	20	5-99	1/0	37.35	3	
Cronje Wessel Johannes ("Hansie")	25.9.1969	1.6.2002	68	*1991–1999*	3,714	135	6	36.41	43	3-14	0/0	29.95	33	188
Cullinan Daryll John	4.3.1967		70	*1992–2000*	4,554	275*	14	44.21	2	1-10	0/0	35.50	67	138

§ *Boucher's figures exclude 17 runs and two catches for the ICC World XI v Australia in the Super Series Test in 2005-06.*

	Born	*Died*	*Tests*	*Test Career*	*Runs*	*HS*	*100s*	*Avge*	*Wkts*	*BB*	*5/10*	*Avge*	*Ct/St*	*O/T*
Curnow Sydney Harry	16.12.1907	28.7.1986	7	*1930–1931*	168	47	0	12.00	–	–	–/–	–	5	
Dalton Eric Londesbrough	2.12.1906	3.6.1981	15	1929–*1938*	698	117	2	31.72	12	4-59	0/0	40.83	5	
Davies Eric Quail	26.8.1909	11.11.1976	5	*1935–1938*	9	3	0	1.80	7	4-75	0/0	68.71	0	
Dawson Alan Charles	27.11.1969		2	2003	10	10	0	10.00	5	2-20	0/0	23.40	0	19
Dawson Oswald Charles	1.9.1919	22.12.2008	9	1947–*1948*	293	55	0	20.92	10	2-57	0/0	57.80	10	
Deane Hubert Gouvaine ("Nummy")	21.7.1895	21.10.1939	17	1924–*1930*	628	93	0	25.12	–	–	–/–	–	8	
de Bruyn Zander	5.7.1975		3	*2004*	155	83	0	38.75	3	2-32	0/0	30.66	0	
de Lange Marchant	13.10.1990		2	*2011*	9	9	0	4.50	9	7-81	1/0	30.77	1	1/2
de Villiers Abraham Benjamin	17.2.1984		82	*2004–2012*	6,012	278*	14	49.27	2	2-49	0/0	49.50	125/2	127‡/44
de Villiers Petrus Stephanus ("Fanie")	13.10.1964		18	*1993–1997*	359	67*	0	18.89	85	6-23	5/2	24.27	11	83
de Wet Friedel	26.6.1980		2	*2009*	20	20	0	10.00	6	4-55	0/0	31.00	1	
Dippenaar Hendrik Human ("Boeta")	14.6.1977		38	*1999–2006*	1,718	177*	3	30.14	0	0-1	0/0	–	27	101‡/1
Dixon Cecil Donovan	12.2.1891	9.9.1969	1	*1913*	0	0	0	0.00	3	2-62	0/0	39.33	1	
Donald Allan Anthony (*CY 1992*)	20.10.1966		72	*1991–2001*	652	37	0	10.68	330	8-71	20/3	22.25	18	164
Dower Robert Reid	4.6.1876	15.9.1964	1	*1898*	9	9	0	4.50	–	–	–/–	–	2	
Draper Ronald George	24.12.1926		2	*1949*	25	15	0	8.33	–	–	–/–	–	0	
Duckworth Christopher Anthony Russell	22.3.1933		2	*1956*	28	13	0	7.00	–	–	–/–	–	3	
Dumbrill Richard	19.11.1938		5	1965–*1966*	153	36	0	15.30	9	4-30	0/0	37.33	3	
Duminy Jacobus Petrus	16.12.1897	31.1.1980	3	*1927*–1929	30	12	0	5.00	1	1-17	0/0	39.00	2	
Duminy Jean-Paul	14.4.1984		17	*2008–2012*	789	166	2	37.57	12	3-89	0/0	42.50	14	94/42
Dunell Owen Robert	15.7.1856	21.10.1929	2	*1888*	42	26*	0	14.00	–	–	–/–	–	1	
Du Plessis Francois	13.7.1984		4	*2012*	445	137	2	111.25	0	0-8	0/0	–	2	26/7
Du Preez John Harcourt	14.11.1942		2	*1966*	0	0	0	0.00	3	2-22	0/0	17.00	2	
Du Toit Jacobus Francois	2.4.1869	10.7.1909	1	*1891*	2	2*	0	–	1	1-47	0/0	47.00	1	
Dyer Dennis Victor	2.5.1914	16.6.1990	3	1947	96	62	0	16.00	–	–	–/–	–	0	
Eksteen Clive Edward	2.12.1966		7	*1993–1999*	91	22	0	10.11	8	3-12	0/0	61.75	5	6
Elgar Dean	11.6.1987		3	*2012*	124	103*	1	41.33	0	0-4	0/0	–	2	5
Elgie Michael Kelsey ("Kim")	6.3.1933		3	*1961*	75	56	0	12.50	0	0-18	0/0	–	4	
Elworthy Steven	23.2.1965		4	1998–*2002*	72	48	0	18.00	13	4-66	0/0	34.15	1	39
Endean William Russell	31.5.1924	28.6.2003	28	1951–*1957*	1,630	162*	3	33.95	–	–	–/–	–	41	
Farrer William Stephen ("Buster")	8.12.1936		6	*1961–1963*	221	40	0	27.62	–	–	–/–	–	2	
Faulkner George Aubrey	17.12.1881	10.9.1930	25	*1905*–1924	1,754	204	4	40.79	82	7-84	4/0	26.58	20	
Fellows-Smith Jonathan Payn	3.2.1932		4	1960	166	35	0	27.66	0	0-13	0/0	–	2	
Fichardt Charles Gustav	20.3.1870	30.5.1923	2	*1891–1895*	15	10	0	3.75	–	–	–/–	–	2	
Finlason Charles Edward	19.2.1860	31.7.1917	1	*1888*	6	6	0	3.00	0	0-7	0/0	–	0	
Floquet Claude Eugene	3.11.1884	22.11.1963	1	*1909*	12	11*	0	12.00	0	0-24	0/0	–	0	

	Born	Died	Tests	Test Career	Runs	HS	100s	Avge	Wkts	BB	5/10	Avge	Ct/St	O/T
Francis Howard Henry	26.5.1868	7.1.1936	2	*1898*	39	29	0	9.75	–	–	–/–	–	1	
Francois Cyril Matthew	20.6.1897	26.5.1944	5	*1922*	252	72	0	31.50	6	3-23	0/0	37.50	5	
Frank Charles Newton	27.1.1891	25.12.1961	3	*1921*	236	152	1	39.33	–	–	–/–	–	0	
Frank William Hughes Bowker	23.11.1872	16.2.1945	1	*1895*	7	5	0	3.50	1	1-52	0/0	52.00	0	
Fuller Edward Russell Henry	2.8.1931	19.7.2008	7	*1952–1957*	64	17	0	8.00	22	5-66	1/0	30.36	3	
Fullerton George Murray	8.12.1922	19.11.2002	7	1947–1951	325	88	0	25.00	–	–	–/–	–	10/2	
Funston Kenneth James	3.12.1925	15.4.2005	18	*1952–1957*	824	92	0	25.75	–	–	–/–	–	7	
Gamsy Dennis	17.2.1940		2	*1969*	39	30*	0	19.50	–	–	–/–	–	5	
Gibbs Herschelle Herman	23.2.1974		90	*1996–2007*	6,167	228	14	41.95	0	0-4	0/0	–	94	248/23
Gleeson Robert Anthony	6.12.1873	27.9.1919	1	*1895*	4	3	0	4.00	–	–	–/–	–	2	
Glover George Keyworth	13.5.1870	15.11.1938	1	*1895*	21	18*	0	21.00	1	1-28	0/0	28.00	0	
Goddard Trevor Leslie	1.8.1931		41	1955–*1969*	2,516	112	1	34.46	123	6-53	5/0	26.22	48	
Gordon Norman	6.8.1911		5	*1938*	8	7*	0	2.00	20	5-103	2/0	40.35	1	
Graham Robert	16.9.1877	21.4.1946	2	*1898*	6	4	0	1.50	3	2-22	0/0	42.33	2	
Grieveson Ronald Eustace	24.8.1909	24.7.1998	2	*1938*	114	75	0	57.00	–	–	–/–	–	7/3	
Griffin Geoffrey Merton	12.6.1939	16.11.2006	2	1960	25	14	0	6.25	8	4-87	0/0	24.00	0	
Hall Alfred Ewart	23.1.1896	1.1.1964	7	*1922–1930*	11	5	0	1.83	40	7-63	3/1	22.15	4	
Hall Andrew James	31.7.1975		21	*2001–2006*	760	163	1	26.20	45	3-1	0/0	35.93	16	88/2
Hall Glen Gordon	24.5.1938	26.6.1987	1	*1964*	0	0	0	0.00	1	1-94	0/0	94.00	0	
Halliwell Ernest Austin (*CY 1905*)	7.9.1864	2.10.1919	8	*1891–1902*	188	57	0	12.53	–	–	–/–	–	10/2	
Halse Clive Gray	28.2.1935	28.5.2002	3	*1963*	30	19*	0	–	6	3-50	0/0	43.33	1	
[2] **Hands** Philip Albert Myburgh	18.3.1890	27.4.1951	7	*1913*–1924	300	83	0	25.00	0	0-1	0/0	–	3	
[2] **Hands** Reginald Harry Myburgh	26.7.1888	20.4.1918	1	*1913*	7	7	0	3.50	–	–	–/–	–	0	
Hanley Martin Andrew	10.11.1918	2.6.2000	1	*1948*	0	0	0	0.00	1	1-57	0/0	88.00	0	
Harris Paul Lee	2.11.1978		37	*2006–2010*	460	46	0	10.69	103	6-127	3/0	37.87	16	3
Harris Terence Anthony	27.8.1916	7.3.1993	3	1947–*1948*	100	60	0	25.00	–	–	–/–	–	1	
Hartigan Gerald Patrick Desmond	30.12.1884	7.1.1955	5	1912–*1913*	114	51	0	11.40	1	1-72	0/0	141.00	0	
Harvey Robert Lyon	14.9.1911	20.7.2000	2	*1935*	51	28	0	12.75	–	–	–/–	–	0	
Hathorn Christopher Maitland Howard	7.4.1878	17.5.1920	12	*1902–1910*	325	102	1	17.10	–	–	–/–	–	5	
Hayward Mornantau ("Nantie")	6.3.1977		16	*1999*–2004	66	14	0	7.33	54	5-56	1/0	29.79	4	21
[1,2] **Hearne** Frank	23.11.1858	14.7.1949	4†	*1891–1895*	121	30	0	15.12	2	2-40	0/0	20.00	2	
[1] **Hearne** George Alfred Lawrence	27.3.1888	13.11.1978	3	*1922*–1924	59	28	0	11.80	–	–	–/–	–	3	
Heine Peter Samuel	28.6.1928	4.2.2005	14	1955–*1961*	209	31	0	9.95	58	6-58	4/0	25.08	8	
Henderson Claude William	14.6.1972		7	*2001–2002*	65	30	0	9.28	22	4-116	0/0	42.18	2	4
Henry Omar	23.1.1952		3	*1992*	53	34	0	17.66	3	2-56	0/0	63.00	2	3
Hime Charles Frederick William	24.10.1869	6.12.1940	1	*1895*	8	8	0	4.00	1	1-20	0/0	31.00	0	

	Born	Died	Tests	Test Career	Runs	HS	100s	Avge	Wkts	BB	5/10	Avge	Ct/St	O/T
Hudson Andrew Charles	17.3.1965		35	1991–1997	2,007	163	4	33.45	–	–	–/–	–	36	89
Hutchinson Philip	25.1.1862	30.9.1925	2	1888	14	11	0	3.50	–	–	–/–	–	3	
Imran Tahir	27.3.1979		11	2011–2012	88	29*	0	12.57	26	3-55	0/0	50.19	4	5
Ironside David Ernest James	2.5.1925	21.8.2005	3	1953	37	13	0	18.50	15	5-51	1/0	18.33	1	
Irvine Brian Lee	9.3.1944		4	1969	353	102	1	50.42	–	–	–/–	–	2	
Jack Steven Douglas	4.8.1970		2	1994	7	7	0	3.50	8	4-69	0/0	24.50	1	2
Johnson Clement Lecky	31.3.1871	31.5.1908	1	1895	10	7	0	5.00	0	0-57	0/0	–	1	
Kallis Jacques Henry (*CY 2013*)	16.10.1975		159§	1995–2012	12,965	224	44	56.61	284	6-54	5/0	32.38	189	316‡/25
Keith Headley James	25.10.1927	17.11.1997	8	1952–1956	318	73	0	21.20	0	0-19	0/0	–	9	
Kemp Justin Miles	2.10.1977		4	2000–2005	80	55	0	13.33	9	3-33	0/0	24.66	3	79‡/8
Kempis Gustav Adolph	4.8.1865	19.5.1890	1	1888	0	0*	0	0.00	4	3-53	0/0	19.00	0	
Khan Imraan	27.4.1984		1	2008	20	20	0	20.00	–	–	–/–	–	1	
[2] **Kirsten** Gary (*CY 2004*)	23.11.1967		101	1993–2003	7,289	275	21	45.27	2	1-0	0/0	71.00	83	185
[2] **Kirsten** Peter Noel	14.5.1955		12	1991–1994	626	104	1	31.30	0	0-5	0/0	–	8	40
Kleinveldt Rory Keith	15.3.1983		3	2012	27	17*	0	13.50	8	3-65	0/0	42.50	1	0/5
Klusener Lance (*CY 2000*)	4.9.1971		49	1996–2004	1,906	174	4	32.86	80	8-64	1/0	37.91	34	171
Kotze Johannes Jacobus ("Kodgee")	7.8.1879	7.7.1931	3	1902–1907	2	2	0	0.40	6	3-64	0/0	40.50	3	
Kuiper Adrian Paul	24.8.1959		1	1991	34	34	0	17.00	–	–	–/–	–	1	25
Kuys Frederick	21.3.1870	12.9.1953	1	1898	26	26	0	13.00	2	2-31	0/0	15.50	0	
Lance Herbert Roy ("Tiger")	6.6.1940	10.11.2010	13	1961–1969	591	70	0	28.14	12	3-30	0/0	39.91	7	
Langeveldt Charl Kenneth	17.12.1974		6	2004–2005	16	10	0	8.00	16	5-46	1/0	37.06	2	72/9
Langton Arthur Chudleigh Beaumont	2.3.1912	27.11.1942	15	1935–1938	298	73*	0	15.68	40	5-58	1/0	45.67	8	
Lawrence Godfrey Bernard	31.3.1932		5	1961	141	43	0	17.62	28	8-53	2/0	18.28	2	
le Roux Frederick Louis	5.2.1882	22.9.1963	1	1913	1	1	0	0.50	0	0-5	0/0	–	0	
Lewis Percy Tyson	2.10.1884	30.1.1976	1	1913	0	0	0	0.00	–	–	–/–	–	0	
Liebenberg Gerhardus Frederick Johannes	7.4.1972		5	1997–1998	104	45	0	13.00	–	–	–/–	–	1	4
[1] **Lindsay** Denis Thomson	4.9.1939	30.11.2005	19	1963–1969	1,130	182	3	37.66	–	–	–/–	–	57/2	
[1] **Lindsay** John Dixon	8.9.1908	31.8.1990	3	1947	21	9*	0	7.00	–	–	–/–	–	4/1	
Lindsay Nevil Vernon	30.7.1886	2.2.1976	1	1921	35	29	0	17.50	–	–	–/–	–	1	
Ling William Victor Stone	3.10.1891	26.9.1960	6	1921–1922	168	38	0	16.80	0	0-20	0/0	–	1	
Llewellyn Charles Bennett (*CY 1911*)	26.9.1876	7.6.1964	15	1895–1912	544	90	0	20.14	48	6-92	4/1	29.60	7	
Lundie Eric Balfour	15.3.1888	12.9.1917	1	1913	1	1	0	1.00	4	4-101	0/0	26.75	0	
Macaulay Michael John	19.4.1939		1	1964	33	21	0	16.50	2	1-10	0/0	36.50	0	
McCarthy Cuan Neil	24.3.1929	14.8.2000	15	1948–1951	28	5	0	3.11	36	6-43	2/0	41.94	6	
McGlew Derrick John ("Jackie") (*CY 1956*)	11.3.1929	9.6.1998	34	1951–1961	2,440	255*	7	42.06	0	0-7	0/0	–	18	

§ Kallis's figures exclude 83 runs, one wicket and four catches for the ICC World XI v Australia in the Super Series Test in 2005-06.

	Born	Died	Tests	Test Career	Runs	HS	100s	Avge	Wkts	BB	5/10	Avge	Ct/St	O/T
McKenzie Neil Douglas (*CY 2009*)	24.11.1975		58	2000–*2008*	3,253	226	5	37.39	0	0-1	0/0	–	54	64/2
McKinnon Atholl Henry	20.8.1932	2.12.1983	8	1960–*1966*	107	27	0	17.83	26	4-128	0/0	35.57	1	
McLaren Ryan	9.2.1983		1	*2009*	33	33*	0	–	1	1-30	0/0	43.00	0	13/8
McLean Roy Alastair (*CY 1961*)	9.7.1930	26.8.2007	40	1951–*1964*	2,120	142	5	30.28	0	0-1	0/0	–	23	
McMillan Brian Mervin	22.12.1963		38	*1992*–1998	1,968	113	3	39.36	75	4-65	0/0	33.82	49	78
McMillan Quintin	23.6.1904	3.7.1948	13	1929–*1931*	306	50*	0	18.00	36	5-66	2/0	34.52	8	
Mann Norman Bertram Fleetwood ("Tufty")	28.12.1920	31.7.1952	19	1947–1951	400	52	0	13.33	58	6-59	1/0	33.10	3	
Mansell Percy Neville Frank MBE	16.3.1920	9.5.1995	13	1951–1955	355	90	0	17.75	11	3-58	0/0	66.90	15	
Markham Lawrence Anderson	12.9.1924	5.8.2000	1	*1948*	20	20	0	20.00	1	1-34	0/0	72.00	0	
Marx Waldemar Frederick Eric	4.7.1895	2.6.1974	3	*1921*	125	36	0	20.83	4	3-85	0/0	36.00	0	
Matthews Craig Russell	15.2.1965		18	*1992–1995*	348	62*	0	18.31	52	5-42	2/0	28.88	4	56
Meintjes Douglas James	9.6.1890	17.7.1979	2	*1922*	43	21	0	14.33	6	3-38	0/0	19.16	3	
Melle Michael George	3.6.1930	28.12.2003	7	*1949–1952*	68	17	0	8.50	26	6-71	2/0	32.73	4	
Melville Alan (*CY 1948*)	19.5.1910	18.4.1983	11	*1938–1948*	894	189	4	52.58	–	–	–/–	–	8	
Middleton James	30.9.1865	23.12.1913	6	*1895–1902*	52	22	0	7.42	24	5-51	2/0	18.41	1	
Mills Charles Henry	26.11.1867	26.7.1948	1	*1891*	25	21	0	12.50	2	2-83	0/0	41.50	1	
Milton *Sir* William Henry	3.12.1854	6.3.1930	3	*1888–1891*	68	21	0	11.33	2	1-5	0/0	24.00	2	
Mitchell Bruce (*CY 1936*)	8.1.1909	1.7.1995	42	1929–*1948*	3,471	189*	8	48.88	27	5-87	1/0	51.11	56	
Mitchell Frank (*CY 1902*)	13.8.1872	11.10.1935	3†	1912	28	12	0	4.66	–	–	–/–	–	0	
Morkel Denijs Paul Beck	25.1.1906	6.10.1980	16	*1927–1931*	663	88	0	24.55	18	4-93	0/0	45.61	13	
[2] **Morkel** Johannes Albertus	10.6.1981		1	*2008*	58	58	0	58.00	1	1-44	0/0	132.00	0	56‡/42
[2] **Morkel** Morne	6.10.1984		47	*2006–2012*	649	40	0	13.80	171	6-23	6/0	29.70	12	55‡/31
Murray Anton Ronald Andrew	30.4.1922	17.4.1995	10	*1952–1953*	289	109	1	22.23	18	4-169	0/0	39.44	3	
Nel Andre	15.7.1977		36	*2001*–2008	337	34	0	9.91	123	6-32	3/1	31.86	16	79/2
Nel John Desmond	10.7.1928		6	*1949–1957*	150	38	0	13.63	–	–	–/–	–	1	
Newberry Claude	1889	1.8.1916	4	*1913*	62	16	0	7.75	11	4-72	0/0	24.36	3	
Newson Edward Serrurier OBE	2.12.1910	24.4.1988	3	*1930–1938*	30	16	0	7.50	4	2-58	0/0	66.25	3	
Ngam Mfuneko	29.1.1979		3	*2000*	0	0*	0	–	11	3-26	0/0	17.18	1	
Nicholson Frank	17.9.1909	30.7.1982	4	*1935*	76	29	0	10.85	–	–	–/–	–	3	
Nicolson John Fairless William	19.7.1899	13.12.1935	3	*1927*	179	78	0	35.80	0	0-5	0/0	–	0	
Norton Norman Ogilvie	11.5.1881	27.6.1968	1	*1909*	9	7	0	4.50	4	4-47	0/0	11.75	0	
[1] **Nourse** Arthur Dudley (*CY 1948*)	12.11.1910	14.8.1981	34	1935–1951	2,960	231	9	53.81	0	0-0	0/0	–	12	
[1] **Nourse** Arthur William ("Dave")	25.1.1879	8.7.1948	45	*1902*–1924	2,234	111	1	29.78	41	4-25	0/0	37.87	43	
Ntini Makhaya	6.7.1977		101	*1997–2009*	699	32*	0	9.84	390	7-37	18/4	28.82	25	172‡/10
Nupen Eiulf Peter ("Buster")	1.1.1902	29.1.1977	17	*1921–1935*	348	69	0	14.50	50	6-46	5/1	35.76	9	
Ochse Arthur Edward	11.3.1870	11.4.1918	2	*1888*	16	8	0	4.00	–	–	–/–	–	0	

	Born	*Died*	*Tests*	*Test Career*	*Runs*	*HS*	*100s*	*Avge*	*Wkts*	*BB*	*5/10*	*Avge*	*Ct/St*	*O/T*
Ochse Arthur Lennox	11.10.1899	5.5.1949	3	*1927*–1929	11	4*	0	3.66	10	4-79	0/0	36.20	1	
O'Linn Sidney	5.5.1927		7	1960–*1961*	297	98	0	27.00	–	–	–/–	–	4	
Ontong Justin Lee	4.1.1980		2	*2001–2004*	57	32	0	19.00	1	1-79	0/0	133.00	1	27‡/11
Owen-Smith Harold Geoffrey ("Tuppy") (*CY 1930*)	18.2.1909	28.2.1990	5	1929	252	129	1	42.00	0	0-3	0/0	–	4	
Palm Archibald William	8.6.1901	17.8.1966	1	*1927*	15	13	0	7.50	–	–	–/–	–	1	
Parker George Macdonald	27.5.1899	1.5.1969	2	1924	3	2*	0	1.50	8	6-152	1/0	34.12	0	
Parkin Durant Clifford	20.2.1873	20.3.1936	1	*1891*	6	6	0	3.00	3	3-82	0/0	27.33	1	
Parnell Wayne Dillon	30.7.1989		3	*2009*	34	22	0	17.00	5	2-17	0/0	45.40	1	27/17
Partridge Joseph Titus	9.12.1932	6.6.1988	11	*1963–1964*	73	13*	0	10.42	44	7-91	3/0	31.20	6	
Pearse Charles Ormerod Cato	10.10.1884	7.5.1953	3	*1910*	55	31	0	9.16	3	3-56	0/0	35.33	1	
Pegler Sidney James	28.7.1888	10.9.1972	16	*1909*–1924	356	35*	0	15.47	47	7-65	2/0	33.44	5	
Petersen Alviro Nathan	25.11.1980		21	*2009–2012*	1,514	182	5	42.05	1	1-2	0/0	62.00	15	17/2
Peterson Robin John	4.8.1979		9	2003–*2012*	207	61	0	20.70	25	5-33	1/0	31.08	7	60/19
Philander Vernon Darryl	24.6.1985		13	*2011–2012*	267	61	0	20.53	74	6-44	8/2	17.40	3	8/7
[2] **Pithey** Anthony John	17.7.1933	17.11.2006	17	*1956–1964*	819	154	1	31.50	0	0-5	0/0	–	3	
[2] **Pithey** David Bartlett	4.10.1936		8	*1963–1966*	138	55	0	12.54	12	6-58	1/0	48.08	6	
Plimsoll Jack Bruce	27.10.1917	11.11.1999	1	1947	16	8*	0	16.00	3	3-128	0/0	47.66	0	
[1,2] **Pollock** Peter Maclean (*CY 1966*)	30.6.1941		28	*1961–1969*	607	75*	0	21.67	116	6-38	9/1	24.18	9	
[2] **Pollock** Robert Graeme (*CY 1966*)	27.2.1944		23	*1963–1969*	2,256	274	7	60.97	4	2-50	0/0	51.00	17	
[1] **Pollock** Shaun Maclean (*CY 2003*)	16.7.1973		108	*1995–2007*	3,781	111	2	32.31	421	7-87	16/1	23.11	72	294‡/12
Poore Robert Montagu (*CY 1900*)	20.3.1866	14.7.1938	3	*1895*	76	20	0	12.66	1	1-4	0/0	4.00	3	
Pothecary James Edward	6.12.1933		3	1960	26	12	0	6.50	9	4-58	0/0	39.33	2	
Powell Albert William	18.7.1873	11.9.1948	1	*1898*	16	11	0	8.00	1	1-10	0/0	10.00	2	
Pretorius Dewald	6.12.1977		4	*2001*–2003	22	9	0	7.33	6	4-115	0/0	71.66	0	
Prince Ashwell Gavin	28.5.1977		66	*2001–2011*	3,665	162*	11	41.64	1	1-2	0/0	47.00	47	49‡/1
Prince Charles Frederick Henry	11.9.1874	2.2.1949	1	*1898*	6	5	0	3.00	–	–	–/–	–	0	
Pringle Meyrick Wayne	22.6.1966		4	*1991–1995*	67	33	0	16.75	5	2-62	0/0	54.00	0	17
Procter Michael John (*CY 1970*)	15.9.1946		7	*1966–1969*	226	48	0	25.11	41	6-73	1/0	15.02	4	
Promnitz Henry Louis Ernest	23.2.1904	7.9.1983	2	*1927*	14	5	0	3.50	8	5-58	1/0	20.12	2	
Quinn Neville Anthony	21.2.1908	5.8.1934	12	1929–*1931*	90	28	0	6.00	35	6-92	1/0	32.71	1	
Reid Norman	26.12.1890	6.6.1947	1	*1921*	17	11	0	8.50	2	2-63	0/0	31.50	0	
Rhodes Jonathan Neil (*CY 1999*)	27.7.1969		52	*1992*–2000	2,532	117	3	35.66	0	0-0	0/0	–	34	245
[2] **Richards** Alfred Renfrew	14.12.1867	9.1.1904	1	*1895*	6	6	0	3.00	–	–	–/–	–	0	
Richards Barry Anderson (*CY 1969*)	21.7.1945		4	*1969*	508	140	2	72.57	1	1-12	0/0	26.00	3	
[2] **Richards** William Henry Matthews	26.3.1862	4.1.1903	1	*1888*	4	4	0	2.00	–	–	–/–	–	0	

	Born	*Died*	*Tests*	*Test Career*	*Runs*	*HS*	*100s*	*Avge*	*Wkts*	*BB*	*5/10*	*Avge*	*Ct/St*	*O/T*
Richardson David John	16.9.1959		42	*1991–1997*	1,359	109	1	24.26	–	–	–/–	–	150/2	122
Robertson John Benjamin	5.6.1906	5.7.1985	3	*1935*	51	17	0	10.20	6	3-143	0/0	53.50	2	
Rose-Innes Albert	16.2.1868	22.11.1946	2	*1888*	14	13	0	3.50	5	5-43	1/0	17.80	2	
Routledge Thomas William	18.4.1867	9.5.1927	4	*1891–1895*	72	24	0	9.00	–	–	–/–	–	2	
[2] **Rowan** Athol Matthew Burchell	7.2.1921	22.2.1998	15	1947–1951	290	41	0	17.05	54	5-68	4/0	38.59	7	
[2] **Rowan** Eric Alfred Burchell (*CY 1952*)	20.7.1909	30.4.1993	26	1935–1951	1,965	236	3	43.66	0	0-0	0/0	–	14	
Rowe George Alexander	15.6.1874	8.1.1950	5	*1895–1902*	26	13*	0	4.33	15	5-115	1/0	30.40	4	
Rudolph Jacobus Andries	4.5.1981		48	2003–*2012*	2,622	222*	6	35.43	4	1-1	0/0	108.00	29	43‡/1
Rushmere Mark Weir	7.1.1965		1	*1991*	6	3	0	3.00	–	–	–/–	–	0	4
Samuelson Sivert Vause	21.11.1883	18.11.1958	1	*1909*	22	15	0	11.00	0	0-64	0/0	–	1	
Schultz Brett Nolan	26.8.1970		9	*1992–1997*	9	6	0	1.50	37	5-48	2/0	20.24	2	1
Schwarz Reginald Oscar (*CY 1908*)	4.5.1875	18.11.1918	20	*1905*–1912	374	61	0	13.85	55	6-47	2/0	25.76	18	
Seccull Arthur William	14.9.1868	20.7.1945	1	*1895*	23	17*	0	23.00	2	2-37	0/0	18.50	1	
Seymour Michael Arthur ("Kelly")	5.6.1936		7	*1963–1969*	84	36	0	12.00	9	3-80	0/0	65.33	2	
Shalders William Alfred	12.2.1880	18.3.1917	12	*1898*–1907	355	42	0	16.13	1	1-6	0/0	6.00	3	
Shepstone George Harold	9.4.1876	3.7.1940	2	*1895–1898*	38	21	0	9.50	0	0-8	0/0	–	2	
Sherwell Percy William	17.8.1880	17.4.1948	13	*1905–1910*	427	115	1	23.72	–	–	–/–	–	20/16	
Siedle Ivan Julian ("Jack")	11.1.1903	24.8.1982	18	*1927–1935*	977	141	1	28.73	1	1-7	0/0	7.00	7	
Sinclair James Hugh	16.10.1876	23.2.1913	25	*1895–1910*	1,069	106	3	23.23	63	6-26	1/0	31.68	9	
Smith Charles James Edward	25.12.1872	27.3.1947	3	*1902*	106	45	0	21.20	–	–	–/–	–	2	
Smith Frederick William	31.3.1861	17.4.1914	3	*1888–1895*	45	12	0	9.00	–	–	–/–	–	2	
Smith Graeme Craig (*CY 2004*)	1.2.1981		106§	*2001–2012*	8,612	277	26	49.78	8	2-145	0/0	110.62	149	185‡/33
Smith Vivian Ian	23.2.1925		9	1947–*1957*	39	11*	0	3.90	12	4-143	0/0	64.08	3	
Snell Richard Peter	12.9.1968		5	*1991–1994*	95	48	0	13.57	19	4-74	0/0	28.31	1	42
[2] **Snooke** Sibley John ("Tip")	1.2.1881	14.8.1966	26	*1905–1922*	1,008	103	1	22.40	35	8-70	1/1	20.05	24	
[2] **Snooke** Stanley de la Courtte	11.11.1878	6.4.1959	1	1907	0	0	0	0.00	–	–	–/–	–	2	
Solomon William Rodger Thomson	23.4.1872	13.7.1964	1	*1898*	4	2	0	2.00	–	–	–/–	–	1	
Stewart Robert Burnard	3.9.1856	12.9.1913	1	*1888*	13	9	0	6.50	–	–	–/–	–	2	
Steyn Dale Willem (*CY 2013*)	27.6.1983		62	*2004–2012*	839	76	0	13.75	312	7-51	19/4	23.28	18	64‡/29
Steyn Philippus Jeremia Rudolf	30.6.1967		3	*1994*	127	46	0	21.16	–	–	–/–	–	0	1
Stricker Louis Anthony	26.5.1884	5.2.1960	13	*1909*–1912	344	48	0	14.33	1	1-36	0/0	105.00	3	
Strydom Pieter Coenraad	10.6.1969		2	*1999*	35	30	0	11.66	0	0-27	0/0	–	1	10
Susskind Manfred John	8.6.1891	9.7.1957	5	1924	268	65	0	33.50	–	–	–/–	–	1	
Symcox Patrick Leonard	14.4.1960		20	*1993–1998*	741	108	1	28.50	37	4-69	0/0	43.32	5	80
Taberer Henry Melville	7.10.1870	5.6.1932	1	*1902*	2	2	0	2.00	1	1-25	0/0	48.00	0	

§ G. C. Smith's figures exclude 12 runs and three catches for the ICC World XI v Australia in the Super Series Test in 2005-06.

	Born	*Died*	*Tests*	*Test Career*	*Runs*	*HS*	*100s*	*Avge*	*Wkts*	*BB*	*5/10*	*Avge*	*Ct/St*	*O/T*
[2] **Tancred** Augustus Bernard	20.8.1865	23.11.1911	2	*1888*	87	29	0	29.00	–	–	–/–	–	2	
[2] **Tancred** Louis Joseph	7.10.1876	28.7.1934	14	*1902–1913*	530	97	0	21.20	–	–	–/–	–	3	
[2] **Tancred** Vincent Maximillian.	7.7.1875	3.6.1904	1	*1898*	25	18	0	12.50	–	–	–/–	–	0	
[2] **Tapscott** George Lancelot ("Dusty")	7.11.1889	13.12.1940	1	*1913*	5	4	0	2.50	–	–	–/–	–	1	
[2] **Tapscott** Lionel Eric ("Doodles")	18.3.1894	7.7.1934	2	*1922*	58	50*	0	29.00	0	0-2	0/0	–	0	
Tayfield Hugh Joseph (*CY 1956*).	30.1.1929	24.2.1994	37	*1949–* 1960	862	75	0	16.90	170	9-113	14/2	25.91	26	
Taylor Alistair Innes ("Scotch")	25.7.1925	7.2.2004	1	*1956*	18	12	0	9.00	–	–	–/–	–	0	
[2] **Taylor** Daniel.	9.1.1887	24.1.1957	2	*1913*	85	36	0	21.25	–	–	–/–	–	0	
[2] **Taylor** Herbert Wilfred (*CY 1925*).	5.5.1889	8.2.1973	42	1912–*1931*	2,936	176	7	40.77	5	3-15	0/0	31.20	19	
Terbrugge David John	31.1.1977		7	*1998–2003*	16	4*	0	5.33	20	5-46	1/0	25.85	4	4
Theunissen Nicolaas Hendrik Christiaan de Jong	4.5.1867	9.11.1929	1	*1888*	2	2*	0	2.00	0	0-51	0/0	–	0	
Thornton George	24.12.1867	31.1.1939	1	*1902*	1	1*	0	–	1	1-20	0/0	20.00	1	
Tomlinson Denis Stanley.	4.9.1910	11.7.1993	1	1935	9	9	0	9.00	0	0-38	0/0	–	0	
Traicos Athanasios John	17.5.1947		3†	*1969*	8	5*	0	4.00	4	2-70	0/0	51.75	4	0‡
Trimborn Patrick Henry Joseph	18.5.1940		4	*1966–1969*	13	11*	0	6.50	11	3-12	0/0	23.36	7	
Tsolekile Thami Lungisa	9.10.1980		3	*2004*	47	22	0	9.40	–	–	–/–	–	6	
Tsotsobe Lonwabo Lennox	7.3.1984		5	2010–*2010*	19	8*	0	6.33	9	3-43	0/0	49.77	1	35/11
[1] **Tuckett** Lindsay	6.2.1919		9	1947–*1948*	131	40*	0	11.90	19	5-68	2/0	51.57	9	
[1] **Tuckett** Lindsay Richard ("Len")	19.4.1885	8.4.1963	1	*1913*	0	0*	0	0.00	0	0-24	0/0	–	2	
Twentyman-Jones Percy Sydney	13.9.1876	8.3.1954	1	*1902*	0	0	0	0.00	–	–	–/–	–	0	
van der Bijl Pieter Gerhard Vintcent	21.10.1907	16.2.1973	5	*1938*	460	125	1	51.11	–	–	–/–	–	1	
van der Merwe Edward Alexander	9.11.1903	26.2.1971	2	1929–*1935*	27	19	0	9.00	–	–	–/–	–	3	
van der Merwe Peter Laurence.	14.3.1937	23.1.2013	15	*1963–1966*	533	76	0	25.38	1	1-6	0/0	22.00	11	
van Jaarsveld Martin	18.6.1974		9	*2002–2004*	397	73	0	30.53	0	0-28	0/0	–	11	11
van Ryneveld Clive Berrange.	19.3.1928		19	1951–*1957*	724	83	0	26.81	17	4-67	0/0	39.47	14	
Varnals George Derek.	24.7.1935		3	*1964*	97	23	0	16.16	0	0-2	0/0	–	0	
Viljoen Kenneth George	14.5.1910	21.1.1974	27	*1930–1948*	1,365	124	2	28.43	0	0-10	0/0	–	5	
Vincent Cyril Leverton	16.2.1902	24.8.1968	25	*1927*–1935	526	60	0	20.23	84	6-51	3/0	31.32	27	
Vintcent Charles Henry	2.9.1866	28.9.1943	3	*1888–1891*	26	9	0	4.33	4	3-88	0/0	48.25	1	
Vogler Albert Edward Ernest (*CY 1908*).	28.11.1876	9.8.1946	15	*1905–1910*	340	65	0	17.00	64	7-94	5/1	22.73	20	
[2] **Wade** Herbert Frederick.	14.9.1905	23.11.1980	10	1935–*1935*	327	40*	0	20.43	–	–	–/–	–	4	
[2] **Wade** Walter Wareham ("Billy")	18.6.1914	31.5.2003	11	*1938–1949*	511	125	1	28.38	–	–	–/–	–	15/2	
Waite John Henry Bickford	19.1.1930	22.6.2011	50	1951–*1964*	2,405	134	4	30.44	–	–	–/–	–	124/17	
Walter Kenneth Alexander	5.11.1939	13.9.2003	2	*1961*	11	10	0	3.66	6	4-63	0/0	32.83	3	
Ward Thomas Alfred	2.8.1887	16.2.1936	23	1912–1924	459	64	0	13.90	–	–	–/–	–	19/13	
Watkins John Cecil.	10.4.1923		15	*1949–1956*	612	92	0	23.53	29	4-22	0/0	28.13	12	

	Born	Died	Tests	Test Career	Runs	HS	100s	Avge	Wkts	BB	5/10	Avge	Ct/St	O/T
Wesley Colin	5.9.1937		3	1960	49	35	0	9.80	–	–	–/–	–	1	
Wessels Kepler Christoffel (*CY 1995*)	14.9.1957		16‡	*1991*–1994	1,027	118	2	38.03	–	–	–/–	–	12	55‡
Westcott Richard John	19.9.1927	16.1.2013	5	*1953–1957*	166	62	0	18.44	0	0-22	0/0	–	0	
White Gordon Charles	5.2.1882	17.10.1918	17	*1905*–1912	872	147	2	30.06	9	4-47	0/0	33.44	10	
Willoughby Charl Myles	3.12.1974		2	2003	–	–	–	–	1	1-47	0/0	125.00	0	3
Willoughby Joseph Thomas	7.11.1874	11.3.1952	2	*1895*	8	5	0	2.00	6	2-37	0/0	26.50	0	
Wimble Clarence Skelton	22.4.1861	28.1.1930	1	*1891*	0	0	0	0.00	–	–	–/–	–	0	
Winslow Paul Lyndhurst	21.5.1929	24.5.2011	5	*1949*–1955	186	108	1	20.66	–	–	–/–	–	1	
Wynne Owen Edgar	1.6.1919	13.7.1975	6	*1948–1949*	219	50	0	18.25	–	–	–/–	–	3	
Zondeki Monde	25.7.1982		6	2003–*2008*	82	59	0	16.40	19	6-39	1/0	25.26	1	11‡/1
Zulch Johan Wilhelm	2.1.1886	19.5.1924	16	*1909–1921*	983	150	2	32.76	0	0-2	0/0	–	4	

WEST INDIES (296 players)

	Born	Died	Tests	Test Career	Runs	HS	100s	Avge	Wkts	BB	5/10	Avge	Ct/St	O/T
Achong Ellis Edgar	16.2.1904	30.8.1986	6	*1929–1934*	81	22	0	8.10	8	2-64	0/0	47.25	6	
Adams James Clive	9.1.1968		54	*1991–2000*	3,012	208*	6	41.26	27	5-17	1/0	49.48	48	127
Alexander Franz Copeland Murray ("Gerry")	2.11.1928	16.4.2011	25	1957–*1960*	961	108	1	30.03	–	–	–/–	–	85/5	
Ali Imtiaz	28.7.1954		1	*1975*	1	1*	0	–	2	2-37	0/0	44.50	0	
Ali Inshan	25.9.1949	24.6.1995	12	*1970–1976*	172	25	0	10.75	34	5-59	1/0	47.67	7	
Allan David Walter	5.11.1937		5	*1961*–1966	75	40*	0	12.50	–	–	–/–	–	15/3	
Allen Ian Basil Alston	6.10.1965		2	1991	5	4*	0	–	5	2-69	0/0	36.00	1	
Ambrose Curtly Elconn Lynwall (*CY 1992*)	21.9.1963		98	*1987*–2000	1,439	53	0	12.40	405	8-45	22/3	20.99	18	176
Arthurton Keith Lloyd Thomas	21.2.1965		33	1988–1995	1,382	157*	2	30.71	1	1-17	0/0	183.00	22	105
Asgarali Nyron Sultan	28.12.1920	5.11.2006	2	1957	62	29	0	15.50	–	–	–/–	–	0	
[2] **Atkinson** Denis St Eval	9.8.1926	9.11.2001	22	*1948–1957*	922	219	1	31.79	47	7-53	3/0	35.04	11	
[2] **Atkinson** Eric St Eval	6.11.1927	29.5.1998	8	*1957–1958*	126	37	0	15.75	25	5-42	1/0	23.56	2	
Austin Richard Arkwright	5.9.1954		2	*1977*	22	20	0	11.00	0	0-5	0/0	–	2	1
Austin Ryan Anthony	15.11.1981		2	2009	39	19	0	9.75	3	1-29	0/0	51.66	3	
Bacchus Sheik Faoud Ahamul Fasiel	31.1.1954		19	*1977–1981*	782	250	1	26.06	0	0-3	0/0	–	17	29
Baichan Leonard	12.5.1946		3	*1974–1975*	184	105*	1	46.00	–	–	–/–	–	2	
Baker Lionel Sionne	6.9.1984		4	*2008*–2009	23	17	0	11.50	5	2-39	0/0	79.00	1	10/3
Banks Omari Ahmed Clemente	17.7.1982		10	*2002*–2005	318	50*	0	26.50	28	4-87	0/0	48.82	6	5
Baptiste Eldine Ashworth Elderfield	12.3.1960		10	*1983–1989*	233	87*	0	23.30	16	3-31	0/0	35.18	2	43
Barath Adrian Boris	14.4.1990		15	*2009*–2012	657	104	1	23.46	0	0-3	0/0	–	13	14/2

	Born	*Died*	*Tests*	*Test Career*	*Runs*	*HS*	*100s*	*Avge*	*Wkts*	*BB*	*5/10*	*Avge*	*Ct/St*	*O/T*
Barrett Arthur George	4.4.1944		6	*1970–1974*	40	19	0	6.66	13	3-43	0/0	46.38	0	
Barrow Ivanhoe Mordecai	16.1.1911	2.4.1979	11	*1929*–1939	276	105	1	16.23	–	–	–/–	–	17/5	
Bartlett Edward Lawson	10.3.1906	21.12.1976	5	1928–*1930*	131	84	0	18.71	–	–	–/–	–	2	
Baugh Carlton Seymour	23.6.1982		21	*2002–2011*	610	68	0	17.94	–	–	–/–	–	43/5	47/3
Benjamin Kenneth Charlie Griffith	8.4.1967		26	*1991–1997*	222	43*	0	7.92	92	6-66	4/1	30.27	2	26
Benjamin Winston Keithroy Matthew	31.12.1964		21	*1987–1994*	470	85	0	18.80	61	4-46	0/0	27.01	12	85
Benn Sulieman Jamaal	22.7.1981		17	*2007–2010*	381	42	0	15.87	51	6-81	3/0	41.41	7	25/17
Bernard David Eddison	19.7.1981		3	*2002*–2009	202	69	0	40.40	4	2-30	0/0	46.25	0	20/1
Bess Brandon Jeremy	13.12.1987		1	2010	11	11*	0	11.00	1	1-65	0/0	92.00	0	
Best Carlisle Alonza	14.5.1959		8	*1985–1990*	342	164	1	28.50	0	0-2	0/0	–	8	24
Best Tino la Bertram	26.8.1981		18	*2002–2012*	291	95	0	13.22	46	6-40	2/0	36.00	4	15
Betancourt Nelson	4.6.1887	12.10.1947	1	*1929*	52	39	0	26.00	–	–	–/–	–	0	
Binns Alfred Phillip	24.7.1929		5	*1952–1955*	64	27	0	9.14	–	–	–/–	–	14/3	
Birkett Lionel Sydney	14.4.1905	16.1.1998	4	*1930*	136	64	0	17.00	1	1-16	0/0	71.00	4	
Bishoo Devendra	6.11.1985		11	*2010–2011*	143	26	0	13.00	40	5-90	1/0	39.55	8	13/4
Bishop Ian Raphael	24.10.1967		43	*1988–1997*	632	48	0	12.15	161	6-40	6/0	24.27	8	84
Black Marlon Ian	7.6.1975		6	*2000–2001*	21	6	0	2.62	12	4-83	0/0	49.75	0	5
Boyce Keith David (*CY 1974*)	11.10.1943	11.10.1996	21	*1970–1975*	657	95*	0	24.33	60	6-77	2/1	30.01	5	8
Bradshaw Ian David Russell	9.7.1974		5	*2005*	96	33	0	13.71	9	3-73	0/0	60.00	3	62/1
Brathwaite Kraigg Clairmonte	1.12.1992		9	*2010–2011*	363	68	0	21.35	1	1-43	0/0	50.00	5	
[2] **Bravo** Dwayne John	7.10.1983		40	2004–*2010*	2,200	113	3	31.42	86	6-55	2/0	39.83	41	129/32
[2] **Bravo** Darren Michael	6.2.1989		21	*2010–2012*	1,637	195	4	46.77	–	–	–/–	–	16	45/8
Breese Gareth Rohan	9.1.1976		1	*2002*	5	5	0	2.50	2	2-108	0/0	67.50	1	
Browne Courtney Oswald	7.12.1970		20	*1994–2004*	387	68	0	16.12	–	–	–/–	–	79/2	46
Browne Cyril Rutherford	8.10.1890	12.1.1964	4	1928–*1929*	176	70*	0	25.14	6	2-72	0/0	48.00	1	
Butcher Basil Fitzherbert (*CY 1970*)	3.9.1933		44	*1958*–1969	3,104	209*	7	43.11	5	5-34	1/0	18.00	15	
Butler Lennox Stephen	9.2.1929	1.9.2009	1	*1954*	16	16	0	16.00	2	2-151	0/0	75.50	0	
Butts Clyde Godfrey	8.7.1957		7	*1984–1987*	108	38	0	15.42	10	4-73	0/0	59.50	2	
Bynoe Michael Robin	23.2.1941		4	*1958–1966*	111	48	0	18.50	1	1-5	0/0	5.00	4	
Camacho George Stephen	15.10.1945		11	*1967–1970*	640	87	0	29.09	0	0-12	0/0	–	4	
[2] **Cameron** Francis James	22.6.1923	10.6.1994	5	*1948*	151	75*	0	25.16	3	2-74	0/0	92.66	0	
[2] **Cameron** John Hemsley	8.4.1914	13.2.2000	2	1939	6	5	0	2.00	3	3-66	0/0	29.33	0	
Campbell Sherwin Legay	1.11.1970		52	*1994–2001*	2,882	208	4	32.38	–	–	–/–	–	47	90
Carew George McDonald	4.6.1910	9.12.1974	4	*1934–1948*	170	107	1	28.33	0	0-2	0/0	–	1	
Carew Michael Conrad ("Joey")	15.9.1937	8.1.2011	19	1963–*1971*	1,127	109	1	34.15	8	1-11	0/0	54.62	13	
Challenor George	28.6.1888	30.7.1947	3	1928	101	46	0	16.83	–	–	–/–	–	0	

	Born	Died	Tests	Test Career	Runs	HS	100s	Avge	Wkts	BB	5/10	Avge	Ct/St	O/T
Chanderpaul Shivnarine (*CY 2008*)	16.8.1974		146	1993–2012	10,696	203*	27	51.67	9	1-2	0/0	98.11	62	268/22
Chang Herbert Samuel	2.7.1952		1	1978	8	6	0	4.00	–	–	–/–	–	0	
Chattergoon Sewnarine	3.4.1981		4	2007–2008	127	46	0	18.14	–	–	–/–	–	4	18
2 **Christiani** Cyril Marcel	28.10.1913	4.4.1938	4	1934	98	32*	0	19.60	–	–	–/–	–	6/1	
2 **Christiani** Robert Julian	19.7.1920	4.1.2005	22	1947–1953	896	107	1	26.35	3	3-52	0/0	36.00	19/2	
Clarke Carlos Bertram OBE	7.4.1918	14.10.1993	3	1939	3	2	0	1.00	6	3-59	0/0	43.50	0	
Clarke Sylvester Theophilus	11.12.1954	4.12.1999	11	1977–1981	172	35*	0	15.63	42	5-126	1/0	27.85	2	10
2 **Collins** Pedro Tyrone	12.8.1976		32	1998–2005	235	24	0	5.87	106	6-53	3/0	34.63	7	30
Collymore Corey Dalanelo	21.12.1977		30	1998–2007	197	16*	0	7.88	93	7-57	4/1	32.30	6	84
Constantine *Lord* [Learie Nicholas] MBE (*CY 1940*)	21.9.1901	1.7.1971	18	1928–1939	635	90	0	19.24	58	5-75	2/0	30.10	28	
Croft Colin Everton Hunte	15.3.1953		27	1976–1981	158	33	0	10.53	125	8-29	3/0	23.30	8	19
Cuffy Cameron Eustace	8.2.1970		15	1994–2002	58	15	0	4.14	43	4-82	0/0	33.83	5	41
Cummins Anderson Cleophas	7.5.1966		5	1992–1994	98	50	0	19.60	8	4-54	0/0	42.75	1	63
Da Costa Oscar Constantine	11.9.1907	1.10.1936	5	1929–1934	153	39	0	19.12	3	1-14	0/0	58.33	5	
Daniel Wayne Wendell	16.1.1956		10	1975–1983	46	11	0	6.57	36	5-39	1/0	25.27	4	18
2 **Davis** Bryan Allan	2.5.1940		4	1964	245	68	0	30.62	–	–	–/–	–	1	
2 **Davis** Charles Allan	1.1.1944		15	1968–1972	1,301	183	4	54.20	2	1-27	0/0	165.00	4	
Davis Winston Walter	18.9.1958		15	1982–1987	202	77	0	15.53	45	4-19	0/0	32.71	10	35
De Caires Francis Ignatius	12.5.1909	2.2.1959	3	1929	232	80	0	38.66	0	0-9	0/0	–	1	
Deonarine Narsingh	16.8.1983		14	2004–2012	588	82	0	29.40	19	4-37	0/0	27.94	12	20/7
Depeiza Cyril Clairmonte	10.10.1928	10.11.1995	5	1954–1955	187	122	1	31.16	0	0-3	0/0	–	7/4	
Dewdney David Thomas	23.10.1933		9	1954–1957	17	5*	0	2.42	21	5-21	1/0	38.42	0	
Dhanraj Rajindra	6.2.1969		4	1994–1995	17	9	0	4.25	8	2-49	0/0	74.37	1	6
Dillon Mervyn	5.6.1974		38	1996–2003	549	43	0	8.44	131	5-71	2/0	33.57	16	108
Dowe Uton George	29.3.1949		4	1970–1972	8	5*	0	8.00	12	4-69	0/0	44.50	3	
Dowlin Travis Montague	24.2.1977		6	2009–2010	343	95	0	31.18	0	0-3	0/0	–	5	11/2
Drakes Vasbert Conniel	5.8.1969		12	2002–2003	386	67	0	21.44	33	5-93	1/0	41.27	2	34
Dujon Peter Jeffrey Leroy (*CY 1989*)	28.5.1956		81	1981–1991	3,322	139	5	31.94	–	–	–/–	–	267/5	169
2 **Edwards** Fidel Henderson	6.2.1982		55	2003–2012	394	30	0	6.56	165	7-87	12/0	37.87	10	50/20
Edwards Kirk Anton	3.11.1984		9	2011–2012	665	121	2	39.11	0	0-19	0/0	–	7	9
Edwards Richard Martin	3.6.1940		5	1968	65	22	0	9.28	18	5-84	1/0	34.77	0	
Ferguson Wilfred	14.12.1917	23.2.1961	8	1947–1953	200	75	0	28.57	34	6-92	3/1	34.26	11	
Fernandes Maurius Pacheco	12.8.1897	8.5.1981	2	1928–1929	49	22	0	12.25	–	–	–/–	–	0	
Findlay Thaddeus Michael MBE	19.10.1943		10	1969–1972	212	44*	0	16.30	–	–	–/–	–	19/2	
Foster Maurice Linton Churchill	9.5.1943		14	1969–1977	580	125	1	30.52	9	2-41	0/0	66.66	3	2

	Born	Died	Tests	Test Career	Runs	HS	100s	Avge	Wkts	BB	5/10	Avge	Ct/St	O/T
Francis George Nathaniel	11.12.1897	12.1.1942	10	1928–1933	81	19*	0	5.78	23	4-40	0/0	33.17	7	
Frederick Michael Campbell	6.5.1927		1	1953	30	30	0	15.00	–	–	–/–	–	0	
Fredericks Roy Clifton (*CY 1974*)	11.11.1942	5.9.2000	59	1968–1976	4,334	169	8	42.49	7	1-12	0/0	78.28	62	12
Fudadin Assad Badyr	1.8.1985		3	2012	122	55	0	30.50	0	0-11	0/0	–	4	
Fuller Richard Livingston	30.1.1913	3.5.1987	1	1934	1	1	0	1.00	0	0-2	0/0	–	0	
Furlonge Hammond Allan	19.6.1934		3	1954–1955	99	64	0	19.80	–	–	–/–	–	0	
Gabriel Shannon Terry	28.4.1988		1	2012	13	13	0	6.50	4	3-60	0/0	21.50	0	
Ganga Daren	14.1.1979		48	1998–2007	2,160	135	3	25.71	1	1-20	0/0	106.00	30	35/1
Ganteaume Andrew Gordon	22.1.1921		1	1947	112	112	1	112.00	–	–	–/–	–	0	
Garner Joel MBE (*CY 1980*)	16.12.1952		58	1976–1986	672	60	0	12.44	259	6-56	7/0	20.97	42	98
Garrick Leon Vivian	11.11.1976		1	2000	27	27	0	13.50	–	–	–/–	–	2	3
Gaskin Berkeley Bertram McGarrell	21.3.1908	2.5.1979	2	1947	17	10	0	5.66	2	1-15	0/0	79.00	1	
Gayle Christopher Henry	21.9.1979		95	1999–2012	6,691	333	14	42.08	72	5-34	2/0	42.00	88	236/31
Gibbs Glendon Lionel	27.12.1925	21.2.1979	1	1954	12	12	0	6.00	0	0-2	0/0	–	1	
Gibbs Lancelot Richard (*CY 1972*)	29.9.1934		79	1957–1975	488	25	0	6.97	309	8-38	18/2	29.09	52	3
Gibson Ottis Delroy (*CY 2008*)	16.3.1969		2	1995–1998	93	37	0	23.25	3	2-81	0/0	91.66	0	15
Gilchrist Roy	28.6.1934	18.7.2001	13	1957–1958	60	12	0	5.45	57	6-55	1/0	26.68	4	
Gladstone Morais George	14.1.1901	19.5.1978	1	1929	12	12*	0	–	1	1-139	0/0	189.00	0	
Goddard John Douglas Claude OBE	21.4.1919	26.8.1987	27	1947–1957	859	83*	0	30.67	33	5-31	1/0	31.81	22	
Gomes Hilary Angelo ("Larry") (*CY 1985*)	13.7.1953		60	1976–1986	3,171	143	9	39.63	15	2-20	0/0	62.00	18	83
Gomez Gerald Ethridge	10.10.1919	6.8.1996	29	1939–1953	1,243	101	1	30.31	58	7-55	1/1	27.41	18	
[2] **Grant** George Copeland ("Jackie")	9.5.1907	26.10.1978	12	1930–1934	413	71*	0	25.81	0	0-1	0/0	–	10	
[2] **Grant** Rolph Stewart	15.12.1909	18.10.1977	7	1934–1939	220	77	0	22.00	11	3-68	0/0	32.09	13	
Gray Anthony Hollis	23.5.1963		5	1986	48	12*	0	8.00	22	4-39	0/0	17.13	6	25
Greenidge Alvin Ethelbert	20.8.1956		6	1977–1978	222	69	0	22.20	–	–	–/–	–	5	1
Greenidge Cuthbert Gordon MBE (*CY 1977*)	1.5.1951		108	1974–1990	7,558	226	19	44.72	0	0-0	0/0	–	96	128
Greenidge Geoffrey Alan	26.5.1948		5	1971–1972	209	50	0	29.85	0	0-2	0/0	–	3	
Grell Mervyn George	18.12.1899	11.1.1976	1	1929	34	21	0	17.00	0	0-7	0/0	–	1	
Griffith Adrian Frank Gordon	19.11.1971		14	1996–2000	638	114	1	24.53	–	–	–/–	–	5	9
Griffith Charles Christopher (*CY 1964*)	14.12.1938		28	1959–1968	530	54	0	16.56	94	6-36	5/0	28.54	16	
Griffith Herman Clarence	1.12.1893	18.3.1980	13	1928–1933	91	18	0	5.05	44	6-103	2/0	28.25	4	
Guillen Simpson Clairmonte ("Sammy")	24.9.1924		5†	1951	104	54	0	26.00	–	–	–/–	–	9/2	
Hall *Sir* Wesley Winfield	12.9.1937		48	1958–1968	818	50*	0	15.73	192	7-69	9/1	26.38	11	
Harper Roger Andrew	17.3.1963		25	1983–1993	535	74	0	18.44	46	6-57	1/0	28.06	36	105
Haynes Desmond Leo (*CY 1991*)	15.2.1956		116	1977–1993	7,487	184	18	42.29	1	1-2	0/0	8.00	65	238
[3] **Headley** George Alphonso MBE (*CY 1934*)	30.5.1909	30.11.1983	22	1929–1953	2,190	270*	10	60.83	0	0-0	0/0	–	14	

	Born	Died	Tests	Test Career	Runs	HS	100s	Avge	Wkts	BB	5/10	Avge	Ct/St	O/T
[3] **Headley** Ronald George Alphonso	29.6.1939		2	1973	62	42	0	15.50	–	–	–/–	–	2	1
Hendriks John Leslie	21.12.1933		20	*1961*–1969	447	64	0	18.62	–	–	–/–	–	42/5	
Hinds Ryan O'Neal	17.2.1981		15	*2001*–2009	505	84	0	21.04	13	2-45	0/0	66.92	7	14
Hinds Wavell Wayne	7.9.1976		45	*1999–2005*	2,608	213	5	33.01	16	3-79	0/0	36.87	32	119/5
Hoad Edward Lisle Goldsworthy	29.1.1896	5.3.1986	4	1928–1933	98	36	0	12.25	–	–	–/–	–	1	
Holder Roland Irwin Christopher	22.12.1967		11	*1996–1998*	380	91	0	25.33	–	–	–/–	–	9	37
Holder Vanburn Alonzo	10.10.1945		40	1969–*1978*	682	42	0	14.20	109	6-28	3/0	33.27	16	12
Holding Michael Anthony (*CY 1977*)	16.2.1954		60	*1975–1986*	910	73	0	13.78	249	8-92	13/2	23.68	22	102
Holford David Anthony Jerome	16.4.1940		24	1966–*1976*	768	105*	1	22.58	51	5-23	1/0	39.39	18	
Holt John Kenneth Constantine	12.8.1923	3.6.1997	17	1953–1958	1,066	166	2	36.75	1	1-20	0/0	20.00	8	
Hooper Carl Llewellyn	15.12.1966		102	1987–2002	5,762	233	13	36.46	114	5-26	4/0	49.42	115	227
Howard Anthony Bourne	27.8.1946		1	*1971*	–	–	–	–	2	2-140	0/0	70.00	0	
Hunte *Sir* Conrad Cleophas (*CY 1964*)	9.5.1932	3.12.1999	44	*1957–1966*	3,245	260	8	45.06	2	1-17	0/0	55.00	16	
Hunte Errol Ashton Clairmore	3.10.1905	26.6.1967	3	*1929*	166	58	0	33.20	–	–	–/–	–	5	
Hylton Leslie George	29.3.1905	17.5.1955	6	*1934*–1939	70	19	0	11.66	16	4-27	0/0	26.12	1	
Jacobs Ridley Detamore	26.11.1967		65	*1998*–2004	2,577	118	3	28.31	–	–	–/–	–	207/12	147
Jaggernauth Amit Sheldon	16.11.1983		1	*2007*	0	0*	0	0.00	1	1-74	0/0	96.00	0	
Johnson Hophnie Hobah Hines	13.7.1910	24.6.1987	3	*1947*–1950	38	22	0	9.50	13	5-41	2/1	18.30	0	
Johnson Tyrell Fabian	10.1.1917	5.4.1985	1	1939	9	9*	0	–	3	2-53	0/0	43.00	1	
Jones Charles Ernest Llewellyn	3.11.1902	10.12.1959	4	*1929–1934*	63	19	0	9.00	0	0-2	0/0	–	3	
Jones Prior Erskine Waverley	6.6.1917	21.11.1991	9	*1947–1951*	47	10*	0	5.22	25	5-85	1/0	30.04	4	
Joseph David Rolston Emmanuel	15.11.1969		4	*1998*	141	50	0	20.14	–	–	–/–	–	10	
Joseph Sylvester Cleofoster	5.9.1978		5	2004–2007	147	45	0	14.70	0	0-8	0/0	–	3	13
Julien Bernard Denis	13.3.1950		24	1973–*1976*	866	121	2	30.92	50	5-57	1/0	37.36	14	12
Jumadeen Raphick Rasif	12.4.1948		12	*1971–1978*	84	56	0	21.00	29	4-72	0/0	39.34	4	
Kallicharran Alvin Isaac (*CY 1983*)	21.3.1949		66	*1971–1980*	4,399	187	12	44.43	4	2-16	0/0	39.50	51	31
Kanhai Rohan Bholalall (*CY 1964*)	26.12.1935		79	1957–*1973*	6,227	256	15	47.53	0	0-1	0/0	–	50	7
Kentish Esmond Seymour Maurice	21.11.1916	10.6.2011	2	*1947–1953*	1	1*	0	1.00	8	5-49	1/0	22.25	1	
King Collis Llewellyn	11.6.1951		9	1976–1980	418	100*	1	32.15	3	1-30	0/0	94.00	5	18
King Frank McDonald	14.12.1926	23.12.1990	14	*1952–1955*	116	21	0	8.28	29	5-74	1/0	39.96	5	
King Lester Anthony	27.2.1939	9.7.1998	2	*1961–1967*	41	20	0	10.25	9	5-46	1/0	17.11	2	
King Reon Dane	6.10.1975		19	*1998–2004*	66	12*	0	3.47	53	5-51	1/0	32.69	2	50
Lambert Clayton Benjamin	10.2.1962		5	1991–*1998*	284	104	1	31.55	1	1-4	0/0	5.00	8	11
Lara Brian Charles (*CY 1995*)	2.5.1969		130§	*1990–2006*	11,912	400*	34	53.17	0	0-0	0/0	–	164	295‡
Lashley Patrick Douglas ("Peter")	11.2.1937		4	*1960*–1966	159	49	0	22.71	1	1-1	0/0	1.00	4	

§ *Lara's figures exclude 41 runs for the ICC World XI v Australia in the Super Series Test in 2005-06.*

	Born	*Died*	*Tests*	*Test Career*	*Runs*	*HS*	*100s*	*Avge*	*Wkts*	*BB*	*5/10*	*Avge*	*Ct/St*	*O/T*
Lawson Jermaine Jay Charles	13.1.1982		13	*2002–2005*	52	14	0	3.46	51	7-78	2/0	29.64	3	13
Legall Ralph Archibald	1.12.1925	2003	4	*1952*	50	23	0	10.00	–	–	–/–	–	8/1	
Lewis Desmond Michael	21.2.1946		3	*1970*	259	88	0	86.33	–	–	–/–	–	8	
Lewis Rawl Nicholas	5.9.1974		5	*1997–2007*	89	40	0	8.90	4	2-42	0/0	114.00	0	28/1
Lloyd Clive Hubert CBE (*CY 1971*)	31.8.1944		110	*1966–1984*	7,515	242*	19	46.67	10	2-13	0/0	62.20	90	87
Logie Augustine Lawrence	28.9.1960		52	*1982*–1991	2,470	130	2	35.79	0	0-0	0/0	–	57	158
McGarrell Neil Christopher	12.7.1972		4	*2000–2001*	61	33	0	15.25	17	4-23	0/0	26.64	2	17
McLean Nixon Alexei McNamara	20.7.1973		19	*1997–2000*	368	46	0	12.26	44	3-53	0/0	42.56	5	45
McMorris Easton Dudley Ashton St John	4.4.1935		13	*1957*–1966	564	125	1	26.85	–	–	–/–	–	5	
McWatt Clifford Aubrey	1.2.1922	20.7.1997	6	*1953–1954*	202	54	0	28.85	1	1-16	0/0	16.00	9/1	
Madray Ivan Samuel	2.7.1934	23.4.2009	2	*1957*	3	2	0	1.00	0	0-12	0/0	–	2	
Marshall Malcolm Denzil (*CY 1983*)	18.4.1958	4.11.1999	81	*1978*–1991	1,810	92	0	18.85	376	7-22	22/4	20.94	25	136
[2] **Marshall** Norman Edgar	27.2.1924	11.8.2007	1	*1954*	8	8	0	4.00	2	1-22	0/0	31.00	0	
[2] **Marshall** Roy Edwin (*CY 1959*)	25.4.1930	27.10.1992	4	*1951*	143	30	0	20.42	0	0-3	0/0	–	1	
Marshall Xavier Melbourne	27.3.1986		7	2005–*2008*	243	85	0	20.25	0	0-0	0/0	–	7	24/6
Martin Frank Reginald	12.10.1893	23.11.1967	9	1928–*1930*	486	123*	1	28.58	8	3-91	0/0	77.37	2	
Martindale Emmanuel Alfred	25.11.1909	17.3.1972	10	1933–1939	58	22	0	5.27	37	5-22	3/0	21.72	5	
Mattis Everton Hugh	11.4.1957		4	*1980*	145	71	0	29.00	0	0-4	0/0	–	3	2
Mendonca Ivor Leon	13.7.1934		2	*1961*	81	78	0	40.50	–	–	–/–	–	8/2	
Merry Cyril Arthur	20.1.1911	19.4.1964	2	1933	34	13	0	8.50	–	–	–/–	–	1	
Miller Nikita O'Neil	16.5.1982		1	2009	5	5	0	2.50	0	0-27	0/0	–	0	39/7
Miller Roy	24.12.1924		1	*1952*	23	23	0	23.00	0	0-28	0/0	–	0	
Mohammed Dave	8.10.1979		5	*2003–2006*	225	52	0	32.14	13	3-98	0/0	51.38	1	7
Moodie George Horatio	26.11.1915	8.6.2002	1	*1934*	5	5	0	5.00	3	2-23	0/0	13.33	0	
Morton Runako Shakur	22.7.1978	4.3.2012	15	2005–*2007*	573	70*	0	22.03	0	0-4	0/0	–	20	56/7
Moseley Ezra Alphonsa	5.1.1958		2	*1989*	35	26	0	8.75	6	2-70	0/0	43.50	1	9
Murray David Anthony	29.5.1950		19	*1977–1981*	601	84	0	21.46	–	–	–/–	–	57/5	10
Murray Deryck Lance	20.5.1943		62	1963–1980	1,993	91	0	22.90	–	–	–/–	–	181/8	26
Murray Junior Randalph	20.1.1968		33	*1992–2001*	918	101*	1	22.39	–	–	–/–	–	99/3	55
Nagamootoo Mahendra Veeren	9.10.1975		5	2000–*2002*	185	68	0	26.42	12	3-119	0/0	53.08	2	24
Nanan Rangy	29.5.1953		1	*1980*	16	8	0	8.00	4	2-37	0/0	22.75	2	
Narine Sunil Philip	26.5.1988		5	2012–*2012*	38	22*	0	9.50	15	5-132	1/0	48.06	2	20/13
Nash Brendan Paul	14.12.1977		21	*2008*–2011	1,103	114	2	33.42	2	1-21	0/0	123.50	6	9
Neblett James Montague	13.11.1901	28.3.1959	1	*1934*	16	11*	0	16.00	1	1-44	0/0	75.00	0	
Noreiga Jack Mollinson	15.4.1936	8.8.2003	4	*1970*	11	9	0	3.66	17	9-95	2/0	29.00	2	
Nunes Robert Karl	7.6.1894	23.7.1958	4	1928–*1929*	245	92	0	30.62	–	–	–/–	–	2	

	Born	Died	Tests	Test Career	Runs	HS	100s	Avge	Wkts	BB	5/10	Avge	Ct/St	O/T
Nurse Seymour MacDonald (*CY 1967*)	10.11.1933		29	*1959–1968*	2,523	258	6	47.60	0	0-0	0/0	–	21	
Padmore Albert Leroy	17.12.1946		2	*1975*–1976	8	8*	0	8.00	1	1-36	0/0	135.00	0	
Pagon Donovan Jomo	13.9.1982		2	*2004*	37	35	0	12.33	–	–	–/–	–	0	
Pairaudeau Bruce Hamilton	14.4.1931		13	*1952*–1957	454	115	1	21.61	0	0-3	0/0	–	6	
Parchment Brenton Anthony	24.6.1982		2	*2007*	55	20	0	13.75	–	–	–/–	–	1	7/1
Parry Derick Recaldo	22.12.1954		12	*1977–1979*	381	65	0	22.41	23	5-15	1/0	40.69	4	6
Pascal Nelon Troy	25.4.1987		2	2010–*2010*	12	10	0	6.00	0	0-27	0/0	–	1	1
Passailaigue Charles Clarence	4.8.1901	7.1.1972	1	*1929*	46	44	0	46.00	0	0-15	0/0	–	3	
Patterson Balfour Patrick	15.9.1961		28	*1985–1992*	145	21*	0	6.59	93	5-24	5/0	30.90	5	59
Payne Thelston Rodney O'Neale	13.2.1957		1	*1985*	5	5	0	5.00	–	–	–/–	–	5	7
Permaul Veerasammy	11.8.1989		2	*2012*	23	13	0	11.50	8	3-32	0/0	31.62	1	3
Perry Nehemiah Odolphus	16.6.1968		4	*1998–1999*	74	26	0	12.33	10	5-70	1/0	44.60	1	21
Phillip Norbert	12.6.1948		9	*1977–1978*	297	47	0	29.70	28	4-48	0/0	37.17	5	1
Phillips Omar Jamel	12.10.1986		2	2009	160	94	0	40.00	–	–	–/–	–	1	
Pierre Lancelot Richard	5.6.1921	14.4.1989	1	*1947*	–	–	–	–	0	0-9	0/0	–	0	
Powell Daren Brentlyle	15.4.1978		37	2002–*2008*	407	36*	0	7.82	85	5-25	1/0	47.85	8	55/5
Powell Kieran Omar Akeem	6.3.1990		13	2011–*2012*	784	134	3	32.66	–	–	–/–	–	8	11
Powell Ricardo Lloyd	16.12.1978		2	*1999–2003*	53	30	0	17.66	0	0-13	0/0	–	1	109
Rae Allan Fitzroy	30.9.1922	27.2.2005	15	*1948–1952*	1,016	109	4	46.18	–	–	–/–	–	10	
Ragoonath Suruj	22.3.1968		2	*1998*	13	9	0	4.33	–	–	–/–	–	0	
Ramadhin Sonny (*CY 1951*)	1.5.1929		43	1950–*1960*	361	44	0	8.20	158	7-49	10/1	28.98	9	
Ramdass Ryan Rakesh	3.7.1983		1	2005	26	23	0	13.00	–	–	–/–	–	2	1
Ramdin Denesh	13.3.1985		49	2005–*2012*	1,825	166	3	25.00	–	–	–/–	–	144/3	94/33
Ramnarine Dinanath	4.6.1975		12	*1997–2001*	106	35*	0	6.23	45	5-78	1/0	30.73	8	4
Rampaul Ravindranath	15.10.1984		18	*2009–2012*	335	40*	0	14.56	49	4-48	0/0	34.79	3	73/19
Reifer Floyd Lamonte	23.7.1972		6	*1996*–2009	111	29	0	9.25	–	–	–/–	–	6	8/1
Richards Dale Maurice	16.7.1976		3	2009–2010	125	69	0	20.83	–	–	–/–	–	4	8/1
Richards *Sir* Isaac Vivian Alexander (*CY 1977*)	7.3.1952		121	*1974*–1991	8,540	291	24	50.23	32	2-17	0/0	61.37	122	187
Richardson Richard Benjamin (*CY 1992*)	12.1.1962		86	*1983*–1995	5,949	194	16	44.39	0	0-0	0/0	–	90	224
Rickards Kenneth Roy	22.8.1923	21.8.1995	2	*1947–1951*	104	67	0	34.66	–	–	–/–	–	0	
Roach Clifford Archibald	13.3.1904	16.4.1988	16	1928–*1934*	952	209	2	30.70	2	1-18	0/0	51.50	5	
Roach Kemar Andre Jamal	30.6.1988		21	2009–2012	291	41	0	10.39	82	6-48	5/1	27.69	6	44/11
Roberts Alphonso Theodore	18.9.1937	24.7.1996	1	*1955*	28	28	0	14.00	–	–	–/–	–	0	
Roberts Anderson Montgomery Everton CBE (*CY 1975*)	29.1.1951		47	*1973–1983*	762	68	0	14.94	202	7-54	11/2	25.61	9	56
Roberts Lincoln Abraham	4.9.1974		1	*1998*	0	0	0	0.00	–	–	–/–	–	0	

	Born	Died	Tests	Test Career	Runs	HS	100s	Avge	Wkts	BB	5/10	Avge	Ct/St	O/T
Rodriguez William Vicente	25.6.1934		5	*1961–1967*	96	50	0	13.71	7	3-51	0/0	53.42	3	
Rose Franklyn Albert.	1.2.1972		19	*1996*–2000	344	69	0	13.23	53	7-84	2/0	30.88	4	27
Rowe Lawrence George.	8.1.1949		30	*1971–1979*	2,047	302	7	43.55	0	0-1	0/0	–	17	11
Russell Andre Dwayne	29.4.1988		1	*2010*	2	2	0	2.00	1	1-73	0/0	104.00	1	30/12
[2]**St Hill** Edwin Lloyd	9.3.1904	21.5.1957	2	*1929*	18	12	0	4.50	3	2-110	0/0	73.66	0	
[2]**St Hill** Wilton H	6.7.1893	d unknown	3	1928–*1929*	117	38	0	19.50	0	0-9	0/0	–	1	
Sammy Darren Julius Garvey	20.12.1983		31	2007–*2012*	1,082	106	1	21.64	76	7-66	4/0	34.31	49	87/37
[2]**Samuels** Marlon Nathaniel (*CY 2013*)	5.1.1981		44	*2000–2012*	2,690	260	5	37.36	24	3-74	0/0	69.00	19	142/23
[2]**Samuels** Robert George	13.3.1971		6	*1995–1996*	372	125	1	37.20	–	–	–/–	–	8	8
Sanford Adam	12.7.1975		11	*2001–2003*	72	18*	0	4.80	30	4-132	0/0	43.86	4	
Sarwan Ramnaresh Ronnie	23.6.1980		87	*1999*–2011	5,842	291	15	40.01	23	4-37	0/0	50.56	53	173/18
Scarlett Reginald Osmond	15.8.1934		3	*1959*	54	29*	0	18.00	2	1-46	0/0	104.50	2	
[1]**Scott** Alfred Homer Patrick	29.7.1934		1	*1952*	5	5	0	5.00	0	0-52	0/0	–	0	
[1]**Scott** Oscar Charles ("Tommy")	14.8.1892	15.6.1961	8	1928–*1930*	171	35	0	17.10	22	5-266	1/0	42.04	0	
Sealey Benjamin James	12.8.1899	12.9.1963	1	1933	41	29	0	20.50	1	1-10	0/0	10.00	0	
Sealy James Edward Derrick.	11.9.1912	3.1.1982	11	*1929*–1939	478	92	0	28.11	3	2-7	0/0	31.33	6/1	
Shepherd John Neil (*CY 1979*)	9.11.1943		5	1969–*1970*	77	32	0	9.62	19	5-104	1/0	25.21	4	
Shillingford Grayson Cleophas.	25.9.1944	23.12.2009	7	1969–*1971*	57	25	0	8.14	15	3-63	0/0	35.80	2	
Shillingford Irvine Theodore	18.4.1944		4	*1976–1977*	218	120	1	31.14	–	–	–/–	–	1	2
Shillingford Shane	22.2.1983		8	2010–2012	116	31*	0	11.60	29	6-119	1/1	44.79	4	
Shivnarine Sewdatt.	13.5.1952		8	*1977–1978*	379	63	0	29.15	1	1-13	0/0	167.00	6	1
Simmons Lendl Mark Platter	25.1.1985		8	*2008–2011*	278	49	0	17.37	1	1-60	0/0	147.00	5	42/14
Simmons Philip Verant (*CY 1997*).	18.4.1963		26	*1987–1997*	1,002	110	1	22.26	4	2-34	0/0	64.25	26	143
Singh Charran Kamkaran	27.11.1935		2	*1959*	11	11	0	3.66	5	2-28	0/0	33.20	2	
Small Joseph A.	3.11.1892	26.4.1958	3	1928–*1929*	79	52	0	13.16	3	2-67	0/0	61.33	3	
Small Milton Aster	12.2.1964		2	*1983*–1984	3	3*	0	–	4	3-40	0/0	38.25	0	2
Smith Cameron Wilberforce.	29.7.1933		5	*1960–1961*	222	55	0	24.66	–	–	–/–	–	4/1	
Smith Devon Sheldon	21.10.1981		33	*2002–2011*	1,384	108	1	24.71	0	0-3	0/0	–	28	42/6
Smith Dwayne Romel	12.4.1983		10	*2003–2005*	320	105*	1	24.61	7	3-71	0/0	49.14	9	87/17
Smith O'Neil Gordon ("Collie") (*CY 1958*) . . .	5.5.1933	9.9.1959	26	*1954–1958*	1,331	168	4	31.69	48	5-90	1/0	33.85	9	
Sobers *Sir* Garfield St Aubrun (*CY 1964*)	28.7.1936		93	*1953–1973*	8,032	365*	26	57.78	235	6-73	6/0	34.03	109	1
Solomon Joseph Stanislaus.	26.8.1930		27	*1958–1964*	1,326	100*	1	34.00	4	1-20	0/0	67.00	13	
Stayers Sven Conrad ("Charlie").	9.6.1937	6.1.2005	4	*1961*	58	35*	0	19.33	9	3-65	0/0	40.44	0	
[2]**Stollmeyer** Jeffrey Baxter	11.3.1921	10.9.1989	32	1939–*1954*	2,159	160	4	42.33	13	3-32	0/0	39.00	20	
[2]**Stollmeyer** Victor Humphrey	24.1.1916	21.9.1999	1	1939	96	96	0	96.00	–	–	–/–	–	0	
Stuart Colin Ellsworth Laurie.	28.9.1973		6	*2000–2001*	24	12*	0	3.42	20	3-33	0/0	31.40	2	5

	Born	Died	Tests	Test Career	Runs	HS	100s	Avge	Wkts	BB	5/10	Avge	Ct/St	O/T
Taylor Jaswick Ossie	3.1.1932	13.11.1999	3	*1957–1958*	4	4*	0	2.00	10	5-109	1/0	27.30	0	
Taylor Jerome Everton	22.6.1984		29	2003–*2009*	629	106	1	15.72	82	5-11	3/0	35.64	5	66/17
Thompson Patterson Ian Chesterfield	26.9.1971		2	*1995–1996*	17	10*	0	8.50	5	2-58	0/0	43.00	0	2
Tonge Gavin Courtney	13.2.1983		1	*2009*	25	23*	0	25.00	1	1-28	0/0	113.00	0	5/1
Trim John	25.1.1915	12.11.1960	4	*1947–1951*	21	12	0	5.25	18	5-34	1/0	16.16	2	
Valentine Alfred Louis (*CY 1951*)	28.4.1930	11.5.2004	36	1950–*1961*	141	14	0	4.70	139	8-104	8/2	30.32	13	
Valentine Vincent Adolphus	4.4.1908	6.7.1972	2	1933	35	19*	0	11.66	1	1-55	0/0	104.00	0	
Walcott *Sir* Clyde Leopold (*CY 1958*)	17.1.1926	26.8.2006	44	*1947–1959*	3,798	220	15	56.68	11	3-50	0/0	37.09	53/11	
Walcott Leslie Arthur	18.1.1894	27.2.1984	1	*1929*	40	24	0	40.00	1	1-17	0/0	32.00	0	
Wallace Philo Alphonso	2.8.1970		7	*1997–1998*	279	92	0	21.46	–	–	–/–	–	9	33
Walsh Courtney Andrew (*CY 1987*)	30.10.1962		132	*1984–2000*	936	30*	0	7.54	519	7-37	22/3	24.44	29	205
Walton Chadwick Antonio Kirkpatrick	3.7.1985		2	2009	13	10	0	3.25	–	–	–/–	–	10	2
Washington Dwight Marlon	5.3.1983		1	*2004*	7	7*	0	–	0	0-20	0/0	–	3	
Watson Chester Donald	1.7.1938		7	*1959–1961*	12	5	0	2.40	19	4-62	0/0	38.10	1	
Weekes *Sir* Everton de Courcy (*CY 1951*)	26.2.1925		48	*1947–1957*	4,455	207	15	58.61	1	1-8	0/0	77.00	49	
Weekes Kenneth Hunnell	24.1.1912	9.2.1998	2	1939	173	137	1	57.66	–	–	–/–	–	0	
White Anthony Wilbur	20.11.1938		2	*1964*	71	57*	0	23.66	3	2-34	0/0	50.66	1	
Wight Claude Vibart	28.7.1902	4.10.1969	2	1928–*1929*	67	23	0	22.33	0	0-6	0/0	–	0	
Wight George Leslie	28.5.1929	4.1.2004	1	*1952*	21	21	0	21.00	–	–	–/–	–	0	
Wiles Charles Archibald	11.8.1892	4.11.1957	1	1933	2	2	0	1.00	–	–	–/–	–	0	
Willett Elquemedo Tonito	1.5.1953		5	*1972–1974*	74	26	0	14.80	11	3-33	0/0	43.81	0	
Williams Alvadon Basil	21.11.1949		7	*1977–1978*	469	111	2	39.08	–	–	–/–	–	5	
Williams David	4.11.1963		11	*1991–1997*	242	65	0	13.44	–	–	–/–	–	40/2	36
Williams Ernest Albert Vivian ("Foffie")	10.4.1914	13.4.1997	4	1939–*1947*	113	72	0	18.83	9	3-51	0/0	26.77	2	
Williams Stuart Clayton	12.8.1969		31	*1993–2001*	1,183	128	1	24.14	0	0-19	0/0	–	27	57
Wishart Kenneth Leslie	28.11.1908	18.10.1972	1	*1934*	52	52	0	26.00	–	–	–/–	–	0	
Worrell *Sir* Frank Mortimer Maglinne (*CY 1951*)	1.8.1924	13.3.1967	51	*1947*–1963	3,860	261	9	49.48	69	7-70	2/0	38.72	43	

NEW ZEALAND (258 players)

	Born	Died	Tests	Test Career	Runs	HS	100s	Avge	Wkts	BB	5/10	Avge	Ct/St	O/T
Adams Andre Ryan	17.7.1975		1	*2001*	18	11	0	9.00	6	3-44	0/0	17.50	1	42/4
Alabaster John Chaloner	11.7.1930		21	*1955–1971*	272	34	0	9.71	49	4-46	0/0	38.02	7	
Allcott Cyril Francis Walter	7.10.1896	19.11.1973	6	*1929–1931*	113	33	0	22.60	6	2-102	0/0	90.16	3	
Allott Geoffrey Ian	24.12.1971		10	*1995–1999*	27	8*	0	3.37	19	4-74	0/0	58.47	2	31
[1] **Anderson** Robert Wickham	2.10.1948		9	*1976*–1978	423	92	0	23.50	–	–	–/–	–	1	2

	Born	Died	Tests	Test Career	Runs	HS	100s	Avge	Wkts	BB	5/10	Avge	Ct/St	O/T
[1] **Anderson** William McDougall	8.10.1919	21.12.1979	1	1945	5	4	0	2.50	–	–	–/–	–	1	
Andrews Bryan	4.4.1945		2	1973	22	17	0	22.00	2	2-40	0/0	77.00	1	
Arnel Brent John	3.1.1979		6	2009–2011	45	8*	0	5.62	9	4-95	0/0	62.88	3	
Astle Nathan John	15.9.1971		81	1995–2006	4,702	222	11	37.02	51	3-27	0/0	42.01	70	223/4
Astle Todd Duncan	24.9.1986		1	2012	38	35	0	19.00	1	1-56	0/0	97.00	0	
Badcock Frederick Theodore ("Ted")	9.8.1897	19.9.1982	7	1929–1932	137	64	0	19.57	16	4-80	0/0	38.12	1	
Barber Richard Trevor	3.6.1925		1	1955	17	12	0	8.50	–	–	–/–	–	1	
Bartlett Gary Alex	3.2.1941		10	1961–1967	263	40	0	15.47	24	6-38	1/0	33.00	8	
Barton Paul Thomas	9.10.1935		7	1961–1962	285	109	1	20.35	–	–	–/–	–	4	
Beard Donald Derek	14.1.1920	15.7.1982	4	1951–1955	101	31	0	20.20	9	3-22	0/0	33.55	2	
Beck John Edward Francis	1.8.1934	23.4.2000	8	1953–1955	394	99	0	26.26	–	–	–/–	–	0	
Bell Matthew David	25.2.1977		18	1998–2007	729	107	2	24.30	–	–	–/–	–	19	7
Bell William	5.9.1931	23.7.2002	2	1953	21	21*	0	–	2	1-54	0/0	117.50	1	
Bennett Hamish Kyle	22.2.1987		1	2010	4	4	0	4.00	0	0-47	0/0	–	0	12
Bilby Grahame Paul	7.5.1941		2	1965	55	28	0	13.75	–	–	–/–	–	3	
Blain Tony Elston	17.2.1962		11	1986–1993	456	78	0	26.82	–	–	–/–	–	19/2	38
Blair Robert William	23.6.1932		19	1952–1963	189	64*	0	6.75	43	4-85	0/0	35.23	5	
Blunt Roger Charles (CY 1928)	3.11.1900	22.6.1966	9	1929–1931	330	96	0	27.50	12	3-17	0/0	39.33	5	
Bolton Bruce Alfred	31.5.1935		2	1958	59	33	0	19.66	–	–	–/–	–	1	
Bond Shane Edward	7.6.1975		18	2001–2009	168	41*	0	12.92	87	6-51	5/1	22.09	8	82/20
Boock Stephen Lewis	20.9.1951		30	1977–1988	207	37	0	6.27	74	7-87	4/0	34.64	14	14
Boult Trent Alexander	22.7.1989		10	2011–2012	133	33*	0	16.62	30	4-42	0/0	31.43	3	7
[1,2] **Bracewell** Brendon Paul	14.9.1959		6	1978–1984	24	8	0	2.40	14	3-110	0/0	41.78	1	1
[1] **Bracewell** Douglas Alexander John	28.9.1990		15	2011–2012	271	43	0	10.42	46	6-40	2/0	31.89	5	6/13
[2] **Bracewell** John Garry	15.4.1958		41	1980–1990	1,001	110	1	20.42	102	6-32	4/1	35.81	31	53
[1] **Bradburn** Grant Eric	26.5.1966		7	1990–2000	105	30*	0	13.12	6	3-134	0/0	76.66	6	11
[1] **Bradburn** Wynne Pennell	24.11.1938	25.9.2008	2	1963	62	32	0	15.50	–	–	–/–	–	2	
Brown Vaughan Raymond	3.11.1959		2	1985	51	36*	0	25.50	1	1-17	0/0	176.00	3	3
Brownlie Dean Graham	30.7.1984		9	2011–2012	547	109	1	34.18	1	1-13	0/0	52.00	9	3/4
Burgess Mark Gordon	17.7.1944		50	1967–1980	2,684	119*	5	31.20	6	3-23	0/0	35.33	34	26
Burke Cecil	27.3.1914	4.8.1997	1	1945	4	3	0	2.00	2	2-30	0/0	15.00	0	
Burtt Thomas Browning	22.1.1915	24.5.1988	10	1946–1952	252	42	0	21.00	33	6-162	3/0	35.45	2	
Butler Ian Gareth	24.11.1981		8	2001–2004	76	26	0	9.50	24	6-46	1/0	36.83	4	26/15
Butterfield Leonard Arthur	29.8.1913	5.7.1999	1	1945	0	0	0	0.00	0	0-24	0/0	–	0	
[1] **Cairns** Bernard Lance	10.10.1949		43	1973–1985	928	64	0	16.28	130	7-74	6/1	32.91	30	78
[1] **Cairns** Christopher Lance (CY 2000)	13.6.1970		62	1989–2004	3,320	158	5	33.53	218	7-27	13/1	29.40	14	214‡/2

	Born	*Died*	*Tests*	*Test Career*	*Runs*	*HS*	*100s*	*Avge*	*Wkts*	*BB*	*5/10*	*Avge*	*Ct/St*	*O/T*
Cameron Francis James MBE	1.6.1932		19	*1961*–1965	116	27*	0	11.60	62	5-34	3/0	29.82	1	
Cave Henry Butler	10.10.1922	15.9.1989	19	1949–1958	229	22*	0	8.80	34	4-21	0/0	43.14	8	
Chapple Murray Ernest	25.7.1930	31.7.1985	14	*1952–1965*	497	76	0	19.11	1	1-24	0/0	84.00	10	
Chatfield Ewen John MBE	3.7.1950		43	*1974–1988*	180	21*	0	8.57	123	6-73	3/1	32.17	7	114
Cleverley Donald Charles	23.12.1909	16.2.2004	2	*1931–1945*	19	10*	0	19.00	0	0-51	0/0	–	0	
Collinge Richard Owen	2.4.1946		35	*1964*–1978	533	68*	0	14.40	116	6-63	3/0	29.25	10	15
Colquhoun Ian Alexander	8.6.1924	26.2.2005	2	*1954*	1	1*	0	0.50	–	–	–/–	–	4	
Coney Jeremy Vernon MBE (*CY 1984*)	21.6.1952		52	*1973–1986*	2,668	174*	3	37.57	27	3-28	0/0	35.77	64	88
Congdon Bevan Ernest OBE (*CY 1974*)	11.2.1938		61	*1964*–1978	3,448	176	7	32.22	59	5-65	1/0	36.50	44	11
Cowie John OBE	30.3.1912	3.6.1994	9	1937–1949	90	45	0	10.00	45	6-40	4/1	21.53	3	
Cresswell George Fenwick.	22.3.1915	10.1.1966	3	1949–*1950*	14	12*	0	7.00	13	6-168	1/0	22.46	0	
Cromb Ian Burns	25.6.1905	6.3.1984	5	1931–*1931*	123	51*	0	20.50	8	3-113	0/0	55.25	1	
[2]**Crowe** Jeffrey John	14.9.1958		39	*1982–1989*	1,601	128	3	26.24	0	0-0	0/0	–	41	75
[2]**Crowe** Martin David MBE (*CY 1985*)	22.9.1962		77	*1981–1995*	5,444	299	17	45.36	14	2-25	0/0	48.28	71	143
Cumming Craig Derek	31.8.1975		11	*2004–2007*	441	74	0	25.94	–	–	–/–	–	3	13
Cunis Robert Smith.	5.1.1941	9.8.2008	20	*1963–1971*	295	51	0	12.82	51	6-76	1/0	37.00	1	
D'Arcy John William	23.4.1936		5	1958	136	33	0	13.60	–	–	–/–	–	0	
Davis Heath Te-Ihi-O-Te-Rangi	30.11.1971		5	1994–*1997*	20	8*	0	6.66	17	5-63	1/0	29.35	4	11
de Groen Richard Paul	5.8.1962		5	*1993–1994*	45	26	0	7.50	11	3-40	0/0	45.90	0	12
Dempster Charles Stewart (*CY 1932*)	15.11.1903	14.2.1974	10	*1929–1932*	723	136	2	65.72	0	0-10	0/0	–	2	
Dempster Eric William MBE.	25.1.1925	15.8.2011	5	*1952–1953*	106	47	0	17.66	2	1-24	0/0	109.50	1	
Dick Arthur Edward	10.10.1936		17	*1961*–1965	370	50*	0	14.23	–	–	–/–	–	47/4	
Dickinson George Ritchie	11.3.1903	17.3.1978	3	*1929–1931*	31	11	0	6.20	8	3-66	0/0	30.62	3	
Donnelly Martin Paterson (*CY 1948*)	17.10.1917	22.10.1999	7	1937–1949	582	206	1	52.90	0	0-20	0/0	–	7	
Doull Simon Blair.	6.8.1969		32	*1992–1999*	570	46	0	14.61	98	7-65	6/0	29.30	16	42
Dowling Graham Thorne OBE	4.3.1937		39	*1961–1971*	2,306	239	3	31.16	1	1-19	0/0	19.00	23	
Drum Christopher James	10.7.1974		5	*2000–2001*	10	4	0	3.33	16	3-36	0/0	30.12	4	5
Dunning John Angus.	6.2.1903	24.6.1971	4	*1932*–1937	38	19	0	7.60	5	2-35	0/0	98.60	2	
Edgar Bruce Adrian	23.11.1956		39	1978–1986	1,958	161	3	30.59	0	0-3	0/0	–	14	64
Edwards Graham Neil ("Jock")	27.5.1955		8	*1976–1980*	377	55	0	25.13	–	–	–/–	–	7	6
Elliott Grant David	21.3.1979		5	*2007–2009*	86	25	0	10.75	4	2-8	0/0	35.00	2	37/1
Emery Raymond William George	28.3.1915	18.12.1982	2	*1951*	46	28	0	11.50	2	2-52	0/0	26.00	0	
Fisher Frederick Eric.	28.7.1924	19.6.1996	1	*1952*	23	14	0	11.50	1	1-78	0/0	78.00	0	
Fleming Stephen Paul	1.4.1973		111	*1993–2007*	7,172	274*	9	40.06	–	–	–/–	–	171	279‡/5
Flynn Daniel Raymond	16.4.1985		24	2008–*2012*	1,038	95	0	25.95	0	0-0	0/0	–	10	20/5
Foley Henry	28.1.1906	16.10.1948	1	*1929*	4	2	0	2.00	–	–	–/–	–	0	

	Born	Died	Tests	Test Career	Runs	HS	100s	Avge	Wkts	BB	5/10	Avge	Ct/St	O/T
Franklin James Edward Charles	7.11.1980		31	2000–2012	808	122*	1	20.71	82	6-119	3/0	33.97	12	98/33
Franklin Trevor John	15.3.1962		21	1983–1990	828	101	1	23.00	–	–	–/–	–	8	3
Freeman Douglas Linford	8.9.1914	31.5.1994	2	1932	2	1	0	1.00	1	1-91	0/0	169.00	0	
Fulton Peter Gordon	1.2.1979		10	2005–2009	314	75	0	20.93	–	–	–/–	–	12	49/12
Gallichan Norman	3.6.1906	25.3.1969	1	1937	32	30	0	16.00	3	3-99	0/0	37.66	0	
Gedye Sidney Graham	2.5.1929		4	1963–1964	193	55	0	24.12	–	–	–/–	–	0	
Germon Lee Kenneth	4.11.1968		12	1995–1996	382	55	0	21.22	–	–	–/–	–	27/2	37
Gillespie Mark Raymond	17.10.1979		5	2007–2011	76	27	0	10.85	22	6-113	3/0	28.68	1	32/11
Gillespie Stuart Ross	2.3.1957		1	1985	28	28	0	28.00	1	1-79	0/0	79.00	0	19
Gray Evan John	18.11.1954		10	1983–1988	248	50	0	15.50	17	3-73	0/0	52.11	6	10
Greatbatch Mark John	11.12.1963		41	1987–1996	2,021	146*	3	30.62	0	0-0	0/0	–	27	84
Guillen Simpson Clairmonte ("Sammy")	24.9.1924		3†	1955	98	41	0	16.33	–	–	–/–	–	4/1	
Guptill Martin James	30.9.1986		30	2008–2012	1,714	189	2	30.60	5	3-37	0/0	43.40	31	65/38
Guy John William	29.8.1934		12	1955–1961	440	102	1	20.95	–	–	–/–	–	2	
1, 2 **Hadlee** Dayle Robert	6.1.1948		26	1969–1977	530	56	0	14.32	71	4-30	0/0	33.64	8	11
1, 2 **Hadlee** *Sir* Richard John (*CY 1982*)	3.7.1951		86	1972–1990	3,124	151*	2	27.16	431	9-52	36/9	22.29	39	115
1 **Hadlee** Walter Arnold CBE	4.6.1915	29.9.2006	11	1937–1950	543	116	1	30.16	–	–	–/–	–	6	
Harford Noel Sherwin	30.8.1930	30.3.1981	8	1955–1958	229	93	0	15.26	–	–	–/–	–	0	
Harford Roy Ivan	30.5.1936		3	1967	7	6	0	2.33	–	–	–/–	–	11	
1 **Harris** Chris Zinzan	20.11.1969		23	1992–2002	777	71	0	20.44	16	2-16	0/0	73.12	14	250
1 **Harris** Parke Gerald Zinzan	18.7.1927	1.12.1991	9	1955–1964	378	101	1	22.23	0	0-14	0/0	–	6	
Harris Roger Meredith	27.7.1933		2	1958	31	13	0	10.33	–	–	–/–	–	0	
2 **Hart** Matthew Norman	16.5.1972		14	1993–1995	353	45	0	17.65	29	5-77	1/0	49.58	9	13
2 **Hart** Robert Garry	2.12.1974		11	2002–2003	260	57*	0	16.25	–	–	–/–	–	29/1	2
Hartland Blair Robert	22.10.1966		9	1991–1994	303	52	0	16.83	–	–	–/–	–	5	16
Haslam Mark James	26.9.1972		4	1992–1995	4	3	0	4.00	2	1-33	0/0	122.50	2	1
Hastings Brian Frederick	23.3.1940		31	1968–1975	1,510	117*	4	30.20	0	0-3	0/0	–	23	11
Hayes John Arthur	11.1.1927	25.12.2007	15	1950–1958	73	19	0	4.86	30	4-36	0/0	40.56	3	
Henderson Matthew	2.8.1895	17.6.1970	1	1929	8	6	0	8.00	2	2-38	0/0	32.00	1	
Hopkins Gareth James	24.11.1976		4	2008–2010	71	15	0	11.83	–	–	–/–	–	9	25/10
2 **Horne** Matthew Jeffery	5.12.1970		35	1996–2003	1,788	157	4	28.38	0	0-4	0/0	–	17	50
2 **Horne** Philip Andrew	21.1.1960		4	1986–1990	71	27	0	10.14	–	–	–/–	–	3	4
Hough Kenneth William	24.10.1928	20.9.2009	2	1958	62	31*	0	62.00	6	3-79	0/0	29.16	1	
How Jamie Michael	19.5.1981		19	2005–2008	772	92	0	22.70	0	0-0	0/0	–	18	41/5
2 **Howarth** Geoffrey Philip OBE	29.3.1951		47	1974–1984	2,531	147	6	32.44	3	1-13	0/0	90.33	29	70
2 **Howarth** Hedley John	25.12.1943	7.11.2008	30	1969–1976	291	61	0	12.12	86	5-34	2/0	36.95	33	9

	Born	Died	Tests	Test Career	Runs	HS	100s	Avge	Wkts	BB	5/10	Avge	Ct/St	O/T
Ingram Peter John	25.10.1978		2	*2009*	61	42	0	15.25	–	–	–/–	–	0	8/3
James Kenneth Cecil	12.3.1904	21.8.1976	11	*1929–1932*	52	14	0	4.72	–	–	–/–	–	11/5	
Jarvis Terrence Wayne	29.7.1944		13	*1964–1972*	625	182	1	29.76	0	0-0	0/0	–	3	
Jones Andrew Howard	9.5.1959		39	*1986–1994*	2,922	186	7	44.27	1	1-40	0/0	194.00	25	87
Jones Richard Andrew	22.10.1973		1	*2003*	23	16	0	11.50	–	–	–/–	–	0	5
Kennedy Robert John	3.6.1972		4	*1995*	28	22	0	7.00	6	3-28	0/0	63.33	2	7
Kerr John Lambert	28.12.1910	27.5.2007	7	1931–1937	212	59	0	19.27	–	–	–/–	–	4	
Kuggeleijn Christopher Mary	10.5.1956		2	*1988*	7	7	0	1.75	1	1-50	0/0	67.00	1	16
Larsen Gavin Rolf	27.9.1962		8	1994–*1995*	127	26*	0	14.11	24	3-57	0/0	28.70	5	121
Latham Rodney Terry	12.6.1961		4	*1991–1992*	219	119	1	31.28	0	0-6	0/0	–	5	33
Lees Warren Kenneth MBE	19.3.1952		21	*1976*–1983	778	152	1	23.57	0	0-4	0/0	–	52/7	31
Leggat Ian Bruce	7.6.1930		1	*1953*	0	0	0	0.00	0	0-6	0/0	–	2	
Leggat John Gordon	27.5.1926	9.3.1973	9	*1951–1955*	351	61	0	21.93	–	–	–/–	–	0	
Lissette Allen Fisher	6.11.1919	24.1.1973	2	*1955*	2	1*	0	1.00	3	2-73	0/0	41.33	1	
Loveridge Greg Riaka	15.1.1975		1	*1995*	4	4*	0	–	–	–	–/–	–	0	
Lowry Thomas Coleman	17.2.1898	20.7.1976	7	*1929*–1931	223	80	0	27.87	0	0-0	0/0	–	8	
McCullum Brendon Barrie	27.9.1981		72	*2003–2012*	4,180	225	6	35.12	0	0-18	0/0	–	174/11	206/57
McEwan Paul Ernest	19.12.1953		4	*1979–1984*	96	40*	0	16.00	0	0-6	0/0	–	5	17
MacGibbon Anthony Roy	28.8.1924	6.4.2010	26	*1950*–1958	814	66	0	19.85	70	5-64	1/0	30.85	13	
McGirr Herbert Mendelson	5.11.1891	14.4.1964	2	*1929*	51	51	0	51.00	1	1-65	0/0	115.00	0	
McGregor Spencer Noel	18.12.1931	21.11.2007	25	*1954–1964*	892	111	1	19.82	–	–	–/–	–	9	
McIntosh Timothy Gavin	4.12.1979		17	*2008–2010*	854	136	2	27.54	–	–	–/–	–	10	
McKay Andrew John	17.4.1980		1	*2010*	25	20*	0	25.00	1	1-120	0/0	120.00	0	19/2
McLeod Edwin George	14.10.1900	14.9.1989	1	*1929*	18	16	0	18.00	0	0-5	0/0	–	0	
McMahon Trevor George	8.11.1929		5	*1955*	7	4*	0	2.33	–	–	–/–	–	7/1	
McMillan Craig Douglas	13.9.1976		55	*1997–2004*	3,116	142	6	38.46	28	3-48	0/0	44.89	22	197/8
McRae Donald Alexander Noel	25.12.1912	10.8.1986	1	*1945*	8	8	0	4.00	0	0-44	0/0	–	0	
[2] **Marshall** Hamish John Hamilton	15.2.1979		13	*2000–2005*	652	160	2	38.35	0	0-4	0/0	–	1	66/3
[2] **Marshall** James Andrew Hamilton	15.2.1979		7	*2004*–2008	218	52	0	19.81	–	–	–/–	–	5	10/3
Martin Christopher Stewart	10.12.1974		71	*2000–2012*	123	12*	0	2.36	233	6-26	10/1	33.81	14	20/6
Mason Michael James	27.8.1974		1	*2003*	3	3	0	1.50	0	0-32	0/0	–	0	26/3
Matheson Alexander Malcolm	27.2.1906	31.12.1985	2	*1929*–1931	7	7	0	7.00	2	2-7	0/0	68.00	2	
Meale Trevor	11.11.1928	21.5.2010	2	1958	21	10	0	5.25	–	–	–/–	–	0	
Merritt William Edward	18.8.1908	9.6.1977	6	*1929*–1931	73	19	0	10.42	12	4-104	0/0	51.41	2	
Meuli Edgar Milton	20.2.1926	15.4.2007	1	*1952*	38	23	0	19.00	–	–	–/–	–	0	
Milburn Barry Douglas	24.11.1943		3	*1968*	8	4*	0	8.00	–	–	–/–	–	6/2	

	Born	*Died*	*Tests*	*Test Career*	*Runs*	*HS*	*100s*	*Avge*	*Wkts*	*BB*	*5/10*	*Avge*	*Ct/St*	*O/T*
Miller Lawrence Somerville Martin	31.3.1923	17.12.1996	13	*1952–1958*	346	47	0	13.84	0	0-1	0/0	–	1	
Mills John Ernest	3.9.1905	11.12.1972	7	*1929–1932*	241	117	1	26.77	–	–	–/–	–	1	
Mills Kyle David	15.3.1979		19	2004–*2008*	289	57	0	11.56	44	4-16	0/0	33.02	4	141/35
Moir Alexander McKenzie	17.7.1919	17.6.2000	17	*1950–1958*	327	41*	0	14.86	28	6-155	2/0	50.64	2	
Moloney Denis Andrew Robert ("Sonny")	11.8.1910	15.7.1942	3	1937	156	64	0	26.00	0	0-9	0/0	–	3	
Mooney Francis Leonard Hugh	26.5.1921	8.3.2004	14	1949–*1953*	343	46	0	17.15	0	0-0	0/0	–	22/8	
Morgan Ross Winston	12.2.1941		20	*1964–1971*	734	97	0	22.24	5	1-16	0/0	121.80	12	
Morrison Bruce Donald	17.12.1933		1	*1962*	10	10	0	5.00	2	2-129	0/0	64.50	1	
Morrison Daniel Kyle	3.2.1966		48	*1987–1996*	379	42	0	8.42	160	7-89	10/0	34.68	14	96
Morrison John Francis MacLean	27.8.1947		17	*1973–1981*	656	117	1	22.62	2	2-52	0/0	35.50	9	18
Motz Richard Charles (*CY 1966*)	12.1.1940	29.4.2007	32	*1961*–1969	612	60	0	11.54	100	6-63	5/0	31.48	9	
Munro Colin	11.3.1987		1	*2012*	15	15	0	7.50	2	2-40	0/0	20.00	0	0/3
Murray Bruce Alexander Grenfell	18.9.1940		13	*1967–1970*	598	90	0	23.92	1	1-0	0/0	0.00	21	
Murray Darrin James	4.9.1967		8	*1994*	303	52	0	20.20	–	–	–/–	–	6	1
Nash Dion Joseph	20.11.1971		32	*1992–2001*	729	89*	0	23.51	93	6-27	3/1	28.48	13	81
Newman *Sir* Jack	3.7.1902	23.9.1996	3	*1931–1932*	33	19	0	8.25	2	2-76	0/0	127.00	0	
Nicol Robert James	28.5.1983		2	*2011*	28	19	0	7.00	0	0-0	0/0	–	2	18/20
O'Brien Iain Edward	10.7.1976		22	*2004–2009*	219	31	0	7.55	73	6-75	1/0	33.27	7	10/4
O'Connor Shayne Barry	15.11.1973		19	*1997–2001*	103	20	0	5.72	53	5-51	1/0	32.52	6	38
Oram Jacob David Philip	28.7.1978		33	2002–2009	1,780	133	5	36.32	60	4-41	0/0	33.05	15	160/36
O'Sullivan David Robert	16.11.1944		11	*1972–1976*	158	23*	0	9.29	18	5-148	1/0	67.83	2	3
Overton Guy William Fitzroy	8.6.1919	7.9.1993	3	*1953*	8	3*	0	1.60	9	3-65	0/0	28.66	1	
Owens Michael Barry	11.11.1969		8	*1992*–1994	16	8*	0	2.66	17	4-99	0/0	34.41	3	1
Page Milford Laurenson ("Curly")	8.5.1902	13.2.1987	14	*1929*–1937	492	104	1	24.60	5	2-21	0/0	46.20	6	
Papps Michael Hugh William	2.7.1979		8	*2003–2007*	246	86	0	16.40	–	–	–/–	–	11	6
[2] **Parker** John Morton	21.2.1951		36	*1972–1980*	1,498	121	3	24.55	1	1-24	0/0	24.00	30	24
[2] **Parker** Norman Murray	28.8.1948		3	*1976*	89	40	0	14.83	–	–	–/–	–	2	1
Parore Adam Craig	23.1.1971		78	1990–*2001*	2,865	110	2	26.28	–	–	–/–	–	197/7	179
Patel Dipak Narshibhai	25.10.1958		37	*1986–1996*	1,200	99	0	20.68	75	6-50	3/0	42.05	15	75
Patel Jeetan Shashi	7.5.1980		19	*2005–2012*	276	27*	0	12.00	52	5-110	1/0	48.46	12	39/11
Petherick Peter James	25.9.1942		6	*1976*	34	13	0	4.85	16	3-90	0/0	42.81	4	
Petrie Eric Charlton	22.5.1927	14.8.2004	14	*1955–1965*	258	55	0	12.90	–	–	–/–	–	25	
Playle William Rodger	1.12.1938		8	1958–*1962*	151	65	0	10.06	–	–	–/–	–	4	
Pocock Blair Andrew	18.6.1971		15	*1993–1997*	665	85	0	22.93	0	0-10	0/0	–	5	
Pollard Victor	7.9.1945		32	*1964*–1973	1,266	116	2	24.34	40	3-3	0/0	46.32	19	3
Poore Matt Beresford	1.6.1930		14	*1952–1955*	355	45	0	15.43	9	2-28	0/0	40.77	1	

	Born	*Died*	*Tests*	*Test Career*	*Runs*	*HS*	*100s*	*Avge*	*Wkts*	*BB*	*5/10*	*Avge*	*Ct/St*	*O/T*
Priest Mark Wellings	12.8.1961		3	1990–*1997*	56	26	0	14.00	3	2-42	0/0	52.66	0	18
Pringle Christopher	26.1.1968		14	*1990–1994*	175	30	0	10.29	30	7-52	1/1	46.30	3	64
Puna Narotam ("Tom")	28.10.1929	7.6.1996	3	*1965*	31	18*	0	15.50	4	2-40	0/0	60.00	1	
Rabone Geoffrey Osborne	6.11.1921	19.1.2006	12	1949–*1954*	562	107	1	31.22	16	6-68	1/0	39.68	5	
[1] **Redmond** Aaron James	23.9.1979		7	2008–*2008*	299	83	0	23.00	3	2-47	0/0	20.66	5	6/7
[1] **Redmond** Rodney Ernest	29.12.1944		1	*1972*	163	107	1	81.50	–	–	–/–	–	0	2
Reid John Fulton	3.3.1956		19	*1978–1985*	1,296	180	6	46.28	0	0-0	0/0	–	9	25
Reid John Richard OBE (*CY 1959*)	3.6.1928		58	1949–1965	3,428	142	6	33.28	85	6-60	1/0	33.35	43/1	
Richardson Mark Hunter	11.6.1971		38	*2000–2004*	2,776	145	4	44.77	1	1-16	0/0	21.00	26	4
Roberts Albert William	20.8.1909	13.5.1978	5	*1929*–1937	248	66*	0	27.55	7	4-101	0/0	29.85	4	
Roberts Andrew Duncan Glenn	6.5.1947	26.10.1989	7	*1975–1976*	254	84*	0	23.09	4	1-12	0/0	45.50	4	1
Robertson Gary Keith	15.7.1960		1	*1985*	12	12	0	12.00	1	1-91	0/0	91.00	0	10
Rowe Charles Gordon	30.6.1915	9.6.1995	1	*1945*	0	0	0	0.00	–	–	–/–	–	1	
Rutherford Kenneth Robert	26.10.1965		56	*1984–1994*	2,465	107*	3	27.08	1	1-38	0/0	161.00	32	121
Ryder Jesse Daniel	6.8.1984		18	*2008–2011*	1,269	201	3	40.93	5	2-7	0/0	56.00	12	39/20
Scott Roy Hamilton	6.3.1917	5.8.2005	1	*1946*	18	18	0	18.00	1	1-74	0/0	74.00	0	
Scott Verdun John	31.7.1916	2.8.1980	10	*1945–1951*	458	84	0	28.62	0	0-5	0/0	–	7	
Sewell David Graham	20.10.1977		1	*1997*	1	1*	0	–	0	0-9	0/0	–	0	
Shrimpton Michael John Froud	23.6.1940		10	*1962–1973*	265	46	0	13.94	5	3-35	0/0	31.60	2	
Sinclair Barry Whitley	23.10.1936		21	*1962–1967*	1,148	138	3	29.43	2	2-32	0/0	16.00	8	
Sinclair Ian McKay	1.6.1933		2	*1955*	25	18*	0	8.33	1	1-79	0/0	120.00	1	
Sinclair Mathew Stuart	9.11.1975		33	*1999–2009*	1,635	214	3	32.05	0	0-1	0/0	–	31	54/2
Smith Frank Brunton	13.3.1922	6.7.1997	4	*1946–1951*	237	96	0	47.40	–	–	–/–	–	1	
Smith Horace Dennis	8.1.1913	25.1.1986	1	*1932*	4	4	0	4.00	1	1-113	0/0	113.00	0	
Smith Ian David Stockley MBE	28.2.1957		63	*1980–1991*	1,815	173	2	25.56	0	0-5	0/0	–	168/8	98
Snedden Colin Alexander	7.1.1918	23.4.2011	1	*1946*	–	–	–	–	0	0-46	0/0	–	0	
Snedden Martin Colin	23.11.1958		25	*1980*–1990	327	33*	0	14.86	58	5-68	1/0	37.91	7	93
Southee Timothy Grant	11.12.1988		21	*2007–2012*	581	77*	0	18.74	65	7-64	3/0	35.04	8	64/31
Sparling John Trevor	24.7.1938		11	1958–*1963*	229	50	0	12.72	5	1-9	0/0	65.40	4	
Spearman Craig Murray	4.7.1972		19	*1995–2000*	922	112	1	26.34	–	–	–/–	–	21	51
Stead Gary Raymond	9.1.1972		5	*1998–1999*	278	78	0	34.75	0	0-1	0/0	–	2	
Stirling Derek Alexander	5.10.1961		6	*1984*–1986	108	26	0	15.42	13	4-88	0/0	46.23	1	6
Styris Scott Bernard	10.7.1975		29	2002–*2007*	1,586	170	5	36.04	20	3-28	0/0	50.75	23	188/31
Su'a Murphy Logo	7.11.1966		13	*1991–1994*	165	44	0	12.69	36	5-73	2/0	38.25	8	12
Sutcliffe Bert MBE (*CY 1950*)	17.11.1923	20.4.2001	42	*1946*–1965	2,727	230*	5	40.10	4	2-38	0/0	86.00	20	
Taylor Bruce Richard	12.7.1943		30	*1964*–1973	898	124	2	20.40	111	7-74	4/0	26.60	10	2

	Born	Died	Tests	Test Career	Runs	HS	100s	Avge	Wkts	BB	5/10	Avge	Ct/St	O/T
Taylor Donald Dougald	2.3.1923	5.12.1980	3	*1946–1955*	159	77	0	31.80	–	–	–/–	–	2	
Taylor Luteru Ross Poutoa Lote	8.3.1984		43	*2007–2012*	3,268	154*	8	43.57	2	2-4	0/0	21.50	68	116/47
Thomson Keith	26.2.1941		2	*1967*	94	69	0	31.33	1	1-9	0/0	9.00	0	
Thomson Shane Alexander	27.1.1969		19	*1989–1995*	958	120*	1	30.90	19	3-63	0/0	50.15	7	56
Tindill Eric William Thomas	18.12.1910	1.8.2010	5	1937–*1946*	73	37*	0	9.12	–	–	–/–	–	6/1	
Troup Gary Bertram	3.10.1952		15	*1976–1985*	55	13*	0	4.58	39	6-95	1/1	37.28	2	22
Truscott Peter Bennetts	14.8.1941		1	*1964*	29	26	0	14.50	–	–	–/–	–	1	
Tuffey Daryl Raymond	11.6.1978		26	*1999–2009*	427	80*	0	16.42	77	6-54	2/0	31.75	15	94/3
Turner Glenn Maitland (*CY 1971*)	26.5.1947		41	*1968–1982*	2,991	259	7	44.64	0	0-5	0/0	–	42	41
Twose Roger Graham	17.4.1968		16	*1995*–1999	628	94	0	25.12	3	2-36	0/0	43.33	5	87
Vance Robert Howard	31.3.1955		4	*1987–1989*	207	68	0	29.57	–	–	–/–	–	0	8
Van Wyk Cornelius Francois Kruger	7.2.1980		9	*2011–2012*	341	71	0	21.31	–	–	–/–	–	23/1	
Vaughan Justin Thomas Caldwell	30.8.1967		6	*1992–1996*	201	44	0	18.27	11	4-27	0/0	40.90	4	18
Vettori Daniel Luca	27.1.1979		111§	*1996*–2012	4,508	140	6	30.25	359	7-87	20/3	34.20	58	268‡/33
Vincent Lou	11.11.1978		23	*2001–2007*	1,332	224	3	34.15	0	0-2	0/0	–	19	102/9
[1] **Vivian** Graham Ellery	28.2.1946		5	*1964–1971*	110	43	0	18.33	1	1-14	0/0	107.00	3	1
[1] **Vivian** Henry Gifford	4.11.1912	12.8.1983	7	1931–1937	421	100	1	42.10	17	4-58	0/0	37.23	4	
Wadsworth Kenneth John	30.11.1946	19.8.1976	33	1969–*1975*	1,010	80	0	21.48	–	–	–/–	–	92/4	13
Wagner Neil	13.3.1986		3	2012–*2012*	50	23	0	8.33	5	2-24	0/0	68.80	1	
Walker Brooke Graeme Keith	25.3.1977		5	*2000*–2002	118	27*	0	19.66	5	2-92	0/0	79.80	0	11
Wallace Walter Mervyn	19.12.1916	21.3.2008	13	1937–*1952*	439	66	0	20.90	0	0-5	0/0	–	5	
Walmsley Kerry Peter	23.8.1973		3	*1994–2000*	13	5	0	2.60	9	3-70	0/0	43.44	0	2
Ward John Thomas	11.3.1937		8	*1963–1967*	75	35*	0	12.50	–	–	–/–	–	16/1	
Watling Bradley-John	9.7.1985		10	*2009–2012*	528	102*	1	33.00	–	–	–/–	–	19	16/3
Watson William	31.8.1965		15	1986–*1993*	60	11	0	5.00	40	6-78	1/0	34.67	4	61
Watt Leslie	17.9.1924	15.11.1996	1	*1954*	2	2	0	1.00	–	–	–/–	–	0	
Webb Murray George	22.6.1947		3	*1970–1973*	12	12	0	6.00	4	2-114	0/0	117.75	0	
Webb Peter Neil	14.7.1957		2	*1979*	11	5	0	3.66	–	–	–/–	–	2	5
Weir Gordon Lindsay	2.6.1908	31.10.2003	11	*1929*–1937	416	74*	0	29.71	7	3-38	0/0	29.85	3	
White David John	26.6.1961		2	*1990*	31	18	0	7.75	0	0-5	0/0	–	0	3
Whitelaw Paul Erskine	10.2.1910	28.8.1988	2	*1932*	64	30	0	32.00	–	–	–/–	–	0	
Williamson Kane Stuart	8.8.1990		20	*2010–2012*	1,090	135	3	30.27	8	2-47	0/0	53.00	16	33/13
Wiseman Paul John	4.5.1970		25	*1997–2004*	366	36	0	14.07	61	5-82	2/0	47.59	11	15
Wright John Geoffrey MBE	5.7.1954		82	*1977–1992*	5,334	185	12	37.82	0	0-1	0/0	–	38	149
Young Bryan Andrew	3.11.1964		35	*1993–1998*	2,034	267*	2	31.78	–	–	–/–	–	54	74

§ *Vettori's figures exclude eight runs and one wicket for the ICC World XI v Australia in the Super Series Test in 2005-06.*

	Born	Died	Tests	Test Career	Runs	HS	100s	Avge	Wkts	BB	5/10	Avge	Ct/St	O/T
Young Reece Alan	15.9.1979		5	*2010–2011*	169	57	0	24.14	–	–	–/–	–	8	
Yuile Bryan William	29.10.1941		17	*1962–1969*	481	64	0	17.81	34	4-43	0/0	35.67	12	

INDIA (275 players)

	Born	Died	Tests	Test Career	Runs	HS	100s	Avge	Wkts	BB	5/10	Avge	Ct/St	O/T
Aaron Varun Raymond	29.10.1989		1	*2011*	6	4	0	6.00	3	3-106	0/0	43.00	0	4
Abid Ali Syed	9.9.1941		29	*1967–1974*	1,018	81	0	20.36	47	6-55	1/0	42.12	32	5
Adhikari Hemchandra Ramachandra	31.7.1919	25.10.2003	21	*1947–1958*	872	114*	1	31.14	3	3-68	0/0	27.33	8	
Agarkar Ajit Bhalchandra	4.12.1977		26	*1998–2005*	571	109*	1	16.79	58	6-41	1/0	47.32	6	191/4
[2] **Amar Singh** Ladha	4.12.1910	21.5.1940	7	1932–1936	292	51	0	22.46	28	7-86	2/0	30.64	3	
[1,2] **Amarnath** Mohinder (*CY 1984*)	24.9.1950		69	*1969–1987*	4,378	138	11	42.50	32	4-63	0/0	55.68	47	85
[1] **Amarnath** Nanik ("Lala")	11.9.1911	5.8.2000	24	*1933–1952*	878	118	1	24.38	45	5-96	2/0	32.91	13	
[1,2] **Amarnath** Surinder	30.12.1948		10	*1975–1978*	550	124	1	30.55	1	1-5	0/0	5.00	4	3
Amir Elahi	1.9.1908	28.12.1980	1†	*1947*	17	13	0	8.50	–	–	–/–	–	0	
Amre Pravin Kalyan	14.8.1968		11	*1992–1993*	425	103	1	42.50	–	–	–/–	–	9	37
Ankola Salil Ashok	1.3.1968		1	*1989*	6	6	0	6.00	2	1-35	0/0	64.00	0	20
[2] **Apte** Arvindrao Laxmanrao	24.10.1934		1	1959	15	8	0	7.50	–	–	–/–	–	0	
[2] **Apte** Madhavrao Laxmanrao	5.10.1932		7	*1952*	542	163*	1	49.27	0	0-3	0/0	–	2	
Arshad Ayub	2.8.1958		13	*1987–1989*	257	57	0	17.13	41	5-50	3/0	35.07	2	32
Arun Bharathi	14.12.1962		2	*1986*	4	2*	0	4.00	4	3-76	0/0	29.00	2	4
Arun Lal	1.8.1955		16	*1982–1988*	729	93	0	26.03	0	0-0	0/0	–	13	13
Ashwin Ravichandran	17.9.1986		12	*2011–2012*	596	103	1	45.84	63	6-31	5/1	32.41	2	43/18
Azad Kirtivardhan	2.1.1959		7	*1980–1983*	135	24	0	11.25	3	2-84	0/0	124.33	3	25
Azharuddin Mohammad (*CY 1991*)	8.2.1963		99	*1984–1999*	6,215	199	22	45.03	0	0-4	0/0	–	105	334
Badani Hemang Kamal	14.11.1976		4	2001	94	38	0	15.66	0	0-17	0/0	–	6	40
Badrinath Subramaniam	30.8.1980		2	*2009*	63	56	0	21.00	–	–	–/–	–	2	7/1
Bahutule Sairaj Vasant	6.1.1973		2	*2000*–2001	39	21*	0	13.00	3	1-32	0/0	67.66	1	8
Baig Abbas Ali	19.3.1939		10	1959–*1966*	428	112	1	23.77	0	0-2	0/0	–	6	
Balaji Lakshmipathy	27.9.1981		8	*2003–2004*	51	31	0	5.66	27	5-76	1/0	37.18	1	30/5
Banerjee Sarobindu Nath ("Shute")	3.10.1911	14.10.1980	1	*1948*	13	8	0	6.50	5	4-54	0/0	25.40	0	
Banerjee Subroto Tara	13.2.1969		1	*1991*	3	3	0	3.00	3	3-47	0/0	15.66	0	6
Banerjee Sudangsu Abinash	1.11.1917	14.9.1992	1	*1948*	0	0	0	0.00	5	4-120	0/0	36.20	3	
Bangar Sanjay Bapusaheb	11.10.1972		12	*2001–2002*	470	100*	1	29.37	7	2-23	0/0	49.00	4	15
Baqa Jilani Mohammad	20.7.1911	2.7.1941	1	1936	16	12	0	16.00	0	0-55	0/0	–	0	

	Born	*Died*	*Tests*	*Test Career*	*Runs*	*HS*	*100s*	*Avge*	*Wkts*	*BB*	*5/10*	*Avge*	*Ct/St*	*O/T*
Bedi Bishan Singh	25.9.1946		67	1966–1979	656	50*	0	8.98	266	7-98	14/1	28.71	26	10
Bhandari Prakash	27.11.1935		3	1954–1956	77	39	0	19.25	0	0-12	0/0	–	1	
Bharadwaj Raghvendrarao Vijay	15.8.1975		3	1999	28	22	0	9.33	1	1-26	0/0	107.00	3	10
Bhat Adwai Raghuram	16.4.1958		2	1983	6	6	0	3.00	4	2-65	0/0	37.75	0	
Binny Roger Michael Humphrey	19.7.1955		27	1979–1986	830	83*	0	23.05	47	6-56	2/0	32.63	11	72
Borde Chandrakant Gulabrao	21.7.1934		55	1958–1969	3,061	177*	5	35.59	52	5-88	1/0	46.48	37	
Chandrasekhar Bhagwat Subramanya (*CY 1972*)	17.5.1945		58	1963–1979	167	22	0	4.07	242	8-79	16/2	29.74	25	1
Chauhan Chetandra Pratap Singh	21.7.1947		40	1969–1980	2,084	97	0	31.57	2	1-4	0/0	53.00	38	7
Chauhan Rajesh Kumar	19.12.1966		21	1992–1997	98	23	0	7.00	47	4-48	0/0	39.51	12	35
Chawla Piyush Pramod	24.12.1988		3	2005–2012	6	4	0	2.00	7	4-69	0/0	38.57	1	25/7
Chopra Aakash	19.9.1977		10	2003–2004	437	60	0	23.00	–	–	–/–	–	15	
Chopra Nikhil	26.12.1973		1	1999	7	4	0	3.50	0	0-78	0/0	–	0	39
Chowdhury Nirode Ranjan	23.5.1923	14.12.1979	2	1948–1951	3	3*	0	3.00	1	1-130	0/0	205.00	0	
Colah Sorabji Hormasji Munchersha	22.9.1902	11.9.1950	2	1932–1933	69	31	0	17.25	–	–	–/–	–	2	
Contractor Nariman Jamshedji	7.3.1934		31	1955–1961	1,611	108	1	31.58	1	1-9	0/0	80.00	18	
Dahiya Vijay	10.5.1973		2	2000	2	2*	0	–	–	–	–/–	–	6	19
Dani Hemchandra Tukaram	24.5.1933	19.12.1999	1	1952	–	–	–	–	1	1-9	0/0	19.00	1	
Das Shiv Sunder	5.11.1977		23	2000–2001	1,326	110	2	34.89	0	0-7	0/0	–	34	4
Dasgupta Deep	7.6.1977		8	2001	344	100	1	28.66	–	–	–/–	–	13	5
Desai Ramakant Bhikaji	20.6.1939	27.4.1998	28	1958–1967	418	85	0	13.48	74	6-56	2/0	37.31	9	
Dhoni Mahendra Singh	7.7.1981		73	2005–2012	3,883	148	5	38.06	0	0-1	0/0	–	203/31	211‡/42
Dighe Sameer Sudhakar	8.10.1968		6	2000–2001	141	47	0	15.66	–	–	–/–	–	12/2	23
Dilawar Hussain	19.3.1907	26.8.1967	3	1933–1936	254	59	0	42.33	–	–	–/–	–	6/1	
Divecha Ramesh Vithaldas	18.10.1927	11.2.2003	5	1951–1952	60	26	0	12.00	11	3-102	0/0	32.81	5	
Doshi Dilip Rasiklal	22.12.1947		33	1979–1983	129	20	0	4.60	114	6-102	6/0	30.71	10	15
Dravid Rahul (*CY 2000*)	11.1.1973		163§	1996–2011	13,265	270	36	52.63	1	1-18	0/0	39.00	209	340‡/1
Durani Salim Aziz	11.12.1934		29	1959–1972	1,202	104	1	25.04	75	6-73	3/1	35.42	14	
Engineer Farokh Maneksha	25.2.1938		46	1961–1974	2,611	121	2	31.08	–	–	–/–	–	66/16	5
Gadkari Chandrasekhar Vaman	3.2.1928	11.1.1998	6	1952–1954	129	50*	0	21.50	0	0-8	0/0	–	6	
[1] **Gaekwad** Anshuman Dattajirao	23.9.1952		40	1974–1984	1,985	201	2	30.07	2	1-4	0/0	93.50	15	15
[1] **Gaekwad** Dattajirao Krishnarao	27.10.1928		11	1952–1960	350	52	0	18.42	0	0-4	0/0	–	5	
Gaekwad Hiralal Ghasulal	29.8.1923	2.1.2003	1	1952	22	14	0	11.00	0	0-47	0/0	–	0	
Gambhir Gautam	14.10.1981		54	2004–2012	4,021	206	9	44.18	0	0-4	0/0	–	38	142/37
Gandhi Devang Jayant	6.9.1971		4	1999	204	88	0	34.00	–	–	–/–	–	3	3

§ *Dravid's figures exclude 23 runs and one catch for the ICC World XI v Australia in the Super Series Test in 2005-06.*

	Born	Died	Tests	Test Career	Runs	HS	100s	Avge	Wkts	BB	5/10	Avge	Ct/St	O/T
Gandotra Ashok	24.11.1948		2	*1969*	54	18	0	13.50	0	0-5	0/0	–	1	
Ganesh Doddanarasiah	30.6.1973		4	*1996*	25	8	0	6.25	5	2-28	0/0	57.40	0	1
Ganguly Sourav Chandidas	8.7.1972		113	1996–*2008*	7,212	239	16	42.17	32	3-28	0/0	52.53	71	308‡
Gavaskar Sunil Manohar (*CY 1980*)	10.7.1949		125	*1970–1986*	10,122	236*	34	51.12	1	1-34	0/0	206.00	108	108
Ghavri Karsan Devjibhai	28.2.1951		39	*1974–1980*	913	86	0	21.23	109	5-33	4/0	33.54	16	19
Ghorpade Jayasinghrao Mansinghrao	2.10.1930	29.3.1978	8	*1952*–1959	229	41	0	15.26	0	0-17	0/0	–	4	
Ghulam Ahmed	4.7.1922	28.10.1998	22	*1948–1958*	192	50	0	8.72	68	7-49	4/1	30.17	11	
Gopalan Morappakam Joysam	6.6.1909	21.12.2003	1	*1933*	18	11*	0	18.00	1	1-39	0/0	39.00	3	
Gopinath Coimbatarao Doraikannu	1.3.1930		8	*1951–1959*	242	50*	0	22.00	1	1-11	0/0	11.00	2	
Guard Ghulam Mustafa	12.12.1925	13.3.1978	2	*1958–1959*	11	7	0	5.50	3	2-69	0/0	60.66	2	
Guha Subrata	31.1.1946	5.11.2003	4	1967–*1969*	17	6	0	3.40	3	2-55	0/0	103.66	2	
Gul Mahomed	15.10.1921	8.5.1992	8†	1946–*1952*	166	34	0	11.06	2	2-21	0/0	12.00	3	
2 **Gupte** Balkrishna Pandharinath	30.8.1934	5.7.2005	3	*1960–1964*	28	17*	0	28.00	3	1-54	0/0	116.33	0	
2 **Gupte** Subhashchandra Pandharinath ("Fergie")	11.12.1929	31.5.2002	36	*1951–1961*	183	21	0	6.31	149	9-102	12/1	29.55	14	
Gursharan Singh	8.3.1963		1	*1989*	18	18	0	18.00	–	–	–/–	–	2	1
Hafeez Abdul (*see* Kardar)														
Hanumant Singh	29.3.1939	29.11.2006	14	*1963–1969*	686	105	1	31.18	0	0-5	0/0	–	11	
Harbhajan Singh	3.7.1980		99	*1997–2012*	2,191	115	2	18.56	408	8-84	25/5	32.27	42	227‡/25
Hardikar Manohar Shankar	8.2.1936	4.2.1995	2	*1958*	56	32*	0	18.66	1	1-9	0/0	55.00	3	
Harvinder Singh	23.12.1977		3	*1997*–2001	6	6	0	2.00	4	2-62	0/0	46.25	0	16
Hazare Vijay Samuel	11.3.1915	18.12.2004	30	1946–*1952*	2,192	164*	7	47.65	20	4-29	0/0	61.00	11	
Hindlekar Dattaram Dharmaji	1.1.1909	30.3.1949	4	1936–1946	71	26	0	14.20	–	–	–/–	–	3	
Hirwani Narendra Deepchand	18.10.1968		17	*1987–1996*	54	17	0	5.40	66	8-61	4/1	30.10	5	18
Ibrahim Khanmohammad Cassumbhoy	26.1.1919	12.11.2007	4	*1948*	169	85	0	21.12	–	–	–/–	–	0	
Indrajitsinhji Kumar Shri	15.6.1937	12.3.2011	4	*1964–1969*	51	23	0	8.50	–	–	–/–	–	6/3	
Irani Jamshed Khudadad	18.8.1923	25.2.1982	2	*1947*	3	2*	0	3.00	–	–	–/–	–	2/1	
Jadeja Ajaysinhji	1.2.1971		15	*1992–1999*	576	96	0	26.18	–	–	–/–	–	5	196
Jadeja Ravindrasinh Anirudhsinh	6.12.1988		1	*2012*	12	12	0	12.00	3	2-58	0/0	39.00	0	60/14
3 **Jahangir Khan** Mohammad	1.2.1910	23.7.1988	4	1932–1936	39	13	0	5.57	4	4-60	0/0	63.75	4	
Jai Laxmidas Purshottamdas	1.4.1902	29.1.1968	1	*1933*	19	19	0	9.50	–	–	–/–	–	0	
Jaisimha Motganhalli Laxmanarsu	3.3.1939	6.7.1999	39	1959–*1970*	2,056	129	3	30.68	9	2-54	0/0	92.11	17	
Jamshedji Rustomji Jamshedji Dorabji	18.11.1892	5.4.1976	1	*1933*	5	4*	0	–	3	3-137	0/0	45.66	2	
Jayantilal Kenia	13.1.1948		1	*1970*	5	5	0	5.00	–	–	–/–	–	0	
Johnson David Jude	16.10.1971		2	*1996*	8	5	0	4.00	3	2-52	0/0	47.66	0	
Joshi Padmanabh Govind	27.10.1926	8.1.1987	12	*1951–1960*	207	52*	0	10.89	–	–	–/–	–	18/9	
Joshi Sunil Bandacharya	6.6.1969		15	1996–*2000*	352	92	0	20.70	41	5-142	1/0	35.85	7	69

	Born	Died	Tests	Test Career	Runs	HS	100s	Avge	Wkts	BB	5/10	Avge	Ct/St	O/T
Kaif Mohammad	1.12.1980		13	*1999–2005*	624	148*	1	32.84	0	0-4	0/0	–	14	125
Kambli Vinod Ganpat	18.1.1972		17	*1992–1995*	1,084	227	4	54.20	–	–	–/–	–	7	104
[1] **Kanitkar** Hrishikesh Hemant	14.11.1974		2	*1999*	74	45	0	18.50	0	0-2	0/0	–	0	34
[1] **Kanitkar** Hemant Shamsunder	8.12.1942		2	*1974*	111	65	0	27.75	–	–	–/–	–	0	
Kapil Dev (*CY 1983*)	6.1.1959		131	*1978–1993*	5,248	163	8	31.05	434	9-83	23/2	29.64	64	225
Kapoor Aashish Rakesh	25.3.1971		4	*1994–1996*	97	42	0	19.40	6	2-19	0/0	42.50	1	17
Kardar Abdul Hafeez	17.1.1925	21.4.1996	3†	1946	80	43	0	16.00	–	–	–/–	–	1	
Karim Syed Saba	14.11.1967		1	*2000*	15	15	0	15.00	–	–	–/–	–	1	34
Karthik Krishankumar Dinesh	1.6.1985		23	*2004–2009*	1,000	129	1	27.77	–	–	–/–	–	51/5	52/9
Kartik Murali	11.9.1976		8	*1999–2004*	88	43	0	9.77	24	4-44	0/0	34.16	2	37/1
Kenny Ramnath Baburao	29.9.1930	21.11.1985	5	*1958–1959*	245	62	0	27.22	–	–	–/–	–	1	
Kirmani Syed Mujtaba Hussein	29.12.1949		88	*1975–1985*	2,759	102	2	27.04	1	1-9	0/0	13.00	160/38	49
Kishenchand Gogumal	14.4.1925	16.4.1997	5	*1947–1952*	89	44	0	8.90	–	–	–/–	–	1	
Kohli Virat	5.11.1988		14	2011–*2012*	891	116	3	38.73	0	0-3	0/0	–	18	93/20
[2] **Kripal Singh** Amritsar Govindsingh	6.8.1933	22.7.1987	14	*1955–1964*	422	100*	1	28.13	10	3-43	0/0	58.40	4	
Krishnamurthy Pochiah	12.7.1947	28.1.1999	5	*1970*	33	20	0	5.50	–	–	–/–	–	7/1	1
Kulkarni Nilesh Moreshwar	3.4.1973		3	*1997–2000*	5	4	0	5.00	2	1-70	0/0	166.00	1	10
Kulkarni Rajiv Ramesh	25.9.1962		3	*1986*	2	2	0	1.00	5	3-85	0/0	45.40	1	10
Kulkarni Umesh Narayan	7.3.1942		4	*1967*	13	7	0	4.33	5	2-37	0/0	47.60	0	
Kumar Praveen	2.10.1986		6	2011	149	40	0	14.90	27	5-106	1/0	25.81	2	68/10
Kumar Vaman Viswanath	22.6.1935		2	*1960–1961*	6	6	0	3.00	7	5-64	1/0	28.85	2	
Kumble Anil (*CY 1996*)	17.10.1970		132	1990–*2008*	2,506	110*	1	17.77	619	10-74	35/8	29.65	60	269‡
Kunderan Budhisagar Krishnappa	2.10.1939	23.6.2006	18	*1959*–1967	981	192	2	32.70	0	0-13	0/0	–	23/7	
Kuruvilla Abey	8.8.1968		10	*1996–1997*	66	35*	0	6.60	25	5-68	1/0	35.68	0	25
Lall Singh	16.12.1909	19.11.1985	1	1932	44	29	0	22.00	–	–	–/–	–	1	
Lamba Raman	2.1.1960	22.2.1998	4	*1986–1987*	102	53	0	20.40	–	–	–/–	–	5	32
Laxman Vangipurappu Venkata Sai (*CY 2002*)	1.11.1974		134	*1996–2011*	8,781	281	17	45.97	2	1-2	0/0	63.00	135	86
Madan Lal	20.3.1951		39	1974–1986	1,042	74	0	22.65	71	5-23	4/0	40.08	15	67
Maka Ebrahim Suleman	5.3.1922	7.9.1994	2	*1952*	2	2*	0	–	–	–	–/–	–	2/1	
Malhotra Ashok Omprakash	26.1.1957		7	*1981–1984*	226	72*	0	25.11	0	0-0	0/0	–	2	20
Maninder Singh	13.6.1965		35	*1982–1992*	99	15	0	3.80	88	7-27	3/2	37.36	9	59
[1] **Manjrekar** Sanjay Vijay	12.7.1965		37	*1987–1996*	2,043	218	4	37.14	0	0-4	0/0	–	25/1	74
[1] **Manjrekar** Vijay Laxman	26.9.1931	18.10.1983	55	*1951–1964*	3,208	189*	7	39.12	1	1-16	0/0	44.00	19/2	
[1] **Mankad** Ashok Vinoo	12.10.1946	1.8.2008	22	*1969–1977*	991	97	0	25.41	0	0-0	0/0	–	12	1
[1] **Mankad** Mulvantrai Himmatlal ("Vinoo") (*CY 1947*)	12.4.1917	21.8.1978	44	1946–*1958*	2,109	231	5	31.47	162	8-52	8/2	32.32	33	

	Born	*Died*	*Tests*	*Test Career*	*Runs*	*HS*	*100s*	*Avge*	*Wkts*	*BB*	*5/10*	*Avge*	*Ct/St*	*O/T*
Mantri Madhav Krishnaji	1.9.1921		4	*1951–1954*	67	39	0	9.57	–	–	–/–	–	8/1	
Meherhomji Khershedji Rustomji	9.8.1911	10.2.1982	1	1936	0	0*	0	–	–	–	–/–	–	1	
Mehra Vijay Laxman	12.3.1938	25.8.2006	8	*1955–1963*	329	62	0	25.30	0	0-1	0/0	–	1	
Merchant Vijay Madhavji (*CY 1937*)	12.10.1911	27.10.1987	10	*1933–1951*	859	154	3	47.72	0	0-17	0/0	–	7	
Mhambrey Paras Laxmikant	20.6.1972		2	1996	58	28	0	29.00	2	1-43	0/0	74.00	1	3
[2]**Milkha Singh** Amritsar Govindsingh	31.12.1941		4	*1959–1961*	92	35	0	15.33	0	0-2	0/0	–	2	
Mishra Amit	24.11.1982		13	*2008*–2011	392	84	0	23.05	43	5-71	1/0	43.30	6	15/1
Mithun Abhimanyu	25.10.1989		4	2010–2011	120	46	0	24.00	9	4-105	0/0	50.66	0	5
Modi Rustomji Sheryar	11.11.1924	17.5.1996	10	1946–*1952*	736	112	1	46.00	0	0-14	0/0	–	3	
Mohanty Debasis Sarbeswar	20.7.1976		2	*1997*	0	0*	0	–	4	4-78	0/0	59.75	0	45
Mongia Nayan Ramlal	19.12.1969		44	*1993–2000*	1,442	152	1	24.03	–	–	–/–	–	99/8	140
More Kiran Shankar	4.9.1962		49	1986–*1993*	1,285	73	0	25.70	0	0-12	0/0	–	110/20	94
Muddiah Venatappa Musandra	8.6.1929	1.10.2009	2	*1959–1960*	11	11	0	5.50	3	2-40	0/0	44.66	0	
Mukund Abhinav	6.1.1990		5	2011	211	62	0	21.10	0	0-14	0/0	–	5	
Mushtaq Ali Syed	17.12.1914	18.6.2005	11	*1933–1951*	612	112	2	32.21	3	1-45	0/0	67.33	7	
Nadkarni Rameshchandra Gangaram ("Bapu")	4.4.1933		41	*1955–1967*	1,414	122*	1	25.70	88	6-43	4/1	29.07	22	
Naik Sudhir Sakharam	21.2.1945		3	1974–*1974*	141	77	0	23.50	–	–	–/–	–	0	2
Naoomal Jeoomal	17.4.1904	28.7.1980	3	1932–*1933*	108	43	0	27.00	2	1-4	0/0	34.00	0	
Narasimha Rao Modireddy Venkateshwar	11.8.1954		4	*1978–1979*	46	20*	0	9.20	3	2-46	0/0	75.66	8	
Navle Janaradan Gyanoba	7.12.1902	7.9.1979	2	1932–*1933*	42	13	0	10.50	–	–	–/–	–	1	
Nayak Surendra Vithal	20.10.1954		2	1982	19	11	0	9.50	1	1-16	0/0	132.00	1	4
[2]**Nayudu** Cottari Kanakaiya (*CY 1933*)	31.10.1895	14.11.1967	7	1932–1936	350	81	0	25.00	9	3-40	0/0	42.88	4	
[2]**Nayudu** Cottari Subbanna	18.4.1914	22.11.2002	11	*1933–1951*	147	36	0	9.18	2	1-19	0/0	179.50	3	
[2]**Nazir Ali** Syed	8.6.1906	18.2.1975	2	1932–*1933*	30	13	0	7.50	4	4-83	0/0	20.75	0	
Nehra Ashish	29.4.1979		17	*1998–2003*	77	19	0	5.50	44	4-72	0/0	42.40	5	117‡/8
Nissar Mohammad	1.8.1910	11.3.1963	6	1932–1936	55	14	0	6.87	25	5-90	3/0	28.28	2	
Nyalchand Sukhlal Shah	14.9.1915	3.1.1997	1	*1952*	7	6*	0	7.00	3	3-97	0/0	32.33	0	
Ojha Pragyan Prayish	5.9.1986		20	*2009–2012*	86	18*	0	12.28	95	6-47	5/0	31.62	8	18/6
Pai Ajit Manohar	28.4.1945		1	*1969*	10	9	0	5.00	2	2-29	0/0	15.50	0	
Palia Phiroze Edulji	5.9.1910	9.9.1981	2	1932–1936	29	16	0	9.66	0	0-2	0/0	–	0	
Pandit Chandrakant Sitaram	30.9.1961		5	1986–*1991*	171	39	0	24.42	–	–	–/–	–	14/2	36
Parkar Ghulam Ahmed	25.10.1955		1	1982	7	6	0	3.50	–	–	–/–	–	1	10
Parkar Ramnath Dhondu	31.10.1946	11.8.1999	2	*1972*	80	35	0	20.00	–	–	–/–	–	0	
Parsana Dhiraj Devshibhai	2.12.1947		2	*1978*	1	1	0	0.50	1	1-32	0/0	50.00	0	
Patankar Chandrakant Trimbak	24.11.1930		1	*1955*	14	13	0	14.00	–	–	–/–	–	3/1	
[1]**Pataudi** Iftikhar Ali Khan, Nawab of (*CY 1932*)	16.3.1910	5.1.1952	3†	1946	55	22	0	11.00	–	–	–/–	–	0	

	Born	Died	Tests	Test Career	Runs	HS	100s	Avge	Wkts	BB	5/10	Avge	Ct/St	O/T
[1] **Pataudi** Mansur Ali Khan, Nawab of (*CY 1968*)	5.1.1941	22.9.2011	46	*1961–1974*	2,793	203*	6	34.91	1	1-10	0/0	88.00	27	
Patel Brijesh Pursuram	24.11.1952		21	1974–*1977*	972	115*	1	29.45	–	–	–/–	–	17	10
Patel Jasubhai Motibhai	26.11.1924	12.12.1992	7	*1954–1959*	25	12	0	2.77	29	9-69	2/1	21.96	2	
Patel Munaf Musa	12.7.1983		13	*2005*–2011	60	15*	0	7.50	35	4-25	0/0	38.54	6	70/3
Patel Parthiv Ajay	9.3.1985		20	2002–2008	683	69	0	29.69	–	–	–/–	–	41/8	38/2
Patel Rashid	1.6.1964		1	*1988*	0	0	0	0.00	0	0-14	0/0	–	1	1
Pathan Irfan Khan	27.10.1984		29	*2003–2007*	1,105	102	1	31.57	100	7-59	7/2	32.26	8	120/24
Patiala Maharajah of (Yadavendra Singh)	17.1.1913	17.6.1974	1	*1933*	84	60	0	42.00	–	–	–/–	–	2	
Patil Sadashiv Raoji	10.10.1933		1	*1955*	14	14*	0	–	2	1-15	0/0	25.50	1	
Patil Sandeep Madhusudan	18.8.1956		29	*1979–1984*	1,588	174	4	36.93	9	2-28	0/0	26.66	12	45
Phadkar Dattatraya Gajanan	12.12.1925	17.3.1985	31	*1947–1958*	1,229	123	2	32.34	62	7-159	3/0	36.85	21	
Powar Ramesh Rajaram	20.5.1978		2	2007	13	7	0	6.50	6	3-33	0/0	19.66	0	31
Prabhakar Manoj	15.4.1963		39	*1984–1995*	1,600	120	1	32.65	96	6-132	3/0	37.30	20	130
Prasad Bapu Krishnarao <u>Venkatesh</u>	5.8.1969		33	1996–2001	203	30*	0	7.51	96	6-33	7/1	35.00	6	161
Prasad Mannava Sri Kanth	24.4.1975		6	*1999*	106	19	0	11.77	–	–	–/–	–	15	17
Prasanna Erapalli Anatharao Srinivas	22.5.1940		49	*1961–1978*	735	37	0	11.48	189	8-76	10/2	30.38	18	
Pujara Cheteshwar Arvind	25.1.1988		9	*2010–2012*	761	206*	3	58.53	–	–	–/–	–	9	
Punjabi Pananmal Hotchand	20.9.1921		5	*1954*	164	33	0	16.40	–	–	–/–	–	5	
Rai Singh Kanwar	24.2.1922		1	*1947*	26	24	0	13.00	–	–	–/–	–	0	
Raina Suresh Kumar	27.11.1986		17	2010–*2012*	768	120	1	28.44	13	2-1	0/0	40.92	22	154/36
Rajinder Pal	18.11.1937		1	*1963*	6	3*	0	6.00	0	0-3	0/0	–	0	
Rajindernath Vijay	7.1.1928	22.11.1989	1	*1952*	–	–	–	–	–	–	–/–	–	0/4	
Rajput Lalchand Sitaram	18.12.1961		2	*1985*	105	61	0	26.25	–	–	–/–	–	1	4
Raju Sagi Lakshmi <u>Venkatapathy</u>	9.7.1969		28	*1989–2000*	240	31	0	10.00	93	6-12	5/1	30.72	6	53
Raman Woorkeri Venkat	23.5.1965		11	*1987–1996*	448	96	0	24.88	2	1-7	0/0	64.50	6	27
Ramaswami Cotar	16.6.1896	1.1990	2	1936	170	60	0	56.66	–	–	–/–	–	0	
Ramchand Gulabrai Sipahimalani	26.7.1927	8.9.2003	33	1952–*1959*	1,180	109	2	24.58	41	6-49	1/0	46.31	20	
Ramesh Sadagoppan	16.10.1975		19	*1998*–2001	1,367	143	2	37.97	0	0-5	0/0	–	18	24
[2] **Ramji** Ladha	10.2.1900	20.12.1948	1	*1933*	1	1	0	0.50	0	0-64	0/0	–	1	
Rangachari Commandur Rajagopalachari	14.4.1916	9.10.1993	4	*1947–1948*	8	8*	0	2.66	9	5-107	1/0	54.77	0	
Rangnekar Khanderao Moreshwar	27.6.1917	11.10.1984	3	*1947*	33	18	0	5.50	–	–	–/–	–	1	
Ranjane Vasant Baburao	22.7.1937	22.12.2011	7	*1958–1964*	40	16	0	6.66	19	4-72	0/0	34.15	1	
Rathore Vikram	26.3.1969		6	1996–*1996*	131	44	0	13.10	–	–	–/–	–	12	7
Ratra Ajay	13.12.1981		6	*2001*–2002	163	115*	1	18.11	0	0-1	0/0	–	11/2	12
Razdan Vivek	25.8.1969		2	*1989*	6	6*	0	6.00	5	5-79	1/0	28.20	0	3
Reddy Bharath	12.11.1954		4	1979	38	21	0	9.50	–	–	–/–	–	9/2	3

	Born	Died	Tests	Test Career	Runs	HS	100s	Avge	Wkts	BB	5/10	Avge	Ct/St	O/T
Rege Madhusudan Ramachandra	18.3.1924		1	*1948*	15	15	0	7.50	–	–	–/–	–	1	
Roy Ambar	5.6.1945	19.9.1997	4	*1969*	91	48	0	13.00	–	–	–/–	–	0	
[1] **Roy** Pankaj	31.5.1928	4.2.2001	43	*1951–1960*	2,442	173	5	32.56	1	1-6	0/0	66.00	16	
[1] **Roy** Pranab	10.2.1957		2	*1981*	71	60*	0	35.50	–	–	–/–	–	1	
Saha Wriddhaman Prasanta	24.10.1984		2	*2009–2011*	74	36	0	18.50	–	–	–/–	–	2	3
Sandhu Balwinder Singh	3.8.1956		8	*1982–1983*	214	71	0	30.57	10	3-87	0/0	55.70	1	22
Sanghvi Rahul Laxman	3.9.1974		1	*2000*	2	2	0	1.00	2	2-67	0/0	39.00	0	10
Sarandeep Singh	21.10.1979		3	*2000–2001*	43	39*	0	43.00	10	4-136	0/0	34.00	1	5
Sardesai Dilip Narayan	8.8.1940	2.7.2007	30	*1961–1972*	2,001	212	5	39.23	0	0-3	0/0	–	4	
Sarwate Chandrasekhar Trimbak	22.7.1920	23.12.2003	9	1946–*1951*	208	37	0	13.00	3	1-16	0/0	124.66	0	
Saxena Ramesh Chandra	20.9.1944	16.8.2011	1	1967	25	16	0	12.50	0	0-11	0/0	–	0	
Sehwag Virender	20.10.1978		101§	*2001–2012*	8,476	319	23	50.15	40	5-104	1/0	47.35	84	241‡/19
Sekhar Thirumalai Ananthanpillai	28.3.1956		2	*1982*	0	0*	0	–	0	0-43	0/0	–	0	4
Sen Probir Kumar ("Khokhan")	31.5.1926	27.1.1970	14	*1947–1952*	165	25	0	11.78	–	–	–/–	–	20/11	
Sen Gupta Apoorva Kumar	3.8.1939		1	*1958*	9	8	0	4.50	–	–	–/–	–	0	
Sharma Ajay Kumar	3.4.1964		1	*1987*	53	30	0	26.50	0	0-9	0/0	–	1	31
Sharma Chetan	3.1.1966		23	*1984–1988*	396	54	0	22.00	61	6-58	4/1	35.45	7	65
Sharma Gopal	3.8.1960		5	*1984–1990*	11	10*	0	3.66	10	4-88	0/0	41.80	2	11
Sharma Ishant	2.9.1988		47	2007–*2012*	444	31*	0	10.09	137	6-55	3/1	38.00	11	50/13
Sharma Parthasarathy Harishchandra	5.1.1948	20.10.2010	5	*1974–1976*	187	54	0	18.70	0	0-2	0/0	–	1	2
Sharma Sanjeev Kumar	25.8.1965		2	*1988*–1990	56	38	0	28.00	6	3-37	0/0	41.16	1	23
Shastri Ravishankar Jayadritha	27.5.1962		80	*1980–1992*	3,830	206	11	35.79	151	5-75	2/0	40.96	36	150
Shinde Sadashiv Ganpatrao	18.8.1923	22.6.1955	7	1946–1952	85	14	0	14.16	12	6-91	1/0	59.75	0	
Shodhan Roshan Harshadlal ("Deepak")	18.10.1928		3	*1952*	181	110	1	60.33	0	0-1	0/0	–	1	
Shukla Rakesh Chandra	4.2.1948		1	*1982*	–	–	–	–	2	2-82	0/0	76.00	0	
Siddiqui Iqbal Rashid	26.12.1974		1	*2001*	29	24	0	29.00	1	1-32	0/0	48.00	1	
Sidhu Navjot Singh	20.10.1963		51	*1983–1998*	3,202	201	9	42.13	0	0-9	0/0	–	9	136
Singh Rabindra Ramanarayan ("Robin")	14.9.1963		1	*1998*	27	15	0	13.50	0	0-16	0/0	–	5	136
Singh Robin	1.1.1970		1	*1998*	0	0	0	0.00	3	2-74	0/0	58.66	1	
Singh Rudra Pratap	6.12.1985		14	*2005*–2011	116	30	0	7.25	40	5-59	1/0	42.05	6	58/10
Singh Vikram Rajvir	17.9.1984		5	*2005*–2007	47	29	0	11.75	8	3-48	0/0	53.37	1	2
Sivaramakrishnan Laxman	31.12.1965		9	*1982–1985*	130	25	0	16.25	26	6-64	3/1	44.03	9	16
Sohoni Sriranga Wasudev	5.3.1918	19.5.1993	4	1946–*1951*	83	29*	0	16.60	2	1-16	0/0	101.00	2	
Solkar Eknath Dhondu	18.3.1948	26.6.2005	27	*1969–1976*	1,068	102	1	25.42	18	3-28	0/0	59.44	53	7
Sood Man Mohan	6.7.1939		1	*1959*	3	3	0	1.50	–	–	–/–	–	0	

§ Sehwag's figures exclude 83 runs and one catch for the ICC World XI v Australia in the Super Series Test in 2005-06.

	Born	Died	Tests	Test Career	Runs	HS	100s	Avge	Wkts	BB	5/10	Avge	Ct/St	O/T
Sreesanth Shanthakumaran	6.2.1983		27	2005–2011	281	35	0	10.40	87	5-40	3/0	37.59	5	53/10
Srikkanth Krishnamachari	21.12.1959		43	1981–1991	2,062	123	2	29.88	0	0-1	0/0	–	40	146
Srinath Javagal	31.8.1969		67	1991–2002	1,009	76	0	14.21	236	8-86	10/1	30.49	22	229
Srinivasan Thirumalai Echambadi	26.10.1950	6.12.2010	1	1980	48	29	0	24.00	–	–	–/–	–	0	2
Subramanya Venkataraman	16.7.1936		9	1964–1967	263	75	0	18.78	3	2-32	0/0	67.00	9	
Sunderam Gundibali Rama	29.3.1930	20.6.2010	2	1955	3	3*	0	–	3	2-46	0/0	55.33	0	
Surendranath	4.1.1937	5.5.2012	11	1958–1960	136	27	0	10.46	26	5-75	2/0	40.50	4	
Surti Rusi Framroze	25.5.1936	13.1.2013	26	1960–1969	1,263	99	0	28.70	42	5-74	1/0	46.71	26	
Swamy Venkatraman Narayan	23.5.1924	1.5.1983	1	1955	–	–	–	–	0	0-15	0/0	–	0	
Tamhane Narendra Shankar	4.8.1931	19.3.2002	21	1954–1960	225	54*	0	10.22	–	–	–/–	–	35/16	
Tarapore Keki Khurshedji	17.12.1910	15.6.1986	1	1948	2	2	0	2.00	0	0-72	0/0	–	0	
Tendulkar Sachin Ramesh (*CY 1997*)	24.4.1973		194	1989–2012	15,645	248*	51	54.32	45	3-10	0/0	54.64	114	463/1
Umrigar Pahlanji Ratanji ("Polly")	28.3.1926	7.11.2006	59	1948–1961	3,631	223	12	42.22	35	6-74	2/0	42.08	33	
Unadkat Jaydev Dipakbhai	18.10.1991		1	2010	2	1*	0	2.00	0	0-101	0/0	–	0	
Vengsarkar Dilip Balwant (*CY 1987*)	6.4.1956		116	1975–1991	6,868	166	17	42.13	0	0-3	0/0	–	78	129
Venkataraghavan Srinivasaraghavan	21.4.1945		57	1964–1983	748	64	0	11.68	156	8-72	3/1	36.11	44	15
Venkataramana Margashayam	24.4.1966		1	1988	0	0*	0	–	1	1-10	0/0	58.00	1	1
Vijay Murali	1.4.1984		12	2008–2011	609	139	1	30.45	–	–	–/–	–	10	11/7
Vinay Kumar Ranganath	12.2.1984		1	2011	11	6	0	5.50	1	1-73	0/0	73.00	0	22/8
Viswanath Gundappa Rangnath	12.2.1949		91	1969–1982	6,080	222	14	41.93	1	1-11	0/0	46.00	63	25
Viswanath Sadanand	29.11.1962		3	1985	31	20	0	6.20	–	–	–/–	–	11	22
Vizianagram Maharajkumar of (*Sir* Vijaya Anand)	28.12.1905	2.12.1965	3	1936	33	19*	0	8.25	–	–	–/–	–	1	
Wadekar Ajit Laxman	1.4.1941		37	1966–1974	2,113	143	1	31.07	0	0-0	0/0	–	46	2
Wasim Jaffer	16.2.1978		31	1999–2007	1,944	212	5	34.10	2	2-18	0/0	9.00	27	2
Wassan Atul Satish	23.3.1968		4	1989–1990	94	53	0	23.50	10	4-108	0/0	50.40	1	9
[1, 2] **Wazir Ali** Syed	15.9.1903	17.6.1950	7	1932–1936	237	42	0	16.92	0	0-0	0/0	–	1	
Yadav Nandlal Shivlal	26.1.1957		35	1979–1986	403	43	0	14.39	102	5-76	3/0	35.09	10	7
Yadav Umeshkumar Tilak	25.10.1987		9	2011–2012	36	21	0	6.00	32	5-93	1/0	32.50	2	17/1
Yadav Vijay	14.3.1967		1	1992	30	30	0	30.00	–	–	–/–	–	1/2	19
Yajurvindra Singh	1.8.1952		4	1976–1979	109	43*	0	18.16	0	0-2	0/0	–	11	
Yashpal Sharma	11.8.1954		37	1979–1983	1,606	140	2	33.45	1	1-6	0/0	17.00	16	42
[1] **Yograj Singh**	25.3.1958		1	1980	10	6	0	5.00	1	1-63	0/0	63.00	0	6
Yohannan Tinu	18.2.1979		3	2001–2002	13	8*	0	–	5	2-56	0/0	51.20	1	3
[1] **Yuvraj Singh**	12.12.1981		40	2003–2012	1,900	169	3	33.92	9	2-9	0/0	60.77	31	274‡/33
Zaheer Khan (*CY 2008*)	7.10.1978		88	2000–2012	1,146	75	0	11.81	295	7-87	10/1	32.35	19	194‡/17

PAKISTAN (210 players)

	Born	*Died*	*Tests*	*Test Career*	*Runs*	*HS*	*100s*	*Avge*	*Wkts*	*BB*	*5/10*	*Avge*	*Ct/St*	*O/T*
Aamer Malik	3.1.1963		14	*1987–1994*	565	117	2	35.31	1	1-0	0/0	89.00	15/1	24
Aamir Nazir	2.1.1971		6	*1992–1995*	31	11	0	6.20	20	5-46	1/0	29.85	2	9
Aamir Sohail	14.9.1966		47	1992–*1999*	2,823	205	5	35.28	25	4-54	0/0	41.96	36	156
Abdul Kadir	10.5.1944	12.3.2002	4	*1964*	272	95	0	34.00	–	–	–/–	–	0/1	
Abdul Qadir	15.9.1955		67	*1977–1990*	1,029	61	0	15.59	236	9-56	15/5	32.80	15	104
Abdul Razzaq	2.12.1979		46	*1999–2006*	1,946	134	3	28.61	100	5-35	1/0	36.94	15	261‡/30
Abdur Rauf	9.12.1978		3	2009–*2009*	52	31	0	8.66	6	2-59	0/0	46.33	0	4/1
Abdur Rehman	1.3.1980		17	*2007*–2012	289	60	0	15.21	81	6-25	2/0	28.40	6	25/7
[2]**Adnan Akmal**	13.3.1985		16	*2010*–2012	440	61	0	27.50	–	–	–/–	–	47/8	5
Afaq Hussain	31.12.1939	25.2.2002	2	*1961–1964*	66	35*	0	–	1	1-40	0/0	106.00	2	
Aftab Baloch	1.4.1953		2	*1969–1974*	97	60*	0	48.50	0	0-2	0/0	–	0	
Aftab Gul	31.3.1946		6	*1968*–1971	182	33	0	22.75	0	0-4	0/0	–	3	
Agha Saadat Ali	21.6.1929	25.10.1995	1	*1955*	8	8*	0	–	–	–	–/–	–	3	
Agha Zahid	7.1.1953		1	*1974*	15	14	0	7.50	–	–	–/–	–	0	
Aizaz Cheema	5.9.1979		7	*2011*–2012	1	1*	0	–	20	4-24	0/0	31.90	1	14/5
Akram Raza	22.11.1964		9	*1989–1994*	153	32	0	15.30	13	3-46	0/0	56.30	8	49
Ali Hussain Rizvi	6.1.1974		1	*1997*	–	–	–	–	2	2-72	0/0	36.00	0	
Ali Naqvi	19.3.1977		5	*1997*	242	115	1	30.25	0	0-11	0/0	–	1	
Alim-ud-Din	15.12.1930	12.7.2012	25	1954–1962	1,091	109	2	25.37	1	1-17	0/0	75.00	8	
Amir Elahi	1.9.1908	28.12.1980	5†	*1952*	65	47	0	10.83	7	4-134	0/0	35.42	0	
Anil Dalpat	20.9.1963		9	*1983–1984*	167	52	0	15.18	–	–	–/–	–	22/3	15
Anwar Hussain	16.7.1920	9.10.2002	4	*1952*	42	17	0	7.00	1	1-25	0/0	29.00	0	
Anwar Khan	24.12.1955		1	*1978*	15	12	0	15.00	0	0-12	0/0	–	0	
Aqib Javed	5.8.1972		22	*1988–1998*	101	28*	0	5.05	54	5-84	1/0	34.70	2	163
Arif Butt	17.5.1944	10.7.2007	3	*1964*	59	20	0	11.80	14	6-89	1/0	20.57	0	
Arshad Khan	22.3.1971		9	*1997–2004*	31	9*	0	5.16	32	5-38	1/0	30.00	0	58
Asad Shafiq	28.1.1986		16	*2010*–2012	894	104	2	42.57	–	–	–/–	–	13	35/10
Ashfaq Ahmed	6.6.1973		1	*1993*	1	1*	0	1.00	2	2-31	0/0	26.50	0	3
Ashraf Ali	22.4.1958		8	*1981–1987*	229	65	0	45.80	–	–	–/–	–	17/5	16
Asif Iqbal (*CY 1968*)	6.6.1943		58	*1964–1979*	3,575	175	11	38.85	53	5-48	2/0	28.33	36	10
Asif Masood	23.1.1946		16	*1968–1976*	93	30*	0	10.33	38	5-111	1/0	41.26	5	7
Asif Mujtaba	4.11.1967		25	*1986–1996*	928	65*	0	24.42	4	1-0	0/0	75.75	19	66
Asim Kamal	31.5.1976		12	*2003–2005*	717	99	0	37.73	–	–	–/–	–	10	

	Born	*Died*	*Tests*	*Test Career*	*Runs*	*HS*	*100s*	*Avge*	*Wkts*	*BB*	*5/10*	*Avge*	*Ct/St*	*O/T*
Ata-ur-Rehman	28.3.1975		13	1992–1996	76	19	0	8.44	31	4-50	0/0	34.54	2	30
Atif Rauf	3.3.1964		1	*1993*	25	16	0	12.50	–	–	–/–	–	0	
Atiq-uz-Zaman	20.7.1975		1	*1999*	26	25	0	13.00	–	–	–/–	–	5	3
Azam Khan	1.3.1969		1	*1996*	14	14	0	14.00	–	–	–/–	–	0	6
Azeem Hafeez	29.7.1963		18	*1983–1984*	134	24	0	8.37	63	6-46	4/0	34.98	1	15
Azhar Ali	19.2.1985		24	2010–2012	1,811	157	4	45.27	1	1-4	0/0	54.00	15	14
Azhar Khan	7.9.1955		1	*1979*	14	14	0	14.00	1	1-1	0/0	2.00	0	
Azhar Mahmood	28.2.1975		21	*1997*–2001	900	136	3	30.00	39	4-50	0/0	35.94	14	143
[2] **Azmat Rana**	3.11.1951		1	*1979*	49	49	0	49.00	–	–	–/–	–	0	2
Basit Ali	13.12.1970		19	*1992–1995*	858	103	1	26.81	0	0-6	0/0	–	6	50
[3] **Bazid Khan**	25.3.1981		1	*2004*	32	23	0	16.00	–	–	–/–	–	2	5
Danish Kaneria	16.12.1980		61	*2000*–2010	360	29	0	7.05	261	7-77	15/2	34.79	18	18
D'Souza Antao	17.1.1939		6	*1958*–1962	76	23*	0	38.00	17	5-112	1/0	43.82	3	
Ehtesham-ud-Din	4.9.1950		5	*1979*–1982	2	2	0	1.00	16	5-47	1/0	23.43	2	
Faisal Iqbal	30.12.1981		26	*2000–2009*	1,124	139	1	26.76	0	0-7	0/0	–	22	18
Farhan Adil	25.9.1977		1	2003	33	25	0	16.50	–	–	–/–	–	0	
Farooq Hamid	3.3.1945		1	*1964*	3	3	0	1.50	1	1-82	0/0	107.00	0	
Farrukh Zaman	2.4.1956		1	*1976*	–	–	–	–	0	0-7	0/0	–	0	
Fawad Alam	8.10.1985		3	2009–*2009*	250	168	1	41.66	–	–	–/–	–	3	27/24
Fazal Mahmood (*CY 1955*)	18.2.1927	30.5.2005	34	*1952*–1962	620	60	0	14.09	139	7-42	13/4	24.70	11	
Fazl-e-Akbar	20.10.1980		5	*1997–2003*	52	25	0	13.00	11	3-85	0/0	46.45	2	2
Ghazali Mohammad Ebrahim Zainuddin	15.6.1924	26.4.2003	2	1954	32	18	0	8.00	0	0-18	0/0	–	0	
Ghulam Abbas	1.5.1947		1	1967	12	12	0	6.00	–	–	–/–	–	0	
Gul Mahomed	15.10.1921	8.5.1992	1†	*1956*	39	27*	0	39.00	–	–	–/–	–	0	
[1, 2] **Hanif Mohammad** (*CY 1968*)	21.12.1934		55	*1952–1969*	3,915	337	12	43.98	1	1-1	0/0	95.00	40	
Haroon Rashid	25.3.1953		23	*1976–1982*	1,217	153	3	34.77	0	0-3	0/0	–	16	12
Hasan Raza	11.3.1982		7	*1996–2005*	235	68	0	26.11	0	0-1	0/0	–	5	16
Haseeb Ahsan	15.7.1939		12	*1957–1961*	61	14	0	6.77	27	6-202	2/0	49.25	1	
[2] **Humayun Farhat**	24.1.1981		1	*2000*	54	28	0	27.00	–	–	–/–	–	0	5
Ibadulla Khalid ("Billy")	20.12.1935		4	*1964*–1967	253	166	1	31.62	1	1-42	0/0	99.00	3	
Iftikhar Anjum	1.12.1980		1	*2005*	9	9*	0	–	0	0-8	0/0	–	0	62/2
Ijaz Ahmed, sen	20.9.1968		60	*1986–2000*	3,315	211	12	37.67	2	1-9	0/0	38.50	45	250
Ijaz Ahmed, jun	2.2.1969		2	*1995*	29	16	0	9.66	0	0-1	0/0	–	3	2
Ijaz Butt	10.3.1938		8	*1958*–1962	279	58	0	19.92	–	–	–/–	–	5	
Ijaz Faqih	24.3.1956		5	*1980–1987*	183	105	1	26.14	4	1-38	0/0	74.75	0	27
[2] **Imran Farhat**	20.5.1982		39	*2000*–2010	2,327	128	3	31.87	3	2-69	0/0	94.66	40	51/7

	Born	Died	Tests	Test Career	Runs	HS	100s	Avge	Wkts	BB	5/10	Avge	Ct/St	O/T
Imran Khan (*CY 1983*)	25.11.1952		88	1971–1991	3,807	136	6	37.69	362	8-58	23/6	22.81	28	175
Imran Nazir	16.12.1981		8	1998–2002	427	131	2	32.84	–	–	–/–	–	4	79/25
Imtiaz Ahmed	5.1.1928		41	1952–1962	2,079	209	3	29.28	0	0-0	0/0	–	77/16	
Intikhab Alam	28.12.1941		47	1959–1976	1,493	138	1	22.28	125	7-52	5/2	35.95	20	4
Inzamam-ul-Haq	3.3.1970		119§	1992–2007	8,829	329	25	50.16	0	0-8	0/0	–	81	375‡/1
Iqbal Qasim	6.8.1953		50	1976–1988	549	56	0	13.07	171	7-49	8/2	28.11	42	15
Irfan Fazil	2.11.1981		1	1999	4	3	0	4.00	2	1-30	0/0	32.50	2	1
Israr Ali	1.5.1927		4	1952–1959	33	10	0	4.71	6	2-29	0/0	27.50	1	
Jalal-ud-Din	12.6.1959		6	1982–1985	3	2	0	3.00	11	3-77	0/0	48.81	0	8
Javed Akhtar	21.11.1940		1	1962	4	2*	0	4.00	0	0-52	0/0	–	0	
Javed Burki	8.5.1938		25	1960–1969	1,341	140	3	30.47	0	0-2	0/0	–	7	
Javed Miandad (*CY 1982*)	12.6.1957		124	1976–1993	8,832	280*	23	52.57	17	3-74	0/0	40.11	93/1	233
Junaid Khan	24.12.1989		8	2011–2012	19	8	0	3.80	27	5-38	3/0	26.70	1	16/3
Kabir Khan	12.4.1974		4	1994	24	10	0	8.00	9	3-26	0/0	41.11	1	10
[2] **Kamran Akmal**	13.1.1982		53	2002–2010	2,648	158*	6	30.79	–	–	–/–	–	184/22	143/39
Kardar Abdul Hafeez	17.1.1925	21.4.1996	23†	1952–1957	847	93	0	24.91	21	3-35	0/0	45.42	15	
Khalid Hassan	14.7.1937		1	1954	17	10	0	17.00	2	2-116	0/0	58.00	0	
[1] **Khalid Wazir**	27.4.1936		2	1954	14	9*	0	7.00	–	–	–/–	–	0	
Khan Mohammad	1.1.1928	4.7.2009	13	1952–1957	100	26*	0	10.00	54	6-21	4/0	23.92	4	
Khurram Manzoor	10.6.1986		7	2008–2009	326	93	0	29.63	–	–	–/–	–	3	7
Liaqat Ali	21.5.1955		5	1974–1978	28	12	0	7.00	6	3-80	0/0	59.83	1	3
Mahmood Hussain	2.4.1932	25.12.1991	27	1952–1962	336	35	0	10.18	68	6-67	2/0	38.64	5	
[3] **Majid** Jahangir **Khan** (*CY 1970*)	28.9.1946		63	1964–1982	3,931	167	8	38.92	27	4-45	0/0	53.92	70	23
Mansoor Akhtar	25.12.1957		19	1980–1989	655	111	1	25.19	–	–	–/–	–	9	41
[2] **Manzoor Elahi**	15.4.1963		6	1984–1994	123	52	0	15.37	7	2-38	0/0	27.71	7	54
Maqsood Ahmed	26.3.1925	4.1.1999	16	1952–1955	507	99	0	19.50	3	2-12	0/0	63.66	13	
Masood Anwar	12.12.1967		1	1990	39	37	0	19.50	3	2-59	0/0	34.00	0	
Mathias Wallis	4.2.1935	1.9.1994	21	1955–1962	783	77	0	23.72	0	0-20	0/0	–	22	
Miran Bux	20.4.1907	8.2.1991	2	1954	1	1*	0	1.00	2	2-82	0/0	57.50	0	
Misbah-ul-Haq	28.5.1974		36	2000–2012	2,284	161*	3	45.68	–	–	–/–	–	35	109/39
Mohammad Aamer	13.4.1992		14	2009–2010	278	30*	0	12.63	51	6-84	3/0	29.09	0	15/18
Mohammad Akram	10.9.1974		9	1995–2000	24	10*	0	2.66	17	5-138	1/0	50.52	4	23
Mohammad Asif	20.12.1982		23	2004–2010	141	29	0	5.64	106	6-41	7/1	24.36	3	35‡/11
Mohammad Aslam Khokhar	5.1.1920	22.1.2011	1	1954	34	18	0	17.00	–	–	–/–	–	0	
Mohammad Ayub	13.9.1979		1	2012	47	25	0	23.50	–	–	–/–	–	1	

§ *Inzamam-ul-Haq's figures exclude one run for the ICC World XI v Australia in the Super Series Test in 2005-06.*

	Born	Died	Tests	Test Career	Runs	HS	100s	Avge	Wkts	BB	5/10	Avge	Ct/St	O/T
Mohammad Farooq	8.4.1938		7	*1960–1964*	85	47	0	17.00	21	4-70	0/0	32.47	1	
Mohammad Hafeez	17.10.1980		29	2003–2012	1,959	196	5	38.41	29	4-31	0/0	35.00	18	110/42
Mohammad Hussain	8.10.1976		2	*1996–1998*	18	17	0	6.00	3	2-66	0/0	29.00	1	14
Mohammad Ilyas	19.3.1946		10	*1964–1968*	441	126	1	23.21	0	0-1	0/0	–	6	
Mohammad Khalil	11.11.1982		2	*2004*	9	5	0	3.00	0	0-38	0/0	–	0	3
Mohammad Munaf	2.11.1935		4	*1959–1961*	63	19	0	12.60	11	4-42	0/0	31.00	0	
Mohammad Nazir	8.3.1946		14	*1969–1983*	144	29*	0	18.00	34	7-99	3/0	33.05	4	4
Mohammad Ramzan	25.12.1970		1	*1997*	36	29	0	18.00	–	–	–/–	–	1	
Mohammad Salman	7.8.1981		2	*2010*	25	13	0	6.25	–	–	–/–	–	2/1	7/1
Mohammad Sami	24.2.1981		36	*2000*–2012	487	49	0	11.59	85	5-36	2/0	52.74	7	85/5
Mohammad Talha	15.10.1988		1	*2008*	–	–	–	–	1	1-88	0/0	88.00	0	
Mohammad Wasim	8.8.1977		18	*1996*–2000	783	192	2	30.11	–	–	–/–	–	22/2	25
Mohammad Yousuf (formerly Yousuf Youhana) (*CY 2007*)	27.8.1974		90	*1997*–2010	7,530	223	24	52.29	0	0-3	0/0	–	65	281‡/3
Mohammad Zahid	2.8.1976		5	*1996–2002*	7	6*	0	1.40	15	7-66	1/1	33.46	0	11
Mohsin Kamal	16.6.1963		9	*1983–1994*	37	13*	0	9.25	24	4-116	0/0	34.25	4	19
Mohsin Khan	15.3.1955		48	*1977–1986*	2,709	200	7	37.10	0	0-0	0/0	–	34	75
[2] **Moin Khan**	23.9.1971		69	*1990–2004*	2,741	137	4	28.55	–	–	–/–	–	128/20	219
[1] **Mudassar Nazar**	6.4.1956		76	*1976–1988*	4,114	231	10	38.09	66	6-32	1/0	38.36	48	122
Mufasir-ul-Haq	16.8.1944	27.7.1983	1	*1964*	8	8*	0	–	3	2-50	0/0	28.00	1	
Munir Malik	10.7.1934	30.11.2012	3	*1959*–1962	7	4	0	2.33	9	5-128	1/0	39.77	1	
Mushtaq Ahmed (*CY 1997*)	28.6.1970		52	*1989–2003*	656	59	0	11.71	185	7-56	10/3	32.97	23	144
[2] **Mushtaq Mohammad** (*CY 1963*)	22.11.1943		57	*1958–1978*	3,643	201	10	39.17	79	5-28	3/0	29.22	42	10
Nadeem Abbasi	15.4.1964		3	*1989*	46	36	0	23.00	–	–	–/–	–	6	
Nadeem Ghauri	12.10.1962		1	*1989*	0	0	0	0.00	0	0-20	0/0	–	0	6
[2] **Nadeem Khan**	10.12.1969		2	*1992–1998*	34	25	0	17.00	2	2-147	0/0	115.00	0	2
Nasim-ul-Ghani	14.5.1941		29	*1957–1972*	747	101	1	16.60	52	6-67	2/0	37.67	11	1
Naushad Ali	1.10.1943		6	1964	156	39	0	14.18	–	–	–/–	–	9	
Naved Anjum	27.7.1963		2	*1989–1990*	44	22	0	14.66	4	2-57	0/0	40.50	0	13
Naved Ashraf	4.9.1974		2	*1998–1999*	64	32	0	21.33	–	–	–/–	–	0	
Naved Latif	21.2.1976		1	*2001*	20	20	0	10.00	–	–	–/–	–	0	11
Naved-ul-Hasan	28.2.1978		9	*2004–2006*	239	42*	0	19.91	18	3-30	0/0	58.00	3	74/4
[1] **Nazar Mohammad**	5.3.1921	12.7.1996	5	*1952*	277	124*	1	39.57	0	0-4	0/0	–	7	
Niaz Ahmed	11.11.1945	12.4.2000	2	1967–*1968*	17	16*	0	–	3	2-72	0/0	31.33	1	
[2] **Pervez Sajjad**	30.8.1942		19	*1964–1972*	123	24	0	13.66	59	7-74	3/0	23.89	9	
Qaiser Abbas	7.5.1982		1	*2000*	2	2	0	2.00	0	0-35	0/0	–	0	

	Born	Died	Tests	Test Career	Runs	HS	100s	Avge	Wkts	BB	5/10	Avge	Ct/St	O/T
Qasim Omar	9.2.1957		26	*1983–1986*	1,502	210	3	36.63	0	0-0	0/0	–	15	31
[2] **Ramiz Raja**	14.8.1962		57	*1983–1996*	2,833	122	2	31.83	–	–	–/–	–	34	198
Rashid Khan	15.12.1959		4	*1981–1984*	155	59	0	51.66	8	3-129	0/0	45.00	2	29
Rashid Latif	14.10.1968		37	1992–*2003*	1,381	150	1	28.77	0	0-10	0/0	–	119/11	166
Rehman Sheikh Fazalur	11.6.1935		1	*1957*	10	8	0	5.00	1	1-43	0/0	99.00	1	
Riaz Afridi	21.1.1985		1	*2004*	9	9	0	9.00	2	2-42	0/0	43.50	0	
Rizwan-uz-Zaman	4.9.1961		11	*1981–1988*	345	60	0	19.16	4	3-26	0/0	11.50	4	3
[2] **Sadiq Mohammad**	3.5.1945		41	*1969–1980*	2,579	166	5	35.81	0	0-0	0/0	–	28	19
[2] **Saeed Ahmed**	1.10.1937		41	*1957–1972*	2,991	172	5	40.41	22	4-64	0/0	36.45	13	
Saeed Ajmal	14.10.1977		23	2009–2012	250	50	0	10.86	122	7-55	6/2	27.09	8	74/50
Saeed Anwar (*CY 1997*)	6.9.1968		55	*1990–2001*	4,052	188*	11	45.52	0	0-0	0/0	–	18	247
Salah-ud-Din	14.2.1947		5	*1964–1969*	117	34*	0	19.50	7	2-36	0/0	26.71	3	
Saleem Jaffer	19.11.1962		14	*1986–1991*	42	10*	0	5.25	36	5-40	1/0	31.63	2	39
Salim Altaf	19.4.1944		21	1967–*1978*	276	53*	0	14.52	46	4-11	0/0	37.17	3	6
[2] **Salim Elahi**	21.11.1976		13	*1995–2002*	436	72	0	18.95	–	–	–/–	–	10/1	48
Salim Malik (*CY 1988*)	16.4.1963		103	*1981–1998*	5,768	237	15	43.69	5	1-3	0/0	82.80	65	283
Salim Yousuf	7.12.1959		32	*1981–1990*	1,055	91*	0	27.05	–	–	–/–	–	91/13	86
Salman Butt	7.10.1984		33	2003–2010	1,889	122	3	30.46	1	1-36	0/0	106.00	12	78/24
Saqlain Mushtaq (*CY 2000*)	29.12.1976		49	*1995–2003*	927	101*	1	14.48	208	8-164	13/3	29.83	15	169
Sarfraz Ahmed	22.5.1987		1	*2009*	6	5	0	3.00	–	–	–/–	–	4	23/2
Sarfraz Nawaz	1.12.1948		55	*1968–1983*	1,045	90	0	17.71	177	9-86	4/1	32.75	26	45
Shabbir Ahmed	21.4.1976		10	2003–*2005*	88	24*	0	8.80	51	5-48	2/0	23.03	3	32/1
Shadab Kabir	12.11.1977		5	1996–*2001*	148	55	0	21.14	0	0-9	0/0	–	11	3
Shafiq Ahmed	28.3.1949		6	1974–*1980*	99	27*	0	11.00	0	0-1	0/0	–	0	3
[2] **Shafqat Rana**	10.8.1943		5	*1964–1969*	221	95	0	31.57	1	1-2	0/0	9.00	5	
Shahid Afridi	1.3.1980		27	*1998*–2010	1,716	156	5	36.51	48	5-52	1/0	35.60	10	344‡/58
Shahid Israr	1.3.1950		1	*1976*	7	7*	0	–	–	–	–/–	–	2	
Shahid Mahboob	25.8.1962		1	*1989*	–	–	–	–	2	2-131	0/0	65.50	0	10
Shahid Mahmood	17.3.1939		1	1962	25	16	0	12.50	0	0-23	0/0	–	0	
Shahid Nazir	4.12.1977		15	*1996–2006*	194	40	0	12.12	36	5-53	1/0	35.33	5	17
Shahid Saeed	6.1.1966		1	*1989*	12	12	0	12.00	0	0-7	0/0	–	0	10
Shakeel Ahmed, sen.	12.2.1966		1	*1998*	1	1	0	1.00	4	4-91	0/0	34.75	1	
Shakeel Ahmed, jun.	12.11.1971		3	*1992–1994*	74	33	0	14.80	–	–	–/–	–	4	2
Sharpe Duncan Albert	3.8.1937		3	*1959*	134	56	0	22.33	–	–	–/–	–	2	
Shoaib Akhtar	13.8.1975		46	*1997–2007*	544	47	0	10.07	178	6-11	12/2	25.69	12	158‡/15
Shoaib Malik	1.2.1982		32	*2001*–2010	1,606	148*	2	33.45	21	4-42	0/0	61.47	16	206/52

	Born	Died	Tests	Test Career	Runs	HS	100s	Avge	Wkts	BB	5/10	Avge	Ct/St	O/T
[1] **Shoaib Mohammad**	8.1.1961		45	*1983–1995*	2,705	203*	7	44.34	5	2-8	0/0	34.00	22	63
Shuja-ud-Din Butt	10.4.1930	7.2.2006	19	1954–*1961*	395	47	0	15.19	20	3-18	0/0	40.05	8	
Sikander Bakht	25.8.1957		26	*1976–1982*	146	22*	0	6.34	67	8-69	3/1	36.00	7	27
Sohail Khan	6.3.1984		2	*2008–2011*	11	11	0	11.00	1	1-62	0/0	245.00	0	5/3
Sohail Tanvir	12.12.1984		2	*2007*	17	13	0	5.66	5	3-83	0/0	63.20	2	50/28
Tahir Naqqash	6.6.1959		15	*1981–1984*	300	57	0	21.42	34	5-40	2/0	41.11	3	40
Talat Ali Malik	29.5.1950		10	*1972–1978*	370	61	0	23.12	0	0-1	0/0	–	4	
Tanvir Ahmed	20.12.1978		4	*2010*	116	57	0	29.00	16	6-120	1/0	24.56	1	2/1
Taslim Arif	1.5.1954	13.3.2008	6	*1979–1980*	501	210*	1	62.62	1	1-28	0/0	28.00	6/3	2
Taufeeq Umar	20.6.1981		43	*2001*–2012	2,943	236	7	38.72	0	0-0	0/0	–	47	22
Tauseef Ahmed	10.5.1958		34	*1979–1993*	318	35*	0	17.66	93	6-45	3/0	31.72	9	70
[2] **Umar Akmal**	26.5.1990		16	*2009–2011*	1,003	129	1	35.82	–	–	–/–	–	12	71/42
Umar Amin	16.10.1989		4	2010	99	33	0	12.37	3	1-7	0/0	21.00	1	3
Umar Gul	14.4.1984		45	2003–2012	554	65*	0	10.25	158	6-135	4/0	33.66	9	114/51
Wahab Riaz	28.6.1985		7	2010–*2010*	57	27	0	9.50	17	5-63	1/0	34.11	1	25/6
Wajahatullah Wasti	11.11.1974		6	*1998–1999*	329	133	2	36.55	0	0-0	0/0	–	7	15
[2] **Waqar Hassan**	12.9.1932		21	*1952–1959*	1,071	189	1	31.50	0	0-10	0/0	–	10	
Waqar Younis (*CY 1992*)	16.11.1971		87	*1989–2002*	1,010	45	0	10.20	373	7-76	22/5	23.56	18	262
Wasim Akram (*CY 1993*)	3.6.1966		104	*1984–2001*	2,898	257*	3	22.64	414	7-119	25/5	23.62	44	356
Wasim Bari	23.3.1948		81	1967–*1983*	1,366	85	0	15.88	0	0-2	0/0	–	201/27	51
[2] **Wasim Raja**	3.7.1952	23.8.2006	57	*1972–1984*	2,821	125	4	36.16	51	4-50	0/0	35.80	20	54
[2] **Wazir Mohammad**	22.12.1929		20	*1952–1959*	801	189	2	27.62	0	0-2	0/0	–	5	
Yasir Ali	15.10.1985		1	2003	1	1*	0	–	2	1-12	0/0	27.50	0	
Yasir Arafat	12.3.1982		3	*2007–2008*	94	50*	0	47.00	9	5-161	1/0	48.66	0	11/13
Yasir Hameed	28.2.1978		25	2003–2010	1,491	170	2	32.41	0	0-0	0/0	–	20	56
[2] **Younis Ahmed**	20.10.1947		4	*1969–1986*	177	62	0	29.50	0	0-6	0/0	–	0	2
Younis Khan	29.11.1977		79	*1999*–2012	6,565	313	20	51.69	7	2-23	0/0	60.14	88	248/25
Yousuf Youhana (*see* Mohammad Yousuf)														
Zaheer Abbas (*CY 1972*)	24.7.1947		78	*1969–1985*	5,062	274	12	44.79	3	2-21	0/0	44.00	34	62
Zahid Fazal	10.11.1973		9	*1990–1995*	288	78	0	18.00	–	–	–/–	–	5	19
[2] **Zahoor Elahi**	1.3.1971		2	*1996*	30	22	0	10.00	–	–	–/–	–	1	14
Zakir Khan	3.4.1963		2	*1985–1989*	9	9*	0	–	5	3-80	0/0	51.80	1	17
Zulfiqar Ahmed	22.11.1926	3.10.2008	9	*1952–1956*	200	63*	0	33.33	20	6-42	2/1	18.30	5	
Zulqarnain	25.5.1962		3	*1985*	24	13	0	6.00	–	–	–/–	–	8/2	16
Zulqarnain Haider	23.4.1986		1	2010	88	88	0	44.00	–	–	–/–	–	2	4/3

SRI LANKA (123 players)

	Born	Died	Tests	Test Career	Runs	HS	100s	Avge	Wkts	BB	5/10	Avge	Ct/St	O/T
Ahangama Franklyn Saliya	14.9.1959		3	1985	11	11	0	5.50	18	5-52	1/0	19.33	1	1
Amalean Kaushik Naginda	7.4.1965		2	1985–1987	9	7*	0	9.00	7	4-97	0/0	22.28	1	8
Amerasinghe Amerasinghe Mudalige Jayantha Gamini	2.2.1954		2	1983	54	34	0	18.00	3	2-73	0/0	50.00	3	
Amerasinghe Merenna Koralage Don Ishara	5.3.1978		1	2007	0	0*	0	–	1	1-62	0/0	105.00	0	8
Anurasiri Sangarange Don	25.2.1966		18	1985–1997	91	24	0	5.35	41	4-71	0/0	37.75	4	45
Arnold Russel Premakumaran	25.10.1973		44	1996–2004	1,821	123	3	28.01	11	3-76	0/0	54.36	51	180/1
Atapattu Marvan Samson	22.11.1970		90	1990–2007	5,502	249	16	39.02	1	1-9	0/0	24.00	58	268/2
Bandara Herath Mudiyanselage Charitha Malinga	31.12.1979		8	1997–2005	124	43	0	15.50	16	3-84	0/0	39.56	4	31/4
Bandaratilleke Mapa Rallage Chandima Niroshan	16.5.1975		7	1997–2001	93	25	0	11.62	23	5-36	1/0	30.34	0	3
Chandana Umagiliya Durage Upul	7.5.1972		16	1998–2004	616	92	0	26.78	37	6-179	3/1	41.48	7	147
Chandimal Lokuge Dinesh	18.11.1989		5	2011–2012	365	65	0	40.55	–	–	–/–	–	6/1	47/12
Dassanayake Pubudu Bathiya	11.7.1970		11	1993–1994	196	36	0	13.06	–	–	–/–	–	19/5	16
de Alwis Ronald Guy	15.2.1959	12.1.2013	11	1982–1987	152	28	0	8.00	–	–	–/–	–	21/2	31
de Mel Ashantha Lakdasa Francis	9.5.1959		17	1981–1986	326	34	0	14.17	59	6-109	3/0	36.94	9	57
de Saram Samantha Indika	2.9.1973		4	1999	117	39	0	23.40	–	–	–/–	–	1	15/1
de Silva Ashley Matthew	3.12.1963		3	1992–1993	10	9	0	3.33	–	–	–/–	–	4/1	4
de Silva Dandeniyage Somachandra	11.6.1942		12	1981–1984	406	61	0	21.36	37	5-59	1/0	36.40	5	41
de Silva Ellawalakankanamge Asoka Ranjit	28.3.1956		10	1985–1990	185	50	0	15.41	8	2-67	0/0	129.00	4	28
de Silva Ginigalgodage Ramba Ajit	12.12.1952		4	1981–1982	41	14	0	8.20	7	2-38	0/0	55.00	0	6
de Silva Karunakalage Sajeewa Chanaka	11.1.1971		8	1996–1998	65	27	0	9.28	16	5-85	1/0	55.56	5	38
de Silva Pinnaduwage Aravinda (*CY 1996*)	17.10.1965		93	1984–2002	6,361	267	20	42.97	29	3-30	0/0	41.65	43	308
de Silva Sanjeewa Kumara Lanka	29.7.1975		3	1997	36	20*	0	18.00	–	–	–/–	–	1	11
de Silva Weddikkara Ruwan Sujeewa	7.10.1979		3	2002–2007	10	5*	0	10.00	11	4-35	0/0	19.00	1	
Dharmasena Handunnettige Deepthi Priyantha Kumar	24.4.1971		31	1993–2003	868	62*	0	19.72	69	6-72	3/0	42.31	14	141
Dias Roy Luke	18.10.1952		20	1981–1986	1,285	109	3	36.71	0	0-17	0/0	–	6	58
Dilshan Tillekeratne Mudiyanselage	14.10.1976		85	1999–2012	5,255	193	15	40.42	36	4-10	0/0	42.88	88	250/46
Dunusinghe Chamara Iroshan	19.10.1970		5	1994–1995	160	91	0	16.00	–	–	–/–	–	13/2	1
Eranga Ranaweera Mudiyanselage Shaminda	23.6.1986		5	2011–2012	34	12	0	6.80	15	4-65	0/0	38.00	3	4/2
Fernando Aththachchi Nuwan Pradeep Roshan	19.10.1986		4	2011–2012	28	17*	0	5.60	3	2-114	0/0	157.66	0	2
Fernando Congenige Randhi Dilhara	19.7.1979		40	2000–2012	249	39*	0	8.30	100	5-42	3/0	37.84	10	146‡/17

	Born	Died	Tests	Test Career	Runs	HS	100s	Avge	Wkts	BB	5/10	Avge	Ct/St	O/T
Fernando Ellekutige Rufus Nemesion Susil	19.12.1955		5	*1982–1983*	112	46	0	11.20	–	–	–/–	–	0	7
Fernando Kandage Hasantha Ruwan Kumara	14.10.1979		2	*2002*	38	24	0	9.50	4	3-63	0/0	27.00	1	7
Fernando Kandana Arachchige Dinusha Manoj	10.8.1979		2	*2003*	56	51*	0	28.00	1	1-29	0/0	107.00	0	1
Fernando Thudellage Charitha Buddhika	22.8.1980		9	*2001*–2002	132	45	0	26.40	18	4-27	0/0	44.00	4	17
Gallage Indika Sanjeewa	22.11.1975		1	*1999*	3	3	0	3.00	0	0-24	0/0	–	0	3
Goonatillake Hettiarachige Mahes	16.8.1952		5	*1981–1982*	177	56	0	22.12	–	–	–/–	–	10/3	6
Gunasekera Yohan	8.11.1957		2	*1982*	48	23	0	12.00	–	–	–/–	–	6	3
Gunawardene Dihan Avishka	26.5.1977		6	*1998–2005*	181	43	0	16.45	–	–	–/–	–	2	61
Guneratne Roshan Punyajith Wijesinghe	26.1.1962	21.7.2005	1	*1982*	0	0*	0	–	0	0-84	0/0	–	0	
Gurusinha Asanka Pradeep	16.9.1966		41	*1985*–1996	2,452	143	7	38.92	20	2-7	0/0	34.05	33	147
Hathurusinghe Upul Chandika	13.9.1968		26	*1990–1998*	1,274	83	0	29.62	17	4-66	0/0	46.41	7	35
Herath Herath Mudiyanselage Rangana Keerthi Bandara	19.3.1978		45	*1999–2012*	704	80*	0	14.08	186	7-157	14/2	29.95	10	38/6
Hettiarachchi Dinuka	15.7.1976		1	*2000*	0	0*	0	0.00	2	2-36	0/0	20.50	0	
Jayasekera Rohan Stanley Amarasiriwardene	7.12.1957		1	*1981*	2	2	0	1.00	–	–	–/–	–	0	2
Jayasuriya Sanath Teran (*CY 1997*)	30.6.1969		110	*1990–2007*	6,973	340	14	40.07	98	5-34	2/0	34.34	78	441‡/31
Jayawardene Denagamage Proboth Mahela de Silva (*CY 2007*)	27.5.1977		138	*1997–2012*	10,806	374	31	49.56	6	2-32	0/0	49.50	194	381‡/44
Jayawardene Hewasandatchige Asiri Prasanna Wishvanath	9.10.1979		52	2000–*2012*	1,900	154*	4	30.64	–	–	–/–	–	97/32	6
Jeganathan Sridharan	11.7.1951	14.5.1996	2	*1982*	19	8	0	4.75	0	0-12	0/0	–	0	5
John Vinothen Bede	27.5.1960		6	*1982*–1984	53	27*	0	10.60	28	5-60	2/0	21.92	2	45
Jurangpathy Baba Roshan	25.6.1967		2	*1985–1986*	1	1	0	0.25	1	1-69	0/0	93.00	2	
Kalavitigoda Shantha	23.12.1977		1	*2004*	8	7	0	4.00	–	–	–/–	–	2	
Kalpage Ruwan Senani	19.2.1970		11	*1993–1998*	294	63	0	18.37	12	2-27	0/0	64.50	10	86
Kaluhalamulla H. K. S. R. (*see* Randiv, Suraj)														
[2] **Kaluperuma** Lalith Wasantha Silva	25.6.1949		2	*1981*	12	11*	0	4.00	0	0-24	0/0	–	2	4
[2] **Kaluperuma** Sanath Mohan Silva	22.10.1961		4	*1983–1987*	88	23	0	11.00	2	2-17	0/0	62.00	6	2
Kaluwitharana Romesh Shantha	24.11.1969		49	*1992–2004*	1,933	132*	3	26.12	–	–	–/–	–	93/26	189
Kapugedera Chamara Kantha	24.2.1987		8	2006–2009	418	96	0	34.83	0	0-9	0/0	–	6	92/21
Karunaratne Frank Dimuth Madushanka	28.4.1988		4	*2012*	200	85	0	28.57	–	–	–/–	–	2	2
Kulasekara Chamith Kosala Bandara	15.7.1985		1	*2011*	22	15	0	11.00	1	1-65	0/0	80.00	0	4
Kulasekara Kulasekara Mudiyanselage Dinesh Nuwan	22.7.1982		18	*2004–2012*	359	64	0	14.95	41	4-21	0/0	35.51	8	126/25
Kuruppu Don Sardha Brendon Priyantha	5.1.1962		4	*1986*–1991	320	201*	1	53.33	–	–	–/–	–	1	54
Kuruppuarachchi Ajith Kosala	1.11.1964		2	*1985–1986*	0	0*	0	–	8	5-44	1/0	18.62	0	

	Born	*Died*	*Tests*	*Test Career*	*Runs*	*HS*	*100s*	*Avge*	*Wkts*	*BB*	*5/10*	*Avge*	*Ct/St*	*O/T*
Labrooy Graeme Fredrick	7.6.1964		9	*1986–1990*	158	70*	0	14.36	27	5-133	1/0	44.22	3	44
Lakmal Ranasinghe Arachchige Suranga	10.3.1987		13	*2010–2012*	77	18	0	6.41	20	3-55	0/0	62.25	2	15/2
Lakshitha Materba Kanatha Gamage Chamila Premanath	4.1.1979		2	2002–*2002*	42	40	0	14.00	5	2-33	0/0	31.60	1	7
Liyanage Dulip Kapila	6.6.1972		9	*1992*–2001	69	23	0	7.66	17	4-56	0/0	39.17	0	16
Lokuarachchi Kaushal Samaraweera	20.5.1982		4	2003–*2003*	94	28*	0	23.50	5	2-47	0/0	59.00	1	21/2
Madugalle Ranjan Senerath	22.4.1959		21	*1981*–1988	1,029	103	1	29.40	0	0-0	0/0	–	9	63
Madurasinghe Madurasinghe Arachchige Wijayasiri Ranjith	30.1.1961		3	1988–*1992*	24	11	0	4.80	3	3-60	0/0	57.33	0	12
Mahanama Roshan Siriwardene	31.5.1966		52	*1985–1997*	2,576	225	4	29.27	0	0-3	0/0	–	56	213
Maharoof Mohamed Farveez	7.9.1984		22	*2003*–2011	556	72	0	18.53	25	4-52	0/0	65.24	7	104/7
Malinga Separamadu Lasith	28.8.1983		30	2004–2010	275	64	0	11.45	101	5-50	3/0	33.15	7	131/40
Mathews Angelo Davis	2.6.1987		31	2009–*2012*	1,668	105*	1	39.71	11	2-60	0/0	70.45	15	85/36
Mendis Balapuwaduge Ajantha Winslo	11.3.1985		16	2008–2011	164	78	0	14.90	62	6-117	3/1	32.48	2	59/27
Mendis Louis Rohan Duleep	25.8.1952		24	*1981*–1988	1,329	124	4	31.64	–	–	–/–	–	9	79
Mirando Magina Thilan Thushara	1.3.1981		10	2003–*2010*	94	15*	0	8.54	28	5-83	1/0	37.14	3	38/6
Mubarak Jehan	10.1.1981		10	2002–*2007*	254	48	0	15.87	0	0-1	0/0	–	13	38/16
Muralitharan Muttiah (*CY 1999*)	17.4.1972		132§	*1992*–2010	1,259	67	0	11.87	795	9-51	67/22	22.67	70	343‡/12
Nawaz Mohamed Naveed	20.9.1973		1	2002	99	78*	0	99.00	–	–	–/–	–	0	3
Nissanka Ratnayake Arachchige Prabath	25.10.1980		4	2003	18	12*	0	6.00	10	5-64	1/0	36.60	0	23
Paranavitana Nishad Tharanga	15.4.1982		32	*2008–2012*	1,792	111	2	32.58	1	1-26	0/0	86.00	27	
Perera Anhettige Suresh Asanka	16.2.1978		3	1998–2001	77	43*	0	25.66	1	1-104	0/0	180.00	1	20
Perera Narangoda Liyanaarachchilage Tissara Chirantha	3.4.1989		6	2011–2012	203	75	0	20.30	11	4-63	0/0	59.36	1	48/21
Perera Panagodage Don Ruchira Laksiri	6.4.1977		8	*1998–2002*	33	11*	0	11.00	17	3-40	0/0	38.88	2	19/2
Prasad Kariyawasam Tirana Gamage Dammika	30.5.1983		12	2008–*2012*	275	47	0	18.33	22	3-82	0/0	59.00	5	12/1
Prasanna Seekkuge	27.6.1985		1	*2011*	5	5	0	5.00	0	0-80	0/0	–	0	9
Pushpakumara Karuppiahyage Ravindra	21.7.1975		23	*1994–2001*	166	44	0	8.73	58	7-116	4/0	38.65	10	31
Ramanayake Champaka Priyadarshana Hewage	8.1.1965		18	*1987–1993*	143	34*	0	9.53	44	5-82	1/0	42.72	6	62
Ramyakumara Wijekoon Mudiyanselage Gayan	21.12.1976		2	2005	38	14	0	12.66	2	2-49	0/0	33.00	0	0/3
Ranasinghe Anura Nandana	13.10.1956	9.11.1998	2	*1981–1982*	88	77	0	22.00	1	1-23	0/0	69.00	0	9
[2] **Ranatunga** Arjuna (*CY 1999*)	1.12.1963		93	*1981*–2000	5,105	135*	4	35.69	16	2-17	0/0	65.00	47	269
[2] **Ranatunga** Dammika	12.10.1962		2	*1989*	87	45	0	29.00	–	–	–/–	–	0	4
[2] **Ranatunga** Sanjeeva	25.4.1969		9	*1994–1996*	531	118	2	33.18	–	–	–/–	–	2	13

§ *Muralitharan's figures exclude two runs, five wickets and two catches for the ICC World XI v Australia in the Super Series Test in 2005-06.*

	Born	*Died*	*Tests*	*Test Career*	*Runs*	*HS*	*100s*	*Avge*	*Wkts*	*BB*	*5/10*	*Avge*	*Ct/St*	*O/T*
Randiv Suraj (Hewa Kaluhalamullage Suraj Randiv Kaluhalamulla; *formerly* M. M. M. Suraj)	30.1.1985		12	2010–*2012*	147	39	0	9.18	43	5-82	1/0	37.51	1	28/7
Ratnayake Rumesh Joseph	2.1.1964		23	*1982–1991*	433	56	0	14.43	73	6-66	5/0	35.10	9	70
Ratnayeke Joseph Ravindran	2.5.1960		22	*1981–1989*	807	93	0	25.21	56	8-83	4/0	35.21	1	78
Samarasekera Maitipage Athula Rohitha	5.8.1961		4	1988–*1991*	118	57	0	16.85	3	2-38	0/0	34.66	3	39
[2]**Samaraweera** Dulip Prasanna	12.2.1972		7	*1993–1994*	211	42	0	15.07	–	–	–/–	–	5	5
[2]**Samaraweera** Thilan Thusara	22.9.1976		81	2001–*2012*	5,462	231	14	48.76	15	4-49	0/0	45.93	45	53
Sangakkara Kumar Chokshanada (*CY 2012*)	27.10.1977		115	2000–*2012*	10,045	287	30	55.80	0	0-4	0/0	–	169/20	330‡/43
Senanayake Charith Panduka	19.12.1962		3	*1990*	97	64	0	19.40	–	–	–/–	–	2	7
Silva Jayan Kaushal	27.5.1986		3	*2011*	84	39	0	14.00	–	–	–/–	–	5/1	
Silva Kelaniyage Jayantha	2.6.1973		7	*1995–1997*	6	6*	0	2.00	20	4-16	0/0	32.35	1	1
Silva Lindamlilage Prageeth Chamara	14.12.1979		11	*2006–2007*	537	152*	1	33.56	1	1-57	0/0	65.00	7	75/16
Silva Sampathawaduge Amal Rohitha	12.12.1960		9	*1982*–1988	353	111	2	25.21	–	–	–/–	–	33/1	20
Tharanga Warushavithana Upul	2.2.1985		15	*2005–2007*	713	165	1	28.52	–	–	–/–	–	11	158‡/10
Thirimanne Hettige Don Rumesh Lahiru	8.9.1989		8	2011–*2012*	356	91	0	23.73	0	0-7	0/0	–	4	31/11
Tillekeratne Hashan Prasantha	14.7.1967		83	*1989–2003*	4,545	204*	11	42.87	0	0-0	0/0	–	122/2	200
Upashantha Kalutarage Eric Amila	10.6.1972		2	*1998*–2002	10	6	0	3.33	4	2-41	0/0	50.00	0	12
Vaas Warnakulasuriya Patabendige Ushantha Joseph Chaminda	27.1.1974		111	*1994*–2009	3,089	100*	1	24.32	355	7-71	12/2	29.58	31	321‡/6
Vandort Michael Graydon	19.1.1980		20	*2001–2008*	1,144	140	4	36.90	–	–	–/–	–	6	1
Warnapura Bandula	1.3.1953		4	*1981–1982*	96	38	0	12.00	0	0-1	0/0	–	2	12
Warnapura Basnayake Shalith Malinda	26.5.1979		14	2007–2009	821	120	2	35.69	0	0-40	0/0	–	14	3
Warnaweera Kahakatchchi Patabandige Jayananda	23.11.1960		10	*1985–1994*	39	20	0	4.33	32	4-25	0/0	31.90	0	6
Weerasinghe Colombage Don Udesh Sanjeewa	1.3.1968		1	*1985*	3	3	0	3.00	0	0-8	0/0	–	0	
Welagedara Uda Walawwe Mahim Bandaralage Chanaka Asanka	20.3.1981		20	*2007–2012*	191	48	0	8.30	54	5-52	2/0	40.48	4	10/2
[2]**Wettimuny** Mithra de Silva	11.6.1951		2	*1982*	28	17	0	7.00	–	–	–/–	–	2	1
[2]**Wettimuny** Sidath (*CY 1985*)	12.8.1956		23	*1981–1986*	1,221	190	2	29.07	0	0-16	0/0	–	10	35
Wickremasinghe Anguppulige Gamini Dayantha	27.12.1965		3	*1989–1992*	17	13*	0	8.50	–	–	–/–	–	9/1	4
Wickremasinghe Gallage Pramodya	14.8.1971		40	*1991–2000*	555	51	0	9.40	85	6-60	3/0	41.87	18	134
Wijegunawardene Kapila Indaka Weerakkody	23.11.1964		2	1991–*1991*	14	6*	0	4.66	7	4-51	0/0	21.00	0	26
Wijesuriya Roger Gerard Christopher Ediriweera	18.2.1960		4	*1981–1985*	22	8	0	4.40	1	1-68	0/0	294.00	1	8

	Born	Died	Tests	Test Career	Runs	HS	100s	Avge	Wkts	BB	5/10	Avge	Ct/St	O/T
Wijetunge Piyal Kashyapa	6.8.1971		1	1993	10	10	0	5.00	2	1-58	0/0	59.00	0	
Zoysa Demuni Nuwan Tharanga	13.5.1978		30	*1996*–2004	288	28*	0	8.47	64	5-20	1/0	33.70	4	9

ZIMBABWE (84 players)

	Born	Died	Tests	Test Career	Runs	HS	100s	Avge	Wkts	BB	5/10	Avge	Ct/St	O/T
Arnott Kevin John	8.3.1961		4	*1992*	302	101*	1	43.14	–	–	–/–	–	4	13
Blignaut Arnoldus Mauritius ("Andy")	1.8.1978		19	*2000–2005*	886	92	0	26.84	53	5-73	3/0	37.05	13	54/1
Brain David Hayden	4.10.1964		9	*1992–1994*	115	28	0	10.45	30	5-42	1/0	30.50	1	23
Brandes Eddo André	5.3.1963		10	*1992–1999*	121	39	0	10.08	26	3-45	0/0	36.57	4	59
Brent Gary Bazil	13.1.1976		4	*1999–2001*	35	25	0	5.83	7	3-21	0/0	44.85	1	70/3
Briant Gavin Aubrey	11.4.1969		1	*1992*	17	16	0	8.50	–	–	–/–	–	0	5
Bruk-Jackson Glen Keith	25.4.1969		2	*1993*	39	31	0	9.75	–	–	–/–	–	0	1
Burmester Mark Greville	24.1.1968		3	*1992*	54	30*	0	27.00	3	3-78	0/0	75.66	1	8
Butchart Iain Peter	9.5.1960		1	*1994*	23	15	0	11.50	0	0-11	0/0	–	1	20
Campbell Alistair Douglas Ross	23.9.1972		60	*1992–2002*	2,858	103	2	27.21	0	0-1	0/0	–	60	188
Carlisle Stuart Vance	10.5.1972		37	*1994–2005*	1,615	118	2	26.91	–	–	–/–	–	34	111
Chakabva Regis Wiriranai	20.9.1987		2	*2011*	108	63	0	27.00	–	–	–/–	–	2	13/2
Chigumbura Elton	14.3.1986		7	*2003–2011*	192	71	0	14.76	12	5-54	1/0	49.58	2	139‡/22
Coventry Charles Kevin	8.3.1983		2	*2005*	88	37	0	22.00	–	–	–/–	–	3	37/9
Cremer Alexander Graeme	19.9.1986		7	*2004–2011*	58	26	0	4.46	15	3-86	0/0	47.13	3	43/9
Crocker Gary John	16.5.1962		3	*1992*	69	33	0	23.00	3	2-65	0/0	72.33	0	6
Dabengwa Keith Mbusi	17.8.1980		3	*2005*	90	35	0	15.00	5	3-127	0/0	49.80	1	37/8
Dekker Mark Hamilton	5.12.1969		14	*1993–1996*	333	68*	0	15.85	0	0-5	0/0	–	12	23
Duffin Terrence	20.3.1982		2	*2005*	80	56	0	20.00	–	–	–/–	–	1	23
Ebrahim Dion Digby	7.8.1980		29	*2000–2005*	1,226	94	0	22.70	–	–	–/–	–	16	82
[2] **Ervine** Craig Richard	19.8.1985		2	*2011*	96	49	0	32.00	–	–	–/–	–	3	23/5
[2] **Ervine** Sean Michael	6.12.1982		5	2003–*2003*	261	86	0	32.62	9	4-146	0/0	43.11	7	42
Evans Craig Neil	29.11.1969		3	*1996–2003*	52	22	0	8.66	0	0-8	0/0	–	1	53
Ewing Gavin Mackie	21.1.1981		3	*2003–2005*	108	71	0	18.00	2	1-27	0/0	130.00	1	7
Ferreira Neil Robert	3.6.1979		1	*2005*	21	16	0	10.50	–	–	–/–	–	0	
[2] **Flower** Andrew OBE (*CY 2002*)	28.4.1968		63	*1992–2002*	4,794	232*	12	51.54	0	0-0	0/0	–	151/9	213
[2] **Flower** Grant William	20.12.1970		67	*1992–2003*	3,457	201*	6	29.54	25	4-41	0/0	61.48	43	221
Friend Travis John	7.1.1981		13	2001–*2003*	447	81	0	29.80	25	5-31	1/0	43.60	2	51
Goodwin Murray William	11.12.1972		19	*1997*–2000	1,414	166*	3	42.84	0	0-3	0/0	–	10	71

	Born	Died	Tests	Test Career	Runs	HS	100s	Avge	Wkts	BB	5/10	Avge	Ct/St	O/T
Gripper Trevor Raymond	28.12.1975		20	*1999–2003*	809	112	1	21.86	6	2-91	0/0	84.83	14	8
Hondo Douglas Tafadzwa	7.7.1979		9	*2001–2004*	83	19	0	9.22	21	6-59	1/0	36.85	5	56
Houghton David Laud	23.6.1957		22	*1992–1997*	1,464	266	4	43.05	0	0-0	0/0	–	17	63
Huckle Adam George	21.9.1971		8	*1997–1998*	74	28*	0	6.72	25	6-109	2/1	34.88	3	19
James Wayne Robert	27.8.1965		4	*1993–1994*	61	33	0	15.25	–	–	–/–	–	16	11
[1] **Jarvis** Kyle Malcolm	16.2.1989		4	*2011*	37	25*	0	12.33	14	5-64	1/0	36.14	0	16/8
[1] **Jarvis** Malcolm Peter	6.12.1955		5	*1992–1994*	4	2*	0	2.00	11	3-30	0/0	35.72	2	12
Johnson Neil Clarkson	24.1.1970		13	*1998*–2000	532	107	1	24.18	15	4-77	0/0	39.60	12	48
Lamb Gregory Arthur	4.3.1980		1	*2011*	46	39	0	23.00	3	3-120	0/0	47.00	2	15/5
Lock Alan Charles Ingram	10.9.1962		1	*1995*	8	8*	0	8.00	5	3-68	0/0	21.00	0	8
Madondo Trevor Nyasha	22.11.1976	11.6.2001	3	*1997–2000*	90	74*	0	30.00	–	–	–/–	–	1	13
Mahwire Ngonidzashe Blessing	31.7.1982		10	*2002–2005*	147	50*	0	13.36	18	4-92	0/0	50.83	1	23
Maregwede Alester	5.8.1981		2	*2003*	74	28	0	18.50	–	–	–/–	–	1	11
Marillier Douglas Anthony	24.4.1978		5	*2000–2001*	185	73	0	30.83	11	4-57	0/0	29.27	2	48
[2] **Masakadza** Hamilton	9.8.1983		19	2001–*2011*	954	119	2	25.78	5	1-9	0/0	23.40	8	115/22
[2] **Masakadza** Shingirai Winston	4.9.1986		1	*2011*	24	21	0	24.00	1	1-102	0/0	102.00	0	9/4
Matambanadzo Everton Zvikomborero	13.4.1976		3	*1996–1999*	17	7	0	4.25	4	2-62	0/0	62.50	0	7
Matsikenyeri Stuart	3.5.1983		8	*2003–2004*	351	57	0	23.40	2	1-58	0/0	172.50	7	112/10
Mawoyo Tinotenda Mbiri Kanayi	8.1.1986		4	*2011*	314	163*	1	44.85	–	–	–/–	–	3	3
Mbangwa Mpumelelo ("Pommie")	26.6.1976		15	*1996–2000*	34	8	0	2.00	32	3-23	0/0	31.43	2	29
Mpofu Christopher Bobby	27.11.1985		9	*2004–2011*	27	8	0	2.45	20	4-92	0/0	44.45	0	62/11
Mupariwa Tawanda	16.4.1985		1	*2003*	15	14	0	15.00	0	0-136	0/0	–	0	35/4
Murphy Brian Andrew	1.12.1976		11	*1999–2001*	123	30	0	10.25	18	3-32	0/0	61.83	11	31
Mutendera David Travolta	25.1.1979		1	*2000*	10	10	0	5.00	0	0-29	0/0	–	0	9
Mutizwa Forster	24.8.1985		1	*2011*	24	18	0	12.00	–	–	–/–	–	0	17/3
Mwayenga Waddington	20.6.1984		1	*2005*	15	14*	0	15.00	1	1-79	0/0	79.00	0	3
Ncube Njabulo	14.10.1989		1	*2011*	17	14	0	8.50	1	1-80	0/0	121.00	1	1
Nkala Mluleki Luke	1.4.1981		10	2000–*2004*	187	47	0	14.38	11	3-82	0/0	66.09	4	50/1
Olonga Henry Khaaba	3.7.1976		30	*1994–2002*	184	24	0	5.41	68	5-70	2/0	38.52	10	50
Panyangara Tinashe	21.10.1985		3	*2003–2004*	128	40*	0	32.00	8	3-28	0/0	35.75	0	25
Peall Stephen Guy	2.9.1969		4	*1993–1994*	60	30	0	15.00	4	2-89	0/0	75.75	1	21
Price Raymond William	12.6.1976		21	*1999–2011*	243	36	0	8.37	79	6-73	5/1	35.92	4	102/16
Pycroft Andrew John	6.6.1956		3	*1992*	152	60	0	30.40	–	–	–/–	–	2	20
Ranchod Ujesh	17.5.1969		1	*1992*	8	7	0	4.00	1	1-45	0/0	45.00	0	3
[2] **Rennie** Gavin James	12.1.1976		23	*1997–2001*	1,023	93	0	22.73	1	1-40	0/0	84.00	13	40
[2] **Rennie** John Alexander	29.7.1970		4	*1993–1997*	62	22	0	12.40	3	2-22	0/0	97.66	1	44

	Born	Died	Tests	Test Career	Runs	HS	100s	Avge	Wkts	BB	5/10	Avge	Ct/St	O/T
Rogers Barney Guy	20.8.1982		4	*2004*	90	29	0	11.25	0	0-17	0/0	–	1	15
Shah Ali Hassimshah	7.8.1959		3	*1992–1996*	122	62	0	24.40	1	1-46	0/0	125.00	0	28
Sibanda Vusimuzi	10.10.1983		6	*2003–2011*	320	93	0	26.66	–	–	–/–	–	4	96‡/7
[2] **Strang** Bryan Colin	9.6.1972		26	*1994*–2001	465	53	0	12.91	56	5-101	1/0	39.33	11	49
[2] **Strang** Paul Andrew	28.7.1970		24	*1994–2001*	839	106*	1	27.06	70	8-109	4/1	36.02	15	95
Streak Heath Hilton	16.3.1974		65	*1993–2005*	1,990	127*	1	22.35	216	6-73	7/0	28.14	17	187‡
Taibu Tatenda	14.5.1983		28	2001–*2011*	1,546	153	1	30.31	1	1-27	0/0	27.00	57/5	149‡/17
Taylor Brendan Ross Murray	6.2.1986		14	*2003–2011*	791	117	2	29.29	0	0-6	0/0	–	14	132/17
Traicos Athanasios John	17.5.1947		4†	*1992*	11	5	0	2.75	14	5-86	1/0	40.14	4	27
Utseya Prosper	26.3.1985		1	*2003*	45	45	0	22.50	0	0-55	0/0	–	2	139/20
Vermeulen Mark Andrew	2.3.1979		8	*2002–2003*	414	118	1	25.87	0	0-5	0/0	–	6	43
Viljoen Dirk Peter	11.3.1977		2	*1997–2000*	57	38	0	14.25	1	1-14	0/0	65.00	1	53
Vitori Brian Vitalis	22.2.1990		3	*2011*	33	14	0	6.60	6	4-66	0/0	55.66	1	6/2
[1] **Waller** Andrew Christopher	25.9.1959		2	*1996*	69	50	0	23.00	–	–	–/–	–	1	39
[1] **Waller** Malcolm Noel	28.9.1984		2	*2011*	124	72*	0	41.33	0	0-8	0/0	–	1	24/5
Watambwa Brighton Tonderai	9.6.1977		6	*2000–2001*	11	4*	0	3.66	14	4-64	0/0	35.00	0	
Whittall Andrew Richard	28.3.1973		10	*1996–1999*	114	17	0	7.60	7	3-73	0/0	105.14	8	63
Whittall Guy James	5.9.1972		46	*1993–2002*	2,207	203*	4	29.42	51	4-18	0/0	40.94	19	147
Wishart Craig Brian	9.1.1974		27	*1995–2005*	1,098	114	1	22.40	–	–	–/–	–	15	90

BANGLADESH (65 players)

	Born	Died	Tests	Test Career	Runs	HS	100s	Avge	Wkts	BB	5/10	Avge	Ct/St	O/T
Abdur Razzak	15.6.1982		9	*2005–2011*	214	43	0	17.83	18	3-93	0/0	65.83	3	138/24
Abul Hasan	5.8.1992		1	*2012*	120	113	1	120.00	0	0-113	0/0	–	0	2/4
Aftab Ahmed	10.11.1985		16	*2004–2009*	582	82*	0	20.78	5	2-31	0/0	47.40	7	85/11
Akram Khan	1.11.1968		8	*2000–2003*	259	44	0	16.18	–	–	–/–	–	3	44
Al Sahariar	23.4.1978		15	*2000–2003*	683	71	0	22.76	–	–	–/–	–	10	29
Alamgir Kabir	10.1.1981		3	2002–*2003*	8	4	0	2.00	0	0-39	0/0	–	0	
Alok Kapali	1.1.1984		17	2002–*2005*	584	85	0	17.69	6	3-3	0/0	118.16	5	69/7
Aminul Islam	2.2.1968		13	*2000–2002*	530	145	1	21.20	1	1-66	0/0	149.00	5	39
Anwar Hossain Monir	31.12.1981		3	2003–2005	22	13	0	7.33	0	0-95	0/0	–	0	1
Anwar Hossain Piju	10.12.1983		1	*2002*	14	12	0	7.00	–	–	–/–	–	0	1
Bikash Ranjan Das	14.7.1982		1	*2000*	2	2	0	1.00	1	1-64	0/0	72.00	1	
Ehsanul Haque	1.12.1979		1	2002	7	5	0	3.50	0	0-18	0/0	–	0	6

	Born	Died	Tests	Test Career	Runs	HS	100s	Avge	Wkts	BB	5/10	Avge	Ct/St	O/T
Elias Sunny	2.8.1986		3	2011	38	20*	0	9.50	12	6-94	1/0	29.41	1	4/7
Enamul Haque, sen.	27.2.1966		10	2000–2003	180	24*	0	12.00	18	4-136	0/0	57.05	1	29
Enamul Haque, jun.	5.12.1986		14	2003–2009	53	13	0	5.88	41	7-95	3/1	39.24	3	10
Fahim Muntasir	1.11.1980		3	2001–2002	52	33	0	8.66	5	3-131	0/0	68.40	1	3
Faisal Hossain	26.10.1978		1	2003	7	5	0	3.50	–	–	–/–	–	0	6
Habibul Bashar	17.8.1972		50	2000–2007	3,026	113	3	30.87	0	0-1	0/0	–	22	111
Hannan Sarkar	1.12.1982		17	2002–2004	662	76	0	20.06	–	–	–/–	–	7	20
Hasibul Hossain	3.6.1977		5	2000–2001	97	31	0	10.77	6	2-125	0/0	95.16	1	32
Imrul Kayes	2.2.1987		16	2008–2011	549	75	0	17.15	0	0-1	0/0	–	16	48/4
Jahurul Islam	12.12.1986		3	2009–2010	114	46	0	19.00	–	–	–/–	–	3	11/2
Javed Omar Belim	25.11.1976		40	2000–2007	1,720	119	1	22.05	0	0-12	0/0	–	10	59
Junaid Siddique	30.10.1987		19	2007–2012	969	106	1	26.18	0	0-2	0/0	–	11	54/7
Khaled Mahmud	26.7.1971		12	2001–2003	266	45	0	12.09	13	4-37	0/0	64.00	2	77
Khaled Mashud	8.2.1976		44	2000–2007	1,409	103*	1	19.04	–	–	–/–	–	78/9	126
Mahbubul Alam	1.12.1983		4	2008	5	2	0	1.25	5	2-62	0/0	62.80	0	5
Mahmudullah	4.2.1986		14	2009–2012	833	115	1	32.03	24	5-51	1/0	44.66	12	85/21
Manjural Islam	7.11.1979		17	2000–2003	81	21	0	3.68	28	6-81	1/0	57.32	4	34
Manjural Islam Rana	4.5.1984	16.3.2007	6	2003–2004	257	69	0	25.70	5	3-84	0/0	80.20	3	25
Mashrafe bin Mortaza	5.10.1983		36	2001–2009	797	79	0	12.85	78	4-60	0/0	41.52	9	126‡/20
Mehrab Hossain, sen.	22.9.1978		9	2000–2003	241	71	0	13.38	0	0-5	0/0	–	6	18
Mehrab Hossain, jun.	8.7.1987		7	2007–2008	243	83	0	20.25	4	2-29	0/0	70.25	2	18/2
Mohammad Ashraful	9.9.1984		57	2001–2011	2,419	158*	5	22.60	20	2-42	0/0	60.40	24	169‡/22
Mohammad Rafique	5.9.1970		33	2000–2007	1,059	111	1	18.57	100	6-77	7/0	40.76	7	123‡/1
Mohammad Salim	15.10.1981		2	2003	49	26	0	16.33	–	–	–/–	–	3/1	1
Mohammad Sharif	12.12.1983		10	2000–2007	122	24*	0	7.17	14	4-98	0/0	79.00	5	9
Mushfiqur Rahim	1.9.1988		30	2005–2012	1,587	101	1	28.85	–	–	–/–	–	46/9	113/26
Mushfiqur Rahman	1.1.1980		10	2000–2004	232	46*	0	13.64	13	4-65	0/0	63.30	6	28
Naeem Islam	31.12.1986		8	2008–2012	416	108	1	32.00	1	1-11	0/0	303.00	2	53/9
[2] **Nafis Iqbal**	31.1.1985		11	2004–2005	518	121	1	23.54	–	–	–/–	–	2	16
Naimur Rahman	19.9.1974		8	2000–2002	210	48	0	15.00	12	6-132	1/0	59.83	4	29
Nasir Hossain	30.11.1991		6	2011–2012	472	96	0	42.90	3	3-52	0/0	77.66	2	19/11
Nazimuddin	1.10.1985		3	2011–2012	125	78	0	20.83	–	–	–/–	–	1	11/7
Nazmul Hossain	5.10.1987		2	2004–2011	16	8*	0	8.00	5	2-61	0/0	38.80	0	38/4
Rafiqul Islam	7.11.1977		1	2002	7	6	0	3.50	–	–	–/–	–	0	1
Rajin Saleh	20.11.1983		24	2003–2008	1,141	89	0	25.93	2	1-9	0/0	134.00	15	43
Raqibul Hasan	8.10.1987		9	2008–2011	336	65	0	19.76	1	1-0	0/0	17.00	9	55/5

	Born	*Died*	*Tests*	*Test Career*	*Runs*	*HS*	*100s*	*Avge*	*Wkts*	*BB*	*5/10*	*Avge*	*Ct/St*	*O/T*
Robiul Islam	20.10.1986		3	2010–*2011*	21	12	0	5.25	4	2-106	0/0	89.75	2	
Rubel Hossain	1.1.1990		14	2009–*2012*	103	17	0	9.36	21	5-166	1/0	78.90	6	38/6
Sajidul Islam	18.1.1988		2	*2007*	14	6	0	3.50	3	2-71	0/0	58.33	0	
Sanwar Hossain	5.8.1973		9	*2001–2003*	345	49	0	19.16	5	2-128	0/0	62.00	1	27
Shafiul Islam	6.10.1989		6	*2009–2011*	149	53	0	13.54	8	3-86	0/0	71.12	1	46/9
Shahadat Hossain	7.8.1986		34	2005–*2012*	476	40	0	10.12	69	6-27	4/0	50.79	8	50/5
Shahriar Hossain	1.6.1976		3	*2000–2003*	99	48	0	19.80	–	–	–/–	–	0/1	20
Shahriar Nafees	25.1.1986		23	*2005–2012*	1,227	138	1	26.67	–	–	–/–	–	19	75/1
Shakib Al Hasan	24.3.1987		28	2007–*2012*	1,835	144	2	35.98	102	7-36	9/0	32.56	11	126/24
Sohag Gazi	5.8.1991		2	*2012*	30	19	0	7.50	12	6-74	1/0	32.83	2	5/1
Suhrawadi Shuvo	21.11.1988		1	*2011*	15	15	0	7.50	4	3-73	0/0	36.50	0	17/1
Syed Rasel	3.7.1984		6	*2005*–2007	37	19	0	4.62	12	4-129	0/0	47.75	0	52/8
Talha Jubair	10.12.1985		7	2002–*2004*	52	31	0	6.50	14	3-135	0/0	55.07	1	6
[2] **Tamim Iqbal** (*CY 2011*)	20.3.1989		26	*2007–2012*	1,885	151	4	37.70	0	0-1	0/0	–	8	118/24
Tapash Baisya	25.12.1982		21	2002–2005	384	66	0	11.29	36	4-72	0/0	59.36	6	56
Tareq Aziz	4.9.1983		3	*2003–2004*	22	10*	0	11.00	1	1-76	0/0	261.00	1	10
Tushar Imran	10.12.1983		5	2002–2007	89	28	0	8.90	0	0-48	0/0	–	1	41

Notes

In one Test, A. and G. G. Hearne played for England; their brother, F. Hearne, for South Africa.
The Waughs and New Zealand's Marshalls are the only instance of Test-playing twins.
Adnan Akmal: brother of Kamran and Umar Akmal.
Amarsingh, L.: brother of L. Ramji.
Azmat Rana: brother of Shafqat Rana.
Bazid Khan (Pakistan): son of Majid Khan (Pakistan) and grandson of M. Jahangir Khan (India).
Bravo, D. J. and D. M.: half-brothers.
Chappell, G. S., I. M. and T. M.: grandsons of V. Y. Richardson.
Collins, P. T.: half-brother of F. H. Edwards.
Cooper, W. H.: great-grandfather of A. P. Sheahan.
Edwards, F. H.: half-brother of P. T. Collins.
Hanif Mohammad: brother of Mushtaq, Sadiq and Wazir Mohammad; father of Shoaib Mohammad.
Headley, D. W (England): son of R. G. A. and grandson of G. A. Headley (both West Indies).
Hearne, F. (England and South Africa): father of G. A. L. Hearne (South Africa).
Jahangir Khan, M. (India): father of Majid Khan and grandfather of Bazid Khan (both Pakistan).
Kamran Akmal: brother of Adnan and Umar Akmal.
Khalid Wazir (Pakistan): son of S. Wazir Ali (India).
Kirsten, G. and P. N.: half-brothers.
Majid Khan (Pakistan): son of M. Jahangir Khan (India) and father of Bazid Khan (Pakistan).
Manzoor Elahi: brother of Salim and Zahoor Elahi.
Moin Khan: brother of Nadeem Khan.
Mudassar Nazar: son of Nazar Mohammad.
Mushtaq Mohammad: brother of Hanif, Sadiq and Wazir Mohammad.
Nadeem Khan: brother of Moin Khan.
Nafis Iqbal: brother of Tamim Iqbal.
Nazar Mohammad: father of Mudassar Nazar.
Nazir Ali, S.: brother of S. Wazir Ali.
Pattinson, D. J. (England): brother of J. L. Pattinson (Australia).
Pervez Sajjad: brother of Waqar Hassan.
Ramiz Raja: brother of Wasim Raja.
Ramji, L.: brother of L. Amarsingh.
Richardson, V. Y.: grandfather of G. S., I. M. and T. M. Chappell.
Sadiq Mohammad: brother of Hanif, Mushtaq and Wazir Mohammad.
Saeed Ahmed: brother of Younis Ahmed.
Salim Elahi: brother of Manzoor and Zahoor Elahi.
Shafqat Rana: brother of Azmat Rana.
Sheahan, A. P.: great-grandson of W. H. Cooper.
Shoaib Mohammad: son of Hanif Mohammad.
Tamim Iqbal: brother of Nafis Iqbal.
Umar Akmal: brother of Adnan and Kamran Akmal.
Waqar Hassan: brother of Pervez Sajjad.
Wasim Raja: brother of Ramiz Raja.
Wazir Ali, S. (India): brother of S. Nazir Ali (India) and father of Khalid Wazir (Pakistan).
Wazir Mohammad: brother of Hanif, Mushtaq and Sadiq Mohammad.
Yograj Singh: father of Yuvraj Singh.
Younis Ahmed: brother of Saeed Ahmed.
Yuvraj Singh: son of Yograj Singh.
Zahoor Elahi: brother of Manzoor and Salim Elahi.

Note: Teams are listed only where relatives played for different sides.

PLAYERS APPEARING FOR MORE THAN ONE TEST TEAM

Fourteen cricketers have appeared for two countries in Test matches, namely:

Amir Elahi (India 1, Pakistan 5)
J. J. Ferris (Australia 8, England 1)
S. C. Guillen (West Indies 5, New Zealand 3)
Gul Mahomed (India 8, Pakistan 1)
F. Hearne (England 2, South Africa 4)
A. H. Kardar (India 3, Pakistan 23)
W. E. Midwinter (England 4, Australia 8)
F. Mitchell (England 2, South Africa 3)
W. L. Murdoch (Australia 18, England 1)
Nawab of Pataudi, sen. (England 3, India 3)
A. J. Traicos (South Africa 3, Zimbabwe 4)
A. E. Trott (Australia 3, England 2)
K. C. Wessels (Australia 24, South Africa 16)
S. M. J. Woods (Australia 3, England 3)

Wessels also played 54 one-day internationals for Australia and 55 for South Africa.

The following players appeared for the ICC World XI against Australia in the Super Series Test in 2005-06: M. V. Boucher, R. Dravid, A. Flintoff, S. J. Harmison, Inzamam-ul-Haq, J. H. Kallis, B. C. Lara, M. Muralitharan, V. Sehwag, G. C. Smith, D. L. Vettori.

Note: In 1970, England played five first-class matches against the Rest of the World after the cancellation of South Africa's tour. Players were awarded England caps, but the matches are no longer considered to have Test status. Alan Jones (born 4.11.1938) made his only appearance for England in this series, scoring 5 and 0; he did not bowl and took no catches.

ONE-DAY AND TWENTY20 INTERNATIONAL CRICKETERS

The following players had appeared for Test-playing countries in one-day internationals by January 6, 2013, or in Twenty20 internationals by December 31, 2012, but had not represented their countries in Test matches by January 14, 2013. (Numbers in brackets signify number of one-day internationals for each player: where a second number appears, e.g. (5/1), it signifies the number of Twenty20 internationals for that player.)

England

M. W. Alleyne (10), I. D. Austin (9), S. G. Borthwick (2/1), D. R. Briggs (1/3), A. D. Brown (16), D. R. Brown (9), J. C. Buttler (1/18), G. Chapple (1), J. W. M. Dalrymple (27/3), S. M. Davies (8/5), J. L. Denly (9/5), J. W. Dernbach (18/18), M. V. Fleming (11), P. J. Franks (1), I. J. Gould (18), A. P. Grayson (2), A. D. Hales (0/14), G. W. Humpage (3), T. E. Jesty (10), E. C. Joyce (17/2), C. Kieswetter (43/25), G. D. Lloyd (6), A. G. R. Loudon (1), J. D. Love (3), M. B. Loye (7), M. J. Lumb (0/11), M. A. Lynch (3), A. D. Mascarenhas (20/14), S. C. Meaker (2/2), P. Mustard (10/2), P. A. Nixon (19/1), A. U. Rashid (5/5), M. J. Smith (5), N. M. K. Smith (7), J. N. Snape (10/1), V. S. Solanki (51/3), B. A. Stokes (5/2), J. O. Troughton (6), C. M. Wells (2), V. J. Wells (9), A. G. Wharf (13), C. R. Woakes (6/3), L. J. Wright (46/39), M. H. Yardy (28/14).

Note: D. R. Brown also played 16 one-day internationals for Scotland, and E. C. Joyce 15 one-day internationals and 11 Twenty20 internationals for Ireland.

Australia

G. J. Bailey (13/13), T. R. Birt (0/4), G. A. Bishop (2), R. J. Campbell (2), D. T. Christian (17/11), M. J. Cosgrove (3), M. J. Di Venuto (9), B. R. Dorey (4), J. P. Faulkner (0/1), C. J. Ferguson (30/3), A. J. Finch (0/3), P. J. Forrest (15), B. Geeves (2/1), S. F. Graf (11), I. J. Harvey (73), S. M. Harwood (1/3), J. R. Hazlewood (1), M. C. Henriques (2/1), J. R. Hopes (84/12), D. J. Hussey (64/39), B. Laughlin (5/1), S. Lee (45), M. L. Lewis (7/2), R. J. McCurdy (11), K. H. MacLeay (16), J. P. Maher (26), M. R. Marsh (1/3), G. J. Maxwell (4/7), D. P. Nannes (1/15), A. A. Noffke (1/2), S. N. J. O'Keefe (0/7), L. A. Pomersbach (0/1), G. D. Porter (2), L. Ronchi (4/3), J. D. Siddons (1), A. M. Stuart (3), G. S. Trimble (2), A. C. Voges (15/4), B. E. Young (6), A. K. Zesers (2).

Note: D. P. Nannes also played two Twenty20 internationals for the Netherlands.

South Africa

Y. A. Abdulla (0/2), S. Abrahams (1), F. Behardien (0/9), D. M. Benkenstein (23), G. H. Bodi (2/1), L. E. Bosman (13/14), R. E. Bryson (7), D. J. Callaghan (29), D. N. Crookes (32), H. Davids (0/3), Q. de Kock (0/3), T. Henderson (0/1), C. A. Ingram (15/9), J. C. Kent (2), L. J. Koen (5), G. J-P. Kruger (3/1), H. G. Kuhn (0/5), R. E. Levi (0/13), J. Louw (3/2), D. A. Miller (16/11), C. H. Morris (0/1), P. V. Mpitsang (2), S. J. Palframan (7), A. M. Phangiso (0/3), N. Pothas (3), A. G. Puttick (1), C. E. B. Rice (3), M. J. R. Rindel (22), D. B. Rundle (2), T. G. Shaw (9), E. O. Simons (23), E. L. R.

Stewart (6), R. Telemachus (37/3), J. Theron (4/9), A. C. Thomas (0/1), T. Tshabalala (4), R. E. van der Merwe (13/13), J. J. van der Wath (10/8), V. B. van Jaarsveld (2/3), M. N. van Wyk (13/3), C. J. P. G. van Zyl (2), D. J. Vilas (0/1), H. S. Williams (7), M. Yachad (1).

West Indies

H. A. G. Anthony (3), S. Badree (0/6), C. D. Barnwell (0/4), M. C. Bascombe (0/1), N. E. Bonner (0/2), C. R. Brathwaite (1/1), D. Brown (3), B. St A. Browne (4), P. A. Browne (5), H. R. Bryan (15), D. C. Butler (5/1), J. Charles (8/13), D. O. Christian (0/2), R. T. Crandon (1), R. R. Emrit (2), S. E. Findlay (9/2), A. D. S. Fletcher (15/16), R. S. Gabriel (11), R. C. Haynes (8), R. O. Hurley (9), D. P. Hyatt (9/5), K. C. B. Jeremy (6), L. R. Johnson (3), A. Martin (9/1), G. E. Mathurin (0/3), J. N. Mohammed (1), A. R. Nurse (0/2), W. K. D. Perkins (0/1), K. A. Pollard (68/32), M. R. Pydanna (3), A. C. L. Richards (1/1), K. Santokie (0/2), K. F. Semple (7), D. C. Thomas (16/2), C. M. Tuckett (1), L. R. Williams (15).

New Zealand

G. W. Aldridge (2/1), C. J. Anderson (0/3), M. D. Bailey (1), M. D. Bates (2/3), B. R. Blair (14), N. T. Broom (22/9), C. E. Bulfin (4), T. K. Canning (4), P. G. Coman (3), C. de Grandhomme (1/4), B. J. Diamanti (1/1), M. W. Douglas (6), A. M. Ellis (11/3), B. G. Hadlee (2), L. J. Hamilton (2), R. T. Hart (1), R. L. Hayes (1), R. M. Hira (0/12), P. A. Hitchcock (14/1), L. G. Howell (12), T. W. M. Latham (8/3), M. J. McClenaghan (0/3), N. L. McCullum (40/42), P. D. McGlashan (4/11), B. J. McKechnie (14), E. B. McSweeney (16), J. P. Millmow (5), A. F. Milne (2/4), J. D. S. Neesham (0/3), T. S. Nethula (5), C. J. Nevin (37), A. J. Penn (5), R. G. Petrie (12), R. B. Reid (9), S. J. Roberts (2), S. L. Stewart (4), L. W. Stott (1), G. P. Sulzberger (3), A. R. Tait (5), E. P. Thompson (1/1), M. D. J. Walker (3), R. J. Webb (3), J. W. Wilson (6), W. A. Wisneski (3), L. J. Woodcock (4/3).

India

P. Awana (0/2), A. C. Bedade (13), A. Bhandari (2), Bhupinder Singh, sen. (2), Bhuvneshwar Kumar (3/2), G. Bose (1), V. B. Chandrasekhar (7), U. Chatterjee (3), N. A. David (4), P. Dharmani (1), S. Dhawan (5/1), A. B. Dinda (12/9), R. S. Gavaskar (11), R. S. Ghai (6), M. S. Gony (2), Joginder Sharma (4/4), A. V. Kale (1), S. C. Khanna (10), G. K. Khoda (2), A. R. Khurasiya (12), T. Kumaran (8), J. J. Martin (10), D. Mongia (57/1), S. P. Mukherjee (3), A. M. Nayar (3), N. V. Ojha (1/2), G. K. Pandey (2), Pankaj Singh (1), J. V. Paranjpe (4), A. K. Patel (8), Y. K. Pathan (57/22), A. M. Rahane (13/7), Randhir Singh (2), S. S. Raul (2), A. M. Salvi (4), Shami Ahmed (1), R. Sharma (4/2), R. G. Sharma (86/35), L. R. Shukla (3), R. P. Singh (2), R. S. Sodhi (18), S. Somasunder (2), S. Sriram (8), Sudhakar Rao (1), M. K. Tiwary (8/3), S. S. Tiwary (3), S. Tyagi (4/1), R. V. Uthappa (38/11), P. S. Vaidya (4), Y. Venugopal Rao (16), Jai P. Yadav (12).

Notes: By January 6, 2013, R. G. Sharma was the most experienced international player never to have appeared in Test cricket, with 86 one-day internationals and 35 Twenty20 internationals. S. K. Raina appeared in 98 one-day internationals before making his Test debut.

Pakistan

Aamer Hameed (2), Aamer Hanif (5), Ahmed Shehzad (19/10), Akhtar Sarfraz (4), Anwar Ali (0/1), Arshad Pervez (2), Asif Mahmood (2), Awais Zia (0/3), Faisal Athar (1), Ghulam Ali (3), Haafiz Shahid (3), Hammad Azam (8/3), Hasan Jamil (6), Imran Abbas (2), Iqbal Sikandar (4), Irfan Bhatti (1), Javed Qadir (1), Junaid Zia (4), Kamran Hussain (2), Kashif Raza (1), Khalid Latif (5/7), Mahmood Hamid (1), Mansoor Amjad (1/1), Mansoor Rana (2), Manzoor Akhtar (7), Maqsood Rana (1), Masood Iqbal (1), Mohammad Irfan (5/2), Moin-ul-Atiq (5), Mujahid Jamshed (4), Naeem Ahmed (1), Naeem Ashraf (2), Najaf Shah (1), Naseer Malik (3), Nasir Jamshed (22/11), Naumanullah (1), Parvez Mir (3), Rahat Ali (1), Rameez Raja (0/2), Raza Hasan (0/7), Rizwan Ahmed (1), Saadat Ali (8), Saeed Azad (4), Sajid Ali (13), Sajjad Akbar (2), Salim Pervez (1), Samiullah Khan (2), Shahid Anwar (1), Shahzaib Hasan (3/10), Shakeel Ansar (0/2), Shakil Khan (1), Shoaib Khan (0/1), Sohail Fazal (2), Tanvir Mehdi (1), Usman Salahuddin (2), Wasim Haider (3), Zafar Iqbal (8), Zahid Ahmed (2).

Sri Lanka

J. W. H. D. Boteju (2), A. Dananjaya (1/4), D. L. S. de Silva (2), G. N. de Silva (4), L. H. D. Dilhara (8/2), E. R. Fernando (3), T. L. Fernando (1), U. N. K. Fernando (2), J. C. Gamage (4), W. C. A. Ganegama (4), F. R. M. Goonatilleke (1), P. W. Gunaratne (23), A. A. W. Gunawardene (1), P. D. Heyn (2), W. S. Jayantha (17), P. S. Jayaprakashdaran (1), C. U. Jayasinghe (0/5), S. A. Jayasinghe (2), S. H. T. Kandamby (38/5), S. H. U. Karnain (19), H. G. J. M. Kulatunga (0/2), B. M. A. J.

Mendis (27/12), C. Mendis (1), A. M. N. Munasinghe (5), E. M. D. Y. Munaweera (0/3), H. G. D. Nayanakantha (3), A. R. M. Opatha (5), S. P. Pasqual (2), K. G. Perera (1), M. D. K. Perera (4/3), H. S. M. Pieris (3), M. Pushpakumara (3/1), S. K. Ranasinghe (4), N. Ranatunga (2), N. L. K. Ratnayake (2), R. J. M. G. M. Rupasinghe (0/2), S. M. S. M. Senanayake (7/2), A. P. B. Tennekoon (4), M. H. Tissera (3), I. Udana (2/6), M. L. Udawatte (9/5), D. M. Vonhagt (1), A. P. Weerakkody (1), S. Weerakoon (2), K. Weeraratne (15/5), S. R. de S. Wettimuny (3), R. P. A. H. Wickremaratne (3).

Zimbabwe

R. D. Brown (7), T. L. Chatara (0/1), C. J. Chibhabha (60/15), K. M. Curran (11), S. G. Davies (4), K. G. Duers (6), E. A. Essop-Adam (1), D. A. G. Fletcher (6), T. N. Garwe (1), J. G. Heron (6), R. S. Higgins (11), V. R. Hogg (2), A. J. Ireland (26/1), T. Kamungozi (4), F. Kasteni (3), A. J. Mackay (3), G. C. Martin (5), T. Maruma (8/4), M. A. Meman (1), K. O. Meth (11/2), T. V. Mufambisi (6), N. Mushangwe (1), I. A. Nicolson (2), G. A. Paterson (10), G. E. Peckover (3), E. C. Rainsford (39/2), P. W. E. Rawson (10), H. P. Rinke (18), R. W. Sims (3), G. M. Strydom (12), S. C. Williams (47/1), C. Zhuwao (1/5).

Bangladesh

Ahmed Kamal (1), Alam Talukdar (2), Aminul Islam, jun. (1), Anamul Haque (5/1), Anisur Rahman (2), Ather Ali Khan (19), Azhar Hussain (7), Dhiman Ghosh (14/1), Dolar Mahmud (7), Farhad Reza (34/8), Faruq Ahmed (7), Gazi Ashraf (7), Ghulam Faruq (5), Ghulam Nausher (9), Hafizur Rahman (2), Harunur Rashid (2), Jahangir Alam (3), Jahangir Badshah (5), Jamaluddin Ahmed (1), Mafizur Rahman (4), Mahbubur Rahman (1), Mazharul Haque (1), Minhazul Abedin (27), Mominul Haque (5/1), Moniruzzaman (2), Morshed Ali Khan (3), Mosharraf Hossain (3), Nadif Chowdhury (0/3), Nasir Ahmed (7), Nazmus Sadat (0/1), Neeyamur Rashid (2), Nurul Abedin (4), Rafiqul Alam (2), Raqibul Hasan, sen. (2), Saiful Islam (7), Sajjad Ahmed (2), Samiur Rahman (2), Shafiuddin Ahmed (11), Shahidur Rahman (2), Shariful Haq (1), Sheikh Salahuddin (6), Shuvagata Hom (4), Wahidul Gani (1), Zahid Razzak (3), Zakir Hassan (2), Ziaur Rahman (0/9).

PLAYERS APPEARING FOR MORE THAN ONE ONE-DAY INTERNATIONAL TEAM

The following players have played one-day internationals for the **African XI** in addition to their national side:

N. Boje (2), L. E. Bosman (1), J. Botha (2), M. V. Boucher (5), E. Chigumbura (3), A. B. de Villiers (5), H. H. Dippenaar (6), J. H. Kallis (2), J. M. Kemp (6), J. A. Morkel (2), M. Morkel (3), T. M. Odoyo (5), P. J. Ongondo (1), J. L. Ontong (1), S. M. Pollock (6), A. G. Prince (3), J. A. Rudolph (2), V. Sibanda (2), G. C. Smith (1), D. W. Steyn (2), H. H. Streak (2), T. Taibu (1), S. O. Tikolo (4), M. Zondeki (2). (Odoyo, Ongondo and Tikolo played for Kenya, which does not have Test status.)

The following players have played one-day internationals for the **Asian Cricket Council XI** in addition to their national side:

Abdul Razzaq (4), M. S. Dhoni (3), R. Dravid (1), C. R. D. Fernando (1), S. C. Ganguly (3), Harbhajan Singh (2), Inzamam-ul-Haq (3), S. T. Jayasuriya (4), D. P. M. D. Jayawardene (5), A. Kumble (2), Mashrafe bin Mortaza (2), Mohammad Ashraful (2), Mohammad Asif (3), Mohammad Rafique (2), Mohammad Yousuf (7), M. Muralitharan (4), A. Nehra (3), K. C. Sangakkara (4), V. Sehwag (7), Shahid Afridi (3), Shoaib Akhtar (3), W. U. Tharanga (1), W. P. U. J. C. Vaas (1), Yuvraj Singh (3), Zaheer Khan (6).

The following players have played one-day internationals for the **ICC World XI** in addition to their national side:

C. L. Cairns (1), R. Dravid (3), S. P. Fleming (1), A. Flintoff (3), C. H. Gayle (3), A. C. Gilchrist (1), D. Gough (1), M. L. Hayden (1), J. H. Kallis (3), B. C. Lara (4), G. D. McGrath (1), M. Muralitharan (3), M. Ntini (1), K. P. Pietersen (2), S. M. Pollock (3), R. T. Ponting (1), K. C. Sangakkara (3), V. Sehwag (3), Shahid Afridi (2), Shoaib Akhtar (2), D. L. Vettori (4), S. K. Warne (1).

K. C. Wessels appeared for both Australia and South Africa. D. R. Brown appeared for both England and Scotland. E. C. Joyce and E. J. G. Morgan appeared for both Ireland and England.

G. M. Hamilton played Test cricket for England and one-day internationals for Scotland. D. P. Nannes played one-day and Twenty20 internationals for Australia and Twenty20 internationals for the Netherlands.

ELITE TEST UMPIRES

The following umpires were on the ICC's elite panel in February 2013. The figures for Tests, one-day internationals and Twenty20 internationals and the Test Career dates refer to matches in which they have officiated as umpires (excluding abandoned games). The totals of Tests are complete up to January 14, 2013, the totals of one-day internationals up to January 6, 2013, and the Twenty20 internationals up to December 31, 2012.

	Country	*Born*	*Tests*	*Test Career*	*ODIs*	*T20Is*
Aleem Dar	P	6.6.1968	78	*2003–2012*	151	26
Asad Rauf	P	12.5.1956	47	*2004–2012*	95	23
Bowden Brent Fraser ("Billy")	NZ	11.4.1963	72	*1999–2012*	176	19
Davis Stephen James	A	9.4.1952	42	*1997–2012*	111	19
Dharmasena Handunnettige Deepthi Priyantha Kumar	SL	24.4.1971	13	*2010–2012*	43	11
Erasmus Marais	SA	27.2.1964	15	*2009–2012*	43	15
Gould Ian James	E	19.8.1957	33	*2008–2012*	77	20
Hill Anthony Lloyd	NZ	26.6.1951	35	*2001–2012*	94	17
Kettleborough Richard Allan	E	15.3.1973	12	*2010–2012*	25	9
Llong Nigel James	E	11.2.1969	16	*2007–2012*	57	17
Oxenford Bruce Nicholas James	A	5.3.1960	10	*2010–2012*	39	12
Tucker Rodney James	A	28.8.1964	23	*2009–2012*	26	14

Note: B. R. Doctrove and S. J. A. Taufel left the panel in 2012. Their final figures were as follows:

Doctrove Billy Raymond	WI	3.7.1955	38	*1999–2011*	112	17
Taufel Simon James Arthur	A	21.1.1971	74	*2000*–2012	174	34

BIRTHS AND DEATHS

OTHER CRICKETING NOTABLES

The following list shows the births and deaths of cricketers, and people associated with cricket, who have *not* played in men's Test matches.

Criteria for inclusion The following are included: all non-Test players who have either (1) scored 20,000 runs in first-class cricket, or (2) taken 1,500 first-class wickets, or (3) achieved 750 dismissals, or (4) reached both 15,000 runs and 750 wickets. It also includes (5) the leading players who flourished before the start of Test cricket, (6) Wisden Cricketers of the Year who did not play Test cricket, and (7) all others deemed of sufficient merit or interest for inclusion, either because of their playing skill, their present position, their contribution to the game in whatever capacity or their fame in other walks of life.

Names Where players were normally known by a name other than their first, this is underlined.

Teams Where only one team is listed, this is normally the one for which the player made most first-class appearances. Additional teams are listed only if the player appeared for them in more than 20 first-class matches or if they are especially relevant to their career. School and university teams are not given unless especially relevant (e.g. for the schoolboys chosen as wartime Cricketers of the Year in the 1918 and 1919 *Wisdens*).

	Teams	*Born*	*Died*
Adams Percy Webster	Cheltenham College; *CY 1919*	5.9.1900	28.9.1962
Aird Ronald MC	Hampshire; sec. MCC 1953–62, pres. MCC 1968–69	4.5.1902	16.8.1986
Aislabie Benjamin	Surrey, secretary of MCC 1822–42	14.1.1774	2.6.1842
Alcock Charles William	Secretary of Surrey 1872–1907	2.12.1842	26.2.1907
Editor, Cricket *magazine, 1882–1907. Captain of Wanderers and England football teams.*			
Alley William Edward	NSW, Somerset; Test umpire; *CY 1962*	3.2.1919	26.11.2004
Alleyne Mark Wayne	Gloucestershire; *CY 2001*	23.5.1968	
Altham Harry Surtees CBE	Surrey, Hants; historian; pres. MCC 1959–60	30.11.1888	11.3.1965
Coach at Winchester for 30 years.			
Arlott Leslie Thomas John OBE	Broadcaster and writer	25.2.1914	14.12.1991
Arthur John Michael	Griq. W., OFS; South Africa coach 2005–10; Australia coach 2011–	17.5.1968	
Ashdown William Henry	Kent	27.12.1898	15.9.1979
The only player to appear in English first-class cricket before and after the two world wars.			
Ashley-Cooper Frederick Samuel	Historian	22.3.1877	31.1.1932
Ashton *Sir* Hubert KBE MC	Cambridge Univ, Essex; pres. MCC 1960–61; *CY 1922*	13.2.1898	17.6.1979
Austin *Sir* Harold Bruce Gardiner	Barbados	15.7.1877	27.7.1943
Austin Ian David	Lancashire; *CY 1999*	30.5.1966	
Bailey Jack Arthur	Essex; secretary of MCC 1974–87	22.6.1930	
Bainbridge Philip	Gloucestershire, Durham; *CY 1986*	16.4.1958	
Bannister John David	Warwickshire; writer and broadcaster	23.8.1930	
Barker Gordon	Essex	6.7.1931	10.2.2006
Bartlett Hugh Tryon	Sussex; *CY 1939*	7.10.1914	26.6.1988
Beauclerk *Rev. Lord* Frederick	Middlesex, Surrey, MCC	8.5.1773	22.4.1850
Beldam George William	Middlesex; photographer	1.5.1868	23.11.1937
Beldham William ("Silver Billy")	Hambledon, Surrey	5.2.1766	26.2.1862
Beloff Michael Jacob QC	Head of ICC Code of Conduct Commission	18.4.1942	
Benkenstein Dale Martin	KwaZulu-Natal, Durham; *CY 2009*	9.6.1974	
Berry Anthony Scyld Ivens	Editor of *Wisden* 2008–11	28.4.1954	
Berry Leslie George	Leicestershire	28.4.1906	5.2.1985
Bird Harold Dennis ("Dickie") OBE	Yorkshire, Leics; Test umpire	19.4.1933	
Blofeld Henry Calthorpe OBE	Cambridge Univ; broadcaster	23.9.1939	
Bond John David	Lancashire; *CY 1971*	6.5.1932	
Booth Roy	Yorkshire, Worcestershire	1.10.1926	
Bowley Frederick Lloyd	Worcestershire	9.11.1873	31.5.1943
Bradshaw Keith	Tasmania; secretary/chief executive MCC 2006–11	2.10.1963	
Brewer Derek Michael	Secretary/chief executive MCC 2012–	2.4.1958	

	Teams	*Born*	*Died*
Briers Nigel Edwin	Leicestershire; *CY 1993*	15.1.1955	
Brookes Wilfrid H.	Editor of *Wisden* 1936–39	5.12.1894	28.5.1955
Bryan John Lindsay	Kent; *CY 1922*	26.5.1896	23.4.1985
Buchanan John Marshall	Queensland; Australia coach 1999–2007	5.4.1953	
Bucknor Stephen Anthony	ICC umpire	31.5.1946	
Umpire of 128 Tests, a record.			
Bull Frederick George	Essex; *CY 1898*	2.4.1875	16.9.1910
Buller John Sydney MBE	Worcestershire; Test umpire	23.8.1909	7.8.1970
Burnup Cuthbert James	Kent; *CY 1903*	21.11.1875	5.4.1960
Caine Charles Stewart	Editor of *Wisden* 1926–33	28.10.1861	15.4.1933
Calder Harry Lawton	Cranleigh School; *CY 1918*	24.1.1901	15.9.1995
Cardus *Sir* John Frederick Neville	Writer	3.4.1888	27.2.1975
Chapple Glen	Lancashire; *CY 2012*	23.1.1974	
Chester Frank	Worcestershire; Test umpire	20.1.1895	8.4.1957
Stood in 48 Tests between 1924 and 1955, a record that lasted until 1992.			
Clark David Graham	Kent; president of MCC 1977–78	27.1.1919	
Clarke Charles Giles CBE	Chairman of ECB, 2007–	9.5.1953	
Clarke William	Nottinghamshire	24.12.1798	25.8.1856
Founded the All-England XI, Trent Bridge ground.			
Collier David Gordon	Chief executive of ECB, 2005–	22.4.1955	
Collins Arthur Edward Jeune	Clifton College	18.8.1885	11.11.1914
Made the highest score in any cricket, 628 in a house match in 1899.*			
Conan Doyle *Dr Sir* Arthur Ignatius	MCC	22.5.1859	7.7.1930
Creator of Sherlock Holmes; his only victim in first-class cricket was W. G. Grace.			
Connor Clare Joanne OBE	England Women; administrator	1.9.1976	
Constant David John	Kent, Leics; first-class umpire 1969–2006	9.11.1941	
Cook Thomas Edwin Reed	Sussex	5.1.1901	15.1.1950
Cox George, jun.	Sussex	23.8.1911	30.3.1985
Cox George, sen.	Sussex	29.11.1873	24.3.1949
Cozier Winston Anthony Lloyd	Broadcaster and writer	10.7.1940	
Dalmiya Jagmohan	President of ICC 1997–2000	30.5.1940	
Davies Emrys	Glamorgan; Test umpire	27.6.1904	10.11.1975
Davison Brian Fettes	Rhodesia, Leics, Tasmania, Gloucestershire	21.12.1946	
Dawkes George Owen	Leicestershire, Derbyshire	19.7.1920	10.8.2006
Day Arthur Percival	Kent; *CY 1910*	10.4.1885	22.1.1969
de Lisle Timothy John March Phillipps	Editor of *Wisden* 2003	25.6.1962	
Dennett Edward George	Gloucestershire	27.4.1880	14.9.1937
Di Venuto Michael James	Tasmania, Derbys, Durham	12.12.1973	
Eagar Edward Patrick	Photographer	9.3.1944	
Edwards Charlotte Marie MBE	England Women	17.12.1979	
Ehsan Mani	President of ICC 2003–06	23.3.1945	
Engel Matthew Lewis	Editor of *Wisden* 1993–2000, 2004–07	11.6.1951	
"Felix" (Nicholas Wanostrocht)	Kent, Surrey, All-England	4.10.1804	3.9.1876
Batsman, artist, author (Felix on the Bat) *and inventor of the Catapulta bowling machine.*			
Ferguson William Henry BEM	Scorer	6.6.1880	22.9.1957
Scorer and baggage-master for five Test teams on 43 tours over 52 years and "never lost a bag".			
Findlay William	Oxford U., Lancs; sec. MCC 1926–36	22.6.1880	19.6.1953
Firth John D'Ewes Evelyn	Winchester College; *CY 1918*	21.2.1900	21.9.1957
Fletcher Duncan Andrew Gwynne OBE	Zimbabwe; England coach 1999–2007; India coach 2011–	27.9.1948	
Ford Graham Xavier	Natal B; South Africa coach 1999–2002; Sri Lanka coach 2012–	16.11.1960	
Foster Henry Knollys	Worcestershire; *CY 1911*	30.10.1873	23.6.1950
Frindall William Howard MBE	Statistician	3.3.1939	30.1.2009
Frith David Edward John	Writer	16.3.1937	
Gibbons Harold Harry Haywood	Worcestershire	8.10.1904	16.2.1973
Gibson Clement Herbert	Eton College; *CY 1918*	23.8.1900	31.12.1976
Gibson Norman Alan Stanley	Writer	28.5.1923	10.4.1997
Gore Adrian Clements	Eton College; *CY 1919*	14.5.1900	7.6.1990
Grace *Mrs* Martha	Mother and cricketing mentor of WG	18.7.1812	25.7.1884

	Teams	*Born*	*Died*
Grace William Gilbert, jun.	Gloucestershire; son of WG	6.7.1874	2.3.1905
Graveney David Anthony	Gloucestershire, Somerset, Durham	2.1.1953	
Chairman of England selectors 1997–2008.			
Gray James Roy	Hampshire	19.5.1926	
Gray Malcolm Alexander	President of ICC 2000–03	30.5.1940	
Green David Michael	Lancashire, Gloucestershire; *CY 1969*	10.11.1939	
Grieves Kenneth James	New South Wales, Lancashire	27.8.1925	3.1.1992
Griffith Mike Grenville	Sussex, Camb. Univ; president MCC 2012–13	25.11.1943	
Haigh Gideon Clifford Jeffrey Davidson	Writer	29.12.1965	
Hair Darrell Bruce	ICC umpire	30.9.1952	
Hall Louis	Yorkshire; *CY 1890*	1.11.1852	19.11.1915
Hallam Albert William	Lancashire, Nottinghamshire; *CY 1908*	12.11.1869	24.7.1940
Hallam Maurice Raymond	Leicestershire	10.9.1931	1.1.2000
Hallows James	Lancashire; *CY 1905*	14.11.1873	20.5.1910
Hartley Alfred	Lancashire; *CY 1911*	11.4.1879	9.10.1918
Harvey Ian Joseph	Victoria, Gloucestershire; *CY 2004*	10.4.1972	
Hedges Lionel Paget	Tonbridge School, Kent, Glos; *CY 1919*	13.7.1900	12.1.1933
Henderson Robert	Surrey; *CY 1890*	30.3.1865	28.1.1931
Hesson Michael James	New Zealand coach 2012–	30.10.1974	
Hewett Herbert Tremenheere	Somerset; *CY 1893*	25.5.1864	4.3.1921
Heyhoe-Flint Baroness [Rachael] OBE	England Women	11.6.1939	
Hodson Richard Phillip	Cambridge Univ; president MCC 2011–12	26.4.1951	
Horton Henry	Hampshire	18.4.1923	2.11.1998
Howard Cecil Geoffrey	Middlesex; administrator	14.2.1909	8.11.2002
Hughes David Paul	Lancashire; *CY 1988*	13.5.1947	
Huish Frederick Henry	Kent	15.11.1869	16.3.1957
Humpage Geoffrey William	Warwickshire; *CY 1985*	24.4.1954	
Hunter David	Yorkshire	23.2.1860	11.1.1927
Hutchinson James Metcalf	Derbyshire	29.11.1896	7.11.2000
Believed to be the longest-lived first-class cricketer, at 103 years 344 days.			
Ingleby-Mackenzie Alexander Colin David OBE	Hants; president of MCC 1996–98	15.9.1933	9.3.2006
Iremonger James	Nottinghamshire; *CY 1903*	5.3.1876	25.3.1956
Isaac Alan Raymond	Chair NZC 2008–10; president ICC 2012–	20.1.1952	
Jackson Victor Edward	NSW, Leicestershire	25.10.1916	30.1.1965
James Cyril Lionel Robert ("Nello")	Writer	4.1.1901	31.5.1989
Jesty Trevor Edward	Hants, Griq. W., Surrey, Lancs; umpire; *CY 1983*	2.6.1948	
Johnson Paul	Nottinghamshire	24.4.1965	
Johnston Brian Alexander CBE, MC	Broadcaster	24.6.1912	5.1.1994
Jones Alan MBE	Glamorgan; *CY 1978*	4.11.1938	
Played once for England v Rest of the World, 1970, regarded at the time as a Test match.			
Kilburn James Maurice	Writer	8.7.1909	28.8.1993
King John Barton	Philadelphia	19.10.1873	17.10.1965
"Beyond question the greatest all-round cricketer produced by America" – Wisden.			
Knight Roger David Verdon CBE	Surrey, Glos, Sussex; secretary of MCC 1994–2005	6.9.1946	
Knight W. H.	Editor of *Wisden* 1864–79	29.11.1812	16.8.1879
Koertzen Rudolf Eric	Umpire in 108 Tests	26.3.1949	
Lacey *Sir* Francis Eden	Hants; secretary of MCC 1898–1926	19.10.1859	26.5.1946
Lamb Timothy Michael	Middlesex, Northamptonshire; chief executive of ECB 1997–2004	24.3.1953	
Langridge John George MBE	Sussex; Test umpire; *CY 1950*	10.2.1910	27.6.1999
Lee Peter Granville	Northamptonshire, Lancashire; *CY 1976*	27.8.1945	
Lillywhite Frederick William	Sussex	13.6.1792	21.8.1854
Long Arnold	Surrey, Sussex	18.12.1940	
Lord Thomas	Middlesex; founder of Lord's Cricket Ground	23.11.1755	13.1.1832
Lorgat Haroon	Chief executive of ICC 2008–2012	26.5.1960	
Lyon Beverley Hamilton	Gloucestershire; *CY 1931*	19.1.1902	22.6.1970
McEwan Kenneth Scott	Eastern Province, Essex; *CY 1978*	16.7.1952	
McGilvray Alan David MBE	NSW; broadcaster	6.12.1909	17.7.1996

	Teams	*Born*	*Died*
MacLaurin Lord [Ian Charter]	Chairman of ECB 1997–2002	30.3.1937	
Marlar Robin Geoffrey	Sussex; writer	2.1.1931	
Marshal Alan	Surrey; *CY 1909*	12.6.1883	23.7.1915
Martin-Jenkins Christopher Dennis Alexander MBE	Writer; broadcaster; president of MCC 2010–11	20.1.1945	1.1.2013
Mendis Gehan Dixon	Sussex, Lancashire	20.4.1955	
Mercer John	Sussex, Glamorgan; coach and scorer; *CY 1927*	22.4.1893	31.8.1987
Meyer Rollo John Oliver OBE	Somerset	15.3.1905	9.3.1991
Modi Lalit Kumar	Chairman, Indian Premier League 2008–10	29.11.1963	
Moles Andrew James	Warwickshire, NZ coach 2008–09	12.2.1961	
Moores Peter	Sussex; England coach 2007–09	18.12.1962	
Morgan Derek Clifton	Derbyshire	26.2.1929	
Morgan Frederick David OBE	Chair ECB 2003–07, pres. ICC 2008–10	6.10.1937	
Mynn Alfred	Kent, All-England	19.1.1807	1.11.1861
Neale Phillip Anthony	Worcestershire; England manager; *CY 1989*	5.6.1954	
Newman John Alfred	Hampshire	12.11.1884	21.12.1973
Newstead John Thomas	Yorkshire; *CY 1909*	8.9.1877	25.3.1952
Nicholas Mark Charles Jefford	Hampshire; broadcaster	29.9.1957	
Nicholls Ronald Bernard	Gloucestershire	4.12.1933	21.7.1994
Nixon Paul Andrew	Leicestershire, Kent	21.10.1970	
Nyren John	Hampshire	15.12.1764	28.6.1837
Author of The Young Cricketer's Tutor, *1833.*			
Nyren Richard	Hampshire	1734	25.4.1797
Proprietor Bat & Ball Inn, Broadhalfpenny Down.			
Ontong Rodney Craig	Border, Glamorgan, N. Transvaal	9.9.1955	
Ormrod Joseph Alan	Worcestershire, Lancashire	22.12.1942	
Pardon Charles Frederick	Editor of *Wisden* 1887–90	28.3.1850	18.4.1890
Pardon Sydney Herbert	Editor of *Wisden* 1891–1925	23.9.1855	20.11.1925
Parks Henry William	Sussex	18.7.1906	7.5.1984
Parr George	Nottinghamshire, All-England	22.5.1826	23.6.1891
Captain and manager of the All-England XI.			
Partridge Norman Ernest	Malvern College, Warwickshire; *CY 1919*	10.8.1900	10.3.1982
Pawar Sharadchandra Govindrao	Pres. BCCI 2005–08, ICC 2010–12	12.12.1940	
Payton Wilfred Richard Daniel	Nottinghamshire	13.2.1882	2.5.1943
Pearce Thomas Neill	Essex; administrator	3.11.1905	10.4.1994
Pearson Frederick	Worcestershire	23.9.1880	10.11.1963
Perrin Percival Albert ("Peter")	Essex; *CY 1905*	26.5.1876	20.11.1945
Pilch Fuller	Norfolk, Kent	17.3.1804	1.5.1870
"The best batsman that has ever yet appeared" – Arthur Haygarth, 1862.			
Preston Hubert	Editor of *Wisden* 1944–51	16.12.1868	6.8.1960
Preston Norman MBE	Editor of *Wisden* 1952–80	18.3.1903	6.3.1980
Rait Kerr *Colonel* Rowan Scrope	Europeans; sec. MCC 1936–52	13.4.1891	2.4.1961
Reeves William	Essex; Test umpire	22.1.1875	22.3.1944
Rice Clive Edward Butler	Transvaal, Nottinghamshire; *CY 1981*	23.7.1949	
Richardson Alan	Warwicks, Middx, Worcs; *CY 2012*	6.5.1975	
Robertson-Glasgow Raymond Charles	Somerset; writer	15.7.1901	4.3.1965
Robins Derrick Harold	Warwickshire; tour promoter	27.6.1914	3.5.2004
Robinson Mark Andrew	Northants, Yorkshire, Sussex, coach	23.11.1966	
Roebuck Peter Michael	Somerset; writer; *CY 1988*	6.3.1956	12.11.2011
Rotherham Gerard Alexander	Rugby School, Warwickshire; *CY 1918*	28.5.1899	31.1.1985
Sainsbury Peter James	Hampshire; *CY 1974*	13.6.1934	
Scott Stanley Winckworth	Middlesex; *CY 1893*	24.3.1854	8.12.1933
Sellers Arthur Brian MBE	Yorkshire; *CY 1940*	5.3.1907	20.2.1981
Seymour James	Kent	25.10.1879	30.9.1930
Shepherd David Robert MBE	Gloucestershire; ICC umpire	27.12.1940	27.10.2009
Shepherd Donald John	Glamorgan; *CY 1970*	12.8.1927	
Siddons James Darren	Vic., S. Aust.; Bangladesh coach 2007–2011	25.4.1964	
Silk Dennis Raoul Whitehall CBE	Somerset; president of MCC 1992–94, chairman of TCCB 1994–96	8.10.1931	
Simmons Jack MBE	Lancashire, Tasmania; *CY 1985*	28.3.1941	

	Teams	*Born*	*Died*
Skelding Alexander	Leicestershire; umpire	5.9.1886	17.4.1960
First-class umpire 1931–1958, when he was 72.			
Smith Sydney Gordon	Northamptonshire; *CY 1915*	15.1.1881	25.10.1963
Smith William Charles ("Razor")	Surrey; *CY 1911*	4.10.1877	15.7.1946
Southerton Sydney James	Editor of *Wisden* 1934–35	7.7.1874	12.3.1935
Speed Malcolm Walter	Chief executive of ICC 2001–08	14.9.1948	
Spencer Thomas William OBE	Kent; Test umpire	22.3.1914	1.11.1995
Stephenson Franklyn Dacosta	Nottinghamshire, Sussex; *CY 1989*	8.4.1959	
Stephenson Harold William	Somerset	18.7.1920	23.4.2008
Stephenson Heathfield Harman	Surrey, All-England	3.5.1832	17.12.1896
Captained first English team to Australia, 1861-62; umpired first Test in England, 1880.			
Stephenson *Lt-Col.* John Robin CBE	Secretary of MCC 1987–93	25.2.1931	2.6.2003
Studd *Sir* John Edward Kynaston	Middlesex	26.7.1858	14.1.1944
Lord Mayor of London 1928–29; president of MCC 1930.			
Surridge Walter Stuart	Surrey; *CY 1953*	3.9.1917	13.4.1992
Sutherland James Alexander	Victoria; CEO Cricket Australia 2001–	14.7.1965	
Suttle Kenneth George	Sussex	25.8.1928	25.3.2005
Swanton Ernest William ("Jim") CBE	Middlesex; writer	11.2.1907	22.1.2000
Tarrant Francis Alfred	Victoria, Middlesex; *CY 1908*	11.12.1880	29.1.1951
Taylor Brian	Essex; *CY 1972*	19.6.1932	
Taylor Samantha Claire MBE	England Women; *CY 2009*	25.9.1975	
Taylor Tom Launcelot	Yorkshire; *CY 1901*	25.5.1878	16.3.1960
Thornton Charles Inglis ("Buns")	Middlesex	20.3.1850	10.12.1929
Timms John Edward	Northamptonshire	3.11.1906	18.5.1980
Todd Leslie John	Kent	19.6.1907	20.8.1967
Tunnicliffe John	Yorkshire; *CY 1901*	26.8.1866	11.7.1948
Turner Francis Michael MBE	Leicestershire; administrator	8.8.1934	
Turner Robert Julian	Somerset	25.11.1967	
Ufton Derek Gilbert	Kent	31.5.1928	
van der Bijl Vintcent Adriaan Pieter	Natal, Middx, Transvaal; *CY 1981*	19.3.1948	
Virgin Roy Thomas	Somerset, Northamptonshire; *CY 1971*	26.8.1939	
Ward William	Hampshire	24.7.1787	30.6.1849
Scorer of the first recorded double-century: 278 for MCC v Norfolk, 1820.			
Wass Thomas George	Nottinghamshire; *CY 1908*	26.12.1873	27.10.1953
Watson Frank	Lancashire	17.9.1898	1.2.1976
Webber Roy	Statistician	23.7.1914	14.11.1962
Weigall Gerald John Villiers	Kent; coach	19.10.1870	17.5.1944
West George H.	Editor of *Wisden* 1880–86	1851	6.10.1896
Wheatley Oswald Stephen CBE	Warwickshire, Glamorgan; *CY 1969*	28.5.1935	
Whitaker Edgar Haddon OBE	Editor of *Wisden* 1940–43	30.8.1908	5.1.1982
Wight Peter Bernard	Somerset; umpire	25.6.1930	
Wilson John Victor	Yorkshire; *CY 1961*	17.1.1921	5.6.2008
Wisden John	Sussex	5.9.1826	5.4.1884
"The Little Wonder"; founder of Wisden Cricketers' Almanack, *1864.*			
Wood Cecil John Burditt	Leicestershire	21.11.1875	5.6.1960
Woodcock John Charles OBE	Writer; editor of *Wisden* 1981–86	7.8.1926	
Wooller Wilfred	Glamorgan	20.11.1912	10.3.1997
Wright Graeme Alexander	Editor of *Wisden* 1987–92, 2001–02	23.4.1943	
Wright Levi George	Derbyshire; *CY 1906*	15.1.1862	11.1.1953
Young Douglas Martin	Worcestershire, Gloucestershire	15.4.1924	18.6.1993

REGISTER OF CURRENT PLAYERS

The qualifications for inclusion are as follows:

1. All players who appeared in Tests, one-day internationals or Twenty20 internationals for a Test-playing country in the calendar year 2012.
2. All players who appeared in the County Championship, the Sheffield Shield, the SuperSport/Sunfoil Series, the West Indian four-day regional competition for the Headley–Weekes Trophy, or the Duleep Trophy in the calendar year 2012.
3. All players who appeared in a first-class match in a Test-playing country in the calendar year 2012 who have previously played Tests, one-day international cricket or Twenty20 international cricket for a Test-playing country.
4. All players who appeared in a first-class match for a Test-playing country on tour or the A-team of a Test-playing country in the calendar year 2012.

Notes: The forename by which the player is known is underlined if it is not his first name.
Teams are those played for in domestic cricket in the calendar year 2012, or the last domestic team for which that player appeared.

Countries are those for which players are qualified.

The country of birth is given if it is not the one for which a player is qualified. It is also given to differentiate between West Indian nations, and where it is essential for clarity.

* *Denotes Test player.*

	Team	*Country*	*Born*	*Birthplace*
Abbott Kyle John	Dolphins	SA	18.6.1987	*Empangeni*
Abbott Sean Anthony	New South Wales	A	29.2.1992	*Windsor*
***Abdul Razzaq**	ZTBL	P	2.12.1979	*Lahore*
***Abdur Rauf**	Port Qasim Authority	P	9.12.1978	*Renala Khurd*
***Abdur Razzak**	Khulna	B	15.6.1982	*Khulna*
***Abdur Rehman**	Sialkot/Somerset	P	1.3.1980	*Sialkot*
***Abul Hasan**	Sylhet	B	5.8.1992	*Kulaura*
***Adams** Andre Ryan	Nottinghamshire	NZ	17.7.1975	*Auckland*
Adams James Henry Kenneth	Hampshire	E	23.9.1980	*Winchester*
Adams Moegamat <u>Qaasim</u>	W. Province/Cape Cobras	SA	29.4.1984	*Cape Town*
Adkin William Anthony	Sussex	E	9.4.1990	*Redhill*
***Adnan Akmal**	Lahore Ravi	P	13.3.1985	*Lahore*
***Aftab Ahmed**	Chittagong	B	10.11.1985	*Chittagong*
***Agarkar** Ajit Bhalchandra	Mumbai	I	4.12.1977	*Bombay*
Agathangelou Andrea Peter	Lancashire	SA	16.11.1989	*Rustenberg*
Ahmed Abu Nachim	Assam	I	5.11.1988	*Guwahati*
Ahmed Shehzad	Punjab/Habib Bank	P	23.11.1991	*Lahore*
***Aizaz Cheema**	PIA/Lahore Shalimar	P	5.9.1979	*Lahore*
Aldridge Graeme William	Northern Districts	NZ	15.11.1977	*Christchurch*
Alexander Craig John	NW/Lions/Dolphins/KZN	SA	5.1.1987	*Cape Town*
***Ali** Kabir	Hampshire	E	24.11.1980	*Moseley*
Ali Kadeer	Leicestershire	E	7.3.1983	*Moseley*
Ali Moeen Munir	Moors/Worcs/Mat. Tuskers	E	18.6.1987	*Birmingham*
Allenby James	Glamorgan	E	12.9.1982	*Perth, Australia*
Allert Atiba Kerry	Trinidad & Tobago	WI	27.6.1981	*McBean, Trinidad*
***Alok Kapali**	Sylhet	B	1.1.1984	*Sylhet*
Alwitigala Kaniksha Gihan	Colts	SL	7.6.1986	*Homagama*
***Ambrose** Timothy Raymond	Warwickshire	E	1.12.1982	*Newcastle, Australia*
Amla Ahmed Mahomed	Dolphins/KwaZulu-Natal	SA	15.9.1979	*Durban*
***Amla** Hashim Mahomed	Dolphins	SA	31.3.1983	*Durban*
Anamul Haque	Khulna	B	16.12.1992	*Kushtia*
Anderson Corey James	Northern Districts	NZ	13.12.1990	*Christchurch*
***Anderson** James Michael	Lancashire	E	30.7.1982	*Burnley*
Andrew Gareth Mark	Canterbury/Worcestershire	E	27.12.1983	*Yeovil*
Ansari Zafar Shahaan	Cambridge MCCU/Surrey	E	10.12.1991	*Ascot*
Anwar Ali	Sind/PIA	P	25.11.1987	*Karachi*

	Team	Country	Born	Birthplace
Anyon James Edward	Sussex	E	5.5.1983	*Lancaster*
Appanna Kotragada Prabhu	Karnataka	I	20.12.1988	*Virajpet*
***Arnel** Brent John	Northern Districts	NZ	3.1.1979	*Te Awamutu*
***Asad Shafiq**	Habib Bank	P	28.1.1986	*Karachi*
Ashraf Moin Aqeeb	Yorkshire	E	5.1.1992	*Bradford*
***Ashwin** Ravichandran	Tamil Nadu	I	17.9.1986	*Madras*
***Asim Kamal**	Port Qasim Authority	P	31.5.1976	*Karachi*
***Astle** Todd Duncan	Canterbury	NZ	24.9.1986	*Palmerston North*
Athanaze Justin Jason	Leeward Islands	WI	29.1.1988	*Antigua*
***Austin** Ryan Anthony	Comb. Campuses & Colls	WI	15.11.1981	*Arima, Trinidad*
Awais Zia	Federal Areas	P	1.9.1986	*Bhown*
Awana Parvinder	Delhi	I	19.7.1986	*Noida*
Azeem Rafiq	Yorkshire	E	27.2.1991	*Karachi, Pakistan*
***Azhar Ali**	Sui Northern	P	19.2.1985	*Lahore*
***Azhar Mahmood**	Kent	E	28.2.1975	*Rawalpindi*
***Badani** Hemang Kamal	Vidarbha	I	14.11.1976	*Madras*
Badree Samuel	Trinidad & Tobago	WI	8.3.1981	*Barrackpore, Trinidad*
***Badrinath** Subramaniam	Tamil Nadu	I	30.8.1980	*Madras*
***Bahutule** Sairaj Vasant	Vidarbha	I	6.1.1973	*Bombay*
Bailey George John	Tasmania	A	7.9.1982	*Launceston*
Bailey Ryan Tyrone	Free State/Knights	SA	8.9.1982	*Cape Town*
Bailey Tom Ernest	Lancashire	E	21.4.1991	*Preston*
***Bairstow** Jonathan Marc	Yorkshire	E	26.9.1989	*Bradford*
***Baker** Lionel Sionne	Leeward Islands	WI	6.9.1984	*Montserrat*
***Balaji** Lakshmipathy	Tamil Nadu	I	27.9.1981	*Madras*
Balbirnie Andrew	Cardiff MCCU/Middx	Ireland	28.12.1990	*Dublin*
Balcombe David John	Hampshire	E	24.12.1984	*London*
Ballance Gary Simon	Mid West Rhinos/Yorks	E	22.11.1989	*Harare, Zimbabwe*
***Bandara** Herath Mudiyanselage Charitha <u>Malinga</u>	Ragama	SL	31.12.1979	*Kalutara*
***Bangar** Sanjay Bapusaheb	Railways	I	11.10.1972	*Bid*
***Barath** Adrian Boris	Trinidad & Tobago	WI	14.4.1990	*Chaguanas, Trinidad*
Barclay Marlon	Trinidad & Tobago	WI	23.10.1987	*Trinidad*
Barker Keith Hubert Douglas	Warwickshire	E	21.10.1986	*Manchester*
Barnwell Christopher Dion	Guyana	WI	6.1.1987	*McKenzie, Guyana*
Barrow Alexander William Rodgerson	Somerset	E	6.5.1992	*Bath*
Bates Michael David	Auckland	NZ	11.10.1983	*Auckland*
Bates Michael David	Hampshire	E	10.10.1990	*Frimley*
***Batty** Gareth Jon	Surrey	E	13.10.1977	*Bradford*
Batty Jonathan Neil	Gloucestershire	E	18.4.1974	*Chesterfield*
***Baugh** Carlton Seymour	Jamaica	WI	23.6.1982	*Kingston, Jamaica*
Bavuma Temba	Lions/Gauteng	SA	17.5.1990	*Cape Town*
***Bazid Khan**	Federal Areas/KRL	P	25.3.1981	*Lahore*
Beaton Ronsford Rodwick	Guyana	WI	17.9.1992	*Montserrat*
***Beer** Michael Anthony	Western Australia	A	9.6.1984	*Malvern*
Behardien Farhaan	Titans	SA	9.10.1983	*Johannesburg*
Behera Natraj Bhuban	Orissa	I	28.5.1988	*Rourkela*
Behrendorff Jason Paul	Western Australia	A	20.4.1990	*Camden*
***Bell** Ian Ronald	Warwickshire	E	11.4.1982	*Walsgrave*
Bell-Drummond Daniel James	Kent	E	4.8.1993	*Lewisham*
Benkenstein Dale Martin	Durham	SA	9.6.1974	*Salisbury, Zimbabwe*
***Benn** Sulieman Jamaal	Barbados	WI	22.7.1981	*Haynesville, Barbados*
Bennett Bevan Leon	Warriors/Border	SA	9.9.1981	*East London*
Berg Gareth Kyle	Middlesex	E	18.1.1981	*Cape Town, SA*
***Bernard** David Eddison	Jamaica	WI	19.7.1981	*Kingston, Jamaica*
***Bess** Brandon Jeremy	Guyana	WI	13.12.1987	*Rosignol, Guyana*
***Best** Tino la Bertram	Barbados	WI	26.8.1981	*3rd Avenue, Barbados*
Bhatia Rajat	Delhi	I	22.10.1979	*Delhi*

	Team	*Country*	*Born*	*Birthplace*
Bhuvneshwar Kumar	Uttar Pradesh	I	5.2.1990	*Meerut*
Binny Stuart Terence Roger	Karnataka	I	3.6.1984	*Bangalore*
Birch Andrew Charles Ross	Warriors	SA	7.6.1985	*East London*
*****Bird** Jackson Munro	Tasmania	A	11.12.1986	*Paddington*
Birt Travis Rodney	Western Australia	A	9.12.1981	*Sale*
*****Bishoo** Devendra	Guyana	WI	6.11.1985	*New Amsterdam, Guy.*
Bisht Punit	Delhi	I	15.6.1986	*Delhi*
Bist Robin Dinesh	Rajasthan	I	2.11.1987	*Delhi*
*****Blackwell** Ian David	Durham/Warwickshire	E	10.6.1978	*Chesterfield*
Blackwood Jermaine	Jamaica	WI	20.11.1991	*St Elizabeth, Jamaica*
Blake Alexander James	Kent	E	25.1.1989	*Farnborough*
Blizzard Aiden Craig	Tasmania	A	27.6.1984	*Shepparton*
Bodi Goolam Hussain	Gauteng/Lions	SA	4.1.1979	*Hathuran, India*
Bodibe Tumelo Mphunzi	Titans/Easterns	SA	22.6.1987	*Vosloorus*
Bolan Nelson Amos	Leeward Islands	WI	29.11.1990	*Tortola, Brit. Virgin Is*
Boland Scott Michael	Victoria	A	11.4.1989	*Parkdale*
*****Bollinger** Douglas Erwin	New South Wales	A	24.7.1981	*Baulkham Hills*
Bonner Nkruma Eljego	Comb. Campuses & Colls	WI	23.1.1989	*St Catherine*
*****Bopara** Ravinder Singh	Essex	E	4.5.1985	*Forest Gate*
Borrington Paul Michael	Derbyshire	E	24.5.1988	*Nottingham*
Borthwick Scott George	Durham	E	19.4.1990	*Sunderland*
*****Botha** Johan	South Australia	SA	2.5.1982	*Johannesburg*
Bothma Johannes Paulus	W. Province/Cape Cobras	SA	28.3.1988	*Bellville*
*****Boucher** Mark Verdon	Cape Cobras	SA	3.12.1976	*East London*
Boucher Rashidi Hasani	Barbados	WI	17.7.1990	*St Michael, Barbados*
*****Boult** Trent Alexander	Northern Districts	NZ	22.7.1989	*Rotorua*
Boyce Cameron John	Queensland	A	27.7.1989	*Charleville*
Boyce Matthew Andrew Golding	Leicestershire	E	13.8.1985	*Cheltenham*
*****Bracewell** Douglas Andrew John	Central Districts	NZ	28.9.1990	*Tauranga*
Bragg William David	Glamorgan	E	24.10.1986	*Newport*
Brathwaite Carlos Ricardo	Barbados	WI	18.7.1988	*Lodge Rd, Barbados*
*****Brathwaite** Kraigg Clairmonte	Barbados	WI	1.12.1992	*Belfield, Barbados*
Brathwaite Ruel Marlon Ricardo	Durham	WI	6.9.1985	*Bridgetown, Barb.*
*****Bravo** Darren Michael	Trinidad & Tobago	WI	6.2.1989	*Santa Cruz, Trinidad*
*****Bravo** Dwayne John	Trinidad & Tobago	WI	7.10.1983	*Santa Cruz, Trinidad*
*****Bresnan** Timothy Thomas	Yorkshire	E	28.2.1985	*Pontefract*
Briggs Danny Richard	Hampshire	E	30.4.1991	*Newport*
Broad Ryan Andrew	Queensland	A	9.3.1982	*Herston*
*****Broad** Stuart Christopher John	Nottinghamshire	E	24.6.1986	*Nottingham*
Brooks Jack Alexander	Northamptonshire	E	4.6.1984	*Oxford*
Brooks Sharmarh Shaqad Joshua	Barbados	WI	1.10.1988	*St John's Land, Barb.*
Broom Neil Trevor	Otago	NZ	20.11.1983	*Christchurch*
Brophy Gerard Louis	Yorkshire	E	26.11.1975	*Welkom, SA*
Brown Ben Christopher	Sussex	E	23.11.1988	*Crawley*
Brown Karl Robert	Lancashire/Moors	E	17.5.1988	*Bolton*
Brown Odean Vernon	Jamaica	WI	8.2.1982	*Westmoreland, Jam.*
Browne Atticus Jeremy	Windward Islands	WI	12.12.1991	*Bel Air, St Vincent*
*****Brownlie** Dean Graham	Canterbury	NZ	30.7.1984	*Perth, Australia*
Buck Nathan Liam	Leicestershire	E	26.4.1991	*Leicester*
Burger Shane	Lions/Gauteng	SA	31.8.1982	*Johannesburg*
Burns Joseph Antony	Queensland	A	6.9.1989	*Herston*
Burns Rory Joseph	Surrey	E	26.8.1990	*Epsom*
Burton David Alexander	Northamptonshire	E	23.8.1985	*Dulwich*
*****Butler** Ian Gareth	Otago	NZ	24.11.1981	*Middlemore*
Butterworth Luke Rex	Tasmania	A	28.10.1983	*Hobart*
Buttler Joseph Charles	Somerset	E	8.9.1990	*Taunton*
Cameron James Gair	Worcestershire	Z	31.1.1986	*Harare*
Cameron Louis Donald Buckley	Victoria	A	21.5.1992	*Belconnen*
Campbell Jason Arneil	Leeward Islands	WI	30.11.1985	*Charlestown, Nevis*

	Team	*Country*	*Born*	*Birthplace*
***Carberry** Michael Alexander	Hampshire	E	29.9.1980	*Croydon*
Cariah Yannic	Trinidad & Tobago	WI	21.6.1992	*Trinidad*
Carter Andrew	Nottinghamshire	E	27.8.1988	*Lincoln*
Carter Jonathan Lyndon	Barbados	WI	16.11.1987	*Belleplaine, Barbados*
Carter Neil Miller	Warwickshire	SA	29.1.1975	*Cape Town*
Carters Ryan Graham Leslie	Victoria	A	25.7.1990	*Canberra*
Castro Teshwan	Trinidad & Tobago	WI	29.2.1992	*Port-of-Spain, Trinidad*
Cazzulino Steven John	Tasmania	A	1.2.1987	*Riverwood*
***Chakabva** Regis Wiriranai	Mashonaland Eagles	Z	20.9.1987	*Harare*
Chambers Maurice Anthony	Essex	E	14.9.1987	*Port Antonio, Jamaica*
Chand Unmukt	Delhi	I	25.3.1993	*Delhi*
***Chandana** Umagiliya Durage Upul	Nondescripts	SL	7.5.1972	*Galle*
***Chanderpaul** Shivnarine	Guyana	WI	16.8.1974	*Unity Village, Guyana*
***Chandimal** Lokuge Dinesh	Nondescripts	SL	18.11.1989	*Balapitiya*
Chandrika Rajindra	Guyana	WI	8.8.1989	*Enterprise*
Chapple Glen	Lancashire	E	23.1.1974	*Skipton*
Charles Johnson	Windward Islands	WI	14.1.1989	*St Lucia*
Chatara Tendai Larry	Mountaineers	Z	28.2.1991	*Chimaniamani*
***Chattergoon** Sewnarine	Guyana	WI	3.4.1981	*Fyrish, Guyana*
Chaudhary Ishwar Haribhai	Gujarat	I	10.7.1988	*Sagthala*
***Chawla** Piyush Pramod	Uttar Pradesh	I	24.12.1988	*Aligarh*
Chetty Cody	KwaZulu-Natal/Dolphins	SA	28.6.1991	*Durban*
Chibhabha Chamunorwa Justice	S. Rocks/Mash. Eagles	Z	6.9.1986	*Masvingo*
***Chigumbura** Elton	Mashonaland Eagles	Z	14.3.1986	*Kwekwe*
***Chopra** Aakash	Rajasthan/H. Pradesh	I	19.9.1977	*Agra*
Chopra Varun	Tamil Union/Warwicks	E	21.6.1987	*Barking*
Choudhry Shaaiq Hussain	Worcestershire	E	3.11.1985	*Rotherham*
Christian Daniel Trevor	South Australia	A	4.5.1983	*Camperdown*
Christian Derwin O'Neil	Guyana	WI	9.5.1983	*Kilen, Guyana*
Clare Jonathan Luke	Derbyshire	E	14.6.1986	*Burnley*
***Clarke** Michael John	New South Wales	A	2.4.1981	*Liverpool*
***Clarke** Rikki	Warwickshire	E	29.9.1981	*Orsett*
Claydon Mitchell Eric	Durham	E	25.11.1982	*Fairfield, Australia*
Cobb Joshua James	Leicestershire	E	17.8.1990	*Leicester*
Cockbain Ian Andrew	Gloucestershire	E	17.2.1987	*Liverpool*
Coetsee Werner Loubser	Griqualand West/Knights	SA	16.3.1983	*Bethlehem*
Coetzer Kyle James	Northamptonshire	Scot	14.4.1984	*Aberdeen*
Coles Matthew Thomas	Kent	E	26.5.1990	*Maidstone*
***Collingwood** Paul David	Durham	E	26.5.1976	*Shotley Bridge*
***Collins** Pedro Tyrone	Barbados	WI	12.8.1976	*Boscobelle, Barbados*
***Collymore** Corey Dalanelo	Middlesex	WI	21.12.1977	*Boscobelle, Barbados*
***Compton** Nicholas Richard Denis	Somerset	E	26.6.1983	*Durban, SA*
***Cook** Alastair Nathan	Essex	E	25.12.1984	*Gloucester*
Cook Simon James	Kent	E	15.1.1977	*Oxford*
Cook Stephen Craig	Lions/Gauteng	SA	29.11.1982	*Johannesburg*
Cooper Kevon	Trinidad & Tobago	WI	2.2.1989	*Trinidad*
Cooper Tom Lexley William	South Australia	NL	26.11.1986	*Wollongong*
***Copeland** Trent Aaron	New South Wales	A	14.3.1986	*Gosford*
Corbin Kyle Anthony McDonald	Comb. Campuses & Colls	WI	15.5.1990	*Newbury, Barbados*
Cosgrove Mark James	Tasmania	A	14.6.1984	*Elizabeth*
Cosker Dean Andrew	Glamorgan	E	7.1.1978	*Weymouth*
Cotterrell Sheldon Shane	Jamaica	WI	19.8.1989	*Jamaica*
Coughtrie Richard George	Gloucestershire	E	1.9.1988	*North Shields*
Coulter-Nile Nathan Mitchell	Western Australia	A	11.10.1987	*Perth*
***Coventry** Charles Kevin	Matabeleland Tuskers	Z	8.3.1983	*Kwekwe*
***Cowan** Edward James McKenzie	Tasmania/Glos	A	16.6.1982	*Paddington, Australia*
Cox Oliver Benjamin	Worcestershire	E	2.2.1992	*Wordsley*
Coyte Scott James	New South Wales	A	7.3.1985	*Liverpool, Australia*
Craddock Thomas Richard	Essex	E	13.7.1989	*Huddersfield*
Crandon Royston Tycho	Guyana	WI	31.5.1983	*Courtland, Guyana*

	Team	*Country*	*Born*	*Birthplace*
***Cremer** Alexander Graeme	Mid West Rhinos	Z	19.9.1986	*Harare*
***Croft** Robert Damien Bale	Glamorgan	E	25.5.1970	*Morriston*
Croft Steven John	Lancashire	E	11.10.1984	*Blackpool*
Crook Steven Paul	Middlesex	E	28.5.1983	*Modbury, Australia*
Cross Gareth David	Lancashire	E	20.6.1984	*Bury*
Crosthwaite Adam John	South Australia	A	22.9.1984	*Melbourne*
***Cumming** Craig Derek	Otago	NZ	31.8.1975	*Timaru*
Cummins Miguel Lamar	Barbados	WI	5.9.1990	*St Michael, Barbados*
***Cummins** Patrick James	New South Wales	A	8.5.1993	*Westmead*
Currency Romel Kwesi	Comb. Campuses & Colls	WI	7.5.1982	*Mesopotamia, St Vinc.*
Cutting Benjamin Colin James	Queensland	A	30.1.1987	*Sunnybank*
***Dabengwa** Keith Mbusi	Matabeleland Tuskers	Z	17.8.1980	*Bulawayo*
Daggett Lee Martin	Northamptonshire	E	1.10.1982	*Bury*
Dananjaya Akila	Colts	SL	4.10.1993	*Panadura*
Also known as Mahamarakkala Kurukulasooriya Patabendige Akila Dananjaya Perera				
***Danish Kaneria**	Sind	P	16.12.1980	*Karachi*
Darekar Akshay Arun	Maharashtra	I	31.7.1988	*Raigad*
***Das** Shiv Sunder	Vidarbha	I	5.11.1977	*Bhubaneswar*
Das Neves Richard	Gauteng/Lions	SA	18.12.1986	*Johannesburg*
Davey Timothy John	South Australia	A	16.9.1987	*Adelaide*
Davids Henry	Titans	SA	19.1.1980	*Stellenbosch*
Davies Alexander Luke	Lancashire	E	23.8.1994	*Darwen*
Davies Mark	Kent	E	4.10.1980	*Stockton-on-Tees*
Davies Steven Michael	Surrey	E	17.6.1986	*Bromsgrove*
Davis Liam Murray	Western Australia	A	2.8.1984	*Perth*
Dawes Jason O'Brian	Comb. Campuses & Colls	WI	27.12.1988	*Westmoreland, Jam.*
Dawson David Graham	New South Wales	A	7.3.1982	*Weekangeria*
Dawson Liam Andrew	Hampshire	E	1.3.1990	*Swindon*
Deacon Wycliffe Andrew	Lions	SA	23.6.1980	*Kroonstad*
***de Bruyn** Zander	Lions/Surrey	SA	5.7.1975	*Johannesburg*
de Grandhomme Colin	Auckland	NZ	22.7.1986	*Harare, Zimbabwe*
de Kock Quinton	Lions	SA	17.12.1992	*Johannesburg*
de Lange Con de Wet	Northamptonshire	SA	11.2.1981	*Bellville*
***de Lange** Marchant	Titans	SA	13.10.1990	*Tzaneen*
Denly Joseph Liam	Middlesex	E	16.3.1986	*Canterbury*
Dent Christopher David James	Gloucestershire	E	20.1.1991	*Bristol*
***Deonarine** Narsingh	Guyana	WI	16.8.1983	*Chesney Estate, Guy.*
Dernbach Jade Winston	Surrey	E	3.3.1986	*Johannesburg, SA*
***de Saram** Samantha Indika	Ragama	SL	2.9.1973	*Matara*
***de Silva** Sanjeewa Kumara Lanka	Kurunegala Youth	SL	29.7.1975	*Kurunegala*
***de Silva** Weddikkara Ruwan Sujeewa	Lankan	SL	7.10.1979	*Beruwala*
***de Villiers** Abraham Benjamin	Titans	SA	17.2.1984	*Pretoria*
de Villiers Cornelius Johannes du Preez	Northerns/Titans	SA	16.3.1986	*Kroonstad*
Dewan Rahul	Haryana/Sylhet	I	15.7.1986	*Delhi*
Dewar Akeem Mark Anthony	Comb. Campuses & Colls	WI	30.8.1991	*Kingston, Jamaica*
Dexter Neil John	Middlesex	E	21.8.1984	*Johannesburg, SA*
Dhawan Shikhar	Delhi	I	5.12.1985	*Delhi*
Dhiman Ghosh	Rangpur	B	23.11.1987	*Dinajpur*
***Dhoni** Mahendra Singh	Jharkhand	I	7.7.1981	*Ranchi*
Dibble Adam John	Somerset	E	9.3.1991	*Exeter*
Dilhara Loku Hettige Danushka	Moors	SL	3.7.1980	*Colombo*
Also known as Dilhara Lokuhettige				
***Dilshan** Tillekeratne Mudiyanselage	Tamil Union	SL	14.10.1976	*Kalutara*
Dinda Ashok Bhimchandra	Bengal	I	25.3.1984	*Medinipur*
***Dippenaar** Hendrik Human (Boeta)	Knights	SA	14.6.1977	*Kimberley*
Di Venuto Michael James	Durham	A	12.12.1973	*Hobart*
Dixey Paul Garrod	Leicestershire	E	2.11.1987	*Canterbury*

	Team	*Country*	*Born*	*Birthplace*
Dockrell George Henry	Somerset	Ireland	22.7.1992	*Dublin*
Dogra Paras	Himachal Pradesh	I	19.11.1984	*Palampur*
***Doherty** Xavier John	Tasmania	A	22.11.1982	*Scottsdale*
Dolar Mahmud	Khulna	B	30.12.1988	*Narail*
D'Oliveira Brett Louis	Worcestershire	E	28.2.1992	*Worcester*
Doolan Alexander James	Tasmania	A	29.11.1985	*Launceston*
Doropoulos Theo Paul	South Australia	A	25.4.1985	*Subiaco*
Dowrich Shane Omari	Barbados	WI	30.10.1991	*West Terrace*
***Dravid** Rahul	Karnataka	I	11.1.1973	*Indore*
Drew Brendan Gerard	Tasmania	A	16.12.1983	*Lismore*
***Duffin** Terrence	Matabeleland Tuskers	Z	20.3.1982	*Kwekwe*
***Duminy** Jean-Paul	Cape Cobras	SA	14.4.1984	*Strandfontein*
Dunk Ben Robert	Tasmania	A	11.3.1987	*Innisfail*
Dunn Matthew Peter	Surrey	E	5.5.1992	*Egham*
***du Plessis** Francois	Titans	SA	13.7.1984	*Pretoria*
du Preez Dillon	Free State/Knights	SA	8.11.1981	*Queenstown*
Durston Wesley John	Derbyshire	E	6.10.1980	*Taunton*
du Toit Jacques	Leicestershire	SA	2.1.1980	*Port Elizabeth*
Dyili Athenkosi Ziphozihle Madoda	E. Province/Warriors	SA	17.7.1984	*King William's Town*
Eckersley Edmund John Holden	Leicestershire	E	9.8.1989	*Oxford*
***Edwards** Fidel Henderson	Barbados	WI	6.2.1982	*Gays, Barbados*
Edwards George Alexander	Surrey	E	29.7.1992	*Lambeth*
***Edwards** Kirk Anton	Barbados	WI	3.11.1984	*Mile and a Quarter, Barbados*
Edwards Neil James	Nottinghamshire	E	14.10.1983	*Treliske*
***Elgar** Dean	Knights	SA	11.6.1987	*Welkom*
***Elias Sunny**	Dhaka Metropolis	B	2.8.1986	*Dhaka*
***Elliott** Grant David	Wellington	NZ	21.3.1979	*Johannesburg, SA*
Ellis Andrew Malcolm	Canterbury	NZ	24.3.1982	*Christchurch*
Emrit Rayad Ryan	Trinidad & Tobago	WI	8.3.1981	*Mount Hope, Trinidad*
***Enamul Haque, jun.**	Sylhet	B	5.12.1986	*Sylhet*
***Eranga** Ranaweera Mudiyanselage Shaminda	Chilaw Marians	SL	23.6.1986	*Chilaw*
Erlank Michael Nicholas	Free State/Knights	SA	4.7.1990	*Kimberley*
***Ervine** Craig Richard	Matabeleland Tuskers	Z	19.8.1985	*Harare*
***Ervine** Sean Michael	Hants/Mat. Tuskers	Z	6.12.1982	*Harare*
Evans Laurie John	Warwickshire	E	12.10.1987	*Lambeth*
Evans Luke	Northamptonshire	E	26.4.1987	*Sunderland*
***Ewing** Gavin Mackie	Matabeleland Tuskers	Z	21.1.1981	*Harare*
Faisal Athar	United Bank	P	15.10.1975	*Hyderabad*
***Faisal Hossain**	Chittagong	B	26.10.1978	*Chittagong*
***Faisal Iqbal**	Sind/PIA/Karachi B.	P	30.12.1981	*Karachi*
Fallah Samad Mohammed	Maharashtra	I	2.5.1985	*Hyderabad*
Farhad Reza	Rajshahi	B	16.6.1986	*Rajshahi*
Faulkner James Peter	Tasmania	A	29.4.1990	*Launceston*
***Fawad Alam**	Sind/Nat. Bank/Karachi W.	P	8.10.1985	*Karachi*
Fedee Sergio Mendes	Windward Islands	WI	13.1.1983	*Unity Village, Guyana*
Feldman Luke William	Queensland	A	1.8.1984	*Sunnybank*
Ferguson Callum James	South Australia	A	21.11.1984	*North Adelaide*
***Fernando** Aththachchi Nuwan Pradeep Roshan	Bloomfield	SL	19.10.1986	*Negombo*
***Fernando** Congenige Randhi Dilhara	Sinhalese	SL	19.7.1979	*Colombo*
***Fernando** Kandage Hasantha Ruwan Kumara	Moors	SL	14.10.1979	*Panadura*
***Fernando** Kandana Arachchige Dinusha Manoj	Ports Authority	SL	10.8.1979	*Panadura*

	Team	Country	Born	Birthplace
Finch Aaron James	Victoria	A	17.11.1986	*Colac*
***Finn** Steven Thomas	Middlesex	E	4.4.1989	*Watford*
Fletcher Andre David Stephon	Windward Islands	WI	28.11.1987	*La Tante, Grenada*
Fletcher Luke Jack	Nottinghamshire	E	18.9.1988	*Nottingham*
Floros Jason Scott	Queensland	A	24.11.1990	*Woden*
***Flynn** Daniel Raymond	Northern Districts	NZ	16.4.1985	*Rotorua*
Foakes Benjamin Thomas	Essex	E	15.2.1993	*Colchester*
Footitt Mark Harold Alan	Derbyshire	E	25.11.1985	*Nottingham*
Forrest Peter James	Queensland	A	15.11.1985	*Windsor, Australia*
***Foster** James Savin	Essex	E	15.4.1980	*Whipps Cross*
***Franklin** James Edward Charles	Wellington	NZ	7.11.1980	*Wellington*
Franks Paul John	Nottinghamshire	E	3.2.1979	*Mansfield*
Friend Quinton	Knights/Free State	SA	16.2.1982	*Bellville*
Frylinck Robert	Dolphins/KwaZulu-Natal	SA	27.9.1984	*Durban*
***Fudadin** Assad Badyr	Guyana	WI	1.8.1985	*Rose Hall, Guyana*
Fuller James Kerr	Gloucestershire	NZ	24.1.1990	*Cape Town*
***Fulton** Peter Gordon	Canterbury	NZ	1.2.1979	*Christchurch*
***Gabriel** Shannon Terry	Trinidad & Tobago	WI	28.4.1988	*Trinidad*
Gale Andrew William	Yorkshire	E	28.11.1983	*Dewsbury*
Gale Matthew Geoffrey	Queensland	A	28.11.1983	*Box Hill*
***Gambhir** Gautam	Delhi	I	14.10.1981	*Delhi*
Ganegama Withanaarchchige Chamara Akalanka	Nondescripts	SL	29.3.1981	*Colombo*
***Ganga** Daren	Trinidad & Tobago	WI	14.1.1979	*Barrackpore, Trinidad*
Ganga Sherwin	Trinidad & Tobago	WI	13.2.1982	*Barrackpore, Trinidad*
Gannon Cameron John	Queensland	A	23.1.1989	*Baulkham Hills*
Garwe Trevor Nyasha	Mash. Eagles/S. Rocks	Z	7.1.1982	*Harare*
Gatting Joe Stephen	Sussex	E	25.11.1987	*Brighton*
***Gayle** Christopher Henry	Jamaica	WI	21.9.1979	*Kingston, Jamaica*
George Dennis Martin	Windward Islands	WI	3.12.1983	*St Patricks, Grenada*
***George** Peter Robert	South Australia	A	16.10.1986	*Woodville*
Gidman Alexander Peter Richard	Gloucestershire	E	22.6.1981	*High Wycombe*
Gidman William Robert Simon	Gloucestershire	E	14.2.1985	*High Wycombe*
***Gillespie** Mark Raymond	Wellington	NZ	17.10.1979	*Wanganui*
Glover John Charles	Glamorgan	E	29.8.1989	*Cardiff*
Godleman Billy Ashley	Essex	E	11.2.1989	*Camden*
Gony Manpreet Singh	Punjab	I	4.1.1984	*Roopnagar*
***Goodwin** Murray William	Sussex	Z	11.12.1972	*Salisbury*
Goswami Shreevats Pratyush	Bengal	I	18.5.1989	*Calcutta*
Gqamane Ayabulela	Border/Warriors	SA	31.8.1989	*King William's Town*
Gray Alistair John Alec	W. Province/Cape Cobras	SA	8.7.1982	*Johannesburg*
Gregory Lewis	Somerset	E	24.5.1992	*Plymouth*
Griffith Trevon Abashai	Guyana	WI	18.4.1991	*Guyana*
Griffiths David Andrew	Hampshire	E	10.9.1985	*Newport, Isle of Wight*
Groenewald Timothy Duncan	Derbyshire	SA	10.1.1984	*Pietermaritzburg*
Guillen Justin Christopher	Trinidad & Tobago	WI	2.1.1986	*Port-of-Spain, Trinidad*
Gulbis Evan Peter	Tasmania	A	26.3.1986	*Carlton*
***Guptill** Martin James	Derbyshire	NZ	30.9.1986	*Auckland*
Gurney Harry Frederick	Nottinghamshire	E	25.10.1986	*Nottingham*
Haberfield Jake Andy	South Australia	A	18.6.1986	*Townsville*
***Haddin** Bradley James	New South Wales	A	23.10.1977	*Cowra*
Hales Alexander Daniel	Nottinghamshire	E	3.1.1989	*Hillingdon*
***Hall** Andrew James	Northamptonshire	SA	31.7.1975	*Johannesburg*
Hamilton Jahmar Neville	Leeward Islands	WI	22.9.1990	*St Thomas, Anguilla*
Hamilton-Brown Rory James	Surrey	E	3.9.1987	*St John's Wood*
Hammad Azam	Federal Areas/Nat. Bank	P	16.3.1991	*Attock*
Handscomb Peter Stephen Patrick	Victoria	A	26.4.1991	*Melbourne*

	Team	*Country*	*Born*	*Birthplace*
***Harbhajan Singh**	Essex/Punjab	I	3.7.1980	*Jullundur*
Harinath Arun	Surrey	E	26.3.1987	*Sutton*
Harmer Simon Ross	Warriors	SA	10.2.1989	*Pretoria*
Harmison Ben William	Kent	E	9.1.1986	*Ashington*
***Harmison** Stephen James	Durham/Yorkshire	E	23.10.1978	*Ashington*
Harris Daniel Joseph	South Australia	A	31.12.1979	*North Adelaide*
Harris James Alexander Russell	Glamorgan	E	16.5.1990	*Morriston*
Harris Marcus Sinclair	Western Australia	A	21.7.1992	*Perth*
***Harris** Paul Lee	Titans	SA	2.11.1978	*Salisbury, Zimbabwe*
***Harris** Ryan James	Queensland	A	11.10.1979	*Nowra*
Harrison Jamie	Durham	E	19.11.1990	*Whiston*
Harrison Nicholas Luke	Worcestershire	E	3.2.1992	*Bath*
Hartley Christopher Desmond	Queensland	A	24.5.1982	*Nambour*
***Hasan Raza**	Habib Bank	P	11.3.1982	*Karachi*
***Hastings** John Wayne	Victoria	A	4.11.1985	*Nepean*
Hatchett Lewis James	Sussex	E	21.1.1990	*Shoreham-by-Sea*
***Hauritz** Nathan Michael	NSW/Queensland	A	18.10.1981	*Wondai*
Hazlewood Josh Reginald	New South Wales	A	8.1.1991	*Tamworth*
Head Travis Michael	South Australia	A	29.12.1993	*Adelaide*
Hemraj Chanderpaul	Guyana	WI	3.9.1993	*Guyana*
***Henderson** Claude William	Leicestershire	SA	14.6.1972	*Worcester*
Hendricks Beuran Eric	Cape Cobras/W. Province	SA	8.6.1990	*Cape Town*
Hendricks Dominic Andrew	Gauteng/Lions	SA	7.11.1990	*Port Elizabeth*
Hendricks Reeza Raphael	Knights/Griqualand West	SA	14.8.1989	*Kimberley*
Henriques Moises Consantino	New South Wales/Glam	A	1.2.1987	*Funchal, Portugal*
Henry Scott Oliver	New South Wales	A	14.2.1989	*Mudgee*
***Herath** Herath Mudiyanselage Rangana Keerthi Bandara	Tamil Union	SL	19.3.1978	*Kurunegala*
Herrick Jayde Matthew	Victoria	A	16.1.1985	*Melbourne*
***Hettiarachchi** Dinuka	Moors	SL	15.7.1976	*Colombo*
Hildreth James Charles	Somerset	E	9.9.1984	*Milton Keynes*
***Hilfenhaus** Benjamin William	Tasmania	A	15.3.1983	*Ulverstone*
Hill Michael William	Victoria	A	29.9.1988	*Melbourne*
***Hinds** Ryan O'Neal	Barbados	WI	17.2.1981	*Holders Hill, Barb.*
Hira Roneel Magan	Canterbury	NZ	23.1.1987	*Auckland*
Hodd Andrew John	Yorkshire	E	12.1.1984	*Chichester*
Hodge Kaveem Ajoel Rakem	Windward Islands	WI	21.2.1993	*Dominica*
Hodge Montcin Verniel	Leeward Islands	WI	29.9.1987	*Anguilla*
Hogan Michael Garry	Western Australia	A	31.5.1981	*Newcastle*
***Hogg** George Bradley	Western Australia	A	6.2.1971	*Narrogin*
Hogg Kyle William	Lancashire	E	2.7.1983	*Birmingham*
***Hoggard** Matthew James	Leicestershire	E	31.12.1976	*Leeds*
Holder Jason Omar	Comb. Campuses & Colls	WI	5.11.1991	*Rouens Village, Barb.*
Holland Jonathan Mark	Victoria	A	29.5.1987	*Sandringham*
***Hondo** Douglas Tafadzwa	Mashonaland Eagles	Z	7.7.1979	*Bulawayo*
Hope Kyle Antonio	Barbados	WI	20.11.1988	*Field Place*
Hopes James Redfern	Queensland	A	24.10.1978	*Townsville*
***Hopkins** Gareth James	Auckland	NZ	24.11.1976	*Lower Hutt*
Horton Paul James	Lancashire/Mat. Tuskers	E	20.9.1982	*Sydney, Australia*
Housego Daniel Mark	Gloucestershire	E	12.10.1988	*Windsor*
***How** Jamie Michael	Central Districts	NZ	19.5.1981	*New Plymouth*
Howell Benny Alexander Cameron	Gloucestershire	E	5.10.1988	*Bordeaux, France*
Howgego Benjamin Harry Nicholas	Northamptonshire	E	3.3.1988	*Kings Lynn*
Hughes Chesney Francis	Derbyshire	WI	20.1.1991	*Anguilla*
***Hughes** Phillip Joel	NSW/Worcs/S. Aust.	A	30.11.1988	*Macksville*
***Humayun Farhat**	Habib Bank	P	24.1.1981	*Lahore*
Hussain Gemaal Maqsood	Somerset	E	10.10.1983	*Waltham Forest*
Hussey David John	Victoria	A	15.7.1977	*Morley*
***Hussey** Michael Edward Killeen	Western Australia	A	27.5.1975	*Morley*
Hyatt Danza Pacino	Jamaica	WI	17.3.1983	*St Catherine, Jamaica*

	Team	*Country*	*Born*	*Birthplace*
***Iftikhar Anjum**	Fed. Ar./ZTBL/Islamabad	P	1.12.1980	*Khanewal*
***Imran Farhat**	Habib Bank	P	20.5.1982	*Lahore*
***Imran Nazir**	ZTBL	P	16.12.1981	*Gujranwala*
***Imran Tahir**	Dolphins/Lions	SA	27.3.1979	*Lahore, Pakistan*
***Imrul Kayes**	Khulna	B	2.2.1987	*Meherpur*
Ingram Colin Alexander	Warriors	SA	3.7.1985	*Port Elizabeth*
Ireland Anthony John	Gloucestershire	Z	30.8.1984	*Masvingo*
Jackson Simon	Jamaica	WI	18.5.1985	*Jamaica*
Jacobs Arno	Warriors/E. Province	SA	13.3.1977	*Potchefstroom*
Jacobs David Johan	Warriors	SA	4.11.1982	*Klerksdorp*
***Jadeja** Ravindrasinh Anirudhsinh	Saurashtra	I	6.12.1988	*Navagam-Khed*
Jadhav Dheeraj Subash	Assam	I	16.9.1979	*Malegaon*
Jaggi Ishank Rajiv	Jharkhand	I	27.1.1989	*Bacheli*
***Jahurul Islam**	Rajshahi	B	12.12.1986	*Rajshahi*
James Lindon Omrick Dinsley	Windward Islands	WI	30.12.1984	*South Rivers, St Vinc.*
James Nicholas Alexander	Glamorgan	E	17.9.1986	*Sandwell*
***Jaques** Philip Anthony	Yorkshire	A	3.5.1979	*Wollongong*
***Jarvis** Kyle Malcolm	Mash. Eagles/C. Districts	Z	16.2.1989	*Harare*
Jayantha Warushavithana Saman	Colombo	SL	26.1.1974	*Ambalangoda*
Jayaprakashdaran Pradeep Sri	Colombo	SL	13.1.1984	*Colombo*
Jayasinghe Chinthaka Umesh	Bloomfield	SL	19.5.1978	*Kalutara*
***Jayasuriya** Sanath Teran	Air Force	SL	30.6.1969	*Matara*
***Jayawardene** Denagamage Proboth Mahela de Silva	Sinhalese	SL	27.5.1977	*Colombo*
***Jayawardene** Hewasandatchige Asiri Prasanna Wishvanath	Bloomfield	SL	9.10.1979	*Colombo*
Jeffers Shane Melvon	Leeward Islands	WI	12.9.1981	*Sandy Point, St Kitts*
Jefferson William Ingleby	Leicestershire	E	25.10.1979	*Derby*
Jennings Keaton Kent	Durham/Gauteng	SA	19.6.1992	*Johannesburg*
Jewell Thomas Melvin	Surrey	E	13.1.1991	*Reading*
Johnson Delorn Edison	Windward Islands	WI	15.9.1988	*St Vincent*
Johnson Leon Rayon	Guyana	WI	8.8.1987	*Georgetown, Guyana*
***Johnson** Mitchell Guy	Western Australia	A	2.11.1981	*Townsville*
Johnson Richard Matthew	Derbyshire/Warwicks	E	1.9.1988	*Solihull*
Johnston Matt James	Tasmania	A	15.10.1985	*South Perth*
Jones Brady	Tasmania	A	16.9.1988	*Franklin*
Jones Christopher Robert	Durham MCCU/Somerset	E	5.11.1990	*Harold Wood*
***Jones** Geraint Owen	Kent	E	14.7.1976	*Kundiawa, Papua N. G.*
Jones Richard Alan	Mat. Tuskers/Worcs	E	6.11.1986	*Stourbridge*
***Jones** Simon Philip	Glamorgan	E	25.12.1978	*Morriston*
Jones William Stephen	Cardiff MCCU/Leics	E	26.3.1990	*Perth*
Jonker Christiaan	SW Districts/Warriors	SA	24.9.1986	*Rustenburg*
Jordan Christopher James	Barbados/Surrey	E	4.10.1988	*Lowlands, Barbados*
Joseph Robert Hartman	Leicestershire	E	20.1.1982	*St John's, Antigua*
Joyce Edmund Christopher	Sussex	Ireland	22.9.1978	*Dublin, Ireland*
***Junaid Khan**	WAPDA	P	24.12.1989	*Matra*
***Junaid Siddique**	Rajshahi	B	30.10.1987	*Rajshahi*
Junaid Zia	ZTBL	P	11.12.1983	*Lahore*
***Kaif** Mohammad	Uttar Pradesh	I	1.12.1980	*Allahabad*
***Kalavitigoda** Shantha	Ports Authority	SL	23.12.1977	*Colombo*
***Kallis** Jacques Henry	Cape Cobras	SA	16.10.1975	*Pinelands*
***Kamran Akmal**	National Bank	P	13.1.1982	*Lahore*
Kamran Hussain	Habib Bank/Bahawalpur	P	9.5.1977	*Bahawalpur*
Kamungozi Tafadzwa	Southern Rocks	Z	8.6.1987	*Harare*
Kandamby Sahan Hewa Thilina	Sinhalese	SL	4.6.1982	*Colombo*
Kanhai Aneil	Trinidad & Tobago	WI	12.4.1982	*Diego Martin, Trin.*
***Kanitkar** Hrishikesh Hemant	Rajasthan	I	14.11.1974	*Pune*
Kantasingh Kavesh	Trinidad & Tobago	WI	30.9.1986	*Trinidad*
Kapil Aneesh	Worcestershire	E	3.8.1993	*Wolverhampton*

	Team	*Country*	*Born*	*Birthplace*
***Kapugedera** Chamara Kantha	Nondescripts	SL	24.2.1987	*Kandy*
***Karthik** Krishankumar Dinesh	Tamil Nadu	I	1.6.1985	*Madras*
***Kartik** Murali	Railways/Surrey	I	11.9.1976	*Madras*
***Karunaratne** Frank Dimuth Madushanka	Sinhalese	SL	28.4.1988	*Colombo*
***Katich** Simon Mathew	New South Wales/Hants	A	21.8.1975	*Middle Swan*
Kaushik Jagannathan	Tamil Nadu	I	25.10.1985	*Madras*
Keath Alexander Robert	Victoria	A	20.1.1992	*Shepparton*
Keedy Gary	Lancashire	E	27.11.1974	*Sandal*
Kelsall Samuel	Nottinghamshire	E	14.3.1993	*Stoke-on-Trent*
Kemp Alexander Robert	Queensland	A	2.12.1988	*Brisbane*
***Kemp** Justin Miles	Cape Cobras/W. Province	SA	2.10.1977	*Queenstown*
Keogh Robert Ian	Northamptonshire	E	21.10.1991	*Dunstable*
Kerrigan Simon Christopher	Lancashire	E	10.5.1989	*Preston*
Kervezee Alexei Nicolaas	Worcestershire	NL	11.9.1989	*Walvis Bay, Namibia*
***Key** Robert William Trevor	Kent	E	12.5.1979	*East Dulwich*
Khadiwale Harshad Hemantkumar	Maharashtra	I	21.10.1988	*Pune*
Khalid Latif	Port Qasim A./Karachi W.	P	4.11.1985	*Karachi*
***Khan** Amjad	Sussex	E	14.10.1980	*Copenhagen, Denmark*
***Khan** Imraan	Dolphins/KwaZulu-Natal	SA	27.4.1984	*Durban*
Khan Imran	Trinidad & Tobago	WI	6.12.1984	*Port-of-Spain, Trinidad*
***Khawaja** Usman Tariq	NSW/Derbys/Queensland	A	18.12.1986	*Islamabad, Pakistan*
***Khurram Manzoor**	Sind/Port Q. A./Karachi B.	P	10.6.1986	*Karachi*
Kieswetter Craig	Somerset	E	28.11.1987	*Johannesburg, SA*
Kirby Steven Paul	Somerset	E	4.10.1977	*Ainsworth*
***Kleinveldt** Rory Keith	Cape Cobras	SA	15.3.1983	*Cape Town*
Klinger Michael	South Australia/Worcs	A	4.7.1980	*Kew*
***Kohli** Virat	Delhi	I	5.11.1988	*Delhi*
***Krejza** Jason John	Tasmania	A	14.1.1983	*Newtown*
Kruger Garnett John-Peter	North West/Lions	SA	5.1.1977	*Port Elizabeth*
Kruger Nicholas James	Tasmania	A	14.8.1983	*Paddington, Australia*
Kuhn Heino Gunther	Titans	SA	1.4.1984	*Piet Retief*
***Kulasekara** Chamith Kosala Bandara	Nondescripts	SL	15.7.1985	*Mavanalle*
***Kulasekara** Kulasekara Mudiyanselage Dinesh Nuwan	Colts	SL	22.7.1982	*Nittambuwa*
Kulatunga Hettiarachchi Gamage Jeevantha Mahesh	Tamil Union	SL	2.11.1973	*Kurunegala*
***Kumar** Praveenkumar	Uttar Pradesh	I	2.10.1986	*Meerut*
***Lakmal** Ranasinghe Arachchige Suranga	Tamil Union	SL	10.3.1987	*Matara*
***Lakshitha** Materba Kanatha Gamage Chamila Premanath	Air Force	SL	4.1.1979	*Unawatuna*
Also known as Chamila Gamage				
Lalor Joshua Kendall	New South Wales	A	2.11.1987	*Mount Druitt*
***Lamb** Gregory Arthur	Mountaineers	Z	4.3.1980	*Harare*
Lambert Tamar Lansford	Jamaica	WI	15.7.1981	*St Catherine, Jamaica*
***Langeveldt** Charl Kenneth	Cape Cobras/Boland	SA	17.12.1974	*Stellenbosch*
Latham Thomas William Maxwell	Canterbury	NZ	2.4.1992	*Christchurch*
Laughlin Ben	Tasmania	A	3.10.1982	*Box Hill*
***Laxman** Vangipurappu Venkata Sai	Hyderabad	I	1.11.1974	*Hyderabad*
Leach Joseph	Leeds Brad MCCU/Worcs	E	30.10.1990	*Stafford*
Leach Matthew Jack	Cardiff MCCU/Somerset	E	22.6.1991	*Taunton*
***Lee** Brett	New South Wales	A	8.11.1976	*Wollongong*
Leie Eddie	Lions/Gauteng	SA	16.11.1986	*Potchefstroom*
Lesporis Keddy	Windward Islands	WI	27.12.1988	*St Lucia*
Levi Richard Ernst	Cape Cobras	SA	14.1.1988	*Johannesburg*
Lewis Evin	Trinidad & Tobago	WI	27.12.1991	*Trinidad*
***Lewis** Jonathan	Surrey	E	26.8.1975	*Aylesbury*

	Team	*Country*	*Born*	*Birthplace*
Liburd Javier Springteen	Leeward Islands	WI	9.2.1987	*Rawlins, Nevis*
Liburd Steve Stuart Wayne	Leeward Islands	WI	26.2.1985	*Basseterre, St Kitts*
Lineker Matthew Steven	Derbyshire	E	22.1.1985	*Derby*
Linley Timothy Edward	Surrey	E	23.3.1982	*Leeds*
Lloyd David Liam	Glamorgan	E	15.5.1992	*St Asaph*
***Lokuarachchi** Kaushal Samaraweera	Sinhalese	SL	20.5.1982	*Colombo*
Louw Brendon Ivan	Warriors/SW Districts	SA	15.11.1991	*Knysna*
Louw Johann	Cape Cobras/Boland	SA	12.4.1979	*Cape Town*
Lucas David Scott	Worcestershire	E	19.8.1978	*Nottingham*
Ludeman Timothy Paul	South Australia	A	23.6.1987	*Warrnambool*
Lumb Michael John	Nottinghamshire	E	12.2.1980	*Johannesburg, SA*
Lynn Christopher Austin	Queensland	A	10.4.1990	*Herston*
***Lyon** Nathan Michael	South Australia	A	20.11.1987	*Young*
Lyth Adam	Yorkshire	E	25.9.1987	*Whitby*
McCarter Graeme John	Gloucestershire	Ireland	10.10.1992	*Londonderry*
McClean Kevin Ramon	Comb. Campuses & Colls	WI	24.1.1988	*Castle, Barbados*
McClenaghan Mitchell John	Auckland	NZ	11.6.1986	*Hastings*
***McCullum** Brendon Barrie	Otago	NZ	27.9.1981	*Dunedin*
McCullum Nathan Leslie	Otago	NZ	1.9.1980	*Dunedin*
McDermott Alister Craig	Queensland	A	7.6.1991	*Brisbane*
***McDonald** Andrew Barry	Victoria	A	15.6.1981	*Wodonga*
McGlashan Peter Donald	Northern Districts	NZ	22.6.1979	*Napier*
***McGrath** Anthony	Yorkshire	E	6.10.1975	*Bradford*
Machan Matthew William	Sussex	E	15.2.1991	*Brighton*
***McIntosh** Timothy Gavin	Auckland	NZ	4.12.1979	*Auckland*
***McKay** Andrew John	Wellington	NZ	17.4.1980	*Auckland*
***McKay** Clinton James	Victoria	A	22.2.1983	*Melbourne*
***McKenzie** Neil Douglas	Lions/Hampshire	SA	24.11.1975	*Johannesburg*
***McLaren** Ryan	Knights	SA	9.2.1983	*Kimberley*
Maddinson Nicolas James	New South Wales	A	21.12.1991	*Shoalhaven*
***Maddy** Darren Lee	Warwickshire	E	23.5.1974	*Leicester*
Madsen Wayne Lee	Derbyshire	SA	2.1.1984	*Durban*
Magoffin Steven James	Queensland/Sussex	A	17.12.1979	*Corinda*
***Maharoof** Mohamed Farveez	Nondescripts	SL	7.9.1984	*Colombo*
***Mahbubul Alam**	Dhaka	B	1.12.1983	*Faridpur*
Maher Adam John	Tasmania	A	14.11.1981	*Newcastle*
Mahesh Vijaykumar Yo	Tamil Nadu	I	21.12.1987	*Madras*
***Mahmood** Sajid Iqbal	Lancashire/Somerset	E	21.12.1981	*Bolton*
***Mahmudullah**	Dhaka	B	4.2.1986	*Mymensingh*
Majumdar Anustup Prabir	Bengal	I	30.4.1984	*Chandannagore*
Malan Dawid Johannes	Middlesex	E	3.9.1987	*Roehampton*
Malan Pieter Jacobus	Northerns/Titans	SA	13.8.1989	*Nelspruit*
Malik Muhammad Nadeem	Leicestershire	E	6.10.1982	*Nottingham*
***Malinga** Separamadu Lasith	Nondescripts	SL	4.9.1983	*Galle*
Mandeep Singh	Punjab	I	18.12.1991	*Jalandhar*
Maniar Sandeep Manubhai	Saurashtra	I	28.12.1976	*Sihor*
Mansoor Amjad	Sialkot	P	25.12.1986	*Sialkot*
***Maregwede** Alester	Southern Rocks	Z	5.8.1981	*Harare*
Marsh Mitchell Ross	Western Australia	A	20.10.1991	*Armadale*
***Marsh** Shaun Edward	Western Australia	A	9.7.1983	*Narrogin*
***Marshall** Hamish John Hamilton	N. Districts/Glos	NZ	15.2.1979	*Warkworth*
***Marshall** James Andrew Hamilton	Northern Districts	NZ	15.2.1979	*Warkworth*
***Marshall** Xavier Melbourne	Jamaica	WI	27.3.1986	*St Ann, Jamaica*
Martin Anthony	Leeward Islands	WI	18.11.1982	*Bethesda, Antigua*
***Martin** Christopher Stewart	Auckland	NZ	10.12.1974	*Christchurch*
Maruma Timycen	Mountaineers	Z	19.4.1988	*Harare*
***Masakadza** Hamilton	Mountaineers	Z	9.8.1983	*Harare*
***Masakadza** Shingirai Winston	Mountaineers	Z	4.9.1986	*Harare*

	Team	*Country*	*Born*	*Birthplace*
Mascarenhas Adrian Dimitri	Hampshire	E	30.10.1977	*Chiswick*
Masekela Lerutla Matheko Gershon	Northerns/Titans	SA	21.7.1987	*Pietersburg*
***Mashrafe bin Mortaza**	Khulna	B	5.10.1983	*Narail*
Masters David Daniel	Essex	E	22.4.1978	*Chatham*
***Mathews** Angelo Davis	Colts	SL	2.6.1987	*Colombo*
Mathurin Garey Earl	Windward Islands	WI	23.9.1983	*Mon Repos, St Lucia*
Matshikwe Pumelela	Lions/Gauteng	SA	19.6.1984	*Johannesburg*
***Matsikenyeri** Stuart	Mashonaland Eagles	Z	3.5.1983	*Harare*
***Mawoyo** Tinotenda Mbiri Kanayi	Mountaineers	Z	8.1.1986	*Umtali*
Maxwell Glenn James	Victoria	A	14.10.1988	*Kew*
Maynard Thomas Lloyd	Surrey	E	25.3.1989	*Cardiff*
Died 18.6.2012 at Wimbledon				
Mbhalati Nkateko Ethy	Northerns/Titans	SA	18.11.1981	*Tzaneen*
Meaker Stuart Christopher	Surrey	E	21.1.1989	*Durban, SA*
***Mehrab Hossain, jun.**	Dhaka Metropolis	B	8.7.1987	*Rajshahi*
Menaria Ashok Lakshminarayan	Rajasthan	I	29.10.1990	*Udaipur*
***Mendis** Balapuwaduge Ajantha Winslo	Army	SL	11.3.1985	*Moratuwa*
Mendis Balapuwaduge Manukulasuriya Amith Jeewan	Tamil Union	SL	15.1.1983	*Colombo*
Mennie Joe Matthew	South Australia	A	24.12.1988	*Coffs Harbour*
Meschede Craig Anthony Joseph	Somerset	E	21.11.1991	*Johannesburg, SA*
Meth Keegan Orry	Matabeleland Tuskers	Z	8.2.1988	*Bulawayo*
Meyer Lyall	Warriors/E. Province	SA	23.3.1982	*Port Elizabeth*
Mickleburgh Jaik Charles	Essex/Mid West Rhinos	E	30.3.1990	*Norwich*
Middlebrook James Daniel	Northamptonshire	E	13.5.1977	*Leeds*
Miller David Andrew	Dolphins	SA	10.6.1989	*Pietermaritzburg*
Miller Horace	Jamaica	WI	26.10.1989	*Jamaica*
***Miller** Nikita O'Neil	Jamaica	WI	16.5.1982	*St Elizabeth, Jamaica*
Miller Samuel Peter	South Australia	A	12.2.1988	*Ballarat*
***Mills** Kyle David	Auckland	NZ	15.3.1979	*Auckland*
Mills Tymal Solomon	Essex	E	12.8.1992	*Dewsbury*
Milne Adam Fraser	Central Districts	NZ	13.4.1992	*Palmerston North*
Milnes Thomas Patrick	Warwickshire	E	6.10.1992	*Stourbridge*
***Mirando** Magina Thilan Thushara	Nondescripts	SL	1.3.1981	*Balapitiya*
Also known as Thilan Thushara				
***Misbah-ul-Haq**	Sui Northern	P	28.5.1974	*Mianwali*
***Mishra** Amit	Haryana	I	24.11.1982	*Delhi*
Mishra Mohnish Dinesh	Madhya Pradesh	I	9.2.1984	*Bhopal*
Mitchell Daryl Keith Henry	Worcs/Mountaineers	E	25.11.1983	*Badsey*
***Mithun** Abhimanyu	Karnataka	I	25.10.1989	*Dasarahalli*
***Mohammad Ashraful**	Dhaka Metropolis	B	9.9.1984	*Dhaka*
***Mohammad Ayub**	Punjab/WAPDA/Sialkot	P	13.9.1979	*Nankana Sahib*
***Mohammad Hafeez**	Sui Northern	P	17.10.1980	*Sargodha*
Mohammad Irfan	Baluchistan/KRL	P	6.6.1982	*Gaggu Mandi*
***Mohammad Khalil**	Punjab/ZTBL/Lahore Ravi	P	11.11.1982	*Lahore*
***Mohammad Salman**	Port Qasim A./Faisalabad	P	7.8.1981	*Karachi*
***Mohammad Sami**	Sind/Port Q. A./Karachi W.	P	24.2.1981	*Karachi*
***Mohammad Sharif**	Dhaka	B	12.12.1985	*Narayanganj*
***Mohammad Talha**	Port Qasim A./Bahawalpur	P	15.10.1988	*Faisalabad*
Mohammed Gibran	Trinidad & Tobago	WI	31.7.1983	*Barrackpore, Trinidad*
Mohammed Jason Nazimuddin	Trinidad & Tobago	WI	23.9.1986	*Barrackpore, Trinidad*
Mohanty Basantkumar Chintamani	Orissa	I	24.11.1986	*Bhubaneswar*
Mominul Haque	Chittagong	B	29.9.1991	*Cox's Bazar*
Mommsen Preston Luke	Leicestershire	Scot	14.10.1987	*Durban, SA*
Moore Stephen Colin	Lancashire	E	4.11.1980	*Johannesburg, SA*
***Morgan** Eoin Joseph Gerard	Middlesex	E	10.9.1986	*Dublin, Ireland*
***Morkel** Johannes Albertus	Titans	SA	10.6.1981	*Vereeniging*
***Morkel** Morne	Titans	SA	6.10.1984	*Vereeniging*
Morris Christopher Henry	North West/Lions	SA	30.4.1987	*Pretoria*

	Team	*Country*	*Born*	*Birthplace*
Mosehle Mangaliso	Easterns/Titans	SA	24.4.1990	*Duduza*
Mosharraf Hossain	Dhaka	B	20.11.1981	*Dhaka*
Motwani Rohit Heero	Maharashtra	I	13.12.1990	*Pune*
Mpitsang Phenyo Victor	Free State	SA	28.3.1980	*Kimberley*
***Mpofu** Christopher Bobby	Matabeleland Tuskers	Z	27.11.1985	*Plumtree*
***Mubarak** Jehan	Nondescripts	SL	10.1.1981	*Washington, USA*
Muchall Gordon James	Durham	E	2.11.1982	*Newcastle-upon-Tyne*
Muchall Paul Bernard	Gloucestershire	E	17.3.1987	*Newcastle-upon-Tyne*
***Mukund** Abhinav	Tamil Nadu	I	6.1.1990	*Madras*
Mullaney Steven John	Nottinghamshire	E	19.11.1986	*Warrington*
Munaweera Eldeniya Medagedara Dilshan Yasika	Bloomfield	SL	24.4.1989	*Colombo*
***Munro** Colin	Auckland	NZ	11.3.1987	*Durban, SA*
***Mupariwa** Tawanda	Southern Rocks	Z	16.4.1985	*Bulawayo*
Murphy David	Northamptonshire	E	24.7.1989	*Welwyn Garden City*
Murtagh Timothy James	Middlesex	Ireland	2.8.1981	*Lambeth*
Mushangwe Natsai	Mountaineers	Z	9.2.1991	*Mhangura*
***Mushfiqur Rahim**	Rajshahi	B	1.9.1988	*Bogra*
Mustard Philip	Durham/Auckland	E	8.10.1982	*Sunderland*
***Mutizwa** Forster	Mashonaland Eagles	Z	24.8.1985	*Harare*
Nadeem Shahbaz	Jharkhand	I	12.8.1989	*Patna*
Nadif Chowdhury	Sylhet/Dhaka	B	21.4.1987	*Manikganj*
***Naeem Islam**	Rangpur	B	31.12.1986	*Gaibandha*
***Nafis Iqbal**	Chittagong	B	31.1.1985	*Chittagong*
Naik Jigar Kumar Hakumatrai	Leicestershire	E	10.8.1984	*Leicester*
Najaf Shah	PIA/Quetta	P	17.12.1984	*Gujarkhan*
Napier Graham Richard	Essex	E	6.1.1980	*Colchester*
***Narine** Sunil Philip	Trinidad & Tobago	WI	26.5.1988	*Trinidad*
***Nash** Brendan Paul	Jamaica/Kent	WI	14.12.1977	*Attadale, Australia*
Nash Christopher David	Sussex	E	19.5.1983	*Cuckfield*
***Nasir Hossain**	Rangpur	B	30.11.1991	*Rangpur*
Nasir Jamshed	Punjab/National Bank	P	6.12.1989	*Lahore*
Naved Arif	Sussex	P	2.11.1981	*Mandi Bahauddin*
***Naved Latif**	Faisalabad	P	21.2.1976	*Sargodha*
***Naved-ul-Hasan**	WAPDA	P	28.2.1978	*Sheikhupura*
Also known as Rana Naved				
Nayar Abhishek Mohan	Mumbai	I	26.10.1983	*Secunderabad*
***Nazimuddin**	Chittagong	B	1.10.1985	*Chittagong*
***Nazmul Hossain**	Sylhet	B	5.10.1987	*Hobigonj*
Nazmus Sadat	Khulna	B	18.10.1986	*Khulna*
***Ncube** Njabulo	Matabeleland Tuskers	Z	14.10.1989	*Bulawayo*
Neesham James Douglas Sheehan	Otago	NZ	17.9.1990	*Auckland*
***Nehra** Ashish	Delhi	I	29.4.1979	*Delhi*
Neser Michael Gertges	Queensland	A	29.3.1990	*Pretoria*
Nethula Tarun Sai	Central Districts	NZ	8.5.1983	*Kurnool, India*
Nevill Peter Michael	New South Wales	A	13.10.1985	*Hawthorne*
Newby Oliver James	Lancashire	E	26.8.1984	*Blackburn*
Newman Scott Alexander	Kent	E	3.11.1979	*Epsom*
Newton Robert Irving	Northamptonshire	E	18.1.1990	*Taunton*
***Nicol** Robert James	Canterbury/Glos	NZ	28.5.1983	*Auckland*
Nipper Kyle	KZN Inland/Dolphins	SA	25.11.1987	*Pietermaritzburg*
***Nkala** Mluleki Luke	Mid West Rhinos	Z	1.4.1981	*Bulawayo*
***North** Marcus James	W. Australia/Glamorgan	A	28.7.1979	*Pakenham*
Northeast Sam Alexander	Kent	E	16.10.1989	*Ashford*
Norwell Liam Connor	Gloucestershire	E	27.12.1991	*Bournemouth*
O'Brien Niall John	Northamptonshire	Ireland	8.11.1981	*Dublin*
Ojha Naman Vijaykumar	Madhya Pradesh	I	20.7.1983	*Ujjain*
***Ojha** Pragyan Prayish	Hyderabad	I	5.9.1986	*Khurda*

	Team	*Country*	*Born*	*Birthplace*
O'Keefe Stephen Norman John	New South Wales	A	9.12.1984	*Malaysia*
***Onions** Graham	Durham	E	9.9.1982	*Gateshead*
***Ontong** Justin Lee	Cape Cobras	SA	4.1.1980	*Paarl*
***Oram** Jacob David Philip	Central Districts	NZ	28.7.1978	*Palmerston North*
Ottley Khesan Yannick Gabriel	Comb. Campuses & Colls	WI	7.9.1991	*Trinidad*
Overton Craig	Somerset	E	10.4.1994	*Barnstaple*
Overton Jamie	Somerset	E	10.4.1994	*Barnstaple*
Owen William Thomas	Glamorgan	E	2.9.1988	*St Asaph*
***Pagon** Donovan Jomo	Jamaica	WI	13.9.1982	*Kingston, Jamaica*
***Paine** Timothy David	Tasmania	A	8.12.1984	*Hobart*
Palladino Antonio Paul	Derbyshire	E	29.6.1983	*Tower Hamlets*
Pandey Manish Krishnanand	Karnataka	I	10.9.1989	*Nainital*
***Panesar** Mudhsuden Singh (Monty)	Sussex	E	25.4.1982	*Luton*
Pankaj Singh	Rajasthan	I	6.5.1985	*Sultanpur*
***Panyangara** Tinashe	Southern Rocks	Z	21.10.1985	*Marondera*
***Papps** Michael Hugh William	Wellington	NZ	2.7.1979	*Christchurch*
***Paranavitana** Nishad Tharanga	Sinhalese	SL	15.4.1982	*Kegalle*
***Parchment** Brenton Anthony	Jamaica	WI	24.6.1982	*St Elizabeth, Jamaica*
Pardoe Matthew Graham	Worcestershire	E	5.1.1991	*Stourbridge*
***Parnell** Wayne Dillon	Warriors	SA	30.7.1989	*Port Elizabeth*
Parris Nekoli	Comb. Campuses & Colls	WI	6.6.1987	*Lowland Park, Barb.*
Parvinder Singh	Uttar Pradesh	I	8.12.1981	*Meerut*
***Pascal** Nelon Troy	Windward Islands	WI	25.4.1987	*St David's, Grenada*
Patel Harshal Vikram	Haryana	I	23.11.1990	*Sanand*
***Patel** Jeetan Shashi	Wellington/Warwicks	NZ	7.5.1980	*Wellington*
***Patel** Parthiv Ajay	Gujarat	I	9.3.1985	*Ahmedabad*
Patel Ravi Hasmukh	Middlesex	E	4.8.1991	*Harrow*
***Patel** Samit Rohit	Nottinghamshire	E	30.11.1984	*Leicester*
Paterson Dane	Dolphins/KwaZulu-Natal	SA	4.4.1989	*Cape Town*
***Pathan** Irfan Khan	Baroda	I	27.10.1984	*Baroda*
Pathan Yusuf Khan	Baroda	I	27.11.1984	*Baroda*
Patterson Steven Andrew	Yorkshire	E	3.10.1983	*Hull*
***Pattinson** James Lee	Victoria	A	3.5.1990	*Melbourne*
Paulsen Steven James	Queensland	A	3.9.1981	*Ipswich*
Pawar Kaustubh Rawalnath	Mumbai	I	13.9.1990	*Bombay*
Payne David Alan	Gloucestershire	E	15.2.1991	*Poole*
Pelser Brett Jonathan	North West/Lions	SA	23.4.1985	*Durban*
Perera Angelo Kanishka	Nondescripts	SL	23.2.1990	*Moratuwa*
Perera Mahawaduge Dilruwan Kumaluneth	Colts	SL	22.7.1982	*Panadura*
Perera Mathurage Don Kushal Janith	Colts	SL	17.8.1990	*Kalubovila*
***Perera** Narangoda Liyanaarachchilage Tissara Chirantha	Colts	SL	3.4.1989	*Colombo*
***Permaul** Veerasammy	Guyana	WI	11.8.1989	*Belvedere, Guyana*
Peters Keon Kenroy	Windward Islands	WI	24.2.1982	*Mesopotamia, St Vinc.*
Peters Orlando	Leeward Islands	WI	10.5.1988	*Antigua*
Peters Rohel Jaison	Leeward Islands	WI	22.11.1989	*Guyana*
Peters Stephen David	Northamptonshire	E	10.12.1978	*Harold Wood*
***Petersen** Alviro Nathan	Lions/Essex	SA	25.11.1980	*Port Elizabeth*
***Peterson** Robin John	Cape Cobras	SA	4.8.1979	*Port Elizabeth*
Pettini Mark Lewis	Essex/Mountaineers	E	7.8.1983	*Brighton*
Phangiso Aaron Mpho	North West	SA	21.1.1984	*Garunkuwa*
***Philander** Vernon Darryl	Cape Cobras/Somerset	SA	24.6.1985	*Bellville*
Phillips Ben James	Nottinghamshire	E	30.9.1974	*Lewisham*
***Phillips** Omar Jamel	Barbados	WI	12.10.1986	*Boscobel, Barbados*
Phillips Timothy James	Essex	E	13.3.1981	*Cambridge*
Piedt Dane Lee-Roy	Cape Cobras/W. Province	SA	6.3.1990	*Cape Town*

	Team	*Country*	*Born*	*Birthplace*
Pienaar Abraham Jacobus	Knights/Free State	SA	12.12.1989	*Bloemfontein*
***Pietersen** Kevin Peter	Surrey	E	27.6.1980	*Pietermaritzburg, SA*
Pinner Neil Douglas	Worcestershire	E	28.9.1990	*Wordsley*
***Plunkett** Liam Edward	Durham	E	6.4.1985	*Middlesbrough*
Polius Dalton	Windward Islands	WI	12.9.1990	*St Lucia*
Pollard Kieron Adrian	Trinidad & Tobago	WI	12.5.1987	*Cacariqua, Trinidad*
***Ponting** Ricky Thomas	Tasmania	A	19.12.1974	*Launceston*
Porterfield William Thomas Stuart	Warwickshire	Ireland	6.9.1984	*Londonderry*
***Powar** Ramesh Rajaram	Mumbai	I	20.5.1978	*Bombay*
***Powell** Kieran Omar Akeem	Leeward Islands	WI	6.3.1990	*Government Rd, Nevis*
Powell Michael John	Kent	E	3.2.1977	*Abergavenny*
Poynton Thomas	Derbyshire	E	25.11.1989	*Burton-on-Trent*
***Prasad** Kariyawasam Tirana Gamage Dammika	Sinhalese	SL	30.5.1983	*Ragama*
***Prasanna** Seekkuge	Army	SL	27.6.1985	*Balapitiya*
Premaratne Weda Gedara Heeran Nilanka	Ragama	SL	17.6.1988	*Kandy*
Price Michael Lynn	Warriors/E. Province	SA	6.10.1981	*Grahamstown*
***Price** Raymond William	Mashonaland Eagles	Z	12.6.1976	*Salisbury*
***Prince** Ashwell Gavin	Warriors/Lancashire	SA	28.5.1977	*Port Elizabeth*
***Prior** Matthew James	Sussex	E	26.2.1982	*Johannesburg, SA*
Procter Luke Anthony	Lancashire	E	24.6.1988	*Oldham*
***Pujara** Cheteshwar Arvind	Saurashtra	I	25.1.1988	*Rajkot*
Pushpakumara Muthumudalige	Tamil Union	SL	26.9.1981	*Colombo*
Pushpakumara Paulage Malinda	Chilaw Marians	SL	24.3.1987	*Colombo*
Putland Gary David	South Australia	A	10.2.1986	*Flinders*
Puttick Andrew George	Cape Cobras	SA	11.12.1980	*Cape Town*
Pyrah Richard Michael	Yorkshire	E	1.11.1982	*Dewsbury*
***Qaiser Abbas**	National Bank/Quetta	P	7.5.1982	*Muridke*
***Quiney** Robert John	Victoria	A	20.8.1982	*Brighton, Australia*
Rabie Gurshwin Renier	SW Districts/Warriors	SA	26.6.1983	*Oudtshoorn*
Rahane Ajinkya Madhukar	Mumbai	I	6.6.1988	*Ashwi Kurd*
Rahat Ali	Baluchistan/KRL/Multan	P	12.9.1988	*Multan*
***Raina** Suresh Kumar	Uttar Pradesh	I	27.11.1986	*Ghaziabad*
Rainbird Samuel Leigh	Tasmania	A	5.6.1992	*Hobart*
Rainsford Edward Charles	Mid West Rhinos	Z	14.12.1984	*Kadoma*
Rajah Emile	Trinidad & Tobago	WI	3.10.1987	*St Augustine, Trinidad*
***Rajin Saleh**	Sylhet	B	20.11.1983	*Sylhet*
***Ramdin** Denesh	Trinidad & Tobago	WI	13.3.1985	*Mission Rd, Trinidad*
Rameez Raja	State Bank of Pakistan	P	31.7.1987	*Karachi*
***Rampaul** Ravindranath	Trinidad & Tobago	WI	15.10.1984	*Preysal, Trinidad*
***Ramprakash** Mark Ravin	Surrey	E	5.9.1969	*Bushey*
***Ramyakumara** Wijekoon Mudiyanselage Gayan	Chilaw Marians	SL	21.12.1976	*Gampaha*
Also known as Gayan Wijekoon				
***Randiv** Hewa Kaluhalmullage Suraj Randiv	Bloomfield	SL	30.1.1985	*Matara*
Also known as Hewa Kaluhalmullage Suraj Randiv Kaluhalamulla; formerly known as M. M. M. Suraj				
Rankin William Boyd	Warwickshire	Ireland	5.7.1984	*Londonderry*
Raphael Samuel Joseph	South Australia	A	24.5.1987	*Bedford Park*
***Raqibul Hasan**	Dhaka	B	8.10.1987	*Jamalpur*
Rashid Adil Usman	Yorkshire	E	17.2.1988	*Bradford*
***Ratra** Ajay	Tripura	I	13.12.1981	*Faridabad*
Rayner Oliver Philip	Middlesex	E	1.11.1985	*Fallingbostel, Germany*
Rayudu Ambati Thirupathi	Baroda	I	23.9.1985	*Guntur*
Raza Hasan	Punjab/Nat. Bank	P	8.7.1992	*Sialkot*
***Read** Christopher Mark Wells	Nottinghamshire	E	10.8.1978	*Paignton*
Reardon Nathan Jon	Queensland	A	8.11.1984	*Chinchilla*

	Team	*Country*	*Born*	*Birthplace*
Redfern Daniel James	Derbyshire	E	18.4.1990	*Shrewsbury*
***Redmond** Aaron James	Otago	NZ	23.9.1979	*Auckland*
Reed Michael Thomas	Glamorgan	E	10.9.1988	*Leicester*
Rees Gareth Peter	Glamorgan	E	8.4.1985	*Swansea*
***Reifer** Floyd Lamonte	Comb. Campuses & Colls	WI	23.7.1972	*Parish Land, Barbados*
Reifer Raymon Anton	Comb. Campuses & Colls	WI	11.5.1991	*Archer's Rd, Barbados*
***Riaz Afridi**	Khyber Pakhtunkhwa	P	21.1.1985	*Peshawar*
Riazuddin Hamza	Hampshire	E	19.12.1989	*Hendon*
Richards Austin Conroy Lenroy	Leeward Islands	WI	14.11.1983	*Freetown, Antigua*
Richards Rowan Ronaldo	Titans	SA	8.7.1984	*East London*
Richardson Alan	Worcestershire	E	6.5.1975	*Newcastle-under-Lyme*
Richardson Andrew Peter	Jamaica	WI	6.9.1981	*Kingston, Jamaica*
Richardson Kane William	South Australia	A	12.2.1991	*Eudunda*
Richardson Michael John	Durham	E	4.10.1986	*Port Elizabeth*
Riley Adam Edward Nicholas	Lough. MCCU/Kent	E	23.3.1992	*Sidcup*
Rimmington Nathan John	Western Australia	A	11.11.1982	*Redcliffe*
Rizwan Ahmed	Hyderabad	P	1.10.1978	*Hyderabad*
***Roach** Kemar Andre Jamal	Barbados	WI	30.6.1988	*Checker Hall, Barb.*
Robinson Andrew William	Queensland	A	10.6.1981	*Devonport*
Robinson Wesley Michael	Western Australia	A	26.12.1980	*Duncraig*
***Robiul Islam**	Khulna	B	20.10.1986	*Satkhira*
Robson Samuel David	Middlesex	A	1.7.1989	*Paddington*
***Rogers** Christopher John Llewellyn	Victoria/Middx	A	31.8.1977	*St George*
Rohrer Ben James	New South Wales	A	26.3.1981	*Bankstown*
Roland-Jones Tobias Skelton	Middlesex	E	29.1.1988	*Ashford, Middlesex*
Ronchi Luke	W. Australia/Wellington	A	23.4.1981	*Dannevirke, NZ*
***Root** Joseph Edward	Yorkshire	E	30.12.1990	*Sheffield*
Rossington Adam Matthew	Middlesex	E	5.5.1993	*Edgware*
Rossouw Rilee Roscoe	Knights/Free State	SA	9.10.1989	*Bloemfontein*
Roy Jason Jonathan	Surrey	E	21.7.1990	*Durban*
***Rubel Hossain**	Khulna	B	1.1.1990	*Bagerhat*
***Rudolph** Jacobus Andries	Titans/Surrey	SA	4.5.1981	*Springs*
Rupasinghe Rupasinghe Jayawardene Mudiyanselage Gihan Madushanka	Moors	SL	5.3.1986	*Watupitiwala*
Rushworth Christopher	Durham	E	11.7.1986	*Sunderland*
***Russell** Andre Dwayne	Jamaica	WI	29.4.1988	*Jamaica*
Russell Christopher James	Worcestershire	E	16.2.1989	*Newport, Isle of Wight*
Rutherford Hamish Duncan	Otago	NZ	27.4.1989	*Dunedin*
***Ryder** Jesse Daniel	Wellington	NZ	6.8.1984	*Masterton*
***Saeed Ajmal**	ZTBL	P	14.10.1977	*Faisalabad*
***Saha** Wriddhaman Prasanta	Bengal	I	24.10.1984	*Siliguri*
***Sajidul Islam**	Rangpur	B	18.1.1988	*Rungpur*
Sales David John	Northamptonshire	E	3.12.1977	*Carshalton*
Salvi Aavishkar Madhav	Mumbai	I	20.10.1981	*Bombay*
Samantray Biplab Bipin	Orissa	I	14.9.1988	*Cuttack*
***Samaraweera** Thilan Thusara	Sinhalese	SL	22.9.1976	*Colombo*
Samiullah Khan	Sui Northern/Faisalabad	P	4.8.1982	*Mianwali*
***Sammy** Darren Julius Garvey	Windward Islands	WI	20.12.1983	*Micoud, St Lucia*
***Samuels** Marlon Nathaniel	Jamaica	WI	5.1.1981	*Kingston, Jamaica*
***Sangakkara** Kumar Chokshanada	Nondescripts	SL	27.10.1977	*Matale*
Sangwan Pradeep	Delhi	I	5.11.1990	*Najafgarh*
Santokie Krishmar	Jamaica	WI	20.12.1984	*Clarendon, Jamaica*
***Sarfraz Ahmed**	Sind/PIA/Karachi W.	P	22.5.1987	*Karachi*
***Sarwan** Ramnaresh Ronnie	Guyana/Leicestershire	WI	23.6.1980	*Wakenaam Is., Guyana*
Savage Calvin Peter	KZN Inland/KZN/Dolphins	SA	4.1.1993	*Durban*
Saxelby Ian David	Gloucestershire	E	22.5.1989	*Nottingham*
Saxena Jalaj Sahai	Madhya Pradesh	I	15.12.1986	*Indore*
Saxena Vineet Ashokkumar	Rajasthan	I	3.12.1980	*Margao*

	Team	Country	Born	Birthplace
Sayers Chadd James	South Australia	A	31.8.1987	*Adelaide*
Sayers Joseph John	Yorkshire	E	5.11.1983	*Leeds*
Scantlebury-Searles Javon Philip Ramon	Barbados	WI	21.12.1986	*Durants Village, Barb.*
Scott Ben James Matthew	Worcestershire	E	4.8.1981	*Isleworth*
Scullard Brandon Michael	KwaZulu-Natal/Dolphins	SA	22.2.1991	*Durban*
Sebastien Liam Andrew Shannon	Windward Islands	WI	9.9.1984	*Roseau, Dominica*
Second Rudi Stewart	Free State/Knights	SA	17.7.1989	*Queenstown*
***Sehwag** Virender	Delhi	I	20.10.1978	*Delhi*
Senanayake Senanayake Mudiyanselage Sachithra Madhushanka	Sinhalese	SL	9.2.1985	*Colombo*
Serasinghe Sachithra Chaturanga	Tamil Union	SL	13.4.1987	*Colombo*
***Shabbir Ahmed**	United Bank	P	21.4.1976	*Khanewal*
***Shadab Kabir**	Port Qasim Authority	P	12.11.1977	*Karachi*
Shafayat Bilal Mustapha	Hampshire	E	10.7.1984	*Nottingham*
***Shafiul Islam**	Rajshahi	B	6.10.1989	*Bogra*
***Shah** Owais Alam	Essex	E	22.10.1978	*Karachi, Pakistan*
***Shahadat Hossain**	Dhaka	B	7.8.1986	*Narayanganj*
***Shahid Afridi**	Karachi	P	1.3.1980	*Khyber Agency*
***Shahriar Nafees**	Barisal	B	25.1.1986	*Dhaka*
***Shahzad** Ajmal	Yorkshire/Lancashire	E	27.7.1985	*Huddersfield*
Shahzaib Hasan	Sind/Port Qasim A.	P	25.12.1989	*Karachi*
Shakeel Ansar	ZTBL	P	11.11.1978	*Sialkot*
***Shakib Al Hasan**	Khulna	B	24.3.1987	*Magura*
Shami Ahmed	Bengal	I	3.9.1990	*Jonagar*
Shantry Jack David	Worcestershire	E	29.1.1988	*Shrewsbury*
***Sharma** Ishant	Delhi	I	2.9.1988	*Delhi*
Sharma Joginder	Haryana	I	23.10.1983	*Rohtak*
Sharma Rahul	Punjab	I	30.11.1986	*Jullundur*
Sharma Rohit Gurunath	Mumbai	I	30.4.1987	*Bansod*
Sheridan William David	Victoria	A	5.7.1987	*Chertsey, England*
Shezi Mthokozisi	Dolphins/KwaZulu-Natal	SA	9.9.1987	*Imbali*
***Shillingford** Shane	Windward Islands	WI	22.2.1983	*Dominica*
***Shoaib Malik**	Punjab/PIA	P	1.2.1982	*Sialkot*
Shreck Charles Edward	Kent	E	6.1.1978	*Truro*
Shukla Laxmi Ratan	Bengal	I	6.5.1981	*Howrah*
Shuvagata Hom	Dhaka	B	11.11.1986	*Mymensingh*
***Sibanda** Vusimuzi	Mid West Rhinos	Z	10.10.1983	*Highfields*
Siboto Malusi Paul	Knights/Free State	SA	20.8.1987	*Cape Town*
Sidana Mayank	Punjab	I	4.12.1986	*Delhi*
***Siddle** Peter Matthew	Victoria	A	25.11.1984	*Traralgon*
***Sidebottom** Ryan Jay	Yorkshire	E	15.1.1978	*Huddersfield*
Silva Athege Roshen Shivanka	Colts	SL	17.11.1988	*Colombo*
***Silva** Jayan Kaushal	Sinhalese	SL	27.5.1986	*Colombo*
***Silva** Lindamlilage Prageeth Chamara	Bloomfield	SL	14.12.1979	*Panadura*
Simetu Siyabulela	Cape Cobras/W. Province	SA	22.8.1991	*Cape Town*
Simmons Craig Joseph	Western Australia	A	1.12.1982	*Paddington*
***Simmons** Lendl Mark Platter	Trinidad & Tobago	WI	25.1.1985	*Port-of-Spain, Trinidad*
Simpson John Andrew	Middlesex	E	13.7.1988	*Bury*
***Sinclair** Mathew Stuart	Central Districts	NZ	9.11.1975	*Katherine, Australia*
Singh Rituraj Rajeev	Rajasthan	I	19.10.1990	*Jaipur*
Smit Darren	Dolphins	SA	28.1.1984	*Durban*
***Smith** Devon Sheldon	Windward Islands	WI	21.10.1981	*Hermitage, Grenada*
***Smith** Dwayne Romel	Barbados	WI	12.4.1983	*Storey Gap, Barbados*
***Smith** Graeme Craig	Cape Cobras	SA	1.2.1981	*Johannesburg*
Smith Gregory Marc	Essex	SA	20.4.1983	*Johannesburg*
Smith Greg Phillip	Leicestershire	E	16.11.1988	*Leicester*
Smith Jamal	Barbados	WI	16.10.1984	*Deacon Rd, Barbados*

	Team	*Country*	*Born*	*Birthplace*
Smith James David	South Australia	A	11.10.1988	*Murray Bridge*
Smith Jeremy Stewart	Tasmania	A	23.10.1988	*Launceston*
***Smith** Steven Peter Devereux	New South Wales	A	2.6.1989	*Sydney*
Smith Thomas Christopher	Lancashire	E	26.12.1985	*Liverpool*
Smith Thomas Michael John	Middlesex	E	29.8.1987	*Eastbourne*
Smith William Rew	Durham	E	28.9.1982	*Luton*
Smuts Jon-Jon Trevor	Warriors	SA	21.8.1988	*Grahamstown*
Smuts Kelly Royce	Warriors/E. Province	SA	22.1.1990	*Grahamstown*
Snell Stephen David	Somerset	E	27.2.1983	*Winchester*
***Sohag Gazi**	Barisal	B	5.8.1991	*Khulna*
***Sohail Khan**	Karachi Whites	P	6.3.1984	*Malakand*
***Sohail Tanvir**	Federal Areas/ZTBL	P	12.12.1984	*Rawalpindi*
Solanki Vikram Singh	Worcestershire	E	1.4.1976	*Udaipur, India*
***Southee** Timothy Grant	Northern Districts	NZ	11.12.1988	*Whangarei*
Spriegel Matthew Neil William	Surrey	E	4.3.1987	*Epsom*
***Sreesanth** Shanthakumaran	Kerala	I	6.2.1983	*Kothamangalam*
***Starc** Mitchell Aaron	New South Wales/Yorks	A	13.1.1990	*Baulkham Hills*
Stevens Darren Ian	Kent	E	30.4.1976	*Leicester*
Stewart Shanan Luke	Canterbury	NZ	21.6.1982	*Christchurch*
***Steyn** Dale Willem	Cape Cobras	SA	27.6.1983	*Phalaborwa*
Stokes Benjamin Andrew	Durham	E	4.6.1991	*Christchurch*
Stone Oliver Peter	Northamptonshire	E	9.10.1993	*Norwich*
Stoneman Mark Daniel	Durham	E	26.6.1987	*Newcastle-upon-Tyne*
***Strauss** Andrew John	Middlesex	E	2.3.1977	*Johannesburg, SA*
Stray Thomas Dean	South Australia	A	18.1.1987	*Box Hill*
Subrayen Prenelan	Dolphins	SA	23.9.1993	*Tongaat*
Sudhindra Taduri Prakashchandra	Madhya Pradesh	I	24.8.1984	*Hindupur*
***Suhrawadi Shuvo**	Rangpur	B	21.11.1988	*Rajshahi*
Suppiah Arul Vivasvan	Somerset	E	30.8.1983	*Kuala Lumpur, Malay.*
Swanepoel Aubrey Ryan	Griqualand West/Knights	SA	18.6.1989	*Kimberley*
***Swann** Graeme Peter	Nottinghamshire	E	24.3.1979	*Northampton*
***Syed Rasel**	Barisal	B	3.7.1984	*Jessore*
***Taibu** Tatenda	Southern Rocks	Z	14.5.1983	*Harare*
***Talha Jubair**	Dhaka Metropolis	B	10.12.1985	*Faridpur*
***Tamim Iqbal**	Chittagong	B	20.3.1989	*Chittagong*
***Tanvir Ahmed**	Sind/Port Q. A./Karachi B.	P	20.12.1978	*Kuwait City*
***Tapash Baisya**	Sylhet	B	25.12.1982	*Sylhet*
***Tareq Aziz**	Dhaka Metropolis	B	4.9.1983	*Chittagong*
***Taufeeq Umar**	Punjab/Sui Northern	P	20.6.1981	*Lahore*
***Taylor** Brendan Ross Murray	Mid West Rhinos	Z	6.2.1986	*Harare*
Taylor Jack Martin Robert	Gloucestershire	E	12.11.1991	*Banbury*
Taylor Jacques David Chesney	Leeward Islands	WI	19.4.1988	*St Kitts*
***Taylor** James William Arthur	Nottinghamshire	E	6.1.1990	*Nottingham*
***Taylor** Luteru Ross Poutoa Lote	Central Districts	NZ	8.3.1984	*Lower Hutt*
Taylor Robert Meadows Liam	Lough. MCCU/Leics	E	21.12.1989	*Northampton*
ten Doeschate Ryan Neil	Essex/Otago	NL	30.6.1980	*Port Elizabeth, SA*
***Tendulkar** Sachin Ramesh	Mumbai	I	24.4.1973	*Bombay*
Terry Sean Paul	Hampshire	E	1.8.1991	*Southampton*
Thakor Shivsinh Jaysinh	Leicestershire	E	22.10.1993	*Leicester*
***Tharanga** Warushavithana Upul	Nondescripts	SL	2.2.1985	*Balapitiya*
Theron Juan	Warriors	SA	24.7.1985	*Vereeniging*
***Thirimanne** Hettige Don Rumesh Lahiru	Ragama	SL	8.9.1989	*Moratuwa*
Thomas Alfonso Clive	Somerset	SA	9.2.1977	*Cape Town*
Thomas Devon Cuthbert	Leeward Islands	WI	12.11.1989	*Bethesda, Antigua*
Thomas Ivan Alfred Astley	Leeds Brad MCCU/Kent	E	25.9.1991	*Greenwich*
Thomas Shacoya Elrick	Comb. Campuses & Colls	WI	15.9.1988	*St Catherine, Jamaica*
Thornely Michael Alistair	Leics/Mashonaland Eagles	E	19.10.1987	*Camden*
Thorp Callum David	Durham	E	11.1.1975	*Mount Lawley, Aus.*

	Team	*Country*	*Born*	*Birthplace*
Thyssen Craig Andre	Warriors/Border	SA	25.3.1984	*Port Elizabeth*
Tietjens Carl	South Australia	A	25.3.1986	*Adelaide*
Tiwary Manoj Kumar	Bengal	I	14.11.1985	*Howrah*
Tiwary Saurabh Sunil	Jharkhand	I	30.12.1989	*Jamshedpur*
Tomlinson James Andrew	Hampshire	E	12.6.1982	*Winchester*
*__Tonge__ Gavin Courtney	Leeward Islands	WI	13.2.1983	*St John's, Antigua*
Topley Reece James William	Essex	E	12.2.1994	*Ipswich*
Townsend Wade James	Queensland	A	29.1.1986	*Herston*
*__Tredwell__ James Cullum	Kent	E	27.2.1982	*Ashford*
Trego Peter David	Central Districts/Somerset	E	12.6.1981	*Weston-super-Mare*
Tremain Christopher Peter	New South Wales	A	10.8.1991	*Dubbo*
*__Tremlett__ Christopher Timothy	Surrey	E	2.9.1981	*Southampton*
*__Trescothick__ Marcus Edward	Somerset	E	25.12.1975	*Keynsham*
Triffitt Thomas Ian Francis	Tasmania/W. Australia	A	13.11.1990	*Latrobe*
*__Trott__ Ian Jonathan Leonard	Warwickshire	E	22.4.1981	*Cape Town, SA*
Troughton Jamie Oliver	Warwickshire	E	2.3.1979	*Camden*
*__Tsolekile__ Thami Lungisa	Lions	SA	9.10.1980	*Cape Town*
*__Tsotsobe__ Lonwabo Lennox	Warriors	SA	7.3.1984	*Port Elizabeth*
*__Tuffey__ Daryl Raymond	Auckland	NZ	11.6.1978	*Milton*
Turner Mark Leif	Derbyshire	E	23.10.1984	*Sunderland*
*__Tushar Imran__	Khulna	B	10.12.1983	*Kharki*
Tyagi Sudeep	Uttar Pradesh	I	19.9.1987	*Ghaziabad*
Udana Isuru	Tamil Union	SL	17.2.1988	*Balangoda*
Udawatte Mahela Lakmal	Chilaw Marians	SL	19.7.1986	*Colombo*
*__Umar Akmal__	Sui Northern	P	26.5.1990	*Lahore*
*__Umar Amin__	Federal Areas/Port Q. A.	P	16.10.1989	*Rawalpindi*
*__Umar Gul__	Habib Bank	P	14.4.1984	*Peshawar*
*__Unadkat__ Jaydev Dipakbhai	Saurashtra	I	18.10.1991	*Porbandar*
Usman Salahuddin	Punjab/Habib B./Lahore Sh.	P	2.12.1990	*Lahore*
Uthappa Robin Venu	Karnataka	I	11.11.1985	*Coorg*
*__Utseya__ Prosper	Mountaineers/Mash. Eagles	Z	26.3.1985	*Harare*
*__Vaas__ Warnakulasuriya Patabendige Ushantha Joseph Chaminda	Colts/Northants	SL	27.1.1974	*Mattumagala*
Vallie Mohammad Yaseen	Cape Cobras/W. Province	SA	30.9.1989	*Cape Town*
van der Gugten Timm	New South Wales	NL	25.2.1991	*Hornsby*
van der Merwe Roelof Erasmus	Northerns/Titans	SA	31.12.1984	*Johannesburg*
van der Wath Johannes Jacobus	Knights	SA	10.1.1978	*Newcastle*
Vandiar Jonathan David	Lions/Dolphins	SA	25.4.1990	*Paarl*
*__Vandort__ Michael Graydon	Nondescripts	SL	19.1.1980	*Colombo*
*__van Jaarsveld__ Martin	Titans	SA	18.6.1974	*Klerksdorp*
van Jaarsveld Vaughn Bernard	Dolphins	SA	2.2.1985	*Johannesburg*
van Schalkwyk Shadley Claude	Knights/Free State	SA	5.8.1988	*Cape Town*
*__van Wyk__ Cornelius Francoius Kruger	Central Districts	NZ	7.2.1980	*Wolmaransstad, SA*
van Wyk Divan Jaco	KZN Inland/Dolphins	SA	25.2.1985	*Bloemfontein*
van Wyk Morne Nico	Knights	SA	20.3.1979	*Bloemfontein*
van Zyl Stiaan	Cape Cobras	SA	19.9.1987	*Cape Town*
Vardhan Manish Singh	Jharkhand	I	6.10.1983	*Purnea*
Venugopal Rao Yalaka	Gujarat	I	26.2.1982	*Visakhapatnam*
Verma Amit Anil	Karnataka	I	30.6.1987	*Bangalore*
*__Vermeulen__ Mark Andrew	Mid West Rhinos	Z	2.3.1979	*Salisbury*
*__Vettori__ Daniel Luca	Northern Districts	NZ	27.1.1979	*Auckland*
*__Vijay__ Murali	Tamil Nadu	I	1.4.1984	*Madras*
Vilas Dane James	Cape Cobras	SA	10.6.1985	*Johannesburg*
Viljoen Gerhardus C. (Hardus)	Easterns/Lions	SA	6.3.1989	*Witbank*
*__Vinay Kumar__ Ranganath	Karnataka	I	12.2.1984	*Davanagere*
Vince James Michael	Hampshire	E	14.3.1991	*Cuckfield*
*__Vincent__ Lou	Auckland	NZ	11.11.1978	*Warkworth*

	Team	*Country*	*Born*	*Birthplace*
***Vitori** Brian Vitalis	Southern Rocks	Z	22.2.1990	*Masvingo*
Voges Adam Charles	W. Australia/Notts	A	4.10.1979	*Perth*
von Berg Shaun	Titans/Northerns	SA	16.9.1986	*Pretoria*
***Wade** Matthew Scott	Victoria	A	26.12.1987	*Hobart*
Wagg Graham Grant	Glamorgan	E	28.4.1983	*Rugby*
***Wagner** Neil	Otago	NZ	13.3.1986	*Pretoria, SA*
***Wahab Riaz**	National Bank	P	28.6.1985	*Lahore*
Wainwright David John	Derbyshire/Police	E	21.3.1985	*Pontefract*
Wakely Alexander George	Northamptonshire	E	3.11.1988	*Hammersmith*
Wallace Mark Alexander	Glamorgan	E	19.11.1981	*Abergavenny*
***Waller** Malcolm Noel	Mid West Rhinos	Z	28.9.1984	*Harare*
Waller Max Thomas Charles	Somerset	E	3.3.1988	*Salisbury*
Walsh Hayden Rashidi	Leeward Islands	WI	23.4.1992	*St Croix, US Virgin Is*
Walters Basheeru-Deen	Warriors	SA	16.9.1986	*Port Elizabeth*
Walters Stewart Jonathan	Glamorgan	E	25.6.1983	*Mornington, Australia*
***Walton** Chadwick Antonio Kirkpatrick	Comb. Campuses & Colls	WI	3.7.1985	*Jamaica*
Wardlaw Iain	Yorkshire	E	29.6.1985	*Dewsbury*
***Warnapura** Basnayake Shalith Malinda	Colts	SL	26.5.1979	*Colombo*
***Warner** David Andrew	New South Wales	A	27.10.1986	*Paddington*
Warrican Jomel	Barbados	WI	20.5.1992	*St Vincent*
***Wasim Jaffer**	Mumbai	I	16.2.1978	*Bombay*
Waters Huw Thomas	Glamorgan	E	26.9.1986	*Cardiff*
***Watling** Bradley-John	Northern Districts	NZ	9.7.1985	*Durban, SA*
***Watson** Shane Robert	New South Wales	A	17.6.1981	*Ipswich*
Weerakoon Sajeewa	Colts	SL	17.2.1978	*Galle*
Weeraratne Kaushalya	Ragama	SL	29.1.1981	*Gampola*
***Welagedara** Uda Walawwe Mahim Bandaralage Chanaka Asanka	Tamil Union	SL	20.3.1981	*Matale*
Wells Jonathan Wayne	Tasmania	A	13.8.1988	*Hobart*
Wells Luke William Peter	Colombo/Sussex	E	29.12.1990	*Eastbourne*
Wells Samuel Raymond	Otago	NZ	13.7.1984	*Dunedin*
Wernars Kirk Ogilvy	Sussex	SA	14.6.1991	*Cape Town*
Wessels Mattheus Hendrik (Riki)	Mid West Rhinos/Notts	E	12.11.1985	*Marogudoore, Aust.*
Westley Thomas	Essex	E	13.3.1989	*Cambridge*
Westwood Ian James	Warwickshire	E	13.7.1982	*Birmingham*
Wheater Adam Jack	Essex/Badureliya/N. Dist.	E	13.2.1990	*Whipps Cross*
***White** Cameron Leon	Victoria	A	18.8.1983	*Bairnsdale*
White David John	E. Province/Warriors	SA	22.5.1991	*Port Elizabeth*
White Graeme Geoffrey	Nottinghamshire	E	18.4.1987	*Milton Keynes*
White Robert Allan	Northamptonshire	E	15.10.1979	*Chelmsford*
White Wayne Andrew	Leicestershire	E	22.4.1985	*Derby*
Whiteley Ross Andrew	Derbyshire	E	13.9.1988	*Sheffield*
Whiteman Sam McFarlane	Western Australia	A	19.3.1992	*Doncaster, England*
Wiese David	Titans	SA	18.5.1985	*Roodepoort*
Willett Tonito Akanni	Leeward Islands	WI	6.2.1983	*Government Rd, Nevis*
Willey David Jonathan	Northamptonshire	E	28.2.1990	*Northampton*
Williams Cameron Dean	South Australia	A	18.11.1991	*Adelaide*
Williams Gavin Anjez	Leeward Islands	WI	18.11.1984	*Bolans*
Williams Kenroy DaCosta	Barbados	WI	9.8.1984	*Harlington, Barb.*
Williams Lizaad Buyron	Boland/Cape Cobras	SA	1.10.1993	*Vredenburg*
Williams Sean Colin	Matabeleland Tuskers	Z	26.9.1986	*Bulawayo*
***Williamson** Kane Stuart	N. Districts/Glos	NZ	8.8.1990	*Tauranga*
***Willoughby** Charl Myles	Cape Cobras/Essex	SA	3.12.1974	*Cape Town*
Wilson Gary Craig	Surrey	Ireland	5.2.1986	*Dundonald*
Woakes Christopher Roger	Warwicks/Wellington	E	2.3.1989	*Birmingham*
Wood Christopher Philip	Hampshire	E	27.6.1990	*Basingstoke*
Wood Mark Andrew	Durham	E	11.1.1990	*Ashington*

	Team	Country	Born	Birthplace
Wood Samuel Kenneth William	Nottinghamshire	E	3.4.1993	*Nottingham*
Woodcock Luke James	Wellington	NZ	19.3.1982	*Wellington*
Worker George Herrick	Canterbury	NZ	23.8.1989	*Palmerston North*
Worrall Daniel James	South Australia	A	10.7.1991	*Melbourne*
Wright Ben James	Glamorgan	E	5.12.1987	*Preston*
Wright Christopher Julian Clement	Warwickshire	E	14.7.1985	*Chipping Norton*
Wright Luke James	Sussex	E	7.3.1985	*Grantham*
Wyatt Alexander Charles Frederick	Leicestershire	E	23.7.1990	*Roehampton*
Yadav Suryakumar Ashok	Mumbai	I	14.9.1990	*Bombay*
***Yadav** Umeshkumar Tilak	Vidarbha	I	25.10.1987	*Nagpur*
Yardy Michael Howard	Sussex	E	27.11.1980	*Pembury*
***Yasir Ali**	KRL/Quetta	P	15.10.1985	*Hazro*
***Yasir Arafat**	KRL	P	12.3.1982	*Rawalpindi*
***Yasir Hameed**	Khyber P./ZTBL/Abbottabad	P	28.2.1978	*Peshawar*
Yasir Shah	Khyber P./Sui N./Abbottabad	P	2.5.1986	*Swabi*
Young Edward George Christopher	Gloucestershire	E	21.5.1989	*Chertsey*
***Young** Reece Alan	Canterbury/Auckland	NZ	15.9.1979	*Auckland*
***Younis Khan**	Habib Bank	P	29.11.1977	*Mardan*
***Yuvraj Singh**	Punjab	I	12.12.1981	*Chandigarh*
***Zaheer Khan**	Mumbai	I	7.10.1978	*Shrirampur*
Zampa Adam	New South Wales	A	31.3.1992	*Shellharbour*
Zhuwao Cephas	Mashonaland Eagles	Z	15.12.1984	*Harare*
Ziaur Rahman	Khulna	B	2.12.1986	*Khulna*
***Zondeki** Monde	E. Province/W. Province	SA	25.7.1982	*King William's Town*
Zondo Khayelihle	KwaZulu-Natal/Dolphins	SA	7.3.1990	*Durban*
***Zulqarnain Haider**	ZTBL	P	3.4.1986	*Lahore*

REGISTER OF WOMEN PLAYERS

The qualifications for inclusion are as follows:

All players who appeared in an international match, or in the County Championship in England, the Women's National Cricket League in Australia, or the Action Cricket Cup in New Zealand, in the calendar year 2012

AND have scored 1,000 runs/taken 50 wickets in one-day internationals, or scored a hundred/taken five in an innings in a Test, one-day international or Twenty20 international since 2009.

* *Denotes Test player.*

	Team	Country	Born	Birthplace
***Al Khader** Nooshin	Railways	I	13.2.1981	*Tehran, Iran*
***Atkins** Caroline Mary Ghislaine	Sussex	E	13.1.1981	*Brighton*
Bates Suzannah Wilson	Otago/Western Australia	NZ	16.9.1987	*Dunedin*
***Blackwell** Alexandra Joy	New South Wales	A	31.8.1983	*Wagga Wagga*
***Brindle** Arran (née Thompson)	Sussex	E	23.11.1981	*Steeton*
***Browne** Nicola Jane	Northern Districts	NZ	14.9.1983	*Matamata*
***Brunt** Katherine Helen	Yorkshire	E	2.7.1985	*Barnsley*
***Chopra** Anjum	Delhi	I	20.5.1977	*Delhi*
***Colvin** Holly Louise	Sussex	E	7.9.1989	*Chichester*
***Dhar** Rumeli	Railways	I	9.12.1983	*Calcutta*
Dottin Deandra Jalisa Shakira	Trinidad & Tobago	WI	21.6.1991	*Barbados*
***Edwards** Charlotte Marie	Kent	E	17.12.1979	*Huntingdon*
***Farrell** Rene Michelle	ACT	A	13.1.1987	*Kogarah*
***Fields** Jodie Maree (née Purves)	Queensland	A	19.6.1984	*Toowoomba*
Fritz Shandre Alvida	Western Province	SA	21.7.1985	*Cape Town*
***Goswami** Jhulan	Bengal	I	25.11.1982	*Kalyani*
***Greenway** Lydia Sophie	Kent	E	6.8.1985	*Farnborough, Kent*
***Guha** Isa Tara	Berkshire	E	21.5.1985	*High Wycombe*
***Gunn** Jennifer Louise	Nottinghamshire	E	9.5.1986	*Nottingham*

	Team	*Country*	*Born*	*Birthplace*
Hunter Julie Lauren	Victoria	A	15.3.1984	*Box Hill, Melbourne*
***Ismail** Shabnim	Western Province	SA	5.10.1988	*Cape Town*
Jayangani Atapattumudiyanselage Chamari	Air Force	SL	9.2.1990	*Gokarella*
***Joyce** Isobel Mary Helen Cecilia	Ireland A	Ireland	25.7.1983	*Wicklow*
***Kala** Hemlata	Railways	I	15.8.1975	*Agra*
***Keightley** Lisa Maree	Wiltshire	A	26.8.1971	*Mudgee*
Lanning Meghann Moira	Victoria	A	25.5.1992	*Singapore*
***Loubser** Sunette	Boland	SA	26.9.1982	*Paarl*
***McGlashan** Sara Jade	Central Districts	NZ	28.3.1982	*Napier*
***Marsh** Laura Alexandra	Kent	E	5.12.1986	*Pembury*
Mohammed Anisa	Trinidad & Tobago	WI	7.8.1988	*Trinidad*
Syeda **Nain** Fatima **Abidi**	ZTBL	P	23.5.1985	*Karachi*
***Nero** Juliana Barbara	St Vincent	WI	14.7.1979	*St Vincent*
***Perry** Ellyse Alexandra	New South Wales	A	3.11.1990	*Wahroonga*
***Poulton** Leah Joy	New South Wales	A	27.2.1984	*Newcastle*
***Raj** Mithali	Railways	I	3.12.1982	*Jodhpur*
Richardson Eimear Ann Jermyn	Central Districts/Ireland A	Ireland	14.9.1986	*Dublin*
Sana Mir	ZTBL	P	5.1.1986	*Abbottabad*
Satterthwaite Amy Ella	Canterbury	NZ	7.10.1986	*Christchurch*
***Seneviratne** Chamani Roshini	Air Force	SL	14.11.1978	*Anuradhapura*
***Sharma** Amita	Railways	I	12.9.1982	*Delhi*
Shrubsole Anya	Somerset	E	7.12.1991	*Bath*
Siriwardene Hettimulla Appuhamilage Shashikala Dedunu	Navy	SL	14.2.1985	*Colombo*
***Smit** Jane	Nottinghamshire	E	24.12.1972	*Ilkeston*
***Sthalekar** Lisa Caprini	New South Wales	A	13.8.1979	*Poona, India*
Sultana Gouher	Hyderabad/Railways	I	31.3.1988	*Hyderabad*
***Taylor** Sarah Jane	Sussex/Wellington	E	20.5.1989	*Whitechapel*
Taylor Stafanie Roxann	Jamaica/Auckland	WI	11.6.1991	*Spanish Town, Jamaica*

CRICKETERS OF THE YEAR, 1889–2013

1889 *Six Great Bowlers of the Year:* J. Briggs, J. J. Ferris, G. A. Lohmann, R. Peel, C. T. B. Turner, S. M. J. Woods.

1890 *Nine Great Batsmen of the Year:* R. Abel, W. Barnes, W. Gunn, L. Hall, R. Henderson, J. M. Read, A. Shrewsbury, F. H. Sugg, A. Ward.

1891 *Five Great Wicketkeepers:* J. McC. Blackham, G. MacGregor, R. Pilling, M. Sherwin, H. Wood.

1892 *Five Great Bowlers:* W. Attewell, J. T. Hearne, F. Martin, A. W. Mold, J. W. Sharpe.

1893 *Five Batsmen of the Year:* H. T. Hewett, L. C. H. Palairet, W. W. Read, S. W. Scott, A. E. Stoddart.

1894 *Five All-Round Cricketers:* G. Giffen, A. Hearne, F. S. Jackson, G. H. S. Trott, E. Wainwright.

1895 *Five Young Batsmen of the Season:* W. Brockwell, J. T. Brown, C. B. Fry, T. W. Hayward, A. C. MacLaren.

1896 W. G. Grace.

1897 *Five Cricketers of the Season:* S. E. Gregory, A. A. Lilley, K. S. Ranjitsinhji, T. Richardson, H. Trumble.

1898 *Five Cricketers of the Year:* F. G. Bull, W. R. Cuttell, N. F. Druce, G. L. Jessop, J. R. Mason.

1899 *Five Great Players of the Season:* W. H. Lockwood, W. Rhodes, W. Storer, C. L. Townsend, A. E. Trott.

1900 *Five Cricketers of the Season:* J. Darling, C. Hill, A. O. Jones, M. A. Noble, Major R. M. Poore.

1901 *Mr R. E. Foster and Four Yorkshiremen:* R. E. Foster, S. Haigh, G. H. Hirst, T. L. Taylor, J. Tunnicliffe.

1902 L. C. Braund, C. P. McGahey, F. Mitchell, W. G. Quaife, J. T. Tyldesley.

1903 W. W. Armstrong, C. J. Burnup, J. Iremonger, J. J. Kelly, V. T. Trumper.

1904 C. Blythe, J. Gunn, A. E. Knight, W. Mead, P. F. Warner.

1905 B. J. T. Bosanquet, E. A. Halliwell, J. Hallows, P. A. Perrin, R. H. Spooner.

1906 D. Denton, W. S. Lees, G. J. Thompson, J. Vine, L. G. Wright.

1907 J. N. Crawford, A. Fielder, E. G. Hayes, K. L. Hutchings, N. A. Knox.

1908 A. W. Hallam, R. O. Schwarz, F. A. Tarrant, A. E. E. Vogler, T. G. Wass.

1909 *Lord Hawke and Four Cricketers of the Year:* W. Brearley, Lord Hawke, J. B. Hobbs, A. Marshal, J. T. Newstead.

1910 W. Bardsley, S. F. Barnes, D. W. Carr, A. P. Day, V. S. Ransford.

1911 H. K. Foster, A. Hartley, C. B. Llewellyn, W. C. Smith, F. E. Woolley.

1912 *Five Members of MCC's team in Australia:* F. R. Foster, J. W. Hearne, S. P. Kinneir, C. P. Mead, H. Strudwick.

1913 *Special Portrait:* John Wisden.

1914 M. W. Booth, G. Gunn, J. W. Hitch, A. E. Relf, Hon. L. H. Tennyson.

1915 J. W. H. T. Douglas, P. G. H. Fender, H. T. W. Hardinge, D. J. Knight, S. G. Smith.

1916–17 No portraits appeared.

1918 *School Bowlers of the Year:* H. L. Calder, J. D. E. Firth, C. H. Gibson, G. A. Rotherham, G. T. S. Stevens.

1919 *Five Public School Cricketers of the Year:* P. W. Adams, A. P. F. Chapman, A. C. Gore, L. P. Hedges, N. E. Partridge.

1920 *Five Batsmen of the Year:* A. Ducat, E. H. Hendren, P. Holmes, H. Sutcliffe, E. Tyldesley.

1921 *Special Portrait:* P. F. Warner.

1922 H. Ashton, J. L. Bryan, J. M. Gregory, C. G. Macartney, E. A. McDonald.

1923 A. W. Carr, A. P. Freeman, C. W. L. Parker, A. C. Russell, A. Sandham.

1924 *Five Bowlers of the Year:* A. E. R. Gilligan, R. Kilner, G. G. Macaulay, C. H. Parkin, M. W. Tate.

1925 R. H. Catterall, J. C. W. MacBryan, H. W. Taylor, R. K. Tyldesley, W. W. Whysall.

1926 *Special Portrait:* J. B. Hobbs.

1927 G. Geary, H. Larwood, J. Mercer, W. A. Oldfield, W. M. Woodfull.

1928 R. C. Blunt, C. Hallows, W. R. Hammond, D. R. Jardine, V. W. C. Jupp.

1929 L. E. G. Ames, G. Duckworth, M. Leyland, S. J. Staples, J. C. White.

1930 E. H. Bowley, K. S. Duleepsinhji, H. G. Owen-Smith, R. W. V. Robins, R. E. S. Wyatt.

1931 D. G. Bradman, C. V. Grimmett, B. H. Lyon, I. A. R. Peebles, M. J. Turnbull.

1932 W. E. Bowes, C. S. Dempster, James Langridge, Nawab of Pataudi sen, H. Verity.
1933 W. E. Astill, F. R. Brown, A. S. Kennedy, C. K. Nayudu, W. Voce.
1934 A. H. Bakewell, G. A. Headley, M. S. Nichols, L. F. Townsend, C. F. Walters.
1935 S. J. McCabe, W. J. O'Reilly, G. A. E. Paine, W. H. Ponsford, C. I. J. Smith.
1936 H. B. Cameron, E. R. T. Holmes, B. Mitchell, D. Smith, A. W. Wellard.
1937 C. J. Barnett, W. H. Copson, A. R. Gover, V. M. Merchant, T. S. Worthington.
1938 T. W. J. Goddard, J. Hardstaff jun, L. Hutton, J. H. Parks, E. Paynter.
1939 H. T. Bartlett, W. A. Brown, D. C. S. Compton, K. Farnes, A. Wood.
1940 L. N. Constantine, W. J. Edrich, W. W. Keeton, A. B. Sellers, D. V. P. Wright.
1941–46 No portraits appeared.
1947 A. V. Bedser, L. B. Fishlock, V. (M. H.) Mankad, T. P. B. Smith, C. Washbrook.
1948 M. P. Donnelly, A. Melville, A. D. Nourse, J. D. Robertson, N. W. D. Yardley.
1949 A. L. Hassett, W. A. Johnston, R. R. Lindwall, A. R. Morris, D. Tallon.
1950 T. E. Bailey, R. O. Jenkins, John Langridge, R. T. Simpson, B. Sutcliffe.
1951 T. G. Evans, S. Ramadhin, A. L. Valentine, E. D. Weekes, F. M. M. Worrell.
1952 R. Appleyard, H. E. Dollery, J. C. Laker, P. B. H. May, E. A. B. Rowan.
1953 H. Gimblett, T. W. Graveney, D. S. Sheppard, W. S. Surridge, F. S. Trueman.
1954 R. N. Harvey, G. A. R. Lock, K. R. Miller, J. H. Wardle, W. Watson.
1955 B. Dooland, Fazal Mahmood, W. E. Hollies, J. B. Statham, G. E. Tribe.
1956 M. C. Cowdrey, D. J. Insole, D. J. McGlew, H. J. Tayfield, F. H. Tyson.
1957 D. Brookes, J. W. Burke, M. J. Hilton, G. R. A. Langley, P. E. Richardson.
1958 P. J. Loader, A. J. McIntyre, O. G. Smith, M. J. Stewart, C. L. Walcott.
1959 H. L. Jackson, R. E. Marshall, C. A. Milton, J. R. Reid, D. Shackleton.
1960 K. F. Barrington, D. B. Carr, R. Illingworth, G. Pullar, M. J. K. Smith.
1961 N. A. T. Adcock, E. R. Dexter, R. A. McLean, R. Subba Row, J. V. Wilson.
1962 W. E. Alley, R. Benaud, A. K. Davidson, W. M. Lawry, N. C. O'Neill.
1963 D. Kenyon, Mushtaq Mohammad, P. H. Parfitt, P. J. Sharpe, F. J. Titmus.
1964 D. B. Close, C. C. Griffith, C. C. Hunte, R. B. Kanhai, G. S. Sobers.
1965 G. Boycott, P. J. Burge, J. A. Flavell, G. D. McKenzie, R. B. Simpson.
1966 K. C. Bland, J. H. Edrich, R. C. Motz, P. M. Pollock, R. G. Pollock.
1967 R. W. Barber, B. L. D'Oliveira, C. Milburn, J. T. Murray, S. M. Nurse.
1968 Asif Iqbal, Hanif Mohammad, K. Higgs, J. M. Parks, Nawab of Pataudi jun.
1969 J. G. Binks, D. M. Green, B. A. Richards, D. L. Underwood, O. S. Wheatley.
1970 B. F. Butcher, A. P. E. Knott, Majid Khan, M. J. Procter, D. J. Shepherd.
1971 J. D. Bond, C. H. Lloyd, B. W. Luckhurst, G. M. Turner, R. T. Virgin.
1972 G. G. Arnold, B. S. Chandrasekhar, L. R. Gibbs, B. Taylor, Zaheer Abbas.
1973 G. S. Chappell, D. K. Lillee, R. A. L. Massie, J. A. Snow, K. R. Stackpole.
1974 K. D. Boyce, B. E. Congdon, K. W. R. Fletcher, R. C. Fredericks, P. J. Sainsbury.
1975 D. L. Amiss, M. H. Denness, N. Gifford, A. W. Greig, A. M. E. Roberts.
1976 I. M. Chappell, P. G. Lee, R. B. McCosker, D. S. Steele, R. A. Woolmer.
1977 J. M. Brearley, C. G. Greenidge, M. A. Holding, I. V. A. Richards, R. W. Taylor.
1978 I. T. Botham, M. Hendrick, A. Jones, K. S. McEwan, R. G. D. Willis.
1979 D. I. Gower, J. K. Lever, C. M. Old, C. T. Radley, J. N. Shepherd.
1980 J. Garner, S. M. Gavaskar, G. A. Gooch, D. W. Randall, B. C. Rose.
1981 K. J. Hughes, R. D. Jackman, A. J. Lamb, C. E. B. Rice, V. A. P. van der Bijl.
1982 T. M. Alderman, A. R. Border, R. J. Hadlee, Javed Miandad, R. W. Marsh.
1983 Imran Khan, T. E. Jesty, A. I. Kallicharran, Kapil Dev, M. D. Marshall.
1984 M. Amarnath, J. V. Coney, J. E. Emburey, M. W. Gatting, C. L. Smith.
1985 M. D. Crowe, H. A. Gomes, G. W. Humpage, J. Simmons, S. Wettimuny.
1986 P. Bainbridge, R. M. Ellison, C. J. McDermott, N. V. Radford, R. T. Robinson.
1987 J. H. Childs, G. A. Hick, D. B. Vengsarkar, C. A. Walsh, J. J. Whitaker.
1988 J. P. Agnew, N. A. Foster, D. P. Hughes, P. M. Roebuck, Salim Malik.
1989 K. J. Barnett, P. J. L. Dujon, P. A. Neale, F. D. Stephenson, S. R. Waugh.
1990 S. J. Cook, D. M. Jones, R. C. Russell, R. A. Smith, M. A. Taylor.
1991 M. A. Atherton, M. Azharuddin, A. R. Butcher, D. L. Haynes, M. E. Waugh.
1992 C. E. L. Ambrose, P. A. J. DeFreitas, A. A. Donald, R. B. Richardson, Waqar Younis.
1993 N. E. Briers, M. D. Moxon, I. D. K. Salisbury, A. J. Stewart, Wasim Akram.
1994 D. C. Boon, I. A. Healy, M. G. Hughes, S. K. Warne, S. L. Watkin.
1995 B. C. Lara, D. E. Malcolm, T. A. Munton, S. J. Rhodes, K. C. Wessels.
1996 D. G. Cork, P. A. de Silva, A. R. C. Fraser, A. Kumble, D. A. Reeve.
1997 S. T. Jayasuriya, Mushtaq Ahmed, Saeed Anwar, P. V. Simmons, S. R. Tendulkar.

1998	M. T. G. Elliott, S. G. Law, G. D. McGrath, M. P. Maynard, G. P. Thorpe.
1999	I. D. Austin, D. Gough, M. Muralitharan, A. Ranatunga, J. N. Rhodes.
2000	C. L. Cairns, R. Dravid, L. Klusener, T. M. Moody, Saqlain Mushtaq.
Cricketers of the Century	D. G. Bradman, G. S. Sobers, J. B. Hobbs, S. K. Warne, I. V. A. Richards.
2001	M. W. Alleyne, M. P. Bicknell, A. R. Caddick, J. L. Langer, D. S. Lehmann.
2002	A. Flower, A. C. Gilchrist, J. N. Gillespie, V. V. S. Laxman, D. R. Martyn.
2003	M. L. Hayden, A. J. Hollioake, N. Hussain, S. M. Pollock, M. P. Vaughan.
2004	C. J. Adams, A. Flintoff, I. J. Harvey, G. Kirsten, G. C. Smith.
2005	A. F. Giles, S. J. Harmison, R. W. T. Key, A. J. Strauss, M. E. Trescothick.
2006	M. J. Hoggard, S. P. Jones, B. Lee, K. P. Pietersen, R. T. Ponting.
2007	P. D. Collingwood, D. P. M. D. Jayawardene, Mohammad Yousuf, M. S. Panesar, M. R. Ramprakash.
2008	I. R. Bell, S. Chanderpaul, O. D. Gibson, R. J. Sidebottom, Zaheer Khan.
2009	J. M. Anderson, D. M. Benkenstein, M. V. Boucher, N. D. McKenzie, S. C. Taylor.
2010	S. C. J. Broad, M. J. Clarke, G. Onions, M. J. Prior, G. P. Swann.
2011	E. J. G. Morgan, C. M. W. Read, Tamim Iqbal, I. J. L. Trott.
2012	T. T. Bresnan, G. Chapple, A. N. Cook, A. Richardson, K. C. Sangakkara.
2013	H. M. Amla, N. R. D. Compton, J. H. Kallis, M. N. Samuels, D. W. Steyn.

From 2001 to 2003 the award was made on the basis of all cricket round the world, not just the English season. This ended in 2004 with the start of Wisden's *Leading Cricketer in the World award. Jayasuriya in 1997 was chosen for his influence on the English season, stemming from the 1996 World Cup. In 2011, only four were named after an ICC tribunal investigating the Lord's spot-fixing scandal made the selection of one of the five unsustainable.*

CRICKETERS OF THE YEAR: AN ANALYSIS

The special portrait of John Wisden in 1913 marked the 50th anniversary of his retirement as a player – and the 50th edition of the Almanack. Wisden died in 1884. The special portraits of P. F. Warner in 1921 and J. B. Hobbs in 1926 were in addition to their earlier selection as a Cricketer of the Year in 1904 and 1909 respectively. These three special portraits and the Cricketers of the Century in 2000 are excluded from the following analysis.

The five players selected to be Cricketers of the Year for 2013 bring the number chosen since selection began in 1889 to 570. They have been chosen from 40 different teams as follows:

Derbyshire	13	Northants	14	Australians	71	Cheltenham College	1
Durham	5	Nottinghamshire	29	South Africans	29	Cranleigh School	1
Essex	24	Somerset	19	West Indians	25	Eton College	2
Glamorgan	11	Surrey	49	New Zealanders	8	Malvern College	1
Gloucestershire	17	Sussex	21	Indians	14	Rugby School	1
Hampshire	15	Warwickshire	22	Pakistanis	12	Tonbridge School	1
Kent	26	Worcestershire	16	Sri Lankans	6	Univ. Coll. School	1
Lancashire	34	Yorkshire	43	Zimbabweans	1	Uppingham School	1
Leicestershire	8	Oxford Univ.	6	Bangladeshis	1	Winchester College	1
Middlesex	28	Cambridge Univ.	10	Staffordshire	1	England Women	1

Schoolboys were chosen in 1918 and 1919 when first-class cricket was suspended due to war. The total of sides comes to 589 because 19 players played regularly for two teams (England excluded) in the year for which they were chosen.

Types of Players

Of the 570 Cricketers of the Year, 288 are best classified as batsmen, 163 as bowlers, 81 as all-rounders and 38 as wicketkeepers or wicketkeeper-batsmen.

Research: Robert Brooke

PART EIGHT

Administration and the Almanack

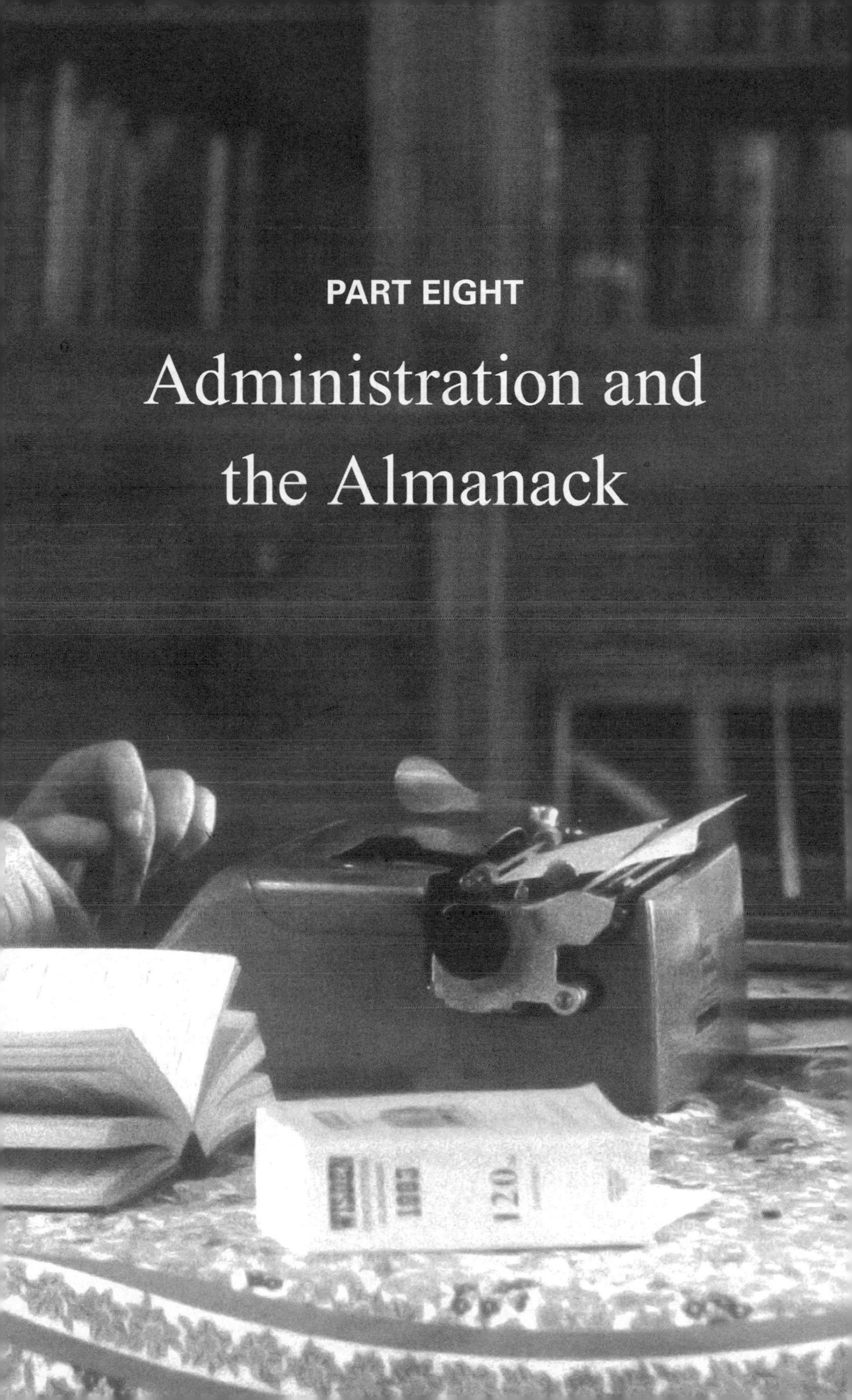

OFFICIAL BODIES

INTERNATIONAL CRICKET COUNCIL

The ICC are world cricket's governing body. They are responsible for managing the playing conditions and Code of Conduct for international fixtures, expanding the game and organising the major international tournaments, including the World Cup and World Twenty20. Their mission statement says the ICC "will lead by promoting and protecting the game, and its unique spirit" and "optimising their commercial rights and properties for the benefit of their members".

Ten national governing bodies are currently Full Members of the ICC; full membership qualifies a nation (or geographic area) to play official Test matches. A candidate for full membership must meet a number of playing and administrative criteria, after which elevation is decided by a vote among existing Full Members. There are also currently 36 Associate Members (non-Test-playing nations or geographic areas where cricket is firmly established and organised) and 60 Affiliate Members (other countries or geographic areas where the ICC recognise that cricket is played in accordance with the Laws).

The ICC were founded in 1909 as the Imperial Cricket Conference by three Foundation Members: England, Australia and South Africa. Other countries (or geographic areas) became Full Members and thus acquired Test status as follows: India, New Zealand and West Indies in 1926, Pakistan in 1952, Sri Lanka in 1981, Zimbabwe in 1992 and Bangladesh in 2000. South Africa ceased to be a member on leaving the Commonwealth in 1961, but were re-elected as a Full Member in 1991.

In 1965, "Imperial" was replaced by "International", and new rules permitted the election of countries from outside the Commonwealth for the first time. The first Associate Members (Fiji and USA), who had diluted voting rights, were admitted. However, Foundation Members retained a veto over all resolutions. In 1989, the Conference were again renamed without changing their initials. The new International Cricket Council adopted revised rules, aimed at producing an organisation which could make a larger number of binding decisions, rather than simply make recommendations to national governing bodies. In 1993, the Council, which had previously been administered by MCC, gained their own secretariat and chief executive, though their headquarters remained at Lord's. The category of Foundation Member was abolished.

In 1997, the Council became an incorporated body, with an executive board, and a president instead of a chairman. The ICC remained at Lord's, with a commercial base in Monaco, until August 2005, when after 96 years they moved to Dubai in the United Arab Emirates, which offered organisational and tax advantages.

Officers

President: A. R. Isaac. *Vice-President:* A. H. M. Mustafa Kamal. *Chief Executive:* D. J. Richardson.

Chairs of Committees – Chief Executives' Committee: D. J. Richardson. *Cricket:* A. Kumble. *Audit and Risk:* A. Zaidi. *Governance Review:* W. J. Edwards. *Human Resources and Remuneration:* A. R. Isaac. *Development:* D. J. Richardson. *Code of Conduct Commission:* M. J. Beloff, QC. *Women's Committee:* C. J. Connor. *Finance and Commercial Affairs:* C. G. Clarke. *Nominations Committee:* A. R. Isaac. *Medical Committee:* Dr P. R. Harcourt. *Anti-Corruption and Security Unit:* Sir Ronnie Flanagan.

Executive Board: The president, vice-president and chief executive sit on the board *ex officio*. They are joined by P. F. Chingoka (Zimbabwe), C. G. Clarke (England), U. Dharmadasa (Sri Lanka), W. J. Edwards (Australia), J. R. Hunte (West Indies), I. Khwaja (Singapore), C. J. D. Moller (New Zealand), Nazmul Hassan (Bangladesh), C. Nenzani (South Africa), C. K. Oliver (Scotland), N. Speight (Bermuda), N. Srinivasan (India), Zaka Ashraf (Pakistan).

Chief Executives' Committee: The chief executive, president and cricket committee chairman sit on the Chief Executives' Committee *ex officio*. They are joined by the chief executives of the ten Full Member boards and three Associate Member boards: D. G. Collier (England), J. A. Cribbin (Hong Kong), W. Deutrom (Ireland), F. Erasmus (Namibia), J. Faul (South Africa), S. Jagdale (India), M. Muirhead (West Indies), W. Mukondiwa (Zimbabwe), Nizam Uddin Chowdhury (Bangladesh), N. Ranatunga (Sri Lanka), Subhan Ahmad (Pakistan), J. A. Sutherland (Australia), D. J. White (New Zealand).

Cricket Committee: The chief executive and president sit on the Cricket Committee *ex officio*. They are joined by A. Kumble (chairman), C. J. Connor, S. J. Davis, D. T. Johnston, D. Kendix, G. Kirsten, R. S. Madugalle, T. B. A. May, K. C. Sangakkara, R. J. Shastri, J. P. Stephenson, A. J. Strauss, M. A. Taylor, D. J. White.

General Manager – Cricket: G. J. Allardice. *General Manager – Commercial:* D. C. Jamieson. *Chief Financial Officer:* Faisal Hasnain. *Head of Legal/Company Secretary:* I. Higgins. *Head of Media and Communications:* C. R. Gibson. *Head of Strategic Management and Support Services:* J. Long. *Anti-Corruption and Security Unit General Manager:* Y. P. Singh. *Global Development Manager:* T. L. Anderson.

Constitution

President: A. R. Isaac of New Zealand succeeded S. G. R. Pawar of India as president in June 2012.

Chief Executive: Appointed by the Council. D. J. Richardson succeeded H. Lorgat in June 2012.

Membership

Full Members (10): Australia, Bangladesh, England, India, New Zealand, Pakistan, South Africa, Sri Lanka, West Indies and Zimbabwe.

Associate Members* (36): Argentina (1974), Belgium (2005), Bermuda (1966), Botswana (2005), Canada (1968), Cayman Islands (2002), Denmark (1966), Fiji (1965), France (1998), Germany (1999), Gibraltar (1969), Guernsey (2005), Hong Kong (1969), Ireland (1993), Israel (1974), Italy (1995), Japan (2005), Jersey (2007), Kenya (1981), Kuwait (2005), Malaysia (1967), Namibia (1992), Nepal (1996), Netherlands (1966), Nigeria (2002), Papua New Guinea (1973), Scotland (1994), Singapore (1974), Suriname (2002), Tanzania (2001), Thailand (2005), Uganda (1998), United Arab Emirates (1990), USA (1965), Vanuatu (1995), Zambia (2003).

Affiliate Members* (60): Afghanistan (2001), Austria (1992), Bahamas (1987), Bahrain (2001), Belize (1997), Bhutan (2001), Brazil (2002), Brunei (1992), Bulgaria (2008), Cameroon (2007), Chile (2002), China (2004), Cook Islands (2000), Costa Rica (2002), Croatia (2001), Cuba (2002), Cyprus (1999), Czech Republic (2000), Estonia (2008), Falkland Islands (2007), Finland (2000), Gambia (2002), Ghana (2002), Greece (1995), Hungary (2012), Indonesia (2001), Iran (2003), Isle of Man (2004), Lesotho (2001), Luxembourg (1998), Malawi (2003), Maldives (2001), Mali (2005), Malta (1998), Mexico (2004), Morocco (1999), Mozambique (2003), Myanmar (2006), Norway (2000), Oman (2000), Panama (2002), Peru (2007), Philippines (2000), Portugal (1996), Qatar (1999), Russia (2012), Rwanda (2003), St Helena (2001), Samoa (2000), Saudi Arabia (2003), Seychelles (2010), Sierra Leone (2002), Slovenia (2005), South Korea (2001), Spain (1992), Swaziland (2007), Sweden (1997), Tonga (2000), Turkey (2008), Turks & Caicos Islands (2002).

* *Year of election shown in parentheses. Switzerland (1985) were removed in 2012 for failing to comply with the ICC's membership criteria.*

Full Members: The governing body for cricket (recognised by the ICC) of a country, or countries associated for cricket purposes, or a geographical area, from which representative teams are qualified to play official Test matches.

Associate Members: The governing body for cricket (recognised by the ICC) of a country, or countries associated for cricket purposes, or a geographical area, which does not qualify as a Full Member, but where cricket is firmly established and organised.

Affiliate Members: The governing body for cricket (recognised by the ICC) of a country, or countries associated for cricket purposes, or a geographical area (which is not part of one of those already constituted as a Full or Associate Member) where the ICC recognise that cricket is played in accordance with the Laws of Cricket. Five Affiliate Member representatives have the right to attend or vote at the ICC annual conference.

Addresses

ICC: Street 69, Dubai Sports City, Emirates Road, PO Box 500 070, Dubai, United Arab Emirates (+971 4382 8800; website www.icc-cricket.com; email enquiry@icc-cricket.com).

Australia: Cricket Australia, 60 Jolimont Street, Jolimont, Victoria 3002 (+61 3 9653 9999; website www.cricket.com.au; email penquiries@cricket.com.au).

Bangladesh: Bangladesh Cricket Board, Sher-e-Bangla National Cricket Stadium, Mirpur, Dhaka 1216 (+880 2 803 1001; website www.tigercricket.com; email office@bcb-cricket.com).

England: England and Wales Cricket Board (see below).

India: Board of Control for Cricket in India, Cricket Centre, 2nd Floor, Wankhede Stadium, D Road, Churchgate, Mumbai 400 020 (+91 22 2289 8800; website www.bcci.tv; email bcci@vsnl.com and cricketboard@gmail.com).

New Zealand: New Zealand Cricket, PO Box 180, Calder Drive, Lincoln University, Lincoln 7647 (+64 3 366 2964; website www.blackcaps.co.nz; email info@nzcricket.org.nz).

Pakistan: Pakistan Cricket Board, Gaddafi Stadium, Ferozpur Road, Lahore 54600 (+92 42 571 7231; website www.pcb.com.pk; email mail@pcb.com.pk).

South Africa: Cricket South Africa, Wanderers Club, PO Box 55009, 21 North Street, Illovo, Northlands 2116 (+27 11 880 2810; website www.cricket.co.za; email info@cricket.co.za).

Sri Lanka: Sri Lanka Cricket, 35 Maitland Place, Colombo 07000 (+94 112 681 601; website www.srilankacricket.lk; email info@srilankacricket.lk).

West Indies: West Indies Cricket Board, PO Box 616 W, Factory Road, St John's, Antigua (+1 268 481 2450; website www.windiescricket.com; email wicb@windiescricket.com).

Zimbabwe: Zimbabwe Cricket, PO Box 2739, 28 Maiden Drive, Highlands, Harare (+263 4 788 090; website www.zimcricket.org; email info@zimcricket.org).

Associate and Affiliate Members' addresses may be found on the ICC website www.icc-cricket.com

ENGLAND AND WALES CRICKET BOARD

The England and Wales Cricket Board (ECB) became responsible for the administration of all cricket – professional and recreational – in England and Wales in 1997. They took over the functions of the Cricket Council, the Test and County Cricket Board and the National Cricket Association, which had run the game in England and Wales since 1968. In 2005, a new constitution streamlined and modernised the governance of English cricket. The Management Board of 18 directors were replaced by a Board of Directors numbering 12, with three appointed by the first-class counties and two by the county boards. In 2010, this expanded to 14, with the appointment of the ECB's first two women directors.

Officers

Chairman: C. G. Clarke. *Deputy Chairman:* vacant at time of publication. *Chief Executive:* D. G. Collier.

Board of Directors: C. G. Clarke (*chairman*), D. G. Collier, M. V. Fleming, C. Graves, B. W. Havill, Lady Heyhoe-Flint, N. R. A. Hilliard, R. Jackson, I. N. Lovett, Lord Morris of Handsworth, J. B. Pickup, J. Stichbury, P. G. Wright.

Chairmen of Committees – Cricket: P. G. Wright. *Commercial:* C. G. Clarke. *Recreational Assembly:* J. B. Pickup. *Audit:* I. N. Lovett. *Remuneration:* N. R. A. Hilliard. *Discipline:* G. Elias QC.

Managing Director, England Cricket: H. Morris. *Managing Director, Cricket Partnerships:* M. W. Gatting. *Managing Director, First-Class Game:* G. Hollins. *Finance Director:* B. W. Havill. *Managing Director of Marketing and Global Events:* S. Elworthy. *Director of Public Policy and International Relations:* P. French. *Director of England Cricket Operations:* J. D. Carr. *Commercial Director:* J. Perera. *Head of Women's Cricket:* C. J. Connor. *Head of Information Technology:* D. Smith. *General Manager of Corporate Communications:* A. J. Walpole. *Head of Operations (First-class cricket):* A. Fordham. *Cricket Operations Manager (Non-first-class cricket):* P. Bedford. *National Selector:* G. Miller. *Other Selectors:* A. Flower, A. F. Giles and J. J. Whitaker.

ECB: D. G. Collier, Lord's Ground, London NW8 8QZ (020 7432 1200; website www.ecb.co.uk).

THE MARYLEBONE CRICKET CLUB

The Marylebone Cricket Club evolved out of the White Conduit Club in 1787, when Thomas Lord laid out his first ground in Dorset Square. Their members revised the Laws in 1788 and gradually took responsibility for cricket throughout the world. However, they relinquished control of the game in the UK in 1968, and the International Cricket Council finally established their own secretariat in 1993. MCC still own Lord's and remain the guardian of the Laws. They call themselves "a private club with a public function" and aim to support cricket everywhere, especially at grassroots level and in countries where the game is least developed.

Patron: HER MAJESTY THE QUEEN

Officers

President: 2012-13 – M. G. Griffith. *Club Chairman:* O. H. J. Stocken. *Treasurer:* R. S. Leigh. *Trustees:* Lady Heyhoe-Flint, D. L. Underwood, A. W. Wreford. *Hon. Life Vice-Presidents:* Lord Bramall, D. G. Clark, E. R. Dexter, G. H. G. Doggart, T. W. Graveney, Lord Griffiths, D. J. Insole, A. R. Lewis, M. E. L. Melluish, Sir Oliver Popplewell, D. R. W. Silk, M. O. C. Sturt, J. J. Warr, J. C. Woodcock.

Secretary and Chief Executive: D. M. Brewer. *Deputy Secretary:* C. Maynard. *Assistant Secretaries – Cricket and Estates:* J. P. Stephenson. *Legal:* H. A-M. Roper-Curzon. *Finance:* S. J. M. Gibb. *Marketing and Catering:* J. D. Robinson.

MCC Committee: J. R. T. Barclay, R. Q. Cake, S. Dyson, D. J. C. Faber, A. R. C. Fraser, M. W. Gatting, W. R. Griffiths, C. M. Gupte, H. J. H. Loudon, T. J. G. O'Gorman, J. A. F. Vallance, K. M. Williams. The president, club chairman, treasurer and committee chairmen are on the committee *ex officio*.

Chairmen of Committees – Arts and Library: A. I. Lack. *Cricket:* M. G. Griffith. *Estates:* C. J. Maber. *Finance:* R. S. Leigh. *Membership and General Purposes:* N. M. Peters. *World Cricket:* J. M. Brearley.

MCC: The Secretary and Chief Executive, Lord's Ground, London NW8 8QN (020 7616 8500; email reception@mcc.org.uk; website www.lords.org/mcc. Tickets 020 7432 1000; email ticketing@mcc.org.uk).

PROFESSIONAL CRICKETERS' ASSOCIATION

The Professional Cricketers' Association were formed in 1967 (as the Cricketers' Association) to be the collective voice of first-class professional players, and enhance and protect their interests. During the 1970s, they succeeded in establishing pension schemes and a minimum wage. In recent years their strong commercial operations and greater funding from the ECB have increased their services to current and past players, including education, legal, financial and benevolent help. In 2011, these services were extended to England's women cricketers for the first time.

President: B. C. Broad. *Chairman:* M. A. Wallace. *President – Benevolent Fund:* D. A. Graveney. *Non-Executive Group Chairman:* A. W. Wreford. *Non-Executive Director:* M. Wheeler. *Chief Executive:* A. J. Porter. *Assistant Chief Executive:* J. D. Ratcliffe. *Legal Director:* I. T. Smith. *Commercial Director:* J. M. Grave. *Financial Director:* P. Garrett. *Commercial Manager:* P. J. Prichard. *Events and Fundraising Manager:* L. A. Michael. *Team England Commercial Manager:* E. M. Barnes. *Team England Partnership Executive:* E. Caldwell. *Team England Account Executive:* L. Cooke. *Member Services Executive:* A. Prosser. *Player Services Liaison:* A. Prosser. *National Personal Development Manager:* I. J. Thomas.

PCA: *London Office* – The Laker Stand, The Oval, Kennington, London SE11 5SS (020 7449 4225; email events@thepca.co.uk; website www.thepca.co.uk). *Birmingham Office* – Box 109, R. E. S. Wyatt Stand, Warwickshire CCC, Edgbaston, Birmingham B5 7QU.

CRIME AND PUNISHMENT

ICC Code of Conduct – Breaches and Penalties in 2011-12 to 2012-13

D. P. M. D. Jayawardene Sri Lanka v Australia, one-day international at Adelaide.
Dissent when umpire no-balled a waist-high full toss. Fined 10% of match fee by B. C. Broad.

T. M. Dilshan Sri Lanka v England, Second Test at Colombo (PSS).
Excessive appealing/celebrating before dismissal made. Fined 10% of match fee by J. Srinath.

O. D. Gibson (coach) West Indies v Australia, Second Test at Port-of-Spain.
Challenged efficacy and implementation of DRS. Fined 20% of match fee by J. J. Crowe.

D. Ramdin West Indies v England, Third Test at Birmingham.
Showing note to public in premeditated fashion. Fined 20% of match fee by R. S. Mahanama.

D. J. Bravo West Indies v England, second one-day international at The Oval.
Criticised umpires after lbw decision against C. H. Gayle. Fined 20% of match fee by J. J. Crowe.

B. B. McCullum New Zealand v India, First Test at Hyderabad.
Dissent at umpire's decision when he was given out lbw. Reprimanded by B. C. Broad.

Umar Akmal Pakistan v Sri Lanka, World Twenty20 semi-final at Colombo (RPS).
Changed batting gloves against orders of on-field umpires. Fined 50% of match fee by J. J. Crowe.

I. Sharma India v Pakistan, first Twenty20 international at Bangalore.
Shouted at Kamran Akmal after beating him outside off. Fined 15% of match fee by R. S. Mahanama.

Kamran Akmal Pakistan v India, first Twenty20 international at Bangalore.
Joined in shouting match with I. Sharma. Fined 5% of match fee by R. S. Mahanama.

D. A. Warner Australia v Sri Lanka, fourth one-day international at Sydney.
Dissent at umpire's decision when given out. Reprimanded by J. Srinath.

Under ICC regulations on minor over-rate offences, players are fined 10% of their match fee for every over their side fails to bowl in the allotted time, with the captain fined double that amount. For major over-rate offences, players are fined 10% for each of the first two overs short and 20% for each additional over not bowled on time, with the captain given an immediate suspension. There were ten over-rate offences in this period:

M. S. Dhoni/India v Australia, ODI at Brisbane, fined 40%/20% of match fee by A. J. Pycroft.
As this was Dhoni's second offence in an ODI in 12 months, he was also suspended for one match.

S. R. Watson/Australia v Sri Lanka, ODI at Adelaide, fined 20%/10% of match fee by B. C. Broad.

Misbah-ul-Haq/Pakistan v Bang., ODI at Mirpur, fined 20%/10% of match fee by D. C. Boon.

D. J. G. Sammy/W. Indies v Eng., Test at Lord's, fined 80%/40% of match fee by R. S. Mahanama.

Misbah-ul-Haq/Pakistan v Sri Lanka, ODI at Colombo (RPS), team fined 40% by B. C. Broad.
Misbah was given two suspension points, which caused him to miss the First Test.

M. S. Dhoni/India v Sri Lanka, ODI at Hambantota, fined 20%/10% of match fee by B. C. Broad.

A. D. Mathews/Sri Lanka v India, ODI at Pallekele, fined 20%/10% of match fee by B. C. Broad.

S. C. J. Broad/England v NZ, World T20 at Pallekele, fined 20%/10% of match fee by J. Srinath.

D. P. M. D. Jayawardene/SL v WI, WT20 at Pallekele, fined 20%/10% of match fee by J. Srinath.

A. B. de Villiers/South Africa v New Zealand, ODI at Paarl, team fined 100% by D. C. Boon.
De Villiers was given two suspension points, which caused him to miss the next two matches.

Details of these and 36 further breaches which took place in Associate Member or Under-19 World Cup matches may be found on the ICC website (www.icc-cricket.com).

INTERNATIONAL UMPIRES' PANELS

In 1993, the International Cricket Council formed an international umpires' panel, containing at least two officials from each Full Member. A third-country umpire from this panel stood with a "home" umpire, not necessarily from the panel, in every Test from February 1994 onwards. In March 2002, an elite panel of umpires was appointed; two elite umpires – both independent – were to stand in all Tests from April 2002, and at least one in every one-day international, where one home umpire was allowed. A supporting panel of international umpires was created to provide cover at peak times in the Test schedule, and to provide a second umpire in one-day internationals. The ICC also appointed specialist third umpires to give rulings from TV replays. The panels are sponsored by Emirates Airlines.

At the end of 2012, the following umpires were on the elite panel: Aleem Dar (Pakistan), Asad Rauf (Pakistan), B. F. Bowden (New Zealand), S. J. Davis (Australia), H. D. P. K. Dharmasena (Sri Lanka), M. Erasmus (South Africa), I. J. Gould (England), A. L. Hill (New Zealand), R. A. Kettleborough (England), N. J. Llong (England), B. N. J. Oxenford (Australia) and R. J. Tucker (Australia). Llong and Oxenford had replaced B. R. Doctrove (West Indies) and S. J. A. Taufel (Australia) during the year.

The international panel consisted of Ahsan Raza (Pakistan), S. Asnani (India), R. J. Bailey (England), G. A. V. Baxter (New Zealand), O. Chirombe (Zimbabwe), J. D. Cloete (South Africa), Enamul Haque (Bangladesh), S. D. Fry (Australia), C. B. Gaffaney (New Zealand), S. George (South Africa), R. K. Illingworth (England), V. A. Kulkarni (India), R. E. J. Martinesz (Sri Lanka), Nadir Shah (Bangladesh), P. J. Nero (West Indies), P. R. Reiffel (Australia), R. B. Tiffin (Zimbabwe), T. H. Wijewardene (Sri Lanka), J. S. Wilson (West Indies) and Zameer Haider (Pakistan).

The specialist third umpires were Anisur Rahman (Bangladesh), G. O. Brathwaite (West Indies), N. Duguid (West Indies), M. A. Gough (England), A. T. Holdstock (South Africa), T. J. Matibiri (Zimbabwe), R. S. A. Palliyaguru (Sri Lanka), S. Ravi (India), R. T. Robinson (England), C. Shamshuddin (India), Sharfuddoula (Bangladesh), Shozab Raza (Pakistan), D. J. Walker (New Zealand) and J. D. Ward (Australia).

There is also an Associate and Affiliate international panel, consisting of N. G. Bagh (Denmark), S. N. Bandekar (USA), M. Hawthorne (Ireland), A. W. Louw (Namibia), D. Odhiambo (Kenya), B. B. Pradhan (Nepal), S. S. Prasad (Singapore), I. N. Ramage (Scotland), Shahul Hameed (Indonesia), R. P. Smith (Ireland) and C. Young (Cayman Islands).

ICC REFEREES' PANEL

In 1991, the International Cricket Council formed a panel of referees to enforce their Code of Conduct for Tests and one-day internationals, to impose penalties for slow over-rates, breaches of the Code and other ICC regulations, and to support the umpires in upholding the conduct of the game. In March 2002, the ICC launched an elite panel of referees, on full-time contracts, to act as their independent representatives in all international cricket. The panel is sponsored by Emirates Airlines.

At the end of 2012, the panel consisted of D. C. Boon (Australia), B. C. Broad (England), J. J. Crowe (New Zealand), R. S. Madugalle (Sri Lanka), R. S. Mahanama (Sri Lanka), A. J. Pycroft (Zimbabwe) and J. Srinath (India).

ENGLISH UMPIRES FOR 2013

First-Class: R. J. Bailey, N. L. Bainton, M. R. Benson, M. J. D. Bodenham, N. G. B. Cook, N. G. Cowley, J. H. Evans, S. C. Gale, S. A. Garratt, M. A. Gough, I. J. Gould, P. J. Hartley, R. K. Illingworth, T. E. Jesty, R. A. Kettleborough, N. J. Llong, J. W. Lloyds, N. A. Mallender, D. J. Millns, S. J. O'Shaughnessy, R. T. Robinson, M. J. Saggers, G. Sharp, P. Willey. *Reserves:* P. K. Baldwin, M. Burns, I. Dawood, B. J. Debenham, M. A. Eggleston, R. Evans, G. D. Lloyd, P. R. Pollard, B. V. Taylor, A. G. Wharf.

Minor Counties: J. Attridge, S. F. Bishopp, T. F. Boston, R. Burn, G. I. Callaway, K. T. Coburn, T. F. Cox, A. Davies, A. D'Leny, M. P. Dobbs, J. Dye, R. G. Eagleton, V. Fallows, K. Fergusson, A. H. Forward, P. R. Gardner, J. C. S. Glynn, D. J. Gower, M. D. Gumbley, R. C. Hampshire, A. Harris, A. Hicks, C. D. Jones, S. Lavis, S. J. Malone, S. Massingham, P. W. Matten, R. Medland, R. J. Newham, P. D. Nicholls, G. Parker, D. Price, C. T. Puckett, M. Qureshi, I. Royle, A. Shaikh, M. I. Southerton, D. M. Warburton, I. Warne, M. D. Watton, C. M. Watts, N. Wheatley, A. J. Wheeler, C. M. B. Williams.

THE DUCKWORTH/LEWIS METHOD

In 1997, the ECB's one-day competitions adopted a new method to revise targets in interrupted games, devised by Frank Duckworth of the Royal Statistical Society and Tony Lewis of the University of the West of England. The method was gradually taken up by other countries and, in 1999, the ICC decided to incorporate it into the standard playing conditions for one-day internationals.

The system aims to preserve any advantage that one team has established before the interruption. It uses the idea that teams have two resources from which they make runs – an allocated number of overs, and ten wickets. It also takes into account when the interruption occurs, because of the different scoring-rates typical of different stages of an innings. Traditional run-rate calculations relied only on the overs available, and ignored wickets lost.

It uses one table with 50 rows, covering matches of up to 50 overs, and ten columns, from nought to nine wickets down. Each figure in the table gives the percentage of the total runs in an innings that would, on average, be scored with a certain number of overs left and wickets lost. If a match is shortened before it begins, for instance to 33 overs a side, the figure for 33 overs and ten wickets remaining would be the starting point.

If overs are lost, the table is used to calculate the percentage of runs the team would be expected to score in those missing overs. This is obtained by reading the figure for the number of overs left and wickets down when play stops and subtracting the figure for the number of overs left when it resumes. If the delay occurs between innings, and the second team's allocation of overs is reduced, then their target is obtained by calculating the appropriate percentage for the reduced number of overs with all ten wickets standing. For instance, if the second team's innings halves from 50 overs to 25, the table shows that they still have 66.5% of their resources left, so have to beat two-thirds of the first team's total, rather than half. If the first innings is complete and the second innings interrupted or prematurely terminated, the score to beat is reduced by the percentage of the innings lost.

The version known as the "Professional Edition" was introduced into one-day internationals from 2003, and subsequently into most national one-day competitions. Based on a more advanced mathematical formula (it is entirely computerised), in effect it adjusts the tables to make allowance for the different scoring-rates that emerge in matches with above-average first-innings scores. Extensive analysis of Twenty20 matches has shown that the same formula can be used for Twenty20 cricket, starting with the row for 20 overs remaining. The former version, now known as the "Standard Edition", is used where computers are not available and at lower levels of the game.

The system also covers interruptions to the first innings, multiple interruptions and innings terminated by rain. The tables were revised slightly in 2009 and 2011, taking account of rising scoring-rates; the average total in a 50-over international is now taken to be 245.

In the one-day international between England and India at Lord's on September 11, 2011, England's run-chase was ended by rain after 48.5 overs, when they were 270 for eight, having lost wickets to the last two deliveries. The computer-produced Duckworth/Lewis tables showed that, with seven balls left and two wickets standing, England had used 96.43% of their run-scoring resources, and 3.57% remained unused. Multiplying India's 50-over total, 280, by 96.43% produced a figure of 270.004. This was rounded to 270 to give the par score (the runs needed to tie), and the score to win became par plus one – 271. Had England not lost wickets to the last two balls bowled, they would have used only 96.07% of their run-scoring resources, par would have been 269 and they would have won by one run. As they had equalled par exactly, the match was tied.

POWERPLAYS

In the first ten "powerplay" overs of an uninterrupted one-day international innings (first six in a Twenty20), only two fieldsmen may be positioned outside the area marked by two semi-circles of 30-yard (27.43 metres) radius behind each set of stumps, joined by straight lines parallel to the pitch. In one-day internationals, there must also be two "close" (and stationary) fielders in this initial period.

After the first mandatory ten-over powerplay in an uninterrupted one-day international, a further block of five overs must be claimed by the batsmen at the wicket, to be completed no later than the 40th over. During these, a maximum of three players may be stationed outside the 30-yard area. If the batting side do not take the powerplay, the umpires will enforce it at the latest available point (i.e. the start of the 36th over). At all other times no more than four fieldsmen (five in Twenty20 internationals) are permitted outside the 30-yard area. In matches affected by the weather, the number of overs in each powerplay is reduced in proportion to the overall reduction of overs, and the restriction on when batting powerplays may be taken does not apply.

MEETINGS AND DECISIONS, 2012

MORGAN REVIEW

The ECB board received David Morgan's report on the domestic game on January 12. A summary of the review and its recommendations appeared in *Wisden 2012*, page 1222.

ECB BROADCASTING DEALS

On January 26, the ECB agreed a new six-year deal with BBC Sport for the radio rights to broadcast live and exclusive ball-by-ball commentary on England's home series from 2014 to 2019 via *Test Match Special*.

On January 31, the ECB announced a further four-year agreement with Sky Sports to show live domestic and international cricket in England and Wales from 2014 to 2017, with an option to extend for a further two years. This would include all England's home games, selected England Lions and England Women's fixtures, plus 60 days of domestic cricket every season. On the same day, the ECB agreed another four-year deal with Channel 5 to screen early-evening highlights of international cricket from 2014 to 2017.

On June 4, the ECB were to renew their contract with ESPN STAR Sports for exclusive multi-platform rights to broadcast the ECB's domestic and home international programme across ESS's territories in Asia, the Middle East and North Africa for seven years from 2013 to 2019.

ICC EXECUTIVE BOARD

The ICC Executive Board met in Dubai on January 31–February 1 and received the Woolf Review (see below). It was agreed that members would discuss it in more detail in April, but it was immediately decided to put one recommendation to June's annual conference, that from 2014 the current role of ICC president should be split between a chairman, to lead the board, and a president, to serve for a single year in an ambassadorial role. Meanwhile an international executive recruitment firm was appointed to find a new chief executive to replace Haroon Lorgat in June.

To promote Test cricket, the prize money shared among the top four in the rankings over the next three years was increased to $US3.8m. The prize for the top team on April 1 each year would rise from $175,000 to $450,000 in 2013, and $500,000 in 2015.

The board approved a $12m Targeted Assistance and Performance Programme to develop more competitive teams among ICC members, with grants for applicants presenting a proper strategy and business plan, and able to match the money.

The Anti-Corruption and Security Unit chairman, Sir Ronnie Flanagan, presented an independent report containing 27 recommendations; seven were judged unworkable, seven consistent with current practice, and the remaining 13 accepted.

The board condemned the Guyanese government's replacement of the Guyana Cricket Board with an interim management committee, and said the only legitimate cricketing authority was that recognised by the West Indies board.

Following the Lahore attack in March 2009 and the introduction of a security task force to review arrangements for international cricket, it was agreed that the ICC and members should adopt a safety and security code. The board also received presentations from Interpol and on the ICC Global Cricket Academy.

WOOLF REVIEW

On February 1, Lord Woolf and PricewaterhouseCoopers presented the conclusions of their independent governance review to the ICC Executive Board. They had been asked to conduct the review in October 2011, and interviewed over 60 individuals from 38 countries, including members of the board, past and present players, officials and journalists. The review contained 65 recommendations, covering five areas:

1. Role of the ICC The ICC's role as leader of the international game should be reinforced; they should own all its elements directly or through appropriate delegation.

2. The ICC Board An independent paid chairman should lead the board, and the president, appointed by rotation from member boards, should become a figurehead with an ambassadorial role.

Independent paid directors (initially three) should augment existing skills, alongside two directors with experience of playing, officiating or commentating on the international men's and women's game, to ensure a greater diversity of views. Each board member's first duty should be to the ICC, and ICC directors should relinquish any executive or leadership roles within their member boards. Board resolutions should be binding on member boards.

3. Ethics Directors should act in the interests of the ICC as a whole, though their secondary duty would be to express the interests of individual stakeholders. They should be excluded from decision-making when they had a potential conflict of interest. Financial assistance between members should be disclosed. Government interference is inappropriate and unacceptable.

A Code of Ethics should apply to everyone involved in the ICC, including member boards, and parties in a significant commercial relationship. An ICC ethics officer should lead a properly resourced ethics function, establish a hotline and be party to member board investigations, while a governance and ethics committee should oversee the ethics officer, the ACSU, the ethics disciplinary committee and the Code of Conduct commission.

4. Membership, Board Structure and Committees There should be only two membership categories: Full and Associate. Full Members should include Test countries and other high-performers, and have the right to representation on the ICC Board. Global competitions should be open to all, with clear qualification routes and limited automatic rights to take part, and Associates should have more chances to compete against Full Members outside ICC events.

The board should be reduced to an optimal size, in which the independent directors would not be the minority, and use one board member, one vote. The strategically important cricket committee should report directly to the board. The Chief Executives' Committee should act as an advisory forum for the chief executive, and the development, women's and medical committee come under the chief executive's auspices. The audit committee should be a committee of the ICC Board, not the IDI (ICC Development International) board, which should take over the activities of the financial and commercial affairs committee.

The ICC Board would be held accountable to all members through the Full Council once a year. The Full Council's role should include ratifying the appointment of the chairman, president and independent board members (but not the chief executive) and changes to membership status.

5. Funding The subscription model should be abolished, and the ICC become self-funding and financially independent. Funds should be distributed to members on the basis of needs, not automatic entitlement, with an appropriate allocation of revenue between distribution to members, funding global development, and targeted assistance to members. All members should provide full financial information before receiving any distributions.

MCC COMMITTEE

The MCC committee met on February 8 and reaffirmed the November decision to focus on developing Lord's Ground on the club's freehold land only, and with MCC's own resources. On February 2, the property developers Almacantar had made a revised offer to proceed with residential development of 275,000 square feet on the club's leasehold land at the Nursery End, an offer amounting to £100m in cash and a contribution of £10m towards supporting young cricketers.

ECB CHAIRMAN

On February 29, Giles Clarke was nominated by the 18 first-class counties and MCC to continue as ECB chairman up to the 2015 AGM. No other nominations were received and the candidacy was put forward to the ECB's 41 full members (the chairmen of the 18 first-class counties, the 21 non-first-class county boards, the Minor Counties Cricket Association and MCC). Clarke's election was confirmed on March 19.

ICC CHIEF EXECUTIVES' COMMITTEE

The Chief Executives' Committee met in Dubai on March 5–6 and received a presentation on the Woolf Review.

Concerning a proposed Bangladesh tour of Pakistan, it was for participating countries to decide whether a particular tour should go ahead but, if the ICC felt it was unsafe to appoint match officials, a special dispensation allowing non-neutral officials could be sought.

The committee agreed to recommend allowing a maximum of 15 Twenty20 internationals for each Full Member, rather than the current 12, in years in which the World Twenty20 tournament was played, to allow full preparation; to increase the 2014 World Twenty20 in Bangladesh to 16 men's teams; to encourage Associate and Affiliate Members to submit propositions to host future World Twenty20 events in a developing country or region; and to keep the World Twenty20 as a joint event for men and women.

A framework of revised regulations on the standards required from international venues was approved. The committee confirmed their confidence in the Test and one-day ranking systems as a means to determine qualification for ICC events, and for promotion and relegation purposes in due course, and recommended a new Future Tours Programme and a revised Anti-Racism Policy to the ICC Board. They were pleased to note an improvement in pitches, leading to a better battle between bat and ball: only 10% of 2011 Tests were drawn, down from 38% in 2010. A workshop for groundsmen would be held in April 2012. They also acknowledged an improvement in over-rates and a more positive interpretation of bad-light regulations by umpires. A report was received on a project to develop technology to monitor bowling actions in match conditions, using inertial sensors.

The committee agreed to investigate a programme for Associates, Affiliates and Full Member A-teams, and to work towards establishing a framework and criteria for different types of disability cricket. They decided to explore an invitation to the 2018 Commonwealth Games in Australia, and to evaluate the pros and cons of taking part in the Olympics.

ECB BOARD

A meeting of the ECB board on March 8 approved the principles of the Morgan Review, including a variety of recommendations and proposals, such as basing the domestic schedule around regular dates (an "appointment to view"). The chairman, Giles Clarke, said many of its recommendations would be implemented immediately, while consumer research and financial analysis of the detailed strategy would be carried out during the summer. Chief executive David Collier and the managing director of the professional game, Gordon Hollins, were asked to produce a financial plan to ensure the long-term sustainability of cricket and its stakeholders from grassroots to Test matches.

ECB SPONSORSHIP DEAL

On March 21, the ECB announced that LV= had agreed to renew their title sponsorship of the County Championship (which began in 2002, under the name Frizzell) for a further four years to 2015.

ENGLAND PERFORMANCE SQUAD

On April 7, the ECB announced a 26-man England Performance Squad for the summer. The England coach would have the right to withdraw any of these players from domestic cricket. The squad consisted of 13 players already on 12-month ECB contracts running from October 2011: England captain Andrew Strauss, James Anderson, Ian Bell, Tim Bresnan, Stuart Broad, Alastair Cook, Steven Finn, Eoin Morgan, Kevin Pietersen, Matt Prior, Graeme Swann, Chris Tremlett and Jonathan Trott; four on increment contracts (Ravi Bopara, Jade Dernbach, Craig Kieswetter and Samit Patel); and nine others (Jonny Bairstow, Danny Briggs, Jos Buttler, Steven Davies, Stuart Meaker, Graham Onions, Monty Panesar, Ben Stokes and James Tredwell). On May 19, James Taylor was added to the squad.

ICC EXECUTIVE BOARD

The ICC Executive Board met in Dubai on April 15, and agreed amendments to the constitution to split the role of the ICC president. The new chairman would be appointed by the board for a maximum of three two-year terms, while the ceremonial role of president would be rotated between member countries each year. Neither would be a voting member of the board.

The board confirmed the Chief Executives' recommendations on Twenty20 internationals (see above).

The board also confirmed that the United Arab Emirates would host a World Twenty20 qualifying tournament in October 2013, and New Zealand a World Cup qualifying event in 2014. They agreed a schedule of events – World Twenty20s, World Cups, World Test Championships, Women's and Under-19 World Cups, and qualifying tournaments – from 2016 to 2023, including the numbers of teams and games (only ten teams were scheduled to play in the 2019 and 2023 World Cups). Women's teams must play at least three one-day or three Twenty20 internationals in a calendar year (excluding ICC-funded events) to retain their one-day and Twenty20 international status.

The board adopted the Bertrand de Speville Report's recommendations on the Anti-Corruption and Security Unit.

MCC ANNUAL GENERAL MEETING

The 225th AGM of the Marylebone Cricket Club was held at Lord's on May 2, with the president, Phillip Hodson, in the chair. He announced that his successor, from October, would be Mike Griffith, the former Sussex captain and Cambridge Blue, whose father, Billy Griffith, was MCC president in 1979-80. In the light of strong feelings on the issue, it was decided not to put to members a resolution preventing residential developments on the club's leasehold land at the Nursery End. The president said that the Ground Working Party would have a free hand to develop a holistic masterplan which would be presented to members later.

Resolutions were passed increasing members' entrance fees and annual subscriptions and amending various rules of the club. Membership of the club on December 31, 2011, totalled 23,634, made up of 17,966 full members, 5,142 associate members, 327 honorary members, 113 senior members and 86 out-match members. There were 10,376 candidates awaiting election to full membership; in 2011, 458 vacancies arose.

ICC CHIEF EXECUTIVE

On May 10, the ICC Executive Board recommended that David Richardson, the former South African Test wicketkeeper and ICC's general manager for cricket since 2002, should succeed Haroon Lorgat as chief executive. The nominations committee put his name forward after interviews with four candidates in Mumbai. The appointment was to be ratified at the annual conference in June.

ICC CRICKET COMMITTEE

The ICC cricket committee held their annual meeting at Lord's on May 30–31. In a discussion of Twenty20 strategy, they said the World Twenty20 tournament should be held every two years and there should not be an Under-19 version. The committee agreed that international cricket was the lifeblood of the world game, and the ICC and member boards must maintain and enhance its attraction compared to other forms.

On one-day internationals, it was noted that the rule compelling teams to take batting and bowling powerplays between the 16th and 40th overs had made little impact. The committee recommended dropping the bowling powerplay, and leaving a batting powerplay to be completed by the 40th over. Outside the powerplay overs, only four (rather than five) fielders would be allowed outside the 30-yard circle. The number of permitted short-pitched deliveries should increase from one to two per over.

Test over-rates were at their highest in five years and the average frequency of no-balls had dropped sharply. There was a reduction in high-scoring draws, and spinners were bowling more often. In the Test rankings, the top five teams were separated by only eight points, but the competitiveness of other countries needed to be improved through the Targeted Assistance Performance Programme and the Future Tours Programme. To raise over-rates further, it was agreed that no drinks should be brought on outside official drinks breaks, including the referral of an umpire's decision; following a referral, all players must be ready to resume as soon as a decision was made; and any delays caused by the batting side should be deducted from the calculation of their own over-rate.

The committee reiterated that, subject to members' ability to finance it, the Decision Review System should be implemented universally in Test and one-day international cricket. Decision-making where the DRS was used was reported to have improved by 4.27% in Tests and 5.01% in one-day internationals, with the overall accuracy rated at 98.26%. Dr Edward Rosten's analysis of ball-tracking in the recent South Africa v Australia series was in complete agreement with the 14 examined sequences. Improved Hot Spot cameras for the England v West Indies series had provided clearer and more accurate results.

The committee considered trials with different coloured balls in day/night conditions. Research suggested day/night cricket might suit certain markets, particularly India, New Zealand and South Africa. Domestic trials should continue, and any requests from countries in a bilateral series to trial day/night Test cricket should be accommodated.

The committee heard about a prototype sensor that could be worn during matches to indicate whether bowlers with suspect actions were straightening their elbows in the delivery swing. This would undergo validation testing at the Under-19 World Cup in August.

A proposal by V. Jayadevan for his calculation of target scores (VJD) to be adopted in place of the Duckworth/Lewis method was considered, but the committee found no evidence of significant flaws in D/L, nor did they believe that VJD offered improvements.

There were reports from the medical committee on heat and extreme weather, helmet research and age determination.

The committee recommended banning suspended players from entering the field of play, and a stricter approach on substitute fielders. They noted that there were still instances of non-strikers leaving their crease before the bowler released the ball and reiterated that this was unfair; bowlers were entitled to run out batsmen who continued to transgress.

ECB ANTI-CORRUPTION TEAM

On May 31, the ECB created a seven-strong team of anti-corruption officials to monitor the Friends Life t20 and CB40 competitions. The team would be overseen by dedicated anti-corruption official Chris Watts and the move followed the establishment in 2011 of the ACCESS (Anti-Corruption, Education and Security) Unit, an advisory body seeking to protect cricket's integrity and enforce its anti-corruption code.

ICC ANNUAL MEETINGS

The ICC annual conference and associated meetings took place in Kuala Lumpur between June 24 and July 1.

The Chief Executives' Committee met on June 24–25. They recommended the universal application of the Decision Review System in all Tests and one-day internationals, subject to finance. Hot Spot cameras should be included in the minimum requirements alongside ball-tracking technology, and there should be a minor amendment to lbw protocols: the margin of uncertainty regarding the point of impact with the batsman should be the same as that for the point of impact with the stumps.

Recommended changes on powerplay regulations and short-pitched balls were accepted. The committee supported the introduction of day/night Test cricket, and noted that extra context would be granted to Test cricket by the planned introduction of a World Test Championship in 2017, and to one-day internationals through the full qualification process for the World Cup from 2015.

Pakistan requested the flexibility to stage a six-match Twenty20 series against Australia in the United Arab Emirates in August, requiring a special dispensation from the usual maximum of three Twenty20s. Because of the extreme daytime heat expected, no objections were raised should the PCB make that switch.

The ICC Board met on June 26–27, and approved the recommended changes on powerplays and short-pitched balls. There was no objection to the introduction of day/night Test cricket if agreed by both teams.

While approving recommendations on Hot Spot cameras in the DRS, and the amendment of lbw protocols, the board rejected the universal application of the DRS and agreed that it would still be up to the two nations in a series to decide whether to use it.

Following the recent decisions of an ECB disciplinary panel in anti-corruption proceedings against Danish Kaneria and Mervyn Westfield, the board unanimously agreed that all members should recognise the sanctions against those players and enforce them within their own jurisdictions. The Bangladesh Cricket Board and Sri Lanka Cricket were told to implement domestic anti-corruption codes by August 15, when the Sri Lanka Premier League was due to begin. Sir Ronnie Flanagan, the Anti-Corruption and Security Unit Chairman, repeated the ACSU's desire for governments to introduce criminal legislation against deliberately underperforming for personal gain, and noted progress in this area in Australia.

The debate on the promotion of international cricket within a changed landscape with a growing number of professional Twenty20 leagues continued.

The board approved grants to Ireland and Scotland from the Targeted Assistance and Performance Programme, which aimed to develop more competitive teams; each would receive $1.5m over three years.

At the ICC annual conference on June 28, Alan Isaac, the former chairman of New Zealand Cricket, was inaugurated as the ICC's eighth president, succeeding Sharad Pawar. David Richardson was confirmed as chief executive. The conference agreed to create the post of ICC chairman, remove the role of vice-president, and make the president a ceremonial figurehead, the changes taking effect from 2014.

Russia and Hungary were confirmed as new Affiliate Members but Switzerland were removed; they had been suspended in 2011 for failing to comply with the ICC's membership criteria and remained unable to do so. ICC membership stood at 106.

ECB SPONSORSHIP ENDS

On August 28, the ECB announced that Friends Life, the sponsors of domestic Twenty20 cricket, would not be renewing their contract beyond 2013. The company had sponsored the competition for the past three years, and the 50-over Friends Provident Trophy for three years before that. Both parties were open to the possibility of a new sponsor taking over for the 2013 season.

ENGLAND TEST CAPTAIN

On August 29, England's Test captain, Andrew Strauss, announced his immediate retirement from professional cricket, after playing 100 Tests and leading England in 50, of which 24 were won. He was succeeded by Alastair Cook, who continued to lead the one-day side.

ENGLAND CENTRAL CONTRACTS

On September 13, the ECB awarded ten central contracts running for 12 months from October 1, 2012, three fewer than the previous year. They went to James Anderson, Ian Bell, Tim Bresnan, Stuart Broad, Alastair Cook, Steven Finn, Eoin Morgan, Matt Prior, Graeme Swann and Jonathan Trott. Compared with September 2012, Kevin Pietersen, Andrew Strauss and Chris Tremlett had been dropped from the list. Incremental contracts were awarded to Jonny Bairstow, Ravi Bopara, Craig Kieswetter and Graham Onions; Bairstow and Onions replaced Jade Dernbach. Players on incremental contracts receive a one-off ECB payment on top of their county salary, whereas centrally contracted players are paid by the ECB rather than their county. Incremental contracts can be earned by amassing 20 appearance points between October and September (five for a Test, two for a Twenty20 or one-day international); Bairstow had previously been awarded a contract on this basis in May, Samit Patel was given one in February and another in December, and Jos Buttler won one later in September. Pietersen signed a full contract in January 2013, having signed a short-term contract in October.

On September 18, the ECB named 17 players for the England Performance Programme, a two-week training programme at the National Cricket Performance Centre in Loughborough followed by training camps and five matches in India. They were Azeem Rafiq, Gary Ballance, Scott Borthwick, Danny Briggs, Jos Buttler, Varun Chopra, Matt Coles, Jade Dernbach, Ben Foakes, James Harris, Simon Kerrigan, Craig Kieswetter, Stuart Meaker, Toby Roland-Jones, Ben Stokes, James Taylor and Chris Wright.

ICC EXECUTIVE BOARD

The ICC Executive Board met in Colombo on October 9–11, and accepted the joint nomination of the Pakistan Cricket Board and Bangladesh Cricket Board of A. H. M. Mustafa Kamal of Bangladesh as ICC vice-president until 2014 and subsequently as president in 2014-15. The board agreed unanimously to appoint former Indian captain Anil Kumble to succeed Clive Lloyd as chairman of the cricket committee.

The board awarded Netherlands $1.5m, Zimbabwe $1.5m and West Indies $3m under the Targeted Assistance and Performance Programme, all over three years. Canada were asked to resubmit their application in 2013.

All ten Full Members had now implemented the domestic anti-corruption and anti-doping codes as instructed.

ECB BOARD

On October 18, the ECB Board agreed a format for the domestic seasons from 2014 to 2017, after hearing the results of market research conducted with more than 25,000 respondents.

The board noted the desire of counties and spectators for regular scheduling of county cricket (known as "appointment to view"), as recommended by the Morgan Review. In particular there was a demand for Twenty20 cricket on regular dates over a longer period, rather than condensed into a few weeks. Consistent with feedback from the players, there was a strong desire to retain the two-division County Championship. There was no compelling preference for 40-over cricket, so from 2014 it was decided to replicate the 50-over format played by the national team.

The board agreed that, from 2014 to 2017, the format of the season should be as follows:

- County Championship – two divisions of nine teams, with two promoted and relegated each season, and the first 14 rounds starting on Sundays.
- 50-over competition – eight group matches per county, with eight teams progressing to a quarter-finals, played in a format consistent with 50-over international cricket.
- Twenty20 competition – 14 matches per county, mostly on Friday evenings, with the top eight progressing to quarter-finals, followed by the finals day (semi-finals and final at one venue).

ENGLAND TEAM DIRECTOR

On November 28, the ECB announced that Ashley Giles had been appointed England's one-day and Twenty20 international coach. He would report directly to Andy Flower, who remained England team director and would continue to tour with the Test team at home and overseas, but would no longer be responsible for the day-to-day management of the one-day and Twenty20 sides. Giles, a former England spinner and most recently Warwickshire's director of cricket, took over for the one-day series in India in January.

DATES IN CRICKET HISTORY

c. 1550 Evidence of cricket being played in Guildford, Surrey.

1610 Reference to "cricketing" between Weald & Upland and North Downs near Chevening, Kent.

1611 Randle Cotgrave's French–English dictionary translates the French word "crosse" as a cricket staff.
Two youths fined for playing cricket at Sidlesham, Sussex.

1624 Jasper Vinall becomes first man known to be killed playing cricket: hit by a bat while trying to catch the ball – at Horsted Green, Sussex.

1676 First reference to cricket being played abroad, by British residents in Aleppo, Syria.

1694 Two shillings and sixpence paid for a "wagger" (wager) about a match at Lewes.

1697 First reference to "a great match" with 11 players a side for fifty guineas, in Sussex.

1700 Cricket match announced on Clapham Common.

1709 First recorded inter-county match: Kent v Surrey.

1710 First reference to cricket at Cambridge University.

1727 Articles of Agreement written governing the conduct of matches between the teams of the Duke of Richmond and Mr Brodrick of Peperharow, Surrey.

1729 Date of earliest surviving bat, belonging to John Chitty, now in the Oval pavilion.

1730 First recorded match at the Artillery Ground, off City Road, central London, still the cricketing home of the Honourable Artillery Company.

1744 Kent beat All England by one wicket at the Artillery Ground.
First known version of the Laws of Cricket, issued by the London Club, formalising the pitch as 22 yards long.

c. 1767 Foundation of the Hambledon Club in Hampshire, the leading club in England for the next 30 years.

1769 First recorded century, by John Minshull for Duke of Dorset's XI v Wrotham.

1771 Width of bat limited to $4^1/_4$ inches, where it has remained ever since.

1774 LBW law devised.

1776 Earliest known scorecards, at the Vine Club, Sevenoaks, Kent.

1780 The first six-seamed cricket ball, manufactured by Dukes of Penshurst, Kent.

1787 First match at Thomas Lord's first ground, Dorset Square, Marylebone – White Conduit Club v Middlesex.
Formation of Marylebone Cricket Club by members of the White Conduit Club.

1788 First revision of the Laws of Cricket by MCC.

1794 First recorded inter-schools match: Charterhouse v Westminster.

1795 First recorded case of a dismissal "leg before wicket".

1806 First Gentlemen v Players match at Lord's.

1807 First mention of "straight-armed" (i.e. roundarm) bowling: by John Willes of Kent.

1809 Thomas Lord's second ground opened at North Bank, St John's Wood.

1811 First recorded women's county match: Surrey v Hampshire at Ball's Pond, London.

1814 Lord's third ground opened on its present site, also in St John's Wood.

1827 First Oxford v Cambridge match, at Lord's: a draw.

1828 MCC authorise the bowler to raise his hand level with the elbow.

1833 John Nyren publishes *Young Cricketer's Tutor* and *The Cricketers of My Time.*

1836 First North v South match, for years regarded as the principal fixture of the season.

***c.* 1836** Batting pads invented.

1841 General Lord Hill, commander-in-chief of the British Army, orders that a cricket ground be made an adjunct of every military barracks.

1844 First official international match: Canada v United States.

1845 First match played at The Oval.

1846 The All-England XI, organised by William Clarke, begins playing matches, often against odds, throughout the country.

1849 First Yorkshire v Lancashire match.

***c.* 1850** Wicketkeeping gloves first used.

1850 John Wisden bowls all ten batsmen in an innings for North v South.

1853 First mention of a champion county: Nottinghamshire.

1858 First recorded instance of a hat being awarded to a bowler taking three wickets with consecutive balls.

1859 First touring team to leave England, captained by George Parr, draws enthusiastic crowds in the US and Canada.

1864 "Overhand bowling" authorised by MCC.
John Wisden's *The Cricketer's Almanack* first published.

1868 Team of Australian aborigines tour England.

1873 W. G. Grace becomes the first player to record 1,000 runs and 100 wickets in a season.
First regulations restricting county qualifications, regarded by some as the official start of the County Championship.

1877 First Test match: Australia beat England by 45 runs at Melbourne.

1880 First Test in England: a five-wicket win against Australia at The Oval.

1882 Following England's first defeat by Australia in England, an "obituary notice" to English cricket in the *Sporting Times* leads to the tradition of the Ashes.

1889 Present Lord's pavilion begun.
South Africa's first Test match.
Declarations first authorised, but only on the third day, or in a one-day match.

1890 County Championship officially constituted.

1895 W. G. Grace scores 1,000 runs in May, and reaches his 100th hundred.

1899 A. E. J. Collins scores 628 not out in a junior house match at Clifton College, the highest recorded individual score in any game.
Selectors choose England team for home Tests, instead of host club issuing invitations.

1900 Six-ball over becomes the norm, instead of five.

1909 Imperial Cricket Conference (ICC – now the International Cricket Council) set up, with England, Australia and South Africa the original members.

1910 Six runs given for any hit over the boundary, instead of only for a hit out of the ground.

1912 First and only triangular Test series played in England, involving England, Australia and South Africa.

1915 W. G. Grace dies, aged 67.

1926 Victoria score 1,107 v New South Wales at Melbourne, still a first-class record.

1928 West Indies' first Test match.
A. P. Freeman of Kent and England becomes the only player to take more than 300 first-class wickets in a season: 304.

1930 New Zealand's first Test match.
Donald Bradman's first tour of England: he scores 974 runs in the five Ashes Tests, still a record for any Test series.

1931 Stumps made higher (28 inches not 27) and wider (nine inches not eight – this was optional until 1947).

1932 India's first Test match.
Hedley Verity of Yorkshire takes ten wickets for ten runs v Nottinghamshire, the best innings analysis in first-class cricket.

1932-33 The Bodyline tour of Australia in which England bowl at batsmen's bodies with a packed leg-side field to neutralise Bradman's scoring.

1934 Jack Hobbs retires, with 197 centuries and 61,237 runs, both records.
First women's Test: Australia v England at Brisbane.

1935 MCC condemn and outlaw Bodyline.

1947 Denis Compton (Middlesex and England) hits a record 3,816 runs in an English season.

1948 First five-day Tests in England.
Bradman concludes Test career with a second-ball duck at The Oval and a batting average of 99.94 – four runs short of 100.

1952 Pakistan's first Test match.

1953 England regain the Ashes after a 19-year gap, the longest ever.

1956 Jim Laker of England takes 19 wickets for 90 v Australia at Manchester, the best match analysis in first-class cricket.

1960 First tied Test: Australia v West Indies at Brisbane.

1963 Distinction between amateurs and professionals abolished in English cricket.
The first major one-day tournament begins in England: the Gillette Cup.

1969 Limited-over Sunday league inaugurated for first-class counties.

1970 Proposed South African tour of England cancelled: South Africa excluded from international cricket because of their government's apartheid policies.

1971 First one-day international: Australia v England at Melbourne.

1973 First women's World Cup: England are the winners.

1975 First World Cup: West Indies beat Australia in final at Lord's.

1976 First women's match at Lord's, England v Australia.

1977 Centenary Test at Melbourne, with identical result to the first match: Australia beat England by 45 runs.
Australian media tycoon Kerry Packer signs 51 of the world's leading players in defiance of the cricketing authorities.

1978 Graham Yallop of Australia is the first batsman to wear a protective helmet in a Test.

1979 Packer and official cricket agree peace deal.

1981 England beat Australia in Leeds Test, after following on with bookmakers offering odds of 500–1 against them winning.

1982 Sri Lanka's first Test match.

1991 South Africa return, with a one-day international in India.

1992 Zimbabwe's first Test match.
Durham become first county since Glamorgan in 1921 to attain first-class status.

1993 The ICC cease to be administered by MCC, becoming an independent organisation.

1994 Brian Lara becomes the first player to pass 500 in a first-class innings: 501 not out for Warwickshire v Durham.

2000 South Africa's captain Hansie Cronje banned from cricket for life after admitting receiving bribes from bookmakers in match-fixing scandal.
Bangladesh's first Test match.
County Championship split into two divisions, with promotion and relegation.
The Laws of Cricket revised and rewritten.

2001 Sir Donald Bradman dies, aged 92.

2003 Twenty20 Cup inaugurated in England.

2004 Lara is the first to score 400 in a Test innings, against England, in Antigua.

2005 England regain the Ashes after 16 years.

2006 Pakistan become first team to forfeit a Test, for refusing to resume at The Oval.
England lose the Ashes after 462 days, the shortest tenure in history.
Shane Warne becomes the first man to take 700 Test wickets.

2007 Australia complete 5–0 Ashes whitewash for the first time since 1920-21.
Australia win the World Cup for the third time running.
India beat Pakistan in the final of the inaugural World Twenty20 tournament.

2008 Indian Premier League of 20-over matches launched.
Durham win the County Championship for the first time.
Sachin Tendulkar becomes the leading scorer in Tests, passing Brian Lara.

2009 Terrorists attack Sri Lankan team bus in Lahore.

2010 Tendulkar scores the first double-century in a one-day international, against South Africa; later in the year, he scores his 50th Test century.
Muttiah Muralitharan retires from Test cricket, after taking his 800th wicket.
Pakistan bowl three deliberate no-balls in Lord's Test against England; the ICC ban the three players responsible.

2011 England complete 3–1 Ashes win in Australia, with three innings victories.
India become the first team to win the World Cup on home soil.
England whitewash India 4–0 to go top of the ICC Test rankings for the first time.
Salman Butt, Mohammad Asif and Mohammad Aamer are given custodial sentences of six–30 months for their part in the Lord's spot-fix.
Virender Sehwag makes a world-record 219 in a one-day international, for India against West Indies at Indore.

2012 Tendulkar scores his 100th international century, in a one-day game against Bangladesh at Mirpur.
Hashim Amla makes 311 not out at The Oval, the first Test triple-century for South Africa, whose 2–0 series victory takes them top of the ICC rankings.
England win 2–1 in India, their first Test series victory there since 1984-85.

ANNIVERSARIES IN 2013-14

COMPILED BY STEVEN LYNCH

2013

April 8 Alec Stewart (Surrey) born, 1963.
Batsman/wicketkeeper who won 133 Test caps, an England record.

May 2 The Gillette Cup begins, 1963.
England's first limited-overs competition started with Lancashire's match against Leicestershire.

May 27 Arthur Mold (Lancashire) born, 1863.
Controversial fast bowler who was eventually no-balled for throwing.

May C. L. R. James's *Beyond A Boundary* published, 1963.
"The finest book written about the game of cricket," said John Arlott, Wisden 1964.

June 25 England draw exciting Lord's Test against West Indies, 1963.
Chasing 234, England finish on 228-9, with Colin Cowdrey at the crease with a broken arm.

July 5 Hon. Alfred Lyttelton (England) dies, 1913.
Wicketkeeper who took four wickets with underarm lobs against Australia at The Oval in 1884.

July 11 Paul Gibb (Essex) born, 1913.
Wicketkeeper/batsman who scored 93 and 106 on Test debut, in South Africa in 1938-39.

July 21 Sir C. Aubrey Smith (Sussex) born, 1863.
Captained England in his only Test, in South Africa in 1888-89; later a Hollywood star.

August 15 R. C. "Jack" Russell (Gloucestershire) born, 1963.
Eccentric wicketkeeper who played 54 Tests for England.

August 28 Lindsay Hassett (Australia) born, 1913.
Diminutive batsman, and 1948 "Invincible", who succeeded Don Bradman as Test captain.

September 13 Robin Smith (Hampshire) born, 1963.
Hard-hitting batsman, born in South Africa, who played 62 Tests for England.

September 21 Curtly Ambrose (West Indies) born, 1963.
Tall and menacing fast bowler who took 405 wickets in 98 Tests.

November 30 J. S. Rao (Indian Services) takes two hat-tricks in an innings, 1963.
A seamer in his second first-class match, and the second (and last) bowler to achieve this.

December 1 Arjuna Ranatunga (Sri Lanka) born, 1963.
Combative left-hander who led his country to World Cup victory in 1995-96.

December 7 Ian Meckiff (Australia) no-balled for throwing in a Test, 1963.
Meckiff retired after being called four times in his only over, against South Africa at Brisbane.

December 30 S. F. Barnes (England) takes 17 wickets in a Test in South Africa, 1914.
Barnes had figures of 17-159 at Johannesburg; he finished the series with 49 wickets in four Tests.

2014

January 28 David "Syd" Lawrence (Gloucestershire) born, 1964
Fast bowler who suffered a terrible knee injury on England's tour of New Zealand in 1991-92.

February 28 Victor Trumper (Australia) scores 293 from No. 9 in New Zealand, 1914.
Trumper and Arthur Sims added 433 (still a record) for the tourists' eighth wicket against Canterbury.

March First edition of *Wisden* published, 1864.
The 116-page volume was due to be published on Feb 8, but actually appeared a few weeks later.

ONE HUNDRED YEARS AGO

from Wisden Cricketers' Almanack 1914

NOTES BY THE EDITOR [Sydney Pardon] On the whole one may look back on the season of 1913 with keen satisfaction. Before the season began there was certainly reason to feel apprehensive… at a private meeting eleven of the leading counties had agreed among themselves to support a proposal by Lancashire to reduce the scope of the Championship by excluding from the competition four or five of the weaker clubs. On the face of it this seemed an unsportsmanlike proceeding, and naturally there was an outcry.

NOTES BY THE EDITOR [Sydney Pardon] As I have said more than once in *Wisden*, it was not until Association Football became such a power in the land that people began to think county cricket could live on gate money. The various committees are now recognising that it is to a larger membership they must look for security. One point, generally overlooked by those who cry out about bad times, is that the expense of running a county club has in these days increased to an extent out of all proportion to the amount of money paid by the public for admission to the matches. For the time it lasts cricket is the cheapest amusement I know of, and there is no safe way of making the general public pay more than they do.

NOTES BY THE EDITOR [Sydney Pardon] With regard to England's position in the cricket world at the present time things could not be better… there is no denying the fact that we are just now very strong. In Hobbs we have, I think, the best bat in the world, Bardsley being at the moment his nearest rival, and in Barnes, beyond all question, the best bowler. That our strength is so largely professional is matter for regret, but this is a state of things that may soon change.

PUBLIC SCHOOL CRICKET IN 1913 Of general interest to school cricket… is the influence of swerve in modern bowling, and the danger of its overcultivation at the expense of spin and length among Public School bowlers. More than once this year I have heard the lament by a cricket master, "Oh! So-and-so was a most promising bowler with a good action and command of length and spin, but he learned to swing, and since then he has lost his length and direction, and has done nothing except get an odd wicket in the first over or two, or after the 200.

THE AUSTRALIAN TEAM IN AMERICA From the end of May [1913] to the end of September an Australian team toured in America. The trip was quite unofficial in character and had no connection whatever with the Australian Board of Control, the side being got up and managed by Mr Benjamin. A huge programme of over 50 matches was completed, the Australians winning nearly all of them and only losing one… Bardsley, Macartney, and J. N. Crawford were in the Australian team, Macartney making seven scores of over a hundred, and Bardsley six.

KENT v WARWICKSHIRE, AT TONBRIDGE, JUNE 19, 20, 21 [1913] The resumption of fixtures between Kent and Warwickshire after a lapse of 14 years yielded the most remarkable day's play during the whole of the season… Warwickshire were left with a lead which looked certain to decide the match in their favour. Blythe and Woolley, however, making the most of the conditions, actually dismissed Warwickshire in 45 minutes for 16, the two famous left-handers being quite unplayable, but after this startling achievement, it was impossible to believe Kent would be capable of hitting off 147 runs. Before lunch Humphreys and Seymour were disposed of for 16, 18 wickets so far having fallen in the day for 60 runs. Afterwards, however, Woolley hit away with such dazzling brilliancy that, under conditions which still placed batsmen at a marked disadvantage, he scored 76 in 80 minutes, Kent gaining a truly memorable victory by six wickets.

LANCASHIRE v YORKSHIRE, AT LIVERPOOL, JULY 10, 11, 12 [1913] The occasion of the King's visit to Liverpool was seized upon to arrange an additional match between Lancashire and Yorkshire. A very interesting contest ended in favour of Lancashire by three wickets, but, of course, the game did not count in the County Championship. The outstanding feature of the match was the bowling of Dean who, taking 17 wickets, accomplished a feat which has only been performed on seven other occasions in modern cricket.

STAFFORDSHIRE IN 1913 As usual Barnes was the outstanding player of the Staffordshire eleven, his doings against some of the second-class county teams being of such a wonderful nature that Staffordshire generally had an easy task when he was in form. He took 65 wickets for just over six runs apiece, and finished up second in the batting figures with an average of over 40 runs an innings.

Compiled by Christopher Lane

FIFTY YEARS AGO

from Wisden Cricketers' Almanack 1964

CRICKET BOOKS by John Arlott   1963 has been marked by the publication of a cricket book so outstanding as to compel any reviewer to check his adjectives several times before he describes it and, since he is likely to be dealing in superlatives, to measure them carefully to avoid over-praise – which this book does not need. It is *Beyond A Boundary*, by C. L. R. James (Hutchinson: 25s.) and, in the opinion of this reviewer, it is the finest book written about the game of cricket.

NOTES BY THE EDITOR [Norman Preston] *Wisden* itself made an indelible contribution to the summer by the appearance on April 19 [1963] of the 100th edition. The newspapers, television and sound radio were lavish in their praise and they treated it as a national event. I don't think I am giving away any secrets when I say that even the publisher was surprised by the public demand for the Almanack. It ran into three impressions by the printers before everyone was satisfied. Naturally, *Wisden*, which specialises in cricket facts and records, established its own record of sales. The firm of John Wisden and Co. Ltd. commemorated the event by launching The Wisden Trophy, with the approval of MCC and the West Indies Cricket Board of Control, to be played for perpetually between England and West Indies in the same way as England and Australia contest the Ashes. West Indies have become the first holders of the trophy, which is being kept permanently in the Imperial Cricket Museum at Lord's.

NOTES BY THE EDITOR [Norman Preston]   Bowlers in England last summer had their first experience of operating with the front foot as the marker for a legitimate delivery. The experiment was confined to county and university cricket and not to the Tests as West Indies did not wish to conform until they had had more practice at it in their own islands. Although some bowlers expressed themselves forcibly as being against it most of them soon became accustomed to the new condition and at the end of the season MCC considered the experiment designed to prevent unfair drag quite successful.

NOTES BY THE EDITOR [Norman Preston]   [1963 was] notable for the successful introduction of the Knock-Out Competition, which in future will be called The Gillette Cup. For years there was talk of introducing such a tournament, but the diehards always had their way because of the obstacles of solving a drawn tie and particularly in finding gaps in the Championship programme and suitable grounds. Happily the modern generation decided to take the bold step, but I doubt if anyone anticipated that the final at Lord's in September would attract, as it did, a full house of 23,000 – the first all-ticket cricket match with a sell-out before the first ball was bowled.

CRICKETER OF THE YEAR, D. B. CLOSE   Because he was senior professional with the club, and the job was his by right, Yorkshire in 1963 offered the captaincy to their all-rounder Brian Close… who hitherto had never quite accomplished what was expected of him. It was a trial appointment. Nobody quite knew how it would work out. The result was astonishing. Almost overnight it seemed that Brian Close matured. He showed a knowledge of his own team and the play of opponents which immediately stamped him as a thinker and tactician. His field placings were as intelligent and antagonistic as any seen in the county for 25 years and, like Brian Sellers before him, if a fieldsman was required in a suicide position the captain himself was first for the job… Determination and purpose came into his own cricket. He regained his place in the England team and won national approval for the unflinching way he played the West Indies fast bowlers, Hall and Griffith. To his own great delight he saw Yorkshire, in their centenary year, to their 28th outright Championship success.

WEST INDIES IN ENGLAND, 1963 No more popular side has ever toured the old country and with so many thousands of the coloured population from the Caribbean having emigrated to the big cities of Great Britain the cricketers received plenty of support from their own people… By their sparkling batting, bowling and fielding they caused the whole nation to follow the progress of the Tests… Worrell's shrewd appraisement of the strength and weakness of the opposition, and his ice-cool control in all types of situation inspired his men and compelled them to give of their best including their last ounce of energy. No wonder they emulated the deeds of the 1950 side and carried off the rubber by the same margin – three victories to one… Sobers was the strong man of the party… in almost every game he played he contributed some outstanding performance. He left his imprint on every field he played… as the outstanding performer and all-rounder in present-day cricket… By the success in the Tests, Frank Worrell was the first captain to receive The Wisden Trophy and he flew home with his men to a tumultuous welcome in Kingston, Jamaica.

ENGLAND v WEST INDIES, SECOND TEST MATCH, AT LORD'S, JUNE 20, 21, 22, 24, 25 [1963] One of the most dramatic Test matches ever to be played in England attracted large crowds and aroused tremendous interest throughout the country. All through the cricket had been keen and thrilling, but the climax was remarkable, Cowdrey having to go in with a broken bone in his arm… When the final over arrived any one of four results could have occurred – a win for England, victory for West Indies, a tie or a draw. The match was drawn with England six runs short of success and West Indies needing one more wicket… When Hall began his last dramatic over eight were needed. Singles came off the second and third balls, but Shackleton was run out off the fourth when Worrell raced from short leg with the ball and beat the batsman to the bowler's end. That meant Cowdrey had to come in with two balls left and six wanted. He did not have to face a ball, Allen playing out the last two. If he had to shape up, Cowdrey intended to turn round and bat left-handed to protect his left arm… Those who saw it, and the millions who followed the game's progress over television and radio, were kept in a constant state of excitement. It was a game to remember.

MCC v WEST INDIES, AT LORD'S, MAY 18, 20, 21 [1963] West Indies won by 93 runs with half an hour to spare… Hunte, acting-captain because of injury to Worrell, did not enforce the follow-on although 186 ahead. When he declared, MCC needed 266 in four and a quarter hours… Substitutes were required for Worrell, Allan and Gibbs. Gibbs was prevented from bowling for a time when he returned to the field and Hunte wanted to put him on immediately. The umpires considered this came under "fair and unfair play", as he came "warm" from the pavilion and all the other players were "cold". When he bowled half an hour later he soon finished the innings.

from Wisden Cricketers' Almanack 1965

AUSTRALIA v SOUTH AFRICA, FIRST TEST MATCH, AT BRISBANE, DECEMBER 6, 7, 9, 10, 11 [1963] The match was made memorable by the no-balling of Meckiff for throwing and his subsequent retirement from first-class cricket… [In a] dramatic over… [he] was no-balled by Egar on his second, third, fifth and ninth deliveries. That was his only over. Egar was booed and Meckiff was carried shoulder high by a section of the crowd at the close… No play was possible on Monday and on the fourth day extra police were sent to the ground because of fears that the umpires, selectors and Benaud might be molested because of the Meckiff incident.

COMMONWEALTH XI IN PAKISTAN, 1963 The Commonwealth team, under the managership of A. R. Gover, made a highly successful tour of Pakistan during November and December. Not surprisingly the side, packed with well-known international cricketers, had considerable spectator appeal. Altogether over half a million people watched the six matches of the tour – 400,000 at the three first-class representative games... T. W. Graveney hit 500 runs in the three major matches for an average of 100 and the West Indies Test players R. B. Kanhai and B. F. Butcher also entertained the huge crowds.

Compiled by Christopher Lane

HONOURS AND AWARDS, 2012-13

In 2012-13, the following were decorated for their services to cricket:

Queen's Birthday Honours, 2012: M. F. Coleman (former secretary to Hambledon CC; services to sport and community in Hambledon) BEM; E. P. Ferebee (former secretary to Battersea Ironsides CC; services to community sports in Battersea) BEM; M. A. Garland (East Yorkshire Cricket Alliance; services to cricket in East Yorkshire) BEM; A. F. W. Grayson (vice-president of York & District Senior League; services to sport in Bedale) BEM.

Queen's Birthday Honours (Australia), 2012: G. J. Anderson (services to dairy and water management in Victoria, and to cricket) OAM; J. P. Geiger (services to cricket in rural Queensland) OAM; M. A. Weatherald (services to cricket and Australian Rules football as coach and administrator) OAM.

Queen's Birthday Honours (Barbados), 2012: W. W. Hall (Barbados and West Indies; services to sport and community) Knight Bachelor.

Queen's Birthday Honours (Grenada), 2012: G. A. Johnson (former umpire; public service and services to sport).

New Year's Honours, 2013: D. A. W. Brazier (Woodmansterne CC groundsman; services to sport) BEM; R. D. B. Croft (Glamorgan and England; services to cricket) MBE; M. H. Denness (Essex, Kent and England; services to sport) OBE; M. R. Ramprakash (Middlesex, Surrey and England; services to sport) MBE.

New Year's Honours (New Zealand), 2013: B. C. Adams (statistician and historian; services to cricket) QSM; H. A. Findlay (Napier junior cricket; services to cricket) QSM; A. R. Isaac (president of ICC; services to cricket and business) CNZM; P. Kanji (vice-patron of Auckland CA; services to cricket and Indian community) QSM.

Australia Day Honours, 2013: J. E. Maxwell (commentator; services to cricket and community) AM; R. H. D. Sellers (South Australia and Australia; services to cricket, particularly as administrator) OAM; B. W. Walker (president of Northern Territory CA; services to indigenous communities and cricket) AM; L. R. Wood (secretary to Maitland District CA; services to cricket and community) OAM.

ICC AWARDS

The International Cricket Council's ninth annual award ceremony, presented in association with the Federation of International Cricketers' Associations, was held in Colombo in September 2012.

Sir Garfield Sobers Trophy (Cricketer of the Year)	**Kumar Sangakkara**
Test Player of the Year	**Kumar Sangakkara**
One-Day International Player of the Year	**Virat Kohli**
Women's One-Day International Cricketer of the Year	**Stafanie Taylor**
Emerging Player of the Year	**Sunil Narine**
Associate/Affiliate Player of the Year	**George Dockrell**
Twenty20 International Performance of the Year	**Richard Levi**
Women's Twenty20 International Cricketer of the Year	**Sarah Taylor**
Umpire of the Year	**Kumar Dharmasena**
Spirit of Cricket Award	**Daniel Vettori**
People's Choice Award	**Kumar Sangakkara**

A panel of five also selected two World XIs from the previous 12 months:

ICC World Test team

1	Alastair Cook (E)
2	Hashim Amla (SA)
3	Kumar Sangakkara (SL)
4	Jacques Kallis (SA)
5	Michael Clarke (A, *captain*)
6	Shivnarine Chanderpaul (WI)
7	Matt Prior (E)
8	Stuart Broad (E)
9	Saeed Ajmal (P)
10	Vernon Philander (SA)
11	Dale Steyn (SA)
12th	A. B. de Villiers (SA)

ICC World one-day team

1	Gautam Gambhir (I)
2	Alastair Cook (E)
3	Kumar Sangakkara (SL)
4	Virat Kohli (I)
5	M. S. Dhoni (I, *captain*)
6	Michael Clarke (A)
7	Shahid Afridi (P)
8	Morne Morkel (SA)
9	Steven Finn (E)
10	Lasith Malinga (SL)
11	Saeed Ajmal (P)
12th	Shane Watson (A)

Stu Forster, Getty Images

A class of her own: England's Sarah Taylor hits out in a Twenty20 international against West Indies at Chester-le-Street in September as Merissa Aguilleira looks on.

Previous Cricketers of the Year were Rahul Dravid (2004), Andrew Flintoff and Jacques Kallis (jointly in 2005), Ricky Ponting (2006 and 2007), Shivnarine Chanderpaul (2008), Mitchell Johnson (2009), Sachin Tendulkar (2010) and Jonathan Trott (2011).

ICC CRICKET HALL OF FAME

The ICC Cricket Hall of Fame was launched in 2009 in association with the Federation of International Cricketers' Associations to recognise legends of the game. In the first year, 60 members were inducted: 55 from the earlier FICA Hall of Fame, plus five new players elected in October 2009 by a voting academy made up of the ICC president, 11 ICC member representatives, a FICA representative, a women's cricket representative, ten journalists, a statistician, and all living members of the Hall of Fame. New members have been elected every year since. Candidates must have retired from international cricket at least five years ago.

The members elected in 2012 were Enid Bakewell (England Women) and Brian Lara (West Indies), with Glenn McGrath (Australia) added in January 2013, bringing the total to 70.

ICC DEVELOPMENT PROGRAMME AWARDS

The ICC announced the global winners of their 2011 Development Programme Awards in February 2012.

Best Overall Cricket Development Programme	**Cricket Ireland**
Best Women's Cricket Initiative	**Cricket Scotland**
Best Junior Participation Initiative	**Cricket Papua New Guinea**
Best Cricket Promotion and Marketing Programme	**Cricket Canada**
Best "Spirit of Cricket" Initiative	**Japan Cricket Association**
Lifetime Service Award	**Kanaksi Khimji** (Oman)
Volunteers of the Year	**Aliya Bauer** (Kenya)
Photo of the Year	**Brunei Darussalam Cricket Association**

ALLAN BORDER MEDAL

Michael Clarke won the Allan Border Medal, for the best Australian international player of the previous 12 months, at a ceremony in February 2012. He also won in 2005 and (jointly with Ricky Ponting) in 2009. Previous winners were Glenn McGrath, Steve Waugh, Matthew Hayden, Adam Gilchrist, Ricky Ponting (four times), Brett Lee and Shane Watson (twice). Clarke received 231 votes from team-mates, umpires and journalists, ahead of Mike Hussey (174) and Watson (166). Clarke was also named Test Cricketer of the Year, while **Shane Watson** was named One-Day International Player of the Year again, and Twenty20 International Cricketer of the Year for the first time. **Rob Quiney** of Victoria was State Player of the Year; **David Warner** was Bradman Young Player of the Year; and **Shelley Nitschke** was named Women's International Cricketer of the Year (now the Belinda Clark Award) for the fourth year running.

SHEFFIELD SHIELD PLAYER OF THE YEAR

The Sheffield Shield Player of the Year Award for 2011-12 was won by **Jackson Bird**, whose 53 wickets at 16 apiece made him the tournament's leading wicket-taker in his debut season and saw Tasmania into the final. The award, instituted in 1975-76, is adjudicated by umpires over the season. The Ryobi One-Day Cup Player of the Year was **Tom Cooper** of South Australia, who scored 366 runs at 73. **Josh Lalor** of New South Wales was the Lord's Taverners Indigenous Cricketer of the Year, and **Simon Taufel** Umpire of the Year. New South Wales team-mates **Leah Poulton** and **Lisa Sthalekar** shared the Women's National Cricket League Player of the Year, and **Meg Lanning** of Victoria won the Women's Twenty20 title. **Queensland** won the Benaud Spirit of Cricket Award for their fair play throughout the season; the women of **New South Wales** won the WNCL Spirit of Cricket Award.

CRICKET SOUTH AFRICA AWARDS

Jacques Kallis was named South African Cricketer of the Year, Test Cricketer of the Year and Fans' Cricketer of the Year at the CSA Awards in June 2012. The one-day international award went to **A. B. de Villiers**, for the fourth time running, as did the Players' Player. The International Twenty20 Cricketer of the Year was **Richard Levi**, who also won the KFC "So Good!" award for his 45-ball century against New Zealand. **Marchant de Lange** was South Africa's Best Newcomer. The SuperSport Series Cricketer of the Year was **Alviro Petersen** of Lions, and **Faf du Plessis** of Titans was the Domestic Players' Player. **Dean Elgar** of Knights was the CSA One-Day Cup Cricketer of the Year, and **Farhaan Behardien** of Titans was MiWay T20 Cricketer of the Year. **Morne van Wyk** of Knights was the SA Cricket Association's Most Valuable Player, and **Eddie Leie** of Lions was Best Domestic Newcomer. **Dolphins** won the CSA Fairplay award. **Matthew Maynard** was Coach of the Year after guiding the Titans to the first-class and Twenty20 titles in his first season. **Shaun George** was Umpire of the Year, and **Karl Hurter** the Umpires' Umpire. **Louis Kruger** of Potchefstroom was best groundsman for the fourth year running and **Gauteng** were the best scorers' association for the fifth. The Women's Cricketer of the Year was **Shandré Fritz**.

ENGLAND PLAYERS OF THE YEAR

England bowler **James Anderson** won the ECB Men's Cricketer of the Year Award in May 2012. In the previous 12 months he had taken 46 Test wickets, including his 250th. The Women's Cricketer of the Year was England captain **Charlotte Edwards**, who averaged over 50 with the bat in one-day internationals and led her team to a clean sweep of series wins at home, in South Africa and in New Zealand. Kent batsman **Daniel Bell-Drummond** was the inaugural winner of the England Development Programme Cricketer of the Year award, after becoming England's overall highest run-scorer in Under-19 one-day internationals. The England Disability Cricketer of the Year award was won by **Callum Rigby**, a 19-year-old bowler from Shropshire who took eight wickets for the Learning Disability Squad during their successful Tri-Series tournament in South Africa and was subsequently selected for a World XI. **Stuart Broad** won the Fans' Moment of the Year award, for his hat-trick against India at Trent Bridge in July 2011.

PROFESSIONAL CRICKETERS' ASSOCIATION AWARDS

The following awards were announced at the PCA's annual dinner in September 2012.

Reg Hayter Cup (NatWest PCA Player of the Year)	**Nick Compton** (Somerset)
John Arlott Cup (NatWest PCA Young Player of the Year)	**Joe Root** (Yorkshire)
ECB Special Award	**Bill Gordon** (Surrey groundsman consultant)
England FTI MVP of the Summer	**Ian Bell**
Investec Test Player of the Summer	**Stuart Broad**
NatWest One-Day International Player of the Year	**Alastair Cook**
Friends Life T20 Player of the Year	**Dimitri Mascarenhas** (Hampshire)
Clydesdale Bank 40 Player of the Year	**Phil Mustard** (Durham)
Sky Sports Sixes League	**Gary Ballance** (Yorkshire)

FTI Team of the Year **Varun Chopra, Chris Nash, Ian Bell, Steven Croft, Darren Stevens, Peter Trego, Phil Mustard, Jeetan Patel, Keith Barker, Chris Wright, Graham Onions.**

WALTER LAWRENCE TROPHY

The Walter Lawrence Trophy for the fastest century in 2012 was won by **Scott Styris**, who hit a hundred in 37 balls, including nine sixes and five fours, for Sussex against Gloucestershire in the Friends Life Twenty20 quarter-final at Hove on July 24. It was the fastest century not boosted by contrived bowling in the Trophy's 75-year history. Styris received £5,000 along with the trophy. This was the fifth time that the competition was extended to cover all senior cricket in England; traditionally, it was reserved for the fastest first-class hundred against authentic bowling (in 2012, this was Graham Napier's 48-ball hundred for Essex against Cambridge MCCU on March 31, the first day of the English season). Oxford MCCU's **Freddie Coleman** won the Walter Lawrence award for the highest score by an MCCU batsman against a first-class county or another university side; he made 141 against Durham MCCU at the Racecourse in April. A new award for the highest score in English women's cricket was won by **Charlotte Horton** after she made 177* off 157 balls, with 28 fours and a six, for Derbyshire against Northamptonshire in the County Championship in May. Coleman and Horton each received a silver medallion and £1,000. The award for the highest score by a school batsman against MCC went to **James Halson**, who scored 132, including 12 fours and six sixes, for Reading Coat School against MCC; he received £250 and a medallion.

CRICKET WRITERS' CLUB AWARDS

The Young Cricketer of the Year was **Joe Root** of Yorkshire, who received the award the day before he was called up for England's Test tour of India. A new trophy for the County Championship Player of the Year went to Somerset's **Nick Compton**, who joined Root in the Test squad. The Peter Smith Memorial Award "for services to the presentation of cricket to the public" was made to the **County Cricket Club Groundsmen** and accepted on their behalf by Stuart Kerrison of Essex. The Cricket Book of the Year award was given to *The Plan: How Fletcher and Flower Transformed English Cricket* by Steve James.

A list of Young Cricketers from 1950 to 2004 appears in Wisden 2005, *page 995. A list of Peter Smith Award winners from 1992 to 2004 appears in* Wisden 2005, *page 745.*

SECOND ELEVEN PLAYER OF THE YEAR

The Association of Cricket Statisticians and Historians named **Will Beer** of Sussex the Les Hatton Second Eleven Player of the Year for 2012, for his contributions across all three formats of the game in a summer when the Second Eleven programme was ravaged by rain. Beer's leg-spin claimed 11 wickets at 18 in five Second Eleven Championship matches, where he also scored 223 runs at 31, with fifties against Hampshire and Middlesex; he took another 14 at nine in the one-day trophy, and 13 at eight in the Twenty20 competition, including five for 24 against MCC Young Cricketers.

GROUNDSMEN OF THE YEAR

Steve Birks of Trent Bridge was named the ECB's Groundsman of the Year for his four-day pitches, with **Stuart Kerrison** of Chelmsford runner-up. There were commendations for **Andy Ward** (Leicester) and **Gary Barwell** (Edgbaston). **Andy McKay** of Hove was awarded the prize for the best one-day pitches, ahead of Andy Fogarty of Headingley, with Ward (Leicester), **Neil Godrich** (Derby) and **David Measor** (Chester-le-Street) all commended. **John Dodds** had the best outground, at Scarborough, with **Vic Demain** named runner-up for Uxbridge. **Gareth Millthorpe** from Leeds/Bradford won the award for the best MCC Universities pitch, with **Will Relf** at Loughborough and **Paul Derrick** from Durham runners-up.

CRICKET SOCIETY AWARDS

Wetherell Award Leading First-class All-rounder	**James Allenby** (Glamorgan)
Wetherell Award for Leading Schools All-rounder	**Tom Abell** (Taunton School)
Most Promising Young Cricketer	**Rory Burns** (Surrey)
Most Promising Young Woman Cricketer	**Tammy Beaumont** (Kent)
Sir John Hobbs Silver Jubilee Memorial Prize (for Outstanding Under-16 Schoolboy)	**Haseeb Hameed** (Bolton School)
A. A. Thomson Fielding Prize for Best Schoolboy Fielder	**Arthur Godsal** (Middlesex Academy)
Christopher Box-Grainger Memorial Trophy (for schools promoting cricket to underprivileged children)	**Joseph Clarke School** (Waltham Forest)
Don Rowan Memorial Trophy (for primary schools promoting cricket)	**Garratt Park School** (Wandsworth)
Ian Jackson Award for Services to Cricket	**Baroness Heyhoe-Flint**
Perry-Lewis/Kershaw Trophy (for contribution to the Cricket Society XI)	**Rob Humphreys**

WOMBWELL CRICKET LOVERS' SOCIETY AWARDS

George Spofforth Cricketer of the Year	**Nick Compton** (Somerset)
Brian Sellers County Captain of the Year	**Jim Troughton** (Warwickshire)
C. B. Fry Young Cricketer of the Year	**Joe Root** (Yorkshire)
Arthur Wood Wicketkeeper of the Year	**Geraint Jones** (Kent)
Learie Constantine Fielder of the Year	**Liam Dawson** (Hampshire)
Denis Compton Memorial Award for Flair	**Gary Ballance** (Yorkshire)
Les Bailey Most Promising Young Yorkshire Player	**Azeem Rafiq**
Ted Umbers Services to Yorkshire Cricket	**Howard Clayton***
J. M. Kilburn Cricket Writer of the Year	**Dr Peter Davies**
Jack Fingleton Cricket Commentator of the Year	**Michael Holding**

** Howard Clayton has been a scorer for 48 years, for teams including England Under-19, Leeds/Bradford MCCU and Yorkshire Second Eleven, and also served 26 years as secretary to the Yorkshire Cricket Board's Pathway to Excellence scheme for boys and girls, and 15 as secretary of the Airedale & Wharfedale Senior Cricket League.*

BRITISH SPORTS JOURNALISM AWARDS

Times cricket correspondent **Michael Atherton** was named Sports Journalist of the Year for the second time in March 2012. He was also Specialist Correspondent of the Year, was highly commended in the Sports Columnist category and took third place in the Broadcaster of the Year poll, while **Sky Sports'** cricket coverage, which features him as a commentator, was the Television Sports Programme of the Year. The best Radio Sports Programme was, for the first time, a single documentary: BBC Radio's ***Depression in Cricket***.

ECB COUNTY JOURNALISM AWARDS

The ECB announced the winners of the second annual County Cricket Journalism Awards, recognising outstanding contributions towards the coverage of domestic cricket, in October. **David Jordan** of the Sportsbeat press agency was named Young Journalist of the Year and received a £5,000 scholarship to report on an overseas cricket event, preferably involving county teams. The ***Daily Telegraph*** was National Newspaper of the Year, the ***Yorkshire Post*** was Regional Newspaper of the Year, **ESPNcricinfo** was Online Publication of the Year and ***The Cricket Paper*** won the Special Award for Outstanding Innovation and Support of County Cricket.

ECB OSCAs

The ECB presented the 2012 NatWest Outstanding Service to Cricket Awards to volunteers from recreational cricket in October. The winners were:

NatWest CricketForce Award — **Amy Rowlinson** (Kent)
Saved Bromley Town CC £36,000 by sourcing supplies and labour to develop club facilities.

Outstanding contribution to disability cricket — **David Townley**
After losing his sight in his forties, helped to found the Blind Cricket England and Wales domestic league; heavily involved with the 2012 T20 Blind Cricket World Cup in Bangalore as president of the World Blind Council.

Building Partnerships Award — **Paul Daniels** (Kent)
Founded the Young Leaders in Cricket programme which in 2012 developed 280 volunteers; set up a £100,000 fund in his son's memory to screen young cricketers' cardiac health; and promoted disability cricket in Bromley.

Young Volunteer Award (for under-25s) — **Carl Tupper** (Sussex)
Captain of West Wittering CC for three years – since he was 19 – he saved the club through fundraising, increasing membership and driving the development of the junior section, while leading them to promotion.

Officiating – umpires and scorers — **Lorraine Elgar** (Kent)
Umpires at many levels from women's internationals to men's Minor Counties games; also trains umpires and works in disability cricket.

Behind the Scenes Award — **Jonathan Jackson** (Herefordshire)
Helped Bartestree and Lugwardine CC at every level from negotiating thousands of pounds' worth of grants from charities to picking up litter.

Leagues and Boards Award — **Phil Williams** (Warwickshire)
Has served Olton and West Warwickshire since 1970; also Midland Club Cricket Conference communications officer, Warwickshire Cricket Board Under-17 league organiser and Solihull District Cricket Board chairman.

Lifetime Achiever — **Frank Wilkinson** (Lancashire)
Over 50 years' service to Morecambe CC, overseeing their ground's transformation, developing a thriving junior section for boys and girls, and creating new junior leagues across the district.

ACS STATISTICIAN OF THE YEAR

In March 2013, the Association of Cricket Statisticians and Historians awarded the Statistician of the Year trophy to **Peter Wynne-Thomas** for his work on *Cricket's Historians*.

DENIS COMPTON SCHOLAR

The Compton Scholar is the overall winner of an award given to the most promising player at each county, organised by NBC Sports Management since 1997. The winner in 2012 was Joe Root, who scored 738 Championship runs for Yorkshire before making his Test debut for England in India.

QUEEN'S DIAMOND JUBILEE VOLUNTEERING AWARD

In December, the ECB was one of 60 organisations – seven of them in sport – recognised by the Queen's Diamond Jubilee Volunteering Awards for "successfully harnessing the hard work, commitment and generosity of volunteers to change Britain for the better".

ECB BUSINESS OF CRICKET AWARDS

The ECB staged the BOCA awards, designed to celebrate Marketing and PR excellence across domestic and international cricket, in October. The winners were: Best Friends Life t20 Campaign – **Essex**; Best Friends Life t20 Matchday Experience – **Kent**; Best Clydesdale Bank 40 Promotion – **Kent**; Best Promotion of an International Fixture – **Hampshire**; Best Sponsorship Activation – **Nottinghamshire**; Best Membership Campaign or Promotion – **Somerset**; Best Community Programme – **Nottinghamshire**; Best Improvement in Customer Engagement – **Essex**; The Innovation Award – **Kent**; Team of the Year – **Essex**.

2013 FIXTURES

Inv Test	Investec Test match
NW ODI	NatWest one-day international
NW T20I	NatWest Twenty20 international
Champs T	ICC Champions Trophy one-day international
LV=CC D1/2	LV= County Championship Division 1/Division 2
YB40	Yorkshire Bank 40-over one-day league
FLt20	Friends Life Twenty20 Cup
Univs	First-class university match
Univs (nfc)	Non-first-class university match
💡	Day/night or floodlit game

Only the first two of each MCCU's three fixtures are first-class.

Sun Mar 24–Wed 27	**Friendly**	MCC	v Warwickshire	Abu Dhabi 💡
Fri Apr 5–Sun 7	**Univs**	Cambridge MCCU	v Essex	Cambridge
		Durham	v Durham MCCU	Chester-le-St
		Glamorgan	v Cardiff MCCU	Cardiff
		Oxford MCCU	v Warwickshire	Oxford
		Sussex	v Loughboro MCCU	Hove
		Yorkshire	v Leeds/Brad MCCU	Leeds
Wed Apr 10–Sat 13	**LV=CC D1**	Durham	v Somerset	Chester-le-St
		Nottinghamshire	v Middlesex	Nottingham
		Warwickshire	v Derbyshire	Birmingham
		Yorkshire	v Sussex	Leeds
	LV=CC D2	Essex	v Gloucestershire	Chelmsford
		Glamorgan	v Northamptonshire	Cardiff
		Hampshire	v Leicestershire	Southampton
		Lancashire	v Worcestershire	Manchester
Wed Apr 10–Fri 12	**Univs**	Kent	v Cardiff MCCU	Canterbury
Wed Apr 17–Sat 20	**LV=CC D1**	Middlesex	v Derbyshire	Lord's
		Surrey	v Somerset	The Oval
		Warwickshire	v Durham	Birmingham
	LV=CC D2	Glamorgan	v Worcestershire	Cardiff
		Leicestershire	v Kent	Leicester
		Northamptonshire	v Essex	Northampton
Wed Apr 17–Fri 19	**Univs**	Durham MCCU	v Nottinghamshire	Durham
		Hampshire	v Loughboro MCCU	Southampton
Wed Apr 24–Sat 27	**LV=CC D1**	Derbyshire	v Nottinghamshire	Derby
		Durham	v Yorkshire	Chester-le-St
		Surrey	v Sussex	The Oval
	LV=CC D2	Gloucestershire	v Northamptonshire	Bristol
		Hampshire	v Worcestershire	Southampton
		Lancashire	v Kent	Manchester
Wed Apr 24–Fri 26	**Univs**	Cambridge MCCU	v Middlesex	Cambridge
		Leicestershire	v Leeds/Brad MCCU	Leicester
Thu Apr 25–Sun 28	**LV=CC D1**	Somerset	v Warwickshire	Taunton
Mon Apr 29–Thu May 2	**LV=CC D1**	Nottinghamshire	v Durham	Nottingham
		Yorkshire	v Derbyshire	Leeds
	LV=CC D2	Essex	v Hampshire	Chelmsford
Tue Apr 30–Fri May 3	**LV=CC D2**	Leicestershire	v Gloucestershire	Leicester

Wed May 1–Sat 4	LV=CC D1	Sussex	v Warwickshire	Hove
	LV=CC D2	Glamorgan	v Lancashire	Colwyn Bay
		Kent	v Northamptonshire	Canterbury
Wed May 1–Fri 3	Univs	Oxford MCCU	v Worcestershire	Oxford
	Univs (nfc)	Somerset	v Cardiff MCCU	Taunton Vale
Thu May 2–Sun 5	LV=CC D1	Middlesex	v Surrey	Lord's
Fri May 3	YB40	Essex	v Hampshire	Chelmsford
Sat May 4	YB40	Leicestershire	v Gloucestershire	Leicester
Sat May 4–Mon 6	Tour match	Derbyshire	v New Zealanders	Derby
Sun May 5	YB40	Durham	v Essex	Chester-le-St
		Glamorgan	v Yorkshire	Colwyn Bay
		Hampshire	v Scotland	Southampton
		Northamptonshire	v Nottinghamshire	Northampton
		Somerset	v Unicorns	Taunton
		Sussex	v Worcestershire	Hove
Mon May 6	YB40	Lancashire	v Durham	Manchester
		Middlesex	v Glamorgan	Lord's
		Surrey	v Hampshire	The Oval
		Unicorns	v Gloucestershire	Wormsley
		Warwickshire	v Kent	Birmingham
Tue May 7–Fri 10	LV=CC D1	Yorkshire	v Somerset	Leeds
	LV=CC D2	Lancashire	v Essex	Manchester
Wed May 8–Sat 11	LV=CC D1	Warwickshire	v Middlesex	Birmingham
	LV=CC D2	Gloucestershire	v Hampshire	Bristol
		Worcestershire	v Leicestershire	Worcester
Wed May 8	YB40	Nottinghamshire	v Kent	Nottingham
Thu May 9	YB40	Surrey	v Durham	The Oval
Thu May 9–Sun 12	Tour match	England Lions	v New Zealanders	Leicester
Fri May 10–Mon 13	LV=CC D1	Surrey	v Durham	The Oval
Fri May 10	YB40	Netherlands	v Kent	Deventer
		Northamptonshire	v Sussex	Northampton
Sat May 11	YB40	Yorkshire	v Somerset	Leeds
Sun May 12	YB40	Derbyshire	v Lancashire	Derby
		Glamorgan	v Unicorns	Cardiff
		Gloucestershire	v Middlesex	Bristol
		Scotland	v Essex	Edinburgh
		Warwickshire	v Sussex	Birmingham
		Worcestershire	v Nottinghamshire	Worcester
Wed May 15-Sat 18	LV=CC D1	Derbyshire	v Sussex	Derby
		Nottinghamshire	v Surrey	Nottingham
		Somerset	v Middlesex	Taunton
		Warwickshire	v Yorkshire	Birmingham
	LV=CC D2	Glamorgan	v Essex	Cardiff
		Northamptonshire	v Leicestershire	Northampton
Wed May 15	YB40	Kent	v Worcestershire	Canterbury
Wed May 15–Fri 17	Univs (nfc)	Cambridge MCCU	v Gloucestershire	Cambridge
Thu May 16–Mon 20	1st Inv Test	**ENGLAND**	**v NEW ZEALAND**	**Lord's**
Fri May 17	ODI	**Scotland**	**v Pakistan**	**Edinburgh**

Fri May 17–Mon 20	**LV=CC D2**	Kent	v Worcestershire	Canterbury
Sun May 19	**ODI**	**Scotland**	**v Pakistan**	**Edinburgh**
	YB40	Glamorgan	v Gloucestershire	Cardiff
		Hampshire	v Durham	Southampton
		Lancashire	v Surrey	Manchester
		Somerset	v Middlesex	Taunton
		Unicorns	v Yorkshire	Chesterfield
Mon May 20	**YB40**	Netherlands	v Sussex	Schiedam
Tue May 21–Fri 24	**LV=CC D2**	Leicestershire	v Glamorgan	Leicester
Tue May 21	**YB40**	Netherlands	v Northamptonshire	Schiedam
Wed May 22–Sat 25	**LV=CC D1**	Durham	v Middlesex	Chester-le-St
		Sussex	v Somerset	Horsham
	LV=CC D2	Essex	v Kent	Chelmsford
		Worcestershire	v Gloucestershire	Worcester
Wed May 22	**YB40**	Hampshire	v Lancashire	Southampton
Wed May 22-Fri 24	**Univs (nfc)**	Oxford MCCU	v Surrey	Oxford
Thu May 23	**ODI**	**Ireland**	**v Pakistan**	**TBC**
Thu May 23–Sun 26	**LV=CC D2**	Hampshire	v Lancashire	Southampton
Thu May 23	**YB40**	Warwickshire	v Nottinghamshire	Birmingham
Thu May 23–Sat 25	**Univs (nfc)**	Loughboro MCCU	v Northamptonshire	Loughborough
Fri May 24–Tue 28	**2nd Inv Test**	**ENGLAND**	**v NEW ZEALAND**	**Leeds**
Sun May 26	**ODI**	**Ireland**	**v Pakistan**	**TBC**
Sun May 26	**YB40**	Gloucestershire	v Unicorns	Bristol
		Leicestershire	v Somerset	Leicester
		Nottinghamshire	v Netherlands	Nottingham
		Scotland	v Derbyshire	Edinburgh
		Sussex	v Kent	Horsham
		Worcestershire	v Northamptonshire	Worcester
Mon May 27	**YB40**	Durham	v Derbyshire	Chester-le-St
		Kent	v Netherlands	Tunbridge Wells
		Middlesex	v Yorkshire	Radlett
		Northamptonshire	v Warwickshire	Northampton
		Scotland	v Surrey	Edinburgh
		Unicorns	v Leicestershire	Wormsley
Tue May 28–Fri 31	**LV=CC D1**	Somerset	v Yorkshire	Taunton
	LV=CC D2	Worcestershire	v Essex	Worcester
Wed May 29–Sat Jun 1	**LV=CC D2**	Kent	v Leicestershire	Tunbridge Wells
		Lancashire	v Gloucestershire	Liverpool
		Northamptonshire	v Hampshire	Northampton
Wed May 29	**YB40**	Derbyshire	v Surrey	Derby
Thu May 30–Sun Jun 2	**LV=CC D1**	Derbyshire	v Surrey	Derby
Thu May 30	**YB40**	Sussex	v Warwickshire	Hove
Fri May 31	**NW ODI**	**ENGLAND**	**v NEW ZEALAND**	**Lord's**
Fri May 31–Mon Jun 3	**LV=CC D1**	Sussex	v Nottinghamshire	Hove
Sat Jun 1	**YB40**	Worcestershire	v Warwickshire	Worcester

Sun Jun 2	**NW ODI**	**ENGLAND**	**v NEW ZEALAND**	**Southampton**
	YB40	Durham	v Lancashire	Chester-le-St
		Essex	v Scotland	Chelmsford
		Kent	v Northamptonshire	Tunbridge Wells
		Leicestershire	v Middlesex	Leicester
		Somerset	v Glamorgan	Taunton
		Yorkshire	v Gloucestershire	Leeds
Mon Jun 3	**YB40**	Essex	v Surrey	Chelmsford
		Netherlands	v Worcestershire	Rotterdam
Tue Jun 4	**YB40**	Middlesex	v Somerset	Lord's
Wed Jun 5	**NW ODI**	**ENGLAND**	**v NEW ZEALAND**	**Nottingham**
Wed Jun 5–Sat 8	**LV=CC D1**	Middlesex	v Sussex	Lord's
		Surrey	v Warwickshire	Guildford
		Yorkshire	v Nottinghamshire	Scarborough
	LV=CC D2	Gloucestershire	v Glamorgan	Bristol
		Hampshire	v Kent	Southampton
		Northamptonshire	v Worcestershire	Northampton
Wed Jun 5–Fri 7	**Univs (nfc)**	Derbyshire	v Durham MCCU	Derby
		Leeds/Brad MCCU	v Lancashire	Weetwood
Thu Jun 6	**Champs T**	**India**	**v South Africa**	**Cardiff**
Thu Jun 6–Sun 9	**LV=CC D1**	Somerset	v Durham	Taunton
Fri Jun 7	**Champs T**	**Pakistan**	**v West Indies**	**The Oval**
Fri Jun 7–Mon 10	**Tour match**	Scotland	v Australia A	TBC
Sat Jun 8	**Champs T**	**England**	**v Australia**	**Birmingham**
Sun Jun 9	**Champs T**	**New Zealand**	**v Sri Lanka**	**Cardiff**
	YB40	Derbyshire	v Essex	Derby
		Surrey	v Lancashire	Guildford
		Unicorns	v Glamorgan	Southend
		Yorkshire	v Leicestershire	Scarborough
Mon Jun 10	**Champs T**	**Pakistan**	**v South Africa**	**Birmingham**
Tue Jun 11	**Champs T**	**India**	**v West Indies**	**The Oval**
Tue Jun 11–Fri 14	**LV=CC D1**	Middlesex	v Yorkshire	Lord's
	LV=CC D2	Leicestershire	v Northamptonshire	Leicester
Wed Jun 12	**Champs T**	**Australia**	**v New Zealand**	**Birmingham**
Wed Jun 12–Sat 15	**LV=CC D1**	Durham	v Warwickshire	Chester-le-St
		Nottinghamshire	v Derbyshire	Nottingham
		Sussex	v Surrey	Arundel
	LV=CC D2	Essex	v Lancashire	Chelmsford
		Hampshire	v Gloucestershire	Southampton
		Kent	v Glamorgan	Canterbury
Thu Jun 13	**Champs T**	**England**	**v Sri Lanka**	**The Oval**
Fri Jun 14	**Champs T**	**South Africa**	**v West Indies**	**Cardiff**
	YB40	Unicorns	v Somerset	Truro
Fri Jun 14–Mon 17	**Tour match**	Ireland	v Australia A	TBC
Sat Jun 15	**Champs T**	**India**	**v Pakistan**	**Birmingham**
	Varsity (T20)	Cambridge Univ.	v Oxford Univ.	Cambridge

Date	Competition	Home	Away	Venue
Sun Jun 16	Champs T	**England**	**v New Zealand**	**Cardiff**
	YB40	Durham	v Scotland	Chester-le-St
		Essex	v Lancashire	Chelmsford
		Gloucestershire	v Yorkshire	Bristol
		Nottinghamshire	v Warwickshire	Nottingham
		Somerset	v Leicestershire	TBC
		Sussex	v Northamptonshire	Arundel
		Worcestershire	v Netherlands	Worcester
Mon Jun 17	Champs T	**Australia**	**v Sri Lanka**	**The Oval**
Tue Jun 18	YB40	Hampshire	v Derbyshire	Southampton
		Lancashire	v Scotland	Manchester
Wed Jun 19	Champs T	**Semi-final**		**The Oval**
	YB40	Kent	v Sussex	Canterbury
		Leicestershire	v Glamorgan	Leicester
		Netherlands	v Nottinghamshire	Truro
Thu Jun 20	Champs T	**Semi-final**		**Cardiff**
Thu Jun 20–Sun 23	LV=CC D2	Lancashire	v Northamptonshire	Manchester
		Worcestershire	v Glamorgan	Worcester
Thu Jun 20	YB40	Derbyshire	v Scotland	Derby
		Yorkshire	v Middlesex	Leeds
	Varsity (o-d)	Cambridge Univ.	v Oxford Univ.	Cambridge
Fri Jun 21–Mon 24	LV=CC D1	Derbyshire	v Somerset	Derby
		Yorkshire	v Surrey	Leeds
	LV=CC D2	Leicestershire	v Essex	Leicester
Fri Jun 21	YB40	Netherlands	v Warwickshire	Amstelveen
		Nottinghamshire	v Sussex	Nottingham
Fri Jun 21–Sun 23	Tour match	Gloucestershire	v Australia A	Bristol
Sat Jun 22–Tue 25	LV=CC D1	Nottinghamshire	v Sussex	Nottingham
Sat Jun 22	YB40	Durham	v Hampshire	Chester-le-St
	Tour match (T20)†	Kent	v New Zealanders	Canterbury
Sun Jun 23	Champs T	**Final**		**Edgbaston**
	YB40	Unicorns	v Middlesex	Southend
Mon Jun 24	YB40	Northamptonshire	v Worcestershire	Northampton
Tue Jun 25	NW T20I	**ENGLAND**	**v NEW ZEALAND**	**The Oval**
Wed Jun 26	FLt20	Hampshire	v Surrey	Southampton
Wed Jun 26–Sat 29	Tour match	Somerset	v Australians	Taunton
Thu Jun 27	NW T20I	**ENGLAND**	**v NEW ZEALAND**	**The Oval**
Fri Jun 28	FLt20	Durham	v Lancashire	Chester-le-St
		Essex	v Hampshire	Chelmsford
		Kent	v Middlesex	Canterbury
		Northamptonshire	v Gloucestershire	Northampton
		Nottinghamshire	v Leicestershire	Nottingham
		Sussex	v Surrey	Hove
		Worcestershire	v Glamorgan	Worcester
		Yorkshire	v Derbyshire	Leeds
Sat Jun 29	FLt20	Leicestershire	v Derbyshire	Leicester
Sun Jun 30	FLt20	Gloucestershire	v Worcestershire	Bristol
		Kent	v Surrey	TBC
		Middlesex	v Sussex	Lord's
		Yorkshire	v Durham	Scarborough

† *Kent v New Zealanders will be cancelled if New Zealand reach the Champions Trophy final.*

Sun Jun 30–Wed Jul 3	**Friendly**	Essex	v England XI	Chelmsford
Mon Jul 1	**FLt20**	Lancashire	v Nottinghamshire	Manchester
Tue Jul 2	**FLt20**	Derbyshire	v Lancashire	Derby
Tue Jul 2–Fri 5	**Tour match**	Worcestershire	v Australians	Worcester
	Varsity	Cambridge Univ.	v Oxford Univ.	Cambridge
Wed Jul 3	**FLt20**	Glamorgan	v Warwickshire	Cardiff
		Surrey	v Sussex	The Oval
Thu Jul 4	**FLt20**	Middlesex	v Essex	Lord's
Fri Jul 5	**FLt20**	Derbyshire	v Nottinghamshire	Derby
		Kent	v Essex	Canterbury
		Leicestershire	v Durham	Leicester
		Northamptonshire	v Warwickshire	Northampton
		Somerset	v Gloucestershire	Taunton
		Surrey	v Middlesex	The Oval
		Sussex	v Hampshire	Hove
		Yorkshire	v Lancashire	Leeds
Sat Jul 6	**FLt20**	Durham	v Nottinghamshire	Chester-le-St
		Warwickshire	v Glamorgan	Rugby
Sun Jul 7	**FLt20**	Lancashire	v Leicestershire	Manchester
		Middlesex	v Kent	Uxbridge
		Somerset	v Northamptonshire	Taunton
		Worcestershire	v Gloucestershire	Worcester
Mon Jul 8–Thu 11	**LV=CC D1**	Durham	v Derbyshire	Chester-le-St
		Middlesex	v Warwickshire	Uxbridge
		Somerset	v Sussex	Taunton
		Surrey	v Nottinghamshire	The Oval
	LV=CC D2	Glamorgan	v Hampshire	Cardiff
		Northamptonshire	v Lancashire	Northampton
Mon Jul 8	**FLt20**	Essex	v Kent	Chelmsford
Tue Jul 9	**FLt20**	Yorkshire	v Leicestershire	Leeds
Wed Jul 10–Sun 14	**1st Inv Test**	**ENGLAND**	**v AUSTRALIA**	**Nottingham**
Wed Jul 10–Sat 13	**LV=CC D2**	Gloucestershire	v Kent	Cheltenham
Fri Jul 12	**FLt20**	Durham	v Yorkshire	Chester-le-St
		Essex	v Middlesex	Chelmsford
		Glamorgan	v Somerset	Cardiff
		Hampshire	v Sussex	Southampton
		Lancashire	v Derbyshire	Manchester
		Leicestershire	v Nottinghamshire	Leicester
		Worcestershire	v Warwickshire	Worcester
Sun Jul 14	**FLt20**	Derbyshire	v Yorkshire	Chesterfield
		Essex	v Sussex	Chelmsford
		Gloucestershire	v Warwickshire	Cheltenham
		Lancashire	v Durham	Manchester
		Middlesex	v Hampshire	Richmond
		Northamptonshire	v Glamorgan	Northampton
		Somerset	v Worcestershire	Taunton
Mon Jul 15–Thu 18	**LV=CC D1**	Warwickshire	v Nottinghamshire	Birmingham
	LV=CC D2	Kent	v Hampshire	Canterbury
		Lancashire	v Glamorgan	Manchester
Mon Jul 15	**FLt20**	Surrey	v Essex	The Oval

Tue Jul 16	**FLt20**	Gloucestershire	v Northamptonshire	Cheltenham
		Sussex	v Middlesex	Hove
Wed Jul 17–Sat 20	**LV=CC D1**	Derbyshire	v Yorkshire	Chesterfield
		Sussex	v Middlesex	Hove
	LV=CC D2	Essex	v Leicestershire	Chelmsford
		Gloucestershire	v Worcestershire	Cheltenham
Wed Jul 17	**FLt20**	Northamptonshire	v Somerset	Northampton
Thu Jul 18–Mon 22	**2nd Inv Test**	**ENGLAND**	**v AUSTRALIA**	**Lord's**
Fri Jul 19	**FLt20**	Nottinghamshire	v Durham	Nottingham
		Somerset	v Glamorgan	Taunton
		Surrey	v Hampshire	The Oval
Sat Jul 20	**FLt20**	Warwickshire	v Northamptonshire	Birmingham
Sun Jul 21	**FLt20**	Derbyshire	v Durham	Chesterfield
		Gloucestershire	v Glamorgan	Cheltenham
		Hampshire	v Kent	Southampton
		Somerset	v Warwickshire	Taunton
		Sussex	v Essex	Hove
		Worcestershire	v Northamptonshire	Worcester
		Yorkshire	v Nottinghamshire	Leeds
Tue Jul 23	**FLt20**	Glamorgan	v Worcestershire	Cardiff
		Leicestershire	v Lancashire	Leicester
		Nottinghamshire	v Derbyshire	Nottingham
Wed Jul 24	**FLt20**	Kent	v Sussex	Canterbury
		Lancashire	v Yorkshire	Manchester
		Warwickshire	v Gloucestershire	Birmingham
Thu Jul 25	**FLt20**	Durham	v Leicestershire	Chester-le-St
		Middlesex	v Surrey	Lord's
Fri Jul 26	**FLt20**	Derbyshire	v Leicestershire	Derby
		Glamorgan	v Northamptonshire	Cardiff
		Gloucestershire	v Somerset	Bristol
		Hampshire	v Essex	Southampton
		Nottinghamshire	v Yorkshire	Nottingham
		Surrey	v Kent	The Oval
		Warwickshire	v Worcestershire	Birmingham
Fri Jul 26–Sun 28	**Tour match**	Sussex	v Australians	Hove
Sat Jul 27	**FLt20**	Worcestershire	v Somerset	Worcester
Sun Jul 28	**FLt20**	Durham	v Derbyshire	Chester-le-St
		Leicestershire	v Yorkshire	Leicester
		Nottinghamshire	v Lancashire	Nottingham
Mon Jul 29	**FLt20**	Kent	v Hampshire	Canterbury
Tue Jul 30	**FLt20**	Glamorgan	v Gloucestershire	Cardiff
		Northamptonshire	v Worcestershire	Northampton
		Warwickshire	v Somerset	Birmingham
Wed Jul 31	**FLt20**	Essex	v Surrey	Chelmsford
		Hampshire	v Middlesex	Southampton
		Sussex	v Kent	Hove
Thu Aug 1–Mon 5	**3rd Inv Test**	**ENGLAND**	**v AUSTRALIA**	**Manchester**

Fri Aug 2–Mon 5	**LV=CC D1**	Middlesex	v Durham	Lord's
		Somerset	v Nottinghamshire	Taunton
		Sussex	v Derbyshire	Hove
		Yorkshire	v Warwickshire	Leeds
	LV=CC D2	Hampshire	v Glamorgan	Southampton
		Leicestershire	v Lancashire	Leicester
		Northamptonshire	v Gloucestershire	Northampton
		Worcestershire	v Kent	Worcester
Fri Aug 2	**YB40**	Surrey	v Essex	The Oval
Sun Aug 4	**YB40**	Surrey	v Scotland	The Oval
Mon Aug 5	**U19 ODI**	Bangladesh U19	v Pakistan U19	Loughborough
Tue Aug 6	**FLt20**	**Quarter-final (2)**		
	Tour match	Hampshire	v Bangladesh A	Southampton
	U19 ODI	England U19	v Pakistan U19	TBC
Wed Aug 7	**FLt20**	**Quarter-final**		
Wed Aug 7	**U19 ODI**	England U19	v Bangladesh U19	TBC
Thu Aug 8	**FLt20**	**Quarter-final**		
Fri Aug 9–Tue 13	**4th Inv Test**	**ENGLAND**	**v AUSTRALIA**	**Chester-le-St**
Fri Aug 9	**Tour match**	Yorkshire	v Bangladesh A	Leeds
	U19 ODI	Bangladesh U19	v Pakistan U19	TBC
Sat Aug 10	**U19 ODI**	England U19	v Bangladesh U19	TBC
Sun Aug 11–Wed 14	**Women's Test**	**ENGLAND W**	**v AUSTRALIA W**	**Wormsley**
Sun Aug 11	**YB40**	Hampshire	v Essex	Southampton
		Leicestershire	v Yorkshire	Leicester
		Middlesex	v Unicorns	Lord's
		Nottinghamshire	v Northamptonshire	Nottingham
		Scotland	v Durham	Glasgow
		Somerset	v Gloucestershire	Taunton
		Surrey	v Derbyshire	The Oval
		Warwickshire	v Netherlands	Birmingham
		Worcestershire	v Kent	Worcester
	Tour match	Lancashire	v Bangladesh A	Manchester
Mon Aug 12	**YB40**	Glamorgan	v Somerset	Cardiff
	U19 ODI	England U19	v Pakistan U19	Leicester
Tue Aug 13	**YB40**	Essex	v Durham	Chelmsford
		Gloucestershire	v Leicestershire	Bristol
		Lancashire	v Derbyshire	Manchester
		Northamptonshire	v Kent	Northampton
		Nottinghamshire	v Worcestershire	Nottingham
		Scotland	v Hampshire	Glasgow
		Sussex	v Netherlands	Hove
		Yorkshire	v Unicorns	Leeds
	U19 ODI	Bangladesh U19	v Pakistan U19	Leicester
Wed Aug 14	**YB40**	Glamorgan	v Middlesex	Cardiff
	Tour match	Nottinghamshire	v Bangladesh A	Nottingham

Thu Aug 15	**YB40**	Derbyshire	v Durham	Derby
		Hampshire	v Surrey	Southampton
		Kent	v Warwickshire	Canterbury
		Leicestershire	v Unicorns	Leicester
		Middlesex	v Gloucestershire	Lord's
		Northamptonshire	v Netherlands	Northampton
		Scotland	v Lancashire	Glasgow
		Somerset	v Yorkshire	Taunton
		Sussex	v Nottinghamshire	Hove
	U19 ODI	England U19	v Bangladesh U19	Worcester
Fri Aug 16–Sat 17	**Tour match†**	Northamptonshire	v Australians	Northampton
Fri Aug 16	**Tour match**	Worcestershire	v Bangladesh A	Worcester
	U19 ODI	England U19	v Pakistan U19	Derby
Sat Aug 17	**FLt20**	**Semi-finals and Final**		**Edgbaston**
Tue Aug 18	**YB40**	Gloucestershire	v Glamorgan	Bristol
Mon Aug 19	**YB40**	Warwickshire	v Worcestershire	Birmingham
	U19 ODI	**Triangular series final**		
Tue Aug 20	**Women's ODI**	**ENGLAND W**	**v AUSTRALIA W**	**Lord's**
Tue Aug 20–Fri 23	**LV=CC D1**	Derbyshire	v Middlesex	Derby
		Warwickshire	v Somerset	Birmingham
	LV=CC D2	Essex	v Northamptonshire	Colchester
	YB40	Lancashire	v Hampshire	Manchester
Tue Aug 20	**Tour match**	England Lions	v Bangladesh A	Bristol
Wed Aug 21–Sun 25	**5th Inv Test**	**ENGLAND**	**v AUSTRALIA**	**The Oval**
Wed Aug 21–Sat 24	**LV=CC D1**	Nottinghamshire	v Yorkshire	Nottingham
	LV=CC D2	Glamorgan	v Leicestershire	Swansea
		Kent	v Gloucestershire	Canterbury
Thu Aug 22–Sun 25	**LV=CC D1**	Durham	v Surrey	Chester-le-St
	LV=CC D2	Worcestershire	v Lancashire	Worcester
Thu Aug 22	**Tour match**	England Lions	v Bangladesh A	Taunton
Fri Aug 23	**Women's ODI**	**ENGLAND W**	**v AUSTRALIA W**	**Hove**
Sat Aug 24	**Tour match**	England Lions	v Bangladesh A	Taunton
Sun Aug 25	**Women's ODI**	**ENGLAND W**	**v AUSTRALIA W**	**Hove**
	YB40	Essex	v Derbyshire	Colchester
		Glamorgan	v Leicestershire	Swansea
Mon Aug 26	**YB40**	Derbyshire	v Hampshire	Derby
		Durham	v Surrey	Chester-le-St
		Gloucestershire	v Somerset	Bristol
		Kent	v Nottinghamshire	Canterbury
		Lancashire	v Essex	Manchester
		Middlesex	v Leicestershire	Lord's
		Warwickshire	v Northamptonshire	Birmingham
		Worcestershire	v Sussex	Worcester
		Yorkshire	v Glamorgan	Leeds
Tue Aug 27	**Women's T20I**	**ENGLAND W**	**v AUSTRALIA W**	**Chelmsford**
Wed Aug 28–Sat 31	**LV=CC D1**	Middlesex	v Somerset	Lord's
		Warwickshire	v Sussex	Birmingham
		Yorkshire	v Durham	Scarborough

† *If Northamptonshire reach FLt20 finals day, England Lions will play the Australians at Northampton.*

Wed Aug 28–Sat 31	**LV=CC D2**	Gloucestershire	v Essex	Bristol
		Lancashire	v Hampshire	Southport
		Leicestershire	v Worcestershire	Leicester
		Northamptonshire	v Glamorgan	Northampton
Thu Aug 29	**NW T20I**	**ENGLAND**	**v AUSTRALIA**	**Southampton**
	Women's T20I	**ENGLAND W**	**v AUSTRALIA W**	**Southampton**
Thu Aug 29–Sun Sep 1	**LV=CC D1**	Surrey	v Derbyshire	The Oval
Sat Aug 31	**NW T20I**	**ENGLAND**	**v AUSTRALIA**	**Chester-le-St**
	Women's T20I	**ENGLAND W**	**v AUSTRALIA W**	**Chester-le-St**
Tue Sep 3	**ODI**	**IRELAND**	**v ENGLAND**	**Dublin**
	ODI	**Scotland**	**v Australia**	**Edinburgh**
Tue Sep 3–Fri 6	**LV=CC D1**	Durham	v Sussex	Chester-le-St
		Nottinghamshire	v Warwickshire	Nottingham
		Somerset	v Derbyshire	Taunton
		Surrey	v Middlesex	The Oval
	LV=CC D2	Essex	v Worcestershire	Chelmsford
		Glamorgan	v Kent	Cardiff
		Gloucestershire	v Leicestershire	Bristol
		Hampshire	v Northamptonshire	Southampton
Fri Sep 6	**NW ODI**	**ENGLAND**	**v AUSTRALIA**	**Leeds**
Sat Sep 7	**YB40**	**Semi-final**		
Sun Sep 8	**NW ODI**	**ENGLAND**	**v AUSTRALIA**	**Manchester**
Mon Sep 9	**YB40**	**Semi-final**		
Wed Sep 11	**NW ODI**	**ENGLAND**	**v AUSTRALIA**	**Birmingham**
Wed Sep 11–Sat 14	**LV=CC D1**	Derbyshire	v Durham	Derby
		Middlesex	v Nottinghamshire	Lord's
		Somerset	v Surrey	Taunton
		Sussex	v Yorkshire	Hove
	LV=CC D2	Kent	v Essex	Canterbury
		Lancashire	v Leicestershire	Manchester
		Worcestershire	v Hampshire	Worcester
Sat Sep 14	**NW ODI**	**ENGLAND**	**v AUSTRALIA**	**Cardiff**
Mon Sep 16	**NW ODI**	**ENGLAND**	**v AUSTRALIA**	**Southampton**
Tue Sep 17–Fri 20	**LV=CC D1**	Durham	v Nottinghamshire	Chester-le-St
		Warwickshire	v Surrey	Birmingham
		Yorkshire	v Middlesex	Leeds
	LV=CC D2	Essex	v Glamorgan	Chelmsford
		Gloucestershire	v Lancashire	Bristol
		Leicestershire	v Hampshire	Leicester
		Northamptonshire	v Kent	Northampton
Sat Sep 21	**YB40**	**Final**		**Lord's**
Tue Sep 24–Fri 27	**LV=CC D1**	Derbyshire	v Warwickshire	Derby
		Nottinghamshire	v Somerset	Nottingham
		Surrey	v Yorkshire	The Oval
		Sussex	v Durham	Hove
	LV=CC D2	Glamorgan	v Gloucestershire	Cardiff
		Hampshire	v Essex	Southampton
		Kent	v Lancashire	Canterbury
		Worcestershire	v Northamptonshire	Worcester

ERRATA

Wisden 1974 Page 63 Peter Sainsbury attended Bitterne Park Secondary Modern School.

Wisden 1978 Page 479 In Middlesex's match with Kent, Asif Iqbal should have the captain's asterisk and A. P. E. Knott the wicketkeeper's dagger.

Wisden 2009 Page 1667 The Third Test between West Indies and England at St John's was played in February 2009 not January.

Wisden 2010 Page 1294 The Fourth Test between South Africa and England at Johannesburg took place in January 2010 not 2009.

Wisden 2012 Page 604 The leading bowlers for Yorkshire in the CB40 had the following figures (wickets–best bowling–average–economy-rate): S. A. Patterson 12–4-28–18.66–5.60; A. U. Rashid 21–3-30–20.33–5.33; R. J. Sidebottom 11–2-19–24.81–5.46; O. J. Hannon-Dalby 5–2-22–28.80–6.64; R. M. Pyrah 7–3-41–30.42–6.26; D. J. Wainwright 10–2-27–35.00–5.34.

Page 576 Warwickshire's academy director is D. R. Brown.

Page 634 The match at Tunbridge Wells on June 3 was not floodlit.

Page 640 Lancashire's defeat was their tenth in 11 limited-overs semi-finals between 2000 and 2011.

Page 656 In Leicestershire's CB40 match with Northamptonshire, Malik's three-wicket opening burst came at the start of the match, not after Cobb's 91*.

Page 666 In Nottinghamshire's CB40 match with Lancashire, it was Smith's bowling, not his batting, which kept down Nottinghamshire's run-rate.

Page 702 Reman Services, not Roman, won the Shropshire League.

Page 886 In Tasmania v Victoria on February 11–14, Bailey came in at 21-2, not 213-5.

Page 956 Ashwin had also dismissed Gayle cheaply in the IPL's first qualifying final, not the elimination final.

Page 975 As stated on pages 991 and 995, Wagner was the fifth man to take five wickets in six balls, but this was the first instance in a single over.

Page 1179 In Afghanistan's first one-day match with Canada, Shabir Noori scored 95, as in the scorecard, not 94, as in the note.

Page 1514 Under Sky Sports Coach Awards, Andy McCrea coaches at Templepatrick CC, not Temple CC.

Page 1545 In the *Shrewsbury Chronicle* entry, Martin Board scored his century for Beacon First XI and Jamie Board for Shrewsbury Third XI, not vice versa.

CHARITIES IN 2012

ARUNDEL CASTLE CRICKET FOUNDATION – over 300,000 disadvantaged youngsters, many with special needs, mainly from inner-city areas (and London's boroughs in particular), have received instruction and encouragement at Arundel since 1986. In 2012, more than 90 days were devoted to activities; over 5,000 young people benefited. Director of cricket: John Barclay, Arundel Park, Sussex BN18 9LH. Tel: 01903 882602; website: www.arundelcastlecricketfoundation.co.uk

THE BRIAN JOHNSTON MEMORIAL TRUST supports cricket for the blind, and aims to ease the financial worries of talented young cricketers through scholarships. The BJMT elite spin-bowling programme, in support of the ECB, was launched in 2010 to provide expert coaching to all the first-class county Academies and the MCCUs. Registered Charity No. 1045946. Trust administrator: Richard Anstey, 178 Manor Drive North, Worcester Park, Surrey KT4 7RU. Email: contact@lords-taverners.org; website: www.lordstaverners.org

BRITISH ASSOCIATION FOR CRICKETERS WITH DISABILITIES was formed in 1991 to promote playing opportunities for cricketers with physical and learning difficulties. We work in close partnership with the ECB. Chairman: Bill Higginson. Tel: 01544 260315 (home/office), 07776 067350 (mobile); email: b.higgi4@yahoo.co.uk

BUNBURY CRICKET CLUB has raised more than £15m for national charities and local good causes for over 26 years, although it is not a registered charity. In 2012, the Bunbury-sponsored ESCA Under-15 festival – which has produced 64 England players, and 318 first-class cricketers – was held at Monmouth School. Founder: Dr David English, CBE, 1 Highwood Cottages, Nan Clark's Lane, London NW7 4HJ; website: www.bunburycricket.com

CAPITAL KIDS CRICKET, formed in 1990, delivers cricket tuition to boys and girls in state schools throughout inner London, assists emerging clubs, organises competitions in local communities and offers out-of-London residential festivals, frequently at Arundel Castle in Sussex. Its British Land Kids Cricket League involves 2,500 primary schoolchildren. William Greaves, 5 The Courtyard, London N1 1JZ. Tel: 020 7609 1988; website: www.capitalkidscricket.co.uk

CRICKET FOR CHANGE has used sport to change young lives since 1981, developing pioneering projects aimed at disadvantaged young people, running its Street20 version of the game with Chance to Shine's "StreetChance" and the Metropolitan Police in London, and various county boards across the UK. Its disability programme Hit the Top is run in London in conjunction with the Mayor of London Participation Fund, and now nationally with various county boards. Overseas work includes initiatives in Afghanistan, Israel and the West Bank, Jamaica, Barbados, France, Serbia, Rwanda, Uganda, Sri Lanka, India, Bangladesh and New York. Chief executive: Andy Sellins, The Cricket Centre, Plough Lane, Wallington, Surrey SM6 8JQ. Tel: 020 8669 2177; email: office@cricketfor-change.org.uk; website: www.cricketforchange.org.uk

THE CRICKET FOUNDATION – Chance to Shine, the Foundation's campaign to regenerate competitive cricket in state schools, is one of the biggest sport-for-development programmes in the UK. It is now running in 6,500 schools: 1.8m children have enjoyed cricketing opportunities as a result. Chief executive: Wasim Khan, Lord's Cricket Ground, London NW8 8QZ. Tel: 020 7432 1259; website: www.chancetoshine.org

THE CRICKET SOCIETY TRUST's principal aim is to support schools and organisations to encourage enjoyment of the game and to develop skills. Particular effort and concentration is given to children with special needs, through programmes arranged with the Arundel Castle Cricket Foundation and the Belvoir Castle Cricket Trust. Hon. secretary: Ken Merchant, 16 Louise Road, Rayleigh, Essex SS6 8LW. Tel: 01268 747414; website: www.cricketsocietytrust.org.uk

THE DICKIE BIRD FOUNDATION, set up by the former umpire in 2004, helps financially disadvantaged young people under the age of 18 to participate in the sport of their choice. Grants are made towards the cost of equipment and clothing. Chairman of the trustees: Les Smith, 47 Ripon Road, Earlsheaton, Dewsbury, West Yorkshire WF12 7LG. Tel: 01924 430593 or 07904 440367; website: www.thedickiebirdfoundation.org

ENGLAND AND WALES CRICKET TRUST was established in 2005 to aid community participation in cricket, with a fund from which to make interest-free loans to amateur cricket clubs. In its latest financial year it incurred costs on charitable activities of £15.9m – primarily grants to

THE BRADMAN INTERNATIONAL CRICKET HALL OF FAME

The Don's legacy lives on

MIKE COWARD

Perhaps as a reaction to contemporary cricket's preoccupation with the trifling and transient, the legend of Sir Donald Bradman has thrived rather than diminished since his death in 2001. His name is now emblazoned on the International Cricket Hall of Fame at Bowral in the southern highlands of New South Wales, where he took his first steps to becoming the game's greatest batsman.

As with the Bradman Museum it has replaced, the Bradman International Cricket Hall of Fame was inspired by Sir Donald's vision, and the museum continues to fulfil his wish that the game be "honoured and strengthened" in his name. Where the Bradman Museum existed to collect, preserve and exhibit Australia's cricketing heritage, the international cricket hall – conceived in 2008 to mark the centenary of Sir Donald's birth – celebrates the history of the game and its diversity.

Built within metres of Bowral's Bradman Oval, it also provides the only formal display of the legendary names inducted into the ICC's Hall of Fame, which was established in 2009. Financially supported by the Australian and New South Wales governments, and marketed as a tourist destination, it is the only exhibition of its kind in the world. Leading architects, designers and sound engineers have pooled their resources to create an interactive experience which entertains and educates in equal measure. Bradman's place in Australian history is taught in Australian primary schools, and an interactive classroom programme has been devised to connect the establishment to global educational institutions.

With the use of the latest technologies, dedicated galleries showcase every aspect of the game. The World of Cricket gallery, with its state-of-the-art touch tables and graphics, provides the visitor with an unparalleled interactive learning experience. Monolithic screens exploring cricket's evolution against a backdrop of global events are the focus of attention in the main area of the building. Visitors also have access to exclusive interviews with more than 130 of the world's foremost players, officials and enthusiasts. This archive is arguably the richest research resource in the game.

The Bradman Foundation, which regularly host exhibition matches and special events on the ground outside, are committed to youth development through cricket. In addition to offering university scholarships in Sir Donald's name, and organising coaching camps, they are a major sponsor of Dream Cricket, for children with disabilities.

cricket charities and county boards to support their programmes. Trustee: Brian Havill, Lord's Cricket Ground, London NW8 8QZ. Tel: 020 7432 1201; email: brian.havill@ecb.co.uk

FIELDS IN TRUST is the only national charity protecting and improving outdoor space for sport, play and recreation. Protect your sites for ever through Fields in Trust. The Fit Fields toolkit provides information and advice on everything to do with managing outdoor recreational space, such as funding, site improvements and more. Chief executive: Helen Griffiths, 15 Crinan Street, London N1 9SQ. Tel: 020 7427 2110; website: www.fieldsintrust.org and www.fit-fields-toolkit.org

THE HORNSBY PROFESSIONAL CRICKETERS' FUND, established in 1928 from a bequest from the estate of J. H. J. Hornsby (Middlesex, MCC and the Gentlemen), supports former professionals and their families, both through regular financial help or one-off grants towards healthcare or similar essential needs. Secretary of trust: The Rev. Prebendary Mike Vockins OBE, Birchwood Lodge, Birchwood, Storridge, Malvern, Worcestershire WR13 5EZ. Tel: 01886 884366.

THE LEARNING FOR A BETTER WORLD (LBW) TRUST, established in 2006, provides tertiary education to disadvantaged students in the cricket-playing countries of the developing world. In 2012 it was assisting 450 students in India, Pakistan, Nepal, Uganda, Sri Lanka and South Africa, a commitment which will expand to 750 over the course of 2013. Chairman: Darshak Mehta, GPO Box 3029, Sydney, NSW 2000, Australia; website: www.lbwtrust.com.au

THE LORD'S TAVERNERS is the official charity of recreational cricket, and the UK's leading youth cricket and disability sports charity, whose mission is "to give young people a sporting chance". This year the charity will donate over £3m to help young people of all abilities and backgrounds to participate in cricket and other sporting activities. Registered Charity No. 306054. The Lord's Taverners, 10 Buckingham Place, London SW1E 6HX. Tel: 020 7821 2828; email: contact@lordstaverners.org; website: www.lordstaverners.org

THE OVAL CRICKET RELIEF TRUST assists in areas affected by natural disasters. In 2010, it assisted with educational projects in Barbados, contributed to the Haiti earthquake appeal, and supported Magic Bus, a charity that works with children living in poverty in India. Chairman of trustees: Paul Sheldon, The Oval, Kennington, London SE11 5SS. Tel: 020 7582 6660; website: www.britoval.com/about/csr/charity

PCA BENEVOLENT FUND is part of the commitment of the Professional Cricketers' Association to aid current and former players and their dependants in times of hardship and upheaval, or to help them readjust to the world beyond the game. Assistant chief executive: Jason Ratcliffe, PCA, The Kia Oval, Kennington, London SE11 5SS. Tel: 07768 558050; website: www.thepca.co.uk

THE PRIMARY CLUB provides sporting and recreational facilities for the blind and partially sighted. Membership is nominally restricted to those dismissed first ball in any form of cricket; almost 10,000 belong. In total, the club has raised £3m, helped by sales of its tie, popularised by *Test Match Special.* Andrew Strauss is president of the Primary Club Juniors. Hon. secretary: Chris Larlham, PO Box 12121, Saffron Walden, Essex CB10 2ZF. Tel: 01799 586507; website: www.primaryclub.org

THE PRINCE'S TRUST CRICKET PROGRAMMES harness the power of the game to support the engagement and positive development of young people aged 14–25 who are unemployed or struggling with education. Through partnerships with the county boards and clubs, they gain cricket qualifications, complete work placements and attend coaching sessions, motivational talks, competitions and workshops. National programme manager: Rebecca Pike, The Prince's Trust, 18 Park Square East, London NW1 4LH. Tel: 020 7543 7315; website: www.princes-trust.org.uk

THE PROFESSIONAL CRICKETERS' ASSOCIATION CHARITY: there are many worthy and needy cases among cricketers (and their dependants) who played in the era before professionalism; working with the PCA, the trustees visit beneficiaries of the charity to do all they can where necessary. Chairman of trustees: David Graveney OBE, PCA, The Kia Oval, Kennington, London SE11 5SS; website: www.thepca.co.uk

YOUTH TRUSTS – most of the first-class counties operate youth trusts through which donations, legacies and the proceeds of fundraising are channeled for the development of youth cricket and cricket in the community. Information may be obtained from the county chief executives.

CRICKET TRADE DIRECTORY

BOOKSELLERS

AARDVARK BOOKS. Email: pete@aardvarkcricketbooks.co.uk. Peter Taylor specialises in *Wisdens*, including rare hardbacks and early editions. Catalogues sent on request. *Wisdens* purchased. Restoration, cleaning and gilding undertaken. Please contact me via email (relocating to North Yorkshire in 2013).

ACUMEN BOOKS, Nantwich Road, Audley, Staffordshire ST7 8DL. Tel: 01782 720753; email: wca@acumenbooks.co.uk; website: www.acumenbooks.co.uk. Everything for umpires, scorers, officials, etc. MCC Lawbooks, open-learning manuals, Tom Smith and other textbooks, Duckworth/Lewis, scorebooks, equipment, over & run counters, gauges, heavy and Hi-Vis bails, etc; import/export.

BOUNDARY BOOKS, The Haven, West Street, Childrey OX12 9UL. Tel: 01235 751021; email: boundarybooks@btinternet.com. Rare and second-hand books, autographs and memorabilia bought and sold. Catalogues issued. Limited-editions published. Unusual and scarce items always available.

CHRISTOPHER SAUNDERS, Kingston House, High Street, Newnham-on-Severn, Gloucestershire GL14 1BB. Tel: 01594 516030; email: chris@cricket-books.com; website: www.cricket-books.com. Office/bookroom open by appointment. Second-hand/antiquarian cricket books and memorabilia bought and sold. Regular catalogues issued containing selections from over 12,000 items in stock.

JOHN JEFFERS, The Old Mill, Aylesbury Road, Wing, Leighton Buzzard LU7 0PG. Tel: 01296 688543; mobile: 07846 537 692; e-mail: edgwarerover@live.co.uk. *Wisden* specialist. Immediate decision and top settlement for purchase of *Wisden* collections. Why wait for the next auction? Why pay the auctioneer's commission anyway?

J. W. McKENZIE, 12 Stoneleigh Park Road, Ewell, Epsom, Surrey KT19 0QT. Tel: 020 8393 7700; email: mckenziecricket@btconnect.com; website: www.mckenzie-cricket.co.uk. Specialist since 1971. Antiquarian and second-hand cricket books and memorabilia bought and sold. Regular catalogues issued. Large shop premises open regular business hours, 30 minutes from London Waterloo. Please phone before visiting.

KEN FAULKNER, 65 Brookside, Wokingham, Berkshire RG41 2ST. Tel: 0118 978 5255. Email: kfaulkner@bowmore.demon.co.uk; website: www.bowmore.demon.co.uk. Bookroom open by appointment. My stall, with a strong *Wisden* content, will be operating at the Cheltenham Cricket Festival in July 2013. We purchase *Wisden* collections which include pre-1946 editions.

MARTIN WOOD CRICKET BOOKS, 1c Wickenden Road, Sevenoaks, Kent TN13 3PJ. Tel: 01732 457205; email: martin@martinwoodcricketbooks.co.uk; website: www.martinwoodcricketbooks.co.uk. Established 1970.

ROGER PAGE, 10 Ekari Court, Yallambie, Victoria 3085, Australia. Tel: (+61) 3 9435 6332; email: rpcricketbooks@unite.com.au; website: www.rpcricketbooks.com. Australia's only full-time dealer in new and second-hand cricket books. Distributor of overseas cricket annuals and magazines. Agent for Association of Cricket Statisticians and Cricket Memorabilia Society.

ST MARY'S BOOKS & PRINTS, 9 St Mary's Hill, Stamford, Lincolnshire PE9 2DP. Tel: 01780 763033; email: info@stmarysbooks.com; website: www.stmarysbooks.com. Dealers in *Wisdens* 1864–2012, second-hand, rare cricket books and *Vanity Fair* prints. Book-search service offered.

SPORTSPAGES, The Oast House, Park Row, Farnham, Surrey GU9 7JH. Tel: 01252 727222; email: info@sportspages.com; website: www.sportspages.com. Large stock of *Wisdens*, fine cricket books, scorecards, signed material and other cricket memorabilia. Books and memorabilia also purchased, please offer.

TIM BEDDOW, 66 Oak Road, Oldbury, West Midlands B68 0BD. Tel: 0121 421 7117; mobile: 07956 456112; email: wisden1864@hotmail.com. Wanted: cash paid for football, cricket, speedway and rugby union memorabilia, badges, books, programmes (amateur and professional), autographed items, match tickets, yearbooks and photographs – anything considered.

WILLIAM H. ROBERTS, Long Low, 27 Gernhill Avenue, Fixby, Huddersfield, West Yorkshire HD2 2HR. Tel: 01484 654463; email: william.roberts2@virgin.net; website: www.williamroberts-cricket.com. Second-hand/antiquarian cricket books, *Wisdens*, autographs and memorabilia bought and sold.

WILLOWS PUBLISHING, 17 The Willows, Stone, Staffordshire ST15 0DE. Tel: 01785 814700; email: jenkins.willows@ntlworld.com. *Wisden* reprints 1864–1946.

WISDEN DIRECT, website: www.wisden.com. Various editions of *Wisden Cricketers' Almanack* since 2001 and other Wisden publications, all at discounted prices.

WISDENS.ORG, Tel: 07793 060706; email: wisdens@cridler.com; website: www.wisdens.org. The unofficial *Wisden* collectors' website. Valuations, guide, discussion forum, all free to use. We also buy and sell *Wisdens* for our members. Email us for free advice about absolutely anything to do with collecting *Wisdens*.

WISDENWORLD.COM, Tel: 01480 819272; email: info@wisdenworld.com; website: www.wisdenworld.com. A unique and friendly service; quality *Wisdens* bought and sold at fair prices, along with free advice on the value of your collection. The UK's largest *Wisden*-only seller.

AUCTIONEERS

ANTHEMION AUCTIONS, 15 Norwich Road, Cardiff CF23 9AB. Tel: 029 2047 2444; email: anthemions@aol.com; website: www.anthemionauctions.com. Sporting memorabilia specialists with an international clientele and extensive dedicated database of buyers.

BONHAMS AUCTIONEERS, New House, 150 Christleton Road, Chester CH3 5TD. Tel: 01244 353117; email: sport@bonhams.com; website: www.bonhams.com. Valuations can be arranged at our offices throughout the UK; please visit our website for further information.
Bonhams, the world's leading auctioneer of sporting memorabilia.

DOMINIC WINTER, Specialist Auctioneers & Valuers, Mallard House, Broadway Lane, South Cerney, Gloucestershire GL7 5UQ. Tel: 01285 860006; website: www.dominicwinter.co.uk. Check our website for forthcoming specialist sales.

GRAHAM BUDD AUCTIONS in association with Sotheby's, PO Box 47519, London N14 6XD. Tel: 020 8366 2525; website: www.grahambuddauctions.co.uk. Specialist auctioneer of sporting memorabilia.

KNIGHTS WISDEN, Norfolk. Tel: 01263 768488; email: tim@knights.co.uk; website: www.knightswisden.co.uk. Established and respected auctioneers; two specialist *Wisden* auctions and three major cricket/sporting memorabilia auctions per year. World-record *Wisden* prices achieved in 2007. *Wisden* auctions: April and September. Entries invited.

MULLOCK'S SPECIALIST AUCTIONEERS & VALUERS, The Old Shippon, Wall under Heywood, Church Stretton, Shropshire SY6 7DS. Tel: 01694 771771; email: info@mullocksauctions.co.uk; website: www.mullocksauctions.co.uk. For worldwide exposure, contact Europe's No. 1 sporting auction specialists. Regular cricket sales are held throughout the year and are fully illustrated on our website.

T. VENNETT-SMITH, 11 Nottingham Road, Gotham, Nottinghamshire NG11 0HE. Tel: 0115 983 0541; email: info@vennett-smith.com; website: www.vennett-smith.com. Auctioneers and valuers. Regular sales of cricket and sports memorabilia. The cricket auction is run by cricketers for cricket-lovers worldwide.

WISDENAUCTION.COM. Tel: 07793 060706; email: wisdenauction@cridler.com; website: www.wisdenauction.com. A specially designed auction website for buying and selling *Wisdens*. List your spares today and bid live for that missing year. No sale, no fee. Many books ending daily. Built by collectors for collectors, with the best descriptions on the internet. See advert on page 188.

BOOKBINDING AND RESTORATION

SOVEREIGN BOOKCARE, The Book Factory, 28-30 Hartshill Road, Stoke-on-Trent, Staffs. ST4 8NQ. Tel: 01782 414805; email: clubprinta@aol.com; website: www.bookfactory.org.uk. Bookbinding presentation volumes, repair and restoration of books and ephemera to museum standards. Hard and soft cover books produced from manuscript. Reprints a speciality.

SYSTON BINDERY, Unit 5a, St Marks Works, Foundry Lane, Leicester LE1 3WU. Tel: 01162 539552; email: paul@systonbindery.co.uk. Restoration, repairs and complete bindings; private commissions welcome. *Wisdens* restored or case bound in either half-bound or full-bound leather.

CRICKET ART

DD DESIGNS, 62 St Catherine's Grove, Lincoln, Lincolnshire LN5 8NA. Tel: 01522 800298; email: denise@dd-designs.co.uk; website: www.dd-designs.co.uk. Official producers of *Wisden's* "Five Cricketers of the Year" limited edition postcards and prints (many signed by cricketers) and other signed cricket portfolios.

CRICKET COACHING

CRICKETCOACH. Website: www.cricketcoachapp.com; Twitter: @cricketcoachapp; Facebook: cricketcoachapp. Batting, Bowling and Fielding coaching on iPhone, Android and Blackberry. Removing the boundaries associated with cricket coaching, putting affordable professional cricket coaching in the palm of your hand. "You be the coach".

CRICKET DATABASES

CSW DATABASE FOR PCs. Contact Ric Finlay, email: ricf@netspace.net.au; website: www.tastats.com.au. Men's and Women's International, IPL, Australian and English domestic. Full scorecards and over 2,000 records. Suitable for professionals and hobbyists alike.

CRICKET EQUIPMENT

BARRINGTON SPORTS, Northgame House, Haig Road, Parkgate Industrial Estate, Knutsford WA16 8DX. Tel: 01565 650269; website: www.barringtonsports.com. Barrington Sports, the cricket specialist, has been providing cricketers of all levels first-class products for 30 years. For a 10% discount, go to our website and use the code WISDEN13.

CHASE CRICKET, Dummer Down Farm, Basingstoke, Hampshire RG25 2AR. Tel: 01256 397499; email: info@chasecricket.co.uk; website: www.chasecricket.co.uk. Chase Cricket specialises in handmade bats and hi-tech soft goods. Established 1996. "Support British Manufacturing."

CRICKETSUPPLIES.COM – The Definitive Cricket Supplies Website. Tel: 0800 023 5043 (freephone in the UK); email: info@cricketsupplies.com; website: www.cricketsupplies.com; Twitter: @cricketsupplies; Facebook: CricketSupplies

DUKE SPORTSWEAR, Unit 4, Magdalene Road, Torquay, Devon TQ1 4AF. Tel: 01803 292012; email: dukeknitwear@btconnect.com. Test-standard sweaters to order in your club colours, using the finest yarns.

FORDHAM SPORTS, 81/85 Robin Hood Way, Kingston Vale, London SW15 3PW. Tel: 020 8974 5654; email: fordham@fordhamsports.co.uk; website: fordhamsports.co.uk. Cricket, hockey and rugby equipment specialist with largest range of branded stock in London at discounted prices. Mail order available.

MILLICHAMP & HALL, Somerset County Cricket Ground, Taunton, Somerset, TA1 1YD. Tel: 01823 327755, email: info@millichampandhall.co.uk; website: www.millichampandhall.co.uk. Finest Handmade Cricket Bats. New range of Bats, Pads, Gloves, Bags and accessories for 2013. Repairs, alterations to existing bats and soft goods.

OWZAT-CRICKET, 72 Mansfield Road, South Normanton, Derbyshire DE55 2ER. Tel: 0800 542 8711; email: info@owzat-cricket.co.uk; website: www.owzat-cricket.co.uk. Everything for the cricketer's bag at permanently discounted prices including all of the top names and more. Quote WISDEN 2013 for a 10% discount.

STUART & WILLIAMS (BOLA), 6 Brookfield Road, Cotham, Bristol BS6 5PQ. Tel: 0117 924 3569; email: info@bola.co.uk; website: www.bola.co.uk. Manufacturer of bowling machines and ball-throwing machines for all sports. Machines for professional and all recreational levels for sale to the UK and overseas.

THE CRICKET GROUND SHOP, c/o total-play Ltd, Quinton Green Park, Quinton Green, Northampton NN7 2EG. Tel: 01604 864643; email: sales@thecricketgroundshop.co.uk; website: www.thecricketgroundshop.co.uk. The one-stop, online shop for the cricket club; offering pitch covers, non-turf pitch supplies, pitchcare products, netting, batting cages & many more cricket ground essentials.

WORLD CRICKET STORE, c/o Unit 6, 72 Mansfield Road, South Normanton, Derbyshire DE55 2ER. Tel: 0800 030 2440 (freephone in the UK); email: info@worldcricketstore.com; website: www.worldcricketstore.com. World Cricket Store is UK based and serves the world online. We supply the Fan, Player, Team, Coach and Umpire with a huge range at unbeatable prices.

CRICKET TOUR OPERATORS

GULLIVERS SPORTS TRAVEL, Fiddington Manor, Tewkesbury, Gloucestershire GL20 7BJ. Tel: 01684 878943; email: gullivers@gulliverstravel.co.uk; website: www.gulliverstravel.co.uk. The UK's longest established and leading cricket tour operator offering a great choice of packages for the most exciting events around the world.

TRAVELBAG. Website: www.travelbag.co.uk. Worldwide tailor-made travel experts, specialise in creating bespoke holidays to Asia, Australasia, North America, the Middle East, Indian Ocean, Latin America, Caribbean and the Mediterranean.

WISDEN SUPPORTERS' TOUR to Australia for the Ashes Tests in Melbourne and Sydney, December 22, 2013 to January 8, 2014. For more information, see www.wisden150club.com

PITCHES AND GROUND EQUIPMENT

CRICKET CARPETS DIRECT, Standards House, Meridian East, Meridian Business Park, Leicester LE19 1WZ. Tel: 08702 400 700; email: sales@cricketcarpetsdirect.co.uk; website: www.cricketcarpetsdirect.co.uk. Installation and refurbishment of artificial cricket pitches. Save money. Top quality carpets supplied and installed direct from the manufacturer. Over 20 years' experience. Nationwide service.

HUCK NETS (UK) LTD, Gore Cross Business Park, Corbin Way, Bradpole, Bridport, Dorset DT6 3UX. Tel: 01308 425100; email: sales@huckcricket.co.uk; website: www.huckcricket.co.uk. Alongside manufacturing our unique knotless high quality polypropylene cricket netting, we offer the complete portfolio of ground and club equipment necessary for cricket clubs of all levels.

NOTTS SPORT, Innovation House, Magna Park, Lutterworth, LE17 4XH. Tel: 01455 883730; email: info@nottssport.com; website: www.nottssport.com. With over 25 years' experience, Notts Sport is the world's leading supplier of non-turf cricket pitch systems for coaching, practice and matchplay.

PLUVIUS, King Henry VIII Farm, Myton Road, Warwick CV34 6SB. Tel: 01926 311324; email: pluviusltd@aol.com; website: www.pluvius.uk.com. Manufacturers of value-for-money pitch covers and sightscreens, currently used on Test, county, school and club grounds throughout the UK.

TILDENET, Hartcliffe Way, Bristol BS3 5RJ. Tel: 0117 966 9684; email: enquiries@tildenet.co.uk; website: www.tildenet.co.uk. Extensive range of equipment – grass germination sheets, mobile practice nets, fixed nets and frames, portable practice nets, netting and fabric, layflat and mobile rain covers, ball-stop fencing, boundary ropes, and sightscreens.

TOTAL-PLAY LTD, Quinton Green Park, Quinton Green, Northampton, NN7 2EG. Tel: 01604 864575; email: info@total-play.co.uk; website: www.total-play.co.uk. Cricket-playing surface expert total-play designs, constructs and maintains non-turf and natural pitches for clubs of all levels; including its ECB-approved tp365 non-turf system.

SPEAKERS AND SOCIETIES

CRICKET MEMORABILIA SOCIETY. Honorary Secretary: Steve Cashmore, 4 Stoke Park Court, Stoke Road, Bishops Cleeve, Cheltenham, Gloucestershire GL52 8US. Email: cms87@btinternet.com; website: www.cricketmemorabilia.org. For collectors worldwide: magazines, meetings, auctions, speakers, and – most of all – friendship.

LOOK WHO'S TALKING (Ian Holroyd), PO Box 3257, Ufton, Leamington Spa CV33 9YZ. Tel: 01926 614443; email: ian@look-whos-talking.co.uk; website: www.look-whos-talking.co.uk. A company specialising in providing first-class public speakers for cricket and other sporting events. Contact us to discuss the event and type of speaker. All budgets catered for.

THE CRICKET SOCIETY, c/o David Wood, Hon Secretary, PO Box 6024, Leighton Buzzard, LU7 2ZS. Email: davidwood@cricketsociety.com; website: www.cricketsociety.com. A society that promotes a love of cricket in all its spheres for all ages and interests – playing, watching, reading and listening.

CHRONICLE OF 2012

JANUARY

5 Michael Clarke scores 329 not out in the Second Test against India, the 100th played at Sydney; Australia win by an innings next day. **6** South Africa complete 2–1 victory over Sri Lanka at Cape Town, their first home series win since 2008. **10** Sri Lanka, bowled out for 43 in one-day international at Paarl, lose to South Africa by 258 runs. **12** Former Essex fast bowler Mervyn Westfield convicted of spot-fixing; later jailed for four months. **15** M. S. Dhoni banned for one Test for India's slow over-rate during another heavy defeat, at Perth. **19** Pakistan complete three-day defeat of England in First Test in Dubai; Saeed Ajmal takes ten wickets. **23** Tillekeratne Dilshan resigns as Sri Lanka's captain after less than a year; Mahela Jayawardene returns. **25** Graham Ford replaces Geoff Marsh as Sri Lanka's coach. **28 England, set 145, collapse for 72 to lose Second Test to Pakistan in Abu Dhabi.** Australia complete 4–0 whitewash of India at Adelaide after double-centuries from Ricky Ponting and Clarke. New Zealand bowl Zimbabwe out twice in a day to win one-off Test at Napier. **31** ECB confirms new four-year broadcast deal with Sky TV.

FEBRUARY

1 Mohammad Aamer released from jail after his sentence for spot-fixing; Mohammad Asif and Salman Butt released in May and June. **2** Woolf Report into workings of the ICC suggests conflicts of interest must be "declared, assessed and addressed". **6 Pakistan complete 3–0 whitewash of England in Dubai, despite being bowled out for 99 in their first innings.** **9** Mashrafe bin Mortaza reports approach "from a fellow cricketer" about spot-fixing during Twenty20 Bangladesh Premier League. **20** Ponting dropped from Australia's 50-overs team, and concedes his one-day career is over. **21** England turn tables on Pakistan, completing 4–0 whitewash in their one-day series. **29** Dhaka Gladiators, including five Pakistan Test players, win inaugural BPL.

MARCH

1 Doug Bracewell and Jesse Ryder dropped by New Zealand after "breach of team protocol" in South Africa. **4** Dav Whatmore confirmed as Pakistan's new coach. West Indies Test batsman Runako Morton, 33, killed in car crash in Trinidad. **6** Allen Stanford found guilty in US court of $7bn fraud; later sentenced to 110 years in jail. **9** Rahul Dravid announces his retirement, after scoring more than 24,000 runs in 164 Tests and 344 one-day internationals. **16 Sachin Tendulkar scores his 100th international century – against Bangladesh at Mirpur in the Asia Cup – more than a year after the 99th.** **17** South Africa win Second Test against New Zealand at Hamilton; the other two are drawn. **22** Pakistan beat Bangladesh by two runs to win Asia Cup final. **23** Former Hampshire wicketkeeper Neil McCorkell celebrates his 100th birthday. **24** Ireland win the World Twenty20 qualifying competition in Dubai; Afghanistan also progress to the tournament itself. **29** Rangana Herath takes 12 wickets as Sri Lanka win First Test against England at Galle. **31** Earliest start to first-class season in England; Sam Robson of Middlesex scores the first-ever century in March.

APRIL

7 England square series in Sri Lanka by winning Second Test in Colombo, after 151 by Kevin Pietersen and ten wickets from Graeme Swann. **8** Durham MCCU bowled out for 18 by Durham at Chester-le-Street. **11** Australia win First Test at Bridgetown by three wickets, after declaring behind. **16** Stuart Law quits as Bangladesh coach for personal reasons. Jamaica win West Indies' domestic first-class competition for the fifth season running, a record. **27** Australia win Third Test in Dominica to take series against West Indies 2–0.

MAY

10 Former South Africa wicketkeeper Dave Richardson named ICC chief executive. **17** England captain Charlotte Edwards is first woman to join MCC World Cricket Committee. **21** Led by a century from Andrew Strauss and 11 wickets from Stuart Broad, England beat West Indies in the First Test at Lord's. **27** Kolkata Knight Riders win IPL for first time. **28** England win Second Test against West Indies at Trent Bridge to claim the Wisden Trophy. **30** Richard Pybus named Bangladesh coach. **31 Pietersen announces short-lived retirement from limited-overs international cricket.**

JUNE

1 Nick Compton completes 1,000 first-class runs for the English season. **5** Chris Gayle's 15-month international exile ends, after he is selected for West Indies' one-day games in England. **10** Tino Best of West Indies hits 95, the highest Test score by a No. 11, in drawn Third Test at rain-affected Edgbaston. **18 Surrey batsman Tom Maynard, 23, found dead on railway line in south London.** **22** Pakistan leg-spinner Danish Kaneria banned for life from cricket in England after ECB panel finds him guilty of corruption. **25** Sri Lanka, for whom Kumar Sangakkara scored 199 not out, beat Pakistan in First Test at Galle; the other two are drawn. **28** New Zealander Alan Isaac starts two-year term as ICC president. **30** Indian board ban five players for spot-fixing in domestic matches.

JULY

4 Sangakkara narrowly misses a double-century for the second Test running – out for 192 in Colombo. **5** Mark Ramprakash announces retirement from county cricket, ending a 25-year career. **9 South African wicketkeeper Mark Boucher requires surgery after an eye injury at Taunton; he is later forced to retire, stranded on 999 international dismissals.** **13** Australian fast bowler Brett Lee announces retirement from international cricket. **20** Mike Hesson, recently in charge of Kenya, is named as New Zealand's coach. **23** South Africa crush England in First Test at The Oval; their total of 637 for two includes a national-record 311 not out from Hashim Amla. **25** In his first Test for more than 18 months, Gayle scores 150 not out and 64 as West Indies beat New Zealand in Antigua.

AUGUST

4 Superb 149 from Pietersen helps England draw Second Test. He is later accused of sending inappropriate texts to South African players, and eventually excluded from the Third Test and (after withdrawing his earlier retirement) the World Twenty20. **5** West Indies defeat New Zealand by five wickets in Second Test at Kingston to clinch series victory. **18** India's V. V. S. Laxman announces retirement from international cricket, after 8,781 runs in 134 Tests. **20 South Africa win Third Test to go No. 1 in the world rankings.** **26** India win Under-19 World Cup, beating Australia in the final in Queensland. Hampshire win the Friends Life t20, beating Yorkshire at Cardiff. **29** England captain Andrew Strauss announces his retirement from all cricket, after 100 Tests.

SEPTEMBER

3 India complete 2–0 victory over New Zealand, winning the Second Test at Bangalore by five wickets. **6 Warwickshire win the County Championship. 11** Yuvraj Singh returns to international cricket after cancer treatment, scoring 34 from 26 balls in Twenty20 game against New Zealand at Chennai (India lose by one run). **13** Ramnaresh Sarwan awarded $161,000 in damages in legal case against West Indies board, which had made incorrect claims about his fitness. **14** Derbyshire win second division of the County Championship for the first time. **15** Hampshire complete a domestic limited-overs double, winning the CB40 final at Lord's. **26** Simon Taufel, 41, announces his retirement as an international umpire after standing in 74 Tests.

OCTOBER

2 Pakistan spinner Abdur Rehman is banned for 12 weeks by the ECB after testing positive for cannabis while playing for Somerset. **3** Pietersen signs a new central contract and is added to England team for forthcoming Indian tour. **7 West Indies beat Sri Lanka in the World Twenty20 final in Colombo. 11** Former Indian captain Anil Kumble appointed chairman of ICC cricket committee. **19** Cricket South Africa chief executive Gerald Majola is dismissed after being found guilty of misconduct. **28** Sydney Sixers win Champions League Twenty20. **30** ICC regulations changed to allow two bouncers an over in one-day internationals, while powerplay overs cut from 20 to 15.

NOVEMBER

1 Graeme Smith signs three-year deal to lead Surrey. **13** Michael Clarke scores 259 not out as First Test against South Africa is drawn at Brisbane. Gayle uniquely hits first ball of a Test for six, against Bangladesh at Mirpur; West Indies go on to win by 77 runs. **19 India, for whom Cheteshwar Pujara scores a maiden double-century, win the First Test against England at Ahmedabad.** New Zealand lose their fifth successive Test, against Sri Lanka at Galle. **22** Australia pile up 482 for five on opening day of Second Test at Adelaide, with Clarke scoring his fourth double-century of the year, a record. **25** West Indies complete 2–0 Test series win over Bangladesh at Khulna, despite Abul Hasan's century from No. 10 on debut. **26 Monty Panesar and Graeme Swann share 19 wickets as England square series in India with a ten-wicket victory at Mumbai.** Faf du Plessis bats through last day at Adelaide, scoring a century on debut to help South Africa save the match. **28** Ashley Giles appointed head coach of England's one-day and Twenty20 teams. **29** Ponting announces that the next Test at Perth, his 168th, will be his last. New Zealand square short series in Sri Lanka.

DECEMBER

2 Bangladesh beat West Indies at Khulna by 160 runs, their biggest one-day victory, and go on to win series 3–2. **3** South Africa win Third Test at Perth by 309 runs to take series 1–0; Amla scores 196, Ponting four and eight. **9** England win Third Test at Kolkata, with Alastair Cook making 190. **17** England win series in India 2–1 – their first victory there since 1984-85 – after Fourth Test at Nagpur is drawn. **23** Tendulkar announces retirement from one-day internationals, after scoring 18,426 runs, with 49 centuries, from 463 matches (all records). **28** Australia beat Sri Lanka by an innings at Melbourne to go 2–0 up in three-match Test series. **29 Former England captain Tony Greig dies, aged 66.** Mike Hussey announces he will retire from international cricket at the end of the Australian season.

The following items were also reported during 2012:

SKY NEWS January 1

Australian Test players were irritated when their prime minister, Julia Gillard, told an official reception for the Indian team that her country's cricket fans were "looking forward to what may be a very special hundred made in Australia" – meaning Sachin Tendulkar's 100th international century. Michael Clarke said his team hoped the century would come somewhere else. His team-mate Mike Hussey called the prime minister's comment "strange".

NDTV.COM January 6

The newly elected chief of Sri Lanka Cricket, Upali Dharmadasa, said he had held a puja to drive out demons he held responsible for the board's cash crisis and the team's poor results. "I am a businessman and I know the effects of these evil spirits."

DAILY TELEGRAPH January 20

The German footballer Didi Hamann claimed to have lost £288,400 on a single cricket spread bet. In his autobiography, Hamann – best-remembered as a defensive midfielder with Liverpool – said he had "bought" an Australian innings against South Africa at 340 for £2,800 a run. Australia collapsed for 237, thus costing him 103 x £2,800. "The next day, when I looked at the mess that was me in the mirror, I said, 'Didi, things have got to change.'"

SOUTH MANCHESTER REPORTER January 26

Manchester City Council approved a plan to turn Longsight Cricket Club, where the touring Australians were beaten in 1878, into a housing estate. Eighteen men of Longsight (including G. F. Grace and W. R. Gilbert) overcame the Australian XI by two wickets. A century later, the club was one of the strongest in the area, but the East Road ground had been closed since 2004 because they could no longer afford the upkeep. The bowling green will stay, alongside 65 houses and 18 flats.

SOUTH ASIAN TIMES January 30

An umpire killed a 15-year-old spectator after he ran on to the field to dispute a decision, according to police in Kishoreganj, Bangladesh. The youth, named as Nazrul Islam, rushed on after a batsman was given not out, and accused the umpire of bias. An argument ensued, then the umpire took a bat and hit the boy, who showed no immediate signs of injury but died of internal bleeding next day. The umpire, who was not named, was in hiding.

THE AGE February 12

The waiting list for the Melbourne Cricket Club has now surpassed the population of Hobart and stands at 217,000. It is estimated that it now takes 22–23 years to join the 61,500 full members and gain full privileges at major MCG occasions. About 3,000 vacancies occur each year, but the list is growing inexorably because there are 15,000 new applicants. However, the club have lost contact with many of those waiting because they have moved so often.

THE AGE February 13

The Melbourne Premier match between Prahran and Richmond at Toorak Park was halted after just nine balls when a fielder became suspicious about the length of the pitch. It turned out to be at least two metres too long. This was the second such incident in Australian club cricket in the 2011-12 season, and both involved Test players. Ryan Harris was playing in the first match (see *Wisden 2012,* page 1547). This time it was Cameron White, who made 147 – on a re-marked pitch.

THE ISLAND February 17

World Cup-winning captain Arjuna Ranatunga condemned the treatment of the trophy Sri Lanka won under his leadership in 1996. It was apparently damaged when on display at an exhibition, and two gold rivets went missing.

THE ISLAND March 1

Thirty Colombo schoolboys were arrested after climbing the walls of a nearby girls' school and demanding money to support their "Big Match". The contests between rival schools are an important part of Sri Lankan cricket tradition and have long been accompanied by a student-rag atmosphere. However, police had specifically issued a warning through the media that girls' schools were off limits. The boys were given a further warning and released without charge.

BBC March 3

The Afghan National Army beat a British military team to win a two-day tournament in war-torn Helmand Province. The British also lost to a team of Afghan interpreters. Lt-Col Tim Law of the Royal Artillery said the Afghan side turned out to be "absolutely fantastic". More than 1,500 supporters ran on to the pitch after the soldiers dismissed the British for 75, a 90-run win.

MUMBAI MIRROR March 11

Cricket Australia flew a cup to mark Sachin Tendulkar's 100th international hundred to every venue where he played in Australia in 2011-12, awaiting the moment for presentation, which never came.

ITV NEWS March 23

Seven-year-old Charlie Allison from Colchester has become an internet sensation after the release on YouTube of a video of him batting in the nets, driving, pulling and reverse-sweeping with near-professional aplomb.

SPORT 360° March 27

A painting depicting the highlights of Tendulkar's career, by the British-based artist Sacha Jafri, has been sold for $750,000. The proceeds will go to the M. S. Dhoni Foundation to support poor children.

PRESS TRUST OF INDIA April 2

The Mumbai Cricket Association intends to shower Tendulkar with a hundred gold coins for reaching 100 international centuries.

INDO-ASIAN NEWS SERVICE April 13

Former Indian captain Mohammad Azharuddin, now an MP, scored a century for the Indian Parliamentarians in Dharmasala to beat a rather less expert team of their British equivalents, the Lords and Commons, by 56 runs.

ESPNCRICINFO April 24

Ratilal Parmar, 56, whose hobby is collecting banknotes that have special associations with Sachin Tendulkar, has acquired a new prize: a ten-rupee note numbered 240412, the date of Tendulkar's 39th birthday. Parmar wants to present his hero with the notes connected with his milestones, especially 160312, the date of the 100th international hundred. He estimates he has spent a million rupees building his collection, sometimes by pleading with bank clerks for help.

ORMSKIRK ADVERTISER April 26

An off-duty nurse, watching the Second XI match between Burscough and Rainsford in Lancashire, went to the rescue after Burscough's Carl Lydiate left the field with chest pains. His team-mates assumed he had indigestion. "I could tell he was in trouble," said Hayley McCullough, "because he was grey, sweating and saying his chest was feeling crushed." She stayed with him until the ambulance arrived and Lydiate could receive treatment for a heart attack. John Williams, chairman of the Liverpool Competition, said: "This is a timely reminder to us all that coaches need to keep their first-aid certificates up to date."

THE TIMES EDUCATIONAL SUPPLEMENT April 27

Teachers have posted hundreds of complaints on an online forum about the idiocy of school inspectors from the British inspection body OFSTED. One PE teacher was allegedly told the lesson was "unsatisfactory as there were children doing nothing". The judgment was overturned after it was pointed out that the pupils were fielding in a cricket match.

DAILY RECORD April 27

Taxpayers have paid £3,000 over the past two seasons so a worker could be employed to throw back balls hit over the fence at Dunfermline Knights' ground in Scotland. The club lost part of their McKane Park pitch due to flood prevention work, and the land was never reinstated. Fearful that fielders would injure themselves fetching the balls, Fife Council paid a member of the contractors' staff £10 an hour to throw them back. Robert Oxley of Taxpayer Scotland said the affair was "barmy".

BBC May 7

The former England one-day captain Adam Hollioake, 40, achieved a draw on his debut as a mixed-martial-arts cage fighter in Queensland. Hollioake said he loved every minute of his brawl with Joel Miller in front of a 1,500 crowd on the Gold Coast, though his wife Sherryn did not. After a bad first round, Hollioake outfought his opponent in the final two. He has been through many travails following the death of his brother Ben, including bankruptcy. He said of Sherryn: "She is a beautiful person and she wants me to follow my dreams. But I just think at the moment she wishes my dreams were something else."

SOUTHERN DAILY ECHO May 8

David Taylor, Totton & Eling's new captain/coach, scored 330 not out for the second team against bewildered Southern Premier League Division Three rivals Trojans, having turned out to get some batting practice when the first team's match was called off. He hit 31 sixes and 19 fours off 160 balls in a total of 412 for three; Trojans mustered 103. Taylor, 37, had played for Worcestershire and Derbyshire.

DAILY TELEGRAPH May 12

British prime minister David Cameron told how he had found his wife Samantha playing French cricket with a bat signed for him by Sachin Tendulkar in the grounds of Chequers and had to warn her: "No, darling, put it down; this is probably the most valuable possession I have." He donated the bat for an auction at Lord's raising £3,400 for the Rwanda Cricket Stadium Foundation.

SYDNEY MORNING HERALD May 17

Australian captain Michael Clarke and his girlfriend Kyly Boldy married in secret in the Blue Mountains, announcing the news on Twitter, and taking friends and Cricket Australia by surprise. This disappointed magazine editors, who would have paid substantially for exclusive rights to the wedding pictures, but won praise from other quarters. "No deals, no media, no $$$s, just family and class," tweeted one fan.

SUNDAY EXPRESS, MUMBAI May 27

Arjun Tendulkar, the 12-year-old son of Sachin, hit his maiden century in the Mumbai Cricket Association's Under-14 trials, scoring 124 for Khar Gymkhana against Goregaon Centre.

CRAVEN HERALD & PIONEER May 28

Settle beat Stacksteads in Division Two of the Ribblesdale League by 452 runs in a 45-over match. Settle captain Nick Cokell scored 275 not out in a total of 467 for one. Stacksteads were then bowled out for 15, the lowest score in the league since 1931. "I'd never even scored a century before," said Cokell. "To be fair, Stacksteads were gracious in defeat."

ESPNCRICINFO May 30

The theory that moisture makes a cricket ball swing is false, according to researchers at Sheffield Hallam and Auckland Universities. Tests using 3D laser scanners and an atmospheric chamber, reported in the journal *Procedia Engineering,* found no link between humidity levels and sideways movement. Altitude and the age of the ball did have an effect, however.

AUSTRALIAN ASSOCIATED PRESS June 2

Actor Jason Alexander, best known for playing George in *Seinfeld*, posted a thousand-word apology after repeatedly calling cricket "a gay sport" on an American chat show. Some of his followers on Twitter had told him they were both gay and offended. There were no reports of complaints from cricketers.

THE HINDU June 5

Sachin Tendulkar has been sworn in as a member of the Indian upper house, the Rajya Sabha. "It has been my dream to be remembered as someone who worked for all sports instead of just cricket statistics," he said after taking the oath. However, he warned that, as an active player, he would continue to focus on his own game. Tendulkar was chosen as one of the 12 members of the parliament the president is allowed to nominate, although some critics claimed that a sportsman did not fulfil the criterion of "special knowledge or practical experience in… literature, science, art and social service" specified for selection under the constitution.

DVLAREGISTRATIONS.DIRECT.GOV.UK June 9

Lot 1706, W15 DEN, was sold for £1,500, almost four times its reserve price of £400, at the regular British auction of personalised car registrations. The buyer would also have been liable for a further £524 in extra fees and tax.

BBC June 11

Barrington were bowled out for six by Huish & Langport in Somerset League Division Two. They had safely reached three for nought, but eight batsmen fell for ducks in reply to their opponents' 195 for seven. Huish & Langport captain Dominic Shillabeer took seven for two.

PETERBOROUGH TELEGRAPH June 11

In Division Four of the Huntingdonshire League, Ramsey Third XI were bowled out for 12 by Yaxley Second XI. There were six ducks and a top score of three in reply to a Yaxley total of 105. "It's not as though we had a bad team out either," Ramsey player Richard Clarke said. "We had three experienced second-team cricketers in the side, but they were all given out lbw, which was crucial."

SCARBOROUGH NEWS June 13

An Under-13 match between Scarborough and Bridlington was halted when a seagull stole one of the bails. The Scarborough players were coming out to field when the bird swooped on its prize, which was lying just behind the stumps. Umpire Barry Rudd tried to chase the bird but it flew off. Scarborough coach John Green said: "Our lads must have been traumatised by what they'd seen as we lost the game."

PRESS ASSOCIATION June 17

Three nine-year-old boys were injured when a tree fell on them on a windy day as they waited to use the nets at Spencer CC in south-west London. The senior team were playing against Cheam when the incident happened. Cricketers and spectators freed the boys before an air ambulance arrived. The boys were named as Lewis Gaston, Aidan Oakley and George Roberts.

BOLTON NEWS June 19

Elton and Edgworth of the Bolton Association played each other at first- and second-team level on Sunday, and both games were tied. In each case, the chasing team needed two off the last ball, but could manage only a single.

HEYWOODCC.CO.UK June 21

Heywood fast bowler Humza Naeem had figures of 5–3–9–8 in an Under-18 match against Oldham, who were all out for 15. Heywood won by 127 runs.

DONCASTER FREE PRESS June 22

Rossington Main CC were banned from the South Yorkshire Senior League until the end of 2013 because players had abused league officials on Twitter.

TIMES OF INDIA June 23

An animal-rights group has lodged a legal complaint against the Indian Test-player-turned-politician Navjot Sidhu after he arrived at a court hearing on an elephant.

THE CRICKETER/CLUB-CRICKET.CO.UK July

Left-arm pace bowler Gareth Fisher had an analysis of 4–1–4–9 for Colchester & East Essex in the Essex Premier League, news that might have delighted the former England left-armer John Lever – had his son James not been playing for the opposition. The young Lever was one of seven Woodford Wells batsmen out for nought in a total of 24 after they had reached ten without loss in the first over. Fisher's figures, which included four in four balls, and six lbws, beat the 45-year-old club record of nine for five, held by the former Ipswich footballer Ted Phillips. Almost the only spectator in 2012 was Ray Hollingsworth, who was operating the scoreboard when Phillips achieved his feat in 1967.

DOWN RECORDER/CRICKETEUROPE July

Dundrum's Indian professional Raviraj Patil hit six sixes in an over in the Ulster Shield for Dundrum at Sion Mills. In all, 39 came off the over: three deliveries were called wides as the bowler, Andy Lucas, tried to stop Patil getting near the ball. The previous day he had scored 53 from 15 deliveries, and team-mates had started goading him into trying for six sixes. This time he scored 167 off 78. The Sion Mills ground is best known as the scene of West Indies' humiliation in 1969, when Ireland bowled them out for 25.

DAILY MAIL July 1

England team members could be investigated by HM Revenue and Customs as part of an inquiry into the use of image-rights companies by the players. According to the Companies House register, 11 of the 13 contracted England players had companies of this kind.

CLUB-CRICKET.CO.UK July 2

The Club Cricket Conference have asked members for ideas about how to deal with flying cricket balls after Dymchurch CC in Kent became the latest club to be ordered by a local council to erect high nets – or move.

ESPNCRICINFO July 3

The record for the longest continuous match has been broken again, this time by Loughborough University staff, who battled atrocious weather for 150 hours 20 minutes. One substitute fielder was allowed per side. "We had torrential rain and hailstones the size of golf balls but, in true British tradition, we kept calm and carried on," said organiser Chris Hughes.

ESPNCRICINFO July 4

Eleven-year-old Kieran Gray of Maidenhead & Bray's Under-13s took the first six Taplow wickets in an over – and was then taken off to allow his team-mates to bowl. His figures thus remained 1–1–0–6. His first five victims were bowled, the last caught at cover. Taplow, 21 all out, lost by 131 runs.

LANCASHIRE TELEGRAPH July 17

The Worsley Cup quarter-final between East Lancashire and Enfield, supposedly a one-day game, stretched for more than a month owing to continual rain. East Lancashire captain Ockert Erasmus finally settled the game by 11 runs with a hat-trick on July 12, just when Enfield appeared to be heading for victory, 33 days after the match should have started. This was the

12th scheduled day and the fifth actual playing day of a match staged on two different grounds – along the way it was switched to Enfield, which was slightly drier. The Warwickshire all-rounder Keith Barker began the game playing for his home club Enfield and took an early catch but, when it rained after four overs, had to leave – and could not be replaced.

NORTHERN STAR, LISMORE July 18

A father and son took five wickets each in an innings for Goonellabah Workers Sports against Southern Cross University at Bexhill, New South Wales. Michael Mansfield, 56, took the first five wickets for five. He was replaced after his maximum five overs by his 17-year-old son Kody, who claimed the remaining wickets for 16. The university were 51 all out and lost the 30-over match by 29 runs.

COLOMBO PAGE July 19

A teachers' union protested when 117 schools in Hambantota postponed exams because of two one-day internationals between Sri Lanka and India being held in the town.

COURIER-MAIL, BRISBANE July 24

The former Test batsman Dean Jones, 51, dislocated his finger when his golf club hit a tree root in his first tournament since he gained his professional card to compete in the Australian senior tour. He popped the finger back in and carried on. His caddy was Graeme Hick.

MUMBAI MIRROR July 26

King's Circle in Mumbai was closed for an hour as bomb disposal units and dogs examined a cricket ball embedded with the dial of a watch which had been left by a tree. It turned out to be an IPL souvenir.

DECLARATION GAME August

With the weather so wet that play was obviously impossible, Bournemouth and Oxford decided to settle their British Universities & Colleges quarter-final without either side travelling. The tie was decided by a long-distance bowl-out, staged in their own home-town indoor schools, and watched by umpires who kept in contact by mobile phone. Bournemouth won.

MALVERN GAZETTE August 27

Liz Hurley and her partner Shane Warne are believed to have bought Donnington Hall, a £6m mansion near Ledbury, Herefordshire. "I think Shane would get a game for us," said Jim Sandford, chairman of nearby Eastnor CC.

THE SPIN September 12

Rock star Alice Cooper, 65, visited the *Test Match Special* box at Lord's during the South Africa Test. On being introduced, Geoff Boycott shook hands with Cooper's wife.

THE GUARDIAN September 18

Officials at Trent Bridge strategically wheeled a sightscreen into position to protect Nick Clegg, the unpopular deputy prime minister, from protesters when he arrived for a meeting with colleagues.

THE INDEPENDENT September 19

Lifeboats had to rescue 11 people and a dog after the annual Brambles cricket match in the middle of the Solent. The sandbar pitch, normally exposed for about an hour at the lowest tides of the year, remained waterlogged because of a strong westerly wind, and the match had to take place with the players, from two rival yacht clubs, at least ankle-deep in the sea. One boat ran aground, and another had engine trouble on the return journey.

MAIL ON SUNDAY September 23

The England fast bowler Graham Dilley, who died of cancer in 2011, aged 52, left nothing in his will once debts and outstanding matters had been settled. Dilley, twice divorced, had hoped his money would be divided equally between his four sons. One of them, Paul, said: "Money was never part of our relationship. He was a top-class bloke and was there when you needed him."

DAILY MAIL September 26

Former England opener John Edrich, 75, said he was cured of cancer by injections of mistletoe extract recommended by Stefan Geider, a doctor near his home in Aberdeenshire. Edrich was diagnosed with a rare blood cancer in 2000, and five years later appeared close to death. Seven years after that, he was back playing golf three times a week and saying he felt on top of the world. The plant has been known for decades to have some anti-cancer properties, but researchers say it can have terrible side-effects, and even Dr Geider admits: "It does not work for everybody. It's not a miracle cure."

ESPNCRICINFO October 12

Jade Child from Launceston, Tasmania, set a world record for the longest net session, batting for 25 hours and facing 15,701 deliveries from a bowling machine and local bowlers. The previous record stood at 12,353 balls.

SYDNEY MORNING HERALD October 17

Australian prime minister Julia Gillard made Sachin Tendulkar an honorary member of the Order of Australia on a visit to India, but the award came under fire for not meeting the rule that such awards for non-Australians should reflect "extraordinary service to Australia or humanity at large". Independent MP Rob Oakeshott said: "I love Sachin, I love cricket, but I just have a problem with soft diplomacy. It's about the integrity of the honours list."

THE HARVARD CRIMSON October 25

The United States' two most famous universities, Harvard and Yale, met for their first-ever cricket match, under floodlights in front of a crowd of 15. Although Harvard had a team in the 19th century, Yale did not, and Harvard cricket had been moribund for more than 80 years. Harvard won by 177 runs.

THE INDIAN EXPRESS November 1

Nine-year-old Aman Tiwari may have been saved from losing an arm because he was hurt when playing cricket. Though hit by only a tennis ball, he was in extreme pain, and doctors were able to diagnose bone cancer far earlier than would have otherwise happened.

THE TIMES November 2

Charles Fenton, 92, and believed to be the oldest umpire in the country, may be able to continue in the job in 2013 after all. He was originally forced to announce his retirement after 61 years officiating in the Derbyshire and Cheshire League because without an extra premium insurers refused to provide cover for anyone over 85. However, publicity-minded bookmakers Paddy Power offered to pay the extra. "What kind of skipper declares with his batsman on 92?" said a spokesman.

HINDUSTAN TIMES November 2

Bone-density tests initiated by India's cricket board, which are supposed to be able to measure young people's age accurately, have shown that many Under-16 players are over-age. Of 32 probables for Mumbai's Under-16 team, 11 were said to be ineligible; similar numbers were reported elsewhere.

SUN HERALD, SYDNEY November 11

Sydney High were bowled out for nought by King's School in a Fourth XI match, with King's bowler Brad Thomas taking six wickets, his victims forming two separate hat-tricks. King's hit the winning run off a dropped sitter first ball. The sides then split into two scratch teams and played a far more satisfying Twenty20 fixture.

THE TIMES November 17

The pavilion at Malpas CC, on the outskirts of Newport, South Wales, achieved an unbeatable niche in political history when it was used as a polling station in Britain's first elections for police commissioners, and no voters at all turned up. Council officials waited in vain for 14 hours for any of the 8,278 electors in Bettws Ward to exercise their democratic rights. Turnout nationally was about 15%, a record low.

DAILY TELEGRAPH/THE GUARDIAN December

Andrew Flintoff had an operation to repair a torn shoulder ligament after his first fight as a professional boxer. It was unclear whether the injury was sustained during his points victory over the American, Richard Dawson. Flintoff took a standing count in the second round, but held firm to win a narrow decision. The bout, much-hyped and much-criticised, looked, said *The Guardian*, "more like two burly farmhands trying to fend off a swarm of invisible bees than a boxing match".

PRESS TRUST OF INDIA December 10

A 15-year-old was allegedly beaten to death by two of his friends after dropping a catch in a game at Lakhimpur, near Lucknow, police said.

DAILY TELEGRAPH December 12

Civil servants in the Department of Communities and Local Government accessed leading websites 54 million times in the previous month, according to a survey by officials. This included 383,000 hits for ESPNcricinfo.

SYDNEY MORNING HERALD December 19

Australia's Transport Accident Commission defended their choice of Shane Warne to front a road-safety campaign less than a year after he was involved in a road-rage dispute with a cyclist.

BURY TIMES December 27

Brooksbottom won their 50th anniversary Boxing Day match against Tottington St John's by nine wickets. Alan Fletcher, who started the fixture in 1963, bowled the ceremonial first ball. "We were really lucky with the weather," said Tottington official Kieran Coe. "It stayed dry and mild until we had finished playing, then it poured down."

MUMBAI MIRROR December 28

Thirteen-year-old Bhupen Lalwani of Don Bosco School, Matunga, became the latest addition to the list of players who have made extreme scores in Mumbai's annual Giles Shield. Lalwani scored 398 out of 715 for five against IES Modern English School (Dadar), who lost by an innings and 590. He said "it hurt" to miss a quadruple-century.

We welcome contributions from readers, especially items from local or non-UK media. Items from club or school websites are also accepted. Please send newspaper cuttings to Matthew Engel at Fair Oak, Bacton, Herefordshire HR2 0AT (always including the paper's name and date) and weblinks to almanack@wisden.com

INDEX OF UNUSUAL OCCURRENCES

INDEX OF ADVERTISEMENTS

PART TITLES

1	Portrait of John Wisden by William Bromley, *c.* 1850 (page 13)	MCC Museum
2	Mark Ramprakash (page 55)	Graham Morris
3	Tony Greig's hat at the SCG, January 3, 2013 (page 153)	Cameron Spencer, Getty Images
4	Jimmy Anderson hides the ball, December 5, 2012 (page 253)	Graham Morris
5	Kent v Essex, Canterbury, August 9, 2012 (page 413)	Ady Kerry
6	Hashim Amla, January 12, 2012 (page 823)	Anesh Debiky, AFP/Getty Images
7	Michael Clarke reaches 300, Sydney, January 5, 2012 (page 1235)	Brett Costello, Newspix
8	John Arlott at work, 1984 (page 1511)	Patrick Eagar